260.00

D1106556

REFERENCE
ONLY

The Dictionary of Art · volume thirty-one

The Dictionary of Art

31

Tinoco

TO

Varna

GROVE

The Dictionary of Art

edited by JANE TURNER, in thirty-four volumes, 1996

This edition is distributed within the United Kingdom and Europe
by Macmillan Publishers Limited, London, and within the United States and Canada by
Grove's Dictionaries Inc., New York.

_____

Text keyboarded by Wearset Limited, Sunderland, England
Database management by Pindar plc, York, England
Imagesetting by William Clowes Limited, Suffolk, England
Printed in the United States of America by RR Donnelley & Sons Company, Willard, Ohio

British Library Cataloguing in Publication Data

The dictionary of art
  1. Art - Dictionaries 2. Art - History -
    Dictionaries
  I. Turner, Jane
  703

ISBN 1-884446-00-0

Library of Congress Cataloging in Publication Data

The dictionary of art / editor, Jane Turner.
  p. cm.
  Includes bibliographical references and index.
  Contents: 1. A to Anckerman
  ISBN 1-884446-00-0 (alk. paper)
  1. Art—Encyclopedias.
  I. Turner, Jane, 1956–
N31.D5 1996   96–13628
703—dc20   CIP

Contents

General Abbreviations

The abbreviations employed throughout this dictionary, most of which are listed below, do not vary, except for capitalization, regardless of the context in which they are used, including bibliographical citations and for locations of works of art. The principle used to arrive at these abbreviations is that their full form should be easily deducible, and for this reason acronyms have generally been avoided (e.g. Los Angeles Co. Mus. A. instead of LACMA). The same abbreviation is adopted for cognate forms in foreign languages and in most cases for plural and adjectival forms (e.g. A.= Art, Arts, Arte, Arti etc). Not all related forms are listed below. Occasionally, if a name, for instance of an artists' group or exhibiting society, is repeated within the text of one article, it is cited in an abbreviated form after its first mention in full (e.g. The Pre-Raphaelite Brotherhood (PRB) was founded...); the same is true of archaeological periods and eras, which are abbreviated to initial letters in small capitals (e.g. In the Early Minoan (EM) period...). Such abbreviations do not appear in this list. For the reader's convenience, separate full lists of abbreviations for locations, periodical titles and standard reference books and series are included as Appendices A–C in vol. 33.

A.	Art, Arts	Anthropol.	Anthropology	Azerbaij.	Azerbaijani
A.C.	Arts Council	Antiqua.	Antiquarian, Antiquaries	B.	Bartsch [catalogue of Old Master prints]
Acad.	Academy	app.	appendix		
AD	Anno Domini	approx.	approximately	b	born
Add.	Additional, Addendum	AR	Arkansas (USA)	BA	Bachelor of Arts
addn	addition	ARA	Associate of the Royal Academy	Balt.	Baltic
Admin.	Administration			bapt	baptized
Adv.	Advances, Advanced	Arab.	Arabic	BArch	Bachelor of Architecture
Aesth.	Aesthetic(s)	Archaeol.	Archaeology	Bart	Baronet
Afr.	African	Archit.	Architecture, Architectural	Bask.	Basketry
Afrik.	Afrikaans, Afrikaner	Archv, Archvs	Archive(s)	BBC	British Broadcasting Corporation
A.G.	Art Gallery	Arg.	Argentine	BC	Before Christ
Agrar.	Agrarian	ARHA	Associate of the Royal Hibernian Academy	BC	British Columbia (Canada)
Agric.	Agriculture			BE	Buddhist era
Agron.	Agronomy	ARIBA	Associate of the Royal Institute of British Architects	Beds	Bedfordshire (GB)
Agy	Agency			Behav.	Behavioural
AH	Anno Hegirae	Armen.	Armenian	Belarus.	Belarusian
A. Inst.	Art Institute	ARSA	Associate of the Royal Scottish Academy	Belg.	Belgian
AK	Alaska (USA)			Berks	Berkshire (GB)
AL	Alabama (USA)	Asiat.	Asiatic	Berwicks	Berwickshire (GB; old)
Alb.	Albanian	Assist.	Assistance	BFA	Bachelor of Fine Arts
Alg.	Algerian	Assoc.	Association	Bibl.	Bible, Biblical
Alta	Alberta (Canada)	Astron.	Astronomy	Bibliog.	Bibliography, Bibliographical
Altern.	Alternative	AT&T	American Telephone & Telegraph Company	Biblioph.	Bibliophile
a.m.	ante meridiem [before noon]			Biog.	Biography, Biographical
Amat.	Amateur	attrib.	attribution, attributed to	Biol.	Biology, Biological
Amer.	American	Aug	August	bk, bks	book(s)
An.	Annals	Aust.	Austrian	Bkbinder	Bookbinder
Anatol.	Anatolian	Austral.	Australian	Bklore	Booklore
Anc.	Ancient	Auth.	Author(s)	Bkshop	Bookshop
Annu.	Annual	Auton.	Autonomous	BL	British Library
Anon.	Anonymous(ly)	Aux.	Auxiliary	Bld	Build
Ant.	Antique	Ave.	Avenue	Bldg	Building
Anthol.	Anthology	AZ	Arizona (USA)		

Bldr	Builder	Chin.	Chinese	Cur.	Curator, Curatorial, Curatorship
BLitt	Bachelor of Letters/Literature	Christ.	Christian, Christianity	Curr.	Current(s)
BM	British Museum	Chron.	Chronicle	CVO	Commander of the [Royal] Victorian Order
Boh.	Bohemian	Cie	Compagnie [French]		
Boliv.	Bolivian	Cinema.	Cinematography	Cyclad.	Cycladic
Botan.	Botany, Botanical	Circ.	Circle	Cyp.	Cypriot
BP	Before present (1950)	Civ.	Civil, Civic	Czech.	Czechoslovak
Braz.	Brazilian	Civiliz.	Civilization(s)	$	dollars
BRD	Bundesrepublik Deutschland [Federal Republic of Germany (West Germany)]	Class.	Classic, Classical	*d*	died
		Clin.	Clinical	d.	denarius, denarii [penny, pence]
		CO	Colorado (USA)		
Brecons	Breconshire (GB; old)	Co.	Company; County	Dalmat.	Dalmatian
Brez.	Brezonek [lang. of Brittany]	Cod.	Codex, Codices	Dan.	Danish
Brit.	British	Col., Cols	Collection(s); Column(s)	DBE	Dame Commander of the Order of the British Empire
Bros	Brothers	Coll.	College		
BSc	Bachelor of Science	collab.	in collaboration with, collaborated, collaborative	DC	District of Columbia (USA)
Bucks	Buckinghamshire (GB)			DDR	Deutsche Demokratische Republik [German Democratic Republic (East Germany)]
Bulg.	Bulgarian	Collct.	Collecting		
Bull.	Bulletin	Colloq.	Colloquies		
bur	buried	Colomb.	Colombian	DE	Delaware (USA)
Burm.	Burmese	Colon.	Colonies, Colonial	Dec	December
Byz.	Byzantine	Colr	Collector	Dec.	Decorative
C	Celsius	Comm.	Commission; Community	ded.	dedication, dedicated to
C.	Century	Commerc.	Commercial	Democ.	Democracy, Democratic
c.	*circa* [about]	Communic.	Communications	Demog.	Demography, Demographic
CA	California	Comp.	Comparative; compiled by, compiler	Denbs	Denbighshire (GB; old)
Cab.	Cabinet			dep.	deposited at
Caerns	Caernarvonshire (GB; old)	Concent.	Concentration	Dept	Department
C.A.G.	City Art Gallery	Concr.	Concrete	Dept.	Departmental, Departments
Cal.	Calendar	Confed.	Confederation	Derbys	Derbyshire (GB)
Callig.	Calligraphy	Confer.	Conference	Des.	Design
Cam.	Camera	Congol.	Congolese	destr.	destroyed
Cambs	Cambridgeshire (GB)	Congr.	Congress	Dev.	Development
can	canonized	Conserv.	Conservation; Conservatory	Devon	Devonshire (GB)
Can.	Canadian	Constr.	Construction(al)	Dial.	Dialogue
Cant.	Canton(s), Cantonal	cont.	continued	diam.	diameter
Capt.	Captain	Contemp.	Contemporary	Diff.	Diffusion
Cards	Cardiganshire (GB; old)	Contrib.	Contributions, Contributor(s)	Dig.	Digest
Carib.	Caribbean	Convalesc.	Convalescence	Dip. Eng.	Diploma in Engineering
Carms	Carmarthenshire (GB; old)	Convent.	Convention	Dir.	Direction, Directed
Cartog.	Cartography	Coop.	Cooperation	Directrt	Directorate
Cat.	Catalan	Coord.	Coordination	Disc.	Discussion
cat.	catalogue	Copt.	Coptic	diss.	dissertation
Cath.	Catholic	Corp.	Corporation, Corpus	Distr.	District
CBE	Commander of the Order of the British Empire	Corr.	Correspondence	Div.	Division
		Cors.	Corsican	DLitt	Doctor of Letters/Literature
Celeb.	Celebration	Cost.	Costume	DM	Deutsche Mark
Celt.	Celtic	Cret.	Cretan	Doc.	Document(s)
Cent.	Centre, Central	Crim.	Criminal	Doss.	Dossier
Centen.	Centennial	Crit.	Critical, Criticism	DPhil	Doctor of Philosophy
Cer.	Ceramic	Croat.	Croatian	Dr	Doctor
cf.	confer [compare]	CT	Connecticut (USA)	Drg, Drgs	Drawing(s)
Chap., Chaps	Chapter(s)	Cttee	Committee	DSc	Doctor of Science/Historical Sciences
Chem.	Chemistry	Cub.	Cuban		
Ches	Cheshire (GB)	Cult.	Cultural, Culture	Dut.	Dutch
Chil.	Chilean	Cumb.	Cumberland (GB; old)	Dwell.	Dwelling
				E.	East(ern)

EC	European (Economic) Community	figs	figures	Heb.	Hebrew
Eccles.	Ecclesiastical	Filip.	Filipina(s), Filipino(s)	Hell.	Hellenic
Econ.	Economic, Economies	Fin.	Finnish	Her.	Heritage
Ecuad.	Ecuadorean	FL	Florida (USA)	Herald.	Heraldry, Heraldic
ed.	editor, edited (by)	*fl*	*floruit* [he/she flourished]	Hereford & Worcs	Hereford & Worcester (GB)
edn	edition	Flem.	Flemish		
eds	editors	Flints	Flintshire (GB; old)	Herts	Hertfordshire (GB)
Educ.	Education	Flk	Folk	HI	Hawaii (USA)
e.g.	*exempli gratia* [for example]	Flklore	Folklore	Hib.	Hibernia
Egyp.	Egyptian	fol., fols	folio(s)	Hisp.	Hispanic
Elem.	Element(s), Elementary	Found.	Foundation	Hist.	History, Historical
Emp.	Empirical	Fr.	French	HMS	His/Her Majesty's Ship
Emul.	Emulation	frag.	fragment	Hon.	Honorary, Honourable
Enc.	Encyclopedia	Fri.	Friday	Horiz.	Horizon
Encour.	Encouragement	FRIBA	Fellow of the Royal Institute of British Architects	Hort.	Horticulture
Eng.	English			Hosp.	Hospital(s)
Engin.	Engineer, Engineering	FRS	Fellow of the Royal Society, London	HRH	His/Her Royal Highness
Engr., Engrs	Engraving(s)			Human.	Humanities, Humanism
		ft	foot, feet	Hung.	Hungarian
Envmt	Environment	Furn.	Furniture	Hunts	Huntingdonshire (GB; old)
Epig.	Epigraphy	Futur.	Futurist, Futurism	IA	Iowa
Episc.	Episcopal	g	gram(s)	ibid.	*ibidem* [in the same place]
Esp.	Especially	GA	Georgia (USA)	ICA	Institute of Contemporary Arts
Ess.	Essays	Gael.	Gaelic		
est.	established	Gal., Gals	Gallery, Galleries	Ice.	Icelandic
etc	*etcetera* [and so on]	Gaz.	Gazette	Iconog.	Iconography
Ethnog.	Ethnography	GB	Great Britain	Iconol.	Iconology
Ethnol.	Ethnology	Gdn, Gdns	Garden(s)	ID	Idaho (USA)
Etrus.	Etruscan	Gdnr(s)	Gardener(s)	i.e.	*id est* [that is]
Eur.	European	Gen.	General	IL	Illinois (USA)
Evangel.	Evangelical	Geneal.	Genealogy, Genealogist	Illum.	Illumination
Exam.	Examination	Gent.	Gentleman, Gentlemen	illus.	illustrated, illustration
Excav.	Excavation, Excavated	Geog.	Geography	Imp.	Imperial
Exch.	Exchange	Geol.	Geology	IN	Indiana (USA)
Excurs.	Excursion	Geom.	Geometry	in., ins	inch(es)
exh.	exhibition	Georg.	Georgian	Inc.	Incorporated
Exp.	Exposition	Geosci.	Geoscience	inc.	incomplete
Expermntl	Experimental	Ger.	German, Germanic	incl.	includes, including, inclusive
Explor.	Exploration	G.I.	Government/General Issue (USA)	Incorp.	Incorporation
Expn	Expansion			Ind.	Indian
Ext.	External	Glams	Glamorganshire (GB; old)	Indep.	Independent
Extn	Extension	Glos	Gloucestershire (GB)	Indig.	Indigenous
f, ff	following page, following pages	Govt	Government	Indol.	Indology
		Gr.	Greek	Indon.	Indonesian
F.A.	Fine Art(s)	Grad.	Graduate	Indust.	Industrial
Fac.	Faculty	Graph.	Graphic	Inf.	Information
facs.	facsimile	Green.	Greenlandic	Inq.	Inquiry
Fam.	Family	Gr.-Roman	Greco-Roman	Inscr.	Inscribed, Inscription
fasc.	fascicle	Gt	Great	Inst.	Institute(s)
fd	feastday (of a saint)	Gtr	Greater	Inst. A.	Institute of Art
Feb	February	Guat.	Guatemalan	Instr.	Instrument, Instrumental
Fed.	Federation, Federal	Gym.	Gymnasium	Int.	International
Fem.	Feminist	h.	height	Intell.	Intelligence
Fest.	Festival	ha	hectare	Inter.	Interior(s), Internal
fig.	figure (illustration)	Hait.	Haitian	Interdiscip.	Interdisciplinary
Fig.	Figurative	Hants	Hampshire (GB)	intro.	introduced by, introduction
		Hb.	Handbook	inv.	inventory

Inven.	Invention	m	metre(s)	Moldov.	Moldovan
Invest.	Investigation(s)	m.	married	MOMA	Museum of Modern Art
Iran.	Iranian	M.	Monsieur	Mon.	Monday
irreg.	irregular(ly)	MA	Master of Arts; Massachusetts (USA)	Mongol.	Mongolian
Islam.	Islamic			Mons	Monmouthshire (GB; old)
Isr.	Israeli	Mag.	Magazine	Montgoms	Montgomeryshire (GB; old)
It.	Italian	Maint.	Maintenance	Mor.	Moral
J.	Journal	Malay.	Malaysian	Morav.	Moravian
Jam.	Jamaican	Man.	Manitoba (Canada); Manual	Moroc.	Moroccan
Jan	January	Manuf.	Manufactures	Movt	Movement
Jap.	Japanese	Mar.	Marine, Maritime	MP	Member of Parliament
Jav.	Javanese	Mason.	Masonic	MPhil	Master of Philosophy
Jew.	Jewish	Mat.	Material(s)	MS	Mississippi (USA)
Jewel.	Jewellery	Math.	Mathematic	MS., MSS	manuscript(s)
Jord.	Jordanian	MBE	Member of the Order of the British Empire	MSc	Master of Science
jr	junior			MT	Montana (USA)
Juris.	Jurisdiction	MD	Doctor of Medicine; Maryland (USA)	Mt	Mount
KBE	Knight Commander of the Order of the British Empire			Mthly	Monthly
		ME	Maine (USA)	Mun.	Municipal
KCVO	Knight Commander of the Royal Victorian Order	Mech.	Mechanical	Mus.	Museum(s)
		Med.	Medieval; Medium, Media	Mus. A.	Museum of Art
kg	kilogram(s)	Medic.	Medical, Medicine	Mus. F.A.	Museum of Fine Art(s)
kHz	kilohertz	Medit.	Mediterranean	Music.	Musicology
km	kilometre(s)	Mem.	Memorial(s); Memoir(s)	N.	North(ern); National
Knowl.	Knowledge	Merions	Merionethshire (GB; old)	n	refractive index of a medium
Kor.	Korean	Meso-Amer.	Meso-American	n.	note
KS	Kansas (USA)			N.A.G.	National Art Gallery
KY	Kentucky (USA)	Mesop.	Mesopotamian	Nat.	Natural, Nature
Kyrgyz.	Kyrgyzstani	Met.	Metropolitan	Naut.	Nautical
£	libra, librae [pound, pounds sterling]	Metal.	Metallurgy	NB	New Brunswick (Canada)
		Mex.	Mexican	NC	North Carolina (USA)
l.	length	MFA	Master of Fine Arts	ND	North Dakota (USA)
LA	Louisiana (USA)	mg	milligram(s)	n.d.	no date
Lab.	Laboratory	Mgmt	Management	NE	Nebraska; Northeast(ern)
Lancs	Lancashire (GB)	Mgr	Monsignor	Neth.	Netherlandish
Lang.	Language(s)	MI	Michigan	Newslett.	Newsletter
Lat.	Latin	Micrones.	Micronesian	Nfld	Newfoundland (Canada)
Latv.	Latvian	Mid. Amer.	Middle American	N.G.	National Gallery
lb, lbs	pound(s) weight	Middx	Middlesex (GB; old)	N.G.A.	National Gallery of Art
Leb.	Lebanese	Mid. E.	Middle Eastern	NH	New Hampshire (USA)
Lect.	Lecture	Mid. Eng.	Middle English	Niger.	Nigerian
Legis.	Legislative	Mid Glam.	Mid Glamorgan (GB)	NJ	New Jersey (USA)
Leics	Leicestershire (GB)	Mil.	Military	NM	New Mexico (USA)
Lex.	Lexicon	Mill.	Millennium	nm	nanometre (10^{-9} metre)
Lg.	Large	Min.	Ministry; Minutes	nn.	notes
Lib., Libs	Library, Libraries	Misc.	Miscellaneous	no., nos	number(s)
Liber.	Liberian	Miss.	Mission(s)	Nord.	Nordic
Libsp	Librarianship	Mlle	Mademoiselle	Norm.	Normal
Lincs	Lincolnshire (GB)	mm	millimetre(s)	Northants	Northamptonshire (GB)
Lit.	Literature	Mme	Madame	Northumb.	Northumberland (GB)
Lith.	Lithuanian	MN	Minnesota	Norw.	Norwegian
Liturg.	Liturgical	Mnmt, Mnmts	Monument(s)	Notts	Nottinghamshire (GB)
LLB	Bachelor of Laws			Nov	November
LLD	Doctor of Laws	Mnmtl	Monumental	n.p.	no place (of publication)
Lt	Lieutenant	MO	Missouri (USA)	N.P.G.	National Portrait Gallery
Lt-Col.	Lieutenant-Colonel	Mod.	Modern, Modernist	nr	near
Ltd	Limited	Moldav.	Moldavian		

Nr E.	Near Eastern	Per.	Period	Ptg(s)	Painting(s)
NS	New Style; Nova Scotia (Canada)	Percep.	Perceptions	Pub.	Public
n. s.	new series	Perf.	Performance, Performing, Performed	pubd	published
NSW	New South Wales (Australia)	Period.	Periodical(s)	Publ.	Publicity
NT	National Trust	Pers.	Persian	pubn(s)	publication(s)
Ntbk	Notebook	Persp.	Perspectives	PVA	polyvinyl acetate
Numi.	Numismatic(s)	Peru.	Peruvian	PVC	polyvinyl chloride
NV	Nevada (USA)	PhD	Doctor of Philosophy	Q.	quarterly
NW	Northwest(ern)	Philol.	Philology	4to	quarto
NWT	Northwest Territories (Canada)	Philos.	Philosophy	Qué.	Québec (Canada)
NY	New York (USA)	Phoen.	Phoenician	*R*	reprint
NZ	New Zealand	Phot.	Photograph, Photography, Photographic	*r*	*recto*
OBE	Officer of the Order of the British Empire	Phys.	Physician(s), Physics, Physique, Physical	RA	Royal Academician
Obj.	Object(s), Objective	Physiog.	Physiognomy	Radnors	Radnorshire (GB; old)
Occas.	Occasional	Physiol.	Physiology	RAF	Royal Air Force
Occident.	Occidental	Pict.	Picture(s), Pictorial	Rec.	Record(s)
Ocean.	Oceania	pl.	plate; plural	red.	reduction, reduced for
Oct	October	Plan.	Planning	Ref.	Reference
8vo	octavo	Planet.	Planetarium	Refurb.	Refurbishment
OFM	Order of Friars Minor	Plast.	Plastic	*reg*	*regit* [ruled]
OH	Ohio (USA)	pls	plates	Reg.	Regional
OK	Oklahoma (USA)	p.m.	post meridiem [after noon]	Relig.	Religion, Religious
Olymp.	Olympic	Polit.	Political	remod.	remodelled
OM	Order of Merit	Poly.	Polytechnic	Ren.	Renaissance
Ont.	Ontario (Canada)	Polynes.	Polynesian	Rep.	Report(s)
op.	opus	Pop.	Popular	repr.	reprint(ed); reproduced, reproduction
opp.	opposite; opera [pl. of opus]	Port.	Portuguese	Represent.	Representation, Representative
OR	Oregon (USA)	Port.	Portfolio	Res.	Research
Org.	Organization	Posth.	Posthumous(ly)	rest.	restored, restoration
Orient.	Oriental	Pott.	Pottery	Retro.	Retrospective
Orthdx	Orthodox	POW	prisoner of war	rev.	revision, revised (by/for)
OSB	Order of St Benedict	PRA	President of the Royal Academy	Rev.	Reverend; Review
Ott.	Ottoman	Pract.	Practical	RHA	Royal Hibernian Academician
Oxon	Oxfordshire (GB)	Prefect.	Prefecture, Prefectural	RI	Rhode Island (USA)
oz.	ounce(s)	Preserv.	Preservation	RIBA	Royal Institute of British Architects
p	pence	prev.	previous(ly)	RJ	Rio de Janeiro State
p., pp.	page(s)	priv.	private	Rlwy	Railway
PA	Pennsylvania (USA)	PRO	Public Record Office	RSA	Royal Scottish Academy
p.a.	per annum	Prob.	Problem(s)	RSFSR	Russian Soviet Federated Socialist Republic
Pak.	Pakistani	Proc.	Proceedings	Rt Hon.	Right Honourable
Palaeontol.	Palaeontology, Palaeontological	Prod.	Production	Rur.	Rural
Palest.	Palestinian	Prog.	Progress	Rus.	Russian
Pap.	Paper(s)	Proj.	Project(s)	S	San, Santa, Santo, Sant', São [Saint]
para.	paragraph	Promot.	Promotion	S.	South(ern)
Parag.	Paraguayan	Prop.	Property, Properties	s.	solidus, solidi [shilling(s)]
Parl.	Parliament	Prov.	Province(s), Provincial	Sask.	Saskatchewan (Canada)
Paroch.	Parochial	Proven.	Provenance	Sat.	Saturday
Patriarch.	Patriarchate	Prt, Prts	Print(s)	SC	South Carolina (USA)
Patriot.	Patriotic	Prtg	Printing	Scand.	Scandinavian
Patrm.	Patrimony	pseud.	pseudonym	Sch.	School
Pav.	Pavilion	Psych.	Psychiatry, Psychiatric	Sci.	Science(s), Scientific
PEI	Prince Edward Island (Canada)	Psychol.	Psychology, Psychological	Scot.	Scottish
Pembs	Pembrokeshire (GB; old)	pt	part	Sculp.	Sculpture

SD	South Dakota (USA)	suppl., suppls	supplement(s), supplementary	Urb.	Urban
SE	Southeast(ern)	Surv.	Survey	Urug.	Uruguayan
Sect.	Section	SW	Southwest(ern)	US	United States
Sel.	Selected	Swed.	Swedish	USA	United States of America
Semin.	Seminar(s), Seminary	Swi.	Swiss	USSR	Union of Soviet Socialist Republics
Semiot.	Semiotic	Symp.	Symposium	UT	Utah
Semit.	Semitic	Syr.	Syrian	*v*	*verso*
Sept	September	Tap.	Tapestry	VA	Virginia (USA)
Ser.	Series	Tas.	Tasmanian	V&A	Victoria and Albert Museum
Serb.	Serbian	Tech.	Technical, Technique	Var.	Various
Serv.	Service(s)	Technol.	Technology	Venez.	Venezuelan
Sess.	Session, Sessional	Territ.	Territory	Vern.	Vernacular
Settmt(s)	Settlement(s)	Theat.	Theatre	Vict.	Victorian
S. Glam.	South Glamorgan (GB)	Theol.	Theology, Theological	Vid.	Video
Siber.	Siberian	Theor.	Theory, Theoretical	Viet.	Vietnamese
Sig.	Signature	Thurs.	Thursday	viz.	*videlicet* [namely]
Sil.	Silesian	Tib.	Tibetan	vol., vols	volume(s)
Sin.	Singhala	TN	Tennessee (USA)	vs.	versus
sing.	singular	Top.	Topography	VT	Vermont (USA)
SJ	Societas Jesu [Society of Jesus]	Trad.	Tradition(s), Traditional	Vulg.	Vulgarisation
Skt	Sanskrit	trans.	translation, translated by; transactions	W.	West(ern)
Slav.	Slavic, Slavonic			w.	width
Slov.	Slovene, Slovenian	Transafr.	Transafrican	WA	Washington (USA)
Soc.	Society	Transatlant.	Transatlantic	Warwicks	Warwickshire (GB)
Social.	Socialism, Socialist	Transcarpath.	Transcarpathian	Wed.	Wednesday
Sociol.	Sociology	transcr.	transcribed by/for	W. Glam.	West Glamorgan (GB)
Sov.	Soviet	Triq.	Triquarterly	WI	Wisconsin (USA)
SP	São Paulo State	Tropic.	Tropical	Wilts	Wiltshire (GB)
Sp.	Spanish	Tues.	Tuesday	Wkly	Weekly
sq.	square	Turk.	Turkish	W. Midlands	West Midlands (GB)
sr	senior	Turkmen.	Turkmenistani		
Sri L.	Sri Lankan	TV	Television	Worcs	Worcestershire (GB; old)
SS	Saints, Santi, Santissima, Santissimo, Santissimi; Steam ship	TX	Texas (USA)	Wtrcol.	Watercolour
		U.	University	WV	West Virginia (USA)
		UK	United Kingdom of Great Britain and Northern Ireland	WY	Wyoming (USA)
SSR	Soviet Socialist Republic			Yb., Y.-b.	Yearbook, Year-book
St	Saint, Sankt, Sint, Szent	Ukrain.	Ukrainian	Yem.	Yemeni
Staffs	Staffordshire (GB)	Un.	Union	Yorks	Yorkshire (GB; old)
Ste	Sainte	Underwtr	Underwater	Yug.	Yugoslavian
Stud.	Study, Studies	UNESCO	United Nations Educational, Scientific and Cultural Organization	Zamb.	Zambian
Subalp.	Subalpine			Zimb.	Zimbabwean
Sum.	Sumerian	Univl	Universal		
Sun.	Sunday	unpubd	unpublished		
Sup.	Superior				

A Note on the Use of the Dictionary

This note is intended as a short guide to the basic editorial conventions adopted in this dictionary. For a fuller explanation, please refer to the Introduction, vol. 1, pp. xiii–xx.

Abbreviations in general use in the dictionary are listed on pp. vii–xii; those used in bibliographies and for locations of works of art or exhibition venues are listed in the Appendices in vol. 33.

Alphabetization of headings, which are distinguished in bold typeface, is letter by letter up to the first comma (ignoring spaces, hyphens, accents and any parenthesized or bracketed matter); the same principle applies thereafter. Abbreviations of 'Saint' and its foreign equivalents are alphabetized as if spelt out, and headings with the prefix 'Mc' appear under 'Mac'.

Authors' signatures appear at the end of the article or sequence of articles that the authors have contributed; in multipartite articles, any section that is unsigned is by the author of the next signed section. Where the article was compiled by the editors or in the few cases where an author has wished to remain anonymous, this is indicated by a square box (□) instead of a signature.

Bibliographies are arranged chronologically (within a section, where divided) by order of year of first publication and, within years, alphabetically by authors' names. Abbreviations have been used for some standard reference books; these are cited in full in Appendix C in vol. 33, as are abbreviations of periodical titles (Appendix B). Abbreviated references to alphabetically arranged dictionaries and encyclopedias appear at the beginning of the bibliography (or section).

Biographical dates when cited in parentheses in running text at the first mention of a personal name indicate that the individual does not have an entry in the dictionary. The presence of parenthesized regnal dates for rulers and popes, however, does not necessarily indicate the lack of a biography of that person. Where no dates are provided for an artist or patron, the reader may assume that there is a biography of that individual in the dictionary (or, more rarely, that the person is so obscure that dates are not readily available).

Cross-references are distinguished by the use of small capital letters, with a large capital to indicate the initial letter of the entry to which the reader is directed; for example, 'He commissioned LEONARDO DA VINCI . . .' means that the entry is alphabetized under 'L'.

T

[continued]

Tinoco. Portuguese family of architects.

(1) Pedro Nunes Tinoco (*fl* 1604; *d* 8 Feb 1641). The head of a distinguished family of architects, he was an exponent of the 'Plain Style', a term used by Kubler to define the rather austere interpretation of Renaissance architecture that occurred in Portugal, to which Tinoco brought an increased rigour. In 1604 he was appointed to one of the three royal apprenticeships to study architecture at the Aula dos Paços da Ribeira in Lisbon, the school created by Philip I of Portugal (Philip II of Spain) in 1584, under Nicolau de Frias. Tinoco's first commission as a Royal Architect was the reformation of the convent of S Clara (destr. 1755), Lisbon. Other assignments included the church and convent of S Marta (1616–36), and the church of Salvador (1616–17), both in Lisbon. The works were well received as being 'sumptuous' and 'modern', and contributed to his high contemporary reputation. In 1622 Tinoco designed the impressive sacristy of the monastery of Santa Cruz, Coimbra, completed in 1624. This is a single barrel-vaulted space, its severe architecture offset by sumptuous decoration on the walls in coloured marble and *azulejos* (glazed tiles). Tinoco's vaulting is more rigorously in the manner of Alberti than the informal version characteristic of those Portuguese buildings that immediately followed the introduction of his style by Filippo Terzi. The compartments of the vault at Santa Cruz are carried across the wide entablature and down the walls in the form of broad pilasters, so unifying the internal volume. In 1624 Tinoco took over work on the completion of Terzi's S Vicente de Fora (begun 1582), Lisbon, in succession to Baltasar Alvares. He also made drawings for *Roteiro das Águas Livres*, a study for the water supply to Lisbon, published by his son (2) João Nunes Tinoco in 1671.

(2) João Nunes Tinoco (*fl* 1631; *d* 1689). Son of (1) Pedro Nunes Tinoco. He became regarded as the leading exponent of the 'Plain Style' (*see* (1) above). In 1631 he was appointed to one of the three royal apprenticeships to study architecture at the Aula dos Paços da Ribeira in Lisbon. In 1641 he succeeded his father as Master of Works at S Vicente de Fora (begun 1582), Lisbon, designed by Filippo Terzi. He also designed two small convents for the Order of S Agostinho, Grilo (1663; destr. 1755) and Monte Olivete (1666; destr. 1755) both in Xabregas,

Lisbon. His first major work was the church of the Jesuit Seminary (1676–87), Santarém. This influential design followed the box-nave type used by Afonso Alvares at S Roque (1567), Lisbon, one that suited the Jesuits' liturgical programme. The broad, undivided nave has a flat wooden painted ceiling; a giant order carried around the nave unifies the arcaded chapels and glazed tribunes. The severe compartmented façade, of Flemish origin, with enormous volutes on the upper level, became a model widely imitated in Portugal and Brazil.

In 1682 Tinoco began work on S Engrácia, Lisbon, the most ambitious architectural project in late 17th-century Portugal (*see* PORTUGAL, fig. 4). The work was continued by JOÃO ANTUNES, who was recorded as Master in 1697. The building reflects the growing Portuguese awareness of Italian Baroque architecture after the end of the period of Spanish dominance in 1640, although it is 'Plain Style' in its interpretation. Two early drawings for the plan exist (both Lisbon, Acad. B.A.), one showing an enlarged version of an hexagonal hall plan, between corner towers, the other based loosely on S Agnese (1652–7), Rome, by Girolamo Rainaldi, Carlo Rainaldi and Francesco Borromini. The final plan, a Greek cross with a central dome and four apses, constrained by an enormous tower at each corner, is usually compared to Bramante's scheme (*c*. 1505–14) for St Peter's, Rome, but the monumental treatment is closer to Michelangelo's later revisions (1546–64). The entrance façade has four great Doric columns that frame a triad of arches and pedimented niches, recalling those at S Vicente de Fora. The façades are compartmented in a Portuguese manner, while the apses are expressed forcibly on the exterior, with re-entrant curved walls to the towers. The spacious interior with its four semi-domes is sumptuously decorated with coloured marble and *azulejos* (glazed tiles) in a scheme typical of the late 17th century. Carvalho suggests that Francisco Tinoco da Silva (*fl* 1683; *d* 1730), who was then master of the Aula dos Paços da Ribeira, with whom João Antunes trained, rather than Tinoco, was responsible for the design. Santos, however, points out that Tinoco was the most prominent architect at the time, and Kubler notes that in 1667 João Nunes Tinoco had surveyed a small Greek-cross-plan church, the Piedade in Santarém (1644) by Jácome Mendes. Work stopped on S Engrácia in 1730 when the building reached the dome, because funds were being diverted to more secular Royal works. It was used as a magazine and works were concluded only in 1966; it is now the national pantheon of Portugal. Tinoco also produced two illustrated books on military architecture, one on Pernambuco and Bahia in Brazil, *Desenhos e plantas illuminades do Recife de Pernambuco . . . e Barra da Bahia . . .* [Illuminated designs and plans of Recife de Pernambuco . . . and Barra da Bahia . . .] (1631–3; MS., Rio de Janeiro, Bib. N.), and the other on Portugal, *Livro das praças de Portugal com suas fortificações . . . Delineadas por João Nunes Tinoco . . .* [A book on the strongholds of Portugal and their fortresses . . . Plans by João Nunes Tinoco] (1663; MS., Lisbon, Bib. Ajuda). In addition he was the author of the first topographical plan of Lisbon (1650; pubd Lisbon, 1851 and in França, 1965). He also published *Roteiro das Aguas Livres*, a study on the water supply to Lisbon, with drawings by his father (1671).

BIBLIOGRAPHY
Viterbo
J. A. França: *Lisboa Pombalina* (Lisbon, 1965)
R. dos Santos: *Oito séculos de arte portuguesa*, ii (Lisbon, 1966)
A. de Carvalho: *As Obras de Santa Engrácia e os seus artistas* (Lisbon, 1971)
G. Kubler: *Portuguese Plain Architecture: Between Spices and Diamonds, 1521–1706* (Middletown, 1972)
J. F. Pereira and P. Pereira: *Dicionário de arte barroca em Portugal* (Lisbon, 1989)

ZILAH QUEZADO DECKKER

Tinoco, José Martins (*fl c.* 1741–55). Portuguese wood-carver. In 1741 he was contracted to carve the pulpit and main altarpiece of the church of the convent of S Domingos in Aveiro (destr.). In 1746 he was contracted to make two side and two lateral altarpieces for the nave of the church of Avanca, Estarreja, giving Miguel Francisco da Silva as a reference. Between 1747 and 1748 he made carvings for the sacristy of the church of S Nicolau, Oporto. In 1748 he carried out the decoration of the Casa do Despacho, including the boardroom of the Third Order of S Francisco, Oporto, probably to the designs of Nicolau Nasoni. In 1755 he collaborated with José da Fonseca Lima on carving two altarpieces for the transept of the Benedictine monastery of S Bento da Vitória, Oporto. In a separate contract of 1755 Tinoco carried out the work on one of the altarpieces, that of the Exile, one of the finest examples of carving in the late Joanine style in Oporto.

BIBLIOGRAPHY
R. C. Smith and D. P. Brandão: *Alguns retábulos e painéis de igrejas e capelas do Porto* (Oporto, 1963), pp. 72–4, 213–20, 290–91
A. M. Basto: *Apontamentos para um dicionário de artistas e artífices que trabalharam no Porto do século XV ao século XVIII* (Oporto, 1964), p. 397
R. C. Smith: *Alguns artistas que trabalharam para a Venerável Ordem Terceira de S. Francisco no Porto, 1657–1800* (Oporto, 1965), pp. 12–13

NATÁLIA MARINHO FERREIRA ALVES

Tino di Camaino (*b* Siena, *c.* 1280; *d* Naples, 1337). Italian sculptor. He led an itinerant career, working in Siena, Pisa, Florence and Naples for some of the most powerful Guelph and Ghibelline patrons of the day. The roots of his style lie in late 13th-century Siena, but during his long stay in Ghibelline Pisa it gradually grew nearer to that of Giovanni Pisano. Tino's return to Siena and the change in his political affiliation in 1315 were accompanied by a new artistic orientation, in which he drew inspiration

from painting, particularly the work of Simone Martini. This period of artistic maturity extended also to his time in Florence (1318–1323/4). He was the most important and inventive sculptor of funerary monuments in Tuscany at this time, and in this capacity he was summoned to Naples by the House of Anjou, the leaders of the Guelph party in Italy. Through his influence on local sculptors, the innovations of Tuscan Gothic sculpture were spread throughout southern Italy, and his influence there was felt long after his death. His style is characterized by powerful figures in which are united an impression of substantial volume and geometric structure with a sense of grace and a rhythmic flow of form.

1. Siena and Pisa, to 1315. 2. Siena and Florence, 1315–1323/4. 3. Naples, 1323/4–1337.

1. SIENA AND PISA, TO 1315. Tino may have been trained in Siena by his father, the sculptor Camaino di Crescentino. During this period Giovanni Pisano was creating statues for the façade of Siena Cathedral (1284–97) that are startling for their expressive and powerful style, and an independent sculptural tradition was being formed under the influence of local Sienese painting and French Gothic art. Tino probably accompanied Giovanni Pisano to Pisa in 1297. He appears to have collaborated with him on the pulpit (1298–1301) in S Andrea, Pistoia, and was probably largely responsible for the relief of the *Three Magi*, because the ample, ponderous forms, their broad surfaces and their arrangement in planes so as to create an impression of depth are unlike Pisano's work. The first work generally attributed entirely to Tino is the altarpiece and tomb of *St Ranierus*, once in Pisa Cathedral (now Pisa, Mus. Opera Duomo). Here Tino arrived at a new solution in which the altarpiece is combined with the tomb in a unified ensemble, the sarcophagus resting on consoles above the altar and its three carved relief panels serving also as a kind of predella to the altarpiece. The reliefs resemble 'paintings of the contemporary Sienese style translated into stone relief' (Seidel), in contrast to those of Pisano. The relief fragments (1312) from the signed and dated font in Pisa Cathedral (Pisa, Mus. N. & Civ. S Matteo) and a signed statue of the *Virgin and Child* datable to 1313–14 (Turin, Mus. Civ. A. Ant.) show, however, that Tino later moved much closer to Giovanni Pisano, both in the conception of his reliefs and in his statuary.

On 12 February 1315 Tino, mentioned as Giovanni Pisano's successor as Master of the Works of Pisa Cathedral, was commissioned to erect the tomb of the *Emperor Henry VII* (*d* 1313; *see* LUXEMBOURG, (1)) in the choir of Pisa Cathedral. This work was largely completed by July 1315, when Tino suddenly left Pisa for Siena. The tomb was dismantled in 1494 and a smaller monument in the south transept was pieced together from fragments; the group of statues originally consisting of the Emperor enthroned between six advisers was placed in the Camposanto (now Pisa, Mus. Opera Duomo). According to one reconstruction (Kreytenberg, 1984) the monument was fixed to the apse wall behind and high above the free-standing altar. The base, carrying the unadorned sarcophagus, was supported at the back by massive consoles, and its front corners were carried on spiral columns. At the front of this structure, in the centre, was the recumbent effigy of the Emperor in a low death chamber flanked by reliefs, each bearing three figures; four more figures were carved on the reliefs at either end, making a total of 14 figures representing the Apostles and Evangelists. Above was a majestic baldacchino sheltering the group of statues flanking the enthroned Emperor. Even with the help of a workshop, this monument could not have been executed in the half year to July 1315, and it is therefore not surprising that the hand of a second Master is discernible. Compared with the statue of the Emperor, those of the advisers are rougher and heavier in construction, the design of the draperies is less imaginative, and the faces are plumper and more solidly modelled. Although features characteristic of Tino can certainly be recognized, and the statues are often attributed to him, it seems more likely that they were carved by another master, possibly his successor as Master of the Cathedral Works, Lupo di Francesco.

2. SIENA AND FLORENCE, 1315–1323/4. In Siena Tino immediately received the important commission for the tomb of *Cardinal Riccardo Petroni* (*see* TOMB, fig. 10), who died in Genoa in 1314 and was buried in Siena Cathedral on 17 March 1317. Standing on the tomb base, supported by massive consoles, are four figures carrying the sarcophagus, which is decorated with reliefs carved with the appearances of Christ after the Resurrection. Above the sarcophagus are two figures that hold open the curtains of a tent-like death chamber in which the effigy of the deceased lies on a bed. The death chamber is crowned by a tabernacle containing the Virgin and Child enthroned with SS Peter and Paul. The use of a baldacchino to bind the various elements together was replaced by a looser arrangement in which the components of the tomb were more freely disposed, yet still formed a harmonious, rhythmic and well-proportioned composition. The sculptures show a change in style compared to those on the tomb of *Henry VII*, the sarcophagus sculptures and the caryatid figures in particular indicating Tino's mastery of the Sienese formal vocabulary, characterized by a soft yet vigorous modelling, a serene composure in pose and bearing and by the rhythmic flow of the draperies. This change is to be explained less by a direct study of Sienese sculpture than by the decisive influence of Simone Martini. These characteristics are even more evident in the three monumental statues of *Apostles*, which Tino may have contributed *c.* 1317–18 to a cycle for the nave of Siena Cathedral (Siena, Mus. Opera Duomo, Cripta delle Statue). He may also have at least participated in the creation of the shrine of S Bartolo (1317–18) for S Agostino in San Gimignano, but only a few fragments survive.

Tino di Camaino was active in Florence from the autumn of 1318 to the end of 1319. In Santa Croce he erected the tomb of *Gastone della Torre*, Patriarch of Aquileia, who had died in Florence in 1318 ; this was dismantled in 1566 (fragments in Florence, Mus. Opera Santa Croce; Bargello; Pal. Vecchio; Frankfurt am Main, Liebieghaus). He probably also produced the modest tomb in S Maria Maggiore for a member of the Barucci family, who were the patrons of the Patriarch's tomb, and perhaps executed a third tomb, from which only a caryatid figure

(Florence, Fond. Romano) and two angels from the death chamber (London, V&A) survive. The decoration of the sarcophagus of the *della Torre* monument suggests that Tino had received instructions from the patron to model the tomb on that of *Cardinal Petroni* in Siena, although according to one reconstruction (Kreytenberg, 1979) Tino made several significant modifications to this design. The death chamber over the sarcophagus resembled a shrine more than a tent, and the group of statues above, representing the presentation of the deceased by angels to the Virgin and Child (see fig. 1), was framed not by a small tripartite tabernacle but by a large baldacchino that rested on the console platform, enclosing the ensemble. Compared to the *Petroni* tomb, the *della Torre* monument was more architectonic in design, but although its sculptures are stylistically related to those in Siena, the reliefs show a change in conception. While the figures in the Sienese reliefs stand or recline on the lower border of the frame in front of a plain, flat background, here a floor formed of clods of earth gives the illusion of an independent space

1. Tino di Camaino: *Virgin and Child*, probably from the tomb of *Gastone della Torre* (*d* 1318), marble, h. 780 mm (Florence, Museo Nazionale del Bargello)

in front of the figures. This move to an illusionistic rather than a physical representation of space was accompanied, however, by a slight flatness and loss of solidity in the figures.

For the first nine months of 1320 Tino di Camaino appears in the accounts of the Cathedral Works in Siena, although the nature of his work there is unknown. It is possible that the circular reliefs that formed part of the shrine of S Ottaviano in Volterra Cathedral (Volterra, Mus. Dioc. A. Sacra; Raleigh, NC Mus. A.), which are based on those of the shrine of S Bartolo in San Gimignano, date from this period. Tino probably returned to Florence in October 1320 in order to erect the tomb of *Bishop Antonio d'Orso* on the interior west wall of the new cathedral (the Bishop was buried in the tomb on 18 July 1321). Much of the tomb, which is signed, is preserved *in situ* and comprises a base supported on consoles, a sarcophagus above borne by lions, and the seated figure of the deceased on top of the sarcophagus. The dead Bishop may originally have been seated on a throne under a small canopy, which would have provided the setting for a monumental representation of the upward journey of his soul (flanking angels in Florence, Torrigiani priv. col.; central portion untraced); this structure would have been surrounded by a baldacchino to tie the ensemble together (Kreytenberg, 1979). The poet Francesco da Barberino, executor of the Bishop's will, had an influence on the design and programme of the tomb, the themes of which were death and both personal and universal judgement. The reliefs in the spandrels of the supports represent the Triumph of Death, and the sarcophagus relief depicts personal judgement, which takes place at the moment of death: the dead man, kneeling, is commended by the Virgin to Christ, beside whom stands St John the Baptist; on either side of this central group are angels and saints. The unique motif of the deceased sitting under a baldacchino awaiting Resurrection and the relief of the soul borne by angels must refer to the separation of body and soul after death. The gable of the larger baldacchino would have alluded to the Last Judgement. In the *d'Orso* tomb reliefs Tino succeeded in recapturing that sense of solidity of form that had been lost in his attempts to represent space in the reliefs of the *della Torre* monument. After the completion of the Bishop's tomb he executed a number of closely related sculptures: the statue of *Charity* (Florence, Mus. Bardini), of unknown provenance, a statue of a monk (once in Berlin but destr.) and a figure in adoration (Florence, Fond. Romano), the last two works suggesting that he made a fifth tomb in Florence. Finally, in 1322–3, he carved three life-size statues for each of the three portals of the baptistery in Florence, a few fragments of which survive (Florence, Mus. Opera Duomo).

3. NAPLES, 1323/4–1337. Tino di Camaino probably went to Naples towards the end of 1323 or early in 1324, although he is not documented there until May 1325. This change of residence had profound consequences for him, as can be seen in his earliest works there: the tombs of *Catherine of Austria* in S Lorenzo Maggiore and *Mary of Hungary* (*see* NAPLES, fig. 4) in S Maria Donnaregina, both of whom had died in the spring of 1323. The tomb of *Catherine of Austria* is free-standing, set between the piers

of the choir arcade; the sarcophagus is carried by two piers with allegorical figures, and two saints stand at both head and foot of the recumbent effigy, the whole being covered by a large baldacchino. The tomb of *Mary of Hungary* (see fig. 2) is set against a wall; the sarcophagus is supported by caryatid figures beneath a death chamber with recumbent effigy, and the ensemble is crowned by the Virgin and Child and other figures under a monumental baldacchino, an arrangement that became the prototype for many subsequent tombs. Simpler versions of the tomb of *Mary of Hungary* are to be seen in the monuments for *Charles, Duke of Calabria* (*d* 1328) and his second wife *Mary of Valois* (*d* 1331) in S Chiara, Naples. In the artistic environment of Naples, Tino di Camaino adopted the highly prized, polychrome decorative style of Roman Cosmati work and attempted to combine it with his own, Tuscan style. The sculptures of his last period do not show any new creative impulse, however, and they have been called, not unfairly, a 'weak epilogue'. The proportions of the figures are more elongated, the modelling harder, the drapery more angular and the facial features more schematic. In his last years he was largely occupied with designing and directing royal building projects, for example the construction of the Castello di S Elmo, the enlargement

2. Tino di Camaino: tomb of *Mary of Hungary*, marble, *c.* 1325–6 (Naples, S Maria Donnaregina)

of the arsenal, a harbour extension and the erection of the Certosa di S Martino (completed 1337).

BIBLIOGRAPHY

E. Carli: *Tino di Camaino scultore* (Florence, 1934)
W. R. Valentiner: *Tino di Camaino* (Paris, 1935)
O. Morisani: *Tino di Camaino a Napoli* (Naples, 1945)
G. Brunetti: 'Note sul soggiorno fiorentino di Tino', *Commentari*, iii (1952), pp. 97–107
——: 'Two Reliefs from the Orso Monument', *A. Q.* [Detroit], xvii (1954), pp. 135–8
W. R. Valentiner: 'Tino di Camaino in Florence', *A. Q.* [Detroit], xvii (1954), pp. 117–32
L. Becherucci and G. Brunetti: *Il Museo dell'Opera del Duomo a Firenze*, i (Milan, 1969), pp. 228–31
G. Previtali: 'Un'arca del 1272 ed il sepolcro di Bruno Beccuti in Santa Maria Maggiore di Firenze', *Studi di storia dell'arte in onore di Valerio Mariani* (Naples, 1971), pp. 81–9
M. Seidel: 'Studien zu Giovanni di Balduccio und Tino di Camaino', *Städel-Jb.*, v (1975), pp. 37–84
K. Bauch: *Das mittelalterliche Grabbild* (Berlin, 1976), pp. 169–72
N. Dan: 'Su un capolavoro tinesco del Museo del Bargello', *Michelangelo*, vi/21 (1977), pp. 19–28
——: 'Ricostruzione della tomba di Arrigo VII di Tino di Camaino', *Michelangelo*, vi/22 (1977), pp. 24–37
——: 'Intorno alla tomba d'Orso di Tino di Camaino', *Annu. Ist. Giappon. Cult. Roma*, xiv (1977/8), pp. 45–77
G. Kreytenberg: 'Giovanni Pisano oder Tino di Camaino', *Jb. Berlin. Mus.*, xx (1978), pp. 29–38
E. Carli: *Il Duomo di Siena* (Siena, 1979), pp. 56–8
G. Kreytenberg: 'Tino di Camaino Florentiner Grabmäler', *Städel-Jb.*, vii (1979), pp. 33–60
N. Dan: 'Tino di Camaino: Le colonne tortili di Pisa e di Londra', *Prospettiva* [Florence], xx (1980), pp. 16–26
G. Kreytenberg: 'Das Marmorbildwerk der Fundatrix Ettalensis', *Wittelsbach und Bayern*, i/1 (Munich, 1980), pp. 445–52
N. Dan: *Ommaggio al VII centenario della nascita di Tino di Camaino* (Florence, 1981)
G. Kreytenberg: 'Fragments of an Altar of St Bartholomew by Tino di Camaino in Pisa Cathedral', *Burl. Mag.*, cxxiv/951 (1982), pp. 349–53
N. Dan: *La tomba di Arrigo VII di Tino di Camaino e il rinascimento* (Florence, 1983)
——: 'Riconsiderazioni sul periodo pisano di Tino di Camaino', *Annu. Ist. Giappon. Cult. Roma*, xix (1983–4), pp. 7–58
G. Kreytenberg: 'Das Grabmal von Kaiser Heinrich VII. in Pisa', *Mitt. Ksthist. Inst. Florenz*, xxviii (1984), pp. 33–64
E. Carli: 'Giovanni Pisano e Tino di Camaino', *Il Museo dell'Opera del Duomo di Pisa* (Milan, 1986), pp. 83–101
G. Kreytenberg: *Tino di Camaino* (Florence, 1986)
——: 'Tino di Camaino: Frammento dell'arca di San Bartolo', *Capolavori e restauri* (exh. cat., Florence, Pal. Vecchio, 1986), pp. 94–5
——: *Die Werke von Tino di Camaino* (Frankfurt am Main, 1987)
——: 'Tino di Camaino: Madonna col Bambino, Anghiari', *Scultura dipinta: Maestri di legname e pittori a Siena, 1250–1450* (exh. cat., Siena, Pin. N., 1987), pp. 42–5
——: 'Zum gotischen Grabmal des heiligen Bartolus von Tino di Camaino in der Augustinerkirche von San Gimignano', *Pantheon*, xlvi (1988), pp. 13–25

G. KREYTENBERG

Tinsel print. *See under* FLOCK AND TINSEL PRINTS.

Tintore, Simone del (*b* Lucca, 7 May 1630; *d* Lucca, 16 Feb 1708). Italian painter. He trained at the painting academy opened in Lucca by Pietro Paolini in the mid-17th century and was acknowledged to be an excellent painter of still-lifes. He bequeathed to his third wife, Caterina del Testore, 13 paintings, almost all of them of religious subjects, which may represent evidence of a still unknown aspect of Simone's painting. There are numerous records of still-lifes by him in collections in Lucca: fruit, fungi, flowers, animals, fish and kitchens are among the most common subjects. Attempts to recreate his oeuvre were inspired by a *Still-life with Mushrooms and Cabbage* (priv. col., see 1960 exh. cat., pl. 57), which has an old inscription with the name of the painter on the back of the canvas. On the basis of that picture, Gregori (1964 exh. cat.) also attributed to Simone two *Still-lifes with Fruit and Vegetables* (both Milan, Castello Sforzesco), one of which bears the initials ST, which had previously been attributed to Tommaso Salini. The same exhibition (Naples, 1964) contained two still-lifes with the monogram ST and the date 1645 (both Lucca, Mazzarosa priv. col.), and there is also another similarly monogrammed painting, dated 1671, depicting a *Still-life with Animals and Fruit* (Milan, priv. col., see Gregori in 1964 exh. cat.). A more complicated painting, *Two Figures in a Landscape with Animals, Fruit and Vegetables* (see Salerno, p. 284), was identified by Salerno (1984), who advanced the hypothesis that the works of Bernardo Strozzi provided Simone with an early source of inspiration.

BIBLIOGRAPHY

Mostra dei tesori segreti delle case fiorentine (exh. cat., Florence, Pal. Borghese, 1960), p. 34
G. Maggi: 'Attualità della natura morta', *Ant. Viva*, 1 (1962), pp. 9–13
La natura morta italiana (exh. cat., Naples, Pal. Reale, 1964), pp. 86–9
C. del Bravo: 'Lettere sulla natura morta', *An. Scu. Norm. Sup. U. Pisa*, 3rd ser., iv/4 (1974), pp. 1565–91
L. Salerno: *La natura morta italiana* (Rome, 1984), pp. 79–85
F. Porzio, ed.: *La natura morta in Italia* (Milan, 1989)

FRANCO MORO

Tintoretto [Robusti]. Italian family of painters and draughtsmen. They were active in Venice, where the career of (1) Jacopo Tintoretto spanned the mid- to late 16th century. Criticized for his unorthodox professional practices, Jacopo developed a style that was highly idiosyncratic and worked with astonishing rapidity. By 1553 he had married Faustina, daughter of Marco Episcopi (or dei Vescovi), a prominent figure in the Scuola Grande di S Marco in Venice. Three of their eight children, (2) Marietta Tintoretto, (3) Domenico Tintoretto and Marco Tintoretto (1561–1637), became artists and were among the many assistants in their father's busy workshop. Marietta, though her career is only scantily documented, seems to have specialized in portrait painting. Domenico adopted his father's style and assisted him on some of his most prestigious commissions, such as that for decorations in the Doge's Palace. He also received several independent commissions, but after Jacopo's death his painting declined.

(1) Jacopo Tintoretto (*b* Venice, 1519; *d* Venice, 31 May 1594). He was the most prolific painter working in Venice in the later 16th century and is recorded away from his native city only in 1580 in connection with a commission for the ruling Gonzaga family at Mantua. In his early career he struggled to achieve recognition, which finally came in 1548 with a work commissioned by the Scuola Grande di S Marco. In his mature years he worked extensively on decorations for the Doge's Palace (*see* VENICE, §IV, 6(ii)) and for the meeting-house of the Scuola Grande di S Rocco, on which he was occupied from 1564 until 1567 and between 1575 and 1588 (*see* VENICE, §V, 4). In addition to his religious and mythological works, Jacopo also painted many portraits of prominent Venetians. He was, however, never wholly accepted by the leading aristocratic families that dominated Venetian cultural life, and to some extent this hindered his patronage. The swift, abbreviated style that characterizes much of his work caused controversy among contemporaries, and the lack of conventional finish was seen by some as merely a result of carelessness or overhasty execution. Despite a long and busy career, Jacopo Tintoretto apparently never became rich, and in 1600 his widow submitted a plea to the Venetian State for financial help to support her family.

I. Life and work. II. Working methods and technique. III. Character and personality. IV. Critical reception and posthumous reputation.

I. Life and work.

1. Before 1548. 2. 1548–55. 3. 1556–74. 4. 1575 and after.

1. BEFORE 1548. His father, Giovanni Battista Robusti, was a cloth-dyer, a common and respectable occupation in Renaissance Venice. Nonetheless, the Robusti do not appear to have enjoyed higher citizen (*cittadino originario*) status. Jacopo's adopted nickname, meaning 'the little dyer', advertised rather than concealed his artisan background. The details of Tintoretto's artistic training are not known, although early sources report that he was expelled from Titian's workshop after a short period, as a result either of the jealousy (Ridolfi, 1642) or incomprehension (Boschini, 1660) of his master. The marked distance from

Titian's chromatic idiom in Tintoretto's earliest works (e.g. the *Holy Family with St Jerome and the Procurator Girolamo Marcello*, 1537–40; ex-priv. col., Lucerne, see Pallucchini and Rossi, p. 292; and the *Holy Family with SS ?Jerome, ?Elizabeth, John, Catherine and Francis*, 1540; London, priv. col., see Pallucchini and Rossi, p. 295) suggests that these romanticizing elaborations have a factual basis. The linear and dynamic values of the paintings indicate that Tintoretto was apprenticed to an artist working in Venice, but influenced by central Italian Mannerism. Bonifazio de' Pitati, Paris Bordone and Andrea Schiavone have variously been suggested as his teachers.

Jacopo Tintoretto was practising as an independent master as early as 1539. Ridolfi mentioned his collaboration with Andrea Schiavone and other 'painters of lesser fortune' in the production of cassone panels. While the connection with Schiavone is certainly important on a formal level, it is also indicative of Tintoretto's lack of artistic standing at this stage. The sets of cassone panels attributable to Tintoretto (e.g. those depicting six scenes from the *Old Testament*, *c.* 1543–4; Vienna, Ksthist. Mus.; see fig. 1) are characterized by a rapid, rough technique in which all form is radically abbreviated. This visual shorthand was, to some extent, an established feature of cassone

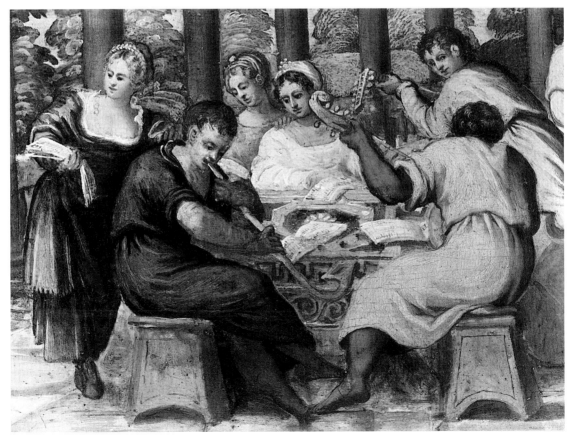

1. Jacopo Tintoretto: *Belshazzar's Feast* (detail), oil on panel, 290×1560 mm, *c.* 1543–4 (Vienna, Kunsthistorisches Museum); one of a series of cassone panels depicting scenes from the *Old Testament*

painting in 16th-century Venice and reflected the economic strictures governing the production of this type of work. Tintoretto's introduction of an analogous technique into the realm of monumental painting distinguished him from his contemporaries.

Tintoretto's *prestezza* (rapid, abbreviated technique) is prominent in the sequence of large religious narrative paintings, including *Christ among the Doctors* (*c.* 1540–42; Milan, Mus. Duomo), the *Adoration of the Shepherds* (*c.* 1544–5; two versions, Cambridge, Fitzwilliam; Verona, Castelvecchio), the *Supper at Emmaus* (*c.* 1545–6; Budapest, Mus. F.A.) and *Christ and the Adulteress* (*c.* 1546–7; Dresden, Gemäldegal. Alte Meister). These *laterali* (horizontal paintings) were probably made to hang on the side walls of Venetian chapels, and Tintoretto's art is at its most progressive in his early period within this relatively new picture type in Venice. These works typically feature active figure groups, set in a forward plane to maximize an effect of formal monumentality and narrative intensity. The figures are shown in dynamic, twisting or foreshortened poses reminiscent of contemporary Mannerist painting but typically have more mass and energy and lack the courtly elegance of, for example, Parmigianino or Francesco Salviati. The earlier compositions are symmetrical, with the protagonists placed centrally. In subsequent works, such as *Christ Washing the Feet of the Disciples* (*c.* 1547–8; Madrid, Prado), the insistent off-centre perspective reflects Tintoretto's concern to make his painting respond to its intended location. It originally hung on the right wall of the presbytery at S Marcuola, Venice, and the perspective assumes that the viewer is positioned to the right, that is, in the nave. The central dramatic exchange between Christ and the Apostle Peter is, accordingly, placed at the extreme right of the pictorial field, at the point nearest the congregation.

Although Tintoretto produced as many as 11 façade frescoes in Venice (L. Foscari, *Affreschi esterni a Venezia* (Milan, 1936), pp. 61–7, 132), knowledge of this activity is limited to the surviving fragments from the Palazzo (Ca') Soranzo (1540–45; Venice, Cojazzi priv. col., see Pallucchini and Rossi, p. 299) and some 18th-century engravings by Anton Maria Zanetti (ii) of the paintings on this building and on the Ca' Gussoni. Nonetheless, the evidence again suggests a concern with formal monumentality at the expense of more traditional Venetian decorative and chromatic values. The Ca' Gussoni frescoes were closely based on Michelangelo's sculptures of *Dawn* and *Dusk* in the Medici Chapel in S Lorenzo, Florence, and it is likely that Tintoretto owned small models of these works. A group of early drawings after the Medici figures (*Day*, Oxford, Christ Church Lib. and Paris, Louvre; *Dusk*, U. London, Courtauld Inst. Gals and Florence, Uffizi) and other sculptures by Michelangelo (*Samson and the Philistines*, eight sheets, including Cambridge, MA, Fogg, and Berlin, Kupferstichkab.; *St Damian*, Sarasota, FL, Ringling Mus. A.) confirms Tintoretto's early interest in the Florentine artist. His complementary concern with Classical and contemporary sculpture is stressed by early sources (Borghini; Ridolfi, 1642; Boschini, 1660).

When Tintoretto was commissioned to produce paintings of a more mainstream type, his style was comparatively timid. The *Apollo and Marsyas* (1545; Hartford, CT,

Wadsworth Atheneum) is probably identifiable with one of the two ceiling paintings commissioned by Pietro Aretino for his house and for which he thanked Tintoretto in a letter of 15 February 1545. The work is relatively conventional, as are Tintoretto's earliest portraits, which typically utilize schemes that recall Titian (e.g. the *Portrait of a Man Aged 25*, 1545; London, Hampton Court, Royal Col.). Their small size and non-official character (e.g. the head and shoulders *Portrait of a Bearded Man*, 1546; Florence, Uffizi; and the *Portrait of a Gentleman*, 1546–8; Madrid, Prado) indicate the limited social range of Tintoretto's portrait clientele at this stage.

Tintoretto painted very few altarpieces before 1548. The conservative *Christ Blessing with SS Mark and Gall* (1540–45; Venice, Mus. Dioc. S. Apollonia) and *St Demetrius with Zuan Pietro Ghisi as Donor* (1544–7; Venice, S Felice) feature static figures set in the traditional vertical space. Ridolfi mentioned the artist's exhibition of ready-made paintings at the Rialto, a common strategy for struggling painters. Tintoretto did, however, gain early support from the smaller, non-noble confraternities. The *Presentation in the Temple* (1540–43; Venice, S Maria del Carmelo) may have been commissioned by the Scuola dell'Arte dei Pescivendoli (the trade guild of the fishmongers), and a frieze (destr.) in the meeting-house of the Scuola dell'Arte dei Sartori (the trade guild of the tailors) also dates from this period.

In 1547 Tintoretto painted his earliest known version of the *Last Supper* (Venice, S Marcuola), a subject he depicted at least eight times during his career. With the exception of the versions for the Scuola di S Rocco (1578–81) and the Benedictines of S Giorgio Maggiore (1592–4), these paintings were commissioned by parish-based Scuole del Sacramento. These small, socially humble confraternities were committed to the upkeep of the reserved sacrament. The paintings they typically commissioned were *laterali* to decorate either the chapels where the sacrament was kept or the Scuola's church meeting-place. The S Marcuola *Last Supper* follows established models and has a symmetrical composition, with the table parallel to the picture plane. However, the newly popular location—in a small parish church—is reflected in the figure types of the apostles. Tintoretto's rapid brushwork emphasizes the rough textures of their drapery, flesh and hair. Comparisons with Leonardo's prototype (1494–8; Milan, S Maria delle Grazie) show that Tintoretto de-individualized the apostles in order to stress their shared social and spiritual characteristics. This, like the limits set on the apostles' vocabulary of expression and gesture, allowed the painter to create a convincing image of popular religious experience.

2. 1548–55. The canvas of *St Mark Rescuing the Slave* (1547–8; Venice, Accad.; see fig. 2), commissioned from Tintoretto by the Scuola Grande di S Marco, was initially rejected and sent back to the painter. This reaction suggests the unprecedented nature of the image in the Venetian tradition, and it was this work that finally brought the artist recognition throughout Venice. Every element in the picture serves to amplify the subject's dramatic and emotional impact. Full bodily movement replaces facial expression as the prime indicator of individual response,

2. Jacopo Tintoretto: *St Mark Rescuing the Slave*, oil on canvas, 4.16×5.44 m, 1547–8 (Venice, Galleria dell'Accademia)

while different incidents within the story are shown simultaneously so as to reinforce narrative meaning. In *St Roch Healing the Plague Victims* (1549; Venice, S Rocco), commissioned by the rival Scuola Grande di S Rocco, Tintoretto used chiaroscuro for the first time as an important compositional device. The distribution of light draws attention to the sick at the expense of St Roch himself, and while this inversion of accepted pictorial convention has formal precedents in central Italian Mannerism, here its significance is expressive and ascetic rather than arbitrary and aesthetic. More generally, the essentially communicative and moral intention of Tintoretto's formal manipulations distance his work from contemporary Mannerism.

Tintoretto's work in the following years has been described as 'an expression of orthodoxy' (Tietze), and a new deference to established pictorial values in Venice is already noticeable in, for example, *St Martial in Glory with SS Peter and Paul* (1548–9; Venice, S Marziale), which uses a conservative pyramidal design. In the paintings decorating the organ shutters at the church of the Madonna dell'Orto, Venice (outer doors: the *Presentation of the Virgin*, 1552–3; inner doors: the *Martyrdom of St Paul* and *St Peter's Vision of the Cross*, 1556), glowing reds and golds replace the cool colours that predominate in earlier works. The *Presentation of the Virgin* is also typical of this phase

in its explicit reference to Titian's well-known version of the subject (1538; Venice, Accad.). Ridolfi's anecdote about Tintoretto's eclectic ambition to combine Michelangelo's *disegno* with Titian's *colore* is relevant only in this period. Paintings such as the *Original Sin* and *Cain Killing Abel* (both 1550–53; Venice, Accad.), from the cycle of paintings commissioned by the Scuola della Trinità, demonstrate a continuing Michelangelesque interest in the nude in movement, but the figures are set in Venetian-style landscapes that bind them within a naturalistic ambience of light and air.

A group of cabinet paintings with mythological or apocryphal subjects (e.g. *Susanna and the Elders*, 1550–55; several versions, including Paris, Louvre, and Vienna, Ksthist. Mus.; the *Rescue of Arsinoë*, 1554–6; Dresden, Gemäldegal. Alte Meister; *Venus, Vulcan and Mars*, 1550–55; Munich, Alte Pin.) also draws on established Venetian models. The female protagonists typically assume complex, diagonal postures, abandoning the traditional arrangement of form in order to accord with the underlying axis of the picture frame, and the paintings are generally highly finished and detailed, employing bright and varied colours. Tintoretto's portraits from this period are characterized by precise individualization, bold chiaroscuro and the suggestion of rapid movement (e.g. the *Portrait of a Man Aged 35*, 1553; Vienna, Ksthist. Mus.). Portraits of important patricians (e.g. that of the *Soranzo Family*, *c.* 1550; Milan, Castello Sforzesco, and *Nicolò Priuli*, *c.* 1549; Venice, Ca' d'Oro) testify to the increasing social range of his patronage.

By 1553 Tintoretto had contributed *Pope Alexander III Excommunicating Barbarossa* (*c.* 1553; destr. 1577) to the prestigious Alexander cycle in the Sala del Maggiore Consiglio in the Doge's Palace and assumed the task of supplying votive pictures for retiring officials of the Magistrato del Sale at the Palazzo dei Camerlenghi (e.g. *St Louis of Toulouse with St George and the Princess*, 1552; Venice, Accad.). Paolo Veronese, however, dominated the field of official commissions at this time, and his success elicited a prompt response from Tintoretto, who, in a series of small ceiling paintings (*Susanna and the Elders*, *Esther and Ahasuerus*, *Judith and Holofernes*, *Solomon and the Queen of Sheba*, *Joseph and Potiphar's Wife* and the

Finding of Moses, all *c.* 1554–5; Madrid, Prado) and in several portraits (e.g. the *Portrait of a Bearded Man*, *c.* 1553–5; Montreal, Mus. F.A.), showed his willingness to experiment with the newcomer's decorative use of colour. Tintoretto's interest was not merely aesthetic, however, and Ridolfi reported that he 'stole' Veronese's commission for an altarpiece for the church of the Crociferi by promising to paint in his rival's manner. The resulting painting, the *Assumption of the Virgin* (*c.* 1554–5; Venice, Accad.), distinctly recalls the work of Veronese in style, employing opaque patches of strong local colour to connect planes and deny movement into depth.

3. 1556–74. In the later 1550s Tintoretto renewed his experiments with pictorial space, as can be seen in a number of portraits that combine complex, foreshortened architectural settings and landscape backgrounds, for

3. Jacopo Tintoretto: *Finding of the Body of St Mark*, oil on canvas, 4.05×4.05 m, 1562–6 (Milan, Accademia di Belle Arti di Brera)

example the *Portrait of a Soldier Aged 30* (1555–60; Vienna, Ksthist. Mus.). In the *Pool of Bethesda* (1559; Venice, Scu. Grande S Rocco), the compressed space becomes a metaphor for the sufferings of the crowd of lepers who struggle within it. The painting demonstrates Tintoretto's increasing interest in large-scale compositions in which individual form is subordinated to the broader sequences, where the overall sense is articulated by a reduced number of key movements or gestures. In the enormous choir paintings (*c*. 1560–63) at the Madonna dell'Orto this devaluation of individual form is implemented through chiaroscuro. In the *Last Judgement*, from this cycle, free-floating figures are arranged in contrasting subgroups of twos or threes, with broken strips of light closely following their forms. Their illuminated movements thus act as directional pointers, encouraging the eye to move quickly across them.

In the cycle of paintings commissioned by Tommaso Rangone for the Scuola Grande di S Marco in 1562—the *Finding of the Body of St Mark* (Milan, Brera; see fig. 3), the *Removal of the Body of St Mark* and *St Mark Saving the Saracen* (both Venice, Accad.)—space is created solely to enhance the scenic or dramatic effect. In both the *Finding* and the *Removal* the linear logic of the emptied, boxlike perspective vistas is undermined by an irrational play of light and shade. Both paintings suggest the simultaneous existence of different levels of reality through the use of a range of pictorial techniques. The detailed modelling of the foreground group in the *Removal* contrasts strikingly with the sketchily rendered piazza and the fleeing Alexandrians beyond, while in the *Finding*, the most commanding physical presence is that of the visionary figure of St Mark, whose miraculous appearance brings about a radical confusion of material and spiritual realities.

Tintoretto further developed this visionary-epic style of religious narrative in the paintings (1565–7) for the Sala dell'Albergo of the Scuola Grande di S Rocco and in such other Scuola paintings as the *Descent into Limbo* and the *Crucifixion* (both 1568; Venice, S Cassiano). Vasari reported that Tintoretto gained the initial commission for the Sala dell'Albergo paintings only by 'illegal' means: he donated and installed the ceiling canvas of *St Roch in Glory* (1564; *in situ*), so undermining the proposed competition. The painting's overt reference to Titian's famous *Assumption of the Virgin* (1516–18; S Maria Gloriosa dei Frari; *see* ALTARPIECE, fig. 4) perhaps reflects an attempt to appeal to the conservative tastes of the members of the Scuola. In the following year Tintoretto was admitted to membership of the confraternity and thereafter played an active role in its organizational and devotional life. The security of his position seems to have encouraged the experimental style in such subsequent paintings as the *Crucifixion* (1565; *see* VENICE, fig. 28), the *Road to Calvary*, the *Ecce homo* and *Christ before Pilate* (all 1566–7; *in situ*). The composition of the enormous *Crucifixion* is conceived as a flattened circle, arranged around the iconic figure of Christ. The picture holds in suspension different realities: the naturalistic depiction of physical effort in the groups raising the thieves' crosses contrasts with the spiritual effort embodied in the hieratic group of mourners at the centre. The combination of idealized pathos with raw artisan action allows the painting the socially inclusive,

epic quality that became a feature of Tintoretto's subsequent work at S Rocco.

In this period Tintoretto also received further commissions from the Scuole del Sacramento for paintings of the *Last Supper*. In the S Felice version (1559; Paris, St-François-Xavier) one edge of the table continues to lie parallel to the picture plane, but its form recedes into depth, with Christ removed to the further end. Despite the apparent symmetry of the composition, important concessions are made to the painting's location—on the left wall of the Cappella Maggiore—and to its patrons. The gesture of the apostle at the foreground left facilitates visual entry from that point, and the traditionally sacred space is used to include contemporary portraits of the Scuola's Guardian (erased probably as early as June 1560; Pallucchini and Rossi, i, p. 179), Scrivener and Vicar. In the S Simeon Grande painting (*c*. 1561–3), the asymmetry is much more radical, with the table set at an oblique angle to the picture plane and Christ removed from his traditional central position. In the versions at S Trovaso (*c*. 1564–6; see fig. 4) and S Polo (*c*. 1570) Tintoretto most radically broke with the compositional frontality that traditionally reinforced in the Last Supper the quality of a hieratic and timeless icon.

In the S Trovaso painting, made to hang on the right wall of the chapel, the shift in compositional axis is undertaken in accordance with an imagined viewer positioned obliquely to the picture plane, at the chapel entrance. This subjectivizes the image, suggesting that the composition unravels as an extension of the observer's own sight line. The Last Supper is set in a dingy basement, crowded with apostles who are shown less as biblical patriarchs than as contemporary Venetians of the lower classes. This reflects the expected social scope of the painting's viewing public. However, other planes of reality are also suggested. The artisan apostles are set in the foreground, nearest to the transition point between fictive and real space. As the eye moves into depth, gestures, responses and figure types are increasingly removed from these naturalistic coordinates. In the S Polo version the intrusion of the outside world into the hieratically fixed space of the Last Supper is again emphasized, by the inclusion of a servant, two beggars, a donor portrait and a landscape. The centrifugal composition explodes outwards from the dynamic central figure of Christ, forcing the viewer's attention back to the subsidiary figures towards the edges of the picture.

In the context of patrician patronage Tintoretto's mature style was very different. After the election of Doge Girolamo Priuli (*reg* 1559–67), who was a friend of Rangone, Tintoretto's career as a state painter flourished. He took over from Titian the role of producing ducal portraits (e.g. *Doge Girolamo Priuli*, *c*. 1559; two versions, Malibu, CA, Getty Mus.; Detroit, MI, Inst. A.) and was subsequently commissioned to produce a whole range of official imagery. Tintoretto's first ceiling decoration for the Venetian State, the canvases depicting *Doge Girolamo Priuli with ?St Mark, Peace and Justice*, surrounded by four *Old Testament* scenes and the *Seasons* (*c*. 1564–5, Venice, Doge's Pal., Sala dell'Atrio Quadrato), is characterized by a tightness of handling and high finish that combine with

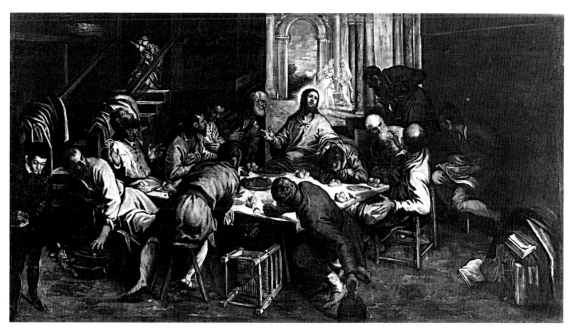

4. Jacopo Tintoretto: *Last Supper*, oil on canvas, 2.21×4.13 m, *c.* 1564–6 (Venice, S Trovaso)

strong local coloration to generate a primarily decorative effect. A similar restraint is evident in such official votive pictures as the *Virgin and Child with SS Sebastian, Mark and Theodore, Venerated by Three Treasurers* (*c.* 1567; Venice, Accad.), which utilize orderly, decorous compositions and where relatively static forms are placed parallel to the picture plane.

The style of Tintoretto's mature portraits is as varied as that in his narrative paintings. The public context of the official portraits (e.g. *Doge Pietro Loredan*, *c.* 1567–70; two versions, Melbourne, N.G. Victoria; Budapest, Mus. F.A.) precluded expressive experimentation, but the portraits of figures from the Venetian intellectual–artistic milieu (e.g. *Jacopo Sansovino*, *c.* 1566; Florence, Uffizi) are less formal, and their style and technique are adapted to the personality and interests of the sitter. Nonetheless, the public–private distinction increasingly broke down. In the *Venetian Senator* (*c.* 1570; Lille, Mus. B.-A.), the focusing of concentration on the face and the simplicity of pose and setting newly suggest an inwardness that stands in expressive contrast to the sitter's public office.

4. 1575 AND AFTER. Tintoretto's most prolific period was the final two decades of his life. In addition to his extensive work at the Scuola Grande di S Rocco (1575–88), he played a major role in the redecoration of the Doge's Palace after the fires of 1574 and 1577. The range of his patronage also broadened following Titian's death in 1576, with commissions from the courts at Prague (*c.* 1577–8), Mantua (1578–80) and the Escorial (1583 and 1587). While such foreign expansion may have been an attempt to take on Titian's mantle as Venetian painter to the aristocracies of Europe, Tintoretto's production of religious paintings, mythologies and portraits for a local clientele did not diminish.

(i) The meeting-house of the Scuola Grande di S Rocco. (ii) Other works.

(i) The meeting-house of the Scuola Grande di S Rocco. Following his work (1565–7) on the Sala dell'Albergo, Tintoretto was commissioned to decorate the rest of the meeting-house in a piecemeal fashion. The artist himself played an active role in generating a demand for paintings and developing an iconographic programme. His series of petitions (July 1575–March 1577) offering to provide paintings for the Sala Superiore ceiling at a greatly discounted price culminated with a proposal (Nov 1577) to execute paintings for the walls and any further work the Scuola might require. He undertook to produce three paintings a year in return for an annuity of 100 ducats. The production of cheap paintings at speed played an important role in determining the style and technique subsequently employed. The irregular development of the commission meant that the iconographic programme underwent a series of reorientations. It was apparently Tintoretto's suggestion that the initial ceiling painting should show the *Brazen Serpent* (1575–6), an Old Testament type of the *Crucifixion* that could stand as an introduction to the Sala dell'Albergo *Passion* cycle. The large ceiling canvases that followed allude to the Christian Sacraments of Baptism (1577; *Moses Striking the Rock*) and the Eucharist (1577; *Gathering of the Manna*). The placing of the latter nearest to the altar, however, suggested a new longitudinal emphasis orientated away from the Sala dell'Albergo. The paintings feature complex, foreshortened figure groups silhouetted against a broken, flickering light that emanates from a supernatural source deep within the picture. Space is arbitrary, with local recessions replacing any continuous perspective system. Landscape is reduced to a schematic minimum, with the effect of further loosening naturalistic form.

5. Jacopo Tintoretto: *Flight into Egypt*, oil on canvas, 4.22×5.79 m, 1583–7 (Venice, Scuola Grande di S Rocco, Sala Terrena)

The decision to commission paintings for the walls necessitated a further iconographic reorientation, five transversal axes being established by the correspondences between the *Old Testament* scenes on the ceiling and those from the *Life of Christ* on the walls (1578–81). The iconographic connection was reinforced by the partial repetition in the wall sequence of the compositional schemes in the central ceiling paintings. The rotating composition of the *Brazen Serpent* is broadly repeated in the *Ascension* and *Resurrection* below, while the diagonal horizon in the *Gathering of the Manna* is picked up in the related wall scenes showing the *Miracle of the Loaves and Fishes* and the *Raising of Lazarus*. Moreover, individual forms originating in the three central ceiling canvases reappear, albeit with variations, in thematically related wall scenes (e.g. God in the *Brazen Serpent* is partially repeated in the Christ of the *Ascension*).

The iconographic and formal dominance of the ceiling also has the effect of freeing the paintings on the walls from the lateral scansion traditional to narrative cycles in Venice, allowing each painting an unprecedented independence from its neighbour. In many paintings, compositional dislocation is taken to new extremes (e.g. the *Nativity* and the *Agony in the Garden*). Working in conjunction with the dominant chiaroscuro, which subdues local colour and simplifies form throughout the cycle, the episodic space subdivides each composition into distinct temporal and narrative units, isolating separate moments within the text. Thus, conventional sequential representation is replaced by narrative simultaneity, requiring the viewer to reconstruct the connecting links.

The wall scenes are, typically, heavily populated, while individual figures are radically abbreviated. Facial expression is concealed through foreshortenings and cast shadows, and the range of movements and gestures employed is relatively limited and repetitious. These formal devices negate any individuality and generate a sense, instead, of the shared material and spiritual status of those who experience Christ's miracles. In many of these works the figure of Christ, displaced from the compositional centre, occupies a secondary position towards the picture margins, while the role of the recipients of miraculous salvation is promoted (e.g. the *Pool of Bethesda* and the *Last Supper*). As in the earlier S Polo version of the *Last Supper*, that in the Sala Superiore also includes beggars, one of whom is, by a trick of perspective, placed next to Christ. An ideal of sacred poverty is a leitmotif throughout the cycle.

The prominence given to groups of the sick, poor and hungry in the wall paintings of this room was probably designed to refer to the charitable activities of the Scuola, but the pictorial inversions also suggest Tintoretto's reformist insistence on the essential equality of man in Christ. The form of Christianity conceived in the Sala Superiore overturns all social distinctions and is, in this sense, both open and popular. In keeping with this emphasis, the eight wall scenes in the Sala Terrena (July 1583–Aug 1587) stress the poverty of the Holy Family. The confused ordering of the six larger paintings suggests that the cycle was initially conceived as a history of Christ's infancy and, finally, as a *Life of the Virgin*. The *Assumption of the Virgin*, along with the smaller canvases showing *St Mary Magdalene* and *St Mary the Egyptian*, were probably late additions to the cycle (*c.* 1586–7), re-emphasizing its Marian iconography. This kind of iconographic inconsistency, found throughout the meeting-house, suggests that Tintoretto and his patrons were concerned with visual power rather than doctrinal coherence.

In the *Annunciation* visionary spirituality dynamically obtrudes into the context of artisan life, and analogous social relocations of the sacred narrative inform the *Flight into Egypt* (see fig. 5) and the *Adoration of the Magi*. Fluid variations of style and technique characterize the Sala Terrena cycle, suggesting the interpenetration of different levels of reality. The sketchy treatment of the visionary landscapes in the Marian paintings contrasts with the closely detailed naturalism of the *Flight into Egypt*. Colour and light are also manipulated with a new expressive freedom. The drained, monochromatic tones of the *Massacre of the Innocents* contrasts with the explosive golds of the *Assumption*.

The detailing of physiognomy and costume in the *Adoration of the Magi* and the *Presentation in the Temple* suggests workshop participation. However, unlike in the contemporary cycles painted for aristocratic patrons, Tintoretto's own hand remained dominant at the Scuola. In his final petition of 1577 he stressed that his work was undertaken 'to show my great love for this venerated Scuola of ours, and the devotion I have for the glorious St Roch'. His personal involvement in the life of the confraternity continued long after the decorations were complete. But concerted opposition to Tintoretto within the Scuola is recorded as late as February 1578. This may have had a basis in artistic taste and cultural position rather than private animosity. The *cittadini originarii* who dominated the Venetian Scuole typically emulated their aristocracy in artistic matters, and it seems likely that Tintoretto's assertively independent style, with its popularizing emphasis on the original communal ideals of the confraternity, was not to the taste of certain of the more socially ambitious members. In addition to the total of two painted ceilings and twenty-eight wall paintings executed for the meeting-house, Tintoretto also painted the altarpiece of the *Vision of St Roch* (1588; *in situ*).

(ii) Other works. A new degree of stylistic and technical variability is evident in Tintoretto's later work. In *laterali* for Venetian parish churches (e.g. six histories of *St Catherine*, 1582–5, Venice, Patriarcato, on deposit; *Christ Washing the Feet of the Disciples*, 1588–90, Venice, S Moisè), Tintoretto utilized a broken chiaroscuro, disjointed spatial arrangements, a limited, sombre palette and a rough surface finish. At the Doge's Palace, he developed a richly coloured decorative modification of this style, using heavy forms set in a forward plane to control spatial recession and emphasize the highly polished picture surfaces. In four political allegories depicting the *Three Graces*,

and *Mercury, Bacchus, Ariadne and Venus, Minerva Rejecting Mars* and the *Forge of Vulcan* (1577–8; Sala dell' Anticollegio), which were originally painted for the Atrio Quadrato, relief-like forms generate complex decorative patterns that are read at the picture surface. Similarly conservative stylistic modulations were exacted in the sequence of votive and ceiling paintings subsequently executed in the important State rooms of the Doge's Palace (1577, Sala delle Quattro Porte; 1579–*c.* 1582, Sala del Maggiore Consiglio; *c.* 1581–2, Sala del Collegio; *c.* 1582, Sala del Senato). The large-scale votive pictures emulate the static prototypes of Giovanni Bellini and Titian. *Doge Andrea Gritti before the Virgin and Saints* in the Sala del Collegio is broadly dependent on Titian's painting of the same subject (1531; destr. 1574). Analogous restrictions on expressive movement, volume and depth are evident in the large ceiling canvases showing *Jupiter Proclaiming Venice Queen of the Adriatic* (Sala delle Quattro Porte), the *Triumph of Doge Nicolò da Ponte* (Sala del Maggiore Consiglio) and the *Triumph of Venice as Queen of the Sea* (Sala del Senato). The lucid colour, compositional symmetries and an elegance reminiscent of Veronese in the figure types stand in sharp contrast to the energy, obscurity and instability that characterize the main ceiling paintings in the Sala Superiore at S Rocco.

Similar variations are evident in his altarpiece commissions. The *Temptation of St Anthony* (1577; Venice, S Trovaso), painted for Antonio Milledonne, Secretary to the Senate, utilizes the 'patrician' modulation of Tintoretto's style and is very close in its formal arrangement to the *Origin of the Milky Way* (*c.* 1577–8; London, N.G.), painted for Rudolf II, Holy Roman Emperor. The complex but studied contrapposto poses of the figures in the former are clearly articulated within a confined forward plane. The altarpiece depicting *St Agnes Reviving Licinio* (*c.* 1578–9; Venice, Madonna dell'Orto), commissioned by the patrician Tommaso Contarini, has been mistakenly attributed to Tintoretto's early period on account of its lucid coloration of turquoises, pinks and yellows and high surface finish. In contrast, the *Baptism* (*c.* 1580; Venice, S Silvestro), commissioned by the Scuola dell'Arte dei Peateri (trade guild of the bargemen), is a radically abbreviated composition, all detail and colour in the landscape being dissolved in an explosion of heavenly light. The chiaroscuro achieves an equivalent simplification in the figures of the two protagonists, broad masses of light and shade reducing their forms to expressive silhouettes.

When Tintoretto adopted a similarly abridged style in an altarpiece for the patrician Bonomo family at S Francesco della Vigna, Venice, his work was substituted for one by the conservative painter Francesco Santacroce (1516–84). Tintoretto's rejected painting, probably identifiable with the *Martyrdom of St Lawrence* (*c.* 1570–76; priv. col.), utilizes roughly sketched forms dissolved by an arbitrary and broken chiaroscuro, within an amorphous, irrational space. Late works such as the *Flagellation* (1585–90; Vienna, Ksthist. Mus.), the *Crowning with Thorns* (1585–90; London, priv. col., see Pallucchini and Rossi, p. 599) and *St Michael and Satan* (1585–90; Dresden, Gemäldegal. Alte Meister) are in a similar style, although their original patrons and locations are not known.

The variety of Tintoretto's late style is indicative of his relatively unimpeded movement among different classes of patrons, institutions and picture types in a desire to fulfil the maximum number of commissions. His avoidance of exclusive relationships with patrons is apparent in the lack of priority accorded to socially exalted clients. Around 1580, for example, Tintoretto himself painted the altarpiece for the Scuola dell'Arte dei Peateri but left the series of battle paintings for Guglielmo Gonzaga, 3rd Duke of Mantua, to his workshop. Titian and Veronese rarely ignored the privileges of rank in such a manner. One possible reason for Tintoretto's independent policy might lie in his continuing distance from the more fashionable sectors of the aristocratic cultural establishment in Venice and abroad. Tintoretto's expected State stipend (*sansaria*), granted in 1574, was apparently never paid, and despite his extensive employment in an official capacity during his late period, he failed to achieve a dominance comparable to Titian's in this area. Veronese was generally more successful with aristocratic patrons and won the competition (1579–82) to paint the huge *Paradise* in the Sala del Maggior Consiglio of the Doge's Palace. Documents reveal that Tintoretto worked under very restrictive conditions for the Gonzaga and, although he produced two paintings for Philip II, King of Spain (*Nativity*, 1583, Madrid, Escorial; and '*Judgement*', 1587, untraced), it was Veronese who was invited to take up a lucrative position at the Spanish court in 1585.

While both Titian and Veronese extended their private portrait clientele beyond the confines of Venetian territory, the vast majority of Tintoretto's later portraits were commissioned by local sitters to hang in public buildings. When he visited Venice, Sir Philip Sidney chose to have his portrait painted by Veronese. In his later portraits of elderly Venetian officials, Tintoretto managed to turn the constraints of their public function to artistic advantage. In those of unknown sitters in the Prado, Madrid (*c.* 1580), and the National Gallery of Ireland, Dublin (1575–80), and those of *Vincenzo Morosini* (1511–88) painted *c.* 1580 (London, N.G.; see fig. 6) and the *Procurator Alessandro Gritti* (1578–82; Barcelona, Mus. B.A. Cataluña), Tintoretto suggested a tension between personal frailty and public power, his uncompromising attention to the lined and pasty flesh of his sitters contrasting with the rich brocades and ermines denoting their high office.

Tintoretto's career ended on a note of triumph. After Veronese's death in 1588, he finally gained the coveted commission for the painting of the *Paradise* (1588–90), which Veronese had not begun, in the Doge's Palace and between 1592 and 1594, he was commissioned to produce a series of important paintings for Palladio's S Giorgio Maggiore (the *Deposition*, the *Last Supper* and the *Gathering of the Manna*; see VENICE, §IV, 2(ii)). The *Last Supper* (1592–4), in the choir, brings to a climax the series of works Tintoretto had painted of the subject. It followed the version from S Margherita (*c.* 1585; Venice, S Stefano), which combines formal elements from the S Polo and S Rocco paintings. Traditionally, depictions of the Last Supper were made for monastic refectories, where the non-liturgical context mitigated against explicit sacramental meanings. In the chapel setting, however, these could come to the fore. In Tintoretto's earlier Last Suppers (S

6. Jacopo Tintoretto: *Vincenzo Morosini*, oil on canvas, 845×515 mm, *c.* 1580 (London, National Gallery)

Trovaso, S Felice) the traditional moment of the Annunciation of the Betrayal was maintained as the central focus, but in subsequent versions (S Polo, S Rocco, S Margherita), this was replaced by the Institution of the Eucharist. At S Giorgio the swirling angels and flickering, supernatural light stress the ritual moment. As in earlier versions, the table is positioned in accordance with the oblique viewpoint of the congregation. However, its recession parallel to the altar wall now serves to enhance the painting's liturgical meaning. The table appears as an extension of the High Altar itself, while Christ and the Apostles become prototypes for the priest and the communicants. Tintoretto's final *Last Supper* is, then, not wholly representative of his earlier, popularizing versions painted for the lay Scuole del Sacramento. The shifts in emphasis, however, suggest his ability once again to modulate the style and content of his paintings according to their specific contexts.

II. Working methods and technique.

Ridolfi reported Tintoretto's practice of arranging 'little models of wax and clay' in artificially illuminated 'little houses', sometimes suspending them from strings, in order to generate compositional ideas. The use of such models was by no means peculiar to Tintoretto, but when seen in relation to the marked lack of surviving compositional drawings attributable to him, it seems likely that the technique was a particularly important one. Such compositional drawings as are known probably followed, rather than preceded, the use of stages and figurines, given their closeness to the finished paintings, as in the drawing (Berlin, Kupferstichkab.) related to *Venus, Vulcan and Mars* (1550–5; Munich, Alte Pin.). In most cases, however, Tintoretto probably bypassed this stage altogether.

The majority of the *c.* 130 sheets of drawings attributable to Tintoretto show single figures in dynamic poses, presumably made at an intermediate point, after the arrangement of the composition but before the painting stage. Most of these figure studies were produced with a specific painting in mind, the poses being repeated fairly closely in the finished work (e.g. *Two Clothed Male Figures*, Florence, Uffizi; *Clothed Male Figure*, Windsor Castle, Berks, Royal Lib.; *Seated Male Figure*, U. London, Courtauld Inst. Gals, all in relation to the *Crucifixion, c.* 1555; Venice, Accad.). It would be easy to exaggerate the importance of drawings such as these in Tintoretto's artistic process. The complex poses were probably dependent on the given narrative invention and for each crowded composition only a few subsidiary figures were drawn. Their peripheral or transitional function is suggested again by their increasingly radical formal abbreviations (e.g. compare *Walking Male Nude*, Florence, Uffizi, with *Male Nude*, Vienna, Albertina).

As with compositional drawings, the number of known *bozzetti* by Tintoretto is small. He seems only to have produced oil sketches on demand. The three sketches (*c.* 1564–7, Madrid, Mus. Thyssen-Bornemisza; *c.* 1579–82, Paris, Louvre; *c.* 1588–9, copy, Madrid, Prado) for the *Paradise* in the Doge's Palace resulted from the series of competitions organized by the Venetian State. Recent technical examination of Tintoretto's paintings has confirmed his abridgement of the process of production. The *Last Judgement* (*c.* 1560–3; Venice, Madonna dell'Orto) and *Christ Washing the Feet of the Disciples* (*c.* 1563–5; London, N.G.) were constructed using complex, uneven paint layers, the random irregularity of the paint structure suggesting that compositional arrangement was simultaneous with the act of painting. In this process the brushstroke itself took on an integral, form-creating significance rather than passively recording prior artistic decisions. However, Tintoretto's use of this abbreviated technique was by no means constant. The *ad hoc* treatment of the *Last Judgement* wholly contrasts with the orderly paint structure and high finish in the *Presentation of the Virgin* (1552–3; Venice, Madonna dell'Orto), in which gold leaf on the risers of the steps reasserts a connection with traditional methods of picture making.

Picture type and patron seem to have played an important role in creating this discontinuity. Many of Tintoretto's upright, round-topped altarpieces have a more traditional technical construction, employing relatively tight handling and high finish (e.g. *St George and the Dragon, c.* 1555–60; London, N.G.), while within the new horizontal format, the technique employed is more experimental. Paintings for aristocratic clients are typically highly finished (e.g. the *Origin of the Milky Way, c.* 1577–8; London, N.G.), while

those for more humble patrons are looser in execution. Expensive ultramarine pigment is extensively used in paintings for aristocratic patrons, while in the cut-price works for S Rocco this prestigious pigment is much less in evidence.

Tintoretto apparently used such technical adaptability to gain coveted commissions. In June 1564 he conceived, executed and installed the ceiling painting depicting *St Roch in Glory* (Venice, Scuola di S Rocco) in under three weeks. In defence of accusations of subverting the proposed competition, Tintoretto pleaded that 'this was his way of designing and he knew no other, and that designs and models ought to be done thus in order to avoid deception' (Vasari). In 1571 the Venetian Senate commissioned Titian to produce a picture commemorating the Battle of Lepanto (1571) for the Doge's Palace. His characteristic delay allowed Tintoretto a chance to submit a petition for the commission, proposing as his sole reward the expectation of the next available State stipend. In a second petition Tintoretto drew attention both to his forfeited fee (500 ducats) and to his completion of the work in just ten months. The contrast between Tintoretto's rapid and cheap production of the battle painting (destr. 1577) and the expensive delays in Titian's completion of his *Battle of Spoleto* (1537; destr. 1577) cannot have been lost on the Senate.

Tintoretto's low pricing was evidently made viable by his rapidity of execution, and he employed many assistants to achieve his prolific output. However, while Titian's pupils were closely dependent on their master, reproducing successful autograph works or working closely from his designs, the personal control exercised by Tintoretto in his workshop was much less strict. The structure and organization seems to have been unusually fluid and devolved, the resultant autonomy facilitating the rapid production and vast output. Tintoretto's assistants were encouraged to produce independent remodellings and enlargements, albeit within the master's idiom. Although workshop replicas do exist, enlarged variants are more common (e.g. *St John the Baptist, c.* 1554–6; St Petersburg, Hermitage, based on the original painting in S Zaccaria, Venice). Few complete autograph designs for paintings undertaken by the workshop are known, and those that do survive differ so markedly from the final works that they cannot be considered as working models (e.g. *Alvise Mocenigo Adoring the Redeemer*, preparatory study, *c.* 1571–4, New York, Met.; painting, *c.* 1581–2, Venice, Doge's Pal., Sala del Collegio). After 1580 relatively few paintings can be attributed to Tintoretto alone.

Foremost among Tintoretto's assistants were his children, Domenico, Marco and Marietta. He also employed an amorphous group of local painters, including Antonio Vassilacchi, Lionardo Corona and Andrea Michieli, and Netherlandish artists, including Pauwels Francke and Lodewyk Toeput. The Netherlandish painters seem to have developed Tintoretto's penchant for naturalistic detail, landscape and still-life. His Italian followers, on the other hand, executed large, heavily populated compositions using a pictorial language based on Tintoretto's but typically incorporating elements derived from the work of other leading masters in Venice, such as Veronese, Jacopo Bassano and Palma Giovane. Tintoretto's reliance on his workshop reflected the traditional craftsmanlike assumption of the lack of distinction between the products of master and workshop.

Tintoretto's style lent itself to rapid replication and expansion, given its economy of form. A single drawing could supply formal ideas for more than one painting (e.g. *Male Nude with a Staff*, Rotterdam, Mus. Boymans–van Beuningen, in relation to both the *Martyrdom of St Lawrence*, 1585–90, Oxford, Christ Church Pict. Gal.; and the *Rape of Helen*, *c.* 1588–9, Madrid, Prado). The figure in *St Jerome* (*c.* 1574–5; Vienna, Ksthist. Mus.) reverses that of one of those in the *Philosophers* (1570–71) in the Libreria Marciana (*see* VENICE, §IV, 7(ii)), itself a variant on another painting.

It is often assumed that Tintoretto was fundamentally opposed to the mass production of paintings. However, the evidence suggests that, on the contrary, he specifically organized his artistic practice to increase his potential output. Nevertheless, his appetite for work was less a matter of eccentricity than is often assumed. Owing to his lack of ready support from powerful groups within the aristocracies in Venice and abroad, the artist seems to have adopted policies of low pricing, rapid production and increased output, which eventually secured him artistic dominance.

III. *Character and personality.*

Tintoretto's private life conformed in many ways to the type of the respectable Venetian citizen. He was a stable, family man running a successful local business. In marrying the daughter of a leading figure in the Scuola Grande di S Marco, Tintoretto gained entry to the pious, civic-minded and essentially conservative world of the non-noble confraternities. He became an active member of the Scuola di S Rocco himself, and the majority of his religious paintings were commissioned by Venetian confraternities. His special relationship with the Scuole del Sacramento, however, suggests that he shared their more progressive commitment to Catholic reform.

Tintoretto was also recorded as a member of two literary academies (the Accademia Pellegrina in 1551 and the Accademia Veneziana Seconda in 1593–4), indicating an active participation in the intellectual life of the city. Both of these organizations were, like the Scuole, dominated by non-nobles, and most of Tintoretto's known friends also came from this social rank. Ridolfi (1642) mentioned Vincenzo Riccio (*d* 1567), Paolo Ramusio (1532–1600) and Bartolomeo Malombra who, despite their exclusion from the patrician Libro d'Oro (Golden Book), won considerable fame in middle-class humanist literary circles. Tintoretto was also friendly with the Florentine polymath Antonio Francesco Doni and the playwright Andrea Calmo (1510–70). These men developed a spontaneous literary style, analogous to Tintoretto's painting technique. The work of both men was aimed at a wider public than was the case with writers enjoying patrician or aristocratic patronage. An indication of Tintoretto's attitude to aristocratic pretensions was given in an anecdote reporting that his ambitious wife insisted on his dressing in patrician regalia. In order to tease her, the painter

deliberately dragged his toga in the muddy street (Ridolfi, 1642; Mariette).

Like Doni, Tintoretto experienced a difficult relationship with the influential circle of artists, writers and connoisseurs who gathered around the older and more established figures of Pietro Aretino and Titian. The latter's opposition to Tintoretto is constantly reiterated in Ridolfi's account, and Aretino's relations with the painter seem to have markedly deteriorated after 1548. Vasari praised Tintoretto's artistic and social accomplishments, stating that 'he has delighted in all the arts, and particularly in playing musical instruments, besides being agreeable in his every action', but he attacked his individualism in art, complaining that he worked 'in a fashion of his own and contrary to the use of other painters'. An indication of this disjunction between social conformity and artistic unorthodoxy can be seen in Tintoretto's surviving self-portraits. The artistic *enfant terrible* (*c.* 1547–8; London, V&A; Philadelphia, PA, Mus. A.) becomes a self-effacing confraternity member (1573; Venice, Scuola di S Rocco), while in a final self-image (*c.* 1588–90; Paris, Louvre) the earlier postures of artistic revolutionary and social conformist are finally abandoned in the name of spiritual withdrawal.

IV. *Critical reception and posthumous reputation.*

Tintoretto's reputation has always been controversial. While opposition from patrons was probably generated by his unusual painting style, that among his fellow artists was a result of his professional conduct. Criticisms of Tintoretto in the contemporary literature derive from these controversies. Pietro Aretino commended Tintoretto's realism in two letters to the painter (1545, 1548), but his interest did not disturb his fundamental commitment to Titian. The second letter ends on a negative note, advising the painter to control his undue 'haste to have done'. The suggestion that Tintoretto's *prestezza* was the product of carelessness was repeated by Aretino's friends and followers. Francesco Sansovino criticized (1556, 1561) the lack of finish in Tintoretto's *Pope Alexander III Excommunicating Barbarossa* as 'the result of his great speed', while Lodovico Dolce criticized (1557) a number of Tintoretto's works, his supposed follies acting as a foil to offset the splendours of Titian's genius.

Vasari clearly drew on the critical consensus of the circle of Aretino in Venice in his account of Tintoretto, which was destined to become the cornerstone of the academic–classical censure in the following centuries. Vasari criticized Tintoretto as 'swift, resolute, fantastic and extravagant', asserting that he worked 'haphazardly, without *disegno*, as if to prove that art is but a jest'. Vasari's negative reaction to Tintoretto's lack of finish contrasted with his positive assessment of Titian's late style. While Titian's loose brushwork could be understood in terms of a progressive courtly aesthetic, and its apparent randomness interpreted as a product of sophisticated dissimulation (*sprezzatura*), Tintoretto's spoke only of an undignified desire to save time and effort. Like Vasari, Federico Zuccaro was particularly concerned to raise the social status of artists. He also shared Vasari's identification of Tintoretto as a potential enemy to this process. Reflecting his concern to preserve the social exclusivity of art, Zuccaro mocked Tintoretto's depiction of the saints in the depiction of *Paradise*, stating that they 'appear like common people in the market place'.

Other contemporaries, however, evaluated Tintoretto's work more positively. For Andrea Calmo and Cristoforo Sorte his *prestezza* was taken as being indicative of special artistic competence, distinguishing artistic creation from the mechanical act of painting. The celebrations offered by the Venetians Carlo Ridolfi (1642, 1648) and Marco Boschini (1660, 1664, 1674) were more selfconsciously polemical, being adopted in reaction to the strictures of central Italian theorists. Ridolfi's *Vita* became (and remains) the single most important historical source for Tintoretto, while Boschini was the first to offer a coherent aesthetic challenge to the classical–academic criticisms. However, Boschini ultimately remained dependent on the image of the painter developed by his arch-enemy Vasari, merely reversing the latter's negative judgements of Tintoretto's artistic unconventionality. In the process, Boschini further exaggerated the academic projection of Tintoretto as an eccentric and instinctual individualist, describing his artistic personality in terms of 'a flash of lightning, a thunderbolt or an arrow'.

Outside Venice, the negative or lukewarm comments of a succession of writers, including Joachim von Sandrart and André Félibien, indicated Tintoretto's low standing within the academic theoretical framework that considered central Italian *disegno* superior to Venetian *colorito*. Even Roger de Piles, whose commitment to painterly Rubénisme in art might have generated a sympathetic response, had mixed feelings, suggesting that 'from the inequality of his mind came the inequality of his works'.

During the Enlightenment the notion that Tintoretto lacked intellectual and artistic control became a commonplace. Even the Venetian Anton Maria Zanetti the younger did little more than elucidate the theme (1771), suggesting that Tintoretto's 'furious enthusiasm' had caused him to go beyond the limits of truth and reality. Critics such as Joshua Reynolds resurrected Vasari's careful distinction between Tintoretto and Titian.

In the earlier part of the 19th century Tintoretto was rehabilitated by writers with new aesthetic interests and sensibilities. For Ruskin (1846, 1853), Tintoretto epitomized 'Imagination Penetrative', the highest formative principle by which the greatest artists transform outward circumstance. Those in possession of this faculty do not 'stop at outward images of any kind' and thus Ruskin celebrated the non-naturalistic aspects of Tintoretto's art. Ruskin's stress on the moral and spiritual content of Tintoretto's work—on his imaginative transformation of the real—allowed him to affirm the painter as a 'purist' illustrator of the central Christian texts, akin to the Gothic artists he idolized. Tintoretto's imagined commitment to spiritual values in the context of the secular, materialist world of late Renaissance Venice could thus stand as a romantic paradox bearing analogies to the experience of Ruskin and other intellectuals and artists in Victorian England.

Ruskin's theoretical division between the spiritual–moral and the material–aesthetic presupposed an analogous division between the artist and his society. This dual division proved essential to the many subsequent writers who rediscovered Tintoretto within the Ruskinian framework. John Addington Symonds likened Tintoretto to a poet for whom 'the intellectual life is paramount, and the body subordinate'. Even the positivist Hippolyte Taine reverted to the language of romantic hyperbole in his description of Tintoretto's 'habits' as 'those of all savage, violent geniuses out of harmony with the world'.

In the 20th century the romantic projection of Tintoretto's artistic personality has proved hard to dislodge. While in England the Ruskinian tradition was extended by Newton, German criticism emphasized aspects of Tintoretto's painting style, such as light (Thode) and colour (von der Bercken) as the agents through which his art exacted a 'spiritualization of reality' (Thode). Other writers, however, were more concerned to establish a precise position for Tintoretto in the history of art, stressing his debt to central Italian Mannerism (Dvořák). Nevertheless, this switch of critical attention from content to form did not prove incompatible with earlier, essentially non-historical models of the artist, and in some cases led to an intellectually myopic concern to locate Tintoretto's work within an abstracted stylistic network (Freedberg).

Marxist analyses of Tintoretto have attempted to explain the artist in terms of class conflict and social alienation (Vipper; Hauser, 1952, 1965), projecting him as 'the rejected champion of a bourgeoisie attacking the patrician aesthetics of fixity and being' (Sartre, 1964, 1966). This position—still dependent in certain ways on Ruskin's romantic outsider—contrasts strongly with the findings of a number of late 20th-century historians who, through concentrating on specific aspects of Tintoretto's activity, emphasized his cultural centrality in the context of 16th-century Venice (de Tolnay, 1960; Levey; Rosand; Hills). It is possible, though, to argue for a reconciliation of these contrasting views, allowing Tintoretto to have played a central role within Venetian culture, while emphasizing his primary connection with those non-noble sections of society that in the later 16th century remained more faithful to the traditional, communal ideals of the Republic than their patricians. The opposition that Tintoretto faced in an age dominated by the aristocracy can thus be understood as a response to the non-exclusive social values permeating his artistic practice.

EWA; Mariette

BIBLIOGRAPHY
EARLY SOURCES

P. Aretino: *Lettere sull'arte* (Venice, 1545–9); ed. E. Camesasca, intro. F. Pertile, ii (Milan, 1957)

A. Calmo: *Il rimanente de le piacevole et ingeniose littere* (Venice, 1548); ed. V. Rossi (Turin, 1888)

G. Vasari: *Vite* (1550, rev. 2/1568); ed. G. Milanesi (1878–85), vi, pp. 587–94

A. F. Doni: *Tre libri di lettere* (Venice, 1552)

F. Sansovino: *Tutte le cose notabili e belle che sono in Venetia* (Venice, 1556, rev. 3/1663)

L. Dolce: *Dialogo della pittura . . . intitolato l'Aretino* (Venice, 1557); Eng. trans. by M. W. Roskill in *Dolce's 'Aretino' and Venetian Art Theory of the Cinquecento* (New York, 1968)

C. Sorte: *Osservazioni nella pittura* (Venice, 1580)

R. Borghini: *Il riposo* (Florence, 1584); ed. M. Rosci (Milan, 1967)

F. Zuccaro: *Lettera a prencipi e signori amatori del disegno, pittura, scultura et architettura . . . con un lamento della pittura* (Mantua, 1605); ed. P. Barocchi in *Scritti d'arte del cinquecento*, II/iv (Milan and Naples, 1971)

C. Ridolfi: *Vita di Giacopo Robusti detto il Tintoretto* (Venice, 1642); Eng. trans. by C. Enggass and R. Enggass (University Park, PA, 1984)
——: *Meraviglie* (1648); ed. D. von Hadeln (1914–24)
M. Boschini: *La carta del navegar pitoresco* (Venice, 1660); ed. A. Pallucchini (Rome and Venice, 1966)
——: *Le minere della pittura* (Venice, 1664)
——: *Le ricche minere della pittura veneziana* (Venice, 1674)
J. von Sandrart: *Teutsche Academie* (1675–9); ed. A. R. Peltzer (1925)
A. Félibien: *Entretiens*, iii (Paris, 1679)
R. de Piles: *Abrégé de la vie des peintres* (Paris, 1699)
J. Reynolds: *Discourses on Art* (London, 1771); ed. R. R. Wark (San Marino, 1959/*R* New Haven and London, 1975)
A. M. Zanetti: *Della pittura veneziana e delle opere pubbliche de' veneziani maestri* (Venice, 1771, rev. 1792)

GENERAL

J. Ruskin: *Modern Painters*, ii (London, 1846); ed. E. T. Cook and A. Wedderburn (London, 1903)
——: *The Stones of Venice*, ii (London, 1853); ed. E. T. Cook and A. Wedderburn (London, 1903)
H. Taine: *Voyage en Italie*, 2 vols (Paris, 1866); Eng. trans. by J. Durand (New York, 1869)
J. A. Symonds: *The Renaissance in Italy*, 7 vols (London, 1875–86)
M. Dvořák: 'Über Greco und den Manierismus', *Jb. Kstgesch.*, i (1921–2), pp. 22–42; Eng. trans. by J. Coolidge as 'El Greco and Mannerism', *Mag. A.*, xxxxiv (1953), pp. 14–23
L. Coletti: 'La crisi manieristica nella pittura veneziana', *Convivium*, xiii (1941), pp. 109–26
H. Tietze and E. Tietze-Conrat: *The Drawings of the Venetian Painters in the Fifteenth and Sixteenth Centuries*, 2 vols (New York, 1944)
A. Hauser: *The Social History of Art*, ii (London, 1952)
——: *Mannerism: The Crisis of the Renaissance and the Origin of Modern Art* (London, 1965)
S. J. Freedberg: *Painting in Italy, 1500–1600*, Pelican Hist. A. (Harmondsworth, 1971)
S. Sinding-Larsen: *Christ in the Council Hall: Studies in the Religious Iconography of the Venetian Republic* (Rome, 1974)
D. Rosand: *Painting in Cinquecento Venice: Titian, Veronese, Tintoretto* (New Haven and London, 1982)

MONOGRAPHS

H. Thode: *Tintoretto* (Bielefeld and Leipzig, 1901)
D. von Hadeln: *Zeichnungen des Giacomo Tintoretto* (Berlin, 1922)
L. Coletti: *Il Tintoretto* (Bergamo, 1940/*R* 1951)
E. von der Bercken: *Die Gemälde des Jacopo Tintoretto* (Munich, 1942)
H. Tietze: *Tintoretto: The Paintings and Drawings* (London, 1948)
B. R. Vipper: *Tintoretto* (Moscow, 1948); Italian trans., abridged, as 'Tintoretto e il suo tempo' in *Rass. Sov.* (1951), viii, pp. 50–57; ix, pp. 63–73; x, pp. 52–77; xi, pp. 53–60
R. Pallucchini: *La giovinezza del Tintoretto* (Milan, 1950)
E. Newton: *Tintoretto* (London, 1952)
C. Bernari and P. de Vecchi: *L'opera completa del Tintoretto* (Milan, 1970)
P. Rossi: *Jacopo Tintoretto: I ritratti* (Venice, 1974)
——: *I disegni di Jacopo Tintoretto* (Florence, 1975)
R. Pallucchini and P. Rossi: *Tintoretto: Le opere sacre e profane*, 2 vols (Venice, 1982)
K. M. Swoboda: *Tintoretto: Ikonographische und stilistische Untersuchungen* (Munich and Vienna, 1982)
A. L. Lepschy: *Tintoretto Observed: A Documentary Survey of Critical Reactions from the 16th to the 20th Century* (Ravenna, 1983) [with extensive bibliog.]

SPECIALIST STUDIES
The Scuola di S Rocco

R. Berliner: 'Forschungen über die Tätigkeit Tintorettos in der Scuola Grande di San Rocco', *Kstchron. & Kstmarkt*, xxxi (1920), pp. 468–97
C. De Tolnay: 'L'interpretazione dei cicli pittorici di San Rocco', *Crit. A.*, vii (1960), pp. 341–76
E. Huttinger: *Die Bilderzyklen Tintorettos in der Scuola di S. Rocco zu Venedig* (Zurich, 1962)
K. M. Swoboda: 'Die grosse Kreuzigung Tintorettos in Albergo der Scuola di San Rocco', *A. Ven.*, xxv (1971), pp. 145–52
J. Grabski: 'The Group of Paintings by Tintoretto in the "Sala Terrena" in the Scuola di San Rocco in Venice and their Relationship to the Architectural Structure', *Artibus & Hist.*, i (1980), pp. 115–31
F. Valcanover: *Jacopo Tintoretto and the Scuola Grande di San Rocco* (Venice, 1983)

Others

D. F. von Hadeln: 'Beiträge zur Tintorettoforschung', *Jb. Kön.-Preuss. Kstsamml.*, xxxii (1911), pp. 1–58
J. Wilde: 'Die Mostra del Tintoretto zu Venedig', *Z. Kstgesch.*, vii (1937), pp. 140–53
D. R. Coffin: 'Tintoretto and the Medici Tombs', *A. Bull.*, xxxiii (1951), pp. 119–25
J.-P. Sartre: 'Le Séquestré de Venise', *Temps mod.*, no. 141 (1957), pp. 762–800; Eng. trans. by W. Baskin in *Essays in Aesthetics* (London, 1964)
C. Gilbert: 'Tintoretto and Michelangelo's St. Damian', *Burl. Mag.*, ciii (1961), pp. 16–20
M. Muraro: 'Affreschi di Jacopo Tintoretto a Ca' Soranzo', *Scritti di storia dell'arte in onore di Mario Salmi*, iii (Rome, 1963), pp. 103–16
M. Levey: 'Tintoretto and the Theme of Miraculous Intervention', *J. Royal Soc. A.*, cxiii (1965), pp. 707–25
J.-P. Sartre: 'Saint-Georges et le dragon', *L'Art*, xxx (1966), pp. 33–52
P. Eikemeier: 'Der Gonzaga-Zyklus des Tintoretto in der alten Pinakothek', *Münchn. Jb. Bild. Kst* (1969), pp. 75–137
C. De Tolnay: 'Il Paradiso del Tintoretto: Note sull'interpretazione della tela in Palazzo Ducale', *A. Ven.*, xxiv (1970), pp. 103–10
C. Gould: 'The Cinquecento at Venice, III: Tintoretto and Space', *Apollo*, xcvi (1972), pp. 32–7
K. M. Swoboda: 'Die Apostelkommunion in den Bildern Tintorettos', *Jb. Österreich. Byz.*, xxi (1972), pp. 251–68
N. Penny: 'John Ruskin and Tintoretto', *Apollo*, cxlvi (1974), pp. 268–73
J. Plesters and L. Lazzarini: 'The Examination of the Tintorettos', *The Church of Madonna dell'Orto*, ed. A. Clarke and P. Rylands (London, 1977), pp. 7–26
C. Gould: 'An X-ray of Tintoretto's "Milky Way"', *A. Ven.*, xxxii (1978), pp. 211–13
J. Plesters: 'Tintoretto's Paintings in the National Gallery', *N.G. Tech. Bull.*, iii (1979), pp. 3–24; iv (1980), pp. 32–48; viii (1984), pp. 24–34
S. Marinelli: 'La costruzione dello spazio nelle opere di Jacopo Tintoretto', *La prospettiva rinascimentale*, ed. M. Dolai (Florence, 1980), pp. 319–30
J. Schulz: 'Tintoretto and the First Competition for the Ducal Palace "Paradise"', *A. Ven.*, xxxiii (1980), pp. 112–26
P. Hills: 'Piety and Patronage in Cinquecento Venice: Tintoretto and the Scuole del Sacramento', *A. Hist.*, vi (1983), pp. 30–43
D. Knopfel: 'Sui dipinti di Tintoretto per il coro della Madonna dell'Orto', *A. Ven.*, xxxvii (1984), pp. 149–54
H. MacAndrew and others: 'Tintoretto's "Deposition of Christ" in the National Gallery of Scotland', *Burl. Mag.*, cxxxvii (1985), pp. 501–17
F. Valcanover: 'Il restauro del Paradiso di Jacopo Tintoretto', *Venezia A.*, i (1987), pp. 96–9
The Cinquecento (exh. cat., ed. C. Whitfield; London, Walpole Gal., 1991), pp. 44–7
P. Hills: 'Tintoretto's Marketing', *Venedig und Oberdeutschland in der Renaissance*, ed. B. Roeck, K. Bergdoff and A. J. Martin (Venice, 1993), pp. 107–20
T. Nichols: 'Tintoretto's Poverty', *New Interpretations of Venetian Renaissance Painting*, ed. F. Ames-Lewis and A. Bednarek (London, 1994)
——: 'Tintoretto, *prestezza del fatto*, and the *poligrafi*: A Study in Literary and Visual Culture of Cinquecento Venice', *Ren. Stud.*, x/2 (in preparation)

TOMAS NICHOLS

(2) Marietta Tintoretto (*b* Venice, *c*. 1554; *d* Venice, *c*. 1590). Daughter of (1) Jacopo Tintoretto. She was taught by her father and assisted him in his workshop. It is said that while young, he had her dress like a boy and follow him everywhere. As his favourite daughter, Jacopo also had her married to a local jeweller to keep her near him. Marietta does not appear to have received commissions for major religious paintings, and, like other women artists in this period, she worked primarily as a portrait painter. Apart from a *Self-portrait* (Florence, Uffizi), no work can be assigned to her with certainty. The three portraits attributed to her in Madrid (Prado) include a possible self-portrait. The only surviving painting that may be signed by her is a *Portrait of Two Men* (Dresden, Gemäldegal. Alte Meister), which bears the initials MR. Ridolfi wrote that her portrait of the antiquarian and collector Jacopo Strada attracted the attention of Emperor

Maximilian II, who enquired about her employment as court painter. However, this may be a mistaken reference to her father's portrait of Strada's son *Ottavio Strada* (Amsterdam, Stedel. Mus.). Philip II of Spain apparently showed a similar interest in Marietta's work. A few small religious paintings are attributed to her, including two pictures of the *Virgin and Child* (both Cleveland, OH, Mus. A.), and her work as an assistant is thought to be evident in certain of her father's paintings (e.g. *St Agnes Reviving Licinio*, c. 1578–9; Venice, Madonna dell'Orto). Two drawings after models (Milan, Rassini priv. col.) are also assigned to her and were probably executed while she was in her father's workshop.

BIBLIOGRAPHY

C. Ridolfi: *Vita di Giacopo Robusti detto il Tintoretto* (Venice, 1642); Eng. trans. by C. Enggass and R. Enggass (University Park, PA, 1984)

E. Conrat-Tietze: 'Marietta, fille du Tintoretto', *Gaz. B.-A.*, ii (1934), pp. 258–62

P. Rossi: *Jacopo Tintoretto: I ritratti* (Venice, 1974), pp. 138–9 [details of attributions to Marietta]

D. Bachmann and S. Piland: *Women Artists: An Historical, Contemporary, and Feminist Bibliography* (Metuchen, NJ, 1978), pp. 65–6

E. H. Fine: *Women and Art* (Montclair, NJ, 1978), pp. 13–14

(3) Domenico Tintoretto (*b* Venice, 1560; *d* Venice, 1635). Son of (1) Jacopo Tintoretto. He was taught by his father and assisted him in his workshop. At the age of 17 he was admitted to the Venetian painters' guild, and he is recorded in the confraternity of painters from 1594. He began his career by helping his father to execute the paintings in the Sala del Collegio and Sala del Senato in the Doge's Palace, Venice. Following this he worked independently at the palace, on the Sala dello Scrutinio and the Sala del Maggiore Consiglio. His training with his father helped him in his own compositions, several of which, such as the *Battle of Salvore*, or the *Second Conquest of Constantinople*, are heroic battle themes with complex groupings and dramatic poses. In the last two decades of the 16th century Domenico concentrated on religious commissions in Venice, including a *Last Supper* and *Crucifixion* (both *c.* 1583) for S Andrea della Zirada (both *in situ*), a *Marriage of the Virgin* for S Giorgio Maggiore (*in situ*) and a *Crucifixion* for the Scuola dei Mercanti. During this early period as an independently commissioned painter he continued to collaborate with his father on occasions, notably on the *Paradise* (1588–90) in the Sala del Maggiore Consiglio in the Doge's Palace.

Domenico was also an accomplished portrait painter (e.g. *Portrait of a Young Man*, 1585; Kassel, Schloss Wilhelmshöhe) and in 1591 the Scuola dei Mercanti in Venice ordered two large portrait groups from him (both Venice, Accad.). In 1592 he went to Ferrara to paint a portrait of Margaret of Austria, later Queen of Spain, and in 1595 he went from Venice to Mantua at the invitation of Vincenzo I Gonzaga, 4th Duke of Mantua, to execute a portrait commission. Some of his most impressive civic portraits were also painted in the last decade of the 16th century, such as that of *Doge Marino Grimani* (*c.* 1595; Cincinnati, OH, A. Mus.). Like many of his others, this is framed by landscapes and vegetation and reveals the influence of his father's assistants, Lodewyk Toeput and Pauwels Francke. In secular works of this period, such as *Venus, Adonis and the Three Graces* (1585–90; Chicago, IL, A. Inst.), Domenico translated his father's structures and compositions into his own individual language, allowing more room for landscape and background details. In these mythological scenes he displayed the same preoccupation with the topography of Veneto that is evident in his portraits of this period. Domenico's style is furthest from that of his father in his drawings, in which the quick, expressive lines that Jacopo used to suggest figures are replaced in Domenico's drawings with clearly rounded limbs and torsos in chiaroscuro. A good example is his *Recumbent Nude* (Ames priv. col.; see Sutton, p. 276) in which he experimented with light as a means of defining form.

At the end of Domenico's career, after the death of his father, there is a notable change in his style. The phosphorescent colours and intricate compositions that he had so aptly borrowed from Jacopo in earlier works gradually disappeared. Later paintings, such as the altarpiece of the *Virgin Interceding with Christ for the Cessation of the Plague* (1631; Venice, S Francesco della Vigna), lack the vitality of the religious panels of the 1580s. Nevertheless, they effectively communicated Counter-Reformation messages and coincided with the naturalism popular in Rome in the 17th century.

BIBLIOGRAPHY

C. Ridolfi: *Vita di Giacopo Robusti detto il Tintoretto* (Venice, 1642); Eng. trans. by C. Enggass and R. Enggass (University Park, PA, 1984)

W. Suida: 'Clarifications and Identifications of Works by Venetian Painters', *A. Q.* [Detroit], ix/4 (1946), pp. 282–99

D. Sutton: 'Sunlight and Movement: Splendours of Venetian Draughtsmanship', *Apollo*, c (1974), pp. 274–81

P. Rossi: 'Per la grafica di Domenico Tintoretto', *A. Ven.*, xxix (1975), pp. 205–11

R. Pallucchini: *La pittura veneziana del seicento* (Milan, 1981)

R. Pallucchini and P. Rossi: *Tintoretto: Le opere sacre e profane* (Milan, 1982)

P. Rossi: 'Per la grafica di Domenico Tintoretto, II', *A. Ven.*, xxxviii (1984), pp. 57–71   □

Tintype. *See under* PHOTOGRAPHY, §I.

Tioda (*fl* 812). Spanish ?architect. He has traditionally been regarded as the first known Spanish architect, building at the request of Alfonso II of Asturias (*reg* 791–842) the Cathedral of S Salvador in Oviedo. Other buildings ordered by Alfonso in Oviedo have also been attributed to him, and it has been arbitrarily suggested that he was of eastern origin, which could explain certain links between Asturian and Armenian architecture. It has also been proposed that his origins were Visigothic and even that he came from Aachen.

Tioda's name appears with other signatures in a document of Alfonso II, the Testament of 812, but without specifying his profession. In a 12th-century version of the Testament he appears as *Tioda edificator predicte ecclesie Sancti Salvatoris. Confirmans* (Tioda appointed builder of the church of S Salvador. Ratified). The most serious problem with this attribution is that the 12th-century document was issued at a time when there was a great movement in Oviedo to mythologize events in 9th-century Asturias. If one were to accept the 12th-century identification of Tioda as an architect, one could also take the name Tioda or Theoda as of Visigothic origin, which would match the Visigothic character of the architecture attributed to him.

Thieme–Becker

BIBLIOGRAPHY
I. G. BANGO TORVISO

Tiranë. Capital city of Albania and centre of production for furniture, glass, wood-carving and ceramics. The 'Misto Mame' Woodwork Combine was initially established in 1947 as a small workshop for furniture production. By 1951 it had changed its name to Ndërmarrja e Përpunimit të Drurit 'Misto Mame' ('Misto Mame' woodworking enterprise) and had greatly increased in size. In 1973 the combine adopted its present name and opened a group of factories. The most important sector within the combine is the furniture production unit, which produces complete suites of bedroom furniture, bookcases, sideboards, tables etc. The majority of products have matt or semi-matt veneer finishes of beech, maple, walnut, poplar, elm and cherry. The Milde Furniture Factory produces armchairs, sofas and wall panelling for domestic interiors and public buildings. Many of the products are covered with textiles such as damask, produced locally. The Factory of Furniture for Institutions produces one-off, usually commissioned, pieces of furniture and decorative items. The Department of Parquet Tiles produces flooring for many different interiors. The combine has its own Technological Bureau and collaborates with such institutes of interior design as the Institute of Building Project Studies and Designs No.1 and the Bureau of Wood Project Studies and Design in Tiranë. Some of the combine's production is exported.

The Glass Factory was founded in November 1957 as a cooperative of master craftsmen. It has four departments—carving, painting, cut glass and artistic glass—and produces such objects as drinking glasses, vases, jugs and figurines, decorated with designs based on archaeological discoveries or folk patterns. The majority of stained-glass production consists of pictures depicting themes from Albanian history. The factory's Technological Project Bureau includes painters, sculptors and technicians.

The 'Migjeni' Artistic Products Enterprise, originally the Kooperativa e Artizanatit të Tiranës (Artisan cooperative of Tiranë), was created in 1957; it adopted its present name in 1966. The Department of Artistic Woodwork had sectors for carving, pyrography, decoration, inlaying and straw application work, which produced simple ornaments: chairs and tables, jewellery and boxes made from beech, pine, walnut and maple veneer and traditional cigar and cigarette holders from brier-wood. The Department of Artistic Ceramics uses plaster moulds to produce figurines, ashtrays, cups, vases etc. The Department of Artistic Bone Work (est. 1970) produces necklaces, earrings and figurines. The Department of Alabaster Objects (est. 1970) produces such items as vases, boxes, dishes and figurines. The production process involves sawing off a piece of alabaster block, which is then shaped on a lathe, finished by hand-carving and lacquered. In the Department of Wood Mosaics (est. 1981) olive, brier, strawberry and oak-wood are carved into cubes, which are then joined together to produce such objects as boxes, ashtrays and fruit-dishes. The Department of Non-ferrous Metals (est. 1966) produces a wide range of objects in silver, iron, brass and copper, most of which are made by traditional techniques, including some skilful filigree work. The decorative motifs are stylized versions of traditional folk ornament, based mainly on geometric and floral patterns, although some contemporary designs are used. All items are produced for export.

In 1958 the Porcelain Factory was created as a state industrial enterprise for the production of goods made from porcelain, faience, maiolica and gesso for domestic use. The small artistic objects and larger ceramic goods, all of which are made by techniques involving plaster moulds, range from copies of archaeological artefacts to modern designs.

BIBLIOGRAPHY
Albanian Alabaster Products (Tiranë, n.d.)
Albanian Artistic Bone Articles (Tiranë, n.d.)
Albanian Artistic Ceramic Articles (Tiranë, n.d.)
Albanian Artistic Handicraft Articles (Tiranë, n.d.)
Albanian Artistic Handicraft Products (Tiranë, n.d.)
Albanian Filigree Silver Items (Tiranë, n.d.)
Wooden Articles (Tiranë, n.d.)
The National Exhibition of the Material Culture of the Albanian People (Tiranë, 1980)
Prodhimet e Kombinatit të përpunimit të Drurit 'Misto Mame' [Products of 'Misto Mame' woodworking combine: a catalogue] (Tiranë, 1986)
GJERGJ FRASHËR

Tiraz [Arab. *ṭirāz*]. Inscription band in Islamic textiles, or fabric with an inscription band added in a technique different from the ground weave. Derived from the Persian word for embroidery, the term originally designated any embroidered ornament. In the early Islamic period textiles were often decorated with inscriptions containing good wishes and the caliph's name and titles, and these fabrics were made up into robes of honour worn by the caliph or bestowed by him as official gifts. Hence the word came to refer to inscription bands done in embroidery or any other technique and the fabrics or garments on which they were found. Tiraz also referred to the workshops in which these fabrics were made, a synecdoche for *dār al-ṭirāz* ('factory for tiraz'). In later times the word tiraz was also used to refer to the long bands inscribed with the ruler's name and titles that were written across the façades of major buildings, as at the mausoleum of Sultan Qala'un in Cairo (1284–5).

The institution of the tiraz—the production of textiles under state supervision in royal factories—flourished in the Islamic world under the patronage of the Abbasid and Fatimid caliphs from the late 9th century to the 13th, when a new taste evolved for patterned silks and all-over embroidered or printed cottons. Most surviving pieces come from the burial grounds at Fustat (Old Cairo), for these were prized and expensive textiles and many were used for shrouds. A few have been preserved in European church treasuries. Major collections are in the Museum of Islamic Art in Cairo (with nearly 1000 inscribed pieces), the Victoria and Albert Museum in London and the Textile Museum in Washington, DC. Studies of tiraz have concentrated on their historical value, since the inscriptions sometimes name the ruling caliph, an amir or local governor, the vizier who supervised the work and the intendant at the workshop as well as the place and date of manufacture, sometimes specified as private or royal (*khāṣṣa*) or public (*'āmma*), but these textiles are also important for documenting changes in weaving techniques, sartorial taste and epigraphic style.

1. TECHNICAL CHARACTERISTICS. The numerous literary texts describing court vestments and furnishings speak primarily of silks, but surviving tiraz are mainly linens and other light-weight fabrics. Most are fragments from mantles, summer outfits and undergarments, turbans, shawls, sashes, napkins, presentation towels and such furnishing fabrics as curtains. The only complete garment is the Veil of St Anne (1096–7; Apt Cathedral; see fig.), which is made of bleached linen tabby adorned with three parallel bands of tapestry-woven ornament in coloured silk and some gold filé. In the centre is a wide band of interlacing circles joining three medallions containing pairs of addorsed sphinxes encircled by kufic inscriptions naming the patron, the Fatimid caliph al-Musta'li (*reg* 1094–1101), and the supervisor of the work, his vizier al-Afdal. The side bands contain birds, animals and another inscription saying that the textile was woven in the royal factory at Damietta in 1096–7. The piece was probably worn as an overgarment or mantle, with the small slits at the side for the hands and the central band containing the medallions falling down the back. Other mantles and simple tunics popular under the Abbasid and Fatimid caliphs were constructed from two narrow widths. Produced on simple vertical looms, these garments needed only a little stitching along the selvage. Fabrics from the eastern Islamic world, however, were typically woven on horizontal looms, and garments were constructed from narrow widths of cloth with many seams.

Until the 12th century there was a dichotomy in the nature of the ground fabric: cotton was used in Iraq, Iran, India and the Yemen, while linen was used in Egypt. Although threads were traded across the Islamic world, imported ones were used sparingly, being reserved for special purposes, particularly decorative bands. The cotton fabrics from the eastern Islamic world were finely woven with undyed Z-spun yarn in tabby weave and were often glazed so that they look like polished paper. Cotton was also combined with silk in a delicate, light fabric known as *mulham* ('half-silk') in which warps of fine, raw silk floss were woven with wefts of heavier, Z-spun cotton in tabby weave (usually weft-faced). Medieval geographers mentioned Khwarazm in western Central Asia, Merv and Nishapur in Khurasan, and Isfahan in central Iran as places where *mulham* was manufactured. Surviving cotton and mulham fabrics are decorated with short inscriptions, mostly embroidered in coloured silk floss. The main band is worked in chain stitch on the free-drawn lines of the lettering, and a small band, not always decipherable, may be added in blanket or back stitch or worked on counted threads. Some of the cotton pieces have painted, printed or gilded inscriptions, which were a cheaper imitation of embroidery. A distinct group of cottons manufactured in the Yemen are ikats. The thick, Z-spun warps were resist-dyed before weaving in shades of blue, brown and white, and the fabrics have characteristic stripes with splashed arrow patterns and embroidered or painted inscriptions. Some mention San'a as a place of manufacture, but there were probably other sites as well.

Egyptian linen was traditionally S-spun, but in the late 9th century the Z-spinning typical of the eastern Islamic world was introduced. The fabric was usually bleached, but occasionally dyed blue or green. At first, silk inscriptions were embroidered on linen in imitation of pieces from the eastern Islamic world, but silk tapestry appeared in the second quarter of the 10th century. In the 12th century tapestry woven bands were in turn supplanted by embroidered decoration of conventionalized ornaments and cursive inscription bands. Embroidered inscriptions were done with coloured silk floss in various counted thread stitches, and tapestry bands were woven in coloured silk wefts and occasionally gold filé on a yellow silk core. The factories at Alexandria, Tinnis and Misr (Old Cairo) produced on such a large scale that the specific characteristics of each centre can be identified.

2. STYLISTIC EVOLUTION. The institution of the tiraz was modelled on Byzantine and Sasanian precedents, although it is not certain whether pre-Islamic workshops were taken over and kept in operation. Pieces inscribed with the caliph's name were already produced under the Umayyads (*reg* 661–750), the first Islamic dynasty. One of

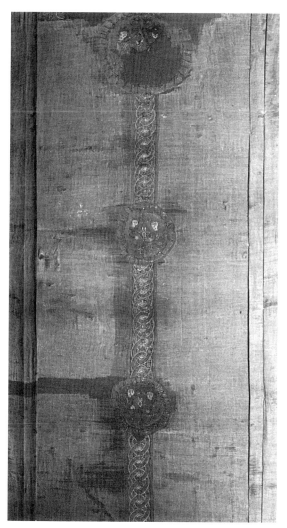

Veil of St Anne, linen with coloured silk and gold filé, 3.1×1.5 m, from Damietta, Egypt, 1096–7 (Apt Cathedral)

the earliest surviving is a fragmentary silk twill (London, V&A; New York, Brooklyn Mus.; Brussels, Mus. A. Anc.) found in Egypt. The main field is decorated with an all-over pattern of circles containing bunches of grapes and flowers with heart-shaped petals. An inscription embroidered along the edge in yellow silk indicates that it was woven for Marwan, the Commander of the Faithful, in the tiraz of Ifriqiya. The patron was an Umayyad caliph, either Marwan I (reg 684–5) or, more probably, Marwan II (reg 744–50), and the factory was located somewhere in Tunisia, probably at Kairouan.

The output of state factories for the production of tiraz can be clearly documented in Egypt from the 9th century, and over time both the titles and the style used in the inscriptions became more elaborate. A typical piece made for an Abbasid caliph in the late 9th century or early 10th has one long line of text written in a simple form of angular kufic script. The text begins with the invocation to God and blessings for the caliph under whose authority the textile was made. The inscription continues with the name of the vizier who ordered the piece, the place of production, the name of the supervisor and the date. Variations in wording may indicate different places of manufacture or different rulers. The phrase *'alā yaday* ('through the agency of'), for example, was used on Egyptian pieces before the name of the factory supervisor, while in the eastern Islamic world it preceded the name of the government official who ordered the textile to be made. The Fatimid caliphs, who were Isma'ili Shi'ites, often invoked such sectarian phrases as 'the People of the House' (*ahl al-bayt*) or 'their pure ancestors' (*āba'ih al-ṭāhirīn*).

In the 10th century scripts became more mannered in style, as the shafts of the letters became taller and the tails of the letters were floriated. The text was sometimes written in two facing bands. A linen textile (Washington, DC, Textile Mus., 73.432) made for the Fatimid caliph al-'Aziz (reg 975–96), for example, has a tapestry-woven inscription of large angular script with arabesques forming discs at the heads of the high (85 mm) letters. The text invokes God's blessing on his servant and friend the Imam, al-'Aziz bi'llah; it was ordered by the vizier ibn Kilis in AH 370 (AD 980–81), and probably made at Tinnis.

In the 11th century inscriptions became shorter and more decorative as non-historical texts, which repeated a single word or phrase such as 'blessing' or 'good fortune', were introduced. The crescent or shovel-shaped tails of the letters were extended below the base line. In pieces (e.g. Ann Arbor, U. MI Mus. A., 22528, and Cleveland, OH, Mus. A., 82.109) made for al-Zahir (reg 1021–36), the terminals are still attached correctly to descending letters, but gradually the large endings were applied at regular intervals and attached indiscriminately to any letter, thereby obscuring the text and making it more difficult to read. The text on a linen woven a century later (Washington, DC, Textile Mus., 73.461), probably for al-Mustansir (reg 1036–94), is almost impossible to read because of the capriciously disposed shovel-shaped terminals. Legible texts were eventually replaced by a decorative 'kufesque' script (e.g. Boston, MA, Mus. F.A., 30.676). The decline of historical inscriptions was accompanied by an increased use of decorative bands, either small-scale geometric

patterns or designs of animals in cartouches. These narrow bands were executed in a variety of colours and generally occur in pairs, with one decorative band framed by inscribed bands and the other decorative band isolated on the ground some distance away (e.g. Washington, DC, Textile Mus., 73.543, made for al-Mustansir). In the 12th century these hard-to-read angular scripts were replaced by cursive ones, as on a linen woven under the supervision of the vizier al-Afdal (Washington, DC, Textile Mus., 73.680). The decorative bands became wider and more elaborate. They often contain medallions with animals or geometric motifs and are themselves framed by narrower bands with inscriptions or pseudo-inscriptions (e.g. Toronto, Royal Ont. Mus., 961.107.3). A wide variety of colours was used, but yellow–gold often predominates, perhaps in imitation of luxury textiles which used gold-wrapped thread.

The most remarkable inscriptions are those in interlaced kufic script on the ikat cottons made in the Yemen. One group made at San'a between 883 and 923 have embroidered decoration with numerous arcs inserted for decorative purposes in the base line of the inscription and in the vertical staffs. A second group dating from the late 9th century to the late 10th have painted and gilded inscriptions in elaborately plaited and foliated kufic. On the four pieces with historical inscriptions (Athens, Benaki Mus., 15603; Cleveland, OH, Mus. A., 50.353; Cairo, Mus. Islam. A.; Washington, DC, Dumbarton Oaks, 33.37), legibility was important and the interlacing was restricted to single letters and decoration confined to occasional trilobed rising tails or heart-shaped ornaments. Those with pious texts (e.g. Boston, MA, Mus. F.A., 31.962) are much more elaborate and have an extraordinary number of arcs, bumps, triangles, curls and other decorative devices inserted between and around the letters. These pious texts are extremely laborious to read, and only their limited repertory of phrases renders them decipherable.

BIBLIOGRAPHY

Enc. Islam/1

G. Marçais and G. Wiet: 'Le "Voile de Sainte Anne" d'Apt', *Mnmts Piot*, xxxiv (1934), pp. 1–18

R. Pfister: 'Materiaux pour servir au classement des textiles égyptiens postérieurs à la conquête arabe', *Rev. A. Asiat.*, x (1936), pp. 1–16, 73–85

F. Day: 'Dated Tirāz in the Collection of the University of Michigan', *A. Islam.*, iv (1937), pp. 421–48

C. J. Lamm: *Cotton in Medieval Textiles of the Near East* (Paris, 1937)

N. P. Britton: *A Study of Some Early Islamic Textiles in the Museum of Fine Arts, Boston* (Boston, 1938)

R. B. Serjeant: 'Material for a History of Islamic Textiles up to the Mongol Conquest', *A. Islam.*, ix–xvi (1942–51), repr. as *Islamic Textiles: Material for a History up to the Mongol Conquest* (Beirut, 1972)

R. Pfister: 'Toiles à inscriptions abbasides et fatimides', *Bull. Etud. Orient.*, ix (1945–6), pp. 46–90

F. Day: 'The Tirāz Silk of Marwān', *Archaeologica Orientalia in Memoriam Ernst Herzfeld*, ed. G. C. Miles (Locust Valley, 1952), pp. 39–61

E. Kühnel and L. Bellinger: *Catalogue of Dated Tirāz Fabrics: Umayyad, Abbasid, Fatimid*, Textile Mus. cat. (Washington, DC, 1952)

L. Golombek and V. Gervers: 'Tirāz Fabrics in the Royal Ontario Museum', *Studies in Textile History in Memory of Harold B. Burnham*, ed. V. Gervers (Toronto, 1977), pp. 82–125

M. Lombard: *Les Textiles dans le monde musulmane du VIIe au XIIe siècle* (Paris, 1978)

S. S. Blair: 'Legibility Versus Decoration in Islamic Epigraphy: The Case of Interlacing', *Acts of the XXVIth International Congress of the History of Art: Washington, DC, 1986*, ii, pp. 329–34

H. Glidden and D. Thompson: '*Ṭirāz* Fabrics in the Byzantine Collection, Dumbarton Oaks, Part One: *Ṭirāz* From Egypt', *Bull. Asia Inst.*, ii (1988), pp. 119–39

N. Micklewright: '*Ṭirāz* Fragments: Unanswered Questions about Medieval Islamic Textiles', *Brocade of the Pen: The Art of Islamic Writing* (exh. cat., ed. C. G. Fisher; East Lansing, MI State U., Kresge A. Mus., 1991), pp. 31–46

SHEILA S. BLAIR

Tîrgovişte. Principal town in the Dimbovita district of Romania. The earliest documentary references date from 1396, when it became the second capital of Wallachia, after Curtea de Argeş. It maintained this role, together with Bucharest from 1457, until the mid-16th century. The most important monument in the town is Curtea Domnească ('the princely court'), the earliest buildings of which date from the time of Mircea I (*reg* 1386–1418). It is thus the first princely residence in the country; with the adjoining chapel it is now preserved as a ruin. In the mid-15th century a defence tower was built above its western side. According to archaeological researches the ruins of the palace (the vaulted cellars and the lofty ground-floor) also date from the mid-15th century. The palace was renovated by Matei Basarab in 1632–54 and by Constantine Brâncoveanu in 1688–1714. In 1583–5, close to Curtea Domnească, Prince Petru Cercel built a smaller palace, rigorously symmetrical, with cellars, part of the ground-floor and residential upper floor connected by a loggia and a bridge to the princely tribune in the contemporary church. The church is of Greek-cross type, with an open entrance area with brick columns and three towers. The internal painting was commissioned by Constantine Brâncoveanu and executed in 1698 by the team of CONSTANTINOS OF TîRGOVIŞTE. In the pronaos is a remarkable princely votive painting. Outside the main part of the palace is the small Domneasca church (*c.* 1420), on a triconic plan with a tower and open entrance; close to it is an asylum-house, dating from 1656. In the 16th and 17th centuries the palace had Italian-style gardens containing a Turkish bath (*c.* 1640) and a kiosk with sculpted stone columns and stucco decoration.

The church of Old Metropolis (*c.* 1500–20), built by the princes Radu IV (*reg* 1495–1508) and Neagoe Basarab (*reg* 1512–21), was of Greek-cross type with an open exonarthex, also of cross shape, with three towers; it was demolished by the French architect André Lecomte du Nouÿ in 1890 and reconstructed by him, with derogations from the principles of the school of Viollet-le-Duc. The town has many other churches, dating from the 16th to the 18th centuries: the church of the Stelea Monastery (1645), the second to be built on that site, was founded by the Moldavian prince Vasile Lupu (*reg* 1634–53); in design and structure it combines indigenous Wallachian elements with Moldavian influences (recognizable also in the decoration). The old Franciscan monastery (15th century) has been replaced by a new building. A series of characteristic landowners' houses from the late 17th century and the early 18th, and traders' houses of the 18th and 19th centuries have been preserved. The eclectic style of the late 19th century and the early 20th is noticeable in the official buildings (e.g. the town hall, the Tribunal and various schools) and also many private dwellings. The town is given a distinct character by the wide gardens. Its commercial centre, however, was almost completely demolished in the 1970s, when the town centre was systematized. There is an Archaeological Museum, an art collection and the Museum of Printing and Early Printed Books (linked with the printing workshop established at the nearby Dealu Monastery in 1508 and revived in 1640).

TEREZA-IRENE SINIGALIA

Tirmidh. *See* TERMEZ.

Tirol [Tyroll], Hans (*b* ?Augsburg, 1505–6; *d* between Oct 1575 and Oct 1576). German painter and architect. First recorded in Augsburg in 1531, marrying the daughter of Jörg Breu the elder, he became a master painter in 1532. He collaborated on work, including murals (Augsburg, Schaezlerpal.) at the Weberhaus, Augsburg, with his father-in-law and the latter's son, Jörg Breu the younger, developing no separate artistic identity. In 1542 he was appointed to the Augsburg building committee, and afterwards he worked almost exclusively as an architect and commissioner of art. From 1551 he lived in Prague as court architect to Archduke (later King and Emperor) Ferdinand I, being entrusted with extensions to Prague Castle, among other things. In 1555–6 he was in charge of the building of the Star Castle (now Villa Hvězda) outside Prague; its interesting shape is based on a design by Archduke Ferdinand. On Ferdinand's death (1564) Tirol's position in Bohemia became less assured. Even though he was confirmed in his office by Ferdinand's successor, Emperor Maximilian II, he was prosecuted for debt and was soon obliged to leave Prague. From 1570 he was back in Augsburg. Woodcuts, miniatures and drawings in various codices that are linked with Hans Tirol's name are not his work; he only wrote the text for them and acted as publisher.

BIBLIOGRAPHY
Thieme–Becker

J. Białostocki: *The Art of the Renaissance in Eastern Europe: Hungary, Bohemia, Poland* (London, 1976), pp. 78ff

JANEZ HÖFLER

Tiron, Napoleon (*b* Oasele, 26 Feb 1935). Romanian sculptor and teacher. He studied sculpture at the Institute of Fine Arts 'N. Grigorescu', Bucharest (1963–70). From 1970 he took part in exhibitions in Romania and abroad, such as the International Biennial for Small Sculpture, Budapest (1973) and the Venice Biennale (1988). He belonged to a generation that tried to recapture Brancusi's morphology, and to add to it new folkloric elements. Tiron's concern in sculpture was fragmentation, division and a form of collage. Both in his works in wood, which were on the scale of domestic furniture, and in his monumental open-air sculptures, he was concerned to adapt the role of sculpture to the multimedia environment of contemporary art: one way he achieved this was to make the gesture of cutting wood into kindling, as if recreating the ancient process of wood cutting (e.g. 1983; Bucharest, Village Mus.). These fragments of carvings were then laid out on Minimalist fields, according to a planned design (see installation view, Redlow, p. 11), assembled, tied with string and glued, in order to create a monumental self-supporting anthropomorphic structure, through which air and light circulate (see installation view,

Redlow, p. 10). Some of these unconventional sculptures were exhibited in a one-man show at the Galeria de Artà Dalles in Bucharest (1986). Later Tiron concentrated on using piles of stone slabs, coloured and glued together, cut transversely and polished into vaguely phallic forms, paralleling his earlier large anthropomorphic work. In 1990 he was appointed professor at the Fine Art Academy in Bucharest.

BIBLIOGRAPHY

T. Redlow: 'Napoleon Tiron: The Structures of Confidence', *Arta*, xii (1986), pp. 9–12

CĂLIN DAN

Tiruchchapērur [Tiruchchuppērur]. *See* TRICHUR.

Tiruchirapalli [Trichinopoly]. City on the Kaveri River *c*. 400 km south-west of Madras in Tamil Nadu, India. An important Hindu religious centre since the 7th century AD, it is dominated by an immense granite rock some 85 m high, on the summit of which is a modern shrine dedicated to the elephant-headed god Ganesha. Hewn into the rock on the south side are two caves, the uppermost dating from the time of the Pallava king Mahendravarman I (*reg c*. 570–630) and the lower to the Pandya era (*c*. 8th century). The façade of the upper temple is of squat, octagonal pillars bearing Tamil and Sanskrit inscriptions executed in beautiful Pallava script. Inside, at the east end, is a bare cell; opposite this is an important sculpted panel representing the descent of Ganga into the hair of Shiva, who is shown surrounded by devotees (*see* INDIAN SUB-CONTINENT, fig. 207). The lower cave is a columned hall (*maṇḍapa*) containing images of various deities, including Shiva and Vishnu. At the west end of the rock is a Shiva temple, mostly dating from the Vijayanagara and Nayaka periods (16th–17th century). On the island of SRIRANGAM, to the north of the city, are two important Hindu temples, the Vaishnava Ranganatha Temple (9th–20th century) and the Shaiva Jambukeshvara Temple (mostly 17th century). Colonial-period monuments include several churches, notably Christ Church (1765) and St John's Church (early 19th century).

See also INDIAN SUBCONTINENT, §IV, 7(vi)(a).

BIBLIOGRAPHY

G. Michell: *Buddhist, Hindu, Jain*, i of *The Penguin Guide to the Monuments of India* (London, 1989), pp. 475–7

P. Davies: *Islamic, Rajput, European*, ii of *The Penguin Guide to the Monuments of India* (London, 1989), pp. 575–7

Tirupati and Chandragiri. Pilgrimage centre and fortified site in Andhra Pradesh, India. It is divided into three main areas: the town of Tirupati, the sacred hill of Tirumalai (h. 700 m) to the north-west, and the fortified hill of Chandragiri to the south-west. All three benefited from the patronage of the VIJAYANAGARA rulers after 1565, when the Vijayanagara capital (Hampi) was sacked and the capital relocated to Chandragiri. In 1646 Chandragiri was captured by 'Abdallah Qutb Shah of Golconda (*reg* 1626–72), and in 1782 it fell to Haydar 'Ali (*reg* ?1761–82).

The Vaishnava Govindaraja Temple in Tirupati dates mainly from the 15th–17th centuries. Built in the Vijayanagara and NAYAKA styles, the complex comprises three enclosures entered by gate towers (*gopura*s). It contains a number of remarkable sculptures, including a figure of Vishnu reclining on the serpent Ananta (*see* INDIAN SUBCONTINENT, §V, 7(vi)). The principal monument in the Venkatachalam sanctuary on Tirumalai Hill is the Venkateshvara Temple, also dedicated to Vishnu. Dating from the 10th century and later, it is one of the richest temples in India and up to 10,000 pilgrims visit it daily. Comprising two enclosures, the temple is entered through a columned portico containing life-size copper figures of the Vijayanagara kings Krishnadeva Raya (*reg* 1509–30) and Achyutadeva Raya (*reg* 1530–42) and their queens. The inner enclosure contains a shrine to Vishnu as Varadaraja as well as the main shrine, which is probably of the Chola period (*c*. 10th century). The latter enshrines the principal image of the temple, representing Vishnu as Venkateshvara, or Balaji, attended by Lakshmi and the earth goddess Bhudevi. The hill of Chandragiri (h. *c*. 180 m) is surmounted by a fort dating from *c*. 1000 and comprising three enclosures with defensive gateways. Inside are the remains of the Vijayanagara royal palace, built *c*. 1600.

BIBLIOGRAPHY

G. Michell: *Hindu, Buddhist, Jain*, i of *The Penguin Guide to the Monuments of India* (London, 1989), pp. 479–82

P. Davies: *Islamic, Rajput, European*, ii of *The Penguin Guide to the Monuments of India* (London, 1989), p. 535

J. MARR

Tiruvanandapuram. *See* TRIVANDRUM.

Tiruvannamalai [Tiruvannāmalai]. Religious centre in Tamil Nadu, India, dedicated to Shiva in the form of the fiery *liṅga* (an aniconic emblem of the god). The main temple is the 24-acre Arunachaleshvara complex, built between the 10th century and the 17th (*see* INDIAN SUBCONTINENT, fig. 84). Three sets of walls define concentric rectangular enclosures, with the eastern portions of each forming large courts. The complex is entered from the east. In front of the principal gateway are two colonnades with a central walkway. Four *gopura*s (towered gateways) are set in the wall of the outer enclosure; that on the east (for illustration *see* GOPURA) is the largest, rising to about 66 m. These structures date to the 16th and 17th centuries. The lower elements (in granite) consist of profusely decorated base mouldings, pilasters and eaves. Finely carved panels are set into the outer walls of the east *gopura*. The ten diminishing storeys of the superstructure (in brick), soaring in a pyramidal mass above, carry no sculptural imagery. Carvings on the doorjambs and pilasters within the eastern and northern *gopura*s include dancing figures and aspects of Shiva. Related Shaiva themes are carved in the ceiling; there are traces of painting.

Structures in the outermost of the three courts include a 'thousand-pillared' hall (16th century) with a dais in the centre. The piers have rampant animals with riders. A small but ornate shrine dedicated to Subrahmanya has intricate carving that is typical of the later 16th century on the columns and outer walls. A large stepped tank is located near by.

Four smaller *gopura*s with less ornamented walls lead to the intermediate enclosure. These date from the 14th century, though the towers, which carry profuse sculptures, have been renovated in the 20th century. The intermediate enclosure contains a stepped tank, a large columned hall with an open porch, and several small shrines. The innermost enclosure is entered through a single unadorned *gopura* on the east, probably dating to the 11th century. The two principal temples of the complex, located within this enclosure, are dedicated to Shiva and the goddess. The Shiva temple is aligned with the *gopura*; its principal sanctuary, a structure of the CHOLA period, is approached through a long antechamber. The outer walls of the temple carry stone images; a *liṅga* is located in the sanctum. In the 17th century, the temple was surrounded by a corridor with characteristic receding piers overhung by projecting brackets. Housed in the colonnades are stone *liṅga*s and metal images, particularly depictions of Shaiva saints. The temple is flanked by a number of small shrines to Ganapati, Subrahmanya and other divinities. The goddess temple, to the north of the Shiva temple, is of particular interest for the carvings on the piers of the inner hall. These illustrate different aspects of the goddess and are carved in high relief in the typical 17th-century manner. The temple is flanked by a series of small shrines, some of which date to the 13th century.

See also INDIAN SUBCONTINENT, §§III, 5(i)(i) and IV, 7(vi)(a).

BIBLIOGRAPHY
F. H. Gravely: *The Gopuras of Tiruvannamalai* (Madras, 1939)
P. K. Nambiar and K. C. Narayana Kurup: *Census of India 1961, ix, part xi–D, Temples of Madras State, iv North Arcot and Nilgiris* (Madras, 1968)
M. Meister, ed.: *Encyclopaedia of Indian Temple Architecture*, i, pt 1: *South India, Lower Drāviḍadēśa 200 B.C.–A.D. 1324*, 2 vols (New Delhi and Philadelphia, 1983)
C. Guilmoto, M.-L. Reiniche and P. Pichard: *La Ville* (1990), v of *Tiruvannamalai: Un lieu saint śivaïte du sud de l'Inde* (Paris, 1990–)
F. L'Hernault, P. Pichard and J. Delouche: *L'Archéologie du site* (1990), ii of *Tiruvannamalai: Un lieu saint śivaïte du sud de l'Inde* (Paris, 1990–)
M.-L. Reiniche: *La Configuration sociologique du temple hindou* (1990), iv of *Tiruvannamalai: Un lieu saint śivaïte du sud de l'Inde* (Paris, 1990–)
P. R. Srinivasan and M.-L. Reiniche: *Inscriptions* (1990), i of *Tiruvannamalai: A Śaiva Sacred Complex of South India* (Pondicherry, 1990–); review by B. Stein in *J. Amer. Orient. Soc.*, cxiii (1993), pp. 149–50
F. L'Hernault: 'Tiruvannamalai', *Temple Towns of Tamil Nadu*, ed. G. Michell (Bombay, 1993), pp. 40–57

GEORGE MICHELL

Tiruvitāṅkoṭu. See TRAVANCORE.

Tiryns. Site in the Peloponnesus in southern Greece, 10 km south-south-east of Argos and 4 km north of Navplion. Tiryns flourished as a Mycenaean fortress-palace *c.* 1390–*c.* 1200 BC, occupying the summit of a rocky knoll that rises out of the coastal plain (see fig.). The earliest architectural remains date to Early Helladic II (*c.* 2900/2600–*c.* 2400 BC), notably the Rundbau, a circular building (diam. 27.6 m) with stone foundations, mud-brick walls and a terracotta-tiled roof. Successive large buildings of the Middle Helladic period (*c.* 2050–*c.* 1600 BC) and some Early Mycenaean (*c.* 1600–*c.* 1390 BC) remains, including fresco fragments and column bases, also underlie the Mycenaean palace.

Tiryns was the first Mycenaean palace to be excavated. Initial investigations at the site were undertaken by Friedrich Tiersch and A. Rangabé in 1831, and by Heinrich Schliemann in 1876. Schliemann, with Wilhelm Dörpfeld, returned to Tiryns and began systematic excavation there

Tiryns, aerial view, most of the remains dating to Late Helladic IIIB (*c.* 1335–*c.* 1180 BC)

in 1884. The Deutsches Archäologisches Institut has carried out all subsequent excavation at Tiryns, with the exception of the Greek Archaeological Service's seasons there in 1957 and 1962–3. Most of the finds are now in the Navplion Archaeological Museum and the National Archaeological Museum, Athens. An ancient robber's hoard found at Tiryns included, among other rich objects spanning the Late Helladic period (*c.* 1600–*c.* 1050 BC), a large gold ring depicting a seated goddess attended by four daemons (Athens, N. Archaeol. Mus.).

The building of the Mycenaean palace began around the start of Late Helladic (LH) IIIA:2 (*c.* 1360 BC) and was undertaken in three main stages. During the first phase the palace, built on a rocky outcrop rising 18 m above the surrounding plain, covered an area of 67×70 m. It comprised a complex of rooms, incorporating two megara, and a circuit wall built of large, carefully cut blocks of limestone. In its second phase, in LH IIIB:1 (*c.* 1335–*c.* 1240 BC), the area of the palace roughly doubled in size and the circuit wall, strengthened and expanded to incorporate an enlargement of the site, was given a double gateway. The third and final stage dates to LH IIIB: 2 (*c.* 1240–*c.* 1180 BC). The massive Cyclopean walls of this period, built of huge blocks of roughly hewn limestone, were extended to enclose Tiryns's lower town and encompassed an area of *c.* 22,000 sq. m. Casements and galleries were built into the south and south-east sections of the wall, probably for storage. Much building also took place within the walls, and the site as it stands today belongs largely to this final phase.

Access to the palace was by a long, steep ramp leading to the main entrance, a gap of 3 m in the walls. From there one passed along a narrow passage with a double gateway and then through the courtyards and two propyla into the main courtyard of the palace, *c.* 18×20 m in area. On the north side of this colonnaded courtyard lay the façade of the so-called Great Megaron, the architectural focus of the palace complex. The porch, a distyle portico *in antis*, led through a Minoan-style pier and door arrangement into the vestibule, from which one entered the *domos* or main hall, a large rectangular room (*c.* 8×12 m) with a circular central hearth and a raised platform for a throne. Standing around the hearth and supporting the roof were four wooden columns on stone bases. To the east of this building lay a second, smaller megaron, with two rooms and a rectangular hearth. A network of rooms and corridors surrounded these megara, and remains of staircases show that in some areas the palace reached two storeys. The walls of the palatial building had foundations of rubble, lower courses of mud and stones reaching 0.5 to 1 m above ground and a superstructure of mud-brick supported by a framework of vertical and horizontal wooden beams. The walls were then coated in mud, sometimes supplemented by lime or stucco, and decorated with frescoes in the more important rooms (*see* HELLADIC, §IV, 1). The floors, some of which were also decorated, were made of cement reinforced with pebbles.

The palace at Tiryns was destroyed by fire at the end of LH IIIB: 2, but the site continued to be occupied for a further 100 years. In its Post-palatial phase Tiryns was important in pottery terms for its near continuity of LH IIIC (*c.* 1180–*c.* 1050 BC) and Protogeometric (*c.* 1050–*c.* 900 BC) styles. Around 750 BC, in the Geometric period (*c.* 900–*c.* 700 BC), a long narrow building was erected on the site of the Great Megaron. This building, which has been identified as a temple dedicated to Hera. was destroyed about 100 years later, but the site continued as a focus of religious worship well into the Classical period (*c.* 480–*c.* 323 BC).

BIBLIOGRAPHY

H. Schliemann and W. Dörpfeld: *Tiryns, der prähistorische Palast der Könige von Tiryns: Ergebnisse der neuesten Ausgrabungen* (Leipzig, 1886; Eng. trans., London, 1886)

Tiryns: Die Ergebnisse der neuesten Ausgrabungen des Instituts, Bde I–IV (Leipzig, 1912; Eng. trans., 1938)

Tiryns: Forschungen und Berichte, Bde V–IX (Leipzig, 1971; Eng. trans., 1980)

U. Jantzen: *Führer durch Tiryns* (Athens, 1975)

S. Iakovidis: *Late Helladic Citadels on Mainland Greece* (Leiden, 1983)

K. Killian: 'Mycenaeans up to Date: Trends and Changes in Recent Research', *Problems in Greek Prehistory: Centenary Conference of the British School at Athens: Manchester, 1986*

For brief reports on more recent and as yet unpublished excavations at Tiryns see *Archäol. Anz.*

LOUISE SCHOFIELD

Tischbein. German family of artists. Between the early 18th century and the late 19th this family from Hesse produced 28 artists and artisans, a third of them women, who were active throughout Germany and elsewhere in Europe. Johann Heinrich Tischbein (1682–1764), an artisan in Haina, had seven sons: the fifth, (1) Johann Heinrich Tischbein I, was a noted portrait painter in Kassel. The second, Johann Valentin Tischbein (1715–68), had a son, (2) Friedrich Tischbein, who also established himself as a portrait painter, in Leipzig; while the first, Johann Conrad Tischbein (1712–78), was father to Johann Heinrich Tischbein II (1742–1808), the author of a treatise on engraving (*Kurzgefasste Abhandlung über die Ätz-Kunst*, Kassel, 1790) and to (3) Wilhelm Tischbein, who worked in Naples and painted Goethe's portrait. The family's three most famous members are thus known, respectively, as 'der Kasseler', 'der Leipziger' and 'der Neapolitaner' or 'Goethe Tischbein'. Their portrait work contributed to the transition in German art from the Late Baroque and Rococo to Neo-classicism and early naturalism. (4) Christian Wilhelm Tischbein, an architect as well as a painter, was the son of the fourth of the seven brothers from Haina, while the painter (5) August Anton Tischbein was the grandson of the sixth, Jacob Tischbein (1725–91).

BIBLIOGRAPHY

Thieme-Becker

H. Keller: *Die Kunst des 18. Jahrhunderts*, Propylaen-Kstgesch., x (Berlin, 1971)

(1) Johann Heinrich Tischbein I (*b* Haina, 14 Oct 1722; *d* Kassel, 22 Aug 1789). Painter. He was apprenticed to Johann Baptist Zimmermann, Johann Georg von Freese (1701–75) and his brother Johann Valentin Tischbein (1715–68) before training with Carle Vanloo in Paris (1748) and with Giovanni Battista Piazzetta in Venice (1749). He copied the Venetian Masters and visited Rome; he returned to Germany in 1751. The following year he settled permanently in Kassel as court painter to the Landgrave William VIII of Hesse-Kassel. He also served as professor of the Akademie in Kassel from 1762. Among his earliest successes was the Schönheitsgalerie for William VIII, a collection of portraits of aristocratic women painted in a conservative Rococo style (1752–5; Kassel, Schloss Wilhelmshöhe). The amiable charm of his worldly style and technical virtuosity soon established him among the foremost portrait painters, particularly of women, of the period.

Johann Heinrich's portraits of his first wife (1756; Berne, Kstmus.) and second wife (1762; Kassel, Neue Gal.) display the familiar characteristics of his large-scale portraits: opulent textures, inviting openness of demeanour, natural settings and graceful poses. *The Artist with his First Wife at the Spinet* (1769; Berlin, Gemäldegal.) betrays the warm humanity of his art in an intimate double portrait that is also an engaging genre painting of a studio. It also records a shift in contemporary social mores towards bourgeois values and greater psychological sensitivity. In addition to portrait painting, Tischbein produced many decorative paintings with mythological and genre themes for various palaces in Germany, as well as religious works in a style reminiscent of Caravaggio and the Carracci brothers (e.g. the altarpiece *Agony in the Garden*, 1788; Haina, former Kloskerkirche). Neo-classical tendencies appear in his work from the later 1770s.

BIBLIOGRAPHY

Johann Heinrich Tischbein der Ältere, 1722–1789 (exh. cat., Kassel, 1964)

B. Bushart: *Deutsche Malerei des Rokoko* (Königstein im Taunus, 1967), pp. 28, 53

Nationalgalerie, Berlin, Staatl. Museen. Preuss. Kultbes. cat. (Berlin, 1968), p. 213

(2) (Johann) Friedrich (August) Tischbein (*b* Maastricht, 9 March 1750; *d* Heidelberg, 21 June 1812). Painter, nephew of (1) Johann Heinrich Tischbein I. After initial study with his father, Johann Valentin Tischbein, and with his uncle, he studied in Paris (1772–7) with support from a patron, Graf Friedrich von Waldeck. He stayed in Rome from 1777 to 1779, where he was influenced by Anton Raphael Mengs and Heinrich Füger. In 1780 he became court painter to von Waldeck at Schloss Arolsen near Kassel. By the late 1780s he had abandoned his early Rococo style and had adopted a sentimental form of Neo-classicism and a sensitive, proto-Romantic naturalism based on the work of such painters as George Romney, Gainsborough and Elisabeth Vigée-Lebrun. His portrait of *?Herr von Chatelain* (1791; Munich, Neue Pin.), which helped establish his lasting reputation as a portrait painter, attests to his eclectic approach. The young man's leisurely pose, dreamy expression and fashionable dress, and the outdoor setting reveal, moreover, the shift in social values from the dominance of the aristocracy to bourgeois society, with its greater concern with psychological characterization.

Friedrich Tischbein: *Countess Theresia Fries*, oil on canvas, 2.19×1.28 m, 1801 (Hamburg, Hamburger Kunsthalle)

Friedrich's frequent trips to the Netherlands from 1786 probably encouraged his transition from a court painter to portrait painter to the middle classes. His reputation as the foremost German family portrait painter of the period is based on paintings such as *Sophie Tischbein with her Daughters* (1796; Leipzig, Mus. Bild. Kst.), which conveys familial affection and intimacy within a sparing and clear Neo-classical composition. In 1800 he became the Director of the Akademie in Leipzig and continued to paint portraits. In *Countess Theresia Fries* (1801; Hamburg, Ksthalle; see fig.) the festive allure of the classically dressed figure combines with gliding movement, luscious textures and vivacious colour harmonies in a muted atmospheric landscape; the result has an overall unity and sense of timeless charm.

BIBLIOGRAPHY
A. Stoll: *Der Maler Johann Friedrich August Tischbein und seine Familie* (Stuttgart, 1923)
Neue Pinakothek, Munich, Bayer. Staatsgemäldesammlungen cat. (Munich, 1982)

RUDOLF M. BISANZ

(3) (Johann Heinrich) Wilhelm Tischbein (*b* Haina, 15 Feb 1751; *d* Eutin, 26 June 1829). Painter, teacher and theorist. In 1776 he trained under his uncle, (1) Johann Heinrich Tischbein I, in Kassel, and then moved to Hamburg to study with another uncle, Jacob Tischbein (1725–91). From both teachers he imbibed the courtly, late Baroque style then fashionable in Germany. His instruction was mainly in portrait painting with a smattering of landscape painting. In Hamburg he also studied history painting in the company of his cousin Johann Dietrich Lilly (1705–92), who was both painter and art dealer, by copying works by the Old Masters. During the 1770s, Tischbein travelled to the Netherlands and worked in Bremen and Hannover, before finally settling in Berlin in 1777. Over the next two years he established himself as a portrait painter to the Prussian court. From 1779 to 1781 he undertook his first trip to Italy, staying mainly in Rome. There he studied at the private academy run by the Swiss sculptor Alexander Trippel, from whom he learnt the principles of the Neo-classical style of which he subsequently became a leading exponent.

In 1781 Tischbein returned north, first to Zurich, where he became a friend of the physiognomist Johann Kaspar Lavater, then to Kassel; but from 1783 to 1799 he was again in Italy. The earlier part of this second Italian sojourn was spent in Rome, where for several years he enjoyed the close company of JOHANN WOLFGANG VON GOETHE. During his Italian journey (1786–88) Goethe harboured hopes of becoming a visual artist, and to this end took informal instruction from Tischbein. The two friends also travelled together, including an extended visit to Naples and its environs. The most celebrated monument to their friendship is Tischbein's portrait, *Goethe in the Roman Campagna* (1787; Frankfurt am Main, Städel. Kstinst. & Städt. Gal.; for illustration *see* GOETHE, JOHANN WOLFGANG VON). A full-length depiction of the poet resting amidst ancient reliefs and the Roman countryside, this picture deservedly remains both the most famous image of Goethe and the best-known painting by Tischbein. It differs significantly from the typical 18th-century portrait of the tourist in Rome (a genre perfected by Pompeo Batoni), in which the traveller in formal dress is flatteringly surrounded with the pomp and trappings of antiquity. Tischbein's Goethe is wrapped in the simple white cloak of a pilgrim and sits among antique fragments and nearly obliterated ruins. As letters between Tischbein and Goethe make clear, the picture was conceived as a meditation on the transient nature of human accomplishments. One prominent fragment at Goethe's feet is based upon a well-known sarcophagus relief, the *Recognition of Orestes by Iphigenia*, a clear reference to Goethe's as yet unfinished drama, *Iphigenia auf Tauris*.

In 1787 Tischbein settled in Naples, which, under the influence of Queen Caroline, had become a recognized haven for German artists. He soon succeeded Giuseppe Bonito as Director of the Accademia in Naples, imposing on its curriculum his own strict interpretation of Neo-classical style and aesthetics. While Tischbein may be credited with having finally removed the Neapolitan artistic tradition from its lingering Late Baroque style, the Accademia during his years there produced virtually no artists of note. While in Naples, in addition to his teaching duties, Tischbein edited the British envoy Sir William Hamilton's publication, *Collection of Engravings from Ancient Vases mostly of Pure Greek Workmanship . . .* (Naples, 1791–5). He also published a volume of his own, *Têtes de différents animaux dessinées d'après nature pour donner une idée plus exacte de leurs caractères* (Naples, 1796), a study probably influenced by his friendship with Lavater. The paintings Tischbein produced in Naples include *Orestes and Iphigenia* (1788; Arolsen, Residenzschloss), inspired by Goethe's poem *Iphigenia auf Tauris*, and a portrait of *Anna Amalia of Weimar* (1789; Weimar, Goethe-Nmus.), in which the Grand Duchess is represented sitting near the main gateway to the ruins of Pompeii. Both of these pictures, as also others executed during Tischbein's years at Naples, are sophisticated examples of Neo-classical taste.

With the fall of Naples to the French in 1799, Tischbein left the city, and his influence on Neapolitan art did not long survive his departure. He returned to Germany (Kassel, Göttingen, Hannover and Hamburg) and worked on his most complex book, *Homer nach Antiken* (1801–5, and 1821–3), attempting to establish a corpus of ancient works of art representing Homeric scenes. The work included scholarly commentaries by the classical scholar Christian Gottlieb Heyne. In 1808, Tischbein settled at Eutin, where he became court painter and gallery inspector to Duke Peter of Oldenburg. Although relatively unproductive as an artist during the last two decades of his life, and unswerving in his allegiance to the theory of Neoclassicism, Tischbein was highly regarded by the Romantics. His autobiography, *Aus meinem Leben*, was first published in 1861.

WRITINGS

Têtes de différents animaux dessinées d'après nature pour donner une idée plus exacte de leurs caractères (Naples, 1796)
Homer nach Antiken (Göttingen, 1801–4; Stuttgart, 1821–3)
G. W. Schiller, ed.: *Aus meinen Leben* (Brunswick, 1861; rev. Berlin, 1992)

BIBLIOGRAPHY

F. Landsberger: *Wilhelm Tischbein: Ein Künstlerleben des 18. Jahrhunderts* (Leipzig, 1908)
B. Grubert: *Johann Heinrich Wilhelm Tischbein: 'Homer nach Antiken gezeichnet'* (diss., Bochum, Ruhr-U., 1975)
J. F. Moffit: 'The Poet and the Painter: J. H. W. Tischbein's "Perfect Portrait" of *Goethe in the Campagna*', *A. Bull.*, lxv (1983), pp. 440–55

PETER WALCH

(4) Christian Wilhelm Tischbein (*b* Marburg an der Lahn, 2 May 1751; *d* Schmiedeberg, 31 July 1824). Architect, draughtsman and painter, nephew of (1) Johann Heinrich Tischbein I and cousin to (2) Friedrich and (3) Wilhelm. He trained with members of his family in Hamburg and studied architecture in Breslau [Wrocław]. He was drawing-teacher to the children of Reichsgraf Hans Heinrich IV von Hochberg-Fürstenstein in Silesia (1781–2) and served briefly as Gallery Director for Herzog Erdmann von Braunschweig-Oels zu Oels. He was Building Director for the Reichsgraf from 1790; he produced room decorations, portraits, landscape designs and various small decorative structures and utilitarian estate buildings.

(5) August Anton Tischbein (*b* Rostock, 9 Oct 1805; *d* ?Trieste, after 1867). Painter, great-nephew of (1) Johann Heinrich Tischbein I. He trained at the academies in Berlin, Dresden and Munich from 1833, after numerous trips to the Netherlands, London, Rome, Calabria, Milan and Venice. In 1839 he settled in Trieste and painted mostly genre scenes and landscapes with Bavarian and Tyrolean subjects, as well as some portraits. He published a volume of architectural views in 1831.

PRINTS

A. A. Tischbein and J. H. Schlösser: *Denkmale altdeutscher Baukunst in Lübeck* (Lübeck, 1831–2)

RUDOLF M. BISANZ

Tischer, (Carl) Marcus. *See* TUSCHER, MARCUS.

Tisi, Benvenuto. *See* GAROFALO.

Tišnov Abbey. Cistercian convent west of Brno in the Svratka Valley, southern Moravia, Czech Republic. The convent, named Porta Coeli, was founded by Queen Constance, widow of Přemysl Ottakar I (*reg* 1198–1230), as her burial place. She was assisted by her sons King Václav I (*reg* 1230–53) and Přemysl, Margrave of Moravia (*reg* 1227–39), who granted Tišnov extensive privileges. The first reference to the convent occurs in a document issued by Queen Constance on 6 February 1233, but it is clear that the foundations had been laid the previous summer. In a document of 4 April 1238, King Václav I referred to his mother who was 'proceeding unabatedly with the completion of the work that had been begun'. On 5 November of that year Pope Gregory IX (*reg* 1227–41), who had given the convent papal protection in 1235, granted indulgences to all who attended the consecration ceremony. Margrave Přemysl (*d* 16 Oct 1239) was buried at Tišnov, and Queen Constance died there (12 Dec 1240); the convent is last mentioned in decrees issued by King Václav I on the day of his mother's funeral (13 Dec).

Tišnov preserves much of its medieval character. The church, dedicated to the Virgin, comprises an aisled nave (formerly with a narthex at the west end), a transept, and a choir with two flanking chapels. The plan was modelled on Notre-Dame, Dijon, in Burgundy, but the style of the church is derived from that of the early Cistercian Burgundian workshops. During the first construction phase (1232–8) the church, narthex and the eastern and western conventual ranges were built, and shortly afterwards the cloister. At this time, probably during Queen Constance's lifetime, the monumental west portal was installed. In the mid-13th century the transept and central vessel of the nave were vaulted; the tapered, hollow chamfered ribs are typical of this later workshop.

The west portal resembles French Gothic portals of *c.* 1230. On the tympanum the figure of *Christ Enthroned* is in a mandorla borne by the symbols of the *Evangelists*; at either side are the *Virgin* and *St John the Baptist*, whose arms reach out protectively towards the kneeling figures of the founders, who offer a model of the church to Christ: the suppliant king on the left must be Václav I; the figure on the right represents Queen Constance. The archivolts are carved with rich foliate ornament: bands of crockets alternating with scrolls. The embrasures each bear five columns flanking statues of the *Apostles*, who stand above acanthus and vine scrolls; at either side of the portal are statues of the remaining two Apostles, set on columns above guardian lions.

Tišnov was devastated during the Hussite wars in the 1420s but the nuns had returned there by 1454. From 1509 the convent was under the protection of the lords of Pernštejn, and was remodelled in the Baroque style in the second half of the 18th century. It was dissolved in 1782, but the nuns returned in 1899. Restorations were carried out in the late 20th century.

BIBLIOGRAPHY

Codex diplomaticus et epistolarius regni Bohemiae, iii/1 (Prague, 1942); iii/2 (Prague, 1962)

J. Joachimová: 'Fundace královny Konstancie a pražské statky německých rytířů' [The Queen Constance foundation and the German Knights' Prague property], *Umění*, xvi (1968), pp. 495–501

J. Kuthan: 'Fundace a počátky kláštera cisterciaček v Tišnově' [The foundation and beginnings of the Cistercian convent in Tišnov], *Časop. Matice Morav.*, xciii (1974), pp. 361–70

J. Kuthan and I. Neumann: 'Ideový program tišnovského portálu a jeho kořeny' [Sources and programme of the Tišnov portal], *Umění*, xxvii (1979), pp. 107–18 [with full bibliog.]

J. Homolka: 'Sochařství doby posledních Přemyslovců' [Sculpture in the time of the last Premyslids], *Umění doby posledních Přemyslovců* (Roztoky, 1982), pp. 86–90

H. SOUKUPOVÁ

Tišov, Ivan (*b* Viškovci, nr Djakov, 8 Feb 1870; *d* Zagreb, 20 Sept 1928). Croatian painter. He studied at the School of Arts and Crafts in Zagreb, the Kunstgewerbeschule in Vienna and, from 1889 to 1893, the Akademie der Bildenden Künste in Munich. From 1905 he taught at the School of Arts and Crafts in Zagreb and in 1913–14 he attended the Académie Julian in Paris. He painted religious and mythological pictures, allegorical scenes and subjects from folklore, as well as contemporary political portraiture. He also executed a number of purely decorative compositions in public buildings, cultural institutions and churches in Zagreb. Under the influence of the painter Vlaho Bukovac he gradually introduced a luminous quality into his canvases. Among his most accomplished works are a portrait of the politician *Nikola Tomašić*, a *Self-portrait with Wife* and a *Self-portrait*. He produced fresh, directly observed watercolours (e.g. *The Field at Grobnik*) and illustrated the *Österreichisch-Ungarische Monarchie in Wort und Bild* (Vienna, 1886–1902; U. Zagreb, Lib.).

BIBLIOGRAPHY

B. Lovrić: 'Ivan Tišov', *Savremenik*, 4 (1908), p. 249

V. Lunaček: 'Ivan Tišov', *Obzor*, 221 (1918)

A. Jiroušek: 'Ivan Tišov', *Vijenac*, 6 (1923)

L. Babić: *Umjetnost kod Hrvata u XIX. stoljeću* [Art in 19th-century Croatia] (Zagreb, 1934), pp. 112-13

BORIS VIŽINTIN

Tissot, James [Jacques-Joseph] (*b* Nantes, 15 Oct 1836; *d* Château de Buillon, Doubs, 8 Aug 1902). French painter, printmaker and enamellist. He grew up in a port, an experience reflected in his later paintings set on board ship. He moved to Paris *c.* 1856 and became a pupil of Louis Lamothe and Hippolyte Flandrin. He made his Salon début in 1859 and continued to exhibit there successfully until he went to London in 1871. His early paintings exemplify Romantic obsessions with the Middle Ages, while works such as the *Meeting of Faust and Marguerite* (exh. Salon 1861; Paris. Mus. d'Orsay) and *Marguerite at the Ramparts* (1861; untraced, see Wentworth, 1984, pl. 8) show the influence of the Belgian painter Baron Henri Leys. In the mid-1860s Tissot abandoned these tendencies in favour of contemporary subjects, sometimes with a humorous intent, as in *Two Sisters* (exh. Salon 1864; Paris, Louvre) and *Beating the Retreat in the Tuileries Gardens* (exh. Salon 1868; priv. col., see Wentworth, 1984, pl. 45). The painting *Young Ladies Looking at Japanese Objects* (exh. Salon 1869; priv. col., see Wentworth, 1984, pl. 59) testifies to his interest in things Oriental, and *Picnic* (exh. Salon 1869; priv. col., see 1984 exh. cat., fig. 27), in which he delved into the period of the Directoire, is perhaps influenced by the Goncourt brothers. Tissot re-created the atmosphere of the 1790s by dressing his characters in historical costume.

During the Franco-Prussian War Tissot participated valiantly in the defence of Paris, but his abrupt move to London in 1871 has been interpreted as an attempt to escape reprisals for associating himself with the Paris Commune. A more plausible explanation for the move might be his desire for better professional opportunities than existed in a war-ravaged city. His acquaintance with Thomas Gibson Bowles (who owned the magazine *Vanity Fair*, for which Tissot had been drawing caricatures for some time) gave him an important entrée into social and artistic circles in London.

In 1872 Tissot began exhibiting regularly at the Royal Academy, where he had first shown in 1864, and continued to do so until 1881 (except for 1877–9). His early London paintings are in the Directoire manner, as exemplified by an *Interesting Story* (exh. RA 1872; Melbourne, N.G. Victoria), but he soon shifted to scenes of fashionable West End life (*Too Early*, exh. RA 1873; London, Guildhall A.G.), of lovers parting (the *Last Evening*, exh. RA 1873; London, Guildhall A.G.), of festive social occasions (*Ball on Shipboard*, exh. RA 1874; London, Tate; see fig.) and of elegant young people at their leisure (*The Thames*, exh. RA 1876; Wakefield, A.G.). These paintings appear to fall within the English narrative tradition but are often infused with a languorous atmosphere whereby his subjects seem emotionally detached and pensive. This confluence of narrative and non-narrative, or emotive, aspects makes his subject-matter open to different interpretations. His technique remained impeccably craftsmanlike and traditional, particularly in depicting the details of women's fashions.

James Tissot: *Ball on Shipboard*, oil on canvas, 0.84×1.29 m, *c.* 1874 (London, Tate Gallery)

Around 1875 Tissot met Kathleen Newton, a beautiful divorcee, and their relationship represented Tissot's only period of real family life as an adult. Mrs Newton and her family dominated the subject-matter of his paintings, particularly those concerned with domestic life and travel, as in *By Water (Waiting at Dockside)* (watercolour study, *c.* 1881–2; London, Owen Edgar).

In his London works Tissot avoided his previous superficial japonaiserie in favour of more pronounced Oriental qualities, for example *The Gardener* (*c.* 1879; untraced, see 1984 exh. cat., fig. 68). At the same time his skill as a painter reached its peak, and his interest in printmaking, particularly etching, was renewed (e.g. *Summer*, etching, 1878; London, BM).

In the late 1870s Tissot also began producing cloisonné enamels, partly inspired by his interest in Japanese metalwork and partly by artists such as Lucien Falize and Ferdinand Barbedienne. The majority of his enamel work took the form of small objects and plaques, a fine example of which is the oval jardinière *Lake and Sea* (bronze mount, 240×620×310 mm, *c.* 1884; Brighton, Royal Pav.). A popular and successful artist in London, Tissot considered himself to be fully modern, as shown by the title of his last important exhibition at the Dudley Gallery in 1882, *An Exhibition of Modern Art*.

Kathleen Newton's death from tuberculosis in 1882 affected Tissot deeply and marked an important transition in his artistic development. He returned to Paris and held a large one-man exhibition at the Palais de l'Industrie in 1882. In 1885 his exhibition entitled *Femme à Paris*, held at the Galerie Sedelmeyer, included a series of 15 large

paintings presenting modern woman in her various occupations. This was part of an ambitious venture, which, had it been finished, would have combined painting, printmaking and literature in a truly novel scheme. During the 1880s he became popular as a portrait painter and began to experiment with pastel (e.g. *Berthe*, 1882–3; Paris, Petit Pal.).

While working on one of the *Femme à Paris* paintings Tissot claimed to have had a religious revelation; this resulted in *Christ the Comforter* (*c.* 1884; St Petersburg, Hermitage), a large painting showing Christ comforting two downtrodden pilgrims in the ruins of the Cour des Comptes in Paris. Tissot also became interested in spiritualism and in 1885 was convinced that Kathleen Newton had materialized at a séance in London, an event he recorded in a mezzotint after a lost painting: *The Apparition* (1885; priv. col., see 1984 exh. cat., no. 151).

His religious experience led him to devote his remaining years primarily to illustrating the Life of Christ and the Old Testament. Tissot felt impelled to depict the Palestine of Christ's day and he made several trips to the Holy Land to do research. His series of 365 gouache illustrations for the *Life of Christ* (New York, Brooklyn Mus.) were executed at the Château de Buillon, which he had inherited from his father in 1888 and shown to enthusiastic crowds in Paris (1894 and 1895), London (1896) and New York (1898) and then toured North America until 1900. They were published in 1896–7 and in several later editions. Tissot left his Old Testament paintings (New York, Jew. Mus.) unfinished, but they were subsequently completed by other artists and the engravings published in 1904.

These two religious series were the most notable visual summation of the Catholic revival in late 19th-century France.

Tissot was initially remembered as an illustrator of the Bible but his depictions of fashionable 19th-century life and his charming genre scenes are now regarded as his most significant work. In a distinctly personal way his work reflects nearly every important artistic development of his time and reveals the interaction between academic and avant-garde developments in art.

BIBLIOGRAPHY

James Jacques Joseph Tissot (exh. cat., ed. D. Brooke; Providence, RI Sch. Des., Mus. A., 1968)

W. Misfeldt: *James Jacques Joseph Tissot* (diss., U. Washington, 1971)

James Tissot: Catalogue Raisonné of his Prints (exh. cat. by M. Wentworth, Minneapolis, MN, Inst. A., 1978)

W. Misfeldt: *The Albums of James Tissot* (Bowling Green, OH, 1982) [many previously unpubd works]

J. *James Tissot: Biblical Paintings* (exh. cat. by G. Schiff, New York, Jew. Mus., 1982)

M. Wentworth: *James Tissot* (Oxford, 1984) [generously illus.]

James Tissot (exh. cat., ed. K. Matyjaskiewicz; London, Barbican A.G., 1984)

C. Wood: *Tissot* (London, 1986)

WILLARD E. MISFELDT

Tite, Sir William (*b* London, Feb 1798; *d* Torquay, 20 April 1873). English architect. He was the son of Arthur Tite, a wealthy London businessman. William Tite was articled to David Laing (1774–1856) in 1812 and was admitted to the Royal Academy Schools in 1818. He was President of the Architectural Society in 1838, RIBA Gold Medallist in 1856, President of the RIBA, 1861–2 and 1867–9, and knighted in 1869. Tite's work has been largely ignored because, although he was extremely successful, he was not a particularly good architect. He did not adopt wholeheartedly the Ecclesiological Gothic Revival. His best-known building is the Royal Exchange, London, a competent but not outstanding classical design, won in competition against Charles Robert Cockerell in 1839 and completed in 1844. From *c.* 1840 he designed a large number of railway stations in a range of styles chiefly for Caledonian and Scottish Central Railways and the Yeovil and Exeter Railway: classical at Gosport (1841–4), Hants; Tudor Revival at Windsor, (1850) Berks; Gothic Revival at Carlisle (1847), Cumbria. Perhaps his most startling building is his neo-Byzantine St James' Church (1858–9), Gerrards Cross, Bucks. From 1850, due to ill-health, Tite increasingly retired from the practice of architecture, but from 1855 to 1873 he was MP for Bath. In this capacity in the late 1850s he heavily criticized Sir George Gilbert Scott's (*see* SCOTT (ii), (1)) Gothic Revival designs for the new Government Offices, Whitehall, London. In a retrospective look at his career delivered to the RIBA in 1859 he lamented on the contemporary taste for revivalist styles. On his death he endowed the Tite Prize 'to promote the study of Italianate architecture'.

BIBLIOGRAPHY

DNB

Obituary, *Builder*, xxxi (1873), pp. 337–9

M. S. Briggs: 'Sir William Tite, MP. His Life and Work', *Builder*, clxxviii/5578 (1950), pp. 39–42; no. 5579, pp. 95–8

R. Dixon and S. Muthesius: *Victorian Architecture* (London, 1978)

G. Biddle: *Great Railway Stations of Britain* (London, 1986)

DAVID PROUT

Titi, Filippo (*b* Città di Castello, *bapt* 16 April 1639: *d* Città di Castello, 23 Oct 1702). Italian prelate, art historian and cartographer. He was born of a noble family and became a priest in 1658. Afterwards he studied theology and law at the University of Rome, and at the same time learnt drawing from the classical painter Virgilio Ducci (*b* 1623). He acted as a consultant in the building of the Teatro degli Illuminati (1660–68) in his native city, and began (also in the 1660s) a rich production of topographical maps that continued for *c.* 30 years.

His fortunes changed markedly with the patronage of Cardinal Gasparo Carpegna, who was made Vicar of Rome by Pope Clement X and was put in charge of conserving the city's works of art (from 1671). After becoming an abbot, Titi published the first edition of his successful *Studio di pittura, scoltura et architettura nelle chiese di Roma.* Rather than following the antiquated model of the guide to holy places for the devout pilgrim, Titi created an annotated catalogue of Roman artistic treasures, examined objectively. After assisting at the erection of the dome (1680–83) of the cathedral at Città di Castello by Nicola Barbioni (1637–88), Titi produced in 1686 an updated edition of the *Studio*, which was not as well received as the earlier version. Later editions appeared after Titi's death, in 1708, 1721 and 1763.

WRITINGS

Studio di pittura, scoltura et architettura nelle chiese di Roma (Rome, 1674); rev. as *Ammaestramento utile di pittura, scoltura et architettura nelle chiese di Roma* (1686, 3/1708, 4/1721, 5/1763); comp. edn, ed. B. Contardi and S. Romano (Rome, 1987) [incl. essay by M. Lattanzi: 'Per Filippo Titi: La vita, l'opera e la fortuna del libro: Uno studio bio-bibliografico', pp. xix–xxxiv]

Descrizione delle pitture, sculture e architetture esposte al pubblico in Roma (Rome, 1763/*R* 1978) [reprint incl. essay by F. Prinzi: 'Filippo Titi: La prima grande vera guida di Roma', pp. 5–10]

GIUSEPPE PINNA

Titian [Vecellio, Tiziano] (*b* Pieve di Cadore, *c.* ?1485–90; *d* Venice, 27 Aug 1576). Italian painter, draughtsman and printmaker. The most important artist of the VECELLIO family, he was immensely successful in his lifetime and since his death has always been considered the greatest painter of the Venetian school. He was equally pre-eminent in all the branches of painting practised in the 16th century: religious subjects, portraits, allegories and scenes from Classical mythology and history. His work illuminates more clearly than that of any other painter the fundamental transition from the 15th-century tradition (characterized by meticulous finish and the use of bright local colours) to that of the 16th century, when painters adopted a broader technique, with less defined outlines and with mutually related colours.

Titian was based in Venice throughout his professional life, but his many commissions for royal and noble patrons outside Venice and Italy, notably for Philip II of Spain, contributed considerably to the spread of his fame. His work was a vital formative influence on the major European painters of the 17th century, including Rubens and Velázquez.

I. Life and painted work. II. Graphic arts. III. Working methods and technique. IV. Critical reception and posthumous reputation.

I. Life and painted work.

1. Training and early work, to 1515. 2. Early success, 1516–mid-1540s. 3. 'Late style', mid-1540s and after.

1. TRAINING AND EARLY WORK, TO 1515. The evidence for the year of Titian's birth is conflicting and has been much disputed. He was brought to Venice as a child, where, according to Dolce, he was first apprenticed to a painter and mosaicist, Sebastiano Zuccati (*d* 1527), and then successively to Gentile Bellini, Giovanni Bellini and finally was associated with Giorgione. A votive picture of *Jacopo Pesaro Presented to St Peter* (Antwerp, Kon. Mus. S. Kst) is probably the most primitive in style of the undocumented early works and therefore among the very earliest, although the presence in it of Pope Alexander VI does not suffice to date the picture before his death in 1503, as has been claimed. The earliest surviving paintings that are precisely datable are three frescoes of scenes from the *Life of St Anthony* (Padua, Scuola di S Antonio), documented as of 1511. As they are almost Titian's only surviving works in fresco, they are of limited value as touchstones of his early style as a painter of easel pictures. Vasari (1568) mentioned works dating from a little before this, but one, a *Tobias*, is not certainly identifiable, and the other, the *Triumph of Christ*, is not a painting but a woodcut (*see* §II, 2 below). Also before 1511, Titian is stated by Vasari to have shared work with Giorgione on frescoes, now almost entirely destroyed (fragments Venice, Ca' d'Oro), on the exterior of the Venetian headquarters of the German merchants, the Fondaco dei Tedeschi, for which Giorgione was paid in 1508. Titian's altarpiece of *St Mark Enthroned with SS Cosmas, Damian, Roch and Sebastian* (Venice, S Maria della Salute) is roughly datable because it includes St Roch who was invoked against the plague, of which there had been an outbreak in 1510. Probably Titian's earliest surviving masterpiece is the *Sacred and Profane Love* (see fig. 1), which includes the arms of both the Aurelio and Bagaretto families and can therefore be associated with a wedding between members of the families that took place in 1514. Although the precise meaning of the picture is uncertain, its extraordinary and original beauty is not in dispute. The gorgeously dressed girl on the left (presumably representing the bride) is contrasted with the nude on the right, presumably Venus, whose flesh is set off by the crimson cloak that flutters to the right of her. Further contrast is provided by the simulated marble relief between the figures and by the panoramic landscape with horsemen, sheep, picturesque buildings and different formations of cloud (of which Titian was a great master). Three other technically similar and therefore probably roughly contemporary paintings of major importance are the *Noli me tangere* (London, N.G.), the '*Three Ages of Man*' (*Daphnis and Chloe*; see fig. 2) and the *Baptism* (Rome, Mus. Capitolino). In all of these, as in the *Sacred and Profane Love*, the figures and the landscape are lyrically interrelated.

Despite the existence of these few landmarks, it is difficult to define Titian's early work, not only because so few pictures are datable, but also because the contemporary work of such painters as DOMENICO MANCINI, GIULIO CAMPI and GIOVANNI CARIANI is even less defined, and liable to be confused with his. Confusion with the work of GIORGIONE has been particularly controversial. Michiel noted that Titian finished or altered a painting of *Venus* by Giorgione, probably the picture now at Dresden (Gemäldegal. Alte Meister). As Giorgione died unexpectedly in 1510, the *Venus* was presumably a late work, left unfinished. However, his share of it—the figure of Venus and the drapery on which she reclines—shows a sharper touch than the evident work of Titian in the landscape: while the *Portrait of a Man* (*see* GIORGIONE, fig. 2), probably of 1510, suggests that the two painters were already developing on different lines. The portrait is delicate in touch and with thin pigment, while roughly contemporary works undoubtedly by Titian such as the *St Mark Enthroned* or the *Holy Family with a Shepherd* (London, N.G.) have vigorous brushwork and relatively thick impasto. There is an increasing tendency to attribute to the young Titian such pictures as *Christ and the Adulteress* (Glasgow, A.G. & Mus.), the *Concert* (Florence,

1. Titian: *Sacred and Profane Love*, oil on canvas, 1.18×2.79 m, *c.* 1514 (Rome, Galleria Borghese)

2. Titian: 'Three Ages of Man' (Daphnis and Chloe; detail), oil on canvas, 0.90×1.51 m, c. 1514 (Duke of Sutherland: on loan to Edinburgh, National Gallery of Scotland)

Pitti) or the *Concert champêtre* (see FÊTE CHAMPÊTRE, fig. 1), which were formerly regarded as borderline between him and Giorgione. In the one instance where the two worked together, at the Fondaco dei Tedeschi, 16th-century opinion judged Titian's contribution superior.

Giorgione's premature death and the departure in 1511 of his partner, Sebastiano del Piombo, for Rome left the young Titian without a serious rival at Venice except for the very old Giovanni Bellini. Titian's status was confirmed in 1513, when he was granted permission to contribute to the redecoration of the Doge's Palace, which he began only in the 1520s (see §2(i)(a) below).

2. EARLY SUCCESS, 1516–MID-1540s.

(i) Religious and mythological pictures. (ii) Portraits.

(i) Religious and mythological pictures.

(a) Venice. (b) Ferrara and Mantua. (c) Urbino. (d) Elsewhere.

(a) Venice. In 1516 a huge architectural frame of marble was installed behind the high altar of S Maria Gloriosa dei Frari at Venice, and on 20 May 1518 Titian's highly dramatic altarpiece of the *Assumption of the Virgin* (see ALTARPIECE, fig. 4) was placed in it. The great height of the vault of the Gothic church conditioned the proportions of the picture, which is unusually high in relation to its width. The gigantic height of the altarpiece—nearly 7 m—and its dynamic spiral composition were unprecedented

in Venice; and Titian's pre-eminence among Venetian painters can be traced to the impact of this work. Dolce noted, however, that the older painters and the unlettered public were at first outraged at the novelty of the picture. This may well be the first recorded instance of a work of art provoking controversy by virtue of its revolutionary visual qualities. The extreme agitation of the Apostles on the ground was less probably the cause of the offence than the portrayal of the Virgin, whose feminine curves are conspicuous. Titian would have seen Mantegna's large fresco of the *Assumption* (c. 1455) in the Ovetari Chapel in the church of the Eremitani at Padua (*in situ*). Mantegna's treatment was unusually animated for its period and evidently exercised some influence on Titian's rendering. His main inspiration, however, seems to have come through a meeting with Fra Bartolommeo, probably at Ferrara in the spring of 1516. Inspired, in his turn, by the dynamism of Raphael's frescoes in the Stanza d'Eliodoro as well as by Michelangelo's Sistine Chapel Ceiling (both Rome, Vatican), Fra Bartolommeo painted several large and dramatic altarpieces at this period, as well as some very dramatic designs for an *Assumption* (now known only in his drawings; Munich, Staatl. Graph. Samml.).

In the second of Titian's altarpieces for the Frari, the Pesaro *Madonna* (*Virgin and Child Enthroned with Saints and Members of the Pesaro Family*, 1519–26; *in situ*), the main novelty is directed to achieving an effect of dynamism in a static subject by shifting the Virgin's throne to an asymmetrical position in order to catch the gaze of the spectator from the central aisle. This acknowledgment of the spectator's existence was one reason why the picture inspired such Baroque masters as Annibale Carracci and Rubens, who executed variants on it, as did Paolo Veronese. Titian first painted a coffered vault as a background, but replaced it with two huge pillars with clouds, a setting that also proved highly influential (*see also* PESARO).

Although Titian is not known to have visited Rome by this date, some awareness of Raphael's and Michelangelo's work, obtained through intermediaries, is apparent not only in the Frari *Assumption* but also in several other paintings from this time. An obvious instance is the *Virgin and Child with SS Francis and Aloysius and the Donor, Alvise Gozzi* (1520; Ancona, Pin. Com.), which evidently owes the principles of its composition to Raphael's *Madonna of Foligno* (1511–12; Rome, Pin. Vaticana). Similarly, in the last of the three great early altarpices for Venice, the *Death of St Peter Martyr* for SS Giovanni e Paolo (1526–30; destr. 1867, known from copies and prints), the most conspicuous figure apparently derives from a figure in Raphael's fresco of the *Deliverance of St Peter* (c. 1512; Rome, Vatican, Stanza d'Eliodoro). The *St Peter Martyr* altarpiece was considered by Vasari and most writers who saw it to be Titian's greatest work. According to Pino, Palma Vecchio competed against Titian for this commission, and, according to Ridolfi, so also did Pordenone.

The next major undertaking for Venice after the *St Peter Martyr* altarpiece was a huge picture of the *Presentation of the Virgin* (finished by 1538) for the Scuola della Carità (*in situ*, now Venice, Accad.). The composition is of the processional type, which was traditional in Venice for pictures of this subject, and it includes portraits of members of the Scuola. The elaborate architecture in the background was perhaps designed, or at least inspired, by Sebastiano Serlio, who had come to Venice after the Sack of Rome in 1527 and had become a close friend of Titian.

Also dating from the mid 1530s is the altarpiece of the *Virgin and Child with Saints* (Rome, Pin. Vaticana) from S Nicolo ai Frari at Venice. This was originally painted with the Virgin enthroned, but the final form is a two-tiered composition with the Virgin on clouds above the standing saints, who are disposed with striking asymmetry and considerable recession in the picture space. Raphael had used a comparable but less extreme system in his *St Cecilia* altarpiece (*c.* 1513–16; Bologna, Pin. N.).

More important at this time was Titian's work for the Doge's Palace in Venice, nearly all of which was destroyed in the fire of 1577. The appearance of his first painting there, of the humiliation of Frederick Barbarossa (1523) is not recorded. The *Battle of Spoleto* (or *Battle of Cadore* 1538; destr. 1577), for which he was granted permission in 1513, is known from copies, engravings and preliminary drawings (Paris, Louvre). Elements of its design were evidently derived, indirectly, from Leonardo's *Battle of Anghiari* (destr.) for Florence, as well as from the fresco by Raphael's workshop of the *Victory of Constantine at the Milvian Bridge* (Rome, Vatican, Sala di Costantino). Titian's composition became, in its turn, the inspiration for some of Rubens's battle pictures (e.g. Munich, Alte Pin.). One more altarpiece, the dramatic *Christ Crowned with Thorns* (Paris, Louvre), was painted for S Maria delle Grazie, Milan, in 1540–42, and it too owes something to the *Laokoon* group. A second version (Munich, Alte Pin.) dates from the end of Titian's life.

(b) Ferrara and Mantua. Concurrently with his work on the three great early Venetian altarpieces Titian was

working for the courts at Ferrara and Mantua. His début as the preferred painter of princes came in the spring of 1516 when he stayed for more than a month in the Este castle at Ferrara at the expense of Alfonso I, Duke of Ferrara (*see* ESTE (i), (8)). The *Tribute Money* (Dresden, Gemäldegal. Alte Meister), one of the noblest of all depictions of the adult Christ, was probably painted at this time.

For several years before this Alfonso had been planning a series of paintings for his *camerino*, a small room in the castle at Ferrara, evidently in emulation of the *studiolo* of his sister Isabella d'Este (*see* ESTE (i), (6)) at Mantua. Alfonso's scheme consisted of bacchanalian subjects illustrating passages from Ovid and Philostratus the younger, which he selected himself. Like Isabella, he wanted a single contribution from each of the leading contemporary painters. He obtained works from Dosso Dossi and Giovanni Bellini. Michelangelo refused to surrender the promised painting, and Raphael and Fra Bartolommeo both died after planning their contributions. Titian was asked to fill the breach. Two of his pictures were based on the designs of the painters he replaced. The first, the *Worship of Venus* (see fig. 3), follows Fra Bartolommeo's sketch for his unexecuted painting, while the second, *Bacchas and Ariadne* (see fig. 4), derives, at least in part, from Raphael's *modello* for his picture of a similar, but not identical, subject. The third painting for the *camerino*, the *Bacchanal of the Andrians* (see fig. 5), was probably ordered from Titian in the first place. Its main pictorial debt is to Michelangelo's cartoon for the *Battle of Cascina* (destr.), part of which was at Mantua where Titian went in 1519. Titian's dependence on the designs of his predecessors also reflects the fact that there was otherwise no pictorial tradition for the representation of these subjects. His three works are brilliantly painted, with a lavish use of ultramarine pigment and with sensuous painting of both the naked bodies and of the occasional silken garments. The landscape backgrounds are also marvellously vivid and lyrically beautiful. Despite his limited knowledge of Classical art at first hand, Titian's bacchanals are amazingly successful, imaginative evocations of the spirit of antiquity, as well as one of the greatest peaks of Italian Renaissance art. It was probably at the end of the series that Titian repainted most of the background of Bellini's bacchanal, the *Feast of the Gods* (Washington, DC, N.G.A.), in order to make it harmonize with his own.

In addition to these crucial contributions to the *camerino* of Alfonso d'Este, Titian painted portraits of the Duke and of his mistress, *Laura Dianti* (*see* §(ii) below). It was his skill as a portraitist that contributed more than any other factor to his success in his lifetime, his ability to combine a degree of flattery with a good likeness. Since the princely families of Italy were interrelated, success with one led to the patronage of others. Alfonso's sister, Isabella d'Este, and her son Federico II Gonzaga offered him patronage at Mantua as did Isabella's daughter, Eleanora, Duchess of Urbino, at her court. The patronage of other notables was secured, in many cases, through Titian's friendship with PIETRO ARETINO, who from the 1530s had constituted himself, in effect, Titian's publicity agent. Having pleased influential patrons with portraits, Titian followed up his success with religious or mythological

3. Titian: *Worship of Venus*, oil on canvas, 1.72×1.75 m, 1519 (Madrid, Museo del Prado)

4. Titian: *Bacchus and Ariadne*, oil on canvas, 1.75×1.90 m, 1522–3 (London, National Gallery)

pictures. According to Vasari, 'there is hardly any noble-man of repute, nor prince, nor great lady, who has not been portrayed by Titian'.

Federico II Gonzaga, 1st Duke of Mantua (*see* GON-ZAGA, (9)), was one of the most enlightened of 16th-century patrons. In addition to Titian, Federico employed Correggio and Giulio Romano, who was court artist at Mantua from *c.* 1525. Titian's *Entombment* (see fig. 6) is similar in treatment, and in its thundery lighting, to the *Bacchanal of the Andrians* and therefore datable to the same period, the mid-1520s. It would thus have been among Titian's earlier work for Federico. In its drama and the depth of the emotion conveyed, this is one of the greatest Renaissance religious pictures. The most admired of the Mantua Titians, however, was a series of 11 pictures of *Roman Emperors* (a 12th was added by Giulio Romano). Drawing on medals and busts, they dated from 1536–40 and were destroyed in Spain in 1734. Federico inherited a taste for antique subjects from his parents who owned works by Mantegna, such as the *Triumph of Caesar*

(London, Hampton Court, Royal Col.). To judge from copies of the *Emperor* series (e.g. drawings by Ippolito Andreasi; Düsseldorf, Kstmus.), Titian infused great variety into these half-length figures: young and old, in profile, three-quarter face of full face, from the side or the back and with many different arrangements of drapery.

(c) Urbino. Titian's work for the court of Urbino started early in the 1530s. The Duke of Urbino, Francesco Maria I della Rovere (*see* ROVERE, DELLA (i), (3)), like his brother-in-law, Federico II Gonzaga, was on intimate terms with Titian, as their letters indicate. Titian worked for Francesco Maria until his death in 1538 and afterwards for his son, Guidobaldo II della Rovere. Most of Titian's pictures for Francesco Maria were portraits (*see* §(ii) below). A notable execption was the *Venus of Urbino* (Florence, Uffizi). This shows a new attitude towards the nude, no longer generalized to the extent that it was in Giorgione's *Venus* (Dresden, Gemäldegal; *see* GIOR-GIONE, fig. 5). Titian's version is given what is virtually a genre setting, and the sitter is less a goddess than a woman.

5. Titian: *Bacchanal of the Andrians*, oil on canvas, 1.75×1.93 m, mid-1520s (Madrid, Museo del Prado)

She reclines naked on sheets, her head on pillows and her lapdog asleep at the foot of the bed. She wears a ring and a bracelet and turns to look at the spectator. To emphasize that the scene is of the real world there are two servants at the back of the room, inspecting the inside of a chest. There is a pronounced erotic element due to the combination of the naked body and realistic accessories, but the way the body is painted is idealized—the outlines very slightly smoothed, and irregularities in the flesh eliminated.

(d) Elsewhere. Although much of his energy throughout the 1520s and 1530s was given to work for Ferrara, Mantua, Urbino and Venice, Titian occasionally painted works for other cities. These included the Ancona *Virgin and Child* mentioned above and an altarpiece of the *Resurrection* (see fig. 7), dated 1522, for SS Nazaro e Celso, Brescia. One panel of the altarpiece shows an elaborate foreshortened figure of St Sebastian, derived, again through intermediaries, from the antique sculpture group of the *Laokoon* (Rome, Vatican, Mus. Pio-Clementino; *see*

Rome, ancient, fig. 59). Also from the early 1520s is an *Annunciation* for Treviso Cathedral (*in situ*), in which the angel, unusually, advances from the back of the room.

(ii) Portraits. Titian, more than any other painter, was responsible for the development of the art of portraiture in the first half of the 16th century. The change involved enlarging the field from the head-and-shoulders format that was normal in 15th-century portraits, to half-length and full-length figures, thereby permitting the inclusion of adjuncts—furniture, musical instruments, a servant, a horse or a dog—to suggest the sitter's interests or his importance. It also entailed new problems of pose, in particular to do with the sitter's hands. In this, as in every other respect, Titian was pre-eminently resourceful. The hands were occupied with a book, a pair of gloves or the hilt of a sword. The subject was shown frontally, from one side, or even from the back, looking over his shoulder. Whereas most of the surviving portraits from the 15th century are of men, from this period onwards the number of portraits

of female sitters increased. In most of Titian's early portraits the sitters are unidentified—he did not yet move among the great—and the works are not precisely dated. In some, such as the *Portrait of a Man* ('*Ariosto*', London, N.G.), perhaps a self-portrait, Titian retained the device of a ledge in the foreground, which had been used by Giorgione. In the *Portrait of a Woman* ('*La Schiavona*', London, N.G.), the ledge includes a raised portion incorporating a pseudo-antique profile relief of the sitter. Gloves feature prominently in two other early portraits of young men (Garrowby Hall, N. Yorks; Paris, Louvre), while an older male subject at Hampton Court (Royal Col.) fingers a book. In all of these portraits except the female one, the sitter's face is shown at an angle. The colours are generally restrained, although in the Garrowby Hall portrait the glimpses of the sitter's scarlet tunic and sleeves are contrasted effectively with the black silk of his robe.

In the portrait of *Federico Gonzaga* (1520s; Madrid, Prado) the field is extended to three-quarter length. The young ruler is shown with one hand on a dog and the other concealed. The colouring, too, a sumptuous blue velvet doublet and red breeches, is more vivid than in the earlier portraits. In the *Laura Dianti* (Kreuzlingen, Heinz Kisters priv. col.), the colouring is brighter still and a second figure, a Moorish page, is added as a foil. The pair of portraits of *Francesco Maria della Rovere, Duke of Urbino*, and his Duchess, *Eleanora Gonzaga* (both Florence, Uffizi), are datable to the mid 1530s. Both are three-quarter length, but Titian's sketch (Florence, Uffizi) (*see* §II,1 below) for the Duke's portrait—the only surviving study for a Titian portrait—shows the sitter at full length. In contrast with the portrait of the Duchess's brother, *Federico Gonzaga* (Madrid, Prado), who is shown in civilian clothes and with an expression of aristocratic confidence, Francesco Maria is depicted as a soldier, in armour, baton in hand. Titian's portrait of a young woman, '*La Bella*' (Florence, Pitti), and the *Portrait of a Girl in a Fur Cape* (Vienna, Ksthist. Mus) are assumed to represent the same sitter. She was evidently also the model for the *Venus of Urbino* and was presumably Francesco Maria's mistress. Probably the greatest of all the half-length standing portraits, perhaps dating from as late as the 1540s, is the enigmatic '*Young Englishman*' (Florence, Pitti).

The pinnacle of Titian's worldly success was reached when he found favour with Emperor Charles V (*see* HABSBURG, I, (5)), and, some years later, worked for Pope Paul III (*see* FARNESE, (1)). In 1533, three years after their first meeting, the Emperor created Titian Count Palatine and Knight of the Golden Spur and tried in vain to persuade him to come to Spain. The first paintings for the Emperor were portraits (some destr.), of which the full-length portrait of *Charles V with his Hunting Dog* (?1532;

6. Titian: *Entombment*, oil on canvas, 1.48×2.05 m, mid-1520s (Paris, Musée du Louvre)

7. Titian: *Resurrection* altarpiece, oil on panel, 2.78×1.22 m (centre panel), 1522 (Brescia, SS Nazaro e Celso)

Madrid, Prado) seems to be merely a copy of one by Jakob Seisenegger (for illustration *see* SEISENEGGER). In 1543 Titian met Pope Paul III, a devoted patron of Michelangelo, at Bologna. This led in 1546 to the artist's only known visit to Rome. There he met Michelangelo, who, according to Vasari, censured his draughtsmanship but praised his colouring.

3. 'LATE STYLE', MID-1540S AND AFTER. During the mid 1540s a major change can be seen in Titian's painting, marking the beginning of the 'late style'. If the great *Ecce homo* (Vienna, Ksthist. Mus.), finished in 1543 for Giovanni d'Anna, a Flemish merchant resident in Venice, is compared with a similar composition, the *Presentation of the Virgin*, finished only five years previously, the difference is clear. The greater agitation in the intensely dramatic later work can be attributed to the more tragic subject, but the stylistic difference is apparent in the darker tones and more summary handling.

(i) Religious and mythological pictures. (ii) Portraits.

(i) Religious and mythological pictures.

(a) Work for Charles V. (b) Work for Philip II and related late paintings.

(a) Work for Charles V. Before the end of 1547 Titian was summoned by Charles V to join him at Augsburg, a journey across the Alps in winter. There he painted, among other subjects, the *Last Judgement* or *Trinity*, known as '*La Gloria*' (Madrid, Prado), which was not finished until 1554 and was later taken by the Emperor to his retreat at the monastery of Yuste in Spain. It differs fundamentally from Dürer's Landauer Altarpiece (Vienna, Ksthist. Mus.)

and Michelangelo's *Last Judgement* (Rome, Vatican, Sistine Chapel; *see* ROME, fig. 43), both of which have been cited as partial prototypes, in not showing a frontal presentation. Instead, the Old Testament figures in the foreground look up towards the Trinity at an angle, and the spectator follows the direction of their gaze.

During this first visit to Augsburg, Titian was commissioned by the Emperor's sister, Mary, Queen of Hungary, the regent of the Netherlands, to paint four large pictures of legendary Greek figures, *Tityus, Sisyphus* (both Madrid, Prado), *Tantalus* and *Ixion* (both untraced), the '*Furias*'. These were destined for Mary's château at Binche (Belgium). Although intended as wall decoration, they are in an heroic style, with the figures filling most of the canvas, similar to the series of ceiling paintings of Old Testament subjects—*Cain and Abel*, the *Sacrifice of Isaac* and *David and Goliath*— that Titian had painted a few years earlier for Santo Spirito in Venice (Venice, S Maria della Salute). In both series some influence from Giulio Romano's frescoes at Mantua (e.g. Palazzo del Te), as well as from Correggio's cupola paintings at Parma (e.g. in the cathedral), may be traced.

(b) Work for Philip II and related late paintings. On his way back from Augsburg, Titian stopped at Innsbruck to paint portraits (untraced) of the family of Ferdinand I, King of Bohemia and Hungary, the brother of Charles V. Soon after he returned to Venice, he received a further summons, to go to Milan to meet the Crown Prince, the future King Philip II of Spain, who was to be his principal patron for the rest of his life. From this meeting the only result was a portrait (untraced), and it was not until Titian was again summoned to Augsburg, in 1550, that he and the young prince worked out an elaborate programme of pictures that the artist would paint in Venice and send to Spain. The most important was a series of canvases of subjects taken, like the Ferrara bacchanals, from Classical literature (Ovid). Referred to as the '*poesie*', they were evidently planned in pairs. The strong erotic element was presumably also specified. The *poesie*, interspersed with pictures of religious subjects, were sent at intervals throughout the 1550s and first half of the 1560s. As with the Ferrara series Titian drew for inspiration on central Italian models: on Michelangelo in the case of the first,

8. Titian: *Rape of Europa*, oil on canvas, 1.78×2.05 m, *c.* 1560 (Boston, MA, Isabella Stewart Gardner Museum)

the *Danaë* (*see* NUDE, fig. 3; an earlier version is in Naples, Capodimonte), on Raphael for the next, *Venus and Adonis* (1553; Madrid, Prado), and probably on Benvenuto Cellini's relief of *Perseus and Andromeda* from his statue of *Perseus* (Florence, Loggia Lanzi; *see* CELLINI, BENVENUTO, fig. 6) for the picture of that subject (London, Wallace). For the *Diana and Actaeon* (*see* ITALY, fig. 33), which is probably the masterpiece of the series, and the *Death of Actaeon* (*see* OIL PAINTING, fig. 1) he seems to have drawn primarily on Classical sculpture. The other surviving *poesie* are the *Diana and Callisto* (Duke of Sutherland, on loan to Edinburgh, N.G.) and the *Rape of Europa* (see fig. 8). In two of the series, *Diana and Actaeon* and the *Rape of Europa*, Titian made brilliant use of a colouristic device

that he had also used to great effect in the *Bacchus and Ariadne*: a crimson cloak fluttering like a flame against an ultramarine sky.

When the style and technique of the *poesie* for Philip are compared with those of the earlier series for Ferrara, the differences conform with the general trend of Titian's development. The mood in the later series is more fiery, the colours deeper and more closely interrelated and the execution more summary. The dimensions of the canvas in the two series are nearly the same but the figures in the later one are larger in relation to the surround. In the *poesie* as in the earlier series, the landscape element is prominent, and in the last of the series, the *Death of Actaeon*, it is treated with a freedom that no other painter attempted

9. Titian: *Pietà*, oil on canvas, 3.53×3.48 m, 1573–6 (Venice, Galleria dell'Accademia)

again until the 19th century. The religious paintings for Philip included a huge *Last Supper* (Madrid, Escorial, Nuevos Mus.).

Three important altarpieces for churches in Venice and the mainland are datable to the late 1540s and the 1550s. The first, the *Pentecost* (S Maria della Salute), was painted for Santo Spirito (destr. 1656) as a replacement for an earlier altarpiece by Titian, which had deteriorated. The arrangement of the Salute picture is traditional (compare with, for example, the picture of the same subject by Luca Signorelli in Santo Spirito, Urbino), but executed with brilliant, opalescent colours. The second, the *Martyrdom of St Lawrence* (Venice, S Maria Assunta dei Gesuiti), is important as being Titian's first night scene. It dates from the mid- or late 1550s, as does the third, the splendid *Crucifixion* (Ancona, S Domenico).

Throughout his last years and almost to the time of his death Titian continued to send most of his output to Philip II. Some of these paintings, such as the *Venus of Pardo* (Paris, Louvre) and the *Religion Succoured by Spain* (Madrid, Prado), had been started many years previously and were now reworked. Others, such as the *St Lawrence* (Madrid, Escorial), were repetitions of compositions he had delivered to other patrons. Many others were found unfinished in his studio at his death. These included the huge canvas for Doge Antonio Grimani, '*La Fede*' (Venice, Doge's Pal.), which had been commissioned as early as 1555. Not delivered in Titian's lifetime, it escaped the first fire at the Doge's Palace (1574). The figure of the kneeling Doge on the right is magnificently painted in Titian's style of the late 1550s. The standing figure of St Mark on the left also appears to be the work of Titian himself, but from a later date. The central figure of Faith is probably at least in part of studio execution. During his last years Titian also executed a few works for the Venetian mainland, including three paintings of allegorical and mythological subjects for Brescia (1568; destr. 1575).

The technique of Titian's late works has been described as proto-Impressionist. Vasari may have been nearer the mark when he described Titian's final style as looking like *macchie* ('blots'). It is not a systematic exploration of the effects of light on colour and form, rather all forms become blurred. The great last *Pietà* (see fig. 9), for example, composes well from a normal viewing distance, but the brushstrokes make little sense when seen from a few centimetres. To some extent this late style may be due to failing eyesight. Certainly the effects of old age on Titian's painting did not escape comment during his lifetime. A dealer, Niccolò Stoppio, reported in 1568 that Titian's hand trembled so much that he was unable to finish any pictures and left them to assistants. The curious form of signature, *Titianus fecit fecit*, on the late *Annunciation* (Venice, S Salvatore) has been interpreted as Titian's defiant rebuttal of such insinuations (Ridolfi).

Nevertheless, a number of paintings dating from the last 10 or 15 years of Titian's life are recognized as masterpieces: the Salvatore *Annunciation*, the *St Sebastian* (St Petersburg, Hermitage), the Escorial *St Lawrence*, the *Flaying of Marsyas* (Kroměříž Castle) and, above all, the last *Pietà*. The *Pietà*, in particular, is one of the most moving of all representations of the subject. All the paintings are very dark in tone, fiery in mood and appear to be unfinished when seen from close quarters. His art was truly humanist. His figures, whether in a religious or a secular context, tend to be slightly more handsome and graceful than the average, but are still creatures of flesh and blood. To see this, they need only be compared with those of his two great successors: the aristocratic abstractions of Paolo Veronese or the faceless figures of Jacopo Tintoretto.

The same is true of his exquisitely beautiful background landscapes. They are more freshly observed than those of previous painters with the possible exception of Giovanni Bellini, but the incidental irregularities of nature have been softened.

As Titian's career spanned more than 65 years he was certainly very old when he died. There was plague in Venice at the time of his death, but the fact that he was buried the following day, in S Maria Gloriosa dei Frari, suggests that he did not die of the plague. Several other members of the VECELLIO family were painters, including one of Titian's sons, Orazio Vecellio. Titian kept a large workshop, and Jacopo Tintoretto and El Greco were among the artists said to have trained there.

(ii) Portraits. In the 1540s Titian produced the three most elaborate of all his portraits: the group of *Pope Paul III with his Grandsons* (1546; Naples, Capodimonte), the larger group of the male members of the *Vendramin Family* (London, N.G.) and the life-size equestrian portrait of *Charles V at Mühlberg* (Madrid, Prado), painted on the occasion of the Emperor's victory over the Lutherans at Mühlberg early in 1547. In the earlier, more modest group portrait, *Bishop Georges d'Armagnac and his Secretary* (late 1530s; Alnwick Castle, Northumb.), the kneeling secretary is allowed only a subordinate place; most of the picture is occupied by the ample form of the seated bishop. The Vendramin group—three adults, six children and a dog—is more complex, and the design suffered somewhat when it was truncated on the left. The contrasts of psychology between the members of the different generations of the family are very effective, however, as well as pictorial contrasts of different colours, mainly red and black, and different textures of the robes.

Painted during Titian's visit to Rome, the design of the group of *Pope Paul III with his Grandsons* evidently derives from that of Raphael's *Pope Leo X and Two Cardinals* (Florence, Uffizi; for illustration *see* MEDICI, DE', (7)). At this time Titian would not have seen Raphael's original, which was already in Florence, but would have known Andrea del Sarto's copy (Naples, Capodimonte) at Mantua. Titian's picture is more vivid and also more loosely constructed. The stooping figure, Ottavio Farnese, has been seen as sycophantic, and as an indication of unreliability. However, since the Pope is known to have been very softly spoken, a more likely explanation is that Ottavio Farnese was trying to hear what he was saying, and Titian brought out the irritation and impatience of old age in the expression of the Pope. In this portrait, which is unfinished, the range of colours is restricted, the white of the Pope's robe setting off the different shades of crimson.

In comparison with the grandiloquence and bravura of equestrian portraits of rulers painted in the 17th century, Titian's great portrait of Charles V appears a model of verisimilitude and restraint. No allegorical figures underline the Emperor's victory, even though Aretino has advocated their inclusion. The enemy is not even shown. Like the Christian champion he felt himself to be, the Emperor rides undaunted from the wood, assured of sufficient divine protection to challenge and defeat the forces of hell.

Of the later single portraits, mention should be made of an oddity, the full-length portrait of *Giovanni Acquaviva, Duca d'Atri* (*c.* 1552; Kassel, Schloss Wilhelmshöhe). The work is splendid in execution and in its scarlet and gold colouring, but the sitter appears so grotesquely overdressed as to suggest some satirical intent on Titian's part. Three single portraits from the later period are outstanding, both visually and psychologically. Titian's first portrait of *Pope Paul III* (see fig. 10) follows the type created by Raphael in his portrait of *Pope Julius II* (London, N.G.), with the sitter shown from an angle, at three-quarter length, in an armchair. By using a slightly higher viewpoint than Raphael, Titian was able to look down on the Pope's outstretched right hand, which seems to claw the velvet pouch he wears, thereby complementing the suspicious mood suggested by the facial expression. The colours are restricted to a combination of whites and marvellous dull reds with light highlights. The full-length *Philip II in Armour* (for illustration *see* HABSBURG, §II(2)) is an official image, since Philip, unlike his father, was not primarily a soldier. The richly damascened black and gold armour is painted with extraordinary virtuosity, but the very free technique, almost anticipating impressionism, was not appreciated by the sitter who attributed it to haste in a letter to his aunt Mary of Hungary. Of the very late portraits, the most arresting is that of the antiquarian *Jacopo Strada* (1567–8; Vienna, Ksthist. Mus.), a man Titian apparently disliked. The sitter's fiery expression is emphasized by his gesture, brandishing a statuette so that his left arm, with its brilliant scarlet satin sleeve, cuts diagonally across his body.

II. Graphic arts.

1. DRAWINGS. Dolce mentioned Titian's facility as a draughtsman during his student days, but, as he made little use of them in the preparatory stages of painting (*see* §III below), there are relatively few drawings from his maturity. As with other Old Masters, the touchstone of authenticity consists of those drawings that connect with authentic paintings, while not corresponding so closely as to be considered sketch copies by later artists after the paintings. In Titian's case these include two in pen and ink: one for the Brescia *St Sebastian* (Berlin, Kupferstichkab.) and the other for the portrait of *Francesco Maria della Rovere* (both Florence, Uffizi). There are two drawings mainly in black chalk: one (London, BM) is for an apostle in the Frari *Assumption of the Virgin*, the other (Paris, Ecole B.-A.) is for the *Sacrifice of Isaac* (Venice, S Maria della Salute). In addition, there are studies for lost paintings, including the *Battle of Spoleto* (e.g. Florence, Uffizi; Paris, Louvre) and the votive picture of Doge Andrea Gritti (Florence, Uffizi), formerly in the Doge's Palace, and a few others possibly connected with known paintings.

The main category of drawings for which the attribution to Titian is still controversial consists of finished studies in pen and ink representing undulating landscapes with prominent bushes in the middle distance, buildings in the far distance and relatively small figures in the foreground. This genre seems to have started in the circle of Giorgione and to have been connected with the production of woodcuts. Two drawings of this type (both London, BM) are signed Domenico Campagnola, who appears to have been the most active exponent of it. The example of this type most confidently attributed to Titian is a sheet (New York, Met.), which appears to be a study for part of a large composite woodcut of the *Sacrifice of Isaac* (Berlin, Kupferstichkab.), which, in its third state, bears an inscription attributing it to Titian. In certain parts of the Metropolitan sheet there is a lack of continuity in the ink lines, and this seems to support the theory that such works are not drawings but are counterproofs taken from the woodcuts that were later touched up by hand with fraudulent intent (Dreyer). Nevertheless, there can be no doubt that Titian did execute drawings of this type.

2. PRINTS. The success at Venice, early in the 16th century, of the engravings and woodcuts of Jacopo de' Barbari and Dürer evidently fired the young Titian. His *Triumph of Christ* (e.g. Paris, Bib. N., Cab. Est.), a huge woodcut procession made from ten blocks, was dated by Vasari to 1508 and is therefore among Titian's earliest works in any medium. Suggestions that this print dates

10. Titian: *Pope Paul III*, oil on canvas, 1.06×0.85 m, 1543 (Naples, Museo e Gallerie Nazionali di Capodimonte)

from a few years later are not based on solid evidence. The enormous and highly dramatic woodcut of the *Crossing of the Red Sea* (e.g. London, BM), which has been described as the greatest woodcut ever made (1983 exh. cat.), was widely influential. It is known from an inscribed edition dated 1549 but is assumed to have originated many years earlier. A chiaroscuro woodcut of *St Jerome* (e.g. London, BM) is inscribed with the names of Titian as designer and of Ugo da Carpi as cutter. A number of other prints have been attributed to Titian by some writers. Despite his relatively small output, there can be no doubt that Titian's importance in the history of woodcut is almost as great as it is in painting (*see also* WOODCUT, §II, 3(iii) and fig. 4). Late in his career he encouraged the reproduction of his paintings by engravers, including Niccolò Boldrini, Giulio di Antonio Bonasone, Giovanni Jacopo Caraglio, Cornelis Cort (for illustration *see* CORT, CORNELIS), Giulio Fontana and Martino Rota.

III. Working methods and technique.

Most of Titian's early works are on panel, including the enormous Frari *Assumption of the Virgin*. Another large work of this period, the Frari Pesaro *Madonna*, is, however, on canvas. Although later he painted more often on canvas, he did not entirely abandon panel, which he used, for example, for the *Christ Crowned with Thorns* (1546–50; Paris, Louvre). The choice of support was probably determined by the size of the work and its intended location. Canvas, which could be rolled, was more suitable for large works that had to be shipped long distances. Both panel and canvas supports were prepared with a layer of light-coloured gesso.

The painting procedure developed by Titian was revolutionary in its day. Vasari, who disapproved, described it in his *Vita* of Titian as 'working merely with paint, without the intervention of preliminary drawings on paper'. Modern scientific analysis, as well as an eye-witness account of Titian's method of painting by Palma Giovane, support Vasari's contention that drawing played no more than a minor part in Titian's procedure. The transfer from panel, for instance, of the *Madonna of the Cherries* (Vienna, Ksthist. Mus.) in the late 19th century revealed only summary lines of underdrawing. The same proved to be true when a later work, the *Vendramin Family*, dating from the 1540s, was cleaned in 1973–4. In this case there was a great deal of underdrawing in dark paint, but it was very sketchily done and did not always correspond with the final outline as painted. On the other hand, when the *Bacchus and Ariadne* (1522–3) was cleaned in 1967–9, there was hardly any indication of underdrawing. It was found that this picture was painted on a thin gesso ground, originally light in colour, although subsequently darkened. This is evidence against the theory that Titian generally used a red–brown ground. It also became clear that Titian was prepared on occasion to improvise on the canvas. Ariadne's scarlet scarf, for instance, is painted over the blue pigment of the sea behind her. In the Pesaro *Madonna* the architectural background was drastically altered more than once, but the figures were not painted until the architecture had assumed its final form. The definitive colour effects were sometimes obtained by underpainting of a different colour from that of the top layer. In the *Virgin and Child with SS John the Baptist and Catherine* (London, N.G.), for instance, dating probably from the 1530s, St Catherine's yellow dress has a pink underpainting.

Something of Titian's preparations may be seen with the naked eye in the portrait group of *Pope Paul III with his Grandsons*, since this picture is clearly unfinished. Crowe and Cavalcaselle (1881) described the process:

> Laid on first with broad sweeps of brush in the thinnest of shades, the surfaces appear to have been worked over and coloured more highly with successive layers of pigment of similar quality, and modelled in the process to a delicate finish. The shadows were struck *in* with the same power as they were struck *out* in chips in the statues of Michelangelo. The accessories were all prepared in well-marked tints, subject to toning down by glazing, smirch or scumble. White in light, dark in shadow, indicate forms, the whole blended into harmony by transparents, broken at last by flat masses of high light, and concrete touch.

Palma Giovane gave a famous description of Titian's painting method, though being born *c.* 1548 he could have known Titian only at the very end of the latter's life. Palma's account was repeated by Boschini (1674):

> Palma Giovane told me . . . that Titian was in the habit of laying in his pictures with a mass of colour, which served as a bed or base for what he was going to construct above it. And I myself have seen some of these, worked with rapid strokes of a brush steeped in solid colour, in some areas with a mass of red earth, which was intended for the middle tones, in others with white lead. Then with the same brush, and red, black and yellow pigment he modelled a highlight; and in this way he fashioned, with four strokes of the brush, the nucleus of a beautiful figure. . . . When he had completed these expert preliminaries he turned the picture to the wall and sometimes left it there for several months without looking at it; and when at last he wished to resume work he examined it rigorously as though it were a mortal enemy, in order to detect in it some feature which was not in keeping with his lofty intention. . . . For the finishing touches he rubbed the edges of the highlights with his fingers, blending them with the half tones, and harmonising one colour with another. At other times he would slide his finger to make a dark accent in a corner and thereby reinforce it, or a spot of red like a drop of blood to enliven an unaccented passage, and in this fashion he brought his painted figures to a state of perfection. And Palma assured me that in the final stages he worked more with his fingers than his brush.

This description makes no mention either of preliminary sketches or of underdrawing. Instead Titian seems to have evolved a roughly equivalent system in terms of paint. Just as one method of drawing starts with a maze of imprecise lines from which the definitive outline ultimately emerges, so Titian seems to have arrived at the final result by a process of refining both the area and the colour of successive layers of pigment. Early in his career he also compensated for his minimal use of drawing by working from the live model at the painting stage. A letter of 14 October 1522 from Alfonso d'Este's agent in Venice about the *Bacchus and Ariadne* mentions that Titian was still using live models at least six weeks after starting on the canvas. Since Palma makes no mention of this, the conclusion is that by the end of his life Titian had abandoned the practice.

IV. Critical reception and posthumous reputation.

During the 20th century Titian has been among the most generally revered of all Old Masters. In previous centuries, however, Raphael was regarded as the greatest of all painters. The reasons for this reversal are complex and not easy to define, but the most cogent factor has probably been the changing attitude to the art of antiquity. As long as the Antique was considered the fountain-head of all excellence in the visual and literary arts, artists whose practice reflected this view were thought superior to those who were content to copy nature. In the 16th century a dispute began concerning the primacy in painting of draughtsmanship or painting (*see* DISEGNO E COLORE). The exponents of *disegno* looked to the art of antiquity for guidance, whereas those who favoured *colore* modelled their art more directly on nature. Raphael was seen as the purest exponent in modern times of the antique ideal and was idolized by the advocates of *disegno*, who included the leading theorists of art: Vasari in the 16th century, Giovanni Pietro Bellori in the 17th and Anton Raphael Mengs in the 18th.

With the decline in the prestige of antiquity, Raphael's fame also started to decline, and that of Titian, as the exponent of the rival, *colore* faction, rose correspondingly. Titian in fact had also been influenced by the art of antiquity, but he was promoted as the great student of nature by Dolce and others in opposition to the school of Rome and the Antique. Among artists there was, nevertheless, some divergence between theory and practice. Whatever the attitudes towards Raphael of Rubens, van Dyck and Velázquez, for instance, there is no doubt that in their painting all three were more affected by Titian. Similarly, in the 19th century, Delacroix (*Journal*, 1 March 1859) referred to Raphael as 'the greatest of all painters' but wrote with more appreciation of Titian.

Titian's fame and influence were disseminated through the collections of his work located outside Venice as well as in it. The export to Spain of most of his output in the last 25 years of his life made works available to Velázquez and other Spanish painters, as well as to such visiting artists as Rubens; and by the middle of the 17th century this tremendous holding was augmented by examples of Titian's earlier period. Two of the Ferrara bacchanals, the *Worship of Venus* and the *Andrians*, arrived in Madrid in the 1630s from Rome, where, following their confiscation from Ferrara at the end of the 16th century, they had already exerted a vital influence on such resident artists as Poussin. In the 17th century there were likewise important examples of Titian's work in collections in England, France and the Netherlands. Although before the 20th century there were reservations concerning Titian's standing outside Venice, his supremacy in relation to other Venetian painters has never been seriously challenged.

BIBLIOGRAPHY
EARLY SOURCES
M. Sanudo: *I Diarii* (1496–1533); ed. R. Fulin, 58 vols (Venice, 1879–1903)
Anonimo Morelliano [Marcantonio Michiel]: *Notizie d'opere di disegno* (c. 1532); Eng. trans. (London, 1903)
P. Pino: *Dialogo di pittura* (Venice, 1548); also in *Trattati d'arte del cinquecento*, ed. P. Barocchi (Bari, 1960), i, pp. 95–139
G. Vasari: *Vite* (1550, rev. 2/1568); ed. G. Milanesi (1878–85), vii, pp. 425–68
L. Dolce: *L'Aretino, ovvero dialogo della pittura* (Venice, 1557); ed. M. Roskill (New York, 1968)
F. Sansovino: *Venetia città nobilissima et singolare* (Venice, 1581); ed. G. Martinoni (Venice, 1663/R Venice, 1968)
R. Borghini: *Il Riposo* (Florence, 1584); ed. M. Rosci (Milan, 1968)
P. Aretino: *Lettere* (Paris, 1609); rev., abridged as *Lettere sull'arte*, (Milan, 1956–7)
'Tizianello': *La vita del insigne Tiziano Vecellio* (1622/R Venice, 1809)
C. Ridolfi: *Le Maraviglie dell'arte* (Venice, 1648); ed. D. von Hadeln (Berlin, 1914–24)
M. Boschini: *La carta del navegar pitoresco* (Venice, 1660); ed. A. Pallucchini (Venice, 1966)
——: *Le minere della pittura* (Venice, 1664); rev. as *Le ricche minere della pittura* (Venice, 1674)
A. Cloulas, ed.: 'Documents concernant Titien conservés aux archives de Simancas' *Mél. Casa Velazquez*, iii (1967), pp. 197–286

GENERAL
B. Berenson: *Venetian School* (1957)
J. Steer: *Venetian Painting: A Concise History* (London, 1970)
J. Wilde: *Venetian Art from Bellini to Titian* (Oxford, 1974)
D. Rosand: *Painting in Cinquecento Venice: Titian, Veronese, Tintoretto* (New Haven and London, 1982)

MONOGRAPHS
J. A. Crowe and G. B. Cavalcaselle: *Life and Times of Titian* (London, 1877, rev. 2/1881)
G. Gronau: *Titian* (Berlin, 1900; Eng. trans., London, 1904)
W. Suida: *Tizian* (Leipzig, 1933)
H. Tietze: *Tizian* (Vienna, 1936)
G. A. Dell'Acqua: *Tiziano* (Milan, 1955)
R. Pallucchini: *Tiziano*, 2 vols (Florence, 1969)
E. Panofsky: *Problems in Titian: Mostly Iconographic* (London, 1969)
H. E. Wethey: *The Paintings of Titian*, 3 vols (London, 1969–75) [fullest account for reference]
C. Hope: *Titian* (London, 1980) [best short account]

EXHIBITION CATALOGUES AND SYMPOSIA
Tiziano e Venezia. Atti del convegno: Venice, 1976
Titianus Cadorinus. Atti del convegno: Pieve di Cadore, 1976
Disegni di Tiziano e della sua cerchia (exh. cat. by K. Oberhuber, Venice, Fond. Cini, 1976) [drawings]
Tiziano e il disegno veneziano del suo tempo (exh. cat. by W. Rearick, Florence, Uffizi, 1976) [drawings]
Titian and the Venetian Woodcut (exh. cat. by M. Muraro and D. Rosand, Washington, DC, N.G.A. and Int. Exh. Found., 1976)
Tiziano e il manierismo europeo (exh. cat. by R. Pallucchini, Florence, 1978)
Da Tiziano a El Greco: Per la storia del manierismo a Venezia, 1540–1590 (exh. cat., Venice, Doge's Pal., 1981)
The Genius of Venice, 1500–1600 (exh. cat., ed. C. Hope and J. Martineau; London, RA, 1983)
Titian, Prince of Painters (exh. cat., Venice, Doge's Pal.; Washington, DC, N.G.A.; 1990–91)
Le Siècle de Titien (exh. cat., Paris, Grand Pal., 1993)

SPECIALIST STUDIES
Drawings
T. Pignatti and M. A. Chiari: *Tiziano: Disegni* (Florence, 1979)
M. A. Chiari Moretto Wiel: *Tiziano: Corpus dei disegni autografi* (Milan, 1989)

Materials and technique
A. Lucas and J. Plesters: 'Titian's Bacchus and Ariadne: The Materials and Technique', *N.G. Tech. Bull.*, 2 (1978)
F. Valcanover and L. Lazzarini: 'La Pala Pesaro: note techniche', *Quad. Sopr. Beni A. & Stor. Venezia*, 8 (1979)

Other
M. Jaffe: 'The Picture of the Secretary of Titian', *Burl. Mag.*, cviii (1966), pp. 114–26
P. Fehl: 'Realism and Classicism ... in Titian's Flaying of Marsyas', *Czechoslovakia Past and Present*, ii (The Hague, 1969)
C. Hope: 'The Camerini d'Alabastro of Alfonso d'Este', *Burl. Mag.*, cxiii (1971), pp. 641–50, 712–21
D. Goodgal: 'The Camerino of Alfonso I d'Este', *A. Hist.*, i/2 (1978)

P. Dreyer: 'Tizianfälschungen des sechzehnten Jahrhunderts', *Pantheon* (1979); review by D. Rosand in *Master Drgs*, 3 (1981)
C. Gould: 'The Earliest Dated Titian?', *Artibus & Hist.*, 13 (1986)

CECIL GOULD

Titicaca Basin. Region in South America, centred on Lake Titicaca on Peru's south-eastern border with Bolivia. It was an important culture area in Pre-Columbian times (*see* SOUTH AMERICA, PRE-COLUMBIAN, §III), being one of only six areas in the Central Andes large enough to allow important human concentrations. Geographically, it corresponds to the Puno depression of south-eastern Peru and the Bolivian *altiplano* (a small part of the Andean *altiplano* that extends as far south as Argentina). Lake Titicaca is endorheic (its waters do not reach the sea) and has a large plateau catchment area, whose rivers all flow into the lake. It has one outlet, the River Desaguadero, which flows into Lake Poopó (also endorheic) in Bolivia. Titicaca, at *c.* 3809 m above sea-level the highest navigable lake in the world, is surrounded by extensive plains and pastures, which rise gradually to form plateaux (*punas*) at over 4000 m, until they reach the arid areas at the foot of the snow-capped mountain peaks *c.* 4800 above sea-level. Although it is at a great height, the lake's waters never freeze, with the result that the climate of its shores is milder than that of the rest of the plateau, and there is accordingly a greater density of population.

1. Early development, before *c.* 900 BC. 2. Early Horizon (*c.* 900–*c.* 200 BC). 3. Early Intermediate period (*c.* 200 BC–*c.* AD 600) and Middle Horizon (*c.* 600–1000). 4. Late Intermediate period (*c.* 1000–1476). 5. Late Horizon (1476–1534).

1. EARLY DEVELOPMENT, BEFORE *c.* 900 BC. No Pre-Ceramic deposits have been found in the Cuzco region, and pottery does not appear until *c.* 1400 BC. Between *c.* 1500 and *c.* 950 BC there seems to have been contact between the south coast, the south-central Peruvian highlands, sierra and forest in the north, and the hilly lowlands to the south-east of Lake Titicaca. In the Cuzco Valley area to the north-east only two important early sites have been found, Marcavalle and Pikicallepata. They formed part of an exchange network for products between the *altiplano* and the Bolivian forests and other areas of the Central Andes. A related site at Qaluyu, Puno Department, which dates from *c.* 1400 BC, appears to have been sparsely inhabited and was probably used by a scattered and mobile population. The early ceramic deposits in the Cuzco Valley and Qaluyu may be related to the cultures of the Peruvian south coast. The fundamental economic occupation was the herding of camelids, but the remains of felines and cervids in domestic rubbish, and of stone artefacts in excavations, show that hunting continued to be important. Two varieties of beans and perhaps maize were also cultivated.

2. EARLY HORIZON (*c.* 900–*c.* 200 BC). In the southern Central Andes there was a gradual transition from a quasi-sedentary life, with a population pattern established in enclosed sanctuaries, towards sedentarism and the consolidation of local sanctuaries into one large regional ceremonial centre. The Chiripa culture to the south of the lake, in Bolivia, may date back as far as 1300 BC. Its ceramic production is similar to the contemporary pottery of Puno and other areas further north, and the basis of its economy was the exploitation of lake products, the raising of camelids and guinea pigs, hunting and vegetable resources, such as quinoa, cactaceous plants and tubers.

Architectural construction at Chiripa began *c.* 1000 BC, when a platform mound was erected. It was modified several times, then abandoned briefly before being used by Tiahuanaco peoples. The platform was eventually raised to 6 m and extended to 55 m square. It was stone-faced and comprised a central sunken court surrounded by rectangular buildings. This plan was enlarged between *c.* 600 BC and *c.* 100 BC, to include a stone-faced sunken court of 23 m square and 1.5 m deep. Within the court carved stone plaques were erected, with representations of serpents, animals and humans. The court was surrounded by 16 rectangular earth and adobe brick buildings, arranged symmetrically and opening on to the platform and court. Their walls were stuccoed and painted in terracotta and green, in one case in a chevron pattern. The doorways were stepped in along a parallel wall construction, giving a door-within-a-door appearance. Chiripa pottery includes flat-bottomed, vertical-sided bowls, often decorated with incised outlines, then painted in red, cream and black. Appliqué felines, animal heads and human faces were also added. Ceramic trumpets from Chiripa are some of the earliest Andean musical instruments.

To the south of Chiripa, on the semi-desert plain to the north and north-east of Lake Poopó, peoples of the Wankarani culture (*fl c.* 1000–*c.* 300 BC) lived in villages but built no ceremonial centres or public buildings. Their economy was based on agriculture and herding, and they cast small items in copper. After the Early Horizon there was a cultural break in the Titicaca Basin proper, and sites were abandoned for a time.

3. EARLY INTERMEDIATE PERIOD (*c.* 200 BC–*c.* AD 600) and Middle Horizon (*c.* 600–*c.* 1000). During this period one of the most important cultures of the *altiplano* was Pucara, which developed in the areas north and south of Lake Titicaca and flourished between *c.* 100 BC and *c.* AD 300. Pucara was the cultural antecedent of TIAHUANACO. The site of Pucara itself (Lampa Province, Puno Department, Peru) was the most important centre. Its inhabitants constructed both monumental and rustic architecture, and the site has at least six principal nuclei in the form of stepped platforms, organized in a circular pattern. The largest structure is the Calasaya, which seems to have a feline plan. The central enclosure is a semi-subterranean temple whose frontage has a series of walls in the form of a horseshoe around a sunken central courtyard. In the centre of each side of the central courtyard there is a tomb chamber. The outside walls enclose a series of small compartments reached from the courtyard by a stairway. The whole is reminiscent of the Chiripa plan. At a lower level there is a terrace reached by a staircase. Among these structures were found broken stone statues, which perhaps decorated the temple. Examples represent human figures with helmet-like headgear, large round eyes and trophyheads held in their arms (*see* SOUTH AMERICA, PRE-COLUMBIAN, fig. 41). The south enclosure has three platforms with ceremonial enclosures.

1. Ceramic polychrome beaker (*kero*) in the form of a feline head, from the Titicaca Basin at Tiahuanaco, Bolivia, *c.* AD 500–*c.* 1000 (Tiahuanaco, Tiahuanaco Museum)

Little is known of Pucara culture; its economic basis was certainly hunting, fishing, herding and agriculture. According to John Rowe, its influence extended as far north as Cuzco and to the south of Lake Titicaca as well. Pucara pottery is distinctive, the most typical vessels being wide-mouthed beakers and footed bowls. Decoration is limited to incision and painting with yellow and black on a red slip. Vessels with a feline head in high relief are common. Close analysis has shown that this style was the source of conventions and mythical motifs that were later to characterize the styles of HUARI and Tiahuanaco (see fig. 1). It seems likely that the Pucara style was influenced to some extent by styles along the southern Peruvian coast, reaching the Titicaca Basin through the PARACAS culture, which brought with it the influence of the CHAVÍN style. During the latter part of the Early Intermediate period Tiahuanaco to the south began to develop into an important centre, becoming the dominant influence throughout the Titicaca Basin during the Middle Horizon (*see also* TIAHUANACO).

4. LATE INTERMEDIATE PERIOD (*c.* 1000–1476). The evidence for the Titicaca Basin during this period is confusing. Too much emphasis has been given to historical dates that do not always agree with archaeological evidence, because the version of history received by Spaniards was provided by the Incas, who, as victors over earlier cultures, frequently distorted reality.

After the fall of Tiahuanaco *c.* 1300, power in the *altiplano* passed to a culture with marked regional differences. By the time of the INCA conquest in the late 15th century there were two large Aymara-speaking kingdoms, the Colla to the north-west and the Lupaca to the south-west. It is uncertain whether these peoples were the descendants of the Tiahuanaco people or new arrivals. Sixteenth-century documents record the existence of other minor kingdoms and lordships in the Titicaca region, but it is not yet possible to determine whether these were autonomous or dependent on Colla or Lupaca. What is clear is that there was a cultural unity, although with much ethnic conflict. These groups caused the Incas many problems. Archaeologically, the cultural complex of these kingdoms is reflected in two types of pottery, known as Allita Amaya and Collao. The relationship between the two styles is unclear, but they seem to be contemporary. Allita Amaya is found almost exclusively in graves and was apparently confined to Lupaca territory. On the other hand, Collao is found in habitation sites throughout Colla territory. It was on this basis that Luis Lumbreras (1974) accepted the existence of two kingdoms. The products of these highland kingdoms were exchanged for those of lower-lying areas, carried in llama caravans between the coast and the *altiplano*. Such a trading system required colonies in the lowlands, allowing the *altiplano* communities to control the pastures in the *punas* (high Andean grassland plateaux), the production of salt, chilli peppers and coca in the tropical areas, and cotton and maize on the coast (*see also* SOUTH AMERICA, PRE-COLUMBIAN, §III, 1(i)).

Little is known about the Colla kingdom. The heartlands of the kingdom were around the north-west of Lake Titicaca. The cultural frontiers of its colonies extended east–west from the western mountain chain to the Pacific coast, and north–south from Sicuani, Peru, to the salt plains of Chile and Bolivia, perhaps as far east as Cochabamba in Bolivia or even Humahuaca in Argentina. It seems that this was an Aymara-speaking area, while the local ethnic minorities spoke Uru and Puquina. The Colla capital is thought to have been at Hatuncolla, north of Puno, Peru. According to Catherine Julien, the archaeological remains occupy an area slightly larger than the modern town. Distinctive fortified sites were built on hilltops, but these have been little studied. As the pottery continued to be used into the Inca period (*see* §5 below) the archaeological picture is more complicated. Inside the fortified settlement, dwellings were mostly round or oval in plan. Other dwellings in the region were rectangular. Houses were often built in two clusters, suggesting a bipartite social organization. None of the earlier ceremonial traditions of platform mounds, sunken courts or carved gateways persisted.

The Lupaca kingdom occupied the area around the south-west of Lake Titicaca. According to John Hyslop, Lupaca sites were settled in the *puna* or on the edges of it, at over 4000 m, in fortified places where pasturing could be carried on. There is almost no archaeological evidence, and most information on the culture is based on written sources. The economy must have been based on the cultivation of tubers and on herding camelids, supplemented by hunting, gathering and fishing. According to colonial *visita* records compiled some 35 years after the Spanish Conquest, these were rich communities with llama herds of scores of thousands of animals.

Architecturally, the most characteristic and best-known features of the *altiplano* kingdoms are the *chullpas* (see fig. 2). Their characteristic shape has a flattened dome-like crown with a formal, but not structural, extrados, being a false, or corbelled, vault that ends much lower. The best examples comprise a double structure, an internal one of unworked stone and an external one of ashlar. It has been suggested that the *chullpas* are of Inca date, but this is not certain. They are a local phenomenon, and in the Lupaca area they are certainly pre-Inca. The confusion arises probably because of the continuity of tradition, well into the Spanish colonial period. The largest *chullpas*, and the most impressive for their fine finish, are those of Sillustani, Peru, built of perfectly cut and fitted ashlar stone. These have a circular plan and a truncated cone or cylindrical shape, the circumference at the base varying according to the height, which can reach 12 m. Other *chullpas* are square or rectangular in plan, forming a kind of parallelepiped, and there are smaller, less impressive ones of uncut stone or adobe.

Another development of the Late Intermediate period was the spread of tin bronze metallurgy from its origination in Tiahuanaco throughout the *altiplano*, owing to the large quantities of copper and tin found in the Bolivian area south-west of Lake Titicaca.

Two other less well-known *altiplano* cultures were Mollo and Churajón. Mollo culture developed in the north-east of the *altiplano*, in Muñecas Province, Bolivia. Ponce Sanginés considered that Mollo culture was initially under Tiahuanaco influence but that after Tiahuanaco's disintegration it remained autonomous until the arrival of the Incas. The site from which it takes its name consists of buildings on terraces associated with agricultural terraces and canals. Mollo pottery is similar to that of Allita Amaya, but Mollo culture occupies terrain from 1500 to 3700 m above sea-level, which makes possible the use of products of different ecological systems. The Churajón culture spread through the Peruvian provinces of Arequipa and Cailloma, and to the Mollendo, Ilo, Moquegua and Locumba valleys. Its pottery has the same characteristics as Mollo pottery, and according to Lumbreras (1974) they have a common ancestry, although the chronology is not clear. Churajón settlements are extensive but similar to Mollo ones, and are also often associated with agricultural terracing.

5. LATE HORIZON (1477–1534). Historical information is abundant for this period in the Titicaca Basin. Before the reign of the 9th Inca, Pachacutec Yupanqui (*reg c.* 1438–71), the Colla and Lupaca kingdoms were rivals, each trying to incite the Incas against the other, and Inca conquest of the region proceeded only with difficulty, finally being accomplished under Tupac Inca Yupanqui (*reg c.* 1471–93). When the Incas had conquered the *altiplano*, as in their other territories, they imposed their own cultural norms. Nevertheless, in rural areas buildings continued to follow traditional forms except when there was an Inca state programme, when the new buildings were of superior quality. In many cases they are still visible,

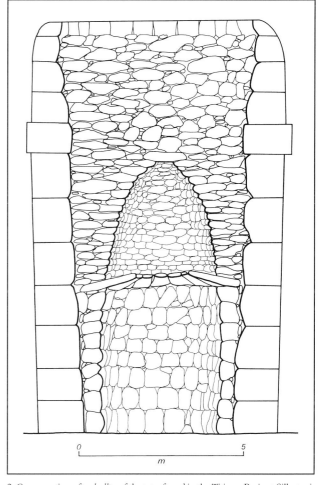

2. Cross-section of a *chullpa* of the type found in the Titicaca Basin at Sillustani, Peru, 14th century; reconstruction drawing

as at Suriqui, on the island of that name in Lake Titicaca. There were also important Inca temples in the *altiplano*, such as those at Copacabana and on various islands in the lake, such as Isla del Sol and Koati. These ruins have never been studied in detail, but are of great importance according to Gasparini and Margolies (1977), because the influence of Tiahuanaco traditions on Inca architecture can clearly be seen in them. An Inca settlement also existed in Tiahuanaco itself.

BIBLIOGRAPHY

A. Kidder II: *Some Early Sites in the Northern Lake Titicaca Basin*, Pap. Peabody Mus. Amer. Archaeol. & Ethnol., xxvii/1 (Cambridge, MA, 1943)

J. H. Rowe: 'Inca Culture at the Time of the Spanish Conquest', *Hb. S. Amer. Ind.*, ii, *Bureau Amer. Ethnol. Bull.*, cxliii (1946), pp. 183–330

J. V. Murra: 'Una apreciación etnológica de la visita', *Visita hecha a la provincia de Chuquito por Garci Diez de San Miguel en el año 1567* (Lima, 1964), pp. 421–44

L. G. Lumbreras and H. Amat: 'Secuencia arqueológica del altiplano occidental del Titicaca', *Actas y memorias, congreso internacional de Americanistas: Buenos Aires, 1966*, ii, pp. 75–106

C. Ponce Sanginés: *Las culturas Wankarani y Chiripa y su relación con Tiwanaku* (La Paz, 1970)

G. R. Willey: *South America*, ii of *An Introduction to American Archaeology* (Englewood Cliffs, 1971), pp. xiv, 559

L. G. Lumbreras: 'Los reinos post-Tiwanaku en el area altiplanica', *Rev. Mus. N.*, xl (1974), pp. 55–85

G. Gasparini and L. Margolies: *Arquitectura inka* (Caracas, 1977)

D. L. Browman: 'The Temple of Chiripa (Lake Titicaca, Bolivia)', *El hombre y la cultura andina*, ii, ed. R. Matos Mendieta (Lima, 1978), pp. 807–13

J. H. Hyslop: 'El area Lupaca bajo el dominio incaico: Un reconocimiento arqueológico', *Histórica*, iii (1979), pp. 13–79

C. Julien: 'Investigaciones recientes en la capital de los Qolla, Hatunqolla, Puno', *Arqueología peruana*, ed. R. Matos Mendieta (Lima, 1979), pp. 199–213

E. Mujica Barreda: 'Excavaciones en Pucara, Puno', *Arqueología peruana*, ed. R. Matos Mendieta (Lima, 1979), pp. 183–97

W. J. Conklin and M. E. Moseley: 'The Patterns of Art and Power in the Early Intermediate Period', *Peruvian Prehistory: An Overview of Pre-Inca and Inca Society*, ed. R. W. Keatinge (Cambridge, 1988), pp. 145–63

J. R. Parsons and C. M. Hastings: 'The Late Intermediate Period', *Peruvian Prehistory: An Overview of Pre-Inca and Inca Society*, ed. R. W. Keatinge (Cambridge, 1988), pp. 190–232

D. Bonavia: *De los orígenes al siglo XV*, i of *Peru: Hombre e historia* (Lima, 1991), pp. xiv, 586

M. E. Moseley: *The Incas and their Ancestors: The Archaeology of Peru* (London, 1992), pp. 202–8, 224–43

DUCCIO BONAVIA

Title-page. Emphasis of a page at the head of a text using large capital letters (for the title and sometimes also for the name of the author), usually contained in a decorative frame. This practice began in the illuminated books of Late Antiquity, and possibly reflects a tradition in earlier Greek and Roman texts.

Evidence for the appearance of such title-pages in Late Antique books is often found in Carolingian or Anglo-Saxon copies, since very few examples from Late Antiquity survive. This is particularly the case for such texts as the *Herbarium* of the pseudo-Apuleius and other medical texts. An example of a title-page in a Late Antique manuscript opens the canon tables (fol. 5*r*) in the fragmentary Rossano Gospels (6th century AD; Rossano, Mus. Dioc.). Its title is set in a circular frame containing small medallions of the four Evangelists. Another Late Antique codex, the *De materia medica* of Dioskurides (AD 512; Vienna, Österreich. Nbib., Cod. med. gr. 1, fol. 7*v*), made in Constantinople, has its title framed in a foliate wreath. An early 11th-century Anglo-Saxon Herbal (London, BL, Cotton MS. Vitell. C. III, fol. 19*v*) also has a wreath surrounding the title; this seems to be an accurate copy of a Late Antique original, possibly through the intermediary of a Carolingian manuscript. In another Late Antique book, the Calendar of 354, known through 16th- and 17th-century copies (Vienna, Österreich. Nbib., Cod. 3416 and Rome, Vatican, Bib. Apostolica, MS. Barb. lat. 2154, respectively) of a Carolingian manuscript (untraced), the title-page incorporates two putti holding a placard or *tabula ansata* (the framed plaque used for carved stone inscriptions). An architectural structure, including an arch with curtains drawn back to reveal a title on a placard, is used for the Ashburnham Pentateuch (early 7th century; Paris, Bib. N., MS. nouv. acq. lat. 2334, fol. 116*v*). A similar motif, derived very probably from a Late Antique model, is in a 13th-century Italian copy of Hippocrates' *De herbis* (Florence, Bib. Medicea-Laurenziana, MS. Plut. 73. 16). The same manuscript has a circular frame for a second title-page.

In the Merovingian period, some 8th-century manuscripts have frames around a title in capital letters (e.g. St Gregory's *Moralia*, London, BL, Add. MS. 11878, fol. 1*v*, and St Jerome's *Tractatus super Evangelia*, Paris, Bib. N., MS. lat. 12155). At the beginning of St Matthew's Gospel in the Gospel book in Trier (mid-8th century; Trier, Domschatz, Cod. 61, fol. 9*r*; see fig. 1), a titulus on a rectangular placard is held above a column by two angels; this follows the schema found in the Calendar of 354, and is continued in later Gospel books (e.g. *c*. 1000; Dublin, Chester Beatty Lib., MS. W. 17, fol. 118*r*). In the 8th and 9th centuries, the opening words of the text were sometimes placed in an elaborate frame, as at the beginning of Prudentius' *Psychomachia*; this does not, however, constitute a proper title-page, and should rather be termed a framed incipit. An alternative form, commonly found in the Carolingian period, is a framed incipit title in which the text's title is preceded by the word 'incipit'. This is more like a title-page than the framing of the opening words. In some cases, the title is contained in a circular, foliate, wreath-like frame, apparently of Late Antique origin. Such framed incipit titles occur frequently in Gospel books before each Gospel. In the Harley Golden Gospels (*c*. 790–800; London, BL, Harley MS. 2788, fol. 12*v*), a circle enframes a general title-page to all four Gospels. There is some continuation of such a system in Anglo-Saxon and Ottonian manuscripts of the 10th and 11th centuries, but title-pages were not provided in books between the 12th and 15th centuries, when the only concession to a title is a rubricated incipit, with larger lettering occasionally placed at the opening line of the first text page. Such incipits are rarely in the form of large illuminated and multicoloured letters as in the early Middle Ages, and are sometimes only distinguishable from the

1. Title-page to St Matthew's Gospel with miniature showing the titulus on a placard held by two angels, from a Gospel book, mid-8th century (Trier, Domschatz, Cod. 61, fol. 9*r*)

2. Title-page with circular, foliate wreath framing the title; from Terence: *Comedies*, 1466 (Oxford, Bodleian Library, MS. E. D. Clarke 28, fol. iii*v*)

text script by the red or, occasionally, blue or green pigment in which they are usually written.

With the revival of humanist scripts and classical ornament and figure style in 15th-century Italy, the title-page re-emerged. The earliest examples occur in the third quarter of the century and place the title in a variety of formats: in a circular wreath, as in the Terence *Comedies* from Florence (1466; Oxford, Bodleian Lib., MS. E. D. Clarke 28, fol. iii*v*; see fig. 2); on the side of a sarcophagus, for example in the *Ducal Oration* by Pietro Baroccio from Venice (before 1471; Cambridge, Fitzwilliam, MS. 188); and on a piece of parchment held by putti in the *Astronomicon* of Basinio de' Basini from Padua (before 1460; Oxford, Bodleian Lib., MS. Bodley 646, fol. 1*v*). The old form of a placard held by two putti was also revived in, for example, the *Polyhistoria* of Solinus from Padua (1457; Oxford, Bodleian Lib., MS. Canon. Class. lat. 161, fol. 7*r*). One final variation is an architectural structure forming the frame to the title, found in such manuscripts as St Augustine's *Commentary on the Psalms* from Naples (1480; London, BL, Add. MS. 14781). These title-pages are usually on the *verso* of a leaf facing the first page of the text; in later practice, the title was placed on the *recto*.

The title-page was adopted in early printed books from 1476 (*see* BOOK, fig. 6) and by the end of the century had become normal practice. The architectural frame was the favoured form for these pages, although some have no frame but reserve a page of large-letter script for the title. In the 16th and 17th centuries, engraved title-pages assume very elaborate forms, rarely excelled in later centuries when simpler decorative systems were more usual. In the Gothic Revival of the late 18th century and the 19th,

medieval architectural forms were often favoured as frames for the title, for example in A. W. N. Pugin's *Contrasts* (London, 1836). The Arts and Crafts movement associated with William Morris used highly decorative frames for title-pages. This tradition has to some degree continued in the 20th century in bibliophile limited editions.

See also CAROLINGIAN ART, §IV, 3; ANGLO-SAXON ART, §IV, 2; and BOOK ILLUSTRATION, fig. 3.

BIBLIOGRAPHY
A. W. Pollard: 'The History of the Title Page', *Univl Rev.*, iv (1889), pp. 204–22, 356–70
——: 'The Title Pages of some Italian Manuscripts', *Prtg A.*, xii/2 (1908), pp. 81–7
W. Koehler and F. Mütherich: *Karolingische Miniaturen*, 5 vols (Berlin, 1930–82)
O. Pächt: 'Notes and Observations on the Origin of Humanist Book Design', *Fritz Saxl, 1890–1948: A Volume of Memorial Essays*, ed. D. J. Gordon (London, 1957), pp. 184–94
M. Corbett: 'The Architectural Title Page', *Motif*, xii (1964), pp. 49–62
H. Grape-Albers: *Spätantike Bilder aus der Welt des Arztes* (Wiesbaden, 1977), pp. 141–3
L. Armstrong: *Renaissance Miniature Painters and Classical Imagery* (London, 1981)
O. Pächt: *Buchmalerei des Mittelalters* (Munich, 1985), pp. 150–54

NIGEL J. MORGAN

Titles. Names by which works of art are known, which may be formulated by their creators, by others dealing with the works, or be labels attached by popular consensus. While the main purpose of titling works is to differentiate them, a title may also be used deliberately to add meaning to a work. The majority of studies on the subject date only from the mid-1960s and concentrate on the modern, Western period of painting, but it is possible also to focus on the titling or earlier works and on titling traditions outside Western art.

1. Western world. 2. East Asia.

1. WESTERN WORLD. Discussions of Western traditions of titling works tend to centre on how titles act as clues to the relationship between words and images, and how they reveal attitudes to art in general. Such analysis stems mainly from the work of scholars such as Ernst Gombrich and Michel Foucault in the 1950s and 1960s, which began to redefine the field of art history within the broader context of the human sciences, and from SEMIOTICS, a field of study concerned with the interpretation of 'sign systems', which has been applied to the humanities, and art history in particular, since the 1960s.

It should be noted that much Western art has been titled only in retrospect and by general description. In such cases, and particularly with regard to Classical works of art, a broad identification of subject-matter usually forms the basis of the title, and this is then often supplemented with a reference to the location where the work was found; the name of the artist to whom the work is attributed; or the name of the individual or museum who owns or has owned the work. Thus the Hellenistic Greek sculpture *Venus of Cyrene* (4th century BC; Rome, Mus. N. Romano) is identified with the name of the ancient city where it was found; Myron's *Diskobolos* (*c.* 450 BC; marble copy in Rome, Mus. N. Romano) is

1. Pieter Bruegel I (attrib.): *Landscape with the Fall of Icarus*, oil on canvas, 735×112 mm, *c.* 1558 (Brussels, Musées Royaux des Beaux-Arts)

identified with the renowned Greek sculptor Myron of Eleutherai; while the *Venus de' Medici* (1st century BC; Rome, Mus. Capitolino), which is attributed to a follower of Praxiteles, and the *Aldobrandini Wedding* (Rome, Vatican, Mus. Sacro), a Roman fresco from the time of Augustus, include the names of the Renaissance patrons who first owned them. Such titles may, of course, change as ownership, location, artistic attribution and even interpretation of the work changes.

During the Middle Ages and into the Renaissance, works were generally commissioned for specific sites, usually churches. Gombrich suggested that because of this assured context, medieval works were usually referred to at the time by subject-matter and location; the reference would usually remain even if the work was later removed from its original context. The titles of many medieval and Renaissance works thus seem similar to those of Classical works, formulated either from the broad type of work (e.g. Book of Hours, Altarpiece, Triptych) coupled with a place-name or perhaps the name of a patron (thus Mérode Altarpiece; Très Riches Heures du Duc de Berry). There are also a large number of generic religious titles for paintings from these periods (e.g. *Virgin and Child, Resurrection, Rest on the Flight into Egypt*), reflecting the subject-matter favoured by the patrons.

As secular works began to grow in popularity from the late 15th century onwards, artists began to have a greater influence on subject-matter. Increasingly formulated only by subject-matter rather than by patron, location or general theme, titles became more varied. Although it is not always clear if a title of a work was created by the artist or used in general reference, for scholars of semiotics the titles of 16th-century works may still provide a particularly good source of analysis, since they would appear to exemplify a concept that words can or should offer a veritable similitude to the created image, an important point in studies of representation. This concept was not, of course, confined to the 16th century, but it was in the 16th century that the relationship between words and images began to be bolder. In Flemish art, for example, a proverb was sometimes used to form the subject-matter of a work— Pieter Bruegel the elder took this to an extreme in *Netherlandish Proverbs* (1559; Berlin, Gemäldegal.), in which over 100 proverbs have been identified. It is also in Bruegel's work and that of some of his contemporaries that we find some of the earliest manipulations of the relationship between title and subject-matter. *Landscape with the Fall of Icarus* (attrib. Bruegel, *c.* 1558; see fig. 1) prompts a search for the subject identified by the title. While we may notice first the plough tracing furrows in the foreground, once Icarus' wildly thrashing legs have been located within the landscape, interpretation of the work changes from that of a bucolic landscape to that of a disturbing landscape that reverberates with indifference to the occurring catastrophe. It is the title that prompts a fuller perusal of the image, provoking the reading of pictorial elements (signs) that may have gone unnoticed, and transforming the overall meaning of the painting. This interactive relationship between titles and works of art was to become more significant in subsequent centuries.

Scholars of semiotics have noted that the meaning of signs and symbols in art began to change in the early 17th century, leading to a duality between titles and images that still persists. The ordering of the arts as characterized by the French and British art academies of the 17th and 18th centuries favoured the discursive over the visual, contesting the reciprocal relation that had earlier existed between images and titles. By 1663 a hierarchy of genres was established, and titles of works of art became one 'element in a hierarchy of names that were fixed by official decree' (Bann). Thus, according to Foucault, instead of conveying meaning through resemblance, signs began to be perceived as having a variable relationship to what they represent (see Foucault, 1966; *see also* SYMBOL). By the 18th century for example, Antoine Watteau's *The Shepherds* (1716; Berlin, Schloss Charlottenburg), as noted by Thomas Crow, contests the vraisemblance of a title to its image through a process of nuanced displacement. Instead of reading the image as a realistic rendition of actual shepherds, the work can be interpreted as portraying Parisian leisure activities, where unofficial theatrical comedians impersonate shepherds for the entertainment of aristocrats. Under such circumstances, both the title and image display a certain artificial mode of representation that questions the relationship between signs and what they represent. As artists began to differentiate between the duality of canonic standards and individual invention, the consensus of opinion that had once made the academies' nomenclature such a viable and formidable force began to

erode. In the 19th century for example, J. M. W. Turner entitled one of his paintings *Snow Storm: Steam-boat off a Harbour's Mouth Making Signals in Shallow Water, and Going by the Lead. The Author Was in this Storm on the Night the Ariel Left Harwich* (1842; London, Tate). In this late work, tension is intentionally created between an image that is abstract, diffuse and individually inventive and a title that is by contrast specific to the point of reporting a historical event, as R. Reed suggested. The juxtaposition between the painting and title thus challenges not only the canonic standard that valued history painting above individual invention, but also suggests the sublimity and preeminence of the visual image over the banality of the verbal title. The renunciation of the academies by leading artists of the 19th century may be seen as part of a larger change in Western society (Ladner). In the visual arts symbolism was explored 'in new ways, in many instances stressing the arbitrariness and subjectivity of signs and symbols rather than their correspondence with an objective reality'.

The effects of this altered perception of titles became pronounced from the mid-19th century onwards. Claude Monet's painting *Impression, Sunrise* (1873; Paris, *see* IMPRESSIONISM, fig. 1), for example, subtly questions the certainty of the relationship between titles and images. Without the title, the painting could be interpreted as either a sunrise or a sunset. Thus, what the painted image

2. René Magritte: *Treachery of Images*, oil on canvas, 622×810 mm, 1929 (Los Angeles, CA, County Museum of Art)

cannot specify, the artist by means of the title does specify, namely that the image is a sunrise. In the language of semiotics, *Impression, Sunrise* points to an understanding of images as open systems that multiply meaning, while language in the form of a title is seen symbiotically as a system that hones meaning down to specifics, here to the specific impression of a sunrise.

The Cubists and the Surrealists also chose titles that question the conventional relationship between titles and works of art. Butor suggested that with Cubism 'there is no longer the resemblance between the object designated by the title and the image [we see]'. In other words, a seemingly straightforward title, such as Pablo Picasso's *Nude Woman* (1910; Washington, N.G.A.) or Georges Braque's *The Portuguese* (1911; Basel, Öff. Kstsamml.) may seem incongruous in the face of a Cubist image. But where in Cubism the correlation between the title and subject-matter seems blocked by the partial abstraction of the image, in the works of various Surrealists just the opposite occurs. The correlation between the two elements is blocked by titles and words that may wilfully misname the recognizable objects presented in the paintings. One of the best examples is Magritte's *Treachery of Images* (1929; see fig. 2), also known by three other titles: *Faithful Image*, *Use of Speech* and the *Air and the Song*. Furthermore, the work is often casually identified by the painted words found on the canvas surface, 'Ceci n'est pas une pipe'. According to Edson ('Confronting the Signs', 1984), the picture of a pipe above the statement 'this is not a pipe' points to a 'disruption of convention and expectation [that] now becomes the starting point for a new kind of response'. Works by Max Ernst and Salvador Dalí also question the assumed function of a title to name the subject of its painting. Ernst's *Two Children Are Threatened by a Nightingale* (1924; New York, MOMA), for example, names two children in the title but presents three children within the image. Likewise, Dalí's *Apparition of a Face and Fruit Dish on a Beach* (1938; Hartford, CT, Wadsworth Atheneum) selectively names only two of many apparitions that appear within the painting, leaving unmentioned the collared dog or the working and sleeping humans shown within the cliffs. These types of incongruities between titles and images expose the arbitrary nature of our systems of representation.

This variable relationship between titles and signification is articulated by thousands of Western works of the mid- to late 20th century. Common devices include the use of letters of the alphabet or numeric symbols instead of words; the deliberate use of '*Untitled*' as a label; and the general use of irony to create or emphasize incongruities between images and words. The most obvious examples are found in abstract and conceptual art, since the framework of signification in such works (*see also* ABSTRACTION) is often dependent on, or deeply affected by, titling traditions. In colour field paintings, for example, the title (even if rendered as *Untitled*) often points to a most intricate interpretation. Barnett Newman's *Adam* (1951–2; London, Tate) or *First Station* (*see* NEWMAN, BARNETT, fig. 1)—each composed formally of simple fields of colour—create an immense difference in signification when title and formal elements are considered together. In another example, Cy Twombly's large, abstract paintings

often bear titles that contrast in their erudition with the childlike scribbles and erasures of the images—with *The Italians* (1961; New York, MOMA) the only recognizable traces of Italians on the canvas are the words 'Italians' and 'Roma' written in faint lettering (see Barthes). It is titles such as these, with their multiple analogies, that highlight the similitudes and incongruities between words and images so fascinating to scholars interested in the semiotics of art.

BIBLIOGRAPHY
R. Jakobson: 'The Phonemic and Grammatical Aspects of Language', *Actes du VIe congrès international des linguistes* (Paris, 1949)
R. Arnheim: *Art and Visual Perception* (Berkeley, 1954)
E. H. Gombrich: *Art and Illusion: A Study in the Psychology of Pictorial Representation* (Princeton, 1960)
T. J. B. Spencer: 'The Imperfect Parallel betwixt Painting and Poetry', *Greece & Rome*, vii (1960), pp. 173–86
D. Mahlow: *Art and Writing* (exh. cat., Baden-Baden, Staatl. Ksthalle, 1963)
M. Foucault: *Les Mots et les choses: Un Archéologie des sciences humaines* (Paris, 1966); Eng. trans. by A. Sheridan as *The Order of Things: An Archaeology of Human Sciences* (New York, 1970)
J. Thuillier: 'The Birth of the Beaux-Arts', *ARTnews Annu.*, xxxiii (1967), pp. 29–37
M. Butor: *Les Mots dans la peinture* (Geneva, 1969)
C. Moncelet: *Essai sur le titre: En littérature et dans les arts* (Le Cendre, 1972)
M. Foucault: *Ceci n'est pas une pipe: Deux lettres et quatre dessins de René Magritte* (Montpellier, 1973; Eng. trans., Berkeley, 1983)
G. B. Ladner: 'Medieval and Modern Understanding of Symbolism: A Comparison', *Speculum*, liv/2 (April 1979), pp. 223–33
R. Barthes: 'The Wisdom of Art', *Cy Twombly: Paintings and Drawings 1952–1977* (exh. cat., New York, Whitney, 1979), pp. 9–22
R. J. Belton: 'Picabia's *Caoutchouc* and the Threshold of Abstraction', *Racar*, ix/1–2 (1982), pp. 69–73
W. Hofmann: 'Ambiguity in Daumier (and Elsewhere)', *A. J.* [New York], xliii/4 (Winter 1983), pp. 361–4
J. V. Mundy: 'Tanguy, Titles and Mediums', *A. Hist.*, vi/2 (1983), pp. 199–213
L. Edson: 'Confronting the Signs: Words, Images and the Reader-spectator', *Dada Surrealism*, xiii (1984), pp. 83–93
——: 'Disrupting Conventions: Verbal–Visual Objects in Francis Ponge and René Magritte', *Espr. Créateur*, xxiv (Summer 1984), pp. 23–35
J. Fisher: 'Entitling', *Crit. Inq.*, xi (December 1984), pp. 286–98
S. Bann: 'The Mythical Conception is the Name: Titles and Names in Modern and Post-modern Painting', *Word & Image*, i/2 (1985), pp. 176–90
M. Camille: 'The Book of Signs: Writing and Visual Difference in Gothic Manuscript Illumination', *Word & Image*, i/2 (1985), pp. 133–48
T. Crow: 'Codes of Silence: Historical Interpretation and the Art of Watteau', *Representations*, 12 (Fall 1985), pp. 2–14
E. H. Gombrich: 'Image and Word in Twentieth-century Art', *Word & Image*, i/3 (1985), pp. 213–41
A. Cook: 'The Sign in Klee', *Word & Image*, ii/4 (1986), pp. 363–81
W. J. T. Mitchell: *Iconology: Image, Text, Ideology* (Chicago, 1986)
F. Armengaud: *Titres* (Paris, 1988)
G. Leffin: *Bildtitel und Bildlegenden bei Max Ernst: Ein interdisziplinarer Beitrag zur Kunst des zwanzigsten Jahrhunderts* (Frankfurt am Main, 1988)
R. Read: '"A Name that Makes it Looked after": Turner, Ruskin and the Visual–Verbal Sublime', *Word & Image*, v/4 (1989), pp. 315–25
B. E. Savedoff: 'The Art Object', *Brit. J. Aesth.*, xxix/2 (1989), pp. 160–67

COLLETTE A. CHATTOPADHYAY

2. EAST ASIA.

(i) *China.* In Chinese art, titles are usually reserved for works of calligraphy and painting. They are written on the upper right-hand or upper left-hand corner of a work, some with dedications. They appear in various script styles and may be followed by a signature and date. Literary writings, commemorations, personal letters or fragments that are of calligraphic value in their own right are known by the name of the text, its opening characters, its date or excavation site. The *Han Yongyuan biance*, for example, is thus understood as the title of a scroll of wooden slips inscribed in the Yongyuan era (AD 90–105). During the Tang period (618–907) examples of inscribed titles of the poet Li Bo (701–62) include *Chengxing* ('Riding exhilaration') in running script and *Yongjiushi* ('Poem for intoning wine') and *Zuizhongtie* ('Calligraphy [copybook inscribed] during drunkenness') in a more cursive style. The titles of existing works were also used to make new titles, such as *Zho Mengfu shu Qianhou Chibifu* ('Zhao Mengfu inscribes the former and latter *Odes to the Red Cliff* by Su Shi').

The largely figurative painting from the Han period (206 BC–AD 220) to the Tang period depicted Buddhist and Daoist deities and ancient cultural heroes with corresponding titles. While narrative content continued to thrive, the rise of landscape painting during the Five Dynasties period (907–60) saw titles reflecting the seasonal and natural aspects in two- or four-character descriptions that became generic: *Early Spring*, *Fishing in a Wintry River*, *Snow Clearing at the Mountain Pass* or *Buddhist Temple in an Autumn Grove*. Titles were also inspired by poetry: *Sunset Glow over Fishing Village*, *Autumn Moon over Xiang Xiang* or *Hearing Wind in the Pines*. The titles of ink-plays by scholars (spontaneous painting without draft, stressing superior brushwork) were symbolic of personal moral aspirations or emotions: *Embracing the Qin* (lofty musical erudition) *and Crane* (longevity), *Twin Purities: Bamboo* (purity) *and Plum* (endurance), *Night Watch* and *Rainy Thoughts*.

JOAN STANLEY-BAKER

(ii) Japan. The Oriental love of grouping by numerical series of interrelated subjects is reflected in titles of Japanese illustrated books and prints. ANDŌ HIROSHIGE was one of many artists who produced prints in sets of eight, of which *Eight Views of Lake Biwa* (*Ōmi hakkei no uchi*; c. 1834) is one of the best-known. KATSUSHIKA HOKUSAI's famous series, an exquisite set of prints depicting Japan's sacred mountain, is entitled *Thirty-six Views of Mount Fuji* (*Fugaku sanjūrokkei*; 1831). Hiroshige and Hokusai both produced a series of views along the ancient road between Edo (now Tokyo) and Kyoto with the title *Fifty-three Stations on the Tōkaidō* (*Tōkaido gojūsantsugi no uchi*). An equally famous highway was depicted in the *Sixty-nine Stations on the Kisokaidō* (*Kisokaidō rokujukyūtsugi no uchi*; late 1830s), a collaborative work by Hiroshige and IKEDA EISEN. The Three Metropolises (Edo, Osaka and Kyoto), the Six Jade Rivers (Tamagawa), the Five Chivalrous Commoners of popular lore and the twelve months of the year all featured in print-series titles. However, numbers such as the '32 types' encountered in titles of sets of prints depicting beautiful women (*bijinga*) were notional, the sets actually containing ten designs (*see* JAPAN, §IX, 3(ii)). Hiroshige's *One Hundred Views of Edo* (*Meisho Edo hyakkei*; 1856–9), a series of prints in an upright format, actually numbered 119 prints in the set.

In many series of prints, the title and subject are analogous or in parody (*mitate*). For example, HOSODA

EISHI produced two series depicting courtesans, entitled *Beauties of the Green Houses as the Six Poets* (*Seiro bijin rokkasen*) and *A Fanciful Selection of Six Flowers* (*Ryaku rokkasen*). Similarly, ISODA KORYŪSAI produced *Present-day Geishas as the Six Poets* (*Imayo giju rokkasen*). The titles of some print series are reproduced or imitated by a decorative device within the design. In the series *Twelve Hours of the Green Houses* (*Seirō jūniji tsuzuki*; c. 1795), KITAGAWA UTAMARO places the title between the weight cords of a clock. A poem placed in a small square cartouche forms part of the title of Hokusai's *One Hundred Poems Explained by the Nurse* (*Hyakunin isshu uba ga etoki*; c. 1840). The titles of *surimono* were as opulent as the pictures; *surimono* were small-format prints produced mainly in the first half of the 19th century, in limited editions usually of 50–75. They often bore poems composed by the people who commissioned them.

In books of the Edo (1600–1868) and Meiji (1868–1912) periods, printed title slips (*daisen*), often featuring the title in fine calligraphy, were pasted to the covers. Japanese books were designed to be read from right to left and thus opened to reveal a title-page on the right, pasted on the inside of the front cover and facing the first page of the preface on the left (*see* JAPAN, §IX, 2).

BIBLIOGRAPHY
B. Stewart: *A Guide to Japanese Prints* (New York, 1922, R/1979)
D. Chibbett: *The History of Japanese Printing and Book Illustration* (Tokyo and New York, 1977)
R. Lane: *Images of the Floating World: The Japanese Print* (Oxford, 1978)
J. Hillier: *The Art of the Japanese Book*, 2 vols (London, 1987)
Y. Brown: *Japanese Book Illustration* (London, 1988)
A. Newland and C. Uhlenbeck, eds: *Ukiyo-e to Shin hanga: The Art of Japanese Woodblock Prints* (Leicester, 1990)

JAMES SELF

Tito, Diego Quispe. *See* QUISPE TITO, DIEGO.

Tito, Santi di (*b* Sansepolcro, 6 Oct 1536; *d* Florence, 2 July 1602). Italian painter, draughtsman and architect. His art is of fundamental importance to the history of Florentine painting in the transitional period between Mannerism and Baroque. He rejected the virtuosity of Mannerist painters and returned to an earlier Renaissance tradition that emphasized clear narrative and the expression of a purer, more genuine religious sentiment. His most important works are altarpieces and frescoes; his private commissions included devotional paintings, mythological scenes and portraits. Although he was less important as an architect, here too he upheld an ideal of purity and simplicity that parallels the style of his paintings.

1. LIFE AND PAINTED WORK.

(i) Florence, Rome and Venice, to c. 1575. Santi di Tito completed his training in Florence, where he studied with Bastiano da Montecarlo (dismissed by Vasari as 'uomo senza disegno'), then with Agnolo Bronzino and Baccio Bandinelli. He was admitted to the Compagnia di S Luca in 1554. In 1555 he was in contact with Vasari (then court artist to Cosimo I de' Medici) and as late as 1557 is again documented with Bastiano. In this early period Santi experimented with the different elements that were to determine his style. The first work that may confidently be attributed to him, an *Adoration of the Magi* (before

1558; Fiesole, S Domenico), which had been begun by Giovanni Antonio Sogliani, is deeply indebted to the Florentine tradition of Andrea del Sarto and Fra Bartolommeo.

Between 1558 and 1564 Santi worked in Rome. The first frescoes he painted there, oval medallions of the *Four Seasons* and narrative panels illustrating the *Parable of the Vineyard* (Rome, Giardini Vaticani Casino Pio IV), remain within this Florentine tradition. The later ones—a *Crucifixion*, scenes from the *Acts of the Apostles* (both Rome, Pal. Salviati, chapel) and the stories of *Nebuchadnezzar* (Rome, Vatican, Cortile Belvedere)—show a tendency towards the more Raphaelesque style of Taddeo Zuccaro.

In March 1564 Santi returned to Florence and in July gained admittance to the Accademia del Disegno (founded 1563), for which he thereafter performed a variety of duties. From 1564, with other artists of the Accademia, he was regularly employed by Vasari. Two paintings, a *Virgin with Saints* (Florence, Ognissanti) and an impressive *Nativity* (Florence, S Giuseppe), both done before 1568, indicate a return to local stylistic tradition. In their simplicity and naturalism they are quite distinct from the complex poses and precious colouring advocated by Vasari, whose projects evidently required Santi to modify his style to one that was more sophisticated and graceful. This compromise is seen in his fresco of the *Construction*

1. Santi di Tito: *Resurrection, c.* 1572 (Florence, Santa Croce)

of Solomon's Temple (1571; Florence, Annunziata, Chapel of St Luke), the small paintings the *Discovery of Purple*, the *Origin of Amber* and the *Crossing of the Red Sea* (1571–2), which were painted to decorate the *studiolo* of Francesco I in the Palazzo Vecchio (*in situ*), and in the great altarpiece of the *Resurrection* (*c.* 1572; Florence, Santa Croce; see fig. 1). His court portraits (e.g. *Don Pietro Medici*, Florence, Uffizi), which recall those by Bronzino and Francesco Salviati, show some of his best qualities.

The influence of Venetian art (Santi evidently visited the city in 1571–2) and more particularly of Paolo Veronese may be seen in Santi's *Feast in the House of Simon* (Florence, SS Annunziata, refectory). Having become a member of the oratory of St Thomas Aquinas in 1568, he painted the *Vision of St Thomas Aquinas* (1573; Florence, S Salvi). The dramatic complexity and spatial effects of this work and of his *Supper at Emmaus* (1574; Florence, Santa Croce) similarly point to his Venetian experience, while the realism of the figures perhaps also suggests a first-hand knowledge of Lombard painters.

(ii) Florence, c. 1575–87. After Vasari's death (1574) Santi received fewer court commissions and worked increasingly for the churches of Florence, for private clients and for oratories and confraternities. He was now able to give more time to painting devotional works. The many drawings related to the *Holy Family* and the *Pietà* (e.g. Florence, Uffizi; Munich, Alte Pin.) indicate that these were his preferred subjects. In 1578 he was granted Florentine citizenship and built a house to his own design in the Via delle Ruote (*see* §2 below).

Santi's *Pentecost* (*c.* 1575; Dubrovnik, Dominican church) marks an abandonment of the experimental style of the early 1570s in favour of an increasingly simple and accessible narrative style, in keeping with the demands of the Counter-Reformation church for works that would both instruct and move the most humble spectator. These ideas were promulgated in Florence by the Provincial Synod of 1573 and later supported by critics as influential as Raffaelle Borghini. Many of Santi's paintings exemplify this approach, among them the *Raising of Lazarus* (1576; Florence, S Maria Novella), the *Martyrdom of St Stephen* (1579; Florence, SS Gervasio & Protasio) and the *Assumption* (1587; Fagna, S Maria). Santi's narrative clarity is largely derived from his progression through several preparatory sketches to one or more highly finished drawings, squared for transfer, as in the drawing (Florence, Uffizi) for the *Nativity* (1583; destr., ex-S Maria del Carmine, Florence); other important examples survive (Florence, Uffizi; Rome, Pal. Farnese; Paris, Louvre). Such preparation was standard Mannerist practice and showed Santi's adherence to the ideal of *disegno*, but his striving to achieve greater naturalism led him away from Mannerism and back to the art of Andrea del Sarto and Raphael, which influenced both his style of composition and the poses of individual figures. This return to an early 16th-century tradition constitutes his 'reform' of Florentine painting. He was searching for a means to express a purer religious sentiment, a quest that is clearly demonstrated in a series of drawings of heads (Florence, Uffizi) and in various aspects of his painted works. Simple and devout paintings, such as the *Pietà with Saints* (Scrofania,

2. Santi di Tito: *Agony in the Garden*, oil on panel, 1591 (Florence, S Maria Maddalena dei Pazzi)

Compagnia del Salvatore) and the *Annunciation* (Scrofania, S Biagio), both dating from 1575–80, adopt the clear structures of early 16th-century paintings. The *Circumcision* (1579; Casciana Alta, parish church) includes direct quotations from Albrecht Dürer's prints of the *Life of the Virgin*, and the frescoes of scenes from the *Life of St Dominic* (1570–82; Florence, S Maria Novella) contain echoes of Domenico Ghirlandaio. These references to earlier art accord with the views of Counter-Reformation theorists, such as Giovanni Andrea Gilio da Fabriano and Gabriele Paleotti, who exalted 'primitive' and Nordic paintings as expressions of a more genuine devotion. There is more feeling too in Santi's later portraits (e.g. *Portrait of an Unknown Gentleman*, Florence, Uffizi), which have a humanity and warmth that suggests the art of Bartolomeo Passarotti and Annibale Carracci.

(iii) Florence, 1588–1602. In his final period Santi responded to the new interest in light and colour that was being developed by younger Florentine artists, such as Lodovico Cigoli, Gregorio Pagani, Jacopo da Empoli and Domenico Passignano. Three paintings, all of 1588, herald this new phase: *St Nicholas of Tolentino* (Sansepolcro, Pin.), *St John the Baptist Preaching* (Lima, Ortiz de Zevallos priv. col., see Spalding, 1982, fig. 70) and the *Crucifixion* (Florence, Santa Croce). Monumental in composition, they are also richer in colour and more realistic in their treatment of light and shade. These aspects of his style culminated in the *Agony in the Garden* (1591; Florence, S Maria Maddalena dei Pazzi; see fig. 2), the *Miracle of the Loaves and Fishes* (1592; Florence, SS Gervasio & Protasio) and the *Vision of St Thomas* (1593; Florence, S Marco). The *Miracle of St Clement* (1592; Sansepolcro, Pin.) is among his less careful paintings, which are probably associated with his being overburdened with commissions. A new mood of subdued yet vibrant emotion is present in such works as the *Pentecost* (1598; Prato, S Spirito) and in the series of *Madonnas in Glory* (*c.* 1600; e.g. Montevettolini, S Michele; Dicomano, S Maria; Prato, Cassa di Risparmio; Florence, S Stefano a Ponte). His last known work, an *Annunciation* (*c.* 1602; Florence, S Maria Novella), revives an archaic composition and is tempered by delicate passages of light, in which some critics have seen a reflection of the works of Caravaggio.

(iv) Workshop and critical reception. Santi's importance was universally recognized. He was an acclaimed teacher, admired by artists as diverse as Cigoli and Passignano. Many young Florentine artists entered his workshop, among them Pagani, Agostino Ciampelli, Andrea Boscoli (*fl* 1550–1606), Ludovico Buti (*c.* 1560–1603), Antonio Tempesta and his own son, Tiberio di Tito (1573–1627). When, in 1602, the Accademia del Disegno established rules for the protection of Florence's artistic patrimony, he was mentioned as the foremost of the leading artists whose signatures were required to sanction the exportation of works of art.

2. ARCHITECTURE. Santi's activities as an architect are poorly documented, and much of his work has been distorted by later alterations. Only the original façades survive of the oratory of St Thomas Aquinas (1568–9), his own house in the Via delle Ruote and the Palazzo Dardinelli-Fenzi (both *c.* 1580). The famous door of the artist's house, with its jambs placed at a slanting angle rather like a painterly conceit, was included in Santi's architectural repertory as a concession to the Mannerist love of the bizarre. All the other elements in these early buildings, however, tend towards an ideal of purity and simplicity, directly in conflict with the architectural notions introduced into Florence by Bartolomeo Ammannati and Vasari. The substantially intact Palazzo Anchini (after 1583), Florence, with a courtyard that has been attributed to Michelozzo, clearly exemplifies these characteristics. There are three surviving examples of Santi's villa architecture: the Villa Montrone at Peretola; the Villa Le Corti at San Casciano, Val di Pesa; and the Villa I Collazzi at Giogoli, the grandeur of which has led to its being attributed to Michelangelo. The Capponi tempietto at Semfonte (1594–7) and the convent of S Michele alla Doccia (now Villa Doccia), on which Santi worked in 1599, are the best documented of his architectural works. For the tempietto he planned to embellish an octagonal oratory with a portico, but this was never carried out; for the convent, however, the work of linking and enriching a series of existing buildings was completed in exact accordance with his plan.

BIBLIOGRAPHY

G. Vasari: *Vite* (1550, rev. 2/1568); ed. G. Milanesi (1878–85), v, p. 124; vii, pp. 91, 309–10, 619–20

R. Borghini: *Il Riposo* (Florence, 1584), pp. 106, 115–16, 187–8, 194, 198, 205, 619–23

G. Baglione: *Vite* (1642); ed. V. Mariani (1935), pp. 41, 65, 153–4, 319, 332

F. Baldinucci: *Notizie* (1681–1728); ed. F. Ranalli (1845–7), ii, pp. 534–54

G. Briganti: 'Un libro su Santi di Tito', *Crit. A.*, iii (1938), pp. xvii–xix

R. Chiarelli: 'Contributi a Santo di Tito architetto', *Riv. A.*, xxi (1939), pp. 126–55

G. Fagnoni Spadolini: 'Una villa restaurata: I Collazzi', *Ant. Viva*, i/3 (1962), pp. 30–40

W. Vitzthum: *Lo studiolo di Francesco I a Firenze* (Milan, 1965)

L. Berti: *Il principe dello studiolo: Francesco I dei Medici e la fine del rinascimento fiorentino* (Florence, 1967), pp. 73, 77–8, 179–81, 196

E.R.M.: 'A Deposition of Christ by Santi di Tito', *Minneapolis Inst. A. Bull.*, lvii (1968), pp. 49, 67

S. J. Freedberg: *Painting in Italy, 1500 to 1600*, Pelican Hist. A. (Harmondsworth, 1971), pp. 428–31

P. Moschella: 'L'oratorio di San Tommaso d'Aquino di Santi di Tito a Firenze', *Boll. Ingeg.*, xix/10 (1971), pp. 22–5

J. Spalding: 'A Drawing by Santi di Tito for his Lost Carmine *Nativity*', *Master Drgs*, xiv (1976), pp. 278–80

M. Collareta: 'Tre note su Santi di Tito', *An. Scu. Norm. Sup. Pisa*, vii/1 (1977), pp. 351–69

I. Bigazzi: 'La scala del Palazzo Nonfinito', *Michelangelo*, vii/25 (1978), pp. 25–8

A. Godoli and A. Natali: 'Santi di Tito e la Maestà di Antonio Vecchietti', *Ant. Viva*, xix/4 (1980), pp. 12–17

J. Spalding: *Santi di Tito* (New York and London, 1982)

M. Gregori: 'Ut pictura poesis: Rappresentazioni fiorentine della *Gerusalemme liberata* e della *Divina commedia*', *Paragone*, xxxiv/401–3 (1983), pp. 107–21 (108–11)

J. Spalding: 'Santi di Tito and the Reform of Florentine Mannerism', *Stor. A.*, xlvii (1983), pp. 41–52

S. Lecchini Giovannoni: 'Studi e disegni preparatori di Santi di Tito', *Paragone*, xxxv/415 (1984), pp. 20–36

Disegni di Santi di Tito (1536–1603) (exh. cat. by S. Lecchini Giovannoni and M. Collareta, Florence, Uffizi, 1985)

Il seicento fiorentino, 3 vols (exh. cat., Florence, Pal. Strozzi, 1986–7), i, pp. 82–4; ii, pp. 67–9; iii, pp. 161–3

MARCO COLLARETA

Titon. French family of civil servants, patrons and collectors. Maximilien Titon (*b* 1631; *d* Paris, 29 Jan 1711) supplied arms for the French war effort in Flanders and later established the royal magazines of arms in Paris and the provinces; he also founded a museum of ancient arms, the nucleus of the future Musée de l'Armée at Les Invalides, Paris. With his large fortune he bought estates, titles and a distinguished collection of paintings, which he housed in the residence he had built (*c.* 1673; destr. 1880) in the Rue de Montreuil in Paris. The house, later known as Titonville for its grandeur, was decorated by Jean-Charles Delafosse, Jean Jouvenet, Jean-Baptiste Belin and Charles Poërson, among others. In the gallery, the paintings (principally battle scenes) were flanked by busts; of two globes by the Venetian Vicento Maria Coronelli (1650–1718), one showed the earth and the other the heavens. Ancient sculpture was given some prominence, with replicas of the *Laokoon* and Farnese *Bull*, but the collection was dominated by paintings, including portraits of Titon and his wife (priv. cols) by Hyacinthe Rigaud and Nicolas de Largillierre respectively. The *Adoration of the Magi* (1704; New Orleans, LA, Mus. A.) by Nicolas Colombel and *Christ Carrying the Cross* (ex-Heim Gal., London) by Bon Boullogne represent Titon's penchant for the French school.

Maximilien Titon's son Evrard Titon du Tillet (*b* Paris, 16 Jan 1677; *d* Paris, 26 Dec 1762) kept many works owned by his father for his own collection. After serving in the army until 1697, he became chief steward to Marie-Adelaïde of Savoy, Duchess of Burgundy (1685–1712), and in 1712 provincial war-commissioner. He is remembered as the instigator of an extraordinary monument, the *French Parnassus*, planned in 1708 as a homage to Louis XIV, King of France, and perhaps inspired by Charles Delafosse's painting on the subject (untraced), which his father had owned. He commissioned a bronze model (1718–21; Versailles, Château), over 2 m high, from the sculptor Louis Garnier. His ultimate aim was to erect a colossal group commemorating the Golden Age of Louis XIV at some prominent point in Paris or at Versailles, comprising life-sized figures of major writers and composers. To this end in 1723 he set about raising money by circulating an engraving of the proposed monument (Colton, no. 27) by Girard Audran and in 1727 by publishing *Description du Parnasse français . . .*, reissued in a sumptuous edition in 1732. Titon du Tillet's obsessive attempts were unsuccessful but unremitting. Just before his death he commissioned Augustin Pajou to make supplementary figures of the writers Prosper Jolyot de Crébillon (1674–1762), Jean-Baptiste Rousseau (1671–1741) and François-Marie Arouet de Voltaire (1694–1778), which, together with a statue of Titon himself (all Versailles, Château), were completed in 1766, when Louis XV accepted the model as a gift from Titon's nephew Jean-Baptiste Titon (*b* Paris, 13 June 1696; *d* Paris, 27 July 1768). Titon du Tillet also amassed a celebrated collection of paintings, among them Watteau's *Family* (*c.* 1716; priv. col.) and *Italian Serenade* (1715; Stockholm, Nmus.), and Largillierre's *Mlle Duclos as Ariadne* (*c.* 1714; Louisville, KY, Speed A. Mus.).

BIBLIOGRAPHY
A. Girodie: 'Les Titon, amateurs d'art et le Parnasse français', *Bull. Soc. Hist. A. Fr.* (1928), pp. 60–77

J. Colton: *Le Parnasse français: Evrard Titon du Tillet and the Origins of the Monument to Genius* (New Haven and London, 1979)

V. Lavergne-Durey: 'Les Titon, mécènes et collectionneurs à Paris à la fin du XVIIe au XVIIIe siècles', *Bull. Soc. Hist. A. Fr.* (1989), pp. 77–103

VALÉRIE LAVERGNE-DUREY,
with COLIN HARRISON

Titus (Flavius Vespasianus), Emperor of Rome (*b* Rome, 30 Sept AD 39; *reg* AD 79–81; *d* Cutilia, 13 Sept AD 81). Roman emperor and patron. He was the eldest son of Vespasian, who entrusted him with the command of the Judean campaign (AD 69–70). Titus' building activity was considerable, despite his brief reign. In AD 80 he began to add the third and fourth orders to the Colosseum (*see* ROME, §V, 6). Overlooking the Colosseum, on the slopes of the Fugutal within the grounds of the Domus Aurea, he built the Baths of Titus (AD 80; *see* ROME, ANCIENT, §II, 2(i)(d)), an early example of the Imperial type that was built very quickly, possibly re-adapting the private baths of Nero's palace. In the Forum Romanum, Titus began the hexastyle Corinthian Temple of the Deified Vespasian; this was later finished by Domitian (*reg* AD 81–96), who extended the dedication to include Titus. A triumphal arch for the Judean victory was built to him in the Circus Maximus, of which fragments remain (AD 71); it is possible that he began the better-known Arch of Titus at the head of the Via Sacra (AD 81; *see*

TRIUMPHAL ARCH, §1 and fig. 1). A huge fire broke out in Rome in AD 80, raging for three days and destroying the Serapeum of the Campus Martius, the Saepta, the Poseidonion, the Baths of Agrippa, Agrippa's Pantheon, the diribitorium, the Theatre of Balbus, the stage-building of the Theatre of Pompey, the Portico of Octavia and the Temple of Jupiter Optimus Maximus on the Capitol. Many of these buildings were restored by DOMITIAN.

BIBLIOGRAPHY
P. H. von Blanckenhagen: *Flavische Architektur und ihre Dekoration: Untersucht am Nervaforum* (Berlin, 1940)
M. Pfanner: *Der Titusbogen* (Mainz, 1983)

LUCA LEONCINI

Titus-Carmel, Gérard (*b* Paris, 10 Oct 1942). French painter and draughtsman. He acquired his technical mastery of drawing and engraving through his studies at the Ecole Boulle (1958–62), Paris. His first exhibited works nevertheless were paintings, to which he attached objects made of fake fur, already at this early stage suggesting the distinction between reality and its imitation. His conceptual experiments were in a similar vein, for example the reconstruction of a landscape by what he termed an 'olfactory operation', the re-creation of the scent of virgin forest. From 1970 he devoted himself entirely to drawing and worked in series on a succession of themes. The first series comprised variations on the idea of rupture, or on that of deterioration, and the distortion of a sphere. Each time it is the relation between the model and the copy that is pursued to the point of exhaustion. The model is thus the true pretext for the drawing, whether it be an *objet trouvé* that he has chosen (e.g. a Japanese helmet, or a chromium-plated lamp), or something that he has constructed himself. He often favoured knots and bindings, or the combination of a branch or bit of wood and a piece of cloth, and this approach to an invented reality culminated in the series of 127 drawings based on the *Pocket-size Tlingitt Coffin* (1975–6). Wrestling with this subject for more than a year, Titus-Carmel described a small object replete with significance from every possible angle and by the most varied techniques of drawing until it was almost worn out. In 1984 he returned to painting, favouring more abstract themes on a large scale.

BIBLIOGRAPHY
J. M. Tisserant: *Gérard Titus-Carmel ou le procès du modèle* (Paris, 1974)
Gérard Titus-Carmel: 61 dessins (exh. cat., Paris, Pompidou, 1978)
Gérard Titus-Carmel, Zeichnungen: Folgen & Serien, 1971–1979 (exh. cat., Bielefeld, Städt. Ksthalle, 1980)

ALFRED PACQUEMENT

Titus van Rijn. *See* RIJN, TITUS VAN.

Tivoli. Italian hill town, 37 km east of Rome, set above the cascades of the River Aniene. As Tibur, it was a favourite retreat of wealthy Romans escaping the summer heat. Villas were built there, the most famous being that of the emperor Hadrian (*see* §2 below). It was sacked by the Ostrogoths early in the 6th century AD, but rebuilt and traded to Pope Hadrian I (*reg* 772–95) by Charlemagne in 787. An attack by Emperor Otto III (*reg* 996–1002) was repulsed in 1001, and Tivoli remained an imperial free city until its annexation to the Papal States in 1816. Some

Roman temples were christianized—S Maria della Rotunda, once the Temple of Vesta, has ten extant Corinthian columns and bucrania—and churches from the 11th century onwards attest to a lively patronage of the arts. Romanesque S Maria Maggiore has a 12th-century painting of the *Virgin*, a painting of the *Virgin and Child* by Jacopo Torriti, two triptychs by Bartolommeo Bulgarini da Siena and a rose window attributed to Angelo da Tivoli. A triptych, the 'Macchina del Salvatore' (late 11th century–early 12th, gilded three centuries later) and a 13th-century *Deposition* of five carved wooden figures are preserved in the cathedral of S Lorenzo, rebuilt in 1659. Pius II built the Rocca Pia (1458–64) with four massive round crenellated towers. Pope Julius III granted the governorship of Tivoli to Ippolito II d'Este, who built the fabulous Villa d'Este (*see* §3 below). Tivoli became fashionable again in the 18th century. In the late 20th century, besides tourism, Tivoli supports chemical, paper and hydro-electric production, and the travertine stone that built the Colosseum and St Peter's is still quarried.

For illustration *see* TOWNE, FRANCIS.

BIBLIOGRAPHY
V. G. Pacifici: 'Tivoli nel settecento', *Atti & Mem. Soc. Tiburtina Stor. & A.*, xlv (1972), pp. 97–173; xlvi–xlvii (1973–4), pp. 127–79
M. Vendittelli: 'Testimonianza sulla cattedrale di Tivoli nel medioevo', *Atti & Mem. Soc. Tiburtina Stor. & A.*, lvii (1984), pp. 73–114
S. Carocci: *Tivoli nel basso medioevo: Società cittadina ed economia agraria* (Rome, 1988)

E. B. SAREWITZ

1. Tibur. 2. Hadrian's Villa. 3. Villa d'Este.

1. TIBUR. Because of its geographical position settlements have existed there since prehistoric times. According to one tradition Tibur was founded by Tiburnus and according to another by the Siculi. Along with the other Latins the Tiburtines were defeated by the Romans at Lake Regillus (498 BC), but the town was not fully subject to Rome until 338 BC, when it became a place of exile for important state prisoners, including Zenobia, the queen of Palmyra (AD 273). Among the leading families of Tibur were the Munatii, the most famous of whom was L. Munatius Plancus, consul in 42 BC, who founded Lyon and rebuilt the Temple of Saturn at Rome. After the Tiburtines acquired Roman citizenship (90 BC) the town became a fashionable resort for such notables as Julius Caesar, Brutus, Catullus, Horace, Augustus and Propertius. Finally Hadrian raised its position to that of an official imperial residence.

The topography of Tibur is incompletely known, although parts of the forum came to light in 1883 and 1920, when the office of public weights and measures was discovered as well as the Augusteum, a hall with a seated statue of Augustus in the apse. Two important 2nd-century BC temples survive on the acropolis: a tetrastyle pseudo-peripteral Ionic temple and a circular peripteral structure, the so-called Temple of Vesta (*see* ORDERS, ARCHITECTURAL, fig. 4), 14.25 m in diameter, raised on a high podium, with a cella of *opus incertum* surrounded by 18 Corinthian columns. The capitals, of the Italo-Corinthian type, have two rings of lush acanthus leaves from which spring corkscrew volutes and a large flower (imitated by Sir John Soane in the Tivoli Corner of the Bank of

England, London, 1805). The rectangular and circular temples have been associated with Tiburnus and Albunea (the Tiburtine Sibyl) respectively on the basis of literary sources (e.g. Horace: *Odes* I.vii.12), which record that they were worshipped near a waterfall beside the acropolis.

The most important cult at Tibur was that of Hercules Victor, whose large sanctuary (see fig. 1 and ROME, ANCIENT, fig. 22) was built just outside the walls to the west of the town. Like the Sanctuary of Fortuna at Praeneste, it has an associated theatre (1a) and temple (1b), although here the two are better integrated, since the theatrical *cavea*, 70 m wide, is situated on the lower edge of the rectangular enclosure, with the temple in the middle. The back and sides of the temple precinct are enclosed by a portico (1c) of arches framed by Doric half-columns. Underneath the temple precinct is a remarkable subterranean building complex, comprising a barrel-vaulted tunnel (1d) for the Via Tiburtina to run obliquely underneath the temple enclosure, and a row of shops (1e) accessible from the tunnel. On the Via Tiburtina just west of the sanctuary stands the so-called Tempio della Tosse, a domed rotunda built in the 4th century AD. At floor-level the drum contains four curved and two rectangular niches, as well as two entrances on opposite sides. Higher up are four semicircular and three rectangular windows. The dome, 12.75 m in diameter, has an oculus, and in its envelope are rows of brick ribs. The building, which is set within two rows of parallel walls belonging to an older building, may have been the monumental atrium of a villa.

The plains west of Tivoli contain enormous beds of travertine, one of the most prized building materials used by the Romans. Its earliest known use is in the Milvian Bridge (109 BC), and it was later employed for the façade of the Colosseum. From the 2nd century BC onwards Tibur's magnificent position attracted the villas of wealthy Romans. Just south of the town are the remains of the so-called Villa of Cassius, a large terraced complex of the late 2nd century BC with splendid views over the plains surrounding Rome. A fine series of Hadrianic sculptures (Rome, Vatican, Mus. Pio-Clementino) was found here, including *Apollo and the Muses*, a herm of *Pericles* and a series of other herms; in a nearby villa, which perhaps belonged to the Pisones, were found 16 herms of Greek philosophers and poets (Madrid, Mus. Arqueol. N.). Just north of the town in the former convent of S Antonio are the remains of a Republican villa, once called the Villa of Horace. Its large barrel-vaulted nymphaeum has walls and apse decorated with shells and chips of marble, a technique that was the forerunner of wall mosaic (*see* ROME, ANCIENT, §VI, 2(i)). Horace's Sabine villa, given to him by his patron Maecenas in 33–32 BC, is probably to be found just outside Licenza, *c.* 23 km north-east of Tibur. The villa, first excavated in 1911, has a fountain court overlooked by winter and summer dining-rooms, and a series of living-rooms and bedrooms facing on to a large garden surrounded on all sides by porticos. The situation of the villa in a shady valley accords well with Horace's own description (*Epistles* I.xvi), while the nearby spring may be the *fons Bandusiae* of *Odes* III.xiii.1.

BIBLIOGRAPHY

S. Cabral and F. Del Rè: *Delle ville e de' più notabili monumenti antichi della città di Tivoli e suo territorio* (Rome, 1779)

F. Bulgarini: *Notizie storiche antiquarie statistiche ed agronomiche intorno all'antichissima città di Tivoli e suo territorio* (Rome, 1848)

T. Ashby: 'The Classical Topography of the Roman Campagna, ii: Via Nomentana, via Tiburtina', *Pap. Brit. Sch. Rome*, iii (1906), pp. 3–200 (76–197)

C. Carducci: *Tibur (Tivoli)*, Italia Romana: Municipi e Colonie (Spoleto, 1940)

C. F. Giuliani: *Tibur*, i, Forma Italiae (Rome, 1970)

F. Coarelli: *Lazio*, Guide Archeologiche Laterza (Rome, 1982), pp. 74–122

2. HADRIAN'S VILLA. The summer palace of the emperor Hadrian, built between AD 118 and 134 and situated on an elevated plateau south-west of Tivoli. Its unusual architecture and wealth of sculpture and mosaics have fascinated artists and scholars since the Renaissance.

(i) Architecture. (ii) Sculpture. (iii) Mosaics. (iv) Rediscovery.

(i) *Architecture.* The buildings on the 120 ha site (see fig. 2) were named after such celebrated landmarks as the Lyceum, the Academy and the Stoa Poikile at Athens (see *Augustan History: Hadrian* xxvi.5), although they were not precise copies of these monuments, but followed a Republican tradition established by such men as Cicero, who had an Academy and a Lyceum in his villa at Tusculum. The site was fairly level, but high enough to command views of Rome. The ground fell away to the north-east to form a broad, secluded valley known as the Vale of Tempe. In typical Roman fashion all the elements are a blend of art and nature. Practically every group of buildings is organized around a peristyle garden, ranging from the vast, park-like enclosure of the Poikile (2a) to the small and intimate garden in the nymphaeum (2b), although little is known of their actual plantings (*see* GARDEN, §II, 4). Apart from peripheral monuments, such as the two small theatres, the Underworld and the Temple of Aphrodite, the villa comprises six loosely related groups of buildings on different axes.

The north-east complex incorporates a Republican villa overlooking the Vale of Tempe. To the south-east of this is the Piazza d'Oro (2c), with its complex domed vestibule,

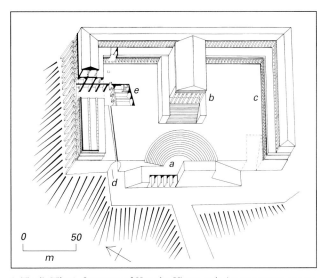

1. Tivoli (Tibur), Sanctuary of Hercules Victor, early 1st century BC, axonometric reconstruction: (a) theatre; (b) Temple of Hercules Victor; (c) portico; (d) tunnel; (e) shops

elaborate nymphaeum and a peristyle court that may be based on a Hellenistic stoa. To the north-west is the Island Villa (2d), Hadrian's private retreat, and adjacent to it, but on a different axis, the Poikile. The latter is certainly a misnomer, as its vast enclosure (232×97 m) has a double running-track along one side, a large pool in the middle and a bath with sun-room near by, which suggests that it was built in imitation of a gymnasium. Adjoining it are the main state apartments of the villa. Facing the mountains of Tivoli is a secluded peristyle enclosing a large pool, while on the other side a suite of rooms with underfloor heating commands a magnificent view towards Rome. These rooms tower above a large nymphaeum in the form of a stadium and the sumptuously marbled square dining-room, on three sides of which were intimate peristyle gardens containing fountains. On a different axis following a long natural depression are the somewhat eccentrically planned Small Baths (2e), the main entrance or vestibule to the palace (2f), the more orthodox Great Baths (2g), the Canopus canal (2h) and the Serapeum (2i; *see also* ROME, ANCIENT, fig. 32). The Serapeum, an enormous nymphaeum with basins in the drum of its half-dome fed by an aqueduct running around its rim, was used for summer banquets. The diners reclined under the half-dome on a vast semicircular couch, while opposite them stretched the canal (119×18 m), built in imitation of the one that linked Alexandria and Canopus, the site of the celebrated Temple of Serapis. Overlooking these, on a higher terrace with a more pronounced east–west orientation, is a complex of buildings culminating in the so-called Academy (2j). At the north-west end of the terrace is the Roccabruna (2k), an isolated square tower surmounted by a circular domed pavilion. Towers of this kind often stood in isolated parts of ancient parks to command panoramic views. They were essentially the equivalent of the follies of the 18th century.

Hadrian himself probably had a hand in the design of the villa, to judge by a remark made by the great architect Apollodoros of Damascus, who criticized him for drawing 'pumpkins' (Dio: *Roman History* LXIX.iv.2), perhaps a reference to the umbrella domes that constitute one of the villa's most striking architectural features. These exotic domes usually consisted of a series of concave segments, as in the vestibule of Piazza d'Oro, while the half-dome of the Serapeum comprised alternate domical and umbrella segments. The domes and most of the fabric of the villa were of concrete (the walls were faced in *opus reticulatum* or brick), since by this date the Romans had mastered the art of concrete construction and were fully aware of its potentialities (*see* ROME, ANCIENT, §II, 1(ii)(c)). The builders of Hadrian's Villa, therefore, were able to execute designs that were as often eccentric as they were complex. For example, they seem to have had an almost obsessive interest in the curvilinear. The Island Villa is a complete miniature villa on a circular site surrounded by a moat. The four main areas of the villa—vestibule, bedroom suite, dining-room and bathing suite—are defined by four sweeping curves, with the result that the central courtyard has four concave sides. The nymphaeum of the Piazza d'Oro has a central octagonal courtyard, 10.35 m in diameter, with alternate convex and concave sides. Similarly, the walls of the domed octagonal hall of the Small Baths are

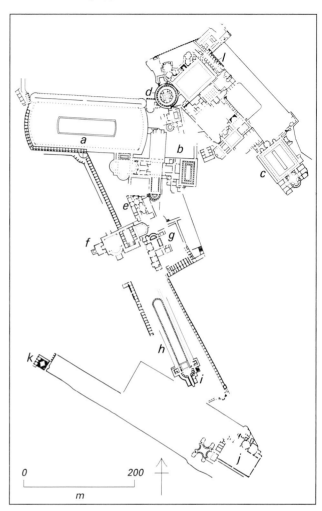

2. Tivoli, Hadrian's Villa, AD 118–34, plan: (a) Poikile; (b) nymphaeum; (c) Piazza d'Oro; (d) Island Villa; (e) Small Baths; (f) vestibule; (g) Great Baths; (h) Canopus; (i) Serapeum; (j) Academy; (k) Roccabruna; (l) Ospitali

alternately rectilinear and concave. Another feature of the architecture, which illustrates a developing trend, can be seen in the vestibule of the Piazza d'Oro. Previously, façade and interior, however complex the shapes involved, were given quite different architectural treatment. Here, however, the curved recesses and complex profiled dome are features of both interior and exterior. (Later interest in internal space became such that an interior could totally dictate the external appearance of a building, as in the Hunting Baths at Leptis Magna.)

See also ROME, ANCIENT, §II, 1(iii)(a).

BIBLIOGRAPHY
H. Winnefeld: *Die Villa des Hadrian bei Tivoli* (Berlin, 1895)
G. Lugli: 'Villa Adriana', *Boll. Comm. Archeol. Com. Roma*, lv (1927), pp. 139–204
W. L. Reichardt: 'The Vestibule Group at Hadrian's Villa', *Mem. Amer. Acad. Rome*, xi (1933), pp. 127–32
H. Kaehler: *Hadrian und seine Villa bei Tivoli* (Berlin, 1950)
L. Vighi: *Villa Hadriana* (Rome, 1958)
S. Aurigemma: *Villa Adriana* (Rome, 1961)
F. L. Rakob: *Die Piazza d'Oro in der Villa Hadriana bei Tivoli* (Munich, 1967)

——: 'Der Bauplan einer kaiserlichen Villa', *Festschrift K. Lankheit*, ed. K. Schauenberg (Bonn, 1973), pp. 113–25

E. Salza Prina Ricotti: 'Criptoportici e gallerie sotterranee di Villa Adriana', *Les Cryptoportiques dans l'architecture romaine* (Rome, 1973), pp. 219–59

C. Giuliani and P. Verduchi: 'Ricerche sull'architettura di Villa Adriana', *Quad. Ist. Top. Ant.*, viii (1975), pp. 3–95

A. C. G. Smith: 'The Date of the "Grandi Terme" of Hadrian's Villa at Tivoli', *Pap. Brit. Sch. Rome*, xlvi (1978), pp. 73–93

A. Hoffmann: *Das Gartenstadion in der Villa Hadriana* (Mainz, 1980)

F. B. SEAR

(ii) Sculpture. Over 300 mythological, portrait and decorative sculptures have been actually or putatively discovered since the 16th century at Hadrian's Villa. Initially prized by antiquarian collectors and esteemed as reflections of Greek masterpieces, current understanding values them for themselves, as documents of a creative age elucidating their settings. Both attitudes are demonstrated by the various statues from Hadrian's Villa of Hercules, for example, the model hero whose fated labours imparted physical and intellectual fortitude. The 'Greek' north theatre reputedly contained a colossal version, along with herms of *Comedy* and *Tragedy* (Rome, Vatican, Mus. Pio-Clementino, inv. nos 262, 265). Another statue of *Hercules* stood in the 'Odeion', the south theatre, joined by a statue of *Minerva* and by Muses (Madrid, Prado, inv. nos 37–8, 40–41, 61–2, 68–9). The Lansdowne *Hercules* (see fig. 3) represents treasures from the villa that were removed beyond papal territory by such agents as Thomas Jenkins in the 18th century, and characterizes the creative retrospection of a classicizing age. The statue combines a Lysippically proportioned long-legged figure, a strongly modelled Polykleitan quadratic torso, and a head and face once termed Skopadic in their pathos. These accentuations would have attracted attention in an open allée or an architectural niche, sculptural settings favoured by Hadrian.

The villa also displayed literary and political portraits, of which only marble examples have survived, including representations of Hadrian, his consort Sabina and most of their successors through the Severans. The Hadrianic examples show the typically crisp facial rendering, emulating bronze, and incipient eye definition executed by drill, which was first undertaken in this period (e.g. *Antisthenes*: Rome, Vatican, Mus. Pio-Clementino, inv. no. 2888). At least 18 statues existed of Antinous, their opposed firm and soft modelling illustrating contrasts inherent in Hadrianic art. A bust of the youth (h. 1 m; Rome, Vatican, Mus. Pio-Clementino, inv. no. 251) juxtaposes sharp delineation around the brow, and typically dreamy eyes, with soft full cheeks, between corkscrews of hair hanging from thick locks. Contradictions characterize such stylistic assimilations as an *Antinous-Osiris* (h. 2.41 m), in which an exaggerated skeletal definition conflicts with a generalized pharaonic and Greek Archaic body, and an idealized portrait head. The Greek marble statue is now in the Museo Gregoriano Egizio in the Vatican, Rome (inv. no. 22795), which also houses an Egyptian collection in dark stone from the Canopus, recalling at Hadrian's Villa a famous pleasure city linked to Alexandria by a canal. Such terms as Canopus, Tempe and Academy enhanced, in conjunction with sculpture, the illusion of distant locales and ages. Excavation of the Canopus in the 1950s revealed

3. Lansdowne *Hercules*, from Hadrian's Villa, Tivoli (Malibu, CA, J. Paul Getty Museum)

its sculptural adornment (replaced at the site by casts). Water flowed from a grotto into a channel, past a *Scylla* (fragments in Tivoli, Mus. N. Archeol., Villa Adriana, storeroom), to an outlet between sculptural personifications of the *Tiber* and the *Nile* (Tivoli, Mus. N. Archeol., Villa Adriana, inv. nos 2261, 2259). Along one side, backs to the water, stood two paired reproductions of the 5th-century BC caryatids from the Erectheion, Athens (inv. nos 2230, 2233, 2238–9), once bearing an entablature, flanked by Silens supporting baskets (both inv. no. 2249). In an arcade skirting the end of the channel two other pairs of statues faced the water. *Hermes* and a *Warrior* (inv. nos 2262, 2257) derive from one 5th-century BC prototype, while *Amazons* (inv. nos 2266, 2255) stem from originals attributed to Pheidias and Kresilas. Contrasting techniques, matching contrasting placements, range from classicizing re-creation to romanticized interpretation. Such groups, reproducing masterpieces of mythical content, some 650 years old, which Hadrian must have seen, engaged him and the villa in a realm of heroic, timeless myth. The settings of two statues of *Aphrodite* coordinated sculpture and architecture: an example of the Crouching Aphrodite type (Rome, Mus. N. Romano, inv. no. 108597), perched by a basin in a bath house, while a version of the *Aphrodite of Knidos* by Praxiteles (Tivoli, Mus. N. Archeol., Villa Adriana, inv. no. 2752) stood in a reconstruction of its shrine at Knidos, in the area of the villa known as the Vale of Tempe. The soft modelling of the first and summary definition of the second illustrate the variety encountered in the sculpture, apparently all Hadrianic in date.

Three works, two signed by sculptors from Aphrodisias, who maintained a workshop in Rome, wittily express the Dionysiac world. Their rich grey or red marble enhances a vivid naturalism of Hellenistic inspiration. Two centaurs, one young and joyful, the other old and pained with hands tied behind his back, both once ridden by cupids, contrast the two faces of love, while a standing smiling satyr, perhaps one of two, raises grapes (Rome, Mus. Capitolino, inv. nos 656–8). These emblems of fertility came from the Academy, where scenes of aspects of nature also appeared in mosaic (*see* §(iii) below). Architectural reliefs of cupids riding sea creatures decorated both the Island Villa and the Piazza d'Oro, where another frieze portrayed cupids hunting. These references to a life beyond care and of aristocratic pleasures give further definition to the villa's purpose.

(iii) Mosaics. Important examples of geometric, botanic and floral, and figural and pictorial *opus vermiculatum* mosaics have been discovered at Hadrian's Villa. The most significant mosaics *in situ* pave the ten rooms of the Ospitali (see fig. 2l above), recording, in black and white over sinopia, the new preference for laying botanic over geometric shapes. In each chamber, mosaics of smaller, repeated, plant-derived forms overlie larger geometric motifs in thresholds and alcoves. A mosaic in the Piazza d'Oro illustrates how more complex geometric patterns endured, while the colouristic richness of its four-patterned sequence of coffers demonstrates the refinement of such polychromy. In the Academy was discovered, among other mosaics, that depicting a metal goblet (Rome, Mus. Capitolino), on the lip of which perch doves, one drinking and casting the shadow of its head on the water. Because Pliny the elder described such a mosaic by Sosos at Pergamon, some see the work at Hadrian's Villa as original, although the bird's shadow is distorted. Pliny failed to record the likeness of a man below the vessel's handle, an apparent allusion to the Homeric Cup of Nestor (*Iliad* XI.632ff.). While the Romans transported emblemata, Pliny's omission and the existence of other versions raises the question of the work's originality. The mosaic's discovery dates from 1737; further excavations in 1779–80 in the Academy revealed others, each giving a different area thematic focus.

The Gabinetto delle Maschere in the Vatican derives its name from three such works from Hadrian's Villa (see fig. 4). An Apolline panel represents a griffin and Apollo's cithara, bow and quiver by a garlanded female mask on a pedestal. A Dionysiac mosaic features a cantharus, a thyrsus and a leopard with a tympanum before an ivy-wreathed mask on a hillock. A third panel displays, on a parapet, comic masks of a female, a young man and an old man above another male mask between a lyre and a broken jug, possibly recalling Menander's *Hydria*. The mosaics' original separate settings, inside garlanded frames on white fields containing twining oak tendrils, were combined into one with a non-theatrical fourth panel. This belongs thematically with another in the Sala degli Animali in the Vatican, each illustrating a deity, one seated female and one standing male, among grazing goats and sheep in spacious, idyllic landscapes. Two other visual allegories manifest divinely fated conflicts in barren, rocky settings with struggling vegetation. One, also in the Sala degli Animali, represents a lion savaging a bull, both impressively foreshortened, distressing a cow seen across a lake, her body reflected in the water. Another, in Berlin (Antiken-mus.), like the dove mosaic suggested as a Hellenistic original, portrays two centaurs battling with wild beasts. A rearing centaur, who has dispatched a lion, ignores a menacing leopard and raises a boulder against a tiger who has felled his mate. All these topoi evoke antecedents in the Greek past that were beloved by Hadrian, yet their tendentious crafting characterizes the Emperor's taste and time.

BIBLIOGRAPHY

W. Helbig: *Führer durch die öffentlichen Sammlungen klassischer Altertümer in Rom*, 4 vols (Tübingen, 1963–72)
J. Raeder: 'Die statuarische Ausstattung der Villa Hadriana bei Tivoli', *Europäische Hochschulschriften*, XXXVIII/iv (Frankfurt am Main, 1983)
M. de Franceschini: *Villa Adriana: Mosaici, pavimenti, edifici* (Rome, 1991)

DERICKSEN BRINKERHOFF

(iv) Rediscovery. Hadrian's Villa ranks among the most influential monuments in the history of architecture, its resonance stemming in significant part from its association with the enigmatic personality of Hadrian himself. After the collapse of the Roman Empire, however, the villa was used as a quarry for more than a millennium, and many local structures were built from its spoils. No descriptions of it survive from this period of neglect, and the earliest account of its ruins is in 1461 by the humanist Pope Pius II (*Commentarii*), in which he meditated on the ephemeral nature of material splendour, thus introducing a topos that artists and poets have continued to explore, with the villa as a focus.

Soon afterwards, Renaissance artists and architects began to visit the villa. At the end of the 15th century Francesco di Giorgio Martini (Florence, Uffizi, 319A, 320, 325 and Turin, Bib. Reale, MS. Saluzzo 148) and Giuliano da Sangallo (Rome, Vatican, Bib. Apostolica, Cod. Vat. Barbeeriniano) made measured drawings that combine accurate observation and imaginative creativity. During the early 16th century DONATO BRAMANTE, RAPHAEL and other High Renaissance architects visited the site, and though none of their drawings has been identified, the influence of the villa may be seen in their designs, notably the former's Tempietto and the latter's Villa Madama, both in Rome. By the mid-16th century references to Hadrian's Villa began to appear in guidebooks and architectural treatises, such as those of Andrea Palladio and Philibert de L'Orme, and PIRRO LIGORIO began to excavate at the site, initiating what has been termed the first large-scale modern archaeological dig. While the primary object of his excavations was ancient statuary for his

4. Mosaics from the Academy, Hadrian's Villa, Tivoli, early 2nd century AD (Rome, Vatican, Museo Pio-Clementino, Gabinetto delle Maschere)

patron, Cardinal Ippolito I d'Este, Ligorio recorded his finds in the first systematic description of the site. He assigned the grandiose names mentioned in the *Augustan History* (*see* §(i) above) to specific parts of the villa and added new names of his own, thereby determining the way later artists and scholars would refer to them. The villa may have influenced his own designs for the Villa d'Este at Tivoli (*see* §3 below) and the Casino of Pius IV in the Vatican. Ligorio's drawings, however, were never published, so that credit for the first comprehensive survey of the site belongs to Francesco Contini. This was completed by 1637 and available for study by Baroque architects such as FRANCESCO BORROMINI and Carlo Rainaldi long before its publication in 1668. Attracted by the numerous departures from Vitruvian classicism embodied in the villa's design, Borromini drew inspiration for some of his greatest works, especially the Oratory dei Filippini and S Ivo alla Sapienza.

The influence of Hadrian's Villa became more diffuse during the 18th century. Artists from all over Europe came to study its remains: in 1755, for example, Charles-Louis Clérisseau, Robert Adam and Giovanni Battista Piranesi drew there together, while in 1760 Jean-Honoré Fragonard and Hubert Robert sketched on the site. Of all the artists, archaeologists and architects who have studied Hadrian's Villa, Piranesi emerges as its most inspired interpreter. At the end of his life he was planning a book on the antiquities of Tivoli, for which his numerous *vedute* of the villa were intended, and his great annotated plan of the villa, issued posthumously by his son Francesco in 1781, is a work of genius. In spite of errors it is still the best site plan and records a wealth of data otherwise unknown.

Since its rediscovery Hadrian's Villa has produced vast quantities of sculpture, mosaics and other works of art. During the 18th century works excavated there found their way into every major European collection; today they are scattered from Malibu to St Petersburg. Knowledge of the villa's décor was further disseminated by the publications of CHARLES CAMERON (*The Baths of the Romans*, 1772), Nicolas Ponce and Piranesi, and its influence may be discerned in countless interiors, ranging from Cameron's Agate Rooms at Pushkin (formerly Tsarskoye Selo) to Robert Adam's Syon House (*see* ADAM (i), (3)). Hadrian's Villa also played a significant role in the formulation of artistic theory at a crucial juncture in the history of Western art, in the controversy over the primacy of Greek and Roman forms. The emphasis placed by JOHANN JOACHIM WINCKELMANN on the noble simplicity and quiet grandeur of Greek sculpture was grounded in no small part on works found at the villa, such as the celebrated *Antinous* relief in the Albani collection (Rome, Villa Torlonia). In contrast, Piranesi's exaltation of the richness and variety of Roman architecture was based largely on its buildings. Similarly, in the 19th century Hadrian's Villa inspired both the beaux-arts Neo-classicists and the Romantics. The acquisition of about half the site by the Italian State in 1870 paved the way for a more systematic archaeological investigation, which is still far from complete. The influence of the villa on Le Corbusier, Frank Lloyd Wright, Louis I. Kahn and, later still, on Charles W. Moore and James Stirling demonstrates its relevance to 20th-century architecture.

BIBLIOGRAPHY

A. Palladio: *L'antichità di Roma* (Rome, 1554)
P. de L'Orme: *Le Premier Tome de l'architecture de Philibert de l'Orme, conseiller et ausmonier ordinaire du roy, abbé de Saint-Serge lez angiers* (Paris, 1567)
F. Contini: *Adriani Caesaris immanem in Tyburtino villam* (Rome, 1668)
P. Ligorio: *Descrittione della superba & magnificentissima Villa Tiburtina Hadriana*, Thesaurus Antiquitatum et Historiarum Italiae (Leiden, 1723)
F. Piranesi: *Pianta delle fabbriche esistenti nella Villa Adriana* (Rome, 1781)
N. Ponce: *Arabesques antiques des bains de Livie, et de la villa Adriana* (Paris, 1789)
P. Gusman: *La Villa impériale de Tibur* (Paris, 1904)
L. C. Gabel, ed.: *Memoirs of a Renaissance Pope: The Commentaries of Pius II*, trans. F. A. Gragg (New York, 1959 and London, 1960), pp. 328–9
E. Salza Prina Ricotti: 'Villa Adriana in Pirro Ligorio e Francesco Contini', *Atti & Mem. Accad. N. Lincei, Atti Cl. Sci. Morali*, xvii (1973–4), pp. 1–47
W. L. MacDonald and J. A. Pinto: *Hadrian's Villa and its Legacy* (New Haven and London, 1995)

JOHN PINTO

3. VILLA D'ESTE. Villa on the edge of the town, famous for its fine gardens with their spectacular fountains and waterworks. In 1550 Ippolito II d'Este (i), Cardinal of Ferrara, was appointed governor of Tivoli. He decided to transform the governor's residence located in a portion of an old run-down Benedictine monastery attached to S Maria Maggiore into a lavish villa with splendid gardens devised by PIRRO LIGORIO. Although some gardens and vineyards were purchased below the monastery at this time, little was accomplished on the project for the next decade as the Cardinal was diverted by political affairs.

The villa itself is, in architectural terms, somewhat plain. Ligorio did, however, execute a fine staircase loggia on the garden front. This is bordered on either side by ranges of private rooms, which are largely frescoed with such works as an *Allegory of Nature* by the school of Federico Zuccaro and the *Labours of Hercules* by the school of Girólamo Muziano. In addition the Audience Hall was frescoed by Muziano himself with views of the gardens.

Between 1560 and 1566 additional land was acquired for the new gardens. In 1560 the first efforts were made to lay on sufficient water for the fountains, which were, and are, the particular glory of the gardens. An aqueduct was built to tap the springs on nearby Monte S Angelo, and in 1564–5 a great conduit was tunnelled under the town of Tivoli to divert water from the Aniene into the garden. The terrain of the valley was remodelled (1563–5) to create a steep slope falling off directly in line with the old monastery and another lesser slope to the north-east. The removed earth was used to form a flat terrace at the south-west, with the existing city wall acting as a retaining wall. A plentiful water supply and a natural gravity flow induced by the different levels provided a play of water for the numerous fountains.

By using ancient statues, some excavated from Hadrian's Villa, and contemporary fountain sculpture, Ligorio devised an elaborate iconographical garden layout celebrating the Cardinal. An ancient statue of *Hercules* standing above the Fountain of the Many-headed Dragon on the hillside along the central walk to the palace identified the garden with the mythological Garden of the Hesperides. According to contemporary historians, Hercules was reputed to be the mythological ancestor of the Estes and had been the ancient deity of Tivoli (*see also* §2(ii) above). A water organ, derived from ancient examples and played by the action of the water, was located in the Fountain of Nature. Another fountain, that of the Owl and Birds, was animated by a water-driven mechanism. Throughout the garden were hidden spurts of water, activated by different devices so as to drench visitors unexpectedly. Water therefore stimulated senses of sight, sound and touch. Work continued on the fountains, pools and grottoes, as well as the formal landscaping, until 1572. In September of that year the Fountain of the Dragons was erected in honour of a visit by Pope Gregory XIII. This is set within a great horseshoe staircase set on the main axis leading from the villa and consists of a group of dragons, set on a circular pool, spouting water. The theme echoes the figure of a dragon on the Pope's coat of arms.

An engraving dated 1573 (see fig. 5) presumably illustrates the original design for the villa and gardens. It depicts features, such as the belvederes rising at the ends of the villa or the Fountain of Neptune in the lower southern corner, that were never realized. In the 17th century a few changes and additions were made in the garden. The great wooden cross-pergola beyond the public entrance, depicted in the 1573 engraving, was replaced by the circle of gigantic cypress trees that is still the major horticultural attraction of the garden. In 1660 Gianlorenzo Bernini designed the Fountain of the Bicchierone on the central axis above the Fountain of the Dragon and added a naturalistic cascade below the Water Organ. With the neglect of absentee owners in the 18th century much of

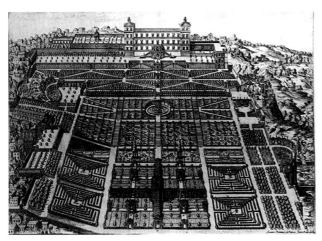

5. Tivoli, Villa d'Este, begun *c.* 1560; from an engraving by Etienne Dupérac, 1573 (London, British Museum)

the garden assumed a more naturalistic appearance appropriate to the taste of the period and charmingly depicted in drawings by Jean-Honoré Fragonard. The villa became the property of the Italian state in 1918 and has since been restored. Its spectacular setting combined with the extravagance of its waterworks has assured the garden a pervasive influence on formal garden design throughout Europe since the 16th century.

BIBLIOGRAPHY

T. Ashby: 'The Villa d'Este at Tivoli and the Collection of Classical Sculptures which it Contained', *Archaeologia*, lxi (1908), pp. 219–56
D. R. Coffin: *The Villa d'Este at Tivoli* (Princeton, 1960)
R. W. Lightbown: 'Nicolas Audebert and the Villa d'Este', *J. Warb. & Court. Inst.*, xxvii (1964), pp. 164–90
C. Lamb: *Die Villa d'Este in Tivoli* (Munich, 1966)
D. R. Coffin: *The Villa in the Life of Renaissance Rome* (Princeton, 1979), pp. 311–40
M. L. Madonna: 'Il genius loci di Villa d'Este: Mito e misteri nel sistema di Pirro Ligorio', *Natura e artificio*, ed. M. Fagiolo (Rome, 1979), pp. 192–226
——: 'Pirro Ligorio e Villa d'Este: La scena di Roma e il mistero della Sibilla', *Il giardino storico italiano*, ed. G. Ragioneri (Florence, 1981), pp. 173–96

DAVID R. COFFIN

Tiwanaku. *See* TIAHUANACO.

Tjakamarra, Michael Nelson. *See* NELSON TJAKAMARRA, MICHAEL.

Tjangala, Wuta Wuta. *See* UTA UTA.

Tjapaltjarri, Clifford Possum. *See* POSSUM TJAPALTJARRI, CLIFFORD.

Tjapaltjarri, Tim Leura. *See* LEURA TJAPALTJARRI, TIM.

Tkachov. Russian family of painters. Sergey (Petrovich) Tkachov (*b* Chugunovka, Bryansk region, 1922) and his brother Aleksey (Petrovich) Tkachov (*b* Chugunovka, 11 Sept 1925) studied in the Surikov Institute in Moscow from 1945 to 1952 under Igor' Grabar', Sergey Gerasimov and Georgy Ryazhsky. The traditions of the Union of Russian Artists had a particular influence on the formation of their style, as well as the paintings of Gerasimov and,

in particular, Arkady Plastov, with their emotional, saturated, impressionistic colouring and keen interest in the themes of rural labour, life and landscape.

The Tkachovs produced paintings after studies from life, working with a free impasted stroke, creating a keen sense of the bright airy surroundings; they also turned special attention to the expressive and realistic treatment of national types and the characteristics of national landscapes. In such genre works as *Mothers* (1961; Moscow, Tret'yakov Gal.) and *Spring 1945* (1980–85; Moscow, Tret'yakov Gal.), they combined an authentic depiction of daily life in the Soviet countryside with a generalized, poetic consideration of the historical period and the personal fates of the people. A number of famous pictures by the Tkachov brothers were dedicated to the years of the formation of the Soviet state, for example the dramatically coloured canvas *Between Battles* (1958–60; Moscow, Tret'yakov Gal.), which depicts a small school where young soldiers master literacy in the days of calm between battles. Historical and everyday genre scenes recur repeatedly in the Tkachovs' works, at times within one painting as in *In Ancient Vshchizh* (1983–4; St Petersburg, Rus. Mus.).

BIBLIOGRAPHY

I. A. Krugly: *Aleksey and Sergey Tkachovy* (St Petersburg, 1979)
Brat'ya Tkachovy [The Tkachov brothers] (Moscow, 1985) [with pls]

N. YA. MALAKHOV

Tkadlík [Kadlik], **František** (*b* Prague, 23 Nov 1786; *d* Prague, 16 Jan 1840). Bohemian painter. He studied under Josef Bergler at the Prague Academy of Fine Arts (1803–16) while studying philosophy at the university. He painted portraits of wealthy citizens and of the family of his patron, Jan Rudolf Czernín, becoming one of the leading Bohemian portrait painters of the time with, for instance, his portraits of the philologist *Josef Dobrovský* (1820; Prague, Hist. Mus.) and the historian *František Palacký* (1821; Maleč Castle, nr Chotěboř), both representatives of the national revival. From 1817 to 1825 he continued his art studies in Vienna and worked as the private painter of Count Czernín and curator of his collection. At the same time he became interested in mythological and historical subjects and identified himself with the Nazarenes and their programme for a new approach to religious art. He often linked this with patriotic themes, as in the *Return of St Vojtěch to Bohemia* (1824; Prague, N.G., Convent of St Agnes). A stay in Rome (1825–32) gave him a greater feeling for monumentality and for the recording of reality. His variant of later Nazarene style found a following in Prague, where he became Director of the Academy in 1836. Many of his pupils, including Josef Mánes, were influenced by his feeling for nobility of form and harmony of expression.

BIBLIOGRAPHY

E. Petrová: 'K vývojové charakteristice Tkadlíkova díla' [The characteristics of the development of Tkadlík's work], *Umění*, iii (1955), pp. 23–31
——: *František Tkadlík* (Prague, 1960) [Fr. summary]
Die tschechische Malerei des XIX. Jahrhunderts (exh. cat., ed. J. Kotalík; Vienna, Belvedere, 1984), pp. 61–2 [entry by M. Nováková]

ROMAN PRAHL

Tlatelolco. Site in the Basin of Mexico, now part of modern Mexico City. It was a ceremonial centre and later a city state, becoming politically and economically incorporated by the Mexica Aztecs of Tenochtitlán in 1473 (*see* MEXICO CITY, §I). Tlatelolco was established on an island in Lake Texcoco, just north of the larger island site of Tenochtitlán. The two islands were eventually connected by canals and *chinampa* agricultural plots (artificial islet fields anchored to the lake bed). The remaining site ruins comprise a large quadrangular plaza, with buildings surrounding it and a series of pyramid-platforms with temples showing several construction phases (see fig.). Notable among them is a building with reliefs of calendrical motifs. After the Spanish Conquest several colonial buildings were erected around the plaza, including the church of Santiago de Tlatelolco and a 16th-century manor house, both using materials from the Pre-Columbian structures. A modern tower houses the Ministry of Foreign Affairs. Residential areas of the ancient city presumably lie beneath the modern housing built by the Mexican government in the 1960s.

Excavations in the 1940s by Pablo Martínez del Río and María Antonieta Espejo identified the principal structures and phases of the ceremonial centre. Further excavations were carried out by Alberto Ruz, in the 1960s and later, during the construction of an underground train line and station. The evidence indicates that Tlatelolco was inhabited by *c.* 1100, although the island was possibly settled earlier. The presence of Lake Texcoco in the centre of the Basin of Mexico would have affected communication patterns in the region, allowing comparatively easy land links in a north–south direction, but requiring transport over water as the shortest east–west route. Tlatelolco island would have provided an important stopover, and eventually the site became the main market town for the western part of the lake, thus acquiring a measure of regional power. The city state was active in regional politics and intervened in disputes, thereby increasing its influence. The founding of Tenochtitlán on the neighbouring island in *c.* 1325 was probably due in part to the proximity and importance of the Tlatelolco market. The Mexica Aztecs, or Tenochca, were closely linked to the market's activities until their liberation from the rule of Azcapozalco, an empire-building city state in the western Basin, and the Tenochca conquest of the Basin of Mexico *c.* 1428. The resulting wars between city states led to the domination of Tlatelolco by Tenochtitlán from *c.* 1431, and the two cities were eventually connected by a causeway.

Tlatelolco became a client of the Mexica, sharing the benefits of Aztec expansion until it was formally conquered in 1473. Sixteenth-century sources state that the conquest was provoked by the ruler of Tlatelolco's mistreatment of his wife, the sister of the Mexica Aztec ruler.

After this conquest the Tlatelolco market became the most important place for exchange in Mesoamerica and one of the main pillars of Aztec commercial power. Special merchants known as *pochteca* dealt with supplies brought in by Aztec war expeditions, tribute and the sale of surplus goods by the central government, thus handling products from all over Mesoamerica and from as far south as Central America. It was active at the time of the Spanish Conquest and its size and variety of goods are described in several early 16th-century sources. Tlatelolco was the scene of the last resistance against Cortés, when Cuauhtémoc, the last Aztec ruler, took refuge on the island and was besieged for 75 days before he surrendered, on 13 August 1521. After the conquest Tlatelolco was selected as the site for a college for the sons of Aztec noblemen, where they were taught Spanish and the Christian doctrine. The important chronicler and historian Fray Bernardino de Sahagún taught at the college and wrote some of his works championing the native cause there. The Spanish colonial government accepted the sovereignty of Tlatelolco for some years, and a native ruler was recognized until the mid-16th century. It later became the Barrio of Santiago, second in importance to Mexico City itself. By the 18th century the part of the lake separating the two islands had been filled in.

Finds from the Tlatelolco excavations include some of the best examples of Late Post-Classic period (*c.* 1200–1521) pottery from the Central Highlands, especially of locally made Tenochtitlán and Tlatelolco black-on-orange wares. These mainly comprise plates, characterized by (presumably symbolic) geometrical designs on the vessel walls, and bowls with naturalistic drawings of flowers, birds and fishes. Also found were highly polished redware jars and bowls with thin black designs, and Cholula polychrome ware, a lacquerware imported from the Puebla region about 100 km to the east (examples of ceramics in Mexico City, Mus. N. Antropol.). The excavators also found a large number of human bones, including artificially deformed crania from a TZOMPANTLI (sacrificial skull rack), one of the best examples of the widespread practice of human sacrifice in Late Post-Classic Mesoamerica.

Tlatelolco, Square of the Three Cultures, with ruins of the great pyramid (15th century) and (behind) the church of Santiago de Tlatelolco (16th century)

BIBLIOGRAPHY

M. A. Espejo: 'Exploraciones arqueológicas en Santiago Tlatelolco', *Tlatelolco a través de los tiempos*, 12 vols (Mexico City, 1944–50), i, pp. 48–69; ii, pp. 9–30; iii, pp. 8–19; iv, pp. 11–15; vi, pp. 19–22; vii, pp. 8–28; viii, pp. 9–16; ix, pp. 7–9; x, pp. 8–13; xi, pp. 5–14; xii, pp. 113–16

P. Martínez del Río: 'Resumen de trabajos arqueológicos', ibid., i, pp. 75–7; ii, pp. 31–6; iii, pp. 18–20; iv, pp. 16–19; vi, pp. 16–18; vii, pp. 29–33

J. Dávalos Hurtado: *La deformación craneal entre los Tlatelolcas* (Mexico City, 1951)

W. T. Sanders: 'El mercado de Tlatelolco: Un estudio de economía urbana', *Tlatoani*, i (1952), pp. 14–16

J. Litvak King: 'Las relaciones entre México y Tlatelolco antes de la conquista de Axayácatl: Problemática de la expansión mexicana', *Estud. Cult. Nahuatl*, ix (1971), pp. 17–20

P. Sánchez Saldaña: 'El tzompantli de Tlatelolco', *Religión en Mesoamérica*, ed. J. Litvak King and N. Castillo Tejero (Mexico City, 1972), pp. 387–91

M. T. Jaén and C. Serrano Sánchez: 'Caracteres morfológicos en craneos de Tlatelolco', *Balance y perspectiva de la antropología de Mesoamérica y del norte de México* (Mexico City, 1975), pp. 73–9

JAIME LITVAK KING

Tlatilco. Pre-Columbian site near the former western shore of Lake Texcoco, now in Mexico City. A village there was occupied *c.* 2000–*c.* 300 BC. Discovered in a brickyard, the site was excavated by Miguel Covarrubias for the Instituto Nacional de Antropología e Historia in 1947, by Román Piña Chan in 1952 and 1960, and by Arturo Romano in the 1960s. The evidence was re-examined by Paul Tolstoy and L. T. Paradis in 1970. Tlatilco is famous as a cemetery site, but finds also included triangular, bottle-shaped storage pits and fragments of wattle-and-daub house walls. Some authorities claim evidence of low one- and two-step platforms, possibly to support temples. Its four developmental phases are related to the archaeological periods of the Basin of Mexico: Ixtapaluca (*c.* 1400–*c.* 800 BC), Zacatenco (*c.* 800–*c.* 400 BC), Ticomán (*c.* 400–*c.* 100 BC) and Patlachique (*c.* 100 BC–*c.* AD 1). In the Museo Nacional de Antropología in Mexico City there is a life-size reconstruction of one of the burials, and a nearby site museum exhibits some of the finds.

Nearly 400 graves were excavated. Many contained few or no artefacts, but others were rich in pottery vessels, figurines, jewellery, clay masks and stone tools. The pottery, some of the earliest found in the Basin of Mexico, included a large variety of shapes and decorations. There were zoomorphic and anthropomorphic vessels, flat-bottomed bowls, *tecomates* (collarless, spherical vessels with a restricted opening), goblets, tripod vessels, long-necked bottles and stirrup-spouted vessels. Decoration included rocker-stamping, geometric painting, slips, differential firing and excisions filled with different-coloured paints or pastes. Notable pieces include the 'life–death' bowl (Mexico City, Mus. N. Antropol.), with a face on one side and a skull on the other, and bowls with excised 'jaguar paw' motifs, filled in with red paint or paste against a black slip (examples in Mexico City, Mus. N. Antropol.).

Tlatilco's figurines are particularly important because of their variety and the information they give on contemporary life. One grave contained as many as 61. There are males, females, couples, figures engaged in daily activities, ball-game players (some of the earliest known), animals and imaginary monsters. The *mujer bonita* ('pretty lady') type is especially numerous, as are mother-and-child groups. Animals represented include peccaries, opossums, bears, armadillos, rabbits, ducks and other birds, frogs, turtles and fish. The figurines are also an important source of information on dress and domestic and ritual activities, as well as providing evidence of trade contacts and influences in the Early and Middle Pre-Classic periods. Some pieces have the OLMEC 'baby face', and one grave yielded an Olmec ground stone axehead. These pieces, together with the 'jaguar paw' vessels and the use of white- and black-slipped pottery, have been used to argue for Olmec presence, possibly even colonization from the Gulf Coast, although most archaeologists point out that the major ingredients of Tlatilco and other Pre-Classic village sites in the Basin of Mexico were locally evolved.

For discussion of the arts of Pre-Columbian Mexico *see also* MESOAMERICA, PRE-COLUMBIAN.

BIBLIOGRAPHY

M. Covarrubias: 'Tlatilco, Archaic Mexican Art and Culture', *DYN*, 4–5 (1943), pp. 40–46

R. Piña Chan: 'Tlatilco y la cultura preclásica del Valle de México', *An. Inst. N. Antropol. & Hist.*, iv (1952), pp. 33–43

M. N. Porter: *Tlatilco and the Preclassic Cultures of the New World*, Viking Fund Publications in Anthropology, xix (New York, 1953)

R. Piña Chan: *Tlatilco*, Serie Investigaciones INAH, i/2 (Mexico City, 1958)

A. Romano: 'Exploraciones en Tlatilco, México', *Bol. INAH*, x (1962), pp. 1–2

——: 'Exploraciones en Tlatilco, México', *Bol. INAH*, xiv (1963), pp. 11–13

P. Tolstoy and A. Guénette: 'Le Placement de Tlatilco dans le cadre du Pré-classique du Bassin de Mexico', *J. Soc. Américanistes*, liv (1965), pp. 47–91

A. Romano: 'Tlatilco', *Bol. INAH*, xxx (1967), pp. 38–42

P. Tolstoy and L. T. Paradis: 'Early and Middle Preclassic Culture in the Basin of Mexico', *Science*, 167 (1970), pp. 344–51

M. P. Weaver: *The Aztecs, Maya and their Predecessors: Archaeology of Mesoamerica* (New York, 1972, rev. 2/1981)

DAVID M. JONES, JAIME LITVAK KING

Tlemcen [Tilimsān; Sp. Tremecén]. Town in north-west Algeria. The earliest settlement at the site was called Pomaria by the Romans; by the 8th century AD it was known as Āgadir and a mosque (destr.) was erected *c.* 790. It later merged with a military camp, established in 1082 by the Almoravid Yusuf ibn Tashufin (*reg* 1061–1106). He founded the congregational mosque, which was enlarged in 1126 by his son 'Ali (*reg* 1106–42), to whose patronage the splendid pierced stucco dome over the bay in front of the mihrab is attributed (*see* ISLAMIC ART, §II, 5(iv)(c)). The Almohads (*reg* 1130–1269) surrounded the town with ramparts and constructed a citadel. Under Muhammad al-Nasir (*reg* 1199–1214), a tomb was erected for the Andalusian mystic Abu Madyan (Sidi Boumedienne; *d* 1197) in the suburb of al-'Ubbad, 2 km south-east of the city. The town, an entrepôt for European and African products and an important religious and cultural centre, became the capital of the Zayyanid dynasty (*reg* 1235–1550). Yaghmurasan, its founder, had the congregational mosque enlarged and a minaret added. Other monuments of this period include the small mosque of the Sidi Bel Hassan (1296; now the Archaeological Museum) with a richly decorated mihrab, the minaret (mid-13th century) added to the Agadir Mosque, and the mosque of Sidi Brahim (1308–18). In 1303 the Marinids (*reg* 1196–1465) constructed al-Mansura (Mansoura), a fortified base 2 km west for the siege of Tlemcen. The ruins of al-Mansura include a palace and a large congregational mosque (85×60 m; before 1336). In 1336 Tlemcen was conquered by the Marinid Abu'l-Hasan 'Ali (reg 1331–48) and the tomb of Abu Madyan transformed into an important shrine complex, including a mosque (1338–9), madrasa (1346), ablution facilities and residence (see ISLAMIC ART, §II, 6(iv)(b)). The small mosque of Sidi al-Halwi (1354) has onyx columns taken from al-Mansura and a finely decorated minaret. The town was taken by the French in 1842 but unlike many Algerian towns, it preserves much of its traditional character and is known for its metal and leather crafts.

BIBLIOGRAPHY

G. and W. Marçais: *Les Monuments arabes de Tlemcen* (Paris, 1903)
G. Marçais: *L'Architecture musulmane d'Occident* (Paris, 1954)
W. al-Akhbar: *Tlemcen* (Algiers, 1971)
R. Bourouiba: *L'Art religieux musulman en Algérie* (Algiers, 1973)
R. I. Lawless and G. H. Blake: *Tlemcen: Continuity and Change in an Algerian Islamic Town* (London, New York and Durham, 1976)
S. S. Blair: 'Sufi Saints and Shrine Architecture in the Early Fourteenth Century', *Muqarnas*, vii (1990), pp. 35–49

S. J. VERNOIT

Tleson. *See* VASE PAINTERS, §II.

Toam. *See* YI CHAE.

Tobago. *See under* TRINIDAD AND TOBAGO.

Tobeian. *See* ITŌ JAKUCHŪ.

Tobey, Mark (*b* Centerville, WI, 11 Dec 1890; *d* Basle, Switzerland, 24 April 1976). American painter. In 1893 the family moved to Jacksonville, TN, but because of the poor educational facilities there they returned a year later to Wisconsin. Moving again in 1906 to Hammond, IN, Tobey attended high school and on Saturdays travelled to Chicago to study the techniques of watercolour and oil painting at the Art Institute of Chicago, this being his only formal art training. In 1909 the family moved to Chicago where, because of his father's illness, he was forced to give up his studies and find employment. After various jobs he eventually became a fashion illustrator. During this period he discovered the great art of the past, first through reproductions and then by visiting the Art Institute of Chicago. He was especially attracted to Italian Renaissance paintings and to works by a variety of artists including Frans Hals, John Singer Sargent and Joaquín Sorolla y Bastida.

In 1911 Tobey moved to New York, where he worked as a fashion illustrator for *McCalls* magazine. Returning in 1912 to Chicago, in 1913 he saw the Armory Show at the Art Institute, though he learnt little from it. From 1913 to 1917 he divided his time between New York and Chicago, still working as a fashion illustrator and developing a reputation for his portrait drawings in charcoal. Numbering the singer Mary Garden, Muriel Draper and Anthony Drexel Biddle among his sitters, he showed his portraits at his first one-man exhibition in 1907 at the Knoedler Gallery in New York. Reluctant, however, to follow this career, he started working as an interior designer while pursuing independent studies in his spare time.

In 1918 Tobey converted to the Bahai faith, to which he had been introduced by the portrait painter Juliet Thompson earlier that year. His adherence to the faith, which took as its central tenets a belief in the unity of all religions and mankind and in the progressive revelation of God through a series of prophets, was profound and permanent. Although its link with his painting took some while to develop fully, it lies behind all his succeeding works. At this time he saw the works of William Blake in the Pierpont Morgan Library in New York; under that influence and that of Michelangelo he painted the violent watercolour *Conflict of the Satanic and Celestial Gods* (1918; Seattle, WA, priv. col., see Dahl and others, p. 60), which points to the danger of ignoring the Bahai quest for unity.

After moving in 1922 to Seattle, where he taught at the Cornish School, Tobey came to understand Cubism. In 1923 he met the Chinese painter Deng Kui, who taught him techniques of Chinese calligraphy. This period was one of great experimentation for Tobey; one of the few surviving works of this period, a pastel *Self-portrait* (early 1920s; Seattle, WA, H. M. Hathaway priv. col., see 1959 exh. cat., fig. 2), reveals his adoption from Cubism of overlapping planes. In 1925, dissatisfied with his work, he travelled to Europe, staying first in Paris. There he met Gertrude Stein, visited the Louvre and produced such works as a portrait in conté crayon of the pianist *Paul McCool* (1925; Seattle, WA, A. Mus.). The following year he travelled to Spain, Greece, Turkey, Lebanon and Egypt. On his return to the USA he divided his time from 1926 to 1930 between New York, Chicago and Seattle, while still working at the Cornish School.

Tobey's teaching job came under threat with the onset of the Depression, and in 1930 he accepted an invitation to teach and paint in England at Dartington Hall, Devon. He remained based there until 1938, meeting, among others, Bernard Leach, Rabindranath Tagore and the novelists Aldous Huxley and Pearl S. Buck. During his time in England he regularly travelled abroad: in 1931 to Mexico; in 1932 to Haifa and Acca, visiting Bahai sites; and with Leach in 1934 to Hong Kong and other parts of China, where he again studied calligraphy with Deng Kui in Shanghai, and to Japan, including a stay at a Zen Buddhist monastery in Kyoto. On his return to England he began using a technique of 'white writing' in works such as the *Broadway* (tempera, 1936; New York, Met.). In this painting, alluding to the colour and activity of New York, he used swift calligraphic brushstrokes, mostly in white, on a variously coloured background.

In 1938 Tobey returned to Seattle via New York. Throughout the 1940s he developed 'white writing' in such frenetic works as *Red Man, White Man, Black Man* (1945; Seattle, WA, A. Mus.). The vast mass of individuals that formed *E Pluribus Unum* (1942; Seattle, WA, A. Mus.) was designed to suggest the latent unity between them, in keeping with the Bahai faith. He continued also to paint in other styles, as in *Still-life with Egg* (1941; Seattle, WA, A. Mus.), which again suggests the influence of Cubism, especially of Juan Gris. Furthermore, in keeping with the Bahai belief in the validity of other religions, Tobey occasionally addressed Christian themes, such as *Deposition* (1947; Seattle, WA, G. Miyake priv. col., see 1974 exh. cat., pl. 13), which consists of highly simplified forms.

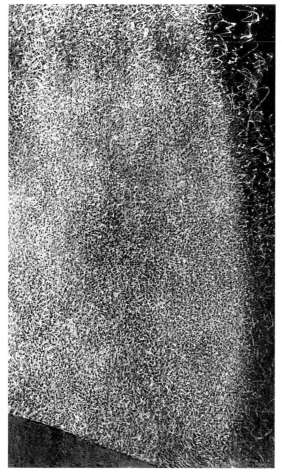

Mark Tobey: *Edge of August*, casein on fibreboard, 1219×711 mm, 1953 (New York, Museum of Modern Art)

From the late 1940s to the early 1950s Tobey tended to paint his works in dark, sombre colours, as in *Biography* (1948; Stanford, CA, U. A.G. & Mus.), though he retained something of his calligraphic style. His 'white writing' soon re-emerged, however, in such classic works as the *Edge of August* (1953; New York, MOMA; see fig.). Here, a mass of fine white brushstrokes covers almost the whole of the canvas, showing the full development of this technique. In 1954 he moved to New York and painted the serene *Meditative Series* (e.g. *Meditative Series VIII*, 1954; priv. col., see Dahl and others, p. 89). In 1955 he visited Europe, where he exhibited with avant-garde artists such as Georges Mathieu and Wols. In 1957 he produced a number of paintings using Japanese black ink, for example *Sumi I* (1957; Stanford, CA, U. A.G. & Mus.), and in the following year he was awarded the Grand International Painting Prize at the Venice Biennale, confirming his reputation in Europe.

After a brief visit to Seattle Tobey decided in 1960 to settle in Basle, where he remained until his death. His style remained constant during the 1960s, although in response to museum pressure he increased the size of his paintings. Among his later works is the monumental *Sagittarius Red*

(1963; Basle, Kstmus.), often claimed as his masterpiece, in which he used densely packed brushstrokes in ink and other media on a red background. He continued to work almost until his death, in spite of being dogged by ill-health in later life, producing such pictures as *Coming and Going* (1970; Buffalo, NY, Albright–Knox A.G.).

Tobey's paintings have often been described as intimate versions of the paintings of Jackson Pollock, because of their elegant gestural quality and small size. In origin, however, they are quite dissimilar, founded not on the artist's individual psyche but on a universalist religion. The comparison, furthermore, suggests that Tobey's style grew out of Pollock's, when in fact the relationship between the two artists was much more reciprocal. In spirit, if not in style, Tobey's paintings are closer to a European tradition of abstract painting that includes the impersonal calm of Mondrian's work. While enjoying great critical support in Europe, notably from Michel Tapié, Tobey's reception in America was somewhat cooler. More specifically his contribution to American art was frequently marginalized by influential New York critics, perhaps because of a lack of sympathy for his religious beliefs and because of his rejection of the substance of Abstract Expressionism.

BIBLIOGRAPHY

C. Roberts: *Mark Tobey* (Paris, 1959)
Mark Tobey: A Retrospective Exhibition from Northwest Collections (exh. cat. by E. B. Thomas, Seattle, WA, A. Mus., 1959)
F. Choay: *Mark Tobey* (Paris, 1961)
Mark Tobey (exh. cat. by F. Mathey, Paris, Mus. A. Déc., 1961)
Mark Tobey (exh. cat. by W. C. Seitz, New York, MOMA, 1962)
W. Schmied: *Mark Tobey* (London, 1966)
Tribute to Mark Tobey (exh. cat. by J. C. Taylor, Washington, DC, Hirshhorn, 1974)
J. Haslem: *Mark Tobey Graphics* (Washington, DC, 1979)
A. L. Dahl and others: *Mark Tobey: Art and Belief* (Oxford, 1984)
Mark Tobey: City Paintings (exh. cat. by E. E. Rathbone, Washington, DC, N.G.A., 1984)
Mark Tobey: Works, 1935–1975 (exh. cat. by M. Bärmann and others, Essen, Mus. Flkwang, 1989)

PHILIP COOPER

Tobol'sk. Russian town on the River Irtysh in the Tyumen' region of Siberia. It was founded in 1587 by a detachment of Cossacks, and remained the military and administrative centre of Siberia until the early 18th century. The Kremlin (late 17th century–early 18th) was the first stone-built citadel in Siberia. It contains the cathedral of St Sophia and the Dormition (Sofiysko-Uspensky; 1681–6), an imposing five-domed building, a *gostinyy dvor* (bazaar; 1703–5, by S. U. Remezov), a pentagon with a covered interior court, and the 'Swedish Palace' (1714–16), the interior of which consists of six halls with barrel vaults. In the lower part of Tobol'sk there are Baroque churches, residential and administrative buildings in the Baroque and Neo-classical styles and a monument (1839, by Aleksandr Bryullov) to Yermak, who began the Russian annexation of Siberia in the 16th century. Local monuments of archaeological and artistic interest are in the Tobol'sk Historical Museum and the Tobol'sk Picture Gallery. The town is famous for the ivory-carvings made there; such carving is first mentioned in 1711, and commercial production began in the 1860s. Mammoth and walrus ivory was used for figurines as well as boxes, pipes and other household objects, sometimes inlaid with darker ivory. Carved miniatures depict scenes from the life of the peoples of Siberia and the animals of the area. The craft continues in the products of the Koopeksport workshop, founded in 1933.

BIBLIOGRAPHY

I. Davydov: *Tobol'skiye kostorezy* [Tobol'sk bone-carvings] (Tyumen', 1954)
V. V. Kirillov: *Tobol'sk* (Moscow, 1984)
S. P. Zavarikhin: *V drevnem tsentre Sibiri* [At the ancient centre of Siberia] (Moscow, 1987)
Yu. Nadtochin: *Tobol'skiy muzey-zapovednik* [The Tobol'sk national park] (Sverdlovsk, 1988)

L. A. D'YAKOV

Tobón Mejía, Marco (*b* Santa Rosa de Osos, nr Medellín, 1876; *d* Paris, 1933). Colombian sculptor, draughtsman, painter and medallist. He studied with Francisco Antonio Cano and co-founded with him the review *Lectura y Arte*, in which he published illustrations and vignettes influenced by the motifs and sinuous style of Art Nouveau. In 1905 he left for Havana, where his talent was more fully recognized. Cuban patronage enabled him to travel to Paris, where he executed delicate life-size marble statues that blend classicism and sensuality, such as *Poetry* and *Silence* (both *c.* 1914; Bogotá, Mus. N.), which are notable for their harmony and ambitious scale.

Tobón Mejía's most personal and interesting works, however, were reliefs in bronze and other alloys in which he gave free rein to his talents as a designer, to his admiration for the subjectivity of the Symbolists and especially to his own imagination and fantasy. In works such as *First Waves* (1915; Bogotá, Mus. A. Mod.), in which a young woman prepares to enter the sea, or *Female Vampire* (*c.* 1910; Bogotá, Mus. N.), he demonstrated a strong inclination towards the supernatural and the mysterious. He also worked, though more sporadically, as a draughtsman and painter, and his production as a medallist was recognized as the first of its kind in Colombia. His work established new standards of quality in Colombian sculpture, introducing a graceful and modern stylization far from the academic Realism that had hitherto predominated.

BIBLIOGRAPHY

Cien años de arte colombiano (exh. cat. by E. Serrano, Bogotá, Mus. A. Mod., 1985)
Marco Tobón Mejía (exh. cat. by M. Acevedo, Bogotá, Mus. A. Mod., 1986)

EDUARDO SERRANO

Toccagni, Callisto de. *See* PIAZZA, (1).

Tocqué, Louis (*b* Paris, 19 Nov 1696; *d* Paris, 10 Feb 1772). French painter and engraver. He studied briefly with the history painter Nicolas Bertin but was more influenced by the portrait painter Jean-Marc Nattier, whose studio he entered *c.* 1718, and whose daughter he married in 1747. In Nattier's studio he executed copies of portraits by van Dyck, Nicolas de Largillierre and Hyacinthe Rigaud (e.g. a copy of Rigaud's portrait of *Cardinal de Fleury*; Hillerød, Frederiksborg Slot). He may have participated in Pierre Crozat's project, begun in 1721, to publish engravings of pictures in the collection of the Regent, Philippe II, Duke of Orléans, making drawings alongside Nattier and Watteau, and he may also have executed engravings after the paintings by Charles Le Brun in the

Grande Galerie at Versailles under the direction of Jean-Baptiste Massé (*c.* 1724).

It was at the relatively late date of 1731 that Tocqué was approved (*agréé*) by the Académie Royale on presentation of the *Family of Peirenc de Moras* (untraced). He was received (*reçu*) as a full member in 1734 with his three-quarter-length portraits of *Louis Galloche* and *Jean-Baptiste Lemoyne* (Paris, Louvre). His talents as a portrait painter were quickly recognized, and he received a number of royal commissions, including the full-length portrait of the *Dauphin, Louis de Bourbon* (1738) and of *Maria Leczinska* (1740; both Paris, Louvre; see fig.). However, the stilted conventionality of such portraits does not reveal Tocqué's true talent for realistic informality and unembellished naturalness, which his contemporaries praised. These qualities are more evident in the private portrait commissions that Tocqué sent regularly to the Salon from 1737 until 1759, such as the full-length portrait of *Mme Harant* (exh. Salon 1738; Paris, priv. col.). Comparisons between Tocqué, Rigaud and Largillierre were drawn by many Salon critics. Yet, while the equal of these artists in the rendition of textures, fabrics and flesh tones, he imbued his sitters with an immediacy that avoids all artificiality or pomposity. His sitters include many aristocrats, but also artists, intellectuals and members of the *haut-bourgeoisie*: subjects who required an informal and objective representation rather than an idealized one.

Louis Tocqué: *Maria Leczinska*, oil on canvas, 2.77×1.91 m, 1740 (Paris, Musée du Louvre)

In 1756, summoned by Count Mikhail Laronovich Vorontsov, the Russian Chancellor, Tocqué left for St Petersburg, where he stayed for nearly two years. His main official commission was a full-length portrait of *Empress Elizabeth I* (St Petersburg, Hermitage), much admired for the realistic treatment of the Empress's features. Tocqué also painted less formal portraits, including that of *Paul Galluccio, Marquis de L'Hospital*, French Ambassador to the Russian Court (untraced; engraved by Teucher), and those of *Count Vorontsov* (1757) and his Countess, *Anna* (1757–8; both untraced). In the 1740s Tocqué painted a number of portraits of Danes in Paris (e.g. the half-lengths of *Joachim Wasserschlebe*, 1746; Copenhagen, Kon. Dan. Kstakad.; and *Frederik Berregard*, *c*. 1745; Copenhagen, Nmus.). In 1758 he spent seven months in Copenhagen, where he was made a member of the newly founded Academy of Fine Arts. He later sent from Paris as his reception piece a half-length portrait of *Nattier*, while Nattier, receiving the same honour, dispatched a portrait of *Tocqué* (both Copenhagen, Kon. Dan. Kstakad.). While in Denmark he executed full-length portraits of *Frederick V* and of his second wife, *Julia-Maria* (Copenhagen, Amalienborg). He also painted portraits of the statesmen *Count Adam Moltke* (untraced) and *J. H. E. Bernstorff* (Hillerød, Frederiksborg Slot).

On his return to France, Tocqué practically ceased to paint but continued to attend the sessions of the Académie Royale. His informal style contributed to the rejuvenation of the portrait in France and in Scandinavia, his influence being visible, for instance, in the work of Carl Gustaf Pilo and Jens Juel.

BIBLIOGRAPHY

A. Doria: 'Tocqué et les commandes royales', *Gaz. B.-A.*, n. s. 4, xviii/2 (1928), pp. 149–66
——: 'Louis Tocqué', *L'Art français* (Paris, [1929])
——: 'Le Discours de Tocqué . . . sur le genre du portrait', *Bull. Soc. Hist. A. Fr.* (1929), pp. 255–92
——: 'Tocqué conférencier', *Gaz. B.-A.*, n. s. 5, vi/1 (1931), pp. 223–37
——: *Le Peintre Tocqué ambassadeur de l'art français auprès des cours du Nord* (Paris, 1953)
B. Lossky: 'Portraits autrichiens dans l'oeuvre de Rigaud et de Tocqué', *Gaz. B.-A.*, n. s. 5, lii (1958), p. 81
E. K. Sass: 'Nattier–Tocqué et vice-versa', *Opuscula in honorem C. Hernmarck, 27.12.1966* (Stockholm, 1966), pp. 181–206 [*Nmus. Skrser*, xv]

PATRICE MARANDEL

Todeschini, Giulio (*b* Brescia, *c*. 1524; *d c*. 1603). Italian architect. He trained initially as a painter in Milan and Venice. He first worked as an architect in Desenzano del Garda, where he designed the porticos of the Palazzo del Comune (*c*. 1560). His Palazzo del Provveditore (1585), with its rusticated arcades, smooth Doric pilasters and entablature without a frieze, resembles a timid reflection of Michele Sanmicheli's Palazzo degli Honorij (later Palazzo Guastaverza; 1553–4) in Verona. Todeschini also rebuilt S Maria Maddalena (begun 1586), Desenzano, an example of severe simplicity in compliance with the principles of the Counter-Reformation, with elegant Doric columns supporting round arches.

In Brescia Todeschini replaced the engineer Ludovico Beretta as Superintendent of Buildings in 1572. He rejected a plan (1575) by Andrea Palladio and Francesco Zamberlan (1529–after 1606) to build a third floor on the Palazzo Comunale della Loggia, where a second floor had already been added (1550–60) to the original scheme (1490–1510), on the grounds that the existing walls were too thin to support the additional load and that the proposed third order would disrupt the strict adherence to the rules of classical architecture and the proportions of the façade. Owing to his technical expertise Todeschini was also consulted on questions of military architecture, such as the restoration of the old castle (1584) and the construction of the new one (1586–8), designed by Giulio Savorgnan (1516–95). He may have designed S Gaetano (1588–98; rebuilt 1692–1745), Brescia, and he drew up the plans for the triumphal arches erected in the city (1595) in honour of Cardinal Giovanni Antonio Morosini.

UNPUBLISHED SOURCES

Venice, Bib. N. Marciana, Cod. it., cl. VII, 1155 (7453) & 1913 (9047) [*Scritture sul vecchio e nuovo castello di Brescia: Preventivo di spesa derivante dal progetto di Giovanbattista Bonhomi* (1586); *Scrittura sullo stato di avanzamento dei lavori* (1588); *Rilievi in qualità di proto del castello* (1589)]

BIBLIOGRAPHY

P. Fontana: *Il sontuoso apparato, fatto dalla magnifica città di Brescia, nel felice ritorno dell'Illu. (et) Reverendiss. Vescovo suo, il cardinale Morosini . . .* (Brescia, 1591)
U. Papa: 'L'architetto Giulio Todeschini da Brescia, 1524–1603', *Emporium*, xiii (1901), pp. 352–65
A. Peroni: 'L'architettura e la scultura nei secoli XV e XVI', *Storia di Brescia*, ed. G. Treccani degli Alfreri, ii (Brescia, 1961), pp. 864–70
A. Manno: 'Un compromesso fra "vecchi" e "giovani": Il nuovo castello di Brescia (1580–1611)', *Stud. Ven.*, n. s., xiii (1997), pp. 255–84
F. Robecchi: 'Fonti inedite per la storia del castello di Brescia e delle fortezze del territorio fra XVI e XVII secolo', *Il colle armato: Storia del castello di Brescia*, ed. I. Gianfranceschi (Brescia, 1988), pp. 187–203

ANTONIO MANNO

T'oech'on. *See* KIM (i), (2).

Toeput, Lodewijk [Lodewyck; Lodewyk] [Pozzoserrato, Pozzo da Treviso; Lodovico, Ludovico; Louis] (*b* Antwerp, *c*. 1550; *d* Treviso, *c*. 1605). Flemish painter and draughtsman, active in Italy. He was apparently a pupil of Marten de Vos and went to Italy probably after 1573. In Venice he presumably joined Tintoretto's workshop. Toeput may have witnessed the event he commemorated in his *Fire in the Doge's Palace* (1577; Treviso, Mus. Civ. Bailo). Either before or after this commission, he made six landscape frescoes (*c*. 1575 or 1577–9) for the abbey of Praglia, which reveal a strong adherence to Flemish conventions. Some years later he painted three frescoes in the church of S Giustina in Padua. He was in Florence in the late 1570s and visited Rome in 1581; by February 1582 he is documented in Treviso, near Venice, where he settled. He remained in close contact with Venetian masters, particularly through another Flemish artist active there, Pauwels Franck (1540–96), whose influence is evident in Toeput's representation of the *Four Seasons* (*c*. 1584; Venice, priv. col., see Crosato, pp. 120–21, pls 1–4), of which two tondi versions exist, which are attributed to Toeput (e.g. Providence, RI Sch. Des., Mus. A., and England, priv. col.). Around 1585 he painted a friezelike series: two canvases (*in situ*), each with two biblical scenes, for the chapel of the Rettori in the church of the Monte di Pietà in Treviso. These compositions were inspired by Netherlandish engravings and works by Tintoretto and Jacopo and Leandro Bassano. Probably dating from the same time is *Susanna and the Elders* (Würzburg, priv. col., see Wegner, 1961, p. 112, fig. 125). One of Toeput's favourite motifs was a formal Mannerist garden containing trellises and sculptures, which he included in *Dives and Lazarus* (Kassel, Schloss Wilhelmshöhe). It also appears in his versions of the *Banquet in the Open Air* (Treviso, priv. col., see Menegazzi, 1961, p. 122, fig. 145) and in his *Outdoor Concert* (see fig.). Only a few of Toeput's church paintings mentioned in early literature survive in Treviso, in the churches of S Leonardo, S Maria Maggiore and S Agostino; similarly the surviving frescoes are scarce and in a poor state of preservation. Around 1590 Toeput painted six landscapes representing *The Months* for the Villa Chiericati-Magna, Vicenza, and in 1593 he decorated the interior of the Scuola dei Battuti in nearby Conegliano with figures of sibyls and prophets and Old Testament scenes.

Toeput's landscape frescoes and canvases are his finest achievements; they are distinctive in their combination of Flemish and Venetian styles, typically showing spacious vistas, full of atmospheric and picturesque effects. This is well shown in such paintings as the *Fall of Phaeton* (1599; Hannover, Niedersächs. Landesmus.), the *Landscape with a Hermit* (1601) and *Town on a River* (both Munich, Alte Pin.). The *View of a Villa* (Venice, Ca' d'Oro), the *Pleasure Garden with a Labyrinth* (London, Hampton Court, Royal Col.) and the *Deer Hunt* (Treviso, Cassa di Risparmio). These developments in the painterly treatment of landscape had a strong influence on the work of Paul Bril, Frederik van Valckenborch, Josse de Momper and Tobias Verhaecht. Toeput also introduced a new kind of genre painting, of well-to-do gatherings, which anticipated the Dutch 17th-century merry company pieces by Willem Buytewech and others. Examples include the *Company in an Interior* (Augsburg, priv. col., see Wegner, 1961, pp. 116–18, fig. 137), the *Ball in a Palace* (sold Christies, London, 9 July 1976, lot 106) and the *Allegory of Autumn* (Prague, N.G., Šternbeck Pal.).

Toeput's interest in topography is reflected principally in his drawings. His *Panorama of Treviso* and *View of Aquapendente* were engraved and included in vol. v (1598) of G. Braun and F. Hogenberg's six-volume atlas, the *Civitates orbis terrarum* (Cologne, 1572–1618). Other drawings depict imaginary landscapes, such as the *Landscape with St John on Patmos* (New York, Pierpont Morgan Lib.), showing his characteristic trees with windswept foliage framing a finely detailed panorama seen from a high viewpoint.

Lodewijk Toeput: *Outdoor Concert*, oil on canvas, 1.71×1.29 m, *c.* 1590 (Treviso, Museo Civico Luigi Bailo)

BIBLIOGRAPHY

K. van Mander: *Schilder-boeck* ([1603]–1604), ii/2, p. 342
C. Ridolfi: *Meraviglie* (1648); ed. D. von Hadeln (1914–24), ii, p. 86
R. A. Peltzer: 'Niederländisch-venezianische Landschaftsmalerei: Pauwels Francken, genannt Paolo Fiammingo; Lodewyck Toeput, genannt Lodovico Pozzoserrato', *Münchn. Jb. Bild. Kst*, i (1924), pp. 143–53
M. Dobroklonsky: 'Further Drawings by Pozzoserrato', *Old Master Drgs*, ix (1934/5), p. 39
S. Sulzberger: 'Le Peintre Louis Toeput (Ludovico Pozzoserrato) et la décoration du Mont de Piété à Trevise', *Bull. Inst. Hist. Belge Rome*, xv (1935), pp. 149–67
R. A. Peltzer: 'Per la conoscenza di Lodewyck Toeput (Pozzoserrato)', *A. Ven.*, v (1951), pp. 122–5
L. Menegazzi: 'Ludovico Toeput (il Pozzoserrato)', *Saggi & Mem. Stor. A.*, i (1957), pp. 167–223
N. Ivanoff: 'Affreschi di Dario Varotari e Lodovico Pozzoserrato nell'appartamento abbaziale di Praglia', *Praglia* (1960)
L. Menegazzi: 'Giunta a Ludovico Pozzoserrato', *A. Ven.*, xv (1961), pp. 119–26
W. Wegner: 'Neue Beiträge zur Kenntnis des Werkes von Lodewyck Toeput', *A. Ven.*, xv (1961), pp. 107–15
——: 'Drawings by Pozzoserrato', *Master Drgs*, i (1963), pp. 27–32
L. Menegazzi: 'Disegni di Lodewijk Toeput', *Mus. Royaux B.-A. Belgique: Bull.*, xiii (1964), pp. 187–96
L. Grossato: *Affreschi del cinquecento in Padova* (Milan, 1971)
L. L. Crosato: 'Di *Quattro Stagioni* del Pozzoserrato e la grafica fiamminga', *Münchn. Jb. Bild. Kst*, xxxvi (1985), pp. 119–30
The Age of Bruegel: Netherlandish Drawings in the Sixteenth Century (exh. cat. by J. O. Hand and others, Washington, DC, N.G.A.; New York, Pierpont Morgan Lib.; 1986–7), pp. 286–7
S. Mason Rinaldi and D. Luciani: *Toeput a Treviso: Ludovico Pozzoserrato/Lodewijk Toeput, pittore neerlandese nelle civiltà veneta del tardo cinquecento: Atti Seminario, Treviso: 1987* [with bibliog.]
T. Gerszi: 'The Draughtsmanship of Lodewijk Toeput', *Master Drgs*, xxx/4 (1992), pp. 367–95

TERÉZ GERSZI

Toesca, Pietro (*b* Pietra Ligure, 1877; *d* Rome, 1962). Italian art historian. He was a student of Adolfo Venturi at Rome University (1900–04). He then became a lecturer at the Accademia Scientifico-Letterario in Milan (1905–6) and was later professor of medieval and modern art history in Turin (1907–14) and Florence (1914–26). He produced several essays, which revealed his perspicacious analysis and vast philological learning. In *I precetti d'arte italiani* he argued that the analysis of works of art should not be based on the notion of 'progress' but rather on the historical conditions that determined their originality and aesthetic value. *La pittura e la miniatura nella Lombardia* was described by Strzygowski as 'a valuable monograph capable of withstanding rigorous scientific examination'. The volume on medieval art in the *Storia dell'arte italiana* remains an indispensable source for the scholar. From 1926 to 1936 Toesca taught medieval art history at Rome University, teaching Renaissance and modern art history from 1936 to 1948. From then onwards he contributed to the *Enciclopedia dell'arte italiana*, established by Giovanni Treccani, editing the medieval and modern sections. During this period he published important works on Italian manuscript illumination (1929) and *Giotto* (1941), as well as the volume on the Trecento in the *Storia dell'arte italiana* (1950).

WRITINGS

I precetti d'arte italiani (Livorno, 1900)
La pittura e la miniatura nella Lombardia: Dai più antichi monumenti alla metà del quattrocento (Milan, 1912, rev. 1966) [rev. ed. contains complete list of Toesca's writings and introductory note by E. Catelnuovo analysing his contribution to art history]
Storia dell'arte italiana, 2 vols (Turin, 1927–50/*R* 1965)
Monumenti e studi per la storia della miniatura italiana (Milan, 1929)
Giotto (Turin, 1941)

MARIO D'ONOFRIO

Toesca y Ricci, Joaquín (*b* Rome, *c.* 1740; *d* Santiago de Chile, 1799). Italian architect, active in Chile. He began his career in the office of FRANCESCO SABBATINI, who at that time was working for the Spanish authorities in Naples. In 1759 Charles IV of Naples assumed the Spanish throne as Charles III (*reg* 1759–88) and took Sabbatini to Madrid as architect to the Crown, together with his best assistants, including Toesca. Toesca's career in Madrid was pursued under Sabbatini's shadow, but he came into his own when he was seconded to Chile in 1778 to rebuild Santiago Cathedral, burnt down in 1769. Reusing the existing foundations, Toesca produced a Neo-classical design, now obscured by late 19th-century additions. His major work was the mint in Santiago, the Real Casa de Moneda (*see* CHILE, fig. 2), now the executive residence. The plan is laid out round several courtyards behind a Neo-classical elevation that features a three-storey central block in three bays flanked by two-storey wings. The central block is articulated below by four sets of coupled columns of a giant order, to which coupled pilasters correspond on the third floor. In lieu of columns, the six-bay wings are marked off by clustered pilasters and surmounted by a heavy balustrade. The composition recalls Luigi Vanvitelli's backdrop to the Piazza Dante, which was going up in Naples while Toesca was working on Sabbatini's schemes there.

Other projects of Toesca's include the rebuilding of the earthquake-damaged church of La Merced (completed 1795) and the design of the hospital of S Juan de Dios. He was also responsible for the embankment of the River Mapocho, and designed a number of parish churches. In the last two years of his life he taught architecture at the Academia de S Luis in Santiago. The influence of his executed work and that of his collaborators and students was far-reaching in Chile.

BIBLIOGRAPHY

R. Toro: 'Toesca, ensayo sobre su vida y su obra', *Bol. Acad. Chil. Hist.* ii/3 (1934)
A. Benavides Rodriguez: *Le arquitectura en el virreinato del Perú y en la capitania general de Chile* (Santiago, 1941, 2/1961; rev. by J. Benavides Courtois, 3/1988), pp. 252–62
E. Pereira Salas: *Historia del arte en el reino de Chile* (Santiago, 1965)
G. Guarda Geywitz: 'El triunfo del neoclasicismo en el reino de Chile', *Bol. Cent. Invest. Hist. & Estét. Caracas*, viii (1967)

RAMÓN ALFONSO MÉNDEZ

Tofanelli, Stefano (*b* Nave, Lucca, 26 Sept 1752; *d* Lucca, 29 Nov 1812). Italian painter. At the age of ten he entered the workshop of Giuseppe Antonio Luchi (1709–74), and in 1767 joined the school of Bernardino Nocchi, who in 1769 took him to Rome, where Tofanelli completed his training with Niccolò Lapiccola. Under the supervision of the latter he took part in the restoration (1772) of Pope Julius II's villa and the decoration of the Palazzo Caffarelli-Vidoni-Stoppani (from 1773; *in situ*), both in Rome. His talent as a draughtsman quickly attracted attention: he was sought after by the engravers Giovanni Volpato and Raphael Morghen to make copies of works by Old Masters, and in 1781 he set up a school of drawing.

Tofanelli was one of the best Neo-classical portrait painters and in Rome he produced such examples as *Count Alessandro Castracane* (1781; Providence, RI Sch. Des., Mus. A.) and *Christopher Hewetson Sculpting the Bust of Gavin Hamilton* (*c.* 1784; Cologne, Wallraf-Richartz-Mus.). He also painted a *Self-portrait* (1783; Rome, Pal. Braschi), showing him with his father and brother Agostino Tofanelli (1770–1834), who was also a painter. However, he achieved fame as a result of his decoration (1784–92) of the Villa Mansi at Segromigno, near Lucca, for which he even designed furniture and paving. The seven canvases depicting the myth of *Apollo* were sent from Rome, but in 1786 the artist went there himself to paint the tempera frescoes (*in situ*). He took advantage of the trip to visit Venice and Parma, where he discovered the work of Correggio. His reputation was formally recognized by his election in 1791 to the Accademia di S Luca in Rome and the commission of 1792 for an *Apotheosis of Romulus* to decorate a ceiling in the Palazzo Altieri, Rome.

From the early 1790s Tofanelli also began to produce religious works. In addition to the frescoes (1794) in the church of S Antonio at Tivoli, he painted altarpieces that were sent from Rome to various Italian towns, including three large canvases for the Benedictine church of S Nicolò dell'Arena at Catania: *Beheading of St John the Baptist*, *Adoration of the Shepherds* and *St Nicholas of Bari Freeing a Slave* (all 1794). Political and economic difficulties obliged Tofanelli to return to his home town in 1801, and in 1802 he was appointed as a teacher at the school of drawing in Lucca.

In 1805 Tofanelli became a member of the Accademia Napoleone and was granted the titles of Senator, and First Painter to the Princess of Lucca and Piombino, Elisa Bonaparte. His activity intensified, though he concentrated on works for Lucca and its environs, including an altarpiece of the *Assumption* (1808; *in situ*) for Lucca Cathedral and murals (1811; *in situ*) for the chapel of the Holy Sacrament in the same cathedral. A period of prosperity brought a great demand for the decoration of buildings in Lucca. Tofanelli painted overdoors in tempera in several rooms of the Palazzo Pubblico (now Palazzo Provinciale; *in situ*) in Lucca, and elsewhere. At Princess Elisa's villa (the Villa Reale) at Marlia he left the decoration, *Dance of the Hours*, unfinished at his death, and this was completed by the French artist Jean-Baptiste Desmarais (1756–1813). He continued to be much in demand as a portrait painter, producing portraits of such important figures as *Elisa Baciocchi and her Husband Felice* (1805; versions Lucca, Pal. Orsetti; Paris, Mus. Marmottan). Several portraits have been destroyed or lost, such as *Princess Napoleone Elisa* (1812), known from a print by Tofanelli's nephew, the engraver Andrea Tofanelli (*b c.* 1778).

Tofanelli also continued to work as a draughtsman for engraving and sculpture projects. He gave unrestrained support to Napoleon by designing a statue (destr. 1814) for the Great Council Room of the Palazzo Pubblico, a work executed in 1804 by Giuseppe Martini. He also designed other statues in 1807 for the Piazza Napoleone in Lucca, and Cesare Lucchesini's oration at Tofanelli's funeral referred to other and diverse works of sculpture: a wax *Christ* and a model (Turin, Mus. Civ. A. Ant.) for a statuette of *Pope Pius VI*, made for the porcelain factory of Giovanni Volpato. Following in the wake of Pompeo Girolamo Batoni, Tofanelli was one of the most accomplished of the Lucca school of painters who went to Rome to find success, but the finesse and precision of his drawing and the excellence of his technique are betrayed by his lack of feeling.

BIBLIOGRAPHY
T. Trenta: *Dissertazioni sullo stato dell' architettura, pittura e arti figurativi in rilievo in Lucca ne' bassi tempi* (Lucca, 1813, rev. 1822)
S. Rudolph: *La pittura del '700 a Roma* (Milan, 1983)
Il principato napoleonico dei Baciocchi, 1805–1814: Riforma dello stato e società (exh. cat., Lucca, Mus. & Pin. N., 1984), pp. 302–13
I. Belli Barsali: 'Per Stefano Tofanelli "Primo pittore di Sua Altezza Imperiale" (1752–1812)', *Il principato napoleonico dei Baciocchi: Atti del convegno internazionale: Lucca, 1984*, pp. 375–403

OLIVIER MICHEL

Tōgan. *See* UNKOKU TŌGAN.

Togansai. *See* HASHIMOTO GAHŌ.

Tōgenshi. *See* KANŌ, (10).

Togo [Togolese Republic; République Togolaise]. Country in West Africa on the Gulf of Guinea. It is bordered by Ghana to the west, Benin to the east and Burkina Faso to the north. Togo is 58,785 sq. km in area, 56 km wide along the coast and extends 579 km north. It has a dry tropical climate and a flat savannah landscape punctuated by several ranges of hills. Its population of 3,349,000 (UN estimate, 1989) consists of 21 major ethnic groups, including the Kabye, Bassari, Kotokoli, Tchokossi, Moba and Gourma in the north; and the Mina and Ewe in the south. The Ewe are the largest group and live on both sides of the Ghana–Togo border. A German colony from 1894 to 1918, Togo was then governed by a joint mandate granted to Britain and France by the League of Nations until independence in 1960. Most Togolese engage in subsistence farming. French is the national language, and 47% of the population speak Ewe. Togo's capital is Lomé. This entry covers art in Togo since colonial times. For the art of the area in earlier times *see* AFRICA, §VII, 4.

The arts of post-colonial Togo, while firmly rooted in tradition and utilitarian in form, show a vitality that reflects the dynamism characteristic of Togolese culture. Artists producing traditional crafts usually devote the bulk of their time to farming and other economic endeavours. Historically they have produced items to order or for sale in local markets and have relied on the community for patronage. In the late 1980s and early 1990s, however, a growing number of craftsmen began to draw on a wider range of African arts for inspiration and to produce objects for Togo's thriving tourist market. Although masks are rare in Togo, calabash and basketry dance-crests are made by the Moba, Batammaliba and Kabye and may take the place of masks; those ornamented with animal horns may also serve as hunting trophies. The crests are worn by men during male funeral celebrations and annual harvest festivals that recall men's prowess in hunting and warfare. Their use has become rarer, due to a decline in hunting and in the population of antelopes and bush cows, whose horns adorn many of the older crests. Carved wooden figures with abstract and attenuated forms are made by the Moba, Gourma, Tchokossi, Kotokoli and Lamba of northern Togo and used in shrine contexts. Such figures are stylistically similar to carvings by people in Ghana, Côte d'Ivoire, Burkina Faso and Nigeria, suggesting some historical and cultural ties. The more naturalistic figure carvings (some commemorating deceased twins, others used in Vodun and Mami Wata cults (*see* IBIBIO, §3) of southern Togo's Ewe and Mina reveal cultural affinities with AKAN and related peoples in Ghana, Benin and south-western Nigeria. Other arts that continue to be practised and developed include the production of ornate calabashes, widely used as containers, which reach a high level of artistic expression in the pyro-engraved products of the Chamba of east-central Togo. Low-fired earthenware pottery is hand built by women in the Agome–Glozou area of south Togo and around Bassari in the north-central region. Among the Moba of northern Togo both men and women are potters, with women responsible for domestic items and men specializing in millet-beer containers. Togo's textiles are dominated by factory-made wax-printed cloth with elaborate, named patterns that function as a means of communication and social commentary. Patterns such as 'mon mari est capable' and 'je cours plus vite que ma rivale' refer to competition among women, particularly acute among co-wives in polygynous households. Distribution and sale of these cloths is controlled by a select group of Ewe and Mina women, the Nana–Benz, whose roles as intermediaries in the cloth trade endow them with considerable economic and political power. (Their title combines the term of respect, Nana, with their preferred mode of transport, the Mercedes–Benz.) The mud architecture of the Batammaliba has been subject to detailed study (Blier; *see* AFRICA, fig. 64).

Few of Togo's late 20th-century artists have received international attention. Despite this, artists of real quality have emerged. Clemclem Lawson and Sokey Edorh (*b* 1955) produced works in acrylic, watercolour, ink and natural pigments that are narrative in content but that explore emotional responses rather than depictions of reality. Drawing on his earlier experience as a weaver of narrow-strip *kente* cloth, fibre artist Kuevi Kangui Akplodjegou (*b* 1951) used specially prepared silk threads in his designs. Based in the southern town of Atakpame, he founded the artists' workshop Venusmerc (Venus and Mercury school) in 1982. The sculptor Agbagli Kossi (*b* 1934) produced figure carvings for the Vodun cult that transcended their traditional domain and achieved international recognition through their display in such exhibitions as *Magiciens de la terre* and *Africa Now* (see bibliography). The Togo-born painter, printmaker and poet El Loko (*b* 1950) also attracted international attention. He was educated in Germany and trained as a textile designer before devoting himself to his art. His works include a number of black-and-white linoleum cuts in which birds' wings, claws and beaks are combined with masks, faces and other elements in striking formal compositions (see Kennedy, 1992, pp. 88–90). Another internationally acclaimed artist, the sculptor Paul Ahyi (*b* 1930), trained at the Ecole des Beaux-Arts, Paris. His sculptures, mosaics and reliefs embellishing banks, supermarkets and boulevards are a familiar part of Lomé's urban landscape (see fig.). Many of his works are in cement, a medium favoured for its practicality and low cost, and they celebrate the importance of the individual and the family in maintaining Africa's traditional values in a modern world.

There are important collections of Togolese paintings and material culture in the Musée National, Lomé (inaugurated 1975); in the regional museum in Aneho (inaugurated 1986); and in the Kponton private collection, Lomé. In the early 1990s plans for an open-air museum in Lomé were under way. Ethnographic museums in Germany (Leipzig, Mus. Vlkerknd.; Hamburg, Mus. Vlkerknd.; Berlin, Mus. Vlkerknd.) and the USA (Chicago, IL, Field Mus. Nat. Hist.) hold important collections of late 19th- and early 20th-century art and material culture from northern Togo.

Togo, Lomé, untitled cement sculpture by Paul Ahyi, 1970s

BIBLIOGRAPHY

B. Benoît-Latour: 'L'Artisanat togolais', *Afrique Lit. & A.*, xxx (1973), pp. 40–42
J. Anquetal: *L'Artisanat créateur au Togo* (Paris, 1980)
L. Bellow: '"Je cours plus vite que ma rivale": Paroles chez les Gen-mina au sud Togo', *Cahiers de littérature orale*, xix (1986), pp. 29–66
S. P. Blier: *The Anatomy of Architecture: Ontology and Metaphor in Batammaliba Architectural Expression*, Res Monographs in Anthropology and Aesthetics (Cambridge, 1987)
R. Cordonnier: *Femmes africaines et commerce: Les Revendeuses de tissu de la ville de Lomé (Togo)* (Paris, 1987)
Magiciens de la terre (exh. cat., ed. J.-H. Martin; Paris, Pompidou, 1989), pp. 174–5
D. Rambert-Hounou: 'Craft in Togo Today', *African Crafts*, ed. E. Melgin (Helsinki, 1990), pp. 94–6, 113–14
P. Amrouche and A. Thiam: *Art moba du Togo* (Paris, 1991)
Africa Now (exh. cat., Las Palmas de Gran Canaria, Cent. Atlantic. A. Mod.; Groningen, Groninger Mus.; Mexico City, Cent. Cult. A. Contemp.; 1991–2), pp. 73–9
J. Kennedy: *New Currents, Ancient Rivers: Contemporary African Artists in a Generation of Change* (Washington, DC, and London, 1992)

CHRISTINE MULLEN KREAMER

Tōgō, Seiji [Tetsuharu] (*b* Kagoshima, 28 April 1897; *d* Kumamoto, 25 April 1978). Japanese painter. He moved to Tokyo at an early age and graduated from Aoyama Gakuin Middle School in 1914. He became familiar with the work of the Futurists, Cubists and Expressionists through the composer Kōsaku Yamada (1886–1965), who had recently returned from studying in Germany. In 1915 Tōgō held a one-man show in Hibiya, Tokyo, of works that revealed the influence of these European styles. On the recommendation of Ikuma Arishima (1882–1974), an oil painter and one of the founder-members of the Nikakai, he showed the Futurist work *Woman with Parasol* (priv. col., see Uemura, pl. 2) in the third exhibition of the Nikakai (Jap. 'second division society'; an association of artists influenced by Western styles founded in 1914) in 1916, for which he was awarded the Nika prize. In 1921 he went to France, also visiting Marinetti in Turin. There he participated briefly in the Futurist movement until his disillusionment with its increasingly political stance led him to return to Paris.

During his stay in France, Tōgō established an individual style depicting figures structured in a Cubist manner suffused with melancholic tone. In 1928 he returned to Japan and showed 23 of the paintings he had done in France, including *Street Performers* (1926; Tokyo, N. Mus. Mod. A.), at the 15th exhibition of the Nikakai. These attracted favourable attention, and in 1930 he became a member of the Nikakai. After this he took the female form as his principal subject and only modified his style in terms of its increased sophistication and decorative qualities. When the Nikakai re-formed shortly after the war, he became active in its management. In 1960 he was appointed a member of the Japanese Academy of Fine Arts.

BIBLIOGRAPHY

T. Uemura: 'Tōgō Seiji: sono geijutsu keisei to gyōseki' [The formation of the art and achievement of Tōgō Seiji], *Tōgō Seiji gashū* [The collected paintings of Tōgō Seiji] (Tokyo, 1981)
J. Tanaka: *Kokorosabishiki kyōjin* [Tōgō Seiji, the lonely leader] (Tokyo, 1983)

TORU ASANO

Tōgo Murano. *See* MURANO, TŌGO.

Togyū Okumura. *See* OKUMURA, TOGYŪ.

Tōhaku. *See* Hasegawa tōhaku.

Toidze, Mose (Ivanovich) (*b* Tiflis [now Tbilisi], 21 Jan 1871; *d* Tbilisi, 17 June 1953). Georgian painter. He studied at the trade school in Tiflis and began working as a master metalworker and blacksmith. His drawing ability was such that he was encouraged to study at the Academy of Arts, St Petersburg. He studied in the studio of Il'ya Repin, whose ideas on Critical Realism in painting had an influence on his work. Toidze's interest in national culture was already perceptible in his diploma work *Festival in Mtskheta* (1900–01; Tbilisi, Mus. A. Georgia). It is a vivid and colourful portrayal of local types enjoying a traditional festive meal.

Toidze was attracted to images of working people and local types before and after the Revolution of 1917. His painting *Revolution* (1918; untraced, sketch in Tbilisi, Mus. A. Georgia) is a dramatic portrayal of social upheaval, but in the 1920s he became concerned with depicting the new public and social conditions. *The Smiths* (early 1920s; Tbilisi, Mus. A. Georgia), in which the twilight interior of the forge is illuminated by a mysterious light pouring from the fire, emphasizes the beauty and energy of the movements and the tense rhythms of the labour of the blacksmiths. During and after World War II, Toidze portrayed the patriotic feelings of the people in such paintings as the *Women of Tbilisi Preparing Gifts for the Front* (1944; Tbilisi, Mus. A. Georgia). He painted many portraits of his contemporaries, as well as landscapes and cityscapes, for example *Moonlit Night* (1903; priv. col.) and *Old Tbilisi* (1935; priv. col.), which are distinguished in their use of colour and their ornamentation. He was well known as a teacher; he founded the People's Art Studio in Tbilisi in 1922 and taught from 1930 to 1953 at the Academy of Arts, Tbilisi.

BIBLIOGRAPHY
Sh. K. Kvaskhvadze: *Mose Ivanovich Toidze* (Moscow, 1965)
O. Piralishvili: *Mose Toidze* (Tbilisi, 1971)

N. YEZERSKAYA

Toke, Brian. *See* Tuke, brian.

Tokelau. Group of three atolls (Fakaofo, Nukunonu and Atafu) in the South Pacific Ocean. Tokelau was proclaimed part of New Zealand in 1948. The population (1690; 1986 census) speaks a distinctive Polynesian language and shares a common culture and history. The major art forms of mat plaiting and canoe building have continued to be practised from the 1840s, when they were first recorded in some detail (Wilkes; Hale), into the late 20th century. While these art forms are basically utilitarian, the best works are judged exemplary by local aesthetic criteria and their makers' expertise recognized. Sources of information on Tokelauan art are limited (see bibliography), and there are no major museum collections.

A skilled female mat maker knows the full range of mat types. These are defined by the diagonal patterns produced by the arrangement of lighter and darker, dyed pandanus fibres. An expert produces a mat with straight sides and a smooth surface through her tight and even plaiting. Durable, often elegant mats are made as domestic furnishings. Pliable, soft mats are made from a particular variety

Tokelau *tufuga* (master canoe maker) shaping the fitted pieces of a canoe, temporarily secured by sennit lashings

of pandanus, processed to produce white, paper-thin fibres. Only very skilled women plait these fine mats.

Men skilled in shaping and fitting wood are called *tufuga* (experts), and every canoe is made by a designated *tufuga* (see fig.). A Tokelau canoe may be described as a three-dimensional jigsaw puzzle. It is constructed of timber from the heartwood of a scarce, slow-growing tree of the Boraginaceae family (*Cordia subcordata*), meticulously shaped, fitted and lashed together. The short trunk portions of three trees are required for the hull of a proper canoe. After hollowing and rough shaping, these sections are aligned, shaped to fit tightly together and joined with sennit lashing. The timbers are finely worked with an adze to produce an even surface and uniform thickness. Upon this base, the sides of the vessel are built up to the required height, with planks shaped to fit exactly the irregular edges of the joined hollowed hull sections, and lashed to it. An outrigger, supported by booms and struts, is attached. Although others assist the *tufuga*, it is he who does the time-consuming work of designing the canoe, positioning the timbers and executing the fine adze work. The finished canoe is his creation and testimony to his reputation.

BIBLIOGRAPHY
EWA: 'Micronesian Cultures'
C. Wilkes: *Narrative of the United States Exploring Expedition during the Years 1838, 1839, 1840, 1841, 1842*, v (Philadelphia, 1844), pp. 5–19
H. Hale: *Ethnography and Philology* (Philadelphia, 1846)
G. H. MacGregor: *Ethnology of Tokelau Islands*, Bishop Mus. Bull., cxlvi (Honolulu, 1937)
L. Hanson and F. A. Hanson: *The Art of Oceania: A Bibliography*, Ref. Pubns A. Hist. (Boston, MA, 1984)

JUDITH HUNTSMAN

Tok-kala [anc. Darsan]. Site in Khwarazm (now in Uzbekistan) that flourished from the 1st century BC to the 11th–12th century AD. The 8 ha site is 14 km north-west of Nukus. The different cultural layers have been studied in varying detail. Of greatest interest is the material from Gudkova's 1962–4 excavations of the early medieval necropolis (7th–8th century; Nukus, Karakalpakiya Reg. mus.; St Petersburg, Hermitage), where all burials were

Tok-kala, plaster ossuary with painted scene of mourning, h. 420mm, 8th century AD (St Petersburg, Hermitage)

conducted according to Zoroastrian rites in small underground crypts (outer size 4×5 m; internal space 2.5×2.5 m). Special niches in these crypts contained sandstone, ceramic and plaster ossuaries with sloping lids and usually on small legs. Many of the ossuaries were decorated with drawings and paintings, from the simplest sun and moon symbols to more complex multi-figural compositions, usually with scenes of mourning (see fig.). In addition, there are over 100 Khwarazm inscriptions on the ossuaries of which more than 20 are complete. Some inscriptions contain, *inter alia*, dates in an unknown era. Livshitz suggested on the basis of the archaeological and numismatic evidence that this unknown era probably began around the first quarter of the 1st century AD, which provides a date range for the inscriptions of 658–738 AD. The inscriptions on the Tok-kala ossuaries, in addition to dated documents from the excavations of the Khwarazm site of Toprak Kala and dated Khwarazm chalices, provide the main chronological evidence for Khwarazm.

BIBLIOGRAPHY
A. V. Gudkova: *Tok-kala* (Tashkent, 1964)
S. P. Tolstov and V. A. Livshitz: 'Decipherment and Interpretation of the Khwarezmian Inscriptions from Tok Kala', *Acta Ant. Acad. Sci. Hung.*, xii/1–2 (1964), pp. 231–51
A. V. Gudkova and V. A. Livshitz: 'Novyye khorezmiyskiye nadpisi iz nekropolya Tok-kaly i problema "khorezmiyskoy ery"' [New Khwarazm inscriptions from the necropolis of Tok-kala and the problem of the 'Khwarazm era'], *Vestnik Karakalpakskogo filiala Akad. Nauk Uzbek. SSR*, xxvii/1 (1967), pp. 3–19
V. A. Livshitz: 'The Khwarezmian Calendar and the Eras of Ancient Chorasmia', *Acta Ant. Acad. Sci. Hung.*, xvi/1–4 (1968), pp. 433–46
YE. V. ZEYMAL'

Tokkuz-sarai Monastery. *See* TUMSHUK.

Tokkuz-tepa. *See* KALA-I KAFIRNIGAN.

Tokoname. Centre of ceramics production in western Chita (Aichi Prefect.), Japan. Tokoname, together with other important centres such as BIZEN, SHIGARAKI, SETO, TANBA and ECHIZEN, is famous for its continuous production to the present day (*see* JAPAN, §VIII, 3(ii)). The origins of the ware can be traced back to the 12th century, when increased agricultural development encouraged the spread of high-fired ceramics techniques from the central SANAGE kiln complex, near the city of Nagoya, to neighbouring districts, including Higashiyama, Atsumi and Tokoname. Evidence for the Sanage lineage is seen in the Tokoname tunnel kilns (*anagama*; *see* JAPAN, §VIII, 1(v)) with a dividing pillar, variously placed at the fire-mouth or inside the kiln at the base of the slope. Unlike the Sanage potters, however, the Tokoname potters made larger vessels by coiling rather than with the potter's wheel.

Before the 16th century, Tokoname kilns made three principal products: narrow-mouthed jars (*tsubo*), used as food containers, cinerary urns or burial containers for *sūtra*s (an important sub-type is a tall jar with three horizontal grooves on the body); wide-mouthed jars (see fig.), also for storage; and bowls, which were produced in two basic sizes. The small bowls, known as YAMACHAWAN, were used as serving dishes, and the larger as mixing bowls and as covers for larger jars. Because of the proximity of the town to the coast, Tokoname ware was shipped all over the country. An enormous number of kilns have been discovered. All produced unglazed wares, although these are often coated by a natural ash glaze deposited during firing.

In the 16th century there was a contraction of the industry, with the remaining kilns clustering around Tokoname. Unlike other prominent early kilns, Tokoname failed to produce significant numbers of wares for the tea ceremony (*see* JAPAN, §XIV), and instead continued to produce utilitarian wares. A significant new development took place at Tokoname in the late 19th century, when local potters began to produce finely crafted vessels for steeped-tea drinking (*sencha*). A white variety of ware was called *hakudei* and a more ubiquitous red variety called *shūdei*. These were sometimes incised or carved with pictorial motifs or poems and then burnished. No glaze was applied. Today's Tokoname production ranges from large-scale production of red-clay pipe and sanitary china to the activities of small workshop potters working in the unglazed stoneware and burnished earthenware traditions.

Tokoname, wide-mouthed jar (*ōgame*), unglazed stoneware, h. 573 mm, 13th–14th centuries (Tokoname, Ceramic Art Research Institute)

BIBLIOGRAPHY
I. Akahane and K. Onoda: *Tokoname, Atsumi* (1975), viii of *Nihon tōji zenshū* [Complete collection of Japanese ceramics], ed. M. Satō and others (Tokyo, 1975–7)
I. Akahane: 'Tokoname', *Nihon yakimono shūsei* [Collection of Japanese ceramics], ii, ed. C. Mitsuoka, S. Hayashiya and S. Narasaki, ii (Tokyo, 1981), pp. 109–15
Y. Sawada: *Tokoname*, Famous Ceramics of Japan, vii (Tokyo, 1982)
Nihon no tōji [Japanese ceramics] (exh. cat., ed. Y. Yabe; Tokyo, N. Mus., 1985)

RICHARD L. WILSON

Tokonoma. Alcove for seating or decorative display in a traditional Japanese room. In the Kamakura period (1185–1333) this space was set aside for the display of devotional objects in a Buddhist monastic setting; typically a hanging scroll or scrolls were placed on the rear wall of the space and a candle, flowerpot and incense burner in front. Monks would recite *sūtra*s in a hall where this altar-like setting was the main decoration. At different times the *tokonoma* was used for a variety of other purposes. The space was sometimes two-thirds the width of a major audience chamber, and a section of its floor was raised above the rest of the room, in some cases by up to 200 mm. It was therefore a suitable place of honour, where high-ranking warriors and aristocrats sat to give audiences to their social inferiors. The *tokonoma* was commonly found in rooms in the *shoin zukuri* ('book hall or study construction') format (*see* JAPAN, §III, 4(ii)(a)), adjacent to a wall space containing a set of *chigaidana* (staggered shelves). Typically, treasured objects were displayed in this style of room, on these shelves, on another shelf at the base of a window and in the *tokonoma*. Later, a *tokonoma* was included, even in very small rooms, not as a space for seating but for the display of objects used to set the tone

for ritual tea consumption (*see* JAPAN, §XIV, 2). When so intended, it often occurred in abbreviated forms, such as a raised platform with *tsudekoko* (storage shelves) beneath it. In some cases, an *oshi ota* (polished board) at the base of a wall was substituted for the raised alcove.

BIBLIOGRAPHY
Kodansha Enc. Japan: 'Flower arrangement'; 'Kakemono'

ROBERT W. KRAMER

Tōkō Shin'etsu [Xin yue; Shōun] (*b* Puyang, nr Hangzhou, Zhejiang Prov., 1639; *d* Mito, Ibaragi Prefect., 1695). Chinese Zen monk, seal-carver, calligrapher, poet and musician, active in Japan. He left his family at the age of seven and entered the Buddhist order, first training in Jiangxi Province and eventually in Hangzhou. In 1677 he emigrated to Japan, at the invitation of the monk Chin'i Dōryō of Kōfukuji, an Obaku-sect Zen temple in Nagasaki. He took up missionary work but found himself at odds with Ōbaku monks and for a short time was held in temple confinement. In 1681 the daimyo of Mito, Tokugawa Mitsukuni (1628–1700), hearing of this situation, invited Shin'etsu to his fiefdom, where in 1692 he became founding abbot of Mitsukuni's temple, Jushōzan Gionji (formerly Tentokuji) in Mito, later the place of his burial. Shin'etsu's school of Buddhism is known as the Jushō or Shin'etsu school of Sōtō Zen.

Shin'etsu is best known as an artist and true literatus. Together with DOKURYŪ SHŌEKI, he is one of the most important figures in the early history of Japanese seal-carving. Through their efforts, seal-carving was accepted as an art form. Shin'etsu himself was adept in the decorative designs of the Modern school of seal-carving (Kindaiha) and was respected for bringing to Japan technically modern Chinese methods of seal-carving (*see also* JAPAN, §XVI, 20). He also brought with him Chinese books of seal script (Jap. *tensho*; Chin. *zhuanshu*), which served as significant reference sources. Many seals carved by Shin'etsu and his two-volume seal album, *Kaizan jikoku inran*, are preserved at Gionji.

Shin'etsu was a talented calligrapher in regular (Jap. *kaisho*; Chin. *kaishu*), running or semi-cursive (Jap. *gyōsho*; Chin. *xingshu*), cursive (Jap. *sōsho*; Chin. *caosho*) and clerical (Jap. *reisho*; Chin. *lishu*) scripts. As a painter he executed studies of religious personalities, such as the Zen patriarch Daruma (Skt Bodhidharma), but excelled at the literati theme of the 'four gentlemen' (bamboo, plum, orchid and chrysanthemum), for example *Bamboo in the Wind* (USA, priv. col.; see Addiss, pl. 43). Shin'etsu was one of the notable exponents of Japanese *Zenga* ('Zen pictures'; *see* JAPAN, §VI, 4(vii)).

BIBLIOGRAPHY
F. Asano, ed.: *Tōkō zenshū* [Complete collection of Tōkō's works], 2 vols (Tokyo, 1911)
K. Nakai: *Nihon in hitozute* [Accounts of Japanese seal carvers] (Tokyo, 1915)
M. Ishizaki: *Kinsei Nihon ni okeru Shina zokugo bungakushi* [Chinese vernacular literature relating to pre-modern Japan] (Tokyo, 1940)
R. H. van Gulik: *Minmatsu gisō Tōkō zenshi shūkan* [Publication of the late Ming devoted Zen master, Tōkō] (Taiwan, 1944)
Y. Nakata, ed.: *Nihon no tenkoku* [Japanese seal-carving] (Tokyo, 1966)
K. Kanda: *Nihon ni okeru Chūgoku bungaku: I* [Chinese literature relating to Japan: I] (1985), vi of *Kanda Kiichirō zenshū* [Complete collection of the works of Kanda Kiichirō] (Kyoto, 1983–93)

The Art of Zen: Paintings and Calligraphy by Japanese Monks, 1600–1925
(exh. cat. by S. Addiss; Lawrence, U.KS, Spencer Mus. A., 1989)

NORIHISA MIZUTA

Tōkō Shinoda. *See* SHINODA, TŌKŌ.

Tokugawa period. *See* EDO PERIOD.

Tokuoka, Shinsen (*b* Kyoto, 14 Feb 1896; *d* Kyoto, 9 June 1972). Japanese painter. He graduated from Kyoto Municipal School of Fine Art in 1917. After considerable success as a student and the expectations of him in *Nihonga* (Japanese-style painting) circles, he was greatly shocked by repeated rejections of his submissions to the Bunten exhibitions. Tormented about his own art, he left the art world in 1919 to live as a recluse in Iwabuchi, on the lower slopes of Mt Fuji. In 1923 he began anew, returning to Kyoto and successfully submitting the painting *Poppy* to the Sixth Teiten exhibition (1925). His subsequent activities centred on the official Teiten, New Bunten and Nitten exhibitions, and in particular the works *Carp*, *Red Pine* and *Harvested Rice Field* (all Tokyo, N. Mus. Mod. A.) were highly regarded for their images based on profound introspection and expressed symbolically in simple forms. He became a member of the Japan Art Academy in 1957 and was awarded the Order of Cultural Merit in 1966.

BIBLIOGRAPHY
Tokuoka Shinsen isakuten katarogu (exh. cat., Tokyo, N. Mus. Mod. A., 1974)
Y. Iwasaki: *Tokuoka Shinsen* (Tokyo, 1979)

YOSHIKAZU IWASAKI

Tokusai. *See* TESSHŪ TOKUSAI.

Tokuyūsai. *See* HON'AMI, (1).

Tokyo [formerly Edo]. Capital city of Japan, on the Musashi Plain on the eastern side of Honshu. This site has been occupied since at least the Jōmon period (*c.* 10,000–*c.* 300 BC). The official date of the founding of the city is taken to be 1457, when the daimyo Ōta Dōkan (1432–86) built a castle on the site. From 1603 to 1867, when it was the seat of the Tokugawa shogunate, the city was known as Edo ('mouth of the river'). By the 1990s Tokyo covered an area of 2168 sq. km and had a population of 11,855,563 (1993).

I. Urban development. II. Art life. III. Buildings and gardens.

I. *Urban development.*

Strategically situated at the head of the Kantō Plain, where the River Sumida flows into Edo (Tokyo) Bay, Tokyo has been the most important city in eastern Japan since 1603, when Tokugawa Ieyasu (1543–1615) made it the seat of his shogunal government (*see* EDO PERIOD). Until that time, Edo had been little more than a provincial backwater dominated by the castle built by Ōta Dōkan. On assuming control in 1590, Ieyasu undertook a vast land reclamation programme that included digging canals and moats and draining the swampy delta area to make it suitable for urbanization. By the 1720s the city had undergone a remarkable population explosion (to *c.* 1.3 million) and physical expansion that made it one of the largest cities in the world. About half this population were samurai and the rest commoners or *chōnin* ('people of the *chō*': a reference to the blocklike divisions of the residential areas; *see* JAPAN, §IV, 3(ii) and fig. 46). Of the samurai, about half were permanent residents of the city, while the other half were single men, travelling retainers of the daimyo, who, in accordance with the policy of *sankin kōtai* ('alternate attendance'), had to spend alternate years in the city. The presence of this large group of affluent transients caused a gender imbalance that affected the cultural character of Edo.

The city's original layout and zoning patterns were designed symbolically to reinforce the Tokugawa government's ideology and prestige. Maintaining the social hierarchy and, especially, establishing visible distinctions between samurai and *chōnin* were important components of this policy. Edo was conceived as a spiral, with an immense castle (*see* §III, 1 below) at its centre and major roads and waterways emanating from it like the spokes of a wheel. The castle's central grounds alone covered some 73 ha, an area deemed large enough to house 260 daimyo and 50,000 standard-bearers in case of attack. Until it was destroyed by fire in 1657, its five-storey donjon (58.6 m from base to top) towered nearly 84 m above Edo Bay. The spiral-shaped moat surrounding the castle merged into the estuary of the River Sumida, one of the city's three major waterways.

The environs of the castle and the hilly area to the west of it, known as Yamanote ('foothills'; sometimes called the High City), were reserved for daimyo and their retainers. Their *Shoin*-style residences (*see* JAPAN, §III, 4(ii)(a)) were situated on large walled estates entered through an imposing gateway. Roughly 70% of the city's land was owned by samurai. The low-lying area to the east, much of it on reclaimed land criss-crossed by canals and bridges, was reserved for merchants and artisans. This part of the city was known as Shitamachi (Low City). Wealthy merchants occupied buildings with large shop-fronts opening directly on to the street and living quarters in the back. Both low-ranking samurai and less affluent *chōnin* lived in terraced houses (*nagaya*), constructed largely of wood, which made fire a constant danger. With the growth of a money economy, this area became the heart of the city's vigorous commercial and artistic life.

The strict segregation of samurai and townsmen began to break down after the Great Meireki Fire of 1657 destroyed two-thirds of the city and more than 100,000 of its inhabitants lost their lives. The less hierarchical pattern of subsequent urban development contributed to the growing interaction between samurai and *chōnin* and in so doing laid the foundation for the popular culture of Edo. Daimyo and their retainers began to build residences in various parts of the city, and shrines, temples and the official brothel district were also moved to the outskirts. Originally the River Sumida formed the eastern boundary of the city, but rebuilding after the fire extended to the far bank as well. As the city sprawled outwards, it absorbed many villages and farms, blurring the separation between urban and rural life.

After the Tokugawa shogunate was overthrown, the Meiji emperor moved his residence from Kyoto to Edo, which was known thereafter as Tokyo (Eastern Capital). During the Meiji period (1868–1912) the appearance of

1. Tokyo, view of old and post-war parts of the city

the city was gradually transformed by the introduction of Westernized innovations. Wheeled vehicles came into use for the first time: rickshaws, replacing palanquins, horse-drawn buses, and trolley-buses, first drawn by horses and later electrified. The dry-goods shops seen in Hiroshige's prints metamorphosed into large, modern department stores. The first railway line, linking Tokyo and Yokohama, was completed in 1872.

Fires continued to be a problem. Following a fire in the Ginza district in 1872, the area was rebuilt with Western-style brick buildings (since destroyed) and gas streetlights. (The Ginza remains the most fashionable shopping area of Tokyo; it is also the location of the most prestigious art galleries.) Plans to fireproof the entire city by rebuilding in brick and cement did not materialize. Wood continued to be the main building material for ordinary purposes. However, an increasing number of large public buildings were constructed in a Western style, partly because they were essential symbols of the new political order. Among the first of these were 300 Neo-classical fire-proof brick and cement commercial structures erected at Ginza to the design of the English architect Thomas J. Waters. At the heart of the Western-style building boom was the English architect JOSIAH CONDER, who was retained by the Ministry of Technology from 1877. Conder was highly eclectic and partial to the grand style in public buildings. His most famous work, the Rokumeikan (completed 1883, destr. 1941) was a splendid two-storey stuccoed brick structure in Italianate style with Mediterranean arcades on each floor. Built to function as a lodging for foreign guests and a gathering-place for the élite, it was intended to demonstrate to the world that the Japanese were civilized

and enlightened. The Mitsubishi office building, a three-storey red-brick structure in the Second Empire style, was completed in Marunouchi in the 1890s by Conder and his former student, Sone Tatsuzo. Other buildings by Conder's students included the Renaissance-style office building of the Bank of Japan (1895) and Tokyo Central Station (1914) by KINGO TATSUNO and the Akasaka Detached Palace (1909), modelled after Versailles, by TOKUMA KATAYAMA (see JAPAN, §III, 5 and fig. 38).

Major buildings constructed in Tokyo during the early 20th century either reflected current trends in Western architecture or attempted to reproduce older Japanese forms in modern materials. The most famous building in the city, Frank Lloyd Wright's Imperial Hotel (completed 1922, destr. 1968), combined Japanese and Western styles; but the Japanese were less impressed by its stylistic qualities than by its technological excellence, dramatically demonstrated by its survival of the great earthquake of 1923. The earthquake and the devastating fire that followed it destroyed most of the old Low City. Ambitious plans for rebuilding were slowed in the 1930s by the worldwide depression and then by the war effort. In addition, the extreme nationalism of the war years limited the permissible range of expression in architecture, as in other art forms.

The city incurred a second round of massive destruction in the fire-bombing of 1945, losing 770,000 buildings. Reconstruction after World War II was slow during the first decade but made dramatic progress during the late 1950s and the 1960s, as showcased at the 1964 Tokyo Olympic Games. The buildings designed for the Games by Kenzō Tange, with their upward-swirling roofs (for illustration *see* TANGE, KENZŌ), are the most famous examples of contemporary Japanese architecture. Near by are the districts of Aoyama and Akasaka, fashionable shopping and residential areas with many more examples of fine modern architecture (*see also* JAPAN, §III, 5). Edo Castle, now the Imperial Palace, was rebuilt in 1968 after destruction by bombing in 1945. The present palace complex, called the Kyūden, maintains some traditional features, with gently sloping roofs (*irimoya zukuri*, 'hip-and-gable roof construction'), and the interiors of the residential facilities incorporate a distillation of the *Shoin* style (*see also* PALACE, §VI, 3).

Although Tange and other architects devised elaborate plans for the development of Tokyo (*see* URBAN PLANNING, fig. 17), the expansion that actually occurred in the 1960s and 1970s was largely unplanned and haphazard (see fig. 1). Tokyo has severe problems of traffic, pollution and congestion. One response to population pressure has been the decentralization of government and commerce, with the creation of secondary city centres in outlying areas, such as Shinjuku to the west, where the new metropolitan government offices are located.

Since the 1980s the number of high-rise skyscrapers has increased enormously, posing a potential hazard in an earthquake zone. New structural engineering techniques have been used with a view to earthquake-proofing, but, since no major earthquake has occurred in recent years in the region, their effectiveness remains untested. Although few physical traces remain, the layout of central Tokyo still reflects the Edo of the shogunate. The Imperial Palace is surrounded by government offices instead of daimyo mansions. Underground and surface train lines follow the paths of the old castle moat. The Tōkaidō route to Kyoto is traversed by the high-speed 'bullet' trains of the Shinkansen (New Trunk Line).

II. Art life.

1. Edo period (1600–1868). 2. Meiji period (1868–1912) and after.

1. EDO PERIOD (1600–1868). In the early decades of its history, Edo was the fountainhead of economic and political power in Japan, but cultural authority was still concentrated in the Kansai (Kyoto–Osaka areas), the nation's traditional centre of artistic production. Nearly a century passed before Edo developed a distinctive identity, largely by drawing on and transforming the culture of the Kansai. The autonomous culture that emerged in Edo in the 18th century was created and supported primarily by merchants, artisans and lower-level samurai living in Shitamachi. Merchants were the lowest of the four classes, but in fact many, especially those who provided cash in exchange for the rice stipends of the samurai, became extremely wealthy. Sumptuary regulations were issued periodically to curb their conspicuous consumption, but to little avail. The energies of the *chōnin* became focused on hedonism, and in particular on the ephemeral pleasures of the 'floating world' (*ukiyo*).

The creative energies unleashed by Edo's urban social mix were given their most eloquent expression in woodblock prints and illustrated books (*see* JAPAN, §IX, 3). These are now commonly known as *ukiyoe* ('pictures of the floating world'), but in the Edo period they were generally known as *Edoe* ('Edo pictures') or *azuma nishikie* ('eastern brocade pictures'; eastern being an allusion to the city's location). Prints celebrated the activities centring around Edo's *kabuki* theatres (*see* JAPAN, §XIII, 2), the Yoshiwara brothel district, and the city's main scenic landmarks (*meisho*).

The theatre district was initially near the Nihonbashi Bridge, in the centre of the Low City, but in 1841, after this area was destroyed by fire, the theatres were relocated in the north-western part of the city, in the vicinity of Asakusa. Izumo no Okuni (*fl* 1600), the legendary founder of *kabuki*, performed at Edo Castle in 1604, and the first *kabuki* theatre in the shogunal city was established in 1624. Following the fire of 1657, four main theatres were licensed: the Nakamuraza, the Ichimuraza, the Moritaza and the Yamamuraza. When the last was closed in 1714 as the result of a scandalous affair between one of its actors and a lady-in-waiting of the shogun's mother, the other theatres became known as Edo Sanza ('three theatres of Edo'). The pre-eminent theatre was the Nakamuraza, where Ichikawa Danjurō I in 1673 premiered a new style of acting known as *aragoto* ('rough stuff'). This flamboyant and exaggerated technique was more popular in Edo than the soft, romantic *wagoto* ('gentle') style associated with the Kansai. The Danjurō line of actors remained the greatest stars of the Edo stage throughout the period and were glorified in numerous woodblock prints.

The origins of the Edo licensed quarter date from 1617 when a group of brothel-owners was granted a tract of land in a marshy area known as Yoshiwara (Field of Reeds). This district, walled and moated, opened in 1618. Prostitution elsewhere in the city was illegal, though nevertheless practised. After the 1657 fire, the Yoshiwara was relocated to a site on the northern edge of the city and rebuilt in the same form as before. Within the walls of the New Yoshiwara (Shin Yoshiwara) the inmates were organized into a strictly regulated hierarchy, like all other groups in society under the Tokugawa regime. At the top were the *tayū*, chosen for their beauty and charm and trained from childhood in traditional arts such as calligraphy and flower arrangement. A courtesan typically began her career as a teenager and retired in her late twenties. Other women associated with the licensed quarter, but not technically prostitutes, included geishas, who entertained with music and witty conversation, and waitresses at the tea houses. Beautiful women, especially the courtesans with their elaborate hairstyles and gorgeous costumes, became one of the most important subjects for *ukiyoe* paintings and prints.

The pursuit of pleasure central to Edo artistic life was given expression in many new aesthetic terms, of which the legacy is felt even in modern Tokyo. Central among these is *iki*, a key concept that captures the essence of Edo chic. Historically, it was a quality acquired by *chōnin* and samurai who frequented the pleasure quarters. Those urban sophisticates who possessed it were designated *tsū* and were noted for dressing in the latest fashion, for skill in the literary and visual arts, and, above all, for knowledge in amatory matters. As Edo eclipsed Kyoto and Osaka in the 18th century, this cultural ideal supplanted the *sui*, the more easygoing Kansai aesthetic ideal. As the embodiment of many of the qualities admired by Edo's inhabitants, the

Edokko ('child of Edo') also played a key role in the city's artistic imagination. An *Edokko* was variously defined as one born between the bridges of Nihonbashi and Kyōbashi, in the heart of the Low City; as a parishioner of either the Kanda Daimyōjin or the Sannō Daigongen shrine, the two Shinto shrines that alternately held an annual festival, which was the major such event in the city; or as one whose family had lived in Edo for three generations. He (for the *Edokko* was typically masculine) was a champion of the popular culture who rejected both the pretensions of the samurai and the frugality of the merchants and enjoyed a fashionable lifestyle regardless of the expense. During the 19th century, when the image of the *Edokko* slipped down the socio-economic scale, firemen and fishmongers, rather than wealthy playboys, came to be regarded as prime examples.

The Yoshiwara and the many tea houses in its environs were the favourite setting for such cultural events as poetry and painting competitions, which attracted participants of both sexes from a wide range of backgrounds. In the 17th century and the early 18th, parties at which participants composed classical *waka* (31-syllable verse) or 17-syllable *haikai* were common, but in the late 18th century these were overshadowed in popularity by *kyōka* ('mad verse') parties. *Kyōka* incorporated the wit, irony and parody that were trademarks of Edo's literary and visual arts. Painting and calligraphy gatherings (*kaigakai* and *shogakai*), where, for a fee, individuals could display their talents before a professional artist and judge, became the rage in the 19th century. The friendships between writers, artists and publishers formed in this convivial setting were the catalysts for the creation of many sumptuously illustrated books and prints as well as for impromptu collaborative paintings by artists from various schools (*sekiga*).

The *sakariba*, open spaces where crowds could gather for recreational activities of all kinds, were as integral to artistic life in Edo as they were in other large cities. The two chief *sakariba* were along the banks of the Sumida in the vicinity of Ryōgoku Bridge and around the temple of Asakusa. These were the settings for carnivals and peep-shows (*misemono*), dramatic and dance performances and painting demonstrations by artists.

The love of the citizens for their city extended to its physical landmarks. The tradition of *meisho* ('famous places'), scenic spots celebrated for centuries in both poetry and painting, was transferred to an urban setting. The Ryōgoku Bridge over the River Sumida, known especially for boating and fireworks on summer evenings, was perhaps the most famous of these sites. Another was Nihonbashi, the central point from which radiated the roads to the various provinces (including the famous Tōkaidō, which linked Edo and Kyoto), the site of the city's famous fish market and the traditional centre of the old *chōnin* area. Other noted spots included the grounds of Shinto shrines and Buddhist temples, such as the Kameidō Tenjin Shrine with its arched bridge and wisteria blossoms, or the gigantic red lantern at the ancient Kinryūzan Temple (founded *c.* AD 628) in Asakusa, on the way to the Yoshiwara. *Meisho* appeared in popular literature and illustrated guidebooks from the 17th century; in the 19th century they were depicted in single-sheet, colour

woodblock prints, such as the series *One Hundred Famous Views of Edo* by ANDŌ HIROSHIGE.

Although colour woodblock prints were celebrated throughout the country as *meibutsu* ('famous products') of the city, artistic production in Edo was not limited to prints. Edo also boasted painters, sculptors, lacquerers and metalworkers, many of whom were employed by the shogunate of the daimyo. Chief among these were the KANŌ SCHOOL and SUMIYOSHI SCHOOL of painting, the Igarashi and Kōami families of lacquerers and the Gotō family of metalworkers.

As the official painters (*gōyo eshi*) to the shogunate, artists of the Kanō school were at the pinnacle of the painting world in Edo. The four main branches of this school are known, after the locations of their studios, as Kajibashi, Kōbikichō, Nakabashi and Hamachō. With the exception of the Kajibashi studio founded by Kano Tan'yū (*see* KANŌ, (11)), which was located outside the gate of Edo Castle, all were in Shitamachi. The artists and publishers of prints and illustrated books also lived predominantly near the city centre, especially around Nihonbashi, so as to be near the clientele of the theatre and amusement districts. In the 19th century, however, when prints featuring scenic landmarks in and around Edo became very popular, publishers whose customers were travellers buying prints as souvenirs moved to outlying districts along roads that connected to the Tōkaidō and Kisokaidō, the two main highways linking Edo with Kyoto.

2. MEIJI PERIOD (1868–1912) AND AFTER. In the Meiji period many of the areas around temples and shrines that had functioned as *sakariba* were officially designated as parks. In 1873 the area around the Tokugawa temple complex of Kan'eiji in Ueno became the first of five public parks in the city and the site of Japan's first art museum, zoo and exposition halls. Domestic industrial exhibitions (Naikoku Hakurankai) were inaugurated in 1882, and annual juried exhibitions of painting (Monbushō Bijutsu Tenrankai), sponsored by the Ministry of Education, in 1907. This so-called Bunten exhibition, which included *Nihonga* (Japanese-style painting), *Yōga* (Western-style painting; *see* JAPAN, §VI, 5(iii) and (iv)) and sculpture, continued until 1947. In 1948, however, the name was changed to Nihon Bijutsu Tenrankai or Nitten (Japan Art Exhibition). Still held annually at Ueno Park, it continues to attract a wide number of contributors from all over the country, ensuring Tokyo's continued role as the nation's pre-eminent artistic centre.

With the establishment of the Tokyo School of Fine Arts (1887) and Tokyo Imperial University (1886), the areas around Ueno and nearby Hongo became lively centres of literary and artistic activity. The founder of the Fine Arts School, TENSHIN OKAKURA, the novelists Ōgai Mori (1862–1922) and Sōseki Natsume (1867–1916) and the Western-style sculptor Fumio Asakura (1883–1964) are only a few of the notable figures who have lived in the vicinity.

Although Tokyo was the most important centre for movements in painting, sculpture and decorative arts that continued into the late 19th century and the 20th, the concerns typically expressed by the artists were either highly individual or national and international in scope.

Modern works do not display the strong consciousness of their city that was seen in the popular art and literature of the Edo period. Within the city itself, the cultural balance of power shifted from the Low City of the *Edokko* to the High City of the old samurai and the new intellectual élite. The remaining traces of Edo-period culture came to seem increasingly shabby, lower-class and old-fashioned, though not without nostalgic charm.

From the Taishō period (1912–26) onwards, a new popular culture emerged, fostered by advances in higher education and publishing and especially by cinema. Pioneer efforts in film making in the 1920s laid the foundation for the films that brought international acclaim to Akira Kurosawa (*b* 1910) and other Japanese directors in the 1950s and for an industry that continues to flourish (see fig. 2). The Taishō was also a period of intense absorption of European ideas, despite the fact that there was no museum of Western art, no permanent exhibition of European works of high quality and no systematic body of literature on art history in the Japanese language. The major sources of information were exhibitions of reproduction and periodicals. The early artistic pilgrims who went to Paris to study before World War I experienced shock and confusion as new styles of French painting challenged the academic standards that they had only recently struggled to master. Those who went after 1918 were confronted by the proliferation of even more disruptive styles. Often, after returning to Japan, they struggled long to integrate their experiences in Europe with their innate aesthetic sensibilities and the Japanese environment.

In 1914 MUNEYOSHI YANAGI took as his special mission the preservation of folk crafts and stimulation of their production and appreciation. This led to the founding in 1926 of the MINGEI (folk art) movement and in 1936 of the Mingeikan (Folk Craft Museum) in Tokyo, followed by a nationwide network of other museums that focused attention on beauty in everyday objects. The *Mingei* movement also brought to the fore the contributions of craftsmen, some of whom were eventually designated National Treasures (*see also* JAPAN, §XV).

Artists habitually established and reinforced their personal identities through group membership in exhibiting associations. By forming and re-forming such associations they defined their artistic aims and created circles of like-minded colleagues. The NIKAKAI (Second Division Society) was formed in 1914 by a group including SŌTARŌ YASUI, RYŪZABURŌ UMEHARA and HANJIRŌ SAKAMOTO in opposition to the conservatism of Bunten. The Shun'yōkai (Spring Season Society) was formed in 1922 to create an open association of painters freed from fixed styles and ideologies. These groups and many others represented varying interests among both *Yōga* and *Nihonga* painters. A proliferation of associations has also represented sculptors, craftsmen and various other kinds of artists.

Because of its extraordinary concentration of money and power, modern Tokyo continues to be the centre of the nation's artistic life. Most of the national literary and artistic organizations have their headquarters in the city, and all but a few artists continue to live within commuting

2. Tokyo, film set in 'movie village'

distance. The strong commercial orientation of Edo's artistic life continues in modern Tokyo, where art exhibitions and sales in department stores often rival those held in museums and galleries.

BIBLIOGRAPHY

T. Yazaki: *Nihon toshi no hatten katei* [The development of the Japanese city] (Tokyo, 1962); Eng. trans. by D. L. Swain as *Social Change and the City in Japan: From Earliest Times to the Industrial Revolution* (New York and Tokyo, 1968)

A. Naitō: *Edo to Edojō* [Edo and Edo Castle] (Tokyo, 1966)

K. Kodama and H. Sugiyama: *Tōkyōto no rekishi* [History of Tokyo] (Tokyo, 1969)

A. Naitō: *Edo no toshi kenchiku* [Edo and its architecture] (Tokyo, 1972)

H. D. Smith II: 'Tokyo and London: Comparative Conceptions of the City', *Japan: A Comparative View*, ed. A. M. Craig (Princeton, 1979), pp. 49–99

W. Coaldrake: 'Edo Architecture and Tokugawa Law', *Mnmt Nipponica*, xxxvi/3 (1981), pp. 235–84

E. Seidensticker: *Low City, High City: Tokyo from Edo to the Earthquake* (New York, 1983)

P. Waley: *Tokyo Now and Then* (New York and Tokyo, 1984)

C. Nakane and S. Ōishi, eds: *Edo jidai to kindaika* [The Tokugawa period and modernization] (Tokyo, 1986); Eng. trans. and ed. by C. Totman as *Tokugawa Japan: The Social and Economic Antecedents of Modern Japan* (Tokyo, 1990)

H. D. Smith II: *Hiroshige: One Hundred Famous Views of Edo* (New York, 1986)

P. Pons: *D'Edo et Tokyo: Mémoires et modernités* (Paris, 1988)

H. Suzuki: *Tokyo no geniusu roki* [Tokyo's *genius loci*] (Tokyo, 1990)

C. S. Seigle: *Yoshiwara: The Glittering World of the Japanese Courtesan* (Honolulu, 1993)

The Floating World Revisited (exh. cat., ed. D. Jenkins; Portland, OR, A. Mus.; Cleveland, OH, Mus. A.; 1993–4)

SARAH E. THOMPSON

III. Buildings and gardens.

1. EDO CASTLE [Edojō]. Edo Castle, in Chiyoda Ward, central Tokyo, was the residential and administrative seat of the Tokugawa shogunate from 1603 to 1868. The interior of the old castle became the imperial palace. Edo was an example of a *hirayamajiro* ('flat mountain castle'; castle on a low-lying plateau on a plain; *see* JAPAN, §III, 4(ii)(c)).

Ota Dōkan (Sukenaga; 1432–89), a vassal of the Uesugi family in Echigo Province and a noted patron of poetry, built the first small castle on the site and made it a major salon for Chinese-style Zen (Chin. Chan) poetry (*kanshi*) in the then culturally remote area of eastern Japan. After Dōkan's death, the castle lapsed into obscurity until 1590, when Tokugawa Ieyasu (1543–1616) received the domain from TOYOTOMI HIDEYOSHI. Ieyasu chose the former castle site for his main castle because of its central location on the Kantō Plain. Major work was carried out on the site between 1590 and 1636, substantially changing the surrounding landscape and creating an almost totally new castle, although the orientation of the defences of the original castle was maintained.

Edo Castle had an unusual spiral-shaped moat, which encircled the castle one and a half times before merging with the River Sumida. Five major highways radiated from its environs, and there were watch-tower gates (*mitsuke*) where they met the moat. The outer complex (*gaikaku*) of the completed castle, marked off by the river on the east and by the moat and stone walls elsewhere, was 15.7 km in circumference, 5.5 km north–south and 3.8 km east–west. It was thus the largest in Japan. The *gaikaku* originally enclosed the major residential, religious and commercial areas of the castle town. The base of the best-preserved section of the outer moat and walls between Kanda and Ichigaya now serves as the railway track for the Chūō line in central Tokyo. The outer wall was topped only by pines and cedars and had no defensive breastworks or towers other than at its 11 gates (destr. 1872). The extent of the old outer defences can still be ascertained on a map of modern Tokyo by following a line from Ryōgoku Bridge on the River Sumida anticlockwise to Ochanomizu, Iidabashi, Yotsuya, Akasakamitsuke, Toranomon and Hama Detached Imperial Palace on Tokyo Bay.

The inner complex (*naikaku*) consisted of six enceintes divided by moats and stone walls forming a series of plateaux surrounding and gradually rising up to the Main Enceinte and covering a total area of just over 1 sq. km. Most of the inner castle is occupied by the modern Imperial Palace and its surrounding parks. Of the Tokugawa defensive structures, only three gates (Sakurada, Uchi-Sakurada, Hirakawa), three towers (Fujimi, Fushimi, Sakurada) and the original stone walls and moats remain. The white plastered walls along the top of the stone walls are reconstructions lacking the original distinctive geometric loopholes such as are preserved in Himeji Castle (*see* HIMEJI, §2). The gates maintain the original double-barbican (*masugata*; 'box-shaped') design, the most impregnable and costly form of Japanese castle gate architecture. Edo Castle was extravagantly endowed with *masugata* gates, all but one of which was a variant on the same design, having few of the secondary turrets and towers that gave the form its proper military function.

The principal buildings of Edo Castle are the donjon and the palaces of the inner complex. The main donjon (*tenshukaku*) of the Main Enceinte (1637–57) was a tower in lavish Momoyama-period (1568–1600) style, with five storeys (58.4 m from ground-level to top). In 1657 the Great Meireki Fire destroyed most of the inner castle, but, for economic and political reasons, the donjon was not rebuilt. An indication of the scale of the building is given by the *Edo zu byōbu* ('Screens of Edo scenes'), the most important of which date from the early 1630s (Tokyo, Gotoh Mus.). The palaces of the Main, Second and Third enceintes and the residence of the heir-apparent in the West Enceinte were all constructed in the *shoin zukuri* ('book hall or study construction') format.

The largest palace was in the Main Enceinte. It served as the residence of the shogun, the venue for major ceremonies of state and the offices of the senior administrators. The one-storey complex covered 3.75 ha and was divided into three sections. The exterior (*omote*) section was the public part of the palace where ceremonies and the business of state were conducted. It consisted of three audience halls—the Ōhiroma (Great Hall), Shiroshoin (White Study) and Kuroshoin (Black Study)—and their adjacent chambers. These were all connected by a series of corridors. The Ōhiroma had some *Shoin*-style elements, for example the decorative alcove (*tokonoma*), staggered shelves (*chigaidana*), writing desk (*tsukeshoin*) and decorative sliding panels (*chōdaigamae*). The middle interior (*naka oku*) was an undivided extension of the exterior section. It served as the living-quarters of the shogun and consisted of sleeping chambers, kitchen, bathroom and rooms for attendants. The interior section (*ō oku*) occupied over half the total area of the Main Enceinte palace (*c.* 2.085 ha) and was the living-quarters for the shogun's wife, concubines and ladies-in-waiting. It was divided from the other sections by a copper-faced wall with only two guarded entrances and was shut off to all males except the shogun himself.

The original main palace was a lavishly decorated building in Momoyama style having multiple gables. However, the complex was burnt down four times and rebuilt seven times before being destroyed by fire for the last time in 1863. While the buildings basically followed the pattern established in 1637, the style of decoration became simpler as the Tokugawa experienced increasing financial difficulties. After the destruction of the palace buildings in 1863, a temporary palace was erected in the Western Enceinte, but this too was destroyed by fire, in 1873.

The garden of the Second Enceinte has been restored and reconstructed. This garden is commonly attributed to KOBORI ENSHŪ, but the discovery in the late 20th century of an early map of Edo Castle confirms that Enshū's original design (1635 or 1637) for the garden and its buildings was markedly different. It proved too idiosyncratic for the taste of the shogun, who had Enshū's buildings demolished in 1641 and the garden relandscaped in 1645 to the more conventional design seen in the modern restoration.

BIBLIOGRAPHY

K. Hirai: *Shiro to shoin* [Castles and palaces], Nihon no bijutsu [Arts of Japan], xiii (Tokyo, 1965); Eng. trans. by H. Sato and J. Ciliotta as *Feudal Architecture of Japan*, Heibonsha Surv. Jap. A., xiii (New York and Tokyo, 1973), pp. 147–52
A. Naitō: *Edo to Edojō* [Edo and Edo Castle], SD sensho [SD select writings], iv (Tokyo, 1966)
C. D. Totman: *Politics in the Tokugawa Bakufu, 1600–1843* (Cambridge, MA, 1967)
W. H. Coaldrake: 'Edo Architecture and Tokugawa Law', *Mnmt Nipponica*, xxxvi/3 (1981), pp. 235–84
M. Murai, ed.: *Edo*, Nihon meijō shūsei [Famous castles of Japan], iv (Tokyo, 1984)
L. Komatsu: *Edojō: sono rekishi to kōzō* [Edo Castle: its history and structure] (Tokyo, 1985)
Edojō: Nihon meijō shūsei [Edo Castle: a collection of famous castles of Japan] (Tokyo, 1986)

J. F. MORRIS

2. KŌRAKUEN. Garden illustrating a Japanese *Kaiyū* ('many pleasures') style created by daimyo literati, in which a variety of scenes are constructed around a central pond (*see* GARDEN, §VI, 3). The present 7 ha garden, in Bunkyō Ward, now a public park, is less than a third its original size, but it retains the flavour of a Japanese stroll garden with some continental features.

Kōrakuen was initially laid out in 1629 by Tokudaiji Sahei on the orders of Tokugawa Yorifusa (1603–61), setting the style for other daimyo mansions in the newly established capital city of Edo. It is noted for its allusions to famous sites in Japan and China. Yorifusa began this tradition by naming several features of the garden after famous places in Kyoto, for example a small stream for the River Ōi north-west of Kyoto and an earth-covered bridge for the Tōgetsukyō, which spans the Ōi at Arashiyama. The stream is lined with large pebbles, which give the surface a swift, rippled effect like the rapids at Arashiyama.

The estate was remodelled in the late 17th century by Yorifusa's son Mitsukuni (1628–1700), the governor of Mito Province (now part of Ibaraki Prefect.), to serve as a retreat where he could study Confucian doctrine. Mitsukuni continued the practice of geographical allusions in the garden, choosing as his theme noted sights in China. With the help of the Chinese scholar Zhu Shunshui (1600–82), Mitsukuni constructed a small Confucian temple and re-created in miniature famous sites of China. Two mounds, each *c.* 10 m high and covered with bamboo grass, represent the forested peaks of Mt Lu in Jiangxi Province in eastern China, where the Tang-period (AD 618–907) poet Bai Juyi (AD 772–846) had his hermitage. Near by, a small pond is crossed by a stone walkway and low-arched bridge, miniature versions of the West Lake near Hangzhou, Zhejiang Province, with its causeway built by the scholar and artist Su Shi. Another stone bridge of Chinese style has a high, rounded arch, which, with its reflection, forms a complete circle, hence the name Full Moon Bridge.

At the centre of the Kōrakuen is a large, irregularly shaped pond edged with an extraordinary collection of stones. Because suitable stones could not be found in the locality, many were brought from other areas of Japan. One squared-off boulder is named after the garden's initial designer, Tokudaiji, and forms the head of a tortoise-shaped island called Hōraijima. Around the shores of the pond and in nearby wooded areas are paths for strolling and pavilions for enjoying the changing views. An iris swamp is crossed by an eightfold bridge in reference to a verse written by the Japanese courtier Ariwara no Narihira (AD 825–80). These and other literary and visual allusions made Kōrakuen one of the most famous gardens of 17th-century Japan. Other daimyo gardens, such as the late 17th-century Genkyūen of the Ii family in the old castle town of Hikone, Shiga Prefecture, and the Ritsurinen in Matsumoto, Nagano Prefecture, have elements clearly modelled on Kōrakuen.

BIBLIOGRAPHY

L. Kuck: *The World of the Japanese Garden: From Chinese Origins to Modern Landscape Art* (Tokyo, 1968, rev. 1980)
Kantō, Tōhoku [Kantō and Tōhoku regions] (1979), x of *Tanbō Nihon no niwa* [Investigation of Japanese gardens], ed. T. Soga (Tokyo, 1978–9), pp. 151–2

BRUCE A. COATS

Toledo. Spanish city, the ancient capital of Castile, now the capital of Castilla-La Mancha. It has a population of *c.* 60,000 and is situated *c.* 70 km south of Madrid on the River Tagus. The styles of its buildings and monuments reflect the occupation of the city by Romans, Visigoths, Muslims, Jews and Christians, and it is particularly noted for its buildings in the Mudéjar and Hispano-Flemish (Isabelline) styles. It is renowned as a centre for the production of steel weapons. Toledo is built on seven small hills and almost encircled by the River Tagus (see fig. 1 and GRECO, EL, fig. 5). As in Islamic townships, the houses are crowded together along twisting, narrow streets in a complex of pathways, of which some are dead ends and others are alleys, covered passages or steep gradients dictated by the topography. The buildings are mostly of brick and *mampostería* (a mixture of pebbles and cement), with brick bonding courses. The Roman walls have been

1. Toledo, aerial view

renovated many times, with various types of gate, the most outstanding of which are the two Puertas de Bisagra, the Puerta del Sol, the Puerta de Alcántara and the Puerta de San Martín.

I. History and urban development. II. Art life and organization. III. Centre of metalwork production. IV. Cathedral.

I. History and urban development.

1. To 1085. 2. 1086–1561. 3. After 1561.

1. TO 1085. In 192 BC, after occupation by the Carpetani and subjection to Carthaginian domination, the town was conquered by the Romans and named Toletum. In the *History of Rome* (xxxv.vii.2) Livy wrote that it was a 'small town, made strong by its location'. There are many traces of Roman villas along the River Tagus in the Vega area, which extends in an arc about the hills that form the steep heights of the central nucleus. Remains can still be found of the walled area of the citadel; some fragments are incorporated in the present-day Puente de Alcántara (begun 1259, rebuilt several times), the most famous of the city's bridges, and there are also the ruins of the great circus (423×101 m) with room for 25,000 spectators. Beneath the church of S Ginés is the so-called Cave of Hercules, the remains of a Roman cistern.

The city was converted to Christianity towards the end of the 3rd century AD, its first bishop being Melancio, who attended the Council of Elvira (300) in that capacity. In 418 Toledo was conquered by the Visigoths. Leovigild I (*reg* 568–86) established it as the 'urbs regia', being both the political capital and metropolitan ecclesiastical see, and the Councils that regulated the life of the Visigothic monarchy were held here. Fragments of Early Christian sarcophagi have been preserved, sometimes set into later constructions, such as that found at the Puerta del Sol. Evidence that in the 6th and 7th centuries Toledo was an important artistic centre can be found in walls throughout the city, and further examples have been collected in the Museo de los Concilios y de la Cultura Visigoda in the church of S Román. Remains of the Visigothic city walls have been preserved, as has abundant documentary evidence concerning the numerous basilicas and the building of the defences and gates. Outstanding among the surviving remains is the stone pilaster carved with *Gospel* scenes in the church of S Salvador.

In 712 the city fell to the Muslims, who named it Tolaitola. The riches and splendour of the Visigothic court astonished the Muslims and were greatly praised by them. Tolaitola always felt some rivalry towards and resistance to Córdoban rule and at times enjoyed complete independence. The large community of Mozarabs (Christians

2. Toledo, synagogue of S María la Blanca, 13th century

to Christian use *c.* 1187; now secularized; *see* ISLAMIC ART, §II, 5(iv)(a)). It is built on a near square plan (7.74×8.60 m) with four central columns dividing it into nine compartments with domical rib vaults in the tradition of caliphal architecture at Córdoba. The use of bricks in the construction of this well-preserved mosque was to prove fundamental to the subsequent development of *Mudéjar* art, and after 1085 the Córdoban influence in the design of its vaults provided the link between the Islamic and Christian worlds.

2. 1086–1561. After the conquest of Toledo by the Christians in 1085 the law provided for the co-existence of the three communities, Christian, Islamic and Jewish, which was fundamental to the city's cultural development. Its strategic position in relation to Andalusia determined its political importance, for it was the scene of many battles that to some extent shaped the future of the Castilian kingdom. In the later Middle Ages the Christians became dominant, with the gradual adaptation of Muslims to Christian customs, and an increasing number of converted Jews. Ever more restrictions were placed on the activities of the Jewish community (the Sephardim), who were expelled in 1492. Owing to the special status enjoyed by the Mozarabic population the renovation of churches respected the existing structures, fusing Islamic and Christian forms and techniques. The effects can be seen in the Mozarabic churches of S Sebastián, S Lucas, S Román and S Eulália. Some buildings were built after the Christian conquest in an archaizing style, as can be seen from the small chapel in the ruins of the church of S Lorenzo, the arch of a house in Calle de Bulas Viejas, and in the curious mosque of Las Tornerías (1159), which was built on two storeys to compensate for the steep gradient of the street and replicates in its upper storey the plan of the Bab-al-Mardum mosque. The domed Capilla de Nuestra Señora de Belén in the Convento de Santa Fe with the *Mudéjar* tomb of the *Infante Don Fernando Pérez* (*d* 1242) is also built in an Islamic style.

Three groups of buildings are particularly significant for medieval Toledo: the *Mudéjar* buildings, the synagogues and the secular buildings. The MUDÉJAR style was developed under strong Islamic influence, characterized by the use of bricks, timber ceilings richly decorated with arabesque work, Islamic friezes in both plaster and wood, with elaborate plaster and stucco work, and the systematic use of horseshoe and lobed arches. The earliest surviving examples of churches built in this style in the 13th and 14th centuries are S Bartolomé, S Antolín, Santiago del Arrabal, Santa Fé, the chevet of El Cristo de la Luz and the church of Cristo de la Vega. In the 14th and early 15th centuries churches such as S Tomé, Magdalena, S Clara and S Miguel el Alto were built with rib-vaulted chevets, and *Mudéjar* towers became more common, as, for example, in Santiago del Arrabal, S Román, S Tomé and S Bartolomé. Outstanding examples of synagogues built predominantly in Islamic styles are S María la Blanca (see fig. 2; converted to Christian use *c.* 1550), with its five aisles, horseshoe arches and 13th-century ceiling; and El Tránsito, built in 1366 by Samuel Leví, finance minister to Peter I of Castile (*reg* 1350–69), and converted to Christian use in 1492. It consists of a large rectangular chamber

living under Muslim rule) must have had some influence in this. The city's history was marked by successive uprisings until the creation of the kingdom of Taifa de Toledo at the end of the first quarter of the 11th century. In 1085 this was conquered by Alfonso VI of León (*reg* 1072–1109), who returned the city to Christianity. The Muslim city was located mainly on the highest part of the citadel, in the eastern zone controlling the routes to the north. A castle or *alcazaba*, dominating the Islamic city, was built on the site of the present-day Alcázar. The city wall and its gates were rebuilt, the Puente de Alcántara renovated and the so-called Puerta Vieja de Bisagra, which was much influenced by Córdoban architecture, was opened. The Great Mosque, on which the cathedral was later built, was constructed at the centre of this sector, and the many remains of the period and documentary evidence are witness to the great flowering of Toledan culture. There are many references to the Palacio de Galiana (destr.) with its many outbuildings, which was situated in the area where the Hospital de Santa Cruz was subsequently built (*see* §2 below), and of other adjoining buildings where Alfonso X of Castile and León (*reg* 1252–84) later established his royal office and in which he dictated some of his writings.

An important Islamic monument is the mosque of Bab al-Mardum (999–1000; now El Cristo de la Luz; converted

surmounted by a magnificent wood-panelled ceiling and a richly decorated chevet wall, whose frieze or *arrocabe* fuses Islamic and Gothic forms.

Islamic forms and techniques were equally prevalent in secular building: the comfort and splendour achieved with few resources and the possibility of obtaining cheap materials and labour must all, given the expense of Gothic building, have favoured their use. From the 14th century many splendid palaces were built, and as they were often converted into convents or monasteries many have survived. Outstanding examples are the large group of mansions including the palaces of Casarrubios and Arroyo-molinos that form the Convento de S Isabel de los Reyes, established in 1477, and the conventos de la Concepción Francisca, Ayala, Seminario Menor and S Clara. Many fine façades also survive, for example that of the incorrectly named Palacio del Rey Pedro and that of the Toledo family mansion. Where façades are lost, the city abounds in ceilings, friezes, door- and window-frames. Other notable 14th-century *Mudéjar* buildings include the so-called Palacio de Galiana (rest.) in the old royal orchard or market garden in the Tagus Valley, the magnificent salons of the Casa de Mesa, and those of the Taller del Moro next to the Palacio de Fuensalida. Also dating from the late 14th century are the magnificent Puerta del Sol, with its horseshoe arches and crenellation, and the Castle of S Servando on the other side of the river, protecting the Puente de Alcántara. Gothic art was introduced to Toledo with the building of the cathedral, which has remained the centre of artistic activity in the city. The predominance of *Mudéjar* architecture in Toledo means that there is very little that is Gothic, apart from a few rib vaults in the chevets of the *Mudéjar* churches and in some chapels.

The most important aspect of Toledan art in the second half of the 15th century was the creation of the HISPANO-FLEMISH STYLE that fused Islamic with Flamboyant forms. The most typical representative of the style was JUAN GUAS, who was responsible for the most important building in Toledo after the cathedral, the Franciscan Convento de S Juan de los Reyes, (*see* GOTHIC, fig. 26), begun in 1476 by Queen Isabella of Castile and León to commemorate the battle of Toro. This building is of an extraordinary decorative richness, especially in the transept, with the repeated motif of the royal coat of arms upheld by the eagle of St John, the elaborately decorated columns supporting the Islamic-style lantern over the crossing and the beautiful arcaded cloister with shouldered arches and carving as fine as gold work (see fig. 3). Many palace façades showing *Mudéjar* influence, such as that of the Casa Posada de la S Hermandad, date from the late 15th century.

Toledo was named the 'Imperial City' after the revolt of the Comunidades (1519–20), led by Juan de Padilla, who was opposed to government by the Flemish agents of Emperor Charles V and to the residence of the Emperor and Isabella of Portugal in the Alcázar. As the Imperial City, Toledo was enriched by many fine buildings. There is a fine example of the PLATERESQUE STYLE, the first period of the Spanish Renaissance, in the Hospital de Santa Cruz (begun *c*. 1500), now the Museo Arqueológico y de Bellas Artes, founded by Cardinal Pedro González de

3. Toledo, cloister of the Convento de S Juan de los Reyes, begun 1476

Mendoza. It was built on a Greek cross plan, with a patio and richly decorated staircase. The façade is one of the most typical examples of Plateresque and was the work of Antón Egas, Enrique Egas (*see* EGAS, (1) and (2)) and ALONSO DE COVARRUBIAS, to this last of whom is attributed the magnificent façade (1534) of the Convento de S Clemente el Reale. Covarrubias, the most representative architect of the second Renaissance period, is associated primarily with the remodelling (from 1543) of the Alcázar (rebuilt several times). This was erected on the site of the medieval alcázar and is remarkable for its commanding monumentalism and for the courtyard with a two-storey Corinthian arcade (1559), on which Francisco de Villalpando collaborated. Covarrubias also worked on the Puerta Nueva de Bisagra (1559), built in homage to Charles V as a great arch flanked by semicircular towers. A similar monumentality is apparent in the Hospital de S Juan Bautista (or de Tavera, 1541–50), now partly the Museo de la Fundación Duque de Lerma, which was built by Covarrubias (*see* COVARRUBIAS, ALONSO DE, fig. 1), with the assistance of HERNÁN GONZÁLEZ DE LARA, and on which BARTOLOMÉ BUSTAMANTE advised on the layout. Its main façade was renovated in the 18th century. The two courtyards, built with the collaboration of other architects, are Mannerist in style. In the chapel is one of the last works of ALONSO BERRUGUETE, the tomb of *Cardinal Juan Pardo de Tavera* (1559), whose effigy is a masterpiece of expressive realism (*see also* TAVERA, JUAN PARDO DE).

3. AFTER 1561. In 1561 Philip II moved his capital to Madrid, and Toledo consequently declined in political importance. JUAN DE HERRERA was employed on a number of projects in Toledo in the late 16th century, including the design of the southern façade (1573–8; destr. 1936; reconstructed) of the Alcázar and that (*c.* 1574) of the Ayuntamiento. In the 17th century a series of richly ornate convent and church buildings were constructed: S Pedro Mártir, the Hospital del Nuncio, and the church of S Juan Bautista (begun in 1625 by Francisco Bautista). Neoclassicism is represented by the work of Ignacio de Haám, who was responsible for the Puerta Llana of the cathedral (late 18th century) and the classical building of the present-day Faculty of Arts of the university. Other works of the 18th century include the arms factory (1777–83) by Francesco Sabatini. The railway station was built in MUDÉJAR REVIVAL style in the 19th century, and 20th-century buildings on the outskirts of the city have enabled Toledo to expand without detriment to the traditional groupings of houses or to the layout of the medieval town centre.

BIBLIOGRAPHY
J. M. Azcárate: *Castilla la Nueva*, 2 vols (Madrid, n.d.)
Amador de los Rios: *Toledo pintoresca* (Madrid, 1845)
S. R. Parro: *Toledo en la mano* (Toledo, 1857)
J. M. Camón: *La arquitectura plateresca* (Madrid, 1945)
L. Torres Balbás: *Arte almohade. Arte nazarí. Arte mudéjar*, A. Hisp., iv (Madrid, 1949)
M. Gómez-Moreno: *El arte árabe español hasta los almohades: Arte mozárabe*, A. Hisp., iii (Madrid, 1951)
B. G. Proske: *Castilian Sculpture: Gothic to Renaissance* (New York, 1951)
F. Chueca Goitia: *Arquitectura del siglo XVI*, A. Hisp., xi (Madrid, 1953)
D. Angulo Iñíguez: *Pintura del renacimiento*, A. Hisp., xii (Madrid, 1954)
J. M. Azcárate: *Escultura del siglo XVI*, A. Hisp., xiii (Madrid, 1958)
J. López de Ayala Cedillo, Alvaros de Toledo y del Hierro, Conde de Cedillo: *Catálogo monumental de la provincia de Toledo* (Toledo, 1959)
L. Moreno Nieto: *La provincia de Toledo* (Toledo, 1960)
J. Porres: *Historia de las calles de Toledo* (Toledo, 1971)
F. Cantera Burgos: *Sinagogas de Toledo, Segovia y Córdoba* (Madrid, 1973)
B. Pavón Maldonado: *Arte toledano: Islamico y mudéjar* (Madrid, 1973)
L. Torres Balbás: *Ciudades hispano-musulmanas*, 2 vols (Madrid, 1973)
B. Martinez Caviró: *Mudéjar toledano: Palacios y Conventos* (Madrid, 1980)
F. Marías: *La arquitectura del renacimiento en Toledo*, 4 vols (Toledo, 1983–6)
Monumentos españoles, iii (Madrid, 1984)
T. Perez Higuera: *Paseos por el Toledo del siglo XIII* (Madrid, 1984)

JOSÉ MARIA AZCÁRATE RISTORI

II. Art life and organization.

1. BEFORE *c.* 1500. There are significant Roman remains in Toledo that indicate an active art life, but Toledo was most creative under Visigothic rule; much material and documentary evidence survives from this period (*see* §I, 1 above and VISIGOTHIC ART). Of particular importance from the Visigothic period is the Treasure of Guarrazar (Madrid, Mus. Arqueol. N.), mainly consisting of crosses and votive crowns. This constitutes one of the most significant groups of European goldwork of this time. With the establishment of the royal court at Toledo and its importance as an ecclesiastical centre, the city acquired a long-lived, central role in the development of the art of Castile. This increased during the Moorish occupation, when Christians, Muslims, Mozarabs and Jews, each with their own artistic traditions, co-existed.

After the Christian conquest (1085) the cathedral provided commissions for numerous painters and sculptors (*see* §IV below). The earliest examples of painting are the Romanesque frescoes in S Román and El Cristo de la Luz. Toledo was associated with the scriptorium that illuminated the *Cantigas de S Maria* (1279; Madrid, Escorial, Bib. Monasterio S Lorenzo, MSS B.I.2 and T.I.1) by Alfonso X, a key work of medieval Castilian art. The paintings in the S Blas Chapel in the cathedral are attributed to the end of the 14th century, while the retable in the chapel of Santiago (or of Alvaro de Luna) is in the Hispano-Flemish style. There are also panels in the chapels of the Bautismo and of S Eugenio. The powerful guilds (indicated by street names), the patronage of some families, especially the MENDOZA family, and the workshops that arose around the cathedral were the principal artistic forces in the later Middle Ages. Some of the manuscripts of Peter IV of Aragon (*reg* 1336–87) and of Isabella, Queen of Castile and León, which were kept in libraries in Toledo, may also have been made there. Sancho de Zamora and Juan de Segovia (both *fl c.* 1488) painted the retable now in the chapel of Santiago, which suggests the existence of a workshop in the city.

Members of the Egas family, notably Egas Cueman, created a tradition of Toledan sculpture of which the finest representative was SEBASTIÁN DE TOLEDO. Ornamental and monumental sculpture are well exemplified in the cathedral portals, retrochoir, and the choir-stalls by Rodrigo Alemán, as well as at S Juan de los Reyes (from 1476) by Juan Guas. Other forms of art connected with the cathedral and the guilds are *rejería* (iron grilles) and gold- and silverwork (*see* GOTHIC, §V, 8). In the mid-15th century the workshop of Master Pablo was responsible for the wrought ironwork of the Puerta del Reloj and the chapel of S Ildefonso in the cathedral.

BIBLIOGRAPHY
M. Gómez Moreno: *Arte mudéjar toledano* (Madrid, 1916)
J. M. Azcárate Ristori: *Arquitectura gótica toledana del siglo XV* (Madrid, 1958)
B. Pavón Maldonado: *Arte toledano: Islámico y mudéjar* (Madrid, 1973)
F. de Olaguer-Feliú y Alonso: 'En torno a la rejería artística toledana', *Bol. Semin. Estud. A. & Arqueol.*, xliii (1977), pp. 223–35
M. T. Perez Higuera: *Paseos por el Toledo del siglo XIII* (Madrid, 1984)
M. A. Piquero Lopez: *La pintura gótica toledana anterior a 1450: El trecento*, 2 vols (Toledo, 1984)

CONCEPCIÓN ABAD CASTRO

2. AFTER *c.* 1500. In the 16th century Toledo was one of the most important cultural centres in Spain, a crucible of native styles, a gateway for the Italian Renaissance and open to both Castilian and Andalusian influences. There was a crafts guild, and the fine arts flourished. This traditional organization, however, was faced with the gradual assimilation of new theories from Italy and the presence of some unconventionally minded artists. Although Philip II established his court in Madrid in 1561, throughout the 16th century Toledo retained its population of nobles, intellectuals, dignitaries and high clergy, and this was given extra strength by the ambitions of the municipal authorities, the establishment of splendid religious foundations during the Counter-Reformation, and such great patrons as cardinals Pedro González de Mendoza and JUAN PARDO DE TAVERA, all of which were sources of commissions for artists between 1500 and 1800.

The decline of the city from the mid-17th century until the end of the 18th was marked by artistic subordination to Madrid and its artists.

The Renaissance reached Toledo at the beginning of the 16th century in the form of the tomb of *Cardinal Pedro González de Mendoza* (1494–1504; Toledo Cathedral), probably by a Genoese artist. Like the tomb of *Francisco Ruiz, Bishop of Avila* in S Juan de la Penitencia (destr. 1936), Toledo, commissioned in 1524 from the Aprile family of Genoa, it reflects the interest of Toledan church dignitaries in the new style, which was also followed by local sculptors such as Vasco de la Zarza. The new style in painting undoubtedly stems from JUAN DE BORGOÑA, whose numerous commissions (e.g. frescoes, *c.* 1509–11, in the cathedral chapter house) led to the establishment of a busy workshop; his combination of Gothic and 15th-century Italian forms attracted many imitators.

Throughout the 16th century the most important sculptors of Castile, for example Alonso Berruguete and Felipe Vigarny, were brought to the cathedral to execute various works (*see* §IV, 2 below). Both Berruguete and Vigarny had followers to succeed them, but the most characteristic mid-16th century Toledan sculpture was that of Berruguete's pupils Isidro Villoldo, Francisco Giralte, Inocencio Berruguete (*fl c.* 1540–63) and Francisco Linares (*d* 1575), who continued to use the dynamic and expressive forms of their master in retables and statues. The work of Gregorio Pardo Vigarny (1517–52) and Juan Bautista Vázquez was more classical. The decorative arts flourished in Toledo from the 16th century. Outstanding examples of gold- and silverwork (*see* §III below) and textiles (lace, embroidery, fabrics), mostly for religious purposes, were produced by Toledan artists. Despite its date, the processional monstrance (1515–24; Toledo Cathedral) by Enrique de Arfe is a superlative example of late medieval Toledan goldsmithing. From 1541 FRANCISCO DE VILLALPANDO and Domingo de Céspedes (*d* after 1570) made grilles for the cathedral that are masterpieces of 16th-century Spanish ironwork (*see* SPAIN, fig. 55).

Italian influence intensified throughout the 16th century, as can be seen in the effect of Raphael's work on Juan Correa de Vivar and Francisco de Comontes (*fl* 1526–65). In the last third of the 16th century there was a general tendency to absorb the style of Michelangelo, but painters in Toledo took other directions. In 1577 EL GRECO arrived in Toledo. His withdrawal to the city was contemporary with the success at the Escorial of other artists of the Toledo school whose style was less personal and more in keeping with the severity and the decorum required by the King in religious painting. LUIS DE VELASCO, Luis de Carvajal and BLAS DE PRADO worked in a more monumental and increasingly naturalistic style. Philip II approved of the work at the Escorial of JUAN BAUTISTA DE MONEGRO, El Greco's pupil, who mainly worked in Toledo. The massive proportions of El Greco's figures and the controlled sentiment of his work marked the transition of sculpture in Toledo to the 17th century. The architecture of retables also developed towards severe classicism, inspired by the work of Juan de Herrera. The new style was represented at the beginning of the 17th

century by GIRALDO DE MERLO, who sometimes worked in collaboration with JORGE MANUEL THEOTOCOPOULOS.

The vitality of the Toledo school continued until the mid-17th century, following the most innovative trends, such as the Venetian naturalism of the Bassano family and Roman Caravaggism. Between 1600 and 1650 there was a surge of activity in Toledo. As El Greco produced his most intense works (*see* GRECO, EL, fig. 5), Juan Sánchez Cotán was painting *bodegones* of ascetic simplicity. The arrival (*c.* 1613) of the canvases of Carlo Saraceni in the cathedral and the paintings (from 1612) of JUAN BAUTISTA MAINO in the monastery of S Pedro Mártir indicate an early awareness of the work of Caravaggio and his followers. The earliest works of Pedro Orrente, influenced by both El Greco and the Bassano family, exemplify developments in art in Toledo in the early decades of the 17th century. The patron Cardinal Bernardo de Sandoval y Rojas (*see* SANDOVAL Y ROJAS, (2)) chose the royal painters Vicente Carducho and Eugenio Cajés (*see* CAJÉS, (2)) to decorate the Virgen del Sagrario Chapel in the cathedral as a family mausoleum. These paintings (1614–16) inaugurated a series of commissions to Madrid painters throughout the 17th and 18th centuries. The most important court painters—sometimes distinguished with the title of Pintor de la Catedral—carried out work for the municipality and for religious institutions, aggravating the crisis in local art and its dependence on Madrid.

Among the followers of El Greco, LUIS TRISTÁN DE ESCAMILLA developed both naturalism and chiaroscuro. His fundamentally religious work is exemplified by the large retable (1623) in S Clara el Real, Toledo. His death in 1624 marked the end of the distinctive Toledo school of painting. While such local artists as Simón Vicente (*fl* 1668–90) and Blas Muñoz (*fl* 1667–1705) satisfied the requirements of popular devotion, Francisco Rizi—sometimes in collaboration with Juan Carreño de Miranda—was occupied from 1653 with commissions, many of which have been destroyed, from the cathedral. Rizi's work introduced Baroque painting to Toledo, which was continued by Claudio Coello and José Jiménez Donoso and culminated in the ceiling fresco (begun 1698) of the cathedral sacristy by Luca Giordano (*see* fig. 4 below). Meanwhile, such goldsmiths as Antonio Pérez de Montalto (*fl* 1677–80) were active. Baroque sculpture in Toledo was fundamentally devotional and followed the models of Madrid; alternatively, patrons commissioned works from outside the city, as with the sculptures by Alessandro Algardi (e.g. *Christ with the Cross* and the three-figure bronze *Flagellation*) and Manuel Pereira (e.g. *Immaculate Conception*, façade of the convent church) for the convent of the Capuchin nuns built (1671–3) by Pascual de Aragón, Archbishop of Toledo, or those in the cathedral and in the Jesuit church (now S Ildefonso) by PEDRO DE MENA from Granada.

In the 18th century the Transparente Chapel (*c.* 1721–32) in the cathedral by NARCISO TOMÉ (*see* §IV, 1 below) and the academic works of Manuel Alvárez (1727–97) and Mariano Salvatierra y Serrano (1752–1814) in the service of the patron Cardinal Francisco Antonio de Lorenzana (1722–1804) indicate the continued dependence on Madrid. This is further exemplified by the retable (1746) of S

Ildefonso, painted by Luis González Velázquez and Alejandro González Velázquez, and the frescoes (1776–83) in the cathedral cloister by Mariano Salvador Maella and Francisco Bayeu, employed on the recommendation of Anton Raphael Mengs. This brilliant succession of Madrid painters working in Toledo was concluded by Francisco de Goya with the *Betrayal of Christ* (1798; Toledo Cathedral, sacristy), among other works.

In the 19th century paintings, of town views were popular and included those of Toledo Cathedral by Pablo Gozalvo (1827–96) and views by Cecilio Pizarro (*d* 1886). In 1882 the Escuela de Industrias Artísticas (destr.) was built in the neo-*Mudéjar* style by Arturo Mélida y Alinari, who also restored (1881–2) the Convento de S Juan de los Reyes. In 1952 the sculptor VICTORIO MACHO settled in Toledo, where he established the Casa–Museo Victorio Macho, a museum of his work.

BIBLIOGRAPHY

D. Angulo Iñiguez and A. E. Pérez Sánchez: *Historia de la pintura española: Pintura toledana de la primera mitad del siglo XVII* (Madrid, 1972)

El Toledo de El Greco (exh. cat. by A. E. Pérez Sánchez and others, Toledo, Hosp. Tavera and S Pedro Mártir, 1982)

P. Revenga Domínguez: *Aproximación a la pintura toledana de la segunda mitad del siglo XVII* (Toledo, 1989)

ISMAEL GUTIÉRREZ PASTOR

III. Centre of metalwork production.

Gold- and silverwork was produced in Toledo from the 14th century, and the ecclesiastical and economic primacy of the archdiocese of Toledo in the 15th century resulted in numerous commissions for gold- and silversmiths active there. The increased political importance of the city in the 16th century led to the influx of craftsmen who worked in various forms of the Renaissance style. At this time metalworkers in Toledo were also noted for their manufacture of sword blades, bronzework and decorative ironwork. Silversmithing in the Mannerist style flourished at the end of the 16th century, when the most prominent silversmith was FRANCISCO MERINO. In the 17th century the city declined in importance as a centre of metalwork production owing to the pre-eminence of Madrid, but a large number of craftsmen continued to operate. Two distinguished goldsmiths—Juan Antonio Dominguez (*d* 1748) and Manuel de Vargas Machuca (*d* 1759)—made a number of Baroque works for Toledo Cathedral and for churches in the archdiocese in the 18th century. Production decreased in the 19th century, although Gothic Revival and Renaissance Revival pieces continued to be made. Hallmarks were used almost continuously on products made in the city from the 15th century; the town mark consists of an abbreviated version of the name (*see* SPAIN, §IX, 1 and 2).

JOSÉ MANUEL CRUZ VALDOVINOS

IV. Cathedral.

The cathedral, the seat of the Primate of Spain, is an important example of Spanish Gothic architecture, structurally unusual and with an innovative liturgical layout. It contains paintings by Giovanni Bellini, El Greco, Luca Giordano (see fig. 4), Anthony van Dyck and others, and stained glass from the mid-14th century to the early 16th.

4. Toledo Cathedral, sacristy, showing the painted ceiling by Luca Giordano, 1698

Among the late medieval and early Renaissance sculptors employed there were Hanequin de Bruselas, Juan Alemán, Alonso de Covarrubias and Alonso Berruguete.

1. ARCHITECTURE. The cathedral was built on the site of a mosque, which occupied that of a Visigothic basilica consecrated in 587. The mosque was converted to Christian use after the conquest of Toledo in 1085, and the present building was started *c.* 1220. The foundation stone was laid in 1226 in the presence of Ferdinand III the Holy (*reg* 1217–52) and Archbishop Don Rodrigo Ximénez de Rada. Building began with the chevet, the mosque being retained for worship on the site of what is now the main body of the church. The ambulatory chapels were founded and the altars endowed in 1238, and the transept was reached towards 1247. In 1289 the remains of Alfonso VII (*reg* 1126–57) and Sancho III the Great (*reg* 1000–35) were moved to the Chapel of the Holy Cross at the back of what is now the presbytery (it disappeared when the Capilla Mayor was enlarged in the early 16th century). Work continued on the south side of the nave and by *c.* 1275 had reached the chapels near the Puerta Llana in the fourth bay; in 1337 the bronze doors were already in place on the west façade. In 1493 the high vault over the *coro* at the end of the nave was put in place. The large number of eastern chapels helped to finance the building by increasing the space for endowments and burials.

The cathedral (113×57 m) is built over a crypt using granite and limestone from Olihuelas, near Toledo. Its structural technique was probably the responsibility of

Master Martín, who is mentioned as Master of the Works in 1227 and 1234. A Petrus Petri, whose epitaph (1291) in the cathedral highly praises his work there, was probably Martín's successor. The design (see fig. 5) was inspired by the cathedrals of Paris (*see* PARIS, §V, 1(i)) and Bourges (*see* BOURGES, §II, 1(i)). It is a five-aisled basilica with a non-projecting transept, a double ambulatory and seven shallow radiating chapels, their interstices filled by small vaulted spaces that brought the number of chapels to 15. The nave has seven bays flanked by chapels, with a triple west portal, and towers on the outer aisles. The cloister, founded in 1389 by Archbishop Don Pedro Tenorio, is off the north side of the nave on the site of the Muslim market.

The nave elevation (see fig. 6) has two storeys, an arcade of compound piers with foliage capitals and sharply moulded arches, and a deep clerestory of six lights, with large oculi containing foiled circles in the window head. The east side of the transept and the chevet have a triforium, but in the nave the triforium is merely implied

6. Toledo Cathedral, view of the interior looking north-west, 13th century

by the transom in the clerestory window. The vault shafts run uninterrupted to the quadripartite main vault. The inner ambulatory, which has twice as many piers as the hemicycle, has three storeys, an arcade, a triforium with cusped arches, and cusped oculi above, which may be Islamic-inspired. The problem of buttressing the chevet and vaulting the double ambulatory was solved, as at Le Mans Cathedral (*see* LE MANS, §1), by creating alternate rectangular and triangular vaulting severies, with quadripartite vaults over the rectangular spaces and bifurcating ribs in the triangular compartments. These ribs descend to the intermediate ambulatory piers and, in the outer ambulatory, to responds on the outer walls. On the outside the two storeys of flying buttresses similarly divide through two levels, so that the vault thrusts are distributed evenly through all the supports.

Petrus Petri may have designed the cusped arches in the ambulatory triforium and probably placed the *coro* in the nave. As the royal burial chapel occupied half of what is now the presbytery, the canons' choir had to be located west of the chevet. In the late 12th century the *coro* in Santiago de Compostela Cathedral had been located in the nave to allow free access for pilgrims to the shrine of St James the Great, east of the crossing. This link with Santiago, which also has cusped arches round the outside of the ambulatory, supports the idea that Petrus Petri was of Galician origin, related to other architects of that name working in Galicia. The location of the *coro* in the nave was to be adopted in most Spanish cathedrals and became a distinct characteristic of Spanish Gothic architecture.

Among later architects employed on the cathedral were JUAN GUAS, who was Maestro Mayor by 1491/2, Antón Egas and Enrique Egas (*see* EGAS, (2) and (3)), who were jointly appointed Maestro Mayor in 1496, ALONSO DE

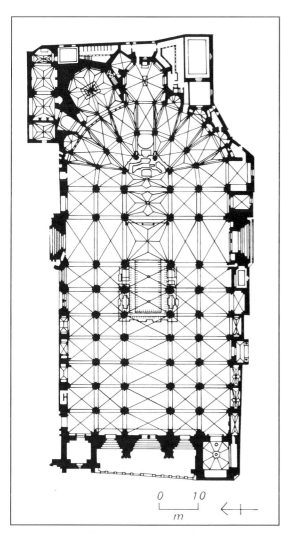

0   10
m

5. Toledo Cathedral, begun *c.* 1220, ground-plan

Covarrubias, Nicolás de Vergara the younger (*see* Vergara, (2)), who was twice Maestro Mayor (1575–82; 1587–1606) and Juan Bautista Monegro, who was appointed Maestro Mayor in 1606. Covarrubias's work included the planning, with Diego de Siloé, of the architectural part of the upper level of the choir-stalls, on the execution of which he was assisted by Esteban Jamete. One of the most remarkable later features of the cathedral is the Transparente Chapel by Narciso Tomé, which fuses together architecture and sculpture. This huge structure represents the culmination of the Baroque retable (*see* Retable, §1).

2. Sculpture. Most of the decoration dates from the 14th century and later, the earliest door being the Puerta de Reloj (*c.* 1300) on the north transept, which is carved with angels and New Testament scenes. The south transept door, the Puerta de los Leones, with lions bearing shields, was begun in 1452 by Hanequin de Bruselas, Egas Cueman (*see* Egas, (1)) and Juan Alemán; they also made the reliefs on the outer walls of the Capilla Mayor from 1490. The Puerta del Perdón, the main west door, was made in the early 15th century, while the north-west cloister door (Puerta de la Presentación) dates from 1586. The Neo-classical Puerta Llana was made by Ignacio de Haám in the late 18th century. Inside the building the lower tier of choir-stalls was made by Rodrigo Alemán in 1495, with reliefs showing the *Conquest of Granada*, while the Old and New Testament scenes of the upper tier (finished in 1543) are by Alonso Berruguete (*see* Berruguete, (2), §3 and fig. 2) and Felipe Vigarny. The principal retable (1498–1504) was commissioned by Cardinal Francisco Jiménez de Cisneros, who was responsible for a number of other architectural and decorative projects in the cathedral. It was designed by Peti Juan (*d* 1503) and made by him and a group of artists including Diego Copín (*d* 1541), Vigarny and Sebastian de Almonacid (*fl* 1494–1527). The choir-screen is decorated with sculptures (1564–74) by Nicolás de Vergara the elder (*see* Vergara, (1)).

In the later Middle Ages several magnificent chapels were added to the cathedral. The Chapel of Santiago was built by Condestable Don Alvaro de Luna (*see* Luna (ii)) in 1450. Inspired by the octagonal 14th-century chapel of S Ildefonso, it became the model for later chapels. Luna's tomb and that of his wife Doña Juana de Pimentel were made by Sebastián de Toledo. The Capilla de los Reyes Nuevos, on which Alonso de Covarrubias worked, was built from 1529 to 1534 as the burial chapel of Henry II (*d* 1379) and his family. The doors are by Hanequin de Bruselas and Juan Alemán.

BIBLIOGRAPHY
G. E. Street: *Some Account of Gothic Architecture in Spain* (London, 1865, 2/1869; rev. by G. G. King, 2 vols, 1914)
M. R. Zarco del Valle: *Documentos de la catedral de Toledo* (Madrid, 1916)
E. Lambert: *L'Art gothique en Espagne aux XIIe et XIIIe siècles* (Paris, 1931)
J. Gudiol Ricart: *La catedral de Toledo* (Madrid, 1948)
L. Torres Balbás: *Arquitectura gótica*, A. Hisp., vii (Madrid, 1952)
J. M. Azcárate: *La arquitectura gótica toledana del siglo XV* (Madrid, 1958)
F. de Olaguer y Alonso: *Las rejas de la catedral de Toledo* (Toledo, 1980)
JOSÉ MARIA AZCÁRATE RISTORI

3. Stained glass. Toledo Cathedral has the most complete medieval glazing scheme surviving in Spain. The windows, dating from the mid-14th century to the early 16th, illustrate the 15th-century development by foreign glaziers of a distinctively Spanish style of rich hues and expressive figures. The earliest window, the 14th-century north rose, has a central *Crucifixion* on a red background, surrounded by two tiers of cusped circles on blue, the inner ring with the Virgin, St John the Evangelist and angels and the outer with prophets. The main programme was begun in 1418 under the master glazier Juan Dolfin (*fl* 1418–27) from France. He was responsible for many of the apse clerestory lancets with angels and saints and for those of the choir. His successors were Loys Coutin (*fl* 1430s), Pedro Bonifacio (*fl* 1450s), who glazed the three chapels of the south aisle with the *Nativity*, *Pentecost* and *Adoration of the Magi*, and, from 1485 to 1492, Enrique Alemán (*fl* 1485–92) from Germany. Alemán used imported glass in his work on the double-tiered nave windows, the six-lancet scheme of which depicts saints, bishops and Apostles under canopies. The dark blues of his north aisle windows deliberately contrast with the brighter reds of the south.

The 15th-century west rose has complex tracery, with a central panel depicting the bishop's insignia surrounded by seven concentric rings of differing designs. The four west windows of the transepts date from the end of the 15th century and are in early Renaissance style. They are the largest in the cathedral, with two tiers of eight lights, the upper showing saints and bishops and the lower heraldic shields, famous scholars and figures representing Virtues, Vices, Arts and Sciences. The south rose, with 16 petals in tones of blue and green, was made by Nicolás de Vergara the elder (*see* Vergara, (1)) in the early 16th century.

See also Gothic, §VIII, 8.

BIBLIOGRAPHY
J. Ainaud de Lasarte: *Cerámico y vidrio*, A. Hisp., x (Madrid, 1952), pp. 374–97
V. N. Alcaide: 'El maestro Enrique Alemán, vidriero de las catedrales de Sevilla y Toledo', *Archv Esp. A.*, clvii (1967), pp. 55–82
L. Lee, G. Seddon and F. Stephens: *Stained Glass* (London, 1976)
CAROLA HICKS

Toledo, Francisco (*b* Juchitán, Oaxaca, 17 July 1940). Mexican painter, sculptor, textile designer, printmaker and collector. He grew up in an area that was rich in legends, rites and beliefs springing from a strong rural tradition predating the Spanish conquest of Mexico. He began to draw and paint at a very early age, studying first in Oaxaca, where he produced linocuts in the graphic workshop run by Arturo García Bustos (*b* 1926). In 1957 he moved to Mexico City to attend the Escuela de Diseño y Artesanía of the Instituto Nacional de Bellas Artes. After holding his first one-man shows of gouaches and prints in 1959 in Fort Worth, TX, and Mexico City, he moved in 1960 to Paris, where until 1963 he studied printmaking under Stanley William Hayter. While continuing to work within western traditions, he became interested in the art of oriental cultures and in ancient Mexican art, especially in those forms that were not officially sanctioned. In his attitude towards the sustaining inspiration of traditions he was particularly close to Paul Klee.

Toledo left France for Mexico in 1965 only to return in 1968, finally settling again in Oaxaca in the following year. He worked in a wide variety of media, including painting, drawing, printmaking, sculpture, tapestry and ceramics, often enriching one technique with discoveries made in another. While his formal vocabulary evolved in response to the demands of each medium, with the forms often based on his appreciation of abstract art, he added consistently to a richly varied iconography of fantastic primordial visions. His work was particularly close in spirit to that of Latin American writers such as Gabriel García Marquéz, Juan Rulfo and Jorge Luis Borges, whose *Manual de zoología fantástica* (Mexico City, 1984) he illustrated. Evoking primordial visions underlying everyday events so ordinary as to pass unnoticed, Toledo's motifs included the imprint of a crab on wet sand, iguana, a woman's large backside, the fur of a cat, the outline of a bat or the scales of an iguana, as in the etchings and aquatints of the *Guchachi Portfolio (Iguana)* (1976; Austin, U. TX, Huntington A.G.; *see* MEXICO, fig. 12). Generally he re-used such images so as to build on their metaphorical meanings, with their identities and interrelationships often clarified by their decorative function.

Although painting and printmaking remained the most important media for Toledo, in the 1980s he also produced polychromed wax sculptures with erotic overtones, such as *Bull Woman*, also known as *Pasifae* (1987; priv. col.), and true fresco paintings on transportable frames. From 1975 to 1983 Toledo lived successively in New York, Oaxaca and Mexico City, finally settling in Paris until 1987 before returning to Mexico. At that time he began to amass a collection of prints by artists from all over the world as the basis for the Instituto de Artes Gráficas de Oaxaca in his former house which he donated to the state. In addition to housing this permanent collection, the museum was intended as a venue for touring exhibitions organized in collaboration with the Museo Nacional de la Estampa in Mexico City.

BIBLIOGRAPHY
L. Cardoza y Aragón: *Toledo: Pintura y cerámica* (Mexico City, 1972)
M. Traba: *Los signos de la vida: José Luis Cuevas, Francisco Toledo* (Mexico City, 1976)
T. del Conde: *Francisco Toledo* (Mexico City, 1981)
C. Monsivais: *Lo que el viento a Juárez* (Mexico City, 1986)

TERESA DEL CONDE

Toledo, Juan Antonio. *See under* EQUIPO CRÓNICA.

Toledo, Juan Bautista de (*b c.* 1515; *d* Madrid, 19 May 1567). Spanish architect. He received his architectural training in the traditional way, working as a stone-cutter. He spent some time in Italy, where he was engaged on projects possibly connected with military engineering for the Holy Roman Emperor Charles V. He may also have worked under Michelangelo at St Peter's in Rome, since a Spaniard named Juan Bautista Alfonsis is recorded as Second Architect of St Peter's, working there between 18 December 1546 and 20 September 1548. It was during this time that the design of Antonio da Sangallo (ii) was rejected in favour of Michelangelo's plans. Juan Bautista subsequently lived in Naples, where he was employed as

a royal architect and engineer, working on fortifications such as the Castel Nuovo (1554; *see* NAPLES, §IV, 4). In 1558 he was put in charge of draining the marshes in the woods of S Arcangelo. He may also have been responsible for the layout of the Strada Toledo in Naples, for urban planning and for the church of S Giacomo degli Spagnuoli, Naples, and the Palace of Pozzuoli.

Recalled to Spain in 1559 by Philip II, Juan Bautista was appointed to the newly established post of Royal Architect for life on 12 August 1561. From this privileged position he completely revolutionized Spanish architecture, introducing a new system of working and innovations to teaching methods, which were used to train his disciple and successor JUAN DE HERRERA. The study of architecture according to Juan Bautista's system was rigorously technical, with a clear distinction between design and execution. Unlike his contemporaries (who described him as the best architect in Spain) Luis de Vega, Gaspar de Vega, Rodrigo Gil de Hontañón and Alonso de Covarrubias, Juan Bautista built in a style that was purely classical, lacking any trace of Gothic and employing spatial and structural solutions unprecedented in Spain. Few examples remain, however, of his extensive production. His buildings for the Hieronymite Monastery in Madrid have disappeared, as has his work on the Madrid Alcázar. At ARANJUEZ PALACE little survives of his design (1561) for the palace and courtiers' quarters; he also devised the hydraulic apparatus to supply water for the splendid flower gardens there. Building advanced slowly, and changes were made, first by Herrera (from 1567) and then in the 17th century by Juan Gómez de Mora (i); more followed in the 18th century, when the Bourbons completed the construction. The palace was conceived as an inverted T-shaped structure of two overlapping volumes. The basic nucleus is a courtyard with rooms on three of its sides, while the fourth side is linked to the unit formed by the front of the building, articulated by the large vestibule and closed by two square tower-like spaces, the one on the right being the chapel. Juan Bautista may also have designed the

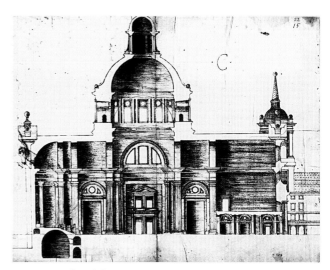

Juan Bautista de Toledo: project 'C' section for the church of Escorial, 1567 (Madrid, Biblioteca del Palacio Real)

façade of the church of the Descalzas Reales in Madrid, although the church itself may have been designed by Francesco Paciotto (1562).

Juan Bautista's masterpiece is his design for the monastery of S Lorenzo El Real at El Escorial (begun 1562; *see* ESCORIAL, §2), which occupied the southern part of the complex. He was also responsible for initial work on the Pantheon and the construction of the private royal apartments, with their intimate courtyard known as the Patio de los Mascarones. His designs for the monastery church (see fig.), however, were greatly modified by Juan de Herrera, as was much of the rest of the building. The parts built from Juan Bautista's designs reveal an unequalled mastery of the distribution and articulation of space and volume, with the virtual elimination of all ornament. Sometimes, as in the case of the austere eastern façades with their storeys of identical unadorned windows, the design is even reminiscent of military architecture, but despite this, Juan Bautista was still able to give particular spaces their own special character, notably in the supremely functional Patios Chicos (the service areas of the monastery) and the enchantingly tranquil Patio de los Mascarones.

BIBLIOGRAPHY
E. Llaguno y Amírola and J. A. Ceán-Bermúdez: *Noticias* (1829)
J. de San Jerónimo: *Memorias*, vii of *Colección de documentos inéditos para la historia de España* (Madrid, 1845/*R* 1984)
F. Iñiguez Almech: *Casas reales y jardines de Felipe II* (Madrid, 1952)
A. Portobales Pichel: *Maestros mayores, arquitectos y aparejadores de El Escorial* (Madrid, 1952)
J. de Sigüenza: *Fundación del Monasterio de El Escorial* (Madrid, 1963)
C. Vicuña: 'Juan Bautista de Toledo, principal arquitecto del Monasterio de El Escorial', *Monasterio de San Lorenzo El Real de El Escorial en el cuarto centenario de su fundación, 1563–1963* (S Lorenzo de El Escorial, 1964), pp. 125–93
F. Iñiguez Almech: *Las trazas del Monasterio de S Lorenzo de El Escorial* (Madrid, 1965)
C. Vicuña: 'Juan Bautista de Toledo, arquitecto segundo de la fábrica de San Pedro de Roma', *Archv Esp. A. & Arqueol.*, xxxix (1966), pp. 1–8
S. Giner Guerri: 'Juan Bautista de Toledo y Miguel Angel en El Vaticano', *Goya*, 126 (1975), pp. 351–9
——: 'Juan Bautista de Toledo, segundo arquitecto de la Basílica Vaticana, junto a Miguel Angel: Estudio crítico sobre su actividad en Italia', *Anlct. Calasanctiana*, xix (1977), pp. 59–121
G. Kubler: *Building the Escorial* (Princeton, 1982)
V. Gerard: *De castillo a palacio: El Alcázar de Madrid en el siglo XVI* (Bilbao, 1984)
J. Rivera Blanco: *Juan Bautista de Toledo y Felipe II: La implantación del clasicismo en España* (Valladolid, 1984)
A. Bustamante and F. Marías: 'El Escorial y la cultura arquitectónica de su tiempo', *El Escorial en la Biblioteca Nacional* (Madrid, 1985), pp. 117–219
J. Rivera Blanco: 'De Juan Bautista de Toledo a Juan de Herrera', *Herrera y el clasicismo* (Valladolid, 1986), pp. 69–83
F. Marías and A. Bustamante: 'De las Descalzas Reales a la Plaza Mayor: Dibujos madrileños en Windsor Castle de la colección de Cassiano del Pozzo', *Terceras Jornadas de Arte* (Madrid, 1991), pp. 73–85
A. BUSTAMANTE GARCÍA

Toledo, Pedro de. *See* MASTERS, ANONYMOUS, AND MONOGRAMMISTS, §I: MASTER OF THE CYPRESSES.

Toledo, Sebastián de. *See* SEBASTIÁN DE TOLEDO.

Tolita. *See* LA TOLITA.

Tollan. *See* TULA.

Tollet, Johann Septimius Jörger von. *See* JÖRGER VON TOLLET, JOHANN SEPTIMIUS.

Tollu, Cemal (*b* Istanbul, 19 April 1899; *d* Istanbul, 1968). Turkish painter. He spent his childhood in the Hijaz (now Saudi Arabia), where he took painting lessons from a retired Ottoman officer while an apprentice in a workshop. In 1919 Tollu enrolled at the Fine Arts Academy in Istanbul but a year later went to Anatolia to join the forces fighting for Turkish independence, serving until 1923 as a cavalry lieutenant. After leaving the army he worked in a railway workshop in Edirne but in 1926 returned to the Fine Arts Academy in Istanbul. In 1927 he was appointed art teacher at the Teacher Training College in Elazig and Erzincan. He made two trips to France and Germany, where for some two years he studied under such painters as André Lhôte, Marcel Gromaire and Hans Hofmann, and such sculptors as Charles Despiau and Marcel Gimond (*b* 1894). In Turkey he contributed to the first exhibitions of the Müstakīl Ressamlar ve Heykeltraşlar Birliği (Association of Independent Painters and Sculptors) and was a founder-member of the D Group in 1933. His works of this period include *The Ballerina* (1935; Istanbul, Mimar Sinan U., Mus. Ptg & Sculp.). Tollu was appointed vice-director of the Museum of Anatolian Civilizations in Ankara and was then selected by Léopold Lévy (1882–1966), head of the department of painting, to teach at the Fine Arts Academy in Istanbul, where he stayed until 1965. In his work he was inspired by Hittite as well as contemporary Western art, and he painted figures, landscapes and portraits in a distinctive fragmented style. His works include *Mother Earth* (1956) and *Fire of Manisa* (1968; both Istanbul, Mimar Sinan U., Mus. Ptg & Sculp.).

BIBLIOGRAPHY
S. Tansuğ: *Çağdaş Türk sanatı* [Contemporary Turkish art] (Istanbul, 1986), pp. 177–9, 189–90, 192, 247, 377–8
G. Renda and others: *A History of Turkish Painting* (Geneva, Seattle and London, 1988), pp. 197–8, 201, 203, 206–8, 210–12, 236, 249–51, 255, 360, 394
□

Tolmeita. *See* PTOLEMAIS.

Tolnay [Tolnai], Charles Erich de [Károly; Vagujhelyi Karoly] (*b* Budapest, 27 May ?1899; *d* Florence, 17 Jan 1981). American art historian of Hungarian birth. He studied at the universities of Berlin (1920–21), Frankfurt (1922), Vienna, where he obtained his doctorate in 1925, and then in Rome. He held lectureships at the University of Hamburg (1929–33) and in art and archaeology at the Sorbonne, Paris (1934–9), among others. In 1939 Tolnay moved to the USA, and from 1939 to 1948 was a staff member of the Institute for Advanced Study at Princeton, New Jersey, becoming an American citizen in 1945. From 1954 to 1964 he was visiting lecturer at Columbia University, New York, and also visited Europe. In 1965 he became Director of the Casa Buonarroti in Florence.

Tolnay's scholarly interests ranged across the field of European Renaissance art. In the 1930s he published a series of influential monographs on Flemish painters, including a study of the Master of Flémalle, which was the first to draw attention to the artist's importance as an innovator, and a book on Hieronymus Bosch, which became a standard work. Tolnay's name is, however, most closely associated with Michelangelo studies. The distinguished series of studies he published over 50 years established his position as the leading authority in the 20th century on the work of Michelangelo.

WRITINGS

Pierre Bruegel l'ancien (Brussels, 1935)
Hieronymus Bosch (Basle, 1937, rev. Baden-Baden, 1966)
Le Maître de Flémalle et les frères van Eyck (Brussels, 1939)
History and Technique of Old Master Drawings (New York, 1943)
Michelangelo (Princeton, NJ): *I The Youth of Michelangelo* (1943, 2/1969); *II The Sistine Chapel* (1945, 2/1969); *III The Medici Chapel* (1948, 2/1970); *IV The Tomb of Julius II* (1954, 2/1970); *V The Final Period: The Last Judgement, Frescoes of the Pauline Chapel, Last Pietàs* (1960, 2/1970); *VI Michelangelo: Architect* (1975)
La Casa Buonarroti (Princeton, 1970)
Michelangelo: Sculptor, Painter, Architect (Princeton, 1975) [condensed edn of *Michelangelo*]

BIBLIOGRAPHY

Contemporary Authors (Detroit, 1978), lxxiii–lxxvi, pp. 164–5

JANET SOUTHORN

Tolomei, Claudio (*b* Siena, 1492; *d* Rome, 1555). Italian diplomat, writer and theorist. He took a degree in law and studied for the priesthood, then travelled to Rome, where he lived from 1516, serving first Ippolito de' Medici, the nephew of Pope Clement VII, and then, after 1541, Pier Luigi Farnese, 1st Duke of Parma. Tolomei was the author of various linguistic studies. From 1541 to 1544 he pursued his interest in architecture and the study of Vitruvius, and under the auspices of the Accademia della Virtù, a private society of intellectuals in Rome, he proposed to publish a definitive edition of Vitruvius's text with a new Italian translation, ample annotations, illustrations, a glossary of technical terms and a verification of the rules as applied to the monuments of ancient Rome (*see* VITRUVIUS, §3(ii)). The project was so ambitious that he and his colleagues were able only to carry out initial studies, and it was never published. Another project of his was for a new city to be built on the promontory of Monte Argentario in Tuscany, which he described in a letter of 1544. This was conceived as an extension of Porto Santo Stefano, using the pool of Orbetello as a new port. Tolomei lacked sufficient experience, however, to carry out his plans. In 1545 Pier Luigi Farnese appointed him Minister of Justice in his Duchy of Parma and Piacenza. After the death of his patron (1547), Tolomei spent a year in Padua and then returned to Rome, where he was given the title Archbishop of Curzola (Dalmatia). In 1552 he went to France, where he was also Bishop of Toulon, in the vain hope of persuading King Henry II to protect the Republic of Siena from falling to the Spanish. He returned to Rome at the end of 1554.

WRITINGS

Delle lettere di M. Claudio Tolomei libri sette (Venice, 1547); ed. G. Lozzi (Naples, 1849)

BIBLIOGRAPHY

J. Schlosser Magnino: *Die Kunstliteratur* (Vienna, 1924)
P. L. Sbaragli: *Claudio Tolomei, umanista senese del cinquecento: La vita e le opere* (Siena, 1939)
P. Barocchi: *Scritti d'arte del cinquecento* (Milan and Naples, 1971–7), pp. 3037–46
S. Benedetti and T. Scalesse: 'Claudio Tolomei. Lettera al conte Agostino de' Landi. Lettera a Gabriele Cesano', *Pietro Cataneo, Giacomo Barozzi da Vignola: Trattati con l'aggiunta degli scritti di architettura di Alvise Cornaro, Francesco Giorgi, Claudio Tolomei, Giangiorgio Trissino, Giorgio Vasari*, ed. E. Bassi and others (Milan, 1985), pp. 33–50
P. N. Pagliara: 'Vitruvio da testo a canone', *Memoria dell'antico nell'arte italiana*, iii, ed. S. Settis (Turin, 1986), pp. 67–74

ADRIANO GHISETTI GIAVARINA

Tolsá, Manuel (*b* Enguera, Valencia, 1757; *d* Mexico City, 24 Dec 1816). Spanish architect, sculptor and teacher. He studied at the Real Academia de Bellas Artes de S Carlos, Valencia, at a time when Baroque forms were being rejected in Spain and Neo-classicism was being promoted. He was apprenticed to the sculptor José Puchol Rubio (*d* 1797), who also taught him extensively about architecture. In 1780 Tolsá moved to Madrid, where he studied under Juan Pascual de Mena and at the Real Academia de Bellas-Artes de S Fernando, where his subjects included painting. There he also designed several reliefs, including the *Entry of the Catholic Kings into Granada* (1784; Madrid, Real Acad. S Fernando). He was selected as an academician in 1789.

Following the endorsement of Juan Adán and Manuel Francisco Alvarez de la Peña, in 1790 Tolsá succeeded José Arias (*c.* 1743–88) as director of sculpture at the Real Academia de S Carlos de la Nueva España in Mexico City. He took with him a collection of plaster casts for sculptures, many books and 154 quintals (7 tonnes) of plaster for the Academia. He arrived in 1791 and set about repairing the statues that had been broken during the voyage. He gave classes on stucco ornament and decorative work in wood and stone and encouraged a change of taste away from the prevailing Baroque style. He also started a ceramics class and prepared the tiles for the convent of Churubusco.

From 1793, when Tolsá was appointed Director de las Obras at Mexico Cathedral, he began to concentrate on architecture, while occasionally undertaking sculptural commissions. In 1796, for example, he was commissioned to design the model for the bronze equestrian statue of *Charles IV* (erected 1803), popularly known as 'El Caballito', which stands beside the Museo Nacional de Arte, Mexico City (*see* MEXICO, fig. 9). The Real Seminario de Minería (1797–1813; now the Palacio de Minería; *see* MEXICO CITY, fig. 3), covering an area of almost 7500 sq. m and built around seven courtyards, is one of his finest architectural works. It is classical in style yet closely integrated with the surrounding contemporary architecture in Mexico City in a way that shows the direct dissemination of form and content to actual buildings at a time when academic architectural studies were important.

Tolsá's contribution to the completion of the cupola (1809) of Mexico Cathedral was paralleled by his replacement of the old Baroque retables by Neo-classical designs. He also made a number of designs in a transitional style, such as the unexecuted design (1808) for a church dedicated to Nuestra Señora de Loreto in Mexico City, and a plan (1797; Seville, Archv Gen. Indias) for the Carmelite convent in Querétaro, which was completed (1807) by Francisco Eduardo Tresguerras. His other projects included the Mexico City cemetery (1808) and a plan for a scale model of such an amenity after a royal decree required its provision in Spanish colonial cities. In 1810 he was appointed director of architecture at the

Academia shortly after the death of Antonio González Velázquez the younger (*b* 1750) but obtained his credentials as an architect only in 1813. His architectural skills are apparent in the residences he built for the Marqués del Apartado (1795) and in the Palacio de Buenavista (1795). His most important late sculptural works were the altar (begun 1799) of S Domingo, Mexico City, and the altarpiece with a baldacchino (1797–1818) for Puebla Cathedral.

BIBLIOGRAPHY

M. Toussaint: *La catedral y el sagrario de México* (Mexico City, 1917)
A. Encontria: *Breve estudio de la obra y personalidad del escultor y arquitecto don Manuel Tolsá* (Mexico City, 1929)
D. Angulo Iñiguez: *Arquitectura neoclásica en México* (Madrid, 1958)

RAMÓN GUTIÉRREZ

Tolstov, Sergey (Pavlovich) (*b* St Petersburg, 25 Jan 1907; *d* Moscow, 28 Dec 1976). Russian archaeologist. He graduated from Moscow University in 1930. From 1929 to 1936 he worked in the Museum of the Peoples of the USSR and simultaneously as academic secretary and then head of the Moscow division of the Institute for the History of Material Culture. In 1937 he became director of the Khorezm archaeological and ethnographical expedition. From 1939 to 1951 he was the professor heading the department of ethnography in the history faculty at Moscow University, and from 1942 to 1966 he also served as director of the USSR Academy of Sciences' Institute of Ethnography, initiating excavations of numerous archaeological sites in Central Asia, including the architectural complexes at TOPRAK KALA and KOY KRYLGAN KALA. He became a corresponding member of the USSR Academy of Sciences in 1953. He was an honorary member of the Italian Institute for the Middle and Far East, the Parisian Asiatic and Anthropological Society and the Royal Anthropological Institute of Great Britain and Ireland.

WRITINGS

Drevniy Khorezm [Ancient Khorezm] (Moscow, 1948)
Po sledam drevnekhorezmiyskoy tsivilizatsii [Retracing the civilization of ancient Khorezm] (Moscow, 1948)
Po drevnim del'tam Oksa i Yaksarta [Along the ancient deltas of the Oks and Yaksart] (Moscow, 1962)

BIBLIOGRAPHY

A. Vinogradov, ed.: *Etnografiya i arkheologiya Sredney Azii* [The ethnography and archaeology of Central Asia] (Moscow, 1979)

V. YA. PETRUKHIN

Tolstoy, Fyodor (Petrovich) (*b* St Petersburg, 21 Feb 1783; *d* St Petersburg, 25 April 1873). Russian sculptor, medallist, painter, draughtsman and printmaker. He came from a distinguished family, and in 1802 he finished his studies in the Naval Cadet Corps in St Petersburg. In the same year he entered the Academy of Arts in St Petersburg as an occasional student and soon began a career as a professional artist. Most surviving examples of his early work are wax reliefs, such as the portrait of *I. I. Golovin* (*c.* 1805–10; St Petersburg, Rus. Mus.) and the *Self-portrait with Family* (1812; Moscow, Tret'yakov Gal.), and drawings.

From 1810 Tolstoy worked in the St Petersburg Mint, where he produced numerous wax medallions devoted to events of the war with Napoleon, such as the *Home Guard* (1818), the *Battle of Borodino* (1818) and the *Battle near Kulm* (1823; all St Petersburg, Rus. Mus.) These were cast as medals between 1814 and 1836. In 1828 Tolstoy became Vice President of the Academy of Arts where he had been professor of the medal section since 1812, and from 1849 he was Professor of Sculpture. At the same time he worked on a series of wax reliefs on the subject of the Odyssey, such as *Mercury Leads the Ghosts of the Suitors into Hades* (1810), the *Feast of the Suitors* (1814) and the *Massacre of the Suitors* (1815; all Moscow, Tret'yakov Gal.). Among his sculptural works, the terracotta bust of *Morpheus* (1822; St Petersburg, Rus. Mus.) is suffused with a fine understanding of the Antique.

Tolstoy also produced gouaches (e.g. *Pastorale*, 1820) and *At the Window on a Moonlit Night* (1822; both Moscow, Tret'yakov Gal.) and paintings, such as the *Family Portrait* (1830; St Petersburg, Rus. Mus.). Between 1820 and 1833 he produced a cycle of 64 pen and Indian ink illustrations to the poem *Dushen'ka* ('Darling') by Ippolit Bogdanovich, which he later engraved. Tolstoy made use of line with great skill and with a great sense of style. He also made drawings for the ballet and silhouettes. His work shows a stylistic duality. His medals, reliefs and the illustrations to *Dushen'ka* are consistently classical, while his gouaches are imbued with Romanticism. But all of Tolstoy's work is notable for its sincerity, poetry and tastefulness.

BIBLIOGRAPHY

E. V. Kuznetsova: *Fyodor Petrovich Tolstoy, 1783–1873* (Moscow, 1977)
——: *Fyodor Tolstoy, 1783–1873* (Leningrad, 1981)

SERGEY ANDROSSOV

Tolstoy, Ivan (Ivanovich) (*b* Luga, St Petersburg province, 18 May 1858; *d* Gaspra, Crimea, 20 May 1916). Russian numismatist and art historian. He graduated from the law faculty of St Petersburg University in 1880 and became a member of the Russian Archaeological Society in 1882; he published his book on the coins of Kievan Rus' in the same year. He also made a study of the coins of medieval Novgorod and Pskov. From 1886 to 1891 he served on the Archaeological Commission in St Petersburg and from 1889 to 1893 he was conference secretary and later vice-president of the Academy of Arts (1893–1905). He served as Minister of Education from 1905 to 1916 and was mayor of St Petersburg from 1913 to 1916. In 1911 he became chairman of the Russian Society of Numismatists. His main works are on Byzantine and Russian numismatics, sphragistics and snake amulets.

WRITINGS

Drevneyshiye russkiye monety Velikogo knyazhestva Kiyevskogo [Old Russian coins of the Grand Principality of Kiev] (St Petersburg, 1882)
with N. P. Kondakov: *Russkiye drevnosti v pamyatnikakh iskusstva* [Russian antiquities in monuments of art], 6 vols (St Petersburg, 1889–99); Fr. trans. as *Antiquités de Russie méridionale* (Paris, 1891)
Vizantiyskiye moneti [Byzantine coins], 1–9 (St Petersburg, 1912–14)

BIBLIOGRAPHY

'K 100-letiyu nauchno-numizmaticheskoy deyatel'nosti I. I. Tolstogo: Novyye numizmaticheskiye issledovaniya' [On the occasion of the centenary of I. I. Tolstoy's scholarly work on numismatics: new numismatic research], *Trudy Gosudarstvennogo Istor. Muz.*, lxi (1986) [whole issue]

V. YA. PETRUKHIN

Tolstoy, Lev [Leo] **(Nikolayevich)**, Count (*b* Yasnaya Polyana, Tula province, 9 Sept 1828; *d* Astapovo, Tambov province, 20 Nov 1910). Russian writer and theorist. He studied at Kazan' University, then served in the army

(1851–4), taking part in the defence of Sevastopol' during the Crimean War. He spent most of his life on his estate, Yasnaya Polyana, although he lived for some time in St Petersburg and Moscow and travelled in Europe. His most productive period was from the 1860s to 1890s, when he published his novels *Voyna i mir* ('War and peace'; 1863–9), *Anna Karenina* (1873–7) and the story *Smert' Ivana Il'icha* ('The death of Ivan Il'ich'; 1886), among others. From the early 1850s, however, in his essays and speeches, as well as in his fiction, he expressed his intense, passionate and troubled thoughts on the purpose and meaning of art, eventually creating his own aesthetic system, which was contradictory and influential.

Tolstoy's artistic talent was in conflict with his idea of the aesthetic purpose of art, which he felt should be readily available to all. He became the prisoner of his own opinion: 'There is one view of art, but it is expressed in two ways—in theory and in practice, in abstract musings on art and in the actual work of so-called artists.' In these 'abstract musings' Tolstoy was arguing not so much with others as with himself. 'Aesthetics are the expression of ethics', he wrote in his diary. His credo, 'in order to create a work of art, one has to know what is good and what is evil', gradually introduced an insistent, preaching tone into his literary work. Almost completely rejecting his own creativity as an artist, he consciously wrote pieces that resembled edifying parables aimed at 'the people'.

In his most famous treatise on aesthetics, *Chto takoye iskusstvo?* ('What is art?'; 1898), Tolstoy denied all art aimed solely at the educated part of society and put forward the suggestion that beauty and good are incompatible. Behind his philosophical and aesthetic thinking lay the passionate fanaticism of the Russian writer 'with an inflamed conscience', which was a general characteristic of Russian literature. While working on *Chto takoye iskusstvo?*, he made a deep and detailed analysis of the ideas of Hegel, Fichte, Schelling and others, largely contrasting them with those of Kant, but he rejected their idea of looking on art purely as spiritual food for the upper classes.

Many of Tolstoy's late works, even the novel *Voskresen'ye* ('Resurrection'; 1899), were produced as embodiments of the aesthetic expression of ethics. He decisively rejected the new trends in art at the turn of the century, seeing in them 'the ultimate level of pointlessness'. His general aesthetic statements, when extrapolated to cover the visual arts, remained the same but often seemed naive, since his verbal preaching destroyed the essence of painting. In spite of the contradictions in his aesthetics, or even perhaps because of their self-destructive force, they became a major element of Russian and international artistic life, a touchstone not only for his supporters but also for his opponents. The dogmatism and intellectual asceticism of Tolstoy the theorist, in perpetual conflict with the greatness of Tolstoy the artist, revealed the true significance and fruitfulness of the unresolved conflicts in the life and work of the writer.

WRITINGS

Polnoye sobraniye sochineniy [Complete collected works], 90 vols (Moscow, 1928–58)
Lev Tolstoy ob iskusstve i literature [Lev Tolstoy on art and literature], 2 vols (Moscow, 1958)

BIBLIOGRAPHY
D. S. Merezhkovsky: *Lev Tolstoy i Dostoyevsky* [Lev Tolstoy and Dostoyevsky] (St Petersburg, 1901–2)
A. Maude: *Tolstoy's View of Art* (London, 1902)
N. Courfinkel: *Tolstoi sans tolstoïsme* (Paris, 1946)
N. Weisbein: *L'Evolution religieuse de Tolstoi* (Paris, 1960)
K. Lomunov: *Estetika L'va Tolstogo* [The aesthetics of Lev Tolstoy] (Moscow, 1972)

MIKHAIL GUERMAN

Toltec. Term applied to Pre-Columbian peoples of Central Highland Mesoamerica, north of the Basin of Mexico, and to their cultural and artistic traditions.

1. Introduction. 2. Architecture and planning. 3. Sculpture. 4. Other arts.

1. INTRODUCTION. The Toltecs were one of the dominant cultural and political groups in Mesoamerica during the Early Post-Classic period (*c.* AD 900–*c.* 1200). They ruled much of central Mexico from their capital at TULA (Tollan) and strongly influenced groups throughout Mesoamerica and beyond, including northern Mexico and present-day Central America. The oldest extant historical records from Pre-Columbian central Mexico describe Tula and the Toltecs in highly exaggerated terms, but careful study of these sources has allowed scholars to use them as a supplement to archaeological discoveries. The annals stress the multiplicity of ethnic groups comprising Toltec society, specifically mentioning the Nonoalca and Tolteca–Chichimeca. The Náhuatl-speaking Nonoalca may have been priests and élites who abandoned TEOTIHUACÁN after *c.* AD 650; the Tolteca–Chichimeca were migrants from the frontier zone of Mesoamerica in north-central Mexico, who perhaps spoke Otomí. The term Toltec (Náhuatl *Toltecatl*) originally meant inhabitant of Tollan (the place of the reeds) and later acquired the additional connotations of 'metropolitan, sophisticated, wise, good and master craftsman'.

Ancient Teotihuacán ruled the future Toltec homeland through the Early Classic period (*c.* AD 250–*c.* 600) until its decline in the early part of the Late Classic period (*c.* AD 600–*c.* 900). The area achieved independence as Teotihuacán's power waned and its final seat of power, nearby Chingu, was abandoned (*see also* MESOAMERICA, PRE-COLUMBIAN, §II, 3(ii)). Toltec Tula, a new settlement *c.* 70 km north-west of Teotihuacán, was established on a ridge overlooking the juncture of the Tula and Rosas rivers. It grew slowly at first, but by *c.* AD 950 covered *c.* 5 sq. km and contained between 15,000 and 20,000 people. Explosive growth during the principal period of occupation, the Tollan phase (*c.* AD 950–*c.* 1200), created one of Mesoamerica's largest cities, with an estimated 35,000 to 40,000 inhabitants.

Toltec culture disintegrated shortly after 1150. Crop failures and famines in the arid land, internal conflicts and pressures from northern immigrants in search of new lands all contributed to Tula's downfall. By 1200 the Toltecs had abandoned Tula and dispersed into central Mexico. However, neither the city nor its people were forgotten: the Aztecs copied and even reused Toltec art, and nobles throughout Mesoamerica claimed Toltec ancestry. In ways large and small, later Mesoamericans credited the Toltecs with founding the civilization of which they were a part.

Toltec wealth was based on agriculture, commerce and tribute paid by conquered peoples. Substantial irrigation was necessary in order to assure harvests and increase yields in this arid land. The Toltecs were self-sufficient in basic foodstuffs but imported cacao, tropical fruits, cotton and other items not locally available. The precise boundaries of Tula's tributary domain are not clear, but, with the possible exception of Yucatán, the area did not extend beyond a compact, contiguous zone in north-central Mexico. The extensive deposits of green-gold obsidian (volcanic glass) near the modern city of Pachuca, Hidalgo, were a crucial resource controlled by the Toltecs. Knappers at Tula produced razor-sharp blades, scrapers and other tools. These and the obsidian cores from which they were struck served for both local use and export.

Toltec merchants travelled far beyond the borders of the Toltec empire into Central America, western Mexico, and the northern desert lands near the modern Mexican–United States border. They returned to Tula with both finished products and raw materials: Plumbate and Papagayo polychrome pottery, feathers, cacao and rubber from Guatemala and northern Central America; rare marine shells from the Pacific Ocean and Gulf of Mexico; and turquoise, serpentine, malachite and other exotic stones from northern Mexico and perhaps even the south-western United States.

Although Toltec art has not received as much attention as other Pre-Columbian styles and traditions, it is important both as an expression of Toltec cultural and political beliefs and as the foundation for later AZTEC art. Buildings and their associated façades and sculptures are the most common durable expressions of Toltec art. Unfortunately Pre-Columbian looters removed many Toltec art works from Tula, leaving relatively little for modern scholars to study. In some cases, however, missing information can be inferred from the much better preserved buildings and sculptures at the Maya–Toltec site of CHICHÉN ITZÁ in Yucatán. There are so many striking similarities in the art, architecture and iconography of the two sites that many scholars believe Toltec merchant-warriors conquered the MAYA centre and initiated a building programme modelled on their own capital. Others argue that Chichén Itzá served as an inspiration for the Toltecs. Although the former argument has much evidence in its favour, the debate continues. Nevertheless, the many traits shared by the two sites are so specific that it is evident that sculptors and architects from one site copied works at the other. It is easy to understand why the Toltecs would have attempted such a conquest so far from their homeland, as Chichén Itzá was in a position to control both Yucatán and the coastal trade route along the peninsula from southern Mexico into northern Central America. Whatever the direction of influence, at Chichén Itzá there was a blend of Toltec and southern Mesoamerican Maya traditions, and most of our knowledge of Toltec art comes from the two sites: Chichén Itzá and Tula.

Miguel Covarrubias has characterized Toltec art as geometric, rigid and austere, and considered it to be technically crude, overstylized and awkward. Nevertheless, he believed that 'it shows vigorous directness and structural simplicity in stone carving based upon cubes and cylinders, with the form contained and subordinated to these geometric shapes' (1957, p. 275).

2. ARCHITECTURE AND PLANNING. Toltec architects blended earlier Mesoamerican forms with new elements to create a distinctive style that quickly became an established architectural tradition for the remainder of the Pre-Columbian Post-Classic period (c. AD 900–1521). Older concepts included the placing of buildings around large open plazas; the construction of solid, multi-tiered platforms as bases for temples and other structures; the occasional enlargement of buildings by erecting new structures on top of the old; painted polychrome designs on both interior and exterior surfaces; and the use of architecture as a visible statement of cosmological beliefs and legends, and of political power. New elements invented by the Toltecs or borrowed from other groups included the extensive use of columns as roof supports; elaborately carved friezes; and new building types comprising colonnaded halls, closed-end ballcourts in the shape of a capital letter I and the TZOMPANTLI (skull rack).

Tula's main civic precinct, Tula Grande, is an impressive complex of temples, colonnaded halls and ballcourts surrounding a large open plaza (100 m along each side) on the summit of the ridge. A terrace on the north side of the plaza supported Pyramid B, the Palacio Quemado and the Vestibule. Pyramid B was a five-tiered temple base constructed of rock and earth rubble. It shows the use of inherited concepts and new ideas in a single structure; the solid platform was enlarged on at least three occasions (the second stage is visible today). Pyramid C, Tula's largest temple mound, occupies the east side of the plaza. Numerous unexcavated temples and other structures surround Tula Grande, and the entire precinct forms part of a larger acropolis defined by huge terrace walls that descend the slopes facing the river. During the Tollan phase the city extended beyond the 2-km-long ridge into adjacent lowlands and covered c. 13 sq. km. Most of this area was filled with stone and adobe houses constructed in groups of two or more around interior courtyards. The house groups were walled off from their neighbours and apparently accommodated several related families.

Residential structures and their associated artefacts show that Toltec society was organized into socio-economic classes and occupational groups including rulers, priests, warriors, merchants, craftsmen, farmers and perhaps slaves. Wealthy individuals occupied spacious, well-built houses with plastered walls, occasionally adorned with painted designs, and used exotic imported goods. Most people, however, lived in unpretentious structures that provided adequate shelter but few amenities, and relied upon local products to fulfil their material needs.

The Palacio Quemado, which forms most of the north side of Tula Grande's main precinct, is a notable example of the Toltec use of columns and other new elements. The roof it shared with the contiguous Vestibule, a colonnaded portico along the front of Pyramid B (see below), was supported by stone columns with wood-beam cores. The use of columns, perhaps adapted from groups living in northern Mexico, allowed Toltec architects to circumvent limitations on room size imposed by the length of single beams resting on structural walls. The sides of the three largest rooms in the Palacio Quemado measure approximately 24 m, and each room contains at least 30 columns. Central roof openings admitted light without weakening the structure. The colonnaded hall based on the Toltec model was quickly adopted by other groups and became a standard building type throughout Mesoamerica. At Chichén Itzá the Temple of the Warriors and the Group of the Thousand Columns on the east side of the site form a similar building complex to Tula's Pyramid B and Palacio Quemado.

Enclosed ballcourts, on which teams played a game with a solid rubber ball, were constructed long before Tula emerged as a major centre, but courts constructed in the shape of a capital letter I were a later innovation, which the Toltecs may have adopted from slightly older examples at Xochicalco or Monte Albán (*see also* Ballcourt, §1). Two such ballcourts excavated at Tula Grande were severely looted after the city's abandonment, but stone marker rings originally placed into the playing field walls were found in both structures. If the Toltec ritual game was similar to that played in later times, the contest was won by propelling the ball through the holes in the rings or into the back of the opponents' court.

The *tzompantli* comprised a masonry platform surmounted by rows of poles to hold hundreds, perhaps even thousands, of perforated human skulls taken from sacrificial victims. Skull racks are frequently associated with ballcourts, and the skulls may have belonged to losers or victims sacrificed during rituals associated with the game. Chichén Itzá's skull rack platform has a carved frieze of human skulls, but Tula's is too badly damaged to know if it shared this feature.

3. Sculpture. Processional friezes showing humans and animals were another Toltec innovation. At times they simply involved repetitions of the same motif, but all seem to portray figures moving towards a central focal point. Similar processions may have occurred in real life while the buildings were in use.

At Tula Grande, Pyramid B had carved panels covering the exterior of each stage. They formed elaborate friezes, which apparently represented a complex cosmological myth (see fig.). The figures on the friezes move from the back of the structure along the sides to the stairway facing the plaza. The remains are too fragmentary to permit an accurate reconstruction of the entire mythic text, but it seems to portray the death and rebirth of Venus as the Morning and Evening stars. Each tier of the platform contains two horizontal registers, and the same imagery is repeated on every tier. The upper ones show jaguars and coyotes, while those below depict eagles and vultures holding human hearts in their beaks, alternating with a composite being that has bird, serpent, jaguar and human features. This creature is thought to be Tlahuizcalpantecuhtli (Venus the Morning Star) or Tlalchitonatiuh (the Sun in the underworld at night). The animals may be avatars for Toltec military orders, perhaps conceived as the god's earthly companions. White paint, symbolic of the underworld into which the sun disappears at night and where Venus resides during conjunction, covers the entire surface.

Toltec carvings on the lower friezes of the east face of Pyramid B, Tula Grande, 10th–11th centuries AD

In the Palacio Quemado a procession of richly attired men, perhaps priests or rulers, adorns masonry banquettes and altars placed against the interior walls. The figures appear to march out of the building and along the Vestibule towards the stairs of Pyramid B. The cornices above them show a procession of serpent deities in which Mixcóatl (the Cloud Serpent) alternates with Quetzalcóatl (the Feathered Serpent). On the nearby Coatepantli at Tula, a free-standing wall decorated with representations of serpents devouring humans, the frieze apparently depicts a similar or related myth (for illustration *see* Coatepantli). The figures face towards a now-missing figure or element in the centre of the wall.

The temple that once stood on top of Pyramid B was destroyed in Pre-Columbian times, but the roof is known to have been supported by the unusual carved stone columns excavated and replaced on the platform of the pyramid by archaeologists. Four of these columns (h. 4.6 m) are carved in the likeness of Toltec warriors and were originally brightly painted. Behind these stand four square pilasters carved in low relief with Toltec warriors on each face. The temple door was flanked by feathered serpents carved on stone drums; their lower jaws rested on the ground while their raised tails served as lintel supports.

4. Other arts. Although few examples have survived the Aztec looting of Tula, the Toltecs also practised lapidary and ceramic arts as well as importing finished pieces. The friezes at Tula show men wearing elaborate jewellery, but none has actually been found. Globular vessels of travertine were made using string and abrasive saws to cut the shape, and bone and abrasive drills to hollow out the interior. Other lapidary objects included utilitarian grinding stones, mortars and pestles, axes and celts, beads and large quantities of obsidian tools and debris.

Toltec ceramics were primarily utilitarian. They included various shallow dishes—either flat-based or with tripod supports, nearly flat circular cooking pans called *comals*, hemispherical bowls, censers, pipes and figurines. Censers were either frying-pan shaped, with long handles, or openwork globular pots with handles. Figurines were made by pressing the clay into flat moulds. Humans with intricate costumes and ornaments are the most common subjects, including women with elaborate coiffures and distinctive long skirts. Other figurines are birds, feline creatures, and dogs and other canids. Some have holes in the legs to hold axles for wheels. The function of the figurines is not clear, but they may have been used as medicinal aids, and some may have been toys, as they have been found most frequently in excavations of household debris.

See also under MESOAMERICA, PRE-COLUMBIAN.

BIBLIOGRAPHY

J. R. Acosta: 'Interpretación de algunos de los datos obtenidos en Tula relativos a la época tolteca', *Rev. Mex. Estud. Antropol.*, xiv (1956–7), pp. 75–110
M. Covarrubias: *Indian Art of Mexico and Central America* (New York, 1957)
C. N. B. Davies: *The Toltecs until the Fall of Tula* (Norman, 1977)
R. A. Diehl: 'Tula', *Hb. Mid. Amer. Ind.*, i, suppl. (1981), pp. 277–95
——: *Tula: The Toltec Capital of Ancient Mexico* (London, 1983)
E. T. Baird: 'Naturalistic and Symbolic Color at Tula, Hidalgo', *Painted Architecture and Polychrome Monumental Sculpture in Mesoamerica*, ed. E. Boone (Washington, DC, 1985), pp. 115–44

RICHARD A. DIEHL

Tołwiński, Tadeusz (*b* Odessa, 18 Jan 1887; *d* Warsaw, 13 Jan 1951). Polish architect, teacher and urban planner. He studied architecture at the Technische Hochschule, Karlsruhe (1904–11), specializing in urban design. He travelled widely in Europe and the USA, and during World War I he worked for the Society for the Protection of Historic Buildings in Warsaw. He helped establish the Faculty of Architecture at Warsaw Technical University in 1915, teaching architectural design and then becoming Head of Urban Design Studies in 1920. Under his direction the Architects Circle prepared a new regulating urban plan for Warsaw (1916), which resulted from progressive developments in urban planning studies and the widening of the city boundaries. Its chief concerns included transport, public health and the development of centres for public life, proposing four different development zones; the plan was used until 1926 when it was replaced by a more detailed plan. Tołwiński also prepared development plans for Greater Lwów (now Lvov, Ukraine) in 1922, as well as Kalisz and Ciechocinek. After World War I, Tołwiński's architectural approach followed the nationalist 'mansion house' style based on traditional Polish country houses. His Stefan Batory School (1924), Warsaw, was in the early Baroque style. He later became one of the principal exponents of a modern form of classicism, which combined new construction methods and forms with the principles of classical composition. He came to public attention with his competition entries for the National Museum (1926) and the Great Theatre Square (1927; unexecuted), both in Warsaw. The former, built in stages (1927–38), broke with the academic tradition of decorative composition; its simple façades were faced with stone and articulated with full-height pilasters. It was one of the largest buildings of the period, reflecting its central role in city life. Tołwiński became Professor of Urban Design at Warsaw Technical University in 1935; under his direction the department became the centre of urban planning studies in Poland. His book on urban design was one of the most important works in its field in Polish.

WRITINGS
Urbanistyka [Urban design], 3 vols (Warsaw, 1934–63)

BIBLIOGRAPHY
Towarzystwo Urbanistów Polskich, 1923–1963 [Society of Polish Town Planners, 1923–1963] (Warsaw, 1963)
J. Minorski: *Polska nowatorska myśl architektoniczna w latach, 1918–1939* [Polish innovative thought in architecture, 1918–1939] (Warsaw, 1970)

WANDA KEMP-WELCH

Toma, Gioacchino (*b* Galatina, Lecce, 24 Jan 1836; *d* Naples, 12 Jan 1891). Italian painter. He was orphaned at the age of six and spent an unhappy childhood and adolescence in convents and poorhouses; these experiences would later provide subjects for his paintings. He was first taught drawing at the art school in the hospice for the poor in the Adriatic town of Giovinazzo, but in 1855 he moved to Naples, where he worked for an ornamental painter named Alessandro Fergola. In 1857 he was mistakenly arrested for conspiracy and exiled to Piedimonte d'Alife, 60 km from Naples, where he was initiated into the secret society of the Carbonari by some local liberal aristocrats who also became his first patrons. His paintings for them were mainly still-lifes, largely in the traditional Neapolitan style. On his return to Naples in 1858 he became a student at the Accademia di Belle Arti, attending the classes of Domenico Morelli, who influenced such early works as *Erminia* (1859; Naples, Pal. Reale). Toma fought for two years with Garibaldi in the campaign for the unification of Italy, then returned to painting, exhibiting *A Revolutionary Priest* at the Esposizione Nazionale in Florence in 1861 (untraced, see Biancale, 1933, pl. 10). In 1862 Toma participated in the first exhibition of the Società Promotrice di Belle Arti di Napoli, showing the *Children of the People* (Bari, Pin. Prov.), a political allegory, and *St Peter's Pence* (Naples, Capodimonte). His work began to treat themes, whether historical or contemporary, from a domestic, everyday viewpoint, focusing more on sentiment and psychology than on the representation of events as such. This youthful phase, influenced by the work of Filippo Palizzi, terminated with *A Stern Cross-examination by the Holy Office* (1864; Naples, Pal. Municipio). Through it the characteristics of Toma's mature style began to show themselves: a harsh perspective, severe composition and the use of all elements for symbolic, never merely decorative, purposes. These elements combined, in the maturer works produced up till 1880, with a control of light achieved through the modulation of cold tones. They keep his paintings from the triteness his chosen themes—derived from minor works of romantic literature—could easily have resulted in. His subtle judgement of effect is particularly evident in his second version of *Luisa Sanfelice in Prison* (Rome, G.N.A. Mod.), where the drama of an incident of Neapolitan history is conveyed through the exploration of light and tone.

Toma taught applied design in a workers' school in Naples from 1865 to 1870, and in an embroidery school that was part of a women's hospice. In 1878 he was invited by Morelli to teach ornamental drawing at the Royal Institute of Fine Art in Naples. Around 1880 he began to feel out of touch with contemporary developments in painting. He entered a period of crisis and radically changed his technique. Stylistically, he moved closer to the painters of the Scuola di Resina, and began to produce works full of luminosity, such as *Nightjars at Torre del Greco* (Naples, Capodimonte). These paintings are characterized by thick, separate brushstrokes, as in an unfinished sketch.

WRITINGS
Autobiografia (Naples, 1886); rev. as *Ricordi di un orfano* (1973)

BIBLIOGRAPHY
G. Tesorone: *Gioacchino Toma e l'opera sua* (Rome, 1905)
M. Biancale: *Gioacchino Toma* (Rome, 1933)
A. De Rinaldis: *Gioacchino Toma* (Milan, 1934)
S. Ortolani: *Gioacchino Toma* (Rome and Bergamo, 1934)
Mostra di Gioacchino Toma (exh. cat., ed. L. Salerno; Rome, 1954)
R. Causa: *La Sala Toma* (Naples, 1962)
P. Ricci: 'Gioacchino Toma, pittore piccolo-borghese', *'Nferta Napoletana* (Naples, 1975), pp. 167–97
L. Galante: *Gioacchino Toma* (Lecce, 1975) [illus. and bibliog.]

MARIANTONIETTA PICONE PETRUSA

Toma de la Suceava (*fl* 1533–41). Romanian painter. Although there is virtually no information about his other projects, it seems probable that he was the principal painter of the mural ensemble (1533) at Humor Church. A document of chancellery mentions 'Toma painter and courtier of His Highness Petru Voyvod of Moldavia', and the name 'Toma' appears in the scene of the *Siege of Constantinople* from the external painting of Humor Church. The decoration of the church, the external walls of which are entirely covered with frescoes, is executed according to a coherent iconographic programme. The internal paintings record the prescriptions of the Orthodox religion, with some noteworthy paintings: the *Embodied Virgin*, surrounded by two concentric circles of angels and prophets with dancing movements (on the pronaos vault), the votive scene of the family of Petru Rares (naos) and the *Last Judgement* (porch). The paintings on the external walls reflect some of the moral and anti-Ottoman ideas of the period. The *Akatistos Hymn* (24 stanzas) surrounds the *Glorification of the Virgin*, and the *Siege of Constantinople*, the *Isaiah Tree* and the *Prayer of All Saints* are painted on the three apses. The frescoes are notable for the rhythm and movement of the figures, the folds of the drapery, the emphasis on facial expressions, the melodious and chromatic lines, and for the fact that the predominating terracotta is enlivened with pinks, blues and greens.

BIBLIOGRAPHY
V. Drăguț: *Humor* (Bucharest, 1973)
S. Ulea: 'Pictura exterioara' [The external painting], *Istoria artelor plastice in Romania* [The history of fine arts in Romania], i (Bucharest, 1988), pp. 364–5

TEREZA-IRENE SINIGALIA

Tomar [Thomar] **Abbey.** Fortified abbey *c.* 45 km southeast of Leiria, Portugal. From 1339 it was the headquarters of the Supreme Order of Christ. In 1159 Alfonso I (*reg* 1139–85) gave the site to Gualdim Pais (*d* 1195), Grand Master of the Order of Knights Templar in Portugal. On 1 March 1160 the Order began work on extensive fortifications, dominated by a castle that preserves its original plan of an irregular pentagon with a detached donjon in the centre of the enclosure: it withstood a siege by the Almohads in 1190. Tomar was the seat of the Portuguese branch of the Templars, which was dissolved in 1312. The Order of Christ was established in 1319 by King Diniz (*reg* 1279–1325) to inherit the Templars' property and traditions.

The rotunda or Charola was also begun in 1160, the typical round church of the Templars (*see* CHURCH, fig. 4). It is a Romanesque–Gothic, centrally planned building against one of the castle walls, and also served as a defensive tower. The work was carried out in two campaigns, interrupted by the siege of 1190, and completed in the mid-13th century. The exterior has 16 sides supported by radial buttresses, with narrow arched windows in each wall. The projecting east bay, which could be called the façade, has a door at ground level and a window above, showing the influence of the west front of the Old Cathedral at Coimbra. The rotunda is crowned by merlons, which were rebuilt and chamfered in the 16th century; the central lantern tower with a pyramidal cupola was destroyed by lightning in 1506. Inside, the circular ambulatory–nave has 16 bays with barrel vaulting and arches, and in the centre an octagonal drum defined by eight pointed arches, the capitals of which are decorated with roughly carved figures of affronted animals, dragons, serpents, basilisks, birds, lions and humans reflecting the theme of Prudentius' *Psychomachia*. There are also biblical scenes with cosmological symbolism in keeping with the character of the central plan, as a 'lantern of the dead' and continuing a tradition of liturgical reference derived from the church of the Holy Sepulchre, Jerusalem.

The Order of Christ made many alterations to the buildings. In the second quarter of the 15th century the palace of the Knights and the Gothic Lavabo Cloister and Cemetery Cloister (the latter influenced by the Batalha Abbey workshop) were constructed by Fernão Gonçalves. These were joined to the Charola by a temporary sacristy and choir. The enrichment of the Order of Christ under the governorship of Manuel I and the magnificence of the General Chapter held at Tomar in 1503 brought a new direction to the abbey: Manuel commissioned Diogo de Arruda to build a spacious, rectangular choir (1510–13) with a new sacristy below, west of the rotunda. The Late Gothic features of this extremely original building are remarkable for the Manueline royal iconography. The west window, between two semicircular buttresses, is an outstanding statement of royal power, combining traditional heraldic and scriptural elements in an eschatological vision of the history of Portugal and the King's life (for illustration *see* ARRUDA, (1)). At the base of the window an old man embraces the roots of an oak tree, the buttresses are carved with symbols of the Order of the Garter and spiritual chivalry, reinterpreting Isaiah's prophecy concerning Emmanuel (Isaiah 7:14) and relating it to the Tree of Life, perhaps connected with the eulogy of Manuel declaimed by Egidio de Viterbo (1469–1532) before the court of Pope Julius II in 1507.

In 1515 João de Castilho added a doorway (see fig.) on the south side, framed by statues in a typological scheme, and a wide arch between the rotunda and the new choir in a style that is more Plateresque than Manueline. At about the same time the interior decoration of the rotunda

Tomar Abbey, south door of church by João de Castilho, 1515

was completed, with gilded stucco (including eight coupled wild men) and painted wooden statues of saints and prophets by OLIVIER OF GHENT and Fernão Muñoz, who were also responsible for the choir-stalls (1511–12; most destr. 1809–10). The ambulatory wall had fourteen panel paintings, of which six remain, attributed to the workshop of the royal painter Jorge Afonso, and the vaults decorated in Hispano-Flemish style with grisaille *trompe l'oeil* frescoes.

After the reforms of 1529, the Order of Christ became enclosed, and the convent was vastly expanded, with a drastic alteration in style and in the organization of interior spaces. Castilho was appointed Master of the Works in 1530 and developed a combination of Late Gothic Plateresque and Renaissance elements, initially experimental and somewhat self-taught, then influenced by Italian theorists (*see* CASTILHO, (1)). An impressive group of buildings was added west of the Manueline choir, surrounding and to some extent constricting it, including a monumental two-storey chapter house (unfinished), a refectory and six cloisters around the Cruzeiro, a two-storey building on a Latin-cross plan. The coffered ceiling of the chapel (1534) at the east end is richly decorated with relief figures of unidentified sacred and secular subjects. The layout may possibly be associated with Neo-Platonic concepts and St Augustine's *City of God* and derived from other hospital and service buildings of tried functionality, such as Antonio Filarete's Ospedale Maggiore (from 1456), Milan, and the Hospital Real de Todos-os-Santos (1492–1504; destr. after 1755), Lisbon. The principal cloister (destr.) had two storeys and revealed the two main influences on Castilho, the Plateresque structure and arrangement being disguised

by classical shapes and forms. Also from the first campaign is the disconcerting St Barbara Cloister, which demonstrates his audacity, inspired by experimentation with hybrid solutions. The four other cloisters are designed on the same lines as the principal cloister, with bays of two semicircular arches with Tuscan columns on both upper and lower floors, but sometimes with a trabeated gallery. The different areas are joined by spiral staircases crowned by domed lanterns. The rooms for the Noviciate (1551) were the last of Castilho's additions, two rectangular rooms of equal size in which four non-canonical Ionic columns support a trabeated timber ceiling. The third room, the larger and square oratory, shows an improved solution with 16 Corinthian columns supporting a groin-vaulted ceiling, which suggests that he knew of the tetrastyle hall illustrated in Cesare Cesariano's Italian edition of Vitruvius (Como, 1521).

In 1558 the new principal cloister, the cloister of John III, was begun by Diogo de Torralva. The cloister has two storeys, the lower Doric, the upper Ionic (*see* TORRALVA, DIOGO DE, fig. 1). In the corners of the cloister are cylindrical turrets containing spiral staircases, the balustrades of which are visible from outside through the windows. Work virtually ceased for 20 years until Filippo Terzi completed Torro's design in 1587. Other benefactions during Philip II's reign provided the new sacristy (*c.* 1593), a Mannerist structure with a coffered ceiling with ornamental relief, and the new monumental entrance to the convent, the Portaria Nova (first third of the 17th century), possibly by Diogo Castro Lucas, announcing the arrival of the Plain Style.

BIBLIOGRAPHY

Definições e Estatutos dos Cavalleiros e Freires da Ordem de Nosso Senhor Jesus Christo (Lisbon, 1746)
An. Mun. Tomar (1920–40)
J. Barreira: *Arte portuguesa: Evolução estética* (Lisbon, 1948–50)
J. W. O'Malley: 'Fulfilment of the Christian Golden Age under Pope Julius II: Text of a Discourse of Giles of Viterbe', *Traditio*, xxv (1969), pp. 265–338
R. Moreira: 'Arquitectura', *Os descobrimentos portugueses e a Europa do renascimento* (exh. cat., 17th Council of Europe, exh.; Lisbon, 1983), pp. 307–52
A. C. Leite and P. Pereira: 'Para uma leitura da simbólica manuelina', *Prelo*, v (1984), pp. 51–74
P. Dias: *A arquitectura manuelina* (Oporto, 1988)
R. Moreira: *A arquitectura do renascimento no sul de Portugal* (Lisbon, 1991)

PAULO PEREIRA

Tomasino da Vimercate (*fl c.* 1390–1415). Italian illuminator. Payment to this artist was recorded on 31 May 1409 for painting the first volume of the *Ambrosianae*, a compilation from the teachings of St Ambrose, made for the Fabbrica of Milan Cathedral. This manuscript survives (Cambridge, Fitzwilliam, MS. C.F.M. 9) and the illumination by Tomasino (see fig.) identifies him as the artist known as the Master of the Modena Hours. He was the most prolific illuminator working in Milan at the turn of the century, illustrating manuscripts for both court and ecclesiastical patrons.

Tomasino was responsible for the decoration of several Books of Hours, including that in Modena after which he was at one time named (*c.* 1390; Modena, Bib. Estense, MS. alpha R. 7. 3, lat. 842). His approach to composition, figure types and bright palette show his dependence on the MASTER OF LATIN 757 (*see* MASTERS, ANONYMOUS, AND MONOGRAMMISTS, §I), although these features are combined with decorative details and an occasional animation, the result of his contact with the De Grassi style. Tomasino's work is at its most polished and inventive in the earliest folios of the Book of Hours later completed for Isabella, Queen of Castile (The Hague, Kon. Bib., MS. 76. F. 6). The delightful full-page borders range from a continuous narrative of the Virgin's journey from her own house to St Elizabeth's, culminating in the historiated initial of the *Visitation* (fol. 14r), to a border composed of two tall and verdant trees with perching birds pursued by climbing naked infants (fol. 24). Not all his output was of this quality or lavish variety and it was the more solid and consistent characteristics of his style—the strong bright colouring and smooth modelling within firm outlines—that were taken up by the Master of the Vitae Imperatorum.

BIBLIOGRAPHY

A. Radaeli: 'Di uno sconosciuto codice lombardo nella Palatina di Parma e il suo miniatore', *Aurea Parma*, xlviii (1964), pp. 245–59

——: 'Nuovi contributi al catalogo del miniatore dell'alfa R 7 3 dell'Estense di Modena', *G. Bord.*, ii (1968–9), pp. 65–7

——: 'Ancora per il miniatore dell'alfa R 7 3 dell'Estense', *G. Bord.*, ii (1968–9), p. 113

M. Bollati: 'Nuove proposte per il Maestro del libro d'ore di Modena', *A. Crist.*, lxxvii (1989), pp. 27–35

K. Sutton: 'The Master of the *Modena Hours*, Tomasino da Vimercate, and the *Ambrosianae* of Milan Cathedral', *Burl. Mag.*, cxxxiii (1991), pp. 87–90

KAY SUTTON

Tomaso [Tommaso] **da Modena** [Barisini, Tomaso] (*b* Modena, 1325–6; *d* before 16 July 1379). Italian painter.

1. LIFE AND WORK. He was the son of a Modenese painter, Barisino Barisini (*fl* 1317; *d* 1343), who probably taught him the craft. Tomaso was absent from Modena in 1346 and has been assumed to have continued his training in Bologna after his father's death, probably in the workshop of Vitale da Bologna: his art shows knowledge of the subject-matter and techniques of Bolognese illumination, as well as dependence on the style and work of Vitale. Two panel paintings probably belong to this period: a small triptych (410×388 mm; Modena, Gal. & Mus. Estense) and the centre of a reliquary triptych (Bologna, Pin. N.). The little triptych is signed with a prayer to the Virgin; its date, repainted and variously interpreted, may be 1345. The subject-matter of holy hermits and martyrs and the *Descent into Limbo* shares the solemn tone of the prayer. The dramatic composition, the facial types and rich brushwork are strongly influenced by Vitale. The reliquary panel has three registers, the central one with three images of the Virgin: showing her pregnant and reading, feeding the Christ Child, and knitting his seamless tunic. The four elegant Virgin Martyrs below are dressed in the latest and finest fashions; such figures are frequently found in Tomaso's work. The damaged *St Agnes* of this panel is the only example to preserve the full richness of his conception of courtly dress.

Tomaso is recorded as a resident of Treviso 1349–54; most of his surviving frescoes date from this period. The earliest is perhaps the *Virgin and Saints* in the Giacomelli chapel, S Francesco, Treviso, which suggests a wide range

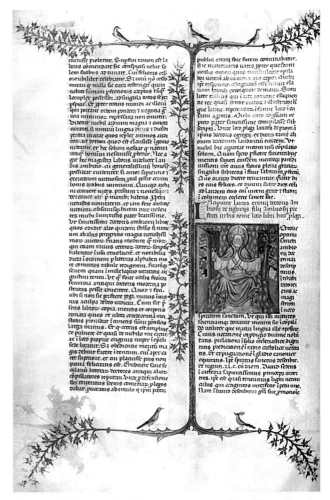

Tomasino da Vimercate: *St Ambrose*, tempera on goatskin; miniature from the *Ambrosianae*, 415×280 mm, 1409 (Cambridge, Fitzwilliam Museum, MS. C.F.M. 9, fol. 4*v*)

of influences, including Vitale, Duccio and Puccio Capanna. In 1352 Tomaso signed and dated the frescoes of the chapter house of the Dominicans of S Nicolò, Treviso, where the provincial chapter was held in 1351. These frescoes are notable for the lifelike representations of 20 canonized and venerated members of the Order and the two popes and 18 cardinals promoted from it. The faces of *Pope Benedict XI*, who came from Treviso, and *St Dominic* are probably copied from their tombs. The friars are shown in their cells studying, writing or turned to the viewer; the composition of their schematically drawn cells, flanking the earlier *Crucifixion* in the centre of the east wall, is related to Bolognese legal illumination and tomb sculpture. Similarly, the meticulous representation of writing materials and books reflects Tomaso's knowledge of the Bolognese book trade. The spectacles worn by *Hugues de St Cher* may be the first ever painted, and the representation of the reading glass of *Nicholas of Rouen* and the scissors of *Pierre de Palud* is equally precocious. On the most prominent pier of the nave of S Nicolò, Tomaso painted *SS Jerome, Romuald, Agnes and John the Baptist. St*

Jerome (see fig. 1), a development of the idea of the scholar shown in the chapter house, is represented commenting on the Gospels and on his own sermons and letters. The depiction of surface textures, Jerome's deep-set eyes, curly beard and eyebrows, and the varying scripts of books and letters are of considerable richness. The writing implements hanging from nails cast shadows on the wall, an early example of this phenomenon.

Tomaso worked in most of the major churches of Treviso, although the frescoes usually attributed to him in S Caterina seem more likely to be by a follower of Altichiero *c.* 1380–85. His most extensive fresco cycle known is from the chapel of S Orsola in S Margherita, the church of the Augustinian Friars (detached; Treviso, Mus. Civ. Bailo). Here he painted the *Legend of St Ursula*, covering a recently painted *Navicella* to which he may himself have contributed. The frescoes probably date from the Hungarian siege of 1356–8, since St Ursula was martyred by the Huns (with whom the medieval Hungarians identified themselves) outside the walls of Cologne during a similar siege. Three rows of two scenes on the side walls related the *Legend*, the last two combined in the single large scene of the *Martyrdom*. Above was the

1. Tomaso da Modena: *St Jerome* (*c.* 1352–5), fresco, S Nicolò, Treviso

Annunciation, an unusual interpretation with Gabriel (destr.) and the Virgin shown frontally looking at each other across the chapel; Mary was accompanied by an early detailed depiction of a herb garden and a scholar's desk of books. The borders and several of the compositions of the *Legend* make deliberate quotations from Giotto's frescoes in the Arena chapel, Padua. Many figures are derived from Vitale, while the *Abdication of Cyriacus* is an adaptation of the standard Bolognese miniature of a papal consistory court. The spectacular costumes probably recall the visit to Treviso of the Empress Anna of Svidnica (*reg* 1353–62) in 1354. The detail of the women's dresses is almost entirely lost, but the English and the Huns appear to be wearing characteristic Hungarian hats.

Tomaso painted two works on panel, both signed, for the Emperor Charles IV's new palace at Karlštejn, Bohemia. The earlier, painted *c.* 1355–60, is a large buttressed diptych (Karlštejn, Imp. Pal.) showing the *Virgin and Child*, the *Man of Sorrows* and the *Archangels Michael and Gabriel* (see fig. 2). Its subject, style and two-tier composition appear to be based on Simone Martini's *St Caterina* polyptych (Pisa, Mus. N. & Civ. S Matteo), which Charles would have seen in 1355, but Tomaso surpasses even his model in the richness of the goldwork and the delicacy of his pinks and ultramarine blues. The second work, a triptych painted *c.* 1359–60, is signed with a Latin couplet. This painting was transferred to the Holy Cross chapel in Karlštejn's Great Tower *c.* 1365; its frame was lost and the background was modified during this process or the 18th-century restoration in Vienna. It shows the *Virgin with SS Wenceslas and Palmatius*; the saints wear richly decorated armour typical of the 1360s. The painting shows a new roundness and plasticity characteristic of Tomaso's later work.

The simplicity and solidity of the Karlštejn triptych are found also in several fragmentary works that survive from Tomaso's later career, which was more productive than is generally recognized. He is recorded in Modena from 1358 to 1360 when he married, and again from 1366 to 1368. He probably resided there continuously apart from working on commissions near by, notably the fresco of *St Augustine* from S Lorenzo, Piacenza (Piacenza, Mus. Civ.). A fresco showing the *Virgin and Child Reading*, a subject typical of Tomaso, survives above the pulpit of Modena Cathedral. There are two small panel fragments, probably both associated with relics: a *cimasa* (altarpiece gabling) of *SS Francis and Clare with the Annunciation* (Modena, Mus. Stor. & A. Med. & Mod.), which dates from the 1360s, and the painted frame with the *Evangelists, SS Michael, Cosmas and Damian* that Tomaso set around the right wing of a *verre églomisé* diptych (Baltimore, MD, Walters A.G.). Judging from Michael's short surcoat and the light, brilliant colours, this dates from the 1370s.

Tomaso's last work was the fresco cycle of the *Lives of Christ and St Louis of Toulouse* in the Gonzaga chapel, S Francesco, Mantua. Most of the cycle was painted by Serafino Serafini, who was summoned to Mantua in 1375, and his assistants, but the earliest fragments of the *St Louis* cycle and the *Ascension* at the bottom of the opposite wall show Tomaso's greater command of modelling and individual expression. A characteristic touch is introduced into the *Ascension*, where Christ is accompanied by angels

2. Tomaso da Modena: *Virgin and Child*, the *Man of Sorrows* and the *Archangels Michael and Gabriel*, tempera on panel, h. 1.61 m, *c.* 1355–60 (Karlštejn, Imperial Palace)

playing fantastic instruments. Tomaso probably designed most of the frescoes, which are composed around pinnacled buttresses typical of his frame designs. They show more elaborate architecture than in his earlier works, perhaps influenced by Altichiero and certainly modified by Serafino. Tomaso may have died soon after the completion of this cycle *c.* 1375–8. His son returned his mother's dowry to her in 1379.

2. WORKING METHODS AND TECHNIQUE. Tomaso appears to have painted fewer standard panel paintings than his Bolognese or Venetian contemporaries. His panels are designed in the Venetian manner with elaborate gables and rich mouldings set on rectangular boards. Their foliate spandrels are a personal development. Tomaso's painting style and technique derive principally from Vitale, notably in his elegant faces with high cheekbones, in the deep brown chiaroscuro of the flesh tone and in the intense, half-closed eyes usually looking slightly sideways. They are modified by many other influences, however, including Simone Martini, Puccio Capanna and the Lorenzetti, and also Roman and 14th-century sculpture. On panel Tomaso used a wide range of colours, but the combination of scarlet, mid-yellow and ultramarine or azurite blue used in the figures of SS Catherine, Agnes or Ursula is particularly

striking. Frequently colour is applied in delicate veils of paint, particularly in the Karlštejn diptych. No oil glaze has been identified in the laboratory, despite the 18th-century misconception that Tomaso invented oil painting, but they may be present in the well-preserved diptych panel in Baltimore. In the *cimasa* (Modena, Mus. Stor. & A. Med. & Mod.) a simplified system of highlights on a dark base tone is used, derived from Bolognese illumination and the cheaper kinds of Venetian panel painting. The Baltimore diptych panel combines a similar but more careful rendering with the brighter tonal painting of the late 14th century. Tomaso's range of punches for goldwork is generally restricted to circles and a 'hexarosette', but the Karlštejn panels employ elaborate incised goldwork and pastiglia. Tomaso's surviving frescoes make use of green and red-brown earth colours and of the contrast of deeply modelled faces and limbs with pale and flat wall-surfaces. In the *St Ursula* cycle and the *St Agnes* (both S Nicolò, Treviso) the plaster is finely hatched, suggesting that metal foils were originally used, and traces of richly patterned draperies added *a secco* are still visible.

3. INFLUENCE AND HISTORICAL IMPORTANCE. While Bolognese painting was dominated by the personality of Vitale in the years 1340–60, Tomaso may well have received commissions because of his receptivity to new ideas. He replaced the dramatic gestures of earlier Bolognese painting with more closely observed details such as the legible texts in paintings of scholars and the detail of the Virgin knitting Christ's seamless tunic on four needles (Bologna, Pin. N.). He also participated in a widespread interest in the description of fashions, objects and their settings, which, with the exception of Andrea de' Bartoli's work, left Bologna otherwise largely unaffected. His late style probably influenced Simone dei Crocefissi, who appears to have followed many of his ideas. Tomaso was evidently regarded as Italy's leading painter in the late 1350s. The panels sent to Karlštejn were a major influence on Bohemian painting *c.* 1360–80, while the master of the frescoes of SS Vittore e Corona, Feltre, and several lesser Trevisan painters show his influence in the province of Treviso, as does Serafino in Modena.

BIBLIOGRAPHY

DBI: Barisini, Tomaso

J. J. Q. Jahn: *Etwas von den ältesten Mahler Böhmens*, Archiv des Geschichte und Statistik (Dresden, 1792)

L. Bailo: *Degli affreschi salvati nella demolita chiesa di S Margherita in Treviso* (Treviso, 1883)

J. Neuwirth: *Mittelalterliche Wandegemälde und Tafelbilder der Burg Karlštein in Böhmen*, Forschungen zur Kstgeschichte Böhmens, i (Prague, 1896)

J. Schlosser: 'Tommaso da Modena und die ältere Malerei in Treviso', *Jb. Ksthist. Samml. Wien*, xix (1898), pp. 240–83

G. Bertoni and E. P. Vicini: 'Tommaso da Modena, pittore modenese del sec. XIV', *Atti & Mem. Reale Deput. Stor. Patria Prov. Moden.*, n. s. 4, v (1903), pp. 287–96

L. Coletti: *Tomaso da Modena* (Bologna, 1932, rev. 2/Venice, 1963)

F. Zava Boccazzi: *Tommaso da Modena*, Maestri Colore (Milan, 1966)

L. Menegazzi, ed.: *Tomaso da Modena* (Treviso, 1979)

Tomaso da Modena e il suo tempo. Atti del convegno: Treviso, 1979

S. M. Newton: 'Tomaso da Modena, Simone Martini, Hungarians and St Martin in 14th-century Italy', *J. Warb. & Court. Inst.*, xliii (1980), pp. 234–8

R. Gibbs: *L'occhio di Tomaso* (Treviso, 1981)

O. Pujmanová: 'Prague, Naples et Avignon: Oeuvres de Tomaso da Modena à Karlštejn', *Rev. A.* [Paris], liii (1981), pp. 56–65

——: *Tomaso da Modena: Painting in Emilia and the March of Treviso, 1340–1380* (Cambridge, 1989)

ROBERT GIBBS

Tomaszewski, Henryk Albin (*b* Siedlce, 1 March 1906; *d* 19 July 1993). Polish glass artist. Between 1926 and 1930 he attended the Municipal School of Decorative Art and Painting in Warsaw and between 1930 and 1936 studied in the sculpture studio of Tadeusz Breyer (1874–1952) and the painting studio of Tadeusz Pruszkowski (1888–1942) at the Warsaw Academy of Fine Arts. Between 1946 and 1950 he worked at Jozefina glassworks in Lower Silesia, during which period he designed both decorative and useful wares, mainly epergnes and thick-walled crystal vases decorated with spherical ornament in the form of circular and oval flutes as well as wavy and oblique lines. In 1950 he started working as a freelance glass artist using only hand-formed glass. In 1963 he settled permanently in Warsaw, working at glassworks in the suburbs of Warsaw, for example Wołomin, Falenica and Ożarów. Initially, Tomaszewski produced very large vases ruffled with large air bubbles and streaks and slender, thin-walled vases with extremely flared rims or long S-shaped necks. Later, he clearly preferred semi-abstract sculptural work in the form of obelisks with slender points, occasionally surmounted with openwork loops, and oval globes filled with fused sheaves of glass rods or with deep, irregular channels of air. All his work was produced from apparently plain, poor-quality glass with a colour spectrum limited to green, bronze and azure hues. He devised a number of original technical solutions based on extensive knowledge of the inherent characteristics of glass. He produced only one example of each design, although certain themes were explored in dozens of variants. Musical inspiration played an important role in his work, and he frequently emphasized the interrelationship between art and music through the titles of his compositions, for example *Rhythms*, *Preludes* and *Fugues* (Warsaw, N. Mus). His expressive and dynamic work resembles pieces by such artists of the American studio glass movement as Dominick Labino (1910–87) and Marvin Lipofsky (*b* 1938). Tomaszewski should be regarded as an important, if under-rated, precursor of this movement in Poland.

BIBLIOGRAPHY

P. Banaś: 'Modern Polish Art Glass', *Glass A. Mag.* (Feb 1975)
I. Huml: *Polska sztuka stosowana XX wieku* [Polish applied art of the 20th century] (Warsaw, 1978)
Henryk Albin Tomaszewski: Szkło artystyczne [Henryk Albin Tomasz-ewski: art glass] (exh. cat., Warsaw, Zachęta Gal., 1980)
P. Banaś: *Polskie współczesne szkło artystyczne* [Modern Polish art glass] (Wrocław, 1982)
P. Banaś and H. Michałowska: *Henryk Albin Tomaszewski* (Warsaw, 1992)

PAWEL BANAŚ

Tomatsu, Shōmei (*b* Nagoya, 16 Jan 1930). Japanese photographer. He graduated from Aichi University in 1954 but was a self-taught photographer. In 1952 he submitted some photographs including *Tsukare* ('Fatigue') and *Utatane* ('A doze') to the monthly contest in the magazine *Camera*, and his talent was recognized by the judges Ken Domon and Ihei Kimura. He became a staff photographer for the Iwanami Photographic Library in 1954 and produced series of works such as *Flood Damage*

and Japanese People and *Seto—Pottery Town*. In 1956 he became a freelance photographer and published works that commented sharply on the life of the lower middle classes, in magazines such as *Chūō kōron* and *Asahi camera*. These photographs of office workers, local politicians and ordinary people were exhibited in the one-man show *Hito—hito* ('People—people') in 1959 at the Fuji Photo Salon, Tokyo. In the same year he formed the group Vivo with Ikkō Narahara and EIKOH HOSOE and became a leading member.

A typical example of Tomatsu's work is *Melted Beer Bottle after the Atomic Explosion, 1945, Nagasaki* (1961; see 1986 exh. cat., p. 39). Highly committed, he published a large number of photographic works, including *Senryo* ('Occupation'; Tokyo, 1960), pictures of American military bases in Japan; *11.02 Nagasaki* (Tokyo, 1966), which examined the post-war period of the town devastated by the atom bomb; *Saraamu areikomu* ('Salaam aleikoum'; Tokyo, 1968), the material for which was obtained in Afghanistan; *Taiyo no enpitsu* ('Pencil of the sun'; Tokyo, 1975), in which the cultural zone from Okinawa to Taiwan and South-east Asia was symbolized in large-scale images. He published an important collection of works in his book *Nippon* ('Japan'; Tokyo, 1967). In his work he consistently examined the relationship between people and society. In 1983 he published in *Asahi Camera* the colour series *Sakura* ('Cherry blossom'), which was later (Osaka, 1990) published as a book of the same name and in which the traditional Japanese sense of beauty was given symbolic expression.

BIBLIOGRAPHY

H. Osada: *Dual Notions: Photographers at Work* (Tokyo, 1969)
New Japanese Photography (exh. cat. by J. Szarkowski and S. Yamagishi, New York, MOMA, 1974), pp. 32–51
Black Sun: The Eyes of Four (exh. cat. by M. Holborn, Oxford, MOMA; London, Serpentine Gal.; Philadelphia, PA, Mus. A.; 1986), pp. 33–48
T. Ito: *In the Ruins* (Tokyo, 1987), pp. 92–103

KOHTARO IIZAWA

Tomažič, France (*b* Ljubljana, 4 Nov 1899; *d* Vienna, March 1987). Slovene architect. He gained his diploma in architecture at Ljubljana University under JOŽE PLEČNIK (1924) and worked as Plečnik's assistant. He also worked with Ivan Vurnik. Tomažič's main buildings in Ljubljana are a semi-detached house (1931), in Dermotova Street, a residential and office building (1934–6), in Miklošičeva Street, and several villas (1932–4), all influenced by Plečnik. After World War II, he was the architectural consultant for the rebuilding of the destroyed village of Borjana. Tomažič was also preoccupied with the problems of low-cost terraced housing, urban planning and the preservation of historic buildings in Maribor.

BIBLIOGRAPHY

F. Šijanec: *Sodobna Slovenska likovna umetnost* [Contemporary Slovene fine art] (Maribor, 1961), pp. 440–42

☐

Tomb. A place of burial or the marking of a grave. As the former it can take the form of a chamber, vault, CRYPT, SARCOPHAGUS or shrine (*see* SHRINE (i)), while as the latter it can take the form of a monument or MAUSOLEUM, usually built of stone, erected over a grave to commemorate the dead. The wide variety of tombs, from the simplest

multiple-grave burial mound to the most elaborate architectural construction, has been determined by historical,
social and geographical factors. Tombs are associated
particularly with cultures that bury rather than cremate
their dead; for this reason there was little incidence of
tomb construction in the Indian subcontinent or South-
east Asia before the spread to these lands of Islam in the
12th and 14th centuries respectively. Whatever the case,
tombs reveal much about the civilizations that produced
them.

I. Ancient world. II. Islamic lands. III. Indian subcontinent and
South-east Asia. IV. East Asia. V. Pre-Columbian Americas. VI.
Western world.

I. Ancient world.

From ancient Egypt to the Mediterranean civilizations of
Greece and Rome, the tombs of the ancient world cover
a broad spectrum of types and include some of the most
impressive architectural monuments of antiquity.

1. Egypt and Mesopotamia. 2. The Greek world. 3. Italy and the Roman
Empire.

1. EGYPT AND MESOPOTAMIA. Egyptian monumental tombs took several forms. The MASTABA was the tomb
type of nobles and early rulers. These low, flat-topped,
rectangular structures of mud-brick (later stone) imitated
houses and were constructed above subterranean tombs
comprising several chambers. Notable examples at Saqqara
are the mastabas of Ti and of both Ptahhotpe and
Akhethotpe, decorated inside with scenes of daily life. The
great age of PYRAMID building was the Old Kingdom (3rd
millennium BC), when more than 80 pyramids were built
for pharaohs and members of their families, beginning in
the 3rd–4th dynasties (c. 2650–c. 2465 BC). These pyramids
are typically of limestone, and most stand at the edge of
the western desert around Giza and Saqqara, forming
parts of funerary complexes. The earliest pyramid-type
tomb, that of Djoser at Saqqara (see SAQQARA, fig. 1),
began as a 63-m square mastaba (h. 8 m) over a deep
burial chamber. A four-stepped stone pyramid was superimposed on this, succeeded by a six-stepped one
(140×118×62 m). Its architect, IMHOTEP, can thus be
credited with the world's first monumental stone building.
It dominated a large walled complex (545×277 m) and
was perhaps intended to symbolize a stairway to 'heaven'.

The first true pyramid was that attributed to Sneferu
(although some ascribe it to Huni) at Maidum (4th
Dynasty; c. 2575–c. 2465 BC). In this case a smooth facing
was added to an earlier stepped pyramid. Pyramids of the
4th–6th dynasties typically included subsidiary complexes
comprising a valley temple at the desert's edge and a
causeway leading west to a funerary temple in front of the
pyramid. An entrance in the north face of the pyramid led
through a descending ramp into the burial chamber, which
might be subterranean, while concerns for security resulted
in elaborate internal passages. The Great Pyramid of
Cheops (reg c. 2551–c. 2528 BC; 230 m sq.×146 m), one of
the three famous pyramids at Giza, has a superb granite
central burial chamber, and outside stood a large cedar
funerary boat (43.4×5.53 m). The pyramid form sometimes recurred in Egypt, but after the Old Kingdom its

use declined and only inferior examples were built. Pyramids were probably symbolic structures representing the
sun-god's protection or his spreading rays.

Rock-cut tombs were constructed for the burial of
almost all the pharaohs of the 18th–20th dynasties (c. 1540–
c. 1075 BC). These formed the New Kingdom necropolis
or 'Valley of the Kings', situated in the limestone hills west
of the capital Thebes (now Luxor; see THEBES (i), §IX).
These long, many-chambered, L-shaped tombs were designed to foil robbers, and there are 62 known examples.
Everywhere decorated with texts, paintings and reliefs (see
WALL PAINTING, colour pl. I, fig. 1), the tombs contain
ramps and stairways descending to crypts with roofs
supported by pillars, and the stone sarcophagi. The fabulously wealthy (because unplundered) tomb of Tutankhamun (reg c. 1332–c. 1323 BC) was architecturally simple,
resembling a noble's. Later tombs, with one exception,
were on a straight rather than L-shaped plan. The tomb
of Sethos I (reg c. 1290–c 1279 BC), for example, is 100 m
long. South of the 'Valley of the Kings' are the simpler
tombs of the 'Valley of the Queens' (Nefertari's is the best
known of more than 70) and the excavated village of the
tomb workers at Deir el Medina, where small pyramids
surmounted some officials' burials. Tombs of noblemen
in the area (more than 400) are rich in paintings of daily
life and government. Notable are the TOMB OF REKHMIRE,
and the TOMB OF RAMOSE with two hypostyle chambers.
(See also EGYPT, ANCIENT, §VIII, 2(ii).)

Contemporary with the pyramids of the 3rd millennium
BC and comparable to them in sheer scale are the Mesopotamian 'royal tombs' at Ur, where large-scale human
slaughter was practised in front of tomb-chambers at the
bottom of deep shafts. Around 2000 BC a mausoleum
complex for three rulers at Ur provided a superstructure
for subterranean vaults, similar to Egyptian practice in
some pyramids. (See also MESOPOTAMIA, §II, 4.)

2. THE GREEK WORLD. Greek tombs developed from
simple burials in dug pits, stone-lined cists or large clay
pots, and these forms persisted throughout antiquity, also
being used by the Etruscans and the Romans. Individual
graves could be grouped together under a large circular
earthen tumulus, sometimes ringed by stones at its base.
Tumuli probably first appeared in the Greek world on the
island of Leukas in the later 3rd millennium BC, and their
use spread down the western coast of Greece and beyond
during the Middle Bronze Age (c. 2000–1550 BC). It is
possible that they originated in the Kurgan culture of the
Russian steppes during the 4th–3rd millennia BC and were
introduced in Greece by Greek-speaking immigrants,
although this is disputed. Tumuli appeared in northern
Greece only towards the end of the Bronze Age (12th
century BC) but persisted in Epeiros and Macedonia,
notably at Vergina, into the Dark Age and even into the
Hellenistic period.

Stone-built tombs occurred in Minoan Crete, especially
in the Mesara plain. These small, round structures (2800–
1700 BC; mostly 3rd millennium BC) contained multiple,
successive burials, perhaps of family members, but the
method of roofing is uncertain, and it is thus difficult to
derive the distinctive corbelled Mycenaean tholos tombs
from these (see below). Rich shaft tombs, grouped in two

1. Lion Tomb, Knidos, h. *c.* 20 m, *c.* 350 BC; reconstruction drawing of restored elevation, from *Die Antike*, iv (Berlin and Leipzig, 1928), fig. 2

circles, occurred at Mycenae. These were, in effect, stone-lined cists at the bottom of shafts (*c.* 1–4 m deep), distinguished from earlier Greek graves by their wealth of offerings and by the practice of multiple burials, both successive and simultaneous. The shafts were filled in with earth and tumuli may once have surmounted the circles. Grave Circle B, the earlier (*c.* 1650–1550 BC), lies just outside the citadel. Grave Circle A (*c.* 1600–1500 BC) (diam. 27 m) contains six shaft tombs (the largest measures 6.4×4.5 m), and was terraced and surrounded by a circle of upright stone slabs in its final phase (13th century BC). This treatment and the rich grave-goods found there may indicate royal tombs in Circle A. Some tombs in both circles were marked by a sculpted stele (examples in Návplion, Archaeol. Mus.). Individual shaft tombs occur at a few other Bronze Age Greek sites, and they continued to be constructed until *c.* 1400 BC.

Rock-cut chamber tombs and stone tholoi (*see* THOLOS TOMB) were generally characteristic of Greece in the Mycenaean period (*c.* 1550–1100 BC). In both cases an entrance passage (dromos) led into the tomb. Both types were used for successive burials, the earlier burials and grave-goods being pushed aside. They were presumably

family vaults. The tholos was usually cut into a hillside, with its lintel at surface level, and covered by an earthen tumulus. The more elaborate tholoi have stone-lined dromoi. Burials within them might be in pits or stone-lined cists. About 200 tholoi are known, and many more chamber tombs.

The origins of the tholos are uncertain; it combines the concepts of chamber tomb and tumulus with a distinctive roofing method. Its beehive-shaped vault was corbelled and buttressed by the earth mound. The earliest tholoi, in Messenia, contain Middle Helladic as well as early Mycenaean pottery. At Mycenae itself the nine tholoi (*c.* 1500–1250 BC) succeed the shaft tombs. The 'Treasury of Atreus' at Mycenae (*c.* 1250 BC) is one of the grandest examples of Greek architecture of any period. Decorated engaged columns (now in London, BM) and reliefs formed part of its façade, and its lintel block weighs 100 tons. Exceptionally, it has a side chamber, as does the 'Treasury of Minyas' at ORCHOMENOS (13th century BC). Both tholoi are unusually large (diam. 14.5 m and 14 m), but many tholoi measure less than 5 m diameter. The height of a tholos was roughly equivalent to its diameter, and large ones contain a relieving triangle (possibly derived from Egypt) above their lintel blocks. One at MARATHON has, uniquely, two facing horses buried in the dromos (*c.* 1400 BC). The unplundered Dendra tholos held a unique bronze suit of armour. By the 12th century BC tholoi had become rare. Examples occur in Dark Age Crete, Messenia and Thessaly (11th–9th centuries BC), when most of Greece had reverted to single burials, although it has been argued that in Thessaly and Thrace tholoi persisted even later.

Phrygian and Lydian tombs date from the 8th–6th centuries BC. Notable Phrygian tombs include some at 'Midas City' with rock-cut, gabled façades adorned with geometric patterns in relief, while others contain facing lions in relief. Tumuli at Gordion covered a wooden chamber, and the largest has plausibly been identified as that of Midas (diam. *c.* 300 m, h. *c.* 53 m). The only larger tumulus is the 'Tomb of Alyattes' in the Bin Tepe cemetery, near Sardis, associated with the kings of Lydia (355×69 m). The 'Tomb of Tantalus', near Smyrna, is in tumulus form although built entirely of stone (29.6×27.6 m). Rock-cut tombs occur often in Caria, while Mycenaean-type chamber tombs continued at Salamis, Cyprus. Some royal or noble tombs at Salamis had façades containing small courtyards, and in their broad dromoi vehicles and teams of horses or asses were buried (*c.* 750 BC–7th century BC).

Archaic and Classical Greek tombs are for the most part less significant architecturally than sculpturally (e.g. carved sarcophagi, stelai and other grave-markers with painted or relief decoration). Tumuli sometimes occur over individual or multiple graves, usually aristocratic. A tumulus burial at BELEVI (6th century BC or later) has a terracotta pipe leading down from the surface for the pouring of libations. Graves grouped below a rectangular enclosing wall (a peribolos) were common. The Dexileos Stele (394 BC) marking a grave belonging to a peribolos tomb (*see* GREECE, ANCIENT, fig. 62) is one of many from the Athenian Kerameikos cemetery, although Athenian monuments were restricted by sumptuary law at the end of the 4th century BC. Monumental Late Classical and Hellenistic tombs developed in the kingdoms of Asia

Minor by combining local forms with Greek architectural elements (Macedonian tombs were essentially different; see below). The basic type was a podium supporting a chamber, which might be constructed in imitation of a Greek temple and be surmounted by a pyramid and crowning sculpture. One possible precursor is the tomb of the Persian king Cyrus at PASARGADAE, a rectangular chamber built on a stepped podium (h. *c.* 11 m; 6th century BC). Another is the Lycian type of tomb, with a chamber or steep-gabled sarcophagus set on a tower-like pillar, such as the misnamed Harpy Tomb at Xanthos (h. 8.87 m; early 5th century BC). The Nereid Monument, also at Xanthos, was the first of the type (*c.* 400 BC; reconstructed in London, BM; for illustration *see* XANTHOS). It comprised a small Ionic temple (6×4 columns) on a high podium (original h. *c.* 13.5 m), with the two upper courses formed by sculpted marble friezes. Usually the podium of such tombs contained the burial. Perhaps the most famous Hellenistic tomb was the Mausoleum at Halikarnassos, begun by Mausolos of Caria (*reg. c.* 377–353 BC) and completed after his death (*see* HALIKARNASSOS, §2 and figs. 2 and 4). Modern reconstructions of it rely heavily on Pliny's description (*Natural History* XXXVI.iv.30–31). It was one of the Seven Wonders of the Ancient World, as much for its sculptures as for its size (h. 57.6 m). As many as 330 statues adorned it, and its 36-column Ionic peristasis was crowned by a 24-stepped pyramid surmounted by a huge four-horse chariot. The Mausoleum, like many such tombs, stood in a spacious built enclosure. Similar, smaller monuments are the Lion Tomb at Knidos (see fig. 1), the Lion Tomb at Amphipolis (*c.* 350 BC), and the mausoleum at Belevi, with a partly rock-cut podium (29.65 m sq.) and a hidden vaulted chamber (h. *c.* 35 m; *c.* 300 BC). A later example is the Mylasa Tomb (2nd century AD).

The other prominent type of Hellenistic Greek tomb is the Macedonian tomb, a rectangular barrel-vaulted chamber covered by a tumulus, approached through a dromos, and often provided with a decorated façade, the best in imitation of temples. They date from the mid-4th to mid-2nd centuries BC. The architectural elements of their solid façades were applied in stucco relief and painted, and are thus purely decorative. Important, well-preserved paintings adorn the frieze of Tomb II at Vergina (*c.* 9.5×5.5× 5.3 m), the interior of the neighbouring 'Tomb of Persephone' (both *c.* 340–310 BC), and the two-storey façade of the 'Great Tomb' at Leukadia (*c.* 300 BC). The tomb of Lyson and Kallikles at Leukadia (mid-3rd century BC) has a fine, painted interior and niches for cremation urns. In other tombs the bodies were laid on stone couches. In Tomb II at Vergina were found a splendid royal burial, associated with either Philip II of Macedon (*d* 336 BC) or a successor, and perhaps the first Greek use of the technique of barrel vaulting, probably learnt from the Near East. Macedonian-style vaulted tombs exist also in other parts of Greece, for example at Eretria, Kassope and Kalydon. (*See also* GREECE, ANCIENT, §II, 1(i)(d).)

Other striking eastern tombs are those with rock-cut architectural façades, especially in Lycia (e.g. at Myra and Telmessos; 4th century BC) and at Petra. The Khazne or 'Treasury' (24.9×38.7×7 m; 1st century BC) and the 'Deir Tomb' (47×42 m; 1st century AD) at Petra both have elaborate two-storey baroque façades, surmounted by a

canopy within a broken pediment. Tower tombs are large pillar-shaped towers on bases. Prominent at Dura Europos and Palmyra (1st century BC–3rd century AD), their use extended through North Africa and the Roman world. The influence of tower tombs and monumental tombs can be seen in the 'Tomb of Absalom' at Jerusalem, the 'Tomb of the Scipios' at Tarragona, Spain, and the canopy-topped Tomb of the Julii at Glanum (St Rémy), France.

3. ITALY AND THE ROMAN EMPIRE. Etruscan tombs were generally grouped in necropoleis, which were often laid out in regular streets, close to the particular city they served. Types of tomb show regional diversity and include rock-cut family chamber tombs and tumuli containing one or more burials. The tumuli at CERVETERI rest on rock-cut drums. One of the earliest burials there is the Regolini-Galassi Tomb (*c.* 700–650 BC); the Tomb of Painted Reliefs (3rd century BC) is among the last elaborate Caeretan tombs. Etruscan chamber tombs usually consist of one or more rectangular rooms, although round tholos-like tombs supported by central pillars are found at Volterra. Interior or exterior decoration often imitated that of domestic architecture. Wall paintings in tombs reached their height at TARQUINIA around 540 BC, with the vivid interiors of, for example, the Tomb of the Bulls (*c.* 540 BC) and the Tomb of Hunting and Fishing (*c.* 510 BC) (*see also* ETRUSCAN, §§II and V, and figs. 7, 25, 27).

Roman tombs typically lined streets leading from a city. Mausolea or house tombs glorifying families or individuals, sometimes grouped in contiguous blocks, stood beside the poorest graves marked by amphorae or covered by stones or roof-tiles. Typical are the tombs lining the Appian Way south of Rome, the Vatican necropolis (2nd–3rd centuries AD), the Via dei Sepolcri outside Pompeii (before AD 79) and the vast Isola Sacra cemetery north of Ostia (AD 100–250). Pompeian tombs, for example, include unroofed enclosures, exedrae, and large altar-shaped tombs. The aedicula type resembles a small shrine. Tumuli continued to be constructed in some places.

An early Roman family tomb is that of the Cornelii Scipiones, cut out of the tufa south of Rome (early 3rd century BC–*c.* 130 BC; reused during the 1st century AD). Shelf-niches (*loculi*) in its walls held sarcophagi. Later tombs, such as the marble-faced pyramid of Gaius Cestius at Rome (h. 36.4 m; late 1st century BC), reflect aristocratic display. A frieze depicting a baker's occupations adorns the large tomb of Eurysaces, also at Rome (late 1st century BC). The marble relief decoration of the Tomb of the Haterii (*c.* AD 100; Rome, Vatican, Mus. Gregoriano Profano) depicts a temple-tomb on a stepped podium, like some 1st-century BC or later examples known from Ghirza, Libya (3rd and 4th centuries AD) and elsewhere. Roman circular mausolea owe something to the Etruscan stone-ringed tumuli of Cerveteri. Possibly the first, that of Augustus by the Tiber (28 BC) contained several imperial family burials in its concentric ring-walls (h. *c.* 44.65 m; diam. *c.* 87 m) surmounted by a mound of some kind and topped by a statue of Augustus. Aristocrats adopted this type; for example the tomb of Caecilia Metella, south of Rome (late 1st century BC), consists of a large round drum on a square podium. Hadrian's tomb, the Castel Sant' Angelo (*see* ROME, §V, 9, and fig. 27), Diocletian's at Split, and Theodoric the Goth's at Ravenna (6th century AD) are other imperial mausolea; their circular or polygonal plan was adopted in Christian church architecture.

During the Roman Empire much use was made of underground necropoleis. A HYPOGEUM is an underground tomb with *loculi* and one or more chambers for multiple burials. The best examples are found at Dura Europos and Palmyra (1st–3rd centuries AD). That of the Aurelii at Rome (early 3rd century AD) was built on several levels and contained both Christian and pagan paintings. The COLUMBARIUM was a large structure, sometimes underground, housing hundreds or thousands of niches for the cremation urns or chests of less prosperous citizens. A burial club might organize such a tomb for its members. The first known is late Republican; notable are the three 'Colombari di Vigna Codini' at Rome (1st century AD) for imperial slaves and freedmen, and two above-ground examples at Ostia.

The CATACOMB was a form of large underground necropolis, found in Hellenistic Alexandria and among the Jewish and Christian communities at Rome (from the 2nd century AD and *c.* AD 200 respectively) and elsewhere, such as at Syracuse. Burials were in niches in corridors or chambers off them. Some, such as the 4th-century AD Via Latina catacombs at Rome, contained elaborate paintings, including pagan motifs, though they were apparently not used for regular worship.

BIBLIOGRAPHY

Å. Åkerström: *Studien über die etruskischen Gräber* (Lund, 1934)
V. Karageorghis: *Salamis: Recent Discoveries in Cyprus* (London, 1969)
K. Branigan: *The Tombs of Mesara* (London, 1970)
D. C. Kurtz and J. Boardman: *Greek Burial Customs* (London, 1971)
J. M. C. Toynbee: *Death and Burial in the Roman World* (London, 1971)
L. V. Grinsell: *Barrow, Pyramid and Tomb* (London, 1975)
O. Pelon: *Tholoi, tumuli et cercles funéraires* (Paris, 1976)
R. Reece, ed.: *Burial in the Roman World* (London, 1977)
J. Brinks: *Die Entwicklung der königlichen Grabanlagen des Alten Reiches* (Hildesheim, 1979)
R. Young and others: *Three Great Early Tumuli* (1981), i of *The Gordion Excavations* (Philadelphia, 1981-)
S. G. Miller: 'Macedonian Tombs: Their Architecture and Architectural Decoration', *Stud. Hist. A.*, x (Washington, 1982), pp. 152–71
M. Torelli: *Necropoli dell' Italia antica* (Milan, 1982)
I. E. S. Edwards: *The Pyramids of Egypt* (rev. Harmondsworth, 1985)
L. Manniche: *City of the Dead: Thebes in Egypt* (London, 1987)
P. J. Watson: *Egyptian Pyramids and Mastaba Tombs of the Old and Middle Kingdoms* (Aylesbury, 1987)
S. Müller: 'Les Tumuli helladiques: Où? Quand? Comment?', *Bull. Corr. Hell.*, cxiii (1989), pp. 1–42
J. Fedak: *Monumental Tombs of the Hellenistic Age* (Toronto, 1990)
S. G. Miller: *The Tomb of Lyson and Kallikles: A Painted Macedonian Tomb* (Mainz am Rhein, 1993)

JOHN R. LENZ

II. Islamic lands.

With the exception of the mosque, the tomb is, in most parts of the Islamic world, the most widespread type of public building, often found as much in villages and the open countryside as in towns. The most celebrated examples are princely tombs, but they are outnumbered by places of pilgrimage or worship marking the actual or supposed graves of saints (*see* SHRINE (i), §II).

1. History. 2. Form.

1. HISTORY. According to Muslim tradition, the Prophet Muhammad was fundamentally opposed to any formal commemoration of the dead, most notably to tombs. He recommended that graves be level with the ground and unroofed, and was himself buried—as he had requested—in simple fashion in his own house. This Islamic orthodoxy, however, ran counter to established practice in pre-Islamic times, both in the Mediterranean world and in western Asia, and was soon challenged. The burial places of Companions of the Prophet or members of his family began to be marked by a staff (still used as a funerary marker in such areas as western Central Asia), a canopy, a tent or some similar form of covering intended to provide shade for the deceased. Such canopies of cloth were interpreted and thereby legitimized, following the Koran, as one of the blessings of Paradise and eventually found monumental form as open-plan tombs. Their legitimacy was defended on the grounds that the burial spot was open to wind and rain. Secular tombs might have a mihrab added (often, appropriately, in the form of a tombstone) to turn them into places of worship, for Islamic tradition asserted that any place could serve for prayer (*see* ISLAM, §II). Another method of rendering a tomb more acceptable in terms of orthodoxy was to decorate it with Koranic inscriptions; although these texts rarely mention judgement and paradise, they often cite Sura xxi.35, stating that every soul must taste death.

The earliest surviving tomb is probably the Qubbat al-Sulaibiyya (mid-9th century AD) at Samarra' (*see* SAMARRA', §2), convincingly identified as a dynastic sepulchre for the Abbasid caliphs. Literary references, however, establish that tombs were built throughout the Islamic world from the previous century onwards. The tomb cult made such spectacular headway against deep-rooted orthodox resistance for several reasons. The most important was the growth of Shi'ism. Graves of the Shi'ite imams (descendants of the Prophet) at Karbala', Najaf, Samarra', QUM and MASHHAD became a natural focus of Shi'ite aspirations and ceremonies commemorating the killing of Husayn, the Prophet's grandson, on 10 Muharram AH 61 (10 October AD 680). As Muharram ceremonies developed, the graves received various marks of respect—grilles and cenotaphs (*see* CENOTAPH, §2)—and these naturally culminated in actual buildings. The custom of visiting these graves, saying prayers and holding Koranic readings there helped to sanctify such buildings, and their upkeep, embellishment and expansion were financed by successive generations of pilgrims and local people alike expressing their piety. Thus, by degrees such tombs (whether at Mashhad in Iran or Mulay Idris in Morocco) became the nuclei of entire shrine complexes, which often extended over several acres and played a major role in the political, social and economic life of the community.

While religious particularism is the most convincing explanation for the phenomenal rise of the tomb cult, other theories are worth considering, including the relationship between the appearance of tombs and the spread of Islam by *jihād*. Along certain Islamic frontiers, such as in western Central Asia, Nubia and India, tombs are found in exceptional quantities, and many of them are anonymous or bear names unknown to historical record. The tombs may well commemorate martyrs to the faith, and if so would illustrate once again the paradox of breaching orthodoxy on impeccably religious grounds. The impact of traditions outside Islamic culture must also be taken into account. In the Mediterranean world the Arabs encountered well-established traditions of funerary architecture, whether the awesome ancient Egyptian monuments, Roman tombs, Palmyrene tomb towers or Early Christian and Byzantine martyria. Such monuments were far more numerous in the past and were already influential from the very beginnings of Islamic architecture, to judge from the Dome of the Rock (*see* JERUSALEM, §II, 1(iii); and ISLAMIC ART, §II, 3(ii) and fig. 17). Sometimes, as in the case of the tombs of Biblical prophets, Islam could appropriately take over site and building alike (e.g. the tomb of Abraham/Ibrahim at Hebron). Another source for the development of tombs was the culture of the nomadic Turkic peoples who inhabited the Eurasian steppe. Their complex funerary rituals included the exposing of the corpse in a tent while mourners processed around it, and the inhumation of the body in a funerary mound (*kurgan*). Tomb towers with crypts containing the body and crowned by an empty room, built from western Central Asia to Anatolia, can be seen as an architectural conflation of these practices.

Thus, the range of traditions on which the medieval Islamic tomb might have drawn in the course of its development was wide, and these traditions reflect an equally wide range of concepts about the commemoration of the dead. The nomenclature employed for tombs in medieval texts and inscriptions reflects the broad range of functions discharged by these buildings in medieval Islamic society. Popular terms include *rawḍa* (Arab.: 'garden'), *qubba* ('dome'), *mashhad* ('martyrium'), *khwābgāh* (Pers.: 'place of sleep'), *qaṣr* (Arab.: 'castle', 'palace'), *'ataba* ('threshold'), *ziyāratgāh* (Pers.: 'place of pilgrimage') and *qabr* (Arab.: 'grave'), to say nothing of a clutch of neutral terms such as *'imāra* ('place') or *binā'* ('building'), or specific ones such as *qadamgāh* (Pers.: 'place of a footstep') or *imāmzāda* ('descendant of an imam'). It is curious that no single word was consistently used to denote simply 'tomb'. The frequency with which tombs were attached to other types of buildings—mosque, MADRASA, *ribāṭ*, *zāwiya*, KHĀNAQĀH—shows how thoroughly funerary architecture permeated medieval Islamic society. Such joint or multiple foundations allowed their high-ranking patrons to perpetuate their names, flaunt their piety and benefit the local community, thereby making atonement for their sins. The tomb itself became at once a symbol of conspicuous consumption and a stamp of ownership for the foundation as a whole. Many such tombs were intended for family or multiple burials and were maintained by carefully defined, inalienable religious endowments (Arab.: *waqf*; *see* ISLAM, §III).

2. FORM. Formal sources for Islamic tombs are easy to find. The core type of Islamic tomb is a domed cube, which has a basic kinship with both Romano-Byzantine funerary monuments and the most common type of fire temple (*chahārṭāq*) in Sasanian Iran, although it was functionally unrelated to the tomb. The domed square probably has even deeper roots and corresponds to a common type of domestic architecture, as suggested by many vernacular marabouts in north-west Africa, and by more ambitious versions, for example at Kairouan and Monastir in Tunisia. In the eastern Islamic world the Buddhist stupa may have played some role, as in the tomb of Sanjar at Merv (*see* MERV, §2 and fig. 2).

From the domed square type there developed numerous other types of tomb, including polygonal, multifoiled, flanged or circular structures, but the most important was the domed octagon, with its distinctive capacity for spatial subtleties, as shown in the great tombs of Mughal India (*see* INDIAN SUBCONTINENT, §III, 7(i)). Direct echoes of the splendid princely tents of the nomadic Turkic peoples as described in medieval sources (*see* TENT, §II, 2) can be recognized in the external elevations of some Iranian tomb towers, such as the two at Kharraqan (1067–8 and 1093–4) and that at Radkan East (1205–6). The Anatolian interpretation of such Iranian models may also have drawn on the tall drums of Armenian churches. Despite these many morphological changes, however, virtually all Islamic tombs are instantly recognizable as such: form, function and symbol are successfully integrated. An innate conservatism, which inhibited radical experiment in this building type, had much to do with this, and such exceptions as the *ḥaẓīra* (funerary compound) or the *imāmbāra* (used both for burial and for Muharram ceremonies) merely prove the rule. The greatest concentrations of the domed square tomb occur in Egypt and Syria. Those in Cairo from the 11th and 12th centuries are the earliest substantial group of tombs to survive in the Arab world, perhaps for the confessional affiliations of their Fatimid sponsors. Nearly 100 tombs survive from the period of Ayyubid rule in Damascus, mostly from the 13th century. The form was equally well adapted to small buildings (e.g. Rukniya Turba, Damascus) as to large ones (e.g. the tomb of Imam Shafi'i, 1211; *see* CAIRO, fig. 5), or the largest such dome in the world, the Gol Gumbaz at Bijapur in central India; *see* INDIAN SUBCONTINENT, fig. 110). While such tombs with four axial entrances are known, those with a single entrance are more numerous.

The domed, centralized form constituted the Islamic tomb par excellence. The prime emphasis was on the exterior, which at the very least made a strong statement in solid geometry, exploiting stark contrasts of square, polygonal and curvilinear forms. Often, however, this powerful basic structure was embellished both within and without by applied ornament. Certain areas were singled out for this purpose. The dome itself might be covered with glazed tiles, either monochrome or patterned; it often bore designs in decorative brickwork or in carved stone, and was sometimes pierced by star-shaped openings (e.g. the tomb in Qus, Egypt, 1120–30) or took on a bulbous melon shape (e.g. the tomb of Zayn al-Din Yusuf, Cairo, 1298). The portal acted as the natural focus of the lower elevation and often bore epigraphic panels or bands giving the date and the name of the patron. In some traditions it was boldly salient from the body of the tomb, acting like a porch. Even when it was flush with the main structure, its importance was signalled by multiple rectangular frames enclosing ornamental bands or inscriptions, a layout recalling the MIHRAB, which was a much-reduced version of the same idea and was often deliberately located on the same axis. This device signalled the sanctity of a tomb to the outside world. Indeed, in some local traditions (e.g. in western Central Asia from the 10th to the 14th century) the portal (see PĪSHTĀQ) came to take up most of the main façade, with the bulk of the building obscured behind it. Gradually such portals acquired *muqarnas* vaulting for their semi-domes (e.g. Qubbat al-Tawrizi, Damascus, c. 1420). Other adjuncts to the nucleus of the domed chamber included ambulatories, internal staircases and subsidiary corner domes or minarets, as at the Taj Mahal (see AGRA, fig. 1).

The choice of a square or polygonal ground-plan for the tomb inevitably implied a zone of transition to carry the dome. While the concept of a dome on pendentives occasionally found favour, notably in Ottoman tombs, the standard solution involved a ring of eight arches, four of them corner squinches. Tombs, along with mosques, were the laboratories in which the structural, formal and decorative implications of this arrangement were worked out. Indeed, in tombs throughout the Muslim world, the zone of transition constitutes the major internal decorative accent, as at the tomb of Arab-Ata at Tim in Uzbekistan (977; see CENTRAL ASIA, fig. 14), while the external significance of the zone of transition is highlighted by means of a highly articulated drum, sometimes furnished with a continuous vaulted gallery (e.g. the tomb of Sanjar at Merv, or the tomb of Uljaytu at Sultaniyya, 1305–15; see ISLAMIC ART, fig. 48) or enlarged to a great height so as to magnify the impact of the dome. Double-shelled domes, especially those with a steep stilt (e.g. Gur-i Mir, Samarkand, 1404; see ISLAMIC ART, fig. 15), had the same purpose. The systematic subdivision of the squinch both laterally and vertically may well have provided the original inspiration for that quintessentially Islamic form, the MUQARNAS, also known as stalactite or honeycomb vaulting. By degrees, *muqarnas* spread to encompass not just the squinches but the entire zone of transition, which was sometimes doubled in both interior and exterior, as in the tomb of Nur al-Din in the Nuriyya Madrasa (1172) in Damascus, and thence expanded to fill the dome itself. In the later stages of the development, such vaults abdicated all pretensions to a structural role, as shown by the astonishingly complex 'squinch-net' vaults found in later Iranian buildings (e.g. the tomb of Gawharshad, Herat, 1417–38), which would effectively have disguised the discrepancy between the shallow inner dome and the lofty outer one. In certain Iraqi domes and their derivatives, the *muqarnas* is externalized into a gigantic articulated sugar-loaf (e.g. Imam Dur, Iraq, 1085–90). In Anatolia a distinctive solution developed in the form of Turkish triangles, which simplify the squinch zone into smoothly faceted prismatic planes (e.g. the tomb of Mehmed I at Bursa, c. 1421).

In the case of a square tomb, the wasted space in the corners encouraged experiments in decoration rather than form, and in the dome chambers of Iranian mosques of the Saljuq period (see ISLAMIC ART, §II, 5(i)(b)) such a space was elaborated as far as possible in that direction. It was a natural development, therefore, to enrich this simple

formula by means of a radiating central plan. In the Iranian world the domed octagon became the preferred choice, evident, for example, at Abarquh (see fig. 2). It contrived to combine the requirements of a central focus—usually provided by an elaborate cenotaph in carved wood, stone or glazed tilework—with those of the maximum space for circumambulation and for spatial experiment, as at Sultaniyya, the tomb of Ruknal-Din 'Alam at Multan (see INDIAN SUBCONTINENT, fig. 86) and the Taj Mahal. Such buildings may have been conceived as interior spaces for practical use as places of pilgrimage and worship. In the Iranian world and India, especially from the 15th to the 17th century, palace kiosks of similar form were sometimes dubbed *hasht bihisht* (Pers.: 'eight paradises') and were set, like the tombs, in garden precincts where umbrageous trees and flowing streams readily evoked the Koranic Paradise (e.g. the tombs of Humayun, Delhi and I'timad al-Daula, Agra; see INDIAN SUBCONTINENT, fig. 99).

Small and structurally unadventurous domed squares could be redeemed from banality by being employed as components in a much larger design. The accumulation of many similar and individually plain structures (as at Chella, nr Rabat, Morocco) makes them interdependent and creates a built landscape of impressive extent. The Marinid royal tombs perched on a hill overlooking Fez are a prime example of such a necropolis, while the tombs straggling down the hillside of the Salihiyya, Damascus, also individually unremarkable, are a looser version of the same idea. Several dozen tombs at Aswan dating from the medieval period (see fig. 3) show that builders blithely experimented with mud-brick as if it were plasticine,

2. Gunbad-i 'Ali, Abarquh, 1056–7

3. Tombs at Aswan, 10th century and later

moulding zones of transition into forms of unprecedented fantasy. Conversely, among several Indian sites with such groups of tombs, the 17th-century Chahar Gunbad at Golconda deserves special attention; indeed, the Indian subcontinent may claim to have more monumental medieval tombs than the rest of the Islamic world put together, some of them bearing Koranic inscriptions hundreds of metres long (*see* §III below). In Turkey the outstanding example is at Ahlat, and in Iran, at Amul and Qum. At the Shah-i Zinda (*see* SAMARKAND, §3(i)) the line of tombs is lifted out of the ordinary by the long processional staircase that leads to the necropolis, by the narrow meandering street along which they are disposed, and by their incandescent tiled ornament. The grandest such necropolis in the Islamic world is probably that formed by the so-called 'tombs of the caliphs' in the Qarafa cemetery, Cairo.

Very different in type was the tomb tower, found throughout the Iranian and Turkish worlds. It was originally a simple, lofty cylinder with a conical roof (e.g. Lajim, 1022–3; Risgit, *c.* 1100), and the emphasis on sheer height was greatly increased by the relative constriction of the interior, making for a ratio of width to height of about 1:3.5 to 1:5.5. Such a building seems to have been intended primarily as an external marker for the grave, with a corresponding neglect of the interior. Iranian architects quickly enriched the primitive formula of the earliest tomb towers by adding flanges (e.g. Gunbad-i Qabus, 1006–7; *see* ISLAMIC ART, fig. 28), engaged columns and corner buttresses to the shaft, and simple cylinders gave way to hexagonal and octagonal prisms, 10- and 12-sided tombs

and various flanged or polyhedral forms over a much lower inner dome. Lavish applied ornament sets off the spartan simplicity of the elevation. The unwavering emphasis on a single attenuated shaft constitutes the main visual impact of such towers, and this illusionistic device enhances the impression of loftiness. Most tomb towers are some 15–20 m high, but seem very much taller. Anatolian tomb towers, the heyday of which was from the 13th to the 15th century, feature a crypt with a sarcophagus for the body, which was sometimes embalmed (*see* ISLAMIC ART, §II, 5(iii)). The crypt was crowned by an empty upper chamber, sometimes reached by an external staircase. The carved stone decoration frequently features animal themes of astrological, totemistic, paradisal and other symbolic intent. Indeed, many tomb towers both in Anatolia (see fig. 4) and Iran are structurally a dead-end, and have become essentially a hoarding for elaborate ornament.

BIBLIOGRAPHY

Enc. Islam/2: 'Ḳubba'

F. Wetzel: *Islamische Grabbauten in Indien aus der Zeit der Soldatenkaiser, 1320–1540* (Leipzig, 1918)

C. Cauvet: 'Les Marabouts: Petits monuments funéraires et votifs du Nord de l'Afrique', *Rev. Afr.*, lxiv (1923), pp. 274–329, 448–522

U. Monneret de Villard: *La Necropoli musulmana di Aswan* (Cairo, 1930)

A. S. Tritton: 'Muslim Funeral Customs', *Bull. SOAS*, ix (1937–9), pp. 635–61

A. Grabar: *Martyrium: Recherches sur le culte des reliques et l'art chrétien antique*, 2 vols (Paris, 1943–6)

E. Esin: 'Al-Qubbah al-Turkiyya: An Essay on the Origins of the Architectonic Form of the Islamic Turkish Funerary Monument', *Atti del terzo congresso di studi arabi e islamici: Ravello, 1966*, pp. 281–309

O. Grabar: 'The Earliest Islamic Commemorative Structures', *A. Orient.*, vi (1966), pp. 1–46

4. Tomb of Hüdavend Hatun, Niğde, 1312

I. Goldziher: *Muslim Studies*, 2 vols, ed. S. M. Stern, Eng. trans. by C. N. Barber and S. M. Stern (London, 1967–71)

C. Kessler: 'Funerary Architecture within the City', *Colloque internationale sur l'histoire du Caire: Cairo, 1969*, pp. 257–68

V. V. Bartol'd: 'The Burial Rites of the Turks and the Mongols', Eng. trans. by J. M. Rogers, *Cent. Asiat. J.*, xiv (1970), pp. 195–222

Y. Ragib: 'Les Premiers Monuments funéraires de l'Islam', *An. Islam.*, ix (1970), pp. 21–36

U. U. Bates: 'An Introduction to the Study of the Anatolian Turbe and its Inscriptions as Historical Documents', *Sanat Tarihi Yıllığı*, iv (1971), pp. 73–84

C. Adle and A. S. Melikian-Chirvani: 'Les Monuments du XIe siècle du Dāmqān', *Stud. Iran.*, i/2 (1972), pp. 229–97

L. Golombek: 'The Cult of Saints and Shrine Architecture in the Fourteenth Century', *Near Eastern Numismatics, Iconography, Epigraphy and History: Studies in Honor of George C. Miles*, ed. D. K. Kouymjian (Beirut, 1974), pp. 419–30

R. Hillenbrand: 'The Development of Saljuq Tombs in Iran', *The Art of Iran and Anatolia, from the 11th to the 13th Century A.D.*, ed. W. Watson, Colloq. A. & Archaeol. Asia, iv (London, 1974), pp. 40–59

L. A. Ibrahim: *Mamluk Monuments of Cairo* (Cairo, 1976)

V. Strika: 'The Turbah of Zumurrud Khatun in Baghdad: Some Aspects of the Funerary Ideology in Islamic Art', *AION*, n. s., xxxviii (1978), pp. 283–96

L. Golombek: 'From Tamerlane to the Taj Mahal', *Essays in Islamic Art and Architecture in Honor of Katharina Otto-Dorn*, ed. A. Daneshvari (Malibu, 1981), pp. 43–50

T. Allen: 'The Tombs of the 'Abbāsid Caliphs in Baghdad', *Bull. SOAS*, xlvi (1983), pp. 421–32

S. S. Blair: 'The Octagonal Pavilion at Natanz', *Muqarnas*, i (1983), pp. 69–94

C. Williams: 'The Cult of 'Alid Saints in the Fatimid Monuments of Cairo, Part II: The Tombs', *Muqarnas*, iii (1985), pp. 39–60

A. Daneshvari: *Medieval Tomb Towers of Iran: An Iconographical Study* (Lexington, 1986)

S. S. Blair: *The Monumental Inscriptions of Early Islamic Iran and Transoxiana* (Leiden, 1992)

R. Hillenbrand: *Islamic Architecture: Form, Function and Meaning* (Edinburgh, 1994), pp. 253–330

ROBERT HILLENBRAND

III. *Indian subcontinent and South-east Asia.*

Because most indigenous Indian belief systems favour cremation, few tombs or burial structures were built in the Indian subcontinent before 1200. Early Islamic doctrine also discouraged the construction of mausolea over graves (*see* §II above), although tombs of the 10th–13th centuries AD have been found in Pakistan. These square, single-domed brick structures are modelled on Iranian prototypes (e.g. Tomb of Muhammad Harun, Bela, Baluchistan; Tomb of an Unknown Woman, Aror, Sind), although the influence of indigenous temple architecture is also evident (e.g. Anonymous Tomb, Aror, Sind). Elsewhere, tombs adhere more closely to local building tradition, for example in Bhadreshvar, Gujarat, where a tomb dated 1159–60 has carved pillars supporting corbelled superstructures. Following the establishment of Islamic authority in the Delhi region at the end of the 12th century, small square or octagonal stone tombs with corbelled or vaulted roofs were erected for rulers and princes (*see* DELHI, §I). Early examples were embellished with elaborately carved ornament and inscriptions or faced with contrasting bands of coloured stone, but from the mid-14th century they became increasingly austere, with stucco over stone rubble replacing the stone facing. Tombs were also erected over the graves of saints. Trends established at Delhi were echoed in tombs erected in provincial centres, although they often reflected local building traditions.

From the late 15th century to the 16th tomb construction in the Delhi region escalated, apparently because they began to be built by the nobility. Hundreds of high, plain, square domed tombs, either stucco-faced or composed of poorly bonded stone, survive in Delhi. After the beginning of Mughal rule in 1526, tomb construction assumed unprecedented importance. The largest mausolea were built by royalty and are characterized by garden settings intended to evoke the gardens of paradise. Many imperial Mughal tombs, such as the Taj Mahal at Agra (1631–47; *see* AGRA, §II, 1, and fig. 1) adhere closely to Timurid prototypes. Others, such as Akbar's tomb at Sikandra (completed 1612–14; *see* SIKANDRA, figs 1 and 2), appear to be modelled on contemporary palace types. The interiors generally comprise a large central chamber surrounded by eight smaller interconnecting rooms. Nearly all the Mughal rulers constructed tombs for Sufi saints, a notable example being the tomb of Shaykh Salim Chishti at FATEHPUR SIKRI (see fig. 5). Members of the nobility not only built such shrines as acts of piety, but also constructed their own mausolea. Often smaller and less lavish than the imperial tombs, they tended to be set in gardens and were commonly used as pleasure pavilions during the owner's life. After the late 17th century an increasing return to orthodox Islam meant that tombs more often comprised simple graves surrounded by stone screens; following Islamic injunction these had no roofs (e.g. the tomb of Jahan Ara, Delhi, 1681).

Although Hindus favoured cremation, Islamic influence began a tradition of erecting commemorative structures (*chatrīs*) among members of the princely houses of Rajasthan (e.g. the Kachhwaha rulers of Amber, and the Sisodiya rulers of Udaipur at Ahar). Often of marble, these rest on a high plinth and consist of pillars supporting domed

5. Tomb of Shaykh Salim Chishti, Fatehpur Sikri, completed 1581

superstructures. The memorial over the cremation site of Mahatma Gandhi in Delhi is a 20th-century form of Hindu commemoration, while the tradition of the Mughal mausoleum was revived in the tomb of Muhammad 'Ali Jinnah in Karachi. Colonial rule in the 18th–20th centuries brought an increasing need for Christian cemeteries in areas where Europeans lived; many contain only simple graves, but some feature monumental sculpture and a few contain small mausolea (e.g. the tomb of J. W. Hessing in Agra). Tombs inside churches (e.g. John Flaxman's monument to *Joseph Webbe* in St Mary's Church, Madras) were often marked by large figural sculptures with allegorical references.

In the Hindu and Buddhist kingdoms of Indianized South-east Asia, as in the Indian subcontinent, the dead were generally cremated, and cremation is still the usual practice in the Theravada Buddhist countries of mainland South-east Asia—Burma, Thailand and Laos—and in Hindu Bali. Consequently, tombs in the strict sense of the term scarcely occur anywhere in South-east Asia until the advent of Islam and Christianity, although reliquary monuments (stupas) and mausolea are major features of the temple architecture of the region, and in sinicized Vietnam there was a long tradition of dynastic tomb building that culminated in the series of tombs built by successive emperors of the Nguyen dynasty (1802–1954) during the 19th century at Hue (*see* VIETNAM, §II, 1(ii)). In several Indonesian islands there is an ancient indigenous tradition of megalithic sculpture, which includes the making of stone sarcophagi and slab graves or tombs on which figures of the ancestors are sometimes carved (*see* INDONESIA, §IV, 3, 4(i) and 5; *see also* SARCOPHAGUS, §IV, 1). In some islands, notably Nias, northern Sumatra and the

Nusa Tenggara islands (Lesser Sunda islands) this tradition has survived to the late 20th century.

See also INDIAN SUBCONTINENT, §III, 6(ii) and 7(i).

BIBLIOGRAPHY
M. Ara: 'The Lodhi Rulers and the Construction of Tomb-Buildings in Delhi', *Acta Asiat.*, xliii (1982), pp. 61–80
A. Welch: 'Qur'an and Tomb: The Religious Epigraphs of Two Early Sultanate Tombs in Delhi', *Indian Epigraphy: Its Bearing on the History of Art*, ed F. M. Asher and G. S. Gai (New Delhi, 1985), pp. 257–67
M. Shokoohy: *Bhadresvar: The Oldest Islamic Monuments in India* (Leiden, 1989)
H. Edwards: *The Genesis of Islamic Architecture in the Indus Valley* (PhD diss., New York U., 1990)
B. Groseclose: 'Imag(in)ing Indians', *A. Hist.*, xiii (1990), pp. 487–515
H. Edwards: 'The Ribat of 'Ali b. Karmakh', *Iran*, xxix (1991), pp. 85–94
C. B. Asher: *The Architecture of Mughal India* (Cambridge, 1992)
CATHERINE B. ASHER

IV. East Asia.

East Asian tombs have two basic forms: deep-shaft tombs and chambered tombs. Deep-shaft tombs were prevalent in ancient China before the 1st century AD, for example the monumental royal tombs of the Shang dynasty (*c.* 1600–*c.* 1050 BC). During the 5th century BC huge pyramidal or tapered rectangular mounds were built over royal and aristocratic tombs (*see* CHINA, §II, 6(i)). Similar tomb forms may be seen in the Korean peninsula dating from before the 4th century AD and Japan dating from before the 5th century AD. A distinctive Japanese tumulus plan of the period is round with a wedge-shaped mound attached (*see* JAPAN, §III, 2(ii)). Early in the 1st century AD deep-shaft tombs in north China were gradually succeeded by chambered tombs. Early examples of the new construction usually consist of a number of interlinked chambers hollowed out from the hillside, a form also seen in 6th–8th-century Japan. Multiple burials in the same tomb were therefore possible. Later chambers were excavated in the ground and could be accessed through a sloping passage over which an earth mound was raised, as can also be seen in 6th-century Paekche. The chambered tombs fully express the Chinese ideal that the dead should be carefully provided for as if they were still living; thus, the spatial organization of the chambers is intentionally modelled on an earthly mansion.

See also BURIAL MOUND.

PUAY-PENG HO

V. Pre-Columbian Americas.

Tombs were used throughout the civilized cultures of Pre-Columbian Mesoamerica and of South and Central America, to contain both interments and cremated remains. In contrast, few cultures in North America used any kind of tomb structure.

Burial in tombs was generally the privilege of the élite, whose bodies were accompanied by personal ornaments, clothing, tools and weapons, and often by such sacrificial victims as wives or concubines, guards and other attendants, and sometimes by dogs in Mesoamerica and South America, or by llamas in the Andean areas. The richness of offerings—jade, turquoise and other hardstones, pearls, valued shells, special ceramics and figurines, artefacts of copper, gold and silver, wall frescoes and stucco sculptures—was scaled according to social rank. The richest known tombs include Tomb 7 at the Mixtec site of MONTE ALBÁN, Mexico (Mesoamerica); the Maya tomb of Lord Pacal at PALENQUE, Mexico (Mesoamerica); the tomb (discovered in 1989) of a Maya lord and scribe, the son of the ruler Smoke Imix, at COPÁN, Honduras (Mesoamerica); two unlooted Moche rulers' tombs (discovered in 1987 and 1989) at Sipán, Peru; and a Sicán/Lambayeque tomb (*see* SICÁN), also unlooted, found near BATÁN GRANDE, Peru, in 1992.

Many forms of burial chamber were used in Mesoamerica and in South and Central America. Most were square or rectangular, but circular and elliptical plans were also used by the central and southern Andean cultures of Nazca, Chancay, Chanka and Tiahuanaco; cruciform plans by the Mixtecs of Mesoamerica; and keyhole-plan mounds by the Tarascans of West Mexico. In north-western South America and in West Mexico several peoples used shaft-and-chamber tombs, possibly indicating contact by sea between the two regions.

The pyramids built by Mesoamerican and Andean cultures were neither primarily nor exclusively for burials but served as temple, palace and ceremonial platforms. Some pyramids, such as those at Maya TIKAL and Palenque, were built as both temple platforms and tombs, while others, such as the numerous Moche *huacas* in the valleys of northern coastal Peru, contain later inserted burial chambers.

1. North America. 2. Mesoamerica. 3. South and Central America.

1. NORTH AMERICA. Among the cultures of North America there was a wide variety of mortuary practices for both interment and cremation, but for the most part burials were in round, oval or elongated pits. The placement of the body also varied among cultures: partly or tightly flexed, extended face up, extended face down, or wrapped as bundles of disarticulated bones. Among most peoples individuals of greater social standing were buried either more elaborately, or with more valuable grave goods, or both. The Hohokam of the US Southwest, whose culture flourished between *c.* 300 BC and *c.* AD 1450, placed the remains of their cremations in pottery jars and buried these in pits in or near their dwellings. Some Plains peoples wrapped their dead in clothing and blankets and exposed them to decay on poled platforms, sometimes also collecting the bones afterwards for burial in bundles in pits. Among some groups in southern California the dead were simply deposited in natural rock shafts or crevices.

Burial chambers were used by several widely distributed cultures of the eastern Woodlands, throughout the vast area of the Ohio–Mississippi river drainage. Between *c.* 1400 BC and *c.* AD 200 the Adena peoples of southern Ohio and neighbouring portions of Indiana, Kentucky, Pennsylvania and West Virginia buried their dead in simple clay-lined basins, sometimes also cremating the body (*see* ADENA MOUND). Other burials were placed in log tombs—holding one, two or three bodies—covered by earthen mounds, some of which had entrances that were kept open for the deposition of later burials. In the more elaborate of these, the bodies were smeared with red ochre or with graphite, and accompanied by more and better grave-goods. Some interments were also accompanied by a severed skull.

The Hopewell peoples, even more widely distributed throughout the Ohio–Mississippi drainage area, and who flourished between *c.* 300 BC and *c.* AD 500, also used log tombs (*see* HOPEWELL MOUNDS). Their burial mounds were normally built in two stages, beginning with a low earthern mound, containing either a log tomb or a series of crematory basins, and surmounted by a larger earthern mound. Hopewell burials were accompanied by lavish grave-goods, including pottery, tubular stone pipes, shell ornaments, stone and bone tools, and artefacts of beaten copper and sheet mica. Further west, near St Louis, MO, and the river valleys to the west, Hopewell influence in the early centuries AD brought with it the use of burial mounds, some of which covered stone-lined burial chambers. After *c.* AD 700 the use of mound burials waned, but peoples of the still more widely distributed Mississippian cultures retained sporadically the custom of mound burial. At CAHOKIA, which flourished between *c.* AD 700 and *c.* 1500, the body in one mound burial wore a robe into which were woven some 12,000 shell beads. Around the body were caches of stone arrowheads and of polished stone and mica artefacts. In a nearby mass grave were buried six male and fifty-three female retainers.

In the cultures of the Northwest, the peoples in the Puget Sound area placed some burials in mounds of earth and rock debris, ringed with boulders. These burials, however, were accompanied by few grave-goods, if any. In some cultures of southern California pit burials had large, obsolete grindstones placed over the grave.

See also NATIVE NORTH AMERICAN ART, §I, 2(i).

2. MESOAMERICA. Mesoamerican peoples preferred to build tombs of stone or to excavate burial chambers into bedrock. Tombs were built within platform mounds and pyramids (either of earth or of earth with stone cladding) that supported important buildings, excavated and built into hills or sunken into ceremonial plazas. Specially designated cemeteries were not common, with the important exception of the island of Jaina, Campeche, off the north-west coast of the Yucatán Peninsula, which became a ceremonial burial place of several hundred tombs for élite Maya in the Late Classic period (*c.* AD 600–*c.* 900). Sites of the Early–Middle Pre-Classic period (*c.* 2000–*c.* 300 BC), such as those of TLATILCO and Copilco, sometimes referred to as 'cemetery sites' by archaeologists, were in fact early village farming settlements where numerous burials have been excavated. At other sites, such as Late Pre-Classic (*c.* 300 BC–*c.* AD 250) and Classic (*c.* AD 250–*c.* 900) Monte Albán or Early Post-Classic (*c.* AD 900–*c.* 1200) XOCHICALCO, tombs were built into the adjacent hills surrounding the ceremonial centres of the cities.

In the Pre-Classic period (*c.* 2000 BC–*c.* AD 250) the Olmecs of the Gulf Coast constructed corbel-vaulted rectangular stone burial chambers, and at the Olmec

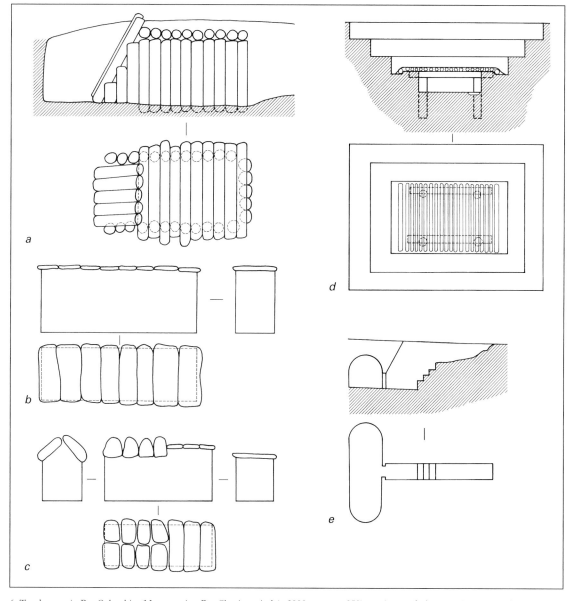

6. Tomb types in Pre-Columbian Mesoamerica, Pre-Classic period (*c.* 2000 BC–*c.* AD 250), sections and plans: (a) La Venta, Olmec tomb of upright and horizontal basalt columns within a mound; (b) Monte Albán, Zapotec rectangular tomb cut into bedrock with flat roof of stone slabs; (c) Monte Albán, Zapotec rectangular tomb cut into bedrock with pitched roof of stone slabs; (d) Kaminaljuyú, Maya rectangular, stepped tomb roofed with beams within a pyramid-platform; (e) El Opeño, West Mexican stepped chamber tomb

ceremonial centre of LA VENTA a tomb was formed by upright and horizontal basalt columns within a mound (see fig. 6a). At Zapotec Monte Albán, in the Southern Highlands, rectangular burial chambers were dug into the bedrock and covered with flat (6b) or pitched (6c) roofs of stone slabs. The inhabitants of early Maya KAMINALJUYÚ inserted stepped rectangular tombs, roofed with beams, into several of the pyramid platforms (6d), and at Maya Tikal several stone burial chambers have remains of frescoes. In West Mexico a separate tradition was developed of shaft-and-chamber tombs: vertical shafts, some with steps, leading to one or more horizontal, stone-lined burial chambers, sometimes with an antechamber, as at El Opeño (6e). Sometimes shaft-and-chamber tombs were covered by mounds, and many were repeatedly opened and reused, as at Ahualulco and ETZATLÁN. Their use continued into the Early Classic period, but died out with the appearance of Teotihuacán influences in architecture (*see also* MESOAMERICA, PRE-COLUMBIAN, §IV, 2(iii)(a)).

In the Classic period (*c.* AD 250–*c.* 900) one of the most famous tombs is that of the ruler of Maya Palenque, Lord Pacal ('Shield'; 615–83). He was buried beneath the Temple of the Inscriptions, in a chamber reached by a vaulted staircase descending to a rectangular vaulted tomb, decorated with sculptured stucco walls. His body was placed in a stone sarcophagus and sealed with a single, ornately carved stone slab (*see also* SARCOPHAGUS, §V). A similar chamber within a pyramid platform has been excavated at Maya Copán. The masonry chamber was roofed with a corbel vault filled with rubble over a rectangular tomb capped with large, rectangular stone slabs. At Copán, however, the tomb was reached by a tunnel with ascending steps at the end, up to the tomb. In the Southern Highlands at Monte Albán numerous tombs were built into the hillsides surrounding the ceremonial centre of the city. The plastered walls were decorated with frescoes in a combination of Zapotec and Teotihuacán art styles, the best preserved being Tomb 104 and Tomb 105 (*see also* MESOAMERICA, PRE-COLUMBIAN, §VI, 2).

In the Post-Classic period (*c.* AD 900–1521) the Zapotec and Mixtec peoples of the Southern Highlands built cruciform tombs with antechambers at MITLA and YAGUL. The chambers were excavated into the ceremonial precincts and capped with huge stone slabs or with beams supporting smaller slabs. At the same time, the Mixtecs reopened and reused many Zapotec tombs at the ceremonial centre of Monte Albán, by then abandoned, including the richly furnished Tomb 7. At the contemporary Mixtec sites of Coixtlahuaca and Tilantongo rectangular tombs were dug into bedrock. The Aztec and related peoples of the Basin of Mexico and the Central Highlands either buried or cremated their dead, depending on the manner of death. Important people were buried in vaulted underground chambers, along with valuable grave-goods and sometimes with sacrificial victims. In West Mexico the Tarascans built monumental keyhole-plan structures (*yacatás*), covering burials beneath a layer of stones, and interred their élite in tombs roofed and walled with beams and planks, as at TZINTZUNTZAN, Ihuatzio and Pátzcuaro.

See also MESOAMERICA, PRE-COLUMBIAN, §II.

3. SOUTH AND CENTRAL AMERICA. In South America natural chambers such as caves and rock shelters were used for burials right through to Inca times. Cemeteries were common, many containing thousands of burial pits.

In the Isthmian region of the Intermediate Area, especially in Costa Rica, stone cist tombs with flagstone lids were common. Large stone slabs with carved borders may have been used for funeral biers. During the second half of the first millennium AD the peoples of SAN AGUSTÍN and TIERRADENTRO in the Cauca Valley and central Columbian Andes practised a tradition of shaft-andchamber tombs, excavating large chambers into the earth at right angles to the shafts, and lining them with stone slab walls and roofs. Shaft-and-chamber tombs 3–6 m deep were also used in the Veraguas culture of central Panama. In the 6th–15th centuries AD the peoples of the MILAGRO-QUEVADO culture of Ecuador built 'chimney tombs' of stacked burial urns with their bottoms broken out.

In the Andean cultures of the late centuries BC and early centuries AD stone-lined pits were used for burial at CHAVÍN DE HUÁNTAR and contemporary sites, bottle-shaped shaft-and-chamber tombs cut into rock at Paracas, and elliptical burials at Tiahuanaco and Salinar in the southern Andes. Deep shaft-and-chamber tombs were also used in the Vicús culture in the far north of Peru, which flourished between *c.* 500 BC and *c.* AD 500. Between *c.* AD 100 and *c.* 750 the Mochica of northern coastal Peru built many rich rectangular tombs of mud-bricks inside their pyramid platforms, roofed with wooden beams. The bodies of the élite were placed in wooden coffins and sacrificed retainers were buried in cane coffins (see fig. 7). In the La Leche Valley of northern coastal Peru, during the Middle Sicán period (*c.* AD 900–*c.* 1100), solid burial vaults were built at the bottom of vertical shafts up to 20 m deep. Such shaft tombs are the southernmost found in the Andes and, when looted, are reported to have contained as many as 200 gold objects or as much as 500 kg of bronze artefacts accompanying up to 17 bodies. In the Recuay culture, inland in the highlands, tombs were subterranean galleries entered by short shafts through holes in the ceilings. Roughly contemporary Nazca burials were usually in simple pits, but some, presumably higher-status individuals, were buried in rectangular, circular or oval chambers lined with mud-bricks and plastered.

During the Middle Horizon (*c.* AD 600–*c.* 1000) and the beginning of the Late Intermediate period (*c.* AD 1000–1476) rock shelters were used in the Huari highlands. Contemporary practice on the coast included the building of true mausolea of subterranean rectangular chambers, with rounded corners, mud-brick linings and roofs of wooden beams and clay.

In the Late Intermediate period and the Late Horizon (AD 1476–1534) the Chimú of northern coastal Peru built tombs that were rectangular shafts, in one case T-shaped, sunk into platforms within walled compounds. Contemporary Chancay tombs were circular or rectangular, lined with mud-bricks and smoothed clay walls, and roofed with canes and wooden poles. The Chanka of the central highlands, traditional rivals of the Inca, buried their dead

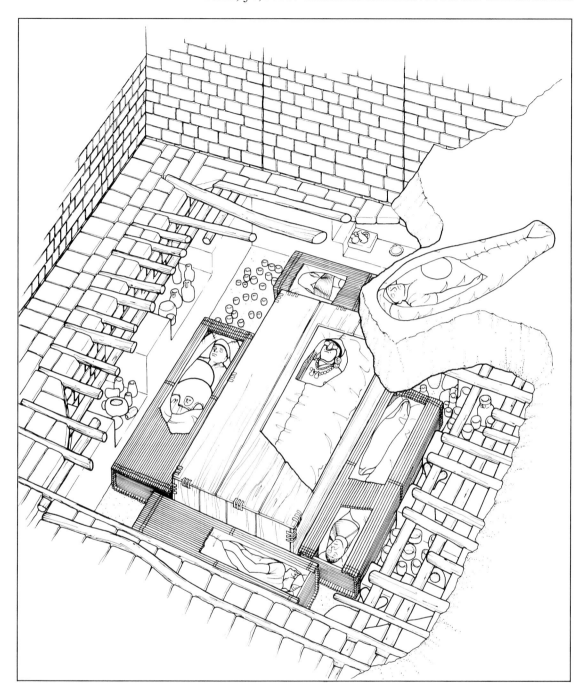

7. Pre-Columbian Moche tomb of a warrior–priest, *c.* AD 290; reconstruction drawing

in circular, corbel-vaulted stone structures (*chullpas*; *see* TITICACA BASIN, fig. 2). The Incas themselves used caves and natural fissures modified with masonry and sealed with stone walls. The bodies of the dead were placed in niches within these semi-natural structures. Inca rulers, however, were mummified and preserved in the Coricancha temple, dedicated to the sun, in Cuzco.

See also SOUTH AMERICA, PRE-COLUMBIAN, §III, 1.

BIBLIOGRAPHY

NORTH AMERICA

D. R. Snow: *The Archaeology of North America: American Indians and their Origins* (London and New York, 1976, rev. 1980)

M. Coe, D. R. Snow and E. Benson: *Atlas of Ancient America* (Oxford, 1986)

MESOAMERICA

I. Marquina: *Arquitectura prehispanica* (Mexico City, 1950, 2/1964/*R* 1981)

J. Soustelle: *La Vie quotidienne des Aztèques à la veille de la conquête espagnole* (Paris, 1955; Eng. trans., London, 1961)

G. Kubler: *The Art and Architecture of Ancient America*, Pelican Hist. A. (Harmondsworth, 1962, rev. 3/1984)

A. Trik: 'The Splendid Tomb of Temple 1 at Tikal, Guatemala', *Expedition*, vi (1963), pp. 2–18

R. Chadwick: 'The Tombs of Monte Albán I Style at Yagul', *Ancient Oaxaca: Discoveries in Mexican Archaeology and History*, ed. J. Paddock (Stanford, CA, 1966), pp. 245–55

M. D. Coe: *The Maya* (London and New York, 1966, rev. 4/1987)

C. Wicke: 'Tomb 30 at Yagul', *Ancient Oaxaca: Discoveries in Mexican Archaeology and History*, ed. J. Paddock (Stanford, CA, 1966), pp. 336–44

B. Bell: 'Archaeology of Nayarit, Jalisco and Colima', *Hb. Mid. Amer. Ind.*, xi (1971), pp. 694–753

R. Chadwick: 'Archaeological Synthesis of Michoacan and Adjacent Regions', *Hb. Mid. Amer. Ind.*, xi (1971), pp. 657–93

M. P. Weaver: *The Aztecs, Maya and their Predecessors: Archaeology of Mesoamerica* (New York, 1972, rev. 3/1993)

A. Oliveros: 'Nuevas exploraciones en El Opeño, Michoacán', *The Archaeology of West Mexico*, ed. B. Bell (Ajijic, Mexico, 1974), pp. 182–201

P. Weigand: 'The Ahualulco Site and the Shaft-tomb Complex of the Etzatlán Area', *The Archaeology of West Mexico*, ed. B. Bell (Ajijic, Mexico, 1974), pp. 120–31

D. Heyden and P. Gendrop: *Pre-Columbian Architecture in Mesoamerica* (New York, 1975)

W. R. Coe: *Tikal: A Handbook of the Ancient Maya Ruins* (Philadelphia, 1976)

J. W. Whitecotton: *The Zapotecs: Princes, Priests and Peasants* (Norman, 1977)

J. S. Henderson: *The World of the Ancient Maya* (Ithaca, 1981)

R. Agurcia Fasquelle and W. L. Fash: 'Copán: A Royal Maya Tomb Discovered', *N. Geog.*, clxxvi (1989), pp. 480–87

W. Fash: *Scribes, Warriors and Kings: The City of Copán and the Ancient Maya* (London, 1991)

SOUTH AND CENTRAL AMERICA

E. G. Squier: 'A Plain Man's Tomb in Peru', *Frank Leslie's Illustrated Newspaper*, xxviii/704 (27 March 1869), pp. 21–2

C. Evans: 'Finding the Tomb of the Warrior-god', *N. Geog.*, xci (1947), pp. 453–82

L. G. Lumbreras: *De los pueblos, las culturas y las artes del antiguo Perú* (Lima, 1969); Eng. trans. by B. J. Meggers as *The Peoples and Cultures of Ancient Peru* (Washington, DC, 1974)

C. B. Donnan and C. J. Mackey: *Ancient Burial Patterns in the Moche Valley, Peru* (Austin, 1978)

R. W. Keatinge, ed.: *Peruvian Prehistory: An Overview of Pre-Inca and Inca Society* (Cambridge, 1988)

W. Alva and B. Ballenberg: 'Discovering the New World's Richest Un-looted Tomb', *N. Geog.*, clxxiv (1988), pp. 510–49 [Sipán]

W. Alva and N. Benn: 'The Moche of Ancient Peru: New Tomb of Royal Splendor', *N. Geog.*, clxxvii (1990), pp. 2–15 [Sipán]

D. Keys: 'Archaeologists Uncover the Golden Secrets of the Tomb', *The Independent* (12 May 1992)

VI. Western world.

1. Introduction. 2. Before *c.* 1600. 3. *c.* 1600–*c.* 1780. 4. After *c.* 1780.

1. INTRODUCTION. Despite the collapse of the Roman Empire in the 5th century AD, important architectural structures continued to be built over the tombs of martyrs and saints (*see* MARTYRIUM), particularly in the areas under Byzantine rule. One of the best-documented examples is the basilica of Hagios Demetrios (*c.* 450 or early 6th century; rebuilt 7th century; *see* THESSALONIKI, §III, 3). Shrines also developed around other kinds of sacred sites, including fragments of a saint's body preserved in a reliquary (*see* RELIQUARY, §I, 1). The tomb or reliquary was usually the location of the shrine's altar. Whole mausolea were also built for rulers in various parts of Europe (*see* MAUSOLEUM, §II), for example the mausoleum of Theodoric (*c.* 526; *see* RAVENNA, §2(iii)). Such buildings developed the already vigorous tradition of free-standing mausolea, which was to continue into the 20th century. From the mid-6th century, however, the practice of locating tombs in or next to churches began to predominate. Sculptural, as opposed to architectural, tombs gained in importance, and it is with these that this survey is principally concerned.

Although constant attempts were made to limit burial within the church, particularly within the choir or sanctuary, almost all churches were surrounded by graveyards. Indeed, notable monuments were erected outside churches in the Middle Ages, in particular the tombs of the DELLA SCALA rulers of Verona, and by the 17th century many handsome carved stone markers adorned graveyards in many parts of Europe. Nevertheless, most of the important Christian tomb sculpture in western Europe after the decline of the Roman Empire and before the 19th century was located within churches. Throughout this period the sculpture was usually erected above the vault where the body was actually buried: before the 18th century the cenotaph (a monument unconnected with an actual burial) was unusual in a European church (*see* CENOTAPH, §1(ii)). Monuments often included a tomb-chest or even, especially after the Renaissance, a Classical sarcophagus or an urn. Whereas the tomb slabs carved with an effigy—a common type of monument in the medieval period—do seem to have served as covers for burial vaults, these tomb chests and sarcophagi seldom contained human remains. Nor did urns contain ashes. They were particularly favoured in 18th-century monuments but cremation was not seriously revived in Europe until the late 19th century. Although grand tombs did not always include effigies before the 14th century, the development of the effigy forms an important part of the history of tomb sculpture. It is much disputed when they began to incorporate the idiosyncrasy of feature that is a prerequisite for portraiture as we understand it, but the effigy of *Charles V* of France (commissioned 1364) by André Beauneveu in Saint-Denis Abbey is a precocious example. Certainly from the Renaissance onwards many effigies had the character of a portrait, while in the 17th and 18th centuries some were shown in action, involved in dramatic scenes with other figures, usually of an allegorical nature. It has often been claimed that European tomb monuments after the Renaissance can be characterized by an increasingly 'retrospective', as opposed to 'prospective', character, looking back at the achievements of the deceased, rather than showing the soul in its ascent, or the deceased kneeling at the Last Judgement or before the enthroned Christ, as in earlier monuments. Biographical allusions were exceptional in medieval monuments: we are not shown the battles in which the Plantagenets fought or the trophies of their enemies, nor do we find references on the tombs of Popes to the reforms that they instituted or the miracles that they enacted. There is perhaps only one type of medieval tomb that was retrospective in emphasis: the monuments commemorating the professors of the northern Italian universities of Bologna and Padua, which can be traced to the early 14th century and which contained representations of the deceased lecturing to students (*see* GOTHIC, §III, 1(iv)(e)). From the late 15th century biographical reliefs were found in the more secular tombs, especially those of military character. Such imagery was to flourish in tomb sculpture in the succeeding centuries.

As well as these iconographical developments in European tomb monuments, important changes in patronage occurred after the Middle Ages. Initially the most important tombs were made for clerics and rulers. From the late 13th century the custom of dividing the body of a prince, which developed in England and France despite Papal opposition, led to some kings and queens having splendid tombs in more than one location: in the 16th century separate and smaller monuments were designed for the hearts of the French kings. Despite the pre-eminence of ecclesiastical and lay tombs, other classes of people became able to purchase prominent spaces for tomb monuments within churches. The funds for much church building and maintenance, especially for that of the great new mendicant churches of the late Middle Ages, came from the sale of family chapels, where monuments were erected; as these buildings increased in number and splendour, so the prohibitions against lay burial and the injunctions against ostentatious commemoration were successively disregarded. Nevertheless there were always controls on the character of tombs erected in churches. These were greatly relaxed in England after the Reformation and the congestion of Westminster Abbey testifies to the opportunities for private enterprise in commemoration that this relaxation—and the Church's need for funds—made possible. While previously most significant tombs were in or near churches, from the 19th century rapid urbanization and population increases led to the growth of large public cemeteries, in which the monuments displayed a wide variety of styles.

2. BEFORE *c.* 1600.

(i) Tomb-chests and slab tombs. (ii) Wall tombs.

(i) Tomb-chests and slab tombs. In the early Middle Ages generally only saints were buried in tomb-chests, which were either raised above ground level or placed in crypts, where they were regularly visited. The tomb-chest of a saint would often serve as an altar. Some tomb-chests were in fact ancient sarcophagi: for example the remains of Mary Magdalene in the basilica of Saint-Maximin-La-Sainte-Beume in Provence rest in a 4th-century sarcophagus. This sarcophagus is carved with Christian imagery, but it is curious how many sarcophagi seem to have been carefully preserved, even those decorated with explicitly pagan subjects. Great rulers coveted these: the Emperor Charlemagne (*d* 814), for example, was buried in the Palatine chapel at Aachen in a late Antonine sarcophagus decorated with the *Rape of Proserpina*. It is possible that this pagan myth would have been interpreted as a pious allegory, as were Ovid's *Metamorphoses* throughout the Middle Ages. It is hard to understand, however, how the pagan nuptials on the large 3rd-century sarcophagus incorporated into the wall tomb of *Cardinal Guglielmo Fieschi* (*d* 1256; see fig. 8) could possibly be thought to relate to the life of the celibate Cardinal, who is depicted in a painting above, kneeling with his uncle, Pope Innocent IV (*reg* 1243–54), before the enthroned Christ.

Many Popes also favoured such Classical sarcophagi, not usually as repositories for their bodies but as part of

8. Tomb of *Cardinal Guglielmo Fieschi*, S Lorenzo fuori le Mura, Rome, mid-13th century, incorporating 3rd-century AD sarcophagus

their tomb-monuments: examples include those of Gregory V (*reg* 996–9; Rome, Grotte Vaticane), *Damasus II* (*reg* 1048; Rome, S Giovanni in Laterano), *Innocent II* (*reg* 1130–43; Rome, S Maria in Trastevere), *Honorius III* (*reg* 1216–27; Rome, S Maria Maggiore) and *Clement IV* (*reg* 1265–8; Viterbo, S Francesco). The appeal of such sarcophagi must have been enhanced by their use of white marble, which by the 6th century had ceased to be quarried. Moreover, porphyry and granite—materials that not only were no longer quarried but also could no longer be carved—enjoyed the highest prestige of all. Pope Anastasius IV (*reg* 1153–4) appropriated the massive porphyry sarcophagus said to have been made for the Empress Helena (Rome, Vatican, Mus. Pio-Clementino); his successor Adrian IV (*reg* 1154–9) chose a roughly worked and probably unfinished red granite sarcophagus (Rome, Grotte Vaticane); and Charles I of Anjou, King of Naples (*reg* 1266–85), searched for such a sarcophagus for the tomb of *Innocent V* (*reg* 1276). Even before the second half of the 15th century, a few attempts were made to imitate ancient sarcophagi (see SARCOPHAGUS, §III, 2). Examples include the columnar tomb-chest of the first Abbot of Airvault, *Pierre de Saine-Fontaine* (*d* 1110; Airvault, St Pierre), and the precocious imitation of antique putti on the tomb-chest of *Ilaria del Carretto* (1405–7/8) by Jacopo della Quercia in Lucca Cathedral (see JACOPO DELLA QUERCIA, fig. 2).

Medieval tombs that re-employed or copied ancient sarcophagi were exceptional, if important. The most common form of tomb from the early Middle Ages was the slab or ledger stone, incorporated into the paving so as to appear to be the actual covering of the vault: it had the same dimensions and often the same shape as the coffin below. The stone was incised or carved in low relief often with a life-size effigy. Tombs of this kind seem to have made their first appearance in western Europe in the 11th century (although the accidents of survival prevent confident generalization) and continued to be produced for several centuries. The effigy of *Rudolf of Swabia* (*d* 1080) made for Merseburg Cathedral, which is remarkable as an early bronze low-relief slab and the earliest known tomb effigy of a layman in the Christian West, represents a type of tomb that was not much modified even in the 15th century: a comparable bronze effigy by Donatello is that of *Bishop Giovanni Pecci* (*d* 1426) in Siena Cathedral, and Nicholas Stone I's black stone slab effigy of *Sir William Curle* (*d* 1619) in his winding-sheet on the floor of St Etheldreda, Hatfield, Herts, belongs to the same tradition. The majority of early slab effigies were those of great princes of the church dating from the 12th century, although other conventions existed for grand carved slabs, most notably the depiction of the soul of the deceased in the form of a child, with hands raised in worship, gathered up in a swag of drapery by angels. This can be seen, for example, on the slab of imported black marble from Tournai that served as the tomb of one of the powerful bishops of Ely (perhaps Bishop Nigellus; see fig. 9). The grandest early examples of slab effigies may also have included mosaic effigies, but these were particularly vulnerable to damage, as indeed were such tombs in all media. It was doubtless for motives of protection and safety, as well as ostentation, that the slabs of great men began to be raised, initially on figures of lions or other animals or on short columns, and then on a tomb-chest. The chest might then be given still more prominence by a canopy, just as the high altar was adorned by a ciborium. The elevation of the slab to the tomb-chest is also intimately connected with the development of the effigy from something carved out of the slab to a wholly three-dimensional figure resting upon it.

In some early slab effigies (e.g. that of *Bishop Roger*, *c.* 1140; Salisbury Cathedral) the effigy is in low relief but more deeply cut, even undercut, around the head. This tendency increased in subsequent centuries, but there were limits to the three-dimensional character that could be achieved when the effigy was cut from a slab of polishable and richly coloured limestone (the black 'marble' of Tournai, the dark brown or grey 'marble' of Purbeck, and the mottled red stones of the Danube or Adige). Pale limestone was more easily quarried in blocks rather than slabs, and masons felt freer to waste this material, permitting such projections as the hands of Eleanor of Aquitaine, Queen of England (*d* 1204), which hold up a small devotional book in her tomb effigy in the church of Fontevrault abbey. The book does not, however, project much higher than her feet or pillow, and it is quite clear that her effigy is fashioned from the same block as the slab upon which she lies, now conceived as a bier and united to the effigy by falling drapery.

The next stage may be represented by effigies of white marble and white alabaster (contemporary documents in

9. Marble tomb of a bishop of Ely, Ely Cathedral, *c.* 1150

northern Europe do not distinguish between the two materials), which were made separately and placed on top of the slab. The earliest example of an effigy made of the prestigious material of marble in northern Europe is that of *Isabella of Aragon* (*d* 1271), first queen of Philip III of France (*reg* 1270–85), completed by 1275 for Saint-Denis Abbey. It is an unusually flat effigy (perhaps cut from the centre of an antique marble column) and one that is sunk into the contrasting black marble slab. The great early 15th-century tomb of *Philip the Bold*, Duke of Burgundy (Dijon, Mus. B.-A.), created by Claus Sluter and others for the Charterhouse of Champmol, near Dijon, is in the same tradition, with its gypsum alabaster effigy on a vast black marble slab: the effigy, however, is now entirely distinct in character from the slab.

The earliest bronze effigies were cast together with the tomb slab, so that an effigy such as that of *Bishop Wolfhart von Roth* (*d* 1302) in Augsburg Cathedral, inscribed 'Made from a wax model by Otto, cast in bronze by Conrad', is really a sort of relief. On the other hand, the impression given by the effigy of *Richard Beauchamp*, Earl of Warwick (*d* 1439), made in the 1450s by William Austen and others for the Beauchamp Chapel in St Mary's, Warwick, is that it is a detachable statue (*see* ENGLAND, fig. 27).

The development of the effigy towards greater substance and autonomy may represent the main episode in the evolution of the medieval tomb, but this statement must be qualified by various considerations. It should be remembered that the effigy was not an invariable adjunct of the grand tomb before the 14th century. No lay effigy in Italy can be dated before the early years of that century: even such a splendid monument as that of *Luca Savelli* (probably 1280s) in S Maria in Aracoeli in Rome features no representation of the deceased. Indeed, some of the 13th-century papal tombs also had no effigy, although it was more unusual in northern Europe for a tomb of an important figure to lack an effigy. Moreover, certain forms of effigies, both on paving-slabs and on slabs raised on tomb-chests, contradict the tendency towards three dimensions that has just been traced—or at least appear to do so at first sight, for in fact they imitate in two dimensions the appearance of three-dimensional figures. As Panofsky observed, 'the three-dimensional effigy ... could be reduced to relative or absolute two-dimensionality again, so that it appeared, if one may say so, in planimetrical projection. This in turn could be effected either by diminishing the height of the relief, or, more radically, by projecting its design onto a perfectly flat surface.' Among the best examples of this are brasses (*see* BRASSES, MONUMENTAL)—flat sheets of metal deeply engraved with texts, effigies or heraldic devices. These became popular in the Rhineland, the Netherlands and Britain in the second half of the 13th century and continued in favour for two or three centuries. Other good examples of two-dimensional effigies are stone slabs with incised decoration filled with black cement, the so-called niello plaques found mostly in France and Italy in the same period.

The question arises as to whether the effigies in tombs of this period represent live or dead bodies. The natural supposition might be that they depict the dead body. The fact that the effigies usually have open eyes in France and elsewhere north of the Alps (closed eyes were common in Spain and Italy), show no sign of physical decay, hold the emblems of high office—orb, sceptre or mitre—and even perform with one hand the action of blessing or even coronation, does not contradict this, since such imagery might reflect the dead body lying in state before burial. This interpretation of the effigy receives some support from the presence of a cushion beneath the head—present, for example, in the effigy of *Bishop Evrard de Fouilloi* (*d* 1220) in Amiens Cathedral—and still more by the presence of figures censing and sprinkling with holy water, in this and many other grand tombs of the 13th and 14th centuries. A close relationship must be presumed between the effigy of wax, covered in real clothes, displayed at a funeral and often preserved for a while afterwards near the place of burial, and the effigy created for the tomb in a more costly and durable material. It should be pointed out, however, that the draperies often fall as if the figures were standing and that the effigies are frequently given some sort of architectural canopy, which implies a vertical position. It may be that the very question as to whether

an effigy of the 12th century or early 13th is conceived of as standing or lying down is irrelevant. Certainly, many of the contemporary upright figures of saints, prophets and ancestors on the portals of Gothic churches appear to have nothing to support them and 'float' in front of the columns to which they are attached, while often resting their feet on animals in just the way that tomb effigies do. But the question certainly does become relevant when some effort is made in effigies of the later 13th century to show drapery falling as it would over a recumbent form.

(ii) Wall tombs. During the 14th century some effigies appear to have been removed from tombs that were presumably congesting the interior of churches, and mounted on the church wall. The effigy of *Pope Clement II* (*reg* 1046–8), carved *c.* 1235–40, was set against a pier in Bamberg Cathedral, and in its vertical position is impressive as a statue of a living man, rather than the effigy of a dead one. It may have been the displacement of effigies of this type that prompted some large tomb effigies actually to be designed for vertical attachment, for example the series of 15th-century effigies of Archbishops of Mainz in Mainz Cathedral.

The free-standing tomb-chest was usually hard to accommodate within an already existing church, and most examples were constructed together with a church or

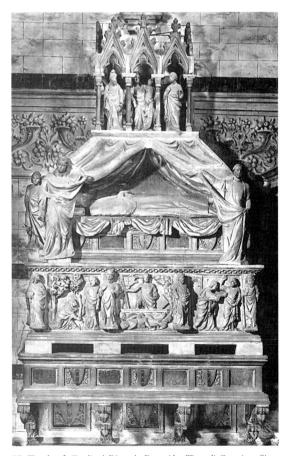

10. Tomb of *Cardinal Riccardo Petroni* by Tino di Camaino, Siena Cathedral, 1317–18

11. Tomb of *John Fitzalan*, St Nicholas, Arundel, West Sussex, mid-15th century

substantial chapel as the tomb of the building's founder. The ambulatories of the choirs of great Gothic cathedrals north of the Alps could also accommodate such tombs; it is noteworthy that they are unusual in Italy, where such ambulatories are rarely found, a rare exception being S Lorenzo Maggiore, Naples, which does have an ambulatory and where there are notable tombs by Tino di Camaino. The most influential solution to the problem of space was to incorporate the tomb-chest and effigy into a niche, which also served as a canopy, attached to the wall or even excavated out of it. This arrangement was known in France as the *enfeu* and was popular there throughout the 12th century. It found favour and took on novel forms

in late 13th-century Italy: early examples there are the tombs of *Pope Clement IV* (*reg* 1265–8) by Pietro di Oderisio and of *Pope Adrian V* (*reg* 1276; both now Viterbo, S Francesco). Such tombs provided opportunities for more sculpture than could be fitted around the effigy on a slab or around a tomb-chest: for example the tomb of *Cardinal Riccardo Petroni* (*d* 1314; Siena Cathedral; see fig. 10) has Virtues supporting a plinth, on which figures of prophets frame narrative reliefs. The next stage is the tomb-chest and effigy with a canopy held back by angels, and above this is a tabernacle containing the *Virgin and Child with SS Peter and Paul*.

The space for large sculptural decoration at different stages in wall tombs of this kind had important consequences, one of which was that it became easier to make religious imagery prominent. In the case of the Petroni tomb such imagery is sculptural, but this was not always the case, especially in Italy: other tombs depicted the deceased kneeling before God the Father, his patron saints or the Virgin and Child in either mosaic or paint. A comprehensive survey of tomb sculpture would claim as effigies some of the best-known frescoes of donors in Italian art, for example the kneeling figures in Masaccio's fresco of the *Trinity* (*see* MASACCIO, fig. 5), or the portraits of Francesco Sassetti and his wife Nera Corsi by Domenico Ghirlandaio in their chapel in Santa Trinita, Florence, on either side of the altarpiece of the *Adoration of the Shepherds* (*see* GHIRLANDAIO, (1), fig. 2). In the case of Masaccio's fresco there is a painting of a skeleton reposing on the chest below the plinth where the couple kneel. It is not certain that it represents either of them after death (some scholars have argued that it represents Everyman or Adam), but it certainly derives from the convention, which appears to have originated in the previous century in France, of representing the deceased as a shrouded and decomposing corpse, sometimes merely cadaverous, often attacked by vermin, frequently skeletal.

These figures 'en transi', as they were termed, were generally contrasted with the effigies of the dead in all

12. Tomb of *Valentine Balbiani* by Germain Pilon, h. 830 mm, *c*. 1580 (Paris, Musée du Louvre)

their worldly pomp and splendour, most commonly by the ingenious conceit of opening the solid tomb-chest below the effigy into a Gothic cage in which the decomposing body could be glimpsed, evident, for example, in the tomb of *John Fitzalan* (*d* 1435; see fig. 11). The most spectacular examples are the French royal tombs of the 16th century: those of *Margaret of Austria* (*d* 1530) and *Philibert II of Savoy* (*d* 1504) in the priory church of Brou, near Bourg-en-Bresse, and those of kings *Louis XII* (1516–31), *Francis I* (begun 1548) and *Henry II* (1559–73) and their queens in Saint-Denis Abbey (*see* SAINT-DENIS ABBEY, figs 7 and 8). In these tombs the higher effigies are no longer recumbent but kneeling. In an aristocratic French wall tomb of the same period, that by Germain

14. Monument to *Pietro Bembo* by Danese Cattaneo, Il Santo, Padua, 1547

13. Tomb of *Doge Pietro Mocenigo* by Pietro Lombardo, SS Giovanni e Paolo, Venice, 1476–81

Pilon of *Valentine Balbiani* (see fig. 12), now without its original architectural setting, the effigy is reclining rather than recumbent, reading, having one hand on her cheek and a lapdog beside her, with the corpse in low relief below.

With the explicit acknowledgement of death and decay, there must have come a desire to contrast the corpse with an effigy of the deceased, not merely presented in his or her physical prime and clad in robes of state or vestments appropriate to the wearer's rank, but also depicted in poses that were explicitly those of a living person. This contrast is apparent in the French tombs mentioned above. It is easy to exaggerate the radical nature of this innovation; after all, some effigies at a much earlier date had been depicted reading (notably that of *Eleanor of Aquitaine*), and the attitude of prayer adopted by the kneeling effigies was characteristic also of earlier recumbent ones. One would not deny that there were ideological implications in the changes in posture, satirized in John Webster's *Duchess of Malfi* (1613) as a 'new fashion' according to which the images of princes 'do not lie, as they were wont, seeming to pray up to heaven, but with their hands under their cheeks as if they had died of the toothache.' All the same, it is obvious that an important motive for these innovations was a practical one of visibility. The architectural frameworks of the tombs in Saint-Denis were so elaborate that if the effigies were to be elevated—as befitted royalty—they would not be visible at all from below if they remained recumbent.

The same problem applies to wall tombs of the Italian type. The first solution, adopted in some 14th- and 15th-century tombs, was the unhappy one of tilting the effigy sideways so that it looks as if it is about to slip down on to the church floor. The next solution was to show the effigy reclining, often supporting its head with a hand under its cheek. It is interesting that in the earliest Italian examples of this, the tombs of *Cardinal Ascanio Sforza* (1505–9) and *Cardinal Girolamo Basso della Rovere* (1507–9) in the choir of S Maria del Popolo, Rome, by Andrea Sansovino, the effigies, although propped up, still have their eyes closed. The fact that the reclining effigy is found in tombs by such sculptors as Sansovino, who were deeply impressed by antique sculpture and who replaced Gothic tomb architecture with a framework modelled on that of the Roman triumphal arch, has prompted speculation that such effigies were inspired by the undeniably similar postures found in many ancient Etruscan effigies as well as in some Roman ones. This seems unlikely, however, considering the evidence of what antique sculpture was then familiar.

Standing effigies made an appearance in Italian wall tombs at a slightly earlier date, as did equestrian monuments to condottieri (*see* STATUE). The tomb of *Doge Pietro Mocenigo* (see fig. 13) by Pietro Lombardo and his workshop may be contrasted with the earlier wall tomb of *Cardinal Petroni* in Siena. It is comparable in size and splendour, but differs in that the figure of the Doge is standing. Moreover, the Christian imagery in Mocenigo's monument is confined to the highest register; the narrative reliefs are not taken from the New Testament but record Mocenigo's victories in the Venetian Republic's wars; the caryatids are soldiers of three generations rather than prophets; and the effigy is attended by nude page-boys in place of angels. Of course, Mocenigo was a secular ruler rather than a prince of the Church, yet no grand tomb in the 14th century had been so secular in theme or pagan in imagery. It is hard to deny that profound changes of outlook had taken place and that these were related to the increasing interest in ancient Rome during the Renaissance. Christian sentiment certainly remained strong in much tomb sculpture, but its frequent subordination was later

15. Epitaph of *Soyer van Marle* (*d* 1578) by Pieter Pourbus, St Jacobskerk, Bruges

to be deplored by the Council of Trent (1545–63). The sternest reformers of the Catholic Church also considered both heraldry and effigies as no more appropriate than nude putti and pagan emblems. Some of the finest Italian funerary chapels of the second half of the 16th century include no effigies at all, only sculpture and paintings of sacred figures.

Pagan Roman emblems and funerary paraphernalia—the pyramid, the obelisk, the trophy and the flaming urn—together with Classical Virtues and personifications—for example Fame and Immortality—were nowhere more enthusiastically displayed than in Protestant England under Queen Elizabeth I and King James I, when a boom in the erection of gigantic monuments of alabaster and coloured marble, embellished with paint and gilding, was permitted within Westminster Abbey, even though they overshadowed the royal tombs. As the demand for monuments in old foundations continued, the consequences were inevitably damaging to the original architecture and often to earlier tombs, although seldom as much as in Westminster Abbey itself. These circumstances may also be connected with the growth in popularity of types of tomb sculpture smaller than any that have so far been discussed.

Some of these smaller monuments incorporated forms of portrait-sculpture, such as the bust, derived from ancient Roman art. These were developed in Italy by such sculptors as Danese Cattaneo, whose bust of *Pietro Bembo* (see fig. 14), was admired by both Pietro Aretino and Titian. Another *all'antica* form used in tomb sculpture was the medallion portrait: this may be regarded as a relief version of the bust but was in fact also related to coins and medals, which were indeed often cast or struck for commemorative purposes. Another important development in the 16th century was the spread of the modest wall-monuments known as epitaphs (*see* EPITAPH), which featured an inscription and a relief of a truncated or diminutive effigy at prayer before either a devotional image (most commonly the *Virgin and Child*) or a narrative (such as the *Resurrection*). These had originated north of the Alps in the 14th century and were adopted chiefly by citizens or clerics of secondary importance, for example Conrad von Busang, who enjoys a convivial relationship with the Virgin and Child in an epitaph of 1464 by Nicolaus Gerhaert in the chapel of St Jean, Strasbourg Cathedral. In this work Busang's half-length figure exemplifies the development of portraiture in tomb effigies. As well as sculpture, epitaphs sometimes also included paintings, as in Pieter Pourbus's epitaph of *Soyer van Marle* (*d* 1578; see fig. 15).

3. *c.* 1600–*c.* 1780.

(i) Formal and iconographical developments. (ii) Changes in patronage.

(i) Formal and iconographical developments. During the 17th century highly innovative and visually rich monuments were produced, often containing a medallion portrait. This was susceptible to more ingenious and lively designs than a bust, for it could more easily be carried by a child angel or an allegorical figure. Bernini, for example, in his tomb of *Maria Raggi* (*c.* 1643) in S Maria sopra Minerva, Rome, showed a gilt bronze medallion of the deceased borne aloft by a pair of child angels against a background of

16. Monument to *Gabriele Fonseca* by Gianlorenzo Bernini, S Lorenzo in Lucina, Rome, *c.* 1668–1670s

agitated drapery in black and yellow marble. He used a similar idea for the monument of *Gabriele Fonseca* (*d* 1668; see fig. 16), in which the deceased, who was physician to Pope Alexander VII, is depicted in a low-relief medallion of white marble carried by a winged skeleton, executed in the same material, against a black marble shroud.

These creations reflected bold ideas first developed in spectacular ephemeral funeral décor, which had become popular in Italy in the second half of the 16th century and sometimes involved whole church interiors being draped with fabric and filled with animated allegorical figures personifying death. The conceit of realizing such decoration in more solid materials was a remarkable one, but it was prompted by practical considerations of space, for, in churches already crowded with monuments, there was a demand for such sculpture that could be fixed on piers and pilasters.

Such considerations did much to condition the inventions of medium- or small-sized monuments in all parts of Europe. An interesting English example is the monument to an eminent naval commander, *Philip de Saumarez* (*d* 1747; see fig. 17). Here, one child angel covers, or, more probably, unveils to posterity, the medallion portrait, while another weeps. Around them are emblems of the achievements and virtues of the deceased—anchor, cable, cannon and books—while below is an inscription on a large shell, flanked by consoles draped with shells, with a low relief of a naval engagement on the base. In this case the tomb is ingeniously designed to fill one of the blind Gothic arcades of the abbey.

The static portrait medallion—a work of art within a work of art—in these sculptures is contrasted with the

17. Monument to *Philip de Saumarez* by Sir Henry Cheere, Westminster Abbey, London, *c.* 1750

the 17th and 18th centuries, from Alessandro Algardi to Antonio Canova, the effigies were accompanied by lively personifications on either side of a sarcophagus or tomb-chest, which served as the base for the effigy and was commonly decorated with a relief. Camillo Rusconi's tomb of *Pope Gregory XIII* (1715–23) in St Peter's, Rome, is one of the finest and most typical in its design (for illustration *see* RUSCONI, CAMILLO). The Pope is seated, his hand raised as if to command as well as to bless the multitudes. A personification of Religion looks up in admiration at her protector and chief representative, while Fortitude, leaning on her shield, uncovers the sarcophagus and views the relief. The heraldic animal of the Pope's family, the Boncompagni, also makes a dramatic appearance, apparently trapped beneath the sarcophagus and howling at Fortitude. The incorporation of personifications in monuments can be traced back to the late Middle Ages, but the animation seen here was a 17th-century innovation.

Another notable feature of Rusconi's tomb is the relief on the sarcophagus depicting the Pope's institution of calendrical reform. This representation of an important event in Gregory XIII's rule recalls the example of Algardi's tomb of *Pope Leo XI* (commissioned 1634), also

activity of the other figures. Both action and narrative of a kind were considered desirable in most ambitious tombs of the 17th and 18th centuries: in some cases the effigy itself could be equally animated and interact with the allegorical figures, as when Cardinal Richelieu, in his tomb (1675–94) by François Girardon in the chapel of the Sorbonne, Paris, dies in the arms of Piety. Other examples of dramatic action include Maurice, Maréchal de Saxe (1696–1750), in Jean-Baptiste Pigalle's great monument (1753–76) in St Thomas, Strasbourg, who strides bravely down into his own tomb, despite the desperate intervention of France (*see* PIGALLE, JEAN-BAPTISTE, fig. 2), and Joseph and Lady Elizabeth Nightingale in Louis-François Roubiliac's monument (1758–61) in Westminster Abbey, London (*see* ROUBILIAC, LOUIS-FRANÇOIS, fig. 2), in which Joseph Nightingale desperately attempts to shield his wife from the dart about to be flung by a skeletal Death.

These examples, however, are exceptional, and in general the effigy seems to inhabit a different level of reality from the other figures, as is usually the case in papal tombs. The seated or praying attitude established for European rulers in the 16th century was taken up by the popes and remained constant until the competitive modesty of the second half of the 20th century. Throughout

18. Monument to *Sir John Dutton* by Michael Rysbrack, St Mary the Virgin, Sherborne, Gloucestershire, 1749

in St Peter's. It exemplifies how tomb sculpture by the 17th and 18th centuries was often 'retrospective' in emphasis. Some monuments, however, were explicitly 'prospective', as when the effigy was represented rising from the dead at the Resurrection: the most dramatic example of this is the series of tombs by Roubiliac, of which the most familiar is that of *General William Hargrave*, erected in Westminster Abbey, London, in 1757, in which the dead man bursts joyously from his winding-sheet. There are, in addition, numerous earlier examples in 17th-century English tomb sculpture, as well as some notable examples in France.

Despite the dynamism of such effigies as that of Hargrave, many sculptors, influenced by the Antique, preferred to present an effigy as though very much alive, but composed, sometimes with an attitude of careless but dignified ease: cross-legged poses were much favoured in 18th-century England and are well exemplified by Michael Rysbrack's monument to *Sir John Dutton* (see fig. 18). The only sepulchral reference here is the large urn on which the deceased leans. Such an effigy may be considered an upright equivalent of the figures that reclined in earlier 18th-century tombs on a classical sarcophagus: the urn here acts as a vertical equivalent of the sarcophagus. The adoption of antique dress for the effigy can be traced back to the 15th century, but it greatly increased in popularity in the 18th century, especially in Britain.

(ii) Changes in patronage. During the 17th and 18th centuries, a dramatic change occurred in the patronage of tombs in Europe. The popes and doges were the only great European rulers to maintain a consistent emphasis on tomb sculpture. For unexplained reasons the kings of France and Spain, who had established such imposing burial places and such grand tombs in the 16th century, ceased to commission tomb sculpture of any consequence, and the kings of England, after the Civil War, are commemorated by ledger stones far more modest in character than those to prosperous tradesmen in the provincial towns of their realm. During this period the new monuments created in Westminster Abbey excited great international interest. To foreign visitors, or at least to the authors of guidebooks and memoirs, it seemed remarkable and usually admirable that such great thinkers as Sir Isaac Newton—commemorated in a monument (1731) by Rysbrack—and even great actors and actresses, as well as naval commanders and statesmen, should be so prominently honoured, whereas in France René Descartes was permitted only a modest wall tomb (*c.* 1667; Paris, Ste Geneviève, destr. 18th century; see Adhemar and Dordor) while Molière was given no tomb at all. Such visitors tended to underestimate the degree to which this national pantheon had grown up without proper planning and the degree to which undistinguished people could buy, or be bought, prominent places within it: burial and monument fees provided vital income for the abbey. The conversion of Westminster Abbey into a national pantheon is also inseparable from the relative weakness of Crown and Church in England as a controlling force; the ease with which the powerful families could convert the chancels of the parish churches of which they provided the living into mausolea filled with monuments is part of the same

phenomenon. Something of a national pantheon was also established in Santa Croce in Florence. The erection in 1737, however, of a monument to *Galileo Galilei* by Giulio Foggini (*fl* 1729–41), Giovanni Battista Foggini, Vincenzo Foggini (*fl* 1736–55) and Girolamo Ticciati had proved far more difficult there than it would have been in Britain, and it would not have been possible, at least not on a comparable scale, in France.

A final point to be made about patronage concerns the increasingly important role of the widow, the bereft family and the grateful heir, who were much more likely to be the people ordering and supervising the erection of a tomb in the 18th century than had previously been the case. This is reflected in the greater popularity of mourning figures, especially female ones, in British and French tombs. Many of these were explicitly widows, others were in fact allegorical, although some of these could easily be mistaken for widows. The theme of mourning had been an important one in European tombs at least since the procession of mourners was placed around the tomb-chest of *Louis IX*, who was buried in Saint-Denis in 1271 (*see* WEEPER). Although the mourners in such tombs represented the dependents of the dead, from high officials at court to minor clerics (and even, occasionally, to the common poor), members of the family were not neglected. Around the tomb-chest (1367) of *Philippa of Hainault*, Queen of England, by Jean de Liège (i), in Westminster Abbey, London, stood the great lords of the realm, including her husband, King Edward III, as well as her own relatives and children. This dynastic emphasis gave way in 17th-century tombs to a closer emphasis on the immediate family: in English tombs a married couple often kneel above a plinth, which is decorated with their kneeling children in relief, sexually segregated and with those who have died holding skulls. A new development in the 18th century was the frequent and prominent expression of domestic sentiment by the figures. The chief motive for the erection of the tomb thus appears to have been the grief of the most intimate mourners, as it was to be so often in funerary art of later years.

BIBLIOGRAPHY

SURVEYS

A. Bride: 'Sépulture', *Dictionnaire de théologie catholique*, ed. A. Vacant and E. Mangenot, xiv/2 (Paris, 1941)
H. Beenken: *Romanische Skulptur in Deutschland* (Leipzig, 1924)
W. Pinder: *Die deutsche Plastik des XV. Jahrhunderts* (Munich, 1924)
A. Gardner: *Medieval Sculpture in France* (New York, 1931)
E. Mâle: *L'Art religieux du XIIe siècle* (Paris, 1940; Eng. trans., 1978)
M. Hubert: *La Sculpture française au moyen âge* (Paris, 1946)
A. Blunt: *Art and Architecture in France, 1500 to 1700*, Pelican Hist. A. (Harmondsworth, 1953/*R* 1970)
J. Pope-Hennessy: *Italian Gothic Sculpture* (London, 1955)
L. Stone: *Sculpture in Britain: The Middle Ages*, Pelican Hist. A. (Harmondsworth, 1955)
J. Pope-Hennessy: *Italian Renaissance Sculpture* (London, 1958)
R. Wittkower: *Art and Architecture in Italy, 1600–1750*, Pelican Hist. A. (Harmondsworth, 1958, rev. 1973)
J. Pope-Hennessy: *Italian High Renaissance and Baroque Sculpture* (London, 1963)
M. Whinney: *Sculpture in Britain, 1530–1830*, Pelican Hist. A. (Harmondsworth, 1964)
T. Müller: *Sculpture in the Netherlands, Germany, France and Spain, 1400–1500*, Pelican Hist. A. (Harmondsworth, 1966)
C. Seymour jr: *Sculpture in Italy, 1400–1500*, Pelican Hist. A. (Harmondsworth, 1966)

W. Sauerländer: *Gotische Skulptur im Frankreich, 1140–1270* (Munich, 1970; Eng. trans., London, 1972)

M. Vovelle: *Mourir autrefois* (Paris, 1974)

P. Ariès: *Essais sur l'histoire de la mort en occident, du moyen âge à nos jours* (Paris, 1975)

——: *L'Homme devant la mort* (Paris, 1977); Eng. trans. as *The Hour of our Death* (Harmondsworth, 1981)

J. Adhemar and G. Dordor: 'Les Tombeaux de la collection Gaignières à la Bibliothèque Nationale. Tome III: Personnages morts entre 1616 et 1714 et supplément', *Gaz. B.-A.*, xc (July–Aug 1977), pp. 1–76 (16)

M. Vovelle: *Piété baroque* (Paris, 1978)

P. Ariès: *Images de l'homme devant la mort* (Paris, 1983); Eng. trans. as *Images of Man and Death* (Cambridge, MA, 1985)

H. Colvin: *Architecture and the After-life* (New Haven and London, 1991)

M. Levey: *Painting and Sculpture in France, 1700–1870* (London and New Haven, 1992)

MONOGRAPHS, EXHIBITION CATALOGUES AND CATALOGUES RAISONNÉS

M. Stephenson: *A List of Monumental Brasses in the British Isles* (London, 1926, rev. 1938/R Ashford, 1964)

R. Montini: *Le tombe dei Papi* (Rome, 1957)

E. Panofsky: *Tomb Sculpture* (New York, 1964/R London, 1992) [only scholarly survey of the subject], p. 53

H. K. Cameron: *A List of Monumental Brasses on the Continent of Europe* (London, 1970, rev. 1973)

Les Pleurants dans l'art du moyen âge en Europe (exh. cat. by P. Quarré, Dijon, Mus. B.-A., 1971)

Le Roi, la sculpture et la mort: Gisants et tombeaux de la basilique de Saint-Denis (exh. cat. by A. Erlande-Brandenburg and others, Saint-Denis, Maison Cult., 1976)

J. Whitlock Blundell and J. Physick: *Westminster Abbey: The Monuments* (London, 1989)

SPECIALIST STUDIES
Tomb sculpture and painting, before c. 1600

C. Ricci: *Monumenti sepolcrali di lettori dello studio bolognese* (Bologna, 1886)

E. Redslob: *Die fränkischen Epitaphien des 14. und 15. Jahrhunderts* (Nuremberg, 1907)

G. Davies: *Renascence: The Sculptural Tombs of the Fifteenth Century in Rome* (London, 1910)

F. H. Crossley: *English Church Monuments, AD 1150–1550* (London, 1921)

A. Gardner: *Alabaster Tombs of the Pre-Reformation Period in England* (Cambridge, 1940)

O. Morisani: *Tino di Camaino a Napoli* (Naples, 1945)

J.-F. Noel and P. Jahan: *Les Gisants* (Paris, 1949)

I. Ragusa: *The Re-use and Public Exhibition of Roman Sarcophagi during the Middle Ages and Early Renaissance* (diss., New York U., 1951)

A. Weckwerth: 'Der Ursprung des Bildepitaphs', *Z. Kstgesch.*, xx (1957), pp. 147–85

K. Bauch: 'Anfänge des figürlichen Grabmals in Italien', *Mitt. Ksthist. Inst. Florenz*, xv (1971), pp. 227–58

C. Dempsey: 'Masaccio's *Trinity*: Altarpiece or Tomb', *A. Bull.*, liv (1972), pp. 279–81

G. Wright: 'A Royal Tomb Program in the Reign of St Louis', *A. Bull.*, lvi (1974), pp. 224–43

A. Erlande-Brandenburg: *Le Roi est mort: Etude sur les funérailles, les sépultures et les tombeaux des rois de France jusqu'à la fin du XIIIe siècle* (Paris and Geneva, 1975)

K. Bauch: *Das mittelalterliche Grabbild* (Berlin, 1976)

H. G. Brand: *Die Grabmonumente Pietro Lombardos* (diss., U. Erlangen, 1977)

B. B. Johannsen: 'Zum Thema der weltlichen Glorifikation des Herrscher- und Gelehertengrabmals des Trecentos', *Hafnia*, 6 (1979), pp. 81–105

R. Grandi: *I monumenti dei dottori e la scultura a Bologna* (Bologna, 1982)

J. Gardner: *The Tomb and the Tiara: Curial Tomb Sculpture in Rome and Avignon in the Later Middle Ages* (Oxford, 1992)

Tomb sculpture, c. 1600–*c.* 1780

K. A. Esdaile: *English Church Monuments, 1510 to 1840* (London, 1946)

A. Chastel: 'Le baroque et la mort', *Troisième congrès international des études humanistes: Rome, 1955*, pp. 33–46

W. C. Kirwin and P. Fehl: 'Bernini's *Decoro*: Some Preliminary Observations on the Baldachin and on his Tombs in St Peter's', *Stud. Iconog.*, vii–viii (1981–2), pp. 323–69

V. H. Minor: 'The Recollection and Undermining of Allegory in Eighteenth-century Roman Sculpture', *Stor. A.*, 57 (May–Aug 1986), pp. 183–91 [discusses papal tombs in St Peter's]

NICHOLAS PENNY

4. AFTER *c.* 1780. In the late 18th century and the early 19th tombs were predominantly Neo-classical in style, or more particularly Greek Revival. Antonio Canova's influence was central, notably through the heroic scale and austerity of his papal tombs in Rome—those of *Clement XIV* (1783–7) in SS Apostoli and *Clement XIII* (1783–92) in St Peter's—and the dramatic composition of his tomb of *Maria Christina of Austria* (1798–1805) in the Augustinerkirche, Vienna (*see* CANOVA, ANTONIO, fig. 3). Heroic Neo-classicism found expression in England in monuments to leading figures of the Napoleonic Wars (1803–15). Those in St Paul's Cathedral, London, feature complex figure groups, variously combining allegory with contemporary references, and include works by Thomas Banks, John Flaxman, Richard Westmacott (ii) and Francis Chantrey. Subsequently Chantrey developed a distinctive manner, which combined Neo-classicism with domestic and sentimental themes—sleeping children, mother-and-child groups, and death-bed scenes—and which strongly influenced later tomb design. Most typical of smaller Neo-classical monuments were wall reliefs, their conventionalized iconography including veiled female mourners, draped urns, inverted torches and shattered columns. They were produced by monumental masons throughout Europe, as well as by such leading sculptors as Bertel Thorvaldsen, Flaxman and Canova himself.

Despite the prevalence of church burial *c.* 1800, during the 19th century, as a result of population growth and rapid urbanization, public cemeteries supplanted churches and their associated graveyards as the usual place of burial in Europe and the USA (*see* CEMETERY, §2). Changes in attitudes towards the dead meant that cemeteries and the family tombs within them became the focuses for a cult of commemoration that lasted into the first half of the 20th century. The core of the cult was urban and middle-class, with the tombs of the bourgeoisie taking on an ostentation that previously had been largely exclusive to the aristocracy. Anonymous burial remained the usual lot of the poor, particularly in northern Europe: by the late 19th century, however, the cult was to extend to working-class families as well. Although cemeteries had already been established in the 18th century (e.g. in Edinburgh and Belfast in the 1770s, and in Sweden from the 1780s), the most important early development took place in France, where Père-Lachaise cemetery, the largest of three on the outskirts of Paris, opened in 1804. Non-denominational, with burial plots for sale in perpetuity, Père-Lachaise gave the affluent the chance to erect permanent tombs expressive of social status, family pride and domestic affection. Most characteristic are the long avenues of house-tombs, which were individual family mausolea. Many other tombs are also monumentally scaled, designed by such architects as Pierre Clochard (1774–before 1855), Vincent Méry and Louis-Tullius-Joachim Visconti. The Neo-classical style dominated until the 1850s, although with a significant admixture of the Egyptian Revival style, appropriate for its funereal connotations. Père-Lachaise was widely emulated: Frankfurt am Main, Munich and Stockholm acquired cemeteries in the 1820s, as did Liverpool. The first cemetery in London, the General Cemetery of All Souls, Kensal Green, opened in 1833, and most British cities had some cemetery provision by the 1840s. These European cemeteries followed the stylistic lead of Père-Lachaise, their tombs predominantly Neo-classical in design and motif, although in German cemeteries the regular re-use of the ground for interment discouraged the building of permanent monuments. The first American cemeteries date from the 1830s: Mt Auburn (1831), Cambridge, MA; Laurel Hill (1836), Philadelphia, PA; and Greenwood (1838), Brooklyn, NY. They have a Romantic, rural quality, later shared by English cemeteries, and distinct from the urban character of their French and southern European equivalents.

From the 1830s Neo-classicism was increasingly challenged by the Gothic Revival: as early as 1810 Karl Friedrich Schinkel had submitted an unexecuted design (Berlin, Staatl. Museen, N.G.) for a Gothic mausoleum for *Queen Louise of Prussia* in the park at Schloss Charlottenburg; in 1817 the bones of Héloïse and Peter Abelard were transferred to a Gothic canopied tomb in Père-Lachaise; Mt Auburn's chapel was Gothic; and in 1837 Norwood, in London, became the first major cemetery where all the buildings were Gothic. English architectural writers, insisting on the Christian significance of Gothic, deplored the paganism of Neo-classical funerary iconography. Gothic-framed wall tablets appeared in English churches from the 1830s; commemorative brasses based on medieval examples from 1841; and recumbent effigies, with Gothic tomb-chests and canopies, from 1843. This last formula came to be widely used in English cathedrals, particularly for ecclesiastics, the tombs often created by leading architects and sculptors. Canterbury Cathedral has a fine sequence, as does Lichfield Cathedral, where there are effigies by Henry Hugh Armstead, Thomas Nicholls and G. F. Watts, among others. Gothic Revival monuments are less common in continental European churches, although there are important examples in the Orléans family's mausoleum, the St Louis Chapel (1816–22), at Dreux. In cemeteries, however, Gothic provided a ready alternative to the continuing tradition of Neo-classical and Egyptian design. From the 1850s Gothic mausolea became common in Britain, France and northern Italy, often assuming the character of private chapels. Other Gothic memorials included pinnacles, tomb-chests and canopied tombs; headstones were shaped like pointed arches; and crosses, variously elaborated, were used everywhere as grave markers.

With continuing urbanization cemeteries increased in both number and size. In Britain, after the Burial Acts of the 1850s, hundreds of cemeteries were built, funded by public rates. In the USA new cemeteries were established in the aftermath of the Civil War, the most famous being Arlington National Cemetery, Washington, DC, in 1864. Burial provision in Paris was supplemented in 1874 by a huge cemetery at Mèry-sur-Oise, connected to the capital by railway. In Vienna the grandly planned Zentralfriedhof dates from 1873. In Italy Rome's Campo Verano opened in 1837, Genoa's Camposanto di Staglieno in 1851, and Milan's Cimitero Monumentale in 1860. Alongside the

historicist styles, sculptural realism emerged in tomb design. An early example is the stark effigy of *Godefroi de Cavaignac* (1845–7) by François Rude in Montmartre Cemetery, Paris. Portrait medallions on monuments, a feature taken from Neo-classicism, took on a new character and intensity: particularly fine are the bronze roundels produced by Auguste Préault for tombs in the cemeteries in Paris. In Italy from the 1840s such *verismo* sculptors as Vincenzo Vela and Giovanni Dupré produced monuments that combined Chantreyesque domestic themes with a minute registration of contemporary dress and detail. In the 1870s such northern Italian cemetery sculptors as Giulio Monteverde, Stefano Saccomanno (1833–1914), Giovanni Scanzi and Giambattista Villa (1832–99) infused *verismo* with a new theatricality. The extraordinary tombs in the Staglieno, for example, feature life-sized tableaux: these range in subject from bourgeois domesticity—a family group around the death-bed, or a father consoling his grief-stricken son—to emotive piety—the risen Christ comforting the bereaved, or angels pointing the way heavenward—or to the grotesque and erotic—a half-naked woman struggling in death's embrace, or a voluptuous nude caressing a sarcophagus. Italian figure sculpture was exported to cemeteries throughout Europe, and monumental masons freely copied designs found in Italian catalogues. In Catholic countries taste in such tombs tended towards the dramatic and erotic: there are fine examples in the Kerepesi Cemetery, Budapest, the Zentralfriedhof, Vienna, and the cemeteries of Barcelona. In northern Europe angels were preferred, along with the figure of a female mourner embracing the cross. Tomb sculpture in the USA was less exuberant, but memorials

19. Tomb of *Queen Victoria and Prince Albert* by Carlo Marochetti, Royal Mausoleum, Frogmore House, Berkshire

to infants showing the child asleep or realistically representing an empty crib or cot were a distinctively American addition to the funerary repertory.

As bourgeois tombs reached unprecedented levels of display, the tombs of royalty took on a commensurate grandeur, often occupying large mausolea (*see* MAUSO-LEUM, §VII, 2). These included the Rundbogenstil Royal Mausoleum (1862–8) at Frogmore House, Berks, by Ludwig Grüner (1801–82) and Albert J. Humbert (1822–77), with Carlo Marochetti's tomb of *Queen Victoria and Prince Albert* (see fig. 19). The great dead of the 19th century were also given public monuments in which nationalist celebration eclipsed commemorative function (*see* MONUMENT, PUBLIC, §6). In the late 19th century Symbolist influences became increasingly apparent in European and American tombs, as also did formal elements drawn from Art Nouveau. Both came together in the fantastic elaboration of the tomb of *Prince Albert Victor, Duke of Clarence* (1892–1928; Windsor Castle, Berks, Albert Memorial Chapel; *see* POLYCHROMY, colour pl. IV), designed by Alfred Gilbert. Made of bronze, marble, brass, aluminium and ivory, the Clarence Tomb also epitomizes the material variety that had developed in monuments by this date. Polychromatic tombs, using polished granites or marbles and designed for both indoor and outdoor settings, had appeared in the 1850s; bronze, particularly for figures, became increasingly common from the 1870s; and terracotta was first used in the 1880s.

By the 1890s, however, opposition to the cult of commemoration was growing, particularly in Britain and northern Europe, and cremation was increasingly advocated as a more rational means of disposing of the dead. Effectively, cremation eliminated the body and with it the need for a tomb. Crematoria were built in major European and American cemeteries in the last decades of the 19th century, often in association with *columbaria*. A profound shift in attitudes towards the dead was underway, and this was confirmed by World War I. Death on such a vast scale undermined the sense of individual uniqueness that was central to the cult of commemoration: the cemeteries of the Western Front, although intensely moving, testify to the impersonality of death in mechanized warfare (*see* CEMETERY, §3). Nonetheless, important individual monuments were still produced in the early 20th century, for example Jacob Epstein's monument to *Oscar Wilde*, installed at Père-Lachaise Cemetery in 1912 (see fig. 20). This work, which included references to Assyrian statuary in the British Museum, London, demonstrates the wide range of sources used by tomb sculptors of the period. Cemetery monuments of the 1920s and 1930s are essentially the final products of the 19th-century commemorative tradition, even though they may borrow formal elements from Futurism or Art Deco. A still older tradition, however, that of glorifying dead leaders, is evident in Lenin's mausoleum (1929–30) in Red Square, Moscow, designed by Aleksey Shchusev (*see* MAUSOLEUM, fig. 6). During World War II, the bureaucratized mass murder of the concentration camps and the experience of total war directed at civilian populations robbed individual deaths of both dignity and significance. Moreover, in the second half of the 20th century, especially in northern Europe and the USA, the tomb was largely reduced to a standardized grave marker or, with cremation far more common than burial, eliminated altogether. More elaborate monuments became rarer, although long-standing traditions of funerary sculpture did survive, as in the tomb of *Pope Pius XII* (*reg* 1939–58) by Francesco Messina (1900–95) in St Peter's, Rome.

Gunnis

BIBLIOGRAPHY

Marty: *Les Principaux Monuments funéraires du Père Lachaise, de Montmartre, du Mont-Parnasse et autres cimetières de Paris* (Paris, n.d.)

J. Strang: *Necropolis Glasguensis, with Observations on Ancient and Modern Tombs and Sepulture* (Glasgow, 1831)

Normand fils: *Monuments funéraires choisis dans les cimetières de Paris et des principales villes de France* (Paris, 1832)

J. C. Loudon: *On the Laying Out, Planting, and Managing of Cemeteries; And on the Improvement of Churchyards* (London, 1843, rev. Redhill, 1981)

A. Hakewill: *Modern Tombs, Gleaned from the Public Cemeteries of London* (London, 1851)

W. Robinson: *God's Acre Beautiful, or the Cemeteries of the Future* (London, 1880)

L. Taft: *The History of American Sculpture* (New York, 1903, 2/1924)

L. Weaver: *Memorials and Monuments* (London, 1915)

C. M. Lerici: *Italia sepolta* (Milan, 1962)

J. S. Curl: *The Victorian Celebration of Death* (Newton Abbot, 1972)

D. Stannard, ed.: *Death in America* (Philadelphia, 1975)

N. Penny: *Church Monuments in Romantic England* (London, 1977)

P. Ariès: *L'Homme devant la mort* (Paris, 1977); Eng. trans. as *The Hour of our Death* (Harmondsworth, 1981)

J. S. Curl: *A Celebration of Death: An Introduction to Some of the Buildings, Monuments and Settings of Funerary Architecture in the Western European Tradition* (London, 1980)

20. Monument to *Oscar Wilde* by Jacob Epstein, Père-Lachaise Cemetery, Paris, 1909–12

B. Read: *Victorian Sculpture* (London, 1982)

H. W. Janson: *Nineteenth-century Sculpture* (London, 1985)

H. Meller: *London Cemeteries: An Illustrated Guide and Gazetteer* (London, 2/1985)

C. Brooks: *Mortal Remains: The History and Present State of the Victorian and Edwardian Cemetery* (Exeter, 1989)

A. Chabot: *Erotique du cimetière* (Paris, 1989)

CHRIS BROOKS

Tomb of Christ. *See under* EASTER SEPULCHRE.

Tombros, Mikhaēl (*b* Athens, 12 Nov 1889; *d* Athens, 28 May 1974). Greek sculptor. He studied at the School of Fine Arts in Athens from 1903 to 1909 and at the Académie Julian in Paris in 1914. After World War I he returned frequently to Paris, exhibiting his work there at the principal Salons until 1928, when he settled permanently in Athens. Stylistically versatile, while living in Paris he was influenced by the classically inspired sculpture of Aristide Maillol, as in *Dancer's Leap* (bronze, 1927; Andros, MOMA, Goulandris Found.). After his return to Athens he acted on other contemporary influences absorbed in Paris, including Cubism, as in *Two Friends* (marble, 1930; Athens, N. Pict. Gal.), and abstract art, which he explored from the 1930s through to the 1950s. Concurrently he produced works with strong classical references, such as a monument to *Eternal Poetry and the English Poet Rupert Brooke* (bronze, 1931; Skiros, Rupert Brooke Square). He received many commissions for war memorials and other public monuments, especially portraits of national heroes; deviating from his modernist course, he rendered these with vivid realism. In 1933–4 he edited the avant-garde magazine *XXe siècle*, which brought him into contact with Le Corbusier, Fernand Léger, Christian Zervos and others. Tombros influenced the development of 20th-century Greek art, and especially its assimilation of European modernism, through both his sculpture and his teaching at the Athens School of Fine Arts, of which he was Director.

BIBLIOGRAPHY

F. Giofillis: *Istoria tēs neoellenikēs tekhnes, 1821–1941* [History of modern Greek art, 1821–1941], ii (Athens, 1963), pp. 465–71

Ellēnas gluptēs ston 20 aiona: Mikhālēs Tombros, 1909–1964: Ta 55 khronia enos ergou [The Greek sculptor in the 20th century: Mikhaēl Tombros, 1909–1964: 55 years of work] (Athens, 1964) [col. of reviews of his work in Greek and foreign press, with bibliog. and biog. inf. and illus.]

S. Lidakis: *Oi Ellenes gluptes: Ē neoellenikē gluptikē* [The Greek sculptors: modern Greek sculpture] (Athens, 1981), pp. 470–72

ATHENA S. E. LEOUSSI

Tombs, The. Aboriginal site *c.* 500 km north-west of Brisbane, on Mt Moffat station in the Carnarvon Range of Queensland, central Australia. It is the site of a rock shelter in the form of a wide amphitheatre with a recessed rock surface at its base, on which is found an extensive collection of stencilled rock paintings. A shallow cave at one end of the overhang also contains some hand-stencilled designs. Unlike many rock shelters in the Central Highlands of Queensland, there is no evidence at The Tombs that the shelter was ever used for burials; instead the paintings are apparently associated with habitation debris. Excavations by Mulvaney and Joyce in 1960 produced slight evidence that the site was used until *c.* 5000 BC and then abandoned, as were several others in

the area. The Tombs was reoccupied no earlier than the 1st millennium AD and it is unlikely that the art is earlier than this, owing to the friable nature of the rock surface.

The stencilled designs at The Tombs are mainly painted in red ochre, but some are in yellow or orange ochre or in a white clay pigment. Most are of hands, including many of children, and there are also human feet, both of adults and children. The most remarkable stencilled image, unique in Aboriginal art, is that of a whole person, standing with arms stretched out near the entrance to the cave. As at other sites, various artefacts were also stencilled: these were exclusively men's objects, such as boomerangs, spear-throwers, a spear and a set of oval stencils with a small hole at one end. This has been identified as the *chekara* shell pendant, which was a valued item traded from the coastal regions of northern Queensland. The placing of the stencils along the rock face appears unstructured, although there is a tendency for similar (sometimes the same) items to be stencilled close together, forming a group of related images. Some stencilled images were superimposed so frequently that the rock face has become an illegible red smear.

Besides the stencilled patterns produced from identifiable objects, there are linear designs that are usually referred to as freehand paintings. They are mainly simple sets of lines or grid patterns and are among the uppermost in the sequence of superimposed paintings; some resemble bird tracks. These more linear designs may also have been made by the stencilling technique (Walsh), for it is possible to create small oval or lozenge-shaped patches by judiciously positioning parts of objects or the fingers. Linear patterns such as grids may therefore be produced by aligning large numbers of small stencilled designs. Thus, instead of representing rapidly sketched, apparently simple motifs, this most recent phase of rock art in the Carnarvon Ranges would have been a painstaking exercise, requiring considerable patience and control.

BIBLIOGRAPHY

D. J. Mulvaney and E. B. Joyce: 'Archaeological and Geomorphological Investigations on Mt Moffat Station, Queensland, Australia', *Proc. Prehist. Soc.*, li (1965), pp. 147–212

G. L. Walsh: 'Composite Stencil Art: Elemental or Specialised?', *Austral. Aboriginal Stud.*, ii (1983), pp. 34–44

ANDRÉE ROSENFELD

Tomé, Narciso (*b* Toro, ?1694; *d* Toledo, 13 Dec 1742). Spanish architect, sculptor and painter. He came from a family of architects and sculptors, which included his father Antonio Tomé (1664–1730) and his two brothers, Andrés Tomé (1688–1761) and Diego Tomé (1696–1732). The family was active in Castile at the beginning of the 18th century; they are first recorded in 1715 as sculptors of the portal of the Universidad de Valladolid, in which a giant order, crowned with statues, dominates the plain façade. The Tomé family was called to Toledo in 1720 to work on the Transparente of the 13th-century cathedral; Narciso appears to have designed the work before his departure on 6 June 1721, when the contract for its execution was issued. He returned to Toledo on 27 October 1721 and was appointed Maestro Mayor of the cathedral. Work was completed by 9 June 1732, when the altar was consecrated.

The Transparente is a *trasaltar*, that is, a sacramental chapel in the ambulatory behind the chancel and high altar, and intended to display the sacrament in both directions, hence 'transparent'. A work of great technical ability, it is one of the most daring and theatrical statements, as well as one of the masterpieces, of Baroque architecture; the formal language was based on Bernini's *Cathedra Petri* (1657–66) in St Peter's, Rome (*see* BERNINI, (2), fig. 2), which Tomé probably knew through prints; it is not related to the work of Pedro da Ribera or the Chirriguera brothers. The Transparente combines architecture, sculpture and painting in an ecstatic affirmation of Catholic mysticism. The extreme nature of its decoration has always been contentious, although at the time it was widely praised.

In order to provide a convincing chapel within the constrained dimensions imposed by the convex wall of the altar, Tomé designed a shallow niche that is made to appear deeper by the use of false perspective: the column bases rise and the entablature declines towards the centre of the chapel. One rib of the Gothic ambulatory was removed to accommodate an enormous clerestory rising over the vault, facing east and filled with golden glass. Streamers and banners of stone seem to peel away from the marble columns, revealing their fluting, and mingle with the sculpture. The paintings and sculpture were all intended to reinforce the importance of the Eucharist: a gilded bronze relief of the *Virgin and Child* occupies the central place over the altar; on the sides are scenes from the *Life of David*; immediately over it lies a 'glory' of gilded bronze rays lighting the *camarín* (chapel) where the Eucharist is displayed; on top is a relief sculpture in alabaster depicting the *Last Supper*. The whole is enlivened by angels and cherubs, and paintings are used to integrate it with the surrounding fabric. No other works by Tomé have survived: the retable of the chapel of the Baronesa convent of Discalced Carmelites in Madrid (1736) is untraced, and of the high altar of León Cathedral (1738), dismantled during the 19th-century restoration, only fragments are preserved in the Capuchin monastery, León.

BIBLIOGRAPHY

E. Llaguno y Amirola: *Noticias de los arquitectos e arquitecturas de España*, iv (Madrid, 1829)
G. Kubler: *Arquitectura de los siglos XVII y XVIII*, A. Hisp., xiv (Madrid, 1957)
G. Kubler and M. Soria: *Art and Architecture in Spain and Portugal and their American Dominions, 1500–1800*, Pelican Hist. A. (Harmondsworth, 1959)
F. Chueca Goitia: 'Narciso Tomé, una incógnita del barroco español', *Goya*, 49 (1962), pp. 12–21
N. A. Mallory: 'Narciso Tomé's Transparente in the Cathedral of Toledo (1721–1732)', *J. Soc. Archit. Hist.*, xxix (1970), pp. 9–23
J. M. Prados: 'Las trazas del Transparente y otros debujos de Narciso Tomé para la catedral de Toledo', *Archv Esp. Arqueol.*, xlix (1976), pp. 387–416

□

Tomimoto, Kenkichi (*b* Ando, Nara Prefecture, 5 June 1886; *d* Kyoto, 8 June 1963). Japanese ceramicist. In 1904 he entered the design department of the Tokyo Bijutsu Gakkō (Tokyo School of Art; now Tokyo University of Fine Arts & Music) and specialized in architecture and interior design. In 1908, after presenting his graduation project early, he went to study at the Central School of Art in London. During his stay he studied the work of William Morris and the collections of the Victoria and Albert Museum, South Kensington. In 1910 he returned to Japan and became closely associated with Bernard Leach. In the following year he was invited to work as an interpreter for Leach, who was a pupil of Kenzan VI (1853–1923), and also experimented with ceramics. In 1913 he built a Raku kiln in Ando. During this period he strengthened his belief in creative production—in 'not making imitations from pre-designed patterns'.

In 1926 he moved to Tokyo and made original forms and designs in stoneware and porcelain. In the same year he participated in the activity of the Mingei ('folk crafts') movement inspired by the philosopher Muneyoshi Yanagi and experimented with the manufacture of mass-produced utilitarian objects. He was active in the Kokugakai (Society for Paintings and Crafts) and government exhibitions. In 1935 he became a member of the Teikoku Bijutsuin (Imperial Fine Arts Academy). In 1944 he assumed the post of Professor at the Tokyo Bijutsu Gakkō. After World War II, however, he withdrew from these societies and declined public positions. In 1946 he moved to Kyoto and the following year founded and became the leader of the newly inaugurated Shinshō Bijutsu Kōgeikai (New Society of Arts and Crafts). In 1950 he became a professor at the Kyoto Municipal College of Fine Arts (now Kyoto Municipal University of Arts). About 1953 he mixed silver with platinum, creating a unique gold and silver colour, thus opening a new area of extreme grace and splendour in enamelled wares. In 1955 he was designated a Living National Treasure for his enamels and in 1961 received the Order of Cultural Merit. In 1963 he became head of the Kyoto Municipal University of Fine Arts. In 1974 his birthplace was rebuilt and opened as the Tomimoto Kenkichi Memorial Museum.

BIBLIOGRAPHY

Kodansha Enc. Japan
B. Shuppansha: *The Masterpiece of Tomimoto Kenkichi* (1971)
A Pageant of Modern Japanese Ceramics. 3. Kenkichi Tomimoto (Shūeisha, 1980)

MITSUHIKO HASEBE

Tominaga, Yuzuru (*b* Taipei, 1943). Japanese architect. He studied at the University of Tokyo, graduating in 1967, and then worked for Kiyonori Kikutake until 1972 when he established his own office, Form System, in Tokyo. Tominaga's architecture is primarily residential and represents a move away from the technologically oriented Metabolist movement in Japan. In his designs he combines a modernist sensibility in his straightforward use of materials, structure, geometry and lack of unnecessary embellishment, with a concern to create spaces with a ritualistic quality, such as complex entry sequences, not complying with modernist functionalism or the optimization of use. The often undulating, white and shiny surfaces of his interiors, reminiscent of those in Hiroshi Hara's 'reflection houses', are juxtaposed with uniquely articulated structural systems such as those that characterize the work of Kazuo Shinohara in the 1970s. The House for a Newlywed Couple (1979) in Odawara and his own house (1983) at Musashishinjō, Kawasaki, feature wooden columns with diagonal braces set within essentially void spaces. The creative use of cheap, readily available materials such as metal, plastic and formica is evident in all

Tominaga's works, including the Residence Hall (1985) in Waseda, Tokyo, and the Kōfuen Nursing Home (1987), Kawasaki.

BIBLIOGRAPHY
C. Fawcett: *The New Japanese House: Ritual and Anti-ritual Patterns of Dwelling* (New York, 1980)
'Tominaga', *Global Archit. Houses*, 14 (1983), pp. 199–207 [special issue: 'Residential Architecture: Japan, pt II']
'Yuzuru Tominaga', *Global Archit. Houses*, 20 (1986), pp. 218–23 [special issue: 'Residential Architecture: Japan, pt III']
B. Bognar: *The Japan Guide* (New York, 1995)

BOTOND BOGNAR

Tominc, Jožef [Tominz, Giuseppe] (*b* Gorizia, 6 July 1790; *d* Gradišče, nr Prvačina, 22 April 1866). Slovene painter. He began his training in Gorizia with a local painter, Karel Kebar (1764–1810). In 1803 Tominc left Gorizia in order to study and in 1809 went to Rome with a letter of recommendation from the Archduchess Mary Anne of Austria. He lived and studied from 1810 until 1817 with the painter Domenico Conti Bazzani (*c.* 1742–1818) and at the Accademia di San Luca, where he won a silver medal in 1914. In Rome he developed a distinctive drawing technique, with plasticity in the figures and objects, and cool colours, producing works in a classicizing style similar to that of Ingres and of Vincenzo Camuccini (e.g. *Self-portrait with the Artist's Brother Francesco, c.* 1818; Gorizia, Mus. Prov. Pal. Attems). In 1818 he visited Naples and then returned to Gorizia before visiting Vienna briefly in 1819. From 1821 until 1823 he painted in Ljubljana, mostly portraits of citizens and members of the Ljubljana Congress and religious paintings, but also a portrait of *Emperor Francis* (untraced). His single figure and group portraits (e.g. the *Family of Dr Frušić, c.* 1830; Ljubljana, N.G.) show a familiarity with Biedermeier painting. In 1830 he left for Trieste, where he remained, and where he had a one-man exhibition. He was famous for his technical facility: in 1836 he painted 25 portraits of English naval officers in 25 days. Tominc's full-length and half-length portraits often include landscapes in the background and objects or views that relate to the profession or property of the sitter. He was particularly skilful at depicting shining surfaces, jewellery, cloth and people's distinctive features, sometimes with humour or irony (e.g. *Self-portrait in the Lavatory, c.* 1830; Trieste, Mus. Civ. Revoltella). He also painted religious scenes in the style of the Nazarenes or after Raphael and Pierre Mignard. In 1855 he returned to Gorizia and then went to Gradišče to his brother's estate, where he had a studio and where he died, nearly blind.

BIBLIOGRAPHY
Jožef Tominc (exh. cat. by A. Morassi, G. Coronini and F. Stelè, Ljubljana, N.G., 1967)
K. Rozman: 'Der Maler Josef Tominz', *Mitt. Österreich. Gal.* (1975–6), pp. 111–32
P. Dorsi: 'Documenti dell'archivio di stato di Trieste di Giuseppe Tominz', *A. Friuli, A. Trieste*, vii (1984), pp. 111–33
S. Tavano: 'Nuovi elementi sulla giovinezza di Giuseppe Tominz', *A. Friuli. A. Trieste*, vii (1984), pp. 93–110
E. Castelnuovo, ed.: *La pittura in Italia: L'ottocento* (Milan, 1991)

KSENIJA ROZMAN

Tomioka Tessai [Tomioka Yūsuke; Tessai; Tetsujin; Yūken] (*b* Kyoto, 1837; *d* Kyoto, 1924). Japanese painter. He is generally considered to be the most brilliant exponent of literati painting (*Nanga* or *Bunjinga*; *see* JAPAN, §VI, 4(iv)(d)) after the Meiji Restoration (1868), and to be responsible for the modernization of the tradition and its integration into the contemporary Japanese painting movement of Nihonga through the introduction of new subject-matter and brush techniques, while also drawing on many other painting traditions such as *Yamatoe* ('Japanese-style painting'; *see* JAPAN, §VI, 3(iii) and 4(ii)); *Ōtsue* ('Ōtsu pictures', popular Edo-period folk paintings from Ōtsu); and the decorative Rinpa school (*see* JAPAN, §VI, 4(v)). The subject-matter of his paintings included landscapes, figures, animals, birds and flowers and, frequently, religious themes, a reflection of his deep commitment to both Buddhism and Shinto. Tessai is estimated to have produced more than 20,000 paintings and on one occasion executed 70 paintings in a single day. The largest collection of his works is owned by the Buddhist temple Kiyoshi Kōjin Seichōji in Hyogo Prefecture, which maintains a public Tessai museum.

1. TRAINING AND EARLY WORK, BEFORE *c.* 1887. Tessai was the second son of an affluent Kyoto merchant family. His father's family had traditionally been involved in scholarly learning, especially the study of the syncretic doctrine of *shingaku* ('heart learning'), which was popular among educated Edo-period townspeople; its moral teachings were rooted in Confucianism but it also combined the principles of Buddhism and Shinto. Tessai was influenced throughout his life on the one hand by his early exposure to philosophical studies and on the other by his mother, who came from a farming family and had a more simple, direct temperament.

Tessai suffered from congenital syphilis, which left him partially deaf and therefore unfit to become a merchant. At the age of six he was sent to a local *terakoya* ('temple school', popular school of the Edo period). While still a youth he may have served the Rikusonnō Shrine in Kyoto. He decided to become a Shinto priest and strove to learn more about the faith. He studied ancient Japanese classics under Nonoguchi Takamasa (1792–1871), a Loyalist (supporter of imperial restoration) and follower of Hirata Atsutane (1776–1843), an important leader in the Kokugaku (National Learning) movement. At the same time he also studied Chinese literature. About the age of 20 Tessai began to learn *waka* poetry (a 31-syllable classical form) from the nun Ōtagaki Rengetsu (1790s–1875), a well-known potter and painter who also encouraged him to paint. In 1856, after his father's death, Tessai became involved in the broadly based, humanistic Yōmeigaku (Chin. Wang Yangming) school of Neo-Confucian philosophy, which emphasized the unity of the three creeds of Buddhism, Confucianism and Daoism. Through his teachers Tessai came to associate with supporters of the Loyalist movement. In 1858 a number of his teachers and friends were arrested for their Loyalist sympathies, and in the following year he embarked on a series of journeys to elude the authorities. In 1861–2 he stayed in Nagasaki to learn about foreign countries from Dutch and Chinese residents there.

Tessai began his formal artistic training under the Chinese-influenced Kubota Setsuyō (*d* 1860) and studied painting theory under Oda Kaisen (1785–1862), an eclectic painter working in the Maruyama–Shijō (*see* JAPAN, §VI, 4(viii)) and literati styles. He also learnt *Yamatoe* from the *Fukko Yamatoe* ('*Yamatoe* revival') artist and Loyalist Ukita Ikkei. Tessai became acquainted with many other prominent scholars and artists of Kyoto and was particularly impressed by the literati painter and calligrapher Nukina Kaioku. While he was in Nagasaki, Tessai continued his education by meeting noted literati artists there and by viewing imported Chinese paintings.

Few of Tessai's early paintings have survived, but they were largely pure ink landscapes following the conventional literati painting styles and composition of his contemporaries, particularly Fujimoto Tesseki (1817–63), Yasuda Rōzan (1830–82) and Yamanaka Shiten'ō (1822–85). His monumental pair of screens, *Mountain Landscape* (1875; Kansas City, MO, Nelson–Atkins Mus. A.), is a fine example of his orthodox Chinese-influenced painting style. The tight composition is dominated by a repetition of sharply pointed mountain forms, delineated by Tessai's typical firm, dry brushstrokes. Although Tessai's artistic intent was scholarly, he often injected humour into pictures, as in *Blind Men Criticizing Beauty* (1884; Yasugi, Shimane Prefect., Adachi A. Mus.), which shows blind men admiring paintings and other art objects.

In 1862 Tessai returned to Kyoto where he opened his own school of philosophy and soon found he was also in demand as a painter. He continued to associate with Loyalist supporters, many of whom, like Fujimoto Tesseki, subsequently lost their lives for the cause. By travelling on foot through most of Japan during the first three decades of the Meiji period, Tessai pursued his scholarly interest in history and observed at first hand many famous scenic spots. He was appointed to official positions at several Shinto shrines, including the Iso no Kami Shrine in Yamato Province (now Nara Prefect.), and helped in the restoration of many others.

Tessai settled permanently in Kyoto in 1881, still attempting to earn a living as a teacher. When this proved unsuccessful, because of a waning public interest in Confucian-influenced classical learning, he turned increasingly to painting. He was involved in the organization of the Kyōtō Bijutsu Kyōkai (Kyoto Art Association, est. 1890) as an exhibition judge and contributor to its journal, the *Kyōtō Bijutsu Zasshi* ('Kyoto art magazine'). Except for his enthusiastic participation in exhibitions sponsored by the Nihon Nanga Kyōkai (Association of Japanese *Nanga* Painters, est. 1896), Tessai largely refrained from entering painting exhibitions and competitions, maintaining that he was principally a scholar who disdained publicity. He supported himself by teaching art theory at the Kyōtōshi Bijutsu Gakkō (Kyoto Municipal Art School) and by selling his work.

2. MIDDLE PERIOD, *c.* 1888–1916. From the 1890s Tessai was patronized by several members of the imperial family and gained acceptance in Tokyo art circles. Soon afterwards, he sequestered himself at his home, to read and to paint prolifically. In 1907 he was honoured by a commission from the emperor, for whom he produced two large hanging scrolls, the *Poet Abe Nakamaro Gazing at the Moon from Mingzhou, China* and *Lofty Meeting of Daoist Immortals* (see T. Kuwahara and others, p. 164).

Tessai's paintings in this period gradually became more personal and less influenced by his elders' works. His brushwork became bolder, and he began defining forms more prominently with colour. He largely retained the detailed, careful compositions that distinguished the works of his early period, but at times the rough freedom of brushwork—the hallmark of his later paintings and of the more individualistic Meiji period literati painters—appeared. Many of his subjects were now drawn from Chinese, Daoist, Confucian and Buddhist philosophies, from classical history and literature or from simple folk beliefs, as well as from direct observation of the places he visited.

3. LATE PERIOD, *c.* 1917–24. Tessai continued to paint in the Taisho period (1912–26); indeed the work he did in his eighties is considered his most original. Although he received several public honours for his paintings, including appointments to the Imperial Art Committee (Teishitsu Gigeiin) in 1917 and to the Imperial Academy of Art (Teikoku Bijutsuin) in 1919, he did not take these seriously.

Most of Tessai's works executed at this time were spontaneously brushed in a variety of colours, applied so that they appeared almost like Western Expressionist artists' oil paintings, and in bold ink on paper. They display a refined integration of the diverse painting styles he studied throughout his life. Favourite subjects from this period included Zen Buddhist themes such as the *bodhisattva* Kannon (Skt Avalokiteshvara) and Daoist symbols of longevity—pine trees, the god of longevity (Jurōjin), cranes and the Immortal Isles. Figures and animals are highly animated, and landscape forms are filled with energy. In the landscape *Sweeping away Worldly Dust* (1918; Nara, Yamato Bunkakan; see fig.), a work of intense emotion, the powerful mountain peaks seem to move around the small figures in the hut. Even the calligraphic inscriptions at the top right of the picture are brushed with wild abandon. Works such as this from his late years instilled new life into the increasingly stagnant literati painting tradition and profoundly influenced his younger contemporaries, including Taikan Yokoyama and Ryūzaburō Umehara, who were working respectively in the tradition of *Nihonga* (Japanese-style painting after the Edo period; *see* JAPAN, §VI, 5(iii)) and its counterpart *Yōga* (Western-style painting; *see* JAPAN, §VI, 5(iv)).

4. OTHER ACTIVITIES. Tessai's wide-ranging scholarly interests included book collecting, seal-carving and the connoisseurship of old paintings. Inscriptions by him are often seen on older *Nanga* school painting boxes and on the backs of albums of paintings. He also continued to study and practise the Chinese method of preparing infused tea (*sencha*), which had been popular among scholars in the late Edo period. Despite his fame and wealth in his later years, Tessai led a modest and frugal life, generously contributing money to assist the needy.

BIBLIOGRAPHY
T. Odakane: *Tomioka Tessai* (Tokya, 1963); Eng. trans. and adaptation by M. L. Hickman as *Tessai: Master of the Literati Style* (Tokyo, 1965)
S. Aoki: *Tomioka Tessai*, Kindai no bijutsu [Modern art], iv (Tokyo, 1971)

Tomioka Tessai: *Sweeping away Worldly Dust*, hanging scroll, ink and colours on paper, 475×285 mm, 1918 (Nara, Yamato Bunkakan)

T. Kuwahara and others: *Tomioka Tessai* (1974), xx of *Bunjinga suihen* [Selections of literati painting], ed. J. Ishikawa and others (Tokyo, 1974–9)

M. Tomioka and others: *Tessai taisei* [Tessai compilation], 5 vols (Tokyo, 1976–82)

Imperial Japan: The Art of the Meiji Era (1886–1912) (exh. cat. by F. Baekeland, Ithaca, NY, Cornell U., Johnson Mus. A., 1980)

S. Addiss: 'Japanese Literati Artists of the Meiji Period', *Essays on Japanese Art Presented to Jack Hillier*, ed. M. Forrer (London, 1982), pp. 10–23

Tomioka Tessai ten [Exhibition of Tomioka Tessai] (exh. cat., Kyoto, City A. Mus., 1985)

PATRICIA J. GRAHAM

Tomitarō Aoki. *See* HARA, SANKEI.

Tomkin, S. N. *See under* HANSON, TOMKIN, FINKEL-STEIN.

Tomkins. English family of artists. William Tomkins (*b c.* 1730; *d* London, 1 Jan 1792) was a landscape painter, known for his views of country houses. He exhibited frequently, becoming an ARA in 1771. His son Charles Tomkins (*b* London, 1757; *d* 1823) began as a topographical painter, exhibiting 1773–9. He later took up aquatint: among other works, he drew and engraved *Eight Views of Reading Abbey* (1791; A1952, 290) and 80 views for a *Tour to the Isle of Wight* (1794–6; A1953, 344). William's younger son Peltro William Tomkins (*b* London, 1760; *d* London, 22 April 1840) entered the Royal Academy Schools in 1775. He trained as a stipple engraver under Francesco Bartolozzi, who allowed him to sign some plates while he was still a pupil and regarded him as one of his worthiest successors: his large plates, such as *Prince Arthur's Vision* (1788), in the first number of Thomas Macklin's *British Poets*, are excellent. The pupils Tomkins took for drawing included the daughters of George III; in 1793 he was appointed Historical Engraver to Queen Charlotte (1744–1818). His major project during the 1790s was a grand edition of James Thomson's *The Seasons* (1793–8; A1953, 252), with stipple engravings after William Hamilton (ii) by Bartolozzi and himself. Between 1795 and 1823 he was established as a print-seller in London but lost heavily on *The Marquis of Stafford's Pictures* (4 vols, 1818; A1953, 210) and the *British Gallery* (1818; A1953, 209). An Act of Parliament was obtained for a lottery of the pictures painted for these works and the more than 16,000 prints made from them. Two other artists believed to belong to this family were Charles Algernon Tomkins (*b* London, 1821; *d c.* 1903), a prominent reproductive engraver, mostly in mezzotint, and his son CHARLES JOHN TOMKINS, likewise an engraver.

BIBLIOGRAPHY
DNB; Engen; Thieme–Becker
A. W. Tuer: *Bartolozzi and his Works* (London, 1882, rev. 1885), pp. 418–20
A. Graves: *The Royal Academy of Arts*, viii (London, 1905–6), p. 4
J. R. Abbey: *Scenery of Great Britain and Ireland in Aquatint and Lithography, 1770–1860* (London, 1952/*R* Folkestone, 1972) [A1952]
——: *Life in England in Aquatint and Lithography, 1770–1860* (London, 1953/*R* Folkestone, 1972) [A1953]

DAVID ALEXANDER

Tomkins, Charles John (*b* London, 1847; *fl* 1869–97). English mezzotint-engraver. He was the son of Charles Algernon Tomkins (1821–*c.* 1903), a mezzotint-engraver, by whom he was probably trained. Between 1869 and 1892 he exhibited five works at Suffolk Street, London, and 12 at the Royal Academy between 1876 and 1894. He and his father were both employed by Henry Graves & Co. to engrave paintings for the *Library Edition of the Works of Sir Edwin Landseer*, published in two volumes (London, 1881, 1893), and he gained a reputation for his reproductions of paintings by Landseer and George Morland. He was also noted for his mezzotint-engravings after photographic portraits which were much in demand as they presented the printer with fewer technical problems than the relatively new process of photographic reproduction. The majority of the 30 plates registered with the Print

Sellers Association are either portraits or engravings after Landseer but towards the end of his career he produced a number of original works, *Lead Kindly Light* (London, V&A), and a pendant, the *Soul's Awakening*, both published by Graves in 1892, and *Ariadne* (1895). His Royal Academy entries from 1880 to 1891 had consisted solely of portraits, but a change of subject can be seen in his later entries, as his two last exhibits, *Little Lord Fauntleroy* (1892) and *The Mirror* (1894) were both after the sentimental genre painter James Sant. His last recorded work was an original mezzotint portrait of *Queen Victoria*, published in 1897, the year of the Diamond Jubilee, presumably with an eye to commercial advantage.

BIBLIOGRAPHY
Engen
H. Beck: *Victorian Engravings* (London, 1973)

DAVID RODGERS

Tomlin, Bradley Walker (*b* Syracuse, NY, 19 Aug 1899; *d* New York, 11 May 1953). American painter. He studied sculpture modelling in the studio of Hugo Gari Wagner from 1913 and painting from 1917 to 1921 at Syracuse University. After graduation he moved to New York and began to work as a commercial illustrator, with many commissions from Condé Nast publications. Tomlin visited France for the first time in 1923 and spent a few months studying in Paris at both the Académie Colarossi and the Académie de la Grande Chaumière. He remained a freelance illustrator until 1929. In 1925 he spent the first of many summers in the emerging colony of Woodstock, NY. Early paintings, such as *Young Girl* (1925; Newark, NJ, Mus.) or the slightly later *Self-portrait* (1932; New York, Whitney), emotionally evocative yet sentimental, soon gave way to a more stylized format.

Tomlin was impressed by the 1936–7 exhibition, *Fantastic Art: Dada and Surrealism*, at the Museum of Modern Art, New York, and returned to it repeatedly. He was both attracted and repelled but found most other art dull and uninteresting after seeing such work. The paintings he produced during World War II, such as *The Goblet* (1940; Washington, DC, Phillips Col.) and *Burial* (1943; New York, Met.), make occasional use of Surrealist-inspired combinations within a decorative late Cubist idiom. He was a founder-member of the American Federation of Modern Painters and Sculptors, an organization dedicated not only to modernism but also to the eradication of artistic nationalism. Other members included Adolph Gottlieb, Mark Rothko and Balcomb Greene (*b* 1904). From the early 1930s he began to share studios with fellow artists, firstly with James Brooks, in Woodstock, and lastly with Robert Motherwell in New York from 1948 to 1949. He also began his teaching career at the Buckley School from 1932 to 1933, before transferring to Sarah Lawrence College (1933–41), both in New York.

Tomlin's mature work can be said to date from *c*. 1947, when his already abstract works ceased to show a direct debt to either Surrealism or Cubism. The use of dots, crosses and other symbols derived from the Surrealist interest in and use of universal images, but, like Gottlieb, Tomlin spread his thickly applied shapes over the entire canvas in a new and more painterly way, as in *Number 3* (1948; New York, MOMA) and *Number 11* (1949; Utica,

NY, Munson–Williams–Proctor Inst.). Although highly textured and richly painted, Tomlin's paintings were more lyrical and less gestural than those of Pollock or de Kooning. They relate more to the work of Philip Guston, Ad Reinhardt and such painters of the 'second generation' of Abstract Expressionists as Joan Mitchell, Helen Frankenthaler and Milton Resnick (*b* 1917).

Clement Greenberg identified 1948 as the year that Tomlin and Guston joined the Abstract Expressionists, and Tomlin quickly became a recognized leader of the group. In 1952 a substantial selection of his recent paintings was exhibited in *15 Americans* at the Museum of Modern Art, New York. Such paintings as *Number 9: In Praise of Gertrude Stein* (1.24×2.59 m, 1950; New York, MOMA) show how his last and by this stage very large canvases were filled with a more uniform and overall pattern of calligraphic brushstrokes than had been the case just two or three years earlier. Because of the changes evident in the paintings of his last years, it is difficult to assign him a firm place in the history of ABSTRACT EXPRESSIONISM, but he remains one of the pioneers of the lyrical branch of the movement of the mid-20th century.

BIBLIOGRAPHY
Bradley Walker Tomlin (exh. cat. by J. I. H. Baur, New York, Whitney, 1957)
H. Geldzahler: *American Painting in the 20th Century* (New York, 1965), pp. 178–9, 193–4, 201
D. Ashton: *The New York School: A Cultural Reckoning* (New York, 1973), pp. 98, 127, 164, 173
Bradley Walker Tomlin (exh. cat. by J. Chenault, Hempstead, NY, Hofstra U., Lowe Gal., 1975)
For further bibliography *see* ABSTRACT EXPRESSIONISM.

DAVID M. SOKOL

Tommaso, Bartolomeo di. *See* BARTOLOMEO DI TOMMASO.

Tommaso da Ravenna. *See* RANGONE, TOMMASO.

Tommaso di Ser Giovanni di Mone Cassai. *See* MASACCIO.

Tommè, Luca di. *See* LUCA DI TOMMÈ.

Tommisen [Thomisen; Tømmisen], **Daniel** (*d* Malmö, before Nov 1603). Swedish sculptor. He was the leading wood-carver and stonemason in Malmö, where he maintained a workshop. He is first mentioned in 1582 working as a journeyman with Mogens Snedker at Malmöhus Castle. The earliest work that may be attributed to him with some certainty is a wooden altarpiece (before 1588; Lund, Kulthist. Mus.), originally in Reng church, Skåne. It would appear that between 1596 and 1599 he carved architectural details in sandstone, probably to the designs of the presumed architect, Hans van Steenwinckel (i), for doors, gables and dormers at Svenstorp Castle, Skåne. Tommisen's finest work was the pulpit (*c*. 1597–1600) in St Peter, Malmö. This was based on the architectonic composition of the pulpit (1592) made by JOHANNES GANSSOG for Lund Cathedral. The Malmö pulpit is made of sandstone and black limestone, with a carved oak baldacchino. Tommisen did not achieve Ganssog's mastery of perspective in relief. Instead the six panels with scenes from the *Life of Christ* are presented in a form of high relief, in which the motifs chiefly unfold on a console along the lower edge of the relief, anticipating the Baroque niche relief (Paulsson). This characteristic style makes it possible to assign to Tommisen both epitaphs in St Peter and its baptismal font (1601), which is the earliest Renaissance font in Skåne and the model for a long series of fonts in the region. In 1600 he was summoned to Copenhagen by Christian IV, King of Denmark, to work on the construction of the Tøjhus (Royal Arsenal; 1598–1604). His name last appears in a document relating to the settlement of his estate in November 1603.

BIBLIOGRAPHY
L. Weibull: 'Bildhuggare och träsnidare i Malmö och Lund under renaissancen' [Sculptors and wood-carvers in Malmö and Lund during the Renaissance], *Hist. Tidskr. Skåneland*, i (1903), pp. 1–48
G. Paulsson: *Skånes dekorativa konst* [Skåne's decorative art] (Stockholm, 1915)
M. Rydbeck: 'Renässanssskulptur i Skåne', *Kun. Vitt., Hist. & Ant. Akad. Hand.*, Antikvariska Studier, iv (1950)
C. A. Jensen: 'Daniel Tommisen', *Weilbachs kunstnerleksikon*, iii (Copenhagen, 1952)
EVA DE LA FUENTE PEDERSEN

Tomon, Toma de. *See* THOMON, THOMAS-JEAN DE.

Toms, Carl (*b* Kirkby-in-Ashfield, Notts, 29 May 1927). English stage designer. He trained at Mansfield College of Art, Notts (1946–9), the Royal College of Art, London (1949–53) and the Old Vic Theatre School, London (1954–7). Between 1952 and 1958, while still a student, he worked as an assistant to Oliver Messel and in 1957 created his first important sets for a production of *Apollo de Bellec* at the Royal Court Theatre, London. Thereafter he worked for leading theatre, opera and ballet companies in Europe and the USA, including the Royal National Theatre, the Young Vic Theatre Co., the Royal Shakespeare Co. and the Royal Opera House, London; the Chichester Festival Theatre, W. Sussex; the Glyndebourne Festival Opera, E. Sussex; the Burgtheater and Staatsoper, Vienna; and the New York City Opera and Metropolitan Opera, New York. Among his most memorable designs were those for productions of *The Merry Wives of Windsor* (1959), *New Cranks* (1960), *Love's Labour's Lost* and *Edward II* (1968), London; *Sleuth* (1970), London, Paris and New York; *Sherlock Holmes* and *Travesties* (1974), London and New York; *The Importance of Being Earnest* (1987), London and Copenhagen; and *Rigoletto* (1988), New York. His film credits include *The Winter's Tale* (1968), *Moon Zero Two* (1970) and *When Dinosaurs Ruled the Earth* (1971). For television he designed productions of *Boule de Suif*, *The Sandcastle* and *Twelfth Night*. In 1969 he was design consultant for the state investiture at Caernarfon Castle of Charles, Duke of Cornwall, as Prince of Wales, and in 1970 he was appointed head of design for the Young Vic Theatre Co. He redesigned and decorated several theatre interiors, notably the Theatre Royal (1982), Bath, and the Garrick Theatre (1986) and Cambridge Theatre (1987), London.

WRITINGS
The Tricks of Scapin (London, 1975) [stage designs]
The Winter's Tale (London, 1975) [stage designs]

BIBLIOGRAPHY
J. Goodwin, ed.: *British Theatre Design: The Modern Age* (London, 1989)

Toms, Peter (*b c.* 1728; *d* London, 1 Jan 1777). English painter. He was trained in the London studio of Thomas Hudson; by November 1748 he was described as an 'eminent painter'. He became a drapery painter for several artists following the death of Joseph van Aken in 1749, but no independent pictures have been unequivocally attributed to him. He may have worked for Hudson and for Allan Ramsay, but it is certain that he worked for Joshua Reynolds between *c.* 1755 and *c.* 1763. Edwards (1808) suggested that Toms was responsible for the drapery in Reynolds's portrait of *Lady Elizabeth Keppel* (1761–2; Woburn Abbey, Beds); another and more convincing claim is that he made a large contribution to Reynolds's *Master Thomas Lister* (early 1760s; Bradford, Cartwright Hall).

After a brief visit to Ireland *c.* 1763 Toms returned to London to work almost exclusively until 1770 for Francis Cotes. There is evidence that he also assisted Thomas Gainsborough in the 1770s, and that he worked for Benjamin West at some time. In 1768 he was made a founder-member of the Royal Academy, where he subsequently exhibited some of his paintings. They were poorly received, however, which may have encouraged the intemperance that led to his death.

BIBLIOGRAPHY
Waterhouse: *18th C.*
E. Edwards: *Anecdotes of Painters who Have Resided or Been Born in England* (London, 1808)
Thomas Hudson, 1701–1779 (exh. cat. by E. G. Miles, London, Kenwood House, 1979)
Reynolds (exh. cat., ed. N. B. Penny; London, RA, 1986)
HUGH BELSEY

Tomsky, Nikolay (Vasil'yevich) (*b* Ramushevo, Novgorod region, 19 Dec 1900; *d* Moscow, 17 Nov 1984). Russian sculptor. He studied at the Art and Industrial Technical College in Leningrad (now St Petersburg) from 1923 to 1927 under Vsevolod Lishev (1877–1960). From 1927 to 1930 he was involved in the restoration of the decorative and monumental sculpture of St Petersburg's classical buildings. His work developed the tradition of the 19th-century Russian school of sculpture and his monumental works combine political ideals with historical and patriotic themes. Expressive gesture and carefully modelled shapes are typical characteristics. Examples of his work include the monument to the World War II commander *I. D. Chernyakhovsky* (bronze, 1950; Vilnius), several monuments to *V. I. Lenin* (e.g. 1977; Tashkent) and the monument to *Mikhail Lomonosov* (bronze, 1953) in front of Moscow University. He also sculpted numerous portraits, gradually intensifying the plastic expressiveness of his modelling, for example of the artist *Diego Rivera* (bronze, 1956; Moscow, Tret'yakov Gal.) and of the *Oldest Flower Grower in Georgia, M. Mamulashvili* (bronze, 1957; Irkutsk, A. Mus.), and he produced monumental reliefs, such as the frieze *Defence, Work and Rest* (reinforced concrete, 1940; St Petersburg, Sov. House). From 1949 to 1984 he taught at the V. I. Surikov Art Institute, Moscow, and from 1968 to 1983 he was President of the USSR Academy of Arts.

WRITINGS
Zametki skul'ptora [Notes of a sculptor] (Moscow, 1965)

BIBLIOGRAPHY
V. B. Minina: *N. V. Tomsky* (Moscow, 1980)
N. V. Tomsky (exh. cat., Moscow, 1981)

A. V. PARAMONOV

Ton, Konstantin (Andreyevich) (*b* St Petersburg, 6 Nov 1794; *d* St Petersburg, 6 Feb 1881). Russian architect. The son of a jeweller, he trained (1803–15) at the St Petersburg Academy of Arts under Andrey Voronikhin. From 1819 to 1828 he worked in Italy, where his research and designs for the restoration of the sanctuary of Fortuna Primigenia in Praeneste, the Palatine palaces in Rome and other monuments made him an expert on Classical buildings. There is some evidence that he studied the theory of vault construction in Paris at the Ecole Polytechnique. On his return to St Petersburg, he began working actively as an architect, executing major state commissions under the direct control of the Emperor Nicholas I (*reg* 1825–55). Among his early works are the Neo-classical ceremonial interiors (1829) of the Academy of Arts in St Petersburg. Ton's design for the Maly Theatre (1837–43) blended well with the late classical ensemble of Theatre Square, Moscow. He built the first railway stations in Moscow (the Nikolayevsky (now Leningrad) Station, 1849) and St Petersburg (the Nikolayevsky (now Moscow) Station, 1851).

In Ton's Great Kremlin Palace (1838–49) and the Armoury Palace (1844–51) in the Kremlin, Moscow, the unavoidable contrast between the picturesque old buildings and the large new complex is softened by the free planning of the latter, by the stepped arrangement of masses and the stylized decoration of the façades (*see* MOSCOW, fig. 10). The sculptural decoration is rich and varied in the interiors, where form is determined by the construction. Ton gave new life to the Roman, Byzantine and Old Russian vault types, using them daringly and rationally. The expressiveness of the structure of the main St George's Hall, covered with a vast barrel-vault, was underlined by white-and-gold wall decoration, ornamentation based on the Classical orders, and low reliefs and panels with the names of knights of the military order of St George.

Ton is particularly well known as the founder of the Russo-Byzantine style, which reflected not only the official ideological programme but also a general interest in the nation's heritage. Ton's first building in this style was the church of St Catherine (1830) in St Petersburg, followed by numerous similar commissions employing the traditional repertory of onion domes, tent roofs and bell-towers in St Petersburg, Moscow, Voronezh, Krasnoyarsk and many other towns. For the first time since the stylistic rule of classicism, ogee arches, elegant mouldings, *kokoshniki* and other elements of the Russian medieval architectural language appeared in the professional repertory adapted by Ton, not without some loss to its free picturesqueness. He transformed the plan of the grandiose cruciform and domed church of Christ the Redeemer (1832–8; destr. 1934; rebuilt 1994–) in Moscow by designing a two-storey gallery on one side of the central block to house a museum. The church was built as a memorial to Russia's victory in the Patriotic War of 1812–14. Ton also combined medieval forms with the Classical orders, developing the traditions that had existed in Russia from the 15th century and finding for them a new opportunity of expression. He thus crowned a Corinthian portico at the elegant Governor's Palace (1843) in Kazan' with ogee gables, which 'echoed' the medieval cathedral opposite. His works gave a strong impulse to the study of Russian architecture. He worked as a restorer on many occasions, for example at the Kremlin, Moscow, and the monastery of Hypatius (Ipat'yevsky Monastery) in Kostroma, although he did not shun stylization and additions to the buildings he was restoring.

The first attempts to create a scientific way of designing buildings are associated with Ton's name. He reworked a series of standard peasant building types, such as houses and shops, using information about methods of construction of national buildings collected and standardized by government establishments in 1840. In his work Ton moved towards advanced constructional devices, including the use of large metal structures.

BIBLIOGRAPHY
T. A. Slavina: *Konstantin Ton* (Leningrad, 1982)
Ye. I. Kirichenko and others, eds: *Khram Khristova Spasitelya v istorii i kul'ture Rossii: Al'bom* [The church of Christ the Saviour in the history and culture of Russia: an album] (Moscow, 1992)

T. A. SLAVINA

Tonalá. Pre-Columbian site in Chiapas, Mexico, 13 km north-east of the modern town of the same name. The ancient site, spread across a mountain slope, was explored by Philip Drucker in 1947 and mapped by Edwin Ferdon in 1949. It comprises five groups of masonry structures, together with various carved stelae, so-called altars and stone sculptures, many of which appear to be earlier than the final masonry structures. Tonalá was occupied from at least the Middle Pre-Classic period (*c.* 1000 BC–*c.* 300 BC) into the Post-Classic period (*c.* AD 900–1521). Throughout its occupation it appears to have been on a major Mesoamerican north–south communication route and to have played a prominent role in the spread of OLMEC ideas and in trade between TEOTIHUACÁN in the Central Highlands and the MAYA region, part of the traffic across the Isthmus of Tehuantepec and down the Pacific Coast to the Maya cities of IZAPA and SANTA LUCÍA COTZUMALHUAPA, to the south on the Pacific slopes of south-eastern Chiapas–Guatemala.

The stelae and sculptures appear to have received influences both from central Mesoamerica and from the south. Monument 5 is a sculptured monolith representing a feline, with long fangs and a crested top, resembling sculptures at the Olmec site of LA VENTA. The sculpture known as Altar 1, representing a jaguar snout, is of a similar 'Olmecoid' style. In contrast, a later carved stele representing the rain god Tláloc (presumed to be from the ancient site but now standing in the main plaza of the modern town), with characteristic goggle eyes and a calendric year sign—an imbricated trapeziform in the headdress—has been variously interpreted as indicative of Central Highlands influence, or of the sculptures at Izapa and Santa Lucía Cotzumalhuapa. Another stele (now in Tuxtla Gutiérrez, Mus. Reg. Antropol. & Hist.), also presumed to be from Tonalá or from near by, is carved in a similar style with the figure of a ball-game player and court, and bears dot and bar glyphs that appear to represent the numbers seven and nine. The massive stone-faced platforms are of Post-Classic date. These vary in height between 1 and 3.5 m and have wide ramps or central staircases, some with side ramps, supporting structures of one to three rooms that are presumed to be temples. Paved ramps connect the central 'acropolis' with other groups of platform ruins, known as precincts, down the slope.

South-east of modern Tonalá, at the site of Tzutzuculi, excavations by Andrew McDonald published in 1977 recovered two roughly cubical, carved volcanic blocks (sides *c.* 1.5 m) representing a were-jaguar and a serpent head flanking the stairway of pyramidal Mound 4, dated *c.* 410 BC (radiocarbon assays from the mound fill gave the dates of 545 BC and 340 BC). Pottery from the site has been dated by comparison with other local pottery to between 550 BC and 450 BC. Both carvings are Olmec in style, although the serpent head is more stylized and abstract than many Olmec pieces. Tzutzuculi comprises some 25 mounds of beaten earth, clay and stones covering an area of *c.* 35 ha. The arrangement of the mounds to form a ceremonial plaza, and the shape of Mound 4 (8 m high and 62 m long, supported by a platform with rounded corners) resemble the arrangement and features at Olmec La Venta. Finds from Tonalá and Tzutzuculi are in the Museo Nacional de Antropología, Mexico City, and the Museo Regional de Antropología e Historia, Tuxtla Gutierrez.

BIBLIOGRAPHY
E. N. Ferdon, jr: *Tonalá, Mexico: An Archaeological Survey*, School of American Research [monographs], xvi (Santa Fe, 1953)
M. P. Weaver: *The Aztecs, Maya and their Predecessors: Archaeology of Mesoamerica* (New York, 1972, rev. 2/1981), pp. 81, 255, 492
A. J. McDonald: 'Two Middle Preclassic Engraved Monuments at Tzutzuculi on the Chiapas Coast of Mexico', *Amer. Ant.*, xlii (1977), pp. 560–66
J. Soustelle: *Les Olmèques* (Paris, 1979; Eng. trans., New York, 1985), pp. 126–8
J. Kelly: *The Complete Visitor's Guide to Mesoamerican Ruins* (Norman, 1982), p. 225
DAVID M. JONES

Tonalism. Style of American painting that appeared between *c.* 1880 and 1920. Though not clearly defined, its main exponents were George Inness, James McNeill Whistler, Thomas Wilmer Dewing, Dwight W. Tryon, Alexander Helwig Wyant and such artists of the Photo-Secession as Edward J. Steichen. The term was used by Isham in 1905 and by Brinton in an essay in a catalogue for an exhibition of American painters held in Berlin in 1910. Brinton named the now virtually forgotten artists J. Francis Murphy, Bruce Crane (1857–1937), Ben Foster (1852–1926) and Henry Ward Ranger (1858–1916) as exponents of the style and as leaders of contemporary art in the USA. The style is characterized by soft, diffused light, muted tones and hazily outlined objects, all of which imbue the works with a strong sense of mood. The term was applied especially to landscape painting in which nature is presented as serene or mysterious, never disquieting or dramatic.

Tonalism grew up alongside American Impressionism yet is distinguished from that (and from French Impressionism) by its restrained palette and strongly subjective aesthetic. Somewhat in the tradition of George Fuller and of the earlier HUDSON RIVER SCHOOL in America, the Tonalists approached nature in a contemplative, Romantic manner, the intention being to capture not so much the appearance of a landscape as its mood as perceived by the artist. This idealistic attitude linked Tonalism to the contemporary Symbolist aesthetic (*see* SYMBOLISM), particularly evident in such paintings as Steichen's *Across the Salt Marshes, Huntington* (*c.* 1905, Toledo, OH, Mus. A.). The outlines of the trees are scarcely visible in the dim, misty atmosphere, lending the scene a strong sense of mystery. Whistler's earlier *Nocturnes*, which date from the 1870s onwards, have similar qualities, as shown by *Nocturne in Blue and Silver: The Lagoon, Venice* (*c.* 1880; Boston, MA, Mus. F.A.). Closer to Impressionism in its lighting and in the brushwork, though still characteristic of Tonalism, is Tryon's *Morning in May* (1911; Oshkosh, WI, Paine A. Cent.) depicting a serene area of tree-lined landscape. Occasionally the Tonalist style was applied to figure and interior subjects, as in Dewing's *The Spinet* (1902; Washington, DC, Smithsonian Inst., Archvs Amer. A.), in which the prominent soft brown hues fuse the foreground with the background, blending the central figure into her surroundings.

BIBLIOGRAPHY
S. Isham: *The History of American Painting* (New York, 1905)
C. Brinton: 'Die Entwicklung der amerikanischen Malerei', *Ausstellung amerikanischer Kunst* (exh. cat., ed. K. Francke; Berlin, Akad. Kst., 1910), pp. 9–42
E. P. Richardson: *Painting in America from 1502 to the Present* (New York, 1956, rev. 1969), pp. 304–7, 368
The Color of Mood: American Tonalism, 1880–1910 (exh. cat. by W. Corn, San Francisco, de Young Mem. Mus., 1972)
R. J. Boyle: *American Impressionism* (Boston, 1974), pp. 76–8
The Paintings of Eduard Steichen (exh. cat. by M. Steichen Calderone and A. C. De Pietro, Huntington, NY, Heckscher Mus., 1985)

Tonauer, Hans, I. *See* DONAUER, HANS, I.

Tondino di Guerrino (*fl* Siena, 1322–8). Italian goldsmith. He was the most important goldsmith in Siena in the first half of the 14th century after GUCCIO DI MANNAIA, to whom he may possibly have been apprenticed. Despite the fact that many contemporary Sienese translucent enamels have been attributed to Tondino, there is supporting evidence for only three objects. A chalice (London, BM) bears his name and that of an associate, Andrea Riguardi, on its knop. A paten representing the *Resurrection* in S Domenico, Perugia, is cited in the church's inventory of 1458 as the mate to a chalice also signed by the two artists. A second paten representing *St James with a Pilgrim* (Perugia, G.N. Umbria), found in 1954 under the choir-stalls of the church (with the *Resurrection* paten), probably corresponds to a second paten mentioned in the inventory of 1458, which is also linked to a chalice signed by the two men; conflicting evidence in an earlier inventory of 1430 makes this attribution somewhat less certain, however. Other works by Tondino mentioned in documents are untraced. In 1322 he sold a silver basin to the Nove family; two years later Andrea Riguardi filed suit on his own and Tondino's behalf against a Florentine goldsmith, Gelino di Geri, for non-payment for a chalice they had sold to him. On 28 December 1327 Tondino was paid for a golden frieze, presumably with repoussé decoration, also for the Nove family. The church of S Francesco, Assisi, once possessed a chalice signed by him, with a paten representing the *Assumption of the Virgin*. In 1853 Pistoia Cathedral still owned a signed chalice, dated 1328, and possibly its paten, since the reference says that it was a chalice for communion under both kinds.

Numerous other works have been attributed to Tondino di Guerrino and Andrea Riguardi or their workshop on the basis of style, including crosses (Paris, Louvre; Matenano, S Vittoria) and a chalice (Rome, Vatican, Mus. Stor. A. Tesoro S Pietro). Too little is known about the work of other Sienese goldsmiths of this period and the organization of their workshops to enable such attributions to be supported, however. Attempts to distinguish Tondino's contribution to the signed chalice in the British Museum from that of Andrea Riguardi are equally problematic.

BIBLIOGRAPHY

G. Milanesi: *Documenti per la storia dell'arte senese*, i (Siena, 1854), p. 104, n. 1–2
P. Leone de Castris: 'Tondino di Guerrino e Andrea Riguardi: Orafi e smaltisti a Siena (1308–1338)', *Prospettiva*, xxi (1980), pp. 24–44 [with bibliog.]
L'Art gothique siennois (exh. cat., Avignon, Mus. Petit Pal., 1983), pp. 149–52 [entries by E. Cioni Liserani and E. Taburet]

BARBARA DRAKE BOEHM

Tondo [It.: 'circle']. Circular painting or relief carving. It developed as an independent form in Florence in the first half of the 15th century. However, earlier examples of the circular form do exist, for example in France with Jean Malouel's *Pietà* (Paris, Louvre) which dates *c.* 1400. Many of the surviving Italian tondi depict themes that also occurred on the *desco da parto*, from which the tondo may have evolved. This was a circular or polygonal painted tray made to celebrate the birth of a child and presented to the mother with gifts of sweetmeats and fruit. Tondi paintings were produced in Florence primarily for domestic settings, with the Adoration of the Magi and the Virgin and Child being particularly popular subjects. Among the earliest surviving tondi are Luca della Robbia's terracotta relief of the *Virgin and Child with Two Angels* (*c.* 1428; Oxford, Ashmolean) and Domenico Veneziano's circular panel painting of the *Adoration of the Magi* (1439–41; Berlin, Bodemus.). The most notable carved marble tondi are Michelangelo's two versions of the *Virgin and Child with St John the Baptist* ('Taddei Tondo', *c.* 1504, London, RA; 'Pitti Tondo', *c.* 1503–5, Florence, Bargello). The tondo form was also used as a decorative motif in architecture (examples in glazed terracotta by Luca della Robbia; Florence, Santa Croce, Pazzi Chapel; Florence, Ospedale degli Innocenti) or to achieve illusionistic effects (e.g. frescoes by Pontormo, 1525–8; Florence, S Felicita, Cappella Capponi; *see* PONTORMO, fig. 2). Donatello also produced a gilt-bronze tondo, the *Virgin and Child with Angels* (London, V&A), the reverse of which was intended to serve as a reusable mould for glass. The circular format continued to be employed by such later artists as Caravaggio, Ingres, Monet, Braque, Picasso and Jackson Pollock.

BIBLIOGRAPHY

M. Hauptmann: *Der Tondo* (Frankfurt am Main, 1936)
A. Cecchi: 'Les Cadres ronds de la Renaissance florentine', *Rev. A.* [Paris], lxxvi (1987), pp. 21–4
R. Carvalho de Magalhàes: 'Il formato del dipinto come elemento compositivo: Il tondo', *Crit. A.*, lv/1 (1990), pp. 77–80

□

Tonga, Kingdom of. Group of 150 islands in the South Pacific Ocean, with a total land area of 699 sq. km and a population of 119,000 (UN estimate, 1989). It lies at the southern point of a triangle formed with its two neighbours Fiji and Samoa. Tonga has been an independent state since 1970. Its parliamentary political system is headed by a monarch, whose ancestry is traced to the Polynesian gods who created and peopled the islands. The primary language is Tongan (which is closely related to other west Polynesian languages), although many Tongans also speak English.

1. Cultural history. 2. Artistic concepts. 3. Bark cloth. 4. Basketry and plaiting. 5. Wood-carving. 6. Figure sculpture.

1. CULTURAL HISTORY. The ancestors of modern Tongans migrated from nearby Fiji *c.* 1200 BC, bringing with them the Lapita cultural complex. Dentate-stamped pottery, the marker of this complex, developed into Polynesian plain ware and eventually died out. It is likely, however, that the Lapita design motifs and the ways in which they were combined in Tonga formed the prototype for such other artistic developments as tattoo, incising on war clubs, bark cloth design and basketry. Tonga is best regarded as part of the west Polynesian cultural complex. Long-distance voyaging between Fiji, Tonga and Samoa developed over time into a tripartite network that included the importation of chiefly spouses and prestige items. The circulation of valuables to and from Tonga makes it difficult for scholars to clarify whether particular items were made or traded from Tonga or Samoa. The hierarchical social structure required outsiders to perform certain functions for those of high rank, such as tattooing, hair cutting and conducting of funerals. In addition, such raw materials as large trees for the production of large canoes were lacking in Tonga but could be obtained from Fiji. The resulting social structure was one of the most hierarchical in Polynesia. Prestige and power eventually became separated and the presentation of prestige goods became an art in its own right. Highest rank is associated with genealogical relationship to the first king of Tonga and the principle that sisters outrank brothers.

2. ARTISTIC CONCEPTS. Art was not a category of traditional Tongan culture. The concept implied by the incorporation of *faiva* ('skill'), however, is important for an understanding of Tongan art and aesthetics. *Faiva* refers to any work, task, feat, trade, craft or performance requiring skill or ability. A second important concept is *heliaki* ('indirectness'), which requires skill based on cultural knowledge to carry out. *Heliaki* is manifested in metaphor and layers of meaning and is developed by skirting a subject and approaching it repeatedly from different points of view. Hidden meanings must be unravelled layer by layer until they can be understood. Thus objects, cultural forms and works of art have meanings that cannot be apprehended simply by examining them. Visual arts can be understood by analysis in relation to poetry and oratory, which incorporate social philosophy and form the structure of the aesthetic system. The visual

arts objectify social and cultural metaphors incorporated through *heliaki* and *faiva* into the oral arts. Male craftsmen, *tufunga*, use their *faiva* to create objects that are works of art because they express the *heliaki* of the poets. Visual arts are integrally related to verbal arts, and both are used in the service of elevating and honouring the prestige or power of individuals or chiefly lines. The most important arts of Tonga were poetry, with its attendant music and dance, scent, bark cloth, mat-making, basketry, wood incising, ornament and sculpture. Bark cloth and mats were most important to the Tongans and were categorized as *koloa* (valuables) and made by women. Other objects were considered either crafts—made by *tufunga*—or decoration—*teuteu*, made by men and/or women. The latter consisted of scented coconut oil, ornaments and, probably, basketry.

Poetry, music and dance have survived into the late 20th century in many traditional as well as modern forms. Bark cloth has continued to be made and to be used for ritual as well as for sale to tourists. Wood incising and sculpture virtually ceased with the end of traditional warfare and the advent of Christianity. Elaborate basketry techniques have given way to quicker ones to produce forms for sale to tourists.

3. BARK CLOTH. Tongan bark cloth is distinguished by its large size and metaphorical designs. Traditionally used for ritual prestations, especially at weddings and funerals, it was also used for clothing and bed coverings. Large finished pieces, sometimes as large as 5×50 m, are categorized by colour and design organization as *ngatu*, *ngatu uli* (black *ngatu*) and *fuatanga*. *Ngatu* designs are organized to run crosswise between crosswise lines that cross a set of long lines that run the entire length of the piece. *Fuatanga* designs are organized to run across the length of the piece, and a series of crosswise lines are used to measure its size. *Fuatanga* are more difficult to make and are used primarily by chiefs. *Ngatu uli* are also used primarily by chiefs, but they derive their high status from the difficulty of making the black dye.

Paper mulberry (*hiapo*; *Broussonetia papyrifera*) is grown and prepared in the usual west Polynesian manner. After beating, the pieces are pasted together and printed by rubbing dye on to the white cloth, which has been laid over a series of stencils. The cloth is then moved and the rubbing of the stencils repeated. Finally, after the piece is dry, the main parts of the design are highlighted by overpainting with a pandanus brush.

The series of stencils form a set with metaphorical meaning. Sometimes these sets are traditional, chiefly designs or have local referents; sometimes they are combined to commemorate specific occasions or to make references to chiefs or their ancestral lines. Thus, a set with pine trees, a coat of arms and a lion refers metaphorically to the monarch, for pine trees form a road on one side of the palace, the coat of arms is the monarch's seal, and the lion as a symbol of the monarch has been adopted from Europe. A set with a feathered hair ornament, a necklace of a certain shell, and a decorative girdle made of sun, moon and stars, metaphorically refers to the late Queen Sālote and commemorates her attendance at the coronation of Queen Elizabeth II of Great Britain in 1953.

Sets of such naturalistic stencils are completed with groupings of traditional geometric designs; these are named and are metaphorical references to chiefs and their deeds. Similar geometric designs have been used since at least the time of the visits of Capt. James Cook (1770s). There are a number of important collections in Europe (e.g. Göttingen, Städt. Mus.; Berlin, Mus. Vlkerknd.; Berne, Hist. Mus.; Oxford, Pitt Rivers Mus.).

4. BASKETRY AND PLAITING. The skills of basketry and plaiting were closely related in Tonga. The products ranged from clothing to baskets, from feathered headdresses to grave decorations, and from combs to fine mats for presentation. Like other Polynesians, Tongans made mats and baskets from varieties of pandanus, but unlike other Polynesians, Tongans had more elaborate techniques for working other plant materials. The highest ranking basket was *kato mosi kaka*. Fibres obtained from the integument at the top of coconut palms, *kaka*, were dyed black and intertwined with those of natural colour into geometric designs outlined with shell beads. The motifs were usually combinations of triangles forming the chiefly *manulua* design, also found on bark cloth. Another important basket, *kato alu*, was made by encircling a vine called *alu* around a coil of midribs of coconut leaflets. Fine pandanus or hibiscus fibre mats were placed in the basket with gourds (and later elaborate imported glass bottles) containing scented coconut oil that was used to anoint both the living and dead.

The technique used to make *kato mosi kaka* was also used to make decorative girdles worn by the highest chiefs on ceremonial occasions (*kātoanga*). They were composed of small pieces in the form of circles, stars, half-moons or rectangles, which were covered with red feathers and which incorporated shell beads, animal teeth and pieces of carved ivory. These were sewn together to form a kind of overskirt. A well-preserved example from Cook's second voyage has survived (Oxford, Pitt Rivers Mus.).

The highest ranking object was a feathered headdress, *pala tavake*, which could be worn only by the highest chief, the Tu'i Tonga. Made of tail feathers of the tropic bird and/or red parakeet feathers, they formed a semicircle over the forehead that stood out *c.* 450 mm. Only one such headdress seems to have survived (Vienna, Mus. Vlkerknd.).

5. WOOD-CARVING. Wood-carvers were specialists known as *tufunga fou vaka* who were primarily canoemakers but who used their skills to make bowls, fly-whisks, neckrests and clubs (for illustrations see 1978 exh. cat.). Bowls were made in a variety of shapes and sizes and were used for mixing kava (an infusion of the root of *Piper methysticum*), serving food and especially for holding scented coconut oil. The carving and use of these oil dishes shows influence from Fiji, where they were used for religious ceremonies. Neckrests were carved in symmetrical and asymmetrical forms, either from a single piece of wood or with the legs lashed to the crossbar with coconut fibre using a technique developed in canoe building. Some examples are inlaid with pieces of ivory. Fly-whisks were status objects comprising a handle of bone or wood and a whisk of partly braided coconut fibre

1. Tongan clubs, incised wood, (top) 1.10 m, acquired 1939; (bottom) 0.97 m, acquired 1884 (Oxford, Pitt Rivers Museum)

bound to the handle with other fibre. The wooden handles varied from straight to curved to zigzag and were sometimes reused objects, such as spear-points or part of the handle of a club, which probably had *mana* in their own right. Other carved and decorated objects included food hooks. These comprised carved hooks surmounted by flat discs, and they were hung inside the house to keep food and other objects out of the reach of rats from above and below. The disc was painted on the underside, and the hook was sometimes made from ivory.

The most numerous wooden objects in collections of Tongan art are clubs (see fig. 1). They have a variety of shapes and serve as the medium for elaborate incising that was done by means of a shark-tooth hafted to a handle of wood. After European contact nails were hafted in the same way, making possible the sharper and deeper incising of many classic examples. Incising was done in sections that were laid out in advance, often using the intersection of a perpendicular line—formed from a diamond-shaped cross-section—and vertical cross lines. Each section so formed was carved to match or contrast with those around it. In the classic form of the clubs, some sections have incised human and animal images set into a geometric background while in others the geometric design is the main element. The designs are the same as those used in bark cloth, and the layout has the same underlying structure. The designs represent metaphorically chiefly attributes and the chiefs themselves. In some cases ivory insets were used instead of the incised naturalistic figures.

6. FIGURE SCULPTURE. Female forms were carved from ivory or wood and seem to represent ancestors or goddesses. Ivory images may represent Hikuleo, a goddess of the afterworld, and may have originally been kept in her god-house hanging from the central ridge-pole either singly or as part of a double-figured hook. They may also have been worn by female chiefs as charms or ornaments. These figures and hooks were also exported to Fiji, where, because they were made of highly valued whale-tooth ivory, they were even more sacred and were also hung in god-houses. Most known examples are quite similar to

each other with broad shoulders, straight, loosely hanging arms, slightly bent knees, the indication of a navel, well-developed breasts, and an ill-defined neck (see fig. 2). Facial features are in low relief except for the ears, which are well carved. Although carved in three dimensions, the figures are reminiscent of the two-dimensional incised or inlaid ivory figures found on clubs and fly-whisk handles. Wooden figures have similar stylistic features and two-dimensional qualities. They, too, were probably part of hooks or were hung from the ridge-pole in god-houses dedicated to them. Examples of Tongan figure sculpture are held in a number of museums throughout the world (e.g. Auckland, Inst. & Mus.; Chicago, IL, Field Mus. Nat. Hist.; London, BM).

BIBLIOGRAPHY

W. Churchill: *Club Types of Nuclear Polynesia*, Carnegie Institution of Washington Publication, cclv (Washington, DC, 1917)

E. W. Gifford: *Tongan Society*, Bishop Mus. Bull., lxi (Honolulu, 1929/R Millwood, NY, 1985)

W. C. McKern: *Archaeology of Tonga*, Bishop Mus. Bull., lx (Honolulu, 1929)

Te Rangi Hiroa: 'Material Representatives of Tongan and Samoan Gods', *J. Polynes. Soc.*, xliv (1935), pp. 48–53, 85–96, 153–62

——: 'Additional Wooden Images from Tonga', *J. Polynes. Soc.*, xlvi (1937), pp. 74–82

K. E. Larsson: *Fijian Studies*, Etnologiska Studier, xxv (Gothenberg, 1960)

A. L. Kaeppler: 'Eighteenth Century Tonga: New Interpretations of Tongan Society and Material Culture at the Time of Captain Cook', *Man*, vi/2 (1971), pp. 204–20, pls 1a–6a

T. Barrow: *Art and Life in Polynesia* (London, 1972), pp. 62–75

S. Kooijman: *Tapa in Polynesia*, Bishop Mus. Bull., ccxxxiv (Honolulu, 1972)

A. L. Kaeppler: 'Exchange Patterns in Goods and Spouses: Fiji, Tonga, and Samoa', *Mankind*, xi/3 (1978), pp. 246–52

——: 'Melody, Drone and Decoration: Underlying Structures and Surface Manifestations in Tongan Art and Society', *Art in Society: Studies in Style, Culture and Aesthetics*, ed. M. Greenhalgh and V. Megaw (London, 1978), pp. 261–74

'*Artificial Curiosities': Being an Exposition of Native Manufactures Collected on the Three Pacific Voyages of Captain James Cook, R.N.*, Bishop Mus. Special Pubn, lxv (exh. cat. by A. L. Kaeppler, Honolulu, Bishop Mus., 1978) [incl. examples of plaiting and basketry, pp. 212–23]

The Art of the Pacific Islands (exh. cat. by P. Gathercole, A. L. Kaeppler and D. Newton, Washington, DC, N.G.A., 1979), pp. 92–3, 173–7

F. Clunie: *Yalo i Viti—Shades of Viti: A Fiji Museum Catalogue* (Suva, Fiji, 1986)

ADRIENNE L. KAEPPLER

2. Tongan figure, whale-tooth ivory, h. 148 mm, 19th century or earlier (Aberdeen, University Marischal Museum)

Tongbong. *See* KIM SI-SŬP.

Tongerloo, Georges van. *See* VANTONGERLOO, GEORGES.

Toniná. Pre-Columbian MAYA site in the mountains of north-east Chiapas, Mexico. Although its elevation is nearly 900 m above sea-level, the culture and art of Toniná belong to the tradition of the Lowland Maya area. Few of the buildings survive, but the originality of the sculptures derives from the outlying situation of the city, which exposed it to artistic trends from diverse sources. Following early visits by various explorers and travellers, including Guillaume Dupaix in 1808 and John L. Stephens in 1840, Frans Blom and Oliver La Farge were responsible for the first systematic study of the site, during the 1920s. Two French expeditions were made to Toniná, in 1972–3 and 1979–80, and subsequent excavations have been carried out by Mexican researchers under the auspices of the Instituto Nacional de Antropología e Historia, Mexico.

Toniná reached its apogee between *c.* AD 600 and *c.* 900. Its ceremonial centre, known as the Acropolis, is built on a hillside with seven terraces supporting the main civic buildings. The highest terrace is 57 m above an esplanade extending from the southern end of the Acropolis, where there are fewer buildings. There are, however, two ball-playing fields within this area. Two large pyramids standing side by side occupy almost all of the upper terraces. One has been explored: it stood 19 m high, with four staircases flanked by ramps with repeated, modelled stucco masks of the jaguar, patron of sacrifice and war. Sculptures from the site are of local sandstone and include free-standing monuments, both in high relief and in the round, as well as low reliefs related to other Lowland styles. In most cases these are statues of dignitaries, usually with a vertical tenon—a feature not of Maya origin—set into a stonework or brickwork pedestal. The statues are generally smaller than other Lowland Maya pieces, and represent the standing sovereign either holding a serpent-rod against his chest or with his hands free and resting on his belt or thighs. These works are intended to be seen either from the front or from the back, where the inscription is found. Dating from AD 909, the most recent known Maya stele was found at Toniná in 1973. The iconography of such pieces draws largely on the themes of war, capture and sacrifice, including scenes of capture, statues of prisoners framing the image of the king and decapitated figures. Most of the sculptures remain at the site, apart from a few pieces which have been removed to the Museo Regional de Antropología e Historia in Tuxtla Gutiérrez and to the Museo Nacional de Antropología in Mexico City.

BIBLIOGRAPHY

F. Blom and O. La Farge: *Tribes and Temples*, 2 vols (New Orleans, 1926–7)

P. Becquelin and C. F. Baudez: *Toniná, une cité maya du Chiapas (Mexique)*, 3 vols (Mexico City, 1979–82)

P. Mathews: *Toniná: Corpus of Maya Hieroglyphic Inscriptions*, vi/1 (Cambridge, MA, 1983)

CLAUDE-FRANÇOIS BAUDEZ

Tonitza, Nicolae (N.) (*b* Bârlad, 13 April 1885; *d* Bucharest, 26 Feb 1940). Romanian painter, draughtsman, illustrator and writer. He studied at the National Academy of Fine Arts in Iași (1902–7), the Akademie der Bildenden Künste in Munich (1908–9), under Hugo von Habermann, and in Paris (1909–10) in the studios of the painters Edmond Aman-Jean and Pierre Laprade. He held numerous exhibitions in Romania and abroad. He taught Byzantine decorative art, painting and drawing at the Academy of Sculpture and Painting, Bucharest (1929), and he was a professor and President of the Iași National Academy of Fine Arts (1933–40). He began working as a graphic artist from 1908, contributing to over 40 periodicals, sketches, drawings and cartoons, as well as reviews and polemical pieces. He decorated 13 churches, and he also wrote and illustrated several books.

Tonitza's early graphic work was mostly political and social in inspiration, in the style of such artists as Olaf Gulbransson, Honoré Daumier and Théophile-Alexandre Steinlen. In the course of time Tonitza achieved a personal style characterized by concision, versatility and elegance in line, with large-scale simplification and with a typical use of decorative accent. Such features were later also integrated into his paintings, following his gradual discarding of the academicism inspired by the Munich School. His palette, initially almost entirely dominated by brownish hues, eventually became lighter, with brighter tones dominated by ochre, yellow, burnt umber and shades of gold interspersed with cobalt and ultramarine. Tonitza's personal style became most apparent in his series of children's portraits, with their characteristically wide, melancholy eyes dominating the entire composition; his series of female nudes and torsos, which display a sensuality full of light, grace and candour, are also distinctive. Portraits of women and children are the main themes of his paintings, but other favourite subjects include still-lifes and panoramic landscapes frequently viewed from an elevated position. His last works, which show his attraction to the beauties of the Black Sea landscapes, have a charming combination of a calm and a sunny, Oriental atmosphere.

BIBLIOGRAPHY

I. Jianu: *Tonitza* (Bucharest, 1945)
K. H. Zambaccian: *N. Tonitza* (Bucharest, 1955)
P. Comarnescu: *N. N. Tonitza* (Bucharest, 1962)
B. Brezianu: 'Les Visages des enfants sont aussi des fleurs', *J. Genève* (15–16 Oct 1966)
——: *Tonitza* (Bucharest, 1967)
Irina Fortunescu: *N. N. Tonitza: Corespondeta 1906–1939* (Bucharest, 1978)
B. Brezianu: *N. N. Tonitza* (Bucharest, 1986)

BARBU BREZIANU

Tonjae. *See* SŎNG SE-CH'ANG.

Tonks, Henry (*b* Solihull, 9 April 1862; *d* London, 8 Jan 1937). English painter and draughtsman. He came to painting from a successful surgical career. From 1887 he studied at Westminster School of Art under Frederick Brown, and in 1891 exhibited his first paintings at the NEW ENGLISH ART CLUB, which he supported all his life. In 1892 he became an anatomy demonstrator at the London Hospital Medical School in order to be free to devote more time to painting. In 1893 he finally abandoned medicine on being invited to join the staff of the Slade School of Art in London, where he taught until 1930, succeeding Brown as Professor in 1919. His overriding concern with draughtsmanship and the structure of the body was apparent in his programme of copying from the Antique, from prints and from life; however, he saw this discipline as the basis for developing each artist's individuality. He influenced such students as Augustus John, Stanley Spencer, Wyndham Lewis, Mark Gertler and Rex Whistler. At the Slade he originated 'Tonking', a method of removing excess oil from canvas with newspaper, which was taught in art schools into the 1950s.

Tonks was himself a fine draughtsman whose knowledge of anatomy complemented his fascination with light effects. His mature works, such as *Spring Days* (1928; London, Tate), combine expressive manipulation of forms with pure, bright colour, while retaining an attraction for implicit anecdote. This led him to deplore the influence of Roger Fry and Post-Impressionism. During World War I he made pastel drawings of wounded soldiers for use in plastic surgery, and painted the large *Advanced Dressing Station in France: 1918* (London, Imp. War Mus.), a government commission. His other commissions include *Founders' Murals* (1922) for University College, London. After retiring from the Slade he continued to defend craftsmanship and observation against modernism as represented by Fry, and he summarized this in a polemical article for *The Times* (1932).

WRITINGS

'Notes from Wander-years', *Artwork*, v/20 (1929), pp. 213–35
'Fifty Years, the Vicissitudes of Art: New Words for Old Ideas', *The Times* (2 March 1932)

BIBLIOGRAPHY

J. Hone: *The Life of Henry Tonks* (London, 1939)
Henry Tonks and the 'Art of Pure Drawing' (exh. cat., ed. L. Morris; Norwich, Sch. A. Mus., 1985)

JUSTINE HOPKINS

Tonnancour, Jacques (Godefroy) de (*b* Montreal, 3 Jan 1917). Canadian painter and writer. He studied painting briefly in the late 1930s at the Ecole des Beaux-Arts, Montreal, and under Goodridge Roberts at the Art Association of Montreal; his early works, mostly landscapes, were strongly influenced by Roberts, Paul-Emile Borduas and Alfred Pellan. In their decorative qualities his paintings of the 1940s, chiefly figure studies and still-lifes (e.g. *Black Table and Rubber Plant*, 1948; Toronto, A.G. Ont.), bear strong similarities to those of Matisse, whose work, with that of Picasso, influenced him. In 1948 de Tonnancour assisted Pellan in forming the short-lived PRISME D'YEUX group in opposition to Les Automatistes. De Tonnancour's restless experimentation with a variety of styles led to a period of artistic crisis from 1950 to 1955, during which he painted little. His interest in landscape was reawakened after a trip in 1956 across northern Ontario to Vancouver. From the late 1950s he produced an extensive series of landscapes of Georgian Bay, Ontario, and the Laurentians, which became progressively simplified; by 1960 he began using a squeegee to allow further abstraction (e.g. *At the Foot of the Mountain*, 1963; U. Toronto, Hart House). In the mid-1960s he turned to producing schematized relief panels in rust, ochre, grey and black, such as *Totemic Figure* (1968; Imperial Oil priv. col., see Duval, p. 96), and he subsequently continued to work with new methods and techniques, producing a series of images of apparently fossilized animals. He also executed several mural commissions in Montreal (e.g. Dow Planetarium, 1966; Université de Montréal, 1968).

WRITINGS

Roberts (Montreal, 1944)

BIBLIOGRAPHY

De Tonnancour: A Retrospective (exh. cat. by D. Shadbolt and R. Simmins, Vancouver, A.G., 1966)
J. Folch-Ribas: *Jacques de Tonnancour: Le Signe et le temps* (Montreal, 1971)
P. Duval: *Four Decades: The Canadian Group of Painters and their Contemporaries, 1930–1970* (Toronto, 1972)

Les Mondes de Jacques de Tonnancour (exh. cat., Montreal, U. Québec, Gal. UQAM, 1985)

ALEXANDRA PEL

Tonne, Jehan de la. *See* TOOLNE, JAN VAN DER.

Tooke, Brian. *See* TUKE, BRIAN.

Tooling. Any work or ornamentation carried out with tools. The term is widely used, from the process of smoothing and finishing a stone block with a chisel (*see* STONE (i), §II) to removing the roughness and blemishes on metalwork after casting. When employed in the sense of decorating metalwork with punches and gravers, the process is also called chasing (*see* METAL, §V). Tooling also describes the process of using heated tools to impress decoration and lettering on to the covers of books or leather (*see* LEATHER, §2(ii)).

□

Toolne [Thoolne]**, Jan van der** [Jonne, Jehan de la] (*fl* c. 1450–64). Netherlandish silversmith. His only surviving work is a silver bust of a man (Bruges, Gruuthusemus.), which can be attributed to him from a document of 1463–4 in the accounts of the Bruges Franc, the autonomous countryside around the city of Bruges. A Pieter van der Gote was sentenced by the court of the Franc to have this bust made at his expense, and it was exhibited in the courtroom of the Franc as an example of justice. In 1458 van der Toolne made two silver basins for Philip the Good, Duke of Burgundy, which the Duke offered as a present for the baptism of his godchild, the son of his adviser Louis de Gruuthuse. In 1459–60 Jan delivered two silver basins to the city government of Bruges, which were presented to Pierre Bladelin, receiver general of the Burgundian court, on the occasion of the consecration of the church in Middelburg, which he had founded. In the same year, van der Toolne also made a silver cup for the city, to be presented to Simon du Carrest, secretary and registrar of the Council of Flanders. In 1460–61, Jan was paid for having repaired some ritual objects from the chapel of the Bruges aldermen. When Guillaume Fillastre made his first official visit to Bruges as the new bishop of the diocese of Tournai in 1461–2, he received a gilt mug, commissioned by the city from van der Toolne.

BIBLIOGRAPHY
M. P. J. Martens: 'Een Gerechtigheidsbuste in het Gruuthusemuseum aan een Brugs Zilversmid van de 15de eeuw toegeschreven' [A justice court bust in the Gruuthusemuseum, and a Bruges silversmith of the 15th century], *Jb. Stad Brugge Stedl. Mus.* (1989–90), pp. 235–42
MAXIMILIAAN P. J. MARTENS

Toorop. Dutch family of artists.

(1) Jan [Johannes] **(Theodorus) Toorop** (*b* Purworedjo, Java, 20 Dec 1858; *d* The Hague, 3 March 1928). He moved to the Netherlands in 1872 and took a course in drawing at the Polytechnische School in Delft (1876–9). He also studied at the Rijksakademie voor Beeldende Kunsten in Amsterdam (1880–82) and at the Ecole des Arts Décoratifs in Brussels (1882–5). In Amsterdam he joined the St Lukas Society, and in Belgium he was a founder-member of Les XX in 1884. Although he had

met Jozef Israëls in 1880 and respected the style of the Hague school, he was more attracted by what he saw in Brussels, particularly work by French artists. His portraits of 1884 are painted in an Impressionist style. With other members of Les XX he trained himself in *plein-air*; he learnt from James Ensor how to apply colours with a palette knife and how to use white with the same intensity as other colours. His style, however, remained austere and his scenes of workmen show a sensitive realism reminiscent of Gustave Courbet's work, for example *Respect for the Dead* (1884; priv. col., see 1978 Kröller-Müller exh. cat., p. 8).

From 1884 Toorop's portraits, interiors, street scenes and landscapes all reflected the prevailing social problems. In his painting he tried to depict real situations with undertones of a universal powerlessness against illness, death, temptation and destructive power. From 1885 he painted bright, colourful landscapes using a pointillist technique, such as *Bulbfields near Oegstgeest* (1885; The Hague, Gemeentemus.). He continued using a personal form of this technique until 1908, not only for symbolic landscapes but also for portraits. In later years his technique tended towards a divisionism of short, powerful brushstrokes, mostly in primary colours.

With his receptive and unbridled artistic nature Toorop felt naturally at home in the non-committal society of the avant-garde. Impressed by a visit to the industrial region of Borinage in Belgium, he became a passionate socialist and developed an interest in literature; after reading works by Maurice Maeterlinck (1862–1949) and Emile Verhaeren, he adopted Symbolism from *c.* 1890, for example in his large drawing *The Three Brides* (780×980 mm, 1893; Otterlo, Rijksmus. Kröller-Müller). In the Symbolist works of the early 1890s he personified the elements of good and evil. Positive and negative powers can be identified in works such as *Song of the Times* (1893; Otterlo, Rijksmus. Kröller-Müller; see fig.). By letting the forms overlap in this work he created only the slightest suggestion of depth; the monumental figures are placed side by side over the length of the surface in a flat, linear Art Nouveau background. He extended the light beams from the auras surrounding the figures beyond the edge of the image and incised the lines into the frame, so that their radiation could be 'felt'. The floating women with wavy hair and blowing draperies, whose stylized shapes may have been borrowed from the Javanese shadow theatre puppets, are typically Art Nouveau. The motif of the opposed forces of good and evil personifed reveals his knowledge of Indonesian culture, which had had such a profound influence on him in his childhood. His Symbolist work, chiefly executed in pencil, black crayon and coloured chalk, was dominated by powerful draughtsmanship. He used geometrical perspective to create spaces, which he filled with fantastic, mysterious vegetation and with figures.

Symbolism also proved an appropriate form of expression for Toorop's cover designs, vignettes, book illustrations and posters. For the catalogue cover of his first exhibition in the Haagsche Kunstkring, which he had founded with Théophile de Bock in 1892, he made a Symbolist lithograph, *Knight in Front of the Gateway* (1892; The Hague, Gemeentemus.). Besides the Symbolist images he continued to draw portraits and to paint landscapes.

Jan Toorop: *Song of the Times*, chalks and blacklead with highlights on dark paper, 320×585 mm, 1893 (Otterlo, Rijksmuseum Kröller-Müller)

He depicted the life of labourers in a series of drawings for an album about the work in the Gouda candle factory (1904; original drawings in Amsterdam, Stedel. Mus.). In the last of three ceramic tableaux that he made for the Koopmansbeurs in Amsterdam (1.4×3 m, 1903–5), his first monumental commission, he placed the figure of the labourer in a biblical setting. His work increasingly became the expression of an outlook on life that he found confirmed by Catholicism. In 1905 Toorop and his daughter (2) Charley Toorop were both baptized into the Catholic Church. Thereafter he painted primarily religious scenes with concrete symbolism, and portraits, often of clergymen. In 1906–7 he joined a Catholic society of artists called De Violier (The Gillyflower), which aimed at a renewal of Roman art and was especially interested in the theories of the Beuroner Kunstschule of Dom Desiderius Lenz (1832–1918). From the manuscript of a lecture given *c.* 1911 it is known that Toorop was sympathetic to Lenz's idea of producing Christian art based on geometrical structures. In 1913 he used a restrained geometrical pattern for the *Apostle's Window* in the St Jozefskerk in Nijmegen, the most famous of the few monumental commissions he was given by the Catholic Church. After 1916 he produced a number of devotional prints, which the public preferred to the industrial pictures then available and which were reproduced repeatedly either individually or in magazines.

After 1900 Toorop's growing interest in decorative arts, stimulated by the British Arts and Crafts Movement, gradually led him to replace ornamental shapes with solid, more concrete forms. He transposed the geometrical designs of his stained-glass work to religious scenes in crayon, creating powerful linear compositions in which the only naturalistic element would, for example, be a head, as in *Christ Guiding the Souls* (1914; The Hague, Gemeentemus.). He attached as much importance to the drawn as to the painted portraits. He was a sharp observer and worked out his portraits in detail. He followed traditional forms of representation, rendering his sitters in a frontal pose or in profile, or in half-profile or full-length, three-quarter-length or head-and-shoulders. From *c.* 1910 he accentuated facial features by means of angular lines and an expressive use of colour. In spite of the rather geometrical style of his later works, each one still conveys a sense of mystical inspiration and of sensitive gravity, which in combination with his complex imagination made him a difficult artist to imitate. Even during his lifetime he was regarded by the Dutch as one of the most progressive Catholic artists of his day.

BIBLIOGRAPHY
R. Siebelhoff: *The Early Development of Jan Toorop, 1879–1892* (diss., U. Toronto, 1973)
Jan Toorop: De Nijmeegse jaren, 1906–1918 (exh. cat. by H. van der Grinten and P. Thoben, Nijmegen, Mus. Commanderie St Jan, 1978)
J. Th. Toorop: De jaren 1885–1910 (exh. cat. by V. Hefting, Otterlo, Kröller-Müller, 1978)
L. M. Reyman: *Selectieve bibliografie van catalogi, boeken, tijdschriftartikelen en voordrachten* [Selective bibliography of catalogues, books, articles and public lectures] (The Hague, 1981)
V. Hefting: *Jan Toorop, en kennismaking* [Jan Toorop, an acquaintance] (Amsterdam, 1989)
Jan Toorop (1858–1928) (exh. cat. by V. Hefting, ed. E. Bergvelt; The Hague, Gemeentemus., 1989)

The Age of van Gogh: Dutch Painting, 1880–1895 (exh. cat., ed. R. Bionda, C. Blotkamp and others; Glasgow, Burrell Col.; Amsterdam, Van Gogh Mus.; 1991)

I. Gerards and E. van Uitert: *Jan Toorop: Symbolisme in de kunst* (The Hague, 1994)

ANNEKE E. WIJNBEEK

(2) Charley [Annie Caroline Pontifex] **Toorop** (*b* Katwijk, 24 March 1891; *d* Bergen, 6 Nov 1955). Daughter of (1) Jan Toorop. She was self-taught as an artist and began to paint in 1909. Her early works are luministic. While she was living in Bergen (1912–15) she painted in a Cubist and Expressionist style. She painted landscapes (of the province of Zeeland and Bergen), figures (her children, friends and portrait commissions) and self-portraits. Also during this period she exhibited at the Moderne Kunstkring and at De Onafhankelijken ('The Independents') in Amsterdam. Between 1915 and 1919 she lived in Laren, Utrecht and Amsterdam. From 1919 to 1921 she frequently stayed in Paris, where she associated with Piet Mondrian.

In 1922 P. L. Kramer built a studio-house, De Vlerken ('The wings'), for her in Bergen. In the same year she travelled to the industrial region of Borinage in Belgium, where she worked in the style of Vincent van Gogh. At this time she began to develop a social-realist style of painting. In 1924–5 she made portraits of psychiatric patients. From 1926 until 1930 she stayed in Amsterdam, where she produced many works on city themes. Through the film maker Joris Ivens (1898–1989) she was influenced by film. In 1928 and 1929 she organized the exhibitions *Architectuur Schilderkunst Beeldhouwkunst* in the Stedelijk Museum, Amsterdam. In 1930–31 she lived in Paris.

Toorop settled permanently in Bergen in 1932. She painted *The Friends' Meal* (Rotterdam, Mus. Boymans–van Beuningen), a group portrait of friends and children, including artists and architects, Gerrit Thomas Rietveld, John Rädecker (1885–1956), Edgar Fernhout, Pyke Koch, Eva Besnyö and the poet Adriaan Roland Holst in 1932–3. Towards the end of the 1930s her work became more lyrical. Between 1940 and 1945 it was heavily influenced by the events of World War II. After the war she painted numerous still-lifes, for example *Still-life with Clogs* (1949; Otterlo, Rijksmus. Kröller-Müller). From 1941 until 1950 she worked on *The Three Generations* (Rotterdam, Mus. Boymans–van Beuningen), in which she depicted herself, a sculpture of her father and her son Edgar Fernhout in her studio.

BIBLIOGRAPHY

Charley Toorop, 1891–1955 (exh. cat.; Utrecht, Cent. Mus.; Stuttgart, Würtemberg. Kstver.; 1982)

Modern Dutch Painting (exh. cat.; Athens, N.G., 1983)

JOHN STEEN

Töpffer. Swiss family of artists.

BIBLIOGRAPHY

D. Plan: 'Les Töpffer du Musée de Genève', *Nos anciens et leurs oeuvres* (Geneva, 1912), pp. 85–106

(1) Adam-Wolfgang Töpffer (*b* Geneva, 20 May 1766; *d* Morillon, nr Geneva, 10 Aug 1847). Painter, caricaturist and engraver. He trained as an engraver in Lausanne and while there illustrated Horace-Bénédict de Saussure's *Voyage dans les Alpes* (Geneva, 1779) in 1786. He studied under Joseph-Benoît Suvée in Paris (1789–91) and was influenced by Jean-Louis Demarne. On his return to Geneva Töpffer went on painting expeditions with Pierre-Louis De La Rive; these studies of the environs of the city inspired his best work. In 1796 he exhibited caricatures at the Salon in Geneva and from 1804 to 1807 was in Paris, where he was Drawing Master to Josephine Bonaparte. From 1810 he concentrated on painting such scenes from local village life as *Open-air Sermon* (*c.* 1810; Geneva, Mus. Rath). His anecdotal, animated landscapes were very popular not only in Switzerland but also in France, where he exhibited at the Salons of 1804 and 1812 in Paris. He won a gold medal at the latter Salon for the contemporary history painting *Re-establishment of Religion in France after the Revolution* (1811; Geneva, Mus. A. & Hist.), a subject he had first treated in 1803 (versions, Geneva, Mus. Rath; Lyon, Mus. B.-A.). In 1816 he visited England, where he exhibited at the Royal Academy. Under the influence of English painting his work became more colourful, vigorous and economical. He also admired Hogarth's work and emulated his style in his own political caricatures (e.g. *La Planche appartient à M. Frédéric Raisin*, 1817). On his return to Geneva in 1816 he began to produce such sparse, sober and balanced paintings as *View of Mont Blanc* (Geneva, Mus. A. & Hist.). After a visit to Italy in 1824, he was inspired to do quick sketches of city life on the streets of Geneva. He was the most comprehensive recorder of the city and its surroundings of any 19th-century Genevese artist.

BIBLIOGRAPHY

SKL

C. Dubois-Melly: *Töpffer le peintre* (Geneva, 1857)

R. Loche: 'Une Fête champêtre d'Adam-Wolfgang Töpffer (1766–1847)', *Genava*, xxxiii (1985), pp. 98–104

A. Rinuy: 'Le Dessin sous-jacent révélé par réflectographie infrarouge', *Genava*, xxxiii (1985), pp. 105–11

RENÉE LOCHE

(2) Rodolphe Töpffer (*b* Geneva, 31 Jan 1799; *d* Geneva, 8 June 1846). Writer, teacher, draughtsman and painter, son of (1) Adam-Wolfgang Töpffer. He was not able to become a professional painter due to an eye disease; therefore, after a period of study in Paris in 1819–20, he returned to Geneva and opened a boarding-house for foreign students in 1823. On holidays with these students he described their excursions in autobiographical accounts that were accompanied by drawings. These were collected and later published as *Voyages en zigzag* (1844). He was Professor of Literature at the Académie de Genève from 1832 and, as well as teaching, wrote novels and short, humorous romantic narratives. In his spare time he drew caricatures, attempting to bring out the character of each subject. They were shown to Goethe, who encouraged Töpffer to publish them; *Albums de caricatures* (1837) is accompanied by captions relating the stories of such figures as M. Crépin ('Mr Frizzy Hair'), M. Vieuxbois ('Mr Woodenhead') and le Docteur Festus ('Dr Broadbottom'). In the 1830s and 1840s some made their first appearance in serial form in various Genevan newspapers. Very popular in his lifetime, they may be seen as precursors of the comic-strip cartoon. He recorded his meditations on drawing and painting in *Essai de physiognomonie* (1845) and *Réflexions et menus propos d'un peintre genevois ou essai sur le beau dans les arts* (1872). His few paintings are mostly local landscapes done in a romantic style (e.g. *Landscape near Meillerie*, 1841; Geneva, Mus. A. & Hist.).

WRITINGS

P. Cailler and H. Cailler, eds: *Oeuvres complètes*, 26 vols (Geneva, 1943–)
E. Wiese, ed., trans. and intro.: *Enter the Comics: Rodolphe Töpffer's Essay on Physiognomy and the True Story of Monsieur Crépin* (Lincoln, NE, 1965)

BIBLIOGRAPHY

SKL
P. Chaponnière: *Caricatures töpffériennes* (Neuchâtel, 1941)
G. Corleis: 'Die Bildergeschichten des Genfer Zeichners Rodolphe Töpffer, 1799–1846', *Ein Beitrag zur Entstehung der Bildergeschichte im 19. Jahrhundert* (Munich, 1973)
D. Kunzle: *The History of the Comic Strip: The Nineteenth Century* (Berkeley, 1990)
Töpffer, l'invention de la bande dessinée: Textes réunis et présentés par Thierry Groensteen et Benoît Peeters Collection Savoir: Sur l'art (Paris, 1994)

JACQUES DROIN

Topiary. Art of cutting or training trees and shrubs into decorative, sometimes fantastic, forms. The term is derived from *opus topiarium* (Lat.: ornamental gardening), by which Pliny the Elder (*Natural History* XII.xiii) meant a wide repertory of garden activities; subsequent misinterpretation led to its identification solely with the art of shaping trees and shrubs. Pliny also described this particular activity, however: he noted how cypress trees were 'clipped and trained to form hedge-rows, or . . . thinned and lengthened out in the various designs . . . which represent scenes of hunting, fleets and various other objects'. He credited Gaius Matius with the invention of clipping arbours 'within the last 80 years' (i.e. towards the end of the 1st century BC). In Roman gardens trees were sometimes even clipped into the shapes of letters, for example so as to spell out the name of the gardener.

Interest in ancient Roman gardening (as described by Pliny) led to a revival of topiary in the 15th century, although the complexity of patterns then in use has been adduced as evidence for the lingering influence of a medieval tradition in which plants were trained on frames. By the second half of the 16th century, the garden at the Palazzo Rucellai in Florence, for example, displayed a collection of trees trained into 'spheres, porticos, temples, vases . . . giants, men, women, warriors, a harpy, philosophers, Popes, Cardinals'; indeed, human and architectural figures had already appeared in the woodcuts that illustrate Francesco Colonna's *Hypnerotomachia Poliphili* (Venice, 1499). During the 16th century the fashion for topiary spread throughout Europe, and in northern Europe especially gardeners employed a wider range of plants— juniper and rosemary among them—than had been used by the Romans. Hans Vredeman de Vries was the first designer to publish garden pattern books, producing illustrated designs for covered walkways and pavilions in his *Hortorum viridariorumque* (1583); topiary played a prominent role in these Mannerist inventions of his. Human and animal forms continued to be popular, though from the late 16th century onwards many writers, for example Sir Francis Bacon (who asserted that such 'images

Topiary work in the Yew Garden, Elvaston Castle, Derbyshire, designed by William Barron, 1830s; engraving from James Veitch & Sons: *A Manual of the Coniferae* (London, 1881)

... be for children'), urged that designs should be greatly simplified. Bacon called instead for further development in the use of architectural forms (he particularly liked pyramids and columns), anticipating the use of topiary to create the forms of entire buildings. Later in the 17th century, what John Evelyn was to call 'hortulan architecture' became an important component of the parterre in France: A.-J. Dezallier d'Argenville recommended cutting and pleaching so as to create galleries and porticos in a 'rustic order' of architecture. In the early 18th century Alexander Pope and others mocked sculptural topiary misleadingly labelling it a Dutch importation into England, and as emphasis on Nature rather than on Art in the garden increased during the century, topiary fell from fashion, first in England and later on the Continent.

A tentative revival occurred in England in the early 19th century: neglected topiary gardens, such as the late 17th-century one at Levens Hall, Cumbria, were restored, while the landscape gardener Humphry Repton and others designed fresh schemes for revivalist gardens. At Elvaston Castle, Derbys, in the 1830s William Barron (1805–91) created a series of hedge-enclosed gardens in which architectural effects, ranging from walls and buttresses to columns, plinths and finials, were imitated in topiary (see fig.). The subsequent publicity given to Barron's work brought architectural topiary back into favour in England, and Lawrence Johnston's example at Hidcote, Glos (laid out from 1907), renewed interest in it in the 20th century. Initially, the more sculptural forms of topiary met with greater resistance, but even these were becoming popular by 1900, promoted by such architects as J. D. Sedding and Reginald Blomfield. The idealistic rhetoric concerning 'Nature', which was strongly associated with the *jardin anglais*, had delayed a parallel renewal of enthusiasm for topiary in France and elsewhere on the Continent, but by 1900 a revival of the Baroque style of André Le Nôtre brought the geometric forms of the late 17th century back into favour.

The popularity of sculptural topiary in Edwardian England was such that specialist nurserymen flourished, as did H. J. Cutbush and Joseph Cheal (who created the topiary chessmen at Hever Castle, Kent, following the purchase of Hever by William Waldorf Astor in 1903), while Nathaniel Lloyd's *Garden Craftsmanship in Yew and Box* (1927) was the first practical manual in English (much of the topiary designed after 1912 by Lloyd (1867–1933) at his own garden, Great Dixter, E. Sussex, still survives). Commercial topiary was dying out by the end of the 1930s, but further recovery of interest began in the 1970s.

BIBLIOGRAPHY

H. Vredeman de Vries: *Hortorum viridariorumque elegantes et multiplicis formae* (Antwerp, 1583)
F. Bacon: 'Of Gardens', *Essays* (London, 1597)
——: *Sylva sylvarum* (London, 1626)
A.-J. Dézallier d'Argenville: *La Théorie et la pratique du jardinage* (Paris, 1709)
A. Pope: 'Catalogue of Greens', *The Guardian*, clxxiii (29 Sept 1713)
C. H. Curtis and W. Gibson: *The Book of Topiary* (London, 1904)
N. Lloyd: *Garden Craftsmanship in Yew and Box* (London, 1927)
M. Hadfield: *Topiary and Ornamental Hedges* (London, 1971)
B. Elliott: *Victorian Gardens* (London, 1986)

BRENT ELLIOTT

Topino, Charles (*b* Paris, 1742; *d* Paris, 13 Dec 1803). French cabinetmaker. He was the son of a Parisian cabinetmaker and was an independent workman before becoming a *maître-ébéniste* on 14 July 1773. He specialized in marquetry, in particular Chinese-style figures, trophies, still-lifes and flower garlands (e.g. Baltimore, MD, Mus. A.). He also used veneers embellished with bronze mounts depicting such subjects as vases on a terrace or children playing with a cat (e.g. New York, Met.). He was also a dealer in ready-made marquetry motifs. He produced very few pieces of furniture, preferring to buy them from colleagues, decorate them and then sell them to the most famous cabinetmakers or *marchand-merciers*. A large number of small and prettily decorated pieces of furniture bear his signature (e.g. New York, Met.; Cincinnati, OH, A. Mus.; Detroit, MI, Inst. A.). He was declared bankrupt in 1789.

BIBLIOGRAPHY

J. Viaux: *Bibliographie du meuble (Mobilier civil français)*, 2 vols (Paris, 1966–88)
G. de Bellaigue: 'Charles Topino (1742–1803)', 'Möbelkunst und Luxusmarkt im 18. Jahrhundert', *Wissenschaftliches Symposium: Erlangen, 1981*

JEAN-DOMINIQUE AUGARDE,
JEAN NÉRÉE RONFORT

Topography. Term for the description, mapping or other representation of the features of a given area. The term is associated with large-scale maps that show both the natural and artificial features of a terrain, although some geographers restrict its use to relief features only. In art-historical terms, it is also closely associated with certain descriptive genres of landscape and townscape views, as represented in paintings, drawings and prints.

1. Mapping. 2. Descriptive art.

1. MAPPING. Since the mid-1970s historians of cartography have become increasingly interested in the concepts involved in mapping; the relation of maps to certain genres of art; and the mapping activities of cultures outside the Western canon, which were previously unexplored or marginalized. Topographical maps form an important part of this research (others being celestial, cosmographical, political etc; *see also* MAP), since they can be regarded as both reflecting and shaping the perception their makers have of the terrestrial space they inhabit and travel through. The study of Asian, Islamic and prehistoric European topographical maps is proving particularly fruitful in this respect, but there are also new angles on the well-studied Western canon of maps from Ptolemy onwards. Ptolemy himself made a fundamental distinction between 'chorographic' (topographical) maps and world maps, calling the latter 'geographic'. His chorography was a representation of parts, a survey and delineation of features over an area of terrain, which did not need to show a relationship to the country or world, whereas his geography was a representation of the whole—the shape of the known world and everything in it, as it were. While Ptolemy's definition of geography could conceivably include topography, the distinction between the two concepts is echoed in the Western development of topographical maps as a more or less separate genre from world maps. This did

not necessarily stem from mapmakers consciously following Ptolemy's distinction; rather, the mapmakers built on existing traditions. For example medieval world maps (*mappae mundi*) were stylistically related to Classical world maps, while medieval topographical maps bear more resemblance to medieval building plans. A modern distinction would be between maps with physical (geographic) features and those with political boundaries of countries, but there is no longer as marked a difference in concept or style.

A historical survey of topographical representation reveals remarkably similar, sweeping changes at various points in the history of major mapmaking cultures—from China to Mexico—although not necessarily changes that became the continuous tradition in that culture. Some scholars have identified these changes in the broadest of terms as from the symbolic to the pictorial and then back to the symbolic. In some Palaeolithic rock-carvings, such as those at Mt Bego in the Italian Alps, lines and dots have been identified as paths, huts and enclosures as seen from above. It is not clear whether these were maps; the answer depends mainly on assumptions about what the function of a map is. The main function of the carvings may well have been symbolic, perhaps mystical, whereas maps are usually regarded primarily as navigational, administrative, military or generally educational aids. It is easier to regard the Palaeolithic carvings simply as topographical and, since they are views from above not from the side, as schematic and symbolic. Another example is the Tepe Gawra 'Landscape' jar (Baghdad, Iraq Mus.) dating from the 5th or 4th millennium BC, on which landscape features are rendered into linear and geometric patterns. Similarly schematic-looking 'maps', both sculptural and graphic, are still found in cultures from the south-west Pacific, notably the Marshall Islands, and in Native American and Inuit cultures.

More literal figures appeared in Mesopotamia, ancient Egypt and, before the 2nd century BC, in China, and these constitute early 'picture-maps'. Features such as buildings and trees were commonly rendered as uniform figures seen in elevation, although orientation is not at all uniform. Easily identifiable features often appear right next to more symbolic figures. The earliest known of these picture-maps is a Mesopotamian clay tablet *c*. 2500–2300 BC (Cambridge, MA, Harvard U., Semit. Mus.). Two ranges of hills are rendered on this as rows of semicircles orientated in opposition to each other; between them is a river marked as four lines running across the tablet, while towns are named and shown as circles. One Chinese military map of the 2nd century BC (Changsha, Hunan Prov. Mus.), found in Tomb 3 of the Mawangdui site, depicts an area in the Nanling Mountains (see fig. 1). In this remarkable rendition of topography, a small image of a military headquarters is easily spotted, while the host of fine lines curling in various directions are, less obviously, the mountains and rivers.

Oblique and BIRD'S-EYE VIEWS for maps, in which topographical features are depicted as if being viewed from a point in space above the terrain, are linked, particularly in European history, with artistic conventions in townscape (*see* §2 below), which themselves can be regarded as a form of mapping or, in another light,

evidence of a human compulsion to map or record one's surroundings. Quite how the bird's-eye perspective was achieved before the advent of flight is a matter for debate; there may have been surveying techniques now unknown. The fictional viewpoint in Jacopo de' Barbari's aerial *View of Venice* of 1500 (*see* VENICE, fig. 1) is an outstanding example, in which buildings are convincingly detailed. The function of such images is, again, sometimes unclear. Jacopo's woodcut is identified more with maps than with descriptive art simply because its decorative features and text are in the mapmaking tradition; however, the print was probably made more to glorify Venice than for any conventional topographical function. In many cases, however, topographical works were made for military purposes. Detailed Islamic maps of cities, such as the beautiful *Siege Plan of Belgrade* (early 16th century; Istanbul, Topkapı Pal. Lib., MS. E. 9440), were probably influenced by the prevalent use of the bird's-eye view in Italian maps.

When strictly from one perspective, the bird's-eye view is not a consistent representation of topography, since to be optically correct the features would have to tail off to the edges of the map, or suggest that they do just beyond. Another common mapmaking device in quite separate cultures was to show importance by size, so certain areas of the map, or single features, were disproportionate to the rest. The development of topographical maps, in which scale as well as orientation were consistent, was necessary for military manoeuvres and important generally as a tool of power and control. The sea-change from picture-maps to scale-maps and surveys, in fact, occurred in various cultures, even in Mesopotamia, and most certainly ancient Rome and China after the 3rd century AD, without continuing as a tradition (Harvey). The tendency towards abstraction and symbolism, rather than literal representation, thus reappears with the scale-map. The scale-map and bird's-eye map were both made in Europe during the 16th century; however, it was the scale-map that prevailed in mapping from the early 17th century, while the bird's-eye view became more associated with descriptive art. The scale-map is a scheme of topography; individual features are shown, often in great detail, but perspective is absent, and any one point on the map is plotted as if from a point directly above it. The first and foremost sense for the viewer is of perceiving the spatial relationship of topographical features to each other, while the features themselves are rendered mainly symbolically, but with literal elements. In the Western world the trend towards uniform orientation—both in north being the top of the map (even more so in world maps) and topographical features all being in one plane—shaped the prevailing modern visualization of a given part of the world as being above, below, to the left or the right of other places. Outside the Western world, topographical features were likely to be orientated more in relation to each other than to the viewer—mountain ranges in opposition to each other, trees following the curve of a river etc—until the homogenizing Western methods were adopted. An Indian map, attributed to Abdur Rahim and no later than 1836, of the *Vale of Kashmir* (London, BL) differs stylistically from the colonial British survey-maps of India, and topographical features, particularly the stylized trees, lie at different angles to the text on the map. Later refinements

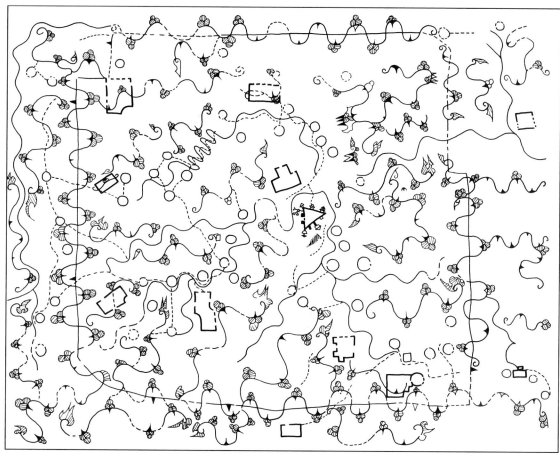

1. Topographical map of an area in the Nanling Mountains, southern China; simplified reconstruction drawing of a damaged silk map, from Tomb 3, Mawangdui site, near Changsha, 2nd century BC (Changsha, Hunan Provincial Museum)

to topographical maps included the invention of hachuring and contour lines to denote the shape of the ground.

Itineraries of routes are a further type of topographical mapping, although images are rare. In civilizations as diverse as ancient Rome and China (from at least the 3rd century AD), texts were written to guide travellers; they would describe topographical features along the route and their distance from one another (*see also* TRAVEL MANU-SCRIPTS). The few surviving examples of these as visual maps often do not resemble the shape of the countries they describe. Rather, the simple concept of the journey being a line through a terrain is rendered pictorially. Thus changes of direction are more likely to be written or marked by the presence of a compass rose than plotted spatially. The *Tabula Peutingeriana* (13th century; Vienna, Österreich. Nbib., Cod. 324) is a copy of an itinerary map from around the 3rd century AD (untraced) of principal routes through the Roman Empire, and it shows Europe in a strip 6.75 m long but only 340 mm wide. Later examples include the mid-13th century AD maps by Matthew Paris of routes through Britain, or in India the *Chahar Gulshan* ('Four gardens'; 1789; New Delhi, N. Mus.), describing routes through northern India, and a scroll map with the features on the road from Kandahar

to Delhi (*c.* 1770; London, BL, Orient. & India Office Lib.). The 'rutters' of the 16th–19th centuries were for maritime navigation, showing the itinerary of a coastline. Some, particularly a few by the Netherlandish maritime mapmaker Lucas Jansz. Waghenaer (1533/4–1606), are a poignant blend of closely observed topographical features as seen in elevation from the sea, but with the shape of the coastline as seen from above to signal the presence and extent of bays, which cannot be seen from the sea. The 20th-century equivalent of the rutters are the striplike diagrams or photographs on pilotage charts, but the development of more technological methods of maritime navigation marked the decline in sophistication of the genre. During the 1980s there was a burgeoning interest in topographical Papunya paintings (*see* ABORIGINAL AUSTRALIA, §IV, 1), in which the significant features on journeys are rendered through colour and symbolic shapes, lines and dots; these are imaginative responses to itineraries rather than navigational aids.

BIBLIOGRAPHY

A. H. Robinson and B. B. Petchenik: *The Nature of Maps: Essays Toward Understanding Maps and Mapping* (Chicago and London, 1976)
A. Bulling: 'Ancient Chinese Maps', *Expedition* (Philadelphia, 1978)

M. J. Blakemore and J. B. Harley: 'Concepts in the History of Cartography: A Review and Perspective', *Cartographica*, vii/4 (Winter 1980) [whole issue]

P. D. A. Harvey: *The History of Topographical Maps: Symbols, Pictures and Surveys* (London and New York, 1980)

R. Rees: 'Historical Links Between Cartography and Art', *Geog. Rev.*, lxx (1980), pp. 60–78

C. Delano Smith: 'The Emergence of "Maps" in European Rock Art', *Imago Mundi: Rev. Early Cartography*, 34 (1982), pp. 9–25

J. B. Harley and D. Woodward, eds: *The History of Cartography* (Chicago and London, 1987–)

D. Woodward, ed.: *Art and Cartography: Six Historical Essays* (Chicago and London, 1987)

S. Gole: *Indian Maps and Plans: From Earliest Times to the Advent of European Surveys* (New Delhi, 1989)

☐

2. DESCRIPTIVE ART. Descriptive topographical art depicts faithfully and exactly in paintings, prints or drawings an identifiable locality and its ambience, most often a building or a cluster of buildings within an urban or rural setting, or a panorama of a town or city. While this definition includes particular landscapes or isolated buildings, such as country houses as well as certain relatively unstudied works that fall outside Western art history, this section focuses on European topographical art, particularly townscape painting, which flourished between the mid-17th century and the end of the 19th. With the latter, the town or city itself—whether viewed from within, with the accent on its rivers, canals, streets or squares, or from without, with the emphasis on the panorama, the profile or the bird's-eye view—became worthy of contemplation and the subject for a work of art. The finest topographical views are, of course, appreciated and collected as works of art, but they are also documents that chronicle the growth and changing appearance of landscapes and townscapes since the Middle Ages, and they reveal contemporary values invested in the places and features depicted. Many townscape artists, moreover, sought to depict the urban experience: the relationship between the physical fabric of the city and Nature brought under control; the creation of a political, social, economic and moral order; and the interaction between transitory human activity and the relatively permanent cityscape (*see also* URBAN LIFE).

(i) Before *c.* 1650. (ii) After *c.* 1650.

(i) *Before* c. *1650.* The development of descriptive topographical art before the mid-17th century can be studied from a Europe-wide perspective, although details varied in specific countries or regions. Townscapes were not uncommon in painting by the 14th and 15th centuries, but until the early 17th century they most often served as backdrops or were imaginary. In the TRÈS RICHES HEURES of Jean, Duc de Berry (*c.* 1413–16; completed *c.* 1486; Chantilly, Mus. Condé, MS 65; *see* FRANCE, fig. 17, and LIMBOURG, DE, figs 2 and 4), and in Ambrogio Lorenzetti's three frescoes on the theme of the effects of good and bad government in the Palazzo Pubblico in Siena (1338–9; *see* SIENA, fig. 12, and LORENZETTI, (1), fig. 2) there are recognizable buildings in characteristic settings, as well as the busy life of town and countryside. Similarly, accurate Venetian townscapes function as stage sets in the series of paintings illustrating the *Miracles of the True Cross* (1500; all Venice, Accad.) by Gentile Bellini, Vittore Carpaccio and others (e.g. Bellini's *Procession of the True Cross in the*

Piazza S Marco; *see* VENICE, fig. 26). Realistic-looking but imaginary cityscapes appear in the background of such Flemish paintings as the Mérode Altarpiece (1425; New York, Cloisters) by the Master of Flémalle and in Jan van Eyck's *Virgin and Child with Chancellor Rolin* (Paris, Louvre). In works such as the *Cervus at Bethlehem* (1566; Brussels, Mus. A. Anc. Preuss. Kultbes.) Pieter Bruegel the elder and his many imitators painted fictional but representative Flemish towns. El Greco's *View and Plan of Toledo* (*c.* 1610; Toledo, Casa & Mus. El Greco) and *View of Toledo* (*c.* 1610; New York, Met.; *see* TOLEDO, §II, 2) stand almost alone as independent cityscapes.

Actual townscapes, by contrast, became popular subjects in illustrated books, maps and prints, as well as in drawings, shortly after the invention of the printing press. Venice was portrayed with reasonable accuracy by Erhard Reuwich in *Peregrinatio in terram sanctum* (1486) for Bernhard von Breydenbach (1450–97). Other volumes with panoramas or profiles of cities followed, from the *Nuremberg Chronicle* (1493) and the six-volume atlas by G. Braun and F. Hogenberg, the *Civitates orbis terrarum* (1572–1618), to the 17th-century townscapes by Matthäus Merian the elder (*see* MERIAN, (1)) and others. Contemporary maps, such as Jacopo de' Barbari's woodcut *View of Venice* (1500), were closely related to townscape traditions (*see* §1 above). Topographical prints of Roman antiquities and ruins were published by Hieronymus Cock (*see* COCK, (3)), while other merchants marketed architectural views and representations of celebrated festivals or recent events. Meanwhile, Anthonis van den Wyngaerde drew panoramas of London and Spanish cities. Other early townscapes include drawings of Nuremberg and Innsbruck by Albrecht Dürer. Such proliferation of townscapes (imaginary as well as real), reflects not only contemporary awareness of the growing number and importance of cities in Europe but also interest in the city itself and the nature of urban life.

(ii) *After* c. *1650.* The topographical townscape thrived in the Netherlands and Italy as an independent motif during the 17th and 18th centuries (*see also* TOWNSCAPE). Later developments in topographical art took place mainly in Britain and France up to the end of the 19th century, when, following the proliferation of photographic images, the making of such images virtually ceased.

(a) *The Netherlands and Italy.* Dutch townscape and architectural painting flourished between the 1650s and *c.* 1700 within a specific historical and cultural context. Emblematic of Dutch prosperity after independence from Spain in 1609 was the tidy appearance of the Republic's expanding towns and cities, with their paved streets, canals and substantial but not ostentatious public and private buildings. Taste for views of such towns as Haarlem, Amsterdam and Delft expressed not just national or civic pride but also quiet satisfaction with the creation of an orderly and aesthetically pleasing built environment and the common political, economic and religious values it represented. As with Dutch traditions in painting church interiors, the topographical townscape, with its confident, serene and detailed description of a harmonious world planned and constructed by man, accordingly mirrored

Dutch perceptions of their urban environment (*see also* ARCHITECTURAL PICTURES, §2). Gerrit Berckheyde, for example, devoted himself almost exclusively to topographical views of cities. His *Grote Markt and the Grote Kerk at Haarlem* (1674; London, N.G.; for illustration *see* BERCKHEYDE, (2)) shows not only elegant buildings harmoniously arranged around an open square but also characteristic human activity integrated with the built environment. The view and the buildings chosen suggest intersecting political, commercial and religious themes, while the painting itself embodies the values of order and decorum. Jan van der Heyden was more influential than Berckheyde but less topographically accurate.

The Italian VEDUTA, associated primarily with Canaletto and his nephew Bernardo Bellotto, as well as with Luca Carlevaris, Michele Giovanni Marieschi and Francesco Guardi, dominated topographical art during much of the 18th century. Indeed, so enduring is the achievement of Canaletto, the finest of the *veduta* painters, that he preserved not only the physical appearance but also the urban ambience of Venice to such a degree and with such captivating light that Arthur Young, an English traveller, measured the city he observed in 1788 against the painted image and found the former wanting. Guardi, on the other hand, often discarded exact topographical descriptions for subjective cityscapes filled with a nervous, almost threatening atmosphere. Unlike the Dutch townscape painters, who celebrated for their compatriots the achievements and values of Dutch urban life, the Italian *veduta* painters worked at a time of political and economic decline, often representing the splendour of a Venice past its prime for those taking Grand Tours, frequently British aristocrats. Examples of CAPRICCIO by Canaletto, Guardi, Giovanni Paolo Panini and others provide a variant of topography, for they create a fanciful and fictitious urban environment composed of arbitrarily juxtaposed topographical representations of actual structures. More in the Dutch tradition was Bellotto, who painted Dresden and other cities for princely patrons. The topographical detail in his Warsaw paintings (*see* BELLOTTO, BERNARDO, fig. 2) assisted in rebuilding the war-ravaged city in the 20th century.

(b) Great Britain. The topographical tradition was perhaps more varied in Great Britain than elsewhere. Commonplace after the 16th century, and certainly after Canaletto's stay in the 1740s and 1750s, are panoramic views of London and the Thames, but also conspicuous are views of country estates, ruined abbeys or castles set in a landscape. Interest in topography accelerated after the 1750s, stimulated by the vogue for THE SUBLIME and Picturesque, and for travel, by a delight in the native English landscape and in medieval antiquities, by patriotic sentiments aroused by the French Revolutionary and Napoleonic wars, and by the transformation of the countryside by the Industrial Revolution, which inspired pictures of railway viaducts and industrial towns. During the next century British artists and publishers produced not only countless watercolours, drawings, prints and illustrated books but also most of the finest examples of the 19th-century tradition of highly commercial, large-scale, walk-in entertainments, such as the PANORAMA and the DIORAMA.

It was at the end of the 18th century that THOMAS GIRTIN and J. M. W. TURNER transformed English watercolour painting. If Girtin's *Peterborough Cathedral* (1794; Oxford, Ashmolean; see fig. 2) or *Rievaulx Abbey* (*c.* 1800; London, V&A) indicate a predilection for antiquities, his *Eidometropolis* (1801–2), a large-scale, 360° topographical panorama of London exhibited in Wrigley's Great Rooms, Spring Gardens (untraced), and a series of soft-ground etchings of Paris demonstrate a fascination with the contemporary city. Topographical watercolours by Turner include Picturesque views of Tintern Abbey and Lincoln Cathedral. Later watercolourists in this tradition include David Roberts, Thomas Shotter Boys and Samuel Prout, the latter much praised by John Ruskin. Topographical plate books and prints, often engravings or lithographs made from the watercolours of Turner, Roberts, Boys, Prout and others, dealt with travel, the countryside, the townscape and antiquities. Among the more celebrated are Roberts's six-volume *Holy Land, Syria, Idumea, Arabia, Egypt and Nubia* (1842–9; for illustration *see* PHILAE), Thomas Malton's two-volume *Picturesque Tour through the Cities of London and Westminster* (1792–1801), Boys's *London as it is* (1842) and John Sell Cotman's *Architectural Antiquities of Norfolk* (1818). Meanwhile, Boys revolutionized lithographic printing with his chromolithographs in *Picturesque Architecture in Paris, Ghent, Antwerp, Rouen etc* (1839). Enthusiasm for topography spread well beyond affluent collectors of watercolours, prints or plate books. The DIORAMA, which originated in Paris in 1821–2,

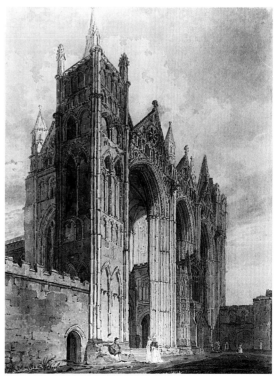

2. Topographical painting by Thomas Girtin: *Peterborough Cathedral*, watercolour, 382×288 mm, 1794 (Oxford, Ashmolean Museum)

supplemented the large-scale panorama in offering topographical views to the general public as inexpensive and instructive entertainment. Furthermore, with the invention of economical methods of printing, such periodicals as the *Illustrated London News* not only included topographical views but also provided subscribers with urban panoramas.

Views of London in the 19th century range from documentary to poetic images. Most artists depicted the modern city, and their work is characterized not by the ordered tranquillity of the Dutch townscapes but by an emphasis on frenetic commercial activity, the erection of new buildings and bridges, and streets congested with traffic. Examples include the *Opening of New London Bridge, 1831* (1832; London, Guildhall) by Clarkson Stanfield and *St Pancras Hotel and Station from Pentonville Road: Sunset* (1884; London, Mus. London) by John O'Connor (1830–89). Better known are the images by Monet, who first painted London in 1870 and 1871. He too focused on the modern city, on the new Houses of Parliament and Westminster Bridge, and on commercial bustle along the Thames; unlike the detailed and somewhat dispassionate British topographers, however, he concentrated on the effects created by buildings or lights seen through a veil of mist and fog. Monet painted a second series of London views at the turn of the century (e.g. *Houses of Parliament, Stormy Sky*, 1904, Lille, Mus. B.-A.), and in them the topography of the city virtually disappears into the fog. James McNeill Whistler was another to depict London in this way.

(c) France. The invention of photography in France during the first half of the 19th century lessened the demand there for topographical drawings, prints and paintings. Before its use became widespread, however, a French topographical tradition had developed, with its origins reaching back to the 17th-century panoramas of Paris and views of its buidings, bridges and quays in the prints of Jacques Callot and Israel Silvestre and in the paintings of Abraham de Verwer (*c.* 1600–*c.* 1650) and others. Alexandre-Jean Noël (1752–1834) and Nicolas Raguenet (1715–93) carried the panoramic tradition to the next century, while Giuseppe Canella (1788–1847), also a painter of markets and traffic along the bridges and quays of the Seine, continued into the 19th century. Other 18th-century views include the *Demolition of Houses on the Pont au Change* (*c.* 1788; Munich, Alte Pin.; see fig. 3) by Hubert Robert. During the 1820s topographical artists turned their attention to French antiquities, the rural countryside and provincial towns, often depicting the street rather than the panorama. Baron Isidore Taylor's 20-volume *Voyages pittoresques et romantiques dans l'ancienne France* (1820–78) includes among its hundreds of lithographed views of churches, abbeys and towns Richard Parkes Bonington's *Rue du Gros-Horloge in Rouen* (1824). Among painters, Corot portrayed *Chartres Cathedral* (1830; Paris, Louvre) and the *Belfry of Douai* (1871; Paris, Louvre), while his *Notre Dame and the Quay des Orfèvres* (1833; Paris, Carnavalet) depicts the Seine panorama. At mid-century, the focus of topographers shifted once again to Paris, and views by the etcher Charles Meryon and the photographer Charles Marville preserved the Old Paris destroyed during the rebuilding campaign of Napoleon III and Baron Haussmann.

The great era of European topographical art ended with the Impressionists. Before it did so, however, artists throughout Europe and the USA were inspired by the British and French traditions to depict faithfully their cities, towns and antiquities. Eduard Gaertner's panorama,

3. Topographical painting by Hubert Robert: *Demolition of Houses on the Pont au Change*, oil on canvas, 0.80×1.55 m, *c.* 1788 (Munich, Alte Pinakothek)

the six-part *View over Berlin from the Roof of the Friedrich-wedersche Church* (1834; Berlin, Schloss Charlottenburg, Schinkel-Pav.), is but one among many examples. Meanwhile, Camille Pissarro, Auguste Renoir and Monet painted the grand boulevards, gardens and railway stations of Haussmann's new Paris, depicting in addition to the city's energy, motion and ceaseless activity, its light and air. Typical is Monet's *Le Pont de l'Europe, Gare St-Lazare* (1877; Paris, Mus. Marmottan; *see* MONET, CLAUDE, fig. 2), with its image of an iron bridge obscured by smoke billowing from a steam locomotive. Such works accurately represent the cityscape and capture a sense of modern life lived within an architectural framework, although they lack the detail of earlier topographical views. By the turn of the 20th century, as Monet's late London views demonstrate, the focus of artists had shifted. The city itself, however, remained an important theme in the work of such photographers as Eugène Atget and Alfred Stieglitz.

BIBLIOGRAPHY

M. Twyman: *Lithography, 1800–1850: The Techniques of Drawing on Stone in England and France and their Application in Works of Topography* (London, 1970)
J. Links: *Townscape Painting and Drawing* (London, 1972)
The Dutch Cityscape in the 17th Century and its Sources (exh. cat., ed. C. van Lakerveld; Amsterdam, Hist. Mus., 1977)
D. Freedberg: *Dutch Landscape Prints of the Seventeenth Century* (London, 1980)
I. Nadel and F. Schwarzbach, eds.: *Victorian Artists and the City: A Collection of Critical Essays* (Elmsford, NY, 1980)
B. Grad and T. Riggs: *Visions of City and Country: Prints and Photographs of Nineteenth-century France* (exh. cat., Worcester, MA, A. Mus., 1982)
B. Adams: *London Illustrated, 1604–1851: A Survey and Index of Topographical Books and their Plates* (London, 1983)
J. Reps: *Views and Viewmakers of Urban America: Lithographs of Towns and Cities in the United States and Canada, Notes on the Artists and Publishers, and a Union Catalog of their Works, 1825–1925* (Columbia, MO, 1984)
R. Hyde: *Gilded Scenes and Shining Prospects: Panoramic Views of British Towns, 1575–1900* (exh. cat., New Haven, CT, Yale Cent. Brit. A., 1985)
B. de Montgolfier: *Le Musée Carnavalet* (Paris, 1986)
M. Warner: *The Image of London: Views by Travellers and Emigrés, 1550–1920* (exh. cat., London, Barbican A.G., 1987)
R. Kagan, ed.: *Spanish Cities of the Golden Age: The Views of Anton von den Wyngaerde* (Berkeley, CA, 1989)
Painters of Venice: The Story of the Venetian 'veduta' (exh. cat., ed. B. Aikema and B. Bakker; Amsterdam, Rijksmus., 1990)
The Impressionist and the City: Pissarro's Series Paintings (exh. cat. by R. Brettell and J. Pissarro, London, RA, 1992)

ROBERT W. BROWN

Toprak Kala. Site on the lower Amu River in Uzbekistan. It was the dynastic seat of the rulers of Khwarazm in the late 2nd century AD and the 3rd, and it appears the site remained occupied, though as a less important town, until the 6th century. Planned as a unified entity and constructed at roughly the same time, the complex comprises a fortified town (see fig. (a)), a citadel with a shrine devoted to the cult of fire (b), a palace on a high platform (c), a group of palaces and temples outside the town (d) and a large enclosure within a high earth framework, evidently for the assembly of troops and ceremonial events (e). It was excavated by the Khorasmian Expedition of the Academy of Sciences of the USSR. The high palace was explored in 1940 and 1945–50 by Sergey Tolstov and was later (1967–72) excavated by Yu. A. Rapoport. The town quarters were excavated in 1965–75 by Ye. Ye. Nerazik. The group

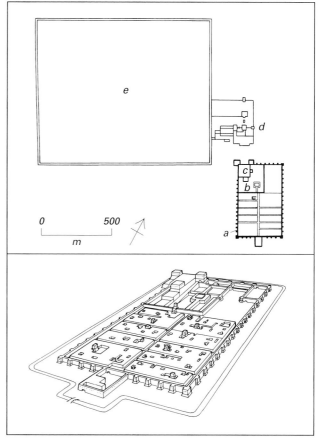

Toprak Kala, 2nd–6th centuries AD, plan and reconstruction of fortified town: (a) fortified town; (b) citadel and shrine; (c) palace on high platform; (d) palaces and temples; (e) enclosure

of palaces and temples outside the town was explored in 1976–85 under the direction of Yu. A. Rapoport. The complex is unusual in that the area occupied by palaces and temples (not including the esplanade attached to them) is larger than that containing the houses of the general population.

The basic material of construction is mud-brick (400×400×100 mm). Arched roofs predominate, and in the larger buildings joists were supported by wooden pillars on stone pedestals. Ancient Near Eastern architectural traditions are dominant. Thus the palace (see fig. (c)) is built on a truncated pyramidal base measuring 80 m square and *c.* 15 m in height. Its white exterior walls, a further 10 m high, were articulated with vertical recesses and buttresses. Within these walls (77×77 m) there were over 100 rooms, the surfaces of the platform forming the floors. Vaults of the rooms arranged along the sides of the palace supported the rooms of the upper floor (partly destr.). The Throne Hall was in the centre of the building and the Hall of Kings in the north-eastern part with an altar by its doorway. On a high dais along the walls were more than 20 large seated statues flanked by secondary figures (examples in Moscow, Mus. Orient. A.). The Hall of Dancing Masques adjoined the Throne Hall. That sanctuary also had a fire-altar in the centre and was decorated with reliefs of masked dancers (example in Moscow, Mus. Orient. A.). Three further spacious rooms contained niche-like wall altars and reliefs of investitive and triumphal scenes, griffins and deer (example of deer in Moscow, Mus. Orient. A.). The zoomorphic forms retain traces of Scythian style, but most reliefs are within the tradition of Hellenistic art. Almost all the halls were painted with depictions of deities, ruling figures, women of the court, warriors, musicians, birds, animals or diverse ornamental motifs. Figural compositions were usually placed in recesses or within frames. Wall paintings also decorated the palaces and temples outside the town. (Other finds are in St Petersburg, Hermitage.) (*See also* CENTRAL ASIA, §I, 3(ii)(c) and 4(iii)(b).)

BIBLIOGRAPHY

S. P. Tolstov: *Po sledam drevnekhorezmiyskoy tsivilizatsii* [An investigation of the civilization of ancient Khwarazm] (Moscow and Leningrad, 1948)
——: 'Les Résultats des travaux de l'expédition archéologique et ethnographique de l'Académie des Sciences de U.R.S.S. au Khorezm en 1951–1955', *A. Asiatiques*, v (1957), pp. 84–112
——: 'Dated Documents from the Toprak-kala Palace, and the Problem of the "Shaka Era" and the "Kanishka Era"', *Bib. Orient.*, xx (1963), pp. 229–38
E. E. Nerazik and Y. A. Rapoport, eds: *Gorodishche Toprak Kala* [The city site of Toprak Kala] (Moscow, 1981)
——: *Toprak-kala: Dvorets* [The palace of Toprak Kala] (Moscow, 1984)
Yu. A. Rapoport: 'The Palaces of Toprak Kala', *Bull. Asian Inst., MI*, n.s., v (1991), pp. 138–42
——: 'Out-of-town Palaces and Temples of Toprak Kala', *Vestnik Drevney Istor.* (1993)

YU. A. RAPOPORT

Toprakkale [Turk.: 'earth castle'; Rusahinili; Toprak Kale]. Site in eastern Turkey on a limestone spur of Mt Zimzim, overlooking modern Van. This Urartian citadel was built by Rusa, probably Rusa II (*reg c.* 680–*c.* 640 BC), and first attracted the attention of European scholars in 1877 when bronzes came on to the antiquities market. The ensuing British Museum excavations by Captain Emilius Clayton, Dr Raynolds and Hormuzd Rassam in 1879, although destructive, provided the first archaeological context for the previously published Urartian cuneiform inscriptions from Van. C. Lehmann-Haupt (from 1898), and subsequent Russian and Turkish expeditions followed. The principal collections of finds are in the British Museum in London, the Hermitage in St Petersburg and the Louvre in Paris.

The fortress was naturally defensible on three sides, with water brought, on the evidence of a contemporary inscription, probably from the artificial 'Lake of Rusa' (Keşiş-Göl). A rock-cut channel also brought water from a spring almost 2 km away into an enormous rock-hewn hall, with basin, drain and benches. A rock-cut spiral staircase, with 56 steps and lit by three windows, led from there into the fortress. The fortification walls are discernible only by the typically Urartian rock-cut ledges serving as base for the masonry.

To the north-east of the citadel's central square stood the temple of the Urartian god Haldi with, to the west, Lehmann-Haupt's 'terrace of the dead', the foundations of which he believed, probably erroneously, to contain thousands of human sacrifices: certainly many animals were slaughtered. Rusticated masonry was used for the temple substructure, alternating limestone and basalt blocks to give contrasting colours in a technique that was possibly introduced from north Syria. The temple of Haldi, which faced south-west and had a forecourt of large sandstone slabs, was of the Urartian square, temple-tower plan, 13.8 m (26 cubits) square overall but only 5.3 m (10 cubits) square within. Soft, white gypsum and hard stones of black, greenish and brownish tone were employed for mosaics decorating both the floor and the walls of the temple in a variety of motifs, among which concentric circles, lozenges and palmettes were popular. Large decorated discs with a central hole may have secured the feet of thrones and footstools. Fragments indicate grey stone reliefs with inlay largely in precious metals, as well as a red marble frieze depicting bulls flanking sacred trees, with decorated roundels inserted in the open areas. Stone limbs hint at the presence of statuary.

Toprakkale is one of the richest Urartian sites for metalwork, mainly in bronze and iron (the latter being abundant), comprising an assemblage of tools and especially weapons closely paralleled at Karmir Blur. Among the military bronzes the decorated shields of Rusa III (*reg c.* 610–*c.* 590 BC), with emaciated or attenuated lions, exemplify the late Urartian style and the bronzesmith's techniques of repoussé for the main forms, and engraving for the details (London, BM; see fig.). By the 7th century BC bronze was rarely used for arrowheads and the few at Toprakkale are votive offerings. Bull's head and siren cauldron attachments, such as those found at Toprakkale, have provoked much discussion on Near Eastern artistic influences and trade. However, research has largely centred on attempts to reconstruct the throne of Haldi, of which 17 bronze elements survive (Berlin, Pergamonmus.; St Petersburg, Hermitage; London, BM; Paris, Louvre); unfortunately the 19th-century excavators failed to record their context *in situ*. Mythical creatures and divine figures support the throne. In its last decades Urartu shared the taste of the 7th century BC for florid ornament and use of colour, but the fashionable proliferation of composite creatures was characteristic of Urartian rather than Assyrian art, especially in bronzes. A much simpler throne is depicted on a gold medallion showing a seated goddess and a female worshipper, perhaps the queen (Berlin, Pergamonmus.).

The storehouse cellar on the east side of the square held 25 jars, each containing 500–600 litres of wine. A silver box with a lid studded with gold nails was part of a treasure also excavated in the storehouse. From another magazine came a bronze candelabrum (h. 1.18 m; Hamburg, Mus. Kst & Gew.), inscribed in cuneiform 'from the magazine of Rusa'. A bronze plaque depicts a fortress with round-topped door, narrow windows and ornate mud-brick parapets (London, BM; *see* URARTIAN, fig. 1), comparable with those on reliefs from Kefkalesi (Adılcevaz). The temple was evidently crowned by masonry with a doubly recessed centre to each panel.

Examples from Toprakkale (e.g. London, BM) indicate that ivory-carving flourished in Urartu; although its antecedents lay in north Syria rather than Mesopotamia, parallels with Urartian bronzework show that it was largely indigenous. Seals and, predominantly, seal impressions

Toprakkale, bronze shield decorated with friezes of repoussé embossed and engraved figures of lions and bulls (detail), diam. 852 mm, *c.* 610–*c.* 590 BC (London, British Museum)

include a sealing with a cult scene depicting a solid-wheeled wagon in which stands a pole with leaves still growing. Lions, bulls, sphinxes and griffins occur frequently on seals. The faceted outline of one seal impression with at least five sides, recorded by Lehmann-Haupt, is paralleled in Neo-Babylonian Mesopotamia (Brussels, Musées Royaux A. & Hist.). Pottery included jugs in typical red polished ware ('palace ware'), imitating metal prototypes. Roped mouldings, impressed chevrons and hieroglyphic and cuneiform notations of contents are common.

BIBLIOGRAPHY
C. F. Lehmann-Haupt: *Armenien einst und jetzt*, ii/2 (Berlin, 1931), pp. 453–605
R. D. Barnett: 'The Excavations of the British Museum at Toprak Kale near Van', *Iraq*, xii (1950), pp. 1–43
——: 'The Excavations of the British Museum at Toprak Kale near Van: Addenda', *Iraq*, xvi (1954), pp. 3–22
H. Hoffmann: 'King Rusa's Candelabrum', *Illus. London News* (19 Nov 1960), pp. 896–7
A. Erzen: 'Untersuchungen in der urartäischen Stadt Toprakkale bei Van in den Jahren 1959–1961', *Archäol. Anz.*, lxxvii (1962), pp. 383–414
R. D. Barnett: 'More Addenda from Toprak Kale', *Anatol. Stud.*, xxii (1972), pp. 163–78
T. B. Forbes: *Urartian Architecture*, Brit. Archaeol. Rep. Int. Ser., clxx (Oxford, 1983)
R.-B. Wartke: *Toprakkale*, Schriften zur Geschichte und Kultur des alten Orients, xxii (Berlin, 1990)
Urartu: A Metalworking Center in the First Millennium B.C.E. (exh. cat., ed. R. Merhav; Jerusalem, Israel Mus., 1991)
R.-B. Wartke: *Urartu: Das Reich am Ararat* (Mainz, 1993)

For further bibliography *see* URARTIAN.

C. A. BURNEY

Toptani, Murad (Said) (*b* Aka, Turkey, 1865; *d* Tiranë, 11 Feb 1918). Albanian sculptor, collector and poet of Turkish birth. His family was in exile in Turkey, and he began his studies in the school of Madame Fyres (1878), finishing them in the Sultanie Lycée of Galatasaray in Istanbul (1894). Toptani's artistic work is intrinsically linked to his efforts in the struggle for Albanian independence. Works such as the bust of *Skanderbeg* (bronze, 1917; Tiranë, A.G.) reveal his realistic style, which is permeated by a naive romanticism. His patriotism and romanticism also infect his poetry. Little of his work and his rich private collection of objects of applied Albanian folk art remains, as his house and gallery in Tiranë were burnt down by the anti-patriotic forces in 1913.

BIBLIOGRAPHY
F. Hudhri: *Murad Toptani, artist dhe patriot* [Murad Toptani, artist and patriot] (Tiranë, 1978)

SULEJMAN DASHI

Toral, Mario (*b* Santiago, 12 Feb 1934). Chilean painter, printmaker and illustrator. He studied under the painter Agustín Calvo (*b* 1878) and then at the Escuela de Bellas Artes in Montevideo, Uruguay, and under Henri-Georges Adam in Paris. While living in Paris from 1950 to 1962 he familiarized himself with techniques of drawing and printmaking. On his return to Chile in 1962 he taught at the Escuela de Arte of the Universidad Católica in Santiago, but he later devoted himself exclusively to his art.

Toral worked first as a printmaker in the late 1950s and early 1960s, and he also received commissions to illustrate volumes of poetry by Pablo Neruda. By the end of the 1960s, however, he worked primarily as a painter. In his *Totem* series initiated in 1967, for example, he depicted human faces as if imprisoned in enormous blocks, introducing a vein of fantasy that became characteristic of his art. A favourite theme was the conflict between the material and the spiritual, as in his series *Captives of Stone* (1976–7; see Galaz and Ivelić, p. 291), in which figures seem to be swallowed up by matter, suggesting a transformation from one state to another. Although there are links with Surrealism in Toral's work, his cultivation of mysterious moods and an almost evanescent line, together with the fleshy eroticism of his figures, are too personal to be aligned with a single movement.

BIBLIOGRAPHY

Mario Toral: Gravuras, desenhos, ilustrações (exh. cat., Rio de Janeiro, Mus. A. Mod., 1964) [leaflet]

G. Galaz and M. Ivelić: *La pintura en Chile desde la colonia hasta 1981* (Valparaíso, 1981), pp. 291–2, 294, 318, 337

Exposición de obras de Mario Toral (exh. cat., intro. L. Castedo; Santiago, Inst. Cult. Las Condes, 1984)

CARLOS LASTARRIA HERMOSILLA

Toral, Tabo [Octavio] (*b* Boquete, Chiriquí, 29 Aug 1950). Panamanian painter. He studied at the Maryland Institute College of Art in Baltimore in 1969 and at the Nova Scotia College of Art in Halifax from 1969 to 1971 before completing his education from 1971 to 1976 at the Escuela de Comunicación Social of the Universidad de Panamá. His first works were delicate and anecdotal drawings and etchings of mysterious, fairy-tale characters in fanciful surroundings. From the late 1970s he produced brightly coloured abstract paintings based on esoteric geometric relationships and inspired by Eastern philosophies; they were usually titled after the date on which they were finished, for example *1–3–1981* (Panama City, Mus. A. Contemp.). Toral moved to the USA in the early 1980s, where he changed to a figurative, neo-expressionist style, returning in the 1990s to his earlier interest in abstraction.

BIBLIOGRAPHY

Tabo Toral: Oleos, 1981 (exh. cat. by C. Alemán and M. E. Kupfer, Panama City, Gal. Arteconsult, 1981)

Tabo Toral, Panama (exh. cat. by E. Camargo and J. Gómez Sicre, Washington, DC, Mus. Mod. A. Latin America, 1983)

MONICA E. KUPFER

Toraldo di Francia, Cristiano. *See under* SUPERSTUDIO.

Toraṇa [Skt: 'gateway']. Free-standing gateway used in the Indian subcontinent, commonly placed before temples and shrines as part of an enclosure. The earliest surviving *toraṇa* was set up in the 2nd century BC in front of the Buddhist stupa at BHARHUT. It was based on timber prototypes, and its mortice-and-tenon jointing is reminiscent of carpentry. Slightly later and more elaborate are the gateways, each about 8.5 m high, at SANCHI. Although there are no other complete *toraṇa*s from ancient India, relief representations in stone and ivory testify to the widespread used of the form.

The Bharhut and Sanchi *toraṇa*s are of a form that influenced later gateways in China and Japan. They consist of a pair of sturdy posts supporting gently arched beams or architraves. At Sanchi the posts have capitals—in the shape of elephants, lions or dwarves—set back to back. The three curved architraves extend beyond the verticals and terminate in volutes. At Bharhut and in some fragments from Mathura the ends of the architraves are treated as curly-tailed *makara*s (crocodile-like monsters). Slender, baluster-like struts link the architraves, and the whole is crowned by sculptures, wheels and other symbolic devices. At Sanchi the arms of the lowest architraves are supported by bracket figures in the form of voluptuous female fertility spirits (*yakṣīs*; *see* INDIAN SUBCONTINENT, fig. 145). Similar brackets, dating to the first two centuries AD, have been recovered from the Mathura area. The posts and architraves at Sanchi are divided into panels and covered with lively reliefs.

There is a long hiatus between the ancient Buddhist *toraṇa*s and the free-standing gates that began to appear in front of temples in the 9th century AD. Examples can be found at GYARASPUR, BADOH, Warangal and elsewhere. The *makara toraṇa*, an ancient motif found all over India, was often used on gateways, as well as doorways and niches. This motif consists of an arch form, generally more vegetal than architectonic, spewed from between the

Toraṇa at Vadnagar, Mehsana District, Gujarat, view from the west, *c.* 1135–40

jaws of a pair of *makara*s or *makara* heads. In the temple halls of western India *makara torana*s of cusped or wavy shape billow up to meet the undersides of beams. *Makara torana*s were commonly combined with the lintels of free-standing gateways, supported by carved pillars set on moulded bases. A fine example is the 12th-century *torana* at Vadnagar in Gujarat, where the crowning *makara torana* rises over an overhanging canopy (see fig.). Below this would have arched another *makara torana*, of which only the supporting *makara*-head brackets remain. Such gateways often formed part of an axial progression of elements, as in the 11th-century Sun Temple at MODHERA, where the surviving pillars of the *torana* stand between an open hall and a stepped tank.

BIBLIOGRAPHY

P. O. Sompura, ed.: *Kshīrārnava* (Ahmadabad, 1957)

P. Brown: *Indian Architecture (Buddhist and Hindu Periods)* (?Bombay [1941], rev. Bombay, 1956)

S. Huntington: *The Art of Ancient India: Buddhist, Hindu, Jain* (New York and Tokyo, 1985)

J. C. Harle: *The Art and Architecture of the Indian Subcontinent* (Harmondsworth, 1986)

ADAM HARDY

Torbido [il Moro], **Francesco (di Marco India)** (*b* Venice, 1482–5; *d* Verona, 1561–2). Italian painter. According to Vasari he was taught by Giorgione. He moved from Venice to Verona around 1500 and was certainly trained in the workshop of Liberale da Verona. In 1514 he is recorded as living with the noble Giusti family in Verona. The *Portrait of a Young Man with a Rose* (Munich, Alte Pin.), signed and dated 1516, displays a soft finish and dreamy countenance, and the *Portrait of a Man and Woman* (Berea Coll., KY) has similar Giorgionesque qualities. The signed *Portrait of a Man* (*c.* 1520; Milan, Brera) is more tightly painted, recalling Lorenzo Lotto rather than Giorgione. In the *Virgin and Child with Five Saints* (*c.* 1520; Verona, S Zeno) the more finished forms, bright colour and twisting poses reveal an interest in Mannerism; the same characteristics are evident in the altarpiece depicting the *Virgin in Glory with the Archangel Raphael and S Giustina* (1523; Verona, S Fermo). Between 1526 and 1530 he produced four frescoes of saints in the Cappella Fontanella, S Maria in Organo, Verona, of which the muscular, energetic forms of *St John the Baptist* and *St Jerome* are similar to those in his slightly earlier altarpieces. In the *Mystic Marriage of St Catherine* (ex-Potsdam, Neues Pal.; see Repetto Contaldo (1984), fig. 15) painted for the same chapel, gesture and pose are agitated and emotional, as found in the work of Correggio. Torbido's frescoes in the choir of Verona Cathedral depicting the *Assumption of the Virgin*, to designs by Giulio Romano, were commissioned by Bishop Giovanni Matteo Giberti (1495–1543) and completed in 1534. Subsequent works in the Abbazia di Rosazzo (1535) reveal powerful forms and sharp foreshortenings. *St Barbara in Glory with SS Anthony and Roch* (late 1530s; Verona, S Eufemia) shows an increased use of chiaroscuro, intense colour, calmer poses and a less polished finish than the altarpieces of the 1520s. At the beginning of 1546 Torbido was back in Venice, where he executed four scenes from *Genesis* (untraced) for the Scuola della SS Trinità. In 1557 he returned to Verona.

Torbido's early assimilation of Mannerism was an important influence on his son-in-law Battista dell'Angolo del Moro and on del Moro's contemporaries Paolo Farinati, Giambattista Zelotti, Anselmo Canneri and Paolo Veronese.

BIBLIOGRAPHY

G. Vasari: *Vite* (1550, rev. 2/1568); ed. G. Milanesi (1878–85), v, pp. 287, 291–6

C. Ridolfi: *Meraviglie* (1648); ed. D. von Hadeln (1914–24), ii, pp. 118–19

B. dal Pozzo: *Le vite de' pittori, scultori e architetti veronesi* (Verona, 1718), pp. 27–8

G. Gerola: 'Questioni storiche di arte veronese, 8: Torbido, Moro e dall'Angolo', *Madonna Verona*, iv/3 (1910), pp. 145–57

D. Viana: *Francesco Torbido detto il Moro, pittore veronese* (Verona, 1933)

B. Berenson: *Central and North Italian Schools* (1968), i, pp. 430–31

M. Repetto Contaldo: 'Francesco Torbido: Da Giorgione alla "Maniera"', *A. Ven.*, xxxvi (1982), pp. 62–80

——: 'Francesco Torbido detto il Moro', *Saggi & Mem. Stor. A.*, xiv (1984), pp. 43–82, 133–68

DIANA GISOLFI

Torcello. Island town in the lagoon 9 km north-east of Venice, Italy. The first inhabitants were refugees from Altinum on the mainland, who fled here after the Lombard invasions of AD 568; in this respect, Torcello's creation mirrors that of Venice. In AD 638 Bishop Paolo moved the bishopric of Altinum to Torcello, bringing with him the relics of St Heliodorus, which are now housed in a 3rd-century sarcophagus below the high altar of the cathedral. From the 7th century to the 13th, Torcello was an island stronghold of considerable importance, and a centre of wool manufacture. At its height it had some 20,000 inhabitants, and dotted over the island are the remains of several churches, as well as the cathedral, dedicated to S Maria Assunta, and S Fosca (*see* §§1 and 2 below). The rich remains inside the cathedral, from the 7th century to the 13th, bespeak its importance and illustrate how it benefited from the acquisitive tendencies of its benefactors: the marble columns of the nave, the pavement, the 11th-century reliefs of the iconostasis and, of course, the mosaics. The lagoons and channels silted up, however; there was endemic malaria, and by the 15th century Torcello had been far outstripped in importance by Venice. In the 17th century only a few hundred people lived there, and by the late 20th century the permanent population numbered about 75; as a result, the churches have survived virtually untouched since the Middle Ages.

1. Cathedral. 2. S Fosca.

1. CATHEDRAL. The first cathedral, consecrated in AD 639 (a foundation stone, discovered in 1895, is set in the wall to the left of the altar), was probably completed under Bishop Adeodatus I (*reg c.* 700), who is recorded as having embellished it in marble. Little is known of this church, but an altar table, discovered in 1929, and the tabernacle 'degli olii santi' now walled into the SS Sacramento chapel, both dated to the 7th century, must have come from it. The restorations carried out by Bishop Adeodatus II (*reg* 864–7) probably involved the reconstruction of the walls and pavements; the remains of a mosaic floor under the pavement of the present church and various sculptural fragments set into its façade and in the museum are attributed to this period; they bear foliate and geometric motifs typical of 9th-century work. The pavement level of the baptistery (destr. 1892) at the west end of the nave is the same as the mosaic fragments,

Torcello Cathedral, interior looking east, founded AD 638

indicating that it was probably also built at this time. Originally circular, with eight columns around the basin, it was rebuilt in octagonal form in the early 18th century.

In 1008 Bishop Orso Orseolo (*reg* 997–1009) was consecrated at Torcello and his father Doge Pietro Orseolo II (*reg* 991–1008) commissioned the restoration of the cathedral. This work is thought to apply to the construction of the present church. Although some scholars have attributed the apses to the 9th-century campaign, the marble plinth (h. 2 m) that continues round the perimeter of the building (except for the annexe on its north side, probably added in the 13th century) indicates that the church, although restored several times and perhaps incorporating earlier fragments, is essentially a homogeneous construction (Polacco, 1984). The synthronon, built at the same time as the crypt vault, covers frescoes of *c*. 1000 and was probably added in the mid-11th century. There is also evidence of early restorations in the triumphal arch, the top of the apse and in the five capitals nearest the sanctuary, which resemble capitals in S Marco, Venice, dating from the second half of the 11th century; these may have been carried out after an earthquake. The extensive restorations undertaken by Bishop Pietro Trani from 1418 to 1426 seem to have included the heightening of the main vessel (later altered), the reconstruction of the

main arcade and clerestory (north side exterior rebuilt 1749), and the three transverse arches over each of the aisles. The present iconostasis, surmounted by 15th-century paintings, may also be Trani's work: it incorporates four fine 11th-century reliefs with peacocks and lions, executed in a fresh, spontaneous style close to sculpture in S Marco. The reliefs were evidently made for a different position, and Polacco suggested that they came from the iconostasis of S Marco, which was replaced in 1394. The ill-fitting pulpit reliefs may also have come from S Marco. Subsequent restorations at Torcello have included those carried out in the late 17th century, in 1855–7 and the late 1970s; the marble shutters on the south side of the nave were added between 1805 and 1827. The tall, square campanile, one of the landmarks of the lagoon, is attributed to the 11th century.

Torcello Cathedral is derived from the type of basilica found at Ravenna. Occidented, it comprises an aisled nave of ten bays, a main apse with an annular crypt and two flanking apsidal chapels; the main arcade, supported by grey marble columns with white marble capitals, stands on a fine *opus sectile* pavement, dated to the 11th century. The bare brick of the interior (see fig.) and the timber tie-beam roof form a marvellous contrast to the rich colours and sheen of the mosaics. On the walls of the main apse are the Twelve Apostles, with St Heliodorus beneath the central window. In the conch is the tall, standing figure of the Virgin holding the Child, set against a plain gold ground, a strikingly beautiful image. Other mosaics include an *Annunciation* on the triumphal arch (fragments from the *Ascension* above it, Torcello, Mus. Torcello) and, in the south apse (i.e. the SS Sacramento chapel), Christ Pantokrator with SS Michael and Gabriel and the Four Fathers of the (Western) Church; on the vault are the angels and the Mystic Lamb. On the west wall of the cathedral are the *Crucifixion* (top), *Christ in Glory* and an immense *Last Judgement*, all on a gold background. The programme has been attributed to the mid-11th century, but the mosaics were executed in two phases. The apse Apostles, the mosaics in the SS Sacramento chapel and part of the *Last Judgement* date from the 11th century; the *Virgin and Child*, the *Annunciation* and *Ascension* fragments and other parts of the *Last Judgement* are all of the second half of the 12th century, perhaps done after earthquake repairs. The iconography shows a mixture of Byzantine and Western features, but the style of the earlier mosaics suggests that the artists were Greek; the later mosaics are more homogeneous and Venetian in style, although they still show close links with Byzantine art (Polacco, 1984). According to Cormack, the mosaics of Torcello may have provided the impetus for S Marco itself.

A precise dating and chronology of the mosaics has been hindered, however, by the restoration campaigns of the 18th and 19th centuries and by the deterioration caused by damp and salt air. A mosaic head sold at Sotheby's, London, in 1987 was identified as being the original of the twelfth Apostle in the *Last Judgement*, demonstrating the extent to which restorations may have disturbed the original appearance of the interior. The head was probably removed by Giovanni Moro during his restorations of 1852–6; in 1859 he was charged with theft on the word of his assistants, who testified that he had deliberately removed original mosaics in order to sell them, replacing them with his own work. The restorers Salviati and Son, who worked at the cathedral in 1872–3, endeavoured to set right the damage, and in 1879 the director of the museum at Torcello reassembled some of the other damaged heads, which were placed back on the west wall in 1895–7. Another campaign of conservation begun in 1980 concentrated on protecting the mosaics and the cathedral from damp.

BIBLIOGRAPHY
M. Brunetti and others: *Torcello* (Venice, 1940)
O. Demus: 'Studies among the Torcello Mosaics', *Burl. Mag.*, lxxxii (1943), pp. 132, 136–40; lxxxvi (1944), pp. 39, 41–5, 195–200
I. Andreescu: 'Torcello I. Le Christ inconnu. II. Anastasis et Jugement: Têtes vraies, têtes fausses', *Dumbarton Oaks Pap.*, xvi (1972)
——: 'Torcello III. Chronologie relative des mosaïques pariétales', *Dumbarton Oaks Pap.*, xxx (1976), pp. 247–341
R. Polacco: *Sculture paleocristiane e altomedievali di Torcello* (Treviso, 1976)
M. Vecchi: *Torcello: Ricerche e contributi* (Rome, 1979)
I. Andreescu: 'Torcello IV: Cappella sud, mosaici', *III colloquio internazionale sul mosaico antico: Ravenna, 1980*, pp. 535–51
J. M. Richards: 'Piecework on a Grand Scale: Restoring the Torcello Mosaics', *Country Life*, clxxi (1982), pp. 1508–10
M. Vecchi: *Torcello: Nuove ricerche* (Rome, 1982)
I. Andreescu: 'Modifiche alla cattedrale di Torcello nel restauro del 1854–58', *Boll. A.*, lxix/25 (1984), pp. 89–122
R. Polacco: *La cattedrale di Torcello* (Treviso, 1984)
X. Barral i Altet: *Les Mosaïques de pavement médievales de Venise, Murano, Torcello* (Paris, 1985)
R. Cormack: 'An Apostle Mosaic from Medieval Torcello', London, Sotheby's: 9 July 1987
C. Hibbert: *Venice: The Biography of a City* (London, 1988)

JACQUELINE COLLISS HARVEY

2. S FOSCA. This church stands next to Torcello Cathedral, at the edge of a burial ground that dates back to the late 10th or early 11th century. Scholars do not agree as to when the church was founded or the timing of the various stages of its development. Three documents from the first half of the 9th century indicate its existence, and in 1011 two sisters left a will donating their goods to S Fosca. It is known for certain that there was a martyrdom of S Fosca in Torcello in the 9th century; it is possible that his remains were taken there at the end of the 10th century. Other evidence is derived from the Romanesque restorations in the late 11th century and the early 12th; the church belonged to a confraternity that was economically independent of the cathedral. The restorations undertaken since the 17th century are documented.

The building is a Greek-cross octagon with short, open aisles that reflect Western architectural traditions. The dome has collapsed, but its first rings and two squinches survive; the eight-sided outer portico was added to the church in the Romanesque period. In plan S Fosca most closely resembles the 11th-century church of Panagia Lykodemou in Athens and Christianou Cathedral east of Filiatra in the Peloponnese (Greece). Elements of its interior decoration, such as the two tiers of niches and the frieze of pendant triangles and saw-tooth bands, are similar to those found in two Constantinopolitan churches, now Kilise Mosque (11th century) and Gül Mosque (12th century) respectively.

BIBLIOGRAPHY
R. W. Schultz: *Die Kirchenbauten auf der Insel Torcellino* (Berlin, 1927)
L. Leciejewicz, E. Tabaczynska and S. Tabaczynski: *Torcello: Scavi 1961–2* (Rome, 1977)
For further bibliography see §1 above

ROBERTO CORONEO

Tordesillas, Gaspar de (*b* ?Tordesillas, before 1494; *d* ?Valladolid, after 1564). Spanish sculptor. He was living in Valladolid in 1554, when he described himself as a carver ('*entallador de ymagineria*') and gave his age as over 60. In 1536 he directed work on the retable of the parish church at Oñate, carried out in collaboration with several sculptors, and in the same year he carved the retable containing paintings for the church of El Salvador, Simancas. He collaborated with Juan de Juni on the retable (1547) for the church of S Benito, Valladolid (fragments, Valladolid, Mus. N. Escul.), as well as carrying out other works in the city. At Tordesillas he carved and assembled the retable of the Capilla de la Piedad, S Antolin, a project on which Juni collaborated from 1564. In 1562 Tordesillas received final payment for the tomb (*in situ*) of one of the founders of S Antolin, *Gaspar de Alderete*, on which instalments had been paid in 1550 and 1560. Tordesillas was essentially a carver and joiner whose work, which generally reflects the current Mannerist style in Spanish sculpture, is of a high quality. He often incorporated medallions in his sculptural decoration and used caryatids at the corners.

Ceán Bermúdez

BIBLIOGRAPHY
J. Martí Monso: *Estudios histórico-artísticos relativos a Valladolid* (Valladolid and Madrid, 1898–1901)
J. Agapito Revilla: 'La obra más antigua de las conocidas del escultor vallisoletano Gaspar de Tordesillas: Retablo de la capilla de la Piedad, Oñate', *Bol. Mus. Prov. B. A. Valladolid*, i (1927), pp. 134–9
C. Candeira: 'Los retablos de Gaspar de Tordesillas', *Bol. Semin. Estud. A. & Arqueol. U. Valladolid*, 8 (1941–2), pp. 111–38
MARGARITA ESTELLA

Torel, William (*fl* 1291–1303). English goldsmith and bronze-caster. In 1291 he was commissioned to cast three life-size effigies: one of *King Henry III* (1292) to stand on the Cosmati work tomb-chest in Westminster Abbey, London, and two of *Eleanor of Castile* (*d* 1290), King Edward I's first wife. The first of the Queen's images was to rest on the Purbeck marble tomb-chest in Westminster Abbey; the other was to lie on the duplicate monument (destr.) provided for her entrails in Lincoln Cathedral. The bronze of the Westminster effigies, which were cast by the lost-wax method, is up to 100 mm thick in places, suggesting that Torel was unfamiliar with casting techniques on such a large scale. His workshop was a shed in the abbey churchyard, where he worked on the project for two years, receiving payment of more than £138 13s 4d. The main figures were cast in one piece; the right hands, sceptres, canopies and foot supports were cast separately, and imitation stones were set in the borders and crowns. The figures were mercury-gilded with gold obtained by melting down florins purchased from Lucchese merchants. Torel's models were possibly provided by ALEXANDER OF ABINGDON, since they adhere to his restrained, elegant French style. The deceased are shown as idealized images rather than as specific portraits. Some unfinished engraving, discovered when the plate underneath the figure of *Henry III* was cleaned, suggests that Torel may have been a skilled brass engraver. The last documentary reference to him, in 1303, states that he had innocently purchased from Richard Podlicote two rings stolen from the king's treasury at Westminster.

BIBLIOGRAPHY
B. Botfield: *Manners and Household Expenses of England in the Thirteenth and Fifteenth Centuries*, ed. T. Hudson Turner, Roxburghe Club (London, 1841)
W. Burges: 'The Tombs in Westminster Abbey', *Gleanings from Westminster Abbey*, ed. G. G. Scott (London, 1863), pp. 143–84
A. P. Stanley: 'On an Examination of the Tombs of Richard II and Henry III in Westminster Abbey', *Archaeologia*, xlv (1880), pp. 309–27
H. J. Plenderleith and H. Maryon: 'The Royal Bronze Effigies in Westminster Abbey', *Antiqua. J.*, xxxix (1957), pp. 87–90
H. M. Colvin, ed.: *The History of the King's Works*, i (London, 1963)
L. Stone: *Sculpture in Britain: The Middle Ages*, Pelican Hist. A. (Harmondsworth, 1972)
PHILLIP LINDLEY

Torelli. Italian family of painters.

(1) Felice Torelli (*b* Verona, 9 Sept 1667; *d* Bologna, 11 June 1748). He began his study of painting in Verona under Santo Prunati (1652–1728). He also pursued an interest in music and moved to Bologna with an older brother, Giuseppe Torelli (1658–1709), who had been appointed violinist at the Cappella di S Petronio and who subsequently became a famous composer. Felice frequented the studio of Giovan Gioseffo dal Sole in Bologna and at the same time followed the conventional training of 17th-century Bolognese painters, studying the wall paintings by the Carracci family in the Palazzo Fava and Palazzo Magnani-Salem in Bologna. During the last decade of the century he became an important member of the artistic community in Bologna. Torelli's early work shows the strong influence of dal Sole in facial types and the style of figures and drapery; for example *St Sebastian* (Bologna, Maccaferri Col.; see 1979 exh. cat., fig. 64) has been assigned to both dal Sole and Torelli, the former attribution being more likely. However, Torelli's style evolved towards a more ponderous, dark-toned, astringent manner of considerable power, clearly inspired by the work of Lodovico Carracci. Torelli's work seems anomalous in comparison with the light-hearted and fluent Italian late Baroque art of the period. However, his style bears some relationship to that of Giuseppe Maria Crespi (ii), who was a colleague at the Accademia Clementina, Bologna, which Torelli co-founded in 1710. Torelli's pupils at the academy included two of the most brilliant Bolognese painters of the second half of the 18th century, Ubaldo Gandolfi and his younger brother Gaetano Gandolfi.

Torelli was chiefly involved with the creation of huge, sombre altarpieces depicting characteristic themes of the Counter-Reformation, including popular saints of the time, in ecstasy, being martyred or ascending to Heaven. These works, with their intense discourses between massive figures with darkly impassioned features, were painted for churches in Bologna (e.g. the *Ecstasy of St Camillus de Lellis*, S Gregorio) and other Emilian cities (e.g. the *Martyrdom of St Maurelius*, Ferrara Cathedral). However, his reputation was sufficiently widespread also to bring him important commissions from such cities as Turin, Milan, Pisa and Verona (e.g. the *Martyrdom of St Peter Martyr*, Verona, S Anastasia). His biblical history painting is represented most impressively in two large horizontal works, *Christ and the Canaanite Woman* and *Christ and the Adulteress* (both now Bologna, S Maria della Grazia). Torelli's portraits, which he painted apparently only rarely, are extremely striking, for example the series of four large oval portraits of members of the Malvezzi family of senators (*c.* 1711–13; Dozza, Rocca). Torelli also painted a *Self-portrait* (Florence, Uffizi). He married Lucia Casalini (1677–1762), also a pupil of dal Sole and a notable painter, by whom he had five children.

(2) Stefano Torelli (*b* Bologna, 1712; *d* St Petersburg, 1784). Son of (1) Felice Torelli. According to Giovan Pietro Zanotti, he executed an altarpiece, *St Ignatius of Loyola Driving out Demons from the Possessed*, for the Jesuit church of S Ignazio, Bologna, although it was removed because of a certain 'suavity and elegance prejudicial to the purity of their noviciate'; the picture was then acquired by the Marchese Sanvittale at Parma. Zanotti further noted that Torelli moved to Venice, where he painted 'in both fresco and oil with much honour'. Luigi Crespi (ii) noted that by the time of his writing (the 1750s), Torelli was in Dresden, where he met Crespi in 1753. Torelli worked for the Elector Frederick-Augustus II and executed altarpieces, ceiling paintings and portraits. He then worked in Lübeck (1759–61) and St Petersburg, where he was appointed Professor of the Academy of Arts in 1762. His son Antonio Torelli (*d* 1754) was also a painter.

UNPUBLISHED SOURCES

M. Oretti: *Notizie de' professori del disegno, cioè pittori, scultori ed architetti bolognesi e de' forestieri di sua scuola* (*c.*1760; Bologna, Bib. Com. Archiginnasio, MS. B.123–35.II) [see extract in MS. B.131; index by R. Landi, 1983]

BIBLIOGRAPHY

C. Malvasia: *Le pitture di Bologna che nella pretesa e rimostrata in hora da altri maggiore antichità et impareggiabile eccellenza nella pittura, con manifesta evidenza di fatto rendono il passaggero disingannato ed instrutto* (Bologna, 1686, rev/1766), pp. 78ff

B. dal Pozzo: *Le vite de' pittori . . . veronesi* (Verona, 1718)

G. P. Zanotti: *Storia dell'Accademia Clementina*, ii (Bologna, 1739/*R* 1977) pp. 75–88, 288

L. Crespi: *Felsina pittrice: Vite de' pittori bolognesi*, iii (Rome, 1769), pp. 243–5

L. Lanzi: *Storia pittorica della Italia*, v (Pisa, 1816), pp. 175–6

D. Miller: 'Felice Torelli, Bolognese', *Boll. A.*, 2nd ser. (Jan–March 1964), pp. 54–66 (includes cat. rais.)

R. Roli: *Pittura bolognese, 1650–1800: Dal Cignani ai Gandolfi* (Bologna, 1977), pp. 168 and 294–5 (includes summary cat. rais.)

La pittura a Verona tra sei e settecento (exh. cat., ed. L. Magagnato; Verona, Gran Guardia, 1978), p. 208 and figs 167–70

L'arte del settecento in Emilia e in Romagna. La pittura: L'Accademia Clementina (exh. cat., intro. E. Riccomini, Bologna, Pal. Podestà and Pal. Re Enzo, 1979), pp. 52–5 and figs 64–6

DWIGHT C. MILLER

Torelli, Filippo [Pippo] **di Matteo** (*b* Florence, 1409; *d* Florence, 2 May 1468). Italian illuminator. He trained in the bottega of Michele di Giovanni Guarducci (1387–1453) between 1438 and 1442. From 1446 he decorated a series of choir-books for the Capitolo di S Marco, among which the Gradual (1456–7; Venice, Fond. Cini, no. 2151) from S Pancrazio is of special interest for its introduction of the 'heroic putto'. He also decorated several manuscripts for Florence Cathedral: for example, two Psalters (Florence, Mus. Opera Duomo, N. II, 3 and O, 4), which were illustrated by Zanobi Strozzi, with whom he continued to collaborate, and an Antiphonary (Florence, Mus. Opera Duomo, U. 46) for which he was paid in 1450–51. Between 1454 and 1463 Torelli worked on the borders of two Graduals (Florence, Bib. Medicea-Laurenziana, MSS Edili 149 and 151), also for the cathedral. Here the figure style recalls the work of Ser Ricciardo di Nanni, who was his pupil, and of Francesco di Antonio del Chierico. In the same period Torelli participated in the decoration of the choir-books (Florence, Archivio del Capitolo di S Lorenzo, Corale K. 209) for the Badia of Fiesole.

The illustration of Livy's *Fourth Decade* (Florence, Bib. Medicea-Laurenziana, MS. Plut. 63.12), documented in 1458 by a letter from Vespasiano da Bisticci to Piero de' Medici, shows that Torelli contributed to humanist as well as liturgical books, although only in the decoration of borders. In 1467–8 he began the decoration of an Evangeliary (Florence, Bib. Medicea-Laurenziana, MS. Edili 115), which was completed by Ser Ricciardo di Nanni. The ornamental friezes, the distortion of the figures and the zoomorphic treatment of plant motifs reflect earlier illumination; but Torelli's images are also sometimes enriched by more sculptural forms and greater naturalism that go beyond the limits of decoration. Torelli thus transformed the conventional white-vine scrolls into arabesques of leaves and fruits with putti and animals (e.g. Brussels, Bib. Royale Albert 1er, MS. IV. 229). This type of decoration, reminiscent of the work of lacemakers, embroiderers and goldsmiths, was widely appreciated throughout the 15th century and the beginning of the 16th, especially in the work of Ser Ricciardo di Nanni, Francesco di Antonio del Chierico and Francesco Boccardi (*d* 1547).

BIBLIOGRAPHY

M. Levi d'Ancona: *Miniatura e miniatori a Firenze dal XIV al XVI secolo* (Florence, 1962), pp. 186–91

A. Garzelli: *Miniatura fiorentina del rinascimento, 1440–1525: Un primo censimento*, i (Florence, 1985)

PATRIZIA FERRETTI

Torelli, Giacomo (*b* Fano, 1 Sept 1608; *d* Fano, 17 June 1678). Italian stage designer, engineer and architect. He may have worked first in Fano, where amateur productions are known to have been performed in the Palazzo della Ragione, but it is more likely that he acquired some theatrical experience in nearby Pesaro or Urbino. The earliest evidence of his activity is in connection with the inaugural performance (Jan 1641) of the Teatro Novissimo in Venice. Torelli had supposedly travelled to Venice to give military advice, but he soon became involved in designing the scenery and stage machinery for *La finta pazza*, an opera with music by Francesco Sacrati, which was followed by productions of *Bellerofonte* (1642) and *Venere gelosa* (1643), also by Sacrati. Torelli was probably also responsible for the design of *Deidamia* in 1644. In the same year, before leaving Venice for Paris, he staged Sacrati's *Ulisse errante* at the Teatro SS Giovanni e Paolo.

In France, troupes of Italian comedians had been popular since the 16th century. In the 1640s, threatened by Cardinal Mazarin's patronage of an opera company, the comedians based in Paris sought the support of the Queen, Anne of Austria (1601–66), who summoned Torelli to Paris in 1645. His first production, *La finta pazza*, held in the Hôtel du Petit Bourbon, was a great success. In 1647, using the superior facilities of the theatre in the Palais-Royal, Torelli staged a new work, *Orfeo*, with a score by Luigi Rossi.

During the civil unrest of the Fronde (1648–53) Torelli was persecuted as one of Cardinal Mazarin's dependants, despite having gallicized his name and married a French woman. It was therefore not until 1650 that his talents were again demonstrated, this time in a French work, *Andromède*, with a score by Charles Dassoucy and a libretto by Pierre Corneille. Following Louis XIV's return to Paris in 1652, Torelli became more involved in *ballets de cour* than in opera, a reflection of the young King's interest in dancing. By the end of the decade, however, Torelli had fallen from favour at the French court and Cardinal Mazarin had summoned Gaspare Vigarini from Modena to build a new theatre in the Tuileries. Torelli did have one last chance to re-establish himself: in 1661 he was chosen by Nicolas Fouquet, the Surintendant des Finances, to stage Molière's *Les Fâcheux* at the celebrated fête given in honour of the King at Vaux-le-Vicomte, near Melun. Fouquet's arrest and imprisonment later that year signalled the end of Torelli's career in France. He attempted to remain in Paris, pleading ill-health, but he was forced to return to his home town, Fano. There, in 1677, he designed the Teatro della Fortuna and produced his last stage setting, for *Il trionfo della continenza*.

Torelli's most significant innovation, which was employed in his very first production, was the use of machinery to change sets. Instead of requiring a stage crew of 16 men, each having to move a single flat at the end of a scene, Torelli devised a system of sub-stage trolleys connected to a central drum that enabled even a 15-year-old boy to change sets quickly and single-handedly. The importance of this was not merely as a labour-saving device, but that it achieved stunning visual effects. The smoothness and swiftness of the transformation was itself dramatic: one scene dissolved and, following a moment of uncertainty, another gradually resolved itself. The speed also allowed changes of setting when the action of an opera required it, rather than restricting them to the ends of acts. Such changes became an integral part of the construction of operas in the second half of the 17th century. Torelli was also the first to create the illusion of enclosed space on the stage. Previously, fixed borders representing the sky had been used to conceal the machinery above the stage. By making these borders exchangeable, he could create the illusion of ceilings of palaces or the roofs of caves. Torelli utilized this to great effect by alternating between open and enclosed sets wherever possible, creating a new sense of rhythm in the sequence of scenery.

Grove 6

BIBLIOGRAPHY

M. Bisaccioni: *Apparati scenici per lo Teatro Novissimo* (Venice, 1644) [with 12 engrs from Sacrati's *Venere gelosa*]

S. Tomani-Amiani: *Del teatro antico della fortuna in Fano* (Sanseverino, 1867)

A. Mabellini: 'L'antico teatro della fortuna in Fano', *Stud. Picena*, vii (1931), p. 161

F. Torrefranca: 'Il "grande stregone": Giacomo Torelli e la scenografia del seicento', *Scenario*, iii (1934), p. 437

P. Bjurström: *Giacomo Torelli and Baroque Stage Design* (Stockholm 1961, rev. 2/1962)

RICHARD JOHN

Toreutics. Term for chased or embossed decorative work on metal vessels, weapons, jewellery etc, used especially on objects made in ancient Greece.

Torgau. German town in Saxony, north-east of Leipzig, on the west bank of the River Elbe. An important centre of the Reformation, it was one of the seats of the electoral princes of Saxony as early as 1456; their castle, which lies in the east of the town, is a notable example of early German Renaissance architecture and became known as Schloss Hartenfels in 1579.

1. INTRODUCTION. Torgau is first documented in AD 973, when a castle there served as a border post for Otto II, Holy Roman Emperor. Having become an urban settlement, it was granted a town charter *c.* 1263 and had developed into an important cultural centre by the time of the Reformation. Lucas Cranach I was active there as court painter from 1503. The Torgau Articles, granting permission to print the first Lutheran Bible, were passed in 1534. Most of the buildings that survive in the old town date from the 16th century, although they have been almost completely restored. Through its patronage of the composer Johann Walter (1496–1570) the court also contributed to the development of Protestant choral music; and the commission to Heinrich Schütz (1585–1672) for a court entertainment resulted in the first

German opera, a setting of *Daphne*, performed at the Schloss in 1627. Because of its strategic position on the Elbe, Torgau developed as a fortress town during the 18th and 19th centuries; on 25 April 1945, just before the end of World War II, it was the area where Soviet and US troops had their first confrontation.

2. SCHLOSS HARTENFELS. Built close to the site of the 10th-century border castle and its successors, the present Schloss was begun *c.* 1470. The layout is in four wings (A–D) set around a courtyard resembling a right-angled triangle with an irregular third side: the apex faces the river crossing. This disposition is significant in that it marks the transition from the Burg to the Burgschloss in Germany, equivalent to the change from the château fort to the château in France, and from the keep to the great manorial house in England.

Construction started with the Albrechtsbau (southern part of wing D), a great hall with four corner towers, on which Arnold von Westfalen probably assisted. It was extended in 1482–5 by Conrad Pflüger, whose scheme included the theatre hall and the Kleine Wendelstein (a tower housing a spiral staircase), completed in 1538 and capped with a fan vault. Although the Albrechtsbau was reworked internally on several occasions, the remains of a Late Gothic ceiling with wooden beams survive at first-floor level. The Johann-Friedrich-Bau (wing C), designed by Konrad Krebs, was built in 1533–6 and closes the courtyard on the south-east side opposite the main entrance. This major work of the early German Renaissance consists of a long three-storey block in 13 bays, articulated by a succession of coupled curtain arch windows, a characteristic of the transitional period from Late Gothic to early Renaissance in Germany; a fourth storey was added *c.* 1820. Horizontality is further stressed by a projecting walkway that runs across the elevation at third-floor level, supported on stone brackets. This horizontality is countered at mid-point by the vertical contrast of the Grosse Wendelstein, a stair-tower that projects from the main block and rises from a simple rectangular substructure with a flight of steps on either side. The walling of the tower is reduced to its framing piers, through which the spiral may be seen, while the crowning gable follows the curvature of the plan.

The Schlosskirche wing (wing B) houses a museum (formerly living-quarters) and the chapel. Between the two, on the courtyard side, is the oriel known as the Schöne Erker (1544), attributed to Stephan Hermsdorf (*fl* 1516–43) and richly decorated with plant motifs and scenic reliefs. The chapel (1543–4), which owes much to the Upper Saxon hall church tradition, is by Nicholas Gromann (*fl* 1537–74). Thought to be the first church built specifically for Protestant worship, it was dedicated by Martin Luther in person. It is in three storeys, two of which have narrow stone galleries. Gothic detailing is everywhere evident, especially in the vaulting. The western wing (wing A) with the entrance gate was completed by Hans Steger (*d* 1637) in 1623.

At the end of the Seven Years War (1756–63), Schloss Hartenfels was variously used as a prison and an orphanage. It became a barracks in 1815 and, after extensive rebuilding and restoration, government offices in 1927. It was further restored in 1952.

BIBLIOGRAPHY

C. Böttcher: *Die Entwicklung des Wendeltreppenbaues bei eingehender Behandlung der altsächsischen Wendeltreppe* (Dresden, 1909)
O. Thulin: *Schloss Hartenfels zu Torgau* (Berlin, 1947)
W. G. Fleck: *Schloss Weikersheim und die hohenlohischen Schlösser der Renaissance* (Tübingen, 1954)
G. Dehio: *Handbuch der deutschen Kunstdenkmäler: Die Bezirke Dresden, Karl-Marx-Stadt, Leipzig* (Berlin, 1965)
F. Mielke: *Die Geschichte der deutschen Treppen* (Berlin, 1966)
P. Findeison and H. Magirius: *Die Denkmale der Stadt Torgau* (Leipzig, 1976)

ERHARD LISSNER

Toribio, Tomás (*b* Villa de Porcuna, Spain, 1756; *d* Montevideo, 23 June 1810). Spanish architect, active in Uruguay. After graduating from the Academia de San Fernando in Madrid, he became a key figure in the colonial architecture of Uruguay, where he introduced Spanish Neo-classical academicism, with some elements of transitional Mannerism. The Cabildo (1804–11), Montevideo, his own house (1804) in Montevideo and the parish church (1808) at Colonia del Sacramento are his major works and constitute one of the most significant legacies of colonial architecture. The architecture is sober and austere in its orderly treatment of space and subtle ornamentation of façades. The Cabildo, which was the seat of city government as well as jail and court-house, has an area of 2000 sq. m. It is a bold, vigorous building, square in plan and with a simple internal layout based on a series of rooms built around large open patios, vaulted galleries and a monumental central staircase. The façade includes rectangular, flat-arched windows, sober moulding and a rhythmic distribution of pilasters and granite columns. The Doric order is used at first-floor level, and Ionic at the second. Toribio's house makes excellent use of a narrow plot. The ground-floor is a covered passageway; the upper floor is divided into two sections separated by a hall. The severe façade features a large central balcony with a wrought-iron balustrade. The church at Colonia del Sacramento was damaged by lightning in 1823 and rebuilt in two phases (1836–41 and 1865–8). Despite some modifications, it clearly reflects the sober character of Toribio's original scheme.

BIBLIOGRAPHY

C. Perez Montero: *El Cabildo de Montevideo: El arquitecto, el terreno, el edificio* (Montevideo, 1950)
J. Giuria: *La arquitectura en el Uruguay*, i (Montevideo, 1955)
A. Lucchini: *Ideas y formas en la arquitectura nacional*, Nuestra Tierra, xi (Montevideo, 1969)

ALICIA HABER

Tori Busshi [Kuratsukuri no Tori; Shiba Kuratsukuribe no Obito Tori] (*fl* early 7th century). Japanese sculptor. He is associated with the inception of Buddhist image production in Japan and is generally considered to be the first great master of Japanese Buddhist sculpture (*see also* JAPAN, §V, 3(i)). Tori Busshi is believed to have worked on the most important monumental sculpture of the Asuka period (*c*. 552–710), the bronze *Great Buddha* (Jap. *Daibutsu*) enshrined in the Asukadera (Japan's first fully fledged temple complex, on the Yamato Plain *c*. 25 km from Nara). In addition, his name is inscribed on the mandorla of the gilt-bronze *Shaka Triad* of the Golden Hall (Kondō) at HŌRYŪJI in Nara (623; *see* JAPAN, fig. 53). He may, however, have operated primarily as a supervisor rather than a craftsman. Scholars usually associate most Asuka period images with his studio, which produced work modelled on the stone sculpture of Chinese Buddhist cave temples of the Northern Wei period (386–535). This is termed Tori style.

Tori's grandfather, Shiba Tatto, his father, Shiba Tasuna, and his aunt, Shiba Shimame, were all directly involved in early Buddhist activities in Japan. The Shiba family has been tentatively traced to various Chinese and Korean roots and undoubtedly had significant connections with the continent, most probably with the Korean kingdom of Paekche (*c*. 350–663), which acted as a channel for the transmission of Buddhism and Buddhist art from China to Japan (*see* §II, 3 above).

BIBLIOGRAPHY

A. C. Soper: 'Notes on Hōryūji and the Sculpture of the "Suiko" Period', *A. Bull.*, xxxiii/2 (1951), pp. 77–94
S. Mizuno: *Hōryūji*, Nihon no bijutsu [Arts of Japan], iv (Tokyo, 1965); Eng. trans. by R. L. Gage as *Asuka Buddhist Art: Horyu-ji*, Heibonsha Surv. Jap. A., iv (New York and Tokyo, 1974)
T. Tsugihito: 'Busshi/Bukkō no Seiritsu to Tori Busshi' [Tori Busshi and the establishment of Buddhist sculptors], *Nihon kōdai busshi no kenkyū* [Research into Buddhist sculptors of ancient Japan] (Tokyo, 1987)

DONALD F. MCCALLUM

Torihama shell-mound. Japanese shell midden in Mikata-chō, Mikata County, Fukui Prefecture, dating from the Jōmon period (*c*. 10,000-*c*. 300 BC). Excavations were conducted in 1962–72 by Doshisha (Kyoto) and Rikkyō (Tokyo) universities and the Wakasa Archaeology Study Association, and in 1975–80 by the Fukui Prefectural Education Committee. The first known cultivars in Japan were found at Torihama, dating from between *c*. 7500 and *c*. 3500 BC. One of these was perilla (Jap. *egoma*), which could be used for oil. The site also yielded the oldest extant pieces of Japanese lacquer, dating from *c*. 6000 BC. About 30 red- and black-lacquered utensils were unearthed at Torihama, as well as red-lacquered trays, a bow and a comb. Two black-lacquered wooden trays were repaired with double-ended nails of deer or boar bone, about 100 of which have been recovered. The larger tray, measuring *c*. 70×120 mm, was in nine pieces, of which four fit together. Holes for the nails had been made with stone drills. Lacquer was probably used as glue and as decoration: one red-lacquered clay pot, for example, bears decorative arcs painted in black lacquer. Bone and stone artefacts found at Torihama include needles, rings (probably thimbles) and polished axes. Some of the heads and handles of the axes were unearthed intact. Bows found at the site are the earliest Japanese examples of such implements. The oldest pieces of rope, mats and reed baskets known in Japan were also found. A narrow, 6 m-long canoe of cryptomeria, with five oars of zelkova and mulberry, is one of the earliest examples of Japanese boat-building. The ceramics recovered at Torihama are of the Kitashirakawa type, which establishes an important link between Torihama and the early Jōmon-period site of Kitashirakawa (now within the campus of Kyoto University).

BIBLIOGRAPHY

'Torihama kaizuka: Jōmon zenki o shutosuro teishichi iseki no chosa' [Torihama shell-mound: excavation of the swampy, chiefly early Jōmon-period site], Torihama Kaizuka Kenkyū Grūppa [Torihama Shell-mound Study Group], *Fukui*, i–v (1979–85)

J. EDWARD KIDDER JR

Torii. Name used by members of a school of Japanese woodblock print designers and book illustrators, active from the Edo period (1600–1868) to the present day. They specialized in the *ukiyoe* ('pictures of the floating world') genre (*see* JAPAN, §IX, 3(iii)). For most of the 18th century the Torii school monopolized the illustrations for the *kabuki* theatre in Edo (now Tokyo). In 1687 Torii Kiyomoto (1645–1702), a painter of theatrical signboards (*kanban'e*; *see* JAPAN, §XV) and a *kabuki* actor playing female roles (*onnagata*), moved from Osaka to Edo, where his son (1) Kiyonobu I established the Torii studio. Kiyonobu I was succeeded by (4) Kiyomasu II, (6) Kiyomitsu I, (8) Kiyonaga and Kiyomitsu II (1788–1868).

BIBLIOGRAPHY

K. Banu: *Torii gakeifu* [Genealogy of the Torii artists] (Tokyo, *c.* 1900)
—: *Gekigashū* [Collection of theatrical elegance] (Tokyo, 1913)
H. Link: 'Speculation on the Genealogy of the Torii Masters', *Ukiyoe geijutsu II* [Ukiyoe art], 34 (1972)
Torii no yakashae [The theatrical prints of the Torii masters] (exh. cat. by H. A. Link, Tokyo, Riccar A. Mus.; Honolulu, HI, Acad. A.; 1977)

(1) Torii Kiyonobu I (*b* Osaka, 1664; *d* Edo [now Tokyo], 1729). Woodblock print designer and founder of the Torii school. He was the son of Torii Kiyomoto (1645–1702). In 1687 the family moved to Edo, where Kiyonobu made a name for himself in 1690 by painting signboards for the Ichimuraza. In 1702 Kiyonobu succeeded his father as head of the family. He produced signboards and playbills for all Edo theatres and established the Torii family as Edo's leading *kabuki* illustrators.

Kiyonobu's work shows the influence of HISHIKAWA MORONOBU, then at the peak of his career. Kiyonobu's first extant works, both dated 1697, are the *ukiyo zōshi* ('Tales from the floating world'; a type of popular fiction), *Kōshoku daifukuchō* ('Album of amorous good fortune'; Nagoya, Ozaki Kyūya Col.) and *Honchō nijūshikō* ('Thoughts on the 24 Japanese poets'; Tokyo, N. Diet Lib.). In that same year *kabuki* script books (*kyōgenbon*) were first published in Edo. Kiyonobu and other artists of the Torii studio are thought to have produced the unsigned illustrations for the plays *Sankai Nagoya* ('Nagoya Sanza's encounter') and *Tsuwamono Kongen Soga* ('Genuine warrior Soga brothers'; both Tokyo U. A., A. Mus.). In the next few years he produced his first broadsheets of actors and untitled collections of *shunga* ('Spring pictures'; erotic prints). Kiyonobu's two representative masterpieces were produced in 1700: *Fūryū shihō byōbu* ('Fashionable folding screen of the four quarters'; Boston, MA, Mus. F.A.), which consists of 43 large-scale illustrations of actors, and *Keisei ehon* ('Yoshiwara picture book'; Chicago, IL, A. Inst.), which depicts 18 named courtesans from Edo's Yoshiwara pleasure quarter. During this period the *aragoto* ('rough stuff') acting style, which had been created by the actor Ichikawa Danjūrō I (1660–1704; *see* JAPAN, fig. 166) in imitation of the puppet theatre, dominated the Edo *kabuki*. From his earliest prints Kiyonobu's works show

a distinctive style, characterized by the drawing conventions of *hyōtanashi* ('gourd [bulbous] legs') and *mimizugaki* ('wriggling-worm line'), to depict the powerful musculature of the actors. Kiyonobu did not only portray *aragoto* in his prints, and the line he used in his *bijinga* ('pictures of beautiful women') shows a careful refinement. However, a comparison of *Fūryū shihō byōbu* with *Keisei ehon* demonstrates that Kiyonobu's forte was the portrayal of actors.

Until his retirement Kiyonobu produced *kyōgenbon* illustrations in collaboration with his students and single-sheet prints of actors and courtesans such as the *sumizurie* ('black-and-white picture'; monochrome print) *Sawamura Kodenji no Tsuyu no mae* ('The actor Sawamura Kodenji as Tsuyu no mae'; Worcester, MA, A. Mus.) and the *tan'e* ('red picture'; two-colour print) *Uemura Kichisaburō no onna San no Miya* ('The actor Uemura Kichisaburō as the woman San no Miya'; Chicago, IL, A. Inst.). His *nikuhitsu ukiyoe* ('original paintings'; polychrome paintings) include *Kasa sashi bijin* ('Beauty with umbrella') and *Kōmenzu*.

Kiyonobu's students included Kiyonobu II (*fl* 1724–60), (3) Kiyotada I, (4) Kiyomasu II, (5) Kiyoshige and Kiyotomo (*fl* 1716–36). His influence can be seen in the work of Kiyomasu I, Kiyoharu (*fl* 1700–30), Hanegawa Chinchō (1679–1754), Kaigetsudō Ando (*see* KAIGET-SUDŌ, (1)) and Nishimura Shigenaga (1697–1756).

(2) Torii Kiyomasu I (*fl* Edo [now Tokyo], 1697–1722). Woodblock print designer, possibly the eldest son or brother of (1) Kiyonobu I. Although his exact artistic lineage has not been clearly identified, his extensive body of work falls into the orthodox Torii style. He excelled at *yakushae* ('pictures of actors'), in particular powerful, large-format prints depicting *aragoto* ('rough stuff'; a *kabuki* acting style). His prints of *Shosei Ichikawa Danjūrō no Takenuki Gorō* ('The actor Ichikawa Danjūrō I as Takenuki Gorō', 1697; Tokyo, N. Mus.), *Shosei Ichikawa Danjūrō no Yamagami Saemon to Shosei Yamanaka Heikurō no Suzuki no Oji* ('The actors Ichikawa Danjūrō I as Yamagami Saemon and Yamanaka Heikurō I as Suzuki no Oji', late 17th century; Kansas City, MO, Nelson-Atkins Mus. A.; *see* fig.) and *Shosei Ichikawa Danjūrō to Shosei Yamnaka Heikurō no Zōhiki* ('The actors Ichikawa Danjūrō I and Yamakawa Heikurō I in Zōhiki'; 1701) exhibit the characteristic Torii *hyōtanashi* ('gourd [bulbous] legs') and *mimizugaki* ('wriggling-worm line') style.

Kiyomasu produced many *bijinga* ('pictures of beautiful women'), as well as outstanding illustrations of eagles and monkeys. Although no signed book illustrations by Kiyomasu have been found, the 61 unsigned illustrated *kabuki* scripts (*kyōgenbon*), published between 1697 and 1711, have been attributed to Torii artists. Kiyomasu may have worked on the first *kyōgenbon*, *Sankai Nagoya* (1697), and for *Tsuwamono kongen Soga* (1697; both Tokyo U. A., A. Mus.), which include illustrations similar to his signed prints. Other works attributed to Kiyomasu include theatre programmes (*shibai banzuke*) and votive picture tables (*hono ema*).

BIBLIOGRAPHY

K. Inoue: 'Torii Kiyonobu to Torii Kiyomasu' [Torii Kiyonobu and Torii Kiyomasu], *Ukiyoe no kenkyū* (1923)

Torii Kiyomasu I: *Shosei Ichikawa Danjūrō no Yamagami Saemon to Shosei Yamanaka Heikurō no Suzuki no Oji* ('The actors Ichikawa Danjūrō I as Yamagami Saemon and Yamanaka Heikurō I as Suzuki no Oji'), hand-coloured woodblock print, 591×324 mm, late 17th century (Kansas City, MO, Nelson–Atkins Museum of Art)

(3) Torii Kiyotada I (*fl* Edo [now Tokyo], *c.* 1720–50). Woodblock print designer, possibly a pupil of (1) Kiyonobu I. Only a few of his works have survived, including *urushie* ('lacquer pictures') and *benizurie* ('pink-printed pictures'; two-colour prints) of actors (*yakusha*) and beautiful women (*bijin*), which have strong similarities with prints by Kiyonobu I and his contemporary OKU-MURA MASANOBU. Masanobu is usually credited with Japan's first *ukie* ('floating pictures'; perspective prints), but Kiyotada's own *ukie*, which may be earlier than Masanobu's, make skilful use of vanishing perspective in the depiction of theatre interiors and genre scenes such as *Yoshiwara ōmon no zu* ('The Yoshiwara grand gate').

(4) Torii Kiyomasu II [Heizaburō] (*b* Edo [now Tokyo], 1706; *d* Edo, 1763). Woodblock print designer and book illustrator, probably the son-in-law of (1) Kiyonobu I. He was the second-generation head of the Torii

school. Once incorrectly identified as Kiyonobu II (*fl c.* 1725–60), he probably married the eldest daughter of the founder of the school, (1) Kiyonobu I, in 1724. While Kiyomasu's work is inferior to Kiyonobu I's, he was a prolific designer and had many students. His extant works include *tan'e* ('red lead pictures'; hand-coloured prints), *benie* ('red pictures'), *urushie* ('lacquer pictures') and *beni-zurie* ('pink-printed pictures'; two-colour prints) of actors (*yakusha*) and beautiful women (*bijin*). Between 1745 and 1760 he produced many illustrations for *kurohon* ('black books') and *aohon* ('blue books'; books intended for children and the semi-literate). His representative works are *Fūryū urozoku taiji* ('Crusade of the fashionable sightseers'; 1745) and *Yakusha meibutsu yatsushi sugata* ('Abbreviated figures of famous actors'; 1757). His students included (7) Kiyohiro, Kiyohide (*fl c.* 1760–75), Kiyotsune (*fl c.* 1760–80) and his second son, (6) Kiyomitsu I, who became the third-generation head of the Torii school.

BIBLIOGRAPHY
The Theatrical Prints of the Torii Masters (Honolulu, 1977)
SUSUMU MATSUDAIRA

(5) Torii Kiyoshige I [?Seichōken] (*fl* Edo [now Tokyo], *c.* 1724–64). Woodblock print designer and book illustrator, pupil of (1) Kiyonobu I. He was listed as member of the Torii studio from 1724 to 1763. His extant works consist of *urushie* ('lacquer pictures') and *benizurie* ('pink-printed pictures'; two-colour prints) of actors (*ya-kusha*) and beautiful women (*bijin*). He worked in the Torii style, but unlike his master's strong fluid line, Kiyoshige's linework is rather weak in its stiffness and hesitant angularity. His compositions often consist of a single figure filling three-quarters of the picture plane, while the upper portion is occupied by a poetic inscription. Kiyoshi-ge also illustrated children's books and *kokkeibon* ('comic novels'). His best works are said to be *hashirae* ('pillar pictures'; 680/730×130/160 mm) in the style of his contemporary OKUMURA MASANOBU, and in which he skilfully arranged the compositional elements to utilize the tall, narrow format.

BIBLIOGRAPHY
H. Link: 'Kiyoshige the First', *Ukiyoeshi* [*Ukiyoe* artists] (1982), ii of *Genshoku ukiyoe daihyakkajiten* [Dictionary of *ukiyoe*] (Tokyo, 1982)

(6) Torii Kiyomitsu I [Kamejurō] (*b* Edo [now Tokyo], 1735; *d* Edo, 1785). Woodblock print designer and book illustrator, second son of (4) Kiyomasu II. He produced his first work, a children's book, *Taimen no biwa* (1747), at the age of 13. His output of illustrated books increased throughout his career, but he is best known for his single-sheet *hosoban* ('narrow format'; *c.* 300×140 mm) *yakushae* ('pictures of actors'). Kiyomitsu was no great innovator, but under his leadership the Torii school dominated the world of *benizurie* ('pink-printed pictures'; two-colour prints) by creating striking images with strong colour contrasts and by refining the bold Torii line. This more elegant Torii style was suited to *abunae* ('dangerous pictures'; erotic prints), which he produced in large numbers. He had many students, including (8) Kiyonaga, whom he adopted as his heir, (7) Kiyohiro and Kiyotada II. Kiyomitsu's influence can also be seen in the work of SUZUKI HARUNOBU.

BIBLIOGRAPHY
K. Yamaguchi and S. Asano: 'Torii Kiyomitsu', *Sakuin ichi Moronobu–Harunobu* [The works of Moronobu and Harunobu] (1982), VI/ii of *Genshoku ukiyoe daihyakkajiten* [Dictionary of *ukiyoe*] (Tokyo, 1982)

JULIANN WOLFGRAM

(7) Torii Kiyohiro [Shichinosuke] (*fl* Edo [now Tokyo], 1751–63; *d* Edo, ?1786). Woodblock print designer, painter and book illustrator. Listed among the members of the Torii studio in 1763, Kiyohiro probably studied under Kiyonobu II (*fl*1725–60), (4) Kiyomasu II or (6) Kiyomitsu I. However, the main influences on his work were (2) Kiyomasu I and ISHIKAWA TOYONOBU. Although a member of the Torii studio, Kiyohiro's extant prints include more *bijinga* ('pictures of beautiful women') than *yakushae* ('pictures of actors'). His single-sheet prints were usually large-format *benizurie* ('pink-printed pictures'; two-colour prints). Kiyohiro's *bijinga* are better than those of Kiyomasu I, and he was a master of *abunae* ('dangerous pictures'; erotic prints). He produced the illustrations for *kurohon* ('black books') and *aohon* ('blue books'; books for chidren and the semi-literate), including *Ise sangū gorishō* ('The divine grace of Ise Shrine', 1755; untraced) and *Meigetsuhime koiuta monogatari* ('The love-poem tale of Princess Full Moon', 1758; Tokyo, Orient. Lib.). He also painted *nikuhistuga* ('original paintings'; polychrome paintings; *see* JAPAN, §VI, 4(iv)(a)) in the style of SUZUKI HARUNOBU.

BIBLIOGRAPHY
The Theatrical Prints of the Torii Masters (Honolulu, 1977)

(8) Torii Kiyonaga [Seki Ichibei] (*b* Edo [now Tokyo], 1752; *d* Edo, 1815). Woodblock print designer, painter and book illustrator, pupil of (6) Kiyomitsu I. He was the son of the bookseller Shirakoya Ichibei. He grew up in one of Edo's liveliest areas, with the Ichimuraza and Nakamuraza *kabuki* theatres close by. Around 1765 he became a student of (6) Kiyomitsu I, and his first work may have been the *hosoban* (narrow-format; *c.* 300× 140 mm) *benizurie* ('pink-printed pictures'; two-colour prints) *Nisei Segawa Kikunojō fun suru Shizuka* ('The actor Segawa Kikunojō as Shizuka', 1767; Hirano). However, no further prints by Kiyonaga are known until the *hosoban benizurie Nisei Yamashita Kinsaku no Tsukisaya to yonsei Iwai Hanshirō no Soga no Gorō* ('The actors Yamashita Kinsaku II as Tsukisaya and Iwai Hanshirō IV as Soga no Gorō', 1770; Mizoguchi), which marked the beginning of a steady production of *yakushae* ('pictures of actors') in the Torii school style.

Katsukawa Shunshō (*see* KATSUKAWA, (1)) and IPPITSUSAI BUNCHŌ introduced *yakusha nigaoe* ('pictures of likenesses of actors') in 1765, and by *c.* 1770 all actor prints

Torii Kiyonaga: *Yoru no okuri* ('Closing time'), *ōban* diptych from the series *Minami jūnikō* ('Twelve seasons of the south'), full-colour woodblock print, each panel 381×354 mm, *c.* 1784 (Honolulu, Honolulu Academy of Arts)

were *nigaoe*, except those of the Torii school. The bulk of the 100 *yakushae* of Kiyonaga's early period are *hosoban* (*c.* 300×140 mm) *benizurie* in the traditional Torii style. It is only between 1776 and 1780 that Shunshō's influence can be seen in his work. Kiyonaga gradually abandoned *yakushae* and began to design *bijinga* ('pictures of beautiful women'). He produced few single-sheet prints, preferring *chūban* (middle format; 260×190 mm) and *koban* (small format; half *aiban* or *chūban* size) *soroimono* (print series), such as the *Fūryū Fukagawa hakkei* ('Eight views of fashionable Fukagawa'; *koban*), *Fūryū Edo hakkei* ('Eight views of fashionable Edo'; *tanzaku*, half *ōban* ('large format') size), *Minami hakkei* ('Eight views of the south'; *chūban*), *Fūryū yatsushi Mutamagawa* ('The fashionable abbreviated six Tama rivers'; *chūban*) and *Fūryū nana Komachi* ('The fashionable seven Komachi'; *chūban*). Some of these show the influence of KITAO SHIGEMASA and ISODA KORYŪSAI, while others suggest attempts to distance himself from them. Kiyonaga was also a prolific illustrator of *kibyōshi* ('yellow covers'; comic novels). His first work in the genre was *Fūryū mono wa zuke* (1775), and his *kibyōshi* illustrations reached their peak in 1780. Of the 70 *kibyōshi* published that year, one-third were illustrated by Kiyonaga.

Frank descriptions of the daily lives of the Edo populace are prominent in the works of Kiyonaga's middle years, as in *Hakone shichitō meisho* ('The seven famous springs of Hakone'; *chūban*). In the *sharebon* ('witty book'; comic novel) *Kyōkun iki hongi* (1784), Kiyonaga was listed among the master illustrators of the period. He continued to use the *chūban* format in his woodblock prints, while at the same time experimenting with *ōban* (380×250 mm) prints, possibly to distance himself from the artists of the KAT- SUKAWA school, who favoured the *hosoban* format. A representative work of this period is *Tōsei yūri bijin awase* ('Beauties of the licensed districts compared'; 1782–4), which depicts courtesans from Edo's pleasure quarters of Shinagawa and Fukagawa. Kiyonaga popularized the use of *ōban* diptychs and triptychs, as in *Fūzoku Azuma no nishiki* ('Brocade of customs and manners of the East'; *ōban*, *c.* 1784) and in possibly his best work, *Minami jūnikō* ('Twelve seasons of the south'; *ōban*, *c.* 1784; see fig.). His first triptych is *Shijōgawara no yūsuzumi no tei* ('Enjoying the evening cool at Shijōgawara'; *c.* 1784). In theatre illustration he improved on Kiyomitsu I's *benizurie degatarizu* ('pictures of theatrical chanters and musicians'), with the first full-colour *ōban degatarizu*. His illustrated books from the period include *Ehon monomi ga oku* ('The hill of sightseeing'; 1785) and *Saishoku mitsu no asa* ('Three mornings of colour'; 1787). In 1785 Kiyomitsu I died and Kiyonaga became the fourth-generation head of the Torii school. He continued to produce *bijinga* until 1788, when his production in the genre suddenly decreased.

Kiyonaga stopped designing prints in 1801, turning to *nikuhistuga* ('original paintings'; polychrome paintings; *see* JAPAN, §VI, 4(iv)(a)). He also painted the *ema* (votive paintings presented to Shinto shrines) *Ya no ne* ('Arrowhead', 1810; Tokyo, Jōjuin) and *Nuregami to hanaregoma* ('Newly washed hair and runaway horse', 1814; Shakujii, Chōmeiji).

BIBLIOGRAPHY

C. Hirano: *Torii Kiyonaga no shogai to geijutsu* [Life and work of Torii Kiyonaga] (Tokyo, 1944)
Y. Mizoguchi: *Ukiyoeshi Torii Kiyonaga* [*Ukiyoe* master Torii Kiyonaga] (Tokyo, 1962)

SUSUMU MATSUDAIRA

Torija, Juan de (*b* Madrid; *bapt* 4 Aug 1624; *d* Madrid, 29 Aug 1666). Spanish architect and writer. In 1652–3 he was the principal architectural assistant for the royal works in Madrid, where he worked on the Alcázar de los Austrias and on the reconstruction of the Palacio del Buen Retiro. In 1657 he built the house of Valdevelada with Juan Fernández and the following year he was commissioned to construct the church of the hospital of Monserrat, both in Madrid. In 1662 he reconstructed the main chapel of Atocha in Madrid, following the design of Sebastián de Herrera Barnuevo. He also participated in the reports on the construction of the sacristy of Seville Cathedral. His greatest prestige came from his authorship of two books, *Tratado breve sobre las ordenanzas de la villa de Madrid y polizia della* and *Breve tratado de todo genero de bobedas . . .* (both Madrid, 1661). The first deals with municipal practices previously promulgated and defends the professional capabilities and competence of masters of the works, masons and bricklayers; it was extremely influential, reprinted several times and used by the royal architect Teodoro Ardemans as the basis of his book on the same theme (Madrid, 1719). The second book, a treatise on vaulting, was polemical, as both San Nicolás (1639) and Ceán Bermúdez (see Llaguno y Amrola) stated that its real author had been Torija's father-in-law, the Madrid architect Pedro de la Peña (*d* 1650), who in turn had plagiarized it from a manuscript version by Andrés de Vandelvira; Torija's study, however, uses different and simpler mathematical calculations, and its practical nature places it much more in the sphere of bricklaying than in that of masonry or stereotomy, offering a broad range of solutions for building and shuttering all types of vaults. The same book announced the publication of another text, the *Libro de trazas de cortes de cantería*, which was not published because of Torija's premature death.

WRITINGS

Breue tratado de todo genero de bobedas asi regulares como yrregulares execución de obrarlas y medirlas con singularidad y modo moderno obseruando los preceptos canteriles de los maestros de architectura (Madrid, 1661); *R* with 'Noticia' by G. Barbe-Coquelin (Valencia, 1981)
Tratado breve sobre las ordenanzas de la villa de Madrid y polizia della (Madrid, 1661)

BIBLIOGRAPHY

L. de San Nicolás: *Arte y uso de arquitectura* (Madrid, 1663)
E. Llaguno y Amrola: *Noticias*, iv (1829)
V. Tovar: *Arquitectos madrileños de la segunda mitad del siglo XVII* (Madrid, 1975)
F. Marías: 'Juan de Torija', *Los tratados de arquitectura*, ed. D. Wiebenson (Madrid, 1988)

JAVIER RIVERA

Torino. *See* TURIN.

Torlonia. Italian family of patrons. Giovanni Torlonia (*b* Rome, 1754; *d* Rome, 1829) and his sons, Marino Torlonia (*b* Rome, 1796; *d* Rome, 1865), Carlo Torlonia (*b* Rome, 1798; *d* Rome, 1847) and Alessandro Torlonia (*b* Rome, 1800; *d* Rome, 1886), were important bankers and used their great wealth to accumulate palaces, villas and collections of paintings and sculpture. Giovanni Torlonia amassed his fortune as banker to the European nobility;

he lent money to Pope Pius VI and bought fiefs and titles from impoverished aristocrats. He was ennobled in 1794 and became a Roman patrician in 1809, with the title of Duca di Bracciano. His children married into the great princely families and inherited large estates in the city of Rome. Giovanni acquired the Palazzo Verospi on the Corso in Rome, opposite the Palazzo Raggi, which housed the Torlonia bank. He bought the Palazzo Nuñes from Jérôme Bonaparte for Marino, the Palazzo Giraud near the Vatican and the Palazzo Bigazzini–Bolognetti, later known as the Palazzo Torlonia, in Piazza Venezia for Alessandro (destr.; see Hartmann, fig. 3). His many other properties included one of the treasures of 18th-century Rome, the Villa Albani in the Via Salaria.

The Torlonia family's collection included such works as Titian's *Diana and Endymion* (untraced) and Hans Holbein the younger's replica portrait of *Henry VIII* (*c.* 1539–40; Rome, Pal. Barberini). However, their main importance lay in their patronage of contemporary artists and architects. They assumed the traditional role of the Roman aristocracy and aided the impoverished papacy by financing the restoration of numerous church buildings. In a Rome weakened by political and fiscal problems, the Torlonia family were responsible for the restoration of S Maria in Via and of Sant' Andrea delle Fratte, the completion of the façade of the SS Apostoli, and the construction of the façade of S Pantaleo, which was endowed with a new high altar. They funded the renovation of the choir of the SS Nome di Gesù, where the *Circumcision* (1842) by Alessandro Capalti (1807–68) was placed, and the Capella della Madonna della Divina Provvidenza in S Carlo ai Catinari. They played a vital role in preserving the artistic heritage of Rome from irremediable decline, respecting traditional values without spurning the new.

The Torlonias employed a variety of architects: Giovanni Torlonia used Giuseppe Valadier, who produced the bare, functional façade for S Pantaleo (1806; for illustration *see* VALADIER) and the theatre of Tor di Nona (1820; destr. after 1870). Marino Torlonia employed Antonio Sarti (1797–1880) to renovate the Villa Torlonia (destr.) at Porta Pia, using borrowings from the Renaissance. Alessandro Torlonia commissioned Giovanni Battista Caretti (1803–78) to rebuild the Villa Torlonia in the Via Nomentana (see Apolloni, p. 5), which received a façade in the style of a Greek temple; Quintiliano Raimondi's (1794–1848) circular theatre, inspired by the Pantheon, still remains, as does the *serra moresca* in the garden design of Giuseppe Jappelli, which was completed in 1840.

The Torlonias commissioned work from an equally wide range of sculptors. They bought Canova's *Hercules and Lichas* (1795–1815; Rome, G.N.A. Mod.) and his pupil Rinaldo Rinaldi (1793–1873) executed the pediment of the Villa Torlonia for Alessandro. Bertel Thorvaldsen produced *The Dancer* and *The Saltarello* (plaster casts, Copenhagen, Thorvaldsens Mus.) and designed the reliefs for the Villa Torlonia in Castel Gandolfo and also for the Palazzo Torlonia, which was decorated with 22 scenes from the life of Diana and 16 scenes of Cupid and Psyche (see Hartmann, figs 14–173). A number of sculptors were also employed on the Torlonia funerary chapel in S Giovanni in Laterano: Pietro Tenerani produced a *Descent from the Cross* (1844) and Luigi Mainoni (1804–50) designed a monument to *Giovanni Torlonia.*

The painters working for the Torlonia family were united by an ideal of formal beauty founded on the primacy of drawing, and they all showed the influence of Vincenzo Camuccini and Tomaso Minardi. Filippo Agricola (1776–1857) provided church paintings, such as the *Redeemer between the Two St Johns* (1839; S Giovanni in Laterano), Francesco Podesti (e.g. *Tasso Reading his 'Gerusalemme' to the Court at Ferrara*, 1835; Brescia, Pin. Civ. Tosio-Martinengo) and Jean-Baptiste Wicar painted historical scenes, while the latter also executed portraits of Giovanni Torlonia and his wife Anna Maria. Above all, however, the Torlonias' patronage revived the tradition of mural painting. Giovanni Torlonia decorated the Palazzo Bolognetti with murals by Domenico del Frate (1765–1821), Pelagio Palagi, Gaspare Landi and Andrea Pozzi (1778–1830). Alessandro Torlonia subsequently replaced these works with murals by Nicola Consoni (1814–84), Podesti and Alessandro Capalti. All these works were destroyed with the demolition of the Palazzo itself in 1902 to accommodate the enlargement of the Piazza Venezia.

BIBLIOGRAPHY
G. Checchetelli: *Una giornata di osservazione nel palazzo e nella villa di S. E. il principe D. Alessandro Torlonia* (Rome, 1842)
O. Iozzi: *Il Palazzo Torlonia in Piazza Venezia, ora demolito* (Rome, 1902)
H. von Hülsen: *Torlonia, 'Krösus' von Rom* (Munich, 1940)
J. B. Hartmann: *La vicenda di una dimora principesca romana: Thorvaldsen, Pietro Galli e il demolito Palazzo Torlonia a Roma* (Rome, 1967)
O. Michel: 'Le mécénat des princes Torlonia de 1830 à 1840', *Actes du colloque Ingres et Rome: Montauban, 1986*, pp. 129–43
M. F. Apolloni and others: 'Villa Torlonia: L'ultima impresa del mecenatismo romano', *Ric. Stor. A.*, 28–9 (1986)

OLIVIER MICHEL

Tormo y Monzó, Elías (*b* Albaida, Valencia, 28 June 1869; *d* 27 Dec 1957). Spanish art historian. He graduated from the law college in Madrid and was a temporary lecturer in natural law at Madrid University. He was a member of the Real Academia de Bellas Artes de San Fernando, of the Asociación Artístico-Arqueológica of Barcelona and of the Sociedad de Amigos del Arte and was also eminent as a Conservative deputy and senator. In 1904, however, he obtained a lectureship in art history at Madrid University, thus abandoning politics and law. His work in this field is characterized by a solid documentary basis and direct knowledge of architectural monuments. Under the Second Republic (1931–9) he abandoned his intentions of promoting Spanish art and turned instead to the study of foreign art. He collaborated with Manuel Gómez Moreno in the Centro de Estudios Históricos, where he was Director of the Archaeology Department, while his follower Francisco Javier Sánchez Cantón continued his work in art history. Tormo y Monzó's research work was wide-ranging and varied. He was especially interested in the iconography of Christian art and in painting of the 15th to 17th centuries, particularly in Valencia. Such works as the *Monasterio de Guadalupe* (1914), which has a documentary basis, and *Las iglesias del antiguo Madrid* (1927), which continues to be reprinted, remain essential sources for the history of art. Tormo y Monzó collaborated on the *Boletín de la Sociedad Española de Excursiones* and was co-founder with Gómez Moreno of the *Archivo Español de Arte*. He was also associated with the literary group Generación del '98.

WRITINGS

Desarrollo de la pintura española del siglo xvi: Las pinturas de Goya y su clasifccación cronológica (Madrid, 1902)
La escultura antigua y moderna (Madrid, 1903)
Catálogo de las tablas de primitivos españoles en la colección de la excma: Señora doña Trinidad Scholtz-Hermensdorff (Madrid, 1911)
Un museo de primitivos: Las tablas de las iglesias de Játiva (Madrid, 1912)
Jacomart y el arte hispano-flamenco (Madrid, 1913)
Don Vicente López y la universidad de Valencia con el decisivo triunfo del pintor ante la Corte (Madrid, 1914)
Monasterio de Guadalupe (Barcelona, 1914)
La Inmaculada y el arte español (Madrid, 1915)
Las viejas series icónicas de los reyes de España (Madrid, 1916)
En las Descalzas Reales: Estudios históricos, iconográficos y artísticos, 4 vols (Madrid, 1917–47)
España y el arte napolitano, siglos xv–xviii, conferencia, etc (Madrid, 1924)
Las iglesias del antiguo Madrid: Notas de estudios (Madrid, 1927)
Monumentos de españoles en Roma y de portugueses e hispano-americanos (Rome, 1940)
Las Murallas y las torres, portales y el Alcázar de Madrid de la Reconquista: Creación del Califato (Madrid, 1945)
Museo Nacional de pinturas y escultura: Catálogo de las esculturas (Madrid, 1949)
Pintura, escultura y arquitectura en España: Estudios dispersos de E. Tormo Monzó (Madrid, 1949)
Contributions to *Cult. Esp.*, *Bol. Soc. Esp. Excurs.*, *Bol. Soc. Castell. Excurs.*, *Bol. Real Acad. Hist.* and *Archv Esp. A. & Arqueol.*

BIBLIOGRAPHY

D. Angulo Iñiguez: Obituary, *Archv Esp. A.* (1958), pp. 85–6

ISABEL MORÁN SUAREZ, J. R. L. HIGHFIELD

Tornabuoni. Italian family of patrons. One of the most powerful merchant families of 15th-century Florence, the Tornabuoni were closely connected with the Medici. Both families were involved in banking and had literary and scholarly interests that brought them into association with the most distinguished humanist scholars of the day.

(1) **Giovanni Tornabuoni** (*b* Florence, 1428; *d* Florence, 1497). He was the son of Francesco Tornabuoni and Selvaggia degli Alessandri and married Francesca Pitti (*d* 1477) in 1466. His sister Lucrezia was the mother of Lorenzo the Magnificent. Around 1450 he had a palazzo built by Michelozzo di Bartolomeo (in the Via Tornabuoni, Florence, but now much altered and known as the Palazzo Corsi). It was modelled on the palazzo that Michelozzo had recently built for the Medici. In 1465 he became head of the Medici bank and supervised the family's financial interests in Rome, where he mainly resided until 1487, for part of that time as treasurer to Pope Sixtus IV. He met Domenico Ghirlandaio in Rome (*see* GHIRLANDAIO, (1)), who in 1481 depicted him with his son, (2) Lorenzo Tornabuoni, in a fresco in the Sistine Chapel. He granted Ghirlandaio a contract, dated 1 September 1485, to paint frescoes of scenes from the *Life of the Virgin* and the *Life of St John the Baptist* in the family chapel in S Maria Novella, Florence. The detailed description of the patron's requirements given in this contract conveys the new interest in richly detailed landscape backgrounds. The frescoes were unveiled in 1490 and include portraits of Giovanni, his wife and numerous relatives and friends. The scene of *Zachariah in the Temple* contains portraits of Marsilio Ficino, Angelo Poliziano and Cristoforo Landino, evoking the humanist circles in which Giovanni moved. Ghirlandaio also designed the stained glass for the chapel

and painted the vast high altarpiece (e.g. central panel of the *Virgin in Glory with Four Saints*; Munich, Alte Pin.). Vasari mentioned many other works commissioned from Ghirlandaio, including a tondo with an *Adoration of the Magi* (Florence, Uffizi) and a cycle of frescoes (untraced) for a villa near Florence then owned by the Tornabuoni, usually identified as the present Villa Lemmi.

In 1477 Giovanni commissioned Verrocchio to create a tomb (e.g. four *Virtues*; Paris, Mus. Jacquemart-André) for his wife, who had died in childbirth in Rome. The low relief of the *Death of Francesca Tornabuoni* that was to be carved on the base (Florence, Bargello) was erroneously said by Vasari to have been commissioned by Francesco Tornabuoni. Similarly it was Giovanni, not Francesco, who had the tomb of *Giovanfrancesco Tornabuoni* carved by Mino da Fiesole in the church of S Maria sopra Minerva, Rome. Giovanni's portrait appears not only in frescoes but also in a medal attributed to Sperandio (Florence, Bargello).

(2) **Lorenzo Tornabuoni** (*b* Florence, 1465; *d* Florence, 1497). Son of (1) Giovanni Tornabuoni. He married Giovanna degli Albizzi (1468–88) in 1486. As a cousin of Lorenzo the Magnificent he moved in Florentine Neo-Platonic circles. He was educated by Angelo Poliziano, who dedicated *L'Ambra* and *La Selva* to him. We know from the Medici archives that at the age of 14 Lorenzo was already reading Greek manuscripts of the *Iliad* and the *Odyssey* (Fahy). According to some critics, the youth depicted in the frescoes painted in the Villa Lemmi (*Youth Presented to the Visual Arts*; Paris, Louvre), attributed to SANDRO BOTTICELLI, was the young Lorenzo. A series of panels depicting the story of *Jason*, painted by Bartolomeo di Giovanni, Biagio d'Antonio and Pietro del Donzello (Paris, Mus. A. Déc.; Cape Town, priv. col., see Fahy, pls 233–9), may have been connected with Lorenzo's marriage, perhaps as decorations for a nuptial chamber.

In 1491 Lorenzo Tornabuoni commissioned from Ghirlandaio an altarpiece representing the *Visitation* (Paris, Louvre) for his chapel in S Maria Maddalena dei Pazzi, Florence. Two portraits of him exist, one on a medal by Niccolò di Giovanni Fiorentino and the other a panel painting, attributed to Francesco Botticini (Stockholm, Kun. Slottet). In 1497, having been accused, with Bernardo del Nero, of plotting to restore Piero de' Medici to Florence, he was tried and beheaded.

BIBLIOGRAPHY

G. Vasari: *Vite* (1550, rev. 2/1568); ed. G. Milanesi (1878–85), ii, p. 444; iii, pp. 118, 258, 260, 262, 269
A. Reaumont: 'Il monumento Tornabuoni del Verrocchio', *G. Erud. A.*, ii (1873), pp. 167–8
G. Milanesi: 'Documenti inediti', *Il Buonarroti*, ser. 3, ii (1887), p. 336 [prints contract between Giovanni Tornabuoni and Ghirlandaio]
R. Ridolfi: 'Giovanna Tornabuoni e Ginevra de' Benci nel coro di S Maria Novella in Firenze', *Archv Stor. It.*, vi (1890), pp. 426–56
V. Chiaroni: 'Il Vasari e il monumento sepolcrale del Verrocchio per Francesca Tornabuoni', *Studi vasariani. Atti del convegno: Firenze, 1952*, pp. 144–5
D. S. Chambers: *Patrons and Artists in the Italian Renaissance* (London, 1970), pp. 170–75
A. Luchs: *Cestello: A Cistercian Church of the Florentine Renaissance* (New York, 1977), pp. 21, 37–64, 159
E. Fahy: 'The Tornabuoni-Albizzi Panels', *Scritti di storia dell'arte in onore di Federico Zeri*, ed. F. Porzio (Milan, 1984), i, pp. 233–48

K. Rådström: 'Un gruppo di dipinti fiorentini nel Palazzo Reale di Stoccolma', *Ant. Viva*, xxv (1986), pp. 9–13

DONATELLA PEGAZZANO

Torner, Gustavo (*b* Cuenca, 13 July 1925). Spanish painter, sculptor and architect. Self-taught as an artist, he showed figurative works at his first exhibition in 1951, but by 1956 he became interested in representing nature for its own sake. He was especially attracted to the mineral world, with its complicated corrugated textures. These interests, partly accounted for by his training in forestry, were also aligned with the aesthetic preference for textured surfaces demonstrated by other painters working within the terms of *Art informel* and especially with the techniques of matter painting. Torner's style matured in the 1960s with the creation of his 'complex images', in which he presented the contrasting qualities of surface, volume, light and colour by giving each a different treatment. *Obsessive Awakening* (1973; Seville, Mus. A. Contemp.) is a good example of the refinement of his later abstract work. It was during this period, too, that he and Fernando Zóbel founded the Museo de Arte Abstracto Español in Cuenca. Torner's varied work also encompassed collages, sculpture, tapestries, interior decoration and exhibition design (e.g. for the Fundación Juan March in Madrid).

BIBLIOGRAPHY
R. Chavarri: *La pintura española actual* (Madrid, 1973)
F. Calvo Serraller: *Torner* (Madrid, 1983)

MARÍA TERESA DABRIO GONZALEZ

Tornioli, Niccolò (*b* Siena, *bapt* 16 June 1598; *d* Rome, after 24 March 1651). Italian painter. His early Sienese training under Francesco Rustici is reflected in the *Crucifixion* (1631; Siena, S Niccolò in Sasso), his first surviving documented work. In Rome in 1634 he won a commission for the *Calling of St Matthew* (1635–7; Rouen, Mus. B.-A.) for the customs-house in Siena. This reveals an interest in the art of Caravaggio, which Rustici and Rutilio Manetti had made known in Siena, yet also an awareness of the new classicism and fluid handling of Andrea Sacchi and Pier Francesco Mola (ii). The highly individual blend of Caravaggesque motifs and the formal language of the Baroque enabled Tornioli to achieve a style analogous to that of Mattia Preti. His most famous work, *The Astronomers* (*c.* 1643; Rome, Gal. Spada), was for many years attributed to Preti. Yet Tornioli's compositions are always more balanced than those of Preti, and his art has a refinement that suggests a familiarity with Florentine painting, particularly that of Sigismondo Coccapani and Cesare Dandini. During the 1640s Tornioli was influenced by the art of Cortona. In 1643 he painted the vigorous *Roman Charity* (Rome, Gal. Spada) and received the commission for the fresco *St Philip Seeing a Vision during his Illness* in the Stanze di S Filippo in S Maria in Vallicella, Rome, and these are his most Baroque works. *Jacob Wrestling with the Angel* and *Cain and Abel* (both Bologna, S Paolo) were painted in 1648, followed shortly afterwards by the *Sacrifice of Iphegenia* (Rome, Gal. Spada), which is probably his last known work.

BIBLIOGRAPHY
M. Ciampolini: 'Niccolò Tornioli', *Bernardino Mei e la pittura barocca senese* (exh. cat., ed. F. Bisogni and M. Ciampolini; Siena, Pal. Chigi-Saracini, 1987), pp. 109–21 [with bibliog.]

MARCO CIAMPOLINI

Tornyai, János (*b* Hódmezővásárhely, 18 Jan 1869; *d* Budapest, 20 Sept 1936). Hungarian painter. He studied at the Budapest Design School from 1886 to 1889 and from 1894 to 1896 at the Académie Julian in Paris. After a study trip to Germany and Italy in 1896–7 he settled in Hódmezővásárhely. Tornyai's early genre pictures were calm, balanced compositions in bright colours. His greatest work, *Inheritance*, is a symbolic depiction of the Hungarian Great Plains peasantry (*see* GREAT PLAINS PAINTING): he worked on variations of this painting for more than 30 years (e.g. *Inheritance*, *c.* 1904; Hódmezővásárhely, János Tornyai Mus.). Some of his genre pictures illustrate the aspects of composition with which he was concerned (e.g. *Taking Off the Boots*, 1906; Budapest, N.G.). In the 1910s he turned to landscape painting, using sombre colours, dramatic contrasts and typical Great Plains motifs in such works as *Louring Sky* (*c.* 1910; Budapest, N.G.). His painting *Woeful Hungarian Fate* (*c.* 1910; Budapest, N.G.) reveals a dramatic passion and expressive tension similar to *Inheritance*, the landscape elements bearing an overemphasized symbolic content. His history pictures, such as *Rakóczi in Rodostó* (1904; Budapest, N.G.), were monumental in conception. In 1912 he moved to Budapest. While at Baja in 1928–9 his style changed, as is shown by the works he painted during his stay in the Szentendre colony in 1933–4. He started using fresh new colours and many new themes based on the colony's park and interior. Tornyai and his artist friends strove to develop the artistic life of their home towns. They established maiolica and clay factories in Hódmezővásárhely and also formed the Great Plains Artists Association in 1928. In 1934 an exhibition of Tornyai's work was held in Hódmezővásárhely and the Tornyai Society was founded. The János Tornyai Museum in Hódmezővásárhely, which houses collections of ethnography, archaeology and Great Plains painting, was founded in 1951. In 1984 a collection of 717 of his paintings and drawings, believed to be lost, was found under the floor of his widow's flat, including more than 300 of his Baja pictures, which were painted in the lighter, brighter colours of his later Szentendre period.

BIBLIOGRAPHY
E. Bodnár: *Az újra felfedezett Tornyai* [Tornyai rediscovered] (Budapest, 1986)
J. Dömötör: 'A Tornyai festménylelet' [The Tornyai discovery], *Művészet*, i (1986), pp. 6–10
F. Kőszegfalvi: *Tornyai János válogatott bibliográfiája* [János Tornyai's selected bibliography] (Hódmezővásárhely, 1986)

JÚLIA PAPP

Toro, Antonio Herrera. *See* HERRERA TORO, ANTONIO.

Toro [Turreau], (Jean-)Bernard(-Honoré) (*b* Dijon, 28 Nov 1661; *d* Toulon, 28 Jan 1731). French sculptor and designer. He was probably taught by the sculptor Pierre Puget, and worked as a sculptor on royal ships from the end of the 1670s. He lived at Arles from 1686 (working notably at the Charterhouse of Villeneuve-les-Avignon), and between 1700 and 1718 at Aix-en-Provence, where most of his extant works are located. In 1718 he obtained the post of Maître Sculpteur au Port de Toulon and was in charge of sculpture for the royal vessels. He was an outstanding draughtsman and is known above all for his work as a designer and sculptor of ornaments (e.g. Paris, Ecole N. Sup. B.-A.; Paris, Mus. A. Déc.; Paris, Bib. N.; Rouen, Mus. B.-A.; Avignon, Mus. Calvet; Berlin, Kstbib. & Mus.; Stockholm, Nmus.). He produced a series of drawings of 25 suites, each comprising 6 plates, of vases, grotesques, tables, liturgical objects, friezes and ceilings, some of which were engraved by Honoré Blanc and Balthazar Pavillon (1649–1729) in Aix, and by Charles-Nicolas Cochin I and Pierre de Rochefort (1673–1728) in Paris. He was inspired by the art of the Renaissance and one of his favourite themes was that of fantastic beings entangled in foliage, from which their angry or sorrowful heads and their helpless wings emerge. Through his engravings, Toro was very influential on French, German and English decorative arts during the first half of the 18th century.

BIBLIOGRAPHY

R. Brun: 'Toro (1672–1731)', *Les Peintres français du XVIIIème siècle sous la direction de Louis Dimier* (Paris and Brussels, 1928)

J. Boyer: 'Une Famille de sculpteurs bourguignons établis en Provence au XVIIème siècle: les Turreau (ou Toro)', *Gaz. B.-A.*, xix (1967), pp. 201–24

N. Volle: 'Toro: Dessins d'ornements', La Donation Suzanne et Henri Baderou au musée de Rouen, *Rev. Louvre*, xxx (1980)

JEAN-DOMINIQUE AUGARDE,
JEAN NÉRÉE RONFORT

Toro, Luis Felipe [Torito]. (*b* Caracas, 1879; *d* 1955). Venezuelan photographer. He photographed the most important political events in Venezuela in the first half of the 20th century. Toro's work appeared in such major newspapers and publications of the period as *El nuevo diario, El cojo ilustrado* and *Billiken.* Aside from his official photography, he was an alert observer of changes in the city of Caracas, and was an exceptional portrait photographer. Much of his work is housed in the Consejo Municipal de Caracas.

Based on information supplied by LELIA DELGADO

Toronto [formerly York]. Capital city of the Canadian province of Ontario. It is situated on the north-western shore of Lake Ontario (see fig. 1) between the mouths of the rivers Humber and Don. Its commercial development, linked to its position as an inland port close to the industrial centres of the USA, led it to become the largest Canadian city in the late 20th century; it is the financial and cultural centre of Canada. The site was first inhabited by native American Indians of the Huron and Petun tribes and was visited by Etienne Brulé, a French explorer, in 1615. The French built forts, which protected the early European community of fur trappers and traders. Control of the area passed to the British in 1759, following the Battle of Quebec. Substantial growth began only after the American Revolution (1776), when settlers loyal to the British moved north from the USA, establishing the province of Upper Canada in 1791. The site of Toronto, known from 1793 to 1834 as York, played a central role in this new province. The first plan (1788), a grid with five open squares, resembles those of other early British colonial settlements, such as Savannah, GA, and Charlottetown, Prince Edward Island. Early buildings included the brick Parliament Building (1797) and garrison, but 'muddy York' remained a rough, primitive outpost. The peace following the end of the War of 1812 accelerated the city's growth, and its role shifted from military fort to regional trading centre.

1. *Toronto, Canada West*, lithograph by Endicott & Company, 1854 (Toronto, Metropolitan Toronto Reference Library); from *Whitefield's Original Views of North American Cities*

The further influx of British Loyalists determined Toronto's Anglo-Saxon character. Few buildings remain from this period; among the best preserved are symmetrical Palladian buildings with porticos: the Grange Mansion (begun 1817; now part of the Art Gallery of Ontario), the Campbell House (*c.* 1822; relocated 1972) and Osgoode Hall (begun 1829) by John Ewart (1788–1856) and others. Brick, either yellow or red, predominated as a building material, with stone not readily available locally. The extensive use of red-and-white brickwork patterns became a favoured device of vernacular architecture.

Growth of commerce in the mid-19th century resulted in a proliferation of building, including the Anglican cathedral of St James (1849–53) by FREDERIC W. CUMBERLAND and Thomas Ridout (1828–1905) and the Roman Catholic cathedral of St Michael (1845–8) by William Thomas (*see* THOMAS (ii), (1)), both in a Gothic Revival style. A number of large residences and commercial blocks from this period are preserved along Queen's Park and St George and Jarvis streets, including Mowat House (1856), 372 Jarvis Street, by Joseph Sheard (1813–83). Other notable public buildings are the Don Jail (1859–64) by Thomas and University College (1856–9) by Cumberland and William Storm (1826–92). Terrace housing *per se* did not predominate; typically dwellings were semi-detached, on lots varying in width from 6 to 8 m and set back from the street. The characteristic design of pattern brick, high gable, bargeboard and ornamental porches set within a small front garden typifies Toronto's older residential neighbourhoods, such as Cabbagetown, the Annex and Yorkville.

Buildings of the late 19th century and the early 20th mark Toronto's rise as a leading centre for commerce and government: the provincial Parliament Building (1886–92) by Richard Waite (1846–1911) and others and Old City Hall (1889–99) by E. J. LENNOX were both built of red sandstone in a robust Romanesque Revival style, with highly ornamented carvings and stained glass. Hart House (1911–24) by SPROATT & ROLPH, on the University of Toronto campus, is in the Late Gothic Revival style. Growing influence, both cultural and commercial, from the USA was reflected in the choice of the classical Beaux-Arts style for public buildings, for example the Royal Ontario Museum (1912–14) and the Art Gallery of Toronto (1918), both by DARLING & PEARSON and others, and Union Station (1911–27) by Ross and McDonald (*see* ROSS, GEORGE), Hugh Jones and JOHN M. LYLE. Beaux-Arts planning was applied at University Avenue, which connects Queen's Park with the city centre, and at the Union Station and Dominion Public Building group (1926–31) by THOMAS FULLER and others. Skyscrapers came relatively late, as conservative attitudes prevailed; an early example is the Canadian Pacific Building (1911–13) by Darling & Pearson.

Attempts at rational planning were undertaken with the introduction of the first comprehensive plan for the city in 1943, which led in 1953 to the establishment of a Metropolitan system of government incorporating the smaller municipalities into the City of Toronto and five boroughs. An underground railway, Canada's first, began operation in 1952. Modernist architecture was introduced against a background of substantial population growth, with 600,000 new immigrants to Canada settling in Toronto between 1945 and 1965. The central monument and symbol of this time is the new City Hall (1958–64; see fig. 2) by Viljo Revell with John B. Parkin Associates. Its neo-Expressionist form of curving, high-rise blocks was a daring departure from the predominantly conservative architecture of the city. It was followed by the Toronto-Dominion Centre (1964–71) by Ludwig Mies van der Rohe with John B. Parkin Associates and Commerce Court (1968–72) by I. M. Pei and Page and Steele. The expansion of the University of Toronto included Massey College (1963) by RON THOM. In the 1970s attention shifted to housing, multi-purpose areas to sustain urban vitality, heritage conservation and the promotion of public transportation, which were addressed in the Official Plan (1976). Significant examples are Sherbourne Lanes (1975), an infill housing project by A. J. Diamond and Barton Myers; the remodelling and expansion (1978) of the Yorkville Library (1906–9) by Barton Myers Associates; the Eaton Centre (1975) by Bregman and Hamann with the Zeidler Partnership; and the construction of the new Spadina subway line. The growth of the city as a cultural centre is marked by the building of Roy Thomson Hall (1976–82), a domed concert auditorium by Arthur Erickson with Mathers and Haldenby, and the Metro Toronto Reference Library (1976–7) by RAYMOND MORIYAMA. Beyond the centre Metropolitan Toronto's expansion was reflected by its boroughs becoming independent cities themselves and the construction of civic centres, notably the Civic Centre (1972–3), Scarborough, by Moriyama.

2. Viljo Revell with John B. Parkin Associates: City Hall, Toronto, 1958–64

Toronto was important for the development of Canadian painting in the 20th century. In the 1920s the painters of the GROUP OF SEVEN were pivotal in establishing the city as a centre for artists. A permanent collection of their work is held at the McMichael Canadian Art Collection in Kleinburg to the north-west of the city. After World War II a new generation of painters in Toronto looked both to Europe and to New York. Among them were HAROLD TOWN and WILLIAM RONALD, who in 1953 formed PAINTERS ELEVEN. Their activities stimulated the development of commercial galleries in Toronto and a new generation of painters, notably MICHAEL SNOW. By the 1970s the pre-eminence of painting was challenged by the development of conceptual art, installation art, sculpture and video, with Toronto at the centre of innovative explorations.

The Ontario College of Art (1867) is Canada's best-known and largest art education institution. The Art Gallery of Toronto (1900) was one of the city's earliest cultural institutions (renamed the Art Gallery of Ontario in 1966). Expansion plans were given impetus by the donation by Henry Moore in 1970 of a significant collection of his sculpture, and the gallery was enlarged in 1971 and 1987. The Royal Ontario Museum, established in 1912 by the provincial government, is the city's oldest museum. The Chinese collection is known internationally, and the ancient Greek and Roman collections are the largest and most representative in Canada. The museum has the only comprehensive collection of Egyptian material and the largest textile and costume collection in Canada. The associated Gardner Museum is devoted to ceramics. Aside from providing a wide range of public programmes, Harbourfront, a non-profit corporation established in 1972 and built on land reclaimed from part of the old port, houses the Powerplant, the city's largest gallery featuring contemporary art. Small, independent, artist-run centres include Art Metropole, A Space, Mercer Union and YYZ.

BIBLIOGRAPHY

E. Arthur: *Toronto, No Mean City* (Toronto, 1964, rev. 1986)
G. P. Glazebrook: *The Story of Toronto* (Toronto, 1971)
J. Spelt: *Toronto* (Toronto, 1973)
W. Kilbourne and R. Christl: *Toronto in Words and Pictures* (Toronto, 1977)
J. M. S. Careless: *Toronto to 1918* (Toronto, 1984)
J. T. Lemon: *Toronto: The English Speaking Metropolis since 1918* (Toronto, 1984)
T. Hendry: *Cultural Capital: The Care and Feeding of Toronto's Artistic Assets* (Toronto, 1985)
P. McHugh: *Toronto: An Architectural Guide* (Toronto, 1986)

GEORGE KAPELOS

T'oros Ṙoslin [Toros Roslin] (*fl* 1256–68). Armenian illuminator. He worked in the kingdom of Cilicia at Hṙomklay, the seat of the Armenian patriarchate. His patrons were King Het'um I of Lambron (*reg* 1226–69) and the Katholikos Constantine I (*reg* 1221–67), whose scriptorium he apparently headed. His richly decorated manuscripts reflect Byzantine, Western and even Chinese models. There are seven known signed manuscripts by T'oros Ṙoslin: the Gospels of Zeyt'oun (1256; Istanbul, Armen. Patriarch., Treasury), the Gospels of 1260 (Jerusalem, Armen. Patriarch., MS. 251), a set of Gospels of 1262 (Baltimore, MD, Walters A.G., MS. 539), a further set of 1262, a set of 1265, a prayer-book of 1266 (all Jerusalem, Armen. Patriarch., MSS 2660, 1956 and 2027) and the Gospels of 1268 (Erevan, Matenadaran Inst. Anc. Armen. MSS, MS. 10675).

Although T'oros Ṙoslin worked within the Cilician school of manuscript illumination, his choice of ornament for the initial letters, margins of the text, headpieces, canon tables and figural scenes was more eclectic. His compositions show a careful observation of contemporary life, for although the main figures are frequently shown in classicizing draperies, the other figures are in contemporary clothing; their faces and gestures are all expressive and carefully executed. He was able to present a religious story in a realistic and dramatic manner without impairing its primary didactic function, as in the *Last Judgement* (in the Baltimore Gospels), *The Jews Crossing the Red Sea* (prayer-book) and the *Raising of Lazarus*, *Last Judgement* and *Incredulity of Thomas* (all in the Gospels of 1268). Another characteristic of his work is the attention paid to secondary themes in the text, which he captures in small and imaginative compositions in the margins, such as the *Angels Praising Christ* (Baltimore Gospels).

A number of illuminated manuscripts by other painters clearly reflect the influence of T'oros Ṙoslin. They include the works of a certain Kirakos, who may have been his pupil, and unsigned works such as a set of Gospels of 1266 (Erevan, Matenadaran Inst. Anc. Armen. MSS, MS. 5458), which was produced in the scriptorium at Hṙomklay. The colour scheme used by T'oros Ṙoslin and his circle is distinguished by the unconstrained use of contrast and harmony and by the skilful use of gold backgrounds in the full-scale miniatures. That T'oros Ṙoslin was also a skilled calligrapher is evident from the colophons of his manuscripts: his output is notable for its treatment of the manuscript as a single artistic entity and indicates an acquaintance with contemporary Byzantine and west European forms of illumination.

BIBLIOGRAPHY

L. R. Azaryan: *Kilikiyskaya miniatyura XII–XIII vv.* [Cilician manuscript illumination of the 12th–13th centuries] (Erevan, 1964)
S. Der Nersessian: *Armenian Manuscripts in the Walters Art Gallery* (Baltimore, 1973)
——: 'La Miniature arménienne au XIIIe siècle', *Archeologia* [Paris], cxxvi (Jan 1979), pp. 18–25
I. R. Drampyan: 'Khudozhestvennyye osobennosti iskusstva Torosa Roslina: Miniatyury Malatiyskogo Evangeliya' [Artistic characteristics of the art of T'oros Ṙoslin: the illuminations of the Malatia's Gospels], *Drevnerusskoye iskusstvo: Rukopisnaya kniga* [Medieval Russian art: manuscripts], iii (Moscow, 1983), pp. 331–41
Armenian Miniatures of the 13th and 14th Centuries from the Matenadaran Collection (Leningrad, 1984), pp. 19–30

NONNA S. STEPANYAN

Torralva, Diogo de (*b* ?1500; *d* before 23 Sept 1566). Portuguese architect. The most prominent architect of the mid-16th century in Portugal, he introduced Italian Renaissance motifs into Portuguese architecture, while retaining such traditional Portuguese features as the immensely thick walls that allowed modelling in depth as well as on the surface. His adaptations were influential in the development of the Plain style, a term used by Kubler (1972) to define the rather austere interpretation of Renaissance architecture in Portugal from the mid-16th century to the beginning of the 18th.

1. EARLY CAREER AND WORK AT TOMAR ABBEY. Due to his Italianate leanings, there is a suggestion that Torralva was of Italian origin; it is more probable, however, that he was of Spanish descent, perhaps the son of the courtier Afonso Fernandes Torralva, who in 1501 had come to Portugal with the court of the Spanish infanta Maria, mother of John III, King of Portugal. Torralva married Catarina, daughter of the architect Francisco de Arruda. He is first documented in 1529 in connection with a house (untraced) near Góis, Coimbra, for Luís de Silveira, Portuguese ambassador to the court of Charles V, King of Spain, which was described by contemporaries as 'in the Roman manner, with monolithic columns'. In 1548 Torralva succeeded his father-in-law, Francisco de Arruda, as Master of Works of the province of Alentejo and assessor (*medidor*) for all royal works in the kingdom.

Torralva's work in the province of Alentejo gave him great authority at the court of John III, such that he was appointed to replace João de Castilho as architect at the monastery of the Ordem de Cristo at Tomar, Santarém, in 1554 (*see* TOMAR ABBEY). The building of the new main cloister (see fig. 1), the cloister of King John, was his main undertaking almost until his death. It is the only work that can be attributed to Torralva with certainty. Castilho, who had been appointed Master of Works in 1530, had already planned the cloister as part of an enormous complex of cloisters and corridors, and the first-floor balustrades were complete when he died in 1552. Torralva visited Tomar in 1554–5 and prepared designs for the new cloister in 1556–7. John III authorized work to begin on 20 May 1558; that same year Castilho's work was demolished. By 1562 Torralva had nearly completed the lower cloister, and had started on the upper walls and made the decision to vault the upper cloister. He retired from the works in 1564, presumably due to infirmity, and work virtually ceased for 20 years. When Filippo Terzi was appointed Master of Works in 1584, the upper storey was still incomplete; he resumed work in 1587 to Torralva's design, making minor alterations.

Torralva's work on the cloister plays a comparable role to that of Andrea Palladio at the Basilica (begun 1548) in Vicenza—clothing a Gothic structure of various dates with a uniform Renaissance façade. It masks, on the north, the Manueline wall of the Templars' church, and, to the east and west, stairways built by Castilho. On each side of the cloister three bays with arched openings alternate with narrower bays faced with pairs of engaged columns; on the ground floor there are single arched openings, while on the upper floor the Serlian motif of a central arch flanked by trabeated openings is adopted. To maintain the rhythmic continuity of the façade, Torralva set the corner bays on the diagonal between the arched bays; in two of the corners these enclose cylindrical stair-towers. Torralva maintained a continuous play of contrasting shapes, with alternating arched and rectangular bays, and oculi on the first floor juxtaposed with rectangular openings in the corresponding position on the floor below.

Although the cloister might appear Palladian in derivation, it in fact comes almost directly from Serlio. The elevations seem to have been derived from illustrations in *Architettura*: Book III, fol. 117, shows a single-storey structure of alternating arched and rectangular bays with

1. Diogo de Torralva: main cloister of Tomar Abbey, Santarém, 1556–64; completed by Filippo Terzi, 1587

attached double columns; Book IV (Venice, 1537), fol. 154, shows a two-storey structure with arched bays almost identical to the Tomar cloister, but with single engaged columns. Furthermore, the proportions and detail would seem to derive from Serlio's rather crude woodcuts. Typically Portuguese, by contrast, is the depth of the walls: the spiral staircases are able to be contained entirely within the walls at the corners. The depth allowed the reveals of the walls on the lower floor to be moulded, and required there to be two sets of Serlian windows, one behind the other, on the upper floor. The multiplicity of openings and the use of *pedra lioz*, a golden-coloured local stone, creates a subtle modulation of space and light. The source for the design of the corner turrets, which made possible the extraordinary continuity of the façade, is unclear. There are similar diagonal corners in the cloister at the monastery of the Jéronimos, Belém, where Torralva was master of works, and the combination of spiral staircase, exposed balustrade and domed roof was Manueline in derivation, although similar corner turrets had been sketched in 1539–40 by Francisco de Holanda at the Villa Imperiale (1530s), designed by Girolamo Genga at Pesaro (for illustration *see* GENGA, (1)), and the drawings could have been known to Torralva. At Tomar the turrets made possible the extraordinary continuity of the façade.

Torralva's cloister at Tomar occupies the same place in Portugal as Pedro Machuca's palace (1527–50) for Charles V in the Alhambra in Granada, Spain (*see* GRANADA, fig. 2), that of introducing Italian Renaissance architecture into the country. Like Charles V's palace, it was without progeny, remaining an isolated masterpiece.

2. ATTRIBUTED WORKS. In 1545 John III referred to Torralva as 'master of my works', apparently at Belém, Lisbon. The chapel of S Amaro, Alcántara, Lisbon (begun 1549), has an unusual configuration that may have been derived from reconstructions of Roman temples in Book III of Serlio's *Architettura*: the nave and sanctuary are in the form of adjoining cylinders, with an enormous semi-circular portico of seven rib-vaulted bays surrounding the nave, vaulted and with a coffered dome. The design of the sanctuary of the church of the monastery of the Jerónimos at BÉLEM is attributed to him; it was executed by Jerónimo de Ruão (see fig. 2). The monastery is one of the master-pieces of Manueline architecture. The nave, begun by Diogo Boitac (1502) and continued by Castilho, has a Gothic ribbed vault supported by extremely slender columns. The sanctuary, in marked contrast, is a simple apsidal barrel-vaulted space with severe rectilinear elevations. However, the enormously thick walls, which permit indirect lateral illumination, are continued from the main body of the church; furthermore, the two parts are united by the use of *pedra lioz*. It is an early example of the tunnel-apse, a form later to be ubiquitous in Portugal.

The attribution to Torralva of several churches with Italian Renaissance details has been made on the basis of his work at Tomar. The design of the church of Nossa Senhora da Conceição (1547), Tomar, has been attributed to Torralva, although it is also given to Castilho (for illustration *see* CASTILHO, (1)). It is rectangular in plan, with pediments on the porch and transepts; the interior is articulated by pure Renaissance design, with Corinthian columns carrying barrel-vaults in the nave and aisles. The church of Bom Jesus de Valverde (1550–60), Mitra, near Évora, has been ascribed to either Torralva or Manuel Pires, who succeeded Torralva in 1566 as Master of Works in Alentejo. The plan is a Greek cross of four domed octagons surrounding a central one; the domes are separated on their diagonal axes by lower flat-ceilinged areas. Torralva's hand may be discernible in the alternating arches and flat lintels.

Torralva was involved in several works in Évora: the church of S Francisco, built to the design of Martim Lourenço (*d* 1524/5) in 1480–1500, where he was Master of Works between 1548 and 1556; improvements for John III to the *mudéjar* royal palace (destr.) built for Manuel I, King of Portugal (*reg* 1495–1521); and the fountain (completed 1556) in the Largo das Portas de Moura, a basin with a column surmounted by a marble sphere. The façade (*c.* 1558) of the church of the monastery of Nossa Senhora da Graça (1524–9; for illustration *see* ÉVORA) is attributed to either Torralva or Miguel de Arruda. The façade is one of the earliest in Portugal to use the Palladian motif of a double pediment, although the bizarre proportions do not imply any direct relationship. The windowed chamber over the loggia would suggest some knowledge of Leon Battista Alberti's church of S Sebastiano (begun 1460), Mantua. The church of S Mamede (*c.* 1566), Évora, has no definite attribution, but the principal element, the *sotocoro* narthex, which resembles one upper bay of the Tomar cloister, is attributed to Torralva. The solution of an open narthex beneath a choir lit by a central window set in the façade became a standard solution for Portuguese churches. The humanist scholar André de Ressende, who translated Alberti's books into Portuguese, was a parishioner of this church.

Viterbo

BIBLIOGRAPHY

G. Kubler and M. Soria: *Art and Architecture in Spain and Portugal and their American Dominions, 1500–1800*, Pelican. Hist. A. (Harmondsworth, 1959)
T. Espanca: *Concelho de Évora, inventário artístico de Portugal*, vii (Lisbon, 1966)
R. dos Santos: *Oito séculos de arte portuguesa*, ii (Lisbon, 1966)
R. C. Smith: *The Art of Portugal, 1500–1800* (London, 1968)
G. Kubler: *Portuguese Plain Architecture: Between Spices and Diamonds, 1521–1706* (Middletown, CT, 1972)

Torre, Macedonio de la (*b* Trujillo, 27 Jan 1893; *d* 13 May 1981). Peruvian painter. He travelled abroad while still very young, visiting Bolivia and Argentina and frequenting the group of artists led by Luis Quinquela Martín in Buenos Aires. On his return to Peru he held his first exhibitions in Arica in 1917 and in Trujillo in 1918. His work matured in France, Belgium, Germany and Italy, and he exhibited in Paris at the Salon d'Automne in 1928 and the Salon des Indépendants from 1927 to 1930. Together with other members of the group Los Independientes, led by Ricardo Grau, he brought Fauvism and abstract art to

2. Diogo de Torralva: sanctuary of the church of the monastery of the Jerónimos, Bélem; executed by Jerónimo de Ruão, 1571–2

Peru in the late 1930s, opening the way to modernism, but his influence was considerably limited by the prevalence at that time of the movement concerned with indigenous subject-matter led by José Sabogal. Torre's expressive strength, original personality and versatility led him to depict diverse subjects, including landscapes, gardens painted in an Impressionist style, portraits, still-lifes and vivid multicoloured compositions that he called 'jungles' because they suggested landscapes dense with plant life. His most important works are to be found in private collections in Lima.

BIBLIOGRAPHY

L. E. Tord: 'Historia de las artes plásticas en el Perú', *Historia del Perú*, ix (Lima, 1980), pp. 169–360

LUIS ENRIQUE TORD

Torre, Pedro de la (*b* Cuenca, *c.* 1600; *d* Madrid, 20 Nov 1667). Spanish retable designer and architect. Although his career as an architect was of minor importance, he was one of the major innovators in retable design. He decisively developed the retable from the classical to the full Baroque style. He unified the components of retables, occasionally with a giant order or Salomonic columns; he broke the monotony of entablatures by creating sharp set-backs and projections. For decoration he used swirling masses of vegetation, which produced a naturalistic and succulent appearance. He also adapted the niche to give his retables greater depth and a theatrical appearance, for example by using a hidden light source. Several of his retables are now lost, such as those in the church of Nuestra Señora de las Maravillas (1624) and the church of the Hospital del Buen Suceso (1633), both in Madrid, and in the parish churches of Pinto (1637), Tolosa (1639) and Begoña (1640), the last in the Basque country. His masterpieces are the retable for the church of Fuencisla, Segovia, which he constructed in collaboration with Francisco Bautista, and those for the parish church of S María (1655) in Tordesillas, Valladolid, and the Benedictine monastery of S Plácido in Madrid. As an architect, together with Bautista, he was involved in the final construction phase of the octagonal reliquary chapel in Toledo Cathedral, which had been begun by Nicolás de Vergara and continued by Pedro Monegro early in the 17th century (completed 1630). Between 1639 and 1654 he presented three designs for ornamental variants to the classical plan, none of which was adopted. In 1641 he won the competition, with plans and detailed technical instructions, for building the chapel to house the relics of St Isidore (patron saint of Madrid), although its construction was entrusted to Juan de Villareal.

BIBLIOGRAPHY

V. T. Martín: 'El arquitecto-ensamblador Pedro de la Torre', *Archv. Esp. A.*, 183 (1973), pp. 261–97

——: *Arquitectos madrileños de la segunda mitad del siglo XVII* (Madrid, 1976)

——: *Arqitectura madrileña del siglo XVII: Datos para su estudio* (Madrid, 1983)

ALFONSO RODRÍGUEZ CEBALLOS

Torre, Susana (*b* Puan, Argentina, 2 Nov 1944). American architect and teacher. She graduated in architecture from the University of Buenos Aires in 1967 and studied at Columbia University, New York (1968–9). She was a principal of the Architectural Studio in New York from 1978 to 1984 and formed an independent practice in 1990.

Torre also held academic appointments at Columbia, Yale and Syracuse universities and at Cooper Union, New York. She became an American citizen in 1989. From the beginning of her career, Torre was concerned with the status of women in architecture, studying the history of the subject and advocating a fuller participation of women in the field. Her work is strongly engaged in a dialogue of Modernist and Post-modernist forms. Fire Station Five (1987), Columbus, IN, for example, is a composition of geometric forms in which pitched roofs appear to form a pediment above a cylindrical tower (containing stairs and fireman's pole), which is reminiscent of Midwestern farm silos. Clark House (*c.* 1980), South Hampton, NY, is a renovation of a shingled carriage house of 1917. This project and a private residence (*c.* 1980) in Amangansett, NY, combine monumentality with intimate domesticity. Torre described the latter house, the circular form of which echoed the path of the sun, as 'a sun porch attached to a tower' (Lorenz). Torre's involvement with architectural history informed her renovation (1985) of Schermerhorn Hall, Columbia University, a structure built by McKim, Mead & White in 1896. To rectify a brutal renovation of 1939, Torre partially restored, or rather evoked, the building's original spacious vestibule and stairway. According to Boles this renovation 'relates new and old through a system of proportional reckoning'.

WRITINGS

Women in American Architecture: A Historic and Contemporary Perspective (New York, 1977)

BIBLIOGRAPHY

P. C. Phillips: 'Susana Torre, Allan Wexler', *Artforum*, xxiii/8 (1985), p. 96

D. D. Boles: 'Teaching Architecture', *Prog. Archit.*, lxvii/9 (1986), pp. 128–31

C. Lorenz: *Women in Architecture: A Contemporary Perspective* (New York, 1990), pp. 120–23

WALTER SMITH

Torreggiani, Alfonso (*b* Budrio, 17 Nov 1682; *d* Bologna, 29 April 1764). Italian architect. He was one of the most important architects in Bologna in the first half of the 18th century. He was a pupil of Giuseppe Antonio Torri (1655–1713) and a contemporary and rival of Carlo Francesco Dotti. His two sons Giuseppe Torreggiani (1718–38) and Antonio Torreggiani (*d* 1738) collaborated with him. Torreggiani's work was characterized by a restrained architectural composition combined with elaborate and stylized decoration, which represents the closest to a Rococo phase in Bolognese architecture. He became Principe of the Accademia Clementina in 1749. His first work was the church of S Lorenzo (1704; completed by Giuseppe Tubertini (1759–1831)) in Budrio. He was also architect to the Curia and to the Jesuit Order, which offered him opportunities for ecclesiastical work in and around Bologna. Such projects included the sacristy (1724) of S Maria del Carmine, Medicina, followed by the Jesuit church of S Ignazio (1726), and the oratory of S Filippo Neri (1731; partly destr. 1944), both in Bologna. He started work in 1743 on the completion of S Pietro, Bologna, which Giovanni Ambrogio Mazenta had started to rebuild in 1605. Torreggiani's design for the façade, with ornate portal and window mouldings, and a curvilinear pediment, was only partly incorporated in the final work, carried out by Francesco Tadolini (1723–1805). The interior portal and *coretti* (small private rooms giving on to the church; 1755) were, however, executed to his design. Of his proposals for the renovation of the church of S Domenico, he was commissioned to execute only the high altar (1745). In the church of the Crocifisso (1748), Medicina, Torreggiani followed the 16th-century Bolognese style of Mazenta, with monochrome interiors lit by thermal windows at the sides, but the wall surfaces are more forcefully articulated with engaged columns and rocaille decoration. The façade of the modest church of S Agostino, Reggio Emilia, was of two storeys, curved in plan, and articulated with engaged columns. Although Torreggiani designed the Jesuit church of S Rocco (1737–54) in Parma, it was executed by Adalberto della Nave (1681–1742).

During a period of economic hardship in Bologna in the first half of the 18th century, architectural commissions from the nobility were largely for improvements to existing palaces. Torreggiani's most important work was the façade and main apartments (1744–52) of the Palazzo Montanari (formerly Aldrovandi), for whose owner he had previously designed the Aldrovandi Chapel (1743) in S Petronio, which was inspired by the works of Francesco Borromini. The façade, with rocaille window pediments and a central curvilinear balcony, has been compared with the contemporaneous remodelling of the Palazzo Doria-Pamphili (1730–35) in Rome by Gabriele Valvassori, but the classical pediment over the central three bays reveals a more sober composition. Other works on palaces included the façade (1753) of the Palazzo Dondini (now Sassoli de'Banchi), and the Palazzo Belloni (completed 1756), both in Bologna. Torreggiani also directed the works of the Palazzo Monti and the Palazzo Davia Bargellini, Bologna, which had been started by Dotti. Outside Bologna, Torreggiani designed the façade (1750) of the Palazzo Montevecchio at Fano, and the façade and interior decoration (1756) of the Palazzo Cavriani, Mantua. Torreggiani executed several important staircases: at the Palazzo Malvezzi (1725; rest. 1934), Bologna, and at the Villa Sampiera (1758), where the staircase was illuminated by a lantern decorated with a *quadratura* painting on its vault.

WRITINGS
D. M. Galeati, ed.: *Diario e memorie varie di Bologna* (Bologna, 1836)

BIBLIOGRAPHY
A. Foratti: *Alfonso Torreggiani* (Bologna, 1935)
R. Wittkower: *Art and Architecture in Italy, 1600–1750*, Pelican Hist. A. (Harmondsworth, 1958, rev. 1991), pp. 390–91
A. M. Matteucci: *Carlo Francesco Dotti e l'architettura bolognese del settecento* (Bologna, 1969)
B. Adorni: 'Alfonso Torreggiani and Adalberto della Nave: L'attribuzione della chiesa di San Rocco a Parma', *Archit.: Cron. & Stor.*, xx (1974), pp. 56–64
J. Varriano: *Italian Baroque and Rococo* (New York, 1986)

Torrelobatón Castle. Castle in the province of Valladolid in Castile, Spain. Built as an expression of the strength of the influential Enríquez family, whose capital was at Medina de Rioseco, the castle is one of the most important and best-preserved fortresses in Valladolid. It was begun *c.* 1406, when Don Alfonso Enríquez, 1st Admiral of Castile, obtained licence from John II to erect a fortress in Torrelobatón; the only fortification there was a modest stone enclosure surrounding the village. The castle was

Torrelobatón Castle, Valladolid, begun *c.* 1406

involved in the Comunera rebellion against Charles I (Holy Roman Emperor Charles V). The rebel army occupied the fortress for a few weeks from February 1521, severely damaging some parts of it. After the decisive Battle of Villalar Charles I ordered an assessment of the damage by master masons and carpenters, with the intention of rebuilding it, and these repairs must have been carried out in the following years. Plays were occasionally performed in the courtyard in the late 16th century, and in the 18th century the administrators of the Duque de Medina de Rioseco lived there. The castle is now used as a store for farm produce.

The castle is situated on the outskirts of the village on almost the same level, as is the case with many 15th-century seigneurial Castilian fortresses. It has a square ground-plan, with circular turrets at three of the corners and the keep set into the fourth, protecting the gate. The castle was surrounded by an enceinte (*c.* 50×48.5 m), of which there are some remains, and a ditch, now mostly filled in. The entrance to the castle courtyard is through a gate with a round-headed arch protected by a portcullis. The keep is the most interesting feature of the fortress. Of considerable height (*c.* 42 m), the upper part is protected by eight turrets supported on accordion brackets, one at each corner and one in the middle of each wall (see fig.). The Enríquez family arms can be seen inside the turrets. The keep is divided into three vaulted storeys. Access to the tower is at ground-floor level from the courtyard. A dark, narrow staircase leads from the barrel-vaulted lower storey to the upper storeys and the flat roof. There was once another access gate from the parapet across a drawbridge. The corner turrets project above the parapet slightly and contain some square rooms. The machicolated parapet has a smooth, rounded top, without crenellations, and must date from the time of the 16th-century restorations.

The castle, constructed in limestone ashlar, belongs to a large group of Castilian fortresses of which the most outstanding feature is the keep, often reaching monumental proportions. Included in this series are the 15th-century castles of Fuensaldaña, Peñafiel, Iscar, Portillo and La Mota, all in Valladolid. In addition to the defensive function, the keep served to intimidate the population and discourage rebellion, especially if sited, as at Torrelobatón, on the side of the castle nearest the village. The sense of ownership of the domain and fortress was proclaimed by the coats of arms of the title holders, usually placed on the keep. Torrelobatón otherwise lies in the tradition of seigneurial fortresses that, except in some older castles or in those built on raised ground, have a quadrilateral ground-plan with the keep set into one of the corners. The most unusual features of Torrelobatón are the turrets on the keep and the straight parapet.

BIBLIOGRAPHY

J. Ortega Rubio: *Los pueblos de la provincia de Valladolid* (Valladolid, 1895/*R* 1979)
Conde de Gamazo: *Castillos en Castilla* (Madrid, 1955)
E. Cooper: *Castillos señoriales de Castilla de los siglos XV y XVI* (Madrid, 1980)

FELIPE VALBUENA

Torrentius, Johannes [Beeck, Jan Simonsz. van der] (*b* Amsterdam, 1589; *d* Amsterdam, 1644). Dutch painter. He was active in Amsterdam, Leiden and Haarlem. In Haarlem in 1627 he was condemned, after severe torture, to 20 years of imprisonment for impiety, blasphemy and his membership of the outlawed Society of Rosicrucians. After having been notified by Sir Dudley Carleton, the British ambassador in The Hague, Charles I of England intervened and brought about Torrentius's release in 1629. Torrentius was subsequently active from 1629 to 1632 in London, which he nevertheless had to leave, again on account of his purportedly immoral mode of life; he returned to Amsterdam. There he was again involved in a trial and died after suffering torture in 1644. His erotic pictures, some of which depicted masterful nudes in mythological settings and are now known only through literary sources, were publicly burnt. A few still-lifes (e.g. *Emblematic Still-life*, 1614; Amsterdam, Rijksmus.) have survived. These carefully composed works, mostly set before a dark background, recall the work of Jan van de Velde II and the circle of Willem Claesz. Heda. In Torrentius's pictures the rendering of physical objects is particularly compelling, and their accurate perspective makes it likely that a camera obscura was used.

BIBLIOGRAPHY

A. Bredius: *Johannes Torrentius* (The Hague, 1909)
A. Rehorst: *Johannes Torrentius* (Rotterdam, 1939)
Stilleben in Europa (exh. cat., Münster, Westfäl. Landesmus., 1979–80), pp. 172, 178–9, 205–6, 575 [with further bibliog.]

IRENE HABERLAND

Torres, Clemente de (*b* Cádiz, ?1662; *d* Cádiz, 1730). Spanish painter. He trained in Seville in the workshop of Juan de Valdés Leal. He probably began to paint *c.* 1680 yet, despite a long career, very little of his work is known. He must have been known at the court in Madrid, as he is documented there in 1724 and was a friend of the writer and Painter to the King, Antonio Palomino y Velasco. The sonnet Torres dedicated to Palomino indicates that he also had some literary training.

Ceán Bermúdez considered Torres to be one of the best painters of the period and praised the exceptional qualities both of his oil and his fresco works. Ceán Bermúdez stated that Torres participated in the decoration of the former church of S Pablo in Seville, now the parish church of La Magdalena. He contracted with the Dominican friars to paint in tempera images of the *Twelve Apostles* on the façades of the pillars in the main nave of the church. According to Ceán Bermúdez, he entered into a lawsuit with the Dominicans when he had completed the first three Apostles and the work was suspended. The completed images portray St Peter, St Paul and St Andrew as solemn, statuesque figures. Ceán Bermúdez cited many other works by Torres, but none is preserved. Paintings attributed to him include a *St Nicholas of Bari* (Seville, Mus. B.A.), which is stylistically similar to the Apostles at S Pablo, and a *St Joseph* (Leningrad, Hermitage).

BIBLIOGRAPHY

Ceán Bermúdez
E. Valdivieso: *Historia de la pintura sevillana* (Seville, 1986), p. 291
A. Pérez Sánchez: *Pintura barroca en España, 1600–1750* (Madrid, 1992), p. 417

ENRIQUE VALDIVIESO

Torres, Francisco Antonio de Guerrero y. *See* GUER-RERO Y TORRES, FRANCISCO ANTONIO DE.

Torres, Martín de (*b* Fuente del Maestro, Extremadura; *fl* 1631; *d* ?Cuzco, 1664 or 1680). Spanish sculptor and architect, active in Peru. He influenced generations of indigenous sculptors in the Cuzco region, where he was resident from about the 1630s until 1664 and where he introduced and developed the Plateresque style. Some of his carved retables are known only from documentation, as is the case with the principal altar (1631; destr. 19th century) at La Merced, Cuzco. Other works in Cuzco include the principal retables in Cuzco Cathedral, executed (1637–?1646) in collaboration with Juan Rodríguez Samanez (*fl* 1626–56), in the monastery of S Clara (1636) and in the monastery of S Agustín (1639; all destr.). He also worked with Rodríguez Samanez on the principal retables for the Monasterio de Nuestra Señora de los Remedios (destr. 1650) and for the Hospital de Españoles de S Juan de Dios in 1637, both in Cuzco. He is best known for the two *ambónes* (1656) in Cuzco Cathedral, pulpits placed either side of the high altar. These combine perfectly with the building's mid-17th-century architecture. They are decorated with paired columns, flanking niches with angular and squared tops, pediments with volutes crowned by a cartouche, and with five carved Apostles on each pulpit. His work as an architect includes that in 1651 for the main entrance to the church of La Merced, Cuzco.

BIBLIOGRAPHY

H. E. Wethey: *Colonial Architecture and Sculpture in Peru* (Cambridge, MA, 1949), pp. 198, 203, 214, 296
E. Harth-Terré: *Perú: Monumentos históricos y arqueológicos* (Mexico City, 1975), pp. 31, 61–2, 130–31
J. de Mesa and T. Gisbert: *Historia de la pintura cuzqueña*, i (Lima, 1982)

Torres, Matías de (*b* Aguilar de Campóo, Palencia, *c.* 1635; *d* Madrid, 1711). Spanish painter. From 1646 he lived in Madrid, where he served a lengthy apprenticeship with his uncle Tomás Torrino (*d* after 1656), painter and merchant. From 1657 he established contact with Francisco de Herrera (ii) and other painters of his circle. According to Palomino he gained respect as a hard-working and efficient artist, although the many paintings of his mentioned by Palomino are either untraced or lost. His few surviving works are all small-scale religious paintings, the earliest being the *Raising of the Cross* (1668; Madrid, Real Acad. S Fernando, Mus.), executed in Herrera's style. He achieved the widest professional recognition for his decorations (destr.) for the canonization of St Rose of Lima in 1671 and for participating, under the direction of Herrera, in painting the ceiling decorations (1679; destr.) in the apartments of Queen Marie Louise of Orléans in the Alcázar (destr. 1734), the latter a project supervised by Herrera and also involving Claudio Coello and José Jiménez Donoso. To celebrate the Queen's entry into Madrid in 1680, Torres executed 18 decorative paintings (destr.) for the arch of the Puerta del Sol, constructed as part of a series of arches for the event; the paintings, traditionally attributed to Coello, have recently been reattributed to Torres through documentary evidence and an examination of his style. Torres's work shares common traits with that of painters of the late Madrid school of the second half of the 17th century. It is especially indebted to Herrera; showing a pronounced contrast of light and shade and a certain nervous agitation in scenes containing small, delicate and fragile, but very lively, figures. These characteristics are seen in such works as *Christ among the Doctors* (Vienna, Gemäldegal. Akad. Bild. Kst.) and *Charles V with SS Matthew and Jerome* (Madrid, Real Acad. S Fernando, Mus.), the latter his largest surviving painting. A late work, the *Purification* (or *Presentation of the Infant in the Temple*, 1697; St Petersburg, Hermitage), is less agitated in composition than earlier works. Torres's son Gabriel de Torres (*b c.* 1665) was also a painter.

BIBLIOGRAPHY
A. A. Palomino de Castro y Velasco: *Museo pictórico* (1715–24)
A. E. Pérez Sánchez: 'Don Matías de Torres', *Archv Esp. A.*, xxxviii (1965), pp. 31–42
T. Zapata Fernández de la Hoz: 'Proyecto del ayuntamiento madrileño para el libro de la entrada en la corte de la Reina María Luisa de Orleans (1680)', *Villa Madrid*, cv–cvi (1991), pp. 3–27

ISMAEL GUTIÉRREZ PASTOR

Torres García, Joaquín (*b* Montevideo, 28 July 1874; *d* Montevideo, 8 Aug 1949). Uruguayan painter and theorist. His father was a Catalan emigrant from Mataró and his mother was Uruguayan. Financial problems forced the family to return to Catalonia in 1891 and he entered the Escuela de Artes y Oficios in Mataró. In 1892 he went to Barcelona, where he attended the Academia Baixas and became involved in the Cercle Artistic, also working as an illustrator for magazines and participating in various exhibitions. In 1903–4 he collaborated with Antoni Gaudí on the Templo Expiatorio de la Sagrada Familia (begun 1882) in Barcelona and on renovating the stained glass in the cathedral of Palma de Mallorca. In 1905, through the works he exhibited at the Sala Parés, his talent as a muralist was recognized by Eugenio d'Ors. He became involved in teaching and met Manolita Piña, whom he married in 1909. In 1910 he provided decorations for the Uruguayan pavilion at the Exposition Universelle et Internationale in Brussels. In 1911 he was commissioned to paint frescoes in the Salón de Sant Jordi in the Palau de la Generalitat, Barcelona (*in situ*), a task that took four years and gave rise to considerable controversy.

Having isolated himself in Tarrasa, Torres García began to paint local scenes and landscapes, as in *Street Scene* (1916; priv. col., see Jardí, p. 93). His desire to convey the dynamism of street life is apparent in a series of works exhibited in 1917 at the Dalmau Galeries, Barcelona, for example *The Fair* (1917; priv. col., see Jardí, p. 95). At this time he met the Uruguayan painter Rafael Barradas, who was also working with urban themes. In June 1917 *Un enemic del poble*, a magazine founded by the Catalan poet Joan Salvat Papasseit, published an untitled drawing by Torres García which depicts the hubbub of Barcelona life (priv. col., see Jardí, p. 102). The picture is divided into squares, an early indication of his approach to spatial organization that led to his Constructivist period a decade later.

As an extension of his teaching endeavours, Torres García began making wooden toys. In 1920 he moved to New York, where he also designed toys, which were manufactured in Fiesole and Livorno after he returned to Europe in 1922. In 1924 he moved to Villefranche-sur-Mer in France, and two years later settled in Paris. In 1928 he submitted works to the Salon d'Automne, but they were rejected. Jean Hélion, also rejected, organized a successful show that November: entitled *Cinq peintres refusés par le jury du Salon d'Automne*, it was held at the Galerie Marck. Torres García's stay in Paris brought him into contact with Mondrian, an encounter that proved decisive. In late 1929 he and Mondrian were among the founders of CERCLE ET CARRÉ, whose single group exhibition, incorporating works by 46 essentially Constructivist artists, took place in April 1930 at Galerie 23 in Paris; he left the group in July 1930 after disagreements with his colleague Michel Seuphor (*b* 1901). A call from friends in the newly formed Spanish Republic led him to move to Madrid in 1932. He held exhibitions at the Museo de Arte Moderno and the Sociedad de Artistas Ibéricos, organized the Grupo de Arte Constructivo, which exhibited at the Salón de Otoño in 1933, gave lectures and returned to teaching. He also established the compartmentalizing linear grid that would become his most familiar compositional device. Yet the period was discouraging for him, and in April 1934 he decided to return to Uruguay after a 43-year absence.

In Uruguay Torres García set out on a formidable educational undertaking: he gave 600 lectures and organized 24 exhibitions of his work. In 1935 he founded the Asociación de Arte Constructivo and from 1936 to 1943 he published *Círculo y cuadrado* (10 numbers), which was modelled on a short-lived periodical of Cercle et Carré. It was followed in 1944 by *Removedor* (26 issues), the official publication of his workshop, the TALLER TORRES GARCÍA. Torres García introduced Cubism, Neo-plasticism and Constructivism to Uruguay. In his own work after his return he often achieved a balance between nature and reason, through a combination of Constructivist elements and signs referring to nature (see fig.). Although conveyed frontally, his motifs have an inner three-dimensionality, as in *Untitled* (1938; Buffalo, NY, Albright–Knox A.G.). These structures, and the reduced signs they contain, echo the work of indigenous South American cultures, such as the walls of the Pre-Columbian Incan fortress of SACSA-HUAMAN. In 1938 Torres García finished his *Cosmic*

Joaquín Torres García: *Composition*, 1943 (Montevideo, Museo Nacional de Artes Plasticas e Visuales)

Monument (Montevideo, Mus. N. A. Plást.), a wall of granite blocks inscribed with figurative and emblematic signs, and in collaboration with his followers painted the 27 murals at the Colonia Saint Bois sanatorium in Lezica, near Montevideo; 20 of the murals are extant, depicting a variety of themes. In 1944 he published the most extensive of his books, *Universalismo constructivo*, in which he summed up his ideas about plastic art. His followers include his two sons, Augusto Torres (1913–92) and Horacio Torres (1924–76), Julio Alpuy (*b* 1919), Gonzalo Fonseca, Manuel Pailós (*b* 1918), José Gurvich (1927–74) and Francisco Matto (*b* 1911).

WRITINGS
Historia de mi vida (Montevideo, 1934)
Metafísica de la prehistoria indoamericana (Montevideo, 1935)
La tradición del hombre abstracto (Montevideo, 1938)
Universalismo constructivo (Buenos Aires, 1944)
Lo aparente y lo concreto en el arte (Montevideo, 1947)
La recuperación del objeto (Montevideo, 1952)

BIBLIOGRAPHY
J. P. Argul: *Joaquín Torres García* (Buenos Aires, 1966)
J. Torres García (exh. cat., ed. D. Robbins; Providence, RI Sch. Des., Mus. A.; Ottawa, N.G.; New York, Guggenheim; 1970)
E. Jardí: *Torres García* (Barcelona, 1973; Eng. trans., New York, 1973)
Torres-García: Grid–Pattern–Sign: Paris–Montevideo, 1924–1944 (exh. cat. by M. Rowell, London, Hayward Gal.; Barcelona, Fund. Miró; Düsseldorf, Städt. Ksthalle; 1985–6)
A. Kalenberg: *Arte uruguayo y otros* (Montevideo, 1990), pp. 69–92
R. Pereda: *Torres García* (Montevideo, 1991)
Torres García (exh. cat., ed. T. Llorens; Madrid, Mus. N. Cent. A. Reina Sofía, 1991)
ANGEL KALENBERG

Torres García Studio. *See* TALLER TORRES GARCÍA.

Torres i Clavé, Josep (*b* Barcelona, 31 Aug 1906; *d* Mombrió de la Marca, Tarragona, 12 Jan 1939). Spanish Catalan architect. He had an academic training in the School of Architecture of Barcelona from 1923 to 1928 and came from a family of architects and builders. He was the co-founder in 1930 of GATCPAC (the Grupo de Arquitectos y Técnicos Catalanes para el Progreso de la Arquitectura Contemporánea) and a colleague of Josep Lluís Sert, with whom he shared the leadership of this group (*see* GATEPAC). He was editor-in-chief of the group's magazine, *A.C. Documentos de Actividad Contemporánea*, and took part in some meetings of the CIAM. His architecture was Rationalist and clearly influenced by Le Corbusier. However, he also tried to root it in the popular indigenous tradition, a result of research into Mediterranean architecture. His projects, consisting of housing, schools and hospitals, were intended to put architecture at the service of the mass of the population, and were either commissions from the Catalan regional government or prototype projects with public backing. A few of them were finished, including the simple 'weekend houses' of Garraf, Barcelona (1935), and the 'Casa-Bloc', Sant Andreu, Barcelona (1934–6), a block of maisonettes for the working class, with communal services. Torres i Clavé collaborated on the latter building with Sert and Juan Baptista Subirana (1904–79), with whom he also worked on Barcelona's Dispensario Antituberculoso (1934–7), the best Rationalist work of the period. This put into practice Le Corbusier's 'five points of a new architecture'.

As an urban planner, Torres i Clavé worked with other GATCPAC members and Le Corbusier in the studies for Barcelona that constituted the Plan Macía, named in honour of the President of the Catalan Government. This examined the city functionally, proposing a new regulatory system for traffic, new zones for industry, residential buildings and services, and a cleaning-up of the old city. From 1936 to 1939, during the Spanish Civil War, Torres i Clavé was Secretary-General of the new Sindicato de Arquitectos de Cataluna and held various other responsible positions, such as Director of the Escuela de Arquitectura in Barcelona and member of the Comisión de Control de la Propiedad Urbana, in charge of municipalizing land. Working from the town hall, he carried out part of the Plan Macià in the most run-down areas. He died at the battle front.

BIBLIOGRAPHY
J. Oliveras: 'Architecture and Revolution in Catalonia', *Lotus Int.*, 23 (1979)
'Josep Torres Clavé arquitecto y revolucionario', *2C: Constr. Ciudad*, 15–16 (1980)
'Homentage a J. Torres Clavé', *Cuad. Arquit. & Urb.*, 140–41 (1980)
JORDI OLIVERAS

Torres Strait Islands. Group of some 100 rocky islands, atolls, cays and exposed reefs in the shallow seaway between Australia and New Guinea. Formerly *c.* 20 were consistently or intermittently inhabited by no more than a few thousand people. By the late 1980s only 10 islands were permanently occupied by *c.* 5000 Islanders, while *c.* 15,000 had settled on the Australian mainland. Politically Torres Strait is part of Australia. The Torres Strait Islanders are predominantly Melanesian, although they have had extensive contact and some intermarriage with Australian Aborigines at Cape York and with Papuans to the north. The eastern Islanders speak a derivative of the Trans-Fly dialects of Western Papua, whereas the remaining population speaks an Australian Aboriginal language with an overlay of Papuan vocabulary. Although some horticulture was practised, the traditional economy of the Islanders was sea-based. Islanders ranged far in their double-outrigger sailing canoes, exploiting the reefs and channels for turtle, fish, crustacea, shellfish and dugong (a large sea-mammal).

Little archaeological work has been done in the area, and it is not known how long the Islanders have been there (though certainly for more than 2000 years) nor where they came from. Cave paintings on some of the western islands are so deteriorated that it is impossible to assess their quality. They seem to be mainly stylized representations of human and animal figures in red and white ochre. Douglas Fraser classified Torres Strait art with what he called the 'aquatic tradition' of the rivers and lakes of East Asia. The distance involved, the time span of 3000 years and the absence of connecting links would seem to render this diffusionist hypothesis extremely tenuous. Torres Strait culture is better seen as a self-contained and unique entity that absorbed minor outside influences from Papua.

Decorative motifs that appear frequently and in varying combinations in Torres Strait art include series of triangles or diamonds, concentric inverted U-shapes, incised or fretted continuous V-shapes, chevrons, star and moon shapes and stylized human and animal outlines. All of these motifs can be seen in the wood and fibre constructions of the people of the Gulf of Papua and in the carved and painted wood carvings of the Marind-Anim of Irian Jaya. This, then, is the likely direction of influence on Torres Strait art. Influences from Torres Strait can be traced down both coasts of Cape York Peninsula where large masks and grass costumes, similar to those of the Islanders, were formerly in use, as were similar double-outrigger canoes, harpoons and other artefacts.

Torres Strait art has been relatively well recorded and studied (see bibliography). There are also a number of important museum collections (e.g. London, BM; U. Cambridge, Mus. Archaeol. & Anthropol.; Sydney, Austral. Mus.; Brisbane, Queensland Mus.).

The most elaborate art works of the Islanders were their double-outrigger sailing canoes. Up to 15 m in length and capable of carrying a dozen or more people, they demonstrated a high degree of technical achievement in their construction and rigging. They were adorned with engraved and painted decorations. Carved figureheads and staffs were set up at stem and stern, as well as numerous other ornaments of wood, shell and plaitwork, to which were added trailing plumes of fresh palm leaves and grasses. The canoes were refurbished and decorated anew each year. No example of a fully rigged and decorated Torres Strait canoe has survived, though there are some mid-19th-century drawings by, for example, O. W. Brierly (see Moore, 1979) and H. S. Melville (see Jukes), and a few photographs taken by members of the Cambridge Anthropological Expedition to Torres Straits in 1898 (see Haddon).

Spectacular turtle-shell and wooden masks and head-dresses were used, together with long grass costumes, in ceremonies concerned with initiation, fertility and death. Performed at night by the light of flickering fires to a slow drum beat and chanting, these ceremonies commemorated

Torres Strait Islands headdress, turtle-shell and other materials, h. 266 mm, Central Islands, collected 1888 (London, British Museum)

the actions of mythical ancestors who travelled through the islands creating natural features and teaching the people about horticulture and hunting. Most masks have a large, elongated human face with a long softwood nose attached. They are often painted and embellished with feathers, goanut rattles and shells. The turtle-shell headdresses often combine animal and human figures in representations of mythical ancestors and their associated totems. They are constructed from turtle-shell plates, shaped by heating and lashed together, and are generally embellished with incised and painted decorations, fringes of fretted turtle-shell and cassowary-feather, shell and goa-nut attachments. A simpler than average example in the British Museum, London, represents a fish (possibly a shark) and has wings, which may represent rain clouds, attached (see fig.).

A wide range of anthropomorphic and zoomorphic stone and wood carvings, often of high quality, were also made, mainly in the eastern and central islands. Soft, grey volcanic stone was most common, although granite and coral were also used. Such sculptures were used in magical practices to protect gardens, to increase food species and to control the weather. Small naturalistic human figures carved in hard, dark wood were employed in both love and revenge magic. Larger anthropomorphic and zoomorphic softwood carvings and constructions, elaborately painted and decorated, were carried in dance ceremonies. Presumably they also represented ancestors and totemic species.

The Islanders' vivid decorative sense extended also to such artefacts of daily use as shell and turtle-shell body adornments, feather headdresses, woven baskets and mats, and even to drums, spears, arrows and harpoons. The Islanders particularly admired and valued their polished conus-shell armlets (*waiwi* or *wauri*), half-moon pearl-shell breast ornaments (*mai*) and pendants made from the ground tip of a conus shell (*dibi-dibi*). All these featured in trade exchanges and bridewealth prestations.

BIBLIOGRAPHY

J. B. Jukes: *Narrative of the Surveying Voyage of H.M.S. 'Fly'. . . during the Years 1842–1846*, 2 vols (London, 1847)

A. C. Haddon, ed.: *Arts and Crafts* (1912), iv of *Reports of the Cambridge Anthropological Expedition to Torres Straits* (Cambridge, 1901–35) [basic source with detailed accounts of tech., des. and contexts]

D. F. Thomson: 'The Hero Cult, Initiation and Totemism on Cape York', *J. Royal Anthropol. Inst. GB & Ireland*, lxiii (1933), pp. 453–537, pls xxvii–xxxvi

——: 'Notes on a Hero Cult from the Gulf of Carpentaria, North Queensland', *J. Royal Anthropol. Inst. GB & Ireland*, lxiv (1934), pp. 217–35, pls xxvi–xxviii

D. Fraser: *Torres Strait Sculpture: A Study in Oceanic Primitive Art* (New York and London, 1978)

D. R. Moore: *Islanders and Aborigines at Cape York: An Ethnographic Reconstruction Based on the 1848–1850 'Rattlesnake' Journals of O. W. Brierly and Information he Obtained from Barbara Thompson* (Canberra, 1979)

——: *The Torres Strait Collections of A. C. Haddon: A Descriptive Catalogue* (London, 1984)

——: *Arts and Crafts of Torres Strait*, Shire Ethnography, 10 (Aylesbury, 1989)

DAVID R. MOORE

Torres & Velázquez. Mexican architectural partnership formed in 1953 by Ramón Torres (*b* Pachuca, Hidalgo, 22 Nov 1924) and Héctor Velázquez (*b* Mexico City, 25 Dec 1923). Both partners studied at the Escuela Nacional de Arquitectura at the Universidad Nacional Autónoma de México, graduating in November 1949. They both then spent a period studying abroad before establishing themselves in private practice. Their first works as a partnership were in the International Style, making free use of glass and metal but nevertheless achieving high-quality, attractive structures, such as a house (1959; in collaboration with Victor de la Lama) in Cuernavaca, Morelos, and the Centro Comercial Jacaranda (1956) in Mexico City, in which the various shop units shared a glass façade. The Lotería Nacional tower (1969–71), however, designed in collaboration with David Muñoz Suárez and 102 m high, marked the end of this stylistic period; built on a slender isosceles triangle plan, its foundations made innovative use of cryogenic construction techniques. In many of their other works Torres & Velázquez were by this time adopting a style more obviously responsive to the Mexican environment. They executed a number of buildings faced with rough textures and using warm colours, in which the wall space predominated over window openings, and they also started to introduce more welcoming interiors. Their designs from the 1960s included several private houses, as well as the Conjunto Habitacional S Juan de Aragón (1964–6), with 10,000 dwellings, and the Unidad Habitacional Villa Olímpica, in collaboration with Agustín Hernández, Manuel González Rul and Carlos Ortega, for the Olympic Games of 1968 in Mexico City. The design of their housing projects (1986; in brick) in Villahermosa Tabasco, for over 1000 apartments, reflects their concern with climate, including thorough ventilation and areas of shade. They also executed the Natural History Museum there in 1987.

BIBLIOGRAPHY

L. Noelle: 'Retrospectiva de la obra de Ramón Torres', *Arquit. México*, 117 (1978), pp. 16–36

——: 'Ramón Torres', *Arquitectos contemporáneos de México* (Mexico City, 1988)

——: 'Héctor Velázquez', *Arquitectos contemporáneos de México* (Mexico City, 1988)

LOUISE NOELLE

Torretti [Torretto], **Giuseppe** (*b* Asolo, Treviso, 29 Aug 1664; *d* Venice, 13 Dec 1743). Italian sculptor. He was a distinguished representative of the classical trend in 18th-century Venetian sculpture. His first career was as a stonecutter. The first works in marble ascribed to him, such as the altar of the *Pietà* (Udine, Monte di Pietà) and the altar (Nimis, Udine) made for S Silvestro, Venice, reveal the influence of Arrigo Merengo (*fl* 1688–98). The *Holy Family* in the church of the Scalzi, Venice, which may be placed among his earliest works, also shows elements of Merengo's style, but Torretti soon moved towards the more classical art of Pietro Baratta (1668–1729). In 1710 he went to Rome with Baratta, Domenico Rossi (1678–1742) and Giovanni Antonio Scalfarotto (*c.* 1670–1764), all of whose work was characterized by classical tendencies united with a Baroque theatricality. Between 1717 and 1719 Torretti completed a series of sculptures for Udine Cathedral, among them a distinguished *Annunciation* group on the high altar, which Domenico Rossi had reconstructed. A series of reliefs showing scenes from the *Life of the Virgin* for the Cappella

Manin at Udine dates from 1732–6. Other important works by Torretti are to be found in Venice, at Alamocco, in Friuli and the Veneto and at St Petersburg. His workshop was inherited by his nephew Giuseppe Bernardi (called il Torretti; 1694–1774) and then by Giovanni Ferrari (1754–1826).

BIBLIOGRAPHY
C. Semenzato: 'Giuseppe Bernardi detto il Torretto', *A. Ven.*, xii (1958), pp. 169–78
——: *La scultura veneta del seicento e del settecento* (Venice, 1966), pp. 38–40, *passim*

CAMILLO SEMENZATO

Torri, Flaminio (*b* Bologna, 1620; *d* Modena, 1661). Italian painter. He was first a pupil of Giacomo Cavedoni and then studied under Simone Cantarini, whose workshop he inherited in 1648. He was attracted both by the idealizing art of Guido Reni and by the sensual and expressive power that Cantarini had developed. Torri's first works reflect this heritage: they include the *Adoration of the Magi* (Bologna, S Giuseppe), which in the past has been attributed to Cantarini, the *Deposition* (Bologna, Pin. N.) and the *Vision of St Anthony* in the church of the Osservanza di Imola, both datable to *c.* 1650. These works are characterized by an emphasis on strong shadows. The altarpiece executed for the Fontana–Bombelli chapel in S Maria della Carità, Bologna, has been destroyed, but a vigorous *bozzetto* survives (Modena, Gal. & Mus. Estense); the figures are derived from the altarpiece of *St Alo* (Bologna, Pin. N.) by Cavedoni, an artist whose originality and modernity Torri admired. In 1658 Torri was in Modena, where he worked for Alfonso IV as superintendent of the Galleria Estense. His curatorial duties included copying the works of other painters, and his study of the art of Mattia Preti, who had worked in Modena (1651–2), encouraged him to develop a weightier naturalism. He also left a considerable number of cabinet paintings, such as the *Holy Family* and the *Ecstasy of St Francis*, which are known in several versions (e.g. Rome, Gal. Pallavicini).

BIBLIOGRAPHY
Maestri della pittura del seicento emiliano (exh. cat., ed. F. Arcangeli, M. Calvesi and G. C. Cavalli; Bologna, Pal. Archiginnasio, 1959), pp. 129–35
A. Colombi Ferretti: 'Bilancio su Flaminio Torre', *Paragone*, xxviii/301 (1977), pp. 8–28
C. Volpe: 'Ancora sul Torre per un' importante aggiunta', *Paragone*, xxviii/301 (1977), pp. 28–36
L. Peruzzi: 'Torri, Flaminio', *La pittura in Italia: Il seicento*, ed. M. Gregori and E. Schleier, ii (Milan, 1988, rev. 1989), p. 903 [with bibliog.]
F. Caroli: 'Aggiunte a Flaminio Torri', *Not. Pal. Albani*, xviii/2 (1989), pp. 61–4
A. M. Ambrosini: 'Flaminio Torre', *La scuola di Guido Reni* (Modena, 1992), pp. 391–8

DANIELE BENATI

Torricelli, Giuseppe Antonio (*b* Florence, 10 March 1659; *d* Florence, 2 March 1719). Italian craftsman. He came from a dynasty of artisans who had been active for some time in the Medici workshop in Florence; an ancestor called Bartolomeo is mentioned among the craftsmen employed at the Cappella dei Principi, Florence, during the reign of Ferdinand I. According to a manuscript (1739; Florence, Bib. N. Cent., MS. E.B.9.5.III, p. 1442) by his contemporary, the collector Francesco Maria Nicolo Gabburri, Torricelli studied drawing with Alessandro Rosi (1627–1707) and modelling with Gaetano Zumbo and was employed by Cosimo III at the Grand Ducal workshop to carve cameos and reliefs. The cameos he created include one of the elderly Grand Duchess *Vittoria della Rovere* (London, V&A) and another, unusually large, of *Cosimo III and Tuscany in front of the Temple of Peace* (chalcedony, h. 180 mm; Florence, Mus. Opificio Pietre Dure).

Torricelli's relief sculptures in pietre dure are sometimes carved masterfully from a single block, as in the chalcedony cherubs' heads that adorn the prie-dieu of the Electress Palatine (1706; Florence, Pitti). Following the practice of the Grand Ducal workshop, Torricelli was responsible solely for the execution of works, the majority of which were designed at that time by Giovanni Battista Foggini. Many of Torricelli's finest works came of this collaboration, including the Electress Palatine's prie-dieu, a cabinet presented to the Prince Elector of the Palatinate (1709; Florence, Pitti) and a series of reliquaries commissioned by Cosimo III (Florence, S Lorenzo). With all their variety of invention, these works share an ebullient, tactile hedonism and a sensuous delight in the nature and qualities of such different but equally splendid and luminous materials as ebony, gilt bronze or silver, and hardstones.

Torricelli's most famous work in Florentine mosaic is a bust of *Vittoria della Rovere* (Florence, Conserv. Quiete), which he mentioned with satisfaction in his *Trattato dell gioie e pietre dure e tenere*. Inspired by a marble bust (1680–92; Florence, Uffizi) by Foggini and of nearly life size (exceptionally large for a pietre dure sculpture), the head was carved from one block of Volterra chalcedony weighing 84 libbre (*c.* 27.5 kg). Torricelli reduced this to 6 libbre (*c.* 2 kg) by hollowing it out from the back to insert the eyes and lips, carved in different coloured stones.

Torricelli's son Gaetano Torricelli (1691–1759) was also employed in the Grand Ducal workshop; the taste for carved pietre dure combined with landscape, however, declined at the end of the Baroque period.

WRITINGS
Trattato delle gioie e pietre dure e tenere (1714; Florence, Bib. N. Cent., II, I, Misc. Palagi 478) [part published in Giulianelli, 1753]

BIBLIOGRAPHY
A. P. Giulianelli: *Memorie degli intagliatori moderni in pietre dure, cammei e gioie dal secolo XV fino al secolo XVIII* (Livorno, 1753)
A. Zobi: *Notizie storiche sull'origine e progressi dei lavori di commesso in pietre dure che si eseguiscono nell' I. e R. Stabilimento di Firenze* (Florence, 2/1853)
U. Baldini, A. M. Giusti and A. Pampaloni Martelli: *La Cappella dei Principi e le pietre dure a Firenze* (Milan, 1979)
Splendori di pietre dure: L'Arte di corte nella Firenze dei Granduchi (exh. cat., ed. A. M. Giusti; Florence, Pitti, 1988–9)

ANNAMARIA GIUSTI

Torriente, Fernando de la (*d* 1886). Spanish architect. There is little biographical information on him, but his name is associated with the headquarters building of the Exposición Nacional de la Industria y las Artes (1881), Paseo de la Castellana, Madrid. His design replaced that of the English architect Peck, which had been awarded first prize in an international competition in 1862. Torriente's design is one of the most notable examples of 19th-century iron architecture in Spain. It combines classicizing elements articulated in red brick and ceramics with structures of iron and glass in an eclectic mix. The iron structures were the work of the Belgian company Braine-le-Conte. Federico Villalva collaborated in the building and, after the death of Torriente, Emilio Boix Merino completed it in 1887. It was later partly modified to become the Escuela Técnica Superior de Ingenieros Industriales and subsequently became the Museo Nacional de Ciencias Naturales.

BIBLIOGRAPHY

P. Navascués: *Arquitectura y arquitectos madrileños del siglo xix* (Madrid, 1973)
Guía de arquitectura y urbanismo de Madrid (Madrid, 1982–3)

ALBERTO VILLAR MOVELLÁN

Torrigiani, Bastiano (*b* Bologna; *d* Rome, 5 Sept 1596). Italian sculptor. He was active in the Roman workshop of Guglielmo della Porta after 1573, and assumed control of the studio after della Porta's death in 1577. He executed bronze sculptures for the Cappella Gregoriana in St Peter's, the Cappella del Presepio in S Maria Maggiore, both in Rome, and the Capella del Coro in S Agostino in Bologna. His best-known works are the colossal bronze figures (1585–7) of *St Peter* and *St Paul* cast for the tops of the columns of Trajan and Marcus Aurelius. Perhaps Torrigiani's greatest contribution was in portraiture, notable examples being a bust of *Gregory XIII* and three busts of *Sixtus V* (Berlin, Bodemus.; Macerata Cathedral; London, V&A). These and other works by Torrigiani are generally regarded as among the most significant sculptures produced in Rome between the death of Paul III in 1549 and the sculpture of Bernini, capturing the zeal of the early years of the Council of Trent. The busts demonstrate an indebtedness to Michelangelo's art and 16th-century Venetian painted portraits, such as those by Titian, in their emphasis on surface texture and the strong presence of the sitter—influences that Torrigiani would have inherited through his training and association with della Porta.

BIBLIOGRAPHY

Thieme–Becker
J. Pope-Hennessy: *Italian High Renaissance and Baroque Sculpture*, iii (London, 1963), pp. 305–6
U. Schlegel: *Italienische Skulpturen* (Berlin, 1989)

STEVEN BULE

Torrigiani, Pietro [Piero] **(di Torrigiano d'Antonio)** [Thoryson, Peter; Torrejano, Pedro; Torrisani, Petrus; Torrisany, Petir; Tourrisan, Pierre; Turrisan, Petrus; Turrizani, Petrus; Master Peter; Magistro Petro] (*b* Florence, 22 Nov 1472; *d* Seville, July or August 1528). Italian sculptor. He is famous both as the man who broke Michelangelo's nose and as the Florentine artist who is generally credited with introducing the Italian Renaissance style to England. He was a brilliant and versatile sculptor and also one of the first Italian Renaissance artists to work in France, the Netherlands, Spain and perhaps Portugal.

1. Life and work. 2. Critical reception and influence.

1. LIFE AND WORK.

(i) Italy and Avignon, to 1506. (ii) Northern Europe, *c.* 1506–*c.* 1522/5. (iii) Iberian peninsula, *c.* 1522/5–8.

(i) Italy and Avignon, to 1506. Pietro was the son of Torrigiano Torrigiani, a member of a family of wine producers (*vinatieri*) in the area around Florence. According to Giorgio Vasari, the young Torrigiani was a pupil of Bertoldo di Giovanni, in the 'academy' of Lorenzo de' Medici, where he studied drawing and marble, bronze and

terracotta sculpture. Vasari considered Torrigiani's early works 'very beautiful', but described his personality and appearance as haughty (*superbo*), powerful and robust, violent and overbearing. Torrigiani's envy of Michelangelo, his contemporary and rival in the academy, led to the famous fight (recorded twice by Vasari and by Benvenuto Cellini) while the two sculptors were boasting about whose skill was greater in drawing Masaccio's figures in the Brancacci Chapel in S Maria del Carmine, Florence. Vasari records that this incident (which must have occurred before 1492) so incensed Lorenzo de' Medici that Torrigiani was forced to flee Florence.

On 18 August 1492 in Bologna Torrigiani promised to make a terracotta bust (untraced) of the physician Stefano della Torre. Shortly afterwards, according to Vasari, he settled in Rome to work with Andrea Bregno and Bernardo Pinturicchio and their workshops on the stucco decorations of the Torre Borgia in the Vatican Palace for Pope Alexander VI (*reg* 1492–1503). During this period Torrigiani must have encountered the Florentines Piero and Antonio del Pollaiuolo, who were responsible for the tombs of *Pope Sixtus IV* (completed 1493) and *Pope Innocent VIII* (completed 1498; both Rome, St Peter's) that influenced Torrigiani's later tombs in England. By 1498 Torrigiani was resident in the house of Stefano Coppi, then rector of S Salvatore alla Suburra, Rome, who came from San Gimignano, Tuscany. Torrigiani's will, dated 18 September 1498, appoints Coppi his executor and mentions that 50 ducats were due to Torrigiani for a head (*testa*) he made of *Pope Alexander VI*; this piece Ferrajoli tentatively, but probably incorrectly, associated with a terracotta bust in Berlin (Berlin, Bodemus.). About this time Torrigiani probably made the earliest surviving works attributed to him, the marble busts of *Christ* (San Gimignano, Mus. A. Sacra) and *St Fina*, and a terracotta bust of *St Gregory*, the last two presented by Coppi to the Ospedale di S Fina in San Gimignano (both *in situ*).

Documents discovered in Florence, Rome and Avignon (Darr, 1992) establish that between 1493 and 1506 Torrigiani remained active in Rome, Florence and elsewhere in Italy and southern France and that he may not have left for northern Europe and England until after early 1506. Between 1496 and 1502, Cardinal Adriano Castellesi, the Papal Secretary for the Spanish Pope Alexander VI, commissioned one 'Magistro Petro, Scarpelino Florentino', also called 'Petrus Scarpelinus florentinus' (Pietro Torrigiani), and other Florentine artists to complete various marble monuments for S Giacomo degli Spagnoli, now called Nostra Signora del Sacro Cuore, on Piazza Navona in Rome. This was founded in 1450 by Bishop Alfonso Paradinas of Seville (*d* 1485) and was the first church built in Rome after the papacy left Avignon and returned to Rome. Documented over seven years, the works Magistro Petro scarpelino florentino created include the church's marble doorways (1499–1500) now on the Piazza Navona façade, a polychome and gilded marble Cantoria (1500–02), a marble altar dedicated to Francisco Gundisalvo de Valladolid (1501), various wall tombs and monuments to Pietro Suarez Guzmán (*c.* 1500), to Don Diego Valdes (*c.* 1501), and probably the heraldic putti on that to Ferdinando de Córdoba (*c.* 1490–95), all three now removed to the cloister of S Maria di Monserrato. A stairway, a royal coat of arms for Spain, and stone window frames for the church (all destr.) are also documented to the same Magistro Petro. His patrons, two of them cardinals influential with England and Spain, help explain the important commissions Torrigiano would later receive.

Vasari states that in order to earn better wages during these years Torrigiani enlisted in Cesare Borgia's army in the war of Romagna (1499–1500); he then joined the Florentines in the battle against Pisa (autumn 1499) and later fought at Garigliano (28 Dec 1503) with Piero de' Medici and the French forces. Heralded as a valiant soldier, he returned to Florence, presumably in early 1504. Several works have been attributed to him during this period, for example a polychrome *Virgin and Child* in SS Annunziata degli Zoccolanti, Fossombrone (on loan to Palazzo Ducale, Urbino), which is associated with a commission for an altarpiece that Torrigiani received on 13 January 1500. Some works attributed to the MASTER OF THE UNRULY CHILDREN and the MASTER OF THE DAVID AND ST JOHN STATUETTES (*see* MASTERS, ANONYMOUS, AND MONOGRAMMISTS, §I) may be by Torrigiani. The earliest surviving documented work identified as 'Pietro Turrisani' is the marble life-size statue of *St Francis* carved by 5 June 1501 for Cardinal Francesco Todeschini-Piccolomini for the Piccolomini Altar in Siena Cathedral (*in situ*; was completed by Michelangelo). Piccolomini was Cardinal Protector of England from 1492 to 1503, when he was elected Pope as Pius III (*d* 1503). He maintained close contacts with the Tudor court, and he and his family were probably instrumental in securing Torrigiani's English appointment. Vasari reports that, before going to England, Torrigiani made for Florentine merchants numerous drawings, some in competition with Michelangelo, and many small marble and bronze sculptures 'with nobility and good style' (all untraced). In 1503 Torrigiani married Felice di Francesco Mori (*d* 1541) in Florence, and they had their only child there, a son Torrigiano (*b* 29 Aug 1503; *d* 1528).

Through his contacts with Cardinals Castellesi, Piccolomini and others in Rome, and the Baroncelli and other Florentine merchants, Torrigiani found employment which led to his journey to northern Europe. On 19 February 1504 he was commissioned by Francesco and Giovanni Baroncelli to sculpt with Clement Delamotte, a local painter and glazier, three statues for a *Crucifix with the Virgin and St John* (untraced) in Avignon. Torrigiani may have met Francesco Baroncelli in Rome in 1503–4, when Baroncelli, head of the Florentine 'nation' in Avignon, led a papal delegation to Rome to meet with the new Pope, Julius II. Documents in Avignon indicate, however, that 'Petrus Torrissani' did not continue to travel north, but returned to Rome and on 26 January 1505/6 purchased two large blocks of marble which Michelangelo owned. These new documents and attributed works establish that Torrigiani travelled regularly between Florence, Bologna and Rome, and the more distant Romagna, the Marches, and even Avignon, before he departed for the Low Countries and England.

(ii) Northern Europe, c. 1506–c. 1522/5. In 1509–10 Torrigiani was recorded in the service of Margaret of Austria, Regent of the Netherlands; on 26 April 1510 he

is mentioned in Bruges as repairing and rejoining the neck of a bust of 'ma dame Marie d'Angleterre'—i.e. Mary Tudor (1496–1533), daughter of Henry VII—and as advising Margaret on the tomb of Mary of Savoy and other funerary complexes, presumably including that at the priory church of Brou. The first reference to his activity in England is the commission to make the tomb of Henry VII's mother *Lady Margaret Beaufort* (*d* 1509) in Westminster Abbey, awarded on 23 November 1511 and guaranteed by Leonardo Fristobaldo and Giovanni Cavalcanti, 'merchauntes of florence'. It is probable, however, that Torrigiani arrived in London by 1507 and that he worked for Henry VII before the King's death in April 1509, modelling the bust of Mary Tudor (untraced) for her proposed marriage of 1507–8 to Margaret of Austria's nephew Charles I (later Emperor Charles V). This theory would support an early date of *c.* 1509–11 (rather than *c.* 1510–12) for the polychrome terracotta busts of *King Henry VII* (London, V&A), the young *Henry VIII* and *John Fisher, Bishop of Rochester* (New York, Met.), all three convincingly attributed to Torrigiani. It would also enable the polychrome plaster and wood *Death-mask and Funeral Effigy of Henry VII* (1509; London, Westminster Abbey Museum) to be attributed to him, suggesting that Henry VII was Torrigiani's first patron in England.

Torrigiani's documented sculptures in England were all produced for Westminster Abbey between 1511 and *c.* 1522/5, when he presumably left England for Spain. The first was Lady Margaret's tomb, a collaborative project involving various northern craftsmen, but made of black touchstone, gilt bronze and white marble, a new combination of elegant and precious materials. According to Scott, the surviving contract and various documents indicate that, although Torrigiani designed and carved a timber model of the tomb chest (employing distinctive Italian Renaissance decorative motifs) and executed work for the tomb, including the veristic portrait, the subtle drapery and hands, and the flanking pinnacles and canopy, much of the two-dimensional design for the effigy and tabernacle was the work of the London painter Maynard Vewicke. The traditional medieval collaborative process resulted, however, in an unbalanced design and created a rather unsuccessful visual tension between the Gothic tabernacle, reminiscent of other Late Gothic English tombs, and the new Italianate-inspired tomb chest.

Possibly as a result of the English admiration for Torrigiani's work, on 26 October 1512 Henry VIII commissioned Torrigiani to design and execute the tomb of *Henry VII and Elizabeth of York* (see fig. 1), the central monument of the newly built chapel of Henry VII in Westminster Abbey. Torrigiani agreed 'to make and worke, or doo to be made and wrought, well, surely, clenly, workemanly, curiously and substancyally, for the sum of £1,500 sterling, a tombe or sepulture of whit marbill and of black touchstone wt. ymags, figures, beasts and other things of cuppure gilt'. Earlier, in 1506, Guido Mazzoni had submitted an estimate, and probably a design for the tomb, which was to be based on that of *Charles VIII of France* at Saint-Denis. The kneeling figures are omitted in Torrigiani's design, however, and the corners are adorned by seated angels holding the epitaph and the royal arms. The effigies rest on a sarcophagus decorated with antique motifs (garlands, grotesques, birds and acanthus-leaf decoration), naked putti in the style of Verrocchio, bearing the royal arms and six roundels containing reliefs of the King's patron saints, arranged in pairs. The head of the Queen is idealized, but that of the King is based on a death mask. The form of the monument reflects the tomb of *Pope Sixtus IV* in St Peter's, Rome, but certain features conform to English rather than Italian traditions—for example the tall tomb chest, the overall gilding and the composition of the bronze, although the casting and gilding methods employed were more advanced. The device of paired saints in relief (rather than statuettes in tabernacles) may derive from Donatello's bronze doors in the Old Sacristy at S Lorenzo, Florence, but the elegant figure style shows the influence of Lorenzo Ghiberti and Verrocchio. The monument has been called 'the finest Renaissance tomb north of the Alps' (Pope-Hennessy); Torrigiani had more freedom in its creation, and it is markedly more Italianate than the Beaufort tomb.

On 5 January 1519 Torrigiani received the commission to make a monumental tomb (later abandoned) for Henry VIII and Catherine of Aragon. It was to be larger than the Henry VII tomb by one quarter, and the artist was to be paid £2000. On 5 March 1516/17 Torrigiani was commissioned for £1000 to create the high altar (mainly destr. 1644 but reconstructed 1932–5) of Henry VII's chapel. Originally this featured rectangular gilt bronze reliefs of the *Resurrection* (front), the *Nativity* (back), and on the front a recumbent polychrome terracotta statue of the *Dead Christ*, and also incorporated black touchstone,

white and coloured marbles and large white glazed terracotta kneeling angels.

Other documents indicate that in order to pursue these commissions Torrigiani left for Italy in June 1519, where he recruited the painter Antonio Toto del Nunziata and the sculptors Antonio di Piergiovanni di Lorenzo da Settignano and Giovanni Luigi di Bernardo di Maestro Jacopo da Verona, all of whom returned with him to England. The sculptor Benedetto da Rovezzano also left Florence for London, probably in 1519, to collaborate with him on the royal tombs. In his *Autobiography* Cellini records that Torrigiani unsuccessfully attempted to enlist him to make 'a great work for my king', and boasted of his 'gallant feats among those beasts of Englishmen'.

Other works have been attributed to Torrigiani and his workshop in England. They include the marble and polychrome terracotta wall tomb of *Dr John Yonge*, or *Young* (*d* 1516) for the Rolls Chapel, Chancery Lane (London, PRO), the first entirely Renaissance-style monument in England; the terracotta bust of *Sir Gilbert Talbot* (*d* 1517; London, V&A); the elaborate marble and polychrome terracotta wall tomb of *Dean John Colet* (*d* 1519) in Old St Paul's (destr. 1666; 17th-century plaster casts of Colet's bust survive, e.g. London, N.P.G.; see Grossmann); the bronze roundel and profile bust of *Sir Thomas Lovell* (*d* 1524; formerly Norfolk, East Herling estate, now London, Westminster Abbey, Undercroft Mus.); the marble head and painted limestone roundel of *Christ the Redeemer* (*c*. 1522; before 1532 set in the western exterior

1. Pietro Torrigiani: tomb of *Henry VII and Elizabeth of York*, gilt bronze, white marble and black touchstone, 1512–18 (London, Westminster Abbey)

wall of Abbot Islip's chapel, Westminster Abbey; since the 19th century London, Wallace); and the restored terracotta panel of two winged putti holding the arms of Cardinal Wolsey above the (possibly later) date of 'MDXXV' (which was originally placed over the Clock Tower at Hampton Court), which is of such characteristic high quality to suggest that this was at least designed, and quite possibly modelled, by Torrigiani himself. This theory would reasonably account for Torrigiani's direct involvement during the early 1520s on his commissions for the Henry VII High Altar, the Henry VIII monument and the other convincingly attributed works in England (above), before departing for Spain. The eight terracotta portrait roundels at Hampton Court, once attributed to Torrigiani, are by his Florentine follower Giovanni da Maiano (ii) who, with Benedetto da Rovezzano and other Italian sculptors, continued to work during the 1520s and 1530s in the area of Torrigiani's workshop and foundry in Westminster Abbey on the tombs of Cardinal Wolsey and Henry VIII (later abandoned) and on other projects (see Higgins; Lindley, 1991).

(iii) Iberian peninsula, c. 1522/5–8. Torrigiani moved to Spain either *c.* 1522, when Charles V visited his aunt, Catherine of Aragon, and Henry VIII in London, or *c.* 1525, when he made a terracotta bust (untraced) of Empress Isabella of Portugal, according to Francisco d'Hollanda, presumably for her marriage in 1526 to Charles V in Seville. On his way to Seville, Torrigiani may have worked in Portugal for Isabella of Portugal (1503–39) and in Granada Cathedral on the royal tombs. He must have worked at the royal monastery of Guadalupe, Extremadura, where a document indicates that in 1526 a polychrome terracotta statue of *St Jerome* (now in the sacristy and attributed to Torrigiani) was placed on the high altar. In Seville Torrigiani modelled imposing life-size statues of the *Penitent St Jerome* (see fig. 2), which is related to the version at Guadalupe, and two *Virgin and Child* groups, one for the Hieronymite convent of Buena Vista outside Seville (both now Seville, Mus. B. A.). These influenced later Spanish sculptors and painters, e.g. Montañes, Zurbaran and Goya. According to Vasari, Torrigiani was so incensed over an inadequate payment from the Duque de Arcos that he destroyed a terracotta statue of the *Virgin and Child*; he was imprisoned for the sacrilege and then starved himself to death. The tale remains unsubstantiated, but estate documents referring to Torrigiani's widow indicate that he died in the summer (July or August) of 1528.

2. CRITICAL RECEPTION AND INFLUENCE. An unsympathetic image of Torrigiani and his work has largely been created by Vasari and other supporters of Michelangelo and by the dispersal and relative inaccessibility of Torrigiani's mature sculptures. His monuments in England and Spain are significant for Italian art, however, in their continuing reflection of the sculptural styles of such Florentine sculptors as Verrocchio, Pollaiuolo, Benedetto da Maiano, the della Robbia and Bertoldo. Torrigiani's modelled and carved works, especially his sepulchral monuments in Westminster Abbey, and his *St Jerome* in

2. Pietro Torrigiani: *Penitent St Jerome*, polychrome terracotta, h. 160 mm, 1525 (Seville, Museo de Bellas Artes)

Seville, are among the best Florentine Renaissance sculptures anywhere and demonstrate the talent of this artist and his role in disseminating disparate Italian Renaissance styles, techniques and new uses of materials throughout Europe.

BIBLIOGRAPHY

Thieme–Becker

F. de Hollanda: *Da pintura antigua* (Lisbon, 1548); Eng. trans. by A. F. G. Bell as *Four Dialogues on Painting* (London, 1928)

G. Vasari: *Vite* (1550, rev. 2/1568); ed. G. Milanesi (1878–85), iv, pp. 255–65

B. Cellini: *Vita* [*c.* 1558–67]; Eng. trans. based on various editions by J. A. Symonds, 2 vols (London, 1887/*R* 1959), pp. 18–19

A. Higgins: 'On the Work of Florentine Sculptors in England in the Early Part of the Sixteenth Century: With Special Reference to the Tombs of Cardinal Wolsey and King Henry VIII', *Archaeol. J.*, li (1894), pp. 129–220, 367–70

A. Venturi: *Storia* (1901–40), x, pp. 278–83

C. Justi: 'Torrigiano', *Jb. Preuss. Kstsamml.*, xxvii (1906), pp. 249–81

R. S. Scott: 'On the Contracts for the Tomb of the Lady Margaret Beaufort, Countess of Richmond and Derby', *Archaeologia*, xlvi (1914/15), pp. 365–76

A. Ferrajoli: 'Un testamento dello scultore Pietro Torrigiano e ricerche sopra alcune sue opere', *Boll. A.*, ix (1915), pp. 181–92

C. Cochin: 'Un lien artistique entre l'Italie, la Flandre et l'Angleterre, Pietro Torrigiano en Flandre', *Rev. A. Anc. & Mod.*, xxxvi (1915–19), pp. 179–82

C. R. Beard: 'Torrigiano or Da Maiano', *Connoisseur*, lxxxiv (1929), pp. 77–88

L. Dimier: 'Pierre Torrigiani: Artiste florentin en Avignon', *Bull. Soc. N. Antiqua. France* (1937), pp. 95–6

F. Grossmann: 'Holbein, Torrigiani and Some Portraits of Dean Colet', *J. Warb. & Court. Inst.*, xiii (1950), pp. 202–36

J. Pope-Hennessy: *Italian Renaissance Sculpture* (New York, 1958, rev. 3/1985), pp. 304–5, 359

H. J. Dow: 'Two Italian Portrait Busts of Henry VIII', *A. Bull.*, xlii (1960), pp. 291–4

J. Pope-Hennessy: *Catalogue of Italian Sculpture in the Victoria and Albert Museum*, ii (London, 1964), pp. 399–401

J. Hernández Díaz: 'Presencia de Torrigiano en el cinquecento europeo', *Archv Hispal.*, lvi (1973), pp. 311–27

B. H. Meyer: 'The First Tomb of Henry VII of England', *A. Bull.*, lviii (1976), pp. 358–67

A. P. Darr: 'The Sculpture of Torrigiano: The Westminster Abbey Tombs', *Connoisseur*, cc (1979), pp. 177–84

——: *Pietro Torrigiano and his Sculpture for the Henry VII Chapel, Westminster Abbey* (diss., New York U., 1980)

——: 'From Westminster Abbey to the Wallace Collection: Torrigiano's *Head of Christ*', *Apollo*, cxvi (1982), pp. 292–8

——: 'Santa Fina', *Capolavori e restauri* (exh. cat., Florence, Pal. Vecchio, 1986), pp. 96–8

C. Galvin and P. G. Lindley: 'Pietro Torrigiano's Portrait Bust of King Henry VII', *Burl. Mag.*, cxxx (1988), pp. 892–902

——: 'Pietro Torrigiano's Tomb for Dr Yonge', *Ch. Mnmts*, 3 (1988), pp. 42–60

P. G. Lindley: 'Una grande opera al mio re: Gilt-bronze Effigies in England from the Middle Ages to the Renaissance', *J. Brit. Archaeol. Assoc.*, 143 (1990), pp. 112–30

——: 'Playing Check-mate with Royal Majesty? Wolsey's Patronage of Italian Renaissance Sculpture', *Cardinal Wolsey: Church, State and Art*, ed. S. J. Gunn and P. G. Lindley (Cambridge, 1991), pp. 261–85

A. P. Darr: 'New Documents for Pietro Torrigiani and Other Early Cinquecento Florentine Sculptors Active in Italy and England', *Kunst des Cinquecento in der Toskana*, ed. M Cämmerer (Munich, 1992), pp. 108–38

——: 'Verrocchio's Legacy: Observations Regarding his Influence on Pietro Torrigiani and Other Florentine Sculptors', *Verrocchio and Late Quattrocento Italian Sculpture*, ed. S. Bule, A. P. Darr and F. S. Gioffredi (Florence, 1992), pp. 125–39

ALAN PHIPPS DARR

Torriti, Jacopo [Iacobus] (*fl c.* 1270–1300). Italian painter and mosaicist. Two mosaics in Rome are signed by him: one, on the apse of S Giovanni in Laterano, that once bore the date 1291 (or, according to some sources, 1290 or 1292); and another on the apse and triumphal arch of S Maria Maggiore, now replaced by a 19th-century restoration but at one time dated 1295 or 1296. Torriti is also known to have executed a mosaic for Arnolfo di Cambio's tomb of *Pope Boniface VIII* (1296; destr.; *see* ARNOLFO DI CAMBIO) in Old St Peter's, Rome. Torriti was active during the same period as Cimabue and Giotto, Pietro Cavallini and Arnolfo di Cambio, but his fame has been obscured by theirs, no doubt because of his closer links with Byzantine art. He was nevertheless one of the most important artists working in Rome during the papacy of Nicholas IV (1288–92) and was entrusted with some of the most prestigious commissions of the day.

Frescoes in the Upper Church of S Francesco, Assisi, have been convincingly attributed to Torriti on the basis of stylistic comparisons with his mosaics in S Maria Maggiore: the first three *Genesis* scenes on the north nave wall (*see* ASSISI, fig. 4) and the vault fresco depicting *Christ, the Virgin and SS John the Baptist and Francis*. They reveal an artist already fully developed in his powers of expression, and it is probable that Torriti was the leader of the Roman artists working at Assisi during this period (his assistants were responsible for the frescoes on the opposite wall, with scenes from the *Annunciation* to the *Resurrection*). In their monumentality and classical sense of proportion, the paintings demonstrate a knowledge of mid-14th-century Byzantine art, but the iconography is typically Roman or central Italian, as are the facial types (e.g. that of the Virgin on the vault) and decorative vocabulary. If, as seems probable, Torriti's activity at Assisi was interrupted by a call to Rome to work on the Lateran mosaics, these frescoes must be dated to the 1280s. Torriti may perhaps have worked at Assisi earlier, on the frescoes of the upper levels of the north transept, which are also by Roman artists; of controversial date, they were probably executed between the early 1260s and the second half of the 1270s.

The Lateran mosaics, showing a *Head of Christ the Redeemer with the Virgin, Pope Nicholas IV and Saints*, with figures of the Apostles below between the windows of the apse, convey only a poor idea of Torriti's capabilities, since they were largely reworked during their transfer to the new apse in 1883–4 (*see* ROME, §V, 15(ii)), but their compositions and iconography show a debt to the Roman school, while Byzantine influence, perhaps through a knowledge of illuminated manuscripts, is apparent in the Apostle figures. The question of how Torriti acquired such skill in the technique of mosaic in Rome, where it had not been practised on a grand scale for many generations, remains unanswered, but the extreme technical refinement of the well-preserved mosaics at S Maria Maggiore, executed immediately after those at the Lateran, makes it unlikely that Torriti was solely responsible for them, especially as he had hitherto, as far as is known, been exclusively a fresco painter. In view of the differences between these mosaics and the essentially non-figurative work of the Cosmati marble workers of Rome, it seems probable that Torriti employed Byzantine craftsmen to carry out his designs and to teach their techniques to his Roman assistants, some of whom must also have worked on the façade mosaic of the church, under Filippo Rusuti's direction.

Torriti's patron at both the Lateran and S Maria Maggiore was the Franciscan pope Nicholas IV, which explains the unusual presence of the figures of SS Francis and Anthony of Padua in the apse mosaics of these churches. The dedication of S Maria Maggiore no doubt combined with the Franciscan emphasis on the Marian cult to influence the iconographic programme devised for the apse, which features as its principal scene the *Coronation of the Virgin* (see fig.), with scenes from the *Life of the Virgin* below (*see* ROME, §V, 20). The general organization of the scheme—the composition with lateral saints and naturalistic background, as well as certain details (e.g. the splendid river landscape, in the Classical tradition)—is indebted to Roman precedents, but the stylistic formulae reveal the influence of Byzantine art. This is demonstrated by Torriti's use of contrasts between blues and reds (seen

Jacopo Torriti: *Coronation of the Virgin* (1295 or 1296), apse mosaic, S Maria Maggiore, Rome

in the work of many icon painters) and the construction of his figures (the Apostles closely resemble the frescoed figures at the monastery of Sopócani in Serbia). The sculptural appearance of the Virgin (whose face is modelled on the icon of the *Salus populi romani* in the same church) approaches Arnolfo di Cambio's work, but Torriti's figure style is very different from that of his other Roman contemporary Pietro Cavallini, even though both artists would have been subjected to similar influences; the narratives on the apse of S Maria Maggiore in fact influenced Cavallini's decoration of the mosaic band around the base of the apse in S Maria in Trastevere. A number of minor mosaics in other Roman churches have been attributed to Torriti, as have some panel paintings, but these are better seen as part of the vast output of the late 13th-century Roman school.

BIBLIOGRAPHY
G. Matthiae: *Mosaici medioevali delle chiese di Roma*, i (Rome, 1967), pp. 347–66
J. Gardner: 'Pope Nicholas IV and the Decoration of Santa Maria Maggiore', *Z. Kstgesch.*, xxxvi (1973), pp. 1–50
H. Belting: *Die Oberkirche von San Francesco in Assisi* (Berlin, 1977)
V. Pace: 'Pittura del duecento e del trecento a Roma e nel Lazio', *La pittura in Italia: Le origini*, ed. E. Castelnuovo (Milan, 1985, 2/1986)
A. Tomei: *Iacobus Torriti pictor* (Rome, 1990)
V. Pace: 'Dieci secoli di affreschi e mosaici romani', *Boll. A.*, lxviii-lxix (1991)

VALENTINO PACE

Torroja (Miret), Eduardo (*b* Madrid, 27 Aug 1899; *d* Madrid, 15 June 1961). Spanish engineer, theorist and teacher. He graduated from the Escuela de Ingenieros de Caminos, Canales y Puertos in Madrid in 1923, having inherited an interest in calculus and experimentation with structures from his father, the mathematician Eduardo Torroja Caballé. He went on to become one of the most innovative engineers of the early 20th century, notable particularly for his designs for laminated roofs. Particularly characteristic of his work was the use of continuous surfaces, as light as possible and with a sense of their intrinsic elasticity, eliminating the need for ribs. He used this type of surface as roofing in the stand and glass roof of the Hipódromo de la Zarzuela (1935), Madrid, produced in collaboration with Carlos Arniches Moltó and Martín Domínguez Esteban; these were conceived as two monumental bird's wings in cross-section, with elegant longitudinal undulations. Other notable works include the aqueduct (1939) at Alloz, Navarre, the bridge (1940) over the River Esla, León, and the church of Pont de Suert (1952), Lerida. Although his aesthetic was based on the truth and objectivity of technique, Torroja understood that a work was better if sustained by its form and not by the hidden resistance of its material, and this led him to establish anatomical analogies to explain resistant behaviour and to the use of organic forms in his designs (*see* SHELL STRUCTURE). From 1939 he taught at the Escuela de Ingenieros de Caminos, and he also founded the Instituto Técnico de la Construcción y Edificación, also in Madrid.

WRITINGS

Razón y ser de los tipos estructurales (Madrid, 1957); Eng. trans. as *The Philosophy of Structures* (Berkeley, 1958)
The Structures of Eduardo Torroja (New York, 1958) [autobiog.]

BIBLIOGRAPHY

R. Moneo: 'Un viejo tema', *Nueva Forma*, ii (1968), pp. 14–19
F. del Pozo: 'Eduardo Torroja visto por uno de sus discipulos', *Nueva Forma*, ii (1968), pp. 3–13
M. G. Salvadori: 'Torroja, pionero de la moderna arquitectura', *Nueva Forma*, ii (1968), pp. 61–2
F. Arredondo and others: *La obra de Eduardo Torroja* (Madrid, 1977)
La modernidad en la obra de Eduardo Torroja (exh. cat., Madrid, Min. Obras Púb. & Urb., 1979)

JORDI OLIVERAS

Tortillon. *See under* STUMPING.

Tortoiseshell. Semi-transparent or translucent material of mottled patterns of brown pigmentation, obtained from the enlarged scales or plates that form the protective outer shell of certain species of tropical and sub-tropical marine turtles. These scales are joined to form the carapace or back and the plastron or belly of the turtle. The plates from the carapace are heavily pigmented in shades of dark brown, amber and red, whereas those of the plastron are usually clear and yellow in colour and provide 'blonde' plates. The three species of turtle associated with providing tortoiseshell for decorative art objects are the Hawksbill turtle (*Chelone imbricata*), which provides the finest scales, the Loggerhead (*Thalassochelys caretta*) and the Green turtle (*Chelone mydas*). The plates from these turtles vary considerably in colour, size and working characteristics. The shell of some land tortoises has also been used to make objects, but 'tortoiseshell' refers almost exclusively to the scales from marine turtles.

1. PROPERTIES AND TECHNIQUES. Tortoiseshell's colour, transparency and brilliant shine when polished have made it a highly prized material for both making and decorating objects. Its principal chemical constituent is keratin, a protein complex secreted by the epidermis of the skin of vertebrates. In marine turtles this keratinous outer layer has developed to a great thickness acting as a protective armour. The protein chains that make up keratin have a high proportion of the amino acid cysteine, which can form disulphide bonds between parallel protein chains.

These disulphide bonds account for the major working characteristics of tortoiseshell. It can be easily sawn and worked with basic hand tools. Due to its chemical make-up it also possesses thermoplastic properties, which means that the normally hard and rigid tortoiseshell can be softened and made pliable by either boiling in salted water or applying direct heat. In this softened state it can be bent, shaped or impressed, and when it cools back to room temperature it will retain its new shape or form. The softening process breaks some of the chemical bonds

Tortoiseshell workbox, carved with figures and landscapes, 305×114×203 mm, from China, 19th century (London, Victoria and Albert Museum)

between the protein chains and allows a rearrangement of them. When the tortoiseshell cools, the bonds re-form to make it rigid again. Sheets of tortoiseshell can be welded together to form larger sheets or bent into a circular shape and welded together on itself, such as for circular boxes. Heat and moisture are used, and pressure is applied over the area to be welded, so that the two pieces become fused together. The tortoiseshell is heated in water until it is pliable, and the two edges to be joined together are overlapped or scarf-jointed, then clamped between heated tongs.

2. USES. Tortoiseshell has been employed for a wide range of decorative effects. Due to the thinness of the scales, one of its major uses is as an inlay or veneer. The shell of the Loggerhead turtle was used, for instance, for furniture inlay in China, and it was imported for the same purpose by the Romans and later the Ottomans. Since the 16th century softened tortoiseshell veneer has been used to decorate European furniture and picture frames by bending it to the desired curve before gluing it in place on a wood groundwork. Tortoiseshell veneer was also used in conjunction with exotic woods and ivory to decorate musical instruments. One of its most celebrated uses as a veneer was in combination with brass veneers in decorative patterns, a technique refined and brought to a high degree of perfection by ANDRÉ-CHARLES BOULLE. This type of work, a special form of marquetry, has since been termed boullework. From the 17th century onwards it was used on a variety of furniture types, such as cabinets, commodes and bracket clocks.

In its slightly thicker form, tortoiseshell has been used to make smaller objects such as combs, hairbrush backs, snuff and tobacco boxes, spectacle frames and pieces of jewellery (e.g. in ancient Egypt). The surface of these objects is often decorated by pressing the softened tortoiseshell with a decorated relief mould or by pressing metal pins or wire into it. Occasionally thicker sheets of tortoiseshell have also been carved, for example into netsuke in Japan and in low relief for decorated boxes and other objects made in China in the 19th century, principally for export to the European market (see fig.). Tortoiseshell has been imitated by stained horn and since the late 19th century by celluloid (cellulose nitrate).

BIBLIOGRAPHY
C. Ritchie: *Carving Shells and Cameos* (London, 1970)
——: *Shell Carving: History and Techniques* (London, 1974)
S. O'Connor: *The Identification of Osseous and Keratinaceous Materials at York*, United Kingdom Institute for Conservation (UKIC), Occasional Papers, v (1987)
GORDON HANLON

Tortolero, Pedro (*b* Seville, *c*.1700; *d* Seville, 1766). Spanish painter and engraver. He was a pupil of Domingo Martínez, but his engravings do not show great skill in drawing or technique. He produced devotional engravings and portraits, and his illustrations for the reports of Lorenzo Bautista de Zúñiga, *Annales eclesiásticos i seglares ... de la ciudad de Sevilla* (Seville, 1747), are mainly of iconographic interest. They include two large plates representing *Philip V and his Court Entering Seville in 1724* and the *Transfer of the Remains of Ferdinand III* (the Saint; *d*1252), to their new resting-place, with the procession passing Seville Cathedral. The frontispiece was engraved by Juan Fernández (*fl*1747) after a drawing by Tortolero. Other engravings of 1738 are of buildings and views of Seville.

BIBLIOGRAPHY
Ceán Bermúdez
A. Sancho Corbacho: *Iconografía de Sevilla* (Seville, 1975), p. 40
A. Gallego: *Historia del grabado en España* (Madrid, 1979), p. 257
E. Paez Rios: *Repertorio de grabados españoles en la Biblioteca Nacional* (Madrid, 1981–5)
J. Carrete, F. Checa and V. Bozal: *El grabado en España: Siglos XV al XVIII*, Summa A., xxxi (Madrid, 1987)
J. M. Serrera and others: *Iconografía de Sevilla, 1650–1790* (Madrid, 1989)
BLANCA GARCÍA VEGA

Toruń [Ger. Thorn]. City in Poland, located on the north bank of the River Vistula. It is the principal city of the Chełmno region, which belonged to Poland from the 11th century, to the order of the Teutonic Knights between 1231 and 1454, and later to the Polish Crown as part of the Kingdom of Prussia. From 1793 it was annexed by Prussia in the Second Partition of Poland, becoming part of Poland in 1920.

In 1233 the Teutonic Order built a castle and established a city on the site of an earlier Polish settlement. It became a commercial centre, trading with Russia, Hungary and Poland. From 1251 to 1259 it was enlarged and given a grid layout. A new settlement, the New Town, was located alongside it in 1264. From the mid-13th century the suburbs expanded and a port was built on the Vistula, making Toruń accessible to seagoing vessels until the 16th century and enabling trade with the Netherlands, England and northern Germany. From the mid-14th century it was part of the Hanseatic League, becoming one of the main exporters of Polish grain in the 15th century. The character of the city's art was influenced by its changing national identity, distant trading partners and, from the 15th century, by an increasing rivalry with Gdańsk.

In the Middle Ages Toruń played a major role in the development of *Backsteingotik* (brick architecture) within the lands of the Teutonic Knights. The castle, the oldest brick fortification in Prussia, was modernized in the late 13th century, destroyed in 1454 and excavated from 1958 to 1966. It had an irregular plan of curved walls with a series of ring defences. Its latrine tower, outside the precinct and joined to it by a corridor, was the earliest built by the Order. St John's Church was built in the second half of the 13th century as a Westphalian/Mecklenburg type of hall church, of square profile; a tower was added 1407–33. In the last quarter of the 15th century it was heightened on the model of St Mary's, Gdańsk. The mid-14th-century Franciscan church of St Mary is also of the Westphalian type. The New Town parish church of St James (1309–40) is a basilica, following German models, but built of brick, with a finely moulded east gable, and decorative tiles around the exterior. The brick town hall (1259–74) was based on Hanseatic models, such as that of Stralsund; between 1385 and 1399 it was transformed under the influence of south Netherlandish town halls and castles of the Teutonic Knights (see fig.). Merchants' houses were arranged in narrow terraces, each house with its own gable, either stepped or decorated with blind arcading. The ground floor consisted of a large vestibule, with a storage floor above. From the second

Toruń, town hall, begun 1259

half of the 14th century to the end of the 15th merchants' houses were modelled on those in Baltic cities such as Lübeck and Stralsund, as were 15th- and 16th-century granaries.

Medieval church fittings followed the Teutonic Order's artistic preferences. At first these were based on imports from the Rhineland, for example the architectural sculpture (c. 1310–30) and a Dominican Crucifix (second half of the 14th century) in St John's, and a wooden Crucifix (1330) from the Town Hall courtroom, and also from the southern Netherlands, such as the bronze tomb-slab of *Jan of Soest*, mayor of Toruń (d 1361). From 1380 these influences were replaced by that of the Bohemian imperial court, for example in the frescoes and stained glass (c. 1380) in St Mary's. Many local workshops adopted the Bohemian style, such as the painter of the altarpiece (c. 1380) in St Mary's. The sculptor known as the Master of the Beautiful Madonnas (fl 1390–1415) worked in Toruń from c. 1400; his surviving work includes the 'Sancta Maria Gravida' (ex-Toruń, Distr. Mus.). Netherlandish paintings were imported during the last quarter of the 15th century, such as a panel in the altarpiece of St John's (c. 1480) and a *Descent from the Cross* (1495), but in the early 16th century they were superseded by south German examples, including the altarpiece of St Wolfgang (1505) in St John's and a portrait of *Nicolaus Copernicus* (first quarter of the 16th century; Toruń, Town Hall).

During the second half of the 16th century some works were produced under the influence of German Protestant art, such as the epitaphs of *Anna Pirnesius* (1576) and *Nicolaus Copernicus* (c. 1580), and of Augsburg and Nuremberg goldsmithery, such as the work of Jan Chrystian Bierpfaff (fl late 16th century). At the turn of the 17th century Catholic reaction was introduced with the arrival of some Netherlandish Mannerists via Gdańsk. Examples

of their work include the Neisser family epitaph (1594), the extension of the Town Hall in 1603 by Antonis van Obberghen and its interior decoration by Anton Möller I, and the pulpit and organs (1605–9) at St Mary's.

The influence of Gdańsk remained strong on local artistic output in the Baroque period. In some cases, such as the tombstone (1636) of *Anne Vasa* (1573–98) in St Mary's, this took on a Netherlandish style. Some artists were influenced by southern German Baroque, for example in the designs for the Włocławek Bishops' Palace (1693) and the Star House (1697) in the town square; others were influenced by Warsaw workshops, such as in the designs for the Evangelical church (1753–6) by Andrew Adam Baehr (fl 1743–56) and Efraim Szreger.

In the 19th century the development of the city came to a standstill. After its annexation by Prussia in 1815, it became a frontier fortress. It was twice encircled with fortifications (1818–28 and 1878–92), which are an outstanding achievement of 19th-century military engineering. Toruń was given back to Poland in 1920 and the university was established in 1945.

BIBLIOGRAPHY

R. Heuer: *Thorn* (Danzig, 1931)
G. Chmarzyński: 'Sztuka w Toruniu' [Art in Toruń], *Dzieje Torunia* [The history of Toruń], ed. K. Tymieniecki (Toruń, 1933), pp. 469–544
G. Dehio and E. Gall: *Deutschordensland Preussen* (Munich, 1952), pp. 70–83
E. Gall: *Danzig und das Land an der Weichsel* (Munich, 1953), pp. 82–104
M. Gasiorowscy and E. Gasiorowscy: *Toruń* (Warsaw, 1963)
Kultura artystyczna Ziemi Chełmińskiej w czasach Kopernika [Artistic culture of the Chełmno area in the time of Copernicus] (Toruń, 1973)
Sztuka Torunia i Ziemi Chełmińskiej, 1233–1815, praca zbiorowa [The art of Toruń and the Chełmno area, 1233–1815] (Toruń, 1986)

MARIAN KUTZNER

Torus [toros]. Large, convex moulding of semicircular profile used principally at the base of a column.

□

Tőry, Emil. *See under* POGÁNY & TŐRY.

Tory, Geofroy (*b* Bourges, 1480; *d* Paris, 1533). French printer, publisher, book designer and bookseller. He left Bourges in 1503 to study in Rome and Bologna. After returning to France in 1507, he published Classical works and taught at the Collège du Plessis in Paris (1508–11) and then, from 1512, at the Collège de Bourgogne (Paris), before a second stay in Italy from about 1516 to 1518. In 1518 he was admitted to the Paris booksellers' guild. He worked under the sign of the Pot-Cassé, first on the Petit-Pont adjoining the Hôtel-Dieu (1512–23) and then on the Rue St Jacques; finally he settled on the Rue de la Juiverie from 1532 to 1533.

From 1529 Tory was active as a printer. Influenced by Classical art and by Italy, he adopted a new approach to the aesthetics of book production in France, concerning himself with a correct balance between text and illustration. From his first book, *Les Heures de la Vierge* published by Simon de Colines in 1525, his work showed both sobriety and elegance. He used Roman typefaces, illustrations with figures in contemporary Italian style and replaced Gothic borders with Renaissance arabesques. It is not known whether he did engraving himself or merely provided designs for others to engrave. The signature of the Cross of Lorraine, which appears on some of his plates, was used by others throughout the 16th century and does not imply that he himself engraved them.

Tory himself wrote a famous illustrated book, *Le Champfleury*: a treatise on aesthetics, it compared lettering with the proportions of the human body, following Luca Pacioli. With his concern for typographical presentation and the accuracy of texts, and his passion for the emblematic and symbolic, Geofroy Tory succeeded in bringing to book production in France, still strongly Gothic in character, the first breath of the Renaissance.

See also MASTERS, ANONYMOUS, AND MONOGRAMMISTS, §II: THE 1520s HOURS WORKSHOP.

WRITINGS

Le Champfleury (Paris, 1529)

BIBLIOGRAPHY

A. Bernard: *Geofroy Tory: Peintre et graveur, premier imprimeur royal, réformateur de l'orthographie et de la typographie sous François Ier* (Paris, 1857), xv
J. Megret: 'Geofroy Tory . . .', *A. & Métiers Graph.*, 28 (1931), p. 7
J. Adhémar: *Inventaire du fonds français: Graveurs du seizième siècle*, Paris, Bib. N., Dépt Est. cat., ii (Paris, 1938), pp. 138–48
R. Mortimer: *French 16th Century Books*, Cambridge, MA, Harvard Coll. Lib. cat. (Cambridge, MA, 1964), ii, pp. 641–5
R. Brun: *Le Livre français illustré de la Renaissance* (Paris, 1969)

MARIANNE GRIVEL

Tosa. Name used by members of the TOSA SCHOOL of Japanese painters that flourished from the early 15th century to the 19th.

(1) Tosa Mitsunobu (*fl* 1469–?1525). Tosa Mitsunobu and (3) Tosa Mitsuoki became the most famous members of the Tosa lineage of painters. In 1469 Emperor Go-Tsuchimikado (*reg* 1464–1500) appointed Mitsunobu director (*azukari*) of the Imperial Painting Bureau (Edokoro), a post he held for an unprecedented 50 years. His appointment took place during the Ōnin War (1467–77), but his known activities occurred only after hostilities had ended. During his tenure at court, he rose in rank and held a succession of honorary appointments. His talent both in painting and as a poet of 'linked verse' (*renga*) attracted the notice of several prominent noblemen, especially the calligrapher Sanjōnishi Sanetaka (1455–1537), whose diaries record many of Mitsunobu's activities. Mitsunobu also received commissions from the ruling Ashikaga (shogun) family. During the Edo period (1600–1868), admiring descendants and connoisseurs attributed numerous paintings to his hand. His signature does not appear on any extant painting, but modern scholars have succeeded in defining both the scope of his oeuvre and a corpus of accepted attributions.

Mitsunobu is best known today for his picture scrolls (*emaki, emakimono*), many of them formal temple and shrine histories done in close collaboration with Sanetaka. Two sets of three scrolls each correspond closely to Sanetaka's records: *Miraculous Origins of Kitano Tenjin* (1503; Kyoto, Kitano Tenmangu) and *Miraculous Origins of Kiyomizudera* (1517; Tokyo, N. Mus.). Sanetaka also wrote the calligraphy for a newly made fourth scroll (1497), the 14th-century set *Miraculous Origins of Ishiyamadera* (Shiga, Ishiyamadera; see fig.). This scene of Lady Murasaki Shikibu (*c.* 973–*c.* 1025) being inspired to write *Genji monogatari* ('Tale of Genji'; *c.* 1005) while on retreat at Ishiyamadera utilizes the horizontal blue clouds, roofless interior view and subtle court figure style characteristic of Mitsunobu's other picture scrolls. Related works are the *Miraculous Origins of Tsukiminedera* (1495; Washington, DC, Freer) and the *Miraculous Origins of Seikōji* (Tokyo,

Tosa Mitsunobu: fourth scroll (detail) from *Miraculous Origins of Ishiyamadera*, handscroll, ink and colours on paper, 0.34×19.32 m, 1497 (Shiga Prefecture, Ishiyamadera)

N. Mus.), a fine close copy after Mitsunobu and Sanetaka's original of 1487.

Mitsunobu also painted picture scrolls in the 'small-painting' (*koe*) genre, which differed in subject, scale and execution from the more usual products of the court painting bureau. A lost work, *Clouds over Kōya*, was painted for Emperor GoTsuchimikado in 1475–9. Extant examples are the *Broken Inkstone* (1495; priv. col., see Yoshida, pls 24–7), the *Rat* (Cambridge, MA, Fogg) and the *Jizō Hall* (priv. col., see Yoshida, pl. 66).

Mitsunobu also excelled in portraiture (*see* JAPAN, §VI, 3(iii)). In 1488 he painted a memorial portrait of *Empress Karakumon'in* (1411–88), which later served as a model for his contemporary Kanō Masanobu (*see* KANŌ, (1)). The following year Emperor GoTsuchimikado sketched a likeness of his own face and had Mitsunobu finish the composition. Neither work survives, but a posthumous portrait of *Emperor Goen'yū* (*c.* 1492; Kyoto, Unryūin) suggests that Mitsunobu adhered to traditional models for imperial portraits. Less conservative are the portraits of *Momonoi Naoaki* seated under pines (*c.* 1480) and of *Ashikaga Yoshimasa*, the eighth Ashikaga shogun (1436–90), in his residence (both Tokyo, N. Mus.). For his portraits, Mitsunobu occasionally made preliminary sketches from life. An ink sketch of *Sanjōnishi Sanetaka* (1501; priv. col., see Yoshida, pl. 53) apparently displeased the sitter, according to his diary, but was nonetheless retained by him.

Mitsunobu's paintings of Buddhist subjects are represented by a set of ten hanging scrolls, *Ten Kings of Hell* (1489–90; Kyoto, Jōfukuji), which served as the focus of Buddhist services for Emperor GoTsuchimikado. Mitsunobu's compositions closely follow those of an earlier set (Kyoto, Nison'in) by Fujiwara no Yukimitsu (*fl c.* 1352–89), who may have been Mitsunobu's ancestor.

Mitsunobu's work in large formats is less easily documented. Visual evidence appears in his picture scrolls: the screen depicting a crescent moon over a field of autumn grasses (see fig.) provides a valuable glimpse of contemporary screen painting in the so-called *Yamatoe* style (*see* JAPAN, §VI, 4(ii)). Sanetaka's diary records a pair of screens depicting scenes in the capital city (Heian, now Kyoto) in 1506. This is the earliest known reference to this subject, painted on behalf of a provincial warlord, and is often linked to drawings (Tokyo, N. Mus.) made after an early screen attributed to Mitsunobu. A screen of *Pines* (Tokyo, N. Mus.), attributed to him by Tosa Mitsuoki, and the unsigned *Four Seasons Bamboo* screens (formerly sliding doors; New York, Met.) may also preserve Mitsunobu compositions.

Mitsunobu is also recorded as designing in other media. In 1488 he designed a lacquerware service for Hino Tomiko (1440–96), the wife of Ashikaga Yoshimasa. Mitsunobu had a son, (2) Mitsumochi, who succeeded him as head of the court painting bureau, and a daughter said to have married Kanō Motonobu (*see* KANŌ, (2)).

BIBLIOGRAPHY

T. Kimura: *Tosa monjo kaisetsu* [Explanation of Tosa documents] (Tokyo, 1935)
S. Tani: 'Tosa Mitsunobu kō' [Study on Tosa Mitsunobu], *Bijutsu Kenkyū*, 100 (1940), pp. 115–28; 101 (1940), pp. 159–69; 103 (1940), pp. 207–21; also in *Muromachi jidai bijutsushi ron* [Essays on the history of art in the Muromachi period] (Tokyo, 1942), pp. 418–514
Y. Yoshida: *Tosa Mitsunobu*, Nihon bijutsu kaiga zenshū [Complete collection of Japanese painting], v (Tokyo, 1979)
R. Takahashi, ed.: *Sanetaka-kō* [Diary of Lord Sanetaka], 13 vols (Tokyo, 1980)
S. Miyajima: 'Tosa Mitsunobu to Tosaha no keifu' [Tosa Mitsunobu and Tosa school lineage], *Nihon No Bijutsu*, 247 (1986) [whole issue]
S. Sakakibara: 'Seikōji engi shiken' [A personal view of *Origins of the Seikōji*], *Museum*, 423 (1986), pp. 4–26
T. Toda and others, eds.: *Suibokuga to chūsei e maki* [Ink painting and medieval-period picture scrolls] (Tokyo, 1992), xii of *Nihon bijutsu zenshū* [Complete arts of Japan]

KAREN L. BROCK

(2) Tosa Mitsumochi (*fl* 1523–70). Son of (1) Tosa Mitsunobu. He succeeded him as *edokoro azukari* ('head of court painting bureau') in 1523. The latest record of his activity dates to 1569. Like his father, he painted many handscrolls (*emaki*), folding-screen (*byōbu*) paintings, portraits and Buddhist paintings for the court, shogunate and high-ranking members of the warrior class (*see also* JAPAN, §VI, 4(ii)). His style is modelled on that of his father but with greater clarity of pictorial structure and more ambitious depictions of landscape. He probably studied the style of Kanō Motonobu (*see* KANŌ, (2)), the dominant painter in Kyoto during most of his life. Later histories even suggest that Motonobu was a close relative through marriage, and contemporary documents inform us that the two sometimes worked on the same projects. In about 1544 he produced sliding-door paintings (*fusumae*) at the imperial palace, at around the same time that Kanō Motonobu was working there. He also worked at Ishiyama Honganji (Shiga Prefect.), the site of Motonobu's greatest commissions. Mitsumochi's masterpiece is *Kuwanomidera engiemaki* ('Illustrated legends of the founding of Kuwanomidera'; 1532; Shiga Prefect., Kuwanomidera), which had been commissioned by Shogun Ashikaga Yoshiharu (1511–50) and involved the efforts of Emperor GoNara (*reg* 1526–57) and other élite members of the imperial court. His other extant works include *Taimadera engiemaki* ('Illustrated legends of the founding of Taimadera'; 1531; Nara, Taimadera), *Hasedera engiemaki* ('Illustrated legends of the founding of Hasedera'; Kamakura, Hasedera) and a preliminary sketch for a portrait of Yoshiharu (1550; Kyoto City U.A.).

BIBLIOGRAPHY

Y. Yoshida: 'Kuwanomidera engiekō' [Thoughts on legends of the Kuwanomidera handscroll], *Geijutsu Ronkyū*, 4 and 6 (1977), pp. 36–74
—: *Tosa Mitsunobu*, Nihon bijutsu kaiga zenshū [Complete collection of Japanese painting], v (Tokyo, 1979)
Tosaha no kaiga [Painting of the Tosa school] (exh. cat., Tokyo, Suntory Mus. A., 1982)
S. Miyajima: 'Tosa Mitsunobu to Tosaha no keifu' [Tosa Mitsunobu and the Tosa school lineage], *Nihon No Bijutsu*, 247 (1986) [whole issue]

(3) Tosa Mitsuoki (*b* Sakai, 1617; *d* Kyoto, 1691). He was the son of Tosa Mitsunori (1583–1638), the painter who brought the Tosa school back to Kyoto after more than half a century in the merchant town of Sakai (now Osaka Prefect.). In 1654 Mitsuoki became the first Tosa *edokoro azukari* ('head of the court painting bureau') since the end of the Muromachi period (1333–1568). With the renewal of Tosa status at court, the school prospered throughout the Edo period (1600–1868). Mitsuoki is generally considered the last major painter of the Tosa school, although he was succeeded by a long line of painters, beginning with his son, Mitsunari (1646–1710).

Like his contemporaries of the KANŌ SCHOOL, Mitsuoki revitalized the Tosa-school style by incorporating the spaciousness and lightness of touch found in Song- (AD 960–1279) and Yuan-period (1279–1368) Chinese court painting and in some 15th-century Japanese ink painting. He also put greater stress on ink brushwork. He became one of the most renowned Japanese exponents of bird-and-flower (*kachō*) painting in the Chinese court manner and is especially famous for his depictions of quail (*see* CHINA, §V, 4(i)(c)). Mitsuoki also wrote painting criticism and was a respected connoisseur (*see* JAPAN, §XXII). Many paintings bear his inscription of authenticity. Many works attributed to Mitsuoki have survived. Two in the handscroll (*emaki*) format are *Ōdera engi emaki* ('Legends of Ōdera handscroll'; 1690; Osaka, Aguchi Shrine) and *Genji Monogatari emaki* ('Tale of Genji handscroll'; Shiga Prefect., Ishiyamadera), the latter a standard subject in the Tosa repertory. His works in the folding-screen (*byōbu*) format include *Awabo uzura zu byōbu* (*Millet Heads and Quail*; priv. col.) and the particularly fine *Kiku uzura zu byōbu* (*Chrysanthemum and Quail*; priv. col.), which he painted with Mitsunari.

BIBLIOGRAPHY

Y. Yoshida: *Tosa Mitsuoki*, Nihon bijutsu kaiga zenshū [Complete collection of Japanese painting], v (Tokyo, 1979)
Tosaha no kaiga [Painting of the Tosa school] (exh. cat., Tokyo, Suntory Mus. A., 1982)
S. Miyajima: 'Tosa Mitsunobu to Tosaha no keifu' [Tosa Mitsunobu and the Tosa school lineage], *Nihon No Bijutsu*, 247 (1986) [whole issue]

QUITMAN E. PHILLIPS

Tosa Hiromichi. *See* SUMIYOSHI, (1).

Tosa school. School of Japanese painting. It flourished from the early 15th century until well into the 19th. Painters of the school (*see* TOSA) have long been recognized primarily as the supreme latter-day masters of *Yamatoe* (*see* JAPAN, §VI, 3(iii) and 4(ii)), but extant works suggest that they were considerably more versatile. Tosa artists painted Buddhist icons and bird-and-flower subjects based on Chinese models as well as native ones. They also sometimes incorporated the coarser styles of brushwork associated in Japan with Chinese painting of the Song period (AD 960–1279) and later.

1. 15TH AND 16TH CENTURIES. Historians of the 17th and 18th centuries ascribed considerable antiquity to the name Tosa, but the surname probably began early in the 15th century as a title of governorship of the province of Tosa (now Kōchi Prefect.) on the island of Shikoku. The genealogy of the family before the late 15th century is unknown. In the early 15th century, a number of painters of different surname, including Fujiwara, Rokkaku and Tosa, worked at the imperial court and headed the Imperial Painting Bureau; advancement for painters was apparently at that time a matter of skill and political connections rather than lineage.

Fujiwara no Yukihiro (*fl c.* 1400–20) made the earliest recorded use of the Tosa name. He was either the son of a painter named Fujiwara no Yukimitsu or of the latter's son Mitsushige. By the time of Yukihiro the repertory of the early Tosa school was largely established. He painted handscrolls depicting temple legends, portraits, conservative Buddhist icons, designs on furnishings and fans and even patterns for clothing. His best-known extant works, on which he collaborated with five other painters, are sections of the two handscrolls of *Illustrated Legends of the Yūzū Nenbutsu Sect* (*Yūzū nenbutsu engi*; 1414; Kyoto, Seiryōji). Rokkaku Jakusai (1348–1424) was the chief artist.

The next painter in the Tosa line for whom reliable historical records exist was Hirochika [Hirokane] (*fl* 1439–87). He appears to have succeeded Yukihiro as an official painter to the Ashikaga shogunate and may have been his son. Illustrations for the handscroll *Illustrated Tale of the Heavenly Boy* (Berlin, Neue N.G.) probably represent his early style. Attributed to him by a 17th-century successor, Tosa Mitsuoki (*see* §2 below), is a pair of folding screens (Tokyo, Suntory Mus. A.) depicting flowers and birds and showing close study of paintings in the manner of the Chinese Imperial Academy. Many scholars are reluctant to accept this as a Tosa work because of the strong traditional association of the school with *Yamatoe*.

The Tosa name was also used in the late 15th century by Tosa Mitsunobu (*see* TOSA, (1); said to have been the son of another painter, Mitsuhiro), although records suggest that until about 1480 he used the surname Fujiwara. After Hirochika's death, the latter's lands passed to Mitsunobu, who seems in some way to have been his successor. The Tosa name thus appears until then to have been earned or awarded. From Mitsunobu's time, however, it was passed on directly through the generations, and family lineage became the source of authority within the school. Mitsunobu was also one of the first and the most illustrious of the superintendents (*azukari*) of the Imperial Painting Bureau (Edokoro), a prestigious position that also became almost hereditary. At the imperial court Mitsunobu rose to levels of honour unprecedented for a painter, and his successors too generally held court rank and office in Kyoto. In the early days of the school, Tosa painters served the ASHIKAGA shogunate (rulers during the Muromachi period, 1333–1568) as well.

For both court and shogunate, Mitsunobu produced numerous portraits and paintings of Buddhist subjects. His narrative handscroll painting extended in scope from small works created as 'storybooks' for dignitaries among the military to elaborate illustrations of temple legends commissioned as offerings. His early handscroll paintings, in particular, tended to have looser brushwork and less brilliant colour than those painted by his 15th-century predecessors. Screens depicting bird-and-flower subjects are attributed to him as well.

Mitsunobu's late-born son Mitsumochi (*see* TOSA, (2)) succeeded him. Mitsumochi in turn became head of the Imperial Painting Bureau and, like his father, Vice-Minister of Law. He too produced works in a variety of formats and genres for the court, the shogunate and other élite members of the warrior class. Compared with paintings by his father, Mitsumochi's works show precision, clarity and spaciousness. Mitsumochi must have studied the paintings of his extraordinarily successful elder contemporary, Kanō Motonobu (*see* KANŌ, (2)), who, according to later histories, was the husband of his sister. The period of Mitsumochi and his son Mitsumoto (?1530–69) coincided with the Ashikaga shogunate's final loss of power and its consequent inability to provide substantial commissions. The upheavals caused by the ensuing power struggles placed the court in dire straits and imperilled the future of the Tosa school.

2. 17TH CENTURY AND AFTER. After the death of Mitsumoto in battle, Mitsumochi put his grandchildren under the charge of a student named Genji, effectively granting him the stewardship of the school as well. Genji is thought to have been Tosa Mitsuyoshi (1539–1613), younger son or pupil of Mitsumochi. He established his family line as the dominant one. Not long after receiving stewardship, he moved the school (c. 1570) to the great port city of Sakai (now Osaka Prefect.), complying only reluctantly with requests from members of the KANŌ SCHOOL to return temporarily to the capital to help them fulfil commissions. In Sakai the mainstay of his repertory—commissioned by merchants using their great wealth to elevate their level of culture—comprised illustrations of the highly regarded classic of court literature *Genji monogatari* ('Tale of Genji'; c. 1105). From this time onwards 'Genji painting' came to be closely associated with the Tosa school. Mitsuyoshi and his son (or disciple) Mitsunori (1583–1638) often painted in the album format, creating paintings noted for their precise attention to lines and meticulous attention to detail (see fig.). They also continued to produce large-scale works.

In 1634, responding perhaps to the new peace and stability established under the firm rule of the Tokugawa shoguns, Mitsunori returned to the capital with his son Mitsuoki (see TOSA, (3)) but died only four years later. In

1654 Mitsuoki regained the leadership of the Imperial Painting Bureau for the Tosa family. Following the lead of Kanō Tan'yū (see KANŌ, (11)), Mitsuoki altered the Tosa style by incorporating the misty spaciousness and lightness of touch found in court painting of the Song (960–1279) and Yuan (1279–1368) periods (see CHINA, §V, 4(i)(c) and (d)) as well as some 15th-century Japanese ink painting (see JAPAN, §VI, 4(iii)). He also placed more emphasis on ink brushwork. Mitsuoki became a renowned exponent of bird-and-flower painting in the Chinese court manner and is especially famous for his depictions of quail. Mitsuoki was an important connoisseur and critic. He was the first of the Tosa school to sign his works, a custom more common among Chinese painters. Although Mitsuoki is generally considered the last major painter of the Tosa school, he was succeeded by a long line of painters, beginning with his son Mitsunari (1646–1710), and his atelier produced an offshoot in the form of the SUMIYOSHI SCHOOL, which eventually moved to Edo (now Tokyo) to serve the Tokugawa shogunate.

BIBLIOGRAPHY
S. Tani: 'Tosa Mitsunobu kō: Tosaha kenkyū no issetsu' [Tosa Mitsunobu: A report on Tosa school research], three parts, *Bijutsu Kenkyū*, 100, 101 and 103 (1940); 100, pp. 9–22 (Jap.)/115–128 (Eng.); 101, pp. 19–29 (Jap.)/159–69 (Eng.); 103, pp. 11–25 (Jap.)/207–21 (Eng.)
——: 'Tosa Yukihiro kō: Tosaha kenkyū no issetsu' [Tosa Yukihiro: A report on Tosa school research], *Bijutsu Kenkyū*, 127 (1942), pp. 175–84; 128 (1943), pp. 8–14
J. Umezu: 'Suzuriwari emaki sonota: koe no mondai' [Suzuriwari emaki and others: problems on miniature handscroll paintings], *Kokka*, 828 (1961), pp. 97–105
Y. Yoshida: *Tosa Mitsunobu* (1980), Nihon bijutsu kaiga zenshū [Complete collection of Japanese painting], xxiv (Tokyo, 1980–82)
Tosaha no kaiga [Painting of the Tosa school] (exh. cat., Tokyo, Suntory Mus. A., 1982)
S. Miyajima: 'Tosa Mitsunobu to Tosaha no keifu' [Tosa Mitsunobu and the Tosa school lineage], *Nihon No Bijutsu*, 247 (1986) [whole issue]
S. Sakakibara, ed.: *Tosa, Sumiyoshi ha* [Tosa and Sumiyoshi schools] (Tokyo, 1992), v of *Edo meisaku gachō zenshū* [Masterpieces of painted albums of the Edo period]
QUITMAN E. PHILLIPS

Tosa Mitsunori: illustration (detail) from an album of the *Tale of Genji, Barrier House* chapter, ink and gold on paper, 247×203 mm, Edo period, 17th century (Washington, DC, Freer Gallery of Art)

Toscanelli, Paolo (*b* Florence, 1397; *d* Florence, 10 May 1482). Italian doctor, mathematician, astronomer, astrologer and geographer. He studied medicine at Padua University (1417–24) where one of his fellow students was Nicholas (later Cardinal) of Cusa, with whom he forged a close friendship. On his return to Florence he enrolled as a member of the Arte dei Medici e gli Speziali in 1425. In 1464 he went to Rome.

Toscanelli is an important figure in the development of scientific thought in 15th-century Florence. He was acquainted with humanists, scholars and artists, including Regiomontanus (1436–76), Alberti—whose *Intercoenalis* is dedicated to Toscanelli—and Brunelleschi, to whom, according to Vasari, he gave lessons in geometry. Of his mathematical and astronomical work, a manuscript survives (Florence, Bib. Cent. N.) that contains observations of a comet visible in the sky over Florence between 1433 and 1472. Toscanelli was also responsible for producing a gnomon for the sundial on Florence Cathedral. He was interested in the mining industry in Volterra and Montecatini, and ran a commercial business in Pisa with his nephew Ludovico. In particular, Toscanelli was one of the foremost authorities on Ptolemaic cartography. In a letter of 1474 to the Portuguese Canon Fernão Martines, he suggested that the most direct route to the Far East was to be found not by circumnavigating the southern tip of Africa but by crossing the Atlantic at the same latitude as the Iberian peninsula. Christopher Columbus was aware of Toscanelli's hypothesis, although he probably came to know of it only after having developed a similar theory of his own.

Enc. It.
E. Garin: *Ritratti di umanisti* (Florence, 1967)
S. Y. Edgerton: 'Florentine Interest in Ptolemaic Cartography as Background for Renaissance Painting, Architecture, and Discovery of America', *J. Soc. Archit. Historians*, xxxiii/4 (1974), pp. 274–92
A. Parronchi: *Paolo dal Pozzo Toscanelli's 'Della prospettiva'* (Milan, 1991)

PIETRO ROCCASECCA

Toscani, Giovanni (di Francesco) (*b* 1370–80; *bur* Florence, 2 May 1430). Italian painter. He matriculated in the Florentine Compagnia di S Luca in 1424, but it seems that already in 1420 he was inscribed on the rolls of the company (Orlandi). In 1423 and 1424 he received payments for decorating the Ardinghelli Chapel in Santa Trinita, Florence (Milanesi). In the *catasto* (land registry declaration) of 1427, Toscani described himself as a cassone painter ('cofanaio').

Bellosi (1966) realized that the two poorly preserved, but surviving fragments of the fresco decoration in the Ardinghelli Chapel, showing *St Nicholas of Bari in Glory* and the *Pietà*, were close in style to the paintings grouped together (Salmi, Offner) under the name of the Master of the Griggs Crucifixion. However, subsequent work on Toscani has led to the view that the Griggs *Crucifixion* (New York, Met.) after which the anonymous master is named should be excluded from Toscani's work; its painter was evidently interested in early Renaissance innovations and had a close affinity with the youthful works of Fra Angelico, whereas Toscani's documented works are closer to the gothicizing style of Lorenzo Monaco and Lorenzo Ghiberti. Among the assistants who worked with Ghiberti (contracts of 1403, 1407) on the north doors of the Florence Baptistery is a Giovanni di Francesco who could be Toscani. Paintings by Toscani such as the *Virgin and Child* (Buffalo, NY, Albright–Knox A.G.) or the triptych of the *Virgin and Child with Saints* (Florence, Gal. Osp. Innocenti) probably can be dated *c.* 1410–20. While they show the influence of late Orcagnesque models, they also reveal an assimilation of a Gothic style that is more tender and more advanced than that of Lorenzo Monaco. The cassone panel of the *Court of Love* (Madison, U. WI, Elvehjem A. Cent.) and one illustrating a scene from Boccaccio's *Decameron* (Edinburgh, N.G.) are also likely to date *c.* 1410–20. Other cassoni panels attributable to Toscani include two depicting the celebrations of the feast day of St John the Baptist (Cleveland, OH, Mus. A.; Florence, Bargello).

Of the painters active in Florence in the 1420s, Giovanni Toscani was one of the most intelligent and original interpreters of the great changes in style that occurred following Gentile da Fabriano's arrival there and in the wake of Masaccio's revolutionary innovations. Among Toscani's works of that decade the decoration of the Ardinghelli Chapel must have been particularly important.

Some panels from the chapel's altarpiece also survive (dispersed), and attempts to reconstruct it have been helped by the discovery of a 17th-century description of the altarpiece (Padoa Rizzo). Fragments include a predella panel of the *Stigmatization of St Francis and a Miracle of St Nicholas of Bari* (Florence, Accademia), the *Adoration of the Magi* (ex-Dodge priv. col., Italy, see 1988 exh. cat., pp. 70–71), the *Baptism of Christ and the Martyrdom of St James* (Philadelphia, PA, Mus. A.), the right-hand panel of *SS John the Baptist and James the Great* (Baltimore, MD, Walters A.G.) and gables with the *Crucifixion* (Florence, Accademia) and the *Annunciation* (Rome, Carandini priv. col., see Padoa Rizzo).

BIBLIOGRAPHY
G. Vasari: *Vite* (1550, rev. 2/1568); ed. G. Milanesi (1878–85), i, p. 629; ii, p. 20
G. Milanesi: 'Le vite di alcuni artefici fiorentini scritte da Giorgio Vasari', *G. Stor. Archv. Tosc.*, iv/3 (1860), pp. 178–210 (207–9)
M. Salmi: *Masaccio* (Rome, 1932), p. 134
R. Offner: 'The Mostra del Tesoro di Firenze sacra, II', *Burl. Mag.*, lxiii (1933), pp. 170–73
W. Paatz and E. Paatz: *Kirchen* (1940–54), v, pp. 251, 358
S. Orlandi: *Beato Angelico* (Florence, 1964), pp. 171, 181
L. Bellosi: 'Il Maestro della Crocifissione Griggs: Giovanni Toscani', *Paragone*, xix/193 (1966), pp. 44–58
——: 'Due note per la pittura fiorentina di secondo trecento', *Mitt. Ksthist. Inst. Florenz*, xvii (1973), pp. 179–94 (189)
M. Boskovits: *Un'Adorazione dei Magi e gli inizi dell'Angelico* (Berne, 1976), p. 38
M. Eisenberg: 'The Penitent St Jerome by Giovanni Toscani', *Burl. Mag.*, cxviii (1976), pp. 275–83
F. Zeri: *Italian Paintings in the Walters Art Gallery*, i (Baltimore, 1976), pp. 29–31
L. Bellosi: *Il Museo dello Spedale degli Innocenti a Firenze* (Milan, 1977), p. 233
A. Padoa Rizzo: 'Sul polittico della cappella Ardinghelli in Santa Trinita di Giovanni Toscani', *Ant. Viva*, xxi/1 (1982), pp. 5–10
Arte in Lombardia tra Gotico e Rinascimento (exh. cat., Milan, Pal. Reale, 1988), pp. 196–7 [entry by L. Bellosi]

LUCIANO BELLOSI

Toshimitsu Imai. *See* IMAI, TOSHIMITSU.

Toshinari. *See* FUJIWARA (ii), (5).

Tōshōgū Shrine. Japanese shrine in Nikkō, Tochigi Prefecture, 120 km north of Tokyo. It is dedicated to the deified spirit of the first shogun of the Edo-period (1600–1868) military government, Tokugawa Ieyasu (1543–1616). During that period it was the guardian shrine of Edo (now Tokyo) and the most prosperous and powerful of all shrines in Japan. The shrine buildings (*shaden*) at Tōshōgū are not only excellent examples of Edo-period architecture but are also among the most sumptuous works in all Japanese architecture.

1. HISTORY. Tokugawa Ieyasu died in 1616 and his corpse was interred on Mt Kunō in the city of Shizuoka, 150 km south-west of Tokyo. A year later, in accordance with Ieyasu's last wishes, a small shrine was built on Mt Nikkō, where his spirit was to be worshipped, and the imperial court bestowed on him the *kami* (deity) name of Tōshō Daigongen ('the great incarnation who illuminates the east'). The first Tōshōgū, called the Kunōsan Tōshōgū, was built on Mt Kunō, and he was worshipped there as a *kami*. In the same year another Tōshōgū on Mt Nikkō, the Nikkō Tōshōgū, was completed. Thereafter during the

Edo period, over 200 Tōshōgū shrines were built by daimyo throughout the country, but the Nikkō Tōshōgū was the central shrine, and it is to this shrine that the name 'Tōshōgū' generally refers.

Mt Nikkō had long been famous as a sacred place for the practitioners of Shugendō, a syncretic religious movement combining elements of Buddhism, Daoism and Shinto, which prescribes ascetic practices in the mountains (*see* JAPAN, §II, 7). The area had been the site of the Futarasan Shrine, revered by the population of the Kantō region around Edo. When Tōshōgū was built, the Futarasan was moved to an adjacent site and became the *jishushin* ('land-owner *kami*' [shrine]).

The construction of the Nikkō Tōshōgū was under the direct management of the Edo government, one of whose three master carpenters, Nakai Yamato Masakiyo, was appointed architect. The site plan was decided on in the tenth month of 1616, construction began in the eleventh month and the shrine buildings were completed four months later. The remains of Ieyasu were transferred to the shrine, and the following month a *shōsengū* (religious ceremony of installing a spirit in the new shrine) was held.

Although the shrine buildings of 1617 were the most magnificent examples of shrine architecture of the period, the third Tokugawa shogun and grandson of Ieyasu, Iemitsu (1604–51), in his fervent reverence for his grandfather, rebuilt them all, in the hope of making the Tōshōgū still more elegant. The rebuilding of the shrine began in the eleventh month of 1634 and was completed in the fourth month of 1636. Almost all the extant shrine buildings date from this time. Tokugawa Iemitsu was buried as he had wished near the Tōshōgū, where the Taiyūin mausoleum was built for him. The style of the Taiyūin is the same as that of the Tōshōgū but smaller and somewhat more modest. Tōshōgū was again rebuilt in 1654. The thick layers of Japanese cypress (*hinoki*) that had covered the roofs of the buildings were replaced with copper tiles, a rare occurrence reserved for buildings of special importance.

2. ARCHITECTURE.

(i) Layout. The buildings were erected on an area of the mountain slope 250 m north–south and 160 m east–west, divided into four terraces. The shrine entrance is on the lowest area to the south and the *honden* (main shrine, where the *kami* reside) is on the highest point to the north. The grave of Ieyasu is on an isolated hilltop 100 m behind the *honden*. The shrine is entered by a large stone *torii* (gate-like structure placed at key points in a Shinto shrine). Through the *torii* to the left is the Gojū no tō (Five-storey Pagoda), destroyed by fire in 1815 and rebuilt in 1817. This Buddhist pagoda is one of several buildings revealing the syncretic nature of the Tōshōgū, since the erection of such a Buddhist structure within a shrine precinct reveals the unity between Shinto and Buddhism. Stone stairs lead to the second level, at the entrance to which is the Omotemon (Front Gate). The road here turns to the left (west), and then curves to the north. On the right of the road three sacred repositories (*shinko*) stand in a line; behind them is the sacred lavatory (*seijin*; obviously not for use). On the left side of the road is the

stable (*shinkyū*), for the shrine's sacred horse. At the curve of the road stands a *mizuya* ('fountain pavilion'), where visitors to the shrine can purify their hands and mouths in preparation for their approach to the *honden*. To the north of the *mizuya* is a sacred library for Buddhist scriptures (*shinzo*), one of several examples of Buddhist architecture at the shrine.

Between the library and the repositories is a stone stairway leading to the third level, which stretches out in an east–west direction. A bell-tower (*shōrō*) and a drum-tower (*korō*) are symmetrically arranged at the sides of the path, and towards the western interior stands a large Buddhist building called the Honjidō, where Yakushi nyorai (Skt Bhaisha jyaguru; the Buddha of healing) is worshipped. The Honjidō holds a statue of Yakushi Nyorai, who is the *honji* ('original' or 'true form') of the deity Tōshō Daigongen (*see also* SHINTO). Near the drum- and bell-towers is a bronze lantern, donated by the Dutch in 1643. Between these towers is a stone stairway leading to the fourth level, on which stands the most famous of all the structures at the Tōshōgū, the two-storey gate called the Yomei Gate (Yōmeimon; *see* JAPAN, fig. 19). On each side of the gate is a continuous corridor, which enclosed the precinct of the fourth level. A little to the north of the centre of the fourth level is the main shrine, a single building comprising the *honden* (sanctuary), the *ishinoma* ('stone-paved room', a covered stone passageway) and the *haiden* (worship hall, a place where Shinto rites are held). Surrounding the main shrine is a *mizugaki* (sacred fence), with a small *karamon* ('Chinese-style gate') along the southern façade. Outside the sacred fence stand buildings called the Shin'yosha (depository of sacred palanquins), the Kaguraden (sacred dance hall) and the Gomadō (building where the Buddhist fire ritual was held, now used as a Shinto oratory).

From the eastern side of the corridor a narrow path continues into the northern mountain, site of the grave of Ieyasu. The grave measures 60 m north–south and 25 m east–west. Ieyasu's tomb is a *hōtō* (single-storey circular pagoda). The original structure of 1617 was wooden but it was rebuilt in 1641 in stone. The extant bronze structure dates from 1683. In front of the *hōtō* is a bronze *karamon*, rebuilt in 1650, and before that stands a small *haiden*. The *haiden* is a wooden structure but all the columns and walls are covered with bronze sheets, a feature unique in Japanese architecture.

(ii) Main shrine. The Tōshōgū main shrine is an unusually styled building composed of three parts: *honden*, *ishinoma* and *haiden*. The name of this type of structure—*Gongen zukuri*—derives from Ieyasu's *kami* name, Tōshō Daigongen. In front of and parallel to the *honden*, which has *irimoya zukuri* (hip-and-gable roof construction), is the *haiden*, which also has a hip-and-gable roof. The *ishinoma* connects these two buildings. All the structures are wooden. The *honden* (façade 13.8 m, sides 10.6 m, height 12.9 m) is much larger than the average *honden* (façade 4 m, sides 4 m). The *haiden* has a façade of 22.3 m and sides of 8.5 m and the *ishinoma* a façade of 9.5 m and sides of 8.1 m.

Both the façade and sides of the *honden* have six round columns. The interior has wooden floors covered with *tatami* (straw mats), and is divided into three rooms. In the innermost room there is a *kyūden* (a small shrine in the shape of a shrine building) where the deity resides. The interior space is divided in such a way as to express the solemnity of the deity and to separate worshipper strictly from deity. On the exterior of the *honden* is a *mawari'en* (wooden verandah).

The *ishinoma* comprises only one room, its wooden floor, with *tatami*, being set somewhat lower than that of the *honden* and *haiden*. There are stairs leading down from both *honden* and *haiden*. In older examples of *Gongen zukuri* (e.g. the Kitano Tenmangū, Kyoto) the building was paved not with wood but with stone, hence the name *ishinoma* ('stone area'). At the Tōshōgū, as elsewhere, the floor of the *ishinoma* was placed quite low. Religious ceremonies take place at this hall.

The *haiden* has ten round columns along the façade and five along the sides. In the centre of the building is a wide hall, with particularly splendid small rooms to the left and right. The room to the right was for the shogun and that to the left for the prince–abbot. The *haiden* also has a *mawari'en* running along the outside. A wide stairway on the façade leads to the *mawari'en*; to keep the rain off, it is covered by a *hisashi* (forward projection of roof eaves from the façade) supported by four square columns. The roof of the stairway has a *karahafu* ('Chinese gable', ornamental cusped gable). The roof of the *haiden* itself has gables on each side and a *chidorihafu* (ornamental gable on the roof slope). The frequent use of gables is a special feature of *Gongen zukuri*.

The main shrine is the most splendidly decorated of all Japanese shrine buildings and represents an especially early use on shrine *honden* of the *Karayō* style ('Chinese style', characterized by its sumptuous details). The serried *kumimono* (wooden blocks and bolsters to support the eaves on top of the columns) are decorative and unusually complicated examples used on shrine *honden*. The *kumimono* beyond the wall on the *honden* are three-tiered, those on the *haiden* two-tiered. Another important characteristic of the building is the prolific use of sculpture. Incorporated in the *kumimono* are *baku* (imaginary animals believed to eat nightmares), *ryū* ('dragons') and *kumo* ('clouds', here stylized clouds like eddies). On the surface of the *haiden* a sculpted dragon takes the place of a *kōryō* ('rainbow beam'). Compact sculpted images occur also between each *kumimono*, on the small wall above the doors, on the windows and on the *hafu*. These include plants such as peonies, chrysanthemums, plums, pines and bamboo; the Chinese phoenix, crane and various types of small birds; animals such as dragons, *baku*, Chinese lions and a *kirin* (an imaginary composite animal with a single horn, deerlike body and horselike hoofs); and water and cloud patterns. While the columns and *nageshi* (ornamental lintels) are painted white and the *kumimono* black, the sculptures are painted in vivid reds, blues and greens, and much gold leaf has been used.

(iii) Yōmeimon. This is a *rōmon* ('two-storey gate') 11.2 m high, with a façade of 7.1 m and sides of 4.2 m. The façades of both storeys have four circular columns, and on each side there are three. Though not unusually large, the gate is distinguished by its extensive and sumptuous

sculptures, whence its popular appellation Higurashimon ('spend-a-day gate', implying that its beauty will detain visitors until sunset). The ground storey does not have a roof, but the next storey has a hip-and-gable roof (*irimoya zukuri*), a *karahafu* that runs along the four sides of the building, and a *mawari'en*. A pair of statues of samurai, which serve as gate-keepers, stand at the sides of a passageway in the centre of the ground storey. On the ends of the *kumimono* and on top of the columns are sculpted busts of Chinese lions. Between the *kumimono* are figures of Chinese mountain hermits and legendary sacred characters. On the second storey are sculptures of the heads of *ryūba* ('dragon–horses') on top of the columns, dragons on the *kumimono* and *hōō* (Chinese phoenix) between the *kumimono*. On the balustrade of the *mawari'en* are sculpted images of Chinese children. The Yōmeimon is a virtual treasure-house of sculpture.

BIBLIOGRAPHY
Tōshōgū shi [The history of Tōshōgū] (Nikkō, 1927)
E. Inagaki: 'Jinja to reibyō' [Shrines and mausolea], *Genshoku Nihon No bijutsu* [Arts of Japan, illustrated], xvi (Tokyo, 1968)
N. Ōkawa: *Tōshōgū*, SD sensho [SD series], lii (Tokyo, 1970)
——: *Nihon kenchikushi kiso shiryō shūsei* [The basic data on the history of Japanese architecture], iii (Tokyo, 1981), pp. 62–85, 138–65
MASAYUKI MIURA

Tōshūsai Sharaku (*fl* Edo [now Tokyo], 1794–5). Japanese woodblock-print designer. He remains one of the most enigmatic figures in the history of *ukiyoe* ('pictures of the floating world') woodblock prints (*see* JAPAN, §IX, 3(iii)). Sharaku was active for just under one year, from May 1794 to January 1795, during which time he is said to have produced 146 prints, of which 136 are *yakushae* ('pictures of actors'), two are *mushae* ('pictures of warriors'), six are *sumoe* ('pictures of sumo'), one depicts *Ebisu*, one of the seven Gods of Good Fortune (Sohichifukujin), and one is a stencilled image (*kappazuri*) of the folk goddess *Otafuku* (or Okame). All of these except *Otafuku* are *nishikie* ('brocade pictures'; full-colour prints) published by the Edo publisher Tsutaya Jūzaburō (1750–99). Several brush paintings have been tentatively attributed to Sharaku, including preliminary studies for his *yakushae* and *sumoe*.

1. IDENTITY AND BACKGROUND. Several conflicting theories have been put forward concerning Sharaku's identity. The first was proposed by Ōta Nanpo (1749–1823) in *Ukiyoe ruikō* ('Biographical notes on *ukiyoe*'). Ōta stated that Sharaku produced *yakusha nigaoe* ('likenesses of actors') but that his excessive naturalism gave his subjects an unusual appearance and that as a result his works were only published for just over one year. In a later revision of the *Ukiyoe ruikō*, Shikitei Sanba (1776–1822) recorded that Sharaku lived in the Hatchōbori district of Edo under the name Tōshūsai. Other reliable sources state that he produced prints of the actors Godaime Kōshirō, Hanshirō and others, that he was commonly known as Saitō Jūrōbei, lived in Edo Hatchōbori during the 1790s and was a *nō* actor from the Awa domain (now Tokushima and Hyōgo Prefect.). Kurth (1910) was one of the earliest Sharaku scholars to link the artist to the *nō* actor Saitō Jūrōbei. In the 1960s this theory was challenged and attempts were made to identify Sharaku

with other personalities, for example the artists Utagawa Toyokuni, Katsushika Hokusai, Maruyama Ōkyo, Shiba Kōkan, Sakai Hōitsu, the publisher Tsutaya Jūzaburō, the poet Tani Sogai and the actor Nakamura Konozō. None of these alternative identities, however, has been proven. In 1976 new evidence was discovered. A residential roster (*Shoka jinmei Edo hōgakuwari*; 'The names of various people in various thought directions in Edo'), compiled by the actor Segawa Tomitarō III in 1818, carries the signature 'Sharakusai' under the address Hatchōbori Jizō-bashi, and a map of Edo in 1854 records that a man named Saitō Yoemon lived next to the Muratas in the north-east corner of Jizōbashi (Nakano). In 1983 *nō* records revealed that the names Jūrōbei and Yoemon were used by alternate generations of the Saitō family. These records proved that the *nō* player Saitō Jūrōbei was 33 years old in 1794, making it highly likely that he was indeed Sharaku (Uchida).

The *kabuki* theatre during Sharaku's period of activity was stagnating. The three major theatres in Edo, the Nakamuraza, Ichimuraza and Moritaza, were unable to stage plays because of financial difficulties, and performances took place at smaller theatres, such as the Miyakoza, Kiriza and Kawarazakiza. The performances and actors at these theatres provided the subject-matter for many of Sharaku's prints. In November 1794 Osaka's foremost playwright, Namiki Gohei I (1747–1808), moved to Edo and instigated reforms in the Edo *kabuki*, introducing the Kamigata (Kyoto–Osaka region) style to Edo audiences. Kamigata actors such as Nakamura Noshio II (1759–1800) and Kataoka Nizaemon VII (1755–1837) had also moved to Edo, and it is therefore not surprising that Sharaku's work shows the influence of Kamigata artists such as Nichōsai (*fl* 1780–1803), Suifutei (*fl* 1782–3) and Ryūkōsai (*fl* 1772–1809).

Tōshūsai Sharaku: *The Actor Ichikawa Ebizō as Takemura Sadanoshin*, woodblock print, 365×245 mm, 1794–5 (London, British Museum)

2. WORKS. Sharaku's work can be divided into four stylistic periods. The first is represented by 28 pieces from *kabuki* performances in May 1794. The prints depict half-length figures and are large-format (*ōban*) *kirazuri* (prints with mica background). The humorous renderings of figures show no attempt at idealization; Sharaku's manner of emphasizing features is seen in the series *Katakiuchi noriai banashi* ('A medley of tales of revenge'; prints), *Hana ayame Bunroku Soga* ('The iris Soga of the Bunroku'; prints), *Koinyōbō somewake tazuna* ('The loved wife's part-coloured reins'; 100 prints; Tokyo, N. Diet Lib.) and *Yoshitsune senbon zakura* ('Yoshitsune of the 1000 cherry trees'; 100 prints; Tokyo, N. Diet Lib.). These works capture the personality of the actors, and many of Sharaku's most representative works are from this period (see fig.). That Tsutaya Jūzaburō permitted Sharaku to use the expensive *kirazuri* technique for his first works seems to indicate the publisher's unusual expectations of the young artist.

The second period is represented by 38 prints from *kabuki* performances in July and August 1794, all of which are full-figure prints of a quality equal to work from Sharaku's first period. The narrow-format (*hosoe*) works with one figure are excellent, as in 13 of the 17 prints in the Miyakoza, for example *Keisei sanbon karakasa* ('The courtesan and the three umbrellas'). Also outstanding are the large-format prints depicting two actors. Sharaku's strong compositions are exemplified by the tension and contrast created in his two-figure prints. Works from the first two periods are signed 'Tōshūshai Sharaku ga' ('pictures by Tōshūsai Sharaku').

Works from the third period are represented by 64 prints including *sumoe* and *yakushae* for *kabuki* performances during November and lunar November 1794. During this phase of his career Sharaku's work changed dramatically. The prints are all half-figure pieces with solid yellow backgrounds, but in contrast to the opulence of the half-figure prints of the first period, they are characterized by a simplification in the printmaking process, a drastically compromised quality of the imagery and an abrupt waning of his former expressive power. His narrow-format full-figure pieces also changed, and some prints dating from this period have been described as undeveloped and trite. All but six works are signed 'Tōshūsai Sharaku ga'; the remainder are signed 'Sharaku ga' ('pictures by Sharaku').

The final period includes 16 prints depicting the New Year *kyōgen* performances of 1795, *sumoe* and others. These provide further evidence of Sharaku's creative decline, as seen in the mannered and pedestrian quality of the *Nido no kake katsuiro Soga* ('The ever-victorious Soga') series of three narrow-format full-figure prints.

Despite Sharaku's prodigious output, he had little impact on the world of *ukiyoe*. While Kabukidō Enkyō (1794–1803) and Utagawa Kunimasa are considered to resemble him in style, Sharaku remains an isolated figure in the history of *ukiyoe*. He was unrecognized in Japan until the American art historian and educator Ernest Fenollosa commented on the extreme ugliness of his subjects in an *ukiyoe* catalogue (1898).

BIBLIOGRAPHY

Ōta Nanpo [Shokusanjin]: *Ukiyoe ruikō* [Biographical notes on *ukiyoe*] (Tokyo, ?*c*. 1802)
Saitō Gesshin: *Zōho ukiyoe ruikō* [Supplementary biographical notes on *ukiyoe*] (Tokyo, 1833)
Catalogue of the Exhibition of Ukiyoe Painting and Prints (exh. cat. by E. Fenollosa, Tokyo, 1898)
J. Kurth: *Sharaku* (Munich, 1910)
K. Nakata: *Arusu bijutsu sōsho no nai: Sharaku* [From the art series: Sharaku] (Tokyo, 1925)
H. G. Henderson and L. V. Ledoux: *The Surviving Works of Sharaku* (New York, 1939)
K. Nakata: *Ukiyoe ruikō* [Miscellaneous notes on *ukiyoe*] (Tokyo, 1941)
T. Yoshida: *Tōshūsai Sharaku* (?Tokyo, 1943)
M. Nakano: 'Shoka jinmei: Edo hōgaku wakari kō' [The names of various people in various thought directions in Edo], *Ukiyoe Geijutsu*, 49 (1976), pp. 7–15 [Eng. summary p. vii]
C. Uchida: 'Sharaku nōyakushasetsu no shin shiryō' [New material on the theory that Sharaku was a *nō* actor], *Ukiyoe Geijutsu*, 79 (1983), pp. 9–12

SUSUMU MATSUDAIRA

Tosini, Michele [Ghirlandaio, Michele di Ridolfo del] (*b* Florence, 8 May 1503; *d* Florence, 28 Oct 1577). Italian painter. He studied with Lorenzo di Credi and Antonio del Ceraiolo (*fl* 1520–38) before entering the workshop of Ridolfo Ghirlandaio. By 1525 he was frequently collaborating with Ghirlandaio, and their closeness is reflected in Tosini's adopted name. Tosini began painting in the early 16th-century Florentine style of Fra Bartolommeo and Andrea del Sarto (e.g. the *Virgin of the Sacred Girdle*, *c*. 1525; Florence, S Marco). His acceptance of Mannerism was slow, but by the 1540s the influence of Francesco Salviati and Agnolo Bronzino was observable in his work. After 1556 Tosini worked for Giorgio Vasari in the fresco decoration of the Salone dei Cinquecento in the Palazzo Vecchio, Florence. Through Vasari's example, Tosini adopted a vocabulary derived from the work of Michelangelo and painted some of his best-known works in this manner (e.g. *Night*, *c*. 1560; Rome, Gal. Colonna, and *Leda*, *c*. 1560; Rome, Gal. Borghese). He executed several important commissions late in his career: the fresco decoration of three city gates of Florence (1560s), the altar in the chapel at the Villa Caserotta (1561), near San Casciano Val di Pesa, and the paintings on the sides and back of the tabernacle of the high altar of S Maria della Quercia (1570), Viterbo. According to Vasari, Tosini headed a large workshop that executed numerous altarpieces and paintings.

BIBLIOGRAPHY

G. Vasari: *Vite* (1550, rev. 2/1568); ed. G. Milanesi (1878–85), vi, pp. 543–8
C. Gamba: 'Ridolfo e Michele di Ridolfo del Ghirlandaio—II', *Dedalo*, ix (1929), pp. 544–61
B. Berenson: *Florentine School*, i (1963), pp. 149–50

GENETTA GARDNER

Toto del Nunziata, Antonio (*b* Florence; *d* London, *bur* Nov 1554). Italian painter active in England. The son of an artist and a pupil of Ridolfo Ghirlandaio, he was engaged in 1519 by Pietro Torrigiano to travel to England to work on a projected tomb of Henry VIII. The scheme was not realized, but Toto entered the King's service with another Florentine, Bartolommeo Penni, with whom he often appears in the royal accounts. Toto's work in the 1530s included painting religious pictures for Hampton Court Palace, five for the library and four for the King's closet. Although none of his work survives, it was clearly valued by Henry VIII. Toto was perhaps the 'Master Anthony' mentioned in Holbein's will of 1543. In the following year he succeeded Andrew Wright as SERJEANT PAINTER. His duties included embellishing royal ships and doing heraldic work for the funeral of Henry VIII and for the coronation and funeral of Edward VI, during whose reign he supervised the design and execution of costumes and settings for revels at court.

BIBLIOGRAPHY

E. Auerbach: *Tudor Artists* (London, 1954), pp. 8, 16–17, 51, 55–7, 77–80, 92–5, 145
M. Edmond: 'Limners and Picturemakers', *Walpole Soc.*, xlvii (London, 1980), pp. 66, 68, 190

MARY EDMOND

Toulouse [Rom. Tolosa]. French city in Haute-Garonne, the regional capital of the Midi-Pyrénées. It is situated on the River Garonne, *c*. 5 km below its confluence with the River Ariège and is known as the 'ville rose' from its predominant use of brick. Its population in the late 20th century was *c*. 383,000.

1. History, urban development and art life. 2. Buildings.

1. HISTORY, URBAN DEVELOPMENT AND ART LIFE.

(i) Before 1562. Toulouse stands at the meeting-point of several important natural routes, of which the Garonne, when swollen by the Ariège, is the most obvious and uncomfortable symbol. The city is of legendary origin and seems to have been a Celtic village that developed under the Romans into Tolosa, an agricultural centre with a cultured urban patriciate; as the Roman level is some 3.5–5 m below the present ground level, there are few physical traces. The Roman city was organized around the intersection of the *cardo* (marked by Rue Pharaon, Rue des Filatiers, Rue des Changes and Rue Saint Rome) and the *decumanus*, which led to the Garonne. The walls ran eastwards from the Garonne, enclosing an area of *c*. 90 ha within a wide semicircle slightly flattened to the north, joining the river again *c*. 1 km downstream. Tolosa was evangelized in the 3rd century AD; its first bishop, St Saturninus, was martyred *c*. AD 250 and the pilgrimage church of St Sernin (*see* §2(i) below) was built over the apse of the 5th-century church enshrining his body. The octagonal church of La Daurade (*see* §2(ii) below) was built possibly from *c*. 400. The city was taken by the Visigoths in 418 and became the capital of a huge kingdom (*see* VISIGOTHIC ART). It declined under Frankish rule but flourished again under the Carolingians, despite the Arab threat to the Midi.

In the 11th century the city expanded northwards towards the Bourg, around the monastery of St Sernin and St Pierre-des-Cuisines. The modest houses, often of brick, were protected by ditches and a wooden fence.

Ecclesiastical buildings were more elaborate: the cathedral of St Etienne and the churches of St Jacques and St Sernin were built or rebuilt at this time, St Sernin being the largest of the so-called pilgrimage churches on the route to Santiago de Compostela (*see* ROMANESQUE, §II, 5). Toulouse was also a great sculptural centre in the late 11th century and the 12th, with a flowering of architectural and cloister sculpture at St Etienne, St Sernin and La Daurade (now in Toulouse, Mus. Augustins; *see* ROMANESQUE, §III, 1(ii)(g)).

With its outstanding religious life, the city appears to have been the centre of a vast and brilliant feudal state in which commerce flourished. Relations between the counts and the general population were not always easy, the people often demonstrating their concern for independence, as shown by the creation in 1152 of the 'commun conseil de la cité et du faubourg de Toulouse'. The period between 1189 and 1209 was a true golden age, brought to a close by the crisis over the Albigensian heresy. Toulouse was besieged many times and finally lost its independence, remaining hostile to both Church and monarchy; by 1335, however, it had become an administrative centre for the monarchy and completely conformist.

The Inquisition was followed by the foundation of the university (1299), linked to the Dominican Order, which was leading the fight against heresy. The economic expansion of the 13th century was reflected in urban growth, particularly the development of empty land both inside and outside the walls, after the establishment of new religious houses. The 13th century was essentially that of Gothic architecture: the Franciscan church (destr. 1871) and the Carmelite church (destr. 1809) were both started; the façade of St Sernin was hurriedly completed *c.* 1220; and the cathedral of St Etienne was vaulted (1211–13) and received a rose window in its façade in 1229. From 1272 Bishop Bertrand de l'Isle Jourdain started to rebuild the choir, but work was stopped owing to lack of money and the bishop's death in 1286. The greatest Gothic building in Toulouse is the Dominican chapel, now the Jacobin church. It was begun between 1230 and 1250 as a modest chapel, divided into two aisles by a central row of columns (see fig. 1). A polygonal choir was added in 1285–98, its vault supported on a column from which radiate 22 ribs. The rest of the church was vaulted with quadripartite vaults in the 14th century.

The city's appearance improved in the early 14th century, as houses became larger and new bridges were built. The outset of the Hundred Years War in 1336, however, brought unhappiness to the city, which suffered from shortages and epidemics. Yet although the city grew poorer, as is shown by the falling population and the shrinkage of the built-up area back inside the walls, it was during this period that the municipal administration took shape.

Toulouse's most brilliant period was between the great fire of 1463 and the outbreak of the Wars of Religion (1562–98). Only in the 16th century did the city transcend its function as essentially an agricultural centre, and the printing industry developed with the renewal of intellectual life. The Parlement took over municipal administration when necessary, although reconstruction was slow after the fire. Measures against fires were increased, and it was

1. Toulouse, the Dominican chapel (now the Jacobin church), interior looking east, begun 1230–50

decided in 1555 that all new buildings would be in brick or stone. Public works at this time included the Hôtel de Ville (now the Capitole) and the Pont Neuf (1544) near La Daurade. Building work recommenced on the cathedral, the church of La Dalbade and the Augustinian convent, but this was the century of secular architecture, with rich hôtels that overrode earlier land divisions. The Hôtel d'Olmières (now de Jean de Bernuy) was built by Guillaume and Jean Picart (*fl* 1502/3) in the traditional way, although the façades in the entrance courtyard, by Louis Privat (*fl* 1516–30), are Renaissance in style; it was the first private house to have a straight staircase. From 1537 NICOLAS BACHELIER and Antoine de Lescalle worked on the Hôtel de Clary for Jean de Bagis. Its rectangular courtyard, the straight staircase with landings and the combination of brick and stone show the changes in taste and a real mastery of techniques. The finest secular building is the Hôtel d'Assézat, built to Bachelier's design from 1555 under the direction of Jean Castagné, called Nicot; its size and the use of Classical orders was stylistically influential.

(ii) 1562 and after. Throughout the Wars of Religion Toulouse remained isolated in a region dominated by Huguenots. This was followed by two centuries of economic stagnation, as the city once more resumed its role as a large market for the surrounding agricultural region. Despite the completion in 1681 of the Canal du Midi, which now runs through the city, trade alone could not stimulate the necessary development. The fall in population benefited the monasteries, which occupied the empty space. When this trend was reversed, however, there was

limited room for expansion, leading to the final push into the suburbs. Yet this was also the period of monumental civic building, marked by the rebuilding of the Pont Neuf and the laying out of the Place Royale to the west of the Capitole in 1676. A grand project involving the riverside quays was not realized, but other plans for urbanization were completed successfully.

A significant development in the 17th century was the creation of a school of painting after the arrival of Jean Chalette (1581–1643) from Troyes, followed by NICOLAS TOURNIER in 1632. The strict standards that they imposed remained the rule for official paintings, without, however, neglecting the trend towards the Baroque shown in the work of AMBROISE FRÉDEAU, his pupil Jean-Pierre Rivalz and the latter's son Antoine Rivalz (see RIVALZ, (1) and (2)).

The city's ecclesiastical buildings suffered most damage during the Revolution from 1789, indicating its religious importance under the *ancien régime*. Although now of military importance, there was little industry, and most of the cultural institutions became active again only under the Empire. The school of painting and the university continued to attract attention. Interest in the city's old monuments was revived, notably by Alexandre-Louis-Charles-André Du Mège, who gathered together from various buildings the collections of medieval sculpture that became the basis of the Musée des Augustins.

Toulouse became more closely linked to Paris and the rest of France during the 19th century, but it remained profoundly medieval, with noisome streets. It was essentially a city of monastic houses, later used as public buildings, but this did not protect them from demolition and vandalism. The town walls were demolished early in the century. Some projects dating from before the Revolution were carried out, such as the enlargement of the Place du Capitole, but major change was introduced only with the arrival of the railways. Although steamboat services had been introduced on the Garonne in 1830, navigation towards Bordeaux remained difficult until the Canal du Midi was extended in 1856. International airline services were operated from Toulouse after World War I, and this eventually led to the establishment of aviation and advanced technology industries.

BIBLIOGRAPHY

A. Du Mège: *Description du Musée des antiques de Toulouse* (Paris, 1835)
R. Limouzin-Lamothe: *Bibliographie critique de l'histoire municipale de Toulouse des origines à 1789* (Toulouse and Paris, 1932)
P. Wolff: *Commerces et marchands de Toulouse, vers 1350–vers 1450* (Paris, 1954)
P. Mesplé: *Toulouse: Musée des Augustins: Sculptures romanes*, Inventaires des Collections publiques françaises, 5 (Paris, 1961)
P. Wolff, ed.: *Histoire de Toulouse* (Toulouse, rev. 2/1961)
J. Coppolani: *Toulouse au XXe siècle* (Toulouse, 1962)
A. Maistre: *Le Canal des deux mers; Canal royal du Languedoc, 1666–1810* (Toulouse, 1968)
P. Wolff: *Regards sur le Midi médiéval* (Toulouse, 1978)
Le 'Gothique' retrouvé avant Viollet-le-Duc (exh. cat., Paris, Hôtel de Sully, 1979)
M. Eclache: 'Topographie de Toulouse au XVIIe siècle: Du Plan Tavernier au cadastre de 1680 dans le quartier de Saint Sernin', *An. Midi* (1980), pp. 345–55
Urbain Vitry à Toulouse (exh. cat., Toulouse, Pal. A., 1981)
Toulouse et l'art médiéval de 1830 à 1870 (exh. cat, Toulouse, Mus. Augustins, 1982)
Saint Sernin de Toulouse: Trésors et métamorphoses (exh. cat., Paris, Hôtel de Sully, 1990)

YVES BOTTINEAU-FUCHS

2. BUILDINGS.

(i) St Sernin. (ii) La Daurade. (iii) St Etienne.

(i) St Sernin. Soon after consecrating the present church on 24 May 1096, Pope Urban II (*reg* 1089–99) credited the construction to Bishop Petrus Rogerius (*fl c.* 1040), but it is more likely that it was undertaken when Bishop Izarn introduced clerical reforms to Toulouse towards 1073. A hospice was founded there before 1080 by Count William II (*reg* 1060–88) and his wife Mathilda, and was entrusted to RAYMOND GAIRARD, a canon of St Sernin who is credited by his biographer with building the body of the church before his death in 1118. Another consecration took place in 1119. Meanwhile the canons, whose authority was challenged by Cluniac monks from Moissac Abbey in 1082, had been offered the direct protection of Rome by Pope Gregory VII (*reg* 1073–85) a year later. With the support of Count William and, from 1098, of his daughter Philippa and her husband, William IX, Duke of Aquitaine (*reg* 1086–1127), most of the building was completed, the entire perimeter was enclosed and plans were laid for a cloister.

(a) Architecture. (b) Sculpture.

(a) Architecture. Although the monastic buildings were destroyed after the Revolution, the basilica, which was

2. Toulouse, St Sernin, south transept looking south-east, late 11th century

restored from 1860 by Viollet-le-Duc, has survived intact. It has an external length of 115 m and is 21.1 m high. Built over the original burial-place of St Saturninus (*see* §1 above), the arms of the cruciform building, including projecting transepts and a five-aisled nave of 11 bays flanked by towers, radiate from a square crossing surmounted by an octagonal tower, and they open through twin portals. The ambulatory surrounding the hemicycle enclosing the Early Christian shrine opens into five radiating chapels; the aisles are surmounted by tribunes that continue around the entire perimeter of the church (see fig. 2) as far as the west façade. These features were combined here for the first time and were imitated only once, at Santiago de Compostela in Spain. The superstructure is built of a unique combination of stone and brick executed by masons from west-central France: the enclosing wall piers of stone are joined by brick wall spans, and many of the internal piers and archivolts are composed of alternating courses of stone and brick. Traces of wall paintings were uncovered during a restoration completed in 1980. Almost all the engaged columns inside the church are decorated with handsome Corinthian-derived and figured capitals; the building is exceptional for the quality and extent of its carved archivolts, imposts, cornices and portal decoration (*see* §(b) below).

In many respects, St Sernin is retrospective in design and decoration, combining features introduced early in the 11th century in a variety of monastic and pilgrimage contexts. It constitutes, however, the first genuine synthesis of elements that would become familiar in urban Gothic churches. Its structure is also important: chapels and portals are used effectively to buttress a fully vaulted building while quadrant and barrel vaulting is combined to accommodate large tribune windows. The success of the structure also seems to be due to a system of proportions: a rigorous plan based on squares underlies an elevation plotted on equilateral triangles. The result was a very large, spacious and well-lit building designed to accommodate throngs of pilgrims.

Between 1258 and 1285 modifications were made to the crypt and the display of the shrine of St Saturninus. The apsidal area of the crypt was elevated so that the reliquary would become visible to pilgrims in the main ambulatory; and the parts of the crypt further west were made over with rib vaults and other Gothic details. The upper parts of the nave were completed by 1300.

BIBLIOGRAPHY

A. Du Mège and d'Aldéguier: *Monographie de l'insigne basilique de Saint-Saturnin* (Toulouse, 1854)
M. Aubert: 'Saint-Sernin', *Congr. Archéol. France*, xcii (1929), pp. 10–68; as booklet *L'Eglise de Saint-Sernin de Toulouse*, Petites Monographies Grands Edifices France (Paris, 1933)
M. Durliat: 'Les Cryptes de Saint-Sernin de Toulouse: Bilan des recherches récentes', *Mnmts Hist. France* (1971), pp. 25–40
T. W. Lyman: 'Raymond Gairard and Romanesque Building Campaigns at Saint-Sernin in Toulouse', *J. Soc. Archit. Historians*, xxxviii/2 (1978), pp. 71–91
M. Durliat: *Saint-Sernin de Toulouse* (Toulouse, 1986)

(b) Sculpture. Two sculpture programmes were planned for the 11th-century church, one before and another soon after William II pledged support for the canons in 1083. The first was executed in limestone to decorate the choir, ambulatory and chapels set up around the early basilica, as well as the south transept portal, the Porte des Comtes, where William chose to bury his ancestors and two sons. The second, executed in marble and intended for the liturgical space between the shrine and the canons' choir, was related to architectural sculpture in the tribune above the Porte des Comtes. An inscription on the altar table signed by BERNARDUS GELDUINUS indicates that it was contributed by a lay confraternity.

The choir programme remained incomplete when the altar was consecrated on 24 May 1096. Three capitals were used instead to decorate a portal in the eighth bay of the nave facing the city to the south. Called the Porte Miégeville because it was joined by a road to the centre of the city, this and another portal left incomplete at the west

3. Toulouse, St Sernin, *Christ in Majesty*, marble relief by Bernardus Gelduinus, before 1096

façade probably stemmed directly from donations by Duke William IX of Aquitaine in 1098. The rest of the choir programme was remodelled with the late 13th-century alterations to the crypt.

The first workshop produced a homogeneous body of work related to the Porte des Comtes. The so-called Porte des Comtes master, whose work was begun before 1083 and completed well before 1096, is credited with the earliest Romanesque portal programme to have survived. Its focus was the image (destr.) of St Saturninus flanked by lions, and it includes capitals depicting the parable of *Dives and Lazarus* alongside themes of punishment and deliverance. The latter were developed on the historiated capitals inside: *St Michael Slaying the Dragon* appears immediately inside the portal, *Daniel in the Lions' Den* is nearer the burial-place of the martyr, and the *Resurrected Christ* appearing to SS Thomas and Peter faces the opposite portal.

The Porte des Comtes master's style is eclectic, drawing on manuscript as well as stone-carving traditions spanning the 11th century. Stylized lions and eagles are placed consistently either side of a central axis and converge at the corners of the capitals, their heads replacing the volutes. Human figures squat or stand in frontal poses on the axis or at the corner beneath the volutes; they also stride in three-quarter poses in the interval between the axis and corner. Just as consistent as the composition is the treatment of heads, feet and drapery. Heads are oval; large eyes are defined by double incisions and mouths by a single incision; hair is either striated, parted in the centre and drawn over prominent ears, or forms a cap with a cusped outline over the brow. Figures wear either gowns or short tunics with notched necklines, which are generally defined by overlapping vertical folds flanked by symmetrical patterns of arching, double incisions. Ornamental capitals by these carvers were used throughout the eastern part of the basilica, often in pairs and selectively to define thresholds, including many laid out according to the Vitruvian canon for the Corinthian Order. The figure style of the Porte des Comtes does not appear elsewhere and had limited influence, but the style of the ornamental capitals was transmitted northward to such Benedictine abbeys as Moissac and south-westward as far as such collegiate churches as S Isidoro, León.

In addition to the altar table the second workshop produced seven reliefs carved on reused marble slabs. Three of them (more than 1 m high) represent *Christ in Majesty* (see fig. 3) flanked by a seraph and cherub in low relief; four others, two representing angels and two men dressed in togas and holding books, are considerably larger and in deeper relief. Set in the ambulatory since their first mention in the 19th century, the seven reliefs have been identified with the cloister or a west portal, but a good case has been made for their original use in the vicinity of the altar before the canons' choir. Three capitals at the Porte Miégeville, two representing episodes in an *Infancy of Christ* cycle juxtaposed with the *Expulsion from the Garden*, are in the same style and may also have been intended for the same liturgical context.

The style of the marble-carvers reponsible for these reliefs differs from that of the Porte des Comtes master. Firmer contours bound forms articulated by rhythmically

4. Toulouse, St Sernin, Porte Miégeville, *c.* 1100

spaced 'comma' folds, consisting of pairs of incisions, and of a more polished technique involving the careful burnishing of bulging surfaces between parallel folds. Loosely related to early ivory- and marble-carving traditions, the origins of this style have been sought in earlier marble-carving traditions in the Bas-Languedoc and, more recently, in the court circles sponsoring ivory- and wood-carving in Spain (and ultimately Germany) earlier in the 11th century. The influence of Early Christian motifs is also notable on the altar table edge as well as on the three capitals reused on the Porte Miégeville.

These capitals would have juxtaposed an *Infancy* cycle consisting of the *Annunciation, Visitation* and *Massacre of the Innocents* with a *Creation* cycle that now consists only of the *Expulsion from the Garden*. In keeping with this antithesis, sculptors who completed the portal in a related style at the turn of the century juxtaposed true and false prophets on the consoles supporting a lintel and tympanum where the *Ascension* (see fig. 4) between SS James and Peter on the spandrels contrasts with the false *Ascension of Simon Magus* beneath the latter. The portal would thus have conveyed a pointed message to townspeople on behalf of the canons and the holy see in Rome (*see* §2(i) above).

Early descriptions and relief fragments in the Musée des Augustins indicate that a programme at the west façade depicting the mission and martyrdom of St Saturninus remained incomplete. Other capitals in the museum are related to those decorating the west portal. Thought to have come from the destroyed cloister, they have been dated to the second and third decades of the 12th century. Finally, a relief in the museum representing two women holding animals, the 'Signs' relief, was formerly mentioned in the vicinity of the font.

An exceptional capital in the south transept tribune (west side), in the style of carvers working in Jaca and Frómista, attests ties between Count William and Sancho V, King of Aragon (*reg* 1063–94). The influence of the marble-carvers at St Sernin persisted in Spain not only in Aragon and León, however, but also at Santiago de

Compostela, especially during the first decade of the 12th century.

BIBLIOGRAPHY

J. de Lahondes: 'Les Chapiteaux de Saint-Sernin de Toulouse', *Mém. Soc. Archéol. Midi France*, xv (1895), pp. 258–83
A. Marignan: *Etudes sur l'art français au moyen-âge: Histoire de la sculpture en Languedoc* (Paris, 1902)
A. K. Porter: *Romanesque Sculpture of the Pilgrimage Roads*, 11 vols (Boston, MA, 1923)
R. Rey: *La Sculpture romane languedocienne* (Toulouse, 1936)
P. Mesplé: *Toulouse: Musée des Augustins: Les Sculptures romanes*, Inventaires des Collections Publiques Françaises, 5 (Paris, 1961)
D. Scott: *The Miégeville Portal of the Basilica of Saint-Sernin of Toulouse* (diss., Berkeley, U. CA, 1962)
M. Durliat: 'La Construction de Saint-Sernin de Toulouse au XIe siècle', *Burl. Mag.*, cxxi (1963), pp. 149–70
D. Scott: 'A Restoration of the West Portal Reliefs of Saint-Sernin of Toulouse', *A. Bull.*, xlvi (1964), pp. 271–82
T. W. Lyman: 'Notes on the Porte Miégeville Capitals and the Construction of Saint-Sernin in Toulouse', *A. Bull.*, xlix (1967), pp. 25–36
——: 'The Programme of the Porte des Comtes Master at Saint-Sernin in Toulouse', *J. Warb. & Court. Inst.*, xxxiv (1971), pp. 12–39
M. Durliat: *Haut-Languedoc roman*, Nuits Temps (La Pierre-qui-Vire, 1977)
T. W. Lyman: 'Le Style comme symbole chez les sculpteurs romans: Essaie d'interpretation de quelques inventions thématiques à la Porte Miégeville de Saint-Sernin', *Cah. Saint-Michel de Cuxa*, xii (1981), pp. 161–79

THOMAS W. LYMAN

(ii) La Daurade.

(a) Architecture. The church of Sanctae Mariae Deauratae, known as La Daurade, was destroyed in 1761 and replaced by a new building. The original church provided a rare example of Visigothic architecture in France and of mosaic decoration north of the Alps. The original brick decagonal building, provisionally dated *c.* AD 400, had six long and four short sides and a diameter of 12.8 m. Light entered through an *opaion* (opening) in the segmental dome. Three walls were demolished in the late 11th century, when the nave was added at the west end and the decagon became the sanctuary. At the east end an arch and vault were built over the high altar and three chapels were added. A large conventual range was added in the 12th century, after Daurade had become a dependency of Moissac in 1067. Except for six mosaic cubes and some 20 carved capitals (*see* §(b) and (c) below), evidence for the early church is entirely documentary. By the 6th century, Gregory of Tours knew the name La Daurade. A charter of Emperor Charles the Bald mentions a monastery in 844. Later accounts record the dismantling in 1702 of the cupola, its weight having buckled the sanctuary walls. In 1812 the monastic buildings were replaced by a tobacco factory.

(b) Mosaics. A painstaking inventory, made by a monk, Odon Lamothe, when the mosaics were cleaned in 1633, is now the sole means of reconstructing and dating the brilliant mosaics that gave the church its name. These were arranged in three tiers of niches separated by carved columns. The top tier depicted scenes from the *Infancy of Christ*; the middle one had prophets, Apostles and archangels; and the lowest tier patriarchs and prophets. The incomplete series in each tier indicate that alterations were made to the church after the mosaics were installed. A 5th- or 6th-century date is suggested by iconography, including the seated figure of the Virgin in the *Nativity*

and the absence of the designation 'sanctus' before any name. The green field and gold background are also found at S Sabina, Rome, and in the Orthodox and Arian baptisteries at Ravenna, but are not seen in later mosaics. This suggests that those in La Daurade dated from the reign of Theodoric II (*reg* 453–66), the only period when the Visigothic kingdom was closely associated with the empire.

BIBLIOGRAPHY

A. Peigné-Delacourt: *Monasticon Gallicanum: Collection de 168 planches de vues topographiques représentant les monastères de l'Ordre de Saint-Benoît* (Paris, 1871)
R. Rey: 'Notre-Dame de La Daurade', *Congr. Archéol. France*, xcii (1929), pp. 105–8
H. Woodruff: 'The Iconography and Date of the Mosaics of La Daurade', *A. Bull.*, xiii (1931), pp. 80–117
D. O. Lamotte: 'Description des mosaïques de la Daurade à Toulouse', *Cah. Archéol.*, xiii (1962), pp. 261–5
P. D. King: *Law and Society in the Visigothic Kingdom* (Cambridge, 1972)

□

(c) Sculpture. The cloister of La Daurade was decorated with sculpture in the course of several campaigns spanning the 12th century. The plan of the cloister is known from drawings (Toulouse, Mus. Dupuy) of the late 18th century and the early 19th and from plans (Toulouse, Archvs Mun.). The surviving sculpture, all of limestone, is now in the Musée des Augustins. It consists of 41 capitals from the cloister area, many bases and imposts, and 25 elements that once decorated the chapter house façade. The capitals, imposts and bases of uniform size from three of the four cloister galleries, which survived until 1812, constitute three stylistic groups.

A first group of eight historiated capitals portrays *David's Musicians*, *Daniel in the Lions' Den*, the *Death of St John the Baptist*, the *Incredulity of Thomas* (see fig. 5), the *Transfiguration*, another scene perhaps related to the last, the *Entry into Jerusalem* and two aspects of the *Last Judgement*. The imposts of this group are rich in figure decoration, including anecdotal scenes based on court life. Short figures wearing tunics articulated by rhythmic twin incisions stand on the astragal but in a loose relation to the structure of the capital. They are small in proportion to the backgrounds, which are often decorated with stylized trees, castellated buildings and inscriptions. Their style closely resembles that of capitals in the cloister of Moissac Abbey, which was completed in 1100.

The second group includes 13 historiated capitals. One portraying the *Passion*, *Crucifixion* and *Resurrection* has no apparent precedent in Romanesque sculpture. With the capital depicting the *Rivers of Paradise*, the cycle would have brought to mind vividly the places in the Holy Land captured from the Muslims in 1099 and the events that took place there. This group contrasts sharply with the earlier one because of a style characterized by animated figures often forming frieze compositions and set against patterned backgrounds beneath arcading, which involved the elimination of both consoles and volutes. The style has been compared to painting as well as sculpture elsewhere in south-west France and particularly to sculpture from St Etienne, Toulouse (see §(iii) below), which has also been dated between 1115 and 1130, in the absence of documentation.

5. Toulouse, La Daurade, *Incredulity of Thomas* (detail), limestone capital from the cloister, *c.* 1100 (Toulouse, Musée des Augustins)

Although the third group of capitals includes one representing the *Story of Job*, it principally comprises ornamental capitals with lions, birds and densely interlacing rinceaux, some inhabited. The architectonic function of the basket is further denied by the deep undercutting of these forms. The similarity between the foliation of some of these capitals, the baskets of which are again articulated by prominent volutes, relates them to the chapter house façade, which has been dated between 1180 and 1196.

Du Mège's records of the chapter house façade left unclear whether or not the two embrasures flanking the portal were also decorated with sculpture. The collection of seven large figures representing the *Virgin and Child*, *King David*, bearded males and a queen are carved on relief slabs; four other male figures, carved as column statues, decorated the oblique doorjambs. A hypothetical programme would consist of two typological groups: Old Testament prophets, a prophetess or queen and two kings, *Solomon* and *David*, on the left, and the *Adoration of the Magi* on the right, an iconographic scheme also found in Spain, at S Vicente, Avila, for example, and in France. The style, like the organization of the figures against jambs and on columns, reflects contemporary developments in northern France, at the cathedrals of Senlis, Mantes, Sens and elsewhere. The ample drapery, articulated by soft folds and fine striations, seems to stretch between the parts of the well-proportioned bodies.

BIBLIOGRAPHY

A. Du Mège: *Description du Musée des antiques de Toulouse* (Paris, 1835)
E. Mâle: 'Les Chapiteaux romans du Musée de Toulouse et l'école toulousaine du XIIe siècle', *Rev. Archéol.*, xx (1892), pp. 28–38
R. Rey: 'Essai d'explication iconographique de l'ancienne porte capitulaire de la Daurade', *Bull. Soc. Archéol. Midi France*, n. s. 2 (1934–7), pp. 34–40
M. Lafargue: *Les Chapiteaux du cloître de la Daurade* (Paris, 1940)
K. Horste: 'An Addition to the Documentation on the Façade of the Chapterhouse of La Daurade in Toulouse', *A. Bull.*, lix (1977), pp. 618–21
——: 'The Passion Series from La Daurade and Problems of Narrative Composition in the Cloister Capital', *Gesta*, xxi (1982), pp. 31–62
S. Moralejo Alvarez: 'La fachada dela sala capitular de la Daurade de Toulouse: Datos iconograficos para su reconstrucción', *Anu. Estud. Med.*, xiii (1983), pp. 179–204

For further bibliography *see* §(i)(b) above.

(iii) St Etienne. The cathedral of St Etienne was begun in 1077. The 11th-century building was replaced at the beginning of the 13th, but the cloister and monastic buildings, attested to in 1120, survived only to be vandalized in 1794 and then dismantled from 1812 to 1817.

Of the 22 capitals (Toulouse, Mus. Augustins) thought to come from St Etienne, five historiated capitals and one representing a squatting musician have survived intact, with another fragment, an inferior copy of the *Story of Job* capital from La Daurade (*see* §(ii)(c) above). Accounts written soon after the Revolution indicate that all the ornamental capitals came from chapels adjacent to the cloister, but Du Mège described a doorway leading to the chapter house. Eight large reliefs from the cloister representing the Apostles, four carved singly and eight in pairs, constitute an ensemble, the original location of which remains controversial. On the single figures were inscriptions, destroyed accidentally in 1864, that read: VIR NON INCERTUS ME CELAVIT GILABERTUS and GILABERTUS ME FECIT (*see* GILABERTUS).

The original location of the capitals seems unknowable. They are all approximately the same height, but their shapes seem to be incompatible with locations in the corners of interior spaces or in a cloister arcade; some could possibly have come from portal embrasures, if not from the openings into the chapter house. Two historiated capitals, one of which remained unfinished, portray the same subject, the *Wise and Foolish Virgins*. The other three are related because they portray stories with female protagonists: *Salome and the Death of St John the Baptist*, *St Mary of Egypt and the Hermit Zosimus* and the *Adoration of the Magi*. Like the *Resurrection* themes at La Daurade, these subjects have been related to contemporary liturgical drama and literature. The special meaning of the capitals with female protagonists for cloistered canons in this secular context has also been explored (Seidel, 1984). The elegant style of the large figures has led to their being dated after the *Passion* cycle at La Daurade, as late as 1137.

Discussion of both the large reliefs and the capitals has turned on questions of style and the identity of Gilabertus. With the exception of the *Adoration* capital, the capitals have all been ascribed to Gilabertus and an assistant largely on the basis of a supple treatment of the human body enhanced by finely chiselled draperies with richly decorated hemlines. The continuity found within the two series of historiated capitals suggests that one artist, but not necessarily Gilabertus, remained on the scene, although other personalities with various styles were allowed in the well-organized workshop.

The large reliefs representing the *Twelve Apostles* although unified thematically, have given rise to varying opinions about their authorship and original location. Owing to successive installations of the reliefs in the museum as jamb figures of a portal, they have been perceived as such and related to the jamb figures arranged on splayed portals at Saint-Denis Abbey and Chartres Cathedral. The first reference to them in the 19th century inside a chapel, however, has prompted imagining the four single figures in corners and the four double figures under the vault ribs of an oblong space, like the Apostle reliefs inside the Cámara Santa in Oviedo Cathedral. The question of their original location is related to another concerning their authorship and date. Two of the single corner figures representing *St Thomas* and *St Andrew*, on which appeared the lost inscriptions referring to Gilabertus, are executed in a very sober style characterized by supple, frontal poses. Elegant heads and long, vertical folds articulating the body have elicited comparisons with column statues, in particular at Chartres. Even though the reliefs are corner figures rather than column statues, the style of Gilabertus has been considered an antecedent of the Gothic style in the Ile-de-France, especially in view of the earlier date often ascribed to the capitals executed in a related style at La Daurade, as well as at St Etienne. Furthermore, the other Apostle reliefs are more Romanesque in style. The six wearing sandals in particular are broadly drawn with exaggerated hands and feet and rendered in a flat, schematic technique that has suggested comparison with sculpture at Santiago de Compostela and S María, Ripoll. The four other barefooted Apostles have a greater stylistic affinity with those signed by Gilabertus, partly because of techniques that lend an unctuous quality to otherwise stylized, cross-legged poses associated with southern traditions in the Languedoc. The iconographic homogeneity of a programme betraying such differences in style requires the supposition that two or perhaps three artists of very diverse backgrounds were present in Toulouse at about the same time; they partly interacted with each other, but they all respected the overall requirements of a cloister master.

BIBLIOGRAPHY

A. Du Mège: *Description du Musée des antiques de Toulouse* (Paris, 1835)
R. Rey: 'Essai d'identification des apôtres du portail capitulaire de Saint-Etienne', *Bull. Soc. Archéol. Midi France*, n. s. 3 (1934–7), pp. 16–20
L. Seidel: 'A Romanesque Forgery: The Romanesque "Portal" of Saint-Etienne in Toulouse', *A. Bull.*, l (1968), pp. 33–42
——: 'Salome and the Canons', *Women's Stud.*, ii (1984), pp. 29–66
K. Horste: 'A New Plan of the Cloister and Rampart of Saint-Etienne, Toulouse', *J. Soc. Archit. Historians*, lv (1986), pp. 5–19

For further bibliography *see* §(i)(b); (ii)(c) above.

THOMAS W. LYMAN

Toulouse-Lautrec (Montfa), Henri(-Marie-Raymond) de (*b* Albi, Tarn, 24 Nov 1864; *d* Château de Malromé, nr Langon, Gironde, 9 Sept 1901). French painter and printmaker. He is best known for his portrayals of late 19th-century Parisian life, particularly working-class, cabaret, circus, nightclub and brothel scenes. He was admired then as he is today for his unsentimental evocations of personalities and social mores. While he belonged to no theoretical school, he is sometimes classified as Post-Impressionist. His greatest contemporary impact was his series of 30 posters (1891–1901), which transformed the aesthetics of poster art.

1. Life and work. 2. Working methods and technique.

1. LIFE AND WORK.

(i) Family life and early training, to 1882. (ii) Success and decline, 1882–1901.

(i) Family life and early training, to 1882. Many of the defining elements of Toulouse-Lautrec's life and work came to him at birth. His parents, Comte Alphonse-Charles de Toulouse-Lautrec (1838–1912) and Comtesse Adèle Zoë Tapié de Céleyran de Toulouse-Lautrec (1841–1930), were first cousins. From them he inherited wealth, an aristocratic lineage, artistic talent and a genetic disorder that would leave him dwarfed and crippled from early adolescence.

Except for one year, Toulouse-Lautrec was educated at home, by occasional tutors and by his mother, with whom he developed a love–hate relationship that was a continual source of conflict for him. His brother Richard had died in infancy and she served and protected her surviving child with well-meaning but iron-willed vigilance; they slept in the same bed until he was eight or nine years old, and even after Toulouse-Lautrec was an adult, his mother lived much of the year close by his studios. When they were in the same city he dined with her almost daily. His father was nearly always absent. A profoundly eccentric man, subject to unpredictable mood-swings resembling symptoms of manic-depressive disorder, the Count spent his time either living in quasi-isolation, deeply involved in all forms of the hunt, or displaying comically attention-seeking behaviour such as bathing naked in his brother's courtyard or driving his carriage through the streets of Paris with cages of hunting birds—owls and falcons—swinging from the rear axle, so they 'could get some air'. A superb athlete, the Count also was reputed to be an incorrigible womanizer, favouring housemaids and peasant girls. As a child, Lautrec quickly learnt that he could not compete with such a colourful figure. 'If Papa is there,' he commented to a grandmother, 'one is sure not to be the most remarkable.' He was right. No matter how exhibitionistic or scandalous the adult Lautrec chose to be, he could never outdo his father in gratuitous eccentricity. Many of Lautrec's passions—drawing and sketching, non-conformist behaviours such as dressing in costumes, collecting eccentric curios and a fascination with animals and women—reflected his father's habits.

Beginning around age ten Toulouse-Lautrec suffered from severe bone pain and was hospitalized for more than a year. In 1878 he fell from a low chair and broke his left thigh bone and in 1879 the right one. His growth stopped at 1.52 m. By age 16 he was permanently dwarfed, and the bone breaks had crippled him so that as an adult he walked as infrequently as possible, in a kind of duck-like stagger using a cane.

Throughout his childhood Toulouse-Lautrec drew and painted alongside his father or one of his uncles, all talented amateur artists. Art became his strongest weapon: with it he was able to fight the depression of long convalescences and the well-meant but stifling protectiveness of a concerned family. He drew constantly, covering schoolbooks and sketchbooks with drawings of animals and caricatures of people. He lived surrounded by horses and dogs, his father's hunting birds and his grandmother's pet parrots and monkeys. He had a striking talent for accurate observation of animal and human movement, which has been described as the ability to capture progressive stages of motion in one image. Recognizing his talent, his parents arranged for him to have early training from his uncle Charles de Toulouse-Lautrec (1840–1915) and from a deaf-mute sports-artist friend, René Princeteau (1844–1914), who taught him to draw horses. When it was apparent that he was irretrievably handicapped, his parents allowed him to go to Paris to study art.

(ii) Success and decline, 1882–1901. In 1882 Toulouse-Lautrec moved to Paris with his mother to study first with Léon Bonnat (1833–1922) and then with Fernand Cormon (1845–1924). He was close to the Cloisonists Louis Anquetin and Emile Bernard and to Vincent van Gogh, all of whom worked with him at Cormon's. At age 19 he received his first commission, to illustrate Victor Hugo's *La Légende des siècles*, although his work was finally not used. After some five years of formal academic training, he had become expert in rendering perspective and volume, but in his own work he freely abandoned the conventions to explore other possibilities. Unlike many of his friends, Toulouse-Lautrec never joined any formal theoretical school, although his work shows the clear influence of Edgar Degas, Honoré Daumier and Jean-Louis Forain among others. He later befriended the Nabi painters Pierre Bonnard and Edouard Vuillard, whom he met through *La Revue blanche*, a magazine that published their work as well as his own. Toulouse-Lautrec's work also shows the influence of Japonisme.

In January 1884 Toulouse-Lautrec set up his own studio in the Rue Lepic, Montmartre, a *quartier* of Paris his mother considered both scandalous and dangerous. It was a haven for the poorest, most marginal members of society and since the 1850s, due to its low rents, had been a neighbourhood of predilection for artists. By 1880, a series of dubious nightclubs at the foot of Montmartre had earned a reputation for wildness and bohemianism. Toulouse-Lautrec and a group of artist-friends quickly developed a highly visible lifestyle, visiting galleries and museums in groups, meeting in cafés to argue loudly, dressing in costumes to attend the popular *bals masqués*, sharing studios and models and generally enjoying all the excitement Paris had to offer. For the rest of his life Toulouse-Lautrec lived in Montmartre (although he took long trips to the south of France), painting friends and models or working from sketches done in the evenings in the Moulin Rouge and other nightspots.

An early tendency to abuse alcohol quickly led Toulouse-Lautrec into hopeless alcoholism. Often drunk, he behaved outrageously, disrupting the bars and dance-halls. Because of his conspicuous appearance (see fig. 1), unpredictable behaviour and ever-present sketchbook, he became a well-known figure at such places as the Moulin de

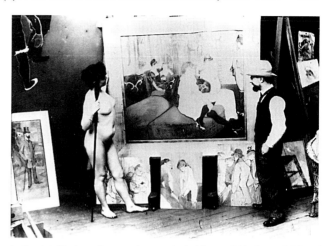

1. Henri de Toulouse-Lautrec photographed with a model in front of *Salon of the Rue des Moulins, c.* 1894 (photograph: Albi, Musée Toulouse-Lautrec)

la Galette, the Elysée Montmartre and the Chat Noir. His raucous lifestyle offended his family, causing constant conflict not only over money, but also over his right to use the family name, his artistic style and even his subjects—more particularly perhaps because they were also his friends. He had intensely loyal friendships with people of widely varying milieux: aristocrats; artists; left-wing intellectuals and writers; side-show, circus and night-club performers; actors; professional athletes; milliners; prostitutes; and coachmen. His father repeatedly tried to convince him to use a pseudonym. Over the years the painter used a series of names, particularly the anagram 'Tréclau'. In the long run he signed himself *H. T. Lautrec* or just with his initials, H. T. L.

Despite his physical handicaps, Toulouse-Lautrec always refused to hide from public view. He had developed a hatred for the hypocrisy and sentimentality that masked people's treatment of him and, as he was coming to realize, all their human relations. Always an aristocrat, he now became an iconoclast, resolutely destroying false pretensions with a sharp word or a sabre slash of pencil on paper. He was increasingly sensitive to anyone's attempts at putting on appearances. His greatest artistic skill perhaps was the psychological acuity with which he portrayed facial expressions and body language: the ability to get behind his models' surface defences and petty vanities to show their vulnerabilities and vices. His portraits capture hidden emotions: hostility, indifference, desire, self-indulgence. His artistic honesty created some tense moments with his models, who sometimes refused to continue posing for him, afraid of his unflattering ability to reveal their true feelings. His subject-matter was almost entirely autobiographical; he primarily depicted the people he knew, often shown in his own studio. After 1886 he tended also to pose them in settings with a social context: in Montmartre's streets, bars and dance-halls or in the circuses, racetracks, sports arenas and brothels of Paris. Today, his images of cancan dancers and nightclub singers, prostitutes lining up for their medical examinations or waiting, bored, for clients, mark our impressions of turn-of-the-century Paris.

In spite of his irregular and distracting lifestyle, and perhaps in part because he was so visible, success as an artist came quickly to Toulouse-Lautrec. As his work began to sell well, he took pride in keeping separate bank accounts for his sales and for his monthly allowance from his parents. Although his allowance (*c.* 15,000 francs per annum) was perfectly adequate, he was always short of money, a by-product of extravagant tastes and lavish generosity. He received critical acclaim from such major art critics as Roger Marx, Gustave Geffroy and Arsène Alexandre. In addition, he was remarkably productive. By age 21 he was selling drawings to magazines and newspapers; he also illustrated books, song sheets, menus and theatre programmes. After being in his first group show (Pau) in 1883, he exhibited in group shows in Paris at the Salon des Arts Incohérents (1886, 1889) and at the Exposition du Petit Boulevard organized by Vincent van Gogh in 1887. He participated a number of times in the annual exhibitions of Les XX in Brussels and at the exhibitions in Paris of the Société des Peintres-Graveurs Français at the Galerie Durand-Ruel, Louis Le Barc de Boutteville's exhibitions of the *Estampe originale* and Impressionists and Symbolists, the Cercle Artistique et Littéraire Volney, the Société des Indépendants and the exhibitions of the *Journal des cent*. Although he exhibited in various places and sold works through a number of dealers, beginning in 1888 he became affiliated to Boussod, Valadon & Cie through Theo van Gogh (1857–91) and he remained with them thereafter. He shared their gallery with Charles Maurin (1856–1914) for his first two-man exhibition in 1893 and had his first one-man show in 1895 at the same gallery, later called MANZI-JOYANT after it was acquired by Michel Manzi and his childhood friend Maurice Joyant (1864–1930). He also exhibited at their London branch in 1898.

Toulouse-Lautrec's success with the artistic avant-garde was equalled by his popular audience. From 1886 his work was placed on permanent exhibition in one of his habitual hangouts, a Montmartre cabaret known as Le Mirliton, and in 1889, for its grand opening, the Moulin Rouge nightclub hung his painting *At the Fernando Circus: The Equestrienne* (1888; Chicago, IL, A. Inst.) in the entrance hall. In 1891 the nightclub itself was the subject of Toulouse-Lautrec's first poster, *Moulin Rouge, La Goulue* (see fig. 2), a work that made him famous all over Paris. Over the next ten years he did a great deal of commissioned work: posters (*see* POSTER, fig. 2), portraits, book illustrations (*see* BOOK ILLUSTRATION, §IV, 2), advertisements, stage décors and the covers of sheet music. He also made brief forays into the Art Nouveau crafts movement, experimenting with ceramics, book-binding and stained-glass windows. The Moulin Rouge continued to feature in a number of works, including *Jane Avril Leaving the Moulin Rouge* (1892; Hartford, CT, Wadsworth Atheneum) and *At the Moulin Rouge* (1896; Chicago, IL, A. Inst.).

By 1893 those who knew Toulouse-Lautrec were aware of his alcoholism and several friends reported that he was also suffering from syphilis. His behaviour became increasingly erratic and eccentric. He lived briefly in several brothels, narrowly escaped violent physical confrontations while drinking and was arrested at least once. He was institutionalized briefly in 1899, an event that caused

2. Henri de Toulouse-Lautrec: *Moulin Rouge, La Goulue*, lithographed poster, 1891 (Paris, Bibliothèque Nationale)

substantial outcry in the newspapers. In 1901 he suffered a stroke while on holiday at Arcachon and was taken to his mother's house, where he died shortly before his 37th birthday.

In his short life Toulouse-Lautrec produced a phenomenal quantity of work. The 1971 catalogue raisonné of his oeuvre, which even before its publication was recognized as incomplete, lists 737 canvases, 275 watercolours, 369 prints and posters and 4784 drawings, including about 300 erotic and pornographic works. Although important original works are held by museums and individuals throughout the world, the largest body of Toulouse-Lautrec's work was donated to form the Musée Toulouse-Lautrec in Albi by his mother after his death. A complete set of his prints and posters (including all states of each work) is in the Cabinet des Estampes, Bibliothèque Nationale, Paris.

2. WORKING METHODS AND TECHNIQUE. Toulouse-Lautrec freely adopted any technique or style that helped him to attain a desired effect, from classical composition to Impressionist colour theory. His artistic goals remained highly eclectic and personal. He was interested in doing art, not talking about it, and he believed rules were to be broken as he desired.

In his painting and drawing, Toulouse-Lautrec worked in oils, watercolour, charcoal, pastel, ink and, very occasionally, coloured pencils. He favoured artificial rather than natural light and seemed to enjoy ironically posing subjects in contexts where they felt ill at ease (e.g. *Golden Helmet*, *c.* 1890–91; Philadelphia, PA, Walter Annenberg priv. col.; *Redhead in a White Blouse*, *c.* 1884; Boston, MA, Mus. F.A.). Working in oils, he often sketched the original outlines with a brush in intense blue or green, allowing those lines to show through subsequent layers of translucent paint to give the finished work a rapid, sketchy quality, which is sometimes enhanced by the presence of bare canvas and undeveloped areas of composition. Imitating a technique developed by Jean-François Raffaëlli, he often painted on raw cardboard *à l'essence* ('with solvent'), using oil greatly thinned with turpentine. The absorbent surface gave the paint a powdery, almost chalky texture as it dried (see fig. 3).

Toulouse-Lautrec made a few monotypes and drypoint engravings, but his important contributions to printmaking are in the field of lithography (*see* MASTER PRINTERS, fig. 1) and most importantly in the colour poster. His experiments in lithography included spattering and the use of gold dust, as in *Miss Loïe Fuller* (1893; *see* PRINTS, §III, 6 and fig. 13), both based on Japanese techniques (*see* JAPAN, §IX, 3(i)). His use of large, flat areas of colour and stylized shapes (e.g. the cape in *Aristide Bruant*, 1893; or the high-kicking legs in *Mlle Eglantine's Company*, 1896)

makes posters that are not only immediately comprehensible to the passer-by but also function as works of social and artistic complexity, full of visual commentary on society and references to other works of art. In some prints his coloured shapes dominate the work as abstractions, moving it beyond the purely representational (*see also* POSTER, §II, 2).

Possibly as a result of his disdain for the kind of art that won prizes at the official Salon, Toulouse-Lautrec developed an absolute hatred for varnished painting, for any surface that was falsely sealed and glossy. To him the varnish and affectation of such works symbolized the hypocrisy and sentimentality that surrounded bourgeois social conventions.

Repetition is characteristic of Toulouse-Lautrec's work. He repeated stories, acts, images. Occasionally he literally traced the same lines over and over. He is said to have gone 20 nights in a row to see Marcelle Lender (1869–1927) dance the bolero in the comic opera *Chilpéric*, because, as he explained, she had a beautiful back. Often his work represents a series of studies of the same model; there are, for example, numerous paintings of 'La Rousse', a model named Carmen Gaudin (?1866–1920). He had a series of 'furias' as he called them—passionate attractions to a person, place or activity, which would dominate his

3. Henri de Toulouse-Lautrec: *In Bed*, oil on cardboard, 531×694 mm, *c.* 1892 (Paris, Musée d'Orsay)

4. Henri de Toulouse-Lautrec: *Jane Avril Dancing*, oil on cardboard, 855×450 mm, *c.* 1892 (Paris, Musée d'Orsay)

life and art for a time and just as suddenly disappear. There are drawings, paintings, posters and lithographs of music-hall performers La Goulue (Louise Weber, 1870–1929), Jane Avril (1868–*c.* 1932; see fig. 4) and Yvette Guilbert (1867–1944; e.g. 1894; Albi, Mus. Toulouse-Lautrec; *see* PORTRAITURE, fig. 8), each in her turn.

After Toulouse-Lautrec was released from the asylum in 1899, his palette moved from the clear, bright colours characteristic of most of his previous work to looming contrasts of dark and light, increasingly marked by blood tones, dense brushstrokes and impasto.

UNPUBLISHED SOURCES
Austin, U. TX, Ransom Human. Res. Cent. [several hundred MS. letters by members of the Toulouse-Lautrec family]
BIBLIOGRAPHY
M. G. Dortu and P. Huisman: *Lautrec by Lautrec* (Seacaucus, NJ, 1964)
L. Goldschmidt and H. D. Schimmel: *Unpublished Correspondence of Toulouse-Lautrec* (London, 1969)
M. G. Dortu: *Toulouse Lautrec et son oeuvre*, ed. P. Brame and C. M. de Hauke, 6 vols (New York, 1971)
M. Melot: *Les Femmes de Toulouse-Lautrec* (Paris, 1985)
C. de Rodat: *Toulouse-Lautrec: Album de famille* (Fribourg, 1985)
W. Wittrock: *Toulouse-Lautrec: Complete Prints* (London, 1985)
The Circle of Toulouse-Lautrec (exh. cat. by P. D. Cate and P. E. Boyer, New Brunswick, NJ, Rutgers U., Zimmerli A. Mus., 1985)
Henri de Toulouse-Lautrec: Images of the 1890s (exh. cat., ed. R. Castleman and W. Wittrock; New York, MOMA, 1985)
G. Adriani: *Toulouse-Lautrec: The Complete Graphic Works, a Catalogue Raisonné, the Gerstenberg Coll.* (London, 1986)
B. Foucart: *La Post-modernité de Toulouse-Lautrec: Tout l'oeuvre peint de Toulouse-Lautrec* (Paris, 1986)
G. Adriani: *Toulouse-Lautrec* (London, 1987)
G. Beaute, ed.: *Toulouse-Lautrec vu par les photographes suivi de témoignages inédits* (Lausanne, 1988)
J. Sagne: *Toulouse-Lautrec* (Paris, 1988)
B. Denvir: *Toulouse-Lautrec* (London, 1991)
G. B. Murray: *Toulouse-Lautrec: The Formative Years, 1878–1891* (Oxford, 1991)
H. Schimmel, ed.: *The Letters of Henri de Toulouse-Lautrec* (Oxford, 1991)
Toulouse-Lautrec (exh. cat. by R. Thomson, C. Frèches-Thory, A. Roquebert and D. Devynck, London, Hayward Gal., 1991; Paris, Grand Pal., 1992)
J. Frey: *Toulouse-Lautrec: A Life* (London and New York, 1994)
JULIA BLOCH FREY

Tour, Georges de La. *See* LA TOUR, GEORGES DE.

Tour, Maurice-Quentin de La. *See* LA TOUR, MAURICE-QUENTIN DE.

Tournachon, (Gaspard) Félix. *See* NADAR.

Tournai [Flem. Doornik]. Belgian city in Hainault, situated on the River Scheldt, with a population of *c.* 67,000.

1. History and urban development. 2. Art life and organization. 3. Centre of production. 4. Cathedral.

1. HISTORY AND URBAN DEVELOPMENT. The site was occupied from a very early date. The city's name, recorded as early as the 3rd century AD, probably derives from the name of a major property owner, combined with the suffix '-acum', giving Turnacum. The site offered fertile land, a river and, most importantly, a stone quarry. As early as the 1st century AD the town was a Roman administrative and military centre in the middle of an important network of routes; by AD 43 Claudius had established a camp in the Loucherie quarter. Under the late Roman Empire a wall was built around the town, enclosing *c.* 6 ha. Two of its towers, linked by a curtain wall, were discovered in 1954–5 in the Loucherie. In about 432 the Franks took control of the town, which had a cathedral complex and a considerable number of churches, for example St Pierre (founded 348), St Piat (founded 369; rest.), St Quentin (founded 421), St Martin (founded ?327) and St Brice (founded after 400); in 1653 the tomb of Childeric I (*d* 481) was found near the last-named. The town soon lost its status as a centre of political and religious authority, however; from 620 to 1146 the bishop lived in Noyon. During the Carolingian period a *castrum* enclosing the episcopal quarter was added to the ancient fortifications, which Charles the Simple (*reg* 898–922) restored in 898.

In the Middle Ages the town's wealth was founded on wool production and the export of stone both as a raw material and in the form of finished pieces (*see* §2 below). Tournai received its first medieval town wall only at the end of the 12th century after the patricians had formed a commune. The wall enclosed land on both banks of the river, including St Brice on the north bank but excluding the Abbey of St Martin (founded 1095; destr.) on the south. The several towers that survive show that the wall was built in two stages; the Tour du Cygne, for example, has a rectangular base and a cylindrical top. Gates with twin cylindrical towers set in front of a *châtelet* and curtain walls mounted on arcades show that the original wall was quickly modernized, doubtless at the initiative of Philip II of France (*reg* 1180–1223), who sought to make Tournai a fortified town. The area enclosed comprised 32 ha on the south bank and 15 ha on the north.

Tournai's growth necessitated the construction of walls (begun *c.* 1277; completed beginning 14th century) to protect new quarters, increasing the area enclosed to *c.* 185 ha. The walls had sixty-five towers and eighteen gates, two of which commanded the river. The enclosure allowed room for projected expansion and also for cultivation and grazing in case of a siege. The political and economic crisis that emerged at the beginning of the 14th century ended hopes of development, however, and consequently the walls survived until 1863–9. Fortifications were added to the earlier walls in the 16th and 17th centuries (see fig. 1). The only parts of this ensemble to survive are the two Tours de Marvis, the two Tours de St Jean, part of the Porte de Marvis and the Pont des Trous (rest.). The town's inhabitants bore considerable expense for the purchase of land, construction and maintenance of the fortifications. The English controlled Tournai between 1513 and 1518, and Henry VIII built a citadel (destr. 1669–88) to the north-west near the church of St

Nicolas; all that survives is the imposing Tour Henri VIII (now Musée d'Armes), a cylindrical donjon with a conical brick vault. The Spanish ruled the city from 1521 to 1667. Between 1667 and 1674 Louis XIV built another citadel (destr. 19th century) to the south-west. In 1713 the Austrians took control of Tournai under the Treaty of Utrecht, until the French regained it in 1792–4. Tournai became part of the independent state of Belgium when it was created in 1831.

Tournai was badly damaged in both world wars, but many buildings that were destroyed have been rebuilt, and sympathetic restoration has been carried out. Consequently, modern Tournai is still dominated by its medieval buildings, including the cathedral (*see* §4 below), a large number of parish churches, the belfry (h. 72 m, 1200–94) in the Grand Place, which inspired many similar constructions, and Romanesque and Gothic houses (*c.* 1172–1200; e.g. 12–14, Rue Barre St Brice). The outer ring of boulevards (*c.* 1860) traces the line of the 13th-century walls.

2. ART LIFE AND ORGANIZATION. The cathedral was a centre of patronage in Tournai in the Middle Ages; for example the Shrine of the Virgin (1205; Tournai Cathedral) by NICHOLAS OF VERDUN was acquired for it. Throughout the Middle Ages such items as bases, capitals, fonts and funerary monuments were produced in Tournai, often made of Tournai marble (*see* BELGIUM, §IV, 1; *see also* §4(ii) below). By the end of this period the iconography and style of these slabs and columns were moving closer to those seen in the works painted by the town's artists. A

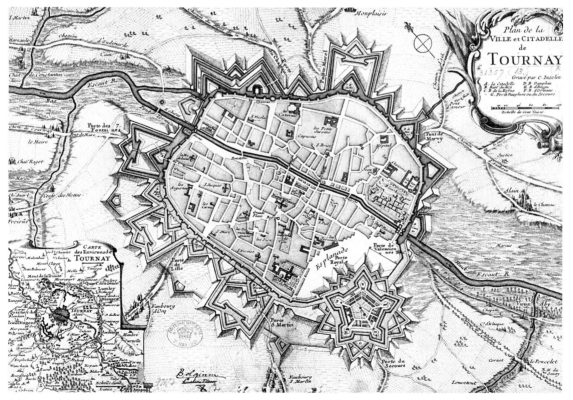

1. Tournai, plan of the city in 1720; engraving by C. Inselin (London, British Library)

famous school of painting flourished in the 15th century, formed by such artists as ROBERT CAMPIN, ROGIER VAN DER WEYDEN, JACQUES DARET and other members of the Guild of St Luke, which supervised the production and distribution of paintings from 1364. Other art forms also prospered; Michel de Gand and the Lefebvre family were well-known goldsmiths (see BELGIUM, §IX, 1), and the illuminator JEAN LE TAVERNIER worked for Philip the Good, Duke of Burgundy. During the 15th century the city took advantage of the decline of Arras and developed tapestry workshops (see §3(ii) below) in order to compensate for the decline of the woollen cloth industry; these became the most important in Europe, and the tapestry merchant PASQUIER GRENIER paid for the ambulatory of St Quentin to be built to give access to his funeral chapel (1474). The town's artistic life was enhanced by the ephemeral works associated with religious festivals. Iconoclasts mutilated much of the sculpture in the city during the Wars of Religion and the French Revolution. A range of ceramics was produced in Tournai in the 18th and 19th centuries (see §3(i) below). A craft school was founded in 1877. Louis Gallait grew up and was trained in Tournai; his painting of *Christ Healing the Blind Man* is in the cathedral, and Guillaume Charlier's monument to *Louis Gallait* (1891) stands in the city. The Musée des Beaux-Arts is the principal museum; the building (1928), by Victor Horta, contains works by many local artists.

BIBLIOGRAPHY
A. de la Grange and L. Cloquet: 'Etudes sur l'art à Tournai et sur les anciens artistes de cette ville', *Mém. Soc. Hist. & Litt. Tournai*, xx, xxi (1887–8) [whole issues]
P. Rolland: *Les Primitifs tournaisiens: Peintres et sculpteurs* (Brussels and Paris, 1932)
——: *Histoire de Tournai* (Tournai, 1964)
Le Patrimoine monumental de la Belgique, vi, 2 vols (Hainault, Tournai and Liège, 1978)
P. H. Schabacker: 'Observations on the Tournai Painters' Guild with Special Reference to Rogier van der Weyden and Jacques Daret', *Acad. Anlct.: Kl. S. Kst.*, xliii/1 (1982), pp. 9–28
Les Enceintes urbaines en Hainaut, Crédit Communal de Belgique (1983)
Les Enceintes de Tournai des origines au XIXe siècle, Publications extraordinaires de la Société royale d'histoire et d'archéologie de Tournai, ii (1985)

JACQUES THIÉBAUT

3. CENTRE OF PRODUCTION.

(i) Tapestry. (ii) Ceramics. (iii) Gold and silver.

(i) Tapestry.

(a) Before 1490. Little is known of the origins of tapestry-making in Tournai, although late 13th-century documents make reference to tapestry-weavers. At the beginning of the 14th century cushion-covers decorated with birds, lions and wild men were woven. As far as good-quality tapestries are concerned, the fact that such a work as the *Story of Piatus and Eleutherius* (Tournai Cathedral) was commissioned (1402) by a canon of Tournai but woven in Arras strongly suggests that the Tournai workshops at that time were quite modest. The industry expanded greatly after 1433, and many beautiful and expensive tapestries were produced.

The principal tapestry-weavers of Tournai produced work of the highest quality. It is known that Robert Dary (*d* after 1458) worked together with Jehan de l'Ortie

(*fl* 1449–53) on a series containing gold thread and depicting the *Story of Gideon* (untraced) after designs by BAUDUIN DE BAILLEUL. It took four years to produce the suite of eight large tapestries, which was designed for the meeting hall of the Order of the Golden Fleece. The suite was preserved in Brussels until the 18th century but was transferred to Vienna in 1794 to protect it from the invading French troops, and it has since disappeared.

One of the most important figures in the industry was PASQUIER GRENIER, who started work *c.* 1447, with the period of his greatest activity dating from 1460 to 1477. (After 1479 his contacts were largely with France: he dealt in wine, and it is possible that he traded tapestries for wine.) He was probably not a weaver himself and is mentioned in documents as 'marchand de tapisserie'. Grenier did business in Bruges, Antwerp, Lyon and the Auvergne and ran a factory in Paris. Several famous series were delivered to the House of Burgundy through his intervention: in 1459 he sold tapestries of *Alexander the Great* (Rome, Gal. Doria-Pamphili) to Philip the Good,

2. Tapestry made in Tournai depicting Penthesilea, Queen of the Amazons, kneeling before Priam (detail), wool and silk, 4.16×7.37 m, series, 1475–90 (London, Victoria and Albert Museum); from the *Trojan War*

3rd Duke of Burgundy, followed in 1461 by the *Passion* (Rome, Pin. Vaticana; Brussels, Mus. A. Anc.) and *Peasants and Woodcutters*. In the following year he sold *Esther and Ahasuerus* and the *Swan Knight* (Kraków, St Catherine; Vienna, Österreich. Mus. Angewandte Kst.) to the King. After Charles the Bold, 4th Duke of Burgundy, succeeded his father in 1467, the City and magistrates of Bruges presented him with a series of Tournai tapestries depicting the *Trojan War* (1475–90; Zamora, Cathedral; New York, Met.; Glasgow, Burrell Col.; Montreal, Mus. F.A.; Worcester, MA, A. Mus.; London, V&A; see fig. 2; *see also* TAPESTRY, colour pl. I, fig. 1).

The best work of Tournai is associated with Pasquier. Such work includes the above-mentioned *Alexander the Great*, three monumental tapestries of wool and silk richly interwoven with gold and silk thread. The *Julius Caesar* tapestries (Berne, Hist. Mus.), once praised as the most beautiful of their time, as well as the tapestries of the *Story of St Peter* (examples, Beauvais Cathedral; Boston, MA, Mus. F.A.; Paris, Mus. Cluny; Washington, DC, N.G.A.) commissioned in 1460 by Guillaume de Hellande, Bishop of Beauvais, and others, were woven in Tournai. These richly illustrated tapestries, with their numerous figures and often with complicated, multiple scenes with rows of tall trees, mountains or buildings, do not differ significantly from the so-called Arras pieces; they are simply a further development of the style. The Tournai pieces, however, contain more rounded leaves than the earlier Arras work, and the plants are laid out more systematically in the composition.

(b) 1490 and after. Towards the end of the 15th century, competition from Brussels ushered in a period of decline, which was worsened by an outbreak of the plague in 1513. The weavers and dealers of Tournai undoubtedly did all they could to retain their clientele, even going so far as to present gifts to such important people as Margaret of Austria, Duchess of Savoy, hoping to tempt connoisseurs of tapestry back to the city. Their efforts were in vain; at the time of the religious disputes many weavers emigrated to other cities. Renewed but fruitless efforts were made to revive the industry by attracting foreign workers.

At the beginning of the 16th century an extremely narrow border was sometimes added around the tapestries from Tournai. The style had gone through considerable evolution, and there was a far greater similarity between Brussels and Tournai tapestries. Notable features include the richly sculptural folds of the garments, and hats crowned with great ostrich plumes. At this time there were still a few important workshops in Tournai. In 1504 Jehan Grenier (*d* 1520), Pasquier Grenier's son, produced a series of tapestries described as *à la manière de Portugal et de l'Indye* (e.g. Glasgow, Burrell Col.), inspired by the voyages made by explorers of the period. It was very successful with the nobility because of the taste for distant, mysterious or exotic countries. In the following year he also sold another suite with the familiar allegorical/historical morality theme of the *Story of the Banquet*.

Clemens Sarrasin (*d* 1514) was the founder of another important weavers' dynasty. His works included armorial tapestries and a *Story of Hercules*. Arnould Poissonnier (De

Visscher; *d* 1522) of Oudenaarde was mentioned in Tournai as early as 1491. In 1510 he supplied Emperor Maximilian I with a suite of tapestries depicting the *Triumph of Julius Caesar*. On his death he left some 3000 square ells of tapestry, including a series of *Judith and Holofernes* (early 16th century; Brussels, Musées Royaux A. & Hist.) and a *Story of Carrabara* (or *The Egyptians*); the latter portrays gypsies with their exotic features, hair and costumes. The tapestries also show dromedaries, elephants, giraffes and other unusual animals.

From 1544 the tapestry-workers were obliged to weave the city arms (a tower) into their work. Two pieces from a *Story of Scipio* with the same city mark (sold London, 1966) date from the end of the 16th century and exhibit a noticeable similarity to Brussels work, which makes it impossible to establish the typical characteristics of Tournai work at this time. On the basis of archival information and a few surviving pieces that form a stylistically, technically and iconographically coherent group, it may be possible to establish such a list of characteristics. The emphasis in this context would be on the great strength of the drawing, the often vivid contrast of the colours and the frequent use of coarse wool, which resulted in the pieces' strength.

In contrast to the Brussels and Antwerp workshops, whose tapestries evolved to suit the changing tastes of the public, the weavers of Tournai continued to use old cartoons. As a result, the craft in Tournai became progressively more obscure, although good works were still being produced. The *Credo* tapestries, for example, are mentioned from the end of the 14th century to the 16th. The first known example was referred to in 1386, at which time the *Story of the Credo* was given to Philip the Fair. Later the inventory of Margaret of Austria refers to three handsome *Credo* tapestries with gold and silver thread. In each case, it was a logical and massively conceived composition in which the prophets and apostles, each speaking one of the articles of the Creed, were portrayed in two facing rows. The *Credo* tapestry of Rome (*c.* 1550–60; Rome, Vatican Mnmt., Musei & Gal. Pont.) is made from wool and silk and attributed to Tournai; the story is shown in a beautiful architectural composition.

Domestic inventories of the 17th century repeatedly mention wall-, table- and hearth-tapestries of Tournai work. It has sometimes been claimed that these are identical to the so-called Bergamo tapestries. A few tapestry-workers were still active in the early 18th century, but the closing in 1712 of the workshop of Jan Baert (*fl* 1682–1724) meant the end of a once-prosperous industry in Tournai.

BIBLIOGRAPHY

E. Soil: 'Les Tapisseries de Tournai: Les Tapissiers et les hautelisseurs de cette ville', *Mém. Soc. Hist. & Litt. Tournai*, xxii (1891)

D. T. B. Wood: ' "Credo" Tapestry', *Burl. Mag.*, xxiv (1914), pp. 247–54, 309–16

La Tapisserie tournaisienne au XVe siècle (exh. cat., ed. J.-P. Asselberghs; Tournai Cathedral, 1967)

J.-P. Asselberghs: 'Charles VIII's Trojan War Tapestry', *V&A Mus. Yb.*, i (1969), pp. 80–84

——: 'Les Tapisseries tournaisiennes de la Guerre de Troie', *Rev. Belge Archéol. & Hist. A.*, xxxix (1970), pp. 93–183

ERIK DUVERGER

(ii) Ceramics. Pottery was produced in Tournai from the 17th century. From 1698 until 1704 Pierre Joseph Fauquez (*d* 1741) operated a factory together with Antoine Beghin (*d* ?1704–8) and then continued production on his own until 1728. In 1718 he set up another factory at Saint-Amand-les-Eaux in France and in 1725 closed the Tournai factory. Pottery was once again produced in Tournai in 1750 when François-Joseph Péterinck (1719–99) set up a pottery and porcelain factory. This produced a considerable amount of everyday pottery, but there are few extant examples. The pottery was decorated in low-fired polychrome colours with flowers inspired by the style of Strasbourg; wares are often confused with the pottery of eastern France.

In 1751 Péterinck obtained the monopoly for the manufacture of porcelain in Belgium for a period of 30 years. In addition to producing everyday blue-and-white porcelain, the factory also developed a range of polychrome, luxury soft-paste porcelain embellished with gold. During the first period (1750–62) the decoration consisted of blue or purple floral sprays on Rococo-style wares. Faults in the paste and the awkwardly placed decoration suggest that there were initial difficulties. During the second period (1763–75) the variety of decorations was more extensive; the most successful were landscapes painted in purple *camaïeu* (several tones of one colour; *see* BELGIUM, fig. 37). This type of ornamentation has been attributed to the painter Henri-Joseph Duvivier (*c.* 1736–1771), who was employed at the factory from 1763 to 1771. Figures and groups depicting such fashionable, contemporary subjects as the Four Seasons or the Elements were also produced at this time, sometimes in biscuit porcelain. During the third period (1775–1800) similar decoration was employed but was contained within reserves. Decoration inspired by botanical or ornithological publications was also introduced. In 1781 Tournai's monopoly expired and was replaced by a 25-year concession, which was limited to Tournai and its environs.

In 1787 Louis-Philippe, Duc d'Orléans (Philippe-Egalité), placed an order for a table-service based on a service from Sèvres decorated with birds copied from *L'Histoire naturelle* (Paris, 1749–1804) by George Louis Leclerc, Comte de Buffon. It comprised 1603 pieces, each decorated with a wide *bleu-de-roi* border, on which were painted gold motifs and polychrome birds in reserves. After Louis-Philippe's death the service was sold, and 600 examples are in the British Royal Collection. The fact that Louis-Philippe ordered the service from Tournai suggests that during this period Tournai was very highly regarded. The factory, however, is best known for its simply decorated blue-and-white wares, which were inexpensive to produce and fared well with their competitors. The decoration comprised Chinese flower patterns or motifs painted in a frieze around the edge, which was very popular and frequently copied by other factories in the 18th and 19th centuries.

After the death of Péterinck the factory was taken over by his daughter Amélie de Bettignies (1757–after 1808). Due to various financial difficulties, however, the production of luxury porcelain was greatly reduced. In 1800 one of Péterinck's sons, Charles Péterinck-Gérard (1756–1815), established another porcelain factory opposite the main one. Production in both factories was similar and plentiful, but due to increasing competition from *faience fine* (creamware) the second porcelain factory was closed *c.* 1880 and the first factory in 1891.

BIBLIOGRAPHY
E. Soil: *Potiers et faïenciers tournaisiens* (Lille-Tournay, 1886)
E. Soil de Moriame and L. Delplace de Formanoir: *La Manufacture impériale et royale de porcelaine de Tournai* (Tournai, 1937)
C. Deroubaix: *Les Porcelaines de Tournai au Musée de Mariemont* (Brussels, 1958)
Faïences tournaisiennes (exh. cat., ed. A.-M. Mariën-Dugardin; Brussels, Musées Royaux B.-A., 1966)
M. Jottrand: *Cent ans de porcelaines de Tournai* (Morlanwelz-Mariemont, 1984)
A. Notter: *Porcelaine de Tournai: Collection du Musée d'Arras* (Arras, 1991)
MIREILLE JOTTRAND

(iii) Gold and silver. As the archives of Tournai were destroyed in World War II, the study and, to an extent, the identification of gold- and silverwork from this city depends on a few valuable academic works published before 1940 and subsequently revised. The tradition of gold- and silversmithing in Tournai dates from the Middle Ages; silversmiths' names are recorded from as early as 1241. The use of makers' marks became obligatory in 1382, and the gold- and silversmiths' guild, with statutes based on those of Paris, was established in 1417. The city mark, stipulated in 1357, is a crenellated tower, derived from the city's coat of arms. This mark underwent several modifications from the second half of the 14th century to the 18th, when an imperial crown was placed above the tower.

See also BELGIUM, §IX, 1(i) and (ii).

BIBLIOGRAPHY
L. Tondreau and others: *L'Orfèvrerie en Hainaut* (Tielt and Antwerp, 1985)
Les Grands Orfèvres du Hainaut (exh. cat. by R. Stilmant, Brussels, Banque-Lambert, 1988)
LEO DE REN

4. CATHEDRAL. The bishopric of Tournai was created at the beginning of the 6th century AD; in the Merovingian period it was endowed as a double cathedral, St Etienne and Notre-Dame. These earlier buildings were replaced in the 12th century by the present cathedral, which with its five towers dominates the city. The building workshop was assembled *c.* 1125; at the time of the consecration of 1171 the nave and transepts were finished except for the vaults over the straight bays of the transepts. There was a second consecration in 1213–14; at that time the cathedral was complete except for the bell-towers on either side of the nave. The choir was rebuilt from 1243. The nave is 60 m long and 26 m high; the choir 61 m long and 33 m high. The cathedral is built of limestone.

(i) Architecture.

(a) Nave and transepts. Nine bays long, excluding the bay forming a gallery inside the façade, the nave introduced a type of elevation new to medieval architecture, the four-storey elevation (see fig. 3). The arcades and gallery are of equal height, followed by a triforium, where the number of arches is doubled, and finally a clerestory. The arcade piers are cruciform with four engaged shafts and four octagonal shafts *en délit* in the re-entrant angles; these

elements correspond to three plain, stepped orders on the arcade arches. The gallery piers look more slender, their octagonal core being flanked by only four shafts and their oblique faces receiving the bevelled order of the gallery arches. The storeys are marked by string courses, but there are no vertical lines to break the horizontals; the bays are marked only by the exact superimposition of the openings, less clear at triforium level. The nave was originally timber-roofed, but groin vaults were substituted in the 18th century. In the 17th century the same had been done in the galleries, where the diaphragm arches had been retained and reused as transverse arches. But the aisles were certainly originally groin-vaulted.

It was also at Tournai that the Anglo-Norman interior wall passage at clerestory level passed to the exterior, appearing in the form of a compact colonnade. The majestic rhythm of arches in the nave accentuating the horizontal lines and the presence of a clerestory passage affirm the Anglo-Norman (and more precisely the English) sources of this design. The same insistence on horizontality is found on the exterior, where blind arches concealing the flat wall-buttresses alternate with the gallery windows.

It is possible that two towers were intended for the façade, but this plan was soon abandoned. From the outset the main façade, its central part surmounted by a gable flanked by two turrets, followed the arrangement of the side walls, the design of each level returning across the façade. At the beginning of the 14th century the base of the façade was decorated with sculpture and covered by a porch; in the 16th century an immense opening was pierced in the central bay, for which an anachronistic rose window was substituted in the 19th century by JUSTIN BRUYENNE. Two side doors, the Porte Mantile and the Porte du Capitole, give access to the last bay but one of the nave.

The transepts are far less homogeneous and are clearly the work of several masters. The first master probably intended to follow the design of the nave but introduced vertical articulation in order to accommodate sexpartite vaults. Apses the width of the central vessel were planned to terminate the transept arms. The second master enlarged the apses and encircled them with a narrow ambulatory surmounted by galleries, which abutted the four flanking towers. A new type of triforium was introduced; the narrow arches in the hemicycle were heightened, so that the arcade is considerably taller than the gallery, giving a strong impression of verticality. The clerestory windows have an exterior passage. The west walls of the transept were adapted to the changed proportions by the insertion of a second triforium linked to the first by shafts. The east transept walls, adapted by a last master, were modified by the construction of the Gothic choir.

Fragments of the Romanesque choir suggest that it had the same design as the east transept walls. The towers at the transept angles probably derive from the abbey church of St Trond or perhaps the bell-turrets associated with Norman apses. The influence of the Romanesque cathedral was great, even if taste was then evolving towards Gothic. The preference for unarticulated walls and for a façade with two small, plain towers was retained; the type

3. Tournai Cathedral, interior of the nave, begun *c.* 1125

of triforium introduced in the transept also continued in use.

(b) Choir. In 1243 Bishop Gautier de Marvis undertook to rebuild the choir (see fig. 4). When the new work was consecrated in 1255, it still lacked vaults and flying buttresses. Toothing stones indicate that a continuation of the work westwards was envisaged, but it was never executed. As at Soissons Cathedral, the vaults of the radiating chapels merge with those of the ambulatory (except for the axial chapel); the radiating chapels are polygonal, their flat surfaces more suitable to accommodate large windows; and the masonry reveals other characteristics of Soissons. But the style is in general a somewhat dry and fleshless version of Rayonnant. In their original state, the piers were very slender, as were those of

4. Tournai Cathedral, view of choir, rebuilt from 1243

the hemicycle; from the end of the 14th century they had to be reinforced with tie rods. Medallions decorate the arcade spandrels in the Norman manner. The triforium is shallow; its back wall is only partially glazed, and it is not linked to the clerestory by mullions. In the straight bays, these two levels have a curious design: two subdivided openings enclose a small central lancet, a design comparable to the middle storey of the nave of Sées Cathedral in Normandy.

Like that of Cambrai, the choir of Tournai had only a limited influence: in the southern Low Countries, the preference was for a less elegant sturdier architecture. The choirs of both Cambrai and Tournai were responsible for the popularity in the region of small, triangular gables crowning the tops of walls and encasing the clerestory windows.

Tournai Cathedral has an important place in the history of medieval architecture, even if the influence of its Romanesque parts was quickly supplanted by that of the cathedrals of Arras and Cambrai; its choir propagated the Rayonnant style in the southern Low Countries until a distinctive style developed there.

BIBLIOGRAPHY

P. Heliot: 'La Cathédrale de Tournai et l'architecture du moyen âge', *Rev. Belge Archéol. & Hist. A./Belge Tijdschr. Oudhdknde & Kstgesch.*, xxxi–xxxiii (1962–4), pp. 3–139

V. Scaff: *La Sculpture romane de la cathédrale Notre-Dame de Tournai* (Tournai, 1971)

JACQUES THIÉBAUT

(ii) Sculpture. Tournai Cathedral is the lone survivor of a group of important 12th century structures in northern France and Flanders. The sculptural decoration of the cathedral, still largely *in situ*, testifies to the richness and vitality of Romanesque sculpture in this region. All carved in the local dark grey limestone known as Tournai stone, the sculpture consists of several hundred capitals in the nave and transept, two portals (the Porte Mantile and the Porte du Capitole) on the north and south sides of the nave, and fragments of a western portal (Cathedral, Treasury). Although the Porte Mantile and the Porte du Capitole are badly weathered, the west door fragments and the interior capitals are well preserved. Most of the exterior capitals have been replaced by modern copies.

The capitals can be divided into three stylistic groups, Nave Groups 1 and 2 and the Transept Group, with a fourth group, Nave Group 3, constituting a transitional stage between Group 2 and the Transept Group. The decorative elements of Group 1, simple variations of the volute capital, appear in the western narthex and along the aisle walls, and belong to the first stage of construction. The Group 2 capitals are mostly located in the main arcades of the nave and in the western two-thirds of the nave gallery. Of a higher quality and more varied than the other capitals, they are roughly cubic and have fleshy ruffled leaves, sometimes inhabited by animals or human heads. The Group 3 capitals, located in the eastern end of the nave galleries, incorporate elements common to Group 2 mixed with motifs of the Transept Group. The Transept Group capitals appear on the interior and exterior of the two easternmost bays of the nave gallery and throughout the transept. They are carved with dry, schematic leaves and volutes.

Four fragments of the western portal were discovered in 1851. The representations of Aries, the Grape Harvest and Temperance suggest that the archivolts contained cycles of the *Zodiac* and *Labours of the Months* and possibly the four *Cardinal Virtues*. The Porte Mantile and the Porte du Capitole both have trilobate archivolts enclosing semicircular archivolts resting on colonnettes. Goldschmidt proposed that each of the three portals was built in two stages, trilobate archivolts being added after the portals had first been completed with a semicircular profile. The Porte Mantile (see fig. 5) is the better preserved in that it still possesses one half of its jamb sculptures, figures carved in shallow relief, including scenes from the *Psychomachia* of Prudentius and the *Punishment of Avarice*. The inner archivolt is carved with a series of scenes from the *Life of David*, probably meant here as a personification of Humility. Interpretation of the reliefs on the other archivolts is uncertain, but they are also likely to refer to the struggle between good and evil. The Porte du Capitole has lost all the original carving on the jambs except for a fragment now preserved in a chapel of the choir. It has two semicircular archivolts, the inner one carved with a *Last Judgement* scene: the dead rising from their tombs.

5. Tournai Cathedral, Porte Mantile, north door, *c.* 1140–55

The winged figures in the second archivolt have not yet been securely identified.

It is difficult to find comparative material for the sculptures of Tournai Cathedral in the surrounding region. Since Rolland, scholars have noted connections with the Anglo-Norman region, the Ile-de-France and Lombardy. Based on fragments from the cathedrals of Arras and Cambrai and the abbey of St Bertin at Saint-Omer, Vanuxem placed the capitals of Tournai within a regional northern French group that he believed to have had an impact on the sculpture of the Ile-de-France. The jamb figures of the Porte Mantile have usually been placed in the general lineage of Saint-Denis Abbey and Chartres Cathedral, but the Tournai sculptures seem more likely to have been influenced by Saint-Denis alone and to belong to an experimental period, before the strictly vertical figure type of the Royal Portal at Chartres became the accepted canon.

Although Goldschmidt's opinion that the three portals and the capitals of the nave arcades were of the same style has been disputed by scholars who date the portals later, study of the architecture, sculpture and the documents supports his view. Whereas the Nave Group 3 and Transept capitals probably date from *c*. 1150–71, both the Group 2 capitals and the portals (except the trilobes) were produced between *c*. 1140 and 1155.

BIBLIOGRAPHY

Scriptores, Mnmt. Ger. Hist., vi (Hannover, 1844), p. 444

A. Goldschmidt: 'Die belgische Monumentalplastik des 12. Jahrhunderts', *Belgische Kunstdenkmäler*, ed. P. Clemen (Munich, 1923), pp. 51–72

P. Rolland: *La Sculpture tournaisienne* (Brussels, 1944)

J. Vanuxem: 'La Sculpture du XIIe siècle à Cambrai et à Arras', *Bull. Mnmtl* (1955), pp. 7–35

V. Scaff: *La Sculpture romane de la cathédrale Notre-Dame de Tournai* (Tournai, 1971)

E. Schwartzbaum: *The Romanesque Sculpture of the Cathedral of Tournai* (diss., New York U., 1977)

——: 'The 12th Century Sculpture of Tournai Cathedral and the Sculpture of Northern Italy', *Romanico Convegno internazionale di studi: Modena and Parma, 1977*, pp. 203–22

ELIZABETH B. SMITH

Tournehem, Charles-François Le Normand de. *See* LE NORMAND DE TOURNEHEM, CHARLES-FRANÇOIS.

Tournier, Nicolas (*b* Montbéliard, Doubs, *bapt* 12 July 1590; *d* Toulouse, before Feb 1639). French painter. His father, André Tournier, was a Protestant painter from Besançon. It has been conjectured that the family moved from the Franche-Comté to Languedoc, where the elder Tournier may have been active in Narbonne. Nicolas Tournier's baptismal record, discovered by Mesuret, is the main source of the few facts known about his life before 1619. He is recorded in Rome from 1619 to 1626, and one early source says that he was a pupil of Valentin de Boulogne. However, none of the paintings that have been attributed to him since Longhi began to disentangle his style of work from that of Caravaggio, or of other Caravaggist painters active in Rome, is documented. Their authorship rests on stylistic comparisons with documented works painted on Tournier's return to south-west France. Nevertheless, he seems to have painted in Rome about 30 pictures in a style close to that of Bartolomeo Manfredi, making him one of the most important French Caravaggists, on a par with Nicolas Régnier and Guy François.

Clearly Tournier was an adept of what Joachim von Sandrart called the 'Manfrediana Methodus'. His Roman pictures, of which the *Banqueting Scene with a Guitar Player* (St Louis, MO, A. Mus.) is a celebrated example, are half- and three-quarter-length genre scenes of drinkers, singers and soldiers grouped around game-tables. On occasion he would seem to have copied Manfredi, as is the case with the *Drinking Party* (Le Mans, Mus. Tessé), once owned by Louis XIV, and the division of works between the two artists is difficult. Some consider, for instance, that the *Lute Player* (St Petersburg, Hermitage) and the *Denial of St Peter* (Dresden, Gemäldegal. Alte Meister) are by Tournier rather than Manfredi.

In 1627 Tournier was back in France, at Carcassonne. Basing himself at Toulouse from 1632, his numerous large altarpieces helped to turn that city into one of the most lively provincial centres of painting in 17th-century France. In such pictures as the *Descent from the Cross* (Toulouse, Mus. Augustins) and the *Crucifixion with the Virgin, Mary Magdalene and St Francis of Paola* (Paris, Louvre) he used effectively the expressive power of strong chiaroscuro and sometimes achieved great dramatic intensity through the simplification of poses and composition. He continued to paint secular subjects, including the *Battle of the Red Rocks* (Toulouse, Mus. Augustins), which he treated in a reserved and serious manner, even when they were genre scenes such as *The Concert* (Paris, Louvre). A painting of *Judas and Joseph* (Narbonne Cathedral) dated 1655 and signed TOURNIER or FOURNIER for a long time led to the erroneous supposition that Tournier died after this date. He made his will in Toulouse on 30 December 1638.

BIBLIOGRAPHY

R. Longhi: 'I pittori della realtà in Francia, ovvero i caravaggeschi francesi del seicento', *Italia Lett.* (19 Jan 1935), pp. 1–6; also in *Paragone*, xxiii/269 (1972), pp. 3–18

R. Mesuret: 'L'Acte de baptême de Nicolas Tournier', *Bull. Soc. Hist. A. Fr.* (1951), pp. 13–18

——: 'L'Oeuvre peint de Nicolas Tournier: Essai de catalogue', *Gaz. B.-A.*, n. s. 4, 1 (1957), pp. 327–50

A. Brejon de Lavergnée: 'Pour Nicolas Tournier sur son séjour romain', *Paragone*, xxv/287 (1974), pp. 44–55

P. Salies: 'Nicolas Tournier peintre en Languedoc, 1590–1639?', *Archistra*, 14/15 (1974), pp. 29–34

Valentin et les Caravagesques français (exh. cat. by A. Brejon de Lavergnée and J.-P. Cuzin, Paris, Grand Pal., 1974), pp. 104–9

J. Bousquet: *Recherches sur le séjour des peintres français à Rome au XVIIe siècle* (Montpellier, 1980)

La Peinture française du XVIIe siècle dans les collections américaines (exh. cat. by P. Rosenberg, Paris, Grand Pal.; New York, Met.; Chicago, IL, A. Inst.; 1982), pp. 324–5

ARNAULD BREJON DE LAVERGNÉE

Tournières, Robert [Levrac-Tournières] (*b* Caen, 17 June 1667; *d* Caen, 18 May 1752). French painter. He began his artistic training with the Carmelite Lucas Delahaye, but a decisive influence on his future development was meeting Bon Boullogne, whom Tournières accommodated in his studio in Paris. There Tournières made copies of paintings of the Dutch School. He also worked as a copyist in the studio of France's most successful contemporary portrait painter, Hyacinthe Rigaud.

In 1702 Tournières was received (*reçu*) as a member of the Académie Royale, on presentation of portraits of the painters *Pierre Mosnier* and *Michel Corneille* (both Versailles, Château). At the Salon of the same year he exhibited

20 portraits. Among these was his *Self-portrait with Pierre de la Roque* (priv. col.; engraving by Isaac Sarrabat, 1703), in which he combined the French formal portrait with a Dutch-inspired feigned oval setting. Tournières also exhibited a group portrait of the goldsmith *Nicolas de Launay and his Family* (Caen, Mus. B.-A.). In this picture he relaxed the formal poses customary in the late 17th century and depicted easy gestures and movements in the intimate setting of de Launay's lodgings at the Louvre. Further portrait commissions came from his patron, the Regent, Philippe I, Duc d'Orléans.

The Dutch influence on Tournière's work is particularly evident in the small, Rembrandtesque *Discovery of Drawing* (1716; Paris, Ecole N. Sup. B.-A.), showing a pair of lovers lit by a single candle; this painting persuaded the Académie to accept him as a history painter also. The heterogeneous character of his work makes him a typical artist of the transitional *Régence* period. Apart from the Dutch elements that give his work a new and more intimate character, his light palette anticipates the Rococo style, as in the portrait of *Graf Ferdinand Adolf von Plettenberg* (1727; Budapest, Mus. F.A.). After his promotion to assistant professor at the Académie in 1737, and a further successful showing at the Salon of 1742, Tournières retired to Caen in 1749 and gave up painting.

BIBLIOGRAPHY
Thieme–Becker
A.-J. Dézallier d'Argenville: *Abrégé de la vie des plus fameux peintres* (1745–52, 2/1762), iv, pp. 361–5
M.-L. Bataille: 'Tournières 1668–1752', in L. Dimier, ed.: *Les Peintres français du 18e siècle*, i (Paris, 1928), pp. 227–43
D. Alcouffe: 'Notes sur un portrait de Tournières, "Nicolas Delaunay et sa famille"', *Rev. Louvre*, xxix (1979), pp. 444–8
CATHRIN KLINGSÖHR-LE-ROY

Tournon, Paul (*b* Marseille, 19 Feb 1881; *d* Paris, 22 Dec 1964). French architect. He studied architecture at the Ecole des Beaux-Arts, Paris, where he won the Deuxième Grand Prix de Rome in 1911; he also taught there from 1925 to 1944, in the last two years as director of the entire school. He was married to the painter Elizabeth Branly (1889–1972) and throughout his career showed a keen interest in the other visual arts. As an architect he was best known for his ecclesiastical work; for example his church (1926) in Villemonble is notable for its steeple, with gigantic angels carved in concrete by the sculptor Carlo Sarrabezolles (1888–1971). His simple yet grandiose Eglise du Saint-Esprit (1928), Paris, echoes the magnitude of Hagia Sophia, Istanbul, while his church (1928) at Elisabethville-sur-Seine and the cathedral (1930) at Casablanca exploited the decorative potential of the concrete frame, with expressionist overtones. The strength of Tournon's architecture is also manifest in his less well-known but equally interesting hall of residence (1930) for female students on the Rue Lhomond in Paris, where furnishings were designed by Jacques-Emile Ruhlmann, and his prize-winning competition entry (1933; with Marcel Chappey) for a Palais des Expositions in Paris, sponsored by the Office Technique de l'Utilisation de l'Acier. Tournon was elected to the Institut de France in 1942.

BIBLIOGRAPHY
A. Louvet: 'Les Eglises modernes: Le Clocher de l'église de Villemonble', *Architecture* [Paris], xl/8 (1927), pp. 233–41
L'Eglise du Saint-Esprit à Paris (Strasbourg, *c.* 1934)
Nouveau Palais des expositions (Paris, *c.* 1934)
Paul Tournon: Architecte, 1881–1964 (Paris, 1976)
ISABELLE GOURNAY

Tournus, St Philibert. Former Benedictine abbey church in Burgundy, France. This is the only large-scale church that exhibits to a significant degree characteristics of both northern and southern Romanesque architecture. Disagreement in the 19th century and the early 20th about the building chronology, with controversy over the date of both the choir plan, with ambulatory and radiating chapels, and the narthex, has led to debate over the building's significance in architectural history. More recently, scepticism has been expressed over the documentary evidence provided in the mid-11th-century Ardain text (see below).

St Philibert is a complex structure, *c.* 80 m long (*see* ROMANESQUE, fig. 13). At the west end is a two-storey narthex of three bays, with a two-tower façade over the western bay (the north tower has an added belfry). The narthex exhibits a wide variety of Romanesque vaulting: the central vessel of the lower storey is groin-vaulted, with transverse barrel vaulting in the aisles; in the upper storey the main vessel has a longitudinal barrel vault, supported by quadrant vaults in the aisles. The vast five-bay nave (see fig.) has massive cylindrical piers, which were coloured pink by the restorer, André Ventre. It was originally covered with a wooden roof, with groin vaults in the aisles. The present transverse barrel vaults were added later. The transept was designed in the early Romanesque period to support a wooden roof, but it was modified to include barrel-vaulted arms, each with an eastern apsidal chapel. The crossing has a dome on squinches beneath a square

Tournus, St Philibert, nave looking east, completed by *c.* 1070; vaults, 12th century

tower. The barrel-vaulted choir, of two bays, has an ambulatory with three radiating chapels, over a crypt of the same plan, all heavily restored.

The building chronology can be established from both documents and examination of the masonry. A fire in 1008 was followed by a consecration in 1019. A famous text announces the burial of Abbot Ardain in 1056 in the north gallery of the cloister, adjoining the south aisle of the nave. There was a burial in the south transept *c.* 1105, and another consecration in 1120. The whole of the narthex and the nave (except the high vaults) are of *petit appareil* construction. Armi's examination of the masonry has confirmed that the lower parts of the narthex precede those of the nave; therefore all of these were up as far as the springing of the aisle vaults by 1056. Nothing in the Ardain text precludes an earlier date for the narthex and nave, which may have been complete when Ardain died, but were almost certainly finished by 1070. Included in this building campaign are the capitals of the north gallery of the cloister. Their secure dating anchors Burgundian, Rhône Valley and Provençal early Romanesque sculpture. No other body of early Romanesque sculpture in these regions can be dated by documentary evidence.

The existing choir, crypt and transept are built of limestone ashlar; but traces of rubble walling in the crypt are evidence of an earlier east end, probably that destroyed in the fire of 1008 and rebuilt for the consecration of 1019. The ambulatory and radiating chapel plan of St Philibert was therefore probably established by the late 10th century. The consecration of 1120 marks the substantive completion of the present east end. The crossing contains Brionnais capitals, frequent in Burgundy, but only from *c.* 1075–1120. The nave vaults, which abut the drum of the crossing dome awkwardly, must post-date it, and were probably the last work on the building.

St Philibert remains a unique monument. From southern First Romanesque architecture came the use of *petit appareil* construction, the massive columnar piers of the narthex and nave, and the complex vaulting system of the narthex. To northern early Romanesque the church owes its immense size, its vast wooden-roofed nave, and the radiating chapel plan of the choir.

BIBLIOGRAPHY
Chronique de Falcon [MS.; 875–1087]; ed. in P. Junien: *Nouvelle histoire de l'abbaye royale de Saint-Filibert, et de la ville de Tournus* (Dijon, 1733), pp. 92–3 [contains the Ardain text]
J. Puig y Cadafalch: *La geografia i els orígens del primer art romànic* (Barcelona, 1930; Fr. trans., Barcelona, 1932)
H. Focillon: *L'Art de l'ouest*, i (Paris, 1938; Eng. trans., London, rev. 1963/*R* 1980)
J. Vallery-Radot and V. Lassalle: *Saint-Philibert de Tournus* (Paris, 1955)
L. Grodecki: *L'Architecture ottonienne* (Paris, 1958)
E. Vergnolle: 'Recherches sur quelques séries de chapiteaux romans bourguignons', *Inf. Hist. A.*, xx (1975), pp. 55–79
E. Armi: *Masons and Sculptors in Romanesque Burgundy*, 2 vols (University Park, PA, [1983])
JOHN CAMERON

Tourrisan, Pierre. *See* TORRIGIANI, PIETRO.

Tours. French city on the River Loire, préfecture of Indre-et-Loire, with a population of *c.* 136,500. It was an important centre for the production of manuscripts in the Carolingian period and for tapestry-weaving in 16th and 17th centuries. The church of St Martin (destr.) was an important pilgrimage site in the medieval period.

1. History and urban development. 2. Centre of production. 3. St Martin.

1. HISTORY AND URBAN DEVELOPMENT. There was a Gallic settlement (Artionis) to the north of the Loire, but the Roman town of Caesarodunum was on the south bank. It was probably an unenclosed settlement covering 40 densely populated hectares. In the 1st century AD a plan provided for settlement, and cemeteries were located at a distance from the town centre to allow Caesarodunum to grow. The settlement, the capital of the Turones, had the status of a free city state (*civitas libera*). It was created to accelerate Romanization and compete with nearby traditional Gaulish settlements. The Roman town remained small; indeed, archaeological research shows that the original site set aside was never fully utilized and that the settlement began to shrink after AD 150.

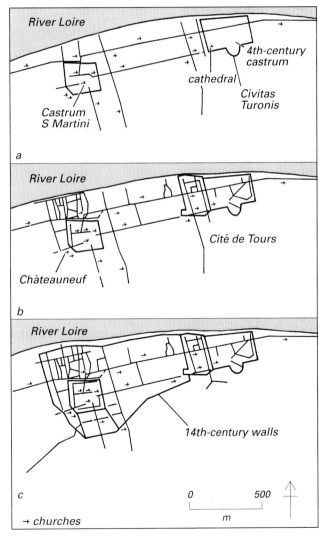

1. Tours, plans showing the development of the city: (a) *c.* 950; (b) *c.* 1250; (c) *c.* 1400

In the 4th century a small *castrum* of 9 ha was built, and the town became the capital of the province of Lugdunensis III. The arrival of Christianity was marked by the construction of a cathedral within the walls, and of a funerary basilica, where the first bishop of Tours, Litorius, was buried, at some distance from the walled town. The second bishop, Martin of Tours (*reg c.* 371–97), however, was buried in a nearby cemetery. The promotion of the cult of St Martin by his successors from the 5th century onwards resulted in the declining importance of Litorius' basilica. In the 6th century GREGORY rebuilt the cathedral and took great interest in local buildings. During the early Middle Ages, St Martin's tomb grew into a monastery, and then a monastic stronghold (*see* §3 below). Thus two opposing centres of power developed: an administrative town, which brought the ecclesiastical and politico-military courts together in the *castrum*, and a religious complex around the tomb of the saint. Between the two was arable land.

The monastery of St Martin erected its own *castrum* (Châteauneuf) against the Viking raids. Its completion in 918 created a territory independent of any civil authority and split Tours into twin towns (see fig. 1a). Medieval Tours and Châteauneuf should be considered as separate (1b), often antagonistic centres, reunited only in 1380 (1c). Tours was ruled by the English in the 12th century but was returned to the French in 1242. Construction of the Gothic cathedral began in the 13th century and continued for over 300 years. Louis XI lived near the city for several years before his death in 1483. A number of 15th- and 16th-century hôtels survive, including the Hôtel Binet and Hôtel Robin-Quantin, and the Palais du Commerce has an 18th-century façade. The town never recovered, however, from the destruction of the religious wars, which also ruined the previously thriving production of silk in the area. Tours had a mint for several centuries before the Revolution; during the Revolution the cathedral's sculpture was largely destroyed.

The city retains traces of its evolution, although it owes its character less to the early Roman town than to the subsequent period of decline. Today, despite the change of axis due to the 18th-century north–south road from Paris to Spain, the rival medieval developments in the east and west are still perceptible. The city was attacked by the Germans in the 1870s and was badly damaged during World War II.

Artists associated with Tours include the 15th-century painter and illuminator JEAN FOUQUET. Jean Bourdichon kept the tradition of manuscript illumination alive in the city. In the 17th century the printmaker Abraham Bosse worked in Tours before moving to Paris.

BIBLIOGRAPHY
L. Pietri: *La Ville de Tours du IVe au VIe siècle: Naissance d'une cité chrétienne* (Paris and Rome, 1983)
B. Chevalier, ed.: *Histoire de Tours* (Toulouse, 1985)
H. Galinie: 'Reflections on Early Medieval Tours', *The Rebirth of Towns in the West, AD 700–1050*, Council Brit. Archaeol. Res. Rep., 68 (London, 1988)

HENRI GALINIE

2. CENTRE OF PRODUCTION.

(i) Manuscripts. During the Carolingian period Tours was a leading centre of book production and may have provided influential models of page layout and script as well as methods of text copying for other writing centres in the Frankish kingdoms (*see* CAROLINGIAN ART, §IV, 3(ii)). The oldest surviving manuscripts written at Tours date from before 750 and were probably copied at the monastery of St Martin. They reveal a script developing from Merovingian cursive and half-uncial towards caroline minuscule (*see* SCRIPT). Anglo-Saxon scribes contributed to books at Tours before and during the abbacy of Alcuin (796–804), but generally Insular influence on Tours script and decorative styles was minimal. The distinctive type of caroline minuscule found at Tours was perfected in the early years of the 9th century, particularly during the abbacy of Fridugisus (*reg* 807–34) and for the rest of the century remained remarkably consistent. The finest examples of book production at Tours date from the lay abbacies of Adalhard (*reg* 834–53) and Vivian (*reg* 844–53), and it was then that some of its most remarkable illuminated manuscripts were produced. Notable among the surviving manuscripts from this highly productive period are four great Bibles, which include the Moutier–Grandval Bible (London, BL, Add. MS. 10546; see fig. 2; *see also* BIBLE, fig. 3) and the Vivian Bible (Paris, Bib. N., MS. lat. 1), and nine Gospel books, for instance the Lothair Gospels (Paris, Bib. N., MS. lat. 266). The page layout typical of Tours books, a masterly hierarchy of scripts, with square capitals, uncial, a special Tours half-uncial and

2. Tours school: decorated initial D to Jerome's preface, with display scripts, from the Moutier-Grandval Bible, *c.* 840 (London, British Library, Add. MS. 10546, fol. 6r)

finally minuscule for the main text, demonstrates the discipline of the scriptorium; the work of many named scribes can be discerned in a number of books, for example Theodegrimus and Fridegaudus, who copied both Bibles and the famous Puteanus Livy (Paris, Bib. N., MS. lat. 5730).

It is clear that manuscripts were produced at Tours on commission and for export, both for other churches and for the Carolingian rulers, for example the splendid copy of Boethius's *De arithmetica* (Bamberg, Staatsbib., MS. misc. class. 5) made for King Charles the Bald, the Marmoutier Sacramentary (Autun, Bib. Mun., MS. 19bis) made for Abbot Raganaldus of Marmoutier and the Gauzlin Gospels (Nancy, Trésor Cathédrale) made for Arnaldus of Orléans, an official at the court of Emperor Louis the Pious (*reg* 814–40). As well as exporting books, Tours specialized in the production of particular kinds of books, notably Bibles and a collection of texts relating to St Martin known as the *Martinellus*. The Bible text disseminated is known as the Tours 'Alcuinian' edition, since Alcuin inaugurated the great enterprise for Bible production with the emphasis on producing a clear and correct text. A major characteristic of this was the copying of pandects (single-volume Bibles) rather than the more customary division of the Bible into separate books or groups of books. These Bibles were produced in quantity in a standard format, consistent layout and a distinctive script, which was followed elsewhere in the west Frankish kingdom.

No 9th-century catalogue of the library at Tours survives. The bulk of the approximately 200 surviving manuscripts produced there were written for other centres rather than for the use of its own school and community, for the library and monastery at Tours appear to have suffered badly in Viking raids in 903 and scribal activity thereafter was limited. As in other Carolingian centres, however, books were acquired from elsewhere for the Tours library throughout its history. This included such older books as a Boethius commentary on Cicero, written on papyrus and borrowed by the Carolingian scholar Lupus of Ferrières (*fl c.* 805–62).

BIBLIOGRAPHY

L. Delisle: 'Mémoire sur l'école calligraphique de Tours au IXe siècle', *Mém. Acad. Inscr. & B.-Lett.*, xxxii (1886), pp. 29–50

E. K. Rand: *A Survey of the Manuscripts of Tours* (Cambridge, MA, 1929)

E. K. Rand and L. W. Jones: *The Earliest Books of Tours* (Cambridge, MA, 1934)

W. Koehler: *Die Schule von Tours* (1935), ii of *Die karolingischen Miniaturen* (Berlin, 1930–82)

B. Bischoff: 'Panorama der Handschriften Überlieferung aus der Zeit Karls des Grossen', *Mittelalterliche Studien: Ausgewählte Aufsätze zur Schriftkunde und Literaturgeschichte*, iii (Stuttgart, 1981), pp. 5–38

ROSAMOND D. MCKITTERICK

(ii) Tapestry. The first documentary evidence of weavers at Tours is an apprenticeship contract dated 1521 that reveals the names of two master weavers, Nicolas Mortaigne and Pasquier Mortaigne. In 1535 the Surintendant des Bâtiments, Babou de la Bourdaisière, in charge of the Fontainebleau tapestry workshop, encouraged the establishment of another workshop, directed by Jean Duval. Examples of the work of the Mortaigne family are the *Story of St Saturnin* (Angers, Château, Col. Tap.; Langeais, Château). Completed in 1527, this was woven to designs by a Florentine painter established at Tours, André Polastron, and bears witness to an Italian influence that can also be seen in the *Life of St Pierre* (Saumur, St Pierre), woven between 1546 and 1548. The name Motheron appears in records in 1565 and again in 1613. With François Cothart, Alexandre Motheron is linked with Marc de Comans (*d* after 1643) and François de La Planche (van den Plancken; 1573–1627) as creating at Tours a branch of the Parisian workshop of Faubourg St Marcel. A number of inventories mention tapestries made at Tours and provide information on the subjects of those produced in the workshop of Faubourg St Marcel. The association of weavers ended in 1625, but a report addressed to Cardinal Francesco Barberini in 1630 mentions the Tours workshop, where weavers from Paris were making sumptuous tapestries for Cardinal Richelieu. Sébastien Motheron continued his father's work until his death in 1674, when the history of tapestry production at Tours comes to an end. Woven on high-warp looms, the tapestries were distinguished by a double pass.

BIBLIOGRAPHY

H. Göbel: *Wandteppiche: Die romanischen Länder* (Leipzig, 1928), pp. 263–9, 549

M. Jarry: 'La Collection de tapisseries du château de Langeais', *Bull. Soc. Hist. A. Fr.* (1973), pp. 44–5

ISABELLE DENIS

3. ST MARTIN. The church, built at the site of the tomb of St Martin, Bishop of Tours, became the most famous pilgrimage sanctuary in France. Venerated during his lifetime, Martin was acclaimed a saint at his death in 397, his remains attracting thousands of pilgrims annually for over a millennium. The earliest basilica, erected shortly after he died, was replaced in the 5th century. This church, known from excavations and contemporary accounts, had an aisled nave 48.77 m long, an apse at the east end and a secure tower at the entrance to hold off Visigothic marauders (see fig. 3). A lantern tower and belfry were added later. The tomb was situated behind the sanctuary and at ground level, rather than in a crypt, an unconventional arrangement made necessary by the high water-table. A constellation of buildings surrounded the basilica, including an atrium built along three sides, a sacristy, refuges for asylum-seekers and the sick and poor, two baptisteries and a little chapel for the community of nuns established there.

Most of this was swept away during the Viking incursions of the late 9th century. Two coins, one from the reign of Charlemagne, the other (893–929) from the time of Charles the Simple (*reg* 898–922), illustrate the transition from a horizontal, self-contained Late Roman basilica to a vertical, confident expression of the Carolingian *renovatio*. The aisled church of 904–18 had two towers, and the canon's choir extended into the nave.

The fire of 994 provided the impetus for a radical building programme, paid for by Hervé de Buzançais, the treasurer of St Martin. The timber-roofed nave of the Capetian basilica measured *c.* 97.0×33.5×23.0 m. Groin-vaulted aisles with tribunes gave on to the transepts, each of which had two two-storey chapels on the east side. Piers supported a lantern tower at the crossing. It is unclear how much of the 11th-century church was a reconstruction, but it incorporated much that was innovative. The

3. Tours, St Martin, late 5th century; reconstruction drawing

unorthodox ground-level 'crypt' corridor evolved into a semicircular arcaded ambulatory with five separate apsidal chapels. There is some debate, however, as to whether this arrangement—imitated by many pilgrimage churches, including Santiago de Compostela and Cluny III—had been introduced in the 10th-century church (see CHURCH, fig. 8).

Part of the chevet and nave were completed at the time of the dedication in 1018. By the mid-11th century the community of canons at St Martin numbered more than 200, and their endowments and estates enabled them to carry on building. In 1050 massive towers were added to the ends of the groin-vaulted transepts, and a new crossing lantern was erected, supported by vaults spanning more than 8 m.

Once again, fire (during the visit of Pope Urban II in 1096) led to renovation. Following the example of other cruciform pilgrimage churches—St Martial, Limoges, Ste Foi, Conques, St Sernin, Toulouse and Santiago de Compostela—the chevet was developed, with clerestory windows added to admit more light and the transepts given rib-vaulting supported by transverse arches. After 1100, the nave walls were replaced with piers, and new external walls were built, to create two more aisles in a revival of the Roman five-aisled basilica. A stone barrel-vaulted roof took the place of the flammable timber one.

Tension between the bourgeoisie of Tours and the canons erupted in 1122 and the church was set ablaze. Makeshift repairs accelerated deterioration until, by 1160, the building was in urgent need of restoration. This programme, initiating the third phase of building, began with the installation of ribbed vaulting in the nave and transept and the completion of two towers at the west end. The Romanesque apse and choir were finally superseded during the 13th-century renovations of the chevet. In imitation of the system developed at Bourges Cathedral, a double ambulatory was built, with piers circling the choir. Work continued into the following century, when chapels were inserted between the wall buttresses.

A miniature by Jean Fouquet depicts the Gothic church in 1450. The aisles rose from heights of c. 9 m and 21 m to the 35.5 m-high nave, and three sets of windows lit the interior. The monumental choir buttresses spanned both ambulatories. The last picture of St Martin, a wash by Pinguet done in 1798, shows the nave in ruins. In 1886–1902 the local architect VICTOR LALOUX built a Romanesque style church on the site.

BIBLIOGRAPHY

Gregory of Tours: *De virtutibus beati Martini episcopi* [6th century]; ed. B. Krusch and W. Levison, Mnmt Ger. Hist., Scriptores rerum Merovingicarum I/1 (Hannover, 1885, 2/1937–51)

——: *Historia Francorum* [early 590s]; Eng. trans. by O. M. Dalton as *The History of the Franks by Gregory of Tours*, 2 vols (Oxford, 1927)

C. K. Hersey: 'The Church of St-Martin at Tours (903–1150)', *A. Bull.*, xxv/1 (1943), pp. 1–39

F. Lesnueur: 'St Martin et les origines de l'art roman', *Bull. Mnmtl.*, cvii (1949), pp. 7–84

K. J. Conant: *Carolingian and Romanesque Architecture, 800 to 1200*, Pelican Hist. A. (Harmondsworth, 1959, 3/1973)

M. Vieillard-Troïekouroff: 'Le Tombeau de St Martin retrouvé en 1860', *Rev. Hist. Eglise France*, xlvii (1961), pp. 151–83

G. T. Rivoira: *Lombardic Architecture: Its Origin, Development and Derivatives*, 2 vols (New York, 1975)

L. Pietri: 'Bâtiments et sanctuaires annexes de la basilique Saint-Martin de Tours, à la fin du VIe siècle', *Rev. Hist. Eglise France*, lxii (1976), pp. 223–34

R. Mark: *Experiments in Gothic Structure* (Cambridge, MA, 1982)

J. Bony: *French Gothic Architecture of the 12th and 13th Centuries* (Berkeley, Los Angeles and London, 1983)

Tousignant, Claude (*b* Montreal, 23 Dec 1932). Canadian painter and sculptor. He studied at the Montreal Museum School of Arts and Design from 1948 to 1952 under Jacques de Tonnancour. In October 1952 he moved to Paris, where he attended the Académie Ranson. His time in Paris was not fruitful, and in 1953 he returned to Montreal where he became associated with an artistic community that included the Canadian painter Rita Letendre (*b* 1929) and Guido Molinari. These artists were then moving away from the Automatism of Paul-Emile Borduas towards Tachism, and Tousignant exhibited 13 Tachist works at the Galerie de l'Echouerie in Montreal in 1955. In 1956, after a brief interest in the works of Sam Francis and Mark Rothko, he began to produce hard-edge painting using two or three contrasted colours, as in *Place of Infinity* (1956; artist's col., see 1973 exh. cat., frontispiece). This move was influenced by the writings of Kazimir Malevich, inspiring Tousignant towards greater simplicity in his work. Colour became increasingly important in his work thereafter.

In 1959 Tousignant created a number of sculptures, reminiscent of Mondrian's work, using brightly coloured planes of wood. From 1961 to 1962 he abandoned primary colours and used colours such as brown, mauve and magenta. The first circles appeared in his work in 1963: these are an important feature of later paintings and allowed him to break completely with classical composition. The circular works employ concentric rings of bright, contrasting colours, as in *Chromatic Accelerator* (1967; Ottawa, N.G.), and were called successively targets, chromatic transformers, gongs and chromatic accelerators. He also used diagonals in his works, as in *Diagonal Triptych* (1971–2; artist's col., see 1973 exh. cat., p. 22, fig. 6).

BIBLIOGRAPHY
Claude Tousignant (exh. cat. by D. Corbeil, Ottawa, N.G., 1973)
Claude Tousignant: Sculptures (exh. cat. by N. Theriault, Montreal, Mus. F.A., 1982)

Tovar, Alonso Miguel de (*b* Higuera de la Sierra, 1678; *d* Madrid, 1758). Spanish painter. He trained in Seville under Juan Antonio Ossorio and executed numerous religious paintings, including *Our Lady of Consolation with SS Francis, James and a Clerical Donor* (1720; Seville Cathedral) and *St Francis Receiving the Stigmata* (*c.* 1720; Madrid, Real Acad. S Fernando, Mus.). In both of these the influence of Murillo is discernible: the colouring is vivid and the drawing precise, if slightly rigid, and both works show a gentle and uncomplicated piety. Tovar was appointed court painter in 1729, when the Spanish court moved to Seville, and he collaborated with Jean Ranc, probably painting replicas of the latter's portraits. His own portraits include *Portrait of a Young Girl* (1732; Meiningen, Schloss Elisabethenburg). In 1733 he travelled with the court when it returned to Madrid, and he may have worked as an assistant to Louis-Michel van Loo. Tovar also probably painted the theme of the Holy Shepherd, popular with Sevillian artists of his time. Of the paintings of the subject attributed to him, however, only the one in the church at Cortelazor, near Aracena, signed in 1748, is considered authentic.

Ceán Bermúdez
BIBLIOGRAPHY
F. Girón María: 'La *Divina Pastora* de Cortelazor', *Archv Hispal.*, viii (1947), pp. 109–11
E. Valdivieso: *Historia de la pintura sevillana* (Seville, 1986), p. 302
JUAN J. LUNA

Tovar y Tovar, Martín (*b* Caracas, 10 Feb 1827; *d* Caracas, 17 Dec 1902). Venezuelan painter. He studied (1839–40) under Antonio José Carranza and in 1841 under Carmelo Fernández and Celestino Martínez at the Colegio La Paz, Caracas. In 1850 he studied at the Real Academia de S Fernando, Madrid, and from 1851 to 1855 he lived in Paris and was taught by Léon Cogniet at the Ecole des Beaux-Arts. Although he continued to travel frequently to Europe, he returned to Caracas in 1855, painting some of his best portraits before 1860 (e.g. *Ana Tovar y Tovar de Zuloaga*, 1858; Caracas, Machado Zuloaga estate). In 1859 he gave drawing classes at the Colegio Roscio, Caracas. Tovar y Tovar became associated with José Antonio Salas in 1864, establishing the art photography studio of Tovar y Salas. In 1867 he directed the painting section of the Academia de Bellas Artes. He was the official painter for the government (1870–88) of Antonio Guzmán Blanco, and was commissioned in 1873 to paint a gallery of

portraits of leading figures for the Capitolio Nacional, Caracas. In 1883 he was awarded first prize in the Exposición Nacional for *Signing of the Independence Act* (Caracas, Col. Concejo Mun.). He was commissioned by the National Executive in 1884 to execute a number of large historical and allegorical paintings, outstanding among which is the *Battle of Carabobo* (1887; Caracas, Col. Pal. Federal). After 1890 he frequently executed landscapes from sketches (e.g. *Macuto Landscape*, *c.* 1890; Caracas, Gal. A.N.).

BIBLIOGRAPHY
E. Planchart: *Don Martín Tovar y Tovar, 1828–1902* (Caracas, 1952)
A. Boulton: *Historia de la pintura en Venezuela: Epoca nacional*, ii (Caracas, 1968/*R* 1972)
J. Calzadilla: *Martín Tovar y Tovar* (Caracas, 1977)
MARÍA ANTONIA GONZALEZ-ARNAL

Tower of Glass [An Túr Gloine]. Irish stained-glass studio. This small cooperative studio was founded in Dublin in 1903 by Edward Martin, a key figure in the Celtic Revival, and Sarah Purser, the Dublin painter, determined to establish a school for the production of stained-glass on the advice of the English Arts and Crafts stained-glass master Christopher W. Whall. The school was funded and directed by Purser, and included two glaziers and selected artists who had trained at the Dublin Metropolitan School of Art under Alfred Ernest Child (1875–1939), a former Whall assistant who also managed the studio. The finest materials were used, to enhance the nature of the glass, and the designs emulated the former glories of Celtic metalwork, manuscript illumination, jewellery, and sculpture in a distinctively modern idiom. The workshop's first recruit, Michael Healy (1873–1941), found his vocation in Byzantine-style stained glass as did Wilhelmina Geddes (1887–1955), while the skilful expressionism is unparalleled. Other artists included Ethel Rhind (*c.* 1879–1952), who notably worked in *opus sectile* (a mosaic of glass embedded in cement), Beatrice Elvery (1883–1968), Hubert McGoldrick (1897–1967) and Catherine O'Brien (1881–1963), who maintained the studio after Purser's death until its closure in 1944.

BIBLIOGRAPHY
25th Anniversary Celebration of An Túr Gloine Stained Glass and Mosaic Works (Dublin, 1928)
J. Piper: *Stained Glass: Art or Anti-Art?* (London, 1968)
M. Wynne: *Irish Stained Glass* (Dublin, 1977)
Christopher Whall, 1849–1924: Arts and Crafts Stained Glass Worker (exh. cat. by P. Cormack, London, William Morris Gal., 1980)
D. Caron: *An Túr Gloine Windows and Mosaic Stations of the Cross in St Brendan's Cathedral, Loughrea, Co. Galway* (diss., Dublin, N. Coll. A. & Des., 1982)
N. Gordon Bowe: *Twentieth Century Irish Stained Glass* (Dublin, 1983)
N. Gordon Bowe, D. Caron and M. Wynne: *Gazetteer of Irish Stained Glass* (Dublin, 1988)
NICOLA GORDON BOWE

Tower house. Type of tall defensive house, originally based on a single, tower-like structure resembling a keep or donjon. Although of a type found elsewhere in Europe, notably in Ireland (*see* IRELAND, §II), the tower house was the predominant form of country residence for noblemen and gentry in Scotland for over three centuries until *c.* 1650; as it evolved there, it acquired a distinctive character, higher and more slender than the comparable peel-towers of Northumbria, barely 50 km south of the

Scottish border. While usually referred to as castles, most tower houses were not military emplacements: frequently built on overlooked sites (probably chosen for proximity to water), they relied for defence on massive strength of structure, difficulty of access and subtlety of internal planning.

The earliest surviving tower house in Scotland is Drum Castle (late 13th century or early 14th; Grampian), but the majority date from after the Battle of Bannockburn (1314), when Scottish nobles were prohibited from owning land in England and north–south cultural exchanges were suspended. Furthermore, the instability of the Scottish economy after 1314 discouraged the erection of traditional castles, and additions to existing royal castles (notably Edinburgh and Stirling), as well as to such buildings as Kildrummy Castle, Grampian, and the archiepiscopal palaces of Glasgow and Spynie, took the form of tower houses. The size and proportions of Scottish tower houses show considerable regional and chronological variations. Threave (1369; Dumfries and Galloway), built for Archibald Douglas the Grim, for example, has a rectangular plan (18.5×12 m) and battlements a sheer 21 m from the ground. Later, as plan forms developed (see below), there was less dominance by a single, massive tower. Occasionally tower houses had fortified enclosures or 'barmkins' (known as 'bawns' in Ireland) for livestock, sometimes turreted, as at Borthwick (*c.* 1430; Lothian), or added for artillery defence, as at Threave (*c.* 1460), although these provided minimal protection. In the late 15th century and after, such enclosures were developed into large and often palatial courtyards, as at Crichton Castle, Lothian, Craigmiller, Edinburgh, and Castle Campbell, Dollar (Central).

Unlike the keep or donjon of the traditional castle, the tower house developed as a complete unit of accommodation, the plan of which was almost invariably determined by the hall on the first floor, supported by stone-vaulted cellars or kitchens below; dimensions were governed by the span of the stone vaults (which also reduced the risk of fire). The entrance was typically designed as a single, narrow opening at ground level, usually guarded by a yett—an interleaved iron gate of such strength that it was later banned—and commanded by a machicolated turret or projection four or five storeys above. This entrance led either to the cellars or kitchens, or to a narrow and easily defended staircase. The great hall above was usually a huge chamber, sometimes with screens, and well lit with large windows; later examples had fine plasterwork decoration. On the second floor were the principal retiring chambers, and on the third floor the guard-house, with access to wall-walk and turrets. Within the wall thickness were staircases, garderobes, chapels, solars, treasuries, minor chambers and, occasionally, guard-rooms.

Variations on the basic square or rectangular plan of Scottish tower houses began with a wing containing the staircase, later developed to provide rooms above, thus forming an L-shaped plan. Not infrequently, the principal public stair rose only up to the principal floor or *piano nobile*, the private stair to the rooms above being corbelled out in the re-entrant.

In the 16th century the vertical plan of the tower house was exchanged for a horizontal one, closely resembling French châteaux, although within the architectural language already formed. The rooms were arranged in apartments in degrees of privacy, from the most public to the most private. A subsidiary tower was usually added to the *corps de logis* on the angle diagonally opposite to the staircase: it almost invariably contains the principal bedrooms stacked above each other and served by their own private staircase. Where existing tower houses were extended vertically—Amisfield (1600; Dumfries & Galloway), Niddry (West Lothian) or Preston (East Lothian)—the additions were clearly identifiable by the regularity of the windows, the use of well-cut ashlar, and the flamboyance of the superstructure. The Renaissance period thus transformed the plan, converting the dominance of the main tower with its defensive features into a mock-military country house, whose gunloops, battlements, towers and superstructures were purely decorative. The principal rooms on the *piano nobile* became grander with, at first, painted plaster walls and vivid tempera painted ceilings, with a vigorous use of Renaissance detail and mythology. In the early 17th century such decoration gave way to heavily modelled plasterwork. A group of tower houses in Grampian, attributed to the Conn family of masons, have anachronistic groin vaulting in their halls, best represented by Towie Barclay, Turriff (1587).

The change in lifestyle and flamboyance symbolized by the move from the tower house to the château was reflected in the disposition of the buildings. During the 16th and 17th centuries these buildings took the general form of a harled plinth (the harling could be tinted in any one of eight pigments imported from Europe) and a flamboyant superstructure, frequently in dressed stone. Roofscapes became wilder with corbelled and conically roofed turrets, balconies, caphouses, gargoyles, balustraded viewing platforms, crenellations, armorial panels and gilt finials. Viewing platforms were normally at the head of the staircase. The most outstanding, by far, were the two enormous structures erected by George Gordon, First Marquess of Huntly, from 1602, the House of Strathbogie (now the Palace of Huntly; Grampian) and Bog of Gight (Fochabers, Grampian). These astonishing irruptions into the sky, with their loggias and arcades, viewing galleries and platforms, gazebos, oriel and decorative dormer windows, conical, ogee and flat roofs, represent the finest flowering of Scottish Renaissance architecture, as an integral part of the developing European architecture. The finest surviving examples of this uniquely Scottish exuberance—Fyvie (Turriff, Grampian) and Craigievar (completed 1626; Alford, Grampian; see fig.) the most noteworthy of four tower houses in Grampian by the Bell family of masons, with Renaissance plasterwork decoration to the hall ceiling—seem pale by comparison. The European-inspired legacy of the Scottish Renaissance remained dominant in Scotland until the end of the 18th century (principal rooms still on the *piano nobile*, and a fondness for striking roofscapes and soaring chimneys). These then provided the direct inspiration for the SCOTTISH BARONIAL architecture of the second Scottish Revival in the mid-19th century; the direct inspiration for Charles

Tower house of Craigievar, Alford, Grampian, completed 1626

Rennie Mackintosh in the third Scottish Revival at the *fin-de-siècle*; and again for the fourth Scottish Revival and a search for Scottish Modernism during the 1930s.

See also CASTLE, §II, 1 and 3.

BIBLIOGRAPHY
D. MacGibbon and T. Ross: *The Castellated and Domestic Architecture of Scotland*, 5 vols (Edinburgh, 1887–92)
S. Cruden: *The Scottish Castle* (Edinburgh, 1963)
J. Dunbar: *The Historic Architecture of Scotland* (Edinburgh, 1966)
G. Stell: 'The Scottish Medieval Castle: Form, Function and Evolution', *Prospect*, xiv (1983)

CHARLES MCKEAN

Town, Harold (*b* Toronto, 13 July 1924; *d* Peterborough, Ont., 27 Dec 1990). Canadian painter, draughtsman and printmaker. He studied at the Ontario College of Art in Toronto from 1943 to 1945. He exhibited widely, holding over 100 one-man shows beginning in 1954. He was a founder-member in 1953 of PAINTERS ELEVEN and was responsible for coining the group's name and for writing the statements for its catalogues. His inventiveness, technical facility and independence of spirit were channelled into a prodigious output in drawing, printmaking, painting and collage. His work ranged from large-scale abstract paintings such as *Banners* (oil and lucite on canvas, 1.84×1.83 m, 1960; U. Regina, Mackenzie A.G.) to figure drawings of great sensitivity (e.g. *Oskar Kokoschka Draws Ezra Pound*, pencil, 1985; see 1986 exh. cat., p. 208), and from biting satirical works, such as his *Enigma* drawings (1964–72; see 1986 exh. cat., pp. 143–52), to eccentric assemblages of found materials, for example *The Weather Report (A Paean to Inaccuracy)* (mixed media collage on door, 1984–5; see 1986 exh. cat., p. 195).

Town worked principally in series, often developing variations on a chosen theme or technique over a number of years and in scores and even hundreds of individual works. Notable early series include *Single Autographic Prints*, a group of monotypes made in the 1950s, and paintings of the 1950s and 1960s, some in an Expressionist style, including the series *Tyranny of the Corner* (e.g. *Tyranny of the Corner: Judge Set*, 1962; Montreal, Mus. F.A.). These were followed in the early 1970s by the *Park* and *Snap* paintings and in the late 1970s and 1980s by three series of works on paper: *Toy Horses, The Famous* and the *Stages*. Town represented Canada at the Venice Biennale in 1956 and 1964; on the latter occasion two of his *Enigma* drawings were withdrawn on the orders of an Italian cardinal. He was one of the most controversial and impressive presences in Canadian art, matching his refusal of conformity with creative surprise and a peerless command of visual language.

WRITINGS
Silent Stars, Sound Stars, Film Stars (Toronto, 1971)
BIBLIOGRAPHY
R. Fulford: *Harold Town Drawings* (Toronto, 1969)
Harold Town: The First Exhibition of New Work (exh. cat., text D. P. Silcox; Oshawa, McLaughlin Gal., 1973)
Indications: Harold Town, 1944–75 (exh. cat., Windsor, Ont., A.G., 1975)
Town (exh. cat., text D. Burnett; Toronto, A.G. Ont., 1986) [retrospective, comprehensively documented]

For further bibliography *see* PAINTERS ELEVEN.

DAVID BURNETT

Town, Ithiel (*b* Thompson, CT, 3 Oct 1784; *d* New Haven, CT, 13 June 1844). American architect and writer. He was born in the years when architecture was just beginning to become a profession in America. His father, a gentleman farmer in north-east Connecticut, died in 1792. His mother soon remarried, and Town was sent to live with an uncle in Cambridge, MA. He later recalled being fascinated at the age of eight by the engraved diagrams in *The Young Man's Best Companion*. The passion for books never left him.

The nature of Town's schooling and training is not known. His biographer, Roger Hale Newton, suggested that he attended Asher Benjamin's architectural school in Boston between 1804 and 1810, but there is no proof that such a school ever existed. He was probably apprenticed as a housewright. In 1810 Town, Solomon Willard and several housewrights founded the Boston Architectural Library. By 1813 Town had moved to New Haven, CT, where he seems to have functioned as superintendent of Asher Benjamin's Center Church, a Federal-style interpretation of James Gibbs's St Martin's-in-the-Fields, London (1722–6). In 1814 Town designed and built the 'Gothick' Trinity Church on the New Haven green. Trinity is derived, like the nearby Center Church, from plates in James Gibbs's *A Book of Architecture* (London, 1728). Town's early romantic eclecticism seems to have been inspired by his enthusiasm for architectural books.

In 1816 Town became involved in bridge construction with Isaac Damon, the builder of Center Church. They created a wooden span over the Connecticut River at Springfield, MA; others followed at Northampton, MA, and at Fayetteville, NC. Based on these experiences Town patented in 1820 a new bridge truss, based on the lattice principle, that was both simpler and more efficient than its predecessors. The Town truss was employed for at

Ithiel Town: Indiana State Capitol, Indianapolis, 1831–5 (destr.); lithograph (New York, Metropolitan Museum of Art)

least 33 major bridges in eastern North America during Town's lifetime. The royalties from these works enabled Town to indulge increasingly his passion for collecting architectural books, prints and paintings. Town travelled to Europe with Samuel F. B. Morse and Nathaniel Jocelyn in 1829, and made a second journey in 1843; in each case he bought books and artefacts copiously. By the end of his life Town's collection is said to have included over 11,000 books, 20,000 to 25,000 separate engravings, 117 portfolios and 170 paintings. In 1834 William Dunlap described the library as 'magnificent and unrivalled by anything of the kind in America'.

Despite his precocious interest in the Gothic style at Trinity Church, New Haven, Town's work during the 1820s in New Haven, New York, and elsewhere remained resolutely in the Greek Revival manner, with details informed by the books of Stuart and Revett and their followers. Town's villas for Henry G. Bowers at Northampton, MA (1825–6), James Abram Hillhouse at New Haven (1828) and for himself at New Haven (1833–7) each have a two-storey central mass flanked by symmetrically placed one-storey wings, a configuration that can be traced to English Regency architecture, probably known to Town through the writings of James Elmes.

In 1825 Town established an additional office in New York which broadened his practice and enabled him to become involved in the city's flourishing artistic community. He was an original member of the New York Drawing Association and a member of the National Academy of Design. Between 1826 and 1829 he designed a variety of Greek Revival buildings including, most notably, the pseudo-peripteral Doric Connecticut State Capitol building in New Haven (1828), which stood between and slightly behind Center and Trinity churches. The demands of his growing practice may have led him to become

associated with Martin Thompson (1786–1877), a conservative architect, for several New York area commissions during this period.

Town's celebrated partnership with ALEXANDER JACKSON DAVIS, a highly accomplished draughtsman 19 years his junior, began in 1828 and lasted six years. Together, and with the occasional involvement of James Dakin and James Gallier sr, they created some of the finest Greek Revival buildings in America, including the Indiana State Capitol, Indianapolis (see fig.), the North Carolina State Capitol (1833–40), Raleigh, the New York Custom House (1833–42), the French Church du Saint Esprit (New York, 1831–4) and many distinguished town houses, villas and commercial buildings.

Ithiel Town's involvement with the Gothic Revival was limited but significant. With Robert Gilmore, a client who had visited and admired Sir Walter Scott's Abbotsford House in the Scottish Borders, Town planned Glen Ellen, Baltimore, America's first Gothic villa (1833–4); details were designed by Davis. Town, Davis and Dakin also designed the New York University building (1833–7) in the Gothic style.

The Town and Davis firm was dissolved in 1835, perhaps because Town was awarded a second bridge patent that year that would re-involve him in engineering projects, and perhaps because Davis was emerging as a major Gothic Revivalist while Town preferred to adhere to the Grecian mode. In 1835 Town began a fireproof Greek Revival house in New Haven featuring a vast second-storey space for his collection of books and art works. He moved there from New York in 1836 although the house was not complete.

Town's architectural output diminished after 1836, although he competed for the Illinois State Capitol commission with Davis in 1837 and they had an important coordinating role in the design of the Ohio State Capitol, Columbus (1839–61). A nationwide financial panic in 1837 interfered with some of Town's bridge construction projects. In 1842 he returned to New York and briefly resumed his partnership with Davis. In 1843 he travelled to England and France for the second time, but on his return he began selling his collections. He died the following year.

Ithiel Town's role in the development of architecture and the fine arts in America is underappreciated, and it is unfortunate that so few of his fine Greek Revival buildings have survived to bear witness to his taste and ability as an architect.

WRITINGS
Improvement in the Construction of Wood and Iron Bridges (New Haven, 1821)
The Outlines of a Plan for Establishing in New York an Academy and Institution of the Fine Arts (New York, 1835)
Important Notice to All Colleges, State and Other Public Libraries, Athenaeums & Other Institutions (New York, 1842)

BIBLIOGRAPHY
W. Dunlap: *History of the Rise and Progress of the Arts of Design in the United States*, 3 vols (New York, 1834/*R* 1965), iii, p. 77
L. H. Sigourney: 'The Library of Ithiel Town, esq.', *Ladies Companion*, x (1839), pp. 123–6
G. D. Seymour: 'Ithiel Town: Architect', *A. & Prog.*, iii (1911–12), pp. 714–16
——: *The Residence and Library of Ithiel Town* (1930)
H. W. Congdon: *The Covered Bridge: An Old American Landmark* (Middlebury, VT, 1941)
J. F. Kelly: 'A Forgotten Incident in the Life of Ithiel Town', *Old-Time New England*, xxxi (1941), pp. 62–9
R. H. Newton: *Town and Davis, Architects: Pioneers in American Revivalist Architecture* (New York, 1942)
T. Hamlin: *Greek Revival Architecture in America* (New York, 1944)
H. A. Brooks: 'The Home of Ithiel Town: Its Date of Construction and Original Appearance', *J. Soc. Archit. Historians*, xxiv (1954), pp. 27–8

C. Condit: *American Building Art: The Nineteenth Century* (New York, 1960), pp. 89–92
W. Pierson: *American Buildings and Their Architects: The Colonial and Neo-classical Styles* (New York, 1970)
H.-R. Hitchcock and W. Seale: *Temples of Democracy: The State Capitols of the USA* (New York, 1976)
W. Pierson: *American Buildings and Their Architects: Technology and the Picturesque: The Corporate and Early Gothic Styles* (New York, 1978)

JACK QUINAN

Towne, Francis (*b* ?Exeter, 1739–40; *d* Exeter, 7 July 1816). English painter. He began to paint in oils at the age of 14, probably at Shipley's Academy in the Strand, London, where he studied at the same time as Ozias Humphrey, Richard Cosway and William Pars. In the late 1750s he returned to Exeter and set up as a drawing-master. There, Towne taught wealthy amateurs, including the lawyer John Herman Merivale (1799–1844), as well as JOHN WHITE ABBOTT, who became an accomplished follower and collector of his works. From 1759 when he won a First Premium from the Society of Arts, Towne exhibited in London, though these were mostly oil pictures. In 1772 he joined the Society of Artists and the following year exhibited *Exeter from Exwick* (Exeter, Royal Albert Mem. Mus.) there. This picture is typical of his landscape oils, workmanlike and rather heavy, imitating Claude in its repoussoir of trees and glistening river winding towards a bright horizon.

By the 1770s Towne was firmly established in Exeter as a painter of landscapes and country houses and, according to Abbott, earning £500 a year from teaching. In 1777 he toured Wales with his patron, the lawyer James White (1744–1825), Abbott's uncle. The *Salmon Leap,*

Francis Towne: *Tivoli from below the Waterfalls*, pen and ink and watercolour, 254×394 mm, 1781 (London, British Museum)

from Pont Aberglaslyn (priv. col., see Bury, fig. vii), produced on this tour, typifies Towne's strength and idiosyncracies as a watercolourist: the initial pen-and-ink outlines were brushed with broad, economical washes of pale colour to suggest the sublimity of the rocky landscape, while tiny figures on the road indicated the vast scale of the ravine.

In autumn 1780 Towne travelled to Rome via Geneva. The clarity of his watercolour style was especially suited to depictions of Roman architecture, as in *SS Giovanni e Paolo, Rome* (London, BM), where he captures the play of bright Roman light over stone. He made many watercolours out of doors, carefully noting time and light conditions, and these became the basis for studio repetitions, for example the *Claudian Aqueduct, Rome* (1781; London, BM; replica, 1785; New Haven, CT, Yale Cent.) which is inscribed *From 10 till 12 o'clock*. His Roman watercolours include *Tivoli from below the Waterfalls* (see fig.); in some he abandoned pen outline and used deep greens, purples and blues, in emulation of the work of his sketching companion John 'Warwick' Smith. Before returning to England with Smith in 1781, Towne visited Thomas Jones in Naples in the spring; by September, when travelling through the Alps, he made several fine watercolours, including the *Source of the Arveiron* (priv. col., see Bury, fig. xl), in which jagged, tipping planes and broad, cool-toned washes convey the awesome nature of the scenery. Towne's response to Sublime landscape is also apparent in bold watercolours such as the *Vale of St John Looking towards Keswick* (Leeds, C.A.G.), the result of his tour of the Lake District with John Merivale and James White in 1786. His appreciation of nature on a more intimate scale can be seen in his studies of trees, delineating the intricacy of branches dappled in sunlight, as in the *Fir Tree* (priv. col., see Bury, fig. xxxviii).

Towne continued to paint in oil and between 1776 and 1803 was eight times an unsuccessful candidate for Associateship of the Royal Academy. He found it difficult to become well known in London and his patrons were largely Devonians, whom he charged 25 guineas for an oil picture and between 8 and 10 guineas for a watercolour. In 1805 he held a one-man exhibition at the Gallery in 20 Lower Brook St, Grosvenor Square, London, of over 190 watercolours painted out of doors in Italy, Switzerland, Wales and the Lake District. Two years later he moved to London, marrying Jeannette Hilligsberg, a dancer, but she died the following year. In 1809 he toured Devon and Cornwall; in 1813 he made a series of drawings of Oxford (Oxford, Ashmolean). A frugal man, Towne left nearly £3000 at his death and bequeathed three albums of his Italian watercolours to the British Museum, to be deposited with the Roman drawings of his friend William Pars. Towne created a powerful and idiosyncratic style but, as a Devon-based painter, he had little influence on the London artistic mainstream and was largely forgotten until rediscovered by A. P. Oppé in the 1930s. At that period his spare, geometric work was hailed as revolutionary for its time.

BIBLIOGRAPHY

W. Jones: *Francis Towne, Landscape Painter* (Exeter, 1890)
A. P. Oppé: 'Francis Towne, Landscape Painter', *Walpole Soc.*, viii (1919–20), pp. 95–126
Francis Towne (exh. cat., London, Burlington F.A. Club, 1929–30)
A. Bury: *Francis Towne: Lone Star of Water-colour Painting* (London, 1962)
M. Hardie: *The Eighteenth Century* (1966), i of *Watercolour Painting in Britain* (London, 1965–9)
English Landscape, 1630–1850 (exh. cat., ed. C. White; New Haven, CT, Yale Cent. Brit. A., 1971), pp. 29–30
Paintings and Drawings by Francis Towne and John White Abbott (exh. cat., Exeter, Royal Albert Mem. Mus. & A.G., 1971)
British Landscape Watercolours, 1600–1860 (exh. cat., ed. L. Stainton; London, BM, 1985), pp. 27–9

SUSAN MORRIS

Townesend. English family of masons. John Townesend I (1648–1728), a labourer's son, was apprenticed in 1664 to Bartholomew Peisley, a mason of St Giles's Parish, Oxford, and became a freeman of the city in 1674. By the 1690s he had emerged as the most important of several relatively minor Oxford masons. In 1691–4 at Pembroke College he built part of the front range and the classical gate-tower (gothicized in 1829–30), in 1692–5 at Queen's College the library, presumably to designs by Henry Aldrich, and in 1695 at Pembroke again the Master's Lodgings. In 1701–3 at Exeter College he made part of the front range and the classical gate-tower (gothicized in 1834), the design of which was probably shared with his oldest son William Townesend (*b* Oxford, 1676; *d* Oxford, 1739). In 1705–11 John I built the kitchen-yard of John Vanbrugh's Blenheim Palace and in 1707, at Queen's College again, the north range of the Back Quadrangle. John I followed traditional forms and used classical motifs naively. The Pembroke lodgings had six small gables, cross-windows and an off-centre, shell-headed doorway, while the Exeter tower, set in a battlemented Gothic range, had a balustrade above a curved pediment. William Townesend may have contributed the high rusticated base and paired Ionic pilasters, or Aldrich himself may have suggested these. Known as Old Pincher by his men, John Townesend I was elected to the City Council in 1700, retired from building in 1712 and was Mayor of Oxford in 1720/21. He is buried in St Giles's churchyard beneath an elaborate altar-tomb topped with a strange mitre-like device, no doubt of his own design.

John I took William as his own apprentice in 1693 but probably sent him on to Edward Strong (1652–1724) or some other great London mason. William Townesend emerged as a Baroque designer in 1701 when he made a drawing for the hall-screen at Corpus Christi College, Oxford. Trained also as a carver, he cut the bold pendants and was paid for making the fine double-domed vault under the tower at Exeter College, the design of which he must have been partly responsible for. When John I worked at Blenheim, William came to dominate the Oxford building boom of the early 18th century. He constructed the Peckwater Quadrangle at Christ Church in 1706–14 to Aldrich's advanced Ionic Palladian design. With Nicholas Hawksmoor and George Clarke he designed and built Queen's College (1710–35) and Worcester College (1720–46), both sober derivatives of Salomon de Brosse's Luxembourg Palace. He built, to Clarke's recension of Aldrich's version of Michelangelo's side wings of the Capitol, Rome, the library at Christ Church in 1717–39. For Hawksmoor and the University Press he built the fine Doric Clarendon Building in 1712–13 and also the highly original Gothick north quadrangle of All Souls

College in 1716–35. He built old-fashioned Gothic ranges in 1717–19 for University College and 1719–20 for Oriel College. In 1728 he gave Trinity College a range that showed the style of Vanbrugh on one side and that of Wren on the other. He loved to mass blocks and used rustication with solid dignity while delighting in experiment, as in his double-canted projection in the Botanic Garden greenhouses of 1727. Townesend's temple at Rousham, reduced from a design by William Kent, shows all his quirks.

John I's second son, John Townesend II (1678–1742), moved to London. He was joint contractor for the Lord Mayor's Mansion House, built to the design (1735) of George Dance (i), and for the Bank of England. John I's third son, George Townesend (1681–1719), built Vanbrugh's Kings Weston House in Bristol. William's son John Townesend III (1709–46) resurfaced and raised the early Tudor main front of Corpus Christi College, Oxford. A kinsman, John Townesend IV (*d* 1784), continued building in Oxford on a large scale, completing Queen's College, giving Convocation House a fine fan vault, Exeter College a graceful Ionic library and commemorating Lady Pomfret—donor of the Earl of Arundel's Classical statues—with a delightful Gothick plaque in St Mary's church.

BIBLIOGRAPHY

W. G. Hiscock: 'William Townesend, the Christ Church Master Mason', *A Christ Church Miscellany* (Oxford, 1946), pp. 38–62

DAVID STURDY

Town hall. Municipal building used for assemblies and to house the offices of local government. It is distinguished by its civic function, and this most frequently demands a degree of display to ensure that civic symbolism competes appropriately with examples of private, corporate or even royal patronage, and often with neighbouring or rival towns. Two common, although not universal, features of a town hall are the incorporation of a large hall and the occupation of a prominent site in, or near, the town centre. Town halls, almost by definition, provide a symbolic and ceremonial focus of local urban identity. As such they reflect not only the differing status of individual towns but also the radical changes over the centuries in urban organization and the varied patterns of municipal freedom in different countries.

1. Introduction. 2. Guildhalls and town halls, 12th–18th centuries. 3. Town halls in the 19th century. 4. Municipal building in the 20th century.

1. INTRODUCTION. Historically, the town hall has always been closely linked to the control of local administration; indeed the first building type recognizable as a town hall was the basilica, developed in the highly centralized Roman Empire, suggesting that some necessary tension between local and central government may underlie the expression of municipal pride in town halls. There is also a close connection with the judiciary deriving from the development of municipal freedoms and the growth of local self-government. The town hall has almost always been a place of assembly, and a large hall has been a feature of the building type since Roman times. In many town halls the assembly hall actually doubles as a courtroom and council-chamber. There has also been a long-standing connection with trade, and a market space was

often incorporated in or linked to the town hall. In the Islamic lands, the separate functions of the town hall were filled by the market (*see* MARKET, COVERED), the MOSQUE and the *dār al-imāra*, or governor's palace (*see* PALACE, § III).

Since the title of town hall, or its equivalent, has over the centuries been given to a wide variety of buildings, it is probably inadvisable to try to establish any narrow description of function beyond that of expressing civic pride. The changes or developments in function reflect the whole history of urbanization, and a long, wide-ranging history precedes the polite architecture of early modern town halls.

The earliest recognizable type of town hall, the Roman basilica, was linked to the function of the forum as a market place. The earliest extant town halls date from the 13th century, when the growth of trade led to increased power among merchants in Italy and the Low Countries. Although many of these buildings included a public open space, or market space, the principal apartment was a grand hall or council-chamber, often located on the first floor. Since the councillors were almost always, as in Florence, prominent members of the trade guilds, their town halls frequently resembled the guildhalls that were erected throughout Europe during the late Middle Ages. Indeed, they do not always surpass the guildhalls in grandeur; and in Britain some guildhalls were adapted to form town halls. Later, the title 'guildhall' was sometimes adopted for the principal civic building in a city, as in London or Bath.

Given the independence of many Italian city states, the cosmopolitan character of the trading towns of the Low Countries and the Baltic coast, and the way in which towns in Britain developed by means of individual charters, it is not surprising that the forms of town hall buildings varied greatly. Any attempt to define town halls by function has to take account of historical development, the varying status of different municipalities (and of the town councils within them) and the varied nature of the services offered by various forms of local government. Only the French mairie, which housed the administration of the commune and closely depended on central government, shows any regular pattern of form or function; but it is the hôtel de ville that is the true town hall in France, and such buildings do show more variety. Elsewhere, the functions of local parliament, court-house (often with prison attached), entertainment hall, market- and service centre all jostle for inclusion. At a later date many town halls included such features as an art gallery, museum, library and even a police or fire station.

Town halls, though not necessarily in the form of a single building, are specified in theoretical treatises from Francesco di Giorgio Martini's *Trattato di architettura, ingengeria ed arte militare* (*c.* 1480; Turin, Bib. Reale) to *Une cité industrielle* (1917) by Tony Garnier. They can be seen as monuments to urban self-consciousness, and are often exact indicators of commercial prosperity and the comparative strength of local self-government. The earliest examples adopted many of the features of the seigneurial buildings that they were replacing; and some 17th- and 18th-century town halls (sometimes incorporating mayoral living accommodation) deliberately aped palace architecture. Their symbolic function as the focus of urban life remained unchanged for centuries and was commonly expressed in the elaboration of a main façade and a tower. The enormous spread of present-day suburbia has, however, diminished the impact of these single buildings, and there has been a corresponding growth of civic centres and a multiplication of suburban centrepieces, usually now dominated by shopping malls.

Although there is a clear distinction of status between a town hall and a city hall, the functions of each may be almost identical in nature, if not in extent, and it seems sensible, therefore, to consider city halls as large town halls; but the upper limits of the class are more difficult to establish, and large town halls may be little different in grandeur from the executive buildings of national government. Thus the Doge's Palace (begun 1309) in Venice, although it functioned like a town hall, must be classed as a building of state government in view of the extent of the Republic's dominion by the 14th century. On the other hand, the Palazzo dei Trecento (1207–17) at Treviso, built before the city's capture by Venice, seems to belong among town halls; but where a city is the capital of an independent state, the distinction remains debatable. The growing power of a mercantile bourgeiosie and of local governments independent of feudal lords provides sufficient justification for categorizing government buildings of city states as town halls. Thus, the Bargello in Florence, as the seat of the Capitano del Popolo and later as the Palazzo del Podestà, would certainly rank as a town hall. The form of the building is closely related to that of the seigneurial town palace; but it is a form that appears in other Tuscan town halls of the period. The Palazzo Vecchio (begun 1299), a much grander edifice, could be seen either as a town hall or as a state capitol; but the 16th-century Palazzo degli Uffizi can be more easily excluded on the grounds that it housed the administration of a monarchic state rather than any form of local democracy (see FLORENCE, §IV, 8 and 10).

North of the Alps, the political position of free cities within the Holy Roman Empire allowed for more obvious forms of municipal building, which were related directly to the economic development of each town. Such cities as Nuremberg (see NUREMBERG, fig. 9) and Rothenburg ob der Tauber built fine town halls from the 13th century onwards. The main focus of these buildings was usually a grand council chamber, and although, like their Italian counterparts, they frequently had towers, these were more for ornament than defence. In England there was a much closer connection between early town halls and market buildings, which resulted in a type of building different from those on the Continent.

A further problem of definition lies in the specifically municipal roots of the town hall. Many 19th-century county halls in Britain show all the symbolic characteristics of a town hall, and they are definitely municipal structures, incorporating most of the functional elements of a town hall. The county hall often lacks only a great assembly hall and a market space; but neither of these is to be found in every town hall. In a less densely urban country than Britain, the distinction may be even more problematic, and there are obvious parallels at a symbolic level between town halls and the many fine state capitols in the USA (so many of which, in turn, bear a formal relationship to the Capitol in Washington, DC). These cannot, however, be properly classed as town halls, any more than can so highly symbolic a city centre as that at Chandigarh, India, planned by Le Corbusier from 1951.

In formal terms, town halls have sometimes, especially in 19th-century Britain, been judged secondary to the architecture of the aristocracy or central government. As a result only a minority of 19th-century British town halls were designed by architects of high standing. At other times, especially in the Low Countries in the 15th and 16th centuries, political and commercial status meant that town halls were often exemplars of the best and richest in contemporary architecture.

2. GUILDHALLS AND TOWN HALLS, 12TH–18TH CENTURIES. The development of the town hall as a recognizable building type is usually linked to the growth of trade and, especially in northern Europe, to the increasing power of the guilds. In Italy, by the end of the 12th century, quite substantial structures were being built (e.g. at Bergamo, before 1198); the Palazzo Broletto (1215; see fig. 1) at Como is one of the earliest dated buildings that is known to have functioned as a town hall. It is distinguished by an open arcade (for festival assemblies, proclamations and probably also for markets), a large upper hall and a tall bell-tower. The later Palazzo Communale (1280–82) at Piacenza, with an open arcade on the ground floor, a first-floor hall and battlemented attic, typifies the north Italian high medieval town hall. Civic buildings in Tuscany and Umbria, although sharing similar simple plans, retained more of the fortress-like elements of the palaces of the feudal lords, whose powers they were assuming. The oldest surviving example is the Palazzo dei Priori (begun 1208) in Volterra, which is marked out by its corner bell-tower and machicolated battlements. Similar forms occur in the Bargello (begun 1255) in Florence and even in the little Palazzo Communale (c. 1460) at Pienza, while the corner bell-tower is also part of the much larger Palazzo Pubblico (1298–1348) at Siena. By the end of the 13th century Italian town halls were often substantial structures, and the Siena building contained accommodation for the Podestà and the Council of the Nine as well as two great assembly halls and extensive warehouse space (see SIENA, §III, 3(i)).

Such buildings as the Palazzo Vecchio at Florence retain strong echoes of their fortress antecedents, but the provision of a central bell-tower added to the formality of that structure. Central towers were to become a common feature: the best-known example is the campanile (a replacement of 1578 by Martino Longhi I) of the Palazzo Senatorio in Rome. Yet the tower was never de rigueur. The original Palazzo dei Priori (1293–7) at Perugia had no tower and the Palazzo dei Consoli (1322–48) at Gubbio (see GUBBIO, §1) has only a small asymmetrical bell-turret. At Gubbio civic expression comprises the whole of the Piazza della Signoria, with the Palazzo dei Consoli, Palazzo Pretorio and a large part of the piazza itself all part of a single construction. This expression of civic pride in a whole piazza is the precursor of the 20th-century civic centre, but it reached its peak in the layout of the Piazza

1. Palazzo Broletto, Como, Italy, 1215

del Campidoglio in Rome, projected in 1450 and finally begun by Michelangelo in 1538. The designer, as well as the special position of Rome, both historically and politically, give this example a unique status; and while its classification as a town hall building may be questioned, it did house the local administration and Michelangelo's great staircase rising from the piazza is a feature to be found at many town halls in Italy, where much civic ceremonial took place out of doors, from the 14th century onwards. The staircase of the Palazzo dei Consoli at Gubbio is a particularly fine example. Such stairways, not always symmetrical, were a dynamic element in the composition and were often supplemented by raised platforms, balconies and even separate loggias, such as the Loggia dei Lanzi (1376–82) in Florence. These ensembles performed a vital function in the ceremonial and processional life of the townspeople.

Older town halls were continually adapted to meet developing needs. In the mid-15th century the Palazzo Vecchio in Florence (*see* FLORENCE, §IV, 8) had its courtyard renewed by Michelozzo di Bartolommeo, with gilded stucco columns that surpassed the splendour of many of the private palazzi. Later, in 1495, Cronaca constructed the vast Salone dei Cinquecento, which was designed to carry frescoes by Michelangelo and Leonardo da Vinci. Renaissance styles of architecture, which offered both grandeur and novelty, seemed to suit the increasingly palatial Italian town halls. Several new ones were built in the Veneto in the 15th and 16th centuries. The Loggia del Consiglio (1476–93) at Verona is a fine Early Renaissance

work, while Brescia has a magnificently ornamented Palazzo del Comune (1492–1508; completed 1574) that includes decorations by Jacopo Sansovino.

A considerable surge of town hall building in the Low Countries, the German principalities and central and eastern Europe followed the growth of trade and the advent of more settled conditions in the 14th and 15th centuries. They do not have strong regional characteristics; the German Rathaus, for instance, does not radically differ in form from its Flemish counterpart. There are differences, however, in the materials used, in the availability and sophistication of local craftsmen, and even greater variety of wealth. All this is reflected in display portals, oriel windows, gables and towers. The earliest examples retain much of the fortress character also evident south of the Alps, for instance the town hall of TORUŃ in Poland, which has a massive tower (1309–85) and solid brick walls with ribbed buttresses rising full to the eaves.

Longer periods of stability encouraged changes in the form of the town hall, away from relative severity towards a more florid display of municipal selfconsciousness. This is particularly evident in the Main Town Hall of Gdańsk (for illustration *see* GDAŃSK), which was begun in 1379 as a severe castellar block and given an exuberant spire in 1560. The growing status of the citizens is also reflected in the elaboration of the Council Chamber: the 14th-century town hall at Munich had an elaborate hall with a vaulted wooden ceiling; and that of Regensburg, begun in the 13th century, had a hall with an oriel window, the hall itself being decorated with frescoes by Melchior Boxberger in 1573.

In the Low Countries a number of early civic buildings had open arcades used for markets. The gradual abandonment of these and the elaboration of façades and halls seems to have occurred at the time when the civic leaders were becoming aware that they formed an urban aristocracy. The development over the course of the 14th century can be clearly seen by comparing the market and belfry (begun c. 1280) at Bruges, which may class as a town hall, with the town hall of 1377–1420 (see BRUGES, §IV, 1 and 2). At the beginning of the 14th century, however, the most striking municipal statements were still to be found in the buildings of individual guilds, such as the Lakenhalle (Cloth Hall; 1200–1304) at Ypres, which dwarfed the town hall built beside it from 1575 to 1621. Individual guildhalls and trade buildings continued the tradition of grandeur, as in the Lonja de la Seda (Silk Exchange; 1482) in Valencia; and the row of guild houses in the Grande Place in Brussels demonstrates their competitive display. The general growth in the centralized power of the municipalities, however, led to such splendid and rich structures as the town halls of Brussels (1401–55; see BRUSSELS, §V, 2) or Leuven (1439–69; rest. 1824–41; see fig. 2).

The town halls of the 15th century in the Low Countries have a strong claim to be regarded as the apogee of municipal building; and the tradition continued into the 16th century at Oudenaarde (1525) and elsewhere. In 15th-century France only a few comparable buildings were erected; but the 16th-century hôtels de ville show a delight in ornament similar to their counterparts in the Low Countries. They have, however, generally been considered less important in French architectural history owing to the great flowering of contemporary château architecture. The hôtel de ville (1502–10) at Compiègne is a fine example, with Franco-Flemish Flamboyant decoration and a central belfry. The Gothic tradition was continued in the next decade at Arras; but at Orléans, the former hôtel de ville (1503–13), since 1790 the Hôtel des Créneaux, provides a more sophisticated example: a new town hall built as a separate structure (the old belfry was retained to the rear) with Early Renaissance detail. The stylistic translation was complete by about 1525 when the little town hall of Beaugency, Loiret, was built with full Renaissance detailing and dormers in the manner of the earlier châteaux.

A number of town halls were also built in Germany, Switzerland and parts of eastern Europe in this period. Kraków had a Cloth Hall (1340–98; see KRAKÓW, fig. 2) with an impressive loggia, which was rendered even more striking by florid Renaissance additions of 1556–60 by Santi Gucci. The town hall (1592) of Konstanz has a particularly fine inner court, and those of Lübeck (for illustration see LÜBECK) and Münster have imposing towers. Wrocław has a town hall (for illustration see WROCŁAW) with a rich series of oriels and gables with Flamboyant decoration dating from the 13th to the 16th century. Even the small town of Stargard, near Szczecin, boasts a town hall of 1569, the modest façade of which is capped by a gable covered in rich blind tracery.

The chief characteristic of all the municipal buildings of this period was the use of carved stone or stucco for exterior display, and fine woodwork and occasionally mural painting inside. Classical motifs and the compositional forms of the Renaissance were easily absorbed into municipal display. The continuing or growing prosperity of many towns meant, however, that building was frequently in the form of an extension, often in a contrasting style. Ghent Stadhuis, begun 1482 (see GHENT, §III, 3), was given a Gothic façade in 1518–33 and a classical wing in 1595–1618. This continuity and the sense of history it imparted became increasingly important aspects of the symbolic function of these buildings, and the construction of entirely new buildings became increasingly rare. Andrea Palladio's encasing from 1549 of the mid-15th-century Palazzo della Ragione or basilica at Vicenza is an example of the process of expansion and recasting that resulted.

There were, however, a few outstanding examples of entirely new town halls in the 16th century, such as that built in Antwerp by Cornelis Floris in 1565 (see ANTWERP, §IV, 2). Probably the most important and grandiose town hall of its period, it occupies one whole side of the square, rising a full storey above the older houses around and dominating them in a way that is relatively rare among town halls. The rusticated arcade recalls the tradition of open market space; but above this are two prominent floors of large apartments that include the rich Salle de Mariage, an arcaded third floor and a roof with exaggerated eaves and tiered dormers. The principal accent is the three-bay centrepiece, with Renaissance detail, and statuary in niches.

In England the situation was rather different. In spite of the growth and independence of various boroughs, few

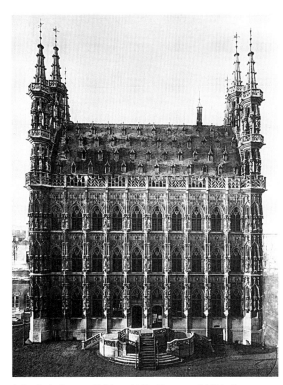

2. Stadhuis, Leuven, Belgium, 1439–69; restored 1824–41

towns had the resources to indulge in building on the Continental scale. Only London produced a building of any scale, the Guildhall, enlarged from 1411 (*see* LONDON, fig. 2), although elsewhere small guildhalls of some quality were built. That at Exeter (rebuilt 1468–70), with its elaborate arch-braced roof and a richly carved Renaissance façade added in 1592, is perhaps the best example.

During the 17th and 18th centuries town halls were built in many smaller towns in Britain that continued the tradition of an assembly hall above an open market arcade. In these buildings the need for a market space was paramount, as can be seen in the market halls of Ledbury (Hereford and Worcs; 1633) and Tetbury (Glos; 1655). Among more elaborate examples was Hereford Old Town Hall (early 17th century; destr. 19th century), in which municipal pride was clearly evident in such features as extravagant half-timbering. The town hall (1670s) of Abingdon, Oxon, built by Christopher Kempster (?1626–1715), perhaps with the assistance of Christopher Wren, was one of the first to introduce a more polite style, making full use of classical details, with composite pilasters rising through both storeys. Yet it, and others like it, simply continued the earlier type, which appeared until the mid-18th century. Meanwhile, an increasing number of court-houses were built, sometimes in conjunction with large halls, which restored the function of a public assembly hall as a dominant feature in English municipal building. Worcester Guildhall (1721–4) by Thomas White (*c.* 1674–1748) is an outstanding example, the carved trophies and stucco ornament on its façade revealing the growing desire for extravagant display. This tradition continued until the early 19th century, when assembly halls, markets and court-houses were often combined to form the centrepiece of a growing industrial town, such as at Mansfield, Notts (1835–6, by J. Nicholson and W. Nicholson (1872–1949)).

There was an equally vigorous flowering of civic architecture in the towns and burghs of Scotland, particularly in the Lowlands and the prosperous east coast. The Tolbooth (1706–8, by Alexander Stronach) at Tain, Ross and Cromarty, represents a determined traditionalism, while the Cromarty Court House (1782, by George Ross) is an elegant classical composition. Among leading architects, William Adam produced designs for Haddington Town House in 1742.

In general the emphasis in Britain was on providing accommodation for both townspeople and the neighbouring gentry—the latter increasingly seeing themselves as a local aristocracy with a corresponding desire for elegant spaces for social gatherings rather than business. The greater cities were able to afford town halls in a grand classical style that would have surpassed many of the smaller mansions of the aristocracy. That at Liverpool, built 1749–51 by John Wood I, had reception rooms and a ballroom added by James Wyatt in 1790, the later work soon ousting the exchange that had been part of the original structure.

Much town hall building on the Continent was still in the form of additions and extensions to older buildings: Haarlem Stadhuis (remodelled and extended in 1620) is a good example (*see* HAARLEM, fig. 1); but there was little development in the pre-industrial period as a whole. The introduction of a more ordered and splendid classicism in

3. Stadhuis (now the Royal Palace), Amsterdam, by Jacob van Campen, 1648–55

the 17th century was easily accommodated. Elias Holl I (*see* HOLL (i), (2)) built a town hall for Augsburg in 1615–20 with a handsome but undecorated Palladian exterior (*see* AUGSBURG, fig. 2); but it also had a sumptuous Golden Hall on the second floor, with Baroque decoration and painted ceilings that rivalled those in the Doge's Palace at Venice. In the 17th and 18th centuries some French mairies were built in the style of large, conventional town houses; but in comparison with the previous period there was little outstanding building.

There were very few examples of completely new structures. By far the grandest is the Stadhuis (1648–55; see fig. 3) in Amsterdam, by Jacob van Campen. It was conceived on an extravagant scale and in a fully developed classical style, with a basement and two orders of pilasters. The grandest interior space was the huge *Burgerzaal* or Council Chamber of the main floor, which effectively claimed palatial status for this citizens' assembly room. Indeed, the building was later converted into the royal palace without extensive reconstruction. This building was probably as close as municipal architecture ever came to the forms of architecture traditionally associated with aristocratic patronage.

3. TOWN HALLS IN THE 19TH CENTURY.

(i) *Britain.* Since Britain was the first fully industrialized nation, it is in British towns that one can most clearly see the next development in town hall architecture. There was a close link between the progress of industrialization and the resurgence of civic consciousness, backed by municipal wealth, which ushered in the second, and best documented, great phase of town hall building. The Municipal Reform Act (1835) created the possibility of building; and by the mid-1840s town halls formed a significant proportion of public building contracts. Styles and plans were more varied than before, reflecting the different services offered and the wide disparity of resources available.

The first town halls continued into the new era the traditional form of council chamber, often doubling as a magistrates court, an assembly hall and attached market, with one or two offices: a typical example is the original town hall (1846, by William Lambie Moffat (1808–82); now a community centre) in the new town of Middlesbrough, Cleveland. Many large towns were still run by the vestry meetings of the Anglican parishes (the Vestry Halls of London performed identical functions to town halls in the semi-independent boroughs of the capital until the municipal reorganizations of 1888 and the establishment of the London County Council). Some fine buildings gave prominence to a single function, such as a concert hall (e.g. Birmingham Town Hall, 1832, by J. A. Hansom (1803–82) and E. Welch (1806–68)) or law courts (e.g. St George's Hall, Liverpool, 1841, by HARVEY LONSDALE ELMES). Such structures were usually supplemented by later buildings that housed the municipal functions (in Birmingham the Council House, 1879, by Yeoville Thomason (1826–1901); in Liverpool the Municipal Buildings, 1861, by John Weightman (1801–72) and E. R. Robson).

The growth in size of British town halls corresponded to the gradual assimilation of the many independent regulatory bodies. By the 1870s municipal bureaucracy was extensive and complex and had to be housed in town halls, in which the office accommodation now equalled, or surpassed, in extent the ceremonial space, as in Manchester Town Hall (1868, by ALFRED WATERHOUSE; see fig. 4). Increasing bureaucracy led to the provision of

extensions and subsidiary office buildings: the design for Sheffield Town Hall (1890, by E. W. Mountford) was specifically commissioned with future extensions in mind, which were executed to Mountford's designs in 1911.

The increase in size in turn made demands on developing technology. The need for complex heating systems, for example, had a significant impact on the external form, as at Leeds Town Hall (1853–8) by Cuthbert Brodrick. A few unusual roof structures were developed; but the most far-reaching technical development was the adoption of fireproof construction, for which the system of concrete floors invented by Dennet and Ingle was the most popular. Their fireproof floor spanning 15 m for the second town hall (1882, by G. G. Hoskins) at Middlesbrough was particularly unusual. For the most part, however, British architects were slow to adopt new materials or techniques, possibly because it was easier to express ideas of civic stability in traditional materials. Stone, as an indicator of wealth, was the preferred facing, although some minor town halls of the mid-19th century, such as the vestry hall (1876) at Hampstead, London, by H. E. Kendall (1805–85) and Frederick Mew (d 1898), and the corn exchange and town hall (1853, by Bidlake and Lovatt) at Kidderminster, Hereford & Worcs, were built in coloured brick with stone or stucco facing.

Since a major function of town halls was to display civic pride, budgets could be stretched to pay for elaborate

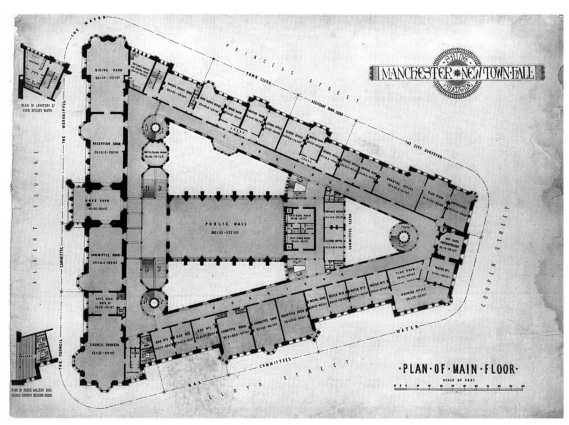

4. Manchester Town Hall, plan of first floor, competition drawing by Alfred Waterhouse, pen and black ink with coloured washes, 560×780 mm, 1868 (London, Royal Institute of British Architects)

ornament, both inside and out. There was usually at least one grand façade, and in most instances a tower, which could be justified as a support for the public clock. An element of rivalry between towns tended to foster variety in design, and architects drew freely on all available styles. Their choice was almost always conservative rather than experimental since the former was appropriate to the need to establish the traditions and history of municipal control. Classicism, most common in the early decades of the 19th century, remained popular for decades (e.g. Todmorden Town Hall, W. Yorks, 1870, by John Gibson (ii)). The style was valued for its palatial associations and for parallels with the world of commerce and banking. There were a few unscholarly Gothic structures (e.g. Wokingham, Berks, 1860, by Poulton & Woodman), which gave way relatively early to varieties of Renaissance-inspired designs (e.g. Tiverton Town Hall, Devon, 1862, by H. Lloyd). Following the rebuilding of the Houses of Parliament, however, there was a growing interest in Gothic, which was seen as a suitably national style; and as there was also a nostalgic link with the great medieval guildhalls, the town halls of the Low Countries were frequently cited as exemplars. Gothic could more easily accommodate the tall towers or spires to compete with the increasing scale of urban buildings. (Halifax Town Hall, W. Yorks, 1859–62, by Sir Charles Barry (see BARRY, (1)) and E. M. Barry, is a rare experiment with a classical spire.) It was also thought that Gothic styles allowed more flexible planning, which was ideal for the often cramped sites of city centres and the need to house rapidly growing bureaucracies. A form of Ruskinian Gothic introduced by E. W. GODWIN at Northampton (1861) and Congleton, Ches (1864), was widely copied, although it was soon succeeded by the Gothic of such practitioners as Waterhouse (Manchester, see MANCHESTER, fig. 1; Reading, Berks, 1877; and Hove, W. Sussex, 1880). In the latter part of the century Gothic gave way to eclectic Renaissance styles, of which Sheffield Town Hall is the best example. Finally, the Edwardian Baroque revival gave an imperial dimension to the town halls of what were increasingly large cities (e.g. Stockport Town Hall, Ches, 1903, by Alfred Brumwell Thomas). These grandiose constructions were occasionally enlivened by details influenced by the Arts and Crafts Movement, for instance at Deptford Town Hall, London (1902, by Lanchester, Stewart and Rickards), where the ironwork of its stair rail is particularly impressive. The internal stylistic traditions of the genre also became important: the design of Leeds Town Hall, for instance, was used as the basis for designs at Bolton, Lancs (1866, by William Hill (1827–89) and G. Woodhouse), Oldham, Lancs (1879, by E. Potts and Woodhouse), Portsmouth, Hants (1887, by Hill), and Morley, W. Yorks (1892, by Holtom and Fox).

The exteriors of many town halls provided rich opportunities for sculptural decoration. Among the leading sculptors were MATTHEW NOBLE (e.g. at Leeds) and Frederick William Pomeroy (e.g. at Sheffield), but commercial stone-carvers, such as Farmer and Brindley and Thomas Earp (1828–93), were also widely employed. Interior decoration could be equally lavish with stained glass, often by Heaton, Butler and Bayne, and painted decoration by such designers as J. D. Crace (1840–1916). Large-scale mural decoration, such as that by FORD MADOX BROWN at Manchester (1878–92), was, however, all too rare. A good deal of furniture and fittings (sometimes even including dinner services), expressly designed for the town hall by its architect, also survives from this period: Godwin's Gothic furniture for Northampton Town Hall is a fine example. The tradition of custom-built furniture continued into the 20th century, although all too often such fittings were later removed.

(ii) British empire. Town halls were built in major cities of the British colonies (later empire), particularly fine examples surviving in India. Early town halls were in the classicist styles favoured by the military engineers who designed them: Calcutta Town Hall (1811, by Col. John Garstin) is a Palladian building, while the town hall (built 1820–35 to designs by Col. Thomas Cowper (1781–1825)) of Bombay is raised on a podium with an octastyle Doric façade. Some later buildings responded to contemporary British fashions, the town hall (c. 1910) of Simla being in Arts and Crafts style, with bay windows and half-timbered gables. The New Municipal Buildings of Bombay, however, completed in 1893 by Frederick William Stevens, included 'Indo-Saracenic' details in its Gothic design. Elsewhere, as at Durban, South Africa (1904–10, by S. G. Hudson (1877–1928)), classicism was retained for municipal buildings; and Melbourne, Australia, produced a fine set of town halls in its separate townships, all of which were classical, perhaps partly in imitation of the parliament building. This suggests that an imperial rather than a municipal image was being projected. Outside the British empire, it is, of course, possible to trace other influences arising from colonialism, such as the Spanish influence in the town halls of Mexico and South America; but the classical language remained paramount as the expression of power.

(iii) Continental Europe. Town halls built in the 19th century in continental Europe can be seen as following in the wake of the British, although there were significant differences. In the German-speaking countries, in spite of the strong classical tradition established by Leo von Klenze and Karl Friedrich Schinkel for government buildings in Munich and Berlin respectively, the most striking municipal monuments were produced in the Gothic Revival style. The design of 1855 for Hamburg Rathaus by George Gilbert I Scott (ii) was not built; but there are equally significant built examples in Erfurt (1876, by Sommer) and Vienna (1872, by FRIEDRICH VON SCHMIDT), the latter distinguished by a grand mural cycle by HANS MAKART and others. In Italy municipal organization was not strong enough to result in new town hall building on any wide scale; and centralized government also inhibited municipal display in France. Nevertheless, a number of new hôtels de ville were built in the latter half of the century (e.g. that at Tours, 1897–1904, by VICTOR LALOUX). These buildings often had high-quality sculptural and painted decoration. The finest municipal creation was unquestionably the rebuilding in 1874 of the Paris hôtel de ville by THÉODORE BALLU and P.-J.-E. de Perthes (1833–98), which was completed by a notable series of murals by PIERRE PUVIS DE CHAVANNES (see FRANCE, fig. 40). There was also a distinguished group of mairies in the arrondissements of Paris, for example at Neuilly

5. Town Hall, Stockholm, by Ragnar Ostberg, 1893 and 1913–25

(built 1886, with sculptural decoration by Tony Noel (1845–1909) and Louis-Ernest Barrias; *see* BARRIAS, (2)). All these buildings adopted versions of the French Renaissance style that had first appeared at Orléans, and each is characterized by a rich skyline of decorative gables and dormers. Smaller town halls and mairies usually had only a single façade to street or square, although it was often richly decorated; but the importance of the Salle de Mariage and other reception rooms generally gave the opportunity for lavish interior decoration, although never on the scale of those in the capital.

In northern Europe, particularly Scandinavia, a further development took place with the self-conscious adoption of nationalistic motifs. Copenhagen Town Hall (1892, by MARTIN NYROP) was probably the first major building to show this trend; but it reached its peak in Stockholm Town Hall (1893 and 1913–25, by RAGNAR ÖSTBERG; see fig. 5), in which much use was made of decorative motifs from Scandinavian history. The short-lived and limited democracy in imperial Russia under the Duma is also linked to the building of a number of town halls, all in the mainstream nationalist style, pioneered by A. A. Semyonov at the Moscow State Historical Museum (1874–83). That at Vladimir (1907, anon.) is a fine and typical example. This nationalistic attitude was eagerly adopted by architects of a number of smaller town halls built in the 20th century.

4. MUNICIPAL BUILDING IN THE 20TH CENTURY. Following the creation in Britain of a county-based bureaucracy in 1888, county halls were built, aping the form and style of town halls, but omitting the assembly hall. Although effectively office blocks, they are often good examples of municipal building. The West Riding County

Hall (1894–8, by J. G. S. Gibson (1861–1951) and S. B. Russell (1864–1955)) at Wakefield, W. Yorks, was furnished and decorated throughout by the architects. In the early 20th century, County Hall (1908–22, by Ralph Knott (1878–1929)), London, was the grandest, a simplified Edwardian Baroque composition of Piranesian scale. The pyramidal project for Northampton County Hall (1973, by Jeremy and Fenella Dixon) is perhaps the most exciting later 20th-century example of this subgroup.

The huge growth in the size of cities in the 20th century and the expansion of local bureaucracies led to the emergence of the city hall as a distinct type. In the USA town halls had mostly developed from court-house buildings, 18th-century examples being invariably classical in style. Classicism remained popular, such examples as San Francisco City Hall (1871, by Thomas Fuller (1822–98) and Augustus Laver (1834–98); destr.) continuing the formal tradition of the state capitols, with a columnar frontispiece backed by a central dome. The increasing size of cities produced correspondingly large city halls, such as that of Chicago (1911, by HOLABIRD & ROCHE), which covered an entire city block, but still looked back to the 19th century, with a monumental Corinthian order on the exterior. The production of a skyscraper for New York City Hall (1907–16, by McKim, Meade & White), however, marked the future direction of the building type. It was probably inevitable that as American cities developed vertically their municipal structures would follow suit; yet the city councils seem to have been slower than the big corporations to use the skyscraper for display. Only after the Modern Movement had banished ornament were municipal skyscrapers—such as the Richard J. Daly Center (1965, by SKIDMORE, OWINGS & MERRILL) in Chicago— to be among the finer examples of that form.

From the early 20th century there was a parallel growth of civic centres, particularly in smaller towns. These are either collections of small buildings or linked complexes containing an assembly hall, offices, courts and service buildings. The function of display was still important, and, since the public clock retained its importance at least until World War II, clock-towers frequently formed the principal element of external display.

A considerable range of styles was still felt to be appropriate. In Japan, with the westernization policies of the Meiji government (1868–1912), local government offices had been built in an appropriate Western style. After 1912 town halls, as symbols of government power and civic pride, were built by leading architects and often represented the most prestigious style of the day. Until 1931 Japanese town halls were built in styles ranging from Beaux-Arts to Gothic Revival, but after that date until 1945, with a change in the status of municipal government under Imperial control, the law stipulated that government buildings must be constructed in Imperial Roof style (*teikan yōshiki*), a tiled and gabled design.

In the 1920s and 1930s in Europe, various forms of stripped classicism were widely popular and were adopted and repeated in Italy in the new towns of the Campagna. Britain has some more individualized interpretations, such as the town hall (1930, by Percy H. Thomas (*d* 1960)) of Swansea, W. Glam., or Southampton Civic Centre (1932, by E. Berry Webber). Under the influence of Stockholm

6. City Hall, Kurashiki, Japan, by Kenzō Tange, 1958

Town Hall, a number were built, particularly in Britain, in which classicism was tempered with Scandinavian elements: a good example is Norwich City Hall (1932, by C. H. James and Rowland Pierce). The adoption of the International style in Britain (as at Poplar, east London, 1938, by E. G. Culpin (1879–1947) & Sons) reflects a deliberate political decision. Elsewhere in Europe architects of the Modern Movement produced some fine buildings, for example the town hall (1931–4, by Tony Garnier and Jacques Debat-Ponson) of Boulogne-Billancourt. Yet modernism does not seem to have offered a sufficiently clear statement of tradition and stability, or a rich enough language of display, to satisfy the still largely conservative tastes of local authorities. Significantly, no town hall was selected for inclusion in *The International Style: Architecture since 1922*, published by Henry-Russell Hitchcock and Philip Johnson in 1932. There were, however, some outstanding town halls: Hilversum Stadhuis (1928) by W. M. DUDOK has long been recognized as a classic. There Dudok adopted the undecorated rectangular forms of modernism, but gave the building its particular quality with elegantly laid brick facing and the use of water and planting at the entrance. It also relies for emphasis on the traditional tall clock-tower. This Dutch version of Modernism had considerable influence on later municipal building, most notably Hornsey Town Hall (1933, by Reginald Uren), London. This version of the modernist approach to municipal architecture produced its next really significant statement in Finland, with the Säynätsalo Civic Centre built by ALVAR AALTO in 1952. Much use was made of brick, wood and copper, and civic and commercial buildings were grouped round courts on different levels, with the careful involvement of surrounding trees to produce a complete centrepiece on a very human scale. A similar approach was developed in the Hillingdon Civic Centre (1976, by Robert Matthew, Johnson-Marshall & partners), London, probably the first Postmodern town hall. A more unusual yet imaginative hold on local history was created in the town hall (1964) of

Bensberg, near Cologne, which Gottfried Böhm partially inserted into the medieval castle.

A few conscious attempts were made to introduce postwar Modernism to Britain (e.g. Harlow Town Hall, 1947, by Sir FREDERICK GIBBERD); but several buildings in continental Europe, such as Oslo City Hall (1930–55, by Arnstein Arneberg and MAGNUS POULSSON; see OSLO, fig. 1), make a much more dramatic impact. There too, partly through the involvement of national pride, the city hall was expressly designed to include large-scale mural and other decoration. Among the other large city halls built since World War II, those at Kurashiki, Japan (1958, by Kenzo Tange; see fig. 6), Toronto, Canada (1958, by VILJO REVELL and John B. Parkin Associates; *see* TORONTO, fig. 2), and Boston, MA (1962–8, by G. M. Kallmann (*b* 1915), N. M. McKinnell (*b* 1935) and E. F. Knowles (*b* 1929)), are among the best examples; yet with the possible exception of the Brutalist Kurashiki, none is really distinct from the great corporate buildings of the age. Indeed it may be argued that the size of modern conurbations makes individual expressions of community difficult within municipal bureaucratic structures. If so, one necessary characteristic of the town hall, the expression of a specifically local civic pride, has been lost. The true descendants of the medieval town hall may better be sought in the suburban civic centres and village halls that have become the province of community architecture. In the absence of strong local pride or local control of finance, however, such buildings have tended to lack the elements of display and ceremonial functions that are distinguishing features of the true town hall.

BIBLIOGRAPHY
R. Anderson: 'The Ancient Town Halls of Europe', *Builder*, lxxi (19 Dec 1896), pp. 517–19
R. Ostberg: *The Stockholm Town Hall* (Stockholm, 1929)
A. C. Cotton: *Town Halls* (London, 1936) [functional analysis of contemporary requirements in Britain]
W. Braunfels: *Mittelalterliche Stadtbaukunst in der Toskana* (Berlin, 1953, 3/1966)
N. Pevsner: *A History of Building Types* (London, 1976), pp. 27–62
C. Cunningham: *Victorian and Edwardian Town Halls* (London, 1981)

E. de Bievre: 'Violence and Virtue: History and Art in the City of Haarlem', *A. Hist.*, ii/3 (1988), pp. 303–34

R. Tittler: *Architecture and Power: The Town Hall and the English Urban Community, c. 1500–1640* (Oxford, 1991)

COLIN CUNNINGHAM

Townley, Charles (*b* Towneley Hall, near Burnley, Lancs, 1 Oct 1737; *d* London, 3 Jan 1805). English collector and antiquary. In the last three decades of the 18th century he formed the most important collection of Classical antiquities in England, representing an important link between the antiquarian milieux of London, Rome, Naples and Paris; with his friend RICHARD PAYNE KNIGHT he became an arbiter of taste on all matters concerning the art of Antiquity. He differed from most other English collectors of Antique marbles in that he devoted his life to learning and sought the company of experts. He supplemented his collection of Graeco-Roman marbles by significant collections of antique bronzes, coins, gems, pastes and drawings.

Townley inherited huge estates at an early age. His family was Roman Catholic and he was educated in France, at Douai and then in Paris (1753–6). Between 1757 and 1767 he lived the life of a country squire; in 1767–8 he made his first Italian tour. In Rome he began to collect, and developed a serious interest in the Antique, being introduced to Johann Joachim Winckelmann. He bought some pictures, but concentrated on Antique marble sculpture. He formed a special relationship with Thomas Jenkins, who for 30 years remained his principal dealer and adviser. The most important marble that Townley acquired at this time came from the Palazzo Barberini: it was *Astragalizontes*, the figure of a youth playing at knucklebones, which enjoyed a brief (and erroneous) celebrity as an original work by Polykleitos. Townley also bought from other dealers and sculptor-restorers, such as Giovanni Battista Piranesi and Pietro Pacilli (*b* 1716; *fl* 1757–69). He engaged the young architect Vincenzo Brenna as his draughtsman and assistant. He also visited Naples, and the excavations at Herculaneum and Pompeii, where he first made the acquaintance of Pierre-François Hugues, Baron d'Hancarville; with Brenna and the painter Pierre-Jacques Volaire he undertook an expedition to Paestum.

Townley made a second, extended visit to Italy in 1771–4, at which time his standing as a connoisseur and expert grew. As well as from Jenkins, he bought extensively from Gavin Hamilton (acquiring marbles from Hamilton's excavations at Hadrian's Villa, Genzano and later Ostia), from James Byres and from a host of minor dealers and sculptor-restorers; through Jenkins he developed a close relationship with the sculptor-restorer Carlo Albacini (*fl* 1780–1807). Townley spent much time in Naples; in 1773 he undertook a journey through Calabria with Sir William Young and the Scottish draughtsman John Brown (ii), and a journey through Sicily, where he greatly increased his collection of Greek coins. In 1774 he returned to London via Paris, where he swapped duplicates of Greek

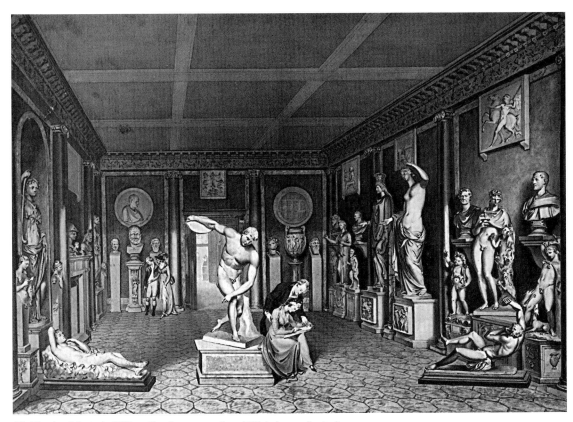

The Townley Collection by William Chambers, watercolour, 1794 (private collection)

coins with the Cabinet des Médailles; he was acquainted with Jean-Jacques Barthélemy and his nephew Barthélemy de Courçay. Townley made his third and final Italian tour in 1776–7, at which time he purchased the important *Venus* (London, BM), excavated by Gavin Hamilton at Ostia.

Townley's new house at 7 Park Street, Westminster (now 14 Queen Anne's Gate), designed for him by Samuel Wyatt, was completed in 1774. It did not have a sculpture gallery, Townley's collection being distributed throughout all the rooms; the largest and finest statues were in the dining room (recorded in a watercolour of 1794 by William Chambers, a minor draughtsman; see fig.). Johan Zoffany's famous conversation piece *Charles Townley's Library in Park Street* (Burnley, Towneley Hall A.G. & Mus.; for illustration *see* ZOFFANY, JOHAN) shows Townley, d'Hancarville, Charles Greville and Thomas Astle the palaeographer surrounded by the collection. Zoffany's arrangement was, however, ideal rather than actual: he painted all the famous sculptures into the room, regardless of their actual location, and the picture, begun in 1781, was repainted several times to include new acquisitions; the *Diskobolos* (purchased from Jenkins in 1792 for £400; see fig.) was added as late as 1798. Townley's house became a centre for artists and scholars, frequented, amongst others, by Joshua Reynolds, Joseph Banks, Richard Payne Knight, John Campbell, 1st Baron Cawdor and Richard Worsley. Zoffany, Joseph Nollekens, Nathaniel Marchant, Joseph Bonomi and Richard and Maria Cosway were all Townley's close friends. In the 1790s, following the French Revolution, learned emigré society began to gather at his house and in his later years he gave encouragement to young scholars and connoisseurs such as William Young Ottley and Samuel Rogers. Anyone who applied could visit the collection. From 1777 to 1785 d'Hancarville lived in London largely under Townley's protection. His learned, esoteric and sometimes fanciful *Recherches sur l'origine, l'esprit, et les progrès des arts de la Grèce* (London, 1785) was written with the support of Townley, who was influenced by d'Hancarville's theories on ancient systems of religion and mythology (including Indian and Egyptian), and in particular on their emphasis on generative symbolism, which they both believed to underlie much of the overtly sexual imagery of ancient art. Townley also shared Hancarville's views on the usefulness of gems and coins as evidence in tracing the history of ancient art.

In 1786 Townley was elected a member of both the Society of Dilettanti and the Society of Antiquaries. He played a leading role in the affairs of the Dilettanti, and in the 1790s, together with Payne Knight, he planned the publication of the Society's *Specimens of Antient Sculpture*. In 1791 he was elected a Fellow of the Royal Society and, more importantly, a Trustee of the British Museum, for which he worked assiduously. Thanks to Payne Knight's efforts, the Townley collection of marble sculptures was acquired by the British Museum for £20,000. In 1814 the British Museum acquired Townley's bronzes and gems from his heir's estate.

BIBLIOGRAPHY

J. Dallaway: 'Biographical Memoirs of the Late Charles Townley', *Gen. Chron. & Lit. Mag.*, v (1812), pp. 33–9, 281–9; privately printed as a pamphlet (London, 1814)

H. Ellis: *The Townley Gallery of Classic Sculpture in the British Museum*, 2 vols (London, 1846)

A. Michaelis: *Ancient Marbles in Great Britain* (Cambridge, 1882), pp. 97–9

M. Webster: 'Zoffany's Painting of Charles Towneley's Library in Park St Westminster', *Burl. Mag.*, cvi (1964), pp. 316–23

B. Cook: 'The Townley Marbles in Westminster and Bloomsbury', *BM Yb.* (1977), pp. 34–78

——: *The Townley Marbles* (London, 1985)

G. Vaughan: *The Collecting of Classical Antiquities in England in the 18th Century* (diss., Oxford, 1988)

GERARD VAUGHAN

Townley & Matheson. Canadian architectural partnership formed in Vancouver in 1919 by Fred Laughton Townley (*b* Winnipeg, 17 July 1887; *d* Vancouver, 15 Oct 1966) and Robert M(ichael) Matheson (*b* Prince Edward Island, 21 Feb 1887; *d* Vancouver, 30 June 1935). Both partners of this highly productive firm graduated from the University of Pennsylvania, Townley in 1910 and Matheson a year later. From 1911 Townley established a successful domestic practice at Vancouver, clothing commodious plans in a variety of styles, such as the Georgian Revival used at Deerholm (1913), Burnaby, British Columbia, and, with Matheson, the H. McLean house (1924), Vancouver, which combined Neo-classical and Arts and Crafts elements. Before Matheson's death, Townley also completed several blocks of flats, notably Tudor Manor (1927), Vancouver. Founder-members of the Architectural Institute of British Columbia (1914), the partners expanded into commercial and institutional design. Their Capitol Theatre (1921; destr. 1974), Vancouver, was in a simplified classical vein, while the Vancouver Stock Exchange (1928–9) echoed the then current quasi-functional Gothic of Raymond Hood.

Townley and Matheson became regional architects to the Imperial Oil Company and Famous Players Theatre group, while Townley completed a number of schools typified by the utilitarian Point Grey Junior High School (1928–9), Vancouver, in Gothic Revival style. In 1935 he designed the new City Hall. Built of reinforced concrete this remains a good example of the 'Stripped Classical' style, having a tight cross-axial plan, hierarchical cubic massing and severe geometrical articulation; the annexe was erected posthumously (1968–70). Townley later evolved a proto-modernist style, retaining residual classical features, represented by the Education Building (1940), Vancouver General Hospital (from 1942), including the Health Centre for Children (1944) and radial Centennial Pavilion (1956–8), and the City Gaol (1954). Elected a Fellow of the Royal Architectural Institute of Canada in 1952, Townley's obituaries (*Vancouver Sun* and *Province*, 17 Oct 1966) credited the firm with *c.* 1000 commissions.

BIBLIOGRAPHY

B. C. Palmer: 'Development of Domestic Architecture in British Columbia', *J. Royal Archit. Inst. Canada*, v/11 (1928), pp. 405–16

A. Gowans: *Building Canada* (Toronto, 1966), p. 205

H. Kalman: *Exploring Vancouver 2* (Vancouver, 1978), pp. 111, 137, 151, 156, 178–9

A. Rogatnick: 'Everything Was Up-to-date in the 1930s', *Vancouver: Art and Artists, 1931–1983* (Vancouver, 1983), pp. 42–8

S. Rossiter: 'Hall around Town', *Vancouver Mag.*, xviii (Jan 1986), pp. 77–8

R. WINDSOR LISCOMBE

Town planning. *See* URBAN PLANNING.

Townscape. Broadly speaking, any painting, print or drawing that contains a certain amount of information on the visual appearance of a town; more narrowly, a genre of painting that flourished in the Netherlands and Italy in the 17th and 18th centuries. For the broader context of this genre *see* TOPOGRAPHY, BIRD'S-EYE VIEW, ARCHITECTURAL PICTURES, LANDSCAPE PAINTING, VEDUTA, CAPRICCIO and URBAN LIFE.

1. Early examples, before *c.* 1650. 2. Development, *c.* 1650–*c.* 1750. 3. Decline, after *c.* 1750.

1. EARLY EXAMPLES, BEFORE *c.* 1650. Late medieval paintings from the southern Netherlands contain very detailed depictions of cities: towns seen from a distance, besides renderings of streets and squares in their centres. Among these are the view through the window in the right wing of the Mérode Altarpiece (1425, New York, Cloisters) and the city in the background of Jan van Eyck's *Virgin and Child with Chancellor Rolin* (*c.* 1430; Paris, Louvre). The evocation of everyday life in these works is so convincing that they have often been taken as a form of documentary realism, although hardly any verifiable topographical information can be obtained from them.

In the 16th century increased travel stimulated the publication of books and prints on lands and cities both near and far. Topography became the main component of print collections. Town silhouettes emerged as a standard type of print, typically in the work of Joris Hoefnagel, as did the bird's-eye view—half map and half aerial survey. There were also prints of individual buildings, which may be characterized as 'state portraits' of architectural monuments. In Netherlandish art factual documentation was long confined mainly to printmaking; the influence of topography on painting remained limited. Urban architecture was depicted in the backgrounds of many paintings but hardly ever became the main subject before *c.* 1650. The Italian townscape appears to have developed almost without contact with the Netherlands but nevertheless has many close parallels. Its antecedents are partly to be found in Venice, where northern artists depicted the colourful festivities on the canals and the lagoon.

2. DEVELOPMENT, *c.* 1650–*c.* 1750.

(i) The Netherlands. The genre of the townscape properly speaking emerged in the Natherlands in the third quarter of the 17th century, in the work of Jan van der Heyden and Gerrit Berckheyde (for illustration *see* BERCKHEYDE, (2)). Most commonly it depicts a public space within the city limits—a street, a square or canal, surrounded by trees and buildings. Occasionally 'portraits' of buildings occur. Another type of townscape, showing harbours and city gates where the city meets the outside world, tends to be more open in composition, incorporating landscape elements. Lastly there are views of a town taken from a certain distance: the *veduta*. Various elements contributed to this genre. Hoefnagel's town silhouettes probably inspired Esaias van de Velde's *Veere* (Berlin, Gemäldegal.)

and Vermeer's *View of Delft* (*c.* 1662; Amsterdam, Rijksmus.; *see* DELFT, fig. 2). Vermeer's *Street* (*c.* 1660; Amsterdam, Rijksmus.) and the related views of backyards and walled gardens in Delft by Pieter de Hooch did not on the other hand noticeably influence van der Heyden. Scenes in streets and markets occur among the repertory of genre painters such as Sybrand van Beest or Hendrick Sorgh and must have influenced the work of Gerrit Berckheyde and his brother Job Berckheyde; they also knew the work of Pieter van Laer and other Dutch Italianates very well. Turning town architecture from background to main subject was only a small step, especially since existing buildings had already been depicted by genre painters, as in Jan Steen's *Fish Market* (The Hague, Gemeentemus.). City gates and harbours were among the favourite subjects of topographical printmakers such as Reinier Nooms. Once these genre elements and landscape compositions were combined into a new specialism, a new vocabulary of themes, motifs and formulae was developed. This novel form, the last to emerge in Dutch painting, came into being as the Dutch predilection for hidden symbolism or 'mock realism' was diminishing. It had apparently become acceptable to make paintings without clear literary content or moral message. The townscape could simply be the image of a city dear to the heart of its owner.

Civic pride and local chauvinism must have been great stimuli for van der Heyden and his patrons; it may be indicative of their intentions that all signs of poverty, crime, noise, stench and other unpleasant phenomena are completely omitted. Cities are shown at their best, in good weather, with attention paid to historic and picturesque buildings, impressive new structures (mostly fantasized) and famous landmarks; at the same time the texture of the historically developed town holds divergent elements together. Van der Heyden masterfully gives the viewer the sense of entering an organic whole that could not possibly have been otherwise. This is done through creating spaces of a rather limited depth, opening out only towards the viewer (as in the *Drawbridge over a Canal in an Imaginary Town*, Amsterdam, Rijksmus.; see fig. 1), partly through choosing low viewpoints—some of his sketches must have been taken from a boat on the Amsterdam canals. The procedure involves so much manipulation of observed forms, however, that the results can hardly be called 'realistic', for all their meticulous rendering of details.

The topographical reliability of Gerrit Berckheyde seems somewhat greater. He suppressed details in his work, rather than over-elaborating them. Italianate sunlight brings out the main forms and overall lines, contours are straightened and simplified, and large buildings tend to be kept apart from each other. Monumentality rather than intimacy seems to have been Berckheyde's aim. Both he and van der Heyden did much work in north-west Germany; these works, tourist souvenirs after a fashion, often cram many 'sights' into one composition, along with people in quaint regional costume or monks in hoods and habits. Some compositions deserve to be called capriccios from their capricious mingling of fantasy with realistic elements, but there is no clear distinction between these and regular townscapes.

1. Townscape by Jan van der Heyden (with figures by Adriaen van de Velde): *Drawbridge over a Canal in an Imaginary Town*, oil on panel, 360×445 mm (Amsterdam, Rijksmuseum)

Van der Heyden lived well into the 18th century, the early decades of which were difficult for Dutch artists, so that many specialisms were discontinued. It was only around the mid-century that townscape painting began to revive. The works of Paulus La Fargue, Isaak Ouwater and others are among the most charming aspects of 18th-century Dutch art. For all of them van der Heyden, with his meticulous execution of detail, formed the chief model, rather than the forceful monumentality of the Berckheydes.

(ii) Italy. In 17th-century Rome, the Classical ruins, the pilgrimage churches and other points of attraction for an increasing crowd of travellers appear in miniatures by Johann Wilhelm Baur (for illustration *see* BAUR, JOHANN WILHELM) and carefully detailed drawings by Lieven Cruyl, both of whom were northerners. However, topographical prints formed the bulk of travelling collectors' souvenirs. The first painter to develop topography into a painterly specialism in Italian art was the Dutch-born Gaspar van Wittel. He arrived in Rome *c.* 1674, before he had begun his independent development as an artist and apparently without knowledge of van der Heyden's townscapes. His work evolved from that of the Dutch Italianates, whose paintings incorporate well-known Roman ruins and other sights in Rome and the Campagna. In van Wittel's work, as in theirs, the architecture is always embedded in the surrounding landscape, with its hills, streams and trees. The artist's viewpoint, therefore, was never very close to a building, and large complexes are shown in overall views (for illustration *see* WITTEL, GASPAR VAN). His works are mostly labelled *vedute*, and they should be considered as a mixture of landscape and urban architecture. Even his overview of the *Piazza Navona* (Rome, Gal. Colonna), taken from a third-floor window, seems to widen this already broad space. Van Wittel was a prolific draughtsman, and some of his sheets reveal the care with which he prepared the perspective construction of building groups. It is possible that he used a camera obscura in preparing his *vedute*. Some other Dutch landscape painters active in Rome also specialized in *vedute*, although van Wittel was the first and most influential. He was also the only one to work in tempera, which demonstrates the connection of his early work with that of Baur—a technical and commercial rather than a stylistic connection.

Giovanni Paolo Panini met van Wittel when he came to Rome as a young man. He soon became one of the most prominent painters of architecture in the city, but even his townscapes proper retain a strong element of genre in their staffage (*see* PANINI, GIOVANNI PAOLO, fig. 2). The difference between Rome, spread out over its hills and still with large areas of unstructured open space, and Venice, crowded on its islands, may partly explain why the *veduta* flourished in Rome and the townscape in Venice. The first Italian specialist to paint townscapes that place the viewer in a public space surrounding him completely was Luca Carlevaris (for illustration *see* CARLEVARIS, LUCA). The best and largest part of his oeuvre is his topographical prints, showing the sights of Venice, and a thorough knowledge of the rules of architecture and of perspective provided this moderately gifted artist with a solid base for his work. The rendering of buildings with the help of mathematical perspective became one of the main concerns of all Italian townscape painters, most of whom were trained as painters of stage sets or in the workshops of *quadraturisti*. Carlevaris is of importance for making the step from printed to painted topography and even more so for being the teacher of Canaletto.

Canaletto extended the limited repertory of his predecessors into a broad range of views in which not only the great festivals but also the major monuments of Venice are recorded (e.g. *Entrance to the Grand Canal, Venice*, 1730; Windsor Castle, Berks, Royal Col.; see fig. 2; *see also* CANALETTO, figs 1, 2 and 3). His successful career depended almost completely on the admiration of foreign travellers, mostly British, for the picturesqueness of Venice. As with van der Heyden, the semblance of realism

and topographical reliability came from skilful manipulation. The painter made innumerable sketches on the spot, made use of a camera obscura and even seems to have painted oil sketches in the open air. His compositions, however, were carefully constructed in his studio, and often the traces of ruler and compass are recognizable. Perspectival effects were heightened, the scale of open spaces adapted to the demands of the composition and the relation between height and width in façades altered. Strong contrasts between light and shade enhance the theatrical effect of perspective constructions in Canaletto's early work; his later compositions tend to be more open, his light a softer and all-pervading sunshine. His characteristic staffage figures are small in scale but carefully executed and full of witty detail.

Canaletto's immense success with foreign collectors compelled him to leave part of his production to studio assistants, and he had a number of imitators, among whom was Michele Giovanni Marieschi (for illustration *see* MARIESCHI, MICHELE GIOVANNI). The career of Bernardo Bellotto, a nephew, pupil and assistant of Canaletto, mostly evolved outside Italy; the vogue for Venice and for the work of his uncle paved the way for him in Dresden, Vienna, Munich and Warsaw (*see* BELLOTTO, BERNARDO, figs 1 and 2). The commissions he executed for Frederick-Augustus II, Elector of Saxony (*reg* 1733–63), translate the intimate urban poetry of Canaletto into the grandeur and monumentality suitable for a central European court.

It was only after Canaletto's death that the townscape became Francesco Guardi's main field of activity (*see* GUARDI, FRANCESCO, figs 1 and 2). Both artists treated the same themes in their views of Venice, but their styles were widely different. Guardi was not greatly concerned

2. Townscape by Canaletto: *Entrance to the Grand Canal, Venice*, oil on canvas, 1.34×1.70 m, 1730 (Windsor Castle, Berks, Royal Collection)

with perspective, nor with the recording of architectural detail; his works conjure up a dreamlike vision of a city that existed more in the imagination of its visitors than in reality. His staffage figures are suggested by specks of colour, which seem to have no contour. Surfaces of water and stone walls seem to be there only to reflect the soft sunlight in Venice's moist atmosphere. Buildings, sky and water are unified by a very free, almost calligraphic handling of the brush.

3. DECLINE, AFTER *c.* 1750. The hierarchy of subjects that had developed in classicizing art theory placed the townscape on a very low level, if it was willing to acknowledge its existence at all; for example, it was only late in his life that Canaletto was admitted to the Accademia in Venice. Such considerations did not affect Canaletto's foreign patrons, nor had they influenced Berckheyde, van der Heyden and their buyers. Not long after Canaletto's death, the Accademia realized the necessity of distinguishing between his oeuvre and the works of his imitators. Not much later the emergence of Romanticism upset all academic rules, obliterating not only the hierarchy of subjects but also the distinction between the traditional specialized genres. Townscape was practised in the 19th century, but it became one of the subjects in which artists expressed their nostalgia. Many took the past as their inspiration, preferring the 17th-century Dutch example to that of the 18th-century Venetian townscape specialists. With the advent of the railway, an innocuous form of nostalgia for historic beauty became a standard ingredient of mass tourism. In the later 19th century topography again became a safe source of income for printmakers and painters, most of whom produced rather traditional work. The combined effects of photography and of stylistic changes in avant-garde painting brought a slow and painless end to the development of townscape painting as a genre.

BIBLIOGRAPHY

R. Fritz: *Das Stadt- und Strassenbild in der holländischen Malerei des 17. Jahrhunderts* (n.p., n.d.)

The Dutch Cityscape in the 17th Century and its Sources (exh. cat. by B. Bakker and others, Amsterdam, Hist. Mus.; Toronto, A.G. Ontario; 1977); review by L. de Vries in *Simiolus*, ix (1977), pp. 187–9

L. de Vries: *Jan van der Heyden* (Amsterdam, 1984)

C. de Seta, M. Ferretti and A. Tenenti: *Imago urbis* (Milan, 1986)

C. Lawrence: *Gerrit Berckheyde (1638–98): Haarlem Cityscape Painter* (Doornspijk, 1991)

LYCKLE DE VRIES

Townsend. American family of cabinetmakers. This talented Quaker family, at least 15 of whom worked as cabinetmakers in Newport, RI, left a rich legacy of some of the most extraordinary furniture produced in America during the 18th century. Although they did not invent the block and shell form, in their hands it reached its highest level of development.

Job Townsend (1699–1765) and his brother Christopher Townsend (1701–73) were both prominent cabinetmakers in Newport. In 1736 JOHN GODDARD became Job's apprentice. Goddard married Job's daughter, Hannah Townsend, in 1745, opened his own shop and, together with John Townsend, became one of the leading cabinetmakers of the famous Newport school.

John Townsend (1732–1809) was born in Newport and, after serving an apprenticeship with his father Christopher, opened his own shop at the age of 21. By the 1760s he was prospering and owned major tracts of land in the city. The best of more than 30 labelled John Townsend pieces (e.g. long-case clock, h. 2.53m, 1789; New York, Met.) were executed in rich, highly figured, Santo Domingo mahogany. His cousin Edmund Townsend (1736–1811) also opened his own shop after an apprenticeship with his father, Job Townsend. Job died before the Revolution, but both John and Edmund suffered during the British occupation of Newport between 1776 and 1779. Despite his Loyalist sympathies John was even taken prisoner for a short while in 1777. They reopened their shops by 1781, turning out furniture in the traditional Chippendale style and, by the 1790s, in the Federal style as well.

The fame of the Townsend family rests on their carved block-front and shell furniture, including chests, kneehole desks, slant-front desks, clockcases and high chests-of-drawers. Their customers included many distinguished citizens of Newport, including Aaron Lopez (1731–82), William Channing (1780–1842) and Governor Joseph Wanton (1705–80).

BIBLIOGRAPHY

W. Garrett: 'The Goddard and Townsend Joiners of Newport', *Antiques*, cxxi (1982), pp. 1153–5

M. Heckscher: 'John Townsend's Block and Shell Furniture', *Antiques*, cxxi (1982), pp. 1144–52

OSCAR P. FITZGERALD

Townsend, Charles Harrison (*b* Birkenhead, 13 May 1851; *d* Northwood, Middx, 26 Dec 1928). English architect and designer. He was educated at Birkenhead School and articled to the Liverpool architect Walter Scott (?1811–75) in 1870. He moved to London with his family in 1880 and was associated with William Eden Nesfield. By 1883 he was working for Thomas Lewis Banks (*c.* 1842–1920) with whom he entered partnership in 1884. He was practising on his own account in 1888 and in that year he was elected a Fellow of the RIBA and a member of the Art Workers' Guild: he maintained ties with both throughout his career. He arranged Guild trips to northern Europe and northern Italy, gathering information on mosaics on which he lectured and wrote extensively.

Townsend expressed his attitude to design in two articles: 'The Value of Precedent' and '"Originality" in Architectural Design'. He stated in the first 'Better too much precedent, that is—Copyism, than too little, that is—Ignorance', but the second paper launched a diatribe against the copyism characteristic of Victorian architecture. Both papers supported historical study, but the second recommended it as an aid rather than a copybook. Townsend himself used precedents in Romanesque and contemporary American architecture, sharing the latter interest with his brother Horace, a journalist who had visited H. H. Richardson in New York and had written on his work. Townsend recognized these precedents but developed his own compositional formula for the public façades of the Bishopsgate Institute, London (1891–4), and the Whitechapel Gallery, London (1896–1901), disposing a single round arch between flanking turrets and using relief decoration and a careful selection of material and colour to heighten the effects. The asymmetrical placement of the arch and the plain surfaces of the Whitechapel façade lent greater power to the composition. The suburban site of the Horniman Museum, Forest Hill, London (1901–12), presented a different problem, and he used a single tower, asymmetrically placed, to anchor both the elevation and the plan. The difficulties of all three sites were solved by economical plans, attentive to functional necessities and the requirements for lighting exhibition spaces. The Bishopsgate and Whitechapel buildings both provided cultural services for the poor in London's East End.

Townsend intended mosaic panels to be incorporated into the Whitechapel and Horniman façades, but only the design by Robert Anning Bell for the latter was carried out. The mosaics indicate Townsend's devotion to the Arts and Crafts ideals of craftsmanship and the unity of architecture with the decorative arts. Townsend himself practised craft metalwork. He went further in his collaborative efforts than many contemporary architects, as illustrated at St Martin's Church, Wonersh, Surrey (1892–7), which incorporated frescoes by Anna Lea Merritt, and at St Mary the Virgin, Great Warley, Essex (1904), where William Reynolds-Stephens was responsible for the decorative scheme in association with Townsend and artists such as Heywood Sumner.

A dominant motif at St Mary the Virgin, Bishopsgate and Whitechapel, was the tree of life. Townsend's use of natural forms and curved surfaces and his rejection of copyism has led historians to characterize his work as Art Nouveau, but he shared the Arts and Crafts distrust of style. To focus on these characteristics would discount his strongly held Arts and Crafts beliefs about site, climate, materials and function, which were evident in his modest residential designs even where Art Nouveau was not. He summed up his design approach in an article on his project for Cliff Towers, Salcombe, Devon (1897; unbuilt), where he stated that the architect's work 'is interesting so far, and only so far, as it is the outcome of necessities moulded by invention'. Critics of his paper on '"Originality"', including Hermann Muthesius, G. F. Bodley and Leonard Stokes, recognized Townsend's individuality but defended precedent against the dangers of a 'free treatment' in less capable hands.

WRITINGS

'The Value of Precedent', *The Studio*, iv (1894), pp. 88–92
'"Cliff Towers": A House on the Devonshire Coast', *The Studio*, xiii (1898), pp. 239–46
'The Art of Pictorial Mosaic', *RIBA J.*, viii (1901), pp. 221–41
'"Originality" in Architectural Design', *The Builder*, lxxxii (1902), pp. 133–6

BIBLIOGRAPHY

H. Townsend: 'An Artistic Treatment of Cottages', *The Studio*, vi (1896), pp. 29–34
'"Originality" in Architectural Design', *Archit. Assoc. Notes*, xvii (1902), pp. 33–9 [disc.]
J. Malton: 'Art Nouveau in Essex', *The Anti-Rationalists*, ed. N. Pevsner and J. M. Richards (London, 1973), pp. 159–69
A. Service: 'Charles Harrison Townsend', *Edwardian Architecture and its Origins*, ed. A. Service (London, 1975), pp. 162–82

VALERIE MCLAUCHLAN

Toyen [Čermínová, Marie] (*b* Prague, 21 Sept 1902; *d* Paris, 9 Nov 1980). Bohemian painter, draughtsman and illustrator. She attended the School of Fine Arts in Prague (1919–20). In 1922 she met the painter Jindřich Štyrský with whom she collaborated until his death in 1942. In 1923 the couple joined the avant-garde Devětsil group in Prague. The group numbered artists, photographers, writers and architects among its members. During a three-year stay in Paris from 1925 to 1928 Toyen abandoned the Cubist syntax of her early work and began a series of impastoed semi-abstract paintings. *Fjord* (1928; Prague, N.G., Šternberk Pal.), along with other works of those years, attempted to realize visually the doctrines of poetic Artificialism in which impressions, feelings and images leave their imprint in abstract traces and vibrating colour sensations. Work of this type was given its label by Toyen and Štyrský to differentiate it from their earlier work and from other abstract forms of contemporary art. They exhibited their first Artificialist compositions in Paris at the Galerie de l'Art Contemporain in 1926.

After 1928 Toyen's work became more Surrealist. Her illustrations for a Czech translation of the Marquis de Sade's *Justine*, which appeared in Štyrský's *Edition 69* in 1932, signalled the beginning of an interest that she never lost in the erotic as a poetic principle and as the basis of a new language of psychological association. Paintings such as *The Abandoned Corset* (1937; Prague, N. G., Šternberk Pal.) combine eroded surfaces suggesting strange visions with images of latent eroticism. As a founder-member of the Czech Surrealist group she helped organize its first exhibition in 1935. During the German occupation her work was banned, and she went into hiding until 1945. In this period she produced several cycles of drawings. She published, among others, the series of 1939–40 for *Střelnice* ('The rifle-range'; Prague, 1946) with J. Heisler (poem) and K. Teige (text) and the series of 1944 for *Schovej se válko* ('Hide yourself war'; Prague, 1946; Paris, 1947) with J. Heisler (poem). Both were powerful indictments of war. Toyen settled in Paris in 1947 where she remained an active participant in post-war Surrealism. She continued to work in the same style, producing paintings, collages and drawings and illustrating books such as *Sur le champ* (Paris, 1967) by Annie Le Brun. For this she produced six collages and three drypoints.

BIBLIOGRAPHY

A. Breton, J. Heisler and B. Peret: *Toyen* (Paris, 1953)
R. Ivsic: *Toyen* (Paris, 1974)
Štyrský, Toyen, Heisler (exh. cat., ed. J. Claverie; Paris, Pompidou, 1982), pp. 32–71
W. Chadwick: *Women Artists and the Surrealist Movement* (London, 1985), pp. 111–17, 162–3, 233–4

WHITNEY CHADWICK

Toyoaki. *See* KITAGAWA UTAMARO.

Toyoharu. *See* UTAGAWA, (1).

Toyohiro. *See* UTAGAWA, (4).

Toyo Ito. *See* ITŌ, TOYŌ.

Toyok [Toyuq]. Site of Buddhist monasteries in a narrow river valley *c.* 20 km south-east of Khocho, in the Xinjiang Uygur Autonomous Region of China. At the northern end of the gorge Buddhist monasteries were made by excavating into the sides of the mountain. Almost nothing was found in the monastic site on the right river-bank, as it had been badly damaged by melted snow and ice from the mountains. The monastery on the left bank, consisting of free-standing buildings and cave temples, contained wall paintings, paintings on paper and fabric, wooden sculptures and clay objects. Like the majority of the cult objects, they showed Chinese influence (8th–10th century AD). The Indo-Iranian style (6th–7th century AD) is present in only a few examples. The silk paintings demonstrate great artistic skill and are usually of Buddhist themes, such as two female donors (Berlin, Mus. Ind. Kst, MIK III 6341). A carved wooden standing image (h. 380 mm) of the *bodhisattva* Avalokiteshvara with eleven heads was particularly skilfully executed; the head is crowned with nine small *bodhisattva* heads and a Buddha head (Berlin, Mus. Ind. Kst, MIK III 7204; see Yaldiz, pl. 104). The piece is totally in keeping with the style of sculpture of the Chinese Tang period (AD 618–907).

An Islamic shrine, the mosque of the Seven Sleepers (Arab. *aṣḥāb al-kahf*), probably dating from the 17th century, is built on one of the western hills (*see also* SHRINE, (i) §IV, 2).

BIBLIOGRAPHY

A. Grünwedel: *Bericht über archäologische Arbeiten in Idikutschari und Umgebung im Winter 1902–03* (Munich, 1906)
——: *Altbuddhistische Kultstätten in Chinesisch-Turkistan* (Berlin, 1912)
A. von Le Coq: *Chotscho* (Berlin, 1913/*R* Graz, 1979)
M. A. Stein: *Innermost Asia: Detailed Report of Explorations in Central Asia, Kan-su and Eastern Iran*, 4 vols (Oxford, 1928/*R* Delhi, 1980–83)
M. Yaldiz: *Archäologie und Kunstgeschichte Chinesisch-Zentralasiens (Xinjiang)* (1987), iii/2 of *Handbuch der Orientalistik*, ed. B. Spuler and others (Leiden, 1978–)

M. YALDIZ

Toyokuni I. *See* UTAGAWA, (2).

Toyokuni III. *See* UTAGAWA, (5).

Toyonobu. *See* ISHIKAWA TOYONOBU.

Tōyō Sesshū (*b* Bitchū [now Okayama Prefect.], 1420; *d* 1506). Japanese Zen monk and painter.

1. LIFE AND WORK. Sesshū began his religious training as an acolyte attending to the eminent Zen master Shunrin Shūtō (*d* 1463); he is known to have been in Kyoto by 1430. Records show him also to have been a disciple of the prominent monk Ryūko Shinkei (*fl c.* 1433–62) at the Zen temple Shōkokuji in Kyoto. Later in his career, Sesshū held the temple post of *shika* (official greeter of guests). He is considered one of the two most accomplished ink-painting (*suibokuga*) students of TENSHŌ SHŪBUN, the official painter to the shogunate at Shōkokuji. He later chose the characters of his *gō* (art name) Sesshū to refer to JOSETSU, Shūbun's teacher, and to Shūbun himself, in an effort to inscribe himself in this illustrious ink-painting lineage. After Shūbun's retirement or death in 1463, however, he was replaced by his other main disciple, OGURI SŌTAN. In 1465, Sesshū left Kyoto and established a painting studio in Suō (now Yamaguchi Prefect.) Scholars have attributed Sesshū's refusal of Shūbun's mantle and hasty departure to his anti-academic stance and his preference for an itinerant lifestyle. It is more likely that

he left Kyoto because of the growing political fragmentation preceding the Ōnin War (1467–77), which led to the razing of the city and to a dissemination of Kyoto's cosmopolitan culture, with the creation of 'little Kyotos', regional cultural centres supported by local lords (daimyo).

Sesshū established his studio, the Unkokuan, under the patronage of the Ōuchi family who were actively involved in trade with Ming-period (1368–1644) China. Having expressed an interest in painting China from first-hand experience and in studying Chinese painting at source, he was authorized to travel to the continent with his disciple Shūgetsu Tōkan (*c.* 1427–*c.* 1510) on an Ōuchi-sponsored vessel as part of a shogunal diplomatic mission. Upon his arrival in 1467, Sesshū became involved with a group of literati painters in Ningbo, from whom he is believed to have learnt the celebrated bird-and-flower painting tradition (*kachōga*). The ebullient work of the Ming-period painter LÜ JI is also often considered significant in the development of Sesshū's style.

After returning from China in 1469, Sesshū maintained the Unkokuan and by 1476 had established another studio called Tenkai Togarō in Bungo Province (now part of Ōita Prefect.). Until the end of his life, Sesshū travelled extensively throughout Japan, often making topographical sketches of famous sites (*meishōe*) such as the immense hanging scroll *Amanohashidate* (*c.* 1503; Kyoto, N. Mus.; see fig.). Sesshū spearheaded an immensely popular school of large-scale bird-and-flower screen painting (*byōbue*) in Japan, which appealed to daimyo patrons because of its references to China in subject and medium, its associations with Zen, its manifestations of power through the use of a large format, its potential for dramatic imagery and the fact that it was being actively collected by the shogunate. A pair of screens (Tokyo, Kosaka Col.; before 1483) reveals Sesshū's approach and his ultimate inclination towards monochrome landscape painting rather than the full decorative nature of polychrome bird-and-flower painting.

In his inscription on the hanging *shigajiku* ('poetry–painting scroll') *Haboku sansui* ('Splashed-ink landscape'; 1495; Tokyo, N. Mus.), one of his most celebrated works, Sesshū wrote directly about his experiences in China, claiming to have studied with the well-known Chinese academic painter LI ZAI and the unknown artist Zhang Yousheng, who may have been a member of the Ningbo artistic circle. Sesshū's four large-scale hanging scrolls of monumental landscapes in the four seasons (1467–9; Tokyo, N. Mus.; for *Winter, see* BRUSHLINE, fig. 2) were certainly influenced by Li Zai (whom Sesshū described as the most important master of the period) and by painters of the ZHE SCHOOL. In fact, scholars believe that these works were executed while Sesshū was still in China because they are signed 'Nihon Zenjin Tōyō' ('the Japanese Zen man Tōyō').

2. CONTEXT AND INFLUENCE. Sesshū's career marks an important stage in the development of Japanese ink painting (*see* JAPAN, §VI, 4(iii)). He is one of the first Japanese artists who is known as an individual through contemporary sources. Extant personal correspondence between Sesshū and his circle of acquaintances and inscriptions and the regular appearance of his signature

Tōyō Sesshū: *Amanohashidate* ('Scene at Ama no Hashidate'), hanging scroll, ink and light colour on paper, 894×1685 mm, *c.* 1503 (Kyoto, National Museum)

on his own works indicate a profound transformation of the artist's social position in Japan. In addition, Sesshū's ability to work in a variety of styles, choosing from an accomplished repertory according to the site or occasion of a painting, reflects the emergence of a new painting trend in the late 15th century. There was a gradual shift in emphasis from the use of brush methods associated with one artist or model to a less specific, reified conception of style. In this system, styles were divided into the calligraphy-derived categories of *shin* (regular script), *gyō* (semi-cursive), *sō* (cursive), depending on their degree of formality. Sesshū's attempts to master a multiplicity of painting techniques is displayed in his series of fan-shaped paintings in the styles of Chinese masters (1470s), including styles associated with LIANG KAI, MA YUAN, XIA GUI, LI TANG and YUJIAN, which he probably learnt from copying works in the shogunal collection while at Shōkokuji.

Despite the adherence to predefined stylistic categories, Sesshū's work is highly interpretative and offers his own personal artistic vision. Moreover, certain pictorial concerns are evident in all Sesshū's works, regardless of style. For example, he was consistently concerned with expressing the solidity of forms and clearly articulating the spatial relations between them. This was achieved through the observant volumetric description of forms and the dissipation of the misty atmosphere that characterized Shūbun's paintings. Sesshū employed sharp outlines and dark ink washes, techniques generally considered to be derived from the study of later academic artists such as the Yuan-period (1279–1368) painter Sun Junze (*fl* early 14th century). For dramatic effect, he also exploited sharp tonal contrast. Sesshū focused almost entirely on the foreground

elements, tending to monumentalize them, and displayed little concern for indicating recession into the distance or the background forms. The foreground thus often appears to deny the painting's borders, serving as a bridge to draw the viewer into the picture.

The two styles for which Sesshū is best known are the formal Ma–Xia academic mode (named after Ma Yuan and Xia Gui) and the looser, more atmospheric manner inspired by Yujian. The former is exemplified by the *Sansui chokan* ('Landscape handscroll'; 1485; Hōfu, Mōri Mus.), which employs a rich, vigorous combination of strongly outlined 'axe-cut' strokes (sharp jabs of the brush) and dark ink washes reminiscent of Li Zai and Zhe-school artists such as DAI JIN. The latter style is typified by the *Haboku sansui*, which was dedicated to his disciple Josui Sōen (*fl c.* 1489–1500) as a kind of certificate of approbation (*inkajō*) from Zen master to disciple. Sesshū's brush method is clearly indebted specifically to Yujian's *Shōshō hakkei* ('Eight views of the Xiao and Xiang rivers'), which was in the shogunal collection at the time (three scrolls extant: Tokyo, Idemitsu Mus. A.; Nagoya, Tokugawa A. Mus.; Katayamazu, Matsutarō Yata Col.), and more generally to the long-standing tradition of Yujian-style painting in Japan practised by painters of the Shūbun school. However, Sesshū used broad, square brushstrokes to suggest mass and solidity. His forms are abstracted but still readable and unblurred, and the ground plane is asserted through the use of bold horizontal strokes at the bottom of the picture (*see also* BUDDHISM, §III, 10).

Of Sesshū's many disciples and stylistic followers, the two whose style was closest to his were Shūgetsu and Shūtoku (*fl* 15th century). The latter eventually took over Sesshū's Suō studio. Josui Sōen, Tōetsu (*fl c.* 1474–1500) and Tōshun (*fl* first half of the 16th century) are also reputed to have studied with Sesshū. The eccentric ink painter SESSON SHŪKEI was not Sesshū's pupil but drew on his work. Already in the 16th century, a dispute arose between HASEGAWA TŌHAKU and UNKOKU TŌGAN over the legitimate succession to Sesshū; according to one source, the case was decided at law in favour of Tōgan. Tōgan's followers in the Unkoku school often made direct copies of Sesshū's paintings and frequently adapted his styles and subjects in other paintings. Another enduring claim to artistic descent from Sesshū came from the KANŌ SCHOOL, which continued his bird-and-flower painting techniques. Even in the late 19th century, when the incursion of Western-style painting (*Yōga*; *see* JAPAN, §VI, 5(iv)) threatened to supplant more traditional modes, the Kanō-school painters Kanō Hōgai and Hashimoto Gahō made reference to the legacy of Sesshū in their effort to create a new type of Japanese-style painting called *Nihonga* (*see* JAPAN, §VI, 5(iii)).

BIBLIOGRAPHY

I. Tanaka: *Shūbun kara Sesshū e*, Nihon no bijutsu [Arts of Japan], xii (Tokyo, 1969); Eng. trans. by B. Darling as *Japanese Ink Painting: Shubun to Sesshu* (1972), Heibonsha Surv. Jap. A., xii (New York and Tokyo, 1972–7)
T. Nakamura: *Sesshū*, Nihon bijutsu kaiga zenshū [Complete collection of Japanese painting], iv (Tokyo, 1976)
Y. Shimizu and C. Wheelwright, eds.: *Japanese Ink Paintings* (Princeton, 1976)
S. Shimada and I. Yoshitaka, eds.: *Zenrin gasan: chūsei suibokuga o yomu* [Inscriptions on Zen-sect paintings: reading medieval ink painting] (Tokyo, 1987)
R. Stanley-Baker: 'Marching in Time: Muromachi Ink Painting and the Zhe School', *Painters of the Great Ming: The Imperial Court and the Zhe School*, ed. R. Barnhart (Dallas, 1993), pp. 333–48

GENNIFER WEISENFELD

Toyota Hokkei [Iwakubo Kinemon; Kikō; Kyōsai] (*b* Edo [now Tokyo], 1780; *d* Edo, 1850). Japanese print-maker and book illustrator. He initially studied painting with Kanō Yōsen (1735–1808), the head of the Kobikichō branch of the KANŌ SCHOOL and *okaeshi* (official painter) to the Tokugawa shogunate. Together with Teisai Hokuba (1771–1844), Hokkei was one of KATSUSHIKA HOKUSAI's best students (*see* JAPAN, §IX, 3(iii)(d)). He made his artistic debut in *ukiyoe* ('pictures of the floating world') circles *c*. 1800, producing illustrations for *sharebon* (comic novels, usually licentious), *hanashibon* (story books) and *kyōkabon* (books of 'crazy verse'). His main period of activity, however, was in the 1820s and 30s. He continued to illustrate *kyōka* books, but his most outstanding works are *kyōka surimono* ('printed objects'; deluxe prints). His representative piece from this period is his illustrated edition of Rokujuen's [Ishikawa Masamochi] (1753–1830) *kokkeibon* (humorous tales of urban life), *Hokuri jūniji* ('The twelve hours of the northern village', a euphemism for the Yoshiwara pleasure quarter). Hokkei produced few *nishikie* ('brocade pictures'; polychrome prints) and his most celebrated work in that genre is *Shokoku meisho* ('Famous places of the provinces'), a series of 15 full-colour prints in the large vertical *tanzaku* (half-*ōban*; 380×170 mm) format, which was published in 1835–6, slightly after Hokusai's acclaimed landscape series, *Fugaku sanjū rokkei* ('The Thirty-six views of Mount Fuji'). Hokkei's own series, which illustrated a popular theme,

shows Hokusai's influence, but his style is characterized by an almost unobtrusive simplicity and lightness of tone that sets him apart from other *ukiyoe* artists.

BIBLIOGRAPHY

Genshoku ukiyoe daihyakkajiten [Encyclopedia of *ukiyoe*, illustrated], Genshoku ukiyoe daihyakka jiten iinkai, 11 vols (Tokyo, 1980–82)

MASATO NAITŌ

Toyotomi Hideyoshi (*b* ?1537; *d* Fushimi [now in Kyoto], 18 Sept 1598). Japanese military leader and patron. He helped to unify Japan, ending the turmoil of the last century of the Muromachi period (1333–1568). Hideyoshi sought to mythologize his obscure but plebeian origins; of the five family names he used, none was his own, and Toyotomi was the name of an 'aristocratic' house created at his behest by the imperial court in 1585. In the service of ODA NOBUNAGA, the prime mover of Japan's unification, Hideyoshi rose from a minor attendant to a general entrusted with the pursuit of major campaigns. When Nobunaga was murdered in 1582, Hideyoshi thrust himself forward as leader of the 'realm' established by Nobunaga in central Japan. In the next few years he consolidated and extended his primacy, and by 1591, as a result of his conquests and appropriations, all of traditional Japan was subjected to his regime, which laid down the foundations of Japan's early modern social order. To legitimize this regime, Hideyoshi resurrected patrician forms of government: in 1585, he had himself appointed *kanpaku* (imperial regent), and in 1587 he was additionally named Daijō Daijin (Grand Chancellor). In the same year he confiscated the settlement of Nagasaki and instituted the first ban on Catholicism in Japan. He made conscious efforts to dress his supreme authority with a veneer of culture and avidly pursued the aristocratic pastimes of the day, including *waka* (31-syllable classical) poetry, *nō* drama and the tea ceremony. He was also an enthusiastic art patron.

Hideyoshi is known for his ambitious building projects, most notably Osaka Castle, a grand citadel begun in 1583 and occupied by him the following year; the sumptuous Juraku no Tei (destr. 1595), built in Kyoto as the *kanpaku*'s official residence, to which he moved in 1587; and the palatial castle at Fushimi (destr. 1600), his main residence between 1594 and 1598. These projects were decorated in a monumental style by the leading painters of the day. For instance, Kanō Eitoku (*see* KANŌ, (5)) and his studio executed large-scale commissions at Osaka Castle and Juraku no Tei, and at residences built for members of the imperial family. None of these architectural monuments, and very few of their contents, survived for long after Hideyoshi's death. Osaka Castle, supposed to be impregnable, was stormed, reduced and destroyed in 1615 by the Tokugawa forces, whose regime succeeded his, and Hideyoshi's son and heir Hideyori (*b* 1593) died in the fire.

Several 16th- and 17th-century buildings in various locations in Japan are claimed to be associated with Hideyoshi, but only one or two attributions are plausible, for example the Kyakuden (Reception Hall) at the temple Saikyōji in Sakamoto, Shiga Prefecture. Two extant masterpieces of Japanese painting were unquestionably commissioned by Hideyoshi: *Maple Tree and Autumn Plants* and *Flowering Cherry Tree* (1592; gold and colours; Kyoto, Chishakuin) executed by HASEGAWA TŌHAKU and his atelier for Shōunji, Kyoto, a temple built by Hideyoshi in memory of his first-born son, Tsurumatsu (1589–1591). This patron's only lasting contribution to the arts of Japan had an ignoble source: some of the most famous types of Japanese ceramics, including ARITA ware and SATSUMA ware, originated among Korean artisans forcibly brought to Japan during Hideyoshi's bloody Korean campaigns (1592–8).

BIBLIOGRAPHY

G. Elison: 'Hideyoshi, the Bountiful Minister', *Warlords, Artists, and Commoners: Japan in the Sixteenth Century* (Honolulu, 1981), ed. G. Elison and B. L. Smith, pp. 223–44

J. W. Hall: 'Japan's Sixteenth-century Revolution', *Warlords, Artists, and Commoners: Japan in the Sixteenth Century*, ed. G. Elison and B. L. Smith (Honolulu, 1981), pp. 7–21

JURGIS ELISONAS

Toyotomi Kiminobu. *See* UKITA IKKEI.

Toys and games. Objects designed as playthings and intended to divert and amuse. Although there are examples of toys and games for both adults and children from early civilizations, it was not until industrialization that they became widely available. Early toys generally reflect the contemporary view of children as miniature adults; during the late 19th century and the early 20th the emergence of child psychology and the educational theories of Friedrich Froebel (1782–1852) and Maria Montessori (1870–1952) resulted in a range of toys and games designed specifically for the different physical and intellectual developmental stages of childhood. Also from the early 19th century new materials, new methods of construction and new technologies produced an enormous variety of play objects, ranging from simple traditional wooden toys to electronic games. Two major developments in the late 20th century were the American film and television industry's mass merchandising of toys and accessories based on successful films and programmes, and the growth of computer and electronic technology, which enabled Japanese manufacturers in particular to produce a range of sophisticated electronic games that appealed equally to adults and children.

See also AUTOMATA.

I. Toys. II. Dolls. III. Doll's houses, miniature rooms and shops and doll's furniture. IV. Games and puzzles.

I. Toys.

1. Ivory, wood, glass and clay. 2. Metal. 3. Paper, composition and plastic.

1. IVORY, WOOD, GLASS AND CLAY. The earliest toys were carved of ivory, bone or wood or modelled in clay. While some are quite crude, others reflect a highly developed artistic sensibility. An extraordinary mechanical toy in the form of a running dog carved from ivory dates to Egypt's 18th Dynasty (*c.* 1550–*c.* 1307 BC: New York, Met.; see fig. 1) and compares favourably to larger sculptures from the same period. Smaller-scale carved ivory animal-form game counters (polar bear, walrus and seal) were produced by Alaskan Inuit craftsmen of the Okvik period *c.* 500–100 BC. Surviving examples of stone and glass toys are a carved limestone porcupine and lion (both *c.* 1100 BC; Paris, Louvre) from Susa (now Shùsh, Iran) and the mosaic marbles found in 4th-century AD Roman ruins and tombs. Clay whistles, miniature items and wheeled animal toys have been found dating from the Late Classic period (*c.* AD 600–*c.* 900) in Central and South America. Fewer carved wooden toys have survived; one example, however, is an Egyptian carved wooden toy tiger with a movable jaw (*c.* 1000 BC; London, BM). These examples represent but a tiny portion of the toys produced by early civilizations. Other evidence is provided by, for example, Greek vase paintings of a boy playing with a yo-yo and children playing with wooden handcarts (Attic vase, 400 BC, London, BM) and a piece of Song-period pottery (AD 960–1279; New York, Met.) decorated with a picture of a boy riding a wooden hobby-horse.

Archaeologists have found 9th-century wooden toys produced by the eastern Slavic tribes who lived on the Volkhov River, and there are surviving examples of 13th- and 14th-century clay toy figures (Strasbourg, Mus. Hist.). Further evidence of medieval toys is provided by margin decoration in such manuscripts as the *Roman d'Alexandre*, which shows boys playing with spinning tops, while a French Psalter of *c.* 1300 (Oxford, Bodleian Lib.) shows children playing with hobby-horses and what may be an

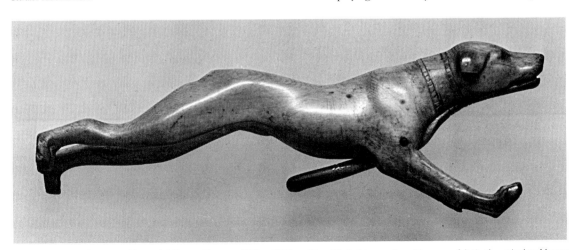

1. Mechanical toy dog, carved ivory, l. 180 mm, Egypt, *c.* 1550–*c.* 1307 BC (New York, Metropolitan Museum of Art); the articulated lower jaw is actuated by the rod

2. Stick and ball toy (bilboquet), carved ivory, France, late 18th century (New York, Cooper-Hewitt Museum)

early version of the stick and ball game that became so popular in France in the late 16th century. Pieter Bruegel the elder's painting of *Children's Games* (1560; Vienna, Ksthist. Mus.) shows children playing with a wide range of traditional carved wooden toys: tops, dolls, hobby-horses and a variety of ball games. In China small clay animal-form toys were produced (*see* CHINA, §XIV, 4). There are later surviving examples of such medieval games as bilboquet—a French stick and ball game (e.g. of late 18th century; New York, Cooper-Hewitt Mus.; see fig. 2)—and battledore and shuttlecock (e.g. painted and gilt-wood battledore, ?17th–18th century; Tokyo, N. Mus.), which was played in both Europe and East Asia.

By the early 1700s the tradition of carving and painting wooden playthings had begun to develop into a cottage industry. Wood-carvers in the Berchtesgaden and Sonneberg areas of what is now Germany began to assemble groups of small animal and human figures (late 18th-century examples; Sonneberg, Dt. Spielzeugmus.); first the traditional Christmas crèche (known as early as 1400) and later farm and village scenes and the ever-popular Noah's ark (e.g. German ark with animals, 1900–10; London, Bethnal Green Mus. Childhood). Jobbers and middlemen located in Nuremberg marketed the toys (often known as Nuremberg ware), and by the late 1800s craftsmen in other areas such as Bogorodskoye in Russia (19th-century examples; St Petersburg, Rus. Mus.) and Slovakia (19th-century examples; Prague, Hist. Mus.) were selling similar wares. Early examples, some 600–900 mm in height, are fine examples of folk sculpture. Later, these toys were semi mass-produced, with jigsaw cutting replacing carving and a decline in the quality of the painting. The next major technical advance took place in the USA where such manufacturers as the R. Bliss Manufacturing Co. (*c.* 1871–1914) of Pawtucket, RI, and McLoughlin Bros (*c.* 1855–1920) of New York applied lithographed paper to jigsaw cut wooden forms. The use of mechanical saws facilitated mass production, and the colourful lithographed decoration eliminated the need for hand-painting. Most American and European firms adopted the same system, and the lithographed paper decoration often faithfully mirrors such period vehicles as circus wagons, fire engines and omnibuses. In Britain such companies as

those established by Paul and Marjorie Abbatt in 1932, and later James Galt, continued and even renewed the tradition of using wood as a material for toymaking. Their sturdy wooden playthings, often in plain, unpainted wood, ranged from building blocks and hammer and peg sets to handcarts and tricycles. They were mass-produced but well-designed and built to last.

2. METAL.

(i) Tin. Cast silver and bronze figures of knights were made for children of the wealthy during the late Middle Ages. A later, documented example is the group of 300 silver foot soldiers that Marie de' Medici had made for the future Louis XIII. In the mid-18th century Andreas Hilpert, a Nuremberg tin manufacturer, began to produce modestly priced lead or small, flat tin soldiers as well as other figures and animals (examples of *c.* 1780; Munich,

3. 'Papal Guard' military miniatures, cast lead, hand-painted, h. 65–75 mm, manufactured by Britains Ltd, London, *c.* 1950–60 (New York, private collection)

Bayer. Nmus.). Other European makers entered the field, and military miniatures have become valuable collectors' items. The best examples are cast in exact detail and meticulously hand-painted (see fig. 3); particularly prized are those produced by William Britain's Ltd (est. 1893), London, which was the first firm to produce hollow-cast figures, the 19th-century French firms of Mignot (est. 1825) and Lucotte (c. 1795–1850) and the Spanish manufacturer Portolli (c. 1830–50). Most firms also turned out a variety of interesting civilian types, including complete circus trains, farm scenes with appropriate flora and fauna and numerous figures suitable for use with miniature railway equipment. Accurate detail and high-quality decoration characterize all these pieces.

(ii) Tin-plate. Tin-plate (thin sheets of iron coated with tin) proved an excellent and durable medium for toy production: the surface readily accepted decoration (first hand-painting and, by the 1870s, printed lithography), and its light weight facilitated the introduction of the clockwork motors that powered most mechanical toys from the 19th century. Mathias Hess, whose business was established at Nuremberg c. 1826, was the first manufacturer to produce such toys in great quantity. He was followed by a number of important German manufacturers, chief among whom were Bing and Märklin. Ignaz and Adolf Bing opened their shop in Nuremberg c. 1865, and production continued until 1932. Bing is probably best known for its wind-up (and later electric) trains introduced in 1882; the company also made spectacular cars (e.g. open car with driver and officer, c. 1900; Nuremberg, Ger. Nmus.) and buses as well as large tin-plate ships. Presence rather than historical accuracy was the goal, and the company's standard ship model reflected an almost worldwide trade, often being painted to represent naval or commercial vessels of many different nations. The firm of Märklin was established in Göppingen in 1859 and was still active in the late 20th century. Famous for its clockwork, steam and electric trains, Märklin specialized in detail. Trains, cars, battleships and even Zeppelins were carefully designed and decorated to resemble full-size models (see fig. 4).

Other well-known German firms that made sheet-tin toys are Georges Carette & Cie (c. 1886–1917) of Nuremberg, which was admired for its highly realistic touring cars, and E. P. Lehmann (est. c. 1881) of Brandenburg, which produced numerous small, inexpensive tin clockwork toys. Tiny tin 'penny toys', only a few centimetres long and designed to be sold for pennies, were produced by J. P. Meier (c. 1880–1910) of Nuremberg and other manufacturers.

The main competition for the German toymakers came initially from the USA, where as early as 1838 the firm of Francis, Field & Francis in Philadelphia was making tin pull toys, and in 1856 George W. Brown, who appropriately enough combined the talents of toy designer and clockmaker, began to produce mechanical toys in Forestville, CT. Other important early manufacturers included Althof Bergmann (est. 1856) of New York and E. R. Ives and Co. (1868–1929) of Bridgeport, CT. Althof Bergmann was one of the first American makers of tin-plate trains and produced a variety of clockwork playthings including ingenious hoop toys. Ives produced some of the first electric trains as well as numerous clockwork toys and competed successfully with the major European tin-toymakers. Louis Marx and Co. (1921–76) in New York was the first firm to capitalize on the popularity of film and comic-strip characters, producing lithographed tin toys featuring such popular American figures as Popeye, Dick Tracey and Li'l Abner.

4. Toy train, lithographed tin and sheet metal, manufactured by Gebrüder Märklin, Göppingen, Germany, c. 1912 (Rochester, NY, Strong Museum)

5. Mechanical toy robots, battery-operated, polychrome plastic and pot-metal, h. 90–205 mm, Japan, c. 1950–60 (New York, private collection)

In Britain Frank Hornby (d 1936), inventor in 1901 of the Meccano construction kit, which remained popular until the 1950s (examples in London, Bethnal Green Mus. Childhood, and Edinburgh, Mus. Childhood), introduced the Hornby tin-plate train in 1920 and the Hornby clockwork train c. 1925. The other major British manufacturer of tin-plate trains and train sets was Bassett-Lowke & Co. (est. 1899). After 1920 Japanese manufacturers began to produce cheaper versions of European toys; in particular demand are battery and clockwork robots and space toys from c. 1950 to 1960 (see fig. 5).

(iii) Cast-iron. Cast-iron toys were first produced in the late 19th century. Although European companies used cast-iron wheels for their tin-plate vehicles, complete cast-iron toys were made almost exclusively in the USA. The most important categories are banks and vehicles. There are two types of what are commonly referred to as 'penny-banks': still and mechanical. The former consists of cast animal and human figures such as lions, cats, pigs, sailors, Santa Claus figures and even a representation of Teddy Roosevelt, all of which have a coin slot and serve simply as depositories. Mechanical banks have moving parts and springs so that depositing a coin triggers a reaction. In the 'Dark Town Battery' the coin is flung past the flailing baseball bat of a perpetually hitless batter (see ,fig. 6). Among the rare European examples is a 'Golliwog' form from Britain. The best of these banks are a form of kinetic sculpture. The more prolific manufacturers in this field were J. & E. Stevens (c. 1843–1935), Cromwell, CT, the

Sheppard Hardware Co. (c. 1882–92), Buffalo, NY, and the A. C. Williams Co. (c. 1920–40), Ravenna, OH.

American manufacturers such as the Hubley Manufacturing Co. (c. 1894–1965), Lancaster, PA, and the Dent Hardware Co. (c. 1895–1940), Fullerton, PA, produced vast quantities of cast-iron vehicles: cars, trucks, buses, aeroplanes, ships and horse-drawn wagons. While the least expensive of these might be poorly cast and painted only a single colour, finer examples mimicked in great detail contemporary American and sometimes European transportation. Among the more interesting survivals are topical vehicles such as the Yellow Cab made famous through the *Amos 'n' Andy* radio programme. In Britain in 1931 the Hornby Modelled Miniatures range of cast-iron vehicles was launched, renamed Dinky Toys from 1934. The enormous success of Dinky Toys led to the launch of competing ranges of model vehicles: Corgi (by Mettoy in 1956) and Matchbox Toys (by Lesney). Original models (examples in London, Bethnal Green Mus. Childhood) in all three ranges are now avidly collected. Other cast-iron toys included the cast-iron and chrome-steel bell-toys, in which the bell rang when the toy was pulled along the floor. Unusual bell-toy forms include Columbus standing in a shell-like vessel and a young woman in a sleigh (both Rochester, NY, Strong Mus.). Though such large firms as J. & E. Stevens made some bell-toys, the most innovative producer was the Gong Bell Manufacturing Co. (c. 1866–1939), East Hampton, CT.

3. PAPER, COMPOSITION AND PLASTIC. Among the best-known early examples of paper toys are shadow

6. Mechanical 'Dark Town Battery' penny-bank, polychrome enamelled cast iron with steel spring, l. 215 mm, USA, *c.* 1910–20 (New York, private collection)

puppets—jointed, stiff paper or cardboard figures, which were employed in sophisticated Chinese theatrical productions (*see* CHINA, §XIII, 20). Related, highly artistic examples are still made by hand and used in traditional Indonesian shadow theatre. By the 1700s French and Italian storytellers were employing simple articulated paper figures to dramatize their renditions of such traditional tales as *Don Quixote*. In the 19th century these home-made figures were gradually replaced by the commercial products of such manufacturers as the German company Georg H. Bestelmeier (*c.* 1800–25). Among innovations were French *pantins* or 'jumping jacks', jointed cardboard dancing figures (e.g. Polichinelle pantin, designed late 19th century, reprinted 1979; London, Bethnal Green Mus. Childhood). In England the peep-show or toy theatre, which was primarily composed of paper and cardboard and was designed to be painted and assembled by the purchaser, was sold in sheets by mid-19th-century manufacturers such as Webb & Pollock, London. A complete set engraved in black was sold for a penny; a hand-coloured set was sold for twopence (hence the phrase 'penny plain, tuppence coloured'). Toy soldiers were also made of paper. Early examples were hand-painted, while such later ones as those produced by the American firm of McLoughlin Bros were lithographed and often backed by cardboard or thin strips of wood. Similar examples were made in France, Spain and Germany during the

1800s. The best of these are faithful reproductions of period regimental costumes. Considerably more complex are the wonderful lithographed paper creations marketed by the French firm of Pellerin (*c.* 1890–1910) in Epinal. It produced detailed coloured construction sheets ranging from railway stations and villages to incredible flying machines and submarines. Other very popular paper toys include dolls (see §II, 1 below) and kites (*see* JAPAN, §XVI, 14).

Composition materials used in toy manufacture include ground stone, which was cast to produce building blocks by several German firms, best known of which is Richter (*c.* 1880–1920) of Rudolstadt. The firm's Anchor Building Bricks (e.g. of 1886; London, Bethnal Green Mus. Childhood) were stained in several colours and included columns, arches and various geometric forms, allowing the builder to create fanciful classical structures. In Britain, Lott's Bricks Ltd (1917–65) produced a similar range of 'stone' bricks. Another form of composition, sawdust and glue, was used (often in combination with metal) to manufacture mechanical toys, for example early 20th-century Japanese nodding toys, which have heads attached by a spring so that they bob up and down at the slightest touch. Earlier examples include animals and figures from Japanese mythology, but by the 1950s these were largely replaced by characters from comics. Composition material was also used in American wind-up toys of the 1920s to

1960s, for example the series of handcars featuring Donald Duck, Mickey Mouse and Peter Rabbit produced in the 1930s by the Lionel Corp. of New York.

In the 1940s plastic replaced the flimsy and highly flammable celluloid that had been used by Japanese toymakers. Initially, plastic toys were of poor quality, lacking both detail and colour variation. By the 1960s, however, Japanese manufacturers were producing robots and space toys that captured the imagination of buyers throughout the world. (Production has since largely shifted to Hong Kong and South Korea.) In Britain, Hilary Page (1904–57) used plastic to manufacture hygienic washable and virtually unbreakable toys for small children, launching the Bri-Plax range in the 1940s. The advantages of plastic as a material for toys for very young children has since been exploited most successfully by such firms as Fisher-Price Toys in the USA. Another very successful use of plastic in toy manufacturing is the Lego building and construction kits launched in Denmark by Ole Kirk Christiansen. Originally a carpenter and joiner who produced carved wooden toys in a small workshop, in 1947 Christiansen invested in a plastic injection moulding machine. The success of the building blocks it produced meant that by 1960 his company decided to concentrate solely on Lego, diversifying into a vast range of models and accessories with worldwide sales. Plastic has also been the major material used to produce another toy marketing phenomenon of the late 20th century—the worldwide merchandising of small figures and accessories to accompany such successful film and television programmes as *Star Wars* and *Teenage Mutant Ninja Turtles*.

II. Dolls.

Almost every culture has produced miniature human figures. It is, however, often difficult to know whether these were intended as play objects or as accessories in some social or religious ritual. Indeed, some doll figures, having served their original ritualistic purpose, were then given to children as playthings. Such 'dolls' have over time become transformed in both form and function into objects produced for commercial trade. An example is the Native North American Hopi *Kachina* figures, which now have fully articulated bodies and are painted in bright colours to make them more attractive to tourists. Early examples of dolls found in Egyptian tombs include not only simple representations consisting of papyrus rolls wrapped in linen but also extremely sophisticated examples carved from wood (e.g. of *c.* 2160–1788 BC; New York, Met.) and resembling larger sculpture from the same period. There are Greek dolls (e.g. terracotta doll from Corinth, *c.* 500 BC; London, BM) and even earlier ones from Peru and Mexico, as well as Roman rag dolls dating to AD 400 (e.g. London, BM) and Inuit dolls of carved ivory dating from *c.* 1100. Japan is one of the few countries that has a history of the early development of dolls, with doll types ranging from simple *Kokeshi* folk dolls to sophisticated ornamental dolls (*see* JAPAN, §XVI, 6).

1. Wood, paper, fabric and other natural materials. 2. Porcelain, pottery, composition and plastic. 3. Tin, wax and papier mâché.

1. WOOD, PAPER, FABRIC AND OTHER NATURAL MATERIALS. In England and in continental Europe, peg dolls, carved of wood with jointed, peg-fastened arms and legs, high foreheads, human hair and painted features, appeared in the 17th century. These dolls were often made in the Netherlands and were commonly referred to as 'Dutch dolls' (German examples of 1925–50; London, Bethnal Green Mus. Childhood). They were sold in Britain for a penny each, hence the term 'penny woodens'. Carved wooden dolls were produced in Germany during the 18th century, and Albert Schoenhut (*c.* 1872–1934), the grandson of one of these German doll-carvers, became one of the major American producers of not only wooden dolls but also turned and painted circus animals and performers.

Each European country, and often individual areas within a country, produced its own wooden folk dolls, characteristically dressed in regional costume. Originally intended only for local consumption, by the mid-19th century they had become export items. Among the best known are the Russian *Matryoshka* nesting dolls, which consist of brightly painted figures that pull apart to reveal ever smaller dolls within. Dolls produced on the Indian subcontinent in the 19th century were roughly carved of wood covered with gesso and then brightly painted; they depicted tradesmen, officials and citizens of India under the Raj. The dolls produced by the Mossi of West Africa are carved in a variety of styles and are regarded as art objects (*see* MOSSI, §4 and fig. 2). Chinese wooden dolls with finely shaped and painted features, clad in silk and cotton clothing typical of the period, were produced in Shanghai during the early 20th century (see King, pl. 27). They were made at and sold by the Door of Hope Mission, which rescued and housed slaves and abandoned children; sale of the dolls defrayed a portion of Mission costs. From *c.* 1850 Chinese exports included elaborate carved and painted, jointed wooden dolls, with aristocratic long fingers and tiny bound feet, clothed in silk brocades.

Paper dolls (or dressing dolls as they are known in Britain) originated in England in the late 18th century. The cut-out figures with changeable costumes proved particularly popular in France, where they served as inexpensive fashion illustrations (and subsequently as valuable records of period costume). By 1850 most European countries were producing paper dolls, some based on popular stage and music-hall figures. Typically, paper dolls were sold in sheets and subsequently cut apart. The earliest examples were engraved and hand-tinted; later, stencils and chromolithography made them available to a wider audience. As with paper theatres and toy soldiers, uncoloured dolls were cheaper than those already decorated. An interesting variation was the fortune-telling doll, which had a carved and painted wooden body and a skirt made of numerous cut and folded pieces of coloured paper, each bearing an individual printed or handwritten fortune. Most were made in Germany from the mid- to late 1800s. Manufacturers rarely marked these pieces, and their origins are often hard to determine. During the early 1900s Polish craftsmen produced delicate paper dolls, the clothing for which was made of individual strips of paper decorated with tiny appliquéd flowers. The Japanese produced flat-bodied, coloured paper figures, known as *anesamaningyō* ('elder sister dolls'), with three-dimensional heads crowned by elaborate hairstyles (*see* JAPAN, §XVI, 6). Among the best-known paper-doll manufacturers was

Raphael Tuck (est. *c.* 1865), London. By the late 19th century paper dolls were being mass-produced by such manufacturers as Milton Bradley (*c.* 1860–1920) of Springfield, MA, and by numerous French and German makers.

Fabrics and other natural materials have long been used to make dolls. Cloth dolls, sometimes stuffed with sawdust, rags or grass, have probably existed in every culture, but they were not produced commercially until the 19th century. Among the finest examples are Japanese 'shelf dolls' (so-called because they were to be displayed rather than played with) made of stiffened fabric over a padded wire framework and elaborately clothed in silk brocades. Much simpler in construction are the Raggedy Ann and Andy dolls patented in 1915. Commercially printed materials from which rag dolls could be constructed became so popular in the early 20th century that such firms as Dean's Rag Co. in Britain and the Arnold Print Works in the USA were commissioned to produce examples advertising everything from breakfast cereal to canned soups. The Italian firm of Lenci (*c.* 1920–40), Turin, produced pressed felt dolls and developed a range of dolls dressed in authentic national costumes, which were sold throughout Europe. The English pedlar doll had face and hands of painted white kid and wool and cotton clothing. She carried a variety of objects, imitating the dress and manner of a 19th-century street merchant. Among the better-known makers of such figures was the firm of C. & H. White (*c.* 1820–40) of Milton, Hampshire.

Many other natural materials have been employed in doll-making. In North America, Plains Indian tribes such as the Sioux and the Cheyenne made dolls of deerskin. Early 19th-century examples were often little more than a roll of skin decorated with feathers. By the late 1800s, however, leather bodies stuffed with dried grass and with horse- or human-hair wigs were dressed in buckskin clothing with beaded decoration mimicking tribal appearance. Similar dolls were produced during the late 19th century and the early 20th by the Inuit of Alaska, Siberia and the north-west American coast. Typically, these dolls have leather faces with embroidered features and are clothed in fur-trimmed seal-hide parkas (e.g. in New York, Mus. Amer. Ind.). Little girls often carried these dolls in their parka hoods, just as they themselves had been carried by their mothers. Inuit boys played with boy dolls equipped with harpoons, kayaks and fishing gear.

Dolls are often made specially to celebrate specific festivals. Egyptians prepare moulded sugar dolls decorated with coloured paper for sale during the feast day of Muhammad's birth. In England and the USA the corn-maiden doll was traditionally prepared from the last shucks, an ancient tradition honouring the goddess of fertility and seeking a rich harvest in the coming year; in the republic of Montenegro the corn-maiden takes the form of an elaborate crowned doll made from oats, while plaited palm-leaves provided the material for the Balinese fertility maiden. In Peru ethnic folk dolls were made from varnished leather, and in Sweden dolls were also made from birch bark (e.g. of 19th century; Stockholm, Nordiska Mus.). In the late 20th century many of these traditional doll forms were produced mainly for the tourist trade, as local children prefer factory-made dolls.

7. Teddy bear with swivel head and limbs, Yorkshire cloth, h. *c.* 220 mm, manufactured by Steiff, Germany, *c.* 1920 (London, Bethnal Green Museum of Childhood)

In 1844 the American Charles Goodyear patented a technique for producing hard rubber, a waterproof material that could be used to make dolls that could be bathed or even 'wet' themselves. Early Goodyear dolls had moulded rubber heads and kid bodies; Italian makers produced all-rubber dolls from the 1860s, and by 1890 the New York Rubber Co. was also producing them. As rubber dolls tend to dry out and crack over time, early examples are quite rare.

In 1903 Morris Mitchom of the Ideal Toy Corp. in the USA launched a range of soft toys known initially as Teddy's Bear (allegedly named after a cartoon showing Theodore Roosevelt refusing to shoot a small bear cub) and subsequently as teddy bears. Also in 1903 the German firm run by Margarete Steiff (1847–1909), which had been producing dolls since 1879, started to produce bears (e.g. of *c.* 1920; London, Bethnal Green Mus. Childhood; see fig. 7). Teddy bears have been perennially popular ever since on both sides of the Atlantic, where they have been produced in a wide variety of shapes, sizes and colours. Steiff bears in particular have become valuable collectors' pieces, and there are regular teddy bear auctions.

2. PORCELAIN, POTTERY, COMPOSITION AND PLASTIC. By 1840 European manufacturers were casting lifelike porcelain heads, hands and feet, which were first joined to bodies of cloth or kid and later to ones of jointed wood

or composition. The earlier preference was for moulded hairstyles and for painted, realistic features that were then given a clear glaze. By the 1870s unglazed, or bisque, heads were preferred, and these matt, natural-looking faces were crowned with wigs of real hair or mohair. Initially, doll heads proved a profitable sideline for such famous porcelain manufacturers as Meissen, but by the 1880s a group of specialized manufacturers emerged. In France the firms of Jumeau, Bru, Fleischmann & Bloedel and Danel & Cie combined in 1899 to form the Société Française de Fabrication de Bébés et Jouets, the purpose of which was to wrest market shares from such dominant German manufacturers as Simon & Halbig, Kestner and Kämmer & Reinhardt. A by-product of this competition, which extended from the 1860s well into the 20th century, was a remarkable variety of beautiful porcelain dolls ranging from the sophisticated 'lady dolls' or fashion dolls dating back to the 1700s to a plethora of bébés or baby dolls (see fig. 8). These, in turn, culminated in the early 20th century with the production in Germany of the first so-called character dolls—realistically modelled figures with expressive, lifelike features that often mirrored ethnic diversity. For the first time black, brown, Asian and even Native American dolls appeared alongside the traditional brunettes and blondes.

It was not until World War I, when wartime embargoes cut off the traditional supplies of porcelain dolls, that non-European manufacturers emerged. In the USA the Fulper Pottery Co. of Flemington, NJ, made attractive bisque dolls from 1918 until 1921; in Japan several manufacturers produced similar porcelain bébés, all of which appear to have been based on German or French moulds. However, the quality of materials and workmanship was generally inferior to the European product. Better examples were produced by such English companies as Hewitt's Willow Pottery, Staffordshire, which manufactured shoulder-head bisque dolls from 1915 to 1920.

Pottery dolls, though of great antiquity (early examples from Egypt, Africa and South America are known), are of considerably less importance than those of porcelain. In Europe high-fired white earthenware was used to manufacture tiny doll's house dolls less than 125 mm high, while in the USA some rare 19th-century moulded stoneware and redware doll heads, clearly copied from European porcelain examples, have survived. In both Spain and Portugal there is a long tradition of painted hand-made low-fired red clay dolls. Spanish examples were still being produced in the 1960s (they are now produced in plastic), often in the guise of local characters such as the fishmonger, priest and train conductor. The Iberian tradition spread to Central and South America, where unusual ethnic dolls (often incorporating native Indian elements) continue to be made in such countries as Mexico, Peru and Guatemala.

Composition materials, including such varied ingredients as sawdust and plaster mixed with glue and water, offered a less costly but equally ductile moulding material for dollmakers. Composition bodies were often combined with heads of other materials, and, in many cases, entire dolls were made of the material. In China the commercial manufacture of dolls was forbidden until 1860. During the 1890s highly realistic peasant figures were created for

8. Doll, porcelain head, hands and feet, kid body and artificial hair, h. 355 mm, Germany, c. 1880–1910 (New York, private collection)

export. These composition figures were carefully cast with sculpted details and hand painted. Costumes of cotton and silk were highly accurate reflections of country garb. In Japan late 19th-century Girls' and Boys' Day Festival dolls were also made from composition. Displayed on stepped shelves, these figures, customarily 15 in number, include the emperor and empress and attendants. Faces are typically covered with *gofun* (white ground powder) or polished oyster shell paste (e.g. of c. 1890; London, Bethnal Green Mus. Childhood).

Though many European manufacturers employed composition material (usually for bodies and limbs), it was used most creatively in the USA. In 1936 the New York firm of Madame Alexander (est. 1923 by Beatrice Behrman) created the Dionne Quintuplets in composition, and Joseph Kallus used it for the Betty Boop doll, which was made in the early 1930s by the Cameo Doll Co. of Allegany, PA. EFFanBEE (Fleischaker & Baum of New York City) produced such composition character dolls as Charlie McCarthy and W. C. Fields in the 1930s and 1940s. Other well-known American makers, all in New York, were the Ideal Toy Co. (c. 1930–50), maker of the Mortimer Snerd and Baby Snooks dolls as well as one of the first Superman figures, the Crown Toy Co. (c. 1940–50), producer of a Pinocchio doll, and the Knickerbocker Toy Co. (c. 1935–45), which manufactured a popular set of Snow White and the Seven Dwarfs.

In 1958 Mattel Co. in the USA launched a plastic 'teenage' Barbie doll, with a constantly changing range of models and endless accessories, ranging from clothes to houses, cars and even a boyfriend (Ken). The success of Barbie resulted in the launch of a British rival, Sindy, by the Pedigree doll range of Lines Bros, while in the USA the Action Man series of dolls and accessories for boys was produced by Hessenfeld Bros. All three ranges continue to sell steadily, with new accessories and models being launched at regular intervals.

3. TIN, WAX AND PAPIER MÂCHÉ. Tin dolls should be more accurately described as tin-headed dolls, as their bodies and limbs were made of other materials such as wood, cloth and composition. The tin heads, purchased from tinsmiths, were either decorated with lithographs or hand painted. Though fragile, they were often quite lifelike. Among the better-known manufacturers were the German firms of Vischer (*c.* 1870–1900) and Buschow & Beck (*c.* 1890–1920), whose attractive dolls had jointed wood or composition bodies.

In the 18th century French designers began to make and export wax fashion dolls, and by the mid-18th century wax dolls were popular in Europe with the finest examples being produced in England by the family firms of Pierotti (*c.* 1850–1920) and Montanari (*c.* 1870–1900), both originally from Italy. They specialized in highly naturalistic figures (e.g. Princess Louise doll by Mme Augusta Montanari, 1853, and crèche baby doll by Henry Pierotti, *c.* 1870; both London, Bethnal Green Mus. Childhood; see fig. 9), and Henry Pierotti is said to have urged young ladies to send samples of their own hair to be implanted

in their new dolls! From the 1850s wax dolls were manufactured in the Sonneberg area of Germany, and French firms such as Lafitte & Desirat (*c.* 1900–15) produced many excellent examples. The best-known American manufacturer was Francisco Vargas, a Mexican resident in New Orleans, who created sensitive models of the common people: street vendors, musicians and cotton-pickers. His business was continued into the 1920s by a granddaughter, Lucy Rosado.

Most early wax dolls were cast in moulds and hand-tinted. However, the fragility of wax doll heads encouraged manufacturers to employ a wax mask over a stronger composition head to produce a longer lasting, though not necessarily more attractive, figure. Among the better-known producers of these dolls were the Sonneberg firms of Charles Motschmann (*c.* 1850–70) and Cuno & Otto Dressel (*c.* 1863–95).

By the early 19th century papier mâché was a popular material for doll manufacture. Although early examples of dolls with papier-mâché heads are rarely marked, most were made in France or Germany *c.* 1820–50. French models have delicate, aristocratic features, while German examples have broad faces and boldly painted features. Both have kid bodies and carved wooden extremities. The first manufacturer to patent a papier-mâché head was Ludwig Greiner (*fl* 1858–72) of Philadelphia in 1858.

III. Doll's houses, miniature rooms and shops and doll's furniture.

1. DOLL'S HOUSES. The earliest surviving doll's houses are German in origin and date to the 16th century (e.g. *c.* 1600; Nuremberg, Ger. Nmus.). Known as cabinets, they were really adult toys designed to hold collections of miniatures in precious metals and exotic woods. By the mid-1700s wealthy Dutch families were displaying houses mounted on stands (examples in Amsterdam, Rijksmus.), which had doors that could be opened to display the detailed contents. Italian craftsmen also produced fine examples (e.g. of late 17th century; Bologna, Pin. N.). In England, the doll's houses (referred to then as 'baby houses') produced for the court of Queen Anne in the early 18th century were the equal of the finest being produced in Nuremberg. These lavish pieces had little to do with children, however, and it was not until the mid-19th century that the doll's house as a plaything emerged. The primary manufacturers were located in France, Germany, England and the USA. In most cases the commercially produced houses were designed to resemble contemporary architecture and were composed of relatively lightweight materials such as thin plywood or cardboard, either covered with lithographed paper or painted. Details were of turned and painted wood, and windows, if any, of glass. French examples were more delicately constructed with fanciful balconies and elaborate doorways. Since many of these houses were exported, they were frequently designed so that they could be taken apart, packed for shipment and later reassembled. The German firm of Benda & Hipauf advertised in 1910 a 'house of the collapsible kind, to be erected upon the box containing it', and Raphael Tuck of London took out a

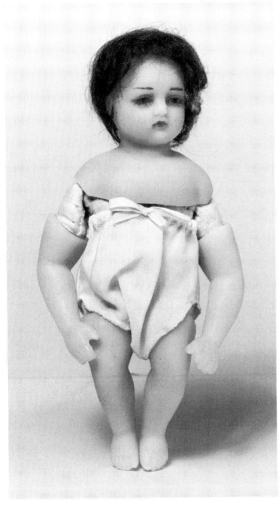

9. Crèche baby doll by Henry Pierotti, wax, England, *c.* 1870–84 (London, Bethnal Green Museum of Childhood)

10. Toy 'Nuremberg Kitchen', wooden framework with utensils and accessories of tin and other metals, Germany, *c.* 1867 (New York, Museum of the City of New York)

copyright for an accordion-like stiff paper house that could be folded up into a book.

The earliest-known surviving doll's house manufactured in the USA is dated 1744 (New York, Van Cortlandt House Mus.). Once colour lithography was perfected in the late 19th century, firms such as the R. Bliss Manufacturing Co. employed it to produce brightly decorated Victorian houses (e.g. of 1890–1910; Rochester, NY, Strong Mus.), barns and even skyscrapers. Rivals in the field included the Morton E. Converse Co. (*c.* 1900–20) of Winchendon, MA, which lithographed decoration directly on to the wooden components of its doll's houses, and Albert Schoenhut & Co. (*c.* 1917–34) of Philadelphia, better known as a maker of jointed wooden figures.

Folding cardboard houses were also an American speciality. In 1894 McLoughlin Bros patented its 'New Folding Doll's House', which consisted of four rooms with printed wallpaper, floor coverings and even a few pieces of furniture. Another later McLoughlin building (*c.* 1911; Rochester, NY, Strong Mus.) had a front wall that folded down to create an elegant formal garden. Other folding doll's house manufacturers included Stirn & Lyon (*c.* 1880–90) of New York and the New Jersey firm of Grim & Leeds (*c.* 1880–1900), which offered examples with windows of isinglass.

2. MINIATURE ROOMS AND SHOPS. The best-known miniature rooms are the 'Nuremberg Kitchens', which were open, three-sided box-like structures packed with every imaginable type of kitchen utensil, usually made from tin although some might be of wood, glass or pottery. The most elaborate examples were produced in Germany from the 18th century until well into the 20th (see fig. 10). From *c.* 1850 English makers produced colourful butcher-shop models of carved and painted wood complete with butcher, block and hanging joints of meat (e.g. London, Bethnal Green Mus. Childhood). Far more elaborate were the German millinery and haberdashery shops produced from 1840 to 1880, which were staffed by porcelain-headed dolls and had bolts of real fabric as well as miniature wood and metal fixtures (e.g. haberdasher's shop, *c.* 1840; Nuremberg, Ger. Nmus.). Among other shop types produced are tobacconist's, chemist's, baker's, poulterer's, fishmonger's and grocer's. The Pet's Grocery Store model made by the American firm of Mason & Parker (*c.* 1914–30) was stocked with well-known American brands—a clever bit of advertising! There were also folding-paper shops. The French firm of Pellerin at Epinal produced complex models, with a wealth of detail, on thick paper, which was often glued to cardboard for further strength (examples in London, Bethnal Green Mus. Childhood).

11. Doll's house furniture, iron, h. 52–155 mm, American, 1920–30 (New York, private collection)

In Mexico, Peru and Chile potters construct small vignettes depicting local craftsmen and shopkeepers surrounded by their wares; in Japan larger scenes featuring fishermen, artisans and shopkeepers have been made for many years.

3. DOLL'S FURNITURE. Doll's house furnishings were produced as early as the 16th century, and some were more valuable than the buildings that housed them. The Dutch filled their miniature bedrooms with burl walnut inlaid bombé chests-of-drawers and commodes, while English dolls ate at mahogany Chippendale tables set with delicate sterling-silver table services embellished with family monograms. German baby houses might contain sets of miniature Meissen porcelain. Blown glass goblets and delicate silk napkins would further enhance the feeling of authenticity and luxury. Examples of miniature furniture found in ancient Egyptian and Chinese tombs are thought to have served ritual or religious purposes.

With the rise of the commercial doll's house industry, furniture became less costly but even more varied. Furnishings, like houses, followed period styles, and there are examples of miniature parlour, bedroom or dining-room sets in every 19th-century revival style. Much of the better furniture was made in the Walterhausen area of Germany, where from 1825 until well into the 20th century numerous manufacturers produced detailed sets in three sizes so as to allow buyers to select a suitable scale. Rose-wood was the preferred material, and the tiny pieces closely resemble full-size parlour, dining-room and bedroom furniture. One of the later manufacturers was Gebrüder Schneegas (*c.* 1880–1910), which, during the early 1900s, produced a line of Art Nouveau style furnishings including longcase clocks, marble-topped wash-stands and ornate cupboards. There was also a variety of cheaper jigsaw cut furnishings gilded and covered with lithographed paper. The high quality and efficient export system of German doll's house furniture virtually eliminated competition. English and French doll's houses of *c.* 1900 are often furnished almost entirely with German furniture. Nevertheless, there was some competition: the Japanese made delicate cane and wicker chairs, settees and tables, which mimicked the popular Victorian porch and garden furnishings. Also, in 1888 the R. Bliss Manufacturing Co. patented a set of painted wood bedroom furniture decorated with lithographed paper in the style of the so-called 'cottage furniture' so popular at the time.

The use of the jigsaw and lithography reflected a change in market direction. While some European firms continued to sell hand-crafted doll's house furnishings or to import such exotic examples as the Indonesian furniture made from feathers, most went over to mass production, which to a great extent meant the use of metal. British and American manufacturers of cast-metal toys were especially well-situated for this market (see fig. 11; *see also* §I, 2 above). William Britain's Ltd (est. *c.* 1893), London, offered cast-spelter kitchen sets, as did Meccano Ltd (*c.* 1901–64) of Liverpool on a more limited scale. American manufacturers produced both cut or stamped tin and cast-metal furnishings (see fig. 11). Francis, Field & Francis made hand-painted tin chairs, chests-of-drawers and even clocks; George Brown (*c.* 1856–68) of Forestville, CT, produced similar examples painted to resemble oak or rose-wood; J. & E. Stevens (*c.* 1870–1930) of Cromwell, CT, made miniature cast-iron furniture, sometimes modelled on the full-size pieces that they also produced. At a much later date (*c.* 1930–40) the Dowst Manufacturing Co. in Chicago, makers of Tootsietoy vehicles and figures, produced a line of die-cast pot-metal household furnishings including refrigerators, stoves and bathroom fixtures. Even pewter, which had replaced silver during the late 19th century for such things as miniature tablewares and tea sets, was utilized in doll's house furniture design by such manufacturers as Peter F. Pia (*c.* 1848–60) of New York, who made ornate filigree-type wares similar to what was then being made in Germany from spelter. Some German firms produced delicate Rococo style gilt furnishings in thin pot-metal; others, led by Märklin of Göppingen, produced household furniture of painted and lithographed tin-plate. Märklin, although better known for its trains and model boats (see §I, 2(ii) above), was an important exporter of doll's house furniture throughout Europe and the Americas.

IV. Games and puzzles.

Simple gambling devices such as dice or knucklebones have often been found in ancient graves, and a wall frieze from Pompeii (Naples, Mus. Archeol. N.) shows a group of women playing astralagus or knucklebones. Game-pieces in a variety of materials have survived from many ancient civilizations (e.g. rock crystal lion gaming-piece, *c.* 3000 BC; Cairo, Egyp. Mus.; walrus ivory chess rook, 12th century; *see* IVORY, fig. 2), as have game- and gaming-boards. As far back as the reign of Ammenemes IV (*c.* 1770–*c.* 1760 BC) Egyptians were playing a complex board-game known as 'Hounds and Jackals' (see fig. 12). Dominoes and playing cards are also known from antiquity.

1. BOARD-GAMES. Board-games, which are found in most cultures (*see* INDIAN SUBCONTINENT, §IX, 6), are generally played on a prepared flat surface, which usually contains a track about which the contestants proceed from start to finish, their movements being determined by throwing dice or spinning a dial or teetotum. The earliest printed board-games were made from copper or steel plates and then hand coloured. By 1840 games were being lithographed, mounted on cardboard and packaged in boxes rather than simply being sold in sheets. By the 1870s both the boxes and the game-boards had become works of art, with high-quality printing and designs reflecting contemporary advertising materials such as theatrical posters and product packaging. Board-games were initially produced by book publishers as a sideline, a fact that contributed to both their artistic quality and their rather pronounced literary bent. The earliest-known children's board-game, *A Set of Squares*, was issued in England during the 1740s and was instructional in nature. Game designers sought to teach history, geography and the classics. There was also a strong moralistic tone, as with *The Reward of Merit* published in 1801 by George Fox of London. Such games originally offered the player the choice between good and evil; by the mid-19th century the choice was extended to one between riches (obtained through honesty and hard work) and poverty. Among the better-known British manufacturers are Bowles & Carver, publishers of *Journey through Europe, or the Play of Geography* (1759), John Harris (1756–1846), John Betts, who published many games including *Roman History* and *Royal Tiger Hunt* during the 1860s and 1870s, and

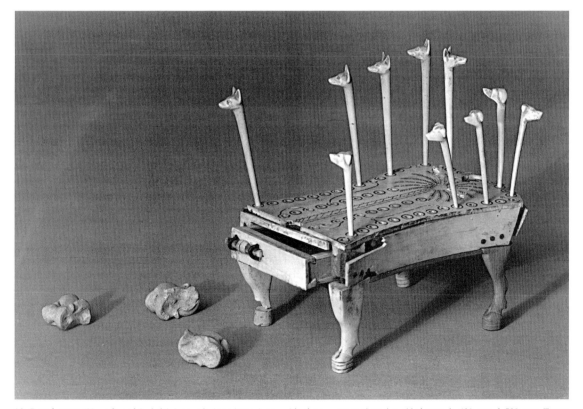

12. Board-game, 'Hounds and Jackals', ivory playing-pieces, ivory with ebony veneer, three knuckle-bones, h. 630 mm, l. 520 mm, Egypt, *c.* 1799–1787 BC (New York, Metropolitan Museum of Art)

A. N. Myers & Co., a large firm active throughout much of the late 19th century. The earliest-known game published in North America is *The Traveller's Tour through the United States* published in 1822 by Frederick and Roe Lockwood of New York. By the end of the 19th century, however, American manufacturers were turning out thousands of different games each year. The two major manufacturers were Parker Bros (est. 1883, Salem, MA) and Milton Bradley. In 1935 the former produced *Monopoly*, the property game that has sold millions of copies in more than 40 languages and, in 1949, *Clue* (known as *Cluedo* in Britain). The firm of Milton Bradley remained active well into the 20th century and published many games based on historical events, especially the various wars in which the USA engaged. The most successful board-game in the latter half of the 20th century was *Trivial Pursuit*, in which contestants' progress round the board was determined by their ability to answer general knowledge questions on a variety of topics.

2. CARD GAMES. Card games are thought to have developed in East Asia. The use of playing cards was already widespread in Europe when it was prohibited by authorities at Regensburg, Germany, in 1378. The earliest producers of playing cards were located in Germany, and by the 15th century they were producing decks of hand-painted cards. These were often works of art created by professional artists, but they were also expensive. Though the Germans attempted to produce less costly cards through the use of stencils and engraving, by the early 16th century French and Belgian manufacturers dominated the field, both because of the quality of their product and because they standardized card design. The figures they chose are essentially the ones used today. Steps were also taken to dissociate card playing from gambling. By the early 1600s packs of instructional cards were appearing on the market, one of the most famous being that devised by the French scholar Jean Desmarests to educate the young Louis XIV in the history of France. Among the notable French manufacturers was B. P. Grimaud & Cie (est. 1748). Like many of its contemporaries the firm specialized in cards bearing elaborately costumed medieval figures.

Cards first appeared in Britain *c.* 1400, and by 1628 a guild, the Worshipful Makers of Playing Cards, had been established. By the end of the 17th century English makers were issuing sets focusing on geography, though remaining mindful of political and religious issues, as in a set captioned somewhat ponderously 'All the Popish Plots from the Armada in 1588 to the Popish Plot of 1678'. The educational nature of children's playing cards reached a peak in the 1850s, but subsequently the emphasis became more on enjoyment with the emergence of such games as *Old Maid*, *Snap* and *Happy Families*. All three games appeared in numerous editions, but *Happy Families* in particular has appeared in such well-known editions as that issued by John Jacques & Son of London (e.g. *c.* 1860; London, Bethnal Green Mus. Childhood) and that illustrated by John Tenniel (e.g. *c.* 1860; London, Bethnal Green Mus. Childhood). The alphabet card games of *Lexicon* and *Kan-U-Go*, which combine learning and

entertainment, were the forerunners of the highly successful word board-game *Scrabble*. Devised by Alfred Butts in 1931, *Scrabble* was first manufactured in Newton, CT, in 1948, and from 1952 sales began to soar. It continues to sell worldwide.

The first American playing-card manufacturer was Jazaniah Ford of Milton, MA, active in the late 18th century; the most distinguished was Lewis I. Cohen, whose firm, established in 1835, continued under various managements into the 20th century. The best-known American games are *Dr Busby*, invented *c.* 1840 by Ann Abbot of Beverly, MA, and *Rook*, copyrighted by George Palmer in the late 19th century.

3. TABLE GAMES. The earliest table games—chess, draughts, backgammon and knucklebones—are of great antiquity and were produced in different materials to suit different ranks of players. For example ivory, ebony or gold were regarded as suitable for royalty, while other players used pieces made of carved or painted wood or, more rarely, clay or polished stone (*see* CHESS SET). Similarly, dominoes might be made of ivory and stored in elaborately carved and inlaid boxes, and even spillikins or 'pick-up sticks' were made in ivory. Knucklebones appear in many variations throughout Africa and Central and East Asia. The Inuit of North America played with animal figures of carved bone, while in Polynesia fish bones sufficed.

In the late 19th century these traditional pastimes were augmented by a variety of factory-made games designed to be played on a table or on the floor. Some of these were miniaturized versions of such outdoor activities as cricket, croquet, table tennis, model golf and the German game of *Kick*, which mimicked football. In 1949 the British company Subbuteo launched a sophisticated version of table association football (followed later by table cricket and rugby), incorporating miniature players and a wealth of constantly changing accessories.

Another popular table game that has been adapted over the years is *Fish*. In the original version contestants attempted to catch porcelain or cardboard fish with hooks dangling from miniature poles. Numerous variations of the game have been issued in a variety of materials by British, German and American manufacturers, including a version in which plastic hippopotamuses try to catch balls and sharks try to catch smaller fish. The game of nine pins or bowling was adapted as a table version in the form of skittles, in which players roll, swing or fire a ball at a line of figures. Skittles targets were carved and painted or jigsaw cut and faced with lithographed paper and are found in a great variety of forms; some are excellent examples of folk art.

4. PUZZLES. Jigsaw puzzles (named after the jigsaw used to cut them into their component units) were invented in the mid-18th century, probably by John Spilsbury (*c.* 1739–69), a London cartographer and engraver. Spilsbury also taught geography, and the first puzzles were teaching tools designed to help children recognize natural and political boundaries. Originally called dissected puzzles, they were made from engraved (later

lithographed) sheets laid down on wood or heavy cardboard and then cut apart. By the 1780s publishers had added picture puzzles to those based only on maps. This gave greater variety and offered children something more interesting to assemble. However, the pedagogical emphasis was maintained with puzzles designed to teach everything from Bible history to multiplication and the alphabet. After 1850 inexpensive lithography and the development of a die that could cut out an entire sheet of printed cardboard facilitated mass production, and a new emphasis on pleasure as opposed to learning allowed for the development of many new puzzles. Children's stories, contemporary events, animals and numerous other subjects found their way on to the puzzle board. Most puzzles were produced by board-game manufacturers. In England these included John Betts and William Darton of London as well as the prolific firm of J. R. & J. W. Barfoot (*c.* 1840–70) in London, and in the USA Milton Bradley, Charles M. Crandall (active at several locations in Pennsylvania, *c.* 1867–90) and the McLoughlin Bros.

BIBLIOGRAPHY

GENERAL

A. M. Earle: *Child Life in Colonial Days* (New York, 1899)
K. Groeber: *Children's Toys of Bygone Days* (New York, 1928)
R. Bayne-Powell: *The English Child in the 18th Century* (London, 1939)
L. Daiken: *Children's Toys throughout the Ages* (New York, 1953, rev. London, 1963)
F. G. Roe: *The Georgian Child* (London, 1961)
P. Aries: *Centuries of Childhood: A Social History of Family Life* (London, 1962)
D. Foley: *Toys through the Ages* (Philadelphia, 1962)
A. Fraser: *A History of Toys* (New York, 1966, rev. London, 1972)
K. E. Fritzsch and M. Bachmann: *An Illustrated History of Toys* (London, 1966, rev. New York, 1978)
M. Hillier: *Pageant of Toys* (New York, 1966)
J. Remise and J. Fondin: *The Golden Age of Toys* (Greenwich, CT, 1967)
R. Culff: *The World of Toys* (Feltham, 1969)
L. H. Hertz: *The Toy Collector* (New York, 1969)
K. M. McClinton: *Antiques of American Childhood* (New York, 1970)
A. L. Haskell and M. Lewis: *Infantilia: The Archaeology of the Nursery* (London, 1971)
J. J. Schroeder: *The Wonderful World of Toys, Games & Dolls* (Northfield, IL, 1971)
G. White: *Antique Toys and their Background* (New York, 1971)
B. Cadbury: *Playthings Past* (New York, 1976)
F. N. Jackson: *Toys of Other Days* (London, 1976)
J. Mackay: *Nursery Antiques* (London, 1976)
C. E. King: *The Encyclopedia of Toys* (London and New York, 1978)
W. C. Ketchum: *Toys and Games* (Washington, DC, 1981)
——: *Collecting Toys For Fun And Profit* (Tucson, 1985)

TOYS

G. Craig: *Gordon Craig's Book of Penny Toys* (London, 1899)
L. H. Hertz: *Mechanical Toy Banks* (Wethersfield, CT, 1947)
E. Hercík: *Folktoys of Czechoslovakia* (Prague, 1952)
J. G. Garratt: *Model Soldiers: A Collector's Guide* (London, 1959)
J. D. Meyer and L. Freeman: *Old Penny Banks* (Watkins Glen, NY, 1960)
C. H. Ellis: *Model Railways, 1838–1939* (London, 1962)
H. Harris: *Model Soldiers* (London, 1962)
G. Speaight: *The History of the English Toy Theatre* (London, 1962)
K. E. Fritzsch and M. Bachmann: *An Illustrated History of Toys: A Contribution to the History of Toy Making in Germany* (London, 1966)
J. Greilsamer and B. Azema: *Catalogue of Model Cars of the World* (Lausanne, 1967)
P. Murray: *Toys* (London, 1968)
N. V. Taranovskoi: *Russkaya derevyannaya igrushka* [Russian wooden toys] (Moscow, 1968) [Eng. summary]
L. H. Hertz: *The Toy Collector* (New York, 1969)
P. Baumann: *Collecting Antique Marbles* (Leon, IA, 1970)
G. White: *Antique Toys and their Background* (New York, 1971)
G. Reder: *Clockwork, Steam and Electric: A History of Model Railways* (Shepperton, Surrey, 1972)
R. Pearsall: *Collecting Mechanical Antiques* (London, 1973)
A. Levy: *A Century of Model Trains* (London, 1974)
K. Harman: *Comic Strip Toys* (Des Moines, 1975)
M. Hillier: *Automata and Mechanical Toys* (London, 1976)
D. Pressland: *The Art of the Tin Toy* (New York, 1976)
C. G. Rogers: *Pennybanks* (New York, 1977)
A. Weltens: *Mechanical Tin Toys in Colour* (Poole, Dorset, 1977)
K. E. Fritzsch and M. Bachmann: *Illustrated History of German Toys* (New York, 1978)
C. Bartholomew: *Mechanical Toys* (Secaucus, NJ, 1979)
J. Milet and R. Forbes: *Toy Boats, 1870–1955* (New York, 1979)
N. K. Spong: *Flywheel Powered Toys* (New York, 1979)
B. Whitton: *American Clockwork Toys, 1860–1900* (Exton, PA, 1979)
B. Barenholtz and I. McClintock: *American Antique Toys, 1830–1930* (New York, 1980)
J. Cieslik and M. Cieslik: *Lehmann Toys: The History of E. P. Lehmann, 1881–1981* (London, 1981)
A. Moore: *The Penny Bank Book* (Exton, PA, 1982)
M. Schiffer, ed.: *Matchbox Toys* (Exton, PA, 1983)
B. Whitton: *Toys* (New York, 1984)
——: *Paper Toys of the World* (Cumberland, MD, 1986)

DOLLS AND DOLL'S HOUSES

R. S. Freeman: *American Dolls* (New York, 1952)
A. K. Early: *English Dolls, Effigies and Puppets* (London, 1955)
V. Greene: *Some English Dolls and Doll's Houses* (London, 1955)
S. Ozawa: *Dolls of Japan* (Tokyo, 1957)
A. Chapuis and E. Droz: *Automata* (New York, 1958)
T. Yamada: *Japanese Dolls* (Tokyo, 1959)
F. G. Jacobs: *A History of Dolls' Houses* (New York, 1965)
F. G. Jacobs and Faurholt: *Dolls and Doll Houses* (Rutland, VT, 1967)
D. S. Coleman: *The Collector's Encyclopedia of Dolls* (New York, 1968)
M. Hillier: *Dolls and Doll Makers* (London, 1968)
J. Latham: *Doll's Houses: A Personal Choice* (London, 1969)
J. G. Anderton: *Twentieth Century Dolls* (Des Moines, 1971)
J. Noble: *A Treasury of Beautiful Dolls* (New York, 1971)
M. U. von Boehn: *Dolls* (New York, 1972)
C. Fox: *The Doll* (New York, 1973)
F. Walker and M. Whitton: *Playthings by the Yard: The Story of Cloth Dolls* (South Hadley, MA, 1973)
F. G. Jacobs: *Dolls' Houses in America* (New York, 1974)
B. W. Jendrick: *A Picture Book of Paper Dolls and Paper Toys* (Pittsford, NY, 1974)
F. Eaton: *Dolls in Color* (New York, 1975)
G. White: *Dolls, Automata, Marks and Labels* (London, 1975)
M. E. Buser and D. Buser: *Guide to Schoenhut Dolls, Toys and Circus* (Paducah, KY, 1976)
D. S. Coleman: *The Collector's Book of Doll Clothes* (London, 1976)
——: *Collector's Encyclopedia of Dolls* (New York, 1976)
I. S. Jones: *Early North American Dollmaking* (San Francisco, 1976)
C. E. King: *A Collector's History of Dolls* (London, 1977)
P. Smith: *Oriental Dolls* (Paducah, KY, 1978)
B. Whitton: *Bliss Toys and Doll Houses* (New York, 1979)
J. Foulke: *Kestner: King of Dollmakers* (Cumberland, MD, 1980)
J. A. Robinson and K. F. Seller: *Advertising Dolls* (Paducah, KY, 1980)
P. A. Rustam: *Cloth Dolls: A Collector's Guide* (Cranbury, NJ, 1980)
M. Whitton: *The Jumeau Doll* (New York, 1980)
J. Young: *A Collector's Guide to Paper Dolls* (Paducah, KY, 1980)
G. Angione: *All-bisque and Half-bisque dolls* (Exton, PA, 1981)
M. B. Howard: *Those Fascinating Paper Dolls: An Illustrated Handbook for Collectors* (New York, 1981)
W. Lavitt: *American Folk Dolls* (New York, 1982)
J. Axe: *Encyclopedia of Celebrity Dolls* (Cumberland, MD, 1983)

GAMES AND PUZZLES

H. J. R. Murray: *A History of Board Games other than Chess* (Oxford, 1952)
R. C. Bell: *Board and Table Games* (London, 1960)
L. Hannas: *The English Jig Saw Puzzle* (London, 1962)
F. R. B. Whitehouse: *Table Games of Victorian and Georgian Days* (Birmingham, 1971)
R. Tilley: *A History of Playing Cards* (London, 1973)
B. Love: *Playing the Game* (Los Angeles, 1978)
R. C. Bell: *The Board Game Book* (London, 1979)
B. Love: *Great Board Games* (New York, 1979)
J. Slocum and J. Botermans: *Puzzles Old and New* (Amsterdam and Seattle, 1986)

A. D. Williams: *Jig Saw Puzzles: An Illustrated History and Price Guide* (Radnor, PA, 1990)

L. Dennis: *Warman's Antique American Games, 1840–1940* (Elkins Park, PA, 1991)

R. Polizzi and F. Schaefer: *Spin Again: Board Games of the '50s and '60s* (New York, 1991)

B. Whitehill: *American Boxed Games and their Makers, 1822–1992* (Radnor, PA, 1992)

The Board Game: America at Play (exh. cat. by W. C. Ketchum, Katonah, NY, Mus. A., 1992)

WILLIAM C. KETCHUM JR

Tozzi, Mario (*b* Fossombrone, Pesaro, 30 Oct 1895; *d* Saint Jean-du-Gard, Provence, 8 Sept 1979). Italian painter. From 1913 he was a student at the Accademia di Belle Arti in Bologna, where he was taught by the Italian painters Augusto Majani (*b* 1867) and Aleardo Terzi (1870–1943). His fellow students included Giorgio Morandi and Osvaldo Licini. In 1919, after fighting at the front during World War I, he married a French woman and moved to Paris. In 1922 he exhibited at the Salon d'Automne and in 1923 at the Salon des Indépendants. He appears at this date to have been fully integrated in the Parisian art world and in particular with the group that met at the Café du Dôme, which included Massimo Campigli, Alberto Giacometti, Amédée Ozenfant, Le Corbusier, Alberto Magnelli, Ossip Zadkine, Max Jacob and Leonor Fini.

Tozzi's contact with Purism in France helped him to define the terms of an artistic language that was to remain fairly coherent throughout the years that followed. He was concerned with a lucid and rational expression of plasticity and the multiplication of perspective planes, with the aim of creating a sort of parallel universe that fuses in an original way two major artistic currents of the time: metaphysics and classicism.

From 1924 Tozzi began again to exhibit in Italy, at the Venice Biennale and at the *Mostra di venti artisti italiani* organized by Ugo Ojetti at the Galleria Pesaro in Milan. He also participated in the activities of the Novecento Italiano, and together with the French art critic Waldemar George he organized the activity of the Italiani di Parigi, with shows in 1928 at the Salon d'Escalier in Paris and in 1930 at the Galleria Barbaroux in Milan and the Venice Biennale. As part of an attempt to strengthen artistic ties between Italy and France, he wrote an article published in *Italia letteraria* (3 Feb 1929) and in 1932 helped organize an exhibition, *22 artisti italiani moderni*, at the Galerie Georges Bernheim in Paris. Tozzi showed his own work in Italy at a one-man show held at the Galleria Sabatello in Rome in 1934, and he was awarded a prize at the second Quadriennale, held in Rome in 1935. Between 1935 and 1938 he worked in Rome and Milan, where among other things he painted frescoes; in 1942 he went to live in Suna, on Lake Maggiore. World War II and the profound changes that followed in its wake left Tozzi in a certain isolation, from which he did not emerge until after 1958. In 1961 he held an exhibition in the Galleria Annunciata in Milan, marking the beginning of a final period of serene activity.

BIBLIOGRAPHY

E. D'Ors: *Mario Tozzi* (Paris, 1932)

M. Pasquali, ed.: *Mario Tozzi* (Ferrara, Gal. Civ. A. Mod., 1984)

VALERIO RIVOSECCHI

Tozzo, il. *See* LARI, ANTONIO MARIA.

Traballesi, Giuliano (*b* Florence, 2 Nov 1727; *d* Milan, 14 Nov 1812). Italian painter and engraver. He trained in Florence with Agostino Veracini (1689–1762) and Francesco Conti (1681–1760), and studied architecture and stage design under Antonio Galli-Bibiena. His earliest known painting is a fresco of 1758: *Heavenly Father in Glory* in the Dominican church in Livorno. He enriched his art by the study of Correggio's works in Parma, and also those of Bolognese painters, making engravings (1764–7) after paintings by Guido Reni, Agostino Carracci, Annibale Carracci, Guercino and others. These were praised in 1765 by Pierre-Jean Mariette and were later collected in an album entitled *Venticinque quadri ai maestri eccellenti incisi da Giuliano Traballesi* (Milan, 1796).

In 1764 he won a competition at the Accademia di Belle Arti di Parma with the painting *Furius Camillus Liberating Rome from the Gallic Senones*, a work that is deeply influenced by the Bolognese tradition and by the Roman classicism of Nicolas Poussin. The success of this painting won Traballesi major commissions in his native Tuscany, where the transition from Rococo to Neo-classicism had been encouraged by the reforms initiated by Leopoldo II Habsburg-Lorraine when he became Grand Duke of Tuscany in 1765. The fresco of *Augustus Sacrificing to Celebrate the Peace of the Empire* (1769–70) in the salon of the Villa di Poggio Imperiale outside Florence retains a Rococo illusionistic framework, yet the bold perspectives, the narrow range of colours and the concretely realized figures anticipate the later development of his art in Tuscany. From this date he turned increasingly to the Roman art of Corrado Giaquinto and Gregorio Guglielmi, and to that of the Florentine Giovanni Domenico Ferretti. On the cupola of the Sanctuary of Montenero he painted the boldly illusionistic *Virgin in Glory* (1771–4). In 1772 he completed the vault fresco in S Maria della Misericordia, Siena, with scenes from the *Life of the Virgin* in four medallions framed in feigned stucco, and in the same year he decorated a bay of a corridor in the Uffizi with an *Allegory of Philosophy*. Another significant Florentine work is the fresco of *Venus Interceding with Jove for Aeneas* in Palazzo Montauti Niccolini. The last dated work of his Florentine period was the airy and expansive decoration (1775) of the vault of the oratory of S Firenze with the *Assumption of the Virgin*.

In 1775 Traballesi was summoned to Milan to collaborate with the Neo-classical architect Giuseppe Piermarini, and from 1775 to 1807 he was Professore del Disegno at the newly established Accademia di Brera, where Andrea Appiani was one of his pupils. He also frescoed (1778–80) the new salons of the Palazzo Arciducale (now known as the Palazzo Reale), where Piermarini was the architect, with *Aurora Fleeing the Night*, *Jove's Repose*, *Cupid and Psyche* and the *Triumph of Hygeia* (all destr. 1943). Sketches and a preparatory drawing (Milan, Brera; Milan, Ambrosiana; Milan, Castello Sforzesco) survive for these frescoes.

Traballesi's frescoes at the palazzi Fontana–Silvestri (where he collaborated with Appiani), Negroni-Prata and Moriggia have also been destroyed. The large fresco of *Juno Commanding Aeolus to Destroy Aeneas's Fleet* (1784; Milan, Pal. Serbelloni) is known through an engraving made by Traballesi in 1794. The surviving pictorial evidence suggests that Traballesi's Milan frescoes lost the airy and luminous qualities of his Tuscan works and were characterized by a compositional rigidity influenced by Neo-classical doctrine. Such rigidity is certainly evident in his only known large Milanese work on a religious subject, the canvas of the *Assumption* (Milan, S Gottardo al Palazzo). As to the feigned low reliefs of mythological subjects in Neo-classical style that formed part of his decoration of palazzi, all that remains is a set of four overdoors from the Casa Silvestri (later Palazzo Fontana-Silvestri; Milan, priv. col., see Bandera Viani, pp. 184–5). Traballesi's smaller paintings include the *Transfiguration* (1801; Rome, priv. col., see Bandera Viani, p. 183) on copper and the *Self-portrait* (Milan, Brera).

Traballesi's many drawings are mainly in Florence (Uffizi) and Milan. Noteworthy among them are two versions of the *Adoration of the Shepherds*, one dated 1794 (Milan, Castello Sforzesca) and the other (Washington, DC, N.G.A.) probably of a later date, in which the religious theme is rendered in a classical language with rich chiaroscuro effects.

BIBLIOGRAPHY

Bolaffi; Thieme–Becker
G. Gori Gandellini: *Notizie istoriche degl'intagliatori* (Siena, 1771), iii, pp. 315–18
C. Bianconi: *Nuova guida di Milano* (Milan, 1787)
G. Rosa and F. Reggieri: *La Casa Silvestri* (Milan, 1962)
Painting in Italy in the 18th Century: Rococo to Romanticism (exh. cat., ed. J. Maxon and J. J. Rishel; Chicago, IL, A. Inst.; Minneapolis, MN, Inst. A.; Toledo, OH, Mus. A.; 1970–71)
O. Panichi: 'Il rinnovamento dell'architettura e della decorazione a Firenze nell'età leopoldina', *Actes du colloque: Florence et la France, 1977*, pp. 15–38
M. C. Bandera Viani: 'Profilo di Giuliano Traballesi', *A. Crist.*, lxxvi/725, pp. 119–38; lxxvi/726 (1988), pp. 117–96
S. Coppa: 'Giuliano Traballesi', *La pittura in Italia: Il settecento*, ed. M. Gregori and E. Schleier (Milan, 1989, rev. 1990), ii, p. 883 [with bibliog.]
Settecento lombardo (exh. cat., ed. R. Bossaglia and V. Terraroli; Milan, Pal. Reale, 1991), pp. 236–8 [by A. Guarnaschelli]

MARIA CRISTINA BANDERA VIANI

Trabeated construction [post and lintel]. Structural system based on the use of columns or posts and beams. It contrasts with arcuated construction, involving the use of arches and vaults. Trabeated construction is an inherent characteristic of framed structures, from the traditional timber-framed architecture of China and Japan to steel-framed buildings of the 20th century. It played a particularly important role in the architecture of ancient Greece, where it was directly related to the development of the architectural orders, a system in which the columns surrounding temples and other public buildings were surmounted by an entablature formed by rectangular architrave blocks, a frieze and cornice (*see* ORDERS, ARCHITECTURAL, §I and fig. 1; *see also* GREECE, ANCIENT, fig. 2). The Temple of Hephaistos in Athens, the best preserved of all Doric temples, illustrates its principles (see fig.). It was also the usual type of structure in the architecture of both ancient Egypt and southern Arabia, where columns or piers were crowned by rectangular blocks (*see* EGYPT, ANCIENT, §VIII and ARABIA, PRE-ISLAMIC, §II); in ancient Roman architecture, however, extensive use was made of arches and vaults, and in such buildings as the Colosseum, Rome (*see* ROME, ANCIENT, fig. 28), the trabeated system of the architectural orders was used only as a means of articulation for an essentially arcuated structure.

In Greek architecture the use of the trabeated system was appropriate to the local limestone, as in the temples of Hera and Zeus at Olympia, or later to marble, as in the Parthenon and Erechtheion on the Acropolis at Athens. It also reflected an approach to architecture in which there was no break between structure and appearance: loads were clearly carried by carefully proportioned columns and rectangular entablature blocks, while non-structural and other architectural elements, including pilasters, were rarely introduced. The plans of buildings were usually rectangular to fit the principles of trabeated construction, and the use of arches in Greek architecture above ground was rare, although examples exist in the entrance to the

Trabeated construction of the Temple of Hephaistos, Athens, *c.* 450–*c.* 445 BC

stadium at Olympia and the entrance to the agora at Priene. Roman architecture was liberated from this essentially rectangular style by its use of arches and vaulting.

The Classical style of trabeated construction was revived in the Renaissance and after, for example in such colonnaded buildings as the circular Tempietto di S Pietro in Montorio (after 1502), Rome (*see* BRAMANTE, DONATO, fig. 4), and in Neo-classical and Greek Revival architecture, and it was echoed in the innumerable buildings that were articulated by the architectural orders in the Roman manner.

BIBLIOGRAPHY

J. Summerson: *The Classical Language of Architecture* (London, 1963, rev. 1980)

D. S. Robertson: *A Handbook of Greek and Roman Architecture* (Cambridge, 1929, rev. 2/1943); repr. as *Greek and Roman Architecture* (London, 1969)

A. W. Lawrence: *Greek Architecture*, Pelican Hist. A. (Harmondsworth, 1957, rev. 4/1983)

A. Boëthius: *Etruscan and Early Roman Architecture*, Pelican Hist. A. (Harmondsworth, 1978)

J. B. Ward-Perkins: *Roman Imperial Architecture*, Pelican Hist. A. (Harmondsworth, 1981)

MARGARET LYTTELTON

Trabzon. *See* TREBIZOND.

Tracery. Stone framework to hold sheets of glass in place within a window opening. Tracery is a particularly characteristic feature of Gothic architecture, appearing first in the late 12th century as a means of creating enlarged window openings. The term is derived from the stage in the construction process in which a window pattern was traced out on a bed of plaster laid on a tracing floor (*see* TRACING FLOOR, TRACING HOUSE), as can still be seen at York Minster (*see* YORK, §III, 1(i)). Individual tracery bars were then cut and laid in position on this surface before being inserted into the window-frame. By the early 13th century the patterns created for windows were extended

to decorating wall surfaces. Construction techniques were perfected by *c.* 1230, allowing architects to concentrate on developing increasingly complex patterns. Tracery remained in widespread use until the end of the 16th century. Though initially and primarily a technique in stone, it also appeared in wood in medieval domestic buildings and even in iron during the 19th century.

1. History. 2. Types.

1. HISTORY. From the mid-12th century architects in northern France sought ways to increase the size of church windows, initially grouping a number of individual windows in each bay, a solution that was succeeded by the most primitive form of tracery, plate tracery (*see* §2(i) below). This was applied equally to the windows of standard bays and to rose windows, both of which expanded in size as a result. Owing to the simplicity of its construction, however, relatively few patterns could be created. The invention of bar tracery (*see* §2(ii) below) at Reims Cathedral between 1210 and 1220 was the key development in the evolution of tracery. Bar tracery enabled both larger and more complex windows to be designed using a system of long, thin stone bars to create the pattern. The principles of bar tracery construction were perfected in northern France *c.* 1230, as a result of which windows increased in size, the number of lights into which they could be divided grew, and the forms in the heads of the window openings became more complex. An unforeseen effect was that by the mid-13th century the architecture of northern France had begun to evolve to provide a more suitable framework for these elaborate tracery patterns. As the fashion spread to other countries, the architecture similarly evolved to accord with developments in tracery.

Tracery designs in the 13th century were based on a range of relatively simple geometric forms; but in the 14th century experiments in pattern-making became one of the principal preoccupations of architects throughout Europe. By the early 14th century the centre of tracery development had shifted to England, where first curvilinear and later Perpendicular forms were invented. Flamboyant tracery, in many essentials similar to some earlier English curvilinear tracery, first appeared in France during the last quarter of the 14th century. In Germany from the later 13th century onwards tracery design was concerned mainly with the use of relatively stark geometrical forms; from the mid-14th century the PARLER family were developing more complicated forms, and by the 15th century patterns similar to the latest French and English designs had appeared. In the 16th century new tracery forms developed to accord with the appearance of Renaissance architectural forms.

2. TYPES.

(i) Plate. (ii) Bar. (iii) Blind.

(i) Plate. The simplest form of tracery (see fig. 1), in which the pattern is constructed in masonry blocks similar in height to the courses of the wall surrounding the window. Its simplicity of construction permitted the creation of two- or three-light windows with one or three oculi or small multifoiled forms in the head of the window opening.

1. Plate tracery in the rose window of the west façade of Chartres Cathedral, *c.* 1205

Rose window designs were limited to accumulations of oculi, multifoiled forms or simple arcades, but always with a large amount of masonry between the openings.

Plate tracery first appeared in northern France for the construction of rose windows, the north transept rose of Laon Cathedral (probably 1170s) being the earliest surviving example. By the 1190s plate tracery was used for windows in standard bays (e.g. the cathedrals of Laon and Chartres). It spread throughout Europe in the first half of the 13th century, but was superseded by bar tracery techniques in northern France in the 1220s and in England after 1245. When plate tracery appeared after the middle of the 13th century it was usually confined to lesser ecclesiastical or domestic structures.

(ii) Bar.

Curvilinear [Flowing]. Tracery with patterns based on the OGEE (reversed) curve, which gives unbroken, sinuous lines (see fig. 2a). It developed *c.* 1300 in England, where it was the most popular form until *c.* 1350. In a curvilinear window the vesica (a bladder shape) defines the larger divisions of the window head, which are filled with patterns based on modifications of the forms of geometric tracery (see below): the mouchette (dagger), a directional shape, and the squashed, foiled soufflet.

Curvilinear tracery developed from reticulated (see below). Although adopted all over England (and eventually the British Isles), it was especially popular in the north and east. Patterns were devised for windows with both even and odd numbers of lights. The most distinctive patterns were those based on foliate designs, such as the four-petal flowers of East Anglia (the cathedrals of Ely and Norwich, 1320s; and associated buildings) and the leafstem designs of Lincoln and Yorkshire (Lincoln Cathedral, south transept, *c.* 1330; York Minster, west window, *c.* 1335; and associated buildings). Curvilinear tracery was commonly used on tombs and screens, such as at Beverley Minster (*c.* 1340; *see* BEVERLEY MINSTER, §2).

Curvilinear motifs were not established in continental Europe until the late 14th century: their use developed in France perhaps as a result of contacts with the earlier English designs. The tomb of *Archbishop Guy d'Auvergne* (*d* 1373) and two of the nave chapels of Amiens Cathedral (*c.* 1375) are the earliest examples of tracery using flowing lines rather than the stricter geometric forms. Curvilinear tracery was designed for Prague Cathedral by the Parler family (e.g. the south transept, upper levels, *c.* 1400) and continued in use on the Continent into the 16th century (Freiburg im Breisgau Minster, choir chapels, 1518–24). The mouchette-wheel motif was especially popular (Bamberg Cathedral, west choir-stalls, *c.* 1390). Curvilinear tracery should be distinguished from the Flamboyant style that developed from it in France (see below).

Fan. Tracery applied as surface ornament to the cone of a fan vault (see fig. 2b; *see also* VAULT: FAN). A series of rectilinear tracery panels follows the shape of the cone from the base, each panel dividing until the top of the cone is reached. Flattened out, the visual effect is fanlike. Primarily an English form, fan tracery is mostly coterminous with fan vaulting, that is from *c.* 1360 to the 16th century, with some notable revival in 17th-century Oxford

(Christ Church, staircase to the hall, 1640). It was also popular in 18th-century Gothick decoration (Strawberry Hill, Twickenham, Gallery, 1761–3) and in the Gothic Revival (St George's Cathedral, London, Petre Chantry, 1848–9). The earliest surviving fan tracery is painted on the tomb canopy (*c.* 1360) of *Hugh, Lord Despenser* in Tewkesbury Abbey (Glos), but the earliest certain stone forms are in the Trinity Chapel (after 1375), Tewkesbury, and the cloister of Gloucester Cathedral (after 1381; *see* GLOUCESTER, §1).

Flamboyant. Form in which the pattern is drawn using sinuous ogee curves to create a series of flame-shaped panels (see fig. 2c). It was the dominant tracery form in France from the late 14th century until the 16th. Before then tracery in France was composed of a series of clear, relatively simple geometric forms in the head of a window opening and a series of distinct lights below. Some Flamboyant tracery designs, especially earlier ones, retain the hierarchical arrangement of geometric tracery but employ the new motifs of the style, the curvilinear soufflets and mouchettes. However, in much Flamboyant tracery this was often rejected in favour of a net of soufflets and mouchettes of equal size and status. This treatment was applied to blind tracery and arcades as well as to rose windows and the windows of standard bays. As Flamboyant tracery developed, the forms became more fluid (as at St Maclou, Rouen, 1436; *see* ROUEN, §IV, 3), while in the 16th century mouchettes and soufflets were sometimes combined with Renaissance motifs.

For illustration *see* FLAMBOYANT STYLE.

Flowing. See Curvilinear above.

Geometric. The simplest form of bar tracery (see fig. 2d), which was named from the small range of simple geometric forms used in the tracery pattern. The window heads are filled with patterns of oculi, multifoiled forms, squares with curved sides or curved triangles. It was invented at Reims Cathedral after 1210 (*see* REIMS, §IV, 1(i)) and was the dominant tracery form in France until the late 14th century. It had spread throughout Europe by the middle of the 13th century and remained in use in England until the early 14th and elsewhere even into the 15th. Geometric tracery was developed particularly for the windows of standard bays, but from Reims onwards an allied technique was developed to create blind tracery (*see* §(iii) below). From the 1220s rose windows were built in geometric bar tracery. The earliest geometric windows had heads filled with single oculi perhaps containing a multifoiled form. By 1230 larger windows had appeared with more complicated patterns. Multifoiled forms free of ocular frames, which first appeared in triforia in the 1220s, were found in tracery windows by 1240. The curved triangle first appeared in French and English tracery patterns from *c.* 1250 (e.g. Paris, Sainte-Chapelle; *see* PARIS, §V, 2(i)), while the square with curved sides was in use by *c.* 1300 (e.g. Howden, N. Humberside, St Peter's). These forms became a particular preoccupation of German architects in the 14th century (e.g. Oppenheim, Katharinenkirche, *c.* 1360).

2. Bar tracery: (a) curvilinear, St Botolph, Boston, Lincolnshire, *c.* 1340; (b) fan, Henry VII's Chapel, Westminster Abbey, London, 1503–9; (c) Flamboyant, St Jean, Caen, after 1417; (d) geometric, Amiens Cathedral, *c.* 1230; (e) intersecting, Exeter Cathedral, *c.* 1310; (f) Kentish, St Mary, Chartham, Kent, *c.* 1296; (g) rectilinear, King's College Chapel, Cambridge, 1446–1515; (h) reticulated, All Saints, Faringdon, Berkshire, 1320

Intersecting. Form of Y-tracery (see below) used in multi-light windows, in which each mullion divides into curves struck on the same radii as the window opening, and the tracery head is made up of intersecting curves (see fig. 2e). Most often found in Britain, Germany and Scandinavia, the earliest surviving example is the north window of the chapel of the Nine Altars (*c.* 1280), Durham Cathedral. Foiled motifs sometimes filled the interstices, as in the east window of St Etheldreda (1284–6), Holborn, London. Intersecting tracery survived into the 15th century in Ireland (Limerick Cathedral, *c.* 1450), and had a long life in continental Europe (Essen, Collegiate Church, *c.* 1375), but it died out in England *c.* 1340.

Kentish. Tracery in which the main motif, a trilobe or quadrilobe, has spikes between the lobes in the form of elongated split cusps (see fig. 2f). The spiked quatrefoil was a ubiquitous decorative device in medieval Europe, found on relief sculpture, in metalwork and in painting. Traceable in France to at least *c.* 1190 in the stained glass of Sens Cathedral, lobed motifs appeared early in Islamic art (Fustat, Egypt, *c.* 900; Tlemcen, Algeria, Great Mosque, *c.* 1136). The form developed in tracery in England, apparently in Kent: the earliest surviving example of true Kentish tracery is on the tomb of *Bishop Bradfield* (*c.* 1283) in Rochester Cathedral. It appeared *c.* 1294 at St Mary, Chartham, and as late as *c.* 1336 in St Anselm's Chapel, Canterbury Cathedral. The design is also found in northern England (Kirkham Priory, N. Yorks, gate-house, *c.* 1296).

Rectilinear. Tracery made up of oblong or rectilinear panels, usually cusped at the top corners (see fig. 2g). Adumbrated in large transomed windows about the middle of the 13th century (e.g. Saint-Martin-aux-Bois, France, after 1245), it was used blind to decorate wall surfaces in Rayonnant architecture (e.g. Saint-Germer-de-Fly, France, Lady Chapel, *c.* 1260). In England a form of it appeared in the lower chapel of St Stephen's, Palace of Westminster (*c.* 1292–7; *see* LONDON, §V, 3(i)(a)), and related works; in a mature form it came to define Perpendicular architecture, with which it is particularly associated (e.g. as surface decoration in Gloucester Cathedral choir, after 1337; *see* GLOUCESTER, §1). It flourished all over Europe in both ecclesiastical and secular buildings until Gothic designs ceased to be made.

Reticulated. The earliest form of curvilinear tracery (see above), made up of linked ogival quatrefoils (soufflets) giving an effect of netting (see fig. 2h). It appears in a bay of Westminster Abbey cloister, which was rebuilt after the fire of 1298, and on the shrine of St Alban in St Alban's Cathedral, *c.* 1305–8. It flourished all over Britain until the late 14th century, surviving into the 15th in Ireland (Sligo, Dominican friary, after 1414); it was not very popular elsewhere.

Y-tracery. Tracery in which a single mullion splits to form a Y-shape in the window head. Used in triforium designs at Whitby Abbey (*c.* 1200) and Bayeux Cathedral (*c.* 1230), it is first found in windows in the nave chapels of Lincoln Cathedral (*c.* 1230s; *see* LINCOLN, §2(i)). Some form of it may also have been used at Lincoln in the great west window (*c.* 1240; replaced 15th century). Its developed form is intersecting tracery (see above).

(iii) Blind. Term used to describe tracery applied to blank surfaces rather than glazed areas. It was first used decoratively on a large scale in French Rayonnant buildings (Reims, St Nicaise, façade, after 1231, *see* REIMS, §IV, 2; Amiens Cathedral, transepts, before 1269) and was thereafter ubiquitous in medieval Europe, decorating architecture, monumental sculpture, metalwork and carpentry.

BIBLIOGRAPHY
E. Sharpe: *Decorated Windows*, 2 vols (London, 1849)
E. A. Freeman: *An Essay on the Origin and Development of Window Tracery in England* (London, 1851)
L. Behling: *Gestalt und Geschichte des Masswerkes* (Halle, 1944)
H. G. Leask: *Medieval Gothic: The Last Phases* (1960), iii of *Irish Churches and Monastic Buildings* (Dundalk, 1955–60/*R* 1971)
D. Etherton: 'The Morphology of Flowing Tracery', *Archit. Rev.* [London], cxxxviii (1965), pp. 172–80
S. Marks: *A School of Kentish Tracery* (diss., U. London, 1967)
R. Sanfaçon: *L'Architecture flamboyante en France* (Laval, 1971)
N. Coldstream: *The Development of Flowing Tracery in Yorkshire, 1300–70* (diss., U. London, 1973)
G. Russell: *Decorated Tracery in the London Basin* (diss., U. London, 1973)
R. Fawcett: 'Sutton in the Isle of Ely and its Architectural Context', *Medieval Art and Architecture at Ely Cathedral: British Archaeological Association Conference Transactions: Ely, 1976*, ii, pp. 78–96
Die Parler und der Schöne Stil, 1350–1400: Europäische Kunst unter den Luxemburgern (exh. cat., ed. A. Legner; Cologne, Schnütgen-Mus., 1978)
J. Bony: *The English Decorated Style* (Oxford, 1979)
W. Leedy: *Fan Vaulting* (London, 1980)
ALLAN M. BRODIE, NICOLA COLDSTREAM

Trachtenbuch. *See* FASHION PLATE AND COSTUME BOOK.

Tracing. Practice of transferring an image from a drawing on to a support (canvas, wood, board, metal etc) or from a finished image to a copy by working over the outlines with a pen, pencil or stylus. One method of tracing is to rub the *verso* or back of the drawing with a soft-leaded pencil or coloured chalk. The drawing is then placed against the support, face up, and the contours of the original drawing are traced using a pencil or stylus (for illustration *see* STYLUS). If required, the traced image on the new support can be reinforced by drawing over it again, though a faint outline is often sufficient.

If the artist wishes to preserve the original drawing from the damage caused by this direct method of tracing, a second drawing may be made using 'tracing paper' to record the main outlines of the original work. The tracing paper version is then lightly rubbed on the back with a soft pencil or coloured chalk and its outlines are then transferred to the new support. A tracing taken from an original drawing can also be used to enlarge or reduce the design by SQUARING UP or to reverse the image by turning it over and redrawing it from behind. This is usually done by holding the sheet up to the light and laying it flat against a transparent surface, such as a pane of glass.

Before the 1820s tracing papers were usually made from gelatine (e.g. fish size brushed and peeled off a marble slab once it dried) or by impregnating a fine, smooth white rag paper with various oils (e.g. linseed) and resins until it became transparent, but the result was not entirely satisfactory. Good tracing paper must be semi-transparent, smooth and free from knots, patterns or irregularities and this was possible only after the introduction of machine-made paper. In the 19th century tracing paper became an

Traced design by Raymond McGrath: *Fisher's Restaurant and Long Bar, New Bond Street, London*, pencil, coloured crayon and gouache on tracing paper, 270×335 mm, 1932 (London, Victoria and Albert Museum)

increasingly useful material for artists, designers, architects and engineers, since it was the most straightforward and accurate technique available for reproducing drawings and designs until photographic copying processes came into use. Moreover, with the development of these photographic reproductive methods, tracing became even more important. A full-sized copy of a drawing could be made quickly by sandwiching a layer of sensitized paper below a tracing and exposing it to light, thus allowing many copies to be made from one master copy.

A wide range of materials can be used on tracing paper, including pencil, crayon, coloured inks, watercolour, gouache (see fig.) and various stamp forms (e.g. oil- and water-based red, blue and black ink stamps and those produced by embossing and sealing wax). Because of their utilitarian purpose, tracings are usually subjected to considerable wear and tear, and this, combined with the effects of the impregnation materials and the methods of giving the paper its translucency, makes them discolour and become brittle on ageing.

BIBLIOGRAPHY

C. Cennini: *Il libro dell'arte* (c. 1390); Eng. trans. and notes by D. V. Thompson jr as *The Craftsman's Handbook: 'Il libro dell'arte'* (New Haven, 1933/R New York, 1954), pp. 13 and 14

J. Watrous: *The Craft of Old Master Drawings* (Madison, WI, 1957)

The Art of the Engineer: Two Hundred Years in the Development of Drawings for Design of Transport on Land, Sea and Air (exh. cat. by K. Baynes and F. Pugh, Cardiff, Welsh A.C., 1978)

J. Stephenson: *The Materials and Techniques of Painting* (London, 1989)

SHIRLEY MILLIDGE

Tracing floor. Area on a building site where full-scale drawings of architectural details to be used in construction were laid out. Such spaces proliferated in Europe during the late 13th century and early 14th, although they probably existed earlier, and were sometimes located within tracing houses set aside for the purpose. They must once have been more common than the few remaining and recorded examples indicate. Some tracing houses, such as those at York and Strasbourg, lasted into the 16th and 17th centuries. They were practical in function and directly connected with the building process. The exact location, character and use of tracing floors and tracing houses varied. Tracing houses, such as those of York Minster, Wells Cathedral and the vanished tracing house at Strasbourg, were separate spaces in the building; they functioned as design 'offices' and storage facilities and were used over long periods. Continuity of use may explain why the tracing floors in these houses were composed of reusable plaster, which could be smoothed over, leaving a clean, fresh surface on which master masons could work out details of mullions, tracery, ribs and mouldings. Mazes of overlapping lines remaining on the floors attest to their continuous use and to the dependence on grids and geometry in the laying out of the designs.

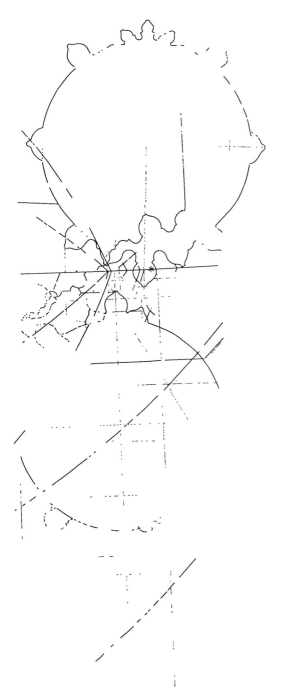

Tracing floor showing plans for piers and attached mouldings, Narbonne Cathedral, axial chapel, late 13th century

In contrast to the floors of the tracing houses, tracing floors such as those at the cathedrals of Limoges, Narbonne (see fig.), Clermont-Ferrand, Soissons, Troyes and Orléans were not necessarily intended for prolonged use. Although the designs occasionally overlap, indicating that a particular floor was used for several years, in general the floors were abandoned when the particular portion of the building in which they were located was put into service. They are frequently (although not always) found in the vicinity of the details depicted in the drawings and are located in aisles, chapels and towers, and on terraces above aisles, chapels and ambulatory vaults. Sharp instruments were used to incise patterns for ribs, mouldings, piers, tracery, arches and flying buttresses into the paving stones as permanent references for design control during the building's construction. These drawings also served as references for masons during a master's absence or provided evidence of the original design for subsequent masters.

Tracing floor and tracing house drawings were full-scale and two-dimensional. Tracery details, mouldings, arches, pier sections and even buttresses and portals were represented by outlines that provided the main dimensions but not specific ornamental details. Occasionally, as at Narbonne and Soissons, secondary lines indicate the projection of a sloping plane, but only very simply. Drawings for mouldings, ribs, piers and splays were horizontal, not vertical, in section; the sections must have been used in the preparation of templates. Full-scale drawings of arches, tracery, portals and flying buttresses were used to work out the proportions of the architectural elements and to visualize their final form, as cartoons for checking the alignment of cut stones before positioning and as guides in the fabrication of centering.

The development of tracing floors corresponded to the increasing complexity of the design process, of architectural detail and of the structures themselves; also to a general increase in the use of architectural drawings. They are related to wall and parchment drawings but must be distinguished from them. Although wall drawings may have been used in the design of templates, more frequently they must represent preparatory sketches. Drawings on parchment tended to be presentation drawings, preparatory sketches, a means of recording design and construction methods or a way of visually documenting observations and ideas. Tracing floor and tracing house drawings were, on the one hand, building aids actually used in the construction process and, on the other, the primary method by which medieval masters formulated and transmitted ideas to their masons before the use of scaled drawings was widespread.

BIBLIOGRAPHY

F. de Verneilh: 'Construction des monuments ogivaux: Épures de la cathédrale de Limoges', *An. Archéol.*, vi (1847), pp. 139–44

O. Kletzl: *Plan-Fragmente aus der deutschen Dombauhütte von Prag in Stuttgart und Ulm*, Veröffentlichungen des Archives der Stadt Stuttgart, iii (Stuttgart, 1939), p. 9

R. Branner: 'Villard de Honnecourt, Reims and the Origin of Gothic Architectural Drawing', *Gaz. B.-A.*, lxi (1963), pp. 129–46

J. Harvey: 'The Tracing Floor in York Minster', *Fortieth Annual Report of the Friends of York Minster* (York, 1968) pp. 9–13

C. Barnes: 'The Gothic Architectural Engravings in the Cathedral of Soissons', *Speculum*, xlvii (1972), pp. 60–64

L. S. Colchester and J. H. Harvey: 'Wells Cathedral. Appendix: The Wells Tracing Floor', *Archaeol. J.*, cxxxi (1974), pp. 209–14

F. Bucher: 'A Rediscovered Tracing by Villard de Honnecourt', *A. Bull.*, lix (1977), pp. 315–19

J.-C. Bessac: 'Tracés et épures gravés dans l'ancienne cathédrale Saint-Just de Narbonne (Aude)', *Actes du colloque international de glyptographie de Cambrai: Cambrai, 1985*, pp. 35–51

VIVIAN PAUL

Tradescant. English family of gardeners and collectors. John Tradescant the elder (*b* London, 1590s; *d* Lambeth, 1638) was gardener in turn to Robert Cecil, 1st Earl of Salisbury, Edward, 1st Baron Wotton (1548–1626), George Villiers, 1st Duke of Buckingham, and Charles I. In 1611 he travelled in France and the Low Countries, collecting plants for Salisbury; it was probably on this journey that he also began to collect 'curiosities'. In June 1618 he travelled to Russia in the suite of Sir Dudley Digges (1583–1639), the Ambassador to Russia, returning the following September; his diary of this voyage (Oxford, Ashmolean) records, *inter alia*, his acquisition of a coat from Greenland made of fish entrails. In 1626 Tradescant bought a house in South Lambeth where he established his renowned 'Closett of Rarities', enhanced by gifts from Charles I and Queen Henrietta Maria, Buckingham and William Laud, Archbishop of Canterbury. His son, John Tradescant the younger (*b* Meopham, Kent, 4 Aug 1608; *d* London, 22 April 1662), succeeded him as Keeper of the Royal Garden and custodian of the collection. In 1656, assisted by ELIAS ASHMOLE, he published the *Musaeum Tradescantianum*, the first printed catalogue of a British museum. After his death, Ashmole successfully disputed the ownership of the collection with Hester Tradescant, John's widow, and presented it to Oxford University, to which it was transferred in 1678, thereby immortalizing Ashmole's name rather than Tradescant's.

BIBLIOGRAPHY
M. Allan: *The Tradescants* (London, 1964)
A. Macgregor, ed.: *Tradescant's Rarities: Essays on the Foundation of the Ashmolean Museum, 1683* (Oxford, 1983)

DAVID RODGERS

Tragurio, Ioannes Stephani Duknovich de. *See* GIOVANNI DALMATA.

Traiectensis, Jacobus. *See* JACOB VAN UTRECHT.

Train, Eugène (*b* Toul, 1832; *d* Annecy, 1903). French architect. He came from a humble background, but through his talent as a draughtsman he secured a grant from the authorities at Nancy to study architecture in Paris at the Ecole des Beaux-Arts, which he entered in 1851. There he studied with Charles-Auguste Questel and Adolphe-Marie-François Jay (1789–1871), architect to the City of Paris and a teacher also at the Ecole de Dessin. When Jay left the Ecole de Dessin in 1853 he appointed Train as a tutor on his course, with particular responsibility for industrial design, and he later also made him his clerk of works. At the same time Train continued his studies and won second prize in the competition for the Prix de Rome in 1858.

In 1861 Train was recommended to Victor Baltard, Director of Public Works to the City of Paris, and worked on the church of St Augustin in the Boulevard Malesherbes, which Baltard began in 1862. On completing his training in 1863, Train married Baltard's niece, who was also the daughter of the architect Paul-Eugène Lequeux (1806–73), and thus joined one of the great architectural families in French history. That same year he was made chief architect to the 8th arrondissement in Paris. In this capacity, he designed one of his most important buildings, the Collège Chaptal (1866–76) in the Boulevard des Batignolles. Designed to accommodate 1000 students, the Collège was built around three courtyards, each reserved for a different age group and distinguished by varying motifs, materials and colours. It was particularly by using colours that Train sought to brighten the slightly austere late medieval and Renaissance formulae that the typology of French schools still demanded. Although slightly shocked by his lively use of colour, Train's contemporaries were unanimous in praising his candour in employing such materials as iron and ceramics, which had hitherto been used sparingly in schools. Train's Lycée Voltaire in the Avenue de la République, built a few years later, is similar but less radical. As well as building other schools in Paris, Train also developed a private practice, which brought him commissions for private houses, hotels and tombs. He also designed altars for several churches in Paris, including the Madeleine and St Philippe-du-Roule, and for St Joseph's Chapel in Baltard's church of St Augustin.

WRITINGS
'Etudes d'écoles', *Croquis Archit.*, v (1884), pp. 1–6; ix (1885), pp. 1–6

BIBLIOGRAPHY
P. Vauthier: 'Collège municipal Chaptal', *Rev. Gén. Archit.* (1878), col. 5–11, pls 3–9
F. Narjoux: *Paris: Edifices édifiés par la ville, 1850–1880* (Paris, 1883), ii, pp. 21–5
E. Rivoalen: 'L'Architecture moderne à l'Exposition Universelle'. *Constr. Mod.* (9 Nov 1889), pp. 49–50
J. Lovegrove: 'Eugène Train', *Architecture* (3 Oct 1903), pp. 377–8
——: *Amer. Architect*, 82 (1903), p. 26
L. Hautecoeur: *Architecture classique*, vii (Paris, 1957), pp. 372–5

MARIE-LAURE CROSNIER LECONTE

Traini, Francesco (*fl* 30 Aug 1321–15 Jan 1345). Italian painter and illuminator. He was the most accomplished Pisan artist in the second quarter of the 14th century, although his career is controversial. On 20 July and 23 August 1322 he was paid for painting the Palazzo Anziani in Pisa. On 2 December 1337 he took an apprentice, Giovanni, for a three-year period. Documents of 12 December 1340 and 19 February 1341 deal with a dispute over a banner Traini had painted for the confraternity of the Laudi of Pisa Cathedral. Only one signed and documented work survives: the altarpiece of *St Dominic* (1344–5; Pisa, Mus. N. & Civ. S Matteo; *see* DOMINICAN ORDER, fig. 2), painted for the Dominican church of S Caterina, Pisa.

Traini's work shows the impact of both Sienese and Florentine art, but so little is known about early 14th-century Pisan painting that it is impossible to assess his debt to the indigenous Pisan tradition. The earliest panel painting attributed to him is the damaged *Virgin and Child* in S Giusto in Cannicci, Pisa, which probably dates from the 1320s. An altarpiece of unusual subject-matter, originally containing *St Anne with the Virgin and Child* (Princeton U., NJ, A. Mus.; *see* fig.), a *St Paul* (Nancy, Mus. B.-A.) and a *St Gregory* (untraced), should be dated to the 1330s. Variations in quality between the *St Gregory*

Francesco Traini: *St Anne with the Virgin and Child*, tempera on panel, 870×690 mm, 1330s (Princeton, NJ, Princeton University, Art Museum)

and the *St Paul*, as well as the significant number of Pisan panels that show his influence, suggest that Traini maintained a large workshop or trained a series of apprentices.

Traini's influence on manuscript illumination is seen as early as 1326–7 in the miniatures of a Benedictine Breviary (Florence, Bib. Medicea–Laurenziana, MS. Strozzi 11), and the same artist was responsible for an Antiphonal (Pisa, Mus. N. & Civ. S Matteo, Antiphonal A). Traini and his shop illuminated a copy of Dante's *Inferno* (Chantilly, Mus. Condé, MS. 1424) *c.* 1328–30 for Lucano Spinola of Genoa. A number of Pisan manuscripts showing his influence have been identified (Dalli Regoli).

Although there is some disagreement among scholars about autograph and shop works, the principal controversy over Traini's career relates to the authorship of the frescoes in the Camposanto, Pisa: the *Thebaid*, the *Last Judgement* and the *Triumph of Death* on the south wall, and the adjoining *Passion* scenes on the east wall, all of which probably date from the mid-1330s. Their attribution to Traini was first made by Supino and subsequently argued by Meiss (1933) on the basis of stylistic comparisons with the altarpiece of *St Dominic*, the *St Anne with the Virgin and Child* in Princeton and the miniatures of the Chantilly *Inferno* and those of Antiphonal A (for alternative attribution *see* MASTERS, ANONYMOUS, AND MONOGRAMMISTS, §I: MASTER OF THE TRIUMPH OF DEATH).

Traini's miniatures in the Chantilly *Inferno* are of extraordinary narrative power and refined beauty. The *St Anne with the Virgin and Child*, a panel that may well have been known to Masaccio, shows a sophistication of conceit rivalling the best productions of Florence and Siena, while the pictorial effects and compositional subtlety of the altarpiece of *St Dominic* testify to the quality of the early 14th-century Pisan school.

Thieme–Becker
BIBLIOGRAPHY
I. B. Supino: 'Il trionfo della morte e il guidizio universale del camposanto di Pisa', *Archv Stor. A.*, vii (1894), pp. 21–40
G. Dalli Regoli: *Miniatura pisana del trecento* (Milan, 1963)
M. Meiss: *Francesco Traini*, ed. H. B. J. Maginnis (Washington, DC, 1983) [contains articles first pubd 1933, 1960, 1965 and 1971]
H. B. J. MAGINNIS

Trajan [Marcus Ulpius Trajanus], Emperor (*b* Italica, eastern Spain, AD 53; *reg* 98–117; *d* Selinus, Turkey, 117). Roman emperor and patron. He was the adopted son of Nerva, whom he succeeded. From AD 101 to 107 he conducted the two Dacian campaigns that are depicted in the spiral reliefs on the great column that bears his name (ded. AD 113; *see* ROME, §V, 7 and ROME, ANCIENT, fig. 76). It was erected as the crowning glory of the great Forum of Trajan, built between AD 107 and 113, which completed the vast urban complex of Imperial Fora (*see* ROME, §V, 2). Both the arch that marked its entrance and the Basilica Ulpia at its west end—the largest ever constructed in Rome—displayed a wealth of relief sculpture: a long frieze in high relief covered the attic of the basilica for its whole length, probably on all four sides of the building. On the slopes of the Quirinal Hill, which was cut to make room for the forum, Trajan built an extensive and articulated system of shops on two levels, culminating in the great hall (*c.* AD 100–12; *see* ROME, ANCIENT, §II, 2(i)(e) and fig. 30). The Markets of Trajan must have been planned together with the forum, and thus probably by the Emperor's military architect Apollodoros of Damascus. Among other major works completed were the Baths of Trajan on the Oppian Hill (ded. 109; *see* ROME, ANCIENT, §II, 1(i)(d)), the arch without reliefs that concluded the work on the port of Ancona (AD 115), and the arch at Benevento (*c.* AD 117), with its highly decorated reliefs. Indeed, relief sculpture above all other art forms reached new heights of achievement under Trajan (*see* ROME, ANCIENT, §IV, 2(v)).

BIBLIOGRAPHY
W. Gross: *Bildnisse Traianus* (Berlin, 1940)
P. Zanker: *Das Trajansforum als Monument imperialer Selbstdarstellung* (Berlin, 1970)
K. de Fine Licht: *Untersuchungen an den Trajansthermen zu Rom* (Copenhagen, 1974)
S. Settis and others: *La Colonna Traiana* (Turin, 1989)
LUCA LEONCINI

Tramello, Alessio (*b* Piacenza prov., before 1470; *d* Piacenza, *c.* 1528). Italian architect. He may have trained under Giovanni di Domenico Battagio, whose style was derived from Donato Bramante; Tramello's own monumental works belong to the same school. Two of his most impressive and original buildings are the Benedictine church of S Sisto (1499–?1511) and the Olivetan monastery of S Sepolcro (?1498–1510/11), both in Piacenza and

Alessio Tramello: S Sepolcro, Piacenza, interior of nave looking west, 1513

both erected by Tramello to his own designs. The Benedictines stipulated that he must respect the existing foundations of the medieval church of S Sisto and incorporate the eight granite columns (which now support the vaults of the nave and aisles) remaining from an earlier project of 1494. The church is a cruciform basilica with a barrel-vaulted nave of five bays flanked by aisles and outer chapels. The aisle bays are square and surmounted by domes; the arcade leading to the outer chapels is supported on cruciform piers, and each chapel consists of a straight bay with an apse. The main transept has apsed arms, but there is a second transept just behind the façade, with a central dome, and here the arms are planned as domed Greek crosses.

The Olivetan monastery of S Sepolcro has three features of particular interest: a three-aisled library, a secret passage (a covered walk parallel to the loggias of the cloisters) and its entrance (known as the 'House of the Commendatory Abbot'), which has an incomplete façade characterized by enormous lozenges and circles. The church of S Sepolcro was rebuilt by Tramello from 1513. Like S Sisto, it has a nave flanked by aisles and apsed outer chapels, but here the nave consists of two square groin-vaulted bays separated by narrow barrel-vaulted bays (see fig.). The square aisle bays behind the latter are domed. There is an apse at each end of the transept, as at S Sisto, and the use of piers without capitals in the main elevation, which stresses the verticality of the composition, was also foreshadowed in the earlier building.

Between 1502 and 1507 Tramello built the smaller court of Palazzo Landi in Piacenza. For the Olivetans he planned and built the church and monastery of the Annunziata (begun 1517; destr.) at Villanova near Lodi, Milan. In 1520–23 he erected the church of S Benedetto (or S Marco) in Piacenza, which in 1547 was incorporated in the pentagonal fortress (destr.) built for Pier Luigi Farnese, 1st Duke of Parma. It is likely that Tramello also built the church of S Benedetto (from 1527; destr.) in Crema, near Cremona, possibly to a design by Paolo Sacca (d 1537). Tramello's last surviving work, which he both designed and supervised, is the civic church of Piacenza, S Maria di Campagna (1522–6). The plan, in the form of a Greek cross, is developed from the scheme he used at S Sepolcro. A square, domed central bay is surrounded by pairs of shallower bays, with small domed square chapels at the corners. The exterior presents a strong contrast between the bare arms of the Greek cross and the complexity of the central lantern, with its two tiers of windows, and the four smaller lanterns of the corner chapels. The interior shows Tramello's ability to play the smaller spaces of the four chapels against the larger space of the Greek cross and to exploit the luminosity of the dome frescoed by Pordenone. One of the finest provincial architects of the Renaissance in Italy, Tramello was made syndic of the Guild of Builders of Piacenza (1508) and in 1527 received a special tribute from the city to which he had contributed so many palazzi and churches.

BIBLIOGRAPHY

Macmillan Enc. Architects
P. Gazzola: *Opere di Alessio Tramello architetto piacentino* (Rome, 1935)
J. Ganz: *Drei Sakralbauten in Piacenza und die oberitalienische Architektur um 1500* (Frauenfeld, 1968)
L. H. Heydenreich and W. Lotz: *Architecture in Italy, 1400–1600*, Pelican Hist. A. (Harmondsworth, 1974)
B. Adorni: *Alessio Tramello* [in preparation]

BRUNO ADORNI

Trani [Lat. Tirenum; Turenum]. Town in Puglia, south-eastern Italy. It was founded by the Romans, probably in the 3rd or 4th century AD, and became important as one of the principal outposts of the Roman Church in the south-east. Trani was ruled for a time by the Byzantines, and the Romanesque churches of S Andrea and S Francesco display Byzantine influence. Under the Normans from the late 11th century, the port became a flourishing commercial centre and an important embarkation point for the eastern Mediterranean. The town expanded with the settlement of colonies of merchants from Genoa, Pisa and Ravello. A number of fine churches date from the Romanesque period; most notable is the cathedral. Trani's greatest period of prosperity was under Frederick II, and for a time the town rivalled Bari in importance. The castle, begun under Frederick II, was remodelled in the 15th and 16th centuries. The town's decline began during the period of Angevin rule (1266–1435), and in 1481 it was devastated by the Turks. It is now an important centre of the wine trade.   □

1. CATHEDRAL. Dedicated to S Nicola Pellegrino, the cathedral was begun in 1099 on the site of the existing episcopal church, which enclosed the chapel of S Leucio. Construction started with the hall crypt, divided into bays by marble columns, to which the relics of the titular saint were translated in 1143. Over this a broad transept with three projecting apses was built in the first half of the 12th century. The nave was begun after the previous church was destroyed in the second half of the 12th century and completed in the late 13th. Its central vessel, divided from the aisles by twin columns supporting galleries, is raised over a longitudinal lower church, which is dedicated to St

Mary and opens to the exterior through a large arch in the two-storey façade. The latter was completed in the 13th century and joined to the campanile (begun by Nicolaus Sacerdos *c.* 1229 but finished in the late 14th century).

The rich sculptural decoration includes some fragments of marble church furniture from S Maria: the reused remains of a Byzantine pergola, fragments (an elephant) of an episcopal throne, three relief panels with fantastic animals and an archivolt from a tomb or ciborium typical of the orientalizing Apulian style of the 11th century (Trani, Mus. Dioc.).

The early 12th-century crypt capitals of S Nicola are based on Early Christian models but enriched with delicately carved human and animal masks. The magnificent main portal of the church dates from the end of the 12th century and frames the bronze doors (*c.* 1180) signed by BARISANUS OF TRANI. It is round-headed with a continuous moulding resting on crouching lions, surrounded by an archivolt with colonnettes supported by caryatids. Among the dense ornament on the inner face of the jamb are the prophets *Isaiah* and *Jeremiah* (right) and the *Sacrifice of Isaac, Jacob's Dream* and *Jacob Wrestling with the Angel* (left). Islamicizing elements are combined with forms that have suggested comparisons with sculpture in south-west France. A common source in Anglo-Norman manuscript illumination or ivories and connections with contemporary Dalmatian sculpture have also been proposed.

The 12th-century decoration of the rose window and of other windows opened in the façade and apse was partly modelled on that of the portal. Two monumental groups of figure sculpture of uncertain subject and the animal figures on the transept façades date from the time of Emperor Frederick II (*reg* 1219–50). In the second half of the 13th century, the transept, which is higher than the nave, was decorated with a heavy frieze of Late Antique inspiration, supported by figured Gothic corbels.

BIBLIOGRAPHY

C. Fiskovic: 'Fragments du style roman à Dubrovnik', *Archaeologia jugoslavico* (Belgrade, 1954), i, pp. 117–30

W. Kroenig: *Contributi all'architettura pugliese del medioevo: Atti del IX congresso nazionale per la storia dell'architettura: Bari, 1955*

R. Piracci: *Per il ripristino del ciborio e dell'ambone nel duomo di Trani* (Trani, 1958)

R. Mola: 'Scavi e ricerche sotto la cattedrale di Trani: Notizie dei ritrovamenti', *Vetera Christ.*, ix (1972), pp. 361–86

S. Schwedhelm: *Die Kathedrale S Nicola Pellegrino in Trani und ihre Vorgängerkirchen* (Berlin, 1972) [with bibliog.]

J. Raspi Serra: 'Presupposti ravennati nella prima decorazione del duomo di Trani', *Felix Ravenna* (1973), pp. 199–208

P. Belli d'Elia: *Alle sorgenti del romanico: Puglia XI secolo* (Bari, 1975, 2/1987)

M. D'Elia: 'A proposito della cattedrale di Trani', *Scritti di storia e d'arte pugliese in onore dell'Arc. Monsignor G. Carata* (Fasano, 1976), pp. 119–48

P. Belli d'Elia: 'Scultura pugliese di epoca sveva', *Atti III settimana di studi di storia dell'arte dell'Università di Roma: Federico II e l'arte del duecento italiano: Rome, 1978*, i, pp. 256–87

L. Pani Ermini: 'Rilievi altomedioevali nel Museo Diocesano di Trani', *Puglia Paleocrist.*, ed. A. Quacquarelli, iii (Bari, 1979), pp. 305–18

M. R. Salvatore: 'Un nuovo sarcofago paleocristiano rinvenuto a Trani', *Puglia Paleocrist.*, ed. A. Quacquarelli, iii (Bari, 1979), pp. 319–29

P. Belli D'Elia: 'Aggiunte tranesi al maestro della cattedra di Elia: Nuove precisazioni sul romanico pugliese', *Studi e ricerche di storia dell'arte in onore di L. Mallè* (Turin, 1980), pp. 49–60

M. S. Calò Mariani: 'La scultura in Puglia durante l'età sveva e protoangioina', *La Puglia tra Bisanzio e l'occidente*, ed. C. D. Fonseca (Milan, 1980), pp. 254–316 [with bibliog.]

——: 'Scultura pugliese del XII secolo: Protomagistri tranesi nei cantieri di Barletta, Trani, Bari e Ragusa', *Studi di storia dell'arte in memoria de M. Rotili* (Naples, 1984), pp. 177–91

T. Garton: *Early Romanesque Sculpture in Apulia* (New York, 1984)

B. Ronchi: *La cattedrale di Trani* (Fasano, 1986)

P. Belli d'Elia: *La Puglia*, Italia Romanica, viii (Milan, 1987), pp. 270–306

For further bibliography *see* ROMANESQUE, §III, 1(vi)(i), and BARISANUS OF TRANI.

PINA BELLI D'ELIA

Trani, Anseramo da. *See* ANSERAMO DA TRANI.

Tranquebar [Taramgambadi]. Town in Tamil Nadu, India. It was granted to the Danish East India Company in 1620 and held by them until its sale to the English East India Company in 1845. The earliest Danish building, Fort Dansborg (1620–21), a simple square structure with corner bastions, housed barracks, warehouses, a church and two-storey quarters for the governor, chaplain and merchants. The Indian township with its temples and mosque at first lay open; battlements and a moat were added piecemeal later in the 17th century and allowed a European exodus from the cramped fort. A plan of Tranquebar dated 1733 shows streets laid out on a grid plan, box-like houses with pitched roofs of country tiles, tree-filled squares, two churches and the commander's residence, a three-storey building with a blind arcaded ground floor, a first floor with a verandah and a top floor with a central dormer. Zion Church (1701), an oblong hall, has a square tower with a parapet, pinnacles, vaulted, Indian-style roofs, quoins and coupled pilasters setting off colour-washed walls. In 1718 Lutherans from Halle in Germany built New Jerusalem Church. Constructed on a Greek-cross plan, it has paired pilasters articulating the sides; the gable ends are enlivened with curving volutes and pinnacles, and there is a large cartouche over the west door. Late 18th-century prosperity enabled military engineers to adorn both fort and town with monumental gates. Many houses were refashioned in Neo-classical style with the addition of pillared verandahs and porticos, flat roofs and parapets: Governor Peter Anker (1788–1806) gave his house a double verandah with a bow-fronted centre. 'Correct' Tuscan pillars, meander friezes and dentil mouldings also appeared at this time. The 'Old Hospital', with its long façade of 11 windows articulated into bays by quoins whose verticals are echoed by the pillars and balcony colonnettes of a central portico, makes a very formal architectural statement.

BIBLIOGRAPHY

S. Nilsson: *European Architecture in India, 1750–1850* (London, 1968), pp. 47–63

Arkitekten [Copenhagen], xxiii (1979) [whole issue]

O. Feldbaek: 'The Development of an Indo-European Town in Mughal India: Tranquebar in the Seventeenth and Eighteenth Centuries', *Changing South Asia*, ed. K. Ballhatchet and D. Taylor (Hong Kong, 1984), pp. 11–20

J. B. HARRISON

Transept. Transverse structure, comparable in height and width with the nave, that crosses the main body of a church of basilican type. The most common position for the transept is at the choir, immediately to the west of the chancel, but transepts also occur at the western ends of naves.

The earliest type of transept is the continuous transept (see fig. (a)), first used at Old St Peter's (*c.* AD 319–29; *see* ROME, §V, 14(i)(a)). It consisted of a transverse space between the apse and the double-aisled nave, entered through a triumphal arch to the nave and through screened entrances corresponding to the four aisles. Its function was to create a separate area around the tomb of St Peter, which stood directly in front of the apse. A second continuous transept in Rome was built in imitation of St Peter's for S Paolo fuori le Mura (begun AD 385; rebuilt after 1823).

Varied attempts at transeptal arrangements with no common thread were made between the 4th and 6th centuries AD. Particularly worthy of mention is S Simpliciano (late 4th century), Milan, which has a long transept subsidiary to the nave. The Holy Apostles (now S Nazaro Maggiore; begun 382; rebuilt 11th century) in Milan has a prominent transept divided from the nave by colonnades. In both buildings the naves are only slightly longer than the transepts, and they tend towards the centralized plan. The same might be said about certain developments in Asia Minor: the church of St Babylas (begun 379) at Antioch consisted of four equal, aisleless arms converging on a central square tower (*see* ANTIOCH (i), §3). The 5th-century church of St John at Ephesos had a similar aisled arrangement, while the most sophisticated version survives in the ruined martyrium (*c.* 480–90) at Qal'at Sim'ān, Syria, around the column of St Simeon the Stylite.

Conventional basilicas with widely differing types of transept were constructed in the Near East. An aisled type at Abu Mina, Egypt, dedicated to St Menas, replaced an early 5th-century continuous transept *c.* 490. Basilica A (5th century) at Perge, Turkey, also had a short, continuous transept enveloped by aisles. Hagios Demetrios (mid-5th century) in Thessaloniki has a subsidiary transept (reconstructed) screened from the nave and with aisles on two sides (*see* THESSALONIKI, §III, 3(i)).

By the 6th century the independent culture and identity of the eastern Roman Empire was reflected in the gradual abandonment of the basilica in favour of centralized church plans. Developments in western Europe during the 6th and 7th centuries remain obscure, but the Carolingian *renovatio* of Constantinian imperial ideals is identifiable in architecture through the reference to Early Christian buildings in Rome, in particular Constantine the Great's St Peter's (*see* CAROLINGIAN ART, fig. 1). A continuous transept was built at Saint-Denis Abbey (*c.* 754–75; *see* SAINT-DENIS ABBEY, §I, 1), together with colonnades and aisles of the Early Christian basilican type. During the reign of Charlemagne the abbey church (now cathedral) at Fulda was extended (802–19) with an exact copy of the transept and apse of St Peter's. This was a deliberate association between the old Empire and new Roman Empire of Charlemagne. Under the Ottonian and Salian emperors the continuous transept, which was very obviously archaic, continued to be employed occasionally, for example at St Emmeram (1020s), Regensburg, and Hersfeld Abbey (1037).

Until the 11th century, however, the subsidiary or low transept (see fig. (b)) was the most common type. The transept arms were narrower and shorter than the nave, and the entrances into the nave were barely more than doorways. A good surviving example is Steinbach Abbey (consecrated 827), where small transept arms are entered from the nave through arches only slightly larger than those of the main arcades.

By the 11th century developments had already taken place that were to lead to the full integration of the transept into the architectural scheme of a church. This was achieved through the introduction of the crossing, which defines, through the introduction of one or two arches across the nave, the bay where the transept arms meet the nave. The final development of the transept and crossing is the regular crossing (see fig. (c)), wherein the transept arms are the same height and width as the nave, and the crossing is defined by four arches of equal height, normally supporting a tower. An early example is at St Michael (1010–33), Hildesheim, which has two identical transepts,

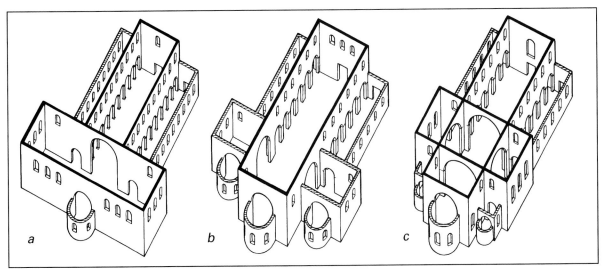

Transept types: (a) continuous; (b) low; (c) with a regular crossing

each with a crossing tower. The regular crossing proved one of the most important innovations of the Romanesque style and became a standard element in basilican church design.

In the valley of the River Meuse the low transept survived well into the 11th century, but it differs from its Carolingian precedents in that the crossing is introduced through the addition of a diaphragm arch defining the transept bay. The best examples of this type are in Belgium at St Hadelin (mid-11th century), Celles-les-Dinant, and Hastière-par-delà (1033–5), and in England at Holy Trinity (c. 1050), Great Paxton.

During the 11th and 12th centuries, with the increasing demand for altar space, transepts became more complex with the addition of chapels and the integration of aisles. Orléans Cathedral (early 11th century; destr. 1568) had aisles on at least the east and west sides of the transept. Surviving examples of aisles on all three sides of each transept arm can be seen at Santiago de Compostela (begun c. 1080) and Winchester Cathedral (begun 1079; see ENGLAND, fig. 2), and there are aisles on the east side alone at Durham Cathedral (1093–1133). At St Maria im Kapitol, Cologne, the transept arms are apsidal, forming a trefoil with the main apse, a design found in the 12th century at the cathedrals of Noyon, Soissons (see SOISSONS, §1) and Cambrai (destr.).

The double transept plan initiated at Cluny III in the late 11th century, with a second, eastern transept placed between the monks' choir and the presbytery (see CLUNIAC ORDER, §III, 1(ii)(a)), may have been devised to create a complete cruciform church east of the main crossing to accommodate large numbers of monks in some privacy. This was adopted elsewhere, notably at Canterbury Cathedral (see CANTERBURY, §III, 1), and the eastern transept became a feature of many great churches, especially in England. Sited sometimes at the upper entrances to the choir, for example at the cathedrals of Lincoln (see LINCOLN, §2(i)(a)) and Salisbury (see SALISBURY, §2(i)), or level with the high altar, for example at York Minster (see YORK, §III, 1(i)) and Worcester Cathedral (after 1218), they could also be associated with a great shrine, as at Beverley Minster. Their main purpose, however, seems to have been to provide extra space for altars following the requirement at the Fourth Lateran Council (1215) that a priest say mass every day.

From the 12th century attention was also directed to the decoration of transept façades, which, starting in the 1170s with the north transept of Laon Cathedral (see LAON, §1(i)), were developed with impressive windows and portals after the manner of main west façades to reflect their function as ceremonial entrances for the clergy or royalty (as at Westminster Abbey; see LONDON, §V, 2(i)). The non-projecting 12th-century transepts of Notre-Dame, Paris, were extended with show façades from c. 1250.

Although in later Gothic buildings there was a tendency to reduce the internal emphasis on the crossing, transepts continued to be architecturally significant, although their functions continued to vary; there is evidence that a transept arm could be used as a sacristy (Durham Cathedral). They were significant enough to be rebuilt (e.g. York Minster main transept, c. 1230–c. 1255) or remodelled (e.g.

Lincoln Cathedral, c. 1330), probably in association with episcopal burials. At the end of the 15th century Martin Chambiges added Flamboyant transepts to Sens Cathedral (south begun 1490, north 1500–17) and Flamboyant façades to the transepts of Beauvais Cathedral (c. 1500; for illustration see CHAMBIGES).

BIBLIOGRAPHY
E.-E. Viollet-le-Duc: *Dictionnaire raisonné de l'architecture française du XIe au XVIe siècle* (Paris, 1854–68), ix, pp. 214–39
R. Krautheimer: 'The Carolingian Revival of Early Christian Architecture', *A. Bull.*, xxiv (1942), pp. 1–38; rev. in *Studies in Early Christian, Medieval and Renaissance Art* (New York and London, 1969), pp. 203–56
F. Cabrol and H. Leclercq: *Dictionnaire d'archéologie chrétienne et de liturgie*, xv (Paris, 1953), pp. 2689–93
L. Grodecki: *L'Architecture ottonienne* (Paris, 1958)
K. J. Conant: *Carolingian and Romanesque Architecture, 800–1200*, Pelican Hist. A. (Harmondsworth, 1959, rev. 2/1974)
R. Krautheimer: *Early Christian and Byzantine Architecture*, Pelican Hist. A. (Harmondsworth, 1965, rev. 2/1975)
F. Oswald and others: *Vorromanische Kirchenbauten*, 3 vols (Munich, 1966–71)
P. Draper: 'The Nine Altars at Fountains and Durham', *British Archaeological Association Conference Transactions: Medieval Art and Architecture at Durham Cathedral: Durham, 1977*, pp. 74–86
——: 'Architecture and Liturgy', *Age of Chivalry: Art in Plantagenet England, 1200–1400* (exh. cat., ed. J. Alexander and P. Binski; London, RA, 1987–8), pp. 83–91

STEPHEN HEYWOOD

Transfer. Process of conveying an image from one surface to another. Preparatory drawings or designs can be transferred to another support by several methods: see CARTOON, COUNTERPROOF, POUNCING, SQUARING UP, STYLUS and TRACING. For the history of transfer printing in the decoration of ceramics (a process in which an engraved copperplate is printed on to paper, which is then pressed while still wet against the ceramic surface to be decorated) see CERAMICS, §I, 4. The article below discusses the conservation technique of transferring paint layers on to a new backing following the complete removal of an irretrievably deteriorated support. It concentrates on the use of transfer for panel and canvas supports; for information on the detachment of frescoes see FRESCO, §2.

1. HISTORY AND USES. The process of transfer was developed in France in the mid-18th century by ROBERT PICAULT, a restorer who worked on many of the large altarpieces brought to Paris from Italy. Since then, it has been a regular part of conservation practice, though it is now used only in extreme circumstances, when all other courses of treatment have been tried and found to fail. The transfer of a painting is a long and laborious task, but a relatively straightforward one. The reluctance to carry it out is partly due to the fact that it goes against the conservation principle that all treatment should be reversible. A transfer is clearly not reversible: the panel, board, paper or canvas is removed in little pieces, and an important part of the historical record of the painting is lost. Another reason for caution is that the appearance of the painting is inevitably slightly altered, however carefully the process is carried out. Paintings transferred from wooden supports are worst affected. Old panel paintings are rarely completely flat, as they usually acquire a slightly convex warp; if more than one panel has been used in the construction, the surface can even have an undulating

shape. This has the effect of making the painting reflect light in an irregular and characteristic way. A transferred painting, on the other hand, is uniformly flat and reflects light with an even sheen. The difference is subtle, but can be disturbing if the painting has a smooth and therefore shiny surface finish.

The process was undertaken more frequently in the past, particularly with badly warped or worm-damaged panels. In modern conservation practice alternative solutions are preferred, either consolidating and building up the fragile part of the painting, or placing the work in a sealed display case with a controlled microclimate. However, when the paint and ground layers are as weak as the support, the removal of the damaged support and its replacement with a strong new backing can be a prerequisite of saving the painting.

It is still usually panels that are transferred, especially those that have been destroyed by dry-rot or wood-worm infestation. Pine and poplar, in particular, are soft and easy to tunnel, and within a few years the wood can be reduced to a spongy pulp. Occasionally transfer is necessary because the adhesion between the wood and gesso ground fails, which leads to flaking and paint loss.

Canvas paintings are transferred when the fabric ceases to be of any structural use. This may be brought about by mould, which flourishes in damp conditions, particularly if the canvas has been heavily sized. It breaks down the cellulose in the fibres, and the process is accelerated by acidic conditions brought about by atmospheric pollutants. A more common cause of the destruction of a canvas support is past conservation treatment. When an old lining canvas is removed in preparation for relining, the thick glue layer has to be scraped off. If this is done dry and the glue picked carefully off the strands, then not too much damage occurs, but if the glue is wetted to speed up the process, it sinks further into the original canvas, and as it is scraped off fibres come away with it. Canvas paintings are sometimes relined as often as every 80 or 100 years, and treatment like this can soon make the original canvas too fragile to be of structural use. When this happens, a transfer has to be considered.

2. TECHNIQUES. The technical innovations that have taken place since the 1960s have all been concerned with the reconstruction stage. The processes involved in removing the old support remain unchanged, relying for their success on good craftsmanship, careful handling and a systematic procedure.

In transfer the backing is removed from the paint, not the other way around. This means that there is never any stage at which the paint layer is unsupported: in fact, throughout most of the operation it remains taped face down on to a smooth working surface. To ensure that the paint is not disturbed by the removal of the support, which in the case of panels involves fairly vigorous carpentry, sheets of thin tissue-paper are stuck on to the paint with a readily soluble adhesive. Mulberry tissue is often chosen for this 'facing' because it is strong yet very thin and therefore forms a perfect contact with the paint. Subsequent layers of paper and fine fabric are then built up until the facing has the rigidity needed to hold the paint together and the thickness to act as a cushion for any raised

brushwork. The facing is made to extend beyond the sides of the painting, so that when the work is placed upside down on a lightly padded surface, the paper edges of the facing can be taped down all round. This prevents the painting from moving and keeps dirt from reaching the front.

The back is removed piecemeal. If it is paper or canvas, this can be done quite simply using a sharp scalpel; if it is wood, then the procedure has to be carried out in stages. Shallow grooves about 20 mm apart are cut across the grain of the wood and the ridges between them chiselled away. This is repeated until only a thin layer of wood remains. Some Italian panels made of poplar are as much as 70 mm thick and are reinforced with broad batons. With these it is necessary to use mechanical tools for the first stages, but the final 10 mm are always removed by hand, using first chisels and then a scalpel.

With all the wood (or canvas) taken off, the back of the ground is left exposed. If this is in such poor condition that it cannot be saved by consolidation, then it too can be cautiously scraped away until only the paint layers remain, still firmly stuck to the facing. This stage can provide an interesting insight into the painter's technique, as it reveals the preparatory layers: the drawing and the first blocking in of colour. For example the removal in 1991 of an old backing from Degas's portrait of *Eugène Manet Reclining on the Grass* (priv. col., see *L'opera completa di Degas* (Milan, 1970), no. 371) showed that it had been painted over a life study of a standing male nude.

The painting then has to be rebuilt. The first stage is to ensure that the back of the paint (or ground, if this has been left on) is strong. Very fragile paint or a crumbling ground is consolidated by brushing on several coats of dilute adhesive. A perfectly level surface must then be prepared before the backing can be glued on, otherwise any lumps or depressions will be transmitted through to the paint. This is done with fillers and judicious scraping.

From this point onwards, modern methods vary from traditional transfer techniques. Previously, the painting remained face down on the flat surface while the new support—usually canvas—was glued to the back. Then the whole assembly was placed under pressure to dry. One of two types of adhesive was used. The first was rabbit-skin glue bulked out with flour paste. This mixture has a long history as a conservation adhesive, but if used in transfer its effect can be disastrous. Being aqueous, it causes the chalk or gesso grounds of panels to swell and soften, and as the painting was always kept under weights while it dried, the expanded paint layers were squashed hard against the working surface. When this happened, the paint was irreversibly disfigured by wrinkling, crushed impasto and an unnaturally flattened look. The second common adhesive was red lead or lead white oil paint. This avoided some of the more damaging effects of the glue paste, but had the problem that it was virtually irreversible. A thick layer of lead-based paint is much stronger than the old paint layers to which it is stuck; it is therefore extremely difficult to remove.

The wide range of synthetic polymers that became available from the 1960s enabled conservators to experiment with new materials. Indeed, some of these adhesives were designed to meet conservation specifications: the ideal adhesive is one that can be softened or made soluble for easy removal should a different treatment be found advisable in the future.

There have also been improvements in the type of support used in transfer. Until the 1960s panel paintings were generally transferred to canvas, which would later impress its weave pattern on the paint surface. Also, the painting would gradually but inevitably acquire the kind of craquelure associated with a fabric support. Since then, however, a number of new materials, including perspex, fibreboard, marine ply, chipboard and aluminium, have been experimented with in an attempt to find a replacement support that is satisfactory from both the structural and the aesthetic point of view. The criteria are that it should be strong, rigid, flat and, above all, that it should not expand and contract in response to moisture or temperature change.

The transfer in the 1970s of Cima's *Incredulity of St Thomas* (1502–4; London, N.G.) by the conservation department of the National Gallery in London was the occasion of an exhaustive study into the most appropriate and acceptable materials to be used. It represents, therefore, one of the most carefully researched examples of modern transfer technique. The transfer was made necessary by the complete failure of adhesion between the wood and the gesso ground. Conservation records on the painting, dating back to the 18th century, document repeated and unsuccessful attempts to keep paint and panel together by the traditional method of introducing glue under the paint. Glue does not travel far when fed in through the craquelure, and restorers in the past resorted to puncturing the paint in the worst affected areas and introducing the adhesive by hypodermic syringe. When the painting was cleaned, the little holes could be seen all over the surface. Despite such drastic intervention, the paint continued to lift, and it was decided that the only way to get at the ground and solve the problem once and for all was to remove the wooden panel.

The method can be summarized as follows. After removal of the wood, the exposed paint and ground layers were consolidated with an acrylic sealant, then made level with a vinyl-based filler. The painting, which had been faced, was turned over and laid face up on a linen canvas previously coated with a thermoplastic adhesive. Painting and canvas were then bonded on a lining table, which supplies regulated heat and light vacuum pressure. The painting, now backed by linen, was heat-sealed again, using the same adhesive, on to a composite panel consisting of two sheets of aluminium around a honeycomb core. This structure had itself been previously built up with layers of fibreglass fabric and fillers to ensure a perfectly flawless surface that would not impose its own texture on the early 16th-century paint layers. Nine surface contacts were involved in this elaborate sandwich, the effect of which was to ensure that the paint remained undamaged by the operation and retained the same surface texture it had when resting on the original poplar panel. After a history of at least three centuries of cracking, flaking and loss, it is possible that the paint on the Cima Altarpiece was finally made secure. The pattern of the wood grain and the surface texture of the paint have been left unaltered by the treatment, and it would be impossible to tell that a transfer had been carried out were it not for the fact that the painting no longer has the slight curvature developed by all large panels. Instead it is perfectly flat.

BIBLIOGRAPHY
P. Marot: 'Recherches sur les origines de la transposition de la peinture en France', *An. E.*, i (1950), pp. 241–83
A. W. Lucas: 'The Transfer of Easel Paintings', *Contributions to the IIC Conference: Recent Advances in Conservation: Rome, 1961*, ed. G. Thomson (London, 1963), pp. 165–8
B. Marconi: 'The Transfer of Panel Paintings on Linen by Sidorov (Hermitage Museum, St Petersburg) in the Nineteenth Century', *Applications of Science in Examination of Works of Art: Proceedings of the Seminar 7–16 May 1965, Boston, MA, Mus. F.A.*, ed. W. J. Young (Boston, 1967), pp. 246–54
G. A. Berger: 'Formulating Adhesives for the Conservation of Paintings', *Conservation and Restoration of Pictorial Art*, IIC, ed. N. Brommelle and P. Smith (London, 1972), pp. 161–81
R. Buck and R. Merrill: 'Honeycomb Core Construction for Supporting Panels', *Bull. Amer. Inst. Conserv. Hist. & A. Works*, xii/2 (1972), pp. 62–7
A. Conti: *Storia del restauro* (Milan, 1973, 2/1988)
M. Mecklenburg and J. Webster: 'Aluminium Honeycomb Supports: Their Fabrication and Use in Painting Conservation', *Stud. Conserv.*, xxii (1977), pp. 177–89
Preprints of the IIC Congress: Conservation of Wood in Paintings and the Decorative Arts: Oxford, 1978 [incl. articles by T. Lennon and M. Viana]
M. Wyld and J. Dunkerton: 'The Transfer of Cima's *The Incredulity of S Thomas*', *N.G. Tech. Bull.*, ix (1985), pp. 38–59

CATHERINE HASSALL

Transitional style. Term used to classify an artistic style that is thought to be in the process of evolution from one established style to another. It was, and to some extent still is, applied especially to European art and architecture from the late 12th century to the mid-13th, as styles changed from Romanesque to Gothic.

The idea of transition resulted from the attempts by such 18th-century antiquaries as Thomas Warton (1728–90) to classify architectural styles, and in the first decade of the 19th century it had been taken up by Friedrich Schlegel and James Dallaway. The first scholar systematically to pursue the notion of linking styles by transitional periods seems to have been Arcisse de Caumont in 1824, and by the 1840s the idea was firmly established in the classification of painting and sculpture in addition to architecture. It was well suited to 19th-century approaches to the history of art, which were influenced by the type of evolutionary theory best known from Charles Darwin's *Origin of Species* (London, 1859).

Although the term was used first of buildings that seemed to have adopted such Early Gothic characteristics as pointed arches and rib vaults while remaining structurally Romanesque, the classicizing and Byzantinizing styles of the figural arts in northern Europe around 1200 have also been described as Transitional (*see* MULDENFALTENSTIL and ZACKENSTIL). As the classification starts from a clear scholarly idea of what constitutes a 'Romanesque' or 'Gothic' style, the question remains whether those elements that mark out an object as belonging stylistically to those years form in themselves a discrete, unified style that is neither Romanesque nor Gothic but can be seen to lead logically from the former to the latter. The validity of the notion of Transitional styles was not seriously challenged until the 1960s, and the question remains unresolved in art-historical literature.

1. ARCHITECTURE. In architecture the concept has persisted most strongly in England and Germany (*see* GOTHIC, §II, 1(iii) and (iv)). In France, where the Gothic architectural style was invented *c*. 1140 (*see* SAINT-DENIS ABBEY, §I, 2), there is little question of transition. All the succeeding buildings in the Ile-de-France are recognizably Early Gothic, many exhibiting features of the mature style. The impact of Gothic took time to spread beyond the Paris basin, and often, as at Fécamp Abbey (Normandy; 1160s), the new was blended with the old, and many regional features were to linger in the mature style, so that it should more truly be called early Norman Gothic.

The same is true of Early Gothic outside France. For example the architecture of the German Rhineland was singled out for its Transitional nature as early as the 1830s, both by William Whewell (1794–1866) and by Sulpiz Boisserée, and German interest in the question was sustained by growing nationalism, which, particularly after the foundation of the German empire in 1871, began to equate Rhenish Transitional less with stylistic development than with ethnic characteristics, so that by 1897 Ernst von Mirbach was referring to the style 'German Transitional' (Frowein-Ziroff). Limburg an der Lahn Cathedral (see fig. 1) is a classic example of the adoption of Gothic in Germany, with Gothic forms in arches, vaults and grouped shafts superimposed on an essentially Romanesque structure. If this is a transition, stylistically it must be classified as early German Gothic, being quite distinct from, for instance, Early Gothic in Normandy. The same is true of England, where many of the first centres to absorb Gothic influence (e.g. the cathedrals of Wells and Canterbury) produced buildings that are distinctly un-French in their mixing of Gothic motifs and ideas with characteristic English Romanesque structural and decorative devices. The continuation of the essentially Anglo-Norman thick-wall technique with mural passages might be advanced as evidence of a Transitional style in England, but as this technique lingered until after 1300 most English building before the mid-14th century would have to be classed as Transitional.

2. FIGURAL ARTS. Sculpture, metalwork and painting (including stained glass) manifest the change to more monumental and classicizing modes that are accepted as a significant component of the advent of Gothic (*see* GOTHIC, §IV, 5(i)). The priority of France, perceived clearly in architecture, is less apparent in the figural arts, except in architectural sculpture (*see* GOTHIC, §III, 1(i)(a)), where the earliest manifestation of the new approach is perhaps seen in the *Christ in Majesty* on the Royal Portal of Chartres Cathedral (*see* CHARTRES, §I, 2(i)). The Klosterneuburg pulpit (1181; *see* NICHOLAS OF VERDUN, §1(i) and fig. 1) and the Ingeborg Psalter (*c*. 1195; Chantilly, Mus. Condé, MS 1695; see fig. 2), both representatives of that branch of Transitional known as the *Muldenfaltenstil* or 'trough' style, can be seen as already Gothic in essence if not in detailed delineation. In English painting the WINCHESTER BIBLE (*c*. 1160–90; Winchester, Cathedral Lib.) is the most celebrated example of the stylistic shift that is universally understood as Transitional: the illustrations encompass Romanesque figurework and decoration alongside work by the so-called Master of the Gothic Majesty (*see also* ROMANESQUE, §IV, 2(vi)(g)), which is strongly Gothic. In this manuscript, however, the illumination does not constitute a body of material in one Transitional style, but shows the effect on a major scriptorium of an influx of new ideas. It is merely the difference between the individual styles that attracts the attention of those who wish to justify the idea of transition. Similarly, the 12th-century sculpture fragments from the cloister of Christ Church, Canterbury (*see* CANTERBURY, fig. 11), dated *c*. 1180, are too disparate in style to be termed Transitional and are linked only by the fact that they were reused together.

Attempts to classify medieval styles collapse completely in the face of the manifestly different approaches in Italy. It can be questioned whether Italy contains any real Gothic architecture, and whether it is legitimate to describe Nicola Pisano's sculpture as Gothic merely because it dates from the second half of the 13th century. The crux of the problem is the early division of the art of western Europe throughout the five centuries from 1000 to 1500 into only two stylistic groupings, Romanesque and Gothic, and the subsequent attempts to ascribe everything to one or other. Yet the period includes a vast range of objects and stylistic variations, both regional and material, with many contemporary and co-existing. To say that in the middle of all this there is also another style called Transitional merely complicates an already unsatisfactory situation, as well as implying that only at one stage during the whole period was style actively changing. All styles in all media

1. Transitional style, Limburg an der Lahn Cathedral, west façade, consecrated 1235

2. Transitional style, *Annunciation, Visitation, Nativity*; miniature from the Ingeborg Psalter, *c.* 1195 (Chantilly, Musée Condé, Château de Chantilly, MS. 1695, fol. 15*r*)

are in a constant state of flux. No one willingly reproduced exact copies, whether a building or a manuscript painting. It is true that in the Early Gothic period there was a new, more logical and humanistic approach in all the arts, and it is this that binds them loosely together. To categorize the period immediately preceding Early Gothic, or in the case of some art forms, running alongside it, as another and quite independent style, would seem to ignore that at all times some people have adopted new fashions, while others have kept to the old.

BIBLIOGRAPHY

T. Warton: *Observations on the Faerie Queen of Spenser* (London, 1754, rev. 2/1762)

J. Dallaway: *Observations on English Architecture* (London, 1806)

A. de Caumont: *Essais sur l'architecture religieuse du moyen âge particulière-ment en Normandie* (Paris, 1824, 2/1925)

[W. Whewell]: *Architectural Notes on German Churches* (Cambridge, 1830, rev. 3/1842)

S. Boisserée: *Denkmale der Baukunst vom 7ten bis zum 13ten Jahrhundert am Nieder-Rhein* (Munich, 1833)

F. Schlegel: *Ansichten und Ideen von der christlichen Kunst* (Bonn, 1877)

P. Frankl: *The Gothic: Literary Sources and Interpretations through Eight Centuries* (Princeton, 1960)

J. Bony: 'The Transition from Romanesque to Gothic', *Romanesque and Gothic Art*, Studies in Western Art, i (Princeton, 1963), pp. 81–91

L'Europe gothique: XIIe–XIVe siècles (exh. cat., Paris, Louvre, 1968)

F. Deuchler and K. Hoffmann, eds: *The Year 1200*, 3 vols (New York, 1970–75)

W. Sauerländer: *Gotische Skulptur in Frankreich, 1140–1270* (Munich, 1970; Eng. trans., London, 1972)

L. Grodecki: 'Les Problèmes de l'origine de la peinture gothique et le "maître de Saint-Chéron" de la cathédrale de Chartres', *Rev. A.* [Paris], xl–xli (1978), pp. 43–64

V. Frowein-Ziroff: *Die Kaiser-Wilhelm-Gedächtniskirche* (Berlin, 1982)

English Romanesque Art, 1066–1200 (exh. cat., ed. G. Zarnecki, J. Holt and T. Holland; London, Hayward Gal., 1984)

W. Sauerländer: 'Style or Transition? The Fallacies of Classification Discussed in the Light of German Architecture, 1190–1260', *Archit. Hist.*, xxx (1987), pp. 1–30

FRANCIS WOODMAN

Transmission. *See under* DISSEMINATION.

Transoxiana. *See under* CENTRAL ASIA, §I.

Transparency. *See under* PHOTOGRAPHY, §I.

Trapani. Town in Sicily, Italy, known for its production of coral objects. It was the most important European centre for coral-carving in the 17th and 18th centuries. Although numerous sources record production of coral items on a large scale from the late Middle Ages, the dating of extant figures to the 16th century and their connection to the figures depicting the *Nativity* and the *Epiphany* seen in the well-known coral mountain (Madrid, Patrm. N.)—a display piece comprising a rocky mountain, a cave, figures and boats, all carved in coral in Trapani, acquired by Don Francisco Avalos de Aquino (1489–1525), Viceroy of Sicily, in 1570 for Philip II, King of Spain—cannot be confirmed. It is impossible to attribute any of the surviving works to Antonio Ciminello (*b* 1520), whose speciality is reported as being *delfini*, dragon-like sea creatures. The technique characteristic of coral-carvers in Trapani was developed in the 17th century: coral was cut into small pieces and applied to goldsmiths' work in the style of the period. Geometric and floral motifs were used for both ecclesiastical and secular objects. A large hanging lamp dated 1633 (Trapani, Mus. Reg.) is signed by Matteo Bavera (*b* 1580/81). Among other works attributed to him is a Crucifix (Trapani, Mus. Reg.). During this period numerous other carvers were active in Trapani, such as Sebastiano Domingo, Pietro Gallo and Giuseppe Barocco, although individual styles are not discernible in extant works. Trapani was the seat of the Viceroy of Sicily in the 17th century, and the court was the most important patron. Small, decorative items were particularly in demand, for example coin-cases (e.g. at Longleat House, Wilts), tables (e.g. in Innsbruck, Schloss Ambras), mirror-frames (e.g. in Munich, Bayer. Nmus.) or centrepieces, for example a caravel (Palermo, Bordonaro priv. col., see 1986 exh. cat. *L'arte del corallo*, no. 160). Inlaid stoups and family altars, often similar in style, were made for churches and monasteries; of greater significance are the cribs (Naples, Mus. N. S Martino) in which freely carved coral was used in relief against goldsmiths' work. In the 18th century production continued in the late Baroque style; in addition to ornament for ecclesiastical and secular goldsmiths' work, coral centrepieces and cribs continued to be produced (examples in Trapani, Mus. Reg.). By the first half of the 19th century coral jewellery and ornaments for textiles were also manufactured, but production ceased in the mid-19th century.

For illustration and bibliography *see* CORAL, §2 and fig. 2.

ELISABETH SCHEICHER

Trappists. *See* CISTERCIAN ORDER.

Traú, Giovanni di. *See* GIOVANNI DALMATA.

Traut (von Speyer). German family of artists. Two painters named Hans von Speyer were in Nuremberg between 1477 and 1516. The 'Hans Traut painter' granted citizenship in 1477 may be the 'Hans Drack v. Speyer' recorded as dying in 1488. This artist—Hans Traut I—was probably the father of (1) Hans Traut von Speyer II, whose work is documented only after 1488. The latter in turn was probably the father of (2) Wolf(gang) Traut, who worked in the circle of Albrecht Dürer. No work by Hans Traut I is documented: six wings from a *St Augustine* altar (1482–7; Nuremberg, Ger. Nmus.), formerly ascribed to him, have a monumental style and deep colouring that distinguishes them from the known work of the Traut family, despite the shared element of a rich landscape background.

BIBLIOGRAPHY
C. Rauch: 'Die Trauts', *Stud. Dt. Kstgesch.*, xxix (1907)
W. Hütt: *Deutsche Malerei und Graphik der frühbürgerlichen Revolution* (Leipzig, 1973)

(1) Hans Traut von Speyer II (*fl* Heilsbronn, 1488; *d* Heilsbronn, 1516). Painter and woodcarver. He is first mentioned as working at Heilsbronn between 1488 and 1495, being paid for various contributions to the new Cistercian abbey building. Of these only fragments of a frescoed *Legend of St Bernard* and carvings (1494) of figures and heraldry in the abbey ceiling survive. Nuremberg town register makes note of his 'transgression and repentance' in 1490: he became a citizen in 1491. He is also mentioned in Weimar in 1491–3, Leipzig in 1495 and Eichstätt in 1499. The principal basis for attributions to Traut is the signed and dated altar at Nuremberg-Katzwang (1498; Marienkirche). Around a carved *Virgin* of *c.* 1420 Traut painted scenes from her life in the wings. The light colours and neat doll-like figures are out of kilter with contemporary Nuremberg painting, revealing a Middle-Rhenish influence in their mild, phlegmatic configuration. There is an elaborate landscape background with a town behind the figures in the *Visitation*. Two wings with 14 auxiliary saints (Bamberg, Neue Residenz, Staatsgal.) contain similar doll-like figures.

Traut, in collaboration with his son (2) Wolf Traut, can be attributed with the wings of Hans Sifer's high altar in the Heilsbronn Minister (1502–3), commissioned by Frederick, Margraf von Ansbach (*reg* 1486–1536) and his wife Sophie. Here Traut worked in a grander manner, avoiding the rather haphazard pictorial arrangement of the Katzwang Altar. The golden sky forms a unified background for the skilfully constructed scenes. The Virgin wears a blue cloak and a gold brocade robe, and is contrasted in each scene with a figure in tones of red. In scenes such as the *Circumcision* (see fig.) a steep foreshortening of the picture space draws the groups together. This gives their setting an atmosphere of solemnity and gives the figures a weightless quality. In the outsides of the wings the Markgraf is shown with his nine sons under a *Crucifixion*, and the Markgräfin with nine daughters in the *Mass of St Gregory*. More saints are depicted on the rear.

A second point of reference for attributions to Traut is a drawing of *St Sebastian* (Erlangen, Graph. Samml. Ubib.), authenticated as his by Dürer. His later works in Nuremberg include the epitaph for *Johannes Löffelholz* (*d* 1504) showing the Holy Family (Nuremberg, St Lorenz), as well as the panel of *St Bridget* from the Dominican church in

Hans Traut von Speyer II: *Circumcision*, panel, 2020×825 mm, detail from the outer wings (1502–3) of the high alterpiece (Heilsbronn Minister)

Nuremberg (Nuremberg, Ger. Nmus.). Both works, especially the latter, show Traut's characteristic combination of subtlety and decorative splendour. The saint, who is writing, is fixed in place between a kneeling emperor and pope, imploring her to have pity on miserable Christendom; behind a parapet a wide landscape can be seen, and above, the half-figures of Christ, the Virgin, and St Agnes.

HANS GEORG GMELIN

(2) Wolf(gang) Traut (*b* Nuremberg, *c.* 1480; *d* Nuremberg, 1520). Painter and draughtsman, thought to be the son or nephew and pupil of (1) Hans Traut von Speyer II. He was active in Dürer's workshop by *c.* 1505, providing designs, alongside Hans Baldung and Hans Schäufelein (i), for woodcut illustrations in Ulrich Pinder's *Der beschlossen Gart des Rosenkrantz Marie* (Nuremberg, 1505), including the *Virgin of the Rose Garden* (ii, fol. 94*v*). The lack of atmospheric and perspectival space and the simple contours and lack of cross-hatching are reminiscent of the 15th century. By 1511 he had emerged as a key figure among Nuremberg painters: the wings of the high altarpiece of the Johanniskirche, presumably painted shortly after the death of the donor, Fritz Holzschuher, on 7 January 1511, reveal his debt to the prints of Dürer and Martin Schongauer. Traut's hand has also been identified in the wings of a side altarpiece *c.* 1510 in the same church. His bright palette, which reflects his debt to his father, characterizes the wings of a predella with *St Barbara* and *St John the Evangelist* (both *c.* 1512; Nuremberg, Ger. Nmus.) and the *11,000 Virgins* altarpiece (1513; Heilsbronn Minister).

An artist of modest talent, Traut completed his masterpiece, the *Holy Kinship* altarpiece (Munich, Bayer. Nmus.; see fig.) for the Tuchmacherkapelle near St Lorenz, in 1514. The luminous colours recall Dürer's *All Saints* altarpiece (1511; Vienna, Ksthist. Mus.) and Hans Süss von Kulmbach's *Epitaph for Lorenz Tucher* (1513; Nuremberg, St Sebaldus). Traut's collaboration (1512–15) with Dürer on woodcuts for the *Triumphal Arch of Maximilian I* (Traut presumably designed 12 historical scenes) explains the modern, triple-arched format and the Italianate ornament of the carved frame of the *Holy Kinship* altarpiece. A fragment of an altarpiece depicting *Joachim and Anna at the Golden Gate* dates from *c.* 1515 (Munich, Bayer. Staatsgemäldesamml.). Between 1516 and 1518 his principal patrons were Abbots Sebald Bamberger and Johannes Wenck of Heilsbronn Minster. Traut received payments for the wings of the *SS Vincent and Maurice* altarpiece (Heilsbronn Minister) in 1516 and 1518 and in 1517 for a *St John* altarpiece, of which only the *Baptism* (Nuremberg, Ger. Nmus.) is known. It may have been a *palla* similar to Dürer's *All Saints* altarpiece; its composition and bright palette reflect Dürer's influence. In 1517 and 1518 Traut was paid for the monumental wings of the *SS Peter and Paul* altarpiece (Heilsbronn Minister; sculpted shrine (central panel) and interior wings 1510), which show he was familiar with von Kulmbach's wings of a *SS Peter and Paul* altarpiece (*c.* 1510; Florence, Uffizi). Traut's wings from a *St Catherine* altarpiece (Bamberg, Neue Residenz, Staatsgal.) date from 1516–18. He painted the wings (posthumously dated 1521) of the high altarpiece of

Wolf Traut: *Holy Kinship* altarpiece, central panel, oil on panel, 1.68×1.14 m, 1514 (Munich, Bayerisches Nationalmuseum)

Nuremberg's Rochuskapelle and possibly designed its sculpted shrine (central panel) and ornamental detail.

In his portraits Traut attempted to wed more modern conceptions of Albrecht Dürer and Hans von Kulmbach to an early Netherlandish pictorial structure. He portrayed *Katharina Geygeren* (1510; Madrid, Mus. Thyssen-Bornemisza) and *Abbot Sebald Bamberger* (*c.* 1516–18; Heilsbronn Minister), as well as the *Portrait of a Man* (Vienna, Ksthist. Mus.).

Among the small group of drawings convincingly assigned to Traut on stylistic grounds are a design for an altarpiece *Virgin and Child with SS John the Baptist and John the Evangelist* (*c.* 1512; Berlin, Kupferstichkab.), a design for a stained-glass roundel *SS Paul and Ida of Toggenburg* (*c.* 1515; Nuremberg, Ger. Nmus.), *Virgin and Child with St Anne* (*c.* 1514; Paris, Louvre) and a chiaroscuro drawing with a mythological subject (Oxford, Ashmolean). His oeuvre of stained-glass designs remains to be assessed; tentative attributions include the small panel depicting *SS Erasmus and Felicity* (1517; Nuremberg, Ger. Nmus.) and the windows of the Rochuskapelle in Nuremberg (1520–21), formerly attributed to Hans Suess von Kulmbach (though here Scholz asserts that conclusive arguments are equally lacking for attribution to either artist). His many woodcut designs include two broadsheets, *Nativity, Passion and the Christian Estate* (1511) and *Man of Sorrows and Mater Dolorosa* (1512), 51 illustrations in St Bonaventure's *Die Legend des heyligen Vatters Francisci* (Nuremberg, 1512), and depictions of reliquaries for Cardinal Albrecht von Brandenburg in the *Hallesche Heiltumsbuch* (Halle, 1520). He often dated his works and occasionally used the monogram WT.

Thieme–Becker

BIBLIOGRAPHY

J. Neudörfer: *Des Johann Neudörfer Schreib- und Rechenmeisters zu Nürnberg Nachrichten von Künstlern und Werkleuten desselbst aus dem Jahre 1547 nebst der Fortsetzung des Andreas Gulden*, Quellenschr. Kstgesch. & Ksttech., x, ed. G. W. K. Lochner (Vienna, 1875), pp. 136–7
C. Dodgson: *Catalogue of Early German and Flemish Woodcuts Preserved in the Department of Prints and Drawings in the British Museum*, 2 vols (London, 1903–11), i, pp. 500–523
L. von Baldass: 'Zur Bildniskunst der Dürerschule', *Pantheon*, xiii (1940), pp. 225–9, 253–9
F. Winkler: 'Die Holzschnitte des Hans Suess von Kulmbach', *Jb. Preuss. Kstsamml.*, lxii (1941), pp. 1–31
Meister um Albrecht Dürer (exh. cat., ed. P. Strieder and others; Nuremberg, German. Nmus., 1961) [extensive bibliog.]
J. Rasmussen: *Die Nürnberger Altarbaukunst der Dürerzeit* (Hamburg, 1974)
J. C. Smith: *Nuremberg: A Renaissance City, 1500–1618* (Austin, 1983)
Gothic and Renaissance Art in Nuremberg, 1300–1550 (exh. cat., New York, Met.; Nuremberg, Ger. Nmus., 1986)
H. Scholz and P. van Treeck: 'Die Glasmalereien in der Imhoffschen Grabkapella St Rochus in Nürnberg', *Mitt. Ver. Gesch. Stadt Nürnberg*, lxx (1989), pp. 265–97
P. Strieder: *Tafelmalerei in Nürnberg, 1350–1550* (Königstein im Taunus, 1993)

BARBARA BUTTS

Trautschold, (Carl Friedrich) Wilhelm (*b* Berlin, 2 June 1815; *d* Munich, 7 Jan 1877). German painter and printmaker. He trained first under Wilhelm Herbig (1787–1861) at the Berlin Akademie der Künste, where he remained until 1832. Between 1833 and 1836 he studied in Düsseldorf under Carl Ferdinand Sohn. During this period he treated a variety of subjects, including genre pieces and animal paintings, which he exhibited in Düsseldorf until 1838. He was most prolific, however, as a portrait painter and established his early reputation as a portraitist. From 1843 to 1846 he was drawing master at the Justus-Liebig-Universität in Giessen; during these years he produced a series of delightfully frank and informal portraits (e.g. *Prince Ludwig Carl of Hesse*, Giessen, Oberhess. Mus. & Gail'sche Samml.). He visited England in 1847 and 1849 (marrying an Englishwoman in 1850). While in Berlin in 1848 he painted a portrait of the sculptor *Gustav Bläser* (exh. Berlin, Gal. Ravené). In 1851 he went to Italy, visiting Rome and Florence before returning to Giessen. After living for a while in Berlin, in 1860 Trautschold returned to England and settled in London, occasionally visiting the Continent. He continued painting and between 1862 and 1873 exhibited several times at the Royal Academy, for instance *Scene in the Black Forest* (exh. RA 1866; untraced). His son (Adolf) Manfred Trautschold (*b* Giessen, 27 March 1854) was also a painter.

Thieme–Becker

BIBLIOGRAPHY

COLIN J. BAILEY

Travancore [anc. Vēṇāḍu; Mal. Tiruvitāṅkoṭu]. Kingdom in south India that encompassed the southern third of the modern state of Kerala and most of the Kanyakumari District of Tamil Nadu. The earliest monuments in the region (*c.* 8th–10th century AD) belong to the period when the Ay dynasty ruled southernmost Kerala and the Kulashekhara dynasty (*c.* 800–1124) of central Kerala controlled the areas north of that, which were called Venadu District. The style of the early rock temples (*see* INDIAN SUBCONTINENT, §III, 5(i)(j)), usually dedicated to Shiva, compares with examples excavated by the Pallava and Pandya dynasties of Tamil Nadu and the Chalukyas of Badami; the lack of inscriptional evidence makes ascription uncertain. The cave temple at KAVIYUR comprises a square shrine chamber preceded by a wider, pillared hall with carved reliefs and a pillared façade. The cave temple at Tirunandikkara, near Kanyakumari, of similar date (pre-9th century), is the only example with traces of wall paintings. Although numerous masonry temples originated in the Ay period, generally only the base (Skt *adhiṣṭhāna*) of those that survive is original. Ground-plans include square, rectangular, circular and apsidal types. According to an inscribed copperplate, the Parthasarathi Temple at Parthivashekharapuram was founded by the Ay king Karunandadakkan in the mid-9th century; the square *sāndhāra* ('with enclosed circumambulatory path') shrine with a smaller preceding pillared hall (*mukhamaṇḍapa*) is surrounded by six subsidiary shrines. The temple at Perumpaladur, associated by inscription with the same Ay king, has a circular outer wall enclosing a square shrine chamber surrounded by columns. A number of Buddha images from the region (*see* INDIAN SUBCONTINENT, §V, 7(vi)(b)) bear close stylistic affinities with Sri Lankan images of the 8th–10th centuries. Major Buddhist monasteries (none of which survives) in the region were patronized by Ay kings.

After the fall of the Kulashekharas in the 12th century Venadu became an independent kingdom, absorbing the former Ay territories. Many temples were built in this period, and earlier temples were often renovated. The Sri Rameshvara Temple at the Venadu capital, QUILON, renovated in 1343, closely resembles Pandyan architecture. The Parashuramesvara Temple complex (13th century) at Tiruvallam includes shrines for various Hindu deities with pitcher-shaped (*ghaṭa*), square and circular ground-plans. The continuing importance of the circular shrine was unique in Kerala during this period (*see* INDIAN SUBCONTINENT, §III, 6(i)(h)). The distinctive wooden superstructures with deeply sloping roofs that crown many temples in the region are unlikely to pre-date the Venadu dynasty. The later kings of Travancore (18th–20th centuries) frequently renovated or enlarged existing temples. Marttanda Varma (*reg* 1729–58) rebuilt the main shrine of the Padmanabhasvami Temple at TRIVANDRUM, which was dedicated to the tutelary deity of the ruling family, and added many other structures. He also added to the palace complex at Padmanabhapuram and was probably responsible for the wall paintings there. Many palaces survive, including the well-preserved Krishnapuram Palace near Kayankulam (*c.* 18th century) and more modest examples scattered throughout the territories.

BIBLIOGRAPHY

Enc. Ind. Temple Archit.
V. Nagam Aiya: *Travancore State Manual*, 3 vols (Trivandrum, 1906/*R* New Delhi, 1989)
Travancore Architectural Series, i (1910–13)

S. Kramrisch, J. H. Cousens and R. V. Poduval: *The Arts and Crafts of Travancore* (Oxford, 1940); rev. as *The Arts and Crafts of Kerala* (Cochin, 1970)

S. Kramrisch: *Dravida and Kerala in the Art of Travancore* (Ascona, 1953, 2/1961)

C. Sivaramamurti: *South Indian Paintings* (New Delhi, 1968)

E. P. N. K. Pillai: *Studies in Kerala History* (Kottayam, 1970)

H. Sarkar: *An Architectural Survey of Temples of Kerala* (New Delhi, 1978)

M. B. Heston: 'The Palace Murals at Padmanabhapuram: The Politics of an Image', *Potpourri of Indian Art*, ed. P. Pal (Bombay, 1989), pp. 115–31

G. Michell: *The Royal Palaces of India* (London and New York, 1994)

M. E. HESTON

Travani, (Gioacchino) Francesco (*b* ?Venice; *fl* Rome, *c*. 1634–75). Italian medallist and goldsmith. He is documented in Rome in 1655 as being one of the three consuls of the Goldsmiths' Guild. In *c*. 1655–74 he was employed at the mint as an assayer and may have produced coins but he is known primarily as a medallist. Early signed pieces are of *Pope Innocent X* (1646) and *Cardinal Federigo Cornaro* (1647), but his most productive years were in the late 1650s with various portrayals of *Pope Alexander VII* and a variety of reverse types, such as the enlarged and fortified *Port of Civitavecchia* (1659; design by Bernini). Travani made two medals of *Queen Christina* of Sweden who had settled in Rome after her abdication (1655). Both are idealized representations of her as helmeted Minerva, yet her distinctive features can be recognized. One version is signed and dated 1665 with the reverse showing *Phoenix Rising from the Ashes*; the other, a large uniface medallion (93 mm) with a similar bust, but helmet adorned with a sphinx, is unsigned and undated. Travani's signature appears as F.TRAVANVS, FRAN.TRAVANVS, TRAVANVS, TRAVANI.F., FT.F; several medals are uniface; diameters range up to *c*. 100 mm. He produced cast as well as struck medals; they are mostly of classical design and do not place great emphasis on individual features. A seal dated 1672 for Cardinal Altieri, later Pope Clement X, is also attributed to him.

BIBLIOGRAPHY

Forrer; Thieme–Becker

R. Venuti: *Numismata Romanorum Pontificum* (Rome, 1744), p. 251

P. A. Gaetani: *Museum Mazzuchellianum*, 2 vols (Venice, 1761–3)

B. E. Hildebrand: *Sveriges och Svenska Konungahusets minnespenningar* [Royal Palace of Sweden coin collection], i (Stockholm, 1874), pp. 312, 323

Bertoletti: *Artisti subalpini in Roma nei secoli XV, XVI e XVII* (Mantua, 1884)

Baron de Bildt: *Les Médailles romaines de Christine de Suède* (Rome, 1908), pp. 19, 49–53, 55, 63–4

C. G. Bulgari: *Argentieri, gemmari e orafi d'Italia*, 2 vols (Rome, 1958–9)

A. S. Norris and I. Weber: *Medals and Plaquettes from the Molinari Collection at Bowdoin College* (Brunswick, ME, 1976), pp. 35–6

MARK M. SALTON

Travel manuscripts. Illustrated manuscripts on travel can be divided into those concerned with the peoples of distant lands and accounts of pilgrimages to the Holy Land. Other texts were not illustrated except in the form of accompanying route maps, such as are found in Matthew Paris's itinerary to the Holy Land in his *Chronica maiora* (e.g. *c*. 1240–53; Cambridge, Corpus Christi Coll., MS. 26, fols i*r*–iv*r*).

The texts in the first category display an interest in the exotic and often fantastic and monstrous peoples that were supposed to live in Africa and Asia. The most important of these is a compilation, known as the *Marvels of the East*, which originated in the 4th century AD. The text was largely derived from the geographical lore of antiquity, especially from such works as Pliny's *Natural History* (completed AD 77) and Solinus' *Collectanea rerum memorabilium* (*c*. AD 200). In no sense is the *Marvels* a practical guide or travel book, but rather an account of the extraordinary peoples of Africa and Asia as described, for example, in the anonymous texts the *Mirabilia*, *Liber monstruorum* and *Epistola Alexandri*: Amazons, Troglodytes, Epiphagi, Blemmyae, Anthropophagi, Antipods, Sciopods, Panotii and others. These descriptions were also extracted for inclusion in encyclopedias and bestiaries, for example the *Etymologiae* (completed 630s) of Isidore of Seville, the *De rerum naturis* (840s) of Rabanus Maurus and the *Liber de natura rerum* (before 1244) by Thomas Cantimpré (*see* ENCYCLOPEDIA, MANUSCRIPT and BESTIARY). The *Marvels of the East* was first illustrated in two Anglo-Saxon manuscripts (1st half 11th century; London, BL, Cotton MSS Vitell. A. XV and Tib. B. V), where it appears with other texts. Another English illustrated version is dated *c*. 1120–40 (Oxford, Bodleian Lib., MS. Bodley 614). These manuscripts are illustrated with painted or drawn framed pictures set into the text.

The *Topographia Hibernica* (*c*. 1188) is an account by Gerald of Wales of his travels in Ireland and describes the animals, fish and birds and the habits of the people there. The latter are often of a legendary or historical nature, the writer presenting lore rather than realistic accounts of the behaviour of the contemporary inhabitants. Some passages, however, are directly observed, for example the very precise description, accompanied by an illustration, of the playing of the Irish harp. The text has small marginal coloured drawings, and these are found in most of the surviving copies of the work (e.g. *c*. 1220; Dublin, N. Lib., MS. 700).

From the 14th century there are descriptions of the travels to the Far East of the Italians Marco Polo (1254–1324) and the Franciscan Odoric of Pordenone (whose report dates from 1330), as well as the fictitious journey of the Englishman Sir John Mandeville (*d* 1372); few illustrated copies of these works survive. Mandeville's account (1356–7) is largely derived from other texts and whether he travelled to any of the places mentioned is debatable. As with the Anglo-Saxon examples, copies of his work appear in compilations of works on exotic travel, including, for example, the travels (1307) of the Armenian prince John Hayton (Haytoum). One such manuscript (*c*. 1350; London, BL, Royal MS. 19. D. I) includes an Alexander romance, Marco Polo's *Il milione*, Odoric's work and a handbook of places in the Holy Land; its illustrations are artistically undistinguished. A damaged early 15th-century manuscript (London, BL, Cotton MS. Otho D. II) has Odoric of Pordenone's text with accompanying miniatures; this text is also illustrated in another book of the same period (Paris, Bib. N., MS. fr. 2810).

Two luxury copies of travel accounts were made early in the 15th century. One is a supplement to a romance of Alexander (1346; Oxford, Bodleian Lib., MS. Bodley 264) and contains illustrations of Marco Polo's travels by an English artist. It is significant that these illustrations—small framed miniatures—with their accompanying text should have been considered an appropriate companion to the Alexander romance, whose hero is supposed to have encountered fantastic peoples on his journeys to the East. The other manuscript, the *Livre des merveilles*, is a compilation of Marco Polo, John Hayton, Odoric of Pordenone, John Mandeville and various other authors of travels to Egypt, the Holy Land and the East (Paris, Bib. N., MS. fr. 2810). This lavish manuscript by the Boucicaut Master and his workshop was a gift of Jean, Duc de Berry, to John the Fearless, Duke of Burgundy. With over 260 miniatures, this is the most profusely illustrated travel book to have survived from the Middle Ages. The different costumes, physiognomic types and religious customs of the peoples are presented in fairy-tale-like pictures, often with landscapes containing exotic animals. Buildings are invariably presented in the style of early 15th-century France as the artists clearly had no conception of the appearance of Oriental architecture.

In both the Oxford and Paris manuscripts of Marco Polo the artists depart from the text descriptions, introducing pictorial imagery from the bestiary and encyclopedic traditions or from the Alexander romance. Although Marco Polo's text often refutes the fantastic lore of the *Marvels of the East*, the illustrators seem determined to interpret his account in the light of that tradition. They were also sometimes influenced by the more fantastic accounts of Odoric and Mandeville and introduced them into the Marco Polo illustrations. John Hayton's *Fleur des histoires de la terre d'Orient* was produced in an illustrated copy for Philip the Bold, Duke of Burgundy (Paris, Bib. N., MS. fr. 12201), in 1402–3. Two other copies, no longer surviving, were given by the Duke to his brother Jean, Duc de Berry, and to his nephew, Louis II, Duke of Anjou. The interest in the text at this time was doubtless stimulated by the visit to France in 1402 of the Byzantine emperor Manuel II (*reg* 1391–1425), whose empire was shrinking before the advancing Turks.

Sir John Mandeville's *Travels* were illustrated, without any text or accompanying works, in a fine early 15th-century Bohemian copy with full-page framed coloured drawings on a light-green ground (London, BL, Add. MS. 24189). The first two of 28 illustrations show Sir John on his journey and these are followed by two of the city of Constantinople. The pictures digress from the topographical to illustrate the legends of the relics that he saw on his travels and related biblical subjects, for example the *Crown of Thorns*. Other pictures depict sites in Constantinople, Cyprus, Syria (see fig.) and the Holy Land. Although Mandeville's *Travels* exist in other manuscripts in various languages, there seems to have been no illustrative tradition; this manuscript and the copy made for John the Fearless stand alone in providing numerous illustrations.

A mid-15th-century *Livre des merveilles du monde* (New York, Pierpont Morgan Lib., MS. M. 461), perhaps produced at Angers, includes descriptions and illustrations of peoples and curiosities in Europe as well as in Africa and Asia. The inclusion of material from Europe is unusual as are its illustrations, which seem to be a unique series. Such accounts of journeys to the Holy Land as the *Descriptio Terrae Sanctae* of Burchard of Worms (1000–1025) were a popular genre of late medieval literature, but most copies

Travellers Sailing to Syria and Paying to Enter the City of Tyre; miniature from Sir John Mandeville: *Travels, c.*1410–20 (London, British Library, Add. MS. 24189, fol. 8r)

lack illustrations. The *Viaggio in Terra Santa* (1480) of Santo Brasca, on the other hand, has some illustrations.

With a few exceptions, medieval illustrated travel books remained attached to the tradition of the *Marvels of the East*. They seem to have been expected to emphasize the exotic as a means of entertainment rather than be of practical use to a prospective traveller or present accurate topographical description.

BIBLIOGRAPHY

RDK: 'Fabelwesen'

G. F. Warner: *John de Mandeville*, Roxburghe Club (London, 1889)

H. Cordier: *Les Voyages en Asie au XIVe siècle du bienheureux frère Odoric de Pordenone, religieux de Saint François* (Paris, 1891)

M. R. James: *Marvels of the East*, Roxburghe Club (London, 1929)

R. Wittkower: 'Marvels of the East', *J. Warb. & Court. Inst.*, v (1942), pp. 159–97

——: 'Marco Polo and the Pictorial Tradition of the Marvels of the East', *Oriente Poliano*, Istituto italiano per il medio ed estremo oriente (Rome, 1957), pp. 155–72

L. Olschki: *Marco Polo's Asia: An Introduction to his 'Description of the World' called 'Il milione'* (Berkeley, 1960)

J. W. Bennett: *The Rediscovery of Sir John Mandeville* (New York, 1964)

L. Momigliano Lepschy: *Viaggio in Terra Santa de Santo Brasca, 1480, con l'itinerario di Gabriele Capodilista, 1458* (Milan, 1966)

G. Pochat: *Der Exotismus während des Mittelalters und der Renaissance, IV: Die Reiseliteratur im 13. und 14. Jahrhundert*, Acta U. Stockholm.: Stud. Hist. A., xxi (1970), pp. 75–91

D. O. le Berrurier: *The Pictorial Sources of Mythological and Scientific Illustrations in Hrabanus Maurus' De rerum naturis* (New York, 1978)

J. B. Friedman: *The Monstrous Races in Medieval Art and Thought* (Cambridge, MA, 1981)

J. J. O'Meara: *Giraldus Cambrensis (Gerald of Wales): The History and Topography of Ireland (Topographia Hiberniae)* (Atlantic Highlands and Harmondsworth, 1982)

J. Krasa: *The Travels of Sir John Mandeville* (New York, 1983)

F. Mütherich: 'Geographische und ethnographische Darstellungen in der Buchmalerei des frühen Mittelalters', *Sett. Studio Cent. It. Stud. Alto Med.*, xxix (1983), pp. 709–43

P. Ménard: 'L'Illustration du *Dévisement du monde* de Marco Polo', *Bull. Soc. N. Antiqua. France* (1985), pp. 85–90

J. B. Friedman: 'The Marvels of the East: Tradition in Anglo-Saxon Art', *Sources of Anglo-Saxon Culture*, ed. P. E. Szarmach (Kalamazoo, 1986), pp. 319–41

C. Deluz: *Le Livre de Jehan de Mandeville: Une géographie au 14e siècle* (Leuven, 1988)

NIGEL J. MORGAN

Traversari, Ambrogio (*b* Pórtico di Romagna, nr Forlì, 16 Sept 1386; *d* Florence, 21 Oct 1439). Italian monk and humanist. He was a Camaldolite monk in the closed monastery of S Maria degli Angeli in Florence until 1431 and thereafter a reforming General of his order, and he was deeply involved with the humanists' return to ancient sources. Although versed in the pagan Classics, his special contribution lay in a series of Latin translations of the Greek works of the Church Fathers, besides an influential re-translation of the Neo-Platonic theological works of Dionysius the Pseudo-Areopagite. His grasp of Eastern Christian dogma enabled him to take a leading role in negotiations for the reunification of the Greek and Roman churches, culminating in the Decree of Union signed at the Council of Florence shortly before his death. His letters and travel diary record an interest in antique coins and gemstones, and a sensitivity to the beauties of Ravenna and the Campo Santo, Pisa. He organized writing and manuscript illumination in the new humanist style at his monastery, which was the setting for contemporary works by Lorenzo Monaco and Ghiberti. Traversari knew Ghiberti personally (in 1430 he sought a Greek technical treatise on his behalf), and he had earlier criticized Leonardo Bruni's programme for the sculptor's *Gates of Paradise* (1425–52) for the Baptistery in Florence. Richard Krautheimer convincingly suggested that the iconography finally adopted was based on Traversari's patristic exegesis. His participation in Brunelleschi's plan (1434) for the oratory in the convent of S Maria degli Angeli, Florence, is more conjectural.

BIBLIOGRAPHY

R. Krautheimer: *Lorenzo Ghiberti*, 2 vols (Princeton, 1956, rev. 1970)

C. Stinger: *Humanism and the Church Fathers: Ambrogio Traversari and Christian Antiquity* (Albany, 1977)

——: 'Ambrogio Traversari and the "Tempio degli scolari" at S Maria degli Angeli in Florence', *Essays Presented to Myron P. Gilmore*, i (Florence, 1978), pp. 271–86

P. Castelli: 'Lux Italiae: Ambrogio Traversari monaco camaldolese', *Atti & Mem. Accad. Tosc. Sci. & Lett., 'La Colombaria'*, n. s. xxxiii, xlvii (1982), pp. 41–90

M. C. DAVIES

Traversi, Gaspare (*b* Naples, 1722–4; *d* Rome, ?1770). Italian painter. He was apprenticed to the elderly Francesco Solimena, whose late style, a reinterpretation of the Baroque art of Mattia Preti, influenced his earliest works. At the same time he studied the naturalist painters of the 17th century: Preti himself, Giovanni Battista Caracciolo, Jusepe de Ribera, Filippo Vitale and Francesco Fracanzano. Classical art also attracted him, and in the 1740s he began to make journeys to Rome to study the influential works of Bolognese and Roman classicism: paintings by Guido Reni, Guercino and the Carracci family, and by Carlo Maratti. During one of these visits he copied two pictures

by Maratti, then in S Isidoro, Rome: the *Flagellation* (ex-art market, Rome, see Bologna, 1980, fig. 2) and a *Crucifixion* (1748; Rome, priv. col., see Bologna, 1980, fig. 1). In the following year he was in Naples; three canvases of scenes from the *Life of the Virgin* (Naples, S Maria dell'Aiuto), one of which is signed and dated 1749, show the influence both of Solimena's last period and of Francesco de Mura (1696–1782), who had assumed control of Solimena's large workshop in 1747.

Traversi's next works, while still indebted to Solimena, already reveal a deep and highly individual realism, for example *Job Derided* (Warsaw, N. Mus.), the *Portrait of a Man* (L'Aquila, De Agostini Dragonetti, priv. col., see Bologna, 1980, fig. 5) and *The Schoolmaster* (sold Milan, Finarte, see Bologna, 1980, fig. 4). *The Schoolmaster*, with three-quarter-length figures in a compressed and uneasy space, established the format and subject-matter of his later pictures of contemporary life. In such pictures he transcended the limitations of genre painting: his lucid, at times merciless, portrayals of local people satirize the social aspirations of the emergent bourgeois class in southern Italy.

From 1752 Traversi spent a great deal of time in Rome, from this date onwards apparently residing alternately there and in Naples. In 1752 he painted a series of six canvases for the Roman basilica of S Paolo fuori le Mura, in which he interpreted biblical and apocryphal subjects as scenes from everyday life. Among these paintings is the powerfully realistic *Feast of Absalom*, a turbulent composition characterized by startling contrasts of light and dark and by figures whose dramatic gestures and expressions of pain and fear recall the art of Caravaggio and Ribera. In Rome one of his major clients was Raffaello Rossi da Lugagnano (*d* 1759), a leading member of the Franciscan order. The many religious paintings he commissioned from Traversi include five scenes from the *Passion* (1753; Parma, G.N.), sent to the convent of Castell'Arquato; the fourteen *Stations of the Cross*, sent to the church of S Rocco in Borgotaro, near Parma (*in situ*); and the *Pentecost* (*in situ*), painted in 1757 for the church of S Pietro d'Alcantara, Parma. An awareness of Traversi's work thus spread beyond central and southern Italy, revealing his similarity to northern Italian painters, such as Giacomo Ceruti and Giuseppe Ghislandi, who were also concerned to restore the 17th-century naturalist tradition. In their fuller, more rounded and classical forms these religious works suggest that Traversi was interested in the art of Marco Benefial, while their chiaroscuro and naturalism recalls the style of the Venetian Giovanni Battista Piazzetta, some of whose drawings and paintings he may have known.

In this mature period, from *c*. 1752 into the 1760s, Traversi was producing genre paintings, sometimes sending them from Rome to Naples with his brother Francesco. These include some of his most powerful and savage works: *The Concert* and the *Secret Letter* (both Naples, Banco di Napoli, on dep. Naples, Capodimonte); the *Drawing Lesson* and the painting usually called *Concert 'a voce sola'* (both Kansas City, MO, Nelson–Atkins Mus. A.); *The Fortune-teller*, which revives one of the most popular Caravaggesque themes, and the *Love Letter* (both Naples, priv. col., see 1979–80 exh. cat., figs 115a–b). His

Gaspare Traversi: *Portrait of a Man*, oil on canvas, 970×721 mm, 1760 (Naples, Museo e Gallerie Nazionale di Capodimonte)

famous *Portrait of a Man* (1760; Naples, Capodimonte; see fig.) and the penetrating and vigorous portrait of *Raffaello Rossi da Lugagnano* (two versions: Rome, priv. col.; Bologna, Cassa di Risparmio; see 1979–80 exh. cat., figs 111a–b) are fine examples of his ability to portray strong-willed character and to suggest a social type. Among his last works are the *Portrait of a Canon* (1770; New York, Paul Ganz priv. col., see 1979–80 exh. cat., fig. 117), *Judith* (Genoa, priv. col., see Bologna, 1980, fig. 49), the *Blind Beggar* (London, Cowper Cooper priv. col., see Bologna, 1980, fig. 48) and the *Old Pedant* (Rome, priv. col.). He left no pupils, yet his art was widely influential, particularly on the work of Lorenzo de Caro, on the genre paintings of Giuseppe Bonito and on certain paintings by Orazio Solimena and Giovanni Battista Rossi.

BIBLIOGRAPHY

Thieme–Becker

R. Longhi: 'Di Gaspare Traversi', *Vita Artistica* (1927), pp. 145–67; also in R. Longhi: *Saggi e ricerche* (Florence, 1967), pp. 189–219
A. Ghidiglia Quintavalle: 'Inediti di Gaspare Traversi', *Paragone*, vii/81 (1956), pp. 39–45
M. Gregori: 'Tre opere del Traversi a Castellarquato', *Paragone*, vii/81 (1956), pp. 45–9
A. Ghidiglia Quintavalle: 'Ancora un Gaspare Traversi', *Paragone*, xviii/209 (1967), pp. 27–9
F. Sricchia Santoro: *Arte italiana e arte straniera: Storia dell'arte italiana*, iii (Turin, 1979), p. 169
Civiltà del '700 a Napoli, 1734–1799 (exh. cat., Naples, Capodimonte, 1979–80), i, pp. 143, 214–37
F. Bologna: *Gaspare Traversi nell'illuminismo europeo* (Naples, 1980) [with illus. and bibliog.]
V. Rizzo: 'Notizie su Gaspare Traversi ed altri artisti napoletani del '700', *Napoli Nob.*, xx/1–2 (1981), pp. 19–38
M. Heimburger Ravalli: 'Data on the Life and Work of Gaspare Giovanni Traversi (1722?–1770)', *Paragone*, xxxiii/383–5 (1982), pp. 15–42
Il patrimonio artistico del banco di Napoli (Naples, 1984), pp. 126–33
F. Bologna: 'Ancora di Gaspare Traversi nell'illuminismo e gli scambi artistici tra Napoli e la Spagna alla ripresa "naturalistica" del XVIII secolo', *I Borbone di Napoli e i Borbone di Spagna: Naples, 1984*, ii, pp. 273–350

ROBERTO MIDDIONE

Traverso, Nicolò Stefano (*b* Genoa, 2 Jan 1745; *d* Genoa, 2 Feb 1823). Italian sculptor. He first studied at the Accademia Ligustica di Belle Arti under Francesco Maria Schiaffino and Pasquale Bocciardo (1710–*c.* 1791), from whom he absorbed the late Baroque sculptural traditions of sweeping drapery patterns, open poses and dramatic gestures. He later softened and toned down this highly rhetorical style, known as *Barocchetto*, especially after he came under the influence of Anton Raphael Mengs and Antonio Canova. Nevertheless, he never fully adopted the Neo-classical style.

Traverso's first contact with the work of Mengs and Canova came some time between 1771 and 1775, when he and the sculptor Francesco Ravaschio (1743–1820), a fellow Genoese, went to Rome under the patronage of the Marchese Michelangelo Cambiaso (1738–1813). According to the *Descrizione di Genova e del Genovesato*, the earliest account of Traverso's life, he continued his studies by copying antique sculpture. In 1777 he won the sculpture prize at the Accademia di S Luca in Rome. In the same year the Palazzo Ducale in Genoa burnt down. The loss of Genoese art in the fire, along with renewed patronage in their native city, may have prompted Ravaschio and Traverso to return in 1780 to contribute works to the new Palazzo Ducale and the Palazzo Reale. They both competed for and collaborated on works in Genoa for several decades, but with the revolution of 1797 Traverso fled to Milan. He returned to Genoa in 1800, after the disturbances had died down, and resumed his post as secretary and later *Custode* of the Accademia Ligustica di Belle Arti.

Traverso's *Virgin and Child* (after 1780; Genoa, S Ambrogio) shows a lack of stylistic coherence and combines elements of the *Barocchetto*, the Baroque and Neo-classicism. The Virgin is seated, but her weight is unconvincingly distributed: as the Child pushes her drapery to one side, she leans away from him. The creases and puckers of the cloth seem at odds with the classical, pyramidal grouping. Certain passages are not graceful: the Child's right arm lacks convincing modelling: the Virgin's hair is putty-like, and the articulation of her right wrist is awkward. *St Agnes Supported by Angels* (after 1780; Genoa, S Maria del Carmine), although more successful, especially in the handling of the angels, struggles with a Baroque composition of clouds, angels and a mystical apotheosis expressed in undemonstrative, Neo-classical terms.

By his death, Traverso had for some time been blind and incapable of sculpting. He remains important for having introduced Neo-classicism, although of a timid and somewhat ambivalent character, into Genoese sculpture. Ignazio Peschiera (*d* 1839) continued the style of Traverso and Ravaschio into the mid-19th century.

BIBLIOGRAPHY

Descrizione di Genova e del Genovesato, iii (Genoa, 1846), pp. 89–90
F. Alizeri: *Guida artistica per la città di Genova*, i (Genoa, 1846), pp. 167, 575

G. de Logu: *La scultura italiana del seicento e del settecento*, ii (Florence, 1933), p. 49

V. Golzio: *Seicento e settecento*, ii (Turin, 1960), pp. 1048, 1052

C. Maltese: 'Appunti per una storia del neoclassicismo a Genova', *Neoclassicismo: Atti del convegno internazionale promosso dal comité international d'histoire de l'art: Londra, 1971*, pp. 77–82

VERNON HYDE MINOR

Travi, Antonio [il Sestri] (*b* Sestri Ponente, 1608; *d* Sestri Ponente, 10 Feb 1665). Italian painter and etcher. He worked with Bernardo Strozzi, first as a servant grinding colours and then as a pupil who, like Giovanni Andrea de' Ferrari, copied Strozzi's work in the early 1620s. However, whereas Ferrari was a figure painter, Travi is best known for his landscapes. This expertise is thought to have been acquired from Strozzi's friend the landscape painter Goffredo Wals, whose presence in Genoa is documented in 1623 (not 1630 as cited by Ratti). Wals's delicately painted, circular landscapes with small figures may have stimulated Travi but, before turning to landscapes, the latter aspired to paint large figured compositions, for example his *Marriage of St Catherine* (1629; Sestri Ponente parish church) in the manner of Strozzi and Ansaldo. Another large figure composition, the *Adoration of the Shepherds* (*c*. 1630; Genoa, Pal. Bianco), shows figures more in keeping with those inhabiting his landscapes; they derive from Sinibaldo Scorza and Cornelis de Wael and emphasize Travi's study under Strozzi, whose own interest in north European art is visible in his treatment of the same subject (Oxford, Ashmolean).

Travi's landscapes are distinguished by the naturalistic figures (some of which may derive from pen studies by Scorza), often stout laundrywomen or shepherds with their flocks, and by the many repetitive brushstrokes that define the architectural ruins of his backgrounds. Occasionally he shows considerable imagination and skill, as with the architectural fantasy and gift for narrative demonstrated in the *Miracle of St Anthony*, and in the rocky cliffs of its pendant, the *Temptation of St Anthony* (both ex-Balbi Piovera priv. col., see 1981 exh. cat.). There are certain features of his landscapes (the framing trees, the animals and rolling hills) that suggest an association with Giovanni Benedetto Castiglione. Also suggestive of this is the fact that both artists used the circular format favoured by Wals, that three Travi prints are inscribed 'Castilione' and that there is a monogrammed copy by Travi (priv. col.; see 1981 exh. cat.) of Castiglione's *Adoration of the Shepherds* (1645; Genoa, S Luca). Possibly Travi followed Wals to Rome after Strozzi left Genoa for Venice in 1630/31 and was with Castiglione in Rome and Naples in the mid-1630s. A journey to Naples would account for the similarity of his landscape style with that of Micco Spadaro.

The consistency of style in Travi's landscapes and the lack of dated pictures make it impossible to develop a chronology for his work; nor is the evidence provided in his etchings (for illustrations see 1971 exh. cat.) and drawings helpful in this respect. His distinctive etching technique and its images correspond with the crosshatching brushwork and the genre figures in his paintings, and his few drawings—indebted to Castiglione—are likewise unhelpful in clarifying his development. A Balbi family inventory of 1649 records 18 landscapes in a Balbi palazzo that were painted by Travi in collaboration with Giovanni Angelo Vicino, a student of Valerio Castello (ii). No work that Travi executed after the 1640s is documented; the only date connected with him after that time is for his remarriage in 1658.

BIBLIOGRAPHY

R. Soprani: *Vite* (1674); ed. C. G. Ratti (1768–9), i, pp. 304–7

M. Bonzi: *S. Scorza e A. Travi* (Genoa, 1964)

C. Marcenaro: *Pittori genovesi a Genova* (Genoa, 1969), pp. 63–74

P. Torriti: 'La natura morta e il paesaggio', *Dal seicento al primo novecento*, ii of *La pittura a Genova e in Liguria*, ed. E. Poleggi (Genoa, 1971, rev. 1987), pp. 311–15

G. B. Castiglione (exh. cat. by A. Percy, Philadelphia, 1971)

G. Biavati: *Problematiche sulla pittura di paesaggio tra '600 e '700* (Genoa, 1976–7)

L'officina di Bernardo Strozzi (exh. cat.; Genoa, Pal. Spinola, 1981), p. 64, fig. 35

V. Belloni: *Scritti cose d'arte genovese* (Genoa, 1988), pp. 56–8

A. Orlando: *Genova nell'età barocca* (Genoa, 1992), pp. 270–72

Kunst in der Republik Genua, 1528–1815 (exh. cat. by M. Newcome, Frankfurt am Main, Schirn Ksthalle, 1992), pp. 140–41, 625–6

M. NEWCOME

Traviès, (Charles) Joseph (*b* Wülflingen, Switzerland, 21 Feb 1804; *d* Paris, 13 Aug 1859). French caricaturist and painter of Swiss birth. His family appears to have settled in France by 1809. He lived among the poor, the rag-pickers and the workers of the outlying districts of Paris, sharing their pleasures and miseries. He worked in the manner of Nicolas-Toussaint Charlet, Jean-Ignace-Isidore Gérard and Daumier, and supplied the periodicals *La Caricature* and *Charivari* with their most powerful prints on political subjects. He used his successful character, the hunchback dwarf Mayeux, to caricature violently the Republican petit-bourgeois, depicting him as a braggart, a liar and a sensualist (see Ferment, p. 67). Traviès was the Republican caricaturist who best expressed the working-class sense of having been betrayed by the bourgeoisie, who had 'confiscated' their revolution of 1830.

Traviès espoused Socialism's most radical causes, those of Jean Journet and Flora Tristan. His first lithographs appeared in 1822. Most of his output dates from 1830–35 (*Charivari*'s best period) and from 1839–45; in the latter works he displays the same political commitment and a better grasp of lithography. He executed more than 600 lithographs. After 1845 he tried unsuccessfully to become a painter: he exhibited at the 1848 and 1855 Salons and received a state commission for a version of *Christ and the Woman of Samaria* in 1853. Nothing remains of these attempts, and he died in poverty in his Paris studio.

UNPUBLISHED SOURCES

Paris, Bib. N., Cab. Est., cote Yb3 2774 [typed cat. of Traviès's lithographs by C. Ferment]

BIBLIOGRAPHY

C. Ferment: 'Le Caricaturiste Traviès: La Vie et l'oeuvre d'un "prince du guignon"', *Gaz. B.-A.*, n. s. 6, xcix (1982), pp. 63–78

The Charged Image: French Lithographic Caricature, 1816–1848 (exh. cat. by B. Farwell, Santa Barbara, U. CA, Mus. A., 1989)

MICHEL MELOT

Treasury [Gr. *thesauros*]. Type of building constructed in some ancient Greek sanctuaries between the 7th and 4th centuries BC. Treasuries housed the often valuable offerings for which there was no space in the crowded temples. Among the finest examples is the Athenian treasury at

Treasury of the Athenians, Delphi, *c*. 500–*c*. 485 BC

DELPHI (*c*. 500–*c*. 485 BC; see fig.), built of Parian marble and now completely reconstructed. These costly monuments, usually architectural showpieces and sometimes embellished with exquisite sculptures (e.g. the Athenian treasury and the Ionic treasuries at Delphi), were generally donated by cities. They commemorated victories, either in battle (e.g. the Athenian treasury, probably after the Battle of Marathon in 490 BC, that of Syracuse after the Athenian defeat in 414 BC, and that of the Thebans after Leuktra in 371 BC), or in the games (e.g. the Archaic Treasury of Myron and the Sikyonians at Olympia), or they were thank-offerings for sudden prosperity (e.g. the Siphnian treasury, *c*. 525 BC, after the discovery of gold on Siphnos; *see* GREECE, ANCIENT, fig. 22). Many treasuries were, therefore, tokens of the piety, power and wealth of cities at the height of their prestige. The earliest was the treasury of the tyrant Kypselos and the Corinthians at Delphi (late 7th century BC), and the latest were those of Thebes and Cyrene at Delphi (both early 4th century BC). After the demise of the city state in the later 4th century BC, Hellenistic rulers preferred to endow sanctuaries with large stoas (*see* STOA), which provided shelter for worshippers and, in some cases (e.g. the Stoa of Attalos I at Delphi, *c*. 230 BC), also functioned as treasuries.

Treasuries were markedly smaller than temples (e.g. the Sikyonian treasury at Delphi is 6.33×8.40 m). The simplest consisted merely of a rectangular chamber (e.g. the treasuries of Metapontion, Sybaris and Gela at Olympia, all earlier 6th century BC, and the Corinthian treasury at Delphi), but most comprised a chamber and a porch with two columns *in antis*, normally closed by a grille to protect the door, which was often of precious materials, and to enable visitors to see the rich offerings without entering the building. Being designed to house valuable objects, treasuries had no windows and were not accessible to the general public. The treasuries of Athens and Cyrene at Delphi and the Sikyonian treasury at Olympia (*c*. 500–*c*. 450 BC) have no steps at the front, and the only people intended to have access were the officials responsible for maintaining and guarding the contents (such as the female

neokore at Delos who supervised the treasuries of Mykonos and Karystos), and a few important visitors.

Both treasuries and temples that doubled as treasuries were often erected for the consecration of one or more statues, usually made of precious materials such as gold and ivory. In an inscription at Delphi the Knidians recorded that they had offered their treasury and its statues to Apollo. At Olympia, Pausanias (*Guide to Greece* VI.xix.7, 10, 12) saw a colossal statue of *Zeus* in the 'Carthaginian' (actually Syracusian) treasury, a *Dionysos* with an ivory face, feet and hands in the Treasury of Selinus, and cedarwood statues with gold inlays in the Megarian treasury (treasury buildings are dated *c*. 500–*c*. 475 BC, *c*. 540–*c*. 520 BC and *c*. 510 BC respectively). By the 2nd century AD, however, when Pausanias was writing, most of the treasuries at both Delphi and Olympia had been emptied.

The number of treasuries in a sanctuary and the diversity of their donors indicate not only how wealthy it was but also how genuinely panhellenic. Delphi contained about thirty treasuries, though not all at the same time, Olympia eleven and Delos only five. Delphi's pre-eminence is explained by the fact that the town itself was only modest, forming part of the Amphiktyonic League, which shared the administration of the Sanctuary of Apollo. Other cities, therefore, had no cause to fear that their offerings would enrich a powerful rival. Similarly, Olympia was controlled by lesser cities: first Pisa, then Elis. In contrast, Delos was always subject to important powers: Naxos, Samos and, above all, Athens. The same factor accounts for the absence of treasuries at Isthmia and Nemea: although their sanctuaries were panhellenic, they were controlled by the powerful cities Corinth and Argos respectively. Treasuries thus illustrate the way in which competition between ancient Greek cities stimulated the production of increasingly beautiful and elaborate architecture and sculpture. However, they also reveal the fatal political divisions that precipitated the decline of Greece.

BIBLIOGRAPHY
G. Roux: 'Trésors, temples, tholos', *Temples et sanctuaires* (1984), vii of *Travaux de la Maison de l'Orient* (Lyon, 1980–), pp. 153–71
GEORGES ROUX

Treatise. Written account of the general principles of art or architecture, usually treated systematically or formally.

I. Architectural. II. Painting. III. Sculptural.

I. Architectural.

Treatises on architecture, which include varying amounts of purely technical information, are to be distinguished from pattern books (*see* PATTERN BOOK, §I, 2(ii)), which contain illustrations of architectural details intended for copying by architects and builders in the appropriate situations. The difference between a treatise and a pattern book is sometimes obscured, as when details of the orders illustrated in the treatises of Vignola and Serlio serve as exemplars for the work of modern architects, or when the plans and elevations that Palladio gave of some of his villas were copied or adapted by others.

This article discusses architectural treatises in the Western tradition, although they have played an important role in the formation and development of architecture in other cultures, particularly in India and, to some extent, in China.

See also CHINA, §II, 2(v) and (viii); INDIAN SUBCONTINENT, §I, 10; ORDERS, ARCHITECTURAL, §I, 2(iii).

1. Italy, France and Spain. 2. England and Germany.

1. ITALY, FRANCE AND SPAIN. No traces remain of Greco-Roman architectural treatises pre-dating the 1st century BC except as references in texts by later authors. The earliest surviving treatise is *On Architecture* (*c.* 33–14 BC) by Vitruvius (*see* VITRUVIUS, §§2 and 3(i) and (ii); *see also* GIOCONDO, GIOVANNI), and ever since the Renaissance architectural theories have invariably made reference to the text of this important work, which its author wrote primarily to help patrons become better informed and more discerning.

Among the most significant architectural treatises of an ecclesiastical nature dating from the medieval period are the writings of SUGER, the Abbot of Saint-Denis (*Libellus alter de consecratione ecclesiae Sancti Dionysii*, 1144; *Liber de rebus in administratione sua gestis*, 1145), and the first book of *Mitrale*, written by Sicard (Bishop of Cremona; *d* 1225), the last being more descriptive of construction practice.

The first text to treat not only the allegorical qualities of architecture but also the working process of the architect is the *Livre de portraiture* (*c.* 1235) by VILLARD DE HONNECOURT (*see* HUMAN PROPORTION, fig. 2), which makes geometrical drawing the basis for architectural invention and construction, thus linking architecture to science and, indeed, to the ranks of the liberal arts. This concept found its highest expression in the *De re aedificatoria* of LEON BATTISTA ALBERTI, written *c.* 1455 but not published until 1485, in Florence. The fundamental principle underlying this text is that every operation inherent in architectural practice must be linked to a predetermined and universal rule. Beauty is interpreted as harmony, that is, a unity among all the parts and as part of the whole; this harmony consists of proportional relationships based on the perfection of numbers and pure geometric forms. The text reinforces the idea that form possesses a beauty of its own, as opposed to the medieval idea of beauty as ornament. The *De re aedificatoria*, written in Latin, was not intended so much for architects as for patrons and had only a few tiny illustrations. Its circulation was therefore not widespread, but Alberti's descriptions of columns laid the basis for the Renaissance system of orders that became canonical in the following century.

The *Trattato di architettura* (*c.* 1461–4) by Antonio di Piero Averlino, known as FILARETE, was, on the other hand, written in the vernacular and applied the ideals of Renaissance beauty to the principles of urban planning, as expressed in the layout for an ideal city called Sforzinda (see fig. 1). The text makes continual reference to the illustrations, such that some subsequent architectural theories were based on the illustrations alone. A departure from the strictly theoretical approach of Alberti is also present in the manuscripts of Francesco di Giorgio Martini (*Trattati di architettura, ingegneria, e arte militare, c.* 1476–1501; *see also* FRANCESCO DI GIORGIO MARTINI, and the unpublished writings of Leonardo (*see* LEONARDO DA VINCI, §II, 4), which were probably a first draft for a treatise on architecture.

In 1486 the first printed edition of Vitruvius' treatise appeared (in Rome). It was not until 1511, however, that the important edition by Fra Giovanni Giocondo (*M. Vitruvius, per iucundum solito castigatior factus, cum figuris et tabula, ut iam legi et intelligi*) was published in Venice, containing 136 of Giocondo's own woodcuts, which assisted in an understanding of the work. In 1521 an Italian translation (*Di Lucio Vitruvio Pollione de architectura libri dece traducti de latino in vulgare*) with a commentary by CESARE CESARIANO, was published in Como (*see also* ORDERS, ARCHITECTURAL, §I, 2(i)(c)). The various treatises of the 16th century all revolved around the text of Vitruvius, including those by Antonio Labacco (*Libro d'Antonio Labacco appartenente a l'architettura nel qual si figurano alcune notabili antiquita di Roma*, 1552), Pietro Cataneo (*I quattro primi libri dell'architettura*, Venice, 1554; and *L'architettura*, Venice, 1567) and Giovanni Antonio Rusconi (*Del architettura di Gio Antonio Rusconi . . . secundi i precetti di Vitruvio . . . libri dieci*, Venice, 1590). The nine volumes of the *Regole generali di architettura sopra le cinque maniere degli edifici* by SEBASTIANO SERLIO, published in Venice from 1537 onwards, were the first to

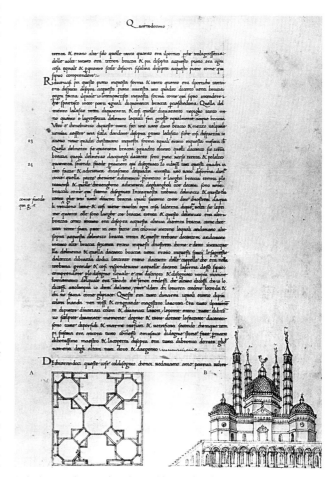

1. Architectural treatise by Filarete: *Trattato di architettura, c.* 1461–4, xiv, folio 108*r* (Florence, Bibliotheca Nazionale Centrale, MS. Magl. II, I, 140)

address systematically the matter of practical building construction, using simple, uncomplicated language (*see* ORDERS, ARCHITECTURAL, §I, 2(iii)(a)). Moreover, in book iv he offers the first explanation of the five orders of architecture, and in book iii, the first systematic account of ancient monuments. As significant and as widely circulated as Serlio's work was the *Regola delli cinque ordini d'architettura* (Rome, 1562) by JACOPO VIGNOLA. The illustrations are of the greatest importance but are limited to the means of constructing the five orders, with reference to the dimensions of ancient buildings and using simpler modules than Serlio's.

ALVISE CORNARO compiled a treatise (*Trattato di architettura*, Milan, *c*.1555) relating to the construction of houses, addressing for the first time the subject of improving the buildings of antiquity and distancing himself from the aesthetic theories of his day, which he considered unnecessary for achieving beauty and comfort. These concepts, quite apart from the use of common language, had a significant effect on *I quattro libri dell'architettura* (Venice, 1570) by ANDREA PALLADIO, who set out rules based largely on his direct studies of ancient monuments, asserting that knowledge of these formed the basis of design. In 1615 Vincenzo Scamozzi (*see* SCAMOZZI, (2)) published *Dell'idea dell' architettura universale* in Venice; it was amply derived from earlier Renaissance treatises and expressed distaste for the emerging Baroque. Of the latter there are, in Italy at least, no theoretical expositions of any significance except for the *Architettura civile* (mid-17th century; pubd Turin, 1737) by GUARINO GUARINI, who proclaimed that 'vaults are the main thing in building'; TEOFILO GALLACCINI's polemic, *Trattato sopra gli errori degli architetti* (1625; pubd Venice, 1767); and the treatise on perspective by ANDREA POZZO, *Perpectiva pictorum et architectorum* (Rome, 1693–1700).

In the 18th century the most significant contributions were those of Ferdinando Galli-Bibiena (*L'architettura civile preparata su la geometria, e ridotta alle prospettive*, Parma, 1711; and *Direzione a' giovani studenti nel disegno dell'architettura civile . . .*, Parma, 1731–2; *see* GALLI-BIBIENA, (1)), BERNARDO ANTONIO VITTONE, Guarini's editor (*Istruzioni elementari per indirizzo de' giovani allo studio dell'architettura civile*, Lugano, 1760; and *Istruzioni diverse concernenti l'officio dell'architetto civile*, Lugano, 1766) and FRANCESCO MILIZIA (*Principj di architettura civile*, Finale, 1781). The *Architettura prattica* (1726, 1750) by G. B. Amico was intended for the education of young architects working in Sicily. The most noteworthy of the theorists of 18th-century architectural rationalism was, however, CARLO LODOLI. He believed that reason should dominate every aspect of design and that function should be interpreted as the use of materials according to their particular properties, proper function and form being 'the only final, scientific aims of civil architecture'. These ideas (the original writings are mostly untraced) found their principal expression in the writings of ANDREA MEMMO (*Elementi d'architettura lodoliana*, Zara, 1834) and to a lesser degree in those of FRANCESCO ALGAROTTI (*Saggio sopra l'architettura*, 1757), who, however, adapted them to his more orthodox views.

In France, the birth of architectural treatise-writing between the end of the 15th century and the beginning of the 16th was influenced solely by the earlier Italian experiences. The first strictly French theory of architecture was based on direct studies of the monuments of antiquity; its exponents, eager to ratify and promote the evolution of a national architectural expression during the second half of the 16th century, were Jacques Androuet Du Cerceau (*De architectura*, 1559–82; and *Les Plus Excellents Bastiments de France*, i, 1576; ii, 1579; *see* DU CERCEAU, (1)), JEAN BULLANT (*Reigle generalle d'architecture des cinq manieres de colonnes . . . a l'exemple de l'antique suivant les reigles & doctrine de Vitruve*, Paris, 1564) and PHILIBERT DE L'ORME (*Le Premier Tome de l'architecture de Philibert de L'Orme, conseiller et ausmonier ordinaire du roy, abbé de Saint-Serge les Angiers*, Paris, 1567), the last adding a French order to the five orders canonized by Serlio (*see* ORDERS, ARCHITECTURAL, §II, 3).

In the 17th century national identity took on a more prominent role, as did constructional reality, involving such considerations as cost, comfort and suitability to the rank of the patron. To these practical matters PIERRE LE MUET gave particular attention in his anthology of models for town houses, *Manière de bastir pour toutes sortes de personnes* (Paris, 1623). Related to such questions and to his teaching experiences at the Académie Royale d'Architecture is the *Cours d'architecture enseigné dans l'Académie royale d'architecture* (Paris, 1675, 1683; pubd 1771 onwards) by FRANÇOIS BLONDEL, who believed that the rules formulated in antiquity could be challenged and that new forms should be developed within the mathematical limits that discipline the imagination; he nevertheless attempted to reconcile his evolutionary ideas with the demands of aesthetic conformity. In contrast, Claude Perrault (*see* PERRAULT, (2)), in his *Ordonnance des cinq espèces de colonnes selon la méthode des anciens* (Paris, 1638; see fig. 2), tried to rise above conformity in architectural expression, maintaining that proportion is an arbitrary concept and promoting use and function as the factors determining beauty in a building (*see also* RATIONALISM (i)).

To the influence of the Académie can be traced the writings of ANDRÉ FÉLIBIEN (*Principes de l'architecture, de la sculpture, de la peinture . . . avec un dictionnaire . . . de ces arts*, Paris, 1676), AUGUSTIN-CHARLES D'AVILER (*Cours d'architecture qui comprend les ordres de Vignole*, Paris, 1693) and Pierre Bullet (*L'Architecture pratique qui comprend le détail du toise et du devis des ouvrages*, Paris, 1691; *see* BULLET, (1)). Perrault's theories were drawn on in turn by JEAN-LOUIS DE CORDEMOY (*Nouveau traité de toute l'architecture ou l'art de bastir utile aux entrepreneurs et aux ouvriers*, Paris, 1706), who emphasized the importance of the functional aspects of building, with free-standing columns and horizontal entablature as the bearers of structure. In 1734 the Académie decreed that good taste was the pre-eminent theoretical concept, but that this must be subject to the exigencies of use and function (good sense and 'noble simplicity'); these theories were expounded by GERMAIN BOFFRAND in his *Livre d'architecture* (Paris, 1745) although he himself was opposed to making taste entirely a matter of subjective judgement. The theory of character as the expressive function of a building introduced by Boffrand was developed by Jacques-François Blondel (*see* BLONDEL, (2)) in his *Cours d'architecture ou traité de la décoration, distribution &*

construction des bâtiments (8 vols; Paris, 1771–7, with P. Patte). An exponent of a new form of functionalism was the Abbé MARC-ANTOINE LAUGIER (*Essai sur l'architecture*, Paris, 1753; and *Observations sur l'architecture*, The Hague, 1765), according to whom architectural expression began with first principles, in imitation of natural processes, and its essence lay in its structural logic. ETIENNE-LOUIS BOULLÉE (*Architecture, essai sur l'art, c.* 1788) and CLAUDE-NICOLAS LEDOUX, whose treatise, *L'Architecture considérée sous le rapport de l'art, des moeurs et de la législation*, was only partially published in Paris in 1802–4, were members of THE ENLIGHTENMENT circle and linked to the cultural reformation that preceded the French Revolution.

The Italian treatises were also very influential in Spain, although their interpretation was altogether different. In certain cases they were treated as absolute authorities (e.g. Francisco de Holanda: *Da fabrica que falece ha cidade de Lysboa*, 1571, pubd 1879), whereas in others attempts were made to legitimize local traditions (e.g. CRISTÓBAL DE VILLALÓN: *Ingeniosa comparación entre lo antiguo y lo presente*, Valladolid, 1539; and the treatise by ANDRÉS DE VANDELVIRA, 1575–91, pubd in 1977 in an edition by G. Barbé-Coquelin de Lisle as *El tratado de arquitectura de Alonso de Vandelvira*). In still other instances, a compromise with local methods was sought: DIEGO DE SAGREDO, in *Medidas del romano* (Toledo, 1526), tried to harmonize the anthropomorphic principles of Vitruvius with the elaborately decorative PLATERESQUE STYLE; along similar lines were the treatise of Rodrigo Gil de Hontañón (*see* GIL DE HONTAÑÓN, (3)) dating to the 16th century, known only in its reworked version of 1681 by Simón García, and Juan de Arfe y Villafañe's *De varia commensuración para la esculptura y architectura* (Seville, 1585; *see* ARFE, (2)). Two original contributions were *Tratado del cuerpo cubico, conforme a los principios y opiniones del 'Arte' de Raimundo Lulio* by JUAN DE HERRERA (pubd Madrid, 1935), influenced by the doctrines of the Jesuits, by mysticism and by the cabbala, and *In Ezechielem: Explanationes et apparatus urbis ac templi Hierosolymitani* (Rome, 1596–1604) by J. del Prado and JUAN BAUTISTA VILLALPANDO, in which ideas derived from the Bible were combined with Vitruvian tradition. In the 17th century the work of Villalpando exerted great influence on theorists in Spain as also in Germany, France and England, but much less so in Italy, where the work was published. The most important treatises written during that century were those of LORENZO DE SAN NICOLÁS (*Arte y uso de architectura*, i, Madrid, 1633; ii, 1663), which influenced architecture in both Spain and Latin America, and *Architectura civil, recta y obliqua, considerada y dibuxada en el templo de Jerusalem* by JUAN CARAMUEL DE LOBKOWITZ (3 vols; Vigerano, 1678–9), in which great importance is laid on the rules of optics. One exponent of the Enlightenment who took a moderately functionalist stance, much influenced by the French and Italians, was Diego de Villanueva (*see* VILLANUEVA, (1)) in his *Colección de diferentes papeles críticos sobre todas las partes de la arquitectura* (Valencia, 1766), although he did not contribute anything new to the critical debate.

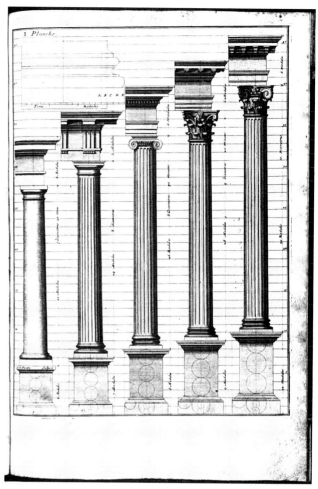

2. *The Five Orders of Architecture*; engraving from Claude Perrault: *Ordonnance des cinq espèces de colonnes selon la méthode des anciens* (Paris, 1638), plan I (London, British Library)

2. ENGLAND AND GERMANY. In England in the 16th and 17th centuries the Italian influence was uppermost: original contributions can be found in the urban concepts expounded in *Utopia* by THOMAS MORE (1516) and in the protofunctionalist position expressed by FRANCIS BACON ('Houses are built to live in, and not to look on; therefore, let use be preferred before uniformity, except where both may be had') in 'On Building' (*Essayes*, 1597, no. xlv). The treatise by Inigo Jones (*see* JONES, INIGO, §1(i)), the precursor of English PALLADIANISM, remained as a draft. JOHN SHUTE'S *The First and Chief Groundes of Architecture* (London, 1563) illustrated the orders after Serlio, with variations of his own, and introduced into printed English the words 'architect', 'architecture' and other architectural terms, but the first book devoted to architecture written in English was that of HENRY WOTTON (*The Elements of Architecture*, London, 1624), in which he emphasized the need to take into consideration the demands of location and stated the three requirements of a good building as 'commodity, firmness and delight'. As in Italy, so too in England, no treatises of any significance were published

in the rest of the 17th century; the writings of CHRISTO-PHER WREN (*Tracts* and *Discourse on Architecture*) were not published until the 18th century. Later publications often referred to COLEN CAMPBELL's three-volume *Vitruvius Britannicus* (printed 1715–25), which was probably the most powerful testimony to English Palladianism. The first full translation into English of Palladio's treatise, the work of JAMES LEONI, who also translated the works of Alberti, came out in 1715, although the English Palladian movement itself produced no literature of any profundity. Palladian elements, along with Baroque and Rococo, were present in JAMES GIBBS's *A Book of Architecture, Containing Designs of Buildings and Ornaments* (London, 1728), which contained designs that 'could be executed by any workman who understands lines', and *Rules for Drawing the Several Parts of Architecture* (London, 1732). ISAAC WARE's *A Complete Body of Architecture* (London, 1756) represented a shift away from Palladian orthodoxy: Ware included certain functionalist examples and expressed the view that an architect must study the works of past masters but then feel free to indulge the fancies of his own genius. A work similar to that of Villalpando was produced by John Wood I (*see* WOOD (ii), (1)) in *The Origin of Building, or, the Plagiarism of the Heathens Detected* (Bath, 1741), which sought to prove that Classical architecture had been revealed to the ancient Hebrews, who used it for Solomon's Temple. A focus on Gothic and Chinese art forms and a further departure from the concepts of Palladianism were found from the 1740s onwards in the writings of BATTY LANGLEY, Paul Decker (*Chinese Architecture, Civic and Ornamental, Adapted to this Climate*, London, 1759; and *Gothic Architecture Decorated*, London, 1759), WILLIAM CHAMBERS and the Adam brothers (*see especially* ADAM (i), (3)). The *Series of Plans for Cottages or Habitations of the Labourer, Adapted as well to Towns as to the Country* (?Bath, 1781) by John Wood II (*see* WOOD (ii), (2)) was, however, the first treatise to deal specifically with dwellings for labourers. The 18th century in England was notable for writings on gardens (*see* GARDEN, §VIII, 4(iv)).

In 16th-century Germany, the writings of Serlio were the primary influence; the only indigenous writings were those of Albrecht Dürer (*see* DÜRER, (1)) on fortifications (*see also* MILITARY ARCHITECTURE AND FORTIFICATION, §III, 4). A pragmatic approach, influenced by Serlio, was prevalent also in the 17th century, as in the work of JOSEF FURTTENBACH the elder, D. Hartmann, J. Wilhelm and Georg Andreas Böckler (*fl* 1644–98), whereas a more religious approach, analogous to that of Villalpando, was present in the writings of Salomon de Bray (*see* BRAY, DE, (1)), of Nikolaus Goldmann and of his editor and commentator Leonhard Christoph Sturm. The most important publications of the 18th century in Germany were those of Paul Decker (*Architectura Theoretica-Practica*, Leipzig, 1720), Johann Bernhard Fischer von Erlach (*see* FISCHER VON ERLACH, (1)), the first to attempt a universal history of architecture, Johann Friedrich Penther (*Ausführliche Anleitung zur bürgerlichen Bau-Kunst*, Augsburg, 1744–8), L. J. D. Suckow and J. B. Izzo.

From the 19th century onwards the conviction that art could be contained within a universal system of teaching began to wane, and treatise-writing declined. Theoretical thought splintered into different sectors each with its own emphasis—the science of art, criticism, aesthetics, poetics and history of architecture—while the practical side was confined to manuals.

See also BIRINGUCCI, (1) and GENTILLÂTRE, JACQUES.

BIBLIOGRAPHY
A. Blunt: *Artistic Theory in Italy, 1450 to 1600* (Oxford, 1940)
N. Pevsner: 'Apollo or Baboon', *Archit. Rev.* [London], civ (1948), pp. 271–9; also as 'The Doric Revival', *Studies in Art, Architecture and Design*, i (New York and London, 1968)
E. Panofsky: 'The History of the Theory of Human Proportions as a Reflection of the History of Styles', *Meaning in the Visual Arts* (New York, 1955), pp. 55–107
E. Forssman: *Säule und Ornament* (Stockholm, 1956)
H. Millon: 'The Architectural Theory of Francesco di Giorgio', *A. Bull.*, xl (1958), pp. 257–61
R. Wittkower: *Architectural Principles in the Age of Humanism* (London, 1962)
L. Heydenreich and W. Lotz: *Architecture in Italy, 1400–1600*, Pelican Hist. A. (Harmondsworth, 1974)
A. Bruschi and others: *Scritti rinascimentali di architettura* (Milan, 1978)
S. Sanabria: 'The Mechanization of Design in the 16th Century: The Structural Formulae of Rodrigo Gil de Hontañón', *J. Soc. Archit. Hist.*, xli (1982), pp. 281–93
D. Wiebenson, ed.: *Architectural Theory and Practice from Alberti to Ledoux* (Chicago, 1982)
L. Lowic: 'The Meaning and Significance of the Human Analogy in Francesco di Giorgio's Trattato', *J. Soc. Archit. Hist.*, xlii (1983), pp. 360–70
J. Caramuel: *Architectura civil recta y oblicua* (Madrid, 1984)
H. W. Kruft: *Geschichte der Architekturtheorie von der Antike bis zur Gegenwart* (Munich, 1985)
A. Tzonis and L. Lefaivre: *Classical Architecture: The Poetics of Order* (Cambridge, MA, 1986)
J. Guillaume, ed.: *Les Traités d'architecture de la Renaissance*, De Architectura (Paris, 1988)
G. Hersey: *The Lost Meaning of Classical Architecture* (Cambridge, MA, 1988)
T. G. Smith: *Classical Architecture: Rule and Invention* (Layton, UT, 1988)
E. Harris: *British Architectural Books and Writers, 1556–1785* (Cambridge, 1990)
R. Adam: *Classical Architecture: A Comprehensive Handbook to the Tradition of Classical Style* (New York, 1991)

ALESSANDRA ANSELMI, TOMMASO MANFREDI

II. Painting.

1. Classical world 2. Middle Ages 3. 15th and 16th centuries: Renaissance and Mannerism. 4. 17th and 18th centuries: Baroque and Neo-classicism. 5. 19th and 20th centuries.

1. CLASSICAL WORLD. Interest in the problems relating to celebrated artistic achievements arose at a very early date in Greece, and originated from technical rather than theoretical issues. Treatises on painting were written as early as the 5th century BC, but nothing is left of these early works, which are known only through references by later authors. One of the earliest commentaries, which discussed problems of perspective in painted stage scenery, was by the scene painter Agatharchos of Samos (*fl* late 5th century BC). The first discussion of theoretical issues is in the philosophical systems of Plato and his pupil Aristotle. Aristotle was mainly interested in technical processes, and regarded the work of art as the product of a particular craft. Characteristic of both philosophers, and of Greek thought in general, was the definition of art as technical skill.

In the period from the late 3rd century BC to the 2nd century AD new concepts emerged. Most important was the idea of the artist himself, who gradually acquired a new prestige; only in this period did philosophical thought seriously attempt to penetrate the mystery of artistic creation. The writings of Xenocrates of Athens in the 3rd century BC were particularly influential on later Roman writers. In the 1st century AD Pliny's *Natural History* embraced the whole of the sciences and their relationship to the arts. In Book 35 he included painting in the ranks of the liberal arts, and drew attention both to technical skills and to the fame that artists could win through their art. In the 3rd century AD these two elements, technical and theoretical, were both present in the work of Philostratos Lemnios. In his *Life of Apollonius of Tyana* he stressed the importance of technical skill, while in the *Imagines*, which includes 65 descriptions of pictures, he put forward the rudiments of a theoretical system of the visual arts and emphasized both the characteristic features of each art and the importance of art's expressive value. Neither of these works attempt a technical discussion of artistic issues; they were intended rather as literary endeavours addressed to an educated public. It was characteristic of the Roman period to relate the visual arts to the wider spheres of rhetoric and poetry; the work of Cicero, Seneca (*c.* 104–65 BC) and Quintilian (*c.* 35–96 BC) established a relationship between the principles of painting and the rules governing literary disciplines.

2. MIDDLE AGES. The Middle Ages inherited from ancient Greece the concept of art as craft and the medieval treatise laid most emphasis on this aspect. In the 8th and 9th centuries, however, the function of art was increasingly stressed, both in the teaching of religious truths and as part of the liturgy. In the 10th and 11th centuries, as workshop practice developed, treatises were written by the master of the workshop and intended exclusively for the use of artists and craftsmen. The first of these technical treatises was the so-called 'recipe book' of Heraclius (10th century), *De coloribus et artibus romanorum*, which deals with the technical processes of illumination, glasswork and goldwork (*see* MANUALS, MANUSCRIPT). The *De diversis artibus* by THEOPHILUS (first half of the 12th century) was the most important workshop treatise of the period; it included a discussion of wall, panel and manuscript paintings, and was intended to aid the artisan rather than to elucidate theoretical problems.

Two important treatises, both original works rather than compilations, date from the late 14th century: the anonymous DE ARTE ILLUMINANDI, which is the most important source on the techniques of manuscript illumination, and CENNINO CENNINI's *Il libro dell'arte*. Cennini continued the medieval tradition of the recipe books, yet also explored ideas that anticipate Renaissance thought. He introduced a new concept, that the purpose of painting was to imitate nature; this belief was developed in 15th-century Florence, and became the cornerstone of the new artistic concept of scientific naturalism.

3. 15TH AND 16TH CENTURIES: RENAISSANCE AND MANNERISM. Leon Battista Alberti's *De pictura* (1540) initiated a new way of thinking on art. For Alberti, the goal of painting was the imitation of nature, which could be achieved if painting was considered to be a science and if the painter studied perspective, proportion and anatomy; the highest form of art was HISTORY PAINTING, which,

like poetry (*see* UT PICTURA POESIS), showed the noble deeds of man. The visual arts were thus elevated to the rank of the liberal arts, and early Renaissance treatises were addressed to a cultivated public rather than to the painter.

The artistic theory of the Renaissance culminated with Leonardo da Vinci's *Trattato della pittura* (in fact an anthology of his writings, compiled after his death), which emphasized the status of painting as natural philosophy; he also stressed the superiority of painting over the other arts, thus establishing the major themes of a debate known as the PARAGONE. In northern Europe, Jean Pélerin's *De artificiali perspectiva* (1505) was important in the development of a humanist culture outside Italy, and Leonardo's ideas were developed by Albrecht Dürer. The main concern of his *Underweysung der Messung* (1525) and his *Vier Bücher von menschlicher Proportion* (1528) was to establish a scientific theory of art.

Towards the end of the 16th century there was an extraordinary flourishing of art treatises, addressed, as were Giorgio Vasari's *Vite*, to an audience that took a refined pleasure in the arts. Vasari defined painting, sculpture and architecture as 'arti del disegno'; *disegno*, which for Vasari was the visual expression of an intellectual idea, was their common root. A crucial concept in Vasari's artistic theory was the definition of the 'maniera' (style), characteristic of the artist; this individual style is assessed according to an absolute criterion of artistic perfection, the 'perfetta regola dell'arte'.

Mannerist art theory attempted to establish artistic rules that would rescue painting from its perceived decline following the death of the great Renaissance masters. The most characteristic works of the period were Giovanni Paolo Lomazzo's *Trattato dell'arte* (1584), Giovanni Battista Armenini's *De veri precetti della pittura* (1587), and Federico Zuccaro's *L'idea de' pittori, scultori ed architetti* (1607); these writers were influenced by Neo-Platonism, and sought the origins of ideal beauty in the divine, as it was revealed to the mind of the artist. Such ideas had been anticipated in the Portuguese Francisco de Holanda's *Da pintura antigua* (1548), which stresses the painter's inner gift and 'divine fury'. Venetian theorists, such as Paolo Pino and Ludovico Dolce, were more interested in *colore* than in *disegno*, and the DISEGNO E COLORE debate was waged until the 19th century.

The Counter-Reformation also produced many ecclesiastical treatises, such as Cardinal Gabriele Paleotti's *Discorso intorno alle immagini sacre e profane* (1582) and Giovanni Andrea Gilio da Fabriano's *Degli errori e degli abusi dei pittori circa l'istorie* (1564), which were intended to ensure that art did not breach DECORUM and would not harm Christian beliefs.

4. 17TH AND 18TH CENTURIES: BAROQUE AND NEO-CLASSICISM. In the 17th century the focus of art theory shifted from Italy to the rest of Europe, especially France. Yet Giovanni Pietro Bellori's *L'idea del pittore, della scultore e dell'architetto*, delivered as a lecture to the Accademia di S Luca in 1664 and later published as a preface to this *Vite* (1672), was the most representative statement of idealist art theory in the 17th century; to Bellori beauty lay not in the divine, but in nature, from

whom the artist, guided by the Antique and by Raphael, should select the most perfect parts. These ideas, anticipated by Giovanni Battista Agucchi, were to be most successful in France, especially within the circles of the Académie Royale de Peinture et de Sculpture (founded 1648). The main aim of the Académie was to codify a set of rules through which the painter, inspired by the sculpture of ancient Greece and Rome, might attain ideal beauty. This Classical theory of art found expression in treatises composed by the Academicians, among them ABRAHAM BOSSE, CHARLES-ALPHONSE DU FRESNOY, ANDRÉ FÉLIBIEN and CHARLES LE BRUN. Félibien elaborated the doctrine of the hierarchy of the genres, by which paintings were classified by subject-matter, with history painting dominant. The unquestioning acceptance of the authority of the Antique led, at the end of the century, to the demand for a greater freedom, and to a renewal of the debate over *disegno e colore*, culminating in the *querelle du coloris*, and the dispute between the Poussinistes (*see* POUSSINISME) and Rubenists (*see* RUBÉNISME); in his *Dialogue sur les coloris* (1673) Roger de Piles gave his support to colour and initiated a dispute with Félibien.

In England, Richard Haydocke translated Lomazzo in 1598, and its influence may be felt in Nicholas Hilliard's *The Arte of Limning* (*c.* 1600; *see* HILLIARD, (1)), a defence of the gentlemanly nature of miniature painting. In Holland the most authoritative art treatise, influenced by Alberti and Vasari, was by Karel van Mander, whose didactic poem 'Het Leerdicht', the first section of *Het schilderboeck* ([1603]–1604), is theoretically orientated, while Samuel van Hoogstraten's erudite treatise, *Inleyding* (1678), was intended as a detailed guide to all that is known about painting. The increased influence of French classicism is evident in Gérard de Lairesse's *Het groot schilderboeck* of 1707.

In the 18th century the reaction against classicism became more fervent, and England replaced France as the centre of art theory. The *Discourses* (1769–90) of Joshua Reynolds perpetuate the classical tradition, but writers such as William Hogarth (*The Analysis of Beauty*, 1753), EDMUND BURKE (*A Philosophical Inquiry into the Origin of our Ideas on the Sublime and the Beautiful*, 1757) and Archibald Alison (*Essay on the Nature and Principles of Taste*, 1790) introduced new concepts such as inspiration, grace, THE SUBLIME and the PICTURESQUE. These treatises laid new emphasis on taste and genius, and on the importance of the imagination, an emphasis characteristic of English aesthetics that did not have a counterpart in Europe. Italian treatises lost the prominent position they had held and simply repeated the principles of French classicism. The heritage of academic classicism was also powerful in Germany, where Anton Raphael Mengs's *Gedanken über die Schönheit und über den Geschmack in der Mahlerey* (1762) represented a rigorously academic standpoint, while Johann Joachim Winckelmann's *Geschichte der Kunst des Alterthums* (1764), the most important theoretical text of Neo-classicism, expressed his belief in the supremacy of the Greek achievement.

5. 19TH AND 20TH CENTURIES. In the 19th century the major movements, such as Realism, Romanticism, Impressionism and Symbolism, and the major aesthetic debates, over the role of authority and the temperament, and the relative importance of the sketch and the finished work, were elaborated in much theoretical writing, but the borders between art criticism and treatise writing became increasingly blurred. The academic Neo-classical treatise, such as Jacques Nicolas Paillot de Montabert's *Traité complet de la peinture* (1828–9), and the writings of Quatremère de Quincy persisted; in England the Royal Academy lectures of such painters as Frederick Leighton and Edward Poynter were published. Artists who were also teachers, such as Thomas Couture and Horace Lecoq de Boisbaudran, wrote treatises directed at their students. There was also a massive rise in production of treatises aimed at the amateur painter, and published by the colour merchants Rowney and Windsor & Newton in England. As the hierarchy of the genres waned, more treatises on landscape were produced, such as those by Pierre Henri de Valenciennes (*Elémens de perspective pratique à l'usage des artistes*, Paris, 1799–1800) and Jean-Baptiste Deperthes (*Théorie du paysage*, 1818), both of which stress the importance of study from nature; Georges Seurat was deeply influenced by Charles Blanc's *Grammaire des arts du dessin* (1867). In England, John Ruskin's *Elements of Drawing* (1857) recommended that the artist should meticulously examine nature and through this aspire to poetry and truth. Realism, initially defined in Gustave Courbet's 'Manifesto of realism', a statement that appeared in the preface to the catalogue of the exhibition of Courbet's works in 1855, and naturalism found an exponent in LOUIS-EDMOND DURANTY, while Symbolist doctrine was elaborated by JOSÉPHIN PÉLADAN.

In the 20th century, with the rise of individualism, the form of the treatise disappeared; its heritage may perhaps be seen in the artist's manifesto, such as those by the Futurist writer Filippo Tommaso Marinetti, the Cubist painters Albert Gleizes and Jean Metzinger (*Du Cubisme*, 1912) and the Purists Amédée Ozenfant and Le Corbusier (*La peinture moderne*, 1925). An echo of the theoretical treatise remains in the prescriptive aesthetic comments of such writers as Roger Fry and Clive Bell, and, above all, CLEMENT GREENBERG.

WRITINGS

Pliny: *Natural History* (1st century AD); ed. H. Rackham, Loeb Classical Library (London and Cambridge, MA, 1952), ix, bks 33–5
Philostratratos Lemnios: *Imagines* (3rd century AD); ed. K. Kalinka and O. Schönberg (Munich, 1968)
Theophilus: *De diversis artibus* (MS., 12th century); ed. and trans. J. G. Hawthorne and C. S. Smith (Chicago, 1963/*R* 1979)
De arte illuminandi (14th century, Naples, Bib. N., MS. XII.E. 27); ed. F. Brunello (Vicenza, 1975)
C. Cennini: *Il libro dell'arte* (MS.; *c.* 1390); trans. and notes by D. V. Thompson (1933)
L. B. Alberti: *De pictura* (MS., 1435) and *De statua* (MS., *c.* 1440s); ed. with trans., intro. and notes by C. Grayson (London, 1972)
J. Pélerin: *De artificiali perspectiva* (Toul, 1505, rev. 1509, 1521)
Leonardo da Vinci: *Trattato della pittura* (compiled after 1519); ed. G. Manzi (Rome, 1817); also in *The Literary Works of Leonardo da Vinci*, ed. J. R. Richter (London, 1888, rev. 1970)
A. Dürer: *Underweysung der Messung* (Nuremberg, 1525); facs. with foreword by A. Wagner (London, 1970); Eng. trans. as *The Painter's Manual*, comment. by W. L. Strauss (New York, 1977)
——: *Vier Bücher von menschlicher Proportion* (Nuremberg, 1528)
F. de Holanda: *De pintura antigua*, bks I and II (1548); Eng. trans. by A. F. G. Bell as *Four Dialogues on Painting* (Oxford, 1928); ed. J. F. Alves (Lisbon, 1984)

P. Pino: *Dialogo della pittura* (Venice, 1548); ed. P. Barocchi in *Trattati dell'arte del cinquecento*, 3 vols (Bari, 1960–62) [P. Barocchi (1960–62)]

G. Vasari: *Vite* (1550, rev. 2/1568); ed. G. Milanesi (1878–85)

L. Dolce: *Dialogo della pittura intitolato Aretino* (Venice, 1557); ed. P. Barocchi (1960–62)

G. A. Gilio da Fabriano: *Due dialogi* (Camerino, 1564); ed. P. Barocchi (Florence, 1986)

G. Paleotti: *Discorso intorno alle immagini sacre e profane* (Rome, 1582); ed. P. Barocchi (1960–62)

G. P. Lomazzo: *Trattato dell' arte de la pittura, scoltura et architettura* (Milan, 1584); Eng. trans. by R. Haydocke as *A Tracte Containing the Artes of Curious Paintinge, Carving & Buildinge* (Oxford, 1598)

G. B. Armenini: *De veri precetti della pittura* (Ravenna, 1587/R New York, 1971; Eng. trans., New York, 1977)

N. Hilliard: *The Arte of Limning* (c. 1600); ed. R. K. R. Thornton and T. G. S. Cain (Manchester, 1981)

K. van Mander: 'Het Leerdicht' ([1603]); ed. H. Miedema in *Karel van Mander: Den Grondt der edel vry Schilder-const*, 2 vols (Utrecht, 1973) [section 1 of *Het Schilder-boeck*, [1603]–1604]

F. Zuccaro: *L'idea de' pittori, scultori ed architetti* (Turin, 1607)

G. B. Agucchi: *Trattato della pittura* (c. 1607–15); trans. and ed. D. Mahon in *Studies in Seicento Art and Theory* (London, 1947); ed. A. Marabottini in *Le arti di Bologna di Annibale Carracci* (Rome, 1966)

A. Bosse: *La Peintre converti aux. . .règles de son art* (Paris, 1667)

C. A. Dufresnoy: *De arte graphica* (Paris, 1667)

G. P. Bellori: *Vite* (1672); ed. E. Borea (1976) [includes *L'idea del pittore* as a preface]

R. de Piles: *Dialogue sur les coloris* (Paris, 1673)

A. Félibien: *Des Principes de l'architecture, de la sculpture, de la peinture et des autres arts* (Paris, 1676)

S. van Hoogstraten: *Inleyding tot de hooge schoole der schilderkonste, anders de zichtbaere weredlt* [Introduction to the academy of painting or the visible world] (Rotterdam, 1678/R Soest, 1969, Ann Arbor, 1980)

C. Le Brun: *Méthode pour apprendre à dessiner les passions* (Paris and Amsterdam, 1698)

G. de Lairesse: *Het groot schilderboek* (Amsterdam, 1707)

W. Hogarth: *The Analysis of Beauty* (London, 1753); ed. J. Burke (Oxford, 1955)

E. Burke: *A Philosophical Inquiry into the Origin of our Ideas of the Sublime and the Beautiful* (London, 1757); ed. J. T. Boulton (London, 1958)

A. R. Mengs: *Gedanken über die Schönheit und über den Geschmack in der Mahlerey* (Zurich, 1762, 3/1771; Eng. trans., London, 1796)

J. J. Winckelmann: *Geschichte der Kunst des Alterthums* (Dresden, 1764); Eng. trans., ed. G. H. Lodge, 4 vols (London, 1849–72, rev. in 2 vols, 1881)

A. Alison: *Essays on the Nature and Principles of Taste* (Edinburgh and London, 1790)

E. Malone, ed.: *The Works of Sir Joshua Reynolds, Knt.*, 2 vols (London, 1797) [inc. first complete col. of *Discourses*]

P. H. de Valenciennes: *Elemens de perspective pratique à l'usage des artistes* (Paris, 1799–1800)

J.-B. Deperthes: *Théorie du paysage* (Paris, 1818)

——: *Histoire de l'art du paysage* (Paris, 1822)

A. C. Quatremère de Quincy: *Essai sur la nature, le but et les moyens de l'imitation dans les beaux-arts* (Paris, 1823)

J. N. Paillot de Montabert: *Traité complet de la peinture* (Paris, 1828–9)

J. Ruskin: *Elements of Drawing* (London, 1857)

C. Blanc: *Grammaire des arts du dessin* (Paris, 1867)

L.-E. Duranty: *La Nouvelle Peinture: A propos du groupe d'artistes qui expose dans la Galerie Durand-Ruel* (Paris, 1876)

J. Péladan: *L'Art idéaliste et mystique* (Paris, 1894)

F. T. Marinetti: *Le Futurisme* (Paris, 1911)

A. Gleizes and J. Metzinger: *Du Cubisme* (Paris, 1912; Eng. trans. London, 1913; rev. Paris, 1947)

A. Ozenfant and C. E. Jeanneret: *La Peinture moderne* (Paris, 1925)

BIBLIOGRAPHY

EWA, xiv, pp. 278–318 [article by L. Salerno with excellent bibliog. of representative treatise writers from the 15th to the 19th century]

E. Panofsky: *Ein Beitrag zur Begriffsgeschichte der älteren Kunsttheorie* (Leipzig, 1924); Eng. trans. as '*Idea*': *A Conception in Art Theory* (New York, 1968)

J. Schlosser: *Die Kunstliteratur* (Vienna, 1924)

A. Blunt: *Artistic Theory in Italy, 1400–1600* (Oxford, 1940)

D. Mahon: *Studies in Seicento Art and Theory* (London, 1947)

E. G. Holt: *Documentary History of Art*, 3 vols (New York, 1957–66)

J. Haystrom: *The Sister Arts: The Tradition of Literary Pictorialism and English Poetry from Dryden to Gray* (Chicago and London, 1958)

P. Barocchi, ed.: *Trattati d'arte del cinquecento*, 3 vols (Bari, 1960–62)

G. Bazin: *Baroque and Rococo* (London, 1964)

B. Teyssedre: *Roger de Piles et les debats sur le coloris au siecle de Louis XIV* (Paris, 1965) [excellent bibliog.]

R. W. Lee: *Ut pictura poesis: The Humanistic Theory of Painting* (New Haven and London, 1967)

L. Eitner: *Neo-classicism and Romanticism, 1750–1850*, Sources & Doc. Hist. A., 2 vols (Englewood Cliffs, NJ, 1970)

M. Baxandall: *Painting and Experience* (Oxford, 1972)

F. Brunello: *De arte illuminandi e altri trattati sulla tecnica della miniatura medievale* (Vicenza, 1974)

L. Grassi and M. Pepe: *Dizionario della critica d'arte*, 2 vols (Turin, 1978)

T. Boase: *Giorgio Vasari, the Man and the Book* (Princeton, 1980)

M. Barash: *Theories of Art from Plato to Winckelmann* (New York, 1985)

The New Painting: Impressionism, 1874–1886 (exh. cat., ed. C. Moffett; San Francisco, CA, F.A. Museums, 1986)

P. Hill: *The Light of Early Italian Painting* (New Haven and London, 1987)

J. C. Taylor, ed.: *Nineteenth-century Theories of Art* (Berkeley, 1987)

Art in the Making: Italian Painting before 1400 (exh. cat. by D. Bomford, J. Dunkerton, D. Gordon and A. Roy, London, N.G., 1989–90)

E. H. Gombrich: 'The Literature of Art', *A. Doc.*, xi (1992), pp. 3–8

P. M. Jones: *Federico Borromeo and the Ambrosiana* (Cambridge, 1993) [bibliog. lists 16th-century ecclesiastical treatises]

ALESSANDRA GIBBA

III. Sculptural.

Until the Age of Enlightenment, treatises on art were predominantly written by artists. In the Western tradition, two of the earliest such treatises (both lost but known from allusions in later writings) were by the sculptors POLYKLEITOS and EUPHRANOR and dealt with sculpture and metalwork. According to Pliny (*Natural History* xxxv.129), Polykleitos designed his celebrated *Doryphoros*, a statue of a male nude carrying a spear, according to a system of proportions that he set out in a treatise called the *Canon*, while Euphranor wrote about proportion and the effects of colour. A type of Classical treatise that dealt with sculpture only incidentally was the travelogue, i.e. observations of the ancient world written by travellers. Best of those is the *Description of Greece* by Pausanias (2nd century AD), who described religious monuments in detail and consequently referred to the sculpture in or near the famous sanctuaries of the Greco-Roman world.

Pliny dedicated several books of his *Natural History* to various aspects of art; those devoted to sculpture are classified by materials, being emanations of the natural world, and this involved a description of the corresponding sculptural techniques. Book xxxiii is about gold and silver as employed by smiths and sculptors and includes a discussion of one of the most famous Greek statues, the colossal *Athena Parthenos* by Pheidias: it was constructed of plaques of carved ivory and beaten gold, attached to a great armature. In book xxxiv Pliny discussed metals, especially bronze, the alloy much used for sculpture on account of its tensile strength, as well as describing the techniques of the foundryman and metal craftsman. Book xxxv deals with soils, minerals and the pigments derived from them, which leads to a discussion of painting and of fictile (modelled) sculpture, since clay is its raw material. In book xxxvi an account of stones leads to the history of carving, especially in marble. Pliny's work continues to be invaluable for its appreciation of many ancient masterpieces of sculpture, in the absence of the originals; his excellent descriptions enable some of them to be identified in later copies. Pliny classified carvers of stone by order of merit, but those who worked in bronze he divided in chronological groups; this had been taken to indicate that he was drawing on earlier sources. In the ancient world, the principal function of art was considered to be the depiction of recognizable beings, human or divine, by means of images drawn from reality, in order to represent more or less abstract ideas. Philosophical discussions of this subject often virtually constituted theoretical treatises on art.

In the Middle Ages it was universally agreed that art must serve Christian aims; treatises therefore tended to give pre-eminence to its practical aspect and, often, to the usefulness of its products. Thus most medieval treatises on sculpture amount to manuals describing technical processes and tricks of the trade, with the aim of training apprentices and passing on mastery of the art. One such treatise, compiled in the first half of the 12th century, is *De diversis artibus*, credited to THEOPHILUS, often identified with the German monk ROGER OF HELMARSHAUSEN. The next famous medieval treatise was *Il libro dell'arte* by CENNINO CENNINI (Florence, late 14th century), which treated art as an application of science. Sculpture was included: Cennini described, for example, the uncomfortable process of taking a life-mask to help in creating a 'scientifically accurate' portrait likeness. Many rather dull Renaissance busts were cast in clay in this manner.

The classic Renaissance treatise on sculpture, Leon Battista Alberti's *De statua* (*see* ALBERTI, LEON BATTISTA, §II, 1), was aimed by its writer, an intellectual aristocrat, at humanists; it was in Latin and was, quite unlike the medieval treatises, purely a work of theory. Being a humanist, Alberti's approach was anthropocentric: he believed that the symmetry and harmony of the human figure reflected those of the universe, all being God's creation, and that the artist–sculptor should emulate this by observing nature but should idealize the particular into a more noble and more universal image. Lorenzo Ghiberti's *I commentarii* (1447–55), especially book iii, are likewise biased towards theory; he, too, was eager to establish his claims to being a humanist intellectual, not just an artist–craftsman. Between 1461 and 1464 the sculptor and architect Filarete wrote the *Trattato di architettura*, a treatise on architecture in the Classical form of a dialogue (*see* FILARETE, §3), in which he propounded his concept of an ideal city; sculpture was to play a part, though not a leading one, in his attempt to apply a rational spirit to the nascent concept of urban planning. In 1504 POMPONIUS GAURICUS, a young Neapolitan art theorist, published in Padua *De sculptura*, a most remarkable treatise. Following Pliny's hierarchy of the materials and techniques of sculpture, he concentrated on sculpture in bronze, which he chose to regard as the true art of sculpture, as distinct from carving in stone. Like Pliny, he listed distinguished sculptors, both ancient and modern, ending with a eulogy of a particular friend of his, the sculptor Severo da Ravenna. According to Gauricus, Severo was universally qualified in all aspects of sculpture, being an 'outstanding sculptor in bronze and in marble, chaser, wood-carver, modeller and painter'. The term 'sculptor' is reserved for one working in bronze.

Leonardo da Vinci also addressed the question of sculpture (Madrid, Bib. N., second Madrid Cod.), an art in which he elsewhere (Milan, Bib. Ambrosiana, Cod.

Atlantico) claimed as great a proficiency as in painting. He was thus perfectly qualified to discuss the respective merits of these two forms of representational art, a topic that became a favourite in the High Renaissance, in the form of debate on Leonardo's famous PARAGONE. Sculpture tended to be looked down on because of its reliance on strenuous manual labour. Benvenuto Cellini, however, asserted in a letter to BENEDETTO VARCHI that sculpture was seven times better than painting because it had eight ideal points of view, whereas painting had only one. Varchi himself published in 1546 his *Due lezzioni* stating his belief that painting and sculpture were equally noble arts (see Barocchi, p. 80). Varchi extolled Michelangelo, who of course practised all three fine arts—architecture, painting and sculpture—with equal proficiency, and probably reiterated several of Michelangelo's ideas on the art of sculpture, notably that a good statue or group should have a serpentine axis, a roughly conical form and a flame-like contour to give movement.

Vannuccio Biringucci's treatise *De la pirotechnia* (Venice, 1540), illustrated with woodcuts, reverted to the time-honoured approach of the manual for practitioners of crafts, in this case bronze-casting and allied activities (*see* BIRINGUCCI, (1)). In his *Vite*, Giorgio Vasari included lengthy passages about artists' techniques, principally as they were practised in his own day and country (*see* VASARI, GIORGIO, §III); he was the earliest writer to expatiate on sculptors' use of preliminary models to plan their compositions, gradually refining and enlarging them from a tiny sketch or 'first thought', often in wax, through medium-sized models and studies made in clay (frequently fired into terracotta), to full-size models, usually too big to be kiln-fired, but strengthened by being built up over an armature of wood. Probably the most famous and most literate late Renaissance treatise on sculpture is that of Cellini (*see* CELLINI, BENVENUTO, §III); it derived from a lifetime's experience in the allied fields of goldsmithing and sculpture (the latter in both bronze and marble), as well as in the manufacture of ornaments and jewellery, for a variety of patrons across Italy and France. His best-known passage about technique also appears in his *Vita*: the dramatic and hazardous casting in one pouring of his monumental bronze *Perseus with the Head of Medusa* (Florence, Loggia Lanzi; *see* CELLINI, BENVENUTO, fig. 6). The theoretical approach to sculpture reappeared in a treatise by the goldsmith and sculptor Vincenzo Danti: the *Trattato delle perfette proporzioni, di tutte le cose che imitare e ritrarre si posano con l'arte del disegno* (Florence, 1567; *see* DANTI, (1), §2).

In the Baroque epoch, the most reasoned approach to the theory of sculpture was that of GIOVANNI PIETRO BELLORI, who in 1644 delivered a lecture to the Accademia di S Luca in Rome, on which he later based the prefatory essay to his *Vite* (Rome, 1672), entitled 'L'idea de pittore, scultore e dell' architetto'. His thesis was that 'the Idea is that reasoned consideration, which applied to nature and imitated in painting, sculpture and architecture gives to the work of art adequate formal and contentual abstraction to make it endure' (see Holt, p. 94). The principal later treatise on sculpture was *Storia della scultura* by LEOPOLDO CICOGNARA (Rome, 1808), in which he defined his aesthetic standards; for him the beautiful in sculpture was epitomized by the statues of Antonio Canova.

EWA

BIBLIOGRAPHY

E. Holt: *A Documentary History of Art*, ii (New York, 1958)
P. Barocchi, ed.: *Tratti d'arte del cinquecento fra manierismo e controriforma* (Bari, 1960)

CHARLES AVERY

Trebizond [Gr. Trapezous; now Trabzon]. Capital of the former Byzantine empire of the Grand Komnenoi from 1204 to 1461, now the Turkish city of Trabzon. The most easterly port on the south coast of the Black Sea, it gives access to central Asia over the Zigana Pass in the Pontic Mountains, which was used by Xenophon and Marco Polo (*c.* 1254–1324), among others. It is the natural capital of the well-watered and forested Pontic littoral.

1. HISTORY AND URBAN DEVELOPMENT. Trebizond was colonized by Milesian Greeks from Sinope in the 7th century BC and remained a free city after its incorporation into the expanded Roman province of Galatia (AD 64). A harbour was built by Hadrian *c.* AD 151, but the city was sacked by the Ostrogoths in 260. It was supposedly evangelized by St Andrew; St Eugenios, martyred under Diocletian, became its patron saint. Under Roman and later Byzantine rule it also served as a supply station to Satala (now Sadak) for campaigns against the Sasanians and Arabs, and in *c.* 824 it became the capital of the *theme* (military province) of Chaldia. From 1204 it reached its greatest importance as the capital of the Byzantine pocket empire of the Grand Komnenoi, who termed themselves 'Emperors and Autocrats of all the East, the Iberians and the Lands Beyond'. Trebizond prospered as an entrepôt for the Mongol Empire, and the Venetians and Genoese established trading bases there. In 1461 the city was conquered by the Ottoman sultan Mehmed II (*reg* 1444–6, 1451–81) and became a minor provincial centre. Its role as a trading post revived between 1829 and 1867, when most Western trade with Iran crossed the Zigana Pass, and the Pontos contributed its own exports. In 1916–18 the city was occupied by the Russians. The Greeks left with the exchange of populations in 1923.

Trebizond, of which prominent physical traces survive in modern Trabzon, was a walled city flanked by an eastern, commercial suburb (see fig.) and a western, garden suburb, hemmed in close to the sea by Mt Minthrion (Boz Tepe). The street plan of the eastern suburb around Daphnous harbour reveals a 'Milesian' grid of blocks of about 100×60 m, with an open four-block agora, the medieval and modern *meydan*. The square is linked to the walled Middle City by a high street (the ancient *cardo*, medieval 'Imperial Street', modern Meraş Caddesi). This *vicus* suburb embraces Trebizond's oldest surviving church, the clerestoried basilica of Hagia Anna (rebuilt 884–5; now Küçük Ayvasıl kilise); the Armenian quarter; the bazaar; and the medieval Venetian and Genoese fortified bases (the Genoese 14th-century Lentokastron survives as Güzel Hisar). The walled city is wedged between two narrow, bridged ravines; the Classical acropolis is at their inland apex, and they run for almost 1 km down to Hadrian's harbour mole. The city's walls, built and rebuilt, enclosed the palace of the Grand Komnenoi, whose chambers clustered, as at Mystras, around a courtyard. A north gate leads to the Middle City and its

Trebizond, view of the city from the east, 1701; engraving from Pitton de Tournefort: *A Voyage into the Levant*, ii (London, 1718)

crossroads cathedral of Theotokos Chrysokephalos, but only 86,400 sq. m were defended until the Grand Komnenos Alexios II completed the walls of the Lower City down to the sea in 1324, enclosing a total of 220,900 sq. m: suburban monasteries still had to be fortified against Muslim attack.

The towns of the Pontos were never large, and Trebizond under the patronage of the Grand Komnenoi numbered only about 4000 souls, but it had over 78 churches. Of these 22 were built or rebuilt before 1204, 56 from 1204–1461 and 24 thereafter. About ten survive today, the most important as mosques. The classic Trapezuntine church is a domed basilica with a pentagonal apse and triple-arched porches on three sides (in the Georgian pattern), with wall painting and *opus sectile* floor. The three major surviving monastery churches, Hagia Sophia, Hagios Eugenios and Theotokos Chrysokephalos (*see* §2 below), share these features. They were also painted, as were at least four other monastery churches. The monastery (destr. 1986) in the village of Manglavita (now Mavlavita) west of Hagia Sophia consisted of several caves and a rock-cut chapel with three phases of painted decoration dating from the 9th or 10th century to the 15th. The main decorative programme was established during the second phase (10th–12th centuries), when the *Nativity, Presentation in the Temple, Crucifixion, Resurrection* and *Dormition of the Virgin* were painted on the chapel ceiling and west wall. Midway between the harbour of Daphnous and the acropolis in the eastern suburb is the cave church of Theotokos Theoskepastos (now closed). It was probably founded by Eirene of Trebizond in the 1340s as part of a nunnery, which continued to function until 1923. Three layers of painting are preserved under soot, and it also contained four painted inscriptions: the three on the north wall of the narthex (repainted 1843) identified the portraits of Alexios III, his wife Theodora Kantakouzenos, whom he married in 1351, and his mother Eirene, who carried a model of the church. The fourth inscription was an epitaph of Despot Andronikos Komnenos (*reg* 1355–76). The now inaccessible cave chapel of St Sabbas (7×12 m), which was painted in 1411, is situated on the north face of Mt Minthrion. On the east slope of the mountain is a rectangular terrace on which stands the main church (a vaulted, single-apsed basilica, now a barn), a small chapel and the arcaded conventual buildings of the Armenian monastery of All Saviour (Amenap'rkich'; now Kaymaklı farm). The church includes several reused *khatchk'ars* (stone slabs engraved with crosses; *see* ARMENIA, §IV, 1(ii)) in the main body. Although it was partly decorated with wall paintings in the 1420s, a remarkable *Last Judgement* probably belongs to the 1640s.

At the Ottoman conquest several churches were converted into mosques. The Hatuniye or Imaret mosque of 1514 contains the tomb (1506) of the mother of Selim I (*reg* 1512–20, governor of Trebizond from 1489 to 1512). Like the Iskender Pasha mosque (1529) it has an adjacent bath. The market (Turk. *bedesten*) dates to the 15th century. Other buildings of the Ottoman period are the Taşhan (16th century) and Alacahan (18th century) inns, respectively south and east of the market, the Sekis Direkli bath (16th century), which takes its name from the eight columns that support its dome, and several traditional wooden houses.

2. BUILDINGS.

(i) Hagia Sophia. Now a museum, it was converted to the Ayasofya Camii before 1609. It is the only surviving monastery church in the city's western suburb and the only Byzantine monument to have been restored. It consists of the main church, a smaller triple-apsed church of which only the foundations survive and a tall bell-tower. The main church was built by the Grand Komnenos Manuel I (*reg* 1238–63), perhaps as his funerary church, on a raised podium into which were inserted 18 vaulted tombs, a unique arrangement. The main church is an elongated cross-in-square with three apses, crowned by a single dome on a twelve-sided drum; three open porches flank the core on its north, south and west sides. The internal decoration reveals a mingling of several traditions: the capitals, columns and relief sculpture under the dome and in the porches include 5th- to 6th-century Byzantine spolia as well as carvings of Armenian, Saljuq and Western inspiration. Although only fragments of the wall paintings survive, the scale and confidence of the angelic host in the dome drum are comparable to work commissioned by contemporary Orthodox rulers in Serbia and were probably executed by artists from Constantinople (now Istanbul). The later four-storey bell-tower (1427; h. 20 m) is also richly decorated. On the east façade is a painted panel showing the *Virgin* holding *Christ* in the centre with *Alexios IV* (*reg* 1416–29) to the right and his son *John IV* (*reg* 1429–48) to the left. Wall paintings also decorate the second-storey chapel, which contains a rare cycle of all 12 Feasts of the Church.

(ii) Hagios Eugenios. This monastery church (Yeni Cuma Camii; converted before 1523) overlooks the acropolis from the eastern suburb and was the focus of the cult of the patron saint (*fd* 24 June). It was endowed *c.* 1021–2 by Basil II (*reg* 976–1025) and was probably rebuilt and its floor (now hidden) laid in 1291. Contrary to received opinion it was not burnt down in 1340 but was repaired and enlarged with the addition of a dome. After 1350 the Grand Komnenos Alexios III (*reg* 1349–90) was responsible for the external dynastic portraits (destr.) and possibly for the vivid internal wall paintings (now whitewashed).

(iii) Theotokos Chrysokephalos. The third surviving monastery church (Ortahisar Camii since 1461) stands in the centre of the Middle City, evidently on an ancient site. It was rebuilt 1214–35 as the coronation cathedral of the Grand Komnenoi, the liturgy for which required unusual *katechoumena* galleries and a *metatorion* robing room. In the 1340s a dome and a narthex were added. Its wall paintings and mosaics are now under plaster, but its fine *opus sectile* floor was briefly exposed in 1988. Reused marble Ionic columns and capitals have been identified in the north porch.

BIBLIOGRAPHY
G. Millet and D. Talbot Rice: *Byzantine Painting at Trebizond* (London, 1936)
D. Talbot Rice: *The Church of Haghia Sophia at Trebizond* (Edinburgh, 1968)
E. Semavi: 'Byzantine Art in Turkey', *The Art and Architecture of Turkey*, ed. E. Akurgal (Oxford, 1980), pp. 48–79

A. Bryer and D. Winfield: *The Byzantine Monuments and Topography of the Pontos*, 2 vols (Washington, DC, 1985)

T. A. Sinclair: *Eastern Turkey: An Architectural and Archaeological Survey* (London, 1987–9), ii, pp. 48–82

M. Yüksel: *Trabzonda Türk-Islam eserleri ve kitabeleri* [Turkish Islamic monuments and inscriptions of Trabzon], 3 vols (Istanbul, 1991)

A. A. M. BRYER, with LALE BABAOĞLU

Treen. Useful and simple items made from wood—especially such hardwoods as maple or burr walnut—carved or turned for domestic purposes and trades. True treen is considered by most to be items made before 1830 or even before the mid-18th century. Wills and family inventories in the 16th and 17th centuries refer to treen objects that include cups, chalices, platters, bowls and spoons. Carving, both professional and amateur, embellished the most varied and inspired part of treen, including Welsh love spoons, although the work of the turner accounted for many early items. The large collection of treen formed by Mr and Mrs Edward Pinto was bought in 1967 by the City of Birmingham Museum and Art Gallery.

BIBLIOGRAPHY

O. Evan-Thomas: *Domestic Utensils of Wood* (London, 1932)

E. Pinto: *Treen or Small Woodware* (London, 1949)

——: *Treen and Other Wooden Bygones* (London, 1969)

J. Toller: *Treen and Other Turned Woodware for Collectors* (Newton Abbot, 1975)

SONIA CORDELL

Trélat, Emile (*b* 6 March 1821; *d* Paris, 30 Oct 1907). French architect, teacher and writer. He trained as an engineer at the Ecole Centrale des Arts et Métiers, Paris, where he later taught (1854–95). After training he ran a ceramics factory before enrolling as a pupil of the architect Louis-Tullius-Joachim Visconti. He developed a particular interest in hygiene in buildings and in 1849 was appointed to a government commission to study the design of public baths. In 1865 he founded the Ecole Centrale d'Architecture in Paris. Set up in opposition to the Ecole des Beaux-Arts, it was intended to lead reform in architectural education, giving it a more practical, scientific basis and relating it to the current debate on such social issues as housing. One of the school's directors was Eugène-Emmanuel Viollet-le-Duc, who had been involved in the ultimately unsuccessful attempts to reform the Ecole des Beaux-Arts in 1863. The school was financed by private shareholders, among them many engineers and industrialists but few architects. The architectural profession was in fact critical of Trélat's venture and ensured that the school never really became established, so that, from 1879, it was agreed that its students could complete their studies at the Ecole des Beaux-Arts. In 1871 Trélat was appointed chief architect of the Seine Départements and in the 1880s he was a regular contributor to congresses on hygiene in buildings, discussing in particular the lighting, heating and ventilation of housing. In 1891 he was elected a deputy, following in the footsteps of his father Ulysse Trélat, a doctor who had devoted himself to treating the poor and who, as an active republican, had served briefly as a minister in 1848 under the Second Empire. Emile Trélat served as a deputy until 1899, concentrating on questions of public health, on which he published a book, *La Salubrité*.

WRITINGS

L'Ecole centrale d'architecture (Paris, 1864)

'Cités ouvrières, maisons ouvrières', *Congrès international d'hygiène: Paris, 1878*, i, pp. 538–52

Ecole spéciale d'architecture, ouverture 1879–80, discours du directeur (Paris, 1879)

Aérage et chauffage des habitations (Paris, 1886)

Images et figures résumant les règles et préceptes professés par l'auteur pour assurer la salubrité dans les édifices (Paris, 1886)

La Salubrité (Paris, 1899)

BIBLIOGRAPHY

Thieme–Becker

J. JAMES READ

Tremanti, Fernando Arbós y. *See* ARBOS Y TREMANTI, FERNANDO.

Tremblay, Barthélémy (*b* Louves-en-Parisis, 1568; *d* Paris, 9 Aug 1629). French sculptor. He is first recorded at the château of Fontainebleau, where, in 1596, he married the sister of Toussaint Dubreuil. The following year he was established in Paris, and in 1601 he is recorded working on the Petite Galerie of the Louvre, Paris. In 1604 his portrait of *Henry IV* was cast in bronze. The official mask of the king, smiling and frontal, is set on an elaborately decorated and finely modelled breastplate (bronze, probably that of 1604; Paris, Mus. Jacquemart-André; marble version, Fontainebleau, Château). From 1605 Tremblay was Sculpteur Ordinaire du Roi, and subsequently curator of the royal marbles.

About 1620 he executed the funerary monument of the *Maréchal d'Ornano* for the church of la Merci, Bordeaux (marble, Bordeaux, Mus. Aquitaine), with a characterful marble effigy of the deceased kneeling before a richly decorated prie-dieu. In 1620 he collaborated with the sculptor Pierre Mansard (*fl* 1618) on the high altar of the church of St Martin-des-Champs, Paris, producing terracotta statues of *St Martin* and *St Benedict*, both with angels (destr.). In 1627 he and his son-in-law, Germain Gissey (1594–1640), were commissioned to execute the funerary monument to *Henri de Lorraine, Duc de Guise* for the former Jesuit church at Eu (marble, *in situ*). The two-tier tomb, with a recumbent effigy of the duke, leaning on one elbow, below, and a praying effigy on top, was devised by Tremblay and completed by Gissey in 1631. Tremblay also provided the model for the tomb of the duke's widow, *Catherine de Clèves*, in the same church; this was executed by Nicolas and Simon Guillain (marble, 1627–31; *in situ*). Gissey also completed ornamental sculpture begun by Tremblay in the chapel at the château of Fontainebleau (1613–29; *in situ*), as well as a large marble statue of *Henry IV* (paid for 1639; Louvre, Paris, on dep. Pau, Château), which reveals Tremblay's characteristic decorative refinement. This commission was probably contemporary with a low relief representing the *Siege of Amiens* (bronze; destr.) intended for the pedestal of Pietro Tacca's equestrian statue of the king on the Pont Neuf, Paris. Gissey erected a tomb decorated with a bust in memory of Tremblay in St Eustache, Paris; it is known through an engraving by Michel Lasne.

BIBLIOGRAPHY

P. Courteault: 'L'Auteur du mausolée du Maréchal d'Ornano', *Rev. Hist. Bordeaux & Dépt Gironde* (1941), p. 103

J. Coural: 'Les Tombeaux du Duc et de la Duchesse de Guise à Eu', *Bull. Soc. Hist. A. Fr.* (1957), p. 251

GENEVIÈVE BRESC-BAUTIER

Tremlett, David (*b* St Austell, Cornwall, 13 Feb 1945). English sculptor, installation artist and draughtsman. He grew up on his parents' farm in Cornwall and attended the Falmouth School of Art (1962–3), afterwards studying sculpture at the Birmingham College of Art (1963–6) and the Royal College of Art, London. He then travelled widely, his experience of different countries and cultures providing inspiration and material for his art. His approach was often similar to that of the exponents of land art, such as Richard Long and Hamish Fulton, showing an interest in temporally based, site-specific works. An early work, the *Spring Recordings* (1971), consist of many copies of an audio-cassette recording of natural sounds of the English countryside, heard on his walks, lined up in a row on minimal shelving along the wall of the gallery. *Hungarian Gypsies* (1972) combined photographs and text. Many of his works from 1980 comprise images drawn on the walls of museums, galleries, old churches and ruined buildings, a notable example being *Working Inside* (1989), in a church at Courmelois, Val de Vesle, France. Many of these works suggest emblematic forms and patterns of African or Aboriginal art, although their context also contributes to their meaning.

BIBLIOGRAPHY

David Tremlett (exh. cat., London, Serpentine Gal., 1989)
David Tremlett: Working Inside Outside (exh. cat. by L. van den Abeele, Val de Vesle, Cent. Création Contemp., 1989)
David Tremlett: Selected Walls (exh. cat., St Priest, Cent. A. Contemp., 1990)
David Tremlett: Written Form (exh. cat. by M. Huys and D. von Dratelin, Brussels, Musées Royaux B.-A., 1990)
The Artspace Drawings (exh. cat., Auckland, Aspace, 1992)
David Tremlett: A Quiet Madness (exh. cat. by C. Ahrens and D. von Dratelin, Hannover, Kestner-Ges., 1992)
David Tremlett (exh. cat. by M. Meneguzzo and A. Commellato, Milan, Padiglione A. Contemp., 1993)

Trémolières, Pierre-Charles (*b* Cholet, 1703; *d* Paris, 11 May 1739). French painter, draughtsman and etcher. In 1719 he began apprenticeship in the Paris studio of Jean-Baptiste van Loo, and thanks to family connections he soon made contact with the influential patron the Comte de Caylus, in whose house he lodged. One of his first commissions was to etch two sets of three plates (1726 and 1728) after drawings by Antoine Watteau for the collection of prints *Figures de différents caractères de paysages et d'études . . .*, published by Jean de Jullienne in 1726. Trémolières also attended drawing lessons at the Académie Royale, and in 1726 and again in 1727 he gained second prize in the Prix de Rome competition. In 1728 he went to complete his artistic education at the Académie de France in Rome with Pierre Subleyras and Louis-Gabriel Blanchet.

In Rome the works of Guido Reni seem to have had a particularly strong influence on Trémolières; in the first year of his stay he made a copy (Grenoble, Mus. Peint. & Sculp.) of Reni's *Virgin Appearing to SS Anthony and Paul* in the Palazzo Giustiniani. In 1732 he painted for Paul-Hippolyte, Duc de Saint-Aignan, the French Ambassador in Rome, an allegory of *Religion* (Paris, Inst. France); Subleyras produced a companion piece, of *Justice*. Trémolières's most important commission in Rome, however, was from Cardinal Pietro Ottoboni for a copy (Rome, S

Maria degli Angeli) after Francesco Vanni's *Fall of Simon Magus* in St Peter's. Ottoboni interceded for the artist with the Directeur des Bâtiments du Roi, the Duc d'Antin, who approved an extension of his stay in Rome until 1734. An intimate, bust-length *Self-portrait* (see 1973 exh. cat., pl. xx), still in the possession of the artist's family, probably dates from that year. In October 1734 Trémolières and his new wife, Isabella Tibaldi (whose sister, the miniaturist Maria Felice Tibaldi, was married to Subleyras), arrived in Lyon, where he painted a series of large-scale oil paintings for the Carmelite church of St Bruno. The most successful of them—the *Ascension of Christ* and the *Assumption of the Virgin* (both Lyon, St Bruno)—were completed in Paris in 1737.

In 1736 Trémolières was approved (*agréé*) at the Académie Royale; and in 1737 he was received (*reçu*) as a full member on presentation of *Ulysses Rescued from Shipwreck by Minerva* (Montpellier, Mus. Fabre), an elegant and harmonious composition.

Trémolières was also active as a decorative painter for private clients. In 1736 he completed a series of overdoors of graceful female figures representing *Music* and *Poetry* (both Switzerland, priv. col., see 1973 exh. cat., pls xxvii, xxviii) and *Tragedy* and *Comedy* (Cholet, Mus. A.). Although the proportions and facial features of the allegories are bounded by academic canons of beauty Trémolières injected a certain amount of Rococo gaiety into the pictures, as he also did in the six mythological compositions (e.g. the *Nuptials of Hercules and Hebe*; *in situ*) painted in 1737–8 for the Hôtel de Soubise, Paris, the greatest decorative ensemble of its period in France. Such graceful and charming compositions were widely admired by contemporaries. At the end of his life he received a royal commission for four tapestry cartoons representing the *Ages of Man*. Only one (Cholet, Mus. A.), however, was begun before his death. There are collections of his drawings at the Musée des Arts at Cholet, at the Musée des Beaux-Arts et d'Archéologie at Besançon, at the Musée des Beaux-Arts et d'Archéologie at Rennes, and in the Louvre, Paris.

BIBLIOGRAPHY

Thieme–Becker

A. J. Dézallier d'Argenville: *Abrégé de la vie des plus fameux peintres* (1745–52, 2/1762), iv, pp. 455–8
A.-C. de Caylus: 'Pierre Charles Trémollière' (1748), *Mémoires inédits sur la vie et les ouvrages des membres de l'Académie royale de peinture et de sculpture*, ed. L. Dussieux and others, ii (Paris, 1854), pp. 442–8
J. Messelet: 'Trémollières', *Les Peintres français du XVIIIe siècle*, ed. L. Dimier, i (Paris, 1928), pp. 267–81
Pierre-Charles Trémolières (Cholet 1703–Paris 1739) (exh. cat. by J.-F. Méjanès and J. Vilain, Cholet, Mus. A., 1973)

CATHRIN KLINGSÖHR-LE-ROY

Trenta, Filippo (*b* Ascoli Piceno, 1731; *d* Foligno, 13 March 1795). Italian bishop, collector, patron and writer. He belonged to a noble family and, having studied law at the University of Bologna, pursued a career in public service and from 1785 was Bishop of Foligno. He had a library of more than 1000 volumes and became a successful poet and tragedian. During his years in Bologna he was an enthusiastic art collector, acquiring more than 150 works, which he himself catalogued in 1784 (MS., Fermo, Bib. Com.). Trenta admired 17th-century Bolognese painters and owned works by Guido Reni, the Carracci, Guido

Cagnacci, Carlo Cignani, Giovanni Andrea Donducci (1575–1655), Pietro Faccini, Francesco Gessi and Elisabetta Sirani. Yet, like other 18th-century Bolognese collectors, he was also drawn to Venetian, Roman and Neapolitan art. The most adventurous aspect of his patronage was his interest in contemporary art, especially in the works of Ubaldo Gandolfi and Gaetano Gandolfi (*see* GANDOLFI, (2)), from whom he commissioned pictures for himself and for some churches in Foligno, for example Gaetano Gandolfi's *Blessed Angel of Foligno* for S Francesco and *St Feliciano Freeing Foligno from the Plague* for the Cathedral (both *in situ*). His collection remained the property of the Trenta family until 1904–5, when it was sold in three public auctions in Fermo. Only a small part of it is still traceable in private collections; several from the original collection were reacquired by a descendant, Filippo Trenta (1892–1976), including Gaetano Gandolfi's *Death of Socrates* (1784) and sketches for his *Adulterous Woman Pardoned by Christ* and *St Paul Preaching to the Athenians*.

BIBLIOGRAPHY
G. Cantalamessa-Carboni: *Memorie intorno i letterati e gli artisti della città di Ascoli nel Piceno* (Ascoli, 1830)
L. Battista: 'Filippo Trenta: Un collezionista dimenticato', *Atti & Mem. Accad. Clementina Bologna*, xxiii (1988), pp. 55–66

LUCIA BATTISTA

Trentacoste, Domenico (*b* Palermo, 20 Sept 1859; *d* Florence, 18 March 1933). Italian sculptor, medallist and teacher. He worked in Palermo in the workshop of Domenico Constantino (1840–*c*. 1915) from *c*. 1870 to *c*. 1877, collaborating for a short while (1874–5) with Benedetto Delisi (1831–75). After a visit to Naples, where he admired the antique sculpture in the Museo Archeologico Nazionale, he went to Florence in 1878 to study 15th-century Tuscan sculpture. In 1880 he was in Paris, where he exhibited his work at the Salons of 1881, 1884, 1885 and 1887. His *Cecilia* (London, Buckingham Pal., Royal Col.) was bought in London in 1891 by the Princess of Wales. He became well known in France and England for his portraits, terracotta pieces depicting genre subjects, and marbles clearly inspired by Tuscan Renaissance sculpture. He was also successful in Italy, participating in the first Venice Biennale in 1895 with the marble *Abandoned Woman* (Trieste, Mus. Civ. Revoltella). He subsequently settled permanently in Florence, where his portraits and female figures were much in demand. His sculpture always maintained a Renaissance-inspired simplicity and rigour and at the same time a grace shadowed with a degree of melancholy, as in the *Meditation* (1896–7), a funerary statue for the grave of his sister in the cemetery at Palermo, or the marble *Sleeping Woman* (1910; Rome, G.N.A. Mod.). Among his important works produced at the beginning of the 20th century are the *Dead Christ* (1905; Florence, Pitti) and *Niobe* (Venice, Pal. Pesaro). In his bronze works, however, he inclined more to a contemporary style between Realism and Impressionism, as in the figure of *Cain* (1902; Rome, G.N.A. Mod.), inspired by Rodin's *The Thinker* (1888; Paris, Mus. Rodin). Trentacoste was also known as a medallist. Many of his medals are in the collection of the Galleria d'Arte Moderna, Florence. From *c*. 1915 he taught at and was Director of

the Accademia di Belle Arti in Florence and in 1932 was nominated an Accademico d'Italia.

BIBLIOGRAPHY
Enc. It.; Thieme-Becker
E. Lavagnino: *L'arte moderna* (Turin, 1956), pp. 666–7
M. De Micheli: *La scultura dell'ottocento* (Turin, 1992), p. 258

STEFANIA FREZZOTTI

Trent Castle. *See* BUONCONSIGLIO CASTLE.

Treppenhaus [Ger. 'stairhouse']. German term for a stairwell and, in Baroque architecture, for the ceremonial hall from which a grand staircase rises.

☐

Très Belles Heures de Notre Dame. *See under* TURIN-MILAN HOURS.

Tresguerras, Francisco Eduardo (*b* Celaya, 13 Oct 1759; *d* Celaya, 3 Aug 1833). Mexican architect, painter, engraver and sculptor. He studied painting under Miguel Cabrera at the Real Academia de las Nobles Artes de S Carlos in Mexico City but did not graduate. He subsequently took up wood-carving and engraving. He learnt the elements of architecture from the Jesuits, who gave him a copy of the writings of Jacopo Vignola. His architecture exhibits a familiarity with the classic treatises, although he never visited Europe. Tresguerras's first major work (1780s) was the reconstruction in Neo-classical style of the convent church of S Rosa, Querétaro, originally consecrated in 1752. The dome over the crossing is set on a drum articulated by rusticated columns, which flank a series of round-headed openings. He is also credited with remodelling the interior of the convent church of S Clara, Querétaro, and with constructing the Neptune Fountain (1802–7) in the plaza in front of it. The god stands under a triumphal arch, while water pours through the mouth of a fish at his feet. Tresguerras also completed (1807) the Carmelite convent in Querétaro, to the designs of Manuel Tolsá.

Tresguerras's most outstanding work was the church of Carmen de Celaya (1803–7), which displayed an emergent Neo-classicism derived from European models (*see* MEXICO, §III, 1). The nave bays are marked externally by buttresses capped by inverted consoles, with square scrolls adapted from ancient Mexican architecture. The crossing dome has a drum set off by coupled columns, in the manner of St Peter's, Rome, but these features are here continued up the dome's tiled exterior with the slightest inflection. The side portal, abutting the transept, has a dished upper storey that serves as a background to the aedicule housing a statue of the Virgin. The main entrance, at the end of the nave, is surmounted by a tower, the upper storeys of which are articulated with various combinations of classical forms, capped by a conical dome. Tresguerras designed all the *retablos* for the church, carved and painted most of the figure sculpture and executed the frescoes.

The most notable secular building by Tresguerras was the palace he designed (1809) for the Condes de Casa Rul in Guanajuato. It features a colossal order above a plinth storey, with a slightly projecting central range surmounted by a pediment, an uncompromising statement of Tresguerras's adherence to Neo-classicism. Other important works include the Teatro Alarcón (1827) in the town of San Luis Potosí, where he also designed the public water supply system. Tresguerras's works set the standard for progressive 19th-century academic Neo-classicism in Mexico, in contrast with the brilliant period of Mexican popular Baroque. He epitomized a certain group of Latin American architects who, although self-taught, were convinced of their creative potential.

BIBLIOGRAPHY

V. M. Villegas: *Francisco Eduardo Tresguerras, arquitecto de su tiempo* (Mexico City, 1964)
Ocios literários (1972)
R. Gutierrez: *Arquitectura iberoamericana, 1800–1850* (Resistencia, 1979)
——: *Arquitectura y fortificación: De la ilustración a la independencia americana* (Madrid, 1993)

RAMÓN GUTIERREZ

Tresham, Henry (*b* Dublin, ?1751; *d* London, 17 June 1814). Irish painter, printmaker, dealer and writer. He first studied at the Dublin Society of Artists drawing school, winning an exhibition prize in 1773. In 1775 he travelled to London and then to Rome, probably in the company of John Campbell, later 1st Baron Cawdor. Tresham spent 14 years on the Continent, chiefly in Rome, and it was there among an international circle of Neo-classical artists that his taste was formed; his acquaintances included Thomas Jones, William Pars, James Northcote, Thomas Banks, Antonio Canova and Henry Fuseli. Tresham supplemented his income by working as a dealer in art and antiquities, while his most ambitious project in Italy was *Le avventure di Saffo* (Rome, 1784), a folio volume of 18 of his aquatints (Josiah Wedgwood's copy now London, BM). In 1789 he returned to London and quickly assumed a prominent position in artistic circles. He exhibited regularly at the Royal Academy, and became ARA in 1791 and RA in 1799. In 1807 he succeeded John Opie as the Academy's professor of painting, resigning after two years through ill health. He was also intermittently active as an editor and poet (publishing five volumes of verse between 1796 and 1810), as well as continuing to work as an art dealer. The annuity on which he depended in his late years was derived from his sale to Frederick Howard, 5th Earl of Carlisle, of a group of supposedly authentic 'Etruscan' vases (for the background to such misattributions *see* ETRUSCAN, §VIII, and ETRUSCAN STYLE).

All Tresham's large-scale history pictures, on which he made his reputation, are untraced. They included ambitious subjects from Classical history undertaken for Frederick Augustus Hervey, 4th Earl of Bristol, at Rome in the 1780s, and his contributions to major history painting projects in London, among them Robert Bowyer's History Gallery, John Boydell's Shakespeare Gallery and Thomas Macklin's *Holy Bible*. The engravings made after Tresham's work indicate that he practised a watered-down version of Füseli's style: elongated and heavily muscled figures, mannered postures and compositions carefully simplified in order to focus attention on emotionally charged incidents. Extant smaller pictures, such as his medievalizing *The Earl of Warwick's Vow before the Battle of Towton* (438×362 mm, exh. RA 1797; Manchester, C.A.G.), confirm this view of his art. His drawings (e.g.

New Haven, CT, Yale Cent. Brit. A., and elsewhere) are more varied in style, and their subject-matter includes landscapes and genre scenes.

PRINTS
Le avventure di Saffo (Rome, 1784)
BIBLIOGRAPHY
DNB; Waterhouse: *18th C.*
The Fuseli Circle in Rome (exh. cat. by N. Pressly, New Haven, CT, Yale Cent. Brit. A., 1979), pp. 101–6

PETER WALCH

Très Riches Heures. Book of Hours produced for the renowned bibliophile and patron Jean, Duc de Berry (*see* VALOIS, (3)). Delisle (1884) identified the manuscript (290×210 mm; Chantilly, Mus. Condé, MS. 65) with a description in an inventory made after the death of the Duc in 1416: 'several gatherings of a very rich Book of Hours, richly historiated and illuminated, that Pol and his brothers made'. This attribution has received general acceptance and has also provided the manuscript with its name.

The first phase of illumination was carried out by the Limbourg brothers, Pol, Jean and Herman, and their assistants *c.* 1411/13–1416 (*see* LIMBOURG, DE). Unfinished at the deaths in 1416 of the artists and the Duc, a mid-15th-century illuminator, possibly Barthélemy d'Eyck, seems to have been employed to work on some of the calendar miniatures. The book was completed *c.* 1485–6 by Jean Colombe (*see* COLOMBE, (2)) for a later owner, Charles I, Duke of Savoy (*reg* 1482–90). Portraits of Charles and his wife Blanche of Montferrat, accompanied by their coats of arms, are on folio 75r. They were married in 1485 and Charles died in 1490, and the second phase of the book's illumination must therefore have taken place between these dates. It has been associated more precisely with an entry in the accounts of Savoy, dated 31 August 1485, of a payment by the Duc of 25 gold pieces to Jean Colombe in Bourges for the illumination of a Book of Hours. The manuscript may have come to Charles through Bonne of Armagnac (*d* 1415), daughter of Jean de Berry and a direct ancestor of the Duke of Savoy. Alternatively, it may have been a gift to the House of Savoy from the Royal Library, since it is known that other books from Jean de Berry entered the King's collections after 1416. The whereabouts of the book from the death of Charles of Savoy up to its purchase in Turin in 1856 by the Duc d'Aumale from the estate of the Marchese Giovanni-Serra are unclear. In 1897 the Duc d'Aumale donated the estate of Chantilly and his collections to the Institut de France, which is responsible for the Musée Condé.

The manuscript consists of 206 leaves of very fine quality parchment. Codicological data indicate that sections are missing and that some of the full-page miniatures were inserted on single leaves (the *Anatomical Man*, fol. 14v; *The Fall*, fol. 25r; the *Meeting of the Magi*, fol. 51v, *see* LIMBOURG, DE, fig. 4; the *Adoration of the Magi*, fol. 52r, *see* FRANCE, fig. 17; the *Presentation*, fol. 54v; the *Fall of the Rebel Angels*, fol. 64v; *Hell*, fol. 108r; the *Map of Rome*, fol. 141v). Meiss and subsequent writers have argued that these miniatures were not originally designed for the Très Riches Heures; however, although the subjects are handled in an innovative manner, they fit within the context of the prayerbook and could well have been part of a developing collaborative plan. There remain in total 65 small miniatures and 66 large ones, which combine with numerous initials and line-endings to orchestrate the text, while a variety of foliate border sprays extend from the initials and decorate some of the margins of the large miniatures. The text is written in two columns in black ink in a regular Gothic script. Traces remain of instructions to the rubricator and illuminators written in fine brown ink in the margins or with a stylus around the arches of the calendar. In addition to the texts characteristic of many 15th-century Books of Hours, the manuscript contains short Hours or Offices for each day of the week and a comprehensive Missal section with masses drawn from both the temporal and sanctoral cycles of the Church's year.

The illumination of the Limbourgs in the Très Riches Heures is a splendid example of the Late Gothic style that flourished in the courts of Europe in the early years of the 15th century (*see* GOTHIC, §IV, 5(x) and (xi)). The fine delineation of mannered, courtly forms and the use of rich, luminous colours combine with a rendering of objects, landscape and natural phenomena to reveal the artist's northern origins and sensibility. In particular, the unusual series of full-page calendar miniatures display the Limbourgs' effective combination of landscape settings and architectural backgrounds with stately pageantry and keenly observed detail. Here the artists adapted and expanded the ancient theme of the changing seasons and their varying activities to allude specifically to the Duc. In the scene of feasting in *January* (for illustration *see* VALOIS, (3)) he is shown surrounded by his colourful court, and in several of the landscapes that follow, ducal châteaux feature in the backgrounds (*see* MILITARY ARCHITECTURE AND FORTIFICATION, fig. 1). It has been convincingly argued, however, that a mid-15th-century artist's hand is recognizable not only in certain figures rendered in distinctively later styles of dress in the months of *October* and *December*, but also in the more naturalistic depiction of such details as cast shadows, individualized facial expressions and atmospheric light effects that characterize, to some extent, the compositions for *March*, *June* and *September* as well. It has further been proposed that in some of the calender miniatures where this later hand is discernible, the buildings may relate to a mid-15th-century royal patron rather than to Jean de Berry (Bellosi, König, Cazelles and 1993 exh. cat.).

Attention has also focused on the Italian influences in the Limbourgs' work in the Très Riches Heures and on their contact with the Classical tradition, evident, for example, in the rendering of the nude torso of Adam in *The Fall* (fol. 25r). Explicit borrowings from Italian compositions have also been identified; most notable is the *Presentation* (fol. 54v), which is an adaptation of Taddeo Gaddi's fresco of the *Presentation of the Virgin* in the Baroncelli Chapel, Santa Croce, Florence (*see* GADDI (i), (2), fig. 1). The innovative treatment of borders by both the Limbourgs and their assistants has also been explained in terms of contact with Lombard illumination. Meiss has distinguished the contribution of the MASTER OF THE BREVIARY OF JEAN SANS PEUR (*see* MASTERS, ANONYMOUS, AND MONOGRAMMISTS, §I) and his assistants to

Très Riches Heures, *Funeral of Raymond Diocrès*, miniature illustrating the Office of the Dead by Jean Colombe to a design by the Limbourg brothers, 290×210 mm folio size, *c.* 1411/13–16 and *c.* 1485–6 (Chantilly, Musée Condé, Château de Chantilly, MS. 65, fol. 86v)

the initial and border decoration of the first phase. Meiss's attempt to differentiate, however, between the three Limbourg brothers has not met with the same measure of acceptance. Scholars agree only that Pol must have been the leader of the team since his name is specified in contemporary documents.

When Jean Colombe assumed the task of completing the book in the 1480s, he had, in some cases, to complete miniatures begun by the Limbourgs, filling in, for example, the foreground figures and faces (see fig.). In other gatherings he was responsible for the whole composition, which he often enclosed in heavy simulated marble and gold frames. His figures are sturdier with more heavily modelled features than those of the Limbourgs, and his weightier draperies are lavishly embellished with gold highlights. While the interest in landscape and architectural settings persists, Colombe's compositions reflect later developments, especially in the progression from foreground through middle ground to distant vistas, often painted in shades of blue.

The Très Riches Heures is the most formal and quasi-liturgical of the extant Hours of Jean de Berry. Its short weekly Offices and series of masses have precedents in earlier Books of Hours made for the Duc and other members of the royal family; but absent from the Très Riches Heures are the suffrages in honour of the saints and the more personal prayers and devotions, which usually intermingle in such prayerbooks with the formally structured Hours and Offices. Instead, the importance of the Psalms for both liturgical and individual prayer is emphasized by a most unusual programme of illustration in which the Psalms and Canticles of the Offices are introduced by small miniatures that illustrate certain verses according to an ancient 'word-picture' tradition. Explanatory *tituli* in alternating lines of gold and blue were originally designed to accompany the illustrations but only seven of these were completed. Even the overtly secular series of calendar miniatures of the Très Riches Heures is imbued with a sense of public ceremonial, and behind its glowing pages lies a world in which patron, artists, scribe and learned adviser worked together to produce an appropriate aid to formal prayer, for use, perhaps, in the ducal chapel, and certainly in a context in which both the sacred and the secular were permeated with a love of rhythmic ritual and colourful splendour.

BIBLIOGRAPHY

L. Delisle: 'Les Livres d'Heures du duc de Berry', *Gaz. B.-A.*, xxix (1884), pp. 97–110, 281–92, 391–405
P. Durrieu: *Les Très Riches Heures de Jean de France, duc de Berry* (Paris, 1904)
O. Pächt: 'Early Italian Nature Studies and the Early Calendar Landscape', *J. Warb. & Court. Inst.*, xiii (1950), pp. 13–47 [40]
E. Panofsky: *Early Netherlandish Painting: Its Origin and Character* (Cambridge, MA, 1958)
J. Longman and R. Cazelles with M. Meiss: *Les Très Riches Heures du Duc de Berry* (London, 1969)
C. Schaefer: 'Oeuvres du début de la carrière de l'enlumineur Jean Colombe', *Cah. Archéol. Hist. Berry*, xxxv (1973), pp. 45–57
M. Meiss with S. O. Smith and E. Beatson: *French Painting in the Time of Jean de Berry: The Limbourgs and their Contemporaries*, 2 vols (New York and London, 1974)
C. Schaefer: 'Les Débuts de l'atelier de Jean Colombe: Jean Colombe et André Rousseau, prêtre, libraire et "escrivain"', *Gaz. B.-A.*, xc (1977), pp. 137–50
R. Cazelles and J. Rathofer: *Les Très Riches Heures du Duc de Berry*, 2 vols (New York, 1984) [facs. and commentary]
——: *Illuminations of Heaven and Earth: The Glories of the Très Riches Heures du Duc de Berry* (New York, 1988)
J. J. G. Alexander: 'The Limbourg Brothers and Italian Art: A New Source', *Z. Kstgesch.*, xlvi (1988), pp. 425–35
——: *Medieval Illuminators and their Methods of Work* (New Haven and London, 1992), pp. 139–43

MARGARET M. MANION

Tress, Arthur (*b* Brooklyn, NY, 24 Nov 1940). American photographer. He studied painting and art history at Bard College, Annandale-on-Hudson, New York (1958–62), but by the mid-1960s was committed to photography. His first published work, for anthropological journals, resulted from travels in Mexico, Japan, India, Europe, Alaska and Africa. In 1971 a more personal direction was demonstrated in his portfolio *Open Space in the Inner City*, which pictures the inhabitants of New York in the squalor and decay of their environment. His first acclaimed book, *The Dream Collector* (Richmond, VA, 1972), consists of re-enactments of children's dreams, showing elements of fantasy and the grotesque that he has continued to explore. In his later work he concentrated on theatrical and psychologically revealing studies of human relationships,

for example in *Theater of the Mind* (New York, 1976), on homo-erotic fantasy in *Facing Up* (New York, 1980) and on the ritualistic aspects of contemporary life. His still-lifes and two major sequences, *Shadow* (New York, 1975) and *The Teapot Opera* (1980; pubd New York, 1988), confirm him as a photographer of great range and imagination.

BIBLIOGRAPHY
M. Tournier: *Arthur Tress: Rêves* (Brussels, 1979)
M. Livingstone: *Arthur Tress: Talisman* (London, 1986)

MARCO LIVINGSTONE

Tressini, Domenico. *See* TREZZINI, DOMENICO.

Tres Zapotes. Pre-Columbian OLMEC site in the southern Gulf Coast of Mexico that flourished *c.* 1000–*c.* 400 BC. It was originally called Hueyapan and extends for about 3.5 km along the right bank of the River Hueyapan at the foot of the Tuxtla Mountains. Tres Zapotes was discovered by José Melgar, who found the first Olmec colossal stone head in 1862. Eduard Seler and his wife visited the site in 1905, as did Albert Weyerstall between 1925 and 1927. Both parties found more sculptures. The site was excavated by Matthew Stirling from 1938 to 1940, when the lower half of Stele C was found, with the Maya Long Count date (*see* MESOAMERICA, PRE-COLUMBIAN, §II) corresponding to 31 BC, then the oldest known inscribed date (Stele 2 at Chiapa de Corzo bears a date of 36 BC, assuming a *baktun* 7). Stirling described and illustrated the site and more than 20 sculpted monuments, while colleagues C. Weiant and P. Drucker studied the ceramics. Ground surveys in and around the site have been done by Alfonso Medellín Zenil and archaeologists from the Universidad Veracruzana. However, studies of Tres Zapotes have been incomplete, and the site is not fully understood. Its oldest part is known to be Middle Pre-Classic Olmec (*c.* 1000–*c.* 300 BC), but occupation by other cultural groups continued until the Early Post-Classic period (*c.* AD 900–*c.* 1200).

Three large terraces can be distinguished. One forms the eastern boundary of the zone and comprises high mounds near the river, Group 2 and the Burnt Mounds Group. The second terrace comprises the Mounds I Group. The third terrace has two levels, the larger, southern one comprising the Small Farm (Village) Group and the New Lands Group, and the northern level comprising the Mounds 3 Group. Unlike the earlier Olmec sites of SAN LORENZO TENOCHTITLÁN and LA VENTA, the architecture at Tres Zapotes lacks both a specific orientation and geometrical arrangement of mounds to form clear ceremonial plazas. Nevertheless, some of the 50 mounds surveyed form plaza-like patterns: next to a mound *c.* 13 m high and 50 m long stands a long, low, narrow mound that measures 150×8×19 m. Smaller lateral mounds are arranged in pairs alongside the main mounds. Most of the mounds are made of clay, but one small platform, two stairways and some floors are faced with cut stone, possibly the earliest use of cut stone for architectural construction in Mesoamerica, although because the dating of the construction cannot be precise, the stone pyramids at CUICUILCO may be earlier. Tres Zapotes overlaps in date and seems to succeed La Venta as the primary Olmec ceremonial centre, but not all its monumental sculptures are of pure Olmec style. Exceptions include two colossal heads—one at the site and one at nearby Cerro Nestepe—and various animal sculptures; and the stelae and busts with human traits on the end of a peg may have been carved towards the end of the Olmec period. These and chests covered with relief carvings show strong links with the Izapan style centred at IZAPA in the Maya highlands. Sculptures from Tres Zapotes are in Santiago Tuxtla (Mus. Reg.), Tres Zapotes village (Tres Zapotes Mus.) and Mexico City (Mus. N. Antropol.).

BIBLIOGRAPHY

P. Drucker: 'Ceramic Sequences at Tres Zapotes, Veracruz, Mexico', *Bureau Amer. Ethnol. Bull.*, 140 (1943) [whole issue]

M. W. Stirling: 'Stone Monuments of Southern Mexico', *Bureau Amer. Ethnol. Bull.*, 138 (1943) [whole issue]

C. W. Weiant: 'An Introduction to the Ceramics of Tres Zapotes, Veracruz, Mexico', *Bureau Amer. Ethnol. Bull.*, 139 (1943) [whole issue]

B. de la Fuente: *Escultura monumental olmeca: Catálogo* (Mexico City, 1973)

BEATRIZ DE LA FUENTE

Tretko, Jan. *See* TRICIUS, JAN.

Tretsch, Aberlin [Albrecht] (*b* Stuttgart, ?1510; *d* Stuttgart, 1577–8). German architect. A bondsman and the son of a poor family, he was self-taught and became adviser to the Dukes of Württemberg on artistic and technical matters. He knew none of the Mediterranean languages but had trained his eye by looking at the architecture of foreign courts. In 1568, with Georg Gadner, a privy councillor, he drew up a set of building regulations for Württemberg. From 1537 he was in the service of Duke Ulrich VI of Württemberg (*reg* 1537–50) and from 1550 in that of Duke Christopher (*reg* 1550–68); after the latter's death Tretsch spent the last years of his own life working for Duke Ludwig VI (*reg* 1568–93).

Tretsch's main work is undoubtedly the Altes Schloss (1553–68), the ducal palace in Stuttgart, on which he collaborated with Blasius Berwart I. The work started with rebuilding the medieval middle section of the Schloss, the Dürnitzbau, which was completed in 1560 with the duchess's chambers. In the same year an outside staircase was constructed in front of the courtyard façade of the Dürnitzbau, probably to designs by Berwart. The building of the three new courtyard ranges began in 1557. All three floors of these ranges are fronted on the courtyard side by arcades with rib vaulting and Corinthian columns (for illustration *see* STUTTGART). In 1559 Tretsch submitted a plan for the new (south) wing of the Altes Schloss, which was to include a chapel. The Schlosskapelle was the first Protestant church in the duchy of Württemberg; the sightline for the church is mentioned in 1557. The church consists of a broad, rectangular transverse chamber with two floors and a polygonal chancel on the outer long side. Its model may have been the church at Schloss Neuburg on the Danube, studied by Blasius Berwart I in 1559. With the three new ranges, the old Dürnitzbau has a four-range layout around a rectangular courtyard. The arcaded ranges are broken up regularly by pavilions at roof level, similar features being found in Schloss Göppingen. The Schlosskapelle, consecrated in 1562, was given stuccoed vaulting in 1566. The chancellery (1564), built adjacent to the

Schloss, is also based on designs by Tretsch. In 1566–7 Duke Christopher added an extra storey to the chancellery.

Tretsch was also involved in many other projects for the dukes. His expertise was particularly in demand for the reinforcement and extension of the fortresses at Hohentwiel (1552–6; 1561–4), Hohenurach (1561–5) and Schorndorf (1565). In addition, he drew up plans for the ducal palaces at Göppingen (1557–65), Pfullingen (1563) and Schloss Neuenstadt (1565) on the Linde. Tretsch also produced plans or prepared reports for other houses of dynasties related or friendly to the Dukes of Württemberg, for example the Schloss at Bad Bergzabern. He also worked for Margrave Georg Friedrich of Ansbach, brother-in-law to Duke Christopher of Württemberg, in the summer of 1563, when he carried out a survey of the Plassenburg. On his homeward journey Tretsch stopped in Munich to make drawings of the latest buildings of Duke Albert of Bavaria (tournament lists at the Mint, the great Georgssaal in the Neuveste). The erection of funeral monuments to the dukes in the chancel of the Stiftungskirche took Tretsch to Tübingen in 1568, 1570 and 1573. In 1574 he was involved in preliminary plans for the new Stuttgart Lusthaus. He retired from service in 1576, on the grounds of failing sight.

BIBLIOGRAPHY

Thieme–Becker

W. Fleischhauer: *Die Renaissance im Herzogtum Württemberg* (Stuttgart, 1971)

K. Merten: *Altes Schloss Stuttgart* (Munich, 1975)

H.-R. Hitchcock: *German Renaissance Architecture* (Princeton, 1981)

H. J. Kadatz: *Deutsche Renaissancebaukunst* (Berlin, 1983)

Die Renaissance im deutschen Südwesten (exh. cat., Karlsruhe, Bad. Landesmus., 1986), pp. 948–9

KAI BUDDE

Tret'yakov, Pavel (Mikhaylovich) (*b* Moscow, 27 Dec 1832; *d* Moscow, 16 Dec 1898). Russian patron, collector, museum founder and curator. A textile magnate, he was one of the first merchants to patronize the arts in Russia. In 1851, after his marriage to Vera Mamontova, the niece of the industrialist Savva Mamontov, the founder of the artistic colony at Abramtsevo, he bought a large mansion in Moscow and began to collect art. Initially he bought western European engravings and 17th-century Dutch paintings, but after seeing the Russian works in Illarion Pryanishnikov's collection in St Petersburg, he switched to Russian art. He collected icons and 18th- and 19th-century works, as well as, most importantly, becoming the main patron of the group that became known as WANDERERS. He appreciated both the Academy of Art in St Petersburg and its rebels. Less concerned with social and moral issues than Vladimir Stasov, who frequently sought his patronage for the Wanderers, his outlook was essentially ethnocentric Slavophile. Diluting the Wanderers' original instinct to reform, he favoured realist landscapes and religious paintings with exclusively devotional content. He commissioned much of their most important work (e.g. Vasily Perov's portrait of *Fyodor Dostoyevsky*, 1872; Moscow, Tret'yakov Gal.) and established close relations with Ivan Kramskoy, Vasily Maksimov, Viktor Vasnetsov and Il'ya Repin.

In 1872, with the growth of his collection and his desire to create a museum of national art that would encapsulate its history, Tret'yakov commissioned a new gallery building on his land. Decorated by Vasnetsov in a style evocative of Old Russia, the gallery opened in 1874. The ground-floor displayed 18th- and early 19th-century canvases by Ivan Nikitin, Aleksey Antropov, Dmitry Levitsky, Vladimir Borovikovsky, Fyodor Rokotov, Aleksey Venetsianov, Karl Bryullov and Ivan Aivazovsky (1817–1900). Upstairs he exhibited the more distinctively Russian school of the Wanderers. This part of the collection grew most rapidly and by 1892 a total of 19 new exhibition halls had been added. The public flocked to see the new Russian art: by 1890 there were 50,000 visitors annually.

After the death of his brother Sergey Tret'yakov (*b* 1834) in 1892, Tret'yakov gave their combined collections of Russian and Western art to the city of Moscow. The gallery that opened in 1893 was called The Pavel and Sergey Tret'yakov Moscow City Art Gallery. It included over 1800 paintings and graphic works from Pavel's collection and 84 paintings that had belonged to Sergey, including works by David, Bastien-Lepage, Courbet, Corot, Millet and other members of the Barbizon school. Pavel remained curator until his death in 1898 when the administration was taken over by a committee appointed by the Moscow Duma (including Tret'yakov's daughter, Aleksandra Botkina (1867–1959), Vladimir Golitsyn (1847–1932) as curator, the collector Ivan Tsvetkov (1845–1912) and the artists Valentin Serov, Igor' Grabar' and Il'ya Ostroukhov). On 3 June 1918 the gallery was nationalized by Lenin and became the State Tret'yakov Gallery. It remains, together with the Russian Museum in St Petersburg, the most important collection of Russian art in the world.

BIBLIOGRAPHY

A. P. Botkina: *P. M. Tret'yakov v zhizni i iskusstve* [P. M. Tret'yakov in life and art] (Moscow, 1951/*R* 1960)
A. N. Tyrsa, ed.: *Gosudarstvennaya Tret'yakovskaya Galereya: Ocherki istorii, 1856–1917* [The State Tret'yakov Gallery: studies in its history, 1856–1917] (Leningrad, 1981)
I. I. Nikonova, ed.: *Gosudarstvennaya Tret'yakovskaya Galereya: Istoriya i kollektsii* [The State Tret'yakov Gallery: its history and collections] (Moscow, 1989)

JEREMY HOWARD

Trevano, Giovanni (*b* Lugano; *fl c.* 1600; *d* Kraków, 1641–5). Italian architect, active in Poland. He appeared in Poland *c.* 1600 and worked almost exclusively for the king and for the bishops of Kraków. From 1607 he was Master of the Royal Works and later (1613) became the king's Surveyor. Between 1606–9 and 1613–19 Trevano supervised the construction, inspired by Il Gesù in Rome, of the Jesuit church of SS Peter and Paul, Kraków, which was begun in 1597 by Giuseppe Brizzio; according to a new design (after 1617) by Matteo Castelli, Trevano added features reminiscent of S Andrea della Valle. The famous ashlar façade (?after 1619) shows the influence of the later works of Carlo Maderno, designed in collaboration with Castelli; it surpasses even contemporary Roman church façades with the perfection of its proportions. However, it is not certain that this was the work of Trevano; on the other hand the two works commissioned by Bishop Marcin Szyszkowski (*d* 1630) in Kraków Cathedral are certainly by Trevano. The bishop's tomb (1629–30) and the enormous baldacchino over the sepulchre of St Stanisław (1626–9) situated on the crossing both evoke late 16th-century artistic traditions of Rome and Maderno's later

period. The baldacchino, realized as an openwork chapel with a dome, was based on Martino Ferabosco's unrealized design (before 1620) for the *confessio* of St Peter's, in Rome. Trevano was the earliest of the group of Italian architects to work for the Vasa dynasty of Polish kings. This group, which included the Castelli family, created the only offshoot north of the Alps of early Roman Baroque architecture, in the style of Maderno.

BIBLIOGRAPHY

A. Bochnak: 'Kościół śś. Piotra i Pawła w Krakowie i jego rzymski pierwowzór oraz architekt królewski Jan Trevano' [The church of SS Peter and Paul in Kraków and its Roman prototype and the royal architect, Giovanni Trevano], *Prace Kom. Hist. Sztuki*, ix (1948), pp. 89–125
A. Małkiewicz: 'Kościół śś. Piotra i Pawła w Krakowie: Dzieje budowy i problem autorstwa' [The church of SS Peter and Paul in Kraków: the history of its construction and the problem of its author], *Prace Hist. Sztuki*, v (1967), pp. 43–86
A. Miłobędzki: *Architektura polska XVII wieku* [Polish architecture of the 17th century] (Warsaw, 1980), pp. 115–17, 121–4, 218 ff
M. Karpowicz: *Artisti ticinesi in Polonia nel '600* (Agno and Lugano, 1983), pp. 20, 27–43

ADAM MIŁOBĘDZKI

Trevi, Temple of Clitumnus. Site of a Roman temple incorporated into an Early Christian or early medieval church, *c.* 15 km north of Spoleto, Italy. The River Clitumnus, with its numerous springs, was sacred in Roman times, and there were many shrines along its course. Spolia from these may have been used in the existing structure. It has some traits in common with Roman temples, most notably its four-columned façade with a pediment above. The framing of the columns with two apparently contemporary square section columns is uncommon, but other aspects of its design mark it out as an Early Christian building (4th or 5th century AD) or an early medieval one (8th or 9th century). The interior has a narrow horseshoe arch in the apse and carved mouldings with early medieval characteristics. The building stands on a podium, but instead of a staircase at the front, a flight of steps on either side leads to a small pedimented doorway giving access to the interior. This unusual arrangement may be due to the siting of the building on a sloping bank, but its bold form, with miniaturized Hellenistic grandeur reminiscent of the Roman sanctuary (late 2nd century BC) at Praeneste, has attracted much interest, including that of Palladio, as seen in his design for the Villa Foscari-Malcontenta (late 1550s). The building is still in use as a church, dedicated to S Salvatore, and there are remains of 8th-century wall paintings of *Christ the Redeemer* between SS Peter and Paul.

BIBLIOGRAPHY

W. Hoppenstadt: *Die Basilica San Salvatore bei Spoleto und der Clitunnotempel bei Trevi* (Halle, 1912)
A. P. Frutaz: 'Il tempietto del Clitunno', *Riv. Archaeol. Crist.*, xvii (1941), pp. 245–64

PATSY VANAGS

Trevisani, Francesco (*b* Capodistria [now Cape of Istra, Slovenia], 9 April 1656; *d* Rome, 30 July 1746). Italian painter. He painted altarpieces and cabinet paintings of biblical and mythological themes in a style that varies between the classicism of Maratti and the softer, sweeter manner of the *Barocchetto*. His portraits, both of noble

Italian patrons and visiting Grand Tourists, are distinguished by their unusual informality and the sense of intimacy between artist and subject.

1. Training and works in Venice and Rome, before 1700. 2. Rome, 1700–20. 3. Late works, 1720–46.

1. TRAINING AND WORKS IN VENICE AND ROME, BEFORE 1700. He trained in Venice, first with Antonio Zanchi and later with Joseph Heintz the younger (1600–78), who specialized in genre painting (Pascoli). No paintings survive from this early Venetian period, and *c.* 1678 Trevisani moved to Rome. There he worked for Cardinal Flavio Chigi until the latter's death in 1693, and is first recorded in the Chigi archives at Ariccia. The titles of documented paintings, such as *Bullfight in Venice, Bertoldo the Goatherd with Goats* and a *Goatherd's Wife with Hens and Turkeys* (all untraced) suggest that, influenced by Heintz, he was producing genre works at this time.

His earliest surviving paintings, however, are orientated towards Emilian and Roman classicism. The *Trinity with St Bernard and St Catherine of Siena* (1684), which was painted for the church at La Cetina, the Chigi–Zandadori villa at Cetinale, near Siena (*in situ*), is derived from prototypes by Guido Reni, interpreted in a soft and mannered style. This was followed by the *Martyrdom of St Stephen* (Rome, Pal. Barberini), based on Filippo Lauri's painting of the same subject (Burghley House, Cambs.). It seems likely that on Lauri's death in 1694 Trevisani inherited his role as a painter of small, delicate pictures in an Arcadian vein.

Other early works, painted for the Chigi family, such as *Christ between St Philip and St James* (1687) and the *Martyrdom of the Four Crowned Saints* (1688; both Siena Cathedral), reveal Trevisani's links with contemporary Roman artists, especially those in the circle of Maratti. However, Trevisani's compositions remain Venetian, reminiscent of those by Antonio Zanchi, as is particularly evident in the *Martyrdom of the Four Crowned Saints*, a lively, dramatic scene placed in an architectural setting and influenced by the works of Veronese. Trevisani's *Martyrdom of St Andrew* (before 1697; Rome, S Andrea delle Fratte), inspired by Mattia Preti's frescoes in S Andrea della Valle, draws closer to the Roman Baroque. His early portraits, such as that of *Jan Jachym, Count of Pachta* (1696; Prague, N.G., Sternbeck Pal.), a Baroque, richly painted work in the tradition of Anthony van Dyck, are extraordinarily intense. Trevisani's first major contribution to Roman art was his decoration of the chapel of the Crucifix in S Silvestro in Capite, Rome, with canvases of the *Passion* and frescoes on the vault and pendentives of *Putti Displaying the Instruments of the Passion*. He may have won the commission through the offices of Cardinal Pietro Ottoboni, whom he probably met shortly after Cardinal Chigi's death, and who became his most important patron. In these works Trevisani drew closer to the art of Giovanni Lanfranco and Guido Reni, as in his *Road to Calvary*, which is indebted both to Reni's *St Andrew Led to Martyrdom* (Rome, S Gregorio al Celio) and also to Lanfranco's *Road to Calvary* in the Sacchetti Chapel in S Giovanni dei Fiorentini, Rome.

1. Francesco Trevisani: *Banquet of Antony and Cleopatra*, oil on canvas, 2.54×2.55 m, 1704 (Rome, Galleria Spada)

Trevisani's response to these works was further modified by his awareness of the art of Lodovico Gimignani and Giuseppe Bartolomeo Chiari, who were also decorating chapels in S Silvestro in Capite. Nevertheless, Trevisani adopted a livelier chiaroscuro than either of these artists and used sharper contrasts. Indeed, there is little doubt that he was also inspired by Francesco Solimena and learned from him how to enrich the rather tired echoes of Maratti's classicism with a new energy and freedom of handling. Thus his lunette painting, the *Agony in the Garden*, while modelled on Maratti's painting in S Isidoro, Rome, has greater dramatic power. A similar development occurs throughout his decorations, and the *Crucifixion* returns to motifs from the art of the Carracci, yet reinterpreted through the more modern vision of Solimena. Trevisani's highly innovative scheme thus marks the beginnings of a new sensibility, of a softer and more sentimental art.

2. ROME, 1700–20. Trevisani was profoundly affected by the Accademia degli Arcadi, with which he became associated through Cardinal Ottoboni, one of its most distinguished members. (By 1698 Ottoboni owned at least two of Trevisani's pictures: the *Dead Christ with Angels* (Stanford, CA, U. A.G. & Mus.) and *Three Marys* (California, priv. col., on loan to Stanford, CA, U. A.G. & Mus.).) In these circles he also met Filippo Juvarra and the musician Arcangelo Corelli, who owned Trevisani's *Virgin and Child* (a copy of an original by Carlo Cignani) and a large portrait of *Cardinal Ottoboni* (both untraced). Another portrait of *Cardinal Ottoboni* (1700–09; Barnard Castle, Bowes Mus.), though spontaneous, is deeply rooted in the Roman portrait tradition that runs from Bernini to Andrea Sacchi, and from Ferdinand Voet to Maratti.

Trevisani was well known at the Accademia by 1704, when Giovan Maria Crescimbeni, its custodian, sang his praises in a poem, and Trevisani himself had some success as a poet (Pascoli). However, it was not until 1712 that he actually became a member of the Accademia, taking the name of Sanzio Echeiano.

The anti-Baroque, rationalistic tendencies of the Arcadians (associates of the Accademia) were expressed in painting in various ways by artists as diverse as Maratti, Gimignani, Daniel Seiter, Bernardo Morando and Trevisani. Nevertheless, they all shared an underlying classicism, even when attracted, as was Trevisani, by the *Barochetto*, and their art looks forward to that of such Venetian painters as Giambattista Crosato as well as to that of François Lemoyne and Charles-Joseph Natoire.

In 1704 Trevisani began the *Mass of Bolsena* (Bolsena Cathedral, Cappella del Miracolo), in which the space is clearly defined and the narrative direct and lucid. The painting is evenly handled, but the colour is vivid, and the rendering of fabrics and highlights rich and brilliant. The classical composition, in the tradition of Sacchi and Maratti, contrasts sharply with the Baroque naturalism of his earlier *Martyrdom of St Andrew*. The *Banquet of Antony and Cleopatra* (1704; Rome, Gal. Spada; see fig. 1) illustrates his achievement as a history painter of biblical and mythological themes. Here too the lucid forms and the attention to detail lend clarity to the narrative. The richly clad figures soberly enact their roles in an elegant architectural interior. Crescimbeni, in his *Breve Notizia dello stato antico e moderno dell'Adunanza degli Arcadi* (Venice, 1730), defined 'gentle birth together with good manners' as an

essential qualification for the Arcadians, and this prescription seems to be reflected in paintings of this kind.

Several other of Trevisani's paintings are stylistically close to this work. Between 1708 and 1717 he painted a series of works for Prince–Bishop Lothar Franz von Schönborn, most of which remain at Pommersfelden in the Schloss Weissenstein. Such religious paintings as the *Repentant Magdalene* (Pommersfelden, Schloss Weissenstein) reflect the style of Maratti and Reni, while in such mythological pictures as *Luna and Endymion* (Pommersfelden, Schloss Weissenstein) Trevisani returned to the art of Lauri, which he interpreted with greater richness. In 1717 Trevisani sent a strikingly immediate *Self-portrait* (Pommersfelden, Schloss Weissenstein) as a gift for the Prince.

Trevisani's style oscillates between the *Barochetto* and the classicism of Maratti, as, for example, in *Dead Christ Supported by Angels* (1705–10; Vienna, Ksthist. Mus.; see fig. 2), which unites Baroque pathos and chiaroscuro with a classical composition. The austere scenes (finished 1715) of the *Life of Saint Joseph* and of the *Death of St Joseph* that decorate the chapel of St Lucy in Narni Cathedral contrast with the more sensuous and colourful *Flight into Egypt* (Dresden, Gemäldegal. Alte Meister), which looks forward to François Boucher, and *Joseph Sold by his Brethren* (1714; Melbourne, N.G. Victoria), which echoes Lauri. Trevisani's art is very different from Maratti's strict adherence to the style of Raphael, a tradition upheld by such contemporary Roman artists as Andrea Procaccini. In fact it has closer parallels with the art of Benedetto Luti and Marco Antonio Franceschini.

3. LATE WORKS, 1720–46. In Trevisani's late works there are no substantial changes in style. Some of his portraits, such as *Prince James Stuart* (Edinburgh, Pal. Holyroodhouse, Royal Col.), are distinguished by a new formality, while a more intimate tone was used for portraits of other members of the Jacobean court visiting Rome, such as the portraits of *David Murray, 6th Viscount Stormont* and *James Murray, Titular Earl of Dunbar* (both Scone Pal., Tayside). Such intimacy is rarely found in Trevisani's female portraits, which are graceful and elegant but often rather conventional in treatment, as in the portrait of *Marjorie Murray* (Scone Pal., Tayside).

In his religious paintings Trevisani's compositions tend to be simpler and more restrained, and space is defined by the positioning of a few sparse figures. Such paintings as the *Vision of St Anthony of Padua* (*c.* 1721–4; Rome, Stimmate di S Francesco), the *Immaculate Conception with St Louis of France and the Blessed Amadeus of Savoy* (1724; Turin, U. Aula Magna), commissioned by Filippo Juvarra for the chapel at Venaria Reale, Victor Amadeus II's hunting-lodge outside Turin, and the *St Turibius* (1726; Rome, S Anastasia) amply document this last phase of the painter's activity.

To the same period belong the cartoons for the mosaics in the Baptismal Chapel of St Peter's, Rome. This project was begun by Giovanni Battista Gaulli, and passed to Trevisani on Gaulli's death in 1709. Trevisani worked on it intermittently from 1710, but with increasing intensity in the 1730s and 1740s. The cartoons (Rome, St Peter's, Loggia delle Benedizioni), of scenes of *Baptism*, attain an

2. Francesco Trevisani: *Dead Christ Supported by Angels*, oil on canvas, 1.38×1.23 m, 1705–10 (Vienna, Kunsthistorisches Museum)

unexpected grandeur through the use of radically simpli-fied, powerful figures. The effects of chiaroscuro strongly suggest the renewed influence of Solimena, and at the same time echo the Baroque art of Lanfranco and Luca Giordano. Here the exquisite refinement of Trevisani's early work yields to a new monumentality, although the modelli for the *Four Continents of the World* (*c.* 1709; Rome, Pal. Barberini) remain subtle and evocative. The mosaics from this design were executed by Giuseppe Ottaviani, Liborio Fattori and Giovanni Battista Brughi (1660–1730).

In Trevisani's last altarpieces we find little innovation: his *St Matthew Resuscitating the Son of the King of Ethiopia* (?after 1730; Pisa) is a magniloquent and original painting, but the *Miracle of St Anthony of Padua* (1734; Venice, S Rocco) reuses earlier ideas, as does the *Martyrdom of St Lawrence* (*c.* 1735; Turin, S Filippo Neri) and the *Family of Darius before Alexander* (1735), commissioned by Juvarra for the throne room at La Granja de San Ildefonso. Here Trevisani, at the height of his success, was occupied on a decorative scheme that included works by Sebastiano Conca, Francesco Imperiali, Placido Costanzi, Donato Creti, Giovanni Battista Pittoni, Solimena and Carle Van-loo. In the *Family of Darius* he returned to a subject treated by Veronese and handles it with a felicitous classicizing touch, in the manner of Charles Le Brun.

BIBLIOGRAPHY

L. Pascoli: *Vite de' pittori, scultori ed architetti moderni*, i (Rome, 1730), pp. 130, 275
F. Moücke: 'Francesco Trevisani', *Serie di ritratti degli eccellenti pittori* (Florence, 1762), iv, pp. 99–103
H. Bodmer: 'Le opere di Francesco Trevisani nella Pinacoteca di Arezzo', *Il Vasari*, vii (1929), pp. 217–22
L. Gasparini: 'Francesco Trevisani', *Pagine Istria*, iv (1950), pp. 103–6
D. Gioseffi: 'L'opera di Francesco Trevisani', *Pagine Istria.*, iv (1950), pp. 107–16
A. Griseri: 'Francesco Trevisani in Arcadia', *Paragone*, xiii/153 (1962), pp. 28–37
——: *Le metamorfosi del barocco* (Turin, 1967)
F. DiFederico: 'Documentation for the Paintings and Mosaics of the Baptismal Chapel in St Peter's', *A. Bull.*, l (1968), pp. 194–8
——: 'Documentation for Francesco Trevisani's Decorations for the Vestibule of the Baptismal Chapel in St Peter's', *Stor. A.*, vi (1970), pp. 155–74
——: 'Francesco Trevisani and the Decorations of the Crucifixion Chapel in San Silvestro in Capite', *A. Bull.*, liii (1971), pp. 52–67
——: 'A Group of Trevisani Drawings in the Uffizi', *Master Drgs*, x (1972), pp. 3–14
——: 'Trevisani's Pictures at Narni and the State of Roman Painting in 1715', *Stor. A.*, xv–xvi (1972), pp. 307–13
——: *Francesco Trevisani, Eighteenth-century Painter in Rome: A Catalogue Raisonné* (Washington, DC, 1977) [incl. hitherto unpubd writings on Trevisani by N. Pio and L. Pascoli]
G. Sestieri: 'Il Francesco Trevisani di Franck DiFederico', *Antol. B.A.*, 4 (1977), pp. 372–9

UGO RUGGERI

Treviso [anc. Tarvisium]. Italian city and capital of the Trevisan Marches, the largest and most important territory in the Veneto. The city (population *c.* 84,000) lies about 30 km north of Venice, to which it is connected by the Terraglio, an ancient road widened and embellished by Napoleon. Treviso stands at the confluence of the Sile and Cagnano (Botteniga) rivers, amid abundant springs at the centre of a fertile alluvial plain famous for its wine production. The original nucleus of the city was expanded to three times its size in the late medieval and Renaissance periods, becoming a rectangular, walled city orientated east–west, with surrounding streams channelled through large moats. The city's picturesque aspect derives from these moats and many smaller canals, as well as from its arcaded streets (e.g. Calmaggiore) of brick buildings with frescoed façades.

Archaeological evidence from the Bronze and Iron ages (from the 13th century BC) as well as substantial finds from Greek and Roman antiquity (Treviso, Mus. Civ. Bailo) attest to the lengthy but modest development of the settlement that became the Roman municipium of Tarvisium by 46 BC; it began to develop a regional importance after the opening of the Via Claudia Augusta (early 1st century AD). A regular grid of roads and irrigation channels was developed, orientated to the north-east, with the city bisected by the *cardo maximus* (now Via Martiri della Libertà), crossed at right angles by the *decumanus* (now Via S Margherita-Indipendenza). Outside the north-west gate (near the Piazza dei Signori, at the centre of the modern city) was a Roman theatre and extensive necrop-olis. The paving and kerbs of a later extramural extension of the *decumanus* provided the foundation for an Early Christian crypt (AD 390s) beneath the present cathedral of S Pietro as the regular grid of Roman streets was gradually replaced by routes that probably existed earlier.

The city grew with surprising consistency during the 4th–6th centuries AD, profiting from a gradual abandon-ment of the Roman cities of Aquileia, Altino and Oderzo in the wake of successive invasions. An increasingly powerful bishopric from at least AD 396, Treviso became a duchy under the Lombards, with a mint founded by AD 773. Charlemagne entered Treviso in AD 776, estab-lishing a hereditary line of Lombard–Frankish counts. The city was sacked by the Hungarians (AD 899, 911); under King Berengarius of Italy (*d* 924) it was briefly capital of the marquisate of Friuli; but in AD 952 its long association with the Holy Roman Empire was reaffirmed by its formal annexation by Emperor Otto I. The first decrees of the essentially independent *comune* date from 1162, and in 1164 Emperor Frederick I granted its civic government important rights, including the construction of houses with covered street arcades and the erection of an enlarged circuit of city walls (completed 1219). The office of Podestà (imperial governor) dates from 1176.

Treviso's cathedral was begun *c.* 1000 and underwent repeated reconstruction in later centuries (see below). Next to the cathedral is the free-standing Romanesque baptismal chapel of S Giovanni (*c.* 1050; rest. 1935). The city's most important period of development, however, was 1200–35, which was marked by the construction of the battlemented Gothic assembly hall, the Palazzo dei Trecento (1207–17; rebuilt 1946–51), which, together with the adjacent Palazzo del Podestà (rebuilt 19th century) and Palazzo Pretorio (*c.* 1490), flanks the Piazza dei Signori. This period was also marked by the arrival (1226) of the Franciscan and Dominican orders, who established themselves respectively in S Francesco (1231–*c.* 1268; rest. 1926–8) and S Nicolò (*c.* 1303–68; continuations to 1856). S Nicolò (see fig.) is the city's largest church and its architectural masterpiece, featuring a triple apse and a ship's-keel ceiling; the Dominican chapter house (now seminary) contains frescoes of *Forty Illustrious Members of*

Treviso, S Nicolò, east end with transept, apsidal chapels and campanile, *c.* 1303–68

the Dominican Order (1352) by TOMASO DA MODENA. The arcaded Loggia dei Cavalieri (1276–7), Piazza Crispi, was built between campaigns on the two monastic churches.

A brief republic was proclaimed in Treviso in 1312–18, but contention between the lords of Verona and Padua for control of the city induced the comune to call in its Austrian overlords, who reaffirmed its rank as an imperial city in 1319. The Trevisan March was subsequently ceded to Venice (1339) as the first of its many mainland territories, among which Treviso enjoyed pride of place for nearly five centuries until 1797. Important churches of the 14th and 15th centuries include S Caterina dei Servi (1346–99; rebuilt 1954) and S Lucia (1355–89; rest. 1919–29), both of which have frescoes by Tomaso da Modena; and the Venetian Gothic basilica of S Maria Maggiore (1473–4; rebuilt 1946–53), with a marble Tempietto (1492) enclosing an early devotional fresco (1352) by Tomaso da Modena.

The history of Trevisan art and architecture is exemplified particularly in the cathedral. Apart from surviving Romanesque portions, it contains work from many subsequent periods, notably the east end (1481–8) by members of the Lombardo family; the chapel of the Holy Sacrament (1501–13) by Antonio Maria da Milano, with sculpture by Giovanni Battista Bregno and his brother Lorenzo Bregno (for discussion and illustration *see* BREGNO, (3) and (4)); and the chapel of the Annunciation (1519–23) by Martino Lombardo, frescoed in 1520 by Pordenone. The nave, aisles and façade were rebuilt *c.* 1760s–1836 to plans by Giordano Riccati (1709–70). Treasures in the cathedral include the tomb of *Bishop Salomone* (1322) by De Santi;

the tomb of *Bishop Zanetti* (late 1480s) by Pietro Lombardo; the altarpiece of the *Virgin and Child Enthroned with SS Sebastian and Roch* (1487) by Girolamo da Treviso (i); a superb *Annunciation* (early 1520s) by Titian; an *Adoration of the Shepherds* (*c.* 1540s) by Paris Bordone; and the marble *St John the Baptist* (*c.* 1565) by Alessandro Vittoria.

The wars of the League of Cambrai (1508–16) caused every able-bodied citizen of Treviso to work throughout the summer of 1509 on a surviving 4.8 km circuit of modernized city walls with 13 bastions (completed 1513) traditionally attributed to Fra Giovanni Giocondo of Verona, supervised by Lorenzo di Ceri and Barolomeo d'Alviano. The Porta S Quaranta (1517) is attributed to Alessandro Leopardi, and the Porta S Tomaso (1518) to Guglielmo Bergamasco (Scarpellino; *fl* 1515–50). Notable buildings of the mid-16th century include the Palazzo Spineda (remodelled early 18th century), with staircase frescoes (from 1747) by Gaspare Diziani. The later church of S Agostino (1751–8) by Francesco Vecelli (*d* 1759) has a Rococo elliptical plan with a convex façade. After a period under Napoleonic rule, Treviso was governed by Austria (1813–66) and was then annexed to the Kingdom of Italy. It suffered badly from aerial bombardment in World War I and was even more severely damaged by bombing in 1944.

Treviso was the birthplace of such Renaissance artists as Girolamo da Treviso (i) and Paris Bordone, while Cima, Giorgione and Titian came from the surrounding area. The city also contains the principal works of TOMASO DA MODENA. Later artists from the city include the 18th-century sculptor Antonio Canova and the 20th-century sculptor Arturo Martini. Most of these masters are well represented in Treviso's fine Museo Civico Luigi Bailo, a complex of historical buildings incorporating also the Biblioteca Comunale (with important manuscript holdings). The Biblioteca Capitolare of the cathedral (catalogued 1135) was one of the richest in northern Italy until its partial destruction in 1944.

BIBLIOGRAPHY

Enc. Catt.; *Enc. It.*

L. Coletti: *Catalogo delle cose d'arte e d'antichità di Treviso* (Rome, 1935)

Veneto, Guida Italia TCI (Milan, 4/1954), pp. 416–31

F. Roiter: *Favolosa Marca: Itinerari nella provincia di Treviso* (Treviso, 1976)

T. Basso and A. Cason: *Treviso ritrovata: Immagini della città scomparsa* (Treviso, 1977)

G. Anselmi: *Treviso: Guida turistica* (Treviso, 3/1985)

I. Sartor: *Treviso lungo il Sile: Vicende civili ed ecclesiastiche in San Martino* (Treviso, 1989)

I. Puccinelli: 'Treviso romana e altomedievale', *Venezia A.*, 4 (1990), pp. 19–28

DOUGLAS LEWIS

Treviso, Dario da. *See* DARIO DA TREVISO.

Treviso, Girolamo da. *See* GIROLAMO DA TREVISO (i) and (ii).

Treviso, Vincenzo da. *see* DESTRE, VINCENZO DALLE.

Trewhiddle Hoard. Collection of late Anglo-Saxon silver, described as the most important ever found. It was discovered in 1774 by tin workers at Trewhiddle, St Austell, Cornwall, hidden under a pile of stones in an old mine working more than 5 m below ground; it was presented to the British Museum in 1880. The term 'Trewhiddle style', after the distinctive decoration of the various objects, is now used to define a phase of 9th-century English art. The associated coins provide a deposition date for the hoard of not later than AD 875, although the silver could have been made some time before this.

The range of silver includes items of secular and ecclesiastical use, suggesting that it may have been the treasure of a church. There was a plain silver chalice, constructed in three pieces with separate bowl, knop and foot, decorated with only a riveted band below the rim. The shape resembles contemporary continental chalices. Another religious item was a ceremonial scourge, the only surviving example of the early medieval period. It was 560 mm long, made of silver chain work in trichinopoly (circular plaiting) technique, ending in a tasselled loop tied with a blue glass bead.

Two patterned silver strips have been identified as the mounts for drinking horns. Their ornament is divided into triangular fields filled with the animals characteristic of the style. A typical creature has a speckled body, distorted into a triangular shape, square muzzle, prominent hip and three-toed feet. There is also foliage ornament. The decoration is achieved by shallow carving against a black niello inlay background. In the same style is a strap end, used perhaps on the end of a silk girdle, and a box-like object with one square and one rounded end. These items are so similar that they were probably made by the same hand.

A long silver pin with a 14-sided head is decorated with trefoil and triquetra designs, as well as angular creatures of more delicate and symmetrical type, with prominent heads. A third animal is seen on another silver strip from a smaller drinking horn mount; it is unspeckled, more attenuated than the others, all four legs shown and with double nicks around the body to give an effect of roundness. There is also more leafy scrollwork.

Undecorated items were two sets of cast silver strap ends and belt loops, one with traces of leather still attached. There was also a plain bronze buckle and plate. A silver penannular brooch was apparently an Irish import; it was decorated with incised lines and had sunken lozenge-shaped fields on the expanded terminals.

The significance of the Trewhiddle Hoard is the information it provides about the styles and techniques of 9th-century metalwork. Silver is the medium preferred rather than the bronze of earlier generations. The animal ornament is a development from the interlacing beasts of pagan Anglo-Saxon art. The style is seen elsewhere, not only on other 9th-century metalwork in the finds from Talnotrie (Dumfries and Galloway), Cuerdale (Lancs), Beeston Tor (Staffs) and Pentney (Norfolk), but also on the contemporary manuscripts of the Canterbury school in their use of speckled contorted beasts and leafy scrolls. The location of the hoard suggests that Cornwall, once a Celtic backwater, was at this time under the artistic influence of the flourishing kingdom of Wessex and contributing to the styles of later Anglo-Saxon art.

BIBLIOGRAPHY
D. Talbot Rice: *English Art, 871–1100* (Oxford, 1952)
D. M. Wilson and C. E. Blunt: 'The Trewhiddle Hoard', *Archaeologia*, xcviii (1961), pp. 75–122
D. M. Wilson: *Anglo-Saxon Ornamental Metalwork, 700–1100* (London, 1964)
——: *Anglo-Saxon Art from the Seventh Century to the Norman Conquest* (London, 1984)
The Making of England: Anglo-Saxon Art and Culture, AD 600–900 (exh. cat., ed. L. Webster and J. Blackhouse; London, BM, 1991)

CAROLA HICKS

Trezzini [Tresini; Tressini; Trezina; Trezini]**, Domenico** (*b* Astano, nr Lugano, Switzerland, *c.* 1670; *d* St Petersburg, 2 March 1734). Swiss-Italian architect, active in Russia. He trained in Switzerland and in Italy. From 1699 to 1703 he was employed by Frederick IV, King of Denmark (*reg* 1699–1733), but no specific Danish projects have been attributed to him, and he is known almost exclusively for his work in St Petersburg. Trezzini was one of the first architects to be hired by Peter I (*reg* 1682–1725) as part of the Tsar's policy to modernize Russia. He arrived in Moscow in September 1703 with nine other craftsmen, and after working on sites there and on the Baltic (fortifications at Kronstadt, 1703–4; gates at Narva, 1705), he settled in St Petersburg in 1706. His first five years there were centred on developing the Peter and Paul Fortress on an island by the north bank of the River Neva. He often referred to himself as 'the architect of the St Petersburg Fortress', since his work there lasted for almost 30 years. From 1706 he supervised the rebuilding of the earthworks in masonry, and the construction of bastions in a layout influenced by Sébastien Leprestre de Vauban. The Peter Gates (1717–18) at the main entrance of the fortress and a triumphal arch with low-relief decoration are among his surviving creations. Acting in the capacity of chief of works, Trezzini also designed model projects for simple dwellings in the city, to be built of wood painted to imitate stone, or faced with clay and stucco. None survives, but the style of the model project of houses for 'distinguished citizens' is visible on a larger scale in Peter I's Summer Palace (1710–12), a two-storey brick structure with a high-pitched roof set in the north-east corner of the Summer Garden. In 1711 Trezzini also built a Winter Palace (destr.).

In 1712, when the court and government departments began to be transferred to St Petersburg from Moscow, and wood and clay structures were replaced by masonry, Trezzini designed the brick-built cathedral of SS Peter and Paul (1712–33; see fig.) in place of the wooden church of the Peter and Paul Fortress. This three-aisled basilica, with a dome at the east end, a tower and a tall gilded spire (122.5 m) over the west entrance, is one of the dramatic landmarks of the city. The exterior has restrained decoration of pilasters and volutes, and the interior an applied Corinthian order and Baroque iconostasis (1722–6) by Ivan Zarudny. The cathedral, which houses the tombs of *Peter I* and his successors, represents a radical departure from the traditional Russian onion-domed style: in the words of a contemporary, it was built 'not after the Byzantine, but after the new taste'. Trezzini's church of the Annunciation (1717–22) in the Alexander Nevsky Lavra (*see* ST PETERSBURG, §IV, 2) is reminiscent of the architect's mansion designs and is capped with a dome. The most ambitious of Trezzini's works in St Petersburg, however, were the Twelve Colleges (1722–41; for illustration *see* ROMANOV, (1)) on Vasil'yevsky Island. These

Domenico Trezzini: cathedral of SS Peter and Paul, St Petersburg, 1712–33; lithograph by André Durand, 1839

premises were built to house the Senate, Synod and ten government departments (and since 1819, the main building of the university). A single line measuring 392.6×17.1 m of identical units three storeys high, each with its own high-hipped roof and entrance portico crowned by an attic, is articulated with a colossal order of white pilasters against a red colour wash. The colleges form the western side of a large square, part of Trezzini's general plan for the eastern tip of Vasil'yevsky Island. In 1715 he had drawn up a plan for the whole island, a symmetrical grid of streets and canals that still forms the basis for its division into regular 'lines'.

During much of the period from 1712 to 1725 Trezzini enjoyed the unofficial status of master of construction and works: a decree of 9 April 1714 stipulated that new arrivals in St Petersburg should 'obtain drawings on the mode of house building from the Architect Trezina'. In 1716 he was temporarily eclipsed by the arrival of the French architect Alexandre-Jean-Baptiste Le Blond, but the latter's death in 1719, together with Peter's rejection of Le Blond's highly abstract and stylized plan for St Petersburg, restored Trezzini's fortunes. In 1723 his name appeared at the head of a list of 59 foreign architects attached to the newly organized Construction Office. After Peter's death, Trezzini continued to work in St Petersburg, although no building from this last period of his career survives intact. In 1726–7 he completed Georg Johann Mattarnovy's

Winter Palace (destr. 1780s), and in 1727 he planned a palace for Peter II (reg 1727–30) on Vasil'yevsky Island, but the new Tsar moved the court back to Moscow. In 1732 Trezzini erected a triumphal arch and pavilion (destr.) for the entry of the new Empress Anna (reg 1730–40) into St Petersburg. At the end of his life he was working on designs for the Academy of Sciences complex (founded 1724) on Vasil'yevsky Island.

Trezzini helped to establish the modern Russian architectural profession. He was, for example, the first foreigner to form a 'team' of Russian apprentice builders (in 1707), his most outstanding pupil being MIKHAIL ZEMTSOV. Trezzini regularly examined architectural students returning from abroad, and in 1732 he was attached to the new élite Army Gentry Corps school in St Petersburg. He was involved in nearly every major building project during the first three decades of the new city, including harbours, bazaars, mansions and hospitals, as well as barracks and fortification works at nearby Kronstadt and Schlüsselburg. His talents were those of a good engineer and practical builder rather than an inspired designer, but these were the skills most prized by his chief patron, Peter I. Trezzini's restrained north European Baroque, rather reminiscent of the style in later 17th-century Holland, was also to Peter's taste.

See also ST PETERSBURG, §§I, 2 and IV, 2.

BIBLIOGRAPHY

E. Lo Gatto: *Gli artisti italiani in Russia* (Rome, 1937)
C. Marsden: *Palmyra of the North* (London, 1942)
M. V. Iogansen: 'Raboty Domeniko Trezini po planirovke i zastroyke Strelki Vasil'yevskogo ostrova v Peterburge' [Trezzini's work on the planning and construction of the spit of Vasil'yevsky Island in St Petersburg], *Russkoye iskusstvo XVIII veka* [18th-century Russian art], ed. T. V. Alekseyeva (Moscow, 1973), pp. 45–55
I. I. Lisaevich: *Pervyy arkhitektor Peterburga* [The first architect of St Petersburg] (Leningrad, 1973); rev. as *Domeniko Trezini* (Leningrad, 1986) [based on archival res., with bibliog.]
E. A. Borisova: 'Arkhitekturnyye ucheniki petrovskogo vremeni i ikh obucheniye v komandakh zodchikh-inostrantsev v Peterburge' [Architectural pupils of the Petrine era and their training in the teams of foreign architects in St Petersburg], *Russkoye iskusstvo pervoy chetverti XVIII veka* [Russian art of the first quarter of the 18th century], ed. T. V .Alekseyeva (Moscow, 1974), pp. 68–79
L. A. J. Hughes: 'Russia's First Architectural Books: A Chapter in Peter I's Cultural Revolution', *Archit. Des.*, liii/5–6 (1983), pp. 4–13
Yu. Ovsyannikov: *Dominiko Trezin* (Leningrad, 1987) [based on archival sources, with chronological tables]
J. Cracraft: *The Petrine Revolution in Russian Architecture* (Chicago, 1988)

LINDSEY HUGHES

Trezzo, Jacopo (Nizolla) da, I (*b* Milan, 1515–19; *d* Madrid, 23 Sept 1589). Italian medallist, sculptor, gemengraver and jeweller. Nothing is known of his background and early life. His family apparently came from Trezzosull Adda but were living in Milan at the time of his birth. By 1550 he had achieved a level of fame that deserved mention in the first edition of Vasari's *Vite*. His activities in Milan, in which city he lived until 1555, included gemengraving and the fabrication of objects in precious and semi-precious stones for Cosimo I, Duke of Florence. Several letters in archives in Florence, dated 1552, 1572 and 1575, describe this work and the difficulties Trezzo experienced in receiving payment. Between 1548 and 1578 Jacopo produced eleven medals, including variants, eight of which are signed. The first of these is the medal of the

Cremonese engineer Gianello delle Torre, of which one example (Florence, Bargello) bears the date 1548. Although not signed, it has been attributed both to Trezzo and to Leone Leoni. Stylistic evidence strongly favours Trezzo as the author of the medal: the portrait is forceful, and the details of hair, beard and drapery are delicately modelled without being fussy. The reverse, showing the *Fountain of the Sciences*, is a masterpiece of relief sculpture with expressive movement, strong modelling, subtle variations in relief and a precise but lively depiction of faces, water, and drapery. While in Milan, Trezzo produced two signed medals (both London, V&A), doubtless commissioned by the Governor of Milan, Ferrante Gonzaga. One was of Gonzaga's wife, Isabella de Capua, Princess of Molfetta (*d* 1559), and the other of their daughter, Ippolita Gonzaga (1535–63), dated by the age of the subject to 1552. The obverse of the latter was copied from a medal made a year earlier by Leoni with some changes in the drapery and jewellery and with a perceptible loss of refinement in the portrait. The reverse, however, showing Aurora in a chariot riding across the heavens, is handled with considerable skill in its modelling and suggestion of space. The medal of Isabella Capua recalls the placid strength of the Gianello delle Torre medal, as well as having similar drapery.

In 1555 Trezzo moved to the Low Countries, probably to Brussels, in the service of Philip II of Spain, who had also become the ruler of Milan. The documentation of Trezzo's move indicates that he carved two seals for Philip in 1557. He also produced his most beautiful medallic portrait, that of Mary I of England (*reg* 1553–8; London, BM), who married Philip in 1554. Her features are given an extraordinary alertness, while the details of her costume are rendered with a precision that is nonetheless subordinate to the form of the body beneath and to the overlapping layers of drapery. The reverse shows Mary in the guise of Peace setting fire to a pile of arms with her left hand and holding aloft palm and olive branches in her right, while suppliants kneel behind her beneath a raincloud. The medal, which is signed, resembles that of delle Torre. Its pendant is a medal of Philip II, signed and dated 1555, of which there are two variants (Florence, Bargello). The portrait of Philip does not have the intensity of that of Mary, nor does its reverse equal that of the Ippolita Gonzaga medal, which it resembles in subject-matter, the *quadriga* of Apollo replacing Aurora's chariot.

In 1559 Trezzo followed Philip to Spain, where he apparently spent the rest of his life. As well as producing cameos and working as a goldsmith, he made two surviving medals in this period: one (signed and dated 1577; Washington, DC, N.G.A.) is of an Italian nobleman, Ascanio Padula; the other (signed and dated 1578; Madrid, Mus. Arqueol. N.) is of the architect Juan de Herrera. Neither of the portraits is particularly distinguished; however, the reverse of the Herrera medal, depicting a personification of Architecture holding measuring instruments, is one of his more successful compositions. The placement of the figure and the surrounding buildings establishes a perspective within which the severe fluting of the piers to the left is contrasted dramatically with the soft contours and richly flowing lines of drapery of the female figure to the right. Trezzo also produced important work on a larger scale, for example a lectern in Plasencia Cathedral and decorative sculpture at the Capilla Mayor at El Escorial, near Madrid (*see* ESCORIAL, §3), for which he carved the great tabernacle of the high altar (1579–86) from designs by Herrera. Trezzo's son Jacopo da Trezzo II (*d* Madrid, 16 Jan 1607) was also a sculptor.

BIBLIOGRAPHY
Forrer

G. Vasari: *Vite* (1550); ed. G. Milanesi (1878–85)
A. Armand: *Les Médailleurs italiens* (2/1883–7), i, pp. 241–3; iii, pp. 114–15
I. B. Supino: *Il medagliere mediceo nel R. Museo Nazionale di Firenze* (Florence, 1899), pp. 140–42
G. F. Hill and G. Pollard: *Renaissance Medals from the Samuel H. Kress Collection at the National Gallery of Art* (London, 1967), pp. 83–4
G. F. Hill: *Medals of the Renaissance* (London, 1920; rev. and enlarged by G. Pollard, 1978), p. 97
V. Johnson: 'La medaglia italiana in Europa durante i secoli XV e XVI', pt 2, *Velia Johnson: Dieci anni di studi di medaglistica, 1968–78* (Milan, 1979), pp. 51–68
Splendours of the Gonzaga (exh. cat., ed. D. Chambers and J. Martineau; London, V&A, 1982), pp. 182–3
G. Pollard: *Italian Renaissance Medals in the Museo Nazionale del Bargello* (Florence, 1985), iii, pp. 1238–51
The Currency of Fame: Portrait Medals of the Renaissance (exh. cat., ed. S. K. Scher; Washington, DC, N.G.A.; New York, Frick; 1994), pp. 158–61, 383–4

STEPHEN K. SCHER

Triad statue. *See* EGYPT, ANCIENT, §IX, 2(i)(e).

Trialeti. Group of Middle Bronze Age archaeological monuments to the south of the Trialeti Range in the valley of the River Tsalka, Georgia. In 1936–40 and 1947 excavations led by Boris A. Kuftin (1892–1953) uncovered large barrows (diam. up to 100 m; first half and middle of the 2nd millennium BC) with various types of burial chamber, including some of massive stone covered by a layer of beams, containing rich funerary artefacts (now Tbilisi, State Mus. Georgia), among them a chariot similar in style to finds at Ur. The pottery consists of large, black-glazed or red-clay vessels with grooved and painted ornament, sometimes in spirals. This spiral design is repeated in filigree on a gold goblet (mound no. 17) that is also decorated with cornelian and paste inlay. Other examples of metalworking show the fusion of local and Ancient Near Eastern traditions, as in a silver goblet (mound no. 17) with two embossed and engraved friezes: the upper frieze shows a procession of 23 masked mummers moving towards a tree, a composition similar to that of Hittite reliefs, while the lower frieze depicts a string of deer and boar. Fragments remain of a small silver bucket with chased images of trees and animals such as goats, chamois, deer and boar, some of them wounded by arrows. The gold and silver vessels and the ceremonial weapons (bronze and silver daggers and a spear) recall similar finds at Ur.

BIBLIOGRAPHY
B. A. Kuftin: *Arkheologicheskiye raskopi v Trialeti* [Archaeological excavations in Trialeti] (Tbilisi, 1941)
——: *Arkheologicheskiye raskopi 1947 g. v Tsalkinskom rayone* [Archaeological excavations in 1947 in the Tsalka region] (Tbilisi, 1948)
L. G. Zhorzhikashvili and E. M. Gogadze: *Pamyatniki Trialeti epokhi ranney i sredney bronzy: Katalog trialetskikh materialov* [Early and Middle Bronze Age monuments in Trialeti: a catalogue of materials from Trialeti] (Tbilisi, 1974)

V. YA. PETRUKHIN

Trianon. *See under* VERSAILLES.

Tribilia, Antonio. *See* TERRIBILIA, (1).

Tribolo, Niccolò [Niccolò di Raffaello de' Pericoli; il Tribolo] (*b* ?Florence, 1500; *d* ?Florence, 7 Sept 1550). Italian sculptor, engineer and garden designer. He was apprenticed in Florence first as a wood-carver with Giovanni d'Alesso d'Antonio and then as a sculptor with Jacopo Sansovino, whom he continued to assist well into the second decade of the 16th century. Vasari listed many works (most now untraced) from Tribolo's youth, among which was his earliest fountain; an old terracotta copy (London, V&A) shows this unpretentious and slightly old-fashioned work to have featured two children and a spouting dolphin that foreshadow the blithe charm of his later masterpieces.

Tribolo was famously unassertive and often adapted his art to suit established or collaborative projects. His plump and lissom putto (marble, *c.* 1523–4) on the lower right of Baldassare Peruzzi's tomb of *Hadrian VI* (Rome, S Maria dell'Anima) indicates his exposure both to antique sculpture and to contemporary Roman work, especially that of Michelangelo's maturity. In 1525–7 he collaborated on façade sculpture for S Petronio, Bologna, where his portal relief of *Joseph Interpreting Pharoah's Dreams* combines recollections of the antique *Laokoon* (Rome, Vatican, Mus. Pio-Clementino) and Michelangelo with an archaizing quality inspired by Jacopo della Quercia's sculptures on the middle portal. Although the influence of Jacopo's grandeur persists in most of Tribolo's later history reliefs, in his next two works he turned away from this epic world: late in 1527 he made the model for a marble angel now at the entrance to the high altar of Pisa Cathedral. This engaging work, which he probably also undertook to carve (though it was finished and signed by Silvio Cosini, who changed the head), is important for its contribution to the development of free-standing sculpture with continuous multiple viewpoints. Enhanced by the sweeping rhythms of the draperies, the figure pushes Michelangelesque contrapposto to an extreme. By contrast his marble statue of *Nature* (Paris, Louvre; *see* ITALY, fig. 105), designed in Florence *c.* 1528 as a stand for an antique vase, is a static, symmetrical composition, intended to be viewed frontally, despite its swarm of animated putti, birds, frogs and other animal and vegetable fantasies; the figure is based on the antique *Diana of Ephesus* (Fontainebleau, Château), and the work can be regarded as a prototype for the great fountains of Tribolo's last years.

Tribolo was among the team of sculptors to work on the Basilica della Santa Casa at Loreto, where he collaborated on several works and in 1533 completed Andrea Sansovino's marble high relief of the *Marriage of the Virgin* (began 1527). He also produced wax models for niche figures of prophets (untraced) in the basilica; these evidently impressed Clement VII sufficiently for him to send Tribolo back to Florence to help Michelangelo complete the Medici tombs in S Lorenzo, though this work was interrupted in 1534 because of the Pope's death. In 1536 Tribolo entered the service of Duke Alessandro de' Medici, producing for him a monumental carved Medici escutcheon with two Victories (marble; Prato, Mus. Com.) and numerous large-scale ephemeral decorations, the latter also for the Duke's successor, Cosimo I. Around this time he was called to Bologna to provide huge marble reliefs of the *Assumption of the Virgin* (payment 1537–8) for the church of the Madonna di Galliera. Tribolo's original arrangement was of a broad lower section depicting the Apostles, with the Virgin soaring above (probably separately compartmented), her smaller scale enhancing the effect of a receding apparition. The reliefs were moved to a chapel in S Petronio in the 18th century and reassembled as a single scene in a coarse and inappropriate Baroque setting. Nevertheless, it remains one of the best history reliefs of the second quarter of the 16th century.

In 1538 Tribolo returned to Florence at the request of Cosimo I to realize the allegorical Mannerist garden at the Medici villa at Castello. Concurrently he worked on a colossal marble Medici escutcheon for one of the bastions of S Miniato, Florence (unfinished; a Victory and some trophies, Florence, Pal. Alessandri), and a model (London, Wallace) for a monument to Cosimo's father, *Giovanni delle Bande Nere* (Florence, Piazza S Lorenzo), the only one of his much-admired models to survive (the commission was later transferred to Baccio Bandinelli). Vasari's account of the elaborate iconographical programme of the gardens at Castello states that a series of portrait and allegorical sculptures was intended to glorify the Medici virtues that nourished the state, the geographical features of which were also to be personified in sculpture. Among the earliest works to be undertaken were marble statues of river gods representing the *Arno* and the *Mugnone* (both untraced), the latter accompanied by a personification of *Fiesole* (Florence, Bargello), one of Tribolo's boldest works. The Fountain of the Labyrinth (Villa Petraia, nr Florence), the first of the two great marble and bronze fountains of the central axis of the garden, initiated the final phase of Tribolo's career, when the demands on his time were such that he had to content himself with making models, leaving much of the execution of the finished works to his pupils. Among the more talented of them was Leonardo's nephew Pierino da Vinci, who was with Tribolo *c.* 1542–6 and carved the exquisite upper part of the fountain.

During his dozen years' service with Cosimo I, Tribolo undertook an extraordinary miscellany of tasks. These included decorations for state occasions, firework displays, theatrical costumes and décor as well as water conservation and other hydraulic projects. More specifically, he was also responsible for the design and supervision of the monumental tomb of *Matteo Corte* (marble, 1544–8; Pisa, Campo Santo), which was executed by Antonio Lorenzi (*d* 1583); the installation of Michelangelo's sculpture in the Medici Chapel at S Lorenzo (1546); the design and installation of the elaborate pavement in the Biblioteca Laurenziana at S Lorenzo; new gardens for the Medici villa at Poggio a Caiano, near Florence; and the continuing work at Castello. The most influential accomplishment of his last years, however, was the laying out of the Boboli Gardens behind the Pitti Palace in Florence (*see* FLORENCE, §IV, 9(iii)). A painting (1599; Florence, Mus. Firenze com'era) by Giusto Utens (*d* 1609) shows this scheme as originally set out before later additions to the south destroyed the logic of the composition. The symmetrical architectonic layout of the big urban palace was continued into the gardens along an impressive receding

Niccolò Tribolo: Fountain of Hercules, marble and bronze, Villa di Castello, near Florence, *c.* 1550

B. H. Wiles: 'Tribolo in his Michelangesque Vein', *A. Bull.*, xiv (1932), pp. 59–70
——: *Fountains of the Florentine Sculptors* (Cambridge, MA, 1933)
J. Holderbaum: 'Notes on Tribolo', *Burl. Mag.*, xcix (1957), pp. 336–43, 369–72
J. Pope-Hennessy: 'A Small Bronze of Tribolo', *Burl. Mag.*, ci (1959), pp. 85–9
M. Ciardi Dupré: 'Presentazione di alcuni problemi relativi al Tribolo scultore', *A. Ant. & Mod.*, 7 (1961), pp. 244–7
J. Pope-Hennessy: *Catalogue of Italian Sculpture in the Victoria and Albert Museum*, ii (London, 1964), pp. 436–9
H. Keutner: 'Niccolò Tribolo und Antonio Lorenzi: Die Äskulapbrunnen im Heilkrautergarten der Villa Castello bei Florenz', *Studien zur Geschichte der europäischen Plastik: Festschrift für Theodor Müller* (Munich, 1965), pp. 235–44
W. Aschoff: *Studien zu Niccolò Tribolo* (Berlin, 1967)
C. Lloyd: 'Drawings Attributable to Tribolo', *Master Drgs.*, vi (1968), pp. 243–5
C. Avery: *Florentine Renaissance Sculpture* (London, 1970)
D. R. Wright: *The Villa Medici at Olmo a Castello* (diss., Princeton U., NJ, 1976; microfilm, Ann Arbor, 1981)

JAMES HOLDERBAUM

Tribune. Raised platform or dais. The term was originally used for the official station of the praetor at one end of an ancient Roman basilica. It later came to refer to the bishop's throne in a Christian basilica and, gradually, to the apse (i.e. the area of the church containing the throne). It is now used for any raised area in a church, such as a pulpit or gallery, and in secular usage for any slightly raised podium or rostrum for a speaker.

See also TRIFORIUM.

central axis. The scheme was to be taken up again in the following century in the gardens of the Tuileries and the Luxembourg Palace in Paris for Maria de' Medici and was to be an essential component in the design of the gardens of the château of Versailles in the 1660s.

So well organized was Tribolo's workshop that his Fountain of Hercules at Castello (see fig.), now judged to be his masterpiece, was executed largely by assistants from his models, much of it posthumously. Larger, more richly decorated and with a more copious flow of water than the Fountain of the Labyrinth, it consists of an octagonal marble basin and two tazze decorated with marble and bronze putti, masks and claws. The whole is topped by a heroic bronze group of *Hercules and Antaeus*, which contrasts in typical fashion with the animated denizens of Tribolo's fairyland below. The monumental bronzes for Castello were cast in a somewhat perfunctory fashion in the 1560s: the *Hercules and Antaeus* and a colossal *Appenine* by Bartolomeo Ammanati's assistants and the small statue of *Florence* by Giambologna's. They nevertheless retain important vestiges of Tribolo's models. His last documented and entirely autograph work is a small, exuberantly twisting figure of *Pan* (1549; Florence, Bargello), shown playing on the pipes. It has been described as one of the most beautiful Florentine bronzes of the Renaissance (Dupré) and should also be seen as an indispensable paradigm for the evolution of the free-standing statue in the art of Giambologna and his contemporaries. Vasari gives his date of death as 7 September 1550; other sources give 20 August 1550.

BIBLIOGRAPHY
G. Vasari: *Vite* (1550, rev. 2/1568); ed. G. Milanesi, vi (1881), pp. 55–117

Trichet de Fresne, Raphaël [De Fresne, Raphaël Trichet] (*b* Bordeaux, April 1611; *d* Paris, 4 June 1661). French scholar, collector and bibliophile. He was the son of the lawyer and bibliophile Pierre Trichet (1586/7–before 1649) and, after studying at the Collège de Guyenne in Paris, he entered the service of Gaston d'Orléans (1608–60), brother of Louis XIII, who on a number of occasions sent him abroad in quest of works of art. He was in Rome in the early 1630s, where he met Sébastien Bourdon and other French artists and intellectuals. In Paris in 1640 he was appointed proof-reader to Cardinal Richelieu's Imprimerie Royale, a role that seems to have been more important than the title suggests. He worked closely with Nicolas Poussin, whom he probably met for the first time at this period, persuading him to modify his frontispiece for Virgil's *Aeneid* and suggesting the subject for his frontispiece to the *Livre des Conciles*. In Rome in 1644 he was intermediary between Poussin and M. des Hameaux, French ambassador to Venice. In 1651 he published Leonardo da Vinci's treatise on painting, *Trattato della pittura*, himself writing the biographies of Leonardo and Alberti. In July 1652 Trichet went to Stockholm, where he served as curator of Queen Christina's collections and later as her librarian also. He followed the Queen to Rome after her abdication in 1654, but subsequently returned to Paris, becoming librarian to Nicolas Fouquet, and then to Jean-Baptiste Colbert. Trichet's own collection included the paintings *Audience Given to a Venetian Embassy in an Eastern Town* (Paris, Louvre) then attributed to Gentile Bellini, which later passed with Fouquet's possessions into the royal collections; *Bacchanal before a Temple* by Poussin (untraced; engraving by Mariette) and a *Dead Christ with*

Angels by Ludovico Carracci (untraced). His remarkable library of more than 1400 volumes was bought by Fouquet for his residence of Saint-Mandé, and then by Colbert for the Bibliothèque Royale.

BIBLIOGRAPHY

R. Dezeimeris: *Pierre Trichet, un bibliophile bordelais au XVIIe siècle* (Bordeaux, 1878)

E. Bonnaffé: *Dictionnaire des amateurs français au XVIIe siècle* (Paris, 1884)

THIERRY BAJOU

Trichinopoly. *See* TIRUCHIRAPALLI.

Tricht, Aert van (*fl* Maastricht, 1492–1501). Netherlandish metal-caster. On 23 October 1492 he finished the monumental and richly decorated copper font of St Janskerk, 's Hertogenbosch, and in the same year he cast a seven-branched candlestand (destr.) for the Franciscans in Maastricht. In 1495–6 he cast some copper railings (destr.) for the Brotherhood Chapel of St Janskerk, 's Hertogenbosch, based on wooden models made by Alart du Hameel. Two signed works by Aert van Tricht survive: an undated brass font originally from the St Nicolaaskerk (destr.) in Maastricht (now in Maastricht, Onze Lieve Vrouwe, stripped of its lid and decorations), and the arched candelabrum of 1501, spanning the choir of Xanten Cathedral. This consists of three Late Gothic traceried arches carrying twenty-four evenly spaced candlesticks. Columns flanking the central arch support statues of the church's two patron saints, *St Victor* and *St Helena* (h. 1 m). A few smaller candlesticks can be attributed to Aert van Tricht on stylistic grounds, as well as some choir lecterns, notably the Eagle lectern from St Pieterskerk, Leuven (now New York, Cloisters), and a bronze tabernacle in Bocholt Church (Belgium).

Aert van Tricht's foundry was still in use on 31 May 1520, when one Arnoldo was paid for the restoration of several pieces of copperwork by the Netherlandish abbey of Averbode. Arnoldo may have been Aert van Tricht's son. There is no basis for his identification with ARNT VAN TRICHT or with the Aerdt van Tricht who was registered in the Antwerp records of 1522.

BIBLIOGRAPHY

BNB, Thieme–Becker

J. Crab: 'The Great Copper Pelican in the Choir: The Lectern from the Church of St Peter in Louvain', *Bull. Met.*, xxvi (1968), pp. 401–6

G. Lemmens: 'Doopvont Aert van Tricht (eind 15de eeuw)', *Openb. Kstbez.*, xiv (1970), pp. 11a–11c

J. J. M. Timmers: *De Kunst van het Maasland*, ii (Assen, 1980), pp. 214–21

A. M. Koldeweij: 'Kunsthistorische en iconografische notities', *De doopvont van Aert van Tricht: St Janskathedraal 's-Hertogenbosch* (exh. cat., 's-Hertogenbosch, St Janskerk, 1981), pp. 8–16, 23–48

Tricht, Arnt van (*fl c.* 1530; *d* Kalkar, 1570). Netherlandish sculptor and wood-carver. He established himself as a sculptor in Kalkar *c.* 1530, succeeding Henrik Douvermann (*c.* 1480–*c.* 1530), by whom he was probably trained. He presumably came from Utrecht, as the style of his work, especially the characteristic heads and the stylish clothing of the figures, is related to that of other Utrecht sculptors, in particular the influential Master of the Stone Female Head (*fl* 1520s).

Arnt van Tricht primarily made religious sculpture; at first he worked mainly in oak but from *c.* 1550 he used stone almost exclusively. A small group of documented works are the basis of the oeuvre attributed to him. All his sculptures are originally from the areas around Kalkar and Xanten, a substantial part being preserved in St Nicolai, Kalkar, and Xanten Cathedral. Oak figures of *St John* (h. 1.035 m) and the *Virgin* (h. 1 m), from a rood dating from *c.* 1540, survive in the Rijksmuseum, Amsterdam; the Westfälisches Landesmuseum in Münster has an oak *Pietà*.

The development of Arnt van Tricht's style can be seen in his surviving works at ST NIKOLAI, KALKAR. The Trinity Altar of *c.* 1530–40, although already showing Renaissance mannerisms, is still broadly influenced by Douvermann; the St John Altar (1541–3) shows his use of forms becoming more independent; and in the last phase, seen in the stone *Pilate Washing his Hands* in the sacristy, the transition to the Renaissance had been fully made. Examples of non-religious work are a painted oak towel-rail depicting a jester embracing a woman (*c.* 1540; Cleve, Städt. Mus. Haus Koekkoek) and the relief portraits of *Wijnand Hackfort* and his wife *Aleid Boshof* of 1557 on the sidepieces of a chimney-breast in the Huis ter Horst (Loenen, Gelderland).

BIBLIOGRAPHY

Thieme–Becker

G. de Werd: 'De Kalkarse beeldhouwer Arnt van Tricht: Een bijdrage tot de kennis van zijn werk', *Bull. Rijksmus.*, xxi (1973), pp. 63–90

——: 'De pendant van Arnt van Trichts Johannesbeeld', *Bull. Rijksmus.*, xxviii (1980), pp. 118–24

——: 'Een handdoekrek door de Kalkarse beeldhouwer Arnt van Tricht (ca. 1540)', *Antiek*, xvi (1981–2), pp. 33–56

——: *St Nicolai, Kalkar* (Munich and Berlin, 1986), pp. 34–8

'Keuze uit aanwinsten: Afb. 3: Arnt van Tricht, *The Mourning Virgin*', *Bull. Rijksmus.*, xxxvi (1988), pp. 343, 348

A. M. KOLDEWEIJ

Trichur [Tricūr; anc. Tiruchchapērur; Tiruchchuppērūr; Tŕśśivapērūr]. Town in the state of Kerala in south-west India, *c.* 60 km north of Ernakulam. According to the *Keralolpatti*, the traditional history of Kerala, it was one of the 32 original Brahman settlements of Kerala. The Vadakkunnatha Temple, dedicated to Shiva and situated in the centre of the town, was associated with that settlement and remains one of the major Hindu institutions of the region. The earliest inscriptions date to the 11th century AD, but the origins of the temple were probably several centuries earlier. The main gateway (Skt *gopura*) of the enclosure faces west; its single-storey stone base follows the south Indian (*drāviḍa*) model, but the triple-roofed, tiled and gabled superstructure is built of wood in the Kerala style (*see* INDIAN SUBCONTINENT, §III, 6(i)(h)). A pavilion for dance, music and drama performances built by the Maharajas of Cochin in the late 19th century stands in the outer enclosure. The main shrines are located within the inner enclosure.

Of the three main shrines, all of which face west, the Vadakkunnatha on the north is ritually predominant. A circular, single-storey structure, the shrine has a conical, copper-clad roof, a square inner shrine of the southern type with an octagonal superstructure and a double row of columns in the circumambulatory path. There are two main entrances—one on the west for Shiva (in his Vadakkunnatha form) and one on the east for his consort—as well as a third functional door on the south. The granite base (*adhishthāna*) survives in its original form and includes an inscription of the 11th or 12th century. The laterite exterior wall may also be original, but the wall paintings in the recessed areas between the pilasters are no earlier than late 19th-century. The shrine is preceded by a detached square pillared hall (*namaskāra maṇḍapa*) with a granite base and stone columns supporting a pyramidal roof. The middle shrine, dedicated to Shankaranarayana (Shiva–Vishnu), is also circular, with a square sanctum and a double circumambulatory path. The paintings on its exterior walls bear a painted inscription indicating that they were replaced in 1731. The square Rama shrine to the south has an attached pillared hall as well as a detached square pillared hall on the west. The style of its wall paintings suggests a late 19th-century date.

BIBLIOGRAPHY

Enc. Ind. Temple Archit.

Annual Report of the Archaeology Department, Cochin State, 1934–35 (1936)

C. R. Jones: *The Temple Theatre of Kerala: Its History and Description* (diss., Philadelphia, U. PA, 1967)

H. Sarkar: *Architectural Survey of Temples of Kerala* (New Delhi, 1978)

M. E. HESTON

Tricius [Tretko], **Jan** (*d* 1692). Painter, active in Poland. He was court painter to three successive Polish kings—John Kasimir, Michael Wisniowecki (*reg* 1669–73) and John Sobieski—but little is known about him, and few of his paintings have survived. He is, moreover, frequently confused with his son Aleksander, likewise a painter. Tricius studied in the studio of Poussin in Paris (*c.* 1641), in that of Jordaens in Antwerp, and also in Gdańsk. He worked in Kraków, where his official duties included looking after the picture gallery in Wawel Castle. His surviving paintings, from the 1670s, indicate that he specialized as a painter of portraits in the specifically Polish Sarmatian manner: for instance his portrait of *John Sobieski* (1677; Kraków, Jagiellonian U., Mus. F.A.) shows the King full-length and standing, in a costume with the insignia of his status, a realistically captured face, with drapes in the background and a small table beside him. The portrait of the same king (1676) in the National Museum, Warsaw, while similar in style to such Sarmatian portraits, introduces new elements into Polish portraiture; these include the exploitation of Classical iconography, depicting the sitter as a Roman emperor, and the use of a seated pose. This classicizing trend also appeared in contemporary architecture and sculpture in Warsaw.

BIBLIOGRAPHY

T. Mańkowski: 'Malarstwo na dworze Jana III' [Painting at the court of John III], *Biul. Hist. Sztuki*, xii (1950), pp. 263ff

M. Walicki, W. Tomkiewicz and A. Ryszkiewicz: *Malarstwo Polskie: Manieryzm, Barok* [Polish painting: Mannerism, Baroque] (Warsaw, 1971), pp. 34,38–9,45,50,347,351–3,374,377–82,395

M. Karpowicz: *Jerzy Eleuter Siemiginowski, malarz polskiego baroku* [Jerzy Eleuter Siemiginowski, painter of the Polish Baroque] (Wrocław, Warsaw, Kraków and Gdańsk, 1974), pp. 109–17

ANDREW STOGA

Triclinium. Dining-room in an ancient Roman house (*see* ROME, ANCIENT, §II, 1(i)(c)).

□

Tridentine style. See ESTILO DESORNAMENTADO.

Trier [anc. Augusta Treverorum]. German city in Rhineland-Palatinate in the valley of the River Mosel. It is the administrative centre of the Trier district, with a population of *c.* 100,000. A Roman foundation of Augusta Treverorum became the seat of a bishopric in the 3rd century AD and an Imperial residence in the 4th. During the early Middle Ages it was a centre for the production of manuscripts (*see* §2 below).

WINFRIED WEBER

1. History and urban development. 2. Centre of manuscript production. 3. Cathedral and Liebfrauenkirche.

1. HISTORY AND URBAN DEVELOPMENT.

(i) Roman foundation. The Roman city of Augusta Treverorum flourished from the 1st to the 5th centuries AD. Before its conquest by the Romans, the site was occupied by the Treveri, a Germano-Celtic people, as attested by nearby burials with late La Tène pottery (first half of the 1st century BC) and the remains of the sanctuary of Lenus–Mars to the west of the River Mosel and the Altbachtal sanctuary to the east. The site's strategic location at the intersection of major roads to Cologne, Koblenz and Mainz attracted the attention of Augustus, who established a military post there during his tour of Gaul in 15–13 BC. Its advantageous position ensured the prosperity of the settlement, which was mentioned as *colonia* by the time of Claudius. More significant, in the later 1st century AD, the city became the administrative centre and perhaps even the residence of the procurator of Gallia Belgica and the Two Germanies.

The city developed mainly during the 1st and 2nd centuries AD. Its irregular rectilinear plan, covering *c.* 80 ha and still partly visible in the layout of modern Trier, was apparently established under Augustus and Tiberius, although parts were first paved later in the 1st century AD. Excavations have identified private residences throughout the city. Several cellar houses, paved with black-and-white mosaic floors in the 1st century AD, stood in the northern and eastern districts, while large villas, including a complex belonging to Victorinus (*reg* AD 269–70), were built within the city walls during the 3rd century AD (*see* MOSAIC, colour pl. III, fig. 1). Harbours and quays doubtless lined the Mosel, and industrial quarters were concentrated along the southern edge of the settlement. Several aqueducts, including a long channel (?late 3rd century AD–early 4th) from the Ruwer Valley to the east, provided the city with its water supply.

The city's primary east–west axis, the *decumanus maximus*, originated at a stone bridge (late 2nd century AD) over the Mosel; its nine iron-clamped piers still support the broad arches of the modern roadway. Traces of two earlier bridges, one in timber dated dendrochronologically to 18–17 BC, the other in stone built by Claudius, have been located slightly upstream. Further south stood the monumental public bath building known as the Barbarathermen (2nd century AD; 170×240 m), which, like the nearby Kaiserthermen (early 4th century AD), was one of the largest baths built outside Rome itself. In addition to an enclosed palaestra, the central bathing block comprised a large rectangular *frigidarium* and *caldarium* linked by a cruciform *tepidarium*. Niches contained elaborate statues,

1. Trier, basilica ('Aula Palatina'), early 4th century AD

of which isolated pieces survive (Trier, Rhein. Landesmus.).

The forum, at the intersection of the *decumanus maximus* with the *cardo maximus*, was apparently established by Augustus and expanded later; in its final form it occupied three broad insulae (*c.* 140×278 m). At its western end stood an open court raised on a cryptoporticus, perhaps with the curia at the centre of the west side. To the east this opened on to a central court flanked by double rows of barrel-vaulted shops to north and south. The organization of the forum's eastern end, which may have contained a basilica, remains uncertain. Further east stood the provincial procurator's residence (mid-1st century AD), of which parts of a cryptoporticus and a mosaic court have been excavated beneath the Constantinian palace (early 4th century AD).

At the eastern edge of the city the *decumanus maximus* terminated at the amphitheatre at Olewig (?*c.* AD 100), which probably replaced a timber predecessor. Its *cavea*, half carved out of the Petersberg hillside and half supported by earthworks, surrounded an arena (50×75 m) with excavated subchambers. Stone seats (destr.) accommodated some 20,000 spectators. Slightly to the south, near the Kaiserthermen, stood the Altbachtal sanctuary, which continued in use into the 4th century AD and contained more than 50 shrines of various Romano-Celtic types (*see* ROME, ANCIENT, fig. 39). Overlooking it stood the monumental Classical temple Am Herrenbrünnchen,

of which isolated limestone fragments survive (late 1st–early 2nd century AD).

By the end of the 2nd century AD Augusta Treverorum was enclosed by a wall with between 48 and 52 towers. Little remains, but the amphitheatre built into its circuit served as the city's eastern gate. The Porta Nigra, a monumental gate with projecting towers (late 3rd century AD or early 4th), stood at the north end of the *cardo maximus*.

The city's period of greatest political importance was the end of the 3rd century AD, after Constantius Chlorus (*reg* AD 305–6) chose it as his Imperial residence in the first Tetrarchic regime (AD 293). Building projects initiated by Constantius, including an enlarged palace quarter and the construction of the Kaiserthermen, were completed by his son Constantine the Great (*see* EARLY CHRISTIAN AND BYZANTINE ART, §II, 2(i)(a)). The audience hall of the palace (the basilica or 'Aula Palatina'; see fig. 1) is a huge rectangular building of solid brick (58×29 m) with a semicircular apse projecting beyond it, where the emperor sat enthroned. A cathedral (*see* §3 below) was founded in the early 4th century. Owing to constant threats to the border by migrating peoples the prefecture was moved to Arles *c.* 395 and the Imperial court to Milan.

BIBLIOGRAPHY

W. Reusch: *Die Kaiserthermen in Trier* (Trier, 1965)
D. Cüppers: *Die Trierer Römerbrücken* (Mainz, 1969)
E. Gose: *Die Porta Nigra in Trier* (Berlin, 1969)
E. M. Wightman: *Roman Trier and the Treveri* (London, 1970)

E. Gose: *Der gallo-römische Tempelbezirk im Altbachtal zu Trier* (Mainz, 1972)

H. Cüppers: 'Die Stadtmauer des römischen Trier und das Gräberfeld an der Porta Nigra', *Trier. Z. Gesch. & Kst Landes & Nachbargebiete*, xxxvi (1973), pp. 133–222

R. Schindler: *Führer durch das Landesmuseum Trier* (Trier, 1977)

Trier: Kaiserresidenz und Bischofssitz: Die Stadt in spätantiker und frühchristlicher Zeit (exh. cat., Trier, Rhein. Landesmus., 1984)

H. Heinen: *Trier und das Trevererland in römischer Zeit* (Trier, 1985)

J. E. James: *Early Christian Cathedral Architecture in Trier* (diss., Bloomington, IN U., 1993)

M. RAUTMANN

(ii) From the Carolingian period. The town was destroyed several times during the 5th century. Large parts of the Roman town were abandoned, and continuity in the early Middle Ages was assured only by the bishop and the Church. After the death of Charlemagne in 814, Trier was first allocated to Francia Media by the Treaty of Verdun (843) and later to Francia Orientalis. In 882 the town was destroyed by the Vikings. The bishop of Trier was granted many royal privileges in 902 and established his secular dominion in the surrounding valley. The see became an archbishopric during the 10th century. The medieval city was confined almost exclusively to the northern area of the former Roman town, the houses lining streets that are related only in a general way to the ancient network. The medieval city walls were built in the 12th–13th centuries; within them the cathedral (*see* §3(i) below) and numerous monastic and parish churches rise above the city's stone houses and timbered buildings. These are encircled like a wreath by the great Benedictine abbeys of St Maria (founded 700; rebuilt 1960–62), St Martin (rebuilt 1626), St Maximin (founded 7th century; rebuilt 1680–98; *see* CHURCH, §II, 3(i) and CRYPT) and St Eucharius (later St Matthias; founded 8th century; rebuilt 1127), and the collegiate church of St Paulin (1148; destr. 1674; rebuilt 1734–54 by Balthasar Neumann), the charterhouse (St Alban) and a number of smaller monasteries and churches.

From the 11th century stone houses intended as defensive towers, for example the Frankenturm, were again to be found in the city. These were often built of reused Roman material, which was also quarried for the many churches, but otherwise the local red or white sandstone was predominantly used down to modern times, with local slate employed for roofing. Timbered buildings were erected between the 13th and 17th centuries, although they were confined to residential use. A type of house peculiar to Trier had an external chimney set in the façade and rising to the top of the gable, which faced the street; nearly all such buildings were destroyed in World War II.

The city flourished in the 14th century, especially after Archbishop Baldwin of Luxembourg (*reg* 1307–54) had founded the electorate of Trier. The first university was opened in 1473. In 1559 there was an unsuccessful attempt to introduce the Reformation to Trier, but the city remained Catholic, its devotion to its patron saint being expressed in the monumental fountain of St Peter (1595) made for the market-place by Hans Rupprecht Hoffmann.

The 17th and 18th centuries were marked by extensive economic decline caused by recurrent wars, although many of the churches were rebuilt (see above). The Residenz was extended from 1753 by JOHANNES SEIZ. In 1794–5 Trier was occupied by the French, who abolished the electorate and made it the capital of the département of the Sarre; many churches and all the monasteries were secularized. In 1815 Trier was allocated to Prussia, and the demolition of the city walls in the 19th century initiated a new phase of development. Large parts of the old town were destroyed in World War II. Rebuilding proceeded with difficulty and economic recovery only followed the canalization of the Mosel, completed in 1964. New residential areas were incorporated into the city in 1969, doubling its area.

BIBLIOGRAPHY

G. Kentenich: *Geschichte der Stadt Trier von ihrer Gründung bis zur Gegenwart* (Trier, 1915/*R* 1979)

E. Zahn: *Trier* (Munich and Berlin, 1976)

Trier, Führer zu vor- und frühgeschichtlichen Denkmälern, 32 (Mainz, 1977) [with contrib. from D. Ahrens, W. Binsfeld, K. Böhner and others]

E. Zenz: *Geschichte der Stadt Trier im 19. Jahrhundert*, 2 vols (Trier, 1979)

——: *Die Stadt Trier im 20. Jahrhundert: 1. Hälfte, 1900–1950* (Trier, 1981)

——: *Trier im 18. Jahrhundert, 1700–1794* (Trier, 1981)

K. Düwell and others: *Trier in der Neuzeit* (Trier, 1988)

WINFRIED WEBER

2. CENTRE OF MANUSCRIPT PRODUCTION. Manuscripts were produced in Trier from the Carolingian period, the oldest of which are from the Benedictine abbeys of St Maximin and St Eucharius–St Matthias, although a scriptorium at the latter is documented only from *c.* 1100. Around 30 9th-century codices survive from St Maximin, some of which were produced by its scriptorium, while others were acquired from elsewhere, for example after the Viking invasion of 882. Those produced in Trier include a Psalter from the second third of the 9th century (Manchester, John Rylands U. Lib., MS. lat. 116) and the Gospels of St Maria ad Martyres (after 800; Trier, Stadtbib., MS. 23), although Echternach has also been suggested as its place of origin.

The most important period for the production of manuscripts was under the Ottonian Archbishop Egbert (*reg* 977–93; *see* EGBERT and OTTONIAN ART, §IV, 2). The books produced under his direction and patronage show the continuation of both antique and Carolingian traditions. An outstanding artist of this period is the MASTER OF THE REGISTRUM GREGORII (for discussion and illustration *see* MASTERS, ANONYMOUS, AND MONOGRAMMISTS, §I), named after fragments of a manuscript in Trier (984; Stadtbib., MS. 117 1626) and Chantilly (Mus. Condé, MS. 14 *bis*). Other manuscripts attributed to him are the Sainte-Chapelle Gospels (before 983; Paris, Bib. N., MS. lat. 8851), the Gospels in Manchester (996 or after ; John Rylands U. Lib., MS. 98) and the Egbert Codex (Trier, Stadtbib., MS. 24). The latter, a book of Pericopes, containing the largest cycle of the *Life of Christ* at this date, was produced with the assistance of monks from Reichenau, and although certainly intended for Egbert in Trier, its original place of production is disputed.

During the first half of the 11th century, manuscript production at the neighbouring abbey of Echternach eclipsed that at Trier, and in the following century there was a decline in activity. A few Romanesque manuscripts survive, for example a Bible (12th century; Bernkastel Kues, St-Nikolaus-Hosp., MS. 8) with numerous line-drawn initials. The next important period was during the archiepiscopate of Baldwin of Luxembourg (*reg* 1307–54), at whose instigation a number of richly illuminated manuscripts were executed, which show stylistic relations with Cologne. Among these books is the picture chronicle of Emperor Henry VII's pilgrimage to Rome (*c.* 1340; Koblenz, Landeshauptarchv., 1c, no. 1), which is extensively illustrated with coloured drawings; three large collections of Baldwin's deeds also survive with decoration (Koblenz, Landeshauptarchiv., 1c, nos 1–3). The workshop of Archbishop Kuno von Falkenstein (*reg* 1363–88) produced a Pericope book (1380; Trier, Domschatz, Hs. 6) in the tradition of the Codex Egberti, while the richly illuminated *World Chronicle* of Rudolf von Ems (1383; Stuttgart, Württemberg. Landesbib., MS. Bib. fol. 5) shows stylistic connections with Metz. In the 15th century monasteries in Trier made numerous manuscripts of little artistic interest. In the 18th century the charterhouse and the abbey of St Matthias produced liturgical pattern books with letters individually painted by hand.

BIBLIOGRAPHY

H. Schiel, ed.: *Armaria Trevensia: Beiträge zur Trierer Bibliotheksgeschichte* (Trier, 1960; rev. G. Franz, Wiesbaden, 1985)

F. J. Ronig, ed.: *Schatzkunst Trier*, Treveris Sacra, iii (Trier, 1984)

R. Frankenberger and A. Habermann, eds: *Literaturversorgung in den Geisteswissenschaften*, Zeitschrift für Bibliothekswesen und Bibliographie, Sonderlieft, xliii (Frankfurt am Main, 1986) [articles by F. Mütherich and F. J. Ronig]

H. Hoffmann: *Buchkunst und Königtum im ottonischen und frühsalischen Reich*, 2 vols, Schriften der Monumenta Germaniae Historica, xxx (Stuttgart, 1986)

G. Franz and others: *Karolingische Beda-Handschrift aus St Maximin* (Trier, 1990)

F. J. Ronig, ed.: 'Egbert, Erzbischof von Trier 977–993: Gedenkschrift zum 1000. Todestag', Trier. Z. Gesch. & Kst Landes & Nachbargebeite (1993) [supplement]

GUNTHER FRANZ

2. Trier Cathedral, west façade, begun 1037

3. CATHEDRAL AND LIEBFRAUENKIRCHE. The cathedral founded in the early 4th century was a double cathedral, consisting of adjacent basilicas (*see* §3(i) below) that underlie the present cathedral (north; *see* §3(ii) below) and the 13th-century Liebfrauenkirche (south; *see* §3(iii) below).

(*i*) *The double cathedral.* The Early Christian double cathedral covered two Roman *insulae* and was constructed in several sections. At the beginning of the 4th century a triple-aisled basilica with a rectangular choir and side chambers (Building I) was built over the remains of houses in the southern part of the west *insula*. In the second quarter of the century a second basilica (Building II) was constructed to the east, again with a rectangular choir and side chambers. A baptistery and numerous annexes also formed part of the complex. Around 330 a three-aisled basilica (Building III) was created to the north of both the earlier buildings, which were now linked together to create two parallel basilica churches (the north and the south church). An atrium may have stood in front of each of them.

Even before the mid-4th century the eastern end of the north church (the present cathedral) was altered: the original rectangular choir was demolished, and in its place work started on a square section (known as the Quadratbau) with four monolithic granite columns as internal supports. Its purpose is uncertain, but it was intended to contain a free-standing, 12-sided 'chapel', which, no doubt owing to changing political conditions, was not completed. It was not until Valentinian I (*reg* 364–75) became emperor that work resumed on the Quadratbau, with a central raised platform instead of the dodecagon. A coin found in the masonry indicates that work was still in progress in the reign of Gratian (*reg* 375–83). The Quadratbau was illuminated by large windows and decorated with marble and mosaic.

The double church was burnt in the Frankish conquest of the 5th century, with only the outer walls of the north basilica left standing. The building was renovated in 'antique' style with the help of 'Italic' builders under Bishop Niketius (*reg* 526/7–61), but it was destroyed by the Vikings in 882. Archbishop Egbert began a reconstruction, encasing the columns of the Quadratbau in masonry to create cruciform piers. Dendrochronological dating of the building timbers to 989–90 shows that work continued after his death, although it was not completed until 1037 under Archbishop Poppo von Babenberg (*reg* 1016–47), when the relics of St Maternus (*d c.* 325) were translated.

(*ii*) *The cathedral after 1037.* In its present form the cathedral of St Peter started to take shape from 1037, when Poppo began a new section west of the Quadratbau. By the time of his death the west façade (see fig. 2) had reached the height of the side staircase towers, a form of westwork with a central apse, two staircase turrets clear of the aisles and set-back square towers. With arcaded wall passages, Lombard bands and hanging arches, this building, which is a fine example of architecture under the Salians, was completed by Poppo's successors, Eberhard (*reg* 1047–66) and Udo (*reg* 1066–78). The legacy of Roman architecture can still be detected both in the structure of the façade and in the spatial disposition.

The east choir, which projected beyond the Early Christian termination, was started under Archbishop Hillin (*reg* 1152–69), and the high altar was dedicated on 1 May 1196. As the new eastern part was vaulted, it was decided in the early 13th century to vault over the nave and aisles; glazed tribunes were created above the side aisle vaults. The cloisters between the cathedral and the Liebfrauenkirche (*see* §(iii) below) were also built in the 13th century. The slender Gothic east towers were given their upper storeys under Archbishop Baldwin of Luxembourg, but the south-west tower was built up only *c.* 1515. Of the medieval furnishings parts of two Romanesque screens, the arches of wall tombs and the Gothic altar tomb of *Baldwin of Luxembourg* have been preserved. In the south transept is a Romanesque tympanum of *Christ* between the *Virgin* and the cathedral's patron, *St Peter*.

Work began on a Baroque renovation of the cathedral interior under Archbishop Carl Caspar von der Leyen (*reg* 1652–76). From 1702, under Archbishop Johann Hugo von Orsbeck (*reg* 1676–1711), a shrine chapel for the Holy Robe was built on to the east choir. In 1717 the roof was destroyed by fire; the building was restored and the transepts built in 1719–23. Post-medieval furnishings include the monumental Renaissance tombs of *Archbishop Johann von Metzenhausen* (1542) and *Archbishop Richard von Greiffenklau zu Vollrads* (1527). The pulpit (1570–72) was built by HANS RUPRECHT HOFFMANN, who went on to make a series of altars, including the 'All Saints' altarpiece (1614). Archbishop Carl Caspar von der Leyen began to renew the cathedral furnishings and had a large altar tomb erected in the west choir between 1664 and 1667. Archbishop Johann Hugo von Orsbeck introduced several new side altars and the large Baroque, altar-like structure (*c.* 1700) in the east choir, which is conceived as the internal façade of the shrine. The altar tomb of *Archbishop Franz Georg von Schönborn* (1756) and the late Baroque monumental tomb of *Archbishop Johann Philipp von Walderdorff* (1768) are also worth noting. The choir-stalls, decorated with expensive intarsia and originally made in 1726 for the charterhouse in Mainz, were purchased for Trier Cathedral in 1781.

From 1793 the cathedral was used by French troops as a storage depot and stables. It was comprehensively renovated in the mid-19th century, when archaeological examinations were also undertaken for the first time, supervised by Johann Nikolaus von Wilmowsky, a member of the cathedral chapter. The second phase of restoration (1884–1910) attempted to reinstate the cathedral's medieval appearance. The building was again restored between 1960 and 1974, both to stabilize the structure and to redesign the interior according to new liturgical requirements. A new 'swallows' nest' organ was installed high on the north wall of the nave, where there was evidence of a medieval predecessor.

(iii) Liebfrauenkirche. A church dedicated to the Virgin that carried out the parochial functions of the cathedral was started *c.* 1235 over the eastern part of the former south basilica. It was completed *c.* 1260. It is a centrally planned building, the two-storey nave and transepts forming an almost equal-armed cross, with a two-bay projecting choir terminating in a five-sided apse; two of the other

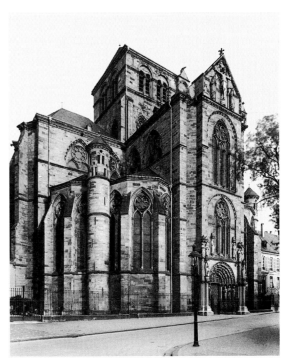

3. Trier, Liebfrauenkirche, west façade, *c.* 1235–*c.* 1260

arms have three-sided apses. Two single-storey chapels set diagonally between each arm create a near-circular ground-plan. The module is based on the crossing square, which also determines the three-storey elevation. Until 1631 the crossing tower culminated in a tall, pointed spire. The window tracery is of typically French geometric form, although the paired openings in the crossing tower and the four round-arched doorways are still reminiscent of Romanesque. The same characteristic hybrid form can also be observed in the cloisters.

The Liebfrauenkirche is indebted to French Gothic for its figural decoration as well as its architectural forms. The main model was Reims Cathedral, without which the figures on the west façade (see fig. 3; originals now in Trier, Bischöf. Dom- & Diözmus.), west doorway and north doorway would be inconceivable. The iconographic theme represents salvation, with emphasis on the Virgin as the patron saint of the church. Very few of the medieval furnishings have been preserved: one remarkable piece is the slab for the tomb of *Jakob von Sierck* (1462; Trier, Bischöf. Dom- & Diözmus.) by Nicolaus Gerhaert of Leyden.

BIBLIOGRAPHY

N. Irsch: *Der Dom zu Trier*, Die Kunstdenkmäler der Rheinprovinz, xiii/1 (Düsseldorf, 1931)

H. Bunjes and others: *Die kirchlichen Denkmäler der Stadt Trier mit Ausnahme des Domes*, Die Kunstdenkmäler der Rheinprovinz, xiii/3 (Düsseldorf, 1938)

T. K. Kempf: 'Grundrissentwicklung und Baugeschichte des Trierer Domes', *Das Münster*, xxi (1968), pp. 1–32

F. J. Ronig, ed.: 'Der Trierer Dom', *Jb. Rhein. Ver. Dkmlpf & Landschaftsschutz* (1978–9) [whole issue]

——: *Der Dom zu Trier* (Königstein im Taunus, 1982)

N. Borger-Keweloh: *Die Liebfrauenkirche in Trier: Studien zur Baugeschichte* (Trier, 1986)

W. Weber: 'Die Anfänge des Trierer Domes', *Trier. Theol. Z.*, xcviii (1989), pp. 147–55

WINFRIED WEBER

Trier, Hann (*b* Kaiserswerth, nr Düsseldorf, 1 Aug 1915). German painter. He studied painting at the Kunstakademie in Düsseldorf (1934–8) and in 1935 became a friend of Joseph Fassbender, who, with Hans Hartung, was to be an important influence on his artistic development. In 1939–41 and 1944–5 he did military service and in 1941–4 was a technical draughtsman in Berlin. Immediately after World War II he worked as a stage designer in Nordhausen, and from 1946 to 1952 he lived at Burg Bornheim, near Bonn, where in 1946 he co-founded the Donnerstagsgesellschaft with Fassbender, Hubert Berke (1908–79), Toni Feldenkirchen (*b* 1907), Hermann Schnitzler (1905–46), his brother Eduard Trier (*b* 1920) and others. As a young artist he was much impressed by the cycles of frescoes in Padua, Assisi, Arezzo, Prato, Florence, Pisa and Rome, in which he perceived 'the creative mental agility of the language of the paintbrush' (see 1985 exh. cat., p. 11). He was also inspired by Abstract Expressionism, producing his first abstract paintings in 1949, and by French Surrealist art, some of which he saw on a visit to Paris in 1950.

In 1951 and 1953 Trier took part in the exhibitions of ZEN 49, which sought to promote non-objective art. In 1952–5 he travelled in Colombia, Ecuador, Venezuela, Mexico, Yucatan and North America. The works relating to his experiences in Colombia were based on line, but the new impressions gained in North and South America, particularly the light, landscape, music and Spanish dances (e.g. *Mambo I*, 1953; artist's col., see Fehlemann, p. 74, pl. 15), encouraged him to re-examine the colour field. This process involved moving colour around on the canvas: 'painting means dancing in a connecting process on a visible surface: the rhythm dances in the legato, the staccato, the pauses, the repeats of the brushstrokes' (Trier, 1959). Trier held his brushes in both hands at the same time, using small sketches, his 'choreography' or 'travel guides', as general instructions. He painted with double, never completely symmetrical strokes, wing-traces, net-like structures and spatial grids that criss-cross the colourful background, surrounding and eventually melting into it (as in *Ambidextro II*, 1959; artist's col., see Fehlemann, p. 240, pl. 33). His 'brush language', derived from body language, became even freer and airier, bolder in its colour intervals (e.g. *Boreas*, 1965; priv. col., see Fehlemann, p. 479, pl. 46).

By the mid-1960s Trier had become one of the leading proponents in Germany of lyrical abstraction. In 1972 he received his biggest commission, to paint the 16×7 m ceiling in the White Hall, the former throne- and dining-room of Frederick II, King of Prussia, in the Schloss Charlottenburg in Berlin. The ceiling had formerly boasted a work by Frederick's court painter, Antoine Pesne, the *Marriage Feast of Peleus and Thetis* (1742), destroyed during World War II. Trier now transcended the space with his abstract media. Over a ground of azure blue, yellow and orange (using secco, egg tempera on plaster), his swinging paint movements complemented the splendid 18th-century atmosphere. The Charlottenburg fresco marked the beginning of Trier's late work, which included

further large-format ceiling and wall paintings in public spaces: among these were the staircase in the Knobelsdorff Wing of the Schloss Charlottenburg (1974), the Bibliothek des Philosophischen Seminars in Heidelberg (1978–9), the Rathaushalle in Cologne (1977–80), the dining-room at the German Embassy in Rome (1984) and the large four-part mural, *Triumph of Painting*, for the Museum Ludwig in Cologne (66 sq. m, 1985–6; see Fehlemann, pp. 762–3).

In his paintings Trier repeatedly referred to the individual colour arrangements of such painters as Tintoretto, Veronese, Tiepolo and Delacroix. This respectful connection with the Old Masters made him liberal and effective as a lecturer at the Hochschule für Bildende Künste in Hamburg (1955–6) and the Hochschule für Bildende Künste in Berlin (1957–80).

WRITINGS
UT POESIS PICTURA? Einige Betrachtungen zur Malerei der griechischen Antike (Heidelberg, 1985)
'Zen', *Die ersten zehn Jahre: Orientierungen: Zen 49* (exh. cat., ed. J. Poetter; Baden-Baden, Staatl. Ksthalle, 1986–7)

BIBLIOGRAPHY
M. de la Motte, ed.: *Dokumentation Hann Trier* (Bonn, 1980)
E. Roters: *Hann Trier: Die Deckengemälde in Berlin, Heidelberg und Köln* (Berlin, 1981)
Georg-W. Költzsch, *Hann Trier: Tatort Malerei* (exh. cat., Saarbrücken, Saarland-Mus., 1985) [incl. autobiographical text by Trier]
S. Fehlemann, ed.: *Hann Trier, Monographie und Werkverzeichnis* (Cologne, 1990)

CHRISTA LICHTENSTERN

Trieste [anc. Tergestel]. Italian city, capital of Friuli-Venezia Giulia. The city (population *c.* 235,000) is situated on the Gulf of Trieste at the head of the Adriatic Sea, about 100 km north-east of Venice. It has been an important port throughout its history, becoming the principal harbour of the Austro-Hungarian empire in the 19th century. A Roman military camp was established in 179 BC near the ancient settlement of Tergeste, which thereafter was gradually assimilated into the Roman world. It became a colony under Julius Caesar in 56 BC, and before 33 BC Octavius ordered the construction of strong walls around the town. The fortifications included a vaulted arch commemorating Augustus that is now known as Arco Riccardo following rumours that Richard I, King of England (*reg* 1189–99), was confined there on his return from the Holy Land. A paved floor and column bases excavated near the cathedral indicate the existence of a Roman basilica and theatre.

Christianity reached the region during the 4th century AD, but with the subsequent decline of the Roman Empire the city suffered 150 years of devastation. In AD 568 it was annexed to the Eastern Empire, together with the Veneto and Istria, and in the late 8th century AD these regions became part of Charlemagne's Holy Roman Empire. The Franks ruled through bishops with various nominal overlords until the beginning of the 13th century, when the independent *commune* of Trieste was established and a long-term rivalry began with Venice for Adriatic trade. The Venetians dominated until 1382, when Trieste came under the protection of the future emperor Leopold III (*reg* 1386–1411). The cathedral (see fig.), dedicated to S Giusto, the city's patron saint, was constructed in the 14th century from two older churches, S Giusto and S Maria Assunta, which had been built between the 6th and

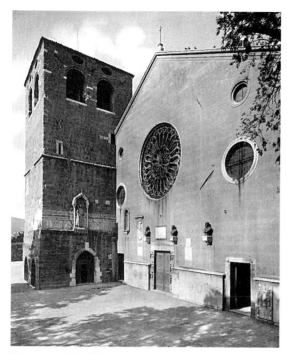

Trieste, cathedral of S Giusto, 14th century

11th centuries on the site of an earlier basilica (destr. AD 568); aisles from each of the two churches were combined to form the nave and aisles of the new cathedral. Five Roman Corinthian columns were reused in the cathedral's campanile, and niches in the pillars of the main portal hold Roman and 15th-century portrait busts. The adjacent baptistery was built in the 16th century.

In 1463 Trieste was saved from a Venetian blockade by the intervention of Pope Pius II, and in 1470 the wasted city was rebuilt by Emperor Frederick III. The castle on Monte S Giusto, constructed on the ruins of an earlier Venetian one (1368), was used by the Habsburgs to maintain control of the city. The oblique porch and chapel of S Giorgio remain, together with the circular rampart added in 1508 by the Venetians. War with Venice continued, but after a short annexation to the kingdom of Spain, Trieste returned to Austrian rule in 1552. In the early 17th century the Jesuits arrived and a Jesuit, Father Giacomo Brinani built the Baroque church of S Maria Maggiore (1627). Andrea Pozza was responsible for the reconstruction and enlargement of the dome and the addition to the façade of giant pilasters, an attic and a broken pediment in the 18th century. The grandeur of the design became particularly apparent after the area was opened up by road-widening work in the late 20th century.

Trieste suffered plague and famine for more than a century but returned to prosperity after 1719, when Emperor Charles VI, needing an additional Austrian trading centre, declared the city a free port. His daughter and heir, Maria-Theresa, Empress of Austria, later drew up a development plan; promoting integration between the old aristocracy and the merchants, she ordered the destruction of the city walls and the reclamation of the salt marshes. This policy was continued by succeeding monarchs and trade flourished, except during three short occupations by the French. From the late 18th century many grand palaces were built and Trieste was transformed into a Neo-classical city, notably through the work of MATTEO PERTSCH; his buildings included the Palazzo Carciotti (1799–1806), one of the finest in the city, with giant Ionic portico, and the Teatro Grande (now Teatro Verdi; begun 1801). Many new commercial buildings were also constructed in the 19th century, including the Neo-classical Borsa Vecchia (1806) by Antonio Mollari and the Tergesteo (1840), which has a glass-roofed arcade. During the 1850s the lavish, Norman-style castle at Miramare, c. 7 km north-west of Trieste, was built for Archduke Maximilian (later Emperor of Mexico, reg 1864–7) to a design by Carl Junker, a Viennese architect working on the railway in Trieste.

In 1918 Italian troops entered Trieste and in 1920 the city was unified with Italy in the Treaty of Rapallo. During the 1930s an urban redevelopment scheme was instigated, but occupation by first German, then Yugoslav troops in 1945–7 brought much destruction. In 1947 Trieste was combined with Istria to form a free territory under Anglo-American trusteeship, and in 1954 the city was reincorporated into Italy. It remained a free port, although its economic structure had been severely damaged. The late 20th century was marked by considerable urban and cultural regeneration and the establishment of several museums, notably the Museo Civico Sartorio and the Museo Civico di Storia ed Arte ed Orto Lapidario, containing the city's principal collections, which include antiquities, medieval icons and 20th-century paintings.

BIBLIOGRAPHY
V. Scussa: *Storia cronografica di Triesta dalla sua origine al 1695* (Trieste, 1885)
S. Benco: *Trieste* (Trieste, 1910)
G. Cuscito: *Muggio guida storico-artistica* (Trieste, 1971)
L. L. Ruaro: *Trieste* (Trieste, 1985; Eng. trans., 1986)
                                        JANET ATTERBURY

Triforium [Lat.: 'three openings'; tribune]. Arcade or shallow passage on the side wall of a church above the nave and below the clerestory. Strictly speaking, the term applies to the three-arched openings that pass through the nave walls into the tribune (for illustration *see* SECTION).

Trigance. Maltese family of bronze-founders. Originally from Haute Provence, they arrived in Malta in 1530 with the Order of St John of the Knights Hospitaller. Between 1700 and 1798 the family was responsible for the Order's foundry in Valletta. The first family member recorded working in Malta was Francesco Trigance (i) (*c.* 1660–1737), who was involved in the casting of the fine bronze statue of *Grand Master Antonio Manuel de Vilhena* (1734) near The Mall in Floriana. The best-known foundry operators were Francesco Trigance (ii) and his brother Gioacchino Trigance (*b* 1746), grandsons of Francesco (i). Francesco (ii) worked in Turin, where he produced a bronze cannon, signed and dated 1769 (now in Great Siege Square, Valletta). The Trigance brothers also cast a number of church bells and made a medal-cutting machine for the Order's mint. When Napoleon expelled the Order from Malta in 1798, work at the foundry was suspended.

UNPUBLISHED SOURCES

K. W. Trigance: *Histoire héroïque de Trigance* (Auckland, 1986) [Typescript distributed privately by author in 1987–8]

BIBLIOGRAPHY

P. P. Castagna: *I i storia ta Malta* (Malta, 1890)
J. Bezzina: 'Il-Qniepen ta' San Gorg t'Ghawdex, 1759–1788' [The bells of St George's church, Gozo], *Festi San Gorg* (July, 1990)

MICHAEL ELLUL

Triglyph [Gr.: 'thrice carved']. Carved ornamental feature of a Doric frieze in the shape of a block or tablet with three parallel, vertical, V-shaped grooves spaced at regular intervals (the precise configuration consists of two full grooves in the middle flanked by half grooves on the outer edges of each block). In such friezes, triglyphs are alternated with metopes (*see* GREECE, ANCIENT, fig. 9g and ORDERS, ARCHITECTURAL, fig. 1xv; *see also* POLYCHROMY, colour pl. I, fig. 1).

Trilithon [trilith; Gk.: 'three stones']. Prehistoric stone monument consisting of three megaliths, two vertical members supporting a horizontal lintel (for illustration *see* STONEHENGE). □

Trinidad and Tobago, Republic of. Country comprising the islands of Trinidad (4828 sq. km) and Tobago (300 sq. km), lying at the southern tip of the Caribbean archipelago (see fig. 1). Trinidad was colonized from 1532 and was united with Tobago in 1889. The country achieved independence in 1962. The capital is Port of Spain, and the official language is English.

1. Map of Trinidad and Tobago

I. Introduction. II. Cultures. III. Architecture. IV. Painting and sculpture. V. Interior decoration and furniture. VI. Ceramics. VII. Patronage and collecting. VIII. Museums. IX. Art education.

I. Introduction.

Unlike many largely volcanic Caribbean islands, Trinidad was until recent geological times a part of the South American mainland and is separated from Venezuela by only 11 km of sea. This island is divided by three mountain ranges running east to west: the Northern Range, a continuation of Venezuela's coastal cordillera; the Central Range, which forms a belt across the middle of the island; and the low hills of the Southern Range. Swamps occur in lowland areas, and tropical rain forest covers much of the island. Tobago lies *c.* 30 km north-east of Trinidad and is dominated by the Main Ridge, running along the northern part of the island. The land flattens out to the lowlands of the south-west.

Prior to Christopher Columbus's arrival in 1498, Trinidad was settled by Amerindian tribes: Caribs and Arawaks. For the next 200 years it remained a colonial backwater, a base for fruitless expeditions in search of El Dorado. Spain, which had colonized Trinidad from 1532, attempted to attract foreign settlers, the Cedula of Population (1783) resulting in an influx of French settlers and their slaves. Under governor Don Chacon, Port of Spain was enlarged and the population tripled to 18,000. In 1797 a British fleet under Sir Ralph Abercromby forced a Spanish surrender. Trinidad then became an experimental Crown colony with Spanish laws and a French-speaking population, controlled directly from London through a governor. With slave emancipation in 1834, a new labour force was needed for the sugar plantations, a problem solved eventually by importing *c.* 144,000 Indian indentured labourers between 1845 and 1917.

Tobago was fought over and settled by the Dutch, French, Spanish, English, pirates and Latvian Courlanders, before it was united with Trinidad, following the collapse of its sugar economy.

After the Depression and the labour unrest of the 1930s, the presence of the USA in Trinidad during World War II revitalized the economy. The most decisive postwar development was the emergence in 1956 of the cohesive People's National Party, led by Dr Eric Williams, which steered Trinidad and Tobago to independence (1962) and then republic status (1973).

BIBLIOGRAPHY

D. Buisseret: *Historic Architecture of the Caribbean* (Port of Spain, 1986)
Caribbean Art Now (exh. cat., London, Commonwealth Inst., 1986)

JERRY BESSON

II. Cultures.

1. Amerindian. 2. Afro-Caribbean.

1. AMERINDIAN. The earliest important art expression of the Amerindians of Trinidad and Tobago is found in the Saladoid, a prehistoric manifestation of the Arawak culture that migrated from Venezuela *c.* 700–600 BC. The earliest pottery, the Cedrosan and the Palo Seco styles of the Saladoid culture, is characterized by a very fine and thin hard-fired ware, with attractive white-on-red painted designs and thin line incisions filled with a white paste on

inverted bell-shaped bowls with flaring rims and D-shaped strap handles. This type of pottery is also characteristic of Pre-Columbian north-eastern Venezuela, the Lesser Antilles and Puerto Rico. Painted decorative motifs consist of straight lines, circles, spirals and other geometric forms applied in ornamental bands on the upper exterior surface. Slip and paints were obtained from mineral oxides, kaolin and occasionally charcoal. The slip-dipped method of painting the entire vessel surface was commonly used. Early Cedros pottery is also characterized by a large percentage of unpainted bowls with cross-hatched, incised flaring rims, which has come to be considered a diagnostic trait of early Saladoid pottery throughout the region.

A cultural change can be seen in such later pottery styles as the Erin Bay (700–1000 AD) and Bontour (1000–1500 AD). These have less artistic merit while still exhibiting continental influences. Erin Bay style is characterized by lack of painted ornamentation, coarse but polished surfaces, and a profusion of modelled, wide incised decorated lugs, similar to the Barrancoid pottery style from Venezuela, from which it derives. Bontour style is characterized by the collared *olla* vessels, hardly ornamented except for some incising, appliqué and a few effigy lugs. As is the case throughout the Antilles, these seem to reflect a decline in the use of pottery for ceremonial and religious objects in favour of wood, shell and stone.

Other artistic objects of possible ritualistic significance, such as polished axes, beads, amulets in the form of bats, birds, frogs or other mythological creatures, were made from mother-of-pearl, shell and polished semi-precious stone. Wood was also used for such ritual objects as snuff-pipes, rattles and masks. Wooden ceremonial four-legged stools (*dujos*), similar to those of the Tainos from the Greater Antilles, have been found in the pitch-lake of Trinidad. By the time of the Spaniards' arrival the Saladoid culture had disappeared. Chroniclers and travellers noted Nepuyos, Aruacos (Arawaks) and Caribs, whose cultures were comparable with the Arawaks and Caribs of South America. The Amerindian population continued to thrive until around the end of the 18th century, when the plantations developed with the arrival of French creole refugees.

BIBLIOGRAPHY

J. W. Fewkes: *A Prehistoric Island Culture Area of America* (Washington, DC, 1922)
S. Loven: *Origins of the Tainan Culture, West Indies* (Göteborg, 1935)
I. Rouse: 'Prehistory of Trinidad in Relation to Adjacent Areas', *Man*, xlvii (July 1947)
J. Bullbrook: *On the Excavation of a Shell Mound at Palo Seco, Trinidad, B.W.I.*, Yale U., Pubns Anthropol., 50 (New Haven, 1953)
A. Boomert and others: 'Archaeological–Historical Survey of Tobago, W.I.', *J. Soc. Americanistes*, lxxiii (1987)
P. Harris: 'Amerindian Trinidad and Tobago', *Proceedings of the 12th International Congress for Caribbean Archaeology: Montreal, 1988*
Proceedings of the International Congresses for the Study of Pre-Columbian Cultures of the Lesser Antilles, 1963–1990: Montreal

RICARDO E. ALEGRÍA, MELA PONS-ALEGRÍA

2. AFRO-CARIBBEAN. Afro-Caribbean culture in Trinidad and Tobago has its origins with the introduction of black slaves and their French owners, whom the Spanish had invited in the late 18th century to settle and economically to develop the two islands. Many slaves were from the Congo region and present-day Nigeria and were Yoruba and Igbo peoples. Many Yoruba and other African settlers who were freed at Freetown in Sierra Leone also made their ways to the shores of Trinidad and Tobago; some came as freed Blacks, and some became owners of sugar estates. African religion and its manifestation in music and performance and African medicine provided a foundation for Afro-Caribbean culture in Trinidad and Tobago. Although it is difficult to reconstruct the historical setting of the importation and adaptation of African culture in these islands, it is known that the Orisa cults of the Yoruba had made inroads in the early 19th century. The Yoruba deity of thunder, Shango (Sango in Trinidad and Tobago), was very strong and remains at the heart of the Afro-Caribbean religious experience, which is interwoven in artistic expression. Worship of this deity was strong in both the rural Trinidad and the primary cities, including Port of Spain. Shango yards flourished in the Belmont and Levantile districts in the east of the capital. Healing rites, dancing, music and feasting were among the activities that took place in the yards. While the old form of Shango worship was becoming a memory for the middle-aged generation of the late 20th century, the cult of Sango had become a focus of the so-called Shouter revivalists, a branch of the Baptists. As in West Africa, Shango is associated with wealth and good luck, which has bolstered his attractiveness in Trinidad and Tobago. The African tradition of medicine is referred to in Trinidad and Tobago as Obeah, and it is found throughout the islands. Obeah men and women may be compared to the healer–diviners of the Yoruba known as the *babalawo*, although the practice may comprise Kongo elements. Obeah magic is a carefully guarded secret on both islands. Its efficacy is based on a programme of sacrifices, divination and the making of medicines to aid patients who need help with a particular task or a challenge that concerns the opposite sex. The use of animal sacrifices, bones, stones and other kinds of materials to make power images has its roots in African medical practices.

Music is an important part of African-derived Caribbean traditions, especially use of the primary instruments of the drum and the gong, and other percussive instruments used in the arts of masquerade. During the late 19th century and early 20th percussive bands known as tamboo bamboo were the mainstay of carnival music. Each band consisted of several individuals who carried hollowed bamboo stocks that were tuned to a certain pitch. Because these instruments could be turned into weapons when aesthetic rivalries became out of control, they were banned. In their place emerged the biscuit tin, kerosine can and other metal containers (pans), which could be tuned. At the centre of a large steel-band orchestra is the percussive ensemble that keeps the pan artists' melodies and harmonies together. Its primary instrument is the double gong, often in the form of two motor car brake-drums, which maintains the rhythm of the other instruments of the ensemble. The double gong, or aggogoo as it is known in Trinidad and West Africa, is also the primary instrument of ceremonial music on the West African coast among the Yoruba and such people as the Asante of Ghana.

The impact of Yoruba culture in the West Indies, and particularly Trinidad and Tobago, has been well documented (e.g. Bascom; Thompson). It is especially evident at carnival. After slave emancipation the British sought a new labour source for the sugar and cocoa estates. The indentureship programme in Sierra Leone resulted in *c.* 6000 Yoruba expatriates, who had settled in Freetown, relocating in Port of Spain, primarily in the Belmont area (formerly known as Freetown in honour of the city they had left). Belmont is an active centre for the worship of Shango, as are the northern rural areas. As in Freetown, the Yoruba introduced the sousou banking system, known in that African city as *asusu*. Trinidadian sousou may have been used to fund the various carnival masquerade groups in the 19th century.

It is difficult to trace the history of specific carnival masking styles, elements and symbols back to Africa. Maureen Warner-Lewis, however, reports that in the early history of Port of Spain the Dahomian Rada peoples all dressed in similar costumes and paraded on carnival day. In Freetown, dressing alike is referred to as *ashoebi* ('we of one dress'). Such dress may be the foundation for the sections of the modern-day large carnival bands where individuals of each section dress alike to convey a theme or idea about the band. In general, the aesthetic of assemblage that guides carnival masquerades may be traced to early migrations from Africa. This aesthetic of display demands the accumulation of such *objets trouvés* as bones, shells, horns and cloth, to create a powerful object similar to obeah power objects. As modern materials became available, plastic ornaments and other fancy materials were added to the pool of items from which this aesthetic could be manifested. With the advent of the Black Power movement of the 1970s, many Trinidadian artists began referring to art books as sources for rendering African-style costumes. Thus both history and a new consciousness help explain African and particularly Yoruba-derived masking elements. Mid-19th century eyewitness accounts of masquerade bands indicate the development of an African and European aesthetic:

> Now we observe the Swiss peasant, in holiday trim, accompanied by his fair Dulcima—now companies of Spanish, Italians, and Brazilians glide along in varied steps and graceful dance . . . But what see we now?—goblins and ghosts, fiends, beasts and frightful birds—wild men—wild Indians and wilder Africans. (Wood, p. 152)

This account shows the development of a dual carnival aesthetic, consisting of the 'fancy' aesthetic as embodied by the Dulcima companies and the 'fierce' aesthetic exemplified by the wild Indians, beasts and fiends. In general the fierce aesthetic derived from African traditions of animal mask presentations and the fancy from the European courtly masking tradition representing kings, queens and courtesans. As carnival developed larger and larger spectacles, the number of principal masquerade characters increased. The Indian character, inspired by the indigenous Caribs, appeared in many styles and spread throughout the Caribbean. Fancy kings and queens, devils, sailors, East Indians, prostitutes, men in women's dress and horse- and cow-head masks were also represented. The important African-derived performer, the Mocu Jumbie or stilt masker, appeared in early carnival in Trinidad and throughout the West Indies. Another masker, Pierrot Grenade, is characterized by his dress of strips of cloth, with bells attached at the ends, and a large heart-shaped

breast-plate that was decorated with mirrors and boa. With a wire-screen mask, this Pierrot character protected his carnival territory against other Pierrots by verbal competitions. The strip-style costume, heart-shaped chest ornament and wire-screen mask appear in many other Caribbean festival costumes including a masquerade of St Kitts–Nevis and Jonkonnu of Jamaica. These convergences suggest a common Afro-Caribbean history for these and other festivals.

There are a few examples of masquerade for which specific African origins, including the Yoruba, can be traced. There has, however, been much controversy about the sources in the case of the Midnight Robber (see fig. 2). The character may have been inspired by late 19th-century illustrations of outlaws in popular literature or by images of the Mexican bandit that were produced by such artists as Frederic Remington. The People's Cultural Association of Trinidad, in a newsletter (1987) about robber history and Trinidad's politics, traces the character back to the Ogboni society and Adamu Orisa plays of the Yoruba city of Lagos in Nigeria. Certainly the use of skulls, feathers, metal and reflective surfaces in robber costumes is paralleled in African costumes and in the practice of Obeah. The fringed hat of the robber, which resembles a fringed platform on which a complex and often tiered superstructure rests, may have its origins in Cross-River costume traditions; such tassel-fringed hats were worn by coastal chiefs of the Niger Delta. Such hats are also found on

2. Trinidad, Midnight Robber masquerade character with Tombstone Headdress

images that adorn the *nduen fobara* of the Kalabari Ijo, again from the Delta area (see Barley, p. 51). The fringe motif may have been adapted by Kru sailors, then introduced to Freetown and the West Indies. The term *nduen* itself may be the origin of the Trinidadian *dwen* or *duen*, which refers to a class of spirits that is sometimes represented in carnival and that Warner-Lewis suggests is of Efik Ibibio origins. The term *nduen* is also an Ijo term for the dead.

Trinidadians have introduced to carnival Yoruba concepts of spiritual force, which reside in the power of the Orisa, the 401 designated deities. The underlying reason for celebrating with carnival bands is to bring in the new year with a fresh start and to clear away the old afflictions, which include hardship, disease and pain. Wayne Berkeley's Rain Forest masquerade of 1983 included a section called 'Lightning' in which the maskers doubled celt (axe) motifs that referred to the god Shango. The Rain Forest band ingeniously transformed the cityscape of Port of Spain into a living rain forest that included sections portraying white and green palms, tropical flowers, hurricanes and the sun (see Nunley and Bettelheim, p. 105). Shango also inspired the designs by Berkeley for the King and Queen sections for the Cocoyea Village band in 1987. The giant robber-shaped king, called Spell of the Cocoyea Broom, was made out of strips of cocoyea palm leaf ribs, which were then dipped in glue and silver glitter. Berkeley explained that the idea for using cocoyea strips came from Shango priests of Trinidad, who dust or clean their altars with a broom made from cocoyea. Thus as the king danced around the Savannah stage, he cleared and purified the Cocoyea Village masquerade band for the new year. Furthermore, in this instance the stage served as the national shrine for the procession of this king, who therefore cleansed the country in its national masquerade festival of 1987.

Since World War II masquerade bands of Trinidad and Tobago have grown considerably, with some having a membership of 4000 masqueraders. The organization of the bands has become thematic, with issues ranging from the political or ecological to social concerns. The Bailey brothers have been important in the development of masquerade bands. George Bailey (1935–71) and his two brothers, Albert and Alvin, grew up in the multi-ethnic Woodbrook district of Port of Spain. As well as having a curiosity for all cultures of the world, George was profoundly aware of his African heritage. With the English school curriculum, he was equally knowledgeable about Greek, Roman and English history, subjects that would play a part in his carnival masquerade. In 1956 he and his brothers produced a masquerade band called Timus Leopard King, which, according to Albert Bailey, was based on research about Africa. George sought to show the variety of African cultures at a time when all Africans were considered black and all the same. He announced the diversity of Africa in a profoundly African manner, through the performance of masquerade. Combining historical research and African adaptations in Trinidad, which included Obeah, Shango and fierce style of masking, he further expanded the thematics of Afro-Caribbean culture in its primary form in Trinidad and Tobago: carnival. In 1957 his band produced Back to Africa, which

stunned the crowds who saw its procession through the streets of Port of Spain and across the various stages where the formal competitions were held. One section of the band included 70 horsemen mounted on bent-wire horses and dressed in robes similar to the professional cavalries of North Africa and the Sudan; other sections included witch-doctors and juju men, who were dressed in the African fierce style of costume. The last section included kings of Nigeria such as the Obas of Benin and the Alafins of the Yoruba; dressed in rich velvets, brocades and capes, these African kings in royal regalia emphasized the point that Africa had a rich history of civilization and kingship in addition to that of Egypt. This newly introduced African monarchy in masquerade paved the way for other bands based on African subject-matter. At the time of Back to Africa other popular band leaders were using themes drawn from Hollywood cinema, creating such masquerades as Quo Vadis and Imperial Rome. Bailey's workshop included many students who have established themselves outside their country, in London, New York and Toronto. Bailey himself has been credited with raising the art of wire-bending to new levels, using light metal substructures that allowed for the creation of large-scale costumes that could be danced in easily by one person. Since his death, other bands have presented African-based themes, drawing on famous types of African art, such as the Bamana antelope headdresses, Dogon masks, Mossi plank masks and Zulu warrior costume for their design and production.

BIBLIOGRAPHY
T. Winterbottom: *An Account of the Native Africans in the Neighbourhood of Sierra Leone* (London, 1803, 2/1969)
M. Deren: *Divine Horseman: The Living Gods of Haiti* (New York, 1953)
D. Wood: *Trinidad in Transition* (London, 1968)
W. Bascom: *Shango in the New World* (Austin, 1972)
E. Hill: *Trinidad Carnival: Mandate for a National Theatre* (Austin, 1972)
B. Brereton: 'The Trinidad Carnival, 1870–1900', *Savacou*, xi–xii (Sept 1975), pp. 46–57
M. T. Drewal: 'Projections from the Top in Yoruba Art', *Afr. A.*, xi/1 (1977), pp. 43–9, 91–2
J. Martin: *Krumen down the Coast*, African Studies Working Papers, 64 (Boston, MA, 1982)
R. F. Thompson: *Flash of the Spirit: African and Afro-American Art and Philosophy* (New York, 1983)
F. Lamp: 'Cosmos, Cosmetics, and the Spirit of Bondo', *Afr. A.*, xviii/3 (1985), pp. 28–43, 98–9
S. A. Boone: *Radiance from the Waters: Ideals of Feminine Beauty in Mende Art* (New Haven, 1986)
V. Comma: 'Carnival in London', *Masquerading: The Art of the Notting Hill Gate Carnival* (London, 1986)
J. W. Nunley: *Moving with the Face of the Devil: Art and Politics in Urban West Africa* (Chicago, 1987)
F. E. White: *Sierra Leone's Settler Women Traders, Women of the Afro-European Frontier* (Ann Arbor, 1987)
People's Cult., 4 (Feb 1987)
J. W. Nunley and J. Bettelheim: *Caribbean Festival Arts: Each and Every Bit of Difference* (Seattle, 1988) [pubd on the occasion of an exh., St Louis, A. Mus., 1988]
N. Barley: *Foreheads of the Dead: An Anthropological View of Kalabari Ancestral Screens* (Washington, DC, 1989)

JOHN NUNLEY
(bibliography with MAUREEN WARNER-LEWIS.)

III. Architecture.

At the time of the Spaniards' arrival the indigenous architectural form was a palm-thatched shelter (*ajoupa*) supported on undressed timbers divided with walls of clay

3. George Brown: Union Club, Port of Spain, Trinidad, 1904

reinforced by straw. The colonizers made use of local skills, for example in the churches and missions set up in the mid-17th century by evangelizing Catalan Capuchin monks. By 1700 the centre of occupation moved from the first capital of San José de Oruna to Puerta de los Hispanioles (Port of Spain), until then little more than a fortified trading post. The rapid rise in population caused by the arrival of the royalist French creole planters was accompanied by the architectural development of the French creole style in Port of Spain with several streets of timber-sided buildings with shingle roofs. A devastating fire in 1808 razed the city to the ground and inspired the colony's first set of building regulations, making it obligatory to use brick or stone and slate roof-tiles. The early 19th century was a period of stability, during which the Anglican Holy Trinity Cathedral was built (1823), facing Woodford Square, and the earlier timber Roman Catholic cathedral (1787) was replaced with the cathedral of the Immaculate Conception (1816–32) on Independence Square in Port of Spain. Both are by Philip Reinagle, working in the Gothic Revival style. The former, wholly constructed in squared Laventille limestone, has a pinnacled tower with a squat octagonal spire and boasts a hammerbeam roof; the latter, with typical brick quoins to dressed, rubble infilling, is more collegiate in style. Neoclassicism was less evident than Gothic Revival, although a few examples of public buildings included the Court House (1822; destr. 1954), Scarborough, Tobago, by

Samuel Hall, which had a pedimented tetrastyle portico, and the General Hospital (1855), Port of Spain, by Lewis Samuel, with windows set in deep reveals giving internal shade and externally an almost layered effect to the elevations.

During the 19th century a number of nationalities and races brought their architectural influences to bear: English, Scottish, French, African, American, Venezuelan, Barbadian and Grenadian. The chattel house-type found throughout the Caribbean islands developed in great numbers, particularly in the suburbs of Belmont, Newtown and Woodbrook, from a small unit to a highly decorative building extended by galleries with high roofs, jalousies and a profusion of fretwork. George Brown (b 1852), an architect recently qualified at the University of Glasgow, went to Port of Spain in 1882. He was employed by Turnbull Stewart & Co. and began almost immediately to transform the city. After a fire in 1895 he rebuilt both sides of Frederick Street using masonry cross-walls at right-angles to the street to support a steel structure and slender cast-iron columns, brackets, lantern lights, grilles and balustrading, imported from Glasgow, to give a unique character to his elegant two-storey terraces. Tall cast-iron columns set at the edge of the pavement gave shaded galleried streets (now mostly destr.) and with lacy verandah rails above bestowed a lightness of touch on their façades. Walls were typically of rubble, stuccoed and painted in light colours and trimmed with red brick quoins to arched openings at ground-floor level. The Union Club (1904), Port of Spain, is an especially well-proportioned surviving three-storey example with open galleries at both upper levels (see fig. 3). Brown was also responsible for some of the many *fin-de-siècle* estate houses and urban mansions. He mixed an uninhibited eclecticism with Arts and Crafts forms already tinged with incipient Art Nouveau, exuberantly decorated: for example the Queen's Park Hotel (1909), Mille Fleurs and Hayes Court, and, strangely out of character, the Romanesque baronial, towered and turreted Archbishop's House. More broadly, as well as dozens of smaller 'gingerbread houses' there are improbable crow-stepped and battlemented mansions such as Killarney (known as Stollmeyers Castle), designed and built by the popular architect–builders Taylor & Gilles, and 12 Queen's Park West (1904), south of the Savannah, by Edward Bowen, where the filigree dormer gable and frilled roofs of the chinoiserie pavilions represent the ultimate achievements of this genre.

In Port of Spain the versatile German architect Daniel Meinerts Hahn completed the free-style museum (1892) and the Italianate Queen's Royal College (1900) and rebuilt Government House (completed 1907; originally the Red House) in a pretentious Second Empire style. A diversity of styles continued in the period leading up to World War II: the Rosary Church by Père Marie Joseph Guillet is a rigid work of Gothic Revival in the style of Pugin; urban buildings included such examples as Bowen's classical store (1923) for C. Lloyd Trestrail on Broadway; the church of the Purification of Our Lady (enlarged and completed 1934), Maraval, is a Romanesque pastiche with a broken curvilinear pedimented gable with Spanish colonial overtones. A local architectural profession developed after 1945, though overseas consultants were employed for some specialized buildings. The local architect W. H. Watkins (later with Watkins, Phillips, Bynoe & Partners) designed an International Style urban block of six storeys (1960) in Port of Spain, a curtain-walled building completely clad in vertical louvres (for some time the city's highest building). John Weeks, then at the Nuffield Foundation Division for Architectural Studies in London, was the designer–consultant of the climate- and context-conscious student halls of residence (1957–60; with Colin Laird) at the Imperial College of Tropical Agriculture, Piarco. With independence and then an oil boom during the 1970s the importance of the local profession grew. Gillespie & Steel Associates (principal architects John Gillespie, *b* 1925, and Colvin Chen, *b* 1941) were responsible for such buildings as the Rhand Credit Union Headquarters (1987), Port of Spain, and for Crown Point Airport (1985; with Colin Laird), Tobago.

BIBLIOGRAPHY

J. M. Richards, ed.: *New Buildings in the Commonwealth* (London, 1961), pp. 161–71

D. Buisseret: *Historic Architecture of the Caribbean* (London, 1980)

R. W. A. Osborne: 'A Review of Some of the Factors Affecting Housing in Trinidad and Tobago in the 1980s', *Int. J. Housing Sci. & Applic.*, vi/3 (1982), pp. 241–54

J. N. Lewis, ed.: *Architecture of the Caribbean and its Amerindian Origins in Trinidad* (Washington, DC, 1983)

L. E. Mitchell: 'Colonial Style: A Look at the Late 19th Century Town Houses of Port of Spain, Trinidad', *Period Homes*, vii (May 1986), pp. 35–7

JOHN NEWEL LEWIS

IV. Painting and sculpture.

The multi-cultural diversity within Trinidad and Tobago has linked the artistic expressions and iconography of not only Africa and Europe but also India, China and the Middle East. In colonial times, imperial social and political systems stunted the growth of an indigenous expression of art. Young West Indian men were educated in Europe. Nevertheless the first formal emergence of a Trinidadian painter, Michel Jean Cazabon (1813–88), took place. Born in Trinidad, the son of Martiniquan 'free coloureds', he studied in Paris under Paul Delaroche and returned to Trinidad *c*. 1850. Closely following the traditions of French landscape painting, he captured the islands and their people in carefully executed watercolours and oils. With the exception of the botanical studies and simple landscapes of Theodora Walter (1889–1959), daughter of a Trinidadian mother and grand-daughter of the English watercolourist Theodore Walter, there are few examples of Trinidadian art from the latter part of the 19th century and early part of the 20th. As West Indian nationalism began to make itself politically vocal in the 1930s, in the arts a growing movement away from a European philosophy was formalized with the emergence of a group that called itself the Society of Trinidad Independents (1929–39). In the work of the Independents can be seen, for the first time, a consciousness of Trinidad's cultural heritage. The influences of Native American iconography and the symbols of African Obeah (*see* §II, 2 above) in the work of Hugh Stollmeyer (1913–81) are two such examples. This spirit was further reinforced by the portraits of exotic black figures by Boscoe Holder (*b* 1920) in the late 1930s, and in the early 1940s by the images of the East Indian by M. P. Alladin (1919–80). Around this time, too, there developed a new appreciation for the country's folklore through the illustrations of Alfred Codallo (1915–70).

The late 1940s and 1950s were dominated by the work of Sybil Atteck (1911–75). She studied in Europe and Peru and later in the USA under the German painter Max Beckmann. Her style developed from a European/Native American neo-classicism to a more Expressionistic style of painting (see fig. 4). The growing political independence of the 1950s and early 1960s created a frenzy of activity in the arts, and Atteck's style formed the nucleus of Trinidad and Tobago's first recognizable school of painting. Few artists from this period did not experiment with expressions of national identity, woven into the strongly geometric composition of the Atteck genre. In the 1950s the Trinidad Art Society (inaugurated 1943) conducted courses in sculpture by Sybil Atteck and Carl Broodhagen of Barbados. The medium does not, however, appear to have been taken seriously by many of the artists. Joan St Louis, Pat Chu Foon (*b* 1931) and later Ralph Baney were, perhaps, the exceptions, although Baney's influences were more directly related to his English training. The introduction of monumental sculpture into mainstream art in Trinidad and Tobago was formalized in the work of Chu Foon. He learnt the fundamentals of sculpting while apprenticed to a manufacturer of handmade toys in the late 1940s. Through Atteck and the 'boys behind the bridge' (Ken Morris with his copper reliefs and Rafael

4. Sybil Atteck: *Stellbandsmen*, oil on canvas, 1949 (Central Bank of Trinidad and Tobago Collection)

Samuel with his naive wood-carvings), he further developed his skills. In 1963 he attended the Universidad de las Américas, Puebla, where he studied Fine Art, and in 1967 the Academia San Carlos, Universidad Nacional de México, where he studied sculpture. In Mexico Henry Moore's work was the major inspiration at that time, having in turn recognized the influence of Pre-Columbian art, in particular the forms of the Aztecs, in his sculpture. Returning to Trinidad in 1968, Chu Foon executed several public sculptures, including a statue of *Gandhi* (1969), *Spirit of Hope* (1971), *Tribute to the Steelband Movement* (1972) and *Mother and Child* (1980) at the new Mount Hope Hospital. Chu Foon is also recognized for his paintings in which, through abstraction, he depicted the relationship of man's inner space to 'outside universal space'. Alongside the more formal development of a Trinidadian Expressionism was the acceptance of intuitive painting as a valid expression through the work of Leo Basso (1901–82).

Following national independence in 1963, experimentation with a range of ethnic and cultural expressions in the quest for a common identity resulted in artistic eclecticism. Following the international wave of Black consciousness in the 1970s, there emerged an important awareness of Trinidad and Tobago's African heritage, best represented by the work of LeRoy Clarke (*b* 1939). Clarke

sought to provide a validity and integrity to the strong religious, cultural and social associations between the Caribbean and Africa. At the same time, the older traditions of landscape painting continued with renewed vigour, as in the watercolours of Jackie Hinkson (*b* 1942). From 1974 Peter Minshall (*b* 1941) developed concepts for carnival by placing the masquerader into highly exaggerated structures. By connecting the feet and arms of the human vehicle to these structures, the movement of the body is echoed by extension, projecting the wearer's energy, to the point where the puppet-structure completely dominates the puppeteer. In combination with the movement of the bodies to the rhythm of the music, enormous dancing mobiles are produced. Such mobiles featured significantly in the opening ceremony of the Barcelona Olympic Games in 1992. Throughout the 1980s the traditional images of Africa, India and Europe continued to provide inspiration for artists, but by the 1990s expressions of anger against historic circumstance were slowly giving way to a new multi-cultural awareness; representations were concerned more with personal, social and environmental statements. Artists preferred to identify themselves within the mainstream of contemporary international expression, rather than with the old values of national, cultural and ethnic identity.

BIBLIOGRAPHY

G. MacLean: *Cazabon: An Illustrated Biography of Trinidad's Nineteenth Century Painter, Michel Jean Cazabon* (Port of Spain, 1986)

N. Guppy, ed.: *A Painter of Living Flowers: Theodora Walter, 1889–1959* (London, n.d. [1988]) [privately pubd cat. of works]

LeRoy Clarke (exh. cat., ed. G. MacLean; Port of Spain, Aquarela Gals, 1991)

G. MacLean: 'L'Art de Trinite et Tobage: Un Héritage bigarré', *1492/1992: Un Nouveau Regard sur les Caraïbes* (exh. cat., ed. P. Bocquet; Courbevoie, 1992), pp. 141–62

——: 'Minshall in Barcelona', *Galerie* [Port of Spain], i/2 (1993), p. 26

——: 'Sybil Atteck', *Galerie* [Port of Spain], i/2 (1993), pp. 28, 325

GEOFFREY MACLEAN

V. Interior decoration and furniture.

The early Spanish settlers appear to have relied heavily on imported materials from Spain. The system of trading in the New World, regulated from Seville, was monopolistic, limiting the colonists to irregular shipments from Spain. Interior decoration and furniture design were therefore largely influenced by contemporary Spanish trends, while at the same time suffering delays, sometimes of long duration, before new designs appeared locally. During the 17th century the first capital of San José de Oruna consisted of *c.* 30 houses; the interiors of these palm-thatched dwellings were described by a contemporary observer as 'rough and unadorned'. In 1763 the Governor of Grenada observed that the timber in Trinidad was 'the best in this part of the world for shipping: besides vast quantities of curious woods for the inside of houses and cabinets'. In Tobago, the isolated estate houses were typically decorated in the English taste and were furnished with imported furniture of the period. Reproductions of the imported furniture were also produced by skilled slave workers, often under the supervision of an indentured craftsman from the home countries. The diaries (1807–12) of Sir William Young record his investigations into the uses of the native trees found on his estates on the island. Under Young's direction, Matthew Hood, 'a very intelligent timber merchant and master carpenter', identified Baleazar, dockwood, yellow sanders, *bois fidèle*, *santa maria* and dogwood as well-known, fine cabinet woods. Silk cotton, 'soft, white and without knotts [sic], suited for ceilings', and wild tamarind, 'a good wainscot wood', were also identified.

By 1783 the Spanish Government recognized that foreign immigrants would have to be accepted if the island was to be developed as a plantation colony. The subsequent influx of French planters and merchants from Grenada, Martinique, Guadeloupe, St Lucia and Cayenne virtually transformed the country into a French colony, and their arrival towards the end of the 18th century injected new life into the building industry. Almost immediately the French creole style became standard for interior decoration and furniture as French creole culture pervaded every aspect of life on the island. Many of these new settlers were farmers who lived in large timber houses on their estates. The interiors of these usually two-storey

5. Trinidad furniture, showing influence of French colonial style, 19th century

dwellings were kept cool and dark by shuttered jalousies on the windows. Simple decoration in the form of pierced fretwork panels were installed above doors or along the tops of interior walls to allow greater airflow. Little survives of furnishings from periods earlier than the 19th century.

In the early years of the 19th century furniture was characterized by French-inspired, Empire-style mahogany pieces imported from Martinique. After slave emancipation (1834), skilled craftsmen from the plantations set up small workshops and continued to produce furniture influenced by French-inspired colonial pieces (see fig. 5), although there is little evidence of a furniture-making industry developing in the colony. By 1860, as the colony flourished, the characteristics of the Trinidadian lifestyle changed. Houses were furnished more lavishly. Nogging came into general use, finished with a lime-plaster rendering. Timber room-divisions were often papered, using imported European designs on a hessian ground. Ceilings were higher and were boarded or beaded, usually flat. All rooms opened on to a gallery and the internal corridors were seldom used. Polished mahogany floors were the norm. Crystal chandeliers might hang from ceilings. Upholstered furniture from England remained a rarity. At the end of the 19th century and the beginning of the 20th there was a significant migration of European merchants to Trinidad. Laird (1954) described their homes as 'vulgarity, gayness, boldness, daring—all mixed with a dash of nostalgia for England, France, Scotland, Spain, Holland, Ireland, Corsica, and yet the houses achieved a very high degree of suitability to the climate'. These styles were mixed with contemporary creole design and resulted in a rich Victorian style of decoration. The Magnificent Nine houses built near Savannah Park in Port of Spain remain the ultimate examples of this affluent lifestyle. Marble floors, cedar, mahogany and greenheart panelling and staircases, high ceilings and wrought-iron fretwork were features often in evidence. Although in the 1990s local furniture continued to be produced, Trinidad made no claims to a recognizably indigenous style; taste continued to be influenced by imports from Europe and the USA. In the latter part of the 20th century young, foreign-trained artists and craftsmen were producing original furniture designs, although these could not yet be described as uniquely Trinidadian in style.

UNPUBLISHED SOURCES
St Augustine, Trinidad, U. W. Indies, Lib. [diaries of 1807–12 of Sir William Young]

BIBLIOGRAPHY
Mrs Carmichael: *Domestic Manners and Social Conditions of the White, Coloured and Negro Populations of the West Indies*, 2 vols (London, 1833)
C. Laird: 'Trinidad Townhouse or the Rise and Decline of a Domestic Architecture', *Carib. Q.*, (Aug 1954), pp. 188–98
A Magnificent Nine: Historical Facts on Nine Buildings in Trinidad and Tobago (Trinidad, 1976)
J. N. Lewis: *Ajoupa* (Trinidad, c. 1980)

VI. Ceramics.

From the earliest settlement of Trinidad by the Spanish colonials, ceramics were probably imported from the Old World for the colony. As attention shifted to Central and South America, however, major shipping often bypassed this small, unimportant outpost. The colonists therefore had to rely on a growing contraband trade, particularly with the Dutch and English. In addition the indigenous Amerindian population probably supplied the major source of domestic wares produced for both their own and later the Spanish community. Deagan (1987) has suggested that by the mid-17th century Mexican maiolica had spread to the Caribbean region, almost completely replacing ceramics from the Old World. Ceramics from the island of Hispaniola may have been another source of supply. It is more probable, however, that such domestic earthenwares as olive jars, cooking pots and bowls were produced by the settlers, since the island was left to its own devices until the 1780s. Despite the influx of African slaves brought by the French landowners, there is little evidence suggesting the development of a distinct, African-influenced form, as created in neighbouring Barbados and in Jamaica.

Following the slave emancipation (1834) new sources of labour were supplied by black creoles as well as immigrants from Sierre Leone, who probably introduced their traditional forms of pottery-making, including the 'monkey' and other domestic wares. By the 1850s East Indian indentured labourers, primarily from Calcutta, were predominant among the artisans in the colony. By the 1870s the Indians had formed their own permanent settlements and reconstituted many of their traditional social institutions. Samaroo (1984) observed that following their indentureship as agricultural labourers many East Indians took to the occupations sanctioned by their caste position, including the Kumars to pottery. The 1891 census of East-Indian population in Trinidad did not list pottery-making as a recognized occupation, which suggests that ceramic production was a secondary occupation and that

6. Gloria Harewood: incised 'calabash' earthenware vase, diam. 230 mm, 1985; terracotta bowl, diam. 300 mm, 1988 (Port of Spain, private collection)

items were probably produced primarily for private domestic use.

During the 20th century Trinidadian East Indians, particularly around Chase Village, in the central Chaguanas region (Trinidad), continued to be the primary producers of local pottery. As well as adopting such traditional Afro-Caribbean forms as the 'monkey jar', decorative flower pots and water-jars, these craftsmen produced traditional Indian forms including the *diya*, a small ceramic lamp, the *loṭa*, a water-jar, and the 'tassa drum'. During the early 1960s Ralph Baney (*b* 1929) was among a small group of Trinidadians awarded British Council scholarships to study at the Brighton College of Art in England; on his return in 1964 Baney, together with his wife Vera Baney, experimented with sculpture and ceramics and pioneered the use of local clays and glazes. Vera produced abstract or totem-like forms. Gloria Harewood (*b* 1927) attended a local training course in ceramics between 1966 and 1968 and then studied under Cecil Baugh at the Jamaica School of Art (1968–70). During the late 1960s and early 1970s she made several visits to Europe and East Asia to observe other ceramic techniques, while continuing to experiment with various clays and glazes, as well as with different forms of ceramic production and kiln construction (see fig. 6). Other contemporary potters included Bunty O'Connor (*b* 1951), Derrick Gay, Margaret Della Costa (*b* 1950) and Mrs Aguiton.

BIBLIOGRAPHY
A. Boomert: *Bibliography of Trinidad and Tobago Pottery* (Trinidad, n.d.)
B. Samaroo: 'East Indian Influences in the British Caribbean', *Conference on Migration and Cultural Contact in the Caribbean: Barbados, 1984*, pp. 12–13
K. Deagan: *Artifacts of the Spanish Colonies of Florida and the Caribbean, 1500–1800* (Washington, DC, 1987)

ALISSANDRA CUMMINS

VII. Patronage and collecting.

During the 19th century and colonial times patronage of art was mainly by the expatriate community: the islands' administrators, planters, wealthy travellers and, to a lesser extent, local plantation owners and merchants. The most important collections of work by Michel Jean Cazabon (1813–88) were commissioned by Lord Harris, then Governor of Trinidad, and by two Scottish plantation owners, William Burnley and James Lamont. Expatriate patronage continued to play a large part in the development of the arts, particularly in the 1930s, with support for the Society of Trinidad Independents (STI) and later in the formation of the Trinidad Art Society in 1943. The most important body of work by members of the STI is now in the private collection of the J. B. Fernandes Trust Company, Port of Spain. Until the mid-1950s the novelty of life in the tropics and colonial decadence determined a preference for island art or native portraiture. Although at the end of the 20th century there was still a general preference for decorative work, intellectual independence and a greater understanding of universal trends, through education and travel, encouraged a more informed market.

Around the time of political independence patronage in the arts was encouraged at all levels. Official participation helped to establish several important collections, in particular those of the Central Bank of Trinidad and

Tobago and Trinidad Hilton Hotel, both in Port of Spain. At this time too, several of the Government Ministries and newly formed national corporations purchased art. Since then many of these collections have not been properly maintained, nor have they been augmented by new purchases. In the case of new acquisitions, the choice of material has often been inappropriate. By the 1990s there existed in both the public and private sectors a growing awareness of art acquisition as an alternative to traditional investment. This led to a more adventurous market, but it became apparent that the need to rationalize collections in terms of quality and content would only be understood clearly through education and with a more formal market. Market stability was slowly assisted by a more professional approach to dealing. In addition, despite differences of language, the Caribbean began to recognize a common cultural heritage, and through regular exchanges and greater regional dialogue the market not only opened up for Trinidad and Tobago's artists but also provided a common voice for international appreciation.

For bibliography *see* §IV above.

GEOFFREY MACLEAN

VIII. Museums.

During the 18th and 19th centuries European interest in tropical archaeology, anthropology and natural history as scientific disciplines served as a catalyst for the formation of the earliest museums in the West Indies. Agricultural, economic and empirical endeavours also led to the development of research collections. At the same time, Victorian philanthropic motives stimulated efforts to educate the newly freed slave population after emancipation. These activities were influential in the establishment of the Victoria Institute in 1887 (later the Royal Victoria Institute, now the National Museum and Art Gallery) in Port of Spain. Built as a memorial for Queen Victoria's Jubilee, it was intended to be a scientific institute with a museum of the colony. The museum began in 1889 with a collection of local fauna presented by the Trinidad Field Naturalists' Club. The Institute opened to the public in September 1892. Examples of local flora, geological and mineral specimens and various archaeological finds were later added, forming the major portion of the collections. Lectures and technical classes in a variety of areas were held, as well as exhibitions of paintings by local artists. Annual horticultural displays were also typical of the period. Plans for an industrial commercial museum and one of hygiene were mooted, but by the 20th century these had not come to fruition. In 1920 the entire structure and contents of the Institute were destroyed by fire. The following decades were devoted to the reconstruction of the buildings and collections. In 1976–7 a UNESCO consultant mission on the development of museums was undertaken at the request of the government. Also during this period the Museum of Tobago History, Mt Irvine, Tobago, was founded by a private trust, and the Coast Guard Marine Museum, Staubles, Trinidad, was also established (both 1977). A UNESCO-sponsored seminar on 'Concepts of Cultural Heritage and Preservation' and other initiatives led to the establishment of a Museum

Task Force in 1980, with a mandate to plan in detail the setting up of a decentralized museum system for Trinidad and Tobago. The Victoria Institute was renamed the Trinidad National Museum and Art Gallery, reflecting the significant growth of its 20th-century art collection. Permanent exhibits now include representative examples of carnival costume, as well as a major exhibit on the island's important oil and energy industry. It also houses a collection of works by Michel Jean Cazabon (1813–88).

BIBLIOGRAPHY

Proc. Victoria Inst. (1894–1902; 1924–8)

F. A. Bather and T. Sheppard: 'Directory of Museums in the West Indies', *The Museums Association Directory of Museums* (London, 1934), pp. 59–63

F. de Carmago e Almeida-Moro: *Trinidad and Tobago: Development of Museums*, UNESCO Technical Report (Paris, 1977)

Concepts of Cultural Heritage and Preservation, Report of UNESCO/Trinidad and Tobago Government (Paris, 1978)

Purpose, Role and Programmes of the Proposed Museum System of Trinidad and Tobago, Museum Task Force (Trinidad, 1980)

J. S. Whiting: *Museum Focused Heritage in the English-speaking Caribbean*, UNESCO Technical Report (Paris, 1983)

A. Cummins: *The History and Development of Museums in the English-speaking Caribbean* (diss., U. Leicester, 1989)

ALISSANDRA CUMMINS

IX. Art education.

Recognition of fine art as a valid profession has been slow to develop in Trinidad and Tobago. Michel Jean Cazabon (1813–88), who studied at the Académie des Beaux-Arts in Paris, was lucky to be born into a family whose cultural values included a serious appreciation of the arts. He was, however, viewed by the majority of the population as an eccentric. Cazabon taught several students but encouraged a general appreciation of painting rather than helping them to make careers as fine artists. Under the guidance of Amy Leong Pang the artists grouped themselves into the Society of Trinidad Independents, an informal alliance that can be considered as Trinidad's first school of painting. The artists gathered in private homes, painted and discussed the arts and developed their ideas. The Independents also published their own philosophical newspaper, intended for the enlightenment of the conservative attitudes born of a strong religious and colonial heritage. Their ideas, however, were considered outrageous and bohemian, and they survived only until 1939. From the Independents the Trinidad Art Society was formed in Port of Spain. The Society's aim was 'to encourage the practice of Fine and Applied Arts and Crafts and to foster their appreciation and practice in Trinidad and Tobago by every possible means such as holding exhibitions, the awarding of scholarships and prizes'. Sybil Atteck, a founder-member, introduced a more formal attitude to the study of painting through a strictly academic appreciation. The Art Society sponsored classes in the many aspects of artistic expression by artists such as the French Neo-Impressionist Pierre Lelong and the Barbadian sculptor Carl Broodhagen and exhibited the work of its members every year. These exhibitions were held first at the Royal Victoria Institute but from 1959 at the old Woodbrook Market. Serious criticism was encouraged, the reviews of Derek Walcott being among the most important commentaries. After political independence scholarships were offered, mainly by the British Council, for artists to study fine art. Most students went to the UK, and for specific training (e.g. ceramics) to continental Europe. Later, scholarships provided by the Ministry of Culture and Commonwealth extended the learning experience to many other countries, including Africa, Canada, India and the USA. Institutions in Trinidad that offer art education include the John Donaldson Technical Institute (established 1963), which provides courses in graphic and applied arts, and the Creative Arts Centre (established 1986), part of the University of the West Indies, St Augustine. By the 1990s, through government loans and scholarships and because of the limited facilities available locally, students of Fine Art continued to be educated outside Trinidad, although a wish to be philosophically closer to Trinidad and Tobago led many to attend the Edna Manley School of Fine Art in Jamaica and the Ecole Régionale d'Arts Plastiques in Martinique.

For bibliography see §IV above.

GEOFFREY MACLEAN

Trinitarians [Order of the Holy Trinity for the Redemption of Captives; Mathurins]. Religious order. The Order was founded by John of Matha (1154–1213) to ransom Christians taken captive by Muslims, chiefly as a result of the Crusades. After a vision of the 'majesty of God', dressed in white robes with a red and blue cross, with hands crossed above a white and a black captive, John joined a community of hermits founded at Cerfroid, near Meaux, by Felix of Valois (1127–1212). Pope Innocent III recognized the Order in 1198 and presented it with the church of S Tommaso in Formis, Rome, in 1203. A roundel (*c.* 1218) of Cosmati work above the entrance of the adjacent hospital represents Christ between two chained captives, below the visionary cross. By 1218 there were more than 30 foundations in France and Spain. The church of St Mathurin (destr.) in Paris was acquired in 1228. The Order continued to expand, establishing itself in Scotland, perhaps as early as 1214 at Aberdeen, in England from 1252, for example at Knaresborough Priory (1257; destr.), and in the Netherlands. At its peak there were more than 200 houses, although the requirement that at least one third of its income be used for ransoms restricted its wealth. There was also strong rivalry between the French and Spanish branches. The Order was in decline by 1529, when the foundation at Fontainebleau was absorbed into Francis I's rebuilding of the château.

A revival in the later 16th century was prompted by the successful campaigns against the Turks and the impetus of the Counter-Reformation. A Reformed branch was founded in France in 1578 and a Discalced branch in Spain in 1599; the Order's established sections became known as the Grands-Trinitaires. At Rome the Discalced Trinitarians founded a chapel at the Quattro Fontane in 1611, with an altarpiece of *St Charles Borromeo in Adoration of the Trinity* by Orazio Borgianni, while the Reformed Trinitarians built S Dionigi (1619–37; destr. 1939) near by. The monastery at Quattro Fontane was enlarged from 1634 and work began on the church of S Carlo from 1637 (see BORROMINI, FRANCESCO, §I, 3 and figs 1, 2 and 3) and on its façade in 1665. Borgianni's altarpiece was replaced by one of the same subject by Pierre Mignard I, the doorway of the monastery was decorated with a

Baroque version of the S Tommaso roundel and S Dionigi was completed with a façade (1686) by Giovanni Antonio Massi. Although the Mathurins were removed from the chaplaincy at Fontainebleau in 1660, Louis XIV commissioned bronze reliefs of *SS John of Matha and Felix of Valois* (now Fontainebleau, St Louis) by François Girardin to flank the *Holy Trinity* on the high altar tabernacle in the château's chapel of the Trinity (for illustration of the vault, from *c.* 1606, *see* FREMINET, MARTIN).

The foundation of Santa Trinità degli Spagnoli (1731–3), Rome, with an oval plan and curved façade (1741) by Manoel Rodrigues dos Santos (*fl* 1733–71), was inspired by a revival of the Grands-Trinitaires. The high altar bears Corrado Giaquinto's *Holy Trinity Freeing a Captive Slave* (1750) and the interior decoration, including Gregorio Guglielmi's *St John of Matha in Glory* (1744–8) on the vault and work by Antonio Gonzalez Velázquez, Gaetano Lapis and Andrea Casali (1775–9), glorifies the Order and its saints. Of similar date are the scenes from the *Life of St John of Matha* (1777–82; Bruges, St Gilliskerk) by Jan Antoon Garemijn. By the 19th century only the Discalced Trinitarians remained; the restored basilica of S Crisogono in Rome was given to the Order in 1866 by Pope Pius IX (*reg* 1846–78).

BIBLIOGRAPHY

P. Deslandres: *L'Ordre des Trinitaires pour le rachat des captifs*, 2 vols (Toulouse and Paris, 1903)
S. Rius: 'Antonio Gonzales Velázquez y los frescos de la iglesia de Trinitarios Calzados de Roma', *Archv. Esp. A.*, xli (1968), pp. 67–70
A. Blunt: *Borromini* (London, 1979), pp. 52–84
——: *Guide to Baroque Rome* (London, 1982)
P.-R. Gaussin: *L'Europe des ordres et des congrégations* (Saint-Etienne, 1984)
S. Tigerman, ed.: *Architecture of Rome: A Nineteenth-century Itinerary by Giovanni Battista Cipriani* (New York, 1986)

Trinquesse, Louis-Rolland [Louis Roland] (*b* ?Paris, 1745; *d c.* 1800). French painter. He was a student at the Académie Royale from 1758 to at least 1770 and worked both as a portrait painter and a genre painter. His portraits are usually gentle and uncomplicated likenesses painted in pastel colours, for example the *Young Girl* (1777; Paris, Louvre). When dealing with older male sitters, however, his style could be grander and more sober, as in the portrait of the *Abbé Gentil* (1783; Bagnols-sur-Cèze, Mus. Bagnols-sur-Cèze) and the *Portrait of an Architect* (formerly identified as Jacques-Denis Antoine; 1780; Paris, priv. col.), the most ambitious of Trinquesse's known works, showing the architect as if measuring a drawing. Trinquesse's genre paintings are in the gallant and bourgeois tradition of Frédéric Schall and Louis-Joseph Watteau de Lille, depicting scenes of love and dalliance in parks and gardens, for example the *Offering to Venus* (1786; Dijon, Mus. B.-A.) and the *Declaration of Love* (1786; Engl. priv. col.). Such works are thoroughly artificial, with a smooth porcelain-like finish; they demonstrate the painter's enjoyment of the depiction of rich materials. Trinquesse was well known among contemporary collectors for his very assured drawings, mostly in red chalk, many of which depict young artists at work, such as the *Drawing Class* (Dijon, Mus. B.-A.). He failed twice to become an Academician and exhibited instead at the Salon de la Correspondance organized by Pahin de la Blancherie.

BIBLIOGRAPHY

Trois Peintres bourguignons du XVIII siècle: Colson, Vestier, Trinquesse (exh. cat., Dijon, Mus. B.-A., 1969)
J. Wilhelm: 'Les Portraits masculins dans l'oeuvre de L. R. Trinquesse', *Rev. A.*, xxv (1974), pp. 55–65
J. Cailleux: 'The Drawings of Louis Roland Trinquesse', *Burl. Mag.*, cxvi/851 (1974), suppl., pp. i–xiv

SIMON LEE

Trip. Dutch family of merchants, patrons and collectors. The family is first recorded in Zaltbommel, but *c.* 1600 Elias Trip (*b* ?1570; *d* Amsterdam, 1636) and his brother Jacob Trip (*b* ?1576; *d* Amsterdam, *bur* 8 May 1661) moved to Dordrecht, where they became successful entrepreneurs, mainly in the iron and munitions trade, with interests in the West India Company. Elias married Maria de Geer and Jacob married Marguerite de Geer (*b* Liège, 10 Nov 1583; *d* Dordrecht, 1672), sisters of their partner, the iron-founder Louys de Geer, who was an important gun manufacturer and dealer. Elias moved to Amsterdam in the early years of the century, and over the years the Trips consolidated their fortunes and became some of the greatest arms suppliers in Europe. Like many other affluent citizens of Amsterdam, the Trips employed Rembrandt to paint a number of portraits for them, including Elias's second wife *Alijdt Adriaensdr.* (1591–1656) (1639; Rotterdam, Mus. Boymans–van Beuningen) and his daughter *Maria Trip* (1619–83) (1639; van Weede Found., on loan to Amsterdam, Rijksmus.). Another portrait of *Maria Trip*, painted in the same year (Aachen, Suermondt-Ludwig-Mus.), although bearing Rembrandt's signature, is possibly by his pupil Ferdinand Bol (although it has been suggested as a work of Govaert Flinck); the Trips gave a number of commissions to Bol, favouring a fellow native of Dordrecht. Rembrandt painted other portraits for the Trips, including a head-and-shoulders of *Marguerite de Geer* and pendant portraits of *Marguerite de Geer* and *Jacob Trip* (all 1661; London, N.G.), although it is uncertain whether the last-named is a copy of another work as Jacob died in May 1661.

Two of Jacob's sons, Louys (1605–84) and Hendrick (1607–66), continued the business and gained entry into the city's ruling circles by marriage into patrician families; Louys was burgomaster three times between 1674 and 1679. The brothers commissioned Justus Vingboons to build them a house on the Kloveniersburgwal in Amsterdam. The Trippenhuis (1660–62) is, in fact, two identical houses behind a single, pedimented front that defines its character. Every feature of classicism inspired by Roman architecture is present: the use of pilasters, rigid divisions of the façade and the pediment. In contrast to the flat, undecorated rear elevation, the front is richly decorated; from the street it was clear how the Trips had made their fortune: there are chimneys on the roof in the shape of mortars, and canons and canonballs sculpted in relief on the façade. The Trippenhuis is the largest house built by a private individual in Amsterdam.

The grandeur of this merchant's palace was also expressed in the interior. The ceilings of each room in both parts of the house were painted by Nicolaes de Helt (1614–62), also known as Stocade (only those in one house now exist). Their allegorical subjects make it clear that peace, freedom and prosperity can only be attained by the movement of weapons. In addition, the brothers commissioned overmantels by Ferdinand Bol (Amsterdam, Rijksmus.) and some overdoors depicting Swedish landscapes by Allart van Everdingen (*in situ*), who had also painted the Trips' *Gun-Foundry at Julietabroek in Södermanland* (Amsterdam, Rijksmus.). Other artists commissioned by the Trips include Nicolaes Maes (a portrait of *Jacob Trip*, The Hague, Mauritshuis), Bartholomeus van der Helst, Jacob Gerritsz. Cuyp, Albert Cuyp and Jan Lievens. In 1808 the Trippenhuis was rebuilt as the Paleis van Wetenschappen en Kunsten (Palace of Science and the Arts); from 1817 to 1855 the Rijksmuseum was housed in it, and it now houses the Koninklijke Academie van Wetenschappen (Royal Academy of Sciences).

BIBLIOGRAPHY

P. W. Klein: *De Trippen in de 17e eeuw: Een studie over het ondernemersgedrag op de Hollandse stapelmarkt* [The Trip family in the 17th century: a study of the behaviour of the entrepreneur on the Dutch staple market] (Assen, 1965) [Eng. synopsis in *Acta Hist. Neerlandica*, i (1966), pp. 187–211]

D. Regin: *Traders, Artists, Burghers* (Assen, 1976), pp. 99–100

S. A. C. Dudok van Heel: 'Het maecenaat Trip: Opdrachten aan Ferdinand Bol en Rembrandt van Rijn' [The Trip family as patrons: commissions to Ferdinand Bol and Rembrandt van Rijn], *Kron. Rembrandthuis*, xxxi (1979), pp. 14–26

R. Meischke and H. E. Reeser, eds: *Het Trippenhuis te Amsterdam* (Amsterdam, Oxford and New York, 1983)

G. Schwarz: *Rembrandt: His Life, his Paintings* (London, 1985), pp. 206–8, 332–5

K. Jongbloed: *Van wapenhandel tot wetenschapbedrijf. De Koninklijke Nederlandse Akademie van Wetenschappen in het Trippenhuis te Amsterdam* [From arms trading to the business of science. The Royal Academy of Sciences in the Trippenhuis in Amsterdam] (Amsterdam, 1993)

J. A. VAN DER VEEN

Tripe, Linnaeus (*b* Devonport, 1822; *d* Devonport, 1902). English photographer. He was an enthusiastic photographer while stationed with the army in India from 1839 to 1875. In the 1850s he initiated and undertook numerous surveys of sites of historical and ethnographical interest: the best-known include commissions for the British East India Company (1855) and the Madras Presidency (1856). The latter resulted in the publication of six volumes entitled *Photographic Views of Indian Scenery: Madura, Tanjore and Trivady, Ryakotta, Seringham, Poodoocottah and Trichinopoly*. Using the calotype process, he enhanced his chosen architectural subject-matter with a dramatic use of available light and a subtly lyrical quality that transcended photography's hitherto purely factual function.

PHOTOGRAPHIC PUBLICATIONS

Photographic Views of Indian Scenery: Madura, Tanjore and Trivady, Ryakotta, Seringham, Poodoocottah and Trichinopoly, 6 vols (1858)

Photographs of the Elliot Marbles and other Subjects in the Central Museum, Madras (Madras, 1858)

ALEXANDRA NOBLE

Tripoli [Ṭarābulus; Aṭrābulus]. Port city in northern Lebanon. Founded by the Phoenicians in the 8th century BC and occupied successively by Greeks (who named it after its three walled quarters), Romans, Arabs and Crusaders, the seaside city was razed in 1289 when it was recaptured by the Mamluk sultan Qala'un (*reg* 1280–90), and a new city built inland. Thirty-five monuments, covering the range of religious, civil and military architecture, survive from the new Mamluk city. The mosques,

spread throughout the city and built by rulers and local residents, include six congregational mosques and three neighbourhood mosques. The madrasas, most of which are clustered around the Great Mosque, range from imposing to modest. Caravanserais were built in the northern part of the city that was most accessible to roads from Syria; they followed the traditional plan of a central courtyard with a ground floor with vaulted rooms and a galleried storey above. Baths, modelled on the Syrian prototype, had a linear arrangement of dressing, cold, warm and hot rooms. These monuments were built of well-cut red or yellow sandstone, often accented by black stone and decorated with polychrome marble in the Syrian and Cairene traditions (*see* ISLAMIC ART, §II, 6(iii)(a)). To this Mamluk core a few buildings were added in the 16th century under the Ottomans. In the 20th century, after a pipe-line was constructed from Kirkuk in Iraq to the Mediterranean, the core has been enveloped by modern concrete structures.

BIBLIOGRAPHY

'Abd al-'Aziz Salim: *Ṭarāblus al-shām fiʾal-tārīkh al-islāmī* [Tripoli of Syria in the Islamic period] (Alexandria, 1967)

'Umar 'Abd al-Salam Tadmuri: *Tārīkh wa āthār masājid wa madāris Tarāblus fī 'aṣr al-mamālik* [History of the mosques and madrasas of Tripoli in the Mamluk period] (Tripoli, 1974)

H. Salam-Liebich: *The Architecture of the Mamluk City of Tripoli* (Cambridge, MA, 1983)

HAYAT SALAM-LIEBICH

Trippel, Alexander (*b* Schaffhausen, 23 Sept 1744; *d* Rome, 24 Sept 1793). Swiss sculptor. He was one of the numerous children of an indigent craftsman. In 1754 his father, with a part of the family, moved to London, where Trippel was first taught drawing and modelling by Johann Christian Ludwig von Lücke. At the age of 15 he moved to Copenhagen; there, with financial support from his elder brother Bernhard Trippel, he was eventually admitted to the Danish Royal Academy and became a pupil of the sculptor and humanist scholar Johannes Wiedeweldt. In 1765, having failed to find employment on new building projects in Berlin and Potsdam, he returned to Copenhagen. He now found work with the sculptor Carl Frederick Stanley. In 1768 he won the gold medal of the Danish Royal Academy for his relief of *Joseph Revealing himself to his Brothers*.

In the absence of further successes Trippel travelled via London to Paris in 1771. There in the course of some three years he produced only a few works, such as a marble *Bacchus* and a terracotta group of *Bacchus and Ariadne*. He made the acquaintance of Christian von Mechel, engraver and art dealer, who arranged for him a number of sales in Switzerland, including that of *Bacchus* to a Gedeon Burckhardt in Basle. Trippel also executed four plaster models of *Hercules in Repose* (version Zurich, Ksthaus), an allegory of Switzerland, to be offered to the four Protestant cantons. Trippel therefore travelled to Switzerland; remaining there for almost a year, he produced a number of works, including a bust of one of his aunts in painted terracotta (Schaffhausen, Mus. Allerheiligen) and one of *Christ* (untraced) for Johann Kaspar Lavater.

With the proceeds from these works and help from a prosperous uncle, Trippel made his first journey to Rome in 1776 but was unable to gain a foothold there. As early as 1778 he returned to Switzerland, where he again worked for Burckhardt. In the autumn of 1778, again supported by his uncle, he returned to Rome, where he remained for the rest of his life. His first years in Rome were difficult; it was only in the 1780s that he began to be known as one of the best artists in Rome. His international commissions increased accordingly. His works from those years included a plaster bust of *Dorothea Schlözer* (1781; U. Göttingen, Kstsamml. U.), and *Agrippina and her Children* and *Mars and Venus* (both terracotta, 1786; Zurich, Ksthaus). Trippel's most famous work was undoubtedly a portrait bust of *Goethe* (Arolsen, Residenzschloss), about which the poet wrote in his *Italienische Reise* (1787), 'Everyone is pleased with it'. It was completed in 1789 and replicated in numerous plaster casts (e.g. Weimar, Landesbib.). Trippel also made over life-size marble busts of *Frederick the Great* (1789; Arolsen, Residenzschloss) and *Johann Gottfried Herder* (1789; Weimar, Kstbib.) and a funerary monument for *Salomon Gessner* (marble, 1792; Zurich, Schweiz. Landesmus.). A good many of Trippel's works were executed only as models or are untraced. The designs he sent to the Prussian court earned him the favour of the minister of state Herzberg, at whose instigation he was made an honorary member of the Königliche Preussische Akademie der Künste on 5 January 1787. Trippel's last major commission was a statue for Catania of *Charles VII, King of the Two Sicilies*, which got only as far as a model. He died suddenly of a fever and was buried near the Pyramid of Gaius Cestius in Rome. His life had been ruled by adverse circumstances, and even though he received wide recognition in his last years and came eventually to be regarded as an important forerunner of Antonio Canova and Bertel Thorvaldsen, his work was neglected for generations.

Thieme–Becker   BIBLIOGRAPHY
C. H. Vogler: 'Der Bildhauer Alexander Trippel aus Schaffhausen', *Neujb. Hist.-Antiqua. Ver. & Kstver. Schaffhausen* (1892–3)
Schaffhauser Kunst und Kultur im 18. Jahrhundert (exh. cat., Schaffhausen, Mus. Allerheiligen, 1983), pp. 77–90
A. Günthardt: *Der Bildhauer Alexander Trippel als Porträtist: Die waldeckischen Idealbüsten* (Lizentiat paper, U. Zurich, 1986)

F. FORTER

Trippenmeker, Heinrich. *See* ALDEGREVER, HEINRICH.

Triptych. Term used to define a picture consisting of three parts and denoting both the object itself and its compositional form. As an object the triptych may vary in size and material, but usually consists of a central panel flanked by wings (or shutters), which may be hinged; as a compositional form it is a tripartite structure, often with an emphasized central element. Although its imagery was, until the 19th century at least, predominantly religious, the object as such was not tied to a specific function.

Although the noun *triptychon* seems to be a relatively modern neologism, triptychs did exist in antiquity as cult images, portraits and independent paintings. The two main functions of the wings, protection and limiting the times when the inside could be viewed, are evident at this early stage. Among the earliest surviving triptychs with Christian imagery are early Byzantine painted icons, middle Byzantine ivories and reliquaries of the Holy Cross. The exterior of these icons and ivories is plain or decorated with a cross. One such reliquary, incorporated in the Stavelot

1. Triptych by Jan van Eyck: *Virgin and Child with SS Michael and Catherine of Alexandria, and a Donor*, oil on panel, central panel 331×275 mm, side panels each 331×136 mm, 1437 (Dresden, Gemäldegalerie Alte Meister)

Triptych (New York, Pierpont Morgan Lib.; *see* ROMAN-ESQUE, fig. 77), shows the type of imagery found later on north European altarpieces; in this case, it is the *Annunciation*, which announces the Redemption, of which the Holy Cross inside is the symbol. The Stavelot Triptych, a work of the 1150s, is the first of a group of reliquaries of the Holy Cross from the Meuse region and adjacent areas. The exterior form of these early triptychs is rectangular, with or without a rounded arch.

The oldest Italian triptychs are Roman panels of *Christ the Redeemer* dating from the middle of the 12th century onwards. As copies of the icon in the Cappella Sancta Sanctorum in the Lateran Palace, Rome, they were primarily processional icons. From the middle of the 13th century there were Tuscan triptychs with a half-length image of the *Virgin* in the central panel. Like the *Redeemer* panels they are rectangular, and may have an inscribed arch. Usually the central panel is twice as wide as the wings; triptychs with three folding panels of equal size have rarely survived (van Os). From the second quarter of the 14th century small triptychs, in central as well as northern Italy, generally had a cusped gable. Such a form persisted well into the 15th century, when rectangular frames became popular again. Small works of this type were used for private devotion in monasteries and homes, or as portable altarpieces. A taste for small DIPTYCHS and triptychs in other media with a similar function spread from France: Gothic ivories, mostly made in Paris, and enamelled objects of precious metal. It can be assumed that such objects were kept in cases, as were small painted panels. Full-scale Italian altarpieces, by contrast, commonly consisted of fixed panels set in an architectural frame: this could have a tripartite structure, and thus be a triptych, but in fact the distinction between a triptych and a POLYPTYCH in Italy at this time is often blurred.

The triptych form was adopted in Germany and the Netherlands from *c.* 1300, and it became the most common form of altarpiece. The wings were almost always movable, and were opened or closed according to the liturgical calendar (see fig. 1; for an example with fixed side panels *see* WEYDEN, VAN DER, (1), fig. 1). The exterior decoration was therefore also important; a combination of painted wings and a sculpted central panel (never the other way round) occurred very frequently. Painted triptychs, particularly those in the Netherlands during the 15th and 16th centuries, usually had grisaille decoration on the exterior of the wings (see fig. 2). The exterior frame was usually rectangular, although in the 14th century it was often enlivened by gables and pinnacles; in the 15th century the central panel could have a rectangular extension in the middle, sometimes with separate shutters. Towards the end of the 15th century ogee-shaped gables occurred as well. On the inside, the panels were generally divided by frames and mouldings, thus creating many compartments with images of saints, narrative scenes, or spaces for relics. From the early 15th century on Netherlandish painted triptychs commonly had one central scene, with saints or narrative scenes appearing on the wings and the *Annunciation* on the exterior. Large-scale altarpieces could have wings with double hinging or two pairs of wings attached to the central panel; in such cases they could be called polyptychs. Donor portraits, sometimes

2. Triptych by Jan van Eyck: *Annunciation*, oil on panel, each panel 331×136 mm, 1437 (Dresden, Gemäldegalerie Alte Meister); exterior of the side panels of the triptych shown in fig. 1

showing whole families, occupied an increasing proportion of the space (e.g. the Moulins Triptych; *see* MASTERS, ANONYMOUS, AND MONOGRAMMISTS, §I: MASTER OF MOULINS, fig. 1); such triptychs were usually memorials, to be placed in private chapels. From the 15th century the triptych form was occasionally also used for portraits or other secular paintings. In the course of the second half of the 15th century painted triptychs tended towards a unified pictorial field. Although this tendency sometimes resulted in a total negation of the tripartite structure, it could hardly have led to the disappearance of the triptych, as is sometimes argued. Throughout the 16th century triptychs remained very common, sometimes reaching enormous proportions, and they were usually treated as three separate pictorial fields; Rubens's great triptychs of the 17th century also follow that convention (e.g. *Elevation of the Cross*, 1610–11; Antwerp Cathedral; *see* BAROQUE, fig. 2). It is more probable that a predilection for frames echoing contemporary architecture was at odds with movable wings, and finally led to the eclipse of the triptych in the second half of the 17th century.

The triptych was revived in the course of the 19th century; with the exception of Gothic Revival altarpieces, most showed secular subjects. The first examples were produced by Nazarene and Pre-Raphaelite painters (e.g. Dante Gabriel Rossetti's the *Seed of David*, 1858–64; Cardiff, Llandaff Cathedral). Towards the end of the century the triptych became popular with Naturalist and Symbolist painters, who intentionally used the tripartite form to give their subjects a religious dimension. This tendency continued with such Expressionist painters as OTTO DIX and Max Beckmann (for illustration *see* BECKMANN, MAX), whose works often follow the tripartite form of a triptych, but with fixed lateral panels. This format continues to arouse interest today. Triptychs by such late 20th-century painters as Francis Bacon are usually composite works consisting of three paintings of equal size, where the triptych format is just a compositional device, comparable to the trilogy in literature.

BIBLIOGRAPHY
E. B. Garrison: *Italian Romanesque Panel Painting: An Illustrated Index* (Florence, 1949)
W. Ehlich: *Bild und Rahmen im Altertum: Die Geschichte des Bilderrahmens* (Leipzig, 1954), pp. 163–85
K. Lankheit: 'Das Tryptychon als Pathosformel', *Abh. Heidelberg. Akad. Wiss., Philos.-Hist. Kl.*, iv (1959)
S. N. Blum: *Early Netherlandish Triptychs: A Study in Patronage* (Berkeley and Los Angeles, 1969)
W. Pilz: *Das Triptychon als Kompositions- und Erzählform in der deutschen Tafelmalerei von den Anfängen bis zur Dürerzeit* (Munich, 1970)
K. Weitzmann: *The Monastery of Saint Catherine at Mount Sinai: The Icons*, i (Princeton, 1976)
H. W. van Os: 'The Discovery of an Early Man of Sorrows on a Dominican Triptych', *J. Warb. & Court. Inst.*, xli (1978), pp. 65–75
D. L. Thompson: 'A Painted Triptych from Roman Egypt', *Getty Mus. J.*, vi–vii (1978–9), pp. 185–92
W. Voelkle: *The Stavelot Triptych: Mosan Art and the Legend of the True Cross* (New York and London, 1980)
D. L. Ehresmann: 'Some Observations on the Role of Liturgy in the Early Winged Altarpiece', *A. Bull.*, lxiv (1982), pp. 359–69
C. Blotkamp: 'Triptieken in Stijl', *Mondriaan in Detail* (Utrecht and Antwerp, 1987), pp. 102–22
Polyptyques: Le Tableau multiple du moyen âge au vingtième siècle (exh. cat., Paris, Louvre, 1990)

VICTOR M. SCHMIDT

Triqueti [Triquetti], **Henri-Joseph-François**, Baron de (*b* Conflans, 24 Oct 1804; *d* Paris, 11 May 1874). French sculptor and designer of Italian descent. He studied painting with Louis Hersent in Paris before embarking on a career as a sculptor. He made his début at the Salon of 1831 with a bronze relief of the *Death of Charles the Bold* (untraced); closely based on 15th-century models, it identified him as one of a new generation of Romantic sculptors who rejected the Neo-classical teaching of the

Henri-Joseph-François Triqueti: monument to *Prince Albert*, Albert Memorial Chapel, Windsor Castle, after 1865

Ecole des Beaux-Arts in favour of learning from medieval and early Renaissance examples.

Triqueti occasionally put his knowledge of medieval art into practice as a restorer, working on the famous bone and marquetry reredos from the abbey of Poissy (Paris, Louvre) in 1831, and in 1840–48 on the restoration of the Sainte-Chapelle, Paris, under the supervision of the architect Félix-Jacques Duban. Numerous drawings provide further evidence of his interest in medieval and Renaissance monuments (e.g. *Romanesque Portal of Basle Cathedral*, 1831, Montargis, Mus. B.-A.; *Chevet of St Pierre in Caen*, 1855, Paris, Ecole N. Sup. B.-A.). During his many travels, especially in Italy, he kept notebooks and made drawings (e.g. Montargis, Mus. B.-A.; Paris, Ecole N. Sup. B.-A.) of paintings and sculptures in Milan, Venice, Padua and most often in Florence. His bronze doors for La Madeleine, Paris (1834–41; *in situ*), decorated with reliefs of the *Ten Commandments*, are clearly inspired by the Baptistery doors of Florence Cathedral. (He received this commission despite being a Protestant convert.) His admiration for such 15th-century Florentine sculptors as Benedetto da Maiano (whom he considered superior to Lorenzo Ghiberti) is also reflected in such works as his marble medallion portraits, bordered by foliage and grotesques (e.g. *Blanche Triqueti*, 1852, untraced; plaster version Montargis, Mus. B.-A.).

In 1842 Triqueti was commissioned to decorate the cenotaph of *Ferdinand Philippe, Duc d'Orléans*, at the Chapelle St Ferdinand, Neuilly-sur-Seine (1842–3; *in situ*), to a design by Ary Scheffer. The recumbent marble figure is surrounded by two angels sculpted by Marie, Princesse d'Orléans, and the base has an *Angel of Death* in shallow low relief. The following year he was commissioned by the architect Louis-Tullius-Joachim Visconti to decorate the crypt of Napoleon's tomb at Les Invalides, Paris; although unexecuted, this led him to experiment with marble intarsia, a technique he used in a panel representing *Peace and Plenty* (1845; Montargis, Mus. B.-A.) and, on a grander scale, in scenes from the *Iliad* and the *Odyssey* for University College, London (1865; *in situ*). It was probably the figure of *Ferdinand Philippe* and Triqueti's later statue of *Edward VI Studying the Holy Scriptures*, sold to Queen Victoria, that led to his being given the most important commission of his career and an opportunity to exploit his experimental intarsia to the full: the cenotaph of *Prince Albert* (after 1865; see fig.) in the Albert Memorial Chapel, Windsor Castle. The Gothic Revival tomb consists of a recumbent figure of the Prince in medieval armour on a base adorned by a delicate colonnette structure; between the columns there are six statuettes of *Virtues* with eight small angels on the corners. There are also marble portraits of all the royal couple's children. The decorations for the walls of the chapel, combining low relief sculpture with variously incised and painted marbles, include scenes from the *Passion*.

Triqueti also produced swords, daggers, hunting-knives, chandeliers, mirrors and vases, both in a Gothic Revival style and, as exemplified by a bronze vase decorated with a Bacchic procession (Paris, Mus. A. Déc.), in a classicizing style derived from antique sculpture and from Roman silverware (drawings in Paris, Ecole N. Sup. B.-A.).

For Pavilioen Welgelegen by Triqueti and J. B. Dubois *see* NETHERLANDS, THE, fig. 9.

Lami

BIBLIOGRAPHY

M. Beaulieu: 'Un Sculpteur français d'origine italienne: Henri de Triqueti', *A travers l'art italien du XVe au XXe siècles* (n.d.)
B. Read: *Victorian Sculpture* (New Haven, 1982), pp. 97, 139, 194
H. W. Janson: *Nineteenth-century Sculpture* (London, 1985), pp. 121, 124–5, 134, 162, 205

ISABELLE LEMAISTRE

Trissino, Giangiorgio [Giovan Giorgio], Count (*b* Vicenza, 1478; *d* Vicenza, 1550). Italian writer, scholar, amateur architect, patron and teacher. He was an active and well-known man of letters who did much to promote the new learning and the principles of Renaissance architecture in the Veneto region, running an informal residential school mostly for the sons of the local aristocracy at his home near Vicenza, where his most famous pupil was ANDREA PALLADIO. Trissino was a keen scholar of linguistics and rhetoric and was very familiar with both Greek and Latin texts. He attempted to revive the Greek epic and introduced Greek tragedy into Italy through his *Sofonisba* of 1514–15. Later he drew on Plautus and Pindar respectively for his comedy *I Simillimi* (1548) and his *Canzoni*. His interest in Greek forms of language culminated in his attempt to hellenize Italian spelling and pronunciation. Trissino also produced books on grammar and an *Ars Poetica* and even tried to develop a common language in Italy. He also translated Horace and wrote pastoral and other poems in Latin. These include the heroic epic poem *Italia liberata dai Goti* which appeared finally in 1547, dedicated to the Emperor Charles V. Trissino states that from his vast knowledge of ancient literature he chose Aristotle and Homer as his two main influences. The poem tells of the expulsion of the Goths from Italy by Belisarius, a commander under Justinian I (*reg* 527–65), which ensured the survival of the classical tradition in Italy. Perhaps more interesting to Trissino was the fact that this act aligned Italy to the Eastern empire, and hence to contact with ancient Greek civilization. Charles V was seen as the new Justinian, charged with the task of ridding the Eastern empire of the infidel. In 1538 Trissino added a loggia of his own design to his villa at Cricoli. This was the first known structure in Vicenza to show an understanding of the principles of Roman Renaissance architecture. This project led to his first meeting with Andrea di Pietro della Gondola, a local stonemason involved in the work, for whom Trissino became both mentor and patron. Trissino set about educating him solely in the theory and practice of Classical architecture and in 1540 renamed him Andrea Palladio. This education made Palladio the first of a new type of humanist architect who was a specialist in his own field.

WRITINGS

S. Maffei, ed.: *Tutte le opere di Giovan Giorgio Trissino* (Verona, 1729)

BIBLIOGRAPHY

J. S. Ackerman: *Palladio* (Harmondsworth, 1966, rev. 1976), pp. 20–25, 31–2
R. Wittkower: *Architectural Principles in the Age of Humanism* (London, 1973), pp. 51–64, 71, 94

DANA ARNOLD

Tristán de Escamilla, Luis (*b* nr Toledo, *c.* 1585–90; *d* Toledo, 7 Dec 1624). Spanish painter. He was born into a family of craftsmen. His father died when he was young, and some years later his mother, Ana de Escamilla, leased an inn in Toledo. He had several brothers, one of whom, Baltasar, was a Dominican friar and another (who called himself 'de Acevedo') was a landscape painter whose work is unknown. Around 1603 Tristán entered the workshop of EL GRECO as an apprentice, where he studied for several years, his name appearing until 1606 as witness in various documents and contracts relating to his master. He was a close friend of El Greco's son, Jorge Manuel Theotocopoulos.

Soon after 1606 Tristán visited Italy, a journey confirmed by autograph notes in a copy of Vasari's *Vite* that had belonged to El Greco. These annotations indicate that he was in Rome and Milan during the pontificate of Paul V (1605–21) and was therefore able to see at first-hand the work of Caravaggio and his followers as well as certain aspects of early 17th-century Lombard painting. According to Jusepe Martínez he also met Jusepe de Ribera in Italy. First from El Greco, Tristán had acquired an ecstatic lyrical Mannerist style with a taste for elongated proportions, the use of broken undulating draperies, stormy skies and angular haloes for figures of Christ. Tristán's awareness of the developments in Mannerism practised at the Escorial, and his introduction in Italy to the naturalism of Caravaggio, transformed his first training. It is also significant that works by Carlo Saraceni were in Toledo after 1614, and that the retable by JUAN BAUTISTA MAÍNO for S Pedro Mártir, Toledo (*Adoration of the Magi*, *Pentecost*, both 1612–13; Madrid, Prado, *Adoration of the Shepherds* and *Resurrection*, both 1611; Madrid, Prado), installed in 1614, gave access to concepts very different from those represented by El Greco. It is evident that at times these opposing currents conflicted in Tristán's work and were not always harmoniously resolved.

In 1613 Tristán signed the *Holy Family* (ex-Contini-Bonacossi priv. col., Florence), in which his knowledge of the work of Caravaggio, and especially that of ORAZIO BORGIANNI, is evident. The same is also apparent in his *St Louis of France Distributing Alms* (1620; Paris, Louvre) painted for the cloister of the Dominican Order of S Pedro Mártir, Toledo. Similarities between this work and Borgianni's *St Carlo Borromeo Succouring Victims of the Plague* (1611–12; Rome, S Carlo alle Quattro Fontane), and with certain works by Antonio d'Enrico Tanzio da Varallo who was in Rome between 1600 and 1611, suggest some direct contact during Tristán's Italian visit. Tristán's *Penitent St Dominic* (c. 1615–20; Toledo, Casa & Mus. El Greco) and both the paintings of *St Francis* (both c. 1615–20; Paris, Louvre, and Seville, Alcázar) again show his sensitivity to the work of Caravaggio and in the latter of contact with Ribera.

In 1613 Tristán contracted to paint a canvas of the *Last Supper* (untraced) for the Bernardine Monastery of La Sisla, Toledo. According to Palomino he owed this commission to El Greco, who was unable to accept it due to old age. In June 1614, two months before El Greco's death, Tristán married Catalina de la Higuera. The death of El Greco left Tristán as the leading painter in Toledo, and he received important commissions and trained pupils in his workshop, including Pedro de Camprobín.

In 1616 Tristán painted the large retable for the high altar in the parish church of Yepes, Toledo. In this, his most important and complete work, there are some signs of opposing influences. In the *Adoration of the Shepherds* (*in situ*; see fig.) the composition is reminiscent of El Greco, but the interpretation is in a naturalistic key, which suggests the early influence of the Bassano family (Jacopo and Leandro dal Ponte), while the group of angels is after an engraving by Guido Reni taken from a drawing by Luca Cambiaso. The *Adoration of the Magi* (*in situ*) echoes the painting of the same subject by Maíno for S Pedro Mártir in 1614. The monumentality of the figures in the *Flagellation* suggests the Escorial masters, as does the solemn and rather cold tonality of the *Ascension* and *Resurrection* (all *in situ*) painted in the tradition of Federico Zuccaro but interpreted with the strong chiaroscuro of Borgianni. From the same commission are the heads of saints, especially *St Monica* and *St Mary Magdalene* (Madrid, Prado), which are conceived as individual portraits and are fine examples of Tristán's naturalistic style.

In 1616 Tristán painted the large canvas of the *Beheading of St John the Baptist* (destr. 1936) for the Discalced Carmelites in Toledo, and in 1619 he painted the portrait

Luis Tristán de Escamilla: *Adoration of the Shepherds*, oil on canvas, 270×162 mm, 1616 (Yepes, Toledo, Parish Church)

of *Cardinal Bernardo de Sandoval y Rojas* (Toledo Cathedral). Tristán and Jorge Manuel Theotocópoulos collaborated in 1621 in designing the catafalque erected for the funeral ceremonies of Philip III in Toledo Cathedral. The *Adoration of the Shepherds* (Cambridge, Fitzwilliam) and *Adoration of the Magi* (Budapest, Mus. F.A.), both signed and dated 1620, are of similar character and quality to those of the Yepes retable and may have been painted for the church of Jerónimas de la Reina, Toledo. In 1623 he painted a retable for the Convento de S Clara el Real, Toledo, a large scheme and the last of his late works to survive in its original setting. These paintings show a surprising fidelity to compositions by El Greco, especially Tristán's *Baptism of Christ* (*in situ*) which reproduces in a simplified version that by El Greco (begun 1608; Toledo, Hosp. Tavera) with its extremely elongated proportions. The same quality is apparent in the *Annunciation*, *Visitation*, *Adoration of the Shepherds*, *Adoration of the Magi* and *Pentecost* (all *in situ*) from the same commission, although the tones of the colours are more subdued than El Greco's, the lighting is tenebrist in style and there are many naturalistic details of remarkable quality, also to be seen in the four half-figures of saints which form part of the same scheme.

Tristán signed various versions of the *Crucifixion* (*c*. 1610–20; Toledo, Mus. Santa Cruz; Toledo, S Tomé; Toledo Cathedral; Toledo, Casa & Mus. El Greco), in which, departing from El Greco's schema, he achieved an expressive intensity, especially in those which depict Christ alive with raised head and an angular halo. There are more poignant and rapt versions that show the dead Christ with his head fallen forwards (Caracas, Gal. A. N.). Other religious subjects include the *Last Supper* (*c*. 1613; Cuerva, Toledo, parish church); *Epiphany* (*c*. 1620; Glasgow, Pollok House); and various versions of the *Trinity* (e.g. 1624; Seville Cathedral), in which the dead Christ is represented in the arms of God the Father and beneath the Holy Ghost in a composition similar to that of El Greco's *Trinity* (1577–9; Madrid, Prado), but Tristán's interpretation emphasizes the more concrete and earthly aspects and has tenebrist lighting. The expressive intensity and strong naturalism in the faces and attitudes of his figures of saints is seen in *St Sebastian* (Toledo Cathedral); *St Bartholomew* (Toledo, Mus. Santa Cruz); *St Peter Repentant* (Cuenca Cathedral and Toledo, Diputación); *St Andrew* (Barnard Castle, Bowes Mus., and Havana, Mus. N., Pal. B.A.); and *St Jerome* (Toledo, Convent of Jerónimas de S Pablo, and Leida, Semin.). It is known that Tristán painted portraits, but the only surviving example is that of *Cardinal Bernardo de Sandoval y Rojas* (1619; Toledo Cathedral, Sala Capitular de Invierno). There is evidence that he painted secular works, such as episodes from Torquato Tasso, *Gerusalemme liberata* (1575), but these are untraced.

Tristán was the outstanding painter of his generation in Toledo, when the extreme Mannerism represented by El Greco was gradually being replaced by a more naturalistic style based in varying degrees on the art of Caravaggio. His own style was an attempt to reconcile these contradictory elements and was most successful in the intensely realistic figures of single saints. His palette was restrained, in contrast with the rich, vibrating colours of El Greco.

He preferred the earthy tones, browns and reds, which were characteristic of early Spanish naturalism and similar to a certain extent to those used by Pedro Orrente and Francisco Ribalta. Since he died young and his activity was confined to Toledo, his influence was slight, although echoes of his style are apparent in the work of minor artists of that city who repeated his subjects, such as *Christ* and *St Francis*, exaggerating their dramatic character. In 1624 Tristán contracted to paint an altarpiece for Alameda de la Sagra (Toledo), but he died on 7 December of that year and was buried in the Convent of S Pedro Mártir.

BIBLIOGRAPHY

J. Martinez: *Discursos practicables del nobilisimo arte de la pintura* (?1675), also in *Fuentes literarias para la historia del arte espanol*, ed. F. J. Sánchez Canton, 3 (Madrid, 1934)

A. A. Palomino de Castro y Velasco: *Museo pictórico* (1715–24)

J. Milicua: 'Observatorio de ángles', *Arch. Esp. A.* (1958), pp. 1ff

D. Angulo Iñiguez and A. E. Pérez Sánchez: *Pintura toledana de la primera mitad del siglo XVII* (Madrid, 1973), pp. 111–99

F. Marías: 'Los anataciones de Luis Tristán a las *Vidas* de Vasari', *El Greco y el arte de su tiempo: Las notas de El Greco a Vasari*, ed. X. de Salas and F. Marías (Madrid, 1992)

X. de Salas and F. Marías: *El Greco y el arte de su tiempo* (Madrid, 1992)

F. Collos de Cáceres: 'Aportaciones a la obra de Luis Tristán', *Anuario del Departemento de historia y teoria del arte*, v (1993), pp. 105–10

ALFONSO E. PÉREZ SÁNCHEZ

Tristram, E(rnest) W(illiam) (*b* Carmarthen, 27 Dec 1882; *d* Newton Abbot, Devon, 11 Jan 1952). English writer and conservator. He trained under Professor W. R. Lethaby at the Royal College of Art, London, and rose to become Professor of Design there from 1925 until his retirement in 1946, when he was made Professor Emeritus. He was an acknowledged expert on medieval wall paintings, particularly their preservation, although his technical methods are now known to have been unsound. He was also a highly influential teacher on the subject and did much to bring the interest and value of medieval painting to public attention. He worked on the preservation and restoration of wall paintings at Westminster Abbey, the Houses of Parliament and Eton College (Berks), among other sites, and in the cathedrals of Norwich, Exeter, Winchester and Christchurch, Oxford, as well as on the Pre-Raphaelite murals in the Oxford Union Library. He gave a large collection of his drawings of medieval wall paintings to the Victoria and Albert Museum, London, and a further collection was bequeathed to Buckfast Abbey, Devon. A keen amateur painter, he worked at York Minster and St Finbarr's Cathedral, Cork, and he illustrated *A Lakeside Anthology* by G. S. Sandiland (1947). He was made honorary D.Litt by the Universities of Oxford (1931) and Birmingham (1946) and in 1935 became an honorary ARIBA; he was a Fellow of the Society of Antiquaries of London.

WRITINGS

with T. Borenius: *English Medieval Painting* (Paris, 1927)

English Medieval Wall-Painting, i (Oxford, 1944); ii, with M. Bardswell (London, 1950); iii, ed. E. Tristram (London, 1955)

BIBLIOGRAPHY

DNB

Obituary, *Antiqua. J.*, xxxii (July–Oct 1952), p. 267

Who Was Who, iv (London, 1961)

JACQUELINE COLLISS HARVEY

Triumphal arch. Monumental arch erected to commemorate national events, especially military victories. Triumphal arches were first used in ancient Rome, the term originally applying to an arch erected to commemorate a formal 'triumph' awarded at Rome to a victorious general, who led his army in procession through the Porta Triumphalis in a chariot drawn by white horses. While many such arches exist, the term is more loosely applied to other commemorative arches, which the Romans erected to mark the founding of colonies, the building of roads and bridges, the death of a member of the imperial family or the accession of a new emperor, and these became potent symbols of Roman Imperial power throughout the Empire. The arches of aqueducts at the point where they crossed an important road were sometimes decorated as if they were triumphal arches, as were important city gates.

Commemorative arches have either a single or a triple opening, or can be placed over a crossroads with arched openings on all four sides. The one-bay arch is the most widespread, and examples range from the very simple type with an opening flanked by pilasters to massive arches with elaborate sculptural decoration. The triple type has a large central aperture over the roadway flanked by lesser openings over the pavements. A commemorative arch usually stands in isolation and has no practical function but is splendidly decorated.

The openings of Roman arches are usually flanked by pilasters, half-columns or free-standing columns. 'Triumphal' arches had sculpted panels illustrating Roman victories or the triumphal procession itself, placed in the passageways, on the attic, on the pylons flanking the passageway or, in the case of a triple arch, over the side apertures. In the spandrels there were usually flying Victories carrying trophies. Dedicatory inscriptions were commonly placed on the attic, and on top of the whole structure there was sometimes a *currus triumphalis*, a bronze statue group showing the emperor in a four-horse chariot. Roman triumphal arches established the general pattern for the architectural and sculptural treatment of similar monuments erected in later times (*see* §2 below; *see also* PAGEANT AND FESTIVAL ARTS).

1. Rome. 2. Later history.

1. ROME. The forerunners of triumphal arches were *fornices* or honorific arches bearing statues, which were erected by victorious generals in public places in Rome during the later Republic. In 196 BC L. Stertinius erected a *fornix* in the Circus Maximus and another in the Forum Boarium from the spoils he brought from Spain; Scipio Africanus erected another on the Capitoline Hill in 190 BC, and Fabianus built one over the Sacred Way in the Forum Romanum in 121 BC. None of these early arches has survived. The earliest extant commemorative arch in Rome is the one that Augustus built next to the Temple of Divus Julius in the Forum Romanum in 19 BC to commemorate the recovery of the standards that the Parthians had captured from Crassus. It has a central arched opening flanked by two lesser apertures covered with horizontal lintels, and it replaced a more modest single-bay arch put up after the victory at Actium in 29 BC. Several notable single arches were erected during the reign of Augustus,

1. Arch of Titus, Forum Romanum, Rome, AD 81

such as those at Rimini (27 BC; *see* ROME, ANCIENT, fig. 25), Aosta (25 BC), Pola (27 BC), Susa (9–8 BC) and Bara (now redated to *c.* 27 BC). The column arrangements and proportions of these arches vary considerably, showing that the form was still in a developmental stage. The classic example of the single-aperture arch is the monumental Arch of Titus in the Forum Romanum (15.4×13.5 m; AD 81; see fig. 1). Relief panels in the passageways depict the triumph of Titus, and a rectangular panel in the soffit of the arch shows his apotheosis. The Arch of Titus seems to have inspired the similar but more richly decorated Arch of Trajan (AD 114) at Benevento, built to commemorate the opening of the Via Traiana; it has a particularly rich series of reliefs decorating its pylons and passageways. The Arch of Trajan (AD 115) at Ancona, built to mark the completion of the new harbour, is of similar design, although it is somewhat taller in proportion and less elaborately decorated.

The earliest surviving triple arch from the Imperial period is the one erected by Tiberius at ARAUSIO (Orange; AD 21), the Arch of Augustus in the Forum Romanum being technically not a triple arch because its side passageways were covered with horizontal lintels. The Arch at Orange has many features of the classic triple arch, such as the dominant central aperture and the four columns framing the three openings. However, the unusual design of its short sides, with four engaged columns supporting an arcuated pediment, the distribution of its sculptural reliefs, the design of its attic and the fact that the columns are partly engaged all reflect its early date. One of the most celebrated triple arches is the massive Arch of Septimius Severus, built in honour of his Parthian victories and situated on a high point of the Via Sacra just below the Capitoline Hill in Rome (20.88×23.27 m; AD 203; *see* ROME, ANCIENT, fig. 34). It is entirely covered with marble, and its passageways are framed by four free-standing columns on each façade. The columns rest on high plinths that carry reliefs of Roman soldiers and Parthian prisoners. Large relief panels (3.92×4.72 m) illustrating Severus's victories are placed above the lateral arches. In the spandrels of the lateral arches are reliefs of river gods, and the spandrels of the main arch depict Victories carrying trophies. The attic bears a large dedicatory inscription that once bore the names of Septimius Severus and both his sons. Geta's name was erased after he was assassinated by his brother Caracalla, and additional illustrious titles for his murderer filled the space. Fixing holes for the bronze chariot have been found on the roof. A pair of column plinths (Florence, Boboli Gardens) probably come from an arch built by Diocletian in Rome *c.* AD 294. The high-relief figure of a Victory on one of them is carved in a self-consciously classicizing manner, reflecting hopes of a revival in Rome's fortunes under the Tetrarchy. The Arch of Constantine (AD 315; *see* ROME, §V, 12, and fig. 30), built to commemorate the victory of Constantine over Maxentius at the Milvian bridge, is similar in design to that of Septimius Severus but is even more extensively decorated with reliefs, many plundered from earlier monuments. Emperors after Constantine generally set up their arches at or near Tiber crossings to St Peter's on heavily travelled pilgrim routes.

The *arcus quadrifrons*, erected over a crossroads and with arched openings on all four sides, was extremely popular in North Africa. The Arch of Marcus Aurelius (AD 163) at Tripoli is an exceptionally complete example of the type. Its slightly broader north and south faces have free-standing columns flanking the aperture and Victories in the spandrels. The arch is entirely sheathed in marble, and the crossing is covered in a dome of stone panels. The Arch of Caracalla (AD 214) at Thevestis is also covered with a dome, and its apertures are flanked by two tiers of paired columns. The arch of Septimius Severus (AD 203) at LEPTIS MAGNA has free-standing columns flanking all four apertures and supporting the corners of pediments with massive gaps at their centres. The sculptural decoration is rich, particularly the panels in the attic. The Arch of Galerius (AD 297–305) at Thessaloniki (*see* THESSALONIKI, §III, 1) is unusual in having triple openings on the Via Egnatia and single openings on the other two sides. Its pylons are elaborately decorated with bands of relief sculpture. Only late examples of the *arcus quadrifrons* survive in Rome. The arch at Malborghetto just north of Rome, probably erected to commemorate the battle *ad Saxa Rubra*, and the Janus arch in the Forum Boarium are both Constantinian. The latter is unusual in that its sides are covered with two or perhaps three tiers of round-headed niches rather than conventional reliefs. Both arches may have had pyramidal roofs.

In Rome and Italy large numbers of commemorative arches were erected up to the time of Trajan (*reg* AD 98–117), but fewer during the Hadrianic and Antonine period. In the provinces, however, the erection of arches continued unabated throughout the 2nd and 3rd centuries AD, many commemorating Imperial visits. North Africa is particularly rich in triumphal arches, although in many cases their design differs somewhat from those in Italy. The Arch of Trajan (AD 116) at Mactaris in Tunisia has a

single opening enclosed within a pedimented aedicula flanked by larger columns. The Arch of Caracalla (AD 216) at Djemila in Algeria has a pair of free-standing columns on separate plinths on each side of the aperture, echoed in the attic by smaller columns framing the inscription. The Arch of Caracalla (AD 216–17) at Volubilis is much squatter but also has pairs of free-standing columns flanking the opening. A similar arrangement occurs in the Arch of Septimius Severus (*c.* AD 200) at Ammaedara and the Arch of Diocletian (*c.* AD 284–*c.* 305) at Sufetula, although in both these cases the columns rest on a continuous podium. The Severan arch at Lambaesis in Algeria and the so-called Arch of Trajan at Thamugadi (*c.* AD 200; *see* ROME, ANCIENT, fig. 52) are triple arches with a similar column arrangement to the Arch of Septimius Severus in Rome. The outer pairs of columns at Thamugadi, however, carry large segmental pediments broken at the bottom. While the triumphal arches of the western provinces and North Africa generally followed Roman fashions, a less massive and architecturally more subtle type of arch is found in some eastern provinces. The Arch of Hadrian at Athens (*c.* AD 131) is a light, elegant structure, with an opening flanked by free-standing columns and a colonnaded upper storey rather than a solid attic. The Hadrianic arch at Jerash in Jordan, however, is of the more massive type, with an extremely tall central opening flanked by two narrow side arches of the same proportions. Each face has four partly engaged columns flanking the apertures, the central pair supporting a broken pediment. Two side pavilions were later built against the arch to buttress it because its tall attic made it unstable.

BIBLIOGRAPHY

Enc. A. Ant.: 'Arco onorario e trionfale'; Pauly–Wissowa: 'Triumphbogen (Ehrenbogen)'
B. Bartoccini: 'L'arco quadrifronte dei Severi a Lepcis (Leptis Magna)', *Africa It.*, iv (1931), pp. 32–142
R. Brilliant: 'The Arch of Septimius Severus in the Roman Forum', *Mem. Amer. Acad. Rome*, 29 (1967) [whole issue]
M. Rotili: *L'arco di Traiano a Benevento* (Rome, 1972)
G. A. Mansuelli and others: *Studi sull'arco onorario romano* (Rome, 1979)
M. Pfanner: *Der Titusbogen* (Mainz, 1983)
F. S. Kleiner: *The Arch of Nero in Rome: A Study of the Roman Honorary Arch before and under Nero* (Rome, 1985)
J. C. Anderson jr: 'The Date of the Arch at Orange', *Bonn. Jb. Rhein. Landesmus. Bonn & Ver. Altertfreund. Rheinlande*, clxxxvii (1987), pp. 159–92
S. De Maria: *Gli archi onorari di Roma e dell'Italia romano*, Bibliotheca Archaeologica (Rome, 1988)
E. Nedergaard: 'Zur Problematik der Augustusbögen auf dem Forum Romanum', *Kaiser Augustus und die verlorene Republik* (exh. cat., Berlin, Martin-Gropius-Bau, 1988), pp. 224–39
F. S. Kleiner: 'The Study of Roman Triumphal and Honorary Arches 50 Years after Kähler', *J. Roman Archaeol.*, ii (1989), pp. 195–206

F. B. SEAR

2. LATER HISTORY. The physical survival of Roman triumphal arches, both in Rome and in the provinces, ensured that they would exert a powerful influence over the creative imagination of later centuries. The adoption of the triumphal arch motif, although sometimes a purely formal borrowing, most frequently performed a commemorative function for a great deed or person, as it had in ancient Rome, but it could also signify ideological aspirations on the part of the patron. An early example of this is the Torhalle or entrance gatehouse at Lorsch Abbey (*c.* AD 800), which led to one of Charlemagne's council

2. Marble Arch, London, by John Nash (i), *c.* 1825–8; from a photograph of before 1908

chambers, thus proclaiming the continuity of the Holy Roman Empire (*see* LORSCH ABBEY, §2 and fig.). Architects did not restrict themselves to using the triumphal arch simply as a model for gateways, however; they also experimented with the motif, embedding it in the façades of churches and palaces, often merely abstracting the rhythm of the arch to articulate a wall. The influence of the ancient arches was strongest in the vicinity of surviving examples, so that the presence of the Roman remains of southern France can be detected in the west front of nearby Saint-Gilles-du-Gard (*c.* 1170).

A rather more reflective revival of the triumphal arch came with the Renaissance and the rediscovery of antique learning. When LEON BATTISTA ALBERTI was commissioned by Sigismondo Malatesta to clothe the small Gothic church of S Francesco, Rimini, with a façade alluding to the warrior-prince's greatness, the humanist architect borrowed the form of the neighbouring Arch of Augustus to create the 'Tempio Malatestiano' (*c.* 1450; *see* RIMINI, §1 and figs 1 and 2). While Alberti was inaugurating the triumphal arch motif in European architecture in general, its original function in military processions was also revived when the entry into Naples of the victorious Alfonso I, King of Naples (Alfonso V of Aragon), was commemorated in a triumphal arch (*c.* 1452–71) at the Castelnuovo (see NAPLES, §IV, 4 and fig. 10; *see also* ARAGON, (1)).

Temporary arches built of lath and plaster continued to feature in civic rituals throughout the Renaissance and Baroque periods, most notably for royal entries. One such was the arch designed for King Henry III of France's visit to Venice (1570) by Andrea Palladio, who also ga-

thered material for an archaeological publication on ancient Roman arches. In the 18th century the arch motif was used increasingly as a purely formal device, two notable examples being the Trevi Fountain, Rome (1732–57; for illustration *see* SALVI, NICOLA), and the garden façade (*c.* 1760) of Kedleston Hall, Derbys (*see* ADAM (i), fig. 1).

The use of the triumphal arch for its royal associations was particularly popular in France, as seen in the tomb of *Francis I* at Saint-Denis Abbey (1547) by Philibert de L'Orme and the arches designed by François Blondel in the 1670s in the city walls of Paris (e.g. Porte St Denis) to honour Louis XIV. Napoleon's imperial aspirations ensured that the motif enjoyed a revival, with a spate of new arches including that in the library of Malmaison (remodelled for the Empress Josephine by Charles Percier and Pierre-François-Léonard Fontaine from 1800). Possibly the most famous modern arch is the Arc de Triomphe (1806–36; *see* PARIS, fig. 8) by Jean-François-Thérèse Chalgrin; its astylar monumentality inspired commemorative monuments across the western world. In London John Nash (i) designed the Marble Arch (*c.* 1825–8; see fig. 2) as the gateway to the new forecourt of Buckingham Palace, which he was enlarging for George IV, and at the same time DECIMUS BURTON designed the Constitution Arch (1827–8), with a single opening, to provide part of the monumental entrance to Hyde Park from the palace (both arches were later moved to new sites around Hyde Park). Twentieth-century examples include the Memorial Arch (1887–1903) at Stanford University, Palo Alto, CA, by

Frederick Law Olmsted and the Jefferson National Expansion Memorial (1948–68) at St Louis, MO, a stainless steel arch by Eero Saarinen.

BIBLIOGRAPHY

D. Watkin: 'The Legacy of Roman Architecture', *The Legacy of Rome* (Oxford, 1990)

RICHARD JOHN

Triumphal cross. *See* ROOD.

Trivandrum [Tiruvanandapuram]. City, capital of the state of Kerala, India. It was named Tiruvanandapuram ('city of the sacred Ananda') after the reclining form of the Hindu deity Vishnu, to whom the Padmanabhasvami Temple at the heart of the original town was dedicated. The temple is mentioned in the *Silappadikkaram*, an early Tamil narrative poem (2nd–5th century AD), and was praised by the Vaishnava saint Nammalvar (*c.* 8th century), although the earliest elements of the present complex seem to date from the 12th century. The Ay dynasty, which claimed Padmanabhasvami as its tutelary deity, ruled over most of southernmost Kerala until the 10th century. These territories, together with the areas north of and including Trivandrum, subsequently became the Venadu district of the Kulashekhara kingdom of central Kerala. After the demise of that kingdom in the 12th century, the former Venadu governors ruled as an independent dynasty, assuming the special prerogatives associated with the temple that were formerly claimed by the Ays. Tiruvanandapuram became the capital of TRAVANCORE in the 19th century.

The walled enclosure of the Padmanabhasvami complex contains numerous shrines built in the Kerala style with sloping roofs covered with copper sheets. The main gateway, on the east, completed in the 18th century, is in the southern (*drāvida*) style, while the other gates are of the local type. According to inscriptions, important phases of building occurred in the 12th and 18th centuries. The Mahadeva complex at Valiashalai, within the modern city, encloses two granite subshrines of the southern type and has been identified by some scholars with Kandalurshalai, mentioned in inscriptions of the Chola ruler Rajendra I (*reg* 1012–44). The fort area surrounding the Padmanabhasvami Temple contains numerous palaces; some remains survive from the 18th century, but most are of the 19th and 20th century. Various late 19th-century structures of interest include the Napier Museum, designed by the English architect Robert Fellowes Chisholm in a style intended to emulate the indigenous architecture and incorporating tiled and gabled roofs, completed in 1880 by the Maharajas of Travancore, and the Gothic-Revival-style Victoria Jubilee Town Hall (*c.* 1897).

BIBLIOGRAPHY

Travancore Archaeological Series, i (1910–13)

E. P. N. K. Pillai: *Studies in Kerala History* (Kottayam, 1970)

H. Sarkar: *Architectural Survey of Temples of Kerala* (New Delhi, 1978)

T. Metcalf: *An Imperial Vision* (Berkeley, 1989)

M. E. HESTON

Trivet. *See under* FIREPLACE FURNISHINGS.

Trivio, Drudus de. *See* DRUDUS DE TRIVIO.

Trivulzio, Gian Giacomo (*b* 1441; *d* 1518). Italian soldier, patron and collector. He was a member of a leading patrician family and inherited considerable estates from his father Antonio Trivulzio, who had been a prominent figure in the Ambrosian Republic. He was a favourite of Galeazzo Maria Sforza, Duke of Milan, and became a noted condottiere, serving, among others, Ferdinand I, King of Naples. In 1495 he transferred his services to Charles VIII, King of France, and in 1499 took the duchy of Milan for Louis XII. Although Trivulzio was considerably rewarded and made Marchese di Vigerano, his relations with the French Crown were strained, due to his own difficult nature and the rivalry within the French regime in Milan. The French continued to rely on his military skills, however, and he remained a prominent and wealthy figure.

Trivulzio's patronage was extensive, although he was considered very mean by his contemporaries. He constructed an elaborate palace (destr. *c.* 1920) in Milan, begun in 1469 and radically altered and lavishly decorated *c.* 1485. He had a considerable interest in antiquity, and his palace was decorated with ancient inscriptions; he also collected and commissioned manuscripts of Classical texts. Trivulzio's leading position in Milan after 1500 is demonstrated by three of his commissions: firstly the set of 12 tapestries (Milan, Castello Sforzesco) illustrating *The Months*, designed by Bramantino and made in a workshop probably established by Trivulzio between 1501 and 1510. The unusual iconography of these tapestries illustrates Trivulzio's interest in the Classical world, his involvement in agriculture and his aim of glorifying his family by the elaborate use of heraldry. He also seems to have been much concerned with the construction of a funerary monument. Leonardo da Vinci made an estimate for an elaborate marble tomb (*c.* 1510), surmounted by a bronze equestrian statue of Trivulzio; a number of extant drawings by the artist (Windsor Castle, Royal Lib.) have been associated with this project, which was not executed. Trivulzio opted instead for a novel kind of funerary chapel, designed by Bramantino and consisting of a complex (*c.* 1512) forming the façade of the church of S Nazaro Maggiore, Milan. This incorporates an octagonal chapel that provided ample space for the family tombs. The complex is an amalgam of traditional Milanese elements and ideas derived from ancient Greek and Roman architecture and illustrates both Trivulzio's empathy with Bramantino's interest in the Antique and his aim of promoting his own interests and those of his family.

BIBLIOGRAPHY

C. de Rosmini: *Dell'istoria intorno alle militari imprese e alla vita di Giano Giacomo Trivulzio detto il Magno*, 2 vols (Milan, 1815)

E. Motta: *Libri di Casa Trivulzio* (Como, 1890)

C. Baroni: 'Leonardo, Bramantino ed il mausoleo di G. Giacomo Trivulzio', *Rac. Vinc.*, xv–xvi (1934–9), pp. 201–70

K. Clark: *The Drawings of Leonardo da Vinci in the Collection of His Majesty the King* (London, 1935); rev. 2 with C. Pedretti as *The Drawings of Leonardo da Vinci in the Collection of Her Majesty the Queen*, 2 vols (London, 1969)

G. Castelfranco: 'Il preventivo di Leonardo per il monumento sepolcrale di G. G. Trivulzio', *Boll. A.*, n. s. 1, iii (1955), pp. 1–8

M. Valsecchi: *Gli arazzi dei Mesi del Bramantino* (Milan, 1968)

N. Forti Grazzini: *Gli arazzi dei Mesi Trivulzio: Il committente, l'iconografia* (Milan, 1982)

CHARLES ROBERTSON

Trnava [formerly Ger. Tyrnau; Hung. Nagyszombat]. Town in western Slovakia, 45 km north-east of Bratislava. Founded in 1211, it was originally a market settlement on an important route between Bohemia and Hungary. In 1238 it became by decree a free royal Hungarian town. It was attacked by Tatars in 1241 and sustained damage during the Czech–Hungarian wars in the 13th century. Around the beginning of the 14th century it began to flourish: a Dominican monastery (destr.) and a Poor Clares' convent were founded, and the whole town was fortified with walls. During the Turkish occupation of Hungary in the 16th century, the town became the seat of the Archbishops of Esztergom. In 1635 Archbishop Petr Pázmány (*reg* 1616–73) founded a university (removed to Budapest in 1777) as a centre for re-Catholicization, led by the Jesuit, Pauline and Trinitarian orders and the Ursuline nuns. Thus, from the 17th century, the town became the intellectual centre of Hungary. During the 19th century factories were built on the outskirts of the town, and it became an important industrial centre. By 1900 it was also one of the centres of Slovak political life.

One of the oldest surviving buildings in Trnava is the parish church of St Nicholas (*c.* 1380), a basilica with a nave and aisles and two towers on its west front. The ceiling of the nave was vaulted in the mid-15th century, side chapels were added in 1629, and the north tower was built after 1666. The interior has a Neo-classical high altar (1776) and an altar of the *Last Supper* (1798) with a painting by A. Zallinger. The chapel of the Virgin was added during the last third of the 18th century. The church of St John the Baptist and the university were both built on the site of the former Dominican monastery. The church, constructed between 1629 and 1637 by Pietro Spezza and Antonio Spezza (both *fl* 1620s–30s), is rectangular in shape and aisleless (see fig.) in the manner of Il Gesù in Rome. The interior has ornate stuccowork, that of 1639–55 by Giovanni Battista Rosso and Jacopo Tornini (both *fl* 1630s–50s) and later work of 1699–1700 by Pietro Antonio Conti. The early Baroque high altar (1637–40) was a collaboration of Balthasar Knillinger from Vienna, the local sculptor Voit Stadler (*fl* 1630s–40s) and the painters V. Knotek, K. Knerr and Ferdinand of Cifer. Rosso, Tornini and Knerr also painted frescoes in the nave. The surrounding university buildings were designed after 1643 by Pietro Spezza. Two four-storey 'L'-shaped wings were built first, and from 1700 to 1718 the west wing was added to enclose the courtyard. A further wing, housing a library and theatre, was also added later, and in 1770–73 the Medical School Faculty was built to a design by Franz Anton Hillebrandt.

The convent and church of the Poor Clares (now the Museum of Western Slovakia), founded in 1240, was originally a Gothic structure rebuilt in the 14th century; in 1683 it was destroyed by fire, and it was rebuilt in 1690–94 in the Baroque style. The interior of the church is Baroque and has a high altar and three side altars of the 18th century. The early Baroque Franciscan church of St James (1633–40) replaced an earlier Gothic church of 1363–6. It has an aisleless nave, a tower on its west front and a polygonal presbytery. The interior is designed in Baroque, Rococo and Neo-classical styles. The monastery building (1619–1749) has four wings enclosing a courtyard

Trnava, St John the Baptist, by Pietro Spezza and Antonio Spezza, interior looking east, 1629–37

and a refectory decorated with stuccowork. The hospital church of St Helen was built in the 14th century in Gothic style but during the second half of the 17th century was transformed into a Baroque church. A statue of *St Catherine* (first half of the 15th century) and Baroque statues of *St Helen* and *St Elizabeth* adorn the portal. The polygonal presbytery has Gothic vaults, a 14th-century auxiliary chamber, wall paintings of the mid-15th century and a neo-Gothic high altar. Other important ecclesiastical buildings include the Protestant church of St Joseph (1646), originally built for the Calvinists and later taken over by the Paulines; the Pauline monastery, rebuilt in 1719 and converted into flats after 1945; the church and monastery of the Trinitarians (both 1710–29); the church of St Anne and the convent of the Ursulines (both 1730–76); and the Marian Seminary (1700), later redesigned as a *Jugendstil* building. The former Archbishop's Palace was originally a Renaissance house built in 1562; its side wings were added in the 17th century, and its façade is Neo-classical.

Trnava has several noteworthy secular buildings, among them the Town Hall, a complex of buildings consisting of a late Renaissance structure (1574) by Master Jakub (*fl* 1570s), a Baroque house rebuilt at the beginning of the 18th century and a main building (1793) in Neo-classical style; a palace (1747–54) built in imitation of Viennese court architecture; and the Albertinum, built in 1623, extended in 1710 and rebuilt between 1886 and 1930. The bridge over the River Trnava was constructed in the first half of the 18th century.

BIBLIOGRAPHY

J. Dubnický: *Ranobarokový Universitný kostol v Trnave* [The early Baroque University Church in Trnava] (Bratislava, 1948)

A. Jursa: *Trnava v Pamiatkach* [Trnava and its monuments] (Trnava, 1956)

Súpis pamiatok na Slovensku [List of historical monuments in Slovakia], iii (Bratislava, 1969), pp. 309–29

M. Štibraniova: 'Trnavskí majstri murári' [Master masons of Trnava], *Problémy umenia 16.–18. storočia* [Problems in 16th–18th-century art] (Bratislava, 1987), pp. 82–5

L. Šášky: *Kunstdenkmäler der Slowakei: Ein Bildkunstführer* (Bratislava, 1988)

IVO KOŘÁN

Troad. Region in north-west Anatolia, now part of Turkey, named after the ancient city of Troy.

1. Introduction. 2. Arts. 3. Museums and collections.

1. INTRODUCTION. The Troad is largely mountainous, and most of its sites are therefore situated on the coast. Stray finds of stone tools indicate the presence of palaeolithic occupation, and a neolithic site has been identified at Coşkuntepe towards the south-west tip of the Troad. The earliest traces of occupation in the region are Late Chalcolithic and were revealed by soundings at the coastal sites of Kumtepe (level Ia) and Beşik-Sivritepe, where pattern-burnished ware is characteristic. Early Bronze Age deposits of Kumtepe (level Ib), Beşik-Yassıtepe and Early Troy I, again on the coast, produced finds partly paralleled at Poliochni on Lemnos. Beşik-Yassıtepe was a fortified site with megara and apsidal structures. Clay model axes found there are paralleled at Ezero. Bronze Age Troadic culture is most fully represented at TROY (c. 3000–1050 BC). This site was fortified throughout most of its existence. The Early Bronze Age settlement of Late Troy II (c. 2465–c. 2150 BC) seems to have been especially wealthy, but the region apparently stagnated in the Middle Bronze Age (Troy IV–V; c. 2000–c. 1700 BC). Surveys suggest denser occupation in the Late Bronze Age (Troy VI–VII; c. 1700–c. 1050 BC), and it is tempting to relate a Mycenaean chamber tomb and cemetery on the ancient shoreline of Beşika Bay to the Achaians of the Trojan War. Continuity of occupation at some sites through the Dark Age of the late 2nd–early 1st millennium BC is suggested by grey wares similar to those of the Late Bronze Age.

In the 8th and 7th centuries BC Greek colonizers from Tenedos, Mitylene, Methymna and Miletos founded cities, mainly on the coast. During the 6th century BC the region came under Persian control, and c. 334–332 BC it was liberated by Alexander the Great. In the ensuing Hellenistic period (323–27 BC) smaller cities were incorporated into the larger foundations of Alexandria Troas and Ilion (Troy IX). At Assos the agora, bouleuterion, gymnasium and theatre are Hellenistic, but the fortifications and Temple of Athena originate earlier. In the late Roman times (2nd and 3rd centuries AD) there was a reversion to village life and, sometimes, to small hilltop settlements, perhaps built in response to Gothic attacks. Churches, monasteries and a few castles are of Byzantine date. The Troad passed to the Turks in AD 1306.

This article concentrates on the Troadic culture of the Bronze Age.

For the wider context of Anatolian art at this time *see* ANATOLIA, ANCIENT; for the art of western Anatolia in the Greek tradition *see* GREECE, ANCIENT.

2. ARTS.

(i) Pottery. Late Chalcolithic wares from Beşik-Sivritepe are mainly brown-red, sometimes pattern-burnished or decorated with shallow zigzag fluting. Shapes include open bowls with incurving profiles or grooved rims, fenestrated pedestals, simple jugs and vessels with horned handles. From Kumtepe (level Ia) also come white-painted wares. In Early Bronze Age (EB I) grey wares became popular, and bowl-rims were decorated with white-filled incision and with long, tubular lugs. Later pottery is best represented by finds from Troy, where grey wares still predominated in EB II (Troy I–Early Troy II). The first wheelmade articles were produced in Early Troy II, but they only became common from EB III (Middle Troy II–Troy III) onwards, when plain wares and two-handled cups were also introduced. Red wares regained their importance in the Middle Bronze Age (MB; Troy IV–V). The EB–MB repertory of shapes is fairly homogeneous. The anthropomorphic jars and lids that occur seem to be purely Troadic designs, and the tall, two-handled flaring goblet (*depas amphikypellon*) is also characteristic. The tripod jars and animal-shaped jugs are typical of north-west Anatolia, as are the pedestalled pyxides that appeared in EB III. Storage jars with vertical wings are of north-east Aegean island inspiration. There are signs of Middle Helladic (MH) influence on certain shapes from Troy III–V: small cups with out-turned rims and a rising loop-handle, jars with disc-like rims, and 'hourglass' tankards. Incised decoration also recalls the patterns of MH matt-painted ware. In the Late Bronze Age (Troy VI–VII) grey wares predominated, and many shapes were borrowed directly from Greece. Mycenaean imports occur at several coastal sites and in quantity at Troy itself. The grey wares of Troy VIII appear to be descended from those of the Late Bronze Age, and there is some originality in the Troad's painted 'East Greek' wares. Thereafter Troadic pottery ceased to be distinctive.

BIBLIOGRAPHY

H. Schliemann: *Ilios: The City and Country of the Trojans* (London, 1881)

C. W. Blegen and others: *Troy: Excavations Conducted by the University of Cincinnati, 1932–1938*, 4 vols (Princeton, 1950–58)

J. M. Cook: *The Troad: An Archaeological and Topographical Study* (Oxford, 1973)

J. W. Sperling: 'Kum Tepe in the Troad', *Hesperia*, xlv (1976), pp. 305–64

Archäol. Anz. (1984–8) [preliminary excav. rep. on the Beşika Bay area by M. Korfmann and others]

J. Seeher: 'Coşkuntepe-Anatolisches Neolithikum am Nordostufen der Ägäis', *Istanbul. Mitt.*, 40 (1990), pp. 9–15

DONALD F. EASTON

(ii) Jewellery. There are two principal sources for surviving Troadic jewellery, most of which dates from c. 2400–c. 2200 BC. These are Troy (level II) and a site on the island of Lemnos, known by its modern name of Poliochni. A third possible source, a collection of jewellery in the University of Pennsylvania Museum, Philadelphia, which is alleged to have come from the Troad, is best excluded as its true provenance is uncertain.

Nearly all Troadic jewellery is of gold. The source of the gold is unknown, though the geographer Strabo (64/3 BC–AD ?21) stated that there were once gold mines in the Troad, which may well have been in use in the Early Bronze Age. Troadic craftsmen, influenced by Mesopotamian and central Anatolian work, were able to exploit a number of sophisticated techniques, including repoussé, filigree, granulation and the making of ornamental chains. Their repertory consisted of diadems, earrings, beads, bracelets, dress-pins and buttons.

The jewellery known from Troy itself consists principally of 'Priam's Treasure'. Although the account of its discovery has been questioned, it still seems probable that 'Priam's Treasure' was indeed excavated by HEINRICH SCHLIEMANN as one hoard in 1873, within or just outside the walls of Troy II. The finest objects were two magnificent diadems with pendant chains that were threaded with gold beads and supported cut-outs of miniature idols (for illustration *see* TROY). Several smaller hoards of the same date also came from Schliemann's excavations, and the American excavations of 1932–8 uncovered a few similar pieces. Nearly all Schliemann's material, which was in Berlin at the end of World War II, disappeared in 1945. All that survives are a few pieces given by Mrs Schliemann to the National Archaelogical Museum in Athens and, in Istanbul (Archaeol. Mus.), some jewellery confiscated by the Turkish authorities in about 1873 and the few pieces excavated by the Americans.

The jewellery from Lemnos was excavated by an Italian expedition in 1956 in the ruins of a house. It is now in the National Archaeological Museum in Athens. It bears a strong resemblance to the Troy material.

Troadic earrings take several forms. Among the most popular were basket-shaped earrings decorated with applied rosettes or with rows of granulation. Some have a short chain hanging from them; others have longer chains threaded with gold leaves and hung with stylized idols resembling those on the diadems from 'Priam's Treasure'. Another type of earring is in the shape of stylized cockle shells. Gold beads were abundant, over 10,000 being recorded at Troy alone. Most take simple forms: spherical, disc, cylindrical, barrel-shaped or floral. More elaborate is the quadruple-spiral. Bracelets were mostly composed of spiralled wire, but a more ornate variety consists of a gold band richly decorated with filigree spirals. Dress-pins in both gold and silver were also popular. Many have heads of two or four spirals, or heraldic arrangements of spirals and small figures of jugs. From Poliochni comes a pin with a head composed of a symmetrical arrangement of two birds.

BIBLIOGRAPHY

K. R. Maxwell-Hyslop: *Western Asiatic Jewellery* (London, 1971), pp. 48–60

L. Bernabo Brea: *Poliochni: Città preistorica nell'isola di Lemnos*, ii (Rome, 1976), pp. 284–90, pls ccxl–cclii

REYNOLD HIGGINS

(iii) Gold and silver plate. All the known material from the Troad is probably of EB III date (*c.* 2465–*c.* 2000 BC), and most comes from a single hoard found in Troy II. Gold, silver and electrum were used, occasionally in combination. Shapes include ovoid pedestalled flasks with vertical

Silver cup with electrum overlay on the rim and foot, from Troy, *c.* 2200 BC (New York, Norbert Schimmel Collection)

tubular lugs, a globular flask, two-handled tankards, a two-handled pedestalled cup, conical cups, a globular jar with flaring rim, a globular jar with cylindrical neck and stand, hemispherical bowls, a spoon comparable with much larger long-handled bronze pans of the same period, a flanged cylindrical lid with string-holes, and a two-handled sauceboat with a flaring mouth at each end. The simpler items, such as the bowls, conical cups and globular flask, were made in one piece with bases of ring, omphalos (i.e. navel) or lozenge shape, punched out as required, and rims, if present, produced by hammering. Handles were hollow, with a soldered seam along the inner edge, and attached to the vessel either by soldering or with rivets. Soldering was also used to attach the cylindrical stand to the globular jar and to reattach the foot of a golden conical cup. The commonest decoration was fluting, which could be vertical, horizontal or diagonal, though incised zigzag and fern designs also occur. One vertically fluted silver cup has electrum overlay on the rim and foot (New York, Norbert Schimmel Col.; see fig.). The shapes and decoration have parallels or at least close analogies in the pottery of the Troad and the north-east Aegean islands, so that the material is probably indigenous.

BIBLIOGRAPHY

H. Schmidt: *Heinrich Schliemanns Sammlung Trojanischer Altertümer* (Berlin, 1902)

O. W. Muscarella: *Ancient Art: The Norbert Schimmel Collection* (Mainz, 1974)

P. S. de Jesus: *The Development of Prehistoric Mining and Metallurgy in Anatolia*, 2 vols, Brit. Archaeol. Rep., Int. Ser. (Oxford, 1980)

3. MUSEUMS AND COLLECTIONS. The histories, present locations and contents of collections of objects from the Troad are not fully documented. Part of the Calvert Collection, from many small-scale excavations, was sold at Sotheby's in 1877 and bought by the British Museum;

a catalogue of the remainder by H. Thiersch (1902) is in the Archaeological Museum in Istanbul, but much of the original collection apparently perished in the fire of 1922 in Smyrna. The Schliemann Collection, sent to Berlin in 1881, was augmented from Schliemann's estate after his death; but in 1895 it was broken up, and duplicates were sent to 37 other museums, universities and academies in Europe. How far this material survived the two world wars is not recorded. Some of the collection remains in Berlin (Bodemus. and Schloss Charlottenburg), but much of the material once in Berlin is now destroyed or lost, although 'Priam's Treasure' once believed lost, has now been located in the Pushkin Museum of Fine Arts, Moscow. Additional pieces were given by Schliemann's widow to the Smithsonian Institution, Washington, DC, and his coins were bequeathed to the National Archaeological Museum at Athens. Valuables stolen by workmen at Troy in 1873 are in the Archaeological Museum at Istanbul, which also received material from the excavations at Assos, from the excavations of Dörpfeld and Blegen at Troy, and from the American excavations at Kumtepe and elsewhere. There are also representative pieces from Blegen's excavations in the Archaeological Museum in Çanakkale; the latter also houses the principal finds from the recent excavations around Beşika Bay. Some secondary Beşika Bay finds are in a temporary depot at Troy. The Archaeological Institute of America received one third of the finds from Assos, of which some, at least, are in the Museum of Fine Arts at Boston. Some of the temple reliefs from Assos are in the Louvre in Paris.

BIBLIOGRAPHY

F. Geupel: 'Das Schicksal der Sammlung Trojanischer Altertümer von H. Schliemann', *Troja und Thrakien: Katalog zur Ausstellung Berlin und Sofia*, ed. E. Hühns (Berlin, 1981)

K. Goldmann: 'Der Schatz des Priamos. Zum Schicksal von Heinrich Schliemanns Sammlung Trojanischer Altertümer', *Heinrich Schliemann: Grundlagen und Ergebnisse moderner Archäologie 100 Jahre nach Schliemanns Tod*, ed. J. Hermann (Berlin, 1992), pp. 377–90

DONALD F. EASTON

Trochilus. *See* SCOTIA.

Trockel, Rosemarie (*b* Schwerte, 13 Nov 1952). German conceptual artist. She studied from 1974 to 1978 at the Werkkunstschule, Cologne, which was then heavily influenced by Joseph Beuys. In the early 1980s she came into contact with the Mülheimer Freiheit, a Cologne-based group of painters that included Walter Dahn (*b* 1954) and Jiří Georg Dokoupil, and she exhibited at the Cologne gallery of Monika Sprüth, who at that time showed only women artists. In 1985 Trockel produced her first 'knitting pictures', consisting of lengths of machine-knitted woollen material stretched on to frames. The material is patterned with computer-generated geometrical motifs or recognizable logos, for example the hammer-and-sickle motif of the Soviet Union ironically superimposed on a background of red-and-white stripes that recall the US flag (*Untitled*, 1986; see 1991–2 exh. cat., pl. 9). The knitted works are ironic comments on the traditionally feminine occupation of knitting placed in a context of mass production. Other works by Trockel also have a feminist theme. A piece consisting of a steel cube fitted with six hot plates in two parallel diagonal lines (*Untitled*, 1988; Cologne, Mus.

Ludwig) establishes a bridge between the feminine domain of cooking and the masculine domain of industrial production. Trockel's *Painting Machine and 56 Brush Strokes* (1990; see 1991–2 exh. cat., pl. 53) is a mechanical contraption of wires and steel rollers, in which 56 paint brushes make small marks on a roll of paper. The brushes are made of human hair and engraved with the names of the hair's donors, who include Georg Baselitz, Cindy Sherman and Barbara Kruger.

BIBLIOGRAPHY

J. Koether: 'Interview with Rosemarie Trockel', *Flash A.*, 134 (1987), pp. 40–42

Rosemarie Trockel (exh. cat., ed. S. Stich; Boston, MA, ICA; Berkeley, U. CA, A. Mus.; Chicago, IL, Mus. Contemp. A.; and elsewhere; 1991–2)

NINA LÜBBREN

Troffamondo [Trofamonti], **Teofilo.** *See* BIGOT, TROPHIME.

Troger, Paul (*bapt* Zell unter Welsberg, South Tyrol [now Monguelfo, Italy], 30 Oct 1698; *d* Vienna, 20 July 1762). Austrian painter, draughtsman and printmaker. Through his fresco-work and his draughtsmanship, which adapt a vast range of Italian influences, as well as his teaching, he is one of the foremost figures of 18th-century Austrian art.

1. LIFE AND WORK. He was the son of a village tailor and sexton and was first taught by Matthias Durchner (1675–1741), a local painter. When young he entered the service of Freiherr Franz Alphons von Firmian, who recommended him to Giuseppe Alberti (1640–1716), a Venetian-trained painter in Cavalese, and, after Alberti's death in 1716, to a Count Giovanelli in Venice. Through the latter Troger studied with Silvestro Maniago (1670–1734), Giovanni Battista Piazzetta and his circle and Federico Bencovich, absorbing their feeling for chiaroscuro realism. But the contemporary Venetian taste for lighter colours, shown by Sebastiano Ricci, Antonio Pellegrini, Giovanni Battista Pittoni and in particular by Gaspare Diziani (1689–1767), also influenced him. Diziani's smoothly propelled draughtsmanship was close to Troger's youthful style. Troger also came into occasional contact with Giambattista Tiepolo, who combined both trends, as a draughtsman and etcher of mythological capriccios and landscapes. The more sombre influences show in Troger's first independent altarpiece, the *Crucifixion* (1722; Caldaro, nr Bolzano, church of the Calvary), the lighter style in the expressive movements and slender forms of the angels carrying Christ's cross in the fresco above it.

Through a grant from Jakob Maximilian, Graf Thurn, the Prince-Bishop of Gurk, who was related by marriage to the Firmians, Troger continued his studies in Italy, firstly in Rome (1723–5), then in Naples and Bologna. In Rome he sought out Sebastiano Conca and Marco Benefial as models, and drew studies of the work of Bernini, Giovanni Battista Gaulli, Carlo Maratti, Lazzaro Baldi and Francesco Trevisani. He also met Martin van Meytens, with whom he sketched antique ruins. One of his finest etchings is a fantasy based on ruins in the spirit of Poussin, Pietro Testa, Salvator Rosa and Giovanni Pannini, the *Apotheosis of Pallas Athene* (1724), and many of the landscape studies made at this time are close to the poetic concepts of nature found in works by Claude, Gaspard Dughet and Herman van Swanevelt, whose etchings Troger collected. In Naples he chiefly studied the work of Francesco Solimena, among contemporaries; Luca Giordano's work also clearly influenced him. Among Bolognese artists, Troger encountered Giuseppe Maria Crespi and learnt from the work of the Carracci, Domenichino, Guercino and Guido Reni. His drawings of the time have been confused with those of his Bolognese contemporary Donato Creti, echoing his elegant sweep of line and slightly Mannerist figures. In all, Troger's knowledge of 17th-century and contemporary Italian painting was greater than that of virtually any other northern artist. Yet in his drawings he was able to convey or alter his models in such a way as to suggest that they were the product of his own imagination.

In 1726 the Prince-Bishop of Gurk asked Troger to return to Austria to paint several altarpieces and the dome fresco (completed 1728) in the Kajetanerkirche, Salzburg. This is a glorification of the Holy Trinity with St Cajetan and the Virgin, with saints and angels resting or going about their business on banks of clouds—all in the style of dome frescoes by Correggio or Giovanni Lanfranco, though freer and less crowded—in line with the dome fresco for the Dreifaltigkeitskirche in Salzburg, in which 30 years earlier Johann Michael Rottmayr had introduced to central Europe an ideal celestial sphere free of illusionistic architecture. Troger's colours are darker, cooler and more solemn than those of Rottmayr, a follower of Rubens, and his style of figure painting is more restrained and classicizing, in the Bolognese tradition. The noble bodies bring to mind Georg Raphael Donner's sculptures, which Troger encountered while working in Salzburg. He also painted Donner's portrait (untraced), of which Jakob Matthias Schmutzer (1733–1811), a pupil of both men, later made an engraving.

Donner's Baroque–classical ideal of the figure with its depth-creating eurhythmy inspired Troger's subsequent painting, even if his figures often appear more tempestuous. Troger was based in Vienna from 1728. In the frescoes executed in the following years, for instance at Hradisch Monastery, near Olomouc (1731), Zwettl Abbey (1732–3), the castle chapel of Heiligenkreuz-Gutenbrunn (1739), the convent church of the Sisters of St Elizabeth of Hungary at Bratislava (1742) and at St Ignatius, Győr (1744, 1747), Troger's colouring becomes lighter, his figures seem to evolve in an airy firmament, and red, gold and blue form the main harmonies, with blue both predominating as the background colour of the sky and creating the solemn, cool overall mood suited to Troger's concept of figures. From this is derived the term 'Troger blue'.

The fresco on the interior of the dome of St Lambert, Altenburg Abbey (see fig.), is one of the supreme achievements of Austrian Baroque painting. Based on the Apocalypse, it represents the *Mission of Christ and the Persecution of the Virgin by the Dragon*. Troger has inserted an area of landscape along the rim of the cupola in the style of Giordano. He was to do so again in the summer refectory at Geras (1738) and in the banqueting-room of the prelacy at Melk (1739). The ceiling frescoes of the marble room

Paul Troger: *Mission of Christ and the Persecution of the Virgin by the Dragon* (1733–4; detail), fresco, St Lambert, Altenburg Abbey

and the library at Seitenstetten Abbey depicting the *Harmony of Faith and the World of Science* (1735) and the *Adoration of the Lamb by the Twenty-four Elders* (1740–41) are of a similarly high standard, as is the grand ceremonial ceiling fresco above the imperial staircase in the Benedictine abbey of Göttweig, the *Apotheosis of Emperor Charles VI* (1739).

These last compositions are again set in an ideal celestial sphere without earthly zones. From about 1738, however, figures move away from the classical form towards a heightening of expression also to be seen in the later drawings and oil paintings. The oil paintings with their marked chiaroscuro show the renewed influence of Piazzetta, Bencovich, Solimena and other tenebrists. This highly expressive, dramatic style peaked in the frescoes at Bressanone Cathedral (1748–50), particularly in the *Worship of the Lamb* above the nave, which has links with Gaulli's ceiling painting in Il Gesù in Rome. In an illusionistic dome fresco (known only through a sketch in oils) Troger even reverted to the *quadratura* of Andrea Pozzo. The last surviving ceiling painting by Troger, the fresco (1752) on the dome of the pilgrimage church at Maria Dreieichen in Lower Austria, is lighter and freer in effect than the Bressanone frescoes; its Rococo-like grace and colourfulness herald the age of Johann Wenzel Bergl and Franz Anton Maulbertsch.

2. WORKING METHODS AND TECHNIQUE. Troger was the first Austrian Baroque painter for whom drawing was an end in itself and not simply preliminary to oil paintings and frescoes. In his drawings, as in his paintings, he started from the single figure, which he outlined with a

sure touch, often using hatching and cross-sections to convey modelling. The 'firm lines' in his *disegno* differ considerably from the drawing methods of most of his immediate predecessors and contemporaries in both Italy and central Europe; they preferred freer forms suggestive of painting, *disegno pittorico* as Giulio Mancini and Marco Boschini called it. Troger's method was more modelled on or akin to Tuscan and Roman art of the 16th and 17th centuries or the allied art of Bologna than to that of Venice, coming close to the classical aspirations in the drawings and etchings of Pietro Testa. Besides the influences assimilated while in Italy from the draughtsmanship of Diziani and Creti, the Roman caricaturist Pier Leone Ghezzi, with his confident drawing, also influenced Troger's work.

It was in fact Troger's style that made its mark on the next generation of Austrian artists, in both drawing and painting; this was partly through his teaching at the Akademie der Bildenden Künste, Vienna, which he joined in 1745. He was its Rector from 1754 to 1757. His pupils and close colleagues included Josef Ignaz Mildorfer, Franz Sigrist, Martin Knoller, Johann Jakob Zeiller and Franz Anton Zoller (*d* 1768); but Bergl, Maulbertsch, Johann Christian Thomas Winck and Franz Anton Palko also learnt from him, even if in their drawings and etchings they often softened his severity and reverted to a more pictorial form. The impact of Troger's work thus extended beyond Austria to Bavaria, Bohemia, Moravia and Hungary.

Troger's etchings and copper engravings, which mostly belong to his early years, and engravings by others based on his work played an important role in the creation of the Vienna Kupferstich-Akademie; its founder, Jakob Matthias Schmutzer (1733–1811), was a pupil of Troger.

UNPUBLISHED SOURCES

Innsbruck, Tirol. Landesmus., MSS Dipauli 1031–2 [A. Roschmann: *Tyrolis pictoria et statuaria* (1742; 1755)]; MS. 230 [J. von Sperges: *Collectanea de artificibus Tirolensibus*, i (1791)]; MS. 1104 [P. Denifle: *Nachrichten von den berühmtern tirolschen bildenden Künstlern* and A. A. von Dipauli: *Nachrichten von Tiroler Künstlern*]

BIBLIOGRAPHY

Kindler; Thieme–Becker
Obituary, *Wien. Diarium*, xciv (24 Nov 1762)
F. Endl: 'Paul Troger: Ein Künstler der Barockzeit', *Ordo Sancti Benedicti: Stud. & Mitt. Benediktiner- & Cisterzienser-Orden*, xvi (1895), pp. 452, 684; xvii (1896), pp. 83, 278
H. Tietze: 'Programme und Entwürfe zu den grossen österreichischen Barockfresken', *Jb. Ksthist. Samml. Allhöch. Ksrhaus.*, xxx (1911), p. 3
H. Hammer: *Die Entwicklung der barocken Deckenmalerei in Wien* (Vienna, 1921)
J. Weingartner: 'Der Umbau des Brixener Domes im 18. Jahrhundert', *Jb. Ksthist. Inst. Staatsdkmlamt.*, xiv (1923)
R. Jacobs: *Paul Troger* (Vienna, 1930)
N. Michailov: *Österreichische Malerei des 18. Jahrhunderts* (Frankfurt am Main, 1935), pp. 5–19, 21–6
J. Ringler: 'Paul Trogers Herkunft und bürgerliche Existenz', *Veröff. Mus. Ferdinandeum*, xxxi (1951), pp. 567–81
H. Tintelnot: *Die barocke Freskomalerei in Deutschland* (Munich, 1951), esp. pp. 90–99
B. Heinzl: 'Die Freskomalerei Paul Trogers', *Wien. Jb. Kstgesch.*, xix (1962), p. 165
Paul Troger (exh. cat. by W. Aschenbrenner, Innsbruck, Tirol. Landesmus.; Stift Altenburg, 1962–3)
E. Knab: 'Über den Zeichenstil und einige Zeichnungen Paul Trogers', *Albertina-Stud.*, i/1 (1963), p. 21; i/2, p. 80
W. Aschenbrenner and G. Schweighofer: *Paul Troger: Leben und Werk* (Salzburg, 1965) [with sources, cat. and bibliog.]
C. Wolf: *Paul Troger: Zeichnung und Graphik* (diss.; Vienna, 1971)
E. Knab: *Daniel Gran* (Vienna, 1977), p. 152
E. Baum: *Katalog des Österreichischen Barockmuseums*, ii (Vienna, 1980), pp. 700–724
E. Hubala: *Johann Michael Rottmayr* (Vienna and Munich, 1981)
K. M. Swoboda: *Die Kunst des 18. Jahrhunderts*, viii of *Geschichte der bildenden Kunst* (Vienna, 1982), p. 231

ECKHART KNAB

Troger, Simon (*b* Abfaltersbach, Osttirol, 13 Oct 1683; *d* Haidhausen, nr Munich, 25 Sept 1768). Austrian sculptor. In 1721 he joined the workshop of the sculptor Schmiedecker in Merano; *c.* 1723–5 he moved to Innsbruck and worked for Nikolaus Moll (1676–1754), and probably also spent some time in Italy. It was probably at this period that he created a large group in wood and ivory of *St Michael Vanquishing Satan* (Florence, Pitti), which consequently may be his earliest known work. By 1726 he had settled in Munich, first to work for Andreas Faistenberger (1647–1736); he then set up his own large workshop in Haidhausen. For one of his patrons, Maximilian III Joseph, Elector of Bavaria, he carved many figures and groups, in a manner characteristic of his workshop; often referred to as 'Troger figures', these were of a combination of materials, such as ivory and wood stained black. Troger made use of other materials, such as metal, and enamel or glass eyes, and of highly polished or textured surfaces, to produce illusionistic effects. The Baroque movements given to these figures display the artist's virtuosity, but also the influence of a variety of sources, including Mannerism, Fürstenberg porcelain and individual artists, such as Faistenberger.

The exact chronology of Troger's work has not been fully established. Two early pieces, the *Martyrdom of St Lawrence* and the *Martyrdom of St Theodore*, which bear the monogram S.T., may have been carved *c.* 1726, after Troger had settled in Haidhausen. The 1733 inventory of the Dresdener Kunstkammer recorded a series of genre figures, all of similar size (less than 350 mm in height, including pedestal). Two of these survive in private collections (see Theuerkauff, 1986): *A Charlatan* and a *Street Vendor of Mussels*. In 1736 Troger was recorded as making a group of the *Rape of Proserpina* (untraced) for the Sardinian court; on this he modelled a later work on the same subject (*c.* 1745; Munich, Bayer. Nmus.). He also executed groups of *Drunken Silenus on a Three-wheeled Carriage* and *Cain and Abel* (both Munich, Bayer. Nmus.); of the latter work there exists a signed lime-wood *bozzetto* (Vienna, Ksthist. Mus.). The Victoria and Albert Museum, London, owns a group of the *Judgement of Solomon* in ivory and walnut on a rose-wood and satin-wood base. There is a stylistic discrepancy between the early works and the pieces carved between 1733 and 1768. Theuerkauff has suggested that Troger's close collaboration during his formative years with Faistenberger, and the knowledge he thus acquired of the master's multi-figured compositions, influenced his own highly theatrical manner of handling poses and the arrangement of garment folds.

BIBLIOGRAPHY

Thieme–Becker
E. von Philippovich: *Elfenbein: Ein Handbuch für Sammler und Liebhaber* (Brunswick, 1961, rev. Munich, 1982)
——: 'Simon Troger und andere Elfenbeinkünstler aus Tirol', *Schlern Schr.*, 216 (1961), pp. 5–11

——: 'Kombinationsfiguren aus Elfenbein und Holz', *Kst Hessen & Mittelrhein*, xvii (1977), pp. 27–35
C. Theuerkauff: *Die Bildwerke in Elfenbein des 16.–19. Jahrhunderts*, Die Bildwerke der Skulpturengalerie Berlin (Berlin, 1986), pp. 267–73

HANNELORE HÄGELE

Trogir [Gr. Traguiron; Lat. Tragurium; It. Traù]. Croatian city on the Adriatic coast, 15 km west of Split. Dating back to prehistoric times, when its oval plan was probably established, the ancient centre is on an islet between the mainland and the island of Čiovo. The first city was the Greek colony of Traguiron (3rd and 2nd centuries BC), of which the most significant surviving feature is the relatively regular network of streets. Roman Tragurium became dependent on nearby Salona. Trogir survived the migrations of peoples following the collapse of the Roman Empire and was taken over by Slavs in the early medieval period. Most of its present-day churches stand on Early Christian foundations; from the 9th–11th centuries survive the miniature basilica of St Barbara (St Martin) and the remains of St Mary, a centralized church on a sexfoil plan.

Between the 12th and 15th centuries Trogir was autonomous but subject to the rule of the Hungaro-Croatian kings, under whom it remained longer than any other city on this coast. This was the period of its greatest prosperity, when most of the houses, with Romanesque details, the city walls and towers, churches, monasteries, the 'loggia' and the palace were built. The cathedral of St Lawrence (*see* §1 below) was started *c.* 1200. Under the Venetians from 1420 to 1797 (*see* VENETIAN EMPIRE) the palace and 'loggia' were rebuilt and the town was given two new fortresses—Kamerlengo (1424–37) and St Mark (1470–72). The town attracted many prominent artists, including Giovanni Dalmata, Andrea Alessi and Niccolò di Giovanni Fiorentino. In the period of French dominance (1808–13) a 'gloriette' was raised in honour of Marshal Auguste Frédéric Louis Viesse de Marmont (1774–1852). The town retains traces of all building styles down to the Gothic and Renaissance revivals that characterized the region under Austro-Hungarian rule to 1918.

1. CATHEDRAL. Begun *c.* 1200, most of the building was finished during the 13th century; the campanile was completed in 1605 by Trifon Bokanić. The cathedral, dedicated to St Lawrence, is especially notable for its sculptural decoration. The west portal bears a signed and dated inscription of 1240 (*see* RADOVAN). Supported on telamons, it is profusely decorated with reliefs. The tympanum and archivolts bear New Testament scenes, while on the jambs are carved the *Labours of the Months*, saints and Apostles, fantastic creatures and animals, and a wide range of decorative motifs. Flanking the portal are statues of *Adam* and *Eve* standing on lions.

The pulpit and ciborium, with their richly carved capitals, are also attributed to Radovan and his circle. The ciborium is crowned with 14th-century statues of the *Annunciation* by the otherwise unknown Master Maurus, recalling those on a ciborium now in the Treasury of S Marco, Venice. The decoration of the exterior includes the waterspouts (from 1417) by Petar Pozdančić (*fl* 1405–17), the corbel heads of the campanile, probably by Lorenzo Pincino (*fl* 1398; *d* after 1452), who worked on the decoration of the Ca d'Oro in Venice and Šibenik

Cathedral, and the four statues of its summit, commissioned from Alessandro Vittoria.

The baptistery, by ANDREA ALESSI, was added to the north side of the portico in 1467. It has a pointed barrel vault but predominantly Renaissance sculptural decoration. A relief of the *Baptism* is set over the entrance; a statue of *St John the Baptist* stands on the altar and above, in the lunette, is a relief of *St Jerome in the Desert*. The chapel of the Blessed Giovanni Orsini was added to the north side of the cathedral in 1468. NICCOLÒ DI GIOVANNI FIORENTINO here collaborated with Alessi, the former being responsible for the highly original design of the chapel and most of its sculpture. On the dado are torch-bearing putti; above are niches containing statues of saints and Apostles (*St John the Evangelist* is signed by Giovanni Dalmata), with *Christ*, the *Virgin* and *St John the Baptist* on the altar wall. Above is a band of oculi. In the lunette is a relief of the *Coronation of the Virgin*, and the coffered, barrel-vaulted ceiling bears angel heads with *God the Father* in the centre.

BIBLIOGRAPHY
G. Lucio: *Memorie istoriche di Tragurio, ora detto Traù* (Venice, 1673)
V. Cega de Celio: *La chiesa di Traù* (Split, 1855)
T. G. Jackson: *Dalmatia, the Quarnero and Istria*, ii (Oxford, 1887)
P. Andreis: *Storia della città di Traù* (Split, 1908)
C. Fisković: *Opis trogirske katedrale iz XVIII stoljeća* [A description of Trogir Cathedral from the 18th century] (Split, 1940)
——: 'Trogirski majstor Mavar' [Master Maurus of Trogir], *An. Hist. Inst. JAZU Dubrovnik*, xii (1970)
R. Ivančević: 'Slikarski predložak renesansnog reljefa krštenja u Trogiru' [Painted originals of Renaissance baptismal reliefs in Trogir], *Peristil*, xxvii–xxviii (1984–5)
——: 'Kronološka analiza ranorenesansne Kapele sv Ivana Ursinije u Trogiru' [Chronological analysis of the early Renaissance chapel of St John Orsini at Trogir], *Prilozi Povijesti Umjetnosti Dalmac.*, xxv (1986–7)
I. Babić and others: *Trogir* (Zagreb, 1987)

IVO BABIĆ

Troili [Trogli], **Giulio** [Paradosso] (*b* Spilamberto, nr Modena, ?1613; *d* ?Bologna, after 1683). Italian painter and writer. Although he claimed to have been self-taught, Malvasia states that he was a pupil of Francesco Gessi. He went to Rome in 1628 and worked with oil and fresco painters. He settled in Bologna before 1653, where he specialized in *quadratura* and perspective painting. In 1672 he described himself as painter to the Bolognese Senate, in which capacity he had produced designs for public festivals. In 1681 he was among ten Bolognese painters invited to Parma to work for Ranuccio II Farnese, 6th Duke of Parma. In 1653 Troili published an account of the copying device known as the parallelogram (*see* PANTOGRAPH). This was followed by his principal work on drawing in perspective, the *Paradossi* (Bologna, 1672). This offers practical guidance on the means of drawing plans and elevations in perspective and the use of such devices as the *velo* (Lat. *velum*: 'veil' or 'net'). The text is illustrated with comprehensive diagrams, and many references are made to other books and to the works of such painters as Titian, Rubens and Simon Vouet. The edition of 1683 also includes observations on the design of fortifications. The *Paradossi* is a practical book rather than a scholarly treatise and is addressed to painters, sculptors, architects and all who delight in drawing. Its especial interest lies in the light that it sheds on the techniques of Bolognese *quadratura* painting.

WRITINGS
Prattica del parallelogrammo da disegnare del P. Christophoro Scheiner della Compagnia di Gesù, di nuovo data in luce da Giulio Troili alias principe pittore di Spilimberto (Bologna, 1653)
Paradossi per pratticare la prospettiva senza saperla (Bologna, 1672, rev. 1683)

BIBLIOGRAPHY
Thieme–Becker
A. Masini: *Bologna perlustrata* (Bologna, 1650, rev. 1666), p. 630
C. C. Malvasia: *Felsina pittrice* (1678); ed. G. Zanotti (Bologna, 1841), ii, pp. 253, 363, 366
G. Tiraboschi: *Biblioteca modenese*, v (Modena, 1784), pp. 299–301

JANET SOUTHORN

Trois crayons. *See* AUX TROIS CRAYONS.

Trois-Frères. Cave site in France, forming part of a cave system around the River Volp in Ariège in the foothills of the Pyrenees. It is known for its cave art of the Late Upper Palaeolithic period (*c.* 20,000–*c.* 10,000 BP; *see also* PREHISTORIC EUROPE, §II, 1 and 2). It was discovered in 1914 by the three sons of Count Henri Bégouën, who had discovered the cave of TUC D'AUDOUBERT two years earlier. Trois-Frères, which is far more richly decorated, comprises a complicated set of galleries, measuring 800 m in all; the only known entry was via the cave of Enlène, which is rich in portable art, Magdalenian (*c.* 18,000–

c. 10,000 BP) hearths and other evidence of human occupation. The material from these sites is housed in the Bégouën family's private museum and the Musée de l'Homme, Paris.

About 130 m into the Enlène cave, a long, narrow corridor leads into the Trois-Frères system. This was full of occupation debris and portable art, even though the ceiling is so low that it is necessary to crawl. The Trois-Frères cave itself has yielded little evidence of occupation, but its walls are covered with a profusion of figures, making it easily the richest Palaeolithic cave art site in the Pyrenees, indeed one of the richest anywhere. One estimate put its content at over 1100 'graphic units', but new figures have since been found, and it is known that more are covered by clay. Many seasons of work by the abbé HENRI BREUIL between 1920 and 1938 were necessary to make tracings of the art, particularly the often very complex palimpsests of engravings. According to the French scholar ANDRÉ LEROI-GOURHAN, the art of Trois-Frères is attributable to his styles III (*c.* 20,000–*c.* 16,000 BP) and especially IV (*c.* 16,000–*c.* 11,000 BP; *see* PREHISTORIC EUROPE, fig. 9). Its close analogies, both in style and in the precise pigment-mixture used, with the dated portable art of Enlène allow much of it to be assigned to the 14th millennium BP.

The figures include five stencilled hand outlines and a few paintings, including a claviform (clublike) sign on a

Trois-Frères, cave painting of a 'Sorcerer' or 'God of the Cave', Late Upper Palaeolithic period, Magdalenian culture, *c.* 18,000–*c.* 10,000 BP

scraped area of wall and some full-face lion heads. The vast majority of figures, however, are engravings, sometimes enhanced with paint or by scraping the rock to produce a light colour. Some limestone surfaces that had been rubbed to a high polish by the bears that formerly occupied the cave were used for very fine engravings. Other well-known images are some large owl-like birds, seen full-face, and a lioness in its own 'side-chapel'. The richest area is a cul-de-sac known as the Sanctuary, which has profusely engraved panels, each dominated by a species—bison, horse or reindeer. It is overlooked by its only painted and engraved figure, placed 4 m above floor-level and nicknamed the 'God of the Cave' or the 'Sorcerer' (see fig.). Its upright stance, hands and legs are human, but the rest is a mixture of different animals—the back and ears of a herbivore, the antlers of a reindeer and the tail of a horse, with the phallus in a feline position.

BIBLIOGRAPHY

H. Bégouën and H. Breuil: *Les Cavernes du Volp: Trois-Frères—Tuc d'Audoubert* (Paris, 1958)

R. Bégouën and J. Clottes: 'Grotte des Trois-Frères', *L'Art des cavernes* (Paris, 1984), pp. 400–09

——: 'Le Grand Félin des Trois-Frères', *Ant. N.*, xviii–xix (1986–7), pp. 109–13

——: 'Les Trois-Frères after Breuil', *Antiquity*, lxi (1987), pp. 180–87

PAUL G. BAHN

Troisi. Maltese family of silversmiths, architects and designers. The first recorded family member is Carlo Troisi (*fl* 1697–1736), followed by Andrea Troisi (*fl* 1750), Pietro Paolo Troisi (?1700–50) and Massimiliano Troisi (*fl* 1794). A silver sugar bowl (1775–97; London, Mus. Order St John) is attributed to Aloisio Troisi, probably a member of the same family. During the 17th and 18th centuries various members of the Troisi family filled the post of Master of the Mint of the Order of St John of the Knights Hospitaller. The Mint was established in Valletta, Malta, in 1566. The best-known Troisi silversmith is Pietro Paolo, who was also an architect. His best work is the Altar of Repose, which he designed for Mdina Cathedral, and which was constructed by the Maltese painter Francesco Vincenzo Zahra in 1750. It is a magnificent Baroque scenographic creation in wood executed in a masterful *trompe-l'oeil* effect. A silver tabernacle, made by Pietro Paolo's brother Andrea, forms its central feature. Between 1721 and 1743, as Master of the Mint, Pietro Paolo designed and minted what have been considered some of the finest coins in the history of the Order (e.g. Valletta, N. Mus.; Mdina, Cathedral Mus.).

BIBLIOGRAPHY

P. P. Castagna: *Li storia ta Malta* (Malta, 1890)

V. F. Denaro: *The Goldsmiths of Malta and their Marks* (Florence, 1972)

E. Sammut: *Guide to Mdina Cathedral and its Museum* (Malta, 1986)

MICHAEL ELLUL

Trojer, Ingenuin Albuin. *See* EGGER-LIENZ, ALBIN.

Trökes, Heinz (*b* Hamborn, Duisburg, 15 Aug 1913). German painter. He attended the Kunstgewerbeschule in Krefeld (1934–6) where he studied under Johannes Itten. His earliest work was pointillist, but little survives. Next he adopted a figurative expressive style, applying the colour straight from the tube and spreading it with his fingers. From 1936 to 1939 he earned a living by designing textiles in Augsburg. After meeting Vasily Kandinsky in 1937 he painted abstract works. His first one-man show (1938), held at the Galerie Nierendorf in Berlin, was closed by the Nazis, and he was expelled from the Reichskulturskammer. Afraid of being banned altogether from exhibiting, he moved to Zurich (1939). His plans to move to the Dutch Indies were shattered by the outbreak of World War II. At this time his work became Surrealist (e.g. *With the Opening Door*, 1943; priv. col., see 1979 exh. cat., p. 78), and he became interested in the work of Max Ernst, Marc Chagall and Paul Klee. On his return to Germany (1940) he began to study under Georg Muche in Krefeld but was called up in the same year. Although he served in an anti-aircraft unit until 1945, he was also able in his spare time to attend the art school headed by Max Dungert (1896–1945) in Berlin.

Trökes made linear figurative drawings using nude models. From 1943 he filled many sketchbooks with part scurrilous, abstract, part Surrealist fantasies. There were also periods when he painted and drew, the drawings being executed in their own right and not as sketches for paintings. Many were based on the motif of flying. After the war he helped Gerd Rosen found the Galerie Rosen in West Berlin and acted as its artistic director until 1946. In 1947 he was appointed to the Staatliche Hochschule für Architektur und Kunst in Weimar but left after only one semester. During the Allied blockade he was in Rodenbach; he later returned to Berlin. His surrealistically conceived images of this time were dominated by two groups of motifs: cosmonautic-futuristic utopias, and landscapes with ruins (e.g. *Blind City*, 1949; priv. col., see 1979 exh. cat., p. 97). In the latter his intention was partly to make ironic reference to the artistic cult of ruins.

In Paris between 1950 and 1952 Trökes struck up a friendship with Wols, joined the circle of artists grouped around Roberto Matta and took part in André Breton's weekly meetings. During the early 1950s he used vivid colours, and his technique had similarities with psychic automatism. In 1952 he settled in Ibiza, to which he always returned between his travels. There he created the *Island* paintings, for example *Island Town* (1952; Gerolstein, U. and H. Hahn priv. col., see 1979 exh. cat., p. 105), which were often topographical. In 1957–8 he executed the *White* paintings, for which he used a double, white, strongly structured grounding, which enabled him to mix different layers. In the 1960s his palette became more subdued, and *c.* 1966 he began to include folkloric elements in paintings of flat geometrically-confined space. This style was superseded in 1971 by one that used two basic colour tones and in smaller format. Besides these he made black-and-white collages as well as gold and enamel pictures. Trökes also designed carpets, church windows, book illuminations and tapestry wall-hangings after World War II.

WRITINGS

Tage Nacht Buch, foreword C. Linfert (Cologne, 1963)

BIBLIOGRAPHY

Heinz Trökes: Bilder, Zeichnungen, Collagen und Skizzenbucher, 1938–1979 (exh. cat., W. Berlin, Akad. Kst.; Duisburg, Lehmbruck-Mus.; 1979)

Heinz Trökes: 31 Skizzenbucher (exh. cat., W. Berlin, N.G., 1983)

DOMINIK BARTMANN

Trolle-Bonde, Count **Gustaf** (*b* Vibyholm, Södermanland, 28 March 1773; *d* Stockholm, 3 Jan 1855). Swedish patron and collector. In 1791 he inherited from his father, Count Karl Bonde, several estates in Sweden, including Sävstaholm in Södermanland. After studies at Uppsala University (1790–92), he embarked in 1794 on a two-year tour of Europe (diary, Sävstaholm archvs), which marked the beginning of the formation of one of Sweden's most remarkable private collections. The itinerary included Denmark, Germany, Belgium and a year in London, during which Count Gustaf sought out Swedish painters, for example Carl Fredrik von Breda, from whom he commissioned his portrait (1795). In November 1795 he moved to Paris, where he acquired, among other paintings, a portrait by Philippe de Champaigne wrongly thought to be of *Blaise Pascal* (untraced), bought through the Swedish Count Sparre. His return to Sweden was via Switzerland and Germany.

In 1800 Count Gustaf was appointed chamberlain to the Swedish queen Fredrika Dorothea, but despite this and other public positions he withdrew from public life to concentrate on his collecting and the management of his estates. Between 1801 and 1804 he made significant acquisitions of modern Swedish paintings, including works by Elias Martin, among them *View of Hanover Square* (1769; London, White's Club), and by Niclas Lafrensen, as well as works by foreign Old Masters, which were hung in his newly decorated gallery at Sävstaholm. However, between 1806, when he inherited the estate of Trolleholm in Skåne from his paternal grandmother, and 1816 there was a hiatus in his collecting, due partly to his restorations and additions to Sävstaholm and partly to his divorce from his wife in 1809 (the year in which he was given permission to use the title of Trolle-Bonde). In 1826, however, he bought Frans Hals's *Merry Lute-player* (*c.* 1625; England, priv. col.). His greatest subsequent acquisition, and the most costly, was the purchase in Vienna in 1828 of 20 Italian Old Master paintings from the miniature painter Giovanni Domenico Bossi (1765–1853), to whom he contracted to pay a yearly stipend of 100 gold ducats until the artist's death. The quality of Trolle-Bonde's Old Master collection was uneven and included several paintings with attributions (e.g. to Giorgione, van Dyck and Boucher) that have since been discredited. Nonetheless it also included works of great quality, including Titian's *Portrait of a Gentleman in Black Beret* (*c.* 1515–18; Copenhagen, Ny Carlsberg Glyp., on dep. Stat. Mus. Kst). He also owned contemporary marble sculpture such as Johan Niklas Byström's *Venus and Cupid* (1823) and Bengt Erland Fogelberg's *Mercury about to Kill Argus* (1825; both Trolleholm, Count Gustaf Trolle-Bonde priv. col.). Although struck blind in the 1830s, he continued to collect until his death.

BIBLIOGRAPHY
L. Looström: *Konstsamlingarna på Sävstaholm* [The art collections at Sävstaholm] (Stockholm, 1882)
O. Granberg: *Svenska konstsamlingarnas historia* [The history of Swedish art collections], iii (Stockholm, 1931), pp. 127–37
S. J. Kjellberg, ed.: *Slott och herresäten i Sverige, Skåne* [Palace and country house in Skåne, Sweden], i (Malmö, 1966) [incl. illus. of Trolleholm interior], pp. 284, 286–7
G. Trolle-Bonde: [unpubd diss. on Trolle-Bonde cols] (in preparation)
ANTONIA BOSTRÖM

Trometta [Trombetta; Martinelli, Niccolo] (*b* Pesaro, *c.* 1540; *d* Rome, *c.* 1610). Italian painter. He probably began his apprenticeship in his native Pesaro, but, while young, he moved to Rome, where he studied in the workshop of Taddeo and Francesco Zuccaro. The work of Taddeo most influenced his style, and, with Cherubino Alberti, Giovanni Maria Ricci and Cesare Nebbia, Trometta became one of the leading members of the Zuccaro workshop, participating in the decoration of the Casino of Pope Pius IV in 1561–3. By January 1565 he was established as an independent master, when he was commissioned to decorate a chapel in S Maria della Consolazione. In the same month he agreed to fresco the choir vault in S Maria in Aracoeli, Rome, as part of the restoration of that church ordered by Pius IV in 1561. Trometta's decorative scheme, executed between 1566 and 1568, is one of the best-preserved and most extensive of mid-16th-century ecclesiastical decorations in Rome and comprises a central oval of the *Virgin and Child with Angels* flanked by rectangular sections depicting *Augustus and the Sibyl* and *Augustus Sacrificing at the Altar*, as well as subsidiary sections. The style reflects the Mannerism of the Zuccaros and of Francesco Salviati, but retains a provincial naivety of Trometta's own. In about 1570 he returned to Pesaro, where he painted a series of large altarpieces, including the *Last Supper* for the Chiesa del Sacramento (now Tavullia, S Lorenzo) and the *Virgin and Child with SS John the Baptist and Nicholas of Bari* for S Maria della Scala della Porta (Budapest, Mus. F.A.), which betray the additional influence of Federico Barocci. After his final move to Rome *c.* 1580, he undertook further ecclesiastical decorations, notably the chapel of the Crucifix (*c.* 1591) and the chapel of St Francis (1595), both in S Maria dell'Orto, but the works of his last period show a marked decline.

BIBLIOGRAPHY
J. A. Gere: 'Drawings by Niccolo Martinelli, il Trometta', *Master Drgs*, i/4 (1963), pp. 3–18
A. Szobon: 'Un Tableau de Pesaro retrouvé de Niccolo Martinelli dit le Trometta', *Bull. Mus. Hong. B.-A.*, xxxiv–xxxv (1970), pp. 85–92
M. Frattarelli: 'Gli affreschi della volta del coro della chiesa di S Maria in Aracoeli in Roma di Niccolo Trometta', *Not. Pal. Albani*, x/2 (1981), pp. 49–53
B. Montevecchi: 'Un ommaggio ai della Rovere', *Quad. Gal. N. Marche*, iii (1981), pp. 65–9

Trompe l'oeil. *See under* ILLUSIONISM.

Tronchin, François (*b* Geneva, 23 Oct 1704; *d* Geneva, 7 Feb 1798). Swiss financier, civic leader, writer, collector and patron. Early in life he became enamoured of literature and the arts. As a young man he was drawn to Paris, where he met Diderot and Voltaire. Tronchin's tragedy *Marie Stuart* was performed in Paris in 1734. He returned to Geneva in 1736; after a brief career in finance he came to hold various civic offices in Geneva. He renewed his friendship with Voltaire, who in 1754 settled in Switzerland, and in 1765 bought from him the estate of Les Délices, near Geneva. He had begun to acquire Old Master paintings around 1740, favouring Dutch and Flemish works, but in 1770 sold 95 of these to Catherine II, Empress of Russia. They included Gabriel Metsu's *Prodigal Son* (*c.* 1650) and Jan Steen's *Jeu de tric-trac* (1667; both St

Petersburg, Hermitage). In 1772 he inventoried and negotiated the purchase of the Crozat de Thiers collection by Catherine. He immediately started a second collection. One of Jean-Etienne Liotard's finest portraits, *François Tronchin Looking at a Painting by Rembrandt* (1757; Cleveland, OH, Mus. A.), represents Tronchin with the jewel of his first ensemble, Rembrandt's *Sarah Awaiting Tobias on her Wedding Night* (*c.* 1645; Edinburgh, N.G.). Liotard also painted a portrait of *Mme Tronchin* (1758; priv. col., see 1974 exh. cat., nos 347–8). Around 1760 Tronchin began to patronize local talent, including Liotard, Jean Huber, and Jean's son Jean-Daniel Huber. He also provided critical support for the latter's contemporaries Pierre-Louis De La Rive and Jean-Pierre Saint-Ours. When Saint-Ours won the Prix de Rome of the Académie Royale in Paris, but was denied French funding, Tronchin supported his sojourn in Italy. He may thus be regarded as the 'godfather' of the Geneva school that, with encouragement from Liotard and the elder Huber, matured around 1780. Genevese artists as well as foreign visitors had ready access to Tronchin's collections. Between 1787 and 1789 he delivered four lectures on painting at the Société des Arts of Geneva (founded 1776). After his death 226 pictures from his collection were sent to Paris to be auctioned in 1801 by Jean-Baptiste-Pierre Le Brun.

UNPUBLISHED SOURCES

Geneva, Bib. Pub. & U. [Archives Tronchin: contains the bulk of his papers, including correspondence with European art-world figures; other manuscripts are in the private Archives de Lavigny, Canton of Vaud]

WRITINGS

Catalogue des tableaux de mon cabinet (Geneva, 1765)
Mes Récréations dramatiques, 5 vols (Paris, 1779–84)
Catalogue des tableaux de mon cabinet (Geneva, 1780)
Discours relatifs à la peinture (Geneva, 1788)
Catalogue raisonné du cabinet de tableaux de feu M. François Tronchin des Délices, Ancien Conseiller d'Etat de la République de Genève: Fait par lui-même (Geneva, 1798)

BIBLIOGRAPHY

H. Tronchin: *Le Conseiller François Tronchin et ses amis Voltaire, Diderot, Grimm etc* (Paris, 1895)
Voltaire: *Lettres inédites aux Tronchin avec une introduction de Bernard Gagnebin* (Geneva and Lille, 1950)
M. Benisovich: 'Les Collections de tableaux du Conseiller François Tronchin et le Musée de l'Ermitage', *Genava*, n. s. 1, i (1953), pp. 25–51
De Genève à l'Ermitage: Les Collections de François Tronchin (exh. cat., ed. R. Loche; Geneva, Mus. Rath, 1974) [also: *Genava*, n. s. 1, xxii (1974), pp. v–xv, 1–217]
M. Natale: 'François Tronchin et la "patience flegmatique" des Hollandais', *Le Goût et les collections d'art italien à Genève du XVIIIe au XXe siècles* (Geneva, 1980), pp. 15–25

GARRY APGAR

Trondheim [formerly Nidaros; Nidaroskaupang; Trondhjem; Trondhjem]. Town and seat of a bishopric on Trondheim Fjord, Norway.

1. HISTORY AND URBAN DEVELOPMENT. According to the documentary sources, Trondheim was founded by King Olaf Tryggvesson (*reg c.* AD 995–1000) in 996 or 997 by the mouth of the River Nid on Trondheim Fjord. There he built a palace and a church (?dedicated to St Clement), laying out plots of land for intending settlers.

In 1030 the body of King Olaf II Haraldsson (*reg* 1015–30), killed at the Battle of Stiklestad, was brought to the Nidaroskaupang. In 1031 Olaf was canonized and, through

his rapidly increasing popularity as a miracle-working saint, the town developed into one of the most important north European pilgrimage centres of the Middle Ages. The town rapidly expanded, and new churches were built, dedicated to SS Olaf, Gregory, Mary and Margaret. At the end of the 11th century King Olaf III Kyrre ('the Gentle'; *reg* 1066–93) built Christ Church as St Olaf's shrine church (the shrine was destroyed in 1537). After the creation of the bishopric *c.* 1100 Christ Church became a cathedral (*see* §2 below).

In the 11th century the town was the country's 'capital' and an important religious and cultural centre. Each of the town properties already consisted of several wooden buildings with turf roofs, positioned in a row along the street and within the block. The houses had a two-room plan, for living and storage, and were originally single storey, but by the 13th century there were some with several storeys. Through the building activities of the kings and Church, techniques of stone building were introduced to the region in the second half of the 11th century. The town is believed to have been an early centre for, among others, professional wood-carvers: excavations have, for example, uncovered a large number of wooden objects decorated in accomplished Urnes style.

In 1152/3 the archbishopric of Nidaros was established, including, besides Norway, Greenland, Iceland, the Hebrides, Shetland, the Orkneys and the Isle of Man. During the next 20–30 years Christ Church was rebuilt, and the Archbishop's Palace (1173–1203) was started. This is Scandinavia's oldest surviving secular stone building complex. In the 13th century the town had about fifteen religious institutions, of which five were abbeys. Owing to the international nature of religious institutions the external influences on the town had a considerable impact on national art and literature. With the Reformation in 1536 the last archbishop fled the country, greatly weakening the town's economic structure and political influence. In 1681 Trondheim burnt down, but it was rebuilt by Caspar von Cicignon as one of Scandinavia's most strongly fortified towns. Kristiansten fort was built on a hill to the east with another on an island in the fjord, the latter with a central tower and curtain wall (partly destr.). The streets were wide and were laid out on a grid pattern, which has survived more or less untouched. During the 18th century a merchant aristocracy emerged, which built, among other things, a number of grandiose wooden mansions in a local Neo-classical style known as 'trønder-empir'. These are among the finest examples of wooden architecture in Scandinavia. The town's name was formally changed from Trondhjem to Trondheim in 1931.

BIBLIOGRAPHY

J. Schreiner, ed.: *Trondheim bys historie*, 4 vols (Trondheim, 1955–62)
G. Kavli: *Trønderske trepaleer: Borgerlig panelarkitektur Nordenfjells*, Norske Minnesmerker (Oslo, 1966)
O. Lunde: *Trondheims fortid i bygrunnen: Middelalderbyens topografi på grunnlag av det arkeologiske materialet inntil 1970*, Riksantikvarens Skrifter, ii (Trondheim, 1977)

AXEL CHRISTOPHERSEN

2. CATHEDRAL.

(i) *Architecture*. Christ Church Cathedral is the principal Gothic building in Norway. Its most striking feature is the octagonal east end, built over the first burial place of St

Olaf and possibly intended to combine the functions of a shrine church and choir. The present building is largely a reconstruction: a devastating fire in 1531 left the west end in ruins, and when the restoration started in 1869 only the octagon and transepts were relatively intact. With the exception of the west front, however, the restoration is based on thorough research. The cathedral is referred to in the Sagas, which are a valuable source if used with care. Many archaeological and topographical records made in the 19th century, together with earlier sources dating back to 1567, are indispensable for details that have since vanished. The major modern contribution to the building history is the archaeological and structural research published by Fischer (1965).

The first church, dedicated to Christ and the Holy Trinity, was founded by King Olaf III Kyrre c. 1070. The excavated walls indicate that its nave corresponded approximately to the central vessel of the present choir. The chancel had a chapel on each side, and a great tower to the west was flanked by smaller structures. This tower either marked the west end of the church or was the central tower of a later extension planned with an aisled choir and nave.

The earliest surviving work in the present building is the Romanesque transept, built after 1140, each arm with

Trondheim Cathedral, *Head of a Young Man*, soapstone, h. 109 mm, c. 1210–35 (Trondheim, Domkirkens Skulptursamlig)

an eastern chapel and a wooden, raftered roof. The foundations of the west front were laid by Bishop Sigurd in 1148, but major building activity took place under Archbishop Eystein Erlendsson (1157–88). Built of soapstone with marble shafting, the present church (l. 100 m) consists of the octagon, which has an ambulatory and three square radiating chapels, a six-bay aisled choir, a lantern tower over the crossing, the transept and an aisled nave of eight bays fronted by a screen façade (w. 39 m), with the bases of two western towers. The main vessel of the choir was probably planned to have sexpartite vaults, but they are now quadripartite; the nave has a tierceron vault with a ridge rib. When restoration began in the 19th century the façade had two storeys of blind arcading with stiff-leaf capitals and three relatively small, simple doorways. It has been reconstructed with three storeys and a taller central window surmounted by a gable. The internal elevation has three storeys, arcade, gallery with twin-arched openings and a clerestory with a wall-passage; the most significant structural feature, however, is the relative thinness of the main vessel of the nave and the use of flying buttresses. The nave clerestory has two layers of geometric tracery, and other decorative details range from chevrons in the transepts to diaper-work in the nave. The screen across the entrance to the octagon, which has Kentish tracery and ogee arches in the English Decorated style, was inserted after a fire in 1328.

The chapter house (or sacristy) north of the choir is a harmonious soapstone building (l. 17 m), with two quadripartite-vaulted bays and an apse preceded by a little pseudo-transept marked by four columnar piers. It has been disputed whether the transept was started in the 1130s, but, with the chapter house, it was presumably completed by the 1180s: according to an inscription on the wall the south transept chapel was consecrated in 1161. The stylistic influence of the cathedral is detectable in local stone churches up to about 1200, after which the demand for new churches declined.

The octagon and choir, which may have been complete by 1230, were vaulted in the 1250s, and the cathedral interior was probably finished before the fire of 1328. The main campaign on the cathedral reveals a close relationship with contemporary English architecture, especially St Hugh's choir at Lincoln Cathedral (*see* LINCOLN, §2(i)(b)), but with its own identity among European cathedrals Trondheim offers a splendid example of the fusion of foreign influences with high-quality local work.

BIBLIOGRAPHY

A. P. Beyer: *Om Norgis rige* (1567); ed. G. Storm in *Historisk-topografiske skrifter om Norge og norske landsdele, forfattede i Norge i det 16de aarhundrede* (Christiania, 1895), p. 14

J. M. Masch [Maschius]: *Norvegia religiosa in dei montem Templum Nidrosianum* (Christiania, 1661)

G. Schøning: *Beskrivelse over den tilforn meget prægtige og vidtberømte Dom-Kirke i Trondhjem, egentlig kaldet Christ-Kirken* (Trondheim, 1762/R 1959)

P. A. Munch: *Throndhjems domkirke* (Christiania, 1859) [Norw. and Eng. texts]

Trondhjem Cathedral: Papers Concerning the Designs for the Restoration, Office of the Restoration of Trondhjem Cathedral (Trondhjem, 1919)

G. Fischer: *Domkirken i Trondheim*, 2 vols (Oslo, 1965) [Eng. summary]

H.-E. Lidén: 'Middelalderens steinarkitektur i Norge', *Norges kunsthistorie*, ii (Oslo, 1981), pp. 7–126

(ii) Sculpture. Most of the original copious sculptural ornament of Trondheim Cathedral has been systematically replaced by copies from 1869 onwards; all the surviving pieces are carefully preserved, but many were destroyed in a fire in 1983. Fragments survive from the Romanesque cathedral (now in the Archbishop's Palace), and in the transept scalloped capitals and corbel heads are still *in situ*. The most varied and interesting sculpture belongs to the octagon: the interior wall arcading has extravagant foliage capitals and corbels, while the exterior string course has medallions with naturalistically carved heads. A carved head (see fig.) preserved in the cathedral stone collection shares these stylistic characteristics. Heads from the cornice are more summarily executed. The Bishop's door on the north side of the octagon has grotesque masks, animals and an Early Gothic variant of the inhabited scroll, its graphic details taking advantage of the soft soapstone. Fragments from the south door to the choir include details from the story of *Adam and Eve* set in deeply carved intertwining foliage stems. Some heads, again more summarily executed, survive above the choir gallery. The reliefs of angels from the spandrels of the nave arcade indicate work of high quality. The best preserved of the sculptures from the original screen front are in the style combining naturalism with idealism that is characteristic of European sculpture of the time. The sculpture of the cathedral as a whole reveals French influence perhaps transmitted via England.

BIBLIOGRAPHY

M. Blindheim: *Norwegian Romanesque Decorative Sculpture, 1090–1210* (London, 1965)

E. B. Hohler: 'The Capitals of Urnes Church and their Background', *Acta Archaeol.* [Copenhagen], xlvi (1975), pp. 1–60

P. Anker: 'Høymiddelalderens skulptur i stein og tre', *Norges kunsthistorie*, ii (Oslo, 1981), pp. 126–85

Age of Chivalry: Art in Plantagenet England, 1200–1400 (exh. cat., ed. J. Alexander and P. Binski; London, RA, 1987), nos 299–306

MARIT NYBO

Trony. Term for a painted character study of a head in exotic dress. Tronies were produced mostly in the Netherlands in the 17th century, mainly in Leiden by such artists as Rembrandt, Jan Lievens and Gerrit Dou.

Troost, Cornelis (*b* Amsterdam, 8 Oct 1696; *d* Amsterdam, 7 March 1750). Dutch painter, draughtsman and printmaker. He was the most important Dutch artist of the 18th century; he received many commissions (the catalogue by Niemeijer contains 925 numbers). Although he generally looked back to the genre scenes of the Dutch 17th-century masters, his satirical paintings earned him the nickname 'the Dutch Hogarth' after his English contemporary. His work shows no stylistic development, despite his versatility in choice of subject-matter and technique.

Information about Troost's life is restricted to 20th-century archival investigations and the information Troost gave to his biographer van Gool (1750–51). His father was a goldsmith. Troost was an actor at the Amsterdam Theatre (*c*. 1717–20 and 1721–4), and after 1724 he was a painter by profession. He married Susanna Maria van (der) Duyn in 1720 in Zwolle, and they had eight children;

he made many portraits of his daughters (his two sons died young) and gave drawing instruction to two of them, Sara and Elisabeth (who later married Cornelis Ploos van Amstel). His only pupil outside his family was Jacobus Buys, who stayed with him for two years. Troost's last known painting dates from 1749. He was buried in the Nieuwe Kerk in Amsterdam.

1. Life and work. 2. Critical reception and posthumous reputation.

1. LIFE AND WORK.

(i) Portraiture, c. *1723*–c.*1732.* Troost began his artistic career *c*. 1723 as a portrait painter, having studied for two-and-a-half years with Arnold Boonen, in his day a much sought-after portrait painter who had been taught by Godfried Schalcken. Boonen was a good teacher who had many pupils, including Jan Maurits Quinkhardt, Philip van Dijk and Cornelis Pronk, to whom he passed on characteristics of Schalcken's style; vestiges of Schalcken's candlelight and chiaroscuro effects are evident in Troost's work. It is not known whether Troost had any additional training, but he did study independently, making copies after Abraham Bloemaert, Anthony van Dyck, Rubens, Jacob de Wit, Philip Wouwerman and Jan Steen.

Troost soon developed a personal style of lively portraiture, combining fine brushwork in imitation of Schalcken and his own free use of colour. The pose of the sitters is usually relaxed, the expression on their faces alert and their setting informal. His subjects were diverse: men, women, children, families (in particular conversation pieces), double portraits, group portraits and self-portraits. His first commission was for the *Inspectors of the Collegium Medicum* (1724; Amsterdam, Rijksmus.) and group portraits were to form a considerable part of his commissioned work. His *Anatomy Lesson of Professor Roëll* (1728; Amsterdam, Hist. Mus.) is compositionally very similar to Rembrandt's *Anatomy Lesson of Dr Joan Deyman* (Amsterdam, Rijksmus.), which was then in its original state. In all his portraits his models were Dutch, with the exception of the Italian composer and violinist Pietro Antonio Locatelli, who lived in Amsterdam much of his life and whose portrait Troost included in a mezzotint of 1733–6. Drawn and painted studies exist for many of his portraits, and he also frequently worked with pastel, developing his own technique of applying pastel to a preliminary drawing in chalk, which he then filled in, heightened or worked up with either gouache or watercolour. Troost used this mixed technique throughout his career.

(ii) Other works, c. *1732*–c. *1749.* After 1732 Troost concentrated more on drawing and painting theatrical scenes. As a former actor he had first-hand experience of the theatre, and he was also connected with the Amsterdam Theatre as a painter of stage sets, none of which has survived. The bold brushwork appropriate to this type of work is also visible in his other work, combined with his usual, more subtle technique. Many 17th-century Dutch artists had preceded Troost in 'illustrating' farces and comedies, notably Steen, an important source of inspiration to Troost who revived the genre. Troost placed his sitters in an everyday setting, such as a domestic interior, a town, inn or country house, which gives them the

appearance of 17th-century genre scenes rather than contemporary stage sets.

Occasionally Troost satirized established literature, as in the undated drawing of the *Death of Dido* (Haarlem, Teylers Mus.), a parody of Virgil's *Aeneid* and presumably based on Pieter Langendyk's satirical play *De Eneas van Virgilius in zyn zondagse Pak: Vierde boek* ('Virgil's Aeneas in his Sunday best: fourth book'). For his theatrical illustrations, Troost probably consulted Charles Lebrun's *Méthode pour apprendre à dessiner les passions* (1698; Dutch trans., 1728), to depict characteristic features of actors. Lebrun's book was considered a standard reference for artists as well as actors.

Troost also painted interiors and outdoor scenes. His genre paintings, like his theatrical scenes, are, via Boonen, based on 17th-century masters; his *Feast of St Nicholas*, known only by a print after the original, is unmistakably based on a similar depiction by Steen (Amsterdam, Rijksmus.). Troost's outdoor scenes, the first dating from 1737, depict parks, country inns or city gardens, rather than extensive landscapes. One of the finest examples of these is his *Amsterdam House Garden* (Amsterdam, Rijksmus.; see fig. 1).

Military subjects feature prominently in Troost's work: battles, attacks, cavalry or infantry standing guard and, especially, officers in the guard-room, smoking and playing cards, their martial behaviour providing him with ample material for satire. The first of these is a drawing of 1736 (Haarlem, Teylers Mus.). After 1740 he painted military scenes more frequently, possibly due to increased military

activity as a result of the Austrian War of Succession. Again, the subject originated with Dutch 17th-century painters such as Willem Duyster, Pieter Codde and Hendrick Pot. But whereas these artists depicted such scenes as if from everyday life, encouraging a direct link between the spectator and the scene, Troost created a certain distance by appearing to set his scenes on a stage.

Troost made several large-scale decorative works, of which only one finished piece, from the house at Herengracht 214, and several designs have survived. This finished piece was restored after the demolition of the house in 1917 and transferred to the bank now occupying the same site. The decorations, a ceiling (signed and dated 1734) and two overdoors, are compositionally reminiscent of de Wit's work, although the colouring and detail are Troost's own. The theme has not been satisfactorily identified: an unknown Roman hero is conducted into heaven by Venus (on the ceiling), while his mourning widow is comforted by Minerva. On each overdoor is a painted bust being adorned with garlands by cherubs and set against a marbled ground. Troost also painted series of seasons and months of the year, but these are no longer intact.

It is known that Troost made other history paintings: biblical and mythological subjects and scenes from ancient history, fragments from literature (e.g. several drawings of Don Quixote) and allegories. It is not clear how much Troost valued this genre, which at the time was so highly respected by the academies and classicists, but the existence of such works does raise questions about his theory of art, especially as he excelled in less exalted subjects. The one remaining clue as to Troost's theoretical attitude is obscure: in the gouache *Two Kinds of Art* (Amsterdam, Rijksmus.) Troost depicted a confrontation between the *imitatio insipiens* ('ignorant imitation') of vulgar realism and the *imitatio sapiens* (' "knowing" imitation') of Classicism, the meaning of which is no longer clear.

One of Troost's best-known works is a series of five pastels, commissioned by the lawyer and poet Theodoor Snakenburg and depicting seven friends who are getting drunk (1739–40; The Hague, Mauritshuis). The title of the series, *NELRI*, is formed by the initial letters of the Latin titles of each scene, which together chart the stages of the convivial evening: *Nemo loquebatur* ('No-one spoke'), *Erat sermo inter fratres* ('The friends engaged in a conversation'), *Loquebantur omnes* ('Everyone spoke'), *Rumor erat in casa* ('It became tumultuous in the house') and *Ibant qui poterant, qui non potuere cadebant* ('Those who could walk, went; the others fell'; see fig. 2). It has been suggested that through this Troost meant to make fun of some of his friends, but the identity of the drinkers is unproven. Neither is the series related to any known play; possibly it depicts a story in its own right. In the penultimate pastel, the influence of Hogarth's print *A Midnight Modern Conversation* (1734; New Haven, CT, Yale Cent. Brit. A.) is striking; Troost obviously knew many of Hogarth's prints and here he has freely copied some of Hogarth's characters.

Hogarth is one of the few foreign artists whose influence can be seen in Troost's work. Otherwise, foreign influence is restricted to that of French classicist architectural and ornamental designers such as Daniel Marot (in the *NELRI* series). There are several striking parallels in the

1. Cornelis Troost: *Amsterdam House Garden*, oil on canvas, 660×560 mm, *c.* 1743 (Amsterdam, Rijksmuseum)

2. Cornelis Troost: *Ibant qui poterant, qui non potuere cadebant* ('Those who could walk, went; the others fell'), pastel and gouache, 565×725 mm, from *NELRI*, 1739–40 (The Hague, Koninklijk Kabinet van Schilderijen 'Mauritshuis')

careers of Hogarth and Troost: both began as portrait painters and revived the conversation piece and the comical genre; both were interested in theatre and favoured significant details in their scenes. Yet there are many differences between the two: Hogarth depicted human vice moralistically, whereas Troost's treatment was humorous; Hogarth was fierce, Troost a good-natured man; Hogarth made prints after his paintings, Troost engraved seldom. Furthermore, there seem to be few borrowings from Hogarth in Troost's work. It is unfortunate that Troost's series of pastels *Five Scenes from the Life of a Libertine*, which was possibly based on Hogarth's *Rake's Progress* (London, Soane Mus.), disappeared after 1847 as this could have shed more light on the relationship between the two artists. There is, nevertheless, one other tentative link between Troost and English art: he produced the drawing for the title page of the Dutch edition (1744) of Samuel Richardson's *Pamela*.

2. CRITICAL RECEPTION AND POSTHUMOUS REPUTATION. In his lifetime Troost's paintings sold easily and sometimes he even had to make several copies. Much of his work ended up in collectors' cabinets, notably that of Gerrit Braamcamp. But not only was his work bought in Amsterdam: Snakenburg was a citizen of Leiden. Soon after Troost's death, his paintings were copied into engravings. These prints, manufactured by Jan Punt, Pieter Tanjé, Jacob Houbraken, Simon Fokke and others, were published by Pieter Foucquet jr and were very popular in the Netherlands and abroad. Some of the prints were copied again in Germany and England with adapted texts.

Foreign collectors greatly valued this type of print. Nevertheless, outside the Dutch Republic, Troost's paintings were less popular than the flower-pieces of van Huysum and other contemporary artists.

BIBLIOGRAPHY
J. van Gool: *De nieuwe schouburg der Nederlantsche kunstschilders en Schilderessen*, 2 vols (The Hague, 1750–51/*R* Soest, 1977), ii, pp. 241–59
J. Knoef: *Cornelis Troost* (Amsterdam, 1947)
J. W. Niemeijer: *Cornelis Troost, 1696–1750* (Assen, 1973); review by E. de Jongh in *Simiolus*, vi (1972–3), pp. 76–80
F. Gryzenhout: *Cornelis Troost NERLI* (Bloemendaal, 1993)
P. KNOLLE

Troost, Paul Ludwig (*b* Elbersfeld, 17 Aug 1879; *d* Munich, 21 Jan 1934). German architect and interior designer. He studied under Ludwig Hoffmann at the Technische Hochschule in Darmstadt. After 1901 he worked in Giessen until becoming head of the Munich office of Martin Dülfer. Most of his works in this period were designs for the remodelling of the interiors of private houses. His first work was the interior (*c.* 1905) of the house of the painter Benno Becker at Maria-Theresien Strasse in Bogenhausen, Munich, where Troost designed the complete interior. In 1906, with Carl Jäger and August Biebricher, he won second prize in the competition for the Deutsches Museum, Munich, with a geometrical Biedermeier design. The house that he designed for Rudolf Chillingsworth (1910; destr.) at Prinzregentenufer 24, Nuremberg, was notable for its simple but elegant exterior and the elaborated and colourful, slightly historicist interiors. In 1897 Troost had been one of the founders of the Vereinigte Werkstätten für Kunst im Handwerk, Munich, modelled on English Arts and Crafts precedents. He worked closely with the workshops that executed many of his furniture designs. From 1910 Troost was the principal interior designer of the shipbuilders Lloyds in Germany. He designed the interiors of such luxury liners as the *Europa*, and they were executed by the Vereinigte Werkstätten. He was also responsible for the interiors of Haus Heineken (1917) in Bremen and the Jacobihalle (1925) in Bremen. As an architect he made his reputation in 1931 with the remodelling of the former Palais Barlow, Munich, into the Brown House. Troost had been a National Socialist since 1924 and as a close friend of Adolf Hitler was promoted by him as the first architect of the Reich. Troost's work after 1931 was a celebration of the Nazi party and its ideology. In 1933 work began on the Haus der Deutschen Kunst in Munich (for illustration *see* NAZISM), which was to be a showpiece of Nazi painting and sculpture, and which became an icon of Nazi architecture. Its construction and eventual completion were accompanied by a huge publicity and various ceremonies and festivities, where it was always described as 'Hitler's work'. The large classical colonnade at the front was reminiscent of the Greco-Prussian austerity of Karl Friedrich Schinkel's Altes Museum in Berlin. Although rooted in early 20th-century neo-classicism, Troost was not oblivious to modernist developments, as can be seen from the almost cubist forms and the flat unornamented surfaces of the museum. Troost's remodelling of the Königsplatz, Munich, into a centre for a cult of the dead was begun in 1934. His two Temples of Honour (destr. 1947), commemorating the fallen of the abortive putsch in 1923, were large open classical pavilions, austere and almost barren. Troost did not live to see the completion of these two works. His unfinished works were completed by his wife Gerdy, an interior designer, who remained a close confidante of Hitler and who published *Das Bauen im Neuen Reich* (Bayreuth, 1938–43) in two volumes.

BIBLIOGRAPHY

Thieme–Becker; Wasmuth

B. Miller Lane: *Architecture and Politics in Germany, 1918–1945* (Cambridge, MA, 1968)

R. R. Taylor: *The Word in Stone* (Berkeley, 1975)

W. Durth: *Deutsche Architekten: Biographische Verflechtungen, 1900–1970* (Brunswick, 1986)

                                                                    ☐

Troostwijk, Wouter Johannes [Joannes] **van** (*b* Amsterdam, 28 May 1782; *d* Amsterdam, 20 Sept 1810). Dutch painter, draughtsman and etcher. In 1803 he was admitted to the Amsterdam Tekenacademie where he was a pupil of the director, Jurriaan Andriessen. Despite a highly successful student career that culminated in a gold medal from the Felix Meritis Society in 1807, he was unable to establish himself as a professional artist during the remainder of his very short working life in Amsterdam. Andriessen's studies from nature seem to have been an important influence; van Troostwijk was one of the earliest artists to paint *en plein air*. Although he looked back to 17th-century Dutch landscape art and to the work of his contemporaries, in such paintings as *Landscape in Gelderland* (*c.* 1808; Amsterdam, Rijksmus.; *see* NETHERLANDS, THE, fig. 21) he achieved a totally new lyricism in the rendering of atmospheric effects. *The Raampoortje* (1809; Amsterdam, Rijksmus.) displays a fresh colouristic touch rare in Dutch painting of this period. His *Self-portrait* (*c.* 1810; Amsterdam, Rijksmus.) is equally original in composition and colour. He also produced animal paintings in the manner of Paulus Potter, drawings and a few etchings towards the end of his life. Van Troostwijk died before his considerable talents could be recognized, and, although he has come to be seen as an important precursor of much late 19th-century Dutch painting, he had little influence on his immediate successors.

BIBLIOGRAPHY

J. Knoef: 'Wouter Joannes van Troostwijk', *Elsevier's Geïllus. Mdschr.*, lxviii (1929), pp. 363–74

——: *Tusschen Rococo en Romantiek* (The Hague, 1943), pp. 111–35

S. J. Gudlaugsson: 'Twee onbekende schilderijen van Wouter Johannes van Troostwijk', *Ned. Ksthist. Jb.*, xxi (1970), pp. 371–5

Op zoek naar de Gouden Eeuw: Nederlandse Schilderkunst, 1800–1850 (exh. cat. by L. van Tilborgh and G. Jansen, Zwolle, 1986), pp. 167–9

                                                                    JOOST WILLINK

Trophy. Dedication of the remains of a defeated enemy, usually on or near the battlefield. This custom was practised by the Egyptians and the Sumerians as well as other peoples of the Mediterranean region and the Ancient Near East. Except in the case of some Egyptian and Mesopotamian monuments celebrating important victories, however, it was never accompanied by any special artistic production in these areas. In Greece and Rome, however, the artistic commemoration of a victorious battle became very popular.

The first trophy documented with certainty is Greek: the trophy of the Aiginetans in the Temple of Aphaia, celebrating their victory over Samos (520 BC). Trophies were mentioned with increasing frequency throughout the 5th century BC, but they became less popular in the 4th century BC and the Hellenistic age (323–31 BC). Among some of the Greeks, however, including the Spartans and the Macedonians, the custom of dedicating everything that remained on the battlefield to the gods remained for some time. For the rest of the Greeks the trophy was at once a symbol of victory, an ex-voto and a warning to the enemy. Two types of trophies are known. In the first and more common type the enemy's arms were suspended from a post or cross, arranged as they had been worn by the soldier. This 'anthropomorphic trophy' was commonly connected with the figure of Victory. The second type, the 'cumulus trophy', was a stack of arms often placed on a pile of stones; the earliest form of trophy appears to have been a simple cone of stones. The array of enemy arms displayed in the two types symbolized the dedication

became widespread. The so-called Dacian captive, seated on a pile of stacked arms, may have been used on a triumphal arch in the Forum of Trajan; a variant of this theme was popular during the Renaissance. The two surviving pilasters of the Armilustrium on the Aventine (where arms were consecrated) depict in low relief an impressive display of arms, armour and naval trophies amounting to more than 800 pieces (see fig.). The two so-called Marius trophies, which were brought to the Piazza del Campidoglio, Rome, by Michelangelo, may also date from the Flavian age (AD 69–96).

Arms and trophies became a motif in friezes and metopes at the end of the Roman Republic. The fragments in the Museo Capitolino, Rome, which may have come from the area of the Circus Flaminius, represent naval trophies with the usual repertory of prows, anchors and rudders, together with sacrificial symbols. Innumerable types of trophies are represented on coins. From the 15th century a marrying of the iconography of the panoply and the grotesque was to be popular in Renaissance architecture and painting, for example the three carved marble doorframes of the Porte della Guerra in the Palazzo Ducale, Urbino (late 15th century; see URBINO, §4).

BIBLIOGRAPHY

J. Durm: *Die Baukunst der Römer* (Stüttgart, 1905), pp. 733–45

K. Woelcke: 'Beiträge zur Geschichte des Tropaions', *Bonn. Jb. Rhein. Landesmus. Bonn & Ver. Altertfreund. Rheinlande*, cx (1911), pp. 127–235

E. Pottier and G. Lafaye, eds: *Dictionnaire des antiquités grecques et romaines*, v/2 (Paris, 1919), pp. 497–518

G. Picard: *Trophées d'Auguste à Saint-Bertrand-des-Comminges* (Toulouse, 1947)

——: *Les Trophées romains* (Paris, 1959)

LUCA LEONCINI

Trophies represented on two pilasters from the Armilustrium on the Aventine Hill, Rome, marble, h. 3.2 m, *c.* AD 69–*c.* 96 (Florence, Galleria degli Uffizi)

of the defeated who had worn them to the gods who had given the victory. The first example of Victories connected with trophies was possibly the one on the balustrade of the Temple of Athena Nike on the Acropolis at Athens (late 5th century BC). In the Hellenistic period naval trophies were given a special monumentality through the display of the great bronze beaks from the prows of captured ships. Later, the cumulus trophy entered the artistic repertory.

The trophy was imported into the Roman world from Greece; there is no evidence of its existence in Etruscan art. The column in the Forum Romanum commemorating the victory of C. Duilius at Mylae in 260 BC and the trophy erected on a battlefield by Cn. Domitius and Q. Fabius Maximus in 121 BC (Florus: *Epitome* I.xxxvii.6) are the first isolated examples of a custom alien to the Latin world. It became popular as an art form in the Roman world mainly because it lent itself well to the celebratory and commemorative purposes dear to Roman art. In particular it was naturally suited to the decoration of the two main types of Roman commemorative architecture, the triumphal arch and the spiral column. The anthropomorphic trophy appeared both in reliefs and sculpture in the round, the latter form documented by numismatic evidence. A scheme often repeated in arches, early examples being those at Carpentras (1st century AD) and Glanum (?1st century BC), was the statue of the defeated barbarian; this

Tropinin, Vasily (Andreyevich) (*b* Karpovo, Novgorod province [now Novgorod region], 30 March 1776; *d* Moscow, 15 May 1857). Russian painter. He was born a serf and in 1790 was apprenticed to a pastrycook in St Petersburg. From 1793 he attended classes at the Academy of Art there, in 1799 becoming a pupil of the portrait painter Stepan Shchukin (1762–1828). In 1804 he was sent to work as a pastrycook and manservant on an estate in the Ukraine owned by his master, General Morkov. Tropinin's Ukrainian period (1804–21) was interrupted by frequent, often protracted, visits to Moscow. During these years he copied a great deal, drew landscapes from nature and also painted religious subjects. His early style is painterly and distinguished by freedom of execution and skill in the use of colour, but the compositions are derivative and the drawing weak: *The Spinner* (1820s), *The Lacemaker* (1823), *Wedding in the Village of Kukavka, Podolsky Province* and *Girl with a Bird* (all Moscow, Tret'yakov Gal.). Portraiture, however, began to take on a more important place in his work; the best of this period is the *Portrait of Arseny, the Artist's Son* (1818; Moscow, Tret'yakov Gal.), especially notable for its use of colour. Tropinin captured perfectly the child's spontaneous vision of the world, his sensitive spirit and openness. While in Moscow from 1813 to 1818, he portrayed a series of important cultural figures that brought him great popularity. He was freed from serfdom on 8 May 1823 and shortly thereafter he became a nominee to the Academy for his paintings *The Lacemaker*, the *Old Beggar Man* (1823; St Petersburg, Rus. Mus.) and *Portrait of the Engraver Yegor Skotnikov*. In 1824 he became an Academician with *Portrait of the Medallist Karl Leberecht*.

Tropinin then settled in Moscow, where he remained until the end of his life. Most of his subsequent work consists of portraits of his contemporaries: art critics and the bourgeois intelligentsia, merchants, businessmen and the common people. His portraits are imbued with a sense of the Russian national character and his images are full of goodwill, creative energy and artistry. He depicts human nature not critically but poetically, emphasizing the positive side of humanity. The concept of the creative personality is particularly convincing in the portrait of *Aleksandr Pushkin* (1827; Pushkin, A. S. Pushkin Mus.). In spite of the poet's ordinary dress (unfastened shirt and loose dressing gown), the image is clearly one of a sublime intelligence. The disorder of his clothes and informality of his pose express an air of independence and hint at an extraordinary character. During the 1820s and 1830s Tropinin produced several notable portraits, including *Guitarist in a Russian Blouse* (1820; Moscow, Glinka Cent. Mus. Musical Cult.) and the painter *Karl Bryullov* (1836; Moscow, Tret'yakov Gal.). These are characterized by freely applied paint, complex elaboration of colour, precise composition and naturalism.

Notable among the portraits of merchants is that of *V. M. Yakovlev* (1830; Moscow, Tret'yakov Gal.). Tropinin also painted a whole range of lesser known figures: cultured patrons, energetic entrepreneurs and eager philanthropists. From 1830 to 1849 he produced large group portraits, but some of these are lacking in compositional coherence.

During the last phase of his career, Tropinin tended to repeat compositional devices, such as the motif of the window opening on to a landscape used as the background to a portrait. His colours were less bright, but there was an increase in plasticity and a thorough attention to detail. The most important work of this time is the well-known *Self Portrait by a Window with View of the Kremlin* (1844–6; Moscow, Tret'yakov Gal.), an informal depiction of the artist, dignified by particular details of composition and chiaroscuro modelling. The view of the Kremlin suggests Tropinin's quintessentially Russian character. He was also a master of female portraiture; poetry, lyricism and simplicity are characteristic of his early style, while in later works there is greater realism (e.g. *Portrait of N. Zubova*, 1834; Moscow, Tret'yakov Gal.). In the female portraits of the final period the element of genre painting is more marked, with attention to accessories and idealization of types, as in the *Treasurer's Wife* (1841; St Petersburg, Rus. Mus.) and *Girl with a Candle* (1850; Moscow Tret'yakov Gal.). In 1971 the Museum of V. Tropinin and the Moscow Artists of his Time was opened in Moscow.

BIBLIOGRAPHY
A. Amshinskaya: *Vasily Andreyevich Tropinin, 1776–1857* (Moscow, 1970)
——: *V. A. Tropinin* (Moscow, 1976)
M. Rakova, ed.: *Vasily Andreyevich Tropinin: Issledovaniya i materialy* [Vasily Andreyevich Tropinin: research and documentation] (Moscow, 1982)
E. Petinova: *Vasily Andreyevich Tropinin* (Leningrad, 1986)

G. A. PRINTSEVA

Troppa, Gerolamo (*b* Rocchette, Sabina, 1630; *d* ?Rome, after 1710). Italian painter. Though evidently an artist of some standing in late 17th-century Rome, with the title of 'cavaliere' and several documented pupils, little is now known of his life and work. His training, both from his teacher Lazzaro Baldi and at the Accademia di S Luca (where he was a pupil in 1664), was in the Carracci tradition. This is evident in the *Adoration of the Shepherds* (Dublin, N.G.). His style shows affinities with that of Carlo Maratti, but he was also interested in Giacinto Brandi, and still more so in Pier Francesco Mola and in Salvator Rosa, whose influence can be seen in such works with a romantic flavour as *Virgil and Homer* (*c*. 1668; Copenhagen, Stat. Mus. Kst). The *Flora* in the Palazzo Chigi in Rome and the two canvases of scenes from the *Life of St Thecla* at S Giuseppe in Ferrara also date from *c*. 1668. The artist's later style shows him moving towards the Baroque, intensifying his relationship with Brandi and with the artists who developed Bernini's later art, such as Giovanni Battista Gaulli. Troppa collaborated with the latter in the decoration of the oratory of S Marta in Rome (1672), producing two tondi representing *Miracles of St Martha* (*in situ*). His later works in the church of SS Ambrogio e Carlo on the Via del Corso in Rome (1678) are similar in style and approach, as is a painting at Cittaducale (1692) and a banner at Torri in Sabina (1700). His much deteriorated frescoes (after 1710) in S Agata in Trastevere are impossible to evaluate.

BIBLIOGRAPHY
S. Rudolph: 'Un episodio del barocco romano a Ferrara e alcune considerazioni su Gerolamo Troppa', *Mus. Ferrar.: Boll. Annu.*, vii (1977), pp. 22–36
A. Busiri Vici: 'Un dimenticato pittore del tardo seicento: Gerolamo Troppa', *L'Urbe*, vi (1980), pp. 22–8
M. Gregori and E. Schleier, eds: *La pittura in Italia: Il seicento*, ii (Milan, 1989), p. 906

UGO RUGGERI

Troppau, Johann von. *See* JAN OF OPAVA.

Troschel [Tröschel]. German family of draughtsmen and engravers. There is no documentary evidence to confirm that (1) Hans Troschel was the brother of the painter Jakob Troschel (1583–1624), but he is presumed to have been the father of (2) Peter Paul Troschel.

(1) Hans [Johann; Johannes] **Troschel** [Dreschell; Dröschel; Tröschell; Troschell] (*b* Nuremberg, 21 Sept 1585; *d* Rome, 19 May 1628). He trained in Nuremberg with Peter Isselburg, for whom he later worked. *Emperor Matthias's Entry into Nuremberg on 3 July 1612* was one of his first works. Signed and dated engravings and drawings increased after 1616. He worked partly from his own drawings and partly after drawings by Jacques Callot, Bernardo Castello, Matthäus Greuther (1564/6–1638), Hans Hauer (1586–1600), Justinus Hein, Antonio Pomarancio (*c*. 1567–1629), Lorenz Strauch, Alexander Vajani (*c*. 1570–*fl* 1613) and Simon Vouet. As well as portraits and coats of arms he engraved views of Nuremberg, such as the *Town Hall* and *Town Hall with the Wedding Procession of a Nuremberg Patrician*, both after Strauch, occasional prints, genre scenes and themes such as the print commemorating the *Celebration of the Centenery of the Reformation* (1617). His drawings consist mainly of studies of heads and figures, but there are also biblical and allegorical subjects. In the red crayon drawing of a *Head of a Youth* (1618; Erlangen, Ubib.) spiritual tension permeates the form, which has been elaborated with powerful sculptural effect. In 1624 Troschel moved to Rome, where his work was influenced by Francesco Villamena.

BIBLIOGRAPHY

E. Bock: *Die Zeichnungen in der Universitätsbibliothek Erlangen*, 2 vols (Frankfurt am Main, 1929), nos 626–35

F. Redenbacher: 'Deutsche Barockzeichnungen in der graphischen Sammlung der Universitätsbibliothek Erlangen', *Beiträge zur Kunstpflege in Erlangen, 50 Jahre Kunstverein Erlangen, 1904–1954* (Erlangen, 1954), pp. 42–51

W. R. Deusch and F. Gerke: 'Sechzig Handzeichnungen des 16.–18. Jahrhunderts aus einer süddeutschen Privatsammlung' (exh. cat., Mainz, Johannes Gutenberg-U. Kstgesch. Inst., 1964), *Kleine Schr. Ges. Bild. Kst Mainz*, xxi (1964), no. 40

B. Chandler and C. Vincent: 'Three Nürnberg Compassmacher, Hans Troschel the Elder, Hans Troschel the Younger, and David Beringer', *Met. Mus. J.*, ii (1969), pp. 211–19

SONJA WEIH-KRÜGER

(2) Peter Paul Troschel (*b* Nuremberg, *c.* 1620; *d* after 1667). Presumed son of (1) Hans Troschel. Little is known of his artistic career: his only known signed drawing, depicting the *Elisabethkirche* in Breslau [Wrocław, Poland], suggests that he was then living in that city. His work between 1638 and 1667 can be reconstructed by means of engravings dated and signed P. A signed engraving, in the *Reitschule* by G. S. Winter (Nuremberg, 1643), was probably published posthumously.

Troschel produced illustrations for numerous books, for example *Der Römischen Keyser . . .* by Friedrich Hortleder (Gotha, 1645), which includes a copy after Lucas Cranach I's altar in the Stadtkirche at Weimar, and the *Historia Universalis* by C. A. Ruperti, with a title page after Georg Strauch. He also produced portrait engravings, such as those of the Nuremberg citizens *Johann Neudörfer*, *Joachim Nützel*, *Caspar Kress von Kressenstein* and *Johann Volckamer*, church dignitaries, including *Pope Clement IX*, and secular princes, including *Albrecht Alcibiades, Margrave of Brandenburg*. Many of his works were based on originals by Strauch, C. Richter, Lucas Cranach I, Hieronymus Fux and Johann Andreas Graff. The equestrian portrait of *Max Heinrich, Archbishop of Cologne*, for example, and the title page of *Isarcus Academicus* (1643) by Johann Michael Dilherr (1604–69) are based on works by Strauch.

BIBLIOGRAPHY

Bénézit; Thieme–Becker

THOMAS KLIEMANN

Trost, Ottó. *See* KOROKNYAI, OTTÓ.

Trotsky, Leon [Bronstein, Lev (Davidovich)] (*b* Yanovka, Ukraine, 26 Oct 1879; *d* Mexico City, 21 Aug 1940). Russian politician, writer and theorist of Ukrainian birth. He was a leader of the Bolshevik revolution in October 1917 and the People's Commissar of War (1918–25) while intermittently writing on literature and art. As an exile in Siberia between 1900 and 1902 he wrote under the name of Antid Oto (from the Italian *antidoto*) for the Irkutsk newspaper *Eastern Review*, covering figures such as Nietzsche, Zola, Hauptmann, Ibsen, Ruskin, Maupassant, Gogol and Gorky. In 1924 he published his most important work, *Literature and Revolution*, which analysed

in a dazzling rhetorical style the current state of Soviet art and letters. Critical of the experimentalism of Futurists such as Vladimir Mayakovsky and Formalist literary theorists such as Viktor Shklovsky, he also castigated the Proletkult movement on the grounds that it could be no more than a preparatory stage in the evolution of Socialist and eventually Communist culture, which would be classless. 'We stepped into the Revolution', wrote Trotsky, 'while the Futurists fell into it'. He also opposed Vladimir Tatlin's model for a *Monument to the Third International* (1919–20; destr.; *see* TATLIN, VLADIMIR, fig. 2) on the grounds of its Utopianism. Yet he was not wholly unsympathetic to Futurist and avant-garde art and supported the principle that art should make its own way by its own methods, within a framework of sympathy for Communist politics. He was also committed to the idea that the party should not command art. He was heavily attacked in the later 1920s for both his aesthetic and his political views, and he was eventually hounded out of the country by the Stalin faction, for whom 'Trotskyism' was a term of abuse. Finally settling in Mexico, he continued to write on culture and by the late 1930s he had become an influential figure for the American left, publishing important statements in *Partisan Review* in 1938 that emphasized the emancipatory possibilities of art and the importance to art of freedom from bureaucratic control. His defence of a dialectical and social role for art contributed, posthumously, to the discussion of Abstract Expressionism, both in the 1940s and later.

WRITINGS

Literatura i revolyutsiya [Literature and revolution] (Moscow, 1924; Eng. trans., New York, 1925)

'Art and Politics: A Letter to the Editors', *Partisan Rev.*, v/3 (1938), pp. 3–10

A. Breton and D. Rivera [unsigned by Trotsky]: 'Manifesto Towards a Free Revolutionary Art', *Partisan Rev.*, vi/1 (1938), pp. 49–53

BIBLIOGRAPHY

P. N. Siegel, ed.: *Leon Trotsky on Literature and Art* (New York, 1970)

F. Frascina, ed.: *Pollock and After: The Critical Debate* (London, 1985)

B. Taylor: *Art and Literature under the Bolsheviks*, 2 vols (London, 1991–2)

BRANDON TAYLOR

Trotsky, Noy (Abramovich) (*b* St Petersburg, 27 March 1895; *d* Leningrad [now St Petersburg], 19 Nov 1940). Russian architect. He studied (1913–19) at the Academy of Arts, St Petersburg, under Ivan Fomin, who was an influence throughout his career. From 1919 to 1921 he attended the Second Polytechnical Institute, Petrograd, where he was taught by Andrey Belogrud. As a student he successfully took part with L. M. Tverskoy (1899–1972) in competitions in Petrograd, producing for example designs for the Crematorium (1919), people's platforms (1919) and the *thermae* on Vatny Island (1920), all of which verge on the extreme of romantic symbolism and reveal the influence of Piranesi's etchings. His design (1923; unexecuted) for the Palace of Labour, Moscow, was awarded first prize and earned wide recognition for his revolutionary style.

In the mid-1920s Trotsky sought to reconcile his ideal of romantic monumentality with Constructivism, filling plain outlines with intensely dynamic and symbolic elements, in the manner of Suprematism. He achieved this link between functional logic and the impact of dynamically organized forms in a series of industrial projects, such as the Bely Bychok Glassworks (1925–9), near Cherepovets, and the Leningrad Meat Combine (begun in 1927). The House of Soviets of the Moskovsky–Narvsky District (1931–4), St Petersburg, which spreads horizontally along a spacious square, recalls the expressive combination of plain shapes that he had used in the refrigeration block in the Leningrad Meat Combine. The logic of the asymmetrical composition is determined by the context of the surroundings, while the dynamic quality of the contrasting extended horizontals and vertical towers is romantic and closer to the 'arkhitektona' of Malevich than to the analytical methods of the Constructivists.

In the Kirov Palace of Culture (1930–37; with S. N. Kazak (1899–1949)) on Vasil'yevsky Island, St Petersburg, the complex functional structure is clearly expressed by the formation of the blocks into three spatial planes, all interconnected but with their own internal consistency. The huge middle plane, connected to the main hall, is symmetrical, while the sprawling mass of the first plane, and the third plane, which includes a tall tower, are asymmetrical. During construction, in response to changing taste, heavy decorative forms were added, but the Suprematist principles remain perceptible. In the late 1930s Trotsky adopted the pervasive historicism, particularly a grotesque exaggeration of Piranesian forms exemplified by the public centre (1937–41) in Moskovsky Prospect, St Petersburg, where the dramatization of form apparent during his period of revolutionary romanticism becomes a hard geometrical regularity, characterized by the dense, eight-storey columns of the façade.

WRITINGS
'Tvorcheskiy otchyot' [Creative account], *Arkhit. SSSR*, 4 (1935), pp. 59–63

BIBLIOGRAPHY
L. A. Il'in: 'N. A. Trotsky', *Arkhit. SSSR*, 2 (1941), pp. 22–33
N. M. Ol': 'Pocherk bol'shogo mastera' [The hand of a great master], *Stroitel'stvo & Arkhit. Leningrad.*, xi (1975), pp. 46–8

A. V. IKONNIKOV

Trotti, Giovanni Battista [il Malosso] (*b* Cremona, 1556; *d* Parma, 11 June 1619). Italian painter and architect. He was the last important exponent of Cremonese Mannerism. He was a pupil of Bernardino Campi and inherited his workshop. The cold, brilliant colours and enamel-like surfaces of Trotti's first recorded works, the *Sacrifice of Melchisedek* and the *Gathering of Manna* (both Pralboino Parish Church), closely follow Bernardino's style. More influential, however, were the works of Antonio Campi, seen, for example, in the detailed use of light in the *Beheading of St John the Baptist* (1590; Cremona, Mus. Civ. Ala Ponzone), and especially Bernardino Gatti. From the latter Trotti derived the elements of Correggio's style that appear in his work from the early *Annunciation* (Casalmaggiore, S Chiara). First-hand knowledge of Correggio's work in Parma is reflected in the *Nativity* (1584; Carate Brianza, SS Ambrogio e Simpliciano). He also absorbed a special interest in landscape from the Flemish painters he met in Parma. From 1587 he participated in the decoration of S Pietro al Po, Cremona. His busy workshop executed an impressive series of commissions in Cremona and the neighbouring regions, for example at Salò Cathedral (*c.* 1590) and S Sisto, Piacenza (1603). To cope with the

enormous quantities required many of his designs were executed by pupils, but he signed the finished paintings. In the early 17th century he was employed as a painter, architect and interior designer by members of the Farnese family in Parma, for example on the decoration of the Palazzo del Giardino (now Palazzo Ducale), and was awarded the title Cavaliere. He often returned to Cremona, for example to work on the cathedral's altar of the Holy Sacrament, design decorations in honour of Philip III, King of Spain, and Margaret of Austria, and supervise his workshop, especially in the decoration of the Oratory of the Risen Christ in S Luca, Cremona.

BIBLIOGRAPHY
C. Baroni: 'Il Malosso e il suo ambiente', *Emporium*, 615 (1946), pp. 109–22
A. Puerari: *La Pinacoteca di Cremona* (Florence, 1951), pp. 97–102
M. di Giampaolo: 'Per il Malosso disegnatore', *A. Illus.*, vii (1974), no. 57, pp. 18–35
——: 'Una scheda per il Malosso', *Ant. Viva*, xv/5 (1976), pp. 20–21
——: 'A Drawing by Malosso at Oxford and Some Additions to his Oeuvre', *Master Drgs*, xv (1977), pp. 28–31
I Campi e la cultura artistica cremonese del cinquecento (exh. cat., ed. M. Gregori; Cremona, Mus. Civ. Ala Ponzone, 1985), pp. 238–48
M. Tanzi: 'Qualche aggiunta al Malosso e alla sua cerchia', *Prospettiva*, 40 (1985), pp. 82–5
——: 'Malosso e "dintorni": Dipinti e disegni', *Prospettiva*, 61 (1991), pp. 67–74

MARCO TANZI

Trouard, Louis-François (*b* Paris, 1729; *d* Paris, 1794). French architect. He studied at the Académie d'Architecture, Paris, and after winning the Prix de Rome in 1753 he travelled to Italy, where he was interested in both Classical and Baroque architecture. On his return to France his father, Louis Trouard (*d* 1763), a prosperous marble supplier in the offices of the Bâtiments du Roi, commissioned him to build a large house (1758) in the Rue du Faubourg-Poissonnière, Paris. Its plain ashlar façade was one of the first in Paris to feature Néo-Grec ornament, here in the form of panels decorated with the Greek key pattern.

By the early 1760s Trouard was working as Inspecteur of external works at the château of Versailles, dealing with some 40 buildings occupied by court staff. Later he served as municipal architect of Versailles and worked for the Economats, a state department presided over by Louis-Sextus de Jarente de la Bruyère, Bishop of Orléans, through whom he received several commissions. These included St Symphorien (1765–70) at Montreuil, near Versailles, an early example of the trend towards an austere, Early Christian type of basilica without transepts; it has an uninterrupted coffered barrel vault carried by a Doric colonnade continued as engaged columns around the apse, above which the coffered vault is decorated with rosettes. Trouard also built the austere Chapelle des Catéchismes in the apse of St Louis in Versailles. His other main church commission was the reconstruction (1766–73) of the façade of Orléans Cathedral in a modified Gothic style, begun by Robert de Cotte at the instance of Louis XIV and continued by Jacques Gabriel V, among others. Trouard's scheme for the portals was based on a study of the cathedrals at Beauvais, Rouen, Strasbourg and Toul.

Trouard was elected to the Académie d'Architecture in 1767 and promoted to Contrôleur of external works at Versailles in 1769. He lived in the old Hôtel de Seignelay there, which he had altered both externally and internally, and he carried on an ambitious double career as Contrôleur and architect. Other work included supervising the repairs to the hydraulic Machine de Marly, designed to raise water from the Seine to carry it by acqueduct to Versailles, and he built a small barracks for the Gardes Françaises. Trouard's authoritarianism, however, and his propensity for mixing his own interests with those of the State attracted criticism and he was replaced by Antoine-François Legrand and transferred to Paris. Here he laid out a hôtel behind a façade by Ange-Jacques Gabriel to the west of the Place Louis XV (now Place de la Concorde). He also taught Claude-Nicolas Ledoux, for whom he is said to have obtained his first commissions at Sens and Auxerre.

BIBLIOGRAPHY
M. Gallet: 'Louis-François Trouard et l'architecture religieuse dans la région de Versailles au temps de Louis XVI', *Gaz. B.-A.*, n. s. 6, lxxxviii (1976), pp. 201–18
A. Braham: *The Architecture of the French Enlightenment* (London, 1980, 2/1989)
                              GÉRARD ROUSSET-CHARNY

Troubadour style. A branch of history painting that flourished in the late 18th century and early 19th, primarily in France. Born out of the historical and aesthetic interests of the 18th century, the Troubadour style in France preceded Romanticism, with which it shared its devotion to the past and its most famous exponents: Ingres, Bonington and Delacroix. It adapted the 18th-century fashion for Neo-classical pastiche and prefigured the historicism of 19th-century art in its taste for scenes and characters drawn from the art and history of the Middle Ages. The style was at first confined to the fine arts and appeared in the Paris Salon from *c.* 1800. Later it merged into Romanticism and influenced the decorative artists of the Restoration (1814–30). It was distinct from the Cathedral style, which was manifested primarily in the decorative arts, and from the Gothic Revival, which followed it.

The term 'troubadour' was first applied by the last contemporaries of Romanticism (e.g. Privat d'Anglemont in 1880) to the art of the previous generation. The style arose out of the vogue for medieval literature that was encouraged around 1780 by Louis-Elizabeth de la Vergne, the Comte de Tressan, and his imitators. To illustrate their works, Clément-Pierre Marillier (e.g. *Amadis de Gaule*, 1787) and Jean-Michel Moreau (e.g. *Figures de l'histoire de France*, 1779–85) invented pretty scenes of chivalry, which already combined all the clichés of the Troubadour style: sentimental anecdote, elegant costume and references to earlier art.

The revival of genuine medieval practice in gardening and pageants and the portrayal of French history presented distinct alternatives to earlier antiquarian models. C. Collé's *La Partie de chasse d'Henri IV* (Paris, 1766) and M.-J. Chénier's *Charles IX* (Paris, 1790), incontestably the two most successful illustrated books on 'historic' theatre, make apparent the universality of old costume in the Spanish style, such dress being common to the *fête galante* and to the heroes of the 18th-century French dramatist Pierre Augustin Caron de Beaumarchais. The accuracy of medieval costumes became general under the Empire (Jean Simon Berthélemy, *Costumes de l'Opéra*, 1804; Paris,

Bib.–Mus. Opéra), particularly in the case of Moreau (*Costumes du XIIIe siècle*; Rouen, Mus. B.-A.). The statues of great men (e.g. *Jean de La Fontaine*; Paris, Louvre) and the cartoons of the *Tapestry of the History of France* commissioned by Louis XVI for the Louvre brought early popularity to the heroes of Troubadour iconography, chief among whom was Henry IV.

On the eve of the Revolution, activity in the art dealing world and the tastes of art lovers encouraged a retrospective vein, which Jean-Baptiste Mallet and Nicolas-Antoine Taunay, among others, were to exploit for 40 years. The Revolution interrupted these activities, but revolutionary vandalism, notably at Saint-Denis Abbey, hastened the growing awareness of an artistic heritage that needed to be preserved. It was from Alexandre Lenoir's Musée des Monuments Français and from their studios in the Convent of the Capucines that the first Troubadour painters drew their inspiration. The Louvre, whose collections were swollen with the booty of the French wars, became a fabulous museum of masterpieces, which widened Troubadour influences to include the masters of the Renaissance and, to a lesser extent, early Italian painting. Troubadour painting also grew out of a continuing northern tradition; this developed through Watteau's parodies of Rubens, the *Conversations espagnoles* of Carle Vanloo and the 'fantasy' portraits of Jean-Honoré Fragonard and culminated in pastiches of Dutch and Flemish genre scenes by Jean-Louis Demarne, Mallet and Taunay.

The relationship of Troubadour artists with the past was tinged with ambiguity, for they sought to evoke it as much by the application of medieval artistic techniques (e.g. precision of line) as by the events and customs they depicted, for instance in Pierre Révoil's oil *The Tournament* (1812; Lyon, Mus. B.-A.). But Troubadour paintings were not limited, as has often been supposed, to small-format works on copper or on wood demanding a very refined technique, such as Ingres's *Paolo and Francesca* (1819; Angers, Mus. B.-A.). Such works as François-Marius Granet's *Blanche of Castille Freeing Prisoners* (1801; Paris, Petit Pal.) and Fleury Richard's *Valentine of Milan* (1802; St Petersburg, Hermitage) were planned as large-format works. There were also ambitious compositions which ostensibly represented historic monuments or sites but which were primarily imaginative re-creations animated by characters who might have inhabited them, such as in the *History of Saint-Denis* (1813; Paris, sacristy of St Denis), with scenes by, among others, Etienne-Barthélemy Garnier, Gros and Pierre Guérin. In the same way the Troubadour style was introduced into heroic landscape painting by Alexandre Millin Du Perreux (1764–1843), Hippolyte Lecomte, Taunay and Auguste, Comte de Forbin, who drew the subjects of their paintings from old chronicles. After 1820 François-Alexandre Pernot (1793–1865) specialized in painting 'historiated' monuments.

Equally equivocal is the feminine strain to Troubadour art. It derives in part from the work of such women artists as PAULINE AUZOU, Hortense Haudebourt-Lescot, Sophie Lemire (*b* 1785), Henriette Lorimier (*fl* 1800–14) and Eugénie Servières (*b* 1786) and their famous clients, who included the Empress Josephine (an important patron of Troubadour art) and Caroline, Duchesse de Berry. But Troubadour art more often involved male artists idealizing women in their search for heroines from the past to give their contemporaries some respite from the masculine subject-matter of ancient and modern wars. Such themes included women as the inspiration of creativity (e.g. Louis Ducis's *Arts under the Sway of Love*; Limoges, Mus. Mun.); the mother of heroes (e.g. Jean-Antoine Laurent's *Du Guesclin as a Child*; lithograph by Pierre Laurent, 1739–1809); the unflinching warrior (e.g. Révoil's *Captivity of Joan of Arc*; Rouen, Mus. B.-A.); the troubled lover (e.g. Paul Delaroche's *Filippo Lippi and Lucrezia Buti*; Dijon, Mus. B.-A.); and the tearful queen (e.g. *Death Sentence of Mary Stuart*; Arenenberg Schloss, nr Steckborn, by Jean-Baptiste Vermay (*d* 1833)). As artists often drew their inspiration from historical novels and fictionalized biographies intended for the female public, so women were more often depicted.

The Troubadour iconography was as varied as the historical and literary curiosities of the century in which the illustrated book reached its zenith. Printmakers perhaps gave the most perfect expression to the Troubadour style. Alfred and Tony Johannot produced engravings for the complete works of Sir Walter Scott (1826), Eugène Lami for the *Histoire des ducs de Bourgogne* (1838) by Baron Brugière de Barante and the *Histoire et chronique du petit Jehan de Saintre* (1830) by Antoine de Lasalle.

The Troubadour style, almost the exclusive speciality of Marie-Philippe Coupin de la Couperie (1773–1851), Laurent, Révoil and Richard, affected most Romantic artists at least briefly, particularly the sculptors of historic figures (Edmé-Etienne-François Gois (1765–1836), Félicie de Fauveau, Marie-Christine-Caroline d'Orléans, James Pradier and Mme de Sermezy (1767–1850)). Among these painters the result was very uneven: the works of Antoine Ansiaux (1764–1840), Pierre-Nolasque Bergeret, Merry-Joseph Blondel and Pierre-Auguste Vafflard were often laborious on the large scale that was so well suited to Delaroche (e.g. *Death of Queen Elizabeth*; exh. Paris Salon 1827), to Eugène Devéria (e.g. *Birth of Henry IV*; exh. Paris Salon 1827) and to Alexandre-Evariste Fragonard (e.g. *Francis I and Bayard*, 1819; all Paris, Louvre). The range and essence of the Troubadour style might best be summed up by contrasting the work of Ingres and Delacroix in this manner: the highly elaborate technique of the former in the *Death of Leonardo da Vinci* (1818; Paris, Petit Pal.) against the freer technique of the latter in his *Self-portrait at Ravenswood* (1821; Paris, Louvre), which probably echoes that of *Henry III and the Ambassadors* (1828; London, Wallace) by his friend Richard Parkes Bonington (*see* BONINGTON, RICHARD PARKES, and fig.). Themes taken from the lives of the great artists gave rise to some undeniable masterpieces, for example Fragonard's *Raphael and the Model of the Virgin and Child* (Grasse, Mus. A. & Hist. Provence), in which the Troubadour painters expressed a genuine poetic meditation on the art of their predecessors. Later in the 19th century the painters of the Lyon school such as Claudius Jacquand, Révoil and Richard exploited the historical vein in a systematic but less interesting manner. The Rococo revival exemplified by the work of such artists as Diaz de la Peña brought a more subtle revival of the Troubadour spirit.

BIBLIOGRAPHY
H. Jacoubet: *Le Comte de Tressan et les origines du genre troubadour* (Paris, 1923)
R. Lanson: *Le Goût du moyen âge en France au XVIIIe siècle* (Paris, 1926)
H. Jacoubet: *Le Genre troubadour et les origines du romantisme* (Paris, 1929)
Le Style troubadour (exh. cat., Bourg-en-Bresse, Mus. Ain, 1971)
R. Strong: 'And When Did you Last See your Father?': The Victorian Painter and British History (London, 1978)
M.-C. Chaudonneret: *La Peinture troubadour, deux artistes lyonnais: Pierre Révoil (1776–1852): Fleury Richard (1777–1852)* (Paris, 1980)
Raphaël et l'art français (exh. cat., ed. J. P. Cuzin; Paris, Grand Pal., 1983)
F. Pupil: *Le Style troubadour ou la nostalgie du bon vieux temps* (Nancy, 1985)
M. Pointon: ' "Vous êtes roi dans votre domaine": Bonington as a Painter of Troubadour Subjects', *Burl. Mag.*, cxxviii (1986), pp. 10–17
FRANÇOIS PUPIL

Troubetzkoy [Trubetskoy; Trubetzkoy], Prince **Paolo** (*b* Intra, nr Lake Maggiore, 15 Feb 1866; *d* Suna di Novara, 12 Feb 1938). Italian sculptor. He was the second son of the Russian prince Peter Troubetzkoy and the American lyric singer Ada Winans. He grew up in a family open to the influence of the Milanese '*scapigliatura*' tendency of the artistic avant-garde (*see* SCAPIGLIATI, GLI). Among the visitors to the family villa was the painter Daniele Ranzoni, whose portraits included *Gigi, Piero and Paolo Troubetzkoy* (1873; for illustration *see* RANZONI, DANIELE). Though basically self-taught, he was influenced by the sculptor Giuseppe Grandi who belonged to that school. In such notable early works as his portrait of *Giovanni Segantini* (1896; Verbania, Mus. Paesaggio), Troubetzkoy took from Grandi the busy modelling and impastoed surfaces designed to catch the air and light in different ways. In 1898 he moved to Russia, where his work was close stylistically to that of the Wanderers. He also made friends with Leo Tolstoy, whose portrait he made in busts and small equestrian statues. In Moscow he taught sculpture at the Academy of Fine Arts, and in St Petersburg he produced the equestrian monument (1899–1909) to *Tsar Alexander III* in Znamenskaya Square (now in the State Russian Museum). He won the Grand Prix at the Exposition Universelle of 1900 in Paris and in 1904 contributed a group of bronzes to the Salon d'Automne.

From 1905 to 1914 Troubetzkoy lived in Paris, where he knew and made portraits of many figures of the contemporary cosmopolitan society, including Auguste Rodin, Anatole France, Henry de Rothschild, George Bernard Shaw and Gabriele D'Annunzio. He was most successful in portraiture (of people and animals), and generally in small-scale 'salon' sculpture, producing works of great elegance and refinement. In contrast, his large public monuments show a certain coldness of approach. Between 1914 and 1920 he resided in the USA, where his portrait subjects included Franklin Delano Roosevelt, Enrico Caruso and Mary Pickford. He exhibited in Chicago, Detroit, Washington, San Francisco and Los Angeles. For the latter city he produced a monument (1919–20) to *Gen. Harrison Gray Otis*. In 1921 Troubetzkoy returned to Paris, but finally moved to Italy in 1932. During this period he made portraits of well-known public figures and several female figures characterized by a rigid solidity. In 1923 he produced the World War I memorial for the town of Pallanza (now Verbania).

BIBLIOGRAPHY
V. Pica: 'Artisti contemporanei: Paolo Troubetzkoy', *Emporium*, xii (1900), pp. 2–19
R. Giolli: *Paolo Troubetzkoy* (Milan, 1913)

Sculture del principe Paolo Troubetzkoy (Milan, 1933) [with note by George Bernard Shaw]
Paolo Troubetzkoy (exh. cat., Verbania, Mus. Paesaggio, 1990)

MARICA MAGNI

Troup, F(rancis) W(illiam) (*b* Huntly, Grampian, 11 June 1859; *d* London, 2 April 1941). Scottish architect. Following an apprenticeship with Campbell Douglas & Sellars of Glasgow, he came to the London office of J. J. Stevenson (1883). While there he studied at the Royal Academy Schools, winning the First Silver Medal for Measured Drawings in 1885. After brief spells in the offices of J. M. Brydon and Sir Rowand Anderson, Troup became an Associate of the RIBA in 1889 and set up practice around a year later at 14 Gray's Inn Square, London, from where he practised until his death. Up to World War I Troup's practice was modest, yet of consistently high quality. His early clients were family and friends, and the houses that he built for them always seemed suited to their locality. The Scottish houses were rugged, granite or roughcast (e.g. Rowanlea and Howglen, Huntly, Grampian, 1898; Blucairn, Lossiemouth, Grampian, 1906), whereas the houses in the south of England were looser and more relaxed, often of patterned brickwork, plain tile and natural oak (e.g. Sandhouse [now Kingswood], Witley, Surrey, 1902; Belcoombe, Saxlingham Nethergate, Norfolk, 1904; 20 Old Queen Street, Westminster, London, 1909). It is in some of these English buildings that the influence of J. J. Stevenson is most apparent.

Following the War Troup obtained many consultancies, including King's College, London (1925) and the Royal Albert Hall, London (1928) and thus became a rather more public figure. His most important consultancy was to the Bank of England for which he built a number of facilities in London from 1918. When Sir Herbert Baker was commissioned to rebuild the Threadneedle Street buildings of the Bank of England (1921–36), Troup was retained as consultant. Although Baker never gave Troup any credit for his involvement, it is clear that Troup exercised a steadying influence and that without his presence the destruction of the old buildings would have been more complete. Dedicated to building and skilled in crafts, he was the epitome of the Arts and Crafts architect. Troup's activities included teaching leadwork at the Central School of Arts and Crafts. Master of the Art Workers' Guild and elder statesman of the Society for the Protection of Ancient Buildings, he outlived nearly all his Arts and Crafts contemporaries but never abandoned their principles.

WRITINGS

'Plasterwork', *The House and its Equipment*, ed. L. Weaver (London, n.d.)
'The Influence of Material on Design in Woodwork', *The Arts Connected with Building*, ed. T. R. Davison (London, 1909), pp. 63–79
'External Leadwork', *The Arts Connected with Building*, ed. T. R. Davison (London, 1909), pp. 187–203
'A Distinction between the Crafts and the Arts', *RIBA J.*, xxxi (1923), pp. 107–11

BIBLIOGRAPHY

L. Weaver: 'Sandhouse, Witley, Surrey', *Country Life*, xxviii (27 Aug 1910), pp. 296–302
Obituary, *Builder*, clx (1941), p. 382
N. Jackson: *F. W. Troup, Architect: 1859–1941* (London, 1985)

NEIL JACKSON

Trova, Ernest (*b* St Louis, 19 Feb 1927). American sculptor and painter. An entirely self-taught artist, in 1944 he began to draw and paint in watercolours and in 1946 produced his first casein and latex pictures. Following this, he began to experiment with a variety of media, often incorporating printed words, and also produced collages, assemblages and sculptures. He had his first one-man show in 1959 at the Image Gallery in St Louis, and in 1960 he designed stage sets for plays by Samuel Beckett. His paintings of this period were often of violently distorted human forms, influenced by Willem de Kooning, as in *Egyptian* (1957; artist's col., see Kagan, pl. 11).

In the early 1960s Trova produced a number of triptychs incorporating junk materials, for example *Man, Woman, Child and Dog* (1961; Jerusalem, Israel Mus.). This soon led into the *Falling Man* series, which dominated most of his later career. This figure, which appeared as an androgynous, mechanical object, was initially treated pictorially, as in *Falling Man/Painting* (1963; Washington, DC, N. Mus. Amer. A.), but soon afterwards also in highly polished sculptures such as *Study/Falling Man (Walking Man)* (1964; New York, MOMA), in which the man has a mechanical device attached to his chest. In the early 1970s, developing the theme, Trova began producing hinged figures, such as *Study/Falling Man (A.W.F.)* (1970; New Orleans, LA, Mus. A.), thereby suggesting the dissection of the body. These were followed by a series of open sculptures using planar metal elements, *Profile Cantos*, for example *Profile Canto IV-A* (1973; Wichita, State U., KS, Edwin A. Ulrich Mus. A.). Concurrent with this series was a series of sculptures, including *Gox #9* (1975; St Louis, MO, Laumeier Sculp. Park), consisting of flat geometric shapes intended to be seen frontally.

The *Falling Man* theme again became dominant in Trova's sculpture in the 1980s, and he also made works concerning troubadours and poets, such as *Poet Standing with Skulls and Bird* (1983; priv. col., see Kagan, pl. 156), which incorporated human figures represented in an impressionistic manner. In 1986 the Trova Studio opened in St Louis as a permanent collection for the display of Trova's work.

BIBLIOGRAPHY

L. Alloway: *Trova: Selected Works, 1953–1966* (New York, 1966)
M. H. Bush: *Edward Trova* (Wichita, 1977)
A. Kagan: *Trova* (St Louis, 1987)

□

Troy [Gk. Ilion; Turk. Hisarlık]. Bronze Age and Classical site on the Asiatic side of the south end of the Dardanelles, north-west Turkey. It was excavated by John Brunton (very briefly, 1855–6), Frank Calvert (1863 and 1865), HEINRICH SCHLIEMANN (1870–73, 1878–9, 1882, 1890), Wilhelm Dörpfeld (1893–4), and Carl Blegen for the University of Cincinnati (1932–8). In 1983 excavation of Bronze Age Troy resumed under Manfred Korfmann of Tübingen University; Brian Rose of the University of Cincinnati resumed work on Roman levels in 1988.

The prehistoric mound and later acropolis, now largely dug away, had *c*. 15 m of deposit and a diameter of *c*. 200 m; the lower town, mostly Hellenistic and Roman, covered an area *c*. 1200×800 m. The sequence of nine 'cities' distinguished by Schliemann and Dörpfeld must be understood as a sequence of 9 broad bands within a history of 50 or more building phases. Attention was focused on the site by Schliemann's contention that it was the Homeric city of Troy. He sought the remains of Priam's city in the second city of Troy (some 1000 years too early), with its megara and impressive fortifications, and discovered in 1873 a rich hoard of tools, weapons, vessels and jewellery, which he called 'Priam's Treasure'. Trojan chronology is a matter of some dispute among archaeologists; the dates used here are those established by Blegen.

See also TROAD and fig.

1. EARLY AND MIDDLE BRONZE AGE, TROY I–V (*c.* 3000–*c.* 1800 BC). A promontory in a natural harbour, since silted up, provided plentiful fishing, command of the Dardanelles and the site of the citadel, which was surrounded by a stone wall 5 m thick with a mud-brick superstructure. During Troy II (*c.* 2600–*c.* 2200 BC) the wall stood on top of a stone-faced glacis. Other features of the fortifications varied in different periods: rectangular towers up to 20 m wide, sometimes enclosing gateways, projected from it during Troy I–II; in later periods gates were set further back. Outside the wall of Troy I was a broken stone stele 790 mm high with a heart-shaped human face in low relief, and beside it were two other vertical slabs with saucer-shaped indentations, all three perhaps reused. Adjoining the gate of Late Troy II was a shrine with a horned altar. Knowledge of the area within the walls is incomplete at all periods. The buildings were chiefly of mud brick and built to two traditions, dominant before and after the destruction of Middle Troy II by fire. The earlier tradition had free-standing rectangular buildings subdivided into hall and porch (megara). Some megara reached stately dimensions (up to *c.* 40×13 m) and so probably had a public use. These, with a forecourt, were enclosed within a walled colonnade broken by a formal gateway. More complex buildings lay outside the colonnade. The buildings of the later tradition had small rooms (e.g. 4×4 m), party walls and internal courtyards, all arranged in large blocks separated by narrow streets. The pattern suggests domestic use.

The pottery was adventurous but not highly accomplished. The principal wares were red and black. Characteristic shapes included shallow wheel-made plates (from Troy II onwards), tankards with one and two handles, tall goblets with two flaring handles (wrongly identified by Schliemann as the Homeric *depas amphikypellon*), jugs with rising, even beaked, spouts sometimes cut away above the handle, and a wide range of flasks. These often had two upraised arms and three knobs representing breasts and a navel, with ears, eyes, eyebrows and nose on the neck of the flask or on the cylindrical lid. A few fanciful jugs were in animal shapes. Incised decoration on bowls and plates was common in Troy I.

Tools and weapons were of copper or bronze. Small items of jewellery, such as pins, rings and bracelets, were of copper, bronze, silver or gold. Besides tools and weapons, 'Priam's Treasure' included cups of gold and electrum, gold and silver bottles, bowls and dishes of silver and bronze, a bucket, vat and shallow pan of copper or bronze, six silver ingots, six gold bracelets, three gold

Troy, 'Priam's Treasure', jewellery from Troy IIg, *c.* 2400 BC; as worn by Mrs Heinrich Schliemann in a steel engraving from *The Queen and Lady's Newspaper* (31 March 1877)

headdresses (two with elaborate pendant decoration), four gold basket-earrings with pendant decoration and 56 gold shell earrings (including six with gold granulation), together with sequins, studs and, apparently, 8700 beads of gold (see fig.). The authenticity of the discovery has been questioned, but excavations since 1873 at Troy and elsewhere have shown all the material to be stylistically correct for the period. The circumstances and records of the discovery tend to confirm its authenticity, although the jewellery could conceivably have been an addition. Most of the objects disappeared from the Pergamonmuseum, Berlin, in 1945, and in 1993 the Pushkin Museum of Fine Arts in Moscow admitted that it held them. Bone and stone were important materials to the ancient Trojans, but only four magnificent shaft-hole axes (one of lapis lazuli) are of artistic interest. More than 15 contemporary sites are known in the Troad, the vicinity of Troy.

2. LATE BRONZE AGE, TROY VI–VII (*c.* 1800–*c.* 1100 BC). By the early 2nd millennium BC the citadel was twice the size of Troy II, with a finely built circuit wall. Its substructure of large blocks of masonry stood 6 m high with a mud-brick superstructure and internal parapet. Shallow offsets marked its outer face at regular intervals of 9 m, and four gates provided access to the interior. Flanking the main gate on the south side was a tower, entered from the top of the wall, containing two

pillars on a stone base that probably had cultic significance; four stelae stood against the outside of the same tower. Two further towers adjoined the circuit wall; the one at the north-east corner contained a staircase leading down to a rock-cut well. Buildings within the citadel stood on concentric terraces of which the highest were removed by levelling in Roman times. All the buildings were of stone, and in level VI they were free-standing. A few were in megaron style, up to 25×17 m, but others were rectangular, with the entrance in the long side, or even L-shaped. Staircases suggest the presence of second storeys or flat roofs; one building, 13×15 m with twelve stone column bases, may have had a central nave, clerestory and two aisles. Towers and some interior buildings were trapezoidal in plan, their sides converging towards the centre of the citadel. Troy VI was destroyed c. 1300 BC. In the succeeding periods Troy VIIa and VIIb the citadel walls remained standing but the interior was rebuilt. The interior rebuilt in VIIa recalled its handsome predecessor, but it was destroyed c. 1250 BC. During VIIb the site was covered with multi-chambered houses with small rooms, thin walls and narrow, winding streets; it was abandoned c. 1100 BC or later.

The indigenous pottery was in two principal wares, Gray and Tan 'Minyan' ware. There was some legacy from the Early Bronze Age, but much was new. Ring bases and pedestals appeared under cups, bowls and jars. Bowls acquired a characteristic concave profile; rising spouts and beak spouts on jugs virtually disappeared. Decoration was infrequent, the most common form being incised wavy lines. Mycenaean imports appeared c. 1500 BC, inspiring clumsy local imitations; they became numerous during Troy VI, but sharply decreased in Troy VII. Handmade pottery with south-east European affinities appeared in VIIb: first a coarse ware with finger-impressed decoration, and later a ware ornamented with pointed, upturned knobs and fluting. Little metalwork survives from this period, although there is evidence for arrowheads, double axes, pickaxes, sickles and a small scale of armour. Luxury goods included alabaster sword-pommels, faience and ostrich egg.

The historical identification of the site with Troy and the historicity of the Trojan War remain unproven, and neither archaeology nor contemporary records provide direct confirmation. Blegen ascribed the destruction of Troy VI to an earthquake, and that of Troy VIIa to an Achaean attack; but recent work suggests that, if an earthquake occurred, it was VIIa that suffered, and that only VI, not VIIa, antedates the fall of the Mycenaean palaces. At least 16 contemporary sites are known in the Troad, including a burial ground, possibly Mycenaean, on the shore of Beşika Bay.

3. CLASSICAL SITE, TROY VIII–IX (c. 700 BC–c. AD 400). The citadel walls of Troy VI–VII, still visible in VIII, were added to and repaired, but little remains of the citadel interior. The Hellenistic and Roman site, Troy IX, is better known. On the western half of the acropolis were a sanctuary, a grandstand, a possible temple on the summit and other buildings. The eastern half was redesigned in the period from Augustus to Claudius (30 BC–AD 55). A paved enclosure (110×90 m) was surrounded by a stoa

and contained a Doric temple of Athena, a well with circular lantern and subterranean access, and cultic buildings now too fragmentary to be identified. To the south lay a theatre, the bouleuterion, agora, palaestra and a built-up town area; to the east was a Roman theatre set in the hillside. The temple of Athena had been almost entirely plundered long before Schliemann's arrival, but architectural fragments show it to have had a triglyph frieze depicting scenes of combat between Greeks and barbarians, and Helios in a horse-drawn chariot. There was a rosette frieze around the doors and walls of the interior.

The pottery and metalwork are unremarkable, although the site has produced its own variety of East Greek Geometric pottery, 'G2–3 ware'. Pyramidal loomweights occur in clay, stone and lead, and discoid or lentoid weights of clay, often stamped with gem impressions, are common. There is a good series of terracotta figurines: Kybele is a frequent subject, often with a lion, but other cultic and secular subjects were also found, and detached female heads are numerous. Votive terracotta plaques show the horseman hero, a heroine, or divine symbols. Coins and inscriptions prove the site to have been Classical Ilion, believed by its inhabitants to occupy the site of ancient Troy.

At some time after AD 350 the Temple of Athena was destroyed, and some of its stones were used in later buildings. Pottery and coins show that the site was re-occupied on a modest scale in the late 12th century and the early 13th. Numerous other sites of Classical and Byzantine date are known in the Troad, of which the most important are Alexandria Troas, Abydos, Dardanos, Gergis, Scepsis, Cebren, Neandria, Assos, Lamponia, Gargara and Antandrus.

BIBLIOGRAPHY
H. Schliemann: *Troy and its Remains* (London, 1874)
——: *Ilios: The City and Country of the Trojans* (London, 1881)
——: *Troja: Results of the Latest Researches and Discoveries on the Site of Homer's Troy, 1882* (London, 1884)
W. Dörpfeld: *Troja und Ilion* (Athens, 1902)
H. Schmidt: *Heinrich Schliemanns Sammlung trojanischer Altertümer* (Berlin, 1902)
C. W. Blegen and others: *Troy: Excavations Conducted by the University of Cincinnati*, 4 vols in 8 pts (Princeton, NJ, 1950–58) and 4 suppl. monographs (Princeton, NJ, 1951–82)
F. W. Goethert and H. Schleif: *Der Athenatempel von Ilion* (Berlin, 1962)
C. W. Blegen: *Troy and the Trojans* (London, 1964)
J. M. Cook: *The Troad: An Archaeological and Topographical Study* (Oxford, 1973)
D. F. Easton: 'Priam's Treasure', *Anatol. Stud.*, xxxiv (1984), pp. 141–69
——: 'Has the Trojan War Been Found?', *Antiquity*, lxix (1985), pp. 188–96
L. Foxhall and J. K. Davies, eds: *The Trojan War: Its Historicity and Context* (Bristol, 1985)
M. J. Mellink, ed.: *Troy and the Trojan War* (Bryn Mawr, PA, 1986)
D. Easton: 'Reconstructing Schliemann's Troy', *Heinrich Schliemann nach hundert Jahren*, ed. W. Calder III and J. Cobet (Frankfurt am Main, 1990), pp. 431–47
——: 'Schliemanns Ausgrabungen in Troja', *Archäologie und historische Erinnerung nach 100 Jahren Heinrich Schliemann* (Essen, 1992), pp. 51–72

DONALD F. EASTON

Troy, de. French family of painters. Antoine de Troy (*b* Toulouse, 1608; *d* Toulouse, 15 Sept 1684) was a painter of modest renown in the Languedoc region. His elder son Jean de Troy (*b* Toulouse, 4 April 1638; *d* Montpellier, 25 June, 1691) established an academy of art in Montpellier.

He was long known only as an academic history painter, but 20th-century research has identified several fine portraits by him on the basis of style, of which the most remarkable is that of *Jeanne de Juliard, Dame de Mondonville* (*c.* 1675–80; priv. col., see Mesuret, 1955, p. 39). Antoine's younger son (1) François de Troy became a fashionable portrait painter in Paris, with a style of portraiture based on Flemish and Dutch models that included van Dyck and Rembrandt. The son of François, (2) Jean-François de Troy, made his name as a painter of portraits, history subjects and tapestry designs, but he is known chiefly for his Rococo 'tableaux de modes', representing fashionable life and amorous encounters.

(1) François de Troy (*b* Toulouse, 9 Jan 1645; *d* Paris, 1 May 1730). He was taught the rudiments of painting by his father, and probably also by the more accomplished regional painter Antoine Durand. Some time after 1662 he moved to Paris to study with the portrait painter Claude Lefebvre and with Nicolas-Pierre Loir, whose sister-in-law, Jeanne Cotelle, he married in 1669. Two years later he was approved (*agréé*) by the Académie Royale and in 1674 was received (*reçu*) as a history painter with a *morceau de réception* that depicted *Mercury and Argus* (Paris, Ecole N. Sup. B.-A.). His known works of this period include tapestry designs for Mme de Montespan, mistress of Louis XIV, and several unexceptional religious and mythological paintings (e.g. *Susanna and the Elders* and *Lot and his Daughters*, both St Petersburg, Hermitage). Early in his career he became friendly with Roger de Piles, who first introduced him to Dutch and Flemish painting. After Lefebvre's death in 1675 de Troy dedicated himself to portraiture in the hope of attracting the same clientele as his late teacher. In 1679 he received his first important commission, for a portrait of the Swedish ambassador *Nils Bielke*, and a year later was commissioned for the portrait of *Anne-Marie of Bavaria*, the bride of the Grand Dauphin. Following these successes, his clients included Mme de Montespan and her descendants, especially her son by Louis XIV, Louis-Auguste de Bourbon, Duc du Maine, and his wife (e.g. *Louise-Bénédicte de Bourbon, Duchesse du Maine*; 1694; Sceaux, Château, Mus. Ile de France). Henceforward de Troy worked continuously in court circles for nearly five decades and was highly praised for his ability to capture the nobility's preoccupation with manners, sartorial modes and social position.

By the mid-1690s de Troy had acquired a reputation as a painter of women. As Dézallier d'Argenville observed, women favoured him for his ability to make them look beautiful. A superb example is his portrayal of *Anne-Marie de Bosmelet, Duchesse de la Force* (1714; Rouen, Mus. B.-A.; see fig.), which is often considered his masterpiece. The somewhat heavy features of the sitter in this painting are enhanced by shimmering silk draperies and the presence of an exotically garbed servant. De Troy's style derived in composition and palette from van Dyck, but was tempered by a French classicizing reserve and grandeur that still characterized the transitional period of the early 18th century. During the Regency his most admired works were the mythological portraits in which he disguised his patrons as Olympian deities such as Venus or Hebe (e.g. *Ceres*, 1724; Paris, Knoedler priv. col.). By

François de Troy: *Anne-Marie de Bosmelet, Duchesse de la Force*, oil on canvas, 1.44×1.11 m, 1714 (Rouen, Musée des Beaux-Arts)

using sensual costuming and attributes, he created an aura of charm and prettification without sacrificing the sitter's individual likeness. Mythological portrayals had existed previously, but his were novel in their combination of realism and sensuality, and therein provided important prototypes for the Rococo portraiture of Hubert Drouais and Jean-Marc Nattier. His other important paintings for the court included *Marie-Adélaïde of Savoy*, bride of the Duc de Bourgogne (1697; Moscow, Pushkin Mus. F.A.); *James Edward Stuart*, pretender to the English throne (1700; Hannover, Niedersächs. Landesmus.); and the *Banquet of Dido and Aeneas* (exh. Salon 1704; priv. col., see Cailleux, p. xv), a historiated portrait depicting more than 40 members of the Duc and Duchesse du Maine's family.

De Troy also executed portraits of the Parisian bourgeoisie. Unlike his competitors and friends Hyacinthe Rigaud, who concentrated on painting for the court, and Nicolas de Largillierre, who painted almost exclusively for the bourgeoisie, he worked readily and frequently for both classes. His portraits of the bourgeoisie, however, differ from those of the court in their greater naturalism, intimacy and reliance on Dutch rather than Flemish formulae. For example, his *Self-portrait* (*c.* 1702; Châlons-sur-Marne, Mus. Garinet) derives its enframing window treatment from the works of Gerrit Dou and the deep, shadowy lighting from Rembrandt. Among other notable portrayals are Watteau's protector *Jean de Jullienne* (1722; Valenciennes, Mus. B.-A.); the famous lute player of the Chambre du Roi *Charles Mouton* (1690; Paris, Louvre); and, commissioned by the Académie, *Jules Hardouin Mansart*, Surintendant des Bâtiments (1699; Versailles, Château).

Around 1700 de Troy began to produce northern-inspired group and family portraits, thus helping to initiate the popular 18th-century subject of figures intimately arranged in contemporary settings, as in the *Family of François de Troy* (c. 1708–10; Versailles, Château, on dep. Le Mans, Mus. Tessé) and the *Magistrate's Family at Home* (c. 1722–5; Paris, Cailleux priv. col., see Cailleux, p. v). He also commemorated historical events such as the Peace of Utrecht of 1715 and the Peace of 1719 for the Echevins of the City of Paris; and to mark the end of the famine in 1709, he produced an ex-voto of Ste Geneviève that was based on an earlier work by Largillierre (the *Echevins of the City of Paris Kneeling before Ste Geneviève*, 1696; Paris, St Etienne-du-Mont).

François de Troy received numerous honours. He advanced in the hierarchy of the Académie, becoming Adjunct Professor in 1692, Professor in 1693, Director from 1708 to 1711 and Assistant Rector in 1722. He participated in the Salons of 1699 and 1704, where he exhibited no less than 24 and 31 works respectively. He ranks, moreover, among the best portrait painters of the late Baroque period, along with Rigaud and Largillierre, with whose works his own are often confused. De Troy's many students included André Bouys (1656–1740), Alexis-Simon Belle and Drouais, as well as his son Jean-François de Troy.

BIBLIOGRAPHY
Mariette
A.-J. Dézallier d'Argenville: *Abrégé de la vie des plus fameux peintres* (1745–52, 2/1762), iv, pp. 219–23
P. Lespinasse and R. Mesuret: 'Documents inédits sur Antoine de Troy et ses fils', *Mém. Acad. Sci., Inscr. & B.-Lett. Toulouse*, vi (1944), pp. 33–61
R. Mesuret: 'L'Age d'or de la peinture toulousaine', *Rev. Hist. & Litt. Languedoc* (1947), pp. 25–32
P. Mesplé: 'Une école de peinture provinciale française au XVIIe siècle: L'Ecole de Toulouse', *Gaz. B.-A.*, xxxv (1949), pp. 187–212
Le Dessin toulousain de 1610 à 1730 (exh. cat. by R. Mesuret, Toulouse, Mus. Dupuy, 1953), pp. 72–9
P. Detroy: *Une Famille de peintres au XIIème et au XVIIIème siècles—Les Detroy* (diss., U. Algiers, 1955)
R. Mesuret: 'Jean de Troy', *Gaz. B.-A.*, xlv (1955), pp. 35–44 [Eng. trans. by R. Mesuret, pp. 64–6]
P. Detroy: 'François de Troy, 1645–1730', *Etud. A.*, xi–xii (1955–6), pp. 213–58 [résumé of dissertation]
J. Cailleux: 'Some Family and Group Portraits by François de Troy (1645–1730)', *Burl. Mag.*, cxiii (1971), pp. (suppl.) i–xviii
The Age of Louis XV: French Painting 1710–1774 (exh. cat. by P. Rosenberg, Toledo, OH, Mus. A; Chicago, IL, A. Inst.; Ottawa, N.G.; 1975–6), p. 74
Largillierre and the Eighteenth-century Portrait (exh. cat., ed. M. N. Rosenfeld; Montreal, Mus. F.A., 1981), pp. 79–81
La Peinture de Langue d'Oc (Aspects de la peinture dans les sociétés de Langue d'Oc de 1700 à 1735) (exh. cat., ed. J. Penet; Flaran, Cent. Cult. Départ. Abbaye Flaran, 1984), pp. 21–4
G. Poisson: 'La Leçon d'astronomie de la duchesse du Maine par François de Troy', *Rev. Louvre*, 34 (1989), pp. 239–44

LAURIE G. WINTERS

(2) Jean-François de Troy (*bapt* Paris, 27 Jan 1679; *d* Rome, 26 Jan 1752). Son of (1) François de Troy. He was first taught by his father, and attended lessons at the Académie Royale de Peinture et de Sculpture. Although he failed to win the Prix de Rome, he was sent to Italy at his father's expense, probably arriving in Rome at the beginning of 1699 and finally returning to Paris in 1706

after long sojourns in Florence and Pisa. None of his paintings from this early Italian period survives. On 28 July 1708 he was both approved (*agréé*) by the Académie Royale and also received (*reçu*) as a history painter, his *morceau de réception* being *Niobe and her Children* (Montpellier, Mus. Fabre). Although officially a history painter, he worked across the genres, with the exception of still-life. As one of the leading painters of the Parisian élite, he satisfied the fashionable demand for erotically charged scenes from the Bible with such paintings as *Susanna and the Elders* (c. 1725; Rouen, Mus. B.-A.). In his *tableaux de modes*, a genre with whose invention he has been credited, he replaced the ambiguity of Antoine Watteau's *fêtes galantes* with a more authentic portrayal of contemporary manners, fashions (*see* UPHOLSTERY, colour pl. XIV, fig. 1) and pastimes, and these paintings (e.g. *Declaration of Love*, 1731; Berlin, Schloss Charlottenburg; see fig.) are now considered his most representative works.

De Troy's contemporary reputation as one of France's finest history painters was built on such works as the *Plague at Marseilles* (Marseille, Mus. B.-A.), commissioned in 1722 by the city of Marseille and popularized in a print by Simon Thomassin in 1727, and *Ste Geneviève and the Aldermen of Paris* (Paris, St Etienne du Mont), painted in 1726 in commemoration of the flooding and resultant famine of the previous year. In 1724, he was commissioned by the Bâtiments du Roi to provide two decorative paintings, *Zephyrus and Flora* and *Acis and Galatea* (both *in situ*), for the Hôtel du Grand Maître (now Hôtel de Ville), Versailles. Numerous other commissions followed, including, in 1734 and 1737, decorative genre paintings for the *petits appartements* of the châteaux of Versailles and Fontainebleau, including the *Oyster Breakfast* (Chantilly, Mus. Condé), *Allegory in Honour of the Children of France* (Versailles, Château) and *Hunt Breakfast* (Paris, Louvre).

In 1736 De Troy was commissioned by the Gobelins factory for a tapestry series of scenes from the story of *Esther*, in which he replaced narrative clarity and readability with a profusion of picturesque and anecdotal detail and brilliant colour effects. The seven large cartoons (two, Paris, Louvre; five, Paris, Mus. A. Déc; oil sketches, Paris, Gal. Cailleux) were exhibited to great acclaim. The tapestry series, first produced between 1738–45, was rewoven at least eight times during the 18th century (e.g. Compiègne, Château). A second commission was the series *Jason and Medea*, begun in 1742, the seven large canvases for which were exhibited at the Salon of 1748.

In January 1738 De Troy was nominated Director of the Académie Française in Rome, where he was not only a popular teacher but also a rich and genial host; the portrait of the *Marquis de Vandières* (1751; Versailles, Château), for example, commemorates the Marquis's stay at the Académie de France during his Grand Tour to Italy in 1750.

BIBLIOGRAPHY
C. Guillaume Baillet de Saint Julien: 'Examens des principaux ouvrages exposés au Louvre, 1748, seconde édition . . ., augmentée de nouvelles notes, et de réflexions sur les tableaux de M. de Troy, in *M**** *Lettre sur la peinture, sculpture et architecture, à M**** (Amsterdam, 1749)
H. Watelet and P. C. Levèsque: *Beaux Arts*, 3 vols (Paris and Liège, 1788–1802), ii

Jean-François de Troy: *Declaration of Love*, oil on canvas, 730×925 mm, 1731 (Berlin, Schloss Charlottenburg)

L. Dussieux and others: *Mémoires inédits sur la vie et les ouvrages des membres de l'Académie Royale de peinture et sculpture*, 2 vols (Paris, 1854–6)
A. de Montaiglon and J. J. Guiffrey, eds: *Correspondance des Directeurs de l'Académie de France à Rome, 1666–1793* (Paris, 1887–1912), iii
G. Brière: 'Jean-François de Troy', *Les Peintres français du XVIIIe siècle*, ed. L. Dimier, ii (Paris and Brussels, 1930) [includes a cat. of de Troy's paintings]
P. Rosenberg: 'Le Concours de peinture de 1727', *Rev. A.*, 37 (1977)
P. Conisbee: *Painting in Eighteenth-century France* (Oxford, 1981)
F. Hamilton Hazlehurst: 'The Wild Beasts Pursued: *The Petite Galerie* of Louis XV at Versailles', *A. Bull.*, lxvi (1984)
M.-C. Sahut: [review of an exhibition of Jean-François de Troy's *L'Histoire d'Esther* at the Palais de Tokyo, Musée d'Art et d'Essai], *Rev. Louvre*, 3 (1985)
E. Goodman-Soellner: *Simiolus*, 17–18 (1987–8)
J.-P. Cuzin: '*Le Déjeuner de chasse* de J.-F. de Troy (1679–1752) peint pour Fontainebleau', *Rev. Louvre*, 1–3 (1991)

□

Troya, Rafael (*b* Caranqui-Imbabura, 25 Oct 1845; *d* Ibarra, 15 March 1920). Ecuadorean painter. He was self-taught as an artist. Between 1870 and 1874 he was appointed as the sole illustrator to a team of German scientists, including the naturalist Wilhelm Reiss and the geologist Alfons Stübel, who undertook volcanic surveys in Ecuador. Stübel trained him to make scientific oil paintings of landscapes *in situ*, emphasizing the details of flora and the exact location of mountains and rivers. A few of the 66 works executed during these years are in the Städtische Reiss-Museum, Mannheim. This scientific vision of the Andean landscape, combined with the freedom of the contemporary Romanticism, created a personal style that changed little and made him one of the most important 19th-century landscape painters in Ecuador. His scientific paintings served as models for such later works as the

Eastern Mountain Range from Tiopullo (1874; Quito, Banco Cent. del Ecuador) and the *Deer Hunt* (1918; Guayaquil, Mus. Antropol. & Mus. A. Banco Cent. del Ecuador). Troya executed portraits of notable Ecuadorean society figures, including the politician and historian *Pedro Moncayo Esparza* (before 1904; Ibarra, Bib. Mun.), and continued to receive commissions from the Church (e.g. *Twelve Apostles, c.* 1912; Ibarra, Metropolitana Cathedral).

BIBLIOGRAPHY
J. M. Vargas: *Los Pintores quitenos del siglo XIX* (Quito, 1971), pp. 64–7
Historia del arte ecuatoriano, 3 (1977), pp. 187–9, 235–6
A. Kennedy Troya: *El pintor Rafael Troya (1845–1920): Catálogo razonado* (Quito, 1984, rev. 1991)
——: *Rafael Troya (1845–1920): Un paisajista ecuatoriano* (MA thesis, New Orleans, Tulane U. LA, 1984)
——: 'Arte y ciencia: Rafael Troya (1845–1920) y los geólogos alemanes Reiss y Stübel', *Bol. Acad. N. Hist.*, cli–ii (1988), pp. 421–55

ALEXANDRA KENNEDY TROYA

Troye, Edward (*b* Lausanne, 12 July 1808; *d* Georgetown, KY, 25 July 1874). American painter of Swiss birth. Before 1822, his father, Jean-Baptiste de Troy, a sculptor of minor fame, moved his family to England, where Edward was instructed in drawing and perhaps painting. The animal painter Jacques-Laurent Agasse knew the family well. Troye wrote in 1857 that he was trained in London by the best masters and stated that he followed the style of George Stubbs and John N. Sartorius. In 1831 Troye arrived in Philadelphia, where he was employed as a magazine illustrator. The following year he exhibited animal subjects at the annual Pennsylvania Academy of Fine Arts exhibition and rapidly found patrons among racehorse owners. His typical works show motionless, unsaddled and riderless animals against a low horizon (e.g. *The Undefeated Asteroid*, 1864; Richmond, VA, Mus. F.A.). Light glistens across the body surface, detailing muscle and bone structure with a skill that received critical acclaim. Many of his works were engraved for publication in the media. From 1849 he taught French and drawing at Spring Hill College, Mobile, AL. In 1855 he left to spend 18 months travelling in Europe and the Near East. His large landscape views of Syria and the Holy Land went on exhibition and were well received. Thereafter he spent 19 years travelling between the major horse breeding centres in Kentucky, Virginia, Ohio and New York.

BIBLIOGRAPHY

J. W. Coleman jr: *Edward Troye: Animal and Portrait Painter* (Lexington, 1958)

K. Barron: 'Edward Troye, Sporting Artist', *Antiques*, cv (1974), pp. 799–807

A. Mackay-Smith: *The Race Horses of America, 1832–1872: Portraits and Other Paintings by Edward Troye* (Saratoga Springs, 1981)

DARRYL PATRICK

Troyen, Rombout van (*bapt* Amsterdam, 15 Dec 1605; *d* Amsterdam, 1656). Dutch painter. He was apprenticed for seven years from *c.* 1615 to Jan Pynas, who influenced his development and introduced him to the painting tradition of Adam Elsheimer. Other artists who affected his style were Jan Pynas's brother Jacob Pynas, and Bartholomeus Breenbergh. After his apprenticeship, van Troyen probably established himself in Amsterdam.

Some 230 paintings have been attributed to van Troyen, many of them biblical or mythological scenes set inside wild grottoes decorated with statues (e.g. *Solomon's Idolatry*, priv. col., see 1979 exh. cat., no. 32). His early work is balanced and well organized both in composition and in the handling of paint, with the figures occupying a relatively large portion of the picture surface. Gradually his compositions become more dramatic in character, with numerous figures set against the background of some imaginary landscape or ghostly cave. Houbraken's *De groote schouburgh* (1718–21) states incorrectly that van Troyen died in 1650 (Marijnen).

BIBLIOGRAPHY

I. Q. van Regteren Altena: 'Apollon cryptogène imaginé par un petit maitre d'Amsterdam, 1641', *Gaz. B.-A.*, lxxxiv (1974), pp. 215–22

Seventeenth-century Dutch Painting: Raising the Curtain on New England Private Collections (exh. cat., ed. J. A. Welu; Worcester, MA, A. Mus., 1979)

M. Marijnen: *Romb. J. van Troyen, een 17e eeuwse meester uit de vergetelheid gehaald* [Romb. J. van Troyen, a 17th-century master rescued from oblivion] (diss., U. Utrecht, 1983)

L. J. WASSINK

Troyes. French city in a loop of the River Seine, préfecture of the Aube département, with a population of 75,000.

1. History and urban development. 2. Art life and organization. 3. Buildings.

1. HISTORY AND URBAN DEVELOPMENT. The Roman settlement of Augustobona was the capital of the Gallic Tricassi, conveniently situated on the road from Lyon to Boulogne. Converted to Christianity in the 3rd century AD, Troyes was ruled by its bishops until the 9th century, when it passed into the hands of the counts of Champagne. They were generous benefactors—Henry I (*reg* 1152–81) 'the Open-handed' endowed 13 churches and 13 hospices. A fortified wall was built around the growing city, canals were dug, and a textile industry and viticulture developed. The Romanesque cathedral was rebuilt from *c.* 1200 after a fire (*see* §3(i)(a) below). The two annual fairs placed Troyes at the hub of European trade in the 12th and 13th centuries and brought it exceptional wealth. The collegiate church of St Urbain, founded in 1262 by Pope Urban IV (*reg* 1261–4), is an example of Champenois Gothic (*see* §3(ii) below). Troyes was the capital of the counts of Champagne until its union with France in the 14th century. It was renowned for its glass-painting workshops, which flourished from the 15th to the 17th centuries, and, in the 16th and 17th centuries, for its sculpture (*see* §2 below). Outstanding examples of local sculpture and glass painting from this period survive in the cathedral, St Urbain, Ste Madeleine (early 13th century; rebuilt 1495–1508), St Pantaléon (1508–50), and in city museums. The fire of 1524 devastated much of the medieval city, but nascent local industry, especially hosiery, financed extensive new building in an imported Italianate style (e.g. the Hôtel de Vauluisant; now Musée Historique de Troyes et de la Champagne) alongside the last flourish of Flamboyant Champenois Gothic (e.g. the Hôtel Jean de Mauroy, *c.* 1550; now Musée de l'Outil). Despite wars, taxation and religious persecution, substantial municipal and ecclesiastical art and architecture, for example the 18th-century Hôtel Dieu (now Musée de l'Hôtel Dieu), attest to the affluence of subsequent centuries. Hosiery manufacturing, rationalized at the Revolution, brought even greater prosperity. Boulevards subsequently replaced the city walls, and the old city has been preserved as a conservation area.

BIBLIOGRAPHY

H. Focillon: *Art d'occident: Le Moyen Age roman et gothique* (Paris, 1938); Eng. trans. as *The Art of the West in the Middle Ages*, ii (London, 1963)

T. W. West: *History of Architecture in France* (London, 1969)

E. A. Gutkind: *Urban Development in Western Europe: France and Belgium*, International History of City Development, v (London, 1979)

La Vie à Troyes sous Louis XIII: Une Ville de province pendant la première moitié du 17e siècle, Centre Troyen de Recherche et d'Etudes Pierre et Nicolas Pithou (Troyes, 1984)

2. ART LIFE AND ORGANIZATION. Some late 12th-century stained glass from the original cathedral is still preserved (*see* §3(i)(b) below). The stained glass in the choir of the present cathedral, which recalls contemporary Parisian work, and, above all that in the choir and transept windows (*c.* 1270; *see* GOTHIC, fig. 69) of St Urbain, are exceptional in their quality and harmony with the architecture. The cathedral preserves three windows with 14th-century glass on the east side of the west transept. In the 15th century the first Troyes workshops appear in the archives. The earliest material evidence of their activity, however, is the stained glass (1485 and 1493) by Girard Noquart in the cathedral. Stimulated by the enterprising and generous merchant class that flourished under Charles VIII and Louis XII, numerous workshops were established in the city. During the first half of the 16th century the city's 111 painter–glaziers responded to this considerable demand, which extended widely beyond southern Champagne.

The fame of Troyen glass was due to its distinctive characteristics: intense, strong, almost violent colours; narrative panels in bands within architectural frames; and a virtuoso technique that revelled in engraved glass and masterpieces of assemblage. The infiltration of Renaissance motifs began in the 1530s. Despite the remarkable creation of the west rose (1547) of the cathedral by Jean Soudain (*fl* 1516–47), the increasing use of GRISAILLE on a clear background encouraged the disappearance of traditional polychromy, such that local production virtually ceased after 1570. LINARD GONTIER, however, introduced the use of enamels in his secular glass, which combined a small-scale format with a disciplined monumental composition. The large grisaille figures (1662–72) in St Pantaléon by Jean Barbarat (*fl* 1653–94) and Léonard Fourché (*fl* 1691) provided a fitting epitaph to Troyes glass.

Sculpture produced in Troyes was abundant, if of uneven quality. Medieval north European influences persisted; over a third of the sculptors known from the 14th and 15th centuries were Flemish. About 1520 the work of the St Martha workshop (named after a statue preserved in Ste Madeleine; see fig. 1) stands out. Jacques Bachot (*see* BACHOT) was a major Troyen Gothic sculptor. The choir-screen (*c.* 1508–15) of Ste Madeleine by JEAN GAILDE is still Flamboyant. In the first quarter of the 16th century local artists' preference for depicting women culminated in a type called a Troyenne Virgin, characterized by luxurious ornamentation and a mannered pose. Domenico del Barbiere, who worked at Fontainebleau, lived in Troyes periodically. Equally talented were François Gentil (1520–81/3) and the Juliot family (*fl* 16th century), who returned from Fontainebleau and received important commissions in their native city. Although François Girardon came from Troyes, he mostly worked elsewhere. Sculpture later declined in the city; PIERRE-CHARLES SIMART left Troyes to train in Paris, and it was at nearby Nogent-sur-Seine, rather than at Troyes, that the sculptors Marius Ramus (1805–88), Paul Dubois (i), Alfred Boucher (*b* 1850) and his pupil Camille Claudel gathered in the last decades of the 19th century.

Local painting flourished in the second quarter of the 16th century. The relative proximity of Fontainebleau made Troyes a pool of labour for the great royal workshops: about 20 painters from Troyes followed Domenico del Barbiere there. The many paintings on canvas and panel, often in grisaille, executed at that time for the churches of the city and its vicinity reveal the influence of Fontainebleau. Jean d'Hoey, grandson of Lucas van Leyden, nephew of Domenico del Barbiere and father-in-law of Martin Fréminet and Ambroise Dubois, was active in Troyes from 1572 to 1585. In the 17th century, especially after 1640, the renown spread of artists associated with Troyes, such as Pierre Mignard I, Nicolas Mignard, Jacques de Létin, Jean Chalette and Rémy Vuibert, resulting in numerous local commissions. In 1773 an art school, the Ecole Royale Gratuite de Dessein à l'Ecole des Beaux-Arts de Troyes, was founded; it still exists.

The city's industrial past is preserved in the Musée de la Bonneterie, part of the Musée Historique de Troyes et de la Champagne, which also houses a collection of sculpture and stained glass. In addition to the eclectic collection of the Musée des Beaux-Arts et d'Archéologie,

1. Troyes, Ste Madeleine, *St Martha*, h. 1.55 m, *c.* 1520

the city's holding of art was supplemented by the donation by Pierre Lévy and Denise Lévy (*see* LÉVY) of part of their collection of modern art, installed in the Musée d'Art Moderne in the former bishop's palace in 1976.

BIBLIOGRAPHY

J. B. Coffinet: *Les Peintres-verriers de Troyes pendant trois siècles, 1375–1690: Documents, nomenclatures, monogrammes* (Paris, 1858)

R. Koechlin and J. J. Marquet de Vasselot: *La Sculpture à Troyes et dans la Champagne méridionale au 16e siècle: Etude sur la transition de l'art gothique à l'italianisme* (Paris, 1900)

A. Babeau: *La Peinture à Troyes au 16e siècle* (Troyes, 1903)

P. Biver: *L'Ecole troyenne de peinture sur verre*, i (Paris, 1935)

Les Trésors d'art de l'école troyenne: 12e–16e siècles (exh. cat., ed. M. Aubert; Troyes, Mus. Hist. Troyes & Champagne, 1953)

Jacques de Létin: Troyes, 1597–1661 (exh. cat. by J.-P. Sainte-Marie, Troyes, Mus. B.-A. & Archéol., 1976)

J.-P. Sainte-Marie: 'Regards sur l'école troyenne de sculpture du 16e siècle', *Vie Champagne*, cccix (1981), pp. 1–40

J.-P. Sainte-Marie and C. Rouquet: 'Les Sculpteurs du 19e siècle dans l'Aube', *Vie Champagne*, cccxxiv (1982), pp. 1–32

J.-P. Sainte-Marie: 'De l'Ecole royale de dessin à l'Ecole des beaux-arts de Troyes: 210 ans d'une institution', *Vie Champagne*, cccxxxiv (1983), pp. 1–28

N. Hany: 'Un Peintre-verrier troyen de la Renaissance: Jean Joudain', *Rev. A.*, lxiii (1984), pp. 17–34

Le Vitrail dans l'Aube du 12e au 17e siècle (exh. cat. by A. Marsat and N. Hany, Troyes, Cent. Cult. Thibaud de Champagne, 1984)

ISABELLE BALSAMO

3. Buildings.

(i) Cathedral. (ii) St Urbain.

(i) Cathedral. The Gothic cathedral of SS Peter and Paul was begun after a fire damaged the old cathedral, an 11th- and 12th-century structure, in 1188. The fire-damaged remains were demolished in a piecemeal fashion from east to west to make way for the new work, which was begun *c.* 1200. The Romanesque west tower survived until the 1530s.

(a) Architecture. The Gothic cathedral was conceived on a grand scale with a main vessel, *c.* 14 m wide and 28 m high, flanked by double aisles. At the east end the seven-bay hemicycle is ringed by a single ambulatory with spacious radiating chapels. The transept has limited projection and no towers. At the west end the five-aisled nave is terminated by a three-bay façade. The interior is particularly harmonious, with proportions (height equals twice the span of the central vessel) that are modest and stable and a three-storey elevation of arcade, glazed triforium and a lofty clerestory linked to the triforium by continuous mullions (see fig. 2). The interior lighting is unified by the deeply coloured glass of the clerestory, but this superficial impression of unity is dispelled on closer inspection, which reveals a sequence of building campaigns extending over three and a half centuries. This prolonged construction reflects inadequate funding, multiple structural disasters and the depopulation and distress of the Hundred Years War (1337–1453) and Black Death. The different phases of building reflect the changing architectural ideas of successive masters.

Work began at the base of the choir hemicycle *c.* 1200. Many details of the ambulatory and radiating chapels may be compared with local buildings (such as Meaux Cathedral and Notre-Dame-en-Vaux at Châlons-sur-Marne), lending a distinctly regional (Champenois) character to the work. A second master began to construct the straight bays of the choir and the lower transept *c.* 1210 in the High Gothic

2. Troyes Cathedral, interior looking east, begun *c.* 1200

style of cathedrals such as Chartres and Reims. A violent storm toppled the unfinished upper choir in 1228 and a third master re-erected this part of the building and built the upper eastern sides of the transept arms. Here the early use of the glazed triforium relates the work to the contemporary Parisian style of the abbey church of Saint-Denis. The triumph of this style reflects the increasing domination of the Capetian monarchs over the county of Champagne.

The fourth phase is the most enigmatic and prolonged one, involving the start of work on the first three bays of the nave and the completion of the upper transept (1270s–1380s). A succession of masters, some of whom are known by name (Master Jacobus, 1290s; Master Henricus, 1330s), worked in a range of styles reflecting both the influence of existing forms and the desire to introduce innovations, derived mainly from Paris and the collegiate church of St Urbain in Troyes. In the 1350s Master Jean de Torvoie worked on the upper parts of the first two bays of the nave (vaults and flying buttresses), but his work was found to be defective by a visiting expert, Pierre Faisant, who in 1362 recommended that Jean de Torvoie's flying buttresses should be taken down and reconstructed at a lower level. This work was undertaken in the 1360s and 1370s by Master Thomas and Masters Michelin de Jonchery, Michelin Hardiot and Jean Thierry. In 1372 an additional bay was built projecting beyond the old provisional west wall that closed in the three nave bays. However, further efforts to complete the cathedral were halted because the clergy decided to concentrate their meagre resources on the construction of a new choir-screen (designed and built by Henry de Bruisselles and Henry Soudan). There was also a series of structural disasters, which included the collapse of the crossing tower in 1365 and the upper nave in 1389, followed by that of the north transept rose window. A low-level provisional roof was then improvised (1390) and major construction efforts were abandoned for 60 years. A crossing tower was built in the first half of the 15th century but it has not survived.

The beginning of the fifth campaign was made possible through an indulgence granted by Pope Nicholas V in 1450. Master Jaquet le Vachier founded the seven piers at the west end of the nave and started to build one chapel, but in 1455 an outside mason was employed to begin work on the new west front: Bleuet, master mason of Reims Cathedral. Bleuet designed a five-bay façade that would have resembled the transept arms of Saint-Denis. His massive tower-supporting pier at the west end of the northern aisles of the nave has multiple sharp-edged fillet mouldings continuing into the arches and ribs without capitals in a distinctly Late Gothic idiom. Bleuet began two such tower-supporting piers and returned to Reims, leaving his 'companion', Anthoine Colas, in charge of the Troyes workshop. Colas, who remained master mason until his death in 1483, installed the vaults of the western bays of the nave aisles, reinforced the north transept façade and began the upper parts of the western nave bays. In order to support the western piers of the nave against the outward thrust generated by the arcade and vaults, he constructed provisional flying buttresses against the masonry of the old west tower, bequeathing to his

successors the problem of demolishing this tower, now part of the support system of the western end of the nave. Colas was succeeded by Jehançon Garnache, who came from Reims in 1485 to repair the broken choir-screen but remained as master mason. Garnache completed the upper nave, building vaults and flying buttresses in a style very close to that of his predecessor. In constructing the clerestory wall, he built two more flying buttresses against the old west tower. The Parisian Martin Chambiges (see CHAMBIGES, (1)) was subsequently invited to Troyes to resolve the problem of demolishing the tower to make way for the new west façade. He designed a three-bay frontispiece that was deep enough to encircle the old tower and to replace the flying buttresses against the nave with new supports. In his design for the new frontispiece Chambiges combined practical expediency, rational geometric planning based on a system of squares and vigorous Flamboyant articulation on a scale that is appropriate to the overall mass of the monument. The west front is the triumphant last flourish of Gothic; its popularity with contemporaries is attested by the numerous local churches that embody elements of Chambiges's stylistic vocabulary.

UNPUBLISHED SOURCES

Troyes, Archvs Dépt. l'Aube, G 1564–1600 [Fabric accounts, 1294–1550. Contains some gaps; other accounts in Paris, Bib. N., London, BL, etc]

BIBLIOGRAPHY

L. Pigeotte: *Etude sur les travaux d'achèvement de la cathédrale de Troyes, 1450 à 1630* (Paris, 1870)

V. de Courcel: 'La Cathédrale de Troyes', *Congr. Archéol. France*, cxiii (1955), pp. 9–28

R. Branner: 'Les Débuts de la cathédrale de Troyes', *Bull. Mnmtl*, cxviii (1960), pp. 111–22

J. Roserot de Melin: *Bibliographie commentée des sources d'une histoire de la cathédrale de Troyes*, 2 vols (Troyes, 1966–70)

S. Murray: 'The Completion of the Nave of Troyes Cathedral', *J. Soc. Archit. Hist.*, xxxiv (1975), pp. 121–39

N. Bongartz: *Die frühen Bauteile der Kathedrale in Troyes: Architecturgeschichtliche Monographie* (Stuttgart, 1979)

S. Murray: *Building Troyes Cathedral: The Late Gothic Campaigns* (Bloomington, 1986)

STEPHEN MURRAY

(b) Stained glass. Stained glass is preserved in the cathedral from each of the major building campaigns from the 13th to the 17th centuries. The earliest glazing, *c.* 1200–40, is located in the ambulatory chapels. The subject-matter of the 13 windows includes a *Tree of Jesse*, typological scenes of the *Infancy of Christ* and scenes from the lives of *SS Peter and Andrew*. Among the most unusual subjects are two windows of the *Public Life of Christ*, a rare subject in 13th-century stained glass, which reflects the influence of popular *bibles moralisées*. A number of grisaille windows survive: their position at the entrance to each chapel indicates that they were used to offset the coloured historiated windows and to supply additional light to the chapels. While most of the ambulatory windows are painted in the classicizing MULDENFALTENSTIL, the later windows in the series show the influence of the Parisian court style, a trend that was continued in the choir clerestory windows of the later 13th century. The important ensemble of later glass in the nave shows influences from Alsace (end of the 15th century) and from the 16th-century French Mannerist style of the FONTAINEBLEAU SCHOOL. The 17th-century glass is dominated by the work of Linard Gontier, whose *Mystical Wine Press* of 1625

commands the last bay on the north side of the nave. Approximately 20 12th-century panels dispersed among collections in France (Paris, Mus. Cluny), England (London, V&A) and North America (Bryn Athyn, PA, Glencairn Mus.) had been thought to belong to the pre-Gothic cathedral, but it has been shown that the associations of this series with the cathedral are circumstantial. It is more likely that the panels belonged to the nearby palace chapel of the counts of Champagne, destroyed during the French Revolution.

BIBLIOGRAPHY

J. Lafond: 'Les Vitraux de la cathédrale Saint-Pierre de Troyes', *Congr. Archéol. France*, cxiii (1955), pp. 29–62
L. Grodecki: 'Nouvelles découvertes sur les vitraux de la cathédrale de Troyes', *Intuition und Kunstwissenschaft: Festschrift für Hanns Swarzenski*, ed. P. Bloch (Berlin, 1973), pp. 173–203
N. Hany: 'Troyes, haut-lieu du vitrail', *Doss. Archéol.*, xxvi (1978), pp. 86–101
E. C. Pastan: *The Early Stained Glass of Troyes Cathedral: The Ambulatory Chapel Glazing, c. 1200–40* (diss., Providence, RI, Brown U., 1986)
——: 'Fit for a Count: The Twelfth-century Stained Glass Panels from Troyes', *Speculum*, lxiv (1989), pp. 338–72
——: 'Process and Patronage in the Decorative Arts in the Early Campaigns of Troyes Cathedral, ca. 1200–1220s', *J. Soc. Archit. Historians*, liii (1994), pp. 215–31
——: ' "Tam haereticos quam Judaeos": Shifting Symbols in the Glazing of Troyes Cathedral', *Word and Image* x/1 (Oct–Dec 1994), pp. 66–83

ELIZABETH PASTAN

(ii) St Urbain. The collegiate church of St Urbain epitomizes the high degree of refinement and sophistication achieved by French Rayonnant architecture during the third quarter of the 13th century. The building summarizes the character of contemporary developments in architecture, while future trends are foreshadowed by the innovative handling of structural elements and the evolution of forms during the period of construction.

St Urbain was founded by Pope Urban IV in May 1262 on the site of his birthplace, and the project was financed by his bequest of 10,000 marks sterling. After Urban's death in 1264 his nephew, Cardinal Ancher, became the main benefactor and guardian of the enterprise. Although attempts have been made to attribute St Urbain to Jean Langlois, mentioned as 'magister operis' in a fabric account, it seems more likely that he was a financial official charged with disbursing papal funds. Thus the identity of the gifted master of this exceptional monument remains unknown. Extensive documentation for St Urbain survives in the church's cartularies as well as in those of the convent of Notre-Dame-aux-Nonnains in Troyes. The extant fabric accounts for 1264–6, with a number of papal bulls, foundations, donations and legal papers, allow a relatively detailed account of the church's construction and tumultuous history to be made.

St Urbain was erected in two main campaigns. During the first campaign, conducted between 1262/3 and 1266, the choir, the ground storey of the transept and eastern bay of the nave and the lower zone of the façade were built. Work was halted abruptly in the spring of 1266 because of two destructive attacks from Notre-Dame-aux-Nonnains, whose abbess was enraged by the location of the church within her area of jurisdiction. St Urbain was further seriously damaged by a fire during the summer of 1266, and the exhaustion of funds prevented the resumption of building. The partial recovery of the fabric's finances provided the opportunity to complete the transept and its porches, the western bays of the nave arcade and a small portion of the façade. This building campaign has been variously dated to the years immediately preceding the consecration of 1389 and as late as the 15th century, but analysis of its forms, combined with documentary evidence, indicates that construction was restarted during the 1270s. In 1276 Charles I, King of Sicily and Count of Anjou, donated wood for three vaults, probably those of the transept, and stone from Tonnerre to complete the building. However, St Urbain remained incomplete throughout the Middle Ages; the nave clerestory and west front were finished only in 1905 as part of the general restoration of the building. The second Master of St Urbain maintained the complex elegance of the first campaign on the exterior but radically simplified the forms of the interior. Probably due to financial constraints, he eliminated tracery screens and elaborately carved capitals and mouldings, simplified the scheme of the façade and developed compact pier forms, the components of which could be easily carved.

The plan of St Urbain, 44.5 m long internally, is composed of a three-bay nave with side aisles, a non-projecting transept fronted by porches, a two-bay choir with aisles terminating in five-sided chapels, and a five-sided apse (see fig. 3). This basilican plan was widely used in the 12th and 13th centuries, for example at St Lazare, Autun. The first St Urbain Master, however, designed a variant that subtly creates the impression of a centralized building. The nave and choir appear to be of equal volume on either side of the spacious crossing, while the unusual use of quinquepartite vaults in the aisles gives the illusion that the main vessel is ringed by a series of polygonal chapels.

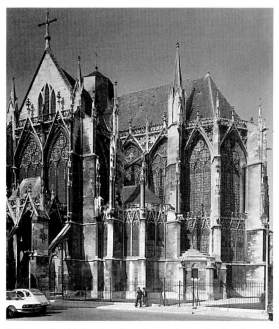

3. Troyes, St Urbain, view from the south-east showing the apse, 1262–76

The interior elevation is designed to two different patterns. The apse rises in two glazed storeys above an unadorned masonry base: at the lower level a walkway is set behind an open screen of tracery, the mullions of which ascend into the clerestory above. Its preciosity and the extensive glazing, which creates a luminous area around the altar, suggest that it may have been conceived as a monumental monstrance, an architectural reflection of Urban IV's devotion to the Eucharistic Sacrament and his institution of the Feast of Corpus Christi. The sanctuary, transept and nave are formed by a powerfully moulded arcade supported by composite piers and a clerestory zone of equivalent dimensions. These two patterns are unified by the consistent treatment of the wall as a series of rectilinear panels set into the gridded framework of vertical pier and vault shafts and horizontal mouldings, and by the overall, delicately scaled linear texture that is underscored by the cool light that streams through the grisaille window glass (*see* GOTHIC, fig. 69).

On the exterior, sharply pointed perforated gables, slim buttresses bristling with pinnacles, and openwork flying buttresses impart a brittle, metallic nature to St Urbain, stressing its shrinelike character. The repetition of the same number of window units and gables draws the various levels together. Yet the disposition of rectangular and pointed forms in depth and the slightly discordant juxtaposition of curving tracery motifs introduce a design of great visual complexity. In order to ensure stability while paring masonry mass to a minimum, the architect employed a resistant limestone from Tonnerre for major structural elements instead of the soft local chalk, which was restricted to the infilling wall masonry.

St Urbain shows knowledge of a wide range of contemporary stylistic trends. The designer drew upon Burgundian sources, particularly Notre-Dame, Dijon, for the use of passages that honeycomb the elevation. He was also influenced by the style of Hugues Libergier, incorporating into the design some of the mannerisms of the façade of St Nicaise at Reims. The handling of space and structure reveals close ties to the vestibule of the Lady chapel of the church of St Germer-de-Fly Abbey (Oise). St Urbain's links to Parisian developments are discernible in the use of the pointed tracery motifs and gabled triplets that appear on the transept façades of Notre-Dame, while its visual opulence connects it to the Sainte-Chapelle in Paris. The impact of the forms of the second campaign was felt at nearby Mussy-sur-Seine and at St Germain, Auxerre. The fluid and boldly polygonal style directly anticipates the architecture of the Late Gothic period.

BIBLIOGRAPHY

C. Lalore: 'Documents sur l'abbaye de Notre-Dame-aux-Nonnains de Troyes', *Mem. Soc. Acad. Agric., Sci., A. & B.-Lett. Dépt Aube*, xxxviii (1874), pp. 113–29

——: *Collection des principaux cartulaires du diocèse de Troyes*, v (Troyes, 1875–90)

——: *L'Eglise Saint-Urbain de Troyes* (Arcis-sur-Aube, 1880)

A. Babeau: *Saint-Urbain de Troyes* (Troyes, 1891)

E. Lefèvre-Pontalis: 'Jean Langlois: Architecte de Saint-Urbain de Troyes', *Bull. Mnmtl*, lxviii (1904), pp. 93–108

O. F. Jossier: *Compte-rendu de la restauration et de l'inauguration de l'église Saint-Urbain de Troyes* (Troyes, 1905)

E. Lefèvre-Pontalis: 'Note', *Bull. Mnmtl*, lxxxii (1922), p. 480

N. Pevsner: 'Bristol, Troyes and Gloucester: The Character of the Early Fourteenth Century in Architecture', *Archit. Rev.*, cxiii (1953), pp. 89–104

L. Grodecki: 'Les Vitraux de Saint-Urbain de Troyes', *Congr. Archéol. France*, cxiii (1955), pp. 123–38

F. Salet: 'Saint-Urbain de Troyes', *Congr. Archéol. France*, cxiii (1955), pp. 96–122

R. Branner: *Saint Louis and the Court Style in Gothic Architecture* (London, 1965), pp. 106–8

M. Davis: 'On the Threshold of the Flamboyant: The Second Campaign of Construction of Saint-Urbain, Troyes', *Speculum*, lxix (1984), pp. 847–84

C. A. Bruzelius: 'A Note on the Second Campaign of Construction of Saint-Urbain, Troyes', *Speculum*, lxxii (1987), pp. 635–40

MICHAEL T. DAVIS

Troyon, Constant (*b* Sèvres, 28 Aug 1810; *d* Paris, 20 March 1865). French painter. He was brought up among the Sèvres ceramics workers and received his first lessons in drawing and painting from Denis-Désiré Riocreux (1791–1872), a porcelain painter who was one of the founders of the Musée National de Céramique. Troyon began his career as a painter at the Sèvres factory while also studying landscape painting in his spare time. He became a friend of Camille Roqueplan, who introduced him to a number of young landscape painters—especially Théodore Rousseau, Paul Huet and Jules Dupré—who were later to become members and associates of the BARBIZON SCHOOL. After an unremarkable début at the Salon of 1833, where he exhibited three landscapes depicting the area around Sèvres (e.g. *View of the Park at Saint-Cloud*; Paris U., Notre-Dame), he took up his career in earnest and made several study trips to the French provinces. Following the example of contemporary collectors, he began to take a great interest in 17th-century Dutch painting, particularly the work of Jacob van Ruisdael, whose influence is seen in such early paintings as *The Woodcutters* (1839; La Rochelle, Mus. B.-A.). At the Salon of 1841 he exhibited *Tobias and the Angel* (Cologne, Wallraf-Richartz Mus.), a biblical landscape that attracted the attention of Théophile Gautier. The subject was intended to satisfy the critics, but the painting served as a pretext for portraying a realistic and sincere representation of nature, even though its ordered and classically inspired composition perfectly fitted the requirements of a genre, the origins of which were the 17th-century paintings of Claude and Poussin and their followers.

At the Salon of 1846 Troyon was awarded a First Class medal by Louis Napoleon (later Napoleon III) for the four paintings he exhibited there, all landscapes inspired by the countryside around Paris, confirming a reputation that continued to grow year by year. In 1847 he travelled to the Netherlands and Belgium, where he discovered the work of the painters Paulus Potter and Aelbert Cuyp; this trip was to have a profound influence on the direction of his career. He was made Chevalier de la Légion d'honneur in 1849, and it was from this time that he devoted himself almost exclusively to the painting of animals, a genre that ensured him substantial financial success due to its popularity with his admirers. He was extremely prolific, and his canvases are often large in format, usually depicting farm animals and labourers in the extreme foreground against a low horizon with dramatic, cloud-filled skies or splendid sunrises or sunsets; examples are *Oxen Going to Plough*:

Constant Troyon: *Oxen Going to Plough: Morning Effect*, oil on canvas, 260×400 mm, 1855 (Paris, Musée du Louvre)

Morning Effect (see fig.), shown at the Exposition Universelle in Paris of 1855, and *View from the Suresnes Heights (Hauts-de-Seine)* (Paris, Mus. d'Orsay), painted in 1856 and exhibited at the Salon of 1859. Troyon was no innovator, but his painting technique was excellent, and he had a sensitive, yet broad-based and solid mastery of his craft. His more exploratory paintings were executed on the coast of Normandy during his last years. These paintings reveal that he was looking closely at variations of light and was expressing a sensitivity not too far removed from that of the precursors of Impressionism.

BIBLIOGRAPHY
C. Blanc: *Les Artistes de mon temps* (Paris, 1876)
A. Hustin: 'Troyon', *L'Art*, xlvi (1889), pp. 77–90; xlvii (1889), pp. 85–96
L. Souillié: *Peintures, pastels, aquarelles, dessins de Constant Troyon relevés dans les catalogues de ventes de 1833 à 1900* (Paris, 1900) [biog. entry by P. Burty]
W. Gemel: *Corot und Troyon*, Künstler Monographien, lxxxiii (Bielefeld and Leipzig, 1906)
The Realist Tradition: French Painting and Drawing, 1830–1900 (exh. cat. by G. P. Weisberg and others, Cleveland, OH, Mus. A.; New York, Brooklyn Mus.; Glasgow, A.G. & Mus.; 1980–82)

A. DAGUERRE DE HUREAUX

Tršar, Drago (*b* Planina, nr Rakek, 27 April 1927). Slovenian sculptor. He completed his studies at the Ljubljana Academy of Fine Arts and taught there after 1960. His early works, autonomous human or animal figures, had already indicated his tendency to synthesize the sculptural volume into a monumental, rudimentary mass suggestive of the subject's character. Soon he began to group his human figures in a manner not unlike modern British sculptors such as Henry Moore, Lynn Chadwick and Kenneth Armitage. In 1957 he began to execute statues described by critics as sculptural ensembles; these were large, usually flattened volumes, in which he carved outlines, shapes and individual parts of the body, to form a single mass of human figures grouped together. These clusters of often rhomboidal figures with a multitude of stylized legs below and raised pointed arms, evoke demonstrators, rioters or the like.

Tršar was one of the most successful monumental sculptors. In 1962 he designed the monument to the *Revolution* in Ljubljana (executed 1975), its impressive composition harmoniously incorporated in the memorial site. He was also an excellent portrait sculptor, capable of capturing the main traits of the sitter in the seemingly shapeless, roughly handled sculptural mass.

BIBLIOGRAPHY
Z. Kržišnik: *Drago Tršar* (1975)

JURE MIKUŽ

Trubert, Georges (*b* ?nr Troyes, *fl* 1467–99; *d* before 1508). French illuminator. There are numerous mentions of him in the accounts of René, Duke of Anjou, between 1467 and 1480. In 1476 René provided Trubert with funds for a journey to Rome and two years later conferred on him the title of Valet de Chambre, an office he had granted to only one other painter, Barthélemy d'Eyck. Trubert lived mainly in Provence and seems to have continued working there after René's death in 1480. By 1486 he was receiving gifts from René's grandson, René II, Duke of Lorraine, and from 1491 until 1499 he was part of the Duke's household in Lorraine. In documents of 1508 he is mentioned as dead.

A Breviary (Paris, Bib. Arsenal, MS. 601 and Petit Pal., MS. 42) and a Diurnal (Paris, Bib. N., MS. lat. 10491), made for René II between 1492 and 1494, have been identified as Trubert's work, and on this basis nine other manuscripts have been attributed to him (Reynaud). These are all liturgical manuscripts, and there is no evidence to suggest that he either illustrated secular books or painted on a larger scale. Nonetheless, the outstanding characteristic of his style is a breadth of conception and a monumentality of form more usually associated with panel or mural painting. In the larger and more lavish books decorated for René II the scenes from biblical history allowed Trubert wide scope, and figures are confidently grouped within spacious surroundings. In many of these compositions the easy relationship of figures to one another and to their setting echoes the work of Jean Fouquet and other illuminators of the Loire valley, which was probably where Trubert trained. Although none of Trubert's surviving works was demonstrably made for René of Anjou, emblematic motifs in the decoration show his awareness of the personal iconography of his first patron and there are compositional links with the work of the illuminator known as the Master of King René of Anjou as well as with Provençal painting in general. Trubert used Italian early Renaissance architectural forms in all but the earliest or humblest manuscripts. Although the motifs are limited and are far simpler than those painted by Fouquet, the interiors represented vary endlessly and are shown from a variety of angles, often with striking illusionism. Faces are very distinctive. In early works, such as the Chester Beatty Hours (sold London, Sotheby's, 24 June 1969, lot 71), they are finely modelled and rounded; later examples are more elongated, with wide, high foreheads, recalling the facial types of Netherlandish and Franco-Flemish painters such as Hugo van der Goes and the Master of Moulins.

Trubert's choice of colour is distinctive: he combined acid green, yellow and orange in effective contrast with sharp blues and a rich range of pinks and mauves. Unlike his contemporaries Jean Colombe or Jean Bourdichon, he did not saturate colours but used a wide tonal range. His sensitivity to tone is seen in a subtle form of grisaille in which whites and greys with touches of pastel colour are set against darker blues, as exemplified in some of the small vignettes in the frames around the miniatures or, more dramatically, within the main illustrations. The sculptural quality of these grisailles and the contexts in which they are found suggest that besides earlier French grisaille painting Trubert may have been impressed by the glazed terracotta of the Florentine Luca della Robbia: grisaille three-quarter figures appear around some miniatures as though they are statues within niches (see fig.); around others, profile heads against a blue ground simulate Antique cameos. Like the *all'antica* architectural features, these may show the impact of Trubert's Italian trip.

Trubert's greatest originality lies in the design of the decorative frames around the miniatures of the more elaborate manuscripts. They range from simple rectangles

Georges Trubert: *David and the Prophets*, 210×145 mm; from the Diurnal of René II, Duke of Lorraine, 1492–4 (Paris, Bibliothèque Nationale, MS. lat. 10491, fol. 7*r*)

simulating tooled leather, wood or stone, sometimes studded with jewels, to others in the form of small reliquaries or elaborate Italianate tabernacles, some of them with complex permutations of marble-insets, inscriptions, putti and garlands. In others the wide base of the frame, below the miniature and around the text, has strewn flowers, jewels, skulls and bones, indicating the influence of Ghent–Bruges illumination. Although Trubert drew upon a restricted range of naturalistic motifs he made full use of illusionistic devices such as cast shadows or, in the case of cartouches carrying the text on decorated pages, simulated parchment rolls appearing as if nailed to the surface of the frame. In some cases the miniatures, three-quarter or half-length compositions, recall the 'dramatic close-up' of contemporary Netherlandish painting and illumination. Trubert's approach to such compositions differed from that of his contemporaries. The high bases beneath some miniatures suggest sufficient space to accommodate the figures behind them as though he had assimilated Alberti's principle of regarding a painting as a view through a window. In this as in his choice of motifs and iconography Trubert was typical of late 15th-century French painters in combining elements from Italy and the Netherlands and assimilating them within an essentially rational vision.

BIBLIOGRAPHY

P. Durrieu: 'La Peinture en France depuis l'avènement de Charles VII jusqu'à la fin des Valois (1422–1589)', *Histoire de l'art*, ed. A. Michel, IV/ii (Paris, 1911), pp. 747–8

V. Leroquais: *Les Bréviaires manuscrits des bibliothèques publiques de France* (Paris, 1934), ii, pp. 345–7, 436–40; iii, pp. 216–21

L. M. J. Delaissé, J. Marrow and J. de Witt: *The James A. de Rothschild Collection at Waddesdon Manor: Illuminated Manuscripts* (London, 1977), pp. 446–70

N. Reynaud: 'Georges Trubert, enlumineur du Roi René et de René II de Lorraine', *Rev. A.*, xxxv (1977), pp. 41–63

Ecriture et enluminure en Lorraine au Moyen Age (exh. cat. by S. Collin-Roset, M. Parisse and M. Paulmier-Foucart, Nancy, Mus. Hist. Lorrain, 1984), pp. 199–202

F. Robin: *La Cour d'Anjou-Provence: La Vie artistique sous le règne de René* (Paris, 1985), pp. 61–5

A. Demarquay Rook: 'Georges Trubert, the René Master and Waddesdon Ms 21', *Burl. Mag.*, cxxx (1988), pp. 352–5

A. DEMARQUAY ROOK

Trubetskoy, Paolo. *See* TROUBETZKOY, PAOLO.

Trübner, (Heinrich) Wilhelm (*b* Heidelberg, 3 Feb 1851; *d* Karlsruhe, 21 Dec 1917). German painter. The son of a goldsmith and jeweller, he began an apprenticeship as a goldsmith. The intervention of Anselm Feuerbach enabled him to overcome his father's resistance and train as a painter. In 1867 he began to study at the Kunstschule in Karlsruhe, where his tutors included Karl Friedrich Schick (1826–75). Trübner also met artists outside the school, such as Hans Canon, who were very influential. Trübner moved to Munich in 1869 to study with Alexander von Wagner (1838–1919) at the Akademie der Bildenden Künste, where he also met Wilhelm Leibl. He continued his studies with Wilhelm von Diez (1839–1907) and met Hans Thoma, with whom, for a while, he shared a studio and models. Trübner acknowledged his debt to Feuerbach, Canon, Leibl and Thoma, whom he described as his 'leaders and guiding stars', throughout his life.

In the winter of 1870–71 he met Carl Schuch and with him and other friends worked in Bernried on the Starnberg Lake, where Leibl championed them, praising Trübner in particular. Summer 1871 marked the real beginning of the Leibl circle (*see* LEIBL, WILHELM). Encouraged by Leibl, Trübner, Schuch and Albert Lang (1847–1933) left the academy and hired a studio together in winter 1871–2. Some of Trübner's most striking works were produced during this period, such as *Boy at the Sideboard* (1872; Stuttgart, Staatsgal.) and *The Sofa* (1872; Berlin, Staatl. Museen, N.G.).

Trübner reached his relatively brief artistic peak between 1872 and 1876, during which time he made some of the most important contributions to the Leibl circle's achievement and produced the most effective examples of what he called 'purist painting', painting that disregards the expectations of the public to concentrate on formal qualities rather than content. *Horse and Beech Trees* (1874; Karlsruhe, Staatl. Ksthalle) and the stark *Carpenters on the Banks of Wessling Lake* (1876; Hamburg, Ksthalle) reject the conventions of picturesque landscape to produce low-key and unglamorous images of rural life and labour painted in sombre tones. After this time Trübner's objectives and achievements began to flag. He felt neglected by the public and tried to achieve popularity by tackling literary subjects and by intensifying the colour-range of his palette.

During his period in Munich Trübner was also involved in the Secession, which was founded in April 1892. After 1896, when he left the city, he travelled widely, visiting Italy, the Netherlands, Belgium, France, Switzerland and England. In London he met important academicians such as Lawrence Alma-Tadema, Hubert von Herkomer and Frederic Leighton. In 1896 he became Director of the Städelsches Kunstinstitut in Frankfurt am Main, and the following year he founded a private art school there. In 1903 he was appointed Director of the Kunstschule in Karlsruhe, and in 1917 he obtained a post at the Akademie der Künste in Berlin but died before he could accept it.

BIBLIOGRAPHY

G. Fuchs: *Wilhelm Trübner und sein Werk* (Munich, 1908)

J. A. Beringer: *Trübner: Des Meisters Gemälde* (Stuttgart and Berlin, 1917)

E. Ruhmer: *Das Rein Malerische* (diss., Halle U., 1940)

K. Rohrandt: *Wilhelm Trübner: Kritischer und beschreibender Katalog sämtlicher Gemälde, Zeichnungen und Druckgraphik* (diss., Kiel U., 1972)

E. Ruhmer: *Der Leibl-Kreis und die Reine Malerei* (Rosenheim, 1984)

EBERHARD RUHMER

Trubshaw. English family of architects, master builders and engineers. At least 18 members of this family are recorded as architects or civil engineers, from Thomas Trubshaw, who built the tower of Armitage Church, Staffs, in 1632, to Wolstan Vyvyan Trubshaw, ARIBA (1893–1981). The family was associated with Staffordshire, of which James Trubshaw (1746–1808) and his grandson Charles (1811–62) were both County Surveyors. The first to be of any importance as an architect was Richard Trubshaw (1689–1745), whose works included several churches and a country house, Emral Hall (1724–7; destr. 1936), Clwyd, in a provincial Baroque style. His son Charles Cope Trubshaw (1715–72) trained in London under the sculptor Peter Scheemakers (ii) and subsequently carried on an extensive business as a mason and monumental sculptor. James Trubshaw (1777–1853) had a considerable reputation as a civil engineer, designing canals and bridges besides continuing the family business as an architect and builder. His eldest son Thomas Trubshaw, FSA (1802–42), had a successful practice as an architect and landscape gardener and designed some churches in an idiosyncratic Gothic style (e.g. Knightley, 1840–41; Salt, 1840–42; both Staffs). James Trubshaw's elder brother John had three sons, all of whom were in practice in Ashton-under-Lyne, Staffs, in the early 19th century. Of these, John Trubshaw (1809–77) subsequently practised as a civil engineer in Normandy, while James Trubshaw (*b* 1817) became Government Architect in India. Although none of the Trubshaws designed major buildings, they figure prominently in the architectural history of Staffordshire, and as builder–architects of the Midlands rank second only to the Smiths of Warwick (*see* SMITH, FRANCIS).

BIBLIOGRAPHY

Colvin; Gunnis

A. Bayliss: *The Life and Works of James Trubshaw (1777–1853)* (Stockport, 1978)

HOWARD COLVIN

Trucial States. *See* UNITED ARAB EMIRATES.

Trudaine. French family of patrons. Charles-Louis Trudaine de Montigny (1765–94) and Charles-Michel Trudaine de la Sablière (1766–94) were the sons of Jean-Charles-Philibert Trudaine de Montigny (1733–77) and the grandsons of Daniel-Charles Trudaine de Montigny (1703–69), both of whom were *intendants de finance*. Charles-Louis built up a rich library and maintained relations with scholars and artists, including the poet André Chénier. Many of them had been friends of his father, himself a man of letters and a collector. The painter Jacques-Louis David also frequented the salon held by the Trudaine brothers in their hôtel in Paris, and it was there that he reflected on topics surrounding his monumental *Oath of the Horatii* (1784; Paris, Louvre). He also painted the *Death of Socrates* (1787; New York, Met.) for Charles-Michel and a portrait of Charles-Louis's wife, *Marie-Josèphe-Louise de Courbeton* (unfinished; Paris, Louvre).

As both brothers subscribed for copies of the engraving intended to finance David's painting of the *Oath of the Tennis Court* (frag. Versailles, Château), they must have remained on good terms with the painter until 1791. The Trudaines were members of the Société de 89, a club for the aristocratic element of the revolutionary party, and supported the French Revolution until the Reign of Terror. However, they were arrested in 1794 and their appeals to the influential David for his support were refused, David even going so far as to threaten to have their representative arrested. On the eve of their execution, charged with being accomplices in a conspiracy within the St Lazare prison, Charles-Michel wrote to David reminding him of their former friendship and asking for clemency for his brother, but the painter did not respond. The brothers perished on the scaffold on 26 July, the day before the fall of Robespierre, the last hours of the elder Trudaine being recorded in a portrait by Joseph-Benoît Suvée (untraced). Suvée later painted a portrait of Charles-Michel from memory (untraced). Both portraits were exhibited at the Salon of 1795.

The paintings of Jean-Charles-Philibert Trudaine de Montigny were sold on 20 December 1777, and six are now in the the Wallace Collection, London: François Boucher's *Autumn Pastoral* and *Summer Pastoral* (both 1749) and four overdoors by Jean-Baptiste Oudry, *Hawk Attacking Partridges and a Rabbit* (1747), *Dog Pointing Pheasants*, *Fox in the Poultry Yard* and *Spaniel Pursuing Ducks* (all 1748).

BIBLIOGRAPHY

E. Choullier: *Les Trudaine* (Arcis-sur-Aube, 1884)
A. Schnapper: *David: Témoin de son temps* (Fribourg, 1980)
P. Bordes: *Le Serment du Jeu de Paume de Jacques-Louis David: Le Peintre, son milieu et son temps de 1789 à 1792* (Paris, 1983)
Jacques-Louis David, 1748–1825 (exh. cat., ed. A. Schnapper and A. Sérullaz; Paris, Louvre; Versailles, Château; 1989–90)

M.-E. HELLYER

Trufemondi. *See* BIGOT, TROPHIME.

Trujillo, Guillermo (*b* Horconcitos, Chiriquí, 11 Feb 1927). Panamanian painter, draughtsman, ceramicist, printmaker, tapestry designer and landscape architect. He studied both architecture and painting in Panama, holding his first exhibition in 1953; he then continued his studies in Madrid (1954–8) at the Real Academia de Bellas Artes de San Fernando, at the Escuela de Cerámica de la Moncloa and at the Escuela Superior de Arquitectura. In 1959 he returned to Panama, where he began a long teaching career at the Universidad de Panamá. In the early 1960s Trujillo painted social satires, such as *The Commissioners* (1964; Panama City, Mus. A. Contemp.) with small monstrous figures in cavernous settings. Later his palette brightened as he turned to new subjects based on nature, including numerous still-lifes and semi-abstract paintings with botanical allusions, for example *Still-life with Fruit* (1975; Washington, DC, MOMA Latin America).

Always a versatile and prolific artist, in the 1970s and 1980s he based his subjects both on his rich imagination and on his knowledge of Panama's indigenous cultures. He made recurring reference to the patterns of pre-Columbian ceramics, natural and biomorphic forms, mythological and primitive figures, and Indian symbols and ceremonies, all treated as elements of an iconography strongly related to his Panamanian origin. Although generally classified as belonging to the return to figuration among Latin American artists, he ranged stylistically from realism to abstraction.

BIBLIOGRAPHY

I. García Aponte: *Guillermo Trujillo* (Panama City, 1964)
M. E. Kupfer: *A Panamanian Artist, Guillermo Trujillo: The Formative Years* (diss., New Orleans, Tulane U. LA, 1983)
P. L. Prados: 'Guillermo Trujillo's Lost Paradise', *Trujillo* (Caracas, 1990)

MONICA E. KUPFER

Trumbauer, Horace (*b* Philadelphia, 1868; *d* Philadelphia, 1938). American architect. He served a six-year apprenticeship in the office of George and William Hewitt in Philadelphia before opening his own firm in 1890. He was the designer of many residences for wealthy families in the suburbs of Philadelphia as well as town houses there, in New York and at Newport, RI, in addition to a number of commercial buildings, churches and clubs. His work was invariably based on careful adaptations of historic precedents, most often from the Renaissance, but also drawing on Gothic and ancient Greek sources. His large-scale works included the Harry Widener Library (1914) at Harvard University, Cambridge, MA, the Free Library (1917–27) of Philadelphia and the Museum of Art (1931–8; with C. Clark Zantzinger and Charles Borie), Philadelphia. The library is almost a copy of one of the 18th-century classical buildings by Ange-Jacques Gabriel on the Place de la Concorde in Paris, while the museum is developed as a linked group of Greek temples. His Irvine Auditorium (1927) for the University of Pennsylvania in Philadelphia was an effort (widely regarded as failed) to adapt the supposed design of the Elizabethan Globe Theatre in London to a large college hall. His major work was the design of the campuses (1927–38) of Duke University in Durham, NC, in Gothic style. Although Trumbauer was highly successful professionally in his eclectic work, his reputation always suffered from the critical view that his slavish respect for historic precedents robbed it of creativity.

BIBLIOGRAPHY

J. T. Maher: *The Twilight of Splendor: Chronicles of the Age of American Palaces* (Boston, 1975)
A. Branam jr: *Newport's Favorite Architects* (Long Island City, 1976)

JOHN F. PILE

Trumbull, Alice. *See* MASON, ALICE TRUMBULL.

Trumbull, John (*b* Lebanon, CT, 6 June 1756; *d* New York, 10 Nov 1843). American painter, architect and diplomat. His importance lies in his historical paintings memorializing events in the American War of Independence. Applying Benjamin West's and John Singleton Copley's realistic innovations in history painting to American subjects, he created a series of images, reproduced in countless illustrations, that have become icons of American nationalism. They are also symbolic of his lifelong political and artistic identity.

Born into a well-to-do and politically prominent Connecticut family, Trumbull was the youngest child of Jonathan Trumbull, later governor of Connecticut, and his wife Faith, a descendant of the Pilgrim leader John Robinson. Despite blindness in one eye (the result of a childhood accident), Trumbull was inclined from early boyhood towards art. His father intended that he prepare for one of the learned professions, either the ministry or the law, and in 1771 sent him to Harvard College. On his way to Cambridge, MA, Trumbull met Copley in Boston and was impressed by the artist's personal elegance as well as by his paintings. At Harvard, Trumbull tutored himself in the fine arts both by studying the Copley portraits that hung there (he copied at least one, *Rev. Edward Holyoke*; untraced) and by reading extensively on the history, theory and practice of art. He graduated in 1773 (the first American artist to be college-educated) and returned home to Lebanon, CT, to take up painting. His early efforts were based on engravings, generally scenes of ancient Roman heroism (e.g. the *Death of Paulus Aemilius at the Battle of Cannae*, 1773; New Haven, CT, Yale U. A.G.). Trumbull's father strongly opposed his artistic ambitions, considering a manual craft beneath the family's station. When war with Britain broke out at Lexington, MA, on 19 April 1775, his father, by now governor, arranged for him to become an aide to General Joseph Spencer. In this capacity, Trumbull saw, from a distance, the Battle of Bunker Hill; it was the closest he came to any of the events he later depicted.

Following the British evacuation of Boston in March 1776, Trumbull moved to New York. His skill at drawing maps brought him to the attention of Generals George Washington and Horatio Gates for whom he served briefly as aide-de-camp and adjutant-general respectively, attaining the rank of colonel. Always hypersensitive, he resigned from military service in 1777 when his expected commission did not arrive on time. He returned to Lebanon and resumed painting, mainly executing family portraits in the style of Copley (e.g. *Governor and Mrs Jonathan Trumbull, Sr*, 1778; Hartford, CT Hist. Soc. Mus.). Trumbull moved to Boston in June 1778, renting the former studio of the artist John Smibert. Since he could not study with Copley, who had gone to England, he taught himself by studying Smibert's copies of Old Master paintings by van Dyck, Poussin and Raphael, which had remained in the studio.

In 1780 Trumbull went to France on a speculative commercial venture for his family. The enterprise was unsuccessful and he continued on to England, where he sought out Benjamin West, who had become Painter of Historical Pictures to George III. West agreed to accept him as a pupil. Perhaps in retaliation for the execution in New York of Major John André as a British spy, or because he may have had a clandestine diplomatic mission, Trumbull was soon arrested as a spy and charged with treason. Thanks to West's influence with the King, Trumbull's life was spared but he was imprisoned for almost eight months and then deported. After hostilities ceased, he returned to London in January 1784 to resume his studies with West and to attend classes at the Royal Academy.

At West's suggestion, and further encouraged by Thomas Jefferson, then American Minister in Paris, Trumbull began in 1785 what was to become his life's work—a series of paintings depicting events from the American War of Independence. (His original plan called for thirteen subjects, eight of which were completed.) By 1786 he had finished the first two, the *Death of General Warren at the Battle of Bunker's Hill* (which West called the best picture of a modern battle that had been painted) and the *Death of General Montgomery in the Attack on Quebec* (both New Haven, CT, Yale U. A.G.), and shortly afterwards he started three other Revolutionary War battle scenes. West's paintings served as theoretical and pictorial sources, while the active compositions, animated brushwork, rich colours and dramatic lighting were derived from Copley's *Death of Major Peirson* (1782–4; London, Tate). A high moral tone pervades the series: officers on opposing sides are shown to display courage, dignity and kindness; and American history is raised to the level of timeless example. The best-known picture in the series is the *Declaration of Independence* (New Haven, CT, Yale U. A.G.; see fig.), which Trumbull began in July 1786 in Paris, Jefferson having provided a first-hand account of the event. Jefferson, Benjamin Franklin and John Adams were painted from life directly on to the canvas in 1787, but the majority of the likenesses in this and in the other history paintings were added from small pencil studies or miniature oil on mahogany panels made several years later (the largest number of studies is in the Yale University Art Gallery, New Haven, CT). These miniature portraits show Trumbull's talent at its best, the fluid brushstrokes and subtle glazes, spontaneity and sensitive renderings of personality, a mark of his work during the 1790s.

In 1789 Trumbull returned to America where he hoped to make his fortune from the sale of engravings after his history paintings, but he was able to sell few subscriptions. Discouraged, he ceased painting and in 1794 returned to Europe, where he remained for almost seven years, serving the new American government in various diplomatic and administrative posts. After his marriage to the Englishwoman Sarah Hope Harvey in 1800, Trumbull once again determined to paint for a living. In 1804 the Trumbulls moved to New York, where he soon became the city's pre-eminent portrait painter. Despite his dislike of the 'mere copying of faces', portraits ultimately constituted the largest part of his oeuvre, the sitters being among the foremost political and cultural figures of New York society (e.g. *Robert Lenox* and *Mrs Robert Lenox*, both 1805; New York, Pub. Lib.). For the most part, these later works are uninspired. Trumbull had a short-lived interest in landscape, which led him to create a number of compositions whose structure anticipates the wilderness landscapes of the later Hudson River school (e.g. *Falls of the Yantic at*

John Trumbull: *Declaration of Independence*, oil on canvas, 536×791 mm, begun 1786 (New Haven, CT, Yale University Art Gallery)

Norwich, *c*. 1806; Norwich, CT, Slater Mem. Mus.). Throughout his career he painted religious and literary subjects. During a stay in England (1808–16), prolonged because of the War of 1812, he produced a series of monumental subjects (e.g. *Woman Taken in Adultery*, 2.39×1.71 m, 1811; New Haven, CT, Yale U. A.G.), which show the influence of West's late paintings.

Upon returning to New York he was elected a director of the new American Academy of Fine Arts, and from 1817 to 1835 he served as its president, an important position that he used largely for his own advancement. He considered the commission of 1817 from Congress to paint four life-size Revolutionary War scenes for the Rotunda of the US Capitol in Washington, DC, to be his crowning achievement. He chose as subjects replicas of his original versions of the *Declaration of Independence* and the *Surrender of Lord Cornwallis at Yorktown, October 19, 1781* (New Haven, Yale U. A.G.) and added the *Resignation of General Washington, December 23, 1783*, and the *Surrender of General Burgoyne at Saratoga, October 16, 1777*. The paintings were installed in the Rotunda in November 1826.

Trumbull's art had a relatively limited impact on other artists. Despite his desire to be a mentor to younger artists, his increasingly intransigent ideas about artistic training alienated most younger members of the New York art world and resulted in the founding in 1826 of the National Academy of Design. By 1830 Trumbull received few commissions, and he was in poor health and difficult financial circumstances. Feeling unappreciated for his

artistic contributions and concerned that the complete history series should find a permanent exhibition space, in 1831 he sold most of the works he possessed, including the Revolutionary War series, to Yale College in return for an annuity and the establishment there of a Trumbull Gallery, designed by himself with the help of Ithiel Town and A. J. Davis. Of his architecture, which included unexecuted plans for the expansion of Yale College, only the Meeting House in Lebanon, CT (1804–6), in an unadorned Neo-classical idiom, survives. At his death he was buried, as he had requested, beneath his life-size portrait of *George Washington at the Battle of Trenton* (1792; New Haven, CT, Yale U. A.G.) in the Trumbull Gallery.

WRITINGS

Autobiography: Reminiscences and Letters by John Trumbull from 1756 to 1841 (New York, 1841)

BIBLIOGRAPHY

T. Sizer: *The Works of Colonel John Trumbull* (New Haven, 1950, rev. 1967)
I. B. Jaffe: *John Trumbull: Patriot-artist of the American Revolution* (Boston, 1975)
John Trumbull: The Hand and Spirit of a Painter (exh. cat. by H. A. Cooper, New Haven, Yale U. A.G., 1982)

HELEN A. COOPER

Trumeau (i) [Fr.: 'pier']. Pier or stone mullion supporting the lintel and tympanum of a large medieval doorway. The term is more generally applied to any pillar or small section of wall between openings (e.g. windows).

Trumeau (ii) [Fr.: 'pier-glass']. Mirror with a decorative surround, typically placed over a chimney-piece.

Tryavna school. Art school in Tryavna, northern Bulgaria, that flourished from the end of the 17th century to the end of the 19th. The organization of the educational process was medieval in character and skills and traditions were handed down from father to son, so that whole families were occupied with art. The first Tryavna artists worked in the environs of the neighbouring town of Tărnovo, the last capital of the independent Bulgarian state. They were the heirs of medieval Bulgarian orthodox traditions, which they developed and modernized. Representatives of the school worked in religious painting, wood-carving and architecture over a wide area of north and south-east Bulgaria and Romania. In Tryavna several extensive families were occupied with religious painting, including the Vitanov (e.g. Vitan Tsonyuv (*d* 1820s): *Jesus Christ*, icon, 1748, Sofia, N.A.G.; and Simeon Tsonyuv (*c.* 1790–1853): *St Nicolas*, icon, 1798, Sofia, N.A.G.), Zakhariev (e.g. Krustyo Zakhariev (*c.* 1785–1850): *St Pachomios*, icon, 1824; Tsanyu Zakhariev (*c.* 1790–1886); and Zakhari Tsanyuv (*c.* 1816–86)) and Minev (e.g. Peter Minev (*c.* 1800–59) and Nikola Genkov (*b c.* 1825)) families. They confined themselves almost exclusively to icons, creating a distinct style using light, warm colours to produce calm, clear faces and balanced movements of the figures, and using ornament frugally. Tryavna church wood-carving (e.g. Church of St John the Baptist, Gabrova, see Drumev, figs 40, 51; Church of the Holy Archangels, Tryavna, see Drumev, figs 2–10; and Church of the Prophet Elijah, Sevlievo, see Drumev, figs 52–72) developed during the 18th and 19th centuries, the artists producing iconostases and church furniture, and in some cases even building wooden churches. Their characteristically symmetrical compositions featured deeply cut and abundant plant motifs, which sometimes included birds and animals and only rarely religious scenes. Some compositions show elements of Baroque, Rococo and Empire style. Most of the Tryavna builders were also sculptors. They decorated the churches and bridges with stone reliefs and the interiors of the houses with wood-carvings.

BIBLIOGRAPHY
D. Drumev: *Trevnensko rezbarsko izkustvo* [Tryavna wood-carving] (Sofia, 1962)
A. Bozhkov: *Trevnenska zhivopisna shkola* [Tryavna painting school] (Sofia, 1967)
A. Bozhkov, ed.: *Trevnenska khudozhestvena shkola* [Tryavna art school] (Sofia, 1985)
IVANKA GERGOVA

Tryggvadóttir, Nína (*b* Seyðisfjörður, east Iceland, 16 March 1913; *d* New York, 18 June 1968). Icelandic painter, designer and illustrator. She studied at the Kongelige Danske Kunstakademi in Copenhagen in 1935–9 under Kræsten Iversen, before going to New York in 1943, where her chief teachers were Hans Hofmann and Fernand Léger. Tryggvadóttir held her first one-woman exhibition in Reykjavík in 1942, in which semi-Cubist models predominated, and the subjects were simplified into an interplay of flat and curved forms, as in *Reykjavík Harbour* (1939; priv. col., see Schram, 1982, p. 52). Her portraits aroused particular attention; in these she combined her ability to simplify the subject with her sensitive psychological insight.

Over the following years Tryggvadóttir gradually dissolved her figurative depiction (e.g. *On the Way*, 1946; Reykjavík, N.G.), and by 1948, when she exhibited purely abstract works at the New Art Circle in New York, she had entirely abandoned direct visual references. After a short geometrical period at the beginning of the 1950s she adopted lyrical abstraction, and her work became predominantly inspired by Icelandic nature, especially in her expressive use of colour. From 1952 until her death she lived in Paris, London and New York, painting in Iceland over the summers. During these years reference to the Icelandic landscape became stronger. The forms became bigger and more powerful and at the same time more defined as she set about applying the colour with a palette knife. In works from the period the picture sections overlap and lie on different planes, and the colours are fuller and deeper, with a concentration on natural earth tones and light colours. She also designed decorations for public buildings in stained glass and in mosaic (e.g. *Christ*, 1964–5; Skálholt, Church), and she wrote and illustrated five children's books.

BIBLIOGRAPHY
B. Th. Björnsson: *Íslensk myndlist á 19. og 20. öld* [Icelandic art in the 19th and 20th centuries], ii (Reykjavík, 1973), pp. 273–89
H. Schram: *Nína Tryggvadóttir: Serenity and Power*, prologue H. Laxness (Reykjavík, 1982)
VIDEOS AND FILMS
H. Schram: *Nína Tryggvadóttir: Her Life and Work*, Íslenska Ríkissjónvarpið (1983) [TV film]
HRAFNHILDUR SCHRAM

Tryon, Dwight W(illiam) (*b* Hartford, CT, 13 Aug 1849; *d* South Dartmouth, MA, 1 July 1925). American painter. From 1876 to 1879 he studied in Paris with Jacquesson de La Chevreuse (1839–1903), a pupil of Ingres. Tryon also knew and was influenced by the Barbizon painters Henri-Joseph Harpignies and Daubigny. Study of their work as well as that of Whistler resulted in the poetic and darkly tonal orientation of many of Tryon's earlier landscapes, for example *Moonlight* (1887; New York, Met.). The lighter palette and broken brushstroke of the Impressionist painters led Tryon to develop a subtle style, now known as Tonal Impressionism, which by the late 1890s concentrated on transient atmospheric effects as in *Early Spring, New England (Springtime)* (1897; Washington, DC, Freer). It is a pastoral scene of a brook in a pasture, with a plough team and hills in the distance and leafless trees across an open sky, which warms to the horizon. 'People think of atmosphere as somehow less real than the other facts of Nature,' Tryon commented, 'but to the painter it is simply a more subtle truth, which he can no more disregard than the rocks in his foreground' (quoted in J. Pearce: *American Painting, 1560–1913*, New York, 1964, p. 47).

In 1879 Tryon donated a gallery to Smith College, Northampton, MA, to house a collection of his own work and that of his contemporaries. His work is also well represented in the Freer Gallery, Washington, DC, since Charles Lang Freer had been an important patron of the artist.

WRITINGS

'Charles François Daubigny', *Modern French Masters*, ed. J. C. van Dyck (New York, 1896/*R* New York, 1976), pp. 153–66

BIBLIOGRAPHY

C. H. Caffin: *The Art of Dwight W. Tryon: An Appreciation* (New York, 1909)
H. C. White: *The Life and Art of Dwight William Tryon* (Boston, 1930)
Dwight W. Tryon: A Retrospective Exhibition (exh. cat., ed. P. F. Rovetti; Storrs, U. CT, Benton Mus. A., 1971)
D. F. Hoopes: *The American Impressionists* (New York, 1972)
M. E. Yehia: *Dwight W. Tryon* (diss., U. Boston, 1977)
Tonalism: An American Experience (exh. cat., ed. J. Davern; New York, Grand Cent. A. Gals, 1982)

ROBERT S. OLPIN

Trzebnica [Ger. Trebnitz], **Abbey Church.** Cistercian nuns' church dedicated to the Virgin and St Bartholomew, near Wrocław, Poland, containing significant remains of an Early Gothic sculptural programme. It was founded in 1202 by Henry I, Prince of Silesia (*reg* 1201–38), and his wife, Hedwig (1174–1243), and colonized in 1203 by nuns from St Theodore's Convent in Bamberg, Germany. A document of 1203 records that the Duke sent one of his masons, Dalemir from Zajączkowo, near Legnica, who presumably began the building. The documents of 1208 and 1234 that mention *lapicida Jacobus magister operis* are medieval forgeries.

The church was consecrated in 1219, but building work continued for many years. It is built of brick with granite and sandstone details. The traditional ground-plan consists of an aisled nave, a transept and a choir terminating in an apse. The choir was originally flanked by two apsed chapels. A three-aisled crypt beneath the choir had columnar supports and still has groin vaults (in one bay a rib vault). The nave and aisles were constructed in the so-called *gebundenes* system, whereby two aisle bays correspond to each of the larger square bays in the nave. The east end and the aisles have quadripartite vaults, while the main vessel of the nave has sexpartite vaults. The vault ribs and transverse arches descend to compound piers. These, with circular and oval windows in the nave and decorative masonry including suspended 'stalactite' bosses, show the influence of Rhenish workshops, introduced through Lubiąż Abbey and the mother abbey in Pforta. There was a nuns' choir gallery in the two eastern bays of the nave and half the crossing. Initially there was a west porch in front of the three façade portals.

Building began at the east end with the crypt, choir and side chapels; in the second building phase the chapel floors were raised to bring them level with the main choir, and the transept, nave and aisles were built. The west porch and the interior and exterior sculpture were probably added during a third campaign. In 1269, when the founder's wife Hedwig was canonized, the south chapel was replaced by a larger, single-cell Gothic chapel dedicated to her. The chapel is elongated and strongly buttressed, with lancet windows, and is the earliest Polish example of a developed Gothic building with a clearly defined skeletal construction. The naturalistic foliage sculpture of the

Trzebnica, Abbey Church, west façade, north portal tympanum showing *David and Bathsheba*

bosses and capitals, and the double-sided tympanum of the entrance door, depicting the *Crucifixion* on one side and the *Coronation of the Virgin* on the other, were carved by a workshop from the cathedrals of Naumburg and Meissen (Germany).

The church suffered fire damage in 1464, 1486 and 1595, but the greatest changes were made from *c*. 1680, when an alabaster and black marble mausoleum was built within St Hedwig's Chapel, and a tomb carved in an anachronistic style was placed in front of the main altar for the founder, Duke Henry I, and for the Grand Master of the Teutonic Order, Conrad von Feuchtwangen. After 1741 the church was completely recased with Baroque decoration. The choir apse walls were heightened to accommodate a new high altar carved by the Moravian sculptor Franz Joseph Mangold (*fl* 1725–53), who was at Trzebnica between 1739 and 1745. He also made most of the altars in the aisles, the figures of SS Hedwig and Elisabeth at the entrance to the choir and a pulpit. About 1765 the 13th-century nuns' gallery was replaced by a new one in the south transept, supported on consoles, and a similar organ gallery was built in the north transept; these have fine Rococo ornament covering the stucco and timber. The new west tower, added in 1780, almost concealed the medieval portals and represents the final phase of the change to Baroque. Between 1697 and 1726 a large monastic complex with two internal courtyards, two new portals and a west façade flanked by two pavilions replaced the medieval one. The portal leading to the abbess's apartments is particularly notable for its very rich architectural form and figure sculpture.

Trzebnica Abbey was planned with important sculptural programmes both inside and outside the church, permitted by its function as a ducal necropolis, although the function and extent of the interior sculpture are obscure. A document of 1515 mentions 'Old Testament figures' linked with the nuns' gallery. On the exterior, carvings were set in the jambs of the three west façade portals and in the tympanum of the former *porta mortuorum* in the north transept wall. The tympana of the north transept and the north portal of the west façade are the only carvings from this Early Gothic programme to survive *in situ*: the north transept tympanum shows the *Virgin Enthroned between Kneeling Angels*, and the north-west façade tympanum depicts *David and Bathsheba*, with inscribed figures of David playing a stringed instrument and Bathsheba accompanied by her servant (see fig.). Numerous fragments with figurative and decorative sculpture (now in the west porch) are evidence of a well-developed sculptural programme linked primarily with the west façade, the nuns' gallery and possibly also the choir. Themes include Old and New Testament figures, New Testament scenes and parables.

The sculpture of Trzebnica Abbey is by at least three hands, of whom the artist of the *David* tympanum was the most talented. He was influenced by Byzantinizing German manuscript painting of the first quarter of the 13th century, a style represented by the Missal of Abbot Berthold of Weingarten (New York, Pierpont Morgan Lib., MS. 710). Many of the figurative fragments, however, show the influence of French Early Gothic sculpture. In some cases there are analogies with the workshop of Bamberg Cathedral, where the sculptural programme was

carved between 1220 and 1237 to a commission by Bishop Eckbert, brother of St Hedwig.

BIBLIOGRAPHY
D. Frey, G. Grundmann and A. Zinkler: *Die Klosterkirche in Trebnitz* (Breslau, 1940)
Z. Świechowski: *Architektura na Śląsku do połowy XIIIw.* [Architecture in Silesia up to the first half of the 13th century] (Warsaw, 1955), pp. 68ff
J. Rozpędowski: 'Die Architektur der Zisterzienserkirche in Trebnitz', *Z. Ostforsch.*, xxxvi (1987), pp. 161–74

ZYGMUNT ŚWIECHOWSKI

Ts'ai Ching. *See* CAI JING.

Ts'ai Hsiang. *See* CAI XIANG.

Ts'ao Chih-pai. *See* CAO ZHIBAI.

Tsaparang [rtsa pa brang; Tsapakang]. Site of the second capital of the kingdom of Guge, Tibet, founded *c.* AD 900 in the Sutlej Valley, west of Tholing. Under King Yeshe Ö (*reg* mid-10th century), the kingdom prospered and Buddhism flourished. The monk Rinchen Sangpo (958–1055) is said to have had more than 100 temples built in the area. During the following centuries the seat of power shifted between Tsaparang and Tholing until the mid-17th century, when Tsaparang and its temples were abandoned. This once imposing town, built on the slopes and summit of a steep, rocky formation, is now in ruins. Five temples have survived, however, including—in the lower part of the town—the so-called White Temple, where some of the earliest examples of Tibetan Buddhist wall paintings can be found. Thought to date back more than a thousand years, they feature various Buddhas and major Tantric deities. Below this temple is a small chapel dedicated to Tsong Khapa (1357–1419). Above the White Temple is the Red Temple, which also contains numerous Tantric wall paintings, including the *Five Jinas* and the *Eight Great Bodhisattvas*. On the walls of another small sanctuary, the Yamantaka Temple, are painted with gold on a dark ground the images of all the major meditation deities (*yidam*s), including Hevajra and Chakrasamvara. Within the ruined citadel on the crest of the cliff is the Chakrasamvara Temple (Demchok Mandala), which once contained a large three-dimensional *maṇḍala*. The 15th-century wall paintings in the temple are surprisingly well preserved and of extremely fine quality. Deities depicted include Mahakala, Samvara and Guhyasamaja.

BIBLIOGRAPHY
G. Tucci: *Indo-Tibetica*, iii/2 (Rome, 1935; Eng. trans. as *The Temples of Western Tibet and their Artistic Symbolism: Tsaparang*, ed. L. Chandra, New Delhi, 1989)
D. L. Snellgrove and H. E. Richardson: *A Cultural History of Tibet* (Boston, 1986)
S. Batchelor: *The Tibet Guide* (London, 1987), pp. 375–8
H. Weyer and J. Aschoff: *Tsaparang* (Freiburg im Breisgau, 1987)

HENRIK H. SØRENSEN

Tsaritsin. *See* VOLGOGRAD.

Tsaritsin Grad. *See* CARIČIN GRAD.

Tsarouhis [Tsarouchis], **Yannis** (*b* Piraeus, 13 Jan 1910; *d* Athens, 20 July 1989). Greek painter, stage designer, illustrator and writer. From 1928 to 1934 he worked as an apprentice in the workshop of Fotis Kontoglou, studying from 1932 to 1934 at the Higher School of Fine Arts in Athens, where he was taught at the Asylon Technis Gallery. Like most of the avant-garde intellectuals of his generation, he became actively involved with the popular art movement and the search for a Greekness in art. He travelled extensively in Greece, and went to Constantinople (now Istanbul) and Asia Minor studying Byzantine music, painting, textiles and the traditional shadow theatre. In 1935 he went to Paris where he was influenced by Matisse, in particular by such works as *Cyclist in a Mauve Singlet* (1936; see *Tsarouchis*, pl. 23), and by Demetrios Galanis. After 1938 he contributed costume and set designs for both the National and the Karolos Koun Theatre in Athens. While serving in World War II he executed numerous sketches of soldiers; these men were to become his favourite subject. From 1941 to 1944 he worked as a professional stage designer to earn his living. He also designed operatic sets for Franco Zeffirelli's production of Cherubini's *Médée* at Epidaurus in Greece, and for productions at La Scala in Milan, Covent Garden in London and the Avignon Festival in France. He contributed illustrations for literary works and published numerous essays on art and drama. In 1967 he moved to Paris and in 1973 returned to live in Athens. After his death his studio home in Maroussi was converted into a museum.

Tsarouhis was widely acclaimed as a painter of Greek people. His painting and his writings testify to his attempt to reconcile Western and Eastern pictorial traditions. Up to the mid-1960s he worked on stage-like compositions of traditional buildings and peasant women in their native dress, urban scenes, as well as portraits and semi-naked male figures. The predominant subject in his work after the 1960s is that of sensual semi-naked male figures. A fervent admirer of Caravaggio and Vermeer, as can be seen, for example, in the *Painter and his Model* (1974; priv. col., see *Tsarouchis*, p. 103), he went against the current of European abstraction. Despite their figurative content his works show a mastery of brushwork which makes them realistic and evocative.

WRITINGS

Tsarouchis (Athens, 1978)

FANI-MARIA TSIGAKOU

Tsarskoye Selo. *See* PUSHKIN.

Tscharner, Johann (Wilhelm Jan) von (*b* Lemberg, Austria [now Lviv, Ukraine], 12 May 1886; *d* Zurich, 20 June 1946). Swiss painter. He attended secondary school in Russia, and from 1905 to 1907 he studied philosophy at Jagiellonian University, Kraków, as well as studying under the history painter Florent Cynk (1838–1912) and the portrait painter Theodor Axentowicz (1859–1938) at the Academy of Fine Arts. In 1908 he attended both the private school in Munich run by Simon Hollósy, and the summer school at Nagybánya (now in Romania); it was there that he met the artist Ilona Spiegelhalter (1889–1971), whom he married. Tscharner attended Matisse's school in Paris, probably from 1909 to 1910, but no work from this period survives. He left Russia in 1914 and by 1916 had settled permanently in Zurich. From 1914 to 1917 Tscharner's style was clearly inspired by the French

Cubists. He took part in, among other things, the Dada exhibition at the Dada Galerie, Zurich (1917). While continuing to show Cubist influence, from 1917 he adopted muted colours and a more academic manner evocative of Jean-Siméon Chardin, principally in the choice of such subjects as lemons, pitchers and books, which concentrated his attention on form and colour. His work *c.* 1925 strongly evoked that of Derain, Braque, and especially that of Giorgio Morandi. He tended towards intimism, depicting subjects as denuded geometrical forms in sombre tones (e.g. *Still-life with Guitar, c.* 1930; Basle, Schweiz. N.-Versich.-Ges. Kol.), and this cocoon-like atmosphere was the dominant characteristic of his work. Between 1930 and 1940 he executed most of his portraits and he increasingly painted landscapes, often depicting lakes in stormy weather; some of these works, particularly those depicting the Rhône near Geneva, have been compared with Corot's paintings.

BIBLIOGRAPHY

I. Meier and G. Jedlicka: *Johann von Tscharner* (Zurich, 1986)

VINCENT LIEBER

Tschichold, Jan [Johannes] (*b* Leipzig, 2 April 1902; *d* Locarno, 11 Aug 1974). German graphic designer and writer. He was the son of a sign painter and studied at the Academy of Book Design, Leipzig (1919–22), before working as a freelance designer. Influenced by Soviet Constructivism (especially the work of El Lissitzky) and the Bauhaus exhibition in Weimar in 1923 (*see* TYPOGRAPHY, fig. 5), he published 'Elementare Typographie' (*Typographische Mitteilungen*, Oct 1925) and *Die neue Typographie* (Berlin, 1928), widely read among young designers, in which he promoted the functional use of sans serif typefaces and asymmetrical layouts (*see* TYPOGRAPHY).

Having been appointed in 1925 to teach at the Meisterschule für Deutschlands Buchdrucker in Munich, Tschichold was arrested by the Nazis in March 1933, accused of advocating radical ideas (*Kulturbolschevismus*), and dismissed from teaching. Released from 'protective custody' after six weeks, he moved to Basle, Switzerland, worked as a book designer and published what he later called a 'more prudent' manifesto, *Typographische Gestaltung* (1935). Re-examining his earlier writings, he decided that he should abandon the new typography because it reminded him of the totalitarian severity of National Socialism and fascism. In addition, he decided that some serif typefaces were often more appropriate and more legible than sans serif. Invited to England in 1947, he redesigned Penguin Books, using classical serif typefaces and symmetrical designs. As a designer of typography, he was the inventor of Sabon. He returned to Switzerland in 1949, where he continued to write and design.

WRITINGS

Die neue Typographie (Berlin, 1928)
Typographische Gestaltung (Basle, 1935); Eng. trans. as *Asymmetric Typography* (New York, 1967)

BIBLIOGRAPHY

R. McLean: *Jan Tschichold: Typographer* (Boston, 1975)
P. B. Meggs: *A History of Graphic Design* (New York, 1983)
E. M. Gottschall: *Typographic Communications Today* (Cambridge, MA, 1989)

ROY R. BEHRENS

Tschudi, Hugo von (*b* Vienna, 7 Feb 1851; *d* Bad Cannstatt, 26 Nov 1911). German art historian and museum curator of Austrian birth. His father, Johann Jakob von Tschudi, worked in Vienna as a researcher and doctor, and from 1860 to 1863 as a Swiss diplomat; his mother was a daughter of the painter Julius Schnorr von Carolsfeld. After finishing his legal studies and holding a post at the Österreichisches Museum für Kunst und Industrie in Vienna, in 1884 Tschudi became the assistant of Wilhelm von Bode at what subsequently became the Kaiser-Friedrich-Museum (now the Bodemuseum) in Berlin. There Tschudi devoted himself to the art of Dutch Old Masters and of the Italian Quattrocento. In 1895 he became director of the Königliche National-Galerie in Berlin, which meant that from then on he dealt with 19th-century art. Tschudi entered effortlessly into this area and soon published fundamental works on Edouard Manet (1902) and Adolph von Menzel (1905). His main preoccupation, in association with other scholars, was the preparation of the great Berlin *Jahrhundertausstellung* of 1906; this exhibition was designed to give a perspective on the German contribution to art over the previous century and to establish its position in relation to French art of the same period.

As director of the Königliche National-Galerie, Tschudi concerned himself with nurturing German artists, and he bought numerous valuable works by Menzel, Wilhelm Leibl, Carl Schuch, Hans Thoma and Max Liebermann, as well as Arnold Böcklin and Hans von Marées, who were the most important representatives of a specifically German variant of the Symbolist movement. His real objective, however, was to acquire works by modern French painters. Tschudi purchased important works by Gustave Courbet, Edouard Manet, Auguste Renoir and Claude Monet. It was when he proposed the purchase of a painting by Eugène Delacroix, however, that rumblings of discontent broke out among Berlin artists, who felt neglected, and also from Emperor William II (*reg* 1888–1918), who prided himself on being an unerring connoisseur of art. Relations in Berlin became so difficult that in 1909 Tschudi decided to accept the appointment he had meanwhile been offered as general director of the Bayerische Staatsgemäldesammlung in Munich.

Tschudi tried to proceed with greater tact in Munich than in Berlin. He consistently avoided using public funds for his purchases of French works of art, applying instead for donations from private collections and wealthy art lovers. While he tried from then on by these means to give Munich the benefit of valuable paintings by modern French artists such as he had previously secured for Berlin, he outwardly applied himself to other tasks such as the rearrangement of the Alte Pinakothek; he also planned to link it spatially with the Neue Pinakothek. When purchasing works by more recent artists he at first restricted himself mainly to German painters, especially the progressive 'Leibl-Kreis' (group centred on Leibl). Then he also began to buy the work of such earlier French painters as Théodore Géricault and Courbet. But he really had his sights set on modern French painters, going beyond the Impressionists to include still more recent artists such as Paul Gauguin and Vincent van Gogh. He was not able to accomplish most of his objectives during his lifetime, but he lived to see such a major work as Manet's *Luncheon in the Studio* (1868; Munich, Neue Pin.) secured for his museum.

It was not long before the disappointments experienced in Berlin began to be repeated in Munich. A reactionary co-director, the painter August Holmberg (1851–1911), and a ponderous, uncooperative purchasing committee increasingly hampered Tschudi's initiatives and thwarted many an ambitious plan. On top of this came a disfiguring illness, which ultimately broke his spirit. After barely two years in Munich he died of a cardiac complaint. Tschudi's colleague, Heinz Braune, succeeded in bringing his ambitious plans to fruition.

WRITINGS
Edouard Manet (Berlin, 1902)
Adolph Menzel: Abbildungen seiner Gemälde und Studien (Munich, 1905)

BIBLIOGRAPHY
H. Uhde-Bernays: 'Die Tschudispende', *Kst & Kstler*, x (1912), pp. 379–88
——: 'Hugo von Tschudi im zehnten Jahr nach seinem Tode', *Ganymed*, iii (Munich, 1921), pp. 70–73
——: *Im Lichte der Freiheit* (Wiesbaden, 1947), pp. 187, 194, 307, 327, 343, 367, 380, 403, 419, 432
K. Martin: *Die Tschudi-Spende* (Munich, 1962)
E. Ruhmer: 'Hugo von Tschudi: Seine Vorgänger und seine Nachfolger', *Festgabe zur Eröffnung der Neuen Pinakothek in München am 28. März 1981* (Munich, 1981), pp. 28–41
P. Paret: 'The Tschudi Affair', *J. Mod. Hist.*, liii (1981), p. 589
H. Ludwig: 'Die Tschudi-Spende', *Kunst, Geld und Politik um 1900 in München* (Berlin, 1986), pp. 236–43

EBERHARD RUHMER

Tschumi, Bernard (*b* Lausanne, 25 Jan 1944). French architect. He was the son of a well-known Modernist architect and he graduated in architecture (1969) from the Eidgenössische Technische Hochschule, Zurich. In the 1970s he taught at the Architectural Association school in London and during this period he developed the 'strategy of disjunctions', a theory based on his belief that contemporary culture and architecture were best expressed by fragmentation as opposed to the classical ideal of unity. Tschumi advocated a 'post-humanist' architecture stressing not only dispersion but also its effect on the entire notion of unified, coherent architectural form. This attempt to deconstruct the components of architecture must be seen in relation to the linguistic theories of the French philosopher JACQUES DERRIDA (*see also* DECONSTRUCTION). Tschumi exhibited drawings in Europe and North America and designed a number of small experimental constructions that he called 'follies', playing on the double meaning of the French word *folie* as a state of mental imbalance and a small pleasure pavilion. In 1981 he published *The Manhattan Transcripts* in which he exploited the cinematographic themes of frame and sequence. In 1983 Tschumi won the international competition for the planning of the Parc de la Villette, an ill-defined site of 35 ha in a working-class suburb on the northern outskirts of Paris. Regarding as obsolete the picturesque landscaping tradition derived from Frederick Law Olmsted, he proposed an 'urban park for the 21st century', designed as much for urban entertainment and social interaction as for individual contact with nature. His scheme, which paid little attention to existing structures, was based on the superimposition on the site of a series of theoretical points, lines and surfaces, a geometrical concept reminiscent of Vasily Kandinsky's theories. The programmatic requirements were placed at the intersections of this 'self-referential' grid, which was marked by red, neo-constructivist follies. Two long, covered galleries were placed at right angles to each other, while a winding pathway revealed a 'cinematic' promenade of thematic gardens. Tschumi built several of the follies and other facilities, as well as coordinating work by other architects and landscape designers. The project gave his career an enormous boost; he was subsequently a finalist in many international competitions including those for the National Theatre and Opera House, Tokyo, and the County Hall, Strasbourg (both 1986), and Kansai International Airport, Osaka (1987). He was appointed Chairman (1987–9) of the Task Force for Flushing Meadows, New York, and in 1988 he became Dean of the Graduate School of Architecture and Planning at Columbia University, New York.

WRITINGS

The Manhattan Transcripts (London and New York, 1981)
'Disjunctions', *Perspecta*, 23 (1987), pp. 108–19
Cinégramme Folie: Parc de la Villette (New York, 1988)
Architecture and Disjunction (Cambridge, MA, 1994)
Event-cities: Praxis (Cambridge, MA, 1994)

BIBLIOGRAPHY

'Works of Bernard Tschumi', *A + U*, 216 (1988), pp. 9–68
S. S. Richardson: *Bernard Tschumi: A Bibliography* (Monticello, IL, 1989)
ISABELLE GOURNAY

Tschusiya, Tilsa (*b* Supe, nr Paramonga, 1936; *d* Lima, 23 Sept 1984). Peruvian painter. She studied at the Escuela Nacional Superior de Bellas Artes in Lima, graduating in 1959 with the school's Gold Medal; she had already received second prize in the Salón Municipal in 1957 and represented Peru at the first Biennale des Jeunes in Paris in 1958. Working in a figurative idiom indebted to Surrealism, she created a unique dream-like universe that made her paintings among the most intense and rich in modern Peruvian art. Although she reached her imagery through intuition, she arrived at forms connected iconographically both with Andean and oriental traditions. The diaphanous quality of her draughtsmanship and her smooth, finely gradated play of blended colours combined to create an atmosphere in which myths take root, fantastic creatures appear and strange metamorphoses take place, ensuring the originality of her work.

BIBLIOGRAPHY

J. E. Wuffarden: *Tschusiya* (Lima, 1981)
LUIS ENRIQUE TORD

Tsereteli, Zurab (Konstantinovich) (*b* Tbilisi, 4 Jan 1934). Georgian decorative artist. He studied (1952–8) at the Academy of Art, Tbilisi, under Ucha Dzhaparidze (1906–91), Iosif Sharleman' (1880–1957) and Vasily Shukhayev, from whom he gained a feeling for colour and high standards in painting. His works at the academy were primarily decorative landscapes with brilliant and contrasting colours. Tsereteli's acquaintance with ancient art, in particular with the mosaics of the 5th-century basilica at Pitsunda (Bichvinta), fostered an interest in monumental art. The study of mosaic technique at the studio of Marc Chagall in France helped Tsereteli to revive the traditions

of smalto mosaic in Georgian art, and he discovered in it new aesthetic and technical possibilities.

Tsereteli's smalto work (two- and three-dimensional) is elegant, decorative and festive in spirit. He used pagan and folkloric motifs lavishly, as well as flora and fauna and Georgian ornamental themes, which he developed into colourful compositions. The mosaics covering the wall of the bar and the decorative walls outside the hotel at the resort of Pitsunda (1966–7) are distinguished by their variety of design. His mosaic (1969) at the pool in front of the V. I. Lenin Museum Complex in Ul'yanovsk creates a colourful picture of the seabed. In the mosaic on the walls of the Trade Union Palace in Tbilisi (1970), the pagan motifs and bright colour emphasize the antiquity of the concept of 'work' itself. Tsereteli made extensive use of wood, metal and glass, and compositions in these materials were erected in public buildings and spaces in Tbilisi, Moscow and elsewhere. The decorative copper installation *Happiness to the Children of the Whole World* (1970s) is in the university campus of Brockport, NY, and the frieze *A Holiday* (engraving on stainless steel) and the stained-glass panel *Salyut* (both 1970s–80s) decorate the embassies of the Russian Federation in Brasília and Tokyo. A number of works, including those in Brasília and Tokyo, are remarkable for their vivid themes, such as the monument in Moscow symbolizing Russo-Georgian friendship (a Pop art composition of gigantic letters created with the poet Andrei Voznesensky in 1980), and an anti-war monument of St George running his sword through a ballistic missile, erected near the UN building in New York in 1990.

BIBLIOGRAPHY

Zurab Tsereteli, intro. Yu. I. Nekhoroshev (Moscow, 1976) [illus., with Eng. summary]
O. Shvidkovsky: *Zurab Tsereteli* (Moscow, 1985) [Rus. and Eng. text]
N. EZERSKAYA

Tsingos, Thanos (*b* Eleusis, 19 Aug 1914; *d* Athens, 26 Jan 1965). Greek painter, stage designer and architect. He studied architecture at the National Technical University in Athens (1931–6). From 1937 to 1939 he worked as an architect. During the second world war he joined the Greek army, serving first in Greece and later in the Middle East. He was imprisoned and sentenced to death for his participation in the Middle East coup, but was pardoned in 1945–6. He moved to Brazil in 1947, where he worked with the architects Oscar Niemeyer, Lúcio Costa and Palumbo on the plans of Brasília; in the same year he worked in Paris on the development of St Cloud. From 1948 to 1961 he lived in Paris, where he painted and made stage designs and costumes (1948–55) for the theatre founded by him and his wife Christine, a leading actress of the avant-garde. In 1953 he had his first one-man show at the Studio Facchetti in Paris; this was followed by others, notably at the Galerie Iris Clert (1956). Between 1961 and 1965 he was mostly in Greece and exhibited in Athens, for example at the Zygos Gallery in 1963. Despite his association with the Ecole de Paris his painting defies classification. Its earlier phase shares the gestures and application of Action Painting, using intense colour in abstract compositions. A marked preference for dynamic and emotionally charged flowers, where the paint is also applied directly from the tube with movements of the whole body, is notable after 1955 and may be interpreted as a move towards the 'New Figuration'.

BIBLIOGRAPHY
Tsingos (exh. cat. by P. Restany and others, Paris, Pompidou, 1980)
Thanos Tsingos (exh. cat., Athens, N.G., 1980)

ANGELA TAMVAKI

Tsiranavor. *See under* ASHTARAK.

Tsonev, Kiril (*b* Kyustendil, 1 Jan 1896; *d* Sofia, 5 April 1961). Bulgarian painter, teacher and critic. From 1915 to 1920 he studied at the National Academy of Arts (Natsionalna Hudozhestvena Academia) in Sofia, in 1921 at the Akademie der Bildenden Künste in Vienna and in 1922–5 under Hugo von Habermann (*b* 1849) at the Akademie der Bildenden Künste in Munich. During the 1930s he travelled extensively in Mexico and Cuba, where he was influenced by the art of the Mexican muralists and by the colour and vitality of Latin American painting in general. At this time he painted landscapes and portraits in oils, in which he balanced the poetic expression of colours and rhythms with simple and monumental, yet decorative, forms, as in *Mulatto Women Picking Citrus Fruit* (1934; Sofia, C.A.G.) and *Sea Gulf* (1940; Sofia, N.A.G.). He became well-known as a painter of portraits (e.g. *Boy with a Soccer Ball*, 1938; Sofia, N.A.G.) and of still-lifes (e.g. *Citrus Fruit in a Green Bowl*, 1936, and *Still-life with Bottles*, 1938). His paintings show his understanding and absorption of several of the trends of modernism prevalent in western Europe in the 1930s. From 1925 to 1940 he was a member of the NATIONAL ART SOCIETY OF BULGARIA and was one of its leading artists. Tsonev was also an art critic and a professor of painting (1945–50) at the National Academy of Arts, Sofia. Many of his works are at the Dimitrov-Maistora museum in Kyustendil.

BIBLIOGRAPHY
Natsionalna Hudozhestvena Galeriya [National Art Gallery], cat. (Sofia, 1970)
I. Mihalcheva: *Portretat v Balgarskara zhivopis* [The portrait in Bulgarian painting], ii (Sofia, 1971)
Kiril Tsonev Album: Anniversary Exhibition (Sofia, 1972)

MARIANA KATZAROVA

Tsuchida, Bakusen (*b* Niigata Prefect., 9 Feb 1887; *d* Kyoto, 10 June 1936). Japanese painter. In 1904 he became a student of Seihō Takeuchi, and in 1911 he graduated from the Kyoto Municipal Professional Painting School. At first he exhibited in official exhibitions, but in 1919, seeking to create a modern form of Japanese-style painting (*Nihonga*), he helped form the unofficial National Creative Painting Society (Kokuga Sōsaku Kyōkai; *see* JAPAN, §VI, 5(iii)). From 1921 to 1923 he travelled and studied in Europe, where he was particularly impressed by early Renaissance frescoes. After returning to Japan, Tsuchida sought with such works as *Maiko Dancer in a Garden* (1924; Tokyo, N. Mus. Mod. A.) to create a style that combined the realistic, logical expression of Western painting with the decorative, traditional Japanese style. In 1928, after the dispersal of the National Creative Painting Society, he again returned to official exhibitions, and in 1934 he became a member of the Imperial Art Academy.

BIBLIOGRAPHY
Murakami Kagaku/Tsuchida Bakusen (Tokyo, 1972)

YOSHIKAZU IWASAKI

Tsuchida, Hiromi (*b* Fukui, 20 Dec 1939). Japanese photographer. He studied dye chemistry at Fukui University from 1959 to 1963 before working in product development for a cosmetics company. From 1965 to 1968 he studied at Tokyo College of Photography where he later became a lecturer (1972) and professor (1993). Taking an interest in the workings of Japanese consciousness, Tsuchida photographed the folk events, festivals and pilgrimages of various regions. These photographs were exhibited as *Jihei kūkan* ('Self-autism space') at the Nikon Salons in Tokyo and Osaka and were later amplified in the collection *Zokushin* ('Gods of the earth'; Yokohama, 1976) and further exhibited in 1977.

Tsuchida's concern with the identity of the Japanese people subsequently developed in a variety of directions, and in the 1970s and 1980s he produced a series of works examining the culture of the lowest social strata of Japan. These include *Aoi hana, Tokyo Doll* ('Blue flower, Tokyo doll'), which focused on transvestites working in the bars and clubs of Tokyo. An interest in the effect of the bombing of Hiroshima at the end of World War II led Tsuchida to put together his series *Hiroshima* (Tokyo, 1986). The three parts of this photographic study included portraits of bomb victims 30 years after the bomb, records of the effect of the bomb blast on the landscape and a survey of the exhibits of the Hiroshima Peace Memorial Museum. Alongside this project Tsuchida's major interest continued to be the photographic investigation of Japanese cultural identity.

BIBLIOGRAPHY
New Japanese Photography (exh. cat. by J. Szarkowski and S. Yamagishi, New York, MOMA, 1974), pp. 64–7
K. Taki: 'The Visible and the Invisible', *Asahi Cam.* (Sept 1977), pp. 182–5
K. Nishii: 'Freedom from the Gods of the Earth', *Cam. Mainichi* (May 1978), pp. 98–100
Japanese Photography Today and its Origin (exh. cat. by A. Colombo and I. Doniselli, Bologna, Gal. A. Mod.; Milan, Gal. A. Mod.; Brussels, Pal. B.-A.; London, ICA; 1979), pp. 138–43

KOHTARO IIZAWA

Ts'ui Po. *See* CUI BO.

Tsuji, Shindō (*b* Tottori Prefect., 28 Oct 1910; *d* Kyoto, 18 Aug 1981). Japanese sculptor. He went to Tokyo in 1931. At first he wanted to be a painter and studied at a private art school. In 1933 he was accepted for the first time into the 20th In Ten (Japan Art Institute Exhibition) with his statue of *Motomaro Senke*, which marked the start of his woodcarving period. In 1939 he exhibited *Seated Woman* (wood, h. 1.28 m, 1939; Kyoto, Mun. Mus. A.) at the 26th In Ten. In 1942 he became a member of the Japan Art Institute. In 1949 he moved to Kyoto, becoming a lecturer at the Kyoto City College of Art, retaining the post until 1976. With sculptor Masakazu Horiuchi, who had become a member of staff in 1950, he trained many students. In 1953 he exhibited *Neck of a Man* at the *Kindai no Chōso—Seiyō to Nihon* (Modern carving and sculpture— The West and Japan) exhibition at the National Museum of Modern Art, Tokyo. Having shown ceramic works at a one-man exhibition in 1956, he began to produce abstract works, showing six ceramic pieces at the 29th Venice Biennale in 1958, including *Horse and Figure* (ceramic, h. 1.015 m, 1958; Kyoto, Mun. Mus. A.). He also exhibited in New York, Pittsburgh, San Francisco and Paris. In 1977 he was selected as Kyoto's Person of Cultural Merit.

BIBLIOGRAPHY
Tsuji Shindō tōchō sakuhinshū [The collected clay sculptures of Shindō Tsuji], essay by S. Kimura (Tokyo, 1978)
Tsuji Shindō—Gendai chōkoku no isai [Shindō Tsuji—a genius of contemporary sculpture] (exh. cat., essay by S. Kimura and M. Horiuchi; Kyoto, N. Mus. Mod. A., 1983)

YASUYOSHI SAITO

Tsuki Katsura. Japanese residential garden in Hōfu (Yamaguchi Prefect.). It was laid out in 1712 by the poet, tea master and Zen practitioner Katsura Tadaharu, a member of the Mōri clan that governed the area. Tadaharu was familiar with the many great Zen gardens of Kyoto, and Tsuki Katsura is unusual in the history of Japanese gardens (*see* GARDEN, §VI, 3) as a residential garden whose bold design was strongly influenced by Zen Buddhism. The name Tsuki Katsura ('moon cinnamon') is derived from the Chinese fable that describes the shadows on the surface of the moon as a rabbit standing beneath a cinnamon tree, and a Zen *koan* (riddle) from the *Blue Cliff Record* (Chin. *Bi yan lu*; Jap. *Hekiganroku*; late 11th century–early 12th), which deals with the inexplicable nature of wisdom.

The garden is L-shaped and encloses the main house on its southern and eastern fronts. It is bounded by a low, yellow plastered wall, raised on a cut-stone base edged with moss and capped by clay tiles. These varied textures are important, since the only other elements are rough boulders, raked gravel and tiny patches of lichen. Nineteen stones, nearly all of which have flat tops, are set into a

Tsuki Katsura, crescent-shaped stone in a dry landscape; garden laid out 1712

gravel bed, while one monolith in the shape of a crescent moon is set on a small stone base in the south-east corner (see fig.). The horizontality of the wall, rocks and raked gravel gives the space a dynamic flow. The only vertical features are the crescent-shaped stone and the nearby rock at which it points. Together they create a visual tension that balances the corner where they stand. The stark simplicity of the space, which is softened only by the trees outside, and the dramatic placement of the stones give Tsuki Katsura a haunting, enigmatic quality. More like a sculptural display than a garden, it had a strong influence on late 20th-century Japanese landscape design.

BIBLIOGRAPHY
T. Soga, ed.: *San'in* (1979), ii of *Tanbō Nihon no niwa* [Investigation of Japanese gardens], 12 vols (Tokyo, 1978–9)

BRUCE A. COATS

Tsukioka Yoshitoshi [Yoshioka Kinzaburō; Taiso Yoshitoshi] (*b* Edo [now Tokyo], 1839; *d* Edo, 1892). Japanese printmaker. At the age of 11 he was apprenticed to the *ukiyoe* artist Utagawa Kuniyoshi (*see* UTAGAWA, (6)), who was to have a pronounced influence on his future work, in both Yoshitoshi's penchant for historical themes and his interest in Western art. In 1853 Yoshitoshi designed his first woodblock print, but no further work is known until 1858, when, following the Utagawa masters, he produced comic and actor prints (*yakushae*). From 1862 he began to produce pictures of warriors (*mushae*) and other historical subjects, which were to be amongst his most important themes. After his father's death in 1863, he seems to have been adopted by the Tsukioka family, for he began to sign works *Tsukioka Yoshitoshi*. His first critical success came with the print series *Wakan hyaku monogatari* ('100 ghost tales from China and Japan'; 1865; e.g. London, V&A). At around this time the lifting of the government ban on illustrating contemporary events allowed Yoshitoshi to depict murders and wars ever more realistically. He produced *Eimei nijuhasshuku* ('28 famous murders with poems'; 1866–7) in collaboration with Utagawa Yoshiiku (1833–1904). Bloodshed and violence were not new to *ukiyoe*, but in answer to the increasing demand for horror and the grotesque towards the end of the 19th century Yoshitoshi's designs show an extreme of gruesome detail, possibly reflecting the artist's own slightly unbalanced and sadistic nature. In the early 1870s he suffered a mental breakdown, but he recovered in 1874 and took the new surname Taiso ('Great Resurrection'). From then on Yoshitoshi produced illustrations of current events for the newspapers, which became his major source of income. By the early 1880s he was the most popular artist of his day; his works after 1885 are generally considered to be his best. His most famous prints include the series of diptychs *Shinsen azuma nishikie* ('A new selection of eastern colour prints'; 1885–9; e.g. Philadelphia, PA, Mus. A.), *Tsuki hyakushi* ('One hundred aspects of the moon'; 1885–92; Amsterdam, Rijksmus.) and *Shinkei sanjūrokkaisen* ('New forms of 36 ghosts'; 1889–92). In contrast to his earlier preoccupation with martial subjects, Yoshitoshi also treated the theme of beautiful women in the series *Fuzoku sanjuniso* ('32 aspects of women'; 1888; e.g. Philadelphia, PA, Mus. A.). Despite his highly individual range of subject-matter, Yoshitoshi is often considered one of the last great masters of the *ukiyoe* tradition (*see* JAPAN, §IX, 3(iii)). There are good collections of Yoshitoshi's works at the Museum of Art, Philadelphia, PA, and the Museés Royaux d'Art et d'Histoire, Brussels.

BIBLIOGRAPHY
R. S. Keyes: *Courage and Silence: A Study of the Life and Colour Woodblock Prints of Tsukioka Yoshitoshi, 1838–92*, 2 vols (Ann Arbor, 1983)
J. Stevenson: *Yoshitoshi's Thirty-six Ghosts* (New York, 1983)
J. Meech-Pekarik: *The World of the Meiji Print: Impressions of a New Civilization* (New York and Tokyo, 1986)
J. Stevenson: *Yoshitoshi's Women: The Woodblock Print Series 'Fuzoku sanjuniso'* (Hong Kong, 1986)
E. van den Ing and R. Schaap: *Beauty and Violence: Japanese Prints by Yoshitoshi, 1839–1892* (Amsterdam, 1992)
J. Stevenson: *One Hundred Aspects of the Moon* (Hong Kong, 1992)

PAUL GRIFFITH

Tsunenobu. *See* KANŌ, (14).

Tsvetayev, Ivan (Vladimirovich) (*b* Talitsy, nr Shuya, Vladimir province, 16 May 1847; *d* Moscow, 12 Sept 1913). Russian art historian and linguist. After studying as a linguist at St Petersburg University in the late 1860s, he was appointed to a series of professorial posts at the universities of Warsaw, Kiev and Moscow, becoming head of the department of the theory and history of fine art at Moscow University in 1889. In addition, he worked at the Imperial Rumyantsov Museum in Moscow (now the Russian Library), first in the department of engravings (1882–9), where he was responsible for the catalogue of the collection published in 1888, and later as director of the museum (1900–10). Simultaneously, he devoted much of his energies to the establishment of the Alexander III Museum of Fine Arts (now the Pushkin Museum of Fine Arts) in Moscow. In 1896 he initiated a competition for the design of the museum, which was built in 1898–1912, in Neo-classical style, on Volkhonka Street by Roman Klein. Envisaged as a complement to the more modern collections of paintings, manuscripts, engravings and sculpture at the Imperial Rumyantsov Museum, the new museum was planned as primarily an educational institution. As such it was affiliated to Moscow University and, initially, modelled on the collections of art and antiquities of the university itself. Tsvetayev was responsible for the museum's collecting policy, and commissioned plaster replicas of the most famous statues in Western European museums; he also bought the exceptional Golenishchev collection of Egyptian antiquities from St Petersburg in 1909. He broadened the scope of the museum by purchasing Italian, French and German Old Masters from private collections in Moscow and St Petersburg. Thus, Tsvetayev's vision and energy ensured that the Museum of Fine Arts, funded by private subscription, became established as the most important collection of pre-Renaissance and Renaissance art in Moscow. His own research and interests were focused on the art, language and culture of the Antique world. A leading member of the Moscow Historical and Archaeological Societies, he was appointed a full member of the St Petersburg Academy of Arts in 1903 and a corresponding member of the Academy of Science in 1904. He was the father of the poet Marina Tsvetayeva (1892–1941).

WRITINGS
ed.: *Moskovskiy i Rumyantsevskiy muzey: Kabinet gravyur: Katalog gravyurnogo otdeleniya* [The Moscow and Rumyantsov Museum: the engravings room: catalogue of the engravings department] (Moscow, 1888)
Uchebnyy atlas antichnogo vayaniya [Educational atlas of Antique sculpture], 3 vols (Moscow, 1890–94)
Iz zhizni vysshikh shkol Rimskoy imperii [From the life of the higher schools of the Roman Empire] (Moscow, 1902)

JEREMY HOWARD

Tuaillon, Louis (*b* Berlin, 7 Sept 1862; *d* Berlin, 21 Feb 1919). German sculptor. It is not known whether his father was his mother's husband (who was killed in the Franco-Prussian war in 1870), as the personal files of the Akademie der Künste in Berlin state, or, as has been conjectured, the Berlin art dealer Lepke. Tuaillon spent his youth in Berlin, attending the French grammar school until 1879. From 1879 to 1881 he studied at the Hochschule für Bildende Künste, before joining the workshop of the most successful Berlin sculptor of the time, Reinhold Begas, as a pupil. With his neo-Baroque style, Begas set the tone for state art under Emperor William II. The following year Tuaillon went to Vienna, where he worked for two years in the studio of the sculptor Rudolf Weyr. He then travelled to Rome where, like his teacher Begas, he became a member of the Deutscher Künstlerverein founded in 1846. One of his first important works was *Girl Tying a Sandal* (1886; Berlin, Neue N.G.), which was already far removed from Begas's idiom.

The sculptor A. J. W. Volkmann introduced Tuaillon to the circle of the painter Hans von Marées, whose tectonic imagery influenced Tuaillon's early work. In this period he completed only a few works, destroying many in his struggle for a new vision and from dissatisfaction with his own approach. After Hans von Marées's death in 1887, Adolf von Hildebrand rejoined the circle of artists in Rome. His formal theories may have influenced Tuaillon. At this time he began to devote himself to preliminary studies for his first major work, *Amazon* (1890), in the Tiergarten in Berlin. After many changes it was completed in 1895.

Tuaillon's breakthrough came when he received major commissions. In his Rome studio he produced the *Victor* for the collector and patron Eduard Arnold in Berlin (now in Reichsstrasse, Berlin); *Chariot Driver* was produced for the Bürgerpark in Bremen (1901). In 1902 Tuaillon returned to Berlin. He joined the Secession in 1903, and his first monument using a mounted figure, the *Emperor Frederick III*, begun in Rome, was presented as a plaster model at their exhibition. In 1905 the striking monument, which showed the Emperor in the semi-naked state of an Imperator, was set up in Bremen (Hermann-Böse-Strasse).

Despite his rejection of modern tendencies in art and their representatives, Emperor William II awarded the sculptor a commission to produce an enlarged version of his *Amazon* for the Tiergarten (1905–6). In addition, two monuments to Prussian rulers were unveiled in Cologne in 1910: the mounted *Emperor William II* (Cologne, Hohenzollernbrücke), begun in 1907, and the mounted figure of his father, *Emperor Frederick III*, on which the artist had been working since 1908. In 1911 the monument to *Frederick the Great* was erected at Beuthen, near

Kraków. These monuments reflected an increasingly conventional outlook in the artist. He prepared preliminary studies for a life-size bull relief in bronze for Krefeld on a trip to Hungary in 1911.

In his time Tuaillon was regarded as a representative of modernism, despite his appointment in 1907 as head of a second studio of sculpture at the Königliche Akademie der Künste in Berlin. This position was undoubtedly of importance to the group of conservative sculptors who produced the official state art, a group to which Tuaillon belonged after several major official commissions. Tuaillon's pupils included Georg Kolbe. His lifestyle placed him among the upper middle-classes, bringing him commissions from the financial upper class of Berlin, and his themes were selected from the traditional mythological stock, as was usual in Begas's time as well. His works were characterized by a severe reduction of form, if not always of content, by a statuesque quality and a closed outer contour.

BIBLIOGRAPHY

Thieme–Becker

W. Grzimek: *Deutsche Bildhauer des 20. Jahrhunderts* (Munich, 1969)

P. Bloch and W. Grzimek: *Das klassische Berlin* (Berlin, 1978), pp. 314–17

Abbilder–Leitbilder: Berliner Skulpturen von Schadow bis heute (exh. cat., W. Berlin, Neuer Berlin. Kstver., 1978)

B. Mielsch: *Denkmäler, Freiplastiken, Brunnen in Bremen, 1800–1945* (Bremen, 1980)

Was ist Kleinplastik? (exh. cat., Bremen, Ksthalle, 1981)

Rheinland Westfalen und die Berliner Bildhauerschule des 19. Jahrhunderts (exh. cat., ed. B. Hüfler; Berlin, Staatl. Museen Preuss. Kultbes., 1984)

G.-D. Ulferts: *Louis Tuaillon, 1862–1919: Ein Bildhauer Wilhelminischer Zeit zwischen Tradition und Moderne* (diss., U. Göttingen, 1987)

Kunst in Berlin, 1648–1987 (exh. cat., E. Berlin, Altes Mus., 1987), p. 338

SIBYLLE EINHOLZ

Tuam. Town in Co. Galway, Ireland, notable for its monastery and cathedral. The monastery was founded in the 6th century by St Jarlath and came into prominence in the 12th century, when it benefited from the patronage of the O'Connor kings of Connaught. In 1152 Tuam was chosen as the seat of an archbishopric. In addition to some architectural sculpture in the cathedral, there are fragments of at least two crosses erected under the patronage of King Turlough O'Connor (*reg* 1106–56). The names of Turlough and Abbot O'Oissin are recorded on an inscription on the market cross (1128–56), originally on the western side of the market place, now at the Church of Ireland cathedral. Its square base with sloping sides bears the figures of two ecclesiastics modelled in bold relief. The shaft above is divided into panels, each filled with delicately incised animal and interlace ornament. The animal designs are fine examples of the Irish Urnes style, a distinctive blend of Irish and Scandinavian elements, popular in Hiberno-Romanesque art. The patterns are comparable with those on the bronze reliquary Cross of Cong (Dublin, N. Mus.) made under Turlough's patronage between 1119 and 1136. When the carved ornament was painted, the analogies with metalwork must have been very obvious. The ringed cross head now surmounting the shaft comes from a different monument, but again there are hints of influence from metalwork, most notably the use of bosses or rivets and the laying of the intermediary cross over the head of the main cross. On the south face is a *Crucifixion* in which the curved patterns on the torso,

Tuam Cathedral, east window, carving on embrasure showing interlace pattern and unidentified figure scene, *c.* 1184–90

coupled with the v-folds of the loin cloth, are distinctly Romanesque in character. The model would appear to have been an imported crucifix of the Winchester school, although no examples survive. On the reverse is an ecclesiastic, probably a bishop, surrounded by six smaller ecclesiastical figures, each holding a bell and crosier and all modelled in a distinctively Irish style. The juxtaposition of a bishop and a *Crucifixion* on the 12th-century crosses was evidently a means of asserting episcopal authority at a time when new diocesan structures were being established in Ireland.

A further cross shaft in the cathedral, decorated with interlace, stylized animals and frets, bears an inscription referring to Turlough, Abbot O'Oissin and the sculptor Gillachrist O'Toole, a name that suggests a Wicklow origin. The quality of Gillachrist's carving, however, is much inferior to that of the market cross.

The architectural sculpture in the cathedral post-dates Turlough's reign by some 30 years. It comes from a church erected after a former cathedral had fallen 'roof and stone' in 1184. Only the chancel survives, sandwiched between an early 14th-century choir and the early Victorian cathedral designed in 1862. The broad chancel arch has a spectacular array of chevrons in six orders, and the block capitals supporting it bear thin but finely detailed grotesque masks. The arch was damaged by fire and exposure to the weather (before 1862), but the three east windows fared better. Here the decorated embrasures, with foliate, interlace and animal patterns, survive in better condition than any other Hiberno-Romanesque sculpture. The stylized animal design, a complex mixture of Irish and Scandinavian elements, defies analysis according to conventional stylistic terminology. The subject of one enigmatic panel with a human figure has been variously interpreted as a Temptation scene or a Virtue conquering a Vice (see fig.). Several designs are interspersed with rivet-like bosses, again suggesting that metalwork served as a model, perhaps items from the cathedral or royal treasury. With its interlace patterns, ribbon-like animals and thin carving technique, the Tuam sculpture is characteristically Irish, but the presence of English influence indicates that this royal site was not isolated from European developments.

BIBLIOGRAPHY

H. G. Leask: *Irish Churches and Monastic Buildings*, i (Dundalk, 1955), pp. 153–4, pl. xvi
F. Henry: *Irish Art in the Romanesque Period, 1020–1170 AD* (London, 1970), pp. 124–5, 132, 140–43, 166, 168, 183, 192–3, pls lxiii–lxiv, lxxxvi–lxxxviii
R. Stalley: 'The Romanesque Sculpture of Tuam', *The Vanishing Past: Studies of Medieval Art, Liturgy and Metrology Presented to Christopher Hohler* (Oxford, 1981), pp. 179–96
P. Harbison: *The High Crosses of Ireland*, i (Bonn, 1992), pp. 175–8

ROGER STALLEY

Tuamotu and Gambier Islands. Archipelagos in the South Pacific Ocean. The sparsely populated archipelago of Tuamotu consists of 64 low coral islands or atolls, stretching *c.* 2500 km to the east of Tahiti, and extending south-east with the Gambier Islands, whose largest island, after which the group is sometimes known, is Mangareva. The islands are part of French Polynesia. The paucity of natural resources and the consequent hardship of daily life have restricted the production of works of art. There were few large trees, so wood was scarce. Before the use of metal became widespread in the 19th century, the inhabitants of western Tuamotu used tools made of hard volcanic stone obtained by exchange, while in the east adzes and chisels were made from large shells (*Tridacna* and *Cassis*).

Traditional architecture consisted mainly of structures, known as *marae*, intended for religious use, built with blocks of coral and upright stone slabs. Inside these the most valuable objects were used, passed down from generation to generation of chiefs. Small wooden houses contained representations of gods and family relics. Effigies carved in wood and coral were invoked during turtle-fishing rituals. A beautiful spear belonging to the chief of Napuka Island with carvings on the tip and the shaft was collected in 1878, although it is probably much older. Made of patinated wood, it is 2.8 m long (Punauaia, Mus. Tahiti & Iles). Canoes were constructed of small planks

lashed together with plaited coir fibre (*sennit*). The Tuamotu Islands' reputation for high-quality basket-work extended as far as Tahiti. In particular, their peoples produced long ornamental belts plaited with leaves, vegetable fibres and hair. Feather ornaments were also made as well as fine mother-of-pearl necklaces. In the late 20th century Tuamotu Islands' handicrafts have been produced mainly for the tourist trade and have been restricted to necklaces and objects made of small shells.

Few works of art from the Gambier Islands are known. In 1835 missionaries ordered the destruction of the statues on the islands of Akamaru, Aukena and Taravai, and again later on Mangareva, where the main *marae* and the meeting-houses belonging to the last great hereditary chief, Maputeoca, once stood. The few sculptures and fragments of objects that survive in museum collections show that the art of the Gambier Islands was very sophisticated and accomplished, and rather closer to European taste than the art of many other Polynesian islands, at least during the 19th century. Nothing is known, however, about the superimposed figures that were used, as in other Polynesian archipelagos, to decorate the rafters of meeting-houses.

Seven free-standing, wooden male figures have survived, all of which are about 1 m high. Four are executed in the same naturalistic style (e.g. London, BM; New York, Met.; La Rochelle, Mus. Hist. Nat. & Ethnog.; Rome, Vatican; for illustrations see exh. cat., 1979, pp. 165–6; Barrow, 1972, pp. 120–21). They are sometimes compared with the statues from Nukuoro (*see* POLYNESIAN OUTLIERS, §1), but the shape and proportion are different. The outline of the Mangareva figures can be framed inside a rectangle. The largest transversal diameter is situated midway along the object, just above the navel, at the point where the arms are folded at the front of the body. The head, which has a rounded crown, rests on a well-defined neck. Under the rectilinear brow ridges, the eyes are framed by a crescent and appear closed, a feature sometimes found in figures from Tahiti and the Austral Islands. The nose, lips and ears are sculptured in relief and appear lifelike; the arms are fairly thin and flat, and are clearly separated from the body. Those that are intact have simplified hands, although the fingers are well-defined. The body is not enlarged, as is often the case in figures from other Pacific archipelagos: it is well-proportioned, as are the sexual organs. The legs are slightly bent; feet and toes are shown. The back is shaped and ends abruptly, forming a transversal line. A fifth sculpture has a similar head and body, but is divided so as to show four legs. The sixth is less well preserved and more primitive: it simply suggests a human figure. (Both Rome, Vatican; for illustrations see *Te Rangi Hiroa* (1938), pp. 464–5.) The seventh sculpture is unique (see fig.). It retains the slender shape of the original pole and has a very stylized upper half, with the head reduced to a prism with a vertical line representing the face. The arms are represented by compact volumes, tapered at the end, and separated from the body. A rhombus, sculptured in relief, depicting the ears and also found on each hip, confirms that the sculpture comes from Mangareva.

All these pieces share a feature not found elsewhere in Polynesian statuary: the legs are wide apart, in an upturned

Tuamotu and Gambier Islands, Mangarevan figure sculpture, wood, h. 1.06 m, before 1835 (Saint-Germain-en-Laye, Musée des Antiquités Nationales)

V, suggesting that the pieces of wood from which they were fashioned were not rectilinear, but Y-shaped.

Two-branch poles, decorated with engravings, have been found in the archipelago. They were used to offer up beaten-bark cloth to the principal divinity. Other supports were used to hold plates and offerings. In the only example to have been preserved, four sculptured arms are raised upwards (Paris, Mus. l'Homme). Very fine herring-bone patterns decorate the surface of the pole, which is 1.8 m high. The base of a single, known drum is decorated with

the same design (Saint-Germain-en Laye, Mus. Ant. N., on dep. Mus. N. A. Afr. & Océan.).

BIBLIOGRAPHY
K. P. Emory: *Tuamotuan Stone Structures*, Bishop Mus. Bull., cxviii (Honolulu, 1934)
Te Rangi Hiroa [P. H. Buck]: *Ethnology of Mangareva*, Bishop Mus. Bull., clvii (Honolulu, 1938)
K. P. Emory: *Archaeology of Mangareva and Neighboring Atolls*, Bishop Mus. Bull., clxiii (Honolulu, 1939)
——: *Tuamotuan Religious Structures and Ceremonies*, Bishop Mus. Bull., cxci (Honolulu, 1947)
T. Barrow: *Art and Life in Polynesia* (London, 1971), pp. 119–21
K. P. Emory: *Material Culture of the Tuamotu Archipelago*, Pacific Anthropological Records 22 (Honolulu, 1975)
The Art of the Pacific Islands (exh. cat. by P. Gathercole, A. L. Kaeppler and D. Newton, Washington, DC, N.G.A., 1979), pp. 86–7, 165–7
ANNE LAVONDÈS

Tuan-fang. *See* DUANFANG.

Tuan Yü-tsai. *See* DUAN YUCAI.

Tuareg. Semi-nomadic pastoralist people of North African Berber origins inhabiting the Sahara Desert, southern Algeria, south-western Libya, Niger, eastern Mali and other adjacent areas. Their language is Tamashegh, and they are nominal Muslims. They are known for their elaborate silver jewellery and leatherwork, their basketry and their woodwork. There are a number of important museum collections of Tuareg art, both in Europe (e.g. Neuchâtel, Mus. Ethnog.; Stuttgart, Linden-Mus.; Offenbach am Main, Dt. Ledermus.; Paris, Mus. Homme) and in Africa (e.g. Niamey, Mus. N. Niger; Algiers, Le Bardo).

1. Introduction. 2. Metalwork and jewellery. 3. Leatherwork. 4. Basketry. 5. Woodwork.

1. INTRODUCTION. The Tuareg are grouped into politically autonomous federations, which may be broadly divided into northern and southern groups. Tuareg class structure comprises noble classes (*ihaggaren*), tributary classes (*imrad*) and ex-servile classes (*iklan*). Marginal classes comprising freedmen include religious leaders (*ineslemen*) and artisan smiths (*inadan*). The Tuareg number *c.* 1,200,000, with *c.* 500,000 living in Niger, 300,000 in Mali and the rest in Algeria and Libya. The *ihaggaren* were once a warrior aristocracy who controlled the caravan trade routes between Mouzourk and Timbuktu and the south-western Sahara into northern Nigeria. To a large extent, Tuareg economy has continued to be based on pastoralism and trade. However, the drought of the 1970s and 1980s and the continuing process of desertification forced many nomadic Tuareg to become sedentary. Tuareg religion and cosmology are thought to represent a layering of Islamic tenets on earlier beliefs because of their mythical and clan associations with certain animals and because of their belief in *kel esouf* spirits. The Tuareg share cultural similarities with other Sahelian peoples.

Tuareg art forms consist of such utilitarian items as household furnishings and more personal objects such as jewellery. Items in general have simple shapes, and almost all decoration comprises linear and geometrical motifs that are endlessly combined to create rich and vibrant patterns. There are no figural motifs in Tuareg art. The artistic traditions are the work of *inadan* smiths. Men carve wooden implements and forge metalwork items, and women are weavers and leatherworkers. Tuareg tents are made of goat skins or straw mats mounted on arched wooden frames and are occupied by one family unit. Furniture includes beds, rugs, cushions, bags and household utensils. Men wear baggy trousers made of cotton cloth, a loose cotton shirt, a turban (*tegelmoust*) and sandals. Women's clothing consists of shirts worn over skirts and underskirts, a head veil and sandals.

While smiths still produced items for Tuareg patrons into the 1990s, their principal source of income lay in the manufacture of innovative items that appealed to foreigners. As a result rattle rings had been transformed into brooches, Maria Theresa thaler silver had been replaced by sterling silver, and leatherworkers had begun to produce cassette holders, picture frames and desk accessories. At the same time some individuals had begun to record older forms and shapes before they became obsolete. Rissa Ixa (*b c.* 1940), a Tuareg painter based in Niamey, used his paintings of scenes of daily life to document the immense inventory of motifs found in jewellery, leather and wooden Tuareg art.

2. METALWORK AND JEWELLERY. Tuareg metalwork includes weapons, tools, objects of daily use, animal trappings and elaborate jewellery forms. Metal items are either forged or cast using moulds or the lost-wax process.

Decorative techniques involve bending, piercing, engraving, stamping, chasing and repoussé work. Since the 1950s swords, spears, and arm daggers are worn mostly for special occasions. Straight blades are made of iron with engraved designs that indicate quality and provenance. Some designs are borrowed from famous European arms manufacturers. The wooden handles have rounded-end knobs or cross shapes. Sheaths are made of leather with incised patterns and woven or punched designs. The bottom portion is rounded and partially encased in silver with pierced circles and engraved triangles.

Sugar tongs and hammers are considered prestige pieces. They are cast in bronze or silver and embellished with zigzags, lines, triangles and ball nails. Tuareg locks are rectangular, of cast iron and decorated with copper or brass overlays. The keys have long handles with intricate openwork designs (fig. 1). Engraved tweezers and needles are used by both men and women to extricate thorns. These are kept in wallets or hung on leather cords around the neck. Camel headstalls are used during festivals for parades and races. These are engraved and have amulets and little bells hanging at the sides.

Both men and women take a special interest in jewellery forms. Jewellery is used as physical adornment and to symbolize protective agents, life-stages and rank. It is also

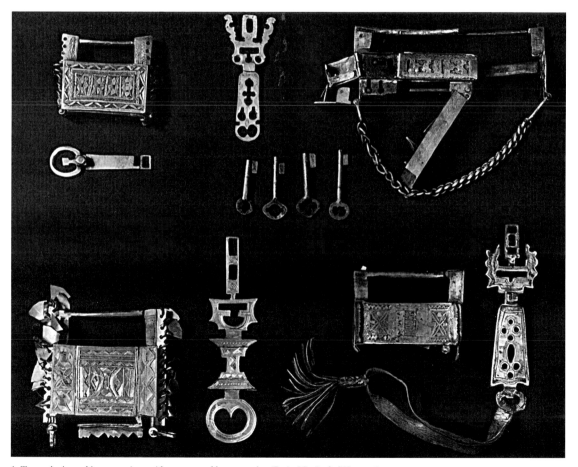

1. Tuareg locks and keys, cast iron with copper and brass overlay (Paris, Musée de l'Homme)

valued for its craftsmanship and monetary worth. Tuareg jewellery is always decorated (for illustrations see Gabus, 1982, iii). Men wear amulet cases, bracelets and rings on a daily basis. Amulet cases are either square, rectangular, triangular or tubular. They usually contain papers bearing Koranic or magical inscriptions prepared by religious leaders. They hang from leather cords and are worn around the neck, on the upper arm or on turbans. The simplest forms are thin, flat cases with two suspension rings. These are sometimes augmented with one or more superimposed cases. Most amulets are hammered, then adorned with repoussé, stamped or engraved geometric motifs, and some have ebony inlay. Tubular models have continuous surface designs, and leather amulets bear incised and stamped decorations. Simple band bracelets made of serpentine are worn singly or in pairs on the upper arm. Men's rings are cast in solid silver and display geometric motifs. Amulet rings have chequer-board patterns with magical letters inside them. Rings are often given as tokens of affection.

Women wear amulets, necklaces, pendants, head ornaments, earrings, bracelets, rings and veil-weights. Women's amulets are similar to men's and are worn on a daily basis with the exception of a very large pectoral triangular amulet, known as the *tereout tan idmarden*. This is composed of a pendant from which hangs a triangular centre-piece decorated with silver ball nails and triangular pendants. The triangle is said to be one of the most important amuletic shapes and decorative designs in all Tuareg art forms (Nicolaisen). It is a stylized representation of an eye and protects the wearer. Other amulets, known as *khomessa*, are made of five silver or bone lozenges joined together and attached to a leather backing, the whole then being decorated with twisted silver wire. These amulets are associated with the protective powers of the number five.

Numerous pendants are used to manufacture necklaces. The Agadez cross has an oval or round ring at the top, joined to a lozenge with curved sides ending in knob ends. Other examples are stone triangles encased in rectangular boxes or elaborate cross forms with openwork motifs. Pendants are often named after the regions from which they come. Head ornaments consist of pendants attached directly to the hair or along the temples. A long triangular construction similar to the *tereout tan idmarden* is worn at the back of the head and is reserved for celebrations. Women wear a profusion of necklaces composed of beads, shells and pendants strung on leather cords. Necklaces are sometimes named after the pendants used to make them, such as the *tadnet*. Silver beads are either tubular or polyhedral squares and have engraved or punched designs.

Bracelets are almost always worn in pairs. These include flat bands with engraved decorations, open circles with ball ends and pieces cast in solid silver with polyhedral end knobs. Earrings consist of large round hoops embellished with small circular motifs and rings with trumpet-shaped polyhedral end knobs. The latter are part of a woman's dowry. Veil-weights are attached to the end of a veil and thrown over a woman's shoulder. They are sometimes in fact keys to locks. Women's rings are simple bands, signet rings or pieces with pyramidal constructions. Rattle rings are particular to the Tuareg and are often decorated with stars or circles.

3. LEATHERWORK. Tuareg leatherwork is distinctive for its vibrant colours (reds, blacks, yellows, whites and greens) and for the intricacy and profusion of its decorated panels, fringes and tassels (for illustrations see Gabus, 1958, iii). The largest production centres for Tuareg leatherwork are in Agadez and Tahoua. Men usually make saddles, weapons, amulets and sandals, while women make bags, satchels, wallets and cushions. Women soak goat or sheep skins several times, then scrape and clean them with knives. Tanned skins are softened with butter or oil and stretched on frames before the dyeing process. Since the 1970s many colours have been obtained with commercial dyes from Nigeria, and women in urban centres sometimes buy skins that have already been dyed (Etienne-Nugue and Saley). Women smiths often work in small groups and use low benches as work tables. The skins are first cut into smaller pieces and are then prepared one at a time. Some decorations are incised, while others are scraped or stamped with metal punches. Panels with perforated triangles, squares or lozenges are fastened over monochrome panels with elaborate stitches and appliqué work. Other panels are adorned with embroidered circles or

2. Tuareg woman's leather saddle bag (Offenbach am Main, Deutsches Ledermuseum)

triangles, then trimmed with white zigzag stitches. Triangular tassels attached to narrow perforated panels hang over red and blue fringes. When all the different elements have been decorated, the pieces are assembled (fig. 2).

Big rectangular bags with long narrow necks are used to hold personal belongings during trips and have heavily decorated front flaps. Smaller bags are used to carry the items needed for making tea, and wallets attached to braided cords are worn around the neck. It has been suggested that the sandal motif often depicted on women's bags has protective properties and indicates prestige and social rank (Gabus, 1982, iii).

There are two styles of Tuareg cushions. Saddle cushions (*sabara*) are elongated rectangles with elaborate decorations used by women on palanquins. These pieces have become scarce since the 1970s, as they are time-consuming to make (taking three months or so) and expensive to buy. Round cushions, trimmed with fringes, are used as pillows.

Saddles are always made by specialists. Horse saddles are made of moulded leather and their pommels and cantles adorned with metal overlays. Camel saddles are made of wooden frames covered with leather panels. There are two types of camel saddle. The *tayast* has a triangular shape, a simple ball pommel, and is covered with colourful blankets. A particularly prestigious type, known as *tamzak*, is made in Agadez. The pommel is a cross shape whose three branches are chest high. The high, oval cantle has a metal point and is made of eight pieces of wood, which are joined and polished and then covered with red leather. Embroidered and perforated panels alternate with metal overlays, which are engraved, pierced or have encased mirrors (Etienne-Nugue and Saley).

4. BASKETRY. Tuareg basketry items are made with fibres from the doum palm and the euphorbia, and acacia bark is used to join bands together (for illustrations see Etienne-Nugue and Saley). Mats are plaited, knotted and twisted, while baskets are coiled. Men make the heavy mats (*tacharabat*) used for transporting goods and the mats used as the outer walls of tents. Women make baskets, tent panels and mats. The Tuareg favour black, red and green, and these colours are now obtained using commercial dyes. Intricate patterns are created by knotting fine leather strands into geometric motifs. It has been suggested that many of the motifs woven in mats are ideograms or pictograms based on Tuareg hunting lore and astronomy. The circle, for example, represents the sun, while an inverted 'v' represents a gazelle's foot and the triangle corresponds to a seated woman seen from the back (Gabus, 1958, iii).

Tuareg mats are rectangular, square or round and have many purposes. They are used as rugs, as the outer and inner walls of tents, and as mattresses. Plaited mats used as tent coverings have alternating black and natural coloured bands joined with zigzag stitches. The mats used as prayer mats and for sitting are more refined. These are often plaited then embellished with black zigzag motifs, parallel lines or stars. Inner tent panels and screens (*firiji*) are very long and require a polished and carefully prepared doum fibre for their manufacture. These mats are decorated with lines, triangles, and lozenges made of coloured leather strands. As they are often part of a wedding dowry, they are made only on commission. Embroidered mats from the Aïr region (*assaber*) are made of twisted fibres. These are very supple and have friezes bordering three of the four edges on both sides of the mat. The frieze is made of red, black and green leather strands that are woven into the mat in geometric motifs.

Coiled baskets are made principally in Agadez and display green and purple geometric motifs. They are made in different shapes and sizes and are used to hold clothing and personal belongings. Cooperatives have been created in the Aïr region to facilitate basket manufacture for the tourist trade.

5. WOODWORK. Because of the paucity of wood in the Sahelian region, wood manufacture is kept to a strict minimum. Most pieces are made with such hard woods as acacia or with such soft woods as *Commiphora africana*. Tuareg wooden articles include furniture, tent armatures and pickets, and camel trappings, as well as household utensils (for illustrations see Gabus, 1958, iii). Smiths use a single piece of wood to make any of these items. They are first shaped with an adze then refined with knives. Pieces are blackened with smoke and decorated with lines and zigzag motifs with the tip of a knife heated in a flame. They are then polished with butter.

Mortars have conical shapes, and they are also used as drums during feasts. Bowls, plates, double cups and funnels have rounded forms and elegant decoration. Spoons and ladles of all sizes are made of a lightweight wood and are prestige items. The handles are elongated and very ornate. Some edges are carved into triangles, and others have cut-out or engraved geometric motifs, which are coloured in with red, green or black. Little metal patches are used to repair cracks and breaks.

Tent accessories include pickets, poles and holders for trays and other items. All of these are carefully engraved and decorated. Shorter pickets with cut-out edges are used to hold mats against the sides of the tent and to hold cushions up. Beds are part of a woman's dowry, and they are made of two long poles ending in pointed finials and joined together with cross poles. They rest on four short feet.

Palanquins (*teraouit*), used by women to ride donkeys and camels, are made of lightweight woods. They consist of a base board attached to lateral support beams. These are joined with two arched beams linked to the saddle bows. The two arches are decorated with richly engraved, pierced metal overlays and are topped off with wooden finials. Women usually fill palanquins with cushions.

BIBLIOGRAPHY

F. R. Rodd: *People of the Veil* (London, 1926)
J. Gabus: *Au Sahara*, 3 vols (Neuchâtel, 1955–8)
H. Lhote: *Les Touaregs du Hoggar* (Paris, 1955, rev. 1984)
Y. Urvoy: *L'Art dans le territoire du Niger* (Niamey, 1955)
L. C. Briggs: *Tribes of the Sahara* (Cambridge, MA, and London, 1960)
J. Nicolaisen: 'Essai sur la religion et la magie touarègues', *Folk*, iii (1961), pp. 113–62
H. T. Norris: *The Tuaregs: Their Islamic Legacy and its Diffusion in the Sahel* (Warminster, 1975)
J. Anquetil: *Niger: L'Artisanat créateur* (Paris, 1977)
J. Keenan: *The Tuareg: People of Ahaggar* (London, 1977)

J. Gabus: *Sahara: Bijoux et techniques* (Neuchâtel, 1982)
C. Beckwith and M. Van Offelen: *Nomads of Niger* (New York and London, 1983)
A. Fisher: *Africa Adorned* (New York and London, 1984)
J. Etienne-Nugue and M. Saley: *Artisanats traditionels en Afrique noire: Niger* (Dakar, 1987)

KRISTYNE LOUGHRAN

Tubières de Grimoard de Pestels de Lévis, Anne-Claude-Philippe de. *See* CAYLUS, Comte de.

Tübke, Werner (*b* Schönbeck, Elbe, 30 July 1929). German painter and printmaker. He studied art at the Hochschule für Graphik und Buchkunst, Leipzig, and art education and psychology at the Ernst-Moritz-Arndt-Universität, Greifswald, from 1948 to 1953. He showed an early inclination to base his work on an emphatic realism. On his own admission he ignored the insights of modernism, absorbing the development of art only up to the 19th century. His first works, showing a conservative rejection of experimental art, were inspired by the German and Netherlandish painting of the 15th and 16th centuries. *Peasant Market in Samarkand* (1963; priv. col., see exh. cat., p. 17), with its multitude of figures, clearly shows the influence of Pieter Bruegel I. Tübke went on to develop a special symbolic language, based on surrealistic effects in pictures from the Middle Ages and the Renaissance, that led to interesting innovations in his painting; an example is *Reminiscences of Dr Schulze III* (1965; Berlin, Neue N.G., see exh. cat., no. 16). In his first diptychs and triptychs, based on medieval multi-panel paintings, he dealt with themes such as the *History of the German Workers' Movement, 1918–45* (1961; Leipzig, Mus. Bild. Kst., see exh. cat., no. 7) and current political events, such as the incomplete *White Terror in Hungary* (1956–7; priv. col., see exh. cat., no. 3). Beside this thematic concern with the present, which also expressed itself in Socialist Realist portraits of workers and groups of workers, for example in *Group Portrait* (1972; Dresden, Gemäldegal. Neue Meister, see exh. cat., no. 36), he showed an increasing tendency to stress his technical skill through his subject-matter. Influenced by several journeys to Italy, he transferred some features of Italian Mannerism to his own work, and by 1971 he was beginning to work on a larger scale. The mural *Working Class and Intelligentsia* (1971–2; Leipzig, Karl-Marx-U.) is one example. In 1983 he began his panoramic painting *Early Bourgeois Revolution in Germany* for a memorial at Bad Frankenhausen; it was completed in 1987.

BIBLIOGRAPHY
E. Beaucamp: *Werner Tübke: Arbeiterklasse und Intelligenz* (Frankfurt am Main, 1985)
K. M. Kober: *Reformation-Revolution. Panorama in Bad Frankenhausen, Monumentalbild von W. Tübke* (Dresden, 1988)
G. Meissner: *Werner Tübke* (Leipzig, 1989)
Gemälde, Aquarelle, Zeichnungen, Lithographien (exh. cat., ed. P. Betthausen; W. Berlin, Neue N.G., 1989)

EUGEN BLUME

Tubuai Islands. *See* AUSTRAL ISLANDS.

Tuby [Tubi], Jean(-Baptiste) [le Romain] (*b* Rome, 1635; *d* Paris, 9 August 1700). French sculptor of Italian birth. He was the son of a French father and was naturalized French in 1666. He is first mentioned in connection with decorative sculpture (destr. 1778) for the Porte Saint-Antoine, Paris, and in 1663 he was received (*reçu*) as a member of the Académie Royale on presentation of the model (untraced) for an allegorical bust of *Joy* (marble version, 1680; Versailles, Château). He had a successful career in the service of Louis XIV, rapidly becoming one of the most eminent sculptors in later 17th-century France.

Tuby's most extensive commissions were for garden sculpture at the château of Versailles (*see* VERSAILLES, §2), where he worked alongside François Girardon, the brothers Gaspard and Balthazar Marsy, and later Antoine Coyzevox, under the direction of Charles Le Brun, Premier Peintre du Roi; Tuby's work here, most of which survives *in situ*, is among the best of its kind. His first commissions were lively marble statues of *Acis* and *Galatea* (1667–74) and the meditative gilded lead fountain group *Apollo in his Chariot* (1668–70; *see* FOUNTAIN, fig. 6). Later he executed the marble statue *Lyric Poetry* (1675–80) for Jean-Baptiste Colbert's scheme for 24 statues at Versailles (the so-called *Grande Commande* of 1674) and a series of highly classicizing works: the allegorical lead fountain *France Triumphant over Spain and the Empire* (1677–83); a marble copy (1684–96) of the antique *Laokoon* group (Rome, Vatican, Mus. Pio-Clementino); bronze figures of the *Rhône* and *Saône* for the Parterre d'Eau (1685); and the elaborate monumental marble *Vase of Peace* (1685–6), a pendant to Coyzevox's *Vase of War*. All these are still at Versailles. In a lighter vein, he contributed lead animals illustrating Aesop's *Fables* to the Labyrinthe (1672–4; fragments, Versailles, Château) and a charming group of *Flora with Putti and Garlands of Flowers* (gilded lead, 1672–4; *in situ*) for the Bassin de Flore. He also executed much decorative sculpture for the façades and interiors of the château.

Tuby was also active as a sculptor of funerary monuments, religious works and decorative schemes for influential private patrons. His earliest funerary monument is that of *Jérôme Bignon* (marble, *c.* 1668; Paris, St Nicolas-du-Chardonnet). Another early work is the wall monument to *Marin Cureau de la Chambre* (marble, *c.* 1670; Paris, St Eustache), designed by Le Brun, which consists of an angel in high relief holding an oval portrait medallion of Marin. He later collaborated with Gaspard Marsy (using designs by Le Brun) on the tomb for Saint-Denis Abbey of *Henri de la Tour d'Auvergne, Maréchal de Turenne* (marble and bronze, 1676–80; Paris, Dôme Hôtel Invalides). Tuby executed the central marble group of the dying Turenne supported by a female personification of Immortality and the gilded bronze relief of the *Battle of Turckheim*. His collaborations with Coyzevox include: the tomb of *Jean-Baptiste Colbert* for St Eustache, Paris, for which he carved the beautiful, seated, draped figure of *Virtue* (marble, 1685–7; *in situ*); that of *Jules, Cardinal Mazarin* for the Collège des Quatre-Nations, Paris (also with Etienne Le Hongre; for illustration *see* COYZEVOX, ANTOINE), to which he contributed a statue of *Peace* (bronze, 1689–92; Paris, Inst. France); and the tomb of *Charles Le Brun* for St Nicolas-du-Chardonnet, Paris, for which he produced all the bronze decorations (1691–6; destr.). Among Tuby's religious works are the marble relief of the *Baptism of Christ* (1680; Sceaux, Hauts-de-Seine, parish church), made for Colbert to designs by Le Brun for the altar of the chapel of his château of Sceaux, and a marble, bronze and wood rood screen to designs by Le Brun and Jules Hardouin Mansart for Orléans Cathedral (1689–95; partially destr., wooden figure of *Christ Crucified* preserved). He is also known to have carried out decorative works at Sceaux and in Paris for Colbert's son Jean-Baptiste Colbert, Marquis de Seignelay, although the precise nature of the commissions is not known. At the end of his career Tuby was involved in the great collaborative project to decorate the Dôme des Invalides (*see* PARIS, §V, 7), carving two monumental stone statues of *Virtues* (1690–91; *in situ*) and stone statues of *St Gregory* and *St Ambrose* (1698; destr. 1790s).

Although he mostly worked within schemes laid down by others, Tuby's work has an emotional generosity, a compositional vigour and a nobility of conception that make him one of the foremost classicizing sculptors of the reign of Louis XIV. He was also a skilled bronze-caster and in 1674 established a foundry at the Gobelins. In 1680 he married Le Brun's niece Suzanne Butay, his second wife. From 1691 he ran the Académie des Gobelins in conjunction with Coyzevox and others. His son, also Jean(-Baptiste) Tuby (1669–1735), was a sculptor of minor talent.

BIBLIOGRAPHY

Guiffrey; Lami; Souchal

L. A. de Bonafous, Abbé de Fontenai: *Dictionnaire des artistes ou notice historique et raisonnée des architectes, peintres, graveurs, sculpteurs, musiciens, acteurs et danseurs, imprimeurs, horlogers et mécaniciens*, 2 vols (Paris, 1777)

FRANÇOISE DE LA MOUREYRE

Tucci, Giuseppe (*b* Macerata, 5 June 1894; *d* San Polo dei Cavalieri, 5 April 1984). Italian scholar and art historian. He is generally considered the 'father' of modern Tibetan studies. His contributions spanned the disciplines of philosophy, philology, archaeology, history, the history of religion and the history of art. His prodigious intellectual gifts were matched by his physical stamina and courage, a rare combination that allowed him to conduct 16 field expeditions to Himalayan India, Tibet and Nepal from 1928 to 1956. After serving in World War I he received his PhD in 1919. From 1926 to 1930 he taught Italian, Chinese and Tibetan at the universities of Shantiniketan and Calcutta in India. For over 30 years he taught the languages, religion and philosophy of India and China at the Istituto Universitario Orientale di Napoli, Naples. His broad educational background in Greek and Roman as well as in Chinese, Tibetan and Sanskrit enabled him to discuss the relationships and distinctive qualities of Western and Eastern civilizations not only in his scholarly works but also in numerous popular books and articles. In 1934 he established the Istituto Italiano per il Medio ed Estremo Oriente (ISMEO), Rome, serving as its president from 1947 to 1978. He also founded the scholarly journal *East and West*. He later founded the Centre of Excavation and the Restoration Centre, both attached to ISMEO. The years following the end of World War II were not without difficulties; unable to continue his field work for some years, Tucci turned his energies to his magnum opus, *Tibetan Painted Scrolls*, still unequalled in the field of Tibetan art history. In 1957 the Italian government founded the Museo Nazionale d'Arte Orientale, Rome, in part to preserve the collections formed through ISMEO excavations in Iran, Afghanistan, Pakistan and elsewhere. The museum also houses Tucci's collections of Tibetan art and his extensive photo archive. In 1969 he became Professor Emeritus at the Università degli Studi di Roma.

Tucci was appointed to distinguished academic societies around the world and received honorary doctorates from the universities of Delhi, Leuven, Tehran and Kathmandu. Honours were awarded him by the governments of Japan, Thailand, Iran, Pakistan, Afghanistan, Indonesia and India (including the Nehru Prize). In Italy he was a member of the Accademia Nazionale dei Lincei; he was awarded the Great Cross of Merit of the Republic of Italy, and he was a fellow of, among other societies, the Accademia delle Scienze di Torino and the Accademia Nazionale di San Luca, and an honorary fellow of the Società Geografica Italiana in Rome.

WRITINGS

Indo-Tibetica, 4 vols (Rome, 1932–41/*R*, ed. L. Chandra, New Delhi, 1988–9)
Tibetan Painted Scrolls, 2 vols (Rome, 1949/*R* Kyoto, 1980)
Transhimalaya (Geneva and London, 1973)
The Religions of Tibet (London and Berkeley, 1980)

BIBLIOGRAPHY

G. Gnoli: 'Giuseppe Tucci (1894–1984)', *E. & W.*, xxxiv/1–3 (1984), pp. 11–21
D. E. Klimburg-Salter: 'The Tucci Himalayan Archive', *E. & W.*, xli/1–4 (1991)
D. E. Klimburg-Salter, O. Nalesini and G. Talamo: *Abbreviated Inventory of the Tucci Himalayan Photographic Archive 1928–1935: Synopsis of the Complete Catalogue Kept in Museo Nazionale d'Arte Orientale Photographic Archives* (Rome, 1994)

DEBORAH E. KLIMBURG-SALTER

Tuc d'Audoubert. Cave site in France, forming part of a cave system around the River Volp in Ariège in the foothills of the Pyrenees. It is important for its cave art of the Late Upper Palaeolithic period (*c.* 20,000–*c.* 10,000 BP; *see also* PREHISTORIC EUROPE, §II, 1 and 2), which was discovered in July 1912, when Count Henri Bégouën and his three sons entered the cave and found engravings on its walls. In October of the same year the three boys, together with a friend, broke through some concretions blocking a passage and made their way to the end of the upper system, where they discovered the famous and unique clay figures of bison. More engravings were discovered between the 1950s and 1970s. The river still flows through the lower cave system, which leads into the 500 m-long upper system. The latter chiefly comprises high, wide galleries, although there are also some low and narrow passages. Evidence for a superficial Magdalenian culture occupation (*c.* 18,000–*c.* 10,000 BP) was found in the cave, but its upper galleries were never occupied and were perhaps visited only once by the maker(s) of the bison. The sparse material recovered from the site is housed in the Bégouën family's private museum and the Musée de l'Homme, Paris. The engravings include bison, horses, imaginary animals and claviform (club-like) signs; most of them are located in small side chambers. In style they all correspond to the middle of the Magdalenian period, and this dating is supported by the fact that the cave's cultural material has yielded an uncalibrated radiocarbon date of 14,350 BP.

The fame of the Tuc d'Audoubert rests primarily on the 'Chamber of Heels' at its far end, where two magnificent clay bison in high relief lean against rocks in the centre (*see* PREHISTORIC EUROPE, fig. 4). The figures measure 610 mm and 630 mm in length; the smaller appears to represent a female, since its raised tail reveals what may be a vulva, while the other, behind it, is more massive and assumed to be male. The eye of the latter is made in relief, whereas the female's is a hollow. Many details of their beards and manes were carefully depicted with parallel incisions, while smoothing was done with fingers and spatula. Most of the artist's detritus seems to have been carefully cleared away. The figures are cracked, but this probably occurred within a few days of their execution, as they dried out. A small engraving on one of the supporting rocks, the only such mark in the chamber, may be a 'signature'. In the past, the bison figures were usually assumed by proponents of fertility magic to be in a precopulatory phase, but in fact the male is not only behind but also beyond the female. A third bison is engraved in the clay floor near by, and a fourth, small, crude clay bison lay next to them. The chamber seems to constitute a real sanctuary, albeit one that may have been used only once: the bison figures were clearly placed in the centre for maximum effect. The many prints around them seem to be those of children walking on their heels—perhaps playing while the artist(s) worked. There are also finger holes and a vague circle of little stalactites stuck into the floor. The working process can be followed: a stalagmite was used to lever slabs of clay out of the floor of a neighbouring chamber, while clay 'sausages' on the ground (often interpreted as phallic symbols or bison horns) were almost certainly made by the sculptor testing the clay's plasticity, as shown by the position of palm- and finger-prints on them.

Since the bison are at the closest point to the cave of TROIS FRÈRES, a few metres away through the wall, it has sometimes been suggested that the two systems were connected, but this is highly unlikely, since any draught or reduced humidity would have destroyed the sculptures. Additionally, the footprints leading to and from the 'Chamber of Heels' can be traced through the upper galleries.

BIBLIOGRAPHY

H. Bégouën and H. Breuil: *Les Cavernes du Volp: Trois-Frères—Tuc d'Audoubert* (Paris, 1958)

R. Bégouën, J. Clottes and H. Delporte: 'Le Retour du petit bison au Tuc d'Audoubert', *Bull. Soc. Préhist. Fr.* lxxiv (1977), pp. 112–20

R. Bégouën: 'Les Bisons d'argile du Tuc d'Audoubert', *Doss. Archéol.* (1984), pp. 77–9

R. Bégouën and J. Clottes: 'Grotte du Tuc d'Audoubert', *L'Art des cavernes* (Paris, 1984), pp. 410–15

B. Beasley: 'Les Bisons d'argile de la grotte du Tuc d'Audoubert', *Bull. Soc. Préhist. Ariège–Pyrénées,* xli (1986), pp. 23–30

PAUL G. BAHN

Tu Chin. *See* DU JIN.

Tucker, Albert (Lee) (*b* Melbourne, 29 Dec 1914). Australian painter. Unable to study at the official art school owing to impoverished circumstances, he attended part-time classes at the Victorian Artists' Society (1933–9) and studied briefly under George Bell. He survived by freelance illustration. His early portraits and street scenes show a tentative exploration of modernism. In 1938 he became a leading member of the group of artists and laymen, including George Bell, Sidney Nolan and John Reed, that established the Contemporary Art Society in Melbourne. From 1939 to 1942 Tucker explored the styles of the Neue Sachlichkeit artists George Grosz and Max Beckmann and became interested in Cubism and Surrealism. A number of his early themes and subjects derived from his interest in the writings of George Orwell and T. S. Eliot. Tucker was friendly with the European expatriate artists Danila Vassilieff and Josl Bergner. Their work helped him break through to more direct and expressive forms of painting, based on primitive and naive art but also on sophisticated European modernist sources. Tucker's early sympathy for radical ideas had dissipated by 1942, but his commitment to a socially critical art continued; he became linked with the anarchist values expressed in the magazine *Angry Penguins*, to which he contributed his important statement 'Art, Myth and Society' (*Angry Penguins*, iv, 1943), in which he demanded unfettered freedom for the individual artist.

In 1942 Tucker married the artist Joy Hester, and between April and October 1942 he served in the Australian army as an official war artist. His depiction of military coercion culminated in a series of drawings for a plastic surgery unit, which emphasize the psychologically destructive side of war. Tucker's mature style dates from 1943, when he began his most important series, *Images of Modern Evil* (1943–7; Canberra, N.G.). In this series of over 30 paintings he wedded all the various influences of the previous years to depict a sinister and threatening night world of psychosexual drama, in the centre of which he located an emblematic female figure formed from an eye and a crescent mouth attached to a fleshy, limbless torso.

In September 1947 Tucker left Australia and over the following 13 years lived and painted in various European locations, as well as New York. In Paris in 1949–50 he discovered the work of Jean Dubuffet, whose influence is present in Tucker's continued development of themes of sexuality and violence. In Italy (1952–6) Tucker turned to biblical subjects, as in such larger allegorical works as *Pilate* (1952; Adelaide, A.G. S. Australia). In Rome, Tucker met Alberto Burri and became interested in the latter's experiments with polyvinyl acetate into which other materials were incorporated; this helped Tucker towards a more experimental approach to the medium of painting.

At this time, partly as a result of renewed contact with Sidney Nolan in Rome in 1955, Tucker turned to Australian themes of bushranging and exploring. While in London and New York he developed out of this national preoccupation the form of a large, cratered, symbolic Antipodean head, for example *Antipodean Head* (1959; New York, Guggenheim). In 1960 Tucker returned to Australia and achieved critical and financial success. His work throughout the 1960s and 1970s was dominated by Australian themes and the Australian landscape. In the 1980s he returned to portrait painting with a large series of works depicting Australian artists and writers. Tucker's art is uncompromising in its concern for the human condition. Together with the work of Nolan and Arthur Boyd, it established the character of Australian symbolic Expressionism that emerged in the 1940s.

WRITINGS
Contributions to *Angry Penguins* (1941–6)
Faces I Have Met (Melbourne, 1986)

BIBLIOGRAPHY
C. Uhl: *Albert Tucker* (Melbourne, 1969)
R. Haese: *Rebels and Precursors: The Revolutionary Years of Australian Art* (Ringwood, 1981)
Albert Tucker: Painting, 1945–1960 (exh. cat., intro. R. Haese; Melbourne, Tolarno Gals, 1982)
Angry Penguins and Realist Paintings in Melbourne in the 1940s (exh. cat., ed. M. Ryan; London, Hayward Gal., 1988), pp. 113–22

RICHARD HAESE

Tucker, William (*b* Cairo, Egypt, 28 Feb 1935). American sculptor of English birth. He returned with his family to England in 1937 and studied history at Oxford University from 1955 to 1958 and sculpture in London, at the Central School of Art and Design and at St Martin's School of Art, from 1959 to 1960. Like Philip King and other British sculptors who took part in the influential exhibition *The New Generation: 1965*, in his early work he favoured simple geometric shapes and industrial materials such as fibreglass and sheet metal painted in bright colours. The works that he showed in this exhibition, such as *Meru II* (fabricated steel, 962×2324×410 mm, 1964; London, Tate), which consists of a series of stepped units rounded on the outside and rectilinear on the inside, bear a superficial resemblance to Minimalist work of the same period. In distinction to the work of Americans such as Donald Judd, however, Tucker suggested an organic development of form and even hinted at narrative, rather than proposing basic geometric forms that could be perceived in their entirety almost at a glance. In the 1970s, with works such as *Cat's Cradle 3* (stainless steel, 1.63×2.62×1.5 m, 1971; London, Tate), he produced more spacious and elegant works that responded to gravity and atmosphere.

Tucker moved to the USA in 1977 and later became an American citizen. By the early 1980s he was particularly interested in creating a tension between mass and open spaces. Later in the decade he returned to modelling after having worked consistently with constructed forms, bringing primordial masses to the brink of figuration in bronzes such as *Gaia* (2.08×1.19×3.23 m, 1986; Rome, Gal. Isola di Milano, see 1987 exh. cat., p. 19), which intimidate by their large scale and mass.

WRITINGS
'Sculpture and Architecture: An Introduction to my Work', *Studio International*, clxxxiii/945 (1972), pp. 241–3
The Language of Sculpture (London, 1974); as *Early Modern Sculpture* (New York, 1974)

BIBLIOGRAPHY
The New Generation: 1965 (exh. cat., intro. B. Robertson; London, Whitechapel A.G., 1965), pp. 65–70
R. Morphet: 'William Tucker', *The Alistair McAlpine Gift* (exh. cat., intro. A. McAlpine; London, Tate, 1971), pp. 88–105
William Tucker: Sculpture, 1970–73 (exh. cat., intro. A. Forge; London, Serpentine Gal., 1973)
William Tucker: Gods: Five Recent Sculptures (exh. cat., intro. D. Ashton; London, Tate, 1987)

DANIEL E. MADER

Tucker China Factory [American China Manufactory]. American porcelain manufactory. William Ellis Tucker (*b* Philadelphia, 11 June 1800; *d* Philadelphia, 22 Aug 1832) made an enormous contribution to the history of American ceramics as the founder of this major porcelain factory in Philadelphia. His interest in ceramics probably stemmed from working with the material in his father's china store, where he occasionally painted European blanks and fired them in a small kiln. Experiments to make porcelain began in 1825. Funding the experiments and later the production of porcelain was so expensive that partners were acquired to help alleviate the financial problems. The factory was known under various titles, chiefly Tucker & Hulme (1828) and Tucker & Hemphill (1831–8). After Tucker's death, production continued with his brother Thomas Tucker (1812–90) as manager. Tableware and decorative pieces in the fashionable French Empire style were the main products of the firm. Although the company stayed in business until 1838, financial stability was always elusive, as European porcelain was cheaper than Tucker's.

BIBLIOGRAPHY
P. H. Curtis: 'The Production of Tucker Porcelain, 1826–1828', *Ceramics in America*, ed. I. Quimby (Charlottesville, 1973), pp. 339–74

ELLEN PAUL DENKER

Tuckerman, Henry T(heodore) (*b* Boston, MA, 20 April 1813; *d* New York, 17 Dec 1871). American writer. Born into a prosperous and intellectually minded merchant family, he attended Harvard College for two years before frail health prevented him from continuing. On advice from a physician, in 1833 he travelled to Italy, where he developed a devotion to literature and art. Returning to Boston in 1834, over the next decade he distinguished himself as a travel essayist, poet and magazine editor. He moved to New York in 1845, finding ready acceptance in the city's social, intellectual and cultural circles. Tuckerman's writings emphasize the aesthetics of the Picturesque, the value of travel and the enrichments afforded by the historical and literary associations of Europe. He balanced his yearning for the refinement of the 'Old World' with an enthusiasm for the budding native school of American artists. As a critic he was both sympathetic and analytical. His most important volume of art criticism, *Book of the Artists: American Artist Life* (1867), written in New York's Tenth Street Studio Building, was based on years of personal association with artists and scores of critical assessments written for such journals as *The Knickerbocker* and *Godey's Magazine and Lady's Book*. It chronicles the achievements and ambitions of American artists by combining contemporary estimation with historical overview.

WRITINGS
Book of the Artists: American Artist Life (New York, 1867/*R* 1966)

BIBLIOGRAPHY
Obituary, *New York Tribune* (18 Dec 1871)
J. Flexner: 'Tuckerman's *Book of the Artists*', *Amer. A.J.*, i/2 (1969), pp. 53–7

SALLY MILLS

Tuckson, Tony (*b* Ismâiliya, Egypt, 18 Jan 1921; *d* Sydney, 24 Nov 1973). Australian painter and museum administrator. He studied at Hornsey School of Art, London, and at Kingston School of Art (1937–40). After serving as a fighter pilot in World War II he continued his studies from 1947 to 1949 at the National Art School, East Sydney Technical College. In 1950 he began working as an attendant at the Art Gallery of New South Wales in Sydney but within a year was appointed assistant to the

Director. He held this position, retitled Deputy Director in 1957, until his death. He painted all his life, but his career as a painter was overshadowed by his administrative job. He was responsible for the curating and building up of the fine collection of aboriginal and Melanesian art in the Art Gallery of New South Wales.

During his lifetime Tuckson had only two one-man exhibitions, in 1970 and 1973 at the Watters Gallery, Sydney. Influenced by Picasso, Klee, and de Kooning, American Abstract Expressionists and aboriginal art, his art progressed from portrait and figurative studies through to Abstract Expressionist works. It is for these later works that he is admired as one of Australia's best action painters. They display a passionate urgency but are contained within a well-balanced composition, as in *Red/Black/White* (1965; Brisbane, Queensland A.G.).

BIBLIOGRAPHY
Tony Tuckson 1921–1973, A Memorial Exhibition (exh. cat. by D. Thomas, Sydney, A.G. NSW, 1976)
Tony Tuckson 1921–1973 (exh. cat. by M. Tuckson, Sydney, Watters Gal., 1982)
D. Thomas, R. Free and G. Legge: *Tony Tuckson* (Sydney, 1989)

CHRISTINE CLARK

Tuculescu, Ion (*b* Craiova, 19 May 1910; *d* Bucharest, 27 July 1962). Romanian painter. He had his first one-man exhibition in Craiova at the age of 15 but studied medicine before taking up painting again in 1935. He visited Paris in 1937 and travelled through Europe for two years. When he returned, his first works were influenced by the local realist tradition, in which strong Impressionist and Post-Impressionist influences mingled with faint echoes of the avant-garde elements that he had encountered in western Europe. His early paintings comprised mainly still-lifes, depictions of peasant homes and landscapes (e.g. *Landscape at Mangalia with Little Donkey*, 1945; Bucharest, Mus. A.), and were characterized by savage gestures and colours. A series of paintings of rape fields (e.g. *Rape Field*, 1943; Bucharest, Mus. A.) showed the influence of van Gogh, while Tuculescu's series of exotic masks was more clearly derived from the work of Paul Gauguin and Maurice de Vlaminck. After 1946 Tuculescu began to explore Romanian folk art: in a rich series of strange landscapes, popular scenes and simplistic compositions, he combined realistic elements with popular, stylized, geometrical forms to produce striking depictions of an elemental nature. From 1957, in his 'totemic' period, he was attracted to pure abstraction. Isolated in his defiance of the dominant and enforced trend towards Socialist Realism, Tuculescu created a world of simple, essential signs, such as crosses, circles and spirals. His last paintings were explosions of pure colour and gesture, representing cosmic visions in which through primeval symbols he sought an abstract, symbolic language of the unconscious (e.g. *Suns*, *c*. 1960; priv. col., see Comarnescu, pl. 55).

BIBLIOGRAPHY
I. Vlasiu: *Ion Tuculescu* (Bucharest, 1966)
P. Comarnescu: *Ion Tuculescu* (Bucharest, 1967)
A. E. Baconsky: *Ion Tuculescu* (Bucharest, 1972)
M. Carneci: *Ion Tuculescu* (Bucharest, 1984)
C. Davidescu: *Ion Tuculescu* (Craiova, 1988)

MAGDA CARNECI

Tudang. *See* CHŎN KI.

Tudor, House of. English dynasty of rulers and patrons. The death of Richard III (*reg* 1483–5), the last Yorkist king, at the Battle of Bosworth (1485) and the accession of Henry Tudor, Earl of Richmond, as (1) Henry VII ended the three decades of civil strife known as the Wars of the Roses. Henry restored strong centralized rule and financial stability. He was succeeded by his second son, (2) Henry VIII. The need for an heir to secure the succession prompted the latter in the late 1520s to seek the annulment of his marriage to Catherine of Aragon (1485–1536). The resulting dispute with Rome led the King to declare himself Supreme Head of the Church in England (1534). Between 1536 and 1540 all monastic houses in England and Wales were dissolved and their property confiscated, enabling him to maintain his enormous expenditure on royal residences and coastal defences. Protestant reformers were prominent during the brief reign of his son Edward VI (*reg* 1547–53), but Henry's elder daughter Mary (*reg* 1553–8) attempted to reimpose Catholic orthodoxy. Under (3) Elizabeth I, the independence of the Church of England was restored. Her reign was marked by extensive private patronage, often associated with rivalry for the Queen's favour. She remained unmarried and was succeeded by James VI, King of Scotland (*see* STUART, House of, (2)).

BIBLIOGRAPHY
H. M. Colvin, ed.: *1485–1660* (1975–82), iii and iv of *The History of the King's Works* (London, 1963–82)
S. Thurley: *The Royal Palaces of Tudor England: Architecture and Court Life, 1460–1547* (New Haven and London, 1993)

☐

(1) Henry VII, King of England (*b* Pembroke, 28 Jan 1457; *reg* 1485–1509; *d* Richmond, Surrey, 21 April 1509). He was the son of Edmund Tudor, Earl of Richmond (1430–56), and Margaret Beaufort. To strengthen his claim to the throne, which passed through his mother's line, he married Elizabeth of York (1466–1503), daughter of Edward IV, King of England, in 1486.

Once he had replenished the royal coffers, Henry became a conspicuous patron. At WINDSOR CASTLE and King's College, Cambridge, he continued, and eventually completed, in an idiom already set down two decades before, the chapels begun by his predecessors. A taste for embellishment emerges at King's with a carved canopy of regal heraldry claiming the nave for the Tudors, while glazing that may date to Henry's reign survives in the Brassie Chapel. His ornate taste found outlet at Windsor in Henry VII's Tower (completed by 1501) by Robert Janyns (ii) (*see* JANYNS, (3)). In addition to the most complex pendant fan vault ever created, all surfaces in Henry VII's Chapel (1503–9) at Westminster Abbey are fretted (*see* LONDON, §V, 2(i) and fig. 28). It was surely designed in emulation of contemporary Spanish extravagances. The exterior was adorned with carved *Apostles*, *Patriarchs* and *Kings of Judah* (removed 18th century) well laced with Tudor emblems. Within, most of the 107 saints around the statue of *Christ* on the east wall have survived, although not the precious image of the *Virgin* for the main altar (*see* LONDON, §V, 2(ii)(a)). The names of many sculptors engaged in this prodigious iconographic display are recorded, and most appear to have been south Netherlandish, probably led by Lawrence Ymber (*fl* 1505–9), who carved the temporary effigy for the Queen's funeral.

To Guido Mazzoni is attributed the amazing terracotta bust of a laughing boy (*c.* 1500; Windsor Castle, Berks, Royal Col.), probably the future Henry VIII. Since PIETRO TORRIGIANI may not have reached England during the King's lifetime, the bust of *Henry VII* (London, V&A) is probably posthumous. 'Patrons' for the effigies of *Henry VIII*, *Elizabeth of York* and *Margaret Beaufort* were made from living likenesses by Meynard Werwicke (*fl* 1502–23), who is thought to be 'Mynour', the painter who took portraits of *Henry VII*, *Elizabeth of York* (Edinburgh, Holyrood Palace), their son *Arthur* and daughter *Margaret* to Scotland in 1503, when Margaret married King James IV of Scotland (*reg* 1488–1513). There was therefore an official likeness of the royal family painted during the Queen's lifetime and many derivatives survive (e.g. London, Syon House, accompanied by an image of *Arthur*). The Mynour type was superseded when, after the Queen's death, a portrait of *Henry VII* (*c.* 1505; London, N.P.G.) was painted by 'Meister Michael' (probably Michel Sittow) for Margaret of Austria.

Guidobaldo I, Duke of Urbino, in response to receiving the Order of the Garter in 1504, sent Baldassare Castiglione to England to be installed as his deputy in 1506. Although the chain of proof is not complete, it is believed that Castiglione presented to Henry VII Raphael's *St George and the Dragon* (*c.* 1505; Washington, DC, N.G.A.), in which St George bears the motto of the Order of the Garter around his left leg. Thus Henry was the first English king to acquire a first-class Italian Renaissance painting. He was also acquainted with contemporary French art. Leaves from a Book of Hours (e.g. London, BL, Add. MS. 35254, T, U, V) may have been given to him by Louis XII, King of France, soon after 1499. The full-page miniatures include the *Virgin Annunciate* opening the Office of the Virgin, a masterpiece of JEAN BOURDICHON of Tours, court painter to four French kings.

Henry was the first English king to appoint a librarian, first at Eltham Palace and subsequently at Richmond Palace (from 1498; destr.). The latter was his major architectural achievement; with its twinned Great Hall and chapel forming equal wings, the basic ground-plan of the main court was symmetrical. Even more spectacular was the tall block of private rooms with ranks of bay windows overlooking the River Thames and surmounted by onion domes. Surviving fenestration at Thornbury Castle (from *c.* 1511), Glos, and in Henry VII's Chapel at Westminster suggest that the fenestration at Richmond was sumptuous. A contemporary heraldic account (*c.* 1501; London, Coll. Arms, MS. M. 13, fols 61–3) records the array of secular rulers, probably statues, who watched over the Great Hall, and of spiritual ancestors in the chapel. The palace's appearance is recorded in drawings (1562; Oxford, Ashmolean) by Anthonis van den Wyngaerde, an engraving (1638) by Wenceslaus Hollar and anonymous 17th-century views (Cambridge, Fitzwilliam; London, Soc. Antiqua.).

Henry's chief act of piety was the building of the Hospital of St John (from 1508; most destr.) on the site of the Savoy Palace (now the site of the Savoy Hotel), London. The great cruciform hospital, the largest in England, with beds for a hundred 'poor, needy people', was directly based on the 14th-century hospital of S Maria Nuova, Florence. The intensity of Henry's personal faith was also expressed in his (unexecuted) intent to bequeath silver-gilt pyxes to every parish in England.

BIBLIOGRAPHY

R. A. Griffiths and R. S. Thomas: *The Making of the Tudor Dynasty* (London and New York, 1985/*R* 1993)

H. G. Wayment: *King's College Chapel, Cambridge: The Side Chapel Glass* (Cambridge, 1988)

Henry VIII: Images of a Tudor King (exh. cat. by C. Lloyd and S. Thurley, London, Hampton Court, 1990–91), pp. 9–20, 57

PAMELA TUDOR-CRAIG

(2) Henry VIII, King of England (*b* Greenwich, 28 June 1491; *reg* 1509–47; *d* Whitehall, London, 28 Jan 1547). Son of (1) Henry VII. He was one of the most significant patrons of all English monarchs and, in building, certainly the most prodigious. Like other European rulers in the 16th century, he can be seen to have turned the production of art to the service of political propaganda. It is difficult to extrapolate a sense of Henry's personal taste from the plethora of luxury goods at his court, where the value of objects was largely determined by their expense and lavishness.

The chief influence on Henry's patronage after 1515 was his rivalry with Francis I, King of France. This ranged from the trappings of chivalric splendour at the Field of Cloth of Gold in 1520 to the length of their respective galleries in palaces under construction around 1540. Like Francis, Henry employed many foreign craftsmen, and a few works of sculpture by them survive, including some by Pietro Torrigiani, who was employed for the tomb (1512–18) of Henry's parents, *Henry VII and Elizabeth of York* (*see* TORRIGIANI, PIETRO, fig. 1), and that of his grandmother *Lady Margaret Beaufort* (1511; both London, Westminster Abbey). Much of the work of these foreigners, however, was produced for court occasions and festivities and was ephemeral. Artists were used for a variety of activities and rarely gained further employment outside the court: for example Girolamo da Treviso (ii), documented at Henry VIII's court as a military engineer, is also credited with an anti-papal painting of the *Four Evangelists Stoning the Pope* (London, Hampton Court, Royal Col.). From the French king, Henry poached the Italian Nicholas Bellin of Modena, who had some responsibility for the programme (and certainly the expertise in manufacture) of the decorative scheme in stucco made for the inner court of Nonsuch Palace, Surrey (begun 1538; destr. 1682; *see* NONSUCH PALACE, §1).

Building was one activity where the scale of production is matched by evidence of Henry's personal involvement and indeed personal discernment. The publication of *The History of the King's Works* has made possible the evaluation of the extent of this activity, though of the more than 60 sites where Henry ordered building, only a handful were either new constructions or substantial additions. Many, including Hampton Court (*see* HAMPTON COURT PALACE and fig. 2), Whitehall (*see* LONDON, §V, 5) and St James's palaces, all in or near London and worked on during the 1530s, were adaptations of older properties; others were conversions of former monastic sites. Henry's interest in building was noted by contemporaries: the

French ambassador Jean Du Bellay informed Francis I in 1532 that, at each of Henry's royal houses, 'he shows it to me and tells me what he has done, and what he is going to do'. Plans are frequently recorded as having been shown to the King for his approval. The cost and drain on Crown resources were noted by Thomas Cromwell as early as 1534, some years before the height of royal building activity.

The characteristic Tudor palace that emerged was predominantly brick, usually gabled and battlemented. However, the visual coherence of these building would have been more apparent to contemporaries through such additions as the painting of brick with ochre and black, gilded weather vanes, heraldry and rich furnishings and decoration, as illustrated in such paintings as *Henry VIII and his Family* (see fig.), than by any architectural similarity. In these buildings significant internal developments took place as the sequences of state and private rooms for the King and Queen developed and became extended to express the functions of royal ceremony and the careful hierarchy (with all its attendant political machinations) of access to the King.

Two other areas of building activity are important: first, the King's completion of royal ecclesiastical work, notably King's College Chapel, Cambridge, in the 1530s (*see* CAMBRIDGE (i), §2), for which he employed leading Netherlandish glass painters; second, the building of coastal fortifications from 1538, where Henry's intervention as 'designer' is even more apparent and often verifiable by the changes of plan that followed his presence on site. Important surviving examples are the castles of St Mawes (*see* MILITARY ARCHITECTURE AND FORTIFICATION, fig. 14), Cornwall, Southsea, Hants, and Deal and Walmer in Kent.

Inventories of the pictures in the royal collection taken in 1542 and 1547 allow for little identification of individual artists. There are pictures celebrating the events of the King's reign: the *Battle of the Spurs* and the *Meeting of Henry and Maximilian* (both London, Hampton Court, Royal Col.) may have been painted by Flemish artists for the King soon after the events took place. Henry appears to have owned a great number of Flemish pictures, both religious and secular, by artists from Antwerp and Bruges, although few of the portraits are identifiable. He certainly dealt with Flemish agents or bought from Netherlanders living in London, but many of the inventoried works may have been gifts. An important aspect of the history of painting at Henry's court was his patronage of the Netherlandish Horenbout family. The miniature of *Henry VIII* (*c.* 1525–6; Cambridge, Fitzwilliam), attributed to Lucas Horenbout (appointed painter to the King in 1534), is probably the earliest example of the distinctively English miniature tradition that developed in the 16th century. Henry was also the first English monarch to be widely known through printed media, for example the title-borders designed for Coverdale's Bible of 1535, the engraving by Cornelis Massys of 1544 and an engraving of the King in Council by Jacob Faber (*fl* 1516–?1550) in 1548.

The results of Henry VIII's employment of Hans Holbein (ii) (*see* HOLBEIN, (3)) from 1536 onwards included two different but equally powerful images of the King that were much copied: one was a regal and dynastic image in a wall painting at Whitehall Palace (1537; destr. 1698; cartoon fragment, London, N.P.G.; *see* ENGLAND, fig. 15), the other is the *Granting of a Charter to the Barber-surgeons Company of London* (1541; London, Guildhall), in which Henry is depicted in state robes, mirroring the more hieratic likenesses found in manuscript illuminations and on royal seals. The only certain Holbein single portrait of *Henry VIII* that survives (1536; Madrid, Mus. Thyssen-Bornemisza) originally may well have been a gift to a foreign prince, since its early provenance is unknown.

It is, however, in the sphere of personal objects, the clothes and gifts he received and gave, that Henry VIII's

Henry VIII and his Family by an unknown artist, oil on canvas, 1.42×3.56 m, 1545–6 (London, Hampton Court, Royal Collection)

personal preferences were most marked. A writing-desk (London, V&A) decorated with the royal arms illustrates the embellished and emblazoned objects with which he was surrounded. In order to rival the technical quality of German and Milanese armour, he set up a workshop at Greenwich in 1516, which produced suits of armour of high quality but with particularly English patterns of badges and scrolling. Jewels produced for him or his wives might indicate personal discrimination; they also reveal a lost world of political propaganda that reached down even to such personal objects. In the New Year's gift, for example, from Henry to Katherine Howard in 1540, one great jewel had inscribed on its reverse: *the pycture of the Busshopp of Rome ronnyng away lamentyng / and divers persons one settyng his fote upon the busshop overthrowen.*

There has been much discussion concerning the the Renaissance or Italianate character of Henry's patronage, with the counter-assertion that his part in the revival of feudal and militaristic values found their best expression in the promotion of late medieval, and particularly 15th-century Burgundian, iconography. The two positions are not in fact incompatible, for the visual splendour of Henry's court was designed both to indulge current fashions and, by reference to the past, emphasize the stability of the Tudor dynasty.

BIBLIOGRAPHY
R. Strong: *Holbein and Henry VIII* (London, 1967)
M. Mitchell: 'Works of Art from Rome for Henry VIII', *J. Warb. & Court. Inst.* (1971)
H. Colvin, ed.: *1485–1660* (1975–82), iii and iv of *The History of the King's Works* (London, 1963–82)
G. Kipling: *The Triumph of Honour* (Leiden, 1977)
Holbein and the Court of Henry VIII (exh. cat., London, Queen's Gal., 1978)
D. Starkey: *The Reign of Henry VIII: Personalities and Politics* (London, 1985)
L. Campbell and S. Foister: 'Gerard, Lucas and Susanna Horenbout', *Burl. Mag.*, cxxviii (1986), pp. 719–27
S. Thurley: *The Royal Palaces of Tudor England* (New Haven and London, 1993)

(3) Elizabeth I, Queen of England (*b* Greenwich, nr London, 7 Sept 1533; *reg* 1558–1603; *d* Richmond, nr London, 24 March 1603). Daughter of (2) Henry VIII. Her mother was Anne Boleyn. Her importance for architecture and painting in England is of an indirect nature. She did not commission any important buildings herself, but since courtiers vied for her favour she can be said to have inspired some of the greatest country houses of the period (e.g. Burghley, Cambs, Holdenby, Northants, and Theobalds, Herts), and some of the best-recorded visual entertainments, presented in her honour at Court and in the country houses and gardens of the nobility. She rationalized the vast number of royal residences inherited from her father, Henry VIII, by maintaining a limited number of the largest of them and relinquishing the rest. She did, however, build a gallery at Windsor Castle (which survives as the Royal Library) and banqueting houses at Greenwich (1559) and Whitehall, London (1572 and 1581; both destr.).

Portraits of Elizabeth played a key role in image-making which, following the Reformation, shifted away from religious subject-matter. The production of both painted and engraved portraits of the Queen was strictly controlled by statute. Some were probably carried out as part of

marriage negotiations—such as the 'Cobham' portrait of *c.* 1575 (London, N.P.G.); others, particularly in her later years, used complex symbolism and classical allusion and avoided the issue of Elizabeth's age to render the virtues she placed at the service of the state. These include the 'Armada' portrait, attributed to George Gower (after 1588; Woburn Abbey, Beds; *see* ENGLAND, fig. 16); and the 'Ditchley' portrait, attributed to Marcus Gheerhaerts II (1592; London, N.P.G.). A rare hint of her personal preference for the flattened, iconic style used in these portraits appears in Nicholas Hilliard's comment in *The Art of Limning*, that she chose to sit to him in 'the open alley of a goodly garden where no tree was near, nor any shadow at all'.

For portrait *see* REGALIA, fig. 4.

BIBLIOGRAPHY
R. Strong: *Portraits of Elizabeth I* (Oxford, 1963)
——: *The Cult of Elizabeth* (London, 1977)
H. Colvin: *1485–1660* (1982), iv of *The History of the King's Works* (London, 1963–82)
J. Arnold: *Queen Elizabeth's Wardrobe Unlock'd* (London, 1988) [on her attire and jewellery]
MAURICE HOWARD

Tufiño, Rafael (*b* Brooklyn, NY, 1918). Puerto Rican painter, printmaker and designer of American birth. He moved permanently to Puerto Rico with his Puerto Rican parents in 1936, initially studying under the Spanish painter Alejandro Sánchez Felipe and with Juan Rosado at his sign-painting workshop in San Juan. In the late 1940s he studied painting, printmaking and mural painting at the Academia de San Carlos in Mexico with José Chavez Morado, Antonio Rodríguez Luna and Castro Pacheco. He joined the staff of the Division of Community Education in Puerto Rico as a poster artist and illustrator in 1950, serving as director of the graphic arts workshop of this division from 1957 until 1963. He was awarded a Guggenheim Fellowship in 1966 and the National Award for the Arts in 1985.

Tufiño's early art was influenced by the social realist currents in Puerto Rican art and by the Mexican nationalist artistic movement. Together with Lorenzo Homar and Carlos Raquel Rivera, Tufiño became a leading printmaker, and like them he worked primarily with woodcuts, linocuts and screenprints. While his expressive emphasis on stark contrasts of black and white can be compared with the production of the Taller de Gráfica Popular in Mexico, he favoured a poetic rather than satirical tone and distinguished himself in his screenprints with his masterly exploitation of the painterly potential of the medium.

Tufiño is often described as the painter of the people of Puerto Rico because of his sensitivity in depicting ordinary places and situations. His subject-matter ranged from intimate interiors and portraits of family and friends to landscapes, nudes and representations of Afro-Caribbean 'bomba y plena' musical festivals. His paintings are characterized by a strong line, richness of colour and spontaneity of touch.

BIBLIOGRAPHY
E. Ruiz de la Mata: 'The Art of Tufiño', *San Juan Rev.*, ii/11 (1966), pp. 18–24

Puerto Rican Painting: Between Past and Present (exh. cat. by M. C. Ramírez, Washington, DC, Mus. Mod. A. Latin America, 1987)

L. R. Cancel and others: *The Latin American Spirit: Art and Artists in the United States, 1920–1970* (New York, 1988)

MARI CARMEN RAMÍREZ

Tugendkhol'd, Yakov (Aleksandrovich) (*b* Moscow, 17 Dec 1882; *d* Moscow, 29 Nov 1928). Russian art historian, theorist and critic. He began his studies in Moscow in 1901, moving in late 1902 to Munich, where he studied in private art schools, among them the studio of Alexei von Jawlensky. In 1905 he went to Paris, where he attended the Ranson Academy and the studio of Théophile Steinlen. His first significant articles, mainly commending Impressionism and Post-Impressionism, are marked by a historicist approach, by the originality of their theoretical interpretation of art and by their literary skill. In the 1910s his studies of Puvis de Chavannes and of a number of the leading Impressionists were published, and he published Van Gogh's letters and Gauguin's *Noa-Noa*, with foreword and notes by himself. In 1913 he returned to Moscow, making a short trip to Germany and France in the spring of 1914 to select contemporary Western paintings for the collector Sergey Shchukin. From 1913 to 1917 he worked on a series of studies of Russian painters such as Viktor Borisov-Musatov, Nikolay Sapunov and Natal'ya Goncharova, in which he made perceptive analyses of the innovative nature of their work. After 1917 Tugendkhol'd worked in arts administration, in particular in the Department for Museum Affairs and the Preservation of Monuments (1918) and in the State Academy of Artistic Sciences (1922–8). He ran the arts sections of the newspapers *Izvestiya*, *Pravda* and the journal *Krasnaya Niva*, in which he published his essays on new trends in contemporary art. He was one of the organizers of the Soviet sections of the Exposition Internationale des Arts Décoratifs et Industriels Modernes in Paris (1925) and of the Anniversary Exhibition of Art of the Peoples of the USSR (1927). During this period he published the books that were to lay the foundation for modern Russian art criticism.

WRITINGS

Frantsuzskoye iskusstvo i yego predstaviteli [French art and its representatives] (St Petersburg, 1911)

'Molodye gody Musatova' [The youth of Musatov], *Apollon*, viii–ix (1915)

'Khudoznik Mark Shagal' [The artist Marc Chagall], *Iskusstvo Marka Shagala* [The art of Mark Chagall], ed. A. Efros and Ya. Tugendkhol'd (Moscow, 1918)

Edgar Dega i yego iskusstvo [Edgar Degas and his art] (Moscow, 1922)

Alexandra Ekster kak zhivopisets i khudozhnik tseny [Alexandra Exter as a painter and theatrical designer] (Berlin, 1922)

Pervy musey novoi zapadnoi zhivopisi [First museum of new western painting] (Moscow and Petrograd, 1923)

Khudozhestvennaya kul'tura Zapada [Western artistic culture] (Moscow, 1928)

Iskusstvo Oktyabr'skoy epokhi [Art of the revolutionary era] (Leningrad, 1930)

Iz istorii zapadnoyevropeyskogo, russkogo i sovetskogo iskusstva: Izbrannyye stat'i i ocherki [From the history of Western European, Russian and Soviet art: selected essays and outlines] (Moscow, 1987) [with articles on Tugendkhol'd by G. Yu. Sternin and T. P. Kazhdan]

ALLA RUSAKOVA

Tughluq. Turkish dynasty that ruled northern India from 1320 to 1413. Ghazi Malik, a nobleman from the Punjab, assumed the title Ghiyath al-Din Tughluq on taking the throne in 1320 after the last KHALJI king had been murdered. During his short reign (1320–25) he constructed a fortified garrison city at DELHI called Tughluqabad and built his own tomb adjacent to it. He also built the tomb in which the saint Rukn-i 'Alam is buried in MULTAN; the congregational mosque there, according to Ibn Battuta, was inscribed with his 29 victories against invaders from Central Asia and Afghanistan.

Muhammad Tughluq (*reg* 1325–51) retained Tughluqabad as his centre but built walls enclosing Siri (the Khalji city) and the older portions of Delhi constructed by the Mamluk dynasty (*see* MAMLUK, §I). This new area, in which Muhammad Tughluq built a palace and a mosque, was named Jahanpanah. He also built the fortress of 'Adilabad on the hills to the south of Tughluqabad. In an effort to consolidate power in the south, Muhammad Tughluq undertook aggressive campaigns in the Deccan and moved the capital to DAULATABAD, forcing the evacuation of Delhi. This expansionist policy, however, ended in failure. In 1336 the residents of Delhi were permitted to return, and by 1347 the BAHMANI dynasty had gained power in the south. Further troubles visited the reign in the form of famines (1334–44) and the Black Death (1335–8).

Firuz Shah (*reg* 1351–88), though not a dynamic leader, brought stability to the Sultanate and was the most active builder of the Tughluq house. In Delhi he established a new urban centre called Firuzabad (now Kotla Firuz Shah). His numerous other projects included palaces, gardens, hunting pavilions, mosques, Islamic colleges, tombs and public works. He also restored older buildings, notably the Qutb Minar. The decade after Firuz Shah was marked by internecine warfare among the nobles. Timur encountered little resistance during his invasion and sack of Delhi in 1398. After this the Tughluqs lingered on as nominal rulers until the death of Mahmud Tughluq in 1413.

See also INDIAN SUBCONTINENT, §III, 6(ii)(b).

BIBLIOGRAPHY

Enc. Islam/2: 'Dilhi Sultanate'

Ziya al-Din Barani: *Tārīkh-i Fīrūz Shāhī* [History of Firuz Shah] (MS. 1358; Calcutta, 1860–62; Aligarh, 1957) [extracts trans. in Eng. in Elliot and Dowson, iii, pp. 93–268 and *J. Asiat. Soc. Bengal* (1869), pp. 181–220; (1870), pp. 1–51, 185–216; (1871), pp. 217–47]

H. Elliot and J. Dowson: *History of India as Told by its Own Historians (The Muhammedan Period)*, 8 vols (London, 1866–77/*R* Allahabad, 1964)

R. C. Majumdar, ed.: *The Delhi Sultanate*, vi of *The History and Culture of the Indian People* (Bombay, 1960/*R* 1967)

I. H. Siddiqi and Q. M. Ahmad, trans.: *A Fourteenth Century Arab Account of India under Sultan ibn Tughluq* (Aligarh, 1971)

A. Welch and H. Crane: 'The Tughluqs: Master Builders of the Delhi Sultanate', *Muqarnas*, i (1983), pp. 123–66

R. NATH

Tughra [Turk. *tuğra*]. Imperial monogram of the Ottoman sultans (*reg* 1281–1924). It consists of the sultan's name, patronymics, titles and the formula 'ever victorious'. Since the Ottoman sultans did not sign their decrees, the tughra was the ultimate authentication, and it fell to the *nişanci*, a high official with the rank of pasha, to draw the tughra after the copy had been checked for accuracy and calligraphed. In the narrowest sense, the tughra is distinguished by three high verticals and one large elliptical curve extending to the left and enclosing a smaller, similar curve. Many theories have been offered to explain the development of this form. The widespread tradition that it represents the three fingers and the thumb of the ruler that Murad I (*reg* 1360–89) allegedly put on a document in Ragusa has been challenged; the tughra has also been connected with the *tūgh*, the yak or horse tail that served in Central Asia as a sign of sovereignty or high military rank and the flourishes at the end of the three verticals do resemble yak tails.

The use of the tughra can be traced back to the Saljuq dynasty in Iran (*reg* 1038–1194); the *nom de plume* of the Saljuq vizier and poet Tughra'i (*d* 1120), for example, shows that a high-ranking member of the bureaucracy was in charge of drawing the tughra. The tendency to place the ruler's name in conspicuous letters at the top of a document began early; the elongation of the vertical letters of the name and sometimes of a benediction is already found on Indo-Muslim documents from the Sultanate period (1206–1555) as well as in Egypt under the Mamluks (*reg* 1250–1517). These verticals are evenly spaced to form a kind of fence, which is often embellished by interlacing the letters with the round endings of the letters *nūn* and *sīn*. Under the Ottomans the tughra was used only in documents sent from the capital to the provinces. High officials, who sometimes used a similarly shaped monogram of their own, did not put it at the top of the document but rather on the right margin, perpendicular to the text.

The earliest Ottoman tughras were rather simple, written in black or gold ink. During the reign of Selim I (*reg* 1512–20), blue ink outlined in gold or blue on a gold ground became fashionable, and fine spiral and arabesque designs filled the curves. Towards the end of the 16th century the decoration around the letters grew into an independent design, which was often triangular but sometimes achieved more fanciful shapes, such as the helmet shape popular *c.* 1600. In the 17th century tughras became very colourful, and the filler decoration, while maintaining the fine spiral design, also included larger, sometimes ungainly vegetal forms. After this Baroque phase the art of drawing tughras deteriorated; from the 19th century black, red and green replaced gold, and the calligraphy declined in quality. In later periods, the sultan's own annotation on the document, 'it shall be acted accordingly', was emphasized in gold, and from the 18th century it became an additional decorative element in the tughra itself.

The tughra was the major decorative element of the firman (Pers. *farmān*), the legal deed, certificate or edict issued by the sultan. The firman was written on long sheets of paper which had been pasted together in strips and often reached several metres in length. In Ottoman firmans, the word *hū* ('He', God) was usually written at the top, and the tughra was drawn after a considerable blank space. The main text was written in a stylized chancellery hand, which is exceedingly difficult to read because of the many ligatures. The lines often rise slightly towards the upper left, creating an elegant curve, and end near the left edge of the paper to exclude later additions. Alternating lines of text may be in gold, black, red and less frequently blue and green ink. Important words, such as the name of God and religious formulas, are written in

gold, and other essential parts can be written in red. The paper is sometimes sprinkled with gold.

As the characteristic sign of sovereignty, the tughra was logically applied to coins and, in the 19th century, to banknotes and postage stamps. These were composed by skilful calligraphers in Ottoman Turkey and other Islamic countries where this decorative style was imitated. The typical tughra shape, with its three verticals and its elliptical curve, is still used for many decorative purposes, including names, titles and religious formulas (e.g. invocations to God or such Sufi saints as Jalal al-Din Rumi). In India the word tughra is applied to any kind of decorative script, such as mirrored sentences or birds and beasts, flowers and faces, buildings and trees, composed of meaningful sentences and invocations. The writing of this type of tughra is subject to strict rules, but the calligrapher is allowed the freedom to write repeated letters as one and to weave various endings into each other. This art was particularly loved in Turkey and India, and numerous architectural and decorative inscriptions show an amazing variety of this type of tughra.

BIBLIOGRAPHY

Enc. Islam/1; *Enc. Islam/2*: 'Diplomatic'
F. Babinger: 'Die grossherrliche Tuğra', *Jb. Asiat. Kst*, ii (1925), pp. 185–96
P. Wittek: 'Notes sur la tughra ottomane', *Byzantion*, xviii (1948), pp. 311–34
E. Kühnel: 'Die osmanische Tughra', *Kst Orients*, ii (1955), pp. 69–82
A. Bombaci: 'Les Toughras enluminés de la collection de documents turcs des archives d'état de Venise', *Atti del secondo congresso internazionale di arte turca: Venezia, 1963*, pp. 41–55
M. Sertoğlu: *Osmanlı Türklerinde Tuğra* [Tughras of the Ottoman Turks] (Istanbul, 1975)
S. Umur: *Osmanlı Padişah Tuğraları* [Tughras of the Ottoman sultans] (Istanbul, 1980)

ANNEMARIE SCHIMMEL

Tuitlán. *See* LA QUEMADA.

Tuke [Toke; Tooke], Sir **Brian** (*d* Layer Marney, Essex, 26 Oct 1545). English courtier and patron. He was made French secretary to Henry VIII in 1522 and was Treasurer of the King's Chamber from 1528 until his death. Tuke's name is associated with two great early Tudor houses. He assumed the property of Layer Marney, Essex, in the 1520s, but he seems not to have completed the courtyard of the house, which was begun by Henry, 1st Baron Marney (1456/7–1523), and John, 2nd Baron Marney (before 1485–1525); only the great gate-house and adjoining ranges (*in situ*) were built. He may well have been responsible, however, for at least the beginning of the building of Weald Hall, also in Essex, a property he assumed in 1541. In his will he left certain building materials to his son George Tuke 'for any buylding or rep[ar]acons at Southwelde'. By *c.* 1550 this brick house consisted of a great hall with cross-wings. Much enlarged subsequently, it was destroyed in 1950.

Hans Holbein II executed a portrait of *Tuke* (Washington, DC, N.G.A.), of which two early copies exist (Munich, Alte Pin.; Pasadena, CA, Norton Simon Mus.). Two dates have been suggested for the original version: one is 1528, which interprets Tuke's wearing of a pendant cross showing the five wounds of Christ as a token of his recovery from a serious illness; the other, *c.* 1538–40, is more widely accepted, since the style of painting accords well with Holbein's later years in England.

DNB

BIBLIOGRAPHY

A. T. Bolton: 'Country Home: Weald Hall, Essex', *Country Life*, xxxvi (3 Oct 1914), pp. 454–61

J. Rowlands: *Holbein* (Oxford, 1985)

MAURICE HOWARD

Tuke, Henry Scott (*b* York, 12 June 1858; *d* Falmouth, 13 March 1929). English painter. He entered the Slade School of Art, London, in 1875, under Alphonse Legros and Sir Edward Poynter. In 1877 he won a Slade scholarship and in 1880 travelled to Italy, where he made his first nude life drawings, an important revelation to him of light, colour and the human form. From 1881 to 1883 he was in Paris and met Jules Bastien-Lepage, who encouraged his studies *en plein air*. Admiring Bastien-Lepage's practice of focusing different areas of a painting by degrees of finish, Tuke adopted this in his own mature work.

In 1883 Tuke settled in Newlyn, Cornwall, and was a founder-member of the NEWLYN SCHOOL. In 1885 he moved to Falmouth, spending the rest of his life based there. During the 1880s he produced anecdotal *plein-air* paintings of the life of the Cornish fishing community. *All Hands to the Pump* (1888; London, Tate), bought by the Chantrey Bequest, is a typical example, showing his alertness to tensions and movements in the human body and his ability to combine classical compositional principles with naturalistic detail, while giving coherence by sensitive rendering of atmosphere.

In 1892 Tuke travelled to Italy, Corfu and Albania; thereafter his palette lightened dramatically, and his technique gained a new Impressionistic freedom. The nude adolescent male emerged as his principal motif in such pictures as *August Blue* (1893–4; London, Tate), another Chantrey Bequest purchase. His admiration of James McNeill Whistler appears in the creation of mood at the expense of narrative and in his preference for evocative titles. An implicit homoerotic element caused some unease at the time.

In 1886 Tuke was a founder-member of the NEW ENGLISH ART CLUB and in 1900 he was elected an ARA. He also acquired a London studio where he spent the winters, usually working on portrait commissions. His work in this field was much admired, and he painted such notable figures as the cricketer *W. G. Grace* (London, Middx Co. Cricket Club; see Wainwright and Dinn, p. 103) and *T. E. Lawrence* (1921–2; Clouds Hill, Dorset, NT). An accomplished watercolourist, in 1911 he became a member of the Royal Watercolour Society. He also worked in pastels and executed a single sculpture, *The Watcher* (1916; see Cooper, p. 58), of which five bronze casts were made.

In 1914 Tuke was made an RA, and his painting style and subject-matter remained substantially unchanged: *Aquamarine* (1928–9; see Cooper, p. 65), probably his last easel painting, closely resembles the earlier *Ruby, Gold and Malachite* (1901; London, Guildhall A.G.). In later pictures, however, the models are no longer portraits, but interchange heads and bodies as vehicles of Tuke's vision. Impersonality and detachment combined with sincere commitment to subject and atmosphere characterize his mature style and challenged artistic expectations of the time, broadening the parameters of British *plein-air* painting.

In 1923 Tuke visited Jamaica and Central America, producing some fine watercolours. Penetrating the interior of Belize, however, he became ill and was forced to return home. He never fully recovered his health, although his passion for travel remained undiminished.

BIBLIOGRAPHY

M. T. Sainsbury: *Henry Scott Tuke: A Memoir* (London, 1933)

E. Cooper: *The Life and Work of Henry Scott Tuke* (London, 1987)

D. Wainwright and C. Dinn: *Henry Scott Tuke, 1858–1929: Under Canvas* (London, 1989)

JUSTINE HOPKINS

Tula [Tollan]. Pre-Columbian city in Hidalgo, Mexico, that flourished as the capital city of the TOLTEC people between *c*. AD 950 and 1150–1200. Tula occupies a ridge overlooking the River Tula in the arid steppes 60 km north-west of Mexico City. Historically, Tula was the second of three major central Mexican urban polities (Teotihuacán, Tula and Tenochtitlán) that exerted political, cultural and artistic influence on other Mesoamerican societies. The Toltecs ruled a small ephemeral empire covering portions of central, north-central and western Mexico, but their commercial and perhaps political influences extended southwards into Yucatán and Central America.

The community, first settled *c*. AD 800, grew into a city with a population of perhaps 10,000 by *c*. 950. Little is known of this early period or Corral phase, but Tula Chico, its largely unexcavated civic–religious precinct, has been identified. Tula Chico consists of platform mounds that once supported buildings arranged around an open plaza in a configuration similar to Tula Grande, the civic–religious precinct of the mature city. Tula Chico was replaced by the much larger Tula Grande zone on the southern edge of the ridge in *c*. 950 (see fig.). In its second stage of development, known as the Tollan phase (from *c*. 950 to *c*. 1150–1200), the city covered 14 sq. km and was home to between 35,000 to 40,000 craftsmen, farmers, merchants, warriors, priests and rulers. By 1200 the abandoned city was already in ruins. The reasons for its decline are not clear, but agricultural problems related to drought, pressure from neighbouring societies and internal conflicts all appear to have been instrumental. Jorge R. Acosta excavated many of the Tula Grande buildings between 1940 and 1957. In the 1970s and 1980s North American and Mexican archaeologists conducted excavations in the Toltec residential zone and surveyed the entire city.

1. ARCHITECTURE. Tula Grande is part of an artificially terraced acropolis, which overlooks the rest of the city. It consists of an open rectangular plaza, 100×100 m, surrounded by pyramids, palaces and ballcourts and, like the rest of the Tollan phase city, is orientated 17 degrees east of north. The pyramids (see fig. (b) and (c)) are stepped temple substructures constructed of stone rubble and adobe blocks mortared with mud. Stairways facing the plaza led to temples or shrines at the summits. Pyramid C

(65×65× *c.* 15 m) was so destroyed by Pre-Columbian looters that little is known about its original appearance. The slightly smaller Pyramid B (40×40×10 m; for illustration *see* CAJA-ESPIGA and MESOAMERICA, PRE-COLUMBIAN, fig. 14), a five-tiered platform north of Pyramid C, was constructed in at least three phases. It also suffered severe destruction, but intact façade fragments show that it was covered with carved stone tablets. The façade includes entablatures depicting a composite being with serpent, avian and jaguar features, thought to be the deity Tlahuizcalpantecuhtli (Venus, the Morning Star), and jaguars, eagles and vultures holding human hearts in their mouths. Friezes above the entablatures portray prowling jaguars and coyotes. Thick white stucco, perhaps symbolic of the Underworld, covered the entire substructure. The temple at the summit was completely destroyed, but the carved stone columns, which depict Toltec warriors and supported the roof, were found by modern archaeologists.

A narrow passageway was created north of Pyramid B by the free-standing COATEPANTLI or Serpent Wall (h. 2.6 m). Each side of the Coatepantli is faced with three bands of carved stone tablets. The top and bottom bands show repetitions of stepped frets thought to represent stylized serpents, while the central panels feature serpents devouring partially skeletonized men. The entire work was painted bright red, blue and yellow. The Palacio Quemado (see fig. (d)) occupies the area west of Pyramid B. Its rectangular platform supported a colonnaded hall covered by a flat roof. Three large rooms on the front apparently functioned as council halls and had benches and rectangular altars lining their interiors. Intact fragments of the bench façades have carved and painted tablets depicting processions of richly dressed male priests or rulers. Undulating serpents portraying Quetzalcóatl, the Feathered Serpent, and Mixcóatl, the Cloud Serpent, slither across the bench cornices. On the same terrace as Pyramid B and the Palacio Quemado is the Vestibule (f), which formed a colonnaded portico in front of both structures.

Two ballcourts (a) have been excavated at Tula Grande. Both consist of platforms surrounding capital letter I-shaped playing fields on which opposing teams played a ritual game with a solid rubber ball. Fragments of stone rings originally placed in the upper walls at the centre of the court have also been found. One way of scoring was to drive the ball through an opening in the ring only slightly larger than the ball itself. One ballcourt also has an associated *tzompantli* (e), a low platform on which the skulls of sacrificial victims, including perhaps defeated ball-players, were displayed.

Although Tula's largest temples and other public buildings are concentrated at Tula Grande, scores of moderately large temple mounds and other élite or special-purpose buildings are found elsewhere in the city. A particularly dense concentration has been noted near the north edge of the city but only the largest, El Corral, has been excavated. This building is a round platform with square appendages and was probably dedicated to Ehecatl, the wind god.

2. ARTEFACTS. Pottery, figurines, onyx bowls, greenstone plaques, carved shell ornaments and beads, and other small portable objects were found at Tula. Hurriedly

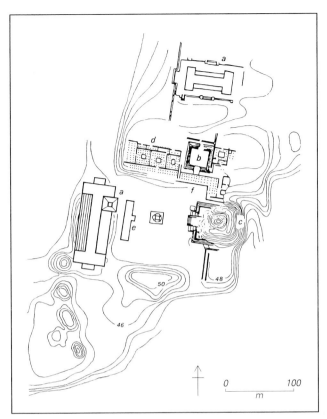

Tula, plan of Tula Grande, *c.* 950–1200: (a) ballcourts; (b) Pyramid B; (c) Pyramid C; (d) Palacio Quemado; (e) *tzompantli*; (f) Vestibule

executed designs on ordinary eating vessels carry the same symbols and cultural messages so proudly displayed on the major public buildings. But the aesthetic qualities of the objects fail to match those of other Mesoamerican civilizations. Indeed the finest pieces are all imports, including pottery from Guatemala and Central America and a carved jadeite plaque thought to come from Oaxaca. In view of this, Toltec objects are not highly prized by collectors and rarely appear in private collections. The Museo Nacional de Antropología in Mexico City and the Museo Regional Jorge R. Acosta at Tula contain numerous pieces of note, and much of the sculpture is displayed at the archaeological site.

BIBLIOGRAPHY

J. R. Acosta: 'Interpretación de algunos de los datos obtenidos en Tula relativos a la época Tolteca', *Rev. Mex. Estud. Antropol.*, xiv (1956–7), pp. 75–110

C. N. B. Davies: *The Toltecs until the Fall of Tula* (Norman, 1977)

R. A. Diehl: 'Tula', *Hb. Mid. Amer. Ind.*, suppl. 1 (1981), pp. 277–95

——: *Tula: The Toltec Capital of Ancient Mexico* (London, 1983)

E. T. Baird: 'Naturalistic and Symbolic Color at Tula, Hidalgo', *Painted Architecture and Polychrome Monumental Sculpture in Mesoamerica*, ed. E. Boone (Washington, DC, 1985), pp. 115–44

RICHARD A. DIEHL

Tulmaythah. *See* PTOLEMAIS.

Tulsi Kalan [Tulsi] (*fl c.* 1560–1600). Indian miniature painter. His work is characterized by an archaic quality, evenly spaced figures and a simple cross-section in architectural design that suggests his training in the indigenous pre-Mughal tradition. The earliest reference to both Tulsi and Tulsi Kalan ('the Elder') appears in the *Razmnāma* ('Book of wars'; *c.* 1582–6; Jaipur, Maharaja Sawai Man Singh II Mus., MS. AG. 1683–1850). Tulsi was given sole charge of three paintings (fols 45, 105 and 62) and Tulsi Kalan fol. 167. As a designer he worked on four folios with other artists, one of whom was Tulsi Khurd ('the Younger'). Tulsi acted as painter for a design by Basawan and Lal and Tulsi Kalan for Daswanth. In the *Timūrnāma* ('History of Timur'; *c.* 1580; Bankipur, Patna, Khuda Bakhsh Lib.) he had sole charge of one painting and worked on five folios as designer/outliner; he also acted as painter for Isar and Madhu Kalan. In the *Khamsa* ('Five poems') of Nizami (*c.* 1585; Pontresina, Keir col.) he was responsible for the design of one folio, which was painted by Kesu Khurd with portraits executed by Nanha. The work of Tulsi Kalan in the *Akbarnāma* ('History of Akbar'; *c.* 1586–90; London, V&A, MS. IS. 2–1896) reveals a conservative, careful painter. The fact that he had charge of the outline and design of several of the first paintings in the manuscript (fols 2–5) suggests that he may have been one of the first artists to join the workshop. Folio 104 is assigned solely to Tulsi Kalan; despite prolific use of gold, bright colours and a busy scene, the painting has an archaic flavour. Four other designs are attributed to Tulsi in the manuscript and fol. 47 bears the appellation Tulsi Kalan. As Tulsi, his name appears in the *'Iyar-i danish* ('Book of fables'; *c.* 1590–95; Dublin, Chester Beatty Lib.), the *Baburnāma* ('History of Babur'; *c.* 1591; London, BL, Or 3714) and the *Jāmi' al-tavārīkh* (dated 1596; Tehran, Gulistan Pal. Lib.) as sole artist and in collaboration with other painters as a designer (fols 171*v* and 195*r*).

BIBLIOGRAPHY

The Imperial Image: Paintings for the Mughal Court (exh. cat. by M. C. Beach, Washington, DC, Freer, 1981)

HEATHER ELGOOD

Tulum, Castillo, *c.* 1200–1520

Tulum. Pre-Columbian MAYA walled site on the east coast of the Yucatán Peninsula, Mexico, which flourished *c.* 1200–*c.* 1520. It lies on the east coast of Quintana Roo *c.* 40 km south-west of the island of Cozumel, on the summit of a limestone cliff *c.* 12 m high, facing the Caribbean Sea. The name 'Tulum', which means 'wall' or 'fortification', is modern, but there is reason to believe that its ancient name was Zama, one of the Maya cities that, according to the chronicles, existed at the time of the Spanish Conquest. The conquistador Juan de Grijalva is generally credited with the discovery of Tulum during his expedition by sea along the coast of Quintana Roo in 1518. It was the American explorer John Lloyd Stephens, however, who first drew widespread attention to the site, in 1843, through his descriptions of its principal buildings, which were illustrated with the excellent drawings of his collaborator, FREDERICK CATHERWOOD. Since 1916 excavation and restoration work have been carried out by the Carnegie Institution of Washington, DC, and by the Instituto Nacional de Antropología e Historia, Mexico City.

The main occupation and construction of Tulum appears to have been limited to the three centuries preceding the Spanish Conquest in 1521, although a sculptured stele found there bears a date in the Maya Long Count calendar (*see* MESOAMERICA, PRE-COLUMBIAN, §II) of 9.6.10.0.0, corresponding to AD 564. Tulum is best known for its enclosing wall, its wall paintings and its architecture, which exemplifies Late Post-Classic period (*c.* 1200–1521) Maya architecture of the east Yucatán coast. The enclosing wall, a thick masonry construction generally assumed to have served as a fortification (*see* MILITARY ARCHITECTURE AND FORTIFICATION, fig. 32), delineates the north, south and west boundaries of the site, while the east side ends at the cliff edge. The enclosure thus formed is roughly rectangular and measures *c.* 380 m north–south and *c.* 165 m east–west. Five entrances through the wall, two each on the north and south sides and one on the west, give access to streetlike spaces along which the principal structures are found. These include the Temple of the Diving God (a term derived from the figure's upside-down position), the Temple of the Initial Series, the Temple of the Frescoes, the Funerary Platform and the Castillo. The largest architectural complex, the Castillo, is perched on the highest point of the cliff (see fig.). The uppermost temple, which faces west, away from the Caribbean, appears to have been modelled after the Toltec–Maya architecture at CHICHÉN ITZÁ, and its doorway features a pair of serpent columns similar to those found in the Temple of the Warriors at that site. Most of the other buildings at Tulum include a mixture of architectural and decorative features that show influences from the Central Highlands of Mesoamerica and from the Maya site of MAYAPÁN, which is also enclosed by a masonry wall. Prominent among the decorative elements on these buildings are the 'diving god' figures found in niches above doorways and profile stucco masks at the corners of the upper façades.

Wall paintings are found on both interior and exterior walls at Tulum. In general, they are more stylized than the paintings found at such Classic period (*c.* AD 250–*c.* 900) Maya sites as BONAMPAK, Chacmultún or Mul-Chic, which show scenes of battles, fiestas and diverse representations of daily life (*see* COLOUR, colour pl. I, fig. 1). In contrast, the paintings at Tulum are symbolic, featuring anthropomorphic deities, intertwined serpents and scenes of offerings involving flowers, fruit and ears of corn. They can best be compared to the pictorial traditions of the surviving Maya codices and painted manuscripts from central Mexico (*see* MESOAMERICA, PRE-COLUMBIAN, §VI). There are several classes of paintings. Some of the simplest and largest are generally painted in red and blue on a white background. Others, which are somewhat smaller, and generally the most detailed, are contained within vertical and horizontal bands formed by intertwined serpents, with turquoise backgrounds and figures partly delineated in red. The smallest paintings, such as those in the Temple of the Frescoes, also show a wealth of detail, with white or black backgrounds and figures rendered in blue.

BIBLIOGRAPHY

J. L. Stephens: *Incidents of Travel in Yucatán*, 2 vols (New York, 1843/*R* 1963)

S. K. Lothrop: *Tulum: An Archaeological Study of the East Coast of Yucatán*, Carnegie Institution of Washington Publication, cccv (Washington, DC, 1924)

M. A. Fernández: 'Las ruinas de Tulum I & II', *An. Mus. N. Arqueol., Hist. & Etnog.*, iii (1945) [whole issue]

W. T. Sanders: *Prehistoric Ceramics and Settlement Patterns in Quintana Roo, Mexico*, Carnegie Institution of Washington Publication, dcvi (Washington, DC, 1960)

G. F. Andrews: *Maya Cities: Placemaking and Urbanization* (Norman, 1975)

A. G. Miller: *On the Edge of the Sea: Mural Painting at Tancah-Tulum* (Washington, DC, 1982)

E. V. Pacheco: 'Consideraciones generales sobre las fortificaciones militares en Tulum, Quintana Roo, México', *Estud. Cult. Maya*, xv (1984), pp. 176–85

GEORGE F. ANDREWS

Tulunid. Islamic dynasty that ruled Egypt and Syria from AD 868 to 905. It was founded by Ahmad ibn Tulun (*b* Iraq, 835; *d* Egypt, 10 May 884), son of a high-ranking Turkish slave at the Abbasid court at Samarra', Iraq. Ahmad received military training there and theological instruction at Tarsus (now in Turkey). He came to the notice of the caliphs, and when his step-father was appointed governor of Egypt in 868 Ahmad went with him as his deputy. He gained control of the financial administration of the country and set up an independent military force, which he used to subdue Syria. In 878 he was formally recognized as governor of both Egypt and Syria. He was the first ruler to secure Egypt's *de facto* independence from the Abbasid caliphs. The country prospered under his rule: for the first time in centuries the surplus funds derived from its rich agricultural base were not sent abroad as tribute, but were used to stimulate commerce and industry. In 870 Ahmad established a new quarter, named al-Qata'i' ('The Allotments'), outside the capital at Fustat (*see* CAIRO, §I, 1). The mosque he built there, known as the Mosque of Ibn Tulun (*see* CAIRO, §III, 2), is one of the glories of medieval Islamic architecture (*see* ISLAMIC ART, fig. 24). Its forms, materials of construction and decoration reflect the contemporary architecture of the Abbasid court at Samarra (*see* ISLAMIC ART, §II, 4(i)).

Ahmad was succeeded by his son Khumarawayh (*b* Samarra, Iraq, 864; *d* Fustat, Egypt, 18 Jan 896). He was

recognized as governor of Egypt by the Abbasid caliph in return for a massive annual tribute, although the workshops producing official textiles (*tirāz*) remained under the caliph's direct control. Court life became more opulent, and Khumarawayh extended the palace his father had built in al-Qata'i' with sumptuous pavilions and gardens. Although Khumarawayh had inherited a stable and wealthy state, such was his profligacy and so large were the amounts of tribute he had to pay that he left the treasury empty when he was assassinated. He was rapidly succeeded by his two teenage sons, Jaysh and Harun, neither of whom was able to maintain authority. The royal palace was looted and burnt in the disturbances that followed, and by 905 both Syria and Egypt had passed back under the direct rule of the Abbasid caliphs.

The production of ceramics and textiles (*see* ISLAMIC ART, §§V, 2(iv) and VI, 2(i)(a)) and the carving of rock crystal, wood and stucco (*see* ISLAMIC ART, §§VIII, 13; VII, 1(i)(a); and II, 9(i)) evidently flourished under the patronage of the Tulunids, although only fragmentary examples have survived. They reflect ABBASID models in the use of Bevelled style ornament, but Egyptian artisans often interpreted the exclusively abstract designs of these models as birds or other representational motifs.

BIBLIOGRAPHY

Z. M. Hassan: *Les Tulunides: Etude de l'Egypte à la fin du IXe siècle, 868–905* (Paris, 1933)

J. Amer. Res. Cent. Egypt, iv– (1965–) [preliminary rep. on the excavations made at Fustat by G. T. Scanlon]

JONATHAN M. BLOOM

Tumaco. *See under* LA TOLITA.

Tumarkin, Ygael (*b* Dresden, 1933). Israeli sculptor, draughtsman and stage designer of German birth. His family left Germany in 1935 to settle in Palestine and there he studied at the Technical School of Tel Aviv until 1949. After serving in the Israeli army he returned to Germany in 1953 to design sets for Bertolt Brecht and the Berliner Ensemble and in 1956 he produced sets for Brecht's *Der gute Mensch von Sezuan*. In 1957 he designed theatre sets in the Netherlands, Germany and Israel, by which time he was sculpting in iron, creating works such as *Chariot* (1956; see 1980 exh. cat.). He had his first one-man show in 1956 at the Santee Landwer Gallery in Amsterdam. In the 1960s he largely used bronze and iron to make his sculptures and assemblages, often incorporating weapon parts into them, as in *Aggression* (1964; see 1967 exh. cat., pl. 55). Other works of this period are similarly disturbing, such as *Agnus Dei* (1967–8; Jerusalem, Israel Mus.), which has screaming heads incorporated into a crucifixion format. At the end of 1969 Tumarkin began using polyhedrons made from stainless steel in his sculptures, as in his public work *Homage to Dürer* (1969; Haifa).

In 1974 Tumarkin travelled to the USA, in 1977 to Egypt and from 1979 to 1980 to Morocco and Tunisia. In his drawings after 1974 he often blended associations derived from travels, books and films, as in *Djerba* (1979; Tel Aviv Mus. A.). The mud huts he saw in North Africa and his experience of the Israeli landscape inspired the use of earth and of tree branches in his later sculpture. His paintings were usually shallow assemblages of various materials such as wood, metal and paper, as in *Rex* (1964; Jerusalem, Israel Mus.).

BIBLIOGRAPHY
Ygael Tumarkin: Sculptures, Assemblages, Plans for Monuments (exh. cat., Jerusalem, Israel Mus., 1967)
Ygael Tumarkin: Journeys into Culture, Works on Paper 1956–80 (exh. cat., Tel Aviv Mus. A., 1980)

Tumm. *See* THUMB.

Tumshuk [Tumšuq; Uygur: 'beak']. Site of Buddhist monastery complexes in the extreme western part of the Xinjiang Uygur Autonomous Region of China. It is not mentioned in the Chinese annals or in reports of journeys by Buddhist pilgrims; it is possible that it was known by an older name. From the archaeological finds it seems that the monastery sites were in use between the 5th and 9th centuries AD. Paul Pelliot led a French expedition in the area in 1906. He discovered two important sites: the Tokkuz-sarai Monastery and Tumshuk-tagh, a site on three cliffs to the south, which he investigated superficially. In 1913 Albert von Le Coq found some exceptional wall paintings and numerous interesting wooden sculptures there.

The ruins of the Tokkuz-sarai Monastery, on a small plateau, covered an area of 300×200 m. The main sanctuary (30×50 m) consisted of a stupa surrounded by a courtyard with many rooms, smaller temples and accommodation for the monks. On the south-western side of the site Pelliot found fragments of paper and silk in a temple, as well as wall paintings and cinerary urns.

The German expedition led by von Le Coq concentrated on Tumshuk-tagh. In one of the temples on the western cliff an octagonal stucco socle for images of worship was discovered; it was decorated with elephant heads, ornamental motifs and Buddhist legends. The more extensive built-up area on the eastern cliff consisted of several freestanding temples. Remains of wall paintings were found in a shrine that had been damaged by fire; the north wall was covered with floral motifs. On the northern transverse wall there was a narrow strip of a sort of miniature painting with varied scenes, possibly depicting a *bodhisattva* escaping from the world (Berlin, Mus. Ind. Kst, MIK III 8717; Yaldiz, pl. XV). The upper section of the west wall was painted with Buddhist preachers; the lower section depicted a row of kneeling monks. Only the remains of two preaching scenes are preserved (Berlin, Mus. Ind. Kst, MIK III 8716; Yaldiz, pl. XIV). In the background two men listen with interest and respect to Buddha preaching; their buckled helmets and armour identify them as warriors. The man standing to the left is of noble rank, as shown by the ellipsoidal halo in concentric circles of different colours. The more complete scene on the right is richer. The Buddha sits in the centre of the picture, his hands raised in a teaching gesture. An elderly bearded brahman ascetic stands on his left, his companion Vajrapani on his right. The halo of the Buddha is made up of several rows of large blossoms, followed by one or more repeated circles. The edge of the nimbus (Skt *maṇḍorla*) is also made up of several circles, while the inner surface is filled with a green, reddish-brown and blue pattern of waves. Such wave motifs and flowers were rare in Central Asia before the middle of the Chinese Tang period (AD 618–907).

Numerous fine wooden sculptures were also discovered at Tumshuk. The figure of Buddha lost in meditation (*see* CENTRAL ASIA, fig. 81) must be dated earlier than the wall paintings, namely to the 5th century AD.

See also CENTRAL ASIA, §II, 3(i) and (ii)(b).

BIBLIOGRAPHY
A. von Le Coq: 'Zwei Bruchstücke alt-buddhistischer Wandgemälde aus Ost-Turkistan', *Jb. Asiat. Kst*, ii (1925), pp. 69–72
——: *Von Land und Leuten in Ostturkistan: Berichte und Abenteuer der 4. deutschen Turfan-Expedition* (Leipzig, 1926)
M. Paul-David, M. Hallade and L. Hambis: *Toumchouq* (1961–4), i–ii of *Mission Paul Pelliot* (Paris, 1961–87)
M. Yaldiz: *Archäologie und Kunstgeschichte chinesisch-Zentralasiens (Xinjiang)* (1987), iii/2 of *Handbuch der Orientalistik*, ed. B. Spuler and others (Leiden, 1978–)
M. YALDIZ

Tu Mu. *See* DU MU.

Tumulus [barrow]. Mound of earth or stone covering a prehistoric tomb chamber or grave.

□

Tuna el-Gebel. *See under* HERMOPOLIS MAGNA.

Tunbridge Wells. English spa town in Kent and centre of decorative woodware production. The chalybeate spring was discovered in 1606, but no major development took place until after 1680, when capital was raised in London to provide shops and amusement rooms. The items that Celia Fiennes, the travel writer, saw being sold on the Parade near the well in 1697 were probably those manufactured in London and sold by tradesmen who visited the town for the season, since there is believed to have been little local manufacturing until the early 18th century. The earliest Tunbridge wares were both turnery and cabinet wares, and some were painted or lacquered in a manner similar to contemporary woodwares produced at Spa in Belgium. Veneered wares decorated with marquetry or parquetry were produced by the late 18th century, and exotic woods used in cubic parquetry designs are distinctive of the period. Prints of Classical and topographical subjects were also extensively employed as decoration. By the late 1820s a technique of producing patterns from small triangular pieces of different-coloured wood had been introduced. From the early 1830s the characteristic tessellated mosaic developed in which such pictorial subjects as birds, butterflies, moths, views of buildings and various types of flower were produced.

The Tunbridge ware industry flourished in the mid-19th century, when there were a number of makers of distinction. William Fenner was selected in 1826 to manufacture a fine work- and writing-table for presentation to Princess (later Queen) Victoria. His business appears to have terminated about 1840. Edmund Nye (1797–1863), a former partner of Fenner, was trading on his own account from 1817. On the retirement of Fenner he took over the latter's factory on Mount Ephraim and displayed at the Great Exhibition in London in 1851. On the death of Nye the business passed to his foreman Thomas Barton (1819–1903), who continued production until the 1890s and was still trading at the time of his death. Many of the wares of Nye and Barton can be identified from paper trade-labels. Henry Hollamby (1819–95) was probably one of the largest manufacturers and as late as 1883 was employing 20 people in his works. He had an extensive wholesale trade and displayed at the Great Exhibition and the International Exhibition of 1862 in London. He was renowned for his production of veneers depicting buildings, mainly in Kent and Sussex. Others include views of the area around Killarney in Ireland, Abbotsford in Scotland, Carew Castle in Wales, and the Warwick, Stratford-upon-Avon and Malvern areas, as well as a view of the Capitol, Washington, DC. When Hollamby retired in 1893, his trade passed to the firm of Boyce, Brown & Kemp, which continued production during World War I. The business then passed through several hands, eventually trading as the Tunbridge Wells Manufacturing Co. Production in Tunbridge Wells ceased in 1927.

Tunbridge ware was also made in the neighbouring town of Tonbridge, Kent, where the main manufactory was run by the Wise family. George Wise jr (1779–1869), who was the most famous member, exhibited at the Great Exhibition in London in 1851 and at the Exhibition of the Industry of All Nations in New York in 1853. He maintained showrooms and probably a factory in Tunbridge Wells between 1832 and 1857. The last business making Tunbridge ware in Tonbridge closed in 1883. Tunbridge ware makers in the main produced such small cabinet wares as tea-caddies, work- and writing-boxes and stamp- and trinket-boxes, as well as various gift and souvenir wares. They also made such items of furniture as game-tables, teapoys and ladies' writing- and work-tables.

BIBLIOGRAPHY
E. H. Pinto and E. R. Pinto: *Tunbridge and Scottish Souvenir Woodware* (London, 1970)
M. A. V. Gill: *Tunbridge Ware* (Aylesbury, 1985)
B. Austen: *Tunbridge Ware and Related European Decorative Woodwares* (London, 1989)

BRIAN AUSTEN

Tung Ch'i-ch'ang. *See* DONG QICHANG.

Tung Yüan. *See* DONG YUAN.

Tun-huang. *See* DUNHUANG.

Tunicle. *See under* VESTMENTS, ECCLESIASTICAL, §1(ii).

Tunis [Tūnis]. Capital city of Tunisia. The site, between a salt lake and a lagoon bordering the Gulf of Tunis, was first settled in the 9th century BC. In 146 BC during the Third Punic War it was destroyed along with nearby Carthage but later prospered under Roman rule. After the Muslim conquest in the 7th century AD and the founding of Kairouan, Tunis became second city of the region. The Zaytuna ('Olive tree') Mosque, founded in 732, was rebuilt between 856 and 864 by Abu Ibrahim Ahmad, sixth ruler of the Aghlabid dynasty (*reg* 800–909; *see* ISLAMIC ART, §II, 4(iii)). The prayer-hall has 15 aisles perpendicular to the qibla; the wide central aisle is surmounted by two cupolas, a gadrooned one (864) over the bay before the mihrab and another with polychrome decoration (11th century) facing the court. The trapezoidal court was lined at a later date with an arcaded gallery, and the square

minaret at the north-west corner is a 19th-century rebuilding of a 13th-century original. An ablution facility was added under the Hafsids (*reg* 1228–1574).

Following the Hilalian nomadic invasions in the mid-11th century, Tunis grew at the expense of Kairouan. The Ksar Mosque was built by the local ruler Ahmad ibn Khurasan *c.* 1106 near his castle (Arab. *qasr*; destr.). Often restored, this simple mosque has a square minaret with elegant polychrome decoration (1647). The nearby Qubba of the Banu Khrissan (1093), the dynastic tomb, is a small cubic chamber with squinches supporting a dome; it stands in the gardens of the Musée Sidi Bou Krissan, a lapidary museum. The mosque of the Kasba (1231–5) was built just before the Hafsid Abu Zakariya declared his independence from the Almohads. Although the mihrab with vertical grooves and voussoirs in two colours continues local traditions, other features of this mosque, such as the *muqarnas*, carved stucco decoration and square minaret, were inspired by Andalusian and Moroccan designs (*see* ISLAMIC ART, §II, 6(iv)(c)). The Hawa (or Tawfiq) Mosque, founded in the suburbs by Abu Zakariya's widow, the princess 'Atf, has brick groin vaults supported on columns. Other buildings from this period include the Haliq Mosque (1375) and the Bab al-Aqwas Mosque (15th century).

In 1535 the Holy Roman Emperor Charles V took possession of Tunis, but in 1574 it was taken by the Ottomans for the third and final time and ruled for them by a series of beys, or governors, until the French protectorate was declared in 1881. During the period of Ottoman rule many other mosques were built in the city; some, such as that of Hammuda Pasha (1655), have a traditional hypostyle plan, while others, such as that of Sidi Mahriz (*c.* 1675), founded by Muhammad Bey, have a domed prayer-hall in the Ottoman style. Among other mosques of this period are those of Sidi Yusuf (1616) and Yusuf Sahib al-Taba' (1812). The medina, or old city, retains much of its traditional aspect, with picturesque narrow streets and vaulted souks, and preserves many fine houses and palaces, such as the Dar al-Bey and Dar Hasan; they are irregular structures comprising patios surrounded by rooms. The Bardo Palace, founded by the Hafsids and enlarged by the beys of Tunis, stands in a park in the northern suburbs; it now houses the Archaeological Museum. The European quarter, which developed to the east of the medina after 1881, contains a variety of buildings in European styles, including the cathedral of St Vincent de Paul, built in 1882 in a Byzantine revival style. Among modern buildings in Tunis, the Hotel Meridien Africa (1970) rises to 21 storeys.

BIBLIOGRAPHY
G. Marçais: *Tunis et Kairouan* (Paris, 1937)
J. Revault: *Palais et demeures de Tunis, I (XVIe et XVIIe siècles)* (Paris, 1967)
A. Lézine: *Deux Villes d'Ifriqiya: Sousse, Tunis* (Paris, 1971)
J. Revault: *Palais et demeures de Tunis, II (XVIIIe et XIXe siècles)* (Paris, 1971)
S. M. Zbiss: *Les Monuments de Tunis* (Tunis, 1971)
J. Revault: *Palais et résidences d'été de la région de Tunis (XVIe-XIXe siècles)* (Paris, 1974)
A. Daoulatli: *Tunis sous les Hafsides* (Tunis, 1976)
D. Hill and L. Golvin: *Islamic Architecture in North Africa* (London, 1976)

J. Revault: *Palais, demeures et maisons de plaisance à Tunis (du XVIe au XIXe siècle)* (Aix-en-Provence, 1984)
J. Woodford: *The City of Tunis* (Outwell, Wisbech, 1988)

Tunisia, Republic of [Al-Jumhūriyyah al-Tūnusiyyah; Tūnis]. Country in North Africa with its capital at TUNIS. It has an area of *c.* 163,600 sq. km, extending from the south shore of the Mediterranean Sea to the Sahara, and it is bordered to the west by Algeria and to the south-east by Libya. The coastal region and fertile plain of the Mejerda River are the most populous; the high plateau of the Tell and the eastern end of the Atlas range descend in the south to an area of salt flats and the sub-Saharan region. Tunisia's geographical position has kept it constantly at the centre of Mediterranean history, with a cultural legacy that is a mixture of Berber, Punic, Roman, Arab, Byzantine, Spanish, Ottoman and French influences. Most of the population (8,094,000, 1990 est.) is Arab, with a small percentage of Berber origin; the rest are French and Italian. The majority are Sunni Muslim, and there are Jewish and Christian minorities. Its main exports are phosphates, chemicals, textiles, crude oil, fish, olive oil and fruit, and there is a growing manufacturing sector; in the early 1990s tourism and remittances sent by migrant workers could not restrain Tunisia's mounting debts. This article covers the art produced in the country from the late 19th century. For its earlier history *see under* AFRICA, §VII, 1; BERBER; PUNIC ART; NUMIDIA; ROME, ANCIENT; EARLY CHRISTIAN AND BYZANTINE ART; ISLAMIC ART; AGHLABID; FATIMID; ZIRID; ALMOHAD; and HAFSID.

1. History. 2. Architecture. 3. Painting and sculpture. 4. Other arts. 5. Archaeology and museums.

1. HISTORY. Although Tunisia was part of the Ottoman empire from 1574, power was held by indigenous rulers, and the dynasty established in 1705 by Husayn Bey lasted until 1957. A policy of modernization in the 19th century resulted in bankruptcy, and French forces invaded the country in 1881. A protectorate was established, with the bey as nominal ruler, and the numbers of Italian and French settlers increased. In 1943 Tunisia came under the control of the Free French, but independence was gained in 1956 under the secularist Habib Bourguiba. The next year the bey was deposed, and Tunisia became a republic, with Bourguiba as president. Conflicts with the French continued into the 1960s, and stormy relations with Libya and internal unrest characterized the 1970s and 1980s. Bourguiba was deposed in 1987. One-party parliaments continued under his successor, Zine el-Abidine ben 'Ali, while the main opposition came from Muslim fundamentalists.

2. ARCHITECTURE. In TUNIS the European quarter developed outside the medina in the mid-19th century, and buildings were erected by the French in European styles. However, the French administration also began to sponsor public buildings in Arab styles. Some were fanciful pastiches, but others attempted to be faithful to what was understood to be the principles of Arab architecture, based on scholarly inquiry. This Arabizing treatment can be seen in railway stations, law courts, schools, post offices and private villas. One outstanding example of a villa was designed by the Italian millionaire Georges Sebastian in 1939–40, just outside Hammamet. It is made of local materials with a vault construction for which Hammamet builders were well known. White colonnades surround a tiled pool, bedrooms contain sunken 'Roman' baths, and doors are studded in Andalusian style. In 1959 the Tunisian government bought Villa Sebastian and converted it into a cultural centre, adding a 'Greek' open-air theatre in 1964. Every summer, Hammamet's International Festival of the Arts is held here and in the grounds.

Some of the Berber underground houses (e.g. at Matmata), first mentioned in the 4th century BC, are still in use. These circular pit homes were dug into the soft earth, with an entrance tunnel that starts some distance away. The inhabitants, however, are beginning to move into modern houses at ground-level, particularly at Haddej, which was devastated by floods in 1969. On Jerba Island the pre-colonial vernacular employs domes and barrel vaults, and after World War II a neo-vernacular style was developed based on this. From the 1970s, blocks of flats, offices and hotels began to abandon indigenous styles in favour of modern Western designs. City-centre skyscrapers, houses that abandoned the tradition of a blank exterior to hide a sumptuous interior and the use of ornate decorative features to create a falsely exotic neo-Moorish architecture have led to a search by both Tunisian and foreign architects to find an architectural style suitable for present-day Tunisia. The Résidence Andalous, an apartment hotel near Sousse, completed in 1980, addressed this problem. The architect Serge Santelli attempted to express the structural principles of Tunisian architectural traditions and arranged the hotel around a series of inner and outer courtyards. The Résidence won an Aga Khan Award for Architecture in 1983. The Tunisian architect Tarak ben Miled (*b* 1945) was also sensitive to these concerns in his designs for industrial buildings, hotels, university complexes and housing (e.g. Dar el-Mannaii in La Soukra, a suburb of Tunis).

From the 1970s there were various conservation schemes and some award-winning redevelopment. In the 1980s UNESCO decided that Tunis was in need of urgent attention; the internal city walls and kasba had been destroyed in the 19th century, and there was more damage in the 20th century because of bombing during World War II, neglect, increased traffic and rapid urban growth. After 1956 the bourgeoisie moved out of the medina to occupy houses in the new town vacated by the Europeans and took with them many architectural details to decorate their new houses. The Association to Safeguard the Medina was formed; one of its plans was for the redevelopment of the Hafsia Quarter, which was by then a slum. The plan was the first large-scale renovation project of its kind in an Islamic country and won an Aga Khan Award for Architecture in 1983. The conservation of the old town of Sidi Bou Said, aided by UNESCO, won this award three years earlier. There are well-preserved medinas in the important Islamic cities of MAHDIA, KAIROUAN, Sfax and Sousse; at Monastir the medina has been replaced by modern buildings and straight streets.

3. PAINTING AND SCULPTURE. In 1894 the French authorities founded the Institut de Carthage, which became the most important scientific and cultural institution

in Tunisia, its function being to assert the cultural and educational legitimacy of the colonial power. In the same year, the Institut organized the first Salon Tunisien in Tunis, marking the formal introduction of Western art into the country. The participants were all French colonial artists. During the first two decades of the 20th century, the Salon Tunisien embraced the Orientalist school of art, generally working within narrow and provincial academic traditions and rejecting modern trends current in Paris.

In 1923 the Centre d'Art opened, the first art school in Tunisia, and in 1930 it became the Ecole des Beaux-Arts. The teaching environment was strictly conservative, and until independence the number of Tunisian pupils was negligible in comparison to foreign students. However, the institution became instrumental in training several generations of artists. Foreign artists who settled in Tunisia collectively influenced the development of local artists by introducing Western styles into the country. Among the French artists who interacted with their indigenous counterparts were Alexandre Fichet (1881–1968), who moved to Tunis in 1902 and became president of the Salon Tunisien from 1913 until his death, Armand Vergeaud (1867–1949), who was associated with the teaching of art in Tunisia after his move there in 1910, and Pierre Boucherle (1895–1988), who was born in Tunisia.

Modern Tunisian art developed either on the periphery or within the framework of the annual exhibitions organized by the French. Ahmed ben Osman was the first local artist to adopt Western painting styles, while Hédi Khayachi (1882–1948) was the first professional artist in the modern sense of the term, known for his portraits of the beys of Tunis and genre scenes of traditional life according to the Orientalist principles. Abdulwahab Jilani (1890–1961), who became the first Tunisian Muslim to exhibit at the Salon Tunisien in 1912, left for Paris in 1921 and joined the Académie Julian and the free ateliers of Montparnasse. He participated in the activities of the Ecole de Paris and worked with Modigliani, Picasso, Soutine, Chagall and others, essentially becoming a European artist. The most important pioneer to influence the formation of modern art in Tunisia was Yahia Turki (1901–68), a self-taught painter who refused a scholarship to the Ecole des Beaux-arts in Paris. His style added an indigenous quality to local painting, and his students included Abdelaziz ben Rais (1903–62), who trained at the Centre d'Art and was known for his peaceful landscapes and an economy in the use of colour that did not detract from the overall richness of his work; Ali ben Salem, who was inspired by painting on glass and miniatures; Hatem el-Mekki (*b* 1918); Amara Debbech (*b* 1918), who emigrated to France; and Ammar Farhat (*b* 1911), who was to become one of the most important figures in the history of Tunisian modern art, his paintings showing the world of the deprived. These early native Tunisian artists attempted to portray a sympathetic and realistic view of North Africa, without the traditional Orientalist clichés.

The earliest artistic group in Tunisia to include Arab Tunisian artists was the Tunis School, founded by Boucherle in the late 1940s. Its members included such pioneers as Yahia Turki and Ammar Farhat, as well as artists from

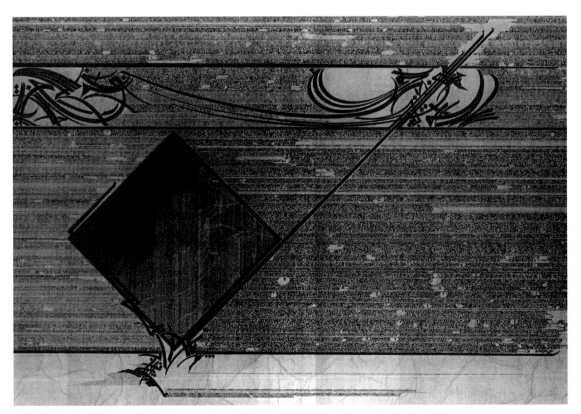

1. Nja Mahdaoui: *Calligramme*, black ink on parchment, 1.0×1.4 m, 1980–85 (Paris, Institut du Monde Arabe)

2. Muhammad ben Meftah: *Benediction*, engraving, 500×325 mm, 1978 (Paris, Institut du Monde Arabe)

the second generation such as Hatem el-Mekki, Jalal ben Abdullah (*b* 1921), Abdelaziz Gorgi (*b* 1928), 'Ali Bellagha (*b* 1925), Safia Farhat (*b* 1924), Zoubeir Turki (*b* 1924) and Hédi Turki (*b* 1922); artists of the third, post-independence generation, among whom were Hassan Soufi (*b* 1937) and Abdelkadir Gorgi (*b* 1949), were also involved. Each developed his or her personal style independently by diverging from contemporary European styles and trying to revive the two-dimensional forms of Islamic miniatures, the popular tradition of painting on glass, Arabic calligraphy and the different techniques of local handicrafts. The Tunis School played a significant role in introducing and developing Tunisian modern art.

The first to break away from the School were Hatem el-Mekki and Hédi Turki, who were less interested in transforming folk values into a symbolic or a thematic painting and sought to benefit from the experiments of international art, notably abstract art, Expressionism and Surrealism. Among the Arab countries abstract art was most practised in Tunisia and helped to push many Tunisian artists into the international arena.

Najib Belkhodja (*b* 1933) adopted a critical attitude towards abstract art and reverted to the use of calligraphic shapes and elements of Islamic architecture such as domes, arches and geometric forms within a two-dimensional perspective, bound together by cursive and angular shapes that recall the rhythm of kufic script. NJA MAHDAOUI (*b* 1937), who was trained at the Accademia S Andrea in Rome, specializing in graphic art, first started creating abstract work through relief paintings. In the early 1970s, he began working on calligraphic compositions under the influence of the Iranian painter Hussein Zenderoudi. The main element in these compositions is the Arabic letter, which he uses within illegible, abstract, visual arrangements in two-dimensional formations (see fig. 1). The abstract

painters were not the only artists to defy the realism of the Tunis School. By the end of the 1970s neo-figurative painters appeared, who rejected both the abstract artists' disregard for realism and the superficialities of classical figuration, preferring Expressionism, Surrealism, neo-realism and primitivism. By the early 1980s several abstract artists were experimenting with Pop art.

Graphic art is important in the development of Tunisian art but is less popular. Significant artists include Ibrahim Dahak (*b* 1931), Khelifa Cheltout (*b* 1939), Hedi Labban (*b* 1946), Gouider Triki (*b* 1949), who studied under Hédi Turki and then in Paris, and Muhammad ben Meftah (*b* 1946; see fig. 2), who studied engraving in Paris and became a professor of graphic design in Tunis.

4. OTHER ARTS. In the traditional arts of pottery and weaving there has been little modern development, although the ceramicist and painter Khalid ben Suleiman (*b* 1951) produces notable work. Since the Roman period Moknine and Jerba Island have been centres for earthenware pottery, and rural traditions of modelled pottery continue, with geometric patterns that date back thousands of years. Potteries at Tunis and Nabeul, the largest ceramic centre in Tunisia, have revived the 17th-century Andalusian style of wall tiles with their green, yellow and blue floral designs. Dar Chaabane, near Nabeul, is the centre for sculpted stonework, with geometric and floral designs; much of the intricate stonework on buildings in northeast Tunisia was carved there.

Kilims are woven at Kairouan following a tradition that probably originated in the 18th century, inspired by imported Anatolian rugs. However, when Europeans began to buy Kairouan carpets in large numbers from the late 19th century, the quality declined as the demand increased. Knotted carpets are controlled by the Office National de l'Artisanat Tunisien, which has set a number of standard patterns based on old tribal and Persian designs. Although geometric patterns predominate, there is a tradition of pictorial designs in the south (e.g. Gafsa). As elsewhere in the Arab world, jewellery was traditionally a Jewish speciality, and the craft has been affected by the migration of most craftsmen to Israel. Carved olive-wood, such as bowls and boxes, are of a high standard (e.g. in Sfax; *see* ISLAMIC ART, §VIII, 9(ii)), metal birdcages are a speciality of Sidi Bou Said, and traditional leather crafts are made. The government has tried to preserve many of the country's old crafts, and there are craft schools (e.g. in the Muradia Medersa, Tunis).

5. ARCHAEOLOGY AND MUSEUMS. Tunisia has an intensive concentration of historical sites. The first objects of artistic interest date from the 7th millennium BC in southern Tunisia, and there are Neolithic cave paintings at Henchir Souar (north-west of Kairouan). The best-preserved architectural remains before the Arab conquest in the 7th century AD come from the Phoenician, Roman, Early Christian and Byzantine periods. The most significant Phoenician remains are at Kerkouane in the Cap Bon Peninsula, discovered in 1952. There are numerous Roman remains, particularly at CARTHAGE (the Phoenician city was destroyed), the amphitheatre at El Djem (anc. Thysdrus), the underground villas at Bulla Regia (first excavated

in 1906 and continuing in the 1990s), the evocative ruined city of DOUGGA, the site of SUFETULA at Sbeitla, Haidra (which also has a Byzantine fortress), Makhtar (anc. Mactaris, first excavated in the late 19th century) and Thuburbo Maius (which German prisoners of war helped excavate during World War I). From 1881, excavations and restoration were encouraged by the French authorities, who set up a Department of Antiquities, housed in the Attarine Barracks in Tunis (now the National Library). Excavations are overseen by the Institut National de l'Art et de l'Archéologie.

Several of the sites have museums. There are also particularly rich archaeological museums at Nabeul, Sfax, Sousse and, above all, in Tunis: the Musée National du Bardo, founded in 1888, contains one of the greatest collections of mosaics in the world as well as numerous Carthaginian, Roman and some Islamic objects. There are a few museums concentrating on Islamic art, such as at Monastir (opened 1958), and several arts and crafts museums that display costumes, pottery, craft techniques and jewellery, such as the museums of popular arts and traditions in Tunis, El Kef (opened 1979), Gabès (opened 1969) and Houmt Souk on Jerba Island (opened 1969), and in the Dar Jalluli in Sfax (opened 1966), a 17th-century palace that also contains good examples of painting on glass. Commercial art galleries and state-run exhibition halls are concentrated at or near Tunis, such as at Sidi Bou Said (which has a reputation as an artists' colony), Carthage and Sousse. The Centre d'Art Vivant (1980) in the Belvedere park in Tunis has exhibitions of contemporary Tunisian and Arab art.

BIBLIOGRAPHY

R. Guy: *L'Architecture moderne de style arabe* (Paris, n.d.) [good pls]
P. Eudel: *L'Orfèvrerie algérienne et tunisienne* (Algiers, 1902)
V. Valensi: *L'Habitation tunisienne* (Paris, 1923)
L. Golvin and A. Louis: *Artisans sfaxiens: Tamis, dalous, cardes* (Tunis, 1945)
——: *Les Tissages décorés d'El-Djem et de Djebeniana: Etude de sociologie tunisienne* (Tunis, 1949)
L. Poinssot and J. Revault: *Tapis tunisiens*, 4 vols (Paris, 1950–57)
J.-L. Combès and A. Louis: *Les Potiers de Djerba* (Tunis, 1967)
J. Revault: *Arts traditionnels en Tunisie* (Tunis, 1967)
Z. Turki: *Tunis naguère et aujourd'hui* (Tunis, 1967)
R. Saïd: *Cultural Policy in Tunisia* (Paris, 1970)
G. Pillement: *La Tunisie inconnue: Itinéraires archéologiques* (Paris, 1972)
J. Kesraoui: *Peintres naïfs tunisiens* (Tunis, 1977)
M. Poncet: *Les Bijoux d'argent de Tunisie* (Tunis, 1977)
C. Sugier: *Bijoux tunisiens: Formes et symboles* (Tunis, 1977)
M. Masmoudi, ed.: *Les Costumes traditionnels féminins de Tunisie* (Tunis, 1978)
J. Revault: *L'Habitation tunisoise: Pierre, marbre et fer dans la construction et le décor* (Paris, 1978)
M. Yacoub: *Chefs-d'oeuvre des musées nationaux de Tunisie* (Tunis, 1978)
M. A. Lesage: *Formes et analogies de la villa tunisoise contemporaine* (Paris, 1982)
F. Béguin: *Arabisances: Décor architectural et tracé urbain en Afrique du Nord, 1830–1950* (Paris, 1983)
I. Reswick: *Traditional Textiles of Tunisia and Related North African Weavings* (Los Angeles, 1985)
P. Signoles: *L'Espace tunisien: Capitale et état-région* (Tours, 1985)
Tunisia, Egypt, Morocco: Contemporary Houses, Traditional Values (exh. cat. by B. B. Taylor, London, Zamara Gal., 1985)
S. Gargouri-Sethom: *Le Bijou traditionnel en Tunisie: Femmes parées, femmes enchaînées* (Aix-en-Provence, 1986)
Six peintres tunisiens contemporains (exh. cat., Paris, Mus. A. Mod. Ville Paris; Villeneuve d'Ascq, Mus. A. Mod. Nord; Paris, Mus. N.A. Afr. & Océan.; 1986–7)
G. S. Golany: *Earth-sheltered Dwellings in Tunisia: Ancient Lessons for Modern Design* (Cranbury, London and Mississauga, 1988)
W. Ali, ed.: *Contemporary Art from the Islamic World* (London, 1989)
I. Serageldin: *Space for Freedom: The Search for Architectural Excellence in Muslim Societies* (London, 1989)
W. Ali: *A Survey of Modern Painting in the Islamic World and the Development of the Contemporary Calligraphic School* (diss., U. London, SOAS, 1993)

☐

Tunja [Hunza]. City in the central region of Colombia and capital of the department of Boyacá, situated at an altitude of 2793 m and with a population in the late 20th century of *c.* 180,000. In Pre-Columbian times it was the site of the Muisca village of Hunza, whose wood and straw houses were decorated with gold rattles and hanging plates on the doors and windows. The area was notable for its production of fine cotton blankets. In 1527 the Spanish conquistadors arrived, and in 1539 Gonzalo Suárez Rendón took possession of the land and drew up a conventional Spanish grid plan for the city. The region attracted many Spaniards, who built their houses of lime and rock with clay roofs and decorated the entrances with escutcheons. Between 1541, when it acquired city status, and 1610 Tunja enjoyed similar status to Bogotá. A wide knowledge of humanistic and classical culture is evident in the ambitious cathedral (begun 1569); with its three naves and stone façade (*see* COLOMBIA, fig. 3) created by Bartolomé Carrión, it is an unusual and outstanding example of Renaissance architecture in Latin America. The same classical interest is evident in the mural paintings of the early 17th century in some houses (*see* COLOMBIA, §IV, 1), but the city's most significant exponent of Renaissance painting was the Italian painter ANGELINO MEDORO, active in Tunja in the late 16th century (e.g. the *Annunciation*, 1588; Tunja, Templo de Santa Clara). The single-nave monastic churches built in the 17th century represented the culmination of Baroque decoration in Latin America, with abundant retables, carved panels and *Mudéjar* panelling on the ceilings, as in the church of S Clara (1613) by Juan Bélmez and Antonio de Alcántara, and the Dominican Capilla del Resario (1563). Museums in the city include the Museo Eclesiástico Colonial and the Colección de los Padres Dominicanos.

See also SOUTH AMERICA, PRE-COLUMBIAN, §II, 1.

BIBLIOGRAPHY

R. Correa: *Historia de Tunja* (Tunja, 1948)
E. Marco Dorta: *Arquitectura del renacimiento en Tunja* (Bogotá, 1957)
S. Sebastián López: *Album de arte colonial de Tunja* (Tunja, 1963)
P. Vandenbroeck: 'Missionary Iconography on Both Sides of the Atlantic', *America, Bride of the Sun* (Antwerp, 1992), pp. 84–96

NATALIA VEGA

Tunnard, John (Samuel) (*b* Sandy, Beds, 17 May 1900; *d* Penzance, 18 Dec 1971). English painter. After studying design (1919–23) at the Royal College of Art, London, he worked as a textile designer and adviser, and was also active as a jazz musician. In 1929 he took up painting and became a part-time design teacher at the Central School of Arts and Crafts in London. Tunnard first painted romantic landscapes such as *The Farm Pond* (1933; Bradford, Cartwright Hall), but from the mid-1930s, under the influence of Klee and Miró, his work became more abstract and began to reflect his interest in plant and animal life and geology. After settling in the Lizard peninsula in Cornwall in 1933, he studied local wildlife and became an expert field botanist, collecting rare insects for the British Museum. The rhythmical designs in his work were inspired by these natural forms and perhaps also by his experience as a musician. Such paintings as *Fulcrum* (1939; London, Tate), which included shapes reminiscent of both Surrealist sculpture and modern technology, represented an invented world of his own. His later paintings frequently reflect his interest in space exploration, as in *Messenger* (1969; priv. col., see exh. cat., p. 35).

BIBLIOGRAPHY
John Tunnard (exh. cat., ed. M. Glazebrook; London, ACGB, 1977)

ANN JONES

Tunner, Josef [Joseph] **(Ernst)** (*b* Obergaden, Styria, 24 Sept 1792; *d* Graz, 10 Oct 1877). Austrian painter, draughtsman and teacher. From 1810 to 1817 he studied portrait painting at the Akademie der Bildenden Künste in Vienna and later travelled in Styria and Carinthia and to Trieste. Inspired by such artists as Joseph von Führich, Leopold Kuppelwieser and Wilhelm August Rieder (1796–1880), he became interested in medieval art and worked in Vienna both as a portrait painter and as a copyist of religious subjects in the museums. In 1821 he married Josephine Pichler, who died the following year. Tunner's painting (Graz, Neue Gal.) of her with her two sisters is in the tradition of a Nazarene family portrait with Biedermeier overtones. In 1823 he moved to Rome, where he was accepted into the circle of the Nazarenes and where, under their influence, he began the most productive part of his career. Two years later he took charge of organizing their communal composition exercises in which they painted mainly biblical and legendary themes, and he himself made copies (Graz, Neue Gal.) after prints by Dürer and paintings by Fra Angelico, Perugino and Raphael. He was a close friend of Eduard Jakob von Steinle, and they worked together on the frescoes of *The Visitation* and *The Annunciation* in Trinità dei Monti, Tunner doing the sketches and Steinle the paintings. He also produced landscape drawings (Graz, Neue Gal.) that are full of atmosphere and that convey his experience of nature surely and spontaneously while at the same time expressing religious spirituality. He won the competition for a painting of *The Crucifixion* (1836–8) for the altar of the Cross in S Antonio Nuovo, Trieste (drawings, Graz, Neue Gal.) and for this was accepted, along with Ingres, into the Congregazione dei virtuosi al Pantheon. Henceforth, he decided to put his art at the service of the Catholic Church and to do no further paintings or drawings of nude figures. In 1840 he was appointed Director of the Steinisch-Ständische Zeichnungsakademie in Graz, where he methodically taught the principles of Nazarene art to aspiring students. He painted portraits of the local aristocracy and received commissions for numerous altarpieces, an important example being that of the *Family of Mathias Constantin Graf von Wickenburg* (1844) for the altar of the Kirche des Kurorts, Bad Gleichenberg. This was rendered in the manner of a Venetian *sacra conversazione*, with the donor's family expressing adoration. In 1870 he was dismissed from the directorship because of strong criticism of his dogmatic teaching methods; he had closed his mind to all contemporary naturalistic trends and had totally rejected landscape as a genre.

BIBLIOGRAPHY
F. Klabinus: 'Der steirische Nazarener Joseph Tunner: Sein Leben und seine Kunst', *Z. Hist. Ver. Steiermark* (1934) [whole issue]
C. Steinle and W. Skreiner: *Die Nazarener in Österreich, 1809–1939: Zeichnungen und Druckgrafik* (exh. cat., Graz, Neue Gal., 1979)
H. Schindler: *Nazarener, romantischer Geist und christliche Kunst im 19. Jahrhundert* (Regensburg, 1982)
C. Steinle: 'Zur Entwicklung und Tradition der nazarenischen Bildkunst in der Steiermark am Beispiel von Josef Tunners Gleichenberger Altarbild der *Familie Mathias Constantin Graf von Wickenburg*, 1844', *Festschrift für Wilfried Skreiner: Kontinuität und Identität*, ed. P. Weibel, C. Steinle and G. Pochat (Vienna, 1993)

CHRISTA STEINLE

Tupac Inca, Juan Tomás Tuyru. *See* TUYRU TUPAC INCA, JUAN TOMÁS.

Tura, Cosimo [Cosmè] (*b* Ferrara, ?1430; *d* Ferrara, April 1495). Italian painter. He was court painter to the Este family of Ferrara from 1458 until the mid-1480s. He was the first and one of the greatest representatives of the Ferrarese school of painting, but many of his most important works, including the decoration of the library of Pico della Mirandola (1463–94), have been either destroyed or dismantled, and some of his large-scale altarpieces are divided between collections. His career is well recorded and provides a vivid illustration of the role and duties of a 15th-century court artist.

1. Life and work. 2. Critical reception and posthumous reputation.

1. LIFE AND WORK.

(i) To 1459. (ii) 1459–70. (iii) 1471–95.

(i) To 1459. Tura is first recorded in Ferrara in a notarial act of 28 July 1431, in which 'Cosimo, the son of Domenico, the shoemaker' is described as an infant, which would set the date of his birth some time within the previous year. The first indications of an artistic career occurred in 1451 when, in association with the painter Galasso di Matteo Piva, Tura was called in to appraise a set of trumpet banners painted by Jacopo Turolo. The following year his name appeared among the regular salaried members of the Este household where he is documented as having designed a jousting helmet decorated with Borso d'Este's *imprese* of the unicorn and palm tree for the St George's Day horse race; he also painted a banner for the tailors' guild (which he was asked to repaint four years later), and worked with the manuscript illuminator Giorgio d'Alemagna and the carver Giovanni Carlo di Bretagna on 17 small coffers (*coffinetti*) decorated with, among other things, religious scenes and heraldic devices of Duke Borso.

Between 1453 and 1456 Tura is absent from the ducal records. Venturi proposed that he had spent this time in Padua and, perhaps, Venice. The former suggestion is based on the observation that several aspects of Tura's painting style seem to be derived from the mannered classicism of Francesco Squarcione and the Paduan school. Specifically, there are similarities with the work of Mantegna and Niccolò Pizzolo in the Ovetari Chapel in the church of the Eremitani, Padua, which has prompted some critics to suggest that Tura worked on or, at least, carefully studied these paintings. The proposed stay in Venice is surmised from a passage in Tura's first will (14 January 1471), in which he leaves money to the poor of Venice. It has also been suggested that during this visit he was influenced by the recently completed mosaic designed by Andrea Castagno in the Mascoli Chapel in S Marco.

In 1456 Tura was in Ferrara and by 1457 he is listed as living in the Castello and earning a regular salary from the court of 15 lire per month. His only documented ducal commission for this year is for tapestry designs containing the coat of arms and devices of the Duke, which were subsequently woven by the Fleming Livino di Giglio. Tura's first documented painting was a *Nativity* (1458; untraced), commissioned by the ducal bailiff Vincenzo de' Lardi, and placed in the Old Sacristy of Ferrara Cathedral. The work must have been part of a portable altar since it was transferred to the main sacristy of the cathedral during the 18th century. According to 18th-century descriptions it consisted of several small figures.

In 1458 Borso d'Este appointed Tura official court painter, doubled his salary and placed him in charge of the decoration of the ducal villa at Belfiore. It is difficult to assess Tura's contribution to the fresco cycle of the *Nine Muses* (destr.), originally intended for the *studiolo* of Borso's father Leonello d'Este. Three contemporary documents relate to the project: a letter of 5 November 1457 from Guarino da Verona to Leonello d'Este, offering a series of iconographic suggestions regarding the form and attributes of the Muses; Cyriac of Ancona's description of 1449 of the finished paintings of *Clio* and *Melpomene* he had seen in the studio of the former court painter, Angelo del Macagnino; and the statement made by the Ferrarese humanist Ludovico Carbone that Tura was responsible for finishing the series of the Muses begun by Angelo del Macagnino. Unfortunately the information contained in these letters is not wholly consistent, thus making it difficult either to make connections with extant works of art or to reconstruct the iconographic programme. However, two panels have been proposed as possible components of the decorative scheme: Tura's *Enthroned Goddess* (London, N.G.; see fig. 1), variously identified as Venus, Spring and the nymph Erato; and the painting usually called *Charity* (Milan, Mus. Poldi Pezzoli) but perhaps intended to represent the muse Terpsichore. (The lower half of the latter painting, showing three dancing children, appears to be by Tura.) Resting on these suggestions is the identification of Tura's first datable works and our understanding of the whole chronology of his oeuvre. If the two paintings in London and Milan are characteristic of Tura's early work, they show him to be an artist much more closely linked to the local tradition of Ferrarese painting and the style of Angelo del Macagnino and Michele Pannonio than had hitherto been suspected. As a result, stylistically similar works such as the *Virgin and Child with SS Apollonia and Jerome* (Ajaccio, Mus. Fesch), dated by Longhi and Ortolani to the 1490s, should be radically redated to the late 1450s or early 1460s. The transition from this softer, and slightly awkward style—via perhaps the *Pietà* (Venice, Corror), the *Crucifixion* (Washington, DC, N.G.A.), the *Ecce homo* (Vienna, Kunsthistorisches Mus.) and the *Portrait of a Young Man* (New York, Met.)—to the highly formalized structure and figures

1. Cosimo Tura: *Enthroned Goddess*, oil on panel, 1160 × 710 mm, 1459–63 (London, National Gallery)

of Tura's earliest extant documented work, the organ shutters (1469; Ferrara, Mus. Duomo) for Ferrara Cathedral, seems plausible.

(ii) 1459–70. In 1459 Tura made designs for tapestries that were probably commissioned as part of the festivities surrounding the visit of Galeazzo Maria Sforza to the Este court. It is also possible that Borso d'Este, constantly beseeching Papal favour, may have been making preparations in the hope of receiving a much grander guest, since Galeazzo Maria was travelling in the cortège of Pope Pius II. On 6 August 1462 Tura was paid for two tournament costumes for Alberto Maria d'Este, which were covered with gold lilies, silver daisies and images of sieves with water running through them (the last probably being one of Alberto Maria's *imprese*). On 7 March and 14 July 1464 he was paid for further tournament costumes for Alberto Maria d'Este and Niccolò d'Este and the following year he decorated three pairs of horse trappings to be given as a gift by Duke Borso to his favourite, Cavaliere Teofilo Calcagnini.

Tura's absence from the ducal records between 1466 and 1467 suggests that during this period he was engaged in the decoration of the library (destr.) of Pico della

Mirandola in the castle of Mirandola. A detailed description of the cycle is given in a dialogue by the Ferrarese humanist Lelio Gregorio Giraldi. The decoration was apparently arranged in six panels, each divided into three registers and surmounted by a lunette. It depicted the history of poetry arranged chronologically from ancient to modern times. The lunettes contained triumphs of the different poetical ages, and the scheme was bound together by a frieze consisting of crowns, armorial devices and foliage.

By 31 December 1467 Tura had returned to Ferrara, involved, again, with tapestry decoration. Late in 1467 he also received a commission from the brothers Uberto Sacrati, Bartolommeo Sacrati and Pietro Sacrati to decorate the walls of their family chapel in S Domenico, Ferrara, with the 'entire story of the New Testament' and provide an altarpiece of the *Adoration of the Magi* (both frescoes and altarpiece destr.).

On 11 June 1469 Tura was paid for painting the organ shutters (Ferrara, Mus. Duomo) for the great organ in Ferrara Cathedral. Together with the severely damaged frescoes of the Salone dei Mesi in the Palazzo Schifanoia, Ferrara (see below), the organ shutters represent the best of Ferrarese painting during the last half of the 15th century. On the outside of the doors is an emotionally turbulent and pictorially dynamic depiction of *St George and the Dragon* (see fig. 2) set in a landscape. On the inside is a dramatically different, serene image of the *Annunciation*, set beneath a classicizing triumphal arch. Stylistically

2. Cosimo Tura: *St George and the Dragon*, 349×305 mm, 1469 (Ferrara, Museo del Duomo); outside of the organ shutters from Ferrara Cathedral

related to the organ shutters, and therefore probably also datable to the late 1460s, are the *Virgin and Child* (Venice, Accad.) and two tondi (both Ferrara, Pin. N.) depicting scenes from the life of St Maurelius, painted for the chapel of St Maurelius in S Giorgio fuori le Mura, Ferrara.

On 30 May 1469 Tura signed a contract to decorate the chapel of Belriguardo (destr.) near Voghiera. The terms are interesting not only because they stipulate wages and provisions for Tura and his two anonymous assistants, the responsibility for materials and a time schedule, but also because they indicate that the patron, Borso d'Este, intended to devise the iconographic programme himself. The progress of Tura's work is well documented, including notations of his various trips to Venice to buy gold and colours. Six months after beginning the project Tura was sent by Borso to Brescia to look at the Malatesta Chapel in the Broletto (town hall). It is unclear whether Borso intended Tura to study the decoration of the chapel as a whole or just the frescoes by Gentile da Fabriano. Either way, it is a reflection of Borso's conservative taste that he chose to send his court painter to study work painted some fifty years earlier.

An accurate picture of the subject-matter and disposition of the decoration, in what appears to have been a free-standing, centrally-domed, cruciform building, is given in a contemporary description (31 March 1471) of the programme, supplied by Baldassare d'Este and the Venetian artist Antonio Orsini when they were called upon to evaluate the project. The paintings were executed in oil and represented God the Father, in the small dome of the lantern, with eight semi-circular half-lengths of Evangelists and Doctors of the Church arranged beneath. The architectural components of the chapel were heavily decorated with animal and vegetal reliefs, and highlighted by a continuous frieze of 145 sculpted and gilt seraphim.

Despite repeated attempts to attach Tura's name to some aspect of the Salone dei Mesi frescoes in the Palazzo Schifanoia, Ferrara, the stylistic evidence of Tura's oeuvre makes this unlikely. Baruffaldi's suggestion was based on the assumption that as court painter Tura must have played a role. He proposed that Tura was responsible for the cartoons and that the rest of the work was executed by other painters. However, this overlooks the fact that between 1468 and 1470, the probable date for the Schifanoia cycle, Tura was engaged in a number of other projects, including the decoration of the Belriguardo chapel. Moreover, stylistically, compositionally and, more tentatively, conceptually, the Schifanoia frescoes bear no more than a generic resemblance to any of Tura's known works.

(iii) 1471–95. On 14 January 1471 Tura made the first of his three wills. His instructions indicate unexpected wealth and properties. In 1464 Tura had bought a two-storey house between the Via Centoversuri and Via Boccanale in Ferrara. In his first will he made provision for the erection and decoration of a church dedicated to SS Cosmas and Damian in which he wanted to be buried, stipulated that his 50 books and all of his drawings were to be left to a certain 'Domenicus filius Jacobi Valerij' and left large legacies to the poor of Venice and to those nearest to him. In August 1471 Borso d'Este died, and Tura was paid 20 lire for constructing the ducal catafalque. His official court

title seems to have been changed or augmented to court portrait painter with the succession of Ercole I d'Este. Tura's first recorded duty for the new Duke was to supply designs for a 36-piece silver set (to be executed by the Venetian goldsmith Giorgio Alegretto da Ragusa), intended for the celebration of the Duke's impending marriage to Eleanora of Aragon. The decoration, recorded in detail in the register of the Guardaroba, consisted largely of ducal *imprese* and devices, but two of the flasks had the unusual iconography of 'wild men', and the garlands used were described as *all'antica*. In 1472 Tura executed portraits of *Ercole I* and of *Lucrezia d'Este* (both untraced) to be sent to Eleanora of Aragon in Naples. During the late summer he provided a coloured sketch for a tapestry, to be woven by Giovanni Mille and Rubinetto da Francia for the marriage bed of Ercole I and Eleanora. Between 1472 and 1474 he seems to have been occupied almost exclusively with tapestry designs.

The year of the death of Bishop Lorenzo Roverella (1474) provides the approximate date for Tura's next major commission, the Roverella altarpiece for S Giorgio fuori le Mura, Ferrara. Baruffaldi records the original location (on the wall in front of the chapel containing Tura's St Maurelius tondi) and the disposition of the panels within the altarpiece. The *Virgin and Child with Music-making Angels* (London, N.G.; see fig. 3) comprised the central portion of the altarpiece and the *SS Paul and Maurelius with the Kneeling Niccolò Roverella* (Rome, Gal. Colonna) was the right wing of the polyptych. The left wing illustrated SS George and Peter, below whom the kneeling Bishop Roverella was shown knocking on the Gates of Paradise. Only a fragment of this, the *Head of St George* (San Diego, CA, Mus. A.), has survived. The central panel was surmounted by the lunette of the *Lamentation* (Paris, Louvre). Two additional half-lengths of SS Benedict and Bernardo have been lost. In his reconstruction of the Roverella altarpiece, Longhi suggested that the *Circumcision* (Boston, MA, Isabella Stewart Gardner Mus.), the *Adoration of the Magi* (Cambridge, MA, Harvard U., Fogg) and the *Flight into Egypt* (New York, Met.) are three of a proposed seven tondi that formed the predella of the altarpiece. In addition to the fact that this contradicts Baruffaldi's observation that the predella was composed of scenes from the lives of SS Benedict and Bernardo, the use of historiated roundels in a predella is unprecedented. Thus, although these tondi belong to the same stylistic period as the Roverella altarpiece, it seems unlikely that they existed as a part of it. In the altarpiece, Tura's painting technique has become appreciably harder and more stylized. The figures seem to have lost all trace of human warmth both in their colouring and their emotional states. Other paintings which can be dated to this period are the *St Jerome* (London, N.G.; see fig. 4) with its corresponding fragment, the *Crucified Christ* (Milan, Brera), the *Annunciation, St Francis* and *St Maurelius* (all Washington, DC, N.G.A.), the *Virgin and Child* (Rome, Gal. Colonna) and the *St John on Patmos* (Genoa, Gnecco priv. col.; see Molajoli, pp. 86–7, no. 27).

In 1475 Tura made further tapestry designs. Between 1475 and 1483 the weaver Rubinetto da Francia is recorded as working on an altarcloth; it is possible that Tura's Lamentation antependium (Cologne, Neven-Dumont

3. Cosimo Tura: *Virgin and Child with Music-making Angels*, oil on panel, 2.34×1.01 m, *c.* 1474 (London, National Gallery); central panel of the Roverella altarpiece

priv. col., see Molajoli, p. 88, no. 28; copy, Cleveland, OH, Mus. A.) dates from this period. Also in 1475 he was commissioned by Ercole I d'Este to make a series of paintings for a small portable altar. The frame was carved by Bernardo da Venezia and the niello decoration executed by Amadio da Milano. Apparently Ercole was dissatisfied with Tura's work and ordered him to repaint it. The

4. Cosimo Tura: *St Jerome*, oil on panel, 1010 × 572 mm, 1471–95 (London, National Gallery)

contract stipulates a central Virgin and Child flanked by four standing saints. Several suggestions have been offered as to which extant panels might have belonged to this altar. These include the four panels in Washington mentioned above and the *Madonna and Child* (Bergamo, Gal. Accad. Carrara). In 1476 Tura was involved in a lawsuit with the Ferrarese notary Giacomo Pinzerna.

In 1477 Tura was commissioned to paint three portraits of the year-old prince, *Alfonso I d'Este* (all untraced). The first was completed on 27 July, while the other two were not finished until October. One of these portraits passed via the Canonici Collection into the collection of Baruffaldi's father, and the critic recalls it as 'exemplary above all others'. In the same year Tura was asked to complete a set of seven female nudes (untraced), four of which had been worked on previously. It is unclear if this is another case of Tura having to repaint, or perhaps 'update' work of his own or of others. Ruhmer suggested that these figures might relate to work Tura had done previously at Belfiore and proposed that the brush drawing of a *Seated Winged Female Figure* (Berlin, Kupferstichkab.), which he

called *Charity*, might be a preliminary study for one of the paintings from this series.

In addition to supplying tapestry cartoons for a door curtain to be woven by Giovanni Mille, and a mule blanket, to be woven in several copies by Rinaldo da Bretagna, in 1479 Tura was paid by Eleanora of Aragon for a portrait of *Lucrezia d'Este* (untraced) to be sent to Lucrezia's fiancé, Annibale Bentivoglio. In 1480 Tura painted a portrait of *Isabella d'Este* (untraced) for her intended spouse, Francesco Gonzaga, Marchese of Mantua, and was paid for a cartoon depicting a story of Solomon. In 1481 he is recorded collaborating with the intarsia worker Tasto Tortoletto and, between 1483 and 1485, he was engaged in making designs for an elaborate silver service for Ludovico Sforza, Duke of Milan.

In a letter to Ercole I (8 January 1490), complaining of poverty and the unpaid debts due to him, Tura mentions two paintings for which payment is outstanding. The first, a *St Anthony of Padua* (untraced), was painted for the Monsignor of Adria and cost 25 ducats, which indicates either that the painting was small or that Tura's reputation as an artist had suffered to the extent that he was no longer able to command adequate fees. The second, an altarpiece for S Niccolò, Ferrara, commissioned by the ducal secretary Francesco Nasello and worth 60 ducats, has been identified with Tura's *St Anthony of Padua* (formerly called *St Giacomo della Marca*, Modena, Gal. & Mus. Estense). This association is slightly problematic as Tura does not mention the subject of his painting for Nasello. He claimed to have painted 'similmente' for Monsignor of Adria, but it is doubtful that this refers to the subject-matter of the painting. Moreover, Tura mentioned that Nasello's picture had been coloured with gold at his own expense and the Modena *St Anthony* has neither gold ground nor details. In support of this attribution, however, the painting can be dated stylistically to *c*. 1484, thereby complementing Tura's note recording that he finished these paintings six years before the date of his letter, and the painting's provenance can be traced back to the church of S Niccolò, Ferrara. If the painting is part of the altarpiece painted for Nasello, it is Tura's last documented work and shows him as having developed a style of painting so mannered and tense as to verge on the repellant. A number of small panels, stylistically related to the Modena *St Anthony*, although not quite so austere, have been variously arranged by critics to form reconstructions of the dispersed altarpieces Tura painted during the mid-1480s. These include *St James the Great* (Caen, Mus. B.-A.), *St Dominic* (Florence, Uffizi), *St Anthony of Padua* (Paris, Louvre) and perhaps *St Christopher* and *St Sebastian* (both Berlin, Bodemus.).

In 1485 Tura received his last court commission for a bust-length portrait of Beatrice d'Este to be sent to her betrothed, Ludovico Sforza. In 1486 he was moved from his lodgings into one of the gate-towers of the city wall near Porta Cosmaria, Ferrara, and lived with a certain Teofilo di Jacopo Cesena, apparently a painter or apprentice. From this time until his death virtually all the documents pertaining to Tura centre on his complaints about poverty. In 1487 he wrote a second will, asking to be buried in S Giorgio. On 18 April 1491 he wrote his third and final will. He was buried, according to the request in his third will, in S Lorenzo, Ferrara.

2. CRITICAL RECEPTION AND POSTHUMOUS REPU-TATION. At the height of his career Tura's fame had spread as far as the courts of Milan and Urbino. Filarete, in his *Trattato di architettura* (1458–64), listed Tura with Fra Filippo Lippi, Piero della Francesca, Squarcione and Vincenzo Foppa as one of the masters fit to paint in the courtyard of the Casa Regia of his imaginary city of Sforzinda. Giovanni Santi, in his *La vita e le geste di Federico da Montefeltro* (*c.* 1488–92), named Tura and Ercole de' Roberti as the two exemplars of Ferrarese painting. Tura's fortunes, however, were directly linked to his patron Borso d'Este, after whose death in 1471 the artist progressively lost commissions to his more fashionable contemporaries. By the middle of the 16th century, only some 50 years after his death, his name was all but forgotten and he was only summarily mentioned by Vasari. Girolamo Baruffaldi was the first to restore his reputation during the 18th century, citing him as the founder and greatest representative of the Ferrarese school. Despite the relative paucity of surviving works, now scattered in different collections, archival work by scholars such as Cittadella, Campori and Venturi has contributed greatly to our understanding of his career.

BIBLIOGRAPHY

EARLY SOURCES

A. Averlino [il Filarete]: *Trattato di architettura* (1458–64); ed. A. M. Finoli and L. Grassi (Milan, 1972), i, p. 258

G. Santi: *La vita e le gesta di Federico di Montefeltro duca d'Urbino* (MS.; *c.* 1488–92); ed. Luigi Michelini Tocci (Rome, 1985), p. 674

T. V. Strozzi: 'Ad Cosmum pictorem', *Carmina, eroticon libri iv* (Venice, 1513)

G. Vasari: *Vite* (1550, rev. 2/1568); ed. G. Milanesi (1878–85), ii, p. 142; iii, p. 92

L. G. Giraldi: *Opera, quae extant omnia* (Basle, 1580)

G. Baruffaldi: *Vita di Cosimo Tura pittore ferrarese del secolo XV scritta dall'Archiprete Girolamo Baruffaldi, corredata di note* (MS.; 1702–37); ed. G. Petrucci (Bologna, 1836)

C. Cittadella: 'Cosimo Tura', *Catalogo istorico de' pittori e scultori ferraresi* . . . (Ferrara, 1782), i, pp. 47–57; ii, pp. 210–12; iv, p. 308

G. Baruffaldi: *Vite de' pittori e scultori ferraresi*, ed. G. Boschini (Ferrara, 1844–6), pp. 63–85

GENERAL WORKS

Enc. It.; *EWA*; Thieme–Becker

L. N. Cittadella: *Notizie relative a Ferrara* . . . (Ferrara, 1864)

——: *Documenti ed illustrazioni risguardanti la storia artistica ferrarese* (Ferrara, 1868)

G. Campori: *L'arazzeria estense* (Modena, 1876)

G. Gruyer: *L'Art ferrarais à l'époque des princes d'Este* (Paris, 1897)

A. Venturi: *Storia* (1901–40), VII/iii, pp. 506–58

E. Gardner: *The Painters of the School of Ferrara* (London, 1911)

J. A. Crowe and G. B. Cavalcaselle: *The History of Painting in Northern Italy*, ed. T. Borenius (London, 1912), pp. 221–31

N. Barbantini: *Catalogo della esposizione della pittura ferrarese del Rinascimento* (Ferrara, 1933), pp. 44–63

S. Ortolani: *Cosmè Tura, Francesco del Cossa, Ercole de' Roberti* (Milan, 1941)

B. Nicolson: *The Painters of Ferrara* (London, 1951), pp. 9–12, 18

C. Padovani: *La critica d'arte e la pittura ferrarese* (Rovigo, 1954)

B. Berenson: *Central and North Italian Schools* (1968), i, pp. 55–60, 297–8

R. Longhi: *Officina ferrarese* (Florence, 1975) [incl. *Officina ferrarese* (1934), *Ampliamenti nell'officina ferrarese* (1940), *Nuovi ampliamenti* (1940–55) and *Note brevi* (1955)]

MONOGRAPHS

L. N. Cittadella: *Ricordi e documenti intorno alla vita di Cosimo Tura detto Cosmè, pittor ferrarese del secolo XV* (Ferrara, 1866)

A. Neppi: *Cosmè Tura* (Milan, 1953)

M. Salmi: *Cosmè Tura* (Milan, 1957)

E. Ruhmer: *Tura Paintings and Drawings* (London, 1958)

P. Bianconi: *Tutta la pittura di Cosmè Tura* (Milan, 1963)

E. Riccomini: *Cosmè Tura* (Milan, 1965)

R. Molajoli, ed.: *Cosmè Tura e i grandi pittori ferraresi del suo tempo: Francesco Cossa e Ercole de' Roberti*, Opera Completa (Milan, 1974)

SPECIALIST STUDIES

A. Venturi: 'L'arte nel periodo di Borso d'Este', *Riv. Stor. It.*, ii/4 (1885)

——: 'Cosmè Tura e la Capella di Belriguardo', *Buonarroti*, 3rd ser., ii (1885), pp. 55–64

G. Campori: 'I pittori degli Estensi nel secolo XV', *Atti & Mem. RR. Deput. Stor. Patria Prov. Moden. & Parm.*, 3rd ser., iii (1886), pp. 526–604

F. von Harck: 'Verzeichnis der Werke des Cosma Tura', *Jb. Preuss. Kstsamml.*, ix (1888), pp. 34–40

A. Venturi: 'Cosma Tura genannt Cosmè, 1432 bis 1495', *Jb. Preuss. Kstsamml.*, ix (1888), pp. 3–33

——: 'L'arte ferrarese nel periodo di Ercole d'Este', *Atti & Mem. Stor. Patria Prov. Romagna*, vi (1888), pp. 91–119, 350–422; vii (1889), pp. 368–412

G. Gruyer: 'Cosimo Tura (1432?–1495)', *Art*, liii (1892), pp. 141–8, 173–9

A. Venturi: 'Documento per la determinazione approssimativa della data della nascità di Cosmè Tura', *Archv. Stor. A.*, vii (1894), pp. 52–3

H. J. Hermann: 'Die Gemälde des Cosimo Tura in der Bibliothek des Pico della Mirandola', *Jb. Ksthist. Samml. Allhöch. Ksrhaus.*, xix (1898), pp. 207–16

C. Padovani: 'Cosmè Tura', *Riv. Ferrara*, xi (1933), pp. 11–21

A. Neppi: 'Alla mostra della pittura ferrarese del Rinascimento: Rettifiche di attribuzione, relative al Tura, al Cossa, all'Ortolano, e al Garolfalo', *Riv. Ferrara*, ii (1934), pp. 185–91

O. Härtzsch: *Katalog der echten und fälschlich zugeschriebenen Werke des Cosimo Tura* (Hamburg, 1935)

H. Beenken: 'Angelo del Maccagnino und das Studio von Belfiore', *Jb. Preuss. Kstsamml.*, li (1940), pp. 147–62

O. Härtzsch: 'Cosimo Tura', *Pantheon*, xxvi (1940), pp. 153–61

D. G. Shepherd: ' "The Lamentation": A Tapestry Antependium Designed by Cosimo Tura', *Bull. Cleveland Mus. A.*, xxxviii (1951), pp. 40–42

E. Ruhmer: 'Zur plastischen Tätigkeit des Cosimo Tura', *Pantheon*, xviii (1960), pp. 149–53

M. Baxandall: 'Guarino, Pisanello and Manuel Chrysolaras', *J. Warb. & Court. Inst.*, xxviii (1965), pp. 183–204

W. Zanini: 'Les Tapissiers franco-flamands à la cour des Este', *Vasari*, xxii–xxiii (1965), pp. 1–3

M. Guidoni and A. Marino: 'Cosmus Pictor. Il nuovo organo di Ferrara: Armonia, storia e alchimia della creazione', *Stor. A.*, iv (1969), pp. 388–416

A. K. Eörsi: 'Lo studiolo di Lionello d'Este e il programma di Guarino da Verona', *Acta Hist. A. Acad. Sci. Hung.*, xxvi (1975), pp. 15–52

M. Boskovits: 'Ferrarese Painting about 1450: Some New Arguments', *Burl. Mag.*, clxxviii (1978), pp. 370–85

J. Bentini, ed.: *San Giorgio e la principessa di Cosmè Tura: Dipinti restaurati per l'officina ferrarese* (Bologna, 1985)

KRISTEN LIPPINCOTT

Tura, Pietro del. *See* ARETINO, PIETRO.

Tur 'Abdin [Turk. Mazi Dağ; Mt Masius, Mt Izla]. Plateau in south-eastern Turkey, in what was northern Mesopotamia, to the south and west of the Tigris River between Diyarbakır (anc. Amida) and Nusaybin (anc. Nisibis'). The Syriac name Tur 'Abdin means 'the mountain of the servants (of God)'. It is a rural area noted for its Early Christian and medieval architecture and for its medieval illuminated manuscripts. From *c.* AD 300 onwards its culture was influenced by that of the surrounding and nearby cities of Amida, Nisibis, Dara (now Oğuz), Resh'aina (Theodosiopolis), Martyropolis (now Silvan), Constantina (now Viranşehir) and the more distant city of Edessa (now Urfa; *see* EARLY CHRISTIAN AND BYZANTINE ART, §II, 2(i)(d) and (ii)(c)). The nearest large city is Mardin, a medieval foundation.

1. Architecture. 2. Illuminated manuscripts.

1. ARCHITECTURE. The Tur 'Abdin preserves many of the churches and monasteries from which it derives its name. Some of these structures, which remain in the hands of Christian, Syriac-speaking communities, still serve their original purpose. Others stand abandoned or lie in ruins; still others entered the archaeological record (*see* BELL, GERTRUDE MARGARET LOWTHIAN) before disappearing in the course of the 20th century. The continual use of some churches has led to alterations and additions that often obscure the original architecture. Unfortunately, very little ancient military or domestic architecture has been recorded in the area.

(i) c. AD 300–640. Until the Arab Conquest of 640, most of the Tur 'Abdin was a frontier territory on the eastern edge of the Byzantine empire. After the defeat of Jovian (*reg* 363–4) in 363, the southern and eastern flanks of the plateau were ceded to the Persians, together with the city of Nisibis. Further threatened by the Persians in the late 5th century and the 6th, the Byzantines strengthened or built new forts along their eastern frontier. Prokopios (*Buildings* II.iv.14–19; v.1–5) recorded for the reign of Justinian fortification work undertaken in the Tur 'Abdin at Rhabdios, Sauras, Margdis (now Mardin), Banasymeon and Sinas (now Fafi), as well as at the surrounding cities of Dara, Amida, Martyropolis, Cepha and Constantina. The Persians may have built the fort of Sargathon, which stands just south of the Tur 'Abdin.

While churches built in the larger, Byzantine part of the Tur 'Abdin were presumably Monophysite or Chalcedonian, those erected along the plateau's southern flank fell within the cultural sphere of Nestorian Nisibis. The Byzantine *Notitia Antiochena* of AD 570 lists 'Turabdion' as a suffragan bishopric under the metropolitan see of Dara. The bishop of the Tur 'Abdin may have sat at Hah (now Anıtlı), where there are the remains of the large church of Mar Sovo (?*c.* 530), until *c.* 614, from which time onwards the bishop is known to have sat in the monastery at Kartmin (now Yayvantepe). Much of the ecclesiastical building attested in the Tur 'Abdin during this period was monastic, the earliest such foundation being that of the monastery of Mar Gabriel (397) at Kartmin. This monastery was later endowed with a church, apparently by Anastatios in 512; its sanctuary retains a vault mosaic, an *opus sectile* pavement and fragments of its Proconnesian marble wall revetment. Other recorded monastic foundations include that of Mar Yaqub (421) at Salah (now Barıştepe), Mar Yohannen Tayaya (*c.* 550), Deir Zafaran (*c.* 530) near Mardin, Deir Saliba and Mar Aha (before 556), Mar Abraham of Kashkar (*c.* 571), Qarqaphta at Magdal (635) and those of Mar Sergius and the Theotokos (both *c.* 640). Prokopios (*Buildings* V.ix.31–8) ascribed to Justinian's generosity several Mesopotamian monasteries, at least two of which (those of Zebinus and Begadeus) may have lain in or near the Tur 'Abdin.

The ecclesiastical architecture of the Tur 'Abdin is distinguished by certain local features, including two church types known from their apparent functions as 'parochial' and 'monastic', a centralized church type and elaborate sculpture. The basilica, which is prevalent in rural northern Syria and elsewhere in the empire, is unknown in the Tur 'Abdin. The prototype of the parochial church is represented by the large church (*c.* AD 530; 27.3×11.1 m) of Mar Sovo at Hah, which may be identified as the episcopal church of the Tur 'Abdin (see above). The building is an oblong hall church orientated along its long axis with an apsed sanctuary and an entrance through a narthex on the south side; a large cross is carved in relief in the apse semi-dome. Outside the entrance of most churches of this type stands an oratory (*beth slotha*) in the form of an open apse usually with a large cross carved in relief in the semi-dome. Mar Sovo was apparently constructed with a timber roof, as was another early parochial church (*c.* 571) at the Nestorian monastery of Mar Abraham (pillaged 1926) of Kashkar. The timber roof in both churches was subsequently replaced by a masonry barrel vault, which sprang from lateral stone arcades added flush to the interior side walls of the nave. The vault and arcades became standard features of the parochial churches from the 8th century onwards. Both Mar Sovo and Mar Abraham are noted for their elaborately carved mouldings and garlanded capitals, which were also used in another parochial church at Deir Mateina as well as in Mesopotamian city churches. Additionally, the apse wall of Mar Abraham was ringed by a series of niches faced with colonnettes.

By comparison, monastic churches are somewhat more austere in their sculptural decoration. This second group of churches includes that built at the monastery of Kartmin in AD 512, and another of uncertain date in the monastery at Salah; the earliest may have been constructed in 507 at Ambar outside Dara. This church type is nearly square in plan and has a long nave axis running north–south, a tripartite sanctuary with straight eastern wall and an entrance through the narthex on the west side. The nave is covered by a broad barrel vault, in stone at Ambar and mainly in brick in the other two churches. A related church type is known in the area of Edessa and was, apparently, exported to northern Syria.

The centralized church type is represented by the main church (?*c.* 530) in the monastery of Deir Zafaran. Its

1. Tur 'Abdin, monastery church of Deir Zafaran, near Mardin, ornamented niche on the façade, *c.* AD 530

inscribed triconch plan may reflect contemporary city architecture, such as the cathedral of St Sophia at Edessa, and its thick walls may have originally supported a masonry dome on squinches (the present vaulting is a later replacement). The church is decorated inside and out with elaborate mouldings and capitals, similar to those of contemporary parochial churches, as well as with ornamented niches (see fig. 1) and, on the upper façade, an animated frieze. A contemporary centralized chapel beside the main church at Deir Zafaran is decorated with less elaborate ornament.

(ii) AD 640–c. 800. The Arab Conquest of the eastern Byzantine provinces eliminated the frontier zone from the Tur 'Abdin and thereby created the peaceful conditions conducive to building activity. For the first time there was widespread construction in unfortified villages rather than in the walled monasteries and forts that apparently predominated before 640. In the 20th century travellers have noted numerous churches or small monasteries in, for example, the villages of Ba Sebrina (25), Hah (7) and Killith. Two local building patrons emerged in this period: Mar Gabriel (593–667), eponymous abbot of the monastery at Kartmin, and Symeon d-Zayte ('of the olives'), bishop of Harran (700–734). The former was reportedly given authority to build churches in the Tur 'Abdin by Caliph 'Umar ibn al-Khattab (*reg* 634–44), and the latter used a silver hoard he discovered to finance extensive building of churches, monasteries, mills and villages; his name derives from his numerous and profitable olive plantations. The Tur 'Abdin under the Umayyad caliphs (661–750) thus came, apparently, to resemble the Limestone Massif in northern Syria (*see* EARLY CHRISTIAN AND BYZANTINE ART, §II, 3(iii)), as it had been in the pre-Islamic period.

The main architectural types of the earlier period continued in use after AD 640. At Habsenas (now Mercimekli), Symeon d-Zayte built both the parochial church of Mar Symeon and the monastic church of Mar Lazarus. The latter honoured a local stylite whose tower-like column still stands in the village. The sculpture of the Mar Symeon church continued in desiccated form the classical-style architectural moulding and capitals as well as the large cross in relief in the apse, all prevalent features in the Tur 'Abdin before 640. This later sculpture reappears in other village churches and may therefore be considered contemporary (i.e. *c.* 700–34): Mar Cyriacus at Arnas (now Bağlarbaşi), Mar Azaziel at Kefre Zeh (now Altintaş) and the el-Hadra church at Hah. The last has some additional sculptural features that echo carvings done in the 8th century for the Lebanese city of Anjar, where masons from northern Mesopotamia worked, indicating building contacts outside the Tur 'Abdin region. The el-Hadra church (see fig. 2) has a dome on squinches and animated carvings on the exterior apparently continuing the architecture of the Deir Zafaran church, while its interior series of elaborate apse niches echoes that of Mar Abraham. Other churches built at Hah include the monastic-type church of the monastery of SS Sergius and Bacchus and that of the Theotokos (740). Parochial churches were also erected in the villages of Heshterek (now Ortaca; 772) and Kefre Beh (now Güngören; 779).

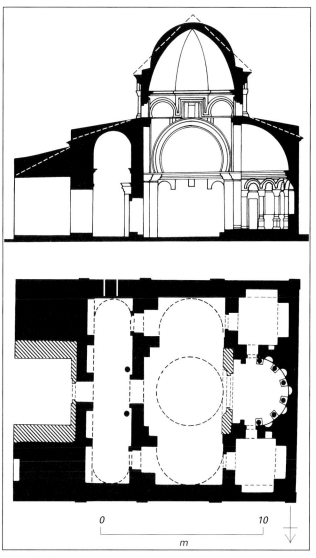

2. Tur 'Abdin, section and ground-plan of el-Hadra church, Hah, early 8th century AD

The building of monasteries is recorded at Mar Awgen (AD 643–64), Qaluq (*c.* 700), and Tell Beshmai (*c.* 750), while Deir Zafaran was refounded as Mar Hananiya (793–811).

(iii) c. 800–c. 1500. Relatively little building is documented in the Tur 'Abdin for the period immediately after 800, a break that coincides with a ban on church building introduced in 853 by the Abbasid caliph al-Mutawakkil (*reg* 847–61). Between 800 and 1100 minor building was carried out in some villages: an oratory of ashlar masonry (934–5) was built at Mar Azaziel at Kefre Zeh, Mar Cyriacus at Arnas was restored in 1014 and its funerary chapel renovated in 1089.

After 1100, written sources and inscriptions record a resurgence of church building that corresponds with the increase in manuscript illumination in the same period.

Unfortunately, these new or renovated buildings have received almost no systematic archaeological attention, and so it is difficult to describe any architectural innovation. The greatest surge of building activity recorded is that undertaken in 1125–66 by John the bishop of Mardin, who built or rebuilt nearly 50 churches and monasteries in the area, a list of which is preserved. Other construction work occurred in the villages of Ba Sebrina (now Haberli; 1199 and 1474) and Kefre Beh (1465), and the monasteries of Mar Awgen (1209 and 1271), Deir Zafaran (1250 and 1496) and Killith (1250–56).

2. ILLUMINATED MANUSCRIPTS. None of the few illuminated Syriac manuscripts surviving from the Early Christian period (*see* EARLY CHRISTIAN AND BYZANTINE ART, §V, 3) is known for certain to have been produced in the Tur 'Abdin. The RABBULA GOSPELS (AD 586) have often been attributed to northern Mesopotamia but were probably copied in northern Syria. An illuminated Nestorian Syriac Bible (6th–7th century; Paris, Bib. N., MS. 341) may have originated at or near Nisibis, and a scribal note states that a 6th-century illuminated Gospel (Paris, Bib. N., MS. 33) was at Deir Zafaran in the 8th century. Between the 11th and the 13th century, however, there was a marked upsurge in the production of illuminated manuscripts in northern Mesopotamia, and some of these are from the Tur 'Abdin, such as the lectionary copied at Hah in 1226 (New York, M. Kevorkian, priv. col.).

BIBLIOGRAPHY

M. C. Mundell: 'The Sixth-century Sculpture of the Monastery of Deir Za'faran in Mesopotamia', *Actes du XVe congrès international d'études byzantines: Athènes, 1976*, ii, pp. 511–28

G. Wiessner: *Christliche Kultbauten im Tur 'Abdin*, 2 vols (Wiesbaden, 1981–3)

M. Mundell Mango: 'Deux Eglises de Mésopotamie du Nord: Ambar et Mar Abraham de Kashkar', *Cah. Archéol.*, xxx (1982), pp. 47–70

M. Mundell Mango, ed.: *The Churches and Monasteries of the Tur 'Abdin* (London, 1982)

J.-P. Fourdrin: 'Les Eglises à nef transversale d'Apamène et du Tûr 'Abdin', *Syria*, lxii (1985), pp. 319–35

MARLIA MUNDELL MANGO

Turcato, Giulio (*b* Mantua, 16 March 1912; *d* Rome, 22 Jan 1995). Italian painter. He trained in Venice from 1928 to 1935 at the Scuola d'Arte dei Carmine, the Liceo Artistico and the Scuola Libera del Nudo. From 1937 to 1939 he worked in Milan for the Novecento Italiano architect Giovanni Muzio. In Milan he was influenced by the expressionistic works of the Corrente movement, which opposed Novecento Italiano. His early landscape painting also showed the influence of the Scuola Romana and in particular of Mario Mafai's colour tones. In 1943 he took part in a group exhibition with such artists as Emilio Vedova in the Galleria Lo Zodiaco in Rome, where he settled. In this period he also attended the studio of Renato Guttuso. After World War II he took part in the artistic debate that took place in Italy between abstract and realist artists. His researches into pure form were characterized by a post-Cubist vocabulary and by a powerful expressive chromatism inspired by Matisse. His attempts to reconcile these qualities with a precise, comprehensible painted image were demonstrated in exhibitions in Rome at the Art Club, which he co-founded, and the Galleria Il Cortile, in 1945 and 1946 respectively. He

also participated in the Forma and FRONTE NUOVO DELLE ARTI groups from 1947, employing a non-geometric abstraction in the *Composition* series of this period. He developed a style of painting where references to political and social themes (as in the *Revolutions*, *Public Meetings*, *Factories* and *Mines* series) were evolved via a complete freedom of formal invention and complete stylistic autonomy (e.g. *Public Meeting*, 1950; Rome, Anna d'Ascanio). In 1952 he took part in the Venice Biennale with the GRUPPO DEGLI OTTO PITTORI ITALIANI, who attempted to overcome the antithesis between representation and non-representation by emphasizing the importance of form.

Turcato's style remained open to a variety of influences including *Art informel*, the Surrealism of Miró and André Masson and also East Asian calligraphy (after a visit to China in 1956). However, his art was modified by a prevailing interest in the nature of signs and material: on this basis in the early 1960s he joined the Continuità group, which was opposed to *Art informel*, and became engaged in a period of intense experimentation with techniques and materials, from collages using sand and asphalt to paintings with phosphorescent pigment on rough sheets of foam rubber. From 1963 he began to experiment with monochrome paintings: these researches continued into the 1970s when he devised paintings and wooden structures employing circular, triangular and oval forms and fluorescent colours.

WRITINGS

'Il colore, il segno', *Letteratura*, 33–4 (1958)

BIBLIOGRAPHY

G. De Marchis: *Turcato* (Milan, 1971)

Giulio Turcato (exh. cat., ed. G. Della Chiesa and I. Mussa; Rome, Pal. Espos., 1974)

Giulio Turcato (exh. cat., ed. A. Monferini; Rome, G.N.A. Mod., 1987)

ANTONELLO NEGRI

Turchi [Veronese], **Alessandro** [l'Orbetto] (*b* Verona, 1578; *d* Rome, 22 Jan 1649). Italian painter. He first studied in Verona with Felice Brusasorci in whose studio he was recorded in 1597 (Brenzoni). Dal Pozzo reported that Turchi completed Brusasorci's *Fall of the Manna* (Verona, S Giorgio) after his master's death in 1605; his early Veronese paintings, such as the *Adoration of the Shepherds* (1608; Verona, S Fermo), are ambitious, with many figures and elaborate backgrounds, echoing the local tradition of which Paolo Veronese was the most distinguished exponent. Turchi may have gone to Venice with his fellow pupil, Marcantonio Bassetti, before moving to Rome *c.* 1614–15. He was paid for work in the Sala Regia of the Palazzo del Quirinale in 1616–17 (Briganti), where he collaborated with a team of artists, among them Giovanni Lanfranco and Carlo Saraceni. His part was to paint an oval medallion with the *Gathering of the Manna* (*in situ*) in a style that suggests Lanfranco's influence. He soon found patrons for altarpieces and cabinet paintings, among them Cardinal Scipione Borghese. By 1619 he had settled permanently in Rome and was a member of the Accademia di S Luca, meetings of which he attended regularly thereafter. He continued to receive commissions

Alessandro Turchi: *Death of Anthony and Cleopatra*, oil on canvas, 2.55×2.67 m, 1640 (Paris, Musée du Louvre)

for altarpieces for churches in Verona throughout his career but if he returned it was only for brief visits.

Turchi's mature work is uneven. His provincial training had been thoroughly absorbed and he was not able to adjust completely to the taste of the capital despite living there for many years. His compositions are often stiffly organized and reveal a poor understanding of the relationship between the setting and the figures, on which he lavished most of his attention. As he became more independent of Brusasorci, he simplified his compositions, reducing the cast of characters in his major altarpieces and placing the emphasis clearly on the figures. The carefully observed faces and hands and the dark, neutral backgrounds echo Caravaggio; the dignified, simply rendered figures owe something to Guido Reni and Lanfranco as well as to earlier 16th-century north Italian artists such as Domenico Morone and Moretto. He painted the *Forty*

Martyrs (*c.* 1619) for S Stefano in Verona and four altarpieces for Roman churches: the *Holy Family with God the Father in Glory* (*c.* 1619; S Lorenzo in Lucina), the *Virgin and Child with St Felix of Cantalice* (*c.* 1630; S Maria della Concezione), the *Flight into Egypt* (*c.* 1632–5; ex-S Romualdo, Rome; versions Madrid, Prado; Manchester, C.A.G.) and the *Madonna in Glory with Angels* (S Salvatore in Lauro). Turchi also made a number of paintings of mythological and religious subjects, on slate and copper as well as on canvas, for Roman collectors. He prided himself on his delicate, *sfumato* modelling of drapery and flesh, and it was the elegant surface polish of such works as *Hercules and Omphale* (*c.* 1620; Munich, Alte Pin.) and *Lot and his Daughters* (Dresden, Gemäldegal. Alte Meister) that appealed to private collectors with a taste for mild eroticism presented as biblical or mythological narrative.

In 1637 Turchi was elected Principe of the Accademia di S Luca after Cortona's four-year term of office, which indicates a certain standing not only among his fellow artists but in papal circles, for the Barberini were closely involved with the Accademia in those years. In the following year he joined the more exclusive Congregazione dei Virtuosi al Pantheon (Gaudenzio). His reputation for mythological pictures was sufficient to attract one powerful French patron, Louis Phélypeaux de La Vrillière, who commissioned a *Death of Antony and Cleopatra* in 1640 (see fig.) along with works by Guercino and Cortona. The compositional study for this (Stockholm, Nmus.), in pen and wash, as are all his known drawings, is characteristic of the light and delicate pen work of his late drawings in this medium. The painting shows Turchi moving towards a clearer, more classical style, which is also evident in such late altarpieces as the austere *Ecstasy of St Francis* (1644; Verona, S Maria in Organo). A comparison of the *Adoration of the Magi* (*c.* 1635; Grezzana, priv. col., see 1974 exh. cat., fig. 130) with the S Fermo altarpiece shows how Turchi accommodated his Veronese taste for densely figured compositions with rich surface pattern and texture to a simpler, grander style indebted to Bolognese idealism and north Italian realism. Yet Turchi remained out of the mainstream of developments in Rome, more akin to later peripheral figures such as Giovanni Domenico Cerrini and Sassoferrato than to the leading artists of the Bolognese school—Domenichino, Lanfranco and Guido Reni.

BIBLIOGRAPHY

Thieme–Becker

G. Mancini: *Considerazioni sulla pittura* (1617–*c.* 1625); ed. A. Marucchi and L. Salerno, 2 vols (Rome, 1956–7), i, p. 255; ii, p. 157

C. Ridolfi: *Meraviglie* (1648); ed. D. von Hadeln (1914–24), ii, pp. 113, 125–6, 241

G. B. Passeri: *Vite* (1679); ed. J. Hess (1934), pp. 177–81

B. dal Pozzo: *Vite de' pittori . . . veronesi* (Verona, 1718), pp. 164–7

La pittura del seicento a Venezia (exh. cat. by P. Zampetti, Venice, Ca' Pesaro, 1959), pp. 31–2

E. Gaudenzio: *Alessandro Turchi: Un pittore veronese nella Roma del seicento* (diss., U. Padua, 1961–2)

G. Briganti: *Palazzo del Quirinale* (Rome, 1962)

E. Schleier: 'Drawings by Alessandro Turchi', *Master Drgs*, ix (1971), pp. 139–53

F. Brenzoni: *Dizionario di artisti veneti* (Florence, 1972)

Cinquant'anni di pittura veronese, 1580–1630 (exh. cat., ed. L. Magagnato; Verona, Gran Guardia, 1974), pp. 107–29

L. Magagnato: 'Alessandro Turchi', *Maestri della pittura veronese*, ed. P. Brugnoli (Verona, 1974), pp. 301–10

Venetian Seventeenth-century Painting (exh. cat. by H. Potterton, London, N.G., 1979), pp. 56–7

ANN SUTHERLAND HARRIS

Tureen [Fr. *terrine*: earthen pot or dish; Lat. *terrenus*: earthen]. A deep circular or oval bowl with a domed lid, handles and three or four short feet, used for serving soup or stew and, in smaller form, sauces. It often has a matching ladle and stand. Made in precious metals, pewter and ceramic, tureens occur singly and in pairs and sets. The tureen, whether of simple or elaborate design, has been in widespread use throughout Europe since the 18th century, and late 17th-century French designs in silver were being copied in Sweden and England from *c.* 1700–10.

☐

Turfan [Turpan]. Oasis city and surrounding region in eastern Xinjiang Uygur Autonomous Region, China. The major sites include KHOCHO, YARKHOTO, BEZEKLIK and ASTANA. Turfan's significance lay in its location on the northern branch of the SILK ROUTE. Its art assimilated concepts from the Indian, Iranian and Chinese cultural traditions and religions disseminated along the Silk Route. Mahayana Buddhism, Nestorian Christianity, Manichaeism and Tantric Buddhism influenced the local style (*see also* CENTRAL ASIA, §II, 1(v)). As political control of the region alternated between China and the nomadic peoples of Central Asia it also influenced artistic production. The best examples of the resulting synthesis are to be found in the wall paintings and painted clay sculptures of the religious complexes and tombs. The spread of Islam in the area effectively ended further development of all art forms except architecture. Natural destruction together with the removal of frescoes and artefacts in the name of archaeological research has left almost nothing to be studied *in situ*, but the major findings are documented in the accounts of AUREL STEIN, ALBERT GRÜNWEDEL and ALBERT VON LE COQ.

See also CENTRAL ASIA, §II, 2(ii)(a), 3(ii)(b) and 4.

BIBLIOGRAPHY

EWA

D. von Klementz: *Turfan und seine Altertümer: Nachrichten über die von der Königlichen Akademie der Wissenschaften zu St. Petersburg im Jahre 1899 ausgerüsteten Expedition nach Turfan* (St Petersburg, 1899)

M. Bussagli: *La Peinture d'Asie centrale* (Geneva, 1963; Eng. trans., London, 1978)

Along the Ancient Silk Routes: Central Asian Art from the West Berlin State Museums (exh. cat. by H. Härtel and M. Yaldiz, New York, Met., 1982)

M. Yaldiz: *Archäologie und Kunstgeschichte Chinesisch-Zentralasiens (Xinjiang)* (1987), iii/2 of *Handbuch der Orientalistik*, ed. B. Spuler and others (Leiden, 1978–), pp. 118–42

Tun-huang t'u-lu-fan wenwu [Cultural relics from Dunhuang and Turfan] (Hong Kong and Shanghai, 1987)

MARY S. LAWTON

Turin [It. Torino; anc. Augusta Taurinorum]. Italian city and capital of Piedmont. It is situated at the confluence of the River Po with Doria Riparia, 120 km north-west of Genoa. The fourth largest city in Italy, Turin (population *c.* 1.2 million) was formerly the capital of the Duchy of Savoy, the Kingdom of Sardinia and the first capital of the Kingdom of Italy. The city is regularly laid out on a Roman grid, which was developed in the 17th and 18th centuries. The city expanded rapidly in the 19th century, when it became an important industrial centre.

I. History and urban development. II. Art life and organization. III. Centre of tapestry production. IV. Cathedral.

I. History and urban development.

1. Before 1800. 2. 1800 and after.

1. BEFORE 1800. Founded under Emperor Augustus in *c.* 28 BC as a colonial settlement for military veterans, the orthogonal street layout of the Roman *castrum* forms the nucleus of modern Turin. The Roman settlement was an almost perfect square, with each of its walls approximately 700 m long and penetrated by at least one gate. The town was divided into four parts by the north–south road (*cardo*) and the east–west road (*decumanus*), which ran from the four main gates to cross at right angles at the

centre of town, which was the site of the forum. The remains of the Roman settlement are few but significant: the ruins of a theatre, the north gate (Porta Palatina) and the street layout. The gate, built of undressed brick, consists of one circular and one octagonal tower connected by a curtain wall pierced by numerous arched openings. Although the Roman achievement was modest, the vigour of the brick construction and the rationality of the street grid were a prominent source of inspiration for subsequent urban development.

During the Middle Ages the regular grid of streets was altered by the introduction of shorter, diagonal passageways connecting such principal buildings as the cathedral and the Palazzo di Città. Most of them were located in the north-west corner of the city. The Roman walls were reinforced with towers under the *comune*. The east gate, which connected the city to the River Po, was radically rebuilt in 1317–19, when it became the fortified Castello degli Acaja (now Palazzo Madama; *see* ITALY, fig. 21). The castle was further enlarged at the beginning of the 15th century. This square fortress with a cylindrical tower at each corner, the fragmented grid of orthogonal streets and the Roman walls were the only distinguishing aspects of the city when Duke Charles V (*reg* 1535–6) lost it to the French in 1536. During their 25-year occupation the French reinforced the fortifications by raising a wall of earth almost as tall as the brick ones and by building a bastion at each of the four corners of the city, with a fifth at the centre on the eastern wall around the castle. In order to build the bastions and defend them effectively, the suburbs and the nearby monasteries were razed. The fortification campaign thus deprived Turin of its suburbs and, through its menacing new walls, endowed it with a ferocious aspect.

In the mid-16th century Turin was still a medieval city, only marginally touched by the ideals of Renaissance architecture. Apart from the French fortification that was built in response to the use of cannon in siege warfare, the only significant Renaissance building was the cathedral (1491–6; *see* §IV below), commissioned by Archbishop Domenico della Rovere from the Tuscan architect Meo da Caprino. Close to the Porta Palatina, the cathedral has a longitudinal nave flanked by aisles and chapels and vaulted with pointed arches. The large, white, undetailed and unadorned upper areas dominate the dark chapels, decorated at a later date. The façade has an insipid silhouette but some successful marble relief decoration around the portals (see fig. 6 below). The east end of the church abutted the bishop's palace, subsequently replaced by the palace of the dukes of Savoy.

The fortunes of Turin changed radically after 1559 with the Treaty of Câteau-Cambresis, which obliged the French to return the duchy of Piedmont-Savoy to the Duke of Savoy. Emanuel-Philibert (*reg* 1553–80) established the capital of his duchy in Turin by transferring the administrative centre from Chambéry, French Savoy. The political and geographical circumstances of the duchy, caught between French and Spanish territories, required able self-defence. One of the Duke's first commissions was the construction of a citadel (1563–6; destr.), designed by FRANCESCO PACIOTTO and built by Francesco Horologgi. Paciotto proposed a pentagonal fortress, placed in the south-west corner of the city. It was to have three bastions orientated towards the countryside, defending the approach to the city from the west, and two bastions facing the city, ready to subjugate it in case of rioting against the Duke's rule. This perfect polygon, influenced perhaps by the Fortezza Alessandra (1533–6; by Antonio da Sangallo

1. Turin, Piazza Castello, by Ascanio Vitozzi, 1606–12

(ii); now Fortezza di Basso) in Florence and by the pentagonal Villa Farnese (from 1521; by Antonio da Sangallo (ii) and Baldassare Peruzzi) in Caprarola, fascinated military architects in the 16th century. It was the first of a number of five-sided citadels, which included Antwerp (begun 1567; destr. 1874), also by Paciotto, Parma (1591) and Ferrara (1618). This splendid fortress established Turin as a mighty *piazzaforte*, and, despite the duchy's neutrality, acted as a provocation to Piedmont's neighbours. It also demonstrated the Duke's interest in architectural and urban renewal, which his successors eventually carried on.

While the strategic defence of the capital was fulfilled by Emanuel-Philibert's citadel, Charles-Emanuel I (*reg* 1580–1630) set himself the task of the structural and aesthetic renovation of the city. Motivated by an ideological need for a large, decorous city worthy of the Duke's residence, plans were made to transform and embellish Turin. The plans made by ASCANIO VITOZZI, ducal architect and military engineer between 1584 and *c.* 1615, proposed circular and elliptical additions to the square perimeter of the city. The demands by Charles-Emanuel I for a renewed capital city, densely populated and disciplined, led to the development of an urban design that conveyed absolute rule. While Vitozzi did not realize completely his plans for the expansion of Turin, he was responsible for several urban interventions, thereby introducing a sober Baroque to this northern city, where the influence of Palladio and Scamozzi persisted. These included the enlargement of Piazza Castello, the square in front of the castle, and its definition with uniform arcaded buildings (1606–12; see fig. 1); the reconstruction of the Palazzo Ducale on the site of the bishop's palace, facing Piazza Castello, the link between the palace and the cathedral; the opening of a street (now Via Roma) south of Piazza Castello (1612–15) on an axis with the portal of the new Palazzo Ducale and connecting it to the castle of Mirafiori; another street (opened 1619; now Via di Palazzo di Città) west of Piazza Castello connecting it to the market place in front of the Palazzo di Città; and a gallery linking the Palazzo Ducale to the castle. The ducal buildings and the new streets altered the hierarchy of the city, underlining the importance of the north-east corner as the new command centre of Turin.

During the first decade of the 17th century plans for the expansion of the city were continued despite the wars in which the Duke was involved. These plans show that Charles-Emanuel I intended to enlarge Turin to the south and to the east, and the foundation stone for this expansion was laid in December 1620. A southern gate, the Porta Nuova, marking the edge of the expansion area, had already been built for the ceremonial wedding entry of Victor-Amadeus (later Duke of Savoy; *reg* 1630–37), the Duke's heir. The principal elements of this first expansion were the elaboration of the bastioned fortification and an extension to the south and east of the orthogonal grid of streets crossed by a few radial ones that connected the main parts of the city to one another (the gate at the Po bridge, the castle and the citadel). The expansion emphasized the castle, which became the centre of the three parts of the town: Città Vecchia, Città Nuova and Borgo di Po. Besides Vitozzi, the expansion was also designed by the Duke, his general of artillery Ercole Negro di Sanfront, and Carlo di Castellamonte.

Very little of this grandiose plan was realized before Charles-Emanuel I's death in 1630, and Victor-Amadeus I readjusted the ambitions of the duchy, both politically and physically; only the expansion south was carried out. Its walls were completed in 1637. Further development was discontinued for the next five years as Victor-Amadeus's widow, Mary Christina, fought to legitimize her regency. In the 1640s ducal construction projects in Turin were again manipulated in an attempt to gain and display power through architecture and urban design. Mary Christina sponsored the construction of the Piazza Reale (now Piazza S Carlo), a residential square that became the spatial focus of the southern expansion. The uniform, long sides of the square, separated by the main north–south street of the southern expansion, linking the south gate to the portal of the Palazzo Ducale, were designed by Castellamonte. They take the form of a three-storey façade with a Doric arcade at ground level, a tall *piano nobile* and a small attic level. The coupled columns of the airy arcade were merged into a pier in the 18th century. The windows of the *piano nobile* feature alternating segmental and triangular pediments. Additional mouldings, cornices and stucco decoration gave the façade a fussy, unfocused quality, worsened by the lack of a bold cornice and parapet. The numerous, closely ranged windows became a highlight of residential architecture in Turin. Castellamonte's design was most influenced by the uniform façades of Vitozzi's Piazza Castello. The short, southern end of the square was defined by the twin churches of S Carlo (1619), designed by Castellamonte, and S Cristina (1639), by his son Amedeo di Castellamonte (their façades were added by Caronesi in 1836 and by Filippo Juvarra in 1715 respectively). The square, unlike most monumental public urban spaces, is not dominated by one single large building but is defined by the long uniform palace façades, behind which several private houses were built. In order to hasten construction work, Mary Christina gave parcels of land along the square to courtiers, who could be relied on to obey building regulations. The crown did not gain financially from this operation, for its motives were ones of symbolic representation rather than speculative development. The courtiers cooperated in this attempt to transform Turin into a visual manifestation of the capital city, the physical counterpart of absolutist government.

The original project to expand Turin to the Po was fulfilled in 1673, when Charles-Emanuel II (*reg* 1638–75) began the second, or eastern, expansion (see fig. 2). While making Turin more decorous, and strengthening it militarily, the expansion was this time also a speculative undertaking. The expansion area was already occupied by suburban inhabitants, who had to pay the crown the difference in value of their property before and after it became part of the city. This legislative instrument successfully blocked speculative efforts that could have stifled growth. In addition, before the expansion became official, Charles-Emanuel II acquired land that he sold at a high price when it became part of the enclosed territory. Despite the greater cost and the lack of such incentives as those offered by both Charles-Emanuel I and Mary Christina, the Borgo di Po expansion grew rapidly. As in the earlier

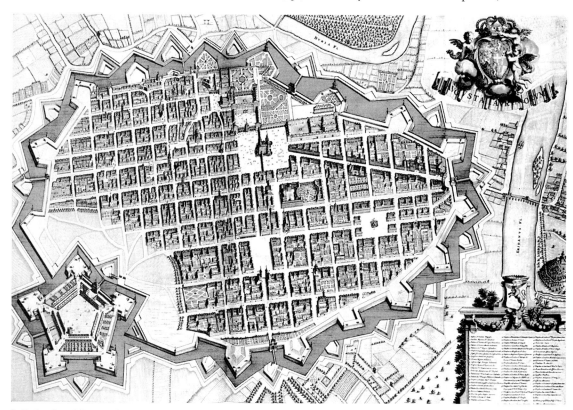

2. Turin, plan of the city after its second expansion in the 17th century; from the *Theatrum statutum regiae celsitudinis Sabaudiae ducis* (1682)

expansion, the streets were straight, wide and framed by buildings of equal height and architectural character. The major spatial elements of the Borgo di Po were the Piazza Carlo Emanuele II (Piazza Carlina) and the Contrada di Po (now Via Po). In its final form, Piazza Carlina was similar to the Piazza Reale, both formally and functionally. They were connected to each other by a major street (now Via Maria Vittoria) that continued to the citadel. Originally designed as an octagonal piazza, its form was reduced to a rectangle in order to facilitate the sale of land and the construction of houses.

The Contrada di Po, a diagonal street, connected the city gate near the Po bridge with the Piazza Castello. It was built on the right of way of an existing suburban street, and its diagonal angle, in relation to the orthogonal street layout, was suggested in part by the siting of the church of S Francesco di Paola, founded in 1632 by Victor-Amadeus I and Mary Christina. In the long row of identical, three-storey, porticoed buildings that frame the wide street, it is the only façade that stands out, although more for its singularity than its architectural excellence. The Piazza Castello was doubled in size with the addition of an identical eastern half, surrounded by uniform porticoed structures, most of which housed ducal agencies (e.g. archives, academy, university, theatre). The façades formed a sombre but stagelike enclosure for the city's public spaces. After the relative dryness and severity of the public exterior, the impact of the highly wrought and personal Piedmontese Baroque interiors, for example Guarino Guarini's church of S Lorenzo (from 1668; *see*

GUARINI, GUARINO, fig. 1), which was designed to match Vitozzi's urban context, must have been even more shocking.

The formal elements adopted in the urban design of the 17th century had a lasting influence. The third expansion west of the Città Vecchia, realized by Victor-Amadeus II (*reg* 1675–1730) after 1706 to a design by Filippo Juvarra, was based on an orthogonal grid of streets, and the military gate became a residential square, as at Piazza Vittoria (now Piazza di Porta Palazzo; completed 1814), and the Quartieri Militari (from 1716; *see* JUVARRA, FILIPPO). Juvarra also restructured the street (now the Via Milano) that runs in front of the Palazzo di Città, widening it and inserting a rhomboidal piazza (Piazza della Repubblica) halfway along it. In the 18th century the rehabilitation of the Città Vecchia followed the restoration of the *cardo* (now Via S Tommaso), which was endowed with a uniform roofline and continuous floor levels for its flanking buildings. Throughout, the local predilection for numerous, large and vertically proportioned windows was amply satisfied, reducing the buildings to a structural skeleton of wall strips.

BIBLIOGRAPHY
C. Promis: *Storia della antica Torino* (Turin, 1869)
A. Cavallari Murat, ed.: *Forma urbana ed architettura nella Torino barocca dalle premesse classiche alle conclusioni neoclassiche*, 3 vols (Turin, 1968)
M. Passanti: *Lo sviluppo urbanistico di Torino dalla fondazione all'unità d'Italia* (Turin, 1969)
V. Comoli Mandracci: *Torino* (Bari, 1983)
M. Pollak: 'The Other Face of the Medal: Turin, 1673', *A. Bull.*, lxix (1987), pp. 256–63

MARTHA POLLAK

2. 1800 AND AFTER. The destruction of the city walls that had confined Turin for more than 1600 years was decided on by Napoleon, but it was not accomplished until 1814, when Duke Victor-Emanuel I (*reg* 1802–21) returned to Turin after the collapse of the Napoleonic empire. The city—which in 1800 had fewer than 80,000 inhabitants—was thus able to expand. The first large urban projects were the construction of the church of the Gran Madre di Dio (1818–31) across the Po by Ferdinando Bonsignore (1767–1843) and the development of the empty space between the Porta di Po and the river. The works included the grandiose, Neo-classical, porticoed Piazza Vittorio Veneto (see fig. 3) by Giuseppe Frizzi (1797–1831), a bridge built by the Napoleonic engineers La Ramée Pertinchamp and Mallet, the church of the Gran Madre and the hill. In the early 19th century Turin was the capital of a regional state with strong military ambitions aimed at the conquest of Italy, and it had the typical productive structure of capital cities: industries linked with state economic initiatives (e.g. military equipment, victuals, tobacco and the Mint) and with the court (e.g. luxury goods, coachmaking and printing). There was, however, little private industry, and entrepreneurs were reluctant to engage in manufacturing activity.

In 1847 work began on the first railway between Turin and Genoa, and the city was soon linked with the principal cities of the kingdom of Sardinia. In its expansion the city largely preserved the regular Roman plan, adding severe new buildings for new services, including the Ospedale dei Pazzerelli (1837) by Giuseppe Talucchi (1782–1863), the main cemetery (1828) by Gaetano Lombardi (1793–1868), the church of S Massimo (1853) by Carlo Sada, and the Stazione di Porta Nuova Centrale (completed 1868) by Alessandro Mazzucchetti (1824–94) and Carlo Ceppi. New houses were constructed in the Piazza Maria Teresa and Borgo Nuovo, with buildings by Alessandro Antonelli, who also designed the Mole Antonelliana (from 1863; for illustration *see* ANTONELLI, ALESSANDRO), reputedly the tallest brick-built edifice in Europe, and a symbol of Turin. Additions were also made by Carlo Promis (1808–72), who designed the Piazza Carlo Felice (1823–55), and buildings were added to Promis's Corso Vittorio Emanuele and Via Nizza. In 1861 the population numbered 205,000, and Turin was proclaimed capital of the new Kingdom of Italy; in 1864, however, the capital was transferred to Florence. It was feared that this would mean the end of Turin's general prosperity, which the presence of the court had assured for three centuries. In

3. Turin, Piazza Vittorio Veneto, by Giuseppe Frizzi, 1825; from a 19th-century photograph

the following decades the civic government made tremendous efforts to provide Turin with the necessary prerequisites for industrialization, from hydraulic energy to public works, trade schools and the Polytechnic.

The Fabbrica Italiana Automobili Torino (FIAT) was founded in 1899. This was not the first car factory to be built in Turin, and for some decades it was not the only one, but it was certainly the most economically important, and it generated a tremendous impact on the political, social and physical conditions of the city. Modern Turin is rightly considered a huge 'factory town'. In the early 20th century extensive workers' suburbs were constructed outside the old city boundary, and a strong and united working class grew up in poor tenements. The closely packed, regular blocks of flats in middle-class areas were marked by the use of *Stile Liberty* architecture and, during the 1930s, *razionalismo*. An early example of Rationalist architecture in Turin was the seven-storey Gualino office building (completed 1929) by Giuseppe Pagano and Gino Levi-Montalcini (1902–74). Influential examples of architecture in the city include two sculptural concrete shell structures designed for the Exhibition Hall (1947–9) by PIER LUIGI NERVI, who also designed the Palazzo del Lavoro (1961) in Turin. In the late 20th century a large, new metropolitan sector took shape with a population of almost two million, due to the enormous influx of migrants arriving from southern Italy in search of industrial work. As a result, the social and political life of the area was affected by serious shortages of housing, amenities and transport.

BIBLIOGRAPHY

P. Spriano: *Storia di Torino operaia e socialista* (Turin, 1958)
F. Cognasso: *Storia di Torino* (Milan, 1959)
A. Cavallari-Murat: *Breve storia dell'urbanistica in Piemonte* (Rome, 1960)
P. Gabert: *Turin, ville industrielle* (Paris, 1964)
Forma urbana e architettura nella Torino barocca. Dalle premesse classiche alle conclusion: Neoclassiche, Istituto di Architettura del Politecnico di Torino (Turin, 1968)
P. Sereno, L. Falco and G. Morbelli: 'Torino', *Stor. Italia*, vi (1976)
Cultura figurativa e architettonica negli Stati del Re di Sardegna, 1773–1861 (exh. cat., Turin, Pal. Reale, 1980)
V. Comoli Mandracci: *Torino* (Bari, 1983)
V. Castronovo: *Torino* (Bari, 1987)

LUIGI FALCO

II. Art life and organization.

The earliest significant evidence of painting in Turin dates from the 14th century and exists in documentation rather than in the works themselves, which remain untraced. During this time in Piedmont painting, unlike other art forms, followed an autonomous trend only partly influenced by the culture of neighbouring Lombardy. Between 1314 and 1348 Giorgio da Firenze (*d* 1348), a Tuscan painter in the service of the ruling Savoy family and about whom little documentation survives, influenced the artistic style in Turin, as can be seen in the frescoes (*c.* 1360) of the Capella delle Grazie in the church of S Domenico, rendered almost unrecognizable, however, by restoration work at the beginning of the 20th century. In the Gothic period painting in Turin was dominated by the figure of GIACOMO JAQUERIO, court painter to Amedeus VIII, 1st Duke of Savoy. He was responsible for the fresco of the *Virgin and Child with Saints* in the medieval church of S

Antonio di Ranverso in Avigliana, near Turin. Also attributed to him are two fresco cycles in the same church, depicting the lives of *St Anthony* and *St Biagio*, a fresco cycle of the life of *St Peter* in S Pietro, Pianezza, near Turin, and some of the decoration of the Castello (now Palazzo Madama). His frequent travels between Turin and Geneva, supported by such important patrons as the dukes of Acaja and Savoy, and by the Church, made him an influential figure in the first part of the 15th century.

Piedmontese art began to be influenced by Renaissance themes and forms with the work of GIOVANNI MARTINO SPANZOTTI, court painter to Charles II, Duke of Savoy, in 1507. Influenced by Vincenzo Foppa, Piedmontese artists continued to work on *vero naturale* (It.: 'natural truth'), of which one of the most important examples is Spanzotti's *Virgin Enthroned with SS Ubaldo and Sebastian* (see fig. 4). Spanzotti's work influenced many Piedmont artists, notably Defendente Ferrari, who trained in the former's workshop and who added to his mentor's style elements taken from wider European Renaissance culture, evident, for example, in the *Assumption of the Virgin* (1516), painted for the Confraternity of the Holy Shroud at Cirliè, near Turin.

The political turbulence in Piedmont during the 16th century hindered artistic development until after 1563, when Emanuel-Philibert, 10th Duke of Savoy (*reg* 1553–80), moved the capital of the duchy from Chambéry to Turin, where the university was reopened and where the most important administrative offices came to be concentrated. During these years the cultural policy of the Savoy dynasty favoured contact with artists from central Italy, facilitating the spread of the Mannerist style. In 1605 Federico Zuccaro moved to Turin, where Charles-Emanuel I, 11th Duke of Savoy (*reg* 1580–1630), entrusted him with the interior decoration of the gallery (1605–7; destr. 1659) that linked the old Palazzo del Vescovo to the Castello (*see* ZUCCARO, (2), §1).

In the last years of the 17th century in Turin stuccoists and well-known engravers were active at the grand architectural sites of the ducal residences, Castello del Valentino and Castello di Rivoli, Venaria. Among them were Alessandro Casella (*fl* 1645–9) and Isidoro Bianchi (1602–90). Bianchi carried out some of the decoration of the Castello di Rivoli and worked also on the Palazzo Reale with the help of his sons, Francesco and Pompeo. With the arrival in Turin of Mary Christina of France, wife of Victor-Amadeus I, 12th Duke of Savoy (*reg* 1630–37), numerous French artists were summoned to the court as portrait painters and decorators. JAN MIEL, a Belgian painter, arrived from Rome in 1658 and was appointed official painter to Charles-Emanuel II, 14th Duke of Savoy (*reg* 1638–75). Also working in the city were GUARINO GUARINI, active in Turin from 1666, and ANDREA POZZO, who, following his decoration (1676) of the church of S Francesco Saverio in Mondovì with a fresco cycle celebrating the church's titular saint, moved to Turin in 1678 to decorate the interior of the Jesuit church of SS Martiri (destr.; fragments survive). In 1688 the Austrian painter DANIEL SEITER arrived from Rome at the invitation of Victor-Amadeus II, 15th Duke of Savoy (*reg* 1675–1730), and carried out some of the decoration of the Palazzo Reale. He was also responsible for the selection and

4. Giovanni Martino Spanzotti: *Virgin Enthroned with SS Ubaldo and Sebastian*, tempera on panel, 1.35×1.33 m, before 1475 (Turin, Galleria Sabauda)

acquisition of works for the royal collection, acquired on visits to Rome in 1691, 1696 and 1698.

In the first decades of the 18th century art in Turin was epitomized by the work of the architect Filippo Juvarra, who entered the service of Victor-Amadeus II in 1714 and collaborated with many Italian artists in his great projects. For interior decoration Juvarra relied principally on the French artist Jean Berain I and on CLAUDIO FRANCESCO BEAUMONT, a decorator from Piedmont whose work at the Palazzo Reale included a painting of the *Judgement of Paris* (1737) for the ceiling of the Gabinetto Cinese, designed by Juvarra. During those same years SEBASTIANO CONCA, FRANCESCO TREVISIANI, Francesco Solimena (*see* SOLIMENA, (2)), Sebastiano Ricci (*see*

RICCI (i), (1)), GIOVANNI BATTISTA CROSATO and the French artist Carle Vanloo (*see* VAN LOO, (3)) were also active at the court. In 1739, four years after Juvarra left Turin for Madrid, BENEDETTO INNOCENTE ALFIERI was appointed first royal architect.

Around 1750 several Italian artists visited Turin; among the most influential were FRANCESCO DE MURA from Naples and GREGORIO GUGLIELMI from Rome, both of whom participated in the decoration of the new apartments of the Palazzo Reale. Meanwhile, as a result of acquisitions by ministers resident in various regions, the Savoy collections were enriched by works of art from central and southern Italy. In 1745 two views of Turin, *Palazzo Reale* and the *Old Bridge over the Po* (both Turin, Gal. Sabauda), were commissioned from the Venetian Bernardo Bellotto by Charles-Emanuel III, King of Sardinia and 17th Duke of Savoy (*reg* 1730–73). During these years landscape painting became particularly popular: after completing part of the frescoes of the Palazzina di Stupinigi, Carle Vanloo established his reputation as a landscape painter. Pietro Bagetti (1764–1831) also gained acclaim as a topographical artist and painter. In the last three decades of the 18th century Victor-Amadeus III, King of Sardinia and 18th Duke of Savoy (*reg* 1773–96), was active as a patron, commissioning works from Giovanni Battista Bernero, who was appointed court sculptor in 1774 and professor at the Accademia Reale in 1778, and Laurent Pécheux (1729–1821), who was appointed court painter in 1777 and the following year summoned to direct the Accademia Reale. Other artists at the court of the dukes of Savoy included the sculptors Ignazio Collino (1724–93) and his brother Filippo Collino (*d* 1800), active at the Palazzo Reale.

In paintings of the early 19th century historical and landscape subjects were extensively treated, for example by GIOVANNI MIGLIARA, who in 1833 succeeded Bagetti in the service of Charles-Albert, King of Sardinia (*reg* 1831–49). At the same time Massimo D'Azeglio was painting landscapes that were clearly influenced by Romanticism, evident, for example, in the *Death of Montmorency* (1825; Turin, Gal. Civ. A. Mod.), in which he introduced into a traditional, detailed, Netherlandish landscape knights and paladins in place of the customary rustic figures, exemplifying the new taste for medievalism and the neo-Gothic.

In the 1830s a number of artists was summoned to court to participate in the major restoration work commissioned by Charles-Albert. In 1832 PELAGIO PALAGI was given responsibility for overseeing the restoration of the Castello di Racconigi and its park; in 1834 he was appointed painter in charge of all the royal residences in Turin. Also at this time the artists FRANCESCO GONIN and Pietro Ayres (1794–1878) were working in Turin. Many sculptures were commissioned by the dukes of Savoy for the town squares, including the equestrian monuments to *Duke Emanuel-Philibert* (1833–7; Piazza S Carlo) and

5. Felice Casorati: *Midday*, oil on canvas, 1922 (Trieste, Museo Civico Revoltella, Galleria d'Arte Moderna)

Duke Charles-Albert (1861; Piazza Carlo Alberto), both by CARLO MAROCHETTI. Also in the 19th century the collections of the Biblioteca Reale were expanded, and the Museo Egizio and Galleria Sabauda were opened, while the private art market developed through the initiatives of the Promotrice di Belle Arte (1842) and the Circolo degli Artisti (1855). Towards the close of the century, in 1895, the Galleria d'Arte Moderna was founded in Turin, the first art gallery devoted to contemporary art to open in Italy. In 1902 the Mostra Internazionale di Arte Decorativa Moderna opened in the city, including work by important 19th- and 20th-century artists. The poster for the event was designed by LEONARDO BISTOLFI, while the exhibition featured *The Fourth Estate* (1898–1901; Milan, Gal. A. Mod.; *see* PELLIZZA DA VOLPEDO, GIUSEPPE, fig. 2) by Giuseppe Pellizza da Volpedo, in which Post-Impressionist techniques were united with new social themes, which the artist moulded to the socialist environment in Turin. A main figure in 'official' painting in the early 20th century was GIACOMO GROSSO, who lectured at the Accademia Albertina for 45 years from 1889. Between 1920 and 1930 the presence in Turin of such intellectuals as Lionello Venturi (*see* VENTURI, (2)) and EDOARDO PERSICO sparked off an intense process of receptiveness to a wider European culture.

In 1923 the artist FILLIA, one of the main protagonists of 'second Futurism' (*see* FUTURISM, §1), founded the Turin Futurist group with the publication of his manifesto *Futurista Torinese—Sindacati Artistici*. From about the same time the paintings of FELICE CASORATI (see fig. 5) became a point of reference for many young artists. Turin was the base for the group Sei a Torino, which comprised Jessie Boswell (1881–1956), Gigi Chessa (1898–1935), Nicola Galante (*b* 1883), Carlo Levi (1902–75), Francesco Menzio (1899–1979) and Enrico Paulucci (*b* 1901). Working in isolation from these artists was LUIGI SPAZZAPAN. During the post-war years some artists from Turin belonged to the Movimento arte concreta. The first exhibition was held in Turin, in the space belonging to the Art Club gallery.

In 1959 the new site of the Galleria d'Arte Moderna was inaugurated, which closed for restoration a few years later and did not reopen until 1994. Also in 1959, at the Circolo degli Artisti, Arte Nuova was inaugurated, with work by such American artists as Jackson Pollock and Willem de Kooning; among the Italian artists showing were Alberto Burri, Emilio Vedova and Giuseppe Capogrossi. In the second half of the 1970s many galleries in Turin began to exhibit work by artists associated with ARTE POVERA, a term coined in 1967 by the Genoese critic Germano Celant. The use of everyday materials, alien to 'official' art, united the Turin phenomenon with that of American Minimalist and conceptual art. In 1984 the Museo d'Arte Contemporanea opened in Rivoli.

BIBLIOGRAPHY

Torino tra le due guerre (exh. cat., Turin, Gal. Civ. A. Mod.,1978)
E. Castelnuovo and M. Rosci: *Cultura figurativa e architettonica negli Stati del Re di Sardegna, 1773–1861* (Turin, 1980)
Materiali: Arte italiana 1920–1940 nelle collezioni della Galleria Civica d'Arte Moderna di Torino (Turin, 1981)
M. Bondini and R. Maggio Serra: *Il museo sperimentale di Torino, arte italiana degli anni sessanta nelle collezioni della Galleria Civica d'Arte Moderna* (Turin, 1985)
Piemonte (Turin, 1991)
Torino, 1950/1970: Un'avventura internazionale (Milan, 1993)

LISA PAROLA

III. Centre of tapestry production.

The dukes of Savoy, like all the leading European families, owned a large collection of French and Flemish tapestries and traditionally employed specialized weavers to maintain them. In 1676 Victor-Amadeus II, 15th Duke of Savoy, gave the French weaver Michele Antonio Demignot (*fl* 1676–1711) this position and the title of usher. The Duke, perhaps already contemplating founding his own tapestry factory, insisted on sending Demignot's gifted son Vittorio Demignot (*fl* 1710; *d* 1742) to apprentice under Jodocus (Josse) de Vos (*fl* 1700-1725), whose workshop was the largest in Brussels. Vittorio returned to Turin in 1711 to take over his father's position caring for the court tapestries. He wove a small *Allegory of the River Po* (untraced) for the apartments of Queen Anne and began a *Charity* (not completed; untraced) before 1714, when he left Turin to work in Rome.

In February 1731 Charles-Emanuel III, King of Sardinia and 17th Duke of Savoy, recalled Vittorio to establish a court factory in Turin. In the same year the painter CLAUDIO FRANCESCO BEAUMONT was recalled from Rome to paint or supervise cartoons for the new enterprise. Weaving on a nine-piece *Story of Alexander* series designed by Beaumont began by 1734 (finished 1742; Turin, Pal. Reale; Rome, Quirinale). By 1736 the high-warp weaver Antonio Dini (*d* 1771) had arrived from Rome. In 1737 official letters were issued to the factory, which, following the model of the Gobelins in Paris, consisted of a low-warp workshop headed by Demignot and a high-warp workshop directed by Dini. In the same year the painter Angela Palanca (*fl* 1737–52) began cartoons for a set of *bambocciate* (e.g. *Country Dance*, 1740–42; Turin, Pal. Reale), which was made in the workshop of Demignot. After Vittorio died, his son Francesco Demignot (*fl* 1742; *d* 1785) headed the workshop, and two other sons, Giuseppe Demignot (*fl* 1741–68) and Antonio Demignot (*fl* 1746-8), also worked there.

The factory's large historical series designed by Beaumont, enlarged into cartoons by assistants and divided between the two tapestry workshops were: ten *Stories of Julius Caesar* (1740–50; Turin, Pal. Reale); the *Story of Pyrrhus* (often incorrectly called the *Story of Cyrus*, 1749–54; Rome, Pal. Quirinale) and *Stories of Hannibal* (1748–78; six pieces, Turin, Pal. Reale). In 1743 a set of landscapes (1743–6; Rome, Pal. Madama; Turin, Rivoli Municipio) on cartoons by Francesco Antoniani (pseud. Lombard; *fl* 1740–75) was begun. From *c*. 1745, when the architect Benedetto Innocente Alfieri was put in charge of the royal decorating schemes with Beaumont, styles became simplified. Tapestries included three architectural subjects (1745–51; Turin, Pal. Caccia and Rivoli Castello) on cartoons by Antoniani; at least three marine subjects (1748–50; two in Turin, Pal. Reale) from cartoons by Antoniani; landscape, with figures (1753–63; Turin, Gal. Sabauda) on cartoons by Vittoria Amedeo Cignaroli (1730–1800); and two small genre scenes (*c*. 1762; Turin, Gal. Sabauda) probably designed by Cignaroli to complete one of the King's Brussels sets. After 1754, when Dini left for Venice, both the low-warp and the high-warp looms were directed by Francesco Demignot. In 1766 Vittorio Blanchery (1735–75) made cartoons for additions to the King's 17th-century *Artemisia* set (1773; Turin, Pal. Chiablese), which had been made in Paris. In 1768 a final large historical set from eight designs by Francesco de Mura enlarged by Giovanni Domenico Molinari (1721–93) of the *Story of the Aeneid* (1768–1802; Turin, Pal. Reale) was ordered and woven by the court workshop, which was run by Antonio Bruno (*fl* 1774–1802) from August 1784. Weaving continued even after the workshop was officially closed in 1799, when the King went into exile as French troops approached. For a short period (1823–32) during the 18th-century revival, encouraged by Charles-Felix, King of Sardinia, tapestry weaving began again with two additions, which had been designed *c*. 1791–5 by Lorenzo Pécheux (1729–1821), to the earlier *Story of Alexander* series, and three of the original subjects were replicated. The accession of Charles-Albert, King of Sardinia, to the throne (1831) ended this revival.

BIBLIOGRAPHY
DBI: 'Demignot'
M. Viale Ferrero: *Arazzi italiani* (Milan, 1961), pp. 64–9
——: 'Arazzi', *Turin: Mostra del Barocco piemontese*, 2 vols (exh. cat., ed. V. Viale; Turin, Pal. Madama and Pal. Reale, 1963), pp. 1–27
Schede Vesme: L'arte in Piemonte, 4 vols (Turin, 1963–82), esp. i, pp. 99–108; iv, pp. 1250–58
O. Ferrari: *Arazzi italiani del seicento e settecento* (Milan, 1968), pp. 31–8, 85–98
M. Siniscalco Spinosa: 'Italia', *Gli arazzi*, ed. A. González-Palacios (Milan, 1981), pp. 23–5
La collezione di arazzi della Galleria Sabauda: Note sulla sua formazione (exh. cat. by E. Ragusa and V. Natale, Turin, Gal. Sabauda, 1984)

CANDACE J. ADELSON

IV. Cathedral.

Until the end of the 15th century the episcopal seat of Turin occupied three churches: S Salvatore, S Giovanni Battista and S Maria. The chair of the first Catholic bishop of Turin was probably in S Maria: in September 398 the council of the Milanese archdiocese was held in that basilica. The basilica of S Salvatore stood on the right-hand side of S Maria, under the left aisle of the present cathedral; between the two was the baptismal church of S Giovanni, under the present nave. S Giovanni was probably the cathedral first mentioned by Gregory of Tours (586–7). It was perhaps in Lombard times that it was enlarged and the three churches were joined together; in 680 a new Catholic bishop, Rusticus, was installed; he died in 691. At the beginning of the 11th century Landolfo, Bishop of Turin, made a pilgrimage to Saint-Jean d'Angely in France, to worship some relics, supposedly of St John the Baptist, that were discovered between 1010 and 1021. He obtained one of these, and when he returned to Turin he reconstructed all or part of the church of S Giovanni to produce a nave-and-aisles structure divided by pillars, with a raised presbytery, a timber roof and a porticoed façade. In 1039 there was evidently a *lipsanotheca* (reliquary) in S Giovanni, and documents dated 1425 and 1434 indicate that it still had its baptistery; a crypt was mentioned in 1435, and the bell-tower was built in 1468. The roof was restored between 1353 and 1379, and the apse was reconstructed in 1395, but the rest of the

6. Turin Cathedral by Meo da Caprino, 1491–6; background right, chapel of the Holy Shroud by Guarino Guarini, 1668–82

Romanesque structures survived until between 1490 and 1492, when S Giovanni, S Salvatore and S Maria were all destroyed.

The first stone of the new cathedral was laid in 1491, and it was finished in late 1496 and consecrated in 1505 (see fig. 6). Its Renaissance design was by MEO DA CAPRINO. The three marble portals are either by Meo himself or by the Florentine Sandrino di Giovanni, who also produced a holy-water basin inside the church. The interior has a nave and aisles, the nave arcade piers faced with half columns, which rise to clerestory level, where they support the transverse arches of a seven-bay barrel vault. There is also an apsidal-ended transept and a deep rectangular choir. Works of art in the cathedral include an important full-size 19th-century copy of Leonardo's *Last Supper*; the late 15th-century tomb of *Giovanna d'Orlie*; the altarpiece of *SS Crispin and Crispinian* (now attributed to Giovanni Martino Spanzotti); a *Baptism of Christ* (1508) by Spanzotti, now in the sacristy; and the tomb of *Bishop Claudio of Seyssel* with sculptures (1526) by Matteo Sammicheli, also in the sacristy. From the ancient church of S Salvatore came the tombstone of Bishop Ursicinus, discovered in 1943, and a mosaic pavement from the Romanesque presbytery, discovered in 1909, depicting the Wheel of Fortune (Kitzinger). Numerous marble fragments with mainly geometrical ornamentation evidently came from the three high-medieval churches (Casartelli Novelli, 1974). Annexed to the cathedral is the Chapel of the Holy Shroud (S Sindone; 1668–82; *see* GUARINI, GUARINO, fig. 2, and ITALY, fig. 20), an integral part of the Palazzo Reale.

BIBLIOGRAPHY
F. Rondolino: *Il duomo di Torino illustrato* (Turin, 1898)
S. Solero: *Il duomo di Torino e la R. Cappella della Sindone* (Pinerolo, 1956)

S. Casartelli Novelli: 'Le fabbriche della cattedrale di Torino dall'età paleocristiana all'alto medioevo', *Stud. Med.*, n.s. 2, xi/2 (1970), pp. 617–58

E. Kitzinger: 'World Map and Fortune's Wheel: A Medieval Mosaic Floor in Turin', *Proc. Amer. Philos. Soc.*, 117 (Oct 1973), pp. 344–73

S. Casartelli Novelli, ed.: *La diocesi di Torino* (1974), vi of *Corpus della scultura altomedievale* (Spoleto)

ROBERTO CORONEO

Turini, Baldassare (*b* Pescia, nr Pistoia, 1486; *d* Rome, 15 Oct 1543). Italian courtier and patron. From an early age he was in contact with the Medici family in Florence, and in particular with the young Cardinal Giovanni de' Medici. When Giovanni was elected Pope Leo X in 1513, he made Turini his chamberlain and, in 1518, Papal Datary. Turini lost this position after Leo's death in 1521, but subsequently became Papal Secretary when another Medici pope was elected (Clement VII, 1523); he retained the post for the rest of his life. From 1535 Turini also received the papal ministry of 'Magister Viarum' and was in charge of road-building and maintenance in Rome.

Turini owned a number of houses in Rome and Pescia and was thus probably quite wealthy. From about 1520 he seems to have lived as an agent of the Medici in their unfinished palace in Rome (now Palazzo Madama). He was in contact with many artists, not only on behalf of the Medici but also to secure works of art for himself, including commissions from Francesco Francia and Leonardo da Vinci. On the Janiculum in Rome he commissioned Giulio Romano to build a villa for him (now Villa Lante), which was decorated by Polidoro da Caravaggio, Maturino da Firenze (*d* 1528) and probably Vincenzo Tamagni. Turini was on good terms with Raphael and acted as his testamentary executor, as appears in the inscription on Raphael's tomb in the Pantheon in Rome. He acquired *c.* 1514 his unfinished panel of the *Madonna and Child Enthroned with Saints* (the '*Madonna del baldacchino*', 1508; Florence, Pitti), which was completed by an unknown painter and served as the altarpiece for the Turini Chapel in Pescia Cathedral. The chapel was designed by Giuliano di Baccio d'Agnolo, while the tomb monument with Turini's statue was executed by Raffaele da Montelupo *c.* 1540.

BIBLIOGRAPHY

C. L. Frommel: 'Der römische Palastbau der Hochrenaissance', *Röm. Forsch. Hrg. Bib. Hertziana*, xxi/2 (1973), p. 228

D. R. Coffin: *The Villa in the Life of Renaissance Rome* (Princeton, 1979)

H. Lilius: 'Villa Lante al Gianicolo: L'architettura e la decorazione pittorica', *Acta Inst. Romani Finland.*, x (1981)

G. Stenius: 'Baldassare Turini e le sue case romane sulla base dei documenti', *Opuscula Inst. Romani Finland.*, i (1981), pp. 71–82

C. Conforti: 'Baldassare Turini da Pescia: Profilo di un committente di Giulio Romano architetto e pittore', *Quad. Pal. Te*, 2 (1985), pp. 35–43

C. Conforti: 'Architettura e culto della memoria: La commitenza di Baldassare Turini datario di Leone X', *Baldassare Peruzzi: Pittura, scena e architettura nel cinquecento*, ed. M. Fagliolo and M. Madonna (Rome, 1987), pp. 603–28

J. L. DE JONG

Turin-Milan Hours. Illuminated manuscript begun in the late 14th century and finished in the mid-15th, the work of French and Netherlandish illuminators and one of the major monuments of northern European art. The identification of the various sections (Paris, Bib. N., MS. nouv. acq. lat. 3093; Paris, Louvre, R.F. 2022–5; section in Turin, Bib. N. U., MS. K. IV. 29, destr. 1904; Turin, Mus. Civ. A. Ant., Inv. no. 47) was established by Durrieu (1902), but the history of the manuscript has been interpreted in various ways. The reconstruction presented here accounts for most, if not all, of the complex evidence.

The original manuscript, a Book of Hours expanded by several other offices and prayers and a nearly complete Missal, was commissioned by Jean, Duc de Berry (*see* VALOIS, (3)), in 1389 at the time of his second marriage, to which the decoration alludes. The text was transcribed in the Parisian shop of Jean L'Avenant, the regular purveyor of liturgical books to the royal family. The decoration was begun by a team headed by the MASTER OF THE PAREMENT DE NARBONNE (traditionally called Hand A; *see* MASTERS, ANONYMOUS, AND MONOGRAMMISTS, §I), who was almost certainly the King's painter, Jean d'Orléans. They painted all the marginal decoration in the book, 19 large miniatures with pictures in the initials and *bas-de-pages*, and the smaller miniatures on several more pages. They also made drawings recently discovered by infrared reflectography for other miniatures that were not painted until a later campaign. For some reason, the work was stopped in 1391, probably by the Duke himself.

The Duc de Berry made another attempt to finish the book around 1400. This time he engaged a team of artists (Hands B and C), one of whom made underdrawing identical to the drawing in an armorial of Guelders (Brussels, Bib. Royale Albert 1er, MS. 15652–56) quite probably by Herman Maelwael or his brother Willem Maelwael (*fl* 1382–*c.* 1400), who seem to have left Nijmegen around 1397. Evidently, they followed Willem's son Jean Malouel to France and were probably accompanied by Willem's grandsons, the young Limbourg brothers. Their contribution was mainly painted on the drawings left by the artists of the first campaign, and they too were stopped, probably by the death of one or both of the elderly painters. The Duke ordered work to begin again in 1405, apparently to test the Limbourg brothers (Hand E), whom he appropriated after their first patron, Philip the Bold of Burgundy, died in 1404. The brothers illustrated only two or three unusual prayers, while the Master of the Holy Ghost (Hand D) painted his eponymous Hours in a style related to theirs. The Duke stopped the work when the first 16 gatherings were complete and put the Limbourgs to work on his Belles Heures (New York, Cloisters), now known to have been started around 1406. A calendar was written and bound with these gatherings as a basic Book of Hours, which was listed in the autumn of 1405 in an inventory of the books in the Duke's castle at Mehun-sur-Yèvre, as 'unes très belles heures de Nostre-Dame'. In 1412 the Duke gave the book to his librarian, Robinet d'Etampes, through whose family it descended down to the late 18th century. In the mid-19th century the manuscript was acquired by Baron Alphonse de Rothschild, whose grandson Maurice gave it to the Bibliothèque Nationale in 1952.

The remaining gatherings, containing several miniatures from earlier campaigns, were acquired by John of Bavaria, Bishop Elect of Liège, who spent time in Paris in the autumn of 1405 and whose armorials appear in two miniatures. The style of the oldest of the new miniatures and the fashionable clothing in one of them indicate that

John made an attempt to have the book finished while he was still in Liège, by a team whose leader may have been Hubert van Eyck (Hand G). This artist painted the first unadorned page in the book, which contained an invocation of the holy virgins, and marked the start of the new work by replacing the original marginal decoration with the new border of inhabited vines (Turin, Bib. N. U., MS. K. IV. 29, fol. 59; destr.). This fourth campaign was suspended, probably when John resigned his office in 1417 in order to take control of Holland. In 1420 John settled in The Hague as Count of Holland, with Jan van Eyck as his painter. The pictorial style and the state of the fashions in the atmospheric *Arrival of a Count of Holland* (Turin, Bib. N. U., MS. K.IV.29, fol. 59*v*; destr.), corresponding to those in Dutch and Rhenish manuscripts of the early 1420s, make it almost certain that Jan painted the rest of the group assigned to Hand G, including the *Mass of the Dead* (see fig.). The attribution is supported by the underdrawing of the extant miniatures, which corresponds to that under the earliest of Jan's accepted works. The small amount of work suggests that Jan was stopped by the death of his patron on 6 January 1425.

The gatherings were taken to Bruges, where an unknown patron made a sixth attempt, around 1440, according to the dress. The new team comprised three principal artists associated with van Eyck, headed by the painter (Hand H) responsible for the copy (Philadelphia, PA, Mus. A.) of Jan's *St Francis in Ecstasy* (Turin, Gal. Sabauda). Two were illuminators: one (Hand F) trained in the shop of the Bedford Master and one (Hand I–J) illuminated later manuscripts probably made in Bruges (Brussels, Bib. Royale Albert 1er, MS. 9015; New York, Pierpont Morgan Lib., MS. M. 421). Their copies of whole paintings by van Eyck, including that of a lost *Crucifixion* (Turin, Mus. Civ., Inv. no. 47, fol. 48), and use of motifs probably from patterns in his shop may imply that Jan supervised their work. This time the gatherings were subjected to a major revision, with repainting of some of the 14th-century miniatures, and subjects for the initials and *bas-de-page* chosen according to a new typological programme based on the *Biblia pauperum* and the *Speculum humanae salvationis*, both of which were popular in Bruges at the time. They painted many pictures, but were stopped, probably by Jan's death in 1441. The book was finally completed in a seventh campaign around 1447, for a patron who was close to Philip the Good, if not Philip himself. A calendar was written, and its margins were decorated with ivy copied from that on the other pages. The illustrations were completed by two artists of Bruges (both, Hand K): the painter of the Eyckian *Virgin and Child* (Covarrubias, Mus. Parroq.) and the most active illustrator of the Hours of Folpard van Amerongen (Malibu, Getty Mus., MS. Ludwig, IX 7). They followed the typological programme of the preceding campaign and copied motifs and compositions not only from the Eyckian collection of patterns but also from miniatures already in the book.

The Turin book exercised a wide influence. Already *c*. 1425 illuminators in Utrecht were copying motifs and compositions by Hands G and G[1]. The style of the Master of Zweder van Culemborg was also modelled on Hand G's small-figured atmospheric scenes, creating a manner that re-emerged in the art of Hieronymus Bosch. The manuscript also influenced the southern Netherlands between 1445 and *c*. 1465. Motifs and compositions by Hands H and K as well as by G and G[1] were used by Hand K in his later manuscripts, two of his followers, Willem Vrelant and late members of the Gold Scrolls Group.

The book may have been among the many pawned or sold from the Burgundian library in the 1470s and 1480s. Entering the possession of the Dukes of Savoy, it remained in Turin until the late 17th century, when it was divided in two. The first part, listed in the university library in 1720, was destroyed in the fire of 1904, but the miniatures are known from reproductions in Durrieu (1902). Several leaves were removed from the first section during the division, and four, containing paintings from several campaigns, are known today (Paris, Louvre, RF 2022–2025). The section of Masses went to a Conte d'Aglië, whose heirs sold it around 1800 to Prince Gian Giacomo Trivulzio. With the nationalization of the Trivulzio collection in 1935, the splendid remnant was given to the city of Turin in compensation for the loss of the other half.

See also DRESS, fig. 30.

Turin-Milan Hours: miniature depicting the *Mass of the Dead*, with *bas-de-page* scene showing the *Blessing of the Grave*, attributed to Jan van Eyck, early 1420s (Turin, Museo Civico d'Arte Antica, MS. 47, fol. 116*r*)

BIBLIOGRAPHY

P. Durrieu: *Heures de Turin: Quarante-cinq Feuillets à peinture provenant des Très Belles Heures de Jean de France, duc de Berry* (Paris, 1902); rev. intro. by A. Chatelet (Turin, 1967)

——: 'Les "Très Belles Heures de Notre-Dame" du duc Jean de Berry', *Rev. Archéol.*, 4th ser., xvi (1910), pp. 30–51, 246–79

G. Hulin de Loo: *Heures de Milan* (Brussels and Paris, 1911)

F. Winkler: 'Zwei Utrechter Miniaturisten aus der Frühzeit der holländischen Malerei und die Heures de Turin', *Jb. Ksthist. Samml. Allhöch. Ksrhaus.*, xxxii (1915), pp. 324–33

M. J. Friedländer: *Von van Eyck bis Breughel* (Berlin, 1916)

F. Lyna: 'Les van Eyck et les Heures de Turin et de Milan...', *Bull. Mus. Royaux B.-A.* [Belgique], iv (1955), pp. 7–20 [Miscellanea Erwin Panofsky]

A. Châtelet: 'Les Etapes de l'enluminure des manuscrits dits de Turin et de Milan–Turin', *Rev. des A.*, vi (1956), pp. 299–306

M. Meiss: *French Painting in the Time of Jean de Berry: The Late 14th Century and the Patronage of the Duke* (London, 1967)

C. Sterling: 'Jan van Eyck avant 1432', *Rev. A.*, 33 (1976), pp.7–28

H. Belting and D. Tichberger: *Jan van Eyck als Erzähler* (Worms, 1983)

M. H. Butler and J. R. J. van Asperen de Boer: 'The Examination of the Milan-Turin Hours with Infrared Reflectography: A Preliminary Report', *Le Dessin sous-jacent dans la peinture. Colloque VII. Géographie et chronologie du dessin sous-jacent: Louvain-la-Neuve, 1987*, pp. 55–76

A. H. van Buren: 'Jan van Eyck and the Hours of Turin and Milan, Approached through the Fashions in Dress', *Masters and Miniatures: ACTA of the Congress on Medieval Manuscript Illumination in the Northern Netherlands: Utrecht, 1990*, pp. 221–43

E. König: *Die Très Belles Heures de Notre-Dame des Herzogs Jean von Berry: Kommentar* (Lucerne, 1992) [facs.]

A. Châtelet: *Jean van Eyck, enlumineur* (Strasbourg, 1993)

E. König: *Die Blätter im Louvre und das verlorene Turiner Gebetbuch: Kommentar* (Lucerne, 1994) [facs.]

A. H. van Buren: *The Turin-Milan Hours: Commentary* (Lucerne, 1995) [facs.]

ANNE HAGOPIAN VAN BUREN

Turino di Sano (*fl* Siena, 1382–1427). Italian sculptor and goldsmith. He was married in 1382 and had three sons: Barna, a wood-carver; Lorenzo (*b* 1407; *fl* 1456), a goldsmith; and Giovanni, or Nanni (*c.* 1385–1455), who was also a sculptor and goldsmith. Mentioned in Pisa in 1394, Turino di Sano's earliest documented work in Siena was the design of an engraved seal with the image of the Virgin (1410; untraced). In 1413 he was commissioned to execute a silver statue of *St Crescentius* (untraced) for Siena Cathedral. On 16 April 1417 he and his son Giovanni were authorized to design two bronze reliefs for the Baptistery font (*in situ*), which were not delivered until July 1427. The two reliefs depict the *Birth of St John the Baptist* (*c.* 1417–18) and *St John the Baptist Preaching* (*c.* 1419–20) and are both relatively conservative in design and eclectic in nature. Evident familiarity with current developments in Florence can be seen in the *Birth of St John the Baptist*, which is replete with motifs borrowed from Lorenzo Ghiberti's first set of bronze doors (1403–24) for the Baptistery in Florence (*see* GHIBERTI, (1), fig. 1). The Turinos then worked on three bronze statuettes representing *Virtues* (completed 1431) for the base of the font, the other *Virtues* having been commissioned from Donatello and Goro di Ser Neroccio. These are among the earliest known bronze statuettes of the Renaissance. Contemporary with them are the two bronze putti designed for the tabernacle of the font: more classicizing in style than the *Virtues*, they are less dynamic and ambitious than neighbouring figures by Donatello. They also made the gilded monogram of Jesus (1425) on the façade of the Palazzo Pubblico, Siena. A number of wooden sculptures tentatively attributed to Turino di Sano include two polychromed statues of *St Anthony Abbot* (Siena, S Domenico, and oratory of the Arciconfraternità della Misericordia) and a figure of *St John the Baptist* (Montalcino, Mus. Dioc. A. Sacra).

Giovanni di Turino also worked independently of his father. In 1426 he completed the marble reliefs of *Evangelists*, begun by Giovanni da Imola, for the new pulpit in Siena Cathedral. He made three bronze statuettes of *Prudence*, *Justice* and *Temperance* for the font in the Baptistery, Siena (all 1430–31; *in situ*). The exuberant and decorative use of line in their draperies shows the influence of Donatello and of Ghiberti, of whom, according to Vasari, Giovanni was a 'faithful friend'. He also made the bronze door with a scene of the *Baptism of Christ* for the font. With his brother Lorenzo he made the bronze *She-wolf with Romulus and Remus* (1429–30; Siena, Pal. Pub.). A water-stoup by Giovanni in the Palazzo Pubblico, Siena, dates from 1438.

BIBLIOGRAPHY
Thieme–Becker

G. Vasari: *Vite* (1550, rev. 2/1568); ed. G. Milanesi, iii, pp. 289, 304–7

G. Milanesi: *Documenti per la storia dell'arte senese* (Siena, 1854–6), ii, pp. 62, 67, 86, 129, 131

P. Schubring: *Die Plastik Sienas im Quattrocento* (Berlin, 1907), p. 21

P. Bacci: *Jacopo della Quercia: Nuovi documenti e commenti* (Siena, 1929), pp. 71, 119, 176, 216, 228

I. Machetti: 'Orafi Senesi', *La Diana*, iv (1929), pp. 67–70

E. Carli: *La scultura lignea senese* (Milan, 1951), pp. 64–7

——: *Gli scultori senesi* (Milan, 1980)

ELINOR M. RICHTER

Turino di Vanni (*b* Rigoli, nr Pisa, 1348; *d* Pisa, after 1438). Italian painter. The style of the altarpiece that is probably Turino's earliest extant work, the *Virgin and Child with Saints, Archangels and Angel Musicians* (*c.* 1380; Palermo, Mus. Reg. Sicilia), suggests he was influenced by Sienese painting, but this may have come via Barnaba da Modena, whose *Madonna dei Mercanti* (Pisa, Mus. N. & Civ. S Matteo) is exactly reproduced in the central group. A *Baptism of Christ* of *c.* 1390 (Pisa, Mus. N. & Civ. S Matteo) is closely based on the panel by Niccolò di Pietro Gerini (London, N.G.). In 1397 Turino signed and dated a panel of the *Virgin and Child with Two Saints and Two Blessed* (Pisa, S Paolo a Ripa d'Arno). In this and panels of the *Virgin and Child with Angels* (Paris, Louvre) and the *Virgin Annunciate* and the *Archangel Gabriel* (both *c.* 1395; Pisa, Mus. N. & Civ. S Matteo) Turino's style is more robust. Figures are larger and more ponderous, recalling earlier Florentine painting. Between 1405 and 1419 Turino was probably in Genoa. He was documented there in 1415 and signed a large triptych of the *Virgin and Child with Saints and Angels* (Genoa, S Bartolommeo degli Armeni). This combines a refinement of handling (possibly associated with contemporary Sienese painting) not always seen in Turino's work with a certain clumsiness of design, especially in the predella with *Scenes from the Life of St Bartholomew*. In 1416 Turino executed paintings (lost) for the Palazzo Pubblico in Savona, and in 1419 he restored frescoes in the Camposanto in Pisa. He was still active in 1438. His work is representative of the competence of late 14th-century Pisan art but also of its diminished vitality. The use of common punches suggests he may have shared a workshop with the Master of the Universitas Aurificum (Frinta).

BIBLIOGRAPHY

A. Da Morrona: *Pisa illustrata nelle arti del disegno* (Pisa, 1787–93)
R. van Marle: *Italian Schools*, v (1924), pp. 240–53
G. Vigni: *Pittura pisana del due e trecento* (Palermo, 1950)
E. Carli: *La pittura pisana del trecento*, ii (Milan, 1961), pp. 76–87 [good pls]
F. R. Shapley: *Paintings from the Samuel H. Kress Collection*, i (London, 1966), p. 74
B. Berenson: *Central and North Italian Schools*, i (1968), p. 434
M. S. Frinta: 'A Seemingly Florentine Yet Not Really Florentine Altarpiece', *Burl. Mag.*, cxvii (1975), pp. 527–35

JOHN RICHARDS

Turkeshi, Muharrem (*b* Tiranë, 25 May 1933). Albanian sculptor. From 1953 to 1963 he worked in the Porcelain Workshops [now the Porcelain Factory] in Tiranë. The influence of his traditional training is clearly evident in the modelling of his maiolica and terracotta pieces of the mid-1960s which have a primitive realism (e.g. *Mälesorja e Razmës* [The woman highlander from Razma], 1956; priv. col.). After graduating from the Department of Sculpture at the Higher Institute of Arts in Tiranë (1963–8) he continued to create works in majolica and terracotta, as individual pieces and for series production. A central theme in his work is the daily life and commonsense philosophy of the Albanian peasantry, and his main body of work is distinguished by a fusion of fable and real life coupled with an ability to convey the best values of folk culture (e.g. *Mundja popullore* [Folk wrestling], 1983; Tiranë, A.G.). Humour and irony are evident in such sculptures as *Gjeli që kërkon të matet me diellin* [The cock that pretended to measure itself against the sun] (1983; priv. col.). As well as sculptures, he made traditional plates and dishes, sets of tableware, ashtrays and pitchers. He has also produced large mural compositions using terracotta tiles, for example *Dasma dibrane* [The wedding of the Dibra region] for the interior of the Historical Museum, Peshkopi.

BIBLIOGRAPHY

K. Krisiko: 'Qeramika artistike në arkitekturë' [Artistic ceramics in architecture], *Drita* (23 Nov 1980)
S. Shijaku: 'Pasioni i artistit për baltën' [The passion of an artist for clay], *Shqipëria*, 9 (1985), pp. 26–7

GJERGJ FRASHËRI

Turkestan [formerly Shavgar, Yasi]. Town in Kazakhstan, north of Tashkent. Located at a ford across one of the tributaries of the middle Syr River, the town was known as Shavgar (Shāvaghar) to medieval Arab geographers, and its remains lie 8 km east of the modern town at the site of Chuy-tobe. It was the administrative and economic centre of the region until the 13th century, when the name disappeared and was replaced by Yasi. Yasi was the home of Ahmad Yasavi (*d* 1166), a Sufi shaykh responsible for the conversion of the Turks to Islam. His epithet, *ḥazrat-i turkistān* (Pers. 'holy man of Turkestan'), has given the modern town its name. In 1399 Timur ordered a magnificent mausoleum to be constructed over the shaykh's grave (*see also* ISLAMIC ART, §II, 6(i)(b) and fig. 50). The building is a compact rectangle (65.5×46.5 m). On the central axis a huge vaulted iwan leads to a central square room covered by a *muqarna* dome. Behind lies the mausoleum, which is also covered by a stunning *muqarna* vault and protected by a blue-tiled melon-shaped dome. The sides of the building are filled with subsidiary service and residential

rooms, including a mosque, kitchen, bath, library and meditation rooms. The core of the building was completed by 1394 and the upper part and the brick and glazed-tile revetment added in a second campaign (1397–9), but the massive entrance portal on the south was never finished. The rich collection of metalwares made for the shrine included an elephantine cast-bronze basin (1399; *see* CENTRAL ASIA, fig. 63) and six inlaid brass oil lamps of baluster shape (h. 900 mm; three *in situ*, others St Petersburg, Hermitage, and Paris, Louvre). Rabiʿa Sultan Begum (*d* 1485), daughter of the Timurid ruler Ulughbeg, added an octagonal mausoleum (diam. 8.55 m; destr.) to the south of the shrine. The shrine had deteriorated by the late 19th century when it was used as a military depot, but it was restored in the 1950s.

BIBLIOGRAPHY

Enc. Islam/2: 'Aḥmad Yasawī'
M. E. Masson: *Mavzoley Khodzha Akhmeda Yasevi* [The mausoleum of Khwaja Ahmad Yasevi] (Tashkent, 1930)
A. A. Ivanov: 'O bronzovykh izdeliyakh kontsa XIV v. iz mavzoleya Khodzha Akhmeda Yasevi' [Bronzewares of the late 14th century from the mausoleum of Khwaja Ahmad Yasevi], *Srednyaya Aziya i eyo sosedi* [Central Asia and its neighbours], ed. B. A. Litvinskiy (Moscow, 1981), pp. 68–84
L. Iu. Man'kovskaya: 'Towards the Study of Forms in Central Asian Architecture at the End of the Fourteenth Century: The Mausoleum of Khvāja Ahmad Yasavi', trans. L. Golombek, *Iran*, xxiii (1985), pp. 109–27
L. Golombek and D. Wilber: *The Timurid Architecture of Iran and Turan* (Princeton, 1988), pp. 284–8, no. 53
B. T. Tuyakbayeva: *Epigraficheskiy dekor arkhitekturnogo kompleksa Akhmeda Yasevi* [Epigraphic decor of the architectural complex of Ahmad Yasavi] (Alma-Ata, 1989)
Timur and the Princely Vision (exh. cat. by T. W. Lentz and G. D. Lowry, Washington, DC, Sackler Gal.; Los Angeles, CA, Co. Mus. A.; 1989)
R. Z. Burnasheva: 'Nekotorye svedeniya o monetnom dvore Yasy-Turkestana, XIII–XVII vv.' [Information on the mint of Yasi-Turkestan, 13th–17th century], *Izvestiya Akad. Nauk Kazakh. SSSR: Seriya Obshchestvennaya*, i (1992), pp. 18–27

A. A. IVANOV

Turkey, Republic of [Türkiye Cumhuriyeti]. Republic in the Middle East that lies 95% in Anatolia (Asia) and 5% in eastern Thrace (Europe), with its capital at Ankara. Turkey has an area of *c.* 779,452 sq. km, bordered in the west by Bulgaria, Greece and the Aegean Sea, in the south by Iraq, Syria and the Mediterranean Sea, in the north by the Black Sea and in the east by Georgia, Armenia and Iran. The economy is based on agriculture, with a significant growth in industrial output since World War II. The land is rich in minerals, and oil was found in south-east Anatolia in the 1960s. Tourism is an important additional source of revenue. The population of *c.* 56,475,035 (1990 estimate) is 99% Muslim, the majority being Sunnis. Over 90% of the population has Turkish as its mother tongue. The principal linguistic minorities are the Kurds and Arabs. Kurdish is the mother tongue of *c.* 7% of the population, spoken predominantly in eastern and south-eastern regions; Arabic is the mother tongue of *c.* 1% of the population. There are also minority communities of Armenians, Greeks and Jews.

Turkey formed part of the OTTOMAN empire from 1281 to 1923, with its capital at Istanbul from 1453. From 1839 the modernization of Turkey began under Abdülmecid (*reg* 1839–61) with a series of judicial, educational and fiscal measures known as the Tanzimat (Reorganization) reforms. After the collapse of the Ottoman empire during World War I, when its territories were occupied and partitioned, there emerged an independence movement led by Mustafa Kemal (later known as Atatürk, 'Father of the Turks') and in 1923 the Turkish Republic was proclaimed. The following year Atatürk abolished the Ottoman Caliphate (religious head), and then proceeded to transform Turkey by such measures as abandoning Arabic for Latin script, abolishing titles and ordering Turks to wear European clothes. On his death in 1938 Atatürk was succeeded by Ismet Inönü (*reg* 1938–50), and in 1950 the Democratic Party under Celal Bayar came to power. On the intervention of the military in 1960 a new constitution was accepted, which gave the presidency a titular role and greater power to the prime minister. After a series of coalition governments in the 1970s, the military again intervened (1980) and a new constitution in 1982 gave more power to the president. This article covers the art produced in Turkey in the 20th century. For the earlier history *see* ANATOLIA, ANCIENT; ANCIENT NEAR EAST; EARLY CHRISTIAN AND BYZANTINE ART; and ISLAMIC ART.

1. Architecture. 2. Painting and calligraphy. 3. Sculpture. 4. Decorative arts. 5. Art education. 6. Museums and galleries. 7. Archaeological sites.

1. ARCHITECTURE. Throughout the 19th century European architectural ideas were introduced to Istanbul (*see* ISTANBUL, §I, 5), especially in the buildings by the BALYAN family of architects. European architects were also commissioned, and during the reign of Abdülhamid II (*reg* 1876–1908) they taught architecture at the Academy of Fine Arts (founded 1883) and the College of Civil Engineering (founded 1884). Late Ottoman architecture

1. Emin Onat and Orhan Arda: Atatürk Mausoleum, Ankara, 1944–53

in Istanbul became dependent on Western capital, technology and ideas. The Public Debts Administration building (1899) by the French architect A. Vallaury and the Sirkeci Railway Terminal (1890) by the German architect A. Jachmund combined Neo-classical and Islamic elements. This revivalist idiom continued in the early 20th century with the eclectic buildings of the Turkish architects VEDAT and KEMALETTIN and became known as the First National Architectural style.

From the late 1920s under the Republican government new styles emerged, inspired by European Modernism. Such European architects as Ernst Egli, CLEMENS HOLZMEISTER, Hermann Jansen and Theodor Post worked in ANKARA and influenced the appearance of the new capital. Post's Ministry of Health building (1927–30) in Ankara stood at the forefront of this development, presenting angular masses and a façade with little ornamentation. In 1931 the first Turkish architectural journal, *Mimar* ('Architect'; from 1935 named *Arkitekt*), was founded, and it published work in the modern style by Turkish architects. During the 1930s, with the encouragement of the Republican government, monumental buildings inspired by German and Italian architecture were commissioned. This phase culminated with Bedri Uçar's Directorate of Turkish State Railways building (1938–41) in Ankara.

From the late 1930s, however, there was a shift in emphasis—known as the Second National Architectural style—as architects began to express in their work an awareness of indigenous Turkish culture, but without a total rejection of modernism. SEDAD HAKKI ELDEM emerged as the influential voice in the defence of local styles over international ones and incorporated local features in his architecture, although some of his designs retained a monumentalism reminiscent of the 1930s. In 1940 Eldem published 'Yerli mimariye doğru' ('Towards local architecture'), which contained his thoughts about a national idiom. The main building of this period, the Atatürk Mausoleum in Ankara (1944–53; see fig. 1) by EMIN ONAT and Orhan Arda, also expressed the preoccupation with evolving a national style.

In the 1950s American and European architectural influences became important in Turkey. The Hilton Hotel (1952) in Istanbul by the American firm SKIDMORE, OWINGS & MERRILL with the collaboration of Eldem was influential as an example of the International Style. A partial liberalization of the Turkish economy led to rapid industrial development and urban growth, especially in Istanbul, Ankara and Izmir. Skyscrapers were introduced into city centres, and unplanned shanty towns developed around cities. From the 1960s increasing use was made of new materials and construction techniques. The campus buildings of the Middle East Technical University (early 1960s) in Ankara by Günay Çilingiroğlu, Altuğ Çinici and Behruz Çinici (*b* 1932), for example, introduced an extensive use of exposed concrete. There also developed a movement towards architectural integration in urban areas. Eldem's Social Security Complex (1962–4) in the Zeyrek district of Istanbul referred to Ottoman architectural traditions by employing corbels, cantilevers and eaves, while retaining a modern structure. Other influential buildings during this period included TURGUT CANSEVER and Ertur Yener's Turkish Historical Society building in

2. Turgut Cansever and Ertur Yener: Turkish Historical Society building, Ankara, 1966

Ankara (1966; see fig. 2), which has a plain exterior and protected interior space, and Sargin and Böke's monumental Iş Bankası Tower (1976) in Ankara. Some buildings displayed an articulation of small fragmented masses (e.g. Çilingiroğlu and Muhlis Tunca's Tercümen Newspaper Offices (1974), Istanbul, while others remained compact (e.g. Cengis Bektaş's Turkish Language Society building, Ankara, 1972–8).

Vernacular architecture in Turkey has several regional variations (*see* VERNACULAR ARCHITECTURE, §II, 7(vii)). The traditional Ottoman house, made of stone or brick on the ground floor and with an upper storey made of a timber frame with stone or brick infill, was diffused from Istanbul throughout the Balkans and Anatolia. Along the Black Sea coast are houses made of wood from the foundations up, with clay packed between beams and roofed with tile or shingle. Wooden houses are also made of rubble packed between laths attached to wooden posts. Although wooden houses can often withstand earthquakes, they are subject to fire. In central and eastern Anatolia houses are built of mud-brick or stone with flat roofs or domes, and may be partially sunk below the ground. Such traditional building techniques, however,

were eclipsed in the 20th century by the introduction of new materials. There also developed an awareness of the need to preserve the architectural heritage and some conservation areas were set up (e.g. at Eyüp in Istanbul).

2. PAINTING AND CALLIGRAPHY. As early as the 18th century European artistic conventions were incorporated in Ottoman miniature painting, and murals depicting landscapes and still-life subjects inspired by European work began to be executed. European conventions in drawing and painting were introduced to the curricula at the Artillery School (1793) and the Military Academy (1835) in Istanbul, and also at high schools (e.g. the Darüssafaka School, Istanbul, founded in 1873). From the 1830s some Turkish students were sent to Paris for their studies. It was as a consequence of these initiatives that easel painting developed in Turkey in the late 19th century.

Among the Turkish painters who were at the forefront of this development were AHMET ALİ and SÜLEYMAN SEYYIT, both of whom studied in Paris in the 1860s; their work consisted predominantly of landscape and still-life paintings. A particularly influential figure was OSMAN HAMDI, who resided in Paris for 11 years and embarked on portrait paintings and figural compositions (*see* ISLAMIC ART, §VIII, 11(ii)). In 1881 he became the director of the Imperial Ottoman Museum at the Çinili Kiosk (Tiled Kiosk), Istanbul, and, two years later, founded and became the first director of the Academy of Fine Arts, Istanbul. At the Academy, which had departments of architecture, sculpture and painting, Europeans were employed on the staff.

In the early 20th century the Çallı Group of painters was prominent in Istanbul, named after IBRAHIM ÇALLI, a graduate of the Academy who trained in Paris and returned to teach at the Academy in 1914. They were inspired by Impressionism and were notable for their landscapes (especially of views along the Bosporus), still-lifes and portraits. Other painters in the group included NAZMI ZIYA GÜRAN, who later became director of the Academy, Feyhaman Duran (1886–1970), Namık Ismail (1890–1935), Avni Lifij (1889–1927) and Hikmet Onat (1886–1977). They formed the ASSOCIATION OF OTTOMAN PAINTERS (renamed the Association of Turkish Painters in 1921), wrote about art in a new monthly magazine called *Naşir-i Efkâr* ('Promoter of Ideas') and exhibited their work annually at the Galatasaray High School, Istanbul. In 1923 they were responsible for the first exhibition of paintings in Ankara.

After World War I younger Turkish painters turned away from the concerns of the Çallı Group to express ideas inspired by the Republic. The Turkish War of Independence resulted in a new consciousness of Anatolian culture, and paintings of this period included scenes of peasants and rural life. Ideas from Europe, however, continued to permeate the work of Turkish artists who trained in France and Germany, such as ALI ÇELEBI and Ahmet ZEKI KOCAMEMI, both of whom studied in the workshop of Hans Hofmann in Munich in the 1920s, and Malik Aksel (1901–87), who studied in Berlin (1928–32).

The formation of the Association of Independent Painters and Sculptors in Istanbul in 1928 was important for the propagation of new ideas. Inspired by developments in European art, the artists in the Association advocated working independently and were unconcerned about creating a common style. The main members of the Association included Çelebi, Kocamemi, REFIK EPIKMAN, NURULLAH BERK and Mahmut Cuda (*b* 1904). In 1933 the D Group was formed in Istanbul by the painters Berk, CEMAL TOLLU, Abidin Dino (1913–93), Zeki Faik Izer (1905–88) and Elif Naci (1898–1987), and the sculptor Zühtü Müridoğlu. Later SABRI BERKEL and BEDRI RAHMI EYÜBOĞLU joined this group. They welcomed ideas from Europe with the result that Cubist, Constructivist and Expressionist ideas entered Turkish painting. TURGUT ZAIM, who painted distinctive scenes of peasant life, also exhibited with the D Group.

During the 1930s there was an increase in exhibitions and articles on art, which encouraged debate. The presence of the French artist Léopold Lévy in Istanbul from 1937 to 1949 as head of the department of painting at the Academy also invigorated Turkish art. Art reflecting Republican ideals was encouraged by the government. In 1933 the tenth anniversary of the Republic was marked by the exhibition *Revolution and the Arts*, held by the Ministry of Education in Ankara. The subjects exhibited included portraits of Atatürk, commemorations of the War of Independence and the modernization of Turkey. In 1939 Inönü's government organized in Ankara the First State Exhibition of Painting and Sculpture, which became an annual event. Folklore themes in painting were also prominent and between 1938 and 1944 were promoted by the government policy of sending artists to the provinces.

By this time Atatürk's decision in 1928 to replace Arabic script with the Latin alphabet had driven a wedge between the new culture of the Republic and the old Ottoman traditions. The art of calligraphy was an immediate casualty. Such masters of the art as HAMID AYTAÇ, HALIM OZYAZICI and NECMEDDIN OKYAY, however, did pass on their knowledge to such younger enthusiasts as Ali Alpaslan (*b* 1925), Hasan Çelebi (*b* 1937), Bekir Pektin (*b* 1913) and others. Some of the traditions of Turkish calligraphy were also kept alive in Egypt and Iraq.

After World War II Turkish painters embraced a variety of styles and groups were formed for the pursuit of different aims. The New Group, founded in Istanbul in 1941, favoured social themes and included such artists as NURI IYEM. From 1947 to 1955 the Group of Ten in Istanbul, led by Eyüboğlu, looked to Anatolian folk arts in the search for a native idiom. In 1959 the New Wing Group was formed in Istanbul; led by Ibrahim Balaban (*b* 1921), it continued many of the ideas of the New Group concerning social themes. An abstract movement in Turkish painting developed in the 1950s, deriving some of its inspiration from calligraphy. Berkel, Izer and Abidin Elderoğlu (1901–74) were important in this area. The abstract trend reached a peak in the 1960s, continuing in the work of Adnan Turani (*b* 1925) and Adnan Çoker (*b* 1925). From the 1970s such styles as Pop art and Hyper Realism influenced Turkish painting. There have also been important Turkish artists active largely outside the country during the 20th century, such as FIKRET MUALLA, FAHRELNISSA ZEID and Burham Doğançay (*b* 1925).

3. SCULPTURE. Under the influence of European art, sculpture developed from the late 19th century. A pioneer in this field was Yervant Oskan (1855–1914), who studied in Rome and taught at the Academy of Fine Arts in Istanbul. He was followed by his pupil Ihsan Özsoy (1867–1944), who trained in Paris, and Mehmet Mahir Tomruk (1885–1954) and Nejat Sirel (1897–1959), both of whom studied at the Akademie der Bildenden Künste in Munich. Sculpture in Turkey grew in importance after the creation of the Republic, when monuments and statues were commissioned to celebrate Atatürk and the War of Independence. Various sculptors were active in this domain, including RATIP AŞIR ACUDOĞU, ALI HADI BARA, HÜSEYIN GEZER, ZÜHTÜ MÜRIDOĞLU, Sabiha Bengutas (*b* 1910), Nusret Suman (1905–78) and Kenan Yontunç (*b* 1904). The appointment of the German sculptor Rudolf Belling as head of the statue department at the Academy of Fine Arts in Istanbul in 1937 ensured that Western influences continued to permeate Turkish work. Belling, who remained in Turkey until 1954, trained such sculptors as Gezer, Ilhan Koman (1921–86) and Hüseyin Özkan (*b* 1909). After 1949 non-figural sculpture began to dominate the output of Hadi Bara, and minimal art was a source of inspiration for Şadi Çalik (1917–79). In 1961

Kuzgun Acar (1928–76) won first prize at the Paris Young Artist Competition.

4. DECORATIVE ARTS. Turkish crafts were affected by a range of factors, including the departure of Armenians—whose traditional skills included metalworking—the emergence of new forms of patronage under the Republic and the adoption of modern industrial techniques. Carpet production remained buoyant, although vegetable dyes were replaced by industrial dyes at the turn of the century and there was a growth of factory workshops. Commercial carpets for merchants were made on upright looms in large factories in such centres as Kayseri, Isparta and Izmir. While the production of knotted-pile carpets was affected by market demands, flatweave techniques—which include the kilim, cicim, zili and sumak—were less affected, because European influence was minimal and the market exerted less pressure. Apart from the kilim, flatweave techniques have been traditionally used to produce such items as saddle bags, bolster and door covers and hearth cushions.

Pottery has continued to be made in such traditional centres as Çanakkale and Kütahya and has been encouraged at such new locations as the Academy of Fine Arts, Istanbul, where ceramic studios were established in 1929. There has also emerged a number of artist–ceramicists, several of whom have won large-scale commissions for public buildings. Füreya Koral (b 1910) carried out work

in 1954 at the Hilton Hotel, Istanbul, and Bedri Rahmi Eyüboğlu produced a 227 sq. m mosaic panel for the façade of the Turkish Pavilion at the Exposition Universelle et Internationale in Brussels in 1958, which won a gold medal; he also worked on ceramic and stained-glass wall panels. Modern industrial demands were met by Atilla Galatalı (b 1936), who designed objects for mass production at the Eczacibasi Ceramic Factory. Other artist–ceramicists include Sadi Diren (b 1927), Candeğer Furtun (b 1936), Güngör Güner (b 1941) and Melike Kurtiç (b 1930); in many cases their works can be regarded as sculpture.

5. ART EDUCATION. The Academy of Fine Arts (Sanayi-i Nefise Mektebi) in Istanbul, which opened in 1883 (now a faculty of Mimar Sinan University), remains one of the main teaching institutions in Turkey for architecture, painting, sculpture and other arts (see ISTANBUL, §II, 3). A separate Academy of Fine Arts for Women (Inas Sanayi-i Nefise Mektebi; see fig. 3), directed by the painter Mihri Müşfik (1886–1954), opened in 1914, and the two merged in 1926. The Academy remained the only institution for European-style art education in Turkey until 1932, when an art department was formed at the Gazi Teachers' College in Ankara. Architecture, however, was also taught at the College of Civil Engineering (Hendese-i Mülkiye Mektebi; now Istanbul Technical University), while Yıldız Technical College (Yıldız Teknik Okulu;

3. Ömer Adil: *Ladies' Painting Atelier*, oil on canvas, 0.81×1.14 m, *c.* 1921 (Istanbul, Mimar Sinan University, Museum of Painting and Sculpture)

founded 1911) established a department of architecture in 1942.

The dual monopoly of the Academy of Fine Arts and the Gazi Teachers' College for education in the arts lasted until the 1950s, when there was a further expansion: the State School of Applied Arts, Istanbul, for example, opened in 1957. In the late 20th century art was taught at a number of universities, including Ege University, Izmir; Hacettepe University, Ankara; and Anadolu University, Eskişehir. There were also private ateliers for practising artists. Meanwhile, the promotion of research into all aspects of Turkish culture was encouraged by the founding of the Turkish Cultural Research Institute in Ankara in 1961, and a Research Centre for Islamic History, Art and Culture (IRCICA) was founded in Istanbul in 1979.

6. MUSEUMS AND GALLERIES. The museum movement began in 1846 when Ahmet Fethi Pasha, the Imperial Marshal of the Arsenal, collected weapons, coins and antiquities at the church of St Irene in the first courtyard of Topkapı Palace, Istanbul. In 1876 the antiquities collection was transferred to the Çinili Kiosk at Topkapı, which became the Imperial Ottoman Museum, while St Irene became a military museum. The Imperial Ottoman Museum developed rapidly after Osman Hamdi was appointed director in 1881. In 1883 he put into effect an order against the traffic in antiquities and began to organize excavations. Upon his death in 1910 his brother HALIL EDHEM ELDEM was appointed director. In the late 20th century three museums were at this location: the Archaeological Museum, the Museum of the Ancient Orient and the Museum of Turkish Ceramics in the Çinili Kiosk. The Topkapı Palace, with its superb collections of Islamic art and manuscripts, Chinese and Japanese porcelains and European items, opened as a museum in 1924 (see ISTANBUL, §III, 13(iv)).

During the 20th century many other museums were established in Turkey. Those in Istanbul included the Islamic Museum founded in 1914 (at the Süleymaniye complex), which reopened in 1927 as the Museum of Turkish and Islamic Art (Türk ve Islam Eserleri Müzesi) at the Ibrahim Pasha Sarayı; the Hagia Sophia Museum (opened 1935); and Christ the Saviour in Chora (Kariye Camii), a Byzantine church with mosaics and wall paintings (see ISTANBUL, §III, 3, and WALL PAINTING, colour pl. II, fig. 1). The Museum of Painting and Sculpture (Resim ve Heykel Müzesi; founded 1937) in Istanbul contains 19th- and 20th-century Turkish paintings and sculptures. In Ankara the Museum of Anatolian Civilizations, which has an important archaeological collection, and the Ethnographical Museum were founded in the 1920s. Many cities now have museums of folk art, while archaeological museums can be found at a range of cities and sites. A Museum of Turkish and Islamic Art was founded in 1975 at Bursa, and Islamic art is displayed in museums at Konya. In Istanbul the Vakıflar Carpet Museum opened in 1979 and the Vakıflar Kilim and Flat-Woven Rug Museum in 1982, both under the General Directorate of Pious Foundations.

Banks and major companies have also funded and acquired art, sometimes for investment. The Iş Bankası, the first national bank of the Republican era, began to collect the work of contemporary artists in the 1920s and by the late 20th century had a rich collection of modern art. Commercial galleries also opened in the major cities in the late 20th century and various private museums were created, such as the Sadberk Hanım Museum at Istanbul and Sabancı Museum at Emirgan.

7. ARCHAEOLOGICAL SITES. Turkey has a vast range of archaeological sites that date from prehistoric times to the Ottoman period. As early as 1834 CHARLES TEXIER drew attention to the ruins at BOĞAZKÖY, later identified as the site of the Hittite capital Hattusass. In 1835 the Hittite site of ALACA HÖYÜK was discovered by William Hamilton; like Boğazköy, it has yielded important objects of art. TROY, PERGAMON and CARCHEMISH were excavated from the 1870s, followed by ZINCIRLI and SAKÇA GÖZÜ (from 1908). After World War I there were foreign and Turkish excavations at a range of sites in Anatolia, including KÜLTEPE and ALIŞAR HÜYÜK. The founding of the Turkish Historical Society in Ankara in 1931, and the Faculty of Languages, History and Geography in 1936, encouraged archaeological research among Turkish scholars. In 1933 a Department of Archaeology was established in the University of Istanbul. After World War II there were further archaeological discoveries in Anatolia. The settlement of KARATEPE, discovered in 1946, yielded evidence on late Hittite architecture and sculpture, and work at the sites of HACILAR and ÇATAL HÜYÜK shed new light on the Neolithic period.

BIBLIOGRAPHY

A. Thalasso: 'L'Art ottoman: Les Peintres de Turquie (Paris, 1910)
S. H. Eldem: 'Yerli mimariye doğru' [Towards local architecture], Arkitekt, 3–4 (1940)
K. Özbel: El Sanatları (Ankara, 1945–9)
N. Berk: La Peinture turque (Ankara, 1950)
R. O. Arık: L'Histoire et l'organisation des musées turcs (Istanbul, 1953)
M. Cezar: Sanatta batı'ya açılış ve Osman Hamdi [Western trends in art and Osman Hamdi] (Istanbul, 1971)
E. Kortan: Türkiye'de mimarlık hareketleri ve eleştirisi, 1950–1960 [Architectural movements in Turkey and their criticism, 1950–1960] (Ankara, 1971)
N. Berk: Istanbul Resim ve Heykel Müzesi [The Museum of Painting and Sculpture, Istanbul] (Istanbul, 1972) [Eng. and Turk. text]
N. Berk and H. Gezer: 50 Yılın Türk resim ve heykeli [Fifty years of Turkish painting and sculpture] (Istanbul, 1973)
M. Tapan and M. Sözen: 50 Yılın Türk mimarisi [Fifty years of Turkish architecture] (Istanbul, 1973)
M. Önder: The Museums of Turkey and Examples of the Masterpieces in the Museums (Ankara, 1977, rev. 2/1983)
W. T. Ziemba, A. Akatay and S. L. Schwartz: Turkish Flat Weaves: An Introduction to the Weaving and Culture of Anatolia (London, 1979)
Rugs of the Peasants and Nomads of Anatolia (exh. cat. by W. Brüggemann and H. Böhmer, trans. E. G. Herzog, G. M. Holmes and G. E. Holmes; Frankfurt am Main, Mus. Ksthandwk; Munich, Staatl. Mus. Vlkerknd.; Krefeld, Dt. Textilmus.; Lübeck, Mus. Kst & Kultgesch., 1980–82)
Ş. Rado: Türk hattatları [Turkish calligraphers] (Istanbul, n.d.)
B. B. Acar: Kilim—Cicim—Zili—Sumak: Turkish Flatweaves (Istanbul, 1983)
N. Berk and K. Özsezgin: Cumhuriyet donemi: Turk resimi [The Republican period: Turkish painting] (Ankara, 1983)
Discoveries from Kurdish Looms (exh. cat. by J. R. Perry and others, Evanston, IL, Northwestern U.; Mary & Leigh Block Gal., 1983–4)
Z. Güvemli: The Sabancı Collection of Paintings (Istanbul, 1984) [Eng. and Turk. texts]
R. Holod and A. Evin, eds: Modern Turkish Architecture (Philadelphia, 1984)
M. Sözen: Cumhuriyet dönemi: Turk Mimarlığı (1923–1983) [The Republican period: Turkish architecture] (Ankara, 1984)
O. Küçükerman: The Art of Glass and Traditional Turkish Glassware (Ankara, 1985) [Eng. and Turk. texts]

Z. Çelik: *The Remaking of Istanbul: Portrait of an Ottoman City in the Nineteenth Century* (Seattle and London, 1986)

G. Renda and C. M. Kortepeter, eds: *The Transformation of Turkish Culture: The Atatürk Legacy* (Princeton, 1986)

S. Tansuğ: *Çağdaş Türk sanatı* [Contemporary Turkish art] (Istanbul, 1986)

S. Bozdoğan, S. Özkan and E. Yenal: *Sedad Eldem: Architect in Turkey* (Singapore, 1987)

W. Eagleton: *An Introduction to Kurdish Rugs and Other Weavings* (Buckhurst Hill, 1988)

G. Renda and others: *A History of Turkish Painting* (Geneva, Seattle and London, 1988)

S. Başkan: *Contemporary Turkish Painters* (Ankara, 1991)

S. Bozdoğan: 'Modernity in the Margins: Architecture and Ideology in Early Republican Turkey', *Proceedings of the XVIII International Congress of the History of Art: Berlin, 1993*

H. Glassie: *Turkish Traditional Art Today* (Bloomington and Indianapolis, IN, 1994)

Turki, Hedi (*b* Tunis, 15 May 1922). Tunisian painter. He was educated at the Lycée Carnot in Tunis from 1936 to 1940, participating in his first group exhibition in 1943, and for two months in 1951 attended art courses at the Académie de la Grande Chaumière in Paris. In 1956 he received a grant to study at the Accademia di Belle Arti in Rome, returned to Tunis in 1957 and taught drawing at the Lycée Technique Emile Loubet. The same year he also visited China, Central Europe and Russia. In 1959 he visited the USA for the first time, where he attended Columbia University, NY, and discovered the work of contemporary American painters. After 1963 he taught at the Ecole des Beaux-Arts, Tunis. He visited Nigeria in 1977, South Korea in 1978, and made a second journey to the USA in 1979, where he met George Segal in California. His early paintings were in a naturalistic style, but after his first visit to the USA he reacted against the pictorialism and folkloric representations of the Ecole de Tunis and pioneered abstract painting in Tunisia. Influenced by the work of Jackson Pollock and Mark Rothko, he evolved a style that was characterized by complex colour compositions within linear or grid frameworks. His abstract paintings include *Organ of Light* (1984; Tunis, Cent. A. Vivant) and *Memory of Finland* (1984–5; Tunis, Cent. A. Vivant).

BIBLIOGRAPHY

Six Peintres tunisiens contemporains (exh. cat., Paris, Mus. A. Mod. Ville Paris; Villeneuve d'Ascq, Mus. A. Mod.; Paris, Mus. N. A. Afr. & Océan.; 1986–7), pp. 64–70

S. J. VERNOIT

Turkish Fine Arts Society. *See* ASSOCIATION OF OTTOMAN PAINTERS.

Turkmenistan. Central Asian republic on the east side of the Caspian Sea, bounded by Kazakhstan to the north-west, Uzbekistan to the north and east, Afghanistan to the south-east and Iran to the south, where the Kopet Dag Mountains form a geographical barrier (see fig. 1). The Karakum Desert occupies much of the country and the Amu River constitutes an approximate or actual north-east boundary for much of its length. The capital, ASHKHABAD, situated close to the southern border with Iran and on both the Transcaspian Railway and the Karakumskiy Canal, is almost entirely a 20th-century city following a sequence of devastating earthquakes. As for most of its history Turkmenistan formed part of the wider nomadic and oasis-based culture of Central Asia, both before and after the Islamicization of the region, for the arts of the period prior to 1800 *see* CENTRAL ASIA, §I, and ISLAMIC ART. This article covers the art of Turkmenistan after 1800.

1. Introduction. 2. Architecture. 3. Painting and sculpture. 4. Decorative arts.

1. INTRODUCTION. Archaeological evidence indicates settlement at key sites in the 5th millennium BC (ALTYN TEPE, Namazga I). MERV, one of the great Central Asian oases, was a major centre by the start of the 1st millennium BC. Khwarazm, centred on Urgench (now Kunya-Urgench) was a prosperous agricultural area from antiquity. Thereafter the territory covered by modern Turkmenistan was successively part of a number of empires starting with the Achaemenid (6th–4th century BC). That of Alexander the Great (*reg* 336–323 BC) and the SELEUCID dynasty (late 4th century–3rd century BC) followed. The Parthians (with their capital at NISA) held power from the 3rd century BC to the 3rd century AD, during which time arose the various strands of the SILK ROUTE linking China with the eastern Mediterranean lands, one of which crossed the Karakum Desert via Merv. From the 3rd century AD the area was dominated by the Sasanians, who held power despite nomadic incursions—the Huns (Hepthalites) drove them back to the Kopet Dag Mountains in the 5th century—until Merv fell to the Arabs in 651.

The region passed into the control of Islamic dynasties, some ruling from afar: the Umayyads and Abbasids, with governors based at Merv; the Samanids (with their capital Bukhara in Uzbekistan); the Qarakhanids (*reg* AD 992–1211) and the Saljuks, who under Sultan Sanjar (*reg* 1118–57) made Merv the capital of one of the most powerful Islamic empires. After his death the city was annexed by the Khwarazmshahs ruling from Urgench, the nominal vassals of the Qara Khitay (Western Liao) of northern China. Turkic tribes had entered south-west Central Asia from the 5th century; a more serious incursion occurred in the 10th century when the Oghuz, originally from Mongolia, arrived in the tract between the Ural Mountains and the Aral Sea. Those on the right bank of the Syr River converted to Islam *c.* 1100. From that time they were referred to as Turkoman (Turkmen) by Arab writers. Mongol invasions were initially deleterious (Merv was destroyed by Genghis Khan in 1221) but comparative peace returned under the Golden Horde (*reg* 1226–1502) and the Ilkhanids of Iran.

From the 16th to the 17th century southern Turkmenistan was controlled by the Safavids, while the north was ruled by the Uzbek *khan*s of Khiva and Bukhara; however, continual shifts in the balance of power meant warfare was frequent. The Shaybanids (descendants of Genghis Khan) and their successors ruled much of Central Asia with varying degrees of success; latterly the area was divided into smaller principalities sometimes called khanates; that based on Khiva was ruled by the Arabshahids, a collateral branch of the Shaybanids, until *c.* 1700.

From *c.* 1500 Turkoman tribes were compelled by water shortages to concentrate near the great oases. By the 19th century the Savik were at Merv, the Yomut at Khiva, the Ersari on the upper Amu Delta. These movements coincided with the drastic decline of the Silk Route and a

1. Map of Turkmenistan; those sites with separate entries in this dictionary are distinguished by CROSS-REFERENCE TYPE

concomitant stultification of the region. In addition Turkoman tribal wars and khanate aggression —the Khan of Bukhara sacked Merv in 1789—left it vulnerable to the increasingly powerful forces of Russia to the north. A series of offensives and campaigns in the late 18th century and the 19th gradually increased Russian influence, but though a treaty of 1791 purported to tie the Turkoman tribes to allegiance to the Tsar, permanent Russian inroads depended on a concerted attack in the 1860s and 1870s that brought about the surrender of the last remaining Central Asian khanate at Khiva in 1873. Anglo-Russian tension over the nebulous frontier between the two powers' spheres of influence increased Russian military expansion into what is now Turkmenistan, and with this came railways, the building of forts and attempts to impose a European-style urban culture on a territory still characterized by its nomadic population. Russian colonization involved the building of new towns adjacent to their predecessors, thereby emphasizing the separation of indigenous and ruling populations.

Following the Revolution of 1917 Russia's Central Asian lands were left in political turmoil until the establishment of Soviet republics there in the 1920s. Turkmenistan, as the Turkmen SSR created in 1924, experienced decades of the imposition of central Soviet policy. This included attempts to establish cotton production on a vast scale: to this end the Karakumskiy Canal was built to irrigate large tracts of land. There was also the penetration of Soviet official art forms such as Constructivism. With the break up of the USSR Turkmenistan declared its independence on 21 October 1991.

2. ARCHITECTURE. The architecture of late feudal Turkmenistan consisted of several types of nomadic dwelling. In areas close to the Kopeg Dag Mountains, two- or three-roomed houses, with slender-columned porches (*ayvan*) and adjacent courtyards, were predominant. Close to Ashkhabad and in Khwarazm, rich Tekke and Yomut semi-nomadic people built small fortress-like dwellings with high walls and towers. In the areas along the Amu River bordering Uzbekistan, dwellings had two enclosed courtyards. Some tribal homes had semicircular domes with openings for the smoke; without any windows, they resembled small mausolea. Houses were normally constructed of pisé (*pakhsa*), with flat roofs of wooden beams. Outside walls were often embellished by ornamentation carved into the clay surface when wet. Nomadic tents (*see* TENT, §II, 2) consisted of wooden frames covered with felt held down on the outside by patterned woven strips; pile carpets covered floors and closed off entrances.

Once Turkmenistan was assimilated into Russia (1860–80) by means of a series of Russian military fortifications (at Askhabad (now Ashkhabad), Krasnovodsk and Merv (a new administrative centre founded near Old Merv)) and by villages at the railway stations of the Transcaspian Railway (at Chardzhuy (now Chardzhou), Kizyl-Arvat and Bayram-Ali), towns designed by Russian engineers appeared. Buildings with façades in the Empire style of provincial Russia were built, such as military assembly halls, barracks, hospitals, churches, stations and schools, alongside traditional single-storey mud-brick houses, mosques and caravanserais. In Soviet times the emphasis was on the construction of industrial facilities (e.g. a textile factory (1925–7) in Ashkhabad in the Constructivist style; *see* CONSTRUCTIVISM). An attempt was made to create a new socialist town, its architecture taking account of local climatic and cultural conditions (Nebit-Dag, founded 1933, general plans 1942 and 1955, with designs for houses with terraces and outside staircases by the workshop of the VESNIN brothers). Until the mid-1950s the architecture of public buildings was dominated by a blend of Neo-classical forms and traditional Central Asian elements, with motifs from Turkoman decoration. The development of new town-building methods in Turkmenistan was decisively influenced by the destructive earthquake that hit Ashkhabad in 1948. Following this disaster designs were drawn up for houses made of reinforced brick, with bands of earthquake-proof monolithic concrete. Town planning provided for industrial zones and public-cum-administrative centres, and wide avenues, large squares and green esplanades. Between 1960 and the 1980s the emphasis was on strict functionalism of form, organic links with the environment and an expressive use of monumental decoration and sculpture (e.g. the Karl Marx Square complex in Ashkhabad, by architects ABDULLA AKHMEDOV, Fikrat Rza-ogly Aliyev (*b* 1933) and others, sculptors Vladimir Sergeyevich Lemport (*b* 1922), Nicholay Andreyevich Silis (*b* 1928), Dzhuma Dzhumadurdy (*b* 1937) and others, 1969–76).

3. PAINTING AND SCULPTURE. Figural art in Turkmenistan dates back to the work of the first professional Turkoman artist, the itinerant (Rus. *peredvizhnik*; *see* WANDERERS) Nazar Yomudsky (1860–97), who studied with Pavel Petrovich Chistyakov (1832–1919) in the Academy of Arts in St Petersburg, and to Russian painters who worked in Turkmenistan at the end of the 19th century and the beginning of the 20th. Two of them, Ruvim Moiseyevich Mazel (1890–1967) and Alexander Pavlivich Vladychuk (*b* 1893), organized the 'Avant-garde School of Arts of the East' in Ashkhabad in 1920. Pupils from this school—Byashim Nurali (1900–65), Sergei Nickitovich Beglyarov (1898–1949) and others—became the founders of a national school of artists. Nurali, who later studied under PAVEL KUZNETSOV in the Moscow Institute for Art and the Theatre ('VKhUTEIN'), expressed through his work an integral world-view in a style imbued with elements from folklore and demonstrated a sensitive approach to national character and a truly national sense of colour (e.g. *The Vintage*, 1929, Moscow, Mus. Orient. A; *Friends*, 1957, Moscow, Tret'yakov Gal.). A special

feature of the figural art of Turkmenistan is the predominance of painting, owing much to folk art traditions of colouring. In the 1960s and 1970s the work of Izzat Nazarovich Klychev (*b* 1923), the brothers Aman Amangeldyyev (*b* 1930) and Chary Amangeldyyev (*b* 1933), Stanislav Gennadyevich Babikov (1937–77), Mamed Mamedov (1938–?1986), Kulnazar Bekmuradov (*b* 1934) and Durdy Bayramov (*b* 1938) was distinguished by its lofty subjects and the rich styles that perpetuate the emotion and energy of folk traditions. In the first years of Soviet rule propaganda graphics began to develop, followed in the 1950s and 1960s by engraving and stage design (Khaky Allaberdy (*b* 1920) and Shamukhamed Akhmukhamedov (*b* 1937)). The first local sculptors (Dzhuma Dzhumadurdy, Klychmurad Yarmamedov (*b* 1941) and Makhtumkuly Nurymov (*b* 1941)) began to work in the 1960s, eventually producing work in a wide variety of styles, though usually maintaining their links with the past. Generalized images of Turkoman people and emotionally expressive monumental forms are common features of the wall low-relief *Motherland* (bronze, 1971; Ashkhabad) by Dzhuma Dzhumadurdy, a sculpted portrait of a Turkoman girl (limestone, 1971) by M. Nurymov and K. Yarmamedov's statue *The Bride* (granite, 1989).

4. DECORATIVE ARTS. Turkoman objects of the 19th century and the beginning of the 20th, reflections of the late feudal structure of the life of the Turkoman tribes, are celebrated, especially in carpets (*see* CENTRAL ASIA, fig. 49), jewellery and embroidery. The making of Turkoman carpets and articles made from them was traditionally undertaken by women. They were woven from sheep's wool coloured with natural dyes (sometimes with the addition of silk in the details of the pattern) on simple

2. Woman's breast ornament, silver gilt set with cornelian, engraved and with fretwork, Tekke tribe, late 19th century (Moscow, Museum of Oriental Art)

vertical or horizontal wooden looms; they varied enormously in shape, size and purpose (bed and wall carpets, door curtains, prayer mats (*see* CARPET, colour pl. III), travelling pouches, mirror-cases, bags for salt and sugar etc). Strict geometrical patterns consisted of multifaceted ornamented medallions—tribal and family signs repeated in chessboard-like or linear order, which are thought to show to which tribe the carpet belonged, hence the national proverb, 'Spread your carpet and I'll know your heart'. In all variants, the typical Turkoman composition features soft tonal colouring, with terracotta, dark red or cherry colour predominating. Elements of carpet ornament partly date back to Parthian times and, with their obviously Turkic motifs, reflect the process of Turkification of the local population.

Jewellery made of silver with grains of cornelian or coloured glass with a cascade of rustling silver pendants, coins and little bells, sometimes covered with gilding and black enamel, were the most costly part of Turkoman national costume (see fig. 2), but embroidery was the dominant element. Using coloured silk on plain (rarely patterned), usually dark, fabric, embroidery emphasized the cut of women's or men's clothing and covered the robes with a bright coloured pattern, while jewelled, interwoven ornaments decorated articles for household use. Carpet horse-cloths and silver harnesses with insets of large cornelians were covered with embroidery; in addition, ornamented hide saddles and straps served as festive trappings for horses and camels.

In the Soviet period, the classical types of carpet of the Turkoman tribes (Tekke, Yomut, Sarak, Ersari (Arabatchi) etc) continued, and new types appeared: portrait and figure carpets were made both in organized carpet workshops and later in the factories of the Turkmenkovyor Company. Early examples, created by the weavers in the 1920s (portraits of Lenin; compositions with propaganda slogans, such as 'Down with bride-money!') exhibited an almost childlike candour as well as a charming primitive quality; from the second half of the 1930s, however, designs for carpets were created by professional artists. Traditional forms of national folk art continue, joined in the late 20th century by forms of decorative and applied arts that are new to Turkmenistan, especially tapestries and ceramics.

See also FELT.

BIBLIOGRAPHY
G. I. Surova: *Iskusstvo Turkmenskoi SSR* [Art of the Turkmen SSR] (Leningrad, 1972) [in Turkoman, Rus. and Eng.]
V. I. Pilyavsky: *Arkhitektura sovetskogo Turkmenistana* [Architecture of Soviet Turkmenia] (Leningrad, 1974) [in Turkoman and Rus.; with Eng. summary]
S. M. Erlashova: *Zhivopis' sovetskoi Turkmenii* [Painting of Soviet Turkmenia] (Leningrad, 1975) [in Rus. and Eng.]
K. Kuraeva: *Sovremennaya turkmenskaya skul'ptura, 1960–1970: Istoricheskiy ocherk* [Contemporary Turkoman sculpture, 1960–1970: historical outline] (Ashkhabad, 1980)
Izobrazitelnoye iskusstvo Turkmenskoi SST [Visual arts of the Turkmen SSR] (Moscow, 1984) [album]
T. Kh. Starodub: 'Iskusstvo sovetskoi Turkmenii: Istoricheskie traditsii i sovremennaya praktika' [Art of Soviet Turkmenia: historical traditions and contemporary practice], *Dek. Isk. SSSR* (1985), no. 4, pp. 3–5
Yu. J. Katsnelson: *Arkhitektura sovetskoi Turkmenii* [Architecture of Soviet Turkmenia] (Moscow, 1987)
E. Medjitova, M. Dzhumaniyazova and E. Grishin, eds: *Turkmenskoye narodnoye iskusstvo* [Turkoman folk art] (Ashkhabad, 1990) [album; with Eng. summary]

T. KH. STARODUB

Turkogeitonia. *See under* ARCHANES.

Türk ressamlar cemiyeti. *See* ASSOCIATION OF OTTOMAN PAINTERS.

Turku [Swe. Åbo]. City in south-west Finland, at the mouth of the River Aura.

1. HISTORY AND URBAN DEVELOPMENT. Turku is Finland's oldest city. There were already trading posts higher up the river at the end of the Iron Age (*c.* AD 800–1150), but a rise in the ground level (*c.* 500 mm in 100 years) gradually forced a move towards the mouth of the river, an area that eventually became the most important district in Finland. Turku is first mentioned in a papal letter of 1229, when it became the only episcopal see in the country, a status that it retained until 1554; in 1280 it became the provincial capital. The medieval plan was partly dictated by the town's position on the so-called 'king's road' between Stockholm and Vyborg, over the Baltic via the Åland islands and crossing the river into Turku. The main square, with the town hall, was established beside the bridge, with the cathedral, consecrated in 1300 (*see* §3 below), close by (see fig. 1). The castle (1280; several times rebuilt; *see* FINLAND, §II, 1), near the mouth of the river, was the most important stronghold of the Swedish crown in Finland in the Middle Ages.

The castle was rebuilt as a less fortified, more palatial structure between 1556 and 1563 under John, Duke of Finland (later John III; *reg* 1568–92), its Renaissance style influencing that of some stone houses in the locality. The Turku Court of Appeal was founded in 1623, and the university (Academia Aboensis) in 1640. The town originally occupied the east bank of the river, but in the 1650s

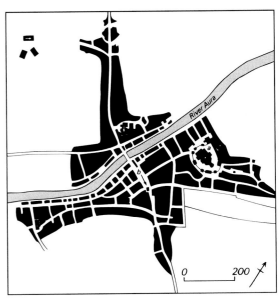

1. Turku, plan, *c.* 1600: (a) cathedral; (b) town hall

a regular grid plan, one of the first in Finland, was set out on the west bank. During the 18th century the town developed greatly, becoming by the end of the century the third in size after Stockholm and Göteborg. Samuel Berner (*d* 1761), the first city architect anywhere in Finland, rebuilt the town hall in 1735–6, a classicist building with a bell-tower. The city architect Christian Fredrik Schröder (1722–89) designed stone buildings for Turku, and early in the 19th century Carl Christopher Gjörwell (1766–1837) built the Academy building (1802–15) in a reduced Neo-classical style.

After Finland became a grand duchy of Russia at the Peace of Fredrikshamn (1809), Tsar Alexander I (*reg* 1801–25), considering Turku to be both too Swedish and too far from St Petersburg, designated Helsinki the new capital. Turku suffered further in 1827, when it burnt down in one of the largest town fires in Scandinavian history, destroying about 2500 houses. One immediate result of the fire was the removal of the university to Helsinki in 1828.

After all previous fires Turku had been rebuilt on the old plans; but now Tsar Nicholas I (*reg* 1825–55) decided on an entirely new town plan. Designed in 1828 by Carl Ludwig Engel, who had designed the university observatory (1814) in the Neo-classical style of St Petersburg, it was, with that of Helsinki, the model for all town plans in Finland, and also to some extent in Sweden. Engel designed a grid plan with main thoroughfares 40 cubits (*c.* 22 m) wide, and lesser streets of 30 cubits (*c.* 16.5 m). Each district was square, consisting of four areas divided by plantations of trees (w. 15 m). Two-storey stone houses only were permitted around the open spaces and along the riverbanks. These directives, which originated in fear of future fires, led at the same time to a homogeneous townscape, of which substantial parts are preserved along the riverbanks and around the cathedral.

In the 1920s ERIK BRYGGMAN and ALVAR AALTO established their offices in Turku, which became the centre of Functionalism in Finland, notable buildings being Aalto's Turun Sanomet building (1928–30) and Bryggman's blocks of flats. In 1929 Turku celebrated its 700th anniversary with an international exhibition, for which Aalto designed a constructivist pavilion. Turku was considerably damaged in World War II.

BIBLIOGRAPHY

Turun kaupungin historia kivikaudesta vuoteen 1970 [History of the city of Turku from the Stone Age to the year 1970], Turun Historiatoimikunta, 13 vols (Turku, 1957–87)

2. ART LIFE AND ORGANIZATION. Turku was already a centre of artistic production in the Middle Ages. The Master of Lieto, a wood-carver, worked there *c.* 1330–50, and his work can be found in several churches (also Helsinki, N. Mus.; Turku, Prov. Mus.). Organized artistic life began in 1830, when the painters' guild founded the Åbo school of drawing, the first art school in Finland, which reached early distinction from 1846, when ROBERT WILHELM EKMAN became its Director. In 1891 the town's first art association was founded, establishing the Art Museum, which was enabled by a private donation in 1904 to move to a new building by Gustaf Nyström in the town centre. The museum is still one of the most important in

the country. It was completed in 1967 with the addition of the Wäinö Aaltonen Museum, designed by the sculptor's architect son Matti Aaltonen, and now has premises on the banks of the River Aura (*see* AALTONEN, WÄINÖ). Owing to its museums and school of drawing, Turku is still the most important art centre in Finland after Helsinki.

3. CATHEDRAL. A forerunner of the present cathedral was built some time after 1229 *c.* 1.6 km upstream at Koroinen, but in the mid-13th century a wooden church was erected, probably by German craftsmen, on a riverside mound at the site of the present building; the river may no longer have been navigable to Koroinen.

After the establishment in 1276 of a permanent cathedral chapter, the Koroinen church was probably too small, and with the shift in focus of the town to the new market square a brick cathedral was built to replace the wooden church. The building consecrated to St Mary and St Henry of Uppsala in 1300 was probably a rectangular, unaisled hall church (35×23 m) with a sacristy on the north side and a small, five-sided choir to the east. The tower and vestibule were added at the beginning of the 14th century. This church was associated with Bishop John (1286–9) from the Dominican friary of Sigtuna (Sweden), and the brick detailing is stylistically akin to contemporary Swedish architecture.

When the Russians plundered Turku in 1318 most of the church was destroyed by fire, and it was not given a new roof until after 1335, when a vault with brick ribs was put on, dividing the nave into three while retaining the hall structure. The original vaulting survives in the aisles, and the main vessel still retains its so-called 'pencil' consoles, cut in limestone, which probably derived from the cathedral and church of St Nicholas in TALLINN.

By the mid-14th century the church was again too small, and a new chancel was built, of the same height and breadth as the main church, with aisles and an ambulatory. When Bishop Hemming, who had initiated this project, died in 1366, the work was already sufficiently advanced for him to be buried in the chancel, but evidence suggests that the work was not finished until the beginning of the 15th century. With its octagonal columns, its passages between the inner buttresses and its rib vaults in the aisles, the chancel is stylistically similar to early 15th-century buildings by HINRICH BRUNSBERG in Pomerania at Stettin (now Szczecin) and Stargard (both now in Poland) and in North Germany at Brandenburg. In the 1460s the nave vault was destroyed, leaving only the consoles intact. By 1466 the hall church had been transformed into a basilica: the nave was raised, with an added clerestory and six bays of star vaulting (see fig. 2). The west tower was increased in height at the same time. The changes may have been prompted by the darkness of the interior, owing to the numerous side chapels that had been added since *c.* 1380, but it is more likely that a basilical cathedral with a spire represented a status symbol among the more important Baltic towns. Much of the brick detailing indicates that the masons now came from Tallinn. The last major work of the Middle Ages was the octagonal chapel (h. 24 m) constructed by 1471 east of the chancel. This, 'the chancel of all saints', probably functioned as a reliquary chapel,

2. Turku Cathedral, nave looking east, consecrated 1300

and with the earlier example at Trondheim (*see* TROND-HEIM, §2(i)), was one of only two such buildings erected in Scandinavia. In 1649 the wall between the chancel and the octagon was removed, giving the chancel its present form.

The cathedral became Lutheran at the Reformation in the 1520s. The decoration was badly damaged in the town fire of 1827. Robert Wilhelm Ekman painted the frescoes (1850–54) in the chancel, depicting *Bishop Henry's Conversion of the Finns*, but the main restoration of the building was undertaken in the 1920s and again between 1976 and 1979; and the cathedral now presents a true reflection of the later medieval period.

BIBLIOGRAPHY
J. Rinne: *Åbo domkyrka till sjuhundraårsminnet* [Turku Cathedral over 700 years] (Helsinki, 1929) [Eng. summary]
——: Tuomiokirken rakennushistoria [The building history of the cathedral] (1941), i of *Turun tuomiokirkko keskiaikana* [Turku Cathedral in the Middle Ages] (Turku, 1941–52)
C. J. Gardberg: 'Åbo domkyrkas tjugo byggnadsskeden' [The 20 phases in the building of Turku Cathedral], *Muistomerkki kirjoituksia Antero Sinisalolle* [Commemorative essays for Antero Sinisalo] (Helsinki, 1987)

CARL JACOB GARDBERG

Turmel, Charles (*b* Quimper, 1 Sept 1597; *d* Quimper, 9 Oct 1675). French architect. He was born into a family of master builders. In 1621 he produced the plans for the Ste-Catherine hospital at Quimper, on which his brother Pierre Turmel also worked. On 2 October 1623 Charles entered the Jesuit novitiate at Rouen. On his return to the college at Quimper in 1626 he put his skills to the service of the Society of Jesus, working initially on the plans of

the Jesuit fathers Etienne Martellange and François Derand and then on his own designs. He was put in charge, in turn, of the supervision of works on the collège de Rennes (1627–31), the Paris novitiate (1630–31) and the college at Orléans (1632–5), all three of which were built to the designs of Martellange. In 1634 and 1637 he produced new designs for the school and church of St-Louis-des-Jésuites (now called St-Vincent) at Blois, modifying the first plan produced by Martellange in 1624. From 1638 to 1641 he worked alongside Derand on St Paul-St Louis church on the Rue St-Antoine in Paris, and in 1643 he was summoned back to Blois, where he remained until 1647. In 1647–8 he made plans for the schools in Alençon and Amiens. He was in Caen in 1653–4, Blois in 1654–5 (where work on the church was resumed), Vannes in 1657–9 and Bourges in 1659–62. Again in Vannes in 1662–7, he was in charge of building the new church there, and then, in 1667, he was called to supervise work on the Jesuit church in Quimper, where he died. His collection of his own designs and those of his teachers Martellange and Derand is kept in the Bibliothèque Municipale, Quimper.

BIBLIOGRAPHY
P. Delattre: 'Notice sur la vie et les oeuvres de Frère Charles Turmel, jésuite et architecte (1597–1675)', *Mem. Soc. Hist. Archéol. Bretagne*, xxii (1942), pp. 29–65
P. Moisy: 'Le Recueil des plans jésuites de Quimper', *Bull. Soc. Hist. A. Français* (1950), pp. 70–84
C. Mignot: 'L'Eglise Saint-Louis-des-Jésuites à Blois', *Congrès archéologique, blésois et vendômois, 1981*, pp. 142–52

CLAUDE MIGNOT

Turnbull, Thomas (*b* Glasgow, 23 Aug 1824; *d* Wellington, New Zealand, 23 Feb 1907). Scottish architect, active in New Zealand. He was employed as Clerk of Works to David Bryce in Edinburgh before travelling to Victoria, Australia, in 1851 where he practised as an architect in the gold-digging townships. He moved to San Francisco in 1861 and over a ten-year period designed many buildings there, none of which is known to have survived. Overwork following the earthquake of 1868 led to a breakdown in his health and his emigration to New Zealand in the early 1870s. He settled in Wellington, establishing an extensive practice there. At the time of his arrival the use of brick for building construction was eschewed by that city's inhabitants who favoured earthquake-resistant wooden structures. Turnbull introduced methods of strengthening brick buildings learnt in San Francisco and was instrumental in transforming Wellington into a brick city of ornate public and commercial buildings in a variety of classical styles.

Turnbull was a pragmatic colonial architect whose work shows a greater concern for practical considerations than for stylistic fidelity. His architecture is representative of the Scottish classical tradition in contrast to the Gothic bias evident in the work of most of his English-trained contemporaries. However, two of his finest surviving Wellington buildings are in the Gothic Revival style. These are the wooden St John's Presbyterian Church (1884–5) and the General Assembly Library (completed 1899), a late example of the use of the style, though finely crafted. His most notable classical building is the Italian Renaissance style former Bank of New Zealand Head Office,

Wellington (completed 1901). This building occupies a prominent triangular site and its main entrance is emphasized by a boldly designed, curved corner section. Much of the design work for these later buildings was carried out by his son, William (1868–1941), whom Thomas had taken into partnership in 1891 under the name Thomas Turnbull & Son.

BIBLIOGRAPHY

The Cyclopedia of New Zealand (Christchurch, 1897), p. 586

J. Stacpoole: *Colonial Architecture in New Zealand* (Wellington, 1976), p. 173

C. Cochran: 'The Architect Thomas Turnbull', *General Assembly Library* (Wellington, 1977), pp. 12–14

JOHN W. F. CATTELL

Turnbull, William (*b* Dundee, 11 Jan 1922). Scottish sculptor, painter and printmaker. He worked as an illustrator for a national periodical publisher in Dundee (1939–41) before wartime service in the RAF. He then studied at the Slade School of Fine Art, London, from 1946 to 1948 before spending two years in Paris. On his return to London he shared a studio with Eduardo Paolozzi, with whom he exhibited at the Hanover Gallery in 1950. Turnbull's reputation grew with the generation of British sculptors acclaimed at the Venice Biennale of 1952. His interest in the interrelationship of blunt, self-evident components differed significantly, however, from the more psychological approach of his co-exhibitor in Venice, Reg Butler, and even, despite certain similarities and their close friendship, the metamorphic interests of Paolozzi. In the early 1950s Turnbull was involved with the INDEPENDENT GROUP at the ICA, whose lectures on recent scientific, sociological and philosophical ideas interested Turnbull.

Turnbull's early work used simple linear elements as basic signs, often implying play and movement. These were followed by paintings in which the motion of groups of figures was suggested by gestural line. The motif of the head as an object became predominant in the mid-1950s, for example in works entitled *Mask* (e.g. 1953–4; London, V&A), which reflected Jean Dubuffet's work of the same period, although lacking his sense of psychological urgency. Turnbull also made free-standing *Heads* (1953–7; see 1973 exh. cat., nos. 20–23) in concentrated ovoid forms with lacerated surfaces, reminiscent of Constantin Brancusi's work. Paintings from the period 1955 to 1957 treated the same motif with a calligraphic handling or heavy use of the palette-knife. Until 1963 his sculpture incorporated several parts in contrasting traditional materials, such as bronze, stone and wood. In a work such as *Janus 2* (rosewood and stone, 1959; London, Tate) he gave more equal importance to stacked elements than Brancusi. Through balancing out the component parts, Turnbull became increasingly interested in the permutations of, and relationships between, diverse elements.

The influence of two exhibitions at the Tate Gallery, London, *Modern Art in the United States* (1956) and *New American Painting* (1959), as well as his first visit to the USA in 1957, had a decisive impact on Turnbull's painting. He began to expunge vestigial imagery. At first he relied on almost monochromatic, heavily worked surfaces, for example *No. 7* (1959; London, Tate), followed by thinly painted colour fields. These were either vertically bisected or incorporated cropped discs that implied an extension beyond the canvas. Later paintings comprised quantities of colour accented by occasional diagonals or bands clinging to the edge. In 1963 Turnbull spoke of being 'concerned with the canvas as a continuous field, where the edge created by the meeting of coloured areas is more the tension in a field than the boundary of a shape'. This stance made him highly influential on the younger British abstract painters who exhibited with Turnbull in the *Situation* exhibition (1960) at the RBA Galleries, London.

Turnbull's painted steel sculptures from 1963 to 1968 often involved irregular zigzag or wavy forms, for example *3/4/5* (1966; London, Tate). In such works as *Parallels* (1967; London, Tate; see fig.), Turnbull's three-dimensional work corresponded with the concerns of the American Minimalists in its repetition or permutation of ready-made geometric units and concern for different responses to identical forms when set in a new context. The influence of American art from the later 1960s continued to be apparent in the increasing variety of materials and more relaxed groupings of forms favoured by Turnbull, although such concerns also followed logically from his earlier preoccupation with process and permutation. In response to the general tendency of the 1970s to express more sensual experiences and historical memory, Turnbull returned *c.* 1977 to small, modelled sculptures. These suggested torsos, masks and small figures, often echoing

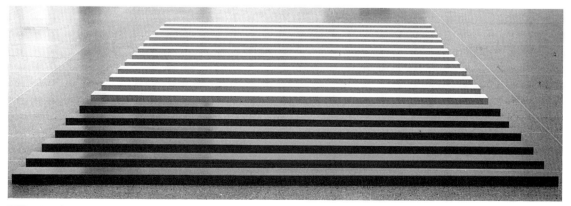

William Turnbull: *Parallels*, printed steel, 18 pieces, each 102×51×2743 mm, 1967 (London, Tate Gallery)

museum objects such as arrowheads and cult figurines. These later works, while evoking his sculpture of the 1950s, were more intimate and less dauntingly imposing.

WRITINGS
'William Turnbull: Painter, Sculptor', *Uppercase*, 4 (1960) [unpaginated; selection of statements, 1949–60]
'Images without Temples', *Living A.*, 1(1963), pp. 14–27

BIBLIOGRAPHY
William Turnbull: Sculpture and Painting (exh. cat., intro. R. Morphet; London, Tate, 1973)
William Turnbull (exh. cat., London, Waddington Gals, 1981)

ADRIAN LEWIS

Turner, Benjamin Brecknell (*b* London, 12 May 1815; *d* London, 29 April 1894). English photographer. He began photographing country churches, trees, family and friends in 1849, using the calotype process. In the early 1850s he became a pioneering amateur photographer of the British landscape and its picturesque monuments. From 1852 he used the paper negative in combination with albumen positives on a large scale (262×381 mm). His work was shown at major exhibitions, including the Society of Arts, London (1852), and International Exhibition, London (1862), bringing him international renown. He was Vice President of the Photographic Society of London and Treasurer and Honorary Secretary of the Photographic Exchange club (1855–7).

Turner's prints are rich and vigorous in tonality, skilful and original in composition. He was a successful tallow-chandler by trade, with premises in the Haymarket. Above these he erected a glass house or studio, in which he made portraits of family, friends and fellow photographers. His landscape and architectural subjects were the only photographs that he exhibited. Inspired by the Great Exhibition of 1851, he made two major views of the interior of the Crystal Palace after the exhibits had been removed, *Transept* and *Nave* (both 1852; see Haworth-Booth, 1982, p. 139).

Among the other monuments and locations photographed by Turner were *Bredicot Court*, *Rievaulx Abbey* and *At Compton, Surrey* (all 1852–4; see Haworth-Booth, 1982, pp. 136–7), in which he translated the motifs favoured by the English watercolour tradition into the new language of photography.

BIBLIOGRAPHY
M. Haworth-Booth: 'The Picturesque Eye: Benjamin Brecknell Turner's Album', *The V&A Album 1* (London, 1982), pp. 135–9
——: *The Golden Age of British Photography* (London, 1984), pp. 50, 52–4
——: 'Benjamin Brecknell Turner: Photographic Views from Nature', *British Photography in the 19th Century: The Fine Art Tradition*, ed. M. Weaver (Cambridge, 1989), pp. 79–94

MARK HAWORTH-BOOTH

Turner, C(laude) A(llen) P(orter) (*b* Lincoln, RI, 1869; *d* 1955). American engineer and writer. He completed a civil engineering degree at Lehigh University, Bethlehem, PA, in 1890 and for the next 12 years he worked for various railway and bridge companies including the New York and New England Railway, the Edgmore Bridge Company of Wilmington, DE, and the Pittsburg Bridge Company where he supervised a group of draughtsmen. In 1901 he opened his own office in Minneapolis as a consulting bridge engineer and a specialist in reinforced-concrete design. During the first decade of the 20th century there was enormous interest in the structural potential of reinforced concrete, both in the USA and Europe. Turner made a major contribution to the field with the development of the mushroom slab system, a method of constructing flat reinforced concrete slabs without using supporting beams. This system was based on Turner's insight that the actions of a slab are different from those of a beam, and that the structural theories evolved by François Hennebique and Ernest L. Ransome were inadequate to describe the behaviour of a slab. Reworking the theory, he found that a reinforced concrete slab could be supported simply on columns with broad 'mushroom' capitals. He originally conceived of his system as a means of simplifying construction and reducing its cost, finding that the heavier the load to be carried, the more economical the system became; but he also realized that it had several other advantages: for example it is easier to install services such as automatic sprinkler systems in buildings that do not have beams running across the ceilings; lighting is more effective and vibration can be minimized. The system could be adapted for almost any type of building, but it was particularly useful for warehouses and factories.

Turner first demonstrated his system in the Lindake-Warner Building, St Paul, MN, in 1908–9, and for the next ten years his business boomed; by 1916 he had opened offices in New York, Chicago, Houston and Danville, VA, as well as Vancouver and Winnipeg in Canada. His firm was responsible for the engineering design of thousands of buildings, while he personally designed many others. His mushroom or flat-slab system was also adopted by many other architects including Kees & Colburn of Minneapolis who used it for the Northern Implement Building (1910) and its Deere-Webber addition (1912), Minneapolis, and Schmidt, Garden & Martin who used it for the Dwight Building (1910), Chicago.

Following the usual practice among the pioneers of structural design in the USA, Turner attempted to patent his slab design; however, a patent for a flat arch resembling the Turner slab had already been purchased and, after prolonged litigation, Turner's claim was disallowed. The financial returns from his invention were thus limited, but he continued working on structural theory and its applications. In 1919 he was co-author of the textbook *Concrete Steel Construction*, which contains in an appendix an account of his legal struggle: 'State of the Art of Reinforced Concrete from the Patent Standpoint and the Menace to Progress by Unscientific Decisions'. He wrote a number of articles about the flat slab and its derivatives for the *Engineering News Record* and the *Transactions of the American Society Civil Engineers*, and in 1922 he published a five-volume work dealing with engineering materials, structural design and the economic theory of steel railway bridge design.

Turner was also a bridge designer of considerable ability; among several works are the three-hinged arch of the railway bridge (1910–11) over the St Croix River, near New Richmond, WI, and, perhaps his best-known work in this field, the swing bridge at Duluth, which he both promoted and designed. His flat slab system was also adapted for bridge construction by other engineers. He eventually abandoned the construction industry and ended his days running a condiments factory in Southern Illinois, but he had made a substantial contribution to the development of the reinforced-concrete flat slab in the USA. Historians of engineering now hold that Turner and Robert Maillart in Switzerland invented their systems of flat-slab design almost simultaneously and quite independently; Maillart's understanding of reinforced-concrete behaviour was perhaps more profound and his expression more elegant.

WRITINGS

with H. T. Eddy: *Concrete Steel Construction* (Minneapolis, 1919)
Elasticity and Strength, 5 vols (Minneapolis, 1922, rev. 1934)

BIBLIOGRAPHY

H. A. Castle: *Minnesota: Its Story and Biography*, ii (New York and Chicago, 1915)
C. W. Condit: *American Building: Materials and Techniques from the First Colonial Settlements to the Present* (Chicago and London, 1968; 2/1982)
H. Newlon, ed.: *A Selection of Historic American Papers on Concrete* (Detroit, 1976)
D. Billington: *Robert Maillart: The Art of Engineering* (Princeton, NJ, 1980)

LEONARD K. EATON

Turner, Charles (*b* Woodstock, Oxon, 31 July 1774; *d* London, 1 Aug 1857). English engraver and draughtsman. In 1789 he was apprenticed to John Jones in London, where from 1795 he studied at the Royal Academy Schools. He began publishing his prints in 1796 and also worked in mezzotint, and occasionally in stipple and aquatint for a variety of publishers, mostly in London but also in Scotland and elsewhere. He was a skilful engraver who could adapt his style to reflect that of the painter; he was also hardworking, reliable and enterprising. The speed with which he worked meant that he was able to engrave many plates of topical interest. His first major success was *Bonaparte Reviewing the Consular Guards* after John James Masquerier (1778–1855), published in 1802 at a time when there were few images of Napoleon available. The painting itself (untraced) was one that he helped Masquerier to paint, and was supposedly painted from life; in fact it was based on secondary images. His plate (1807) of *The Shipwreck* (1805; London, Tate) was the first print after a painting by J. M. W. Turner.

From 1806 Charles Turner engraved many of the early plates of Turner's *Liber Studiorum*, although the two men had a long-standing quarrel. Charles Turner published many prints on his own account, including his largest plate, depicting the *Marlborough Family* (1815), after the painting (exh. RA 1778; Blenheim Pal., Oxon) by Reynolds. The majority of his plates are after contemporary painters: he engraved 76 plates after Lawrence, including Turner's favourite, *Lord Castlereagh* (1810; London, N.P.G.; engraving pubd 1822). He was the outstanding mezzotint-engraver in England between 1800 and 1840, and he sent drawings and prints to the exhibitions of the Royal Academy throughout his career. He was elected Associate Engraver in 1828; he subsequently exhibited prints until 1843. His oeuvre—638 portraits and over 300 subject-plates—is among the largest of any English engraver.

BIBLIOGRAPHY

DNB; Engen; Redgrave; Thieme–Becker
A. Graves: *The Royal Academy of Arts: A Complete Dictionary of Contributors and their Works from its Foundation in 1769 to 1904*, v (London, 1906), pp. 29–30
A. Whitman: *Charles Turner* (London, 1907)
R. Lister: *Prints and Printmaking* (London, 1984), pp. 354–5

DAVID ALEXANDER

Turner, Dawson (*b* Great Yarmouth, Norfolk, 18 Oct 1775; *d* London, 20 June 1858). English banker, antiquarian, patron, collector and botanist. He inherited a fortune on the death of his father, James Turner (1743–94), and in 1796 joined the family bank in Great Yarmouth, where he spent all but the last seven years of his life. He had a serious interest in botany, and his wealth enabled him to publish sumptuously illustrated botanical works between 1802 and 1819. Thereafter he turned his attention mainly to antiquities.

Turner engaged first John Crome and in 1812 John Sell Cotman as drawing-masters for his wife, Mary Palgrave (1774–1850), and daughters (all of whom became proficient watercolour painters in the style of Cotman): Maria (1797–1872), wife of the botanist W. J. Hooker (1785–1865); Elizabeth (1799–1852), wife of FRANCIS PALGRAVE; Mary Anne (1803–74); Harriet (1806–69); and Hannah Sarah (1808–82). Turner put his family to work in producing over 4000 topographical illustrations to his grangerized copy of the *History of Norfolk* by Francis Blomefield (1739–75; London, BL, Add. MSS 23013–62, 23064, 23065). They also illustrated Turner's *Outlines in Lithography* (1840), a catalogue of his picture collection. Turner had purchased the collection from Crome, Thomas Harvey (1748–1819) and dealers such as Alexis Delahante, and it included Jan Steen's *The Christening Feast*, originally entitled *The Gossiping* (1664; London, Wallace), and Giovanni Bellini's *Virgin and Child Enthroned with Saints and a Donor* (1505; Birmingham, Mus. & A.G.).

Dawson Turner's collection was sold at Christie's, London, on 14 May 1852. Turner owned little of Cotman's work, preferring to encourage the artist in etching projects more akin to his own antiquarian tastes, most notably *Architectural Antiquities of Normandy* (1822), for which Cotman produced 100 plates of Gothic architecture in a carefully composed manner to accompany Turner's text.

BIBLIOGRAPHY

DNB
Obituary, *The Athenaeum*, 1603 (17 July 1858), pp. 82–3
S. D. Kitson: 'Notes on a Collection of Portrait Drawings Formed by Dawson Turner', *Walpole Soc.*, xxi (1932–3), pp. 67–104
W. R. Dawson: 'A Bibliography of the Printed Works of Dawson Turner', *Trans. Cambridge Bibliog. Soc.*, iii/3 (1961), pp. 232–56
A. W. Moore: *Dutch and Flemish Painting in Norfolk: A History of Taste and Influence, Fashion and Collecting* (London, 1988)

For further bibliography *see* NORWICH, §2.

ANDREW W. MOORE

Turner [née Monro], **(Annie) Helen (Nairn) Monro** (*b* Calcutta, 1901; *d* Edinburgh, 21 Sept 1977). Scottish illustrator, glass-engraver and teacher. She was educated at George Watson's Ladies College in Edinburgh, Edinburgh University, and later, at Edinburgh College of Art, where she specialized in wood-engraving. During the 1930s and 1940s she illustrated several books for Thomas Nelson & Sons of Edinburgh and designed and illustrated catalogues and advertisements for the Edinburgh & Leith

Flint Glass Co., as well as submitting designs for intaglio work and tablewares. Her first exhibited glass was shown in the exhibition of *British Art in Industry* at the Royal Academy, London, in 1935. In 1938 she studied glass engraving, cutting and etching under Professor Wilhelm von Eiff (1890–1943) at the Kunstgewerbeschule in Stuttgart, returning to Britain at the outbreak of World War II. In March 1940 she established her own studio, and in January 1941 she started the department of Glass Design at the Edinburgh College of Art. In 1943 she married Professor W. E. S. Turner (1881–1963) and in 1947 she was appointed a full-time instructor at the college. By 1965 a furnace was added to the department so that all aspects of glass design and making could be taught. In 1956 she established the Juniper Green Workshop with John Lawrie (*b* 1928) on the outskirts of Edinburgh and for the rest of her career she worked on a wide range of commissions, from small-scale items to such large architectural panels as the windows at the National Library of Scotland (*in situ*).

WRITINGS
H. M. Turner: 'The Art of Glass Engraving', *J. Royal Soc. A.*, cviii (1960), pp. 477–95

BIBLIOGRAPHY
The Art of Glass: An Exhibition of the Works of Helen Monro Turner and John Lawrie (exh. cat., ed by B. J. R. Blench; Dunfermline, Pittencrieff Park, Music Hall, 1972)

BRIAN J. R. BLENCH

Turner, Hugh Thackeray. *See under* BALFOUR & TURNER.

Turner, J(oseph) M(allord) W(illiam) (*b* London, 23 April 1775; *d* Chelsea [now in London], 19 Dec 1851). British painter and printmaker. He dominated British landscape painting throughout the first half of the 19th century. He established a reputation in the Royal Academy, London, first as a topographical watercolourist and then within a few years as a painter of Sublime and historical landscapes.

Turner's ambition was to confirm the status of landscape as a serious art form, in the wake of Richard Wilson, and he always perceived his position as being in direct line from the 17th-century classicists Poussin and, especially, Claude. His later exploration of effects of light in the pursuit of new demonstrations of sublimity has led to his purposes being confounded with those of the Impressionists; but in reality he remained true to earlier conceptions of great art, as formulated by such theorists as Jonathan Richardson and, above all, Joshua Reynolds, never attempting spontaneity or informality on the scale of exhibition pieces as did his contemporary John Constable. The large body of his sketches and studies in oil and watercolour, however, which, after wrangles over his will, was given to the British nation in 1856, testifies to the wide variety of his responses to the world and to the processes of picture-making. His finished work is characterized by a theatrical grandeur and a straining after effect that are offset by an encyclopedic understanding of natural phenomena and a pervasive fascination with human life in all its manifestations.

I. Life and work. II. Bequests. III. Character and professional stance.

I. Life and work.

1. Family and private life. 2. Training and early career. 3. Printmaking, lecturing and poetry. 4. Response to contemporary artists. 5. Experiments with colour and technique. 6. Continental tours and work at Petworth House. 7. Ruskin, Turner and the European tradition. 8. Coupled pictures, modern subjects and last works.

1. FAMILY AND PRIVATE LIFE. Turner's father, William Turner, of a Devon family, was a barber and wigmaker in Maiden Lane, Covent Garden, London. The artist's breadth of intellect, the 'wonderful range of mind' that Constable noted on their first meeting in 1813, was apparent from an early age; his father quickly and proudly recognized that 'my son is going to be a painter'. The illness and death of a younger sister in 1795–6 seem to have occasioned the boy's removal to stay with a maternal uncle at Brentford, Middx, and with other relations of his mother's at Margate, Kent; in both of these places there are records of his making drawings. In 1799 his desire for professional independence led him to rent and later buy a house in Harley Street, London, a move that may also have been precipitated by his liaison with a member of the family of the glee composer John Danby. This was either Danby's widow Sarah or more probably his niece Hannah; she was installed by Turner in a house near by. By her he had two illegitimate daughters, Evelina and Georgiana. Turner probably had a further motive for leaving Maiden Lane in the increasing mental instability of his mother, who in 1800 was committed to the Royal Bethlehem Hospital; she died there in 1804. Thereafter his father became a close companion and studio assistant; he lived with him at Harley Street, then briefly at Isleworth and Hammersmith, and from 1813 to 1826 at Solus (later Sandycombe) Lodge, Twickenham, which had been built to Turner's own designs, possibly with assistance from the architect John Soane. The loss of his father in 1829 was deeply disturbing to Turner and precipitated an increasing sense of isolation. He began to spend frequent weekends at Margate, in the lodgings of Mrs Sophia Caroline Booth, with whom he became intimate after her husband's death (1833 or 1834). In 1846 or earlier he brought her to London to act as housekeeper at 6 Davis Place, Cremorne New Road, Chelsea; this was a small house facing the river, to which he retreated secretly, and it was where he died. His London house, which since 1810 had been at 47 Queen Anne Street West and had latterly become dilapidated, was being presided over at the time by Hannah Danby. Sarah lived on until the 1860s, having apparently long lost contact with Turner. He included a small legacy for her in his first will, of 1829, but not in that of 1831. His daughter Georgiana, also a legatee in the 1829 will, seems to have died shortly afterwards, while her sister Evelina married a diplomat and lived abroad. The will was modified by various codicils, the last in 1849, in which both Hannah Danby and Mrs Booth were bequeathed annuities.

2. TRAINING AND EARLY CAREER. Having acquired some experience in the offices of the architect Thomas Hardwick and of Thomas Malton, an architectural draughtsman, Turner entered the Royal Academy Schools

as a boy of 14, to study in the Plaister and Life Academies. His first exhibited works were watercolours of architectural subjects: in 1790 the *Archbishop's Palace, Lambeth* (Indianapolis, IN, Mus. A.) appeared at the Royal Academy. In 1791 Turner worked briefly as assistant scene-painter at the Pantheon opera house in Oxford Street, London. The building was destroyed by fire in January 1792, and he sent a watercolour of the ruins (London, Tate) to the Academy that spring. He soon began to experiment with other subject-matter, including scenes from literature; a monochrome composition of *Don Quixote and the Enchanted Barque* (1792–3; priv. col., see *Young Turner* exh. cat., 1988, no. 8) competently imitates the graphic style of Philippe Jacques de Loutherbourg. A small oval study of a watermill of the same time is his first extant essay in oil (London, Tate); the first to be exhibited was *Fishermen at Sea* (1796; London, Tate), a nocturnal sea-piece that throws down the gauntlet to Joseph Vernet with unexpected success. It may have been preceded by the little *Moonlight: A Study at Millbank* (London, Tate), which Turner sent in the following year, but which is in the nature of a modest technical exercise preparatory to the larger work. His experiments in oil seem to have also stimulated technical developments in watercolour, and, under the influence of Rembrandt and Piranesi, both perhaps encountered in the collection of Richard Colt Hoare, a patron of his, he produced a number of architectural interiors of grandiose atmospheric effect, including a series of Salisbury Cathedral (Salisbury, Salisbury & S. Wilts Mus.; London, V&A; U. Manchester, Whitworth A.G.; Birmingham, Mus. & A.G.) for Hoare himself.

Through participating in a small 'academy' at the home of Thomas Monro, where he collaborated with THOMAS GIRTIN in copying studies by John Robert Cozens and Edward Dayes, Turner deepened his acquaintance with, respectively, the most subtle of the watercolourists of the preceding generation and a leading modern topographer. These lessons bore fruit in work he did for Hoare and for other patrons. For William Anne Capell, 4th Earl of Essex, he executed views of Hampton Court, of Herefordshire (e.g. U. Manchester, Whitworth A.G.) and of Cassiobury Park, Herts (e.g. Boston, MA, Mus. F.A.). For Edward Lascelles, 1st Earl of Harewood (*d* 1820), he depicted Harewood House, W. Yorks (examples *in situ*). The success of these, and of work shown at the Royal Academy, attracted many other commissions throughout the 1790s.

Turner's paintings of the later 1790s were the product of two factors: the influence of Richard Wilson, and his own experience of the mountains of northern England and of Wales, especially Snowdonia. He was elected an ARA in 1799 and, early in 1802, full RA; his diploma piece was a view of *Dolbadarn Castle, North Wales* (London, RA), which presents sublime scenery in terms even broader than Wilson's, evoking historical associations as an essential part of its meaning. Two Welsh subjects in watercolour demonstrate how that medium, too, could be employed for serious purposes: *Caernarvon Castle* (exh. RA 1799; priv. col., see 1974–5 exh. cat., no. 42) is Turner's first response to one of the most fruitful of all influences on him, the sunset harbours of Claude, examples of which he had encountered that year in the collection of John Julius Angerstein; a more expansive view of *Caernarvon Castle,*

North Wales (exh. RA 1800; London, Tate) is part of an unfinished pair depicting the destruction of the Welsh Bards by Edward I, following Thomas Gray's famous poem *The Bard*.

Turner went on to show a succession of large-scale works in oil and watercolour, often imitating the Old Masters: one that earned him controversial prominence was *Dutch Boats in a Gale: Fishermen Endeavouring to Put their Fish on Board* (exh. RA 1801; Duke of Sutherland priv. col., see 1974–5 exh. cat., no. 71), executed for Francis Egerton, 3rd Duke of Bridgewater, as a pendant to Willem van de Velde the younger's *Kaag Close-hauled in a Fresh Breeze* (Toledo, OH, Mus. A.). Another sea-piece, *Ships Bearing up for Anchorage* (Petworth House, W. Sussex, NT), smaller but even more sophisticated in its formal organization, was purchased at the Royal Academy exhibition of 1802 by George Wyndham, 3rd Earl of Egremont (*see* WYNDHAM, (2)), another important patron, who was to acquire many works by Turner during the ensuing decade. After a tour of Switzerland and France in 1802, during which he closely studied the paintings in the Louvre, Paris, Turner sent to the Royal Academy watercolours depicting the waterfalls and passes of the Alps, as well as paintings imitating Claude, Titian and Salomon van Ruysdael: these were, respectively, the *Festival upon the Opening of the Vintage at Mâcon* (Sheffield, Mappin A.G.), *Holy Family* (London, Tate) and *Calais Pier, with French Poissards Preparing for Sea: An English Packet Arriving* (London, N.G., see fig. 1). This last work extended the range of his ambitious marine paintings and in turn led to the *Shipwreck* of 1805 (London, Tate), which was acquired by an important patron, John Fleming Leicester, and engraved in mezzotint by Charles Turner (no relation).

3. PRINTMAKING, LECTURING AND POETRY. Turner opened his own gallery in Harley Street in 1804, but continued to send to the Royal Academy exhibitions. In 1807 he initiated a further assault on the public with the first issue of the *Liber studiorum* (version, London, BM), a long series of plates after his own designs, including exhibited subjects. It was modelled on the edition of Richard Earlom's mezzotints after Claude's *Liber veritatis*, which had been published in the 1770s. Turner himself etched the majority of the subjects in outline; they were then mezzotinted by Charles Turner and others. The 14 parts, which appeared irregularly until 1819, each contained five plates, categorized as historical, mountainous, pastoral, marine and architectural. They were a deliberate advertisement of Turner's range and adumbrated a penchant for didacticism that was to emerge recurrently in his career. Also in 1807 he put his name forward for the post of Professor of Perspective to the Academy and was duly elected. He prepared himself carefully by wide reading and gave the first series of lectures early in 1811, illustrating them with diagrams and watercolours that were much admired, though the lectures themselves attracted ridicule for their awkwardness of expression and delivery. He continued to offer the course most years until 1828 and resigned the post in 1837.

In the first decade of the century Turner was flexing his creative muscles in another medium: poetry. He seems to have been inspired by the success of fellow Academician

1. J. M. W. Turner: *Calais Pier, with French Poissards Preparing for Sea: An English Packet Arriving*, oil on canvas, 1.72×2.42 m, 1803 (London, National Gallery)

2. J. M. W. Turner: *Snow Storm: Hannibal and Army Crossing the Alps*, oil on canvas, 1.45×2.36 m, 1812 (London, Tate Gallery, Clore Gallery)

Martin Archer Shee, whose *Rhymes on Art* (1806) had been well received. His sketchbooks of this time are filled with drafts, usually related thematically to pictures on which he was working, notably the *Goddess of Discord Choosing the Apple of Contention in the Garden of the Hesperides* (1806; London, Tate), *View of Pope's Villa at Twickenham, during its Dilapidation* (1808; Sudeley Castle, Glos), *Thomson's Aeolian Harp* (1809; Manchester, C.A.G.) and *Apollo and Python* (1811; London, Tate). In 1812 an important historical subject, *Snow Storm: Hannibal and Army Crossing the Alps* (London, Tate; see fig. 2), was accompanied by his own verses in the Royal Academy catalogue; these were attributed to a manuscript poem, *Fallacies of Hope*, fragments of which Turner was to append to selected exhibits throughout his career, but which never materialized as a completed work. A more sustained performance was the long draft poem he intended as text for George and William Bernard Cooke's *Picturesque Views on the Southern Coast of England* (see §5 below); but all his verses betray signs of strain or uncertainty of diction, even though they are often powerful in conception. James Thomson and the minor 18th-century poets remained his principal models. Since 1798, when the Academy first permitted quotations in its catalogues, he had regularly cited them, along with Milton, and after the appearance of *Childe Harold's Pilgrimage* (1812 and 1816) he added Lord Byron to his list of favourite sources.

Turner seems to have offered a wry comment on his own problems with the poetic muse in a picture exhibited in 1809, the *Garreteer's Petition* (London, Tate). It is a gloomy interior, with the single figure of the uninspired poet, and was catalogued with these lines: 'Aid me, ye Powers! O bid my thoughts to roll/In quick succession, animate my soul/Descend my Muse, and every thought refine,/And finish well my long, my *long-sought* line.' The model here was probably Alexander Pope, just as the visual connotations of the genre subject go back to Hogarth, though the picture is equally a pastiche of Rembrandt and the Dutch genre painters of the 17th century.

4. RESPONSE TO CONTEMPORARY ARTISTS. Dutch genre painting had been brought sharply to Turner's attention by the success of David Wilkie, who had exhibited several works modelled on the rustic interiors of Adriaen van Ostade and Jan Steen. The first to appear, *Village Politicians* (1806; Scone Pal., Tayside), prompted an immediate response from Turner, whose *Country Blacksmith Disputing with the Butcher upon the Price of Iron, and the Price Charged to the Butcher for Shoeing his Poney* (London, Tate) appeared in 1807. It initiated a succession of such 'replies' to fellow-artists: Turner was highly susceptible to stimuli of this kind, being all his life ready to imitate the subject-matter, and even occasionally the manner, of a successful contemporary. This sometimes involved him in playful competition with colleagues. His masterly paraphrase of Aelbert Cuyp, the *Dort, or Dordrecht: The Dort Packet-boat from Rotterdam Becalmed* (1818; New Haven, Yale Cent. Brit. A.), was painted in response to the success of his own follower, Augustus Wall Callcott, whose work, like Turner's, was attacked by

Sir George Beaumont for its use of white, instead of earth-coloured, grounds. Thomas Stothard's Watteau-like decorations prompted such pictures as *What You Will!* (1821; London, Michael Sobell priv. col., see Wilton, 1979, no. 137) and *Boccaccio Relating the Tale of the Birdcage* (1828; London, Tate); George Jones's *Shadrach, Meschach and Abednego in the Burning Fiery Furnace* piqued Turner to deliberate imitation with a painting on the same subject (both 1832; London, Tate). Turner's work displays the Rembrandtian influence that affected many of his works around 1830. Similarly the example of C. R. Leslie led him to paint a few small historical genre scenes, notably *Watteau Study by Fresnoy's Rules* (1831; London, Tate); and as late as 1833 Clarkson Stanfield prompted his first Venetian oil painting, *Bridge of Sighs, Ducal Palace and Custom-house, Venice: Canaletti Painting* (London, Tate). Characteristically, this alludes openly not to Stanfield, but to the master of all Venetian viewmakers, Canaletto, who actually appears in a composition that consciously apes his own subject-types.

5. EXPERIMENTS WITH COLOUR AND TECHNIQUE. The tendency for Turner's pictures to become increasingly light in tonality continued throughout the 1810s until his visit to Italy in 1819, when first-hand experience of Mediterranean light seems to have confirmed his preference for a preponderantly brilliant palette dominated by chrome and cadmium yellows, vermilion and white. In practice, however, the dazzling effect of his work in the 1820s and 1830s, ridiculed by the critics as 'yellow fever', was constructed on a sober and carefully controlled chromatic plan, usually based on contrasted blocks of roughly complementary colours, often an ochre or earth colour and indigo or some other blue. He may have been encouraged in these experiments by those of the colour-man George Field, but a crucial factor in his technical advance was the continuing interaction of oil and watercolour practice. His steady output of topographical watercolours, which had tended to be executed on a large scale during the first decade of the century, took a new turn when he was commissioned to contribute to the Cooke brothers' *Picturesque Views on the Southern Coast of England* (1814–26), the designs for which were all executed in a small format, and Thomas Dunham Whitaker's *History of Richmondshire* (1819–23). The culmination of his newly concentrated style, in which watercolour was applied over broadly washed fields of colour in minute and brilliantly saturated touches, is perhaps the series of views of the *Rivers of England and Wales*, published as a set of mezzotints by Thomas Goff Lupton and others between 1823 and 1827, and its sequel, never published in its entirety, the *Ports of England* (both London, Tate).

These projects necessitated tours in the West Country (1811 and 1813) and in the north of England, where he was a frequent traveller between 1808 and 1825. He had become intimate with Walter Ramsden Fawkes (1769–1825) of Farnley Hall, near Leeds, who built up an unparalleled collection of his paintings and watercolours, also commissioning views of his own properties in Wharfedale, N. Yorks, and the Lake District, and studies of birds and family heirlooms for private albums. After Fawkes's death Turner ceased to visit Farnley, but remained on close terms with Fawkes's son Hawkesworth and his sister.

3. J. M. W. Turner: *Bay of Naples with the Castle of the Egg*, pencil and watercolour, 254×406 mm, 1819 (London, Tate Gallery, Clore Gallery)

By 1818 Turner had perfected an idiosyncratic method of painting in watercolours, which Hawkesworth Fawkes observed during the execution for his father of a *First-rate Taking in Stores* (Bedford, Cecil Higgins A.G.): 'He began by pouring wet paint till it [the paper] was saturated, he tore, he scratched, he scrubbed at it in a kind of frenzy and the whole thing was chaos—but gradually and as if by magic the lovely ship, with all its exquisite minutia, came into being and by luncheon time the drawing was taken down in triumph.' In order to marshal the quantities of detailed information that made up the subject-matter of his watercolours, Turner had taken to making preliminary studies in which the broad colour masses of the design were laid out; sometimes several of these, addressing different aspects of a complex composition, succeeded each other before the final drawing was begun (usually on a slightly smaller sheet). He rarely worked directly from the motif in colour. In Italy in 1819 he is reported as saying 'that it would take up too much time to colour in the open air—he could make 15 or 16 pencil sketches to one coloured'; however, he made many handsome colour studies in Venice, Rome and Naples during that stay, presumably at his hotel rather than out of doors (see fig. 3). He also, very occasionally, worked direct from nature in oil. A sequence of studies in both canvas and panel was made from a boat along the Thames and its tributary the Wey in about 1805; and while he was in Devon, probably in 1813, he felt encouraged to make small open-air sketches in oil on paper. One or two of these he gave to friends, but in general his practice was to retain all his sketches, of whatever type, for reference. His sketchbooks likewise were labelled and kept as sources for material that he might draw on decades afterwards. The long and important series of watercolours of *Picturesque Views in England and Wales* that he executed for Charles Heath the elder between 1825 and 1835—Turner's last major published topographical project—relied heavily on drawings made in sketchbooks in the 1790s, although he undertook further tours during the progress of the work.

Another great topographical enterprise of the 1820s and 1830s was a scheme to produce a series of 'Annuals' illustrating the scenery of the great rivers of Europe; this was not realized, but three volumes concerned with French rivers, the Loire and the Seine, appeared in 1833–5. Turner adopted an unusual format for his designs: using small sheets of blue paper, he worked in gouache instead of watercolour, exploiting the capacity of the medium for brilliant effects of saturated colour. Although these paintings were to be translated into the black and white of line engraving, they rank among his most expressionistic essays in unbridled colour. The brilliant little designs that he made about the same date in pure watercolour, illustrating the works of Samuel Rogers, Walter Scott, Thomas Campbell and Lord Byron, are hardly less impressive in this respect. All these projects apparently have a technical corollary in the series of mezzotints in pure black and white that he made in the late 1820s, the so-called 'Little Liber Studiorum', in which he pushed as far as it could go the expressive potential of black as a colour in its own right.

6. CONTINENTAL TOURS AND WORK AT PETWORTH HOUSE. The 'Rivers of Europe' scheme occasioned several further tours on the Continent, which Turner undertook in the 1820s and 1830s; these also gave rise to some important oil paintings, including *Harbour of Dieppe (Changement de Domicile)* (1825) and *Cologne: The Arrival of a Packet-boat: Evening* (1826; both New York, Frick), as well as *Mouth of the Seine, Quille-boeuf* (1833; Lisbon, Mus. Gulbenkian) and an unfinished subject, apparently showing a fortified town on the Meuse (London, Tate), which demonstrates his working methods in pictures of this type in the late 1820s. One of these tours, that of 1835, took him to Copenhagen, Berlin, Dresden and Vienna, as well as, probably, for a second time to Venice. The motive for this journey, which he used hardly at all to expand his repertory of subjects for finished works, may have been to inspect state picture galleries in connection with the building of the National Gallery in London, then in hand. A more practical, and highly unusual, attempt to involve himself in the artistic activity of the Continent took place in 1828, when he set up a studio in Rome and produced a number of oil sketches and finished pictures, some of which he put on public view. They were received with incomprehension and disgust: Turner's manner was certainly out of sympathy with the medievalizing crispness of the Nazarenes, then based in Rome; their style reached England shortly afterwards and (especially after the arrival of Prince Albert of Saxe-Coburg in 1840) rendered Turner's art outdated, as well as impenetrably idiosyncratic.

After Turner's return in early 1829, all the finished Roman pictures were shown again in London. They included *View of Orvieto*, the *Vision of Medea* and *Regulus* and perhaps *Palestrina* (all London, Tate), a canvas executed as a pendant to Claude's *Landscape with Jacob and Laban* (Petworth House, W. Sussex, NT) in the collection of the Earl of Egremont. Turner had already painted a pastiche of this picture, *Apullia in Search of Appulus* (1814; London, Tate), for a competition at the British Institution, London; he now produced an entirely personal complement to it. Egremont did not, however, acquire it, but in 1828 he commissioned Turner to paint four decorative panels for the dining-room at Petworth House, W. Sussex; these eventually comprised two views of the park at Petworth and views of *Chichester Canal* and the *Brighton Chain Pier*, two projects in which Egremont had a financial interest. They remain *in situ* (oil sketches; London, Tate), as do Egremont's other acquisitions of Turner's work. During one of his stays at Petworth (that of 1827) Turner also made numerous small drawings in gouache on blue paper (as in the 'Rivers of Europe' designs), which record the reception rooms and bedrooms of the house, as well as social events and scenes of intimate conversation between guests, among whom were several of Turner's artist colleagues.

Another canvas that seems to have had its origins in the Roman stay is *Ulysses Deriding Polyphemus* (exh. RA 1829; London, N.G.; see fig. 4). It was a subject on which Turner had been pondering since the beginning of the century, as he had the *Parting of Hero and Leander* (exh. RA 1837; London, N.G., on loan to London, Tate).

4. J. M. W. Turner: *Ulysses Deriding Polyphemus*, oil on canvas, 1.33×2.03 m, 1829 (London, National Gallery)

The brilliant colour of *Ulysses* reflects his experiments in watercolour and gouache during the late 1820s, as well, no doubt, as his sharpened awareness of early Italian fresco painting, gained during the Rome stay, though it is still heavily indebted to the painterly Venetians for its rich brushwork and sensuous palette. Both *Ulysses* and *Hero and Leander* also glance in the direction of a successful young painter from York, William Etty, whose classical subjects and Titianesque colour were attracting wide attention.

Egremont's death in 1837 brought to an end the regular visits to Petworth that Turner had enjoyed from 1827 onwards. By then another patron had begun to occupy a place among the artist's intimate friends: the Scottish landowner H. A. J. Munro of Novar, with whom he travelled to Chamonix and the Val d'Aosta in 1836. Apart from a long series of watercolour studies, one painting resulted from the trip: *Snow-storm, Avalanche and Inundation: A Scene in the Upper Part of the Val d'Aout, Piedmont* (exh. RA 1837; Chicago, IL, A. Inst.). The tour was a prelude to a series of return visits (1841–4) to the Alps; Turner stayed each year at Lucerne, making excursions to different regions of Switzerland. His last Continental forays were two brief cross-Channel trips in the spring and summer of 1845, when he confined his travels to the Normandy coast. These restrictions were imposed on him by failing health. Despite this, he continued to produce a large quantity of work, and the tours of the 1840s resulted in some of his most inspired watercolours (*see* WATERCOLOUR, colour pl. VIII, fig. 1: John Ruskin related how in the winter of 1841–2 Turner approached

his agent, Thomas Griffith (*b* 1795), with fifteen watercolour studies, from which patrons, solicited by Griffith, were to choose subjects for a suite of ten finished watercolours. Only nine buyers were forthcoming, and Griffith himself received the tenth drawing as commission. A further six were executed after the following year's tour (e.g. *Lucerne: Moonlight*; London, BM; see fig. 5), and ten more in 1845. There is reason to believe that still further sets were in hand until the end of Turner's life. All the subjects appear to have been Swiss, except for *Koblenz Bridge* (untraced), which was commissioned by Ruskin.

7. RUSKIN, TURNER AND THE EUROPEAN TRADITION. Ruskin had been moved to admiration of Turner by an early acquaintance with the vignette illustrations that he had designed for Samuel Rogers's *Italy* (1834) and *Poems* (1830). When Turner's Royal Academy exhibits of 1835, which included *Juliet and her Nurse* (Argentina, Fortabat priv. col., see Butlin and Joll, pl. 369) and *Rome from Mount Aventine* (Dalmeny House, Lothian, on loan to Edinburgh, N.G.), were attacked in *Blackwood's Magazine*, he penned an eloquent defence, which he sent to Turner, who discouraged him from publishing it. Ruskin expanded his apologia into a weighty volume, which was published in 1843 as the first volume of *Modern Painters*, a survey of landscape painting that was not completed until 1860. It caused a revival of interest in Turner's work of the preceding two decades, which had increasingly baffled the public. A new generation of collectors, industrialists from Birmingham, Manchester or Belfast, such as Joseph Gillott (1799–1872) and Henry McConnel (1801–

71), began to commission pictures or acquire ones that had been languishing in Turner's gallery.

Turner was not anxious to sell everything he had painted and often went to great lengths to repurchase works that came on to the market. Following Soane's decision to make over his house in London to the public as a museum, and more particularly after the gift by Robert Vernon of his important collection of British pictures to the National Gallery, London, in 1847, he formulated the intention of leaving his finished oil paintings to the nation. He had already, in his will of 1831, bequeathed *Sun Rising through Vapour: Fishermen Cleaning and Selling Fish* (1807) and *Dido Building Carthage or the Rise of the Carthaginian Empire* (1815) to the National Gallery. The latter was perhaps the most evolved of his many paraphrases of the Claudian harbour prototype and had originally been bequeathed along with a later 'companion' picture, the *Decline of Carthage* (1817; London, Tate). The 1807 work was perhaps substituted as constituting a greater contrast of type, being modelled on the 17th-century Dutch marine painters. He refused to sell *Dido Building Carthage*, increasing the price to discourage purchasers. He similarly refused to part with a later masterpiece, the *Fighting Temeraire Tugged to her Last Berth to be Broken up, 1838* (1839; London, N.G.), to which he referred in a draft letter as 'my Darling'.

There seems little doubt that Turner perceived his own output as rivalling in range and quality the whole of the national collection of Old Masters as it then existed. His finished paintings include tributes to Titian, van Dyck, Poussin, Salvator Rosa, Jan van Goyen, Ruysdael, Watteau and Canaletto, as well as the grandiloquent homage to Raphael that he showed after his first visit to Italy, *Rome from the Vatican: Raffaelle Accompanied by La Fornarina, Preparing his Pictures for the Decoration of the Loggia* (1820; London, Tate). In this large canvas, which celebrates both the Renaissance Master and the whole city of Rome as a treasure-house of modern art, Turner seems explicitly to identify himself with the European tradition. A companion piece, painted for Soane but not bought by him, *Forum Romanum* (exh. RA 1826; London, Tate), makes a similarly public statement about the continuing value of the ancient civilization of Rome.

8. COUPLED PICTURES, MODERN SUBJECTS AND LAST WORKS. The opposition of ancient and modern occupied Turner repeatedly and stimulated several pairs of works in the 1830s and 1840s. *Modern Italy: The Pifferari* (Glasgow, A.G. & Mus.) and *Ancient Italy: Ovid Banished from Rome* (1838; priv. col., see Butlin and Joll, pl. 377) treat the relationship between art and culture; while *Ancient Rome: Agrippina Landing with the Ashes of Germanicus* (1839; London, Tate) proposes a fantastic reconstruction of a Classical city (perhaps in tribute to Soane, who had died in 1837), as opposed to the ruins of *Modern Rome: Campo Vaccino* (Dalmeny House, Lothian, on loan to Edinburgh, N.G.). *Childe Harold's Pilgrimage: Italy* (1832; London, Tate) summed up the contemporary perception of beauty in decay, as evoked by Byron in his poem. Turner gave a more formal expression to the idea in *Bay of Baiae, with Apollo and the Sibyl* (1824; see fig. 6) and the *Golden Bough* (1834; both London, Tate). The most striking of the coupled pictures are, however, not concerned with Italy. They are *War: The Exile and the Rock Limpet* and *Peace: Burial at Sea* (1842; both London, Tate) and two pictures of 1844, *Shade and Darkness: The*

5. J. M. W. Turner: *Lucerne: Moonlight*, watercolour, 290×476 mm, 1843 (London, British Museum)

6. J. M. W. Turner: *Bay of Baiae, with Apollo and the Sibyl*, oil on canvas, 1.45×2.38 m, 1824 (London, Tate Gallery, Clore Gallery)

Evening of the Deluge and *Light and Colour (Goethe's Theory): The Morning after the Deluge—Moses Writing the Book of Genesis* (both ex-Tate, London, 1994). The former pair contrasts the exile of Napoleon, framed in a blood-red sunset, with the cool moonlit scene of the obsequies of Turner's colleague David Wilkie. The latter pair puts into practice the idea expressed by Goethe in his *Farbenlehre* that colours carry with them emotional connotations, depending on whether they belong to the warm or cool side of the spectrum. Turner's application of the theory is not, as some have maintained, ironic; though he gives his own twist to the exegesis of Christian redemption by involving the whole composition of *Light and Colour* in a huge bubble, which, as his verses pointed out, is 'Hope's harbinger, ephemeral as the summer fly/Which rises, flits, expands, and dies'.

The ambiguous tone of the paired pictures recurs in other works of the late 1830s and the 1840s, notably in the suffused red sunsets of the *Fighting Temeraire* and *Slavers Throwing Overboard the Dead and Dying: Typhon Coming On* (1840; Boston, MA, Mus. F.A.). The Venetian picture *Sun of Venice Going to Sea* (1843; London, Tate) is ominous only through the implication of its verse (partly from Gray's *The Bard*). But other works of the 1840s are joyous celebrations of the present, and modern criticism has seen them as pessimistic only because Ruskin insisted that Turner's world-view should exactly reflect his own. The *Opening of the Wallhalla, 1842* (London, Tate), shown at the Royal Academy in 1843 and at the Munich Congress of European Art in 1845, takes as its subject the Neo-classical Pantheon of Ludwig I, King of Bavaria, on the banks of the Danube, which Turner used to symbolize the re-emergence of the arts in the peaceful state of Europe

following the defeat of Napoleon. He also maintained a keen and appreciative eye for the pictorial qualities of modern industrial and technological subjects, submitting them to his rigorous academic conception of serious art: a view at Tynemouth, Tyne & Wear, *Keelmen Heaving in Coals by Night* (1835; Washington, DC, N.G.A.), is a witty nocturnal variant on the familiar Claudian seaport at sunset, as is *Whalers (Boiling Blubber) Entangled in Flaw Ice, Endeavouring to Extricate Themselves* (1846; London, Tate), one of four whaling subjects executed in 1845–6, apparently under the influence of a patron, the whaling entrepreneur Elhanan Bicknell. *Rain, Steam and Speed: The Great Western Railway* (1844; London, N.G.; for illustration *see* ROMANTICISM, fig. 2) presents one of the most radical developments of the 19th century in terms of a dazzlingly reinvented Poussinesque perspective. An even more emancipated description of modern travel in adverse weather conditions is the *Snow Storm: Steam-boat off a Harbour's Mouth* (1842; London, Tate), which was ridiculed by the press as 'a mass of soap-suds and whitewash'—criticism that Turner found particularly galling. He claimed to have been lashed to the mast of the vessel and painted it 'to show what such a scene was like' (see Leslie, p. 1).

Many of Turner's late pictures were effectively painted on the walls of the Royal Academy during the varnishing days before the exhibitions opened to the public. Turner's 'performances' on these occasions were admired by his colleagues as unique displays of his creative genius (see Leslie, p. 6):

They looked more like some of the transformation scenes at the pantomime than anything else. . . . Turner used to send these pictures into the Academy with only a delicate effect, almost in monochrome, laid onto the canvas, and very beautiful they looked, often like milky ghosts. They had probably been painted for some time, as they were quite dry and hard; all the bright colour was loaded on afterwards, the pictures gradually growing stronger in effect and colour during the three varnishing days.... He must ... have had many works thus commenced laid by in his studio, from which he would take one, from time to time, to send to the Academy exhibition.

The sequence of Venetian subjects that he submitted in the late 1830s and 1840s seems particularly to have been accomplished in this way and epitomizes the brilliant, misty atmosphere that is so closely associated with his late style.

Turner's last exhibits at the Royal Academy were further paraphrases of Claude: four additions to the long series of works relating the story of Dido and Aeneas at Carthage (one destr.; the others London, Tate). They present the well-known harbour composition in an iridescent haze and were received tolerantly by critics aware of the artist's approaching demise.

II. Bequests.

Although Turner died in the obscurity of his Chelsea house, he was buried with great pomp in the crypt of St Paul's Cathedral, London. His family almost immediately contested his will, which was inadequately defended by his executors, among whom Ruskin had decided, apparently on account of a quarrel, not to stand. By a decree of the Court of Chancery of 1856, a compromise settlement was reached whereby all original works remaining in the artist's possession (not simply his hundred finished pictures as he had stipulated) were to go to the National Gallery, while the large sums of money (some £140,000) he had accumulated in property and Government stocks were divided among the plaintiffs. Turner's primary intentions were therefore never realized. These were to found an asylum for indigent landscape painters on a site purchased by him at Twickenham and to endow a professorship in landscape painting at the Royal Academy. Both objects reveal his overriding concern for the art he had practised all his life, and for its exponents, his professional colleagues, whom he regarded as brothers—his true family. Ruskin volunteered his services to sort, select and exhibit paintings and drawings from the 'Bequest', which consisted of some 300 oil paintings on canvas or panel and over 20,000 drawings, including the contents of nearly 300 sketchbooks. Although Turner had stipulated that his work was to hang in a specially built chamber, to be called 'Turner's Gallery', this never happened. Instead, the selected exhibits were shown in London at Marlborough House, at the National Gallery, at the South Kensington Museum (now the V&A) and elsewhere throughout the second half of the 19th century until the new National Gallery of British Art (now the Tate Gallery) was opened on Millbank, London, in 1897. Here selections of the oil paintings have consistently been on view; the works on paper, however, were removed following a flood in 1928 to the Print Room of the British Museum, London, where they remained until the opening of the Clore Gallery for the Turner Collection on Millbank in 1987. Examples of Turner's work in both oil and watercolour are to be found in collections around the world, most notably in the USA.

III. Character and professional stance.

Turner's private life was passed in secrecy; even his family were kept at a discreet distance. His primary loyalties were to his professional colleagues and friends, including a few patrons, and to the Royal Academy itself, of which he was a devoted and conscientious official. It was with such fellow Academicians as George Jones and the sculptor Francis Chantrey that he was able to relax on convivial excursions to Greenwich or Richmond, and with whom he engaged in playful contests at angling, a favourite recreation. He served frequently as a member of the Royal Academy's Council and Hanging Committee and was passionately involved in its administrative as well as social and artistic affairs.

Turner was highly conscious of the relationship between painter and public, exploiting both the traditional pattern of private patronage and the new independent status conferred on painters by the Royal Academy. Between 1790 and his death he showed watercolours and, from 1796, with rare absences, oil paintings at its spring exhibitions, although from 1804 he used his private gallery to amplify the public display of his work. He followed Reynolds's example in building up a team of able engravers, carefully trained by him to interpret his ideas in black-and-white line or mezzotint for a wider audience. For most of his career he was prepared to execute illustrations on a modest scale for publishers who wished to profit from his reputation. By careful investment of his earnings in Government stocks and in property he established a fortune that he husbanded jealously, earning himself the character of a miser. His tight-fistedness in business dealings contributed to this, and his natural reticence and secretiveness, combined with a deficiency in the social graces and an unprepossessing appearance, ensured that he was ridiculed and misunderstood by superficial acquaintance. He perhaps never sought acceptance in elegant society, but he coveted the office of President of the Royal Academy, a post for which, despite his acknowledged eminence, he was not considered suitable. His close friends, however, testified to his warmth of heart, good humour and generosity, and his company was valued by several distinguished patrons as well as by many of his colleagues.

Turner's awkwardness in society is usually attributed to the conditions of his early life, but it is clear that he was by temperament a man little given either to refinement or to insincerity of manner. He was, as Ruskin described him in 1840, 'a somewhat eccentric, keen-mannered, matter-of-fact, English-minded gentleman: good-natured evidently, bad-tempered evidently, hating humbug of all sorts, shrewd, perhaps a little selfish, highly intellectual; the powers of his mind not brought out with any delight in their manifestation, or intention of display, but flashing out occasionally in a word or a look'.

WRITINGS
J. Lindsay, ed.: *The Sunset Ship: The Poems of J. M. W. Turner* (Lowestoft, 1966)
J. Gage, ed.: *The Correspondence of J. M. W. Turner* (London, 1980)

BIBLIOGRAPHY

Extensive bibliographies are given in Butlin and Joll (1977) and in Wilton (1979), cited below; this list gives only major publications and works that have appeared since those bibliographies were published. Important collections of articles, reprinted essays and other matter relating to Turner are to be found in *Turner Studies*, published biannually since 1980; they are not itemized separately here. Further, more recondite material occasionally appears in *Turner Society News* (quarterly from 1975).

GENERAL

G. D. Leslie: *The Inner Life of the Royal Academy* (London, 1914)

CATALOGUES

W. G. Rawlinson: *Turner's 'Liber Studiorum': A Description and a Catalogue* (London, 1878, rev. 1906)

C. F. Bell: *The Exhibited Works of J. M. W. Turner, R.A.* (London, 1901)

W. G. Rawlinson: *The Engraved Work of J. M. W. Turner, R.A.*, 2 vols (London, 1908–13)

A. J. Finberg: *Complete Inventory of the Drawings of the Turner Bequest*, 2 vols (London, 1909)

——: *The History of Turner's 'Liber Studiorum', with a New Catalogue Raisonné* (London, 1924)

L. Herrmann: *Ruskin and Turner*, Oxford, Ashmolean cat. (Oxford, 1968) [drawings]

M. Kitson: *Watercolours by J. M. W. Turner from the Collection of Sir Stephen Courtauld* (London, 1974)

M. Cormack: *J. M. W. Turner, R.A., 1775–1851: A Catalogue of Drawings and Watercolours in the Fitzwilliam Museum, Cambridge* (Cambridge, 1975)

M. Butlin and E. Joll: *The Paintings of J. M. W. Turner*, 2 vols (New Haven and London, 1977, rev. 1984)

J. Dick: *The Vaughan Bequest of Turner Watercolours*, Edinburgh, N.G. cat. (Edinburgh, 1980)

T. Clifford, ed.: *Turner at Manchester: Catalogue Raisonné, Collections of the City Art Gallery* (Manchester, 1982)

C. Hartley: *Turner Watercolours in the Whitworth Art Gallery* (Manchester, 1984)

B. Dawson: *Turner in the National Gallery of Ireland*, Dublin, N.G. cat. (Dublin, 1988)

MONOGRAPHS

W. Thornbury: *The Life of J. M. W. Turner R.A.*, 2 vols (London, 1862, rev. 1876)

W. C. Monkhouse: *Turner* (London, 1879)

W. Armstrong: *Turner* (London, 1902)

B. Falk: *Turner the Painter: His Hidden Life* (London, 1938)

A. J. Finberg: *The Life of J. M. W. Turner R.A.* (London, 1939, rev. 1961)

J. Lindsay: *Turner: A Critical Biography* (London, 1966)

A. Wilton: *The Life and Work of J. M. W. Turner* (London, 1979) [with catalogues of paintings and watercolours]

J. Lindsay: *Turner: The Man and his Art* (London, 1986)

J. Gage: *J. M. W. Turner: 'A Wonderful Range of Mind'* (New Haven and London, 1987)

A. Wilton: *Turner in his Time* (London, 1987)

SPECIALIST STUDIES

A. J. Finberg: *Turner's Sketches and Drawings* (London, 1910)

——: *Turner's Watercolours at Farnley Hall* (London, [1912])

——: *In Venice with Turner* (London, 1930)

J. Gage: *Colour in Turner* (London, 1969)

G. Wilkinson: *Turner's Early Sketchbooks* (London, 1974)

——: *Turner's Colour Sketches, 1820–34* (London, 1975)

——: *The Sketches of Turner, R.A.* (London, 1976)

J. Dixon Hunt: 'Turner and Landscape Painting: Remarks, Aspects, Glosses', *18th C.*, xx (1979), pp. 260–76

E. Shanes: *Turner's Picturesque Views in England and Wales* (London, 1979)

——: *Turner's Rivers, Harbours and Coasts* (London, 1981)

K. H. Stader: *William Turner und der Rhein* (Bonn, 1981)

G. Wilkinson: *Turner on Landscape* (London, 1982)

A. Wilton: *Turner Abroad* (London, 1982)

D. Hill: *In Turner's Footsteps through the Hills and Dales of Northern England* (London, 1984)

A. Wilton: 'Sublime or Ridiculous? Turner and the Problem of the Historical Figure', *New Lit. Hist.*, xvi (1984–5), pp. 343–76

R. Hamlyn: 'An Early Sketchbook by J. M. W. Turner', *Rec. A. Mus., Princeton U.*, xliv (1985), pp. 2–31

M. Omer: *Turner: Die Landschaften der Bibel* (Vienna, 1985)

L. Stainton: *Turner's Venice* (London, 1985)

B. Venning: 'A Macabre Connoisseurship: Turner, Byron and the Apprehension of Shipwreck Subjects in Early Nineteenth-century England', *A. Hist.*, viii (1985), pp. 303–19

N. Bryson: 'Enhancement and Displacement in Turner', *Huntington Lib. Q.*, xlix (1986), pp. 47–65

A. Wilton: 'Turner at Bonneville', *In Honor of Paul Mellon* (Washington, DC, 1986), pp. 403–27

M. Pointon: 'Turner: Language and Letter', *A. Hist.*, x (1987), pp. 467–74

C. Powell: *Turner in the South: Rome, Naples, Florence* (London, 1987)

S. A. Reid: 'A Vaulted Hall *c.* 1835 by J. M. W. Turner: Its Setting Identified', *Burl. Mag.*, cxxix (1987), pp. 393–4

U. Seibold: *Zum Verständnis des Lichts in der Malerei J. M. W. Turners* (diss., U. Tübingen, 1987)

A. Wilton: *Turner Watercolours in the Clore Gallery* (London, 1987, rev. 1988)

D. Hill: *Turner's Birds* (Oxford, 1988)

A. Wilton, ed.: *The 'Wilson' Sketchbook* (London, 1988)

M. Butlin, I. Warrell and M. Luther: *Turner at Petworth: Painter and Patron* (London, 1989)

K. Nicholson: *Turner's Classical Landscape: Myth and Meaning* (Princeton, 1990)

D. Hill: *Turner in the Alps* (London, 1992)

——: *Turner on the Thames: River Journeys in the Year 1805* (New Haven, CT, 1993)

EXHIBITION CATALOGUES AND BOOKS OF PLATES

R. N. Wornum, ed.: *The Turner Gallery* (London, 1875)

J. M. W. Turner, 1775–1851 (exh. cat., London, Agnew's, 1951)

Paintings and Watercolours by J. M. W. Turner, R.A. (exh. cat., London, Agnew's, 1967)

Turner, 1775–1851 (exh. cat. by M. Butlin, A. Wilton and J. Gage, London, RA, 1974–5)

Turner in the British Museum (exh. cat. by A. Wilton, London, BM, 1975)

Turner and the Sublime (exh. cat. by A. Wilton, Toronto, A.G. Ont.; New Haven, CT, Yale Cent. Brit. A.; London, BM; 1980)

Turner in Scotland (exh. cat. by F. Irwin and D. Irwin, Aberdeen, A.G., 1982)

J. M. W. Turner (exh. cat. by J. Gage, E. Joll and A. Wilton, Paris, Grand Pal., 1983)

K. Solender: *Dreadful Fire! Burning of the Houses of Parliament* (Cleveland, 1984)

J. M. W. Turner: Akvareller, målningar, grafik [Watercolours, paintings, graphic art] (exh. cat. by T. Clifford, Stockholm, Nmus., 1984)

Turner in Wales (exh. cat. by A. Wilton, Llandudno, Mostyn A.G., 1984)

J. M. W. Turner: The Foundations of Genius (exh. cat. by E. Shanes, Cincinnati, OH, Taft Mus., 1986)

Turner (exh. cat. by M. Butlin, E. Joll and A. Wilton, Tokyo, N. Mus. W. A.; Kyoto, Mun. Mus. A.; 1986)

A. Wilton: *The Turner Collection in the Clore Gallery: An Illustrated Guide* (London, 1987)

Turner and the Channel: Themes and Variations, c. 1845 (exh. cat. by D. Blayney Brown, London, Tate, Clore Gal., 1987)

Turner and Architecture (exh. cat. by I. Warrell and D. Perkins, London, Tate, Clore Gal., 1988)

Turner and Natural History: The Farnley Project (exh. cat. by A. Lyles, London, Tate, Clore Gal., 1988)

Young Turner: Early Work to 1800: Watercolours and Drawings from the Turner Bequest, 1787–1800 (exh. cat. by A. Lyles, London, Tate, Clore Gal., 1988)

Colour into Line: Turner and the Art of Engraving (exh. cat. by A. Lyles and D. Perkins, London, Tate, Clore Gal., 1989)

Painting and Poetry: Turner's Verse Book and his Work of 1804–1812 (exh. cat. by A. Wilton, London, Tate, Clore Gal., 1989)

Turner and the Human Figure: Studies of Contemporary Life (exh. cat. by A. Chumbley and I. Warrell, London, Tate, Clore Gal., 1989)

Turner: The Second Decade: Watercolours and Drawings from the Turner Bequest, 1800–1810 (exh. cat. by R. Upstone, London, Tate, Clore Gal., 1989)

Turner: The Third Decade: Watercolours 1810–1820 (exh. cat. by D. Perkins, London, Tate, Clore Gal., 1990)

Turner: The Fourth Decade: Watercolours 1820–1830 (exh. cat. by I. Warrell, London, Tate, Clore Gal., 1991)

Turner: The Fifth Decade: Watercolours 1830–1840 (exh. cat. by A. Lyles, London, Tate, Clore Gal., 1992)

Turner: The Final Years: Watercolours 1840–1851 (exh. cat. by R. Upstone, London, Tate, Clore Gal., 1993)

ANDREW WILTON

Turner, William [Turner of Oxford] (*b* Black Bourton, Oxon, 12 Nov 1789; *d* Oxford, 7 Aug 1862). English painter. He probably received his earliest training from William Delamotte, in Oxford. In 1804 he went to London and became a pupil of John Varley, possibly being formally apprenticed. He first exhibited at the Royal Academy in 1807; in January 1808 he was elected an associate of the Society of Painters in Water-Colours, and in November of that year became its youngest full member. He exhibited there annually from 1808 until his death, sending 455 works in all. His passionate, technically complex youthful work was highly acclaimed, yet its promise remained unfulfilled; around 1811 he returned to Oxfordshire and soon established himself as a drawing-master in Oxford, where he lived for the rest of his life.

Turner worked principally in watercolour, occasionally in oils, and experimented in lithography and etching. His output consisted almost entirely of landscape, and he travelled through Britain in search of subjects, visiting the Wye Valley, the Lake District, north Wales and Derbyshire by 1818. His range was later extended beyond the conventionally picturesque to include many detailed panoramic views, remarkable for their combination of breadth and delicacy (e.g. *View from Bow Hill*; 1846; priv. col., see 1984 exh. cat., no. 68). In 1838 he visited Scotland, where he sketched in both familiar and remote areas; the mysterious power of the uncultivated landscape became a major theme of his late work. Turner was initially influenced by Thomas Girtin; his later work was refined, intensely coloured and tinged with nostalgia. The contents of his studio were auctioned at Christie's, London, on 9 March 1863.

BIBLIOGRAPHY

M. Hardie: 'William Turner of Oxford', *Old Wtrcol. Soc. Club*, ix (1931–2), pp. 1–22 [with a transcript of Turner's marginal notes in his Watercolour Society annual exh. catalogues, 1808–59]

L. Herrmann: ' "This Patient and Unassuming Master": William Turner of Oxford', *Connoisseur*, clxii (1966), pp. 242–7

William Turner of Oxford (1789–1862) (exh. cat. by T. Wilcox and C. Titterington, Woodstock, Oxon Co. Mus., 1984) [with full bibliog.]

TIMOTHY WILCOX

Turnerelli, Peter (*b* Belfast, 1774; *d* London, 18 March 1839). Irish sculptor. His family was of Italian origin and settled in Ireland. In 1793 he moved to London and studied sculpture there under Peter Francis Chenu and at the Royal Academy, where he exhibited from 1802. He spent a period in Italy, where he was deeply influenced by Antonio Canova. From 1797 to 1800 he taught modelling to the daughters of George III and was subsequently Sculptor-in-Ordinary to the Royal Family. This led to a large international royal and aristocratic clientele for whom he modelled busts such as those of *George III* (1810; Windsor Castle, Berks, Royal Col.), *Arthur Wellesley, 1st Duke of Wellington* (1815; London, India Office) and *Louis XVIII* (exh. R.A. 1816). He visited Ireland frequently and while there modelled a bust of *Henry Grattan* (1812; Dublin, N.G.), which Canova praised, and one of *Daniel O'Connell* (1829); reproductions of these had a wide circulation.

Turnerelli's busts are Neo-classical in design, often combining realistic description and contemporary dress. He made a number of memorials for Westminster Abbey, Canterbury Cathedral and elsewhere, including the fine memorial to *Robert Burns* (1816; Dumfries). The tomb of *Archbishop Troy* (*c*. 1823) in St Mary's Pro-Cathedral, Dublin, which is attributed to him, and his high altar relief (1823) there are both based on a Roman Renaissance tomb. His marble sculpture, although idealized, has a softness of description characteristic of the tradition of Canova. Socially he had great success in the circle of the Prince Regent and twice refused a knighthood.

BIBLIOGRAPHY

Gunnis; Strickland

J. Gilmartin: 'Peter Turnerelli, Sculptor, 1774–1839', *Bull. Irish Georg. Soc.*, x/4 (1967), pp. 2–19 [with bibliog.]

JOHN TURPIN

Turning. Technique of shaping wood in a lathe with a sharp tool as it rotates. It is used to make chair legs etc (*see* WOOD (i), §III).

Turone (di Maxio da Camenago) (*fl* Verona, *c*. 1356–80). Italian painter. A Lombard, he worked in Verona, where he was first recorded in 1356 and where he ran a productive and locally dominant workshop. The origins of his style are complex, but the staring eyes and the ponderous mass of the principal figures in the signed and dated Holy Trinity polyptych (1360; Verona, Castelvecchio) suggest the influence of the Giottesque painting of Padua, perhaps filtered through the Veronese work of the Master of the Redentore (*fl c*. 1310–20), or of Tuscan strains in the art of Lombardy. A contrasting daintiness characterizes the minor figures of the polyptych. The bright local colours, the assured design and modelling and the sculptural weight of the figures all mark an advance on the unambitious painting of earlier 14th-century Veronese works. The frame design has close affinities with the stone altarpieces produced in Verona at this period, while the iconography of the *Coronation of the Virgin*, with the Virgin kneeling, suggests contact with Bolognese painting.

The design of a fresco of the *Crucifixion* (*c*. 1360) in S Fermo Maggiore, Verona, reflects Florentine models but combines a monumental figure style with a typically northern interest in genre detail. Turone and his workshop painted frescoes in other Veronese churches, including the *Virgin and Child with SS Zeno and John the Baptist (Madonna delle Grazie)* in S Maria della Scala, an important cult image. Turone participated in, and perhaps directed, the illumination of a series of choir-books for Verona Cathedral (Verona, Bib. Capitolare, MSS MXLVIII–MLXV), some dated 1368, several of which show the dawning influence of Altichiero.

BIBLIOGRAPHY

E. Sandberg-Vavalà: *La pittura veronese del trecento e del primo quattrocento* (Verona, 1926), pp. 131–44

——: 'Turone miniatore', *Dédalo*, x (1929), pp. 15–44

Da Altichiero a Pisanello (exh. cat., ed. L. Magagnato; Verona, Castelvecchio, 1958), pp. 2–6

L. Magagnato: *Arte a civiltà del medioevo Veronese* (Turin, 1962), pp. 72–86 [good colour plates]

R. Pallucchini: *La pittura veneziana del trecento* (Venice, 1964), pp. 141–2

M. T. Cuppini: 'Turone di Maxio da Camenago', *Boll. A.*, n.s. li/5 (1966), pp. 33–42

——: 'L'arte gotica a Verona nei secoli XIV e XV', *Verona e il suo territorio*, iii/2 (Verona, 1969), pp. 300–310

G. Zivelonghi: *La vita di Cristo secondo l'anno liturgico miniato dal Turone nei corali della Biblioteca Capitolare di Verona* (Verona, 1983) [fine colour pls]

JOHN RICHARDS

Turpentine. Colourless, volatile SOLVENT commonly used as a thinner for oil paints and as a solvent for varnish. It is derived from distilling balsam, a resin obtained by tapping pine trees, and has been known since at least the 1st century AD. Balsams are occasionally referred to as turpentines, and the distillate is known as oil or spirits of turpentine. Turpentine has been used in oil painting since the 15th century but has now largely been replaced by solvents derived from petroleum. It has slight toxic and irritant properties.

RUPERT FEATHERSTONE

Turpin de Crissé, Lancelot-Théodore, Comte de (*b* Paris, 6 July 1782; *d* Paris, 15 May 1859). French painter, lithographer and collector. Born into a distinguished military family, he inherited from his father a talent for painting, which was encouraged by the Comte de Choiseul-Gouffier, who sent him to Switzerland (1802–3) and then to Italy (1807–8). Turpin de Crissé exhibited for the first time at the Salon of 1806, showing *René's Farewell* (sold London, Sotheby's, 25 Nov 1981), a romantic subject taken from Chateaubriand's *René*, and a *View of the Temple of Minerva at Athens* (untraced), which had probably been commissioned by Choiseul-Gouffier. He was welcomed into Napoleon's court as the protégé of Queen Hortense and later of the Empress Josephine, to whom he became chamberlain in 1809. He accompanied her to Switzerland and Savoy in 1810, returning with an album of 33 sepia drawings (Malmaison, Château N.) that express a delightful 'troubadour' feeling for nature.

His landscapes were highly prized—the *View taken from Civita Castellana* (exh. Salon 1808; Malmaison, Château N.) was bought by the Empress. The *View of Switzerland, the Town of Sion in the Valais* (1806; exh. Salon 1810; Boulogne-Billancourt, Bib. Marmottan) is the product of a subtle decorative gift and is pervaded by a restrained bucolic atmosphere. In 1813 he married his cousin Adèle de Lesparda, a pupil of Pierre-Joseph Redouté.

In April 1816 he was made a *membre libre* of the Académie des Beaux-Arts and then a member of the Beaux-Arts commission for the Seine and of the Conseil des Musées. On his travels to Switzerland (1816) and Italy (1818 and 1824) he devoted himself entirely to the study of landscape and antiquity. His search for pictures, medals and curiosities dates from this period. In this he was principally concerned with the objects' aesthetic value, showing little interest in their history. From 1825 he was a conscientious Inspecteur Général des Beaux-Arts, responsible for supervising the royal manufactures, theatres and the arts. By 1818 he had met Ingres in Rome, who drew in pencil both his portrait and that of the Comtesse (both New York, Met.). In 1819 he obtained Ingres's *Paolo and Francesca* (1819; Angers, Mus. Turpin de Crissé), which he considered the jewel of his collection. In 1825 he directed the preparations for an album commemorating the coronation of Charles X, entrusting Ingres with the most important pages (portraits of the King and of Cardinal de Latil; Paris, Louvre; Angers, Mus. Turpin

de Crissé). Work on the album was interrupted by the revolution of 1830, which 'restored to him at a stroke his liberty, his cabinet, and the mediocrity of his fortune'. He took up painting again and exhibited landscapes and architectural views regularly at the Paris Salon until 1835.

Turpin de Crissé's surviving works reveal a mastery of drawing constantly refined during his travels in Italy, Switzerland and England. They are classical in their assured, if conventional, composition but show the influence of Romanticism in their acute awareness of light. Typical of his historical landscapes are *Hunter in the Apennines* (see fig.) and *Apollo, Turned out of Heaven, Teaches the Shepherds Music* (exh. Salon 1824; Carpentras, Mus. Duplessis). His lithographs are freer in style and abound in picturesque details. In 1828 he wrote *Souvenirs du Golfe de Naples* with lithographs by other artists after his illustrations, and in 1834 *Souvenirs du vieux Paris* appeared with his own lithographs.

A gift from the artist endowed the Musée Turpin de Crissé at Angers with many records of his travels in Italy, for example *The Temple of Vesta at Tivoli* (1831). His links with the monarchy enabled him to paint pictures (untraced) for the Galerie d'Orléans in the Palais-Royal, Paris, and a *Mass in the Expiatory Chapel* (1835; Paris, Mus. Carnavalet). After 1835 Turpin devoted himself entirely to his collection, bequeathed to the town of Angers in 1859, and from 1889 onwards installed in the Hôtel Pincé. His 'cabinet de curiosités' included Egyptian sculptures, Greek vases, maquettes, coins, antique jewels and drawings, engravings and paintings by his contemporaries and even some photographs.

WRITINGS
Lettre au conservateur de ses collections publiques par J. Levron (Angers, 1937)

BIBLIOGRAPHY
F. Deville: 'Notice biographique sur M. le comte Turpin de Crissé', *Rev. Gén. Biog. & Nécrol.*, xii/1 (1846), pp. 219–222
T. L'Huillier: *Une Famille d'amateurs d'art: Les Turpins de Crissé* (Paris, 1896)
M. de la Grandière: *Le Comte Turpin de Crissé: Un gentilhomme artiste* (Angers, 1935)

VIVIANE HUCHARD

Turquerie. French term used to describe artefacts made in Turkey, or in France by Turkish craftsmen, and by derivation the influence on French design of elements from the Byzantine Empire, the Saljuq Islamic period and the Ottoman Empire. Specific motifs, borrowed from the original Turkish carpets, included arabesques or stylized flowers and vegetal scrolls and decorative animal forms—also included within the generic term 'grotesques'—from the Renaissance onwards. From the Middle Ages inventories and accounts record objects *façon de Turquie* imported from the East through the Crusades or the Silk route. In the accounts (1316) of Geoffroi de Fleuri, treasurer to King Philippe V of France, '11 cloths of Turkey' were noted, and in 1471 the inventory of the château of Angers records a wooden spoon and a cushion 'à la façon de Turquie'. In the 16th century Turkish textiles were highly prized, and Turkish craftsmen were employed in Paris to embroider cloth for ladies' dresses: in 1603 Louise de Vaudemont owned 'a piece of blue satin from Turkey'. These fabrics were often listed alongside carpets: in 1653 Cardinal Mazarin's inventory records 'a coverlet

Lancelot-Théodore Turpin de Crissé: *Hunter in the Apennines*, oil on canvas, 1.60×1.25 m, 1822 (Angers, Musée Turpin de Crissé)

from Turkey' together with some 20 carpets among which was a 'carpet made of wool, from Turkey, with a red ground and flowers *à la turque* in different colours'. In the 17th century *tapis de Turquie* was a generic term to describe all carpets from Persia, Egypt and Asia Minor as well as French carpets made in Turkish or Eastern designs. Such carpets were very valuable and were displayed on tables and buffets, as well as on the ground. In the 17th century, under the influence of André Le Nôtre, gardens were designed to imitate East Asian carpets, with flowerbeds known as *parterres de broderie* or *parterres de Turquerie* in which boxwood was cut in arabesque patterns, for example at the châteaux of Vaux-le-Vicomte and Versailles. In the 18th century there was a limited vogue for *cabinets turcs*, for example that of the Comte d'Artois at Versailles (1780s; three surviving panels, Paris, Mus. A. Déc.), for which François Rémond made a gilt-bronze clock with figures of sultans (1780; Paris, Louvre). Queen Marie-Antoinette commissioned a canapé sofa, footstools and a carpet for her *boudoir turc* (see exh. cat.), and a pair of console tables (*c.* 1780) from a *cabinet turc*, showing turbaned negroes and medallions of Turkish heads, are now in the Frick Collection, New York. Apart from the *cabinets turcs*, in the 18th century Turquerie refers more widely to a certain ORIENTALISM in fashion, literature, paintings, prints and decorative motifs for such objects as fans. The fashion for Turkish smoking rooms and other Turkish elements in the revival style of the 19th century is a direct product of the Orientalist aspect of Romanticism, the love of the Orient that had started in the 17th century with the creation of the East India Companies (1660 in France; *see* CHINOISERIE) and culminated in the 19th century in the poetry of Victor Hugo (e.g. *The Orientals*, 1829) and the harem scenes of J. A. D. Ingres (e.g. *Turkish Bath*, 1863; Paris, Louvre).

BIBLIOGRAPHY

H. Havard: *Dictionnaire de l'ameublement et de la décoration* (Paris, 1887)
Exposition de la Turquerie au XVIIIe siècle (exh. cat., Paris, Mus. A. Déc., 1911)
E. de Ganay: *Les Jardins de France et leur décor* (Paris, 1949)

MONIQUE RICCARDI-CUBITT

Turquet de Mayerne, Sir Théodore (*b* Mayerne nr Geneva, 23 Nov 1573; *d* London, 22 March 1655). Swiss physician and writer, active in England. He studied medicine at the universities of Montpelier and Paris and in 1600 was appointed royal physician to Henry IV of France. Unpopular with the Galenist faction at court who opposed his chemical cures, he nevertheless remained in royal favour. In 1611 he moved to London, where he was employed as principal physician to James I (who knighted him in 1624) and later Charles I. Turquet de Mayerne's scientific background no doubt prompted his interest in the technical aspects of painting; the research he carried out is contained in the manuscript *Pictoria sculptoria et quae subalternarum artium*, which he compiled between 1620 and 1646. His chemical experiments involving pigments apparently led to his discovery of a purple pigment that could be used for carnation tints in enamel painting. Practical issues he followed up included priming canvases and the best way to clean brushes without destroying their bristles. Among those whose opinions and technical advice he sought were Peter Paul Rubens (in London from June 1629 to March 1630), who gave him practical advice on varnishes and mixing pigments, Daniel Mijtens I, Anthony van Dyck and the miniature painter John Hoskins. He also encouraged Edward Norgate's work on technical matters concerning painting in miniature; Norgate's notes (MS Oxford, Bodleian Lib.) were eventually edited and published as *Miniatura, or the Art of Limning* by Martin Hardie in 1919.

Turquet de Mayerne's friendship with Rubens (believed to have begun with the latter's visit to London in 1629) resulted in Rubens's portrait of him and the offer to paint a portrait of his second wife. Although there are several portraits of Turquet de Mayerne that have been attributed to Rubens, the autograph version is probably the *Sir Théodore Turquet de Mayerne* in North Carolina (Raleigh, NC, Mus. A.). He is depicted seated beside a window that gives a view out over a stormy bay and a distant lighthouse; behind the sitter is a statue of Asklepios, a Greek god of healing. Rubens presumably painted this portrait in his Antwerp studio, basing it on a drawing in black chalk washed with brown ink and watercolour (London, BM), which he probably executed while in London. The oil portrait was completed in 1631 and sent to the sitter in London.

UNPUBLISHED SOURCES

London, BL, Sloane MS 2052 [*Pictoria sculptoria et quae subalternarum artium*]

BIBLIOGRAPHY

DNB
A. M. Hind: *Drawings by Rubens, Van Dyck and Other Artists of the Flemish School of the XVII Century* (1918), iv of *Catalogue of Drawings by Dutch and Flemish Artists Preserved in the Department of Prints and Drawings in the British Museum* (London, 1915–32)
F. Huemer: *Portraits, I* (1977), xix of *Corpus Rubenianum Ludwig Burchard* (London)
J. Held: *The Oil Sketches of Peter Paul Rubens*, 2 vols (Princeton, 1980)
C. White: *Peter Paul Rubens: Man and Artist* (New Haven, 1987)

SUSAN JENKINS

Turreau,   (Jean-)Bernard(-Honoré). *See* TORO, BERNARD.

Turrell, James (*b* Los Angeles, 6 May 1941). American installation artist. He studied psychology and mathematics at Pomona College, Claremont, CA (1962–5), and then took a course in fine art at the University of California, Irvine (1965–6). His first projects were carried out at the Mendote Hotel, Ocean Park, CA, which he rented as a studio and exhibition space from 1966 to 1972. Here, using cross-projected halogen lights, Turrell created illuminated geometrical shapes that interacted with the bare interior and with the world outside. In *Shallow Space Constructions* (1968; exh. New York, Whitney, 1980) he used screened partitions, allowing a radiant effusion of concealed light to create an artificially flattened effect within the given space. In his many subsequent installations Turrell was concerned to revivify the viewer's perception of the world, using fixed durations of light and colour to convey the experience of 'touching with sight'. Many of his projects went beyond the confines of galleries and museums. In 1977 he purchased the Roden Crater, an extinct volcano north-east of Flagstaff, AZ. In a most ambitious enterprise, not expected to be completed until the end of the 20th century, Turrell planned to infill the mountain to its original form, leaving a cluster of spaces and walkways within the volcano. Apertures to each compartment were designed to filter various degrees of natural light and to capture the subtle changes of the seasons within a cosmic landscape.

BIBLIOGRAPHY

James Turrell: Four Light Installations (exh. cat., ed. L. J. Millin; Seattle, WA, Cent. Contemp. A., 1982)

Occluded Front: James Turrell (exh. cat., ed. J. Brown; Los Angeles, CA, Mus. Contemp. A., 1985)

James Turrell: The Roden Crater Project (exh. cat. by C. Adcock and J. Russell, Tucson, U. AZ Mus. A., 1986)

Mapping Spaces: A Topological Survey of the Work by James Turrell (New York, 1987)

C. Adcock: *James Turrell: The Art of Light and Space* (Berkeley and Los Angeles, 1990)

James Turrell: Behind my Eyes: An Anthology of Perception (Flagstaff, 1994)   ☐

Turrisan [Turrizani], **Petrus**. *See* TORRIGIANI, PIETRO.

Tuscan order. *See under* ORDERS, ARCHITECTURAL.

Tuscany, Grand Dukes of. *See* MEDICI, DE'.

Tuscher [Discher; Tischer; Tüscher; Tyscher], **(Carl) Marcus** (*b* Nuremberg, 30 March 1705; *d* Copenhagen, 6 Jan 1751). German architect, painter, illustrator and engraver. The illegitimate child of a braidmaker, he spent some years in the Nuremberg orphanage before being apprenticed to the director of the academy of drawing and painting, Johann Daniel Preissler. Among his early works are *Views of the Orphanage in Nuremberg* (1723–6; Nuremberg, Stadtbib.) and a plan with elevation, section and groundplan of the Orphanage (1727; Nuremberg, Nmus.). In 1728 the city council financed his study tour to Rome, where he was introduced to the art collector Philipp von Stosch by his former fellow pupil Johann Justin Preissler. Tuscher prepared a series of drawings for a work on Stosch's gemstones, *Description des pierres gravées du feu Baron de Stosch* (Florence, 1760) by Johann Joachim Winckelmann, and drew his medal collection. He also produced drawings of various monuments in Florence and Tuscany, views of newly discovered antiquities and pictures of historic festive decorations. On Stosch's recommendation Tuscher was commissioned by Cardinal Melchior de Polignac, France's ambassador at the papal court, to record in gouache 'the great fireworks on the Piazza Navona' celebrating the birth of the Dauphin in 1729. Tuscher also addressed various architectonic problems, resulting in his *Abecadario dell'architettura civile . . . coll'aggiunta d'un saggio d'un ordine nuovello . . .* (1743), containing drawings of buildings in the so-called 'Noric' order and architectural designs in a variety of styles. In 1741 he visited several Italian cities, including Florence, Cortona, Livorno and Naples, before travelling via Paris and Holland to London, where he intended to establish an academy of art. There he renewed a friendship with Frederik Ludwig Norden (1708–42), for whose *Voyage d'Egypte et de Nubie* (Copenhagen, 1755) he executed copper engravings.

In 1743 Tuscher was summoned to Copenhagen as a court painter. He travelled with Johann Lorenz Natter and Lorenz Spengler, whom he had met in Britain, and on 12 February 1748 was appointed the first professor at the academy of drawing and painting. He had a considerable influence on the large-scale architectural designs of the court architect Niels Eigtved for the new district of Fredriksstad. He also produced a series of paintings, mainly with Antique and allegorical themes, primarily executed for the castles of the Danish kings; most of these have been lost. A sketch of the total composition and detail

Marcus Tuscher: design for an amber chandelier, pen and ink, 1746–53 (Copenhagen, Kongelige Kobberstiksamling, Statens Museum for Kunst); executed by Lorenz Spengler, h. 1.04 m, 1753 (Copenhagen, Rosenborg Slot)

studies convey some impression of the allegory *Christian VI Receiving the Allegiance of Denmark and Norway* (1748; ex-Christiansborg Slot, Copenhagen; destr. 1794). Tuscher's paintings, drawings and engravings were all greatly influenced by the school of Carlo Maratti and by Sebastiano Conca. Pen-and-ink drawings provided the basis for works in amber (Copenhagen, Rosenborg Slot) executed by Lorenz Spengler, including designs for a large chandelier (see fig.), an amber bowl and a vase on a gilded stem (1748).

BIBLIOGRAPHY

F. F. Leitschuh: 'Die Familie Preisler und Markus Tuscher. Ein Beitrag zur Geschichte der Kunst im 17. und 18. Jahrhundert', *Beitr. Kstgesch.*, n. s. ii (1886), pp. 1–85

M. Due: *Carl Marcus Tuscher: Hofmaler og Hofbygmester* (Copenhagen, 1916)

H. Egger: 'Philipp von Stosch und die für seinen "Atlas" beschäftigten Künstler', *Festschrift der Nationalbibliothek in Wien* (Vienna, 1926), pp. 221–33

E. von Philippovich: 'Elfenbeinkunstwerke Nürnberger Provenienz, zugleich ein Beitrag zur Nürnberger Beziehung nach Dänemark', *Mitt. Ver. Gesch. Stadt Nürnberg*, xlix (1959), pp. 339–60

F. Barroni Salvadori: 'Marcus Tuscher, artista norico fra la Toscana e Roma', *Bib. Bibliog. It.*, lxxxvi (1978), pp. 85–118

SONJA WEIH-KRÜGER

Tusculum. *See under* FRASCATI.

Tusŏngyŏng. *See* YI AM (ii).

Tutankhamun [Nebkheperure] (*reg c.* 1332–*c.* 1323 BC). Ancient Egyptian king of the late 18th Dynasty. His virtually intact Theban tomb (numbered KV 62) was discovered at the Valley of the Kings, in 1922, by Howard Carter. The art of Tutankhamun's reign epitomizes the immediate post-AMARNA STYLE. The significance of his tomb's contents (Cairo, Egyp. Mus.) for the cultural history of Ancient Egypt is still largely unstudied. Few of these artefacts—ranging from chariots to canopic vases—have been dealt with as works of art, and many are characterized by excessively ambitious design because of attempts to incorporate a plethora of religious symbols into the structure of a single item, a tendency particularly evident in the jewellery and the ceremonial calcite vessels. The technical precision evinced in the execution of these designs is, however, generally high, as Aldred has demonstrated for the gold work. (For illustration of artefacts *see* JEWELLERY, colour pl. IV, fig. 2 and WOOD, colour pl. III, fig. 1.)

Tutankhamun was probably born in el-Amarna (the city founded by AKHENATEN), where he was known as Tutankhaten, but he abandoned this residence in favour of the traditional capital Memphis, soon after his accession. It is at Saqqara, the Memphite necropolis, that the tombs of his regent, HOREMHEB, and his chancellor, Maya, have been rediscovered. Objects excavated at el-Amarna associated with Tutankhamun are meagre, but one object securely dated to the beginning of his reign is the 'golden throne' (Cairo, Egyp. Mus., JE 62028) from his Theban tomb. Its decoration pictures Tutankhamun and his queen in the style typical of the last phase of the Amarna period. The radiant sun disc of the Aten (the favoured god of Akhenaten) makes its final appearance on this monument.

Representations of the King and Queen in an informal, intimate setting, so characteristic of the Amarna period, are found in the decoration of other pieces from the tomb, such as the small golden shrine (Cairo, Egyp. Mus., JE 61481). For constructing the human figure, sculptors and draughtsmen returned to the traditional 18-unit grid, rejecting the 20-unit grid introduced under Akhenaten (*see* EGYPT, ANCIENT, §IV, 3). Significant for the subsequent development of monumental relief was the creation of new themes that were taken up and elaborated under the Ramesside kings (*c.* 1292–*c.* 1075 BC), such as large-scale battle scenes with the archer–pharaoh in his chariot as the focal point. Thus true narrative relief was already being created in the reign of Tutankhamun, rather than being an innovation of Sethos I (*reg c.* 1290–*c.* 1279 BC) as was previously thought.

A stele bearing the important 'restoration decree' (Cairo, Egyp. Mus., CG 34183) claims that new temple statuary was produced during Tutankhamun's reign; presumably statues depicting the god Amun were commissioned in large numbers, to replace those destroyed by Akhenaten's agents. A notable example is the statue of Amun enthroned with a diminutive (now headless) Tutankhamun standing before him (Paris, Louvre, E. 11609), from Karnak. There is also a quartzite colossus of Amun still standing in Karnak Temple (see fig.). In both of these monumental hardstone figures, the treatment of the eye area (the upper

Quartzite colossus of the god Amun (detail), total original h. *c.* 4.9 m, from the reign of Tutankhamun (*c.* 1332–*c.* 1323 BC), Karnak Temple, Luxor

lid defined by a flattened ridge with a sharp edge) and the slightly smiling mouth are features derived from the statuary of AMENOPHIS III and adapted subsequently in the best works of Ramesses II. The overall impression created by these images is of benign aloofness. Other statues in a softer, more naturalistic style evolved from the late Amarna period are exemplified by another figure of Amun from Karnak (Luxor Mus., J 198).

Tutankhamun ordered the decoration of the Processional Colonnade at Luxor Temple, the largest architectural monument of his reign still standing (*see* THEBES (i), §III). Associated inscriptions assert that Tutankhamun 'renewed' this temple for his 'father' Amenophis III (*reg c.* 1390–*c.* 1353 BC), the last orthodox ruler of the 18th Dynasty. At Karnak, as at Luxor Temple, some of Tutankhamun's monuments served a propagandist purpose, associating the King again with Amenophis III. Figures depicting Tutankhamun were added to the third pylon at Karnak, and restoration work was carried out on a building of Amenophis III whose decoration had been damaged during the iconoclastic phase of Akhenaten's reign. These restorations were executed in fine, low relief, in contrast to the markedly bold style of the original. The crio-sphinx avenue linking the tenth pylon at Karnak with the Mut precinct is attributable to the reign of Tutankhamun, who may perhaps have built on the tenth pylon as well. New projects may have included a structure named the 'mansion' of Tutankhamun at Thebes, left unfinished at his death. The reign also witnessed the first officially sanctioned attacks on monuments erected by Akhenaten.

BIBLIOGRAPHY

LÄ: 'Tutanchamun'

H. Carter: *The Tomb of Tut.ankh.Amen*, 3 vols (London, 1923–33)

P. Gilbert: 'L'Art au tombeau de Tout-Ankh-Amon', *Tout-Ankh-Amon*, ed. J. Capart and others (Brussels, 1950), pp. 185–204

J. R. Harris, ed.: *Tut'ankhamun's Tomb Series I–IX* (Oxford, 1963–90) [monographs on different types of obj. from the tomb]

C. Aldred: *Tutankhamun: Craftsmanship in Gold in the Reign of the King* (New York, 1979)

M. Eaton-Krauss: 'Tutankhamun at Karnak', *Mitt. Dt. Archäol. Inst.: Abt. Kairo*, 44 (1988), pp. 1–11

[C.] N. Reeves: *The Complete Tutankhamun. The King. The Tomb. The Royal Treasure* (London, 1990)

M. Eaton-Krauss: 'Neue Forschungen zum Schatz des Tutanchamun', *Ant. Welt*, 22 (1991), pp. 97–105

——: *The Sarcophagus in the Tomb of Tutankhamun* (Oxford, 1993)

MARIANNE EATON-KRAUSS

Tuthmosis III [Menkheperre] (*reg c.* 1479–*c.* 1426 BC). Ancient Egyptian ruler and patron of the 18th Dynasty. The long reign of Tuthmosis III can be viewed as both a retrospective and a formative period for Egyptian art and architecture of the New Kingdom, a period in which artists endeavoured both to preserve the standards of the past and to experiment with novel ideas. One of the greatest military figures of Egyptian history, Tuthmosis III passed the first half of his reign under the shadow of his stepmother and aunt, HATSHEPSUT (*reg c.* 1479–*c.* 1458 BC). He succeeded his father, Tuthmosis II (*reg c.* 1482–*c.* 1479 BC), at a young age, and although monuments such as the temple of Semna in Nubia were dedicated in his name during these early years, the management of affairs of state was largely in the hands of Hatshepsut acting as queen regent. Throughout his co-regency with Hatshepsut, Tuthmosis was accorded secondary (and occasionally equal) mention on royal and private monuments, and it is only from the beginning of his sole reign, in his regnal year 22, that the policies and, endeavours of the Egyptian throne can be unequivocally ascribed to him.

The sculptural style of the first kings of the 18th Dynasty, natives of Thebes, owes much to the rather severe appearance of royal statuary of the late Middle Kingdom, which must have served as a model for Theban sculptors of the time. In contrast, the sculpture of both Hatshepsut and Tuthmosis III is characterized by a youthful idealism that initiates a clear break with the past and with provincial Theban traditions. The royal physique is typically that of a young athlete: vigorous, slim and lightly muscled, as in the marble statuette of Tuthmosis III from Deir el-Medina (Cairo, Egyp. Mus., JE 43507A). His face is smooth and seamless, the small mouth is curved in a bland smile that expresses a sweet naivety. The eyebrows follow the rounded arc of the eyes, and the nose is often noticeably aquiline; a pointed chin and plump cheeks enhance the youthful image. Remarkably, these traits remained consistent for almost the whole of his reign, in such works as the colossal red granite statue

(New York, Met., 14.7.15) from Medamud and the greywacke statue (Luxor Mus., J2; *see* EGYPT, ANCIENT, fig. 59) from Karnak.

The remains of numerous architectural projects of Tuthmosis III have been identified at sites throughout Egypt and Nubia, but his major surviving monuments are located at Thebes. In expanding the Temple of Amun at Karnak, he rebuilt the court of Tuthmosis I (*reg c.* 1493–*c.* 1482 BC) and the shrine containing the portable bark of the god, added several pylons, dedicated seven obelisks and erected a vast festival complex notable for its imaginative depictions of Syrian flora. An account of his campaigns, apparently extracted from official journals and carved in the hall to the east of the 6th pylon at Karnak, is unique among royal military reliefs for its objective historicity. His tomb in the Valley of the Kings, at western Thebes, is the earliest datable royal tomb that can be termed typical of the New Kingdom, establishing a plan that was to be followed and expanded by his successors of the 18th and 19th dynasties. His temple, named Djeserakhet, at Deir el-Bahri has been excavated by a joint Polish and Egyptian team, yielding thousands of fragments of brilliantly painted relief, which have yet to be completely studied (for further discussion *see* THEBES (i), §IV).

The artistic achievements of the reign of Tuthmosis III were due in no small part to domestic prosperity and to the sudden expansion of an Egyptian empire. The impressive royal and private monuments of the time reflect an awareness of the greatness of Egypt's past as well as a thirst for rediscovering it in the present. The artistic achievements of Tuthmosis III's reign are a result not only of a sudden increase in material wealth but also of the rise of a large administrative and scribal class, a permanent standing army and an extensive workforce associated with temples. They also heralded the dramatic changes that occurred in Egyptian society as a result of the foreign ventures of Tuthmosis III and his successors.

BIBLIOGRAPHY

LÄ: 'Deir el-Bahari III', 'Tuthmosis III'

P. Barguet: *Le Temple d'Amon-Rê à Karnak* (Cairo, 1962), pp. 87–223, 258–272

K. Mysliewic: *Le Portrait royal dans le bas-relief du Nouvel Empire* (Warsaw, 1976), pp. 46–9, pls. xxxii–xli

L. Habachi: *The Obelisks of Egypt* (New York, 1977), pp. 72–7

PETER F. DORMAN

Tutin, Mary. *See* GILLICK.

Tuttle, Richard (*b* Rahway, NJ, 12 July 1941). American draughtsman, sculptor and installation artist. He was a student at Trinity College, Hartford, CT (1959–63), and at the Cooper Union, New York (1963–4), and he worked for a time as assistant to Agnes Martin. His first works, small monochrome reliefs, were followed by such sculptural works as *Paper Cubes* (1963), comprising a group of small (72×72×72 mm) paper objects penetrated with geometric slots. These were followed in turn by a number of works in wood (e.g. *Yellow Dancer*, 1965; priv. col.; *see* 1975 exh. cat., p. 33) that have an almost calligraphic quality and by a series of works in which Tuttle experimented with irregularly shaped pieces of dyed cloth (e.g. *Grey Extended Seven*, 1967; New York, Whitney). These works demonstrated an interest in Minimalism that continued in the 1970s in numerous works that used lines created from pencil marks, wire and shadow effects to investigate three-dimensionality (e.g. *6th Wire Piece*, 1972; artist's col.). Tuttle's interest in small, intimate works with relief-like qualities continued into the 1980s in such works as *Silver Mercury* (1986; New York, Whitney).

BIBLIOGRAPHY
Richard Tuttle (exh. cat. by M. Tucker, New York, Whitney; Los Angeles, CA, Otis A. Inst. Gal.; 1975)
Private Notations, Artist's Sketchbooks II (exh. cat. by J. Kardon and others, Philadelphia, PA, Coll. A., 1976)
Richard Tuttle (exh. cat. by R. W. McKaskell, London, U. W. Ont., McIntosh A.G., 1976)
G. Vema: *List of Drawing Materials of Richard Tuttle & Appendices* (Zurich, 1979)
Richard Tuttle (exh. cat., Amsterdam, Stedel. Mus., 1979)
Richard Tuttle: From 210 Collage-Drawings (exh. cat. by H. Smith, Pasadena, CA, Inst. Tech., 1980)
Richard Tuttle (exh. cat., Calais, Mus. B.-A., 1982)
P. Schjedahl: *Art of our Time: The Saatchi Collection*, i (London and New York, 1984)
Richard Tuttle, Engineer (exh. cat. by S. Ullmann, Portland, OR, Cent. Visual A., 1984)
Richard Tuttle (exh. cat. by D. Stemiler, Mönchengladbach, Städt. Mus. Abteiberg, 1985)   □

Tuttukkudi [Tuticorin]. Town on the south-east coast of Tamil Nadu, India. Founded in 1540 by the Portuguese, it was captured by the Dutch in 1658. By 1700 there was a population of 50,000 according to Jesuit reports. In 1782 it was taken by the British, who restored it to the Dutch in 1785. It changed hands twice more and figured in the Poligar War of 1801, when it was held by the Poligar of Panchalamkuricchi, a petty chief called Kattabomman Wayaka (executed 1799), and his two brothers (both executed 1801). It passed to the British again in 1825. The Catholic church of Our Lady of the Snows dates from the 17th century. There is also an old Dutch cemetery containing some fine Baroque tombstones with armorial bearings.

A few kilometres to the south along the coast is the temple of Tiruchendur, commemorating the spot where the god Subrahmanya or Murugan is said to have leapt ashore after defeating the demon Surapadma in the sea. The nucleus of this temple is a shrine hewn out of the rock, probably under the PANDYA kings in the 9th or 10th century. The principal shrine is to Subrahmanya and his two consorts Teyvayanai (Devasena) and Valli. The entrance tower (*gopura*) is some 42 m high and is visible from a great distance.

BIBLIOGRAPHY
N. Subrahmanian: *History of Tamilnad (AD 1565–1956)* (Madurai, 1977), pp. 190–93
P. Davies: *Islamic, Rajput, European*, ii of *The Penguin Guide to the Monuments of India* (London, 1989), p. 578

J. MARR

Tuva. *See under* RUSSIA, §XII, 4.

Tuvalu [formerly Ellice Islands]. Group of nine low-lying coral atolls in the South Pacific Ocean, situated *c.* 800 km north of Fiji. North to south they are Nanumea, Niutao, Nanumanga, Nui, Vaitupu, Nukufetau, Funafuti, Nukulaelae and Niulakita. The total land area is 26 sq. km and the population *c.* 9000 (UN estimate 1989). The people are predominantly Polynesian and came mainly from Samoa via Tokelau. The name Ellice Islands was conferred on Funafuti in 1819 and applied to the whole group from the 1840s. The group was annexed by Britain in 1892 and governed jointly with the neighbouring Gilbert Islands (now Kiribati) as a protectorate until 1917, and then as a colony. In 1975 the Ellice Islands became a separate administrative region known as Tuvalu, becoming independent in 1978. The capital is Funafuti.

Much of the traditional culture of Tuvalu was destroyed by Samoan pastors of the London Missionary Society. By 1880 they had established a regime intolerant of anything deemed to be a relic of paganism. Many chants, dances and ceremonies fell into disuse, while tattoo and the wearing of ornaments, such as pendants made of shell or from the teeth of dolphin or whale, were discouraged. Thus, the ornaments used by Tuvaluans have come to be made almost exclusively from plants, intended for use on a single occasion. Moreover, sculptures, figures roughly worked in stone, and shrines were destroyed. The shrines (*afu*) took the form of a vault constructed from slabs of coral rock containing the grave of an ancestor. It was the custom for the population to journey around the island in short stages, halting for a day or two at each shrine, where a priest (*vaka atua*) would address the spirit it was believed to contain. With the arrival of the missionaries the Tuvaluans were cut off from their past, even from knowledge of it. Nevertheless, they did maintain much of their material culture, at least until imported manufactured goods became more abundant from the 1940s.

Typically, Tuvaluan material culture was simply constructed, functional, of limited variety and unadorned. For a small population occupying islands that were isolated, infertile, short of timber, and subject to cyclones it could hardly be otherwise. Decoration was confined mainly to patterns woven into pandanus-leaf mats and to those used in tattoo. The standard designs were built around a combination of parallel lines and diamond- or star-shaped devices. It was common for the bodies of both men and women to be tattooed along the sides, from the knees to the shoulders. Houses were constructed on an A-frame of wooden ribs covered with thatch and were meagrely furnished. The main items they contained were mats, wooden backrests, pillows of wood or of woven pandanus-leaf, and woven baskets for holding fighting skirts (*takai*) made from strips of hibiscus bark. The Tuvaluans produced a range of canoes and such fishing equipment as hooks, nets and spears, and lidded wooden boxes for holding the fishermen's hooks and lines while the canoes were at sea. Canoes (*vaka*) characteristically have outriggers and a triangular sail of pandanus-leaf matting, although paddles are also used. They are constructed from a hollowed-out tree trunk, with raised sides made of planks. The largest canoes may reach 11 m in length and may carry up to 20 people on a platform built over the outrigger.

Since independence Tuvalu has frequently issued sets of colourful postage stamps, some of which depict items of local culture. The sale of these stamps internationally has contributed significantly to the national income.

BIBLIOGRAPHY

H. Hale: *Ethnography and Philology* (Philadelphia, 1846), vii of *Narrative of the United States Exploring Expedition during the Years 1838, 1839, 1840, 1841, 1842 under the Command of Charles Wilkes, U.S.N.* (Philadelphia, 1844–74)

C. Hedley: 'General Account of the Atoll of Funafuti', *Mem. Austral. Mus.*, iii/1 (1896), pp. 3–71

——: 'The Ethnology of Funafuti', *Mem. Austral. Mus.*, iii/4 (1897), pp. 229–304, pls xiii–xv

D. G. Kennedy: *Field Notes on the Culture of Vaitupu, Ellice Islands*, Mem. Polynes. Soc., ix (New Plymouth, 1931)

G. Koch: *Die materielle Kultur der Ellice-Inseln*, Veröff. Mus. Vlkerknd., Berlin, n. s. 3/Südsee 1 (Berlin, 1961; Eng. trans., 1984)

B. Macdonald: *Cinderellas of the Empire: Towards a History of Kiribati and Tuvalu* (Canberra and London, 1982)

H. Laracy, ed.: *Tuvalu: A History* (Suva, Fiji, 1983)

L. Hanson and F. A. Hanson: *The Art of Oceania: A Bibliography*, Ref. Pubns A. Hist. (Boston, MA, 1984)

P. McQuarrie: *Tuvalu: A Celebration in Photos of 10 Years Independence* (Funafuti, 1988)

HUGH LARACY

Tuxen, Laurits Regner (*b* Copenhagen, 9 Dec 1853; *d* Copenhagen, 21 Nov 1927). Danish painter. He was instructed in the tradition of academic realism at the Kunstakademiet in Copenhagen between 1868 and 1872, but later studies in Paris, with Léon Bonnat, and Rome (1879–80) guided him towards naturalism. As professor (1880–1905) at the School of Artistic Studies, Copenhagen, founded to counteract the conversatism of the official Royal Academy of Fine Arts there, Tuxen was able to introduce naturalism to Danish students, making the way for 20th-century modernism. Until the end of the century, Tuxen lived and worked a great deal in Paris, where he adopted a cosmopolitan style that set him apart from his Scandinavian contemporaries. His fame rested on his position as one of Europe's leading court painters for over 30 years. He introduced relative freshness and modernity to such royal group portraits as *Christian IX and his Family at Fredensborg Castle* (1886; Copenhagen, Christiansborg Slot, Queen's Reception Rooms) and the British equivalent, *H.M. Queen Victoria and Family at Windsor Castle, Jubilee* (1887; Windsor Castle, Berks, Royal Col.). With his well-developed feeling for colour harmony and virtuoso manipulation of bright hues, he painted directly on to the canvas without preliminary drawing, although he did produce a number of remarkably free oil sketches, for example *Queen Victoria* (1894; Copenhagen, Hirschsprungske Saml.) and a study for *The Duke of York's Wedding* (1894; Windsor Castle, Berks, Royal Col.). His royal sitters are informally grouped as ordinary human beings and not the sublime divinities celebrated in royal portraits of the absolutist era.

The French influence of Jules Bastien-Lepage on Tuxen is apparent in *Paula and Yvonne Rebeque* (1899; priv. col.). After 1900 he was a member of the Scandinavian artists' colony at Skagen. The naturalism characteristic of his work at this time was derived from Claude Monet's paintings of the 1860s and 1870s. In the last decade of Tuxen's life, with the *Artist's Wife and Daughters in Dagminne Garden* (1922; Skagen, Skagens Mus.), his art was reinvigorated with an expressionistic, impasto handling of paint.

WRITINGS

En malers arbejde gennem tredsindstyve aar, fortalt af ham selv [Sixty years of a painter's work, in his own words] (Copenhagen, 1928)

BIBLIOGRAPHY

A. L. Baldry: 'The Work of Professor Laurits Tuxen', *A.J.* [London] (1904), pp. 109–14

L. Svanholm: *Laurits Tuxen* (in preparation) [monograph and cat. rais.]

LISE SVANHOLM

Túy [anc. Tude; Galician Tui]. City situated on the estuary of the River Miño in Pontevedra province, Galicia, Spain. Túy existed before the Roman conquest and grew in importance in the periods of Suevi and Visigothic domination (411–711), when it was the seat of a bishopric and a centre for minting coinage. After the Arab invasion (721), successive raids by Vikings (844–1016) and Arabs (997) frustrated attempts to restore the city. The independence of Portugal (1128) made Túy strategically important as a frontier fortress and the subject of frequent disputes between the new Kingdom and that of Castile and León, since its diocesan boundaries included Portuguese territory until the 15th century. Ferdinand II granted the city privileges (1170) and encouraged the rebuilding of its fortifications.

Medieval sources are unclear as to the site, or successive sites, of the city, although it is now generally agreed that the present location, on a hill dominating the River Miño and crowned by the fortified cathedral, could well be its original one. The restoration of the bishopric in 1071, however, was provisionally located in the suburb of Rebordáns, in the monastery of S Bartolomé, the church of which, with nave and two aisles, is considered one of the outstanding examples of Galician Romanesque. Its sculptural decoration, similar to that of the church of S Martín de Mondoñedo (Lugo), reflects in a rather crude manner the tradition developed on the Santiago pilgrim route between Frómista and Jaca at the end of the 11th century, with parallels especially in the Aragonese church of S María de Iguácel.

1. CATHEDRAL. Begun *c.* 1140, Túy Cathedral was built in two main campaigns. Both the architecture and the sculptural decoration of the first phase reflect Santiago de Compostela, but the second phase, completed between 1218 and 1232, shows the influence of northern French Gothic. The chevet was rebuilt in the 15th century. The west façade portal (*c.* 1225) is one of the first Gothic examples in Spain. Its tympanum is divided into three registers, bearing scenes of the *Annunciation*, the *Nativity*, the *Annunciation to the Shepherds*, the *Magi before Herod* and the *Adoration of the Magi*, surmounted by a representation of the *Heavenly Jerusalem*, the last giving the preceding scenes an eschatological significance. Like the repeated allusions to the Coronation of the Virgin in the scenes of the *Nativity* and the *Adoration of the Magi*, this detail creates an iconographic programme that combines a narrative Infancy cycle with a representation of the Virgin as a type of the Church, as seen in French Gothic portal programmes. The column-statues expand this programme: Solomon with the dwarf Marcolf at his feet, the Queen of Sheba, St Peter, and figures probably representing Daniel and Isaiah are grouped with two representatives of Christ-bearers, SS John the Baptist and Simeon. Simeon holds the crucified Christ in his arms, embodying his prophetic vision of the Passion in a daring piece of iconography, the earliest of three in Galicia, a precedent

for which appeared in the cloister of Notre-Dame-en-Vaux, Châlons-sur-Marne. The iconography of the individual scenes is rendered in an animated and expressive fashion that surpasses the plastic qualities of the sculpture, which suggest a provincial version of sculpture at Laon Cathedral, through St Yved, Braine, as well as recalling work at Sens Cathedral.

The sculpture of the cathedral was influential on both sides of the River Miño, particularly in Portugal.

BIBLIOGRAPHY

A. L. Mayer: 'The Decorated Portal of the Cathedral of Tuy', *Apollo*, ii (1925), pp. 8–12

F. B. Deknatel: 'The Thirteenth Century Gothic Sculpture of the Cathedrals of Burgos and Leon', *A. Bull.*, xxvii (1935), pp. 243–389 (245–52)

A. Duran Sanpere and J. Ainaud de Lasarte: *Escultura gótica*, A. Hisp., viii (Madrid, 1956), pp. 15–17

S. Moralejo: *Escultura gótica en Galicia* (Santiago, 1975), pp. 7–14

I. Bango Torviso: *Arquitectura románica en la provincia de Pontevedra* (Corunna, 1979), pp. 239–45

S. Moralejo: 'La Rencontre de Salomon et de la reine de Saba: De la Bible de Roda aux portails gothiques', *Cah. Saint-Michel de Cuxa*, xii (1981), pp. 79–109 (92–3)

S. MORALEJO

Tuyru Tupac Inca, Juan Tomás (*b* San Sebastián; *d* Cuzco, 1718). Peruvian architect and sculptor. A descendant of the Inca nobility, he was the finest of the indigenous craftsmen who participated in the reconstruction of the old Inca capital, Cuzco, after the earthquake of 1650. He was self-taught as well as being trained in the system of guild artisans and had excellent technical skills, which included gilding and the building of altarpieces. Tuyru Tupac Inca's finest work as an architect is the design of S Pedro, attached to the Hospital de Indias in Cuzco, his plan for which was drawn up in 1688 and is preserved in Spain in the Archivo General de Indias in Seville. In addition he built the tower (1688) of the Recoleta Church, Cuzco, and Belén Church (in construction, 1696) in Cuzco is also attributed to him. Among his finest works as a sculptor are the statue of the *Virgen de La Almudena* (1686) in the Almudena church, Cuzco, a retable (*c.* 1690) in the same church and another in Cuzco Cathedral (1714). In 1679 he carved 26 figures for the principal retable of S Ana, Cuzco, and executed the gilding of this retable and for the principal retables of S Sebastián, near Cuzco, and San Juan de Dios, Cuzco. Dating from the 1690s, the designs of the pulpits of the Almudena church, of S Pedro, Cuzco, and Belén are also by him, and the famous carved pulpit of S Blas, Cuzco, is also attributed to him, but without documentary evidence.

BIBLIOGRAPHY

D. Angulo Iñiguez: *Planos de monumentos arquitectónicos de América y Filipinas en el Archivo General de Indias*, 7 vols (Seville, 1933–9)

P. Kelemen: *Baroque and Rococo in Latin America*, 2 vols (New York, 1951)

E. Marco Dorta: 'La influencia indígena en el barroco del Perú', *XXXVI Congreso internacional de Americanistas; Sevilla, 1966*

RAMÓN GUTIÉRREZ

Tver' [formerly Kalinin]. Russian provincial capital on the River Volga 200 km north-west of Moscow, first documented in 1164. From the 12th century to the end of the 15th it was the capital of an important appanage principality, and after absorption by Moscow it remained a major commercial centre. The oldest surviving architectural monument is the church of the White Trinity (Belaya Troitsa; 1564–84), a massive building that was originally an austere cube with a prominent apse and a single small dome; in the late 16th century and early 17th a further six domes were added. The cathedral of the Assumption (Uspensky; 1722) in the Otroch Monastery, designed in the 'Naryshkin Baroque' style, is typical of the city's architecture throughout the 17th century and the first half of the 18th. In 1762 a fire destroyed a large part of the city; building works undertaken from 1763 to 1790 transformed Tver' into the first example of Russian Neoclassical urban planning. Catherine II (*reg* 1762–96) made it the model for all other provincial centres. I. Betsky wrote a theoretical treatise on the remodelling of Tver'. Aleksey Kvasov and P. R. Nikitin produced different versions of a plan for the town, of which the latter's was implemented. The focal point on the approach road from Moscow is a (semicircular) square with the city's three main streets radiating from it, the central avenue passing through an octagonal square. On the far side of the Volga a regular layout was created, orientated on the embankment, with an adjacent system of small squares opening on to the river. The replanning of all medieval Russian towns was based on the Tver' model, which helped to define the development of urban planning in Russia in the 18th and 19th centuries. Buildings were erected to standardized designs, as can still be seen on the Stepan Razin Embankment (late 1760s). Notable among the buildings of the Neo-classical period are the Putevoy Dvorets (coaching palace) of Catherine II (1760s, by MATVEY KAZAKOV; remodelled by KARL ROSSI, 1804–12) and the house of the merchant Aref'yev (1760s).

The city was badly damaged in World War II, but the reconstruction has preserved its Neo-classical style. The Regional Local History Museum houses local antiquities, and the Tver' Picture Gallery displays 18th- and 19th-century Russian paintings and medieval icons.

BIBLIOGRAPHY

V. Shkarikov: *Russkoye gradostroitel'stvo XVIII–XIX vekov* [Russian urban planning of the 18th and 19th centuries] (Moscow, 1940)

Y. Gerchuk: *Khudozhestvennyye pamyatniki Verkhney Volgi* [Art monuments of the Upper Volga] (Moscow, 1976)

A. Bunin: *Istoriya gradostroitel'nogo iskusstva* [A history of urban planning] (Moscow, 1978)

Kalinin: Putevoditel' [A guide to Kalinin] (Kalinin, 1980)

Tver'. Spravochnik-putevoditel' [A guidebook to Tver'] (Tver', 1993)

D. O. SHVIDKOVSKY

Twachtman, John H(enry) (*b* Cincinnati, OH, 4 Aug 1853; *d* Gloucester, MA, 8 Aug 1902). American painter and printmaker. He began as a painter of window-shades but developed one of the most personal and poetic visions in American landscape painting, portraying nature on canvases that were, in the words of Childe Hassam, 'strong, and at the same time delicate even to evasiveness'. His first artistic training was under Frank Duveneck, with whom he studied first in Cincinnati and then in Munich (1875–7). His absorption of the Munich style, characterized by bravura brushwork and dextrous manipulation of pigment, with the lights painted as directly as possible into warm, dark grounds derived from Frans Hals and Courbet, is reflected in such paintings as *Venice Landscape* (1878;

Boston, MA, Mus. F.A.) and *Landscape* (*c.* 1882; Utica, NY, Munson-Williams-Proctor Inst.).

Twachtman became increasingly dissatisfied with the Munich style's lack of draughtsmanship, so he went to Paris in 1883 to study at the Académie Julian. In the winter he concentrated on drawing, and in the summer he painted in the Normandy countryside and at Arques-la-Bataille, near Dieppe. *Springtime* (*c.* 1885; Cincinnati, OH, A. Mus.) and *Arques-la-Bataille* (1885; New York, Met.) mirror not only his training at the Académie Julian but also the influence of the draughtsmanship and tonal values of Jules Bastien-Lepage. In its emphasis on pattern and economy of form, *Arques-la-Bataille* may also suggest an awareness of Whistler and Oriental art. This period of Twachtman's work was his most popular, and in 1888, three years after his return to the United States, he won the Webb Prize of the Society of American Artists.

Soon after his return from France, Twachtman changed his style, painting with a lightened palette and a modified Impressionist technique, which derived less from Monet and French art than from his friend Theodore Robinson, whom Twachtman first met in Paris. By 1890 Twachtman was developing a mature and personal vision, which can be seen in pastels and etchings and in the subtle poetry of *Winter Harmony* (see fig.) and *Old Holly House, Cos Cob*

(Cincinnati, OH, A. Mus.), both painted *c.* 1890–1900. Twachtman's work is complex, although his myriad brushstrokes and wide range of colours combine to give the impression of great simplicity.

Although he was essentially a private man, Twachtman founded an informal art school at the Holly House, a boarding house for artists at Cos Cob near Greenwich, NY, and he taught at the Art Students League and the Cooper Union in New York. In 1897, along with Childe Hassam and J. Alden Weir, he was one of the principal founders of the Ten American Painters, who were considered to be a kind of Academy of American Impressionism and who left the more conservative Society of American Artists to exhibit on their own. About three years later, Twachtman and his colleagues began painting in Gloucester, MA, where his style changed once again. His painting became more direct, his colour more defined and, as in *Fishing Boats at Gloucester* (1901; Washington, DC, N. Mus. Amer. A.), his brushwork bolder. His overall approach began to be more openly expressive, pointing in the direction later taken by his most famous pupil, Ernest Lawson (1873–1939).

Twachtman's few figure pieces were not very successful. He was more comfortable with nature, and his attitude towards it was basically romantic and contemplative. He

John H. Twachtman: *Winter Harmony*, oil on canvas, 654×813 mm, *c.* 1890–1900 (Washington, DC, National Gallery of Art)

had a small but impressive output of etchings. In a manner similar to that of Whistler, he used just a few lines to suggest an entire scene, as in *Boats on the Maas* (*c*. 1881–3; Philadelphia, PA, Mus. A., see 1966 exh. cat., p. 38).

BIBLIOGRAPHY

T. Dewing and others: 'John Twachtman: An Estimation', *N. Amer. Rev.*, clxxvi/1 (1903), pp. 555–7
C. G. Mase: 'John H. Twachtman', *Studio Int.*, lxxii/286 (1921), pp. lxxi–lxxv
R. J. Wickenden: *The Art and Etching of John Henry Twachtman* (New York, 1921)
E. Clark: *John H. Twachtman* (New York, 1924)
A. Tucker: *John H. Twachtman* (New York, 1931)
J. D. Hale: *The Life and Creative Development of John H. Twachtman*, 2 vols (diss., OH State U., 1957)
A Retrospective Exhibition: John Henry Twachtman (exh. cat., Cincinnati, A. Mus., 1966)
R. J. Boyle: 'John H. Twachtman: An Appreciation', *Amer. A. & Ant.*, i/3 (1978), pp. 71–7
——: *John Twachtman* (New York, 1979)
Twachtman in Gloucester: His Last Years, 1900–1902 (exh. cat., New York, Spanierman Gal., 1987) [essays by J. D. Hale, R. J. Boyle and W. H. Gerdts]

RICHARD J. BOYLE

Tweed, John (*b* Glasgow, 21 Jan 1869; *d* London, 12 Nov 1933). Scottish sculptor. He studied at the Glasgow School of Art before selling his family publishing business and moving to London in 1890, where Hamo Thornycroft engaged him as an assistant while he studied at the Royal Academy Schools. Tweed's admiration for the work of Rodin took him in 1893 to Paris, where he worked under Alexandre Falguière. Later that year he returned to London to execute his first major commission, a bronze relief of *Jan van Riesbeeck* (*in situ*) for Cecil Rhodes's residence, Groote Schuur (Cape Town). Further African commissions followed, including a characterful bronze statue of *Rhodes* (1902; Bulawayo; bronze statuette version, Duke of Westminster priv. col.).

In 1901 Tweed was engaged to complete Alfred Stevens's bronze equestrian figure for the Wellington Monument (London, St Paul's Cathedral; *see* LONDON, fig. 26). His appointment aroused the hostility of Sir Edward Poynter, President of the Royal Academy, who considered Tweed an undesirable exponent of the 'new art', probably because of his allegiance to Rodin. The successful outcome, however, led to further large-scale commissions in London, such as bronze statues of *Lord Clive* (1917) and *Lord Kitchener* (1926; both London, Whitehall), the bronze figures of the *Rifle Brigade Memorial* (1924; London, Grosvenor Place) and the *House of Lords War Memorial* (1932). Although such official works had to be realistic in format, their vigorous modelling reflected Rodin's influence. Tweed's ideal sculptures and busts, in which this influence is even more apparent, include the undated marble bust of *Lendal Tweed* and *Embracing Couple* (bronze, 1909; both Reading, Mus. & A.G.). The latter closely resembles Camille Claudel's *The Embrace* (bronze, 1888; Cambrai, Mus. Mun.).

BIBLIOGRAPHY

DNB
John Tweed: Memorial Exhibition (exh. cat., London, Imp. Gal. A., 1934)
L. Tweed: *John Tweed, Sculptor: A Memoir* (London, 1936)

MARK STOCKER

Twenty, the. *See* ⟨VINGT⟩, LES.

Twentyman, Lawrence Holme (*b* Liverpool, 5 May 1793; *d* London, 8 June 1852). English silversmith, active in South Africa. After qualifying as a clock- and watchmaker, in 1818 he left for the Cape, where he became the most prolific and best-known 19th-century silversmith. Within three weeks of his arrival in Cape Town he opened a shop, and a year later he was advertising for craftsmen and apprentices in the silver and jewellery trade. Within four years Twentyman had established himself as the leading silversmith at the Cape, receiving commissions from the governor, churches and leading citizens. He made a number of presentation vases, all in the prevailing English style, and many small pieces such as snuff-boxes, christening cups, beakers and flatware of varying quality. An astute businessman, he imported large quantities of plated ware, which ultimately led to the death of the silversmith's craft at the Cape. Twentyman returned to England in 1832, leaving what was by then an importing and retailing business in the hands of a manager.

BIBLIOGRAPHY

S. Welz: *Cape Silver and Silversmiths* (Cape Town, 1976)

STEPHAN WELZ

Twickel. Dutch garden near Delden, in the province of Overijssel. In the 17th century the gardens were designed in typical Dutch Renaissance style, with canals, parterres and woodland. In 1676 Jacob van Wassenaer Obdam married a descendant of Herman van Twickelo and commissiond Daniel Marot I to redesign the gardens. Marot's remaining design shows intricate parterres, bordered at the top with a semicircular canal, which appears in a mid-18th-century map of the garden; this also shows that further changes were made, including the introduction of parterres in the Rococo style and a small English garden, probably an early example of such a garden in the Netherlands. In 1765 the garden was opened to the public. Between 1770 and 1794 the garden was increasingly anglicized and the formal design gradually gave way to a landscape (although the older structure remained visible) and Marot's canal became an irregular lake. On the lake was a thatched hut, possibly after a design by Gijsbert van Laar. To the north of the house were an orangery and a game park; to the south was a hermitage, a small polygonal thatched pavilion, possibly also designed by van Laar. The designer of the garden is unknown, but Johan Georg Michael (1738–1800) has been suggested, as has the Baron van Wassenaer Obdam himself or T. A. Hartmeyer, who had worked elsewhere for the same family. Jan David Zocher designed a second landscape garden (1830–35) in the picturesque style derived from 'Capability' Brown. The winding paths were removed and the emphasis was on water and trees. Designs were made for various buildings, including an orangery, a menagerie and a temple. More land was acquired in 1846 and work began on new designs by Zocher and his son Louis Paul Zocher (1820–1915) in 1872. From 1885 to 1891 Carl Eduard Adolf Petzold (1815–1891) designed for Twickel. Views of the house were created by cutting away groups of trees, and the house and landscape were more closely linked. Further individual gardens were designed and built at the beginning of the 20th century, including a rose garden, a topiary garden and a rock garden.

BIBLIOGRAPHY
H. W. M. van der Wijck: *De Nederlandse buitenplaats* [The Dutch country seat] (Alphen aan de Rijn, 1982)
M. E. G. B. Jansen: *Twickel te ambt Delden* [Twickel in the domain of Delden], Bijdragen tot het bronnenonderzoek naar de ontwikkeling van Nederlandse historische tuinen, parken en buitenplaatsen [Contributions to original research into the development of Dutch historical gardens, parks and country seats], xxi (Zeist, 1988)

Twiss. American family of clockmakers, active in Canada. The five Twiss brothers, Austin (*d* ?La Prairie, ?1826), Joseph, Ira, Russell (*bur* ?Rawdon, Quebec, ?1851) and Benjamin, moved at various times between 1821 and 1836 from Connecticut to establish themselves in Montreal. They made longcase clocks in the manner of Thomas Chippendale, with wooden works (usually cherry), grain-painted cases in imitation of mahogany or other fancy woods and gilded wooden finials. The use of wood throughout except for a few elements in the mechanism was an economy typical of American clockmakers. The faces are signed 'Twiss, Montreal' and are decorated with flowers, fruit and occasionally landscape scenes with buildings (e.g. in Montreal, Mus. F.A.; Toronto, Royal Ont. Mus.). Some have been found with labels. One of the first semi-industrial manufactures in Canada, Twiss clocks were inexpensive and were widely distributed in both Upper and Lower Canada. Probably more of these clocks survive than any other single kind of furniture produced in early 19th-century Canada and attributable to one artisan or family group of craftsmen.

BIBLIOGRAPHY
E.-Z. Massicotte: 'Les Horlogers Twiss et les autres', *Bull. Rech. Hist.*, xlii (1936), pp. 453–5
Y. Bergeron: 'Artisans horlogers des régimes français et anglais', *Rev. Ethnol. Québec*, 9 (1979), pp. 21–44

JOHN A. FLEMING

Twombly, Cy (*b* Lexington, VA, 25 April 1928). American painter, draughtsman, printmaker and sculptor. He studied from 1948 to 1951 at Washington and Lee University in Lexington, VA, at the Museum School in Boston, and at the Art Students League in New York. In 1951–2 he spent a semester at BLACK MOUNTAIN COLLEGE, an important period for his involvement with Abstract Expressionism. Action painting, in particular, became his point of departure for the development of a highly personal 'handwriting' that served as a vehicle for literary content. During this period he became friendly with Robert Rauschenberg, travelling with him to North Africa.

In *Untitled* (1952; Basle, Kstmus.) Twombly used long brushstrokes in contrasting tones against a dark background, only to paint partly over them again. This alternation between the visible and the hidden, between clear and murky forms, which became a unifying theme in Twombly's work, has been interpreted by one critic, Gottfried Boehm, as a struggle between memory and oblivion. Twombly's use here of clusters of brushstrokes arranged diagonally across the surface became a recurring feature of his pictures in a variety of forms, for example as perpendicular stripes in the series of lithographs *Gladings (Love's Infinite Causes)* (1973; see Lambert, pp. 35–41).

In the mid-1950s Twombly began working also in chalk and pencil, and his paintings assumed a more graphic character. The stylistic changes in his paintings were subsequently registered more or less simultaneously in his prolific production of drawings and prints, which were often executed in series; often he drew contrasting, gradually dissolving lines on a beige or greyish-black ground, sometimes when it was still damp. *Panorama* (1955; priv. col., see Bastian, 1978, pl. 6), the only surviving dark canvas on a monumental scale, is completely covered with dynamic interweaving white lines truncated by the borders of the picture. The potential of gestural brushwork as a form of handwriting was not exploited by Twombly until he settled in Rome in 1957 and found inspiration in classical landscapes and literature. In *Olympia* (1957; priv. col., see Bastian, 1978, pl. 11), for instance, coloured lines form signs against a light-coloured background with pale yellow spots. In his paintings and drawings Twombly made direct reference to antiquity only in the inscriptions, which at the same time form part of the complex of lines and forms, and he remained committed to a deliberately awkward line verging on a scrawl. The few small sculptures that he produced between 1955 and 1959 are more disciplined, and their forms also suggest references to Classical culture. For example, in *Untitled* (painted resin, 1959; priv. col., see Zurich 1987 exh. cat., pl. 102) a pedestal of three superposed geometrical forms carries a row with interconnected staves suggesting a pan-pipe.

In the first half of the 1960s Twombly made particular use of subjective, erotic signs in his paintings, and he began to use more intense and denser colours. In *Leda and the Swan* (1961; priv. col., see Bastian, 1978, pl. 43), red and pink marks gradually emerge from the concentrated turbulence of the brushwork to assume a recognizable form. In the *Blackboard Paintings* initiated in 1966 Twombly returned to contrasting lines against a light or dark background. Rhythmic marks, spatially projected geometric shapes, words, letters and numbers are characteristically scattered across the painting surface, as in *Untitled* (1969; Basle, Kstmus.).

From 1976 Twombly again produced sculptures, lightly painted in white, suggestive of Classical forms. In the mid-1970s, in paintings such as *Untitled* (1976; priv. col., see Bastian, 1978, pl. 97), Twombly began to evoke landscape through colour (favouring brown, green and light blue), written inscriptions and collage elements, often distributing these features across the surface by means of right angles that emphasize the legibility of the image and its narrative character. In later works such as *Gaeta-Sets* (1986; see Bonn 1987 exh. cat., pp. 131–6, 138–44), however, Twombly treated landscape in a more purely abstract manner, freeing it from a literary context.

BIBLIOGRAPHY
H. Bastian: *Cy Twombly: Bilder/Paintings, 1952–1976* (Frankfurt am Main and Berlin, 1978)
Y. Lambert: *Catalogue raisonné des oeuvres sur papier de Cy Twombly* (Milan, 1979) [with text by R. Barthes]
H. Bastian: *Cy Twombly: Das graphische Werk, 1953–1984: A Catalogue Raisonné of the Printed Graphic Work* (Munich and New York, 1985)
Cy Twombly: Bilder, Arbeiten auf Papier, Skulpturen (exh. cat., ed. H. Szeemann; Zurich, Ksthaus, 1987)

Cy Twombly: Serien auf Papier, 1957–1987 (exh. cat. by K. Schmidt and
    G. Boehm, Bonn, Städt. Kstmus., 1987)

ANNEKE E. WIJNBEEK

291. American art gallery founded in New York in 1905
by Alfred Stieglitz and Edward Steichen. It was located at
291 Fifth Avenue and soon came to be known simply as
291 ('two ninety-one'). The gallery at 291 was an important
early centre for modern art in the USA. Originally called
the Little Galleries of the Photo-Secession, it was founded
to promote photography as an independent art form. In
their first exhibition Stieglitz and Steichen featured the
work of the PHOTO-SECESSION group. However, their
concentration on photography was brief and they soon
broadened the scope of the gallery to include exhibitions
of avant-garde painting, sculpture and graphic arts.

Aptly described by Marsden Hartley as 'the largest small
room of its kind in the world', the gallery became a
pioneering force in bringing European modern art to
American attention even before the Armory Show of
1913. Following the first American exhibition of Auguste
Rodin watercolours (1908), similar début exhibitions were
held for Henri Matisse (1908), Toulouse-Lautrec (1909),
Henri Rousseau (1910), Paul Cézanne (1911), Pablo
Picasso (1911), Francis Picabia (1913), Constantin Brancusi (1914) and Gino Severini (1917).   Equally important
was Stieglitz's promotion, through the gallery, of contemporary American artists. He staged the first exhibitions for
Pamela Coleman Smith (1877–1925; exhibition in 1907),
John Marin (1909), Alfred Maurer (1909), Arthur B. Carles
(1882–1952), Arthur G. Dove, Marsden Hartley and Max
Weber (a group show of 1910), Abraham Walkowitz
(1880–1965; exhibition in 1912), Oscar Bluemner (1915),
Elie Nadelman (1915), Georgia O'Keeffe (1916) and
Stanton Macdonald-Wright (1917). Stieglitz also organized
at the gallery what were possibly the first exhibitions of
children's art in 1912 and, in 1914, of African sculpture as
art rather than anthropological material. In 1915–16 the
gallery gave its name to the short-lived Dadaist magazine
291, edited by Stieglitz and emulated later in the title of
Picabia's magazine, *391*. Over 70 exhibitions had been
held at 291 by 1917, when the building's scheduled
demolition forced Stieglitz to close it down.

BIBLIOGRAPHY
R. Doty: *Photo-Secession: Photography as Fine Art* (Rochester, 1960; rev.
    as *Photo-Secession: Stieglitz and the Fine Art Movement in Photography*,
    New York, 1978)
D. Norman: *Alfred Stieglitz: An American Seer* (New York, 1973)
W. Homer: *Alfred Stieglitz and the American Avant-garde* (Boston, 1977)
The Eye of Stieglitz (exh. cat., New York, Hirschl & Adler Gals, 1978)

ROGER J. CRUM

Tworkov, Jack (*b* Biała, Poland, 15 Aug 1900; *d* Provincetown, MA, 4 Sept 1982). American painter. He was
one of the leading individualists of the New York School,
and taught at universities throughout the United States.
He was Chairman of the Art Department at Yale University, New Haven, CT, 1963–9.

Tworkov went to the USA in 1913 and settled permanently in New York. He studied at Columbia University
(1920–23), at the National Academy of Design (1923–5)
and at the Art Students League of New York (1925–6).
He saw the French painting exhibition of 1921 at the

Brooklyn Museum, New York, where he was introduced
to the work of Cézanne, who was a major formative
influence. From 1923 Tworkov spent his summers in
Provincetown, MA, where, under the guidance of the
painter Karl Knaths (1871–1971), he became familiar with
the work of Kandinsky, Klee and Miró. He became
interested in automatic painting through the influence of
Freudian theory, but was never attracted by Surrealism or
Dada. Tworkov worked for the Works Progress Administration on the Federal Art Project (Easel Division) from
1935 to 1941, and during World War II he worked as a
tool designer.

After the War Tworkov concentrated on still-life subjects for about two years, turning then to abstract work.
His first important exhibition was held in 1947 at the
Charles Egan Gallery, New York. Soon identified with
new ideas in art, he was a founder-member of The Club,
which from 1949 until the late 1950s was the primary
avant-garde forum for art in New York, particularly for
Abstract Expressionism. Tworkov's paintings, then based
on the human figure, were characterized by concrete form
and colour, energetic line and spontaneous application. In
works such as *House of the Sun* (1952–3; New York, IBM
Corp.), theme and painterly means merged: figures represented the reality of paint application, and each brushstroke functioned as a structural unit. Archetypal myths,
such as the *Odyssey*, were interpreted by Tworkov as the
artist's search for self-realization. By 1955 works such as
Watergame (1955; New York, priv. col.) and *Duo I* (1956;
New York, Whitney) showed formal elements interwoven
with more expressive painting. Rhythmic, gestural brushstrokes varied from the atmospheric shimmer of subtle
feathering to forceful diagonal marks. Tworkov did not
consider the action of painting as an end in itself, even for
works closely identifiable with Abstract Expressionism.
What was fundamental was the interplay established
between deliberation and spontaneity, and between the
intuitive and the intellectual.

Tworkov's paintings of the early 1960s, such as the *Red,
White and Blue* series, consisted of a grid-like structure of
unmodulated colour areas; depth was achieved by divisions of the painting surface, rather than by the relationship
between figure and background (e.g. *Souza*, 1961; Franklin,
MI, Mr and Mrs Joel Nosanchuk priv. col., see 1987 exh.
cat., pl. 48). Progressively geometric and severe, this direction in Tworkov's work culminated in the mid-1960s in
his rejection of the subjective focus of Abstract Expressionism for geometry. Using his 'diagonal grid', a systematic approach to harmonic geometrical relationships,
Tworkov imposed an order upon the painting surface,
within which there was a free range of creative possibilities.
Within this linear geometric structure, his brushwork could
still function as a structural component, but also contained
a rhythmic element like a beat in music. These last works
of his career are the high point of his search for an
authentic self-completion (e.g. *Compression and Expansion
of the Square*, 1982; New York, Nancy Hoffman Gal.).
Directed by choice and intuition, their value, as he put it
in an interview with Marcia Tucker, is 'in being, and not
in representing' (see 1979 exh. cat., p. 17).

BIBLIOGRAPHY
Jack Tworkov (exh. cat. by E. Bryant, New York, Whitney, 1964)
P. Tuchman: 'An Interview with Jack Tworkov', *Artforum*, ix/5 (1971), pp. 62–8
K. L. Gula: 'The Indian Summer of Jack Tworkov', *A. America*, lxi/5 (1973), pp. 62–5
Jack Tworkov: Paintings 1950–1978 (exh. cat., ed. R. Demarco; Glasgow, Third Eye Cent., 1979)
L. Fichner-Rathaus: 'Jack Tworkov: A Retrospective View', *Arts* [Paris], lvii/1 (1982), pp. 121–5; lvii/2 (1982), pp. 124–8
S. W. Kroeter: 'Interview with Jack Tworkov', *A. America*, lxx/10 (1982), pp. 82–7
Jack Tworkov: Fifteen Years of Painting (exh. cat., ed. A. Forge; New York, Guggenheim, 1982)
Jack Twarkov: Paintings 1928–1982 (exh. cat. by R. Armstrong and K. Baker; Philadelphia, PA Acad. F.A., 1987)

EDWARD BRYANT

Ty, tomb of. Stone-built mastaba, built for the ancient Egyptian official Ty (*fl c.* 2380 BC), in the Old Kingdom cemetery north of the Step Pyramid of Djoser at Saqqara. Ty, the overseer of the sun temples of Neferirkare and Neuserre, served several 5th Dynasty kings, terminating his career within the most prolific period of tomb sculpture in the Saqqara necropolis. During the later Old Kingdom, Ty's chapel reliefs were imitated by local sculptors and artists working in chapels in southern Egypt. Gradually, however, the superstructure was engulfed by sand and was thus preserved until its discovery in 1860 by the French archaeologist Auguste Mariette.

The tomb incorporates a multi-roomed chapel, burial shafts and a doorless serdab enclosing a life-size statue of the deceased (Cairo, Egyp. Mus., CG 20). The high walls of the chapel are decorated with raised reliefs, many of which are delicately carved illustrations of outdoor activities (such as fishing, fowling and harvesting crops) and symbolic scenes, elaborated by hieroglyphic inscriptions. These are arranged in narrow, horizontal registers, usually before large representations of the tomb owner accompanied by his family or retinue. Some of the reliefs were left unpainted, but others retain traces of pigment, especially red-brown, black, green and yellow against a light ochre background wash. In every room the quality of sculpture is of a consistently high standard. Nevertheless, it is the sheer variety of detail in the scenes and inscriptions and the inventiveness of subject-matter and composition that have earned the chapel its reputation as a masterpiece of ancient Egyptian art.

BIBLIOGRAPHY
G. Steindorff: *Das Grab des Ti* (Leipzig, 1913)
B. Porter and R. L. B. Moss, eds: *Topographical Bibliography* (1927–), iii, pp. 468–78
L. Epron and F. Daumas: *Le Tombeau de Ti* (Cairo, 1939)
H. Wild: *Le Tombeau de Ti* (Cairo, 1953–66)
K. Lange and M. Hirmer: *Ägypten: Architektur, Plastik, Malerei, in drei Jahrtausenden* (Munich, 1967) [serdab statue]

YVONNE HARPUR

Tybrind Vig. Late Mesolithic coastal settlement site now submerged *c.* 200–300 m off the west coast of Fyn Island, southern Denmark. It was the first underwater excavation site in northern Europe. The site's position indicates that the area has sunk *c.* 2–3 m since the Late Mesolithic period. The main part of the settlement area had been eroded when the area was flooded by the sea, but *in situ* finds were preserved in the 'waste zone' in the shallow water off the coastline. Conditions for the preservation of organic materials were the most favourable encountered in the region to date (1994).

The site belongs to the Ertebølle culture, especially the earlier part, which has been dated by radiocarbon analysis to *c.* 4500–*c.* 400 BC. Zooarchaeological analysis demonstrated year-round human habitation, possibly permanent occupation. Finds from a zone *c.* 100×10–15 m along the prehistoric shoreline indicate that the area just off the settlement proper was a combination of an inshore fishing area and a 'dump' for waste. Human remains included those found in the inhumation grave of a young girl (15–17 years old) with a newborn baby (0–3 months) in the settlement proper. The subsistence economy was based on the hunting of red deer, wild boar and roe deer, the fishing of cod, spurdog and eel and the collection of hazelnuts, acorns and certain marine molluscs. Of these, fishing was of the greatest importance. Also many animals (e.g. pine marten) were killed for fur. Implements of flint, bone, antler and pottery of the usual Ertebølle types were found.

Due to the excellent preservation conditions, large quantities of wooden artefacts were excavated, including leister prongs, bows of elm wood, wooden arrows with pear-shaped point, a fish weir and axe-handles. The most numerous wooden objects were long, straight stakes with pointed tips, probably parts of fish traps. Three limewood dugout canoes measuring up to 9.5 m long were also found. The canoe paddles were carved in one piece from ash trunks and have heart-shaped blades. Three of the bigger paddles are decorated with designs cut into the surface and filled with brown colouring matter to give a sharp contrast with the white wood, a technique well known from ornamented objects of bone, antler and amber. The motifs are a mixture of geometric and more fluid elements, the latter of which are completely new and display a hitherto unknown style of Mesolithic art. These decorated paddles are among the first examples of Mesolithic decorated wood in Europe and indicate that this kind of art may in fact have been very common; many more wooden items would probably have been covered with similar designs.

BIBLIOGRAPHY
S. H. Andersen: 'Tybrind Vig: A Preliminary Report on a Submerged Ertebølle Settlement on the West Coast of Fyn', *J. Dan. Archaeol.*, iv (1985), pp. 52–69
——: 'Tybrind Vig: A Submerged Ertebølle Settlement in Denmark', *European Wetlands in Prehistory*, ed. J. M. Coles and A. J. Lawson (Oxford, 1987), pp. 253–80

SØREN H. ANDERSEN

Tŷ Ddewi. *See* ST DAVID'S.

Tyl, Oldřich (*b* Ejpovice, near Rokycany, 12 April 1884; *d* Prague, 4 April 1939). Czech architect. He graduated in architecture (1913) from the Technical University, Prague, and immediately became a member of the Architects' Club. In 1920 he was co-founder of a business organization called the Tekta Society. Tyl was among the first to foster the development of Functionalist architecture in Prague. His numerous commercial and administrative buildings demonstrate a constructional inventiveness with their clarity of composition, balanced proportions and restrained approach. His most outstanding work was the building (1926–8; with Josef Fuchs) for the Trade Fair Palace (damaged by fire 1974; reconstructed 1981–93) in Prague, which was one of the first large Functionalist structures in Europe. His other main work was the Black Rose Shopping Arcade (1931–9), Prague; this is based on two large multi-storey galleries, symmetrically arranged and with an aesthetically pleasing structure of glass and concrete.

BIBLIOGRAPHY
O. Starý: 'Oldřich Tyl', *Architektura*, i (1939), pp. 85–8
Z. Lukeš and R. Švácha: 'Oldřich Tyl', *Archit. ČSR*, xliii (1984), p. 463
R. Sedláková: 'Oldřich Tyl', *Tschechische Kunst der 20er & 30er Jahre: Avantgarde und Tradition* (exh. cat., Darmstadt, Inst. Matildenhöhe, 1988–9), pp. 452–5
The Art of the Avant-Garde in Czechoslovakia 1918–38 (exh. cat., ed. J. Anděl, Valencia, IVAM Cent. Carme, 1993)
Prague 1891–1941 Architecture and Design (exh. cat., Edinburgh, City A. Cent., 1994)
RADOMÍRA SEDLÁKOVÁ

Tylissos. Site in northern Crete, 14 km south-west of Herakleion, in the foothills of the Ida massif overlooking the coastal plain, which flourished *c.* 2900–*c.* 1000 BC. It lay on routes heading both west and south and is mentioned (as tu-ri-so) in the Linear B tablets. The excavations conducted by JOSEPH HAZZIDAKIS (1909–13) uncovered only a fraction of the site.

An Early Minoan (EM) II to Middle Minoan (MM) II settlement (*c.* 2900/2600–*c.* 1675 BC), represented by traces of walls and pottery but of uncertain form, was succeeded *c.* 1650 BC by free-standing, two-storey houses which differed in detail. The irregularly shaped Houses A and C have store-rooms containing pithoi, separated by corridors and stair units from living areas, including halls with pier-and-door screens and adjacent light wells, lustral basins and pillar crypts. Both have multiple access routes. House B is rectangular and only slightly less complex. All three buildings were destroyed by fire *c.* 1425 BC. Linear A tablets, sealings and a copper ingot fragment discovered in the houses attest to some form of estate management, while raw pigments, a potter's wheel, bronze chisels and precision saws/scrapers and stone tools indicate the presence of craftsmen. Linear A also occurs in graffiti on a clay figurine and on walls. Other notable finds include three massive, and one smaller, bronze cauldrons, a remarkable bronze statue representing a plump worshipper, an obsidian rhyton, and faience and ivory inlays, probably from wooden chests. Best finds are held at the Archaeological museum in Herakleion. The houses also contained sophisticated frescoes in the Miniature style, processions and floral subjects (*see* MINOAN, §IV, 2).

The only substantial later house remains on the site date from Late Minoan (LM) III to Subminoan (*c.* 1390–*c.* 1000 BC). A cistern and clay and stone channels indicate an interest in water dispersal. Burials are few: an LM III burial cave, an LM IIIB-C chamber tomb and an early cremation (?LM IIIC). There are also traces of Classical period (*c.* 475–323 BC) occupation, including an altar stone. Other religious sites in the vicinity include a peak sanctuary (EM–MM) and a sacred cave (MM–LM).

BIBLIOGRAPHY
J. Hazzidakis: *Tylissos à l'époque minoenne* (Paris, 1921)
——: *Les Villas minoennes de Tylissos* (Paris, 1934)
S. G. Spanakis: *Kentriki-anatoliki* (1964), i of *I Kriti* (Herakleion, 1964–), pp. 495–503
A. Vasilakis: 'Tylissos', *The Aerial Atlas of Ancient Crete*, ed. J. W. Myers, E. E. Myers and G. Cadogan (Berkeley, 1992), pp. 270–73
D. EVELY

Tylkowski, Wojciech [Adalbertus] (*b* ?near Putusk, 19 April 1625; *d* Warsaw, 14 Jan 1695). Polish scientist, philosopher, teacher and art theorist. He became a Jesuit in 1646 and took holy orders in 1657, working mainly as a teacher in Jesuit colleges. Between 1669 and 1673 he lived in Rome, studying natural science and making contact with the scientific community there, including Athanasius Kircher. Versatile, erudite and polyglot, he published many scientific papers, notably *Philosophia curiosa seu universa Aristotelis philosophia* (Oliwa, 1680–91), of which the second part, *Physica* (ten volumes), features five treatises on the senses, of which the first, on sight (volume vii), contains a theory of painting. In this he discussed technological rules, the problem of light and colour, the principles of geometric perspective (including anamorphosis), colour and aerial perspective, anatomy and the proportions of the human body, the theory of expression and the science of physiognomy, and noted instruments helpful to the painter, such as vellum, the camera obscura and the pantograph. He believed in illusionistic verity to nature, attainable through theoretical knowledge, and close observation of the world. The treatise on sight also contains remarks on the theory of architecture and a short discourse on sculptural technology. The work is among the oldest Polish writings on art theory and, by virtue of its breadth and topicality, represents the best of 17th-century painting theory in Poland.

BIBLIOGRAPHY
A. Małkiewicz: 'Wojciecha Tylkowskiego censura imaginum iuxta doctrinam' [Wojciech Tylkowski's critique of images in the guise of doctrine], *Symbolae historiae artium: Studia z historii sztuki Lechowi Kalinowskiemu dedykowane* [Studies of the history of art dedicated to Lech Kalinowski] (Warsaw, 1986), pp. 447–56
——: 'Wojciech Tylkowski a teoria architektury' [Wojciech Tylkowski and the theory of architecture], *Podług nieba i zwyczaju polskiego: Studia z historii architektury, sztuki i kultury ofiarowane Adamowi Miłobędzkiemu* [According to the climate and custom of Poland: studies from the history of architecture, art and culture offered to Adam Miłobędzki] (Warsaw, 1988), pp. 638–42
ADAM MAŁKIEWICZ

Tylman van Gameren. *See* GAMEREN, TYLMAN VAN.

Tylos. *See* BAHRAIN.

Tympanum. Architectural term used to describe the vertical, triangular space enclosed by the horizontal and raking cornices of a pediment (for further discussion and illustration *see* PEDIMENT); also the space between the square head or lintel of a door or window and the round or pointed discharging arch above it. In Classical architecture, more particularly of the Doric order, the area was filled with sculpted figures, which were adapted in posture to the space available. In Early Christian and medieval architecture it likewise served as the field for sculpture, sometimes arranged in tiers, a genre that reached its apogee in the decoration of the great French cathedrals

Tympanum showing scenes from the *Passion* and *Resurrection*, Porte de la Calende, Rouen Cathedral, France, 1276–1306

(see fig.; *see also* PARIS, fig. 33; AUTUN, fig. 2). The light screen of lath and plaster, or of wood, that fills the space between the rood screen and the chancel arch of a church is also referred to as a tympanum. It is often decorated with a representation of the Last Judgement. Finally, the term is occasionally applied to the dado of a pedestal, that is, to the shaft between the base and cornice. Further information on specific tympana is given in this dictionary within the relevant articles on buildings (where subdivided, under the heading 'sculpture').

For further discussion and illustration of medieval sculpture in tympana *see* ROMANESQUE, §III, 1 and GOTHIC, §III, 1.

BIBLIOGRAPHY
J. Summerson: *The Classical Language of Architecture* (London, 1963, rev. 1980)

Tyng, Anne Griswold (*b* Jiangxi, China, 14 July 1920). American architect, teacher and writer. She graduated from Radcliffe College in 1942 and received her Masters of Architecture degree from Harvard University, Cambridge, MA, in 1944. From 1947 to 1973 she worked with Louis I. Kahn and was closely involved in the design of many of his buildings, notably the Yale University Art Gallery. During this time she was also Associate Consultant Architect for the Philadelphia City Planning Commission and Redevelopment Authority (1952–3) and for the Mill Creek Pennsylvania Redevelopment Plan. From 1968 she was an adjunct professor in the Graduate School of Fine Arts, University of Pennsylvania, Philadelphia; she also taught at several other colleges, and she practised architecture independently after 1973. In 1975 Tyng received a PhD in architecture from the University of Pennsylvania. Her highly theoretical research involved the interrelations between physical, natural and psychic structures and their architectural application. Her dissertation discusses the mathematically based Fibonacci–Divine Proportion as a matrix, 'linking unpredictable information bits in the brain ... to precise proportional mean, or "essence"'. This she related to Jung's theories of the collective unconscious. An early independent building by Tyng, the Walworth Tyng House (1953), Cambridge, MD, utilized triangulated space-frame structural concepts based on the ideas of R. Buckminster Fuller. Unbuilt projects by Tyng, for example 'Spiral Urban Hierarchies' (1970), an integrated complex of 40 dwelling units, explored various types of symmetry—bilateral, rotational and helical—relating to the human body's symmetry, the space around the body, and the human social sphere respectively. Synthesizing organic and geometrical forms, Tyng created highly cerebral yet, it would seem, easily habitable networks of form and space.

WRITINGS

'Geometric Extensions of Consciousness', *Zodiac*, 19 (1969), pp. 163–73
Simultaneous Randomness and Order: The Fibonacci-Divine Proportion as a Universal Forming Principle (PhD diss., University Park, PA State U., 1976)

BIBLIOGRAPHY

A. Sky and M. Stone: *Unbuilt America* (New York, 1976)
J. McGroarty and S. Torre: 'New Professional Identities: Four Women in the Sixties', *Women in American Architecture: A Historic and Contemporary Perspective*, ed. S. Torre (New York, 1977)
C. Lorenz: *Women in Architecture: A Contemporary Perspective* (London, 1990), pp. 124–5

1. Typography of the 15th century from Eusebios of Caesarea: *De praeparatione evangelica* (Venice, 1470), printed by Nicolas Jenson (London, British Library)

D. B. Brownlee and D. G. DeLong: *Louis I. Kahn: In the Realm of Architecture* (New York, 1991)

WALTER SMITH

Typaldos, Nikolaos Xydias. *See* XYDIAS TYPALDOS, NIKOLAOS.

Typography. The art of using type for communication, involving the design or selection of type and its layout.

1. Invention and development. 2. 19th-century technology. 3. Innovative 20th-century typographers.

1. INVENTION AND DEVELOPMENT. Typography began in Europe in the Rhineland (and possibly also in the Low Countries) in the mid-15th century with the invention of a method for casting letters in metal in standard sizes (*see* PRINTING). Letters (types) were assembled into pages that were then inked and printed on to vellum or paper. The object was to produce books and other documents more quickly and in greater numbers (and therefore more cheaply) than was practicable by writing them out by hand. In emulation of manuscripts, aesthetic considerations were present from the beginning.

At first types were copies of the script of the region in which the printed books were to be sold (*see* SCRIPT). In 15th-century Rhineland, that was the lettering now known as black letter or gothic. As the new art spread across Europe towards Italy the style of type design changed, almost imperceptibly, from German black letter to what is now called roman. Gradually scribes became obsolete in book production as books no longer attempted to copy manuscripts and were designed as objects in their own right, and according to their own technology, by printers (typographers). One of the first books of aesthetic importance printed in roman type was Eusebios of Caesarea's tract *De praeparatione evangelica* (see fig. 1), printed by a Frenchman, NICOLAS JENSON. His type was easily readable, mellow in form and with an evenness of colour in mass; the very imperfection of his letter-forms recommended them, since they did not tire the eye. Jenson's roman types have been the accepted models for roman letters ever since.

About 1500 italic type was introduced by the Venetian scholar and publisher ALDUS MANUTIUS. It was based on a cursive hand used in the papal chancery, which he saw would suit the Classical texts he intended to publish; it had the important commercial advantage of being condensed in form, making possible the printing of an increased number of words to the page. It was first used with upright roman capital letters and was an entirely independent type face; it was not until later that it was thought of as an adjunct to roman to be used for differentiation or emphasis. Italic was first used in England by Wynkyn de Worde (*c.* 1456–1535) in 1528. Manutius's italic was cut by Francesco Griffo da Bologna (*c.* 1450–1518), who also cut the roman type used in one of Manutius's most famous books, *De Aetna* (Venice, 1495) by Pietro Bembo. (This was the model chosen by Stanley Morison for the Bembo typeface cut by the Monotype Corporation in 1929.)

In the 16th century printing flourished in France, where the printing of books became established as an art through the work of GEOFROY TORY, ROBERT ESTIENNE, Henri Estiennes (ii) (1528–98), Simon de Colines (*d* 1546), Jean de Tournes (1504–64) and Claude Garamond (*c.* 1500–61). The earliest printing manual in English, *Mechanick Exercises on the Whole Art of Printing* (London, 1683–4) by Joseph Moxon (1627–1700), contains the statement: 'By a *Typographer*, I do not mean a *Printer*, as he is Vulgarly accounted … I mean such a one, who by his own Judgement, from solid reasoning with himself, can either perform, or direct others to perform from the beginning to the end, all the Handy-works and Physical Operations relating to *Typographie*.' *Mechanick Exercises …* was intended for craftsmen; Moxon's use of the term 'typography' implied but did not mention design; nor did he refer to 'layout', although printers had used drawn layouts at least as early as the *Nuremberg Chronicle* (1493) and probably earlier. The first important book about typography, however, was *Manuel typographique* (Paris, 1764–6) by PIERRE-SIMON FOURNIER. Type had until then been cast in a variety of sizes, differing from place to place, with names such as Diamond, Nonpareil, Brevier and Pica, though one printer's Pica would not be exactly the same size as another's. Fournier proposed a table of the dimensions and inter-relationships of type-bodies, thereby introducing the point system. It consisted of expressing type sizes as multiples of units, which he named 'points Typographiques'. His unit was 0.349 mm. Fournier knew that his system would improve the quality of printing, since the absence of standardization of type and other components of the printed page led inevitably to botched work and visual disorder. A slightly different point system (0.3759 mm), introduced later by another Parisian, François-Ambroise Didot (1730–1804), became generally adopted by French and then German type-founders; the American point system (0.3515 mm) was adopted in 1886 by American founders and in 1898 by the British. The credit for this important rationalization is due to Fournier, and the beautiful pages of his *Manuel* (see fig. 2) show him to have been one of the world's greatest typographers.

With the point system typographers knew that, for example, six lines of type set in 12 point ('pica') would be approximately one inch deep, as would one letter cast in 72 point size. Type (which has actually been cast as small as 3 point in size) went up by increments of one point (or more rarely half a point) to 12 point and then in jumps of two points to 24 point; after that, the most popular sizes were 28, 30, 36, 42, 48, 60 and 72. Type cast in metal to these sizes would be the same wherever it was cast, though when printed on paper it might appear slightly different, since paper is non-stable and can shrink or expand. A fount of type consists of one alphabet in capitals and another in lower case. (The latter term, derived from the days when compositors set type by hand standing in front of two cases of which the upper contained capitals and the lower the small letters, is still the accepted name for 'small letters'.) Lower-case letters are of three kinds: those with ascenders (such as h, k, l), those with descenders (such as g, j, q) and those without either (such as a, e, o, u and x). If the ascenders/descenders are long, the bodies of the letters must be smaller in x-height than if the descenders and ascenders are short, so the point size of type does not define the exact size of a type as it appears

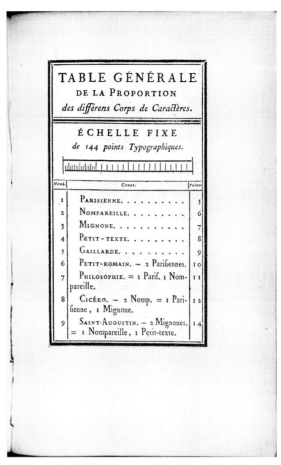

2. Typography of the 18th century from Pierre-Simon Fournier: *Manuel typographique* (Paris, 1764–6)

when printed. However, printers and typographers know well from experience what each face looks like in any given size.

For over 400 years typefaces were designed not by drawing (although a drawing might first be made) but by engraving a punch for each letter in steel. From each punch a mould was made into which molten metal (mostly lead) was poured to cast the letter. The types so cast had to be capable of not breaking when printed under heavy pressure on to handmade paper softened by dampening. Since the process was so laborious and could be done by only a very few men at any one time in any country, the number of types available to printers was limited. Even as late as the 19th century, most book printers had only one kind of roman and italic, in a range of sizes for text setting, a black letter for legal and religious uses, no bold, no script type and no sanserif (a type in which there is no cross line at the end of the strokes). The designing of books was the business of the master printer but would often be left to the compositors, though the master printer might instruct his compositors by means of pencil sketches and/or verbal guidance. JOHN BASKERVILLE in Birmingham, ROBERT FOULIS and Andrew Foulis (1712–74) in Glasgow and GIAMBATTISTA BODONI in Parma were printers whose work is distinctive. The design of books began to move out of the printers' control during the 19th century when publishing became a profession distinct from printing. Publishers, paying for the printing, naturally wished to determine the appearance of their books. Early examples of books designed by publishers rather than printers are those issued in London by William Pickering (1796–1854), John Moore Philp (1819–99) and Joseph Cundall (1818–95).

2. 19TH-CENTURY TECHNOLOGY. The first major change in printing technology to affect typography was the application of the pantograph to type design. The pantograph, the principle of which had been known since the 17th century, is an instrument with which a drawing or map may be enlarged or reduced mechanically; it was used in the 19th century to make wooden type, which had previously been cut by hand. In 1884 the American Linn Boyd Benton (1844–1932) invented a machine that could cut punches mechanically in any size from 2 to 72 point from one drawing; since new types could thus be produced far more quickly and cheaply than ever before, the typographer's choice of typefaces soon greatly increased. (Similarly after *c.* 1950 photographic and then computerized technology enabled typefaces to be not only enlarged or reduced mechanically but also elongated, expanded, condensed, angled in either direction or altered in weight and otherwise distorted, to any degree.)

The mechanical enlargement or reduction of a type design from a single size is not, however, in the interests of good typography. The maxim 'The eye is the sovereign ruler of taste', which had been propounded by N. Jaugeon (*d* 1725), engaged *c.* 1692 by the Académie des Sciences in Paris to state and rationalize the principles of type design, was echoed centuries later by Daniel Berkeley

Updike in *Printing Types* (Cambridge, MA, 1922) and remains true, despite modern technology. Well-designed letters do not follow exact rules, as the lettering on the Trajan Column (AD 113; Rome) shows. Rounded letters, such as capital Os, extend below the other capitals to give the effect of an even line; round lower-case letters must extend above square lower-case letters as well as below to appear to align; Vs and Ws descend below the base of other letters. Small capital letters in a fount of type are approximately the same size as the x-height of the lower-case letters; they are used where capitals are needed to differentiate a word or phrase but where normal 'caps' would look too prominent on the page (if normal capital letters are reduced photographically, the thick strokes become too fine and the resulting letters do not look like the same family).

The invention of the punch-cutting machine made possible, and was closely followed by, the invention in the USA of the Linotype (1884) and Monotype (1885) composition machines. The printing industry, which had not altered to any great extent since the time of Johann Gutenberg and William Caxton, now had to adapt to the advent of steam and electric power, photographic process blocks, offset lithography and many other technical developments (*see* PRINTING).

3. INNOVATIVE 20TH-CENTURY TYPOGRAPHERS. As a result of new inventions and a proliferation of new typefaces, type design and typography became separate professions, although there were no formal qualifications or training for typographers until the 1950s. The first professional freelance type designer, FREDERIC WILLIAM GOUDY (see fig. 3), and the first full-time freelance international typographer, BRUCE ROGERS, were both American. In 1917 Rogers was asked to advise Cambridge

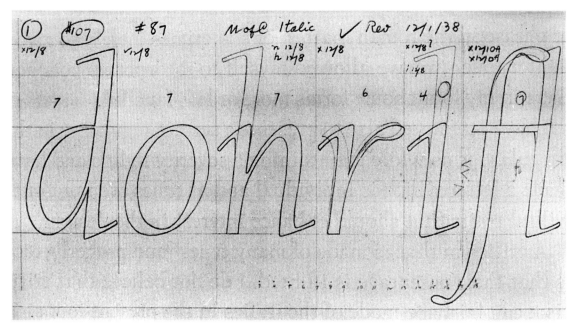

3. Type design by Frederic William Goudy: University of California Old Style, working drawing, 1938; from his *Typologia: Studies in Type Design and Type Making* (Berkeley and Los Angeles, 1940)

University Press on its typography, and his report (not made public until 1950) is a succinct statement of the objectives of typography and book design. It stresses the tactile as well as visual qualities of books, claiming that type set by machine can be as attractive as that set by hand. His opinion opposed that of DANIEL BERKELEY UPDIKE, whose book *Printing Types* (Cambridge, MA, 1922) was entirely hand-set, as Updike did not then believe that machine composition was as good as hand-setting by his own compositors. Rogers's faith in modern technology was best understood in Germany, although there, as elsewhere in the Western world, typography and design were currently influenced by JOHN RUSKIN, WILLIAM MORRIS and the British ARTS AND CRAFTS MOVEMENT. The appointment of the architect PETER BEHRENS as design adviser to AEG in Berlin in 1907 can be seen as the first major industrial design appointment in Europe. Behrens designed, among other things, typefaces, catalogues, posters and books; he is also credited with designing the first company logo, unifying all printed material produced by AEG to create a graphic 'corporate image'. The first Bauhaus exhibition in Weimar in 1923 had a profound influence on JAN TSCHICHOLD, then a young freelance designer, who became one of the most influential typographers of the 20th century. His book, *Die neue Typographie* (Berlin, 1928), proclaimed that typographic form, an expression of the new age of the machine, should be strictly functional. It must also be asymmetric, because symmetry involved putting words and sentences into shapes that were decorative and artificial and had nothing to do with their meaning and were therefore false. The typeface should be sanserif, which was seen at that time, particularly in Germany, as lettering in its purest form, shorn of inessentials (see fig. 4). The first sanserif typeface had been cut by William Caslon IV (1781–1869) in 1816. A century later it was seen as 'modern' when, in 1916, EDWARD JOHNSTON created the distinctive sanserif typeface for London Transport that it still uses (see fig. 5).

ideas of cultural import cannot spread and develop faster than the new society itself which they seek to serve. however, i think it is not an overstatement when i maintain that the community of the bauhaus, through the wholeness of its approach, has helped to restore architecture and design of today as a social art.

the new architecture and the bauhaus
by w. gropius, faber & faber, london, 1935.
"education towards creative design"
by w. gropius, american architect and architecture, new york, may 1937. "the gropius symposium" in the american academy of arts and sciences, arts and architecture, california, may 1952.

4. Typography of the 20th century from *50 Years Bauhaus* (London, 1968)

ABCDEFGHIJKLMN
OPQRSTUVWXYZ
abcdefghijklmnopq
rstuvwxyz 123456
7890 (&£.,:;'!?-*“”)

ABCDEFGHIJKLMN
OPQRSTUVWXYZ
1234567890

ABCDEFGHIJKL
MNOPQRSTUV
WXYZ abcdefgh
ijklmnopqrstuvw
xyz (&£.,:;'!?-*“”)
1234567890

5. A fount of Johnston type for London Transport

Other sanserif faces followed: in Germany, Erbar, designed by Jakob Erbar (1878–1935) in 1922, Paul Renner's Futura and Rudolf Koch's Kabel in 1927; in Britain, Gill Sans designed by ERIC GILL in 1927; and in 1957, Univers, designed by the typographer Adrian Frutiger (*b* 1928), for a time the most widely used typeface in the world. The appropriation of the word 'functional' by proponents of the 'new typography' was perverse, since serifs on type faces are highly functional, distinguishing letters from each other and joining letters into words. A further irony was the belief among some members of the Bauhaus (in which Tschichold never in fact worked) that capital letters, as well as serifs, were dispensable. Tschichold's insistence on sanserif type and asymmetric typography was often modified. After his move to Switzerland in 1933, nearly all his work became centred and 'traditional'. He found that asymmetric typography was inappropriate for works of literature and history, but could be effective for books on modern art and architecture. All Tschichold's work, whether asymmetric or symmetric, is outstandingly elegant; and in his early asymmetric work in particular, the subtlety of his typography is matched by the unexpected use of different papers, embossing and colour. In 1947

Tschichold was invited to Britain to take charge of the typography of Penguin Books—perhaps the most important assignment ever given to a freelance typographer. His insistence on meticulous composition, itemized in his *Penguin Composition Rules* that was circulated to all the leading book printers in Britain, was of crucial importance. He completed his task in three years and returned to Switzerland, having established standards in popular book production that were a lesson to publishers all over the world.

The leading English typographer in the 20th century was STANLEY MORISON. His essay 'First Principles of Typography', first published in the periodical *The Fleuron* in 1930, and in book form in 1936, quickly became a definitive text, although Eric Gill's *An Essay on Typography* (1931) revealed more of the depth and complexity of the subject. Morison exerted enormous influence on day-to-day typographic design in Britain through his work as typographic adviser to the Monotype Corporation (at that time the chief supplier of types for book printing in Britain), Cambridge University Press and other publishers and *The Times* newspaper, for which in 1931–2 he created Times New Roman, as well as redesigning the newspaper itself.

In 1960 Tschichold was commissioned to design Sabon, the first typeface to be designed for the three principal contemporary systems of composition: Linotype, Monotype and hand composition. Type set in Sabon by any of those methods would be identical and interchangeable; the drawings were made expressly for photographic reproduction, and the technical limitations imposed on the drawing by the requirements of the three quite different manufacturing processes were successfully overcome. By the time Sabon was made available (*c.* 1966) new methods of manufacturing type were being developed. By the early 1990s the design of typefaces and text composition was based on such technology as the computer and the laser, which enabled, for example, type to be set with every letter touching or even to be superimposed. In the late 20th century the growth of desk-top publishing has brought an increased awareness of typographical design and perhaps also an increased awareness of the skills it demands.

See also COMMERCIAL ART and CONCRETE POETRY.

BIBLIOGRAPHY

D. B. Updike: *Printing Types: Their History, Form and Use*, 2 vols (Cambridge, MA, 1922/*R* New York, 1980)
H. Carter: *Fournier on Typefounding* (London, 1930)
E. R. Gill: *An Essay on Typography* (London, 1931/*R* 1989)
A. F. Johnson: *Type Design* (London, 1934/*R* 1960)
S. Morison: *First Principles of Typography* (Cambridge, 1936/*R* 1967)
F. W. Goudy: *Typologia* (Berkeley, CA, 1940)
B. Rogers: *Paragraphs on Printing* (New York, 1943/*R* 1979)
S. Morison: *A Tally of Types* (Cambridge, 1953/*R* 1973)
J. Tschichold: *Typographische Gestaltung* (Basle, 1955); Eng. trans. as *Asymmetric Typography* (London, 1967)
H. Zapf: *About Alphabets* (New York, 1960)
H. Spencer: *Pioneers of Modern Typography* (London, 1969/*R* 1982)
J. Blumenthal: *Art of the Printed Book* (Boston, 1973)
J. Tschichold: *Ausgewählte Aufsätze über Fragen der Gestalt des Buches und der Typographie* (Basle, 1975/*R* 1987)
J. Blumenthal: *The Printed Book in America* (Boston, 1977)
J. Lewis: *Typography: Design and Practice* (London, 1978)
R. McLean: *The Thames and Hudson Manual of Typography* (London, 1980/*R* 1988)
W. Tracy: *Letters of Credit* (London, 1986)
S. Carter: *Twentieth-century Type Designers* (London, 1987)
W. Tracy: *The Typographic Scene* (London, 1988)

RUARI MCLEAN

Typological cycles. Pictorial programmes illustrating a system of biblical (occasionally allegorical) typology, especially popular in the medieval West. The typological interpretation of the Bible demonstrates the unity of the two testaments: the Old Testament is shown to announce the New in prophecies and prefigurations, while the New Testament is presented as the fulfilment of the Old, to which it is deemed superior. The history of the world, from its beginning to its approaching end, is thus conceived as a single history divided into stages: in the time before the coming of Christ and the inauguration of the era under grace, all that pertains to Christ and the Church was foreshadowed. Christian commentators on the Bible, seeking to reveal the mysteries that lay hidden in Scripture, identified a wealth of correspondences between things, persons and events in the Old Testament ('types') and in the New ('antitypes'). Christian biblical typology—anticipated in Jewish messianic and eschatological writings in which early events of biblical history were interpreted as prefigurations of events to come—received its mandate from the Gospels. Christ, who announces that his coming is a fulfilment of the Law and the Prophets, identifies Old Testament types for his own crucifixion and resurrection: 'And as Moses lifted up the serpent in the desert [Numbers 21:9], even so must the Son of Man be lifted up' (John 3:14); 'For even as Jonah was in the belly of the fish three days and three nights [Jonah 2:1], so will the Son of Man be three days and three nights in the heart of the earth' (Matthew 12:40). Numerous typological parallels are also drawn in the Pauline epistles. Typological exegesis had a profound impact on Christian art, especially in the later Middle Ages, when the alignment of types and antitypes often gave structure to pictorial programmes.

1. The early medieval period, before the 12th century. 2. 12th century and later.

1. THE EARLY MEDIEVAL PERIOD, BEFORE THE 12TH CENTURY. The practice of typological interpretation of the Bible, witnessed in the earliest extant Christian writings, began to influence the visual arts at an early date. In Early Christian funerary art, isolated Old Testament scenes of miraculous deliverance, for example Daniel in the lion's den, prefigure salvation for the Christian. By the 4th century AD extensive pictorial cycles incorporating both Old and New Testament scenes were being created. Evidence for the appearance of a monumental programme is offered by the *Dittochaeon*, a poem in 48 quatrains by the Latin poet Prudentius, which describes 24 episodes from the Old Testament, beginning with Adam and Eve, and 24 from the New Testament, beginning with the Annunciation. Neither in this poem nor in such contemporary works as the 18 extant panels from the wooden door (*c.* 430) of S Sabina in Rome, are systematic correspondences between Old and New Testament events easy to discover. Eight types and antitypes were carefully aligned, however, in certain tituli surviving from the 6th century, possibly composed by Rusticus Helpidius (*d*?533).

Typological thinking clearly stands behind the programme of the mosaics (c. 547) in the presbytery of S Vitale in Ravenna. Here four types of the eucharist—three of which are named in the ancient mass prayer *Supra quae*—flank the altar, namely *Abel Offering the Firstling of his Flock* (Genesis 4:4), *Melchizedek Bringing Forth Bread and Wine* (Genesis 14:18), *Abraham and the Three Angels* (Genesis 18:1–18) and the *Sacrifice of Isaac* (Genesis 22:1–14; see RAVENNA, fig. 6). A fully fledged typological cycle is described by Bede (673–735) in his *History of the Abbots of Wearmouth and Jarrow*: Benedict Biscop is reported to have brought back from Rome 'paintings demonstrating the concordance of the Old and New Testaments, most cunningly ordered', which included paired images of *Moses Raising the Brazen Serpent* (Numbers 21:9) and the *Crucifixion*. Typological elements are found in surviving early medieval works: Abel and Melchizedek inhabit the initial at the opening of the canon of the mass in the Drogo Sacramentary (c. 850; Paris, Bib. N., MS. lat. 9428; see MISSAL, fig. 1). Monumental programmes may be assumed to have existed: for example, at the request of Archbishop Aribo (d 1031), Ekkehard IV (980–1060) composed Old and New Testament tituli for the decoration of Mainz Cathedral.

2. 12TH CENTURY AND LATER. It was in the 12th century, especially the latter half, that typological programmes began to be produced in number. Episodes from the *Life of Christ* commonly formed the core of these increasingly extensive and systematic cycles: each antitype was often juxtaposed with more than one type. On the pedestal of the great golden cross (consecrated 1147) that Abbot Suger had made for Saint-Denis Abbey, 68 enamels showed 'the history of the Saviour' in alignment with 'the testimonies of the allegories from the Old Testament'. By the 17th century the work was destroyed, but it can be partially reconstructed on the basis of descriptions and a small replica produced c. 1170 (Saint-Omer, Mus. Hôtel Sandelin), which is decorated with eight types of the cross. Suger summoned goldsmiths from Lorraine to produce the piece; in subsequent decades artisans from the region between the Rhine and Meuse rivers would create many works decorated with typological programmes, among them the Stavelot Portable Altar (c. 1150–60; Brussels, Musées Royaux A. & Hist.), the Alton Towers Triptych (c. 1150–60; London, V&A), the Averbode Gospels (c. 1160; U. Liège, Bib. Gen., MS. 363), and numerous altar crosses and reliquaries of the True Cross. A representative Mosan cross (see ENAMEL, colour pl. IV, fig. 2) is adorned on the front with five types of the cross drawn from the standard repertory: *Moses Raising the Brazen Serpent*, the *Widow of Sarepta Picking Up Two Sticks* (1 Kings 17:10), *Jacob Blessing Ephraim and Manasseh* (Genesis 48:12-14), an *Israelite Writing the Sign of the Tau* (Exodus 12:7) and the *Two Spies Returning from Canaan Carrying a Cluster of Grapes* (Numbers 13:24). In 1181 NICHOLAS OF VERDUN completed the greatest of medieval typological works, a pulpit decorated with enamels, which had been commissioned by Provost Werner for the church of the Augustinian monastery of Klosterneuburg, near Vienna. The complicated programme, explained in inscriptions, unfolds in three vertically aligned tiers: episodes from the *Life of Christ* representing the era *sub gratia* occupy the central register, while types drawn from two periods of Jewish history—the era *ante legem* and the era *sub lege*—are placed in the upper and lower registers respectively. The scheme demanded ingenuity on the part of the designer, and some of the combinations are unusual: the *Annunciation* is aligned with the *Annunciation of Isaac* (Genesis 18:1–16) and the *Annunciation of Samson* (Judges 13:2-5). More traditional correspondences were also used: the *Crucifixion* is aligned with the *Sacrifice of Isaac* and the *Two Spies*.

Typological cycles were produced in many parts of Europe in the 12th and 13th centuries. Among the important survivals are the following: from northern France, the *Crucifixion* panel in a window (before 1147) in St Etienne, Châlons-sur-Marne; from Lower Saxony, the Hildesheim Missal (c. 1160; priv. col.); from southwest Germany, the illustrated *Dialogus de laudibus crucis* (c. 1170; Munich, Bayer. Staatsbib., Clm. 14159), a manuscript from Prüfening Abbey (nr Regensburg) containing on its first folios a sequence of 47 Old Testament scenes interpreted as prefigurations of the cross; and from the Rhineland, paintings (mid-13th century) of 12 pairs of Old and New Testament scenes decorating the nave vaults of S Maria Lyskirchen in Cologne, and typological windows (c. 1275) in the former abbey church of St Vitus at Mönchengladbach and in Cologne Cathedral—one in the Three Kings Chapel (c. 1260) and one in the chapel of St Stephen (c. 1280; see also STAINED GLASS, §III, 1).

English artisans produced a strikingly large number of typological cycles in this period, in many media. Three enamelled ciboria from the third quarter of the 12th century (New York, Pierpont Morgan Lib.; the Balfour and (damaged) Warwick ciboria, both London, V&A) are each decorated with six paired types and antitypes in medallions. Inscriptions on the vessels match inscriptions known to have been incorporated in a lost typological cycle in the chapter house at Worcester: here ten clusters of four typologically related scenes appeared in the vaults or windows of the circular room. At Canterbury Cathedral a set of 12 'typological windows' (c. 1180–90), now partially preserved, decorated the choir aisles: episodes from the *Life of Christ* extending from the *Annunciation* to the *Resurrection* were each flanked by two scenes, most of them Old Testament types, which demonstrated the spiritual significance of the New Testament events (see CANTERBURY, fig. 12). In the *Pictor in carmine*, an anonymous text composed c. 1200 to help painters create typological programmes, the author identified two or more types for no fewer than 138 antitypes and supplied for each pairing at least two distichs 'which shortly explain the Old Testament subject and apply it to that of the New'. A cycle of typological paintings (1233–45), which once decorated the choir enclosure at Peterborough Abbey, and which is known from 17th-century descriptions, is echoed in the extensive sequence of typological miniatures in the Peterborough Psalter (early 14th century; Brussels, Bib. Royale Albert 1er, MS 9961–2). Some of the Worcester inscriptions surfaced in later manuscripts, namely one at Eton College (c. 1250; Eton, Bucks, Coll.

Typological scenes, *The Ascension of Christ* and *Jacob's Dream of a Ladder Reaching to Heaven*; tinted drawings from the *Speculum humanae salvationis*, Italy, late 14th century (Paris, Bibliothèque Nationale, MS. lat. 9584, fol. 12*v*)

Lib., MS. 177), where on each of ten pages an antitype in a medallion is surrounded by two prophets and four typological scenes in medallions, and in the richly ornamented Sherbourne Missal (*c*. 1400; London, BL, Loan MS. 83).

Typological picture books of various kinds, containing long cycles of images accompanied by brief explanatory texts, were very popular in the later Middle Ages. The *Bible moralisée*, a genre of illustrated Bible created in Paris in the early 13th century, survives in 14 copies, dating from the 13th to the 15th century. In this work, superposed paired images in medallions illustrate the literal and spiritual senses of passages extracted from the Bible; most of the spiritual interpretations are allegorical or moral, but typological readings also occur. A more purely typological work, the *Biblia pauperum*, was composed in south-west Germany in the last quarter of the 13th century; over 80 manuscripts, produced largely in central Europe, survive, as well as many printed versions, the earliest dated *c*. 1460. The work comprises 34 groups of images: in each, an episode from the *Life of Christ*—enclosed in a roundel in the earliest copies—is encircled by four prophets and flanked by two Old Testament types, which are identified in verse inscriptions and explained in prose passages (*see*

BIBLE, fig. 9). Yet more ambitious was the *Speculum humanae salvationis*, a typological text in verse, composed in the early 14th century by an anonymous author, which was accompanied in almost all copies by an extensive cycle of illustrations; more than 350 manuscripts and early printed books survive (*see* BLOCK-BOOK, fig. 3). In each of 45 chapters (34 in the shorter version), four images in rectangular fields of equal size, appearing above four columns of text, illustrate an event from the *Life of Christ* (see fig.) or the *Life of the Virgin* and three prefigurations of the event. The range of antitypes is expanded and types are here drawn from extra-biblical as well as biblical sources: thus an image of Christ showing his wounds to God the Father, 'praying for us', is aligned with scenes of the unjustly accused soldier Antipater showing his wounds to Julius Caesar, Mary showing her son the breasts that nourished him, and Esther pleading with Ahasuerus on behalf of her people (Esther 7–8). In an even more extensive, but less widely distributed, typological work, the *Concordantia caritatis*, composed after 1351 by Abbot Ulrich of Lilienfeld (*d* 1358), each antitype is juxtaposed with four prophets, two types and two scenes from natural history.

The *Biblia pauperum* and the *Speculum humanae salvationis* provided a large repertory of imagery for use in monumental programmes. Motifs from the latter appear, for example, in windows (*c.* 1330–40) in St Stephen, Mulhouse (Alsace); in wall paintings (mid-14th century) in Königsberg Cathedral; in the great embroidered hanging (*c.* 1430) in the convent of Wienhausen; in Konrad Witz's *Heilsspiegel* altarpiece (*c.* 1435; dispersed; scenes in Basle, Kstmus.; for illustration *see* WITZ, KONRAD); and in the sculptures of the central portal (*c.* 1480) of St Maurice, Vienne.

Typological thinking long continued to play a role in the design of pictorial programmes. Traditional types and antitypes were employed and given new meanings in Michelangelo's ceiling (1508–12) for the Sistine Chapel, Vatican Palace, Rome; in Lucas Cranach the Elder's several allegories of the Law and Grace (from 1529); and in the *Triumph of the Eucharist*, a series of tapestries from cartoons (1625–7) designed by Rubens, commissioned by the Infanta Isabella, Archduchess of Austria (1566–1633), for the convent of the Descalzas Reales in Madrid (tapestries *in situ*).

BIBLIOGRAPHY
J. Daniélou: *Sacramentum futuri: Études sur les origines de la typologie biblique* (Paris, 1950); Eng. trans. as *From Shadows to Reality: Studies in the Biblical Typology of the Fathers* (London, 1960)
R. A. Koch: 'The Sculptures of the Church of Saint-Maurice at Vienne, the *Biblia pauperum* and the *Speculum humanae salvationis*', *A. Bull.*, xxxii (1950), pp. 151–5
M. R. James: 'Pictor in Carmine', *Archaeologia*, xciv (1951), pp. 141–66
F. Goldkuhle: *Mittelalterliche Wandmalerei in St. Maria Lyskirchen*, Bonner Beiträge zur Kunstwissenschaft, iii (Düsseldorf, 1954)
G. Schmidt: *Die Armenbibeln des XIV. Jahrhunderts* (Graz and Cologne, 1959)
F. Unterkircher and G. Schmidt, eds.: *Die Wiener Biblia pauperum: Codex Vindobonensis 1198*, 3 vols (Graz, 1962)
F. Röhrig: 'Rota in medio rotae: Ein typologischer Zyklus aus Österreich', *Jb. Stift. Klosterneuburg*, n. s., v (1965), pp. 7–113
E. Guldan: *Eva und Maria: Eine Antithese als Bildmotiv* (Graz, 1966)
P. Bloch: 'Typologische Kunst', *Lex et Sacramentum im Mittelalter*, ed. P. Wilpert, Miscellanea Mediaevalia, vi (Berlin, 1969), pp. 127–42
L. Freeman Sandler: 'Peterborough Abbey and the Peterborough Psalter in Brussels', *J. Brit. Archaeol. Assoc.*, 3rd ser., xxxiii (1970), pp. 36–49
H. Hoefer: *Typologie im Mittelalter: Zur Übertragbarkeit typologischer Interpretation auf weltliche Dichtung* (Göppingen, 1971)
R. Haussherr: 'Sensus litteralis und sensus spiritualis in der Bible moralisée', *Frühmittelalt. Stud.*, vi (1972), pp. 356–80
M.-L. Thérel: 'Les Différents Types d'illustration des commentaires bibliques', *Doss. Archéol.*, xvi (1976), pp. 28–34
A. C. Esmeijer: *Divina quaternitas: A Preliminary Study in the Method and Application of Visual Exegesis* (Amsterdam, 1978)
H. Buschhausen: *Der Verduner Altar* (Vienna, 1980)
H. Appuhn: *Heilsspiegel: Die Bilder des mittelalterlichen Andachtsbuches Speculum humanae salvationis* (Dortmund, 1981, rev. 1989)
M. Caviness: *The Windows of Christ Church Cathedral, Canterbury*, Corp. Vitrearum Med. Aevi, Great Britain, ii (London, 1981)
N. Stratford: 'Three English Romanesque Enamelled Ciboria', *Burl. Mag.*, cxxvi (1984), pp. 204–16
A. Wilson and J. L. Wilson: *A Medieval Mirror: Speculum humanae salvationis, 1324–1500* (Berkeley, 1984)
A. Henry: *Biblia pauperum: A Facsimile and Edition* (Ithaca, 1987)
——: *The Eton Roundels: Eton College MS 177* (Aldershot, 1990)

ELIZABETH SEARS

Tyre [Gr. Tyrus; Arab. Sur]. Ancient city in south Lebanon, *c.* 30 km south of Sidon, which flourished as one of the leading centres of the Phoenicians (*see* PHOENICIAN). It was originally an island fortress facing Palaetyrus (now Tell el-Rashidiyeh). In 332 BC, after an unsuccessful siege of seven months, Alexander the Great joined the island to the mainland with a causeway, thus turning Tyre into a peninsula. The history of the city spans more than 4000 years. The site was first excavated in 1860 by Ernest Renan, and again briefly in 1903; French expeditions surveyed it in 1921 and 1934–6, and since 1947 excavations have been directed by Maurice Chébab. Most of the finds are in the Louvre in Paris and the Musée National in Beirut.

Excavations have revealed little of the ancient city, but in the first half of the 1st millennium BC the skill of its craftsmen was recorded in the Bible (I Kings 5:18; 7:13–45). The magnificent remains of Roman and Byzantine Tyre, however, prove that the city deserved the title 'Metropolis of Phoenicia'. A splendid avenue bordered with cipollino marble columns and paved with mosaic leads to the southern port. Other remains include a palaestra bordered with grey granite columns from Aswan in Upper Egypt, baths, a rectangular construction with five tiers of steps used for festivals, and cisterns for the flourishing purple dye industry. A monumental archway 20 m high was raised over the principal road leading into Tyre. The city's aqueduct ran perpendicularly to the road. On both sides spread a vast Roman-Byzantine necropolis, which has yielded about 300 sarcophagi (e.g. Beirut, Mus. N.). Several of the sculptured reliefs depict episodes from the *Iliad*, the ransom of Hector being a favourite subject. Other sarcophagi, in marble and limestone, are decorated with scenes from naval battles, a battle of the Amazons, processions of Bacchantes, garlands and cupids. Some sarcophagi are of the *kliné* type with a representation of the dead man reclining, sometimes accompanied by his wife. Inscriptions in Greek give the name of the occupant with the phrase, 'Be comforted, no one is immortal'. The hippodrome (*c.* 500×160 m) was one of the largest in the Roman world. From the covered walk tiered steps, built over a podium, slope down to the race-track; an obelisk and a statue of Herakles stood on the spina.

A large Crusader cathedral (12th century) with four colossal, monolithic granite double columns, each more than 1 m in diameter, was built over a Roman road. After the fall of Jerusalem in 1187 it became the traditional place for Crusader royal marriages, coronations and burials. Tyre was captured by the Mamelukes in 1291.

BIBLIOGRAPHY
E. Renan: *Mission de Phénicie* (Paris, 1864)
L. Lortet: *La Syrie d'aujourd'hui* (Paris, 1884)
A. Poidebard: *Un Grand Port disparu: Tyr* (Paris, 1939)
M. Chébab: 'Tyr à l'époque romaine', *Mél. U. St-Joseph*, xxxviii (1962), pp. 11–40
——: 'Sarcophages à reliefs de Tyr', *Bull. Mus. Beyrouth*, xxi (1968) [whole issue]
N. Jidejian: *Tyre through the Ages* (Beirut, 1969)
H. J. Katzenstein: *The History of Tyre* (Jerusalem, 1973)
J.-P. Rey-Coquais: 'Inscriptions de la nécropole', *Bull. Mus. Beyrouth*, xxix (1977)

NINA JIDEJIAN

Tyrnau. *See* TRNAVA.

Tyroll, Hans. *See* TIROL, HANS.

Tyrsa, Nikolay (Andreyevich) (*b* Aralyk, Armenia [now in Turkey], 10 May 1887; *d* Vologda, 10 Feb 1942). Russian artist and watercolourist of Armenian birth. He did not receive a systematic art education, although he studied with Léon Bakst at the Academy of Arts in St Petersburg from 1905 to 1910. He regarded Bakst, a clear influence in the many nude studies of the early and mid-1910s, as one of his principal mentors. During this period Tyrsa also studied and copied church frescoes, sharing in the general rediscovery and reappraisal of the national traditions of Russian culture, including icons, church architecture and the decorative arts. After the October Revolution of 1917 he was successful as a commercial designer, poster artist and book and magazine illustrator, especially for children's literature. Together with the artists Vladimir Konashevich, Vladimir Lebedev (1891–1967) and Yury Vasnetsov, and the writers Korney Chukovsky (1882–1969) and Samuil Marshak (1887–1964), Tyrsa contributed to the virtual renaissance of the children's book during the 1920s and early 1930s. He also gave much attention to the Russian classics, illustrating Pushkin's *Pikovaya Dama* (The Queen of Spades; Leningrad, 1936), Tolstoy's *Anna Karenina* (Leningrad, 1939) and Lermontov's *Geroy nashego vremeni* (A Hero of Our Time; Leningrad, 1941).

Although remembered primarily as an illustrator, Tyrsa was also active as a studio painter, choosing the most varied subjects for his preferred medium of watercolour—bathers, St Petersburg streets, flowers and portraits (e.g. *The Artist's Daughter (A Sleeping Girl)*, 1929; St Petersburg, Rus. Mus.). Using a free and lyrical style, Tyrsa did not share in the extreme formal experiments of the avant-garde, even though his friends included Vladimir Tatlin (whose portraits he drew in 1923 and 1925 (artist's estate)), Lev Bruni and Nikolay Punin.

PUBLISHED WRITINGS

'Illustratsiya i tvorchestvo' [Illustration and creation], *Literaturnyy Sovremenik*, 1 (1931)

BIBLIOGRAPHY

Nikolay Andreyevich Tyrsa (1887–1942) (exh. cat., Leningrad, Rus. Mus., 1967)
Nikolai Andreyevich Tyrsa (exh. cat., ed. B. Suris; Moscow, Pushkin Mus. F.A., 1967)
E. Kuznetsov: 'Khudozhnik Nikolay Tyrsa' [The artist Nikolay Tyrsa], *Tvorchestvo* [Creative work], 1 (1968)

JOHN E. BOWLT

Tyscher, (Carl) Marcus. *See* TUSCHER, MARCUS.

Tyshler, Aleksandr (Grigor'yevich) (*b* Melitopol', Ukraine, 26 July 1898; *d* Moscow, 23 June 1980). Russian painter, graphic artist, stage designer and sculptor of Ukrainian birth. He was born into a Jewish family of carpenters. From childhood he was fascinated by itinerant showmen, puppeteers, gypsies and market traders who carried their wares in large baskets or their booths on their heads. From 1912 to 1917 he studied at the Kiev school of art. At the time of the 1917 revolution he was working in Alexandra Exter's studio, where he met other young artists interested in the theatre, notably I. Rabinovich (1894–1961) and N. Shifrin (1892–1961). After service in the 12th Army he returned in 1919 to Melitopol', where he created propaganda posters and cartoons for ROSTA (the Russian Telegraph Agency). In 1921 he went to Moscow and undertook some teaching in Vkhutemas (the Higher Artistic and Technical Workshops). He was a

founder member of the SOCIETY OF EASEL PAINTERS where, among other works, he exhibited *War* (1925; Moscow, Tret'yakov Gal.) and *Young Girl and Aeroplane* (1927; former USSR, priv. col.). During the 1930s Tyshler was attacked for his alleged formalism but continued to work, concentrating on theatrical design. In 1935 he designed *Richard III* for the Gor'ky Theatre, Leningrad (now St Petersburg), and *King Lear* for the State Jewish Theatre, Moscow (both designs Moscow, Bakhrushin Cent. Theat. Mus.), the latter production attracting the enthusiasm of Edward Gordon Craig. In the last 20 years of his life he resumed his depictions of itinerant showmen and young lovers, and he executed designs for Shakespeare's plays.

Tyshler's stage designs, often for a stage within a stage, were imaginative evocations of a sinister medieval world. His sculptures consisted of branches and twigs, from which he seemed to release rather than carve the slender bodies of young girls. His paintings and sketches were carried out in short nervous strokes and usually featured an isolated central figure overwhelmed by an enormous headpiece in the shape of a fairground booth, flower stall or candelabrum, as in *Girl of Fashion on a Bench* (1966; exh. London, Grosvenor Gal., 1974). Tyshler's work embodies the joy and tragic burden of the creative gift.

BIBLIOGRAPHY

F. Syrkina: *Aleksandr Grigor'yevich Tyshler* (Moscow, 1966)
Aleksandr Tyshler, 1898–1980, USSR Union of Artists (Moscow, 1983)

ALAN BIRD

Tytgat, Edgard (*b* Brussels, 28 April 1879; *d* Brussels, 10 Jan 1957). Belgian painter, printmaker and writer. He learned to draw in his father's lithography studio. In 1900 Tytgat entered the Académie Royale des Beaux-Arts in Brussels and studied under Constant Montald. His first paintings were influenced by Symbolism and in particular the work of Pierre Puvis de Chavannes, whom he admired. He met Rik Wouters in 1907, and the two became friends. World War I drove him into exile, and he lived as a refugee in England until 1920. There, he not only painted but also made prints, including woodcuts and linocuts with the help of his wife, Maria. She was also his model for the numerous canvases painted in London, for example *The Pose* (1918; Brussels, Mus. A. Mod.). His early work was full of sensitivity, using bright tones that accentuated delicate greys in an impressionistic manner. Towards 1925 Tytgat became aware of Expressionism. His plasticity grew stronger, and his colours darker, and his desire for simplification came to dominate the forms (e.g. *Violinist*, 1929; Ostend, Mus. S. Kst.). Tytgat was a member of the Art Contemporain group in Antwerp, and of Groupe des IX, Le Centaure and Sélection in Brussels. He played an active role in Belgian Expressionism. At the end of his career, Tytgat abandoned the subjects of his youth—merry-go-rounds, childhood, window views, couples—and turned towards more fantastic subjects, drawing inspiration from mythology, history and pure imagination in such works as *Iphigenia Embarking for the Sacrificial Island* (1950; Brussels, Mus. A. Mod.). His literary output was also quite abundant and he also wrote and illustrated accounts of his childhood memories. Only a selection of his writings has been published.

BIBLIOGRAPHY
M. Roelandts: *Edgard Tytgat* (Antwerp, 1948)
A. Dasnoy and G. Ollinger: *Edgard Tytgat: Catalogue raisonné de son oeuvre peint* (Brussels, 1965) [comprehensive bibliog. and illustrations]
Edgard Tytgat, évocation d'une vie (exh. cat., Brussels, Musées Royaux B.-A., 1974)

GISELE OLLINGER-ZINQUE

Tyumen'. Russian town and regional centre in Western Siberia, 2144 km east of Moscow. The Tatar town of Chimgi-Tura, sited on a headland at the confluence of the Tyumenka and Tura rivers, was captured in 1581 by the ataman Yermak Timofeyevich (*d* 1585). A fortress (destr. 18th century) was founded in 1586 and the first Russian town in Siberia developed along the Tura to the south-east. The northern part of the town is dominated by the Baroque Troitsky Monastery, which was founded in 1616 as the monastery of the Transfiguration, with its five-domed Troitsky Cathedral (1709–15), decorated in a late 17th-century Ukrainian Baroque style, the cruciform church of SS Peter and Paul (1755) with a bell-tower (1741), and other ecclesiastical buildings (1739). The Baroque churches of St Iliya (18th century), the Exaltation of the Cross (1791) and the Saviour (1794) are also noteworthy. The wave-shaped façades, stepped domes and bell-tower of the Znamensky Cathedral (1768–1801) are characteristic of the Siberian Baroque style. Buildings of the 19th century show Neo-classical influence and include the town administrative headquarters (first quarter of the 19th century), the post office (1800s) and the town bazaar (Gostinnyy dvor; 1835–8). Single-storey wooden houses of the 19th century and the early 20th with carved window-sills have been preserved alongside two-storey houses, richly decorated with bas-relief carving.

BIBLIOGRAPHY
S. Zavarikhin: *Vorota v Sibir'* [The gateway to Siberia] (Moscow, 1981)
S. Zavarikhin and B. Zhuchenko: *Tyumen' arkhitekturnaya* [The architecture of Tyumen'] (Sverdlovsk, 1984)

M. I. ANDREYEV

Tzanck, Daniel (*b* Tiflis, 1874; *d* 1964). French collector and dentist. Though he practised dentistry, his principal interests were artistic and intellectual. He began collecting before World War I, and had made the acquaintance of Guillaume Apollinaire by 1913. In the 1920s he was extremely active as a supporter of modern art, and in 1923 founded the Société des Amateurs d'Art et des Collectionneurs with his friend Jean Crotti. The society campaigned for a new museum of modern art based on private initiative, and organized several exhibitions, including a Salon de la Folle Enchère which reflected his involvement with the booming auction market of the time. In June 1925, at the Hôtel Drouot in Paris, he held a sale of items from his own collection, in which 63 artists were represented. His tastes were eclectic, although he inclined more to the figurative work of the Ecole de Paris than to either abstract or Surrealist art. He did, however, own at least one 'extreme' work: a false cheque from Marcel Duchamp, drawn on the 'Teeth's Loan and Trust Company Consolidated', payment for his professional services in 1919.

BIBLIOGRAPHY
M. Gee: *Dealers, Critics and Collectors of Modern Painting* (New York and London, 1981), pp. 158–65

P. Read: 'Gestes et opinions du Docteur Tzanck, défenseur de l'art moderne, virtuose de l'art dentaire, ami de Guillaume Apollinaire', *Que Vlo-Vé*, 20 (Oct–Dec 1986), pp. 3–25

MALCOLM GEE

Tzanev, Stoyan (*b* Burgas, 28 Feb 1946). Bulgarian printmaker and painter. In 1973 he graduated in printmaking from the Academy of Fine Arts (Akademia Sztuk Pięknych) in Warsaw. His works, especially his prints, are filled with symbols and visual metaphors that relate to themes from Bulgaria's cultural and historic heritage. There are elements of the grotesque and the phantasmagoric, as well as paradox and irony, in his oils and acrylic paintings (e.g. *Idol*, 1985; Sofia, N.A.G.). Tzanev prefers to employ a variety of techniques in printmaking, favouring soft-ground etching and aquatint (*Embrace*, 1982; e.g. Sofia, C.A.G.), colour lithography and mixed media. As a printmaker he has exhibited in various biennales of graphic art, including the International Biennale of Graphic Art in Kraków and one in Heidelberg. In 1987 he won the Grand Prix at Intergraphic in Berlin.

BIBLIOGRAPHY
Natsionalna Hudozhestvena Galeriya [National Art Gallery], cat. (Sofia, 1980)
Gradska Hudozhestvena Galeriya [City Art gallery], cat. (Sofia, 1988)
J. Nedeva: 'The Art of Stoyan Tzanev', *Kontakti*, 6 (1988)

JULIANA NEDEVA-WEGENER

Tzara, Tristan (*b* Moinești, 16 April 1896; *d* Paris, 24 Dec 1963). French writer of Romanian birth. His first poems were influenced by Symbolism. He went to Zurich in 1915 to study philosophy, and he founded the DADA movement with his friends Marcel Janco, Hans Arp, Richard Huelsenbeck and Hugo Ball. He edited the review *Dada* (1917–22), which served as an interchange and a melting-pot for the different artistic avant-gardes (Futurism, Expressionism, Cubism) isolated in Europe during World War I. It welcomed poets and visual artists with similar views. As early as issue 3, the 'manifeste dada 1918' laid the foundations of a revolutionary art, advocating chaos and the mixing of genres. The page exploded: typography itself was exploited as art. Influenced by the visual discoveries of his friends, including Arp, Janco and Viking Eggeling, Tzara composed poems that are their verbal equivalents, treating the word as sonorous material and attempting to produce an ideographic alphabet. The *soirées nègres* that he organized led him to become interested in the art of the peoples of Africa and Oceania, of which he was a discriminating lifelong collector (collection sold at Drouot, Paris, Nov 1988). He saw in such non-Western art 'l'enfance de l'humanité'—a spontaneity and a *joie de vivre*, which he made the fundamental criteria of Dada. He introduced into his poetry the rhythms and the verbal techniques of negro songs. His collections of poetry and his plays are characterized by a drastic treatment of language and a deliberate confusion of genres (*Mouchoir de nuages*, 1925, for example, introduced pictorial collage to the theatre), but they also affirm a joy in creativity.

Tzara joined Francis Picabia, with whom he felt a deep affinity, in Paris in January 1920. He was welcomed by the group Littérature, which included Louis Aragon, André Breton and Philippe Soupault, who wholeheartedly embraced Dada. After various scandals, provoked by his contempt for institutions, Tzara decided to bring Dada to an end and pursue his poetry. His more intimate collections (especially *L'Homme approximatif*, Paris, 1931) led him back to Surrealism and from 1930 to 1935 he contributed to defining its activities and ideology. His 'Essai sur la situation de la poésie', published in the review *Surréalisme au Service de la Révolution* (4, 1931, pp. 15–23), described the poetic evolution by which a long revolutionary tradition had culminated in Surrealism. An 'experimental dream' 'Grains et issues' (*Surréalisme au Service de la Révolution*, 6, 15 May 1933, pp. 49–56) illuminated the relation between oneiric and controlled thought in automatic writing. He drew closer to the Communist Party, becoming friends with Picasso. Forced into hiding during the occupation, he published occasional, clandestine poems. He upbraided the Surrealists who, in his eyes, had abandoned the struggle, in *Le Surréalisme et l'après-guerre* (Paris, 1947). He was also opposed to Jean-Paul Sartre, whose notion of 'poésie engagée' he refuted. His collections, illustrated by Matisse (*Midis gagnés*, Paris, 1939), André Masson (*Terre sur terre*, Geneva and Paris, 1946), Miró (*Parler seul*, Paris, 1948–50) and Picasso (*De Mémoire d'homme*, Paris, 1950), took up contemporary preoccupations with the nature of humanity and art. Acquainted with the greatest artists of his time, Tzara dedicated many essays to Man Ray, Max Ernst, Henri Rousseau, Kurt Schwitters and especially Picasso, whose progress he analysed by a sort of intuitive complicity. His articles on poetry and painting ('Le Pouvoir des images', *Oeuvres complètes*, iv, pp. 297–440) focus on creative acts in relation to society. They discuss processes that use heterogeneous materials, such as collage, and they are based on the premise that art and life need to undergo transformation through revolt.

For a portrait of Tzara *see* DRESS, fig. 57.

WRITINGS
H. Béhar, ed.: *Oeuvres complètes*, 6 vols (Paris, 1975–82)

Tzintzuntzan, *yácata* I, the northernmost of five *yácatas*, *c.* 1300–1525, view from the south

BIBLIOGRAPHY
Europe, 555–6 (July–Aug 1975) [issue dedicated to Tzara]
For further bibliography *see* DADA.

HENRI BÉHAR

Tzaritchingrad. *See* CARIČIN GRAD.

Tzintzuntzan. Pre-Columbian site on the edge of Lake Pátzcuaro, Michoacán, Mexico. From *c.* 1300 to 1525 it was the capital of the Purépecha kingdom, later called TARASCAN by the Spaniards, of north-western and lowland Michoacán, adjacent Jalisco and north-western Guerrero. The *Relación de Michoacán*, an anonymous 16th-century chronicle recorded by a Franciscan missionary *c.* 1539–41 (Madrid, Escorial, Bib. Monasterio S Lorenzo), relates that the ?14th-century ruler Tariácuri consolidated the Purépecha kingdom and established his capital at Pátzcuaro. He later divided his kingdom, bequeathing Michuacán–Tzintzuntzan to his nephew Tangaxoan I. Thereafter, the site of Tzintzuntzan ('place of humming-birds') soon became the Tarascan capital.

Despite the presence of abundant volcanic stone in the region, the Tarascans created neither an imposing architecture nor a monumental art. Nevertheless, their ceremonial precincts included large platform structures that seem to have been in perfect harmony with the lake-filled landscape in which they were built. The city of Tzintzuntzan had at least three ceremonial precincts: one situated at the foot of Cerro Yahuarato, another on the spurs of Cerro Tariaqueri and a third on the plain bordering the lake. The residential zones of the inhabitants were grouped around these precincts and extended into the hills and along the lake shore. At the time of the Spanish Conquest the population is estimated to have been 40,000. Enormous platforms were built of earth and stone cores clad with rectangular stone slabs set in mud. The platforms, over 400 m long, were terraced and served as stages for temple bases, known as *yácatas*, multi-roomed élite residences built around patios, houses for religious ceremonies, storehouses and other administrative and ceremonial structures.

The most distinctive Purépecha or Tarascan structure was the *yácata* ('a piling-up of stones with mud'). The principal remains of one precinct at Tzintzuntzan comprise a rectangular, terraced platform (*c.* 425×250×18 m) supporting five *yácatas* (see fig.) constructed *c.* 1300–1525. Each *yácata* base included both rectangular and circular elements. In plan they resemble the letter T (each 66×22×12 m), with a large circular platform (diam. 29 m) at the base of the T. The walls were constructed from volcanic stone slabs, and the floors of their bases were made of fire-hardened clay. All faces of the *yácatas* were tiered in narrow steps, and the rectangular top of the T included a stairway for ascending to the round temple, made of perishable materials, on top.

Excavations of the *yácatas* and other structures at Tzintzuntzan have yielded numerous examples of Tarascan ceramic forms, including resist-painted pottery, forms with stirrup handles and 'teapot' spouts, miniature tripods and clay smoking pipes; other artefacts include numerous notched bones and a wealth of small copper axes, bells and other ornaments (Mexico City, Mus. N. Antropol.;

Morelia, Mus. Reg. Michoacano). The painstaking excavation of *yácata* V uncovered several rich multiple burials. In the north-east patio, between the circular and rectangular elements of the platform, there was a primary grave with nine skeletons covered by a layer of stones. Each body had been placed on a woven straw mat, with a pot under each head. The arms of each skeleton were linked to those of its neighbours. Associated grave furniture included a pair of silver tweezers, a pair of simple gold earrings, copper bells from ankle and wrist bracelets, a copper axe with a wooden handle, long-stemmed clay smoking pipes, and obsidian lip and ear plugs. The five burials, probably secondary, in the south-west patio, also between the circular and rectangular elements of the platform, were all of females. The grave offerings comprised miniature ritual objects, and some of the vessels had been ritually 'killed' by knocking a small hole in the base. Copper objects included tiny bells and needles, and brooches with animal heads and dangling bells. A lip plug of rock crystal was also found. Multiple burials excavated in *yácata* IV were accompanied by similar artefacts of gold, obsidian, rock crystal and turquoise.

The nature and accompanying rituals of such burials are described in the anonymous *Relación de Michoacán* and in the *Monarquía indiana* of Juan de Torquemada. These describe the burial of a Tarascan king and the slaying of accompanying servants for his afterlife. The king's body, however, was cremated on a sumptuous bier. It seems likely, therefore, that the multiple burials at Tzintzuntzan are those of the slain retainers, and that the charred bones of Tarascan royal burials, together with their rich grave furniture of metalwork, pottery and clothing, remain to be discovered.

Two types of sculptured works of a functional and religious nature were important in Tarascan ceremonies: thrones, carved in the shape of a coyote, rendered in a sober, angular style, in which the animal's back has become the seat and its feet the supports; and carved basalt figures called *chacmools*, which retain the horizontal, angular style of the coyotes but represent human figures lying on their backs, with rectangular receptacles on their stomachs for offerings to the Tarascan gods—possibly human hearts from sacrificial victims. No examples of either type have actually been found at Tzintzuntzan itself, but rather at the Tarascan city of Ihuatzio, across Lake Pátzcuaro. Examples of coyote 'thrones' and *chacmools* are in the Museo Nacional de Antropología, Mexico City, and in the Museo Regional Michoacano, Morelia.

For discussion of the arts of Pre-Columbian Mexico *see also* MESOAMERICA, PRE-COLUMBIAN.

BIBLIOGRAPHY

Relación de las ceremonias y ritos y población y gobierno de los indios de la provincia de Michoacán (1541); Eng. trans. by E. R. Crain and R. C. Reindorp as *The Chronicles of Michoacán* (Norman, 1970)

J. de Torquemada: *Los veinte y un libros rituales y monarquía indiana, con el origen y guerras de los yndios occidentales, de sus poblaciones, descubrimientos, conquista, conversion y otras cosas maravillosa*, 3 vols (1613; Seville, 1615; Madrid, 1723; facs., Mexico City, 1969)

P. Beaumont: *Crónica de la provincia de los santos apóstoles S. Pedro y S. Pablo de Michoacán de la regular observancia de N. P. San Francisco*, 5 vols (Mexico City, 1873–4)

D. F. Rubín de la Borbolla: 'Exploraciones arqueológicos en Michoacán, Tzintzuntzan, Temporada III', *Rev. Mex. Estud. Antropol.*, iv (1940), pp. 5–20

——: 'Orfebrería tarasca', *Cuad. Amer.*, iii (1944), pp. 125–38

R. Galí: 'Arqueología de Tzintzuntzan', *An. Mus. Michoacano*, ii (1946), pp. 50–62

I. Marquina: *Arquitectura prehispanica* (Mexico City, 1950, 2/1964/R 1981)

R. Piña Chán: *Mesoamerica*, Memorias INAH, vi (Mexico City, 1960)

D. Basalenque: *Historia de la provincia de San Nicolás de Tolentino de Michoacán del Orden de N. P. S. Agustín* (Mexico City, 1963)

M. P. Weaver: *The Aztecs, Maya and their Predecessors: Archaeology of Mesoamerica* (New York, 1972, rev. 2/1981), pp. 469–73

L. González y González: *Michoacán* (Mexico City, 1980)

J. Kelly: *The Complete Visitor's Guide to Mesoamerican Ruins* (Norman, 1982), pp. 34–6

ROMÁN PIÑA CHÁN

Tzompantli [Náhuatl: 'skull rack']. Structure used in PRE-COLUMBIAN MESOAMERICA to display the heads of sacrificed human victims or a stone platform carved with human skulls. Skull racks were usually placed near temples or ballcourts (*see* BALLCOURT, §1). Those displaying real skulls comprised a wooden framework supporting skulls skewered on horizontal poles run through holes drilled through the temples. Skull racks were described by Spanish conquistadors and missionary friars. *Tzompantli*s took a variety of forms and seem to have served several functions: altars and venues for ritual; displays of Aztec prowess; and structures to terrorize subjugated populations. Attempts to calculate the numbers of skulls on them include Diego Durán's report of 80,000 and Andres de Tapía's (a soldier with Cortés) 136,000.

The earliest known *tzompantli* was excavated by Charles Spencer at La Coyotera in Oaxaca, a Late Classic period (*c.* AD 600–*c.* 900) site. Some of the skulls had been drilled through, presumably in order to be skewered on a pole. Several Post-Classic period (*c.* AD 900–1521) *tzompantli*s have been found on Toltec, Maya and Aztec sites; and according to Weigand (1982), a *tzompantli* found at Early Post-Classic (*c.* AD 900–*c.* 1200) ALTA VISTA, Zacatecas, western Mexico, served as a prototype for later structures at the Toltec capital of TULA. At Tula a *tzompantli* base was found near one of the ballcourts. It is thought that skull racks were associated with the ballcourts because the losing team was sometimes sacrificed and their severed heads displayed.

At the Maya site of CHICHÉN ITZÁ, Yucatán, there was strong Toltec influence in the Early Post-Classic period. East of the main ballcourt there is a low platform supporting a carved stone *tzompantli*, the vertical sides of which are covered with rows of sculpted and painted human skulls. At least two real skulls were also found at this *tzompantli*. At contemporary UXMAL a similar low platform is also thought to have supported a skull rack.

In the Late Post-Classic period (*c.* AD 1200–1521) several *tzompantli*s are known from Aztec sites. At the Aztec capital, Tenochtitlán (*see* MEXICO CITY, §I), a platform excavated near the present Mexico City Cathedral seems suitable for the principal skull rack depicted in the Codex Florentino, compiled by the Spanish priest Bernardino da Sahagún. In the northern part of the Templo Mayor (Great Temple), Adatorio B or the Skull-rack Altar is a huge block of grey-black volcanic stone, the sides of which are carved with at least 240 human skulls, originally covered with several coats of stucco and painted red (see fig.). At TLATELOLCO, Tenochtitlán's twin city just to the north, evidence of a skull rack was found in the form of rows of

Tzompantli, skull rack and altar in the Templo Mayor, Mexico City, Aztec, late 15th century–early 16th

160 human skulls with perforated temples. At CALIXTLA-HUACA, to the west in the Valley of Toluca, a small cruciform platform of red and black volcanic stone was found, with small human skulls carved around its sides. This structure is called the Altar of Skulls.

Several other Late Post-Classic stone structures with smaller than life-size carved human skulls are also known, and several structures that appear to be variations on the *tzompantli* theme. A small-scale *tzompantli* model was excavated at Tlatelolco and another is in the Santa Cecilia Acatitlán Museum, Mexico City. Presumably from Te-nochtitlán, a stone block measuring 1.68×1.96 m is carved with skulls, skull profiles and crossed bones (Mexico City, Mus. N. Antropol.). At Aztec TENAYUCA, 10 km north-west of Mexico City, another stone altar is carved with human skulls in high relief; and continuing the skull theme, its interior bears a fresco of skulls and crossed bones. At CHOLULA, south of Mexico City in the Valley of Puebla, there is an altar of skulls made of adobe covered with stucco. Inside were found two skeletons, one male and one female, indicating that the altar was used as a mausoleum.

BIBLIOGRAPHY

A. Caso: 'El Templo de Tenayuca estaba dedicado al culto solar', *Tenayuca* (Mexico City, 1935), pp. 299–301
E. Noguera: *El Altar de los Cráneos esculpidos de Cholula* (Mexico City, 1937)
F. González: 'Trabajos en Tlatelolco', *Bol. INAH*, xv (1964), pp. 17–18
W. Bray: *Everyday Life of the Aztecs* (London, 1968)
E. Matos Moctezuma, ed.: *Trabajos arqueológicos en el centro de la Ciudad de México* (Mexico City, 1979)
C. Vega Soza: *El Recinto Sagrado de México-Tenochtitlán: Excavaciones 1968–69 y 1975–76* (Mexico City, 1979)
E. Matos Moctezuma: *El Templo Mayor: Excavaciones y estudios* (Mexico City, 1980)
C. S. Spencer: *The Cuicatlan Cañada and Monte Albán: A Study of Primary State Formation* (Storrs, 1982)
P. Weigand: 'Mining and Mineral Trade in Prehispanic Zacatecas', *Anthropology*, vi (1982), pp. 87–134
R. A. Diehl: *Tula: The Toltec Capital of Ancient Mexico* (London, 1983)
E. Pasztory: *Aztec Art* (New York, 1983)
E. Matos Moctezuma: *The Great Temple of the Aztecs: Treasures of Tenochtitlan* (London, 1988)

ELIZABETH BAQUEDANO

Tzutzuculi. *See under* TONALÁ.

U

UAE. *See* UNITED ARAB EMIRATES.

U.A.M. *See* UNION DES ARTISTES MODERNES.

Uata Uata Tjangala No. 2. *See* UTA UTA.

Uaxactún. Pre-Columbian site in the northern Petén region, Guatemala. It was a principal MAYA political, cultural and ceremonial centre during the Late Pre-Classic (*c.* 300 BC–*c.* AD 250) and Classic (*c.* AD 250–*c.* 900) periods. Sylvanus G. Morley explored the site in 1916 and made photographs, plans and drawings. Between 1926 and 1937 further plans and reconstructive drawings were made, and excavations were carried out for the Carnegie Institution of Washington, DC, by Morley, Oliver and Edith Ricketson, A. Ledyard Smith, Robert Smith, Robert Wauchope, Edwin Shook and Tatiana Proskouriakoff. Uaxactún's ceramic sequence, which began in the early Middle Pre-Classic period (*c.* 1000–*c.* 300 BC), established the foundations of Lowland Maya chronology and has ultimately been linked to the ceramic chronologies of most of Mesoamerica. In the Middle Pre-Classic period a few low platforms were the principal constructions, but the earliest pyramidal platforms were erected in the Late Pre-Classic period. The earliest stele to be erected has a Long Count date (*see* MESOAMERICA, PRE-COLUMBIAN, §II) corresponding to AD 328 and the latest stele a date corresponding to AD 889.

The Late Pre-Classic and Classic period site comprised six groups of buildings (A–F) on low hills, linked by causeways. Each group consisted of plazas comprising tripartite, vaulted temple complexes with roof-combs and multi-roomed buildings with numerous doorways. Late Pre-Classic Pyramid E-VII-sub, the best-preserved monument, is the principal structure of group E. It comprises five roughly square tiers, with apron mouldings, supporting a platform reached by tripartite staircases on all four sides, the whole covered in white stucco (now discoloured). The inset corners of the tiers and aprons create interlocking vertical and horizontal lines. Each staircase is divided by massive, protruding balks carved with huge masks representing a stylized serpent figure and an anthropomorphic figure. Some authorities detect an OLMEC influence in their style, which resembles a mask on Stele C at TRES ZAPOTES. Similar masks were carved at Late Pre-Classic–Early Classic Maya Acanceh, Cerros, LAMANAI, MIRADOR, PIEDRAS NEGRAS and TIKAL. Remains of four large post-holes indicate that the platform supported a temple of perishable materials. In the Early Classic period Stele 20, carved with a human figure shown full frontal, was erected at the base of the east staircase. Pyramid E-VII-sub was ultimately covered by Pyramid E-VII. Directly east, Structures E-I, E-II and E-III form a line of ruined buildings north to south. These four structures were deliberately sited for viewing, from an observation point on the east stairway of Pyramid E-VII, the positions of the sun that marked the winter and summer solstices and the spring and autumn equinoxes, as it rose behind Structures E-I, E-II and E-III.

The best-preserved building of Group A is a two-storey temple known as Structure A-XVIII. Several *zapote* wood lintels remain, and much of the interior plaster is intact. An internal staircase leads to the second storey beneath unusual bottle-shaped vaulting. Also within Group A the careful excavation of Complex A-5 revealed that it underwent eight construction phases. The first phase comprised three small, vaulted temples with high roof-combs on a low platform. In subsequent phases between the early 4th century AD and the early 9th, the temples were enclosed within a compact mass of new shrines, staircases, subsidiary platforms and elongated, multi-doored buildings.

Group B, directly north of Group A, and Groups C, D and F comprised structures now mostly reduced to rubble mounds. However, in Temple B-XIII Early Classic period wall paintings (the earliest Maya murals known; 3.2×0.9 m; now mutilated) were executed in reds, brown, tan and black, depicting a palace and conversing figures (three female, within the palace, and two male), two lines of at least 21 other figures, including musicians, plus hieroglyphs and 72 calendrical day-signs. The left-hand figure of the two conversing males carries central Mesoamerican weapons, an indication of contact with and influence from that region. Stele 5, erected in Group B, is carved with a figure wearing a helmet-like headpiece, large circular earrings, sandals and what appear to be knee-length trousers. Its hieroglyphic date corresponds to AD 377. The figure is shown in profile, facing right, and carries an *atlatl* (spear-thrower) in his right hand, a weapon previously unknown in the Maya region and constituting further evidence of a brief period of central Mesoamerican influence.

BIBLIOGRAPHY

R. Wauchope: *House Mounds at Uaxactún*, Carnegie Institution Publication, cdxxxvi (Washington, DC, 1934)

O. G. Ricketson and E. B. Ricketson: *Uaxactún, Guatemala: Group E, 1926–1931*, Carnegie Institution Publication, cdlxxvii (Washington, DC, 1937)

R. E. Smith: *A Study of Structure A–I Complex at Uaxactún*, Carnegie Institution Publication, cdlvi (Washington, DC, 1937)

T. Proskouriakoff: *An Album of Maya Architecture*, Carnegie Institution Publication, dlviii (Washington, DC, 1946, rev. Norman, 2/1963), pp. 3–5

I. Marquina: *Arquitectura Prehispanica* (Mexico City, 1950, 2/1964/R 1981), pp. 518–35

A. L. Smith: *Uaxactún, Guatemala: Excavations of 1931–1937*, Carnegie Institution Publication, dlxxxviii (Washington, DC, 1950)

G. Kubler: *The Art and Architecture of Ancient America*, Pelican Hist. A. (Harmondsworth, 1962, rev. 3/1984), pp. 207–14, 227, 271–2

M. D. Coe: *The Maya* (London and New York, 1966, rev. 4/1987), pp. 62, 75–6

J. S. Henderson: *The World of the Ancient Maya* (Ithaca, 1981), pp. 124–6, 134–8, 197–8

J. Kelly: *The Complete Visitor's Guide to Mesoamerican Ruins* (Norman, 1982), pp. 438–41

DAVID M. JONES

Ubac, Raoul (*b* Malmédy, 31 Aug 1910; *d* 24 March 1985). Belgian painter, sculptor and photographer, active in France. He originally intended to become a waterways and forestry inspector. His interest in art was aroused when he made his first visit to Paris in 1928 and met several artists, including Otto Freundlich. After returning to Malmédy he read the *Manifeste du Surréalisme* (1924) by André Breton. In 1930 he settled in Paris and made contact with the Surrealist group, attending the first showing of Luis Buñuel's film *L'Age d'or* (1931). He attended the Faculté des Lettres of the Sorbonne briefly but soon left to frequent the studios of Montparnasse. About 1933–4 he attended the Ecole des Arts Appliqués for more than a year, studying mainly drawing and photography. In the course of a visit to Austria and the Dalmatian coast in 1933, he visited the island of Hvar where he made some assemblages of stones, which he drew and photographed, for example *Dalmatian Stone* (1933; see Bazaine and others, p. 20).

After his return to Paris in 1934, Ubac became friendly with Camille Bryen, for whose collection of poems, *Actuation poétique* (Paris, 1934), he produced a series of photomontages published under the pseudonym Raoul Michelet. They also pasted their poems and images on walls in Paris. From 1936 to 1939 he became closely associated with the Surrealist group and took part in all its activities. He concentrated on photography, making particular use, in photographs such as *Combat* (1937; see Bazaine and others, p. 25), of the technique of solarization (*see* PHOTOGRAPHY, §I), and some of his photographs were published from 1937 in *Minotaure*. In 1936 he studied engraving under S. W. Hayter at Atelier 17.

The Surrealist group broke up following the outbreak of World War II, and Ubac took refuge at Carcassonne in 1940 with René Magritte and Jean Scutenaire. After being repatriated, he divided his time between Paris and Brussels. He gradually distanced himself from Surrealism, his last contribution being photographic illustrations for *L'Exercice de la pureté* (Paris, 1942) by Jean Lescure. Instead he started to make pen drawings of groupings of everyday objects, sometimes with menacing overtones as in *Ink Drawing* (1943; Paris, A. Frenaud priv. col., see Bazaine and others, p. 34), and to paint small gouaches such as *Head* (1949; Brussels, Mus. A. Mod.). In 1946, while staying in Haute-Savoie, he found a small piece of slate whose form appealed to him, and he scratched a design on it; from then on he was fascinated by this material.

In 1947 Ubac resumed painting and began to frequent the group of abstract artists associated with the Galerie Denise René, particularly Jean Bazaine and his friends. His own paintings became abstract, although retaining echoes of such underlying themes as reclining figures, as in *Reclining Forms* (1953; Rio de Janeiro, Mus. A. Mod.), imaginary heads or trees in a forest. In keeping with their grave, reticent character, their colours were usually muted and earthy, their forms weighty and slab-like. Ubac's interest in working with slate developed in parallel with his painting, and he began to use larger pieces, carving into them more and more deeply until they became true reliefs; a few, such as *Torso* (1966; Paris, Pompidou), were free-standing, carved on both sides. In addition he started *c.* 1960 to make relief paintings, such as *Terres* (1967; Paris, Mus. A. Mod. Ville Paris), out of resin-based mortar, which allowed him to combine washes of colour with the relief patterns of rhythmical lines characteristic of his slate carvings. He also carried out a number of commissions for the design of tapestries, such as those for the Nouveau Palais de Justice, Lille (1969), and stained glass, for example a collaboration with Georges Braque for a church at Varengeville (1961), as well as murals in slate or mosaic.

BIBLIOGRAPHY

J. Bazaine and others: *Ubac* (Paris, 1970)

Ubac (exh. cat., ed. C. Esteban; Liège, Gal. St Georges, 1981)

RONALD ALLEY

Ubaid, Tell al- [Tell el-Obeid; Tell al-Ma'abad; Tell al-Abd]. Site near Ur, Iraq. It is noted for the first identification of the prehistoric pottery that bears its name (5th millennium BC) and for a Sumerian temple with elaborate façade ornament (first half of the 3rd millennium BC). The site was excavated by H. R. Hall (1919) and by Leonard Woolley (1923–4). The black painted, greenish buff ceramic now known as Ubaid is one of the most distinctive Mesopotamian wares (*see* MESOPOTAMIA, §V, 1). The decoration is largely geometric, more elaborate in the earliest phases (6th millennium BC, later stratigraphically identified at nearby Eridu) and tending towards broad, sweeping patterns in its latest phase (*c.* 4200 BC), by which time the potter's wheel was in widespread use in Mesopotamia. No stratified material of prehistoric Ubaid date was excavated; the published Ubaid sherds were found either on the surface or out of context in the excavation of the later cemetery at the south end of the tell. These, however, identify the presence of all phases of the prehistoric Ubaid period at the site.

The Early Dynastic temple at the north end of the tell was built by A-ane-pada, a Sumerian king of Ur, for the goddess Ninhursag. Only the platform has survived, but the façade ornament (London, BM; Baghdad, Iraq Mus.), found in adjacent debris, is unique and of considerable artistic merit. It includes a great bronze lintel with a lion-headed eagle, Imdugud, between two stags (London, BM), copper reliefs of bulls, panels of various animals and birds in limestone and shell inlay and stone-petalled rosettes. Several unusual columns have survived, consisting of palm logs covered with bitumen and inlaid with mother-of-pearl and red and black limestone tesserae. Of special interest is a further series of panels, the 'milking scene', modelled in high relief and set in a copper frame (Baghdad, Iraq Mus.). Iconographically related to Uruk period portrayals of the temple or sacred herd, this scene is unusual for its realism and is the earliest pictorial representation of ordinary agricultural practices. A number of pieces of Sumerian sculpture were also found. In 1937 Pinhas Delougaz and Seton Lloyd demonstrated that the Early Dynastic temple was surrounded by an oval precinct wall, similar to that discovered at Khafajeh.

BIBLIOGRAPHY
H. R. Hall and C. L. Woolley: *Al-'Ubaid: Ur Excavations*, i (Oxford, 1927)
P. Delougaz: 'A Short Investigation of the Temple at Al 'Ubaid', *Iraq*, v (1938), pp. 1–11
S. Lloyd: *The Archaeology of Mesopotamia* (London, 1984)

JOAN OATES

Ubaldini, Pietro Paolo. *See* BALDINI, PIETRO PAOLO.

Ubangi Shari. *See* CENTRAL AFRICAN REPUBLIC.

Ubeda. Spanish town in Andalusia, on the edge of a broad slope terminating in a steep cliff (La Loma) in the hilly area between the Guadalimar and Guadalquivir rivers, with a population of *c.* 30,000. During the second half of the 3rd millennium BC a Neolithic settlement of the El Argar civilization occupied the area of the present Piazza Vázquez de Molina. The Roman town was known as Bétula; little information survives concerning the community in the reign of the Visigoths (AD 470–711). Under Muslim domination, and on the initiative of the 4th Amir of Córdoba, 'Abd al-Rahmān II (*reg* 822–52), a new settlement called Ubbadat al-Arab was founded on the site. With the erection of fortifications (from 852) and the Alcázar, the town became one of the principal manufacturing centres trading with the Muslim world; this prosperity lasted for over four centuries. The victory of Alfonso VIII of Castile–León (*reg* 1158–1214) in the battle of Las Navas de Tolosa (16 July 1212) initiated a period during which possession of the city alternated between Christians and Muslims. The decisive conquest by Ferdinand III of Castile–León (*reg* 1217–52) on 29 September 1234 ended this situation. Subsequently, Ferdinand created over 100 *infanzones* (Sp.: 'vavasours') by distributing land, in order to ensure control of the town and its environs. He also granted the city the *fuero* (Sp.: 'charter') of Cuenca, which was to form the basis of its legislation. These provisions, however, caused the vavasours to fight among themselves for control of the town in a series of disputes that was interwoven with greater dynastic struggles from the 13th to the 15th century. The town also participated in the final stages of the Reconquista (1455–7 and 1482–92) under Henry IV of Castile–León (*reg* 1454–74), who granted Ubeda city status, and Isabella the Catholic, who ordered the demolition of the Alcázar, the possession of which was frequently the cause of conflict between citizens.

The layout and architectural history of Ubeda reflects this prolonged state of war. The Muslim town was completely destroyed in several stages; new city walls were constructed on top of the previous ones and, according to a tradition of varying reliability, new Christian churches were built on the ruins of mosques. The Puerta del Losal

(or Puerta de Sabiote), the Puerta de Granada and the Muralla de la Cava (all 14th century) reveal the presence of Arab *Mudéjar* workmen even after the Christian conquest of the town. Only the church of S María de los Reales Alcázares, built on the ruins of the mosque located inside the Muslim fortress and possibly consecrated by Ferdinand III, and the monastery of S Clara (from 1290) retain features dating from the early Christian period. S Pablo (13th century), S Isidoro, S Domingo, S Pedro and S Nicolás (founded 13th century; rebuilt 14th century) are traditionally dated to the same period, although their architecture suggests a later one.

The peace resulting from the Reconquista began a process of social change in which the feudal aristocracy and lesser nobility used the city for self-glorification. In the first two decades of the 16th century many churches were restored and private chapels added; those of S Pablo, for example, display a wide variety of styles. At the same time, such town residences as the Casa de los Salvajes, the Palacio de la Calle Montiel and the Casa de las Torres were built on traditional plans, making use of non-structural, typically plateresque wall decoration. Such innovations were, however, integrated into late medieval urban life without affecting its fundamental organization.

There was a further period of instability due to the involvement of Ubeda in the revolts of the Comuneros (1520–21). Initiatives subsequently undertaken by Francisco de los Cobos, secretary to Charles I of Spain (Emperor Charles V from 1519), and other members of his family during the 16th century remodelled the area

Ubeda, Hospital de Santiago by Andrés de Vandelvira, 1562–75

around S María de los Alcázares with a series of new buildings: the church of El Salvador (1536–56; *see* COBOS, FRANCISCO DE LOS), based on a design by Diego de Siloé (*see* SILOÉ, (2)) and executed by Andrés de Vandelvira (for illustration *see* VANDELVIRA, ANDRÉS DE), was erected as the backdrop to a straight avenue that runs parallel to the façade of S María and terminates in the spacious plaza in front of it. In the centre of the plaza the principal façade of the Palacio Vázquez de Molina (*c.* 1560) by Vandelvira faces that of S María, defining one square and at the same time forming a second square with the contemporary classical loggia built on its north-east side by Vandelvira to complete the Palacio Vela de los Cobos. Vandelvira also built the Hospital de Santiago (see fig.). As an example of urban planning the double open space was not influential, although individual elements of Vandelvira's style were imitated in such town residences as the Palacio del Marquéz de Mancera or the Palacio del Conde de Guadiana, built around the end of the 16th century. This created an exceptional stylistic unity among the monuments that form the historic centre of the town.

The expansion of Ubeda in modern times initially followed the irregular circular limits of the old walls, with some buildings being constructed directly against them. Subsequently, however, to the north and north-east of the town developing areas were laid out in a slightly more regular pattern due to the division of land into lots on a grid basis. The entire belt of suburbs to the north-east and west of the town is contained within a bypass that provides access both to other principal towns of the region and to the historic town centre.

BIBLIOGRAPHY

J. Pasquau Guerrero: *Biografía de Ubeda* (Ubeda, 1958)
J. Molina Hipolito: *Guía de Ubeda* (Madrid, 1965)
R. Vano Silvestre: *Desarrollo histórico del perímetro urbano de Ubeda* (Jaén, 1975)
C. Tessari: 'Autocelebrazione e architettura: La famiglia Cobos y Molina e Andrés de Vandelvira a Ubeda', *Ric. Stor. A.*, xxxii (1987), pp. 45–64

CRISTIANO TESSARI

Übelbacher [Ueblbacher], **Hieronymus**, Prior of Dürnstein (*b* Oberhollabrunn, 31 Oct 1674; *d* Dürnstein, 13 Jan 1740). Austrian prelate and patron. He entered the Augustinian Order of Canons at Dürnstein on 12 March 1693 and after studying philosophy, theology, history and law was unanimously elected prior of Dürnstein on 15 June 1710. He set his stamp on the foundation by extensive alterations and additions to its buildings, taking personal charge of the whole process. He was his own engineer and architect, creating a Baroque unity of style with the carefully planned collaboration of artists and craftsmen.

With the assistance of Jakob Prandtauer, he began by building the Kellerschlössl (1714–20); in 1716 he converted the former church of the Order of St Clare into a granary and from 1715–16 to 1733 rebuilt and extended the monastery building over the Danube. The architects of these projects were Joseph Munggenast and Matthias Steinl, while the following craftsmen and artists executed the work: the stucco workers Domenico Piazoll (*fl* 1686; *d* 1719) and Johannes Piazoll, Santino Bussi (1666–1736) and Michael Bolla; the engineers Antonio Galli-Bibiena and Antonio Beduzzi; the sculptors Matthias Steinl, Peter Thornir, Joseph Babel and Johann Georg Schmidt; the painters Wolfgang Ehrenreich Prieter, Matthias Stainz, Matthias Pichler (*fl* 1766–9), Anton Umsinn and Martin Johann Schmidt; and the goldsmiths Sebastian Somkovsky (*fl* 1720–77) and Johann Caspar Holbein (1677–1742). Records of the building show Hieronymus Übelbacher to have been an example of the Baroque patron-prelate with absolutist leanings. His approach influenced the neighbouring monastery of Göttweig and Melk Abbey, which were also erecting new buildings and were glad to take his advice and use his connections, although his reputation as a patron has been unduly overshadowed by those of the builders of these monasteries. As a patron and teacher of artists he used carefully selected Baroque literature and printed graphics as models and teaching material, notably in the teaching institute that he set up in the priory in 1722. He is buried in the prelates' vault at Dürnstein, and portraits of him are exhibited there. In 1788 the priory was dissolved by Emperor Joseph II (1741–90), with great cultural losses. From that time the Stiftskirche Mariä Himmelfahrt was the parish church of Herzogenburg, and the priory buildings served as exhibition rooms and apartments.

BIBLIOGRAPHY

F. N. Dittel: *Eulogy and Funeral Oration on the Death of . . . Hieronymus Übelbacher . . . of Tiernstein, Held on 16, 17 and 18 February* (Vienna, 1740) [obituary]
Topographie von Niederösterreich, i (Vienna, 1879–85), pp. 376–8
W. Pauker: 'Die Kirche und das Kollegiatstift der ehemaligen regulierten Chorherrn zu Dürnstein: Ein Beitrag zur österreichischen Kunst- und Kulturgeschichte des 18. Jahrhunderts', *Jb. Stift. Klosterneuburg*, iii (1910), pp. 179–344
R. Gnevkow-Blume: *Dürnstein: Die Malerstadt an der Donau* (Vienna and Leipzig, 4/1932)
E. Schmettan: *Das Chorherrenstift Dürnstein* (diss., U. Vienna, 1948)
F. Dworschak and W. Schwengler: *König Richard I. Löwenherz von England (1189–1199)* (Dürnstein and Vienna, 1966)
L. Pühringer-Zwanowetz: 'Die Baugeschichte des Augustiner-Chorherrenstiftes Dürnstein und das "Neue Kloster" des Propstes Hieronymus Übelbacher', *Wien. Jb. Kstgesch.*, xxvi (1973), pp. 96–198
G. Brucher: *Barockarchitektur in Österreich* (Cologne, 1983), pp. 242–9
Dehio-Handbuch der Kunstdenkmäler Österreichs: Niederösterreich nördlich der Donau (Vienna, 1990), pp. 120–33

GREGOR M. LECHNER

Ubeleski [Ubelesqui], **Alexandre** (*b* Paris, 1628; *d* Paris, 1715). French painter of Polish origin. In 1669 he was recorded as being a pupil of the Académie Royale de Peinture et de Sculpture in Paris. In June 1672 he won first prize in the drawing competition and the following October travelled to Rome to study at the Académie de France. He returned to Paris in 1679 and in 1682 was received (*reçu*) as a member of the Académie, on presentation of the painting *Louis XIV Giving Peace to Europe*, a work that shows the influence of Charles Le Brun.

In the following decades Ubeleski received several important official commissions. In 1682 and 1692 he painted the 'May' of Notre-Dame de Paris, the picture which the goldsmiths' guild donated annually to the cathedral. The 1692 composition survives: *Jesus Healing the Sick* (Paris, Louvre). In 1695 he contributed illustrations to Charles Perrault's *Cabinet des Beaux-Arts*, in company with such famous painters as Louis Boullogne (ii), Michel Corneille (ii), Antoine Coypel and Charles de La Fosse. He painted the *Allegory of Poetry*, which was engraved in 1699 by Pierre Lepautre: the composition illustrates Ubeleski's poetically expressive talent, which is also a striking feature of his drawings. He was also engaged by the court, among other works painting for the Ménagerie at Versailles two scenes (1702) from the story of *Arachne* (Fontainebleau, Château), based on Ovid's *Metamorphoses*.

BIBLIOGRAPHY

Mariette; Thieme–Becker

P. Marcel: *La Peinture française au début du dix-septième siècle (1690–1721)* (Paris, 1906), pp. 17ff

P. Rosenberg: 'Un Emule polonais de Le Brun: Alexandre Ubelesqui', *Artibus & Hist.*, xxii (1990), pp. 163–87

CATHRIN KLINGSÖHR-LE ROY

Uberti, Lucantonio degli (*b* Florence; *fl* Venice, 1503; *fl* Florence, 1557). Italian printmaker. In Venice between 1503 and 1526 he engraved numerous woodcut book illustrations: his monogram, known in 17 variations, appears in *c.* 60 different volumes, printed in Venice. Among his most famous works is the edition (*c.* 1517) in nine blocks of Titian's woodcut *Triumph of Christ*. Uberti's return to Florence *c.* 1550 is suggested by the presence of wood-engravings in the Venetian fashion in certain Florentine texts, such as the *Historia di S Antonio di Padova* (1557). Apart from his woodcuts, a further seven copper engravings (and a dubious eighth) are attributed to him (e.g. B. 1, 2 [390] and Patellani, pp. 48–55), which, in a graphic language that is still late 15th century, are inspired by works by Perugino, Leonardo da Vinci, Marcantonio Raimondi and Dürer.

BIBLIOGRAPHY

Bolaffi

G. Patellani: 'Lucantonio degli Uberti', *Quad. Conoscitore Stampe*, xx (1974), pp. 46–55

M. Zucker: *Early Italian Masters*, 25 [XIII/ii] of *The Illustrated Bartsch*, ed. W. Strauss (New York, 1980) [B.]

FELICIANO BENVENUTI

Ubertini, Francesco. *See* BACCHIACCA.

Ubirr [Obiri Rock]. Complex of at least 36 Aboriginal sites in the Kakadu National Park, Northern Territory, Australia, formerly known by the anglicized form of its name. The entire area near the East Alligator River Crossing in Western Arnhem Land is subject to seasonal monsoonal flooding, but there are numerous sandstone outcrops and monoliths containing rock shelters above the maximum flood level. The rock paintings found in these shelters include representative examples from the earliest styles to the most recent (*see* ABORIGINAL AUSTRALIA, §§II, 2(ii)(b) and III, 4). The few examples of the earliest Dynamic-style figures to have been found are located in well-protected crevices. They are believed to be at least 9000 years old and depict in red ochre small human beings wearing large headdresses, carrying boomerangs (see fig.) and using hand-thrown spears. Small, predominantly red, human figures from the subsequent period are more common throughout the complex; these wear headdresses and have distinctive S-shaped bodies. Several paintings depict the thylacine or Tasmanian wolf, and these are likely to date to a minimum of 3000 years ago when the wolf is believed to have become extinct on the Australian mainland. Other figures from more recent

Dynamic-style rock painting of a figure carrying boomerangs, typical of those found in Ubirr, *c.* 7000 BC

periods are painted in a range of colours, including red, yellow, white and black. They are no longer depicted wearing large headdresses, while spear-throwers and an increasing variety of spear types are carried instead of boomerangs.

Although numerous different styles occur within the Ubirr complex, the polychrome X-ray style is visually dominant. The style name is derived from the detailed depiction of internal features such as the backbone and intestines in the painted figures. Whereas land animals are generally the subject of paintings in the earlier styles, aquatic fauna are more common in paintings in the X-ray style. This change in subject-matter is believed to reflect the development of the freshwater wetlands in the Kakadu region from about 3000 years ago. The principal gallery in the Ubirr complex, which has one of the largest and best-preserved concentrations of X-ray-style paintings in the Kakadu National Park, has a wall (*c.* 2–3×15 m) completely covered with heavily superimposed paintings in the style. Most depict a variety of fish species, but there are also representations of turtles, marsupials, birds, goannas, human figures, rifles and steel axes. Contemporary Western Arnhem Land Aborigines recognize them as the product of their own society, and this style is still employed in the medium of bark painting.

BIBLIOGRAPHY

C. P. Mountford: *Australia: Aboriginal Paintings: Arnhemland* (New York, 1954)

R. Edwards: *The Art of the Alligator Rivers Region of the Northern Territory* (Canberra, 1979)

DARRELL LEWIS

Üblher, Johann Georg (*b* Wessobrunn, 23 March 1703; *d* Maria Steinbach, 27 April 1763). German stuccoist. He was active *c.* 1730 as a journeyman with Johann Baptist Zimmermann, collaborating on the stuccowork at Schloss Alteglofsheim to designs by François de Cuvilliés I, and in the Reichezimmer of the Residenz in Munich. At Diessen am Ammersee he worked (1736–7) for the first time with Franz Xaver Feichtmayer (i) and Johann Michael Feichtmayer, and it was here that his first rocaille forms, combined with strapwork, lattice motifs and hanging trophies, were carried out. From 1741 to 1744 he was court stuccoist at the abbey at Kempten. Üblher shared Johann Michael Feichtmayer's workshop until *c*. 1750; thereafter he was in partnership with Franz Xaver Schmuzer II, to whom he was related through his wife Maria Agatha. From 1759 he again worked on projects with Johann Michael Feichtmayer: according to Jocher Üblher was responsible for figurework during this period of collaboration. In 1735–7, working with Johannes Schütz, Üblher decorated the state apartments at the Residenz at Kempten. The throne-room (1740–43) is one of his masterpieces: his splendid rocaille ornaments dominate the room and make the lines of it disappear into the decoration, in which are interwoven the stucco modelling and Egid Verhelst I's sculptures. In the Cistercian abbey church at Wilhering, Üblher was responsible for stuccowork with Johann Michael Feichtmayer and for the stucco figures on the high altar and side altars (1742–51). The tranquil, softly modelled figures, mostly wrapped in flowing draperies, are influenced to a high degree by Verhelst's work. From 1745 to 1751 Üblher worked in the monastic church of Amorbach on figures for both transept altars and for the high altar, developing the types he had created at Wilhering. In 1750–53 he produced the deeply sculpted rocaille ornaments in the rotunda of the monastic church of Ettal while working there with Schmuzer. He executed stuccowork and built altars to his own designs for the pilgrimage church of Maria Steinbach (from 1751) and worked on similar projects for the abbey church of Engelszell (from 1758). His unfinished work at both churches was continued after his death by Franz Xaver Feichtmayer (ii) and the Modler workshop.

BIBLIOGRAPHY
Thieme–Becker

R. Guby: 'Johann Georg Üblher, des Hochstiftes Kempten Hofstukkadorer', *Münch. Jb. Bild. Kst*, xi (1921), pp. 13–29

F. Wolf: 'Johann Michael Feichtmayers Werkverhältnis zu Johann Georg Üblher', *Alte & Mod. Kst*, iv (1964), pp. 24–8

E.-C. Vollmer: 'Neue Erkenntnisse zur Innenausstattung der Wallfahrtskirche Maria Steinbach an der Iller', *A. Bavar.*, xv–xvi (1980), pp. 97–104

L. Dorn: 'Die Wallfahrtskirche Maria Steinbach: Ein Beitrag zu ihrer Baugeschichte', *Allgäu. Geschfreund*, lxxxi (1981), pp. 16–42

N. Jocher: *Johann Georg Üblher (1703–63): Ein Beitrag zur Geschichte des Ornaments und der Stuckplastik Süddeutschlands im 18. Jahrhundert* (diss., U. Munich, 1986)

H. Schnell, U. Schedler and N. Jocher: *Lexikon der Wessobrunner Stukatoren* (Munich, 1987)

ULRICH KNAPP

Ubong. *See* CHO HŬI-RYONG.

Ubriachi. *See* EMBRIACHI.

Uccello, Paolo [Paolo di Dono] (*b* Florence, *c*. 1397; *d* Florence, 10 Dec 1475). Italian painter, draughtsman, mosaicist and designer of stained glass. His work vividly illustrates the principal issues of Florentine art during the first half of the 15th century. Trained within the tradition of the Late Gothic style, he eventually became a leading exponent of the application of linear perspective based on the mathematical system established by Filippo Brunelleschi and Leon Battista Alberti. It is the merging of these two diametrically opposed tendencies that forms the basis of Uccello's style. As well as painting on panel and in fresco (many of his works in this medium have been severely damaged), he was also a master mosaicist and produced designs for stained glass.

1. Life and work. 2. Working methods and technique. 3. Critical reception and posthumous reputation.

1. LIFE AND WORK.

(i) Training and early work, *c*. 1412–43. (ii) Middle years, 1443–*c*. 1460. (iii) Late works, *c*. 1460–75. (iv) Lost works.

(i) Training and early work, c. *1412–43*. The documents are relatively informative about Uccello's life and movements, but less so about his artistic output. His proper name was Paolo di Dono, but he was commonly referred to as Uccello. According to Vasari, this was simply a sobriquet adopted as a result of the painter's love of birds (*uccello*: 'bird'), but it seems that the name also had some legal sanction, since it occurs in official documents and in the signatures on the fresco of *Sir John Hawkwood* (Florence Cathedral; see fig. 1) and on one of the panels of the *Rout of San Romano* (Florence, Uffizi). Uccello's father, Dono di Paolo, was a barber–surgeon from Pratovecchio, who became a Florentine citizen in 1373 and married in 1387. Uccello's date of birth is deduced from his tax returns beginning with that of 1427, when his age is given as 30, although a slight degree of variance is apparent in subsequent returns; discrepancies of this type are not unusual at this date. Uccello spent most of his life in Florence, apart from visits to Venice (1425–*c*. 1430), Padua (1445–6) and Urbino (1465–8/9). He married Tommasa di Benedetto Malifici, apparently rather late in life. A son, Donato, was born in 1453 and a daughter, Antonia, in 1456.

It is usually stated that Uccello was recorded as an assistant (*garzone*) in Lorenzo Ghiberti's workshop in 1404 or 1407, but this is a misreading, and the artist's apprenticeship with Ghiberti is now thought to have been from 1412 until 1416 (Beck, 1980). Uccello's affiliation with Ghiberti undoubtedly established the basis of his early style. The large workshop employed by the sculptor for his many projects in Florence also included Masolino and Donatello. During Uccello's years in the shop, work was proceeding on the first set of bronze doors for the Florentine Baptistery and on the bronze *St John the Baptist* for Orsanmichele (*in situ*). Ghiberti was one of the main Florentine exponents of the Late Gothic style, with its emphasis on decorative quality derived from line, colour and pattern. The figure style of the north door of the Baptistery and the friezes that teem with animal life would have appealed to Uccello, given his proclivity for such subject-matter, as recounted by Vasari. By the time he left Ghiberti's workshop, however, Uccello had gained a certain independence. In 1414 (not 1424 as often interpreted) he joined the Compagnia di S Luca, and in 1415 he was a member of the Arte dei Medici e degli Speziali, being referred to as painter.

Between 1425 and 1427 Uccello was in Venice working as a mosaicist in S Marco. The evidence for this rests in the inquiry made by the authorities of Florence Cathedral in 1432 into the artist's performance while employed as a master mosaicist at S Marco. The full extent of Uccello's work there is not known, and only a figure of *St Peter* (destr.; see Salmi, 1950) is documented. It is sometimes argued that Uccello was involved with the design of the narrative scenes of the *Life of the Virgin* in the Mascoli Chapel, S Marco.

The identification of Uccello's earliest works is difficult because of the dearth of information following his departure from Ghiberti's workshop. Attempts to establish an oeuvre for the artist during the 1420s have not been convincing (e.g. Volpe, 1980). It is likely that the opportunities presented by his work as a mosaicist in Venice reinforced those stylistic tendencies already inculcated by Ghiberti. The earliest works reliably attributed to Uccello, therefore, are the frescoes on the east wall of the Chiostro Verde of S Maria Novella, Florence, which are usually dated to the early 1430s. The frescoes represent scenes from Genesis and are part of an extensive scheme of decoration in the cloister to which Uccello himself further contributed at a later date. From the first campaign, the frescoes of the *Creation of the Animals and the Creation of Adam* and the *Creation of Eve and the Fall* in the opening bay are by Uccello. The style of the figures and the handling of the landscape are not dissimilar to Masolino's, whereas the care taken over the animals and foliage recalls Ghiberti and also to some extent Gentile da Fabriano. The poses of Adam and Eve are inspired by their counterparts in the comparable panel of Ghiberti's second set of bronze doors for the Florentine Baptistery, while ultimately the drapery of the figure of God the Father is dependent on *St Matthew* at Orsanmichele.

The one documented work dating from the 1430s is the commemorative fresco of *Sir John Hawkwood*, painted in 1436 on the north wall of Florence Cathedral (see fig. 1). Uccello's fresco, depicting the English condottiere (*c.* 1320–94) on horseback, replaced the image commissioned from Agnolo Gaddi and Giuliano Pesello in 1395 and was matched in 1456 by Andrea del Castagno's companion fresco commemorating *Niccolò da Tolentino* (*d* 1435; *see* ANDREA DAL CASTAGNO, fig. 4). Uccello in fact painted the fresco of Hawkwood twice, since the cathedral authorities were for some reason dissatisfied with his first attempt. Possibly the problem was one of technique. Nonetheless, the final result is an important link in the evolution of the equestrian monument. In the fresco, Uccello addressed the problems of perspective and three-dimensionality posed by Masaccio in the *Trinity* (Florence, S Maria Novella) or by Donatello in the tondi in the Old Sacristy, S Lorenzo. It demonstrates his growing interest in perspective and his tendency to render natural forms as a series of geometrical shapes, particularly in the horse and rider. The artist used two viewpoints: the horse and rider are seen as if on a level with the spectator, but the sarcophagus is seen sharply from below. Such a discrepancy might have been the result of a change of design requested by the cathedral authorities (Even, 1985).

Uccello made three cartoons (destr.) for circular stained-glass windows positioned in the octagon below the cupola of Florence Cathedral. The work was part of a large project started in the early 1430s in which Ghiberti, Donatello and Castagno were also involved. Uccello was commissioned in 1443 to submit designs for scenes of the *Ascension*, the *Resurrection*, the *Nativity* and, in 1444, the *Annunciation*. Of these only the *Nativity* and the *Resurrection*, executed by the glass painters Bernardo di Francesco

1. Paolo Uccello: *Sir John Hawkwood* (1436), fresco, Florence Cathedral

and Angelo di Lippo respectively, survive; the *Annunciation* (destr. 1828) was executed by Bernardo di Francesco alone, and a design by Ghiberti was used for the *Ascension*. Uccello worked again in partnership with Bernardo di Francesco for the cathedral authorities in 1456.

(ii) Middle years, 1443–c. 1460. Uccello's paintings of the 1440s and 1450s reveal his determination to come to terms with recent developments in Florentine art. The frescoes executed for S Miniato al Monte and a second series for S Maria Novella emphasize his growing preoccupation with the ideas expounded by Alberti regarding the representation of space. Alongside the purely theoretical influence of Alberti, it is likely that Donatello's example profoundly affected Uccello in the matter of translating Alberti's ideas into practice. The bolder modelling of the four saints' heads decorating the corners of the painted clockface at the west end of Florence Cathedral (1443; *in situ*) shows the influence of Donatello's marble sculpture.

In 1445–6 Uccello visited Padua at the behest of Donatello (Vasari). There, he frescoed a series of giants (destr.) in *terra verde* in the entrance to the Casa Vitaliani. These are a serious loss as regards the connection between central and north Italian art at that date. They may have been similar in style to the heads adorning the clockface in Florence Cathedral, and, according to Vasari, they influenced Andrea Mantegna's early work in the Ovetari Chapel (Padua, Eremitani).

The fresco cycle (badly damaged) in the cloister of S Miniato al Monte is devoted to scenes of monastic life and was most probably painted towards the close of the 1440s. The receding lines of the buildings bear witness to Uccello's concern to depict space three-dimensionally, a feature that also characterizes his next frescoes.

Uccello's second fresco cycle in the Chiostro Verde, S Maria Novella, illustrates the story of Noah and decorates the east side of the cloister. Uccello painted the *Flood and the Recession of the Flood* (see fig. 2) in a lunette, with the *Sacrifice of Noah and the Drunkenness of Noah* below. Suggested dating for these scenes varies considerably, ranging between the mid-1440s and the first half of the 1450s. The style of Donatello's relief panels on the altar of the Santo, Padua, with their steep perspective and use of movement to augment the drama, may have been in Uccello's mind as he was painting the *Flood*. This scene shows Uccello's style at its most advanced and no longer dependent on Alberti. Undeniably, however, the establishment of separate vanishing points that yet serve to fuse together two separate incidents, the recession into space, the range of characterization, the display of imagination and even the technique are close to Alberti's prescriptions for compositional procedure. There has been an attempt to identify the figure standing in the right foreground of the fresco as Alberti (Ames-Lewis, 1974; Eisler, 1974), while the figure of Noah leaning out of the ark has been identified as Uccello (Joost-Gaugier, 1974). Vasari was inspired to write one of his most vivid descriptions of the dramatic detail of the scene, where for once Uccello's somewhat academic concept is quickened by a forceful depiction of the cataclysm overwhelming mankind.

During the later stages of his career Uccello explored the tension between the formal decorative aspects of his art and the more scientific principles that he first adopted during the 1430s and developed during the 1440s. Nowhere is this tension more apparent than in the three panels illustrating the *Rout* (or *Battle*) *of San Romano* (London, N.G.; Florence, Uffizi; Paris, Louvre). These were first recorded in a Medici inventory of 1492 and evidently formed part of a decorative scheme in the newly built Palazzo Medici in Florence. They are usually dated to the mid-1450s. The paintings were originally in a room in which two other paintings by Uccello and one by Pesellino were also hung. Later the room was used as a bedroom by Lorenzo de' Medici. The Rout of San Romano was a military action that took place on 1 June 1432 in the war between Florence and Lucca. The panel in London (see fig. 3) shows Niccolò da Tolentino, the Florentine commander, directing the attack against Sienese forces, who had formed an alliance with Lucca. The Uffizi panel depicts the unhorsing of the Sienese commander, Bernardino della Carda, while the panel in Paris portrays another Florentine commander, Michele da Cotignola, bringing up the reserve troops in a surprise attack against the Sienese (Griffiths, 1978). Uccello displayed his finest skills in these three battle scenes. The sightlines are established by the array of weapons, the movement of horses and the debris of war scattered on the ground. Yet, although the eye does

2. Paolo Uccello: *Flood and the Recession of the Flood* (*c.* 1445–55), fresco, Chiostro Verde, S Maria Novella, Florence

3. Paolo Uccello: *Rout of San Romano*, oil on panel, 1.81×3.20 m, mid-1450s (London, National Gallery)

penetrate into the background landscapes, Uccello discouraged any such movement into depth by overlaying the constituent elements, so that lances, banners, assorted headgear, plate armour, horses' flanks and kicking hooves create a network of interlocking shapes across each of the panels. What characterizes these paintings, therefore, is the dualism resulting from an application of geometric principles, which evokes both a unified space and a sense of pattern resulting from a fascination for the geometry contained within individual forms. The means at Uccello's disposal is pre-eminently scientific, but the effect is unrelievedly decorative, to the extent that the panels are often likened to tapestry.

(iii) Late works, c. *1460–75.* A similar dualism underlies those works that are generally considered to be late, including *St George and the Dragon* (*c.* 1465; Paris, Mus. Jacquemart-André), to which a document of 1465 may allude (Beck, 1979). A group of payments made to Uccello in Urbino between 1465 and 1468 almost certainly relates to the predella panels of the *Profanation of the Host* (Urbino, Pal. Ducale), painted for the altarpiece of the *Institution of the Eucharist* (Urbino, Pal. Ducale), which is probably by Justus of Ghent. Another late work is the Hunt In the Forest (Oxford, Ashmolean; see fig. 4). These panels are all considerably smaller in scale than previous works. Their bright colouring and figural types—the heads with pointed noses but no chins—are distinctive, and Uccello's exploration of mathematical principles remains relentless. The *Hunt* best exemplifies the degree of sophistication that Uccello could bring to his compositional

4. Paolo Uccello: *Hunt in the Forest*, tempera on panel, 730×1770 mm, *c.* 1470 (Oxford, Ashmolean Museum)

methods. The wood is neatly divided into equal parts; the orthogonals are represented by branches lying in the undergrowth; the eye is drawn to the central vanishing point by the fleeing stags and galloping hounds but at the same time is presented with a number of secondary viewing points, formed by compartments of space defined by the tree trunks. Within this firmly structured ambience, the huntsmen, some shown running at full stretch like athletes on a Greek vase, create a ribbon of colour intertwined with the trunks of the trees. It would be hard to find a better example of Uccello's dualism in the simplicity of structure and the complicated dramatic invention. It is sometimes suggested that the *Hunt* was painted while Uccello was in Urbino (1465–7), but it is more likely to have been done *c.* 1470 in Florence. Although in many ways these late pictures are the summation of Uccello's art, they are essentially in a style that had fallen behind developments in Florentine art. The *Hunt* and the predella panels in Urbino are supreme works by an experimental artist who had brought the stylistic virtues of the 1440s and 1450s to a pitch of the greatest refinement. Uccello made a vital contribution to the literal realization of space within the confines of a painting, but by the end of his life younger artists were already beginning to find means other than mathematics for this purpose, and the use of aerial perspective was being developed.

The artist made two wills, the first in 1425, presumably before travelling to Venice, and the second in 1475, a month before he died. His final tax return in 1469 includes the plea 'I find myself old and ailing, my wife is ill, and I can no longer work'—a statement that is echoed by Vasari, who added that because of Uccello's predilection for perspective 'he came to live a hermit's life, hardly knowing anyone and shut away out of sight in his house for weeks and months at a time'. Nevertheless, there is some tentative evidence that he may still have been active as a painter during the 1470s (Beck, 1979). He was buried in his father's grave in Santo Spirito, Florence.

(iv) Lost works. Only a few lost works by Uccello are recorded in documents; more are mentioned in the early biographies of the artist. For the early style of Uccello the fresco of the *Annunciation* (destr.), formerly in S Maria Maggiore, Florence, may have been significant because of its possible relationship with paintings of that subject by Masolino and Masaccio (Spencer, 1955). Vasari described the fresco cycle of scenes from the *Life of St Benedict*, formerly in the cloister of S Maria degli Angeli, Florence, in sufficient detail to suggest that in it Uccello made full use of his narrative powers. The *Battle of Dragons and Lions* (untraced), listed in the Medici inventory of 1492 and also described briefly by Vasari, is further testimony to Uccello's interest in animals. It has been argued that contemporary Florentine engravings reflect the type of composition devised by Uccello (Salmi, 1950). The most serious loss is the fresco of giants, formerly in the Casa Vitaliani, Padua, which may have influenced Mantegna.

2. WORKING METHODS AND TECHNIQUE.

(i) Frescoes and panels. Nearly all Uccello's frescoes have been damaged, and understanding of the scenes is often enhanced by reference to 19th-century line-engravings such as those published by Giovanni Rosini (*Storia della pittura italiana*, 1839–54) and Seroux d'Agincourt (*Histoire de l'art*, 1810–23). On the other hand, the parlous condition of the frescoes has necessitated restoration, which in turn has revealed the underlying *sinopie*, thereby providing additional information about Uccello's preparatory methods. In the case of the scenes of the *Creation* in S Maria Novella, the gain is one concerning pictorial content, but in the case of the *Nativity and the Annunciation to the Shepherds* from S Martino alla Scala, the *sinopia* provides a perfect demonstration of the laying-in of grid lines. It is possible that the deterioration of Uccello's frescoes was in some cases, although not necessarily in all, hastened by the use of mixed media. At S Miniato al Monte, for example, oil was adopted as the medium (Saalman, 1964). The frescoes are normally described as having been executed in *terra verde*. It can be seen from surviving examples that this creates a predominantly chiaroscuro effect relieved only by subdued local colours. Uccello seems to have specialized in this monochrome technique, which was advocated by Alberti, and it contrasts strongly with the vivid colours he used for the panels. Technical information for panel paintings is sparse. For the transference of the design to the surface of the painting, Uccello seems to have used both squared drawings for enlargement and pricked cartoons. Given the precise structure of the compositions, it is likely that Uccello relied on such detailed preparatory methods as well as the greater freedom inherent in the *sinopia*.

(ii) Drawings. Few drawings can be firmly attributed to Uccello, although Vasari stated that the painter left 'whole chests full of drawings'. Of particular interest are the squared study for the upper half of the fresco of *Sir John Hawkwood*, the portrait of a man in profile facing left (given by Hartt to Castagno; see *A. Q.* [Detroit], xix (1956), pp. 162–73) and the squared and pricked study of a soldier on horseback (all Florence, Uffizi; see Degenhart and Schmitt, 1960, nos 302, 307, 309). These are drawings made in preparation for paintings, and the portrait study constitutes valuable evidence for the unresolved problem of Uccello's painted portraits. Uccello also made a number of studies of objects seen in perspective amounting to exercises in geometry; these include the drawing of a *mazzocchio* (Florence, Uffizi) and an even more elaborate drawing of a cup (Florence, Uffizi). Several drawings of animals are, not surprisingly, attributed to Uccello. Vasari claimed to have owned several drawings by the artist.

(iii) Perspective. Discussion of Uccello all too often concentrates on the issue of perspective, stressing the mathematical aspects and tending to overlook the general philosophical or intellectual connotations that the term *prospettiva* had in 15th-century Florence. Perspective was not simply a mathematical exercise but a new way of recording, and therefore of looking at the world. Uccello's depiction of himself on the panel known as the *Founders of Florentine Art* (Paris, Louvre) alongside such artists as Filippo Brunelleschi and Donatello as well as the astronomer and geographer Paolo dal Pozzo Toscanelli has a certain significance in this matter. The various ways in which Uccello applied his knowledge of perspective, including bifocal perspective, show that he was not content

to stick rigidly to the system enshrined in Alberti's *Della pittura* (1435). Central to an understanding of Uccello's use of perspective is his concern to assess its theoretical formulation in the context of natural phenomena. His conclusion seems to have been that while one-point perspective assisted in a more convincing pictorial rendering of the world, it was at the same time restricting and ultimately false because it demanded a fixed viewing point not in accordance with nature. Uccello's experiments in perspective and his constant deployment of mathematical principles in his works are in essence an examination of this dilemma.

(iv) Studio practice. Uccello does not seem to have maintained a large studio. Only a single individual, Antonio di Papi, is recorded as an assistant, in the documents for work carried out at S Miniato al Monte (Saalman, 1964). On the whole, Uccello's paintings do not show evidence of collaboration. Yet it is clear that a number of painters were influenced by his distinctive style and, accordingly, may have received some training in his workshop. Of those followers, the Prato Master is perhaps the most individual. His animated style and light tonality are best displayed in the scenes from the *Lives of the Virgin and St Stephen* (Prato Cathedral) or the *Virgin and Child* (Dublin, N.G.). Another hand that can be isolated is that of the painter known as the Karlsruhe Master, named after the panel of the *Adoration of the Child* (Karlsruhe, Staatl. Ksthalle), to whom several works, including *Christ on the Cross with Four Saints* (Madrid, Mus. Thyssen-Bornemisza) and the *Scenes from Monastic Legends* (Florence, Accademia), can be attributed (Pope-Hennessy, 1950). Many of the works by these two masters have at one time or another been incorporated into Uccello's oeuvre, but without any real justification (*see* MASTERS, ANONYMOUS, AND MONOGRAMMISTS, §I: KARLSRUHE MASTER and PRATO MASTER).

3. CRITICAL RECEPTION AND POSTHUMOUS REPUTATION. In Landino's preface (1481) to Dante's *Divine Comedy*, Uccello is described as a 'good composer and varied, great master of animals and landscapes, skilful in foreshortening, because he understood perspective well'. Vasari (2/1568) was more concerned with evaluation than bald description:

> The most captivating and imaginative painter to have lived since Giotto would certainly have been Paolo Uccello, if only he had spent as much time on human figures and animals as he spent, and wasted, on the finer points of perspective. Artists who devote more attention to perspective than to figures develop a dry and angular style because of their anxiety to examine things too minutely; and, moreover, they usually end up solitary, eccentric, melancholy and poor, as indeed did Paolo Uccello himself.

However, Vasari was not totally dismissive of Uccello's art, admiring the painter's facility for landscape and the depiction of animals.

Vasari's analysis of Uccello's art is echoed by Berenson (1896), who declared that Uccello 'almost entirely sacrificed what sense of artistic significance he may have started with, in his eagerness to display his skill and knowledge'. For Berenson, Uccello's achievements lay more in the

realm of mathematics than in art, but, in the light of subsequent research into the use of linear perspective by artists, he missed the essential point. Pope-Hennessy (1950) discerned that the dualism in Uccello's work is not between art and science 'but between two imperfectly reconciled visual traditions and two incompletely synthesized attitudes to art'. He recognized that Uccello was both an imaginative decorative painter and a remarkable naturalist, as is evident in the Chiostro Verde frescoes. Although Uccello's reputation has remained intact since the 15th century, it is true to say that, as with Piero della Francesca, there has been a quickening of interest in his work in the 20th century, mainly because of its appeal to modern sensibilities. Clark (1983) compared Uccello's achievement to that of Georges Seurat and likened his methods to those of the Cubists. He described Uccello as an artist in whose work there is 'a synthesis of his Gothic fantasy and Euclidian logic: a synthesis so complete that we can never be certain whether a happy passage of design is a triumph of taste or of calculation'.

BIBLIOGRAPHY

EARLY SOURCES

C. Landino: *Comento di Cristoforo Landino fiorentino sopra la Comedia di Dante Alighieri poeta fiorentino* (Florence, 1481); preface in *Scritti critici e teorici*, ed. R. Cardini, i (Rome 1974), pp. 100–164; extract in O. Morisani: 'Art Historians and Art Critics III: Cristoforo Landino', *Burl. Mag.*, xcv (1953), pp. 267–70; Eng. trans. of extract in C. Gilbert: *Italian Art, 1400–1500* (Englewood Cliffs, 1980), pp. 191–2

G. Vasari: *Vite* (1550, rev. 2/1568), ed. G. Milanesi (1878–85), ii, pp. 203–17

GENERAL

Colnaghi; *EWA*; Thieme–Becker

J. A. Crowe and G. B. Cavalcaselle: *A History of Painting in Italy* (London, 1864, rev. 2/1911, ed. L. Douglas), iv, pp. 106–22

B. Berenson: *The Florentine Painters of the Renaissance* (London, 1896), pp. 33–41

A. Venturi: *Storia* (1901–40/*R* 1967), VII/i, pp. 331–45

R. van Marle: *Italian Schools* (1923–38), x, pp. 203–50

M. Davies: *The Earlier Italian Schools*, London, N.G. cat. (London, 1951, 2/1961/*R* 1986), pp. 525–33

J. White: *The Birth and Rebirth of Pictorial Space* (London, 1956, 2/1967), pp. 202–7

E. Borsook: *The Mural Painters of Tuscany from Cimabue to Andrea del Sarto* (London, 1960, rev. Oxford, 2/1980), pp. 11–9

B. Degenhart and A. Schmitt: *Corpus der italienischen Zeichnungen, 1300–1450*, I/ii (Berlin, 1960), pp. 379–414 [detailed disc. of Uccello's drgs]

B. Berenson: *Florentine School* (1963), i, p. 209

H. W. Janson: 'The Equestrian Monument from Cangrande della Scala to Peter the Great', *Sixteen Studies* (1970), pp. 159–68 [disc. of *Sir John Hawkwood*]

H. Saalman, ed.: *The Life of Brunelleschi by Antonio Tuccio Manetti* (Philadelphia, 1970), pp. 18–19, n. 24 [identifies Uccello's self-portrait in the *Founders of Florentine Art*]

MONOGRAPHS

W. Boeck: *Paolo Uccello* (Berlin, 1939); review by M. Wackernagel in *Pantheon*, xxvii (1941), pp. 102–10

M. Pittaluga: *Paolo Uccello* (Rome, 1946)

J. Pope-Hennessy: *The Complete Work of Paolo Uccello* (London, 1950, rev. 2/1969); review by C. Gilbert in *A. Q.* [Detroit], xxxiii (1970), pp. 441–3

E. Sindona: *Paolo Uccello* (Milan, 1957)

E. Carli: *Tutta la pittura di Paolo Uccello* (Milan, 1959; Eng. trans., 1963)

P. D'Ancona: *Paolo Uccello* (Eng. trans., London, 1960)

E. Flaiano and L. Tongiorgi Tomasi: *L'opera completa di Paolo Uccello* (Milan, 1971)

F. Borsi and S. Borsi: *Paolo Uccello* (1992); Eng. trans. by E. Powell (London, 1994)

SPECIALIST STUDIES

E. Campani: 'Uccello's *Story of Noah* in the Chiostro Verde', *Burl. Mag.*, xvii (1910), pp. 203–10

G. J. Kern: 'Der Mazzocchio des Paolo Uccello', *Jb. Preuss. Kstsamml.*, xxxvi (1915), pp. 13–38

M. Marangoni: 'Gli affreschi di Paolo Uccello a San Miniato al Monte a Firenze', *Riv. A.*, xii (1930), pp. 403–17

G. Poggi: 'Paolo Uccello e l'orologio di S. Maria del Fiore', *Miscellanea di storia dell'arte in onore di I. B. Supino* (Florence, 1933), pp. 323–36

W. Paatz: 'Una *Natività* di Paolo Uccello e alcune considerazioni sull'arte del maestro', *Riv. A.*, xvi (1934), pp. 112–48

G. Pudelko: 'The Early Works of Paolo Uccello', *A. Bull.*, xvi (1934), pp. 231–59

M. Salmi: *Paolo Uccello, Andrea del Castagno, Domenico Veneziano* (Milan, 1938), pp. 7–49, 101–14

R. G. Mather: 'Documents, Mostly New, Relating to Florentine Painters and Sculptors of the Fifteenth Century', *A. Bull.*, xxx (1948), pp. 62–4

M. Salmi: 'Riflessioni su Paolo Uccello', *Commentari*, i (1950), pp. 22–33

C. Grayson: 'A Portrait of L. B. Alberti', *Burl. Mag.*, xcvi (1954), p. 177

J. K. Spencer: 'Spatial Imagery of the Annunciation in Fifteenth Century Florence', *A. Bull.*, xxxvii (1955), pp. 273–80

D. Gioseffi: 'Complementi di prospettiva, 2', *Crit. A.*, v (1958), pp. 102–39

A. Parronchi: 'Le fonti di Paolo Uccello', *Studi su la 'dolce' prospettiva* (Milan, 1964), pp. 468–532

H. Saalman: 'Paolo Uccello at San Miniato', *Burl. Mag.*, cvi (1964), pp. 558–63

M. Aaronberg Lavin: 'The Altar of Corpus Domini in Urbino: Paolo Uccello, Joos van Ghent, Piero della Francesca', *A. Bull.*, xlix (1967), pp. 1–24

M. Meiss: 'The Original Position of Uccello's *Sir John Hawkwood*', *A. Bull.*, lii (1970), p. 231

H. E. Mittig: 'Uccellos Hawkwood Fresko: Platz und Wirkung', *Mitt. Ksthist. Inst. Florenz*, xiv (1970), pp. 235–9

R. L. Mode: 'Masolino, Uccello and the Orsini *Uomini famosi*', *Burl. Mag.*, xciv (1972), pp. 369–78

E. Sindona: 'Introduzione alla poetica di Paolo Uccello: Relazioni tra prospettiva e pensiero teoretico', *L'Arte*, xvii (1972), pp. 7–100

F. Ames-Lewis: 'A Portrait of L. B. Alberti by Uccello?', *Burl. Mag.*, cxvi (1974), pp. 103–4

C. Eisler: 'The Portrait of L. B. Alberti', *Burl. Mag.*, cxvi (1974), pp. 529–30

C. Joost-Gaugier: 'Uccello's "Uccello": A Visual Signature', *Gaz. B.-A.*, n.s. 6, lxxxiv (1974), pp. 233–8

C. Griffiths: 'The Political Significance of Uccello's *Battle of San Romano*', *J. Warb. & Court. Inst.*, xxxxi (1978), pp. 313–16

J. Beck: 'Paolo Uccello and the Paris *St George*, 1465: Unpublished Documents 1452, 1465, 1474', *Gaz. B.-A.*, n.s. 6, xciii (1979), pp. 1–5

—— : 'Uccello's Apprenticeship with Ghiberti', *Burl. Mag.*, cxxii (1980), p. 837

C. Volpe: 'Paolo Uccello a Bologna', *Paragone*, xxxi (1980), pp. 3–28

C. Lloyd, ed.: *Paolo Uccello's 'Hunt in the Forest'* (Oxford, 1981)

K. Clark: 'Paolo Uccello and Abstract Painting', *The Art of Humanism* (London, 1983), pp. 43–76

Y. Even: 'Paolo Uccello's *John Hawkwood*: Reflections of a Collaboration between Agnolo Gaddi and Giuliano Pesello', *Source*, iv/4 (1985), pp. 6–8

J. O'Grady: 'An Uccello Enigma', *Gaz. B.-A.*, n.s. 6, cv (1985), pp. 99–103

P. A. Rossi: 'La *Madonna* di Dublin', *Crit. A.*, li (1986), pp. 40–50

CHRISTOPHER LLOYD

Uceda Castroverde, Juan de (*b* Seville, *c.* 1570; *d* Seville, 1631). Spanish painter. The earliest reference to Uceda is in 1593, when he began to practise as a master painter, which indicates that his apprenticeship ended around 1590. His painting was strongly influenced by Sevillian Mannerism of the last third of the 16th century, but during the early years of the 17th century it developed towards a more Baroque naturalism. His first known work was executed in collaboration with Alonso Vázquez, who departed for New Spain in 1603, leaving Uceda to complete the unfinished upper part of his *Death of St Hermengild* (Seville, Mus. B.A.). About 1615 Uceda executed paintings for the altar of *St John the Baptist* in the convent church of S María del Socorro, Seville. His *Earthly Trinity*

(1623; Seville, Mus. B.A.) is a work of intense feeling and demonstrates the extent to which the artist had moved away from the cold Mannerist spirit in which he had been trained. *Christ Served by Angels* in the chapel of the Cristo de Maracaibo (Seville Cathedral), the *Immaculate Conception with SS Joseph, Benedict and Francis* (Seville, S Vicente) and the *Adoration of the Shepherds* (Carmona, nr Seville, priv. col., see Valdivieso and Serrera, fig. 169) are all characteristic works. At his death Uceda left unfinished the paintings he had begun in 1629 for the reredos of S Vicente, Seville, including the *Story of the Bed of Roses* and the *Martyrdom of St Vincent* (both *in situ*); they were completed by Francisco Varela.

BIBLIOGRAPHY

D. Angulo Iñiguez: *Pintura del siglo XVII*, A. Hisp., xv (Madrid, 1971), p. 91

E. Valdivieso and J. M. Serrera: *Pintura sevillana del primer tercio del siglo XVII* (Madrid, 1985), pp. 204–27

A. E. Pérez Sánchez: *Pintura barroca española* (Madrid, 1992), p. 169

ENRIQUE VALDIVIESO

Uchii, Shōzō (*b* Tokyo, 1933). Japanese architect. The eldest son of the architect Shin Uchii, in 1956 he graduated in architecture from Waseda University, Tokyo, where he also completed a graduate course in 1958. From 1958 to 1967 he worked for Kiyonori Kikutake. In 1967 he opened his own office in Tokyo; in his designs particular attention was paid to site, materials and building function. After 1980 he developed the view that industrial standardization and excessive personalization (tendencies of Post-modernism) are unhealthy directions for contemporary architecture. His idea of sound architecture is that it should embody the architect's spiritual relationship with nature and craftsmanship. Such buildings as the Setagaya Museum (1986), Tokyo, reveal in their stylistic influences his admiration for the work of Frank Lloyd Wright. Uchii won the Mainichi Art Award for this building; he also received prizes from the Architectural Institute of Japan for the Sakuradai Court Village (1970), Kanagawa, and from the Japan Architects Association for the Kawashima Textile School (1973), Kyoto.

WRITINGS

Kenkō na kenchiku [Healthy architecture] (Tokyo, 1984)

BIBLIOGRAPHY

Uchii Shōzō, Nihon gendai kenchikuka shirizu [Modern Japanese architects series], ii (Tokyo, 1982)

H. Suzuki, R. Banham and K. Kobayashi: *Contemporary Architecture of Japan: 1958–1984* (New York, 1985), pp. 110–11

TOSHIAKI NAGAYA

Uch Tepe. *See under* HAMRIN REGION.

Udaipur. City in south-eastern Rajasthan, India. The earliest settlements were prehistoric. Excavations at Ahar (anc. Aghatapura), 3.2 km east of Udaipur, revealed two periods of occupation, the earlier dating to the second millennium BC; the second period is marked by the introduction of Northern Black polished ware (*see* INDIAN SUBCONTINENT, §VIII, 5(i)) and seals and coins datable to the 3rd century BC and later. Ahar was subsequently important as the capital of the Guhila kings, ancestors of the Rajputs, during the 10th century AD. The ruins of a 10th-century fort, Dhul Kot (Fort of Ashes), survive, as do the temple of Mira Bai (10th century), the Adinatha

Temple (11th century, with renovated tower) and a group of 15th-century Jaina temples. Ahar was the cremation ground of the Rajput rulers, and several elegant *chatris* (pavilion-shaped memorials) were erected there (17th century onwards).

Udaipur was established as the capital of Mewar by Udai Singh (*reg* 1536–72) after the sacking of Chittaurgarh by the Mughal emperor Akbar in 1567 but probably existed some time before this. The artificial Pichola Lake in the heart of the city may have existed in the late 14th century, and another artificial lake, Udai Sagar, was built 14.5 km outside the city by Udai Singh between 1559 and 1565. The great City Palace on the eastern bank of Pichola Lake was begun *c.* 1567. Its earliest phases, completed *c.* 1572, are most clearly seen in the eastern range of Rajya Angam Chowk and the Badal Mahal. There was little building between 1572 and 1614 owing to military conflicts with the Mughals. In 1614 Amar Singh I (*reg* 1597–1620) finally submitted to the Mughals, whose generous terms led to prosperity and renewed building activity. The variety of architectural forms that developed between 1567 and 1734 can be seen on the eastern front of the City Palace, where the solid, fortress-like lower walls are surmounted by balcony-pavilions with slender columns and windows marked by delicate stone interlace (*see* INDIAN SUBCONTINENT, fig. 113). The decoration of the interior, ranging widely in date, is elaborate and at times even whimsical. The walls of the Moti Mahal (*c.* 1700) are inlaid with mirrors and coloured glass. The Chini-ki Chitra Mahal (1711–34) is faced with Dutch and Chinese tiles. Other interior areas decorated in the 19th century include the Krishna Vilas, installed with miniature paintings in 1805.

Numerous additional palaces and gardens include the Gul Mahal (1620–30) and several 18th-century pavilions on Jag Mandir Island in Pichola Lake. The Sahelion-ki Bari (Garden of the Ladies), a small-scale garden palace, was built for the concubines of Sangram Singh II (*reg* 1710–34). One of Udaipur's most sumptuous buildings is the Jag Nivas (1734–51), occupying an entire island on Pichola Lake; the white marble pleasure palace is now a luxury hotel. Udaipur's most outstanding religious structure is the Jagdish Temple (1640), dedicated to Vishnu. It continues traditional temple forms with its tall, curvilinear spire and walls encrusted with figural sculpture.

Udaipur was also the main centre of miniature painting of the Mewar school (*see* INDIAN SUBCONTINENT, §VI, 4(iii)(a)). Museums include the City Palace Museum, with an outstanding collection of miniature paintings, and the Government Museum, also in the City Palace, which has an important collection of stone inscriptions and sculptures from neighbouring sites dating from the 6th to the 14th century. The Bharatiya Lok Kala Museum contains a variety of objects relating to folk theatre: costumes, masks, puppets and musical instruments. The Archaeological Museum at Ahar contains prehistoric materials and 10th-century sculptures.

See also INDIAN SUBCONTINENT, §III, 7(ii)(b).

BIBLIOGRAPHY
K. C. Jain: *Ancient Cities and Towns of Rajasthan* (Delhi, 1972)
B. D. Agarwal: *Udaipur*, Rajasthan District Gazetteers (Jaipur, 1979)
G. H. R. Tillotson: *The Rajput Palaces* (New Haven and London, 1987)
P. Davies: *Islamic, Rajput, European*, ii of Penguin Guide Mnmts India (London, 1989)
G. Michell: *Buddhist, Jain, Hindu*, i of Penguin Guide Mnmts India (London, 1989)

ASOK KUMAR DAS

Udal'tsova [née Prudkovskaya]**, Nadezhda (Andreyevna)** (*b* Oryol, 1886; *d* Moscow, 1961). Russian painter. She received her initial artistic education in Moscow at the School of Painting, Sculpture and Architecture (1905–9), Konstantin Yuon's Art School (1906–9), where she may have met Lyubov' Popova, and in 1909 at the Art School of Istvan Kiss where she met Vladimir Favorsky and Konstantin Istomin (1887–1942). In November 1912 she went to Paris with Popova to see Matisse's work but was influenced by Cubism and studied at the Académie de La Palette under Jean Metzinger, Henri Le Fauconnier and André Dunoyer de Segonzac. From them she assimilated the principles of Cubism, as in the monochrome canvas *Guitar: Fugue* (1914; Moscow, Tret'yakov Gal.), where the instrument is fragmented into broadly defined interpenetrating planes intersected by sheet music and the picture surface is flattened by lettering and numbers. In late 1913 Udal'tsova returned to Russia and worked in Vladimir Tatlin's studio, known as the Tower, in Moscow, together with Aleksandr Vesnin and Popova. Udal'tsova continued working in a Cubist idiom producing such works as *Cubist Composition* (*c.* 1914–15; Cologne, Mus. Ludwig), in which the forms are evoked by interlocking planes within a linear framework. She exhibited at the Jack of Diamonds exhibition in 1914, and at *Tramvay V: Pervaya futuristicheskaya vystavka kartin* ('Tram V: the first Futurist exhibition of paintings') and *Poslednyaya futuristicheskaya vystavka kartin: 0.10* ('The last Futurist exhibition of paintings: 0.10'), both held in Petrograd in 1915. By the end of 1915 she was producing such works as *At the Piano* (1915; New Haven, CT, Yale U., A.G.), in which Cubist lettering and planar fragmentation is combined with a Futurist interest in movement conveyed in the repeated elements of the hands and feet. At this point Udal'tsova may have experimented briefly with Mikhail Larionov's Rayism, but by the end of November 1916 her affiliation to Kazimir Malevich and SUPREMATISM was firmly established and she was one of his collaborators in 1916–17 on the projected Suprematist magazine *Supremus*. Udal'tsova produced abstract Suprematist paintings such as *Untitled* (*c.* 1918; Athens, George Costakis priv. col., see Rudenstine, no. 1128), where the use of overlapping coloured planes is close to Popova, and she also applied Suprematism's geometric vocabulary to designs for handbags, fabrics and dresses. In 1917 Udal'tsova participated in the decoration of the Café Pittoresque in Moscow with Georgy Yakulov and Tatlin.

After the Revolution of 1917 Udal'tsova became active in the Artists' Union and in the art departments of the Moscow Proletkul't (Organization for Proletarian Culture) and of the Moscow Soviet of Peasant, Soldier and Workers' Deputies. She was an energetic expounder of avant-garde ideas, delivering lectures and writing and is thought to have been the author of the brochure *Vladimir Yevgrafovich Tatlin* (Petrograd, 1915). In 1918 she became a member of the Moscow section of the Department of Fine Arts (IZO) within Narkompros (the People's Commissariat for Enlightenment). She taught at the Free Art Studios (Svomas), initially as Malevich's assistant, but later independently (1918–20), continuing to teach painting at Vkhutemas (1921–30) and subsequently at the Textile Institute and the Institute of Printing. She was an active member of the Institute of Artistic Culture, INKHUK, but she and her husband, Aleksandr Drevin, left the Institute in 1921 in protest against the dominating influence of the Constructivists. They argued for the primacy of painting and early in the 1920s became committed to a return to figurative subject-matter. At first this meant a return for Udal'tsova to the vocabulary of Cubism, but by the mid-1920s she was using a more descriptive style. She was strongly influenced by her visits to the Urals and the Altay (1930–31) and to Armenia (1933–4) and in response produced lyrical genre scenes and landscapes such as *Armenia* (1933; Moscow, Tret'yakov Gal.), painted with feathery brushstrokes and in muted tones.

WRITINGS

Zhizn' Russkoy kubistki: Dnevniki, stat'i, vospominaniya [The life of a Russian Cubist artist: diaries, articles and reminiscences] (Moscow, 1994)

BIBLIOGRAPHY

Women Artists of the Russian Avant-garde, 1910–1930 (exh. cat., Cologne, Gal. Gmurzynska, 1979), pp. 285–312

A. Rudenstine, ed.: *Russian Avant-garde Art: The George Costakis Collection* (London, 1983), pp. 484–7

M. N. Yablonskaya: *Women Artists of Russia's New Age, 1900–1935* (London, 1990), pp. 157–72

CHRISTINA LODDER

Udayagiri, Cave 5, Varaha image, h. 3.83 m, early 5th century AD

Udayagiri (i). *See* KHANDAGIRI AND UDAYAGIRI.

Udayagiri (ii). Site of 20 rock-cut cave shrines in Vidisha District, Madhya Pradesh, India, some 4.5 km west of Vidisha. Udayagiri is a low, narrow hill approximately 2.5 km long. Its cave shrines, which can be dated to the 5th century AD on the basis of two inscriptions (on Caves 6 and 7), were first comprehensively published by Alexander Cunningham in the 19th century. Known for their outstanding sculpture, the caves are Brahmanical except for a Jaina cave halfway up the hill and a Jaina image (*c.* 11th century) in Cave 1. The most important and best preserved are Caves 4, 5, 6, 13 and 19.

Cave 4 is remarkable for its early 5th-century doorway with delicately carved lotus scrollwork on the jambs and lintel. Following the conventions of the period, the lintel extends beyond the jambs to create a T-shape. Inside the sanctum is a single-faced (Skt *ekamukha*) Shiva *linga*, which was the main focus of worship.

Cave 5, the most celebrated at the site, is not so much a cave as a shallow niche some 6.7 m wide. It contains a panoramic relief of Vishnu in his incarnation as the Cosmic Boar Varaha (see fig.), the mightiest representation of the theme in all of Indian art. Depicted on the back wall of the cave are the gods and seers who took refuge in Vishnu during his rescue of the world from the ocean's depths, as recounted in *Matsya purāṇa* (248: 65–78). On the sides of the cave are representations of the rivers Ganga and Yamuna. At the foot of Vishnu is the serpent Shesha, representing the cosmic waters, and a battered figure, possibly a royal donor. This cave has been subject to a number of allegorical interpretations that need critical review.

Relief panels decorating the façade of Cave 6 include Durga Slaying the Buffalo Demon (*Mahiṣāsuramardinī*), two images of Vishnu and an image of Ganesha. Two guardian figures (*dvārapāla*s) flanking the doorway are among the finest sculptures of the early Gupta period (for illustration *see* INDIAN SUBCONTINENT, fig. 173). A small inscribed panel (above the image of Durga and an adjacent image of Vishnu) records that this work was done in Gupta year 82 (AD 401). The cave entrance, the oldest dated doorway in India, has a T-shaped frame, similar to that of Cave 4, with decorated jambs. The lintel is flanked by goddesses standing on mythical aquatic animals (*makara*).

Cave 13, a shallow niche like Cave 5 but of smaller proportions, has a damaged image of Vishnu reclining on the serpent Ananta dating to the early 5th century. A donor figure is at the base of the relief.

Cave 19, dating to the mid-5th century and later than the others at the site, has a doorway that is architecturally more complex, featuring wide panels of richly worked floral scrolls and small figures set into the base of the jambs. The middle of three jambs carries amorous couples (*mithuna*s), a theme popular in later temple architecture. Guardian figures carved in high relief flank the door. Over the lintel is a depiction of the *Churning of the Milky Sea*, a mythological subject recorded in the *Mahābhārata* (1[5]16: 1–40). The theme, represented here and at Pawaya for the first time, became common in later Indian art. A ruined forehall (*maṇḍapa*), of which only a few pillars remain, stands in front of the cave. The interior has a raised plinth (*pīṭha*) in the centre and four elaborate pillars. Beams, reflecting wooden architecture, are cut in the cave ceiling.

On top of Udayagiri hill are the ruins of a large structure. A platform (*jagatī*) and a number of fragments (including a door jamb) survive. A ceiling panel (*vitāna*; Gwalior, Archaeol. Mus.) is carved with a large lotus pattern in the centre and signs of the zodiac along the outer edge. Immediately beside the temple is a monolithic stone column, now fallen, which was once surmounted by a lion capital (h. 2.8 m; Gwalior, Archaeol. Mus.). The capital appears to be an early 5th-century work, not a recut Maurya capital as commonly believed (e.g. Williams, 1973).

See also INDIAN SUBCONTINENT, §III, 1(ii)(c).

BIBLIOGRAPHY

A. Cunningham: *Archaeol. Surv. India Rep.*, x (1874–7), pp. 46–56 [numbering system subsequently modified]
K. Jayaswal: 'Candragupta and his Predecessor', *J. Bihar & Orissa Res. Soc.*, xviii (1932), pp. 17–36
D. R. Patil: *The Monuments of Udayagiri Hill* (Gwalior, 1948)
V. Agrawala: *Matsya Purāṇa: A Study* (Varanasi, 1963)
D. Mitra: 'Varāha-cave of Udayagiri, an Iconographic Study', *J. Asiat. Soc.*, v (1963), pp. 99–103
J. Harle: 'On a Disputed Element on the Iconography of Early Mahiṣa-suramardinī Images', *A. Orient.*, viii (1970), pp. 17–36
J. Williams: 'A Recut Aśokan Capital and the Gupta Attitude towards the Past', *Artibus Asiae*, xxxv (1973), pp. 225–40
J. Harle: *Gupta Sculpture* (Oxford, 1974)
P. Granoff: 'Mahiṣāsuramardinī: An Analysis of the Myths', *E & W*, xxix (1979), pp. 139–51
J. Williams: *The Art of Gupta India: Empire and Province* (Princeton, 1982)

MICHAEL D. WILLIS

Udayapur [Udayapura; Udaypur]. Town near Vidisha in Madhya Pradesh, India; flourished from the 11th century AD. It became prominent as a seat of the Nemakas, vassals of the PARAMARA dynasty. During the time of the Para-mara ruler Udayaditya (*reg c.* 1070–86) the celebrated Udayeshvara (anc. Udalameshvara) Temple was con-structed (*see* INDIAN SUBCONTINENT, fig. 57). Dedicated to Shiva, the temple is considered an architectural marvel, ingenious and striking both in plan and elevation. Com-menced in 1059 and consecrated in 1080, it conforms to the type known canonically as *bhūmija* (Skt: 'earth-born'). The temple is the earliest of the *bhūmija* type in central India. The exterior of the sanctum has a stellate configu-ration with the vestibule, halls, porches, ceilings, pillars and doorways all richly embellished with relief sculptures that are predominantly Shaiva in theme. The *bhūmija* superstructure has a central vertical spine (*latā*) on each side. These spines divide the spire into four quadrants, each containing seven storeys of five *kūṭa-stambha*s (min-iature spires resting on pilasters) receding in size as they rise. The arched medallions at the base of each spine contain remarkable sculptures, the most imposing being the Natesha on the east side (*see* INDIAN SUBCONTINENT, fig. 195). A smaller version has been removed to the Archaeological Museum, Gwalior.

Other remains include the 11th-century Bija mandala, or Ghadiyala ka makan, and the Barakhambhi, a pillared hall, also 11th-century. The Pisnari ka mandira is a temple, probably later than the 13th century. A massive 11th-century image of Natesha is located at Ravanapol, 2 km south-east of the town. Inscriptions dated AD 1336 and 1338 (AH 737 and 739) refer to a mosque built immediately to the west of the Udayeshvara Temple during the rule of Muhammad Tughluq (*reg* 1325–51). The mosque was built using temple pillars and other fragments, but the mihrab is a good example of the provincial Tughluq style. In the 15th and 16th centuries Udayapur was a flourishing town, and several small mosques were built, notably the Sher Khan ki Masjid (1488). Portions of the town walls, gates, stepwells, main bazaar and palatial residences survive in various states of preservation.

BIBLIOGRAPHY

H. N. Dvivedi: *Gvāliyar rājya ke abhilekha* [Inscriptions of Gwalior state] (Varanasi, V.S. 2004)
D. R. Patil: *The Cultural Heritage of Madhya Bharat* (Gwalior, 1952)
——: *The Descriptive and Classified List of Archaeological Monuments in Madhya Bharat* (Gwalior, 1952)
K. Deva: 'Bhūmija Temples', *Studies in Indian Temple Architecture*, ed. P. Chandra (New Delhi, 1975), pp. 90–113
M. A. Dhaky: *Indian Temple Forms* (New Delhi, 1977)
Indian Archaeology, 1983–84: A Review (New Delhi, 1986), p. 56

R. N. MISRA

Uden, Lucas van (*b* Antwerp, 18 Oct 1595; *d* Antwerp, 4 Nov 1672). Flemish painter, draughtsman and engraver. He was the son of Artus van Uden (*b* 1544), town painter of Antwerp, and grandson of Pieter van Uden (i) (*fl* 1553), founder of a noted tapestry and silk factory in the city. Lucas was probably trained by his father and in 1626–7 was enrolled in the Antwerp Guild of St Luke as a 'master's son'. On 14 February 1627 he married Anna van Woelput (*d* 1667). On 31 December 1649 he was registered as no longer living in the city, so for a period in 1650 he must have lived elsewhere.

Houbraken, who had high praise for van Uden, wrote that he often set out into the countryside early in the morning to make landscape sketches. This account may be stretching the truth somewhat, for even more important than the observation of nature for van Uden were earlier developments in Flemish landscape painting, and whereas his drawings often appear to follow nature faithfully and seem realistic, his paintings, though fairly successful, frequently seem contrived.

Most of van Uden's works are constructed according to the same plan. The foreground usually has a small bank topped by a few slim birches or other tall trees with transparent foliage; the trees are typically arranged in small groups and are all very straight except for one, which inclines crookedly, usually towards the centre of the panel. In the centre are peaceful fields and meadows, with hamlets, small ponds with reflections of trees and clouds, shrubs and bushes or rows of trees with thick, round foliage. In the background are mountains, which, unlike those in the paintings of many of his predecessors, are not in the least ominous. Include characteristic examples include the *Summer Landscape* (see fig.) and the *River Landscape with Anglers* (Hamburg, Ksthalle). The colours are rather pale, principally dull green, pinkish brown and the yellow tone of the sunbeams, and the whole is bathed in a silvery green haze. Van Uden often depended on David Teniers (ii) for the figures, as can be seen from a number of paintings with both his signature and Teniers's monogram (e.g. *Landscape with Dancing Peasants*; Dublin, N.G.). Most often, however, the staffage—shepherds, walkers, peasants

Lucas van Uden: *Summer Landscape*, oil on panel, 395×580 mm, *c.* 1640–50 (Mainz, Landesmuseum Mainz)

at work, gipsy girls telling fortunes—was van Uden's own work, frequently influenced by Teniers and Rubens.

Van Uden's careful attention to detail, particularly noticeable in the smaller works, and his search for decorative elements in the larger paintings—for example his contrasting of dark, cool zones with clear, warm ones—place him in the same tradition as Jan Breughel I and Josse de Momper II. Another artist who played an important role in the development of his art was Rubens. Van Uden made a number of more or less literal copies of compositions by Rubens (e.g. *Landscape with Ulysses and Nausicaa*; Barnard Castle, Bowes Mus., after Rubens's painting in Florence, Pitti); elsewhere he reworked compositions to form new ones with a pronounced capriccio character. He also introduced Rubensian elements into many of his own works: a woman carrying a round jug on her head and cows at a watering place, for example, or such stylistic devices as foreground trees lit from behind with the tips of the branches highlighted with yellow-orange touches. But van Uden's paintings lack the grand, broad and synthetic vision that characterizes the work of Rubens, and the reduction of the rich Rubensian colours to a monochrome green tends to make the paintings look somewhat dry. On the other hand, he achieved a certain grace, intimacy and tenderness in them. He seems to have lacked the strength to develop a personal style that deviated from the paths opened up by Breughel, de Momper and Rubens. His greatest individual talent is shown in his observation of nature, as revealed in such drawings as the *Landscape with Rock Face* (Berlin, Kupferstichkab.) and a

few straightforward paintings such as the *Landscape with a Gipsy Girl Telling Fortunes* (Berlin, Gemäldegal.), made jointly with Teniers.

In art-historical literature Lucas van Uden and Jan Wildens are usually bracketed together as assistants of Rubens; both are thought to have painted the background landscapes in numerous works by the great master. While this certainly holds true for Wildens, it cannot be so for van Uden. Firstly, his hand is not recognizable in any of Rubens's paintings; secondly, there is no documentary evidence to support the claim. This misconception, already common in the 18th century, was reinforced by Rooses, who not only asserted that he knew a number of pictures on which van Uden had worked but also identified him as the landscape assistant mentioned by Rubens to Dudley Carleton in a letter of 26 May 1618, a reference that is clearly to Wildens. Nonetheless, the error was embellished so that people came to believe that, before becoming a free master, van Uden had worked in Rubens's workshop and had contributed to the landscape backgrounds in the designs for the *Decius Mus* tapestry series. Although van Uden never actually worked for Rubens, he did borrow many motifs from Rubens's paintings and copied several of his compositions. Another misapprehension, first expressed by Gault de Saint Germain and often repeated thereafter, is that Rubens painted the figures in some of van Uden's works. A number of his landscapes do have figures borrowed from Rubens, but these were painted by van Uden himself.

Van Uden's pupils included Philips Augustin Immenraet (1627–79) and Jan Baptist Bonnecroy (1618–76). His brother Jacob van Uden (*fl* 1627–9) was a landscape painter too, and Jacob's son Adriaen van Uden (*fl* 1655–6) and his grandson Pieter van Uden (ii) (*fl* 1673–4), a miniature painter, were also active in Antwerp. The guild records also mention an Arnoldus van Uden in 1695/6.

BIBLIOGRAPHY

A. Houbraken: *De groote schouburgh* (1718–21), p. 158
G. de Saint Germain: *Guide des amateurs de tableaux pour les écoles allemande, flamande et hollandaise* (Paris, 1818), i, p. 239
A. Michaels: *Histoire de la peinture flamande depuis ses débuts jusqu'en 1864*, 10 vols (Paris, 1865–76), viii, pp. 180–92
F. J. Van den Branden: *Geschiedenis der Antwerpsche schilderschool* (Antwerp, 1883), pp. 687–90
M. Rooses and Ch. Ruelens, eds: *Correspondance de Rubens et documents épistolaires concernant sa vie et ses oeuvres* (Antwerp, 1898), ii, p. 170
R. L. Delevoy: 'L'Oeuvre gravé de Lucas van Uden: Contribution à l'étude de la gravure du XVIIIe siècle', *Belg. Tijdschr. Oudhdknd. & Kstgesch.*, x (1940), pp. 47–58
Y. Thiéry: *Le Paysage flemand au XVIIe siècle* (Paris and Brussels, 1953), pp. 62–6
E. Plietzsch: *Holländische und flämische Maler des XVII. Jahrhunderts* (Leipzig, 1960), pp. 214–15
W. Adler: *Jan Wildens: Der Landschaftsmitarbeiter des Rubens* (Fridingen, 1980)
S. Bailey: 'A Preparatory Drawing by Lucas van Uden', *Master Drgs*, xix (1981), p. 441–2
Flemish Drawings in the Age of Rubens (exh. cat. by A.-M. Logan, Wellesley Coll., MA, Davis Mus. & Cult. Cent., 1993–4), pp. 221–2

HANS DEVISSCHER

Udine, Giovanni da [Nanni, Giovanni; Ricamatori, Giovanni dei] (*b* Udine, 27 Oct 1487; *d* Rome, 1564). Italian stuccoist, painter, draughtsman and architect. In 1502 he was apprenticed to Giovanni Martini (also called Giovanni da Udine; *d* 1535), a painter in Udine, and subsequently he may have studied with Giorgione in Venice. According to Vasari, armed with a letter of introduction to Baldassare Castiglione, he decided to go to Rome to seek work with Raphael. He joined Raphael's workshop, where he may have learnt techniques of still-life painting from a Netherlandish colleague. The musical instruments in Raphael's *St Cecilia* altarpiece (1516; Bologna, Pin. N.) are often attributed to Giovanni.

In Rome, Giovanni da Udine was particularly inspired by the decoration of ancient buildings. Excavations revealed rooms then underground (thus called *grotte*) with a style of painted and plastered decoration incorporating foliated scrolls, naturalistic animals and plants and fantastic figures and architecture (hence called *grotteschi*; *see* GROTESQUE). Such motifs had been copied before in Rome (notably by Bernardino Pinturicchio), but it was Raphael, probably with the assistance of Giovanni, who created the first decorative scheme entirely composed of them in the bathroom (*stufetta*) of Cardinal Bernardo Bibbiena (1516; Rome, Vatican Pal.; see fig.). That scheme was entirely painted. At about this time a formula for re-creating the Romans' rock-hard plaster, capable of reproducing minute details, was devised, almost certainly by Giovanni, probably using marble dust and chips of travertine stone. Thus when Raphael and his assistants began decorating the 13 bays of the first of the great Logge of the Vatican Palace (1517–19), Giovanni was able to contribute figured frames and other details in stucco to the scheme, as well as painted grotesques on the pilasters and walls, with a delicate

freshness at least partly due to his inclusion of tempera in the fresco medium. Vasari described Giovanni's work on the Loggia as 'the finest painting ever seen by mortal eye'.

During this period Giovanni was also involved in Raphael's decoration of the villa of Agostino Chigi (1517–18; Rome, Villa Farnesina). In the villa's Loggia of Cupid and Psyche, Giovanni painted festoons of flowers and fruit on the walls, decorative features on the ceiling and grotesques above the windows. In his grotesques he both copied and transformed Roman models and also showed considerable powers of invention. These are evident in the more conventional scheme in the Vatican on which he and Polidoro da Caravaggio collaborated for the ceiling of the corridor below Raphael's Loggia for Leo X (1518–19). In 1520 Giovanni became involved in the decoration of the Villa Madama, Rome, which Raphael had begun some years earlier for Cardinal Giulio de' Medici; on Raphael's death the same year, Giovanni was put in charge of the work, together with Raphael's senior assistant, Giulio Romano. This collaboration was fraught with difficulties, which were the talk of the papal court, but it resulted in the most harmonious decorative treatment of any Renaissance villa. In the garden loggia, which is all that remains of what was built of the project, Raphael's magnificent architecture is sumptuously enriched by its stucco skin of small-scale Classical ornament, more architectonic and sculptural than grotesque (*see* RAPHAEL, fig. 9). The painted decoration of the vault does contain grotesques, as well as small scenes and fields of pure ornament, and the vigorous colouring reflects the taste of Giulio Romano, but this does not detract from the

Giovanni da Udine: fresco decoration (1516) in the bathroom of Cardinal Bernardo Bibbiena, Vatican Palace, Rome

remarkable beauty of the whole, which is the only Renaissance interior fully to reflect the grandeur of Imperial Rome. (Giovanni is also credited with the design of an Elephant Fountain (untraced) in the gardens, *c.* 1526.)

In 1522, during the artistic drought of the pontificate of Adrian VI (*reg* 1521–3), Giovanni left Rome for Udine. The accession of Giulio de' Medici as Clement VII the following year led him to return; it may have been on this journey that he decorated a room (destr.) in the Palazzo Medici, Florence. Again in the Vatican, he collaborated with Perino del Vaga on the ceiling decoration of the Sala dei Pontefici, with celestial motifs and the Medici arms (*c.* 1521; *in situ*). This sojourn was terminated by the Sack of Rome in 1527. On his return to Udine, he designed the campanile in the Piazza Contarena (1527; now Piazza Vittorio Emanuele). In 1531 he was summoned back to Rome by Clement VII to decorate a chapel in St Peter's and was then set to work on Medici projects in Florence. In 1532 Giovanni began work on the stucco decoration for Michelangelo's Medici Chapel in S Lorenzo, Florence, but the project was never completed. It was probably at this time that he designed the stained-glass windows with exquisite grotesques in the Laurentian Library (Florence, Bib. Medicea-Laurenziana), attached to the monastery of S Lorenzo. In 1534, when Clement VII died, Giovanni returned to Udine, where he married and eventually had 12 sons. In 1537 he began to decorate a room in the Palazzo Grimani, Venice, for the brothers Giovanni and Vettor Grimani, with *Myths of Diana* in his most elegant stuccowork; in 1540, in another room of the palace, he created an elaborate stucco framework for painted *Myths of Apollo* by Francesco Salviati (all *in situ*). Over the next decade Giovanni was involved in various unrealized public projects in Udine, where in 1552 he secured an official architectural position. In 1560 he was summoned back to Rome by Pius IV, to undertake the decoration of one of the new Vatican Logge with grotesques and Medici arms. He died while engaged on this work and is buried in the Pantheon.

BIBLIOGRAPHY

Thieme–Becker: 'Udine, Giovanni de'

G. Vasari: *Vite* (1550, rev. 2/1568); ed. G. Milanesi (1878–85), vi

A. Venturi: *Storia* (1901–40), vii/4, ix/2, xi/1

H. Voss: *Die Malerei der Spätrenaissance in Rom*, i (Berlin, 1920)

S. J. Freedberg: *Painting in Italy, 1500–1600*, Pelican Hist. A. (Harmondsworth, 1971)

R. Redig de Campos: 'La stufetta del cardinale Bibbiena in Vaticano', *Röm. Jb. Kstgesch.*, xx (1983), pp. 221–40

E. Bartolini: *Giovanni da Udine* (Udine, 1987)

Udine, Girolamo da. *See* GIROLAMO DA UDINE.

Udine, Martino da. *See* PELLEGRINO DA SAN DANIELE.

Udmurtia. *See under* RUSSIA, §XII, 3.

Udney [Udny]. English family of connoisseurs, collectors and dealers.

(1) Robert Udney (*b* ?Aberdeen, 1722; *d* ?London, 1802). He built up an impressive collection of paintings, which he acquired both through his own purchases and through those of his brother (2) John Udney. His connoisseurial expertise was called upon when he acted as a witness in the dispute between rival dealers Noel Desenfans and Benjamin Vandergucht over a fake Poussin (*see* VANDERGUCHT, (4)). He patronized James Barry and Giovanni Battista Piranesi dedicated two plates in *Vasi, candelabri, cippi, sarcophagi. . .* (Rome, 1778) to him. He appears to have taken great interest in the contemporary art world and in the education of young artists. He regarded his collection as a nucleus of a potential national repository of Old Master paintings, and, according to his will, the Royal Academy was to be given a chance to acquire the collection before it was placed on the open market. The Council declined the offer, however, and the paintings were sold at auction at Christie's (18 and 19 May, 1804). The collection included a large number of works by Flemish and Dutch artists. Among the paintings acquired for him by his brother John were the *Virgin with the Infant Jesus and St John* by Fra Bartolommeo, purchased from the collection of the Marchese Albergotti at Arezzo as a model for Raphael's *Madonna della Seggiola*, the *Holy Family with St John* by Raphael, purchased from Albergotti at the same time, and Correggio's *Danaë* (Rome, Gal. Borghese), which John Udney had acquired on the open market in 1780 and sent to England in 1793. Among a large number of drawings, mainly by 17th- and 18th-century Italian artists, was a series of works by Guercino. Prints, books, books of prints, furniture and sculpture from the collection were sold by Philipe Scott (26 May–10 June 1802; 11 June 1802) and Christie's (9–11 July 1804).

(2) John Udney (*b* ?Aberdeen, 1727; *d* London, Jan 1800). Brother of (1) Robert Udney. Very little is known about his life. He is officially recorded as British Consul in Venice (1773–4) and Livorno (May 1787–February 1788) and probably lived in Venice from the early 1760s to 1775 and in Livorno from 1779 to 1796. Contemporary accounts describe him as a socially adept man of considerable connoisseurship, well-connected both in Venetian and Livornese society as well as with British Grand Tourists, and in possession of a choice collection of Old Master paintings, for example Guercino's *David with the Head of Goliath*, which can be traced back to the collection of Ranuccio II Farnese. In addition to being a discerning collector who acquired works with a provenance from the most prestigious Italian collections, Udney was also a shrewd art dealer. In 1762, he bought works of art from the Gherardo Sagredo collection (*see* SAGREDO, ZACCARIA), managing to obtain 'discounts' on the prices stipulated by the heirs. He also dealt in copies of Old Master paintings. In February 1789 Carlo Cantoni dispatched to Udney in Livorno three cases of pictures which included copies of Andrea del Sarto's *Holy Family with Angels*, Raphael's *Madonna della Seggiola* and Guido Reni's *David*. Around the same period Cosimo Fioravanti is recorded to have copied paintings by Jacopo Bassano, Carlo Maratta and Reni, among others, which Udney intended to ship to London, and on 12 March 1789 he is reported to have encountered difficulties in obtaining export licences for some originals, among them a *Madonna and Child with St John the Baptist*, attributed to Raphael, and a *Martyrdom of St Lawrence* by Baccio Bandinelli. Paintings from the collection sold at auction at Christie's on 25 April 1800 and 28 May 1802, included a large number by or given to such artists as Raphael, Salvatore Rosa, Guercino, the Carracci family, Guido Reni, Domenichino, as well as Parmigianino and Correggio.

UNPUBLISHED SOURCES
London, Christie's Archv
London, Mellon Cent., Brinsley Ford priv. col.

BIBLIOGRAPHY
W. Whitley: *Artists and their Friends 1700–99* (London and Boston, 1928), ii

☐

Ueblbacher, Hieronymus. *See* ÜBELBACHER, HIERONYMUS.

Uecker, Günther (*b* Mecklenburg, 13 March 1930). German sculptor and stage designer. He studied painting at the Kunstakademie in Berlin-Weissensse (1949–53), working first in the style of Socialist Realism. During his period at the Kunstakademie in Düsseldorf he undertook self-imposed repetitive exercises such as archery, and he modelled his first relief-form paintings by hand. In 1957 he made his first relief structures with nails leading to works such as *White Picture* (nails on canvas on wood, 1959; Krefeld, Kaiser-Wilhelm Mus.). He also incorporated corks (e.g. *Cork Picture Light Medium*, 1960; Düsseldorf, Kstmus.) and cardboard tubes set into the surface of the painting. The nailed picture became the antithesis of the painted picture; it allowed Uecker to explore the articulation of light through the shadows created by the nails, the unchanging ritual of hammering and the violation of taboo surfaces. In 1958 he began to work on circular nail formations, leading in 1961 to his rotating nailed illuminated discs.

Within the Zero group, which he joined in 1961 after participating in the exhibition *Das rote Bild* in Otto Piene's studio (1958), Uecker developed fantastic projects to jolt and stimulate the imagination of an ossified society, such as painting a street white as part of the Zero demonstration in 1961 (see Honisch and Haedecke, p. 69). From 1963 he nailed items of furniture such as chairs, pianos and television sets, for example *TV on Table* (artist's col., see Honisch and Haedecke, p. 194). Rotation continued, for example in the nailed fabric sculptures that inflate through centrifugal force, or in the *Sand Mills*. After 1967, influenced by Land art, Body art and Conceptual art, Uecker's work slowly moved towards a critical analysis of prevalent structures, exemplified by *Chichicastenango* (1980; Krefeld, Pax Christi Church), a nailed-up boat symbolic of the martyrdom of South American Indians by the Catholic missions. The *Black Mesa* cycle of 1984 (artist's col.; Kiel, Christian Alberts-U., Ksthalle), exhibited in Mönchengladbach at the Städtisches Museum Abteiburg, takes as its theme the threatening of a table mountain in South Dakota holy to the Indians. From 1974 Uecker made several stage sets for opera productions including *Fidelio* (Bremen), *Parsifal* (1976; Stuttgart) and *Lohengrin* (1979; Bayreuth Festival).

WRITINGS
S. von Wiese, ed.: *Günther Uecker: Schriften, Gedichte— Projektbeschreibungen—Reflexionen* (St Gallen, 1979)
ed.: *Der geschundene Mensch* (exh. cat., Stuttgart, Inst. Auslandsbeziehungen, 1993)

BIBLIOGRAPHY
D. Honisch and M. Haedecke: *Uecker* (Stuttgart, 1983; Eng. trans., New York, 1986) [cat. rais.]
Günther Uecker: Eine Retrospektive (exh. cat., ed. D. Honisch; Munich, Ksthalle Hypo-Kultstift, 1983)

STEPHAN VON WIESE

Uelsmann, Jerry N(orman) (*b* Detroit, 11 June 1934). American photographer. He studied photography with Ralph Hattersley (1886–1971) and Minor White at Rochester Institute of Technology, NY, from 1953 to 1957, and with Henry Holmes Smith (*b* 1909) at Indiana University Graduate School, Bloomington, from 1958 to 1960. From 1960 he taught photography at the University of Florida in Gainsville, and in 1962 he was a co-founder of the Friends of Photography in Carmel, occasionally taking an administrative role. Uelsmann's photography deals with fictions and visions that are close to the imagery of René Magritte; his photograph *Magritte's Touchstone* (1965; see Uelsmann, 1975) depicts the head of a woman asleep in a field, with a rock mysteriously hanging in the sky above her. By combining several negatives to make one picture he confronted various levels of reality; in works such as *Rock Tree* (1969; see Uelsmann, 1975), the foreground ambiguously reads as either a reflection in a pool of the hybrid tree, or a cross-section of the roots below, cryptically playing on the perception of reality and its depiction.

PHOTOGRAPHIC PUBLICATIONS
8 Photographs: Jerry Uelsmann (New York, 1970)
Jerry N. Uelsmann, intro. P. C. Bunnell (New York, 1970/*R* 1973)
Jerry Uelsmann: Silver Meditations (New York, 1975)

BIBLIOGRAPHY
J. Szarkowski: *Jerry N. Uelsmann* (New York, 1967)
J. Ward: *The Criticism of Photography as Art: The Photographs of Jerry Uelsmann* (New York, 1970)
Jerry N. Uelsmann: Photographs from 1975–79 (exh. cat., intro. S. Klindt, essay J. Enyeart; Chicago, Cent. Contemp. Phot., 1980)

REINHOLD MISSELBECK

Uemon. *See* NISHIKAWA SUKENOBU.

Uemura, Shōen (*b* Kyoto, 23 April 1875; *d* Nara Prefect., 27 Aug 1949). Japanese painter. In 1887 she entered the Kyoto Prefectural Art School and studied under Shōnen Suzuki, but in 1888 she left the school and studied the techniques of Japanese-style painting (*Nihonga; see* JAPAN, §VI, 5(iii)) in the works of Shōnen Suzuki, Bairei Kōno and Seihō Takeuchi. In 1907 she exhibited powerful works at the first Bunten, the Ministry of Education exhibition, where she later exhibited annually and won a number of prizes. As a painter of *bijin* ('beautiful women'), Uemura's works were important in establishing a modern, refined style that broke away from the popular images of *bijin* established by *ukiyoe* ('pictures of the floating world') and was based on the realistic techniques of the Maruyama–Shijō school (*see* JAPAN, §VI, 4(iv)(b) and (vii)). Among her most important works is *Mother and Child* (1934; Tokyo, N. Mus. Mod. A.). In 1941 she became a member of the Imperial Art Academy, and in 1948 she was the first woman to receive the Order of Cultural Merit.

BIBLIOGRAPHY
Uemura Shōen (Kyoto, 1990)

YOSHIKAZU IWASAKI

Uffelen, Lucas van (*b* Amsterdam, after 1575; *d* Amsterdam, 1637). Flemish merchant, patron and collector. He belonged to an Antwerp family which had moved to Amsterdam for religious reasons. Working for the family firm, by 1616 he was established in Venice, dealing in armaments and the fitting-out of ships. He returned to Amsterdam in the early 1630s. Like other foreign residents of the day in Italy, such as Jan Reynst and Daniel Nys in Venice and Gaspare Roomer in Naples, van Uffelen developed a taste for art patronage and collecting. He owned work by Jusepe de Ribera and is said to have commissioned paintings from, among others, Francesco Albani, Domenichino and Guercino with the object of comparing styles. As a focus for north European artists in Italy, he was the dedicatee of prints by Aegidius II Sadeler and Abraham Casembroot (a marine painter in Messina), and by Anthony van Dyck, who may have painted his portrait: two portraits (New York, Met.; Brunswick, Herzog Anton Ulrich-Mus.) have been identified as of either van Uffelen or Daniel Nys. He was in contact with the Flemish painter and art dealer in Genoa, Cornelius de Wael, and knew Joachim von Sandrart I in Venice in 1627–8. It was Sandrart who arranged van Uffelen's purchase of the marble statue *Cupid Carving his Bow* by François Du Quesnoy. Van Uffelen's collection of 16th-century pictures included Raphael's portrait of *Baldassare Castiglione* (Paris, Louvre) and, among many Venetian paintings, Lorenzo Lotto's portrait of *Andrea Odoni* (1527; London, Hampton Court, Royal Col.). Some paintings may have been sent to members of the family still resident in Antwerp but the remainder were dispersed at sales in Amsterdam, one on van Uffelen's death and another on 9 April 1639, when the Castiglione portrait was sold to the dealer Alfonso Lopez for 3,500 florins, an event recorded by Rembrandt.

BIBLIOGRAPHY

C. Ridolfi: *Meraviglie* (1648); ed. D. von Hadeln (1914–24)
J. von Sandrart: *Teutsche Academie* (1675–9); ed. A. R. Peltzer (1925)
M. Vaes: *Le Séjour d'Antoine Van Dyck en Italie* (Rome, 1924); extract from *Bull. Inst. Hist. Belge Rome*, iv (1924), pp. 163–234
——: 'Corneille de Wael', *Bull. Inst. Hist. Belge Rome*, v–vii (1925), pp. 137–247

JANET SOUTHORN

Uffenbach, Philipp (*b* Frankfurt am Main, *bapt* 15 Jan 1566; *bur* Frankfurt am Main, 6 April 1636). German painter, engraver, etcher and cartographer. He was the most renowned painter in Frankfurt *c.* 1600, but little of his work has been preserved or studied. He is most often cited as the teacher of Adam Elsheimer and for his reports to Joachim von Sandrart about Grünewald. He had inherited a volume of Grünewald's drawings from Adam Grimmer (*d* Mainz, *c.* 1598), believed to be the son of Grünewald's only known pupil, Johann Grimmer; these drawings were sold in 1639 by Uffenbach's widow to the collector Abraham Schelkens (1606–48). Uffenbach's work is typical of the German painters of the so-called Dürer-Renaissance, who took a renewed interest in the work of their early 16th-century forebears.

Sandrart said that Uffenbach was trained by Adam Grimmer. By 1592 he had returned to Frankfurt, where he took over the workshop of the painter Elias Hoffmann and married his daughter. He only became a citizen in 1598; the document cites him as *Philips Ofenbach, Maler*, spelt like the neighbouring town on the River Main. He received numerous municipal commissions for cartographic work and for the prestigious project of mural decorations for the bridge tower (1609–10; destr. 1801). His early work, for instance *St Mary Magdalen Lamenting under the Cross* (1588; Frankfurt am Main, Städel. Kstinst.) reflects careful study of early 16th-century German art. Grünewald's influence is especially obvious in the engraving *Resurrection* (1588; Andresen, no. 2) and in a watercolour drawing of *St Anthony Abbot Receiving Bread from a Raven* (1590; Göttingen, Kstsamml. U.). His most important extant work, the *Ascension* altarpiece (1599; Frankfurt am Main, Hist. Mus.), commissioned by the Pithan family for the Dominican church, was clearly based on Dürer's famous Heller Altarpiece in composition, dimensions and individual figures, and was placed near it as a type of pendant altarpiece. The panel includes a self-portrait of the artist in the left background.

Uffenbach's extant graphic oeuvre is small, consisting of five signed and dated single-sheet etchings (A 1–5), a variety of book illustrations and a series of signed etchings of 1596 illustrating military history (A 6–11). With his pupil Adam Elsheimer, Uffenbach supplied most of the illustrations for the Frankfurt *Messrelationen*, news-sheets reporting on world events that were published twice a year for the Frankfurt fairs in the spring and autumn. Among about a dozen preserved paintings, the *Adoration of the Magi* (1587; Weimar, Schlossmus.) and a tiny panel on the same theme, executed in a miniaturist style (1615; Frankfurt am Main, Hist. Mus.), are of particular interest. Beginning in 1618 Uffenbach executed the ceiling decorations (destr. *c.* 1818) in Schloss Butzbach for Philipp III of Hesse, illustrating 31 scenes from Hessian and Thuringian history, for which he was paid 5000 gulden. In 1630 he was a founding member of Frankfurt's Malergesellschaft. Uffenbach also pursued a scientific career. His knowledge of astronomy, mathematics, geography and cartography is evident in his publications, *Zeitweiser der Sonnen über die ganze Welt* (Frankfurt am Main, 1598) and *De quadratura circuli mechanici* (1619).

BIBLIOGRAPHY

Thieme–Becker
J. von Sandrart: *Teutsche Academie* (1675–9); ed. A. R. Peltzer (1925)
A. Andresen: *Der deutsche Peintre-Graveur*, iv (Leipzig, 1874), pp. 313–24 [A]
O. Donner von Richter: 'Philipp Uffenbach', *Archv Frankfurt. Gesch. & Kst*, n. s. 2, vii (1901), pp. 1–220
H. Weizsäcker: *Die Kunstschätze des ehemaligen Dominikanerklosters in Frankfurt am Main*, 2 vols (Munich, 1923), pp. 260ff, nos xxxii–xxxiv
——: *Adam Elsheimer: Der Maler von Frankfurt*, i (Berlin, 1936), pp. 19–20, 31–7, nos 2–4
W. Prinz, ed.: *Gemälde des Historischen Museums Frankfurt* (Frankfurt am Main, 1957), pp. 84–5
K. Andrews: *Adam Elsheimer: Paintings, Drawings, Prints* (New York, 1977), pp. 13–16
G. F. Koch: 'Adam Elsheimers Anfänge als Maler in Frankfurt', *Jb. Berlin. Mus.*, n. s. xix (1977), pp. 114–71, esp. pp. 117–19, 127–68, nos 4, 7, 11, 13, 14, 17, 44, 46, 52

CHRISTIANE ANDERSSON

Uffington Horse. Figure of a horse cut into the chalk downland at Uffington in the Vale of the White Horse, Oxfordshire, England (see fig.). It is the most distinctive and possibly the earliest extant British HILL-FIGURE. This flowing figure of a slender horse, 120 m long, lies close to

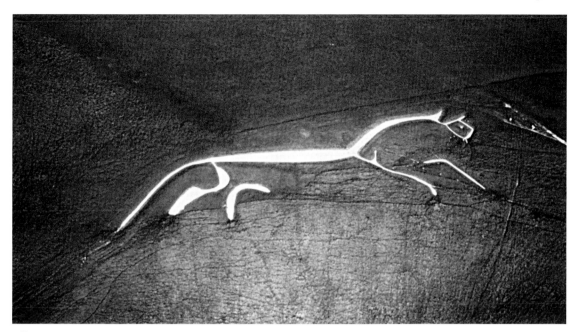

Uffington Horse, chalk hill-figure, l. 120 m, probably 1st century BC, Uffington, Oxfordshire

the ramparts of the Iron Age hill-fort of Uffington Castle. The horse faces right, its exaggerated thin neck supporting a head with a large eye and beak-like mouth. The slim, lightly curved line of the body leads to a tail the length of the hind legs. Two of the horse's legs are attached to the body; one foreleg is separate, emphasizing the feeling of perspective, and the second hindleg is represented as a separate curve under the horse's hip.

A 13th-century manuscript included this horse as one of the wonders of Britain, second only to Stonehenge; but there has been considerable debate as to whether it has always taken its present form. There are 18th-century representations of the Uffington Horse drawn in a more conventional manner, but these may have been the result of alterations made to a type of image unfamiliar to the artist recording it. In its present disjointed form the horse bears a strong resemblance to horses shown on British coins of the 1st century BC. These coins, based ultimately on the gold stater of Philip of Macedon, show Celtic versions of the images of a head on the obverse and a chariot and horses on the reverse: the original designs are broken up and individual elements, such as the laurel wreath and the horse, are isolated. The leaping, loosely defined horses on these coins are closely replicated by the Uffington Horse, lending strength to the claim that the hill-figure was cut in the 1st century BC. Archaeological work on the figure has shown that, though the belly may once have been 1 m wider than at present, it never attained the width portrayed in the 18th century, and that the horse's shape has remained essentially unchanged. Examination of the 'beaked' mouth showed a succession of four beaks interspersed with colluvium (accumulated material). The material below the first beak is prehistoric, and the figure could thus be genuinely early.

BIBLIOGRAPHY
S. Piggott: 'The Uffington White Horse', *Antiquity*, v (1931), pp. 16–18
M. Marples: *White Horses and Other Hill Figures* (London, 1949)
SARA CHAMPION

Ugalde, Manuel (*b* Cuenca, Ecuador, *c.* 1805; *d* Cochabamba, Bolivia, after 1888). Ecuadorian painter, active in Bolivia. He arrived in Bolivia a few years after it gained independence in 1825. He worked in Cuzco (Peru), La Paz, Potosí and Sucre and spent the last years of his life in Cochabamba. His painting of the *Valley of Cochabamba* (1830; Cochabamba, City Hall), portraying the valley and the city, ushered in a new era in landscape painting in Bolivia, replacing the imaginary landscapes and conceptual perspective of the painting of the preceding colonial period with a greater concern for accuracy. He also painted portraits of important dignitaries, such as *Marshal Andrés de Santa Cruz* (*c.* 1839; La Paz, priv. col.) and *President Gregorio Pacheco* (1884; La Paz, Bib. Mun.). His painting is academic in style, with grey and unemotional colours.

BIBLIOGRAPHY
M. Chacón Torres: *Pintores del siglo XIX*, Bib. A. & Cult. Boliv.: A. & Artistas (La Paz, 1963)
P. Querejazu: *La pintura boliviana del siglo XX* (Milan, 1989)
PEDRO QUEREJAZU

Uganda, Republic of. Land-locked country in East Africa, bordered by Sudan to the north, Kenya to the east, Tanzania and Rwanda to the south, and Zaïre to the west. The total area is 236,036 sq. km and the population 17,500,000 (UN estimate, 1990). The capital is Kampala. Uganda's high altitude modifies a tropical climate, preventing extremes of temperature or rainfall. The official language is English. After 70 years of British rule, Uganda became independent in 1962, and was instituted as a republic in 1967. Uganda continues to be a multi-ethnic, multi-cultural state incorporating such culturally vibrant kingdoms as those of Buganda, Bunyoro, Toro and Ankole. As in many other African countries, however, this cultural vibrancy has been greatly scarred by the effects of colonialism, and later neo-colonialism. The development of traditional arts have been overshadowed by the forceful development of new art forms. This article covers the art produced in Uganda since colonial times; for art of the area in earlier times *see* AFRICA, §VII, 7.

1. CONTINUING TRADITIONS. Many of Uganda's traditional arts are still widely practised, especially such performing arts as dance, theatre and music. Traditional architecture also continues to be made in the villages. Right across the country, each family or group of families construct their own houses using such readily available materials as mud and stone, as well as wood and grass. In so doing, families are not just concerned with the functional aspects of their future homesteads. The often cylindrical, rectangular or square-shaped dwellings embody highly pronounced aesthetic characteristics in their shapes and decorative appearance. Indeed, in many villages, families compete in beautifying their homes, and the best-decorated homesteads are accorded public acknowledgement.

The traditional decorative arts continue to be popular in some parts of Uganda. For example, pottery is decorated with varieties of incised patterning, and, in some areas, the art of body decoration is highly developed. Pottery, basketwork, printed textiles, wood and ivory carvings, and other traditional crafts made from skin and bark-cloth continue to be produced in various parts of the country.

Traditional musical instruments also continue to be produced. These include the xylophone and the thumb piano, the lyre, harp, lute and stick zither, and wind instruments, made from reeds, bamboo, animal horns, metal or even pots and gourds. The most widespread musical instrument, however, is the drum, which is found throughout the country.

2. PAINTING, GRAPHIC ARTS AND SCULPTURE. A number of Ugandan artists have established successful careers and gained international recognition. Gard Okello (*b* 1941) studied fine arts at the University of Nairobi, Kenya, and later took a postgraduate Diploma in Education at Makerere University. Before working full time as an artist and designer, Okello taught design at the University of Nairobi. Okello's screenprints and batiks on cotton have been widely exhibited. The printmaker Richard Ndabagoye (*b* 1937) has lived in Uganda since 1960, having grown up in Kigoma, Tanganyika. His interest in art was first aroused through doing odd jobs at the Makerere School of Art. The lecturers Jonathan Kingdon and Michael Adams taught him lithography and etching. Ndabagoye first exhibited at the Nommo Gallery in Kampala, and has since become one of Uganda's better-known artists. His lithographs most commonly feature birds and animals in a naive style, and occasionally landscapes and people.

Francis Nnaggenda (*b* 1936) trained at the Akademie der Bildenden Künste in Munich, gaining the title Meisterschüler in 1967, living before and after in Uganda. He is best known for his large sculptures and carvings made from metal and palm-wood, which often deal with themes of destruction and dehumanization. Nnaggenda has exhibited internationally, including shows at the African Art Gallery, Santa Monica, CA, in 1975, and the University of Texas in 1977, and locally at Uganda's Nommo Gallery in Kampala. Mordechai Ochungo Buluma graduated from the Makerere School of Art in 1960 and continued his studies in Canada. He taught art at the Uganda Technical College before heading the education division of the Uganda Museum. As well as working in the Ministry of Culture, Buluma has been the administrator of the Nommo Gallery in Kampala.

While training at the Makerere School of Art, Francis Musango won the Margaret Trowell Prize for best performance. He has since gone on to study for a number of postgraduate degrees, including a Master of Education from Makerere University. Musango is a fellow of the Royal College of Art, London. His work has been exhibited throughout Africa, Britain and the USA, and examples of his work are held in many private collections.

Among successful Ugandan artists using the medium of batik are Katongole Kakooza Wasswa and W. Lukange. Using the craft techniques in the most intricate ways to depict Ugandan scenes, their works have been exhibited widely, including the opening exhibition at the African Art Gallery in Santa Monica, CA, in 1974. Muhammad Kamulegeya (*b* 1944) also works in batik. He trained at the Makerere School of Art, majoring in painting. His batiks and paintings have been exhibited in Uganda, Kenya, Tanzania, and at 'Festac 77' in Nigeria. Francis Sekitoleko (*b* 1939) works mainly in batiks and oil. Sekitoleko studied graphic design at the University of Nairobi, later taking a postgraduate Diploma in Education at Makerere University. He paints scenes of Ugandan daily life, often with Christian themes.

3. ART INSTITUTIONS. Many of Uganda's most successful artists, as well as many from other East African countries, have trained at Makerere University's Margaret Trowell School of Fine Arts (often referred to as the Makerere School of Art). The first formal art classes were held there in 1939, and a four-year degree course was later established. Students there have continued to produce work throughout the times of Uganda's political upheaval and confusion. In the early 1990s the practical courses included sculpture and modelling, graphics, screen printing, lithography, photography and ceramics. The first colour-illustrated magazine printed in Uganda, *Roho*, was written and produced at the art school. Art is also taught at secondary school level in many schools. (*See also* AFRICA, §IX, 3.)

Attached to the Makerere School of Fine Arts is the Makerere Art Gallery, which opened in 1968, funded initially by the Calouste Gulbenkian Foundation. The gallery holds outstanding works by staff and artists associated with the art school in a collection that was begun by Margaret Trowell in 1940. The Nommo Gallery in Kampala is one of the most popular cultural centres in the city. Funded in part by the government, and also privately, it promotes Ugandan and East African contemporary art and is much patronized by tourists. The Uganda Museum in Kampala was founded in 1908. The collections mainly comprise ethnography, music, archaeology and history. A temporary exhibition gallery often exhibits the work of Ugandan artists.

BIBLIOGRAPHY

K. M. Trowell: 'Modern African Art in East Africa', *Man*, xlvii/1 (1947), pp. 1–7

M. Trowell and K. P. Waschmann: *Arts and Crafts in Uganda* (London, 1953)

M. Trowell: *African Tapestry* (London, 1957)

——: *A Handbook of the Museums and Libraries in Uganda* (Kampala, 1957)

M. Posnansky: 'The Uganda Museum', *Mus. J.: Organ Mus. Assoc.*, lix/11 (1960), pp. 253–9

——: 'The Uganda Museum, Kampala: The Programme and Organization', *Museum* [Kampala], xvi/3 (1963), pp. 149–53

V. Vowles: 'The Uganda Museum, Kampala: The Public', *Museum* [Kampala], xvi/3 (1963), pp. 153–5

G. Kwanai: 'Nommo Gallery', *Transition* [Kampala], iv (1965), p. 39

S. Ntiro: 'The Future of East African Art', *East Africa's Cultural Heritage* (Nairobi, 1965), pp. 55–69

Uganda Crafts, Ministry of Culture and Community Development (Kampala, 1965)

S. L. Kasfir: 'Nnaggenda: Experimental Ugandan Artist', *Afr. A.*, iii/1 (1969), pp. 8–13, 88

J. von Daler: 'A New Gallery in Kampala', *Afr. A.*, iv/1 (1970), pp. 50–52

A. M. Lugira: *Ganda Art* (Kampala, 1970); review by D. Banabakintu in *J. Afr. Relig. & Philos.*, i/2 (1990), pp. 137–40

W. Enwaku: 'Exhibition of Uganda Prints', *Afr. A.*, iv/2 (1971), p. 74

E. Nankya: '1970 Prizewinners', *Afr. A.*, iv/2 (1971), pp. 8–17

S. L. Kasfir: 'Richard Ndabagoye: Kampala Printmaker', *Afr. A.*, v/3 (1972), pp. 32–6

E. Kyekune: 'Art in Uganda and its Relationship to Other Aspects of Culture', *Mawazo*, iv/1 (1973), pp. 29–35

R. W. Freeman: 'Gandan Batiks', *Afr. A.*, viii/1 (1974), p. 70

J. von D. Miller: *Art in East Africa: A Guide to Contemporary Art* (Nairobi and London, 1975)

J. Povey: 'Francis Nnaggenda', *Afr. A.*, viii/3 (1975), p. 75

M. Lawrence: 'Francis Nnaggenda', *Afr. A.*, xi/1 (1977), p. 78

R. Coates: 'Gard Okello', *Afr. A.*, xii/2 (1979), p. 64

E. C. Burt: *An Annotated Bibliography of the Visual Arts of East Africa*, Trad. A. Africa (Bloomington, IN, 1980)

J. Agthe: *Wegzeichen: Kunst aus Ostafrika, 1974–1989/Signs: Art of East Africa, 1974–1989*, Frankfurt am Main, Mus. Vlkerknd. cat. (Frankfurt am Main, 1990) [includes interviews with artists]

S. Peters and others, eds: *Directory of Museums in Africa/Répertoire des musées en Afrique* (London and New York, 1990)

N. Guez: *L'Art africain contemporain/Contemporary African Art: Guide Edition, 92–94* (Paris, 1992)

PAULINOS VINCENT MAGOMBE

Ugarit [Ougarit; now Ras Shamra]. Canaanite city on the Mediterranean coast of Syria, 11 km north of Latakia, which flourished in the 2nd millennium BC. The tell of Ras Shamra rises 20 m above a fertile plain bounded to the east by the Jabal al-Nusaytiyya Mountains and to the north by the Jabal Akra (the Mount Cassius of the Ancients, or Mount Sapun of the Ugarit texts). The plain is watered by a large number of wadis, the mouths of which form well-sheltered bays. The site of ancient Ugarit was discovered by chance in 1929. A French archaeological expedition under the direction of Claude Schaeffer first explored the harbour area of Minet el Beida and later the tell, 1 km inland at Ras Shamra. Exploration has continued at Ras Shamra and, from 1974, at a neighbouring site on the Ibn Hani headland. Large sections of the town (which covered 30 ha) were excavated, enabling much of its plan to be reconstructed, including the layout of a sprawling palace and several temples. Many votive stelae have been found, and Ugarit's workshops produced a variety of artefacts, such as bronze figurines, ivories, faience objects, jewellery and metal vessels. Foreign goods from Mesopotamia, inland Syria, the Aegean, Cyprus and Egypt were traded through the neighbouring port of Minet el Beida, and many have been found in the city's vaulted tombs. Finds are mostly in the National Museum in Damascus and in the Louvre in Paris.

Exploration of the tell revealed a Neolithic settlement of the 7th millennium BC. From the Middle Bronze Age (18th–17th centuries BC) onwards, diplomatic and economic texts from other large Syrian centres such as Mari show that the city's name was Ugarit. Its last phase, in the 13th century BC, has been the most thoroughly investigated and has given a clear idea of Ugarit's urban plan. The settlement discovered at Ras Ibn Hani, 6 km further south, was built during this period of intense activity, and the ruins of two palaces or residences were discovered there. Ugarit and this settlement were pillaged, then destroyed and burnt towards 1180 BC, possibly by invaders known as the 'Sea Peoples'. There is some evidence of reoccupation at Ras Ibn Hani, characterized by the ceramics attributed to these peoples, but Ras Shamra was abandoned until the Persian period when, after the 6th century BC, a small settlement was built on top of the tell using the ruins as a quarry. At this time the port of Minet el Beida was given the Greek name of Leukos Limen.

1. Planning and architecture. 2. Sculpture and decorative arts.

1. PLANNING AND ARCHITECTURE. Only that small part of the city walls adjacent to the royal palace survives. A postern with corbelled vaulting, later replaced by a monumental gateway with a ramp, gave access to the palace complex. Nothing is known of the other city gates. A network of narrow streets followed the curves of the tell's contours. Short culs-de-sac or transverse alleys led to the heart of the blocks of buildings. Breaks in the alignment of the roads show that they were laid down progressively as new building expanded on to open land. Individual water systems of wells and basins, drains and cesspools show the care taken with water storage and drainage. Inside the palace complex an enormous sewer with corbelled vaulting took waste water towards the outside of the tell, passing under neighbouring buildings.

(i) The palace. The royal palace of Ugarit (see fig.) was a vast complex entirely surrounded by an irregular defensive wall that isolated it from the rest of the city. Only two gates gave access to this enclosure: one in the west from the direction of the city wall, and one in the east from the city centre. The complex was built with one or more upper storeys, where the residential areas were situated. A large pool of fresh water and a vast courtyard garden embellished the ground level, which was otherwise occupied by the guards' and servants' quarters and the arsenal. Texts written in cuneiform on clay tablets mention stores of arms such as chariots, bows and lances. Supplies for the royal family and their household were stored there, and also goods intended for trade, as the palace was an economic and industrial centre. There were probably workshops, as in the northern palace of Ras Ibn Hani, where a metal-casting installation and a mould in the shape of an oxhide (used to cast copper ingots) were found.

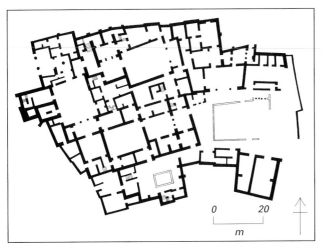

Ugarit, royal palace, 14th–13th centuries BC, plan

Accounts were kept of all these activities, which were overseen by civil servants known as 'the king's men'.

(ii) The temples. Two large sanctuaries, probably erected during the 18th and 17th centuries BC, stood on the summit of the acropolis. One, the Temple of Dagon, was identified by an inscribed stele. The other has revealed a rich collection of objects connected with its cult, including a stone stele representing Baal, the storm-god (*see* §2 below). These sanctuaries have the characteristic shape of 2nd-millennium BC Syrian temples and have numerous parallels in the Levant and at Ebla, Maskana, Emar and Tell Atchana. They consist of free-standing buildings with an antechamber and an axial cella, within a walled perimeter or temenos. The very thick walls and the presence of a stairway indicate an upper storey. The Temple of Baal, on the very summit of the acropolis, probably served as a landmark for sailors entering the bay of Minet el Beida. Numerous stone anchors placed within the temple enclosure as votive offerings strongly suggest that the temple was the object of particular veneration by sailors.

The existence of other places of worship is indicated by texts, which mention a 'house' for each of the many divinities in the Ugarit pantheon. Excavation has uncovered, in the middle of the tell, a 'sanctuary of the rhyta' with a very different layout. A vast hall, surrounded by stone benches on three sides and terracing on the fourth, opens on to a small cul-de-sac off a main street. A small room lies on one side. A dozen stone or pottery rhytons, the latter either local or imported from Cyprus and Mycenae, were found in this section of the sanctuary. There was also a fragment of a cult stand carved with the figure of a king in prayer.

(iii) The settlement. More than 50 years of excavations have uncovered a large area of the settlement. There is no apparent spatial division by social rank or activity; vast dwellings built in ashlar masonry stand side by side with smaller houses made of rubble stone. Furthermore, small houses (e.g. those identified by texts found in them as occupied by Rapanu or Rashapabu) had extremely refined ashlar masonry bonds, while enormous residences like the

'house of the alabasters' were built of ordinary masonry. The periphery of the tell, where polluting industries may have been located, is badly ruined, but there does not seem to have been a special neighbourhood devoted to craft or industry. On the contrary, it appears that these activities took place on the ground floors of houses, where domestic storerooms were also situated. Small oil presses, jars, mortars and grinders used to prepare food have been found, as well as quantities of flints, which were used in sickles to cut reeds, probably for thatching. Everything suggests that the city lived in symbiosis with the surrounding countryside, and that some agricultural activities could be carried out on the city's edge or even within it.

The inhabitants of Ugarit lived in close proximity to the world of the dead. Nearly every house was built with a family vault in the basement, a custom also found in the royal palace, which had its own necropolis within the walls. The most recent tombs, built in the 13th century BC, have superb corbelled roofs.

2. SCULPTURE AND DECORATIVE ARTS. The figurative arts illustrate the refinement achieved by the workshops of Ras Shamra. They are striking in the profoundly religious character of their iconography, which constitutes a precious source of information for the reconstruction of Ugarit's pantheon. Votive stelae with curved tops and a trapezoidal shape bear images of the major gods of the local pantheon. The stele of the Temple of Baal (*see* SYRIA-PALESTINE, fig. 7) represents Baal as a storm-god and protector of royalty; he is slender and dressed in a short kilt, which allows him to stride forward. He holds a mace and a thunderbolt in the shape of a sprouting spear. The king, shown on a smaller scale, is enveloped in a long robe with rolled borders and appears under the protection of the god's arm. The balance of the composition and the grace and dynamism of the figures combine to make this low relief one of the masterpieces of Ancient Near Eastern art. Another stele (Aleppo, N. Mus.) shows El, the father of the gods, enthroned on a chair with arms and back, and wearing a ceremonial robe and an Egyptian-style composite headdress. Before him, a royal figure is carrying out a ritual. The importance of official and royal religion appears here very clearly, as it does in the literature. Bronze figurines were placed in small chapels or in deposits in Ras Shamra and Minet el Beida. These figurines are divided into iconographic archetypes, of which two are analogous with those of the stelae: the young smiting god, of which one of the finest examples, from Minet el Beida, wears a gold-covered Egyptian-style headdress (Paris, Louvre), and the father-god, illustrated by a seated figure (Damascus, Mus. N.), found in the southern part of the city. The father-god's long draped robe and crown are covered in gold leaf, and he is making a gesture of peace, as on the stele. A standing goddess appears as a 'peace figure', wearing the same robe with rolled borders. It is not easy to identify this divinity in the Ugarit pantheon, and her image is rarer than that of Baal. On gold and silver jewellery, however, the 'naked goddess' (perhaps Astarte) is much more popular. She appears in stylized form, reduced to a human mask, breasts and pubic triangle. This jewellery commonly associates her with her astral form—the planet Venus—on star-shaped pendants.

Two decorated bowls discovered near the Temple of Baal, and probably made locally, are among the most perfect examples of the goldsmith's art in the Levant. One of them (Aleppo, N. Mus.), in the shape of a hemisphere, has scenes of monsters and wild animals fighting heroes or royal ancestors in a stylized landscape. The hero appears here as the regulator of the world. The other, a flat-bottomed bowl (Paris, Louvre), shows the royal huntsman in a chariot drawn by two horses. He is shooting with his bow at bulls and stags, which are escaping in a flying gallop. The style harmoniously blends both Syrian and Aegean elements. These two precious bowls with their royal iconography, doubtless princely offerings to Baal, demonstrate yet again the close bonds that united the king to the divine world. Terracotta and glazed earthenware figurines, however, were the expression of a more popular devotion; they include 'naked goddesses' in the local style as well as idols imported from Mycenae, known as 'phi' or 'psi' idols according to the way they hold their arms.

Works in faience and ivory are among the most refined in the Levant. Faience, which appeared in the Middle Bronze Age, at first imitated Egyptian models and their blue glazes. Later, a more individual polychrome style developed, with goblets in the form of flowers, or decorated with female faces in relief (see ANCIENT NEAR EAST, fig. 32). Cakes of Egyptian blue pigment indicate its use in local production of beads, small vases and cylinder seals. Large numbers of make-up boxes, spindles and personal items of high quality were produced in hippopotamus ivory (the hippopotamus survived on the coast of Syria-Palestine until the 1st millennium BC). Make-up boxes in the form of ducks are the purest expression of this craft. Exceptional works intended for the temples or the palace, such as a bed decorated with hunting and mythological scenes expressing royal iconography, were carved in elephant ivory, which had to be imported. One of the panels of this bed (Damascus, Mus. N.) shows a goddess in Egyptian-style dress nursing two royal children, while another shows the victorious king transfixing a fallen enemy with his sword. In addition, many works of art were imported: painted ceramics from Mycenae, alabaster vases from Egypt, amber beads from the Baltic and amulets and lapis lazuli beads from Afghanistan all show how cosmopolitan and artistically aware Ugarit became during the 2nd millennium BC.

For further illustration see ANCIENT NEAR EAST, fig. 27.

BIBLIOGRAPHY
Syria, x– (1929–) [excav. rep. from Ugarit by C. F. A. Schaeffer and others]
Ugaritica, 7 vols (Paris, 1939–78)
J.-C. Courtois and others: 'Ras Shamra', *Supplément au Dictionnaire de la Bible*, ix (1979), cols 1124–1466
G. Saade: *Ougarit: Métropole cananéenne* (Beirut, 1979)
Ebla to Damascus: Art and Archaeology in Ancient Syria (exh. cat., ed. H. Weiss; Washington, DC, Smithsonian Inst., 1985)
M. Yon, ed.: *La Centre de la ville* (1986), iii of *Ras Shamra-Ougarit* (Paris, 1983–6)

ANNIE CAUBET

Ugarte Eléspuru, Juan Manuel (*b* Lima, 11 May 1911). Peruvian painter, sculptor, teacher and critic. His adolescence was spent in Germany and Spain. In 1929 he went to Buenos Aires, studying first (until 1932) at the Escuela Superior Nacional de Artes and then (1933–6) at the Escuela Superior de Bellas Artes 'Ernesto de la Cárcova'. In 1940 he returned to Lima, where he struggled against being absorbed into the Indigenist movement and joined the group Los Independientes, whose members promoted European styles, although not to the exclusion of Peruvian subject-matter (see also PERU, §IV, 2). In 1944 he began teaching at the Escuela Nacional de Bellas Artes, Lima, becoming its Director in 1956. Ugarte Eléspuru's paintings are characterized by rich textures and colours and are often purely abstract (e.g. *Death of Pachacamac the Bullfighter*, 1961; Lima, Mus. A.), although in such murals as *Urban Education* (5.0×6.0 m, 1956; Lima, Ministerio de Educación) he refers broadly to the strong figures and social comment of Mexican murals by Diego Rivera and others. His sculptures include the bust of *Túpac Amaru* (bronze, 1964; Quito, Plaza de los Próceres). He also wrote a number of books about Peruvian art and architecture and acted as a juror and commissioner for a number of international exhibitions.

WRITINGS
Lima y lo limeño (Lima, 1966)
Ignacio Merino y Francisco Laso (Lima, 1968)

BIBLIOGRAPHY
J. Villacorta Paredes: *Pintores peruanos de la República* (Lima, 1971), pp. 85–7
J. A. de Lavalle and W. Lang: *Pintura contemporánea*, Colección arte y tesoros del Perú, ii (Lima, 1976), pp. 100–103

W. IAIN MACKAY

Uglich. Russian town *c.* 200 km north of Moscow on the River Volga, first mentioned in AD 937. From the 12th to the 17th century Uglich consisted of a kremlin on the bank of the Volga, surrounded by the trading quarter fortified with ditches and ramparts, with artisans' settlements beyond. The oldest surviving building is the prince's palace (second half of the 15th century) in the kremlin. It is stone-built, which was unusual in Russia at that time, since almost all secular buildings were constructed of wood. The three-storey palace is square in plan; the smooth stone walls of the lower storeys contrast with the richly decorated brick facing of the upper part of the building. Beside it is the cathedral of the Transfiguration (Spaso-Preobrazhensky; 1485; rebuilt 1713) with its five domes. Uglich is known for its 17th-century religious architecture, including the monastery of the Resurrection (Voskresensky; 1674–7) and the churches of St John the Baptist (1690) and of Dmitry's Blood (1692), built on the site of the murder of Tsarevich Dmitry, son of Ivan IV (*reg* 1547–84). The church of the Dormition, called the Miraculous (Uspenskaya/Divnaya; mid-17th century), in the Alekseyev Monastery is an outstanding example of a hipped-roofed building, with three imposing and well-proportioned hipped roofs that seem to enhance its size. The Smolenskaya (1700) and Korsunskaya (1730) churches are in traditional Russian style while extant 18th-century secular buildings, such as the Kalashnikov and Ovsyannikov houses, are in Baroque style. Rare examples survive of wooden 18th-century urban mansions (e.g. the Voronin House), which retain the forms of medieval secular wooden architecture. The Neo-classical style was first introduced in Uglich in the late 18th century and spread in the 1830s (e.g. the Ozhegov and Bychkov houses). Local antiquities are exhibited in the Uglich Historical Museum.

BIBLIOGRAPHY
F. Kissel': *Istoriya goroda Uglicha* [The history of the town of Uglich] (Yaroslavl', 1859)
Ye. Mikhaylovsky: *Uglich* (Moscow, 1948)
Issledovaniya i materialy po istorii Uglichskogo Verkhovolzh'ya [Research and materials relating to the history of the Uglich area of the Upper Volga], 3 vols (Uglich, 1957–65)
I. Kovalyov: *Uglich* (Yaroslavl', 1960)
V. Ivanov: *Rostov, Uglich* (Moscow, 1968)
I. Kovalyov and I. Purishov: *Uglich* (Yaroslavl', 1978)
B. Kirikov: *Uglich* (Leningrad, 1984)

D. O. SHVIDKOVSKY

Uglow, Euan (*b* London, 10 March 1932). English painter. He trained in London at Camberwell School of Art from 1948 to 1951 and from 1951 to 1954 at the Slade School of Fine Art, where he came under the influence of William Coldstream. His early figurative style adapted a form of planar drawing derived from Alberto Giacometti's work of the 1920s and applied it to a Classical structure, derived from Paul Cézanne, with an intensity of colour unrivalled by his teachers of the Euston Road School. *Musicians* (1953; London, Tate) reinterpreted the Impressionist theme of figures in a landscape by combining directly observed elements with a deliberately contrived backdrop painted on the studio wall.

Uglow was consistently concerned with formal relationships within a self-sufficient system, whatever the subject. He graduated colour according to a tonal scale and used drawing to define three-dimensional form and tactile surfaces. The proportions of the images and of the canvas itself are often mathematically derived, as in the *Nude from Twelve Regular Vertical Positions from the Eye* (1967; U. Liverpool). There is a strong conceptual element in Uglow's work, with each picture regarded as a specific project with clearly defined aims. The end product unambiguously reveals the history of its making by a prolonged and entirely conscious process of analysis and synthesis, combining objectivity with a private and often quirky passion.

BIBLIOGRAPHY
Euan Uglow (exh. cat. by M. Murphy, ACGB, 1974)
Hayward Annual 1979 (exh. cat., ACGB, 1979)

KENNETH G. HAY

Ugly Realism. Term coined to describe the work of a number of artists working in Berlin in the 1970s. These artists combined the fine draughtsmanship of Otto Dix and George Grosz with an iconographical treatment of the 'ugly': this could be a pimple, a deformed limb or a terrorist with a machine-gun, all rendered with a chilling photographic clarity that pointed to the brutality, shallowness, alienation and perversion of modern urban humanity. The objects and figures presented to the observer in such detail were designed to provoke in him a mixture of disgust, revulsion and distaste as well as a reluctance to recognize what was being portrayed. Many of the artists associated with Ugly Realism were originally members of the artists' co-operative gallery in Berlin, Grossgörschen 35, founded in 1964. In 1966 a rift developed between the expressionist faction represented by K. H. Hödicke, Markus Lüpertz and Koberling and the so-called critical

realists, Ulrich Baehr (*b* 1938), Charles Diehl, Wolfgang Petrick and Peter Sorge (*b* 1937), who later made the Galerie Eva Poll home to this new brand of realism.

Petrick's work is typical of the genre: he combined photographic images from medical books with obsessive pencil and paint work to depict the alienation of the individual from an environment created by the machine. Indeed, his figures are weighed down by contemporary gadgets. In a pencil drawing entitled *Den Vansinniga, blyerts, Furgpenna* (1973; see 1978–9 exh. cat., p. 269), an elderly woman with a monstrous foot is marooned in a tiled kitchen with an iron, some pliers and a portable television, her moronic expression indicative of her isolation from her physical surroundings. Klaus Vogelgesang also created work belonging to the ugly realist category. His microscopic rendering of material surfaces such as leather, silk, steel and flesh produced an uncomfortable sensation of artificiality, as in *Good Morning* (1980), where the surfaces and smiles hide a shallowness, unnaturalness and perversion that reflects bleakly on the moral vacuity of contemporary life.

BIBLIOGRAPHY
Berlin: A Critical View. Ugly Realism '20s–'70s (exh. cat., London, ICA, 1978–9)
Realism and Expressionism in Berlin Art (exh. cat., Los Angeles, UCLA, Wight A.G., 1980–81)

DEBORAH NASH

Ugo da Carpi. *See* CARPI, UGO DA.

Ugolino di Nerio [Ugolino da Siena] (*fl* Siena, 1317; *d* ?Siena, ?1339 or ?1349). Italian painter. He was probably a pupil of Duccio and perhaps his most faithful follower. He is documented in Siena from 1317 to 1327 and appears to have been an important artist with a successful workshop. None of the documents mentions works of art, however, and it has proved difficult to reconstruct his career.

Ugolino's only surviving autograph work is the polyptych of the *Virgin and Child with Saints* that was painted for the high altar of Santa Croce, Florence, *c.* 1325; until at least the 19th century it bore a signature, which has since disappeared. Between 1566 and 1569 the altarpiece, originally some 4.28 m wide, was dismantled to make way for a ciborium designed by Giorgio Vasari, and at the end of the 18th century it was seen in the upper dormitory of Santa Croce by Filippo della Valle. Scholars have attempted to reconstruct this work on the basis of della Valle's descriptions, and those made by Gustav Friedrich Waagen, who saw the surviving fragments in the collection of William Young Ottley in 1835. There is also an 18th-century drawing (Rome, Vatican, Bib. Apostolica, MS. Vat. lat. 9847, fol. 92*r*), made for Jean-Baptiste Séroux d'Agincourt, which shows the altarpiece in its entirety, although by then some of the panels were in a very poor condition, and there appear to be anomalies concerning the frame. At the centre of the altarpiece was the *Virgin and Child* (ex-Young Ottley priv. col., London, 1835); the surviving spandrel angels (Los Angeles, CA, Co. Mus. A.) give an indication of its original width. Each side panel also had spandrel angels. On the right were *St Peter* (Berlin, Bodemus.), *St Francis* and *St Louis of Toulouse* (both untraced); on the left were *St Paul* and *St John the Baptist* (both Berlin, Bodemus.) and a Franciscan saint, probably *St Anthony of Padua* (untraced). Above the main tier were paired figures of saints and Apostles: on the right were *St James the Greater* and *St Philip* (Berlin, Bodemus.), *St Simon* and *St Thaddeus* (London, N.G.) and *St Matthias* and *St Elisabeth of Hungary* (Berlin, Bodemus.; see fig.); on the left were *St Bartholomew* and *St Andrew* (London, N.G.), *St Matthew* and *St James the Less* (Berlin, Bodemus.), ?*St Clare* and a male saint (untraced). Above the main panel was a *Crucifixion* (untraced), already ruined in the 18th century. Finally, the top pinnacles depicted, on the right, *Moses* (London, N.G.), ?*Jeremiah* (untraced) and *Daniel* (Philadelphia, PA, Mus. A.) and, on the left, *David* (London, N.G.) and *Isaiah* (London, N.G.; for illustration *see* TEMPERA) and ?*Ezekiel* (untraced). All the predella panels survive, although the arms of the Alamanni family (who probably commissioned the altarpiece), which would probably have been on the predella, are missing. The predella consisted of a Passion cycle: the *Last Supper* (New York, Met.), the *Betrayal* (London, N.G.), the *Flagellation* (Berlin, Bodemus.), the *Road to Calvary* and the *Deposition* (both London, N.G.; for illustration *see* PUNCH), the *Lamentation* (Berlin, Bodemus.) and the *Resurrection* (London, N.G.).

The arrangement of the panels of the Santa Croce Altarpiece as shown in the drawing has been confirmed by X-rays, which reveal the patterns of the wood grain and the siting of the dowel holes that locked the vertical tiers together. At the back the panels were joined with interlocking battens. It is likely that the altarpiece was supported by lateral buttresses. It was almost certainly painted in Siena in seven vertical units and one horizontal unit and then assembled *in situ*. In design it derives from the multi-tiered polyptych as developed by Duccio, with a narrative predella based on Duccio's *Maestà* (for locations *see* DUCCIO); Ugolino's technique differs considerably

Ugolino di Nerio: *St Matthias* and *St Elisabeth of Hungary*, tempera on panel, 562×569 mm, from the Santa Croce Altarpiece, *c.* 1325 (Berlin, Bodemuseum, Gemäldegalerie)

from Duccio's, however, particularly in the former's preference for azurite rather than ultramarine, his very complex palette and his sparing use of underdrawing. The Santa Croce Altarpiece must have been one of the most spectacular and influential works to be painted in Florence in the 1320s. It suggests that Ugolino's mature style was one of elegance and refinement. His figures express an intense spirituality and have a smooth, enamelled appearance.

A second altarpiece, attributed to Ugolino by Vasari, was painted for the high altar of S Maria Novella, Florence, *c.* 1320–24. It had a *Virgin and Child* as its centre panel and must have been almost as large as the Santa Croce Altarpiece, since the surviving altar frontal (Florence, Bargello) indicates a maximum width of 4.38 m, close to the original size of the later work. It once bore the arms of the Sassetti family and was probably commissioned *c.* 1320 by Fra Baro Sassetti (*d* 1324). The fact that a Sienese artist had two such major works on the high altars of the two most important churches in Florence indicates the esteem in which Ugolino was held.

Among the most important surviving works attributed to Ugolino are two Franciscan commissions. One of these is a polyptych of the *Virgin and Child with SS Francis, Andrew, Paul, Peter, Stephen and Louis of Toulouse* (Williamstown, MA, Clark A. Inst.). The spandrels of the rounded arches contain angels, and in the gables are figures of prophets holding inscribed scrolls. Stylistically, it still shows the strong influence of Duccio and has been dated *c.* 1317–25. It has been claimed as the earliest known heptaptych, predating Simone Martini's altarpiece of 1319 painted for S Caterina, Pisa (Pisa, Mus. N. & Civ. S Matteo). Another polyptych, depicting the *Virgin and Child with SS Francis, John the Baptist, James and Mary Magdalene* (Cleveland, OH, Mus. A.), appears to have been painted after the Williamstown Polyptych, but the rounded arches suggest that it is earlier than the Santa Croce Altarpiece. Both polyptychs contain ideas that were more fully developed in the later work, including a *Crucifixion* above the central panel, the use of spandrel angels (first used by Duccio in his altarpiece for S Domenico, Perugia) and the iconography of certain figures. A fragmentary *Crucifixion* (Madrid, Mus. Thyssen-Bornemisza) is also attributed to Ugolino, and it has been suggested that it was painted for the Bardi Chapel in Santa Croce.

BIBLIOGRAPHY

G. Vasari: *Vite* (1550, rev. 2/1568); ed. G. Milanesi (1878–85), i, p. 454
P. Bacci: *Dipinti inediti e sconosciuti di Pietro Lorenzetti* (Siena, 1939), pp. 123–51
G. Coor-Achenbach: 'Contributions to the Study of Ugolino di Nerio's Art', *A. Bull.*, xxxvii (1955), pp. 153–65
H. S. Francis: 'An Altarpiece by Ugolino da Siena', *Bull. Cleveland Mus. A.*, xlviii (1961), pp. 195–203
J. Pope-Hennessy: *Heptaptych: Ugolino da Siena* (Williamstown, 1962)
H. B. Maginnis: 'The Literature of Sienese Trecento Painting, 1945–1975', *Z. Kstgesch.*, xl (1977), pp. 282–3
H. Loyrette: 'Une Source pour la reconstruction du polyptyque d'Ugolino da Siena à Santa Croce', *Paragone*, xxix/343 (1978), pp. 15–23
C. Gardner von Teuffel: 'The Buttressed Altarpiece: A Forgotten Aspect of Fourteenth-century Altarpiece Design', *Jb. Berlin. Mus.*, xxi (1979), pp. 21–65
J. H. Stubblebine: *Duccio di Buoninsegna and his School* (Princeton, 1979), pp. 157–89
J. Cannon: 'Simone Martini, the Dominicans and the Early Sienese Polyptych', *J. Warb. & Court. Inst.*, xlv (1982), pp. 69–93
H. B. Maginnis: 'The Thyssen-Bornemisza Ugolino', *Apollo*, cxviii (July 1983), pp. 16–21
D. Gordon and A. Reeve: 'Three Newly Acquired Panels from the Altarpiece for Santa Croce by Ugolino di Nerio', *N.G. Tech. Bull.*, viii (1984), pp. 36–52
Art in the Making: Italian Painting before 1400 (exh. cat. by D. Bomford and others, London, N.G., 1989), pp. 98–123

DILLIAN GORDON

Ugolino di Vieri (*fl* 1329; *d* 1380–85). Italian goldsmith. The first reference to Ugolino is in 1329 when he and his sons, Ugolino the younger and Giovanni, sold a house. In 1332, Ugolino received compensation in connection with the commission of a chalice that the Comune of Siena was to give to the condottiere Guidoriccio da Foligno. In 1337–8 Ugolino produced his most important work, the magnificent reliquary of the Santo Corporale (Orvieto Cathedral; see fig.). The inscription on the reliquary states that it was commissioned by Bishop Tramo Monaldeschi and the canons of Orvieto Cathedral during the pontificate of Benedict XII. It was probably manufactured in Siena; payments date from 7 May 1337 to 27 December 1339, and the total cost was 1374 and a half gold florins.

The reliquary is double-sided and resembles an altarpiece in form, its triple-gabled profile repeating the architectural silhouette of the façade of Orvieto Cathedral (*see* ORVIETO, fig. 3). The form was unprecedented and ran counter to the traditional circular or polygonal reliquaries but may have been dictated by the fact that it had to contain a square of linen fabric, the relic of the Santo Corporale. A total of 23 gilded silver statuettes adorn the reliquary, but its most notable decoration consists of 32 narrative scenes rendered in *basse taille* or translucent enamel, and depicting the *Miracle of Bolsena*, to which the chapel housing the reliquary is dedicated, and scenes from the *Life of Christ*. Of the 24 scenes from the *Life of Christ* and his *Passion*, 14 are based directly on Duccio's *Maestà* (1308–11; for locations *see* DUCCIO), but the episodes from the *Miracle of Bolsena* were depicted for the first time and new iconography had to be devised. A number of these scenes derive from frescoes (*c.* 1338) by Ambrogio Lorenzetti in S Francesco, Siena. The predominant colour of the reliquary is a brilliant blue, with the addition of emerald green, turquoise, violet and purple. Ugolino fully explored the potential of translucent enamel for pictorial representation, and he achieved remarkable technical refinement. The reliquary is inscribed, PER MAGISTRVM VGOLINVM ET SOTIOS AVRIFICES DE SENIS FACTVM FVIT SVB ANNO DOMINI MCCCXXXVIII, indicating that Ugolino had collaborators, although they are not named in the payments. Attempts have been made to distinguish individual hands; Viva di Lando (*fl* 1337; *d* before 1370) and Bartolomeo di Tommé, called Pizzino (*fl* 1375–1404), are traditionally identified as two of the assistants, although it is generally agreed that Ugolino was the principal master. The reliquary was carried to the cathedral in a procession on the festival of Corpus Christi in 1338 and is still paraded annually on this feast day.

Ugolino and Viva were recorded in Siena in April 1343, and in June 1343 Ugolino burnished and repaired a chalice for the officials of the Mercanzia, a gift from the Sienese

Ugolino di Vieri: reliquary of the Santo Corporale, gold and silver with *basse taille* enamel, 1.39×0.63 m, 1338 (Orvieto Cathedral)

Comune to a visiting cardinal. On 27 November 1356 he worked with Viva on another chalice for the Comune. In 1357 Ugolino, acting as ambassador, travelled to Pistoia and San Gimignano and in the same year the Pistoiese nominated him to arbitrate in a dispute between the Opera di S Jacopo and Master Pietro, a Florentine goldsmith. The final document that refers to Ugolino is dated 1358, when the goldsmith pledged a chalice and paten of gilded silver and enamel to the monastery of San Prospero. His only other signed work, made in collaboration with Viva, is the very fine reliquary for the cranium of S Savino (Orvieto, Mus. Opera Duomo), inscribed VGHOLINVS . ET . VIVA . D[E] . SENIS . FECIERV[N]T . ISTVM . TA[B]ERNACVLV[M]. The reliquary is more traditional in form and comprises a dodecagonal base resting on six crouching lions and supporting a polygonal cupola that bears a statuette of the *Virgin and Child*, beneath an elaborate, tiered Gothic canopy.

Documents attest to further works by Ugolino. An entry for 4 August 1458 in an inventory of the sacristy of S Domenico, Perugia, records the existence of a chalice, with paten, inscribed ISTE.CALIX.VGHOLINVS.ET.VIVA. DE.SENIS. The paten, decorated with an enamel of the *Annunciation*, is identified with the one (Perugia, G.N. Umbria) discovered in 1955 in S Domenico, Perugia; the high quality of the enamel work points to the authorship of Ugolino and Viva. Other works have been linked to Ugolino on the basis of their high quality. The crown of S Galgano (Siena, Mus. Opera Duomo), from the abbey of S Galgano, near Chiusdino, is attributed to a Sienese goldsmith in Ugolino's circle. The crown comprises eight rectangular gilt plaques decorated with translucent enamel. The reliquary of S Galgano (Frosini, nr Siena, parish church) has also been attributed to Ugolino.

Other attributions have included a plaque depicting the *Nativity* (London, BM) and a rock crystal mounted in silver gilt and enamel, showing *Tristan and Isolde* (Milan, Mus. Poldi Pezzoli). The influence of the reliquary of the Santo Corporale is seen in the enamelled cope clasp with the *Annunciation* (London, V&A). It was formerly thought that Ugolino died shortly after 1358, but one of his sons is referred to as 'di maestro Ugolino' in a marriage contract document of 1380, while in 1385 his daughter, Niccola, is described as 'del fu Ugolino di maestro Vieri . . .'. This suggests that Ugolino died sometime between 1380 and 1385.

BIBLIOGRAPHY

G. Milanesi: *Documenti per la storia dell'arte senese*, i (Siena, 1856), pp. 210–13

E. Carli: *Il Duomo di Orvieto* (Rome, 1964)

——: *Il Reliquiario del Corporale ad Orvieto* (Milan, 1964)

P. dal Poggetto: *Ugolino di Vieri: Gli smalti di Orvieto*, Forma e colore: I grandi cicli dell'arte, ix (Milan, 1965)

Il Gotico a Siena: Miniature, pitture, oreficerie, oggetti d'arte (exh. cat., Siena, Pal. Pub., 1982), pp. 117, 189–97

HELEN GEDDES

Ugonio, Pompeo (*b* ?Brescia; *fl* 1572; *d* Rome, 1614). Italian antiquary and writer. In 1572 he accepted a clerical office in the Basilica Vaticana, Rome. During the 1570s he served as librarian and antiquary to the patron and collector Cardinal Ascanio Colonna (1560–1608). He subsequently held the post of Professor of Rhetoric and Theology at the Archiginnasio Romano and at the Collegio Salviati, Rome, where he delivered numerous orations, beginning with *De lingua Latina Oratio* (Rome, 1586). His fellow antiquary Fulvio Orsini called Ugonio 'giovane Romano et assai incaminato nelle lettere'. In 1587 Ugonio commemorated Sixtus V's removal of the obelisk of Nero to Piazza S Pietro in a collection of poems entitled *De sanctissima cruce in vertice obelisci vaticani*. The following year he completed his most important work, the *Historia delle stationi di Roma* (Rome, 1588), which was dedicated to Sixtus's sister Camilla Peretti. Unlike Onofrio Panvinio's earlier *Sette chiese* it was composed in the form of a guide for pilgrims. Ugonio's later role at the papal court was primarily as eulogist.

In the 17th century Ugonio's voluminous notebooks on the topography of ancient and medieval Rome were assembled by Fioravante Martinelli, who believed Ugonio had used them as preparatory notes for his lectures at the Sapienza. The main manuscripts (Rome, Vatican, Bib. Apostolica, MSS Barb. lat. 1994 and 1995) bear the title 'Compendium rerum memorabilium urbis romae/ Monumenta sacra et profana romanae urbis/Antiquitates urbis. Theatrum urbis Romae'; an addendum to this volume (the pagination continues) is in Ferrara (Civ. Bib. Ariostea, Cl. I. 161). Two other manuscripts (Rome, Vatican, Bib. Apostolica, MSS Barb. lat. 2160 and 2161) concern the urbanization of Rome from Classical to modern times and include copious sketches of medieval wall paintings, liturgical furniture and sarcophagi. Ugonio was also one of the first scholars to re-examine critically the *Mirabilia* and other topographical texts from the later Middle Ages. An apograph of Niccolò Signorili's catalogue (Pesaro, Bib. & Mus. Oliveriani) bears copious marginal notes in Ugonio's hand.

UNPUBLISHED SOURCES

Ferrara, Civ. Bib. Ariostea, Cl. I. 161 [notebooks]

Rome, Vatican, Bib. Apostolica, MSS Barb. lat. 1994, 1995, 2160 and 2161 [notebooks]

WRITINGS

De lingua Latina Oratio (Rome, 1586)

De sanctissima cruce in vertice obelisci vaticani (Rome, 1587)

Historia delle stationi di Roma (Rome, 1588)

BIBLIOGRAPHY

G. V. Rossi: *Pinacotheca imaginum, illustrium, doctrinae vel ingenti laude, virorum* (Cologne, 1643)

F. Cancellieri: *De secretariis Basilicae Vaticanae*, iv (Rome, 1786)

P. de Nolhac: *La Bibliothèque de Fulvio Orsini: Contributions à l'histoire des collections d'Italie et de la Renaissance* (Paris, 1887)

K. Waetzoldt: *Die Kopien des 17. Jahrhunderts nach Mosaiken und Wandmalereien in Rom* (Vienna and Munich, 1964)

F. J. McGinness: 'The Rhetoric of Praise and the New Rome of the Counter Reformation', *Rome in the Renaissance: The City and the Myth*, ed. P. A. Ramsey (Binghamton, 1982), pp. 355–70

I. Herklotz: '*Historia Sacra* und mittelalterliche Kunst während der zweiten Hälfte des 16. Jahrhunderts in Rom', *Baronio e l'arte. Atti del convegno internazionale di studi: Sora, 1984*, pp. 23–74 (39–45)

P. Jacks: *The Antiquarian and the Myth of Antiquity: The Origins of Rome in Renaissance Thought* (Cambridge, 1993), pp. 241–56

PHILIP J. JACKS

Ugryumov, Grigory (Ivanovich) (*b* Moscow, 11 May 1764; *d* St Petersburg, 18 March 1823). Russian painter. He attended the Academy of Arts in St Petersburg from 1770 to 1785, studying history painting under Gavriil Kozlov (?1738–92), Ivan Akimov (1755–1814) and Pyotr Sokolov. From 1785 to 1790 Ugryumov held an Academy scholarship in Italy, where he copied the works of the Old Masters and studied at both the French and Roman academies. He returned to Russia in 1791 and for the rest of his life taught history painting at the St Petersburg Academy, where he became Rector in 1820. He attached great importance to drawing as part of the students' training.

Ugryumov chiefly painted pictures on themes from Russian history; Anton Losenko was an early influence on his career. Ugryumov was made an Academician for his painting on a legendary heroic theme, the *Trial of Strength of Yan Usmar'* (1796–7; St Petersburg, Rus. Mus.). The internal dynamism of the composition, with the folk hero in the centre restraining an angry bull, is conveyed with a vigour of line and a richness of colour that recalls the palette of Peter Paul Rubens. In the late 1790s Ugryumov painted two large canvases for the Mikhaylovsky Palace in St Petersburg, the *Capture of Kazan' by Ivan the Terrible in 1552* and the *Invitation to Mikhail Fyodorovich Romanov to Ascend the Throne in 1613* (both St Petersburg, Rus. Mus.). His works are notable for their brilliance of design and mastery of colour, the precision of their somewhat theatrical composition and the endeavour to depict events as accurately as possible. They are also strongly patriotic in tone. He is generally regarded as the first Russian history painter.

In his last years Ugryumov turned to portraiture and recorded, always in a realistic manner, his friends and acquaintances, chiefly from merchant circles (e.g. portraits of *A. I. Serebryakov* and his wife, both 1813; Moscow, Tret'yakov Gal.). He exerted a strong influence on both the development of Russian history painting and the academic system of teaching. Among his pupils were Andrey Ivanov (1776–1848), Vasily Shebuyev and Aleksey Yegorov (1776–1851).

BIBLIOGRAPHY

Z. Zonova: *Grigory Ivanovich Ugryumov* (Moscow, 1966)
N. Yakovleva: *Grigory Ugryumov* (Leningrad, 1982)

G. KOMELOVA

Uğura. *See* OLBA.

Uhde, (Friedrich Hermann Karl) Fritz von (*b* Wolkenburg, 22 May 1848; *d* Munich, 25 Feb 1911). German painter. He came from a family of civil servants with artistic interests. In 1866 he briefly attended the Hochschule der Bildende Künste in Dresden, but he was bored by the teaching and in 1867 he joined the army. In 1877, despite being an officer, he took leave of absence, having decided after all to be an artist. He was determined to succeed rapidly in order to justify his late start and almost to the end of his life, therefore, his work revealed a tension between innovation and conformity.

Rejected as a pupil by Hans Makart, Karl Theodor von Piloty and Wilhelm von Diez (1839–1907), Uhde studied 17th-century Dutch painters in Munich on his own. On the invitation of Mihály Munkácsy he went to Paris in 1879 and attended Munkácsy's painting school for five months. His last work painted at the school, *The Chanteuse* (1880; Munich, Neue Pin.), a genre painting aiming at popular success, received honourable mention at the Salon.

In Paris Uhde first discovered his abiding interest in painting from nature.

In 1880 he returned to Munich, where he was based for the rest of his career. Encouraged by Max Liebermann, he experimented with *plein-air* painting in the Netherlands. *Fishermen's Children in Zandvoort* (1882; Vienna, Belvedere) was painted entirely *en plein air*, yet Uhde only dared to exhibit a much more conventional version, the *Hurdygurdy Man is Coming* (1883; Hamburg, Ksthalle), in which the immediacy of the study was lost. In *Drum Practice* (1883; Dresden, Gemäldegal. Neue Meister), a subject from military life given a *plein-air* treatment, Uhde adopted a provocative Naturalism, which he abandoned after receiving harsh reviews by conservative critics. *Suffer the Little Children to Come unto Me* (1884; Leipzig, Mus. Bild. Kst) shows Jesus as an itinerant preacher receiving timid peasant children at a village school. The critics accepted this work by the 'painter of filth' because of its important religious content. Thus Uhde found a way to pursue what really interested him—the rendering of natural light and realistic settings—under the guise of religious subject-matter.

Against the current of 19th-century historicism, Uhde's updated versions of events from the life of Jesus set among the contemporary poor were very successful, for example *Last Supper* (1886; Stuttgart, Staatsgal.) and *Holy Night* (1888/9; Dresden, Gemäldegal. Neue Meister). In *Heavy Gait* (see fig.) the secularization is taken so far that only the initiate can discern the religious subject, the journey to Bethlehem. Like all of Uhde's works, this depiction of a wretched, homeless craftsman's family does not accuse, but rather arouses pity. Nevertheless, setting episodes from the Gospels in the context of contemporary poverty was explosive; it suggested that the Christian demand of equality for all men had not been met politically or socially. Conservative elements of the public condemned the paintings for degrading holy subjects and unleashed a controversy, which paradoxically made the artist the most popular of his day.

Until the early 1890s Uhde was regarded as the head of the Naturalist movement in Munich. He was one of the founders of the Munich Secession in 1892 (*see* SECESSION, §1). The cultural liberalization in Germany in the 1890s caused Naturalism to lose some of its force as an oppositional movement. Uhde's religious paintings became more conventional, authoritarian rather than egalitarian. In 1903–05 he painted his only commissioned religious work, the altarpiece (*Das Volk, das in der Finsternis sass, hat ein grosses Licht gesehen*, Matthew 4:16; *in situ*) for the Lutheran church at Zwickau. The Protestant church began to accept Uhde's work, and in 1908 he was awarded an honorary doctorate by the theological faculty at Leipzig.

It was in his unofficial work that Uhde expressed his personality most clearly; his private family pictures, showing his home life and his three daughters (his wife died in 1886), such as *Nursery* (1889; Hamburg, Ksthalle) and *In the Bower* (1896; Düsseldorf, Kstmus.), eventually won public recognition. Uhde showed much sensitivity as a painter of children, to whom, as a shy man, he felt close, for example in *Little Princess of the Heath* (1889; Berlin, Alte N.G.). Summers spent at Dachau and at a country house at Starnberg in the 1890s influenced his steady

Fritz von Uhde: *Heavy Gait*, oil on canvas, 1.17×1.26 m, *c.* 1890 (Munich, Neue Pinakothek)

development towards an Impressionistic rendering of light. From the late 1890s he produced fresh, glowing paintings of his daughters in the garden, which became his refuge when he withdrew from the art world after 1900: *In the Garden* (1901; Frankfurt am Main, Städel. Kstinst. & Städt. Gal.) and *In the Garden* (1906; Mannheim, Städt. Ksthalle).

BIBLIOGRAPHY
F. von Ostini: *Uhde* (Bielefeld and Leipzig, 1902)
H. Rosenhagen: *Fritz von Uhde* (1908), xxii of *Klass. Kst. Gesamtausgaben* (Stuttgart and Leipzig, 1904–37)
A. Mochon: *Fritz von Uhde and Plein-air Painting in Munich, 1800–1900* (diss., New Haven, CT, Yale U., 1973)
B. Brand: *Fritz von Uhde: Das religiöse Werk zwischen künstlerischer Intention und Öffentlichkeit*, Heft des Kunstgeschichtlichen Instituts der Universität Mainz, vii (Heidelberg, 1983)

BETTINA BRAND

Uhde, Wilhelm (*b* Friedeberg in der Neumark [now Strzelce Krajeńskie, Poland], 28 Oct 1874; *d* Paris, 17 Aug 1947). German writer, collector and dealer. After studying law and breaking off his studies of art history, he moved to Paris in 1904, where he joined the circle of German artists and those interested in art that gathered at the Café du Dôme (*c.* 1907). In 1908 he opened a small gallery, in which he exhibited work by Picasso, Braque and Derain, among others, and from 1909 he was a member of Sonderbund, which was an important supporter of Expressionism in the western part of Germany (*see* COLOGNE, §II, 5). Through Sonia Terk (later Delaunay), to whom he was married from 1909 to 1910, he met Robert Delaunay and Henri Rousseau in 1907. He wrote the first monograph on Henri Rousseau in 1911 and organized his retrospective at the Galerie Bernheim Jeune, Paris, in 1912. With Terk he initiated a broader understanding of the work of such other 'naive' painters as Camille Bombois, Séraphine and Louis Vivin. His contact with Julius Meier-Graefe, the museum director Harry Graf Kessler (1868–1937) and particularly Alfred Flechtheim encouraged an interest in more recent French art in Germany before

World War I. As a German, in 1914 he was forced to leave France. His collection, which had been open to the public twice weekly, was seized and sold by auction in 1921. After the war Uhde initially lived with the painter Helmut Kolle (1899–1931) in Burg Lauenstein, where they organized educational events for the young as part of the movement for cultural reform. Their objectives were embodied in the almanac *Die Freude* (1921). In 1922 Uhde worked in the Galerie Gurlitt in Berlin for a year. From 1924 he lived with Kolle again in France, where he renewed his involvement with the work of naive artists. He was disturbed by other modern developments in the art world. His outlook, which was shaped by the ideas of Nietzsche and can be found in all his writing, became very pessimistic. *Fünf primitive Meister* (1947) summarizes his opinions.

WRITINGS

Henri Rousseau (Paris, 1911)
Henri Rousseau (Düsseldorf, 1914, rev. Dresden, 2/1921)
Die Freude (Das flammende Reich: Ein Bekenntnis zum heimlichen Deutschland) (Burg Lauenstein, 1921)
Picasso et la tradition française (Paris, 1926)
Von Bismarck bis Picasso: Erinnerungen und Bekenntnisse (Zurich, 1938)
Fünf primitive Meister: Rousseau, Vivin, Bombois, Bauchant, Séraphine (Zurich, 1947)

BIBLIOGRAPHY

Kürschners deutscher Literaturkalender: Nekrolog 2, 1936–1970 (Berlin, 1973), pp. 688–9
H. Thiel: 'Wilhelm Uhde: Ein offener und engagierter Marchand-Amateur in Paris vor dem Ersten Weltkrieg', *Avantgarde und Publikum*, ed. H. Junge (Cologne, 1992), pp. 307–20

BARBARA LANGE

Uhl, Ottokar (*b* Wolfsberg, 2 March 1931). Austrian architect and theorist. He studied at the Akademie der Bildenden Künste, Vienna, where he attended Lois Welzenbacher's masterclass (1950–53). During this period Uhl designed a room for worship, in which worshippers would be able to arrange the Catholic liturgy according to their needs. Processes such as this, whereby fixed hierarchical structures are broken down, subsequently became important in his work, for example the Demontable Kirche (1963), Siemensstrasse, Vienna. The restorational development following the second Vatican Council in 1963 resulted in the ending of a series of commissions of this nature. Thereafter he turned his interests more to housing. Here he had the opportunity of publishing works on participatory processes in architecture, supported by the Austrian government, which passed a law (1968) requiring the approval of designs by future occupiers of buildings. In 1973 Uhl became Professor of Planning and Design in the Architectural Faculty of Karlsruhe University, but he retained his architectural office in Vienna and links with the SAR Team in Eindhoven and Austrian colleagues in order to study the possibility of building flats and even designing towns with a minimum of predetermined structural elements. Uhl was convinced that an architectonic response to the changing needs of the users, in other words process-oriented planning, is a socio-political necessity for the emancipation of the underprivileged. Two examples of his work in this field are the residential developments 'Wohnen mit Kindern' (1984), Jeneweingasse, Vienna, and Gemeinschaft BROT (1990), Geblergasse 78, Vienna. His rejection of authoritarian methods echoed the work of Emil Steffann (1899–1968) and Josef

Frank (1885–1967) and his use of structural systems that of Konrad Wachsmann, whom he met at the International Summer Academy in Salzburg. Unlike the latter, however, he did not wish to make decisions himself but to leave planning and responsibility to others. This reflected his view of a new role for architects, involving mainly delegation and publication. He received several awards, including the Preis der Stadt Wien für Architektur (1973).

WRITINGS

with R. Dirisamer and G. Figlhuber: *Wohnen: Ein Handbuch* (Vienna, 1984)
with K. Freisitzer and R. Koch: *Mitbestimmung im Wohnbau* (Vienna, 1987)
ed.: *Wohnen mit Kindern: Ein Erfahrungsbericht* (Vienna, 1992)

BIBLIOGRAPHY

E. Lucie-Smith, S. Hunter and A. M. Vost: *Kunst der Gegenwart*, Propyläen-Kstgesch. (Frankfurt am Main, 1978), pp. 116, 269
I. Bohning: 'Autonome Architektur' und 'partizipatorisches Bauen': Zwei Architekturkonzepte (Basle, 1981)
F. Achleitner: *Österreichische Architektur im 20. Jahrhundert*, ii (Salzburg and Vienna, 1983)
H. Muck: *Gegenwartsbilder: Kunstwerke und religiöse Vorstellungen des 20. Jahrhunderts in Österreich* (Vienna, 1988)

THOMAS SPERLING

Uhle, Max (*b* 1856; *d* 1944). German archaeologist. His pioneering work in Peru and Bolivia between 1892 and 1912 revolutionized the archaeological study of Pre-Columbian South America. Uhle was trained as a philologist but later took up archaeology. His interest in Peru began when he was curator of the Dresden Museum. From 1892 he conducted field research for the universities of Pennsylvania and California, excavating on the Peruvian coast at Pachacamac and on Moche and Chimú sites. He worked in the valleys of the Chincha and Ica, discovering the production sites of Nazca ceramics. He later extended his work into the Peruvian highlands and to Bolivia, Ecuador and Chile; he also made a notable contribution to North American archaeology with his excavations of the Emeryville shell-mound in San Francisco Bay. His rigorous approach, influenced by the systematic excavations of FLINDERS PETRIE in Egypt, emphasized stratigraphic excavation and the ordering of finds in an evolutionary sequence as a means of establishing chronology. The basic chronological framework he established for Pre-Columbian South America has only been superseded in the later 20th century.

WRITINGS

Pachacamac (Philadelphia, 1903)
'Die Ruinen von Moche', *J. Soc. Américanistes*, x (1913)
Explorations at Chincha, U. CA Pubns Amer. Archaeol. & Ethnol., xxi (1924)   □

Uhlig, Max (*b* Dresden, 23 June 1937). German draughtsman, printmaker and painter. Between 1951 and 1954 he trained in Dresden as a sign-painter and draughtsman. His first free artistic work, drawings, painting, woodcuts, was done during this period. He studied at the Hochschule für Bildende Künste in Dresden (1955–60) under Max Schwimmer (1895–1960) and Hans Theo Richter, then attended the Deutsche Akademie der Künste (1961–3) under Richter. From the outset drawing had a crucial role in Uhlig's work. Richter was responsible for making him first see graphics as a black-and-white art, thus opening up to him the wide range of shades of grey. Until the mid-1960s the tension between the differing characteristic structures of graphic art and painting, between elements suggesting depth and those emphasizing flat surfaces with a mediating effect, was often explored using a combination of aquatint and line etching. He brought together Schwimmer's linear vitality and Richter's reduced, concentrated form, latching on to the meditative aspect of the latter's work. After the mid-1960s Uhlig started to develop his own independent artistic concept: rather than fulfilling the function of describing contours, lines were used in bundles and in a network of strokes to construct form by working from the inside to the outside, becoming conveyors expressing inner processes. In portraits the experience of the physiognomy is subservient to the visionary analysis of mental processes. With portraits such as *Max Butting* (etching, 1964; Dresden, Kupferstichkab.) or *Pukall* (aquatint, 1964) he gave the first signs of a new dimension in portraiture in East Germany. Getting to know Alberto Giacometti's work confirmed Uhlig in his chosen direction. His emphasis on the line led him away from the use of aquatint.

In the following years Uhlig produced large-format lithographs, mainly intense portraits, of which *Portrait of the Mother* (1967), *Hans Theo Richter* (1969), *Willy Wolff* (1971) and *Hans Jüchser* (1975; all Dresden, Kupferstichkab.) are among the most important. Spiritual and mental movements are captured in the rhythm of the lines. At the same time he strove to encapsulate the whole being of the person. From the 1970s he also turned his attention to landscape. He again used interweaving lines to convey the rhythmic tensions of organic forms, their inner movements and the atmospheric changes of nature. The micro-world of segments of nature is filtered out and at the same time grasped in its totality as a unified entity. Around 1970 he started to produce a large number of watercolours and paintings. Transferring his individual style, which had evolved in black and white, to multi-coloured painting was a daring act that the public was reluctant to accept. In the early 1980s he produced several two-figure works using graphic techniques, in which the inner tension of interpersonal relationships became a key factor.

BIBLIOGRAPHY

Max Uhlig (exh. cat., text by K. Werner; E. Berlin, Gal. Arkade, 1979)
Max Uhlig (exh. cat., W. Berlin, Gal. Brusberg, 1984)
Max Uhlig (exh. cat., text by W. Schmidt; Kiel, Gal. Eichhof, 1986)
Max Uhlig: Malerei, Arbeiten auf Papier (exh. cat., text H. Liesbrock; Ravensburg, Gal. Döbele, 1989)
Max Uhlig: Gemälde und Aquarelle, Zeichnungen und Grafiken (exh. cat., Bielefeld, Städt. Ksthalle, 1990)
Max Uhlig: Gemälde, Aquarelle, Zeichnungen, Graphik, Skizzenbücher (exh. cat., Dresden, Staatl. Kstsammlungen, 1993)
Max Uhlig: Am Mont Ventoux. Bilder aus Südfrankreich, 1991–93 (exh. cat., Esslingen, Gal. Stadt, 1994)

ANITA KÜHNEL

Uhlmann, Hans (*b* Berlin, 27 Nov 1900; *d* W. Berlin, 28 Oct 1975). German sculptor and draughtsman. After studying engineering at the Technische Hochschule in Berlin, he began making sculpture in 1925. Self-taught, he spent the next 20 years evolving the basic artistic ideas that shaped his work, although engineering remained his main profession. Uhlmann's chief subject was the human head, stimulated by the Constructivist principles of Naum

Gabo and by Alexander Calder's early wire sculptures, leading him simultaneously to confront two divergent formal problems. He first produced fully sculpted female portrait heads based on traditional concepts, although the faces were simplified to stylized geometrical forms. Parallel with these from the mid-1930s he produced soldered wire sculptures, for example *Head* (1936–7; Duisburg, Lehmbruck-Mus.). In these, solid volume was for the first time abolished in favour of linear constructions in which the thin wires cleave through space while retaining figural forms. The head sculptures that he made from sheet-iron occupy a position between material structures and the incorporeal shapes of the wire heads, as in *Head, Woman, Aeroplane* (1937; priv. col., see 1978 exh. cat., pl. 3). They are composed of metal planes following a principle of construction that mediates between closed and open forms. After 1945 Uhlmann redefined the spatial volumes inherent in the wire sculptures, which became increasingly free of objective references. He developed a transparent, almost weightless treatment of form in which the lines of iron wire unfold freely in space, which were related in their expressive gesture to *Art informel*, as typified by the paintings of Hans Hartung in the late 1940s. The idea of tension-charged sequences of movement is expressed in the organic flow of the wire lines, with their strongly graphic effect and the extreme vertical orientation of the works, as in *Bird* (1947; priv. col., see 1978 exh. cat., pl. 10). The wires rise in rotating loops and rhythmical angles, the whole structure based on the interpenetration of positive, space-excluding and negative, space-permeable forms. In complexity these works are allied to the 'space' sculptures of Norbert Kricke.

In 1950 Uhlmann was appointed to teach at the Hochschule für die Bildenden Künste (now Hochschule der Künste) in Berlin, a post that opened up new and exciting possibilities of personal expression. He dispensed with maquettes and applied himself to the direct manipulation of steel strips in stereometric, abstract sculptures, indicative of and extending far into the surrounding space; their statue-like quality was attained by the balance of repeated parts. He freely inserted solid planes and perforated triangular and circular plates to stabilize these linear structures (e.g. *Bird*, 1951; priv. col., see 1978 exh. cat., pl. 18), which were based on an enlargement of format. In 1954 Uhlmann executed his first large-scale outdoor sculpture, entitled *Concerto*, at the Hochschule für Musik in Berlin. Like bundles of rays, the sculpture seems to draw in the space of the public square; creating an impression of extreme density. In the late 1950s he produced a series of fantastic, figural metal 'fetishes'. From 1967 his work took on themes of 'tower' and 'column'. In an attempt to comprehend the tension between envelope and core, he trod new ground in his exploration of space and architectural sculpture. In one example, over a ground-plan ranging between a square and an octagon, he erected a spatial box that resembles a casket or a stele, which, as in a peep-show, gives a view of a symmetrical arrangement of rods and wall-compartments. The parts interlock in such a way that light and space flow through them; the resulting mirror-effects also include coloured elements (e.g. *Head-Fetish*, 1967; see 1968 exh. cat., pl. 116). Uhlmann's extensive work as a draughtsman is characterized by graphically structured rhythms of light and dark comparable to his sculptural forms. They focus on the relationship of the static and the mobile.

BIBLIOGRAPHY

F. Baumgart: *Uhlmann, Handzeichnungen* (Frankfurt am Main, 1960)
Hans Uhlmann (exh. cat., E. Berlin, Akad. Kst. DDR, 1968)
W. Haftmann: *Hans Uhlmann, Leben und Werk* (Berlin, 1975)
Hans Uhlmann, 1900–1975, Plastik und Zeichnungen (exh. cat. by H. Fuchs, Mannheim, Städt. Ksthalle, 1978)
Hans Uhlmann (exh. cat. by C. Brockhaus and J. Merkert, Duisburg, Lehmbruck-Mus.; Berlin, Berlin. Gal.; 1991) [incl. cat. rais. of wtrcol. and drgs]

GOTTLIEB LEINZ

Uhyang. *See* CHŎNG TAE-YU.

Ŭijae [Ŭijaesanin, Ŭidoin]. *See* HŎ PAEK-NYŎN.

Uilenburg, Gerrit. *See* UYLENBURGH, GERRIT.

Uiterwijk, John, & Co. *See* ARTS AND CRAFTS, JOHN TH. UITERWIJK & CO.

Uitz, Béla (*b* Temes-Mehala, nr Timişoara, 8 March 1887; *d* Budapest, 26 Jan 1972). Hungarian painter, draughtsman and writer, active in Russia. He registered at the School of Crafts and Design, Budapest, in 1907, and went on to attend the Academy of Fine Arts (1908–12). In 1914 he showed his loosely executed drawings at the third Young Artists exhibition, and in the same year travelled to Italy. In 1915 he joined the ACTIVISTS, the avant-garde artists grouped around his brother-in-law Lajos Kassák. Uitz's expressive ink drawings appeared in the Activist periodical *A Tett* ('The Act', 1915). In April 1916 he took part in an exhibition at the National Salon in Budapest of work by The Young (Fiatalok) and the Seven (Hetek). He spent summer 1916 at the Kecskemét colony, where his painting became richer in colour. It was here that he painted *Apple Pickers* (1916; Budapest, N.G.), his first significant oil painting, influenced by Hungarian followers of Cézanne. In 1917 he became co-editor with Kassák of the periodical *MA* (*see* MA GROUP), which had succeeded *A Tett* as the forum for The Activists after the latter was banned. He published his own drawings and exhibition reviews in *MA*, as well as works by József Nemes Lampérth. His expressive and monumental style of ink drawing was influenced by Cézanne, Goya, Picasso and The Eight (iii).

By 1919 Uitz's style had completely matured. During the period of the Soviet Republic in Hungary (1919), he designed murals for the parliament building (e.g. *Builders, Fishermen, Humanity*, 1919; Budapest, N.G.). He became head of the Proletarian Fine Arts Workshop and produced such posters as *Red Soldiers, Forward!* (1919; Budapest, N.G.) to promote Kún's Communist regime. In early 1920 he went to Vienna, where the activities of *MA* continued in exile. He was impressed by Dada and Futurism, and was preoccupied by the problems of Cubist forms and the use of cold and warm colours. His themes were derived primarily from his immediate environment. An exhibition of his work was organized at the *MA* premises in Vienna, and his album *Versuche*, containing eight etchings, was published. In 1921 he left *MA* and went to Moscow (via Berlin), where he was influenced by Soviet Constructivism. Back in Vienna, he painted compositions with dynamic brushwork influenced by Aleksandr Rodchenko's linear

Béla Uitz: *Icon Analysis*, watercolour, 397×296 mm, 1921 (Budapest, Hungarian National Gallery)

style (e.g. *Analysis Series*, 1922; Edinburgh, N.G.) and introduced Constructivist elements into coloured ink drawings and watercolours of Vienna and Moscow. His abstract works were inspired by Russian icon art (e.g. *Icon Analysis*; see fig.). In 1922 he and Kassák's former associate, the writer Aladár Komját (1894–1963), started the ultra-left periodical *Egység* (Unity), in which Soviet Constructivist ideas were promoted. Uitz's *General Ludd* series (1923; Budapest, N.G.) was inspired by the English Luddite movement, in which workers had protested at job losses brought on by industrialization. Hoping for a commission for a monumental fresco, he set off for London, but instead ended up working for two years in France, from October 1924. He continued his wide-ranging proletarian cultural activities within Parisian émigré organizations, and these experiences appear in his expressive series of ink drawings of urban scenes and Gothic studies (e.g. *Parisian Gothic*, 1925; Budapest, N.G.), executed in purple ink, and influenced by Japanese woodcuts. He spent summer 1926 in Collioure in southern France, where he painted Fauve-inspired large-scale works in primary colours (e.g. *Collioure*, 1925; Moscow, Pushkin Mus. F.A.); his works and articles appeared in Paris under the pseudonym B. U. Martel. Failing to gain residency, he was obliged to leave France later that year.

In October 1926 Uitz settled in the USSR and taught composition at the Vkhutemas (later Vkhutein) work-shops in Moscow. He worked on the decorations for the Culture and Leisure Parks Exhibition, but he was given little opportunity for traditional fine art activities. He was one of the founder-members of the October group, which aimed for the organic unity of a 'proletarian realism', or art for the masses, and whose artists were later branded as formalists. From 1930, after the closure of Vkhutein, he worked for five years as secretary to the Revolutionary Artists International Bureau. He also started drawing again and made a monumental series of studies of heads on newspaper (e.g. *Woman's Profile*, 1932; Moscow, Pushkin Mus. F.A.). In 1933 he completed his last series of expressive landscape drawings, on blotting paper in the Crimea. He also painted murals that met the Stalinist demands of Socialist Realism. In autumn 1936 Uitz was commissioned to paint a mural of the *Kirgiz Uprising, 1916* in the governmental palace in Frunze, Kirgizia (now Bishkek, Kyrgyzstan): Kirgizian folk art and Renaissance traditions served as the starting point for his design (sketches, 1936; Budapest, N. Mus.). In 1938 he was arrested on false charges, and 18 months later he was sent back to Moscow. He was a committed designer of works immortalizing the struggle of the proletariat, but the constraints of the dogmatic Soviet cultural policy are most noticeable in his murals for the Moscow Agricultural Exhibition (1950–55). In 1970 he returned to Hungary, and in 1978 the Uitz Museum was dedicated to him in Pécs.

WRITINGS
Versuche (Vienna, 1920)
Analizis (Vienna, 1922)
Ludditenbewegung, preface by E. Bettelheim (Vienna, 1923)
B. U. Martel [B. Uitz]: *La Guerre impérialiste*, preface by M. Cachin (Paris, 1926)
Uitz, intro. by F. Münnich (Budapest, 1967)

BIBLIOGRAPHY
Uitz Béla (exh. cat. by L. Kassák; Vienna, *MA*, 1920)
I. Hevesy: 'Uitz Béla', *Nyugat*, 20 (1922), pp. 1205–11
Béla Uitz (exh. cat. by L. Bazalgette, Paris, Gal. A. Clarté, 1925)
J. Mácza: *Béla Uitz* (Moscow, 1931)
E. Kholostenko: *Béla Uitz* (Khar'kov, 1933)
É. Bajkay: *Uitz Béla* (Budapest, 1974)
S. Kontha: *Vár egy új világ* (Budapest, 1975)
É. Bajkay: *Uitz Béla* (Budapest, 1987) [with cat.]
Standing in the Tempest: Painters of the Hungarian Avant-garde, 1908–1930 (exh. cat. by S. Mansbach, Santa Barbara, Mus. A., 1991), pp. 61, 63, 69, 119–21, 133, 157–62, 237

For further bibliography *see* ACTIVISTS.

ÉVA BAJKAY

Ujjain [anc. Ujjayinī; Ujjeni; Ozene; Visala]. Sacred city and ancient astronomical centre on the Shipra River in Madhya Pradesh, India. It was already an important centre in MAURYA times (4th–3rd centuries BC) and flourished under the GUPTA rulers of the 4th–5th centuries AD. From the 9th to the 13th century Ujjain was the capital of the PARAMARA kings but was sacked by Muslim forces in 1235. The city subsequently flourished under MUGHAL and Maratha rule (16th–19th centuries), especially during the governorship of Raja Jai Singh in the early 18th century.

The site of the ancient city is marked by a substantial mound known as Garh-kalika on the bank of the Shipra River to the north of the present town. Excavations (1938–9, 1955–8 and 1964–5) have dated the foundation of the city to *c.* 700 BC. Finds included objects of pottery, iron and stone, beads, coins and terracotta figurines. The earliest buildings found at Ujjain are a brick-lined tank of the 4th century BC and a stupa belonging to the first centuries AD. Other notable monuments include the Paramara-period Dhaneshvara Temple, the 11th-century Chaubis Khambha Gate, the Bina Nava-ki-Masjid (1397), the 16th-century Kaliadah Mahal, the Observatory (1725) and the Mahakala Temple, an 18th-century reconstruction of an 11th–12th century structure. The Chaubis Khambha Gate, also reconstructed, contains a number of carved pillars of black stone and may have been a supplementary structure of the original Mahakala Temple. The mosque was constructed from temple spoil by Dilavar Khan Husayn Ghuri (*reg* 1401–5), one of the sultans of Malwa. About 9 km north of the city, the Kaliadah Mahal, a palace dating from *c.* 1500, emulates the style of MANDU and is noteworthy for its water system. The palace was used and repaired by the Mughal rulers and finally the Scindias. Because of its location in the centre of the country, Ujjain became the most important astronomical centre in India and was used as the meridian for astronomical calculations. The Observatory was built by Sawai Jai Singh (*reg* 1699–1743) of Amber and is comparable to the others he built in Delhi, Jaipur and Varanasi. Its four structures served, among other things, to calculate time, to fix the position of particular stars and to measure the declination of the sun. However, by far the most significant monument at Ujjain is the temple dedicated to Shiva as Mahakala, the great destroyer of time; on an ancient site, the temple (see fig.) is regarded as one of the seven most sacred places in India. It has a three-tiered elevation with two storeys of colonnaded porches topped by a high, conical spire (*śikhara*). Rows of small spires, diminishing in size as they rise, face the body of the spire and accentuate its vertical ascent. The temple is also embellished with perforated

Ujjain, Mahakala Temple, view from the east, rebuilt 1745

screens and carved pillars, which recall late Mughal and Maratha stonework.

Extant remains of sculpture include very few pieces pre-dating the 10th century. However, an 8th-century Nataraja or Dancing Shiva (Gwalior, Cent. Archaeol. Mus.) and a Shiva (*in situ* at Okhaleshvara) are notable for their simplicity of form and iconography. In the 10th century there was an upsurge in art activity at Ujjain, exemplified by images of Parvati performing penance and a standing female, possibly the goddess Ambika (Ujjain, Dist. Archaeol. Mus.). Other loose sculptures include those found on the outskirts of Ujjair in a dilapidated cell at Okhaleshvara and in the reconstructed niches at the Rama–Janardana Temple at Ankpat; they exhibit a range of stylistic idioms and dates. Among these, the image of Krishna lifting Mt Govardhana (*in situ* at Ankpat) is distinguished by its sensitive modelling and flowing volume. An 11th-century image of Vishnu carved on four sides of a block (*caturmūrti*) is an example of singular iconographic significance in that it delineates Vasudeva and his emanations Sankarsana, Pradyumna and Aniruddha. The image is preserved in an independent enclosure close to the Garh-kalika.

BIBLIOGRAPHY
B. C. Law: *Ujjayini in Ancient India* (Gwalior, 1944)
H. N. Dvivedi: *Gvāliyar rājya ke abhilekha* [Inscriptions of the Gwalior kingdom] (Gwalior, 1946)
D. R. Patil: *The Cultural Heritage of Madhya Bharata* (Gwalior, 1952)
Indian Archaeology, 1955–56: A Review (New Delhi, 1956), pp. 19–20
Indian Archaeology, 1956–57: A Review (New Delhi, 1957), pp. 20–28
Indian Archaeology, 1957–58: A Review (New Delhi, 1958), pp. 32–6
D. C. Sircar: *Ancient Malwa and Vikramaditya Tradition* (Delhi, 1965)
Indian Archaeology, 1964–65: A Review (New Delhi, 1969), p. 18
P. Davies: *Islamic, Rajput, European*, Penguin Guide Mnmts India, ii (London, 1989)
G. Michell: *Buddhist, Jain, Hindu*, Penguin Guide Mnmts India, i (London, 1989)
D. C. Bhattacharya: *Pratimālakṣana of the Viṣṇudharmottara* (New Delhi, 1991)
H. V. Trivedi: *Inscriptions of the Paramaras*, Corpus Inscriptionum Indicarum, vii/2 (New Delhi, n.d.)
R. N. MISRA

Ukhaydir. Early Islamic palace in Iraq, located in the desert on the Wadi'Ubayd almost 200 km south of Baghdad. The ruins of this fortified palace provide important evidence for Islamic architecture and its decoration in the late 8th century AD. The site, known to several 18th-century travellers, was rediscovered by L. Massignon in 1908 and quickly visited and studied by Bell, Reuther and others, who dated it to the Sasanian (AD 226–645) or early Islamic (7th century AD) period. Creswell (1932–40) circumstantially identified it as the palace of 'Isa ibn Musa (*d* 783/4), a powerful member of the ruling Abbasid family, but Caskel later argued that it was the palace of 'Isa ibn 'Ali and dated it AD 762. The outer enclosure (175×169 m) is built of slabs of limestone rubble set in heavy mortar. Its walls, which once had a parapet, were originally about 19 m high. A round tower marks each corner, with half-round towers spaced regularly between. A gate in the centre of each side is flanked by quarter-round towers, except on the north, where the main entrance is expanded with a projecting block. The north entrance leads to the palace proper (112×82 m), which is adjacent to the outer enclosure on the north. The palace

consists of an entrance complex, with a small mosque to its right, a large open court with engaged pilasters, a great vaulted iwan leading to a square hall and flanking apartments. On either side of this central tract are two self-contained residential units arranged around smaller courts. Excavations by the Iraqi Department of Antiquities in 1963 revealed a bath complex constructed of baked brick to the south-east of the palace, which was added slightly later than the main construction. The palace at Ukhaydir is notable for the variety of its vaults, particularly the early use of transverse vaulting, and the extensive use of carved stucco and brick laid in geometric patterns. These features point to the increased importance of Mesopotamian and Iranian architectural traditions at the end of the 8th century and foreshadow the emergence of a distinctive regional style.

BIBLIOGRAPHY
L. Massignon: 'Note sur le château d'al Okhaïdir', *Acad. Inscr. & B.-Lett.: C. R. Séances* (1909), pp. 202–12
O. Reuther: *Ocheïdir* (Leipzig, 1912)
G. L. Bell: *The Palace and Mosque at Ukhaidir* (Oxford, 1914)
K. A. C. Creswell: *Early Muslim Architecture*, 2 vols (Oxford, 1932–40; i R and enlarged, 1969)
——: *A Short Account of Early Muslim Architecture* (Harmondsworth, 1958, rev. Aldershot, 1989)
W. Caskel: 'Al-Ukhaidir', *Der Islam*, xxxix (1964), pp. 28–37
T. Alyawir: *Versuch einer neuen stilistischen Einordnung des Wüstenschlosses al-Ukhaidir* (diss., Mainz, Johannes Gutenberg-U., 1968)
B. Finster and J. Schmidt: 'Sasanidische und frühislamische Ruinen in Iraq', *Baghdad. Mitt.*, viii (1976) [whole issue]

Ukhtomsky, Dmitry (Vasil'yevich) (*b* Moscow, 1719; *d* Arkhangel'skoye, nr Tula, 1774). Russian architect. He was an exponent of the Baroque of the Moscow school, but was greatly influenced by St Petersburg masters. Ukhtomsky occupies a special place in the history of Russian architecture as the founder, in 1749, of the first Russian architectural school. Special accommodation and money for the purchase of drawing equipment were set aside for the school, and many well-educated masters graduated from it, including ALEKSANDR KOKORINOV and MATVEY KAZAKOV.

Ukhtomsky came from an impoverished noble family and studied at the School of Mathematical and Navigational Sciences in Moscow. In June 1733 he was sent to train under the Moscow architect Ivan Michurin, and in 1741 he was transferred to a pupillage under Ivan Korobov (1701–47), who had moved to Moscow from St Petersburg. With Korobov, Ukhtomsky built the Triumphal Gates (1742) at the end of Tver' Street in honour of the coronation of the Empress Elizabeth. From 1744 he was Korobov's main assistant. On 16 September 1745 Ukhtomsky was appointed architect to the Moscow police, and until 1760 he was engaged in drawing up plans for districts of Moscow that had been destroyed by fire. He prepared designs for their reconstruction and chose sites for new residential blocks, offices and industrial buildings. In 1751, after Michurin left Moscow, Ukhtomsky completed the restoration of the church of St Nikita the Martyr.

In connection with the arrival of the Empress Elizabeth for a prolonged stay in Moscow, Ukhtomsky received two important commissions in 1753: to construct the Senate

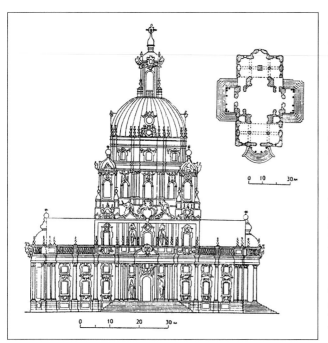

Dmitry Ukhtomsky: design (1758–9) for the north façade of the Invalid Hospital, Moscow (unexecuted)

foundations, successively diminishing in size and pierced on all sides by arches. The total height was 86 m and the whole was surmounted by a gilded, four-sided cupola with a cross. The gradual reduction in size of the tiers and the identical span of the arches gave the bell-tower a light quality and underlined its upward thrust. Niccolò Michetti's unexecuted design (1721–2) for the lighthouse at Kronshtadt harbour and Rastrelli's bell-tower in the Smol'ny Convent in St Petersburg (1748–64; see ST PETERSBURG, §IV, 3) had an undoubted influence on this work.

From the mid-1750s Ukhtomsky was also engaged on a wide range of relatively minor projects, the majority in Moscow. In 1754 Ukhtomsky rebuilt the interior of the Central Pharmacy building on Red Square to house the lecture rooms of the first Russian University. From 1754 to 1760 he repaired and remodelled the buildings of various offices in the Kremlin. In 1755 he was involved in the restoration of the bell-tower of Tver' Cathedral. In 1756 he built the three-arched Kuznetsky Bridge across the Neglinka, Moscow, and the following year he prepared a design for the nine-span Kozmodem'yansky Bridge. Ukhtomsky's most important work, however, would have been the Invalid Hospital in Moscow (see fig.), designed in 1758–9 but never built. Four two-storey blocks, each over 200 m long, were planned to form a cruciform area, with a huge five-domed cathedral at its centre. The envisaged decoration of the blocks is severe, intended to prepare for the splendid Baroque decoration of the cathedral. The blocks are interconnected by curved galleries and result in an enclosed ensemble, a form characteristic of Russian monasteries. Ukhtomsky here seemed to be competing with the ensemble of the Smol'ny Convent. He even repeated its scheme for the disposition of the cathedral's domes, with four small ones closely abutting the large one in the centre. The ensemble was to have been built in south-west Moscow, at the bend of the river. In 1760 Ukhtomsky built the Armoury Palace (Druzheyneya Palata; destr. late 18th century) in the Kremlin, but in the same year he became a victim of intrigue. He was dismissed from all works and a financial inquiry was instituted. The examination lasted two years, at the end of which Ukhtomsky was acquitted. In 1762 Empress Catherine II ascended the throne, the Baroque was deemed to be old-fashioned and vulgar, and Neo-classicism became fashionable, leaving Ukhtomsky without work.

building and to replace with stone gates the wooden Krasnyye Vorota (Beautiful or Red Gates), which he had built in 1742 and which had suffered in a fire. On both sides of the Senate building Ukhtomsky built two administrative blocks (completed 1757; destr.), which projected to form a spacious, rectangular *cour d'honneur*. The blocks were united with the main building by covered galleries. The layout recalls that developed for country houses by Francesco Bartolomeo Rastrelli in the 1740s. The centre of the building was emphasized by a large pediment crowned by a bell-shaped dome. The ends of the administrative blocks were surmounted by smaller pediments and cupolas, and the lavish decorative mouldings, statues, vases and the shallow profile of the entablature were all characteristic of the mature Baroque. The elegant Krasnyye Vorota (completed 1757; destr. 1930s) was pierced in the middle by a large archway through which traffic passed, and by two smaller side arches. The upward thrust of the building was accentuated by a tall, narrow attic, crowned by a figure of *Fame*. Paired columns enhanced the corners of the piers, while vases, cartouches and 55 pictorial panels gave a festive appearance to the whole. The Krasnyye Vorota successfully continued the tradition of Russian triumphal arches that dated back to the reign of Peter I. In 1753 Ukhtomsky prepared designs for a country house for Prince Nikita Trubetskoy (1699–1767). Ukhtomsky successfully combined stylistic elements of the severe 'Dutch' Baroque of the time of Peter I with an imposing quality that was characteristic of the period of Empress Elizabeth. The same year Ukhtomsky submitted a design for the construction of a new bell-tower at St Sergius Monastery at Sergiyev Posad. Work began in 1754, when four tall rectangular tiers were built on the original

BIBLIOGRAPHY

I. Grabar': 'Shkola i komanda arkhitektora kn. D. V. Ukhtomskogo' [The school and team of the architect Prince D. V. Ukhtomsky], *Arkhit. SSSR*, 3–5 (1923), pp. 5–15

V. Nechayev: 'Chertyozhi kn. D. V. Ukhtomskogo v Senatskom arkhive' [Drawings by Prince D. V. Ukhtomsky in the Senate archives], *Arkhit. SSSR*, 3–5 (1923), pp. 16–21

S. Zombe: 'Novyye materialy o D. V. Ukhtomskom' [New material on D. V. Ukhtomsky], *Arkhit. SSSR*, 6 (1939), pp. 76–80

A. Mikhaylov: *Arkhitektor D. V. Ukhtomsky i ego shkola* [The architect D. V. Ukhtomsky and his school] (Moscow, 1954)

Istoriya russkogo iskusstva [History of Russian art], v (Moscow, 1960), pp. 244–56

Arkhitektor D. V. Ukhtomsky [The architect D. V. Ukhtomsky] (exh. cat. by T. Geider, Moscow, Shchusev Res. & Sci. Mus. Rus. Archit., 1973)

YURI OVSYANNIKOV

Ukita Ikkei [Toyotomi Kiminobu; Sekinan Shōja; Tameushi (Igyū)] (*b* Kyoto, 1795; *d* Kyoto, 1859). Japanese painter and poet. He was an official painter for the imperial court in Kyoto, a *waka* (31-syllable form) poet and a fervent loyalist, supporting the re-establishment of imperial rule against the Tokugawa shogunate. Ikkei was active at the close of the Edo period (1600–1868). He expressed his political opinions in his paintings, which, though closely modelled on *Yamatoe* paintings of the Heian (794–1185) and Kamakura (1185–1333) periods (*see* JAPAN, §VI, 3(iii)), included explicit satires on the contemporary political scene. As a result of his paintings and a speech he wrote questioning the future of the country, he was imprisoned in 1858. Released in 1859, he died shortly afterwards from an illness he had contracted in prison.

Ikkei studied painting under Tanaka Totsugen (1760–1823), founder of the *Fukko Yamatoe* ('*Yamatoe* revival') movement. Ikkei's painting style is close to Totsugen's, being modelled after earlier *Yamatoe*-style works, while also exhibiting close stylistic links with later inheritors of the *Yamatoe* tradition: the TOSA SCHOOL, Sumiyoshi school and, at times, *Rinpa* painting (*see* JAPAN, §VI, 4(v)). KANŌ SCHOOL mannerisms are also present, derived from Totsugen's training in a Kanō atelier. The aim of the *Fukko Yamatoe* painters was to glorify the imperial age of Japan through paintings of historical and Buddhist subjects in the classical *Yamatoe* style associated with the court. By reviving this style, *Fukko Yamatoe* intended to re-establish a link between imperial and cultural supremacy. Particularly in Ikkei's case, however, the intention was also to make subtle criticism of the present political situation. The style created by these artists was an important precedent for 'Japanese-style' paintings (*Nihonga*) of historical subjects in the Meiji period (1868–1912) (*see* JAPAN, §VI, 5(iii)). In this regard, Ikkei is credited with furthering the spread of the *Fukko Yamatoe* movement from Kyoto to various parts of Japan.

BIBLIOGRAPHY

Fukko Yamatoe: Tanaka Totsugen to sono shūhen [*Yamatoe* revival: Tanaka Totsugen and his surroundings] (exh. cat., Nagoya, Tokugawa A. Mus., 1978)

N. Tsuji, ed.: 'Ukita Ikkei to seno daihyōsaku *konkesoshi emaki* ni tsuite' [Regarding Ukita Ikkei and his representative work, the Konke handscroll], *Bunjinga shoha* [Various schools of literati painting] (1980), vi of *Zaigai Nihon no shihō* [Treasures of Japanese art abroad], ed. S. Shimada, M. Akiyama and Y. Yamane (Tokyo, 1979–81)

The Great Japan Exhibition: Art of the Edo Period, 1600–1868 (exh. cat., ed. W. Watson; London, RA, 1981)

Konoike Collection ōgie zuroku 3, Tosa, Kanōha hen [A pictorial record of fan illustration in the Konoike collection 3: Tosa and Kanō schools] (Tokyo, Ōta Mem. Mus. A., 1983)

Reizei Tamechika, fukko yamato-e no gajintachi, Uemaro Wado korekushion [Reizei Tamechika and the revived *Yamatoe* school from the Uemura Wado collection] (exh. cat., Tokyo, Nezu A. Mus., 1993)

PATRICIA J. GRAHAM

Ukon. *See* KANŌ, (14).

Ukraine. Country in Europe located in the steppes to the south of the central Russian upland. It covers an area of 603,700 sq. km and borders Moldova, Romania, Hungary, the Slovak Republic and Poland to the west, Belarus' to the north, Russia to the east, and the Black Sea to the south. The name Ukraine means 'borderlands'. Although predominantly a plain, it contains a portion of the Carpathians to the west and the Crimean Mountains to the south. The plain is divided into east and west by Ukraine's largest river, the Dnepr (Ukr. Dnipro), which flows from the Valdai Hills west of Moscow to the Black Sea (see fig. 1). Not only is the river an important trade route, but the fertile black-earth soil on either side has attracted dense settlement since ancient times. In 1989 it had a population of *c.* 51,700,000. Its capital is Kiev.

I. Introduction. II. Architecture. III. Painting. IV. Sculpture. V. Decorative arts. VI. Patronage and collecting. VII. Museums and institutions.

I. Introduction.

The earliest traces of material culture in Ukraine have been recovered from early Palaeolithic sites such as Kiik–Koba in south Crimea, Zhitomir, and Luka Vrublets'ka (Rus. Luka Vrublevetskaya) on the Dnepr. There is evidence of a tribal society evolving in the Mesolithic period (10th–7th millennia BC), which became more complex in the Neolithi period (6th–4th millennia BC) with the portrayals of animals and humans on the walls of caves at Kameneva Mogyla (Kamennaya Mogila) on the north shore of the sea of Azov. Further development in the 3rd and 2nd millennia BC is attested by the remains of the Tripole, Pit-grave and Chernole cultures. In the 7th century BC the art and architecture of the Ukrainian steppe began to be influenced by that of the migrating Scythian tribes (*see* SCYTHIAN AND SARMATIAN ART) and, from the 6th century BC, by that of the Greek cities that were established on the northern Black Sea coast (*see* BLACK SEA COLONIES, §1). The development of an indigenous variant of Classical art continued until the invasions of the north Black Sea by the Goths, Huns and Avars (3rd–6th centuries AD) and the occupation of the middle Dnepr region by an alliance of Slav tribes (4th–7th centuries AD).

In the 9th–10th centuries AD the eastern Slav tribes were united, and during the joint reign (*c.* 866–82) of the princes Askol'd and Dir, Kievan Rus' became one of the leading states of the medieval world. Large cities were built in Ukraine: Kiev, Chernihiv, Pereyaslav, Belgorod and Volodymyr Volyns'ky (Vladimir Volynsky). It was the beginning of the great period in Old Russian art, in which, after the adoption of Christianity in 988–9, Byzantine techniques of stone construction, wall painting, mosaic decoration and carving were adapted and combined with local traditions to form the basis of Ukrainian medieval art.

The dissolution of Kievan Rus' into several independent principalities from the late 11th century led to Kiev's decline and, with the Tatar-Mongol invasions of 1239–40, Kievan control of the steppes was brought to an end. From the late 14th century to the early 19th century the territory of Ukraine was fought over by and divided between Poland, Lithuania, the Crimean Tatars (later the Ottoman Turks) and Russia. In 1596 the Union of Brest–Litovsk divided the Ukrainians into Orthodox and Roman Catholic; already by this date the influence of Roman Catholic taste is evident in the use of Renaissance and western Baroque forms and motifs in Ukrainian art. Religious dissent was accompanied by social and political strife,

1. Map of Ukraine; those sites with separate entries in this dictionary are distinguished by CROSS-REFERENCE TYPE

including the uprising of the Zaporozhian Cossacks against Poland. In 1654 the area controlled by the Cossacks was united with Russia, while in 1667 and 1686 Poland–Lithuania recognized Muscovite suzerainty over Kiev and the lands east of the Dnepr. In the 18th century the victory of Peter I (*reg* 1682–1725) over Charles XII (*reg* 1697–1718) at Poltava in 1709 and the subsequent partitioning of Poland led to Russia's acquisition of Ukrainian lands west of the Dnepr except for Galicia, which went to the Austro-Hungarian empire.

Between 1917 and 1920 several attempts were made to establish an independent Ukrainian state, ending in a bloody civil war. In 1924 Ukraine became part of the USSR; after World War II its boundaries were extended with the acquisition of Galicia. It remained a Soviet republic until December 1991, when it declared its independence. During the period of Soviet domination the Ukraine's ties with Russia were emphasized and its art tended to represent the people's revolutionary struggle, and various historical, military and patriotic subjects. Folk art, however, adhered more closely to traditional forms.

JANA HOWLETT

II. Architecture.

1. *c.* AD 860–1239. 2. 1240–1550. 3. After 1550.

1. *c.* AD 860–1239. After the adoption in 988–9 of Christianity in Kievan Rus', already a major medieval state

since the reign (*c.* 866–82) of the princes Askol'd and Dir, Byzantine architectural techniques were combined with local traditions, particularly in wooden construction, to produce the great period of Kievan architecture that was halted by the Tatar–Mongol invasions of 1239–40.

(i) Building materials and techniques. (ii) Secular architecture. (iii) Religious architecture.

(i) Building materials and techniques. Wood was the most common building material in Kievan Rus': the Arab writers Ibn Miskawayh (*d* 1030) and Ibn Fadlan (10th century) both noted that Russian warriors and merchants always carried the tools of a joiner on them. Builders' workshops were already established by the 11th century and in the same period the first known builder, Zhdan-Nikolay, constructed the church of SS Boris and Gleb (destr. 1240) in the upper city of Kiev. Stone was introduced, first for the construction of the gateways and towers of fortifications and monasteries (*see* KIEV, §1(i)) and subsequently for churches and princely palaces, which are known from excavations at Kiev, Chernihiv and Pereyaslav. Byzantine architects were brought in to work side by side with local craftsmen, whose knowledge of traditional wood construction techniques is reflected in many extant stone buildings, such as the towers that gave access to the galleries and service rooms of churches. The walls were made of courses of local stone and flat, almost square bricks bound together with a mixture of lime and crushed brick, creating a striped

surface on the building façades. Pink slate was used for external ornament.

In the 12th century growing international contacts between individual principalities and the countries to the east and west stimulated the development of different schools of architecture and led to the introduction of new principles of urban planning and new building techniques. Stone-carving and the use of potters' wares, such as glazed ceramic tiles for flooring, became widespread. Individual marks and stamps on bricks identify the work of different masons, such as Ivan, who built the monastery of St Euphrosyne in Polotsk; Avdey, who decorated a church in Kholm with carving; and the Kievan architect Pyotr Mil'oneg, who built the breast wall of the church of the Vydubetsky Monastery (1180–1200; destr.; *see* KIEV, §1(i)).

(ii) Secular architecture. The names of several settlements (e.g. Ol'zhichi, Berestiv (Berestovo) and Predslavyn (Predslavin)) belonging to princely estates are recorded from as early as the 10th century AD; they contained the court of the feudal lord, accommodation for his retainers and a storehouse for produce. According to the archaeological evidence, until the 11th century these settlements were established along rivers. In the north of Kievan Rus' single-room peasant houses were built of logs, while in the south the timber frames were filled with daub.

During the 11th century Old Russian towns gained their definitive form: an upper town fortified with ditches and ramparts, where the main cathedral was located together with the living quarters for the prince, boyars, the members of the prince's bodyguard and the artisans who served them; a lower town or trading quarter, defended by a stockade, which contained a market-place, churches, monasteries and the houses of merchants and craftsmen; and suburbs, also inhabited by merchants and craftsmen. Archaeology and literary records indicate that these towns had radial plans with wooden paved streets that usually met either at the city gate, as at Kiev, or at the kremlin, as at Pereyaslav.

Most of the population lived in single-room, single-storey wooden houses, the floor of which lay 300–600 mm below ground-level. The princes and boyars had luxurious town houses with gold-roofed towers, intricate carved gates and lofty reception halls. The houses were built of a framework of logs; larger residences, in two storeys, consisted of several log-framed units comprising a central reception hall and a warm and a cold chamber. Defensive walls were made of a wooden frame filled with earth and reinforced from the outside with earthen embankments that were replaced by wooden buttresses in the 11th century. Later, under Vladimir I Svyatoslavich (*reg* 980–1015) and Yaroslav the Wise (*reg* 1019–54), defences were built of wood and unbaked brick, as at Belgorod (991) and Pereyaslav (992). These were surmounted by log walls with loopholes, and there were towers at the corners. From the 11th century princely palaces were built of stone.

(iii) Religious architecture. The other principal building type to be made in stone was the urban cathedral, the most common form being the cross plan with four or six piers supporting a central dome (a domed cross). The first stone church was that of the Tithe of the Most Holy Mother of God (Desyatina Presvyatoy Bogoroditsy; 989–96; destr. 1240) in Kiev; only its foundations survive. The two earliest extant stone churches are the cathedral of St Sophia (begun 1037) in Kiev (*see* KIEV, §3(i)) and the cathedral of the Transfiguration (Spaso-Preobrazhensky; *c.* 1036) in the centre of the kremlin in Chernihiv. St Sophia has been much altered but the cathedral of the Transfiguration preserves its domed-cross plan and external surfaces decorated with symmetrically arranged niches.

In the second half of the 11th century the break-up of Kievan Rus' into separate principalities with their own capitals enabled the Church to grow more powerful as the principalities' economic potential and political horizons became more confined. Small parish churches were built in towns and villages while monasteries acquired a particularly important role, often of a strategic nature. Several of the latter were founded in Kiev in the late 11th century and the early 12th, including the Pecherskaya Lavra (*see* KIEV, §3(ii)), St Michael with the Golden Roofs (Zlatoverkhy; 1108; destr. 1935) and the Vydubetsky; these all had churches of the domed-cross type, but without a tower or galleries. Unlike earlier examples, the interiors of these churches were subdivided rather than remaining open. Other buildings erected during this period include a four-piered baptistery, a refectory hall and the tiny church of the Trinity (Troitskaya; 1108; rebuilt 1722–9), all in the Pecherskaya Lavra. The definitive simplified form of a cubical mass surmounted by a central dome is represented by the mid-12th-century cathedral of the Yeletsky Monastery in Chernihiv. The decoration of the exterior walls became more restrained. Although pilasters continued to divide the walls vertically, the striped effect formed by the brick and stone courses was replaced by the use of brick only.

Pereyaslav was another centre of considerable building activity from the late 11th century. Excavations (1949–53) have revealed that although the town had a traditional

2. Kiev, Ukraine, church of the Holy Trinity (Troitskaya) in the monastery of St Cyril, south façade, mid-12th century

Russian plan, its commercial and cultural links with the Byzantine world clearly influenced the development of its architecture, as in the five-aisled cathedral of St Michael (1090; destr. 1239) and the church (1098; destr. 1239) erected in the palace. Small churches with two central piers were also built in the principality, for example the church of the Saviour (11th century; destr. 1239). In general, Pereyaslav's churches appear to have had a rectangular interior preceded by a narrow narthex. A similar arrangement is also found in the chapel of St George (1098) at Ostra, which is decorated with wall paintings, and the Letskaya Chapel (1106), which was founded by Vladimir II Monomakh (*reg* 1113–25) at Kyivshchyna (Kiyevshchina).

During the second quarter of the 12th century religious architecture tended towards modesty of scale and harmony of proportions. Among the alterations to the cathedral of the Dormition (Uspensky Sobor; 1073–8) in the Pecherskaya Lavra, for example, the stairs to the gallery were incorporated into the thickness of the wall; the half-columns with simple capitals that divided the external walls were surmounted by *zakomary* (semicircular arches), and the expensive mosaic decoration was supplanted by wall paintings. The same tendency towards simplicity of design can be seen in the cathedral of St George or the Dormition (1144) in the small town of Kaniv (Kanev), the church of the Holy Trinity (Troitskaya) in the monastery of St Cyril (mid-12th century; 17th- and 18th-century additions; see fig. 2) and the church of the Mother of God (Bogoroditsa Pirogoshchi) in Kiev and the remains of a church found at Pereyaslav. Architecture in the principality of Chernihiv developed along slightly different lines. For example, the cathedral of SS Boris and Gleb (1170s; rest. 1954–7; see fig. 3), which served as the prince's mausoleum, is a more compact version of the six-pier, dome-in-cross type of structure than is the church of St Cyril in Kiev. In the Dnepr region the only Old Russian church to have survived is the 12th-century church of the Prophet Elijah. The drum of its single dome rests on four piers, which are connected by arches to pilasters on the walls, thus increasing the space under the dome. In style this church is similar to the main cathedral and the cathedral of the Dormition (both mid-12th century) in the city of Volodymyr Volyns'ky. They are distinguished by the simplicity of their design and architectural decoration.

As the economic power of the towns grew in the late 12th century, the artisans and craftsmen became the dominant class; their tastes were reflected in a new style of architecture. In the trading quarters outside the city walls they erected churches in honour of the patroness of commerce, St Paraskeva Pyatnitsa. The external appearance of these churches became all important. Their designs imitated traditional wooden folk architecture, with its pyramidal arrangement of forms and emphasis on upward movement. Influences from Gothic architecture are evident in the pointed arches and brickwork, which remained the principal building material; ceramic decorative details were also widely used. The fact that the same craftsmen worked in Kiev, Smolensk, Belgorod and Ovruch led to the development of a certain uniformity of style. The decoration of the façade and the elegant proportions of the church of St Basil (late 12th century; rest. 1908–12) at

3. Chernihiv, Ukraine, cathedral of SS Boris and Gleb, 1170s; restored 1954–7

Ovruch differentiate it from 11th-century churches but introduce certain stylistic traits that were most clearly expressed in the church of St Paraskeva Pyatnitsa (late 12th century or early 13th; destr. 1941; rebuilt 1967) in the market-place at Chernihiv. While its lower part is a four-pier, domed-cross church with three entrances and steps up to the choir, its upper part is different from any form that had come before. The barrel vaults covering the aisles are lower than the arches linking the four central piers that support the drum and dome. This interior arrangement of vaults and arches is reflected in the decoration of the exterior with arches on pilasters surmounted by a tier of *zakomary*. At the base of the drum there are an additional four *kokoshniki* (arches shaped like women's head-dresses), thus reinforcing the impression of upward movement. The influence of wooden folk architecture is evident in the brick patterns of latticed ornament and the simplified meander, both of which are reminiscent of embroidery. Similar churches were built (1180–90) in Novgorod-Seversky, Putyvl' (Putivl') and Grodno (now in Belarus'), where bricks with the marks of craftsmen who had worked in Chernihiv have been found in the monuments of the 12th century and the early 13th.

In the mid-12th century the principality of Halich in the south-west of Rus' reached a peak in its development. Its close links with the lands along the Danube, Poland and Moravia had resulted in the creation of a Galician school of architecture. Excavations in 1939–41 and the 1950s in the capital city, HALICH, revealed the remains of the white-stone cathedral of the Dormition (Uspensky Sobor; 1157), of the 12th-century monastery of SS Boris and Gleb 12 km outside the city, and of many other churches built of well-cut blocks of limestone; sculptural details and carved capitals decorated the façades and portals. Their architecture is varied and includes plans with four-pier or single-cell types with extended apses or circular central sections. The only surviving church is that of St Panteleymon (before 1200; rebuilt 17th century), which retains its detailed carvings in a Romanesque style. Similar churches of white stone with sculptural decoration were built at Kholm between 1230 and 1254.

BIBLIOGRAPHY

G. Lukomsky: *O proiskhozhdenii form drevnerusskogo zodchestva Chernigova* [On the origins of the forms of the Old Russian architecture of Chernigov] (St Petersburg, 1912)

M. Krasovsky: *Plany drevnerusskikh khramov* [The plans of Old Russian churches] (Petrograd, 1915)

N. Petrov: *Chernigovskoye zodchestvo XI–XII vv.* [The architecture of Chernigov in the 11th–12th centuries] (Chernigov, 1915)

G. Loukomsky: *L'Architecture religieuse russe du XIe siècle au XVIIe* (Paris, 1929)

N. Voronin: *Ocherki po istorii drevnerusskogo zodchestva X–XII vekov* [Studies in the history of Old Russian architecture of the 10th–12th centuries] (Moscow, 1934)

M. K. Karger: 'Zodchestvo Galitsko-Volynskoy zemli v XII–XIII vv.' [The architecture of Galicia and Volynia in the 12th and 13th centuries], *Kratkoye Soobshcheniye Inst. Istor. Mat. Kul't.*, ii (1940), pp. 14–21

B. A. Rybakov: 'Drevnosti Chernigova' [The antiquities of Chernigov], *Mat. & Issledovaniya Arkheol. SSSR*, 11 (1949), pp. 7–92

N. I. Brunov: *Mastera drevnerusskogo zodchestva* [Masters of Old Russian architecture] (Moscow, 1953)

M. G. Hamilton: *The Art and Architecture of Russia*, Pelican Hist. A. (Harmondsworth, 1954, rev. 2/1975)

Yu. S. Aseyev: *Drevniy Kiyev* [Ancient Kiev] (Moscow, 1956)

P. A. Rappoport: *Ocherki po istorii russkogo voyennogo zodchestva, X–XIII vv.* [Studies in the history of Russian military architecture, 10th–13th centuries] (Moscow, 1956)

M. K. Karger: *Drevniy Kiyev* [Ancient Kiev], 2 vols (Moscow, 1958–61)

K. P. Afanas'yev: *Postroyeniye arkhitekturnoy formy drevnerusskimi zodchimi* [The construction of architectural form by Old Russian architects] (Moscow, 1961)

Yu. S. Aseyev: *Dzherela: Mystetstvo u Kyïvs'kyy Rusi* [Origins: the art of Kievan Rus'] (Kiev, 1980)

——: *Arkhitektura drevnego Kiyeva* [The architecture of ancient Kiev] (Kiev, 1982)

For further bibliography see KIEV, §1(i).

2. 1240–1550. During the Tatar–Mongol domination of Kievan Rus' from *c.* 1240, building in stone temporarily ceased except in the Volhyn' principality, where the princes retained their independence. Although churches were constructed, Volhyn''s strategic position on the western frontier meant that defensive architecture predominated. With the return of stone architecture to the rest of Ukraine, many churches and monasteries there, too, were designed or adapted to withstand attack.

(i) Secular architecture. In the late 13th century the towns of Berestya (now Brest, Belarus') , Kaminets' (Kamenets) and Lyubomyl (Lyubomil) in Volhyn' were protected by stone towers of over 35 m. They were square or round with a wooden gallery in the middle to accommodate the defenders; similar towers were also built at Drogobych and Chartoryys'k. In the 14th century such Gothic features as buttresses began to appear in the architecture of Volhyn', for example in the remnants of the castle at Luts'k (Lutsk), the principality's political and cultural centre. Stone walls connect its rectangular towers, which have small loopholes and windows adorned on the inward side with Gothic shafts. Other decorative elements include a moulded frame around the main gates and bricks with glazed borders in the masonry. Simplicity of form and decoration is even greater at Kremenets' (Kremenets) Castle (11th century), originally wood but rebuilt in white limestone between the late 13th century and the beginning of the 14th. It occupies a hill site some distance from the city, which had its own fortifications. The castles of Khuts'k (Khutsk) (14th century; partially destr.) and Mukachevo (14th century; rebuilt 16th–17th centuries) were also built on hills but were not connected to the fortifications surrounding their towns in the valleys. The towns themselves were built according to the new principles of urban planning, with regular, radially arranged streets centred on a market square with a town hall and a cathedral.

4. Fortress at Belgorod, Ukraine, 1438–54; rebuilt 16th–17th centuries

In the 15th century and the first half of the 16th the wooden and stone castles and fortifications of the 12th and 13th centuries ceased to be suitable for the new military equipment: the walls were not thick enough, and there were too few embrasures. Luts'k, Kremenets', Mukachevo and Khuts'k castles were all rebuilt and made more picturesque by the addition of sculptured door and window frames and glazed stone and brick ornament. Another 15th-century reconstruction was undertaken at Khotyn', when it became part of the Moldovian principality in the reign of Stephen III (reg 1457–1504). The thickness of its walls was increased to 8 m and the height of its towers to 30 m. The great Belgorod fortress (1438–54; rebuilt 16th–17th centuries; see fig. 4) was mainly the work of the Galician mason Fyodorko and consisted of three parts: the citadel, the fortified city and the fortified approach. The walls (l. 2 km) were guarded by 26 rectangular, square, octagonal or round towers without any ornament. In the 16th century the influence of Italian Renaissance architecture can clearly be seen in the fortresses of Kaminets'-Podil's'ky and Berezhany. The former, founded before the Tatar–Mongol invasions, was rebuilt several times in wood; reconstruction in stone began in the 15th century. In 1545, under the guidance of the architect Iov Pretvich the walls were extended and overhanging embrasures added to the round and rectangular towers. These were adorned with architectural decoration such as carved figures on the buttresses of the overhanging embrasures and an ornamental frieze on the Rozhanka Tower. The two main entrance gates were overlooked by several towers connected by a covered gallery. Among other similar castles is Medzhibozh (c. 1545).

At Berezhany Castle (1534–54) the features that most clearly reflect the influence of Renaissance architecture are the pentagonal plan, the large windows of the living-quarters, the two-storey arcaded galleries around the courtyard, and the southern building with its high attic and blind arcading.

(ii) Religious architecture. In the late 13th century and the early 14th churches in Volhyn' were built in the traditional domed-cross form, as in the church of St Basil at Volodymyr Volyns'ky, and in the rotunda form, as in the two examples at Volodymyr Volyns'ky and Goryany. Church building became more widespread in the second half of the 14th century, and some Gothic features were introduced, especially in western Ukraine, which was then part of Poland. Thus, in the aisled church of the Nativity of Christ (Rozhdestvo Khristova; late 14th century–early 15th) in Halich the central aisle and transept were higher than the side aisles, while in the church of the Birth of the Mother of God (Rozhdestvo Bogoroditsy; late 14th century) in Rogatin Gothic buttresses replaced the plain pilasters of the façades. At L'viv, Drogobych and other cities in western Ukraine, numerous Catholic churches were built entirely in the Gothic style: but, with the strengthening of Ukrainian national consciousness, the influence of the traditional wooden architecture on stone buildings became particularly marked.

By the 15th century the largest landowners were the monasteries, where grand building schemes were developed. In Kiev the Pecherskaya Lavra (see KIEV, §3(ii)) was completely restored in the late 15th century. To the cathedral of the Dormition were added Gothic stepped pediments, buttresses and high sloping roofs. The wooden living and service structures and the wooden fortified walls, which converted the monastery into a fortress, were built according to a regular plan. Other monasteries, such as those at Mizhrichehya (Mezhirech'ye) and Derman', were also carefully planned around the church. Settlements were often linked to the monasteries by a system of fortifications. The churches themselves were equipped for defensive purposes, as in the church of the Dormition (Usperskaya) at Zimno, the cathedral of the Nikolayev Monastery at Mil'tsy and the church of the Protecting Veil of the Mother of God (Pokrovskaya) at Sutkovtsi. Intimate interiors were combined with severe defensive architecture: windows are small, and a huge central pillar supports the internal system of arches.

In the 15th and 16th centuries the wooden church architecture in the western regions of Ukraine became more complex. The various types included squat structures of three-framed units built of logs or planks with multiple roofs, often of different pitches, found in Volhyn'; high and well-proportioned three- and five-framed structures in L'viv; and churches with abundant horizontal articulation in Transcarpathia. These frameworks were adapted to form churches with three chambers corresponding to the apse, nave and narthex or to make domed-cross churches. These were built as a cube, for example the church of the Holy Spirit (Svyatoy Dukh; early 16th century) in Potelich; with an octagonal upper storey, as in the cathedral of the Annunciation (Blagoveshcheniye; 1505) at Kovel', or with a pyramidal upper storey as in the church of the Mother of God (Bogoroditsa; 1580) at Sukhodillya (Sukhodolya). A characteristic feature of Ukrainian wooden churches is the combination of pyramidal and square frames for the upper storey and roofing. Another typical feature of the 16th century was the faceting of the main apses and upper storeys of the high central tower, which rose above the arched roofs over the altar and subsidiary rooms. The combination of different forms is also evident in the small stone churches founded by groups of craftsmen and peasants, as in the church of the Trinity (Troitsa) in the Znamens'ky (Znamensky) Monastery (1465–75), where the polygonal drum of the dome rises from the central square. A type of triple-apsed church, which was derived from churches in the Balkans and Moldavia, also became widespread in the foothills of Carpathia, as in the church of St Onufrios at Lavriv (Lavrov) near Sambor.

The Jewish communities in Ukraine also erected their own places of worship. Their synagogues were square in plan with groin vaults supported in the centre by four closely placed pillars surrounding a platform from which the Torah was read (see JEWISH ART, §II, 1(iii)(a)); any decoration was painted, as for example in the stone synagogue (15th century) at Shargorod.

BIBLIOGRAPHY
M. Grushevsky: *Yuzhnorusskiye gospodarskiye zamki v polovine XVI veka* [Southern Russian landowners' castles in the middle of the 16th century] (Moscow, 1890)

G. G. Pavlutsky: *Derevyannyye i kamennyye khramy* [Wooden and stone churches] (Kiev, 1905)

G. K. Lukomsky: *Galitsiya v yeyo starine: Starinnaya arkhitektura Galitsii v ocherkakh i risunkakh* [Galicia in the old days: the old architecture of Galicia in sketches and pictures] (Petrograd, 1915)

A. S. Grushevsky: *Goroda velikogo knyazhestva litovskogo v XIV–XVI vv.* [The cities of the Great Lithuanian Principality between the 14th and 16th centuries] (Kiev, 1918)

V. Sichins'ky: *Rotondy na Ukraïni* [Rotundas in Ukraine] (Kiev, 1929)

S. V. Bezsonov: *Arkhitektura zapadnoy Ukrainy* [Architecture of western Ukraine] (Moscow, 1946)

P. P. Sova: *Arkhitekturni pam'yatniki Zakarpattya* [Architectural monuments of Transcarpathia] (Uzhgorod, 1958)

G. Logvin: *Po Ukraïni* [In Ukraine] (Kiev, 1968)

G. Ostrovsky: *L'vov* (Moscow, 1975)

3. AFTER 1550. In the second half of the 16th century and the early 17th buildings in stone began to combine the techniques and forms typical of wooden architecture with those of the Renaissance. Peter I's victory in 1709 at Poltava opened a new period of architectural development in Ukraine, with the rapid growth of the old towns of Kiev, Chernihiv and Pereyaslav and the founding of the new towns of Sumy, Lebedyn (Lebedin) and Kharkiv. The accumulation of wealth and lands by the monasteries, Cossack leaders and ruling nobility stimulated the construction of religious and secular buildings and the development of new building techniques. For the next 150 years much of this activity was dominated by a spirit of Neo-classicism in the planning of cities. Since the second half of the 19th century, however, various styles have been adopted and developed in the search for a national style.

(i) Secular architecture. (ii) Religious architecture.

(i) Secular architecture. Architectural development during the late 16th century and the 17th was particularly intense in the western Ukraine, and especially in L'viv. Among the numerous buildings erected there were several residences near the market square, the L'viv Brotherhood building and the Kornyakta tower (1578). As with the churches in the city (*see* §(ii) below), these buildings were the work of local and Italian architects. From the late 16th century until the early 18th the most common house type had a single interior space, with thick walls surmounted by a cylindrical roof. The size of brick used for the walls determined the nature of the architectural decoration of the façade. Only rebuilt examples of such house have survived, such as the Lizogub house at Syndiv (Sednev) and the metropolitan's house (early 18th century) in the precincts of the cathedral of St Sophia in Kiev. Another particularly noteworthy building is the Ya. Lizogub house (1680–90) at Chernihiv. The façades of the rectangular house are divided by half-columns and pilasters, which lie between the windows and niches and are surmounted by architraves. This sculptural approach to architecture is typical of the 17th century and early 18th and is found on the refectory buildings of the Vydubetsky and Trinity (Troitsky) monasteries in Kiev and Chernihiv respectively. By 1700, following the union with Russia in 1654, the Russian Baroque style had begun to influence Ukrainian architecture, as in the two-tiered Borisoglebsky Collegium (1700–02) at Chernihiv. Numerous other secular buildings were erected in this style by Russian and Ukrainian architects during the 18th century, including the palace and park (1760s; by Andrian V. Kvasov (1718–72)) at

Baturyn (Baturin), the offices of the Kiev Regiment (1765; by Ivan Grigorovich-Barsky) in Kozolets' (Kozelets), the Klovsky Palace (1754–8; by P. I. Neyelov) in Kiev, the collegium in Novgorod-Seversky, the seminary (1763–7; by M. Yurasov) in the precincts of the St Sophia Cathedral in Kiev and the Kiev Academy (begun 1703; completed by Gottfried Schädel in 1740).

In addition to the popularity of the Baroque style, many buildings erected in the cities and towns of Ukraine in the 18th century and early 19th formed part of government-approved urban plans that followed Classical models. Public and administrative buildings were constructed around the central squares in Kherson (1778), Sevastopol' (1784) and Odessa (1794). Additions were made to the old centres of Kiev, Chernihiv and Poltava. Another characteristic feature of this urban architecture was the symmetrical arrangement of the building façades, as in the magistrates' courts (late 18th century; by Ivan Starov) at Mykolaïv (Nikolayev) and the structures (1805–11; by U. D. Zakharov) around the circular open space at Poltava. Commercial buildings were often placed in key urban locations, as for example were the Contracts Building (1815–17; by William Hastie) in Kiev and the hotels at Bila Tserkv (Belaya Tserkov'; 1809–14) and Kiev (1809–28; by Aloizy I. Ruska (1758–1822) and Andrey I. Melensky (1766–1833)). The theatres of Kiev (1804–6; by Andrey I. Melensky) and Odessa (1809; by J. Thomas de Thomon; destr. 1873) and institutes of learning such as the Nezhinsky Lyceum (1824; by Aloizy I. Ruska (1758–1822)) of Prince I. A. Bezborodko, the schools for the daughters of the nobility in Poltava (1832) and Kiev (1832–42; by Vikenty I. Beretti (1781–1842)) and the university in Kiev (1837–42; by Vikenty I. Beretti; *see* KIEV, fig. 3) are all examples of this new planning, with corridored interiors and rigidly composed façades and colonnades using the Classical orders.

In the second half of the 19th century town construction became more varied, with many buildings adopting eclectic and stylized approaches to Gothic and Renaissance designs, as in the Trade Building (1880; by B. G. Mikhalovsky) at Kharkiv and the theatres at Odessa (1884–7; by Ferdinand Fellner (*b* 1847) and Herman Helmer (1849–1919)) and Kiev (1901; by Viktor A. Shreter). The search had also begun for a 'national' style, and in the early 20th century this led in three directions. The first was based on Ukrainian folk art and is represented by the work of Vasyl' Krychevs'ky in Kiev (e.g. the Poltava City Council building; 1900) and Ivan I. Levinsky (1851–1919) in L'viv. The second direction was towards the neo-Baroque and the third, common to the whole of the Russian empire, stemmed from the architecture of Kievan Rus' of the 10th–12th centuries. At the same time, Ukraine, in common with Europe and Russia, was affected by the Art Nouveau style as represented by the City Museum of Antiques and Art (now the Museum of Ukrainian Art; 1897–1900; by Vladislav V. Gorodetsky (1863–1930) and G. P. Boitsov) in Kiev.

In the years immediately following the Russian October Revolution and Civil War (1917–20), the appearance of new construction materials and methods, together with the growth of industrial towns and centres (e.g. Kryvy

Rog (Krivoy Rog), Zaporizhzhya (Zaporozh'ye) and Kramoyors'k (Kramatorsk)), led to the development of the Soviet Rationalist and Constructivist styles. The power station at Dneprgas represents a major achievement in industrial architecture of the 1920s and early 1930s. Standardized housing for workers was introduced (e.g. in Zaporizhzhya and Kharkiv), and many hospitals, clubs, schools, theatres and cinemas were built, often along the main streets of towns (e.g. Donets'k (Donetsk)). Among the best examples of Constructivist town architecture are the House of Doctors (1927; by Pavel F. Alyoshin (1881–1961)) in Kiev, the Dynamo stadium (1934–5; by Vasily A. Os'mak (1870–1942) and Nina D. Manucharova (1900–88)) and restaurant (1934; by Iosef Yu. Karakis and Nina D. Manucharova) in Kiev and the buildings centred on Kiev's Dzerzhinsky Square. There were two other stylistic tendencies: the first developed Ukrainian Baroque and wooden architecture (e.g. the complex of the Ukrainian academy of agriculture in Kiev; 1925–30; by Dmitry M. D'yachenko (1869–1921)); the second developed Neoclassical forms (e.g. Hospital No. 3 in Kharkiv; 1924–7; by V. A. Yestrovich). A national architectural style was developed in certain projects (e.g. the Shevchenko Memorial Museum near Kaniv; 1931–4; by Vasyl' Krychevs'ky and Pavel F. Kostyrko).

During World War II serious damage was inflicted on many Ukrainian towns, houses and public monuments. A general plan of restoration was undertaken between 1943 and 1954. Urban planning was based on districts, and the façades of houses were extensively decorated with Neoclassical and Ukrainian Baroque motifs. National architectural styles continued to be used in rural areas. From the mid-1950s architecture changed direction, focusing on new materials and methods of construction. In the 1960s–80s urban planners paid more attention to historical monuments. A typical approach in the design of new towns was to use limited amounts of new land and to rebuild and reshape town centres (the general plan for Kiev, 1986). Standardized housing projects were improved by a move away from factory-style construction to the introduction of a variety of house types. Among the cities that acquired new residential districts were Kiev, Kharkiv and L'viv. Underground railways were built in both Kiev and Kharkiv, with leading artists and architects involved in the design of the stations.

(ii) Religious architecture. The Chapel of the Three Prelates (Kaplitsa Tryokh Svyatiteley; 1578–91) and the church of the Dormition (Uspenskaya; 1598–1631) in L'viv are among Ukraine's most important examples of late 16th- and early 17th-century church architecture in the Renaissance style and are richly decorated with sculpture and carving. Similar but less ornate churches include those of the Protecting Veil of the Mother of God (Pokrov; 1622–9) in Sulymivka (Sulimovka), the Prophet Elijah (1653) in Subbotovo and Nikola Pritiska (18th century) in Kiev. Wooden churches continued to be constructed in three sections surmounted by roofs and towers of different heights, as in the church of the Holy Spirit (Svyatoy dukh; 17th century) in Rogatin and the churches of the Exaltation of the Cross (Vozdvizheniye, before 1636; rebuilt 1661; see fig. 5) and St George (1654), both in Drogobych. More complex forms for the upper sections and roofs of churches were developed in the different regions of Ukraine. For example, the Galician school is characterized by the use of a variety of cupolas, as in the church of the Nativity (Rozhdestvo; 1705) in Zholkva (now Nesterov), while the Podil's' school favoured hipped roofs, as in the church of the Ascension (Vozneseniye; 1738) in Chortkiv (Chortkov).

An early example of a stone church in the Baroque style is the Roman Catholic church (1600–30; by A. Prikhil'ny and Pavel Rimlyanin (*d* 1618); see fig. 6) in the Bernardine monastery in L'viv. By the late 17th century most stone churches were built in the Baroque style, for example the church of the Prophet Elijah (1679–89) in the Trinity Monastery at Chernihiv. The style continued to dominate Ukrainian religious architecture into the 18th century, with the result that in the 1720s–50s Russian and Ukrainian architects produced numerous fine monuments that combined European Baroque architecture with the characteristically Russian elements of belfries, cupolas, porches and slender columns. Many of the most important examples from this period are in Kiev (*see* KIEV, §1(iii)), such as the church of St Andrew (1747–53; by Bartolomeo Francesco Rastrelli and Ivan F. Michurin (*c.* 1703–63)) and that of Nikolay Naberezhny (1772–5; by Ivan Grigorovich-Barsky). The Kovnirovsky building (1744–5; by Stefan D. Kovnir) in the Pecherskaya Lavra and the Brama Zaborivs'ka (1746–8; by Gottfried Schädel) in Kiev are geometrically precise and make use of rich ornamentation, carved decorative detail and glazed ceramics. The cathedral of St George in L'VIV (1745–64; by Bernard Meretyn (*d* 1759)) is one of several churches outside Kiev that contain Baroque features.

In the late 18th century and the 19th large domed-cross city churches were built rather than monasteries or small wooden churches. Colonnaded porticos abutting on to the north and west sides of a church became a common

5. Drogobych, Ukraine, church of the Exaltation of the Cross (Vozdvizheniye), before 1636; rebuilt 1661

6. L'viv, Ukraine, church of the Bernadine Monastery by A. Prikhil'ny and Pavel Rimlyanin, 1600–30

I. Sventsitsky: *Derevyannyye tserkvi Galitskoy Rusi XVII–XVIII vekov* [Wooden churches in Galician Rus' in the 17th and 18th centuries] (Lemberg, 1915)

D. Antonovich: *Z istorii tserkovnogo budivnytstva na Ukraïni* [From the history of church architecture in Ukraine] (Prague, 1925)

V. Shcherbakivs'ky: *Bukovyns'ki i galyts'ki derev'yani tserkvy, nadgrobni, prydorozhni khresty, fygury i kaplytsi* [Bukovinian and Galician wooden churches, tombs, roadside crosses, figures and chapels] (1926), ii of *Ukraïns'ke mystetstvo* [Ukrainian art] (Kiev, 1913–26)

S. Taranushenko: *Mystetstvo Slobozhanshchyny XVII–XVIII vv.* [The art of the Slobozhanshchina of the 17th and 18th centuries] (Khar'kov, 1928)

S. V. Bezsonov: *Arkhitektura zapadnoy Ukrainy* [The architecture of western Ukraine] (Moscow, 1946)

P. T. Yurchenko: *Derev'yane zodchestvo Ukrainy (XVIII–XIX st.)* [Ukrainian wooden architecture of the 18th and 19th centuries] (Kiev, 1949)

M. Tsapenko: *Arkhitektura Levoberezhnoy Ukrainy XVII–XVIII vekov* [The architecture of eastern Ukraine of the 17th and 18th centuries] (Moscow, 1967)

S. A. Taranushenko: *Monumental'na derev'yana arkhitektura Livoberezhnoï Ukraïny* [Monumental wooden architecture in eastern Ukraine] (Kiev, 1976)

Pamyatniki gradostroitel'stva i arkhitektury Ukrainskoy SSR: Illyustrirovannyy spravochnik-katalog [Monuments of town building and architecture in the Ukrainian SSR: illustrated guidebook and catalogue], 4 vols (Kiev, 1983–6)

III. Painting.

The wall paintings, mosaics, icons and manuscript illuminations of Kievan Rus' were all closely related to Byzantine art but soon acquired stylistic traits of their own. The Tatar–Mongol domination curtailed artistic development from the mid-13th century until the 14th, when there was renewed activity in local centres. By the end of the 16th century the spread of humanistic ideas had led to an increasingly secular approach to art.

1. *c.* AD 860–1239. 2. 1240–*c.* 1600. 3. After 1600.

1. *c.* AD 860–1239.

(i) Monumental painting and mosaic. (ii) Icons. (iii) Manuscripts.

(i) Monumental painting and mosaic. As in Byzantine churches, the interiors of churches in Kievan Rus' were completely and richly decorated with wall paintings and mosaics; examples from the 11th and 12th centuries have been preserved in Kiev. As the Kievan state declined, fresco gradually replaced and finally ousted altogether the more expensive mosaics.

The first artists were Greeks brought by Vladimir I Syvatoslavich (*reg* 978–1015) to decorate the church of the Tithe of the Most Holy Mother of God (Desyatina Presvyatoy Bogoroditsy; 989–96; destr. 1240) in Kiev. Only a few fresco fragments of their work survive (Kiev, Hist. Mus.), but the chronicles attest to the church's elaborate decoration with marble, slate, porphyry, mosaic and wall painting. Whereas in the Byzantine empire these last two art forms were never used in the same building, in Kievan Rus' mosaic and wall painting existed side by side. The best-preserved fragment of wall painting from the Tithe church depicts the upper part of a young saint's face; its large eyes, sharp shadows and heavy lines are reminiscent of the 2nd-century AD mummy portraits (London, BM) from Faiyum (*see* FAIYUM, §2).

One of the most outstanding extant schemes of combined mosaic and wall painting is in the cathedral of St Sophia (1037) in Kiev (*see* KIEV, §3(i) and fig. 5). The mosaics are organized in a hierarchical scheme that follows the standard system of Constantinople. The iconographical

---

feature, as in the church of All Saints (Vsekhsvyatskaya; late 18th century) in Nizhyn (Nezhin) and of St Nicholas (1816) in Romny. Round churches with an adjoining refectory and belfry, as in the cathedral of the Transfiguration (Preobrazhensky; 1830–35; by Andreyan D. Zakharov) in Yekaterinoslav (now Dnipropetrovs'k), and square, five-domed churches such as the Transfiguration of the Saviour (Spaso-Preobrazhensky; 18th century; by D. Kvarengi) in Novgorod-Seversky were also built. As a result of a decree of the Synod of 1801 prohibiting the construction of churches in the 'lesser Russian style', wooden churches ceased to be built in the eastern regions of Ukraine. In the west, however, they retained their traditional appearance, as evidenced by the church (1824) in the village of Yasyn' (Yasin').

Church architecture of the latter half of the 19th century and the beginning of the 20th shows the same tendencies as secular architecture. The architectural traditions of the Kievan Rus' are evident in Vladimirsky Cathedral (1862–82; by Ivan V. Shtorm, Pavel I. Sparro, Aleksandr V. Beretti and others) in Kiev; in the residence of the Metropolitan of Halich (1864–82; by Iosif Glavna (1831–1908)) in Chernovtsy; and in the Trinity (Troitsky) Cathedral in Pochayevskaya Lavra (1906; by Alexey V. Shchusev). Vasily Maksimov (1844–1911), who designed a memorial church (1912–14) above a Cossack graveyard near Berestechko, was inspired by Ukrainian Baroque architecture. In Roman Catholic churches, borrowings from Gothic architecture are evident (e.g. church of St Elizabeth, L'viv; 1912; by Teodor Talovsky (1857–1910)).

BIBLIOGRAPHY

G. K. Lukomsky: *Ukrainskiy barokko* [Ukrainian Baroque] (St Petersburg, 1911)

V. Shcherbakivs'ky: *Derev'yane budivnytstvo i riz'ba na derevyni* [Wooden architecture and wood carving] (1913), i of *Ukraïns'ke mystetstvo* [Ukrainian art] (Kiev, 1913–26)

sequence of the compositions in the main part of the church became a model for subsequent Russian wall painting.

In style the mosaics and wall paintings in St Sophia followed Hellenistic traditions in art that are especially evident in the portraits of bishops in the central apse and were matched in quality by the wall paintings in the cathedral of the Transfiguration of the Saviour (Spaso-Preobrazhensky) in Chernihiv, as illustrated by a copy of a fragment of the portrait of *St Thekla* (*c.* 1036–40; destr. World War II; copy Kiev, St Sophia Hist. & Archit. Mus.). An important school of painting began to develop at the Pecherskaya Lavra (founded 1051) in Kiev (*see* KIEV, §3(ii)) in the second half of the 11th century, producing ALIMPY, the first recorded Russian icon painter. He probably worked with the Greek artists who were brought in to decorate the monastery's cathedral of the Dormition (Uspensky; 1073–89; destr. 1941), the paintings of which reflect the combined influences of contemporary schools of art on Mt Athos, in Thessaloniki and in Constantinople. Greek artists were also responsible for the mosaics in the church in the Kiev monastery of St Michael with the Golden Roofs (Zlatoverkhy; 1108; destr. 1935). All that survives of the decoration are some fragments of wall painting, a mosaic of the *Eucharist* (all Kiev, St Sophia Hist. & Archit. Mus.; see fig. 7) and the mosaic of *St Dmitry Solumsky* (Moscow, Tret'yakov Gal.). The predominant colours are rose-reds, greens and gold, while the linear treatment of form reflects the influence of manuscript painting. Of the same date and style but much better preserved are wall paintings (1098–1125) in the church of St Michael at Ostyor.

By the mid-12th century various schools of wall decoration had begun to develop in the individual principalities of Kievan Rus', primarily in the medium of wall painting rather than in the more costly mosaic. Overpainted on several occasions, the cycle of paintings (second half of 12th century) in the church of the Holy Trinity (Troitskaya)

in the monastery of St Cyril in Kiev have now been partially uncovered. Although they continued to be influenced by those in the cathedral of St Sophia, they also reflect the growing influence of Bulgarian and Romanesque art. The iconography is complex and departs in several instances from the thematically rigid Byzantine system of church decoration. Bishops are portrayed in rounded frames with a painted loop on top in imitation of an icon hanging on the wall, as in Balkan churches, while in the diakonikon are scenes from the lives of St Cyril of Alexandria (*d* 444) and of St Afansy. Balkan saints, for example Cyril (Constantine), Methodius, Clement of Bulgaria, John of Macedonia, are depicted beside Byzantine and Russian military saints, and Slavonic inscriptions accompany many of the scenes. A representation of the *Day of Judgement* decorates the vaults and walls of the narthex.

Fragments of frescoes depicting the *Martyrs of Sebaste*, and the *Baptism of the Prelates* (late 11th century–early 12th) survive in the baptistery of the cathedral of St Sophia, Kiev, which, like those in the church of the Holy Trinity, are painted on a white background. In CHERNIHIV the cathedral of SS Boris and Gleb (1123), the church of Paraskeva Pyatnitsa (12th century; rebuilt 1962) and the cathedral of the Dormition (Uspensky; 12th century; rest. 1960) in the Yeletsky Monastery preserve remnants of their 12th-century painted decoration, composed of a fine layer of paint over a single layer of limestone whitewash. In style the paintings reflect the growing impact of local traditions on painting and the waning influence of the artistic heritage of Constantinople. The increasingly linear treatment of form and reduced range of colours imparted greater power and spontaneity to the pictures. Although monumental painting in the cities of the western Ukraine is recorded, no examples from this period have survived.

BIBLIOGRAPHY

D. Aynalov and Y. Redin: *Drevniye pamyatniki iskusstva Kiyeva* [Ancient monuments of Kievan art] (Khar'kov, 1899)
D. V. Aynalov: *Ocherki i zametki po istorii drevnerusskogo iskusstva* [Essays and notes on the history of Old Russian art] (St Petersburg, 1908)
F. I. Shmit: *Mystetstvo staroï Rusi–Ukraïny* [The art of Old Rus'-Ukraine] (Khar'kov, 1919)
A. I. Nekrasov: *Drevnerusskoye izobrazitel'noye iskusstvo* [Old Russian fine art] (Moscow, 1937)
N. I. Voronin: *Drevnerusskoye iskusstvo* [Old Russian art] (Moscow, 1962)
M. K. Karger: *Drevnerusskaya monumental'naya zhivopis' XI–XIV vekov* [Old Russian monumental painting of the 11th–14th centuries] (Moscow, 1964)
V. N. Lazarev: *Old Russian Murals and Mosaics from the XIth to the XVIth Century* (London, 1966)
Yu. S. Aseev: *Mystetstvo Kyivs'koï Rusi* [The art of Kievan Rus'] (Kiev, 1980)

(ii) Icons. According to chronicle sources the first icons were brought from Chersonesos by Prince Vladimir I Svyatoslavich (*reg* 980–1015) to decorate his church of the Tithe of the Most Holy Mother of God (Desyatina Presvyatoy Bogorditsy) in Kiev. Greek icons were also imported for the Pecherskaya Lavra in Kiev, where in the late 11th century and the early 12th the icon painter and mosaicist Alimpy is thought to have worked. Also in the early 12th century an icon of the *Virgin and Child* (Moscow, Tret'yakov Gal.) was brought to Vyshgorod near Kiev. In 1155 this icon was taken by Prince Andrey

7. Mosaic depicting the *Eucharist* (detail) from the church in the monastery of St Michael with the Golden Roofs (Zlatoverkhy), Kiev, 1108, destr. 1935 (Kiev, St Sophia Historical and Architectural Museum)

I Bogolyubsky (*reg* 1157–75) to Vladimir, where he subsequently placed it in his cathedral of the Dormition (Uspensky; 1158–60; rest. 1185–9). By the late 14th century the *Virgin of Vladimir*, as it became known, had become the most venerated of all Russian icons. Despite frequent damage and many repairs, the surviving original fragments in subdued ochre and olive hues represent one of the earliest and most important images of the Virgin of Tenderness (Rus. *umileniye*), which is derived from a Byzantine type of the early 12th century showing the Virgin embracing the Child.

Between the 12th and 14th centuries Kievan icons were widely disseminated, and among those attributed to Kievan artists are the *Virgin Orans* or *Great Panagiya* (early 13th century; Moscow, Tret'yakov Gal.; *see* ICON, colour pl. II, fig. 2), discovered in 1919 in the monastery of the Transfiguration of the Saviour (Spaso-Preobrazhensky; late 12th century) in Yaroslavl'. The Virgin stands with her arms raised in prayer and a medallion of Christ on her breast, as in the apse mosaics in the cathedral of St Sophia, in the Pecherskaya Lavra and in St Michael with the Golden Roofs, all in Kiev. One of the icon's most distinctive features is the predominantly brown and purple range of colours set against a white background: the masterly use of a few bright and complementary hues became a characteristic trait of Russian painting. Two other icons that may be attributed to the Kievan school are the Ustyug *Annunciation* (early 12th century; Moscow, Tret'yakov Gal.; see fig. 8), which Ivan IV (*reg* 1533–84) is said to have brought from the monastery of St George (Yur'yevo) in Novgorod to the cathedral of the Dormition in Moscow's Kremlin; and the head of an Archangel (*c.* 1150; St Petersburg, Rus. Mus.). All three icons reflect the continued influence of the classical canon of form in early Russian painting; it is particularly evident in the linear regularity of the face and clothing, and in the range of colour, from bright hues to dark red and gold.

As a result of constant internecine warfare in the 12th century, the depiction of warrior saints became widespread. One of the earliest to be adopted by the Russian church was St Demetrios of Thessaloniki, as in the icon (after 1150; Moscow, Tret'yakov Gal.) from Dmitrov, which may also be attributed to the Kievan school. The saint is shown frontally, seated on a throne, recalling the consuls on Early Christian and Byzantine ivory diptychs (*see* CONSULAR DIPTYCH). The two-dimensional design is underscored by the repeated use of curved lines. Shapes are formed by vigorous masses of light set against a dark green background.

One of the most popular images of the Virgin in Russian art is the Virgin of the Protective Veil (Rus. *Bogomater' pokrova*), which was based on the mosaic of the Virgin in the church (6th century; destr.) in the Blachernai monastery in Constantinople, where her veil was said to have been preserved. The earliest surviving Russian version of this Virgin type is a 13th-century icon from Galicia (Kiev, Mus. W. & Orient. A.). It is rare in depicting all the characters in the 8th-century legend in which Andrew the Fool saw a miraculous apparition of the Virgin spreading her veil over the people.

8. Icon of the *Annunciation* (known as the Utyuzhnoye blagoveshcheniye), tempera on panel, 2.29×1.44 m, early 12th century (Moscow, Tret'yakov Gallery)

BIBLIOGRAPHY

M. I. Uspensky and V. I. Uspensky: *Zametki o drevnerusskom ikonopisanii* [Notes on Old Russian icon painting] (St Petersburg, 1901)

A. I. Anisimov: 'Domongol'skiy period drevnerusskoy zhivopisi' [The pre-Mongol period of Old Russian painting], *Voprosy restavratsii* [Questions of restoration], 2 (Leningrad and Moscow, 1928), pp. 102–8

V. I. Antonova and N. Ye. Mneva: *Katalog drevnerusskoy zhivopisi XI–nachala XVIII vekov: Opyt istoriko-khudozhestvennoy klassifikatsii* [Catalogue of Old Russian painting of the 11th century to the early 18th: an attempt at a historical and artistic classification], 2 vols (Moscow, 1963)

L. S. Milyayeva: 'Pamyatniki Galitskoy zhivopisi XIII veka' [Monuments of Galician painting of the 13th century], *Sov. Arkheol.*, iii (1965), pp. 240–57

S. Hordynsky: *Die ukrainische Ikone, 12. bis 18. Jahrhundert* (Munich and Graz, 1981)

A. I. Anisimov: *O drevnerusskom iskusstve* [On Old Russian art] [col. articles] (Moscow, 1983)

(iii) Manuscripts. With the spread of literacy in Kievan Rus' the art of manuscript illumination also developed. The earliest books were produced at the metropolitan's court in Kiev and in the large monasteries. They acquired a special prominence under Yaroslav I (*reg* 1019–54), whose library was housed in the cathedral of St Sophia in Kiev. Although, like other types of Old Russian painting, manuscript illumination was influenced by Byzantine art in the depiction of characters, the surroundings of the

compositions and the ornament during the 11th century motifs and figures from everyday life began to appear: portraits of princes and scenes depicting artisans, merchants and people working. The oldest surviving illuminated manuscript is the Ostromir Gospels (St Petersburg, Rus. N. Lib.), which was written in 1056–7 by Deacon Grigory for the mayor of Novgorod, Ostromir, a kinsman of the Kievan Prince Izyaslav I (*reg* 1054–8; 1069–73; 1076–8). The book's borders and headpieces are decorated with multicoloured vegetal motifs on a gold background. The decorated initials are similar to pieces of notched enamel jewellery, with busts in profile above. Many initials are also embellished with fantastic beasts, for example the lower flourish of the letter B in the form of a massive two-bodied winged monster (fol. 18*v*). The stylized vegetal designs are similar to those in the wall paintings in the cathedral of St Sophia in Kiev.

Another early illuminated manuscript is the *Miscellany of Svyatoslav* (1073; Moscow, Hist. Mus.), which includes a group portrait of the *Family of Prince Svyatoslav I Yaroslavich* (*reg* 1054–76) in frontal poses (see fig. 9). It has been suggested that the poorly preserved depiction of a monster with the head of a dog represents Simurgh, protector of the Tree of Life. The *Miscellany* also contains four frontispieces showing stylized churches fronted by saints; it is decorated with fantastic plants, animals and birds, and drawings of the signs of the zodiac using familiar images. For example Sagittarius (fol. 250*v*) has a face with

9. *Family of Prince Svyatoslav I Yaroslavich*; miniature from the *Miscellany of Svyatoslav*, 1073 (Moscow, Historical Museum, fols 1*v* and 2*v*)

a bushy beard and long hair, and Virgo (fol. 251*r*) is depicted as a round-faced girl wearing a *kokoshnik* (arched headdress). These images recall the secular painted scenes (11th century) in the stair-towers of the cathedral of St Sophia in Kiev.

The production of illuminated manuscripts, which had been established in the 11th century, developed further in the 12th and 13th centuries. The Gospels (12th century; Moscow, Hist. Mus.) from the monastery of St George (Yur'yevo), Novgorod, were probably produced in Kiev. The volume contains 65 initials painted in vermilion and often decorated with animals, birds and humans. The initials and headpieces are also notable for their linear treatment of form. Another illumination that has been attributed to Kievan artists is that of a Russian prince in a book entitled the *Lay of Hippolyte* (12th century or early 13th; Moscow, Hist. Mus.). The colours are restrained (greens, reds, browns and blacks), the figure drawings flattened but correctly proportioned and there is a lack of decorative detail. The Egbert Psalter (Codex Gertrudianus, 11th century; Cividale del Friuli, Bib. Civ.) has miniatures that combine the Russian–Byzantine and Roman styles and may have been executed at the Monastery of St Jacob on the Danube. One of the miniatures depicts *Prince Yaropolk Izyaslavovich* and his wife; above them there is an inscription in Cyrillic that mentions the name Yaropolk. The ornamental and linear styles are combined in the illuminations in the Dobromilov Gospels (1164; Moscow, Rus. Lib.), which were imitated by Galician artists of the late 13th century and the 14th. During the late 12th century and early 13th miniatures were used to illustrate chronicles and historical narratives and became more secular in character, even in religious books such as the Orshanka Gospels (12th–13th centuries; Kiev, Cent. Lib. Acad. Sci.).

BIBLIOGRAPHY

V. V. Stasov: *Slavyanskiy i vostochnyy ornament po rukopisyam starogo i novogo vremeni* [Slavonic and Oriental ornamentation in old and new manuscripts], 3 vols (St Petersburg, 1884–7)
N. P. Kondakov: *Izobrazheniye russkoy knyazheskoy sem'i v miniatyurakh XI veka* [Portrayal of the Russian princely family in 11th-century miniatures] (St Petersburg, 1906)
I. S. Sventsits'ky: *Kyrylychni pergamenty XII–XV vv.* [Cyrillic parchments of the 12th–15th centuries] (L'vov, 1933)
Ye. E. Granstrem: *Opisaniye russkikh i slavyanskikh pergamennykh rukopisey* [Account of Russian and Slavonic parchment manuscripts] (Leningrad, 1953)
Ya. P. Zapasko: *Ornamental'noye oformleniye ukrainskoy rukopisnoy knigi* [Ornamentation in Ukrainian manuscripts] (Kiev, 1953)

2. 1240–*c.* 1600.

(i) *Monumental painting.* In the late 13th century and the first half of the 14th stone construction was limited and the development of monumental painting was arrested. The chronicles, however, record the decoration with wall paintings (destr.) of the churches of L'viv, Lutsk, Khotyn' and of other cities. Although wall painting techniques remained virtually unchanged between the 14th and 16th centuries, compositions contained some Gothic features but are particularly notable for their large-scale modelling of form and rich colour schemes, as in the wall paintings (1360–70) in the Goryany Rotunda (mid-13th century) near Uzhhorod and the wall paintings (1360–70) in the church (14th century) at Zmeivki in Transcarpathia. During the 14th century representations of the Virgin either developed along the more intimate, expressive lines of the *Virgin* at Goryany or imitated Byzantine Virgin types, for example the wall paintings of Lavrov.

In the 14th and 15th centuries numerous Ukrainian painters worked outside their homeland. They included the Kievan artist Friar Anthony, who painted the cathedral of the Holy Trinity (Troitsky; 12th century; rebuilt 1365–7 and 1682–99) in Pskov, and many other artists who worked in Poland, for example in the royal bedchamber in Wawel Castle (11th–12th centuries) in Kraków (*see* KRAKÓW, §I, 1) and in the third collegiate church of WIŚLICA (second half of the 14th century). One of the most renowned and extensive programmes of wall painting decoration (1418) is in the Gothic chapel of the Holy Trinity in the royal castle LUBLIN. The painter was a certain Andrew, who, together with his team of three helpers, probably came from Ukraine. The latest dated works by a Ukrainian artist in Poland are the wall paintings (1470) in the chapel of the Holy Cross in Wawel cathedral in Kraków, which decorate the arches and comprise approximately 50 scenes from the Gospels, along with portraits of saints, angels and prophets. The scene of the *Eucharist* is particularly reminiscent of contemporary Kievan painting, and the *Entombment* is distinguished by its expressive lines.

Among surviving examples of 15th-century wall paintings in the Ukraine are those in the church of St Onufrios in Lavrov, which completely cover the walls and include much ornament, and in the church of the Dormition (Uspenskaya; 1453–8) in the village of Luzhany. Fragments of wall paintings (1390–1437) also survive in the Armenian cathedral (1363) in L'viv. They combine the flattened forms of the 11th and 12th centuries with the more naturalistic modelling of the 15th century and early 16th achieved through the use of tempera, as in the figures of the Apostles. There was a general attempt in painting during this period to achieve greater realism and more original compositions; and the ornamental aspect was also emphasized, as in the small castle chapel (1541–6) in Khotyn'.

(ii) Icons. Icon painting after the Tatar–Mongol invasions (1239–40) was primarily connected with the decoration of iconostases. Although icons continued to be produced in the Pecherskaya Lavra and in the Galician and Volhynian monasteries, the lack of centralized patronage hampered the development of new significant centres of icon production. The icons adhered to the general rules governing iconography but tended to reflect individual tastes. A few icons have survived from the 13th and 14th centuries, and the spirit that prevailed during the grim period following the Tatar–Mongol invasions is still evident, as in *St George the Dragon Slayer* (14th century; Lembergeri, St Clements U., Ukrain. Mus. & Lib.) from Stanyl' and the *Virgin and Child* (13th–early 14th century; Kiev, Mus. W. & Orient. A.) from Lutsk. The latter icon is thought to be by Pyotr Ratensky (*d* 1326).

By the 15th century city and village fraternities had become the main patrons of icon painters, whose works are distinguished by their simple compositions with elements of the fantastic and with rich colour schemes. The restrained style of 14th-century icons is also evident in such icons as the *Transfiguration* from Busavisk and *SS Cosmas and Damian* (L'viv, Mus. Ukrain. A.) from Tilich (both 15th century). In the second half of the 15th century a more expressive linear style began to prevail in Galician icons, as in the *Saviour-Teacher* from Milik and the *Council of Joachim and Anne* (1466; both Lembergeri, Mus. Ukrain. Theol. Acad.) from the village of Stanyl'. Icons also became more decorative, and gold backgrounds were sometimes added with carved or stamped ornament. The realistic representation of subsidiary details is most evident in icons with a complex subject-matter, for example in the *Birth of Christ* (mid-16th century; L'viv, Mus. Ukrain. A.) from the village of Trushevichi. One of the few signed icons from this period is the *Assumption of the Virgin* by a certain Aleksey of Lys'k (1547; Lembergeri, Mus. Ukrain. Theol. Acad.), which, together with a group of related icons (L'viv, Mus. Ukrain. A.) from Bagnovatoye (16th century), reflects the move away from traditional icon painting towards the representation of detailed scenes from everyday life in a palette of contrasting ochre-browns and blacks with bluish-green hues. The icons by Dmitry have a similar picturesque quality, as in *Christ and the Twelve Apostles* (1565; L'viv, Mus. Ukrain. A.) from Dolina.

Icons from the L'viv area can be divided into three styles of painting: archaic, as in the icon of *St Nicholas* (15th century) from Radruzh (now in Poland); linear, as in the *Virgin Who Points the Way* (*Hodegetria*; 15th century) from Krasov; and folk, as in the icon of *Archangel Michael* (mid-16th century) from Yablonevo, which is distinguished by its original treatment of the figures and its emphatically decorative content (all L'viv, Mus. Ukrain. A.). Many other icons of the first half of the 16th century are characterized by their restrained grey ochre-brown hues and linear forms, as in the *Day of Judgement* (1575; L'viv, Mus. Ukrain. A.) from Kamenka-Buzkaya. One of the greatest works from the L'viv area is the Nakonechy iconostasis (1560s; nr Yavorovo); a similar style of painting is evident in the icons (L'viv, Mus. Ukrain. A.) from Potelich and in those by Fedusko of Sambor (e.g. the *Annunciation*, 1579; Kharkiv, Mus. F.A.). Icons of the 16th century from Volhynia, such as the *Exaltation of the True Cross* from Dubno (early-16th century; L'viv, Mus. Ukrain. A.), remain more faithful to the painting traditions of Kievan Rus'. Although icons from Galicia also follow traditional forms of composition, certain scenes are depicted with greater realism and the figures appear more solid (e.g. the *Transfiguration* from Yablonevo; church of the Archangel Michael).

(iii) Manuscripts. During the 14th to 16th centuries the illumination of manuscripts became one of the most popular art forms, with artists increasingly depicting scenes from the world around them. In 1397 the Deacon Spiridony of Kiev decorated a Psalter (the 'Kievan Psalter'; St Petersburg, Rus. N. Lib.) with ornament and scenes that are reminiscent of the painting traditions and format of the *Miscellany of Svyatoslav* (*see* §III, 1(iii) above) with its gold background and vegetal designs. The Psalter's illuminations are in three shades of green, which became a distinguishing feature of book decoration; certain pictures, such as the *Dance before Saul* (see fig. 10), recall the wall paintings on the stair-towers of St Sophia Cathedral in

10. *Dance before Saul*; miniature by Deacon Spiridony of Kiev, from the 'Kievan Psalter', 1397 (St Petersburg, Russian National Library, fol. 204*v*)

Kiev. In the Kievan Gospels (1393; St Petersburg, Rus. N. Lib.) and Lutsk Gospels (14th century; Moscow, Rus. Lib.) fantastic animals appear alongside plant ornament, imparting a fairytale quality to the books. The only surviving illuminated manuscript from the 15th century is the *Teaching of Yefrem Sirin* (1492; St Petersburg, Rus. N. Lib.), which also reflects the influence of monumental painting.

During the 16th century the representation of worldly subjects became increasingly pronounced, as in the Pere-sopnitsky Gospels (1556–61; Kiev, Cent. Lib. Acad. Sci.). There was also widespread use of motifs from folk art: the garland and circular ornament. Despite the emergence of the printing press in the late 16th century manuscript illumination continued to develop, as can be seen in the pictures in the *Tale of Varlaam and Joseph* (16th century; L'viv, Mus. Ukrain. A.) and in the Grimensky Gospels (1602; St Petersburg, Rus. N. Lib.).

BIBLIOGRAPHY
G. K. Bugoslavsky: 'Volynskiye rukopisnyye evangeliya i apostoly' [The illustrated Gospels and Epistles of Volhynia], *Trudy IX arkheologiches-kogo syezda: Vil'na, 1897* [Works of the ninth archaeological congress: Vilnius, 1897], ii, pp. 277–307
A. Gruzinsky: 'Persopnitskoye evangeliye, kak pamyatnik iskusstva epokhi vozrozhdeniya v yuzhnoy Rossii v XVI v.' [The Persopnitsky Gospels as a monument of the art of the Renaissance in southern Russia in the 16th century], *Iskusstvo* [Kiev], i (1911), pp. 1–48
U. Sventsits'ky: *Galyts'ko-rus'ke tserkovne malyarstvo XV–XVI st.* [15th–16th century Galician–Russian church painting] (L'vov, 1914)
M. Golubets': *Galits'ke malyarstvo* [Galician painting] (L'vov, 1926)
M. O. Makarenko: 'Ornamentarstvo ukraïns'koï knyzhky XVI–XVIII st.' [Ukrainian book ornamentation of the 16th–18th centuries], *Ukraïns'ka knyga XVI–XVIII st.* [Ukrainian books of the 16th–18th centuries], ed. M. O. Makarenko and S. I. Maslov (Kiev, 1926), pp. 153–218
P. M. Zholtovs'ky: *Ukraïns'ka rukopysna knyga ta ïï ozdoblennya* [The Ukrainian manuscript book and its ornamentation] (Khar'kov, 1926)
I. Sventsits'ky: *Ikonopys Galits'koï Ukraïny* [Icon-painting of Galician Ukraine] (L'viv, 1928; Ger. trans., 1928)
J. B. Konstantinowicz: *Ikonostasiis* [Iconostases], i (L'viv, 1939)
Ya. P. Zapasko: *Ornamental'noye oformleniye ukrainskoy rukopisnoy knigi* [Ornamention in Ukrainian manuscripts] (Kiev, 1960)
L. I. Batig: 'Galyts'kyy stankovyy zhyvopys XIV–XVIII st. u zbirkakh derzhavnogo muzeyu ukraïns'kogo mystetstva u L'vovi' [Galician painting of the 14th–18th centuries: anthologies from the State Museum of Ukrainian Art in L'vov] (Kiev, 1961), *Materialy z etnografiï ta mystetstvoznavstva*, ed. I. F. Simonenko, 5 vols (Kiev, 1954–63), iv, pp. 144–67
G. Logvin, L. Mylyaeva and V. Sventsits'ka: *Ukraïns'kyy seredn'ovichnyy zhyvopys* [Medieval Ukrainian painting] (Kiev, 1976)
S. Hordynsky: *Die ukrainische Ikone, 12. bis 18. Jahrhundert* (Munich and Graz, 1981)
V. A. Ovsiychuk: *Ukraïns'ke mystetstvo drugoï polovyny XVI-pershoï polov-yny XVII st.* [Ukrainian art of the second half of the 16th century to the first half of the 17th century] (Kiev, 1985)
V. I. Svents'itska and O. F. Sifor: *Spadshchyna vikiv: Ukraïns'ke maliarstvo XIV–XVIII stolit' u muzeinykh kolektsiyakh L'vova* [The legacy of centuries: Ukrainian painting of the 14th–18th centuries in the museum collections of L'viv] (L'viv, 1990)

3. AFTER 1600. The spread of humanistic ideas and the development of education in the late 16th century and the early 17th and the growing understanding by artists of anatomy and the technique of oil painting resulted in fundamental changes to Ukrainian art of this period. Portrait painting emerged as an independent art form, as evidenced by the portrait of a certain *K. Kornyatka* (*c.* 1603; L'viv, Hist. Mus.) by an unknown artist, and a more humanistic spirit entered icon painting, for example in the *Hodegetria with the Akathistos* (1599; Church of Rep-nyovo) by Fyodor of L'viv. Manuscript illuminations are notable for their diversity and are reminiscent of the images found in wall paintings. A Service Book of 1635 (Kiev, Acad. Sci.), for example, shows the influence of the Italian Renaissance. In wall and icon painting the tradi-tional iconography of religious compositions was disrupted by the expressive depiction of specific landscape back-grounds, individualized figures and scenes from the Pas-sion, as in the paintings (1620–40) of the church of the Holy Spirit in Potelich and the icon of the *Day of Judgement* (end of 17th century) from the village of Bagnovato.

In the second half of the 17th century, following the union of Ukraine with Russia (1654), painting was distin-guished by elements taken from both folk and Baroque art. Wall painting became more narrative in character, and icons also developed a more secular appearance, often depicting individual founders and patrons of churches, for example in the *Crucifixion* accompanied by a portrait of *Colonel Leonty Svechko* (late 17th century; Kiev, Mus. Ukrain. A.) from Pyratyn' (Piryatin). The representations of saints were often distinguished from portraits only by the ornamental gold background, as in the icons (L'viv, Mus. Ukrain. A.) by two renowned artists from L'viv, I. Kondzelevich and U. Rutkovich (*fl* late 17th century).

During the 18th century the icon painting school at the Pecherskaya Lavra in Kiev, which was well acquainted with western European painting, was significant in the development of Ukrainian art. Baroque and Old Russian styles were combined with realistic representations of scenes from daily life, as on the iconostasis (1732; *in situ*) in the church of the Transfiguration (Preobrazhenskaya) in the village of Velyko Sorochintsi (Velikiye Sorochintsy). Depictions of ordinary people and portraits of individual members of the Cossack élite, such as that of *D. Yefremov* (1752; Kiev, Mus. Ukrain. A.), became widespread. In folk art the image of the legendary Cossack Mamay accompanied by verses and humorous sayings also became popular.

With the spread of the ideas of the Enlightenment and the strengthening of ties with Russia, Ukrainian art became increasingly secular. After the opening of the St Petersburg Academy of Fine Art (1757), many gifted artists, such as Vladimir L. Borovikovsky, who had begun their careers in Ukraine, went to the Russian capital. Baroque traditions in painting were ousted by Neo-classicism; highly individualized portraits became fashionable, as for example the *Self-portrait* (1830) by Kapiton S. Pavlov (1792–1852), the *Boy from the Tomara Family* (1847; both Kiev, Mus. Ukrain. A.) by Gavrila A. Vas'ko (1820–86) and the *Self-portrait* (1846; Kharkiv, Mus. F.A.) by Dmitry I. Bezperchy (1825–1913). In landscape painting urban scenes became popular with works by Ivan M. Soshenko (1806–76) (e.g. *Selling Hay on the Dnieper*; Kharkiv, Mus. F.A.) and M. M. Sazhin (e.g. *River-crossing on the Dnieper*, 1846; Khar'kiv, Mus. F.A.). The paintings of the Russian landscape artist V. I. Shternberg (1818–45), who spent many years in Ukraine, had a profound influence on the development of Ukrainian painting, particularly with his *Windmills on the Steppe* (1836; St Petersburg, Rus. Mus.). He was among the precursors of TARAS SHEVCHENKO, the founder of the school of Ukrainian painting that was connected with the spread of revolutionary democratic ideas and the development of realism. Shevchenko devoted his artistic and poetic work to exposing the system of serfdom in Tsarist Russia, as in the picture of *Katerina* (1842; Kiev, Shevchenko Mus.). His art exercised a considerable influence on subsequent generations of Ukrainian and Russian artists, including Lev M. Zhemchuzhnikov (1828–1912), Konstantin A. Trutovsky (1826–93) and Ivan I. Sokolov (1823–1912), who continued to represent the life and sufferings of the peasants and to denounce social injustices, as for example Trutovsky's *Collecting Arrears in the Village* (1886; Kazan', Mus. F.A. Tatarstan).

In the second half of the 19th century art schools were established in which instruction was given by artists of the realist school: in Kiev by Mykhaylo Murashko (1844–1909), in Odessa by Kiriak Kostandi and in Kharkiv by S. M. Prokhorov (1873–1948). They were associated with the WANDERERS (Rus. *Peredvizhniki*), founded in 1863 to take art to the people in travelling exhibitions and as a counterweight to the St Petersburg Academy of Art. Nature and peasant life were portrayed by Nikolay Kuznetsov (1850–1930), Sergey Svetoslavsky (1857–1931), Pyotr A. Nilus (1869–1943), Pyotr A. Levchenko (1856–1917), Vladimir D. Orlovsky (1842–1914) and Sergey I. Vasil'kovsky (1854–1917). The early 20th-century works of the landscape painters Abram A. Manevich (1881–1942) and Nikolay G. Burachek (1871–1942) and the portraits of Aleksey Kh. Novakivsky (1872–1935) reflect the influence of Impressionist and Post-Impressionist art, and the portrait painting of Oleksandr A. Murashko was

influenced by the works of various groups in southern Germany, including the Munich Secession (*see* SECESSION, §1). Murashko's faithful representation of the figures was combined with a decorative use of colour, as in *A Peasant Family* (Kiev, Mus. Ukrain. A.). In the early 20th century various Ukrainian artists, including Alexandra Exter, responded to new developments in Russian art during the formative years.

In the 1920s monumental painting became the most important art form in Ukraine. Artists, headed by Mikhail L. Boychuk, drew on the work of Giotto, ancient Ukrainian icons and Ukrainian folk art in their paintings of new Soviet subjects on the walls of clubs, sanatoria (e.g. that on Khadzhibei Estuary in Odessa; destr. 1928) and other public buildings (e.g. Lutsk Barracks in Kiev, 1919; destr.). Easel painting, however, regained popularity, and artists worked in the Cubist, Futurist and Expressionist styles, evident, for example, in *Invalids* (1924; see fig. 11) by ANATOLI PETRITS'KY, *Sawyers* (1926) by Oleksandr Bohomazov and *Red Banner* (1927; all Kiev, Mus. Ukrain. A.) by Viktor N. Pal'mov (1888–1929); others worked in the more traditional realist style, such as Fyodor G. Krychevsky (1879–1947). His works include *The Bride* (1910) and the *Merry Milkmaids* (1937; both Kiev, Mus. Ukrain. A.), which are noteworthy for the expressive portrayal of character, large forms and emotionally intense colours. Realism emerged as the dominant style in the 1930s, as seen in the works of Vladimir N. Kostetsky (1905–68), for example *Presentation of the Party Card* (2nd variant, 1959; Kiev, Mus. Ukrain. A.), and of K. Trokhimenko (1885–1979), for example *Female Kolkhoznik Activists* (1940; Vinnista, Local Mus.).

Among the notable artists to appear after World War II are Viktor G. Puzyr'kov (*b* 1918) and TAT'YANA YABLONSKAYA, whose landscape and thematic works are executed in a style based on traditional folk wall painting, exhibiting a rich use of colour and decorative quality. In

11. Anatoli Petrits'ky: *Invalids*, oil on canvas, 167×194 mm, 1924 (Kiev, Museum of Ukrainian Art)

the 1960s Valery Lamakh (1925–78), Ernest Kotkov and Ivan S. Litovchenko were employed to decorate the walls of new cultural and administrative buildings. Following reunification with the western areas, the traditions of Ukrainian folk art also developed under the influence of painters from that area, such as F. F. Manaylo (1910–78), Al'dabert M. Erdeli (1891–1955) and I. I. Bokshaya (1891–1975). Landscape painting holds a special place in Ukrainian art; works by Nikolay P. Glushchenko (1901–77), Ilya M. Shtil'man (1902–66) and Aleksey A. Shovkunenko (1884–1974) combine the romance characteristic of 19th-century Ukrainian painting with the decorative traditions of folk art and Impressionist techniques. Avant-garde developments and experimental approaches typify the later 20th-century generation of Ukrainian painters, for example Lamakh, Grigory I. Gavrilenko (1927–84), Kotkov, Galina A. Nelevda (*b* 1938), Viktor Grigoryev (*b* 1939), Vladimir Pasivenko (*b* 1939), Tiberiy Silvashi (*b* 1947), and the young artists Gleb Vysheslavsky (*b* 1962), Aleksandr Zhivotkov (*b* 1964) and Oleg Golosy (1965–92).

BIBLIOGRAPHY

D. Shcherbakovs'ky and F. Ernst: *Ukraïns'kyy portret: Vystavka ukraïns'kogo portretu XVII–XX st.* [The Ukrainian portrait: the 17th–20th century Ukrainian portraiture exhibition] (exh. cat., Kiev, Mus. Ukrain. A., 1925)
Ukraïns'ke malyarstvo XVII–XX stopichchya [Ukrainian painting of the 17th–20th centuries] (exh. cat., ed. F. Ernst; Kiev, Mus. Ukrain. A., 1929)
E. Kholostenko: *Monumental'ne malyarstvo radyans'koï Ukraïny* [Monumental painting in Soviet Ukraine] (Khar'kov, 1932)
P. M. Zholtovs'ky: *Vyzvol'na borot'ba ukraïns'kogo narodu u pam'yatkakh mystetstva XVI–XVIII st.* [The liberation struggle of the Ukrainian people in the art of the 16th–18th centuries] (Kiev, 1958)
V. Pavlov and L. Popova: *Ukraïns'ke radyans'ke mystetstvo 20–30-kh rokiv XX st.* [Ukrainian Soviet art of the 1920s–1930s] (Kiev, 1966)
V. Sventsits'ka: *Ivan Rutkovych i stanovlennya realizmu v ukraïns'komu malyarstvi XVII st.* [Ivan Rutkovych and the development of realism in Ukrainian painting in the 17th century] (Kiev, 1966)
P. O. Bilets'ky: *Ukrainskaya portretnaya zhivopis' XVII–XVIII vekov* [Ukrainian portrait painting of the 17th–18th centuries] (Leningrad, 1981)
——: *Ukraïns'ke mystetstvo drugoï polovyny XVII–XVIII st.* [Ukrainian art of the late 17th and early 18th centuries] (Kiev, 1981)
P. M. Zholtovs'ky: *Ukraïns'kyy zhyvopys XVII–XVIII st.* [17th–18th-century Ukrainian painting] (Kiev, 1978; Leningrad, 1981)
V. P. Pavlov: *Ukraïns'ke radyans'ke mystetstvo 1920–1930-kh rokiv* [Ukrainian Soviet art of the 1920s–1930s] (Kiev, 1983)
V. A. Afanas'yev: *Ukraïn'ske radyans'ke mystetstvo 1960–80-kh rokiv* [Ukrainian Soviet art of 1960–1980] (Kiev, 1984)

IV. Sculpture.

1. *c.* AD 860–1240. 2. After 1240.

1. *c.* AD 860–1240. The development of early sculpture in Kievan Rus' was hampered by the Greek church's prohibition of graven images at the end of the iconoclastic controversy (843). This was understood to mean carved rather than painted likenesses of holy figures, and as a result the churches in Kievan Rus' lacked large-scale figural sculpture. That there was a tradition in pre-Christian Ukraine of carving three-dimensional forms in wood or stone is evident from a stone post (Kraków, Acad. F.A.) discovered in 1848 near Gusyatyn (Gusyatin), which is carved with a standing pagan figure on each of its four sides.

The chronicles record the marble decoration of the church of the Tithe of the Most Holy Mother of God (Desyatina Presvyatoy Bogoroditsy; 989–96, destr. 1240), and in the 17th century Paul of Aleppo, Archdeacon of Antioch, was still able to see the carved crosses alternating with plant motifs on the columns, capitals and cornices of the cathedral of St Sophia in Kiev. Among the few

12. Slate slab with reliefs of *St George of Cappadocia* and *Fyodor Stratilates*, 216×111 mm, from the monastery of St Michael with the Golden Roofs, Zlatoverkhy, Kiev, late 11th century–early 12th (Kiev, Historical Museum)

surviving pieces of sculpture from the 11th and 12th centuries are fragments of stone sarcophagi discovered in the ruins of the church of the Tithe and a marble sarcophagus of Yaroslav I the Wise (*reg* 1019–54) preserved in St Sophia. The sarcophagi were probably brought from Byzantium and are decorated with carvings of Christian symbols such as fish, trees and crosses. Slate slabs (late 11th century–early 12th; Kiev, St Sophia Hist. & Archit. Mus.), with reliefs that are less canonical, have also been preserved. One example (Kiev, Hist. Mus., see fig. 12) from the monastery of St Michael with the Golden Roofs (Zlatoverkhy; 1108; destr. 1935) in Kiev shows *St George of Cappadocia* and *Fyodor Stratilates*. Their weapons and clothing are represented in considerable detail in a flat style based on the traditions of Slav wood carving. Other slabs (Kiev, Hist. Mus.) have images of *Hercules Fighting the Nemean Lion* and *Cybele*, which combine certain fantastic elements, familiar from wood-carving, with a classicizing style.

In the 12th century local schools of architecture were formed outside Kiev. Finely carved garlands decorated the cathedral of SS Boris and Gleb (1123) in Chernihiv, and reliefs resembling those on Romanesque buildings were found on the white stone cathedral of the Dormition (Uspensky; 1157) and on the church of St Panteleymon (built before 1200; reconstructed 17th century), both in Halich. In the 12th and 13th centuries ceramic slabs with ornamental and representational reliefs were used for facing. There was also a trend towards working clay and stone with the same precision as jewellery, for example in the reliefs of the *Conversion of Thomas* (13th century; Kiev, Hist. Mus.) from Kiev and the *Crucifixion with the Angels* (12th–13th centuries; Kiev, Hist. Mus.) from Knyazhaya Gora, near Kaniv. The sculpture of Kievan Rus' exerted a great influence on the development of the exceptional VLADIMIR-SUZDAL' school of sculpture.

BIBLIOGRAPHY
F. C. Belfour (tr.): *The Travels of Macarius, Patriarch of Antioch; Written by his Attendant Archdeacon, Paul of Aleppo, in Arabic*, 2 vols (London, 1829)
O. Nekrasov: 'Rel'efni portrety XI stolittya' [Relief portraits of the 11th century], *Naukovyy zbirnyk za 1925 rik* [Scientific anthology, 1925], ed. M. Grushevs'ky (Kiev, 1926), pp. 16–40
M. Makarenko: 'Skul'ptura i rizbyarstvo Kyïvskoï Rusi peredmongol'skikh chasiv' [Wood-carving in Kievan Rus' in the pre-Mongol period], *Kyïvski zbirnyky istoriï v arkheologii: Pobutu i mystetsva* [Kievan anthology of history and archaeology: life and art], i (Kiev, 1930), pp. 27–96
G. K. Vagner: *Dekorativnoye iskusstvo v arkhitekture rusi X–XIII vv.* [Decorative art in the architecture of Rus' in the 10th–13th centuries] (Moscow, 1964)

2. AFTER 1240. The Tatar–Mongol invasions of 1239–40 mark a hiatus in the development of Ukrainian sculpture. During the 15th and 16th centuries sculptural relief developed along lines laid down in the 12th century and the early 13th. In the 16th century the trend towards more expressive representation of worldly subjects is evident in the reliefs in the Armenian Cathedral in L'viv. The trend towards a more immediate, emotional representation is also represented by carved tombstones, which combine decorative embellishment with portraits of the deceased, as in the tombstone of *Prince K. I. Ostrozhsky* (1579; destr. 1713; copy Kiev, Pechersky Hist. Mus.). In the late 17th century and the 18th there were two predominant

trends: one followed the traditions of carving found in folk art, as in the figure of *St Paraskeva* in the church of the village of Polonne (Khmelnitsk); the other made use of the motifs and forms in Baroque art, as on the wooden iconostasis in the church of the Nativity of the Virgin (Rozhdestvo Bogoroditsy; 1763) in Kozelets'. The iconostases (1661; 1669–75) in the church of St Nicholas in Buchach and in the cathedral of the Dormition (Uspensky) in the Yeletsky Monastery in Chernihiv combine elements from Baroque and folk art. In the early 18th century buildings were decorated with ceramic sculptural reliefs, as for example those of *Christ* and the *Mother of God* in the school (1702) at Chernihiv. Carved reliefs and three-dimensional sculptures, such as the relief portrait of *Tsar Peter I* (1756–61) by Ivan A. Ravich (1677–1762) and the sculpture of *Archangel Michael* (*c.* 1697) from the cathedral of St Michael with the Golden Roofs (Zlatoverkhy), were also used to decorate the Baroque buildings of Kiev. L'viv was another centre of sculpture in the Baroque and Rococo styles, as is shown by the complex and dynamic compositions (1760–70) by Pinzel' and Filevich on the façades of the Baroque cathedral of St George (1740–70).

The classical revival of form that is found in Ukrainian and Russian architecture of the late 18th century and early 19th is also evident in Ukrainian monumental and free-standing sculpture of the period and reflects the region's closer ties with western Europe. Examples include the sculptures by Feodosy Shchedrin on the Column of Glory (1811) in Poltava; the monument to *Armand Emmanuel Richelieu* in Odessa (bronze, 1823–8) by Ivan Martos; and the statue of *Prince Vladimir* in Kiev (bronze, 1850–53), cast by Pyotr Klodt after a design by Vasily Demut-Malinovsky.

In the second half of the 19th century and the early 20th sculpture became more representational, as exemplified by the bronze and granite equestrian statue of *Bogdan Khmel'nitsky*, the Cossack who freed Ukraine from the Poles. It was cast by MIKHAIL MIKESHIN in St Petersburg in 1880 and erected in Kiev in 1888. Following the October Revolution of 1917 Lenin's Plan for Monumental Propaganda stimulated the development of sculpture; many monumental and free-standing statues were erected in honour of the Revolution and its heroes in the cities of Ukraine. Despite the difficult conditions for the development of art in the 1930s sculptures continued to be produced, such as the bronze statues of the artist and poet *Taras Shevchenko* in Kharkiv (1935) and Kiev (1938) by Matvey Manizer and the equestrian statue (bronze, 1949–54) in Kiev of *N. A. Schors* by Mikhail G. Lysenko (1912–72). Ukrainian sculptors who since World War II have received recognition include Aleksandr A. Kovalev (*b* 1915), whose momument to *Pushkin* was erected in Kiev in 1962, Nikolay L. Ryabinik (1919–91), Vasily Z. Boroday (*b* 1917), Emmanuil P. Mis'ko (*b* 1929), Mikhail Ya. Gritsyuk (1929–79), Makar K. Vronsky (*b* 1910), Anatoly S. Fuzhenko (*b* 1936) and Galina N. Kal'chenko (1926–75).

BIBLIOGRAPHY
A. V. Nimenko: *Ukrains'ka skul'ptura drugoï polovyny XIX-pochatku XX st.* [Ukrainian sculpture of the late 19th century and the early 20th] (Kiev, 1963)
Yu. A. Varvarets'ky: *Stanovlennya ukrains'koï radyans'koï skul'ptury* [The development of Ukrainian Soviet sculpture] (Kiev, 1972)

V. F. Lyubchenko: *L'vivs'ka skul'ptura XVI–XVII st.'* [L'viv sculpture in the 16th–17th centuries] (Kiev, 1981)

V. Decorative arts.

Some of the earliest and finest pieces of jewellery and metalwork from Ukraine have been found in the numerous tombs of the Scythian and Sarmatian period (*c.* 600 BC–*c.* AD 300) in the Crimean peninsula (*see* SCYTHIAN AND SARMATIAN ART). This was followed by a distinct decline in artistic standards, which do not appear to have revived until the rise of Kievan Rus' in the late 9th century. Other decorative arts include objects made from clay, wool, flax, wood and glass.

1. Jewellery. 2. Metalwork. 3. Other.

1. JEWELLERY. Surviving items of male and female jewellery from the 9th to the 11th century are mostly in gold and silver, which was worked in a variety of techniques including filigree, as in the 10th-century ornaments from Kopivky (Kopivki; Kiev, Hist. Mus.). These typically include heavy, hooped necklaces made either from a single strand or from two or three interwoven strands. Round temple pieces (*kolty*) were suspended from women's caps. These were matched by chains with pendants, bracelets and rings; their shapes and ornamentation are frequently derived from the traditions of eastern Slav art, such as geometric designs and interlaced plant and animal motifs.

In the 11th century the Byzantine art of cloisonné enamelling was brought to Ukraine and used to decorate all types of jewellery. Temple pieces from Kiev and the Zhitomir region (e.g. St Petersburg, Hermitage) are decorated with enamelled female bust portraits, sirens (e.g. 12th century; St Petersburg, Hermitage; see fig. 13) and birds on the Tree of Life. The last image is also found on

13. Temple piece (*kolt*) depicting sirens, gold and enamel, 50×31 mm, from Kiev, 12th century (St Petersburg, Hermitage Museum)

silver bracelets with niello designs (11th century–mid-13th; Kiev, Hist. Mus.) and is similar to that used in manuscript illumination and stone-carving. Among other subjects are the pre-Christian images of gryphons and lions symbolizing power and strength, as on a diadem with a portrait of *Alexander the Great* from Sakhnovs'ke (Sakhnovskoye; 10th–12th centuries). The purely Christian representation of Christ and saints appears on an enamelled, gold medallion from Kaminnyy Brid (Kamenny Brod; 12th–13th centuries).

In the 11th and 12th centuries cast moulds were taken of precious items of jewellery, such as earrings with a simurgh design, and the newly cast objects were set with cut, ground and faceted gemstones and hardstones. Jewellery making was curtailed during the Tatar–Mongol invasions in the 13th century but revived in the 14th, particularly in L'viv, where some 200 craftsmen are documented between the 14th and 18th centuries; one L'viv workshop founded in 1595 employed 30 goldsmiths. In the second half of the 17th century Kiev, Chernihiv, Nizhyn and Hlukhiv (Glukhov) also became centres of jewellery production, mainly making objects for the Church and the Cossack officer class. The predominant technique was low-relief chasing with a contrasting use of both gold and silver.

In the late 18th century and early 19th jewellery production, which had until then been the prerogative of craftsmen belonging to urban guilds, spread to the countryside. Instead of gold and silver, rural craftsmen used copper, brass and bronze to create rings, earrings, ornamental buttons and necklaces from which a gold or silver coin dangled. In the Hutsul'shchyna (Gutsul'shchina) district, buckles and necklaces of the 18th century to the early 20th were decorated with engraved designs and embossed crosses (L'viv, Mus. Ukrain. A.).

2. METALWORK. A wide range of objects, including richly adorned weapons and items for domestic and liturgical use, survive in gold, silver and base metals. Together with the examples of jewellery (see above), they indicate that by the 11th century metalworkers were familiar with the basic techniques of forging, punching, engraving, encrustation with gemstones, gilding and the use of niello, for example on the 10th-century, silver-mounted horn of an aurochs (Kiev, Hist. Mus.) from the Black Tomb at Chernihiv. As on jewellery, typical designs include representations of people, real and fantastic animals and plants. One frequently recurring pattern consists of four interlaced lilies, for example on a plaque from a horse harness set found at the burial ground of Shestkovits'ky and on the handle of a sword recovered near the Golden Gates in Kiev (both 10th century; Kiev, Hist. Mus.).

In the 12th century the use of niello became widespread, initially as background and, by the mid-13th century, for outline drawings. Plates and drinking vessels are often decorated with scenes of battle and hunting, for example on a 12th-century silver goblet from Chernihiv (Chernihiv, Hist. Mus.). Punching was another popular technique, as in a copper fish platter (second half of the 11th century; Kiev, Hist. Mus.) from Shchuchynka (Shchuchinka), which bears the depiction of a saint. During the 11th and

12th centuries chandeliers for churches, weapons and other objects were often cast and frequently gilded.

The development of metalworking was interrupted in the 13th century by the Tatar–Mongol invasions. Traditional techniques were revived in the 14th and 15th centuries, particularly in the Galitsko–Volynskoye principality. Icon mountings and Gospel covers were made of silver inlaid with pearls and enamels (e.g. Kiev, Hist. Mus. and L'viv, Mus. Ethnog., A. & Crafts Ukrain. Acad. Sci.). Numerous silver spoons (L'viv, Mus. Ethnog, A. & Crafts Ukrain Acad. Sci.) engraved with mottoes and aphorisms have also survived. From the 15th century L'viv served as an important centre for the production of arms and armour, attracting craftsmen of various nationalities. Many of their products are gilded with ornamental designs. Locksmiths and blacksmiths also settled here, manufacturing goods that are shaped and decorated according to traditional designs. The decoration on crosses worked by blacksmiths and intended to be fitted to church domes is closely related to popular styles and incorporates pre-Christian elements.

In the 16th century Gothic, Renaissance and Baroque motifs were combined with traditional designs, for example on the Mikhaylovsky Cross (1546; untraced). The influence of Renaissance decoration is also evident in the ornament and coats of arms found on 16th- and 17th-century cannon, such as the Oryol Gun (1570–71), which was cast by Leonhard Herle (*fl* 1529–71). Many of these cannons were cast in the principal foundries at Halich and Volhyn'. Bells were also cast there and decorated in low relief. The designs could be figurative, for example the St George on a bell (L'viv, Mus. Ethnog., A. & Crafts Ukrain. Acad. Sci.) cast in 1643 by the L'viv craftsman Andrey Frankovich, or purely ornamental, as on a 16th-century bell from the church of the Transfiguration (Preobrazhenskaya) in Dubno.

In the second half of the 17th century and the 18th, Chernihiv, Nizhyn, Hlukhiv and especially Kiev became centres of metalwork production. As with jewellery production, gold and silver was sometimes used, for example for the Holy Doors (1747, by Pyotr Volokh and Ivan Zovodovsky; *in situ*) of the iconostasis in the cathedral of St Sophia, Kiev, and for the icon mounting of the *Il'inskaya Virgin* (18th century; Chernihiv, Hist. Mus.). The casting of goblets, collection boxes, dishes and crosses in pewter also became common at this time. Examples of Jewish metalwork for ritual and domestic use, including candlesticks and pointers for reading the Torah, have been preserved from Halich, Volhyn' and Podillya (Podoliya; e.g. Kiev, Hist. Mus. and L'viv, Mus. Ethnog., A. & Crafts Ukrain. Acad. Sci.).

During the same period the iron foundries at Kiev and in its vicinity achieved high standards in the casting of bells and cannon. By the 18th century the products of each foundry bore a mark for identification. Copper, brass and sometimes pewter and silver were used for candlesticks, candelabra and chandeliers, many of which are decorated with the Tree of Life (e.g. L'viv, Mus. Ethnog., A. & Crafts Ukrain. Acad. Sci.). The increasingly solid appearance of these objects from the late 18th century and the early 19th, particularly the chandeliers, reflects the contemporary classicizing trend in art. By this period, however, the technique of die-stamping wares from moulds predominated, leading to the decline of the traditional decorative techniques of metalworking.

3. OTHER. Although most objects date from the 14th century AD onwards, weaving, embroidery, pottery, glassmaking and wood-carving were long-established art forms. Among the few surviving examples are the moulded earthenware utensils (3rd–2nd millennia BC) of diverse shapes and intricate designs discovered on the banks of the Dnepr River, and fragments of Kievan glass (11th–12th centuries AD; Kiev, Mus. Ukrain. Pop. & Dec. A.). Despite the destructive blow of the Tatar–Mongol invasions, traditional forms of decorative art continued to be produced in rural areas as folk art. Three main phases can be distinguished: the 14th century to the first half of the 16th, when the items produced were strictly for private domestic use; the mid-16th century to the first half of the 17th, when crafts began to be sold and workshops established; and the second half of the 17th century to the early 20th, during which cottage industries were gradually overtaken by factory-based industries. Objects came increasingly to serve a decorative rather than a utilitarian purpose. Since the 1930s, however, artists have produced works on an individual basis or as part of small folk art workshops.

The numerous forms of glazed and unglazed ceramics reflect the wide range of colours, designs and techniques used in the different regions of Ukraine. In the districts around Poltava, Chernihiv and Kharkiv, for example, traditional polychrome tableware, including vessels in animal or human shapes (Kiev, Mus. Ukrain. Pop. & Dec. A.), were particularly popular. Designs include floral motifs, birds, animals and narrative scenes, which are usually incised by means of a truncated cowhorn and are often painted. Since the 19th century Oposhnya and Kosiv have been the main centres of folk art ceramics, with such renowned artists as Aleksandr Bakhmatyuk (1820–82) producing pottery typical of the Hutsul'shchyna district with a white slip painted with green and yellow glazes (e.g. a tile depicting stags; second half of the 19th century; Kolomyya, Mus. Hutsul Flk A.). In the early 20th century a new style of decoration was introduced with the addition of animal and human miniatures, as in the hunting scene around the neck of a green-glazed vase (1935; Kiev, Mus. Ukrain. Pop. & Dec. A.) by Ivan Gonchar (1888–1944).

Although glass workshops are first recorded in the 15th century, free-blown glassmaking reached its peak in the 17th and 18th centuries and was centred in Volhyn', Chernihiv and Kiev. Various techniques were used for decorating a vast range of coloured and colourless glasswares including bottles, jugs, bowls, plates, cups and vessels in the form of animals (e.g. prunted bear decanter; 18th century; Kiev, Mus. Ukrain. Pop. & Dec. A.). More expensive objects such as chandeliers, mirror frames, carafes of cut and engraved glass and goblets were also produced. In the late 19th century large factories replaced the free-blown glass workshops; it was not until 1945 that the traditional techniques of glassmaking were revived in and around L'viv.

Three widespread art forms are weaving, embroidery and carpet-making. Patterned textiles of wool, linen and cotton were handwoven in virtually every Ukrainian village, with regional variations reflected in the choice of techniques, ornament and colour schemes. The fabrics were used for garments as well as for such household items as tablecloths, pillowcases, blankets and 'rushnik' towels, which served both as towels and as decorative hangings inside houses. A distinctive feature of rushniks is their predominantly red colouring, which may be combined with geometrical and floral designs, bird motifs or alternating black-and-white horizontal stripes (Kiev, Mus. Ukrain. Pop. & Dec. A.). Handwoven textiles continue to be produced in such major centres as Reshetilovka, Boguslav and Krolevets'.

The earliest extant samples of embroidery work (17th and 18th centuries) reveal the use of various techniques (e.g. cross-stitch, satin stitch, drawn-thread work) for embellishing garments, household linen, priestly vestments and even saddle-cloths. Different regions continue to produce their own distinctive embroideries, as in the area around Poltava, which is renowned for the white satin-stitched and buttonhole-stitched geometrized floral designs on shirts and blouses.

Another method of decorating broadcloth and linen was by block-printing, which was practised as early as the 12th century but flourished between the 18th century and early 19th. Wooden blocks were carved with small geometrical motifs or with inhabited floral designs. These blocks were then coated with oil paints and the pattern impressed on the fabric by a roller in monochrome colours of blue, black or brown, or in combinations of dark brown and terracotta, or dark brown and bottle green (Kiev, Mus. Ukrain. Pop. & Dec. A.).

In the mid-16th century the weaving of rugs and carpets became more widespread. They were made with and without a nap; cut-pile carpets known as kotsa carpets were common around Kharkiv until the mid-19th century. A characteristic feature of carpets from the Poltava, Kiev, Chernihiv and Zaporizhzhya districts is the use of floral motifs which in the latter three areas are more geometrized (Kiev, Mus. Ukrain. Pop. & Dec. A.; L'viv, Mus. Ethnog., A. & Crafts Ukrain. Acad. Sci.). In the Bokovian, Hutsul' shchyna and Volhyn' districts, geometrical designs (e.g. lozenges, star-shaped rosettes, stripes) predominate.

The use of decorative wood-carving in secular and ecclesiastical architecture goes back to the region's early Slav tribes. Wood was also used for household items and utensils; designs were either engraved or carved. Since the late 19th century wood carvers in the Hutsul'shchina district have also decorated such small items as caskets, plates, cigarette cases and miniature chests with intarsia, bugle-bead and mother-of-pearl inlay. Among the renowned exponents of this style of decorated wood-carving are members of the Skriblyak and Korpanyuk families (e.g. Kolomïa, Mus. Hutsul Flk A.; Kiev, Mus. Ukrain. Pop. & Dec. A.).

Another traditional art form found in most Ukrainian peasant houses were the hand-painted designs and scenes on walls, furniture, toys and Easter eggs. In the late 19th century the commercialization of this kind of painting resulted in the creation of a new art form known as decorative pictures on paper, in which birds, animals, fish and village scenes are represented in a stylized manner and in vividly contrasting colours. Examples of this type of work include *Happy Time* (gouache and watercolour on paper, 1965) by Anna Sobachko-Shostak (1883–1965), *Galya Comes to Fetch Water and Waits for Vasya* (1975) and *Ukrainian Puss-in-Boots* (1975) by Mariya Prymachenko (*b* 1909) and *Flowers behind the Fence* (all Kiev, Mus. Ukrain. Pop. & Dec. A.) by Kateryna Bilokur.

BIBLIOGRAPHY

W. Zozinski: *Złotnictwo lwowskie* [L'viv goldsmithery] (L'viv, 1912)
K. Sherotsky: *Ocherki ob istorii dekorativnogo iskusstva Ukrainy: Khudozhestvennoye ubranstvo v proshlom i nastoyashchem* [Essays on the history of decorative art in Ukraine: artistic house decoration in the past and present] (Kiev, 1914)
V. N. Perets: *O nekotorykh osnovaniyakh dlya datirovki drevnerusskogo mednogo litiya* [Sources for the dating of Old Russian copper castings] (Leningrad, 1933)
P. N. Sobolyev: *Ocherki po istorii ukrasheniya tkaney* [Essays on the history of fabric decoration] (Moscow, 1934)
A. Gushchin: *Pamyatniki khudozhestvennogo remesla drevney Rusi XI–XIII vv.* [Leading works of the artistic handicrafts in Old Rus' of the 11th to 13th centuries] (Moscow, 1936)
M. V. Babenchikov: *Narodnoye dekorativnoye iskusstvo Ukrainy i yego mastera* [Decorative folk art of Ukraine and its masters] (Moscow, 1945)
B. Rybakov: *Remeslo drevney Rusi* [The crafts of Old Rus'] (Moscow, 1948)
N. D. Manucharova: *Dekorativno-prykladne mystetstvo Ukraïns'koï RSR* [Decorative/applied arts of Ukrainian SSR] (Kiev, 1952)
B. Kolchin: *Tekhnika obrabotki metalla v drevney Rusi* [Metalworking techniques in Old Rus'] (Moscow, 1953)
I. M. Matyasyak: *Hutsul's'ki khudozhni metalevi vyroby* [Hutsul artistic metalware], vii (Kiev, 1954)
Yu. P. Lashchuk: *Hutsul's'ka keramika* [Hutsul ceramics] (Kiev, 1956)
——: *Zakarpats'ka narodna keramika* [Transcarpathian folk ceramics] (Uzhhorod, 1956)
P. M. Zholkovs'ky: 'Khudozhne lytya na zakhidnykh zemlyakh Ukraïny XVII–XIX st.' [Artistic foundry work in western areas of Ukraine in the XVII–XIX centuries], *Materialy z ethografiï ta mystetstvoznavstva* [Material on ethnography and the study of art], v (Kiev, 1959), pp. 136–59
Khudozhni metalevi vyroby zakhidnykh oblastey Ukraïns'koï RSR (XVI–XIX st.) [Artistic metalware from western provinces of the Ukrainian RSR (XVI–XIX centuries)] (Kiev, 1959)
A. M. Zhuk: *Ukraïns'ki narodni kylymy* [Ukrainian folk carpets] (Kiev, 1966)
L. P. Zapasko: *Ukraïns'ke narodne kylymarstvo* [Ukrainian folk carpet-weaving] (Kiev, 1973)
P. M. Zholtovs'ky: *Khudozhne lytta na Ukraïni XIV–XVII st.* [Artistic metal-casting in Ukraine in the 14th–17th centuries] (Kiev, 1973)
N. D. Manucharova: *Suchasne Ukraïns'ke narodne mystetstvo* [Ukrainian folk art] (Kiev, 1976)

L. I. POPOVA

VI. Patronage and collecting.

Until the mid-19th century patronage and collecting in eastern Ukraine was almost exclusively the province of the Church. A few collections of art and sculpture, mainly decorative in purpose, were held in the country palaces of the nobility. The Sanguszko palace in Pidluvtsi is among the few 17th-century examples of domestic interiors still surviving, although much altered. Among 18th-century palaces were those belonging to the Zavadovskys in Lyialichi, and the Rozumovskys in Pochep and Baturin. In the first half of the 19th century the Vorontsov palace in Odessa and the Galagan palace in Sokoryntsi were furnished with eclectic collections of European art. The palace of Khan Mengli Giray (*reg* 1478–1514 with interruption) in BAKHCHISARAY preserves examples of Islamic art from as early as the 16th century.

Serious private collecting began in the 1880s when T. V. Kibal'chich and I. A. Khoyonovsky established private museums. The growing emphasis on Ukrainian national identity meant that most new collectors concentrated on gathering material documenting Ukrainian culture (e.g. artefacts discovered in privately funded excavations of Scythian burials), examples of Ukrainian folk art (e.g. embroidery, carpets), arts associated with specific ethnic groups (e.g. the Zaporozh'ye Cossacks), and works by 19th- and 20th-century Ukrainian artists. The prominent collections of Ukrainian antiquities formed by Vasyl Khrychevsky, F. Vovk, Venyamin Tarnovsky (1837–1906), O. Pol and K. Skarzhynska now form part of major state collections.

The first major collection of Western art was begun by Bohdan Khanenko (1848–1917). It contained works by 18th-century Dutch graphic artists and painters as well as European porcelain of the late 18th century and the early 19th. In 1882 Khanenko commissioned the Neo-classical architect Roman Mel'tser to build his house and a private museum for his collection in Kiev. Over the next 20 years Khanenko enlarged his collection with the addition of Slavonic antiquities, icons and 19th-century Russian furniture. The museum later became the Kiev Museum of Western and Oriental Art, which also incorporated the collection of Flemish art created in the last years of the 19th century by V. Shchavinsky.

In 1880 the industrial magnate M. Tereshchenko commissioned a building to house his family's collection of works, mainly by Ukrainian and Russian artists belonging to the WANDERERS (Rus. *Peredvizhniki*). It included paintings by Il'ya Repin, Nikolay Ge, Mikhail Vrubel' and Vladimir Borovikovsky. In the late 19th century the painter IVAN AYVAZOVSKY founded the Ayvazovsky Picture Gallery in Feodosiya, based on his own collection. This was one of the few to survive the October Revolution (1917) and civil war period (1919–20) intact.

After the Revolution all private collections were nationalized and most of their contents were dispersed among several state museums. Patronage and private collecting were not considered worthy of record and only in the late 20th century did Ukrainian scholars begin to study these subjects.

BIBLIOGRAPHY

I. Lazarevsky: *Sredi kollektsionerov* [Among collectors] (Petrograd, 1917)
K. A. Akinsha: *Kul'turnaya zhizn' Kieva vtoroy poloviny XIX–nachala XX vekov* [The cultural life of Kiev in the late 19th century and the early 20th] (Moscow, 1990)

VII. Museums and institutions.

Until the 19th century, when the first public museums and art galleries in Ukraine were established, only religious foundations had exhibited objects from their collections. In 1878 religious art from the cathedral of St Sophia in Kiev was exhibited in the Kiev Church and Archaeological Museum. In the 1880s paintings by the Wanderers were exhibited in Kiev and formed the core purchases for such collectors as M. Tereshchenko, whose private museum became the Kiev State Museum of Russian Art (*see* §VI above), and was later supplemented by icons, 18th-century Russian art, collections of porcelain and glass, and 20th-century works, especially of SOCIALIST REALISM.

Following the incorporation of Ukraine into the USSR (1924) the cathedral complex of St Sophia was secularized and renamed the St Sophia Historical and Architectural Museum, with more than 60,000 works of religious art. The cathedral has since been reconsecrated, but icons, enamels and other treasures of applied art from the 11th to the 19th centuries are still displayed. The Kiev–Pechersky State Historical Museum contains the most important collection of Scythian gold outside the Hermitage, St Petersburg, as well as Ukrainian goldsmiths' work from the 14th to the 19th centuries.

In 1904 the Art and Industrial Museum was opened in Kiev for the display of Russian and Ukrainian paintings, sculpture and crafts, as well as examples of local industrial production; from 1906, however, it became primarily a centre for Ukrainian folk art. It was later renamed the State Museum of Ukrainian Popular and Decorative Art and houses a large collection of textiles, carpets, embroidery, carvings, ceramics and porcelain from the 18th century to the present. The State Museum of Ukrainian Art in Kiev contains icons dating from the 12th to the 18th centuries, 17th- and 18th-century portraits, and important paintings of the 19th century and the early 20th, including works by Dmitry Levtsky, TARAS SHEVCHENKO and VLADIMIR BOROVIKOVSKY. It also contains posters from the civil war (1919–20) and the period of Soviet rule (1924–91), including many examples of Socialist Realism.

The Kiev Museum of Western and Oriental Art was largely created from the private collections of Bohdan Khanenko (1848–1917) and V. Shchavinsky and mainly consists of western European art up to the mid-19th century. 'Ancient Kiev' is a museum founded on the site of Kiev's old town to conserve its architecture and to provide an open-air exhibition of ancient and medieval sculpture.

Outside Kiev, the Khar'kiv Historical Museum has brought together exhibits from several local private and public collections, including folk art from the former museums of Slobidska Ukraine and of Art and Industry, icons and religious objects from the former Khar'kiv University Museum of Art and Antiquities and the Khar'kiv Church Museum, and works by Taras Shevchenko and other Russian and Ukrainian painters, sculptors and graphic artists.

The collection in the State Museum of Ukrainian Art in L'viv is based on 19th-century ethnographic and archaeological collections designed to document the development of Ukrainian culture. It also contains portraits from the 16th to the 18th centuries, religious art (mainly Orthodox) and illuminated manuscripts from the holdings of the former Stauropegion Institute. Works of the 19th and 20th centuries are housed in the L'viv Picture Gallery, including some by Aleksander Archipenko (1887–1964) and V. Manastyrski.

BIBLIOGRAPHY

A. Danyliuk: 'Muzei na Ukrainy' [Museums in Ukraine], *Ukrainsky kalendar* [Ukrainian yearbook] (Warsaw, 1974)
I. Nanov'skyi and others: *L'vivsky muzei ukrainskoho mystetstva* [The L'viv museum of Ukrainian art] (L'viv, 1978)
B. Buyanovskaya: *Muzei Kieva* [Museums in Kiev] (Moscow, 1984)
Derzhavnii arkhitenkturno-isotorichnii zapovednik 'Sofiskii muzei' [The state architectural and historical monument 'Sophia museum'] (Kiev, 1984)

A. Miletskyi and P. Tolochko: *Park-muzei 'Drevniy Kiev'* [The 'old Kiev' open-air museum] (Kiev, 1989)

JANA HOWLETT

Ukyōnoshin. *See* KANŌ, (13).

Ul, Sebastiano d'. *See* VALENTINIS, SEBASTIANO DE'.

'Ula. *See under* ARABIA, PRE-ISLAMIC, §§I; II; III; IV, 1.

Ulenborch, Gerrit. *See* UYLENBURGH, GERRIT.

Ulitin, Vasily (Ivanovich) (*b* Serpukhov, 1888; *d* Moscow, 1976). Russian photographer. After graduating from a school of commerce and chemical technology he worked in Ivan Sytin's zincographic workshop. In 1911 he joined Karl Fisher's photographic studio, where he trained as a portrait photographer. In 1917–20 he was a photographer at the Armoured Vehicles Academy. From 1922 to 1930 he exhibited at photographic shows and received numerous awards in Europe, North America and Japan. He was a member of the Russian Photographic Society and an editor of the journal *Fotograf*. In 1928–30 he taught basic photography to trade union groups and in 1931 founded the Moscow Industrial Union's first school of photography. From 1934 he taught photography at the Moscow Printing Institute, where he developed the 'bromochromotype', a three-colour positive printing technique (which he used in his photograph *Red Flag*, 1930s), and he experimented in the design of photographic equipment. He was known for his psychological portraits, such as *Old Man* (1925), and for soft-toned landscapes (e.g. *Pines at Tsaritsyno*, 1925) that were often reminiscent of the work of 19th-century photographers, themselves influenced by paintings by the Wanderers.

WRITINGS

Rezinotipiya [Resin-printing] (1927)

BIBLIOGRAPHY

Antologya sovetskoy fotografii, 1917–1940 [Anthology of Soviet photography] (Moscow, 1986)
D. Elliot, ed.: *Photography in Russia, 1840–1940* (Berlin, 1992)

A. N. LAVRENTIEV

Ullman, Micha (*b* Tel Aviv, 1939). Israeli sculptor, painter, draughtsman, printmaker and conceptual artist. He studied at Bezalel Academy of Arts and Design in Jerusalem and in 1965 at Central School for Arts and Crafts in London. After painting abstract pictures in an expressionist technique he began to make etchings and (from the early 1970s) drawings. He also became involved in land art and conceptual art projects, some of them politically oriented, such as the *Messer-Metzer Project* in 1972, which involved an exchange of earth between an Arab village and an Israeli *kibbutz*. On some of these projects he collaborated with other artists, among them Moshe Gershuni and Avital Geva.

From 1978 Ullman evoked graves, archaeological excavations or trenches both in drawings and in sculptures in earth such as *Lot's Wife* (1984), a six-foot deep pit dug in Har Sedom, Israel. As Israel's representative at the Venice Biennale in 1980 he showed a large work, the *Third Watch*, entirely dug in the ground. Similar references were made in his drawings, through the use of mud. From 1980 he made allusion to fortifications erected by the British during the Palestinian mandate, concentrating on systems of defence and fortification in sculptures made of earth and cement with a firm upright stance, such as *Up to Here* (cast earth, 1980; see 1980 exh. cat., pp. 16–17). The reductive structure of, for example, *Chariot* (iron and red sand, 1985; Tel Aviv Mus.) is reminiscent of military shelters or can be seen as a spiritual entity derived form Ezekiel's vision of the chariot.

BIBLIOGRAPHY

Borders (exh. cat., Jerusalem, Israel Mus., 1980)
Micha Ullman: The Surface: Drawings, 1970–1980 (exh. cat., foreword M. Scheps, text S. Breitberg-Semel; Tel Aviv Mus. A., 1980–81)
Micha Ullman: Works, 1981–1986 (exh. cat., text A. Ofek; New York, Bertha Vardang Gal., 1986)
Micha Ullman, 1980–1988 (exh. cat., text Y. Zalmonq; Jerusalem, Israel Mus., 1988) [in Eng. and Heb.]
Two Israeli Artists: Micha Ullman, Danny Shoshan (exh. cat., text M. Omer; Ramat Gan, Beit Immanuel Mun. Mus., 1989) [in Eng. and Heb.]

SUSAN T. GOODMAN

Ullmann, Gyula. *See under* KÁRMÁN & ULLMANN.

Ullrich, Dietmar. *See under* ZEBRA.

Ulm. German city, the regional capital of Baden-Württemberg, with a population of 100,000 and a university. It is situated on the Danube, near the mouths of the Blau and the Iller, on important commercial routes.

1. History and urban development. 2. Buildings.

1. HISTORY AND URBAN DEVELOPMENT. Although the area was inhabited as early as Neolithic times, a settlement on the site of the present city has been traced only from the Germanic period. Ulm was first documented in AD 854 as the site of a Carolingian royal palace (situated on the Weinhofberg), of which only the Heiligkreuzkapelle has been excavated. Ulm developed quickly into the principal town of the Swabian duchy and in 1027 was documented as a fortified *oppidum*. From the late 11th century, the Staufen made it their capital. In 1134 it was destroyed by the Guelphs.

From 1140 the town was rebuilt, fortifications were constructed, and the palace complex in the south-west corner of the rectangular town plan was restored and elaborated. On several occasions from the 1260s Ulm was the leading member of alliances between regions and towns. In 1274 it became an Imperial Free City. From 1316 it was extended in the course of a comprehensive reinforcement, quadrupling its former circumference. The textile industry, especially the production of fustian and linen, led to an enormous economic boom in the 14th century. Ulm reached its political peak in the two *Schwörbriefen* of 1345 and 1397, which established a breakthrough in guild constitution.

As a result of its economic prosperity, Ulm developed into one of the leading artistic centres of the German-speaking region. The erection of the minster from 1377 and the alteration of the Rathaus from 1397 created the means of livelihood for numerous artists (*see* §2 below), among them Jörg Syrlin the elder, Michel Erhart, Hans Multscher and BARTHOLOMÄUS ZEITBLOM. Numerous timber-framed buildings were constructed in the 16th century, and from 1527 the medieval city wall was remodelled, according to Albrecht Dürer's system, by the Nuremberg master builder Hans Beheim the elder.

During the Reformation Ulm became Protestant, and in 1531 iconoclasm began. The religious wars led in 1548 to the abolition of the constitution; patrician rule was reestablished, and the guilds were suppressed. The fortification of the ramparts (1604–22) under GIDEON BACHER and the Dutch engineer Johann van Valckenburg (*d* 1625) included the construction of the Soldatenstädtlein (small town for soldiers) on the new Glöcklerbastion. (*See also* FURTTENBACH, JOSEF.)

In 1702–4 Ulm came under Bavarian occupation. As a result of the Napoleonic wars it lost its status as an Imperial Free City and was incorporated into Bavaria in 1802 and Württemberg in 1810. The construction of a federal, polygonal fortress (1842–59) in Ulm was followed by its development into an important railway junction. Subsequently the city expanded, especially to the north. The Gymnasium (grammar school) was built in 1876–8, and the Justizgebäude for the district and county courts in 1894–9. From *c.* 1900 the demolition of the ramparts facilitated the further expansion of the city. Military and commercial areas developed outside the walls, but the old city centre remained untouched until World War II, when it was almost completely destroyed (1944–5). Only the minster survived, albeit severely damaged. The city was later largely rebuilt in its earlier form.

BIBLIOGRAPHY

H. E. Specker: *Ulm: Stadtgeschichte* (Ulm, 1972)
Tradition und Wagnis: Ulm, 1945–1972. Festschrift Theodor Pfizer (Ulm, 1974)
Ulmer Handwerk in Mittelalter und Neuzeit (exh. cat., ed. H. E. Specker; Ulm, Stadtarchv, 1975)
H. Wiegandt: *Ulm: Geschichte einer Stadt* (Weissenhorn, 1977)
O. Schäuffelen: *Die Befestigung Ulms und ihre Geschichte: Europas grösste Festungsanlage* (Ulm, 1980)
H. Koepf: *Ulmer Profanbauten: Ein Bildinventar* (Ulm and Stuttgart, 1982)

ULRIKE LIEBL

2. BUILDINGS.

(i) Minster. (ii) Rathaus.

(i) Minster. The parish church was planned from the mid-14th century on an enormous scale and was one of the most ambitious projects for a religious building promoted by townspeople in the late Middle Ages; as such, it assisted the Imperial Free City in staking its claim to political primacy in Swabia. The city council's plan to transfer an older building outside the city walls—'*ennet veldes*' (in the fields)—into the city itself met with success in 1377, and the burgomaster Lutz Krafft laid the foundation stone of the new parish church of the Heilige Jungfrau Maria. In 1446 Ulm acquired the advowson and parish rights from the monastery of Reichenau.

(a) Architecture. (b) Sculpture.

(a) Architecture. The fragmentary written records reveal several phases of design and construction. A statement of account from 1387 names the first three consecutive architects as members of the family of PARLER VON ULM: Heinrich the elder (1377–83/4), Michael (1383/4–7) and Heinrich the younger (1387–91). Based on the evidence of the building, an early design for a single-aisled polygonal

choir, with radiating chapels and choir towers on the sides, and an exceptionally wide three-aisled hall nave with a west tower, must have been modified under Heinrich the elder by the omission of the radiating chapels. Michael must have effected the change to the basilical cross-section in the nave. The dimensions of the nave have been established by the time of Heinrich the younger at the latest.

Ulrich von Ensingen became Master of the Works in 1392, by which time eight bays of the nave had probably been built, and he presided over the most important building phase (1392–1419; *see* ENSINGEN, (1)). He replanned the west end, inserting the impressive tower into the nave, as is shown by a fragment of a plan, 'drawing A' (Ulm, Stadtarchv). To accommodate its ground-plan within the existing nave dimensions, the span of the arches of the last two nave bays was extended. Later Ensinger versions of the tower elevation (see below) also indicate that Ulrich originally intended the nave to be 4 m lower. By 1419 the tower was level with the porch eaves (*c.* 19 m). The consecration had taken place in 1405 when the minster was still only partially complete.

Under the architect Hans Kun (appointed 1417) and his son Kaspar Kun, who succeeded him in 1435, work continued mainly on the first upper storey of the tower (St Martin window) and the west part of the nave (*see* KUN). The Besserer chapel by the south choir tower was built *c.* 1420–30 (*see* GOTHIC, §VIII, 5). The arch between the space at the base of the west tower and the central nave dates from 1435, and the Neithart chapel by the

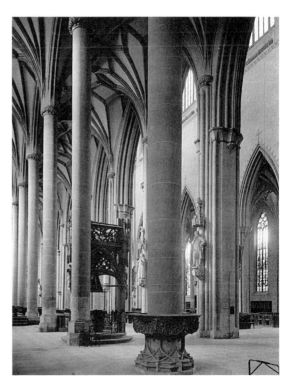

1. Ulm Minster, south double side aisle (1502) by Burkhard Engelberg, view from the south-east corner, with the holy water stoup (*c.* 1507) in the foreground

north choir tower was begun *c.* 1444. Matthäus Ensinger, Master of the Works from 1446 (*see* ENSINGER, (2)), added a chapel (1447; destr. 1817) endowed by the Roth family in the south aisle. He vaulted the choir (1449) and the two west bays of the side aisles on either side of the tower. In 1452 Matthäus completed the vaulting of the north aisle and, in 1455, that of the south aisle. In the first upper storey of the tower the tripartite decorative arch in front of the St Martin window and the blind arches on the tower buttresses were constructed.

Moritz Ensinger (*see* ENSINGER, (4)) became Master of the Works in 1465, and his position was confirmed in 1470. Between 1469 and 1471 he completed the upper walls, the east end of the nave and the nave vault. Flying buttresses were later constructed to stabilize the nave. The new design for the completion of the tower, 'drawing B' (*c.* 1470; parts Ulm, Evangel. Gesamt-Kirchgemein., and London, V&A), must be ascribed to Moritz. After Moritz Ensinger's premature departure in 1477, Matthäus Böblinger from Esslingen was appointed and (1480) given life tenure. Böblinger presented a new design for the tower, 'drawing C' (after 1477; Ulm, Evangel. Gesamt-Kirchgemein.; for illustration *see* BÖBLINGER, (3)), with proposals for the completion of the upper storeys. Apart from constructing pinnacles on the pier buttresses at the southwest corner of the minster, however, Böblinger contributed only the second upper storey of the tower, with the quadrangular gallery, and about 5 m (later dismantled) of the lower part of the octagon (but see also below).

In 1492–4 the unfinished west tower threatened to collapse, as a belated consequence of inadequate foundations for the load-bearing piers installed in Ulrich von Ensingen's time. The Augsburg mason Burkhard Engelberg was consulted in 1493 and replaced Böblinger as minster architect (1494/5–1511). He made good the foundations and consolidated the tower by walling up the open arches at the base and renovating some of the pillars in the western arcading of the nave. The side aisles were unstable because of the heavy vaulting erected by Matthäus Ensinger and the failure to complete the buttressing; Burkhard solved this by converting them into graceful double-aisled hall-type spaces (1502) and replacing the earlier vaulting by light net and star vaulting supported by slender round columns (see fig. 1). He entrusted the supervision of work on the site to his foreman Lienhard Aeltlin (*fl* 1493–*c.* 1517) and to Bernhard Winkler (*fl* 1499–1532) from Rosenheim; from 1518 the latter was appointed minster Master of Works. Under Winkler only peripheral work relating to the repair and extension of the tower octagon was undertaken. The Reformation put an end to construction work in 1531.

The next important phase of building did not occur until a builders' yard was set up in 1844. Under Ferdinand Thrän (1811–70; architect 1844–70), 20 m post-stressing pinnacles were installed above the pier buttresses of the side aisles, and a system of flying buttresses (1856–70) was added. Thrän's successor (1871–80), Ludwig Scheu (1830–80), completed the recently begun tracery-work gallery above the choir as well as the east choir towers, although no medieval design for these has survived. August von Beyer (1834–99; architect 1881–99) completed the west tower (1885–90; see fig. 2), which had been abandoned

2. Ulm Minster, west tower, h. 161.6 m (possibly the highest church tower in the world), completed 1885–90 by August von Beyer to a design (after 1477) by Matthäus Böblinger

for centuries as a stump, on the basis of Matthäus Böblinger's drawing. Despite its post-medieval date, it must be considered an important 14th- to 15th-century tower design in the tradition of the towers of the cathedrals in Freiburg im Breisgau, Strasbourg and Esslingen.

World War II damage (1944–5) to the choir area was repaired and the vaulting renewed (work completed 1956) under Karl Friedrich (1906–89). The comprehensive restoration of the interior of the nave was undertaken from 1965 to 1970. General restoration (1970–) has since been carried out on the exterior by Gerhard Lorenz.

The Minster is a five-aisled basilica with no transepts, the nave extending over ten bays. The single-aisled choir of four bays is the same width as the nave, and the east end is formed by five sides of a decagon. The dimensions are exceptional, the overall length being *c.* 124 m, of which the choir accounts for *c.* 29 m. The nave (h. *c.* 41.6 m) is twice the height of the double side aisles (h. 20 m), and the nave and aisles have a combined width of 79.5 m. The impressive west tower, with a height of 161.6 m, is believed to be the tallest church tower in the world. The building is mainly of brick, stone being used for distinctive features and for the tower. Its external appearance is principally characterized by the work of the late 19th century. The post-stressing pinnacles and the flying buttresses enliven the huge expanses of wall, window and roof. The completion of the west tower in accordance with the medieval designs was an outstanding achievement. The square storeys of the lower part, surmounted by a gallery running around the edge, support the octagon with its four newels. The final stage consists of a powerful open tracery-work pyramidal spire.

BIBLIOGRAPHY

K. D. Hassler: 'Die zwei ältesten Münster-Urkunden', *Verhand. Ver. Kst & Altert. Ulm & Oberschwaben*, vii (1850), pp. 25–9

H. Bazing and G. Veesenmeyer: *Urkunden zur Geschichte der Pfarrkirche in Ulm* (Ulm, 1890)

R. Pfleiderer: *Das Münster zu Ulm und seine Kunstdenkmale* (Stuttgart, 1905)

V. K. Habicht: 'Das Ulmer Hüttenbuch von 1417–1421', *Repert. Kstwiss.*, xxxiii (1910), pp. 412–17

K. Friedrich: 'Die Risse zum Hauptturm des Münsters', *Ulm & Oberschwaben*, xxxvi (1962), pp. 19–38

R. Wortmann: 'Zur Baugeschichte des Münsterchores', *Z. Württemberg. Landesgesch.*, xxviii (1969), pp. 105–17

——: *Das Ulmer Münster* (1972), iv of *Grosse Bauten Europas*, ed. E. Adam (Stuttgart, 1968–74)

H. Koepf: 'Die gotischen Planrisse der Ulmer Sammlungen', *Forsch. Gesch. Stadt Ulm*, xviii (1977)

G. Lorenz: 'Aus der Ulmer Münsterbauhütte von 1844–1977', *600 Jahre Ulmer Münster*, ed. H. E. Specker (Ulm, 1977, rev. 1984), pp. 503–20

R. Wortmann: 'Hallenplan und Basilikabau der Parler in Ulm', *600 Jahre Ulmer Münster*, ed. H. E. Specker (Ulm, 1977, rev. 1984), pp. 101–25

E. Schmitt: 'Münsterbibliographie', *Das Münster in Literatur und Buchillustration* (exh. cat., ed. E. Schmitt and R. Breidenbruch; Ulm, Stadtbib., 1977), pp. 9–59; rev. as *Münsterbibliographie: Kommentiertes Gesamtverzeichnis aller Schriften über das Ulmer Münster* (Weissenhorn, 1990)

Les Bâtisseurs des cathédrales gothiques (exh. cat., Strasbourg, Musées Ville, 1989), pp. 205, 409–11

F. Bischoff: 'Anmerkungen zum Umbau der Seitenschiffe des Ulmer Münsters unter Burkhard Engelberg', *Geschichte des Konstruierens IV: Wölbkonstruktionen der Gotik 1* (Stuttgart, 1990), pp. 15–91

H. Koepf: 'Die Ulmer Münstergründung und die Parlerfrage', *Ulm & Oberschwaben*, xlv–xlvi (1990), pp. 199–226

FRANZ BISCHOFF

(b) Sculpture. The figural decoration of the exterior is confined essentially to the main west portal and the tympana of the four aisle portals. The latter were partly produced for the old parish church. They are not uniform in style. The *Nativity* and *Adoration of the Kings* on the north-west portal (1356) are characterized by a few clearly outlined figures against a flat ground. By contrast, the reliefs on the other three portals show congested scenes with small figures: on the south-east portal the *Last Judgement* (*c.* 1360); on the north-east the *Passion* (*c.* 1370–80); and on the south-west the *Life of the Virgin* (*c.* 1370–80; partly after 1380). The influence of lodges from the Upper Rhine (Strasbourg and Freiburg im Breisgau cathedrals) and Swabia (Kapellenturm, Rottweil; Heiligkreuzkirche, Schwäbisch Gmünd; and Augsburg Cathedral) is evident.

The double west portal and three-arched narthex have remarkable figural ornamentation (1380–1430; *c.* 1500; see fig. 3). The tympanum (*c.* 1383–91) illustrates the opening scenes of Genesis. The archivolt figures (*c.* 1415) represent *Apostle Martyrs* and the *Wise and Foolish Virgins*; the 12 seated *Apostles* (*c.* 1410–15) on the archivolts of the two doorways bear the sign of the Master of the Kreuzwinkel. On the jambs and trumeau of the portal are 21 carved wooden *Saints* (*c.* 1500; two now inside) from the workshop of Niklaus Weckmann. Also on the trumeau is the magnificent sandstone *Man of Sorrows* (1429; *see* GOTHIC, fig. 37; original inside) by Hans Multscher. The 19 figures (1420–22) above the arches of the narthex and those (1418–19; originals inside) on its piers are by MEISTER HARTMANN. Eight *Prophets* (1383–7) on the chancel buttresses and two figures (*c.* 1390–1400) on the sacristy buttresses (originals inside), in common with all the architectural sculpture of the minster from 1383 to 1400, show the influence of the sculptures produced in Prague under Peter Parler.

Although many of the original furnishings were destroyed in the iconoclasm of 1531, several important works survive. Most of the 35 consoles of the nave piers, now carrying new statues, are still original. Seven of them (1387–91), with excellent figural ornamentation embedded in foliage, are signed by the Master of the Reissnadel. The same master executed the oldest parts of the stone pulpit (before 1391; remodelled 1498–9; modern reliefs, 1937); the baldacchino (1510), a masterly work of joinery, was made in the workshop of Jörg Syrlin the younger. The 26 m high tabernacle (1467–71), possibly designed by Moritz Ensinger, is richly sculpted. The font (1470) is

3. Ulm Minster, west portal with narthex

covered by an unfinished triangular ciborium. A holy water stoup (*c.* 1507; see fig. 1 above), adorned with foliate ornamentation, ingeniously encircles an aisle pier.

The Dreisitz (1468) and choir stalls (1469–74) are by Jörg Syrlin the elder (*see* SYRLIN, (1)). The busts of the stalls have been attributed to MICHEL ERHART and other Ulmish sculptors. Most of the more than 50 altars of the Middle Ages created for the minster, including the high-altar retable (1474–81; 1499–1503) by Syrlin the elder and Michel Erhart, were destroyed or removed during the iconoclasm. The most important surviving retable, the Hutz Altar (1521), shows a *Holy Family* when it is open. The carved group in the shrine is ascribed to Weckmann; the paintings of the predella and the wings are by Martin Schaffner. The stone Karg Retable (1433; mutilated) by Multscher constituted a major contribution to the development of the south German altar retable.

BIBLIOGRAPHY

I. F. Schultz: 'Beiträge zur Baugeschichte und zu den wichtigsten Skulpturen der Parlerzeit am Ulmer Münster', *Ulm & Oberschwaben*, xxxiv (1955), pp. 7–38

H. E. Specker, ed.: *600 Jahre Ulmer Münster* (Ulm, 1977, rev. 1984), pp. 183–322, 330–76

R. Wortmann: 'Die Parlerplastik des Ulmer Münsters', *Die Parler und der Schöne Stil, 1350–1400* (exh. cat., ed. A. Legner; Cologne, Schnütgen-Mus., 1978), i, pp. 328–32

H. Meurer: 'Das unvollendete Retabel: Zum ehemaligen Hochaltar des Ulmer Münsters', *Heilige Kst*, xxiv (1988–91), pp. 13–16

G. Fischer: *Figurenportale in Deutschland, 1350–1530* (Frankfurt am Main, 1989), pp. 447–72

E. Schmitt: *Münsterbibliographie: Kommentiertes Gesamtverzeichnis aller Schriften über das Ulmer Münster* (Ulm, 1977, rev. Weissenhorn, 1990) [publication issued by Ulm Stadtbib.]

Meisterwerke massenhaft: Die Bildhauerwerkstatt des Niklaus Weckmann und die Malerei in Ulm um 1500 (exh. cat., Stuttgart, Württemberg. Landesmuseum, 1993)

KARL HALBAUER

(ii) Rathaus. The town hall on the market-place evolved out of a municipal building, to the south of which an extension, the Kaufhaus, was added in 1370. In 1397 the number of councillors was increased by 40, and a larger council chamber was built on the second floor of the Kaufhaus (first called the Rathaus in 1419). The council chamber is distinguished on the outside by monumental windows, the fine sculptural decoration (originals, Ulm, Ulm. Mus.) of which expressed the town's status as an Imperial Free City. Each of the three windows on the south side is flanked by two *Electors* (*c.* 1425) executed by the minster workshop under Meister Hartmann. In contrast, the figures (1427–30) of *Charlemagne* and the *Kings of Bohemia and Hungary* on the jambs of the two eastern windows, and the two *Squires* on the central mullions, are early works of Hans Multscher, notable for their elegance and subtle realism.

From the pulpit (1473) on the east façade, the burgomaster and council paid homage to the emperor. In 1539 the north wing (before 1357) was demolished and replaced by an arcade. The east and south façades were painted in 1540 by Martin Schaffner: didactic biblical and mythological scenes (rest. 1905), after woodcuts by Hans Schäufelein the elder, Hans Burgkmair I the elder and others, illustrate virtues and vices within an illusionistic architectural framework. The Late Gothic astronomical clock on the east side was restored (1580–81) by Isaak Habrecht

(1544–1620). At about this time the stepped terracotta sides of the east and south gables were added.

BIBLIOGRAPHY

M. Schefold: *Ulm: Das Bild der Stadt in alten Ansichten* (Weissenhorn, 1967)

H. Koepf: *Das Ulmer Rathaus* (Ulm, 1983)

H. E. Specker: *Ulm a.d. Donau* (Munich and Zurich, 1985)

HERIBERT MEURER

Ulmann, Doris (*b* New York, 29 May 1882; *d* New York, 28 Aug 1934). American photographer. She studied at Columbia University, New York, but did not take up photography until 1914, when she studied it with Clarence H. White. She became his best pupil and then worked for several years as a portrait photographer, concentrating on professional people in New York. Around 1925 her attitude towards photography changed: she wished to become involved with social affairs and began to travel around the country—particularly the Appalachian region—in order to photograph the less privileged classes and to give an impression of their character and circumstances. She showed particular interest in highlighting the problems of black people, photographing them most memorably in South Carolina. Despite this, her photographic work is not documentary. The people pose in front of the camera, and in this respect her work still belonged to the 'pictorialist tradition' of an earlier generation.

PHOTOGRAPHIC PUBLICATIONS

A Portrait Gallery of American Editors (New York, 1925)

Roll, Jordan, Roll (New York, 1933)

Handicrafts of the Southern Highlands (New York, 1937)

BIBLIOGRAPHY

J. J. Niles and J. Williams, eds: *The Appalachian Photographs of Doris Ulmann* (Penland, 1971)

ERIKA BILLETER

Ulocrino (*fl c.* 1485–1530). Italian sculptor. The identification of this artist, who signed his bronze plaquettes VLOCRINO, has prompted a number of proposals, the most ingenious (Molinier) being that his name was formed from the Greek *oulos* and the Latin *crinis*, meaning 'curly-haired', and is therefore a pseudonym for Andrea Briosco, known as Andrea Riccio on account of his curly hair; this identification has been refuted on stylistic grounds, while it is accepted that this artist may also have been curly-haired.

Ulocrino's classicizing and clearly modelled compositions include religious plaquettes of *St Jerome*, *St Cecilia* and *St Gerasimus* and mythological scenes of *Apollo and Marsyas* and the *Death of Meleager* (all Berlin, Bodemus.). A plaquette showing *Aristotle and Alexander of Aphrodisias* (London, V&A) is a rare treatment of a literary subject, and it has been suggested that the composition depends on an illuminated frontispiece to an edition of Aristotle's *Works* (Venice, 1483; New York, Pierpont Morgan Lib. ChL 907), probably executed by Girolamo da Cremona. Stylistically, Ulocrino's compositions are related to Paduan plaquette sculpture of the early 16th century.

BIBLIOGRAPHY

E. Molinier: *Les Plaquettes: Catalogue Raisonné*, i (Paris, 1886), pp. 176–84

E. F. Bange and F. Goldschmidt: *Reliefs und Plaketten* (1922), ii of *Die italienischen Bronzen der Renaissance und des Barock* (Berlin, 1914–22), pp. 57–8, nos 418–27, 430

J. Pope-Hennessy: 'The Italian Plaquette', *Proc. Brit. Acad.*, 1 (1964), pp. 63–76

D. R. Morrison: '*Aristotle and Alexander of Aphrodisias* by Ulocrino', *Aristotle Transformed: The Ancient Commentators and Their Influence*, ed. R. Sorbi (London, 1990), pp. 481–4

☐

Ulrich, Johann Jakob (*b* Andelfingen, nr Winterthur, 28 Feb 1798; *d* Zurich, 17 March 1877). Swiss painter. He first studied under his father and then in Paris in 1822 in the studio of Jean-Victor Bertin. As a student he concentrated on unusual lighting effects in his landscape paintings well before they became a hallmark of the precursors of the Impressionists. In 1824 at the Salon in Paris he first saw paintings by Constable. On a trip to Italy in 1828 he did studies *en plein air* as preliminary sketches for his studio paintings. His early paintings emphasize brilliant colour, low horizons and scientific observation of cloud formations in a manner similar to Constable's studies, which he actually saw on visits to England in 1832 and 1835. Like Eugène Boudin, Ulrich was interested in poetic evocations of sun, water and effects of atmosphere rather than in the precise delineations of topography typical of Swiss art of that period. From 1824 he showed regularly at the Salons in Paris and in 1837 he returned to Zurich. Because the Swiss public was reluctant to accept his freer, more adventurous style, he often painted traditional landscapes for exhibitions (e.g. *Port of Rotterdam*, 1844; Berne, Kstmus.), while at the same time executing more innovative charcoal drawings (e.g. *Storm at Sea*, 1849; Zurich, Ksthaus) that resemble those of Turner. In his paintings of the 1850s he was able to combine conventional compositions and sensitive lighting effects, as in *Waterfall in the Forest* (1853; Zurich, Ksthaus) and *Moonlight in Sorrento* (1858; Winterthur, Kstmus.), both of which are poetic images removed from the banality of similar themes treated by his contemporaries.

BIBLIOGRAPHY

V. Meyer-Huber: *Die Entwicklung des 'paysage intime' in der schweizer Landschaftsmalerei des 19. Jahrhunderts* (diss., U. Zurich, 1946), pp. 67–75

H. A. Lüthy: *Der Zürcher Maler Johann Jakob Ulrich II, 1798–1877* (Zurich, 1965)

WILLIAM HAUPTMAN

Ulrich von Ensingen. *See* ENSINGEN, (1).

Ulster. *See* IRELAND, NORTHERN.

Ultvedt, Per Olof (Jörgensen Hungerholt) (*b* Kemi, 1927). Finnish sculptor, painter, printmaker and stage designer. In 1938 his family moved to Sweden, where in 1945 Ultvedt enrolled at the Konsthögskola in Stockholm; the following year he attended Sven Erixson's decorative art school in Stockholm. In 1947 and 1948 he visited Paris, and in 1950 he had his first one-man show at the Galleri Noa-Noa in Copenhagen. At this time he was producing drawings, watercolours and engravings. In 1954 he designed the décor for the ballet *Spiralen*, performed at the Konserthus in Stockholm. From the mid-1950s he turned to collage, welded-metal sculptures and wood-and-paper assemblages, producing such works as *Pig Trough* (1958; see 1988 exh. cat., p. 16), a rectilinear object made from fragments of wood. In the early 1960s he made a number of shallow relief works using open layers of wood, as in *Mobile* (1961; Stockholm, Mod. Mus.). From the same period were a number of installations using wood, wire and other materials that were loosely assembled and often included moving parts, as in that for the *Körelse i konsten* (Movement in art) show at the Moderna Museum in Stockholm in 1961. In 1962 he collaborated with Robert Rauschenberg, Jean Tinguely, Niki de Saint Phalle and others on the large installation *Dylaby* at the Stedelijk Museum in Amsterdam; for this a labyrinth of rooms was built, each filled with assemblages and other objects. Ultvedt also produced small-scale assemblages using moving parts and sometimes electric motors, as in . . . *Life* (1961; Stockholm, Mod. Mus.). In 1966 he collaborated with Saint Phalle and Tinguely on the huge installation *She: A Cathedral* for an exhibition at the Moderna Museum in Stockholm. This consisted of a vast reclining woman 25 m long, between whose legs the spectator could walk to reach a series of interconnecting rooms with environmental assemblages, a bar and a cinema. After the exhibition the installation was destroyed. He continued to produce assemblages and sculptures, as well as installations that often had moving parts triggered by the movements of spectators. In 1972 he started drawing satirical cartoons that were later collected in *Lag och ordning* (1986). He travelled to France in 1973 and to Mexico in 1977. In the 1980s he designed a number of public sculptures, such as the *Déjeuner sur l'herbe* (1984) for the Folkets Park in Motala. These were simplified two-dimensional figurative designs cut into slabs of stone or concrete.

BIBLIOGRAPHY

Hon: En katedral [She: a cathedral] (exh. cat., Stockholm, Mod. Mus., 1966)

Lag och ordning [Law and order] (Stockholm, 1986)

Per Olof Ultvedt: Tvivel och övermod: Arbeten fran 1945 till 1988 [Per Olof Ultvedt: doubt and presumption: works from 1945 to 1988] (exh. cat., ed. C. Erikson and others; Malmö, Ksthall, 1988)

☐

Ul'yanov, Nikolay (Pavlovich) (*b* Yelets, 1 May 1875; *d* Moscow, 5 May 1949). Russian painter and graphic artist. He went to school in Yelets until the family moved to Moscow. In 1888 he studied for several months with an icon painter and then with Vasily Meshkov (1866/7–1946), who trained him for entry into the Moscow College of Painting, Sculpture and Architecture. There Ul'yanov studied under Nikolay Nevryov and Illarion Pryanishnikov and from 1899 to 1901 under Valentin Serov, who had a strong influence on him. A very close relationship developed between Serov and Ul'yanov, who attended Serov's studio even after graduating from College right up to 1904, and who taught with Serov from 1901 to 1907 at the Zvantseva Academy in Moscow.

From 1905 he moved closer to Symbolist groups in art and literature. He became friendly with many future participants of the Blue Rose group, contributed drawings to the journals *Iskusstvo* in 1905 and *Zolotoye runo* in 1906–9 and exhibited with the Moscow Society of Artists, the Union of Russian Artists and the World of Art group. A typical work of the period, *The Princess* (1905; Moscow, Tret'yakov Gal.), was clearly painted under the influence of Viktor Borisov-Musatov and future Blue Rose artists. His early stage designs show the influence of Art Nouveau, in particular those for Vsevolod Meyerhold's production of Gerhart Hauptmann's *Schluck und Jau* (1905) for the Mkhat (the Moscow Art Theatre) studio theatre (sketches in Moscow, Mkhat Mus.). The portraits of this period show the same stylistic influences, for example that of *Konstantin Bal'mont* (1905–9; Moscow, Tret'yakov Gal.) and the drawing of *Aleksey Nikolayevich Tolstoy* (1912; Moscow, Tret'yakov Gal.), which are constructed using a break in the contour line, reminiscent of Serov's late style, and, in the case of the painted portraits, with ornamental and flat unmodulated areas of colour.

Between 1907 and 1912 Ul'yanov visited Italy, France and Germany in order to study contemporary artistic trends. His work of the 1910s frequently contains both Cubist and Expressionist elements, as in *A Paris Window* (1911; Moscow, Tret'yakov Gal.) and *Café* (1911; Moscow, Tret'yakov Gal.). In 1923–4 he took part in the activities of the Zhar-tsvet (Fire-colour) Society, and in 1925 he joined the Four Arts Society of Artists. He continued producing stage and costume designs, for example for Mikhail Bulgakov's *The Days of the Turbins* at Mkhat in 1926 (sketches in Moscow, Mkhat Mus.) and for Bizet's *Carmen* at the Opera Theatre of Konstantin Stanislavsky and Vladimir Nemirovich-Danchenko in 1935 (sketches in Moscow, Bakrushin Cent. Theat. Mus.).

Aleksandr Pushkin was particularly important as subject-matter in Ul'yanov's work of the 1930s (e.g. the series of paintings and drawings *Pushkin in Life*, Moscow, Tret'yakov Gal., St Petersburg, Rus. Mus. and Pushkin, A. S. Pushkin Mus.). The painted works of the series are characterized by great colouristic variety and free and spirited brushwork, while the drawings are notedly concise.

WRITINGS
Vospominaniya o Serove [Recollections of Serov] (Moscow, 1945)

BIBLIOGRAPHY
P. Muratov and B. Griftsov: *N. P. Ul'yanov* (Moscow, 1925)
M. P. Sokol'nikov, ed.: *N. P. Ul'yanov: Moyi Vstrechi: Vospominaniya* (Moscow, 1952, 2/1959)
O. Lavrova: *N. P. Ul'yanov, 1875–1949* (Moscow, 1953)
Nikolay Pavlovich Ul'yanov, intro. O. Roytenberg (Moscow, 1953)
V. A. Lenyashin: *N. P. Ul'yanov* (Leningrad, 1976)

MIKHAIL F. KISELYOV

Umayyad. Islamic dynasty of rulers and patrons descended from the Meccan clan of Umayya. One branch ruled from Syria from AD 661 to 750; following their defeat by the Abbasids, the surviving Umayyad founded another branch that ruled in Spain from 756 to 1031.

1. SYRIAN BRANCH. The founder of the dynasty, Mu'awiya (*reg* AD 661–80), had been governor of Syria for two decades before he seized power following the death of 'Ali ibn Abi Talib (*reg* 656–61), the Prophet's cousin, son-in-law and fourth caliph. Under Umayyad rule the early Muslim conquests were consolidated and expanded, so that Islam found its furthest initial borders from central France to India and the borders of China. The Umayyads ensured that a distinctively Arab and Islamic culture spread throughout this vast empire, the internal frontiers of which gradually melted away. This political and, by degrees, cultural unity encouraged the large-scale movement of people and goods, including sea trade across the Indian Ocean. Arabic displaced Greek, Latin, Coptic and Pahlavi

as the language of the bureaucracy, court, ruling élite and religious establishment. Arab descent was vaunted and secured preferential treatment in fiscal matters, military pensions and land allocation. This racial pride, coupled with their espousal of the spectacularly victorious Islamic faith, made the Umayyads largely impervious to the blandishments of the Christianized Classical culture of the Mediterranean world and the millennial Near Eastern culture of Sasanian Iran, both of which were supplanted. Such independence was symbolized by the choice of Damascus (*see* DAMASCUS, §1(ii)) as capital in preference to other, hitherto more important, eastern Mediterranean cities. Reforms in the administrative structure and coinage of the empire (692–7) finalized this break with the past.

The Umayyad rulers, of whom the three greatest were Mu'awiya, 'Abd al-Malik (*reg* 685–705) and Hisham (*reg* 724–43), took the title *khalīfat allāh* ('God's deputy'), thereby claiming religious as well as political authority. Yet their reign was punctuated by religious revolts (notably in 680 and a civil war lasting intermittently from 683 to 692), while their attempts to hold the balance between conflicting tribal factions (especially Quda'a vs. Qays) made for inherent political instability. Ultimately the dynasty was brought down *inter alia* by disaffected tribal groupings and non-Arab Muslims (Arab. *mawālī*) enraged at their treatment as second-class citizens.

The effective administrative system developed by the Umayyads can be seen in the planning and execution of vast building projects, such as the refurbishing of the Haram al-Sharif with the Dome of the Rock and the Aqsa Mosque (*see* JERUSALEM, §§I, 2; II, 1(iii) and (iv)) and the Great Mosque of Damascus (*see* DAMASCUS, §3). Organized levies of labour and materials brought these projects to remarkably speedy completion. Public works were undertaken on a grand scale. Roads were built and provided with way-stations; travel was made safe; canals, dams, aqueducts and other irrigation works were constructed or repaired; and provision was made for the poor, the disabled and lepers.

Umayyad art survives principally in the form of architecture and its decoration, supplemented by the occasional textile (*see* ṬIRAZ), metalware (*see* ISLAMIC ART, §IV, 2(i)(b)), ceramics (*see* ISLAMIC ART, §V, 2(i)) or ivory (*see* ISLAMIC ART, §VIII, 7). There is also a rich sequence of coins with increasingly bold and imaginative reworkings of Byzantine and Sasanian originals, culminating in a radically new, purely epigraphic type which accords pride of place to Koranic inscriptions and religious formulae (*see* ISLAMIC ART, §VIII, 2). Umayyad religious buildings in Jerusalem, Damascus, MEDINA and SAN'A show—in their precise location, sheer scale, epigraphy and fabulously rich decoration, much of it in wall mosaic (*see* ISLAMIC ART, §II, 9(iv))—an acute awareness of the psychological, political and propaganda dimensions of architecture and self-consciously symbolize the new *imperium* (*see* ISLAMIC ART, §II, 3(ii)). Sometimes direct comparisons with Christian monuments (as in Jerusalem and San'a) drive the message home.

The many Umayyad secular establishments—hunting lodges, minor residences and full-scale palaces—erected for the most part in the hinterland of the major cities of the Levant speak the same language of power but with a

Umayyad frieze of heads in interlace, stucco, from Khirbat al-Mafjar, second quarter of the 8th century AD

rather different vocabulary (*see* ISLAMIC ART, §II, 3(iii)). They draw on the Sasanian world for the notion of royal authority expressed through a luxurious lifestyle of feasting, revelling and hunting. The figural themes so obviously absent for theological reasons in Umayyad religious architecture are ubiquitous here and attest, as does much of the architectural detail, to the persistence of Classical and Byzantine stylistic conventions (see fig.). Thus East and West merge in a new dispensation. But the Umayyad use of borrowed motifs is anything but reverential. It may veer into parody or burlesque; it yokes together disparate ideas with wilful and unpredictable originality, changing the effect of familiar motifs by giving them an unexpected setting, enlarging or miniaturizing them, and boldly transferring ideas from one medium to another. This inexhaustible inventiveness, this sheer *élan*, is the abiding hallmark of Umayyad art.

BIBLIOGRAPHY
K. A. C. Creswell: *Early Muslim Architecture*, i (Oxford, 1932; rev. 1969 in 2 vols/*R* New York, 1979)
E. Kühnel and L. Bellinger: *Catalogue of Dated Tirāz Fabrics: Umayyad, Abbasid, Fatimid: The Textile Museum, Washington, D.C.* (Washington, DC, 1952)
K. A. C. Creswell: *A Short Account of Early Muslim Architecture* (London, 1958); rev. by J. W. Allan (Aldershot, 1989)
U. Monneret de Villard: *Introduzione allo studio dell'archeologia islamica: Le origini e il periodo omayyade* (Venice, 1966)
O. Grabar: *The Formation of Islamic Art* (New Haven and London, 1973, rev. 1987)
F. M. Donner: *The Early Islamic Conquests* (Princeton, 1981)
R. Hillenbrand: 'Islamic Art at the Crossroads: East Versus West at Mshatta', in A. Daneshvari, ed.: *Essays in Islamic Art and Architecture in Honor of Katharina Otto-Dorn* (Malibu, 1981), pp. 63–86
——: 'La *dolce vita* in Early Islamic Syria: The Evidence of Later Umayyad Palaces', *A. Hist.*, v (1982), pp. 1–35
M. L. Bates: 'History, Geography and Numismatics in the First Century of Islamic Coinage', *Rev. Suisse Numi.*, lxv (1986), pp. 231–62
R. Hamilton: *Walid and his Friends: An Umayyad Tragedy* (Oxford, 1988)
J. Raby and J. Johns, eds: *Bayt al-Maqdis: 'Abd al-Malik's Jerusalem* (Oxford, 1993)

2. SPANISH BRANCH. Extreme political instability had reigned for the first few decades after the Muslim armies entered Spain in AD 711, but following the arrival of the Umayyad amir 'Abd al-Rahman I (*reg* 756–88) the country was substantially pacified. A lucky survivor of the massacre of the Umayyad princes in Syria by their Abbasid rivals, he established in the Muslim West an implacable hostility to the Abbasid caliphate in Baghdad. Helped by numerous refugees from Syria, he set about creating an alternative centre of power in Spain. An obsessional fidelity to things Syrian is said to have expressed itself in place names and dialects, in the importation of Syrian trees and plants, in literary genres and tribal rivalries, and in the hydraulic techniques that made the barren lands of Andalusia verdant. The Great Mosque of Córdoba (*see* CÓRDOBA (i), §3(i)(a), and ISLAMIC ART, §II, 4(iv) and fig. 26), which he founded in 786, is the most important building of the period. A marked conservatism in architecture and decoration was complemented by the adherence of Muslim Spain to the Maliki school of law and a lack of interest in Sufism.

Successive Umayyad rulers, keeping Córdoba as their capital, gradually extended their power over most of the peninsula apart from the Christian kingdoms in the north. By the late 10th century Spain had become the dominant culture of the western Islamic world, although the impact made by the aesthete Ziryab, a refugee from the *beau monde* of Baghdad, in such fields as music, poetry and dress, suggests that in these fields respect for Abbasid culture counted for more than did political enmity. The apogee of Umayyad rule came with the dazzlingly successful reign of 'Abd al-Rahman III (*reg* 912–61). Following the example of the Fatimid rulers of North Africa, he took the title of caliph and made Córdoba the greatest city in Europe, perhaps ten times the size of Rome and complete with such amenities as street lighting, running water and public libraries. His palace city outside Córdoba, MADINAT

AL-ZAHRA', with its antique statues, quicksilver pond and other exotica, was the most splendid of several such medieval Islamic foundations in Spain. Despite occasional persecution, the Christian and Jewish minorities were allowed to play their full part in a tolerant, multi-confessional society. The Great Mosque of Córdoba (see ISLAMIC ART, §II, 5(iv)(a)), enlarged for the fourth time in 981, was the second largest mosque after that of Samarra' in Iraq, and it provided a model for such buildings as the Bab Mardum Mosque (999–1000) at Toledo.

Many arts flourished in the later Umayyad period, including woodwork (see ISLAMIC ART, §VII, 1(iii)) and stone-carving (e.g. two marble troughs, dated 987–8; Madrid, Mus. Arqueol. N., and 1002–7; Marrakesh, Ben Yusuf Madrasa). Rich textiles of silk and gold tapestry inwoven in a tabby ground are represented by the celebrated Veil of Hisham II (reg 976–1013 with interruption; Madrid, Real Acad. Hist.; see ISLAMIC ART, §VI, 2(i)(c)). Pride of place must go to ivory-carving (see ISLAMIC ART, §VIII, 7 and fig. 237). Inscribed caskets and pyxides, often with self-apostrophizing dated inscriptions identifying royal patrons, draw on a rich repertory of scenes of princely life and revelry. After the death of Hisham II, power slipped from Umayyad hands, and increasing factional unrest erupted in 1010 in a savage civil war during which Córdoba was sacked. This heralded the advent of the Party Kings (Arab. mulūk al-ṭawā'if; Sp. Reyes de Taifas) under whose rule Spain broke up into a patchwork of rival principalities.

BIBLIOGRAPHY

E. Lévi-Provençal: Histoire de l'Espagne musulmane, 3 vols (Paris, 1950–53)
M. Gómez-Moreno: El arte arabe español hasta los Almohades: Arte mozárabe, A. Hisp., iii (Madrid, 1951)
J. Beckwith: Caskets from Córdoba (London, 1960)
J. M. Bloom: 'The Revival of Early Islamic Architecture by the Umayyads of Spain', The Medieval Mediterranean: Cross-cultural Contacts, ed. M. J. Chiat and K. L. Reyerson (St Cloud, MN, 1988), pp. 35–41
J. D. Dodds: Architecture and Ideology in Early Medieval Spain (University Park, PA, and London, 1990)
Al-Andalus: The Art of Islamic Spain (exh. cat., ed. J. D. Dodds; Granada, Alhambra; New York, Met.; 1992)

ROBERT HILLENBRAND

Umbach, Jonas (b Augsburg, 1624; d Augsburg, 1693). German painter, draughtsman and etcher. He was the son of a beltmaker in the service of the Fuggers and his year of birth is known from an inscription on an engraved portrait (1652; Hollstein) by Melchior Küsel I. His studies included years of travel in the Netherlands and north and central Italy: a drawing of Three Men and a Boy by the Fire (1645; Berlin) shows a knowledge of Dutch art, and a Roman Capriccio with Antique Circular Temple (before 1652; Augsburg, Schaezlerpal.), in charcoal on brown-tinted and oiled paper, has been accredited (Biedermann) to his stay in Italy. By 1652 he had returned to Augsburg, where in 1654 he was licensed as a painter.

Although Umbach is known to have executed several paintings, of religious subjects, such as the Death of St Benedict (1665; ex-SS Ulrich und Afra, later Augsburg Cathedral; destr. 1944), his landscape drawings are accounted the most significant part of his work. As few are dated and he used diverse techniques (though retaining characteristic lines, flourishes and washes, often replaced by hatching), no clear artistic development is apparent. His preference was principally for the format of a show-piece or miniature, using broad or sharply pointed black chalk or charcoal, sometimes on a tinted ground or even oiled paper of very uneven composition, as if he deliberately intended to use this medium as a plastic structuring; white highlighting is also used in the pen-and-ink drawings to intensify the effects of light and shadow in a sensitive way.

Convincing attributions include the Visit of St Eustace (Augsburg, Schaezlerpal.), a sketch for a round-arched altar panel executed in brown ink over black pencil, with a grey wash and white highlighting, and a Mountain Landscape with Path (Augsburg, Schaezlerpal.), a charcoal drawing on yellow-tinted paper. The latter is entirely in the style of a Romantic ideal landscape, as is his Rocky Landscape with Path and Ruin (Munich, Staatl. Graph. Samml.), executed in brown ink on blue clay-paper and reminiscent of Tobias Verhaecht. A drawing entitled In the Riess (Berlin, Kupferstichkab.) also belongs to this 'tradition of universal landscape' (Kuhrmann). The charcoal drawing Ascent to a City Tower (Augsburg, Schaezlerpal.) depicts in the background a Gothic mitre roof, thus revealing local architectural tradition. An Italian Landscape with Ruin (Augsburg, Schaezlerpal.) is done in charcoal on yellowish, fibrous, unusually coarse paper. The Narrow Pass with Footbridge (Augsburg, Schaezlerpal.), with concealed staffage figures, uses a similar technique on yellow clay-paper.

Diogenes (red chalk over pencil, 1658; Augsburg, Schaezlerpal.), an important drawing in that it is dated, shows the influence of Johann Heinrich Schönfeld in both style and theme: the seclusion of mankind after the horror of the Thirty Years War. Related to its technique but unusual in its composition is Susanna Bathing (Augsburg, Schaezlerpal.), after an etching by Agostino Carracci. Umbach represented a mythological theme in his red-chalk drawing Satyr in Chains with River Nymphs (1653; Augsburg, Schaezlerpal.). An important part of his oeuvre, a bundle of papers (Augsburg, Staats- & Stadtbib., on loan to Schaezlerpal.) consisting of 345 bound, small-format (110×85 mm), pen-and-ink drawings, served as designs for the Heiligem-Benedictiner Jahr (4 vols; Augsburg, 1710) by Aegidius Rambeck, representing saints surrounded by borders of maxims distributed over the year. The drawings, executed in a variety of techniques (red chalk, pencil, brown ink), clearly show the marks of tracing with sharp graphite. Those pages with an inscription are signed Jon.umbach delin, Barth.Kilian or J.G.Waldreich sculp.

The standard tally of Umbach's etchings is now established (Thieme–Becker: Thöne) as 300. Engravers following his manner include Bartholomäus Kilian II, Philipp Andreas Kilian, Matthäus Küsel and Melchior Küsel I.

BIBLIOGRAPHY

Hollstein: Ger.; Thieme–Becker
G. Lill: Hans Fugger und die Kunst (Leipzig, 1908), p. 148
E. Haas: Jonas Umbach: Ein Augsburger Maler-Radierer (diss., U. Würzburg, 1921)
Deutsche Maler und Zeichner des 17. Jahrhunderts (exh. cat., Berlin, Staatl. Museen Preuss. Kultbes., 1966), no. 207 [H. Möhle]
H. Geissler and R. Biedermann: 'Ausgburger Handzeichnungen und Druckgraphik, 1620–1720', Augsburger Barock (exh. cat., Augsburg, Rathaus and Holbeinhaus, 1968), nos 385–99

N. Lieb: *Octavian Secundus Fugger und die Kunst* (Tübingen, 1980), p. 162
Zeichnungen aus der Sammlung des Kurfürsten Carl Theodor (exh. cat., Munich, Staatl. Graph. Samml., 1983), no. 127 [D. Kuhrmann]
Meisterzeichnungen des deutschen Barock (exh. cat. by R. Biedermann, Augsburg, Zeughaus, 1987), nos 76–7

BERNT VON HAGEN

Umbdenstock, Gustave (*b* Colmar, 24 Dec 1866; *d* Paris, 16 Nov 1940). French architect and teacher. He was a student of Julien Azais Guadet at the Ecole des Beaux-Arts, Paris, where he won second prize in the Prix de Rome (1896). In partnership with Marcel Auburtin (1872–1926) he designed two buildings (destr.) for the Exposition Universelle, Paris (1900), and then built the French Pavilion at the Louisiana Purchase Exposition (1904) in St Louis, MO. He produced many public buildings, including railway stations and churches, and as a member of the Conseil des Bâtiments et Lycées de France he was responsible for such schools as the Lycée Pasteur (1912), Neuilly, and the Lycée Claude-Bernard (1938), Auteuil. He also erected a number of offices and residential buildings, for example for the Banque d'Algérie and for railway and mining companies. Umbdenstock's architectural styles ranged from 17th-century French classicism to regional and exotic styles; in the 1930s he even made some forays into Modernism. Umbdenstock also taught at the Ecole Polytechnique, where he was a reader from 1901 and Professor of Architecture from 1919 to 1937, and he opened an *atelier libre* at the Ecole des Beaux-Arts in 1906. A tireless orator, he was convinced that the abandonment of ornament would endanger social harmony. He is best known for his public controversy with Le Corbusier in 1932–5, when he participated in the campaign against the latter mounted by *Art National*, a revue published by the Association des Architectes Anciens Combattants, of which he was honorary president. Alongside the art historian Louis Hourticq (1875–1944), the art critic Camille Mauclair and the architect René Clozier (1886–1965), he championed the cause of regionalism and traditional building crafts against burgeoning internationalism. Le Corbusier's *Croisade ou le crépuscule des académies* (Paris, 1933) was a direct response to the lecture given by Umbdenstock at the Salle Wagram (14 March 1932) in defence of manual building crafts and craftsmen.

WRITINGS

Cours d'architecture (Paris, 1930)
L'Evolution architecturale au XXème siècle (Paris, 1932) [lecture given at the Rotary Club on 21 Oct 1931]
'La Défense des métiers de main des artistes et artisans français', *Architecture* [Paris], xlv (1932), pp. 134–8 [extracts from lecture of 14 March 1932]
'La Défense de nos traditions artistiques dans le domaine architectural', *A. N.* (Dec 1933), pp. 25–6; (Jan 1934), pp. 5–6; (Feb 1934), pp. 9–10; (March, 1934), pp. 9–10; (June 1934), pp. 25–7
La Lutte contre le chômage: La Défense des qualités artistiques françaises (Paris, 1935)

BIBLIOGRAPHY

J. Favier: 'M. G. Umbdenstock: Membre de l'Institut', *Constr. Mod.*, 1 (1935), pp. III–IV
——: 'Le Lycée de garçons "Claude Bernard", Avenue du Parc des Princes à Auteuil', *Constr. Mod.*, liv (1939), pp. 178–87
J.-C. Vigato: *Le Jeu des modèles, les modèles en jeu: Doctrines architecturales dans l'entre deux guerres* (Villers-les-Nancy, 1980)
——: *L'Architecture régionaliste: France, 1890–1950* (Paris, 1994)

JEAN-CLAUDE VIGATO

Umberto II, King of Italy. *See under* SAVOY, §I, 2.

Umehara, Ryūzaburō (*b* Kyoto, 9 March 1888; *d* Tokyo, 16 Jan 1986). Japanese painter. In 1903, wanting to be a painter, he left school and studied at various institutions, including from 1906 the Kansai Academy of Art, which had been founded in Kyoto by Chū Asai. In 1908 he went to Paris, where he studied initially at the Académie Julian. Soon after his arrival, however, he was inspired by the works of Renoir that he saw at the Musée du Luxembourg. He visited Renoir in Cagnes-sur-Mer and was permitted to study with him for two months. He returned to Paris and, on Renoir's recommendation, entered the Académie Ransom. He travelled throughout Europe before returning to Japan in 1913 and was especially impressed by the ancient remains and classical paintings that he saw on a trip to Naples. Such works as *Gold Necklace* (1913; Tokyo, N. Mus. Mod. A.) reveal the influence of Renoir and the brightness and sensuality of Naples.

After Umehara returned to Japan he was troubled by the differences in customs between Japan and Europe, and his work stagnated for several years. In 1919 he visited for the first time Beijing, which he later depicted in numerous works throughout his career (e.g. *Ch'ang-an Streets, Beijing*, 1940; Tokyo, N. Mus. Mod. A.). In 1920 he returned to Europe and travelled through Cannes, Paris and Naples, returning the following year to Japan. In 1922 he participated in the formation of the Spring Season Society (Shunyōkai), but in 1925 he left the group and was invited to join the National Creative Painting Society (Kokuga Sōsaku Kyōkai). From this time he focused on the painting of nudes (e.g. *Nude with Fans*, 1938; Kurashiki, Ohara Mus. A.) and landscapes (*see* JAPAN, fig. 111) and returned to the use of rich colours. Using simple flat forms and thick paint, he formulated an individual decorative style that made him Japan's most popular oil painter in the period after World War II. From 1944 to 1952 he also taught in the *Yōga* (western-style painting) department of the Tokyo School of Fine Art.

WRITINGS

Teni muhō [Perfect beauty with no trace of artifice] (Tokyo, 1984)

BIBLIOGRAPHY

Paris in Japan: The Japanese Encounter with European Painting (exh. cat. by S. Takashima, J. T. Rimmer and G. D. Bolas, Tokyo, Japan Found.; St. Louis, MO, Washington U.; 1987), pp. 67–8, 112–13, 232–43, 271–2
Umehara Ryūzaburō isakuten [Retrospective exhibition of Umehara Ryūzaburō] (exh. cat., Tokyo, N. Mus. Mod. A.; Kyoto, N. Mus. Mod. A.; 1988)

ATSUSHI TANAKA

Umělecká Beseda. *See* ARTISTIC FORUM.

Umm al-Nar [an-Nar]. *See under* ARABIA, PRE-ISLAMIC, §§II, 2; III, 1(i)(a); IV, 3 and 8.

Umm al-Qaywayn. *See under* UNITED ARAB EMIRATES.

Umm Dabaghiya [Umm Dabaghiyah]. Prehistoric site in the Jazira in northern Iraq, *c.* 100 km south-west of Mosul. Umm Dabaghiya was a specialized settlement and trading post that flourished *c.* 6200–*c.* 5750 BC and is an early ceramic site with distinctive architectural features. Many of the finest objects from the site are now to be found in the Iraq Museum, Baghdad. Diana Kirkbride conducted four seasons of excavation (1971–4), clearing a large area (*c.* 3000 sq. m). Periods of abandonment separated the four levels of occupation (IV–I). In the better-preserved earlier levels (IV–III) three blocks of double or triple rows of small, well-built, rectilinear compartments (each *c.* 1.5×2.0 m) defined three sides of a large open area. Their size and lack of household features indicate they were used for storage; the overall layout suggests a planned construction. Beyond these were small, irregular one- to three-roomed houses. Exterior ovens opened into the interior for hearths that had chimneys. Plastered steps and toeholds in the upper walls and the absence of doorways suggest that entry was from the roof. Some of the white-plastered interiors, especially in levels IV–III, had painted bands around the floor and naturalistic frescoes on the walls, one of which seems to depict an onager hunt (Baghdad, Iraq Mus.; *see* MESOPOTAMIA, §VI, 1). The pottery is coarse and simple, with burnish, painting, incising, impressions or applied decoration, which in the later levels has parallels to early Hassuna culture (*see* MESOPOTAMIA, §V, 1). Ground stone artefacts include limestone and alabaster bowls, 'maceheads', beads and small basalt axes. The chipped-stone tool assemblage and predominance of onager and gazelle remains over those of domesticated animals suggest a hunting rather than an agricultural or herding economy and the processing of hides and meat for trade.

See also MESOPOTAMIA, §I, 2(i)(a) and (b).

BIBLIOGRAPHY

D. Kirkbride: 'Umm Dabaghiyah, 1973: A Second Preliminary Report', *Iraq*, xxxv (1973), pp. 1–7
——: 'Umm Dagaghiyah, 1974: A Fourth Preliminary Report', *Iraq*, xxxvii (1975), pp. 3–10
——: 'Umm Dabaghiyah', *Fifty Years of Mesopotamian Discovery*, ed. J. Curtis (London, 1982), pp. 11–21

ROBERT C. HENRICKSON

Umm el-Ebeida. *See under* SIWA OASIS.

UMS [Utrechtsche Machinale Stoel- en Meubelfabriek; Pastoe]. Dutch furniture factory established in 1913 by Frits Loeb (1889–1959) to provide furniture for his small department store in Utrecht. Under the management of the furniture-maker Dirk Lubertus Braakman (1887–1966) UMS quickly developed into a mass-production furniture manufacturing company that supplied trademarked items to retailers. Originally UMS designs differed little from the period furniture produced by the average manufacturer in response to public taste. However, *c.* 1930 UMS took advantage of the greater demand for furniture with modern styling, and the designers W. coni, A. A. M. Grimmon (1884–1953) and Herman Frederik Mertens (1885–1960) produced some designs for wood and tubular-steel furniture (e.g. Barnasconi, sideboard, 1930, see A. H. Jansen: *Het industrieel uitgevoerde meubel*, Rotterdam, 1935, p. 55; and Grimmon, small oak-dresser, *c* 1932; Utrecht, Cent. Mus.), a forerunner of the later Pastoe storage cupboards). The modernist-inspired collection designed by Braakman sold well, and UMS was regarded as one of the few companies able to mass-produce good-quality Dutch modern design.

After World War II UMS concentrated on modern design. The firm produced simple, functionalist furniture, related by style and adjusted by measure, so the items fitted easily into any combination. UMS expressed this 'passe-partout' principle in their trademark 'Pastoe', introduced in 1948 and meaning 'apply', 'combine' or 'put together'. The pieces were designed primarily by Braakman's son Cees Braakman jr (*b* 1917). Central to the Pastoe collection was the storage cupboard; seating and associated items were modelled around it. Meanwhile, although the factory remained UMS, the company itself became known as Pastoe. At the end of the 1970s outside designers offered the firm new inspiration. A resounding success was the Amsterdammer series of cupboards in synthetic materials with roll-down shutters (*see* NETHERLANDS, THE, fig. 45), designed by Aldo van den Nieuwelaar (*b* 1944) and introduced in 1979. In the 1990s Pastoe worked with various designers, including Pierre Mazairac (*b* 1943) and Karel Boonzaaijer (*b* 1948) of the design group Mazairac & Boonzaaijer (est. 1980), Wolfram Peters (*b* 1952) and Peter Krouwel (*b* 1952) of the design group Peters & Krouwel (est. 1979), Shiro Kuramata (*b* 1934) and Rob Eckhardt (*b* 1953).

BIBLIOGRAPHY

UMS Pastoe: Een Nederlandse meubelfabriek, 1913–1983 (exh. cat., ed. G. Vreeburg and H. Martens; Utrecht, Cent. Mus., 1983)
G. Vreeburg: 'UMS', *Industrie en vormgeving in Nederland, 1850–1950* (exh. cat., Amsterdam, Stedel. Mus., 1985–6), pp. 276–8
M. Boot, T. Asselbergs and B. Vreeken: 'Ontworpen voor de woning', *Holland in vorm, 1945–1987*, ed. G. Staal and H. Wolters (The Hague, 1987), pp. 139–79

PETRA DUPUITS

Un. Temple site in West Nirmar District, Madhya Pradesh, India. Six Shaiva and two Jaina temples were built at Un in the 11th–12th centuries under the PARAMARA dynasty and the Chalukyas of Kalyana (*see* CHALUKYA, §2). Inscriptions mentioning Udayaditya Paramara (*reg c.* 1070–80) were found in two temples at the site. All the buildings have superstructures of the *bhūmija* type, a mode of construction characterized by vertical rows of miniature spires set on pilasters (Skt *kūṭa-stambha*; *see* INDIAN SUBCONTINENT, §III, 5(i)(g)). The exterior walls, divided by an ornate median band, are devoid of carving except for pilasters on the projections and recesses. Those in the recesses are capped by miniature spires and thus replicate the *kūṭa-stambha* elements in the superstructures. This configuration is elaborated in the later architecture of Karnataka. The cardinal projections (*bhadra*) support prominent niches with images of Chamunda, Tripurantaka and Nataraja. The Jaina temples display divinities of the Jaina faith. The halls, with fine circular ceilings, are surmounted by pyramidal roofs covered by miniature bell-shaped spires (*saṁvaraṇā*s).

BIBLIOGRAPHY

Archaeol. Surv. India, Prog. Rep., W. Circ. (1918–19), pp. 54 and 61–3; (1920–21), p. 87
D. R. Patil: *Cultural Heritage of Madhya Bharat* (Gwalior, 1952), pp. 132–4
Krishna Deva: *Temples of North India* (New Delhi, 1969)
——: 'Bhūmija Temples', *Studies in Indian Temple Architecture*, ed. P. Chandra (New Delhi, 1975), pp. 90–113
——: 'Central India, Paramāra Zone—Un', *Jaina Art and Architecture*, ii, ed. A. Ghosh (New Delhi, 1975), pp. 295–7

K. K. CHAKRAVARTY

Uncastillo, S María. Former collegiate, now parish, church in Saragossa Province, Aragon, Spain. A church existed on the site by AD 934, to judge by a document of donation of the 10th century, but the present church was founded in 1135 with a grant of land by Ramiro II, King of Aragon (*reg* 1134–7). It was consecrated by Juan, Bishop of Pamplona, in 1246. The church, with a single-cell nave of seven bays, spanned by a pointed barrel vault, and an eastern apse, is notable for its Romanesque sculpture, especially that of the south portal. Dating from the mid-12th century, the sculpture shows the distant influence of St Pierre, Moissac (*see* ROMANESQUE, §III, 1(iii)(b)). On the north side of the nave is a Plateresque cloister with three chapels by Master Larrandi (1557). The lower of the two upper storeys added to the square south-west tower in the 15th century has machicolation and bartizan turrets; the top storey is octagonal, crowned by a pinnacled spire.

The south portal of S María has three orders, profusely decorated with sculpture. The archivolts have radial voussoirs with a varied repertory of subjects including combat scenes, birds, animals, a miser with a purse around his neck, two actors on a curtained stage, a ram being shorn, a dancing scene with musicians, a man carrying fish, and birds with entwined necks. On the second archivolt the roll moulding covers the bodies of the figures so that only their heads, arms and feet are visible. There is no tympanum, but the subjects of the six capitals include the *Expulsion of Adam and Eve*, the *Flight into Egypt* (with five figures), scenes of *Damned and Blessed Souls* and an equestrian figure being attacked by two enemies. Four of the columns are twisted; the other two are decorated with interlace and foliate motifs. Above the portal are two reliefs, *Christ in Majesty* and an upright standing figure probably representing St John the Baptist; they may come from another church or from the lost Romanesque west portal. The *Adoration of the Magi* tympanum relief set above the present west portal has been identified as the source of a whalebone relief of the same subject (London, V&A).

The well-preserved apse corbels, once protected by a Gothic sacristy, are carved with acrobats, dancing girls and musicians. There are several groups of sculpture inside the church. The apse arcade capitals are mostly foliate, with some replacements. The choir includes capitals with lions and griffins and such figured scenes as *Samson and the Lion*, the *Punishment of the Damned* and children fighting. Most of the nave capitals are decorated with foliate motifs and fruit, except for two on the south wall, which bear eagles and jugglers. Those of the interior of the south portal are carved with hybrid birds, and a man between vines.

BIBLIOGRAPHY

A. K. Porter: *Spanish Romanesque Sculpture*, 2 vols (New York, 1928)

F. Abbad Rios: *Catálogo monumental de España: Zaragoza*, 2 vols (Madrid, 1957)

J. Beckwith: *The Adoration of the Magi in Whalebone* (London, 1966)

A. Canellas-Lopez and A. San Vicente: *Aragon romane*, Nuit Temps (La Pierre-qui-vire, 1971)

P. Williamson: *The Medieval Treasury: The Art of the Middle Ages in the Victoria and Albert Museum* (London, 1986)

J. R. L. HIGHFIELD

Unch'ŏn. *See* KIM TU-RYANG.

Underdrawing. Preliminary drawing made before the application of an overlying layer. Although most commonly understood as the preliminary sketch on a panel, canvas or parchment, the term is also applicable to works on paper that have multiple layers of drawing in different media, such as a black chalk underdrawing for a metalpoint or pen-and-ink sketch. Underdrawings are discussed as a working stage of a finished drawing or painting in early artist's manuals and technical treatises by Cennino Cennini, Karel van Mander, Vasari, Paolo Pino and Albrecht Dürer, among others. Some underdrawings have always been visible to the naked eye, especially in drawings and in thinly painted or unfinished pictures. However, the actual detection and documentation of many only became possible through the use of infra-red techniques, specifically infra-red reflectography (*see* TECHNICAL EXAMINATION, §II, 2), which was developed for application to paintings by J. R. J. van Asperen de Boer in the early 1970s. In this method, portions of the underdrawing may be documented by photography from a monitor screen or recorded and assembled by computer (see fig.). The most substantial body of published information on underdrawing is associated with paintings of the Renaissance period. This is because the underdrawing on an early panel painting is more easily detected due to the painting technique, typically a carbon black drawing on a white-ground preparation, superimposed by thin overlying paint layers. By the 16th century certain artists, including Jan Gossart, began

Underdrawing (detail) from Gerard David: *Adoration of the Magi*, oil on panel, 597×584 mm (whole), *c.* 1519–23 (London, National Gallery); infra-red reflectogram computer assembly of 70 source images

to use a grey undermodelling that obscures the underdrawing; paint layers became more opaque and the colour of the ground preparation began to change. Moreover, the purpose and function of the underdrawing was considerably altered by the introduction of the independent oil sketch, which originated in Venice after 1550 and came into common usage in northern Europe in the 17th century. Underdrawings have nonetheless been discovered beneath the paintings of later artists: for example in works by such 17th-century artists as Rubens, van Dyck, Caravaggio, Jan van Goyen and Jan Saenredam, in 18th-century works by Watteau and in the 19th century in those by Ingres. Such American painters as Winslow Homer or William Michael Harnett and such 20th-century artists as Picasso and Klee also made underdrawings on their chosen painting support. In fact most artists presumably made some kind of preliminary sketch on their panels or canvases; it is simply that the detection of them by current techniques is not always possible and thus warrants further investigation. Equally fruitful would be the study of underdrawings in manuscript illumination.

From the evidence that has been gathered it is clear that underdrawings vary in their state of finish and complexity as well as in their medium. They range from the most summary sketch roughly laying out the composition to fully worked-up drawings that include hatching and cross-hatching for the description of volumes and the tonal modelling of forms (Dürer and Giovanni Bellini, for example, share this latter feature in their underdrawings). The form of some underdrawings indicates that they were transferred from a pre-existing design, or cartoon, by means of tracing, pouncing or squaring (for illustration see CARTOON). Since these cartoons rarely survive due to repeated use, the underdrawing gives the only evidence of their previous existence and appearance.

Artists of the 15th century generally followed the instructions of Cennini, making use of a preliminary black chalk or charcoal underdrawing, which was gone over and 'fixed' in its details in brush or pen and an aqueous black pigment. As this first sketch in charcoal or black chalk was then brushed away, it is far more difficult to detect than is the much more prevalent brush or pen underdrawing. Metalpoint lines may also have been employed for preliminary designs of early 15th-century paintings. Incised stylus lines used to indicate the perspective system of a composition occasionally appear in northern Renaissance paintings but are more commonly used for the contours of the entire design on Italian panels of the same period. Other materials, such as red chalk or brown ink, cannot be detected by infra-red reflectography but are sometimes visible to the naked eye or through the microscope. In the 16th century both liquid and dry media underdrawings are found, but after c. 1520 black chalk became the favoured medium and the character of the underdrawing became less finished and more sketchy. With the introduction of coloured ground preparations on canvases in the 17th century, the traditional underdrawing media also changed, to white chalk (as is found in Vermeer's *Allegory of Painting*, c. 1666–7; Vienna, Ksthist. Mus.) or brown paint, or simply to palette scrapings, as in Rembrandt's underpainted sketches. Underdrawings of the 18th and 19th centuries were executed using a variety of materials, among them pencil or graphite.

The function of the underdrawing can be self-evident but is further discerned by its relationship both to the overlying painted layers and to other existing preparatory drawings on paper. The underdrawing may show reworking in certain forms or that the alterations occurred in the paint layers alone. For many northern Renaissance artists, underdrawings are the only indication of their drawing style, for relatively few drawings on paper by them survive, and of these the preparatory nature of the drawings is questionable. The case is different for Italian Renaissance artists, as the opportunity exists more often to compare drawings with underdrawings. That some underdrawings were meant to be seen or approved by others may be deduced by the discovery of colour notations (combinations of letters found mostly on northern Netherlandish and German paintings) and other identifying words (as of characters or locations) in the underdrawing. Such annotations would also have been useful if part or all of the final painting was to be carried out by a workshop assistant. Furthermore, in the first quarter of the 16th century tonal washes were sometimes added to already very finished-looking underdrawings, and it has been suggested that these chiaroscuro underdrawings (as in works by Lucas van Leyden, Bernard van Orley, Hans Schaufelein and Pontormo, among others) may have served as a kind of *vidimus* for the patron to approve.

BIBLIOGRAPHY

J. R. J. van Asperen de Boer: *Infrared Reflectography: A Contribution to the Examination of Earlier European Paintings* (diss., Amsterdam U., 1970)
——: 'The Study of Underdrawing: An Assessment', *Le Dessin sous-jacent dans la peinture, colloque V: Louvain-la-Neuve, 1983*, pp. 12–24
M. Ainsworth and M. Faries: 'Northern Renaissance Paintings: The Discovery of Invention', *Bull. St Louis A. Mus.*, xviii/1 (1986) [whole issue]
J. R. J. van Asperen de Boer, M. Faries and J. P. Filedt Kok: 'Painting Technique and Workshop Practice in Northern Netherlandish Art of the Sixteenth Century', *Kunst voor de Beeldenstorm: Noordnederlandse kunst, 1525–50* [Art before the iconoclasm: northern Netherlandish art, 1525–50] (exh. cat., Amsterdam, Rijksmus., 1986), ii, pp. 106–16
M. Ainsworth: 'Northern Renaissance Drawings and Underdrawings: A Proposed Method of Study', *Master Drgs*, xxvii/1 (1989), pp. 5–38
MARYAN WYNN AINSWORTH

Underground station. *See* METRO STATION.

Underwood, Paul Atkins (*b* Aguadilla, Puerto Rico, 22 Feb 1902; *d* Knoxville, TN, 22 Sept 1968). American archaeologist and art historian. He gained BSc and MFA degrees in architecture from Princeton University (NJ) in 1925 and 1928 respectively and practised as an architect in New York from 1929 to 1931. In 1931–4 he travelled in Greece, developing his knowledge of its Classical and medieval monuments. He returned to Princeton in 1935 and became a graduate student in the Department of Art and Archaeology, specializing in Early Christian and Byzantine art. He taught at Cornell University (Ithaca, NY) from 1938, and in 1943 he obtained a fellowship at Dumbarton Oaks (Washington, DC), where he remained for the rest of his career, becoming a full professor in 1960. In 1950 he also became Field Director of the Byzantine Institute and supervised archaeological and restoration projects in Istanbul and Cyprus. When the institute was taken over by Dumbarton Oaks, Underwood was elected its chairman, a post he held until 1968. His major work for the institute was the restoration project undertaken in the church of St Saviour in Chora (Kariye Camii) in Istanbul, where he supervised the cleaning and consolidation of the mosaic decoration and uncovered the remarkable cycle of early 14th-century wall paintings in the parekklesion. The results of his exceptionally thorough and systematic study were published in the three-volume *The Kariye Djami* (1966). The fourth volume, published posthumously, set his study of the mosaics and wall paintings in the wider context of the art and culture of the period. Underwood contributed considerably to the preservation and study of Byzantine churches, mosaics and wall paintings in Istanbul and published numerous reports on the fieldwork of the Byzantine Institute and Dumbarton Oaks. He also initiated a fieldwork programme on the medieval painted churches of Cyprus.

WRITINGS
'A Preliminary Report on Some Unpublished Mosaics in Hagia Sophia: Season of 1950 of the Byzantine Institute', *Amer. J. Archaeol.*, lv (1951), pp. 367–70
'The Mosaics of Hagia Sophia at Istanbul: The Portrait of the Emperor Alexander. A Report on Work Done by the Byzantine Institute in 1959 and 1960', *Dumbarton Oaks Pap.*, xv (1961), pp. 187–215
The Kariye Djami, 3 vols (New York, 1966)
ed.: *The Kariye Djami: Studies in the Art of the Kariye Djami and its Intellectual Background* (Princeton, 1975)

BIBLIOGRAPHY
E. Kitzinger: Obituary, *Dumbarton Oaks Pap.*, xxiii–xxiv (1969–70), pp. 1–6 [with bibliog.]
                         A. N. PALMER, J. VAN GINKEL

Underworld Painter. *See* VASE PAINTERS, §II.

Unga, De. *See* YOUNG ONES.

Ungaro, Michele. *See* PANNONIO, MICHELE.

Ungegenständlichen, Gruppe der. *See* ZEN 49.

Unger, (Christian) Wilhelm (Jacob) (*b* Kirchlotheim, Hesse, 25 Feb 1775; *d* Neustrelitz, Mecklenburg, 18 Aug 1855). German painter and printmaker. He was a nephew of Johann Heinrich Tischbein II (1742–1808), under whom he first trained at the Akademie der Künste in Kassel. His earliest known works include paintings of the countryside around Kassel and landscape etchings. In 1795 he was appointed court painter to Prince Friedrich von Waldeck in Arolsen. At this time he developed an interest in portrait miniatures, travelling to Paris to study under Jean-Baptiste Isabey. From 1799 until 1801 he taught in Hannover at the ladies' drawing school founded by his cousin Wilhelm Tischbein. Between 1801 and 1806 he lived in Hamburg, where he executed a large number of etchings, including a series of animal subjects after Paulus Potter and others after Adriaen van Ostade. In 1806 he moved to Paris, where he exhibited a miniature, *Portrait of a Seated Woman* (untraced), at the Salon of 1812. He returned to Hamburg in 1814, and in 1815 he was appointed to teach at the Kassel Akademie. By this time he was already specializing as a portrait painter.

In 1817 Princess Marie von Hesse-Kassel, Grand Duchess of Mecklenburg-Strelitz, one of Unger's pupils, took him to Neustrelitz to be her court painter. In 1820 she conferred on him the title of professor. While in her service he executed a series of portrait silhouettes of her friends and the members of her court. In his later years he energetically pursued the practice of landscape painting, and in 1837 he undertook a tour of Mecklenburg-Strelitz, recording in his sketchbook 16 views of the towns through which he passed.

Thieme–Becker
BIBLIOGRAPHY
                         COLIN J. BAILEY

Ungers, Oswald Mathias (*b* Kaisersesch, near Koblenz, 7 Dec 1926). German architect. After completing his studies with Egon Eiermann at the Technische Hochschule in Karlsruhe (1947–50), he established his own architectural office in Cologne. The practice prospered in the 1950s, mainly on the strength of commissions for domestic architecture in the Cologne area. In addition to a series of one- and two-family houses in the Cologne suburbs, which included the architect's own house at Müngersdorf (1958–9), he designed larger housing projects, such as the scheme (1959–61) at Eckewartstrasse, Mauenheim, Cologne. There were also industrial buildings in Braunsfeld, Cologne: a clothing factory (1951) at Aachener Strasse and a printing works (1960–64) at Stolberger Strasse.

A project that occupied Ungers for many years was the Oberhausener Institut (1953–8; 1967–9), Wehrstrasse, Oberhausen. These early works have a certain affinity to the New Brutalism prevalent at the time in Britain. Although involved in two large-scale housing schemes in the early 1960s—the Neue Stadt (1961–4) at Chorweiler/Seeberg, Cologne, and the infamous Märkisches Viertel (1962–7) in Wittenau, Berlin—Ungers substantially abandoned architectural practice in the 1960s in favour of theory. In 1960 he and Reinhard Gieselmann wrote the manifesto *Zu einer neuen Architektur* as a protest against Functionalism and the anonymous technology of the curtain wall. They insisted that architecture was 'a vital penetration of a multi-layered, mysterious, evolved and structured reality' and suggested that architecture should abandon the self-imposed anonymity and rootlessness of Neues Bauen and return to the *genius loci*.

From 1963 to 1968 Ungers held the Chair of Architecture at the Technische Universität, Berlin, and exercised considerable influence not only through his teaching but also through a series of important competition designs, which included the Enschede student housing project in the Netherlands (1964) and the German Embassy at the Vatican in Rome (1965). As Chairman of the Department of Architecture at Cornell University (1969–75), Ithaca, NY, he continued to produce influential competition projects, including a redevelopment plan (1973; with Rem Koolhaas, P. Allison and D. Allison) for the Tiergartenviertel, Berlin; a design (1975) for the Wallraf-Richartz-Museum, Cologne; housing (1976) for the Ritterstrasse, Marburg; and the Hotel Berlin (1977), Budapester Strasse, Berlin. For the Marburg scheme he developed a series of housing types in which the individual rooms, the houses and the block are related to each other as a series of elements in a typology derived from the site and the historical context. While the theme of the room within the house and the house within the block reflects Ungers's belief in the generation of form out of the *genius loci*, his

Oswald Mathias Ungers: interior of the Badische Landesbibliothek, Karlsruhe, 1980–92

perception of a fragmented cityscape led him to the strictly defined perimeters of the Tiergarten scheme or the Hotel Berlin, which isolate the specific site from the surrounding chaos.

In the late 1970s Ungers's practice as an architect gathered new momentum, and he produced a series of widely varying works in which he continued to explore his chosen themes: the house within the house; the transformation of the given architectonic element through a series of variations; the 'assemblage' of contrasting elements; and the adaption of the built work to the *genius loci*. While his formal vocabulary is Rationalist, his intellectual premises are wide-ranging and have a strong emotional attachment to particular historical sites, such as Schinkel's Schlosspark at Glienecke near Berlin, or Trier Cathedral. Among his works of the 1970s and 1980s are a block of flats (1978–9) at Schillerstrasse, Berlin; the Deutsches Architekturmuseum (1979–84), Frankfurt am Main; the Alfred-Wegener-Institut für Polarforschung (1980–84), Bremerhaven; a terrace-housing development (1979–83) at Lützowplatz, Berlin; three large buildings—Messehalle 9, Galleria (both 1980–83) and Torhaus (1983–4)—on the Frankfurt Fair site; and the Badische Landesbibliothek at Karlsruhe (1980–92; see fig.). This last-named project might be seen as an archetypal Ungers building, with the characteristic features of a rectilinear grid, a core surrounded by a shell, a vigorous dialogue with Friedrich Weinbrenner's adjacent Stephanskirche, careful detailing and a preference for red sandstone and stucco on the exteriors. Among prize-winning competition projects of the 1980s were schemes for a Media-Park in Cologne, for a Rathaus, Bremen, for the 'Campanile' tower in Frankfurt am Main, and for modern art museums in Vienna and

Hamburg. In the 1990s Ungers enjoyed further competition successes, most notably with the urban design competitions for the Potsdamer Platz and for Spreeinsel, both in Berlin. In 1991 he was commissioned to design one of the three blocks for Berlin's new commercial centre on Friedrichstrasse. Among his most recent buildings are the library extension (1989–90) to his own house in Cologne, and the residence (1988–94) of the German ambassador in Washington, DC. While the former explores the theme of square and cube in a single building, the latter returns to an old Ungers topic, that of the city within a city.

WRITINGS

'Für eine lebendige Baukunst', *Bauwelt*, lii/8 (1961), pp. 193, 196
with R. Gieselmann: 'Zur einer neuen Architektur', *Programme und Manifeste zur Architektur des 20. Jahrhunderts*, ed. U. Conrads (Frankfurt am Main and Berlin, 1964); Eng. trans. as *Programmes and Manifestoes on 20th-century Architecture* (London, 1970), pp. 165–6
with K. Frampton and G. Brown-Manrique: *O. M. Ungers: Works in Progress* (New York, 1981)
Die Thematisierung der Stadt (Stuttgart, 1983)

BIBLIOGRAPHY

'Ein Werkstattbericht: Bauten und Projekten von O. M. Ungers', *Bauwelt*, li/8 (1960), pp. 204–17
L. Bisogli: 'Germania di oggi: O. M. Ungers', *Casabella*, 305 (1966), pp. 35–59
H. Klotz, ed.: *O. M. Ungers, 1951–1984: Bauten und Projekte* (Brunswick and Wiesbaden, 1985)
H. Klotz: *The History of Postmodern Architecture* (Cambridge, MA, 1988), pp. 213–19
M. Kieren: *O. M. Ungers Architektur, 1951–1994* (Zurich, 1994)
Oswald Mathias Ungers Architekt (exh. cat., Hamburg, Ksthalle, 1994)

IAIN BOYD WHYTE

Ungewitter, Georg Gottlob (*b* Wandbek, 9 Sept 1820; *d* Kassel, 11 June 1864). German architect and writer. He was among the foremost architects of the German Gothic Revival and played a major role in applying the ideas of the Rhenish Gothic Revival to Protestant church architecture. Ungewitter was one of the first doctrinaire Gothic Revivalists to teach in a German architectural school, and his students figured prominently in the movement in the late 19th century. His buildings, books and published projects helped to establish high standards of workmanship and archaeological exactitude in church design.

Ungewitter studied at the Akademie der Bildenden Künste in Munich (1838–42) and afterwards worked in the office of Friedrich Bürklein. He moved to Hamburg after the great fire of 1842, working first for the architect J. H. Klees-Wülbern and later forming a partnership with Gustav Martens. He gradually progressed beyond the *Rundbogenstil* training of his Munich years (which favoured an eclectic mix of Romanesque and Renaissance elements) to work in an indigenous north German brick idiom. He developed a personal style, more dependent on forms of brick construction (corbelling, diapering, jambs and friezes of moulded brick, pilaster strips and recessed blind arches) than on Gothic ecclesiastical architecture and inspired by the local work of Alexis de Chateauneuf and Theodor Bülau. Influenced by August Reichensperger, Ungewitter renounced the *Rundbogenstil* for the Gothic and spent most of 1849 reorienting himself by studying the medieval architecture of Lübeck. After two years unsuccessfully trying to practise Gothic architecture in Leipzig, Reichensperger's recommendation gained him a professorship at the Höhere Gewerbeschule in Kassel, which he helped convert into one of Germany's principal centres of Gothic instruction.

Ungewitter's prize-winning entry in the 1853 Vienna Votivkirche competition, a creative synthesis of elements from regional centres of German Gothic architecture, established him as a major church architect, although it remained unbuilt. Despite being a Protestant, Ungewitter looked to the Gothic Revival in the Catholic Rhineland for inspiration, and he established strong ties with Reichensperger and the Cologne architect Vincenz Statz. Ungewitter's church designs, along with those of his colleague Conrad Wilhelm Hase in Hannover, marked the ecumenical high point of the German Gothic Revival and the culmination of Reichensperger's influence. Ungewitter's first successful commission was in Neustadt, for which he designed his finest small church (1856–61). Entirely vaulted in masonry, its robustly sculpted buttresses and plate tracery adhere to the 13th-century German models that Reichensperger prescribed. Ungewitter's churches are invariably symmetrical compositions, dominated by western entrance towers that terminate in octagonal stone spires. Only in small flanking sacristies or stair-turrets did he permit asymmetrical accents. Although conservative in his choice of form, Ungewitter was fiercely original in detail. He articulated the exterior walls of his church at Hundelshausen (1863–7) into an alternating pattern of blind arches and projecting cross-gables, divided by thick buttresses.

During the 1850s Ungewitter diverted much of his energy to publishing his unbuilt Gothic designs. The most remarkable of his books is his *Entwürfe zu Stadt- und Landhäusern*, a collection of designs for half-timbered houses. The striking difference between his rugged stone churches and these rambling, original domestic designs reveals creative tensions central to the German Gothic Revival. On the one hand his churches showed a deep-seated German concern for systematizing and regularizing, reinforced by Reichensperger's notion of Gothic geometry and by the structural canon described in Ungewitter's *Lehrbuch der gothischen Construction* (1859–64). On the other hand, Ungewitter's houses evoked rustic and picturesque values, appealing to German folk tradition. Just as his manual of Gothic construction was reprinted several times, the restless invention of Ungewitter's pattern books provided German architects with motifs into the 20th century.

WRITINGS
Vorlegeblätter für Ziegel- und Steinarbeit (Leipzig, 1849, rev. 3/1899)
with V. Statz: *Gothisches Musterbuch*, 2 vols (Leipzig, 1856–61; Eng. trans., 1858–62)
Entwürfe zu Stadt- und Landhäusern, 2 vols (Glogau, 1858–64)
Lehrbuch der gothischen Construction, 2 vols (Leipzig, 1859–64, rev. 4/1901–3, ed. K. Mohrmann)
Land- und Stadtkirchen (Glogau, 1866)
Sammlung mittelalterlicher Ornamentik in geschichtlicher und systematischer Ordnung dargestellt (Leipzig, 1866)

BIBLIOGRAPHY
A. von Reichensperger: *Georg Gottlob Ungewitter und sein Wirken als Baumeister* (Leipzig, 1866)
J. Schuchard: *Carl Schaefer, 1844–1908: Leben und Werk des Architekten der Neugotik* (Munich, 1979)

MICHAEL J. LEWIS

Unghero, Nanni [Giovanni d'Alesso d'Antonio] (*b* Florence, *c.* 1490; *d* Florence, 31 May 1546). Italian carpenter, wood-carver, architect and military engineer. He trained in carpentry with his father and by 1510 had his own workshop. Through the patronage of Baccio d'Agnolo, architect of the Florentine Opera del Duomo, Nanni may have gained his first known commission, for two altars (1510; destr.) in the cathedral, as well as work on the palace and villas that Baccio built for the Bartolini family in the second decade of the century.

Nanni also became known for his sculpture in wood; Vasari related that he carved a number of figures after designs by Jacopo Sansovino, with whom he carved his one surviving statue, the *St Nicholas of Tolentino* (Florence, Santo Spirito). This formed the centrepiece of an altar (1513–18) containing wooden putti (destr.) after designs by Sansovino and painted panels by Franciabigio. Nanni and Sansovino also worked together at the Bartolini family's suburban villa of Valfonda in those years, and Sansovino took on Niccolò Tribolo as an apprentice after he had worked with Nanni.

From the 1520s Nanni concentrated more exclusively on architecture and engineering. In 1520 he restored the choir-stalls of the cathedral (destr.) and later renewed those of SS Annunziata, Florence (1528–39; destr.). The best example of his architectural style is the organ-case and altar of S Salvatore in SS Annunziata. The marble framework employs a basic architectural vocabulary derived from Giuliano da Sangallo and resembles Baccio d'Agnolo's Palazzo Serristori façade (1523) in its decorative motifs.

The uncertain state of Tuscan politics in the 1520s and 1530s gave scope for Nanni's abilities as a military architect: he was engaged on fortifications for Pisa (the citadel), Pistoia (Palazzo Capitano, Fortress of S Barbara), Arezzo and Borgo San Sepolcro and built the Fortezza da Basso in Florence (1535–7) after designs by Antonio da Sangallo the younger. He was made master builder of the Parte Guelfa in 1531 and was an engineer for Cosimo I from 1538 to 1544. Nanni's development from carpentry to sculpture and architecture mirrored that of Baccio d'Agnolo and the Sangallo family and illustrates the lack of rigid divisions between the guilds in Florence at the time.

BIBLIOGRAPHY
G. Vasari: *Vite* (1550, rev. 2/1568); ed. G. Milanesi (1878–85), vi, pp. 56–7
P. Tonini: *Santuario di SS Annunziata di Firenze* (Florence, 1876), p. 59
J. Balogh: 'Nanni Unghero', *Az Országos Magyar Szépművészeti Múzeum Évkönyvei* [Yearbook of the Museum of Fine Arts, Budapest], iv (1924–6), pp. 91–115
F. Gurrieri: 'La fortezza rinascimentale di S Barbara a Pistoia: Una conferma per Nanni Unghero', *Boll. A.*, lxi (1976), pp. 12–20
L. B. Salimbeni: 'Una "fabbrica" fiorentina di Baccio d'Agnolo', *Palladio*, xxvii/2 (1978), pp. 7–28
M. Gianneschi and C. Sodini: 'Urbanistica e politica durante il principato di Alessandro de' Medici, 1532–37', *Stor. Città*, x (1979), pp. 5–34

BRUCE BOUCHER

Union des Artistes Modernes [U.A.M.]. French group of architects and designers founded in Paris in 1929 and active until 1958. Its founder-members included Charlotte Perriand, Robert Mallet-Stevens, Francis Jourdain, René Herbst (1891–1982) and Jean Puiforcat. During the group's existence membership varied widely. The activities of the U.A.M. may be divided into two periods. Between 1929 and 1939 the group represented a centre of activity for a broad range of tendencies within the French avant-garde, from advanced technology to fine craftsmanship. Although spokespersons for the group at times claimed to be creating a 'movement', in reality the U.A.M. was not doctrinaire; it was essentially devoted to the idea of the unity of the arts common to the ideology of applied arts reform from the mid-19th century. Le Corbusier was a member of the U.A.M., and his Pavillon de L'Esprit Nouveau for the Exposition Internationale des Arts Décoratifs et Industriels Modernes (Paris, 1925), intended as a mass-produced dwelling, was in keeping with the U.A.M.'s aim to design prototypes for mass production.

The world economic crisis hit France in 1931 at the exact moment when the U.A.M. was formulating its identity and social role, thus limiting important design commissions and forcing the group to become a defender of modernism against bitter attacks by the designer Paul Iribe (1883–1935) and the critics Thiébault-Sisson, Camille Mauclair and Waldemar George, among others. Critics claimed that the clean lines and smooth surfaces of modern architecture and design were responsible for the crisis in French building and decoration industries. In response to these criticisms, the group published *Pour l'art moderne: Cadre de la vie contemporaine* (1934), one of the few manifestos published by French artists in the 1930s. It praised modern art's accessibility, claiming it to be a socially aware art. Despite financial difficulties and attacks by conservative critics, the group organized an important series of exhibitions during the 1930s, both independently (1930–33) and within the Salon d'Automne (1934, 1936) and the Salon de la Lumière (1935). The U.A.M. was also responsible for a steel-and-glass pavilion in the *Exposition internationale des arts et techniques dans la vie moderne* (Paris, 1937).

The second period of the U.A.M.'s activities (1944–58) was animated principally by the architects Georges-Henri Pingusson and André Hermant (1908–78), as well as Herbst and Perriand. Post-war reconstruction fostered a change in the orientation of the U.A.M. towards a stricter emphasis on technology and series production marked by the formation of a new section of the group: Formes Utiles. From 1949 to 1958 the latter's annual exhibitions, held in the Salon des Arts Ménagers, Paris (beginning in 1951), formed the group's principal activity. Each year the group chose a specific task related to domestic equipment, such as 'the Easy Chair' (1957), presenting a selection of the best international design solutions. As the Formes Utiles section progressively dominated the U.A.M. to the exclusion of exhibitions of new works by U.A.M. members, the original ideals of the group were lost. The U.A.M. became increasingly disunited and disbanded in 1958.

WRITINGS
F. Jourdain: 'Origin and Raison d'Etre of the New Society: The First Salon of the Union des Artistes Modernes at the Pavillon Marsan', *Creative A.*, vii (1930), pp. 368–71
L. Cheronnet: *Pour l'art moderne: Cadre de la vie contemporaine* (Paris, 1934) [manifesto]
'U.A.M.', *Archit. Aujourd'hui* (1937) [issue devoted to the U.A.M. and the exhibition of 1937; articles by R. Mallet-Stevens, F. Jourdain and M. Barret]
G.-H. Pingusson: *Manifeste* (Paris, 1949) [second manifesto]

BIBLIOGRAPHY
A. Barré-Despond: *Union des artistes modernes* (Paris, 1987)
Les Années UAM, 1929-1958 (exh. cat., Paris, Mus. A. Déc., 1988)
SUZANNE TISE

Union of Bulgarian Artists. *See* NATIONAL ART SOCIETY OF BULGARIA.

Union of Russian Artists [Soyuz Russkikh Khudozhnikov]. Russian exhibiting society, active from 1903 to 1923. It was set up when the WORLD OF ART group, based in St Petersburg, amalgamated with the Moscow artists who had participated in the Exhibitions of the Work of 36 Artists held in Moscow in December 1901 and 1902. United by their hostility to old forms and the desire for exhibitions that were not controlled by juries, the two groups nevertheless embraced widely divergent aesthetic stances. While former World of Art artists, such as Alexandre Benois and Léon Bakst, attacked the Wanderers, some Moscow artists, including Abram Arkhipov and Konstantin Korovin, continued to exhibit with them. The Union's exhibitions were held in Moscow. Inevitably, they were not stylistically unified: academically lyrical landscapes by Nikolay Klodt (1865–1918) and Arkady Rylov were shown alongside 'impressionist' paintings by Igor' Grabar', 'symbolist' canvases by Viktor Borisov-Musatov, more experimental works by Valentin Serov and Mikhail Vrubel', as well as elegantly decorative pictures by Ivan Bilibin and Konstantin Somov. After the seventh exhibition in 1910 the Union split precisely because of such aesthetic differences, exacerbated by Benois's review of the show, which praised the St Petersburg artists but castigated the majority of works as 'fussy, tasteless and lifeless'. The Moscow artists remained within the Union, but the St Petersburg artists seceded and began to exhibit again under the name World of Art. By 1917 the Union represented outdated artistic concerns: it held its 18th and final exhibition in 1923, after which many former members, including Rylov, Arkhipov and Isaak Brodsky, joined AKhRR, the ASSOCIATION OF ARTISTS OF REVOLUTIONARY RUSSIA.

BIBLIOGRAPHY
V. P. Lapshin: *Soyuz Russkikh Khudozhnikov* [The Union of Russian Artists] (Leningrad, 1974)
CHRISTINA LODDER

Union of Soviet Socialist Republics [Rus. Soyuz Sovetskikh Sotsialisticheskikh Respublik; USSR; Soviet Union]. Former political union formed in 1922 and consising originally of ARMENIA, AZERBAIJAN, BELARUS', GEORGIA, KAZAKHSTAN, KYRGYZSTAN, RUSSIA, TAJIKISTAN, TURKMENISTAN, UZBEKISTAN and the UKRAINE. At the outbreak of World War II ESTONIA, LATVIA, LITHUANIA and MOLDOVA were acquired. The union ceased to exist in 1991, when the union republics gained their independence and formed the Commonwealth of Independent States.

Union of the Societies of Artists of Bulgaria. *See* NATIONAL ART SOCIETY OF BULGARIA.

Union of Youth [Rus. Soyuz Molodyozhi]. Association of Russian avant-garde painters, active in St Petersburg from 1910 to 1914. It was financed by the businessman Lerky Zheverzheyev, who was also its president. The core of the group comprised the artists Pavel Filonov, Ol'ga Rozanova, Iosif Shkol'nik (1883–1926) and Eduard Spandikov (1875–1929) and the painter and art critic Vladimir Markov (Waldemar Matvejs, 1877–1914). The musician and painter Mikhail Matyushin and his wife, the poet Yelena Guro (1877–1913), were also associated with the group, as were the artists Kuz'ma Petrov-Vodkin (in 1910), Jean Pougny (1912–14) and Natan Al'tman and Ivan Klyun (both 1913–14). The Union functioned principally as an exhibiting society, holding five annual exhibitions in St Petersburg and one in both Riga and Moscow. A reaction against the conservatism of the contemporary art and exhibition societies, Union of Youth was the first major organized group of young avant-garde painters in Russia. Members of the Union had a rather free aesthetic ideology in distinction to other groups of the period (such as Donkey's Tail) and painted in a variety of styles. Pavel Filonov's Neo-primitivism and Rozanova's Cubo-Futurism with Rayist elements typified the breadth of stylistic aspirations within the group. The Union was a microcosm of the rich and varied picture of Russian avant-garde art in the pre-war years.

The importance and strength of the Union lay in its ability to harness the forces of the Russian avant-garde as a whole and to organize collaborative ventures. It succeeded in particular in drawing together the warring factions of the Muscovite avant-garde. Both the Jack of Diamonds and Donkey's Tail groups were invited to exhibit with them in 1912. In fact Mikhail Larionov, Natal'ya Goncharova, Kazimir Malevich, Vladimir Tatlin, David Burlyuk and Il'ya Mashkov frequently exhibited with the group and could be counted as supporting members. The Union also provided a neutral forum for debates on contemporary art and publicized the views of Donkey's Tail and Jack of Diamonds.

In 1912 the Union published two numbers of an important literary and artistic journal edited by Markov. The first was devoted to eastern art forms and contemporary Russian painting, while the second dealt with contemporary western art and included translations of two Italian Futurist manifestos, a text by Le Fauconnier and an article on van Dongen. Markov's important essay 'The Principles of the New Art' was also serialized in these two numbers. Acting as spokesman for the group, Markov advocated 'the principle of free creation'—the artist's right to paint intuitively according to his inner impulses rather than the dictates of stylistic convention. The Union was always ready to collaborate with other avant-garde groups and in 1913 invited David Burlyuk and his group of poets, including Vladimir Mayakovsky, Aleksey Kruchonykh (1886–1969) and Velimir Khlebnikov (1885–1922), to participate in its third journal. Rozanova's essay 'The Bases of New Creation', a reply to the critics of the avant-garde, was published here, as was Matyushin's influential review of Albert Gleizes's and Jean Metzinger's book *Du Cubisme* (Paris, 1912).

Before its demise in 1914, members of the Union also collaborated with other poets and painters in illustrating and publishing more than a dozen Russian Futurist books. It also extended its activities into the theatre, financing and organizing both the opera *Victory over the Sun* (with score by Matyushin, libretto by Kruchonykh and designs by Malevich) and the play *Vladimir Mayakovsky: A Tragedy* (written and performed by Mayakovsky himself, with stage designs by Shkol'nik and painted properties by Filonov). These were performed in the Luna Park Theatre in St Petersburg in December 1913.

WRITINGS

Obshchestvo khudozhnikov 'Soyuz Molodozhi' [The society of artists 'Union of Youth'], i, ii (1912)
'Soyuz Molodozhi' pri uchastii poetov 'Gileya' ['Union of Youth' with the participation of the 'Hylaean' poets], iii (1913)

BIBLIOGRAPHY

Soyuz Molodozhi [Union of Youth] (exh. cats, St Petersburg, 1910, 1911, 1912, 1913, 1914; Riga, 1910; Moscow, 1912)
C. Douglas: 'Birth of a Royal Infant: Malevich and *Victory over the Sun*', *A. America*, lxii/2 (1974), pp. 45–51
V. Markov: 'The Principles of the New Art', *Russian Art of the Avant-garde*, ed. J. Bowlt (New York, 1976), pp. 23–37
O. Rozanova: 'The Bases of the New Creation', *Russian Art of the Avant-garde*, ed. J. Bowlt (New York, 1976), pp. 102–10
J. Howard: *The Union of Youth: An Artists' Society of the Russian Avant-garde* (Manchester, 1992)

ANTHONY PARTON

Union Porcelain Works. American porcelain factory. Originally founded in Greenpoint, NY, as William Boch & Bros in 1850 to make porcelain hardware trimmings, it was bought by Thomas Carll Smith (1815–1901) *c.* 1861. The wares were first made of bone china, but in 1864 Smith began to experiment with a hard-paste formula, and his firm is considered the first in America to have used this material. In 1875 Smith hired Karl Müller (1820–87), a German sculptor, to create models for the Centennial International Exhibition of 1876 in Philadelphia, and his work includes the 'Century' vase (New York, Met.), 'Liberty' cup and 'Keramos' vase. In addition to artwares, the firm also made porcelain tiles for fireplaces and decorative wainscoting, hardware trimmings and tableware. The factory closed *c.* 1922.

BIBLIOGRAPHY

E. A. Barber: *The Pottery and Porcelain of the United States* (New York, 1893, rev. 3/1909/*R* 1976), pp. 252–8

ELLEN PAUL DENKER

Unitarianism. Christian doctrine denying the doctrine of the Trinity. A belief in one God, the humanity of Jesus and universal salvation was first propounded during the Reformation and believers were persecuted by both Catholics and Protestants: Miguel Serveto (1511–53), for example, was burnt at the stake in Geneva. A Unitarian tradition was founded in Transylvania by David Ferencz (1510–79). In Poland, a summation of Unitarian belief known as the Racovian Catechism was published in 1605 by followers of Fausto Socinus (1539–1604). London's first avowedly Unitarian church, Essex Hall (1774; destr. 1944), was established in Essex Street, off The Strand, by an Anglican clergyman, Theophilus Lindsey (1723–1808). The growth of rationalism, represented by Joseph Priestley (1733–1804), became associated with the movement in Britain and the USA. Unitarians are presently active in Romania, western Europe and Britain, the USA, Canada and India.

Transylvanian churches, for example at Toroçko (17th century), near Cluj-Napoca, are simple, barn-like structures with a tower. Earlier British chapels are unadorned, symmetrical 'preaching boxes': at Norwich the Octagon Chapel (1754–6), designed by Thomas Ivory (1709–79), has been a Unitarian church since 1820. A new spirit of religious aestheticism, encouraged by James Martineau (1805–1900) and his friends, is evident at Mill Hill Chapel (1848, by Bowman & Crowther), Leeds. Ullet Road Chapel (1896–9), Liverpool, designed by Percy Scott Worthington (1864–1939; see also WORTHINGTON, THOMAS), contains Art Nouveau metalwork and murals by Gerald Edward Lobb Moira (1867–1967). Twentieth-century buildings include Cambridge Memorial Church (1928, by Ronald Potter Jones, 1876–1965), in the Wren Revival style, and Notte Street Chapel (1959, by Louis De Soissons), Plymouth. American Unitarian-Universalist churches include such notable examples as Unity Temple (1905–8, by Frank Lloyd Wright), Oak Park, IL, the first public building in the USA for which poured reinforced concrete was adopted. The First Unitarian Church, Rochester, NY (1964, by Louis Kahn) has a typical arrangement of social spaces.

BIBLIOGRAPHY

E. M. Wilbur: *A History of Unitarianism*, 2 vols (Cambridge, MA, 1945–52)

G. Hague and others: *The Unitarian Heritage: An Architectural Survey* (Sheffield, 1986)

C. Stell: *Inventory of Nonconformist Chapels and Meeting-houses in Central England, Southwest England and Northern England* (London, 1986–94)

M. J. Hamilton: *The Meeting House: Heritage and Vision* (Madison, WI, 1991)

JUDY HAGUE

Unitas Fratrum [Unity of Brethren]. *See* MORAVIAN BRETHREN.

United Arab Emirates [Arab. Al-Imārātt al-'Arabiyya al-Muttaḥida; formerly the Trucial States]. Federation of seven states in the eastern Arabian peninsula, with coastlines along the Gulf: Abu Dhabi (comprising 88% of the territory), Dubai, Sharjah (Arab. al-Shariqa), Ra's al-Khayma, Fujayra, Umm al-Qaywayn and 'Ajman (the smallest emirate); each emirate is named after its main city. Salt flats along the coast give way to sand desert and gravel plains, with the Hajar mountain range dividing the east and west coasts. The indigenous population (*c.* 2,200,000) is mainly Sunni Muslim and there is a large expatriate workforce. In prehistoric times the people were sea traders on the route between the east (e.g. Indus Valley, Iran) and Mesopotamia. They were at the height of their prosperity in the 3rd millennium BC when greater Oman (including the UAE) can possibly be identified as the copper-producing land of Magan, known from Mesopotamian cuneiform tablets. Islam arrived in this region *c.* AD 630. The Portuguese occupied the main Gulf ports from the 16th century to the mid-17th. The origins of the present-day states lie in the 18th century when relations with Britain also began. In the late 19th century and early 20th the pearl industry reached its height, which helped make Dubai a major entrepôt. In 1971 Britain withdrew from the region and the UAE was founded. Revenue comes largely from oil and gas. Oil was found from 1958 onwards in Abu Dhabi, Dubai, Sharjah and Ra's al-Khayma. This article mainly covers the art and architecture of the 20th century. For the earlier history of this area *see* PRE-ISLAMIC ARABIA and ISLAMIC ART, which also covers the modern period in a more general context.

Oil revenues, particularly in the 1970s, financed intensive urban development and the destruction of many old buildings in Abu Dhabi, Dubai and Sharjah. Because of the need to provide for a modern state with an international business community, Western architects were commissioned to design International Style high-rise buildings; these dominate, for example, the Corniche in Abu Dhabi and the Creek in Dubai. Islamic motifs were occasionally incorporated, such as arched entrances, but from the late 1970s attempts were made to find styles that related more to the local environment and the region's history, and Arab architects were also commissioned. An awakened interest in the past also led to the restoration and preservation of various old buildings, such as watch-towers and forts.

In Abu Dhabi town the only remaining building from the pre-oil past, dwarfed by modern skyscrapers, is the restored al-Husn Palace, also known as the White or Old Fort (1793). It houses the Centre for Documentation and Research, which collects manuscripts and archives covering the Islamic history of the Emirates. In Dubai there are houses with wind-towers in the Bastakiya district that were built in the early 20th century by Iranian immigrants and are being preserved. Shaykh Sa'id's palace (late 19th century) in the Shindagha district of Dubai was converted to a museum in 1986. It had been abandoned in 1958 and was rebuilt using the old coral blocks. It is a courtyard house with wind-towers and such traditional features as pierced plaster screens and carved woodwork. Al-Fahidi Fort (early 19th century) is the oldest building in Dubai. Formerly the seat of government, it was re-opened in 1971 to house the Dubai Museum. It is built of plastered coral blocks and has been given an extensive face-lift. Forts of coral stones or baked mud are also to be found in Fujayra, Ra's al-Khayma and 'Ajman. Many of the old souks have been pulled down and modern shopping malls erected. However, souks that combine modern and traditional elements have been built, such as the monumental Sharjah or New Souk (also known as the Central Market) in Sharjah, with its blue-tiled round roofs and wind-towers, designed by the British architects Michael Lyell Associates (1978). One of the first modern buildings in the region to use an Islamic vocabulary, it incorporates traditional tile designs and *muqarnas* niches under a barrel-vaulted roof. Many of the old mosques have been replaced by new buildings commissioned either by the State or by private individuals. The huge King Faisal Mosque in Sharjah and the Jumayra Mosque in Dubai (1983) underline the centrality of the Muslim faith in the UAE.

The art movement in the Emirates dates to the mid-1970s, when artists sent on scholarships returned from Egypt, Iraq, Syria, Britain, France and the USA. As in neighbouring countries, the strongest artistic trend in the Emirates is a figurative one that records traditional scenes. Among its adherents are Abdul Qadir al-Rayis (*b* 1948), Muhammad al-Qasab, Ibrahim Mustafa (*b* 1953), Abdar Rahman al-Zainal, Muhammad Mundi, Issam Shreida

(b 1953), Abd al-Karim Sukar, Obaid Srour (b 1955) and Muna al-Khaja. The Surrealists include Salih al-Ustadh (b 1957), who has studied in California and produces Daliesque works, and Hisham al-Mazloum, a graduate of the Al-Ain University. Other notable artists in the Emirates include Muhammad Yousif (b 1954) and Hassan Sharif (b 1956). The Emirates Fine Arts Association founded in 1980 in Sharjah has been instrumental in arranging exhibitions in the UAE and abroad. The first Sharjah Biennale (the first in the Arabian Peninsula) was held in 1993 by the Department of Culture and Information in Sharjah and the Emirates Fine Arts Association. It included works by 132 artists from 22 countries.

Many traditional crafts are still practised, often supported by the government, such as pottery (figurines as well as pots), weaving, braiding (using date-palm fibres for baskets etc), embroidery and making bride chests of wood and brass. Jewellery in the lower Gulf has traditionally employed coral and small polished pebbles from the shores. The government-run Women's Craft Centre in Abu Dhabi teaches and promotes traditional craft skills.

Most of the Emirates have museums. The Al-Ain Museum, Abu Dhabi, is in the grounds of a fort built in 1910. It has objects from several archaeological excavations, as well as silver bedouin jewellery and a collection of weapons, such as *khanjars* (small ornamented daggers); it also houses the Department of Antiquities. In Abu Dhabi town the Cultural Foundation holds exhibitions of foreign and local artists. Dubai Museum contains archaeological finds, traditional weapons, dress, crafts, jewellery and other artefacts from the 1st millennium BC to the 20th century AD. Ra's al-Khayma has a museum in a restored mid-18th-century fort with objects from the sites at Shimal and Julfar (the old port abandoned in the 17th century in favour of Ra's al-Khayma) as well as traditional silver jewellery. 'Ajman's museum (opened 1981) is in a late 18th-century fort and includes archaeological finds and weapons. The museum at Fujayra opened in 1991 and also displays archaeological finds, traditional weapons and dress, and there is a collection of local archaeological finds in the Sharjah Archaeological Museum.

BIBLIOGRAPHY
G. Bibby: *Looking for Dilmun* (London, 1970)
M. M. Abdullah: *The United Arab Emirates* (London, 1978)
R. S. Zahlan: *The Origins of the United Arab Emirates* (London, 1978)
P. Mansfield: *The New Arabians* (Chicago, 1981)
J. Whelan, ed.: *UAE: A MEED Practical Guide* (London, 1982, rev. 1990)
W. Dostal: *The Traditional Architecture of Rās al Khaimah (North)* (Wiesbaden, 1983)
A. Salman: *Al-tashkīl al-mu'āṣir fī duwal majlis al-ta'āwun al-khalījī* [Contemporary art in the countries of the Gulf Cooperation Council] (Kuwait, 1984)
J. Hansman: *Julfār, an Arabian Port: Its Settlement and Far Eastern Ceramic Trade from the 14th to the 18th Centuries* (London, 1985)
A. Al-Tajir and A. J. Ahmed, eds: 'The Arts in the United Arab Emirates: A Special Supplement', *A. & Islam. World*, iii/4 (1985–6), pp. 57–96
W. Ali: ed.: *Contemporary Art from the Islamic World* (London, 1989)
S. Kay and D. Zandi: *Architectural Heritage of the Gulf*, Arabian Heritage (Dubai and London, 1991) [series also incl. bks on individual Emirates]
'Architecture, Archaeology and the Arts in the United Arab Emirates', *A. & Islam. World* (1993) [special issue 23]

United Kingdom (of Great Britain and Northern Ireland). Country in north-western Europe, comprising

Map of the United Kingdom; all of the countries have separate entries in this dictionary

the formerly independent nations of ENGLAND, WALES and SCOTLAND as well as the six counties of NORTHERN IRELAND. With the exception of the territory belonging to the Republic of Ireland, the UK comprises all of the group of islands known as the British Isles. Most of England, Wales and Scotland are contained within the largest of these (Great Britain), but the UK also includes numerous small groups of islands, especially off the coast of Scotland (see fig.). The capital is LONDON, and in the late 20th century the population was c. 58 million.

From AD 43 most of Great Britain was absorbed into the Roman Empire, although Scotland resisted colonization. After the Norman invasion of 1066, Norman lordships were established not only in England but also in southern Wales, as well as in the eastern part of Ireland. It was not until the late 13th century, however, under the English king Edward I (*reg* 1272–1307), that the northern parts of Wales were brought under English rule, with Edward appointing his son Prince of Wales, a title subsequently adopted by each eldest surviving son of the monarch. In 1603, when the English queen Elizabeth I died, the English throne passed to her cousin James VI of Scotland (James I of England), but Scotland remained constitutionally independent. In 1707, however, an Act of Union was passed, by which the Scottish parliament was abolished (new Scottish seats being established in the House of Commons in London), although the Scots retained an independent legal system. In 1800, after several centuries of settlement in Ireland, a further Act of Union was passed, quashing the Irish parliament in Dublin. In 1922, 26 of the 32 counties of Ireland left the UK and established the REPUBLIC OF IRELAND, the remaining 6 counties remaining under British rule. While their histories are inextricably linked, and while there has been much reciprocation of artistic influences, each of the constituent nations of the UK has broadly retained a distinct artistic identity.

United Society of Believers in Christ's Second Appearing. *See* SHAKERS.

United States of America. Country composed of 50 states, 48 of them contiguous and stretching between the Atlantic and Pacific Oceans and between the borders of Canada to the north and Mexico to the south (see fig. 1). Of the other two states, Alaska is on the north-western tip of the North American land mass, while Hawaii comprises a group of islands in the Pacific Ocean, *c.* 3800 km off the western American coast (for a full discussion *see* HAWAII). The total land mass of the USA is *c.* 9,370,000 sq. km. Its rich and varied array of natural resources, including minerals, oils, forests and fertile soil, led to its rapid development and prosperity, especially in the 19th and 20th centuries. The country became the United States of America in 1781 during the American Revolution. The first inhabitants of North America, however, came *c.* 15,000 BC from Asia in a series of migrations across the Bering Strait and established distinct cultural and linguistic units (*see* NATIVE NORTH AMERICAN ART, §I, 2(i)). Although Vikings explored North America in the 10th and 11th centuries AD, it was Christopher Columbus's voyage of 1492 that signalled the beginning of intensive exploration and settlement by numerous European countries, most notably Spain, Great Britain, France and the Netherlands, which created an enduring diversity of cultures. The importation of slaves from Africa in the 17th and 18th centuries added to this cultural diversity (*see* AFRICAN AMERICAN ART), as did the arrival later of political refugees, for instance from Nazi Germany, and others attracted by the country's economic success, especially from such nearby countries as Mexico, Puerto Rico and Cuba (*see* LATIN AMERICAN ARTISTS OF THE USA).

I. Introduction. II. Architecture. III. Painting and graphic arts. IV. Sculpture. V. Interior decoration. VI. Furniture. VII. Ceramics. VIII. Glass. IX. Metalwork. X. Jewellery. XI. Textiles. XII. Patronage. XIII. Collecting and dealing. XIV. Museums. XV. Art education. XVI. Art libraries and photographic collections. XVII. Historiography.

DETAILED TABLE OF CONTENTS

I. Introduction.

The history of the visual arts in the USA is intimately tied to the political, social and cultural histories of the European

1. Map of the United States of America; those sites with separate entries in this dictionary are distinguished by CROSS-REFERENCE TYPE

nations that initially explored and colonized North America. This close relationship with Europe was crucial not only to the stylistic development of all the arts (*see* §§II–XI below) but also to the establishment of public cultural institutions and the character of patronage (*see* §§XII–XVI below). The first Europeans were Spanish settlers and explorers who arrived in Florida and New Mexico during the early 16th century. By the early 17th century several other European countries, including France, the Netherlands and Great Britain, had settlements in the New World. The earliest British settlements were Jamestown, VA (1607), and Plymouth, MA (1620). The British were by far the most successful of the colonists and built up a distinctly British provincial culture. By the late 18th century, however, dissatisfaction with British rule and taxation led to the American Revolution and the War of Independence (1776–83), after which the USA set out on a path of aggressive expansionism. The Louisiana Purchase (of land from France), secured by Thomas Jefferson in 1803, nearly doubled the size of American territory, and westward expansion to the Pacific coast became America's goal. Conflicts with the French, British and Spanish continued throughout early 19th-century American history, and in 1845 Texas, which had declared its independence from Mexico in 1835–6, was annexed, leading to the Mexican War (1846–8). The displacement of Native American people also continued, while huge waves of European immigrants, mostly German and Irish, arrived between 1830 and 1850. Throughout this period the northern states were becoming increasingly industrial, while the southern ones remained agricultural. The South's continued use of African slaves amid growing calls for abolition led to the Civil War (1860–65). The South's defeat resulted in the preservation of the Union and the emancipation of slaves, although segregation continued to be officially sanctioned in some parts of the South until the 1960s. The second half of the 19th century was marked by increased industrialization, westward expansion and immigration from Europe and Asia. This growth and prosperity resulted, however, in greater injustices to Native Americans: their numbers dwindled through armed conflict, and their lands were confiscated. At the end of the 20th century they remained, for the most part, relegated to 'reservations' in underdeveloped areas of the country.

Despite the remarkable growth and prosperity of the 19th century, however, in the early 20th century the USA remained culturally insular and provincial. The shock, disbelief and ridicule that met the European works in the Armory Show (1913), an exhibition of contemporary European and American art (*see* §III, 3 below), testified to America's cultural backwardness. This changed dramatically in the 1940s, however, when many European intellectuals and artists came to the USA as refugees from Nazism. The period of the late 1940s is often thought of as a turning-point, at which the USA, and specifically New York, became the new centre of Western culture, at least in regard to the visual arts (*see* §III, 4 below). From the late 1940s the USA's relative material wealth was accompanied by various political and social crises. The 'Cold War' with the USSR, which began after World War II, only ended with the latter's dissolution in 1991. The Vietnam War (1955–75) created deep wounds in America's

psyche, as did the political assassinations of President John F. Kennedy (1963), Robert Kennedy and Martin Luther King (both 1968). Violence became and continued to be a constant preoccupation. In the 1970s the Watergate scandal, which brought about the resignation of President Richard Nixon in 1974, led to widespread cynicism regarding the honesty of politicians. The radicalism of the late 1960s gave way to growing conservatism in the 1980s, while deepening economic difficulties in the 1990s led to a mood of uncertainty.

BIBLIOGRAPHY
D. M. Mendelowitz: *A History of American Art* (New York, 1960, rev. 1970)
J. Wilmerding: *American Art*, Pelican Hist. A. (Harmondsworth, 1976)
M. Brown and others: *American Art* (New York, 1979)
M. Baigell: *Dictionary of American Art* (London, 1980)
R. B. Morris, ed.: *Encyclopedia of American History* (New York, 1982)
M. Baigell: *A Concise History of American Painting and Sculpture* (New York, 1984)
A Proud Heritage: Two Centuries of American Art (exh. cat., ed. T. A. Neff; Chicago, IL, Terra Mus. Amer. A., 1987)
W. H. Gerdts: *Art across America: Two Centuries of Regional Painting, 1720–1920*, 3 vols (New York, 1990)

II. Architecture.

1. The Colonial period, before 1776. 2. The Federalist period and eclectic revivalism. 3. The Civil War and late 19th-century eclecticism. 4. The Chicago school, the Prairie school, academic eclecticism and the rise of Modernism. 5. After World War II: Modernism, Neo-expressionism, Post-modernism.

1. THE COLONIAL PERIOD, BEFORE 1776. The architecture of the Colonial era in the USA reflects the wide variety of influences brought by the European settlers, adapted to the needs imposed and the resources afforded by the local environment. The oldest surviving building of the period is the Governor's Palace at Santa Fe, NM. Begun in 1610, it formed the south range of the *presidio*. The walls are built of adobe, which had been used by the Pueblo Indians for centuries. The Spanish, however, introduced the technique of making adobe into bricks (see fig. 2), which greatly facilitated the church-building programme undertaken by the Franciscan friars who began the conversion of the Pueblos in the early 17th century. In many of their churches a transverse clerestory window was placed between the roof of the sanctuary and the lower roof of the nave, a feature apparently unique to New Mexico; these Franciscan buildings constitute a most remarkable regional development. In Florida, although the town of St Augustine was founded 44 years before Santa Fe, its major Spanish monument, the Castillo de San Marcos (for illustration *see* ST AUGUSTINE), the last of a succession of three structures bearing the same name, was not begun until 1672, as the northernmost of a chain of fortresses built to protect the Spanish fleet against the British. Its design has been attributed to the Cubans Juan Síscara (*fl* 1664–91) and Ignacio Daza. Of the bastioned type invented in the early 16th century in Italy and perfected in the 17th by Sébastien Leprestre de Vauban, it was built of a local shell-limestone, the special qualities of which enabled it to withstand three British sieges.

In the British Colonies the vast majority of buildings in the 17th century were of wood, the ready availability of which attracted settlers from a land where its price had been rising disproportionately since the 13th century. In Puritan New England the central building of each community was the meeting-house, which served both religious and secular functions. The earlier meeting-houses were indistinguishable externally from dwellings, but in the second half of the century a distinctive new building type, derived from the English market hall, appeared. The Old Ship Meeting-house (1681; enlarged 1729 and 1755), Hingham, MA, with its square plan and hipped roof, contrasts tellingly with the most important survival of 17th-century Anglican church architecture in the South, the Old Brick Church (*c.* 1660), Isle of Wight County, VA, whose antiquated Gothic features can also be seen in English churches of the time. Most Anglican churches in the South were simple wood-frame structures; none has survived.

In domestic architecture too there were marked regional differences. In New England the typical middle-class house was of two storeys, with two rooms to a floor and a central chimney. It was never more than one room deep under the main roof, although extra rooms might be provided in a lean-to at the rear. Its equivalent in the South was of one or one-and-a-half storeys, with end chimneys and two rooms (hall and parlour) on the ground floor; from *c.* 1700 the rooms were divided by a central passage containing the stairs to the rooms in the roof. Each type was suited to the climate of the region in which it was built, but while the New England type had first appeared in England in the 16th century, the Southern type had no English antecedents. The grander Southern houses, however, such as Bacon's Castle, Surry County, VA, designed by Arthur Allen in 1664–5, remained purely English. Another innovative type of house was built in southern New York (including Long Island) and northern New Jersey, both of which from 1626 to 1664 were parts of New Netherland, in which the Dutch influence was

prominent. This was a single-storey or one-and-a-half-storey house with end chimneys and a gently sloping roof with flared eaves of unusual projection; early in the 18th century a distinctive form of gambrel roof came to be substituted for the two-slope roof of the 17th century (see fig. 3), and towards its end a raised platform (*stoep*) along the front of the house, sheltered by the eaves, became a frequent feature. In New Amsterdam (now New York City) and Albany the Dutch built narrow-fronted houses with stepped gables facing the street, continuing to do so under British rule. The Swedes also made an invaluable contribution to the settling of the continent in bringing to the USA the log cabin, built with horizontal logs notched at the corners; however, Sweden profited less than its European rivals from its American venture. Another log-building technique, of disputed origin, was employed by the French in the Mississippi Valley, with vertical logs trimmed flat on two sides and either set in the earth (*poteaux en terre*) or on a sill (*poteaux sur sole*).

In the 18th century, outside New Mexico, where the indigenous 17th-century style continued unchanged, Spanish Colonial architecture followed Mexican precedents. Thus the unfinished façade of S Antonio de Valero (1744–after 1777; now church of the Alamo), San Antonio, TX, is a naive imitation of the north transept façade of Durango Cathedral; that of S José y S Miguel de Aguayo (1768–77), near San Antonio, by Pedro Huizar belongs to the final phase of the Mexican Baroque; and that of S Xavier del Bac (1775–97), near Tucson, AZ, is a belated example of the *estípite* style. There are no surviving mission churches in California from before 1776. In Louisiana the French developed a type of house well suited to the climate, with a hipped roof spreading out to shelter a *galerie* surrounding the principal rooms on the first floor; Parlange (1750), Pointe Coupée Parish, is a fine early example. The British, on the other hand, showed little concern for climate: in

2. Church and convent of S Estevan, Acoma, New Mexico, 1629–42; view from the south-east before restoration

3. Ackerman House, Hackensack, New Jersey, 1704

their colonies porches of any kind were conspicuous by their absence. In the early 18th century the influence of Christopher Wren became evident for the first time in the church of St Philip (1711–23; destr. 1835), Charleston, SC, and the double pile was generally adopted for grander houses (see fig. 4). The Governor's Palace, Williamsburg, VA, probably designed by Henry Cary and Alexander Spotswood in 1706–20 (destr. 1781; reconstructed 1931–4), was the grandest early 18th-century double pile. It was as English as Bacon's Castle, as was the typical Virginian plantation house of *c.* 1720–*c.* 1760, five bays wide, of two or two-and-a-half storeys with a hipped roof, whose antecedents are to be found in the brick vernacular of south-eastern England. Exceptional houses of the second quarter of the century include Stratford Hall (1725–30),

Westmoreland County, VA, which has been seen both as an imitation of the first Capitol (1701–5; destr. 1747; reconstructed 1931–4) at Williamsburg, VA, because of its E-plan, and as a product of the English Baroque school of Vanbrugh and Hawksmoor because of its grouped chimneys linked by arches. Another example is Drayton Hall (1738–42), Charleston, SC, whose two-storey portico makes it the first unequivocally Palladian house in British America.

By mid-century architectural books from England were beginning to make an impact, and there was an American building—the Redwood Library (1749–50), Newport, RI— of which the most doctrinaire Palladian could have approved. Its architect, PETER HARRISON, followed it with other buildings, of which the King's Chapel (1749–58), Boston, MA, influenced by James Gibbs, was the finest, showing Harrison to be adept in the intelligent use of printed sources. As a rich merchant with a gift for design, he was an exceptional figure in the Colonial scene. Most of those who are named as architects of Colonial buildings, such as ROBERT SMITH (i) in Philadelphia and WILLIAM BUCKLAND in Virginia and Maryland, had a craft training. Thanks to them, and the books they used, British Colonial architecture of the quarter of a century before Independence, although very rarely original, attained a high level of competence in craftsmanship and design.

BIBLIOGRAPHY
S. F. Kimball: *Domestic Architecture of the American Colonies and of the Early Republic* (New York, 1922/R 1966)
G. Kubler: *The Religious Architecture of New Mexico in the Colonial Period and since the American Occupation* (Colorado Springs, 1940/R Albuquerque, 1972)
T. T. Waterman: *The Dwellings of Colonial America* (Chapel Hill, NC, 1950)
H. S. Morrison: *Early American Architecture from the First Colonial Settlements to the National Period* (New York, 1952)
H. W. Rose: *The Colonial Houses of Worship in America* (New York, 1963)
M. C. Donnelly: *The New England Meeting House of the Seventeenth Century* (Middletown, 1968)
W. H. Pierson jr: *The Colonial and Neo-classical Styles*, i of *American Buildings and their Architects* (Garden City, NY, 1970)
A. L. Cummings: *The Framed Houses of Massachusetts Bay, 1625–1725* (Cambridge, MA, 1979)
M. Whiffen and F. Koeper: *American Architecture, 1607–1976* (Cambridge, MA, 1981)
D. D. Reiff: *Small Georgian Houses in England and Virginia: Origins and Development through the 1750s* (London, 1986)

MARCUS WHIFFEN

2. THE FEDERALIST PERIOD AND ECLECTIC REVIVALISM. American architecture began a new phase at the time of the Revolution with a general desire to establish identifiable American models following political independence. After the signing of the Treaty of Paris, the writing of the Constitution and the creation of the federal form of government, the first requirement was for a seat for the new government. In 1791 the site for a new capital was selected on the Potomac River, roughly midway between the northern and southern states. A ten-mile (16-km) square was set aside as the District of Columbia for a federal city, named Washington in honour of the first US President (*see* WASHINGTON, DC). PIERRE-CHARLES L'ENFANT was appointed to plan the new city. He employed a series of radiating diagonals (inspired by Versailles, where he had spent his childhood) and a grid-plan to encourage land sale and development. The two principal government

4. North front of Westover, Charles City County, Virginia, *c.* 1730–35

buildings, for the legislature and the president, were designed by WILLIAM THORNTON, a gifted self-trained amateur, and an Irish emigrant, JAMES HOBAN. Thornton's Capitol (begun 1793) incorporated a classical Roman rotunda on the centre axis. Hoban's presidential residence, the White House (1792–1803), was modelled on 18th-century Irish country houses.

After 1795 New England architecture began to develop its own identity, although it was still strongly indebted to such contemporary English practitioners as William Chambers. Samuel McIntire of Salem, MA, was typical of the self-taught architects who had begun as craftsmen and who were still common in the early 19th century. Trained as a wood-carver and cabinetmaker, he designed such residences as the Gardner-Pingree House (1805), Salem, which have a tautness and linearity of ornament characteristic of Federalist work in New England.

In Boston CHARLES BULFINCH was even more influential. He pursued architecture as a gentlemanly avocation until investment losses forced him to make his living by designing buildings. His best work included elegant brick houses for prominent Boston merchants as well as rows of brick town houses built speculatively, the most notable being the Tontine Crescent (1793; destr.). Bulfinch is perhaps best known for his domed, brick-built Massachusetts State House (1795–8), Boston. Although designed to house the legislature of the newly independent state, the building was based on William Chambers's Somerset House (1776–1801), London.

In the more southerly states, architects and designers attempted to develop an architecture appropriate to the character of the new nation. THOMAS JEFFERSON, the last and perhaps the most skilled of the gentlemen amateur architects, was well known among Virginians for his architectural accomplishments, most notably his hill-top home, Monticello (begun 1770). In 1785 Jefferson was asked to provide a design for a new Virginia State Capitol at Richmond. His solution (see fig. 5), developed in collaboration with Charles-Louis Clérisseau, was the earliest Neo-classical building in the USA and a characteristic example of the emerging Federal style (*see* FEDERAL STYLE, §1) and it was based on the ancient Roman Maison Carrée, Nimes. Jefferson also used a Roman model, the Pantheon, for his library rotunda of the University of Virginia (1823–7), Charlottesville.

Jefferson exerted a marked influence on the development of early American architecture, but he was even more influential through his sponsorship of one of the first professional architects to arrive in the USA, BENJAMIN HENRY LATROBE. Jefferson obtained for him the commission for the Virginia State Penitentiary (1797–8). Also trained as an engineer, Latrobe designed the waterworks system (1798–1801; destr.) for Philadelphia. Like Jefferson, Latrobe advocated Neo-classicism as the style for the new nation, best represented in his Greco-Roman Bank of Pennsylvania (1798–1800; destr.), Philadelphia. Latrobe's most acclaimed design, Baltimore Cathedral (1804–18), MD, has solid ashlar masonry vaulting, with precise Greek detailing in the Ionic porch (*see* FEDERAL STYLE, fig. 1). Like the architecture of John Soane, Latrobe's used the stark geometries of ancient Greece and Rome as a

5. Thomas Jefferson: Virginia State Capitol, Richmond, 1785–99; from a photograph *c.* 1900, before the addition of the wings and front steps in 1906

point of departure for the creation of an original and consciously modern idiom.

Unlike Great Britain, the USA had only a few trained professionals throughout the country trying to meet the needs of a burgeoning westward-moving population. Inexpensive architectural manuals aimed not at educated amateurs but at builders were published to meet the challenge. ASHER BENJAMIN was most successful in this enterprise, publishing a series of books from 1797. His most popular include *The American Builder's Companion* (1806), presenting designs for houses and for a county court-house, a building-type invented for the American frontier.

American architecture entered a new and increasingly nationalist phase *c.* 1815 with the beginnings of revivalism. Latrobe's inventive variations on Greco-Roman classicism were replaced with increasingly accurate recreations not only of ancient Greek and Roman buildings but also of a broad range of styles, from Ancient Egyptian through medieval to Italian Renaissance. One aspect of this historicism that soon acquired nationalistic connotations was the GREEK REVIVAL. Many Americans saw a parallel between their recent struggle for freedom and the struggle of the Greeks to free themselves from Turkish domination. Ancient Greek temples were reproduced almost exactly, as in the Second Bank of the United States (1818–24) in Philadelphia, designed by William Strickland. The white marble exterior was inspired by the recently published restoration drawings of the Parthenon by JAMES STUART and NICHOLAS REVETT. The Greek Revival soon established itself as the style for public and government buildings, for example Alexander Parris's Quincy Market (1825–6) in Boston, MA, and Robert Mills's US Treasury Building (1836–42), Washington, DC.

The adaptation of the Greek temple for white-painted wood-frame houses was uniquely American. Many were built in upper New York state and throughout the developing Northwest Territory. Unlike the earlier Federal style house, the Greek Revival house was more nearly square

6. Daniel D. Badger and John P. Gaynor: Haughwout Building, New York, 1856–7

in plan, with a low pitched roof, and the entrance through a portico on one of the gable ends. One example is the Boody House, called Rose Hill (*c.* 1835), outside Geneva, NY. One reason for the widespread popularity of such houses was the availability of engravings of the classical orders, especially in the new pattern books produced by MINARD LAFEVER. His most influential book, *The Modern Builder's Guide* (1833), contains detailed plates of the orders, elaborate house plans, and even a design for a simpler Grecian house that could be built with plain wooden boards, eliminating costly carved ornament. Thus popularized, the Greek Revival spread throughout the USA, especially in the ante-bellum South (*see also* PATTERN BOOK, §I, 2(ii)).

During the late 1830s, however, a broadly interpreted medieval idiom began to be used for country houses. This style was popularized by A. J. DOWNING in his two books, *Cottage Residences* (1842) and *The Architecture of Country Houses* (1850). A horticulturist, Downing advocated the fusion of the building and its landscape. For him the most appropriate setting was one in which plants and topography asserted their own character rather than having a geometric shape imposed. The architecture complementing such a landscape was to have similar irregularity and roughness; thus Downing preferred medieval vernacular and Gothic forms. The houses illustrated in his books, designed by such prominent architects as Alexander Jackson Davis, often had irregular, L-shaped plans, elaborate

medieval details, steeply gabled roofs and dormers, and broad porches from which to survey the surrounding landscape. A characteristic example is the Nicholls-McKim House (1858–9), Llewellyn Park, West Orange, NJ. This is doubly significant for being built in a utopian suburb outside New York. Llewellyn Park, begun by manufacturer Llewellyn Haskell in 1852, was an ideal retreat from the city made possible by the rapidly expanding railway. The site for Llewellyn Park was a steeply rolling hillside in which the streets were laid out to follow the topography, leaving a strip of public park along a stream, and realizing Downing's recommended reciprocal relationship between buildings and landscape.

The various historical styles became invested with associational meanings, so that Roman or Greek classicism was deemed appropriate for public and commercial buildings, and Downing's medievalism was viewed as suitable for country residences. A more 'correct' Gothic idiom became established for churches (especially Episcopalian) through the efforts of Richard Upjohn (*see* UPJOHN, (1)). Although he employed a variety of stylistic idioms, he became best known as an advocate of 14th- and 15th-century English Gothic for churches. His best-known application is Trinity Church (1839–46), New York, which is reminiscent of A. W. N. Pugin's work.

A more generic medievalism was established for prisons and was promoted by JOHN HAVILAND in his Eastern State Penitentiary (1821–5), Philadelphia, PA. If the heavy medievalism of the outer walls was retardataire compared to European historicism, the arrangement of individual cells in radiating arms for easier central control was radically new, and established a system of prison design named after Haviland, and which was closely studied by European penal experts. Haviland also used Egyptian motifs for some of his prisons, such as the Halls of Justice (1835; destr.) in New York, popularly known as The Tombs, but Egyptian motifs were more commonly used for cemeteries, for example Henry Austin's massive pylon gate (1845–8) for the Grove Street Cemetery, New Haven, CT.

Other stylistic idioms employed in the early 19th century included the round-arched Romanesque Revival used in THOMAS TEFFT's expansive Union Passenger Railroad Station (1848–55; destr. 1896), Providence, RI, and JAMES RENWICK's Smithsonian Institution (1847–55) in Washington, DC. It is significant that these were new building-types that had appeared in the early part of the century. Romanesque details were used for such buildings, as this style had less firmly established associational links than did Greek or Gothic. However, in the USA at this time the connections between historic detail and function were far less fixed than in Europe.

Industrialization had a major influence on American architecture. As in Britain, manufacturers quickly turned to making parts of buildings in cast iron. One example is the Haughwout Building (1856–7), New York, designed by JOHN P. GAYNOR but better known as the work of its manufacturer, DANIEL D. BADGER (see fig. 6; *see also* NEW YORK, fig. 1). Entire façades of such buildings were assembled from identical prefabricated pieces of cast iron bolted together, with wide glazed window-openings. The Haughwout Building was also notable for containing the first steam-operated passenger lift, which made feasible the construction of higher commercial buildings. Mechanization made an even more dramatic impact on house construction. Standardized, machine-cut pieces of timber were assembled rapidly into a complete house-frame held together by cheap, machine-made wire nails. A carpenter could hammer together such a balloon frame in the space of one day, needing none of the skills of a traditional joiner in cutting mortice-and-tenon joints.

3. THE CIVIL WAR AND LATE 19TH-CENTURY ECLECTICISM. The limits of literal replication gradually became apparent, and architects needed to use historical references more inventively for new building-types. In the USA this shift coincided with the outbreak of the Civil War, although little civil building took place between 1860 and 1866. Just before the war Americans had become aware of the new French mode of classical design exemplified by the additions (1852–7) of Visconti and Lefuel to the Musée du Louvre in Paris, just as they also read avidly the views of John Ruskin. The result was that almost immediately after the war, fully developed versions of both the French Second Empire style and the English High Victorian Gothic appeared in the USA.

The Second Empire style was employed for similar building-types to those previously designed in the Greek Revival style—commercial buildings, banks, office blocks, and especially governmental buildings. The Second Empire style was characterized by pavilions with mansard (gambrel) roofs, connected by lower wings also with mansard roofs. Such a composition allowed these buildings to be built on large irregular sites, for example Alfred B. Mullett's triangular post office (1869–75; destr. 1939), New York. Other examples include Mullett's Executive Office Building (1871–6; originally the State, War and Navy Building) next to the White House in Washington, DC, and the Philadelphia City Hall (1871–1901), by John McArthur jr. The tall mansard-capped tower also became identified with the houses of the growing upper middle class in the 1870s and 1880s.

High Victorian Gothic developed from the writings of John Ruskin, who advocated the development of a new Gothic idiom suited to modern needs but inspired by the commercial Gothic of Venice. This was to be a boldly irregular and colourful Gothic architecture, freed of archaeological dependence in its massing and details. Like the Gothic Revival of the 1840s and 1850s, however, this idiosyncratic High Victorian Gothic was used for churches, collegiate buildings and some houses. Two examples illustrating the use of variously coloured materials are the Old South Church (1876), Copley Square, Boston, by CUMMINGS & SEARS and the Memorial Hall (1870–78) at Harvard University, Cambridge, MA, by William Robert Ware and Henry Van Brunt. This style allowed the architect an almost unprecedented margin for invention, and FRANK FURNESS was perhaps the most successful in exploiting this. Several of his extant buildings have been restored, most notably his Pennsylvania Academy of the Fine Arts (1871–6), Philadelphia, a combined public gallery and art school. Furness was one of a new group of architects who began to redirect the course of American architecture in the 1870s and 1880s. Their extensive formal training was strongly influenced by the academic programme of the Ecole des Beaux-Arts in Paris. In Furness's case, this influence was indirect, through his teacher Richard Morris Hunt (see HUNT, (2)), who had been a student at the Ecole des Beaux-Arts for nine years, and who had supervised construction of the additions to the Louvre under Lefuel. Hunt returned to the USA in 1855 and established in New York a studio where he trained some of the most important architects active at the end of the century, including Furness and George Browne Post. The French influence is most apparent in Hunt's command of historical detail, unparalleled at the time. This was demonstrated in his French Renaissance-style residence for William Kissam Vanderbilt (1879–82; destr.), Fifth Avenue, New York, which established Hunt as the architect for the very wealthy.

After the Civil War domestic architecture became the focus of stylistic experimentation. The New Jersey coast and Newport, RI, became the settings for the creation of two new informal residential styles. The STICK STYLE (c. 1870–80) developed out of High Victorian Gothic and employed multiple, intersecting steep roofs with prominent gables and exposed timbers. Such houses were usually completely surrounded by verandahs. The basic elements of this style are evident in the Jacob Cram House (1872) of Middletown, RI, believed to be by Dudley Newton. The spiky appearance of the Stick style soon gave way to the greater integration and stylistic unity of the SHINGLE STYLE (c. 1880 to 1895), which exploited long sweeping roofs and wall surfaces covered with wooden shingles. Windows and porches were grouped more harmoniously than in the Stick style. Shingle style houses had large rooms grouped around a spacious central hall dominated by a hearth and a staircase, ascending by means of various landings. A particularly good example is the Isaac Bell House (1881–3; see MCKIM, MEAD & WHITE, fig. 1), Newport, RI, by McKim, Mead & White, who were leading practitioners of this idiom. Although these styles were at first used in houses for the very wealthy, they soon appeared in such popular pattern books as those of Paliser & Paliser and thus spread across the USA.

Commercial architecture after the Civil War was usually either Second Empire style or High Victorian Gothic, but increasingly in the major commercial centres the emphasis was on size and height. In New York new records were quickly set in building height, with the Equitable Life Assurance Company Building (1868–70; destr.) by Gilman, Kendall & Post, which rose to 39 m, then superseded by Richard Morris Hunt's *New York Tribune* Building (1873–6; destr.), which rose to an astonishing 78 m. Boisterous assertiveness in these commercial blocks was characteristic in the post-Civil War period, but a measure of authoritative calm was introduced by the most influential architect of this period, H. H. RICHARDSON. By 1872 he had developed a highly individual style that employed great masses of solid masonry with stylized Romanesque ornament. His architecture was not of a Romanesque revival, but rather the result of careful analysis of functional requirements in dense building masses. Richardson's buildings had a monumental quality, an early example being his massive pyramidal Trinity Church (1875–7), Boston, MA,

7. Louis Sullivan and Dankmar Adler: Wainwright Building, St Louis, Missouri, 1890–91

but his best work was done towards the time of his early death, for example the Marshall Field Wholesale Store (1885–7; destr. 1930), Chicago, and Allegheny County Courthouse and Jail (1885–7), Pittsburgh, PA.

A detailed knowledge of history, honed by training in Paris studios, marked the last phase of eclecticism in the 19th century. After new schools of architecture were established in the USA (see §XV below), architects increasingly began to consider their designs as integrated wholes rather than a collection of historic details, the result of their intensive educational programme. They also began to devise new structural elements to enclose the spaces they desired, including metal and concrete frames and Gustavino tile vaults.

Perhaps the most important creation of American architects during this period, exceeding even the balloon frame in its social impact, was the metal-framed commercial SKYSCRAPER. Richard Morris Hunt had provided the conceptual model in his soaring tower for the *New York Tribune*, but the traditional load-bearing wall construction of such early skyscrapers limited their height. In Chicago WILLIAM LE BARON JENNEY was the first to substitute an internal metal skeleton to support all the wall and floor loads of a commercial office block in his Home Insurance Building (1883–5; destr. 1931; see CHICAGO, fig. 1). The technology of these first hybrid skeletons of cast- and wrought-iron and steel members was quickly perfected,

resulting in frames made entirely of steel in such towers as DANIEL H. BURNHAM and JOHN WELLBORN ROOT's Reliance Building (1889–95; see SKYSCRAPER, fig. 1). The architect who did most to determine the form of these metal-framed skyscrapers was LOUIS SULLIVAN, briefly a student at the Ecole, working with his partner, DANKMAR ADLER. Their trend-setting office towers included the Wainwright Building (1890–91; see fig. 7), St Louis, MO, and the Prudential (now Guaranty) Building, Buffalo, NY, in which continuous vertical lines stress the height of these skyscrapers (see SULLIVAN, LOUIS, fig. 1). Among important contributors to the developing Chicago school was the firm of HOLABIRD & ROCHE, founded in 1883. Another significant development in American building in this period was the long-span suspension bridge using twisted cables of steel wire, a method perfected by John Augustus Roebling and Washington Augustus Roebling (see ROEBLING) in their Brooklyn Bridge (1869–83; see NEW YORK, fig. 4). Bridge construction also influenced the technique and materials of metal-frame skyscraper design.

In the face of industrial expansion and social disruption during the 1870s, American architects and clients sought a sense of cultural continuity, admiring the balance and repose of Colonial and Federal style architecture. The result, beginning c. 1880 and widespread by the early 1890s, was a resurgence of academic classicism, in the form of a COLONIAL REVIVAL in domestic architecture. The leading advocate of this classicism was the firm of McKim, Mead & White, who introduced the Colonial Revival in their 18th-century style house (1883–5; destr. 1952) at Newport, RI, for H. A. C. Taylor. They also developed a more generic Italian Renaissance classicism for urban buildings in their six-house complex (1882–6; altered, 1975–6) for Henry G. Villard in New York and in the magisterial Boston Public Library (1887–95).

By the mid-1890s academic classicism had become the preferred idiom for urban buildings across the country, and the most influential event in popularizing this civic classicism was the World's Columbian Exposition (1893), Chicago. The team of architects who designed its buildings decided in favour of a unified ensemble of buildings in a Renaissance style (the only style all of them knew equally well; see BURNHAM, DANIEL H., fig. 1). The white plaster buildings of the Columbian Exposition spurred the CITY BEAUTIFUL MOVEMENT, which swept the USA at the turn of the century and led to the creation of scores of neo-classical civic centres. It also led Daniel H. Burnham to devote his energies to urban planning, then in its infancy.

4. THE CHICAGO SCHOOL, THE PRAIRIE SCHOOL, ACADEMIC ECLECTICISM AND THE RISE OF MODERNISM. Among the most potent agents shaping American architecture in the early 20th century were the progressive architects now labelled the CHICAGO SCHOOL. Although the movement had reached maturity by the turn of the century, its most incisive thinker, Louis Sullivan, had by then separated from Dankmar Adler, and had begun a slow decline into virtual obscurity. During his enforced leisure, however, he wrote his theoretical study *A System of Ornament According with a Philosophy of Man's Powers* (1922–4) and his *Autobiography of an Idea* (New York, 1924) among other essays. The further development of

the Chicago skyscraper was carried on by Burnham & Root, particularly by the younger partners. Burnham's planning projects included a master plan for Chicago, finished in 1909. The firm of Holabird & Roche was especially active, developing a standardized form for their office towers, as characterized by their white terracotta-clad Republic Building (1905–9; destr. 1961).

The other principal focus of the progressive Chicago architects was the suburban family house. The most revolutionary changes in its design were made by Frank Lloyd Wright (*see* WRIGHT, (1)). For his own house (and later studio) in the Chicago suburb of Oak Park (1889), Wright drew on the Shingle style favoured by J. L. Silsbee, then popular along the eastern seaboard. Wright's goals of ridding the house of applied ornament and of opening up and connecting its spaces were realized in a series of houses built around the turn of the century, particularly in the expansive Willits House (1902–6) in the suburb of Highland Park (see fig. 8; for plan *see* WRIGHT, (1), fig. 1). Scores of houses followed, all with these characteristics, relating the house to the flat Midwestern prairie by emphasizing the horizontal line. In his few non-residential buildings—most notably the Larkin Building (1903–6; destr. 1950), Buffalo, NY, and the Unity Temple (1905–8), Oak Park (*see* WRIGHT, (1), figs 2 and 3)—Wright turned the cubic masses in upon themselves, creating inwardly focused spaces.

Wright attracted to his studio a number of associates (most of whom soon left to set up their own practices) including Marion Mahony (later Mahony Griffin) and Walter Burley Griffin. These disciples, together with Wright, established a PRAIRIE SCHOOL, which existed until World War I. Their work should also be considered part of the Arts and Crafts Movement, whose chief American proponent was GUSTAV STICKLEY. Also related to this Arts and Crafts aesthetic is the work of the brothers Charles Sumner Greene and Henry Mather Greene (*see* GREENE & GREENE) of Pasadena, CA. Their masterwork, the David B. Gamble House (1908), Pasadena, synthesizes elements of the Stick style, the Shingle style, Japanese architecture and construction methods, with Arts and Crafts interiors and furnishings (*see* ARTS AND CRAFTS MOVEMENT, fig. 2).

The Chicago skeletal metal frame for commercial skyscrapers was quickly adopted in New York. By 1900 office towers in New York were being built higher than those in Chicago. Because of greater height and smaller building sites, New York skyscrapers took on the form of a slender spire rising from a lower block. This profile was used by ERNEST FLAGG in his soaring Singer Building tower (1906–8; destr. 1967–8), whose 47 storeys rose 186.54 m, and by CASS GILBERT in his even higher Woolworth Building (1910–13), whose 55 storeys rose 231.95 m and held the record for height until 1930.

After 1915 civilian construction slowed down in the USA as World War I dominated political and economic developments. After the war, in contrast to the spirit advocating a revolutionary modern architecture in Europe, there flourished an academic eclecticism, which paralleled American political isolationism. The inspiration for this lay in the work of such architects as MCKIM, MEAD & WHITE. Their major building of the early years of the

8. Frank Lloyd Wright: Ward Willits House, Highland Park, Illinois, 1902

century was Pennsylvania Station (1902–11; destr. 1963–5), New York, which formed a node of majestic order at the end of the railway line into the city.

Academic eclecticism also prevailed in church design. The Gothic Revival was vigorously championed by RALPH ADAMS CRAM together with BERTRAM GOODHUE and was taken up by other architects. Cram & Goodhue's work is well represented in St Thomas's (1905–14), Fifth Avenue, New York. Cram later developed an immense Gothic scheme for St John the Divine, Amsterdam Avenue, New York, on which he worked from 1912 until 1941, and which was still under construction in 1988.

In city centres the continuing City Beautiful Movement inspired classical city halls, court-houses and public libraries until the mid-1930s, but as before the spirit of American inventiveness focused on the creation of a new generation of office skyscrapers. Some of these office towers had historical trappings, such as the Gothic competition-winning design for the Tribune Tower (1922–5), Chicago, by JOHN MEAD HOWELLS and RAYMOND HOOD; its grey limestone exterior was closely based on the 15th-century Tour de Beurre at Rouen by Guillaume Pontis. Eliel Saarinen's design, which won second prize, had an even stronger influence on subsequent skyscraper design, however, despite remaining unexecuted. He achieved the legally required reduction in area by means of many subtle setbacks and used ornament in traditional but original ways. After emigrating to the USA (1923) Saarinen founded the Cranbrook Academy of Art (1925) at Bloomfield Hills, MI, with a curriculum derived from the Finnish Arts and Crafts Movement.

With the strong recovery of business in the 1920s, architects were called on to design stately suburban homes as, increasingly, the wealthy fled the urban core. A characteristic example, which also documents another change radically affecting American social patterns, is the residence for Edsel Ford (1927), Grosse Pointe, MI, designed by ALBERT KAHN. This house is an amalgam of medieval elements evoking an English manor house. Similar houses were built in the 1920s in suburbs outside every major city, in styles inspired by medieval or Italian Renaissance or English Baroque models.

9. Albert Kahn: Dodge Half-Ton Truck Plant, Detroit, Michigan, 1937

In the late 1920s in office tower designs American architects drew on European Art Deco to create bold geometric ornamental and coloured patterns. Almost every major city acquired at least one Art Deco skyscraper, of which the Chrysler Building (1928–30; *see* SKYSCRAPER, fig. 2), New York, by WILLIAM VAN ALEN is a characteristic example. Height was still paramount, and Van Alen's building was soon overtopped by the Empire State Building (1929–31) by SHREVE, LAMB & HARMON, whose height of 381 m was unsurpassed until 1965.

Another new building type in which American architects revelled was the CINEMA. This quickly became a rich field for inventive escapism with the creation of elaborate environments of fantasy that rivalled the films themselves. French Baroque and Spanish Renaissance were favoured styles, often combined in wondrously florid extravaganzas. Several have been restored to their original brilliance, often serving new uses, such as the huge Chicago Theater (1920–21), by Cornelius and George Rapp, now used for popular music concerts.

While individual houses, urban and public buildings were treated with emblematic eclecticism and richly elaborate ornament, factories and other utilitarian buildings were designed in lean, functional modernism. A leading architect in this field was Albert Kahn. Among his earliest factory designs were concrete-frame factories for car manufacturers in Detroit, such as the Packard and Ford plants of 1905 and 1908–10. These and similar factories were much admired by Walter Gropius and Le Corbusier. Kahn continued to pioneer such new construction methods as wide-span steel trusses and single-level factories in his Dodge Half-Ton Truck Plant (1937; see fig. 9), Detroit. During the Depression of the 1930s, lean functional utilitarianism was also employed in public works projects. Among the best examples are the massive dams and electrical generating plants of the Tennessee Valley Authority, including the Kentucky Dam (1938–44), designed by ROLAND WANK and his team of architects and engineers. The architect Bertram Goodhue attempted to bring these disparate elements of historicism and functionalism together, as seen, for example, in his competition-winning design for the Nebraska State Capitol (1919–32), Lincoln,

with a broad cross-in-square plan (reminiscent of well-established Beaux-Arts schemes) and a metal-framed skyscraper tower rising from its centre. Inside and out, boldly abstracted sculpture and tile mosaic create an environment that is at once both traditional and modern.

In 1911 at Spring Green, WI, Frank Lloyd Wright built his house, Taliesin, a culmination of the Prairie-house type. During the 1920s he explored other expressions, using his own form of prefabricated concrete block for houses in California that referred to Pre-Columbian sources. In 1936 a new phase in his career was inaugurated by two designs: the weekend house, Fallingwater (1936–9) in western Pennsylvania, and the Johnson Wax Administration Building (1936–9), Racine, WI. In both Wright exploited the possibilities of reinforced concrete, using spreading cantilevered floor-trays in Fallingwater (for illustration *see* CANTILEVER), and tall columns with broad capitals like lily pads in the spacious central office of Johnson Wax (for illustration *see* OFFICE BUILDING). Having rejected the idea of the traditional city, Wright modelled his version of the future, with individual houses spread across the landscape, in 'Broadacre City' (early 1930s). Out of this emerged his concept of the single-family Usonian house, compact and exploiting methods of prefabrication to reduce the cost. A number of such houses were built in Wisconsin and Michigan during the 1930s. A high point in his long career was the Solomon R. Guggenheim Museum (designed 1943; built 1957–60), New York. Like his other urban buildings, this was inwardly focused, formed by a huge spiral ramp in reinforced concrete that defined a central glass-domed space.

5. AFTER WORLD WAR II: MODERNISM, NEO-EXPRESSIONISM, POST-MODERNISM. Although Wright enjoyed significant notoriety in his later years, by far the greater impact was made by European emigrant architects who espoused a radically new architecture. Wright had in fact helped start this trend, for publication of his designs attracted two Viennese architects to the USA: RUDOLPH SCHINDLER and RICHARD NEUTRA. Both worked briefly for Wright and then settled in Los Angeles, where they developed their own variants of Modernism filtered through the influence of Wright. Another immigrant was PIETRO BELLUSCHI, who, after working briefly as a mining engineer in Idaho, worked in the architectural office of A. E. Doyle (d 1928) in Portland, OR. After 1930 he gradually moved away from the academic eclecticism practised by Doyle and developed his own variant of modern functionalism, signalled by the Portland Art Museum (1931–8). During the next 25 years he developed an open house-type, touched perhaps by the influence of Wright, exploiting wood construction and unique to the Pacific Northwest. Belluschi's Northwest residences were paralleled by a regional style in the San Francisco Bay Area advanced by WILLIAM WILSON WURSTER in the 1950s. The greatest European influence on American architecture began with the flight of artists and intellectuals from Nazi Germany. By 1938 Walter Gropius had left the Bauhaus and was head of the Graduate School of Design at Harvard University, Cambridge, MA. In the USA Gropius's influence was felt primarily through the scores of young

architects whom he trained and through the new curriculum he instituted at Harvard, which spearheaded the abandonment of the Beaux-Arts method of design instruction in American architectural schools.

Even more decisive was the influence of Gropius's successor as head of the Bauhaus, Ludwig Mies van der Rohe, who gave definitive form to the post-war American office skyscraper. (The only earlier example of an American Modernist skyscraper was the Philadelphia Savings Funds Society Building (1929–33), by GEORGE HOWE in collaboration with the Swiss architect WILLIAM EDMOND LESCAZE.) Mies came to the USA in 1937 and accepted the position of Director of Architecture at the Armour (later Illinois) Institute of Technology. Although he was a teacher like Gropius, Mies's profound influence came through his austere buildings, reduced to a bare minimum of metal frame and glass, and beginning with the Lake Shore Drive Apartments (1948–51; see fig. 10), Chicago, and the elegant Seagram Building (1954–8), Park Avenue, New York.

The principal agent in spreading this new architectural language of the International style world-wide was the architectural firm SKIDMORE, OWINGS & MERRILL (SOM), based in Chicago and then with branch offices in New York, San Francisco, Portland, OR, and elsewhere; by the mid-1980s there were 47 partners and more than 1400 architects in this giant multi-national firm. The original partnership rose to prominence with Gordon Bunshaft's design for the Lever House (1950–52; see INTERNATIONAL STYLE, fig. 2), New York, based closely on the glass towers of the Lake Shore Drive Apartments. Subsequently the firm specialized in metal and glass corporate headquarter towers, of which the Chase Manhattan Bank (1957–61),

New York, is but one example. In the mid-1960s SOM introduced a new scale to urban office building with the design of the John Hancock Center (1965–79) and the Sears Tower (1970–74; see SKYSCRAPER, fig. 3), both in Chicago. These buildings used the new principle of a vertical cantilevered tube to withstand enormous wind pressure and to reduce the amount of structural steel.

PHILIP JOHNSON was also important in preparing the way for Mies. He helped to organize the exhibition of *Modern Architecture of Europe* at MOMA, New York, in 1932, the first presentation of such architecture in the USA. Johnson modelled his own Glass House (1949) at New Canaan, CT, on Mies's design for a residence for Dr Edith Farnsworth (executed 1945–50), Plano, IL. For the next few years Johnson and Mies worked closely together, Johnson collaborating with Mies in the design and construction of the Seagram Building (1954–8; with Kahn & Jacobs). The move away from Mies came in 1960, when Johnson designed a memorial church in New Harmony, IN, the moulded shingled roof of which contrasted with Mies's reductivism.

One architect who endeavoured to find the single most expressive form for each of his commissions was Eero Saarinen (*see* SAARINEN, (2)), the son of Eliel Saarinen. After finishing his architectural education at Yale University, Eero began practice in partnership with his father, and together in 1948 they won the competition for the Jefferson National Expansion Memorial in St Louis, MO, with their scheme for a gigantic reverse catenary arch (completed only in 1968). For the General Motors Technical Center (1945–55), Warren, MI, the Saarinens used a variation of Mies's purism (with brilliantly coloured glazed brick end-walls), but for the Kresge Auditorium and interdenominational chapel at the Massachusetts Institute of Technology (1950–55), Eero used a spherical shell and a cylinder. Two of his most expressive buildings, suggesting the levitation of flight, were designed for airports, first the wing-like cantilevered concrete shells for the Trans World Airlines (TWA) Terminal (1956–62; *see* ROOF, fig. 3) at Idlewild (now Kennedy) Airport, New York, and then the suspended-roof structure of the Dulles International Airport (1958–62) outside Washington, DC (for illustration *see* SAARINEN, (2)).

Louis Kahn established a position similar to that of Goodhue a generation earlier, seeking to resolve the Beaux-Arts interest in didactic form with the modernist insistence on structural precision and expression. His first major success was the Richards Medical Research Laboratories (1957–61) at the University of Pennsylvania, Philadelphia, in which 'served spaces' of research laboratories were defined by the 'servant spaces' comprising all the utilities, every element being expressive of the constructive process. This was followed by his Salk Institute for Biological Studies (1959–65) at La Jolla, CA, in which the constituent elements were even better articulated and the construction process more clearly revealed. A principal concern of Kahn's was admitting and manipulating natural light in his interiors, and frequently his buildings were shaped by their need for light, for example his Kimbell Art Museum (1966–72; for illustration *see* KAHN, LOUIS I.), Fort Worth, TX.

10. Ludwig Mies van der Rohe: Lake Shore Drive Apartments, Chicago, Illinois, 1948–51

Around 1965 a reaction began against the strictures of the International Style represented in the uniformity of the work of Mies van der Rohe. The galvanizing agent was a small book published by architect Robert Venturi (*see* VENTURI, RAUCH & SCOTT BROWN) called *Complexity and Contradiction in Architecture* (New York, 1966), which celebrates the multiple and ambiguous meanings of architecture, thereby criticizing the singularity of intent and the deliberate absence of understandable imagery of international modernism. Venturi demonstrated how this philosophy might be realized in such early works as Vanna Venturi House (1962), Chestnut Hill, Philadelphia.

By the early 1970s a number of alternative approaches to international Modernism had begun to emerge. In the area of corporate and speculative building, the endlessly repeated Miesian glass-box tower was replaced with experiments by architects to find recognizable images for office towers, like those of the Art Deco skyscrapers of the 1920s, giving form to corporate identities. Philip Johnson, with his partner John Burgee (*b* 1933), was among the first to play with form in this way, in his Pennzoil Place (1976), Houston, TX, and the classically inspired AT&T company headquarters (1983) in New York, with its so-called 'Chippendale' pediment (*see* POST-MODERNISM, fig. 1).

By far the most austere reaction was the minimalism espoused by PETER D. EISENMAN, who created an ascetic architecture of pure geometry expressing what he interpreted as the self-contained and non-referential language of architecture (readable only to a handful of initiates). A more derivative approach was that taken by RICHARD MEIER, whose geometrically abstract residences of the early 1970s (for illustration *see* MEIER, RICHARD), rendered in pure white, borrowed heavily from Le Corbusier's house designs of the late 1920s. In the various public buildings designed by Meier in the late 1970s, the geometries became more complex and ambiguous, and the historical references more inclusive, but the purity of surface and colour was made more emphatic by making use of white enamelled metal panels. These developments are well illustrated in Meier's High Museum of Art (1980–84; for illustration *see* ATLANTA), Atlanta, GA.

Another reaction to the universal prototypes of international Modernism was the new emphasis architects now gave to contextual response, a development that first appeared in California in the work of CHARLES W. MOORE and his associates. One of the earliest manifestations was the stylized Second Empire style massing of his firm's Citizens' Federal Savings and Loan Association (1962), San Francisco, which reiterated the principal forms of the original bank next door. A parallel approach was taken in his firm's Sea Ranch condominium complex (1965–72), designed for a coastal bluff north of San Francisco. The design was carefully studied in wind-tunnel models to find the optimum living conditions for this environment, and the results were rugged wood siding and sharply angled shed roofs. In his work of the late 1980s Moore moved in a direction similar to that of Robert Venturi, since both took up the use of abstracted ornament, another Postmodernist response, either inventing ornamental patterns when the immediate context reveals no prevailing motif, or deriving their motifs from local sources to maintain contextualism. Venturi's shingled Trubeck and Wislocki homes (1970), Nantucket Island, MA, show his high regard for local early 19th-century models; and Moore, in his proposal for the Beverly Hills Civic Center (1982), made reference to the then-prevailing Spanish Renaissance historicist themes, long popular in southern California.

Revivalism was another reaction to international Modernism, for example of neo-classicism for public buildings, or of the 19th-century Shingle style for residences. ROBERT A. M. STERN was particularly successful in his references to the Shingle style in a number of summer and weekend houses on Long Island, NY, built in the 1970s and early 1980s. Even such advocates of Modernism as SOM adopted neo-classicism when the context suggested it was appropriate (e.g. competition entry, 1986, for the extension of McKim, Mead & White's classical Brooklyn Museum, begun 1894). However, designing a meaningful public architecture became more challenging, particularly because of the high cost of elegant durable materials such as marble and bronze, the high cost of artisans to shape these materials, and the stringent budgets made available by a public unwilling to regard architecture as a long-term investment. The Portland Building (1978–82; see fig. 11), Portland, OR, by MICHAEL GRAVES won a design competition partly because it alone met the tight city budget. Responding to the adjoining older classical City Hall and Court House, Graves attempted to allude to their classical language; the ornament is of paint and plaster. By the late 20th century American architects were struggling to frame a coherent view of their art and the direction it should take.

11. Michael Graves: Portland Building, Portland, Oregon, 1978–82

BIBLIOGRAPHY

G. H. Edgell: *The American Architecture of Today* (New York, 1928)

F. Lloyd Wright: *An Autobiography* (New York, 1932, rev. 4/1977)

T. Hamlin: *Greek Revival Architecture in America* (New York, 1944/*R* 1966)

E. Mock, ed.: *Built in the USA since 1932* (New York, 1945)

J. M. Fitch: *American Building: The Historical Forces that Shaped it* (Boston, MA, 1948, 2/1966)

H.-R. Hitchcock and A. Drexler, eds: *Built in the USA: Post-war Architecture* (New York, 1952)

H. Morrison: *Early American Architecture, from the First Colonial Settlements to the National Period* (New York, 1952)

L. Mumford: *Roots of Contemporary American Architecture* (New York, 1952)

W. Andrews: *Architecture, Ambition and Americans* (New York, 1955, 2/1964)

V. J. Scully jr: *The Shingle Style and the Stick Style* (New Haven, CT, 1955, 2/1971)

H.-R. Hitchcock: *Architecture, Nineteenth and Twentieth Centuries* (Harmondsworth, 1958, 4/1977)

E. McCoy: *Five California Architects* (New York, 1960)

V. J. Scully jr: *Frank Lloyd Wright* (New York, 1960)

J. Burchard and A. Bush-Brown: *The Architecture of America: A Social and Cultural History* (Boston, 1961, 2/1967)

W. von Eckardt, ed.: *Mid-century Architecture in America* (New York, 1961)

P. Heyer, ed.: *Architects on Architecture: New Directions in Architecture* (New York, 1966)

C. W. Condit: *American Building* (Chicago, 1968, 2/1982)

P. B. Stanton: *The Gothic Revival and American Church Architecture: An Episode in Taste, 1840–1856* (Baltimore, 1968)

V. J. Scully jr: *American Architecture and Urbanism* (New York, 1969)

R. A. M. Stern: *New Directions in American Architecture* (New York and London, 1969, rev. 1977)

W. H. Pierson jr: *The Colonial and Neo-Classical Styles*, i of *American Buildings and their Architects* (Garden City, NY, 1970)

W. H. Jordy: *The Impact of European Modernism in the Mid-twentieth Century*, iv of *American Buildings and their Architects* (Garden City, NY, 1972)

——: *Progressive and Academic Ideals at the Turn of the Century*, iii of *American Buildings and their Architects* (Garden City, NY, 1972)

L. Cummings: *The Framed Houses of Massachusetts Bay, 1625–1725* (Cambridge, MA, 1974)

C. Robinson and R. Haag Bletter: *Skyscraper Style: Art Deco in New York* (New York, 1975)

W. H. Pierson jr: *Technology and the Picturesque, the Corporate and early Gothic Styles*, ii of *American Buildings and their Architects* (Garden City, NY, 1978)

G. Ciucci, F. Dalco, M. Manieri-Elia and M. Tafuri: *The American City: From the Civil War to the Deal* (Cambridge, MA, 1979, 2/London, 1980)

L. M. Roth: *A Concise History of American Architecture* (New York and London, 1979, 2/1988)

M. Whiffen and F. Koeper: *American Architecture, 1607–1976* (Cambridge, MA, 1981)

L. M. Roth: *America Builds: Source Documents in American Architecture and Planning* (New York, 1983)

D. P. Handlin: *American Architecture* (London and New York, 1985)

LELAND M. ROTH

III. Painting and graphic arts.

1. The Colonial period, to 1820. 2. 19th-century developments. 3. Modernism: To World War II. 4. Abstract Expressionism, Pop, Minimalism and late 20th-century developments.

1. THE COLONIAL PERIOD, TO 1820. The opportunistic nature of early explorations and the impermanence of ill-fated settlements that characterized the period between 1492 and 1600 did not encourage elaborate artistic production among European colonists. It was not until the mid-17th century, after permanent civilian communities had begun to thrive in Philadelphia, New York, Boston and elsewhere, that notable paintings and prints were produced by artists resident in the colonies. However, the constant importation of paintings and reproductive prints, and the regular presence of artists trained in Europe—who emigrated, worked itinerantly throughout the colonies or made art in some official capacity such as that of military draughtsman—meant that in the 17th and 18th centuries Americans were accustomed to western European traditions and continued to be aware of the contemporary artistic developments in such centres as London, Paris and Rome. Political patterns of colonization, concentrated along the Atlantic seaboard, affected the visual arts in that they determined settlers' immediate sources of cultural training and conventions. As Britain secured control of North America in the 18th century, and as cities with strong economic and political ties to London—such as Boston, New York, Philadelphia and Charleston—simultaneously grew and prospered, British art and aesthetic sensibilities dominated American cultural development throughout the North American colonies. Consequently, French influence along the Mississippi and the St Lawrence rivers and the Spanish presence in Florida and the far Southwest had little lasting impact on the development of the fine arts.

Most works produced during the Colonial period were commissioned or purchased for domestic situations, and this dictated the predominance of modestly sized easel paintings and of such subjects as portraits, still-lifes and landscapes, rather than grandiose religious or historical images. Indeed, when attempted soon after independence, history painting met with little enthusiasm. Prints designed and produced in the USA were published in books or general digest-type magazines, individually on speculation to be sold in art-supply and stationery shops, or in portfolios by subscription from private individuals. Portraits and landscape scenery were the most common subjects. While American printmakers most frequently employed simple line engraving, they also worked with aquatint and mezzotint.

The painters responsible for most extant 17th-century New England portraits remain anonymous, although scholars have identified individual artists at work in discrete groups of images. The finest of these was the painter of *Mrs John (Elizabeth) Freake and her Baby Mary* (1670; Worcester, MA, A. Mus.; see MASTERS, ANONYMOUS, AND MONOGRAMMISTS, §I: FREAKE PAINTER). This image of a prosperous Boston matron and her child exemplifies the transatlantic migration of late Elizabethan style and form in its flat, straightforward presentation, dark background punctuated by rudimentary drapery and close attention to intricate decorative patterns. The only contemporary painter whose name is known is THOMAS SMITH (ii), to whom a number of Boston portraits have been attributed, including a *Self-portrait* (1670–91; Worcester, MA, A. Mus.) with *memento mori* objects. Smith's more robust tone and occasional insertion of narrative scenery behind his sitters anticipated the relative sophistication and complexity introduced to American portraiture by the Scottish-born John Smibert. Smibert settled in Boston in the early 1730s, bringing with him the portrait style of Godfrey Kneller and Peter Lely then current in London. His large conversation piece *Bermuda Group* (1729–31; New Haven, CT, Yale U. A.G.) demonstrates an easy competence in handling full figures and natural scenery unprecedented in the

12. John Singleton Copley: *Mrs Ezekiel Goldthwait (Elizabeth Lewis)*, oil on canvas, 1.27×1.01 m, 1771 (Boston, MA, Museum of Fine Arts)

The careers of the native-born colonials JOHN SINGLETON COPLEY and BENJAMIN WEST mark the beginning of an efflorescence of American art. Although both men, natives of Boston and Pennsylvania respectively, spent most of their careers in London, their work was certainly strongly flavoured by their Colonial origins and had an immense impact on the young Americans who went abroad to study with them. Copley, who educated himself with imported prints and closely studied the work of Smibert and such travellers as Blackburn, had by the 1760s and early 1770s attained a personal style in portraiture, distinguished by a crisp light full of subtle colour, sumptuous textures and a penetrating appraisal of his sitters, a style exemplified in his portrait of *Mrs Ezekiel Goldthwait (Elisabeth Lewis*; 1771; see fig. 12). Although his work became grander after he moved to London with his Loyalist in-laws in the 1770s, Copley never surpassed the individualistic boldness of his late Boston portraits. West, influenced by the itinerant Williams and sent to Italy and England for study by a group of Philadelphia educators and philanthropists in 1760, became history painter to the court of George III and in 1792 second President of the Royal Academy of Arts, London. West's early work is marked by a smooth, almost Neo-classical manner, but as his career progressed his hand became increasingly loose and almost romantic in its emotional drama. Although much of his work depicts standard mythological and scriptural subjects, West made a major innovation in history painting with the *Death of General Wolfe* (1770; Ottawa, N.G.), in which contemporary clothing and a realistic setting rather than timeless classical accessories commemorate the British victory at Quebec (*see* WEST, BENJAMIN, fig. 1).

Painters who came to maturity during the Revolution sought to blend the European sophistication of their models—Smibert, Copley and West—with fresh, distinctly American subjects and approaches. Charles Willson Peale, a Philadelphia portrait painter with an astonishing range of interests from natural history to progressive agriculture, infused his likenesses with both tender familial sentiment and adamant political commentary, as did other members of his family (*see* PEALE). A student also of landscape and still-life, he often included these as personally symbolic elements in portraits, as in *William Smith and Grandson* (1788; Richmond, VA, Mus. F.A.). GILBERT STUART, a contemporary whose informal, loose style, imitative of Gainsborough and his followers, is very different from Peale's simplicity, returned in the early 1790s from a lengthy period in England and Ireland to become the most popular portrait painter of the nation's emerging Federalist élite. Persuaded by West that the new nation should glorify and preserve the pivotal episodes of its birth, Connecticut native John Trumbull sought to launch an indigenous tradition of history painting. Deviating from his master's dignified reserve towards a more personally felt, earnest interpretation of events that his generation had experienced closely, Trumbull planned a series of Revolutionary images commemorating key battles and political debates, such as the *Declaration of Independence* (1786; New Haven, CT, Yale U. A.G.; for illustration *see* TRUMBULL, JOHN). History painting was likewise the principal occupation of John Vanderlyn, who trained in Paris and brought the cool

colonies (for illustration *see* SMIBERT, JOHN). Smibert's London training, his collection of paintings gathered in Italy and fine prints imported from London, and his richly coloured portraits for prosperous mercantile families provided models for several generations of American painters. His most immediate heir was ROBERT FEKE, a native of Long Island who was active in Rhode Island and Boston, and whose facility for opulent textures and imitation of English portrait compositions and poses (e.g. *James Bowdoin*, 1748; Brunswick, ME, Bowdoin Coll. Mus. A.) rivalled Smibert's own.

Smibert was the first and best of a number of painters who left Europe and spread simplified and sometimes awkward versions of their native late Baroque styles throughout the colonies in the early 1700s. English and Dutch portrait painters active in Manhattan Island and the Hudson River Valley remain anonymous. Simplicity and realism characterize the work of Gustavus Hesselius, a Swedish artist active in the Middle Atlantic region, while the work of the German immigrant Justus Engelhardt Kuhn, active in Maryland, is marked by intricate, elaborate backgrounds and an emphasis on ornate costume. Portraits by Jeremiah Theus, a Swiss who settled in Charleston, show an incipient Rococo lightness in colour and form. This form of pretty elegance found its fullest expression in the colonies at mid-century in the work of the itinerant, wide-ranging Englishmen John Wollaston, Joseph Blackburn and William Williams.

sharpness of French Neo-classicism to peculiarly American subjects. In such works as the *Murder of Jane McCrea* (1804; Hartford, CT, Wadsworth Atheneum) Vanderlyn sought to marry the drama of frontier settlement to ennobling, Classically inspired figures and monumental composition (for illustration *see* VANDERLYN, JOHN). America's pioneer Romantic painter was WASHINGTON ALLSTON, also a student of West. Concentrating on the realm of the imagination, the emotions and the soul, as in *Hermia and Helena* (*c.* 1818; see fig. 13), Allston's work is distinguished by lush colours, complex glazes and loose brushwork. He was particularly interested in literary subjects that broached the intricate connection between vision and the spoken word.

Although landscape did not become a major theme in American art until the 1830s, the subject had been pursued and appreciated for decades. Immigrant painters and printmakers trained in England brought with them the soft, graceful Picturesque modes then current. Peale, Trumbull and Allston all experimented with native landscape subjects, but American-born painters THOMAS DOUGHTY and ALVAN FISHER were the first to specialize in the genre. Their work, sometimes marred by an inarticulate haziness or a cloying charm, at least recognized American scenery as a legitimate subject and at best introduced the identification of nationalism with place, which became a central inspiration of subsequent landscape painters.

The work of native-born printmakers, generally trained as artisans (such as the silversmith and printmaker PAUL REVERE), is generally coarse and awkward. Subjects included original themes, as in Revere's engraving *Boston Massacre* (1770; New York, Pub. Lib.), copies after American painters and the quasi-industrial decoration of banknotes and business documents. As in painting, immigrant artists contributed considerably to the overall quality of American printmaking. The elegant cityscapes and views of country houses of William Russell Birch (1755–1834), for example, were notable examples for Americans to emulate. Magazines published in Philadelphia and New York provided such fledgling American printmakers as James Trenchard (*b* 1747) and CORNELIUS TIEBOUT with an outlet for original, if rather crudely executed, compositions. ASHER B. DURAND, the most accomplished native-born and trained engraver of the early 1800s, later turned to painting.

While scholars seeking to identify the distinguishing features of American art in this period have noted a fascination with tangible reality and a resultant focus on realistic texture and form (as in Copley's Boston portraits) or a willingness to challenge tradition (as in West's contemporary heroes), American art was to establish a distinctive and independent character. This process had only just begun by 1820, and the art of the USA before that time is often marked by a distinct simplicity or literalness in its interpretation of contemporary styles. Although Peale and Trumbull certainly attempted to address specifically national concerns in their work, it was not until the generation of Allston and Vanderlyn that Americans began confidently to innovate in aesthetic terms.

13. Washington Allston: *Hermia and Helena*, oil on canvas, 737×635 mm, *c.* 1818 (Washington, DC, National Museum of American Art)

BIBLIOGRAPHY

W. Dunlap: *History of the Rise and Progress of the Arts of Design in the United States*, 3 vols (New York, 1834)
D. M. Stauffer and M. Fiedling: *American Engravers upon Copper and Steel* (New York, 1907/*R* Philadelphia, 1917)
F. Weitenkampf: *American Graphic Art* (New York, 1912)
——: 'Early American Landscape Prints', *A. Q.* [Detroit], viii (1945), pp. 40–67
G. C. Groce and D. H. Wallace: *The New York Historical Society's Dictionary of Artists in America, 1564–1860* (New York, 1957)
J. Dolmetsch: 'Prints in Colonial America: Supply and Demand in the Mid-18th Century', *Prints in and of America to 1850*, ed. J. D. Morse (Charlottesville, 1970), pp. 53–74
The Flowering of American Folk Art, 1776–1876 (exh. cat. by J. Lipman and A. Winchester, New York, Whitney, 1974)
H. Honour: *The European Vision of America* (Cleveland, 1975)
J. Dolmetsch, ed.: *Eighteenth Century Prints in Colonial America: To Educate and Decorate* (Charlottesville, 1979)
J. L. Fairbanks and R. F. Trent, eds: *New England Begins*, 3 vols (Boston, 1982)
N. Harris: *The Artist in American Society: The Formative Years, 1790–1860* (Chicago, 1982)
J. Poesch: *The Art of the Old South: Painting, Sculpture, Architecture and the Products of Craftsmen, 1550–1860* (New York, 1983)
E. J. Nygren, ed.: *Views and Visions: American Landscape before 1830* (Washington, DC, 1986)
J. Yarnall and W. H. Gerdts: *The National Museum of American Art's Index to American Art Exhibition Catalogues from the Beginning through the 1876 Centennial Year*, 6 vols (Boston, 1986)
R. H. Saunders and E. Miles: *American Colonial Portraits, 1770–1776* (Washington, DC, 1987)

KAROL ANN PEARD LAWSON

2. 19TH-CENTURY DEVELOPMENTS. As the USA expanded in the first half of the 19th century, artists shared in this process of nation building by developing an

American style and mythology. Although portraiture and history painting were vehicles for nationalistic sentiments, landscape and genre played a particularly active role in defining the country and its people. From 1821 to 1825 the *Hudson River Portfolio* was published in New York by the watercolourist William Guy Wall and the engraver John Hill. Charting the river from its source to New York harbour, this series of 20 aquatints is one of the early masterpieces of American graphic art. The prints reveal a debt to British practice and theory, particularly the aesthetic concepts of the Sublime, the Beautiful and the Picturesque.

With the rise to prominence of THOMAS COLE in 1825, landscape painting began to glorify the wilder aspects of American scenery. Among his first works was *Falls of Kaaterskill* (1826; Tuscaloosa, AL, Warner Col. Gulf States Paper Corp.), in which a Native American overlooks a cascade in the Hudson River Valley, vibrant with autumnal colours. Like many of Cole's compositions, this painting depicts a primeval America untouched by civilization and alludes to the changing of the wilderness, a theme treated in the novels of James Fenimore Cooper. Such works as *Oxbow on the Connecticut River* (1836; New York, Met.) present a transcendental view of nature. In the composition the artist serves as an intermediary between nature and the divine, a concept later embodied in Asher B. Durand's *Kindred Spirits* (1849; New York, Pub. Lib.). Painted a year after Cole's death, this homage to the deceased artist portrays him on a precipice in the wilderness with the poet William Cullen Bryant. Cole fostered the HUDSON RIVER SCHOOL, which included Albert Bierstadt, Frederic Edwin Church, Jasper Francis Cropsey, Sanford Robinson Gifford and John Frederick Kensett, among many others. Their works often treated awe-inspiring scenery and emphasized the country's manifest destiny. This is particularly evident in such monumental canvases as Church's *Niagara* (1857; Washington, DC, Corcoran Gal. A.; see fig. 14) with the river and falls under a protective rainbow, symbolizing the potential and power of the New World. These artists also recorded the USA's

pastoral character, presenting the country as an earthly paradise. Such painters as Martin Johnson Heade and Fitz Hugh Lane, meanwhile, focused on scenes in which light and atmosphere are the subjects. This development became known as LUMINISM.

While landscape painting extolled the potential of the American land, genre painting glorified working people and the ideals of democracy. Paintings of people engaged in everyday activities, which had their roots in 17th-century Dutch art and were treated in Britain by David Wilkie and his contemporaries, inspired such artists as John Lewis Krimmel of Philadelphia. It was, however, in the work of WILLIAM SIDNEY MOUNT of New York and GEORGE CALEB BINGHAM of Missouri that genre painting found its finest expression in the decades before the Civil War. Some of their paintings were translated into popular prints by Currier & Ives and others.

Genre scenes tended to idealize life in America even as they underscored regional differences. Many also embodied racial and social attitudes characteristic of the time but offensive today. For example, Mount's *Farmers Nooning* (1836; Stony Brook, NY, Mus.) can be seen as a visual essay on the carefree nature of rural America, but the portrayal of the sleeping Afro-American, undoubtedly a slave, is ambivalent. Although sympathetically presented in a classical pose, he is nonetheless to some extent the butt of the white man's joke. Compositions by FREDERIC REMINGTON, William Ranney, John Mix Stanley, Arthur Fitzwilliam Tait and others often give stereotypical views of Native Americans as blood-thirsty savages or noble primitives (*see* WILD WEST AND FRONTIER ART). Bingham's exuberant series depicting grass-roots politics in Missouri, while critical of the democratic process in the depiction of drunken voters in, for example, his two versions of the *County Election* (1851 and 1852; version in St Louis, MO, A. Mus.), still expresses the vitality of the USA's political system in the years following the collapse of republican movements in Europe.

The Civil War allowed such photographers as Mathew Brady and Timothy O'Sullivan to establish themselves

14. Frederic Edwin Church: *Niagara*, oil on canvas, 1.08×2.30 m, 1857 (Washington, DC, Corcoran Gallery of Art)

through their documentary work. It also brought with it rapid industrialization, which eventually led to the urbanization of the USA and the internationalization of its economy. The arts also underwent a transformation. Although landscape and figure painting remained dominant, with black artists such as Robert S. Duncanson, Edward Mitchell Bannister (1828–1901) and Grafton Tyler Brown (1841–1918) becoming prominent for the first time through their treatment of landscape, the tone of many compositions became intimate and reflective. Styles also changed from contact with Europe as well as through exhibitions of European works in the USA. While academies had been established in New York, Philadelphia and elsewhere in the early 19th century (see §XV below), these were small institutions, and many artists went abroad for study. In the second part of the century, as travel increased, American art responded to European developments. Pre-Raphaelitism, Realism, Impressionism and Symbolism all had American phases. Hundreds of American artists settled abroad, and their choice of subjects frequently reflected their new surroundings: Thomas Hovenden and Daniel Ridgway Knight (1840–1924), for example, painted European peasants, while Frederick A. Bridgman (1847–1927) and Edwin Lord Weeks (1849–1903) depicted exotic scenes in the Near East and North Africa.

American painters, once they had adopted European styles and themes, saw themselves as part of an international community wherever they lived. Many, such as JAMES MCNEILL WHISTLER and MARY CASSATT, stayed in Europe, while others, such as JOHN SINGER SARGENT and HENRY OSSAWA TANNER, lived there for extended periods. Their reputations and influence transcended national boundaries. For example, Whistler's Art-for-Art's-Sake aesthetic was embraced by artists on both sides of the Atlantic, and his etchings and lithographs were widely imitated. Cassatt was aligned with the most progressive forces in Paris, and, like the work of some of the Impressionists, her compositions show the influence of Japanese prints in motif, design and patterning. Sargent, a fashionable portrait painter, was in great demand in both Europe and the USA, while Tanner gained an international reputation for his religious paintings.

In the last quarter of the century, still-life painting emerged as an important art form in the USA. Following the example of the Peale family at the beginning of the century and of the American Pre-Raphaelites, who had treated related subjects, especially in watercolour, a number of artists, using a heightened realism, created trompe l'oeil paintings of extraordinary verisimilitude in the final decades of the century (e.g. Music and Good Luck, 1888; New York, Met.; see ILLUSIONISM, fig. 2). Most notable were William Michael Harnett, whose trophy pieces frequently contain references to the past, John F. Peto, whose imagery includes personal allusions, and John Haberle, whose works often jokingly refer to his own paintings. One peculiarly American subject was the representation of paper money, as in Haberle's Bachelor's Drawer (1890–94; New York, Met.). Such images commented on the materialism of the society as well as on monetary issues also treated in contemporary literature.

Figurative art during this period often alluded to social and demographic changes. Rural subjects tinged with nostalgia continued to attract such artists as Eastman Johnson and Winslow Homer, but urban themes became commonplace. Such realists as Thomas Anshutz, John George Brown and Charles Ulrich (1858–1908) depicted the working classes and portrayed their country as a melting-pot society. Middle- and upper-class women engaged in genteel pastimes often appear in compositions by such American Impressionists as William Merritt Chase, Childe Hassam and Edmund Tarbell. Although generally not appreciated at the time, Thomas Eakins's portraits of doctors, sportsmen and musicians actively engaged in their pursuits offer psychological insights into human activity. Painted in 1875 and intended for the Centennial International Exhibition of 1876 in Philadelphia, The Gross Clinic (Philadelphia, PA, Thomas Jefferson U., Medic. Col.) is a powerful, if brutally realistic, homage to modern science and affirms the artist's commitment to anatomical training (see EAKINS, THOMAS, fig. 2). Eakins's interest in science was further manifested in his photographs, which he used to study motion and to develop such compositions as the Swimming Hole (1883; Fort Worth, TX, Amon Carter Mus.; see fig. 15).

While Church, Thomas Moran, Thomas Hill (1829–1908) and Albert Bierstadt continued to produce monumental views of Sublime scenery (for illustration see BIERSTADT, ALBERT; see also LANDSCAPE PAINTING, colour pl. IV, fig. 1), landscape painting after the Civil War generally became more modest in scale and subject. It also underwent stylistic shifts, for example in the work of GEORGE INNESS, who rejected the meticulous manner of the Hudson River school for painterly handling in the style of the Barbizon school. His late paintings are reflections on a spiritual landscape rather than depictions of specific places. Internalization of nature is even more apparent in the darkly poetic compositions of Albert Pinkham Ryder and Ralph Albert Blakelock. On the other hand, the contemporary light-filled landscapes of Willard Leroy Metcalf, Theodore Robinson, John H. Twachtman and Julian Alden Weir, as well as those of Chase and Hassam, are buoyantly optimistic; their impressionistic style survived well into the 20th century.

The shift from objective observation to subjective interpretation of nature is particularly noticeable in the work of Winslow Homer. His depictions of the Civil War, growing out of his work as a journalist illustrator, gave way, by the end of the century, to such intensely symbolic compositions as the Fox Hunt (1893; Philadelphia, PA Acad. F.A.) in which natural enemies engaged in a life-and-death struggle become metaphors for human existence (see HOMER, WINSLOW, fig. 1). Homer also emerged in the closing decades of the century as a gifted watercolourist. Earlier, such artists as William Guy Wall had practised a variation on British topographical art, and such painters as John William Hill had produced brilliant Pre-Raphaelite watercolours. However, it was not until Homer that the full potential of the medium was realized in the USA. His loose and quick application of washes, particularly after 1880, created expressive works of crystalline colour unequalled by any other American until Charles Prendergast (1863–1948) and Sargent at the turn of the century.

15. Thomas Eakins: *Swimming Hole*, oil on canvas, 685×915 mm, 1883 (Fort Worth, TX, Amon Carter Museum of Western Art)

By 1900 the expansion of the USA and the growth of its population from just over five million in 1800 to almost seventy-six million, together with increased wealth and improved transportation, all encouraged internationalization in the arts as well as in commerce. Major collections were formed by American millionaires, and American art began to outgrow its provincialism.

BIBLIOGRAPHY

A. Frankenstein: *After the Hunt: William Harnett and Other Still-life Painters, 1870–1900* (Berkeley and Los Angeles, 1953, rev. 1969)
J. Flexner: *That Wilder Image: The Painting of America's Native School from Thomas Cole to Winslow Homer* (Boston, 1962)
B. Novak: *American Painting of the Nineteenth Century: Realism, Idealism and the American Experience* (New York, 1969, rev. 1979)
W. Gerdts and R. Burke: *American Still-life Painting* (New York, 1971)
H. Williams jr: *Mirror of the American Past: A Survey of American Genre Painting, 1750–1900* (Greenwich, CT, 1973)
The Flowering of American Folk Art, 1776–1876 (exh. cat. by J. Lipman and A. Winchester, New York, Whitney, 1974)
American Art in the Barbizon Mood (exh. cat., ed. P. Bermingham; Washington, DC, N. Mus. Amer. A., 1975)
American Expatriate Painters of the Late Nineteenth Century (exh. cat., ed. M. Quick; Dayton, OH, A. Inst., 1976)
American Master Drawings and Watercolors (exh. cat., ed. T. Stebbins jr; New York, Whitney, 1976)
P. Marzio: *The Democratic Art: Pictures of a 19th Century America* (Boston, 1979)
B. Novak: *Nature and Culture: American Landscape and Painting, 1825–1875* (New York and Toronto, 1980)
American Light: The Luminist Movement, 1850–1875 (exh. cat., ed. J. Wilmerding; Washington, DC, N.G.A., 1980)
A New World: Masterpieces of American Painting, 1760–1910 (exh. cat., ed. J. Silver; Boston, MA, Mus. F.A.; Washington, DC, Corcoran Gal. A.; Paris, Grand Pal.; 1983–4)
The New Path: Ruskin and the American Pre-Raphaelites (exh. cat., ed. L. Ferber; New York, Brooklyn Mus., 1985)
American Paradise: The World of the Hudson River School (exh. cat., ed. J. Howat; New York, Met., 1988)
W. Gerdts: *American Impressionism* (New York, 1989)
M. Lovell: *A Visitable Past: Views of Venice by American Artists, 1860–1915* (Chicago, [1989])
H. B. Weinberg: *The Lure of Paris: Nineteenth Century American Painters and their French Teachers* (New York, 1991)
The West as America: Reinterpreting Images of the Frontier, 1820–1920 (exh. cat., ed. W. Truettner; Washington, DC, N. Mus. Amer. A., 1991)

EDWARD J. NYGREN

3. MODERNISM: TO WORLD WAR II. Despite the exemplary technical and aesthetic qualities of the work of such artists as Homer, Eakins and Albert Pinkham Ryder, in the early 20th century many American artists sought to go beyond the depiction of landscape, portrait and genre scenes and looked to Europe for inspiration, not so much in deference to their European roots as from a sense that American art was still parochial and backward in comparison with contemporary European work. While a similar sentiment had already drawn such artists as Whistler, Cassatt and Sargent to Europe (*see* §2 above), a more influential figure in stimulating the growth of an indigenous modernist movement in the USA was ROBERT HENRI. When he returned to Philadelphia in 1891 from an

extended European study journey, Henri found a group of young artists anxious to learn what he had absorbed of European painting movements. John Sloan, William J. Glackens, George Luks and Everett Shinn had studied art at the Pennsylvania Academy of Fine Arts and were earning their livings as political cartoonists for various newspapers in Philadelphia. They were inspired by Henri to use their journalistic instincts to record the exciting and colourful spectacle of the noisy, crowded city. With Henri they gravitated to New York, where they were joined by Arthur B. Davies, Ernest Lawson and Maurice Prendergast. Although they called themselves the Eight (*see* EIGHT, THE, (ii)), the group became known as the ASHCAN SCHOOL, because of their defiance of existing academic principles in ignoring classical themes and high moral messages in their work and their depiction instead of backstreets, popular entertainments and humble events in the lives of ordinary working people, as in Luks's *Closing the Café* (1904; Utica, NY, Munson–Williams–Proctor Inst.).

With Walt Kuhn (1877–1949), who painted acrobats and circus performers in a rich realist manner, the group also instigated and organized an exhibition that radically changed the face of American art. Officially entitled the International Exhibition of Modern Art, the ARMORY SHOW was staged from 17 February to 15 March 1913 in the 69th Regiment Armory in New York. Comprising more than 1600 works of art by contemporary European and American artists, the exhibition had two purposes: the first was to stimulate an interest in new American painting and to create a market for it, while the second was to introduce American audiences to European modernism. It was for its pursuit of this second aim that the exhibition was most memorable, as the introduction of the work of the Impressionists, Post-Impressionists, Fauves and Cubists to unprepared American audiences almost caused riots, and conservative critics ridiculed in particular Matisse's works and Marcel Duchamp's *Nude Descending a Staircase No. 2* (1912; Philadelphia, PA, Mus. A.). Selections from the exhibition moved on to Chicago and Boston, where the criticism was even more strident. In 1915 a similar exhibition, but including also work by the German Expressionists and the Italian Futurists, was presented at the Panama–Pacific International Exposition in San Francisco, so that the audiences of the most sophisticated American cities and the artists who lived there were all exposed to European modernism.

After the Armory Show ALFRED STIEGLITZ, who had earlier opened his 291 (*see* ⟨TWO NINE ONE⟩) or PHOTO-SECESSION gallery in New York to fight conservatism in American photography, assumed the mantle of defender of all that was new and exciting in the visual arts. He exhibited work by the Americans John Marin and Max Weber, who had studied abroad and absorbed Cubist, Futurist and primitivist methods (see fig. 16), and he also showed work by such Europeans as Brancusi, Matisse, Cézanne and Picasso. The gallery became a meeting-place for artists sympathetic to the modernist ideal, who were venerated by Stieglitz. His magazine *Camera Work* defended all new artistic currents and began to educate a small but sympathetic audience. Although his difficult manner sometimes led to arguments, even with artists

whose work he exhibited, Stieglitz was undoubtedly the single most important influence on the advent of modernism in American art, and he helped establish the careers of Arthur Dove, Charles Demuth and Marsden Hartley, and Georgia O'Keeffe, whom he later married.

In 1915 Duchamp arrived in the USA, still notorious from the Armory Show but given international credibility by his association with Fauvism, Cubism and Futurism and his innovative use of ready-mades. Duchamp's influence on American art was profound, its most concrete manifestation being the SOCIÉTÉ ANONYME, which he founded with Katherine S. Dreier and his American disciple Man Ray in 1920 in support of avant-garde art. Most of the few American artists who espoused modernism in the 1920s and 1930s had spent time in Europe during the critically formative years from 1900 to 1910, even if the European influence did not become evident until their return to the USA at the beginning of World War I. Of all the contemporary European styles, Cubism was undoubtedly the most influential, perhaps because of its rationalism. Only a few American artists could accept the raw qualities of Fauvism and Expressionism, which seemed contrary to their aesthetically naive and inhibited nature. Surrealism was then even more foreign to the American puritan heritage. Until the mid-1920s, when he was joined by Stuart Davis, the single consistent exponent of abstract art, based on a reverence for the mysteries of nature, was ARTHUR DOVE. The modernist fervour created by the Armory Show largely died down, and in a mood of disenchantment American artists stopped judging their work by European standards. A renewed interest in the American scene as a reassuring source of common experience was revived. A generation after the Ashcan school,

16. Max Weber: *Rush Hour, New York*, oil on canvas, 921×775 mm, 1915 (Washington, DC, National Gallery of Art)

17. Ben Shahn: *Unemployed*, tempera, 338×422 mm, 1938 (La Jolla, CA, Museum of Contemporary Art)

romantic realists such as Edward Hopper and Charles Burchfield presented a country filled with loneliness and deep shadow, reflecting a failure of the spirit in contrast to the USA's phenomenal economic success: isolated people and empty and decaying buildings, bathed in raking and storm-drenched light, gave their work a unique if disquieting tone. Charles Sheeler, Niles Spencer and Preston Dickinson (1891–1930) on the other hand, with Demuth, O'Keeffe and others, used a rudimentary awareness of Cubism to illustrate the cool geometry of the American industrial environment and to pay homage to the machine as an extension of the puritan work ethic in what later became known as PRECISIONISM. The Harlem Renaissance of the 1920s in New York, meanwhile, was the first self-consciously black art movement and represented a very different form of introversion by American artists (*see* AFRICAN AMERICAN ART).

The worldwide economic depression of 1929 forced American artists to search again for their cultural identity. The Federal Art Project (*see* §XII below), established by President Franklin D. Roosevelt in 1934, encouraged mural decoration in the nation's libraries, schools and post offices. While there was no restriction on subject-matter, the majority of works had a distinct regional flavour and embodied a naive form of social realism, inspiring Americans to reflect on their heritage of revolution, hard work and religion in an attempt to bring back prosperity. Thomas Hart Benton and Grant Wood among others tried to create an American idiom dealing with myth and reality that denied European influence (*see* AMERICAN SCENE PAINTING). Cheerful and conservative by nature, this art disturbed more radical and socially conscious artists and goaded them towards artistic exposition of the nation's shortcomings. Reginald Marsh and Raphael Soyer depicted the problems of the urban middle class humanely, while the graphic work especially of William Gropper (1897–1977) probed at American political life more satirically, and Ben Shahn, whose artistic influence was more enduring, highlighted social problems (see fig. 17) and attacked social injustice. Jack Levine and his pupil Hyman Bloom developed an interest in the harsh social themes and brilliant colour of the German Expressionists and of Chaïm Soutine, Levine striking out against the courts, high society and mob rule while Bloom dealt with the literal decay of humanity. Another scheme instigated during Roosevelt's presidency (1933–45) was the Farm Security Administration Photographic Project, in which Shahn, Dorothea Lange and Walker Evans, among others, were involved, which documented the problems of the USA's rural poor (*see* PHOTOGRAPHY, §II).

Apart from Dove, the only American artist to persist with the lessons of modernism was Stuart Davis, who also participated in the Federal Art Project. Throughout the 1930s he looked to the Cubists and to Fernand Léger to develop a form of flat, colourful and witty abstraction that synthesized the sense of American life (for illustration *see* DAVIS, STUART). Continuing to work against the grain of the sombre regional realists and the romantic expressionists, he developed a following among a younger generation of American artists. In 1936 the AMERICAN ABSTRACT ARTISTS group was formed, and their exhibitions became a source for advanced ideas based on European Constructivism and especially on the work of Piet Mondrian, who moved to New York in 1940. As well as Davis, Fritz Glarner and Burgoyne Diller were important members.

During the 1930s, much of the considerable art activity outside New York was undocumented, since there was little provincial art publishing, except by daily newspapers. The national popularity of regional realism enabled Grant Wood and Thomas Hart Benton to make a living in Iowa and Missouri, but the common practice was for artists to leave their native environment to work in New York, where there was an art market and opportunity for criticism. In Chicago, however, an interest in romantic Surrealism developed, and Ivan Albright received recognition for his meticulous paintings of human life in decay, while in the San Francisco Bay Area, during the 1920s and early 1930s, an abiding interest in the natural beauty of the local landscape developed and was adopted by the Oakland-based Society of Six, a colour-centred modernist idiom which referenced the landscape, but which was inspired by their exposure to the new European art of the Post-Impressionists. A form of clean-edged organic abstraction also developed around the brothers Charles Howard (1899–1978) and Robert Howard (1896–1982) and the latter's wife, Adeline Kent (1900–57). In Los Angeles a flurry of pure abstraction developed, based on the return to the city of Stanton Macdonald-Wright after his successful launching with Morgan Russell of SYNCHROMISM in Paris in 1912. Macdonald-Wright's modernist colour theories found favour with a group of independent artists, including Peter Krasnow (1890–1985), Oskar Fischinger and Knud Merrild (1894–1954), who experimented with colour and light. Other modernists included Lorser Feitelson (1898–1978) and Helen Lundeberg (*b* 1908), who in 1933 co-founded Post-Surrealism, a form of romantic classicism, and were included in important national exhibitions. Los Angeles was also the national centre for the film industry, and a large community of directors, composers, writers and artists gathered there after escaping from Nazi Germany. In the Seattle area Mark Tobey and Morris Graves developed highly personal and poetic work that was indebted to Asian philosophy and calligraphy. Tobey invented 'white writing', a delicate web of non-representational script based on his calligraphic studies and used in such works as *Broadway* (1936; New York, Met.), while Graves concerned himself with tender, psychological images of birds and trees.

4. ABSTRACT EXPRESSIONISM, POP, MINIMALISM AND LATE 20TH-CENTURY DEVELOPMENTS. Almost immediately after World War II, a revolution in American painting occurred. A group of mature artists, seasoned by the economic depression and international conflict, recognized that the prevailing American isolationist and regional sentiment looked provincial in the face of world events. These artists had also had the advantage of a ten-year-long interaction with many of the best-known European artists who had settled in the USA before or during the war. Marc Chagall, Fernand Léger, Piet Mondrian, Josef Albers, Hans Hofmann and the Surrealists André Breton, Yves Tanguy, Max Ernst, André Masson and Arshile Gorky were all grouped, like their American counterparts, around Peggy Guggenheim's Art of This Century gallery in New York. Many of the American artists now saw Surrealism, in which they had previously shown little interest, as an alternative to the pure geometry of the American Abstract Artists and the newly established Museum of Non-objective Painting. Surrealism offered spontaneity and unpremeditated impulse leading to creative freedom, and American artists were drawn to the automatic writing of André Masson rather than the carefully executed fantasies of Salvador Dalí and Yves Tanguy.

The first American artist fully to realize the possibilities was Jackson Pollock, who moved from intensely personal and expressive figurative work to pouring and dripping pigment on large canvases, which were laid out on the floor so that he could attack the surface from all sides. This technique was known as ACTION PAINTING, and the result was an informed but fresh and underivative form of abstraction known as Abstract Expressionism, exemplified by such works as Pollock's *Number 2, 1949* (*see* ABSTRACT EXPRESSIONISM, fig. 1).

In 1952 MOMA in New York organized an exhibition at the Musée National d'Art Moderne, Paris, entitled *12 peintres et sculpteurs américains contemporains*, which for the first time established American painting as having international validity. This was uniquely possible since most European art was still attached to traditional movements or recovering after the war. The exhibition introduced European audiences to contemporary work by William Baziotes, James Brooks (ii), Sam Francis, Arshile Gorky, Adolph Gottlieb, Philip Guston, Hans Hofmann, Franz Kline, Willem De Kooning, Robert Motherwell, Barnett Newman, Ad Reinhardt, Mark Rothko and Clyfford Still, as well as Pollock. Other artists associated with the group included Lee Krasner and Helen Frankenthaler. Gorky developed a cryptographic, abstract organic form of Surrealism inspired by the work of Joan Miró and Roberto Matta. Gottlieb, Rothko, Baziotes and Still were all concerned with myth and primitivism, and all used elements of chance to give vitality to their work. De Kooning, the leading figure of the group after 1952, had derived his early work from the fluid shapes of Miró and Picasso in the 1930s, but after 1948 elements of violence and erotic fantasy were subdued in favour of concern for the autonomy of the act of painting itself (*see* ABSTRACT EXPRESSIONISM, fig. 2).

Around Los Angeles in the early 1950s such artists as Lorser Feitelson and John McLaughlin (1898–1976) were moving towards a more geometric form of abstraction for which the term HARD-EDGE PAINTING was later coined, while in the San Francisco Bay Area during the 1950s a group of artists experimented with abstraction before reintroducing the figure into American art. Elmer Bischoff (1916–1991), David Park and Richard Diebenkorn were the primary members of the Bay Area figurative school, whose rich brushwork was expressionist in style, but whose subjects were lonely humans, isolated in a passive environment, as in Diebenkorn's *Figure on Porch* (1959; Oakland, CA, Mus.). Both Diebenkorn and Bischoff, however, later returned to sophisticated abstract images. Some Afro-American artists in the 1950s were influenced by Abstract Expressionism, but others remained in the realist tradition.

The stability of the USA during World War II enabled artists to prosper while in much of post-war Europe and Asia creative development was suspended until after reconstruction. The economic centre of the art world moved from Paris to New York, where galleries proliferated and major auction houses established a viable American market. Prompted by the international success of the Abstract Expressionists, Americans and Europeans began to collect American art seriously for the first time (*see* §XIII below), and this surge, combined with the GI Bill, which entitled all American war veterans to a free four-year college education, filled the nation's art schools with budding talent. By the mid-1950s such artists as Robert Rauschenberg and Jasper Johns were ready to challenge the art of the previous generation. These two played an important part in the transition from Abstract Expressionism to Pop art through their free and expressive handling of paint and by employing images derived from popular culture. Rauschenberg used collaged comic strips, newspaper headlines and advertising images, while Johns introduced heraldic images such as the American flag and the target (*see* COLOUR INTERACTION, colour pl. VIII, fig. 1b and JOHNS, JASPER, fig. 1). Both also began to incorporate *objets trouvés* into their work, breaking down the barriers that had existed between painting and sculpture and recalling Marcel Duchamp's dictum that the mere selection of material could itself transform a useless or obsolete object into art. Their use of *objets trouvés* and residual material, for example in the 'combine' paintings of ROBERT RAUSCHENBERG, coincided with the early work of Jim Dine and with the work of Wallace Berman (1925–1975), Edward Kienholz and Bruce Conner (*b* 1933) in California and promoted the growth of assemblage as an art form, which was fuelled also by the sense of alienation of the 'Beat' generation to which they belonged.

The first large-scale American Pop art paintings were by Andy Warhol and were derived from Popeye comic-strip images (e.g. *Saturday's Popeye*, 1960; Mainz, Landesmus.). Warhol's works were followed by those of Roy Lichtenstein, first using Walt Disney images and then enlarged interpretations appropriated from single panels of comic strips. Warhol meanwhile moved on to multiple images of such international icons as Marilyn Monroe, Elizabeth Taylor or Coca-Cola bottles, emphasizing the ephemeral and disposable nature of American culture (for illustration *see* POP ART). Both artists often used mass reproduction techniques such as screenprints and stencils

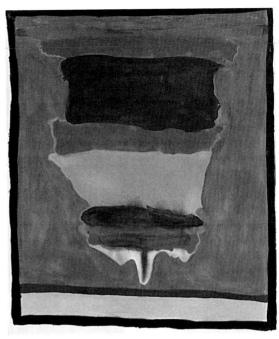

18. Helen Frankenthaler: *Cape (Provincetown)*, acrylic on canvas, 2.78×2.37 m, 1964 (Melbourne, National Gallery of Victoria)

and denied the uniqueness of paint, the handling of which had been so important to previous generations: their images were clearly defined, with flat surfaces. Another Pop artist, James Rosenquist, used his experience as a sign painter to make sophisticated recompositions of billboard images (e.g. *President Elect*, 1960–61; Paris, Pompidou). Pop art also took root on the West Coast: Edward Ruscha experimented with the depiction of key words from popular culture, such as 'Boss' and 'Noise'; Joe Goode (*b* 1937) looked at such common household items as milk bottles, staircases and the California bungalow itself; Wayne Thiebaud painted elegant pies, cakes and hot dogs (e.g. *Cut Meringues*, 1961; New York, MOMA); and Mel Ramos (*b* 1935) turned to such comic book heroes as the Phantom and Batman. Each artist had a unique and identifiable image and style, but there was nevertheless a shared acceptance of the culture in which they had all grown up, with its comics, television and film.

While Johns and Rauschenberg were reintroducing narrative elements, another group of artists were working with abstraction to investigate the ethereal nature of colour and develop the ideas of Mark Rothko and Barnett Newman. This movement, which arose in the late 1950s when it was known as COLOUR FIELD PAINTING (*see* COLOUR, colour pl. III, fig. 2 and COLOUR INTERACTION, colour pl. VII, fig. 2d), came to prominence in 1964 in an exhibition at the Los Angeles County Museum of Art, entitled *Post-Painterly Abstraction* and curated by critic and theorist Clement Greenberg. Artists associated with the movement rejected the illusion of depth and the gestural brushwork of the Abstract Expressionists and accepted the two-dimensional nature of the canvas surface. Colour was applied flat or sometimes stained into the surface.

Frank Stella, Kenneth Noland and Jules Olitski worked with loose geometric shapes and bright colours, while Helen Frankenthaler and Morris Louis poured their thinned pigment on to the canvas, staining the surface in bold abstract shapes and colours (see fig. 18). The introduction of high-intensity, water-soluble acrylic pigment helped these artists in their staining process without leaving spots of oil that would bleed through the canvas fibres (*see* ACRYLIC PAINTING, §1). Stella, Noland and Ellsworth Kelly also broke away from the traditional, rectangular format and introduced shaped canvases, making the wall on which they hung into an active component (for illustration *see* NOLAND, KENNETH).

An exhibition at the Leo Castelli Gallery in New York in 1960 of 'notched' pinstripe paintings by Frank Stella was the precursor to another, more austere direction in American art. Looking back to the work of Mondrian and the Soviet Constructivists, a number of artists in the 1960s chose to see their art in the context of a classical ideal that had been recently exemplified by the clarity of Barnett Newman and Ad Reinhardt. MINIMALISM in painting and the graphic arts eliminated representational imagery in favour of a single, unified group of forms, often composed on a geometric grid. Even at its most reductive, however, there was room for identifiable, individual variation ranging from the quiet, almost monochromatic works of Brice Marden, Robert Ryman and Agnes Martin to the spare geometry of Sol LeWitt and Robert Mangold.

While Minimalism dominated the art of the American East Coast during the 1960s (*see also* §IV, 2 below), art in the San Francisco Bay Area during this period was dominated by Funk art, which derived its energy from the improvisational style of jazz musicians. Pungently playful painting by William Wiley (*b* 1937), Robert Hudson (*b* 1938) and Robert Arneson (1930–93) typified the movement, which closely paralleled a Chicago group known as the Hairy-Who, to which James Nutt (*b* 1938), Ed Paschke (*b* 1939) and others belonged. Chicago was also one of the main centres of Black Expressionism, which flourished during the 1960s, and the birthplace of the Black Neighborhood Mural Movement, which addressed political and social issues. Artists in Los Angeles in the 1960s rejected the tenets of New York's Abstract Expressionism and chose instead to experiment with the high colour and technological materials that dominated their environment. A group that included Billy Al Bengston (*b* 1934), Larry Bell and Craig Kauffman (*b* 1932) became known as the Fetish–Finish school, because of their use of new plastics, glass and lacquer and the attention to surface. The involvement with new industrial materials led to a deeper investigation of light and of its perception by Robert Irwin, James Turrell (*b* 1943) and Maria Nordman (*b* 1943). This movement, entitled Light and Space, took its art beyond painting and into the realm of illumination.

With the exception of those artists associated with PHOTOREALISM, such as Chuck Close, artists at the end of the 1960s appeared to be being led away from painting by Minimalism on the East Coast and Light and Space on the West Coast. Moreover, such artists as Nancy Spero and Judy Chicago were seeking to investigate their status as women in an art world from whose traditional forms and institutions they felt excluded. Many women chose to work in media other than painting, which they associated with the male-dominated establishment. During the 1970s and 1980s, however, a number of outside forces coincided to change American attitudes to painting and to the purpose of art itself. Extended involvement in the Vietnam War depressed and aggravated the creative spirit, as did the spectre of increased urban unrest and the devastating impact of the AIDS virus, leading many artists towards using painting as a political and social weapon. Leon Golub, for example, produced huge canvases that criticized American foreign policy, such as his *Vietnam* series, Peter Saul (*b* 1934) attacked social injustice in wild, cartoon-like paintings, and Sue Coe (*b* 1951) dealt with issues of dehumanization in society. Other artists, however, critical of the intense materialism of the art world, turned towards performance, video art and other forms that defied commercialism by virtue of their transient nature. Still others, such as Jeff Koons (*b* 1955) and Mark Kostabi (*b* 1960), created cynical work that catered in a blatant and provocative way to the market place, while David Salle, Julian Schnabel and Eric Fischl tried to reintroduce the concept of the artist as hero. For a brief period graffiti art emerged from the New York subways on to museum walls. Keith Haring (1958–90) used his simplistic graffiti style not only in large canvases that dealt with the human condition but also to reach a worldwide audience through sales of posters and T-shirts. Other artists, including a number of women, also explored the idea of art beyond the traditional museum or gallery siting. Jenny Holzer (*b* 1950) and Barbara Kruger (*b* 1945), for example, used large pictorial spaces such as sides of buildings and hoardings, or illuminated signs, often carrying comments on their cultural environment (see fig. 19). The paintings and collages of Sherrie Levine (*b* 1947) also often take as

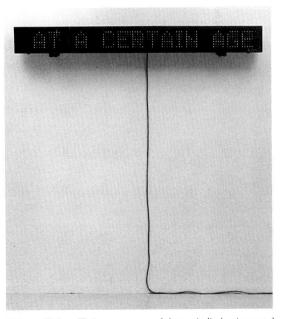

19. Jenny Holzer: *Truisms*, programmed electronic display sign, metal and plastic, 169×1539×162 mm, 1984 (London, Tate Gallery)

their subject-matter aspects of their own artistic context in their recurrent references to other painters and photographers (e.g. *Untitled (After Alexander Rodchenko)*, 1987; New York, Mary Boone), while Cindy Sherman's parodic photographs also took up the theme of the relation between women and the pictorial arts. At the end of the 20th century the diversity of approaches taken by young artists and the growing acceptance of the validity of previously neglected or marginalized artistic traditions constituted, therefore, an irresistible challenge to the modernist orthodoxy.

BIBLIOGRAPHY

M. W. Brown: *American Painting from the Armory Show to the Depression* (Princeton, 1955)
I. Sandler: *The Triumph of American Painting: A History of Abstract Expressionism* (New York, 1970)
S. Hunter: *American Art of the Twentieth Century* (New York, 1972)
D. Shapiro: *Social Realism: Art as a Weapon* (New York, 1973)
M. Baigell: *The American Scene: American Painting of the 1930s* (New York and Washington, 1974)
D. Tashjian: *Skyscraper Primitives: Dada and the American Avant-garde, 1910–1925* (Middletown, CT, 1975)
H. T. Hopkins: *California Painting and Sculpture: The Modern Era* (San Francisco, 1976)
R. Hobbs and G. Levin: *Abstract Expressionism: The Formative Years* (New York, 1978)
I. Sandler: *The New York School: The Painters and Sculptors of the Fifties* (New York, 1978)
B. Rose: *American Painting* (London, 1980)
A. A. Davidson: *Early American Modernist Painting, 1910–35* (New York, 1981)
D. Ashton: *American Art since 1945* (New York and London, 1982)
S. Guilbaut: *How New York Stole the Idea of Modern Art: Abstract Expressionism, Freedom and the Cold War* (Eng. trans., Chicago and London, 1983)
W. Seitz: *Abstract Expressionist Painting in America* (Cambridge, MA, 1983)
C. Robins: *The Pluralist Era: American Art, 1968–1981* (New York and Toronto, 1984)
Blam! The Explosion of Pop, Minimalism and Performance, 1958–1961 (exh. cat. by B. Haskell, New York, Whitney, 1984)
T. Albright: *Art in the San Francisco Bay Area, 1945–1980* (Berkeley and Los Angeles, 1985)
H. Wooden: *American Art of the Great Depression* (Kansas, 1985)
The Advent of Modernism: Post-Impressionism and North American Art, 1900–1918 (exh. cat. by P. Morrin, J. Zilczer and W. Agee, Atlanta, GA, High Mus. A., 1986)
C. De Noon: *Posters of the WPA, 1935–1943* (Los Angeles, 1987)
R. Pincus-Witten: *Postminimalism into Maximalism: American Art, 1966–1986* (Ann Arbor, 1987)
H. A. Harrison: *Women Artists of the New Deal Era* (Washington, DC, 1988)
L. K. Hammond: *Black Printmakers and the WPA* (New York, 1989)
R. Atkins: *Art Speak* (New York, 1990)
E. Doss: *Benton, Pollock and the Politics of Modernism: From Religionalism to Abstract Expressionism* (Chicago and London, 1991)

HENRY T. HOPKINS

IV. Sculpture.

1. The Colonial period to World War I. 2. After World War I.

1. THE COLONIAL PERIOD TO WORLD WAR I. During the 17th and 18th centuries American sculpture was predominantly produced by craftsmen: indigenous stonecutters satisfied the steady demand for burial markers, and local wood-carvers decorated everyday objects. The earliest gravestones, made principally from slate, were low in relief and modest in design, with a mere inscription forming the overall composition. Later, intricate geometric and floral motifs were superseded by a variety of symbols

of death, such as crossed bones, skeletons, hour-glasses and winged souls' heads, but the most significant innovation was the portrayal of the deceased. As stonecutters experimented with a wider selection of materials and developed a facility in carving them, they were able to gratify the increasing worldliness of the colonists and the consequent desire for more elaborate and less grim imagery. Nevertheless, it was not until the beginning of the 19th century that the quality of the tombstones was elevated to a fine art by American sculptors whose awareness of sophisticated European works helped foster the transformation.

For wood-carvers, too, the social, religious and economic character of the first 100 years in the colonies offered little opportunity for ornamentation of a high style and on a grand scale. They confined their efforts to incising shallow geometric and floral patterns on utilitarian boxes and other items of furniture that they made. In time figurative sculpture found expression in shop signs, ships, bureau bookcases and chest-on-chests. The most versatile of these craftsmen were Simeon Skillin sr and his sons John Skillin and Simeon Skillin jr. Samuel McIntire was equally talented, especially in architectural and furniture decoration, but he had less command of figuration. Of all the wood-carvers of the late 18th century and the early 19th, it was William Rush who best exemplified the transition from artisan to sculptor. His experience of clay modelling was the key to his achieving a confident air in his portraiture in plaster and terracotta, a medium rarely chosen by American sculptors. Further, the natural ease of his rendering surpassed the typically stiff handling of his fellow carvers. His life-size, pine *George Washington* (1815; Philadelphia, PA, Indep. N. Hist. Park) demonstrates this mastery of wood and reflects his knowledge and assimilation of English late Rococo statuary.

While many aspiring sculptors at the turn of the 19th century had access to books, engravings and plaster casts of Greek and Roman sculpture, it was the War of Independence that served as perhaps the single most important stimulus for these artists by creating an immediate need to commemorate the new national heroes with portrait busts and statues. The paucity of native sculptors qualified to supply marmoreal tributes was exposed, and orders were awarded to foreigners. The enormous publicity surrounding the marble statue of *George Washington* (1788; Richmond, VA, Capitol Bldg) by Jean-Antoine Houdon, who actually travelled to the USA to sketch the General, and those (also in marble) by Antonio Canova (unveiled in Raleigh, NC, in 1821; destr. 1830) and by Francis Chantrey (1826; Boston, MA, Capitol Bldg) had a telling effect on young Americans who dreamt of major commissions.

It became clear to Horatio Greenough, Hiram Powers and Thomas Crawford, the leading figures of the first generation to adopt Neo-classicism, that extensive travel was essential to compete with the finest sculptors of the era and to escape from provincialism. The prevailing attitude in Europe that a period of study in Italy was fundamental to a sculptor's education had a massive impact in the USA. Between 1824, when Greenough left Boston, and *c.* 1875, if a sculptor did not stay at home—as did John Frazee (1790–1852), Erastus Dow Palmer, Clark Mills

(1815–83) and William Rimmer—Rome or Florence was the destination necessary for the training, practice and cultural enrichment of countless American artists, many of whom remained abroad permanently.

In Italy they found a conducive artistic milieu, in which studios were readily available, marble was plentiful and skilled marblecutters were indispensable assistants. Like most 19th-century sculptors, Greenough relied on portrait busts to support himself, but he and others preferred literary, mythological, religious or historical themes. His masterpiece, installed in the US Capitol rotunda in 1841, was the monumental seated marble *George Washington* (1832–41; see fig. 20), the bare chest, robe and sandals revealing how thoroughly steeped in classicism Greenough had become. The American public, however, received it poorly, being ill-prepared for so Olympian a reference and preferring their heroes to be shown less grandly.

The delicate balance between satisfying typical middle-class taste and illustrating narratives that reflected the sculptor's lofty ideals was achieved by Hiram Powers in his internationally acclaimed life-size standing marble figure the *Greek Slave* (*c.* 1843; for illustration *see* POWERS, HIRAM). Although a few condemned the figure's nudity,

20. Horatio Greenough: *George Washington*, marble, 3.45× 2.59×2.09 m, 1832–41 (Washington, DC, National Museum of American History)

Powers succeeded in ensuring that the rendering of the pathetic story of the slave being held captive by the Turks militated against a prurient response. For the rest of the century similar judgements were delivered by a puritanical society: nudity was acceptable if justified by the context.

A second generation of Neo-classical sculptors settled in Italy between *c.* 1850 and 1875 and was far more numerous, including Richard Greenough, William Wetmore Story, Harriet Hosmer, Emma Stebbins (1815–82), William Rinehart (1825–74), Randolph Rogers and Larkin Mead (1835–1910). Frequently Victorian in spirit and mood, the work of these artists bore little relation to the urgent political and social issues of slavery, the preservation of the Union and the Civil War. The sentimental content of much of the sculpture lacked the force of its antecedents and was matched in its decline by the Neo-classical style itself, which was being emasculated and replaced by a vigorous naturalism.

By the second half of the 19th century, patrons wanted greater realism in their sculpture, in the form of either portrait busts or monuments in public parks and squares. For outdoor statuary bronze was more suitable than stone, as it easily survived the harsh North American climate, was lighter and reflected contemporary stylistic changes. Henry Kirke Brown (1814–66), Clark Mills, Thomas Ball, Anne Whitney (1821/2–1915), Launt Thompson (1833–94), George Bissell (1839–1920) and Martin Millmore (1845–83) were transitional figures using bronze; they presented their subjects with a straightforward and accurate, if not always exciting or even memorable, execution. John Quincy Adams Ward belongs in this period of objective naturalism, although his later works in particular are more animated and endowed with a keener psychological insight than those of his contemporaries.

Plaster was explored for its inexpensiveness rather than for its inherent properties by John Rogers (ii), who was acclaimed for his statuette groups depicting genre scenes of American life. These were so popular that Rogers sold thousands of plaster copies by mail order. The Civil War was a source for many of his pieces, and after 1861 it provided a powerful inspiration for innumerable artists. In fact AUGUSTUS SAINT-GAUDENS and DANIEL CHESTER FRENCH, his Yankee compatriot, are remembered not least for their monuments and memorials celebrating Civil War heroes. Saint-Gaudens's portrayals of *Admiral David Glasgow Farragut* (1876–81, New York, Madison Square Park), *Abraham Lincoln* (1884–7, Chicago, IL, Lincoln Park; 1897–1906, Chicago, IL, Grant Park), *General William Tecumseh Sherman* (1892–1903, New York, Grand Army Plaza) and *Colonel Robert Gould Shaw* (see fig. 21), and French's versions of *Abraham Lincoln* (e.g. seated marble figure for the Lincoln Memorial, ded. 1922; Washington, DC) are unmistakably American in content despite bearing the stylistic imprint of mid- to late 19th-century French sculpture. During the late 1860s several American sculptors, including Saint-Gaudens and Olin Levi Warner, understood that Paris had replaced Rome and Florence as the city where the most rigorous artistic instruction could be obtained. The prestige attached to residing in Paris, enrolling in the Ecole des Beaux-Arts and exhibiting in the annual Salons was so pronounced that it gave enterprising sculptors a distinct advantage on their return home

21. Augustus Saint-Gaudens: *Colonel Robert Gould Shaw*, bronze relief, 3.35×4.27 m, 1884–97, Boston Common

in gaining commissions over those lacking in Parisian experience.

The flickering and lively surfaces that Saint-Gaudens and Warner learnt to use in their bronze portrait reliefs, or that Frederick William MacMonnies lavished on his picturesque, decorative and highly expressive bronze groups, such as *Bacchante and Infant Faun* (1893; New York, Met.), were not the only elements adapted from the French for American consumption. These three and such other sculptors as Frederic Ruckstull (1853–1942), Francis Edwin Elwell (1858–1922), Herbert Adams (1858–1945), Charles Grafly (1862–1929), George Grey Barnard, Paul Wayland Bartlett (1865–1925) and Karl Bitter (1867–1915), who all worked in the richly modelled, spontaneous and seemingly unlaboured manner that came to be known as the Beaux-Arts style, also imported ideas on the teaching of sculpture, implementation of studio systems, expansion of foundries and the establishment of organizations, exhibitions and collaborative projects for the display of their art.

Figurative French-derived sculpture was the dominant strain for the last quarter of the 19th century and was carried over into the early 20th century with offshoots as dissimilar as works reminiscent of Auguste Rodin and a virtual school of 'cowboy and Indian' themes, executed with a French-influenced technique. Frederic Remington, Cyrus Dallin (1861–1944), Charles M. Russell and Hermon Atkins MacNeil (1866–1947) captured a nostalgia for the American frontier in their bronzes and implied that a unique facet of the nation's life had been lost forever (*see* WILD WEST AND FRONTIER ART). The genteel Beaux-Arts mode survived but was sent a death knell by the convulsions of World War I and its aftermath, which quickly made artists of a traditional vein seem antiquated. In its place, a modern art was being born that reflected the dynamism of the by this time firmly industrialized, internationalized and urban-centred USA.

KATHRYN GREENTHAL

2. AFTER WORLD WAR I. During the early 20th century young American sculptors anxious to break with Beaux-Arts academicism sought new sources of inspiration. Europe still provided the dominant point of reference. Some artists were attracted to Auguste Rodin's expressive interpretations of the figure, while others were drawn to Cubism, Futurism and Constructivism. In 1915 Max Weber produced a number of non-objective sculptures related to the new concepts of space and dynamism

found in Italian Futurist manifestos, such as *Spiral Rhythm* (New York, Forum Gal.) and *Air, Light and Shadow* (New York, MOMA). In 1916 ROBERT LAURENT, who had migrated from France, made abstract wood-carvings indebted to Brancusi. Man Ray was inspired by Marcel Duchamp's ready-mades to produce his own Dada-related constructions. His *New York* (1917; Paris, priv. col.) featured metal rods restrained by a carpenter's vice, and *Obstruction* (1920; destr.) included wooden coat-hangers as a suspended mobile construction that presaged Alexander Calder's works. Morton Livingston Schamberg used a plumbing trap attached to a mitre box for his only sculptural work, *God* (*c.* 1917; Philadelphia, PA, Mus. A.) as his response to Duchamp's *Fountain*, an altered urinal exhibited in 1917 at the Society of Independent Artists Inc. exhibition in New York. Many Americans, however, including GASTON LACHAISE and ELIE NADELMAN, remained committed to the figure while exploring modernist interpretations. Lachaise's monumental 'goddesses' were based on fertility artefacts from the ancient world, while Nadelman was inspired by folk art in his creation of circus figures and dancers of painted wood trimmed with wrought iron.

During the 1920s and early 1930s Americans produced abstract and non-objective sculpture composed of a variety of industrial materials. John Storrs (1885–1956) created some of the most refined non-objective works. By the mid-1920s he was creating geometric constructions in various metals with a strongly architectonic quality, resembling the skyscrapers of the American urban landscape and featuring machine-like surfaces (e.g. *Forms in Space*, *c.* 1924; New York, Whitney). One of the most important abstract sculptors was ISAMU NOGUCHI, who worked in Paris as a studio assistant to Brancusi in 1927. The young Japanese–American produced more than 20 abstract works, inspired by Brancusi and by Picasso's metal constructions. *Sphere Section* (1927; untraced) is among his most elemental: the highly polished marble sphere was followed by abstractions of female forms in wood and marble. In *Abstraction in Almost Discontinuous Tension* (1928; artist's estate.) Noguchi used sheets of brass and zinc, cutting and bending them into various shapes, and using tension and gravity, rather than welding, to afford the pieces a sense of motion.

Alexander Calder (*see* CALDER, (3)) is significant as the first American to combine Constructivist aesthetics with biomorphic imagery, forming a personal style of great inventiveness. Calder's non-objective constructions in a variety of industrial materials and his invention of kinetic works represent a unique achievement. At a time when only a few American sculptors of his generation were experimenting with Constructivist methods, seeking places to exhibit and desperately trying to support themselves, Calder already had an international reputation and was beginning to sell his works to such American museums as MOMA, New York, and such private collectors as James Johnson Sweeney.

Calder credited his visit to Mondrian's studio in Paris in 1930 for his change to an abstract idiom, but his friendship with Joan Miró, whom he had first met two years earlier, was also significant. Coupled with these artistic influences were Calder's innate mechanical ingenuity, his training as an engineer and his fascination with popular science. His earliest kinetic works were confined within a wire 'frame' and included a number of elements that were activated by small motors. The term 'mobile', which was given to these devices, was coined by Marcel Duchamp on his initial visit to Calder's studio in 1932. The word was in fact a generic designation that Duchamp had earlier given to one of his ready-mades, *Bicycle Wheel* (1913; untraced), which was mounted on a stool. One of Calder's best-known motorized devices is *Universe* (1934; New York, MOMA), a work that documents his enduring interest in the cosmos. Spheres of different sizes follow trajectories on wires, and the construction suggests Calder was inspired by mechanized orreries, scientific instruments that show the varying orbits of planets in the solar system. From the mid-1930s Calder continued to produce works in a variety of media. His wind-driven mobiles became his predominant interest through the 1940s and 1950s (for illustrations *see* CALDER, (3) and MOBILE), and his monumental stabiles of the 1960s and early 1970s were created primarily for public sites in the USA and France.

Other American sculptors were aware of Surrealism from as early as 1926. In the work of DAVID SMITH, for example, the appearance of Surrealist-related imagery resulted in part from direct exposure to relevant artists and works in Paris. Smith assimilated not only the formal appearance of Surrealism, however, but also its thematic

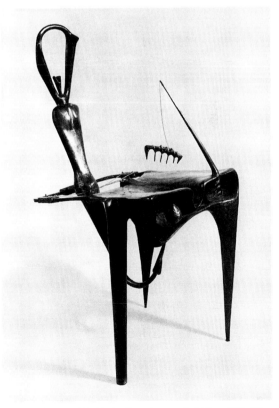

22. David Hare: *Magician's Game*, bronze, h. 1.02 m, 1944 (New York, Museum of Modern Art)

content. Even when he was a young artist in the 1930s the expressive imagery of Smith's mature years was already in evidence, while links with the Surrealist-related works of Alberto Giacometti, Picasso and Julio González appeared in his work. In 1933 Smith began to produce welded sculptures, but while the Surrealists often made visual puns on the correspondence of manufactured objects, shapes to human anatomy or to animal forms, Smith showed little interest in retaining the original function of the mechanical part in relation to new subject-matter. Smith's *Interior for Exterior* (1939; USA, Orin Raphael priv. col.) is derived from one of Giacometti's best-known sculptures, *Palace at 4 a.m.* (1932–3; New York, MOMA). Again Smith adopted not only the cage-like formal structure of Giacometti's Surrealist work but also the notion of symbolic elements of a very personal (and frequently sexual) nature. The formation of the AMERICAN ABSTRACT ARTISTS in 1936 provided a forum for links with such European artists as Léger and Mondrian, but Ibram Lassaw, Theodore Roszak, Gertrude Greene (née Glass; 1904–56) and others continued to be influenced also by Surrealism, mainly through various pioneering exhibitions and publications. The impact of Surrealism is particularly evident in the early works of David Hare (see fig. 22) and in the work of Joseph Cornell, whose sculptural 'constructions' (for illustration *see* CORNELL, JOSEPH) are particularly reminiscent of the work of Max Ernst.

In the 1940s Smith used welded metals in expressive forms that continued earlier interests. After World War II, however, many sculptors sought new directions, inspired by the radical experiments of the Abstract Expressionist painters and by a new feeling of confidence in the international significance of American art (*see* §III, 4 above). From the 1950s, when he became the most renowned sculptor of the Abstract Expressionist generation, Smith developed such series as the *Tanktotems* and *Sentinels* (e.g. *Lectern Sentinel*, 1961; for illustration *see* SMITH, DAVID). These monumental figures represent Smith's most powerful version of the standing human figure. Made of steel and incorporating the ends of boiler tanks, the works are simultaneously abstract and anthropomorphic. Like many of Smith's mature works, *Tanktotem IV* (1953; Buffalo, NY, Albright–Knox A.G.; see fig. 23) is both expressive and enigmatic. The geometry is animated by the suggestion of a figure, while the steel surfaces are manipulated by the artist into large abstract patterns. Smith also removed the work from the pedestal and placed it directly on the ground.

In the late 1950s a number of artists were interested in enlarging the possibilities of sculpture as a medium and, with an enduring interest in *objets trouvés*, experimented with assemblage. These included Louise Nevelson (e.g. *Dawn's Wedding Chapel*, 1959; for illustration *see* NEVELSON, LOUISE), Louise Bourgeois, Richard Stankiewicz, John Chamberlain and others, such as Robert Rauschenberg, who had hitherto been more closely associated with painting. Nevelson's mysterious 'walls', such as *Sky Cathedral* (1958; Buffalo, NY, Albright–Knox A.G.), have a unified, architectural presence but are filled with wooden fragments, representing the detritus of urban existence. Bourgeois also created a deeply personal art, often with sexual references, primarily totemic forms fashioned from

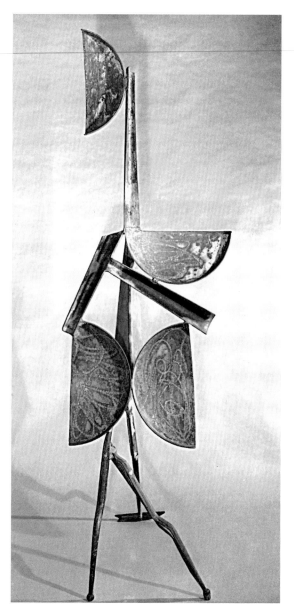

23. David Smith: *Tanktotem IV*, steel, h. 2.36 m, 1953 (Buffalo, NY, Albright–Knox Art Gallery)

wood. Stankiewicz welded scrap materials, including pipes, bolts and boiler plates to create witty personages in the tradition of Dada and Surrealism (for illustration *see* ASSEMBLAGE), while Chamberlain assembled crushed motor car parts, which were brilliantly painted to parallel the powerful brushstrokes of Willem De Kooning. MARK DI SUVERO was also compared to the Abstract Expressionist painters, particularly Franz Kline, for the counterbalancing of roughly surfaced railway components. His *Hankchampion* (1960; New York, Whitney) features thrusting beams and logs held in tension by rope and chains, and he was later acclaimed for monumental steel works on public sites.

In the 1960s there was a continuation of neo-Dada interests in the use of popular culture and mass consumerism associated with Pop art. JASPER JOHNS created a meticulously rendered cast-bronze version of beer cans (*Painted Bronze*, 1960; Basle, Kstmus.), and Rauschenberg continued to make assemblages from scrap materials (for illustration *see* RAUSCHENBERG, ROBERT). Pop imagery can also be found in the provocative gigantism of Claes Oldenburg, who gave anthropomorphic presences to food items and consumer products (for illustration *see* OLDENBURG, CLAES). GEORGE SEGAL and EDWARD KIENHOLZ created Pop-related environments, including some with political commentaries. In the late 1960s sculptors based in the San Francisco Bay Area, such as Robert Hudson (*b* 1938) and Robert Arneson (*b* 1930), made playful works in clay, but more significant were the primary structures associated with Minimalism. DONALD JUDD, ROBERT MORRIS and CARL ANDRÉ used wood and industrial materials to create elemental forms that often created their own environment (for illustration *see* MINIMALISM). Tony Smith's monumental black constructions are among the most complex and rigorous outdoor works of the period. Related to such developments was an interest in works that addressed conceptual issues about the nature of art and of its production, of which Richard Serra's works provide an example (for illustration *see* PROCESS ART). EVA HESSE was the successor to the static industrialism of primary structures with her use of latex and fibreglass in quirky, personalized exaggerations of Minimalist works (see fig. 24). Others, such as Nancy Graves (*b* 1940),

experimented with new materials; Graves used animal skin, bones and feathers in her *Camel* series (1968–9).

Conceptual and environmental issues combined in the wrapping projects of CHRISTO AND JEANNE-CLAUDE, but land projects became the major achievement of the 1970s. Robert Smithson's renowned *Spiral Jetty* (1970; for illustration *see* LAND ART) set a new direction for American sculpture, increasing the scale to that of the landscape itself and offering many new options in relating sculpture to a specific site and its history. Alice Aycock (*b* 1946), Nancy Holt (*b* 1938), Mary Miss (*b* 1944) and Siah Armajani (*b* 1939) studied the relationship of site, situation and architecture. Charles Simonds's works experimented with ideas about human habitation and with questions of scale and situation, for example in his *Floating Cities* series in the late 1970s, while also showing Smithson's influence. DAN FLAVIN and others, on the other hand, continued to explore the possibilities of Minimalism, for example in Flavin's use of fluorescent light tubes (e.g. *Untitled (for Robert with Kind Regards)*, 1977; New York, Whitney). The most remarkable achievements of the 1980s and 1990s were not in the creation of sculptural objects so much as in the building of site-specific projects as public sculpture. Among the most significant is *Vietnam Veterans' Memorial* (1980–82) by Maya Lin (*b* 1959) in Washington, DC. In the 1990s American sculpture continued to be characterized by its diversity, ranging from bronzes through conceptualism to site-related public monuments, with political issues and multicultural expressions also becoming prominent.

JOAN MARTER

BIBLIOGRAPHY
L. Taft: *The History of American Sculpture* (New York, 1903, rev. 1924)
D. Ashton: *Modern American Sculpture* (New York, 1968)
W. Craven: *Sculpture in America* (New York, 1968, rev. Newark, DE, 1984)
W. Andersen: *American Sculpture in Process, 1930–1970* (Boston, MA, 1975)
200 Years of American Sculpture (exh. cat. by T. Armstrong, New York, Whitney, 1976)
Vanguard American Sculpture, 1913–39 (exh. cat., texts J. Marter, R. Tarbell and J. Wechsler; New Brunswick, NJ, Rutgers U., Zimmerli A. Mus., 1979)
J. Beardsley: *Earthworks and Beyond: Contemporary Art in the Landscape* (New York, 1984)
G. B. Opitz: *Dictionary of American Sculptors* (Poughkeepsie, 1984)
The Third Dimension: Sculpture of the New York School (exh. cat. by L. Phillips, New York, Whitney; Fort Worth, TX, A. Mus.; Cleveland, OH, Mus. A.; Newport Beach, CA, Harbor A. Mus.; 1985–6)
Sitings (exh. cat., texts H. M. Davies, R. J. Onorato and S. Yard; La Jolla, CA, Mus. Contemp. A.; 1986)
Sculpture since the Sixties: From the Permanent Collection of the Whitney Museum of American Art (New York, 1989)
C. Rubinstein: *American Women Sculptors* (Boston, MA, 1990)
KATHRYN GREENTHAL, JOAN MARTER

V. Interior decoration.

The surviving examples of American interiors are to be found mostly in museum re-creations that use rooms salvaged from historic houses, which are then furnished in the appropriate manner. For early interiors these re-creations are based on information gleaned from inventories and literary records or adapted from European sources. In the USA, unlike France and England, few early interiors survive with their original setting and contents,

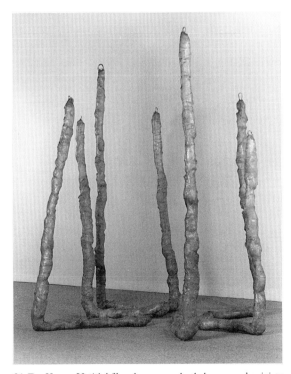

24. Eva Hesse: *Untitled*, fibreglass over polyethylene over aluminium wire, seven units, h. of each unit *c.* 2.18–2.82 m, 1970 (Paris, Pompidou, Musée National d'Art Moderne)

and there is little other visual evidence for interior decoration in the early years of the colonies. Museums where room re-creations can be seen include the Metropolitan Museum of Art and the Brooklyn Museum, both in New York, the H. F. Du Pont Winterthur Museum in Delaware and the American Museum in Britain at Claverton Manor, Bath.

1. Before 1730. 2. 1730–90. 3. 1791–1830. 4. 1831–1900. 5. After 1900.

1. BEFORE 1730. In the 17th century American houses were usually relatively simple structures. Few grand houses were built, and these were probably furnished in the manner of their English models, but little survives of their interiors. More typical were clapboard, brick or stone houses divided into a few rooms by panelling made of simple vertical boards, very much like 15th-century northern European dwellings. The exterior walls of these rooms were finished with whitewashed plaster and punctuated by small windows with diamond-shaped panes set in lead frames. The structural beams that formed the framework of the house were visible in each room, and the ceiling was usually made up of the floorboards of the upper storey. The overall appearance of these rooms was not very different from the simple, functional interiors of medieval European houses.

The amount of furniture in early rooms has been disputed and obviously varied, though some inventories suggest that there was very little. As in Europe in this period, rooms were multipurpose, with beds a feature of almost every one. The other furniture, generally made of oak and embellished with motifs of classical or Renaissance derivation, consisted of blanket chests, cabinets, cupboards for display as well as storage, small and large tables, chairs and stools. The furniture made by Colonial craftsmen was based on English provincial models rather than on the more fashionable Baroque styles that had been introduced in London by 1650. Candles were a common source of light and were preferred by those who could afford them to the oil lamps (now known as Betty lamps), which were easily supplied with fuel from fish oils. In the simple home, ceramics included basic, functional earthenware along with decorative tin-glazed wares from England, the Netherlands, Italy and Spain. Archaeological excavation has also uncovered stoneware of German origin and even a few pieces of Chinese porcelain. Metalware included pewter, brass and silver, some of which was produced locally. The silver that was produced in Boston and New York in the 17th century is conservative in design, mostly following English examples. Early room descriptions suggest that the simple furnishings and panelling were occasionally enlivened with japanning, which first became popular in the 1670s and was particularly favoured in Boston and New York.

A few textiles would have been found in these interiors, including plain curtains attached to poles by rings sewn on tapes, cupboard cloths, and cushions of plain woollen fabric, needlework or imported turkeywork. The most conspicuous, and often the most valuable items listed in

25. Wentworth Room, from Portsmouth, New Hampshire, c. 1690 (New York, Metropolitan Museum of Art)

inventories, would have been bed-hangings and coverlets. Most of these textiles would have been home-produced from wool, linen or a mixture of the two known as linsey-woolsey, but costly silks, chintzes and embroideries were occasionally imported. Bedrugs were popular throughout the 17th and 18th centuries; they were made of heavy canvas through which strands of wool were pulled to form loops or cut pile.

Carpets were used on tables and cupboards but not on floors, which were generally bare. Where Dutch influence was strong, the floor was sanded and the sand swept into patterns. The existence of Colonial portrait painters and the availability of prints based on paintings suggest that, at least in some interiors, pictures were to be found on the walls.

A change in fashion is discernible at the end of the 17th century, when such interiors as the Wentworth Room (c. 1690; reconstruction, New York, Met.; see fig. 25) in Portsmouth, NH, began to reflect the WILLIAM AND MARY STYLE. More emphasis was placed on elaborate ornament and fine craftsmanship. The profusion of design books, illustrating objects and interiors, that appeared in Europe at the end of the 17th century left its mark on American rooms. An interest in classical design was demonstrated in room panelling that was made of wood but modelled on classical stonework. One likely source of inspiration for the panelling and the bold mouldings around chimney-pieces was the work of the Huguenot designer Daniel Marot the younger. In more elegant interiors the panelling was stained, painted in stone colours or, in rare instances, marbled. Ceilings were usually plastered; when the beams showed they were often cased in panels cut in the same patterns as the wall panelling. Larger houses were built on a central plan, with a central hall and an elegant staircase, and the use of rooms became more specialized: the kitchen, for example, was separated from the living quarters. Many different activities—eating, entertaining and sleeping—still took place in the same room, and special forms of furniture, such as trestle tables, gate-legged tables and chair-tables, were devised to save space and to fulfil several functions.

Greater elegance was a factor in every aspect of room decoration. Comfort was provided by upholstered day-beds and wing-chairs, and, to complement the classicism of the panelling, furniture design became more refined and ornate, often emulating London fashions rather than the provincial models that had been used earlier. If not japanned, surfaces could be painted to look like japanning, veneer or grained wood. Curtain styles became more elaborate and included festoons similar to those illustrated by Marot. Carpets continued to be used on tables not floors. Prints, portraits and, occasionally, townscapes or landscapes were hung on the walls. Interiors were lit by candles in holders that were shaped as balusters or as richly detailed classical columns.

2. 1730–90. The sixty years between 1730 and 1790 were marked by increasing affluence and ease. This, and the growing demand for intimacy, comfort and convenience, led to more elegant interiors. Few, if any, Colonial houses rivalled the English country house in size; they compared instead with English merchant homes of the same period. Many of the interiors, however, were just as well appointed as those in Europe—inventories of the grander American houses testify to that. They contained a great profusion of objects for eating, drinking and writing, and at the same time rooms came to be used for more specific purposes. Another trend was towards regionalization: Boston, New York, Philadelphia and Newport, RI, developed their own tastes, while in Connecticut, which was more conservative, the Queen Anne style in furniture persisted until the 19th century. In rural areas many householders retained the customs of their Dutch, German and Scandinavian ancestors, preferring simple, heavy furniture with painted decoration to more fashionable styles.

In sophisticated homes new influences became apparent. The Palladian style, which was introduced in England in the 1720s, reached America through architectural handbooks, including that of William Kent; these provided suggestions for the treatment of windows, doors and chimney-pieces. The European taste for Rococo and chinoiserie also extended to America. Chinese goods, including wallpaper, porcelain and lacquer panels, were imported via England from the mid-18th century, and Chinese influence can be seen in locally made furniture and porcelain.

Panelling design continued to be based on classical stonework, but mouldings became smaller in proportion, and colours that were not associated with stone or wood, such as pink, tan, green and blue, were introduced to paint the woodwork. Some clients and builders preferred simple surrounds and delftware tiles for fireplaces, while others chose designs from handbooks. Wallpapers were introduced, in floral patterns inspired by painted cottons or with chinoiserie scenes. Many were simply painted or printed, but flock was not unknown; some were locally made, others imported.

An ever-increasing number of furniture forms appeared: the tea-table became popular as tea-drinking became a social ritual, and a number of tables, desks and chests for varied purposes were introduced. Mirrors and longcase clocks were elegant embellishments to an affluent interior. Upholstery became more widely used on chairs and settees, but the finer fabrics were still imported and therefore expensive. Plain, strong colours—reds, blues, greens and yellows—were preferred, and the curtains would often be in a matching fabric. Printed cottons became fashionable in the mid-18th century, and chintz reproductions of Indian calicoes were imported from England. Crewelwork and flamestitch embroidery was popular for beds. Candles continued to be the favoured source of lighting; although metal was more common, ceramic holders were to be found.

In the 1760s greater flamboyance in design was introduced as the Rococo entered its second phase. Essentially the change was not radical since it involved the same combination of classical and chinoiserie elements, but more relief ornament was employed on furniture, wall decoration and decorative objects. This taste, which can be seen in the Powel Room (built in Philadelphia, 1765–

26. Powel Room, from Philadelphia, 1765–6, remodelled 1769–71 (New York, Metropolitan Museum of Art)

6; remodelled 1769–71; reconstruction, New York, Met.; see fig. 26), became fashionable at the same time that Thomas Chippendale's *Gentleman and Cabinet Maker's Director* (London, 1754) brought new furniture designs to the American colonies. Other architectural handbooks published in London in the mid-18th century, for example those by Batty Langley and Abraham Swan, provided ideas for architectural details, mainly chimney-pieces and doors. Although American craftsmen were able to do the elaborate carving, records show that mouldings were sometimes ordered from London.

Americans did not follow Chippendale's book as closely as Londoners, but they did enjoy its suggestions for greater and more obvious elegance, and they achieved the desired effects in rooms by adding the appropriate embellishments. In furniture design, however, Americans were conservative. While chair forms, at least in part, were inspired by engravings in the *Director*, such pieces as the tallboy, which was not included in the *Director* because it had gone out of fashion in England, continued to be popular in the colonies. In fact, 'Chippendale' is simply the popular name for the style that is the American equivalent of the Rococo and a version of what is known as Georgian in England. Even the colours are related, featuring the same pastel palette, slightly greyed, that was used in England between 1760 and 1790. Wallpaper patterns reflected this more elaborate Rococo style by

including complex designs in which architectural elements were used in surprising juxtapositions. Also, with the greater demand for chinoiserie, Chinese landscapes became an increasingly popular subject for papers.

3. 1791–1830. In design, the Federal era was marked by a preference for classicism that was characterized at first by its delicacy and later by a grander, heavier look (*see* FEDERAL STYLE). In the early work the influence of English designers, led by Robert Adam (i), is discernible. Later it was French designers, particularly Charles Percier and Pierre-François Fontaine, whose influence was important. Other fashionable stylistic elements of the period derived from Napoleon's Egyptian campaign of 1798–1802, which inspired the Egyptian designs popularized in England by Thomas Hope, and from the opening of direct trade between the USA and East Asia in the 1790s, which stimulated a renewed craze for chinoiserie.

Neo-classicism came into fashion in the USA several decades after its advent in England and France, its arrival coinciding with the publication in London of the popular furniture design books of George Hepplewhite (1788) and Thomas Sheraton (1791). The new style was characterized by a classical revival in which the ornament was directly inspired by Greek and Roman decoration, but the forms were adapted to 18th-century taste. This decoration was delicate and flat or in low relief, and it was in the decoration rather than the plan that the American house of the Federal era differed from what had been popular earlier. However, there were more big houses and more rooms segregated for such specific purposes as dining, sewing or reading. Bedrooms now received special attention, with elaborately dressed toilet-tables and beds.

The introduction of mass-production techniques transformed interior design. Bands of ready-made decoration were available for furniture and silver; classical architectural trim could be bought by the yard, moulded rather than carved; wallpaper became cheaper due to technical advances and therefore more widespread; and the introduction of the Jacquard loom brought down the price of textiles and allowed windows to be extravagantly draped.

Furniture of the period before about 1815 was made with the same delicacy as before, but the decoration was flatter. Veneers and inlays were used to emphasize surfaces, and carving, if present at all, was generally in lower relief. For the newly fashionable dining-room, cabinetmakers designed tables to stay open in the centre of the room. They were supported by either a pedestal or by straight legs; in the case of the latter, the tables were made up of separate units that could be added when needed or used independently as side tables. The sideboard with ample storage space was a new form introduced by English furniture design books. All around the house there was an increasing number of small tables with a single drawer or a set of drawers. For furnishing textiles cotton became more popular, as did horsehair. The small sprigs and stripes of the late 18th century were gradually replaced by bolder versions of these patterns and by medallion designs. Similarly, light colours were followed by strident reds, yellows, greens and blues.

Decorative objects reflected the same taste for delicate, classical design. Lighting was brighter as chandeliers were used more widely, and a variety of oil lamps offering brighter light than candles was introduced. An oil lamp with special construction to provide a draught and so increase the light was patented by the French inventor Louis Argand. Silver design tended to be restrained, with elegance achieved not in decoration but through form, inspired, at least in part, by ancient models. Carpets became more popular in the Federal era, but oriental patterns were less fashionable than classical ones. Contemporary paintings of interiors often show boldly patterned carpets or painted floor cloths covering the entire floor or, more simply, floors stencilled or painted in overall patterns.

Around 1815 interior decoration shifted from delicacy to monumentality. The second phase of the Federal style, which is commonly called the Empire style, was clearly the result of French influence, but this could have come through London as well as directly through Paris. In architecture the equivalent of the Empire style was the Greek Revival: both styles had political implications for the newly independent nation, and it was no accident that the main source of influence became France rather than England. The Greek Revival was most important between 1825 and 1860, when houses were built on a grander scale, with high-ceilinged rooms finished with elegant but heavy and simple classical trim. It appears, however, that the new fashion was introduced first in objects. The design books and magazines that were influential in the USA

showed people in the latest Empire clothing sitting on chairs in the same taste, but architects and builders did not respond to this trend for a while. The first furniture-makers to follow the more monumental style were such French emigrants as Charles-Honoré Lannuier who embellished their work with handsome gilt swans, caryatids and eagles. Silver design was influenced further by the publications of collections of ancient Greek and Roman works as well as by designs made for the court of Napoleon. This second phase of classicism was characterized by heavy forms and very prominent, large-scale decoration, as evident in ceramics as it was in metalwork. The first interiors in the new style were strikingly simple in detail, with several of the most notable examples reflecting the influence of English Regency architects. Large rooms with bold classical detailing were characteristic. Doors might be crowned with pediments, and in the ceilings there were elaborate plaster rosettes from which were suspended chandeliers. The ideal mantelpiece was white or black marble, either very simple or with carved caryatids supporting the shelf. Scenic wallpapers were popular because they were considered to be in the spirit of ancient Roman mural decoration.

4. 1831–1900. The commonly held view that 19th-century design was eclectic and unimaginative is unfortunate. There was indeed a tendency all through the period to exploit tradition and seek inspiration in historic styles, but there were also changes in approach. The manner in which early design was used varied, as did the eras or areas that provided inspiration: it is possible to see a succession of revivals in which ancient, medieval, Renaissance and Rococo models were adapted to 19th-century use. This was encouraged by the growing number of interior decorating firms. By the last quarter of the century designers had divided into two camps. There were those dedicated to reform, architect–designers whose work lay at the foundations of the Modern Movement, and those whose work in historic styles, until closely inspected, bears at first sight a convincing resemblance to its models. It is possible therefore to trace historicism and reform as parallel trends. This was a period of great social advancement, which naturally had an impact on interior design. The growth of an affluent middle-class market was accompanied by increasing demands for comfort and style in the home. Mass production encouraged a proliferation of ornate furniture and decorative knicknacks; the development of interior springing transformed the role of upholstery; the invention of aniline dyes introduced brighter, harsher tones to vie with the prevailing dull greens, reds and browns; and by the 1870s such modern conveniences as gas lighting and central heating were widespread. It must not be forgotten, however, that away from the affluent urban centres there was a very different approach to home life. The SHAKERS were the most extreme proponents of rural simplicity, but until the 1860s many country interiors were sparsely decorated with locally made textiles and boldly painted furniture and ceramics. At the end of the century this folk art and other vestiges of Colonial life, including Spanish influence in the Southwest, provided inspiration for designers who sought alternatives to European historicism.

Although Greek Revival was considered particularly appropriate to public buildings, it was also used freely for domestic architecture. The leading practitioner of the style was Alexander Jackson Davis, who frequently took overall control of interiors and furnishings as well as exteriors. Grand, temple-like porticos gave access to a central hall off which the main rooms were symmetrically arranged. Double parlours on one side and a dining-room and library on the other constituted a particularly popular ground-floor plan. The rooms were high-ceilinged with heavy classical detailing in the form of cornices, pilasters and architraves. The furniture was equally imposing and characterized by bold shapes, particularly large-scale pillar and scroll motifs.

A reaction against the Greek Revival inspired more romantic designs in the 1840s. The Italianate villa, based on 16th-century Tuscan prototypes, was introduced, though it was rarely Italian on the inside, and the picturesque Gothic villa was popularized by A. J. Downing's books *Cottage Residences* (1842) and *Architecture of Country Houses* (1850). Both these styles allowed for more freedom in internal planning than the Greek Revival. The pointed arch and tracery of Gothic architecture were used as motifs to embellish furniture, and in some instances walls and ceilings were decorated with similar Gothic elements. The

most extreme reaction against classicism can be seen in the extravagantly curved and ornamented Rococo Revival furnishings of the 1840s to 1860s (e.g. the Richard and Gloria Manney Rococo Revival Parlour by JOHN HENRY BELTER, *c.* 1852; reconstruction, New York, Met.; see fig. 27). These historical styles were sometimes associated with certain rooms: the Gothic with the library, for example, and the Rococo with entertaining. The severe and classical lines of a Greek Revival room could be modified to a Gothic or Rococo concept by the addition of the appropriate wallpaper, mantelpieces and furniture. Ingrain carpeting, made to cover the entire floor, was available in detailed Rococo or classical patterns; but 'Brussels' pile carpeting with scroll patterns and floral motifs was also favoured for Rococo interiors.

In the 1860s a renewed burst of French influence in the USA brought flatter ornament in incised linear patterns to replace the relief decoration on chimney-pieces and door surrounds; sometimes the woodwork was stained rather than painted. The straight lines of this Renaissance Revival are to be found on furniture as well, but a close look at objects reveals a fascinating juxtaposition of Neo-classical and Renaissance motifs. The larger furniture manufacturers provided sets of furniture in a particular style, but in the grander homes there tended to be a mixture of styles.

27. Richard and Gloria Manney Rococo Revival Parlour by John Henry Belter, New York, *c.* 1852 (New York, Metropolitan Museum of Art)

28. Mr J. Taylor Johnston's parlour, New York, early 1880s; from *Artistic Houses* (New York, 1884)

This can be seen in the portrait of the *Brown Family* (priv. col.) by Eastman Johnson, where the furniture is in several styles to suggest wealth over a long period.

The publication in London in 1868 of Charles Locke Eastlake's *Hints on Household Taste* introduced a new approach to design that was soon adopted in the USA. After 1875, rather than reviving historic styles, designers began to use historic motifs in distinctively different designs, embellishing rich, elegant interiors with exotic decoration. Although Eastlake had followed William Morris in advocating reform and a return to the functionalism of medieval design, designers who seemed to base their work on his suggestions for new forms embellished them in ways he detested, resulting in a rich eclecticism. In New York several cabinetmaking establishments expanded their businesses to include decorating and took on the responsibility of providing everything necessary for the interior. In 1879 Louis Comfort Tiffany (*see* TIFFANY, §2) and CANDACE WHEELER were two of the founder-members of the Louis C. Tiffany & Associated Artists, a decorating firm that created Aesthetic Movement interiors. Christian Herter and Potier & Stymus were two of the most prominent firms to offer furnishings carefully selected from a variety of sources, and in parlours designed by them old and new were tastefully combined. While the lines of furniture were restrained, inlays, painting and

gilding were popular. By the 1880s the use of elegant antiques or finely made furniture in 17th- and 18th-century styles began. The interiors of elegant homes were embellished with exotic patterns on the walls as well as in the designs of the objects that filled the rooms (see fig. 28). Tapestries for period interiors were supplied by such studios as that of William Baumgarten (*see* §XI, 3(i) below).

5. AFTER 1900. At the turn of the century, when the Arts and Crafts Movement flourished, such designers as Gustav Stickley began to produce simple oak furniture. Amateur cabinetmakers were encouraged to imitate the style with the aid of such publications as Stickley's *The Craftsman*, a magazine that was published monthly from 1901 to 1916. The magazine, which had great appeal among the reform-minded, reported on adventurous European designs and reviewed Art Nouveau exhibitions, although Americans did not use that style to any great degree. It was the Arts and Crafts Movement that inspired the foundation of a few magazines specifically focusing on home decoration: *House Beautiful* (est. 1896) and *House and Garden* (est. 1903) were started as publications advocating reform in design and continued to reflect popular taste in the late 20th century.

Also at the beginning of the 20th century traditionalists became somewhat more aware of authentic historical design, and they introduced furnishings that combined original period work with their own designs in the spirit of the 16th century to the early 19th. In such houses as the Breakers, built for Cornelius Vanderbilt in Newport, RI, by Richard Morris Hunt, the mixture of old and new works so well that there is sometimes confusion in distinguishing what was designed specifically for the house. The grander town houses of *c.* 1900 were designed in the Georgian style, but country or suburban houses were more frequently made classical by exploiting American antecedents, a style generally called Colonial Revival, even when the model was a late Federal style house. In each variation equal attention was devoted to the decorative and functional aspects, and houses were equipped with the latest conveniences to make living comfortable. Servants' quarters were done simply but efficiently, whereas reception rooms and those reserved for the family were decorated in the appropriate styles. Such architects as H. H. Richardson, Louis Sullivan and Frank Lloyd Wright led the reform trend in interiors (see fig. 29), while Richard Morris Hunt and McKim, Mead & White head the list of traditionalists.

After 1920 interior decoration continued to follow the traditional and the reform, more often called modern, and each had a certain range from the pure to the conciliatory. Purists in traditional design became increasingly careful in reproducing the period that they admired and in finding original material from that period, so that, for example, the finest 18th-century style room had walls of 18th-century panelling to surround furnishings of the period and lighting consisted of simulated candles. Reformist designers divided into two schools: some followed the example of German designers from the Bauhaus by attempting to create new forms and by using either new materials or old materials in new ways; other modernists, working in the Art Deco idiom, were keen on modifying design and simplifying shapes to suit the taste of those who enjoyed traditional forms.

After World War II these two basic, opposing trends continued to be significant, although an increasing effort was made towards a blending of the so-called modern and the traditional. Americans were much influenced by the Bauhaus innovators who moved to the USA just before or just after the war, and the functionalist tradition of the Bauhaus proved to be more influential than the Art Deco approach. In the 1980s experiments in Post-modernism inspired designs that combined bright colours and traditional elements. Houses in 18th-century American styles,

29. Living-room of the Francis W. Little House by Frank Lloyd Wright, Wayzata, Minnesota, 1912–14 (New York, Metropolitan Museum of Art)

with either period furniture or reproductions, continued to be popular.

BIBLIOGRAPHY

A. J. Downing: *Cottage Residences* (New York, 1842)
——: *Architecture of Country Houses* (New York, 1850/*R* 1969)
H. H. Holly: *Dwellings in Town and Country* (New York, 1878)
E. Wharton and O. Codman: *The Decoration of Houses* (New York, 1897)
R. R. Meyric: *American Interior Design: The Traditions and Development of Domestic Design from Colonial Times to the Present* (New York, 1947)
M. D. Schwartz: *American Interiors, 1675–1885: A Guide to the American Period Rooms in the Brooklyn Museum* (New York, 1968)
H. L. Peterson: *Americans at Home: From the Colonists to the Late Victorians: A Pictorial Sourcebook* (New York, 1971)
W. Seale: *The Tasteful Interlude: American Interiors through the Camera's Eye, 1860–1917* (New York, 1975)
E. De Noilles Mayhew with M. Myers jr: *A Documentary History of the American Interior* (New York, 1980)
R. Bishop and P. Coblenz: *American Decorative Arts: 360 Years of Creative Design* (New York, 1982)
M. B. Davidson and E. Stillinger: *The American Wing in the Metropolitan Museum of Art* (New York, 1985)
C. Gere: *Nineteenth-century Decoration: The Art of the Interior* (London, 1989)

MARVIN D. SCHWARTZ

VI. Furniture.

1. Before 1730. 2. 1730–90. 3. 1791–1840. 4. 1841–1900. 5. After 1900.

1. BEFORE 1730. During this period American furniture changed markedly both in style and construction. Colonial furniture of the mid-17th century, like its English models, was characterized by simple, heavy forms with architectural, geometric and floral decoration derived from northern European Mannerism. By the end of the century American furniture reflected the Baroque style that was then fashionable in Europe. This furniture, with its exuberant carving, turnings and elaborately veneered surfaces, is known as WILLIAM AND MARY STYLE, after the English monarchs whose reign (1685–1702) brought about an influx of new ideas from the Continent.

In the early Colonial period furniture was made by local joiners who also applied their skills to the building of houses. In the 1690s, however, with the arrival in New England of such London-trained cabinetmakers as John Brocas (*d* 1740), joinery gave way to cabinetmaking. Where joiners used framed panels for the sides of their case pieces, cabinetmakers fastened the solid sides to the top and bottom with dovetails. Where joiners ornamented the surfaces of their work with carving and applied geometric mouldings and half-spindles, or in New Haven with inlay, cabinetmakers applied rich veneers.

Until the mid-17th century the colonists had very few chairs with backs; instead they sat on stools or long benches called forms. By mid-century, however, three types of 'back-stools' were common: turned, wainscot and 'Cromwell'. Turned chairs were produced on a lathe and had a rush or splint seat. Instead of vertical spindles some had slats across the back, a design that originated in Germany and the Netherlands. Wainscot chairs were made by joiners. They had plank seats and solid, carved backs and were fitted with a cushion. The large oak boards from which they were made were also used for wainscoting, hence the name of the chairs. By the end of the 17th century sets of upholstered side chairs (later called Cromwell chairs after Oliver Cromwell, the Protector of England from 1649 to 1658) were found in the homes of prosperous merchants. They were usually made of maple and oak with ball-turned legs and stretchers and upholstered backs and seats. Occasionally spiral turning was substituted, particularly on chairs made in New York and New Jersey. They were upholstered in leather or brightly coloured Turkey work. Fringe or brass nails at the edges of the upholstery heightened the appearance of these chairs.

The impact of East Asian culture in England in the mid-17th century substantially altered the appearance of chairs in the William and Mary style. The elaborate carving and turning were predominantly Baroque, but the frequent use of caning and the curved backs that replaced the stiff, straight backs of 17th-century chairs were all derived from Chinese prototypes. Banister-back chairs, which were less expensive than caned ones, repeated the shape of turned back posts in half-balusters across the back. Another variation with leather backs and seats, turned legs and stretchers, Spanish feet and moulded top rails (crest rails) developed in Boston. These were imitated in other major cabinetmaking centres, notably New York and Philadelphia. Also by 1700 a new type of chair, the easy chair, with turned legs, an arched cresting and upholstered wings, became common. Associated with invalids and the elderly, these chairs were used for sleeping in an upright position. Also, day-beds or couches, fitted with a long cushion or squab, appeared for the first time.

Tables were rare in the 17th century, and only a few trestle- and chair-tables in the medieval tradition survive. By the end of the century gate-leg tables began to appear. By the early 18th century these tables were made of walnut instead of oak, and their turnings had become lighter and more complex. Some had gates in the shape of a butterfly supported from a single point on the stretcher. Another innovation was the toilet or dressing table (lowboy).

Chests were also used as tables in the 17th century. They sometimes had drawers that ran on side runners and were fitted with wooden handles. The most popular form of decoration was shallow relief carving highlighted with red, blue, white, black, brown or green paint. Panelled chests were made by joiners and fall into three major categories, depending on the type of carved decoration. The most elaborately carved chests with tulips, first discovered in the Hadley area of Massachusetts, were made in the Connecticut River Valley. Another group, from the Wethersfield area of southern Connecticut, has stylized Tudor roses and tulips. Chests from Guilford and Saybrook, CT, feature painted tulips, thistles, urns and roses based on stylized Dutch and English designs.

The chest-of-drawers gradually replaced the chest by 1700. Originating in London and evolving from the chest-of-drawers with doors, these were found in Boston by the 1640s. They usually had turned feet, ball- or turnip-shaped, or feet formed by extending the sides or corner stiles below the bottom drawer. By 1700 they were often adorned with japanning, veneer or inlay. Single- or double-arched mouldings typically outlined each drawer. By 1700 drawers ran on the bottom edge of the drawer side instead of on grooves cut into the drawer sides. The earliest drawer handles were usually of wood, but by the end of the 17th century brass pear-shaped drops hung in front of rosette-shaped back plates, and matching cartouche-shaped brass escutcheons protected the wood around the keyholes.

30. Cupboard, oak with pine and maple, 1.42×1.27×0.58 m, from Massachusetts, c. 1675–90 (New York, Metropolitan Museum of Art)

Such variations as brass knobs or ring pulls were also found. Related to chests-of-drawers were bureaux, which developed when the so-called bible box of the 17th century was placed on a frame. Later the frame was replaced with more serviceable drawers. When closed, the slanting lid provided a convenient lectern; when open and supported by slides or small drawers, it formed a writing surface. As merchants expanded their accounts the need for handy storage of ledgers was filled by the addition of a bookcase on top of the desk.

The splendid cupboards that graced the best rooms of many colonists' homes by the mid-17th century were used to display expensive silver, glass and tin-glazed earthenware, and so to impress visitors with the wealth of the household. The enclosed upper sections, on which a length of brightly coloured cloth was often laid, were framed by massive turned pillars; the panels were elaborately carved or, later, fielded, and further decoration was applied in the form of bosses and half-balusters. The lower sections often contained drawers (e.g. a cupboard from Massachusetts, c. 1675–90; New York, Met.; see fig. 30). By the end of the 17th century these cupboards went out of fashion and were replaced by the tallboy (highboy) as the best piece of furniture in the house. This, along with the corner cupboard, assumed the role of the cupboard as a place to display finery.

Even more valuable than the tallboy was the fourposter bed with its canopy, expensive hangings and mattresses stuffed with as much as 30 kilos of feathers. Tent and field beds could easily be taken apart and folded. Cots, hammocks and simple, low-post frames were even more common. By the beginning of the 18th century bed rails were fastened with screws in a departure from the 17th-century practice of using mortice and tenon joints, making them easy to dismantle.

Only clocks rivalled fine beds as the greatest luxury a gentleman could own. Most clocks were imported from London. The earliest had only an hour hand: minute hands were unnecessary since clocks were not accurate to the minute. By the beginning of the 18th century longer pendulums were added to clocks that had formerly hung on the wall, and a tall wooden case was required to protect the pendulum. Although by the early 18th century American clockmakers were turning out brass works and faces in such major cities as Philadelphia and Boston, most works continued to be imported from England. Few colonists could afford looking-glasses before 1700. Virtually all the glass was imported, as were most of the frames. William and Mary style looking-glasses were usually square or rectangular with an angular cresting and ogee curves often pierced with hearts and geometric designs. The appearance of such luxury items as expensive looking-glasses and longcase clocks attested to the growing wealth of the colonists and to their desire to display that wealth through the most fashionable furniture.

BIBLIOGRAPHY

I. Lyon: *The Colonial Furniture of New England* (Boston and New York, 1891/*R* 1977)
P. Kane: *Furniture of the New Haven Colony: The Seventeenth Century*, (New Haven, 1973)
V. Chinnery: *Oak Furniture: The British Tradition* (Woodbridge, 1979)
R. H. Randall: 'Boston Chairs', *Old-Time New England*, liv (May 1980), pp. 12–20
New England Begins: The Seventeenth Century (exh. cat. by J. Fairbanks and R. Trent, Boston, MA, Mus. F.A., 1982)
B. Forman: *American Seating Furniture, 1630–1730: An Interpretive Catalogue*, Winterthur, DE, Du Pont Winterthur Mus. cat. (New York and London, 1988)

2. 1730–90. With increasing prosperity colonists built grand houses and decorated them with luxurious furnishings in the latest fashion, which by the 1730s was the Queen Anne style. This had been popular in England for more than a decade before it appeared c. 1730 in Boston, the largest Colonial city in the first half of the 18th century, and in other major American cities. The best pieces were executed in walnut and later in mahogany, replacing the coarser oak used in the 17th century.

The new style combined classical and oriental elements. The classical proportions, architectural details and carved motifs, such as scallop shells and acanthus leaves, reflected European Renaissance traditions. The cabriole leg, called a 'housebone' or 'crook'd foot' in the 18th century, the hallmark of the new style, was a universal form found in Classical, European and East Asian cultures. The claw-and-ball foot, which appeared for the first time on Queen Anne furniture and became even more popular in America in the Chippendale period, had clear oriental antecedents. Japanning, a decorative technique that imitated oriental lacquer work, was most popular in Boston but was known in all the colonies. Queen Anne brass drawer handles on case furniture imitated the simple batwing handles found on oriental furniture.

Although Queen Anne curves continued to grace some furniture until after the Revolution (and remained popular in rural areas until the 19th century), the more angular Chippendale style gradually gained ascendancy between 1755 and 1790. The elements of the new style were set out in Thomas Chippendale's *Gentleman and Cabinet Maker's Director*, first published in London in 1754. Chippendale understood the importance of classical proportions and admonished his readers to study the classical columns that he displayed in the front of his book. His designs show three major influences, Chinese, Gothic and Rococo, grafted on to furniture with classical proportions. The most obvious influence in Chippendale was the Rococo style with such asymmetrical motifs as rocks, shells, vines, leaves and flowers. The rounded top rail of the Queen Anne chair was replaced by an angular one with projecting ears similar to those on Chinese chairs. The pierced baluster splat had occasionally appeared on Queen Anne chairs, but in the Chippendale period carvers turned the splat into a panoply of ribbons, cusps, arches and scrolls (e.g. an armchair from Philadelphia, *c.* 1756; New York, Met.; see fig. 31). Densely grained and richly figured imported mahogany was the perfect wood for the beautiful carving of the Chippendale period. It was first imported from the West Indies soon after 1700 but was not widely used until the mid-18th century, for example in the shop of BENJAMIN RANDOLPH, when carving became so important. Veneer and inlay, which were occasionally found on American Queen Anne furniture particularly from Boston, were rarely used in the Chippendale period.

In the 18th century strong regional variation, arising from disparate cabinetmaking traditions learnt in various parts of England or the Continent, could be seen in furniture, particularly chairs. The persistence of the apprentice system and such closely knit communities of cabinetmakers, many of them Quakers (*see* SAVERY, WILLIAM), helped perpetuate these differences. One particularly good index of this was the shaped or carved foot characteristic of each major cabinetmaking centre (*see* BOSTON, §III, 1 and PHILADELPHIA, §3). This work was often done by a few specialist craftsmen. The pad foot was associated with Massachusetts, the slipper foot with Newport, RI, and the trifid foot with Philadelphia. The elongated ball and finely sculpted talon of Newport work contrasted with the squashed ball and webbed talon of Philadelphia examples. The retracted or raked talon of Boston differed from the square, blockish balls and talons of New York. Brightly upholstered easy chairs in the Queen Anne style but now with smoothly curving cresting and cabriole legs, also showed distinctive regional variation. Arms on New England chairs rested on vertical cones, whereas in Philadelphia they were supported by C-scrolled blocks. By the mid-18th century carved acanthus leaves and claw-and-ball feet were often grafted on to the Queen Anne form. By the 1770s straight Marlboro' legs replaced cabriole legs on both easy chairs and sofas. As large parlours became more common early in the 18th century sofas and settees proliferated and day-beds declined in popularity.

Windsor chairs also exhibited regional variation, though they did not follow the stylistic progression characteristic of other furniture in the 18th and 19th centuries. American Windsors were made in Philadelphia by the 1740s but did not surpass the cheaper rush-seated chairs in popularity until after the Revolution. The low-backed chair, precursor of the type known in 19th-century America as a Captain's chair, was the earliest. Soon a horizontal top rail evolved, supported on spindles rising from the seat through a rail following the curvature of the seat. The double bow back (sack back), particularly popular in New England, was similar but had a rounded top rail. Such makers as Ebenezer Tracey (1744–1803) of Lisbon, CT, made Windsor settees, stools, cradles, high chairs and tablet chairs (writing armchairs) using several different woods in their construction.

Some of the most distinctive American furniture was produced outside the major centres of Boston, Newport, New York and Philadelphia. While city cabinetmakers made fashionable furniture, often as close to London styles as possible, craftsmen in rural areas, where the majority of the population lived, followed traditional designs that survived long after they had been abandoned in the cities. Notable work was produced by relatively isolated craftsmen, such as Eliphalet Chapin (1741–1807) in the Connecticut River valley, the brothers John Dunlap (1746–92) and Samuel Dunlap (1752–1830) of southern New Hampshire and the Dominy family, Nathaniel Dominy (i) (1737–1812), Nathaniel Dominy (ii) (1770–1852) and Felix Dominy (1800–68), on Long Island. In Pennsylvania, German craftsmen perpetuated their peasant folk traditions, particularly in the construction of highly painted chests.

31. Walnut armchair, h. 1.12 m, from Philadelphia, *c.* 1756 (New York, Metropolitan Museum of Art)

Among the most impressive pieces of furniture produced in the urban areas were the high chest-of-drawers or tallboy (highboy) and the matching dressing table (lowboy). The flat tops of Queen Anne tallboys, with their heavy cornice mouldings often derived from architectural design books, gave way to ogee or cove mouldings and frets, which were popular until the end of the century. Triple-arched aprons (skirts) were fitted with drop finials, vestiges of the multiple front legs on earlier pieces. By the 1740s tallboys were fitted with broken arches over central drawers with carved fans or scallop shells copied from architectural designs. As the century progressed the gentle arches of the Queen Anne pediment (bonnet) often with a closed top, gave way to the more abrupt thrust of the Chippendale pediment, carved and ornamented with elaborate finials and a central cartouche. The Queen Anne chest-on-stand tallboy had been replaced in England by the chest-on-chest form by about 1740 but continued to be popular in America where the best examples carried

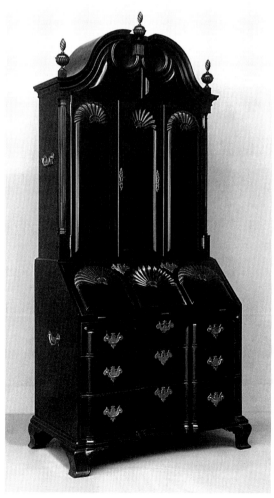

32. Bureau bookcase, mahogany with chestnut, pine and cedar, h. 2.52 m, from Newport, Rhode Island, c. 1760–90 (New York, Metropolitan Museum of Art)

elaborately carved Rococo and classical motifs. Only in Charleston, SC, was the chest-on-chest form widely popular. On bureau bookcases (desk and bookcase) the pediments followed the same progression. Glass panes or sparkling looking-glass added elegance, but wooden panel doors, usually with rounded arches, were more common in the Queen Anne period. Chippendale pieces had square-hinged doors, the frames of which had ogee mouldings around wood or glass panels.

Newport and Boston favoured block-front furniture that depended on three panels alternately concave and convex in a Baroque fashion for their pretensions to elegance (e.g. a bureau bookcase from Newport, c. 1760–90; New York, Met.; see fig. 32). The earliest documented block front, a walnut bureau bookcase (Winterthur, DE, Du Pont Winterthur Mus.), was made by Job Coit (1692–1742) and his son Job Coit the younger (1717–45) in Boston in 1738. Later the idea was executed with paramount success by a talented group of craftsmen working in Newport, principally the TOWNSEND and GODDARD families, who produced more than twenty cabinetmakers, including JOHN GODDARD, in that city before the Revolution. In addition to block fronts, customers in Boston, Newport and adjoining areas enjoyed serpentine or reverse serpentine fronts on case furniture. However, the height of elegance in Boston was the bombé chest or bureau bookcase. BENJAMIN FROTHINGHAM made the earliest dated bombé form in 1753, a bureau bookcase (Washington, DC, State Dept) possibly copied from an imported English example.

Whereas Boston and Newport excelled in making outdated Baroque forms, Philadelphia carried the Rococo aesthetic of the second half of the 18th century to its highest pitch. Tallboys with flat tops continued to be made, but such Philadelphia craftsmen as William Savery (1721–88) and THOMAS AFFLECK added pediments for their best customers. These were most often designed as scrolls or pitched in a triangular shape. Fluted columns on the corners of the case and richly carved pediments and aprons enhanced the finest pieces (e.g. a tallboy, c. 1762–90; New York, Met.; see fig. 33). Sculptural finials and cartouches in the form of urns and flames, carved busts or baskets of fruit and flowers added unexcelled richness. The pieces were finished off with imported English brass handles, the best with Rococo detailing.

A variety of tables proliferated. In the Queen Anne period serving tables were fitted with tile, slate or marble. Cabriole legs and pad feet gave way in the Chippendale period to straight legs. Tea-tables became more common as the price of tea dropped to a level where it was no longer a luxury. Card-tables and games-tables with fold-over tops were common even in Philadelphia, where the Quakers frowned on gambling. By the mid-18th century a characteristic five-legged table with a serpentine apron and square corners for candles developed in New York. Plainer card-tables with four straight legs were made in all the colonies. As the century progressed, wealthy merchants filled their houses with an ever-increasing array of forms, such as fire screens, slab, dining- and corner-tables, and candle, basin and kettle stands.

Looking-glasses in the Queen Anne style often had solid walnut, veneered or japanned frames surmounted by

the most desirable. Press beds were used until the middle of the century when houses became larger and the need for fold-up furniture lessened. Octagonal posts indicate an earlier date, whereas round posts were used throughout the century.

The American Revolution drastically curtailed the production of fine furniture as the war affected both cabinetmakers and their patrons. Many of the best customers were wealthy Tories who fled to Britain or Canada. Supporters of the Revolution found that extra money that might have been spent on furniture was taxed away to finance the war effort, and many cabinetmakers turned their talents to supporting the war. By the 1760s Neoclassicism was developing in England, but in America, on account of the war, the Chippendale style lingered well into the 19th century. However, the Neo-classical taste had found its way into the more stylish homes by the 1790s.

BIBLIOGRAPHY
W. Hornor: *Blue Book, Philadelphia Furniture: William Penn to George Washington* (Philadelphia, 1935/*R* Washington, DC, 1977)
J. Downs: *American Furniture: Queen Anne and Chippendale Periods*, Winterthur, DE, Du Pont Winterthur Mus. cat. (New York, 1951)
R. Randall: *American Furniture in the Museum of Fine Arts, Boston* (Boston, 1965)
C. Hummel: *With Hammer in Hand: The Dominy Craftsmen of East Hampton, New York* (Charlottesville, 1968) [cat. rais.]
The Dunlaps & their Furniture (exh. cat by C. Parsons, Manchester, NH, Currier Gal. A., 1970)
J. Kirk: *American Chairs: Queen Anne and Chippendale* (New York, 1972)
B. Greenlaw: *New England Furniture of Colonial Williamsburg* (Williamsburg, 1974)
W. Whitehill: *Boston Furniture of the Eighteenth Century* (Boston, 1974)
D. Warren: *Bayou Bend: American Furniture, Paintings and Silver from the Bayou Bend Collection* (Houston, 1975)
D. Fales: *The Furniture of Historic Deerfield* (New York, 1976)
R. Trent: *Hearts & Crowns* (New Haven, 1977)
C. Santore: *The Windsor Style in America, 1730–1830* (Philadelphia, 1982)
B. Jobe and M. Kaye: *New England Furniture: The Colonial Era* (Boston, 1984)
M. Herckscher: *American Furniture in the Metropolitan Museum of Art: Late Colonial Period: Queen Anne and Chippendale Styles* (New York, 1985)
G. Ward: *American Case Furniture*, New Haven, CT, Yale U. A.G. cat. (New Haven, 1988)
C. Venable: *American Furniture in the Bybee Collection*, Dallas, TX, Mus. A. cat. (Dallas, 1989)

33. Tallboy, mahogany with yellow pine, tulip and cedar, h. 2.33 m, from Philadelphia, *c.* 1762–90 (New York, Metropolitan Museum of Art)

hoods with carved and gilded shells or feathers. Vertical pier glasses were designed to hang between two windows and horizontal looking-glasses for use over a fireplace. Chippendale's *Director* illustrated a new type with a tabernacle frame, so-called because of its relationship to architectural niches in Gothic and Renaissance buildings. These frames were gilded and surmounted with triangular or scrolled pediments topped by a central eagle or phoenix. Carved vines and flowers and later acanthus leaves and C-scrolls streamed down each side of the frame. By 1775 oval looking-glasses with Rococo ornament were particularly popular. Throughout the 18th century most looking-glasses and frames were imported from England.

The most expensive piece of furniture continued to be the elaborately hung beds, which became more common in the early 18th century as houses were built with bedrooms. Low posted beds were frequently surrounded by hangings strung from hooks. Field beds with arched canopies were also common, but fourposter beds were

3. 1791–1840. Between the 1790s and 1840s furniture-makers in the USA, as in Europe, interpreted and reinterpreted the designs found on Classical artefacts and architectural remains. The initial phase of Neo-classicism, the FEDERAL STYLE, was followed about 1815 by a new interpretation called the *style antique* or American EMPIRE STYLE. The subtle geometrical and classical inlay of the largely two-dimensional Federal style (e.g. a bureau bookcase from Baltimore or Philadelphia, *c.* 1811; New York, Met.; see fig. 34) was supplanted by the three-dimensional sculptural carving of the Empire style.

American Federal furniture was derived largely from English sources, which in turn were inspired by Robert Adam's reinterpretation of Classical design. English books containing Neo-classical furniture designs by George Hepplewhite, Thomas Sheraton and Thomas Shearer (*fl* 1788) were available in the USA and helped to popularize the Adam designs. Immigrant cabinetmakers, such as John Seymour and Thomas SEYMOUR, who had been trained in the new style also brought the new ideas to the

34. Bureau bookcase, mahogany and satin-wood, h. 2.31 m, from Baltimore or Philadelphia, *c.* 1811 (New York, Metropolitan Museum of Art)

USA (*see* WOOD, colour pl. II, fig. 2), while imported furniture served as models for local cabinetmakers. The Empire style that followed originated in France, but came to the USA by way of both England and France. Thomas Hope's *Household Furniture and Interior Decoration*, first published in London in 1807, was particularly important in spreading the new style.

Specialization in the woodworking trade was known even in the 17th century, but the trend accelerated at the end of the 18th century as shops, such as that of STEPHEN BADLAM, grew larger. Rarely did a single craftsman working in a large urban cabinetmaking shop both design and construct a single piece of furniture. The efficiency of specialization allowed the cabinetmaker to meet the demands of a rapidly expanding population and a growing export trade. Various workshops of carvers, inlay makers, upholsterers and turners contributed to the final product, which was then warranted by the seller who might not have done any of the work on the furniture himself.

After the Revolution many of the cabinetmakers settled in New York, which by 1815 was the centre of furniture manufacturing in the new nation. Foremost among the city's cabinetmakers was DUNCAN PHYFE, who dominated the trade from 1792 until his retirement in 1847. Other important makers included the French-born CHARLES-HONORÉ LANNUIER and the New York firm of Joseph Meeks & Sons (active 1797–1868). Boston and Philadelphia continued to be important into the 19th century (*see* BOSTON, §III, 1 and PHILADELPHIA, §3), but Newport

declined. Neighbouring Salem, MA, even though it was less than half the size of Boston, produced some of the finest Federal furniture, which was then shipped to major East Coast ports and to many foreign countries. Salem work is particularly known for the fine carving of eagles, fruit baskets, cornucopias and wheat sheaves. These have often been attributed to SAMUEL McINTIRE. After the Revolution Baltimore became the fastest growing city in the USA. Its cabinetmakers (*see* BALTIMORE, §2) produced some of the most elegant Federal furniture, often with distinctive bellflower inlay and inset *verre églomisé* panels. Although the art of painted furniture was popular everywhere in the early 19th century, the technique was used to spectacular effect by Baltimore painters.

Neo-classical dining chairs had either a square, tapered leg and an oval- or shield-shaped back, or a round, tapered leg, usually reeded, and a square back with small columns. Easy chairs, now with tapered or turned legs, continued to be popular along with upholstered barrel-back chairs and lolling or Martha Washington chairs. The latter evolved from the mid-18th-century upholstered armchair but had a higher back and tapered or turned and reeded legs reflecting the new Federal styling. By 1815 chairs based on actual classical examples, such as the sabre-legged Klismos, were popular. A horizontal rail, often painted or carved with cornucopias, anthemia, eagles and lyres, replaced the vertical splat common in the 18th century. An innovation in chair design in the 1830s was the gondole chair, in which the rear stiles curved down and forward. Cheaper chairs had rush seats, turned legs and stiles and stencilled decoration instead of expensive upholstery, carving and brass mounts. The best-known maker of these 'fancy chairs' was LAMBERT HITCHCOCK, who opened his Connecticut factory in 1818.

Before 1800 sofas were seen only in the richest homes. Cabinetmakers in the Federal period softened the bold lines of the Chippendale sofa, tapered the legs and accented the top rail and legs with delicate carving, veneer or inlay. Also popular were the square-backed sofa and the cabriole sofa with a delicately curved back. By the Empire period the sofa had become more widespread. It was heavier in style, and the Grecian couch with lion's paw feet and double scrolls on the cresting was among the most popular.

In addition to sofas, the parlour contained an assortment of tables. The Pembroke table, now with tapered legs and delicate inlay, continued in use, as did the fire screen, lighter now with classical and patriotic embellishments. The centre table first became popular in the Empire period and served much like the coffee-table of the 20th century. Card-tables were ubiquitous. Work tables both for writing and sewing grew in number. Pier tables, used as serving or hall tables, rested on supports carved in the form of caryatids, dolphins, swans, lion-footed scrolls, eagle monopodia and simple Doric and Ionic columns. In the dining-room large banquet tables seated up to 20 guests. 'Pillar-and-claw' pedestal tables with curved legs and brass feet were found in the finest houses. These, along with tables with tapered or turned legs, were made in sections and set against the wall when not in use. The most impressive piece in the dining-room was the sideboard: Federal examples stood on delicate turned or tapered legs, while

Empire ones rested on carved feet and had doors extending almost to the floor.

Other luxury items included pianofortes, mirrors and clocks. Longcase clocks continued to be among the most expensive pieces of furniture. The so-called Roxbury type, made in the Roxbury suburb of Boston, had spaghetti-like scrolls on the rounded hood (bonnet), brass finials, fluted corner columns and an inlaid case. Longcase clocks were gradually replaced by less expensive mass-produced wall or shelf clocks by the second quarter of the century. Pillar-and-scroll shelf clocks made by Eli Terry (1772–1852) were particularly sought after and were widely imitated. Mirrors, rectangular with painted top sections, had ball-hung cornices or lightly scrolled pediments with Neo-classical motifs or were made with round frames often topped by a carved gilt eagle and fitted with a convex glass. Horizontal chimney glasses framed by heavy, turned balusters exhibited standard Empire motifs.

Desks and bureau bookcases changed radically in the Federal period. The slant-front type of the 18th century, updated with Neo-classical carving or inlay, continued to be made into the first quarter of the 19th century, but the fashionable desk was now fitted with an escritoire or secretary drawer. This pulled out and its front folded down to form the writing surface. Another design had hinged flaps that folded down and rested on sliding supports to make the writing surface. Bookcase sections on these were often fitted with tambour doors made by gluing thin strips of wood on to a canvas backing. By the Empire period the French-inspired *secrétaire à abattant* had become popular. This had a flat-topped case flanked by classical columns and a large door in the upper section that folded down to form the writing surface.

Beds continued to carry a high value. Like other Federal furniture, the bedstead featured delicately turned, reeded or carved posts and occasionally carved or inlaid cornices. Empire ones had massive carved or turned posts and tall, carved headboards. The French bed, today called a sleigh bed, with headboard and footboard the same height, became popular about 1815. The typical chest-of-drawers had flaring French feet with a scrolled apron and a straight, bowed or serpentine front. Oval brass handles, often embossed with patriotic images, enlivened drawer fronts. By the early 19th century the looking-glasses that hung above the chest in most bedrooms were supplanted by chests with the looking-glass attached, similar to modern dressing-tables. Other bedroom furniture included large wardrobes.

By the 1830s Neo-classicism in furniture design entered a third and final stage dominated by massive pillars and scrolls. Imported ormolu mounts were replaced by wooden knobs, and gilding and stencilling no longer enlivened the broad expanses of mahogany veneer. This style developed in France after the restoration of the monarchy in 1815, and the advertising broadside of Joseph Meeks & Sons published in 1833 illustrates a number of such pillar-and-scroll pieces. Shortly before he retired in 1847, Duncan Phyfe referred to the current style as 'butcher furniture'. Its popularity, however, was so great that it continued to appear throughout the 19th century, alongside the Victorian revivalist styles.

BIBLIOGRAPHY

N. McClelland: *Duncan Phyfe and the English Regency, 1795–1830* (New York, 1939/*R* 1980)

L. Waxman: 'The Lannuier Brothers, Cabinetmakers', *Antiques*, lxxxii (Aug 1957), pp. 141–3

Classical America, 1815–1845 (exh. cat. by B. Tracy, Newark, NJ, Mus., 1963)

C. Montgomery: *American Furniture: The Federal Period*, Winterthur, DE, Du Pont Winterthur Mus. cat. (London, 1966)

D. Fales: *American Painted Furniture, 1660–1880* (New York, 1972)

M. Clunie: 'Joseph True and the Piecework System in Salem', *Antiques*, cxi (May 1977), pp. 1006–13

B. Hewitt: *The Work of Many Hands: Card Tables in Federal America, 1790–1820* (New Haven, 1982)

G. Weidman: *Furniture in Maryland, 1740–1940* (Baltimore, 1984)

4. 1841–1900. From the end of the 1840s American furniture was characterized by a succession of revivalist styles, notably Gothic, Rococo, Renaissance and Eastlake. These were popularized by the great world fairs, beginning in 1851 with the Great Exhibition in London and followed in 1853 by a similar exhibition in New York. Their dissemination was made possible by the Industrial Revolution, which by the mid-19th century was well established in the USA. Throughout the century the shift accelerated from small cabinetmaking shops selling to a local market to large-scale factories that distributed their products nationally from their bases in Chicago, Grand Rapids, MI, and other Midwestern centres. Using steam-driven band saws and new manufacturing techniques, these factories could produce furniture by the train load in every conceivable revivalist style to satisfy the demands of a booming consumer market.

Another innovation was the use of new and exotic materials. Wicker was exhibited at the Great Exhibition and steadily grew in popularity. Like animal horn, it was used for chairs, tables and sofas, and it appealed because of its novelty and its association with frontier life. Rustic furniture made of roots and branches had a similar novelty value and was used in gardens and rural retreats. Other innovative materials included papier mâché, cast iron and wire.

The first revivalist style to be used in the USA was Gothic, complete with crockets, quatrefoils, cusps, pointed arches, cluster columns and rose-window forms. This was particularly popular in the 1840s but continued throughout the century. Even though the USA had no medieval heritage, American manufacturers, drawing on the work of such English designers as Augustus Charles Pugin and his son A. W. N. Pugin produced a wide variety of Gothic furniture for use in halls and libraries. The Gothic style, however, was never as popular as the Rococo, or Louis XIV as it was inaccurately called in the 19th century. This style was first revived in France during the reign of Louis-Philippe (*see* ROCOCO REVIVAL). Furniture designers of the period looked back to the 18th century as the great age of French design, and such French cabinetmakers as Alexander Roux (*fl* 1837–81) and CHARLES A. BAUDOUINE brought the style to the USA in the 1850s. Numerous French publications available in the USA reinforced its popularity. Its best-known exponent was JOHN HENRY BELTER, who used lamination and steam-moulding to make strong, heavy, curved boards that could sustain deep and intricate carving (e.g. sofa, *c.* 1850–60; New York, Met.; see fig. 35).

Several design sources were plundered for Renaissance Revival furniture, which was particularly favoured for dining-rooms. Sixteenth-century French models inspired the Baroque cartouches, animal and human figures, flattened arches and roundels, while 18th-century Louis XVI prototypes gave rise to straight, turned legs, straight backs and gilt and ebonized surfaces. Many of these motifs can be seen in a cabinet (*c.* 1860–70; New York, Met.; see fig. 36) by Alexander Roux. This style had been originally promoted in France by Empress Eugénie, wife of Napoleon III. Another group of furniture known as Néo-Grec features such Greek, Roman and Egyptian motifs as columns, paterae, acroteria, sphynxes, anthemia and lions' paws.

By the 1870s there was a reaction against the complex and extravagant Rococo and Renaissance revival styles. Drawing on the ideas of such English reformers as John Ruskin, William Morris and Charles Locke Eastlake, American furniture manufacturers produced lines featuring turnings and plain oak surfaces, sometimes enlivened by reeding and incised decoration (*see* EASTLAKE STYLE). Reflecting its medieval inspiration the style was sometimes called 'Modern Gothic'. Another strain, contributed by such English designers as E. W. Godwin, arose from a fascination with East Asia, particularly Japan. Oriental elements, such as ebonized surfaces and exotic inlay, characterized exclusive custom-made furniture produced by such cabinetmakers as CHRISTIAN HERTER in New York. Just as Eastlake's followers drew on medieval England for inspiration, some American designers referred back to the American Colonial style, which loosely included the Federal and Empire styles as well. Colonial Revival furniture manufactured after the Centennial International Exhibition of 1876 in Philadelphia thrived on the need for Americans to express their cultural nationalism.

New forms of furniture proliferated in the Victorian period. By mid-century every household required a seven-piece matching suite, consisting of an armchair, a lady's chair, a sofa and four armless parlour chairs. Some of the best Rococo Revival suites were produced by Belter (see fig. 27 above). Rococo Revival chairs had cabriole legs and balloon backs. Naturalistic carving of flowers, vines, birds and animals evoked French culture and aristocratic pretensions. In addition to carving, the elegance of these Rococo suites depended on rich upholstery of satin, silk and plush, tufted, pleated and finished by tassels and fringes. Renaissance Revival suites had square-backed chairs and sofas, bulging U-shaped seats, incised designs and triangular pendants on the seat rails, applied roundels and turned legs. Eastlake chairs were less ornate and even more angular. Turned spindles, echoing turned legs, often supported the top rails. Shallow carving, reeding, geometric or floral marquetry and incised decoration enlivened the seat rails and other exposed wooden parts. By the 1880s elaborate fretwork inspired by Japanese design offered an acceptable alternative for top rails and the area beneath the arms. The Morris chair, based on a reclining chair produced by William Morris, was widely copied in the USA. The Eastlake sofa was a pale reflection of bold Empire models. A few squiggles were incised into bracket

35. Rose-wood sofa attributed to John Henry Belter, l. 2.28 m, *c.* 1850–60 (New York, Metropolitan Museum of Art)

feet, and carving on angular, stepped-down crests flanked by wheel-like crowns and simple scrolls repeated the shallow work on the feet. In the 1870s and 1880s Turkish corners were set up, with overstuffed chairs and sofas trimmed with fringe and tassels, to achieve an exotic effect. Simple chairs sold by the Shakers (*see* SHAKERS, §3) offered a sharp contrast to such ornate parlour furniture.

Many creative designers patented unique furniture in the 19th century. The first patent for folding chairs was issued in 1855. Those of George Hunzinger (1835–98), with their vertical stretchers and pipe-like frames, looked as if they should fold but often did not. By the 1870s the distinctive American form, the rocking chair (rocker), was redesigned as a stationary platform that rocked quietly on coil springs.

Chairs were often grouped around a centre table in the parlour. Rococo Revival tables, often topped with white marble, were circular, oval or oblong and rested on cabriole legs. Renaissance Revival examples took on a characteristic angular and jagged outline; their roundels, panels of veneer and incising related to similar embellishments on chairs. Oval tops continued to be made, but rectangular shapes with rounded ends gradually became more stylish. Giant cup-like finials were sometimes placed beneath the tables to add interest. A new type of table, the étagère or whatnot, emerged. Made in Rococo and Renaissance styles, it usually consisted of four or five shelves either free-standing or surmounting a table or cabinet. It held the personal knicknacks through which Victorians expressed their individuality in an age of increasingly standardized factory production. Other parlour furniture included easels for the display of paintings, sewing tables, music racks and library or writing tables.

Among the most impressive pieces of furniture were Renaissance Revival sideboards and cabinets. They consisted of two or three drawers above two doors resting on a raised plinth that sat directly on the floor. Above the top of the cabinet rose a wooden back that supported shelves and was topped with a Renaissance pediment. Cheaper versions had incised gilded lines and burl veneer, a highly figured veneer cut from a growth on the trunk of a tree, instead of costly carving or abundant applied ornament. The more expensive Eastlake cabinets had ebonized and painted geometrical or floral decoration, but even the cheapest ones were often crowned with the familiar gallery of spindles.

In the 1870s many prominent industrialists owned desks of an ingenious design patented by William S. Wooton (1835–1907). They consisted of a case of pigeonholes with a drop-front writing top. Large doors, also with pigeonholes and shelves, were hinged to the central section so that the owner could close up the entire cabinet when not in use. Eastlake-style desks and secrétaires of the cylinder or slant-front varieties were decorated like the Eastlake cabinets. Convertible furniture, such as chest-beds, proliferated in this period as apartment living became increasingly common.

Ornate, richly carved beds continued to be among the most expensive pieces of furniture. In the 1840s massive fourposter ones with Gothic details contrasted with less expensive spool-turned beds later named after Jenny Lind, the Swedish opera star who toured the USA in the 1850s.

36. Rose-wood cabinet by Alexander Roux, h. 1.36 m, *c.* 1860–70 (New York, Metropolitan Museum of Art)

The naturalistic carving of the best Rococo Revival beds was replaced in Renaissance Revival versions by more angular carving dominated by cartouches. Eastlake beds, often made of maple, were less massive and were ornamented with restrained reeding, incising and ebonizing.

BIBLIOGRAPHY

C. Otto: *American Furniture of the Nineteenth Century* (New York, 1965)
Eastlake-influenced American Furniture, 1870–1890 (exh. cat. by M. J. Madigan, Yonkers, Hudson River Mus., 1974)
W. Seale: *The Tasteful Interlude: American Interiors through the Camera's Eye, 1860–1917* (New York, 1975)
The Gothic Revival Style in America, 1830–1870 (exh. cat. by K. Howe and D. Warren, Houston, TX, Mus. F.A., 1976)
E. Denker and B. Denker: *The Rocking Chair Book* (New York, 1979)
D. Hanks: *Christian Herter and the Aesthetic Movement in America* (New York, 1980)
M. Schwartz, E. Stanek and D. True: *The Furniture of John Henry Belter and the Rococo Revival in America* (New York, 1981)
A. Axelrod, ed.: *The Colonial Revival in America* (New York, 1985)
Herter Brothers: Furniture and Interiors for a Gilded Age (exh. cat., Houston, TX, Mus. F.A.; Atlanta, GA, High Mus. A., New York, Met.; 1994–5)

5. AFTER 1900. For the American furniture industry the 20th century was a time of innovation and change. In 1900 furniture manufacturing centred in the northern and Midwestern cities of New York, Chicago and GRAND RAPIDS. After World War II southern centres in Virginia and North Carolina dominated large-scale furniture production, although New York and Chicago continued to turn out speciality work.

By the turn of the century many Americans were breaking away from the revival styles of the 19th century and were purchasing the new Mission furniture. The principal purveyor of this style was GUSTAV STICKLEY and his Craftsman Workshops near Syracuse, NY. Heavily influenced by John Ruskin, William Morris and the Arts and Crafts Movement in England, the best of his furniture depended on rich grained oak, good proportion and avoidance of ornament. Stickley had many imitators including his own brothers, Leopold Stickley (1869–1957) and J. George Stickley (1871–1921). Others, including the Roycroft Shops of ELBERT HUBBARD and Charles P. Limbert's Grand Rapids factory (1902–44), offered their

37. Lounger and ottoman designed by Charles Eames, moulded plywood and rose-wood veneers on cast aluminium base, black leather upholstery, 851×851×806 mm (chair), 425×654×527 mm (ottoman), manufactured by Herman Miller Inc., 1956 (New York, Museum of Modern Art)

own interpretations of Mission furniture. Charles Rohlfs (1853–1936), an actor turned cabinetmaker, enjoyed international fame with his idiosyncratic designs. Such avant-garde architects as Frank Lloyd Wright and other Prairie school members in Chicago and Charles Sumner Greene and Henry Mather Greene in California commissioned custom-made Mission furniture for their clients (see ARTS AND CRAFTS MOVEMENT, fig. 2).

By 1915 Stickley was bankrupt, a victim of overexpansion and shifting public taste. Even at the height of Mission's popularity, revivals of 18th- and early 19th-century styles, both American and European, commanded the lion's share of the furniture market. Throughout most of the 20th century a majority of Americans preferred traditional reproductions to modern styles. Wallace Nutting (1861–1941), one of the best-known exponents of the Colonial Revival, began manufacturing furniture in 1917. The opening of the American wing of the Metropolitan Museum of Art, New York, in 1925 and Colonial Williamsburg, VA, in 1932 added impetus to the demand for copies of traditional Americana. At the end of the 20th century high-quality Williamsburg reproductions by the Baker Furniture Co. and low-end furniture from the Ethan Allen firm still dominated a major portion of the furniture business.

By the 1930s, however, modern design was making significant inroads. At the beginning of the decade MOMA in New York exhibited modern furniture. The *Century of Progress Exposition* of 1933–4 in Chicago further boosted modern styles with its ten 'Design for Living' houses by GILBERT ROHDE. The work of such European-trained architects and designers as Joseph Urban, Paul Frankl, Rudolph Schindler, Richard Neutra, Kem Weber (1889–1963) and William Lescaze also promoted the new fashion. Influenced by such European design and art movements as Constructivism, Futurism, Cubism and Expressionism, American designers brought out successful modern furniture lines. Their modular, geometrical furniture—typically with low, horizontal lines—used polished metal and exotic woods. Rich materials substituted for ornament derived from historical styles.

Many architects were forced to design their own furniture because good modern lines were not available commercially. In 1930 Herman Miller Inc. of Zeeland, MI, hired Rohde, who convinced the company to adopt modern designs to fill this need. Rohde, along with Donald Deskey (b 1894) and Lescaze, experimented with tubular furniture based on German Bauhaus precedents. British-trained Terence Harold Robsjohn-Gibbings (1905–76) conceived a line for the Widdicomb firm that reflects Art Deco classicism of the 1920s. In California Weber, working for the Barker Brothers Furniture Co., designed popular laminated furniture knocked down for ease of shipping. In 1935, for the Conant Ball Co., Russel Wright (1904–76) designed blond maple furniture influenced by the Scandinavian modern style. This Modern Living line included the first widely available sectional sofa, a form created by Rohde. Edward Wormley (*b* 1907), who began his long career in the 1930s working for the Dunbar Furniture Co., created another modern line. At the end of the 1930s and in the early 1940s furniture with biomorphic curves by such designers as Frederick Kiesler (1890–1965) and Isamu Noguchi replaced the earlier geometrical look.

The World's Fair in New York in 1939 showcased modern design. Soon after, however, World War II virtually halted furniture manufacturing as factories turned to war production. Following the war the way was paved for mass acceptance of modern design. To meet the pent-up demand for housing, developers rushed to build modern houses, and customers furnished them with modern furniture.

Among the creative designers of the post-war era were Charles and Ray Eames (*see* EAMES). They experimented with such 20th-century materials as plywood and plastic and with new methods of joining metal, rubber and wood developed during the war, primarily in the aircraft industry. Their bent plywood 'Eames' chair produced after the war was based on designs submitted in collaboration with Eero Saarinen (*see* SAARINEN, (2)) that won first place in the MOMA contest in 1940 for Organic Design in Home Furnishings. Other influential Eames designs, including wire, aluminium and plastic furniture and stacking chairs, were produced by Herman Miller in the 1950s. Another classic, the lounger of 1956, features a moulded plywood shell, a leather seat, a cast aluminium base and a matching ottoman (see fig. 37).

Charles Eames began his collaboration with Saarinen while teaching at the Cranbrook Academy of Art, Bloomfield Hills, MI, where they, along with many of the most influential designers of the post-war period, had worked in the 1930s. Although Saarinen turned his attention to architecture after the war, he retained an interest in furniture. In 1946 he designed his famous 'Womb' chair, which was produced by Knoll Associates. In 1957 his quest for new furniture forms resulted in his 'Tulip' pedestal chairs and tables.

The architect GEORGE NELSON was persuaded to become the chief designer at Herman Miller after Rohde's death in 1944. His 'Marshmallow' sofa and 'Coconut' and 'Kangaroo' chairs became classics of modern design. He also pioneered modular, metal furniture, such as the Comprehensive Storage system introduced by Herman Miller in 1959.

Competing with Miller was Knoll Associates, started in 1937 to provide furniture compatible with modern architecture. After the war the company president, Hans Knoll (1914–55), married Florence Schust (*b* 1917), a Cranbrook Academy graduate. She promoted the work of many prominent architects and designers, including Mies van der Rohe, George Nakashima (*b* 1905), Isamu Noguchi and HARRY BERTOIA. While working for Knoll in 1952, Bertoia created his 'Diamond' chair made of wire.

From the 1960s both Knoll and Herman Miller concentrated on office furniture, finding corporate designers more willing than individuals to experiment with modern design. With the advent of the open office concept in the 1960s Herman Miller promoted the Action Office system designed by Nelson and Robert Propst (*b* 1921) to furnish

these open spaces with modular, specialized furniture. The interest in health in the 1970s fostered the development, by William Stumpf (*b* 1936) at Herman Miller and Niels Diffrient (*b* 1928) at the Sunar Hauserman firm, of ergonomic chairs, which support the back well during long hours at a desk. Stumpf updated the open office concept in the mid-1980s with the flexible Ethospace system produced by Herman Miller. Knoll responded with a modular collection designed by Andrew Morrison (*b* 1939).

Since the 1950s austere modern furniture had dominated offices, although it was not universally accepted for the home. By the 1960s a reaction began to set in, led by Robert Venturi (of Venturi, Rauch & Scott Brown), Michael Graves and other architects who believed that design once again should incorporate interesting detail, colour and classical ornament. In 1984 Venturi designed a bent plywood line for Knoll, parodying Thomas Sheraton and early 19th-century classical ideas. About the same time Graves incorporated Art Deco, Biedermeier and Neoclassical elements into his furniture made with exotic woods and inlay for the Memphis group and Sunar Hauserman (see fig. 38).

By the 1960s much of the modern furniture for both home and office commonly used metal and plastic. Frank Lloyd Wright had introduced all metal furniture for his Larkin Building (1904–6; destr.), Buffalo, NY; by the

38. Side table and chair designed by Michael Graves, hardwood with polyurethane finish, h. 730 mm (table), h. 750 mm (chair), manufactured by Sunar Hauserman, 1984 (Elkart, IN, DoMore/DO3)

1960s metal was used in mass-produced furniture, particularly for kitchens and offices. Likewise, plastic was at first seen merely as a substitute for wood, but soon designers came to appreciate its property of taking any shape imaginable. Manufacturers also experimented with polyurethane foam to shape chair parts or to use as a substitute for traditional upholstery. In the 1980s the Formica Corp. sponsored a design competition to encourage the use of its brightly coloured plastic laminates to produce striking, geometrical furniture similar to that of the Memphis group. The entry of Garry Knox Bennett (*b* 1934)—a desk made of rose-wood, aluminium, Formica and gold-plated brass (priv. col.)—was among the most successful.

For the custom-made furniture market Wharton Esherick (1889–1970) produced furniture from the 1920s in the tradition of the late 19th-century Arts and Crafts Movement. After World War II he had competition from George Nakashima, Arthur Carpenter (*b* 1920), Wendell Castle (*b* 1932), Sam Maloof (*b* 1916), Tage Frid (*b* 1915) and James Krenov (*b* 1920). The rich, smooth wood surfaces and amorphous shapes of their furniture in the 1960s became the geometrical and symbolic designs executed in exotic woods, metal and plastic laminates in the 1980s. While Edward Zucca (*b* 1946), Alphonse Mattia (*b* 1947) and Judy Kensley McKie (*b* 1944) produced humorous and fanciful furniture, Richard Kagan (*b* 1927), Jere Osgood (*b* 1936) and James Schriber (*b* 1952) continued the tradition of fine workmanship and reverence for wood.

BIBLIOGRAPHY

D. Cathers: *Furniture of the American Arts and Crafts Movement* (New York, 1981)
D. Hanks: *Innovative Furniture in America from 1800 to the Present* (New York, 1981)
K. Davies: *At Home in Manhattan: Modern Decorative Arts, 1925 to the Depression* (New Haven, 1983)
Design in America: The Cranbrook Vision, 1925–1950 (exh. cat.; Detroit, MI, Inst. A.; New York, Met.; 1983)
S. Darling: *Chicago Furniture: Art, Craft & Industry, 1833–1983* (New York, 1984)
C. Greenberg: *Mid-century Modern: Furniture of the 1950s* (New York, 1984)
M. Stone: *Contemporary American Woodworkers* (Salt Lake City, 1986)
J. Neuhart and M. Neuhart: *Eames Design: The Work of the Office of Charles and Ray Eames* (New York, 1989)

OSCAR P. FITZGERALD

VII. Ceramics.

1. Before 1800. 2. 1800–*c.* 1900. 3. After *c.* 1900.

1. BEFORE 1800. Although Native Americans had a long-established pottery tradition, Europeans brought their own techniques when they began to colonize North America after 1600. Small potteries in most Dutch, English, French and Spanish settlements successfully made bricks, roof tiles and utilitarian earthenware for kitchen, dairy and tavern use. In the 17th century, Colonial earthenware followed English and Continental models so closely that identification is difficult, and only in the late 20th century have archaeologists begun to develop laboratory techniques for separating indigenous from imported wares found in early Colonial sites. Among the 17th-century potteries known from documentation or archaeological evidence are two identified with the making of tin-glazed earthenware. Wasters of chargers and a single tin-glazed cup (Yorktown, VA, Colon. N. Hist. Park) excavated from Governor William Berkeley's Green Spring Plantation, VA, suggest that a London-trained maiolica potter was working there after 1660. In 1688 Dr Daniel Coxe and others contracted John DeWilde of London and William Gill (*fl* 1688–93) of Lambeth to establish a pottery making tin-glazed earthenware in Burlington, NJ (*see* COXE-DEWILDE POTTERY). Their products were reportedly sold locally and in Barbados and Jamaica. The pottery operated until *c.* 1692.

As the population of the colonies increased, potteries became more numerous, and the wares made were more elaborate. These potteries were generally scattered throughout the countryside wherever there was sufficient demand, and certain urban areas, such as Boston (*see* BOSTON, §III, 3), became important pottery centres from which large quantities of ware were traded inland and along the coast. In the mid-18th century the village of Charlestown, MA, boasted nearly forty potters, who shipped their wares along the New England coast. Production declined when the town was badly damaged during the American Revolution, and its pottery business was undermined by general overproduction in eastern Massachusetts.

From 1730 Danvers in Essex Co., MA, had a large pottery community active for two centuries. Large potteries around New York Bay from Norwalk, CT, to Rahway, NJ, supplied a burgeoning population well into the 19th century. Philadelphia was the major centre farther south. Philadelphia earthenware was traded widely along the coast from New England to Virginia and became a standard to which other potters referred and aspired. In 1773, for example, the potter Jonathan Durrell advertised in a New York newspaper that he could provide 'Philadelphia Earthen-Ware . . . equal to the best of any imported from Philadelphia'. At his pottery on the outskirts of New York, he made such typical Colonial products of this period as oyster and chamber pots, milk pans and porringers.

Decoration of 18th-century American earthenware was usually minimal. Plain lead-glazed and black-glazed redwares were the most common, but simple slip decoration was also used, and some potters, particularly those in the mid-Atlantic region from Connecticut to Philadelphia, used copper-oxide to heighten white slip decoration with 'clouds' of green. In contrast to these common and usually rather plain slip-decorated wares were the special commemorative pieces made with elaborate slip or sgraffito decoration by potters working in the German settlements of south-eastern Pennsylvania and the colourful slipwares made in the Moravian settlements of Bethlehem, PA, and Salem, NC. The inscriptions on many of the pieces are in German dialects, and motifs used include symbolic birds, such as double-headed eagles and pelicans, flowers, horses and figures of men and women. Many of the artists have been identified, including Georg Huebner (1757–1828), John Jacob Stoudt (1710–79) and John Leidy (1764–1846). GOTTFRIED AUST, the master potter of the Moravian communities in North Carolina, used the forms and colourful, elaborate slip decoration with which his brethren had been familiar in Moravia.

Minimal evidence exists to prove the making of fine earthenware in America before 1800. Cream-coloured earthenware in the English manner is mentioned in a Boston newspaper in 1769, although actual examples have not been certainly identified. In Salem, NC, William Ellis introduced the manufacture of creamware in 1773 alongside the flamboyant, traditional redwares of Aust, which remained the principal product. Archaeological evidence from Philadelphia suggests attempts to make refined earthenware at this time, but the relatively inexpensive importation of European finer ceramics hampered the founding of successful enterprises for large-scale production in America.

Stoneware production began during the first half of the 18th century. William Crolius and John Remmey (see CROLIUS AND REMMEY) were probably in the pottery business together shortly after their arrivals in New York, making lead-glazed earthenwares and salt-glazed stonewares. Similarly, Anthony Duché (*fl* Philadelphia, 1700–62) was already making stoneware in Philadelphia in 1730 when he applied to the provincial legislature for a monopoly and subsidy that were eventually denied. The stoneware potters in Manhattan exploited part of the Raritan Formation, NJ, a major bed of blue-stoneware clays; the same resource prompted a large group of stoneware potteries to be established near by, beginning about 1754 with that of JAMES MORGAN and continuing through the 19th century. Clay from this resource supplied many potters from New England to upstate New York via clay-mining operations in New Jersey. In contrast to these northern stonewares in the Rhenish style, as early as the 1730s WILLIAM ROGERS (ii) of Yorktown, VA, was making large quantities of salt-glazed stoneware for home and tavern use indistinguishable from English stoneware of the period. In New England, however, there was a lack of proper clays for stoneware production, which did not begin until after the American Revolution; instead stoneware was imported from England or from other American colonies.

In spite of the difficult conditions in the colonies during the 17th and 18th centuries there was some interest in making porcelain. ANDREW DUCHÉ attempted to produce porcelain with indigenous materials in Savannah, GA, during the 1730s, but it was the porcelain factory of BONNIN & MORRIS that turned out an identifiable body of work between 1770 and 1772 at Southwark in Philadelphia. The bone china body was decorated in underglaze cobalt blue in the style of such English factories as Bow, and ambitious forms were produced, including tiered shell-shaped sweetmeat stands (see fig. 39) and pierced fruit baskets. Despite the high quality of the porcelain, high labour costs and competition from abroad proved to be too extensive to overcome, and the factory closed in 1772.

2. 1800–c. 1900. The American ceramics industry developed dramatically during the 19th century as the population grew and spread to the West and the demand for finer products increased. The centres of ceramic production also moved west to accommodate the growing population, and after 1840 modest cities served by major transportation networks were more likely to become pottery centres than the urban areas of the previous

39. Sweetmeat stand, soft-paste porcelain with underglaze cobalt blue decoration, h. 133 mm, made by Bonnin & Morris, Philadelphia, 1770–72 (New York, Brooklyn Museum)

century. By 1885 a variety of wares was produced, including industrial stoneware, decorative tiles, earthenware for kitchen, table and sanitary uses, art pottery and porcelain.

(i) Earthenware and stoneware. (ii) Art wares.

(i) Earthenware and stoneware. After 1800 red earthenware continued to be made, while an increasing number of potteries adopted salt-glazed stoneware as a viable product. For both wares greater competition engendered more decoration, and regional characteristics can thus be more readily identified in wares made after 1800. New England redware, for example, displays colourful effects obtained by firing the wares in a reducing atmosphere that forced the lead glazes to 'bloom' in contrasting colours around trace imperfections in the body or glaze. The region around New York Bay from coastal Connecticut to north-eastern New Jersey produced wares with a distinctively bold use of trailed white slip on a bright red body. Decorations included geometric ornament, spirals, birds, names, mottoes and aphorisms. The same aesthetic was translated into brilliant cobalt blue slip trailed on to grey, salt-glazed stoneware made during the mid-19th century inland from the bay area in New Jersey, but especially north along the Hudson River and Erie Canal in New York state. A menagerie of animals, whimsical birds and human figures engaged in humorous activities were used on the pots and jugs from this region. Outside Philadelphia, in south-eastern Pennsylvania, the use of highly stylized sgraffito and slip decoration of the previous century continued unabated in the German settlements until at least 1840, especially on presentation pieces.

The consumer interest in redwares, however, began to fade during the early 1800s. Three factors effectively eliminated redware as a popular ceramic product by 1850: the danger of the lead in the glaze was known, the affordability of English white earthenwares increased, and Rockingham-glazed yellow wares emerged as the most popular kitchen crockery. Press-moulding and Rockingham (wares with a brown mottled glaze) were introduced to American potteries by English potters coming from the over-competitive industry in Staffordshire. The transition to press-moulding had already begun on a small scale during the 1810s and early 1820s when some potters in the mid-Atlantic region used moulds to make black-glazed teapots. In 1828 D. & J. Henderson purchased a pottery in Jersey City, NJ, and began making high-quality Rockingham in moulds for the first time in the USA. This operation, renamed the AMERICAN POTTERY MANUFACTURING CO. in 1833, is thought to have been the first true pottery factory in the USA in which a large number of skilled potters, semi-skilled workers and labourers were organized to mass produce good-quality tableware. Their modeller between 1839 and 1850 was the Englishman Daniel Greatbach, who introduced the classic Houndhandle pitcher (e.g. Newark, NJ, Mus.; Trenton, NJ State Mus.) to the American potter's repertory, a form that was popular for the rest of the century. While in Jersey City he also made large, fine Toby jugs, vine-covered tea sets and an 'Apostle' jug. By 1852 he was employed by the United States Pottery Co. in Bennington, VT, to produce exhibition pieces for the Crystal Palace Exhibition of 1853 in New York. In Bennington, Greatbach used the 'flint enamel' glaze developed by Christopher Webber Fenton (1806–65), as in the 'Apostle' pattern water cooler (1849; New York, Brooklyn Mus.; see fig. 40) attributed to him and made at Lyman, Fenton & Co.

Like Rockingham, white earthenwares were press-moulded, but were not made in the USA until the late 1850s. In the second half of the 19th century Rockingham and yellow wares were used primarily in kitchens, while whiteware was considered suitable for dinnerware because of its colour. Both were generally embellished with motifs popular on similar wares in England: hunt scenes, dead game, anchors, putti, scrolls and such simple border patterns as wheat for white dinnerware. Transfer-printed whiteware, sometimes filled with colours, was popular by about 1880, and coloured lithographic decoration began to appear c. 1890. Until 1880 most of these wares were not marked or were marked with pseudo-English makers' devices to confuse buyers who preferred English goods.

The manufacture of press-moulded wares provided the cornerstones for the development of America's two most important ceramic centres in the 19th century and the early 20th: East Liverpool, OH, and Trenton, NJ. Manufacturers in each city were able to take advantage of water and rail transportation networks to serve highly populated areas. In addition, the early success of the first English potters to arrive in these cities during the second quarter of the 19th century attracted more potters and more investment capital from local businessmen. Between 1850 and 1920 most of the American crockery used in the USA was produced in these two cities, and although many of the potteries lasted for fewer than 20 years the wares of such manufacturers as the Homer Laughlin China Co. (see LAUGHLIN, HOMER) in East Liverpool and the Ceramic

40. Stoneware water cooler attributed to Daniel Greatbach, earthenware with flint enamel glaze, h. 597 mm, made by Lyman, Fenton & Co., Bennington, Vermont, 1849 (New York, Brooklyn Museum)

Art Co. (later the Lenox China Co.; see LENOX, WALTER SCOTT) in Trenton were consistently popular with American consumers.

Utilitarian stoneware was used throughout the later 19th century, although more for industrial use than for homes, where such lighter materials as tin and glass were used for storage. After 1850 many of the stoneware potteries switched to industrial products (e.g. drainage tiles) as their mainstays.

Some of the most imaginative stoneware was made in utilitarian potteries during the second half of the 19th century in Ohio and Illinois, at a time when the Renaissance and Rococo revival styles coincided with a decline in handcraft. This dénouement generated some extravagant sculptural work; Wallace Kirkpatrick (1828–96) and Cornwall Kirkpatrick (1814–90) of Anna, IL, for example, made stoneware temperance jugs covered with writhing lifelike snakes. Their pig-shaped whisky flasks with railroad maps inscribed on the side were metaphors for corn production and consumption in the Midwest. A distinctly different tradition in stoneware developed in the southern states, where potters preferred alkaline to salt glaze. Woodash was a commonly used flux in the mixtures with sand and clay that produced glassy green glazes ranging from clear pale celadon to dripping dark effects later called 'tobacco spit'. In the late 20th century North Carolina and Georgia continued to be known for the production of traditional alkaline-glazed stonewares. These wares were also made as far west as Texas.

The manufacture of decorative tiles flourished in the USA between 1870 and 1930 (*see* TILE, §II, 10). Inspired by the public interest in the exhibits of English tilemakers at the Centennial Exhibition of 1876 in Philadelphia, a number of tile companies were established in the late 1870s in Ohio, Pennsylvania, Massachusetts and New Jersey to make fashionable high-glazed, relief-moulded tiles. During the 1890s the fashion in tile decoration shifted to matt glazes in flat stylized patterns.

(ii) Art wares. The making of decorative ceramics in the USA received little encouragement until the 1880s: before 1800 Americans depended on English merchants to supply fine ceramics, and after the American Revolution, when trade conditions were more favourable to manufacturers, consumers already preferred wares from England, Europe and China. Porcelain was rarely produced with much commercial success until after the Civil War. In the early 19th century Dr Henry Mead (1774/5–1843), a New York physician, Abraham Miller (?1799–1858), a Philadelphia potter, and William Ellis Tucker (*see* TUCKER CHINA FACTORY), also of Philadelphia, all made table and decorative porcelains in the fashionable Empire style, but only Tucker was successful for any period.

In 1849 Christopher Webber Fenton established the United States Pottery Co. in Bennington, VT, which made parian figures, pitchers, vases and trinkets. Charles Cartlidge & Co. in Greenpoint, NY (1848–56), made soft-paste porcelain doorknobs and buttons, but is best known for the parian portrait busts and porcelain pitchers in his display in the New York Crystal Palace Exhibition of 1853. In 1863 William Boch and Bros' Union Porcelain factory became Thomas C. Smith's (1815–1901) UNION PORCELAIN WORKS, where the first hard-paste porcelain was made c. 1865.

In Trenton porcelain was produced at least as early as 1854 by William Young (1801–71), who had worked for Cartlidge, but his stock-in-trade remained hardware trimmings. In the 1860s William Bloor (1821–77) introduced parian manufacture to East Liverpool. Although this venture was a false start, his partnership in the late 1860s with Joseph Ott and John Hart Brewer in Trenton bore fruit. Ott & Brewer (1863–93) continued to make parian portrait busts after Bloor's departure, and in 1875 they hired the sculptor ISAAC BROOME to prepare models for exhibition pieces to be shown at the Centennial International Exhibition of 1876.

In a similar move, Thomas Smith hired German sculptor Karl Müller (1820–87) for the Union Porcelain Works. Each sculptor produced several models for exhibition and sale, but for size and complexity Müller's 'Century' vase (e.g. Atlanta, GA, High Mus. A.; New York, Brooklyn Mus.; New York, Met.; Trenton, NJ State Mus.) and Broome's 'Baseball' vase (1875; Trenton, NJ State Mus.; see fig. 41) were their principal contributions and rank as the USA's first major ceramic exhibition sculpture. Müller's vase is historical in terms of the modelled decoration, which celebrates the virgin land and early republic. In

Broome's large covered vase, which honours contemporary sport, throwing, catching and batting are depicted by three figures arranged around a cone-shaped faggot of bats topped by a baseball on which an American eagle sits. Ott & Brewer persisted in the development of American art porcelain by producing a version of Belleek beginning in 1883. This was decorated in the Aesthetic taste with gold encrustations, delicate flowers and flying cranes. In 1887, after his success as art director at Ott & Brewer, Walter Scott Lenox took the same concept for art porcelain

41. Parian porcelain 'Baseball' vase by Isaac Broome, h. 864 mm, made at Ott & Brewer, Trenton, New Jersey, 1875 (Trenton, New Jersey State Museum)

to the Willets Manufacturing Co., a rival Trenton firm, where his famous nautilus-shell ewer was first produced. In 1889 Lenox founded the Ceramic Art Co., which specialized exclusively in porcelain art wares, a radical idea in the American ceramics industry. In East Liverpool, KNOWLES, TAYLOR & KNOWLES produced a version of Belleek during the late 1880s, and they also introduced 'Lotus Ware', a bone china that was slip cast in lacy shapes, in 1890.

During the 1870s Maria Longworth Nichols, later Mrs Storer (1849–1932), and Mary Louise McLaughlin (1847–1939), both from Cincinnati, OH, were learning to decorate china and were impressed with the painterly style of the slip-decorated pottery exhibited by Haviland & Co. of Limoges at the Centennial Exhibition of 1876. In 1878 McLaughlin successfully imitated the effect, though not the process, and in 1880 Nichols established the ROOKWOOD POTTERY in Cincinnati to produce the wares (see fig. 42). Although lesser-known firms were doing similar work, Rookwood survived and was often copied by such later Ohio companies as the Weller Pottery (1888–1948) and the Roseville Pottery (1898–1954). The painterly slip

decoration of Rookwood contrasted with the Chinese-style wares with monochromatic glazes that were produced by HUGH CORNWALL ROBERTSON in his family's Chelsea Keramic Art Works (1872–89) in Chelsea, MA. In 1895 a new pottery was established in Dedham, MA, using Robertson's distinctive crackled glaze for dinnerware, decorated in cobalt blue with stylized flowers and animals.

Other important American art wares of the late 19th century included those made by WILLIAM HENRY GRUEBY between 1894 and 1913. Inspired by the work of the French art potter Auguste Delaherche, Grueby's art wares combined monochromatic flowing matt glazes with organic low-relief decoration. The Newcomb Pottery in New Orleans, LA, developed a distinctive regional style by rendering local flora in stylized patterns in a limited colour palette. The pottery employed art graduates from the Newcomb College for Women, to which it was connected, from 1895 to 1940. Master potter George E. Ohr (1857–1918), of Biloxi, MS, produced artistic redwares of unusual character between 1890 and 1910. His work was wheel-thrown to exquisite thinness and then adeptly altered with twists and frills.

3. AFTER *c*. 1900. American ceramics matured as both industry and art during the 20th century, and much of this development came from the institutionalization of ceramics education. Industrial art education in the USA began in the late 19th century; although initially based on the English system, which for potteries had begun much earlier, it focused instead on education within a university setting, segregated from the workplace. Important ceramics and clayworking courses were established in the late 19th century and the early 20th at such universities as Ohio State University, Columbus; Alfred University, Alfred, NY; Rutgers University, New Brunswick, NJ; and the University of Illinois, Urbana–Champaign. Such courses trained engineers, chemists and industrial designers to develop original forms and to improve the quality of the product for commercial potteries. Independent potters began to think of themselves as artists in the same way as painters and sculptors; they were associated primarily with small, hand-production potteries, serving a giftware market created by the American Arts and Crafts Movement, and later operated their own studios.

The American Ceramic Society, founded in 1899, also contributed greatly to the development of commercial ceramics. Unlike its predecessor, the American Potters' Association, which consisted of pottery owners and focused primarily on management and labour issues, the American Ceramic Society was open to anyone associated with the pottery industry. Meetings provided forums for sharing technical research and design concerns that addressed common problems in the potteries.

(i) Production ceramics. (ii) Art wares.

(i) Production ceramics. By the end of the 19th century the composition of domestic whitewares was so refined that it was closer to stoneware or proto-porcelain than to earthenware. By 1920 this low-cost, high-quality product dominated the American market, but modernization of factory technology was necessary to meet increased demand profitably, and careful attention to design was

42. Earthenware vase with underglaze slip-painted portrait of *Chief Joseph of the Nez Percés* painted by William P. McDonald, h. 356 mm, made by the Rookwood Pottery, Cincinnati, Ohio, 1895 (New York, Metropolitan Museum of Art)

needed to meet increased competition from foreign manufacturers after World War I. For the most part earlier American potteries were content to copy foreign wares, but the post-war environment required greater creativity.

One of the most successful tableware firms to respond to these pressures was the HOMER LAUGHLIN CHINA CO. In 1927 FREDERICK HURTEN RHEAD became its art director. He advocated the combination of formal industrial art education and factory apprenticeship and suggested that knowledge of advanced technology, design and marketing methods would help manufacturers create inexpensive, serviceable products for the American mass market.

Rhead's advice was not closely followed by many potteries that hired design-school graduates with little practical experience and/or consultant designers who created a single product or product line that could be promoted for its artistic design qualities. The streamlined 'American Modern' dinnerware line (1939) designed by Russel Wright for the Steubenville Pottery Co. (1879–1960), Steubenville, OH, is probably the best-known example of the latter type of relationship. Similarly, the 'Museum' dinner service designed in 1942–3 by Eva Ziesel (*b* 1906) and produced by the Castleton China Co., New Castle, PA, for MOMA in New York had the added cachet of recognition by an arts institution.

Other mass-market potteries that were significant during the second quarter of the 20th century were the Sebring Pottery Co. (1887–*c.* 1934), Sebring, OH; the Onondaga Pottery Co. (1871–), makers of Syracuse China, Syracuse, NY; the Shenango Pottery Co. (1901–), parent of Castleton China; the Flintridge China Co. (1945–70), Pasadena, CA; and the Gladding-McBean Co., which produced Franciscan China from 1934 to 1979 in Glendale, CA. Beginning in the late 1920s many of these firms produced off-white, semi-vitreous china or earthenware, probably following on the success of Lenox China's ivory china formula, which had evolved from the Belleek body formulated in Trenton, NJ, in the 19th century. Prior to World War II Lenox took a position apart from mass production in its merchandise, which was made to compete with the finest English and Continental chinas for the wealthy American customer. After the war, however, Lenox capitalized on the new affluence of the American middle class and by the early 1960s had, along with Japanese and English manufacturers, effectively eliminated the other large American china firms from the fine dinnerware market.

(ii) Art wares. In the early 20th century art ceramics were still made largely by the small art potteries that were founded under the Arts and Crafts Movement. Such pioneering firms as the ROOKWOOD POTTERY, the Newcomb Pottery (1895–1931) and the Dedham Pottery (1896–1943) survived until at least the middle of the 20th century. In contrast a host of small art potteries were established and capitalized for a short time on the distinctive artistic inventions of their founders: Clewell Metal Art (1906–*c.* 1920), Canton, OH, produced earthenwares covered in a patinated metal, a process developed by Charles Walter Clewell (*c.* 1876–1965); the Tiffany Pottery (1904–*c.* 1919), Corona, NY, of Louis Comfort Tiffany

(*see* TIFFANY, §2), made wares with matt, crystalline and iridescent glazes; the Clifton Art Pottery (1905–11), Newark, NJ, specialized in shapes and decorations modelled after early Native American Indian pottery; the Markham Pottery of Ann Arbor, MI (1905–13), and National City, CA (1913–21), produced redware vases with applied finishes that made them resemble archaeological relics; in 1909 the Fulper Pottery (1860–1935), Flemington, NJ, began using its 19th-century utilitarian stoneware body to make 'Vasekraft' wares, created by the German designer J. Martin Stangl (*d* 1972), which were covered with colourful crystalline, flambé and monochromatic glazes.

Several art potteries founded during the early 20th century operated for many years because their products filled particular market niches. The work of the Van Briggle Pottery (1901–) in Colorado Springs, CO, is based on the artistic concepts of Artus Van Briggle (1869–1904), who modelled Art Nouveau vases with designs based on American flora. Many of his original designs continued to be used after his death. The Pewabic Pottery (1903–61) was founded by Mary Chase Perry (1868–1961) in Detroit, MI, and specialized in the development of iridescent glazes on flat tiles or simply shaped vases. The firm's broad, flat, pictorial designs for tile installations were particularly popular with ecclesiastical customers.

About 1920 Jacques Busbee and Juliana Busbee founded the Jugtown Pottery as a way of preserving the dying craft of pottery-making in rural North Carolina. Although most of this pottery's earthenware and stoneware was of a traditional American character, the potters also made elegant Chinese-inspired forms with white or transmutational turquoise and red glazes.

Several individual potters were important figures during the first quarter of the 20th century because of their roles in the evolution of art potters into studio potters and in the recognition of clay as a legitimate medium for art. CHARLES FERGUS BINNS was the first director of the New York State School of Clayworking and Ceramics at Alfred University, which continues to be one of the foremost American schools for ceramic artists following its foundation in 1900; ADELAIDE ALSOP ROBINEAU had a distinguished career as a potter, publisher, editor and teacher and in 1932 inspired the establishment of the Ceramic National Exhibitions; and R. GUY COWAN believed that art and industry could be profitably united. In Cowan's Rocky River Pottery, near Cleveland, OH, such young ceramic artists as Waylande Gregory (1905–71), Victor Schreckengost (*b* 1906) and Edris Eckhardt (*b* 1910) designed limited edition vases and figures. After the firm closed in 1930 each of these artists continued to work in clay: Gregory worked as a sculptor in New Jersey, and his Fountain of Atoms (figure, estate of the artist's wife, see Anderson and Perry, fig. 1:8–11) for the World's Fair of 1939 in New York is considered the largest single work in modern ceramic sculpture; during the 1930s Schreckengost was a designer for the production dinnerware potteries in Sebring, OH, but continued to produce small clay sculptures; and Eckhardt, although later a glass artist, led a distinguished sculpture programme (1933–41) for the Works Progress Administration in Cleveland, OH.

Prior to World War II American potters continued to draw from English and European models and aesthetic

43. Pierced and glazed stoneware stack pot by Peter Voulkos, h. 762 mm, 1964 (Detroit, MI, Institute of Arts)

ideas. Vally Wieselthier (1895–1945) and Susi Singer (1895–1949) settled in the USA and brought with them a playful, colourful, figural style, which they had learnt from Michael Powolny of the Wiener Werkstätte. Henry Varnum Poor (1888–1971) explored Cubism in ceramic decoration, using the sgraffito technique on earthenware. Charles M. Harder (1889–1959) at Alfred University and ARTHUR EUGENE BAGGS at Ohio State University adhered to the emphasis on a technically proficient vessel style that they had learnt as students under Charles Fergus Binns at Alfred University. In 1939 the Austrian potters Otto Natzler (*b* 1908) and Gertrude Natzler (1908–71) settled in Los Angeles and concentrated on combining elegant, classical forms with colourful and textural glaze effects. The Finnish potter MAIJA GROTELL exerted a profound influence on American art ceramics as an experimental, vessel-oriented potter and as an instructor (1938–66) at the Cranbrook Academy of Art in Bloomfield Hills, MI. Her foremost students included Toshiko Takaezu (*b* 1929), Richard DeVore (*b* 1933), John Glick (*b* 1938),

Suzanne Stephenson (*b* 1935) and John Stephenson (*b* 1929), who remained major figures in late 20th-century art ceramics as artists and teachers.

After World War II influences on American art ceramics were more varied. The group of young potters who were associated with Peter Voulkos (*b* 1924) at the Otis Art Institute in Los Angeles (1954–8) produced a large and diverse body of work that drew inspiration from Japanese ceramics, American Abstract Expressionist painting and improvisational jazz. As a result of the high level of expressive experimentalism that Voulkos brought to his work, such as his stoneware stack pot (1964; Detroit, MI, Inst. A.; see fig. 43), he was a very influential figure in post-war American ceramics. Many of his students, including Paul Soldner (*b* 1921), Jim Melchert (*b* 1930), Stephen De Staebler (*b* 1933), Kenneth Price (*b* 1935), Michael Frimkiss (*b* 1937) and Ron Nagle (*b* 1939), became successful potters in the late 20th century. Melchert and Price preferred to work in porcelain, exploiting its whiteness, fine texture and translucent nature. Porcelain was also preferred by such potters as Rudolf Staffel (*b* 1911), Herbert Sanders (*b* 1909), Robert Hudson (*b* 1938), Richard Shaw (*b* 1941) and Adrian Saxe (*b* 1943). David Gilhooly (*b* 1943) and Robert Arneson (*b* 1930) were the central force behind a ceramic genre called 'Funk', which was inspired by Dada and Surrealist sculpture and was a protest against conventional notions of subject-matter and propriety. Such potters as Robert Turner (*b* 1913), Karen Karnes (*b* 1920), Val Cushing (*b* 1931), Kenneth Ferguson (*b* 1928), David Weinrib (*b* 1924) and Daniel Rhodes (*b* 1911) were trained at Alfred University and had a more reserved approach to the medium.

BIBLIOGRAPHY

E. A. Barber: *The Pottery and Porcelain of the United States: An Historical Review of American Art from the Earliest Times to the Present Day* (New York, 1893, rev. 3/1909/*R* New York, 1976)
——: *Tulip Ware of the Pennsylvania-Germans: An Historical Sketch of the Art of Slip-decoration in the United States* (Philadelphia, 1903)
——: *Marks of American Potters* (Philadelphia, 1904)
L. W. Watkins: *Early New England Potters and their Wares* (Cambridge, MA, 1950)
R. C. Barrett: *Bennington Pottery and Porcelain* (New York, 1958)
Abstract Expressionist Ceramics (exh. cat., Irvine, U. CA, 1966)
D. B. Webster: *Decorated Stoneware Pottery of North America* (Rutland, 1971)
P. Evans: *Art Pottery of the United States: An Encyclopedia of Producers and their Marks* (New York, 1974, rev. 1987)
R. Kovel and T. Kovel: *The Kovels' Collector's Guide to American Art Pottery* (New York, 1974)
G. Clark: *A Century of Ceramics in the United States, 1878–1978: A Study of its Development* (New York, 1979)
S. S. Darling: *Chicago Ceramics and Glass: An Illustrated History from 1871 to 1933* (Chicago, 1979)
American Decorative Tiles, 1870–1930 (exh. cat. by T. P. Bruhn, Storrs, U. CT, Benton Mus. A, 1979)
H. V. Bray: *The Potter's Art in California, 1885 to 1955* (Oakland, 1980)
L. Lehner: *Complete Book of American Kitchen and Dinner Wares* (Des Moines, 1980)
S. H. Myers: *Handcraft to Industry: Philadelphia Ceramics in the First Half of the Nineteenth Century* (Washington, DC, 1980)
G. H. Greer: *American Stonewares: The Art and Craft of Utilitarian Potters* (Exton, 1981)
A. K. Winton and K. B. Winton: *Norwalk Potteries* (Norwalk, 1981)
W. C. Gates jr and D. Ormerod: 'The East Liverpool Pottery District: Identification of Manufacturers and Marks', *Hist. Archaeol.*, xvi (1982), pp. 1–358
R. I. Weidner: *American Ceramics before 1930: A Bibliography* (Westport, 1982)

R. Anderson and B. Perry: *Diversions of Keramos: American Clay Sculpture, 1925–1950* (Syracuse, NY, 1983)

J. D. Burrison: *Brothers in Clay: The Story of Georgia Folk Pottery* (Athens, GA, 1983)

S. R. Strong: *History of American Ceramics: An Annotated Bibliography* (Metuchen, 1983)

J. Poesch: *Newcomb Pottery: An Enterprise for Southern Women, 1895–1940* (Exton, 1984)

E. Denker and B. Denker: *The Main Street Pocket Guide to North American Pottery and Porcelain* (Pittstown, 1985)

J. Liebowitz: *Yellow Ware: The Transitional Ceramic* (Exton, 1985)

C. G. Zug III: *Turners and Burners: The Folk Potters of North Carolina* (Chapel Hill, 1986)

R. Blaszczyk: *Product Development in the American Tableware Industry, 1920–1945* (MA thesis, Washington, DC, George Washington U., 1987)

M. L. Branin: *The Early Makers of Handcrafted Earthenware and Stoneware in Central and Southern New Jersey* (Rutherford, 1988)

A. C. Frelinghuysen: *American Porcelain, 1770–1920* (New York, 1989)

S. J. Montgomery: *The Ceramics of William H. Grueby: The Spirit of the New Idea in Artistic Handicraft* (Lambertville, 1993)

ELLEN PAUL DENKER

VIII. Glass.

1. Before 1800. 2. 1800–80. 3. After 1880.

1. BEFORE 1800. The first permanent English settlement in North America, at Jamestown in the colony of Virginia, was founded in 1607 principally to furnish the English market with raw materials for industry, but the merchant investors who made up the Virginia Company of London were also alert to profitable manufactures that could be carried on there. One obvious choice was glassmaking: as the land was heavily wooded, fuel for the furnaces—in short supply in England—was abundant, and it was assumed that the raw materials necessary for glassmaking could be found near by. Although two different attempts at glassmaking were tried during the first quarter of the 17th century, the primitive conditions and the distance from the customers in England meant failure for this first effort to found an industry in America. Glassmaking, unlike cabinetmaking, silversmithing and other Colonial crafts that supplied the populace with goods, required a few skilled workmen—at least one person with experience in mixing the raw materials and with knowledge of furnace construction—and a considerable amount of raw material and fuel before any saleable products could be made. These requirements made a substantial capital outlay a necessity for any potential glassmaker, and they explain why other crafts flourished in the colonies well before glassmaking did.

There was considerable demand for both window and bottle glass, and the immense tracts of forest, which were a hindrance to agriculture, encouraged glassmaking. Between 1732 and 1780 nearly twenty glasshouses were started. The three most ambitious and commercially successful factories were founded by German entrepreneurs, and most of the workers were German as well. Investors found it easier to induce German rather than English glassblowers to come to America, because the Germany economy was less stable than that of England.

In 1738 CASPAR WISTAR brought over four German glassblowers and financed the building of a glasshouse in what came to be known as Wistarburgh, near Alloway in Salem Co., NJ. By 1739 it was in production, using wood from nearby forests for fuel and local sand and wood

ashes as the principal raw materials. The glass produced was typical *Waldglas*, an impure greenish glass common throughout northern Europe from the Middle Ages. Wistar's advertisements indicate that he produced mainly window glass and bottles, the glass commodities most needed by the colonists. Tablewares were still largely supplied from abroad; however, some sugar bowls, cream baskets, mugs and candlesticks in green, blue and colourless glass were probably made at the factory for sale in Wistar's store and for the use of his family. The manufacture of glass and similar goods was officially discouraged by the British authorities, who viewed the colonies solely as producers of raw materials for British manufacturers. By the mid-18th century, however, there was considerable interest in the domestic manufacture of glass in several colonies, particularly in Massachusetts, New York and Pennsylvania.

Among Colonial glass factories, the most famous is that of HENRY WILLIAM STIEGEL. In 1764 he opened his first

44. Lead-glass goblet, h. 172 mm, made by Henry William Stiegel's American Flint Glass Manufactory, Manheim, Pennsylvania, 1773; wheel-engraved by Lazarus Isaacs in commemoration of the marriage of Stiegel's daughter Elizabeth to William Old (Corning, NY, Museum of Glass)

glasshouse at Manheim, PA, a village he had founded for his workers. Although he manufactured principally bottles and window glass there, Stiegel was determined to produce fine lead-glass tableware in the English tradition. By 1769 he was advertising an extensive assortment of 'white and blue flint' glass tablewares, including tumblers and decanters in several sizes, water bottles, wine and water glasses, serving glasses for salt and cream, cruets for vinegar and mustard, and vials for chemists and apothecaries, all produced at his American Flint Glass Manufactory. Some of Stiegel's tableware was decorated with wheel engraving (see fig. 44). His factory prospered for several years, but his continued expansion led to increasing debt and by 1774 he was forced to close.

In 1784 JOHN FREDERICK AMELUNG moved from Germany to Maryland with equipment and workmen for three furnaces. Within a few months he advertised that window glass and green and white hollow-ware were for sale at his New Bremen Glassmanufactory in Frederick, MD. In one of the first planned industrial villages in the USA, he built homes for his workmen near the factory and a school for their children. By 1789 Amelung claimed to manufacture 'all kinds of Flint-Glass, such as Decanters, and Wine Glasses, Tumblers of all Sizes, and any other Sort of Table Glass. He also cuts Devices, Cyphers, Coats of Arms, or any other Fancy Figure on Glass.' Probably as a means of attracting public notice, Amelung presented a pair of elaborately engraved goblets (untraced) to President George Washington, a goblet (New York, Met.) to Governor Thomas Mifflin of Pennsylvania and other pieces to some influential citizens. Many of these glasses are dated and signed, which aids in the identification of similar, unsigned pieces. Although a little old-fashioned by contemporary European standards, Amelung's presentation pieces are the most ambitious and elegant tableware produced in the USA in the 18th century.

With the end of the Revolutionary War in 1783 official restraints on manufacturing were removed, thus encouraging the development and growth of new industries. Manufacturers still had to compete with imported goods, and the British were especially eager to preserve their markets and to discourage American manufacturing. Except for Amelung's ambitious venture and a short-lived factory in Philadelphia, the managers of glasshouses started in the 1780s and 1790s were content to manufacture windows and bottles, leaving the tableware market to importers.

2. 1800–80. After the American Revolution settlers flowed west, lured by the promise of free land. The price of the commonest household goods sold in the western communities was greatly increased by freight charges, thus providing an irresistible impetus for manufacturers in the West to compete with goods shipped in from coastal cities. Window glass was especially prone to breakage during shipment, and it was thus one of the products made in the first glasshouses west of the Allegheny mountains in Pennsylvania. While window and bottle glasshouses continued to be concentrated in the heavily forested areas of New England, upstate New York and southern New Jersey, the factories that produced fine tablewares were in cities, closer to the centres of population.

American manufacturers were not freed from foreign competition until the Acts of Embargo (1807) and the Napoleonic Wars (1803–15) cut off the supply of imported British goods. This was only a temporary respite; the glass industry did not really flourish until it was protected by the Tariff Act of 1824. The first successful manufactory of lead-glass tablewares in the USA was located in Pittsburgh, PA. The distance from foreign competition, as well as the availability of customers and of coal for fuel, may have prompted Benjamin Bakewell, a Pittsburgh merchant, to start a glasshouse, BAKEWELL & CO., in 1808. Anxious to show off his cut glass, Bakewell presented a pair of decanters (Washington, DC, White House Col.; priv. col., on loan to Corning, NY, Mus. Glass) to President James Madison and another pair (untraced) to President James Monroe when they visited Pittsburgh in 1816 and 1817. President Monroe then ordered a set of English-style cut glass (untraced) for the White House, Washington, DC, from the Bakewell glasshouse in 1818. These early products of the American glass industry are astonishingly well cut and are difficult to distinguish from English cut glass of the same period: English glass was the standard by which American glass was judged, most of the glasscutters had learnt their trade in England, and such motifs as strawberry diamonds, fine diamonds, arches, fans, circular facets and flutes were fashionable in both places.

By the 1820s Bakewell had competitors in Pittsburgh and western Virginia, as well as in Boston, New York and Philadelphia. In 1818 a group of investors opened the NEW ENGLAND GLASS CO. in East Cambridge, MA. It eventually became one of the largest and most successful glass factories in the USA, making all types of tableware and lighting devices. In 1825 Deming Jarves (1790–1869) started the BOSTON & SANDWICH GLASS CO. in Sandwich, MA, which made similar products. These two factories dominated the market in New England. By 1830 three glasshouses in the New York area were producing fine tablewares, two of which had been started by workmen from the New England Glass Co. There were several independent cutting shops, which used glass blanks made in the New York factories or abroad. In Philadelphia the Union Flint Glass Co. was started in 1826 by a group of workmen from the New England Glass Co. It is difficult to make any stylistic distinctions among the products of the various factories making wares for the luxury market, as all the factories were producing blown and cut wares in the English style.

Although the largest factories often made tableware and containers, it was during the early 19th century that factories began to specialize. The raw materials and skills necessary to make refined, colourless tableware differed from those for commercial green-glass containers and flat glass. The blowers in the window- and bottle-glass factories were allowed to use their free time to make whatever they wished from the unrefined glass left in the pots at the end of the shift. Most of these were utilitarian household wares, such as milk pans, sugar bowls, creamers and large jugs. Although composed of many shades of green, amber and aquamarine, they are often attractive and skilfully made. They are usually simple in shape and often decorated

45. Pressed glass (from left to right): covered sugar bowl, h. 152 mm, probably from Providence Flint Glass Works, Providence, Rhode Island, *c.* 1830–33; bowl (on stand), h. 47 mm, 1830–45; cup plate, diam. 88 mm, *c.* 1835; salt dish, h. 50 mm, probably from Boston & Sandwich Glass Co., 1830–40; plate, h. 40 mm, 1835–50 (Corning, NY, Museum of Glass)

with applied threading and extra gathers of glass tooled into leaflike decorations called lily pads. The making of these wares flourished throughout the first half of the 19th century.

By the mid-19th century the growth in population meant a greater demand for glassware, and because the manufacture and decoration of hand-blown glassware was slow and costly manufacturers sought ways to speed production and to decorate their glass more cheaply. In the early 19th century the technique of mould-blowing glass, which produced the shape and surface pattern in one operation, was introduced in the manufacture of European and American tablewares. The first patterns used were copies of the cut glass then in vogue, but later manufacturers made use of other decorative elements. Although this was an efficient method of mass production, a number of American glassmakers experimented further in the 1820s with new methods to reduce costs and speed production. The result was the pressing or casting of glass into moulds. This was not a new technique: its origin can be traced back to ancient Rome (*see* GLASS, §II, 1(ii)). The principle of forcing rather than blowing glass into a shape had also been practised in Europe since the early 18th century. The process, however, of pressing molten glass into metal moulds by machine was perfected first in the USA by a series of improvements between 1820 and 1825, and within a few years many companies were using the new technique. Large quantities of American pressed-glass tableware were exported to Europe, the Caribbean and

South America. By 1840 the patterned, mould-blown tableware was completely outmoded by pressed glass.

Some of the earliest pressed patterns were probably copied from cut glass, still the most fashionable tableware. Designs of Gothic arches, acanthus leaves, scrolls and other elements fashionable to interior decoration were copied from architectural pattern books, and stylized floral designs may have been copied from English transfer-printed ceramics. Identifying the manufacturers of many of the earliest pressed patterns is difficult because so few pieces are marked, and many firms copied one another's popular patterns, thereby making absolute identification of early pressed glass nearly impossible; the examples in fig. 45 are all from New England. The development of the mechanical press and improved technology also gave rise to a greater variety of new shapes; this was accompanied by a shift in taste to simpler panelled and fluted decorative patterns that emphasized the purity of the glass and related to the new fashion in cut glass. Copies of every shape of the more expensive cut glass were suddenly available to people of lesser means, and the popularity of pressed-glass table sets was a tremendous boost for glass factories. By the mid-19th century machine pressing had become so efficient that a team of five men could make one hundred tumblers in an hour. This was much faster than producing blown wares in similar shapes. For the first time the American glass industry was stable and prosperous, able to fill the demands of an expanding market with quality products. Mass-production was thus the most important American contribution to the glass industry.

The development of a cheaper, non-lead formula for glass pressing, combined with the availability of coal and natural gas for fuel in the Midwest, gave the western factories an economic edge that gradually shifted the centre of the American glass industry westwards. Most of the eastern companies, such as the New England Glass Co., stopped making pressed glass in the 1870s and concentrated on the market for luxury wares, where the higher manufacturing costs could be more easily passed on to the buyer.

In the 1860s, after two decades of heavy pieces cut in simple patterns, tableware became lighter and thinner, and the cutting finer. This style did not remain popular for long as the glass was more fragile, and heavier, thicker glass, more deeply cut in intricate patterns, regained popularity in the 1870s. This change was heralded at the Centennial International Exhibition of 1876 in Philadelphia, where the East Coast glass companies exhibited cut and engraved glasses in both the new, heavier style and the older lightweight one. Gillinder & Co. of Philadelphia operated a complete glass factory on the exhibition grounds, making and selling popular pressed souvenir pieces as well as cut and engraved glass. The attention that Gillinder's displays of cut glass attracted, combined with the growing middle-class prosperity in the USA, led to a boom in the cut-glass industry. A new class of millionaires whose fortunes were made in railways, steamships, oil, steel and other industries created a large market for luxury goods. The entire surface of an object was decorated with intricate cutting—a style that went well with the heavy furniture, patterned fabrics and rich colours popular at that time.

Copper-wheel engraving was used increasingly to embellish glassware, especially presentation pieces. Many of the engravers were Germans or Bohemians who had been trained in highly organized apprenticeship systems, although by the end of the 19th century the demand for skilled cutters and engravers was so high that a number of Americans were able to find both training and employment in the indigenous glass industry. Although monograms and inscriptions of various sorts were popular on glass throughout the 1800s, mid-19th-century engravers added elaborate floral patterns, views of American scenery and buildings and naturalistic motifs of plants and animals.

3. AFTER 1880. Several firms in New England and the Midwest in the 1880s and 1890s sought new methods and styles of decoration for their products. Some of the varicoloured art glass of this period imitates such substances as mercury glass, which resembles silver, and tortoiseshell glass. Other glassmakers created new and dramatic colour effects; the addition of special ingredients to the raw materials meant that the finished product could be shaded or particoloured, and reheating portions of the glass caused them to strike or change colour. This became a popular method of decoration when in 1883 the New England Glass Co. introduced 'Amberina'. It inspired a host of imitators, the most famous of which is 'Peachblow', an 'Amberina' glass lined with opaque white to give it a porcelain-like appearance. The name was adopted after the sale in 1886 of a Chinese porcelain peach-bloom vase for £18,000. The sale made national headlines, and such

glass factories as HOBBS, BROCKUNIER & CO., the LIBBEY GLASS CO. and the Mount Washington Glass Co. (see MT WASHINGTON GLASS WORKS), as well as pottery manufacturers, rushed to capitalize on the publicity by making objects in the same shape with vaguely related colours. These pieces of art glass came in a variety of shapes and colours, some with elaborate applied decoration and crimped edges, others with silver or silver-plated stands. Because most of the decoration was done at the furnace, while the glass was hot, it cost less to make and sold for half the price of heavy, cut glass. It is likely that cut glass appealed to more conservative buyers, and that art glass was favoured by buyers interested in something new and more stylish. Both styles, however, suited cluttered, over-decorated Victorian interiors, and they remained widely popular throughout the last two decades of the 19th century.

As the Art Nouveau style gradually made the popular Victorian strongly coloured art glass and the complex, prickly cut glass look fussy, people of discriminating taste began to prefer the work of Louis Comfort Tiffany (see TIFFANY, §2) and his competitors. Tiffany was the leading exponent of the Art Nouveau style in the USA, although it was his chief rival, the painter JOHN LA FARGE, who, in 1879, first perfected a striated, opalescent glass, which was immediately copied by artists in the USA and abroad. Tiffany was fascinated by the possibilities of stained glass and began using it extensively for decorative glass windows and in domestic interiors in the 1880s. Tiffany had his designs made for him in several factories until 1893, when he set up his own plant at Corona, Long Island, NY. From windows Tiffany turned to iridescent glass vessels and was influenced by both the French glass designer EMILE GALLÉ, who was the acknowledged leader of this style, and the English exponents of the Aesthetic Movement. With the introduction of electricity in domestic lighting, Tiffany's firm began to make lamps with mosaic and stained-glass shades, which were immensely popular. In the USA Tiffany's competition in the field of Art Nouveau glass included Victor Durand jr (1870–1931) of the Vineland Flint Glass Works (see fig. 46) and FREDERICK CARDER, who founded the Steuben Glass Works with Thomas G. Hawkes (see HAWKES, T. G., & Co.). Carder's 'Aurene' glass is nearly indistinguishable from Tiffany's in some shapes and colours. Other glass companies in New England, New York and the Midwest began to copy ornamental glass in the style of Tiffany, and soon a flood of cheaper wares, including pressed glass with an iridescent surface, was available. By World War I both art glass and the brilliant cut glass had been eclipsed in popularity by simpler, lighter styles, which were less expensive and suited modern taste.

In the 1920s and 1930s glass was produced in the modern streamlined Art Deco look, first shown at the Exposition Internationale des Arts Décoratifs et Industriels Modernes in 1925 in Paris. Many American designers were influenced by Scandinavian design and the principles of the Bauhaus. Steuben, Inc. (see STEUBEN GLASS WORKS), now a subsidiary of the CORNING GLASS WORKS, developed a flawless, colourless glass with a high lead content and in 1933 began to produce simple heavy pieces often decorated with elaborate copper-wheel engraving.

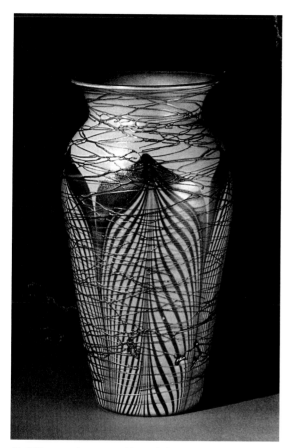

46. Iridescent glass vase with applied thread decoration, signed *Durand*, h. 224 mm, from the Vineland Flint Glass Works, Vineland, New Jersey, *c.* 1924–31 (Corning, NY, Museum of Glass)

This glass was specifically aimed at the affluent buyer. Advances in technology made nearly automatic mechanical pressing possible, and thousands of pieces of glass dinnerware were turned out so cheaply that they were affordable even during the Depression. Many glass companies making the more expensive luxury wares found that their markets nearly disappeared in this period, and many companies were forced to close.

In the late 1940s and early 1950s traditionally styled cut and engraved glass enjoyed a brief boom as consumers rushed to buy wares that had been unavailable during World War II. Most of the remaining factories producing fine tableware were in the Ohio River valley in western Pennsylvania and West Virginia, and nearly all of them had outmoded plants built in the early years of the 20th century. Rising production costs and the high price of modernizing the factories forced many of these companies to close in the 1950s; in the late 20th century Lenox Crystal was one of only two or three glasshouses in the USA that made glass tablewares and ornamental wares of the highest quality lead-crystal glass to compete with the high-quality tablewares made abroad.

In the 1950s a few artists began to experiment with producing glass individually in studios. Edris Eckhardt (*b* 1910), Michael Higgins (*b* 1908), Frances Higgins

(*b* 1912) and Maurice Heaton (*b* 1900) were craftsmen who perfected methods of forming glass, including fusing glass in ceramic kilns, sagging, layering and laminating in kilns and decorating with enamels and applied metals. Many artists felt hindered by their lack of access to factories where it was possible to work with molten glass. HARVEY K. LITTLETON, a professor and potter at the University of Wisconsin at Madison, was especially persistent in his attempts to find a place where he could create blown-glass pieces. In 1962 Littleton established two workshops for glass craftsmen at the Toledo Museum of Art. He found the process of melting glass from raw materials impossible in the small workshop furnace and turned to melting glass marbles that had been developed for the making of fibreglass. Dominick Labino (1910–87), the scientist who had developed the marbles, provided technical advice for the glassblowers and was soon caught up in the movement himself. In 1965 he retired from his job in the glass industry to devote his time to the creation of blown-glass pieces, many of them with extraordinary colour effects made possible by his knowledge of glass chemistry. Littleton offered courses in glassblowing to his students, and from Madison and Toledo the studio glass movement spread to colleges and universities all over the USA in the 1960s and 1970s. Many American glass artists, seeking more opportunities to work in glass factories as well as in their own studios, went to Europe and were influential in exporting their ideas. In these years most of the artists were experimenting with shapes and techniques; as they gained technical skill their pieces became less functional and more sculptural (*see* GLASS, colour pl. VII, fig. 2).

Artists continue to explore the seemingly inexhaustible potential of glass as a sculptural medium, alone, and in combination with other materials. The studio glass artists of the 1960s and 1970s considered themselves craftsmen trying to revive the craft of glassblowing; subsequent creators in this medium are more inclined to view themselves as artists who happen to have chosen glass as their method of expression. In the 1980s there was further refinement in glass production by individual artists. Many found that blowing glass limited their creativity and began making pieces that are a mixture of hot-working and cold-working techniques, combining blowing and moulding with cutting, engraving, sand-blasting, sagging and other methods of forming and decoration (*see* GLASS, §II, 1). Many glass artists worked in stained glass, producing windows and also sculptural pieces that are meant to be hung indoors like paintings rather than actually serving as windows.

BIBLIOGRAPHY

G. S. McKearin and H. McKearin: *American Glass* (New York, 1941/*R* 1989)
——: *Two Hundred Years of American Blown Glass* (New York, 1950)
A. C. Revi: *Nineteenth Century Art Glass: Its Genesis and Development* (New York, 1963, rev. 1967)
R. Koch: *Louis C. Tiffany: Rebel in Glass* (New York, 1964)
A. C. Revi: *American Pressed Glass and Figure Bottles* (New York, 1964)
——: *American Cut and Engraved Glass* (New York, 1965)
——: *American Art Nouveau Glass* (Camden, NJ, 1968)
P. V. Gardner: *The Glass of Frederick Carder* (New York, 1971)
K. M. Wilson: *New England Glass and Glassmaking* (New York, 1972)
L. Innes: *Pittsburgh Glass, 1797–1891: A History and a Guide for Collectors* (Boston, 1976)
D. P. Lanmon and A. M. Palmer: 'John Frederick Amelung and the New Bremen Glassmanufactory', *J. Glass Soc.*, xviii (1976), pp. 14–137

A. M. Palmer: *The Wistarburgh Glassworks: The Beginning of Jersey Glass-making* (Alloway, NJ, 1976)

H. McKearin and K. M. Wilson: *American Bottles and Flasks and their Ancestry* (New York, 1978)

E. S. Farrar and J. S. Spillman: *The Complete Cut and Engraved Glass of Corning* (New York, 1979)

C. U. Fauster: *Libbey Glass since 1818: Pictorial History and Collector's Guide* (Toledo, OH, 1979)

A. Duncan: *Tiffany Windows* (New York, 1980)

J. S. Spillman: *American and European Pressed Glass in the Corning Museum of Glass* (Corning, 1981)

M. J. Madigan: *Steuben Glass: An American Tradition in Crystal* (New York, 1982)

A. Duncan: *American Art Deco* (New York, 1986)

S. K. Frantz: *Contemporary Glass: A World Survey from the Corning Museum of Glass* (Corning, 1989)

A. Palmer: '"To the Good of the Province and Country": Henry William Stiegel and American Flint Glass', *The American Craftsman and the European Tradition*, ed. F. J. Puig and M. Conforti (Minneapolis, 1989), pp. 202–39

J. S. Spillman and S. K. Frantz: *Masterpieces of American Glass* (New York, 1990)

JANE SHADEL SPILLMAN

IX. Metalwork.

1. Silver. 2. Base metals.

1. SILVER. The search for silver and gold was a driving force behind the settlement of the American continent, and silver coins and objects have been an integral part of American art ever since. In Colonial America the silversmith was a leader in introducing the newest and most fashionable styles from abroad, especially from England. His craft was perceived as one of the fine arts in the New World and it received greater attention from patrons in the 17th and 18th centuries than the sister arts of painting, sculpture or architecture. American silver remained responsive to the major artistic movements abroad and it rivals English silver in its skill and elaboration. Americans also introduced their own innovations, particularly in the continuing development of such traditional forms as porringers and tankards long after they ceased to be popular in Europe. In the 19th century American firms and designers became leaders in the development of new designs.

(i) Before 1700. (ii) 1700–50. (iii) 1751–75. (iv) 1776–1820. (v) 1821–1900. (vi) After 1900.

(i) Before 1700. Colonial silversmiths were not regulated by the guild system long present in England, and thus American objects lack hallmarks. The craftsman's touchmark was his guarantee that the work leaving his shop was of sufficient quality. Most silversmiths ran small-scale operations, employing only one or two apprentices and journeymen. Sons often followed their fathers in the trade; notable examples include the Edwards family of Boston, the Richardson family of Philadelphia, and, on a lesser scale, the Lang and Northey families of Salem, MA. Journeymen specializing in such branches of the craft as engraving, chasing and casting often contributed to the definition of regional characteristics, for example the banding and pierced galleries that were used on the products issued by different shops in the Philadelphia–Baltimore area, or by engraving the products of more than one silversmith. Scholars continue to focus attention on the importance of these skilled journeymen, whose contribution to the transfer of styles from England and Europe

47. Silver beaker by Cornelius van der Burch, h. 203 mm, 1685 (New Haven, CT, Yale University Art Gallery)

and to the development of new artistic expressions were significant as early as the 17th century. Colonial silversmiths drew on a wide variety of design sources in their work. Imported English objects provided first-hand knowledge of the latest fashions, and ceramic forms were another frequent source of inspiration. Immigrant craftsmen brought new ideas and fashions with them when they came to America. Dutch and French influence can be seen primarily in the work of silversmiths from New York, northern New Jersey and Albany.

Much of the silversmith's day-to-day work consisted of repairing worn pieces, replacing lost parts and making jewellery or small objects. Raw material was derived from melting down clipped and worn coins and damaged or unfashionable objects. In the early years of Spanish exploration of Central and South America, silver was mined in large quantities at the mines at Potosi in the Andes, and bullion and roughly minted coins were transported to Europe. However, silver in bullion form was rare in the British Colonies of North America, coming only from the occasional Spanish ships captured during periods of war. Most American silversmiths worked in gold as well as silver, and the terms goldsmith and silversmith were used interchangeably in early documents. Gold, rare in the colonies, was used only to fashion such small pieces of jewellery as buttons, lockets and buckles. Many silversmiths practised related crafts, including engraving, making coins and engraving paper currency, cutting seals and medals, making clocks, watches, mathematical, nautical and medical instruments, firearms, swords and other military equipment, and working in other metals.

American silver of the 17th century is notable for its broad proportions, fine engraved detail and flat-chased ornament. Stylish objects, such as cups with cast scroll and caryatid handles by Jeremiah Dummer (1645–1718) and JOHN CONEY of Boston and Bartholomew Le Roux (c. 1663–1713) of New York reveal the influence of the Mannerist style, also seen in the engraved strapwork designs on beakers. The rectilinear and architectural nature of much work in this period is evidenced by Dummer's monumental cluster-column candlesticks (New Haven, CT, Yale U. A.G.). English influence was predominant, as would be true of New England silver throughout the Colonial period. Occasionally, Continental sources seem to have provided prototypes for American work, as with Dummer's Portuguese-inspired two-handled bowl (New Haven, CT, Yale U. A.G.).

Silversmithing in 17th-century America was almost exclusively practised in the major seaports of Boston and New York; only towards the very end of the century did craftsmen practising this luxury trade work in Philadelphia, Charleston, SC, and elsewhere. Boston was the centre of the craft and the source of supply for all of New England (*see* BOSTON, §III, 2). The partnership of John Hull (1624–83) and Robert Sanderson (1608–93) in Boston began in the 1650s; they are the first silversmiths active in America by whom any work survives (e.g. dram cup, c. 1650–60; New Haven, CT, Yale U. A.G.). Both Hull and Sanderson were born in England and came to the Massachusetts Bay Colony in the 1630s. Dummer, one of their apprentices, was the first American-born silversmith to produce a substantial body of work. John Coney was the outstanding Boston craftsman; Timothy Dwight (1654–92) and William Rouse (1639–1705) were other important Boston artisans of this early period.

A rich body of Dutch-related silver was produced in New York, which came under English rule in 1674 but retained a distinctly Dutch air well into the 18th century. Beakers, such as the large example of 1685 (New Haven, CT, Yale U. A.G.; see fig. 47) by Cornelius van der Burch (c. 1653–99), were a distinctive, Dutch-inspired form popular with New York craftsmen. The van der Burch beaker is engraved with designs derived from the engravings of Adriaen van der Venne used as illustrations in a popular Dutch emblem-book by Jacobus Cats (1577–1660). Tankards made by such prominent New York silversmiths as Jacobus van der Spiegel (1668–1708) and Jurian Blanck jr (c. 1645–1714) represent an important hybrid object. Generally English in form, although lower and broader than most New England examples, the New York tankard is often embellished with applied meander wire at the base, a corkscrew-spiralled thumbpiece, ornamental engraving featuring pendent fruit, cast and applied decoration on the handle and, occasionally, with a coin or medal inset in the lid. Late in the century such immigrant Huguenot craftsmen as Bartholomew Le Roux had an impact on New York styles. Members of the Ten Eyck family of Albany and others carried the Dutch tradition into the 18th century.

American silversmiths produced many forms, but spoons, porringers, beakers, dram cups, standing wine cups, two-handled cups, bowls, plates, salts and tankards were among the most common in this period. Silver objects were extremely expensive and were owned only by wealthy members of society or institutions, particularly churches. In the South most large planters traded directly with London merchants and therefore had credit there that could be used to acquire and import English silver.

(ii) 1700–50. The Baroque style, with its undulating lines and contrasting surfaces, is perhaps the most striking of all styles in early American silver. The forms produced were similar to those fashioned in the 17th century, but they were embellished with new ornament. Bold gadrooned bands and distinct mouldings were often used by the silversmith as an artistic foil for the plain shimmering silver surfaces in the creation of such elaborately three-dimensional masterpieces as John Coney's monteith (c. 1705–15; New Haven, CT, Yale U. A.G.; see fig. 48), used for rinsing and cooling wine glasses, and sugar-boxes by Coney and Edward Winslow (1669–1753). Coney's monteith, made for the Colman family of Boston, is stylish by London standards and is testimony to Coney's skill in all areas of the craft. Even the simplest objects were often distinguished by elaborate piercings and exquisite ornamental engraving.

The Baroque style was brought to New England by an influx of immigrant craftsmen who came to Boston to fill the needs of the newly appointed British officials after the Massachusetts Old Charter was replaced by a royal charter in 1692. Boston and New York grew and developed in this period, and Philadelphia began to emerge as a significant port during this era of peace. This new affluence led

48. Silver monteith by John Coney, h. 219 mm, diam. 273 mm, c. 1705–15 (New Haven, CT, Yale University Art Gallery)

to the production of such new forms as teapots, chocolatepots, sugar-boxes, casters for condiments, chafing dishes, inkstands, large covered cups and punch-bowls.

In Boston the craft was dominated, among others, by Coney, Dummer, Winslow and John Edwards (1671–1746). Samuel Vernon (1683–1737) practised the trade in nearby Newport, RI. Craftsmen of Dutch and French descent, including Gerrit Onckelbag (c. 1670–1732), van der Speigel, Cornelius Kierstede (1675–1757), Le Roux and Peter Van Dyck (1684–1751), dominated the trade in New York. Cornelius Kierstede's work, including a pair of monumental candlesticks and a snuffers stand en suite, a tea kettle and a brandywine bowl (all New York, Met.) and numerous tankards, represents perhaps the finest work done in New York at this time. Three two-handled covered cups by Onckelbag (New Haven, CT, Yale U. A.G.; Hist. Deerfield, MA; Winterthur, DE, Du Pont Winterthur Mus.) and an example by Kierstede (Chicago, IL, A. Inst.) are evidence, however, that these Continental makers could also fashion objects in the English tradition. In Philadelphia, Cesar Ghiselin (c. 1663–1733), Johannis Nys (1671–1734), Francis Richardson (1681–1729) and Philip Syng sr (1676–1739) were major silver producers whose work is in the English style.

Characterized by balanced, symmetrical forms that rely on line and form rather than ornament for their visual impact, the Queen Anne style was popular in the colonies from about 1715 to 1750. Such geometric forms as the circle and octagon, smooth surfaces, superb proportions and the subtle interplay of reverse curves, particularly the S-curve, distinguish objects in this style, noted for its simplicity and restraint. The plain surfaces of the Queen Anne style allowed the engraver to display his abilities to great advantage (e.g. a salver by Jacob Hurd (1703–58); New Haven, CT, Yale U. A.G.).

In Boston, Hurd was the leader of his generation, noted especially for his large two-handled presentation cups (e.g. of 1744; New Haven, CT, Yale U. A.G.) and the high quality of engraving on his objects. He received many commissions for church silver, tutorial plate and civic objects. In New York, Charles Le Roux (1689–1745) and Simeon Soumaine (1685–1750) were accomplished masters. Soumaine's sugar bowl (New Haven, CT, Yale U. A.G.), based on East Asian ceramic prototypes, is a sophisticated statement of harmonious proportions and the interplay of circles on various planes, while a two-handled cup by Le Roux (New Haven, CT, Yale U. A.G.) is decorated with the harp-shaped handles and cut-card work characteristic of French Huguenot work produced in London. Philip Syng jr (1703–89) of Philadelphia produced a marvellous capacious tankard (New Haven, CT, Yale U. A.G.) that embodies the best of the Queen Anne style.

More specialized forms of tea equipment began to be made, as tea-drinking became a widespread form of domestic entertainment, and every fashionable hostess sought to acquire her own silver service. Large numbers of teapots, sugar bowls, cream jugs, tea caddies, sugar scissors and teaspoons were produced to fill the demand. The so-called keyhole-handled porringer (a small bowl with one handle for multipurpose domestic use and frequently given to infants and children) was developed in this period and remained a standard design for the rest of the century.

(iii) 1751–75. Silver in the Rococo style is more elaborately embellished and more asymmetrical than its Queen Anne style predecessors. The repoussé ornament popular during this period was expensive, because it required great skill and much time for the maker to produce. Therefore, much American silver of this period is Rococo in form but lacks ornamentation other than engraving. Sugar bowls, teapots and coffeepots share the inverted pear (or 'double-bellied') shape and high centre of gravity characteristic of this style. The full vocabulary of Rococo ornament, including shells, scrolls and flowers, can be seen on a tea kettle with stand (New Haven, CT, Yale U. A.G.; see fig. 49) by Joseph Richardson (1711–84) of Philadelphia, probably based on an English example by Paul de Lamerie owned in Philadelphia. Cast ornament, repoussé decoration and gadrooning were popular techniques used to place emphasis on ornament and small details in this period. Echoing furniture styles, silver objects were sometimes supported on short cabriole legs terminating on claw-and-ball, pad or, as with the Richardson kettle, shell feet. The highest achievements of American Rococo were made in Philadelphia, which by 1775 had become the largest city in America. Imported English silver played an increasingly important role, as silversmiths attempted to satisfy the demands of an increasingly large and affluent population by becoming importers and retailers as well as producers.

Rococo silver from New York is noted for its pierced decoration, as seen on a cake basket and dish ring (New

49. Silver tea kettle with stand by Joseph Richardson, h. 389 mm, c. 1745–55 (New Haven, CT, Yale University Art Gallery)

Haven, CT, Yale U. A.G.) by Myer Myers (1723–95), who also produced important examples of Jewish ritual silver for synagogues in New York and Philadelphia. John Heath (*fl c.* 1760–70) and the Swiss immigrant Daniel Christian Feuter (1720–85) were other New York makers of prominence. Feuter's sophisticated Rococo work includes a cake basket (Boston, MA, Mus. F.A.), a gold coral and bells (New Haven, CT, Yale U. A.G.) and a beaker elaborately engraved with anti-papist propaganda (Winterthur, DE, Du Pont Winterthur Mus.). During the latter part of his years in New York (1754–69), Feuter employed John Anthony Beau (*fl c.* 1769), a specialist chaser who also emigrated from Switzerland and whose work is representative of the importance of such immigrant craftsmen.

In Boston, where the growth in population had slowed, a more restrained type of Rococo was practised, in which engraved ornament often appeared, for example on more traditional forms. The finest wares were produced by Benjamin Burt (1729–1805) and PAUL REVERE, who produced an impressive variety of objects, well documented in his surviving account-books and represented by objects in most major collections. His colleague Nathaniel Hurd (1730–77) is more noted for the high quality of his engraving in the Rococo style on both silver objects and bookplates. They relied on such English sources as Sympson's *New Book of Cyphers* (1726) and John Guillim's *Display of Heraldry* (6th edn, 1724) for their coats of arms and heraldic devices; Hurd, in fact, was painted by John Singleton Copley with these books at his side (*c.* 1765; Cleveland, OH, Mus. A.).

The first production of silver hollow-ware in substantial amounts by southern makers came in the Rococo period. By mid-century Thomas You (*fl* 1753–86) and Alexander Petrie (*d* 1768) were producing fine wares in Charleston, SC, and a teapot (New Haven, CT, Yale U. A.G.) by Gabriel Lewyn (*fl c.* 1768–80) of Baltimore is one of the most sophisticated American expressions of the Rococo.

Tea equipment grew to include large-footed trays or salvers and cream pots, and candlesticks, cruet-stands and large pierced baskets joined the repertory of forms in this period.

(iv) 1776–1820. The Neo-classical style marked a return to elegant simplicity. After a lull during the Revolution, silversmiths emphasized such forms as the urn and the oval and ornament inspired by the art and architecture of ancient Egypt, Greece and Rome. The influence of Classical antiquity came to America through the filter of Robert Adam of England. The style was introduced as early as 1774 in the form of an urn (Philadelphia, PA, Mus. A.; *see* FEDERAL STYLE, fig. 2) fashioned by Richard Humphreys (1750–1832) and engraved by James Smither (1741–97) of Philadelphia, and gained currency in the 1790s, remaining fashionable into the 1820s. Ornament, including pierced galleries, strips of beading and reeding, tended to be used with restraint. Despite the Revolution, English taste continued to be profoundly influential. In the 19th century the making of sterling silver objects evolved from a craft into an industry. Such labour-saving techniques as dropstamping, rolling, spinning and machine-engraving augmented traditional methods of handcraftsmanship. Sheet

silver, used by Revere and others for teapots, made it possible to create objects of thinner-gauge material, with the result that more objects could be made from the same amount of raw material. This factor and the rise of fortunes made in international commerce, particularly with East Asia, that emerged after independence resulted in the production of more extensive tea services, often including coffeepots, two teapots, hot milk and cold cream pitchers and slop or waste bowls, and the first matched sets of silver flatware. The first silver substitute, fused or Sheffield plate, was imported in large quantities from England, and craftsmen from Philadelphia and elsewhere attempted to manufacture their own variety of this less expensive metal. Silver forms became broader and heavier in the 19th century as Neo-classicism developed into the Empire style.

Bright-cutting, a technique in which the silver is gouged or notched to form facets, was an important decorative technique in this period. Matching tea services became fashionable, as represented by a tea set (New Haven, CT, Yale U. A.G.) by Abraham Dubois (*fl c.* 1777–1807) of Philadelphia in which all the vessels are fashioned with urn-shaped bodies. The hot-water urn, used to heat water for diluting tea or coffee, was a characteristic form of the period. Coffeepots, too, became much more common.

Production in Philadelphia and New York eclipsed that of Boston in this period, and silversmiths began to find more work in such smaller cities as Baltimore, MD, Salem, MA, Hartford, CT, Alexandria, VA, and in many small towns on the expanding western frontier.

(v) 1821–1900. Design in the 19th century was characterized by an eclectic medley of successive yet overlapping styles borrowed from the past. The most successful designers avoided imitation and were able to assimilate and transform historical styles into a synthesis that was truly original. As the century progressed, objects were influenced by the French Rococo, Gothic, Greek, Renaissance and many other revival styles. The more exotic flavour of Egyptian, Japanese, Moorish and East Indian taste is also evident. Manufacturers competed for the buyer's attention by creating increasingly fanciful designs, many of which were now being patented at the US Patent Office, founded in 1791. At the end of the century a few manufacturers produced silver in the Art Nouveau style, led by the GORHAM Manufacturing Co. of Providence, RI, and popularized by such firms as Unger Bros of Newark, NJ. Gorham indicated in 1912 that with its Martelé ('hammered') line of silverware and jewellery, 'The form is the important thing, and the decoration, far from being conventional, partakes almost wholly of naturalistic forms: waves of the sea, natural flowers, mermaids, fishes, cloud effects—almost anything can be used provided it is treated in a naturalistic manner.' (Holbrook, pp. 113–14)

Early in the century there was a huge increase in smallshop production, but by mid-century these firms began to consolidate to form large manufacturing companies. New York played an increasingly important role, but as huge fortunes were made in the gold and silver rushes, silversmiths began to move west to provide objects for the new clientele. Small firms opened throughout the country, but these increasingly served as retailers of objects made by the major firms that began in this period, including

Gorham (1831), Tiffany & Co. of New York (1837), Reed & Barton of Taunton, MA (1824), Samuel Kirk of Baltimore (1815) and others. Such significant designers as William Christmas Codman (1839–1923) at Gorham, and Edward C. Moore (1827–91) and Paulding Farnham (*fl* 1889–*c*. 1904) at Tiffany played important roles in shaping taste. The exhibits by Tiffany, Gorham and other American firms at international exhibitions and fairs, including the Exposition Universelle of 1889 in Paris, the World Columbian Exposition of 1893 in Chicago, the Esposizione Internazionale d'Arte Decorativa Moderna of 1902 in Turin, the World's Fair of 1904 in St Louis, MO, and others, established American firms as leaders in international design and provided an opportunity for American companies to publicize their technical and design expertise through exceptional showpieces in a variety of styles.

While large quantities of domestic silver were produced in this period, presentation occasions provided silvermakers with some of their most lucrative commissions. Vases, pitchers and other presentation pieces made for heroes of the war of 1812 by such firms as that of Thomas Fletcher (*fl* 1809–50) and Sidney Gardiner (*fl c*. 1812–38) of Philadelphia were among the first major examples of a tradition that would last the century. Silver objects were used to

50. Vase for Edward Dean Adams, gold decorated with quartz, rock crystal, pearls, spessartites, tourmalines, amethysts and enamel, designed by Paulding Farnham for Tiffany & Co., New York, h. 495 mm, 1893–5 (New York, Metropolitan Museum of Art)

commemorate a wide variety of accomplishments, from swords presented to war heroes, to monumental prizes for yachting and other sports, and full dinner services for use on US Navy battleships. Perhaps the most opulent of all American presentation pieces is the vase (New York, Met.; see fig. 50) for Edward Dean Adams (1846–1931); designed by Farnham and produced by Tiffany in 1893–5, it is made of gold and decorated with quartz, rock crystal, pearls, spessartites, tourmalines, amethysts and enamel. Another particularly impressive example of presentation silver is the 2.6 m high cup (Chicago, IL, Hist. Soc.) made in 1898 by Gorham to honour Admiral George Dewey. Designed by Codman, the enormous cup was fashioned from more than 70,000 dimes donated by men and women throughout the country in grateful appreciation for Dewey's victory at Manila in the Spanish–American War.

With the opening of the great silver mines in the American West in the 1850s and the introduction of electroplating techniques at about the same time, the ownership of silver and silverplate became much more commonplace. Suddenly silver was no longer the province of the few but was made accessible to the many. Silverplated objects were made in a variety of revival styles, closely following forms in silver, and could be cheaply produced and widely marketed. Large factories and increased automation became the rule. Major manufacturers of silverplated wares were located in Connecticut, including Rogers Bros, the Meriden Britannia Co. and others. In 1898 more than twenty companies joined to form the International Silver Co. in Meriden, CT. In the 19th century nearly any article might be fashioned in sterling or silverplate; elaborate dining customs called for many specialized forms of flatware (such as terrapin spoons, fish forks and asparagus tongs) and table services consisted of tureens, trays, dinner plates, serving dishes, candlesticks and large decorative centrepieces, many to hold flowers or fruit. The service made by Tiffany in the 1870s for Mr and Mrs John W. Mackey consisted of about 1250 pieces (dispersed, see Carpenter and Carpenter, figs. 55–64) made from silver taken from Mackey's Comstock Lode mines in Virginia City, NV.

(vi) After 1900. At the beginning of the 20th century opulent naturalistic designs existed alongside the fluid functionalism of the Arts and Crafts aesthetic. Noted practitioners of the Arts and Crafts manner included Karl F. Leinonen (1866–1957) of Boston, Clara Welles (1868–1965), founder of the Kalo Shop in Chicago, Robert Jarvie (1865–1941) of Chicago, and Porter Blanchard (1886–1973) and Clemens Friedell (1872–1963) in southern California. Leinonen's hot chocolate set (1906; New Haven, CT, Yale U. A.G.; see fig. 51), commissioned as a gift for Louise G. Dietrick by the principal patron of the Boston Society of Arts and Crafts Handicraft Shop, Arthur Astor Carey, represents the restraint, sobriety and clean look of much Arts and Crafts work.

The same purity of line carried over into items manufactured by such firms as Tiffany & Co. but did not totally overshadow the prevailing taste for more traditional forms. Scandinavian influence, notably that of Georg Jensen, can be seen in this period in the work of such craftsmen as Hans Christensen (1924–83). Some firms, such as those

51. Silver hot chocolate set by Karl F. Leinonen, h. 205 mm (pot), 1906 (New Haven, CT, Yale University Art Gallery)

of Arthur J. Stone (1847–1938) of Gardner, MA, and George C. Gebelein (1878–1945) of Boston, turned to 18th-century American and English forms for inspiration (e.g. loving-cup by Arthur J. Stone; Cambridge, MA, Fogg; *see* BOSTON, fig. 5). For the first time women silversmiths, such as Marie Zimmerman (1878–1972), Mary Regnier (*b* 1901), Katherine Pratt (1891–1978) and Elizabeth E. Copeland (1866–1957), made major contributions to silver design.

Beginning in the late 1950s a new generation rebelled against mass manufacturing and 'traditional' styling by creating handcrafted objects. Experimentation resulted in a wide variety of artistic expressions, particularly in the production of jewellery and small items, many of which combine silver with gold and other metals and with plastic and acrylics, as well as with gemstones. The silversmith was often a teacher as well as an artist, and metalsmithing became an integral part of the curricula of many American colleges, universities and art schools. Freed from the pressures of the marketplace to some degree, these artists explored many different designs and techniques; John Prip (*b* 1922), Mary Lee Hu (*b* 1943), Stanley Lechtzin (*b* 1936) and Robert W. Ebendorf (*b* 1938) were only a few of the many skilled metalsmiths active in the late 20th century. Much silverware made for the mass market, however, continued to be made in traditional, revival styles. Many flatware patterns popular in the late 20th century, for example, had been in production since the 1870s.

BIBLIOGRAPHY

J. S. Holbrook: *Silver for the Dining Room: Selected Periods* (Cambridge, MA, 1912), pp. 112–19

Colonial Silversmiths: Masters and Apprentices (exh. cat. by K. C. Buhler, Boston, MA, Mus. F. A., 1956)

K. Morrison McClinton: *Collecting American 19th Century Silver* (New York, 1968)

D. T. Rainwater and H. I. Rainwater: *American Silverplate* (Nashville and Hanover, PA, 1968)

K. C. Buhler and G. Hood: *American Silver: Garvan and Other Collections in the Yale University Art Gallery*, 2 vols (New Haven, 1970)

G. Hood: *American Silver: A History of Style, 1650–1900* (New York, 1971)

N. D. Turner: *American Silver Flatware, 1837–1910* (New York, 1972)

M. Gandy Fales: *Early American Silver* (New York, 1973)

C. H. Carpenter jr and M. G. Carpenter: *Tiffany Silver* (New York, 1978)

Silver in American Life (exh. cat., ed. B. McLean Ward and G. W. R. Ward; New York, Amer. Fed. A., 1979–82)

B. McLean Ward: *The Craftsman in a Changing Society: Boston Goldsmiths, 1690–1730* (diss., Boston U., 1983)

Marks of Achievement: Four Centuries of American Presentation Silver (exh. cat. by D. B. Warren, K. S. Howe and M. K. Brown, Houston, TX, Mus. F.A., 1987)

American Rococo, 1750–1775: Elegance in Ornament (exh. cat. by M. H. Heckscher and L. G. Bowman, New York, Met.; Los Angeles, CA, Co. Mus. A., 1992)

GERALD W. R. WARD

2. BASE METALS.

(i) Pewter. (ii) Iron and tinware. (iii) Copper, brass and bronze. (iv) Other.

(i) Pewter. American pewter was based on English forms. The first known American pewterer was Richard Graves, who is recorded as working in Salem, MA, in 1635. By 1700 there were six pewterers working in the colonies, although few examples of their work survive: fragments of a pewter spoon (Jamestown, VA, N. Hist. Site) made by Joseph Copeland (1675–95) were excavated at Jamestown, VA, and the second oldest documented piece is a bowl (Winterthur, DE, Du Pont Winterthur Mus.) made by Edmund Dolbeare (1671–1711) of Massachusetts. After 1700 the number of pewterers increased, with production strongest in the Boston area, supplemented by work in New York, Middleton, CT, Rhode Island and Philadelphia. By the 1760s over 300 tonnes of pewter were shipped annually to America from England. Throughout the Colonial period, England placed strict restrictions on the importation of raw materials in order to discourage local production and to increase the market for English pewter and other goods. The major pewterers in the 18th century were: in Massachusetts, John Skinner (1733–1813) and Nathaniel Austin (1741–1816); in Rhode Island, Lawrence Langworthy (*fl* 1735) and David Melville (*fl* 1755–93); in the Connecticut Valley, Thomas Danforth (*fl* 1733–86) and Thomas Danforth II (*b* 1756); in New York, William Diggs (*fl* 1702), William Horsewell (*fl* 1705), Joseph Liddell (*d* 1754), Francis Basset (1690–1758) and his family, John Will (1696–1770) and William Bradford (1688–1759); and in Philadelphia, William Will (1742–98). Individual makers can sometimes be identified by certain characteristics: Peter Young (1749–95) of Albany, NY, is known for baluster stem chalices, and the work of Johann Christoph Heyne (1715–81) of Philadelphia shows German influence, seen for example in a flagon with angel-head feet (Winterthur, DE, Du Pont Winterthur Mus.).

The pewter made in Colonial America reflected the styles and tastes of the makers' and customers' ethnic origins, usually England, although immigrants from Germany and Sweden exerted some stylistic influence. Pewter forms usually followed silver forms, though often lasted longer. There were regional differences; in New York, for example, tankards usually had a crenated lip, whereas in the Lancaster area of Pennsylvania, German influence was strong. Porringers were made with solid handles in Rhode Island and floral-design handles in the rest of New England. Multi-reeded edged plates were made prior to 1700, followed by single-reeded ones. From 1750 to 1775 hammered booges (the section between the bottom of the plate and the rim) appeared on some plates, while plates made in Boston were thinner.

After the Revolution there was a significant increase in the amount of pewter made in the USA as the English control of commerce ended. Some of the major pewterers active until the first half of the 19th century were: in the Massachusetts Bay area, the Green family (fl 1710s–1790s) and George Richardson (fl 1818–28); in Rhode Island, Samuel Hamlin (fl 1840s) and William Calder (1792–1856); in New York, William Elsworth (fl late 1750s–1780s) and Henry Will (fl 1750s–1780s); in Albany, Spencer Stafford (fl 1794) and Timothy Brigden (fl 1770–1818); and in Philadelphia, Blakeslee Barnes (1781–1823). The largest pewter business in the USA was that of the Boardman and Danforth families of Connecticut (about 14 members; fl until the 1850s).

From about 1825 Britannia metal was produced in the USA; it was cheaper to make than pewter and allowed for more complicated forms because it could be spun. Britannia was used to make, among other objects, pitchers, coffeepots, whale-oil lamps and caster sets. The major makers of Britannia metal were: William Calder; Roswell Gleason (Dorchester, MA, 1799–1865); Reed & Barton (Taunton, MA, 1824–); Babbit Crossman (Taunton, MA, fl 1826–8); Eben Smith (Beverly, MA, fl 1814–56); Philip Lee (Beverly, MA, fl 1807–12); Israel Trask (Beverly, MA, 1786–1867), known for his bright-cut engraving; Capen & Molineaux (New York, fl 1848–53), makers of whale-oil lamps; Crossman, West & Leonard and the Taunton Britannia Manufacturing Co. (Taunton, MA, fl 1828–35); Ashbil Griswold (Meriden, CT, fl 1784–1853); Rufus Dunham (Westbrooke, ME, fl 1815–82); and the Boardman and Danforth families.

The further decline of pewter began in the 1850s when electroplate silver replaced Britannia as a favoured domestic metal, and production essentially ceased by 1875. In 1898 W. F. Cowleshow of Boston made pewter reproductions. In the 1930s Morton Wheelock produced some modern pewter forms, and in the late 20th century Reed & Barton continued to make pewter (see PEWTER, fig. 3).

Touchmarks contained a lion or rose and crown prior to 1776, after which an eagle was used; an 'X' meant high-quality pewter. Touchmarks on Britannia metals were usually a manufacturer's name in intaglio.

(ii) *Iron and tinware.* During the Colonial period large amounts of iron goods were imported. The earliest known blacksmith was James Read (fl 1607–?1624) of Jamestown, VA, in 1607. A large number of craftsmen were making guns, locks, hinges, farm equipment, andirons and other fireplace equipment, cooking utensils, candlesticks and lamps. The first attempt to establish an iron-producing furnace was in 1622 at Falling Creek, VA, but it never went into production because of a Native American attack. The first successful furnace was constructed in 1644 at Saugus, MA, and operated until 1663 (the site has been excavated and restored). Weathervanes were often made of iron; the earliest American one (in the shape of a flag), dated 1673, is at the Meeting House, Concord, MA (see WEATHERVANE).

A furnace was opened in Connecticut in the 17th century, and by the 18th century numerous foundries were operating. Among them were the Principio Furnace in Maryland (1728), a furnace at Ancram, NY (1740), and in New Jersey the Sterling Furnace (1740s) and the Basto Furnace (1766–1876). The Basto Furnace sold work to George Washington and made the fence for Independence Hall in Philadelphia. The Colebrookdale and Hopewell Furnaces (1770s–1930s) were among the large number operating in Pennsylvania.

In 1742 Benjamin Franklin (1706–90) invented a fireplace insert stove made from cast-iron plates. The glassmaker Henry William Stiegel of Pennsylvania made stoves in 1756. In the 18th century they were decorated with Rococo motifs similar to those found on furniture of the period, and in the early 19th century elaborate, tall columnar stoves were made.

Several regional differences in ironwork exist; for example, staghorn hinges were used in Pennsylvania, and L-shaped hinges were used in New England. Samuel Wheeler (1742–1820) made the gate (1785) at Old Church, and an iron railing for Congress Hall, both in Philadelphia. There exists a railing with 13 arrows (1789) made for Federal Hall, New York, and there is an important 18th-century wrought-iron chandelier in the collection of Old Sturbridge Village, Sturbridge, MA.

Tinsmiths created objects by using tin-coated rolled iron. They made weathervanes, lanterns and a range of domestic goods, chiefly cooking utensils. In the 17th and 18th centuries a great deal of tin-faced ironware was shipped from England. Shem Drowne (1683–?1750) of Boston was the first known maker of tinware, producing lanterns, trays and candlesticks. Other early tinsmiths were Edward Pattison (or Paterson) & Sons (1730–?1787) of Berlin, CT; the Oliver Filley family (fl 1784) of Simsbury, CT; Henry Degenhardt (fl 1765) of Reading, PA; Passmore & Williams (est. 1796) of Philadelphia; and the Zachariah Stevens family of Maine.

Pierced tin objects were popular in New England, while punched tin and wriggleware were preferred in Pennsylvania. Tin mirror-frames were popular in the Southwest. By the early 19th century machines increased productivity. Tinsmiths made coffeepots, food warmers, cookie cutters, sconces, trays and boxes among other domestic wares. Prior to 1800 American tinware was usually undecorated. By 1800 Edward Pattison of Berlin, CT, began to paint tin (called 'Japan' ware). Some pieces were stencilled or hand decorated with folk designs of fruit and flowers. Some of the major decorators were the Filleys of Connecticut and New York, the Stevens of Maine, the Butler family (fl 1824–60) of Greenville, NY, and the North family (fl 1806–41) of Fly Creek, NY.

The city of Charleston, SC, is known for its fine ironware, including the gates at St John's church by Jacob P. Roh and the gates (1848) by A. W. Iusti (fl 1840s) at St Michael's. Such whitesmiths as John Long (fl 1832–5) of Pennsylvania made small, fine iron articles. Excellent locks were made by the Rohrer family (*fl* 1808–22) of Pennsylvania.

Iron and tin weathervanes were popular throughout the 19th century. Some major makers were L. W. Cushing Sons (1867–1933) of Waltham, MA; J. W. Fiske (1858–) of New York; W. A. Snow & Co. (1885–1940) of Boston; and E. G. Washburne (1853–) of New York. Designs in weathervanes progressed from animals, flags, angels and Native Americans to such elaborate items as copies of the statue of *Liberty* and steam engines. Production of many of these designs was revived in the late 20th century, using old moulds and forms.

By the mid-19th century large iron manufacturers were making goods based on English forms. During the second half of the 19th century cast iron was used for garden furniture and cemetery fixtures. A major maker of such forms in the ornate Victorian style was Robert Wood (1839–81) of Philadelphia. Fine hand-wrought ironware, gates, railings and candlesticks were made by Samuel Yellin (1885–1940) of Philadelphia.

(iii) Copper, brass and bronze. The earliest European coppersmiths and braziers to move to America settled in New England and Pennsylvania. The first copper mine opened in Simsbury, CT, in 1705, and other early mines were operating in New Jersey and Maryland. Brassworkers, including the earliest recorded one, Joseph Jenks (*fl* 1647–79) of Lynn, MA, melted old brass for reuse, because brass manufacturing was severely restricted by England in order to control the market for English brass in the colonies. Some significant brassmakers working in the 18th century were: William Bailey (*fl* 1720; *d* 1797) of Lancaster, PA, Caspar Wistar (also a glassmaker), John Sarrett (*fl* 1760), Richard Collier (*fl* 1763–79), George Plumly (*fl* 1760), the silversmith Phillip Syng jr (1703–89), Daniel King (1731–1806) and William Wittingham (*fl* 1791; *d* 1821). A notable early copper piece is the weathervane in the shape of a grasshopper made in 1749 by Shem Drowne for Faneuil Hall in Boston (*in situ*; see fig. 52).

While large amounts of copper and brass articles were imported from England, pieces made in the USA have traits that identify them as American, for example straight body copper teapots without spout covers. Brass andirons evolved from those with bold, simple turnings and pad feet of the late 17th century to ones with complicated turnings and ball-and-claw feet of the period from 1740 to 1770. Neo-classical andirons employed columns and urns, while Empire style andirons had bold turnings and ball feet. Richard Collier created andirons with scenic or Neo-classical engravings. Richard Lee (*fl c.* 1800) of Springfield, VT, made brass skimmers and ladles. Philadelphia was a centre for brass production; Baltimore became a centre for copper production after 1800. In the early 19th century Benjamin Harbeson & Son of Philadelphia was a prominent company. The silversmith Paul Revere and his sons in Boston made brass bells and copper articles. Heddeley & Riland of Philadelphia made pewter moulds in 1819, and William C. Hunneman of Boston (*fl* 1798–1845) made andirons. Mass-produced objects were made in the 19th century. Sleigh bells were first made by William Barton (*fl* 1808–32) of Connecticut and New

52. Copper weathervane by Shem Drowne, 1749, Faneuil Hall, Boston, Massachusetts

York. In the 19th century many companies made copper weathervanes, while others produced only utilitarian ware.

Copper, brass and bronze were used extensively in the Arts and Crafts Movement. Hand-hammered pieces with a dark patina (with hammer marks remaining) were made by the Roycroft Shops (1895–1938) of Elbert Hubbard; Leopold and J. George Stickley and Gustav Stickley's Craftsman Workshops; and the workshop (1908–1930s) of Karl Kipp. Bronze lamps and desk sets were made by Tiffany & Co. Dirk Van Erp of Chicago (*fl* 1908–25) made copper lamps and bowls. Bradley & Hubbard of Boston made a large number of brass lamps, desk sets and accessories. After the period of the Arts and Crafts Movement, interest in copper and brass declined.

(iv) Other. Zinc was used in weathervanes and architectural elements. The Chase Brass & Copper Co. (*fl* 1920s–1950s) of Waterbury, CT, employed such prominent designers as Russel Wright and Gilbert Rohde to design chrome-plated accessories. Oscar Bach, active in New York by 1914,

used chrome, aluminium, copper and bronze in his architectural elements. During the 1920s and 1930s furniture was made of chrome tubing, and aluminium tubing was used in the furniture designs of Warren McArthur and Eugene Schoen. Monel metal (nickel–copper alloy) was produced by the International Copper Co. and was used for decorative trim, furniture and architectural details in the 1920s and 1930s. Walter Kantack (*fl* 1920s–1930s) of New York made metal furnishings in an Art Deco Style. In the 1960s there was a resurgence of interest in handcrafted objects of base metals.

BIBLIOGRAPHY

A. Sonn: *Early American Wrought Iron* (New York, 1923)
Bull. Pewter Colrs' Club America (1934–)
L. Laughlin: *Pewter in America: Its Makers and their Marks*, i–ii (Boston and Barre, MA, 1940, rev. 1969), iii (1971) [the most complete book on the subject]
M. Gould: *Antique Tin and Tole Ware* (Rutland, 1958)
J. Lindsay: *Iron and Brass Implements of the English and American House* (Bass River, MA, 1964)
N. Goyne: 'Britannia in America: The Introduction of a New Alloy and a New Industry', *Winterthur Port.*, ii (1965)
J. R. Mitchell: *Marked American Andirons before 1840* (MA thesis, Winterthur, Du Pont Winterthur Mus., 1965)
H. Kauffman: *Early American Ironware* (New York, 1966)
M. Coffin: *The History and Folklore of American Country Tinware, 1700–1900* (Camden, NJ, 1968)
S. DeVoe: *The Tinsmiths of Connecticut* (Middletown, 1968)
H. Kauffman: *American Copper and Brass* (Toronto, 1968)
——: *The American Pewterer: His Techniques and his Products* (Camden, NJ, 1970)
J. Thomas, ed.: *American and British Pewter: A Historical Survey* (New York, 1971)
K. Ebert: *Collecting American Pewter* (New York, 1973)
C. Klamkin: *Weather Vanes: The History, Design and Manufacture of an American Folk Art* (New York, 1973)
C. Montgomery: *A History of American Pewter* (New York, 1973, rev. 1978)
A. C. Revi: *Collectible Iron, Tin, Copper and Brass* (Hanover, NH, 1973)
American Metalsmiths (exh. cat., Lincoln, MA, DeCordova & Dana Mus., 1974)
American Pewter in the Museum of Fine Arts (exh. cat., Boston, MA, Mus. F.A., 1974)
Forms in Metal: 275 Years of Metalsmiths in America (exh. cat. by P. Luck and P. Smith, New York, Mus. Contemp. Crafts, 1975)
J. Thomas: *Connecticut Pewter and Pewterers* (Hartford, 1976)
P. Schiffer: *The Brass Book* (Exton, 1978)
P. H. Schiffer and N. Schiffer: *Antique Iron: A Survey of American and English Forms* (Exton, 1979)
S. DeVoe: *The Art of the Tinsmith* (Exton, 1981)
J. Mulholland: *A History of Metals in Colonial America* (Tuscaloosa, AL, 1981)
C. Goodman: *Copper Artifacts in Late Eastern Woodland Prehistory* (Kampsville, IL, 1984)
T. Groft: *Cast with Style: Nineteenth Century Cast-iron Stoves from the Albany Area* (Albany, 1984)
Pewter in American Life (exh. cat., Lexington, MA, Scot. Rite Mason. Mus. N. Her., 1984)
D. Lamoureaux: *The Arts and Crafts Studio of Dirk Van Erp* (San Francisco, 1989)
B. Sven and G. Hassell: *The Geddy Foundry* (Williamsburg, 1992)
J. B. Whisker: *Pennsylvanian Silversmiths, Goldsmiths and Pewterers, 1684–1900* (Lewiston, NY, 1993)

CHARLES J. SEMOWICH

X. Jewellery.

Although some Colonial silversmiths made and repaired jewellery, its design and manufacture was not properly established in the USA until the mid-19th century. This was prompted by the government's imposition in 1850 of heavy import duties on fashionable, but often inferior-quality European jewellery, much of which came from London and Birmingham. The wealthy, nevertheless, continued to shop in Paris and London for their important jewels. Early American-made jewellery emulated European styles with perhaps a more vigorous approach to form and an extravagant use of materials. A taste for cameos and parures of matching jewellery, set with turquoises, garnets, coral, seed pearls, *millefiori* or dark blue or black enamel, was influenced by European examples. Chased, pierced or engraved gold with stones pavé set or surrounded by rich gold scrolls was popular.

From the mid-19th century the luxury jewellery trade was dominated by Charles Louis Tiffany (1812–1902) of New York. Established as Tiffany & Young in 1837 as a stationer and importer, in 1848 Tiffany set up a goldsmithing workshop on the company premises, which was among the first serious attempts to make high-quality jewellery in the USA. The fashion for archaeological jewellery in Etruscan, Greek and Roman styles that swept Europe and the USA in the 1860s suited such early manufacturers as Tiffany, with its emphasis on gold and sculptural forms rather than on gemstones. In 1861 Abraham Lincoln celebrated his inauguration with the purchase of a Tiffany-made parure of gold and seed pearls for his wife, Mary Todd Lincoln (Washington, DC, Lib. Congr.). Other well-known silversmiths and jewellers included the Gorham Manufacturing Co. (founded 1831) of Providence, RI, which introduced factory methods for casting and stamping out silverware and silver jewellery *c.* 1841 (*see* GORHAM).

From the late 1860s, after the opening of South Africa's diamond mines, until World War II, diamond jewellery was in demand for formal wear, with diamond-studded flower-and-leaf shapes giving way after 1900 to elaborate linear and scrolled patterns set in platinum, a material known since the 16th century but little used before this period. Tiffany & Co., with the New York jeweller Harry Winston (1896–1978), became the country's most prominent dealers in gems, followed by the Linz Bros, established in Dallas, TX, in 1891. An American version of the brilliant-cut for diamonds was developed, allowing more facets and sparkle; the solitaire diamond ring was also an American invention. The popularity of Japonisme in the 1870s and 1880s influenced American jewellers to mix metals or use coloured gold in pieces delicately engraved, appliquéd or enamelled with such motifs as dragonflies, herons and women in kimonos (e.g. Fringe necklace, New York, Tiffany's, *c.* 1880; London, BM). The Centennial Exhibition of 1876 in Philadelphia marked a watershed for American jewellery-makers, who exhibited in strength for the first time and excited international recognition for their distinctive designs, highlighted with native gemstones.

About 1889 Louis Comfort Tiffany (*see* TIFFANY, §2) established the Tiffany Studios for the production of handmade artistic jewellery, inspired by Art Nouveau and using innovative combinations of gold, enamels, gems and hardstones. He delighted in the use of fantastic animal and plant forms (e.g. orchid brooches, 1889; New York, Ruth Sataloff and Joseph Sataloff priv. col., see Loring, p. 88) and later embraced Celtic, medieval and Renaissance

Revival designs (e.g. Peacock necklace, *c.* 1902; Winter Park, FL, Morse Gal. A.). About 1900 a keen interest in the natural world encouraged the production of jewelled insect brooches and pins, as well as hair and dress ornaments of horn and tortoiseshell. Such American stones as river pearls, sapphires, garnets and topazes enriched many pieces (e.g. Chrysanthemum brooch, 1904; priv. col.; see fig. 53), and turquoises and fire opals obtained from Mexico were also used. American Arts and Crafts jewellery was largely influenced by the English movement and gave rise to cooperatives and guilds in Boston, Chicago and Minneapolis, MN. Most notable was the work of Florence Koehler (1861–1944) of Chicago. The Gorham Co. inaugurated their studio-designed Martelé ('hammered') line of Art Nouveau and Crafts Revival mixed-metal jewellery (e.g. brooch, *c.* 1900; priv. col., see Gere, 1975, p. 188). Silver and enamel floral jewellery, buckles and buttons were mass-produced; a typical example is the 'Gibson Girl' silver brooch (*c.* 1903; untraced) sold by Averbeck & Averbeck of New York (*fl* early 1900s).

During the 1920s and 1930s Art Deco and Hollywood styles dominated manufacture, as seen in the 'Shooting Star' diamond bracelet by Paul Flato (1936; ?priv. col., see Hughes, pl. 224). Ivory, jade, coral, crystal and onyx were used with gems for better-quality, Art Deco style jewellery, while lacquer, marcasite, bakelite, paste gems and plastic were used for cheaper kinds. Settings were made of rhodium-plated silver, platinum and, in the 1930s, white gold. Geometric, Cubist or streamlined designs in bold, often chunky pieces for day or evening wear were favoured. Barbaric jewellery of ivory, horn, bakelite or plastic satisfied fashionable notions of Africa, and after 1925 polychromatic jewellery was inspired by Indian, Persian and East-Asian art. In the 1940s designers borrowed ideas from both movie-stars' costume jewellery and a machine-in-motion aesthetic to create sleek, gold cocktail jewellery.

Between *c.* 1933 and 1952 the sculptor Alexander Calder (*see* CALDER, (3)) made whimsical jewellery, mainly from flattened silver and brass coils (e.g. silver necklace, *c.* 1940; New York, MOMA). From 1945 Salvador Dalí designed Surrealistic jewellery and jewelled objects for Carlos Bernardo Alemany (*fl* 1940s–1950s) of New York, sometimes with such moving parts as a pulsing heart or waving fronds. In the 1950s and 1960s designs ranged from exclusive, gem-studded pieces by such designers as Jean Schlumberger (1907–87) for Tiffany's (e.g. diamond-studded Dolphin clip, 1962; Beverley Hills, CA, Elizabeth Taylor priv. col., see Loring, p. 169) and David Webb (*b* 1925) of New York, to work by such craftsmen-jewellers as John Paul Miller (*b* 1918) (e.g. Fruit-bat pendant; ?priv. col., see Hughes, p. 181, no. 344) and mass-produced costume jewellery from simulated materials.

During the 1970s young designers launched body jewellery for men and women. They made such large, sculptural pieces as pectoral necklaces, earpieces, breast- and armplates, headdresses and necklets that cascaded from the shoulder to the hemline from gold, oxidized silver, copper, steel, synthetic stones, leather, wood, feathers, fur, acrylic and plastic. In the 1980s large department stores opened in-house jewellery boutiques where 'designer' costume jewellery by such American couturiers as

53. Chrysanthemum brooch, dogtooth Mississippi river pearls, gold, platinum and diamonds, made by Tiffany & Co., New York, 1904 (private collection)

Donna Karan (*b* 1948) was sold. Established designers, including Elsa Peretti (*b* 1940) and Paloma Picasso (*b* 1949), continued to work solely for Tiffany & Co.

BIBLIOGRAPHY
G. Hughes: *Modern Jewelry: An International Survey, 1890–1963* (London, 1963)
D. J. Willcox: *Body Jewellery* (London, 1974)
C. Gere: *European and American Jewellery, 1830–1914* (London, 1975)
Rattlesnakes: Exhibition of Modern American Jewellery (exh. cat. by G. Hughes, London, Goldsmiths' Co., 1978)
V. Becker: *Antique and Twentieth Century Jewellery: A Guide for Collectors* (Colchester, 1980)
K. Harlow: 'A Pioneer Master of Art Nouveau: The Handwrought Jewellery of Louis C. Tiffany', *Apollo*, cxvi (1982), pp. 46–50
V. Becker: *Art Nouveau Jewelry* (London, 1985)
J. Loring: *Tiffany's 150 Years* (Garden City, NY, 1987)
M. Gabardi: *Art Deco Jewellery, 1920–1949* (Woodbridge, 1989)
C. Gere and G. C. Munn: *Artists' Jewellery: Pre-Raphaelite to Arts and Crafts* (Woodbridge, 1989)
☐

XI. Textiles.

1. Woven and printed fabrics. 2. Needlework. 3. Tapestry. 4. Lace.

1. WOVEN AND PRINTED FABRICS. The first European settlers depended on imported fabrics for clothing themselves and furnishing their homes. The European imperial powers were not interested in promoting textile manufacture in North America, and England, ultimately the dominant European power, actively deterred textile production in the colonies, preferring instead to supply the market with her own textiles. This policy was generally successful, but as early as 1640 Colonial governments began to promote the production of linen, wool and cotton textiles. These efforts were important but they did

54. Cotton and wool coverlet by P. Warner, 2.35×2.03 m, from Carroll County, Maryland, 1848 (North Andover, MA, Museum of American Textile History)

not result in a highly organized or comprehensive manufacturing system. Instead, American textile production developed around individuals and small groups of hand-weavers, who primarily produced staple textiles for local and regional markets. Throughout the Colonial period and into the 19th century the American consumer chose from a mixture of imported and domestically produced textiles, with imports providing the greater volume and a broader range of fabrics. American interest in ending the dependence on imports rose and fell, and textile production increased during periods of political or economic estrangement from Europe.

Textile manufacture in America operated in several different ways, providing domestic versions of some imported fabrics and also supplying speciality items. Although self-sufficient household production of textiles in the pre-industrial period is a myth, many households did participate in the creation of textiles. Household weavers usually made such relatively simple fabrics as tow cloth (coarse linen or hemp), household linens, blankets and, occasionally, decorative furnishing textiles. However, looms were never a common feature of all homes, and families were more likely to do only parts of the textile process. They might spin yarn and use it to knit stockings or send it to someone else for dyeing, weaving into fabric and finishing. Outworkers were used but they were never as important in the USA as in Europe. The mills distributed prepared warps to hand-weavers, including stripes, checks and plaids.

From the 17th century well into the 19th, professional weavers (almost exclusively men) produced a variety of domestic textiles, from simple utilitarian fabrics to decorative dress and furnishing fabrics. Weavers' account-books include entries for gingham, shirting, jean, fustian, stripe, diaper, swan-skin, coverlets, carpets and bed tick,

among many other fabrics. Opportunities for these craftsmen began to diminish in the industrial period, but many urban weavers continued to find work producing such textiles as carpets and silks even after those fabrics could be woven on powered machinery.

Other hand-weavers found a niche for themselves producing decorative bedcovers. These were made in a range of designs, from simple alternating blocks of colour to portraits and elaborate scenes, each design determined by the weave structure and patterning mechanism. The most common materials were undyed cotton and blue wool, but coverlets were also made of linen and wool, all-wool and all-cotton in such colours as red, black, brown, green, gold and lavender. Weave structures included overshot, summer-and-winter, twill, double-weave and tied double-weaves. Harness-controlled structures produced geometric designs imaginatively described as 'roses', 'tables' and 'chariot wheels', but the introduction of the Jacquard loom in the 1820s made it easier for weavers to produce curved lines, flowers, buildings and even faces by mechanizing the creation of hundreds of warp combinations (see fig. 54). Hand-weavers, primarily in the mid-Atlantic and Midwestern states, produced Jacquard coverlets until about the time of the Civil War. The centennial celebration in 1876 sparked a revival of coverlet production, but these textiles, which were made in factories of poor-quality materials, quickly disappeared from the market. Hand-weaving was on the wane and survived, barely, in a few areas such as Appalachia and the Midwest.

As increasing industrialization transformed the English textile-production system, so it radically altered the organization, output and importance of American production. Samuel Slater's success in 1790 in spinning cotton yarn on water-powered machinery patterned after the Arkwright system and Eli Whitney's invention of the cotton gin, patented in 1794, had an important effect on the availability of cotton and of cotton yarn. However, it was not until the introduction of the power loom at Waltham, MA, in 1813–14 that mass production of textiles began. In northern New England cotton manufacture quickly developed in large, fully integrated mills. At Waltham and later at Lowell, MA, the Boston Associates, a group of wealthy merchants who invested heavily in the textile and other industries, used the limited capabilities of their early machinery to produce large quantities of heavy cotton sheeting and drill. This practice of manufacturing long runs of coarse fabrics came to be seen as the standard American approach, but other mills, for example those in Rhode Island and Philadelphia, became very successful in producing a broad range of textiles.

Throughout most of the 19th century, woollen mills were typically smaller and more specialized. In the early years they manufactured broadcloths, as well as jeans and relatively coarse woollens. Of particular importance was satinet, a medium-grade fabric used for outer wear, which looked like wool but was woven on a cotton warp. Flannels, delaines and cassimeres gradually accounted for more of the production, but imported woollen and worsted fabrics maintained their importance in the American market. It was not until the last quarter of the 19th century that American production of worsted fabrics came into prominence.

55. 'Cocheco Furniture Twills XX', printed cotton sample, 263×454 mm, Cocheco Print Works, Dover, New Hampshire, 1888 (North Andover, MA, Museum of American Textile History)

As early as the Colonial period Americans were fascinated by the prospect of developing a domestic silk industry. Although the cultivation of mulberry trees and breeding of silkworms was never successful, the manufacture of silk products increased throughout the 19th century. The industry, which developed dramatically from 1870 to 1890, concentrated initially on the manufacture of sewing silk and machine twist (silk thread for sewing machines), then on ribbons, trimmings and handkerchiefs, and finally on broad silks, velvets and plushes. The products of Connecticut, New Jersey and Pennsylvania, the primary American centres of production, never displaced the finest European luxury silks, but they amply supplied the market for good-quality, medium-grade fabrics.

Block- and plate-printing never became well established in the USA, but copper-roller printing grew steadily from its introduction on a large scale in the 1820s to become the dominant, though not exclusive, supplier of the American market. Printed textiles continued to be imported, and the design of American prints drew heavily on European models. Among the thousands of new patterns that appeared each year were two- and three-colour geometrics and a limited repertory of florals used as shirting fabrics. Variety in both design and colour became important in dress prints, which changed more frequently and completely according to fashion. Furnishing prints were usually larger in scale and more complicated in design than shirting or dress prints (see fig. 55). During the 20th century the variety of designs produced in any one season decreased, and about the middle of the century screen-printing technology began to supersede copper-roller printing.

Woven and printed textiles in the USA have followed a stylistic course parallel to that of Western decorative arts. The Arts and Crafts Movement was of particular importance in its direct effect on style and motif, but even more in its impact on Americans' attitudes to their own decorative arts history. It advanced the development of American textile designers in general and inspired the work of high-style, art-conscious individuals such as CANDACE WHEELER. The Arts and Crafts Movement, along with the retrospection that accompanied the 1876 centennial were factors in the growth of the Colonial Revival. This, in turn, led to a number of revivalist trends in the 1920s and 1930s and stimulated interest in traditional pre-industrial textile production. This interest has manifested itself in three generally distinct groups: the first pursuing hand-weaving as a satisfying pastime; the second producing for the art market; and the third weaving for purchasers interested in securing satisfying, often intangible, qualities in hand-woven fabrics.

The success of the hand-weavers led in the late 1960s and 1970s to a demand for upmarket commercially woven textiles that simulated their effects. Such designers as Jack Lenor Larsen concentrated on textured fabrics in plain, pale colours. In the 1970s and 1980s experiments were done with open weaves and unusual fibres that increased the textural interest. In the late 20th century the computer was introduced to textile production, inspiring a new wave of creative development in print and knit, as well as new approaches to colour in woven textiles.

2. NEEDLEWORK. Until the 20th century plain sewing was the most widely known and practised form of needlework in the USA. Nearly every American female learnt

basic sewing and knitting, which she used in the construction of clothing and the finishing of household textiles. Sheets and other large textiles were usually created by joining two or three widths of fabric with a whip stitch. Hems were generally rolled or very narrow. Household textiles of all types were marked with cross-stitched initials and numbers to differentiate one piece from another; in the 19th century names and numbers inscribed in ink appeared more frequently. With the invention of the sewing-machine in the middle of the 19th century and the development of the ready-to-wear trade, extensive hand-production of clothing and household textiles began to disappear.

Fancy needlework was, by definition, non-utilitarian, but it was sometimes used to decorate useful textiles. During the 17th and 18th centuries fancy work was a prerogative of the rich, but in the 19th and 20th centuries more middle-class needleworkers took an interest in the art. In the 1720s distinctive groups of needlework began to emerge as a result of the influence of particular schools and individual teachers, whose styles are clearly recognizable in surviving needlework. Silk-on-silk embroideries, especially mourning pictures, became very popular in the late 18th century and the early 19th.

The SAMPLER was common. From the 17th century to the end of the 18th, samplers were most often stitched in silk threads on linen or linen/wool grounds. Embroiderers sometimes used the woven structure of the ground fabric as a grid on which to work their letters and designs, but, especially in later years, design motifs were also created by free-hand 'drawing' with embroidery floss. In their most basic form, samplers were used to teach a young girl the basic stitches necessary to mark textiles; later work might include more intricate and decorative stitches, which could be used to embellish clothing or household textiles. In the 17th century American samplers echoed contemporary English work: they were typically long, narrow pieces of fabric with horizontal bands of stitching intended to serve as catalogues of stitches and designs. From the first, however, American samplers included verses, a trait not found this early in English samplers. During the 18th century American samplers became shorter and wider and often included borders. They were used less as reference and more to display the embroiderer's abilities. Simple alphabets began to be combined with more decorative designs, and eventually a completely decorative picture developed as the showpiece of a young woman's accomplishments.

Canvaswork, executed in woollen yarns on a linen ground, always used the ground fabric as the geometric grid on which the design was placed. Colourful geometric shapes or fanciful landscapes decorated pocket-books and upholstery, or were used in a needlework picture. Wool embroidery on a fabric other than canvas and stitched in a more free-hand style is known as crewelwork. Although crewelwork petticoat borders and pockets are known, much of the finest crewel embroidery of the late 17th century and the 18th survives in the form of bed-hangings. In the 19th century, wool embroidery was done on linen canvas in the same style as samplers; because Germany had become a major source of wool yarns, canvas and printed patterns, this type of embroidery came to be called Berlin woolwork. By the middle of the century embroidery using woollen yarns on perforated paper or board became popular. In the late 19th century there was a proliferation of different styles of needlework, followed by a period of selfconscious examination of needlework arts sparked by the American Arts and Crafts Movement. The Deerfield Blue and White Society, a group of embroiderers directed by Margaret C. Whiting and Ellen Miller, was foremost among those who deplored late 19th-century embroidery and looked to Colonial styles and materials for inspiration.

QUILTING, in a variety of forms including quilted petticoats, was brought to America by European immigrants. In the 18th century bed quilts were generally one-piece quilts; that is, the top was made from a single, solid colour fabric. This fabric, often a dark glazed wool, was quilted with fine stitches in an elaborate design, for example flowers, fruits and feather-like leaves. PATCHWORK and appliqué combined printed and dyed fabrics of many different colours and styles (see TEXTILE, colour pl. VI, fig. 3). Sometimes used together in the same quilt, the two techniques differ in that patchwork (or piecing) is the joining of small pieces to create a flat textile, while appliqué is the stitching of fabric pieces on top of an already existing flat textile. One important type of quilt made in the late 18th century often used a central image of an appliqué flower or tree surrounded by pieced borders. Quilts made entirely by piecing sometimes utilized bits of fabric from textiles that were too worn to use any other way. This was not always the case, however, and very often pieced quilts were made with fabrics acquired specifically for the project. Appliqué allowed greater freedom in creating designs on quilts, lending itself to more pictorial images. In the late 20th century both quilting and patchwork became extremely popular, and some traditional pieces, notably the bold patchwork produced by the Amish communities, became collectors' items. They also inspired textile artists to explore the possibilities of these techniques and to develop new designs in relation to other forms of contemporary art.

See also RUG.

BIBLIOGRAPHY

L. R. Brockett: *The Silk Industry in America: A History Prepared for the Centennial Exposition* (New York, 1876)
W. R. Bagnall: *The Textile Industries of the United States, Including Sketches and Notices of Cotton, Woollen, Silk and Linen Manufactures in the Colonial Period*, i (Cambridge, MA, 1893)
J. H. Brown, E. M. Norris and E. E. Foster, eds: *Lamb's Textile Industries of the United States, Embracing Biographical Sketches of Prominent Men and a Historical Résumé of the Progress of Textile Manufacture from the Earliest Records to the Present Time*, 2 vols (Boston, 1911–16)
R. M. Tryon: *Household Manufactures in the United States, 1640–1860* (Chicago, 1917)
A. H. Cole: *The American Wool Manufacture*, 2 vols (Cambridge, MA, 1926)
C. F. Ware: *The Early New England Cotton Manufacture: A Study in Industrial Beginnings* (Boston, 1931)
G. B. Harbeson: *American Needlework* (New York, 1938)
F. M. Montgomery: *Printed Textiles: English and American Cottons and Linens, 1700–1850* (New York, 1970)
P. Orlofsky and M. Orlofsky: *Quilts in America* (New York, 1974)
A. N. Landreau: *America Underfoot: A History of Floor Coverings from Colonial Times to the Present* (Washington, DC, 1976)
S. B. Swan: *Plain & Fancy: American Women and their Needlework, 1700–1850* (New York, 1977)
G. F. Krueger: *New England Samplers to 1840* (Sturbridge, MA, 1978)

C. L. Safford and R. Bishop: *America's Quilts and Coverlets* (New York, 1980)

D. J. Jeremy: *Transatlantic Industrial Revolution: The Diffusion of Textile Technologies between Britain and America, 1790–1830s* (Cambridge, MA, 1981)

P. Scranton: *Proprietary Capitalism: The Textile Manufacture at Philadelphia, 1800–1885* (Cambridge, MA, 1983)

C. Anderson: 'Coverlet Bibliography', *A. Textrina*, ii (1984), pp. 203–15

F. M. Montgomery: *Textiles in America, 1650–1870* (New York, 1984)

B. Ring: *American Needlework Treasures: Samplers and Silk Embroideries from the Collection of Betty Ring* (New York, 1987)

C. M. Sheridan, ed.: 'Textile Manufacturing in American History: A Bibliography', *Textile Hist.*, xviii (1987), pp. 59–86

DIANE L. FAGAN AFFLECK

3. TAPESTRY.

(i) Before 1934. (ii) 1934 and after.

(i) Before 1934. The first large-scale tapestry studio in the USA was that founded by William Baumgarten (1845–1906), the owner of a firm specializing in interior decoration. The studio opened in New York City in 1893, staffed by the Foussadier family, who had originated from and trained in Aubusson, France, and had subsequently been employed at the Royal Windsor Tapestry Factory, England. The tapestries, designed primarily for period rooms in the city homes of the rich, were woven to commission and reflected the prevailing conservative taste. Although Renaissance and Baroque styles were popular, the 18th-century tapestries designed by François Boucher were by far the favourite models. Wall hangings were supplied for state buildings (e.g. Rhode Island State House, Providence; *in situ*), hotels (e.g. Manhattan Hotel, New York; untraced, see Baumgarten, p. 16) and private businesses (e.g. New York Life Insurance Co.; untraced, see Baumgarten, p. 40). Tapestries more contemporary in style and individualized in subject-matter were also made. The tapestries were designed in the New York office but woven on low-warp looms by the French weavers (and later by American apprentices) at the firm's studio in Williamsbridge, the Bronx. The warp was wool or cotton, with wool, silk and metal thread for the weft. Natural dyes were employed. Many of the tapestries bear the initials B (or WB), NY and the year of production. The tapestries were of varying quality, but the best were so fine that two won the grand prize at the World's Fair of 1904 in St Louis, MO. After Baumgarten's death, the studio continued until the 1920s.

The second major American tapestry studio was founded in New York City in 1908 as Aubusson Looms, but changed its name the following year to Herter Looms, after its creator and chief designer, Albert Herter (1871–1950). He had been a student in Paris of Jean-Paul Laurens, a mural painter who designed tapestries for the Gobelins. The workshop initially produced copies and adaptations of old tapestries, as well as new designs for wall hangings and furniture coverings. The hallmark of the company was its innovative subject-matter, interpreted in a style reflecting that of the Middle Ages. Its first major commission (1909; *in situ*), for Arden House, the New York home of E. H. Harriman, included Louis XVI style wall panels, a modern-medieval *millefleurs* panel entitled the *Spirit of Arden House*, and more contemporary pieces showing the surrounding countryside and the building of the house. Herter's most ambitious project is a set of 26 tapestries, the *History of New York* (1912; 21 tapestries, New York,

Met.; 1 tapestry, priv. col., see De Kay, p. 202; 4 tapestries, untraced, see De Kay, pp. 202, 204, and *Good Furn. Mag.*, vi (1916), p. 315) for the Hotel McAlpin, New York. The company also produced transparent tapestries (in which the dyed wool warp was left partially exposed and the piece was finished on both sides), primarily for *portières*. Herter's designs were developed by other studio artists into detailed cartoons for the weavers to follow, as can be seen in the *Great Crusade* cartoon and tapestry (Bloomfield Hills, MI, Cranbrook Acad. A. Mus.). Materials included wool, silk, cotton, mercerized cotton and silver and gold thread. Charles E. Pellew, Viscount Exmouth (1863–1945), was employed as a dye chemist to develop a range of synthetic dyes for the Herter palette. Each tapestry bears the logo HL, a cherry blossom and the date of the design. Herter disassociated himself from the company in 1922, but it remained in business until 1934.

The Edgewater Tapestry Looms, of Edgewater, NJ, was founded by Lorentz Kleiser (1879–1963) in 1913. After training as a painter in Europe, he returned to the USA to work for Baumgarten & Co., where his interest in tapestry was intensified. For his own company he designed tapestries in styles from medieval to Louis XVI, as well as developing a conservative but contemporary manner for depicting themes drawn from American history, literature and everyday life. His most inventive works were fantastic florals and landscapes. From 1926 F. Schumacher & Co. handled the stock tapestries, while Kleiser worked on special commissions and experiments. In addition to those for private clients, tapestries were made for churches (e.g. the Blessed Sacrament, New York; *in situ*), state houses (e.g. Missouri and Nebraska; both *in situ*) and for the Newark Museum in Newark, NJ (*in situ*). Although Kleiser made the initial sketches, the cartoons were developed by others. In addition to the weavers, who were both French and American, there was also a group of assistants or protégés, who could both design and weave, and a dye studio. The tapestries were woven on low-warp looms using cotton, mercerized cotton, wool, silk and silver and gold thread. The company logo changed over the years: until 1915 it was L.K. above U.S.A.; from 1915 to 1920 it was LK with a five-pointed star before and after the initials; and from 1920 it was a diagonally barred L merged with a K. The initial F, for the cartoonist Folstadt, can often be seen. The Edgewater Tapestry Looms was particularly interested in the relationship between art and industry. The company participated in numerous exhibitions, and Kleiser did much to popularize tapestry through lectures and articles. Its period of greatest activity was in the 1920s, when work was also done by associate weavers in Aubusson. The Depression, coupled with changing tastes, caused the studio to close in 1934. Kleiser attempted to revive the tapestry workshop on a much smaller scale in California, but the venture did not flourish.

BIBLIOGRAPHY

W. Baumgarten: *Tapestry* (New York, 1897)

G. L. Hunter: 'Tapestries in America', *Int. Studio*, xlvii (1912), pp. xxviii–xxxvi

C. De Kay: 'Tapestries for Schools and Hotels', *A. & Dec.*, iii (1913)

A. D. Fleetwood: 'The New Home of the Herter Looms', *House Beautiful*, xxxv (1913), pp. 4–9

A. Lee: 'Tapestries Made in America', *Int. Studio*, lxxxi (1925), pp. 297–301

L. Kleiser: 'Arras', *Good Furn. Mag.*, xxxiv (1930), pp. 21–30
A. Zrebiec: *The American Tapestry Manufactures: Origins and Development, 1893 to 1933* (diss., New York U., Inst. F.A., 1980)

A. M. ZREBIEC

(ii) 1934 and after. Following the closure of the Edgewater Tapestry Looms in 1934, there were no commercial tapestry workshops in the USA until the 1970s. This was due partly to the Depression and also to changing attitudes to interior design. Two separate traditions emerged: that of the tapestry artist, who has his designs woven by others, and that of the artist-weaver, who designs and weaves his own work. The latter practice, deriving not only from American hand-weaving but also from French and Scandinavian traditions, has become the more common in the USA, and since the 1960s it has been influenced by the FIBRE ART movement. By the 1970s the distinction between artist-weavers and tapestry artists was acknowledged in *Who's Who in American Art*.

(a) Tapestry artists. The American public was exposed to the work of Jean Lurçat and other French tapestry artists through such exhibitions as the 1939 World's Fair in New York and the *Loan Exhibition of French Tapestries* (1948; New York, Met.); French and Co. also lent tapestries for museum exhibitions. American tapestry artists of this period, especially painters and printmakers, had designs woven by Aubusson and other European workshops; among those following this practice were Arthur B. Davies, MARK ADAMS, Joseph Domjian (*b* 1907), Alexander Calder, Sylvia Carewe (1914–80), Abraham Rattner (1895–1978), Allan Porter (*b* 1934) and June Wayne (*b* 1918).

Exhibitions of tapestries increased interest, which was reflected in the growing number of American studios and workshops. Weavings by the Edinburgh Tapestry Co. of

56. Tapestry designed by Michelle Lester: *Charybdis*, wool, 1.52×1.52 m, 1988 (artist's collection); woven by Mary Ann Sievert

works by contemporary British tapestry artists were first shown in New York in 1953; in the same studios from 1970 Archie Brennan worked with Americans Frank Stella and Gloria F. Ross (*b* 1923) to interpret works by Abstract Expressionist artists as tapestries. In 1950 Jan Yoors (1922–77), a Belgian artist, moved to New York and set up a small studio, weaving his own designs. In Los Angeles beginning in the late 1950s the Dalzell–Hatfield Galleries displayed works of American tapestry artists in their 'Artoramas', and in 1959 the Jeppson Galleries (Washington, DC) held the *Murals of Wool* exhibition. Charles E. Slatkin took works from his Modern Master Tapestries gallery on tour in 1965.

(b) Artist-weavers. The history of the artist-weaver tradition is one of teacher-pupil relationships, through universities and colleges, art schools, summer courses and workshops. While early courses emphasized the designing of handwoven textiles for industry, new approaches were developed at the Cranbrook Academy of Art, MI, Black Mountain College, NC, and the Institute of Design in Chicago by such Europeans as Loja Saarinen, Anni Albers (*see* ALBERS, (2)) and Trude Guermonprez (1910–76), all of whom emigrated to the USA during the 1920s and 30s. Notable among their students were Else Regensteiner and Lili Blumenau. Institutions of higher education played an important role by including fibre art in art and textile departments as well as by arranging exhibitions in campus galleries. Henry Easterwood (*b* 1934) taught at Memphis College of Arts, Janet Taylor (*b* 1941) at Arizona State University, Susan Iverson (*b* 1951) and Michelle Morris (*b* 1956) at Virginia Commonwealth University and Scharon Marcus (*b* 1941) at the Oregon School for Arts and Crafts. These and other teachers also joined summer programmes at crafts schools and colleges. Ronald Cruickshank (1897–1969) came from the Edinburgh Tapestry Co. to the University of Southwestern Louisiana, where he taught French techniques. Among other Europeans who trained overseas and brought their expertise to the USA were Vera Kopecek (*b* 1926) and Sylvia Heyden (*b* 1927).

American artist-weavers began during the 1960s to combine tapestry techniques with other weaves and to incorporate abstract imagery. The monumental abstract tapestries of G. Elayne Bick used traditional materials, but some artist-weavers began to use natural matter and wools, such as those handspun by Paula Simmons. The American Craft Council promoted tapestry-weaving through its periodical *Craft Horizons* (later *American Craft*), through exhibitions held at America House and at the Museum of Contemporary Crafts in New York, and through the Good Design shows and the Pasadena Art Museum's California Design shows. American tapestries were shown in London in 1962 (*Modern American Wall Hangings*, V&A).

During the 1970s such artists as Stephen Thurston (*b* 1944), Winston Herbert (*b* 1942), Nancy Kozikowski (*b* 1943) with Janucz Kozikowski, and Michelle Lester (*b* 1942) opened studio workshops in America. Lester's tapestries include stylized and abstract images based on the landscapes of the American Southwest (see fig. 56). In 1977 the San Francisco Tapestry Workshop was founded by weavers Jean Pierre Larochette (*b* 1942), Ruth Tanenbaum, Phoebe McAfee (*b* 1944), Ernestine Bianchi and Margery Livingston. The workshop had its roots in the 1976 exhibition *Five Centuries of Tapestry from the Fine Arts Museums of San Francisco*, organized by Anna Bennett; Livingston, then chairman of the Textiles Department at San Francisco State University, organized a concurrent tapestry demonstration in which a cartoon by artist Mark Adams, *California Poppies*, was woven (for illustration *see* ADAMS, MARK). Livingston invited Larochette, who had been at Aubusson, to train 12 weavers on the low-warp loom. The training was organized in the French apprenticeship tradition, with beginning- and advanced-level coursework and intensive summer workshops. Tapestries from the workshop were on view in the exhibitions *Modern Tapestries* (1979; San Jose, CA, Mus. A.) and *Contemporary Tapestry* (1983; San Francisco, CA, Glastonbury Gal.). The workshop was also commissioned to produce tapestry banners for Judy Chicago's *Dinner Party* project (1978, San Francisco, CA, MOMA). Artists Mark Adams and Yael Lurie (*b* 1943) designed many of the tapestries woven at the workshop. By 1983 it was unofficially closed due to problems of finance and personnel. Larochette and Lurie have since formed the Lurie-Larochette studio and have continued to use the name of the San Francisco Tapestry Workshop for their teaching programmes. Over 300 of their students have since established their own studios.

American tapestry in the 1980s, notably in Oregon, California and New York City, was characterized by a blossoming of pictorial tapestry-weaving using French techniques, Shannock looms and Paternayan yarns. The abstract works of the 1960s gave way to genre scenes (e.g. by Martha Matthews, *b* 1940), urban and political issues (by Lilian Tyrrell, *b* 1944, and Muriel Nezhnie, *b* 1934), flowers (Mary Lynn O'Shea, *b* 1946), portraits (David Mooney, Deann Joy Rubin) and landscapes (Julia Mitchell, *b* 1950).

The Scheuer Tapestry Studio was established in Greenwich Village (New York City) in 1982 and moved to nearby SoHo in 1987. The owner, Ruth Scheuer (formerly Tanenbaum), had left the San Francisco Tapestry Workshop in 1979 to study for a year at the Gobelins tapestry factory in France, returning to create her own workshop using high-warp techniques. Scheuer employed weavers on a European apprenticeship system, whereby auxiliary work in the studio is exchanged for classes in the technique, design and history of tapestry. Two to three artist-weavers work in collaboration on small unique tapestries, thus sharing ideas as they weave. They weave both their own designs and those of outside artists for commissions or as experimental works, as well as florals and urban scenes for corporations, religious buildings and private homes. In 1989 the Scheuer Tapestry Studio was reorganized as a non-profit organization to become the Center for Tapestry Arts and to include related fibre arts. A new gallery provided space for group shows and public lectures. Tapestries from the studio are in the collections of IBM, Touche-Ross and Nabisco-RJR.

The number of organizations and events to promote American tapestry and encourage its development increased during the 1980s. In 1982 Hal Painter (*b* 1922) and Jim Brown (*b* 1927) created the American Tapestry Alliance, which exhibits with Convergence, the biannual meeting of the Handweavers' Guild of America; the latter organization publishes the periodical *Shuttle, Spindle and Dyepot*. Exhibitions and symposia were held in Flagstaff (1988), Maryland and Mendocino (1989) and Portland (1990), and in 1990 Helga Barry (*b* 1948) founded the International Tapestry Network (ITNET).

BIBLIOGRAPHY
Loan Exhibition of French Tapestries: Medieval, Renaissance and Modern (exh. cat. by M. Constantine and J. L. Larsen, New York, Met., 1948)
J. Lovoos: 'American Tapestries', *Amer. Artist*, xxv (Sept 1961), pp. 45–8, 77
J. Beardsall: 'Tapestries: An Art Reborn', *A.G.: Mag.*, xvii (Dec 1973), pp. 55–8
Five Centuries of Tapestry from the Fine Arts Museums of San Francisco (exh. cat. by A. G. Bennett, San Francisco, CA, F.A. Museums, 1976)
Fiberarts Design, 3 vols (Asheville, NC, 1980–87)
E. Prosser: 'Weaving in San Francisco', *Weaver's J.*, vi (1981), no. 3, pp. 44–7; no. 4, pp. 50–53
K. Rowley: 'San Francisco Tapestry Workshop: A European-style Atelier in the United States', *Fiberarts*, xx/3 (1983), p. 60
R. T. Scheuer: 'The Scheuer Tapestry Studio: Applying Old Techniques to New Designs', *Fiberarts*, xx/3 (1983), pp. 39–41
From American Looms: Scheuer Tapestry Studio (exh. cat. by A. Zrebiec and R. Scheuer, Trenton, NJ State Mus., 1985)
Tapestry: Contemporary Imagery/Ancient Tradition, United States, Canada, United Kingdom (exh. cat. by V. Clausen, Spokane, WA, Cheney Cowles Mus., 1986)
American Tapestry Weaving since the 1930s and its European Roots (exh. cat. by C. A. Shaw, College Park, U. MD A.G., 1989)

COURTNEY ANN SHAW

4. LACE. America's only documented pre-19th-century lace industry of any size was a cottage industry in Ipswich, MA. From the 17th century to the 1820s Ipswich produced white and black silk and thread laces in bobbin techniques characteristic of laces produced in the English Midlands, homeland of the original settlers. By 1790 the industry claimed to produce 38,000 m annually. Thirty years later Ipswich laceworkers were embroidering lacelike designs on mesh fabric. The first machines to manufacture mesh fabric in the USA were apparently constructed from memory by English immigrants in 1818. From these a machine-made lace industry grew, relying heavily on (often illegally) imported European textile technology and machines.

Handmade lace industries reappeared in the late 19th century when American philanthropists, imitating European self-help industries, established schools to teach marketable lacemaking skills to indigent women. In 1890 an Episcopalian missionary, Sibyl Carter, began classes among Minnesota's Ojibwa Indians. By 1908 Indians of ten tribes from New York state to the West Coast were producing bobbin, tape and needlepoint laces, which, except for occasional Indian figures with bow, papoose or canoe, are indistinguishable from European laces. In 1905 an Italian lacemaker from a self-help lacemaking school in Burano, Italy, was imported to teach Italian immigrant women and girls in New York City's Scuola d'Industrie Italiane to copy needle-made antique laces and contemporary European fashion laces. These and similar industries died in the 1930s when fashion interest in lace declined. America's first identifiable 'lace artist' was an English immigrant, Marian Powys (1882–1972), whose Honiton technique design won a gold medal in the 1915 Pan American Exposition. Not until the 1970s were traditional lace techniques again seen in American artists' work, and then often on a large scale, in colour, in non-traditional fibres and sometimes in pieces in no way resembling lace.

The amateur lacemaker has always been part of American domestic life. Early 19th-century ladies' academies routinely offered lace instruction, and later in the century instruction books for a wide range of openwork techniques were readily available. Lacemaking became a late 19th- and early 20th-century fad. After a mid-century decline, interest in lacemaking as a hobby reappeared at the end of the 20th century.

BIBLIOGRAPHY

E. N. Vanderpoel: *American Lace & Lace-makers* (New Haven, 1924)

F. Morris and M. Hague: *Antique Laces of the American Collectors* (New York, 1926)

V. Bath: *Lace* (Chicago, 1974) [Amer. lace artists]

K. Duncan: 'American Indian Lace Making', *Amer. Ind. A.*, v/3 (1980), pp. 28–35, 80

P. P. Grey: 'In these Delicate Constructions', *Amer. Craft*, xxxxi/4 (Aug/Sept 1981), pp. 51ff [on Marian Powys]

M. Sonday: *Lace*, New York, Cooper-Hewitt Mus. cat. (New York, 1982)

S. M. Levy: *Lace: A History* (London, 1983)

J. HEINRITZ BIDNER

XII. Patronage.

Private patronage, both individual and corporate, has played a substantial role in the evolution of American art, while the relatively modest and sporadic levels of public funding for the arts throughout much of American history reflects national wariness of the élitism and constraints inherent in the European examples of ecclesiastical and royal patronage. After the Revolution, patriotism and civic pride prompted members of the educated, professional class to form voluntary societies and academies such as the Columbianum in Philadelphia (founded 1794) and the Boston Athenaeum (founded 1807), which sought to promote the study of the arts. Direct public patronage began meanwhile with Pierre Charles L'Enfant's design for the seat of government and the subsequent construction of federal buildings in the capital city, Washington, DC (*see.* §II, 2 above). The variety of classicizing styles adopted by James Hoban for the president's residence (the White House; 1792–1830), by Robert Mills for the Treasury Department and the Patent Office (now the National Museum of American Art and National Portrait Gallery building; both begun 1836), and by William Thornton for the Capitol (completed 1830) were intended to symbolize the nation's democratic ideals. Funded by Congressional appropriations, the construction, redesign and expansion of the Capitol continued periodically from 1793 until after the Civil War. The building originally entailed commissions to foreign artists for murals and architectural sculpture. By the 1820s, however, merchants such as Luman Reed and Thomas J. Bryan of New York, and Nicholas Longworth of Cincinnati were beginning to form collections and to play a role in the art community. Wealthier, but less educated than the professional class of patrons, these merchants supported and befriended artists, occasionally opened their collections to the public and fostered the growth of a 'native school' of landscape painters (i.e. those who had not studied in Europe, as had hitherto been considered obligatory for aspiring artists).

By the 1830s Congress directed that commissions for the decoration of the Capitol be awarded to American artists, such as John Trumbull, Horatio Greenough and Thomas Crawford.

In the period before the Civil War, subscription organizations broadened the democratic base of support for the arts. The most successful of these, the American Art-Union (1844–51), based in New York, sponsored exhibitions, commissioned engravings, published two art journals documenting its transactions and acquired works of art to be sold by lottery to its members. Before its demise, the union boasted over 16,000 members throughout the nation and had distributed over 150,000 engravings and 2400 paintings by 250 American artists. After the war concentration of industrial wealth produced a new group of entrepreneurial patrons. Less concerned with American art and more enamoured of European culture, the new industrialists not only formed large and sometimes eclectic collections (*see* §XIII below) but also commissioned the building of palatial residences and founded art museums in the cities of the Northeast and Midwest. A few collectors, however, such as Thomas B. Clarke and Charles Lang Freer, continued to collect American art during the late 19th century.

State governments continued to fund construction of Neo-classical, domed legislatures that echoed Thomas U. Walter's monumental dome for the US Capitol until the 1880s, when Italian Renaissance, ornamented architecture became the dominant style for federal, state and municipal buildings, exemplified by City Hall in Philadelphia and the Library of Congress and the Department of Agriculture buildings in Washington, DC. The US Commission of Fine Arts, established by Congress in 1910, and Secretary of the Treasury Andrew W. Mellon carried out the mandate of the 1926 Public Buildings Act by perpetuating the Italian Renaissance tradition in federal monuments and in the complex of government buildings known as Federal Triangle (1926–37) in Washington, DC. The accelerated pace of industrialization in the late 19th century, however, was meanwhile transforming American architecture more radically and altering patterns of architectural patronage. Newly powerful industrial and corporate clients were responsible for the proliferation of a new commercial building type, the SKYSCRAPER, examples of which were erected in such cities as Chicago and New York, soon becoming emblems of corporate enterprise. Corporations not only commissioned prominent architects to design their headquarters but also occasionally gave direct commissions to American artists: for example, in 1927 the Ford Motor Co. employed Charles Sheeler to make a photographic record of its River Rouge factory in Detroit, MI. Patronage of architecture and fine arts were combined in such commercial complexes as Rockefeller Center (1931–40) in New York (for illustration *see* ROCKEFELLER). Corporations extended the scope of patronage by fostering exacting standards of design, sponsoring advertising competitions for the fine arts, eventually subsidizing museum exhibitions and forming art collections. In continuing these practices into the second half of the 20th century, American corporations emulated patterns of individual, private patronage established by late 19th-century entrepreneurs.

While wealthy entrepreneurs and industrialists provided most private patronage, after the turn of the century members of the upper-middle and professional class helped shift the focus of patronage from traditional to modern and avant-garde art. Such influential lawyers as John Quinn in New York and Arthur Jerome Eddy in Chicago, as well as men with modest inheritances such as Walter Arensberg in New York and Duncan Phillips in Washington, DC, participated directly in the growth of the avant-garde through their collections of contemporary European and American art. Albert C. Barnes and Katherine S. Dreier were particularly notable as propagandists for the modernist art they collected, while in 1915 Gertrude Vanderbilt Whitney established the Friends of Young Artists. In 1918 the group became known as the Whitney Studio Club, leading to the foundation of the Whitney Museum of American Art (see §XIV, 2 below). By 1929, with the founding of MOMA in New York, more established families such as the Rockefellers had begun to patronize the avant-garde, while private foundations such as the John Simon Guggenheim Memorial Foundation (founded 1925) began to offer fellowships to individual artists. Artists meanwhile sought to find and develop alternative, more independent forms of financial support. The photographer ALFRED STIEGLITZ patronized the first generation of American modernist painters and sculptors, promoting their work through his Gallery 291, while the painter Arthur B. Davies was active as an arts organizer, collector and adviser to other wealthy collectors, such as Lillie P. Bliss. Such activities anticipated the more radical search for alternative exhibition spaces and cooperative support in the late 20th century

In the 1930s the economic hardships of the Depression brought a fundamental change to public patronage at the national level. Franklin D. Roosevelt (President, 1933–45) initiated a series of unprecedented emergency relief programmes for artists and craftsmen. In 1933 the Civil Works Administration established several state programmes, known collectively as the Public Works of Art Project (1933–4), which became the model for the more far-reaching Federal Art Project (FAP) of the Works Progress Administration (WPA) under Harry Hopkins. Directed by Holger Cahill, the FAP employed more than 5000 American artists from 1935 to 1943 (see §III, 3 above). Under Edward Bruce, the Section of Fine Arts of the Department of the Treasury also commissioned numerous works of art from such artists as Reginald Marsh and Arshile Gorky, including murals and architectural sculpture for the Federal Triangle and for federal buildings, especially post offices, throughout the country between 1934 and 1943. Other projects initiated through Roosevelt's New Deal programme included the Index of American Design, a major research and publishing programme also under Cahill's direction that involved artists in the execution of watercolour renderings of folk art objects, and the Farm Security Administration's photographic documentation of the effects of the Depression on the rural poor, especially in the 'Dust Bowl' area (see PHOTOGRAPHY, §II). Roosevelt's New Deal art programmes did not survive his administration, however, and World War II, post-war prosperity and the tensions of the Cold War undermined the political rationale for federal subsidy of the arts during the late 1940s.

During his presidency (1961–3) John F. Kennedy developed the basis for a national cultural policy that resulted in the establishment in 1965 of the National Endowment for the Arts (NEA) and the National Endowment for the Humanities (NEH) during the administration (1963–8) of his successor, Lyndon B. Johnson. The NEA provided direct subsidy to artists through individual fellowships and indirect support through grants to museums and arts organizations. In 1967 the Endowment initiated an Art-in-Public-Places programme, and five years later the NEA Chairman, Nancy Hanks, was instrumental in reactivating the General Services Administration's Art-in-Architecture programme, which later allocated a percentage of federal construction budgets for fine arts. Artists also expanded the scope of private philanthropy by establishing such non-profit, charitable organizations as the Pollock–Krasner Foundation (established 1984; see KRASNER, LEE). By the late 1970s some contemporary artists were rejecting established forms of individual and corporate patronage and seeking to defy the market system of private patronage through the production of temporary, conceptual and site-specific environmental works, while the NEA and GSA programmes both continued to provide public support for a broad range of contemporary art, including the experimental and avant-garde. In the late 1980s, however, some members of Congress attempted to censor the work of certain artists and sought to reduce if not curtail altogether public funding for the arts. The public debate that ensued continued into the following decade.

BIBLIOGRAPHY

R. Brimo: *L'Evolution du goût aux Etats-Unis* (diss., Paris, Inst. A. & Archéol., 1938)
E. McCausland, ed.: *Work for Artists: What? Where? How? A Symposium* (New York, 1948)
N. Harris: *The Artist in American Society: The Formative Years, 1790–1860* (New York, 1966)
L. B. Miller: *Patrons and Patriotism: The Encouragement of the Fine Arts in the United States, 1790–1860* (Chicago and London, 1966)
W. F. McDonald: *Federal Relief Administration and the Arts* (Columbus, OH, 1969)
F. V. O'Connor: *Federal Support for the Visual Arts: The New Deal and Now* (Greenwich, CT, 1969)
F. V. O'Connor, ed.: *The New Deal Projects: An Anthology of Memoirs* (Washington, DC, 1972)
R. D. McKinzie: *The New Deal for Artists* (Princeton, 1973) [excellent historical analysis of New Deal programmes]
F. V. O'Connor, ed.: *Art for the Millions* (Greenwich, CT, 1973)
G. Berman: *The Lost Years: Mural Painting in New York City under the WPA Federal Art Project, 1935–1943* (New York and London, 1978)
Art Inc.: American Paintings from Corporate Collections (exh. cat. by M. D. Kahan, Montgomery, AL, Mus. F.A., 1979) [definitive bibliog. on corporate collecting]
The Public as Patron: A History of the Treasury Department Mural Program (exh. cat. by V. Mecklenburg, College Park, U. MD A.G., 1979)
K. A. Marling: *Wall-to-Wall America: A Cultural History of Post-office Murals in the Great Depression* (Minneapolis, 1982)
E. C. Banfield: *The Democratic Muse: Visual Arts and the Public Interest*, Twentieth Century Fund Essays (New York, 1984)
G. Gurney: *Sculpture of the Federal Triangle* (Washington, DC, 1985)
Art, Design, and the Modern Corporation (exh. cat. by N. Harris and M. R. Norelli, Washington, DC, Smithsonian Inst., 1985)
A. J. [New York], xlviii/4 (1989) [entire issue on critical issues in public art]

JUDITH ZILCZER

XIII. *Collecting and dealing.*

Apart from such isolated collections of prints or copies as that of John Smibert (*see* §XIV, 1, below), in Colonial times the furnishings of the houses of the wealthy constituted the only significant artistic collections. The only paintings commonly owned were family portraits, which functioned as likenesses rather than works of art. Even after the Revolution a concern for the sciences was at first more apparent than any interest in the fine arts, and collections of art were extremely rare, despite the efforts of such artists as Charles Willson Peale and Rembrandt Peale. It was not until the early 19th century that there were the first signs of collecting activity by such figures as JAMES BOWDOIN III. Collections formed at this time generally included either Dutch and Flemish art and/or works by contemporary local artists, a pattern similar to that in England in the same period. Because opportunities to buy European work in the USA were generally restricted to rather questionable auction sales, such art was generally acquired in Europe by the collectors concerned, or by artists acting as agents, while American art was acquired directly from the artists responsible.

Despite the occasional notable collection, such as those of grocer LUMAN REED and Thomas Jefferson Bryan (1802–70) in New York, the ownership of art works was still regarded as eccentric in the mid-19th century. A landmark in efforts to counter this prejudice, particularly with regard to local artists, was the American Art-Union (1844–51), based in New York. This organization, by holding regular exhibitions of works by American artists and distributing over 150,000 engravings and paintings to its members by means of a lottery, introduced original art into many districts and made ownership of art works more widespread. Other organizations such as the Dusseldorf Art Union attempted to stimulate interest in foreign artists in a similar manner. Art collecting in the USA continued, however, to be circumscribed by the dearth of outlets where potential collectors could obtain works until after the 1850s, when a number of knowledgeable dealers, the most notable of whom were connected with galleries in Paris (e.g. Michel Knoedler), began to appear in New York and a few other East Coast cities. The success of John Rogers (ii) in selling plaster copies of his statuette groups by mail order (*see* §IV, 1 above) is indicative of the expanding market in the second half of the 19th century, but it was not until just after the Civil War that there was significant collecting and dealing in the USA, partly stimulated by the emergence of a new class of wealthy industrialists.

In the third quarter of the 19th century the standard of American collecting underwent a qualitative change as the first American collections to contain works of real art-historical significance began to appear. The new collectors of the time did not share their predecessors' reservations about buying art; instead they wished to advertise their wealth and status by living in opulent surroundings, accompanied by large, dramatic works of art. The works they collected were also very different from those previously sought after, as the dubious Old Masters (mainly of the Italian and northern European Renaissance) or contemporary American works of earlier collections were replaced by contemporary French painting, particularly by such established French Salon favourites as Rosa Bonheur, William-Adolphe Bouguereau, whose work was promoted by SAMUEL P. AVERY, or, from the 1870s, the Barbizon painters, whose work was introduced to the New York public largely by Michel Knoedler (*see* KNOEDLER, M., & Co.). This shift was stimulated partly by a number of European-minded American artists who acted as advisers to collectors, and despite the introduction in 1883 of a heavy import duty on works of art, contemporary American art declined in relative popularity with collectors in the late 19th century. (Duty on works more than 20 years old was only repealed in 1909; in 1913 works less than 20 years old were exempted.) It was not until 1892 that the first gallery specializing in American art opened in New York.

In the mid-1880s Impressionism was introduced to the USA by such dealers as Paul Durand-Ruel (*see* DURAND-RUEL, (2)), and, with the added encouragement of Mary Cassatt, a number of collectors such as BERTHA HONORÉ PALMER and Henry and LOUISINE HAVEMEYER acquired notable groups of Impressionist paintings. However, although these collectors acquired substantial amounts of contemporary art, their collections still also included art of the past. By the 1890s the taste of such tycoons as Andrew W. Mellon (*see* MELLON, (1)), J. PIERPONT MORGAN and SAMUEL H. KRESS, on the other hand, had become synonymous with accredited Old Masters and 18th-century works. Typically these collections were large and historical, including works from the early Renaissance to the 18th century; some were almost encyclopedic, or even acquired in bulk. The USA's new economic and cultural strength was the stimulus behind such collections, which were characterized by an enthusiasm for the most prestigious works and by the remarkably high prices paid for their masterpieces. Another important element was the intention of collectors such as Isabella Stewart Gardner, William T. Walters and others to leave their collections to the public as memorials to their achievements (*see* §XIV, 2 below). The shift in emphasis from contemporary to past art was made possible by improvements in art scholarship and the appearance of the first expert advisers. A number of prestigious European dealers, including JOSEPH DUVEEN and Nathan Wildenstein (*see* WILDENSTEIN, (1)), established themselves in New York and played a crucial part in building these collections. The era of such collections lasted until the late 1920s, when it was curtailed by the Stock Market Crash and the subsequent Depression.

On the whole, American collectors ignored subsequent developments in European art such as Post-Impressionism. Before World War I the only American collectors who showed any enthusiasm for modern art from Post-Impressionism onwards were distinguished by their strong ties to Europe, such as the STEIN family and the CONE sisters, who bought works from European dealers or from the artists themselves. In the early 20th century the Madison Gallery and the 291 Gallery of ALFRED STIEGLITZ were among the first few galleries handling modern European art and contemporary American artists in New York. It was the Armory Show of 1913, which introduced the American public to European avant-garde art, that was most effective in stimulating American collectors in this direction. Among the collectors who built significant holdings of the most radical and recent European and American art in the years immediately after were Walter ARENSBERG, A. E. GALLATIN (who subsequently exhibited his collection as the Gallery of Living Art), JOHN QUINN, ALBERT C. BARNES and KATHERINE S. DREIER. American taste during the 1920s continued to be dominated by the Old Masters, however, and although there was more interest in modern art, the number of those buying it remained tiny, as did the number of galleries exhibiting such work. American art also had few notable buyers at this time, except such dedicated patrons as Gertrude Vanderbilt Whitney (see WHITNEY, (1)). Largely as a consequence of the increasing activity of museums, however (see §XIV below), this situation began to change from the mid-1930s.

After World War II there was an unparalleled increase in the number, variety and quality of American collections. Whereas before the war American collectors of any note could be counted in tens, by the 1960s it was possible to talk of hundreds. Moreover, collecting and dealing became truly nationwide for the first time. The nature of these collectors also underwent a change: whereas in the past collectors had traditionally been of the wealthy social élite, increasingly they were much younger, newly wealthy, well-educated professionals. The range of such collections also diversified considerably, but two notable trends were the increasing scarcity of large eclectic historical collections (NORTON SIMON being a notable exception) and a greater willingness to acquire works representing new developments in art. For the first time very large collections of modern art appeared, such as those of JOSEPH H. HIRSHHORN and Nelson Aldrich Rockefeller (see ROCKEFELLER, (4)). These shifts were influenced by a number of factors, the most significant of which was the heightened critical standing of American art in the postwar era. While such galleries as Peggy Guggenheim's Art of This Century (see GUGGENHEIM, (2)) and the SIDNEY JANIS Gallery initially promoted European artists who had fled from the war, they and such other dealers as BETTY PARSONS were also important in promoting Abstract Expressionism. The acclaim with which such artists as Jackson Pollock were greeted in turn helped establish New York in particular as a centre of the art market, a trend that continued in the 1960s with the commercial success of many Pop artists and the establishment of such galleries as that of LEO CASTELLI (see also §III, 4 above); and whereas in the early 1940s there were c. 70 galleries of all types in New York, 20 years later this number had nearly quadrupled, and by the mid-1970s it had doubled again. Another significant factor was the American taxation system, which encouraged private collectors to give their holdings to museums; this institutional drift in turn created increasing shortages of certain kinds of works, such as major Old Masters or Impressionist paintings, and forced collectors into new fields. A further important development was the growth of corporate art collecting, which in the 1940s was still quite rare, but which became increasingly common from the early 1960s, with corporations such as the Chase Manhattan Bank building up extensive collections of contemporary art. The economic recession

of the mid-1970s brought to an end this great era of expansion, and with some artists experimenting with new media and sceptical of the gallery system, collecting and dealing became less prominent.

BIBLIOGRAPHY
R. Brimo: L'Evolution du goût aux Etats-Unis (diss., Paris, Inst. A. & Archéol., 1938)
A. B. Saarinen: The Proud Possessors (London, 1959)
W. G. Constable: Art Collecting in the United States (London, 1964)
J. Lipman, ed.: The Collector in America (New York, 1970)
W. Towner: The Elegant Auctioneers (New York, 1970)
F. V. O'Connor: 'Notes on Patronage: The 1960s', Artforum, xi/1 (1971)
M. N. Carter: 'The Magnificent Obsession: Art Collecting in the '70s', ARTnews, lxxv/5 (1976), pp. 39–45
Art Inc.: American Paintings from Corporate Collections (exh. cat. by M. D. Kahan, Montgomery, AL, Mus. F.A., 1979)
L. Skalet: The Market for American Painting in New York, 1870–1915 (diss., Baltimore, MD, Johns Hopkins U., 1980)
S. N. Platt: Responses to Modern Art in New York in the 1920s (Ann Arbor, 1981)
L. de Coppet and A. Jones, eds: The Art Dealers: The Powers behind the Scene Talk about the Business of Art (New York, 1984)
A. D. Robson: The Market for Modern Art in New York in the 1940s and 1950s (diss., U. London, 1988)

XIV. Museums.

In the USA the development of the art museum has led to the existence of a museum in almost every major town. It has also grown from being a repository of an eclectic collection of curiosities to a specifically designed building, its commission often offering a prestigious opportunity for national and international architects (see MUSEUM, §II). The general organizational patterns of museums in the USA were laid down in the 19th century and changed little over time. There are two basic kinds of museums, both effectively created by the wish of prominent citizens to commemorate civic and personal pride. The first is the institution initially organized by a committee of prominent and wealthy citizens and/or collectors and run by a board of trustees. A variant on this is the museum that was founded by an art association, which might have been stimulated by a local art exhibition, for example the Detroit Museum of Art, founded in 1885. The second clearly defined strand within the museum sector is that of the museum derived from the collecting activity of a single individual.

1. Early developments: mid-18th century to the mid-19th. 2. Period of expansion and the roles of individual collectors. 3. The museum and society.

1. EARLY DEVELOPMENTS: MID-18TH CENTURY TO THE MID-19TH. During the Colonial period there was little development in the museum sphere as the priorities of settlers lay more towards solving the immediate difficulties of living and working in a new and often hostile land. Only in the middle of the 18th century could Benjamin Franklin suggest that at last 'circumstances that ... afford leisure to cultivate the finer Arts, and improve the common Stock of Knowledge' had been attained (cited in Pach). Unlike Europe, where art institutions generally relied on royal or noble collections, in the New World local associations organized by private citizens to promote learning and culture were responsible for the birth of the first museums. In Boston in the early 18th century John Smibert provided the forerunner of the art

gallery in the USA, when he displayed copies after Old Masters and plaster casts of ancient and modern sculpture in the space above his 'color shop', selling artists' materials.

In the 1750s Harvard College attempted to build a 'repository of curiosities' (destr.) along the lines of the Ashmolean Museum, founded at Oxford University in England in 1683. In 1705 the Library Society of Charleston, SC, began to collect materials for a record of the natural history of the state. In 1791 the Massachusetts Historical Society, the model for many subsequent societies, was founded in Boston and opened a small gallery and library. Other developments included the opening by the Society of St Tammany of a museum on Wall Street, in fact a room in the City Hall (destr.), with a collection consisting primarily of Native North American relics, while the New-York Historical Society opened its doors in 1804 and ran what was for many years the only museum in New York.

Attempts to ameliorate the scientific and historical emphases of most early American collections were made from the 1770s. The first of these was arranged by Charles Willson Peale (see PEALE, (1)), who in 1784 began to exhibit his paintings in his own museum in Philadelphia, PA, with the addition of objects such as minerals, whale bones and stuffed animals. The collection was displayed in various venues until 1820. In 1814 his son Rembrandt Peale (see PEALE, (4)) opened the Baltimore Museum and Gallery of the Fine Arts (now Peale Museum, Baltimore, MD) with a similar collection ranging from paintings to ethnographic specimens. The building, designed by Robert Cary Long sr (1770–1833), was the first in the USA and only the third in the world to be constructed as a museum, preceded by the Ashmolean Museum in Oxford and the Museo del Prado in Madrid. Peale charged an admission fee, and there were lecture programmes and nightly 'Philosophical demonstrations'. Such collections tended to present art as a curiosity: it was not until the foundation of the Pennsylvania Academy of the Fine Arts, Philadelphia, in 1805, intended to be the American counterpart of the Royal Academy in London, that there was any attempt to bring together works of art in a display with the intention of elevating public taste. The academy was organized at the suggestion of Charles Willson Peale, but the 71 founders were mainly from the business and legal community, keen to cultivate the arts as part of a nationalistic consciousness. In 1846 the Smithsonian Institution was founded in Washington, DC, from the bequest of James Smithson, a chemist and mineralogist, for a scientific institution.

By the end of the first quarter of the 19th century the society-organized gallery, with its somewhat heterogeneous collection of natural and historical specimens, was one of only two significant types of museum in the USA. The second was the 'dime' museum or emporium of curiosities operated for profit and entertainment, for example Barnum's American Museum in New York. Despite the paucity of public collections, however, college museums expanded in the early 19th century. These contained mainly zoological and geological specimens that were used for teaching purposes, but a number were open to the general public. By 1852 c. 20 colleges had started their own 'cabinets' along these lines; in the next decade another 25 were founded. Although in 1811 JAMES BOWDOIN III endowed the college in Brunswick, ME, named after him with a collection of Old Master paintings and drawings, the first college museum devoted specifically to art was not opened until 1832, when Yale University, New Haven, CT, opened its Trumbull Gallery to stage temporary exhibitions; it was named after JOHN TRUMBULL, who had sold most of his collection to the college in 1831. In the 1850s Harvard University, Cambridge, MA, acquired its first art collection when it accepted the gift of a group of prints, and the University of Michigan began collecting sculpture casts, while Yale began a permanent collection when in 1871 it purchased the collection of Italian Primitive paintings formed by the writer James Jackson Jarves (1818–88).

The main developments of public art museums during the first half of the 19th century were within the context of libraries that added art galleries: the Boston Athenaeum, founded in 1807 as a library, began to stage art exhibitions in one of its rooms in 1826, while the Wadsworth Atheneum added a picture gallery to its building in 1842 and began to build a collection of paintings. In the 1850s, however, the Brooklyn Museum in New York opened, and, aided by a bequest of £5000, instituted a gallery of fine art. During this period the main alternative to the public galleries were a few public displays of private collections, such as those of both LUMAN REED, which could be viewed at his home during the 1830s, and the lawyer Thomas Jefferson Bryan (1802–70), whose collection was shown as the Bryan Collection of Christian Art in the 1850s.

2. PERIOD OF EXPANSION AND THE ROLES OF INDIVIDUAL COLLECTORS. The first public museums to open in the USA were the Metropolitan Museum of Art, New York (1870), and the Boston Museum of Fine Arts (1875), followed by the Philadelphia Museum of Art (1876) and the Chicago Academy of Fine Arts (1879; Art Institute of Chicago from 1882). The establishment of these and other institutions marked an important period of growth of museums in the USA. In the 50 years after 1876 the national total of museums of all types rose from 233 to nearly 2500. In earlier decades museums had been dominated by historical and scientific collections, but during this later period it was art museums that demonstrated the greatest expansion; from only 11 such museums in 1870, half a century later there were 224 public art museums and 115 college or university art museums. Moreover, the period signalled a change in the nature of museum formation and organization: the societies, academies and lyceums that had played the central role in establishing 'cabinets' and collections in previous decades gave way to formally chartered institutions. These museums were characterized by a new emphasis on their role as a public service that could help to raise the standards of American taste, especially in the context of manufacturing design. The Chicago Academy of Fine Arts, for example, aimed to promote design, holding both exhibitions and classes for this purpose.

An important influence on the establishment of public institutions was the new civic and national pride stimulated by the centennial of the War of Independence, and the urge to rebuild after the bitter divisions of the Civil War.

These forces, coupled with the post-war period of prosperity, which created a considerable number of private fortunes, encouraged persons of private wealth to involve themselves in philanthropy and the foundation of institutions that could serve as monuments to civic pride and personal munificence. For example, the M. de Young Memorial Museum, San Francisco, CA, grew out of the newspaper publisher's role in organizing the California Midwinter International Exposition in 1894, and the decision to create a permanent museum as a memorial to the International Exposition.

The appearance of art museums in the late 19th century was due largely to a change in attitudes towards art; it was no longer regarded merely as a curiosity but was seen as a cultural product with a moral and aesthetic value. This shift, concomitant with improvements in art-historical scholarship, both in Europe and the USA, and the growth in the art market in such cities as New York, helped to lead to an improvement in the standards of private collections in the USA (*see* §XIII above). It is unlikely that American museums and their collections could have been started without a body of individuals willing and able to acquire their own private collections. A factor discernible from the 1870s was that these were built up with a view to being presented to an institution.

Many institutions were founded on large industrial fortunes, for example the Cleveland Museum of Art, OH, which opened to the public in 1916 with the support of LEONARD C. HANNA jr and others. As economic trends shifted, new wealth appeared in the form of museums, whose founders and/or benefactors recognized the value of an institution as a monument to their collecting. The oil magnate J. Paul Getty jr began to collect in the 1930s, and in 1953 he made public his collection in four galleries in his home. In the late 1960s he constructed a new building in Malibu, CA, modelled after the Villa dei Papiri in Herculaneum, which opened to the public in 1974. The John Paul Getty Museum's acquisition of a number of substantial collections in 1984 necessitated further expansion, and a branch of the museum was scheduled to open in Los Angeles in 1997. Until the establishment of the Getty and of the Kimbell Art Museum (opened in 1972) in Fort Worth, TX, named after its benefactor, Kay Kimbell, a millionaire whose fortune also derived primarily from oil, the Cleveland Museum of Art had been the most heavily endowed. Another museum dependent on its city's industry was the Detroit Institute of Art, which became a public institution in 1919, owned by the city of Detroit. It was constantly dependent on the automobile-based economy of Michigan and it therefore sometimes suffered its volatility, being particularly badly hit by the recession of 1974–5.

A characteristic of all American museums founded by boards was the dominant role of the private individual collector since, in the absence of public funding for the purpose, an institution's collection generally grew from works provided or promised by the founding trustees. Moreover, although a museum's direction might be established by its founder, the development of its collection was likely to be shaped significantly by later donations. Museum collections were therefore often a barometer of contemporary taste. On occasion, where civic pride demanded a municipal institution but the question of local private patronage was neglected, the ridiculous situation arose of a museum with empty galleries. For example, the Toledo Museum of Art, OH, founded in 1901 by a group of citizens led by the industrialist Edward Drummond Libbey, had no collections when it opened, and it was thus dependent on loans. Libbey, whose successful LIBBEY GLASS CO. provided the basis of the economy in Toledo, formed a collection of European paintings, however, which he bequeathed to the museum in 1925 and which was supplemented by a trust provided by his estate.

Art collections in American museums were augmented either by complete collections or by individual works. For instance, the Metropolitan Museum of Art, New York, founded by 50 New Yorkers, including Henry G. Marquand, who grouped together to raise an endowment for the museum, was given several collections in the 1880s. Many gifts followed, including parts of the J. Pierpont Morgan collection and the Havemeyer collection; by the 1920s it was the largest and wealthiest art museum in the country. MOMA in New York, founded in 1929, also opened without a collection, but it soon acquired one through the bequest of Lillie P. Bliss. Subsequent gifts to the collection tended to be single or small groups of works, although the dealer Sidney Janis made an important donation of 100 paintings in the 1960s. By the late 1950s the collection included 1200 paintings, ranging from late works by Claude Monet to the Ecole de Paris and the New York school of Abstract Expressionists. The first director, ALFRED H. BARR jr, consciously steered MOMA's development towards a synthesis of the visual arts (including design and architecture) and aimed at providing not only a place to house works of art but also a forum for the experimental avant-garde. The museum's founders were prominent art collectors and scholars rather than business people or simply rich benefactors.

Institutions dependent on private patronage were varied with respect both to scale and to the kind of work they contained. The collections formed at smaller art museums, effectively in many cases by an individual, are sometimes eccentric in scope and taste. The first such institution open to the public was the Corcoran Gallery of Art in Washington, DC, which opened in 1869 displaying the collection built up by its founder, WILLIAM WILSON CORCORAN, in the mid-century. In the 1870s and 1880s a number of American collectors began to amass collections with the aim of eventually presenting them to the public. Among these was that of Isabella Stewart Gardner at Fenway Court in Boston, MA (now Isabella Stewart Gardner Museum, made public in the 1920s), and the Walters collection (now Walters Art Gallery) in Baltimore, MD, formed by William T. Walters and his son Henry Walters and bequeathed in 1931. The Gallery of Living Art, housing A. E. Gallatin's private collection, was opened to the public in 1927 at New York University; it was the first museum in the USA devoted exclusively to modern art. John Ringling, who began buying art in the 1920s, installed his collection in its own museum in Sarasota, FL, by 1929, with the express intention that it become the state art museum of Florida; it was so designated in 1946, opening to the public in 1949. Similarly, Andrew W. Mellon began to collect for his own pleasure but soon sought major works with a view to providing a collection for a national museum; the National Gallery of Art opened in Washington, DC, in 1941 with further support from Samuel H. Kress and Joseph E. Widener.

There are some discernible strands within the category of museum derived from the individual collector. Some of the museums based on a single collection, such as the Gardner Museum and the Frick Collection in New York, founded by Henry Clay Frick, have remained frozen in time, explicit memorials to the taste of their founders, perpetually presented in much the same settings as in the patron's lifetime. In other cases a collection amassed by one person has been memorialized in a more conventional institutional setting, with new acquisitions generally orientated toward the original collector's taste. An important example is the Solomon R. Guggenheim Museum in New York (built 1956–9) to show abstract art as the Museum of Non-objective Painting, with a collection of nearly 800 early 20th-century European paintings formed by Solomon R. Guggenheim (see GUGGENHEIM, (1)); another is the Hirshhorn Museum and Sculpture Garden in Washington, DC, opened in 1974 to house the collection of JOSEPH H. HIRSHHORN. Both collections had been assembled with the idea that they would enter institutions. In the case of other museums owing their existence to a single patron, the individual's collection has been supplemented by a wide range of purchases or gifts, as with the Whitney Museum of American Art, New York (built 1963–6), based on a core collection of 700 works of art provided by Gertrude Vanderbilt Whitney (see WHITNEY, (1)) in 1930. This nucleus quickly grew, however, initially with purchase funds provided by Whitney, later also by gifts from other collectors, until 30 years later it had quadrupled in size. This growth enabled the museum to continue her patronage of contemporary artists while responding to new developments in American art.

3. THE MUSEUM AND SOCIETY. The network of museums in the USA again grew substantially from the 1930s. According to *Museums USA: A Survey Report* (1975), a study conducted for the National Endowment for the Arts, there were 1821 well-established museums in the USA in 1971–2. Generally art museums were the wealthiest: their combined endowments totalled *c.* £484 million, compared with £230 million for history and science museums combined. By the 1970s nearly 70% of all museums and *c.* 45% of art museums had been founded after 1940. The Smithsonian Institution (founded 1846) in Washington, DC, of which the National Gallery of Art was originally a part, illustrates well the growth of the museum sector, being the largest complex of museums and art galleries in the world. Among the institutions under its aegis are the National Museum of American Art and the Renwick Gallery, the National Portrait Gallery, the National Museum of African Art, the Freer Gallery of Art, the Hirshhorn Museum and Sculpture Garden, and the Cooper-Hewitt Museum in New York. This expansion, which was further fuelled by a rise in general educational standards, helped partly by the GI Bill (1945), reflected a shift by American museums from their traditional, more passive interpretation of their roles of acquisition, the

physical care, study and classification of the museum's collection, and the display of works, to a more active stance. The latter, in turn, involves the museum in educational activities, such as practical art classes given to school pupils, art teachers and the general public, and lectures relating to the collection. It also includes museum and gallery publications, touring exhibitions and the encouragement of private collections through collectors' clubs or art lending societies.

The educational role of American museums, which initially reflected the high-minded civic idealism of their founders, became increasingly important since for most museums it was only through such channels that they could obtain public funding. Government in the USA (whether federal, state or city) generally contributed little directly to public institutions, although a number of museums did manage to obtain money towards capital costs and annual running expenses from city or state authorities. Museums operated wholly or mainly with public funds were relatively uncommon. Government, however, effectively provided indirect support via the exemption provisions of the personal taxation code. These allowed private individuals to give (either money or objects) to charitable or educational organizations or institutions and then to deduct the value of their gifts from their taxation liabilities, effectively encouraging such donations. Gifts made in this way were essential in building up the endowments that cover capital and maintenance costs and were also a major source of the growth of museum collections. However, the Tax Reform Act (1969) abolished the full tax deduction of the original cost plus the appreciated value of a work of art up to a limit of 20–30% of a donor's adjusted gross income. Some tax advantages were subsequently available on gifts of works of art to museums, but some of these were revoked during the Reagan administration (1980–88).

After World War II museums in the USA became increasingly influential on public taste through their support not only of the most highly prized art of the past, which had earlier dominated their collections, but also of previously unfashionable fields. For example the foundation in 1930 of the Whitney and of the Addison Gallery of American Art in Andover, MA, did much to raise the critical profile of American art, an area hitherto thought historically unimportant. Similarly, the collecting and exhibiting of modern art by MOMA in New York helped to raise its status and to establish the relative importance of different movements in 20th-century art. In the later half of the 20th century museum collections increasingly focused on new art: indeed, many new museums specialized in it. This tendency blurred the museum's traditional function of providing historical validation, since the purchase of an artist's work by a museum influenced, sometimes controversially, his or her critical and commercial standing and appeared to sanction one tendency over another.

Museum collections, particularly of modern art, grew dramatically after World War II. Some institutions found it increasingly difficult, however, to acquire major works of art as prices escalated and works of the highest quality became scarce; the problem of shortages was in some ways self-inflicted, since it was the purchases by public collections that diminished the pool of available works. In an effort to ensure that private collectors continued to supply works to museum collections, in the post-war years many museums were active in stimulating collecting activity among the public, in contrast to earlier years when they were mainly content to be the passive recipients of existing collections. This was achieved through such tactics as exhibitions of private collections, art lending libraries or special sale exhibitions for museum members. Apart from a few very prosperous institutions, such as the John Paul Getty Museum in Malibu, CA, and in spite of an apparently growing public interest in the arts, most museums faced ever greater difficulties in funding their work, and as a result they increasingly sought sponsorship from the business community.

Financial constraints, especially after c. 1970, increasingly prevented museums from staging substantial exhibitions using only their own resources. One way in which museums began to supplement their funding was through 'blockbuster' exhibitions, which were large shows, usually of prestigious art, that could attract both substantial corporate finance and large attendances. Such exhibitions, however, soon attracted controversy: they were accused of distracting museums from their essential function, that of looking after their collections, and of narrowing a museum's educational potential by restricting the scope of exhibitions to those guaranteed to attract sponsorship and large crowds. In spite of these dilemmas, museums have continued to address themselves to the many functions that they have performed throughout their history.

BIBLIOGRAPHY
L. V. Coleman: *The Museum in America: A Critical Study*, 3 vols (Washington, DC, 1939)
W. Pach: *The Art Museum in America* (New York, 1948)
G. Bazin: *The Museum Age* (New York, 1967)
D. Ripley: *The Sacred Grove: Essays on Museums* (New York, 1969)
E. Spaeth: *American Art Museums* (New York, 1969)
S. Lee, ed.: *On Understanding Art Museums* (Englewood Cliffs, 1975)
Museums USA: A Survey Report, National Endowment for the Arts (Washington, DC, 1975)
N. Burt: *Palaces for the People* (Boston, 1977)
K. E. Meyer: *The Art Museum: Power, Money, Ethics* (New York, 1979)

A. DEIRDRE ROBSON

XV. Art education.

The first institutions to foster training in the visual arts in the USA were academies such as the Pennsylvania Academy of Fine Arts, which was founded in Philadelphia in 1805, the National Academy of Design in New York (founded 1825), the Cincinnati Academy of Fine Arts (founded 1838) and, to a lesser extent, the Art Students League (founded 1875), which were modelled on European academies and were initially dedicated to the display and promotion of the fine arts rather than to education. Until then most aspiring artists were trained in other artists' studios or were self-taught; many still looked to Europe for examples and for guidance; for sculptors in particular a period of study in Italy was considered almost essential during much of the 19th century (*see* §IV, 1 above). Architects usually had a formal university education followed by a period at the Ecole des Beaux-Arts in Paris, before working in the office of a Beaux-Arts trained architect. As industrialization spread in the second half of the 19th century, many of these academies evolved into professional art schools seeking to promote emergent industries by training designers. The Chicago Academy of Design (founded 1866) became the Chicago Institute of Fine Arts in 1879 and the Art Institute of Chicago in 1882. The Rhode Island School of Design (founded 1877) in Providence, RI, offered courses in textile design to support local industries, and the New York State College of Ceramics (founded 1900) administered by Alfred University, was founded to promote the ceramics industry. By the 1870s publicly funded schools were assuming preliminary responsibility for the teaching of drawing, a skill that assumed greater importance as the pace of industrialization increased, especially in the education of working-class pupils. Instruction was largely based on the copying of geometric figures. The first state-wide system of education in industrial drawing was established in Massachusetts in 1871 by Walter Smith, who had trained in South Kensington, London, and emigrated to Boston to establish the programme. The School of Drawing and Painting was attached in 1877 to the Museum of Fine Arts, Boston, and became the School of the Museum of Fine Arts in 1901. By the 1880s architects were able to complete their training by study at one of several new schools of architecture in the USA, most of which were modelled on the Ecole des Beaux-Arts and directed by French architectural teachers. At about the same time in a number of schools, especially those for women, art began to be studied through printed reproductions, copies and plaster casts, as well as through practical instruction in drawing and painting. The establishment of the Art Institute of Chicago as a school of art and design and as a collection was a typical example of this. Charles Eliot Norton introduced art appreciation into Harvard University, Cambridge, MA, in 1874, and the Minneapolis School of Fine Arts (founded 1886) used academic methods under the guidance of Douglas Volk (*b* 1856). By the 1880s and 1890s industrial drawing in public schools was being supplanted by the study of art as objects of refinement and beauty. 'Picture study' and 'schoolroom decoration' were urged by American disciples of John Ruskin, such as Henry T. Bailey (1865–1931), and there was a growing emphasis on the edifying moral effects of aesthetic education. By 1901 it was estimated that one in every three undergraduate college students came into contact with a professor of fine arts, although even professors specializing in the history of art, such as Norton and Samuel F. B. Morse at New York University, rarely gave historical lectures. Formal study in art history in the USA began in the 1880s at Princeton University, NJ, and by 1942 most college art history survey courses had standardized their organization of content as a chronological sequence. This situation changed dramatically in the 1970s and 1980s, by which time a wide variety of approaches to the teaching of art history had come into favour (*see also* §XVII below).

Meanwhile, on the practical side, many American educators in the 1880s and 1890s eschewed industrialism, and, inspired by William Morris, advocated a return to the ideals of good craftsmanship and design. This movement also reaffirmed the importance of manual training, especially when the latter was losing importance as a vocational study. Art and manual training teachers were at this time frequently members of the same professional associations.

At the turn of the 20th century the study of design was promoted by Arthur W. Dow (1857–1922), although interest in discerning universal principles of artistic design had appeared in 1856 in Owen Jones's *Grammar of Ornament*. Dow's *Composition*, first published in 1899, was a significant influence throughout the early 20th century, while the fame of the Bauhaus in Germany also helped promote the importance of design education. The rise of such modernist art styles as Impressionism and Expressionism meanwhile led many educationalists to view the innate expressive artistic ability of the child as a natural resource to be cultivated. The arts were accorded a greatly enhanced role as they came to be taught as self-expression, an emphasis that permeated the pedagogy of the progressive education movement. With the economic Depression of the 1930s, however, and the spectre of totalitarianism in Europe, fine art assumed a new importance as a resource for enhancing home and community and as a power for social cohesion. The most prominent example of this was perhaps the independent BLACK MOUNTAIN COLLEGE in North Carolina, founded by John Andrew Rice in 1933. It inherited many aspects of Bauhaus educational philosophy through the immigrant teachers that it attracted from Germany and elsewhere.

After World War II, spurred by renewed economic prosperity, art teachers were appointed in many elementary schools, especially in expanding suburbs. By contrast, however, urban schools lacked the services of such specialist teachers, and by the mid-1960s the qualitative disparity between inner-city and suburban schools was a recognized problem. Post-war teaching methods were inspired by Viktor Lowenfeld (1903–60), who suggested ways in which children at different stages of artistic development should be stimulated by appropriate media and themes, and art teachers returned to self-expression as a pedagogical ideal, with the curriculum being guided mainly by developmental considerations. The success of the distinctively American Abstract Expressionism also reinforced the ideal of creative self-expression. In the late 1950s Cold War tensions caused educators to undervalue the arts and humanities, and in the 1960s a movement to restructure art education began when M. Barkan (1913–70) and others suggested that art teaching should reflect art's structure, based on characteristic 'modes of inquiry' employed by artists, art historians and art critics. This led to 'discipline-based art education' (DBAE), which was widely espoused and which from 1984 was vigorously supported by the Center for Education in the Arts of the J. Paul Getty Trust in Santa Monica, CA.

In the 1990s American art educators were divided into several overlapping groups. One proclaimed the importance of self-expression and regarded studio studies as the heart of the curriculum. A second structured curricula around a rationally grounded conception of art as a discipline, advocating a greater role for the study of art history, art criticism and aesthetics. A third focused on economic, cultural, political and social concerns, with feminist issues and the need for balanced attention to the art forms originating in many diverse cultures (especially those of oppressed minority groups) forming a central focus.

BIBLIOGRAPHY

I. E. Clarke: *Art and Industry: Education in the Industrial and Fine Arts in the United States*, i (Washington, DC, 1885)
A. W. Dow: *Composition* (New York, 1899)
H. T. Bailey: *The Flush of the Dawn: Notes on Art Education* (New York, 1910)
V. Lowenfeld: *Creative and Mental Growth* (New York, 1947)
L. Cremin: *Transformation of the School* (New York, 1964)
M. Barkan: 'Curriculum Problems in Art Education', *A Seminar in Art Education for Research and Curriculum Development*, ed. E. Mattil (Philadelphia, 1966)
N. Pevsner: *Academies of Art Past and Present* (New York, 1973)
Art in Transition: A Century of the Museum School (exh. cat. by B. Hayes, Boston, MA, Mus. F.A., 1977)
M. Stankiewicz: 'The Eye is a Nobler Organ: Ruskin and American Art Education', *J. Aesth. Educ.*, xviii/2 (1984), pp. 51–64
G. Clark, M. Day and W. D. Greer: 'Discipline-based Art Education: Becoming Students of Art', *J. Aesth. Educ.*, xxi/3 (1987), pp. 129–96
Pike's Peak Vision: The Broadmoor Art Academy, 1919–45 (exh. cat. by G. L. Cuba and E. Cunningham, Colorado Springs, CO, F.A. Cent., 1989)
A. Efland: *A History of Art Education: Intellectual and Social Currents in Teaching the Visual Arts* (New York, 1990)

ARTHUR D. EFLAND

XVI. Art libraries and photographic collections.

The development of art libraries in the USA is closely related to the formation of the great art collections and the growth of art history as an academic discipline, with many libraries being established to support the educational programmes of art schools and academies. Another related factor was the extension of services in public libraries, to which responsibility for cultural education and enrichment increasingly devolved. The first small art libraries were established in the 19th century with the foundation of major museums such as the Boston Museum of Fine Arts (1875) and the Metropolitan Museum in New York (1880). At the same time libraries were also necessarily gradually fostered by art schools and academies: the great collection of the Ryerson and Burnham Libraries of the Art Institute of Chicago began as a shelf of books in the director's office. Meanwhile, in the case of those universities or colleges with their own museums, libraries arose to serve the dual purpose of supporting the museum's collecting activities and of promoting the educational mission of the parent institutions, as with the Fine Arts Library at Harvard University, Cambridge, MA. The changing nature of the contents of the art library during the 19th century and the early 20th reflects the development of the literature of art, which originally comprised primarily biographies, guidebooks, handbooks for collectors and auction sale catalogues, but which was soon augmented by the growth of periodicals (*see* PERIODICAL, §III, 2(ii)), systematic inventories of the great museums and monumental corpora and catalogues raisonnés.

In the 20th century the holdings of many libraries continued to reflect the special interest of the collection of the parent museum, as with the Freer Gallery of Art in Washington, DC, which concentrates on East Asian art and culture, and MOMA, New York, which maintains extensive files on 20th-century artists. An evolution took place in the growth and increasingly sophisticated management of visual arts collections, most of which developed more or less independently of art libraries. Besides large general photographic collections such as those of the Frick Art Reference Library in New York and the National Gallery in Washington, DC, there are specialized visual collections, including the Princeton Index of Christian Art, Princeton, NJ, a card catalogue of images representing Christian themes with accompanying descriptions, the photographic collection of the National Museum of African Art in Washington, DC, or the Peter A. Juley Collection of Photographic Records at the Smithsonian Institution, Washington, DC, documenting 80 years of American art activity. The large photographic archive of the Getty Center for Art History in Santa Monica, CA, is broader in its coverage, and broader still in scope is the Prints and Photographs Division of the Library of Congress, Washington, DC. While most of these visual libraries continued at the end of the 20th century to be arranged according to art-historical categories of medium, school or artist, the curators of many collections were increasingly concerned to provide access to material by subject or theme, as scholars in other disciplines became more reliant on visual resources.

Although from the 19th century photography vastly extended the range of images available to the scholar and connoisseur, technological developments in the late 20th century promised to have still more far-reaching implications. The availability of large microfiche collections of images, such as the Marburger Index, suggested that these miniaturized pictures might obviate the need for individual libraries to continue to maintain their own unique collections. Other possible developments included conversion of printed material to microfiche, to CD-ROM (compact disk-read-only memory), to video disks or to optical digital disks, the images of which could be transmitted electronically. The feasibility of linking image banks with bibliographic data was also being investigated by both art and visual resource librarians.

BIBLIOGRAPHY

W. Freitag: 'Art Libraries and Collections', *Encyclopedia of Library and Information Science*, i (New York, 1968), pp. 571–621
B. J. Irvine: *Slide Libraries* (Littleton, 1974, rev. Littleton, CO, 1979)
P. Pacey: *Art Library Manual: A Guide to Resources and Practice* (London, 1977)
H. Harrison, ed.: *Picture Librarianship* (Phoenix, 1981)
W. Freitag: 'Indivisibility of Art Librarianship', *A. Libs J.*, vii (1982), p. 28
A. B. Lemke: 'Education for Art Librarianship: The First Decade', *A. Libs J.*, vii (1982), pp. 36–41
S. S. Gibson: 'The Past as Prologue: The Evolution of Art Librarianship', *Drexel Lib. Q.*, xix (1983), pp. 3–17
J. Larsen, ed.: *Museum Librarianship* (Hamden, 1985)
L. S. Jones and S. S. Gibson: *Art Libraries and Information Services: Development, Organization, and Management* (Orlando, 1986)
C. C. Freeman: 'Visualizing Art: An Overview of the Visual Resources Profession in the United States', *A. Doc.*, vii (1988), pp. 6–8
H. Roberts: '"Do you Have any Pictures of . . . ?": Subject Access to Works of Art in Visual Collections and Book Reproductions', *A. Doc.*, vii (1988), pp. 87–90

SARAH SCOTT GIBSON

XVII. Historiography.

Throughout much of the 19th century, interest in the arts in the USA was primarily aesthetic rather than historical, and appreciation of art was considered a morally uplifting ingredient of a well-rounded humanist education; it was not until late in the century that this moral aspect was seen

as a focus for formal art education (*see* §XV above). Historical texts on art and design, such as William Dunlap's *History of the Rise and Progress of the Arts of Design in the United States* (New York, 1834), James Jackson Jarves's history of Italian art (1861) and *A Glimpse of the Art of Japan* (1876), and William C. Prime's *The Pottery and Porcelain of All Times and Nations* (1878), were published only occasionally. Charles E. Lester made a major contribution when he published *The Artists of America: A Series of Biographical Sketches of American Artists with Portraits and Designs on Steel* (1846). In the second half of the century the history of art was introduced into American colleges and universities. For the pioneers of art history in the USA, original scholarship was not an issue of great importance, and, as Charles Eliot Norton recognized, American art history students and scholars were reliant on European texts.

Two individuals of note, however, did explore new areas and methodologies in art history. The Leipzig-trained scholar CHARLES C. PERKINS, who helped found the Boston Museum of Fine Arts, wrote five academic books on Italian art. Because he never held a university position, however, Perkins's historical rigour found few disciples. The example of BERNARD BERENSON, on the other hand, was widely followed. Having earnt his degree at Harvard, Berenson settled in Italy, where he adopted the methodology of the connoisseur Giovanni Morelli, who had sought to establish a scientific method to determine the authorship, date and provenance of works of art. Although Berenson's application of Morelli's method of CONNOISSEURSHIP sometimes led him to questionable historical conclusions, his *Drawings of the Florentine Painters* (3 vols, 1903) is an enduring example of his scholarship.

Connoisseurship has had a lasting legacy in American art history, for example in Richard Offner's *Critical and Historical Corpus of Florentine Painting* (1931–81). Most scholars, however, combined it with other modes of inquiry, as in the catalogues raisonnés compiled by galleries and museums. PAUL J. SACHS, an esteemed connoisseur and trainer of museum personnel, epitomized this approach, but similar attempts to integrate techniques were also made by Edgar Richardson in his *Washington Allston: A Study of the Romantic Artist in America* (1948) and by Robert Rosenblum in his *Transformations in Late Eighteenth Century Art* (1967).

Meanwhile, from the early 20th century a number of new approaches evolved, without necessarily preventing existing and very different approaches from continuing to develop. During the first few decades of the century, as leading humanists attempted to model their disciplines on the natural sciences, the positivist compilation and examination of data displaced what was seen by some as an outmoded predilection for aesthetics and interpretation. Younger American art historians pursued such hitherto uninvestigated areas as the della Robbia family, whose works were studied in six volumes (Princeton, 1928) by Alan Marquand, the founder of the Princeton Art Department; *Lombard Architecture* (4 vols, New York, 1915–17) and *Romanesque Sculpture of the Pilgrimage Roads* (Boston, 1923), both by ARTHUR KINGSLEY PORTER, who in the latter work restructured the chronology and theories on the spread of sculpture through Europe; the study of

Spanish art was undertaken by CHANDLER R. POST (in *A History of Spanish Painting*, 12 vols, Cambridge, MA, 1930–66) and Walter W. S. Cook. The concentration on documents also advanced the establishment of specialist manuscript collections and other resources (*see* §XVI above) and contributed to the reputation of American scholarship abroad.

After World War I the study of iconography (*see* ICONOGRAPHY AND ICONOLOGY) began to replace documentary practices and connoisseurship. CHARLES RUFUS MOREY directed iconographic studies at Princeton, publishing surveys on medieval and Early Christian art. Although Morey's stylistic classifications, such as those expounded in his essay 'Sources of Medieval Style' (1924), were controversial, he influenced many students, including Albert M. Friend jr, who did important work on Byzantine and Carolingian manuscript illumination and on medieval ivories and goldwork. Another of Morey's disciples was E. Baldwin Smith, who wrote studies of architecture and sculpture, tackling formal, iconographic and historical issues in such works as *Egyptian Architecture as Cultural Expression* (New York, 1938). Karl Lehman's 'The Dome of Heaven' (1945) and Caroll Meek's *The Railroad Station: An Architectural History* (1956) are other outstanding examples of historical approaches into the context of art.

During the 1930s many distinguished scholars moved from Europe to the USA, including WALTER FRIEDLAENDER and, most notably, ERWIN PANOFSKY. Influenced by Ernst Cassirer and Aby Warburg, Panofsky taught at New York University and Princeton, where he guided the work of many Americans in iconography and in his more interpretive formulation, iconology. Among those inspired by Panofsky's work were W. H. Janson, Frederick Hartt, Millard Meiss, Robert Rosenblum and Meyer Schapiro, although none adhered to a strict iconological methodology. Schapiro, a scholar of medieval, 19th- and 20th-century art, drew on many disciplines, including Marxism, psychology, phenomenology, existentialism and theories of style to determine the relationship between artists and their work, for example in his study of *Paul Cézanne* (1970).

Despite the popularity of iconology, FORMALISM or the analysis of style still preoccupied many critics and scholars in the early 20th century. The theories of Heinrich Wölfflin and Henri-Joseph Focillon were particularly influential in this regard. Wölfflin's *Principles of Art History* (1915), which established 'a history of form working itself out inwardly', prompted many stylistic analyses, including Sydney Freedberg's *Painting of the High Renaissance in Rome and Florence* (2 vols, 1963). In *The Life of Forms* (1934) Focillon added an emphasis on artists' materials and techniques to Wölfflin's and Aloïs Riegl's premises of the perpetual metamorphosis of form. This and Focillon's brief professorship at Yale University helped sway American art history from a documentary approach to a descriptive one. Formalism prevailed especially in the field of modern art, notably in the scholarship of ALFRED H. BARR jr as director (1929–67) of MOMA, New York, and the criticism of CLEMENT GREENBERG. In his essay 'American "Type" Painting' (1955), published in *Art and Culture* (Boston, 1961), Greenberg gave an account of

modernism that rooted Abstract Expressionism in 19th-century European avant-garde movements, an interpretation that continued to be embraced by many scholars.

From the 1930s, scholars of American art sought to establish a native artistic tradition. This was encouraged by the Federal Arts Project's *Index of American Design*, a survey of the crafts and popular arts of Americans of European descent, begun in 1935 and published in 1950, with text by Erwin O. Christensen. The quest for a stylistic American heritage was continued in Barbara Novak's *American Painting of the 19th Century* (New York, 1969), in which the author isolated a stylistic 'Americanness in American art' by linking a national spirit to the characteristic forms of 19th-century painting. Influenced by Wölfflin, Ernst Gombrich and Greenberg, Novak argued that a romantic painterly tradition was dominated by a conceptual linear tradition. Her survey was more advanced methodologically than those by Holger Cahill and Alfred H. Barr jr (1934), Alan Burroughs (1936), Oscar Hagen (1940) and John McCoubrey (1963), although McCoubrey's *American Art, 1700–1960: Sources and Documents* (1965) helped base subsequent works such as Jules Prown's *American Painting from its Beginnings to the Armory Show* and Barbara Rose's *American Painting* (both 1969) on original sources.

In the fields of architecture and design, similar accounts by Fiske Kimball of national stylistic developments were highly influential. Foremost in the investigation of modern architecture was HENRY-RUSSELL HITCHCOCK, whose *Modern Architecture* (1929) attempted to distinguish between the conservative 'new tradition' and the more radical production of certain modernists. *Sticks and Stones* (New York, 1922) by LEWIS MUMFORD used historical architectural analysis and Marxist criticism to urge social and economic reform and, with *The International Style* (1932) by Hitchcock and the architect Philip Johnson, determined much of the ensuing discourse on the subject, as other architectural historians incorporated technical, social, economic and ideological issues into their historical analyses and often demanded change. The technological emphasis of SIGFRIED GIEDION, a student of Wölfflin who taught at Harvard, had a monumental impact in the USA and elsewhere, while George Kubler's *Mexican Architecture of the Sixteenth Century* (New Haven, 1948), integrated Focillon's theories of formal mutation with the contextual issues of demography, ecology and economics. Later, Kenneth Frampton, a British architect and historian teaching in the USA, provided a concise assessment of 20th-century architecture while drawing on Marxism and other critical schools of thought in his *Modern Architecture: A Critical History* (London, 1980).

Earlier examples of works influenced by Marxism, which was more commonly applied to other disciplines at the time, were Milton Brown's *The Painting of the French Revolution* (1938) and Meyer Schapiro's 'The Nature of Abstract Art' (1937). After World War II many scholars chose to study artists in their social environments. Those tracing artistic evolution from a biographical perspective included John Rewald in his *Post-Impressionism from Van Gogh to Gauguin* (New York, 1956), Alfred H. Barr jr's study of *Matisse: His Art and his Public* (1951) and Lloyd Goodrich in his catalogue to the retrospective exhibition at the National Gallery of Art, Washington, DC, in 1961 of the work of Thomas Eakins. Others, such as Oliver Larkin (*Art and Life in America*, 1946), Peter Selz (*German Expressionist Painting*, Berkeley, 1951) and Robert Herbert (*Impressionism: Art, Leisure in Parisian Society*, London, 1988) probed the aesthetic and cultural contexts of artistic production. Significant analyses of artistic patronage and its effects on style were advanced by Frederick Hartt in his study of 15th-century Florence (1964) and Lilian B. Miller in her study of patronage in the USA (*see* §XII above).

Many later scholars reacted against the traditional canons of art, architecture and design. Several, such as the curator of American art at the National Museum of American Art, Joshua Taylor (*America as Art*, 1976), Jules Prown ('Mind in Matter: An Introduction to Material Culture', 1982) and Frank Willet (*African Art: An Introduction*, 1971), undertook the research of previously neglected artists, cultures and art forms. Others looked into the canon of art history anew from the perspectives of MARXISM, psychoanalysis (*see* PSYCHOANALYSIS AND ART), feminism (*see* FEMINISM AND ART) and SEMIOTICS. These included Michael Fried (*Absorption and Theatricality: Painting and the Beholder in the Age of Diderot*, Berkeley, 1980), Svetlana Alpers (*The Art of Describing: Dutch Art of the 17th Century*, London, 1983), Rosalind Krauss (*Passages in Modern Sculpture*, London, 1977), Elizabeth Johns (*Thomas Eakins: The Heroism of Modern Life*, Princeton, 1983) and T. J. Clark (*The Painting of Modern Life*, New York, 1984). Linda Nochlin's essay 'Why Have There Been No Great Women Artists?' (1971) launched a lively feminist challenge to traditional art history, which was elaborated in *From the Center: Feminist Essays on Women's Art* (New York, 1976), edited by Lucy Lippard, and *Feminism and Art History: Questioning the Litany* (1982) by Norma Broude and Mary D. Garrard. The increasing number of multi-contributor exhibition catalogues meanwhile encouraged a plurality of perspectives that characterized late 20th-century art history in the USA. This was also reflected in the annual conferences of the College Art Association of America, a professional association of university-based artists and art historians with offices in New York. It was founded in 1911 to support a commitment to the practice, teaching and research of visual arts. In the 1990s no single orthodoxy dominated a field that was increasingly open to influences from other disciplines and to the urgent pressures of social and cultural forces outside the academy.

BIBLIOGRAPHY

P. Hiss and R. Fansler: *Research in Fine Arts in the Colleges and Universities of the United States* (New York, 1934)
A. Neumeyer: 'Victory without Trumpet', *Frontiers of Knowledge*, ed. L. White jr (New York, 1956), pp. 178–93
R. Wittkower: 'Art History as a Discipline', *Winterthur Seminar on Museum Operation and Connoisseurship: Winterthur, 1959*
J. S. Ackerman and R. Carpenter: *Art and Archaeology* (Englewood Cliffs, NJ, 1963)
C. Eisler: '"Kunstgeschichte" American Style: A Study in Migration', *The Intellectual Migration: Europe and America, 1930–1960*, ed. D. Fleming and B. Bailyn (Cambridge, MA, 1969)
W. E. Kleinbauer: *Modern Perspectives in Western Art History: An Anthology of 20th Century Writings on the Visual Arts* (New York, 1971)
E. Panofsky: 'Three Decades of Art History in the United States: Impressions of a Transplanted European', *Meaning in the Visual Arts* (New York, 1971)
J. G. Schimmelman: 'A Checklist of European Treatises on Art and Essays on Aesthetics available in America through 1815', *Proc. Amer. Antiqua. Soc.*, xciii (1983), pp. 93–195
M. A. Holly: *Panofsky and the Foundations of Art History* (Ithaca, NY, 1984)
T. Gouma-Peterson and P. Mathews: 'The Feminist Critique of Art History', *A. Bull.*, lxix/3 (1987), pp. 326–57
W. Corn: 'Coming of Age: Historical Scholarship in American Art', *A. Bull.*, lxx/2 (1988), pp. 188–207
J. G. Schimmelman: *American Imprints on Art through 1865: An Annotated Bibliography of Books and Pamphlets on Drawing, Painting, Sculpture, Aesthetics, Art Criticism and Instruction* (New York, 1990)

SHANA GALLAGHER

Unit One. English group of architects, painters and sculptors. The group was formed in London in 1933 after discussions between Paul Nash, Wells Coates, Henry Moore and Ben Nicholson. In 1932 Nash had described the need for a 'sympathetic alliance between architect, painter, sculptor and decorator' (*The Listener*, 16 March 1932), which would further the modernization of British artistic culture according to the precedents of the European Modern Movement. The other members were John Armstrong (1893–1973), John Bigge (1892–1973), Edward Burra, Barbara Hepworth, Colin Lucas (1906–84) and Edward Wadsworth. Frances Hodgkins was a member for only a very short time and was later replaced by Tristram Hillier (1905–83). The name of the group was chosen by Nash to express both unity (Unit) and individuality (One).

Nash announced the formation of Unit One in a letter to *The Times* (12 June 1933), describing the group as 'a solid combination standing by each other and defending their beliefs'. Exhibition space and offices were provided by the Mayor Gallery, London. Herbert Read was the group's spokesman and Douglas Cooper its secretary. The members had little in common, however, other than an interest in modern European art and architecture. A book of statements and photographs, *Unit 1*, was edited by Read and published to coincide with the group's only exhibition in London in 1934 at the Mayor Gallery. A tour of municipal galleries in England, Ireland and Wales attracted considerable publicity and served to polarize opinion about modern art in general, although by the time the tour ended in 1935 the sense of common cause had dissipated, and the group had effectively ceased to exist.

WRITINGS

H. Read, ed.: *Unit 1: The Modern Movement in English Painting, Sculpture and Architecture* (London, 1934)

BIBLIOGRAPHY

Unit 1 (exh. cat., Portsmouth, City Mus. & A.G., 1978)
C. Harrison: *English Art and Modernism, 1900–1939* (London, 1981)
Unit One: Spirit of the '30s (exh. cat., London, Mayor Gal., 1984)

☐

Universal Exposition. *See* INTERNATIONAL EXHIBITION.

University palace. University building that served as a centre for teaching, examinations and academic ceremonies. University palaces came into existence in western Europe from the end of the 15th century. Universities were at first mobile communities that, in the event of dissension, could easily migrate to other cities in what were known as *peregrinationes academicae*; they owned no established premises, not even for teaching and conferring degrees. The sources indicate that any area of sufficient size was considered suitable for teaching purposes: this might be in town halls (Bologna, Modena, Pavia, Fano), teachers' homes, shops, or on the streets and squares of university towns.

The earliest university to be granted property for its own use was Cambridge, England. Under Nigel de Thornton's foundation of 1278 the university owned the land on which, a century later, the construction of the Old Schools, the first university palace in Europe, was put in hand (now much altered). The plan was for a closed rectangular court with lecture rooms, libraries, a chapel and a senior common room; there were no living-quarters such as were provided by the colleges. The north wing was built between 1350 and 1400, but the work was only completed by the addition of the south and east wing in 1474.

In Oxford the university acquired in 1426–7 the land on which the Divinity School was subsequently built. A second storey was added to this building after the creation of Duke Humphrey's Library (*see* LANCASTER, (2)) in 1445, the library premises being completed *c.*1482. The university thus possessed two apartments, to which the Bodleian Library was added at the beginning of the 17th century. The building works were completed with the erection of Convocation House, 1634–7. Here again it was only after several centuries that the university possessed a building of its own, enclosing a quadrangle, for tuition and library purposes.

University palaces were much more common in southern Europe. In Italy, where during the Renaissance they were built under the name Palazzo della Sapienza, the earliest palaces combined the functions of college and university building. When Florence University was moved to Pisa, the architect to Lorenzo de' Medici devised a two-storey structure (begun 1472) with lecture rooms on the ground floor and the college, with its living-quarters, above. After 1481 Giuliano da Sangallo planned a similar arrangement, with two institutions superimposed, in a building for the Sapienza in Siena. Although the architectural origin of the university palace plan lies in college buildings, the living-quarters were steadily reduced: at Rome after the remodelling of 1594 the plans provided only for some sets of professors' rooms at the top of the building. Finally, the palaces consisted of an *aula magna* (great hall) and lecture rooms.

Italian universities generally consisted of two independent bodies, one devoted to medicine and the arts, the other for jurisprudence; and they needed two adjoining courts, as in Naples and Pavia. In the remodelled Roman Sapienza (see fig.), single-court extensions were added on the English model, but the existence of two universities in one building was emphasized by the provision of a staircase for each side of the court; moreover, there are two flights of steps at the Archiginnasio at Bologna (1562–3).

University palaces were built most frequently in Spain, particularly in the 16th century: Valencia (1493), Granada (1527), Salamanca (completed 1533), Oviedo (founded 1534; completed 1608), Alcalá de Henares (1535, by Rodrigo Gil de Hontañón), Oñate (after 1540), Tortosa (founded 1544) and Orihuela (begun 1552), both designed by Juan Anglés; Osuna (founded 1548), Seville (begun

University palace, Palazzo della Sapienza, Rome, begun 1497, chapel 1632–70 by Francesco Borromini

1566) and Baeza (1568). An 18th-century group includes Huesca (1690, by Francisco Artiga); Valladolid (façade 1715, by Narciso Tomé), Cervera (1718–51) and Santiago de Compostela (1769–1805). In Germany no quadrangular structures were created after those of Altdorf (1571–4), Helmstedt (begun 1576) and Würzburg (1582–92): university palaces, like Protestant academies, either formed three sides of a rectangle, presenting an imposing spectacle to the city, or confronted the city with a main façade.

As the university palace developed, college architecture was assimilated to meet new demands. Although in Rome after 1594 the chapel (see fig.) occupied a central position, as in college buildings based on the Collegio di Spagna in Bologna (*see* COLLEGE, fig. 2), this was a clear expression of the Counter-Reformation spirit that distinguished the papal university. During the 17th century, except in Jesuit foundations, the chapel generally forfeited its central position. Universities other than the Jesuit ones had no pastoral functions and more space was needed for teaching. Whereas in earlier times the university palace had only one lecture room for each faculty, permanent rooms were needed for the sciences in particular, especially as the equipment could not be constantly moved about. Ultimately nearly every discipline had its own accommodation. The plan for the new university palace in Edinburgh, published anonymously in the *Scots Magazine* in 1785, even included rooms for the university collections. The university palaces of the 18th century no longer had any residential function but served only public purposes, and their use of space was correspondingly distinct from that of the colleges.

See also COLLEGE.

BIBLIOGRAPHY

R. Willis and J. Willis Clark: *The Architectural History of the University of Cambridge*, 4 vols (Cambridge, 1886/*R* 1986)

H. Rashdall: *The Universities of Europe in the Middle Ages*, 2 vols (London, 1895); ed. F. M. Powicke and A. B. Emden, 3 vols (London, 1936)

A. Gray: 'Old Schools and Universities in Scotland', *Scot. Hist. Rev.*, ix (1912), pp. 113–38

C. H. Haskins: *The Rise of the Universities* (New York, 1923/*R* Ithaca, NY, 1957)

An Inventory of the Historical Monuments of the City of Oxford, Royal Comm. Anc. & Hist. Mnmts & Constr. England (London, 1939/*R* 1949)

C. Martinell: 'Las antiguas universidades y colegios españoles, como monumentos arquitectónicos', *Cuad. Arquit.*, v (1948), pp. 2–20

N. Pevsner: 'Universities Yesterday', *Archit. Rev.*, cxxii (1957), pp. 234–9

An Inventory of the Historical Monuments in the City of Cambridge, Royal Comm. Anc. & Hist. Mnmts & Constr. England, 2 vols (London, 1959)

K. Rückbrod: *Universität und Kollegium; Baugeschichte und Bautyp* (Darmstadt, 1977)

M. Kiene: 'Die Grundlagen der europäischen Universitätsbaukunst', *Z. Kstgesch.*, xlvi (1983), pp. 63–114

——: 'Der Palazzo della Sapienza: Zur italienischen Universitätsarchitektur des 15. und 16. Jahrhunderts', *Röm. Jb. Kstgesch.*, xxiii–xxiv (1988), pp. 219–71

——: 'Die italienischen Universitätspaläste des 17. und 18. Jahrhunderts', *Röm. Jb. Kstgesch.*, xxv (1989), pp 329–80

MICHAEL KIENE

Unkei (*b* Nara region, 1151; *d* ?1223). Japanese sculptor. He was the son of KŌKEI and a member of the KEI school of sculptors that flourished in the Kamakura period (1185–1333; *see* JAPAN, §V, 3(iv)). Unkei was the foremost exponent of a new sculptural style of the period. His earliest important work was the wooden statue of the *Dainichi nyorai* (Skt Mahavairocana tathagata; the Buddha who expounded Esoteric Buddhism) made in 1176 under the supervision of his father at the temple of Enjōji in Nara (*in situ*). This early image, with eyes of mounted crystal and deliberately irregular bold carving, already shows something of the naturalism that characterized Kamakura-period sculpture. In 1183 he transcribed the *Hokuekyō* or *Myōhō renge kyō* (Lotus Sutra; Hyōgo Prefecture, Ueno priv. col.). In 1186 he produced wooden statues (all extant) of *Amida* (Skt Amitabha; Buddha of the Western Paradise), *Fudō myōō nidōji* (Skt Acala; the Fudōmyōō Triad) and *Bishamonten* (Skt Vaishravana; Guardian King of the North) at the request of the warrior Hōjō no Tokimasa (1138–1215) for the Ganjōjuin in Shizuoka. In the same year he made the wooden statue of the *Miroku bosatsu* (Skt the *bodhisattva* Maitreya) for the subtemple of Shōgan'in at the Shōryakuji in Nara. In 1189 he was commissioned by the military leader Wada Yoshimori (1147–1213) to make wooden statues (all *in situ*) of the *Amida sanzon* (Amida Triad), *Fudō myōō* and *Bishamonten* for the temple of Jōrakuji in Kanagawa. He was at this time in the priesthood at the Sōōin at Kōfukuji. In 1194 he assisted his brother Jōkaku (*b* mid-12th century) and his colleague KAIKEI with the creation of the *Niten* ('Two devas') for the Chūmon (Middle Gate) of the temple of Tōdaiji in Nara (*see* NARA, §III, 4(i)). He received the ecclesiastical rank of *hōgen* in 1195. In 1196 he worked on the *Shitennō* (Skt Caturmaharajika; Four Guardian Kings) and the *Attendants* of the Tōdaiji Daibutsuden (Great Buddha Hall) together with Kōkei, Jōkaku and Kaikei. In 1197–8 he repaired the statues (completed 839; most *in situ*) in the Early Heian period (794–early 10th century) Kōdō (Lecture Hall) of the Kyōōgokokuji (Tōji) in Kyoto and also made the *Niō* (temple gate guardians) for the Nandaimon (Great Southern Gate) at that temple. He produced the *Niten* ('Two devas'; *in situ*) for the Chūmon at Jingōji in Kyoto. The *Hachidaidōji* ('Eight attendants'; 1197) at Kongōbuji in Wakayama; the 1201 *Shō Kannon* (Skt Arya Avalokiteshvara), the *Bonten* (Skt Brahmadeva) and the extant *Taishakuten* (Skt Shakra, one of the Buddhist tutelary gods) at Takisanji in Aichi, all wooden sculptures, are also attributed to Unkei.

In 1203 he led a team including Kaikei and several lesser Buddhist sculptors in the production of the wooden *Kongō rikishi* or *Niō* (Skt Vajradhara; temple gate guardians; *in situ*) for the Nandaimon (Great Southern Gate) at Tōdaiji. In the same year he was awarded the highest ecclesiastical rank of *hōin*. From 1208 to 1212, during the restoration of Kōfukuji in Nara, Unkei, together with his son and disciples, created for the Hokuendō such wooden masterpieces as the *Miroku bosatsu* and the *Muchaku* (Skt Asanga; a famous Indian priest who lived *c.* 290–360) and *Seshin* (Skt Vasubandhu; *fl c.* 5th century; Indian Buddhist priests who produced some of the leading scriptures of the Hossō sect of Japanese Buddhism). In 1213 he participated in the production of Buddhist images for the nine-storey pagoda at Hōjōji in Kyoto. For a few years after 1216 he made sculpture for important members of the Kamakura shogunate, such as the images for the Jibutsudō ('hall for Buddhist images for personal use') of Minamoto no Sanetomo (1192–1219). During this time, the headquarters of the *Nara busshi* were moved from Nara to Heian (now Kyoto) and Unkei moved the statues of the *Jizō jūrinin* (the cloister of the *bodhisattva* Jizō, Skt Kshitigarbha) in Kyoto, which he had created, to Kōzanji in 1223. This is known to have been his last project. Other attributions to Unkei or other Kei sculptors include the wooden statue of *Dainichi nyorai* at the Kōtokuji in Ibaraki, a temple associated with the Ashikaga family who had strong ties to the shogunate, and the wooden seated *Jizō bosatsu* (a *bodhisattva* in monk's garb who delivers people from the world) at the Rokuharamitsuji in Kyoto.

The elements of Unkei's style and his considerable artistic gifts were already present in the Enjōji and Ganjōjuin statues of his early period, in which he abandoned much of the gentleness of late Heian period sculpture and established a new style, the special traits of which were bulging, rounded facial features, undulating, muscular body form and intricately carved drapery. It may be that Unkei's contact with the samurai of the Kantō region who were his patrons—men of simple and vigorous dispositions—influenced the development of his mature style, which was criticized as being too rough for the Kyoto nobility. After the death of his father, Unkei inherited the title of *Nara busshi*. The style of his later period is represented by works at the Hokuendō at Kōfukuji. Although Unkei's own name does not appear in the inscriptions on these works along with the names of his son and disciples, the superior accomplishment and splendour that imbue each piece indicate that Unkei played a crucial role as project leader. Unlike the *Amida* in the Triad at Jorakuji from Unkei's early period, these works hark back to the Buddhist images of the Nara (710–94) and Heian periods, in such elements as the tension of the slender torsos and the style of the drapery. The images of *Muchaku* and *Seshin* surpass the bounds of simple portrait sculpture, vividly conveying the intellectual and human qualities of their subjects, who are portrayed with individualized features, expressions and stances. These remarkably realistic imaginary portraits are representative not only of Unkei's best work but also of the finest in all Japanese sculpture. A technical innovation developed by Unkei was a special structure that firmly covered the base of seated figures in order that the ashes of the Buddha and *sūtra*s could be inserted in the interior of the image. His Enjōji pieces were the first examples of Buddhist imagery in Japan known to have been signed by an artist in his position as maker, thus indicating the rise in social status of Buddhist sculptors during this time. Formerly, those inscriptions which mention the maker were written by patrons or monks. Unkei's daughter Nyoi (*fl* 1199) married into the aristocracy, becoming the daughter-in-law of one of the court ladies (*nyōbō*). His sons Tankei (1173–?1256), Kōun, Kōben, Kōshō, Unka and Unjo were all active as Buddhist sculptors early in the Kamakura period.

For further discussion *see* JAPAN, §V, 3(iv).

Unkoku Tōgan: *Crows on Snowy Plums* (detail), colours on gold foil, one of a series of sliding-door paintings (*fusumae*), each panel 1665×1565 mm, ?1588 (Kyoto, National Museum)

BIBLIOGRAPHY
EWA; *Kodansha Enc. Japan*, 'Buddhist Sculpture', 'Kei School', 'Unkei'; Thieme–Becker
T. Kobayashi: 'Busshi Unkei no kenkyū' [Research on the *busshi* Unkei], *Nara Kokuritsu Bunkazai Kenkyūjo Gakuhō*, 1 (1954) [whole issue]
K. Mizuno: *Unkei to Kamakura chōkoku* [Unkei and Kamakura sculpture] (Tokyo, 1972)
S. Tanabe, ed.: 'Unkei to Kaikei' [Unkei and Kaikei], *Nihon No Bijutsu*, 78 (1972) [whole issue]
T. Kuno: *Unkei no chōkoku* [Sculpture of Unkei] (Tokyo, 1974)
T. Kobayashi: *Nihon chōkoku sakka kenkyū* [Research on the artists of Japanese sculpture] (Yokohama, 1978)

HIROMICHI SOEJIMA

Unkoku Tōgan [Hara Jihei] (*b* Hizen Province [now Nagasaki Prefect.], 1547; *d* Hagi, Suō Province [now Yamaguchi Prefect.], 1616). Japanese painter. According to the *Hara Jihei Naoyoshi kefuroku* ('Family record of Hara Jihei'; 1765), Tōgan was the second son of the Hara Naoie (*d* 1584), lord of Nokomi Castle in Hizen Province. Although Tōgan was raised with the privileges of a high-ranking samurai, shifting political fortunes and the death of his father ended his military career in 1584. His artistic training is unclear; a mid-17th-century painters' biography lists him as studying with Kanō Eitoku or with Eitoku's father, Shōei (*see* KANŌ, (3) and (5)), yet Tōgan's paintings bear scant evidence of serious study with either man. All Edo period painting histories agree that Tōgan wanted to link his artistic lineage to the seminal Muromachi period (1333–1568) painter TŌYŌ SESSHŪ. The artist's name 'Unkoku Tōgan' amply demonstrates this conscious link: the character Tō of Tōgan comes from the first character of Sesshū's religious name Tōyō, and his 'family' name 'Unkoku' derives from Sesshū's Unkokuan ('Cloud Valley Hermitage') studio in Yamaguchi, which was later taken over by Tōgan. Moreover, when the daimyo Mōri Terumoto (1553–1625) commissioned Tōgan to copy Sesshū's *Sanzui Chokan* ('Long landscape scroll'), Tōgan added a colophon in which he claimed to be the present-day representative of Sesshū's lineage. Finally, Tōgan often signed his works 'painted by Tōgan, descendant of Sesshū' or 'painted by Tōgan, third generation Sesshū'.

None of Tōgan's extant paintings can be dated with any certainty, and this has led to much speculation about the evolution of his painting style. Traditionally the 44 *fusumae* (sliding-door paintings) from three rooms at the Ōbaiin subtemple of Daitokuji in Kyoto have been accepted as Tōgan's earliest paintings. They are thought to have been painted when Ōbaiin was built in 1588. The west room features a *Sansui zu* ('Landscape') in the formal style (*shintai*), the central room depicts the *Chikurin Shichiken zu* ('Seven sages of the bamboo grove') in the running style (*gyōtai*) and the east room shows *Rogan zu* ('Reeds and geese'; now badly damaged) in the cursive style (*sōtai*). The *Chikurin Shichiken zu* displays Tōgan's figural painting at its best. Tōgan does not characterize his sages by creating individualized facial features for each man, but by depicting each of the four groups with a different type of expressive brushwork. Tōgan's brushwork is a reinterpretation of the Chinese Southern Song period (1127–1279) painter LIANG KAI's angular and cursive modes, which were the template for Sesshū's technique a century earlier. In the adjacent *Sansui zu* Tōgan reveals his transformation of an entirely different tradition. Tōgan's sober and deliberate landscapes, often labelled 'conservative', are adaptations from Sesshū's orthodox landscape style. In particular Tōgan adapted the XIA GUI style that was the basis for Sesshū's *Sanzui Chokan*. The horizontal orientation of the handscroll composition is preserved in the strong sideways movement of the Ōbaiin *Landscape*. The many signs of human activity—the profusion of straight-edged dwellings and numerous boats tucked behind large rocks—are reminiscent of Sesshū's *Sanzui Chokan*. Yet, through a process of distillation and magnification, Tōgan transformed the more active landscape handscroll style to meet the needs of wall painting. This same approach to composition and subject is seen in Tōgan's many screens depicting figures in landscapes.

While most of Tōgan's paintings, whether landscapes, figures or horses, are in ink and light colour, he also worked in the *kinpeki* (colour on gold ground) technique, which testifies to the breadth of his skill and the variety of his commissions. The *fusumae Ume ni Karosu zu* ('Crows on snowy plums'; see fig.), the most striking example of Tōgan's *kinpeki* style, may have been painted in 1588 for the audience hall at Najima Castle in Chikuzen Province (now Fukuoka Prefect.). The boldly decorative sensibility of *Crows*, with its jarring angular composition, daring sense of spatial play and assertive contrast of ink and gold, probably reflects an early 17th-century date. In this painting, and in the pair of *kinpeki* folding screens *Shunka Sansui zu* ('Spring and summer landscapes'; priv. col.), Tōgan seems to have turned away from a style derived from Sesshū and looked towards the more innovative painting of his contemporaries HASEGAWA TŌHAKU and KAIHŌ YŪSHŌ.

Tōgan's characteristic style and subjects were taken up by his second son Tōeki (1591–1644), who succeeded him as official painter to the Mōri clan and went on to found the Unkoku school. The school flourished under Tōyō (1612–68), and by 1662, when Tōhan (1635–1724) became its leader, it had more than doubled in size. Its decline in the 18th century paralleled the waning fortunes of the Mōri family. The death-knell of feudal Japan sounded by the Meiji restoration of 1868 was echoed by the demise of the last Unkoku master, Tōyū (1811–82).

BIBLIOGRAPHY
S. Tanaka: 'Unkokuha tokushu ni tsuite' [On the painters of the Unkoku school and their work], *Kokka*, 420 (1960), pp. 249–95
M. Kawai: *Yushō, Tōgan*, Nihon bijutsu kaigai zenshū [Complete collection of Japanese painting], i (Tokyo, 1981)
H. Yamamoto: *Unkoku Tōgan to Momoyama jidai* [Unkoku Tōgan and the Momoyama period] (Yamaguchi, 1984)
S. Kageyama: 'Unkoku Tōeki ko' [Thoughts on Unkoku Tōeki], *Kobijutsu*, 78 (1986), pp. 76–81
H. Yamamoto: *Unkokuha no keifu* [Lineage of the Unkoku school] (Yamaguchi, 1986)
☐

Unovis [Rus. Utverditeli Novogo Iskusstva: 'Affirmers of new art']. Russian group of artists and designers gathered around KAZIMIR MALEVICH at Vitebsk (Viciebsk), Belarus', from 1919–20. Vera Yermolayeva (1893–1938), who became director of the Art Institute in Vitebsk in 1919, appointed Malevich (who had been invited by Marc Chagall) to head a teaching studio. The group, known as Posnovis (Posledovateli Novogo Iskusstva: 'Followers of new art') in January 1920, was soon renamed

Unovis and was formed to explore Malevich's concept of SUPREMATISM. Their work reflected Constructivist techniques and was characterized by mathematical forms, such as the parabola, and by suggestions of construction. This is seen in the work of EL LISSITZKY, who had studied under Yermolayeva's predecessor, Marc Chagall, before becoming a convert to Suprematism. Lissitzky gave to his paintings and prints the name *Proun* ('Affirmation of the new'). He printed 1000 copies of Malevich's book *O novykh sistemakh v iskusstve* ('On new systems in art') at Vitebsk in December 1919, and this was followed in 1920 by Malevich's *Suprematizm: 34 risunkov* ('Suprematism: 34 drawings'). Theatrical productions played an important role in Unovis, and both Vladimir Mayakovsky's *Misteriya-Buff* and Aleksey Kruchonykh's opera *Pobeda nad solntsem* ('Victory over the sun'; February 1920) were produced there. The work of Unovis also extended to utilitarian designs and could incorporate explicit political commitment. The Unovis design for a Lenin tribune (1920; see Kueppers-Lissitzky, pl. 129) and Lissitzky's civil war poster *Beat the Whites with the Red Wedge* (1919; repr. 1960; Eindhoven, Stedel. Van Abbemus., see Kueppers-Lissitzky, pl. 40) are examples of this. Other members of the group included Yermolayeva, Il'ya Chashnik (1909–29), Nikolay Suetin (1897–1954) and Lev Yudin (1903–41). Lazar' Khidekel (1904–86) was also associated with the group. Unovis published two journals, *Aero* (1920) and *Unovis* (1920–21), and organized numerous exhibitions. Branches were organized in Moscow, Petrograd, Smolensk, Orenburg, Saratov, Samara, Perm and Odessa.

Lissitzky moved to Moscow in 1921 and then to Western Europe as an emissary of Russian revolutionary art (1922–5). Malevich and the remaining group, forced out of the Vitebsk Art Institute following disagreements with the authorities over methods, moved to INKHUK at Petrograd, working there on architectural forms and producing designs for the Lomonosov porcelain factory.

BIBLIOGRAPHY
S. Kueppers-Lissitzky: *El Lissitzky: Life, Letters, Texts* (London, 1968)
The Suprematist Straight Line: Malevich, Suetin, Chashnik, Lissitzky (exh. cat., London, Annely Juda F.A., 1977)

JOHN MILNER

Unsong kŏsa. *See* KANG, (2).

Unterberger. Austrian family of artists. They originated in Cavalese in the Italian Tyrol and worked widely in the territories of the Austro-Hungarian empire.

BIBLIOGRAPHY
K. Zimmeter: *Michael Angelo und Franz Sebald Unterberger* (Innsbruck, 1902)
J. Ringler: *Die barocke Tafelmalerei in Tirol* (Innsbruck and Munich, 1973), pp. 123–30

(1) Michael Angelo [Michelangelo] **Unterberger** (*b* Cavalese, 11 Aug 1695; *d* Vienna, 27 June 1758). Painter. He was first taught by Giuseppe Alberti (1640–1716) in Cavalese. He is believed to have spent some time in Venice after this, and to have copied the work of Nicola Grassi (1682–1754). After a short period in Klausen (now Chiusa, Italy) where the *Apostles* in the church of the Twelve Apostles are attributed to him, he was granted citizenship of Bozen (now Bolzano, Italy) in 1726; he painted the

Michael Angelo Unterberger: *Fall of the Rebel Angels*, oil on canvas, 7.0×3.5 m, 1752 (Vienna, Michaelerkirche)

Judgement of Solomon (Bolzano, Mus. Civ.) for the town hall. Around 1730 he worked in Upper Austria near the Inn, and in Passau, where he is known to have created several works for the convent of St Nikola. Among the few works from this period that have survived are the *Baptism* in the monastery church at Vornbach, the altarpiece depicting the *Holy Family* in the Kurhauskapelle at Schärding, the *Martyrdom of St Maurice* (1732) in the parish church at Aurolzmünster and the *Holy Family* and *St Leonard* in the parish church of St Florian am Inn.

Around 1737 Michael Angelo Unterberger moved to Vienna; in 1738 he won first prize for painting at the Akademie der Bildenden Künste, with the *Dismissal of Hagar*. His early works had shown the influence of local artists from the Tyrol and upper Italy, with a certain academicism in composition and painting method, as in the *Judgement of Solomon*. His study at the Akademie in Vienna developed his figure painting and composition along more classical lines, but his works are almost all marked by a warm, full Baroque colourfulness. In the 1740s and 1750s he worked successfully in and around Vienna. He received several commissions from the Jesuits, including paintings for St Leopold in Wiener Neustadt, the altarpiece of *Ignatius* (*c.* 1752) in the Jesuit church of Stuhlweissberg (now Székesfehervár, Hungary) and the *Baptism* (*c.* 1754) for Marosvásárhely in Transylvania (now Tirgu Mures, Romania). He also produced an altarpiece of *St Anthony* for the Stephansdom in Vienna (now Vienna, Dom- & Diözmus.), a *St Sebastian* for the Neu-klosterkirche in the Wiener Neustadt and the *Virgin of the Rosary* altarpiece for the Chiesa dei Dominicani in Bozen, which has been in the Chiesa dell'Assunta, Kaltern (now Caldaro, Italy) since 1785. In 1752 he painted the *Death of the Virgin* for Bressanone Cathedral, his most important early commission, and a work that shows his creative powers at their height. He incorporated a number of different motifs, some his own and some borrowed, to create a unified and expressive work.

Unterberger's election as Rector of the Akademie in Vienna in 1751 was confirmation of his artistic standing. He held this position twice: after Paul Troger's term as Rector he was entrusted with the office again in 1757. The fame this brought him also attracted a number of prestigious commissions, such as the former altarpiece in the Michaelerkirche in Vienna depicting the *Fall of the Rebel Angels* (see fig.) and the *Assumption of the Virgin* (*c.* 1751–2) for the parish church at Postoloprty, Bohemia [now in Czech Republic]. The *Fall of the Rebel Angels* shows his distinctive manner, with its repetition and variation of compositional patterns, at its maturest. Although Michael Angelo Unterberger specialized in religious paintings, he also produced a few secular works, including the *Four Seasons* (Vienna, Ksthist. Mus.) and overdoors on allegorical themes for the Schloss Schönbrunn in Vienna.

BIBLIOGRAPHY

J. Ringler: 'Michelangelo Unterberger: Zu seinem 200. Todestag', *Schlern: Illus. Mhft. Heimat- & Vlksknd.*, xxxiii (1958), pp. 372–83
J. Kronbichler: *Michael Angelo Unterberger (1695–1758)* (diss., U. Vienna, 1976)
——: 'Die Zeichnungen Michael Angelo Unterbergers', *Veröff. Tirol. Landesmus. Ferdinandeum*, lx (1980), pp. 107–53
K. Garas: 'Unbekannte Werke Michelangelo Unterbergers', *Festschrift Kurt Rossacher* (Salzburg, 1983)
J. Kronbichler: 'Die Engelsturz-Darstellungen im Werk von Michael Angelo Unterberger', *Schlern: Illus. Mhft. Heimat- & Vlksknd.*, lix (1985), pp. 395–42

(2) Franz Sebald [Francesco Sebaldo] **Unterberger** (*b* Cavalese, 1 Aug 1706; *d* Cavalese, 23 Jan 1776). Painter, brother of (1) Michael Angelo Unterberger. He probably received his first painting lessons from Michael Angelo and spent some time in Venice, where he became familiar with the works of Giambattista Pittoni. Local Tyrolean painters such as Stephan Kessler I, Ulrich Glantschnigg and Matthias Pussjäger (1654–1734) also influenced his style of painting and composition. Around 1731 he moved to Brixen (now Bressanone, Italy), where he spent most of his life. Among his earliest works are a cycle of 24 paintings depicting the *Life of St Clare* (1731–3), a *Road to Calvary* and other works for the convent of St Clare in Bressanone. He subsequently fulfilled a large number of commissions, almost all on religious themes, and the majority within the Tyrol and Trentino area. He worked mainly on altarpieces, the most representative being the *Baptism* (1741) in S Michele, Bressanone, the *Virgin of the Rosary* in Bressanone Cathedral, *St Catherine* (1758) in the Chiesa dei Cappuccini, Bressanone, an altarpiece depicting the *Holy Family* (*c.* 1750; Trent, Mus. Dioc.) and the very expressive late work, the *Stoning of St Stephen* (1775–6) in S Stefano, Villanders (now Villandro, Italy).

The characteristics of Franz Sebald Unterberger's painting style were already formed when he painted the *Life of St Clare* and showed only minor modifications during the next four decades. His method of painting was spontaneous and flowing, particularly when depicting drapery, decorative details and occasional glimpses of landscape. He also borrowed directly from works by his brother Michael Angelo Unterberger, for example in the *Baptism* (1741), and from Paul Troger (e.g. the *Stoning of St Stephen*).

BIBLIOGRAPHY

Ausstellung Franz Unterberger in Brixen (exh. cat. by K. Wolfsgruber, Bressanone, Mus. Dioc., 1953)

N. Rasmo: *Francesco Unterberger, Pittore, 1706–1776* (Cavalese, 1977)

J. Kronbichler: 'Beiträge zu Franz Sebald Unterberger', *Schlern: Illus. Mhft. Heimat- & Vlksknd.*, lii (1978), pp. 651–63

JOHANN KRONBICHLER

(3) Christoph [Cristoforo] **Unterberger** (*b* Cavalese, 27 May 1732; *d* Rome, 25 Jan 1798). Painter, nephew of (1) Michael Angelo Unterberger and (2) Franz Sebald Unterberger. He studied first in Brixen (now Bressanone, Italy) with Franz Sebald Unterberger, and *c.* 1750 he went to Vienna to work under Michael Angelo Unterberger. In 1754 he won first prize at the Akademie der Bildenden Künste in Vienna and became a member. He then moved to Venice and later to Verona, where he attended the school of Giambettino Cignaroli. In 1758 he settled permanently in Rome, with visits to Cavalese in 1769 and 1796. He lived in the same house as various other artists, including Friedrich Anders (*b c.* 1734, *fl* 1797–1816), Martin Knoller and Nicolas Mosmann (1727–87). In 1772 he was made a member of the Accademia di S Luca, then presided over by Anton Raphael Mengs, and in 1775 he married Ottavia della Valle, the daughter of the sculptor Filippo della Valle, and so became the brother-in-law of the goldsmith Luigi Valadier.

Unterberger sent altarpieces from Rome to Cavalese, a *Transfiguration* (1767) for the cathedral at Bressanone, and for the convent of Novacella in Bressanone, the *Blessed Hartmann* (sketch in Rome, Accad. N. S. Luca) and *St Monica at Prayer at the Side of St Augustine*. His work is particularly well represented at Faenza, in S Andrea (*Visitation* and *St Dominic Guided by the Angels*), S Agostino (the *Flight of the Santa Casa of Loreto*), the church of the Suffragio (the *Sermon of St Anthony at Ezzelino*) and in the chapel of the hospital (the *Virgin Appearing to St James the Apostle and to St John of God*). During this period his style was close to those of Stefano Pozzi, Nicole Lapiccolas and Agostino Masucci.

Christoph Unterberger was in the service of the Apostolic Camera from 1772 to 1780. He decorated the Museo Pio-Clementino: the Sala dei Papiri in 1773 (in collaboration with Mengs), the Galleria delle Statue in 1772 and 1780 and the Atrio del Torso in 1776 (sketches in Montefortino, Pin. Com. and Worcester, MA, A. Mus.). He also worked in the papal palaces: in the Quirinale (these frescoes have since been lost), in the Vatican (restoration work in the Sala di Costantino and in the Sale dei Paramenti) and in Castel Gandolfo in 1774, where he and the painter Giovanni Angeloni (1725–95) decorated the billiard-room. Christoph Unterberger collaborated on a life-size copy in encaustic (St Petersburg, Hermitage) of Raphael's Loggia, working from 1778 to 1788 with Angeloni and his son Vincenzo Angeloni (1752–1815), his pupils Wenzel Peter (1745–1829) and Felice Giani, and with Andreas Nesselthaler (1748–1821), Giovanni Campovecchio (1754–1804), Giovanni Battista dell'Era (1765–98) and Giuseppe Cades.

Unterberger produced decorative paintings for houses belonging to Prince Marcantonio Borghese IV, such as *Apollo and the Pythian Priestess* (1784; destr.; sketch, London, Sir Brinsley Ford priv. col.), and he designed the seahorse fountain in the gardens of the Villa Borghese in 1791 (sculpted by Vincenzo Pacetti). He also drew the plans for the temples of Aesculapius (1785) and of Antoninus and Faustina (1792), both of which were built by the architect Antonio Asprucci. After Mengs's death, Unterberger was supplanted by Bernardino Nocchi, and he ceased to receive major commissions from Pius VI, apart from carrying out additions to his frescoes in the Museo Pio-Clementino (1787) and producing designs for the bronze tables for the Vatican Library (1789). He returned to executing altarpieces, with a prolific output, for example the *Institution of the Eucharist* (1782; Iesi Cathedral), *St Julian* (1786; Macerata Cathedral), *SS Philip Neri and Ignatius Loyola* (mosaic, Loreto, Basilica; sketch, Montefortino, Pin. Com.), the *Crucifixion of St Andrew* (1788; Subiaco, S Andrea), the *Assumption* (Gallese Collegiata; sketch, Montefortino, Pin. Com.) and *St Crescentino and the Blessed Mainard* (1792; Urbino Cathedral; sketch, Urbino, Mus. Duomo). In 1793 he painted *Apollo Entrusting Aesculapius to Cheiron* for the Sala dei Specchi at the Altieri Palace, Rome. Unterberger's style had developed both under Mengs's influence and due to contact with Domenico Corvi, and he may also have been influenced by Giuseppe Cades; like them, he was a member of the first generation of Roman Neo-classical artists. His pupils included Giuseppe Turchi (1759–99) and Luigi Gismondi (1759–1830). His son Giuseppe Unterberger (1776–1846) was also a painter.

BIBLIOGRAPHY

O. Michel: 'Peintres autrichiens à Rome dans la seconde moitié du XVIIIème siècle: 2, Christoph Unterberger', *Röm. Hist. Mitt.*, xiv (1972), pp. 175–98

C. Pietrangeli: *I Musei Vaticani: Cinque secoli di storia* (Rome, 1985)

E. Mich: 'Introduzione ai disegni di Cristoforo Unterberger', *Scritti in onore di Nicolo Rasmo* (Bolzano, 1986), pp. 355–96

OLIVIER MICHEL

(4) Ignaz [Ignazio] **Unterberger** (*b* Cavalese, 24 July ?1742; *d* Vienna, 4 Dec 1797). Painter and engraver, brother of (3) Christoph Unterberger. He trained with Franz Sebald in Brixen (now Bressanone, Italy) and then with Christoph in Rome, where he was influenced by the circle of artists surrounding Anton Raphael Mengs and where he acquired a comprehensive education in the spirit of the Enlightenment. The works of Correggio served as his main model and inspiration. Around 1776 he went to Vienna, where he worked mainly for the nobility; Prince

Wenzel Anton Kaunitz-Rietburg was one of his main patrons. Ignaz was appointed court painter to Emperor Francis II after the Emperor bought *Hebe and the Eagle of Jupiter* for his private art collection. This work typifies Unterberger's style, with its classical, academic method of painting and unusual lighting effects, with clearly differentiated gradations from light to dark areas.

As well as paintings on biblical, historical and mythological subjects, Unterberger produced altarpieces, the most famous of which are the *Miracle of Pentecost* for the cathedral in Königgratz (now Hradec Králové, Czech Republic) and the *Virgin of the Snows Supported by Angels* in the Minoritenkirche in Vienna. He was also a successful portrait painter to the Viennese aristocracy, producing portraits of *Privy Counsellor Franz Georg von Kees*, *Graf Gottfried von Heister* and *Franz Xaver Alexander von Stettner*, among others. Unterberger also worked as an engraver and made several portraits in mezzotint, including an idealized portrayal of *Prince Wenzel Anton Kaunitz-Rietburg*. A versatile artist, he also invented several machines, including one for engraving copper plates.

BIBLIOGRAPHY

BLKO; Thieme–Becker
N. Rasmo: 'Intorno a tre quadri di Ignazio Unterberger', *Trentino*, xiii (1935)
E. Baum: *Katalog des Österreichischen Barockmuseums im Unteren Belvedere in Wien*, ii (Vienna and Munich, 1980), pp. 728–30

JOHANN KRONBICHLER

Unteutsch, Friedrich (*b* Berlin, *c*. 1600; *d* Frankfurt am Main, 1670). German designer and cabinetmaker. He was the son of the gunsmith Hans Unteutsch. After nine years as a journeyman, in 1628 he settled in Frankfurt am Main, where he became a master and cabinetmaker to the city in 1631. He also passed a gunsmith's examination. Between 1635 and 1640 he received several commissions for church pulpits and for furniture from the municipality. Of his many documented works, only the pulpit of the Protestant church in Frankfurt-Oberrad has survived, although lacking its characteristic decoration. Unteutsch also produced a celebrated two-part book of ornament, the *Zieratenbuch*, published in Nuremberg by Paulus Fürst (*fl* 1630–75), possibly in several editions. As Unteutsch described the book as the product of a life's work, it can be dated between 1635 and 1670, but on the basis of style the designs can be dated to *c*. 1640. Unteutsch's designs not only show the Auricular style at the peak of its development but are the most comprehensive series of their kind. Although Unteutsch's work takes its title from the *Neue Zierat Büchlein* (1627) by the painter Nikolaus Rosman (*fl* Magdeburg and Halle *c*. 1650–75), its content and scope are closer to Rutger Kassmann's *Architectur nach antiquitetischer Lehr und geometrischer Ausstheylung* (1630). Unteutsch's *Zieratenbuch* may, thus, be seen as a logical continuation of the tradition of 'Architecturae' inspired by Hans Blum.

For illustration of furniture *see* GERMANY, fig. 46.

BIBLIOGRAPHY

Thieme–Becker
W. K. Zülch: *Entstehung des Ohrmuschelstiles*, Heidelberg. Kstgesch. Abh., xii (Heidelberg, 1932), pp. 115–23
E. Forssman: *Säule und Ornament: Studien zum Problem des Manierismus in den nordischen Säulenbüchern und Vorlageblättern des 16. und 17.*
Jahrhunderts, Acta Universitatis Stockholmiensis (Stockholm, 1956), i, pp. 198ff
R. Zöllner: *Deutsche Säulen-, Zieraten- und Schildbücher, 1610 bis 1680: Ein Beitrag zur Entwicklungsgeschichte des Knorpelwerkstils* (diss., U. Kiel, 1959), pp. 92–106
A.-M. von Graevenitz: *Das niederländische Ohrmuschel-Ornament: Phänomen und Entwicklung dargestellt an den Werken und Entwürfen der Goldschmiedefamilien van Vianen und Lutma* (diss., U. Munich, 1971, Bamberg, 1973), pp. 74, 84ff, 219, 256, 259

JÜRGEN ZIMMER

Unwin, Sir **Raymond**. *See under* PARKER & UNWIN.

Upbargen, Antonis van. *See* OBBERGHEN, ANTONIS VAN.

Updike, Daniel Berkeley (*b* Providence, RI, 1860; *d* Boston, MA, 1941). American typographer, printer and graphic designer. He was advertising manager and layout artist at the publishing house of Houghton, Mifflin & Co. before transferring to the firm's printing works at the Riverside Press, where he worked until 1892. Updike's first freelance commission, the design of a *Book of Common Prayer* (1892) was well received, and in 1893 he set up his own studio, initially with the idea of designing types but then as a printing press, the Merrymount Press. He commissioned a new type called Merrymount from Bertram Goodhue for use on a new *Episcopalian Altar Book* (Boston, 1896). Between 1893 and 1896 Updike produced *c*. 18 books before turning to printing them himself, assisted by John Bianchi (*fl* 1893–1947), his first typesetter and later his partner. The Merrymount Press undertook a wide range of work for publishers, book clubs, libraries, churches and institutions. In 1896 Updike purchased the Caslon face for use at the press; in 1904 Herbert Horne designed Montallegro for him; other types employed included Scotch Roman, Janson, Mountjoye and Oxford; Updike was the first American to use Times New Roman. In 1899 the Merrymount was firmly established by a commission to print Edith Wharton's novels for the publisher Charles Scribner & Sons; however, much of Updike's work was for the private collectors' market and limited-editions clubs. His finest work is thought to be the *Book of Common Prayer* (Boston, 1930), financed by J. Pierpont Morgan and begun in 1928, for which he employed Janson type. His *Printing Types* was first published by Harvard University Press in 1922 and was based on lectures that he had given at the University (1911–16). At his own estimate Updike produced *c*. 14,000 pieces of printing.

WRITINGS

Printing Types: Their History, Forms and Use, 2 vols (Cambridge, MA, 1922)

BIBLIOGRAPHY

The Work of the Merrymount Press and its Founder, Daniel Berkeley Updike (1860–1941) (exh. cat., San Marino, CA, Huntingdon Lib. & A.G., 1942)
K. Day, ed.: *Book Typography, 1815–1965, in Europe and the USA* (London, 1966)
J. Blumenthal: *The Printed Book in America* (Dartmouth, NH, 1989)

LAURA SUFFIELD

Upholstery. Application of textiles to the decoration and furniture of a room. This has traditionally included the provision of all those components of a room that rely principally on textiles or leather for their visual effect. In the 20th century it has come to mean more specifically the stuffing of seat furniture and its covering with textiles. In the ancient world, upholstery appears to have been confined to loose but often highly decorated mattresses, coverlets, cushions and curtains, usually of textiles but sometimes of leather. This article deals with Western aspects of upholstery, from the Middle Ages onwards. Further information on upholstery can be found in this dictionary within country and civilization surveys under the headings 'Interior decoration', 'Furniture', 'Textiles' and 'Other arts'.

For colour plates for this article *see* vol. 30.

I. Introduction. II. History and development. III. Conservation.

I. Introduction.

The heyday of the upholsterer lasted roughly from 1670 to 1890. As his work could transform completely the appearance of a room, the upholsterer gradually also undertook to provide all the furnishings that a room could require, even those that were not primarily textile-based. He played an important role in the dissemination of fashionable styles and eventually came to occupy the position enjoyed by the modern interior decorator, although his social station was undoubtedly less exalted. His work also impinged on that of the architect, who required the upholsterer's services to 'dress' a new room. Here the upholsterer could enhance the architect's spatial creation, or he could spoil it if he were not working in sympathy with the latter's intentions. Moreover, while architects might be called on to extend or alter the fabric of an important residential building perhaps two or three times in a century at most, an upholsterer might be brought in to change the décor of a room much more frequently and, in doing so, could make the basic structure of the room unrecognizable.

The upholsterer's ability to work this miracle—and the creations of the best upholsterers could possess real artistic merit—meant that the leading practitioners acquired such a reputation that clients were prepared to pay enormous sums for the sometimes impressive, often delightful and not infrequently glamorous confections that these craftsmen–entrepreneurs were able to provide. Although it was far more ephemeral, the work of the leading upholsterers of the 17th and 18th centuries deserves similar attention to that of contemporary cabinetmakers. Indeed, it made a far greater impact visually because it was in greater evidence. Their work occupied much more space, it was invariably colourful, and the materials of which it was composed were often of great beauty and very costly. Unfortunately, however, upholstery suffers too readily from fading, wear and grime, and unless carefully protected it soon becomes shabby and is then removed. Until the early 20th century it would be replaced with something of equal richness but in the current fashion. More recently, however, replacements, if any, have generally been meaner, chiefly as a consequence of a change in taste away from rich effects in the mid-20th century.

The ephemeral nature of upholstery has resulted in its having been largely ignored by historians of the decorative arts, who have tended to concentrate on what can be acquired in good condition by collectors, rather than on

the range of what was created in the past. Only in the second half of the 20th century has the growing interest in the details of interior decoration of the past led to a reappraisal of the importance of the upholsterer and his achievements. All too often the only surviving evidence for his work is contemporary visual material and descriptions and the documentary evidence of the enormous bills.

II. History and development.

1. Before 1670. 2. 1670–1800. 3. After 1800.

1. BEFORE 1670. In important households, from early medieval times, it must have fallen on certain servants to be responsible for contriving comfortable domestic arrangements using textiles. Eventually, a senior officer of such households was put in charge of these arrangements, with staff below him. In Boccaccio's *Decameron* (written *c.* 1350), a household official called a *siniscalco* was required to rig up a pleasant ambience in which the storytellers could relate their tales. The title of the official changed over the centuries, but his duties remained much the same.

Until modern times upholstery was rarely left hanging or otherwise exposed day after day. It was either protected with loose covers or removed entirely and stored in a 'wardrobe'. (It. *guardaroba*; Fr. *gardemeuble*), which could be a large room with presses or cupboards for storage and tables at which the specialist wardrobe staff could brush or repair existing items or make up new ones. Such establishments, which became important in the 16th and 17th centuries, were to be found in most households of standing. Later some upholsterers set up as independent suppliers in the principal cities, and it became common, by the second half of the 17th century, even for monarchs to order upholstery work from such tradesmen. In 1660, for example, Charles II appointed to the office of King's Upholsterer the London tradesman Robert Morris, who supplied the court with over £10,000 worth of carpets, chairs, couches and beds over a period of 21 months.

If not working to the dictates of an architect, an upholsterer would call on his customers to measure up the site, might advise on matters of style and taste, and was then prepared to provide whatever was needed to furnish the room concerned.

The furnishings used by the seigneurial classes during the Middle Ages were of necessity portable, as an entire household and most of its possessions would often move from one residence to another, sometimes at short notice. Chairs that folded (*see* CHAIR, §3) were useful under such a regime, as was tapestry (*see* TAPESTRY, §II), which was a decorative and very robust material that could withstand much putting up and taking down. These two types of furnishings later came to symbolize seigneurial or princely status in the 16th century, to the extent that updated versions of folding chairs, such as the X-frame chair, and of tapestries were retained in use long after the practical need for such things had ceased, as the upper classes came increasingly to lead a more static life. Once wall hangings remained in position for months on end, the practical characteristics of tapestry no longer mattered, and there were many other materials, such as velvet, silk damask, brocatelle and several sorts of fine woollen cloth, that were at least as pleasing and did not need to be as robust, as they were not removed once hung in place.

During the late medieval period attention began to be paid to the padding of important pieces of seat furniture, to make them more comfortable for the most exalted ranks of society. Primitive stuffed upholstery was very simple. A heap of some yielding material, such as carded wool or wool flock, was placed on a stout canvas base stretched across the seat-frame; the heap was then kept in place by a second piece of material laid over it and nailed as tightly as possible to the four outer edges of the frame. This produced a domed seat, but the stuffing, being unsecured except by such pressure as the top cover exerted, tended to shift around and lose its shape and resilience. The challenge for makers of upholstered seat furniture lay in getting the stuffing to remain in place and retain its shape, and it is not surprising, therefore, to find indications that early seat upholstery was often made by saddlers who knew how to fix padding so that it stayed in place. A saddler (calling himself *selaro* in his bill) was involved in the making of a chair at Ferrara in 1531, according to the ducal accounts, and a court saddler provided Charles X, King of Sweden (*reg* 1654–60), with some stuffed chairs in 1654. Gradually upholsterers learnt to secure padding more effectively, first with quilting, a type of regular stitching in parallel lines right across the seat or back (backs began to be padded on a few extremely comfortable chairs in the late 16th century) and, later, by introducing 'brides', which were bold stitches inserted where needed, executed with strong twine that linked tightly the base canvas and the cover, thus locking the padding in place. An invalid-chair made in the 1590s for Philip II of Spain, known from a contemporary drawing, was padded with quilted horsehair. During this early phase the wooden members of seat furniture (the arms, their supports and sometimes their legs) were often close-covered with the same material as that covering the padded seat. This close-covering was apparently secured with nails for decorative reasons, but was actually glued to the wooden surface. Because coffer-makers also commonly covered the chests they produced with leather (*see* LEATHER, §3(ii)), velvet and other textile materials, these craftsmen dressed chairs in this manner in the late 16th century, certainly in England but probably elsewhere as well. However, by the time of James I, King of England, purveyors of stuffed seat furniture were often calling themselves 'upholsterers' or 'upholders'.

The Renaissance expectation that the decorative elements of a room should present a unified appearance could be achieved architecturally, but that unity was then easily spoilt if the furnishings that were subsequently introduced did not in themselves match in colour, style and ornament. The upholsterer could play an exceedingly important role in imparting a sense of unity to a room. Although decorative wooden furniture had been made in matching suites already in the 1460s, it was not until about 1570 that unified suites of upholstery became a familiar sight in Italy, then still the leading country in terms of interior decoration. An inventory of Ingatestone Hall, Essex, taken in 1600, indicates that even where chairs were not actually made to match each other, they were at least upholstered *en suite*. Unified schemes achieved by the use of textiles became the norm during the Baroque period all over Europe, as can be seen in the Queen's

Closet (*c.* 1670) at Ham House, Surrey, where the crimson and gold upholstery of the seat furniture matches the wall hangings.

2. 1670–1800.

(i) Beds. (ii) Curtains. (iii) Seat furniture.

(i) Beds. The most important piece of furniture in a great 17th-century house was the formal BED, which stood in the main bedchamber. Monarchs and great lords felt obliged to place a splendid state bed in the principal bedchamber of the house, as a symbol of their authority. Lesser mortals had beds that were correspondingly less imposing, but were still intended to remind visitors that their hosts too were people of standing. In this connection, it is of course important to note that, in former times, visitors of a respectable social standing were commonly shown the rooms in a principal apartment, including the main bedchamber, which therefore acquired an almost public character. Even the most modest of these huge beds was an extremely costly item. They were tall structures requiring a vast yardage of expensive material for the curtains, valances (or pelmets), tester, headboard and coverlet. Every component had to be lined (again, with an expensive material, as the lining was often displayed), and many of the components required stiffening. Every component, moreover, was embellished with trimmings (*see* PASSEMENTERIE) of various kinds (silk or gold lace, for example, as well as fringe, tassels, cords and braid), all of which were made of costly materials. Indeed, the greatest talents of the upholsterer went into making these enormous edifices, which, during the Baroque period, appeared to be made entirely of textiles and heavy trimmings: no part of the wooden structure was visible once the bed had been dressed. Contemporary bills show that the difference in value between the upholstery and the bed frame was considerable. A bill submitted to the Great Wardrobe in London by Francis Lapiere (1653–1714) in 1699 for two beds indicates that, with similar frames, one bed cost £134 7s. 6d., while the other, with extremely lavish hangings and six matching walnut chairs, came to £630 5s. 9d. One of the finest complete Baroque beds still in existence is the Melville state bed (London, V&A), which dates from *c.* 1690 and is over 5 m high.

Increasingly in the 17th century the curtains of beds and canopies (which were rather like beds without the sleeping surface and were suspended over thrones and other seats of honour) might be hitched up, tied back, draped or decorated with bunched or gathered pieces of material to produce wildly flamboyant effects, which were then often echoed in the decoration of the wall hangings of the room (see fig. 1) and, from the 1680s, of window-curtains, after these had become common from about 1670. The valances of bed-testers were frequently cut with fancy profiles (tongues, lappets, scrolling shapes) to their lower edges and were particularly richly ornamented, since they occupied the most eye-catching position when viewed by a visitor advancing into the bedchamber. The most elaborate confections of this type were produced during the last quarter of the 17th century; two beds (see fig. 2) made in the early 1670s for Louis XIV and his mistress to stand in the Trianon de Porcelaine (destr.) at Versailles

1. State bedchamber designed by Daniel Marot the elder; engraving from his *Second Livre Dappartement* (The Hague, 1703)

were among the earliest manifestations of this riotous form of decoration, which required prodigious amounts of very costly material.

The state bed was almost invariably the most expensive piece of furniture in the house, and there might be two or even three important beds in the building, one for each principal apartment. It is not surprising, therefore, that the makers of such costly and impressive objects, which were designed to occupy a focal point in an important building, should themselves have acquired a high standing among the purveyors of luxury goods during the time when the state bed was an essential adjunct to courtly life or life among the rich, from the mid-16th century until about 1770. The lack of interest in the history of upholstery until the late 20th century explains why the names of such masters of their craft as Delobel (who served Louis XIV) and Francis Lapiere (who served William III) are unfamiliar compared with those of such cabinetmakers as André Charles Boulle, John Cobb, Jean-Henri Riesener and George Bullock, whose furniture is today so highly regarded and valuable. It should be added that, in 18th- and 19th-century England, many cabinetmakers, such as Thomas Chippendale (i) and Gillow, could also undertake upholstery work in all its branches. One of the best-known English upholsterers during the 18th century was THOMAS K. BROMWICH, whose trade card of 1748 indicates how wide the definition of upholsterer had become by that date.

(ii) Curtains. Curtains were very rarely fitted to windows before 1600 and were at first purely utilitarian fittings, installed to exclude strong sunlight. Draughts were excluded by wooden shutters or, in bedrooms, by furnishing the bed itself with warm curtains. Indeed, so utilitarian were early window-curtains that no attempt seems to have been made to make them look attractive until after the middle of the 17th century, when the divided form—a pair of curtains to each window—was introduced for the sake of symmetry and balance. But even when the main curtains were divided, it was long common to fit a single subsidiary sun-curtain within, leaving this to be pulled to one side when open, thus destroying the symmetry.

The heavily draped style of late 17th-century state beds was echoed in the pelmets of window-curtains, perhaps as early as the 1680s, and the draped character was compounded when a new form of curtain was introduced that could be pulled up towards the pelmet-board by means of cords, instead of being suspended from rings running on horizontal rods and pulled to the sides. Several variants were devised, but the general impression of such curtains, when pulled up, was of billowing festoons. Apart from suiting the taste of the times, the pull-up or festoon curtain served a practical purpose. It was the habit to place candlestands on either side of pier-tables standing between the windows of grand rooms at this period. It would have been easy to knock over such a stand, and particularly dangerous if it was bearing a lighted candelabrum, when pulling a curtain sideways. Pull-up curtains obviated this

2. Elaborately draped bed in the Chambre des Amours, Trianon de Porcelaine, Versailles, installed 1672; pencil drawing by Nicodemus Tessin the younger, 1677–80 (Stockholm, Nationalmuseum)

particular risk, but they had the disadvantage that they somewhat obscured the upper part of the window. Houses built in the expectation that such curtains would be fitted therefore tend to have taller windows than those designed with divided curtains pulling sideways in mind.

(iii) Seat furniture. In the late 17th century there were great advances in the stuffing of seat furniture, especially in France. For rather more than a century until about 1785, two traditions, the French and the English, ran in parallel, using different upholstery techniques on chair-frames of quite different shapes and producing chairs of very different appearance. After that the two traditions merged, and seat furniture in the two countries came to look very much alike. Other nations followed one or other of the two traditions right through the period of schism.

Materials of many kinds have been used for stuffing the seats and backs of chairs, the requirements being that they should offer a soft or springy seat that remained in position and retained its shape under constant use. Particularly useful in this respect is curled horsehair, which is springy and readily available. While yielding to pressure it springs back into shape once the pressure is removed. Saddlers had known of its properties for a long while.

It was probably in the construction of invalid-chairs that most of the advances in contriving comfortable seating were first made. It is unlikely that there were standard models of such chairs. They were made for wealthy people who became invalids and could afford to buy the comforts that such a piece of furniture offered. Accommodating seats and backs were the first requirement. Adjustable backs and leg-supports came second. Casters, so that the chair could be moved, came third: they were an option about which few people then knew. In some places the less affluent had invalid-chairs of wicker with a large hooded back. Such seats tended to be used in the bedchamber in front of the fire, and this was where 'easy-chairs', which derived from the invalid-chair, were also originally placed. Related to these are sleeping-chairs, of which a pair of English examples of the 1670s survives at Ham House, Surrey (*see* ENGLAND, fig. 50). By using down for the top layer of the stuffing, especially for the seat (which often took the form of a fat cushion resting in a padded well between the arms), a supremely comfortable piece of seat furniture was evolved, but it was intended for informal relaxation, not for show in presentation rooms. Thus the Ham House sleeping-chairs were placed in a private room, the Queen's Closet, rather than in one of the more public rooms.

The Parisian easy-chair (*fauteuil de commodité*) of the late 17th century has probably never been bettered as a seat in terms of bodily comfort. A painting by Jean-François de Troy (see colour pl. XIV, fig. 1) shows a particularly low-slung variant of the French *fauteuil*, showing the domed effect of French stuffing. The characteristics of the easy chair were later extended sideways, as it were, to form the SOFA or *canapé*, which sometimes actually had two backs, set side by side, recalling its origins in the single-back conformation. Sofas, too, must have formed part of private and informal rooms, where one could take advantage of such relaxed comfort. Lolling about in the manner depicted by de Troy would never have been considered polite in rooms of parade.

Chairs for rooms of this more formal type had quite a different character at the end of the 17th century. They were members of the main line of development where the seat was upholstered and there was a back-support that was padded; there was no fully upholstered back, as on the invalid-chair and its voluptuous derivatives. These more formal chairs were much more sparsely treated. Until about 1670 arms were often close-covered along with the rest of the woodwork, but later armchairs had bare, polished wooden arms. Much use was made of trimming or *passementerie* on grand chairs of this class. One could alter the proportions of a chair very considerably by attaching a deep fringe around the edges of the stuffed seat, or by continuing down a flap of the seat-covering to produce a similar effect. Such chairs usually came in sets, which included armless versions that were *en suite* in every way except that they were usually slightly narrower.

French chairs of this principal class became increasingly comfortable, both in the armed and armless versions, and the mid-18th century form, with its sinuously carved frame and its, by then, well-padded seat and back-support (the two elements were still not united at this stage in France), was one of the most comfortable types of chair ever devised for general use. The English equivalent was far less comfortable: it had a harder seat and often no padding at all in the back, which was commonly decorated with openwork carving. A technique that seems to have been developed in England concerned the production of a rigid and square vertical edge to seats and backs by means of tightly stitching a roll of horsehair running along an edge so as to compact it into rigidity. This was needed on English chairs, which, already in the 1740s, had squared forms—at a time when French seats were all domed and yieldingly round without any vertical border. A design by John Linnell (see fig. 3) shows the characteristic English square-edged seat with shallow tufting. Later, after the introduction of Neo-classical forms, French chairs also needed squared edges, and the French quickly adopted the same technique. The silhouette of chairs was largely formed by the outline of their upholstery, which is why it became a matter of importance to get the lineaments right. The elegance of a chair could depend very much on the skill of the upholsterer.

The 18th century was more a period of general refining of known techniques than a time when totally new methods were introduced. There was a certain amount of experimenting with springs and even with inflatable cushions, but this met with little success. One of the daughters of Louis XV insisted that she would certainly not want to retire to a convent, as her sister had just done, because it would mean giving up her sprung easy chair. It is not known what this chair was like, and it was presumably a one-off production by the royal upholsterer in Paris.

3. AFTER 1800. Upholstery reached the height of perfection in the 19th century, in terms of technique and what could be achieved. Never had such ambitious schemes been undertaken and never was the precision of the work so great. The apogee was reached between about 1860 and 1880. Although the upholsterer's creations of that period now seem unattractive or worse, the brilliance of the workmanship must be acknowledged. It is worth noting this because it is widely believed that 17th- and 18th-century upholstery was of far higher quality than that of the 19th century. The opposite is true. Indeed, 17th-century upholstery was technically really very crude, and the same is also true of upholstery produced in the 18th century, at least before about 1770. This refers, of course, to high-class upholstery, for upholstery of poor quality has been carried out at all periods, and a great deal of shoddy work was produced in the 19th century because furniture production overall was so much less exclusive than in earlier centuries. What is true, on the other hand, about 17th- and 18th-century upholstery is that the quality of the textiles was generally far more sumptuous and expensive than it has been more recently, if only because upholstery was then a trade serving almost exclusively the rich. The equivalent level of expenditure in the 19th century could produce comfortable arrangements of the utmost opulence, all executed with finesse and imbued with an assurance that by then rested on a long and substantial tradition (see fig. 4 and colour pl. XVI). This tradition has been maintained, and a modern skilled craftsman, steeped in the Victorian tradition, is inclined when faced with a specimen of high-class 17th-century upholstery, to believe it must be the work of an amateur.

(i) Hangings and draperies. Upholsterers in the mid-19th century invented even more items that required their skills than their predecessors in the 18th century had done. Mantel-shelves might sport a heavily trimmed cover with a pelmet all round, and the fire-opening might in addition be furnished with curtains. Mirrors could have drapery borders, the chains of chandeliers and gasoliers had elaborate sleeves, and some lamps had flounced shades. Doors were fitted with *portières*, again heavily draped, which echoed the no less heavy arrangement of the window-curtains, which were, however, additionally complemented by inner curtains of net or lace. Walls in richly appointed rooms were not merely hung with textiles (more opulent than wallpaper, which was also provided by upholsterers) but might even be quilted (see fig. 5). An infinite variety of seat furniture was evolved, much of it deeply stuffed and heavily trimmed with fringe and sometimes with added drapery as well. Never before had there been an age when textile embellishment could totally dominate a room (see colour pl. XIV, fig. 2). The architecture was often swamped by all this ornament, which, in skilled hands, could be delightful, magnificent or extremely elegant, but which, in the hands of the average upholsterer, all too often presented a confused clutter, where good judgement had not been brought into play and an understanding of the principles of integrated decoration was all

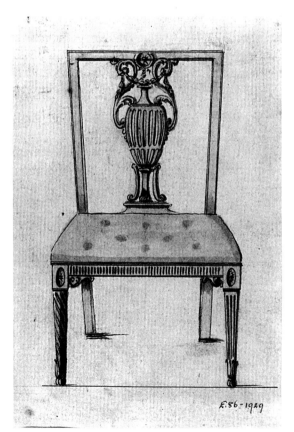

3. Design for a chair by John Linnell, showing square-edged seat and tufting, pencil, pen and wash, with touches of watercolour (London, Victoria and Albert Museum)

4. Design for the Queen of Prussia's bedchamber, Berlin, by Karl Friedrich Schinkel, watercolour, 1810 (Berlin, Verwaltung der Staatlichen Schlösser und Gärten)

too evidently absent. This was to bring about a reaction, which began to manifest itself in the late 1860s, particularly in England (*see* ENGLAND, V, 6), although it was not really until the 1890s that the reformers' recommendations came to be widely adopted. Then the load of ornament, the fussiness of pattern, the heavily draped curtains and the generally suffocating atmosphere of the characteristic High Victorian room yielded to arrangements where the bones were still in place but much of the flesh, or perhaps fat, had been pared away. New and lighter forms of curtain were devised, lighter colours were adopted, and upholstered seating assumed slimmer lines.

(ii) Seat furniture. The highest achievements of the upholsterer in the mid-19th century lay in the stuffing and covering of seat furniture (see colour pl. XV). Stuffing in the 16th century and the early 17th had been so shallow that a quilting technique sufficed to hold it in place (*see* §1 above). As stuffing became deeper in the 18th century, a technique used in mattress-making was adopted. This involved stitching through the padding with a long needle, using strong twine pulled fairly tight, with tufts of twine at each end that prevented the thread under tension pulling through the covering material. This method of securing

the padding could be organized to produce a calculated disposition of tufts in patterns that enhanced the appearance of chair-seats and chair-backs. As the strain put on the thread was not great, the resulting depressions in which the tufts nestled were shallow, and no additional yardage of covering material was needed to accommodate the distortion. When the stuffing grew thicker from the 1830s and the strain on the thread became greater, however, the depression in consequence became deeper, and much ingenuity, and some mathematics, had to be devoted to cutting the cover with ample spare material to take into the folds that were thus generated (these were commonly organized to form a diamond pattern; see fig. 4). As the strain on the tufts increased, moreover, it was found necessary to replace them with rigid buttons. Stuffing that is buttoned is nevertheless still called *capitonné* in French, a reminder that this technique had formerly involved the use of a tuft (or *capiton*) of material.

The depth of the padding and the strain on the buttoning increased greatly when effective upholstery springs were introduced. This occurred in the second quarter of the 19th century even though successful experiments were carried out around 1820. The breakthrough occurred when the double-cone form of spiral spring was adopted, but it

5. Design for a boudoir in Paris; from V. Quetin: *Le Magazin de meubles* (Paris, 1865–7)

took time to devise ways of lashing the cones with twine to anchor them and control their movement. All this was perfected by about 1850.

Spiral springs work in compression. Tension springs, adopted in the 1930s from metal-framed bed-springing, work horizontally (deflected slightly downwards when a sitter's weight presses down on the seat). Rubber webbing, laminated with rayon that limited the stretch, was introduced in the 1940s and worked on the same principle. These methods ushered in a new phase in the history of seat-upholstery. Perhaps of even greater significance was the introduction of rubber latex foam in the 1930s and polyurethane foam in the 1950s, both produced in moulds. As these moulds were in themselves expensive, so moulded latex or polyurethane cushions and seats were most economically manufactured in long production runs. This made the method too costly for small batches and custom-built furniture; its greatest successes were to be seen in contract seating, for cinemas, railways, aircraft and motor cars. It should be noted that some of the greatest advances in comfortable seating technology have been made by the motor industry.

Traditional methods, however, continued to be used everywhere, especially for domestic seating of high quality. Sometimes, especially in the late 20th century, old techniques have been combined with modern materials, notably with foam fillings that can be of different qualities, some possessing more resilience than others. While these developments in technology were taking place, the traditional upholsterer frequently rose to the occasion when new styles demanded new lineaments. For instance, much Parisian Art Deco seat furniture of the 1920s and 1930s

required a slimmer line than furniture of the pre-World War I period had possessed; this was achieved by traditional methods skilfully adapted to the trim elegance of the new style.

III. Conservation.

The study of upholstery is still in its infancy, not having kept pace with the study of other aspects of furniture history. Great advances, however, have been made since the early 1980s. In some quarters the same amount of care is now being taken over the restoration or replacement of old upholstery as over a fine piece of veneered furniture, and much has been learnt about traditional practices and techniques in recent years. The methods of the archaeologist have been applied to the dismantling of surviving old upholstery on chairs and beds, the process often taking as long as its restoration or its replacement. This is in stark contrast to the 'stripping out' of old upholstery by commercial upholsterers, which is usually accomplished in a matter of minutes.

Much has been learnt from this patient dismantling. It has also come to be recognized that some widely accepted methods of repair to old furniture should no longer be used where ancient upholstery is also involved. For example, it is now rather frowned on to fill old nail-holes with glue or similar filling substances, so as to provide a fresh set of nails with a secure ground into which they can be hammered. Conservators have developed a range of what they call 'minimally intrusive' restoration processes, the most striking of which is the fitting of a rigid foam-plastic 'cap' to old seat furniture. Instead of nailing new replacement layers of upholstery on to the old frame, using traditional techniques, the loose 'cap' carefully shaped to the supposed original conformation, is dropped into position on the old seat-frame. The cap is covered with appropriate material so as to present precisely the same contours as the traditionally stuffed seat would have possessed; it can even be given a certain amount of resilient surface-stuffing to make the effect seem less solid and unyielding. Decorative nailing is simulated by affixing nail-heads to the covered surface of the cap. Thus no changes are made to the surviving frame, and all its tell-tale blemishes are retained. Such capped furniture cannot be used, and the method can be applied only to museum objects.

BIBLIOGRAPHY

J.-F. Bimont: *Principes de l'art du tapissier* (Paris, 1770)
H. Havard: *Dictionnaire de l'ameublement et de la décoration*, 4 vols (Paris, 1887–90)
R. Edwards, ed.: *The Dictionary of English Furniture* (London, 1954)
P. Verlet: *Les Meubles français du XVIIe siècle*, i (Paris, 1956, rev. 1982)
H. Lassen: *Sadler og draperier og polstermöblets historie* (Copenhagen, 1960)
E. Stavenow: *Siden, sammet, läder, larft, klädsel på gamla stolar* (Stockholm, 1961, rev. 1993)
The Golden Age of English Furniture Upholstery, 1660–1840 (exh. cat., Leeds, Temple Newsam House, 1973)
J. Fowler and J. Cornforth: *English Decoration in the Eighteenth Century* (London, 1974), pp. 82–173
P. Eames: 'Furniture in England, France and the Netherlands from the Twelfth to the Fifteenth Century', *Furn. Hist.*, viii (1977) [whole issue; see especially sections B and D]
P. Thornton: *Seventeenth Century Interior Decoration in England, France and Holland* (New Haven and London, 1978), chaps IV–VIII
L. White: 'Two English State Beds in the Metropolitan Museum of Art', *Apollo*, cxvi (1982), pp. 84–8
F. Montgomery: *Textiles in America, 1650–1870* (New York, 1984)
P. Thornton: *Authentic Decor: The Domestic Interior, 1620–1920* (London, 1984)
P. Verlet: 'Notes sur quelques tapissiers parisiens du XVIIIe siècle', *Furn. Hist.*, xxi (1985), pp. 19–31
E. Cooke, ed.: *Upholstery in America & Europe from the Seventeenth Century to World War I* (New York, 1987)
A. Westman: 'English Window Curtains in the Eighteenth Century', *Antiques* (June 1990), pp. 1407–17
Upholstery Conservation: Preprints of a Symposium: Colonial Williamsburg, 1990
P. Thornton: *The Italian Renaissance Interior, 1400–1600* (London, 1991)

PETER THORNTON

Uphues, Joseph (Johann Ludwig) (*b* Sassenberg, Westphalia, 23 May 1850; *d* Berlin, 2 Jan 1911). German sculptor. After an apprenticeship as a carpenter and travels (*c.* 1868–70), he took up an apprenticeship as a mason. In 1878 he began to study sculpture at the Königliche Akademische Hochschule für Bildende Künste in Berlin under Reinhold Begas and Fritz Schaper. In 1882 he became Begas's master pupil, and between 1885 and 1890–91 he was his assistant, although he developed his own style and became an extremely successful monumental sculptor.

Uphues's first monument was to *Emperor William I* (1891; Düren), made in the Begas studio. In 1891 he won the commission to produce a monumental bust to *Frederick III* (Bad Homburg, Kurpark). In 1896 he was awarded his first large commission in Berlin, for the group *Margrave Otto II* (1898; Berlin, Lapidarium). He received the title of Professor from Emperor William II for the statue of *Frederick II* (1899; Berlin, Lapidarium).

In 1899 Uphues joined the Berlin Secession, but he was a passive member, and he continued to work on Imperial commissions, such as the Neo-classical monument to *General Moltke* (marble, 1905; Berlin, Grosser Stern) and a monument to *Emperor Frederick III* (1902; Kronberg, Stadtpark). Uphues departed from Begas's style most completely with the statue *Archer* (1884; Melbourne, N.G. Victoria) and the *Sabine Man Defending his Sister* (bronze, 1886; Duren, Stadtpark), an important work he produced while working in Begas's studio. The gravestone for *Heinrich von Stephan* (marble, 1897–9; Berlin, Hallesches Tor cemetery) shows his first use of *Jugendstil* forms, most evident in the later gravestones, such as those for *Philipp Schoeller* and *Anna Schoeller* (Düren, Evangel. Cemetery).

BIBLIOGRAPHY

P. Bloch and W. Grzimek: *Das klassische Berlin: Die Berliner Bildhauerschule im 19. Jahrhundert* (Frankfurt am Main, 1978)
Berliner Kunst von 1770 bis 1930: Studiensammlung Waldemar Grzimek (exh. cat., W. Berlin, Berlin Mus., 1982)
Rheinland Westfalen und die Berliner Bildhauerschule des 19. Jahrhunderts (exh. cat., Bottrop, Mod. Gal.; Cappenberg-Salm, Schloss Cappenberg; 1984)
Von Begas bis Barlach: Bildhauerei im Wilhelminischen Berlin (exh. cat., W. Berlin, Kolbe Mus., 1984)

BRIGITTE HÜFLER

Upjohn. American family of architects of English birth. The principal and best-known member of an architectural dynasty comparable to the Scotts in England, (1) Richard Upjohn, was born in Shaftesbury, Dorset, but enjoyed a successful career in the USA. His most important contribution was Trinity Church, Wall Street, New York (1839–46), which introduced to the USA the phase of the Gothic Revival represented in the work of Pugin and the Ecclesiologists. The most obvious result was the creation of an architecture for the Protestant Episcopal Church in America. The ultimate effect, however, was to dramatize ideas that had played a vital role in American architectural thought since Thomas Jefferson: that the arts have a role in a democracy; that architecture should suit its purpose; that architecture can have a particular psychological impact on the viewer and thus can affect, in a positive way, the morality of the individual and of society.

Richard Upjohn's son (2) Richard Michell Upjohn was also an architect, who perpetuated the Gothic Revival style championed by his father. Richard Michell Upjohn's youngest son, Hobart Upjohn (1876–1949), took up the cause of church architecture, designing Colonial Revival churches especially in the South in the early 20th century. Several other family members of Richard Michell's and Hobart's generations either became Episcopalian priests or had artistic interests in a way that makes the family an embodiment of the 19th-century belief in the moral power of the arts. A member of the fourth generation, Everard Upjohn (1903–78), was trained as an architect at Harvard University but devoted his life to teaching art history.

(1) Richard Upjohn (*b* Shaftesbury, Dorset, 22 Jan 1802; *d* Garrison, NY, 17 Aug 1878). His father was a builder and estate agent, who also taught at Christ's Hospital, London. The daughter of a clergyman, Upjohn's mother also came from an educated family. Despite his family's objections, Upjohn secured an apprenticeship to a cabinetmaker in 1819. In 1829, following his marriage and the birth of his first son, (2) Richard Michell Upjohn,

Richard Upjohn and his family emigrated to the USA. By 1830 he was working in New Bedford, MA.

1. Life and work. 2. Office organization. 3. Influence.

1. LIFE AND WORK.

(i) Early years, before 1837. One of his earliest works was the William Rotch house (1834) in New Bedford, which shows Upjohn's English experience as a cabinetmaker in the Regency details of the interior and his American experience of drawing houses for building speculation in such details of the New England vernacular as clapboarding, the gabled roof and the exterior proportions. Of Upjohn's other early works, those in Boston, MA, where he settled in 1834, proved important because it was through his acquaintance with prominent Bostonians that he acquired a reputation and national contacts that led to the work at Trinity Church, New York. The major work of this period was the country house Oaklands (1835–42) for Robert Hallowell Gardiner and his family in Gardiner, ME. A Tudor-style manor house, it is of additional significance as one of the few houses by Upjohn that remains in original condition. Upjohn's work in Boston also established his place in the continuum of American architecture. Many of his Boston clients were members of Trinity Church, Boston. It was there that Upjohn, after a lapse, reaffirmed his ties with the Episcopal Church, as others did at this time. He also made alterations to the 1829 Trinity Church and designed a new organ-case. The building later burnt down and was replaced by H. H. Richardson's famous Copley Square structure (1872–9).

Both the Reformation and Puritanism had affected the design of English and American ecclesiastical architecture, especially in restraining the use of colour and ornament and in the emphasis in the plan on the congregation and on preaching. Even in the 1830s, the Puritan legacy still contributed to the suspicion with which Americans regarded art in general and their preference for the written word over visual representations as the means for communicating religious truth; this was particularly true in Boston. It may not, therefore, be a coincidence, given the traditions of Boston and New York, that while four people important to the Gothic Revival in the USA (Upjohn, the Rev. John Henry Hopkins, the Rev. George Washington Doane and the Rev. Jonathan Mayhew Wainwright) were at Trinity Church, Boston, in the 1830s, it was in New York, always a more secular city with a more lavish lifestyle, that the English medieval parish church was revived.

(ii) Mature work, 1837 and after.

(a) Trinity Church. In October 1837 the Rev. Wainwright became assistant minister at Trinity Church, Wall Street, New York. When the Building Committee authorized inspection of the 18th-century building in February 1839, it hired Upjohn, who soon moved to New York. After inspecting the roof he recommended extensive renovations, and on 9 September 1839 he submitted plans for a new church (see fig. 1). Several innovations appeared in Upjohn's early longitudinal section. The balconies, as well as the plaster and lath vaults found in the 18th-century church, were gone, to be replaced by an open timber ceiling. Furthermore, the chancel was differentiated from the nave by size, shape and an arch, and thus formed a separate compartment. As opposed to broad naves to emphasize the congregation characteristic of the 18th century, the nave in Upjohn's design is long, accentuating the chancel and the rite of communion. This represents a shift in theological tenets and liturgical practices, which had been the subject of debate in England since the 1830s, a debate that the Ecclesiologists, the group that had codified precise guidelines for church design, carried on with great vigour in the 1840s and 1850s.

A. W. N. Pugin's *True Principles of Pointed or Christian Architecture* (1841) recommended changes in church design, predicated on the belief that the Middle Ages were morally superior to the 19th century and that the use of medieval forms would morally improve modern society. Like Pugin, Upjohn believed that use and circumstances, not arbitrary laws, should dictate the form buildings should take. Their concept of fitness, which emphasized truth in materials, structure and purpose, regarded the deliberate use of past forms as necessary. Upjohn's alterations for Trinity Church, Boston, incorporated these views, and his 1839 section for Trinity Church, New York, is the first representation of these ideas in the USA.

Deemed 'the puny cathedral of Broadway' by Horatio Greenough and praised by others, Trinity Church as built was different from Upjohn's initial plan. It did revive 14th-century English Gothic in its elevations, but the roof timbers were concealed behind imitation plaster vaulting (the antithesis of Pugin's *True Principles*) and the chancel was made more continuous with the nave. Although Upjohn did not carry out as elaborate a decorative scheme on the interior as Pugin and the Ecclesiologists thought ideal, the stained-glass windows over the altar were among the first examples in the USA and represented the collaboration of Upjohn with the painter and stained-glass artist Thomas Hoppin (1816–72). Upjohn designed the church furniture and supervised its carving, along with all other aspects of the building, in a churchyard shed in the tradition of the medieval mason's lodge. Even in its simplified state, Trinity Church allowed the wealthy parishioners to indulge their desire for art in a manner sanctified by the church, in which materialism and morality were effectively blended.

(b) Later churches. Upjohn's success at Trinity and his contact with Episcopal clergymen who supported the reformed liturgy were the basis of future patronage. He first achieved complete expression of Ecclesiological ideals at St Mary's (begun 1846), Burlington, NJ, commissioned by Bishop George Washington Doane. This church has a cruciform plan with a spire over the crossing, and it has the exposed roof timbers that Trinity Church lacks. It was not as lavish in its interior decoration as Pugin might have wished, but Upjohn and Doane carefully worked out a suitable interior scheme. The church of the Holy Communion (1844–6), New York, exhibited all of the attributes advocated by the church reformers.

The parish church was regarded as vital for spreading the Christian word. Its importance in Upjohn's career is evident in the number of parish churches designed by him and his office, as well as in his only book, *Upjohn's Rural Architecture* (1852). In it Upjohn presented a set of

1. Richard Upjohn: Trinity Church, Wall Street, New York, 1839–46; from a watercolour by Richard Upjohn, 526×670 mm (New York, Columbia University, Avery Architectural Memorial Library)

drawings for a small church, comprising the first stage of a commission: a perspective, elevations, plans, sections and diagrams of the structural timbers, as well as drawings for a school and a parsonage. *Upjohn's Rural Architecture* made standardized designs available throughout the USA and spread current architectural idioms to many parts of the country. Churches built according to this book may be found in upstate New York, northern New England, the South and as far west as Wisconsin. Although Upjohn's motivation was religious, the effect was to popularize church architecture.

(c) Domestic architecture and public buildings. Upjohn clearly regarded domestic architecture as the staple of his practice and it accounted for a substantial amount of the office's work. The Edward King house (1845–7), Newport, RI, in the Italianate style, has stood for many years as the main example of Upjohn's domestic architecture and his ability to design in a style other than the Gothic. Like all of Upjohn's house plans, this one is a variation of a plan, with rooms distributed around a central hall, with which he must have become familiar during his New Bedford days. Somewhat earlier and smaller than the King house but close in design was Highlawn (1844–5), Lenox, MA, built for the minor Transcendentalist writer and patron of

the arts Samuel Gray Ward. Although Upjohn used the Italianate style in varied ways throughout the 1840s and 1850s, he soon began to exploit the stylistic possibilities of timber construction. The George Atwater house (1854–5), Springfield, MA, is one of the earliest examples of a conscious revival of American Colonial architecture and one that preceded by 15 years Upjohn's important address to the American Institute of Architects, 'The Colonial Architecture of New York and the New England States'.

Upjohn's exclusive use of the Gothic for Episcopal churches and rectories may have been an article of religious faith: he is remembered for refusing to build for the Unitarians because they denied the Trinity. However, the architectural corollary of this doctrinaire refusal is the strength of his conviction that style and purpose should be in accord. Thus for Congregational institutions, such as Bowdoin College (1845–55), Brunswick, ME, Upjohn used the *Rundbogenstil*. His church of the Pilgrims (1844–6; see fig. 2), Brooklyn, NY, is the first example of that style in the USA and may have been designed in collaboration with the Austrian immigrant Leopold Eidlitz.

2. OFFICE ORGANIZATION. Richard Upjohn's office, one of the largest of its day, was organized as a family practice. In addition to his eldest son, (2) Richard Michell

2. Richard Upjohn: church of the Pilgrims, Brooklyn, New York, 1844–6; engraving (New York, New-York Historical Society)

Upjohn, who worked with his father from a very early age, Upjohn had as many as five draughtsmen and assistants, depending on the amount of work in the office. Between 1843 and 1846 Leopold Eidlitz worked there. Upjohn's collaboration with the younger men in his office was first recognized in 1851 when the first partnership between father and son, Upjohn & Co., was created. Charles Babcock (1829–1913) joined the office in 1850 and three years later was made a junior partner. He married Upjohn's daughter several months after becoming his partner.

3. INFLUENCE. Upjohn gained a strong reputation as the defender of professional ethics at a time when the architect and builder were still closely identified in fact and in the public mind. By insisting that the architect be a man of honour, whom the public could trust to uphold high standards of design and construction, Upjohn sought to distinguish the professional architect from the builder. He led the movement for the founding of the American Institute of Architects (A.I.A.) in 1857 and was made its first president. It is indicative of Upjohn's impact on the evolving profession that a high percentage of the original members of the A.I.A. had either worked in his office or been closely associated with him in some way. As part of the campaign to increase the status of the architect, Upjohn sought to establish a library and a collection of architectural and engineering models in the A.I.A. offices, where young

architects could study them. Yet Upjohn does not appear to have been particularly interested in breaking away from the tradition of training the young in an architect's office. His commitment to the office apprenticeship may be reflected in Babcock's departure from the office in 1858, as a year earlier Babcock had argued strenuously for professional training institutes, criticizing contemporary office training of the sort that he had received from his father-in-law. Babcock subsequently took up this cause at Cornell University, where he became the first professor of architecture.

Despite the size and success of his practice and his careful attention to all aspects of a commission, Upjohn's architecture often appears more successful in elevation than in perspective, as a result of his approach to design and reliance on architectural illustrations. Often austere at its best, his architecture is restrained and carefully, even delicately, detailed, with finely proportioned interior spaces. Nonetheless, Upjohn was instrumental in developing for his clients an American architecture based on the traditions of Europe.

Although he saw himself as crusading for the cause of the architectural profession and the Episcopal Church in America, his achievements had other dimensions. Many of his clients, such as Robert Hallowell Gardiner, Theodore Lyman, Samuel Gray Ward and the Rev. George Washington Doane, had ambitions for the establishment of American culture in a broad sense. But in the period before the Civil War, with industrialism still growing, they lacked the material resources and institutional organization to achieve all their goals. By supporting their ideals, by introducing new styles, by insisting on truth and by advancing the profession, Upjohn furthered the cause of the arts in general. He thereby created the foundations for the achievements of such architects as McKim, Mead & White, H. H. Richardson and Frank Lloyd Wright.

(2) **Richard Michell Upjohn** (*b* Shaftesbury, Dorset, 7 March 1828; *d* Brooklyn, New York, 3 March 1903). Son of (1) Richard Upjohn. He succeeded his father as head of the firm Upjohn & Co. in 1872. He had been very active in the office since the mid-1850s and his work is particularly evident after Babcock's departure. Known as the architect of the Connecticut State Capitol (1872–88), Hartford, in a Gothic Revival style, he also designed many houses, small churches and innumerable grave-markers while working for his father and seems to have introduced Ruskinian motifs to the office's repertory. His later career remains unstudied, except for the Connecticut State Capitol; he did carry on the tradition of designing for the Episcopal Church but was a very difficult personality, who, having been overshadowed by his father as a young man, never achieved equal success in his own right.

UNPUBLISHED SOURCES

New York, Columbia U., Avery Archit. Mem. Lib., Richard and Richard Michell Upjohn Collection [incl. typescript of E. M. Upjohn: 'A Brief Note on Richard Michell Upjohn', *c.* 1971]

New York, Pub. Lib., Manuscripts Division, Richard and Richard Michell Upjohn Papers

Washington, Amer. Inst. Architects, Archvs [MS. of R. Upjohn: *Addresses to the A.I.A.; 1857–1878*]

WRITINGS

Richard Upjohn: *Upjohn's Rural Architecture* (New York, 1852)
Richard Upjohn and others: *Rural Church Architecture* (New York, 1860s/R 1876)
Richard Upjohn: 'Colonial Architecture of New York and the New England States', *Proc. Amer. Inst. Architects*, ii (1869–70), pp. 177–9

BIBLIOGRAPHY

T. U. Walter: 'Richard Upjohn, F.A.I.A., 1802–1878', *J. Amer. Inst. Architects*, viii (1878), pp. 272–6
E. M. Upjohn: *Richard Upjohn: Architect and Churchman* (New York, 1939/R 1969)
W. H. Pierson: *American Buildings and their Architects: Technology and the Picturesque, the Corporate and the Early Gothic Styles* (Garden City, NY, 1978), pp. 159–205
D. P. Curry and P. D. Pierce, eds: *Monument: The Connecticut State Capitol* (Hartford, 1979)
J. S. Hull: *Richard Upjohn: Professional Practice and Domestic Architecture* (diss., New York, Columbia U., 1987)

JUDITH S. HULL

Uplistsikhe. Town on the north bank of the Kura River, 20 km east of Gori in the Republic of Georgia. Excavations have shown that Uplistsikhe was settled in the Early Bronze Age (3rd millennium BC); the name itself (literally translated as 'fortress of the rulers') apparently dates only from the 10th century BC. In successive centuries it became an increasingly powerful city of the east Georgian kingdom of Kartli (Iberia), enjoying contacts with the cultural centres of Urartu, Iran, Armenia, Asia Minor and the Greek and Roman empires. With the Christianization of Georgia in the 330s AD and the appearance of new feudal centres, Uplistsikhe declined in importance, although from the early 11th century until 1122 it served as the residence of the Georgian kings; thereafter it continued to exist as a town until destroyed by the Mongols in the first half of the 13th century.

The town occupies a rocky hillside site of 9.5 ha., which is cut off to the south and west by high precipices; the north and east sides are defined by a channel and a defensive stone wall with towers. There are three main entrances and also a secret tunnel. The principal thoroughfare begins at the southern entrance; streets branch off it on both sides and are lined with houses hewn out of the terraced cliff. Free-standing buildings were also constructed; those dating from the antique period are of trimmed stone blocks held together with metal clamps, while in the medieval structures rubble stone with lime mortar and brick are used. Both rock-cut and free-standing buildings served a variety of residential, religious and commercial purposes.

In the centre of Uplistsikhe is a rock-cut hall with three adjoining rooms and a yard, dating to the 1st century AD and later used as a church. The hall's ceiling imitates the appearance of a wooden roof with parallel beams, and has a cylindrical opening which serves both as window and chimney. Another rock-cut complex at the western end of the town has a central hall with a vaulted ceiling decorated with coffers, and a pediment above the entrance. At the town's highest point stands a three-aisled basilical church of the 10th–11th century.

BIBLIOGRAPHY

T. Sanikidze: *Uplistsikhe* (Tbilisi, 1982)

V. BERIDZE

Upper Peru. *See* BOLIVIA.

Upper Volta. *See* BURKINA FASO.

Uppsala [East Aros]. Swedish city on the River Fyris in the county of Uppland, with a population of *c.* 161,000.

1. HISTORY AND URBAN DEVELOPMENT. North of Uppsala are three large grave mounds dating from the 6th century AD and part of the medieval stone cathedral; these constitute the most obvious remains of Old Uppsala, an important centre during the pagan era. During the Middle Ages the church of St Peter, the church of Our Lady (both destr.) and a Franciscan monastery (of which parts of the walls survive) were built. The two churches were erected *c.* 1300 and the monastery towards the end of the 13th century.

On the ridge west of the river, a separate settlement developed from a royal fortification (late 1100s) on the cathedral mount. Old Uppsala was the first seat of the archbishopric that was established in 1164. In 1258 the Pope agreed to allow the archbishop's seat to move from Old Uppsala to East Aros, the city's present site, which may previously have been a commercial centre. During the 13th century a fortified ring wall with a gate tower (Domtrapptornet, or the cathedral stair tower) was added to the east side of the cathedral area. The present cathedral was constructed in the castle yard (*see* §2 below). With the addition of ecclesiastical buildings, chiefly the archbishop's residence, an enclosed cathedral–castle was created. South of the cathedral, Holy Trinity Church (*c.* 1300), a small basilica in grey stone and brick, was built; a west tower was added probably in the 1400s. At the end of the Middle Ages Uppsala consisted of the commercial area to the east and the cathedral complex to the west. Uppsala University was founded in 1477 and was closely associated with the cathedral.

Under Gustav I (*reg* 1523–60) the archbishop and the church lost their power due to the Reformation, and the university more or less closed. Gustav fortified his local residence, Uppsala Manor (destr.), which was situated on the slope above the archbishop's residence. In 1549 he began a new, large-scale fortification, which commanded the whole city. It consisted of a huge, irregular rectangular castle yard, bounded by walls, ramparts and bastions, and was greatly enlarged by Erik XIV (*reg* 1560–68) and John III (*reg* 1568–92). Franciscus Pahr (*d* 1580) and then Antonius Watz worked on the project. Building was interrupted from *c.* 1616, however, and only two out of three wings and three out of four towers were completed. Uppsala was regarded as Sweden's chief city historically and symbolically; the Vasa kings were crowned and buried in the cathedral and the secular ceremonies took place at the castle.

The university was reconstituted by Gustav II Adolf (*reg* 1611–32), who had KASPAR PANTEN remodel the archbishop's residence into the Gustavianum (1622–3) to accommodate it. Further premises were provided by converting two medieval houses to form the Skytteanum. In 1643–5 the Stockholm city engineer Anders Torstensson (*d* 1674) replaced the earlier irregular street system with a strict grid with two main thoroughfares that crossed each other at right angles in a new central square, in imitation of the plan of a Roman *castrum*. The principles of Torstensson's plan were applied until 1880. From *c.* 1660 to 1702 OLOF RUDBECK effectively worked as city architect, designing the anatomical theatre (1662–3) in the roof of the Gustavianum and so giving it its distinctive cupola.

Most of the houses in 17th-century Uppsala were low and built of wood, but within the cathedral complex brick dominated. Near by, the Oxenstierna Palace was built, while in the commercial district three large stone houses with high saddle roofs were clustered around the new square. The appearance of the city in the second half of the 17th century is seen in woodcuts in Rudbeck's *Atlantica* (1679), in a *huskarta* ('house map') from 1687, and in drawings for and engravings in Erik Dahlbergh's *Svecia antiqua et hodierna* (Stockholm, 1723).

In 1702 much of Uppsala was destroyed by fire. Carl Hårleman completed restoration of the cathedral with new Renaissance-style lanterns on its twin west towers, and he began to rebuild the castle (1744); this project, however, was never completed. He also built the university Senate (1749), a cathedral school connected to the old walls and the orangery in the Linné Gardens east of the river. From 1788 to 1807 the Botany Department, Uppsala University was built in the castle garden to designs by Olof Tempelman (1745–1816) and Louis-Jean Desprez, with a Greek temple façade and strict, geometrical forms (*see* SWEDEN, §II, fig. 5).

The new university library (1819–41) was planned by Carl Fredrik Sundvall (1745–1831) to act as a monument to the first Bernadotte ruler, Karl XIV (*reg* 1818–44). Uppsala preserved its small-town character until the mid-19th century, when large-scale immigration took place and an industrial area developed east of the river. To the west of the river an academic enclave grew up with new institutional buildings and the student association houses: for example, a Renaissance Revival university house (1878–87) was designed by Herman Teodor Holmgren (1842–1914), and the Uppsala School (1867–9; now Katedralskolan) was built by Fredrik Wilhelm Scholander (1816–81). Within the commercial district multi-storey brick houses were built in the early 1850s. During the 1880s large buildings throughout the city (e.g. the town hall on the main square) were given palatial Renaissance Revival façades. There were thus great contrasts between newly built blocks of houses and earlier adjacent low, wooden constructions.

In the early 20th century more large apartment block complexes in restrained Art Nouveau and National Romantic styles were put up. Around 1910 a more expensive quarter of villas was built to the west in Kåbo, which partly resembled the English garden cities. From 1920 to 1954 the city architect Gunnar Leche (1891–1954) exercised great influence over new construction and environmental planning. An extensive project for a new cultural and commercial centre at Vaksala Square remained largely unexecuted, although Leche did build the Vaksala School (1925) on the south side of the square, along with many residential areas. The development of the university area continued; more student association buildings were constructed, including the Värmland House (1930) by Ragnar Östberg and the Västmanlands-Dala House (1960s) by Alvar Aalto. From the mid-20th century extensive student accommodation and residential suburbs were developed.

From the late 1950s extensive demolition of older buildings and a radical widening of the central pedestrian precincts took place. Buildings from the 18th and 19th centuries were replaced with large commercial and residential complexes in reinforced concrete. In the 1980s greater caution and the blending of old and new buildings (e.g. the new city library by Carl Nyrén; *b* 1917) were advocated.

BIBLIOGRAPHY

Å. Stavenow: 'Sjuttonhundratalets Uppsala' [18th-century Uppsala], *Upplands Fornminnesfören. Tidsk.*, xxxviii (1923)

H. Lundh, ed.: *Uppsala stads historia* [Uppsala city history] (Uppsala, 1953–)

N. Sundquist: *De arkitektoniska miljöerna i Uppsala före och efter branden 1702* [The architectural environment of Uppsala before and after the fire of 1702] (Uppsala, 1956)

G. Lindahl: *Universitetsmiljö* [University environment] (Uppsala, 1957)

G. Eimer: *Die Stadtplanung im schwedischen Ostseereich, 1600–1715* (Stockholm, 1961)

S. Lindroth: *Uppsala Universitet, 1477–1977* (Uppsala, 1976; Eng. trans., 1976)

R. Zeitler: *Schweden: Kunstdenkmäler und Museen*, Reclams Kstführer (Stuttgart, 1985)

TORBJÖRN FULTON

2. CATHEDRAL. The shrine church of St Eric (*d* 1160), patron saint of Sweden. Building began *c.* 1270, when the entire plan was laid out, and work went on simultaneously at both ends. Building continued throughout the 14th century, with only a few changes of plan, but the cathedral was consecrated only in 1435. The lower parts are built of

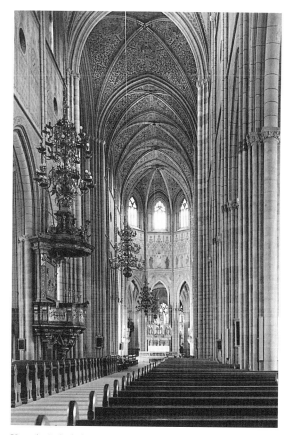

Uppsala Cathedral, interior looking east, late 13th century

stone and the upper, except for the portals and window-frames, in brick. The main stylistic influences on the church are French, presumably brought by ETIENNE DE BONNEUIL, who worked at the site from 1287 to c. 1300, and subsequently north German and Baltic *Backsteingotik*.

The cathedral is c. 118 m long. Its ground-plan is a classic French design of the second half of the 13th century. It comprises a three-bay choir (see fig.) with an ambulatory and five pentagonal radiating chapels, and a sacristy on the north side. The aiseless transept has richly decorated façades. The aisled seven-bay nave has chapels (all burial chapels since the Reformation) between the buttresses, and three storeys. A quadripartite rib vault is supported on triple shafts descending to moulded piers with foliate capitals. There are prominent flying buttresses, and the west front was originally designed to have two squat towers. The north transept portal, with its statue of *Olof the Holy*, can be attributed to Etienne de Bonneuil; at the same period the richly moulded façade with its gables and large rose window was executed, together with several interior capitals. The choir had been vaulted by c. 1300 and the vaulting of the transept and nave continued until c. 1350, when French influences were being replaced by north German and Baltic ones, which are particularly noticeable in the vault and its buttressing system. When the west front with its two towers was completed c. 1450–65 the exterior conformed even more closely to the Baltic tradition of blind decoration.

After a fire in 1572 the exterior was transformed. New flying buttresses with finials and intermediary pinnacles gave the building a 'cathedral' appearance, and high spires were added to the west towers, with a new, taller lantern over the crossing. After another fire in 1702 the roof was substantially lowered and Carl Hårleman (1700–53) redesigned the west towers to make them look more Baroque. The most extensive rebuilding was that undertaken in the restoration of 1885–93, when Helgo Zetterwall (1831–1907) attempted to return the cathedral to its original High Gothic appearance. The restoration coincided with the fashion for neo-Gothic, with tall, pointed spires, buttress finials and a higher roofline. With the exception of the spires, these additions were removed by Åke Porne (*b* 1905) in the most recent restoration, which was followed by a reconsecration in 1976.

The Baroque pulpit was designed by Nicodemus Tessin the younger (1654–1728). The axial chapel is the burial chapel of Gustav I (*reg* 1523–60). His tomb was made in the Netherlands c. 1576; the recumbent effigy of the king is flanked by those of his first two wives.

BIBLIOGRAPHY

G. Boethius and A. Romdahl: *Uppsala domkyrka, 1258–1435* [Uppsala Cathedral, 1258–1435] (Uppsala, 1935)

F. Nordström: *Studier i Uppsala domkyrkas äldsta byggnadshistoria* [Studies in the earliest building history of Uppsala Cathedral] (Uppsala, 1952)

R. Zeitler: 'Die Baugeschichte des Doms zu Uppsala', *Aspekte zur Kunstgeschichte von Mittelalter und Neuzeit, Karl Heinz Clasen zum 75. Geburtstag*, ed. H. Müller and G. Hahn (Weimar, 1971), pp. 359–85

G. Malm: 'Recent Excavations at Uppsala Cathedral, Sweden', *World Archaeol.*, xviii/3 (1986), pp. 382–97

ERLAND LAGERLÖF

Ur [now Tell el Mukayyar, southern Iraq]. Ancient Mesopotamian city occupied from at least 4000 BC. Ur lies 186 km south-east of Baghdad, on an old branch of the Euphrates. J. G. Taylor, who identified the site, first excavated there in 1853 and 1854. The Joint Expedition of the University Museum of Pennsylvania, Philadelphia, and the British Museum, London, led by LEONARD WOOLLEY, undertook full-scale excavations from 1922 to 1934. The site is dominated by a ziggurat, which was cleared, and excavation revealed monumental buildings that had been continuously occupied and rebuilt over the centuries, as well as an area of private housing which gives a rare picture of everyday life 4000 years ago. Most famous of all are the spectacular finds from the Sumerian Royal Cemetery, particularly those from the Death Pits, which contained the richly adorned bodies of high dignitaries and their slaughtered attendants. Finds, including jewellery and the inlaid sound-boxes of lyres, have provided virtually all available evidence for Sumerian expertise in goldwork such as gold vessels, sheet gold cylinder seals and gold weapons and tools. These objects and many from other periods are in the Iraq Museum, Baghdad, the British Museum, London, and the University Museum of Pennsylvania, Philadelphia, PA.

1. History. 2. Architecture. 3. Metalwork and other finds.

1. HISTORY. Ur was occupied during the Ubaid period (c. 5000–4000 BC), when there occurred a great inundation, wrongly identified by Woolley as the Flood of Semitic legend. The succeeding Uruk, Jemdet Nasr and Early Dynastic periods (c. 4000–2300 BC) are represented mainly by graves. The Royal Tombs and foundations on the ziggurat terrace were built in the late Early Dynastic period, in the time of the historical First Dynasty of Ur.

Ur became less important under the Akkadian ruler Sargon (*reg* 2334–2279 BC) but reached its zenith under the rulers of the Third Dynasty of Ur (known as the Ur III period). In 2004 BC the city was destroyed by the Elamites, and in 1740 BC Samsuiluna of Babylon razed the walls and sacked it again. Ur did not fully recover until the Kassite ruler Kurigalzu I (or II?) carried out extensive repairs in the 14th century BC.

The Neo-Babylonian (or Chaldaean) kings Nebuchadnezzar II (*reg* 604–562 BC) and particularly Nabonidus (*reg* 555–539 BC) greatly influenced the architectural history of Ur and gave rise to the name Woolley used for the site, 'Ur of the Chaldees'. Nabonidus was a fanatical antiquarian and restorer of ancient monuments, many of which were destroyed after the Persian conquest of 539 BC. The city had always depended on maritime trading, and as the river began to change course it lost its importance for the last time.

2. ARCHITECTURE. The area enclosed by the defensive wall and rampart of Ur-Nammu (*reg* 2112–2095 BC) formed the nucleus of the city (an area 1200×800 m). After the destruction of the wall in 2004 BC a defensive line was maintained by building houses around the same circuit.

(i) *Temenos*. Within the walled city the most important public buildings were located on a raised temenos (sacred enclosure), around which a wall was built in Ur III times.

Nebuchadnezzar's later and extended version, with but-tressed faces, intramural chambers and monumental gate-ways, enclosed an area of about 350×200 m and is a major feature of the site (see fig. 1). A defensive bastion (1a) in the north-west corner, decorated with niched engaged half columns, dates to Warad-Sin (*reg* 1834–1823 BC). Buildings of a purely religious nature were grouped around the temple platform (called Etemenigur; 1b) with its ziggurat (called Egishirgal; 1c). All were enclosed by a thick wall with intramural chambers, the essential plan varying little through the ages. Other buildings combined residential and religious functions. The ziggurat (*see* MESOPOTAMIA, fig. 9) was built by Ur-Nammu, who created a temple platform, enclosing earlier remains inside it. One stage of the tower survives (*c.* 18 m high), consisting of a solid mass of mud-brick faced and buttressed in baked brick. Its plan is a curved-sided rectangle (62.5×43 m), which is the earliest example of entasis. Three staircases led to the second storey, one to the third. Here it is assumed a special shrine stood, where the 'sacred marriage' fertility rite took place. The structure was restored by subsequent rulers and rebuilt by Nabonidus.

Inside the temenos, over the centuries, there were various enigmatic religious buildings, particularly temples to Nanna, the city god, and his consort Ningal, and this area remained the most important part of the site. Inti-mately connected with the ziggurat enclosure was a large sunken court (Court of Nanna; see 1d) to the north-east, enclosed by a buttressed wall with intramural chambers and monumental decorated gateways. It was founded during the Third Dynasty and was enlarged (from 65.6×43.6 m internally to 71.4×52.6 m) in the Isin-Larsa period (2025–1763 BC) by cutting back the terrace. The outer wall was then faced with engaged decorated half columns as on the bastion of Warad-Sin. This was covered by the repairs of Kurigalzu; though subsequently restored, the plan remained the same.

The Giparu (1e), a complex dedicated to Ningal to the south-east of the ziggurat, was built almost square (79×76.5 m). A corridor ran round three sides inside the thick buttressed outer wall, and another effectively divided the building into two: the high priestesses, often kings' daughters, lived and were buried in the north-west half (with its three courtyard complexes), while the south-east half included a large temple and well-equipped kitchen. Kurigalzu departed from the Ur III/Isin-Larsa plan and moved the main Ningal temple to the ziggurat terrace.

A further complete change occurred in the Neo-Babylonian period, when the site of the building was shifted to incorporate the Great Gate, called Edublalmah (1f). This was built in Early Dynastic times, or before, as an entrance to the ziggurat terrace, and retained its alternative status as a shrine and law-court long after it ceased to provide access. It consisted of a cruciform inner chamber, rectangular outer chamber and paved court beyond. By Kassite times it stood on a high platform.

The Ekhursag of the Ur III period (1g) was apparently a temple to the deified King Shulgi (*reg* 2094–2047 BC). It measured 59 m square and was divided into two distinct halves, religious and residential. It was finally destroyed in Samsuiluna's raid.

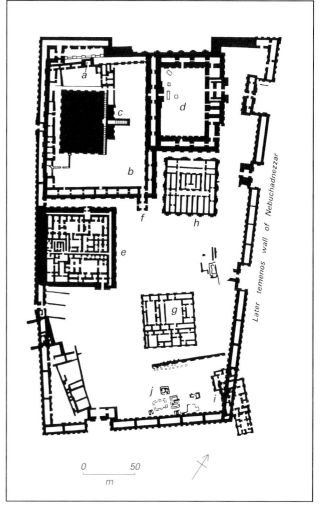

1. Ur, plan of temenos, from *c.* 2100 BC: (a) bastion of Warad-Sin; (b) temple platform (Etemenigur); (c) ziggurat (Egishirgal); (d) Court of Nanna; (e) Giparu; (f) Great Gate (Edublalmah); (g) Ekhursag; (h) Enunmah; (i) mausolea complex; (j) site of earlier Royal Cemetery

The longer-lived Enunmah (1h) was very different. It was 57 m square, with stepped buttresses on the outer walls; its plan was unchanged from Ur III to Kassite times. The core was a five-chambered shrine to Nanna and Ningal, reached only from a surrounding corridor. This also gave access to the magazines and probable priests' living quarters that comprised the rest of the building. Nebuchadnezzar kept only the central shrine in his new building, changing the essentially private nature of worship there by siting a large open area to the south-east.

(ii) Mausolea. Just south-east of the Ur III temenos wall and under the corner of Nebuchadnezzar's wall lay a complex of mausolea (1i) consisting of a central building dated to Shulgi and two annexes of his successor Amar-Suen (*reg* 2046–2038 BC). The central building (35×27 m) had an open court in the middle with surrounding cham-bers, some richly decorated with inlaid gold, and one with an altar and libation places. Two sealed underground

vaults reached by stairways were an integral feature. The annexes were essentially similar. All were stripped by the Elamites, and, though they were clearly burial-places, their occupants are unknown.

(iii) Private houses. Outside the temenos wall Woolley excavated an area of private housing of the early 2nd millennium BC. A typical plan consisted of a courtyard around which a range of rooms were grouped, including a reception hall, kitchen and toilet. The walls on the street side were blank and the thresholds high to counter the ever-rising street levels. Stairways led to a flat roof or possibly to a second storey. There were burial-vaults, under the floors in some cases, and private chapels within houses. There was no concept of urban planning and the streets were narrow and winding. There were occasional wayside shrines, and open-fronted buildings may well have been shops.

3. METALWORK AND OTHER FINDS. The Ubaid levels at Ur contained fine examples of the painted handmade pottery of the period and a number of the typical clay figurines of naked women. Most of the objects from later periods are unexceptional, but the ornaments of gold, silver and other materials found buried with the occupants of the Royal Cemetery (1j) and their slaughtered attendants (*c.* 2650–2550 BC) form a collection unrivalled in western Asia. Most techniques of goldworking are represented: gilding, casting, hammering, repoussé, chasing, granulation, filigree and cloisonné.

There are some spectacular large items, including a helmet from the tomb of Prince Meskalamdug, formed from a single sheet of hammered gold imitating an elaborate chignon hairstyle (Baghdad, Iraq Mus.). Most of the design is executed in repoussé, though some details are chased. A dagger from the same tomb, with solid lapis lazuli hilt, is decorated with complicated filigree tracery on the sheath (Baghdad, Iraq Mus.). There are also some unusual gold vessels, especially from the grave of Queen Pu-Abi. Luxury grave offerings were sometimes imitations

in silver or gold of, for instance, cockle shells for cosmetic paint and larger shells for lamps. Enough gold was available to permit the extravagance of solid-casting. The famous electrum ass which crowns the rein ring of Pu-Abi's sledge was made this way (London, BM).

Silver, copper and bronze survive less well, but there is ample evidence for their use. Strips of gold hammered into engraved grooves on bronze spearheads provide the first known examples of metal inlay-work. Hammered sheet-bronze fitted over a bitumen core was used to make large ornaments, particularly architectural fittings, for instance in the Ur III mausolea. None of these ornaments survives intact, but a similar technique is demonstrated in composite objects such as the well-known 'rams caught in a thicket' (versions, London, BM; Philadelphia, U. PA, Mus.). The rams have gold legs and faces, silver bellies, and horns, shoulder-fleeces and eyes of lapis, all fitted over a wooden core.

There was a thriving miniature art in shell, ivory, mother-of-pearl, lapis, cornelian, limestone and shale. Inlaid gaming-boards were found in the tombs. Elaborate and often fantastic scenes composed of inlay are depicted on the wooden sound-boxes of musical instruments such as lyres and harps. They include typical motifs such as heroes struggling with beasts and lions attacking cervids. Most famous of such pieces is the 'Royal Standard of Ur', a double-sided wooden object inlaid with shell and red limestone against a lapis background (see fig. 2). One side depicts in three registers a Sumerian king standing before his ass-drawn chariot and receiving prisoners and his victorious troops; the other shows the victory celebrations, with feasting, and tribute being carried in.

Fabulous quantities of jewellery, worn by both sexes, were found in the Royal Tombs (*see* ANCIENT NEAR EAST, fig. 30). Only women wore the elaborate headdresses; that of Queen Pu-Abi is the most complex example (Philadelphia, U. PA, Mus.). Long coiled ribbons of gold or silver were worn in the hair and secured by pins. Bands of pendent beaten gold leaves with rows of lapis and cornelian

2. 'Royal Standard of Ur', wood inlaid with red limestone, shell and lapis lazuli, set in bitumen, l. 483 mm, Sumerian, *c.* 2600 BC (London, British Museum)

spacers were worn around the brow. Upstanding comb-like metal ornaments were also worn (though exactly how is unknown); Pu-Abi's consisted of a bunch of beaten gold flowers, inlaid with coloured stones, on stalks. Earrings were of the usual double-lunate form, exceptional for their huge size.

Strings of beads, lapis, cornelian and, in Pu-Abi's case, agate were used in quantity. The gold and silver beads and pendants that were sometimes added to the strings could be very elaborate, for instance double and quadruple spirals, and gold beads decorated with filigree. Characteristic of Early Dynastic jewellery is the 'dog-collar', made of alternating triangles, usually gold and lapis, strung together. Finger rings and metal hairpins are of known Sumerian types; the latter often have decorated heads in forms such as a clenched fist or a horned head.

One item deserving mention is the 'diadem' of Pu-Abi (Philadelphia, U. PA, Mus.). Against a blue background of small lapis beads on what was probably a leather band were fixed tiny, finely wrought gold amulets in the forms of fruit, flowers, ears of corn and animals modelled in the round, some decorated with cornelian beads.

BIBLIOGRAPHY

L. Woolley and others: *Ur Excavations*, 10 vols (Oxford, London and Philadelphia, 1927–76)
——: *Ur of the Chaldees* (London, 1929, rev. 1982)

JANE MOON

Uragami Gyokudō [Uragami Hitsu; Ki Tasuku; Gyokudō, Ryosai] (*b* Ikeda, Bizen Province [now Okayama Prefect.], 1745; *d* Kyoto, 1820). Japanese musician, painter, poet and calligrapher. Although he was more famous in his lifetime as a musician and little appreciated as an artist, Gyokudō has come to be considered one of Japan's great painters in the literati painting tradition (Jap. *Bunjinga* or *Nanga*; see JAPAN, §VI, 4(vi)(e)) and his rough, bold works are among Japan's most powerful and individualistic artistic expressions. He belonged to the third generation of Japanese literati artists, who returned to painting in a more Sinophile, orthodox manner in contrast to the more unorthodox, Japanese approach of second-generation masters such as Ike Taiga and Yosa Buson.

1. BEFORE 1794. He was born to a samurai-official family, and in 1752, a year after his father died, he took up the Ikeda clan duties. He received a Confucian-style education and as a youth studied the Chinese zither (*qin*). He was skilled both as a player and composer on this subtle instrument. The creative processes that he developed for composition, particularly with respect to asymmetry and repetition, were transferred to the calligraphy and painting of his later years. He took his art name (*gō*) from the inscription *Gyokudō seiin* ('jade hall pure tone') on the back of a Chinese *qin* he purchased in 1779, frequently signed his works 'Gyokudō the *qin* player' and eventually named his sons Shunkin ('Spring *qin*', 1779–1846) and Shukin ('Autumn *qin*', 1785–1871). By the early 1780s Gyokudō was producing his first paintings; the first extant example dates from 1780 and is a copy of a sketch of Mount Fuji made by the Chinese visitor Fang Xiyuan (see Hashimoto, pl. 2). His early paintings display his interest in a brushwork technique of overlaying dots,

associated with the Song-period (AD 960–1279) painters Mi Fu and his son Mi Youren. A different brush technique was used in his best-known work from this period, the hanging scroll *Building a Hut in the Mountains* (1792; Tokyo, N. Mus.). As his style developed, he used gradually fewer varieties of brush strokes, the major expressive force evolving instead into rhythmic patterns created by rich ink tonalities, which, although naive in sentiment, contains compositional elements that were to recur throughout his painting career: a sage, often standing on a bridge; a fanciful pavilion; a foreground mass, generally in one corner; a screen of trees leading to a taller mountain; and a poetic inscription or title in running (*gyōsho*) or regular (*kaisho*) script.

2. 1794–1811. At the age of 49 Gyokudō took the unusual step of renouncing his samurai-official position to live as a free-spirited literatus. He spent the next 17 years travelling throughout Japan, staying at the homes of artistically-minded friends. He always carried his *qin* and brushes, ink and paper with him. He continued to write poetry, and his calligraphy gained new vibrancy in the two scripts that he chose to explore: the somewhat archaic clerical script (*reisho*), and the more lively running script, used in *Flower Moon* (1808; Hyogo, K. Yabumoto priv. col., see Addiss, fig. 4.3). He wrote out his own poetry and also occasionally brushed large-character studio names for his friends.

Gyokudō's growth as a painter was slow; he mastered a unique style only gradually. In terms of brushwork, he evolved a style of overlaying rapid black strokes, often with dry-brush technique, over wetter, greyer strokes. The effect is a layering of textures, frequently completed by horizontal or vertical dots 'flying' off the surfaces, as in the painting *Clouds Shield the Layered Cliffs* (1804; Virginia Shōka priv. col., see Addiss, fig. 5.7). By using rhythmically dynamic brushwork in continuous asymmetrical patterns, Gyokudō created a vision of nature that was appreciated by only a few of his artist contemporaries but is now recognized as among the most significant in Japanese history.

Towards the end of this period Gyokudō produced what are considered his most dramatic and energized paintings in the album of 12 landscapes called *Enkachō* ('Album of mist and smoke'; 1810–11, Tokyo, Umezawa Mem. Found.). In this set of landscapes, some with colour and some in ink, mountains reach out beyond the edges of the format, trees seems to burst with life, and the few humans who appear seem dwarfed by the power of their surroundings. At times the brushstrokes were so quickly and dynamically applied that they almost reach abstraction, perhaps as though they were shaking in an earthquake, and colour, where used, appears to have been rubbed into the paper rather than laid on it. The overriding feeling of almost frenzied energy marks the *Enkachō* as unique among literati works.

3. AFTER 1811. In 1811 Gyokudō had settled in Kyoto with his son Shunkin, who was by then a more successful literati artist than his father. In the following decade, Gyokudō devoted much of his time to painting, producing most of the masterpieces for which he is known, such as

Uragami Gyokudō: *Expansive Sky, Distant Roads*, hanging scroll, ink and light colour on paper, 304×466 mm, *c.* 1810–20 (Lawrence, KS, University of Kansas, Spencer Museum of Art)

Expansive Sky, Distant Roads (Lawrence, U. KS, Spencer Mus. A.; see fig.). *Eastern Clouds, Sifted Snow* (Kanagawa Prefect., Yasunari Kawabata priv. col., see Addiss, fig. 5.17) is a large winter landscape in which two dramatically shaped trees dominate the lower composition, looming over a bridge and a small hut, within which a scholar can be seen reading. In the middle ground a few more huts and a tower are almost obliterated by the swirling mist, rendered with free brushstrokes, and over the entire land surface a spidery network of tree shapes emerges here and there from the mist and snow. At the top a mountain peak, in Gyokudō's typical layered brushwork, towers over two pine trees on the right, which seem to be exploding like Roman candles. The artist noted on the picture that he had painted it 'while drunk'. Although Gyokudō's friend the literati painter Tanomura Chikuden had written that Gyokudō often painted after drinking sake, the skill and subtlety of the work preclude his having executed it in a state of anything more than mild inebriation. The painting embodies the essence of Gyokudō's vision of nature, in which man is but a small part of the great energy of creation.

In the last five years of his life, Gyokudō painted with less energized brushwork than before but with a greater clarity and maturity, as in the final leaf—*Geese Aslant in the High Wind*—in his album *Enjoying the Qin and Other Things* (1817; priv. col., see Addiss, fig. 5.27). In this leaf the artist's earlier brushwork technique is unchanged: an initial application of grey ink overlaid with darker and drier strokes and finally a few dots upon, or 'flying off', the surface. The rhythms of the brushwork, still asymmetrical in application, are slower and quieter, but the internal energy of the artist is still apparent in the power of each brushstroke.

BIBLIOGRAPHY
K. Hashimoto: *Gyokudō kinshi ibokushū* [Ink traces of Gyokudō the *qin* player] (Osaka, 1924)
K. Miyake: *Uragami Gyokudō shinseki shū* [A collection of the true works by Uragami Gyokudō], 3 vols (Tokyo, 1955, 1956, 1958)
S. Suzuki: *Uragami Gyokudō gashū* [Uragami Gyokudō painting collection] (Tokyo, 1956)
T. Ishikawa and others: *Uragami Gyokudō* (1974), xiv of *Bunjinga suihen* [Selections of literati painting], ed. J. Ishikawa and others (Tokyo, 1974–9)
C. Yoshizawa: *Gyokudō, Mokubei* [Gyokudō and Mokubei] (1975), xiii of *Suiboku bijutsu taikei* [Compendium of the art of ink painting], ed. I. Tanaka and Y. Yonezawa (Tokyo, 1973–6)
K. Ryūkawa: *Uragami Gyokudō, hito to geijutsu* [The life and works of Uragami Gyokudō] (Tokyo, 1976)
S. Suzuki: 'Uragami Gyokudō', *Nihon No Bijutsu*, 148 (1978) [whole issue]
J. Sasaki: *Uragami Gyokudō* (Tokyo, 1980)
H. Wakida: *Uragami Gyokudō* (1980), xx of *Nihon bijutsu kaiga zenshū* [Complete collection of Japanese painting], ed. I. Tanaka, T. Matsushita and T. Minamoto (Tokyo, 1980–81)
I. Tanaka and others: *Uragami Gyokudō gafu* [A picture album of Uragami Gyokudō], 3 vols (Tokyo, 1982)
S. Addiss: *Tall Mountains and Flowing Waters: The Arts of Uragami Gyokudō* (Honolulu, 1987)

STEPHEN ADDISS

Urang. *See* KWŎN TON-IN.

Urartian. Name given to the inhabitants of the kingdom of Urartu, centred on Lake Van in eastern Anatolia (now Turkey; *see* ANATOLIA, ANCIENT, §I, 2(ii)(c)), and ruled from Tushpa (Van) from the mid-9th century BC until *c.* 590 BC. During this period the Urartians built many fortresses with walls of fine ashlar masonry and produced a distinctive series of artefacts, particularly in bronze, of which the largest collections are in the Museum of Anatolian Civilizations in Ankara, the British Museum in London and the Hermitage in St Petersburg.

1. History. 2. Architecture. 3. Artefacts.

1. HISTORY. It is questionable to what extent the people of Urartu constituted a distinctive Urartian race, although it is clear that they were neither Semitic nor Indo-European. The Urartian language, known from cuneiform inscriptions, probably developed from Proto-Hurrian. Archaeological evidence suggests that the precursor of Urartian civilization was the essentially Hurrian Early Transcaucasian culture of the mid-4th millennium BC to the late 3rd, otherwise termed Kura-Araks, which extended from the Upper Euphrates Valley in the west to the Caucasus in the north and to the Hamadan region of Iran to the east, but there is a frustrating dearth of firm data for this part of the Near East throughout the 2nd millennium BC.

The name Uruadri/Uratri (Bibl. Ararat) first occurs in Assyrian records in the reign of Shalmaneser I (*reg* 1273–1244 BC), when it represented a wide highland region close enough to Assyria to pose some threat to its security. Uruadri probably overlapped the highland region of Nairi, which was far more frequently mentioned by the Assyrian kings. Both regions seem to have been occupied by loosely organized clans under petty princelings—no match, even in alliance, for the sophisticated, determined Assyrian military machine. The final form of the region's name, Urartu, came into common use under Assurnasirpal II of Assyria (*reg* 883–859 BC). Although there is no explicit reference to a kingdom until the reign of Shalmaneser III (*reg* 858–824 BC), it seems reasonable to suggest that Urartu had become established by the end of the 10th century BC or very soon thereafter.

The fortresses that dominate the archaeological record of Urartu are first attested in the detailed representations on the repoussé bronze panels (London, BM) from the doors of a minor Assyrian palace at Imgur-Enlil (Balawat). These date to the reign of Shalmaneser III, who defeated Arame of Urartu (*reg c.* 858–844 BC). Under Sarduri I (*reg c.* 844–832 BC) the centre of government moved to Tushpa, perhaps in the wake of a change in dynasty, and Urartu became permanently established on the basis of royal administration centred on Van. The name Urartu was alien to its rulers, who styled themselves, in the laconic but not uninformative Urartian inscriptions, princes of the city of Tushpa and of the land of Biaina (Van). The land of Van was the nucleus from which a rapid expansion began in the 9th century BC. This essentially centralized administration was the background and support of Urartian civilization.

The new princely line seems to have had close relations with the wealthy city of Muṣaṣir, named Ardini in the Urartian records. The principality of Muṣaṣir controlled a frontier region of crucial interest to both Assyria and Urartu, a fact illustrated by the presence there of two bilingual stelae, inscribed in the cuneiform characters of Assyria. The war-god Haldi, whose main temple was at Muṣaṣir, became head of the state pantheon of Urartu. The Hurrian roots of Urartian civilization are demonstrated by the presence of the god of weather and storms, Tesheba/Teshub, second in rank to Haldi, and followed by the sun-god Shivini. The leading status of these three gods is attested in the lists of offerings of bulls and sheep decreed for these and a host of minor divinities by Ishpuini (*reg c.* 832–810 BC) in the lengthy cuneiform rock inscription of Mehr Kapısı ('Mithra's Gate'), below the later Urartian citadel of TOPRAKKALE near Van. Ishpuini may have instituted extensive religious reforms, and these must have sprung from the expansion and administrative consolidation of the kingdom.

The expansion of Urartu may be briefly summarized as a movement south-east into Iran, initiated by Ishpuini and continued in the next two reigns. Under Menua (*reg c.* 810–786 BC) there were also strong thrusts both north across the River Araxes and west to the Upper Euphrates Valley. Argishti I (*reg c.* 786–764 BC) extended Urartian control of the fertile lands north of the Araxes, founding a major provincial centre at Erebuni (Arinberd; now Yerevan). His successor Sarduri II (*reg c.* 764–734 BC) further extended Urartian control towards the Black Sea, in the region of Colchis, and adopted an expansionist policy in northern Syria. This led him into direct conflict with the resurgent power of Assyria under the able usurper Tiglath-pileser III (*reg* 744–727 BC). The expansion of Urartu received a setback with the defeat of the coalition led by Sarduri II in a battle near the Euphrates (743 BC), followed by a campaign by Tiglath-pileser III through the heart of Urartu to Van itself, although the citadel was not taken (735 BC). The next king of Urartu, Rusa I (*reg* 734–714 BC), annexed new lands along the shore of Lake Sevan, even venturing into the Kura Valley. In so doing, however, he stirred up the Cimmerian tribesmen who, on the evidence of reports sent to Assyria by spies, were eventually to inflict a major defeat on Urartu (715–714 BC). At the same time Sargon II of Assyria (*reg* 721–705 BC) was attempting to thwart Rusa I's policy of containment through alliance with the Medes in the Urmia basin and surrounding areas of north-west Iran. Urartu suffered a major reverse, probably on the slopes of Mt Sahend, east of Lake Urmia, yet won the praise of the Assyrian king for its impressive irrigation canals, skills in horse-training, massive fortresses and the abundant supplies, including wine, stored within. The one later Urartian king of note was Rusa II (*reg c.* 680–640 BC), who seems to have shown both political and military skills in rebuilding his kingdom while avoiding fruitless conflict with Assyria: although few inscriptions survive from his reign, it may well have witnessed a wide-ranging reorganization of government in the provinces, suggested by the construction of major new fortresses at Toprakkale, KEFKALESI (Adilcevaz), KARMIR BLUR and Bastam (*see* BASTAM (i)). Foreign plunder had reached a climax in the campaigns of Sarduri II, recorded at his open-air shrine at Van; under Rusa II more careful exploitation of the kingdom's own resources became essential.

Urartu did not long outlive its ancient rival Assyria. It finally fell to the Medes from Iran *c.* 590 BC. Armenians had probably infiltrated from the west, perhaps peacefully, from as early as the mid-7th century BC and intermarried with the indigenous population. Eventually, during the 6th century BC, they imposed their Indo-European language throughout the old Urartian homeland around and beyond the region of Lake Van. A faint echo of the name remained in the guise of the Alarodians (Ararodians) mentioned by Xenophon (*c.* 428–354 BC).

2. ARCHITECTURE. The fortresses, temples and palaces of Urartu all exhibit a strong indigenous architectural tradition. Several variations of design and differing qualities of masonry can be discerned as styles developed in the earlier reigns. Apart from minor refuges and local centres, many of them built of rough stonework without regular courses, there was a planned network of major fortresses with associated outer towns or walled enclosures. The evidence of centralized planning lies in the siting of these fortresses on natural routes, including the approaches to Van, often in commanding positions on a spur overlooking a stretch of agricultural land. Many are dated by inscriptions. Menua was the most energetic builder, followed later by Rusa II. The steep slopes had to be carefully terraced; the foundations were keyed into the rock by cutting ledges that are often all that remain to show the line of a wall: at Van citadel the full width of the walls along the north side can be measured by their rock-cut bedding. The fortresses were built of mud brick, best preserved where burnt, and the walls were crowned with ornate stepped parapets. Blank windows, carved from a block of basalt, were a popular decorative feature (see fig. 1).

Palaces of the 8th century BC that were built before the defeats inflicted on Rusa I and Argishti II (*reg* 714–*c.* 680 BC), such as that of Argishti I at Erebuni, were open, even dispersed, in plan, with individual units linked by courtyards and passages. Palaces of the 7th century BC were designed, perhaps for greater security, as public rooms

1. Urartian model of the fortifications of a city, bronze, from Toprakkale, h. 280 mm excluding tower, 8th–7th centuries BC (London, British Museum)

built over the storerooms comprising the basement; consequently little survives *in situ*. Some palaces have columned halls, which perhaps were inspired by those in the burnt citadel (*c.* 1100–800 BC) excavated in level IV at HASANLU in north-west Iran. Wall paintings were largely in Assyrian style (*see* ALTINTEPE). One major fortress had reliefs depicting battlements (*see* KEFKALESI). Although palace reliefs in the Assyrian style do not occur in Urartu, there is some evidence for wall paintings based on Assyrian reliefs and painted decoration (e.g. Altıntepe).

2. Urartian lion figurine in the 'Court style', bronze, from Kayalıdere, h. 64 mm, 7th century BC (Ankara, Museum of Anatolian Civilizations)

The standard temple in Urartu was square in plan with massive walls, as thick as the width of the sanctuary within, constructed of fine ashlar to a limited height with mud brick above. It was normally sited on the highest point of the citadel, and its great height gave it the appearance of a tower. The precise form of the roof is uncertain, since the relief (destr.) from Khorsabad in Assyria depicting the looting of the temple of Muṣaṣir showed a gabled façade. The temple of Haldi at Erebuni is of a different plan, with a columned portico, and it would also appear that distinctive regional temple designs were used in the Araxes Valley, alongside the square plan. The temples commonly had associated storerooms. The temples' dimensions depended on the contours of each site. The open-air rock-cut shrine at Van best exemplifies another type of sanctuary. Here the soffits and stelae standing within two tall, deep, round-topped niches are inscribed with the annals of Sarduri II; a platform, part rock-cut and part terraced, gave space for sacrifices.

The annals of Argishti I are inscribed at the entrance to his rock-cut tomb in the south cliff of Van citadel, overlooking the lower city of Tushpa. This tomb, with chambers and wall niches, is the finest example of the rock-cut tombs favoured by the kings and nobility of Urartu, and imitated in masonry where there was no suitable rock. Associated with one group of masonry-built, false-vaulted tombs was a funerary open-air sanctuary area with finely dressed but quite unadorned, uninscribed stelae, discovered at Altıntepe in the north-west of the kingdom. Cremation, with the ashes stored in jars set into crevices in natural rock, seems to have been favoured by those whose status and wealth did not permit a rock tomb.

Perhaps the most outstanding achievement of successive Urartian kings was the extensive system of irrigation canals that converted the 'wilderness' into fertile, productive land for crops, vineyards and orchards. The royal inscriptions reveal the pride taken in these engineering works, especially the longest, the Menua Canal (l. 75 km), which brought water from the south-east to Tushpa. Although only part of the Araxes Valley is arid, one probable explanation for the Urartian irrigation canals is that they increased production for the government storehouses. These are attested in written sources and have been excavated in the citadels: for example, sesame oil and no less than 400,000 litres of wine were stored at Teishebaina (Karmir Blur). These depots were the economic basis of the Urartian state.

3. ARTEFACTS. Since the late 19th century Urartu has been renowned for its elaborately decorated bronzes, including mythical figures, cast by the lost-wax method, which originally decorated furniture from the temple at Toprakkale (London, BM; St Petersburg, Hermitage; for illustration *see* ANATOLIA, ANCIENT, fig. 9). Most prestigious metalwork, however, until the late period of Urartu, was of a military character. By the 8th century BC iron had come into general use for tools and weapons, even for arrowheads, which indicates its abundant supply. The quest for iron may indeed have been a strong motive behind Assyrian aggression in the lands of Nairi and later against Urartu. Outstanding examples of bronzework include helmets, shields, belts and quivers decorated in

repoussé. Assyrian influence is undeniable in early examples in the so-called 'Court style' (see fig. 2), in the form of helmet, and the chariot scenes of war and hunting that decorate the bronzes, but the general design is distinctively Urartian, although whether exclusively so it is hard to judge. Workshops must have flourished under royal patronage in Urartu, but foreign influence is evident, and foreign workmanship cannot be ruled out: cauldrons with ornate protomes, for example, may perhaps have been of north Syrian origin.

Stylistic changes are apparent, most markedly in the closing years of the kingdom, when, for example, lions become attenuated. In the later period, from about the mid-7th century BC, a 'Popular' style in bronzework appeared, some of its pieces being fairly crude in execution. The regular themes, for instance the god Haldi standing on a lion, gave way to mythical creatures such as centaurs and winged horses, scorpion-tailed lions and human-headed birds, barbaric in inspiration yet vigorous in a manner alien to the formal 'Court style'. Local tribes, new arrivals from the west and northerners from the steppes beyond the Caucasus may all have made an impact on the art of Urartu in its declining years. Some belts have overtones of decorative designs found in the Koban culture of the north Caucasus.

The most distinctive type of Urartian pottery is a fine, red-burnished 'Palace' ware that appears in a variety of forms including tulip-shaped footed cups and globular jugs. Huge storage jars, excavated in rows in the storerooms of Urartian fortresses, are often over 2 m high. They are frequently decorated with recessed triangles and bear incised hieroglyphic signs indicating their contents.

Typical Urartian seals are cylinder-shaped like those of their Assyrian neighbours, but with a loop handle and a design on the base so that they could be used both as stamp seals and as cylinder seals. These stamp-cylinders often have concave sides. Designs include processions of mythical creatures, net patterns, the king under his parasol, and genii on either side of a stylized tree, sometimes with a cuneiform inscription. The design on the base, often a winged disk or an animal, can be accompanied by hieroglyphic signs. Many seals and impressions have been excavated at Bastam (Tehran, Archaeol. Mus.).

There is evidence for some ivory-carving, both in the round (*see* ALTINTEPE, fig. 2) and in panels with griffins (e.g. London, BM), which show Assyrian influence.

BIBLIOGRAPHY

F. Thureau-Dangin: *Une relation de la huitième campagne de Sargon* (Paris, 1912)
N. Adontz: *Histoire d'Arménie: Les Origines du Xe au VIe siècle av. J.-C.* (Paris, 1946)
C. A. Burney: 'Urartian Fortresses and Towns in the Van Region', *Anatol. Stud.*, vii (1957), pp. 37–53
B. B. Piotrovsky: *Vanskoye Tsarstvo (Urartu)* [The kingdom of Van (Urartu)] (Moscow, 1959); Eng. trans. as *Urartu: The Kingdom of Van and its Art* (London, 1967)
C. A. Burney: 'Measured Plans of Urartian Fortresses', *Anatol. Stud.*, x (1960), pp. 177–96
B. B. Piotrovsky: *Iskusstvo Urartu: VIII–VI vv. do N. E.* [Urartian art from the 8th–6th century BC] (Leningrad, 1962)
M. N. van Loon: *Urartian Art: Its Distinctive Traits in the Light of New Excavations* (Istanbul, 1966)
M. Salvini: *Nairi e Ur(u)atri: Contributo alla storia della formazione del regno di Urartu*, Incunabula Graeca, xvi (Rome, 1967)
G. Azarpay: *Urartian Art and Artefacts: A Chronological Study* (Berkeley and Los Angeles, 1968)
B. B. Piotrovsky: *The Ancient Civilization of Urartu* (London, 1969)
C. A. Burney and D. M. Lang: *The Peoples of the Hills* (London, 1971), pp. 127–82
M. T. Tarhan and V. Sevin: 'The Relation between Urartian Temple Gates and Monumental Rock Niches', *Belleten*, xxxix (1975), pp. 401–12
Urartu: Ein wiederentdeckter Rivale Assyriens (exh. cat., ed. H.-J. Kellner; Munich, Prähist. Staatssamml., 1976)
W. Kleiss: *Topographische Karte von Urartu* (Berlin, 1976)
S. Kroll: *Keramik urartäischer Festungen in Iran* (Berlin, 1976)
T. B. Forbes: *Urartian Architecture*, Brit. Archaeol. Rep. Int. Ser., clxx (Oxford, 1983)
Urartu: Een vergeten cultuur uit het bergland Armenie (exh. cat., ed. L. Vanden Berghe and L. De Meyer; Ghent, Cent. Kst & Cult., 1983)
P. E. Zimansky: *Ecology and Empire: The Structure of the Urartian State*, Studies in Ancient Oriental Civilization, xli (Chicago, 1985)
R.-B. Wartke: *Toprakkale*, Schriften zur Geschichte des alten Orients, 22 (Berlin, 1990)
Urartu: A Metalworking Center in the First Millennium B.C.E. (exh. cat., ed. R. Merhav; Jerusalem, Israel Mus., 1991)
R.-B. Wartke: *Urartu: Das Reich am Ararat* (Mainz, 1993)

C. A. BURNEY

Ura Tyube [Ura Tepe; Vagkat]. Town in northern Tajikistan. It has been identified by some scholars as ancient Kurushkada [Cyreschata; Cyropolis], an Achaemenid foundation of Cyrus I (*reg* 559–529 BC; *see also* KURKAT). The town contains the Mug Tepe settlement (6 ha), the remains of urban fortified structures on the hilly areas of Tal, Mug and Kallamanora, madrasas, mosques and mausolea (15th–20th centuries), and secular architecture (18th–20th centuries). The earliest finds from Mug Tepe include a bronze seal with a winged griffin on the obverse (4th–2nd centuries BC), a terracotta statuette of a male figure, a fired clay male figure with a triangular face and applied phallus, a ceramic censer stand, a sherd with a lion in relief and a small bronze human face. A hoard of Roman denarii from nearby Mydzhum provides evidence of trade in the first centuries AD.

The earliest structural remains at Mug Tepe comprise part of the clay and mud-brick fortification walls and residential buildings (*c.* 3rd century BC–3rd century AD) and a two-storey tower complex (either a fortress or a religious centre) with two rows of embrasures (5th–8th centuries AD). Ceramic production in this period took place at Sari Kubur on the western edge of the town and included thrown and moulded red, brown or pale burnished slip wares ornamented with applied braiding, stamping or combing. Ceramic spindle-whorls and some jewellery, particularly ceramic and ivory beads, were also found. Noteworthy ceramic objects are an idol with an elongated slanting forehead (5th–7th centuries); a rectangular ossuary (700×360×280 mm) richly ornamented with alternating pilasters and niches containing figures, solar and lunar symbols, trees, stamped circles and merlons (6th–7th centuries); and a sherd with a stamped image of a lion standing in front of an imitation inscription or snake (7th–8th century). Glazed ceramics of the 10th–12th centuries are decorated with red or greenish-brown painting on a light slip ground. Among the fabric, wood and metal items of this period is a 12th-century hoard of *c.* 15 bronze items from Kalaibaland, near Ura Tyube. The hoard includes a cast octagonal base covered with engraved sirens and lionesses, hunting scenes and Arabic inscriptions, a rectangular chased and inscribed tray decorated with two rosettes enclosing winged predators, a medallion with three intertwined figures-of-eight in the centre encircled by kufic inscriptions and birds, and a pear-shaped ewer inscribed in Arabic *Fame and Happiness . . .* and decorated with bird and vegetal ornament.

The town expanded from the 15th century. The Shaybanid sultan 'Abd al-Latif (*reg* 1540–52) constructed the Kok Gumbaz, a monumental mosque–madrasa, and during the 16th to 19th centuries the dominant citadel of the ruler was surrounded by monumental religious, memorial and public buildings and numerous residential, artisan and commercial quarters. Interiors were decorated with wood and plaster carvings and polychrome wall paintings that combined geometric and vegetal designs with inscriptions.

The architectural monuments of Ura-Tyube have been studied by many academics; excavations took place, however, from the 1920s to the 1950s as part of the North Tadjik Expedition by Prof. N. Negmatov. Finds from the excavations are housed in the Ura-Tyube Museum, the Museum of Oriental Art, Moscow, and the Donish Institute of History, Archaeology and Ethnography at the Tajikistan Academy of Sciences, Dushanbe.

BIBLIOGRAPHY

E. Benveniste: 'La Ville de Cyreschata', *J. Asiat.*, ccxxxiv (1947), pp. 163–6

B. V. Veymarn: 'Mechet' Kok-Gumbez v Ura-Tyube' [The Kok Gumbaz Mosque in Ura Tyube], *Novyye issledovaniya arkhitektury narodov SSSR* [New research into the architecture of peoples of the USSR] (Moscow, 1947)

E. V. Kil'chevskaya and N. N. Negmatov: 'Shedevry torevtiki Ustrushany' [Masterpieces of Ustrushana metalwork], *Pamyatniki kul'tury, novyye otkrytiya: pis'mennost', arkheologiya: Yezhegodnik 1978* [Cultural monuments, new discoveries: literature, art, archaeology: 1978 yearbook] (Leningrad, 1979), pp. 458–70

N. N. Negmatov and E. V. Kil'chevskaya: 'The Kalaibaland Hoard of Metal Items', *Isk. Tadz. Naroda*, iv (1979), pp. 34–53

Ye. V. Zeymal': *Drevniye monety Tadzhikistana* [Ancient coins of Tajikistan] (Dushanbe, 1983), pp. 63–8

Drevnosti Tadzhikistana [Antiquities of Tajikistan] (exh. cat., ed. Ye. V. Zeymal'; Leningrad, Hermitage, 1985), nos 332–4, 426–8, 816, 823–6

N. Rahimov: 'The Terra-cotta Figurine from the Mug-Teppa Settlement', *J. Cent. Asia*, ix (1986), pp. 53–60

N. T. Rakhimov: *Istoriya Ura-Tyube po arkheologicheskim dannym* [The history of Ura Tyube from archaeological data] (Samarkand, 1989)

N. N. NEGMATOV

Urban VIII, Pope. *See* BARBERINI, (1).

Urban, Joseph (*b* Vienna, 1872; *d* New York, 10 July 1933). American architect, stage designer, interior designer and illustrator of Austrian birth. He studied at the Akademie der Bildenden Künste in Vienna under Karl Hasenauer. Urban first received recognition as an architect in the USA in 1904 when his design for the interior of the Austrian Pavilion at the World's Fair in St Louis, MO, was awarded a Gold Medal. He subsequently established himself in Europe as a stage designer; in 1911 he emigrated to the USA to assume a position as set designer with the Boston Opera Company.

After the completion of the Ziegfeld Theater (1922), New York, Urban solidified his reputation as an architect with unexecuted proposals for several large theatres. For the Metropolitan Opera House, intended as the focal point of the first schemes for the Rockefeller Center (1926–8), he proposed a semi-circular seating arrangement, to which he added galleries that projected from the proscenium into the seating area to break down the separation between audience and stage. In 1928 he completed a design for the German theatre director Max Reinhardt, which used an oval seating plan reminiscent of Walter Gropius's *Total-theater* concept (1927) and Frederick Kiesler's Space Theater (1916–24). Like the opera house, this design was meant to create a sense of immediacy and action, an idea consistent with the innovations of dramatists such as Reinhardt, who emphasized spectacle and audience engagement. Urban was intent on achieving a similarly spectacular architecture for these projects; the designs for both the Reinhardt Theater and the Metropolitan Opera House had boldly coloured façades and tower-like forms, which derived from the setback buildings of the so-called 'skyscraper style'. The carefully orchestrated illumination of these buildings was intended to produce the atmospheric qualities of the renderings of Hugh Ferris.

Although his early schemes for theatres had been coloured and ornamented generously, toward the end of his career Urban incorporated motifs of the International Style into his work. The New School for Social Research (1929–30) in New York, generally regarded as his most important work, used both a cantilevered façade and horizontal strip windows in a subdued composition. The inspiration of Josef Hoffmann is evident, however, for example in the mixture of black and buff brick. The differentiation of interior spaces through complex level changes suggests that Urban had also looked to the work of Adolf Loos. On the interior walls, murals by José Clemente Orozco and Thomas Hart Benton, each designed to use the space and lighting of their location to encourage a specific perception of the painted work, demonstrate Urban's desire to integrate art with architecture. They clearly show the connections between the concept of *Gesamtkunstwerk*, which he had absorbed from his Viennese architectural training, and the total-theatre projects on which he had been working.

In the last years of his life Urban was responsible for a great number of architectural projects, but few were built. His unexecuted competition design for the Palace of the Soviets (see *Archit. Rec.*, lxxi, April 1932, p. 278) was awarded an honourable mention in 1932. His final executed work, the colour scheme for the *Century of Progress* exhibition in Chicago in 1933, was a further reminder of his love of bold and contrasting coloration. In this, as in his sensual use of 'industrial' materials such as polished metal, his work forms a link between the Vienna Secession and American architects such as Norman Bel Geddes.

WRITINGS

Theaters (New York, 1929)
The New School for Social Research (New York, 1930)

BIBLIOGRAPHY

'The New School for Social Research', *Archit. Rec.*, lxvii (April 1930), pp. 305–9

R. Davison: 'Procedure in Designing a Theater', *Archit. Rec.*, lxvii (April 1930), pp. 457–85

'Prize Winning Design for the Palace of the Soviets in Moscow', *Archit. Rec.*, lxxi (April 1932), p. 278

D. Taylor: 'The Scenic Art of Joseph Urban: His Protean Work in the Theatre', *Architecture* [USA], lxix (May 1934), pp. 275–90

O. Teegan: 'Joseph Urban', *Architecture* [USA], lxix (May 1934), pp. 251–66

—: 'Joseph Urban's Philosophy of Color', *Architecture* [USA], lxix (May 1934), pp. 267–71

PAUL LOUIS BENTEL

Urbania. *See* CASTEL DURANTE.

Urban life. Subject that has been portrayed by artists throughout history. The life of the city-dweller became a major theme especially in the late 18th century. While TOWNSCAPE, URBAN PLANNING, PANORAMA and figural GENRE scenes may include life in the city as an element, this article will focus on the theme of urban life as a depiction of the public life of the city-dweller.

1. Before 1800. 2. The modern city.

1. BEFORE 1800. A survey of the visual record of urban life before 1800 reveals a broad division between two types of scene: formal portrayals of public festival and more informal depictions of work and leisure. Public festivals have been a central feature of urban life throughout history, and, whether religious or political, ceremonial or celebrational, they provide the exemplary expression of the collective experience of life in centres of population. The Panathenaic games, for example, were a focal point of Athenian life, and the procession represented in the frieze from the Parthenon (*c.* 440 BC; London, BM) is the great monument to this aspect of city life. With the rise of cities in Europe in the later Middle Ages and the Renaissance, the pageantry of the urban festival became a significant pictorial subject. A variety of festive events in such cities as Paris and Florence was portrayed (e.g. anon. *Tournament on the Place Royal for the Betrothal of Louis XIII, c.* 1612; Paris, Carnavalet), and a particularly rich spirit of urban pageantry in Venice is reflected in several late 15th-century paintings by Gentile Bellini and Vittore Carpaccio (e.g. *Legend of St Ursula*, 1495; Venice, Accad.). Such pageantry continued to flourish in the capitals of the Baroque period and evolved, in the late 18th century and early 19th, into the *fêtes révolutionnaires*, several of which were staged in Paris in the 1790s by Jacques-Louis David.

Early representations of the more ordinary daily activities of cities can be found in Egyptian tombs such as those at Beni Hasan and on Greek vases, but the most explicitly urban imagery from the Ancient world is that of the frescoes and mosaics of Pompeii (before AD 79). These include scenes in the markets and public fora, along with aspects of street life, shops and entertainment. Similarly, a topographical border on a floor mosaic from Daphne (Antakya, Hatay Mus.) presents a vivid portrayal of the streets, shops and activities of 5th-century Daphne and Antioch.

It is only with the emergence of European cities in the later Middle Ages that a developing imagery of city life can begin to be traced in any detail. An early example is in the manuscript *La Vie de St Denis* (1317; Paris, Bib. N. MS 2090–2), in which a series of scenes from the saint's life is accompanied by vignettes of contemporary life along the Seine in Paris, including depictions of street life and riverfront activity. Although their topography is highly schematic, these scenes are compellingly lifelike. In the same generation Ambrogio Lorenzetti incorporated a

similar diversity of urban life into a more accurate topographical view of Siena in the *Effects of Good Government in the City and the Country* (fresco, 1338–9; Siena, Pal. Pub.). This work initiated a tradition of realistic townscape painting, and soon the backgrounds and settings of many Italian and Flemish paintings reflected a growing attentiveness to the character of the Renaissance city. This increasingly detailed picture of urban life was largely a celebration of the vitality and diversity of the city. A significant exception, however, appeared in the pictorial association of the virtue of charity with the city; for example, the *Seven Acts of Mercy* by the Master of Alkmaar presents the streets and buildings of Alkmaar as the setting for such charitable acts as the feeding of the hungry (see fig. 1) and the care of the injured and sick—an early acknowledgement of the concentration of poverty and need that would become one of the characteristics of modern cities.

1. Master of Alkmaar: *Feeding the Hungry*, detail from the *Seven Acts of Mercy*, oil on panel, 1010×540 mm, 1504 (Amsterdam, Rijksmuseum)

In the 17th century both genre and townscape emerged as important pictorial subjects, and as a result the workday activities of the cities of the time received considerable attention. Such Dutch townscape painters as Jan van der Heyden of Amsterdam and Gerrit Berckheyde of Haarlem were often attentive to details of activity in their cities' streets, squares, markets and ports. This type of painting achieved international popularity in the hands of 18th-century specialists in *vedute*, or view-painting (*see* VEDUTA). Although the emphasis remained topographical, the attention to human activity in the Venice and London of Canaletto or the Vienna, Munich, Dresden and Warsaw of Bernardo Bellotto provides a revealing overview of urban life at the time. The 17th-century Dutch genre painters tended to emphasize a more private, interior world, avoiding public, urban settings except for occasional scenes of markets and shopfronts (e.g. Hendrick Sargh's *Vegetable Market*, 1666; Amsterdam, Rijksmus). A more emphatically urban genre appeared in the 18th century, especially in such moralizing engravings of London as *Gin Lane* by William Hogarth and in the paintings of Parisian street life by Etienne Jeaurat. Printed scenes of popular life and public leisures by such artists as Gabriel-Jacques de Saint-Aubin and Thomas Rowlandson set the stage for an expanding artistic exploration of the life of Paris and London as two of the first great urban centres of the modern, industrial age.

2. THE MODERN CITY. The increasing complexity of the urban experience in the 19th century, in a world transformed by industry and massive population growth, inspired a greater diversity of response on the part of artists (*see* INDUSTRIAL SCENES), and by the end of the century the city was established as a major subject of modern art. The great tradition of the urban festival became a less central theme; however, major artists occasionally portrayed urban celebrations, with highly unconventional results and sharply contrasting attitudes. In Claude Monet's two paintings of Paris streets during the *fête nationale* of 1878 (*Rue Montorgueil*, Paris, Mus. d'Orsay; *Rue Saint Denis*, Rouen, Mus. B.-A.), the exuberant spirit of the event is expressed in vibrant patterns of colour. In the *Entry of Christ into Brussels in 1889* (Malibu, CA, Getty Mus.), James Ensor transformed the press of crowds at a similar urban celebration into a menacing mob. Increasingly, the city inspired both enthusiasm and bitter criticism.

The tradition of depicting everyday urban activities maintained its importance, expanding and enriching its possibilities. Popular prints played a significant role in the growing prominence of urban genre. Many scenes of city life appeared in illustrated journals, such as *Le Charivari* and *L'Illustration* in Paris, and their London counterparts *Punch* and the *Illustrated London News*. Along with many minor illustrators, a few major artists worked for these journals, including Honoré Daumier, one of the greatest artists of early 19th-century Parisian life, and Constantin Guys. The latter was featured in Charles Baudelaire's essay 'The Painter of Modern Life' (*Le Figaro*, 26 Nov, 28 Nov and 3 Dec 1863), in which modern life was equated with the city as the most heroic of artistic themes. Prints also played a significant part in the increasing attention to

urban poverty during the later 19th century. A harshly realistic image of London slum life was presented in several series of prints by Gavarni, and in Gustave Doré's *London: A Pilgrimage* (1872). Such scenes were featured in the journal *The Graphic* throughout the 1870s, a time when the development of the railways caused many homes to be destroyed, which contributed to overcrowding in the cities. Among the painters who explored similar themes were Hubert von Herkomer in London (he also did prints for *The Graphic*) and Jean-François Rafaëlli in Paris. With the publication of Jacob Riis's *How the Other Half Lives: Studies among the Tenements of New York* (1890), photography became an important medium in the case for urban reform.

Other urban themes that achieved new prominence during the 19th century include the barricade and the boulevard. The association of city streets with barricades and popular insurrection was reinforced by countless pictures of revolutions by illustrators as well as painters (e.g. Ernest Meissonier's *Barricade, Rue de la Mortellerie (June 1848)*, 1848; Paris, Mus. d'Orsay). The teeming life of the boulevard was seized by the new, instantaneous lenses of stereoscopic photographers and was celebrated by painters, including such progressive artists as Monet (e.g. *Boulevard des Capucines*, 1873; Moscow, Pushkin Mus.) and Gustave Caillebotte (e.g. *Place de l'Europe on a Rainy Day*, 1877; Chicago, IL, A. Inst.), as well as more fashionable painters such as Jean Béraud. Important painters of urban life during the later 19th century include William Powell Frith (e.g. *Paddington Station*, 1872; Egham, U. London Royal Holloway & Bedford New Coll.) and James Tissot in London, Adolph Friedrich Erdmann Menzel in Berlin, and Edouard Manet, the Impressionists and their contemporaries in Paris. It was especially in Paris, in the circle of the Impressionists, that the theme of city life reached a new level of importance. In his essay on the Impressionist exhibition of 1876, the critic Louis-Edmond Duranty enumerated the themes of this 'new painting', including railways, shops, scaffolds, gaslit boulevards, urban transport, cafés and restaurants. Such artists as Manet (e.g. *The Railroad*, 1873; Washington, DC, N.G.A.) and Edgar Degas were especially probing in their portrayals of these and other aspects of urban life. Their unconventional styles often served to capture the quicker pace and more fragmentary experiences of life in the modern city, as in Degas's depiction of *Women on the Terrace (A Café on the Boulevard Montmartre*; see fig. 2).

One important aspect of the Impressionists' involvement in urban themes was their discovery of Japanese prints. In their devotion to the life and entertainments of Japanese cities, these popular *ukiyoe* prints were part of a rich tradition. Their principal source was the *fūzokuga* (genre) painting that had flourished in Kyoto during the 16th and 17th centuries. The great multi-panelled screens of this era entitled *Scenes in and out of the Capital* (examples in Tokyo, N. Mus.) are all-encompassing portrayals of a city and its inhabitants. Such a balance between topography and figural activity is rare in Western art, but can be found in East Asia as far back as the early 12th century in the Chinese handscroll *Going up the River at the Qing Ming Festival* by Zhang Zeduan (Beijing, Pal. Mus.). The Impressionists' discovery of Japanese prints reinforced their

2. Edgar Degas: *Women on the Terrace (A Café on the Boulevard Montmartre)*, pastel on monotype, 410×600 mm, 1877 (Paris, Musée d'Orsay)

interest in the life of the city, but it also marked a momentous intersection between a rich Eastern tradition of portraying urban life and an important climax in the Western tradition.

With Impressionism, urban life was established as a central theme of the modern artist. This importance persisted into the 20th century, as a variety of styles and attitudes were applied to several major cities. *Fin-de-siècle* Paris remained a major cultural capital, generally celebrated for its vibrancy and diversity. Occasionally an undercurrent of despair was expressed, as in works by Henri de Toulouse-Lautrec and Pablo Picasso. A dynamic vibrancy was reasserted, however, by such artists as Robert Delaunay, who applied the stylistic language of Cubism to the multiplicity of urban experience, notably in his *Eiffel Tower* series (e.g. 1910–11; Basle, Kstmus.).

The portrayal of life in early 20th-century Berlin, however, is generally quite different from that of Paris. As the capital of a new German empire, Berlin had grown and industrialized with tremendous rapidity, and many artists responded with alarm rather than enthusiasm. The harsh and distorted city scenes painted by Ernst Ludwig Kirchner and Ludwig Meidner expressed an aversion to the industrial metropolis, which was a pervasive theme of contemporary Expressionist literature and art. After World War I, such artists as Max Beckmann and George Grosz returned to the subject of urban life. Although their post-war styles had hardened and become more realistic, their portrayals of the city as the scene of corruption, degradation, violence and fear extended the essentially negative view of urban life developed by the Expressionists.

New York, the archetypal 20th-century city, has been the source of a range of artistic responses to modern urban life. Early in the century the members of the Ashcan school were particularly attracted by the theme. In spite of their frank acknowledgements of poverty and overcrowding, the works of such artists as John Sloan and George Bellows are basically enthusiastic about city life. The Cubist-inspired dynamics of urban experience appear in different forms in the works of Joseph Stella and Stuart Davis. During the Depression of the 1930s a variety of more negative attitudes emerged, from the loneliness and alienation of the city scenes of Edward Hopper to the more biting social criticism of Ben Shahn. As New York succeeded Paris as the major centre of progressive art after World War II, the city's attraction as a theme for creative expression was further enhanced. Piet Mondrian demonstrated that the pulsating energies of city life could be expressed abstractly in his painting *Broadway Boogie-woogie* (1942–3; New York, MOMA; *see* MONDRIAN, PIET, fig. 4). Among the younger artists of the New York School, the tense, gestural style of Willem De Kooning and the bold black-and-white configurations of Franz Kline most forcefully embody aspects of modern urban experience.

The streets, parks, theatres and cafés of 20th-century London provided the subject-matter for the members of the Camden Town Group, the London Group and the Euston Road School. Their aesthetic was one of verification, and their objective, honest treatment was often combined with restrained colours and brushwork. A harsher view of life in the capital was found in the Vorticist paintings of Wyndham Lewis and WILLIAM ROBERTS, who depicted the city-dweller stripped of humanity and moving through a mechanical, dehumanized landscape, although Roberts's later works restore an element of humanity. By contrast, the Italian Futurists celebrated the mechanistic concept of the city, concentrating on the energy generated by the urban environment in such works as Boccioni's painting of the *City Rises* (1910; New York, MOMA), in which human and animal tension is conveyed in fragmented colour and thin, rapid brushstrokes, while Antonio Sant'Elia's drawings express the excitement of Milan's industrial growth based on a vision of a city created through contemporary technology and industry (for further discussion and illustration *see* SANT'ELIA, ANTONIO). An altogether different view of city life is conveyed in the series of posters commissioned by London Underground: Rex Whistler's *Tate Gallery* (1928) and E. McKnight Kauffer's The *Flea: Natural History Museum, London* (1928) depicted the city as a cultural centre replete with sophisticated shops and historical treasures; in the late 20th century the posters went on to celebrate the ethnic and cultural diversity of urban life.

The growth of photography as both a poetic and documentary medium has resulted in disparate images of urban life. The French photographer ROBERT DOISNEAU conveyed his attachment to Paris in charming, atmospheric pictures of daily life, in which the combination of chance and naturalness combine in images of slightly unusual but everyday events in such pictures as *Waltzing on Bastille Day* (1949). Henri Cartier-Bresson rejected flash photography and obtrusive lighting in favour of psychological penetration in such studies of city life as *Madrid* (1933; for further discussion and illustration *see* CARTIER-BRESSON, HENRI). By contrast Brassaï's pictures of *Paris de nuit* (Paris, 1933), shot with artificial light, and Bill Brandt's compelling reportage of East End pubs and race tracks in London present the seedier side of city life in a series of striking black-and-white images that lend a temporary dramatic allure. In the 1950s ROGER MAYNE captured the vitality of young children playing in the bleak environment of the streets of post-war London, while in the 1970s GILBERT AND GEORGE used photographic images of urban life in such pieces as *Smash the Reds* (1977; USA, Judy and Harvey Gushner priv. col.) and *Wanker* (1977; London, Anthony d'Offay Gal.) to produce an almost dream-like view of the harsh reality of working-class life.

In the mid- and late 20th century a further development in the depiction of urban life was the focus on the actual detritus of the city, rather than its inhabitants, and the incorporation of it into the paintings and sculpture of Pop art. Such artists as Claes Oldenburg created found-object environments that reflected the colours and textures of decaying urban slums. He later produced painted plaster versions of everyday objects, and produced giant replicas of, for example, hamburgers and lipsticks, installing them

as part of the urban landscape. Edward Kienholz reconstructed tableaux or journalistic and descriptive environmental assemblages, for example *Roxy's* (1961; R. Onnasch priv. col.), a reconstruction of a 1940's brothel, in which the attention paid to period detail contrasts with the dehumanized mannequin figures with their junk features and limbs. Although the desire to record both familiar places and people in the tradition of the Camden Town Group was continued by such British painters as LEON KOSSOFF (e.g. *Children's Swimming Pool, Autumn Afternoon 1971*; London, Tate), younger artists, such as Mark Boyle, focused on the actual fabric of the urban environment, using cast fibre glass, dirt and stone to produce such works as *Holland Park Avenue Study* (1967; London, Tate; for illustration *see* FIBREGLASS).

BIBLIOGRAPHY

M. Poëte: *Une Vie de cité: Paris de sa naissance à nos jours*, iv (Paris, 1925)
E. Magne: *Les Fêtes en Europe au XVIIe siècle* (Paris, 1930)
G. Poisson: *La Vie parisienne vu par les peintres* (Paris, 1953)
P. Lavedan: *Représentation des villes dans l'art du moyen âge* (Paris, 1954)
M. Brunetti and others: *Venice* (Geneva, 1956)
American Artists Paint the City (exh. cat., ed. K. Kuh; Chicago, IL, A. Inst., 1956)
P. Courthion: *Paris, i: In the Past; ii: In our Time* (Geneva, 1957)
J. Wilhelm: *Paris vu par les peintres* (Paris, 1961)
Panorama berlinois: Berlin vu par les peintres (exh. cat., Paris, Gal. Creuze, 1961)
A. Toynbee, ed.: *Cities of Destiny* (London, 1967)
G. Briganti: *The View Painters of Europe* (London, 1970)
J. G. Links: *Townscape Painting and Drawing* (London, 1972)
H. J. Dyos and M. Wolff, eds: *The Victorian City: Images and Realities*, 2 vols (London, 1973)
Y. Yamane: *Momoyama Genre Painting* (Tokyo, 1973)
F. Barker and P. Jackson: *London: 2000 Years of a City and its People* (London, 1974/R 1983)
V. Wylie Egbert: *On the Bridges of Medieval Paris: A Record of Early Fourteenth-century Life* (Princeton, 1974)
Die Stadt: Bilt, Gestalt, Vision: Europaische Stadtbilder im 19. und 20. Jahrhundert (exh. cat., Bremen, Ksthalle, 1974)
Die Stadt: Druckgraphische Zyklen des 19. und 20. Jahrhunderts (exh. cat., Bremen, Ksthalle, 1974)
A. M. Lecoq: 'La città festeggiante: Les Fêtes publiques au XVe et XVIe siècles', *Rev. A.*, xxxiii (1976), pp. 83–100
D. Kuspit: 'Individual and Mass Identity in Urban Art: The New York Case', *A. America*, lxv (Sept-Oct 1977), pp. 67–77
Cityscape, 1910–1939: Urban Themes in American, German, and British Art (exh. cat., ACGB, 1977)
The Dutch Cityscape in the 17th Century and its Sources (exh. cat., Toronto, A.G. Ont., 1977)
R. Lane: *Images from the Floating World: The Japanese Print* (New York, 1978)
R. Heller: 'The City Is Dark: Conceptions of Urban Landscape and Life in Expressionist Painting and Architecture', *Expressionism Reconsidered: Relationships and Affinities*, ed. G. B. Pickar and K. E. Webb (Munich, 1979), pp. 42–59
I. B. Nadel and F. S. Schwarzbach, eds: *Victorian Artists and the City: A Collection of Critical Essays* (New York, 1980)
B. Farwell: *French Popular Lithographic Imagery, 1815–1870*, iii–iv (Chicago, 1981–6)
J. Bumpus and others: 'London: Visions of a City', *A. & Artists*, 188 (1982), pp. 6–33
D. Piper: *Artists' London* (London, 1982)
T. J. Clark: *The Painting of Modern Life: Paris in the Art of Manet and his Followers* (New York, 1984)
P. Hales: *Silver Cities: The Photography of American Urbanization, 1839–1915* (Philadelphia, 1984)
T. Shapiro: 'The Metropolis in the Visual Arts: Paris, Berlin, New York, 1890–1940', *Metropolis, 1890–1940*, ed. A. Sutcliffe (London, 1984), pp. 95–127

DENNIS COSTANZO

Urbano (di Pietro) da Cortona (*b* Cortona, ?1426; *d* Siena, 8 May 1504). Italian sculptor. He was first mentioned working as an assistant to Donatello in September 1447 when he and Giovanni da Pisa (i), Antonio Chellini and Francesco del Valente (*fl* 1446; *d* after 1464) were each paid for the execution of an Evangelist's symbol and a relief of an angel for the high altar of the Santo, Padua (although which sculptor did which pieces is not specified). Soon afterwards Urbano apparently worked in Perugia, designing the tomb of the university professor *Ubaldo Bartolini* (Perugia University) and the wall tomb of *Archbishop Andrea Giovanni Baglioni* (*d* 1451; Perugia Cathedral), before establishing himself permanently in Siena. In July 1451 he was commissioned to design two marble statues of saints for the Loggia di Mercanzia (Loggia di S Paolo), Siena, which were never carved. In 1462 Urbano carved a marble bench for the loggia ornamented with personifications of the four Cardinal Virtues.

In October 1451 Urbano and his brother Bartolommeo began the decoration of the Chapel of the Madonna delle Grazie (destr. 1661) in Siena Cathedral. Sixteen marble reliefs (Siena Cathedral) depicting scenes from the *Life of the Virgin* originally intended to ornament the pilasters, the symbol of St Matthew and a tondo of the Virgin from the pediment survive (Siena, Mus. Opera Duomo). The rigid lines of the drapery and the stereotyped figures reveal an artist of a conservative and eclectic nature, whose manner, influenced by Donatello, was unlikely to have much of a following among his Sienese contemporaries.

In 1456 Urbano designed a terracotta figure of *St Bernardino* (Siena, Osservanza) whose pose is reminiscent of Donatello's statues of saints on the high altar of Il Santo. In 1457 he was sent to Florence by the Sienese authorities to deliver monies owed to Donatello for the bronze *St John the Baptist* (Siena Cathedral). The marble wall tomb (Siena, S Francesco) of Cristoforo Felici, former Operaio of the cathedral, is dated 1462 or 1463, although the final payment was delayed until 1487.

In March 1470 Urbano was paid for a lunette of *St Catherine and Two Angels* for the oratory of Caterina, Siena (*in situ*); together with many other Sienese masters, Urbano had been employed on the decoration of the oratory from 1468 to 1474. In 1470–72 Urbano decorated the newly constructed Palazzo Piccolomini, Siena, and in September 1481 he received his last important commission from the Sienese authorities, to design a marble intarsia of the *Persian Sibyl* for the cathedral pavement; the final payment was made in October 1483. Urbano acted as arbitrator in a dispute between Giovanni di Stefano and his workmen in 1497–8.

Also attributed to Urbano, but with a lesser degree of certainty, are a relief of the *Virgin Suckling the Infanty Christ* (Montarioso, Seminario Archivescovile), formerly in S Francesco, Siena, and a number of polychromed stucco reliefs of the Holy Family based on a prototype by Donatello (Berlin, Skulpgal.; Florence, Mus. Bardini; London, V&A).

BIBLIOGRAPHY
Thieme–Becker
G. Milanesi: *Documenti per la storia dell'arte senese*, 3 vols (Siena, 1854–6)
R. H. H. Cust: *The Pavement Masters of Siena, 1369–1562* (London, 1901)
P. Schubring: *Urbano da Cortona: Ein Beitrag zur Kenntnis der Schule Donatellos und der Sieneser Plastik im Quattrocento* (Strasbourg, 1903)
J. Pope-Hennessy: 'Some Donatello Problems: Three Stucco Reliefs', *Essays on Italian Sculpture* (London, 1959, R/1968), pp. 60–64
V. Herzner: 'Donatello in Siena', *Mitt. Ksthist. Inst. Florenz*, xv (1971), pp. 161–86
E. Carli: *Il Duomo di Siena* (Genoa, 1979)
——: 'Un tondo di Urbano da Cortona', *Antol. B.A.*, xxi–xxii (1984), pp. 11–14
R. Munman: 'Urbano da Cortona: Corrections and Observations', *Verrocchio and Late Quattrocento Italian Sculpture* (Florence, 1992), pp. 225–41
ELINOR M. RICHTER

Urban the Painter [Urban målare] (*fl* late 1520s; *d* ?Stockholm, between 1568 and 1574). Swedish painter, possibly of German birth. He was in the service of the Swedish king Gustav I (*reg* 1523–60) from the late 1520s and of the succeeding kings Erik XIV (*reg* 1560–68) and John III (*reg* 1568–92). The best-known work attributed to him, albeit uncertainly, is the *Vädersolstavlan* (1535) in Stockholm Cathedral. It commemorates a celestial phenomenon believed to be an omen. The importance of the work is due to the fact that it is thought to be the earliest example of Swedish landscape painting and that it contains the earliest depiction of medieval Stockholm. The somewhat fantastical quality of the surrounding hilltops and the high skyline suggest influences from the German Danube school, of which Albrecht Altdorfer is the best-known representative. Urban probably worked as a decorative painter at Gripsholm Castle, in particular on the decorative painting of a ceiling that is otherwise attributed to Anders Larsson.

SVKL   BIBLIOGRAPHY
G. Axel-Nilsson: 'Urban målare', *St Eriks Åb.* (1941), pp. 75–92
TORBJÖRN FULTON

Urban planning [Town planning]. The deliberate application of principles relating to the desirable form and nature of urban settlements. As a distinctive component of the overall process of urban development, it is typically achieved through the use of regulatory policies and coordinating institutions. This survey covers the development of urban planning in the Western world from the medieval period to the late 20th century. Further discussion of significant buildings and of particular instances of urban development is also contained in country surveys and in articles on individual cities; together with entries on ancient cities and sites, these also provide coverage of urban planning traditions in such areas as Africa, the ancient world, East and South-east Asia, the Islamic world and the Pre-Columbian Americas.

I. Introduction. II. Before *c.* 1450: the medieval town. III. *c.* 1450–*c.* 1800: the ideal city. IV. *c.* 1800–*c.* 1890: the industrial city. V. *c.* 1890–1945: the urban metropolis. VI. After 1945: regional development and urban renewal.

I. Introduction.

The form of cities depends largely on the relationships between mass and space, with mass consisting of buildings, their ground coverage, bulk and height, and the space between buildings forming streets of different width, length and direction and open areas of different shape. Urban buildings, streets and open areas provide for a variety of types and intensity of land uses and possess different degrees of permanence. These combinations of mass and space constitute the built form of the city.

Five essential categories of urban built form relationships have been identified by such theorists as Kevin Lynch (*see also* §VI below), and these provide a common language for description and comparison. The categories are: paths (corridors of movement, e.g. streets and canals); edges (built or natural features forming barriers, e.g. waterfronts); districts (distinctly identified areas, e.g. town centres or new residential areas); nodes (meeting places of paths, e.g. squares); and landmarks (built form features with a high symbolic and/or visual identity). The combination of these features at any one time forms an urban pattern or structure. Cities vary in their nature, but common features can be observed. One basic factor is the degree of planning influence exerted on a city's form and structure. At one end of the spectrum is the highly planned city (new town); at the other end is the uncoordinated, unplanned, organic city. In between lies a wide range of greater or lesser planned influences, perhaps covering different areas at different times or being strongly marked in certain structural elements but not in others. The scale of planning may vary from the level of the individual site through to the district level, the city as a whole, and even to groups of towns and cities in a regional system.

The principles guiding urban planning are grounded in cultural values, in power and the structures of authority, in economic and social interests, and in dominant technologies. They are expressed through technical and professional competences (notably those of architecture, engineering and, from the late 19th century, a separately identified discipline of urban planning) and in legal procedures and instruments. Urban planning principles range from the visionary or Utopian through to the practicalities of safety and protection (as in fortified towns), of colonization (as in the European city settlements of North and Latin America) and of political status (as in the Baroque capitals). Other urban planning principles look towards economic development (as in the model industrial settlements) and new standards of local residential environment (in city centre improvements, suburban extensions and garden cities). Late 20th-century planning principles embody wider public interest considerations with those of architectural heritage and nature conservation, the relationship of motor traffic and land uses and the induced regeneration of the inner city together with the managed expansion of the metropolis into a more diffuse regional constellation.

This survey of the historical evolution of the Western planning tradition begins with the origins of planned urban settlements in the later medieval era. In this it excludes the contributions of earlier, most notably Roman, urban development and planning. While not neglecting the continuing strength of inherited urban structure where settlement continued after the end of the Empire, it is important not to strive after presumed continuities where, in practice, sharper discontinuities and new beginnings existed, and where the lessons of antiquity awaited rediscovery in quite new surroundings. The early modern period saw a flourishing of urban planning theories and practical activity. Ideal cities were proposed; new capitals

were constructed. Outside Europe, notably in the Americas, new territories were conquered, settled and administered through networks of planned towns. Separate urban elements of mass and space were brought together in deliberate designs. The 19th century brought massive industrialization and urbanization to much of Europe and the eastern seaboard of North America. New principles, techniques and regulatory mechanisms were developed to restructure city centres, accommodate railways and tramways, regulate factory development and provide basic infrastructure services. Urban planning began to emerge as a separate administrative, professional and academic discipline to tackle neglected urban issues of housing and environmental quality and to help coordinate measures for urban development.

The 20th century saw the emergence of a new scale of metropolitan city and experiments with urban planning principles designed to manage the decentralization of population and activities from the central city or conurbation to the wider metropolitan region. A countervailing set of principles sought to retain population and activities and to take account of the impact of the car in wholly modern built forms in the central cities. The devastation of World War II gave urban planners in Europe immense reconstruction powers and social responsibilities, while elsewhere decentralization and the policy issues of the fragmented metropolis led to more sporadic and unplanned development. In the last two decades of the 20th century there was a strengthening of policies for neighbourhood protection and historic and nature conservation in cities, together with experiments designed to free enterprise from the burden of planning restrictions in an attempt to promote urban regeneration.

BIBLIOGRAPHY

S. E. Rasmussen: *Towns and Buildings* (Liverpool, 1951)
K. Lynch: *The Image of the City* (Cambridge, MA, 1960)
E. N. Bacon: *Design of Cities* (London, 1967, rev. 1975)
K. Lynch: *A Theory of Good City Form* (Cambridge, MA, 1981)

DAVID W. MASSEY

II. Before c. 1450: the medieval town.

Two types of medieval town are generally recognized: those of organic growth, which are generally towns with long histories, and those planned largely in a single period (often called 'planted towns'). The distinction was firmly made by Beresford (1967), who identified 251 English and Welsh towns planted between 1066 and 1368. It seems likely, however, that the majority of medieval towns developed in an organic, uncoordinated manner and were composed of a series of units dating from different periods. Even where new towns were initially laid out systematically, they often spilt over and developed their own idiosyncrasies; such models of regularity as Salisbury (Wilts; founded *c.* 1218; *see* SALISBURY, §1(ii)(a)) and New Winchelsea (E. Sussex; founded *c.* 1280) are therefore extreme and untypical examples. The most significant features in medieval urban planning were the institutional parts of the town—castle, monastery and other defined precincts—and those features that helped to concentrate the settlement in one place or that served it once it was established—such as defences, civic amenities and the market-place.

1. Urban planning in medieval Arles, showing the Roman amphitheatre converted into a fortified enclave; from an engraving after J. B. Guibert, 18th century (London, British Museum)

1. Patterns of development. 2. Improvements. 3. New foundations.

1. PATTERNS OF DEVELOPMENT. In many cases the plans of towns were influenced by the existing landscape. Some were moulded to the contours of hills, which affected the design and development of the place: such towns as Siena, Laon and Edinburgh still display the crags or steep slopes on which they were built. At Edinburgh, the Old Town clings to its narrow ridge of rock, with the High Street forming the spine for properties to either side; settlement spread below it to the south into the Cowgate Valley, since the main approach roads to the citadel were from the south and east (*see* EDINBURGH, §1). Sometimes the units of new settlement were based on field boundaries and ridges, as in the 12th century at Stratford-upon-Avon (Warwicks) and Lichfield (Staffs). Little is known of what existed on the site before the town of Salisbury, but the alignment of some streets may have been influenced by previous drainage ditches. Indeed, the completed plan is not particularly regular: only three of the streets are parallel.

Towns quickly developed on coasts, beside rivers and along major roads. Nearly half of all medieval planted towns in England were ports, on the coast or at estuaries; the majority of these were on the south coast, acting as shipping and landing points with direct access to the Continent. In Wales, 24 towns occupied coastal sites. The majority were English foundations, the garrisons of which

could be landed and supplied by ship. Several also had profitable fishing industries during the medieval period, and the economic life of the town centred as much on the public quay as on the castle. A main road running through a town was probably as important a cause of growth as any other. In some cases major routes were diverted to new boroughs with new bridges, as at New Sleaford (Lincs) or Boroughbridge (N. Yorks); the names Stockbridge (Hants), Uxbridge (Middx) and Brigg (Lincs) emphasize the main reason for the place. The Roman road system contributed to the rebirth of London after each of its periods of destruction or decline; then, as now, it was a hard place to avoid. Bridges were therefore important points for communication and access to markets, and in their own way prompted settlement. In both England and Wales, many medieval towns grew up on or near parts of the Roman road system. Most of the 24 medieval towns of Essex, for example, developed on the radial roads running north and east of London. Development within old Roman towns was restricted to some extent by existing ruins and street-patterns. Although much was lost during periods of decline and covered by scrub and silt, such major Roman features as amphitheatres formed fixed points around which streets had to run, and their shapes can be traced in the modern street-plans of such towns as London and Lucca. In Arles the amphitheatre itself was fortified in the 8th and 12th centuries, and a small town was contained within its walls (see fig. 1).

Two clear influences on the shape and extent of old and new towns were their defences and castles. Defences signified the town limits and the size or the intended size of the settlement. Extensions to circuits might therefore be caused by growth of population or expansion of building beyond original boundaries, as at Abergavenny (Gwent) or Southampton (Hants). In Britain only Bristol, Lincoln (*see* LINCOLN, §1) and Norwich certainly had successive concentric rings of defences as at such continental cities as Florence (*see* FLORENCE, §I, 2 and 3(i)) and Siena. Rebuilding the defences to define a smaller area, which presumably reflected urban decay, was rare, although exceptions include New Winchelsea, where the defences in 1414–15 reduced the area of the town, and Berwick-upon-Tweed (Northumb.), where the Elizabethan circuit covered only two-thirds of the area of the 14th-century town. Roman defensive circuits were reused in medieval towns on the same sites, for example at Canterbury (*see* CANTERBURY, §I, 1), Lincoln (*see* LINCOLN, §1), London (*see* LONDON, §II, 2) and York (*see* YORK, §I, 1). The walls were of masonry, and the Roman gates were formidable structures, so it was usual for the majority of the medieval gates in a town to be on the same sites as their Roman predecessors. Any new gates therefore signify new interests; in the case of Moorgate (1415), London, for example, it was a consequence of the reclamation of the marsh outside the walls to provide an open space for the citizens. At other towns, a defensive circuit originally of Anglo-Saxon date was partly or wholly reused in the medieval town, as at Barnstaple and Totnes (Devon), and at Oxford. New medieval circuits or extensions were built substantially of masonry in the larger towns, including Newcastle upon Tyne and Norwich. Gates of masonry were an essential part of these defences, giving both strength and prestige to the entry points into the town. Sometimes there were gates but no defences, as at Banbury (Oxon) and Glasgow.

The single most important plan-unit in most medieval towns was the castle (*see* CASTLE, §I). A distinction is made between castle-boroughs, in which a castle was the point of attraction for a new town, and truly urban castles, in which fortified centres were inserted into existing settlements. The Norman kings and their followers built new castles that were often powerful stimulants to urban growth. Besides offering security, any aristocratic residence would generate a market, and it is therefore not surprising that 80% of all new towns in Wales and 75% in England before 1150 grew up or were established next to a castle; the association of castle and burgh was even more marked in Scotland, where 31 of the 33 burghs founded by the king before 1286 were beside castles. At some places, for example Pleshey (Essex) and Devizes (Wilts), the design of the town in its defences suggests that both were founded at the same time; occasionally castles moved site, perhaps to encourage settlement in a better location. Although castle-boroughs continued to be the norm in the Welsh Marches, the relative peace that existed in England after the mid-12th century meant that only kings founded new towns with the full defensive armoury of a castle. In castle-boroughs the castle was usually on the edge of the new

town, often with its back to an adjacent river. Castles placed in existing towns were similarly on the edge of the settlement, often incorporated into the Roman or Saxon defences, as at Lincoln and London. This resulted, however, in the destruction of earlier housing, or even, as at Cambridge and Norwich, in sweeping aside a church and a cemetery.

The castle, however, was only one type of building to form a nucleus of public life and traffic in the medieval town. In some towns the meeting of main roads, and the market, were to be found at the gate of the monastery or cathedral church, which took over the castle's role as the focal point of the place, as at Bury St Edmunds (Suffolk), Battle (E. Sussex) and Dunstable (Beds). In many Italian and French cities the cathedral, and the bishop's palace next to it, took the place of the castle and became the dominant force in the town, for example at Florence and Chartres. New boroughs were often sited on the edges of existing parishes, and sometimes the church for the new place was dependent on the mother-church; this often created difficulties (e.g. the distance necessary to conduct funerals) and resentment. But where, as in the majority, there was a parish church, market life was also inextricably mixed with daily religious observance. Markets were held in or near churchyards, as at Llanelli and Haverfordwest (Dyfed); churches in other towns lay in the middle of broad market streets. Generally, planted towns had only one church, which contrasted with the many churches of pre-12th-century towns.

The existence of suburbs does not imply that the space inside the town walls was full; many suburbs grew around a bridge or along a waterfront. The form of suburbs was usually dictated by existing approach-roads and by the location of markets immediately outside the town gates, illustrated most vividly by the space called St Giles outside the north gate of Oxford. Near by is Broad Street, another market that was able to expand over the outer edge of the city ditch. Similar developments also occurred in Stamford (Lincs) and in Worcester. Dangerous or noxious trades were often banned to the extramural areas of a town. Blacksmiths, potters, tanners and fullers were found there, either banned because of their smoke or noise, or in order to take advantage of the relatively open space. When the hospitals and friaries were built in the 12th and 13th centuries, they limited rather than encouraged further growth.

Besides expanding along approach-roads, the medieval town often spread in a rather different manner into the adjacent river or sea. A waterfront zone often developed as a narrow strip of reclaimed land along the riverbank or shore, which was modified to suit the needs of the landing and exporting of goods, and subsequently for housing, warehouses and others buildings, even churches. Thus, many towns actually increased their area during the medieval period, the City of London perhaps by as much as 15%. The waterfront zone was articulated by streets and lanes leading to the water's edge, and in such towns as King's Lynn (Norfolk) and London, by regulated landing-places. At Bristol the river was moved to improve the town's harbour.

2. IMPROVEMENTS. The local ruler controlled the revenues of trade by establishing a market within a town, often on only one site. A central space, often near the main church, would be made available for stalls, which in time became permanent structures, evident, for example, at Salisbury. Covered, specialized markets and civic warehouses for food, grain or cloth were to be found in principal towns, including Paris, London and Bruges. A supply of clean water was essential both for consumption and for such industries as textile production, while running water drove corn- or fulling-mills. In Italy this could be crucial: Siena had tunnels and springs in the hillsides but lost out to its rival Florence because the latter could use the Arno both for easy transport and for its textile industry. Major towns organized a public water supply during the 13th century. At Gdańsk (Danzig), Antwerp and elsewhere canals were built to bring water into the town for drinking and for industrial uses.

By 1300, at least in the larger cities, concepts of basic hygiene and the municipal provision of cleaning facilities were widespread. In London and Paris, householders were obliged by law to clean the pavements in front of their houses, and the removal of household and trade waste was assiduously supervised. In London, building regulations to prevent fire and control drainage were formulated by 1200, thus ensuring a certain quality of construction in housing, at least along boundaries with neighbours. In Florence, Siena and Toledo, street widths and the distance a building or its roof could project into the street were fixed by law. In some Italian cities civic pride was developed to the extent that the aspect of the city was controlled: buildings facing the harbour at Genoa, for example, had their proportions regulated to produce a decorous prospect. In general, therefore, while there was little coordination in the planning of streets or urban areas, there was considerable concern about the provision and improvement of civic amenities.

3. NEW FOUNDATIONS. During the 12th and 13th centuries urban expansion took place in virtually every part of Europe. In the existing, pre-medieval towns this took the form of filling out the unsettled areas within the town and spreading beyond such boundaries as defences into new suburbs. Away from the established centres, completely new towns were founded, or the spread of market rights and fairs prompted the crystallization of a loosely formed place into a town. Kings, lords and bishops promoted the transformation of villages into boroughs, often by adding new areas of settlement. Several regions of Europe have groups of new towns in which ideas of urban planning were expressed, including the Valdarno in northern Italy, where several towns were probably designed by Arnolfo di Cambio (e.g. San Giovanni and Castelfranco), and the towns associated with Edward I, King of England. In northern England, at Berwick-upon-Tweed, and in Wales, at Flint (Clwyd), Conwy and Caernarfon (Gwynedd), Edward hoped not only to keep the peace by establishing garrison towns but also to encourage peace by promoting ports and efficient markets. New towns in Gascony, then held by the English crown, are called *bastides*; the name is related to *bâtir* (Fr.: 'to build'), and the streets, public buildings and market-places

of the new towns, by being constructed afresh on new sites, bring into clearer focus the factors at work in the development of towns. Edward I had gathered together experts in the field of urban planning, as it then existed as a subject; the new towns of *c.* 1300 in Wales and Gascony are the most 'planned' of all the English foundations. At Flint (1277), the first of Edward's *bastides* in Wales, the building of which was supervised by JAMES OF ST GEORGE, work began simultaneously on the castle and the town. The land allowed regular blocks to be laid out, with space for the market inside the walls; the town's defences, although on a large scale, were of earth, however, despite being sited on a sandstone outcrop. It is possible that the design owed something to Edward's recent visits to towns in Gascony, or to the Mediterranean *bastide* of Aigues Mortes, which he would have seen in 1270, when departing on a crusade. A second example, Caernarfon (1283), was to be a fortified town on the edge of the hostile kingdom of Gwynedd (see fig. 2). Streets at right-angles divided the intramural area into eight blocks; the market-place lay outside the walls to the east, on the site of the previous Norman castle, next to which a large mill-pool was crossed by a stone bridge of seven arches. Whether the principles of order and uniformity, evident in the design of streets, extended to house-design remains unknown. Apart from these examples, there is little evidence for widespread thought about urban planning in the modern sense. The medieval town plan was as much the product of the ruling

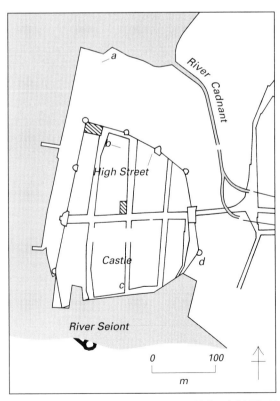

2. Urban plan of medieval Caernarfon, Gwynedd, founded 1283: (a) St Mary; (b) Town Hall; (c) wharf; (d) market-place

authority's attempts to attract tenants to the place as of a particular aesthetic.

BIBLIOGRAPHY

R. E. Dickinson: *The West European City* (London, 1950)
M. Beresford: *New Towns of the Middle Ages: Town Plantation in England, Wales and Gascony* (London, 1967/*R* Gloucester, 1988)
M. G. Conzen: 'The Use of Town Plans in the Study of Urban History', *The Study of Urban History*, ed. H. J. Dyos (London, 1968)
H. Carter: *The Study of Urban Geography* (London, 1972, rev. 3/1981/*R* 1985)
M. W. Barley, ed.: *The Plans and Topography of Medieval Towns in England and Wales*, Council Brit. Archaeol., Res. Rep., 14 (London, 1975)
C. Platt: *English Medieval Towns* (London, 1976)
S. Reynolds: *An Introduction to the History of English Medieval Towns* (Oxford, 1977)
J. Le Goff, ed.: *La Ville médiévale* (1980), ii of *Histoire de la France urbaine*, ed. G. Duby (Paris)
M. D. Lobel, ed.: *Historic Towns: Maps and Plans of Towns and Cities in the British Isles, with Historical Commentaries, from Earliest Times to 1800*, i (Baltimore, 1980); ii (London, 1975); iii (Oxford, 1989)
V. F. Pardo: *Storia dell'urbanistica dal trecento al quattrocento* (Rome and Bari, 1982)
M. Girouard: *Cities and People: A Social and Architectural History* (New Haven and London, 1985)
H. B. Clarke and A. Simms: *The Comparative History of Urban Origins in Non-Roman Europe: Ireland, Wales, Denmark, Germany, Poland and Russia, from the Ninth to the Thirteenth Century*, 2 vols, Brit. Archaeol. Rep., Int. Ser., 255 (Oxford, 1985)
K. Boockmann: *Die Stadt im späten Mittelalter* (Munich, 1986)

JOHN SCHOFIELD

III. *c. 1450–c. 1800: the ideal city.*

By the mid-15th century Europe already had a dense urban network, and few additional centres were created between the 16th and 18th centuries, except in the northern areas. Although the population growth in the cities during this period was impressive, it was only slightly higher than that in rural areas. The sharpest rises were seen in the cities of northern Europe: between the middle of the 15th century and end of the 18th the population of Moscow rose from 30,000 to 200,000, and that of Berlin from 15,000 to 150,000. In southern Europe the population of such cities as Florence, Genoa and Venice tended to remain stable or even shrink, although here too urban life remained vigorous. Generally, however, it was the already established major cities that grew fastest, with the population of London, for example, rising from 150,000 to 850,000, and that of Paris from 200,000 to 500,000. The scale of such cities was entirely new in the Western world, although Beijing and Istanbul constituted examples from outside the West of urban development on a similar scale. It would be misleading, however, to suggest too close a link between developments in urban planning and economic growth, or between urban expansion and population growth: urban improvements sometimes resulted from accumulated wealth rather than current economic prosperity (as in 16th-century Venice), and sometimes urban expansion might be largely or wholly attributable to the development of large residential areas for the wealthy, with any population growth being absorbed by an increasingly densely inhabited city centre. The increased significance of the city was reflected in a new concern for its ideal form, evident in projects for urban expansion, rebuilding and improvements, and in new foundations.

1. Planning theory. 2. Expansion. 3. Rebuilding. 4. Embellishments and improvements. 5. New foundations.

1. PLANNING THEORY. The major innovation in urban planning during the 15th and 16th centuries was the emergence of a new concept of the form that a city should take. Regularity, both geometrical and statutory, was not unknown in the Middle Ages—for example the grid-pattern layout of a number of new towns and the building regulations in the towns of Tuscany (*see* §II, 2 above)—but from the 15th and 16th centuries urban planning was governed by deliberate design. The preliminary drawing began to be used to give expression to planning aims and to imbue regularity of construction with authoritative power: the slightest irregularity, which might be concealed in an actual townscape, is immediately evident in a drawing. Regularity was of course subject to the constraints of the actual size, shape and contours of the existing medieval town and the available land around it, to the characteristics of the individual site and to the unpredictable hazards that might arise when construction work was carried out. Nevertheless, regularity constituted an ideal that found expression both in actual experiments, beginning in Italy, and in treatises.

An early attempt to realize this urban planning ideal was the design of the Piazza SS Annunziata (from 1421) in Florence. The piazza was based on a design by Filippo Brunelleschi, and the area was immediately cleared to form a rectangular piazza flanked by porticos (of the church and the new hospital) on two of its sides; opposite the church a street was opened up, which extended along the same axis as the piazza. Although on the two remaining sides porticos were not built until the beginning of the 16th century, the overall unifying design was planned from the outset and was evident in the original plans (*see* FLORENCE, §I, 3). Such a notion of regularity in construction continued to be developed in a number of theoretical proposals (e.g. Sforzinda, an ideal town designed by FILARETE) as well as in actual experiments. The designs of Francesco di Giorgio Martini (from 1482) and Leonardo da Vinci (1497–1503), and the built works of Fra Giovanni Giocondo (1511) and Pietro Cataneo (1554), all disseminated the image of the ideal city with its grid pattern or sunburst-shaped layout. The models most frequently followed were Sabbioneta (1560–84), built by Vespasiano Gonzaga, Duca da Sabbioneta, and particularly Palmanova (see fig. 3), Venetia, the sunburst-shaped layout of which was designed either by Vincenzo Scamozzi or G. Savorgnan. Usually, however, the regularity resulting from plans to improve or extend existing centres arose out of work carried out at different times; regularity was achieved patiently, as in Rome in the 16th century.

The care taken to introduce regularity in terms of layout was accompanied by a desire to create specific scenic vistas, depicted in the perspective views of Francesco di Giorgio Martini and of other late 15th-century artists. Michelangelo's Piazza del Campidoglio (1561–8; *see* MICHELANGELO, §I, 4) on the Capitoline Hill, Rome, was typical in the desire both to create regularity through symmetry and to arrange spaces in order to create a specific visual impression (in this case setting the scene using a Classical equestrian statue of the Roman emperor

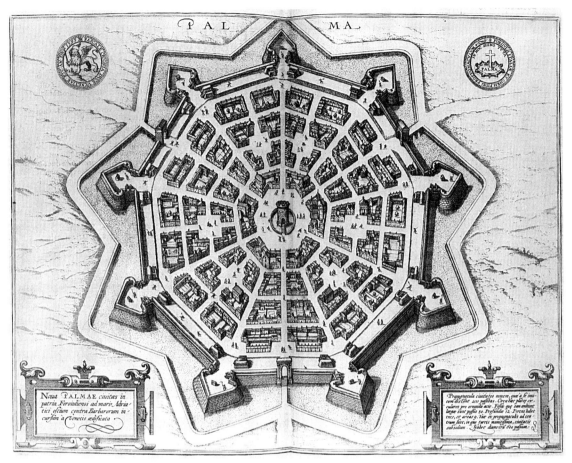

3. Urban plan of Palmanova, designed by G. Savorgnan or Vincenzo Scamozzi; engraving by G. Braun and F. Hohenberg in *Urbium praecipuanum mundi theatrum*, 1573 (London, British Library)

Marcus Aurelius). The Piazza del Campidoglio is an example *par excellence* of symmetry built out of irregularity: the Palazzo dei Conservatori was not parallel to the axis of the piazza, giving the latter its resulting trapezoidal shape. Another symmetrical project in Rome was realized on a larger scale: the street layout on either side of the Via del Corso created by the construction of two new roads running from the Piazza del Popolo, which together with the central axis formed the Tridente. The practicality of having roads converging towards the Porta del Popolo, as well as the layout of the site itself, lent themselves to this design. Pope Leo X had the Via Ripetta built at a tangent to the Tiber between 1513 and 1521, while Pope Clement VII had the Via del Babuino built at the foot of the Pincio Hill between 1534 and 1549. A monumental character was lent to this urban design by the two churches, S Maria dei Miracoli and S Maria in Montesanto (both 1675–8; by Gianlorenzo Bernini and Carlo Fontana; *see* ROME, fig. 7), which marked the two prongs of the Tridente, the outline of which was filled in with speculative developments.

A second important stage in the emergence of new ideas about urban planning occurred during the second half of the 18th century. Although the use of individual improvements to increase the regularity of the city continued (e.g. the opening up in 1727–35 of the Piazza di S Ignazio, Rome, by FILIPPO RAGUZZINI, or the projects designed from 1764 for Metz by Jacques-François Blondel; *see* BLONDEL, (2), §2), from *c.* 1750 a new concern for the ease of circulation in cities emerged, encompassing the movement of people, vehicular traffic and the channelling of water. In all three cases the solution was the same: open up new urban spaces in the form of streets, squares, embankments and distribution networks. Although the new ideas relating to circulation were explored in Britain and the Netherlands, it was in France that the main theories relating to such improvements were published, for example Abbé Marc-Antoine Laugier's *Essai sur l'architecture* (Paris, 1753) and Pierre Patte's *Mémoires sur les objets les plus importants d'architecture* (Paris, 1769). Theories also began to emerge relating to the concept of the industrial town, but although occasionally these were put into practice (e.g. the town designed by CLAUDE-NICOLAS LEDOUX around the Salines de Chaux, 1774–1804, at Arc-et-Senans, nr Besançon, or the industrial town of San Leucio, 1774–89, nr Naples), they had little subsequent influence, and industrial cities in the 19th century never assumed such monumental forms.

2. EXPANSION.

(i) Moderate. The population of many Italian towns fell between the 16th and 18th centuries. Growth had previously been very rapid, however, and this had expressed itself clearly through several large areas of development, for example the San Frediano quarter in Florence, which was built up between 1425 and 1520. Some of Italy's major cities underwent significant expansion, however, such as Ferrara, where from 1491 Ercole I d'Este (*reg* 1471–1505) doubled the surface area of his city with a new quarter laid out along two almost perpendicular axes (*see* FERRARA, §1). In Rome, linked with the opening up of the Tridente, the area between the Corso and the Via di Ripetta was developed (1516–26), as well as to the south around the new Piazza di Monte d'Oro (1523–43) on plots of land bought by Sigismondo Chigi. Among those who bought plots were Baldassare Peruzzi (who may have drawn up the plans for the development), Antonio da Sangallo (ii) and Giulio Romano. On the other side of the Corso, the monks of S Silvestro in Capite developed a vast area; work started in 1547, continued until the end of the century, and included the construction of two major streets: the Via Condotti and the Via Frattina.

In Naples, the monastery of Monte Oliveto developed Pizzofalcone Hill (1530–38) in conjunction with a new city wall (*see* NAPLES, §I, 3). Later, in the middle of the century, the viceroy, the Marqués de Villafranca, developed the Spanish Quarter—a vast chequer-board layout built in line with the Via Toledo. During the first half of the 17th century in Turin, the Città Nuova was added to the original square formation of the ancient Roman town and the 16th-century citadel. This was also built on a square grid layout, with units slightly bigger than those of the ancient town, and it was also surrounded by a modern, fortified, city wall. Work started in 1673 on a second extension to the city, which increased its area by simply extending the streets, thereby forming a new expanse of square grid pattern. A novelty in the form of a diagonal street was added, however, when the Contrada di Po was built to link the Porta del Po to the Piazza Castello, itself cleared in 1587 to relieve congestion around the new royal palace as both the piazza and the palace were built on the earlier 16th-century ramparts. Not all Italian cities, however, undertook such developments. Lucca, for example, saw the addition of only a few small housing developments linked with a new fortified city wall; Venice essentially added nothing more than the modest Fondamente Nuove development. There were, however, several major urban expansions during the 18th century, such as the growth of TRIESTE.

After the Spanish court settled permanently in Madrid in 1610, the city's population more than doubled over some 20 years. As well as the construction of a considerable number of palaces, churches, convents, monasteries and other amenities required by its status as capital city, Madrid also expanded towards the north, east and south during the second half of the 16th century and the first half of the 17th. These expansions consisted of irregular developments on rectangular plots covered in low, generally poorly built, houses. By the mid-17th century, the city had already reached the limits beyond which it did not expand significantly until the 19th century. Paris was the biggest city in Europe at the beginning of the 17th century, and it was expanded partly by adding aristocratic suburbs (e.g. Faubourg Saint-Germain-des-Prés and Faubourg Saint-Honoré), but mainly due to a variety of housing developments. Some of these were large grid-plan layouts (e.g. Pré-aux-Clercs, from 1620; Ile-St-Louis, 1614–45), but most were smaller, less regular developments such as the Marais (throughout the 17th century) or the Quartier Richelieu (1633–7; *see* PARIS, §II, 3(iii)), or the later Chaussée d'Antin (1770–85; *see* PARIS, §II, 4(i)). It was not until the end of the 18th century that developments began on the sites of such existing buildings as earlier, private mansions with gardens, and began either to be laid out in more elaborate patterns of urban design or to be arranged around such monumental works as the Théâtre de l'Odéon or the Couvent des Capucins. These latter developments were planned by such major architects as Alexandre-Théodore Brongniart, Claude-Nicolas Ledoux, Charles de Wailly and François-Joseph Bélanger. Similar extensions were added during the 18th century to the major French ports, including Nantes and Bordeaux, and also to France's second city, Lyon (*see* LYON, §1(ii)(b)).

One of the most interesting cases was that of Antwerp, which became Europe's leading port during the 17th century. While a new bastioned city wall was built (1543–5; *see* ANTWERP, fig. 1), a single entrepreneur—Gilbert van Schoonbeke—planned developments of every kind: both replacing existing buildings (e.g. the new Stadthuis, 1560–64; *see* ANTWERP, §IV, 2), and extending them, both within the city walls (the Nieuwstad) or outside them (the Leikwartier). In the case of the Nieuwstad and the Tapissierspand quarters, van Schoonbeke was working on behalf of the civic authorities, but in the other cases he acted as a private entrepreneur. Most of his developments were simple square grid plans, sometimes with tree-lined avenues (e.g. the Leikwartier), but on at least one occasion his concern with aspects of composition revealed Italian influences, as in the town square and three radiating streets from the Stadthuis. During the 17th and 18th centuries, London provided the paradigm of a particular type of urban housing development: the square. Large properties belonging to the aristocracy were dismembered to form leasehold properties subject to long leases, and housing developments were built around large squares with central gardens, which were surrounded by streets forming an orthogonal network. The forerunners of these squares dated from the early 17th century, including Covent Garden (1618–21, by Inigo Jones), which John Evelyn described in 1644 as inspired by Livorno in Italy. By the mid-18th century, 11 town squares already existed in London, including St James's Square, Bloomsbury Square and King Square (1680–81), the first instance of a central garden being reserved exclusively for the use of those living around it. Those built towards the end of the 18th century were usually designed along similar lines, but with Bedford Square (1775–6) and the work of the Adam brothers (e.g. the Adelphi, begun 1772; rebuilt 1936–8; *see* ADAM (i), (3)) there was a move towards greater architectural ambition and monumentality (*see* LONDON, §II, 3).

The growth of Amsterdam between the 16th and 18th centuries was marked in the 17th century by the creation of two new quarters between the centre and the new bastioned city wall then under construction. Three parallel concentric canals were cut from 1615, and the islands of land they delimited were divided up into regular plots of 6–9 m in width. A middle-class residential neighbourhood was built up there over the following decades, under the direction of Daniël Stalpaert, while another neighbourhood—now known as the Jordaan—was designated for artisans and immigrants (*see* AMSTERDAM, §II, 2).

(ii) Major. In contrast with urban growth rates in other parts of Europe, the north and east saw the foundation of a considerable number of new towns and the birth of true capital cities, particularly during the 18th century. Copenhagen expanded from a medieval core, growing in a series of planning campaigns, each of which was typical of its period. At the beginning of the 17th century Christianhaven was a small new fortified town built on a grid pattern and settled on the far bank of the port by Christian IV (*see* OLDENBURG, (2)). Then, in the middle of the century, a new town was planned in between the old town and the citadel, within a new city wall; the Nye Skipperboder and Nyboder were constructed, made up of regular square or rectangular blocks. Between this ensemble and the port, Frederick V (*reg* 1746–66) had the district of Frederiksstad built from 1749 to designs by Niels Eigtved. It was arranged around a central octagonal square, Amalienborg Slotsplads, with four main radiating streets (*see* COPENHAGEN, fig. 1). Stockholm was no more than a

large village on a small island (Stadsholmen) at the beginning of the 17th century, but work began in 1640 to build new districts on gridded layouts to the north (Norrmalm) and south (Södermalm; *see* STOCKHOLM, §1).

Berlin underwent equally rapid growth towards the end of the 17th century, beginning with the development of Friedrichswerder (1662) to the west, and later incorporating the addition outside the ramparts of Dorotheenstadt (see fig. 4), a quarter laid out in chequer-board fashion to the west of the old town and lying on either side of the Unter den Linden (opened in 1647; for illustration of the street plan *see* BERLIN, fig. 1). The grid-plan layout initiated with Dorotheenstadt was later extended towards the south by Elector Frederick III (later King Frederick I) at the beginning of the 18th century, when Friedrichstadt was enlarged using the same grid for the street layout and with Friedrichstrasse and Liepzigstrasse as its axes. In the 1730s Friedrichstadt was further enlarged and encircled by a monumental composition made up of town squares of every shape, together with the avenues that linked them to the square grid plan (*see* BERLIN, §I, 2). To the north and east of Berlin, districts with less regular layouts (e.g. Spandau and Königstadt) were built. During the same period, Vienna and Moscow also expanded along similar lines, with a system of suburbs less regular in their layout. Even smaller towns such as Stuttgart were also enlarged. Stuttgart was endowed with a new quarter (Turnieracker) laid out on a regular ground-plan as early as the mid-15th century. In fact, it became common practice for German

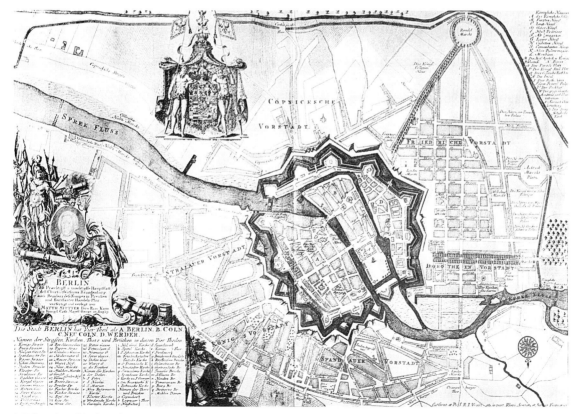

4. Urban plan of Berlin and the new quarter of Dorotheenstadt, by Matthaeus Seutter, *c.* 1750

towns to add this type of planned extension (e.g. Kassel, Oberneustadt, by Paul Du Ry, after 1688; *see* DU RY, (2)).

The principal innovations in extension planning came from Great Britain, with Bath and Edinburgh the most important examples. The new areas in Bath were conceived as small, independent fragments linked to one another only by a street. This concept of the fragment was developed by John Wood II after his father had started the expansion of Bath with Queen Square and its vicinity (1728–36; *see* WOOD (ii), (1)). A new bourgeois monumentality was evident in the Royal Circus (1754–*c.* 1766) and Royal Crescent (1767–*c.* 1775), where one-family houses combined to form a continuous body of building, obliterating all signs of division between the plots. Robert Adam later extended this system to the new neighbourhood of Pulteney (1777–82).

In Edinburgh, faced with the necessity of expanding the city, the civic authorities bought land to the north of the Old Town, built the North Bridge and invited architects to submit planning proposals (*see* EDINBURGH, §1(ii)). The plan by James Craig (1744–95) was made up of two ranges of blocks on either side of George Street, completed by an orthogonal square at each end: Charlotte Square and St Andrew's Square. The blocks were divided lengthwise by mews. Immediately to the north of Craig's New Town (*see* EDINBURGH, fig. 2), R. Reid added another at the end of the century, which was similar, with the exception of two town squares, one of which was circular (Royal Circus) and the other of which ended in a semicircle (Drummond Place).

3. REBUILDING. In the history of urban development, natural and non-natural disasters have necessarily played a significant role, and the great cities—with their houses still often half-timbered—were not spared outbreaks of fire. The Great Fire of London (1666) and the Lisbon earthquake (1755), for example, were two events that prompted significant new developments in the history of urban planning. Such catastrophes provided an opportunity to plan the most extensive renovation or rebuilding of the centres of some major cities. As with the establishment of new towns, these undertakings were also an opportunity to experiment with new designs.

The Great Fire of London could have been the first such opportunity. Charles II wanted to take advantage of the occasion to modernize the capital and issued a proclamation ordering the reconstruction of houses in brick or stone and the construction of new, wider streets. Of the six projects presented to him the King preferred Christopher Wren's, which was the most ambitious (*see* LONDON, §II, 3(i)). Wren's design (see fig. 5) was made up of three parts, one square grid layout in the centre (with St Paul's Cathedral in the middle) and systems of radiating and concentric streets on either side of it, laid out on an octagonal basis. To the west, the Royal Exchange took pride of place in the middle of a square, while an independent neighbourhood was planned for the east, beyond the culverted Fleet Ditch. Given the innovative nature of the design, it is impossible not to look for sources of influence—firstly in Italy, as suggested by the fact that Wren named the squares 'piazzas'. Italian treatises and such projects as Palmanova offered examples of the octagonal layout and of the sunburst layout planned for the Place de France (unexecuted) in Paris under Henry IV. As for the fact that St Paul's was sited at the fork of two diagonal axes, this recalls the siting of the church of S Maria di Montesanto (completed late 1670s, by Carlo Rainaldi; *see* ROME, fig. 7) at the Piazza del Popolo in Rome.

Due to opposition from landowners, Wren's plan was not executed in its entirety. Over a period of 25 years, London was rebuilt on the same layout as before, but with wider, straighter streets, and New Quay was built, opening up the banks of the Thames. Other rebuilding projects enjoyed greater success. The centre of Rennes in France was renovated after the 1720 fire, to a gridded layout

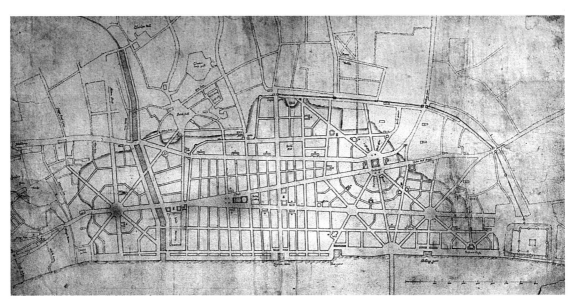

5. Urban plan for the reconstruction of London, by Christopher Wren, 330×698 mm, after 1666 (Oxford, All Souls College)

designed by Isaac Robelin (*fl* 1722–4) and revised by Jacques Gabriel V. The course of the River Vilaine was straightened and a royal square added to embellish the centre (*see* RENNES, §1). In other parts of France (e.g. Châteaudun, Pontarlier, Saint-Dizier) and elsewhere (e.g. Oslo), a considerable number of other towns were rebuilt with a regular layout during the course of the 18th century.

The rebuilding of Lisbon was the most impressive of the 18th-century urban projects (*see* LISBON, §I). Shortly after the earthquake, the Marquês de Pombal commissioned Manuel de Maia to produce a number of designs for the rebuilding work (*see* POMBAL). De Maia came up with three suggestions: to rebuild along the same lines as before while merely widening the old streets; to rebuild on a regular layout, having razed the remains of the central Baixa quarter; or to build a completely new town on the banks of the River Tagus. Pombal chose the second of these three solutions and commissioned six variations on the design, opting for that submitted by the military engineers Carlos Mardel and Eugénio dos Santos. The regularity of the grid-plan layout was complemented by the Neo-classical POMBALINE STYLE architecture (*see* PORTUGAL, §II, 2(ii)). The building of the new Lisbon went on for some 20 years.

A few decades before, in 1693, a serious earthquake had struck south-eastern Sicily. Several towns were rebuilt on their original sites to a grid plan (e.g. Ragusa, Catania), while others were rebuilt on more auspicious sites a short distance away (e.g. Noto, Avola). Among the most elaborate layouts, Avola and Granmichele (both with hexagonal city walls) were both clearly inspired by 16th- and 17th-century treatises, but the ideal layouts decreed by the authority of great noblemen (e.g. the Duca di Camastra, the Prince of Butera) were not always followed by the local officials in charge of their realization. In the case of San Stefano di Camastra in particular, there was considerable difficulty in reconciling a geometrically sophisticated design for the town's layout with the persistent use of terraced housing. It was for the same reason that when towns in Calabria were being rebuilt after an earthquake in 1783, the most elaborate of the plans drawn up by Neapolitan engineers were scarcely adhered to at all (e.g. Cortale, Bagnara, Santa Eufemia), unlike those that were no more than simple square grids (e.g. Mileto, Filadelfia).

4. EMBELLISHMENTS AND IMPROVEMENTS. Embellishments and improvements were the essential means of modernizing cluttered urban centres, and they always involved creating empty spaces in order to ease the flow of both traffic and air. Such improvements therefore often involved the destruction of buildings or changes of use in peripheral zones and the introduction of straight streets and geometrically regular city squares. Improvement was, however, also a question of stylistic modernization; because the old town could not be entirely destroyed, the aim was to give it an appearance more in keeping with contemporary tastes. The new façades, often unified, thus played a role of prime importance by providing a backdrop to existing monuments or new ones where areas had been cleared. The old town with its improvements thus gave the impression of a new city. It is worth noting that apart from such improvements most operations of this type also involved new developments, but these were generally limited to the depth of a single row of buildings.

(i) Street planning. The first straight streets built in Rome were planned with the aim of providing better links between the Vatican and the Field of Mars parade ground. The Via Alessandrina was laid out in the reign of Alexander VI to connect the Castel Sant'Angelo in a straight line with St Peter's. The Via Giulia, which was laid out during the reign of Julius II, was intended to open on to a new bridge (added much later) across the Tiber in order to relieve congestion on the Ponte Sant'Angelo. Straight streets of this kind multiplied in Italian cities during the 16th century and were often flanked by palazzi, which gave them the appearance of avenues of monuments. Examples included the Via Toledo (1536–43) in Naples, the Strada Nuova (1548–71) in Genoa, where a development with a regular layout was arranged along a wide, straight road, administered by the town authorities for the benefit of the aristocratic families, and the Via Cassaro (1560s; now Via Toledo) and the Via Maqueda (1590s) in Palermo, which cut diagonally through the town (*see* PALERMO, §I). This fashion for straight, open streets in the old town centre or on its margins later spread throughout Europe. One example was the Rue Dauphine in Paris, built under Henry IV on the axis of the Pont-Neuf (1599–1603).

(ii) Town squares. The second element in the improvements typical of this period was the prestigious town square. The earliest examples were generally spaces cleared around monuments (e.g. Piazza SS Annunziata, Florence). When PIENZA was rebuilt, a piazza was constructed in front of the cathedral, framed by the Palazzo Piccolomini and the Episcopal Palace (1459–64, by Bernardo Rossellino). Another example was the Piazza S Marco in Venice. In this last case, all that was required was to extend the church piazza before the basilica and to surround it with buildings: the Procuratie Vecchie (rebuilt from 1513, by Pietro Buon) and the Procuratie Nuove (1529–37, by Jacopo Sansovino). The Piazzetta, which was linked with the piazza, was widened, and its building was modified by the Library (1536–7, by Jacopo Sansovino (*see* SANSOVINO, (1)).

Town squares graced by an equestrian statue enjoyed widespread success during the 17th and 18th centuries, particularly in France. The same principles were usually adopted: the squares were built on the edge of town but in contact with the centre, and in some cases they actually replaced part of an ancient town wall (e.g. Place des Victoires, Paris, 1685, by Jules Hardouin Mansart). Once a site had been chosen, a regular town square was designed around an equestrian statue of the king and was then surrounded by unified façades, which might appear only on one side (e.g. Place de la Concorde, Paris). These squares generally played a modest part in the city's traffic-flow scheme, as in the case of the Place Royale (from 1605; now Place des Vosges), inserted between the Rue St-Antoine and the Grands Boulevards, but were also part of housing development operations, where the increase in the value of the land financed such improvements.

Although the Spanish plaza mayor served a similar, decorative function, it also played a more diverse role, particularly because it was surrounded by shops and workshops and because bullfights were held there. At first, these squares were regular in shape and unified, with arcades (e.g. as Plaza Mayor, Valladolid, 1561, by Francisco de Salamanca and Juan Bautista de Toledo; Plaza Mayor, Madrid, 1617–21, by Juan Gómez de Mora). Later, however, they developed into squares that were entirely closed off and accessible only by way of vaulted entrances, as in the case of the Corredera (1683) in Córdoba or that in Salamanca (1729–88, by R. Caballero y Llanes), presumably in order to make them still more suitable for use as bull-rings.

(iii) Linking old and new quarters. Improvements were also often used to resolve difficulties in linking old and new towns, separated by ramparts that were later destroyed. In Aix-en-Provence, for example, the Cours à Carosses (1650; now Cours Mirabeau; for illustration *see* AIX-EN-PROVENCE) was built between the old town and the Quartier Mazarin; in Nancy there was the Place Stanislas (1752–5, by Emmanuel Héré), which extended the 16th-century Place de la Carrière; in Kassel there was the rectangular Friedrichsplatz, designed by Paul Du Ry, and the circular Königsplatz, designed by Louis Du Ry in the mid-18th century. In Stockholm, a system of axes between two town squares and a (partially executed) monumental town centre laid out around the new Royal Palace provided the necessary links between old and new town.

Such embellishments should not, however, obscure the fact that in most cases it was the outlying areas of each town that benefited more from improvements; town centres tended to remain insalubrious areas where traffic was severely restricted.

5. NEW FOUNDATIONS. New towns were, ideally, supposed to give shape to the urban aspirations of the society that created them by means of a specific design; herein lies their cultural interest, as few new urban centres were created, even in northern Europe.

(i) Urban centres. (ii) National borders. (iii) Political seats and centres of refuge. (iv) Colonial towns.

(i) Urban centres. Since the Middle Ages onwards, it had proved necessary to create new towns in central and northern Europe in order to give these regions—which had lain outside Europe's urbanized world since Roman times—a much-needed urban network. This major increase in urban foundations continued, although it was less significant than the planned extensions to medieval city centres.

One of the most representative examples was that of the creation of ZAMOŚĆ in Poland, the foundation of which (1580) was promoted by Jan Zamoyski, who summoned Bernardo Morando to work on it. Zamość was laid out in the middle of a vast estate and took on all the functions required of an urban centre for a considerable area, and it was inspired by Renaissance ideal models. The project consisted of a sophisticated grid-plan layout with a central square emphasizing the town hall (1591; 18th-century additions), and it was built quickly. Zamość was not an isolated example: Poland had already seen the foundation, along the same lines, of Lubortow (1537) and Glogów (1570). Norway and Sweden were home to another wave of new foundations. Christiana (now Oslo),

founded by Christian IV of Denmark, reproduced the canonical model of a town laid out on a square grid plan and flanked by a citadel, the whole being surrounded by a fortified town wall. Christian IV also founded Bredstedt (1616) in Denmark and Kristiansand (1641) in Norway; both had gridded layouts but were not fortified, demonstrating that economic considerations prevailed on some occasions at least. Towns founded in Sweden during the 17th century had similar characteristics in that they too were not always fortified; examples included Uppsala (1643), Kristinehamm (1654), Norrköping (1640–55), Göteborg (1619), Falun (1621) and Helsinki (1640). All these square grid layouts had to be adapted to their sites and to existing structures. A number of small, fortified towns were also built in Denmark and Sweden on square grid layouts, or on radial plans.

The greatest example of such developments in northern Europe was St Petersburg, which was the subject of several plans during the reign of Peter I (*see* ST PETERSBURG, §I, 2 and 3). The city finally took shape during the reign of Elizabeth (1725–62), when three great convergent roads were built on the left bank of the Neva starting from the Admiralty House. The system was completed by two concentric canals outlining, as it were, a new Amsterdam. In 1763, Catherine II organized a European competition to design projects to embellish the centre and develop the outlying areas of the city. Under her long reign (1762–96) St Petersburg was filled out, gradually becoming studded with mansions designed by Italian and French architects.

(ii) National borders. Towards the end of the 17th century there was a revival of the ancient Roman concept of frontier defences, and new fortified towns were built along the borders of several European states. The same idea—together with the importance of maritime trade—also led to the foundation of new ports. However, in some regions with few urban centres (e.g. Andalusia), there was an internal colonization of the marginal areas.

SÉBASTIEN LEPRESTRE DE VAUBAN created a network of small, fortified towns along several French frontiers, including Montlouis (1681) in the Pyrenees. The basic plan was always the same: a polygonal town wall enclosing a regular, chequer-board street layout with a square or rectangular parade-ground in the middle. Nor did the Spanish hold back on their side of the border, founding Charleroi (by 1666) in the Ardennes to face France. During the same period, a line of new ports was also established in France along the Atlantic coast, which included Rochefort (1666), Lorient (1666–1736) and Brest (1631–94). The same policy was adopted in Scandinavia, but here the model was clearly provided by LIVORNO. Built under Francesco I, Livorno was intended as a new maritime trade outlet for the Grand-Duchy of Tuscany after the decline of Pisa. Bernardo Buontalenti designed a regular grid layout surrounded by a fortified pentagonal town wall. The first stone was laid in 1577, and at the end of the century a handsome town square with unified façades was added.

In Spain, many important marginal areas still remained to be urbanized. Charles III's efforts in this respect between 1767 and 1775 amounted to a veritable interior colonization programme, with the foundation of a considerable number of towns including La Carolina and La Luisiana. Some cases of internal colonization also occurred in other countries; one interesting example was San Lorenzo Nuovo (1771–9) on the northern edge of the Papal States, founded by Pius VI, with a handsome, octagonal town square in the centre. In Russia, Catherine II founded a large number of border towns following the colonial type, including Pietroza Wodska (1778), Bogorodizk (1779), Tula (1779), Lucha (1781), Bogorosk (1784), Voskresenk (1784) and ODESSA (1794).

(iii) Political seats and centres of refuge. The foundation of some towns was political in nature. Towns serving as royal or aristocratic seats formed the most obvious group, characterized by the juxtaposition of a château or palace and a town that could be described as existing to serve it. Versailles, founded *c.* 1665–71 (see fig. 6), served as a model for the whole of Europe, although it was not the oldest example: RICHELIEU (i) was built between 1631 and 1642. The links between château and town were particularly skilfully planned, with the converging avenues inspired by the area around the Piazza del Popolo in Rome. Throughout Europe, this combination of square grid developments built close to a château predominated; examples of princely residences with their own towns included Ludwigsburg (from 1704; *see* STUTTGART, §1),

near Stuttgart, POTSDAM (enlarged 18th century), near Berlin, and Aranjuez, near Madrid.

Another group of political foundations comprised the new capitals, with France giving the earliest, handsome examples in the form of Nancy and Charleville. At Nancy, Duke Charles III of Lorraine added a vast Ville Neuve with a square grid layout and fortifications (designed *c.* 1590 by an Italian engineer) to the pre-existing medieval town. In Charleville, Carlo I Gonzaga, Duc de Nevers (later Duke of Mantua), had a handsome town built on a regular layout from 1608; it had a central square with unified façades, built with arcades and designed by Clément Métezeau. The finest example in Germany was MANNHEIM, founded in 1606 as a fortified town, which became a model of its kind. The elector Palatine made it his capital in 1721, destroyed the fortress and redesigned the layout of the town (from *c.* 1699) with a palace and a vast square grid layout studded with regular-shaped town squares.

A separate group of foundations comprised the religious towns of refuge, which were, for the most part, simple square grid layouts designed for those German electors who protected the Protestants. From the point of view of urban development, Freudenstadt and Henrichemont were the most interesting. FREUDENSTADT, founded in 1599 by Frederick I of Württemberg (*reg* 1593–1608), was

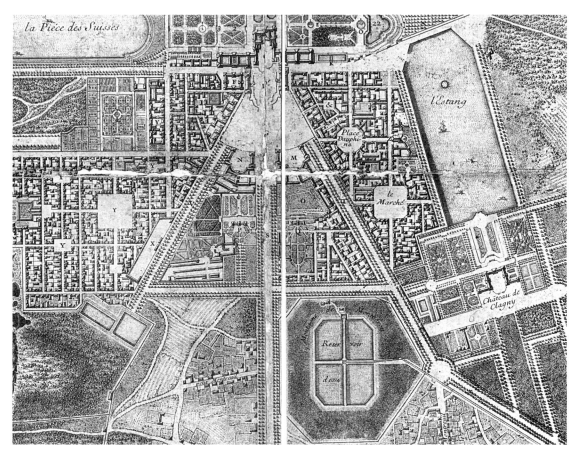

6. Plan of the town and château of Versailles, by Pierre Le Pautre, 1717 (London, British Library)

designed as a square town with a central town square of the same shape, surrounded by parallel, rectangular blocks of buildings. The town's architect, Heinrich Schickhardt II, drew his inspiration from a large number of existing treatises and designs for ideal cities, including those of Dürer (1527), Pietro Cataneo (1554), G. Cataneo (1584) and Jean Perret (1601).

In 1619 Freudenstadt served as the model for many Utopian Protestant towns (e.g. Christianopolis, unexecuted, by J. V. Andrae). Henrichemont (est. 1605–8; partially executed) was also a square town with a sophisticated layout. Eight streets led away from the central town square, and four subsidiary town squares occupied the centre of each of the four quarters of the town, with eight streets leading away from each of these in their turn. The basic concept may have been the work of J. Errard, author of *La Fortification réduite en art* (1600), which contained the plan of a fairly similar fortified town.

Valletta in Malta was founded in 1566 for religious, military and political reasons. Designed by Francesco Laparelli (1521–70), it was laid out on a standard square grid plan possibly inspired by Pietro Cataneo's treatise, but it did not have the fine detail of the idealized Renaissance urban plans (*see* MALTA, §III, 1).

(iv) Colonial towns. The most common aspects of the towns founded in the American colonies reflected the urban planning ideas prevalent in Europe. The Spanish, the British, the French and the Dutch all exported development techniques that were particularly suited to the colonial system (designed for ease of layout and construction, with the allocation of plots of equal size and orientation and with possibilities for expansion). The basic model for such developments ultimately derived—although the Europeans had no precise knowledge of this—from the colonial towns of the Greeks and Romans; ancient urban planning was unknown to archaeologists until the 19th century.

The new towns clearly followed changes in the colonial system as it developed, but the most significant factor was the individual approach taken by each colonizing nation. The Spanish set out to design true cities in their colonies from as early as the beginning of the 16th century, but it was not until the mid- to late 17th century that the other European nations founded anything more than trading posts protected by forts. However, it is now recognized that these towns were founded not in order to absorb existing population growth but in an attempt to attract colonists coming from Europe, so as to create the conditions to populate the colonies—a process that was often

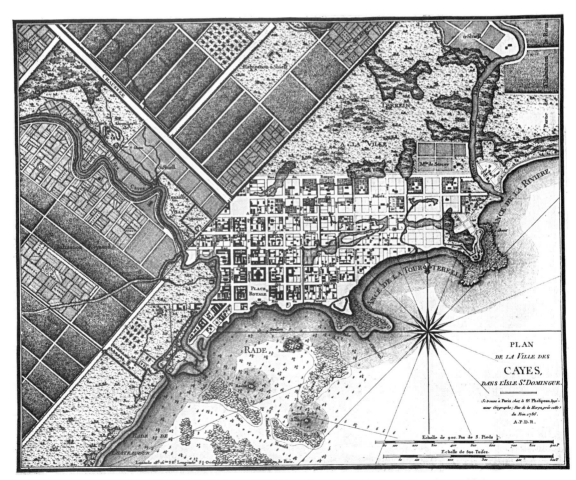

7. Urban plan for Les Cayes, Santo Domingo, by Phelipeau, 1726 (Aix-en-Provence, Centre des Archives d'Outre-Mer)

long in developing. Even before 1576, when Philip II of Spain proclaimed specifications for the foundation of towns in the Americas, several towns had already been established, including Santiago (1504) on the island of Santo Domingo (now Haiti and the Dominican Republic). It is thus clear that the basic design, incorporating a square grid of streets surrounding a plaza mayor, had already been established. This basic plan was to spread throughout Central and South America: HAVANA (1514–19), Veracruz (1519), Mexico City (1524, founded by Hernán Cortés to plans by A. García Bravo; *see* MEXICO CITY, §§I and II, 1), PUEBLA (1530), Panama City (1673; *see* PANAMA, §II, 1), SANTA FE DE BOGOTÁ (1538), Caracas (1567), San Francesco de Quito (1534), La Plata (Sucré, 1538), Buenos Aires (1580), Trujillo (1535) and Lima (1535; *see* LIMA, §2).

The British founded more modest urban centres in North America, including Philadelphia (1682), founded on a rectangular layout of the greatest regularity (*see* PHILADELPHIA, §1(i)); Williamsburg, VA, which was even smaller; and ANNAPOLIS (1694), MD, where a more original plan was used, combining a square grid layout with circular town squares and diagonal avenues. These last two designs, as well as others in Virginia and Maryland, were the work of Francis Nicholson, who was extremely familiar with European urban planning. The great square grid layouts multiplied during the course of the 18th century, with other examples including SAVANNAH (1733, by James Oglethorpe), GA, which had a skilfully executed layout adorned with town squares in a style faintly reflecting those of London, and New Ebenezer (1736), GA, as well as many others inspired by Savannah. Washington, DC, stood in a class of its own, owing to the originality and size of its layout and its role as capital of the USA. Its complex ground plan (*see* WASHINGTON, DC, §I, 2 and fig. 1) was drawn up by Pierre-Charles L'Enfant in 1791, with a vast square grid layout incorporating several modules, studded with town squares with numerous diagonal avenues running from them (up to six from a single square). Despite the French points of reference often suggested as L'Enfant's source of inspiration (e.g. Versailles), the Washington design was basically a new one.

During the 18th century, the French also founded several major cities in Santo Domingo (see fig. 7), which was the chief sugar cane production centre in the Antilles and the pivotal point of the colonial trade triangle. After a number of modest initiatives in the form of small fortified towns (e.g. Léogane, est. 1710; Saint-Louis, 1721, by Amédée-François Frézier), the engineer J.-L. de La Lance designed a series of open, square grid plan towns. These were followed by other foundations (e.g. Port-au-Prince, 1749) and completed an existing network (Le Cap, 1680–1711); their essential aim was to attract a population of colonists capable of defending the island against the neighbouring British.

The 18th century left Europe with an uneven network of urban centres, predominantly made up of towns whose structure was still medieval in spite of the addition of later embellishments or improvements. The towns of southern Europe, in particular, were aging. During the 19th century, these centres had to be adapted to meet new needs with regard to traffic flow and health.

BIBLIOGRAPHY
R. Pernoud: *Les Villes marchandes aux XVe et XVIe siècle* (Paris, 1948)
I. de Wolfe: *The Italian Townscape* (London, 1963)
E. Herzog: *Die ottonische Stadt* (Berlin, 1964)
E. A. Gutkind: *International History of City Development*, 8 vols (London and New York, 1964–72)
G. C. Argan: *The Renaissance City* (New York, 1969)
P. Francastel, ed.: *L'Urbanisme de Paris et de l'Europe, 1600–1690* (Paris, 1969)
P. D. Partner: *Renaissance Rome, 1500–1559* (Berkeley, CA, 1976)
P. Sica: *Storia dell'urbanistica: Il settecento* (Bari, 1976)
F. Braudel: 'Les Villes', *Civilisation matérielle, économie et capitalisme, XVème–XVIème siècle*, i of *Les Structures du quotidien* (Paris, 1979)
E. Guidoni and A. Marino: *Storia dell'urbanistica: Il seicento* (Bari, 1979)
——: *Storia dell'urbanistica: Il cinquecento* (Bari, 1982)
P. Lavedan, J. Hugueney and P. Henrat: *L'Urbanisme à l'époque moderne: XVIème–XVIIIème siècles* (Paris and Geneva, 1982)
D. Thomson: *Renaissance Paris: Architecture and Growth, 1475–1600* (London, 1984)
M. Girouard: *Cities and People: A Social and Architectural History* (New Haven and London, 1985)
P. M. Hohenberg and L. H. Lees: *The Making of Urban Europe, 1000–1950* (Harvard, MA, 1985)
H. W. Kruft: *Die Idealstadt vom 15. bis zum 18. Jahrhundert zwischen Staatsutopie und Wirklichkeit* (Munich, 1989)

PIERRE PINON

IV. c. 1800–c. 1890: the industrial city.

The most remarkable social phenomenon of the 19th century was the concentration of population in cities: so observed Adna Ferrin Weber in a Columbia University, NY, dissertation, subsequently published in 1899. At the beginning of the century the world could boast only 44 urban agglomerations with more than 100,000 inhabitants; by the close the number had increased to 270. European countries accounted for much of this increase, although in the second half of the century there was a marked urban surge in the USA to join other high-income nations. A major contribution to this period of rapid urbanization was made by the rise of the industrial city. The new big cities played a crucial role in the process of capital accumulation that marked the aggressive capitalism of the 19th century and acted as engines of an economic growth that propelled 19th-century societies towards new modes of urban living. This economic growth was often accompanied, however, by severe social and environmental disorders that brought new priorities to the discipline of urban planning. The growth of alternative, Utopian communities during this period was to some extent a response to the changes wrought by industrialization on the urban context.

1. Growth and change. 2. Structural and social aspects. 3. Improvements. 4. Model settlements.

1. GROWTH AND CHANGE. During the 19th century the total population of the developed world rose by rather less than three times; the urban share of that population increased by a factor of nearly ten. It was not just a question of adding population to existing towns; the century saw the emergence of new cities, where an industrial manufacturing base was firmly established, the majority of these being in North America. Europe set the trend, the 1830s being especially marked by urban growth. During this decade the population of European cities rose

from 28 million to 108 million, England and Germany in particular sharing in this increase. Notably in England, the rise of new manufacturing towns changed the old urban hierarchy, but the disruption was less apparent elsewhere, where industrialization more frequently grafted on to old established cities.

The processes of growth, sometimes very rapid indeed, depended very much on population redistribution, notably the transfer from rural to urban. The patterns of relocation were certainly complex, but two points can be made. First, while some long-distance individual movements took place (particularly related to specific employment opportunities), most migration was relatively short-distance, from countryside to town, perhaps in two stages before a final break with the area of origin was made. Further migration streams had 'counter' flows, so that net inward migration was the result of an excess of one stream over another. Secondly, there were trans-national emigration waves, which effected a transfer both from country to town and from city to city. The European heartland of industrial cities was firmly established by mid-century. The second half saw substantial industrialization and urbanization in other countries, in a late attempt to catch up. In Russia, the emancipation of the serfs in 1861 raised the possibility of their moving to the cities, and at the same time an influx of foreign capital stimulated Russian industry and railway development. Urban population increased substantially: from less than 6 million in 1860 to 23 million in 1913. St Petersburg and Moscow grew rapidly, as did smaller cities on the periphery of the empire. The second half of the century also witnessed an industrializing Lombardy, with Milan as its centre.

The USA was an even more dramatic example. Around 1820 perhaps 6% of the population lived in towns with populations of more than 5000, which was less than half of the European figure at the same time. By 1850, however, the urban share had risen to 14%, and shortly after the turn of the century the USA had caught up with Europe. A transportation revolution was critical in this development, the role of railways and steamships assuming great importance and the confluence of water and rail accounting for a large number of successful urban locations: the most notable was Chicago, with a population of under 5000 in 1840, rising by the end of the century to overtake Philadelphia, which itself had been the largest city in the country at the beginning of the century.

The new industrial cities that sprang up in the 19th century were progressively different from those of pre-industrial periods. While cities of earlier societies had been varied in function (administrative, commercial, religious, craft-related and perhaps military), and while capital cities retained a varied occupational mix, the 19th century produced cities where manufacture was pre-eminent. Around 1800 industrial manufacturing in western Europe employed only a little more than 6 million people, and a large proportion of these lived and worked in rural districts; by the end of the century the figure had increased approximately sixfold, and rural industrial labour was much reduced. Thus, while cities grew in size and number, so too did the extent of their share of industrial concentration. However, the link between industrialization and urbanization was neither immediate nor obvious. For example, areas in some European countries proceeded to industrialize, but their growth rates of urbanization were low. Moreover, even in areas of early, rapid town growth, mills and factories were established in the countryside, particularly if water power was a dominant factor in location. The Industrial Revolution in Britain did not just manifest itself in cities; initial advances in cotton textiles and in metal manufacture occurred largely outside the cities. By mid-century, however, except where 'out-working' in satellite villages was still the rule, an urban location had been assured in most areas of manufacture, and the true merger of industrial with urban growth was effected.

The emergence of the industrial city transformed the urban map in most countries. Economic development proved to be spatially selective, some regions industrializing and others failing to do so. Coalfield locations, tidal estuaries and natural trade corridors along waterways proved exceptionally attractive, in both Europe and North America. In Britain the growth of the northern and midland industrial cities quite replaced the earlier geography of manufacture, which had favoured the prosperity of a range of small, historic settlements, largely in the south; London itself was, however, an exception to this. Elsewhere in Europe the major coalfields provided the setting for new industrial agglomerations: north-east France and Belgium, the Ruhr in Germany, Silesia and (latterly) the Donetz in Russia. Capital cities such as Paris maintained their dominance, and Berlin burgeoned. In France, Lyon–St Etienne flourished, but in Germany, particularly, industry was attracted to major regional cities, which succeeded in maintaining an occupational balance with commerce, administration and service trades.

The patterns of location with regard to industrial cities changed during the century. Britain had both urbanized and industrialized first; *c.* 1850 England and Wales could boast 54% of its population living in towns of more than 5000 people. Belgium also became urbanized early, although in a more scattered way. Germany urbanized rapidly once railway construction had begun, with Berlin, the Ruhr and Hamburg emerging as the major concentrations. By mid-century, every part of Europe except Portugal experienced an increased share of urban population. Austria, Switzerland and Sweden made rapid urban gains. On the other hand, in France, outside Paris, most provincial and industrial towns failed to keep pace with other European regions. The Netherlands and northern Italy, regions with a large initial urban population, exhibited a relatively low rate of increase. In eastern Europe, industrial development was pronounced in Moscow, St Petersburg and Warsaw.

2. STRUCTURAL AND SOCIAL ASPECTS. Industrial cities grew by means of a continual process, first of territorial expansion and then of land use reorganization within the existing built-up area, operated through a vigorous speculative land market. The growth mechanism was both additional and transformational, comprising annexation of more land for urban uses and a constant resorting within, with the result that by the end of the century the basic components of the modern city were in place. City centres took on an expanded commercial role as new retail outlets opened, and market-places were often

transformed into market-halls. On the edges of city centres, but sometimes well within them, were the railway stations, accompanied by hotels and adjoining vast warehousing tracts and sidings. An intermixture of land use was typical, but occasionally whole districts were given over to manufacturing industry, particularly where topography provided flat land for factory units. The precise nature of the urban form depended much on particular industrial characteristics. Textile towns such as Manchester featured concentrations around mills (*see* MANCHESTER, §1), whereas mining and metal-working towns tended to be more diffuse. There was also a propensity for nearby towns to grow together, the combined area forming a poly-nucleated industrial city: 'conurbations' were in the making.

City form also came to depend greatly on modes of urban transport. Progression from horse-drawn omnibus to tram, the application of electric power and, by the end of the century in London and Paris, the underground railway were key stages. The innovation of the American streetcar spread to Europe in the form of fixed tracks for tramways and, together with suburban railways, proved particularly significant for extending the opportunities for the labour force to travel greater distances to work. This enhanced mobility encouraged the progressive decentralization of cities, but it was not the only factor influencing suburbanization: the emergence of new cultural values was equally significant. Both the British and the Americans favoured an environment that offered a mixture of urban and rural features, and public parks came to punctuate the urban fabric. While housing spread outwards, especially in Great Britain and most of the USA, this trend highlighted some significant social differences. In the USA, for example, it was noticeable that incomes rose with distance from the city centre, and in Great Britain too by the end of the century, the older, central parts of the industrial city had been largely abandoned to the poor and the working class.

The development of suburban areas for the middle class was to a large extent a response to the social consequences of industrialization, which were particularly profound with respect to housing and the environment. Throughout the century the construction industry was unable to build dwellings either of a sufficient number or of adequate quality for the working class, beset by irregular employment and low wages. Early observers on the industrial city had been quick to condemn its environmental limitations. Chadwick's *General Report on the Sanitary Condition of the Labouring Classes of Great Britain* (1842), built up from surveyors' reports, was painstaking in its investigation; and Engels's *The Condition of the Working Class in England* (1845) described the squalor of the great towns 'from personal observation and authentic sources'. Throughout the century the perceived wretchedness of the worst forms of urban living, in association with widespread poverty, remained a matter for concern and investigation. While considerable improvements were made in housing conditions for the better off, the 19th century was one of hardship and no little degradation for the impoverished sections of the urban working classes. Even when the worst housing stock, such as cellar dwellings and insanitary courts, had gone, the tenements

of Glasgow, the apartments of Paris, the wooden dosshouses of Moscow and the 'dumb-bell' houses of New York remained, contributing to the late 19th-century urban crisis.

It was in Britain that the early facts of correlation between poor sanitation, overcrowding and disease were established and the role of bad housing confirmed. Urban death rates in the industrial cities were high, and survival rates seemed to depend a great deal on geography, the crucial disparity being between country and town, as well as between occupational groups and social class. A dominant impression among informed observers by the end of the century was that the big industrial city was inimical to health. The most feared disease was cholera, with most European countries experiencing epidemics from the 1830s, but typhus was also common in overcrowded conditions. Tuberculosis thrived in circumstances of undernourishment, squalor and lack of ventilation. It was clear that improved health depended on improved sanitation in the first instance; both the provision of pure water and sewers for the removal of waste were important urban priorities. Urban death rates remained high throughout the century, however, only falling in the later decades in more advanced countries, where sanitary precautions were enforced in the cities. Thereafter attention turned to housing. Conditions varied greatly between countries and indeed within the same country. The unifying feature was urban overcrowding, which led to over-concentration and congestion. Housing reform in most countries gathered pace in the movement towards environmental improvement during the second half of the century. It made slow progress, perhaps because it included such a wide range of concerns, from housing construction, layout and design, to health and poverty, but it proved to be a major spur to schemes for municipal improvement.

3. IMPROVEMENTS. In response to the issues that had emerged in studies of the environmental condition of the industrial city, the efforts of the reformers were targeted on the supply of pure water, the removal of filth and waste, and the provision of air, space and sunlight. Other problems included fire control, but the rapidity and the extent of the growth of the industrial city meant that old institutional arrangements were incapable of meeting the new demands. The state, in the form of either local or central units of administration, was slow to engage in these matters and did not do so to any great extent in the new industrial cities until the second half of the century. The further problems of both air and river pollution were tackled belatedly, but only half-heartedly. Other urban services, notably with regard to housing, were long regarded as areas inappropriate for public action. Engagement in the provision of public utilities (e.g. gas and electricity) and transport varied from country to country.

Some European capital cities nevertheless achieved spectacular improvements, especially in road development. The ramparts of Vienna were torn down in 1858 to make way for the new Ringstrasse, which was lined with impressive buildings (*see* VIENNA, §II, 3 and fig. 5). Berlin, on the other hand, was a disappointment, with the city securely in the grip of land speculators. Paris, however, triumphed

8. Design of the Avenue de l'Opéra, Paris, by Georges-Eugène Haussmann, 1853–69

under GEORGES-EUGÈNE HAUSSMANN, who was instrumental in pushing through a massive programme of renewal, whereby imposing avenues and boulevards were cut through the urban fabric (see fig. 8; *see also* PARIS, §II, 5). London had no comparable programme; after John Nash's scheme (1826) to link Regent's Park with Carlton House, the Regent's residence (*see* NASH, JOHN, §2(ii)), it was the Metropolitan Board of Works (1855–88) that assumed responsibility for road improvements, but these were only piecemeal (*see* LONDON, §II, 4). New York, meanwhile, grew under the direction of the Commissioners' Map layout plan of 1811 (see fig. 9), the celebrated city grid being extended again in the 1870s (*see* NEW YORK, §I, 2 and 3).

By and large, city improvements were effected through local initiatives. In the UK, central Newcastle upon Tyne was transformed in the 1830s and 1840s by a local estate developer in association with the City Council Corporation (*see* NEWCASTLE UPON TYNE, §1). Central Glasgow was the subject of municipally directed development after the 1860s, permitted by the City Improvement Act (*see* GLASGOW, §1(ii) and fig. 2). Birmingham had major improvements to its central area from the 1870s, driven by its

reforming mayor Joseph Chamberlain (1836–1914; *see* BIRMINGHAM, §1 and fig. 1). In the USA, improvements in Chicago came with the World's Columbian Exposition in 1893. In France, Lyon and Marseille began ambitious improvement programmes in the enthusiasm of the early years attending the Second Republic. In Spain, ILDEFONSO CERDÀ regularized the urban structure of Barcelona (*see* BARCELONA, §I, 2). German industrial expansion was very rapid after the 1840s, and the pace of urban growth was even more marked than in Britain during its early phase. New towns were founded, including Bremerhaven and, later, Ludwigshaven and Wilhelmshaven; older cities grew by means of planned town extensions, which permitted the proper layout of suburban streets. The biggest of these extension plans was that for Berlin drawn up by James Hobrecht in 1862, which controlled the expansion of the city until 1919 (*see* BERLIN, §I, 3).

During the 19th century, the industrial city witnessed increasing efforts to use public action to regulate urban growth and to take steps to control and enhance the older physical infrastructure. The paving and lighting of streets, water supply, sewerage, waste removal, public health, gas and electricity, transport provision, fire fighting, new highways, street-width regulation, air and water pollution measures, parks and open spaces: all these features of regulation entered to some extent into the purview of city control.

One of the more problematic areas (and hence one of the last to be tackled) concerned housing, particularly the compulsory closure and removal of unfit housing on health grounds. Urban improvements depended on political and cultural attitudes governing slum clearance and public renewal schemes, but the strength of the housing reform movement varied considerably in its effect across the industrialized world. In the USA, codes of urban building regulation were slow to emerge, municipal administrations were weak, and the reformers were divided, showing effectiveness only in the large urban centres of New York and Chicago, where settlement houses were established. In France, interest in housing improvement only really quickened after the turn of the century, a public health law of 1902 signalling new possibilities for improvements to the urban environment. In Germany, the target of concern was the spread of the tenement block, improvements being seen in the move to lower densities made

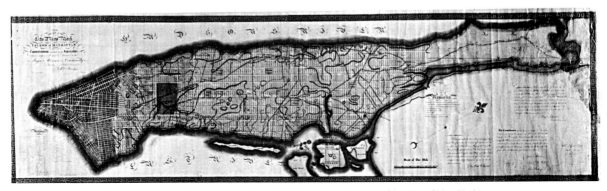

9. Urban plan for New York, known as the Commissioners' Map, 1811 (New York, Museum of the City of New York)

available in the various city extension plans drawn up after the 1870s. British efforts relied heavily on local authority bye-laws prescribing minimum street widths, space around dwellings and standards in building construction; after 1890 the London County Council embarked on municipal clearance and house building programmes (*see* LONDON, §II, 5).

Other forms of urban improvement came as a result of architectural, design or aesthetic influences, which affected not only public authorities but all sectors engaged in forms of urban development. One such was the urban park movement led by JOSEPH PAXTON in Britain and FREDERICK LAW OLMSTED in the USA. New York's Central Park (from 1858), Lincoln Park in Chicago and Boston's park system (*see* BOSTON, §I, 2) were cases in point. Another, later stimulus for improvement, so important for civic identity, was the CITY BEAUTIFUL MOVEMENT, strongly influenced by Philadelphia's centennial exhibition (1876) and the World's Columbian Exposition (1893) in Chicago (*see* §V, 1 below; *see also* CHICAGO, §1). In matters of residential layout, romantic informality was increasingly sought by the suburban wealthy, and this became an aspect of city beautification, as for example at Riverside (after 1870), a suburb of Chicago, and at Bedford Park (begun 1876; *see* LONDON, §II, 4), west London. Curvilinear layouts and green, open spaciousness became models to follow in later decades.

4. MODEL SETTLEMENTS. There was a strong tradition of alternative communities in the 19th century, particularly in Britain and the USA. Small, often short-lived communities, either to promote Utopian and agrarian socialism or to bring together the advocates of sectarian movements and of anarchist persuasion, were recurrent themes. In particular, a number of industrialists, acting as paternalist benefactors for their workforce, planned or built their own model communities (see fig. 10), supplying better dwellings and improved urban services. Robert Owen's experiment was centred on the cotton mill adjoining the Falls on the River Clyde near the country town of Lanark; New Lanark (after 1799) was both an efficient factory and a well-governed community. TITUS SALT, a woollen manufacturer in Bradford, Yorks, built a new mill of huge proportions and from 1851 laid out an adjacent workers' estate (called Saltaire) north of the city in open fields bordering the River Aire and the Leeds–Liverpool canal. Later, attracted to another greenfield site, this time south of Birmingham, the garden village of Bournville (begun in 1895) was developed around the new chocolate works of the Cadbury Brothers, George and Richard, who moved their factory from the centre of Birmingham in 1879 (*see* CADBURY, GEORGE). Later, WILLIAM HESKETH LEVER built his Port Sunlight soap factory and adjoining village (1889–1938) near Liverpool. Both Bournville and Port Sunlight were generous in open space provision and contributed significantly to the ideal of new forms of urban layout for workers' housing at the turn of the century. These constituted merely a few examples in Britain. There were also others in continental Europe and in the USA. In Germany the Krupp family built large-scale satellites, notably Margaretenhöhe, and there were also workers' colonies in France, Italy and the Netherlands. In the USA the Pullman community (after 1880), built up around the railway car premises near Chicago, was perhaps the best-known example (*see* PULLMAN, GEORGE MORTIMER).

10. *Owen's Village of Cooperation*, engraving (1906) after the drawing by R. R. Reinagle that accompanied Robert Owen's plan for the regeneration of society, presented to a Select Committee of the House of Commons, 1817

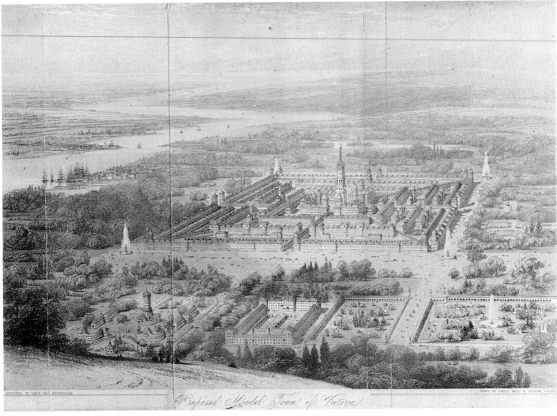

11. View of the proposed model town of Victoria; from J. Silk Buckingham: *National Evils and Practical Remedies* (1849)

These practical improvements to the industrial city towards the end of the century married principles of urban design, dwelling standards, service provision and quality of environment with community building in a social sense. They were to have great significance for later decades. In the meantime, theoreticians were considering ideal forms of urban layout as models for the future industrial city. In mid-century England a Model Town Association was advocated by James Silk Buckingham; in *National Evils and Practical Remedies* (1849) Buckingham described the layout of Victoria, a concept of an ideal settlement for 10,000 people (see fig. 11). Health reformers envisioned ideal cities of health; scientists and engineers sought to build cities with new circulatory systems for traffic; architects and designers rebelled against the ugliness of cities; and new urban forms were postulated. By the end of the century there was widespread demand for radical alternatives.

BIBLIOGRAPHY

A. F. Weber: *The Growth of Cities in the Nineteenth Century—A Study in Statistics* (New York, 1899)
A. Briggs: *Victorian Cities* (London, 1963)
J. W. Reps: *The Making of Urban America: A History of City Planning in the United States* (Princeton, 1965)
E. N. Bacon: *Design of Cities* (London, 1967, rev. 1975)
C. Tunnard: *The City of Man* (New York, 1970)
D. J. Olsen: *The Growth of Victorian London* (London, 1976)
A. Sutcliffe: *Towards the Planned City* (Oxford, 1981)
D. Fraser and A. Sutcliffe, eds: *The Pursuit of Urban History* (London, 1983)
D. A. Kreuckeberg, ed.: *Introduction to Planning History in the United States* (New Brunswick, NJ, 1983)
M. Girouard: *Cities and People* (New Haven and London, 1985)
P. M. Hohenberg and L. H. Lees: *The Making of Modern Europe, 1000–1950* (Cambridge, MA, 1985)
A. Lees: *Cities Perceived* (Manchester, 1985)
P. Bairoch: *Cities and Economic Development: From the Dawn of History to the Present* (London, 1988)
W. Braunfels: *Urban Design in Western Europe* (Chicago and London, 1988)
G. E. Cherry: *Cities and Plans* (London, 1988)
S. Kostof: *The City Shaped: Urban Patterns and Meanings throughout History* (London, 1991)
——: *The City Assembled: The Elements of Urban Form throughout History* (London, 1992)

GORDON E. CHERRY

V. c. 1890–1945: the urban metropolis.

After the great urban projects of the mid-19th century, such as the Ringstrasse scheme in Vienna or Haussmann's work in Paris, a new phenomenon emerged: the urban metropolis, conceived as an economic, territorial and cultural entity. Out of the attempts to come to terms with this new urban type grew the modern professional discipline of urban planning, which united the skills of architects, engineers, sociologists and others involved in determining the structure and shape of towns. If the idea of reordering historic urban centres, based on the arrangements of open spaces and built-up plots of land, can be dated back to the mid-19th century, however, the idea of providing historical unity through the preservation of individual buildings or architectural ensembles was new. By 1914 urban planning had become a complex discipline, involving practical experiments linked to analytic and prescriptive discourse and embodied in legal provisions and professional handbooks. After World War I, reconstruction schemes and colonial developments in particular provided opportunities for the application of urban theory, but new problems of scale raised by urban developments in western Europe and North America prompted a broader regional emphasis in planning and the thorough-going theoretical approach of the Functionalists. The renovation of large town centres remained an important concern, however, and became particularly pressing as a result of the ravages of World War II.

1. Extension policies and the emerging professions. 2. Reconstruction and experimentation. 3. The emergence of regional plans. 4. Functionalism. 5. A new policy for the centre.

1. EXTENSION POLICIES AND THE EMERGING PROFESSIONS. At the end of the 19th century the two major objectives in urban planning were the regulation of urban extensions and the preservation of the historic interest of the city centre. Two main schools of thought emerged, based on contrasting historical paradigms. On the one hand, rules about positioning buildings and streets, grounded on the expansion of classical rules developed at the Ecole des Beaux-Arts in Paris, were the basis of the ideas of the CITY BEAUTIFUL MOVEMENT, whose first product was Daniel H. Burnham's plan for the World's Columbian Exposition (1893) in Chicago. The same approach also influenced Burnham's later project for the Washington Mall and above all his 1909 extension plans for Chicago, which he conceived with Edward Bennett (1874–1954), the principle being both decentralized and focused on a monumental centre (see fig. 12). It was also found in the works of some French architects, whose search for harmony and variety (as opposed to Haussmannian 'monotony') involved a reassessment of 17th- and 18th-century experiments. On the other hand, the method recommended by CAMILLO SITTE in *Der Städtebau nach seinen künstlerischen Grundsätzen* (1889) involved dispensing with the strict grid pattern of cities and adopting a more flexible urban plan, following the examples offered by towns dating from the Middle Ages and the Renaissance. In this urban vision the configuration of squares and the relationship between them dominated the axial relationship between public buildings. This concern for the artistic dimensions of urban plans was continued in the International Congresses of Public Art in Brussels (1898, 1910), Paris (1900) and Liège (1905), at the initiative particularly of CHARLES BULS. There the supporters of 'urban art' formulated a position based on respect for the past and for history, the latter judged alone as the basis for new steps.

However, such interest in the configuration of space for monuments and public buildings in towns did not

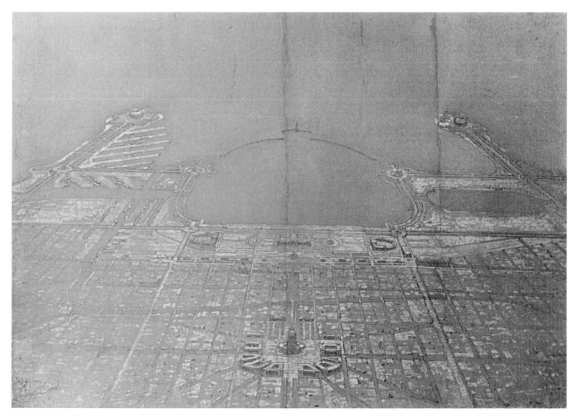

12. Urban plan for the development of the city centre of Chicago, by Daniel H. Burnham and Edward Bennett; illustration by Jules Guérin, tempera and pencil toned paper, 1907 (Chicago, IL, Art Institute of Chicago)

resolve the more general problem of agglomeration growth. Whatever solutions were adopted in the centres, completely different questions were posed as to the structure of the urban metropolises that were developing at the end of the 19th century, both in Europe (e.g. London, Paris, Berlin, Vienna) and in the USA (e.g. Chicago, New York, Philadelphia). The first question was that of their overall shape. Were they destined to spread like a patch of oil, or should they have, in the very course of this growth, discontinuities and rhythms and take the form of a more diffuse whole?

The main alternative to the continuous town was the GARDEN CITY movement. According to the initial scheme proposed in 1898 by the movement's founder, EBENEZER HOWARD, the ideal arrangement was based on the creation of agglomerations limited in size and linked to the centre of the existing town by fast trains but with their own productive resources. The first British garden city was Letchworth, Herts, conceived by Raymond Unwin (from 1904; *see* PARKER & UNWIN, §2). However, thanks to the translation of Howard's writings, the success of the Letchworth and Hampstead Garden Suburb (from 1906), London, projects, and the formation of sympathetic societies in France, Germany, Italy and Russia, the garden city movement rapidly took on a European dimension. Hans Kampfmeyer (1876–1932) was instrumental in the creation of a first German garden city in Hellerau, near Dresden (1907), and of a second, near Strasbourg (1912), but the unceasing publicity given out by Georges Benoît-Lévy (1880–1971) did not have the same effect in France. Only the Cité Paris-Jardins de Draveil (1911) can be compared to contemporary European schemes. In Russia, the Society of Garden Cities originated many projects, including Prozorovskaya Station (1913–14, by Vladimir Semyonov, *see* RUSSIA, §III, 2) on the railway line from Moscow to Kazan. Eliel Saarinen's plan (1918) for Greater Helsinki (*see* SAARINEN, (1)) linked a major use of the garden cities to the redefinition of monuments and public buildings in the centre (*see* HELSINKI, §1). It should be noted, however, that the term 'garden city' was used at this time not only to refer strictly to schemes based on Howard's ideas but also more loosely to designate developments established by benevolent patrons such as the Cadburys or the Krupps.

The garden city was not, however, the only theory formulated to answer metropolitan pressures. Other radical solutions were often based on technical innovations or on transport networks. In 1882, for example, Arturo Soria y Mata (1844–1920) pictured a 'Ciudad Lineal', an arrangement of land 600 m wide, its axis being a central avenue equipped with tramways and intended to link the country's main cities. He undertook to complete an experimental fragment of his system north-east of Madrid (1894). Tony Garnier, who won the Grand Prix de Rome at the Ecole des Beaux-Arts, shocked the academy in 1901 with his Cité Industrielle project, published in 1917, a new town made autonomous by hydro-electric power and with an emphasis on collective space (for illustration *see* GARNIER, TONY). As against these projects, which tended to replace the metropolis with decentralized territorial configurations, many large towns in Europe and the USA were reorganized to incorporate new areas by improved transport networks spreading their reach further afield. The most important examples of this were the gardens and parks created in the USA by Frederick Law Olmsted. Established in Boston, Chicago and New York, the park systems linked play areas, meadows, formal gardens and outdoor nature reserves with parkways, which later proved perfectly adaptable to the spread of the car. The spread of these areas of free space was also linked to the growth of outdoor sporting activities. Similar concepts were introduced into Europe by Jean-Claude-Nicolas Forestier, WERNER HEGEMANN and Martin Wagner. In Germany, ideas from the USA stimulated projects for such large 'Volkspärke' as that in Hamburg (before 1914), created by FRITZ SCHUMACHER, and they also influenced projects submitted to the competition for the plan of Greater Berlin in 1910.

Two key issues in many proposals were mobility and overdevelopment. The first had an effect on the profile of 'arteries', the adoption of this term revealing the power of the organic model in the thought of the architects of the time. The superposition of networks later proposed by Charles Lamb (1860–1942) and HARVEY WILEY CORBETT was already a reality in New York with the construction of Grand Central Terminal (1903–13) by Warren & Wetmore and Reed & Stem (*see* NEW YORK, §I, 2) and the neighbouring areas. The complex networks that also inspired the Italian Futurist Antonio Sant'Elia were the basis of the ideas of the Parisian architect EUGÈNE ALFRED HÉNARD on the 'transformation' of Paris and the 'city of the future', in which aeroplanes and underground transport would cross in all directions. The question of traffic was posed in new terms not only by the rise of the car but also by the growing specialization of urban centres. In order to control this specialization and keep industrial districts at a distance, German urban planners introduced the new notion of functional zoning. Tested in Frankfurt am Main, this practice of dividing up urban land according to use and morphology rapidly spread to the USA, particularly thanks to the architect George Burdett Ford (1879–1930), whose 'City Scientific' was based on the ability to control ground use and traffic flow. Meanwhile, new attention was also given to the sociology of the urban metropolis. Georg Simmel in Germany, Maurice Halbwachs (1877–1945) in France and PATRICK GEDDES in the UK each advanced a theory of urban social relationships, based on historical analysis or, for Geddes, on the study of environmental and social planning, known as the 'civic survey'.

The multiplication of professional, technical treatises in the early 20th century, often linked to theoretical visions of the large city and the consideration of historical aspects, contributed to the creation of a common fund of knowledge. In the decade before World War I, knowledge gained from experiences in European and American large towns was also disseminated by the continuous travels of professionals and by conferences for professional associations or on particular themes (e.g. hygiene, roads) and by comparative exhibitions such as those in Berlin (1910), Düsseldorf (1912) and Ghent (1913). Mainly practical, international competitions also encouraged debate on such issues as the Antwerp extension (1910) or the general plan for the new Australian capital of CANBERRA (1912; for illustration *see* GRIFFIN). The growing number of journals devoted to urban planning, starting with *Der Städtebau*

(1904) and the *Town Planning Review* (1910), also contributed to the continually expanding stock of knowledge. The opening of the first courses in urban planning at the universities of Berlin, Liverpool, Birmingham and Harvard (all before 1914) completed the picture. In addition, the Institut d'Urbanisme was created at the university in Paris in 1919—having been started earlier as the Ecole des Hautes Etudes Urbaines—and the course in Edilizia Cittadina was established in Rome by Gustavo Giovannoni in 1919.

2. RECONSTRUCTION AND EXPERIMENTATION. In the decade separating World War I from the 1929 Depression, urban planning was characterized by the conjunction of reforming policies sketched out before 1914 (but subsequently consolidated and developed) with earlier experiments involving plans and new architectural problems. In France, for example, partly destroyed by fighting, the Cité Reconstituée exhibition (Paris, 1916), George Burdett Ford's work in rebuilding cities in eastern France (e.g. his plan of 1917 for the rebuilding of Reims) and the work of DONAT-ALFRED AGACHE turned reconstruction into an experiment for modernizing urban form. The contribution of LOUIS VAN DER SWAELMEN to Belgian reconstruction had similar effects.

However, some towns in European colonies and dominions had already been places of experimentation for new methods of control and urban design for over a decade. Daniel H. Burnham had worked on the plan for Manila (1905), while the competition for Canberra saw the triumph of Frank Lloyd Wright's pupil Griffin over the Frenchman Agache. New Delhi, British India's new capital, was the subject in 1912 of a project linking gardens, roads and monuments. Its author, Edwin Lutyens, sought to preserve vestiges of the numerous earlier towns on the site if they could serve to highlight the new buildings, a symbol of the colonial Raj (*see* LUTYENS, EDWIN, fig. 3). In French-controlled Morocco, the Protectorate established in 1912 launched an ambitious development policy separate from 'indigenous' towns and new towns (*see* MOROCCO). While the plans of HENRI PROST for Fez and Rabat emphasized the preservation of the historical medinas, his plan for Casablanca (1915) inclined towards regulating an industrial and commercial town through zoning and extensive expropriation measures, which had been unknown in metropolitan France for a long time. At the end of the 1920s Agache's plan for Rio de Janeiro (1927; partially executed) extended these experiments by proposing to base the remodelling of the city on the functional and morphological differentiation of the Brazilian capital.

3. THE EMERGENCE OF REGIONAL PLANS. In the large European and North American towns a new scale of urban planning emerged, as post-war planners had to answer to the expectations of a more numerous and, above all, more turbulent population. The plans then developed for the metropolises revealed a change of scale and of priorities from those that had characterized 'urban art' and the City Beautiful Movement. In New York, the 1916 Zoning Law regulated for the first time in three dimensions the outlines of blocks of buildings. On the metropolitan

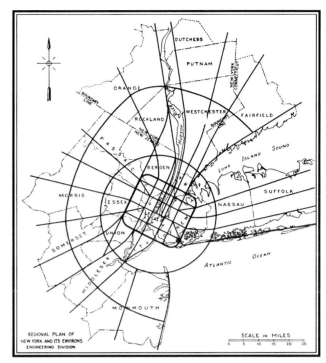

13. Regional plan of New York, by Thomas Adams, 1931, showing in diagrammatic form the principal transport and traffic routes; from T. Adams: *The Building of the City* (New York, 1931), i, p. 179

scale, from 1921 to 1929 the Russell Sage Foundation conducted a study that formed the basis of the first regional plan, entrusted to the Scottish urban planner Thomas Adams (1871–1940; see fig. 13). The plan aimed to reinforce the transport system and to create a network of 'major radical routes' linking, through an ambitious programme of civil engineering works, existing areas and the periphery. In Manhattan, control of urban density involved recasting the Civic Center and a programme transforming riverside monuments and buildings (*see* NEW YORK, §I, 4). The disparate sketches of Corbett, Ford, Francis S. Swales (1878–1962) and HUGH FERRISS clearly set out visually the planners' intentions. The provision of living space away from the city centre and of communities sufficiently removed from the centre to be viable, both missing from the regional plan, was realized in such isolated schemes as the new town of Radburn, NJ, conceived from 1927 by Henry Wright (1878–1936) and Clarence Stein (1883–1975).

In Germany, a merging of previously separate communes made possible the creation of Gross-Berlin in 1918, covering an area of 800 sq. km and forming part of an even larger regional Grossraum, which was the subject of a theoretical study by Martin Mächler (1881–1958). A zoning edict was passed within the new limits in 1925, at which time the agglomeration had more than 4 million inhabitants. The transformation in 1929 of the Alexanderplatz area into a commercial centre linked to all the underground, surface and air transport networks coincided with the reconstruction of the Scheunenviertel, a chaotic and overcrowded area (*see* BERLIN, §I, 4). On the periphery, the modernist and traditional Siedlungen applied a decentralization principle also practised in Frankfurt am Main by Ernst May's team. At around the same time the development plan for the Kohlenbezirk (1928) in the Ruhr provoked the first examples of planning on a regional scale, gathering together agglomerations and diffuse areas. Around London the ideas of the proponents of the Garden City were made evident by the launch of the Welwyn plan (1919), while at that time the London County Council started a policy of satellite cities, the most important being Becontree, Essex. From 1935 this policy was recast into the Green Belt plan around the capital. British urban planners' considerations were directed both at the inter-urban scale, with many regional schemes planned from 1925, and towards those of the local area with the emergence of the 'Neighbourhood Unit' as a planning element (*see* LONDON, §II, 5).

In Paris, however, the municipal perimeter grew only marginally bigger, with the annexation of the fortified wall and parapets; and conflicts between the city and the Conseil Général of the Seine prevented any new initiatives in the heart of an agglomeration of 5 million inhabitants. However, in the competition for a new urban layout, the winning project (1919) by LÉON JAUSSELY proposed making Paris into a tailored, 'self-contained economic organism', its functioning dependent on the articulation of canal and railway networks and parkways. In 1928 Henri Prost began work on the first regional plan, which was approved in 1934. Rather than simply extending the urban agglomeration, the plan aimed to 'give it vertebrae' through simple zoning. 'Incomplete, imperfect' in the words of its own promoters, the Prost plan was nevertheless effective as far as roads were concerned and began to roll back the 'red belt' of working-class areas, whose stranglehold frightened the middle classes (*see* PARIS, §II, 6(ii)).

4. FUNCTIONALISM. Side by side with the new plans developed for large agglomerations, new theoretical and methodological approaches also began to emerge. If the garden city still remained the dominant ideology on the world scale, other more radical projects were also advanced during the 1920s, including Le Corbusier's 'Contemporary City' (1922), LUDWIG HILBERSEIMER's 'Hochhausstadt' (1924) and Richard Neutra's 'Rush City Reformed' (1926). These all consolidated the hegemony of the business centre over the rest of the town's elements and heralded the emergence of service industries as a determining force in urban growth. Even in the USSR, a society determined to turn its back on modern capitalism, it was an ideal of a Fordism-like industrial city that, between 1929 and 1930, inspired such partisans of the linear town as Nikolay Milyutin and encouraged the advocates of the dissolution of those existing agglomerations opposed to urban planning. In practice, however, urban planning in the USSR was more conservative, at least until 1930, when Ernst May and his team began to apply their experience to the study of new industrial towns.

Among those contributing to the increasingly professional and institutional debate on urban planning theory,

the approach of CIAM (the Congrès Internationaux d'Architecture Moderne), created in 1928, was particularly noteworthy. At their third congress in Brussels (1930), CIAM discussed forms acceptable for new neighbourhoods, confronting the issues of high-rise building and horizontal sprawl. At the following congress (Athens, 1933), they proposed their definition of a 'Functional' town. Authentic, practical experiments such as that of CORNELIS VAN EESTEREN, the designer of the Amsterdam extension plans (published 1934) and of doctrinaire visions similar to those of Le Corbusier, were aired there and resulted in conclusions, which Le Corbusier himself published in 1942 as the *Athens Charter*. For the groups that made up CIAM, who implicitly integrated three decades of experiments in zoning, urban planning was based primarily on the distinction and parallel development of the four major 'functions': living, work, leisure and traffic movement.

Around the same time, however, the urban policies of various dictatorial political regimes in Europe were adopting a different approach to the modernization of the infrastructure, dressing it up and even hiding it in a more nostalgic urban monumentalism. After a heated debate between the contradictory currents of Soviet urban planning, which resulted in the rejection of the more radical projects, the Moscow Plan (1932; ratified 1935), developed by VLADIMIR SEMYONOV, gave the capital the extension plan it had lacked since the 19th century. Based on strengthening the city's radial structure, centred on a huge Palace of the Soviets, then in blueprint but never executed, Semyonov's plan depicted a metropolis rich in communal housing developments arranged according to a homogeneous pattern (*see* MOSCOW, §I, 3). A few years later the (unexecuted) plans developed by Albert Speer for Berlin linked the motorway with an axial design arrangement for the city centre (see fig. 14; *see also* BERLIN, §I, 4). The idea of a large north–south axis could be dated back to the days of the Prussian kings but was conceived by Speer as a way of linking a new station to the south with a huge Kongresshalle to the north. The Berlin model, however, which was also applied to Munich and other 'Führerstädte', was far from being the only one in Nazi urban planning practice. In the projects of Otto-Ernst Schweizer (1890–1966) for greater Karlsruhe, for example, or those of Rudolf Schwarz for the occupied region of Lorraine (1940–44), the themes of the linear town and the townscape were used. The theme of the garden city, however, to which Gottfried Feder (1883–1941) had given a nationalist interpretation, clashed with projects for industrial towns such as Herbert Rimpl's city for the Hermann-Göring works.

An even more overt pluralism was implemented in Fascist Italy. The construction of a monumental 'Third Rome', based on a reconstruction of the existing transport network, was accompanied by a state policy for new towns, the main ones being built on the Pontine marshes. Built around a grandiose centre intended for parades, Littoria (1932) and Sabaudia (1933) were in keeping with the generally inventive and rationalist approach of the time. Elsewhere, functionalist groups to the north of the country followed more radical ideas, thanks to the support of the industrialist Adriano Olivetti, who commissioned a village

14. Urban plan for Berlin, by Albert Speer, 1930s

and industrial complex (from 1934) at Ivrea from FIGINI AND POLLINI. At the end of the 1930s BBPR ARCHITECTURAL STUDIO also designed for Olivetti generous landscapes in the Val d'Aosta, on which buildings and infrastructure could spread.

5. A NEW POLICY FOR THE CENTRE. The question of renovating old centres emerged in the early 20th century in all large towns, each with different sets of problems. The appreciation and conservation of historical monuments and open spaces no longer provided the only criteria for intervention, and the issue of improved sanitation was a central concern wherever plans for total renovation were launched, as with the 'insalubrious blocks' in Paris or the German 'Stadtsanierung'. Major plans for road systems were not, however, abandoned in the central metropolitan areas. The last traces of Haussmann's influence were visible in Paris, while in Italy a policy of clearances was launched. The developed projects covered a very large spectrum, from monumentalizing squares in Brescia, to modernizing the plan for the Via Roma (1930) in Turin. At the same time, Giovannoni suggested in his book *Vecchie città e urbanistica nuova* a way forward that respected old remains and buildings.

After 1940 the destructions of World War II focused attention again, and more acutely, on old city centres.

Theories about identical reconstructions of affected towns were extremely marginal in the thoughts of German and French urban planners, although they dominated the work of the Russians. More common was the temptation of the *tabula rasa* visible in various radical plans for the reorganization of urban areas on interlinked systems, such as that for London (1942) by the MARS Group, or the Kollektivplan for Berlin, worked out under Hans Scharoun's supervision (1946). However, these extreme proposals, and those of Le Corbusier at Saint-Dié (1944) or of Marcel Lods at Mainz (1946), remained unexecuted. The schemes that were realized tended to be those that saw the city as a cellular organism, such as the London County Plan of 1943 (see fig. 15), drawn up by PATRICK ABERCROMBIE. This approach, which combined a social vision of urban communities with a concern to modernize space, also took hold in Italy and France, albeit in a more rigid form derived from the Beaux-Arts tradition. In fact, therefore, the strict Functionalism of CIAM had only a limited impact on reconstruction. Nevertheless, the precepts of the *Athens Charter* provoked discussion, and eventually criticism, worldwide. The limitations of the Functionalist ideology became evident when a new wave of urban extensions was outlined in the post-war period.

BIBLIOGRAPHY
J. Stübben: *Der Städtebau* (Darmstadt, 1890, rev. Leipzig, 3/1924)
C. M. Robinson: *Modern Civic Art* (New York, 1903)

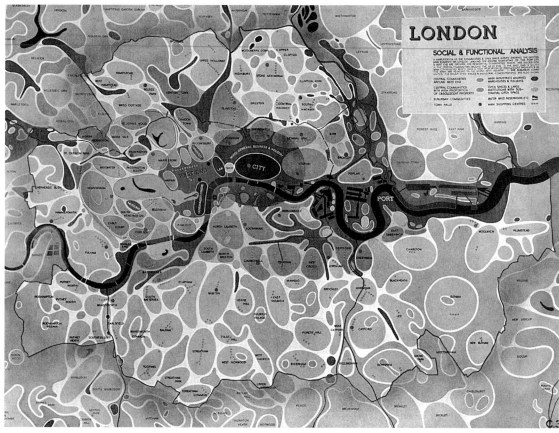

15. London County Plan, by Patrick Abercrombie, 1943

J. C. N. Forestier: *Grandes Villes et systèmes de parcs* (Paris, 1906)
T. Mawson: *Civic Art* (London, 1911)
E. Joyant: *Traité d'urbanisme* (Paris, 1923)
C. B. Purdom: *The Building of Satellite Towns* (London, 1925)
P. Lavedan: *Qu'est-ce que l'urbanisme?* (Paris, 1926)
——: *Epoque contemporaine* (Paris, 1952), iii of *Histoire de l'urbanisme*
F. Choay: *L'Urbanisme: Utopies et réalités* (Paris, 1965)
G. Albers: *Entwicklungslinien im Städtebau: Ideen, Thesen, Auslagen, 1875–1945* (Düsseldorf, 1975)
M. Smets: *L'Avènement de la cité-jardin en Belgique* (Liège, 1977)
F. Mancuso: *Le vicende dello zoning* (Milan, 1978)
P. Sica: *Storia dell'urbanistica: II novecento* (Bari and Rome, 1978)
D. Calabi: *Il 'male' città: Diagnosi e terapia* (Rome, 1979)
J.-L. Cohen, M. De Michelis and M. Tafuri, eds: *URSS, 1917–1978: L'Architecture, la ville* (Paris, 1979)
M. Steinmann, ed.: *CIAM Dokumente, 1928–1939* (Basle and Stuttgart, 1979)
G. Cherry, ed.: *Pioneers in British Planning* (London, 1981)
M. C. Boyer: *Dreaming the Rational City* (Cambridge, 1983)
D. Krueckeberg, ed.: *Introduction to Planning History in the United States* (New Brunswick, NJ, 1983)
A. Sutcliffe, ed.: *Metropolis, 1890–1940* (London, 1984)
J.-P. Gaudin: *L'Avenir en plans: Technique et politique dans la prévision urbaine, 1900–1930* (Seyssel, 1985)
J. Clair, ed.: *Les Années 20: L'Age des métropoles* (Montreal, 1991)
JEAN-LOUIS COHEN

VI. After 1945: regional development and urban renewal.

In the aftermath of World War II, most European countries embarked on programmes of reconstruction. In most cases new housing was an urgent need, but the industrial base and transport infrastructure had also to be re-established. In such countries as the United Kingdom these needs were harnessed to a new political structure, making local authorities responsible for programmes of development and encouraging decentralization. A key element in the British approach was the New Towns programme, which was begun in 1946 and established 28 new towns, housing over 1 million people. Economic decline in the 1970s, however, and a downward revision of population forecasts led to the virtual ending of the programme in 1981. Moreover, a dramatic contrast was beginning to emerge between the relative prosperity of areas away from the city centre and the deprivations of the inner city. Attention at the end of the 20th century, not only in the United Kingdom but in much of the Western world, therefore focused largely on problems of inner-city decay, raising new issues of responsibility and coordination.

1. Post-war construction. 2. Theoretical developments: urban design and townscape. 3. Planning systems. 4. Guidelines and good practice.

1. POST-WAR CONSTRUCTION. Throughout Europe the period immediately after the end of World War II was one of reconstruction. In Great Britain the New Towns Act of 1946 provided for the establishment of development corporations to designate specific areas for new towns and to plan and construct them. The first new

towns were built around London and included Hemel Hempstead, Stevenage, Basildon, Harlow, Bracknell and Hatfield, all built in response to an urgent housing demand caused by large-scale wartime destruction within the capital. Possibly the best-known example was Harlow New Town (from 1946) in Essex, planned by FREDERICK GIBBERD. In Scotland the first new town was East Kilbride, designed to relieve housing pressure in Glasgow. Together with such other examples as Glenrothes in Scotland, Peterlee in the north-east of England and Cwmbran in Wales, all these new towns were designed to meet planning objectives identified by the new regional planning authorities. All were built on garden city principles, with low-density development and architecture emulating post-war Scandinavian design. Cumbernauld New Town, however, begun in 1955 and intended to supplement the role played by East Kilbride, represented a radically different approach. Its linear town centre (see fig. 16), designed by Geoffrey Copcutt in 1961, introduced a new concept of vertical pedestrian/vehicular segregation, and the low-rise/high-density Seafar housing designed by Roy Hunter was equally radical.

Cumbernauld was a major breakthrough in planning ideas and did much to stimulate proposals in such other 'Mark II' New Towns as Runcorn (from 1965), Ches, where the Chief Architect, F. Lloyd Roche, promoted new concepts of housing and traffic circulation as well as having a totally enclosed town centre, designed by David

Gosling and others. Runcorn could be regarded as transitional since, unlike earlier towns built on green field sites, it was attached to an existing industrial community. In the mid-1960s, regional investigations indicated the need for further measures, and in 1967 the first of the 'Mark III' New Towns appeared with the designation of Milton Keynes, Bucks, with a target population of 250,000. Like Irvine New Town in Scotland, designated a year earlier as part of a regional growth strategy, it incorporated a sizeable existing community, but whereas Milton Keynes was initially planned for a car-owning population, Irvine incorporated new methods of integrating public and private transport within the concept of the community route introduced by the Chief Planner, David Gosling, with traffic consultants Jameison & McKay.

During the 1950s and 1960s rapid changes also took place in other parts of the world. In Japan, the reconstruction of the industrial base after World War II resulted in an economic success without parallel in the 20th century, except possibly in Germany. By 1960, Japan's economic growth was reflected in new concerns about population growth and city frameworks. The plan drawn up by KENZŌ TANGE for the expansion of central Tokyo, across Tokyo Bay (see fig. 17), suggested a projection of the infrastructure of the new city directly on to water, revealing the controlling framework of its highway system with startling clarity. Tange's planning contribution formed part of the

16. Urban design for linear town centre, Cumbernauld New Town, near Glasgow, by Geoffrey Copcutt, 1961

17. Urban plan for Tokyo by Kenzō Tange, 1959–60

emerging Japanese Metabolist movement, led by such figures as Kiyonori Kikutake and KISHŌ KUROKAWA, who advanced the notion of differential rates of change in the idea of the city as process (*see* METABOLISM). Individual dwellings were seen to have a shorter life-cycle than the supporting structure and services that sustained them, and the Metabolists used botanical analogies in their proposals.

This vision of the future city was also reflected during the same period (1964–70) in the work of the British group Archigram, whose manifesto proposed the three-dimensional megastructure support system for future urban development epitomized in Peter Cook's *Plug-in City* (1963–4) and Ron Herron's *Walking City in New York* (1964; for illustration *see* ARCHIGRAM).

In France new towns were created as a result of rapid urbanization not only in the Paris region but also in provinces during the late 1950s and early 1960s. The government's response to these problems was important in the fourth and fifth National Plans (1962–5; 1966–70). The Paris Regional Structure Plan (SDAURP) appeared in 1965, and it was in this latter plan that the proposal for new towns, including Ivry and Evry, first appeared in France. In the Netherlands, during the same period, a serious lack of housing resulted in an exodus of population from the major cities. Central government developed a policy of 'channelled deconcentration' to guide migration and identify growth cores. Of these, the two most important were Lelystad (1968; pop. 60,000, 1985) and Almerie, near Amsterdam, which had a final target population of 250,000 inhabitants.

By the 1950s in the USA a new urban problem was beginning to demand attention. Private car ownership had risen to such a level that serious and unexpected side-effects had become apparent. Congestion in the city centres, coupled with the dispersal of some key urban elements to out-of-town sites made accessible by the new regional highway systems, resulted in the construction of the first generation of such huge, new, out-of-town shopping centres as the Northland Shopping Center (1954) near Detroit, MI, designed by Victor Gruen Associates. Among the first proposals for the major reconstruction of a city centre was the 1956 plan for Fort Worth, TX, also by Gruen. Traffic was seen as a generator of design, but it was LOUIS I. KAHN in his plans for Philadelphia (1952–3), PA, who first suggested that this might be more than a mechanical necessity. He drew analogies between traffic flows and river flows as a novel analysis of movement patterns in a large metropolitan area. Kahn's proposals of the 1950s and 1960s were distinguished by an emphasis on the renewal of an existing city by its assimilation of a new circulation infrastructure. The subsequent reconstruction of Philadelphia under the direction of its city planner, Ed Bacon, had less of the radical vision of Kahn's earlier proposals, but it was nevertheless the first American city to incorporate wide-reaching pedestrianization proposals and an integrated public and private transportation network (*see* PHILADELPHIA, §1(iii) and fig. 2).

Pedestrianization of most major cities, particularly in Europe, during the 1970s may be seen as an attempt to reconstruct sections of the inner city and form urban units that would be cohesive in both management and visual terms and able to stimulate economic activity. The pedestrianization of the Kaufingerstrasse and the Neuhauserstrasse in Munich for the 1972 Olympic Games, where improvement continued until 1979, completed a unified public space and spanned the width of the old city core. The Stroget in Copenhagen, started in the late 1950s, was also important. In Britain a major government report, *Traffic in Towns* (1963), was produced by a team led by Colin Buchanan, which recommended a total restructuring of urban environments to guarantee the preservation of environmental quality, threatened by the rapid increase in vehicular traffic. American pedestrianization projects from the same period include the conversion and rehabilitation of buildings around Fisherman's Wharf in San Francisco,

CA, during the late 1960s and early 1970s, the most notable of which was Ghirardelli Square (1962–7; by WILLIAM WILSON WURSTER). In Boston, MA, the pedestrianization and rehabilitation of the Faneuil Hall/Quincy Market area was begun in 1971 by Benjamin Thompson Associates, and by 1988 it formed one of the most comprehensive urban renewal schemes in North America.

2. THEORETICAL DEVELOPMENTS: URBAN DESIGN AND TOWNSCAPE. During the later 1950s, urban design began to emerge as a discipline capable of uniting the diverging professions of architecture and urban planning. The pioneering work of KEVIN LYNCH and Donald Appleyard at the Massachusetts Institute of Technology resulted in Lynch's *Image of the City* (1960), while the influential work of GORDON CULLEN as Art Editor from 1947 of the British journal *Architectural Review* produced the publication in 1961 of *Townscape*. There was a growing interest in the three-dimensional aspects of urban planning and, in the case of Lynch, an attempt to investigate the ways in which the ordinary inhabitant of a city viewed and understood the urban environment. Lynch developed an important innovation in urban design technique through the use of interviews to establish how the city was perceived by its inhabitants, with the analysis of Boston, MA, Jersey City, NJ, and Los Angeles, CA. He identified five key urban design categories or elements—paths, edges, districts, nodes and landmarks. Appleyard, a former student of Lynch's, investigated movement aspects of urban highway design as co-author of *View from the Road* (1964) and developed this further in urban simulation laboratories at the University of California, Berkeley. Jane Jacobs's 'Four Conditions' in *The Death and Life of Great American Cities* (1965) and CHRISTOPHER ALEXANDER with '253 Patterns' in the encyclopedic work *A Pattern Language* (London, 1977) identified interrelated networks of urban elements from the smallest to largest scales. Somewhat later, Robert Venturi, Steven Izenour and Denise Scott Brown produced a subversive version of Lynch's theories with *Learning From Las Vegas* (1972; *see* VENTURI, RAUCH & SCOTT BROWN).

Urban design theory was also developed by the Rationalists: Aldo Rossi, Léon Krier and Rob Krier drew lessons from urban morphology to advance new configurations of the public realm of cities as exemplified in Rob Krier's *Stadtraum in Theorie und Praxis* (Stuttgart, 1979). Urban design began to be seen as a specialist area in development control and inner city regeneration. Possibly the most notable built example of an urban design project in late 20th-century Europe was the Staatsgalerie (see fig. 18) in Stuttgart by JAMES STIRLING and Michael Wilford (*b* 1938), in which the new art gallery was skilfully designed as a major urban link and pedestrian route between the upper and lower city. The same partnership's earlier project (1979) for an administrative centre in Tuscany was a prototypical design of a major urban intervention in an articular and planned landscape, with the buildings themselves forming a sequential urban route. Their later designs, including competition schemes in Japan for the Tokyo International Forum and unbuilt proposals for Canary Wharf (1988), London, show entirely new directions in urban design and architectural imagery. Their entry for

18. Urban design project by James Stirling and Michael Wilford: Staatsgalerie, Stuttgart, 1984

the Kyoto Railway Station competition (1991) in Japan was a masterpiece of urban articulation and followed a much earlier transport interchange proposal for the city of Bilbao.

Townscape is a particular branch of urban design theory that was developed by Gordon Cullen in England about the same time as Lynch, Appleyard and others. An artist of considerable talent, Cullen's work was devalued until comparatively late in the 20th century, ironically because his graphic fluency tended to obscure his theory, which was seen to be more subjective and less scientific than that of Lynch. His book *Townscape* (1961) introduced the concept of 'serial vision', in which sequential images are seen as an important analytical and design tool in experiencing the city either as pedestrian, passenger or motorist. Cullen later produced proposals using analytical systems as serial vision in plans for the new town of Maryculter in Scotland (see fig. 19) and in the rehabilitation of London Docklands in *Isle of Dogs: A Guide to Design and Development Opportunities* (1982), although this latter report was seen by many critics to exemplify its author's romanticism and lack of objectivity.

3. PLANNING SYSTEMS. In the period after World War II both the American and the British planning systems developed sophisticated legislative machinery. Since the Town and Country Planning Act of 1947 the British system (except in Scotland) had been centralized under a government ministry, with plans being subject to local authority planning committee and full local council approval, and with the possibility of public objections resulting in public enquiries. Ministry approval was required for structure plans. In the USA, however, systems of plan preparation and development control were decentralized, with local authorities taking responsibility for

them. No formal review or adoption of urban or metropolitan plans was required by central government, and the state governments did not review plans, on which any extensions of infrastructure must be based. By the 1990s, though, the British system was beginning more closely to resemble that of the USA. However, whereas previously local authorities in Britain had acted simultaneously as planning authority, public transport authority, education authority, highway authority, drainage and water authority, as well as housing authority, government legislation in 1987 and 1988 eliminated the transport authority role in public transport. Further legislation brought about the privatization of water authorities in 1989 and enabled schools and colleges to opt out of local authority control, making planning coordination more difficult. The abolition of the Greater London Council in 1986, with all planning functions reverting to the constituent London boroughs, also created formidable coordination problems in development control, conservation, land use planning and transport strategy. At the same time, public housing authorities were reduced in scope and control. Moreover, the clear definition of boundaries between local authorities in Britain resulted in the polycentric city and the decline of inner city areas. Another enduring difference between the British and American systems in the 1990s was that, whereas in Britain the preparation of plans and the development control were a combined function, in the USA planning and zoning were two separate functions, and zoning control could be exercised either without a plan or contrary to the plan.

In the area of community involvement in urban planning, developments in the United Kingdom again showed similarities to and differences from those in the USA. Poverty and social and economic deprivation were seen as root causes of urban riots in 1967 in many major American cities: advocacy planning and citizen participation thus became an important part of the planning process. Regional and Urban Design Assistance Teams (R/UDAT) were established by the American Institute of Architects, and in 1967 four volunteer teams, each representing a variety of professions, were formed to work with all members of specific communities who requested aid. By contrast, only two similar teams had been organized in Britain before 1988, although two minor studies did take place in Newcastle upon Tyne and Manchester in 1989. Community architecture in Britain—essentially a self-help, self-build system of small housing communities and associations—appeared somewhat later than the American initiatives but became fashionable. More vague and general in its scope than advocacy planning, community architecture's beginnings may be identified with such self-help, self-build housing associations and communities as ASSIST in Glasgow, founded in 1972 by Raymond Young and Jim Johnson to help tenants and owners with the rehabilitation of tenements in the district of Govan. Black Road in Macclesfield, Ches, which was a similar self-help project, also started in 1972, under the leadership of a resident architect, ROD HACKNEY. In Newcastle upon Tyne, Ralph Erskine established a consultative procedure with a shop on site as early as 1968 for tenants to be

housed in the Byker Wall redevelopment (1969–80), the first phase of which was completed in 1973. The movement was given fresh impetus by inner-city riots in London, Manchester, Bristol and elsewhere in the 1980s and received widely publicized support from CHARLES, Prince of Wales, during the same decade.

Among the member-states of the European Community, planning systems in the late 20th century varied greatly. In France there was a decentralized system of planning set out precisely in the Code de l'Urbanisme and with four levels of government (central, regional, departmental and commune). This decentralization was introduced in 1983, with communes being given the power of development control dependent on an approved local plan. Germany also had a system of development plans and development control. The enactment of the Bundesraumordnungsgesetz (BROG) in 1965 established comprehensive regional planning, with later laws requiring each of the Länder to accommodate the provisions of the BROG. The Dutch system was different from that of other European countries in that planning and building control were combined in a single permit within the framework of a legally binding plan. These plans were established by the Physical Planning Act of 1962, but the 1985 Act extended the system into a much more flexible

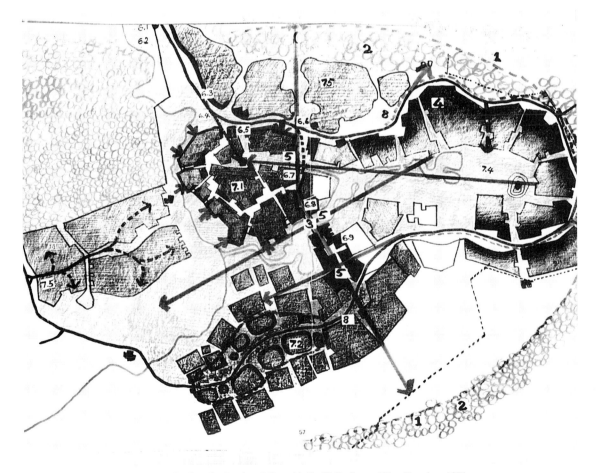

19. Urban plan for Maryculter, near Aberdeen, by Gordon Cullen with David Gosling and Dan Donohue, 1974

framework for the municipalities. Denmark's planning system was established between 1965 and 1975, and statutory policy was controlled by central government through the National Agency for Physical Planning (Planstyrelsen) within the Ministry of the Environment, as well as by counties and municipalities.

In the United Kingdom, urban development corporations were established from 1980 in a number of cities, including Cardiff, Newcastle upon Tyne, Manchester, Liverpool and Sheffield. The most significant was probably the London Docklands Development Corporation (LDDC; est. 1980), the terms of reference for which were set out by the Department of the Environment and included the new planning concept of the Enterprise Zone. This was a 'free' planning envelope with far fewer planning controls than before and with substantial capital and tax benefits for the private sector developer. Unlike previous new town development corporations, the new urban corporations were enablers rather than being responsible for implementation. They did not design and construct housing, industry and commercial facilities but purchased and assembled land and improved infrastructure before selling it to the private sector for development. A formal planning system was lacking, however, particularly in London Docklands, which was charged with the redevelopment of the Port of London area. Although planning reports were produced for this project, they had no statutory powers, and the result was rapid development without effective control, combined with spiralling land values, often resulting in visual anarchy. This resulted in development proposals of extremely high density and high plot ratios. The largest of these developments is Canary Wharf, where some doubt has been expressed as to whether the existing infrastructure, and transportation in particular, can sustain such a development. By the mid 1990s, a number of major cities re-investigated public transport issues. Sheffield and Manchester were the first to build light rail systems utilizing existing streets and new rights-of-way. Manchester was criticized in the architectural press for the clumsiness of its street design and for its light rail system.

4. GUIDELINES AND GOOD PRACTICE. For the first time in the British urban planning system, the private sector developer at Canary Wharf introduced urban design guidelines, which had been in common use in the USA in the 1970s. These provided a prescriptive, three-dimensional design control system that attempted to achieve visual and functional coherence in a large-scale urban development. Of course, the use of design guides in the planning process can be dated back to at least the medieval period, but they assumed a particular importance in the late 20th century. The best-known British design guide of this period was that prepared for Essex County Council in 1973, as a result of public concern over the expansion of suburban housing and its effect on the character of the old towns and villages. The *Essex Design Guide* amounted to a textbook of the aesthetics of town design, road engineering standards and planning for privacy and amenity. Using case studies of acceptable and unacceptable forms of development, it was instrumental in creating a popular form of 'vernacular' architecture in which neither buildings nor landscape dominated, and in which the use of traditional materials, construction details and local landscape species was mandatory. It was followed by many other county design guides, which tended to be less creative and more restrictive.

In the USA, the most significant urban design guidelines were those produced by the San Francisco Department of City Planning in 1970, which created a framework for detailed urban design plans at district and neighbourhood levels. These guidelines depended on the analysis of the city as a set of discrete 'design units' or 'visual districts' indicating the qualities of each part of the city that could be enhanced. Such an approach offered a consensus view of the particular qualities of a city that new developments should respect.

The *Canary Wharf Urban Design Guidelines* were produced in draft in 1986 by the Chicago practice of Skidmore, Owings & Merrill and were a highly prescriptive set of regulations governing not only the volumetric form of the skyscrapers to be designed by different architects on the site but also external materials, cornice lines, sloped massing planes, pedestrian easements and so on. The drawings were, nevertheless, two-dimensional diagrams, whereas the 1988 *Heron Quay Urban Design Guidelines* produced by David Gosling and Stephen Proctor attempted to respond three-dimensionally (albeit on a smaller scale) to the Canary Wharf proposals immediately to the north and included colonnade, arcade and waterfront proposals. However, the London Docklands Development Corporation ignored attempts to introduce such regulatory measures, resulting in rapid and chaotic development. Similar waterfront developments in the USA, however, of which there are extensive examples, have provided many cases of major federal, state, municipal and private sector investment combined within coherent development plans. Waterfront redevelopment in Boston, MA, commenced as early as 1975, and other important later projects include the Embarcadero in San Diego, CA, Portland, OR, and Vancouver, BC. Baltimore, MD, is a good example of user participation in the planning process, resulting from a referendum in 1978.

Although in the 1990s inner-city policies in Britain had replaced regional planning policies as a reflection of government response to socio-economic disparities, a general loosening of planning controls—through the Enterprise Zones, the privatization of many public services and the deregulation of public transport—militated against a rational planning policy. The problems of rail links to the Channel Tunnel (opened 1994) and the traffic congestion on the M25 orbital London motorway reflected a lack of coordination in transport planning. This was further emphasized by the removal of trade barriers between the 12 member states of the European Union to allow the free flow of people, goods, services and capital, which highlighted the clear need for physical planning coordination at a European level.

BIBLIOGRAPHY
P. Abercrombie: *Greater London Plan, 1944* (London, 1945)
K. Lynch: *The Image of the City* (Massachusetts, 1960)
G. Cullen: *Townscape* (London, 1961); rev. as *The Concise Townscape* (London, 1971)
L. Mumford: *The City in History* (Harmondsworth, 1961)

J. Jacobs: *The Death and Life of Great American Cities* (rev. Harmondsworth, 1965)

H. J. Dyos: *The Study of Urban History* (London, 1968)

F. J. Osborn: *Green Belt Cities* (London, 1969)

F. Schaffer: *The New Town Story* (London, 1970)

R. Sennett: *The Uses of Disorder: Personal Identity and City Life* (Harmondsworth, 1970)

G. E. Cherry: *Urban Change and Planning: A History of Urban Development in Britain Since 1750* (London, 1972)

H. Evans, ed.: *New Towns: The British Experience* (London, 1972)

A. Whittick: *Encyclopedia of Urban Planning* (New York, 1974)

D. Gosling and B. Maitland: *Design and Planning of Retail Systems* (London, 1976)

P. Hall: *Great Planning Disasters* (Harmondsworth, 1976)

J. Rykwert: *The Idea of a Town* (London, 1976)

L. Krier and others: 'Architecture rationelle', *Archvs Archit. Mod.* (1978)

G. R. Collins: *Visionary Drawings of Architecture and Planning: 20th Century Through the 1960s* (Massachusetts, 1979)

R. Cresswell, ed.: *Urban Planning and Public Transport* (Lancaster, 1979)

J. B. Cullingworth: *Environmental Planning, 1939-1969* (London, 1979)

H. W. E. Davies: *Development Control in the Netherlands* (London, 1979), pp. 20–23

R. Krier: *Urban Space* (London, 1982)

B. Badcock: *Unfairly Structured Cities* (Oxford, 1983)

D. Gosling and B. Maitland: *Concepts of Urban Design* (London, 1984)

Town and Country Planning: The Report of a Committee of Inquiry Appointed by the Nuffield Foundation: London, 1986

G. E. Cherry: *Cities and Plans: The Shaping of Urban Britain in the 19th and 20th Centuries* (London, 1988)

J. B. Cullingworth: *Town and Country Planning in Britain* (London, 10/1988)

'Planning for Town and Country, 1914–1989', *Planner*, dxxv (1989)

J. Punter: 'Decentralization of the Planning System in France', *Planner*, dxxv (1989), pp. 12–14

G. Broadbent: *Emerging Concepts in Urban Space Design* (London, 1990)

'The New Public Realm Competition', *Prog. Archit.* (1992)

DAVID GOSLING

Urbański [Urbansky], **Jan Jerzy** [Jan Jiří] (*b* Chlumec in the Usti district on the Elbe, *c.* 1675; *d c.* 1738). Bohemian sculptor, active in Silesia. He was a pupil of Jan Brokof in Prague (1693–7); after a disagreement with his master, he moved to Bautzen, where in 1704 he gained a master's degree. In 1708 he settled in Breslau, Silesia (now Wrocław, Poland), where he carved for the cathedral alabaster reliefs on the pulpit (1719–23), and also on the funerary monuments of *Bishop Gottfried* and *Bishop Nanker* (1723–4). He also executed lime and gilt figures of the *Fathers of the Church* for the presbytery balustrade. For St Mary Magdalene, Breslau, he made an organ (1722–5; destr.). Urbański sculpted several sandstone statues of *St John of Nepomuk*: one (1723) to stand in front of the church of St Matthew, and one (1724) for the monastery at Jasna Góra in Częstochowa, Poland. In 1726 he carved a wooden altarpiece with a *Pietà* for the church of Corpus Christi, Breslau (the altar was destroyed in 1945 but the *Pietà* survived); and between 1727 and 1729, an organ for the Evangelical church of God's Grace in Hirschberg (now Jelenia Góra, Poland). Urbański executed another sandstone statue of *St John of Nepomuk* (1730–32) to stand in front of Holy Cross Church, Breslau. His last works were wooden sculptures for the stalls and the high altar (1735–8) in the Benedictine church in Lüben (now Lubin, Poland). Urbański's art is representative of Bohemian Baroque in Silesia and characterized by pathos inspired by the work of Brokof and Gianlorenzo Bernini.

BIBLIOGRAPHY

A. Więcek: *Jan Jerzy Urbański* (Wrocław, 1963)

K. Kalinowski: *Rzeźba barokowa na Śląsku* [Baroque sculpture in Silesia] (Warsaw, 1986)

JERZY KOWALCZYK

Urbino [anc. Urvinum Mataurense]. Italian hilltop city in the Marches. Set in a relatively isolated position east of the Appenines, *c.* 12 km south-west of Pesaro, Urbino (population *c.* 16,000) achieved an extraordinary cultural importance in the 15th and 16th centuries, especially under the rule of Federigo II da Montefeltro (*see* MONTEFELTRO, (1)), who built the great Palazzo Ducale that dominates the walled city.

1. History and urban development. 2. Art life and organization. 3. Centre of maiolica production. 4. Palazzo Ducale.

1. HISTORY AND URBAN DEVELOPMENT. Renaissance tradition held that the city was founded 100 years after Rome by Metaurus Suassus Umbro, who is mentioned in an inscription on the Porta Valbona (1621), but the city's Latin name refers more directly to the nearby River Mataurum (now River Metauro), while its more ancient remains date back to the 3rd and 2nd centuries BC. The Roman city, bisected by its *cardo maximus* and *decumanus*, spread over the summit of the hill surrounded by walls in *opus quadratum* of local stone, of which some traces remain. Of the four city gates, only the northern one was accessible on the flat. Along the *decumanus* were the forum and a theatre, the remains of which may be dated to the first half of the 1st century AD. More Roman remains, including baths, dwellings and a necropolis, exist outside each gate, often beneath later medieval quarters.

Urbino subsequently became the seat of a garrison of Goths and was captured by Belisarius in AD 538. It then became part of the Byzantine province of Ravenna, passing to the Lombards (AD 751) and finally to the Church (AD 774). In the 12th and 13th centuries a new circuit of walls was built, extending the city further to the north-east, the only side on which it could expand within the slopes of the surrounding hills. In 1234 the city came into the hands of the Montefeltro family, and the walls withstood a siege (1284–5) by the papal army. Churches built in the 14th century include: S Domenico, with a Renaissance portal (1449–52) designed by Maso di Bartolommeo and realized by Pasquino da Montepulciano, with Fra Carnevale supervising the building; S Francesco (altered 18th century); and the oratory of S Giovanni Battista (Gothic Revival façade, early 20th century).

At the beginning of the rule of Federigo II da Montefeltro (1444), Urbino was still divided internally into quarters based on the Roman plan, with the Piazza Maggiore (now Piazza Duca Federico) on what may have been the site of the ancient forum, with the supposed medieval Palazzo del Conte Antonio to the south-east and the cathedral on the other side. The Castellare, a medieval building that, in view of its light construction, is unlikely to have served a defensive purpose, occupied the third site of the Piazza Maggiore and was later incorporated into the new Palazzo Ducale. The position of such medieval public buildings as the Palazzo dei Priori and Palazzo del Podestà, which are mentioned in documents, and the ancient cathedral and other buildings, has been credibly reconstructed by Negroni. The city was then radically transformed by the construction of Federigo's great hilltop Palazzo Ducale (begun ?1454; see figs 3 and 4 below; *see also* §4 and fig. 5 below), starting with the east range flanking the built-up area along the road (widened in 1563; now Piazza Rinascimento; see fig. 4s below) where S Domenico stands, and extending west down into the valley on a powerful substructure. At the lower level, looking to the Mercatale, a market square outside the city walls, there is the Data, the great ducal stables extending on two levels along the slope below the palace; the Data were constructed with a wide bastion containing spiral ramp inside by FRANCESCO DI GIORGIO MARTINI as part of his work there.

The Piazza Maggiore was ultimately defined on two sides by the entrance façade of the palace ('Facciata ad Ali'), which was linked by the Castellare to the new cathedral (begun *c.* 1480) by Francesco di Giorgio on the side of the old one, but with a new orientation (see fig. 4 below). Francesco also built the convent of S Chiara on the south-eastern slopes of the city and the church of S Bernardino (*see* FRANCESCO DI GIORGIO MARTINI, fig. 2) facing it on an adjacent hill (both begun *c.* 1482). In addition, the medieval city walls were extended by Federigo, with a new stretch, the Risciolo, extending downhill from his new palace to the 14th-century fortress of Albornoz. New fortifications, begun in 1507 under Federigo's successors, with contributions from Federigo Commandini, perfected his plans; they were mostly completed by 1525, with 12 demi-bastions. The new cathedral (see fig. 4q below) was not completed until 1604, when the dome was added, probably by Muzio Oddi; the structure was later rebuilt following earthquake damage in 1741 and 1781, with a new façade (1784–1801) by Camillo Morigia (1743–95) and a new Neo-classical dome and interior by GIUSEPPE VALADIER, begun in 1789 after the collapse of the dome that year.

Urbino was briefly occupied by Cesare Borgia in 1502–3, and in 1508, on the death of Federigo's son Guidobaldo da Montefeltro, the city passed to his chosen heir, Francesco Maria I della Rovere (ii). It reverted to the Church in 1631, returning to its role as a small commercial centre for a relatively poor agricultural region; almost unaltered, it ultimately became part of the Kingdom of Italy in 1860. Sensitive modern interventions in the historic fabric of the city appear in several works (late 1950s and after) by GIANCARLO DE CARLO, particularly his buildings for the university.

BIBLIOGRAPHY

F. Bianchini: *Memorie concernenti la città di Urbino* (Rome, 1724/*R* Bologna, 1978)

F. Ugolini: *Storia dei conti e duchi d'Urbino*, 2 vols (Florence, 1859)

E. Cabrini: *Urbino e i suoi monumenti* (Florence, 1899)

L. Moranti: *Bibliografia urbinate* (Florence, 1959)

G. De Carlo: *Urbino: La storia di una città e il piano della sua evoluzione urbanistica* (Padua, 1966)

G. Franceschini: *I Montefeltro* (Milan, 1970)

C. H. Clough: *The Duchy of Urbino in the Renaissance* (London, 1981)

F. Mazzini: *I mattoni e le pietre di Urbino* (Urbino, 1982)

L. Benevolo and P. Boninsegna: *Urbino* (Rome and Bari, 1986)

M. Bruscia, ed: *La Data (Orto dell'Abbondanza) di Francesco di Giorgio Martini* (Urbino, 1990)

F. Negroni: *Il duomo di Urbino* (Urbino, 1993)

FRANCESCO PAOLO FIORE

2. ART LIFE AND ORGANIZATION. Artists active in Urbino in the early 1400s included Lorenzo Salimbeni and his brother Iacopo Salimbeni (*fl* 1416–27), who decorated the oratory of S Giovanni Battista in 1416 (for illustration *see* SALIMBENI, LORENZO). The city was, however, renowned above all for the brilliance of its Renaissance court under Federigo II da Montefeltro (*reg* 1444–82; *see* MONTEFELTRO, (1)), which was immortalized in Baldassare Castiglione's eulogy to the ideal courtier, *Il libro del cortegiano* (Venice, 1528). Throughout the reign of the Montefeltro family and their heirs, the della Rovere, until 1631, Urbino was recognized as a centre of learning and culture. According to his librarian and biographer Vespasiano da Bisticci, Federigo encouraged artists from all over Italy and beyond to come to his court and add to the decoration of the city's churches and the embellishment of his new Palazzo Ducale (*see* §4 below), which Castiglione described as the most beautiful palace in Italy.

Several important artists were born in the region of Urbino, studied there or worked there, including Bramante, GIOVANNI SANTI and his son RAPHAEL, Federico Zuccaro, Girolamo Campagna (who produced a controversial marble statue of *Federigo da Montefeltro*, 1604–6; Urbino, Pal. Ducale), and TIMOTEO VITI and FEDERICO BAROCCI, who painted several religious works in the cathedral and elsewhere in Urbino in the early and mid-17th century. Important visitors to the city during the reign of Federigo included Ottaviano Nelli, Leon Battista Alberti, Luca della Robbia, Maso di Bartolommeo, Paolo Uccello, Piero della Francesca, Melozzo da Forlì and Luca Signorelli. Justus of Ghent, the only major Netherlandish painter working in 15th-century Italy, ran a workshop in Urbino in the 1470s and painted portraits of Federigo and his son Guidobaldo (see fig. 1) and an altarpiece of the *Communion of the Apostles* (Urbino, Pal. Ducale; *see* JUSTUS OF GHENT, figs 1 and 2), as well as a series of *Famous Men* (Urbino, Pal. Ducale; Paris, Louvre) in the *studiolo* of the palazzo (*see* §4 below); some of the latter have been attributed to Pedro Berruguete (*see* BERRUGUETE, (1)), who is also thought to have been in Urbino in the 1470s. In the 16th century TITIAN had particularly close relationships with Francesco Maria I della Rovere and Guidobaldo II della Rovere, successors to the Montefeltro; Titian's *Last Supper* and *Resurrection* (1542–4), parts of a standard painted for the Confraternity of Corpus Christi, still hang in the Galleria Nazionale delle Marche at the Palazzo Ducale, together with masterpieces by Piero della Francesca, Raphael and others. This collection also reflects the strong tradition of maiolica work at Urbino during the later Renaissance period (*see* §3 below), as well as the rich blossoming of Baroque art under Barocci and his school.

Many of the art works produced at the Renaissance court of Urbino were later dispersed to Rome, Florence and even further afield. Federigo da Montefeltro's library of Classical, medieval and contemporary texts, a collection of over 1000 manuscripts, was dispersed into papal collections and, through Vittoria della Rovere, Grand Duchess of Tuscany and daughter of Claudia de' Medici, to collections in Florence. Likewise, many of the sumptuous paintings, pieces of sculpture, maiolica, carpets, tapestries and ornate pieces of furniture listed in contemporary inventories of ducal property were removed

1. Justus of Ghent: *Federigo da Montefeltro and his son Guidobaldo*, 1340×755 mm, *c.* 1476 (Urbino, Palazzo Ducale)

when, on the death of Francesco Maria II della Rovere in 1631, the Duchy of Urbino was taken over by the papacy and ducal possessions divided between surviving heirs.

BIBLIOGRAPHY

J. Dennistoun: *Memoirs of the Dukes of Urbino* (London, 1851, rev. 1909)
G. Gronau: *Documenti artistici urbinati* (Florence, 1936)
C. H. Clough: 'Federigo da Montefeltro's Patronage of the Arts, 1468–1482', *J. Warb. & Court. Inst.*, xxxvi (1973), p. 137
G. Cerboni Biairdi, G. Chittolini and P. Floriani, eds: *Federico di Montefeltro: Lo stato/le arti/la cultura*, 3 vols (Rome, 1986)
L. Cheles: *The Studiolo of Urbino: An Iconographic Investigation* (Wiesbaden, 1986)

ANABEL THOMAS

3. CENTRE OF MAIOLICA PRODUCTION. Urbino was a prominent centre for the production of maiolica during the 16th century. Pottery had been produced in Urbino from medieval times but became celebrated in the 16th century for its fine *istoriato* (narrative) maiolica. Although

CASTEL DURANTE served as the training ground for many maiolica painters, the best of them worked in the ducal capital of Urbino. Artists schooled in both places were also active in such other Italian cities as Pesaro and Venice and beyond the peninsula in Lyon and Nevers, where the Urbino style took hold. *Istoriato* wares captured the imagination of both middle-class and aristocratic patrons, including Isabella d'Este. Although these labour-intensive, painted wares constituted only a small percentage of the output of the factories, they have been better preserved and are traditionally more highly valued than any other type of maiolica.

The *istoriato* style developed soon after 1500 and by 1515 had spread throughout central Italy. At first FAENZA was particularly noted for these wares; between 1525 and 1575, however, the potteries in the duchy of Urbino were unsurpassed in this mode. The narrative style became fully developed in the 1520s with the influx into Urbino of such prominent and talented artists as Nicola di Gabriele Sbraghe (formerly incorrectly identified as Nicola Pellipario; *see* URBINO, NICOLA DA) and FRANCESCO XANTO AVELLI of Rovigo. The artist Guido Durantino, who adopted the name Fontana, ran an extremely successful workshop with his sons, Camillo Fontana and Orazio Fontana, and later his nephew, Flaminio Fontana, and may have enjoyed the patronage of Guidobaldo II, Duke of Urbino; in 1565 Orazio founded his own workshop. The only other documented shop that made marked wares in any notable quantity was that of Guido di Merlino, whose circle of painters in the 1540s included the prolific FRANCESCO DURANTINO. Other artists working in the *istoriato* tradition in Urbino included the anonymous 'Milan Marsyas' and 'Coal-Mine' painters, Francesco Urbini and Camillo Gatti (*fl* 1545–51).

Characteristic Urbino *istoriato* wares depict subjects drawn from literature, history, the Bible, Classical mythology and, occasionally, contemporary life. The restricted palette of the 15th century was replaced by a broader range of brilliant colours, including orange, yellow, green, turquoise, blue, purple and black (*see* CERAMICS, colour pl. I, fig. 1). Some *istoriato* wares were sent on to Gubbio for the addition of the red and gold lustres for which that city's workshops were famous. Many painters in Urbino were inspired by woodcuts from illustrated books and engravings after the works of such painters as Raphael, Mantegna, Dürer and Rosso Fiorentino, copying individual figures and even whole compositions from these models (see fig. 2); Xanto was especially noted for this tendency. Other design sources included architecture, painting and sculpture, which artists knew either first hand or from prints and drawings.

Around 1560 a new genre appeared in Urbino in which ornamental grotesques, in the style made popular by Raphael, were spread liberally over the white, tin-glazed surfaces of dishes. They were also applied to more elaborate forms of vases and basins sometimes based on contemporary silverwares, which had become popular in the mid-16th century. Grotesques were frequently used as auxiliary decoration to frame smaller *istoriato* scenes in roundels or cartouches. The production of these wares was dominated firstly by the Fontana workshop and later by that of the PATANAZZI family from *c.* 1580 into the

2. Maiolica dish painted with the *Muses and Pierides* from a print by Giovanni Jacopo Caraglio after Rosso Fiorentino, diam. 460 mm, workshop of Guido Durantino, probably made by Camillo Gatti, *c.* 1545–50 (Cambridge, Fitzwilliam Museum)

17th century (e.g. flask, probably from the workshop of Antonio Patanazzi, *c.* 1579; London, BM). In addition to the *istoriato* and white-ground grotesque wares, both shops produced such sculptural pieces as inkstands and salt cellars decorated with whimsical genre scenes or mythological figures. The Urbino ceramic industry continued into the 18th century at a much reduced level, producing plaques bearing landscapes in the manner of the Abruzzese Castelli workshops.

BIBLIOGRAPHY

G. Vanzolini, ed.: *Istorie delle fabbriche di maioliche metaurensi* (Pesaro, 1879)

C. D. E. Fortnum: *Maiolica: A Historical Treatise on the Glazed and Enamelled Earthenwares of Italy* (Oxford, 1896)

J. V. G. Mallet: 'In botega di Maestro Guido Durantino in Urbino', *Burl. Mag.*, cxxix (1987), pp. 284–98

T. Wilson: *Ceramic Art of the Italian Renaissance* (London, 1987)

Italian Renaissance Pottery: Papers Written in Association with a Colloquium at the British Museum, London: 1987

WENDY M. WATSON

4. PALAZZO DUCALE. The residence of the dukes of Urbino, which dominates the city, was begun by Federigo II da Montefeltro (*see* MONTEFELTRO, (1)) in the mid-15th century and was the work of several masters, notably Luciano Laurana and Francesco di Giorgio Martini. The building now houses the Galleria Nazionale delle Marche. Although Federigo took power in Urbino in 1444, he was not awarded the title of duke until 1474; construction of the palace was provided for in the agreement he signed with the *comune* on entering the city, but its starting date remains uncertain. According to the anonymous *Memorie* (1723), Federigo began his new residence in 1454. In 1466 Laurana sent a model for the building from Mantua.

The Palazzo Ducale developed within clearly defined limits of the existing city (see fig. 3): medieval buildings to the south, S Domenico to the east, the medieval walls towering over the valley to the west, and another medieval building, the Castellare, to the north in the Piazza Maggiore (now Piazza Duca Federico; see fig. 4r below). The originality of the Palazzo Ducale, which was progressively built to fill all the available space, lay in its great size and an articulation that surpassed even that of contemporary Florentine palaces, although it adopted numerous elements of their style and architectural language, especially the arcaded central court. The interior was large enough to accommodate both the state administration and the court. In describing it as a city in the form of a palace, Baldassare Castiglione captured the significance of its form and organization as well as the character of the architectural synthesis which expressed the will of a lord who was both a condottiere and a humanist.

In the *Ordini et offici*, describing the *'famiglia'* of Federigo in the early 16th century, the 'master' architects mentioned are: LUCIANO LAURANA, FRANCESCO DI GIORGIO MARTINI and Baccio Pontelli, besides Fra Carnevale (known as a painter) and Sciro Sciri (a military engineer). Laurana came to the court in 1466 and remained until 1472; Francesco di Giorgio was certainly there from 1476 to 1485; and Pontelli, present from 1479, probably helped him to complete the palace until Federigo's death in 1482. Laurana was appointed supervisor for the project in 1468. Numerous other masters worked on the palace in those years, probably including Bramante; they were engaged in different parts of the work but often collaborated. The precise role of each one is thus unknown; it is particularly hard to distinguish between the work of Laurana and Francesco di Giorgio, and the attribution of the architectural decoration is equally problematical. The most likely hypotheses about the architectural decoration are those by Rotondi, which are referred to here.

(i) Palazzetto della Jole. This refers to the whole southern part of the palace (see fig. 4a), including the wing fronting the Cortile del Pasquino and those on three sides (east, south and west) of the Cortile d'Onore. This, the oldest part of the palace, was mainly built before the arrival of Laurana; before its completion Federigo and his wife lived in the east range facing S Domenico, which was created by joining a central two-storey building with a medieval house to the south. The appearance of this brick wing was not unlike that of other noble residences in north-central Italy. It was crowned with battlements; the first floor has a series of arched two-light windows, of which the last three at the south end were added after 1474, as shown by the carved initials F. D. ('Federicus Dux') and by their more mature design.

Inside, two rooms on the first floor show important decorations: the Sala degli Affreschi (4c) and the Sala della Jole (4d). In the Sala degli Affreschi there are remains of painted decoration representing ancient warriors in Renaissance dress. Below these figures is a band with escutcheons, attributed to Giovanni Boccati. In the whole range the corbels of the vaults embracing lunettes—where they are not replaced by later cloister vaults—appear to be of the oldest type used in the palace. Bartolommeo Genga

3. Urbino, Palazzo Ducale, Facciata dei Torricini, after 1466

later added a suite of rooms (1554–7) on the second floor, begun in the 15th century. The Sala della Jole has a monumental chimney-piece supported by piers featuring *Hercules* and *Jole*, and an architrave carved with a *Triumph of Bacchus and Ariadne* surmounted by a fascia of putti and festoons. A trabeated portal on pilasters leads to the grand staircase, and outside there is a similar portal decorated with military motifs. The Florentine–Riminese taste of the decorations points to Pasquino da Montepulciano as the designer and Michele di Giovanni da Fiesole (*b* 1418) as the sculptor.

(ii) Scalone d'Onore. The construction of the Scalone d'Onore or grand staircase (4e) played a decisive role in determining the width of the main range (north wing of the Cortile d'Onore). Placing the staircase in the corner, however, created major difficulties in designing both the east façade and the north, looking on to the Piazza Maggiore. On the east it was necessary to vary the rhythm of the arched two-light windows, replacing them with differently spaced single-light ones. More importantly, the four rectangular windows introduced to light the staircase on the north façade were not uniform in size and position with the large aediculated windows on the *piano nobile* of the 'Facciata ad ali' (*see* §(viii) below). The negative effect

was minimized by leaving the *piano nobile* façade incomplete, perhaps for that reason.

The interior treatment of the staircase was monumental and novel: for the first time a single entrance flight was built, in line with the north arcade of the courtyard, followed by two exceptionally wide and well-lit flights at right angles to it. A free-standing column faces the main internal wall on the second landing, and the corners are adorned with matching pilasters with candelabra attributed by Rotondi to Ambrogio d'Antonio Barocci and his associates. The staircase is believed to have been built before 1474: the initials F. C. ('Fredericus Comes') appear in the ceiling medallions except for the first and last flights, where the initials F. D. were probably introduced later, as was the complete Montefeltro coat of arms on the second landing.

(iii) Main range. The main range (4f), the north wing of the Cortile d'Onore between the grand staircase and the Facciata dei Torricini, contains the most important public spaces of the court and ends with private quarters, with windows and loggias between the towers facing the valley to the west. In the basement are the main kitchen, the furnace and the duke's bathroom, *calidarium*, *frigidarium* and dressing-room; other service rooms communicate with the lowest loggia between the towers. The plan of

the bathrooms and their simple decoration of Doric pilasters can be attributed to Francesco di Giorgio. On the ground floor are the barrel-vaulted entrance hall, guard room and library; the latter was decorated with four panels representing the *Liberal Arts* (destr.) and still has ceiling decoration of Federigo's eagle radiating flames. Towards the Facciata dei Torricini is an apartment considered by some to be that of Ottaviano Ubaldini, Federigo's 'brother'; it is quite similar to Federigo's on the floor above, except for two small rooms, the Tempietto delle Muse and the Cappella del Perdono, the purpose and attribution of which are problematical. The Tempietto is

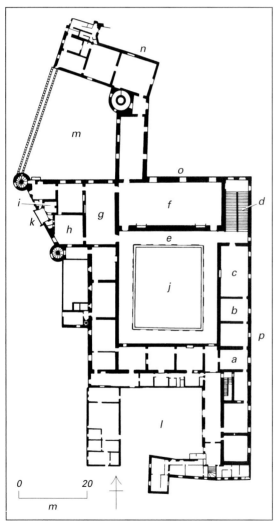

4. Urbino, first-floor plan of the Palazzo Ducale, begun *c.* 1454: (a–c) Palazzetto della Jole: (b) Sala degli Affreschi; (c) Sala della Jole; (d) Scalone d'Onore; (e) main range; (f) Sala Grande; (g) Sala degli Angeli; (h) Sala delle Udienze; (i) *studiolo*; (j) Cortile d'Onore; (k) Facciata dei Torricini, overlooking the Mercatale; (l) Cortile del Pasquino; (m) Giardino Pensile; (n) Castellare; (o) 'Facciata ad Ali', overlooking the Piazza Duca Federico (formerly Piazza Maggiore) and the new cathedral; (p) Piazza Rinascimento (enlarged in 1563); from M. L. Polichetti, ed.: *Il palazzo di Federico da Montefeltro: Restuari e ricerche* (Urbino, 1985)

a small rectangular space with a niche at the end, covered by a barrel vault divided into squares. Until 1632 there were painted panels on the walls representing the *Nine Muses, Apollo* and *Pallas*, some of which are attributed to Timoteo Viti (e.g. the *Muse Thalia with Apollo*; now Florence, Gal. Corsini) and Giovanni Santi. The adjoining barrel-vaulted Cappella del Perdono strongly evoked the Antique in its marble inlay and decoration attributed to Ambrogio Barocci. The inscription in the frieze over the portal suggests a date before 1480. The numerous attributions of the architectural design to Bramante cannot be confirmed.

The first-floor corridors over the courtyard arcades lead to the Sala Grande (4g; erroneously called the Sala del Trono), the Sala degli Angeli (4h) and Sala delle Udienze (4i); this sequence of public spaces leads to the smaller, private spaces of Federigo's apartment, with his bedchamber, *studiolo* and antechamber. At each end of the Sala Grande are side entrance portals framed by pilasters and entablatures, with different designs inside and out. Two Ionic chimney-pieces attributed to Francesco di Giorgio project into the vast rectangular space covered by a vaulted ceiling (see fig. 5); their detailing dates them to 1471–4. The passage from the Sala Grande towards Federigo's apartment is marked by accentuated decoration, which extends to the doors, with their wooden inlays of perspectives and symbolic motifs. In the Sala degli Angeli there is a striking architraved chimney-piece on brackets by Domenico Rosselli, who also designed the room's three doors with segmental pediments and who, with a pupil of Pietro Lombardo, built the chimney-piece in the Sala delle Udienze (probably designed by Francesco di Simone Ferrucci). This latter room is perhaps the most richly decorated, together with that thought to have been Federigo's bedroom.

The Sala delle Udienze leads to the *studiolo* (4j), a small room clad with intarsia work and, up to the ceiling, with panels painted with 28 *Portraits of Famous Men*. These portraits (some now Paris, Louvre) were painted by JUSTUS OF GHENT and Pedro Berruguete in strict unity with the illusionistic architectural framework of the intarsia decoration below, probably executed by the Florentine Giuliano and Benedetto da Maiano, looking to Botticelli for the *Virtù* and to Francesco di Giorgio for the *Squirrel* panel. Within the open doors of the *trompe l'oeil* cupboards created in inlaid wood, objects appropriate for study and war are displayed with great three-dimensional effectiveness; the room has often been interpreted as a humanistic microcosm of the duke. The frieze bears the date 1476, probably indicating the completion of the work (for further discussion and illustration *see* STUDIOLO, fig. 1).

(iv) Cortile d'Onore. The layout of the palace as a whole is determined by Laurana's grand, rectangular courtyard, the Cortile d'Onore (4k), surrounded by arcades or columns (1467–72; for further discussion and illustration *see* LAURANA, LUCIANO). The corners of the courtyard are emphasized by L-shaped piers articulated by half columns set against pilasters of a major order, the capitals of which touch at the angle. The effect is to create a firm and clear

5. Urbino, Palazzo Ducale, interior of the Sala Grande, 1471–4

separation of the court's façades, looking at Brunelleschi's and Alberti's architecture together. On the upper floor, above the arcades, completed by Francesco di Giorgio, pilasters and counter pilasters divide the amply fenestrated walls. According to Rotondi, the eulogy to Federigo inscribed on the frieze was added after 1482. An attic storey above the *piano nobile* was added to the court in the time of Guidobaldo II della Rovere (*reg* 1538–74), by Filippo Terzi and Giulio da Thiene (1551–1619).

(v) Facciata dei Torricini. According to Rotondi, the west wing of the Palazzetto della Jole was already finished when Laurana began construction of the section with the *torricini* after 1466. This façade (4l and see fig. 3 above) was angled outward towards the road leading from Rome, allowing it to be connected to the Castellare. The façade was completed before 1474, as evidenced by the initials F. C. on the arch of the second loggia between the towers. The two cylindrical towers are crowned with corbelled merlons surrounding octagonal spire-capped turrets. Inside are spiral stairways for rapid vertical communication between Federigo's apartment and the lower floors, terminating in a secret escape door. The small size of the towers indicates that they did not have a real defensive function, but they can be clearly seen from a distance, and their intention seems to have been celebratory.

This function is emphasized in the interior, where the loggias, the upper ones having arches on free-standing columns, recall the triumphal arch between the towers of

the Castel Nuovo, Naples, to which Federigo was attached from the beginning of his military career. The architectural decoration is particularly fine, as are the second loggia capitals, executed by Francesco di Simone Ferrucci *c.* 1470. The trabeated windows later used throughout the palace were perhaps first fitted on this façade. On the side overlooking the Terrazza del Gallo is another two-arched loggia on two storeys, contemporary with the body of the towers.

(vi) Cortile del Pasquino. Just behind the medieval structures of the Palazzetto della Jole, at the southern end of the palace, the Cortile del Pasquino (4m) was laid out with loggias on two sides: one at ground level with three arches on pillars, and the other with a loggia on the first floor, which was a later addition, as shown by the masonry. This had seven spans, of which two were originally blocked up and alternated with the open arches (at present the first three exterior bays are also blocked up). The capitals of the pillars with pilasters are similar to those of the corner pilasters on the first floor of the Cortile d'Onore. Baldi believed that a circular tempietto was planned for the centre of the court. An existing underground space has been interpreted as the tempietto's burial chamber (Rotondi) but seems to be a cistern (Polichetti).

(vii) Giardino Pensile and Castellare. When Laurana left Urbino in 1472, only the wing facing the Piazza Maggiore and some foundations for the court could possibly have

been built between the block with the towers and the Castellare. Francesco di Giorgio is therefore credited with the construction of the underground quarters with stables and snow pit, and the mechanism for collecting water under the hanging garden, as well as the regularization of this whole northern part of the palace. The resulting trapezoid court, artificially converted into a garden, the Giardino Pensile (4n), was surrounded by a wall with windows facing the valley, topped by a walkway between the duke's apartment and the new quarters in the Castellare (4o). On the eastern side of the court a portico with simple arches on pillars was completed with a cylindrical structure projecting at the angle with the Castellare, containing a spiral ramp for use by horses; this was a functional counterpart of the grand staircase and solved the difficult problem of the junction with the Castellare, which is at an angle to the palace. The *piano nobile* of the Castellare was remodelled, and from 1477 it became the duchess's apartment.

(viii) 'Facciata ad Ali'. The entrance forecourt (4p), known as the 'Facciata ad Ali' ('façade with wings') because it embraces two sides of what used to be the Piazza Maggiore (on the third side is the new cathedral), is the focus of the whole varied organism of the palace. It is designed in an innovative *all'antica* style, with a plinth storey faced with flat, rusticated stone punctuated by doors and windows. The brick *piano nobile*, with large trabeated windows on stone pilasters, may have been intended to be lightly stuccoed. The walls were originally topped with battlements, which were hidden when the roof was raised under Guidobaldo II della Rovere. The façade displays other unusual features, including a corner pier above which the string course juts out to form a sort of capital; the alternating rhythm of the ground-floor portals and first-floor windows; and the interruption of the stonework with the change in rhythm of the last three windows on the *piano nobile* in line with the end portal of the second wing of the façade. The rhythm was varied not only because of the grand staircase in the corner but also because the Sala Grande is off-centre, as is the palace entrance, on axis with the court, which is also off-centre. The architect nevertheless also had to resort to wholly or partly false windows and doors to balance the composition. The successful result, which inspired numerous imitations in the Renaissance, is attributable to Francesco di Giorgio; it is certainly after 1474, as seen from the inscription FE DUX on the apron below the windows on the *piano nobile*. Francesco di Giorgio is also credited by Vasari with the sculpted panels depicting the *Arts of War*, placed as backrests to the benches at the base of the façade. According to Rotondi, these panels were executed by Ambrogio Barocci, as was probably the architectural decoration of the façade.

BIBLIOGRAPHY

Memorie istoriche concernenti la devoluzione dello stato di Urbino alla sede apostolica (Amsterdam, 1723)

B. Baldi: 'Descrizione del palazzo ducale di Urbino', *Memorie concernenti la città di Urbino*, ed. F. Bianchini (Rome, 1724)

A. Venturi: 'Studi sul palazzo ducale di Urbino', *L'Arte*, xvii (1914), pp. 414–73

L. Serra: 'Le varie fasi costruttive del palazzo ducale di Urbino', *Boll. A.*, x (1931), pp. 1–11, 433–47

M. Salmi: *Piero della Francesca e il palazzo ducale di Urbino* (Florence, 1945)

P. Rotondi: *Il palazzo ducale di Urbino*, 2 vols (Urbino, 1950–51; Eng. trans., London, 1969)

G. Marchini: 'Il palazzo ducale di Urbino', *Rinascimento*, ix/1 (1958), pp. 43–78

——: 'Aggiunte al palazzo ducale di Urbino', *Boll. A.*, i–ii (1960), pp. 73–80

L. H. Heydenreich: 'Federico da Montefeltro as a Building Patron: Some Remarks on the Ducal Palace of Urbino', *Studies in Renaissance and Baroque Art Presented to A. Blunt* (London, 1967), pp. 1–6

G. Eimer: 'Francesco di Giorgio Fassadenfries am Herzogpalast in Urbino', *Festschrift Ulrich Middeldorf* (Berlin, 1968)

P. Rotondi: *Francesco di Giorgio nel palazzo ducale di Urbino* (Novilara, 1970)

Urbino e le Marche prima e dopo Raffaello (exh. cat., ed. M. G. Ciardi Duprè and P. Dal Poggetto; Urbino, Pal. Ducale, 1983)

G. Bernini Pezzini: *Il fregio dell'arte della guerra nel palazzo ducale di Urbino: Catalogo di rilievi* (Rome, 1985)

M. L. Polichetti, ed.: *Il palazzo di Federico da Montefeltro: Restauri e ricerche* (Urbino, 1985)

C. Ceri Via: 'Ipotesi di un percorso funzionale e simbolico nel palazzo ducale di Urbino attraverso le immagini', *Federico di Montefeltro*, ed. G. Cerboni Baiaroli, G. Chittolini and P. Floriani (Rome, 1986), ii, pp. 47–64

L. Cheles: *The Studiolo of Urbino: An Iconographic Investigation* (Wiesbaden, 1986)

F. P. Fiore: 'Le residenze ducali di Urbino e Gubbio: Città in forma de palazzo', *Archit.: Stor. & Doc.*, ii (1989), pp. 5ff

Piero e Urbino: Piero e le corti rinascimentali (exh. cat., ed. P. Dal Poggetto; Urbino, Pal. Ducale, 1993)

F. P. Fiore and M. Tafuri: *Francesco di Giorgio architetto* (Milan, 1994)

FRANCESCO PAOLO FIORE

Urbino (da Crema), Carlo (*b* Crema, *c.* 1510–20; *d* Crema, after 1585). Italian painter, draughtsman and theorist. He has been identified, and is principally of interest, as the author of the Codex Huygens (New York, Pierpont Morgan Lib., MS. M.A. 1139), a collection of studies of proportion and perspective based, in part, on the notebooks of Leonardo da Vinci. Urbino's earliest works were frescoes (destr.) depicting scenes from *Jerusalem Delivered* for the Palazzo Zurla, Crema, and altarpieces painted between 1554 and 1557 in S Maria presso S Celso, Milan. Contact with the school of Leonardo and also with Gaudenzio Ferrari is evident in the decoration of the Cappella Taverna, S Maria della Passione, Milan, and in the organ shutters in the same church. He subsequently worked with Bernardino Campi, for whom he made preparatory drawings for paintings executed by his partner and for fresco cycles in the Palazzo Ducale, Sabbioneta, and the Cappella di Cecilia in S Sigismondo, Cremona. In the frescoes in the Santuario di S Maria in Campagna, Pallanza, executed with Aurelio Luini (1530–93), he demonstrates the skills in perspective seen in the drawings of the Codex Huygens, although the execution in paint is disappointing. His painting technique is generally poor, as is evident both from such earlier works as the *Incredulity of Thomas* (Milan, Brera), influenced by Ambrogio Figino, and such later work as the *Calvary* (Crema, S Maria della Croce). A better executed result is achieved in the frescoes painted in 1580 in S Pietro, Quintano. Drawings for a treatise on terms and caryatids (London, V&A) have been attributed to Urbino.

BIBLIOGRAPHY

E. Panofsky: *The Codex Huygens and Leonardo da Vinci's Art Theory* (London, 1940)

M. Di Giampaolo: 'Bernardino Campi a Sabbioneta e un'ipotesi per Carlo Urbino', *Ant. Viva*, xiv/3 (1975), pp. 30–38

G. Bora: 'Note Cremonesi, II: L'eredità di Camillo e i Campi (continu-azione)', *Paragone*, xxviii/327 (1977), pp. 54–88

S. Gatti: 'Due contributi allo studio del pittore Carlo Urbino', *A. Lom-barda*, 47–8 (1977), pp. 99–107

U. Ruggeri: 'Disegni di Oxford', *Crit. A.*, xlii/154–6 (1977), pp. 98–118

——: 'Carlo Urbino e il Codice Huygens', *Crit. A.* xliii/157–9 (1978), pp. 167–76

G. Bora: 'Un ciclo di affreschi, due artisti e una bottega a Santa Maria di Campagna a Pallanza', *A. Lombarda*, 52 (1979), pp. 90–106

S. Marinelli: 'The Author of the Codex Huygens', *J. Warb & Court. Inst.*, xliv (1981), pp. 214–29

M. Kemp: *The Science of Art: Optical Theories in Western Art from Brunelleschi to Seurat* (New Haven and London, 1990), pp. 74–6

UGO RUGGERI

Urbino, Nicola da [Sbraghe, Nicola di Gabriele; Sbraga di Gabriele; Pellipario, Nicolò] (*fl* 1520–37/8; *d* Urbino, ?1537/8). Italian maiolica painter. He has long been confused with Nicolò Pellipario from Castel Durante, who was the father of the maiolica painter Guido Durantino (later Fontana) of Urbino. Nicola was documented as being in Urbino in 1520, by which time he was already referred to as *maestro*. He was head of his own workshop but also collaborated with others. One of his finest pieces is a large signed plate (1528; Florence, Bargello) decorated with the story of St Cecilia. Four other signed pieces are in the State Hermitage Museum, St Petersburg (1521), the Louvre, Paris (*c*. 1525–8), the church of S Stefano, No-vellara (*c*. 1530), and the British Museum, London (*c*. 1535). Several magnificent armorial services have been attributed to him on the basis of these works. The 'Correr' service (*c*. 1520; Venice, Correr) is noted for its lyrical scenes drawn from mythology and contemporary romances and for its graceful figures and sophisticated colour harmonies. A service of *c*. 1525 for Isabella d'Este, Marchioness of Mantua, was his most prestigious commission, and he also produced another set around the same time for the Calini family of Brescia. Both sets feature imaginative architec-tural settings. In the 1530s he made services for Isabella's son, Federico Gonzaga, 1st Duke of Mantua, and his wife, Margherita Paleologo. Nicola was a pre-eminent figure in the production of Italian Renaissance maiolica and was a major influence on other *istoriato* painters in and around Urbino and Pesaro. Like other artists such as Francesco Xanto Avelli, he drew on prints for inspiration, using woodcuts from Ovid's *Metamorphoses* (Venice, 1497) and engravings by such artists as Marcantonio Raimondi. Nicola's compositions, however, are imbued with a fresh-ness and originality that set them apart from those of his contemporaries and followers. He is often regarded as the most gifted and inventive of the 16th-century *istoriato* artists and was largely responsible for establishing what is thought of as the classic style of Renaissance maiolica.

BIBLIOGRAPHY

H. Wallis: *XVII Plates by Nicola Fontana da Urbino at the Correr Museum, Venice: A Study in Early XVIth Century Maiolica* (London, 1905)

G. Liverani: 'Le "Credenze" maiolicate di Isabella d'Esta Gonzaga e di Federico II Duca di Mantova', *Corriere Cer.*, xvii (1939), pp. 1–17

B. Wallen: 'A Maiolica Panel in the Widener Collection', *National Gallery of Art: Report and Studies in the History of Art* (Washington, DC, 1968), pp. 94–105

J. Rasmussen: 'Zum Werk des Majolikamalers Nicolo da Urbino', *Keramos*, lviii (1972), pp. 51–64

F. Negroni: 'Nicolo Pellipario: Ceramista fantasma', *Not. Pal. Albani*, xiv/1 (1985), pp. 13–20

WENDY M. WATSON

Urfa [Orfa; Gr. Edessa; Arab. al-Ruhā']. Town in south-east Turkey. Lying at the intersection of important trade routes, the town must have existed before the Macedonian conquest, as it was refounded by Seleukos I (*reg* 312–281 BC). Lying on the frontier, the town suffered in the wars between Rome and the Parthians. Christianity was introduced by the 3rd century AD and Edessa became an important centre of Nestorianism. The town changed hands during the Persian–Byzantine wars and was taken by the Arabs in 638. The Mandylion or Holy Image of Edessa was a famous image of Christ that remained in the city until 942–3, when Romanos I removed the image with great ceremony to Constantinople. Arab geographers reckoned the cathedral, which had ceilings decorated with mosaics, one of the four wonders of the world. The city was taken by the crusaders, who there established the County of Edessa (*see* JERUSALEM, LATIN KINGDOM OF), the first Latin state in the east (1098–1144). The capture of Edessa by the Zangids in 1144 led to the proclamation of the Second Crusade (1145–9). Known for its fine stone buildings and masons, the town is said to have supplied the builders of the 12th-century walls of Cairo. The congregational mosque, built on the site of an earlier structure, has a shallow rectangular prayer-hall covered by two rows of cross-vaults with a dome to the east of the central axis. A transverse-vaulted portico opens on to a court; the mosque resembles the congregational mosque at Aleppo in Syria as restored by Nur al-Din. Other notable buildings include the citadel, built on Hellenistic founda-tions, the Hızmalı Bridge (14th century), the Halilürrah-man Mosque and the Abdulrahman Madrasa (18th century).

BIBLIOGRAPHY

Enc. Islam / 1: 'Orfa'

A. Gabriel: *Voyages archéologiques dans la Turquie orientale* (Paris, 1940)

LALE H. ULUÇ

Urgench. *See* KUNYA-URGENCH.

Uri, Aviva (*b* Safed, Palestine [now Zefat, Israel], 1927). Israeli draughtswoman. She studied drawing in Tel Aviv with David Hendler whom she later married. In 1956 she won the Dizengoff prize and in 1957 had her first solo show at the Tel Aviv Museum. This had a strong impact on younger Israeli artists who saw it as a contrast to the contemporary, brightly coloured works of the New Hori-zons group. Uri exhibited with the 10+ group around Raffie Lavie, founded in 1965, which reacted against the New Horizons style and prepared the way for the devel-opments of the 1970s. Her drawings are mostly in black chalk, very sparely used, taking landscape as the starting point. The result is near abstract gestural works such as *Landscape* (1960; Jerusalem, Israel Mus.). She also made limited use of coloured chalk on occasion, as in *Drawing* (1967–8; Jerusalem, Israel Mus.). In addition her later work included purely abstract drawings, such as *Drawing* (1981; Amsterdam, Stedel. Mus.), as well as strongly coloured abstract works such as *Drawing* (1984; Tel Aviv, Givon A.G., see 1984 exh. cat., p. 6).

BIBLIOGRAPHY

Artists of Israel: 1920–1980 (exh. cat., New York, Jew. Mus., 1981), pp. 140–41

Aviva Uri (exh. cat. by D. Le Vitté-Harten, Düsseldorf, Städt. Ksthalle, 1984)

Uric, Gavril (*b* ?1390; *d* after 1442). Romanian illuminator and calligrapher. He was a monk at Neamt Monastery, where he founded a school of book illumination. The development of his cursive, semi-uncial and liturgical scripts reflects the influence of south Slavonic calligraphy. Other characteristic features of his work that continued to mark Moldavian manuscripts until the 17th century include the interwoven geometrical designs of frontispieces, the elegant layout of pages, the refined lines, the unusual forms of certain letters and the balanced presentation of the ensemble. He may also have visited the scriptoria of Constantinople. One of the six manuscripts attributed to him and dated between 1413 and 1447 is the Diatessaron of Princess Marina, wife of Voivode Alexander I (1429; Oxford, Bodleian Lib., MS. can. gr. 122), which has full-page portraits of the Evangelists painted in the Byzantine manner but imbued with the artist's personal style. The Evangelists are shown seated on thrones against schematic grounds in the Hellenistic tradition, with naturalistic proportions, and expressive gestures and faces presented in rhythmic compositions of undulating lines and in a refined palette. These Evangelist portraits served as models for manuscripts of the 15th and 16th centuries and for the wall paintings on the large pendentives below the nave domes of Moldavian churches.

BIBLIOGRAPHY

E. Turdeanu: 'The Oldest Illuminated Moldavian Manuscript', *Slav. & E. Eur. Rev.*, xxix/73 (1951), pp. 342–79

S. Ulea: 'Gavril Uric primul artist român conoscut' [Gavril Uric, the first known Romanian artist], *SCIA*, II/ii (1964), pp. 235–63

——: 'Pictura si manuscrisul' [Painting and the manuscript], *Arta in Moldova din secolul al XIV-lea pină la mijlocul socolului al XV-lea* [Art in Moldavia from the 14th century until the mid-15th century] (1968), i of *Istoria Artelor Plastice in România* [History of the fine arts in Romania] (Bucharest, 1968–), pp. 54–128

——: 'Gavril Uric: Studiu paleografic' [Gavril Uric: a palaeographical study], *SCIA*, III/ii (1981), pp. 35–62

TEREZA-IRENE SINIGALIA

Urlaub, Georg Anton (*bapt* Tüngersheim, nr Würzburg, 20 May 1713; *d* Würzburg, 20 Feb 1759). German painter. He came from a family of painters and probably first studied under his father, Georg Sebastian Urlaub (1685–1763). With the support of Friedrich Karl von Schönborn, Prince–Bishop of Würzburg, he studied at the Akademie der Bildenden Künste in Vienna from 1737 to 1741, after which he returned to work in Würzburg. In 1744 he left for Italy, where he studied (1745–7) at the Accademia Clementina (now Accademia di Belle Arti e Liceo Artistico) in Bologna and was awarded several prizes. In 1749 he went to Venice to study the works of Giambattista Tiepolo. He returned to Germany in 1751 and painted altarpieces and frescoes in Würzburg and its environs. Other than a few drawings from his years in Bologna (Accad. B.A. & Liceo A.) his first documented works are the ceiling fresco of the *Apotheosis of the Cross* (1752; Ipthausen, Wallfahrtskirche Mariae Geburt.) and two altarpieces in the Augustinerkirche in Würzburg, the *Glorification of Christ* and the *Circumcision* (both 1753; destr.), which show the distinct influence of Tiepolo, who was working at the Residenz in Würzburg at that time. Urlaub's frescoes in S Wendelin, Eyershausen (*Adoration of the Magi* and *Last Supper*, both 1753), and in SS Martin and Johann Nepomuk, Königheim (*Adoration of the Magi*, 1759), are mostly without illusionistic construction, the focus of the paintings being concentrated in the area around the balustrades. His several easel paintings of biblical subjects (e.g. *Story of Joseph*; Würzburg, Mainfränk. Mus.) and his few portraits (e.g. *Johann Georg Oegg*; Würzburg, Mainfränk. Mus.) are strong in expression but somewhat dull in colour.

BIBLIOGRAPHY

W. Runge: *Georg Anton Urlaub: Ein fränkischer Schüler Tiepolos* (Würzburg and Munich, 1919)

N. Knott: *Georg Anton Urlaub, 1713–1759: Ein fränkischer Maler* (Würzburg, 1978)

KLARA GARAS

Urnes [now Ornes]. Site of a stave church in Sogn, western Norway. The carved ornament on the exterior of the church gave its name to the last of the Viking-period art styles of Scandinavia.

1. STYLE. The present building is a mid-12th-century stave church (*see* §2 below), but it incorporates decorated timbers from its 11th-century predecessor. These consist of the portal and door, with two planks, in the north wall of the church (see fig. 1), the north-west corner post and the gables at the east and west ends of the church. The portal, planks and corner post are carved in high, rounded relief (up to 120 mm deep), while the gables and door are executed in the contrasting technique of low, flat relief. The composition schemes and motifs used are, however, the same.

Urnes-style designs are composed of open 'interpenetrating loops' consisting of two intersecting loops (or figures-of-eight) or of more complex multi-loop schemes. These patterns of fluent curves are given an additional elegance and sense of movement by the characteristic use of two line widths, which may also gradually swell and taper. The Urnes phase of Viking art represents a reassertion of the native Scandinavian tradition at the expense of the European influences that had been particularly evident in the preceding Ringerike style phase of the first half of the 11th century, with its lavish use of foliate motifs. The Urnes style is dominated by animal motifs in three main varieties, all of which are used by the Urnes sculptor: a standing quadruped, a ribbon-shaped animal and a snake. These animals frequently bite one another so as to complete the loop schemes (see fig. 1).

The Urnes style had developed by the mid-11th century, although its origins have yet to be established in detail; its name is coincidental and was first used by the Norwegian scholar Haakon Shetelig in 1909. It became a pan-Scandinavian fashion during the second half of the 11th century and was introduced into England; its influence was also a factor in the development of Irish art. It is best seen in Sweden, where it was used to decorate numerous rune-stones, notably in Uppland (*see* VIKING ART, fig. 9), among which there are examples with designs transitional between the Ringerike and the Urnes styles as the one is gradually refined into the other (e.g. Ardre III, from the parish of Ardre in Gotland). Swedish scholars have

1. Urnes-style carved wooden portal, door and planks on the north wall of the stave church at Urnes, Norway, 11th century

sometimes found it convenient to group together their ornamented rune-stones in both styles under the one heading of 'rune-stone style', but more recent studies (particularly by Signe Horn Fuglesang) have re-emphasized the distinctive qualities of both, even allowing for a fair amount of stylistic overlap between them. The Urnes phase of Viking art lingered on into the 12th century, while its use waned with the growing influence of the ultimately victorious European Romanesque style.

The superb quality, in both design and execution, of the Urnes carvings themselves, on a small church in a remote area, serves as a reminder for the late Viking period (as do the Oseberg carvings for the early Viking period) of the limitations faced by the student of Viking art, given the accidental survival of wood-carving from this period.

See also VIKING ART, §II, 1(i).

BIBLIOGRAPHY
H. Shetelig: 'Urnesgruppen' [The Urnes group], *Foreningen til norske fortidsmindesmerkers bevaring, aarsberetningen* [The Society for the Preservation of Norwegian Ancient Monuments, Annual Report] (1909), pp. 75–107
D. M. Wilson and O. Klindt-Jensen: *Viking Art* (London, 1966, rev. 1980)
S. H. Fuglesang: *Stylistic Groups in Late Viking and Early Romanesque Art*, Acta Archaeol. & A. Hist. Pertinentia (Rome, 1981), pp. 79–125

JAMES GRAHAM-CAMPBELL

2. STAVE CHURCH. Excavations below the present church at Urnes have revealed the structure of at least one earlier building on the site (Bjerknes, Christie). Four large central post-holes are an unusual feature, and there is disagreement about the relationship between this early structure and the decorated remains (Anker). The 12th-century church, while incorporating early decorated planks in its walls (*see* §1 above), is essentially an ordinary STAVE CHURCH of the aisled type, with the remains of an original pentice to the west and a later sacristy added to the east. The interior posts have cubic capitals (see fig. 2) and large moulded archivolts, however, which is not the normal practice in stave churches. Urnes therefore occupies a key position in any consideration of the possible influence of stone architecture on stave church construction.

The capitals and the abatements above them on the posts are carved in a flat two-plane relief, featuring dragons, lions, grotesque humanoids and plant scrolls, all of a general European Romanesque character. The technique, motifs and details bear little resemblance to the carving in most stave churches; the main influences are early 12th-century soapstone sculpture in Trondheim and mid-12th-century granite sculpture in Jutland (Hohler). The west doorway also has cubic capitals; although decorated with dragons like those in the interior, they are much closer in technique to the 11th-century doorway reused in the north wall and seem to represent a deliberate attempt to adjust the 12th-century work to the earlier style. The quality of both the 11th- and 12th-century carving is extremely high. Historical sources indicate that for centuries this was the

2. Urnes stave church, carved wooden capital in the nave, h. 370 mm, 12th century

demesne and home church of one of the most powerful families in western Norway (Magerøy). As further evidence of their generosity, the building contains a large Romanesque *Calvary* group and a pair of high-quality Limoges candlesticks. The church attracted the notice of the Norwegian painter Johan Christian Dahl, who published a volume of drawings, with text in German (Dresden, 1837).

BIBLIOGRAPHY

J. C. Dahl: *Denkmale einer sehr ausgebildeten Holzbaukunst aus den fruehesten Jahrhunderten in den inneren Landschaften Norwegens*, 3 vols (Dresden, 1837)
L. Dietrichson: *De norske stavkirker: Studier over deres system, oprindelse og historiske udvikling* [Norwegian stave churches: studies of their design, origins and historical development] (Kristiania, 1892/*R* Farnborough, 1971), pp. 212–22
P. Blix: *Nogle undersøgelser i Borgund og Urnes kirker* [Some investigations on the churches of Borgund and Urnes] (Kristiania, 1895)
A. Bugge: 'Drageportalen i Hopperstad kirke' [The dragon portal in Hopperstad Church], *Fortun fra til Sognefest* (Bergen, 1941), pp. 28–43
K. Bjerknes: 'Urnes stavkirke', *Fortidsforen. Åb.* (1958), pp. 75–96
H. Christie: 'Urnes stavkirkes forløper' [Precursors of the Urnes stave church], *Fortidsforen. Åb.* (1958), pp. 49–74
R. Hauglid: 'Urnes stavkirke i Sogn', *Fortidsforen. Åb.* (1969), pp. 34–69
P. Anker and A. Andersen: *The Art of Scandinavia*, i (London, 1970)
R. Hauglid: *Norske stavkirker: Dekor og utstyr* [Norwegian stave churches: decoration and ornament] (Oslo, 1973)
E. B. Hohler: 'The Capitals of Urnes Church and their Background', *Acta Archaeol.* [Copenhagen], xlvi (1975), pp. 1–60
P. Anker: 'Om dateringsproblemet i stavkirkeforskningen' [Researches on dating problems in stave churches], *Hist. Tidsskr.*, lvi (1977), pp. 103–42
H. Magerøy: 'Urnes stavkyrkje, Ornes-ætta og Ornesgodset' [Urnes stave church, the Ornes family and the Ornes property], *Hist. Tidsskr.*, lxvii (1988), pp. 121–44

ERLA BERGENDAHL HOHLER

Urrabieta y Ortiz, Vicente (*b* 1813; *d* Paris, Dec 1879). Spanish draughtsman, engraver and lithographer. A pupil of Inocencio Borghini (1799–1867), he was later associated with the lithographic establishments of Juan José Martinez and Santos González in Madrid. As well as producing wood-engravings, he worked for many Spanish illustrated magazines such as *Semanario pintoresco español* and *El artista*. He illustrated books such as *Historia de Cataluña* by Balaguer; the series *Recuerdos y bellezas de España* (Barcelona, 1839–72) in collaboration with FRANCISCO XAVIER PARCERISA I BOADA and others; *Historia de la marina real española* (Madrid, 1854) by José March y Labores; a collection of lithographs in colour, *Episodios de la guerra de Africa* (Madrid, 1859–60); royal chronicles and novels, as well as making numerous contemporary portraits. His son was the illustrator Daniel Urrabieta y Vierge (1851–1904), who worked in France. In 1882 his *Pablo de Segovia* (Paris) was published, a landmark in pen-drawn book illustration.

BIBLIOGRAPHY

M. Ossorio y Bernard: *Galería biográfica de artistas españoles del siglo XIX* (Madrid, 1868, 2/1883–4/*R* Barcelona, 1975)
A. Gallego: *Historia del grabado en España* (Madrid, 1979), p. 356
E. Paez Rios: *Répertorio* (1981–3)

BLANCA GARCÍA VEGA

Urrea, Francisco Ximénez de. *See* XIMÉNEZ DE URREA, FRANCISCO.

Ursins, Jouvenel des. *See* JOUVENEL DES URSINS.

Urswick, Christopher (*b* Furness, 1448; *d* Hackney, 24 March 1522). English cleric, lawyer, diplomat, patron and collector. Educated probably at Cambridge and subsequently recorded at Oxford, he became chaplain to Margaret Beaufort *c.* 1482, and later her executor, and *c.* 1484 was chaplain to her son, the future Henry VII. Urswick became Dean of Windsor on 20 November 1495, and under his direction parts of the deanery and of St George's Chapel were rebuilt (*see* WINDSOR CASTLE, §2). His arms appear in a boss in St George's; he is depicted in a stained-glass window at the entrance to the Albert Memorial Chapel (1350–54) at Windsor Castle, and there are inscriptions requesting prayers for his soul on a stone screen formerly in the Urswick Chapel (ded. 1507) of St George's. On 5 November 1502 he was inducted to the living of Hackney, where he lived for much of the rest of his life, and embarked on rebuilding St Augustine's (destr. 1798). He was a close friend of Sir Thomas More and John Colet; the latter sent him books from Rome in 1493. He was a benefactor of Desiderius Erasmus, who visited Urswick in 1503 and who dedicated to him his translation (*c.* 1503) of Lucian's *Somnium sive gallus*. Urswick also owned several manuscripts copied by the humanist scribe Peter Meghen (*fl* 1506–9), including a Vulgate New Testament with

Erasmus's translation, written for Henry VIII and Catherine of Aragon.

BIBLIOGRAPHY

A. B. Emden: *A Biographical Register of the University of Oxford to AD 1500* (Oxford, 1957), pp. 1935–6

JEREMY GRIFFITHS

Ursy, Giovanni Domenico. *See* ORSI, GIOVANNI DOMENICO.

Urteaga Alvarado, Mario (Tulio Escipión) (*b* Cajamarca, 1 April 1875; *d* Cajamarca, 12 June 1957). Peruvian painter. Having worked as a journalist, administrator, teacher and farmer, he took up oil painting around the age of 30. Urteaga seems to have been self-taught, using such poor quality materials as old sugar sacks and cheap pigments, as well as making his own brushes. His scenes of the lives of northern Andean Indians are colourful. Their naïve though detailed execution has been described as primitive and unacademic, and has been likened to that of Henri Rousseau. His spontaneity and topicality are reminiscent of the caricatures of Pancho Fierro (?1809–79), yet his representation of the indigenous peoples of Peru and their daily life is serious; he was the first painter to portray Indian people without patronizing them, as can be seen in the *Adobe Makers* (1937; priv. col.) and *Return of the Peasants* (Lima, Mus. A.). A retrospective exhibition of his work was held at the Banco de la Nación, Lima, in 1989.

BIBLIOGRAPHY

J. A. de Lavalle and W. Lang: *Pintura contemporánea: Primera parte, 1820–1920*, Arte y tesoros del Perú (Lima, 1975), pp. 184–95

Mario Urteaga, 1875–1957: Un hombre, un pincel, un mundo (exh. cat., Lima, Banco de la Nación, 1989)

W. IAIN MACKAY

Uruguay, Eastern Republic of [Republica Oriental del Uruguay]. South American country. It is on the east coast of the continent, bounded to the south and east by the estuary of the River Plate and the south Atlantic, to the west by the River Uruguay and Argentina and to the north by Brazil. With an area of *c.* 187,000 sq. km, Uruguay is one of the smallest countries in South America, and 87% of its population is urban, over one third living in the capital city, MONTEVIDEO, a port situated on the River Plate (see fig. 1). Through this river and its tributaries, the Uruguay and Paraná rivers, Uruguay is at the entrance to a vast navigable river system, and Montevideo is one of the ports of entry to Argentina, Paraguay, Bolivia and the Brazilian state of Rio Grande do Sul. Physically, the country consists of undulating grass plains on granite, with chains of low hills. The climate is temperate and humid; agriculture and dairy production dominate in the south but stock-rearing occupies much of the land in the north and centre. Uruguay was colonized by Spain after 1624 and became independent in 1828. About 85% of its population are of European descent.

For the earlier history of the region *see* SOUTH AMERICA, PRE-COLUMBIAN, §§I and VII, 2–4.

1. Map of Uruguay; those sites with separate entries in this dictionary are distinguished by CROSS-REFERENCE TYPE

I. Introduction. II. Indigenous culture. III. Architecture. IV. Painting, graphic arts and sculpture. V. Gold and silver. VI. Textiles. VII. Collections and museums. VIII. Art education. IX. Art libraries and photographic collections.

I. Introduction.

Uruguay was the last area in South America to be colonized by Spain. Juan Díaz de Solís first landed in 1516 during his exploration of the River Plate estuary, and contacts were subsequently made by gauchos who came from Argentina to take charge of increasing herds of cattle introduced by the Spanish. Only in 1624, however, did Spain send missionaries to the territory to begin the conversion of the indigenous population, which was drastically reduced in the colonial period and finally disappeared shortly after independence (*see* §II below). During the 17th century the territory was disputed between the Portuguese in Brazil and the Spanish in Argentina, and this led to the founding of the first settlements of any size—initially by the Portuguese in 1680 at COLONIA DEL SACRAMENTO across the river from Buenos Aires, and then by Spain, which established a more significant settlement in 1726 at San Felipe y Santiago de Montevideo (now Montevideo). However, the territory, known as the Banda Oriental, was not rich or of great appeal to colonizers and hence in general there was limited development and artistic production during the colonial period. In 1811 José Gervasio Artigas led an independence revolution against Spain, and the territory became part of a federation with the newly independent Argentina until 1821, when it was annexed by Portugal. Only after British intervention in the ensuing conflict over possession of the territory did Uruguay finally achieve its independence in 1828.

In 1830, the date of the first constitution, Uruguay had 74,000 inhabitants, a society with few class distinctions, a rural economy, a land ownership that was not clearly defined and political rivalry between two main factions, the liberal Colorados and the conservative Blancos. These conditions led to many years of political instability and civil strife, with Montevideo under siege from 1843 to 1851, followed by war with Paraguay (1865–70). However, in the last quarter of the 19th century and the first three decades of the 20th the population increased rapidly, helped by a substantial influx of immigrants, particularly from Spain, Italy and France; Europeans accounted for half the population of Montevideo between 1840 and 1890, resulting in the predominance of European influences in the arts, which began to flourish amid improved economic prosperity and urban expansion. This continued during the presidency (1903–29) of José Batlle y Ordóñez, which marked a period of advanced social reform, the development of the consumer goods industry and trade with Europe, stimulating further cultural developments in the country. However, lasting economic depression that began with the financial crisis of 1929 led to renewed political unrest and the breakdown of democratic government, first in 1933 and again in 1973 when a harshly repressive military dictatorship took power and large numbers of Uruguayans left the country. Democracy was restored in 1985.

BIBLIOGRAPHY

W. E. Laroche: *Elementos contributos a la historia del arte en el Uruguay* (Montevideo, 1952)
E. Laroche: *Derrotero para una historia del arte en el Uruguay* (Montevideo, 1961)
W. Reyes Abadie and A. Vázquez Romero: *Crónica general del Uruguay*, 4 vols (Montevideo, 1980–86)
L. Castedo: *Historia del arte iberoamericano*, 2 vols (Madrid, 1988), i, p. 358

JOSÉ PEDRO BARRÁN

II. *Indigenous culture.*

At the time of European arrival (1516), three distinct groups of indigenous peoples were living in the territory that became Uruguay. The Guaraní peoples lived on the lower parts of the River Uruguay and on the north shore of the River Plate as far east as the River Santa Lucía, having recently arrived by way of the Paraná River. A characteristic feature of their culture was the practice of secondary burials in large, thick clay pots. However, after colonization they seem to have rapidly disappeared from the region as chronicles of the 17th century no longer include references to them. The Chanáe peoples lived on the banks and islands of the middle section of the River Uruguay, with a transitional culture partly based on hunting and fishing and partly on an incipient agriculture, possibly borrowed from the Guaraní. They developed a ceremonial form of pottery portraying birds. After colonization they were brought into the first *reducciones* (missionary settlements), but they quickly became integrated with Europeans and their culture disappeared around the middle of the 18th century.

The Charrúa peoples were the largest group, whose original culture shared elements in common with those of

the Chaco, Pampean and Patagonian areas (*see* SOUTH AMERICA, PRE-COLUMBIAN, §VII, 2–4). They were hunter-gatherers who used the bow and arrow and the *boleadora* (hunting sling) and demonstrated great skill in making the tips of arrows and spears; they also mastered the technique of stone polishing, which they applied to making multi-edged maces. Pre-Columbian stone tablets engraved with geometric designs based on the circled cross are attributed to the Charrúa; this device also appears in pictographs made on rocks, especially in the Chamangá and the Pintos River area (Flores), the Mahoma Hills (San José) and the Maestre de Campo (Durazno). They made a rough type of incised or burnished clay utilitarian pottery and practised initiation or funeral ceremonies of a shamanistic type. The culture of the Charrúas underwent rapid, profound transformations through contact with Europeans, from whom they adopted the use of iron tools and weapons, cloth, alcohol, tobacco and *mate* (a tea-like plant), all of which they obtained by bartering cowhides. The introduction of the horse increased their mobility and bellicosity, the depredatory features of their economy and probably their numbers. The Spanish waged continual war on them, and although they joined the forces of José Gervasio Artigas during the struggle for independence, they were nearly all massacred in the battle of Salsipuedes (1832) by the forces of the new republic.

For the earlier history of indigenous cultures in the region *see also* SOUTH AMERICA, PRE-COLUMBIAN, §I, 1 and 2.

BIBLIOGRAPHY

A. Serrano: 'The Charrúa', *Handbook of South American Indians*, ed. J. H. Steward, i (Washington, DC, 1946), pp. 191–6
R. Pi Hugarte: *El Uruguay indígena* (Montevideo, 1969)
E. Acosta y Lara: *La guerra de los Charrúas en la Banda Oriental*, 2 vols (Montevideo, 1989)
L. R. González Rissotto and S. Rodríguez Varese: *Guaraníes y paisanos: Impacto de los indios misioneros en la formación del paisanaje* (Montevideo, 1990)

RENZO PI HUGARTE

III. *Architecture.*

The first significant European building activity in the Banda Oriental resulted from the dispute between Spain and Portugal over possession of the territory (*see* §I above), which led to the founding of settlements there by both powers. Following the Spanish incursion into Santo Domingo de Soriano (1624), the first urban settlement of any size was established by the Portuguese in 1680 at Colonia del Sacramento. A fortified base facing Buenos Aires across the River Plate, it was typical of other enclaves set up by the Portuguese along the coast of Brazil, with stone and brick fortifications designed by military engineers and simple dwellings of adobe and thatch. Montevideo (formerly San Felipe y Santiago de Montevideo), situated on a promontory 250 km to the east of Colonia, was a Spanish settlement established in 1726, in response to the Portuguese initiative, by the Governor of Buenos Aires, Don Bruno Mauricio de Zabala, and its early development was also dominated by the construction of fortifications. Other strongpoints, fortresses and guard-houses were developed along the shores of the River Plate and the north-eastern coastal border with Brazil (e.g. the Fortaleza S Teresa), and the military engineers responsible for this work also designed and constructed civil and religious buildings in the urban settlements. In Montevideo, for example, the church of the Immaculate Conception (now the cathedral) was begun *c.* 1784 by a Portuguese military engineer in the service of Spain, José Custodio de Saa y Faría. A large building with a triple nave, it is planned on the Latin cross with a dome at the crossing. Another engineer, José del Pozo y Marquy, was responsible for the parish church (1792) of San Carlos, near Maldonado—a fortified settlement established by the Spanish in 1757 at the entrance to the estuary of the River Plate—and de Saa also built the simple, Neo-classical church of S Fernando (1796) at Maldonado.

European academic Neo-classicism was introduced by the Spanish architect TOMÁS TORIBIO, who studied in Madrid and arrived in the colony around 1799. He designed the façade of the cathedral in Montevideo, said to be influenced by the Neo-classical façade of Pamplona Cathedral; the towers were completed much later (1858) when the façade was renovated by the Swiss architect Bernardo Poncini (1820–63). Toribio also designed the church at Colonia del Sacramento (1808; reconstructed 1836–41) and the Cabildo (1804–11), Montevideo, a Neo-classical town hall and former prison building that faces the cathedral across the city's oldest square, the Plaza Constitución.

In the years following independence in 1828, official Uruguayan architecture continued to be strongly influenced by Neo-classicism and imperial French architecture in works that sought to symbolize the power of the new state. Despite political instability and civil war (*see* §I above), a series of urban developments was begun in Montevideo, the capital of the republic after 1828; the Plaza Independencia (see fig. 2) was laid out in 1837 by the Italian architect Carlos Zucchi (*d* 1856), who had studied in Paris; he also designed the French Beaux-Arts-style Teatro Solís (1841) in the Plaza Independencia (completed 1856 by Francisco Garmendia). More settled conditions in the last quarter of the 19th century led to more widespread urban expansion, with the adoption of contemporary European artistic trends encouraged by an influx of European immigrants as well as by the need for Uruguayan architects to study abroad. The Italian engineer Luis Andreoni (1853–1936), for example, designed some of Montevideo's best-known public buildings in eclectic styles: the Uruguay Club (1885) in the Plaza Constitución, the Umberto I Hospital (1890) and the central railway station (1897); other eclectic buildings were designed by the Uruguayan engineer Juan Alberto Capurro, who was trained in Italy. The construction of rail links stimulated economic growth and led to a speculative building boom that resulted in some surprisingly high-quality housing complexes, for example the Reus districts in the north and south of the city, developed by the Catalan financier Emilio Reus, and the well-planned communities of one- and two-storey standardized terraced houses built around patios (1890s), whose carefully scaled façades created open-spaced 'corridor' streets that are characteristic of large sectors of Montevideo.

In the early 20th century Art Nouveau took root in Montevideo, as in Buenos Aires, for example in school buildings by the Office of Public Works and in a number of private residences designed by the first graduates from

2. Old Government House, Plaza Independencia, Montevideo, by Carlos Zucchi, 1837

the new school of architecture (*see* §VIII below), including the house built for himself (1921) in Montevideo by Juan Antonio Rius (1893–1974). The celebrations of 1930 were marked by a series of competitions, and these resulted in several buildings reflecting the language of European Rationalism, although tinctured with Art Deco for a period. Among these are the Estadio Centenario (1930), with a soaring Art Deco tower, by Juan Antonio Scasso (1892–1975); the Centro Médico (1932) by Carlos Surraco; and the Palacio Municipal by Mauricio Cravotto (1893–1962), all in Montevideo. Notable public buildings by Rius include the Facultad de Ontología (1932–9) for the Universidad de Montevideo, a three-storey 'white' building in the purist spirit of the Modern Movement. A similar character is found in the Clínica Médica (1930), Montevideo, by Ernesto Leborgne (1906–86). These architects were among the pioneers of Modernism in Uruguay.

One of the most widely acclaimed and influential architects of the 1930s and 1940s—although he was not one of the pioneers—was JULIO VILAMAJÓ. His work ranged from the amalgamation of simplified classical features with a Modernist handling of surfaces and materials (e.g. his own house of 1930) to the highly articulate, reinforced-concrete Facultad de Ingeniería (1937–8), Universidad de Montevideo, reminiscent of work by the Perret brothers. In contrast, the buildings of his Villa Serrana (1943–8), a resort centre in the country north of Montevideo, were designed in local stone, timber and thatch in harmony with the environment. Another notable figure was ANTONIO BONET, a Spanish architect who had worked with Le Corbusier; well-known works include Punta Ballena, near Punta del Este, the Casa Berlingieri (1946), which is reminiscent of Le Corbusier's work of the 1930s, and the restaurant-hotel La Solana del Mar (1947), which suggested a new aesthetic, its long single-storey glass façade open to the beach. Vilamajó's pragmatic, almost astylar approach was adopted by his pupil,

MARIO PAYSSÉ-REYES, although in a manner much influenced by the Constructivist painter Joaquín Torres García; this is evident in the structure, proportion and use of such materials as rough, local brickwork in his buildings, for example his own house at Carrasco (1955), Montevideo. ELADIO DIESTE, an engineer who was also a member of Torres García's circle, developed a unique brick and tile technology that resulted in such structural masterpieces as the parish church at Atlántida (1959); its wave-walls and tile-vaulting were repeated in later works (e.g. a shopping centre (1983–4) in Montevideo).

In the 1960s a series of multi-storey curtain-wall buildings was produced (e.g. the Notariado Building (1962–7), Montevideo, by Estudio Cinco), but there was also a renewed interest in Le Corbusier's work after World War II. This appears in later buildings by Payssé-Reyes, for example the Banco de la República (1962), Punta del Este, although it is perhaps most obvious in the work of Nelson Bayardo, whose board-marked concrete Columbarium (1962) at the Cementerio del Norte, Montevideo, provides one of the best-known images of Uruguayan architecture. The increasing pluralism of the decade is particularly evident in buildings at Punta Ballena, for example in the Casa Olle Perez (1966) by Juan Borthagaray (b 1917), who had worked for Mies van der Rohe, and in the *casa-pueblo* settlement of artists' houses designed by the Uruguayan sculptor Carlos Paez Villaro, which continued to grow for 30 years after the early 1960s; its forms climbing the rising ground from the sea are suggestive of Gaudí and reveal a growing sense of formal freedom.

A feature of the 1970s was the construction of many new urban residential developments by cooperatives, encouraged by a new housing law (1968). A notable example is the medium-rise housing complex in Montevideo built of brick in north European realist character (1971–5) for the Savings and Loans Cooperative (COVFI) by the Centro Cooperativista Uruguayo. System building techniques were also developed, as seen in the Hospital Policial (1975–83), Montevideo, by the Benech, Marzano, Sprechman and Villaamil partnership. The last decades of the 20th century were characterized by a growing awareness of the need for conservation of Uruguay's architectural heritage; an example of this work is the rehabilitation (1980s) of the Reus terraces, Montevideo, by the Grupo de Estudios Urbano.

BIBLIOGRAPHY

L. E. Azarola Gil: *Los origenes de Montevideo, 1600–1900* (Buenos Aires, 1933)
F. Ferreiro: *Origenes uruguayos* (Montevideo, 1937)
C. Perez Montero: *El cabildo de Montevideo, el arquitecto, el terreno, el edificio* (Montevideo, 1950)
J. Giuria: *La arquitectura en el Uruguay, 1830–1900* (Montevideo, 1958)
F. Bullrich: *New Directions in Latin American Architecture* (London, 1969), pp. 14–21, 54–8, 90–92
D. Bayón and P. Gasparini: *Panorámica de la arquitectura latino-americana* (Barcelona, 1977; Eng. trans., New York, 1979), pp. 191–214
A. Migdal: 'Dossier Uruguay', *Spazio & Soc.*, 35 (1986), pp. 88–125
R. L. Mourelle: 'Viviendas de arquitectos', *Arquitectura* [Montevideo], 256 (1986), pp. 10–21
J. F. Liernur, ed.: *America latino: Architettura gli ultimi vent'anni* (Milan, 1990), pp. 162–79
A. Toca, ed.: *Nueva arquitectura en América Latina: Presente y futuro* (Mexico City, 1990), pp. 29–41
Arquitectura en Uruguay, 1980–90 (Montevideo, 1992)

MARIANO ARANA, RUBEN GARCÍA MIRANDA

IV. Painting, graphic arts and sculpture.

European artistic production in the territory that became Uruguay, unlike other countries in Latin America, was very limited during the colonial period (*see* §I above), although minor religious statuary flourished in the churches. The first significant artistic views of life in Uruguay were provided by the travelling chroniclers of the 19th century—scientists and explorers as well as artists—who recorded their findings in drawings and lithographs. Among the most important were the Englishmen Conrad Martens (who accompanied Charles Darwin) and EMERIC ESSEX VIDAL; the German Johann Moritz Rugendas (*see* RUGENDAS, (2)); and the Frenchman Alphonse D'Hastrel (1805–70), who was the most significant name for Uruguay. Other European artists who worked or settled in Uruguay included the Spanish calligrapher Juan Manuel Besnes e Irigoyen (1788–1865) and the Italian Cayetano Gallino (1801–84), who produced elegantly drawn portraits. These artists introduced contemporary European styles and movements to Uruguay: the sculpture of José Livi (1820–90), for example, represented European Neo-classicism (e.g. the statue of *Liberty*, 1866; Montevideo, Plaza Cagancha). European influences continued to dominate Uruguayan art: in addition to large numbers of European immigrants, nearly all Uruguayan artists studied and travelled abroad until the establishment of art schools in the 20th century (*see* §VIII below).

Uruguayan historical and social iconography began with the work of JUAN MANUEL BLANES, the country's first important native-born artist, who painted historical subjects (e.g. the *Thirty-three Uruguayan Patriots*, 1878; Montevideo, Mus. N. A. Plást. Visuales), genre scenes, particularly of rural life, and portraits (e.g. *Carlota Ferreira*, Montevideo, Mus. N. A. Plást. Visuales; and an official portrait of *General José G. Artigas*, Montevideo, Casa Gobierno). His imagery found an echo in the work of his elder son, Juan Luis Blanes (1856–95), and other Uruguayan artists, including Horacio Espondaburu (1855–1902), who painted gaucho themes; Diógenes Hequet (1866–1902), who concentrated on military subjects; and Manuel Larravide (1871–1910), a painter of seascapes. Historical subjects were also used in the monumental work of the first important Uruguayan-born sculptor, JUAN MANUEL FERRARI, who was influenced by Auguste Rodin (e.g. the monument to *General San Martin's Liberation Army*, 1914; Mendoza, Argentina, Cerro de la Gloria).

The first signs of modernism in Uruguayan painting appeared in the 1890s in the work of such artists as CARLOS FEDERICO SÁEZ and Carlos María Herrera (1875–1914). Sáez was influenced by the Macchiaioli (Italian luminists) and used techniques later associated with Abstract Expressionism (e.g. *Ciocciaro Head*, 1897; Montevideo, Mus. N. A. Plást. Visuales). Herrera, who specialized in pastel, played an important role as an educator and founder of the Círculo de Bellas Artes in 1905 (*see* §VIII below). Impressionism was introduced into Uruguay by PEDRO BLANES VIALE and Milo Beretta (1870–1935). They developed the art of landscape painting, using a luminous palette that owed more to Spanish painters than the Ecole de Paris (e.g. *Palma de Mallorca* by Blanes Viale, 1915;

Montevideo, Mus. N. A. Plást. Visuales). Immediate followers of this approach included Manuel Rosé (1882–1961) and Carlos Alberto Castellanos (1881–1945), the first maker of tapestry cartoons. The development of Uruguayan imagery is revealed in the work of PEDRO FIGARI, who was influenced by Post-Impressionism and whose paintings portray the lives of blacks and gauchos (see fig. 3). JOSÉ CÚNEO and others followed his example in appropriating and transforming foreign artistic languages by filling them with local content.

Uruguayan printmaking during the early 20th century was marked by the appearance of xylography and the work of Federico Lanau (1891–1929), who did wood-engravings linked to the French school of the 1920s, and Leandro Castellanos Balparda (1894–1967), who worked against the grain and incorporated Latin American motifs, particularly in his later work. CARLOS GONZÁLEZ may perhaps be considered the founder of Uruguayan printmaking in that he reflected the essence of Latin America in a primitive and direct language that showed an affection for rural people. Meanwhile, the sculptor Antonio Pena (1894–1947), a student of Emile-Antoine Bourdelle at the Académie de la Grande Chaumière, Paris, was producing the last works of Uruguayan historical classicism. Other important sculptors of this generation included the naturalist José Belloni (1882–1965); José Luis Zorrilla de San Martin (1894–1978), whose figures revealed an expressive, Baroque strength; Severino Pose (1894–1964), who was a follower of Anton Hanak in Vienna; and Bernabé Michelena (1888–1963), who produced monumental works—the best known is at Montevideo's Carrasco Airport.

The next generation of painters was more interested in geometrization, in some cases leading to Constructivism. Cubism and Futurism were incorporated obliquely into Uruguayan art through RAFAEL BARRADAS, who lived in Spain for most of his career and produced paintings he called *vibracionismo* because of their shimmering appearance (e.g. *Apartment House*, 1919; Montevideo, Mus. N. A. Plást. Visuales). In contrast, Miguel Angel Pareja (1908–84) freed colour from Impressionist naturalism, introducing an abstract conception. By far the most celebrated and influential Uruguayan artist of the late 1930s and 1940s, however, was Joaquín Torres García, who returned to Montevideo from Europe in 1934 at the age of 60. He found a flourishing Uruguay, and there he introduced a radical change to artistic development with a universal type of abstract art. Through his teaching, writing and his studio, the TALLER TORRES GARCÍA, he introduced Cubism, Neo-plasticism and Constructivism as well as his own concept of 'Constructive Universalism', which was highly influential in the creation of a national art (for illustration *see* TORRES GARCÍA, JOAQUÍN). His late works include the *Cosmic Monument* (1938; Montevideo, Mus. N. A. Plást. Visuales). His students and followers included his sons, Augusto Torres (1913–92) and Horacio Torres (1924–76), and GONZALO FONSECA, who is also a sculptor. Others took his Constructivism a stage further, consolidating non-figurative art. Antonio Llorens (*b* 1920) and Rhod Rothfuss (1936–69) were members of the Argentine Arte Madí group, and Rothfuss was also a pioneer of the shaped canvas, theorizing on it as early as 1944. In 1955 José P. Costigliolo (1902–85) and the sculptor María Freire

3. Pedro Figari: *Creole Dance*, oil on cardboard, 521×813 mm, *c.* 1925 (New York, Museum of Modern Art)

(*b* 1917) organized Uruguay's first non-figurative art exhibition.

Uruguayan sculpture also underwent a radical change in the mid-20th century, and this can be seen in the work of Eduardo Díaz Yepes (1909–79), a naturalized Spaniard, who began with abstraction (e.g. *Womb*, onyx, 1958; São Paulo, Parque de Ibirapuera) and ended with a symbolic interpretation of reality (e.g. monument to *Those Who Died at Sea*, 1958; Montevideo, Plaza Virgilio), which he integrated splendidly into the setting. GERMÁN CABRERA produced abstract works in marble, bronze, porous concrete, scrap iron, ceramics, baked clay and wood. Other abstract sculptors included Salustiano Pintos (1905–75), who used wood and sandstone in serialized totem-pole forms; Octavio Podestá (*b* 1929), who resolved iron figures with a mechanistic approach; Wifredo Díaz Valdéz (*b* 1932), who made cuts in commercial wooden products, destroying their cultural use and identity and thus revealing their organic core; and Hugo Nantes (*b* 1933), who followed Yepes's expressionist vein, creating monsters with mimetic forms made of discarded materials.

Other approaches in painting included ALFREDO DE SIMONE's 'arte matérico', in which he used rhythmic brushstrokes and heavy impasto to communicate the vibrancy of the city's streets and tenements (e.g. *Suburb*, 1941; Montevideo, Mus. N. A. Plást. Visuales). WASHINGTON BARCALA and NELSON RAMOS worked with everyday objects and materials, producing what Kalenberg termed an 'Organic Constructivism'. LUIS SOLARI dressed his figures in animal masks, visualizing an indigenous mythology; he also created zoomorphic characters in his drypoint etchings. The work of MANUEL ESPÍNOLA GÓMEZ developed in the same surrealist, dreamlike environment, culminating in *Mid-afternoon Crepe Hangers* (Montevideo, priv. col., for illustration see Kalenberg, p. 177), a funeral symbolizing the end of an era. The Uruguay of the 1960s was not the one encountered by Torres García, and political and economic problems were thereafter reflected in art. Around 1980 JOSÉ GAMARRA began to produce large-format paintings filled with irony and a naive air, addressing the problem of colonialism. The printmaker ANTONIO FRASCONI directly addressed political themes. Carlos Tonelli (*b* 1937) took refuge in a world of symbols consecrated by esoteric tradition, and Clever Lara (*b* 1952) concentrated on a naturalist approach, also inspired by the Taller Torres García. The etchings of Luis Camnitzer (*b* 1937) added a conceptual dimension, provoking an ethical–political reflection linked to the preservation of human rights.

BIBLIOGRAPHY

J. M. Fernández Saldaña: *Pintores y escultores uruguayos* (Montevideo, 1916)
C. S. Vitureira: *Arte simple* (Montevideo, 1937)
J. Romero Brest: *Pintores y grabadores rioplatenses* (Buenos Aires, 1951)
J. P. Argul: *Pintura y escultura del Uruguay: Historia crítica* (Montevideo, 1958)
E. Dieste: *Teseo: Los problemas del arte* (Montevideo, 1964)
F. García Esteban: *Panorama de la pintura uruguaya contemporánea* (Montevideo, 1965)
J. P. Argul: *Las artes plásticas del Uruguay: Desde la época indígena al momento contemporáneo* (Montevideo, 1966); rev. as *Proceso de las artes plásticas del Uruguay* (Montevideo, 1975)
F. García Esteban: *Artes plásticas en el Uruguay en el siglo XX* (Montevideo, 1970)
Arte contemporáneo en el Uruguay (exh. cat., ed. A. Kalenberg; Montevideo, Mus. N. A. Plást., 1982)
Seis maestros del arte uruguayo (exh. cat., ed. A. Kalenberg; Buenos Aires, Mus. N. B.A.; Montevideo, Mus. N. A. Plást.; 1985–7)
Arte dell'Uruguay nel novecento (exh. cat., Rome, Ist. It.–Lat. Amer., 1988–9)
G. Peluffo: *Historia de la pintura uruguaya* (Montevideo, 1989)
A. Kalenberg: *Arte uruguayo y otros* (Montevideo, 1990)

ANGEL KALENBERG

V. Gold and silver.

No goldwork or silverwork made before the 19th century in the region that is now Uruguay appears to have survived. Before this date, silversmiths no doubt concentrated on producing plain, domestic articles; the more ambitious ecclesiastical commissions were ordered from Peru or Buenos Aires (across the River Plate), such as the elaborate lectern (*c*. 1770; Buenos Aires, priv. col.) made for Montevideo Cathedral. During the 19th century, however, the increase in wealth on account of the cattle industry, combined with growing nationalism, led to a tremendous increase in demand for domestic silver articles, specifically those associated with the infusing and serving of the drink *mate*, and with horse trappings and personal adornments for the gaucho. Silver and even gold *mate*s in the form of gourds or sometimes following the shape of chalices were often chased with foliate scrolls and sometimes have stems in the form of birds; they are often accompanied by a *bombilla* or perforated tube. Such European emigré silversmiths as Marcelino Barnech (*fl* 1840–*c*. 1870), Jose Mantegani, Carlos Bellini and Torricella made magnificent silver and even gold horse trappings. Bridles, reins, breastplates and some saddle girths were mounted in silver and were sometimes made of silver mesh. Personal items for the caudillo and gaucho included spurs, whips and daggers, usually decorated with European-inspired cast or chased foliate scrolls and often incorporating such nationalistic symbols as the 'Cap of Liberty'.

BIBLIOGRAPHY
F. O. Assunção: *Uruguayan Folk Art* (Montevideo, 1985)

CHRISTOPHER HARTOP

VI. Textiles.

There is little information available concerning early production of textiles in Uruguay. There was no indigenous tradition, and the colonial inheritance was limited, although from the 18th century there was some production of textiles on domestic looms (also called 'creole looms' or 'pre-looms') in rural areas. Still in use, these vary in size and are made from a rough, simple frame of wood. Coarse woollen cloth, pallets and blankets, in whites, ochres and greys and in simple patterns or in stripes were also produced. From the 19th century, particularly in schools run by Spanish nuns, embroidery work was executed for more refined domestic flags and presidential sashes, as well as crocheting, lace cuff edging, macramé and painstakingly executed Hispanic petit point; this tradition, however, is gradually disappearing.

From 1915 textiles were produced in the workshops of the Escuela Nacional de Artes y Oficios, from 1944 in the Universidad del Trabajo del Uruguay (formerly the Escuela Nacional de Artes y Oficios) and from 1960 in the Escuela Nacional de Bellas Artes, all in Montevideo. Although many items continued to be imported, the manufacture of

4. Ernesto Aroztegui: *Double Portrait of Sigmund Freud with Cancer of the Lower Left Jaw*, high-warp tapestry, plastic and synthetic with cotton warp and crayon on paper, 0.24×0.18 m (Montevideo, Dr Ricardo Bernadi private collection)

textiles became an important industry in the second half of the 20th century. The most significant output was in wool products, promoted, in the late 20th century, by the Secretariado Uruguayo de la Lana (est. 1968), which has organized the Bienales de Tapiz de Lana since 1978.

An important centre of production is Manos del Uruguay (est. 1968), formed of 18 cooperatives producing carpets, curtains, blankets, cushions and tapestry cloth made of wool and natural native fibres (ramie and thistle) based on models from its own department of design. Stylistically, production has evolved from the use of two or three natural colours to more than 90 different shades and from sheepskin wool to refined wool. Batik and tapestry are also produced. Craftsmen of European ancestry, skilled in traditional techniques, execute crochet and macramé work. Products are exported to the USA and Europe. Throughout Uruguay—particularly in Montevideo— there is a limited industrial production of patterned wool and acrylic fibre carpets, for which many of the designs are imported. The quality of wool carpets is supervised by the Secretariado Uruguayo de la Lana. As well as cooperatives and industrial production, there is also a small number of independent craftsmen producing wool and batiks.

The production of tapestry has been of great importance from 1960, thanks to the influence of Ernesto Aroztegui (1930–94), both as craftsman and teacher. He encouraged research and, as the result of his involvement in the Taller Montevideano de Tapices (1967), a large, progressive movement in tapestry work developed that emphasized the importance of each stage in the process of tapestry-making. Aroztegui excelled in the high-warp Gobelin technique (*see* TAPESTRY, §I, 2 and fig. 2) and worked in a style that was both symbolic and hyperrealist, often making use of anamorphic images (see fig. 4). He ended his teaching career managing a workshop at the Escuela Nacional de Belles Artes. From 1960 to 1980 most tapestry was of fine-grain high-warp thread. Thereafter all kinds of materials and fibres were incorporated, and experimental, three-dimensional work in the style of nouvelle tapisserie began to be produced. The Centro de Tapicería Uruguaya, an association of craftsmen established in 1982, which has a membership of 140 tapestry-makers, promotes the production of tapestry in Uruguay.

BIBLIOGRAPHY
A. Martínez Montero and E. Villegas Suárez: *Historia de la Universidad del Trabajo del Uruguay* (Montevideo, 1968)
F. García Esteban: *El arte nuevo* (Montevideo, 1969)
O. Larnaudie: *Artesanía uruguaya* (Montevideo, 1988)
S. Rostagnol: *Las artesanas hablan* (Montevideo, 1988)

ALICIA HABER

VII. Collections and museums.

Uruguay's public collections are primarily devoted to Uruguayan art, with a sprinkling of Latin American and 19th-century European painting. Its private collections, on the other hand, include more examples of European art after the Renaissance. The number of museums in Uruguay grew steadily after the stimulus to the arts provided by the creation of the first formal art schools in the early 20th century (*see* §VIII below). The first museum to be established was the Museo Nacional (1837). Its subsequent reorganization in 1911 resulted in the creation of the Museo Nacional de Bellas Artes, the Museo Nacional de Historia Natural and the Archivo y Museo Histórico Nacional. The first of these became the Museo Nacional de Artes Plásticas, the most important museum of art in Uruguay, which is located in the Parque José E. Rodó in Montevideo. Its complex history was marked by temporary closures, but in 1961 it was permanently reopened, and in 1969 it embarked upon a dynamic policy for the popularization of art, underscored by temporary exhibitions that attracted huge numbers of visitors. The museum underwent a substantial rebuilding programme in 1970, directed by the Argentine architect Clorindo Testa; it was subsequently expanded, tripling the total area of the museum, and in 1986 new, technically advanced galleries and a conference hall were added.

The holdings of the Museo Nacional de Artes Plásticas include the most complete and systematic collection of Uruguayan art in existence, with the most important collection of the works of Rafael Barradas and major collections by Juan Manuel Blanes, Carlos Federico Sáez, Pedro Figari, Joaquín Torres García and José Cúneo. Its European collection comprises mostly 19th-century painting, including works by Giovanni Fattori, Mariano Fortuny y Carbó, Joaquín Sorolla y Bastida, Ignacio Zuloaga and Hermenegildo Anglada-Camarasa. Its Latin-American collection includes paintings by David Alfaro Siqueiros,

Emilio Pettoruti and Jorge de la Vega, and the Cuban painter René Portocarrero (1912–86).

The second most important museum in the country is the Museo Municipal Juan Manuel Blanes, founded in 1928 after the Montevideo City Council approved a proposal by the politician César Batlle Pacheco to create a municipal museum of painting and sculpture. The Morales estate in Montevideo was purchased as a permanent home for the new museum, remodelling and extensions designed by Eugenio P. Baroffio (1877–1956) began in 1929, and the museum was given its name in 1930 on the centenary of the birth of Juan Manuel Blanes. It was transferred to its new site in 1931 but, due to the financial crisis that began in 1929, it was not finally opened to the public until 1935. The holdings of the Museo Municipal Juan Manuel Blanes were based on the collection of European paintings and sculptures donated to the Municipality of Montevideo in 1912 by Alejo Rossell y Rius (1848–1919) and his wife, Dolores Pereira. These works were held initially by the Jardín Zoológico Municipal, the Museo Histórico Nacional and the Museo Nacional de Bellas Artes. Between 1928 and 1953 the museum's initial core of works was increased by purchases from individuals, by donations and, above all, from the Salón Municipal de Artes Plásticas that began in 1940, bringing a contemporary profile to the works entering the museum's collection. Uruguayan works held by the museum include oils, drawings, sketches and documents of Blanes, and oils and drawings by Figari, Torres García, Cúneo, Sáez, Luis Solari, Pedro Blanes Viale and, in particular, Alfredo De Simone. Also of note are some prints by Carlos González, who donated several works to the museum in 1991.

Other important museums in Uruguay include the Museo Juan Zorrilla de San Martín, opened in 1943, which holds works from the collection of the poet Juan Zorrilla de San Martín including some by his son, the sculptor José Luís Zorrilla de San Martín, and the Museo de Arte Precolombino y Colonial, opened in 1975, both in Montevideo. The Museo San Fernando was opened in Maldonado in 1984, partly in response to the cultural and tourist development of the region, which includes Punta del Este, and the Museo Solari was opened in Fray Bentos in 1989 with a collection that includes works by Luis Solari but is also devoted to the promotion of fine arts in the region. Private museums include the Museo de Arte Contemporáneo of the newspaper *El País*, which promotes national and foreign avant-garde art. The Museo Torres García was founded in Montevideo by the Fundación Torres García in 1988, with a view to bringing together the works of the artist that were scattered throughout the world. While Uruguay has no significant Pre-Columbian art of its own, its private collections in this area are of considerable importance; examples include the Francisco Matto collection, which is on display to the public.

BIBLIOGRAPHY
F. García Esteban: 'Valorización crítica del acervo actual del museo', *Rev. Mus. Juan Manuel Blanes*, i/1 (1958), pp. 18–20
Catálogo descriptivo del Museo Nacional de Bellas Artes (Montevideo, 1966)

ANGEL KALENBERG

VIII. Art education.

Applied arts were first taught in Uruguay in the second half of the 19th century, initially in the Talleres de Maestranza and after 1878 in the Escuela Nacional de Artes y Oficios in Montevideo. The Escuela changed radically under the direction of Pedro Figari between 1915 and 1921, when he discarded academicism and created a modern centre of training, in which art and industry were of equal importance and emphasis was placed on regional art and originality of design. This was the basis on which the Universidad del Trabajo del Uruguay, Montevideo, was founded (1942; formerly the Escuela Nacional de Artes y Oficios), where applied arts were taught. Before 1905 professional art education was imparted individually by artists, principally foreign, and most Uruguayan artists travelled to Europe to acquire a complete training. This situation changed in 1905 when the Círculo de Bellas Artes, the first formal institution for art education, was founded. Many of the best-known artists of Uruguay studied and taught there, helping to foster the development of modern art. In 1943 the Escuela Nacional de Bellas Artes was founded; it acquired university status in 1959 and established a new curriculum in 1960. Organized through a series of workshops, its programme involved active teaching, the development of the senses, teamwork, experimentation, spontaneity, empirical learning and integration with the environment.

Private studios and workshops also played an important role in the development of modern Uruguayan art. The most prominent of these, the Asociación de Arte Constructivo and the Taller Torres García, were founded by Joaquín Torres García in 1935 and 1943. After his death in 1949 his pupils continued teaching his principles of Constructivism. Other important private workshops and training centres included the Club de Grabado, which from 1953 offered instruction in the graphic arts; and the Centro de Diseño Industrial, which established a training programme for designers in 1988.

Formal architectural training began in 1888 in the Facultad de Matemáticas y Ramas Anexas in Montevideo; the Facultad de Arquitectura was subsequently founded in 1915. The tuition of the French architect José P. Carré (1870–1941) was particularly influential between 1906 and 1940. A new curriculum was established in 1952, described as a humanistic technical programme based on the concept of the architect as a technician in the service of society. The course was organized in workshops directed by leading architects, among them Julio Vilamajó, Mauricio Cravotto (1893–1962), Mario Payssé-Reyes and Carlos Gómez Gavazzo (1904–87).

BIBLIOGRAPHY
J. P. Argul: *Educación para la belleza y el arte: Del ejercicio de la crítica de arte* (Montevideo, 1956)
——: *Los artes plásticas del Uruguay: Desde la época indígena al momento contemporáneo* (Montevideo, 1966); rev. as *Proceso de las artes plásticas del Uruguay* (Montevideo, 1975)
A. Martínez Montero and E. Villegas Suárez: *Historia de la universidad del trabajo del Uruguay* (Montevideo, 1968)
Proyección de su experiencia educacional, Escuela Nacional de Bellas Artes (Montevideo, 1986)
R. García Miranda: 'Evolución de los estudios de arquitectura', *El País* (Dec 1988)

IX. Art libraries and photographic collections.

Most of the libraries and slide collections with significant art-historical material are found in Montevideo. The most important are the Biblioteca Nacional del Uruguay, the Biblioteca Municipal del Museo de Historia del Arte and the libraries of the Facultad de Arquitectura at the Universidad de la República, the Museo Nacional de Artes Plásticas, the Universidad Católica and the Escuela Nacional de Bellas Artes. These collections cover international and Uruguayan art history from the prehistoric period to the 20th century. There are 30 other libraries with partial collections. Specialist libraries include those at the Centro de Diseño Industrial (design); the Biblioteca Artigas-Washington (American art); the Biblioteca del Instituto Cultural Anglo-Uruguayo (British art); the French Embassy and Alliance Française (French art); and the Instituto Italiano de Cultura (Italian art). The best libraries for the study of Uruguayan art are those of the Círculo de Bellas Artes, the Museo Nacional de Artes Plásticas and the Biblioteca Nacional. The Comisión Nacional de Bellas Artes has a large collection of catalogues on Uruguayan art, and there is a library devoted to Joaquín Torres García at the Museo Torres García.

The most important slide collections, covering international and Uruguayan art, are those of the Facultad de Arquitectura, the Escuela Nacional de Bellas Artes and the Museo Municipal de Historia del Arte. There are also specialist slide collections in the foreign cultural institutes. The Ministerio de Educación y Cultura has a slide collection of Uruguayan sculpture, and the Intendencia Municipal de Montevideo has an important collection of black-and-white photographs of the history of the city. Due to economic problems, the use of microfilm and computers is restricted to a few private libraries, such as the Biblioteca Artigas-Washington.

ALICIA HABER

Uruk [Bibl. Erech; Class. Orchoë; now Warka]. Site in southern Iraq of an important Sumerian city, once situated on a branch of the Euphrates, continuously occupied from the 5th millennium BC to Sasanian times (7th century AD); it is noted especially for remarkable architecture of the 4th millennium BC (Uruk period) and for the world's earliest written documents. The site was excavated in 1850 and 1854 by William Kennet Loftus; since 1912 German teams have worked there under J. Jordan (1912–13, 1928–31), A. Nöldeke (1931–3, 1934–9), E. Heinrich (1933–4) and, since 1954, under H. Lenzen and later J. Schmidt. Most of the finds are in Baghdad (Iraq Mus.), although some of Loftus's are in London (BM) and some from the earlier German excavations are in Berlin (Pergamonmus.).

The city of the legendary Gilgamesh, Uruk is believed to have consisted originally of two settlements, Kullaba and Eanna, of which Kullaba, the site of the later Anu precinct, is believed to be the earlier. Here two temples of the 5th millennium BC (Ubaid period) have been discovered beneath a later building known as the Steingebäude, the construction of which disturbed them. The nearby high Anu terrace is also thought to date from this time. These two temples are 'low temples' (*Tieftempel*), like those at Tepe Gawra, in contrast to the 'high temples' (*Hochtempel*), of which at least seven Uruk-period rebuildings are attested on the Anu terrace, a tradition comparable with that at Eridu and Uqair (*see* MESOPOTAMIA, §II, 1–3). The best-preserved of these 4th-millennium BC high

terrace shrines is the White Temple, now dated to the Late Uruk period.

Also dating to the second half of the 4th millennium BC are the remarkable developments in the Eanna precinct, which came not only to rival Kullaba but ultimately to replace it. Remains of cone mosaic ornament in Eanna level VI (*c.* 3500 BC) suggest the presence of monumental buildings, but there is no evidence here for the long sequence of religious buildings attested in Kullaba (Anu precinct). The earliest excavated building is the Limestone Temple (level V). It was beneath this structure that the deep sounding, which still provides the basis for Uruk chronology, was excavated in 1932 (*see* MESOPOTAMIA, §I, 2(i)(c)). Throughout the three phases of level IV, Eanna was rebuilt several times, culminating in an extraordinary plan, one of the most remarkable and spectacular achievements of ancient times (*see* MESOPOTAMIA, §II, 3 and fig. 8). The earliest known pictographic tablets were recovered from level IVa, in total some 4000 fragments. Small clay tokens, which some see as precursors of the pictographic script, are found as early as Eanna VI, though token containers (hollow spherical clay bullae bearing the impressions of seals), simple numerical tablets and more developed pictographic documents occur together in level IVa. It seems likely, however, on the basis of evidence from Habuba Kabira and Susa, that the numerical tablets and some of the simpler pictographic types pre-date level IVa, including possibly the few *juss* (gypsum) tablets found in the area of the White Temple (*see* ANCIENT NEAR EAST, §I, 3).

Eanna IVa was deliberately razed to create the foundations for a new precinct in level III (*c.* 3000 BC, often called the Jemdet Nasr period). From this time onwards there seems to have been only one central sanctuary in Uruk. This was of the 'high temple' type, covered a smaller area and was more centralized than its Late Uruk predecessor. Some of the most famous objects from Mesopotamia were found in level III, though many of these almost certainly derive from earlier Late Uruk contexts. These include the lion-hunt stele, the Warka Head (see fig.), the Warka Vase (*see* MESOPOTAMIA, fig. 12) and many stone vessels illustrating the vigorous artistic style of the period.

During the Early Dynastic period (*c.* 2900–*c.* 2400 BC) the city wall was built (according to legend the work of Gilgamesh), encompassing a vast area of 5.5 sq. km. The wall was 9.5 km in length, with rectangular (later round) towers. The Stamplehmgebäude, the pisé foundations of a large administrative or palace-like building, also dates from Early Dynastic times. Some archaic tablets were found in it, like those of Eanna IVa almost certainly deriving from an earlier fill. Also in Eanna—and the source of the precinct name—is the 3rd-millennium BC ziggurat originally dedicated by Ur-Nammu of Ur (*reg* 2112–2095 BC) to the goddess Inanna. Unlike his famous ziggurat at Ur, the outer surface of the Uruk example was only plastered, not faced with baked brick; nor was it stepped. In fact, in construction it was no more than an imposing terrace, rising *c.* 14 m above its associated court, comparable with the prehistoric high terrace in Kullaba. The ziggurat and its precinct were renovated by a number of Mesopotamian rulers, down to the Achaemenid Cyrus (*reg*

third complex, the Eanna precinct dedicated to Inanna, had been the site of her high temple shrine for some 1500 years. Among the Hellenistic objects from the site is an extremely fine gold wreath found in a grave outside the walls (Baghdad, Iraq Mus.). Also outside the city wall was a *bit akitu* of Hellenistic date, where the Babylonian New Year was celebrated. Much of the southern sector of the site is covered by Parthian ruins, dominated by a fortified temple of Gareus (before AD 110; *see* BRICK, fig. 6), with an impressive arched and columned façade. A Parthian palace lay to the east.

BIBLIOGRAPHY

Vorläufiger Bericht über die von der Notgemeinschaft der Deutschen Wissenschaft in Uruk unternommenen Ausgrabungen in Uruk-Warka, i–xi, Abhandlung der preussischen Akademie der Wissenschaften, philosophisch-historische Klasse (Berlin, 1929–40)

Ausgrabungen des deutschen Forschungsgemeinschaft in Uruk-Warka, i– (Leipzig and Berlin, 1936–)

H. J. Lenzen: 'Tempel der Schicht IV', *Z. Assyriol.*, xlix (1950), pp. 1–20

Vorläufiger Bericht über die von dem Deutschen Archäologischen Institut und der Deutschen Orient-Gesellschaft aus Mitteln der Deutschen Forschungsgemeinschaft unternommenen Ausgrabungen in Uruk-Warka, xii– (Berlin, 1956–)

W. K. Loftus: *Travels and Researches in Chaldaea and Susiana* (London, 1957)

Baghdad. Mitt., i– (1960–) [regular articles and rep. on the excavations]

M. A. Brandes: *Untersuchungen zur Komposition der Stiftmosaiken an der Pfeilerhalle der Schicht IVa in Uruk-Warka*, Baghdad. Mitt. Beiheft, i (1968)

H. J. Nissen: 'The City Wall of Uruk', *Man, Settlement and Urbanism*, ed. P. Ucko, R. Tringham and G. Dimbleby (London, 1972), pp. 793–8

——: 'The Archaic Texts from Uruk', *World Archaeol.*, xvii (1976), pp. 317–34

E. Heinrich: *Die Tempel und Heiligtümer im alten Mesopotamien* (Berlin, 1982)

R. M. Boehmer: *Uruk Kampagne 38, Ausgrabungen in Uruk-Warka*, Endberichte, i (Mainz, 1987)

JOAN OATES

Uruk, Warka Head of a woman, white marble, h. 201 mm, Uruk period, third quarter of 4th millennium BC (Baghdad, Iraq Museum)

538–530 BC). Under the Seleucids it seems to have been transformed into a fortification.

Near the city wall was the imposing palace of a ruler of the Old Babylonian period, Sinkashid (*reg* 1865–1833 BC). A small temple constructed by the Kassite king Karaindash (late 15th century BC) was dedicated to the goddess Ishtar; its outer wall was ornamented with unusual reliefs made of moulded baked bricks in the shape of deities holding flowing vases. Although façade decoration in mud brick originated in Old Babylonian times (*see* RIMAH, TELL EL), the use of moulded baked-brick ornament was a Kassite innovation that was to inspire the later and even more elaborate tradition of moulded glazed bricks as seen in the Ishtar Gateway at Babylon (*see* ANCIENT NEAR EAST, §II, 5).

At the heart of later Uruk lay three vast buildings. The so-called Bit Resh, or Principal Temple, is an enormous complex dedicated to Anu, god of the heavens, and his wife Antum. This was the area of the prehistoric high terrace sequence and explains its Anu identification. The central shrine of the latest temple, built in the Hellenistic period, continues the form of the Babylonian 'broadroom' (*Breitraum*) shrine, opening off a central courtyard. The complex itself occupies some 213×167 m and contains 22 individual shrines. Near by is a second huge Hellenistic temple, Irigal (205×198 m), dedicated to Ishtar, built in baked brick and containing four separate sanctuaries. The

Urzecze [Radziwiłł] **Glassworks.** Glassworks in Urzecze, Poland (now Urechje, Belarus'), established by Princess Anna Radziwiłł (1676–1746), and in production from 1737 to 1842. The Glassworks was started by a team from Dresden-Friedrichstal and specialized in mirrors. Mirror plates were produced firstly by the 'Lorraine' method (*see* GLASS, §II, 1(ii)) and from 1756 by the casting method. Mirrors were mounted and ornamented with cut and engraved decoration under the artistic supervision of Christian Theodor Scherber (*fl* 1737–65; e.g. Warsaw, N. Mus.; Krakow, N. Mus.). Urzecze products included pier-glasses with glass cresting, sconces, devotional pictures and panels for furniture. Surviving examples date from 1750 to 1780 and reflect the English and Dresden Baroque style. A factory pattern book (Warsaw, Cent. Archvs. Hist. Rec.) dates from 1748. About 1750 Urzecze Glassworks started production of vessels in association with the Naliboki Glassworks. Local craftsmen were employed in both glassworks and contributed to a distinctive local style known as the Urzecze–Naliboki style (*see* NALIBOKI GLASSWORKS). English stylistic influence first reached the area *c.* 1770 and gained prominence in the 1780s, while the Neo-classical style prevailed between 1790 and 1820, particularly in mass-produced glassware for the table.

BIBLIOGRAPHY

K. Buczkowski: *Dawne szkła artystyczne w Polsce* [Old artistic glass in Poland] (Kraków, 1958)

Z. Kamieńska: *Manufaktura szklana w Urzeczu, 1737–1846* [The glass-works at Urzecze, 1737–1846] (Wrocław, 1964)

H. Chojnacka and P. Chrzanowska: 'La Verrerie polonaise baroque et ses contacts avec l'Europe centrale', *Annales du 5e congrès de l'Association internationale pour l'histoire du verre: Prague, 1970*, pp. 187–96

M. M. Janickaja: *Belaruskae mastackae šklo (XVI–XVIII stst.)* [Belarusian artistic glass (XVI–XVIII century)] (Mińsk, 1977)

H. Chojnacka and Z. Kamieńska: 'Influence anglaise sur les formes de miroirs produits en Pologne au XVIIIe siècle', *Annales du 9e congrès de l'Association internationale pour l'histoire du verre: London and Liverpool, 1979*, pp. 271–81

A. Kasprzak: 'Produkcja szkieł rubinowych w Nalibokach w l poł XVIII w.' [Production of ruby glass in Naliboki in the first half of the 18th century], *Roc. Muz. N. Warszaw./Annu. Mus. N. Varsovie*, xxxviii (1995)

HALINA CHOJNACKA

Usermaatre-setepenre. *See* RAMESSES II.

Useynov & Dadashev. Azerbaijani architectural partnership formed *c.* 1929 by Mikael' Useynov (*b* Baku, 19 April 1905) and Sadykh (Alekper ogly) Dadashev (*b* Baku, 15 April 1905; *d* Moscow, 24 Dec 1946). Useynov studied at the Azerbaijan Polytechnical Institute, Baku, from 1921 to 1929. Dadashev completed his studies at the same institution the same year. In their first joint works they applied Constructivist principles within the context of the physical and climatic conditions of Azerbaijan. Examples include the food factory (early 1930s) in Bailov, a suburb of Baku, with numerous terraces and a pergola on the flat roof, and the teaching block (1930–31) of the Azerbaijan Industrial Institute, Baku. In the same style are several residential buildings, some of which were extended into large complexes, such as the Novy Byt complex (early 1930s), Baku. Using reinforced-concrete construction, and occasionally imitating it in stone, Useynov and Dadashev overcame the stark asceticism that characterizes many Constructivist residential blocks of this period.

There followed a short period of neo-classicism, as in the Nizami Cinema (1934), Baku, where neo-Renaissance forms, including pergolas, are imposed on a rationally organized asymmetrical structure. By the mid-1930s, however, Useynov and Dadashev had developed a 'neo-Azerbaijani' style, a synthesis of rationally organized, constructionally functional structures, in an architectural form that was essentially classical with elements of the Azerbaijani vernacular. This style was used in the design of the Conservatorium (1937–9), Baku, the Azerbaijani pavilion at the All-Russian Agricultural Exhibition (1939) in Moscow, and the residential block (1938–41) of the Baku Soviet. It is most strikingly employed in the Museum of Azerbaijani Literature (1940), Baku, where traditional blue, glazed ceramic insets are introduced into the precise, symmetrical composition and the central loggias are formed with pointed arches. From the mid-1940s the façades of their buildings were increasingly overloaded with decorative elements, as in the flats for scientific workers (1946), Gusa Gadzhiyev Street, Baku.

After Dadashev's death Useynov designed the complex of buildings of the Azerbaijan Academy of Sciences (completed 1952), Baku, the restrained decoration of which reveals the rigidly neo-classical arrangement of masses. In the Narimanov and Nizami metro stations (both 1967) in Baku, he used unique decorative devices to form a link between the buildings' Modernist interiors and the traditional architecture of the city. His major late work was the completion of Lenin Square (now the Square of Freedom), which is open to the Caspian Sea on one side and forms the central part of Baku city centre. Here he built two 17-storey hotel buildings, the Azerbaijan (1972) and the Apsheron (1985), placed opposite each other at right angles to the House of Government of Azerbaijan (completed 1951) by Lev Rudnev and V. O. Munts (1903–74), which forms the centre of the ensemble. From 1948 Useynov was head of the institute of architecture and art of the Academy of Sciences of Azerbaijan.

WRITINGS

M. A. Useynov and S. A. Dadashev: *Arkhitekturnyye pamyatniki Baku* [The architectural monuments of Baku] (Moscow, 1946, 2/1955)

M. A. Useynov: *Pamyatniki azerbaydzhanskogo zodchestva* [Monuments of Azerbaijani architecture] (Moscow, 1951)

M. A. Useynov and S. A. Dadashev: *Ansambl' dvortsa shirvanshakhov v Baku* [The ensemble of the Shirvanshakhov Palace in Baku] (Moscow, 1956)

M. A. Useynov, L. Bretansky and A. Salamzade: *Istoriya arkhitektury Azerbaydzhana* [The history of Azerbaijani architecture] (Moscow, 1963)

BIBLIOGRAPHY

E. A. Kasimzade and Y. S. Yaralov: *Dadashev, Useynov* (Moscow, 1951)

A. V. IKONNIKOV

Ushakov, Simon [Pimen] **(Fyodorovich)** (*b* Moscow, 1626; *d* Moscow, 1686). Russian painter and graphic artist. He is a key figure in the late 17th-century 'transitional' period of Russian culture, when signs of Western influence began to make their appearance in an art that was still predominantly religious. He is first referred to in 1648 as working as a designer in the royal silver workshops in the Kremlin. His first authenticated icon was *Our Lady of Vladimir* (Bogomater' Vladimirskaya, 1652; Moscow, Tret'yakov Gal.), a conventional composition based on a famous Byzantine prototype, which nevertheless displays the artist's characteristic highlighting of faces. In the 1650s Ushakov painted a series of icons for the new church of the Trinity in Nikitniki in Moscow's commercial district. They include the *Great Archbishop* (Veliky Arkhiyerey, 1657; Moscow, Hist. Mus.) and the *Saviour Not Made by Human Hands* (Spas nerukotvorny, 1658; Moscow, Tret'yakov Gal.), the form in which the ancient icon of the MANDYLION OF EDESSA was then usually represented. The use of light and shade in these compositions gives the faces a three-dimensional quality, softening and humanizing the ascetic otherworldliness characteristic of figures in earlier icons.

From 1664 until his death Ushakov directed the icon-painting workshop in the tsar's Armoury Chamber (Oruzheynaya Palata). The Armoury enjoyed the status of an early Russian academy of arts, employing leading craftsmen, including foreigners, to make all manner of objects for the royal household. Ushakov had authority as both teacher and theoretician. His treatise *K lyuboshchatel'nomu ikonnogo pisaniya* ('To the lover of icon painting'; *c.* 1667), a rare example of Russian aesthetic writing before the time of Peter I (*reg* 1682–1725), lauded the lifelike alongside the spiritual in religious art. Among the many icons painted and signed (itself an innovation) by Ushakov in the 1660s–1670s, the following are especially noteworthy for the innovative use of shading, perspective and naturalistic detail: *Our Lady of Mercy of Kikkos* (Bogomater'

Eleusa Kikkskaya, 1668; Moscow, Tret'yakov Gal.), an unconventional Virgin and Child composition with rhythmic drapes in unusual pinks and greens; and *Our Lady of Vladimir* (Bogomater' Vladimirskaya; part of the *Tree of the Muscovite State* (Drevo moskovskogo gosudarstva), 1668; Moscow, Tret'yakov Gal.), an original allegorical composition of the Virgin and Child in an oval borne aloft on a vine stem and flanked by branches bearing medallions with Russian saints and clerics. The *Tree of the Muscovite State* is also notable for the portraits (below, left and right) of Tsar Alexis (*reg* 1645–76) and his wife and son and a realistic rendition of the Kremlin walls. The *Old Testament Trinity* (Troitsa, 1671; St Petersburg, Rus. Mus.), depicting three angels at a table, can usefully be compared with the famous early 15th-century icon of the same subject by ANDREY RUBLYOV. Whereas the earlier work shows few items and interprets its subject in spiritual terms, Ushakov's displays more temporal concerns: a precisely drawn arch, a naturalistic tree, moulded faces and clutter of objects on the table. Ushakov also painted portraits (destr.) of members of the royal family, supervised the painting of frescoes in the Kremlin cathedrals and royal palaces and made drawings and engravings, such as designs for the frontispieces, engraved by Afanasy Trukhmensky, for Simeon Polotsky's *Psaltir' rifmotvornaya* ('Psalter in verse'; Moscow, 1680) and *Povest' o Varlaame i Ioasafe* ('Tale of Varlaam and Josaphat'; Moscow, 1680–81).

Ushakov and his school were denounced by traditionalist contemporaries, who associated realism in art with foreign 'heresy'. In the 19th century Ushakov was blamed for initiating the 'decline' of Russian icon painting, a view still expressed today by those who see in his art an uneasy compromise between the religious and the secular. Soviet scholars regarded him as a 'progressive' artistic reformer, a pioneer of secular cultural trends on the eve of the reforms of Peter I. He may perhaps most usefully be considered as one of the chief exponents of 'Moscow Baroque', a hybrid style found also in architecture and the decorative arts, which fused traditional compositions with Western devices.

WRITINGS

K lyuboshchatel'nomu ikonnogo pisaniya [To the lover of icon painting] (*c.* 1667); *Mastera Isk. Isk.*, iv (1939), pp. 27–30

BIBLIOGRAPHY

G. Filimonov: *Simon Ushakov i sovremennaya yemu epokha russkoy ikonopisi* [Simon Ushakov and the contemporary era of Russian icon painting] (Moscow, 1873)

I. E. Grabar', ed.: *Istoriya russkogo iskusstva* [The history of Russian art], iv (Moscow, 1959), pp. 368–402

T. Anna'yeva: *Simon Ushakov* (Leningrad, 1971)

L. A. J. Hughes: 'The Moscow Armoury and Innovations in 17th-century Muscovite Art', *Can.–Amer. Slav. Stud.*, xiii (1979), pp. 204–33

——: 'The 17th-century "Renaissance" in Russia', *Hist. Today* (1980), pp. 41–5

V. G. Bryusova: *Russkaya zhivopis' XVII veka* [17th-century Russian painting] (Moscow, 1984)

L. A. J. Hughes: 'The Age of Transition: 17th-century Russian Icon Painting', *Icons 88* (Dublin, 1988), pp. 63–74

LINDSEY HUGHES

Ushimaro. *See* HANABUSA ITCHŌ.

Ushtur-Mullo. Small Buddhist monastery in southern Tajikistan. Built in the Kushana period (1st–4th century AD), it is situated on the right bank of the Amu River, east of the confluence of the Kafirnigan River and abutting the Tepa-i Shah Oasis. The complex was fully excavated by T. I. Zeymal between 1979 and 1982 (all finds from the site Dushanbe, Tajikistan Acad. Sci., Donish Inst. Hist., Archaeol. & Ethng.). It consists of a rectangular monastery building or *sangharama* (40×30 m) with the main stupa to the south. The monastery had 26 rooms of various types around a square courtyard (20.5×21.0 m). In the middle of the northern side was a temple enclosed by a pi-shaped corridor, with a portico opening on to the courtyard. To the west of the temple was a hall (*c.* 100 sq. m) used by the monks for assemblies. The north-eastern corner of the monastery contained an isolated group of storage and service rooms, while the western, eastern and southern sides comprised 14 monks' cells, all identical in plan and size (*c.* 10 sq. m). Around the perimeter of the courtyard was an iwan supported by wooden columns with stone bases. The courtyard walls were covered with narrative paintings (poorly preserved) on loess stucco, while the lower part of the walls was painted red or dark blue. A passage in the southern façade of the monastery gave access to the main stupa. This structure had an almost square base (16.4×16.7–17.3–17.6 m), with a ramp or staircase on the south side, flanked by rectangular pylons. The stupa was built of unbaked brick and faced with both plain and ornamental limestone tiles. Only the first step of the socle (h. *c.* 400 mm) and the lip of the second step of the base of the stupa have survived, but the dimensions of both the cylindrical drum and hemispherical dome have been precisely calculated using fragments of their stone facing, a stone reliquary in the form of a stupa from the site and analogous examples, particularly the GULDARA stupa, south of Kabul. The reconstructed height of the Ushtur-Mullo stupa was over 15 m (including 0.4 m for the socle, 4.5 m for the second step and 4.5 m for the drum).

The monastery ceased to function during the second half of the 4th century AD, when all the Buddhist structures on the right bank of the Amu River were destroyed and abandoned. In the 6th century, however, when the political and religious climate in northern Tokharistan changed, the main stupa was restored, a flight of steps being built on each of its four façades in place of the original single staircase on the south side. As a result the stupa became cruciform in plan, an important characteristic of later stupas in Central Asia and Afghanistan.

BIBLIOGRAPHY

Ye. V. Zeymal': 'Buddiyskiy kompleks Ushtur Mullo' [The Buddhist complex of Ushtur-Mullo], *Arkheol. Raboty Tadzhikistane*, xix (1979), pp. 186–202

——: 'Raskopki buddiyskogo kompleksa Ushtur-Mullo v 1981' [Excavations of the Buddhist complex of Ushtur-Mullo in 1981], *Arkheol. Raboty Tadzhikistane*, xxi (1981), pp. 227–88

——: 'Buddiyskiy monastyr' Ushtur-Mullo (raboty 1982)' [The Buddhist monastery of Ushtur-Mullo (work in 1982)], *Arkheol. Raboty Tadzhikistane*, xxii (1982), pp. 255–61

——: 'Buddiyskaya stupa u Verblyuzh'yey gorki (k tipologii stup pravoberezhnogo Tokharistana)' [The Buddhist stupa by the Camel Hill (on a typology of stupas on the right bank of Tokharistan)], *Proshloye sredney Azii (arkheologiya, numizmatika i eipgrafika, etnografiya)* [Central Asia's past (archaeology, numismatics and epigraphy, ethnography)] (Dushanbe, 1987), pp. 70–78

YE. V. ZEYMAL'

'Usiyeh. *See under* HADITHA REGION.

Üsküdari. *See* OKYAY, NECMEDDIN.

Uskup. *See* SKOPJE.

Usol'sk [Usol'ye Vychegodskoye]. *See* SOL'VYCHEGODSK.

Uspensky, Pyotr (Dem'yanovich) [Ouspensky, Peter] (*b* Moscow, 5 March 1878; *d* Virginia Water, Surrey, 2 Oct 1947). Russian philosopher. His theories of a four-dimensional 'hyperspace' were highly influential on a number of Russian avant-garde artists and poets, including Mikhail Larionov, Kazimir Malevich, Mikhail Matyushin, Velimir Khlebnikov and Aleksey Kruchonykh (*see* FOURTH DIMENSION). According to Uspensky, man's consciousness was trapped in the illusory world of three dimensions as a result of an incomplete 'space sense'. This needed to be expanded into the fourth dimension, in order to cultivate a new 'cosmic consciousness'. Uspensky described how a three-dimensional being entering four-dimensional space would initially experience horror and a sense of chaos, arising from the fact that the laws of the previous dimension no longer operate in the new, higher dimension.

The concern in *zaum* ('transrational language') to free the word from the confines of accepted meaning and transport it into a new spatial dimension with its own higher system of logic had its source in the hyperspace philosophy of Uspensky, and the illusory world of three dimensions was rejected in the Futurist opera *Pobeda nad solntsem* ('Victory over the sun'; 1913; *see* KRUCHONYKH, ALEKSEY). In 1913, Matyushin juxtaposed excerpts from Uspensky's *Tertium Organum* with his translation of Albert Gleizes and Jean Metzinger's *Du Cubisme* (Paris, 1912), in order to associate the Cubist style of painting with transformation to a higher consciousness in the fourth dimension. The theories of Rayism and Suprematism also embraced the idea of an 'Uspenskian' fourth dimension of space. In 1921 Uspensky settled in England, where he had many followers, although his influence on art was mostly confined to the Russian avant-garde.

See also THEOSOPHY.

WRITINGS

Chetvortoye izmereniye [The fourth dimension] (St Petersburg, 1909; Eng. trans., London, 1960)
Tertium Organum: Klyuch k zagadkam mira [Tertium Organum: a key to the enigmas of the world] (St Petersburg, 1911, 2/1916; Eng. trans., New York, 1970)
A New Model of the Universe: Principles of the Psychological Method in its Application to the Problems of Science, Religion and Art (London, 1960)

BIBLIOGRAPHY

S. Compton: 'Malevich and the Fourth Dimension', *Studio Int.*, clxxxvii/965 (April 1974), pp. 190–5; clxxxviii/968 (July 1974)
L. D. Henderson: 'The Merging of Time and Space: The Fourth Dimension in Russia from Ouspensky to Malevich', *The Structurist*, xv/xvi (1975/6), pp. 47–108
S. Compton: 'Malevich's Suprematism: The Higher Intuition', *Burl. Mag.*, cxviii/881 (1976), pp. 576–85
L. D. Henderson: *The Fourth Dimension and Non-Euclidean Geometry in Modern Art* (Princeton, 1983)

CHARLOTTE HUMPHREYS

Ussher & Kemp. Australian architectural partnership. Beverley Ussher (*b* Melbourne 1868; *d* Melbourne, 9 June 1908) and Henry (Hardie) Kemp (*b* Broughton, Lancs, 10 March 1859; *d* Melbourne, 22 April 1946) formed a partnership in Melbourne in 1899, which lasted until Ussher's death. In his youth Kemp was articled to Corsen and Aitken of Manchester, worked with R. W. Edis in London and with Paull & Bonella. Ussher was articled to Alfred Dunn (1862–94) in Melbourne, and through Dunn was introduced when visiting London to Walter Butler (1864–1949), W. R. Lethaby, Ernest Gimson and Sidney Barnsley (1864–1926) and Ernest Barnsley. Both Ussher and Kemp had strong Arts and Crafts commitments. Both had been in partnerships before forming their own: Ussher with Walter Butler (1889–93); Kemp with Percy Oakden and G. H. M. Addison (1857/8–1922) from 1887 to 1893. They each worked alone during the 1890s after the economic depression ended the earlier partnerships. Kemp subsequently worked with George Inskip (*fl* 1879–1913) until 1913 and then with his nephew F. Bruce Kemp (*b* 1877) between 1918 and 1927 when he retired. Both partners were members of the Royal Victorian Institute of Architects.

Ussher & Kemp's practice specialized in the design of picturesque houses featuring terracotta tiles, red bricks and painted decorative timber details. The large number of their house designs express the various functions within by the use of gables, dormers, bays and chimneys arranged in decoratively picturesque and asymmetrical compositions. Some are dominated by gable roofs but many have sweeping hip roofs from which gables emerge. Two excellent examples are Dalswraith, 99 Studley Park Road, Kew, Melbourne (1906), and 7 Adeney Avenue, Kew (1908). Kemp's own house, Heald Lawn, a fine gabled example, is at 5 Adeney Avenue, Kew (1913). Their commercial buildings included such examples as the former store and office for Metcalfe and Barnard, corner of Russell Street and Flinders Lane (*c.* 1901), in which bold red brick arches and striking decoration suggest Louis Sullivan's influence.

UNPUBLISHED SOURCES

Melbourne, State Lib. Victoria [drawings]
Melbourne, Beaumaris, R. H. Kemp priv. col. [drawings]

BIBLIOGRAPHY

AUDB
G. Tibbits: 'The So-called Melbourne Domestic Queen Anne', *Hist. Envmt*, i/2 (1982), pp. 4–44

GEORGE TIBBITS

Ussi, Stefano (*b* Florence, 3 Sept 1822; *d* Florence, 11 July 1901). Italian painter. He received his formal training at the Accademia delle Belle Arti in Florence (1837–50, expelled 1838–40) under Tommaso Gazzarini (1790–1853), Pietro Benvenuti and Giuseppe Bezzuoli. In 1854 he won a scholarship to study in Rome and for several years worked on the large-scale painting that established his reputation, the *Expulsion of the Duke of Athens from Florence* (1860; Florence, Pitti). This major example of the new realistic tendency in Romantic history painting was acclaimed for its subject—a 14th-century event that alluded to the expulsion in 1859 of Grand Duke Leopold II (1797–1870), in the course of Italian unification—and for the modernity of its realistic representation. It shows the influence of Paul Delaroche and Domenico Morelli, particularly in its dramatic groupings, vivid characterizations and violent colours. In December 1860 Ussi was appointed professor at the Accademia. He favoured historical and literary themes, executed with a realistic academic vocabulary, and portraits. His more private works, such as the portrait of his wife *Linda Ussi* in the garden (*c.* 1858–9; Florence, Pitti), display in their loose brushwork the freshness and luminosity of the style practised by the Macchiaioli, with whom he was acquainted.

Ussi visited Egypt in 1869, receiving several important commissions, and Morocco in 1875. These trips influenced his choice of subject-matter and stimulated him to capture the striking colours and strong contrasts of light in numerous abstract, outdoor sketches (e.g. *Landscape with Poplars* and *Arab in White*; both Florence, Pitti). Though highly celebrated, Ussi was seldom satisfied and reworked his pictures many times. At the end of his life he endowed a prize for painting to bear his name; he bequeathed many of his works to the Accademia and all his drawings to the Galleria degli Uffizi, Florence.

BIBLIOGRAPHY

Cultura neoclassica e romantica nella Toscana Granducale: Sfortuna dell'Accademia (exh. cat., ed. S. Pinto and A. R. Caputo Calloud; Florence, Pitti, 1972)
Romanticismo storico (exh. cat., ed. S. Pinto; Florence, Pitti, 1973–4)
S. Bietoletti: 'Ussi, Stefano', *Pitt. Italia*, ii (Milan, 1991), p. 1052

EFREM GISELLA CALINGAERT

USSR. *See* UNION OF SOVIET SOCIALIST REPUBLICS.

Ustad Mansur. *See* MANSUR.

Usteri, Johann Martin (*b* Zurich, 14 February 1763; *d* Rapperswil, 29 July 1827). Swiss poet and draughtsman. He was introduced to drawing at art school in Zurich by Valentin Sonnenschein, and he was also helped and encouraged by Salomon Gessner. His first published work, 74 sketches illustrating J. J. Bodmer's historical stories, appeared in 1781. However, despite his strong artistic leanings, he had to join his father, a merchant, in his business. In 1783 he set out on a prolonged cultural tour through Europe, visiting Basle, Strasbourg, Frankfurt, Leipzig, Dresden, Berlin and Hamburg. In the course of his travels he made contact with Daniel Chodowiecki and the poets Friedrich Gottlob Klopstock and Matthias Claudius. He spent the winter of 1783–4 in Brussels; in 1784 he made an extended tour of the Netherlands, from which he derived great inspiration. In the summer of the same year he went to Paris where he studied in the royal library, returning to Zurich in the autumn. In 1787 his uncle Heinrich Usteri (1754–1802) founded the Zürcher Künstlergesellschaft for visual artists in Zurich in which Usteri distinguished himself by his initiative and dynamism. In 1793 he wrote the poem 'Freut euch des Lebens', which achieved fame throughout Europe. Financial upsets compelled Usteri to retire from business in 1804, and he thenceforth devoted himself to drawing, poetry and public works. In 1806 the Schweizerische Künstlergesellschaft was established in Zofingen, largely at his instigation.

BIBLIOGRAPHY

Nagler; *SKL*; Thieme–Becker
Historische-biographische Lexikon der Schweiz (Neuenburg, 1934)

CHRISTINA STEINHOFF

Ust'-Poluy. Iron Age site on the River Poluy, near Salekhard, western Siberia. Excavations by Vanda I. Moshinskaya have revealed a sacrificial site of the second half of the 1st millennium BC containing carved antlers and bones (St Petersburg, Peter the Great Mus. Anthropol. & Ethnog.). Knife and spoon handles have end-pieces sculpted in the round. Two knife handles made of antler represent the heads of a deer and of a bird of prey; they are carved in great detail, showing both animals with their mouths open. Of five spoon handles, three represent the head of an animal: one is a stylized head of a walrus; another the head of a Brent goose made of mammoth tusk. Another unusual, carefully modelled piece is of a small duck made of antler, with its feathers carved in relief, sitting on the head of what may be a hare. A common stylistic feature of the carvings is the elongated eye-sockets. More numerous are examples of relief sculpture, mostly decorating flat spoons (11 items). Two-sided reliefs represent the heads of animals, or sometimes whole animals or birds, usually in profile; there are also compositions showing the heads of two wild animals joined at their necks or by their tongues. Generally the reliefs are more schematic than the sculpture in the round. The most expressive head is that of an elk with mouth half-open, while the influence of the Scythian-Siberian Animal Style is visible in a composition showing a bird of prey pecking an elk's head. The rows of relief rectangles representing the bird's wings and tail are typical.

BIBLIOGRAPHY

V. I. Moshinskaya: *Drevnyaya skul'ptura Urala i zapadnoy Sibiri* [Ancient sculpture of the Urals and western Siberia] (Moscow, 1976)

V. YA. PETRUKHIN

Ustyug, Veliky. *See* VELIKY USTYUG.

Utagawa. Name used by members of a school of Japanese painters, woodblock print designers and book illustrators. They are known for their work in the *ukiyoe* ('pictures of the floating world') genre (*see* JAPAN, §§VI, 4(iv)(b) and IX, 2(iii)). The school was founded by (1) Utagawa Toyoharu, who moved from Kyoto to Edo (now Tokyo), where he set up a woodblock print studio. His leading pupils were (2) Toyokuni I and (4) Toyohiro. Both artists designed *bijinga* ('pictures of beautiful women'), but around 1800 Toyokuni began to produce *yakushae* ('pictures of actors') that eclipsed those of the KATSUKAWA school. Other important Utagawa artists include (5) Kunisada I, the master of the landscape print, ANDŌ HIROSHIGE, (3) Kunimasa and (6) Kuniyoshi. The Utagawa school was the most prolific in the field of printmaking, accounting for over half of Japan's extant *ukiyoe* prints. The lineage continued into the modern period in the work of Kaburagi Kiyokata (1878–1973) and Itō Shinsui (1898–1972).

(1) Utagawa Toyoharu [Masaki; Tajimaya Shōjirō, Shinemon; Ichiryūsai, Senryūsai] (*b* Kansai region, 1735; *d* Edo, 1814). Painter, woodblock print designer and founder of the Utagawa school. A native of western Japan, Toyoharu may have studied in Kyoto under the KANŌ SCHOOL painter Tsuruzawa Tangei (1688–1789). In the 1760s he moved to Edo, where he became a student of the book illustrator Toriyama Sekien (1712–88). His earliest work is thought to be a narrow-format polychrome print (*hosoban nishikie*) of the *Actor Sawamura Sōjurō II as Segawa Kikunojō* (*c.* 1768; Tokyo, Riccer A. Mus.). In the 1770s he produced many polychrome *ukie* ('floating pictures'; perspective prints) of interiors and landscapes, improving on OKUMURA MASANOBU's early attempts in the genre. His use of Western techniques of perspective and occasionally of Western subjects can be seen in his *Shin Yoshiwara sōshimai no zu* ('Closing time in the Yoshiwara'; *c.* 1776; priv. col.) and *Ukie Oranda yukimi no zu* ('Snow viewing in the Netherlands'; *c.* 1776; Tokyo, Riccer A. Mus.). The leading exponents of *yakushae* ('pictures of actors') during the late 18th century were the TORII school. With the interruption of the Torii lineage after the death of Torii Kiyomitsu I (*see* TORII, (6)) in 1785, Toyoharu produced signed theatre programmes for the *kaomise* ('face showing'; first *kabuki* performance of a season) at the Kiriza (1786) and Nakamuraza (1798) and also designed *kanban* (theatre signboards; *see* JAPAN, §XV). Although he produced few *bijinga* ('beautiful women') prints, one of his representative works is *Kinki shoga* (*ōban*, large format; polychrome print; 1775; Tokyo, N. Mus.).

(2) Utagawa Toyokuni I [Kurahashi Kumakichi; Ichiyōsai] (*b* Edo, 1769; *d* Edo, 1825). Painter, woodblock print designer and book illustrator. As a boy he was sent by his father, Gorobei (*d* 1786), a doll-maker, to the studio of (1) Utagawa Toyoharu. Toyokuni's first signed works are dated 1786 (Tokyo, Dai Tōkyū Mem. Found.). In the 1790s he began his collaboration with Izumiya Ichibei and other publishers in the illustration of *kibyōshi* ('yellow covers'; comic novels). In 1794–6 he published a series of large-format, full-figure *yakushae* ('pictures of actors'), *Yakusha butai no sugatae* ('Likenesses of actors on stage'; e.g. New York, Met.), but his forte was *ōkubie* ('large-head pictures') portraits of actors, such as the *Actor Kataoka Nizaemon VII as Fujiwara Shihei* (Tokyo, Sakai col.) and the *Actor Onoe Matsusuke I as Kudō Suketsune* (see fig.), which show the influence of his contemporary and rival TŌSHŪSAI SHARAKU. Toyokuni's career reached its zenith in the decade beginning in 1794. In addition to single-sheet prints, he produced many *yakusha ehon* ('picture books of actors'), including *Yakusha gakuyatsū* ('Actors in dressing-room'; 1799), *Yakusha sangaikyō* (1801) and *Yakusha awase kagami* ('Hand-mirrors of actors'; 1804). Toyokuni's *bijinga* ('pictures of beautiful women') show the influence of KITAGAWA UTAMARO, though the subjects depicted in *Fūryū nankomachi yatsushi sugatae* and *Fūryū sanpukutsui* are familiar women engaged in everyday activities, lacking the ripe eroticism of Utamaro's courtesans. After 1800 Toyokuni's designs became increasingly mannered and conventional, as he tried to keep up with increasing demand. He sought new subject-matter in *yakushae* by shifting the focus from the physiognomy of individual actors to the depiction of the entire stage in a scene from a particular play. His *bijinga* shifted from gentle female figures to fiery, stylish beauties. Toyokuni experimented with printing techniques and invented *murasakie* ('purple pictures'), also called *beni-giral* ('avoiding red'). The names of 28 direct students, including (3) Kunimasa,

Utagawa Toyokuni I: *Actor Onoe Matsusuke I as Kudō Suketsune*, polychrome woodblock print, 1799 (London, Victoria and Albert Museum)

(5) Kunisada I and (6) Kuniyoshi, are listed on Toyokuni's funerary monument.

BIBLIOGRAPHY
F. Socco: *Utagawa Toyokuni und seine Zeit* (Munich, 1913)
K. Iijima: *Ukiyoeshio Utagawa Retsuden* (Tokyo, 1941)
S. Kikuchi: *Toyokuni* (Tokyo, 1955)

(3) Utagawa Kunimasa [Jinsuke; Ichijusai] (*b* Aizu Prov. [now Fukushima Prefect.], 1773; *d* Edo, 1810). Woodblock print designer and book illustrator. He went to Edo as a boy to work in a dyer's shop. Showing an early talent for *yakushae* ('pictures of actors'), Kunimasa came to the attention of (2) Utagawa Toyokuni I. He joined Toyokuni's studio and may have been his first student. He began to design *yakushae* in 1795, principally *ōkubie* ('large–head pictures') portraits, and later half- and full-length portraits. His representative *ōkubie* are *Ichikawa Danjurō VI* (Tokyo, Riccar A. Mus.), *Sawamura Sōjurō II* (Chicago, IL, A. Inst.) and the *Actor Ichikawa Ebizō as Shibaraku* (Tokyo, Riccar A. Mus.). He also designed *bijinga* ('pictures of beautiful women'). In 1797 he produced the illustrations for *Kakutsū yūshi* ('Travellers well-versed in the pleasure quarters'; Tokyo, N. Diet Lib.), the first of his four *sharebon* (popular novels, often licentious). He also collaborated with (2) Toyokuni I on the illustrated theatre books, *Yakusha sanjūni sō* ('Thirteen aspects of actors'; 1799) and *Yakusha gakuya tsū* ('Backstage actors'; 1799; both Tokyo, N. Diet Lib.).

(4) Utagawa Toyohiro [Okajima Tōjirō; Ichiryūsai] (*b* Edo, 1773; *d* Edo, 1829). Painter, woodblock print designer and book illustrator. He was a pupil of (1) Toyoharu founder of the Utagawa school, and a fellow student and rival of (2) Toyokuni I. Toyohiro's earliest known work is an *egoyomi* (pictorial calendar) for 1788. In book illustration, his first works are *Jūsanban kyōka awase* ('Thirteen *kyōka* ['crazy verses'] compared'; ex-Urushiyama Col., Tokyo) and *Kyōka michinokugami* ('Michinoku paper in *kyōka*'; both 1793). During 1802–6 he produced many illustrations for *kibyōshi* ('yellow covers'; comic novels) and *hanashibon* ('story books'; collections of short stories). After *kibyōshi* went out of fashion in 1807, he turned to *gōkanbon* ('bound-together volumes'; popular novels, often on historical themes) and *yomihon* (biographical novels). Toyohiro's single-sheet prints date from 1800 and 1820. These consist of *bijinga* ('pictures of beautiful women'), such as *Mawaridōrō* ('Revolving lantern'; Tokyo, Riccar A. Mus.), *Toyokuni Toyohiro ryōga jūnikō* ('The twelve seasons by Toyokuni and Toyohiro'; of which four are by Toyohiro; priv. col.) and the *kakemonoe* ('hanging scroll picture'; vertical woodblock imitations of a hanging scroll), *Kashibune bijin* ('Beauties on a hired boat'), and a series of landscape prints, such as *Ōmi hakkei* ('Eight views of Ōmi'; priv. col.) and *Edo hakkei* ('Eight views of Edo'; Tokyo, N. Mus.), which were to influence the work of his illustrious student, ANDŌ HIROSHIGE. Toyohiro also painted *nikuhitsuga* ('original paintings'; polychrome paintings; *see* JAPAN, §VI, 4(iv)(a)) of *bijin*.

(5) Utagawa Kunisada I [Sumida Shōzō; Gototei, Ichiyōsai, Gepparō, Kinraisha, Kōchōrō, Toyokuni III, Hanabusa Ittei, Fuchō, Sanjin, Kiō, Bukiyō Matahei] (*b* Edo, 1786; *d* Edo, 1864). Woodblock print designer and book illustrator. As a child he was gifted at drawing and produced *yakushae* ('pictures of actors') without formal training. Around 1801 he became a student of (2) Utagawa Toyokuni I. Kunisada's earliest works are the illustrations for *gōkan* (popular novels), *Oisenukado keshō no Wakamizu* ('Fresh water for make-up'; 1807; Tokyo, Dai Tōkyū Mem. Found.). In the following year he became famous for his illustrations of KITAO MASANOBU's *gōkan*, *Kagamiyama homare no adauchi* ('Honourable revenge of Kagamlyama'; Tokyo, Waseda U.). A narrow-format (*hosoban*) *bijinga* ('picture of beautiful women'), *Fūryū mitate Ōtsue* ('Fanciful analogy of Ōtsue'; 1809; Tokyo, Sakai Col.), is his earliest known single-sheet print, which he signed Kunisada. From 1811 he began to use the artist's name Gototei. The taut, powerful lines of the high-spirited five-piece *bijinga* series *Hokkoku goshikizumi* and the *yakushae* series *Ōatari kyōgen no uchi* are evidence of a maturing style in this period. In the early 1820s Kunisada's career reached its peak, with the *bijinga* series *Hoshi no shimo tōsei fūzoku* ('Starry frost modern manners'; see fig.), *Tōsei sanjūni sō* ('Thirty-two modern faces'; Tokyo, Seikadō Bunko) and *Imafū keshō kagami* ('Modern make-up mirror'; priv. col.). After the death of Toyokuni I in 1825, Kunisada became the *de facto* head of the Utagawa studio, supplanting Toyokuni I's adopted son, Toyoshige (Toyokuni II; 1802–35). Kunisada's prints were admired more

Utagawa Kunisada I: *Andon* from *Hoshi no shimo tōsei fūzoku* ('Starry frost modern manners'), woodblock print, 369×249 mm, *c.* 1820 (London, British Museum)

for their superb technique than for their feeling or warmth. The works of his later period are marred by conventionality caused by overproduction. He continued to be popular, however, working until the year of his death. He was succeeded by Kunisada II (1823–80).

BIBLIOGRAPHY
Y. Hayashi: *Kunisada* (Tokyo, 1960)
J. Suzuki: *Kunisada, Kuniyoshi, Eisen* (Tokyo, 1974)

SUSUMU MATSUDAIRA

(6) Utagawa Kuniyoshi [Igusa Yoshisaburō, Magosaburō; Ichiyūsai, Chōōrō] (*b* Edo, 1797; *d* Edo, 1861). Painter, woodblock print designer and book illustrator. He was born into the urban artisan class of Edo (*Edokko*), the son of a silk dyer. As a child he showed a flair for drawing. Biographies mention his boyhood fascination for picture books by KITAO SHIGEMASA and Kitao Masayoshi (1764–1824) and his contact with the works of Katsukawa Shun'ei (*see* KATSUKAWA, (3)) and Katsukawa Shuntei (1770–1820). Kuniyoshi's formal training took place from 1811 to 1814, when he was apprenticed to (2) Toyokuni I, from whom he learnt the Utagawa style of *yakushae* ('pictures of actors') and *bijinga* ('pictures of beautiful women'). Kuniyoshi launched his career in 1814 with the illustrations of *Gobuji Chūshingura* (e.g. Tokyo, N. Diet Lib.). Single-sheet actor prints followed in 1815, and his first triptych was published in 1818. His early work is indistinguishable from that of Toyokuni's other students, who included (5) Kunisada I and ANDŌ HIROSHIGE. He achieved a professional breakthrough in 1827 with the publication of the first five designs for the series *Tsūzoku Suikoden gōketsu hyakuhachinin no hitori* ('The 108 heroes of the popular *Suikoden*'; 1827; parts in Springfield, MA, Mus. F.A.; *see* JAPAN, fig. 248). In these dynamic *mushae* ('pictures of warriors'), Kuniyoshi found his *métier*. His series was inspired by the Japanese translation of the *Suikoden* (Chin. *Shuihu zhuan*; 'Tales of the water margin'; late 16th century) by Takizawa Bakin (1767–1848). That serial publication began in 1805 but was halted two years later. Kuniyoshi's polychrome designs show the influence of KATSUSHIKA HOKUSAI's monochrome illustrations for the novel. It may have been due to the popularity of Kuniyoshi's prints that the project was restarted in 1829, with Takai Ranzan as the translator and Hokusai as illustrator.

During the 1830s–1850s Kuniyoshi was a leading print artist. The full range of *ukiyoe* subjects is represented in his oeuvre, estimated at *c.* 20,000 designs. He produced *yakushae*, *bijinga*, landscapes, studies of marine life, *mitatee* ('parody pictures') and illustrations of combat and horror stories, in both single-sheet series and triptychs. He was fined under the Tenpō Reforms (1841–3) for violating a short-lived prohibition against *yakushae*. A triptych of 1843, *Minamoto no Yorimitsu-kō no tachi ni tsuchigumo yōkai nasu no zu* ('Minamoto Yorimitsu and the earth spider'; e.g. London, V&A), also earned him mild censure from the authorities when it was deemed to contain political satire. On the whole, however, his depictions of historic warriors were welcomed by the public and shogunate alike. His most significant students were Yoshitoshi (1839–92), Yoshitora (*fl c.* 1850–80) and Yoshikazu (*fl c.* 1850–80).

BIBLIOGRAPHY
B. W. Robinson: *Kuniyoshi* (London, 1971)
——: *Kuniyoshi: The Warrior Prints* (Ithaca, 1982)
M. Takeuchi: 'Kuniyoshi's *Minamoto Raikō and the Earth Spider*: Demons and Protest in Late Tokugawa Japan', *A. Orient.*, xvii (1987), pp. 5–22
MARK H. SANDLER

Utagawa Hiroshige. *See* ANDŌ HIROSHIGE.

Utamaro. *See* KITAGAWA UTAMARO.

Uta Uta (Jangala) [Wuta Wuta Tjangala; Uata Uata Tjangala No. 2] (*b* Kintore Ranges, N. Territory, ?1915–20; *d* Alice Springs, N. Territory, 14 Dec 1990). Australian Aboriginal painter. He was a Pintupi elder and senior custodian of the important site of Yumari; his encyclopedic knowledge of the Dreaming made him a dominant force in the Papunya painting movement from its inception (*c.* 1971). He was one of the first of the Pintupi to make his desire for art materials known to the art teacher Geoff Bardon (*b* 1940), precipitating the involvement of other men from the Pintupi encampment at Papunya. For most of the 1970s Uta Uta lived on outstations established west of Papunya, painting always with a vigour and dynamism that inspired those around him. In the late 1970s and early 1980s he emerged as a master of the mature Pintupi style, producing six large canvases that are among the most powerful works of the Papunya movement. His paintings,

usually of subjects from the Tingari cycle, were all different, fearlessly tackling unusual approaches such as the incorporation of huge figurative representations of ancestral and land forms, infilled with contour-like dotting similar to a traditional design, as in *Yumari* (1981; Sydney, Aboriginal A.) and *Old Man Dreaming at Yumari* (1983; Adelaide, A.G., S. Australia). In 1985 he won the National Aboriginal Art Award. His work has been internationally acclaimed and is included in most major public and private collections in Australia. Uta Uta returned to his homelands in the early 1980s, settling on his outstation at Muyinnga, west of Kintore.

BIBLIOGRAPHY
Dreamings: The Art of Aboriginal Australia (exh. cat., ed. P. Sutton; New York, Asia Soc. Gals; U. Chicago Smart Gal.; Melbourne, Mus. Victoria; Adelaide, S. Austral. Mus.; 1988–90), pp. 37, 97, 105, 130–32, 135–7, 139, 241
East to West: Land in Papunya Painting (exh. cat., ed. J. Kean; Adelaide, Tandanya Aboriginal Cult. Inst. (1990)
G. Bardon: *Papunya Tula: Art of the Western Desert* (Melbourne, 1991), pp. 95–8
VIVIEN JOHNSON

Utenwael, Joachim. *See* WTEWAEL, JOACHIM.

Uther, Johan Baptista van (*fl* Sweden, 1562; *d* Oct 1597). Netherlandish painter, active in Sweden. No signed works by van Uther are known, but, as court painter in Sweden from 1562, he is attributed with portraits of *Catherine Stenbock, Dowager Queen of Sweden* (1570s; Torpa Slott), *John III Vasa, King of Sweden* (1582; Siena, Pal. Reale) and *Prince Sigismund of Sweden* (*c.* 1585; Florence, Uffizi), all of which show the influence of the reserved, elegant court style of Antonis Mor. Van Uther's court duties also included teaching portrait painting. Among his pupils were Holger Hansson, who became his assistant, and possibly John III's son Sigismund. Van Uther may also have influenced the style of Cornelius Arendtz (Steneberg).

BIBLIOGRAPHY
SVKL; Thieme–Becker
K. E. Steneberg: *Vasarenässansens porträttkonst* [Portraits of the Vasa renaissance] (Stockholm, 1935)
TORBJÖRN FULTON

Utili, Giovanni Battista dei. *See* BERTUCCI, (1).

Ut pictura poesis [Lat.: 'as is painting so is poetry']. The phrase is derived from the *Ars poetica* (361) of Horace (65–8 BC). It has subsequently been used to suggest a general similarity between the arts of painting (and sometimes, by extension, sculpture) and poetry. From the 16th to the 18th centuries it was the motto of theorists who wished to elevate the status of painting to that of poetry and the other liberal arts.

See also PARAGONE and POETRY AND ART.

1. ANTIQUITY. In Horace the phrase *ut pictura poesis* introduces a specific analogy: repeated pleasure is afforded not by pictures that have to be scrutinized closely, but by those that can be appreciated at a distance; the same, Horace suggests, is true of poetry, in which broad effects are most successful. The distinction between paintings that are to be seen from different distances may have been

derived from Aristotle, who used it as a parallel to the different forms of rhetoric appropriate to judicial enquiries and public assemblies (*Rhetoric* 1447a7–14). Occasional references to painting are also found in Aristotle's *Poetics*, in which, having distinguished arts that use colour and form from those that rely on the voice (1447a15–25), he draws parallels between painting and poetry on the basis of the common practice of imitation; the shared tendency to heroize the subject, and the analogy between design in painting and plot in drama.

The parallel between painting and poetry is more explicitly articulated in the formulation attributed by Plutarch to Simonides (556–468 BC): 'painting is mute poetry and poetry a speaking picture' (*Moralia* 346). Plutarch used the saying to commend writers of vivid historical prose whose colourful narrative allowed the reader to picture the events described. But the parallel could also be to the disadvantage of painting, as in the *Republic*, in which Plato dismisses painters along with poets as the purveyors of an inferior reality. Although the aesthetic writings of PHILOSTRATOS (*Imagines*) and Lucian of Samosata (*Imagines*) imply that paintings may be read like poetry, the comparison of the two arts was employed in antiquity chiefly to elucidate the qualities of literary language.

2. THE RENAISSANCE. It was only during the 15th century in Italy that painting and poetry came to be considered on a more equal footing and the parallel between them used for their mutual explication. Leon Battista Alberti (*Della pittura*) noted that painters and poets have many ornaments in common and advised artists to emulate the inventions of poets as the sculptor Pheidias had learnt from Homer. Leonardo da Vinci considered invention and measure to be principles that governed both poetry and painting. But in his *Paragone* he drew out the implications of Simonides' maxim to the advantage of painting: 'Poetry is the science of the blind and painting of the deaf. But painting is nobler than poetry in that it serves the nobler sense' (*Trattato della pittura* 15). Leonardo's comparison of the two arts emphasizes that the function of both is to imitate nature, and it was primarily on this basis that the analogy continued to be employed.

In the 16th century the kinship of painting and poetry was a commonplace. But while Florentines, such as Benedetto Varchi in his *Due lezzioni* of 1549, used the comparison primarily as a means of contrasting the two arts, Venetian writers emphasized their unity. Lodovico Dolce, the friend and spokesman of Pietro Aretino, published his *Dialogo della pittura intitolato l'Aretino* in 1557. Dolce had published a translation of the *Ars poetica* in 1537 and was influenced by the work of Bernadino Daniello (*d c.* 1565) on poetry; he thus emphasized the reciprocal nature of the relationship between painting and poetry and even suggested that the *Aretino* might be of value to students of literature as well. The dialogue argues that practitioners of both arts may draw with equal benefit from one another's work because they are alike committed to the imitation of nature, to the use of invention, design and colouring, and to the maintenance of decorum. Giovanni Paolo Lomazzo, in his *Trattato dell'arte de la pittura* (Milan, 1584), asserted that the sisterhood of painting and poetry lay in the shared need for inspiration in the rendering of the emotions. But he went beyond previous authors in specifying practical ways in which painters might learn from poets in depicting the actions of animals and the emotions of men.

3. 17TH AND 18TH CENTURIES. The work most effective in disseminating the *ut pictura poesis* theme outside Italy was the *De arte graphica* (1668) of CHARLES-ALPHONSE DU FRESNOY. Du Fresnoy, who had worked as a painter in Rome from 1633 to 1654, opened his poem with the declaration: 'Ut pictura poesis erit; similisque poesi/sit pictura ...' ('As a painting so a poem will be, and likewise let a painting be as poetry'). Despite echoes of Dolce's *Aretino*, the rest of the poem presents a theory of painting that makes few references to literature. But the opening lines prompted critics and translators to more expansive treatments of the topic: in his commentary on the poem published in 1668, Roger de Piles provided a brief review of the literature comparing the two arts, and John Dryden's English translation of 1695 was prefaced with an essay containing 'A parallel betwixt painting and poetry', a comparison that he had already elaborated in a number of poems, including his ode *To Sir Godfrey Kneller* (1694). The *De arte graphica* influenced both poetry and painting in the 18th century, and the new English translation of 1783 was annotated by Sir Joshua Reynolds, who was of the opinion that 'Poetry addresses itself to the same faculties and the same dispositions as Painting, though by different means' (*Discourses* XIII.172–3).

The Abbé Jean-Baptiste Dubos, in the *Réflexions critiques sur la poésie et sur la peinture* (1719), argued that painting has a greater impact than poetry, on account not only of its appeal to the sight, but of its employment of natural rather than artificial signs. This distinction, later elaborated by James Harris in 1744, suggested that painted figures have, through resemblance, a natural relation to their subject, while words are merely symbols, intelligible only as the result of tacit agreement among language-users. As Harris observed: 'Poetry is forced to pass through the medium of compact, while painting applies immediately through the medium of nature' (*Three Treatises*, p. 77).

The enumeration of the differences between the sister arts prepared the way for a direct attack on the notion of *ut pictura poesis*. Gotthold Ephraim Lessing's *Laokoon* (1766) is an extended polemic on the confusion of the visual arts with poetry. According to Lessing, painting and poetry operate in different dimensions, employ incommensurable means and have distinct subject-matters. Painting extends through space and uses form and colour to depict material entities; poetry extends through time and uses articulated sounds to represent sequential action and abstract ideas.

4. 19TH AND 20TH CENTURIES. Lessing adhered to the tradition that art was essentially imitative. The Romantics thought of the arts in terms of expression rather than imitation, and in the middle years of the 19th century John Ruskin reformulated the concept of *ut pictura poesis* accordingly: 'Painting is properly to be opposed to *speaking* or *writing* but not to poetry. Both painting and speaking

are methods of expression. Poetry is the employment of either for the noblest purposes' (*Modern Painters*, v, p. 31). But despite the interaction between the arts in the 19th century, the *ut pictura poesis* motif ceased to be of central importance. Painters no longer needed to align themselves with poets to enhance their professional status for the academies had achieved that goal, and the new paradigm of genius emphasized spontaneity rather than learning.

In the 20th century, the development of SEMIOTICS reawakened interest in the kinship of painting and poetry. The distinction between natural and artificial signs was reformulated in terms of the iconic and the symbolic, but with a new emphasis on the role of convention in the formation of visual imagery. The critical strategies derived from semiotics and STRUCTURALISM can be employed with reference to any signifying practice, and the *ut pictura poesis* theme gained fresh currency among critics who wished to apply to the visual arts techniques first used in literary criticism.

BIBLIOGRAPHY

L. Dolce: *Dialogo della pittura intitolato l'Aretino* (Venice, 1557)
G. P. Lomazzo: *Trattato dell'arte de la pittura* (Milan, 1584)
C.-A. Du Fresnoy: *De arte graphica* (Paris, 1668; Eng. trans. with a preface by J. Dryden, London, 1695; Eng. trans. by W. Mason with notes by Sir J. Reynolds, Dublin, 1783)
J.-B. Dubos: *Réflexions critiques sur la poésie et sur la peinture*, 3 vols (Paris, 1719)
J. Harris: *Three Treatises* (London, 1744)
G. E. Lessing: *Laokoon* (Berlin, 1766; Eng. trans., New York, 1962)
J. Ruskin: *Modern Painters*, v (London, 1860)
J. P. Richter, ed.: *The Literary Works of Leonardo da Vinci*, 2 vols (London, 1883, 2/1939)
W. G. Howard: '*Ut pictura poesis*', *Pubns Mod. Lang. Assoc*, xxiv (1909), pp. 40–123
J. H. Hagstrum: *The Sister Arts* (Chicago, 1958)
R. G. Saisselin: '*Ut pictura poesis*: Dubos to Diderot', *J. Aesth. & A. Crit.*, xx (1961), pp. 145–56
R. W. Lee: '*Ut pictura poesis*': *The Humanist Theory of Painting* (New York, 1967)
N. Goodman: *Languages of Art* (New York, 1968)
M. W. Roskill: *Dolce's 'Aretino' and Venetian Art Theory of the Cinquecento* (New York, 1968) [contains text and trans. of the *Aretino*]
R. Park: '*Ut pictura poesis*: The Nineteenth-century Aftermath', *J. Aesth. & A. Crit.*, xxviii (1969), pp. 155–69
G. P. Landow: *The Aesthetic and Critical Theories of John Ruskin* (Princeton, 1971)
S. Alpers and P. Alpers: '*Ut pictura poesis*? Criticism in Literary Studies and Art History', *New Lit. Hist.*, iii (1972), pp. 437–58
C. Grayson, ed.: *Leon Battista Alberti on Painting and on Sculpture* (London, 1972)
N. Schweizer: *The 'Ut pictura poesis' Controversy in Eighteenth-century England and Germany* (Frankfurt, 1972)
W. Trimpi: 'The Meaning of Horace's *ut pictura poesis*', *J. Warb. & Court. Inst.*, xxxvi (1973), pp. 1–34
W. Steiner: *The Colors of Rhetoric* (Chicago, 1982)
R. Wendorf, ed.: *Articulate Images: The Sister Arts from Hogarth to Tennyson* (Minneapolis, 1983) [contains 'A checklist of modern scholarship on the sister arts']
D. Wellbery: *Lessing's 'Laocoon': Semiotics and the Age of Reason* (Cambridge, 1984)
W. J. T. Mitchell: *Iconology: Image, Text, Ideology* (Chicago, 1986)

MALCOLM BULL

Utrecht. City in the Netherlands at the confluence of the rivers Rhine and Vecht.

1. History and urban development. 2. Art life and organization.

1. HISTORY AND URBAN DEVELOPMENT. Utrecht was originally founded as a Roman *limes* fort in AD 47. Remains of the tufa outer wall of its last phase (*c.* 200–75)

are still extant. Excavations in and around the *castellum* have shown continuous occupation during the Frankish and early Merovingian periods. The first church, dedicated to St Martin, was burnt by the Frisians *c.* 650. In 695 St Willibrord settled inside the remains of the *castellum* and built a double cathedral, with separate buildings dedicated to St Martin (later Utrecht Cathedral) and St Salvator (later the Oud Munster). The Merovingian kings gave the *castellum* and its surroundings to Willibrord and his successors, and after the Viking invasions the power of the bishops of Utrecht grew through generous gifts of lands and rights by the emperors from the 10th to the 12th century. During the same period a trading settlement, called Stathe, grew beside the River Rhine north-west of the episcopal settlement. Because the westward course of the Rhine had silted up *c.* 1000 AD, Stathe was connected to the River Vecht by a canal that is now the northern part of the Oude Gracht (Old Canal).

Bishop Bernold (*reg* 1027–54) devised a so-called cross of churches with the cathedral of St Martin as its centre. These churches were dedicated to St John, St Peter, St Paul and St Mary, the saints of the four great basilicas of Rome. The St Pauluskerk was a Benedictine abbey, but the others were collegiate churches within large closes that were exempt from both civil jurisdiction and parochial control. The first three, built of tufa, were nearly completed during Bernold's episcopate, and the St Janskerk and the St Pieterskerk are still largely extant: they are columnar basilicas with the choir elevated over a crypt, and transepts with eastern chapels. The nave of the St Pieterskerk retains its monolithic red sandstone columns with block capitals, and its crypt, in which Bernold was buried, has grooved columns of yellow sandstone. The crypt of the St Janskerk was demolished after a fire in the late 13th century, and the nave, transepts and crossing were roofed with a painted wooden barrel vault, parts of which were revealed during restoration. Both churches originally had twin western towers, the St Pieterskerk with an internal gallery, the St Janskerk with a western apse. They now have late 17th-century gables. During the early 14th century the choir of the St Pieterskerk was remodelled, with a new south chapel, in which parts of a rectilinear mosaic tile floor of a common Utrecht type survive. Four 12th-century relief slabs carved in Mosan style with scenes of the *Crucifixion* and *Resurrection* have been placed at either side of the choir steps. A late 13th-century brick coffin, found, like the slabs, during restoration, is painted inside with figures of saints and of the deacon, who was buried in the coffin. A similar painting of the *Crucifixion* with a canon, dating from 1563, is *in situ* on the wall of a burial vault in the St Janskerk, where the choir was rebuilt in the 16th century. The Mariakerk, which was built between 1080 and 1160 to a design initially inspired by Speyer Cathedral but also showing some Italian influence, is well known from drawings by Pieter Saenredam; only part of its cloister has survived.

Utrecht received its charter in 1122. The east and west edges of the city were determined by the collegiate closes, while to the north a riverine settlement was incorporated, the River Vecht serving as the city moat. There was a similar arrangement to the south. Two straight canals were dug between the northern and southern parts of the Vecht, lined inside by an earthen rampart and a short stretch of tufa wall. Square towers, also of tufa, gave added defence, but during the 13th century a brick wall, with circular towers, was built. There were four gates, the east and west ones spanning an old land route, the north and south ones alongside the Oude Gracht overlooking the river. With an area of *c.* 140 ha enclosed, major extensions outside the walls were not necessary until the 19th century.

Before 1127 a canal had been dug between Stathe and the southern part of the Vecht, incorporating a part of the River Rhine in the south, which was silted up. During the 13th and 14th centuries cellars with brick barrel vaults were built between the houses alongside the canal and its waterfront, the public road running over them. An open space called 'wharf' lay between the cellars and the water. This arrangement survives on both sides of the Oude Gracht (see fig.) and along the late 14th-century Nieuwe Gracht (New Canal).

Between 1122 and 1173 the parishes of St Nicholas, St James and St Gertrud were separated from the old Utrecht parish of the Buurkerk (church of the Neighbours), which extended well outside the city boundaries. The St Nicolaikerk retains its twin-towered Romanesque west front. The other parish churches were completely rebuilt during the 14th and 15th centuries. The Buurkerk (see SAENREDAM, (2), figs 1 and 2) has a number of fine wall paintings of lesser-known saints dating from these centuries.

After 1122 the political power of the bishops gradually declined, while that of the leading citizens rose. The latter were often divided into factions supporting the Counts of Holland and the Counts of Guelders. During the second

Utrecht, view of the Oude Gracht with wharfs and cellars in the foreground and the Oudaen 'town-castle' (built *c.* 1276) in the background

half of the 13th century the citizens built large brick houses along the Oude Gracht, known from their crenellated exteriors as 'town-castles'. This type of house hardly occurs in the northern Netherlands outside Utrecht. It is highly unlikely that they were really meant to be defensible; rather, their function was probably just to look imposing. The ground floors of the town-castles are up to 7 m high. In the early 14th century power passed to the aldermen of the craft guilds. From then most of the houses and churches were built of brick, of which enormous amounts were fired on the banks of the rivers and canals near the city. There was also another flourishing ceramics industry producing—partly for export—roof- and floor-tiles and household pottery along the River Vecht to the north of Utrecht.

In 1251 fire destroyed part of the 11th-century cathedral. Rebuilding started after 1288, but a plan had already been made in 1254 (see NETHERLANDS, THE, §II, 2(ii) (a)). The choir is heavily influenced by French Rayonnant churches. About 1315 the transepts were reached, but not built. Between 1321 and 1381 a single tower 112 m high (see GOTHIC, fig. 21) was erected to the west of the old Romanesque nave. The Gothic transepts and the nave were built during the 15th century and early 16th, but the nave collapsed during the storm of 1674 and was never rebuilt.

In 1528 the Bishop of Utrecht lost his temporal power to Emperor Charles V, who built a mighty citadel, the Vredenburg (for illustration see KELDERMANS, (4)), to keep the townspeople under control, while the aldermen lost their powers to the central Habsburg administration. In 1579 Utrecht joined the rebellious Dutch provinces against Philip II. The subsequent adoption of the Reformation led to the suppression, and, in some cases, demolition, of the more than 20 monasteries and other religious houses. Some monastic buildings survived because they were used for other purposes: for example the convent of the Knights Hospitaller remained the city (and after 1636 also the university) hospital until the early 19th century. Its church (now the Catholic cathedral), main building and magnificent cloisters date from the late 15th century and the first half of the 16th.

New streets and houses were built on the monastic and collegiate closes. A number of fine, large, mid-17th-century houses survive, as well as rows of almshouses, which were built along the street and not around courtyards, as in Holland. As the United Provinces did not have a strong central administration, the city council regained more power but lost it after 1674, when the Prince of Orange as Stadholder retained the nomination of the most important city officers. Ambitious plans to enlarge the city in the mid-17th century did not materialize owing to economic decline, which lasted into the 19th century. The Maliebaan was built outside the city in 1636 for the convenience of the university students. During the second quarter of the 19th century the medieval town defences were torn down and replaced by a 'green belt' along the southern and eastern side of the city, designed by J. D. Zocher the younger.

The development of the railways in the third quarter of the 19th century brought increased prosperity, and Utrecht expanded outside its medieval limits. At first this was rather haphazard, but later more systematic urban planning was introduced. The most famous single building in the Utrecht suburbs is the Schröder House (*see* MODERN MOVEMENT, fig. 2), built in 1924 by Gerrit Rietveld. It is the purest architectural example of De Stijl.

After World War II three large, planned parts of Utrecht were built: Kanaleneiland, Overvecht and Lunetten. Plans for large-scale through roads and the filling-in of the city moat were only partly realized. Huge office and residential blocks were built around the Central Station, with a covered shopping precinct (Hoog Catharijne) that partly overflows into the old city. The north-west of the inner city was almost entirely redeveloped, but the rest retains its medieval structure and old buildings. In the mid-1990s Utrecht was the fourth largest town in the Netherlands, with *c.* 235,000 inhabitants. Although heavy industry (e.g. steel) was no longer important, there was a great variety of light industry.

BIBLIOGRAPHY

E. J. Haslinghuis: *De gemeente Utrecht* (1956), i of *De provincie Utrecht*, Ned. Mnmt. Gesch. & Kst (The Hague, 1956–)

E. J. Haslinghuis and C. J. A. C. Peeters: *De dom van Utrecht*, Ned. Mnmt. Gesch. & Kst (The Hague, 1965)

R. Blijstra: *2000 jaar Utrecht: Stedebouwkundige ontwikkeling van castrum tot centrum* (Utrecht, 1969)

J. E. A. L. Struick: *Utrecht door de eeuwen heen* (Utrecht, 1971)

A. Becker-Jordens and R. de Vries: *Wandelingen van Jan David Zocher in Utrecht, 1829–1861*, Gemeentelijke Archiefdienst (Utrecht, 1973)

E. Taverne: 'In't land van belofte: In de nieuwe stad': Ideaal en werkelijkheid van de stadsuitleg in de Republiek, 1580–1680* (Maarssen, 1978)

E. Cremers, F. Kaay and C. M. Steenbergen: *Bolwerken als stadsparken: Nederlandse stadswandelingen in de 19e en 20e eeuw* (Delft, 1981)

L. C. van der Vlerk: *Utrecht ommuurd: De stedelijke verdedigingswerken van Utrecht* (Vianen, 1983)

T. J. Hoekstra: 'Vredenburg Castle: Medieval Castle or Modern Fortress?', *Archéologie des temps modernes: Actes du colloque international de Liège: Liège, 1985*, pp. 53–93

M. Dolfin, E. M. Kylstra and J. Penders: *Utrechtse: De huizen binnen de Singels*, Ned. Mnmt. Gesch. & Kst (The Hague, 1988)

T. J. Hoekstra: 'The Early Topography of Utrecht and its Cross of Churches', *J. Brit. Archaeol. Assoc.*, cxli (1988), pp. 1–34

K. Jacobs and L. Smit, eds: *De ideale stad: Ideaalplannen voor de stad Utrecht, 1644–1988* (Utrecht, 1988)

J. de Meyere: *Utrecht op schilderijen: Zes eeuwen topographische voorstellingen van de stad Utrecht* (Utrecht, 1988)

A. J. J. Mekking, ed.: *Utrecht: Kruispunt van de middeleeuwse kerk* (Zutphen, 1988), pp. 13–54, 95–108 [articles by J. M. van Winter, A. J. J. Mekking and T. J. Hoekstra]

C. L. Temminck Groll: *De romaanse kerken van Utrecht* (Utrecht, 1988) [with Eng. summary and captions]

L. R. P. Ozinga and others, eds: *Het romeinse castellum te Utrecht: De opgravingen in 1936, 1938, 1943/44 en 1949* (Utrecht, 1989)

M. Donkersloot-de Vrij: *Kaarten van Utrecht: Topographische en thematische kartografie van de stad in vijf eeuwen* (Utrecht, 1989)

B. van Santen: *Architectuur en stedebouw in de gemeente Utrecht, 1850–1940* (Zwolle, 1990)

M. W. J. de Bruijn: *Husinge en de hofstede: Een institutioneel-geografische studie over de rechtspraak over onroerend goed in de stad Utrecht in de middeleeuwen*, Stichtse historische reeks, 18 (Zutphen, 1994)

H. L. de Groot: 'De Heilig Kruiskapel te Utrecht: Die Tatsachen bleiben, die Interpretation schwankt', *Kon. Ned. Oudhdknd. Bond: Bull. KNOB*, xciii (1994), pp. 135–48

TARQ HOEKSTRA

2. ART LIFE AND ORGANIZATION. As an episcopal see, Utrecht was an important centre for architecture and sculpture as well as painting and crafts. The earliest surviving examples of Utrecht school painting date from the 14th century (e.g. the anonymous *Calvary of Hendrik van Rijn, c.* 1363; Antwerp, Kon. Mus. S. Kst.), and towards the middle of that century the first painters

appeared in the records of the Saddlers' Guild. By 1448 the city had a Brotherhood of St Luke, with an altar in the chapel of the Dominican friary. In the 15th century Utrecht became a centre for the production of illuminated manuscripts. The principal workshop was that of the Master of Zweder van Culemborg. During the 16th century the workshop of Jan van Scorel became particularly influential, and his pupil Anthonis Mor was one of the leading portrait painters of his time.

In 1611 the city's painters and sculptors demanded an organization independent of the Saddlers' Guild. This led to the foundation of the Guild of St Luke, which, apart from painters, included framemakers, art dealers and wood-carvers. Within 30 years of the Guild's foundation, painting in Utrecht flourished as never before or since. Such artists as Abraham Bloemaert, Joachim Wtewael, Paulus Moreelse, Roelandt Savery, Hendrick ter Brugghen, Gerrit van Honthorst and Cornelis van Poelenburch turned the city into an artistic centre of international importance (*see also* UTRECHT CARAVAGGISTI). After founding the Guild, the most prominent of these artists established a drawing school, which, in imitation of the Accademia in Rome, is occasionally referred to in the sources as 'akademie'. It is not known how long this school continued to exist.

In 1639 the painters decided to dissociate themselves from the sculptors and wood-carvers, and in 1644 the new College of Painters received its statutes. Although the College existed until 1815, it underwent considerable changes. Until 1717 it had the character of a guild; it then became a society for the encouragement of the arts, allowing in amateurs, but with a maximum membership of 25. The College played an important role in art education in Utrecht. From at least 1696, with one or two short interruptions, it once again governed a drawing school, the Tekenacademie, where artists drew from life, including nude models. After 1750 drawing classes were also offered by two of the city's orphanages: from 1761 to 1863 orphans were trained as painters and sculptors at the Renswoude Foundation, and between 1769 and 1863 the Dutch Reformed Civic Orphanage (Gereformeerd Burgerweeshuis) provided art education for apprentices.

In 1807 the College of Painters was succeeded as the main artists' organization by a society, later named Kunstliefde (Love of Art), founded by Pieter Christoffel Wonder and Jan Kobell the younger. The society included artists and connoisseurs and is still the most important artists' organization in Utrecht. Kunstliefde took over both its predecessor's premises and its art collection, and from the beginning the society provided drawing classes, including life drawing. With donations from the members, the society built up a collection of paintings by local masters. In 1873 this collection, together with the city's own collection, part of which had previously belonged to the College of Painters, was housed in the Kunstliefde Museum. After its closure in 1920, the core of the collection went to the Centraal Museum (where the best survey of the history of Utrecht painting is still to be seen).

Since the 19th century Utrecht has produced only two artists of more than national importance: Gerrit Rietveld and the painter Pyke Koch. After World War II art education in Utrecht was taken over by the art academy Artibus, now the Hogeschool voor de Kunsten.

BIBLIOGRAPHY

S. Muller: *De Utrechtsche archieven: Schildersvereenigingen te Utrecht* [The Utrecht archives: painters' societies in Utrecht] (Utrecht, 1880)

D. P. R. A. Bouvy: *Middeleeuwsche beeldhouwkunst in de Noordelijke Nederlanden* (diss., U. Amsterdam, 1947)

J. W. C. van Campen: *Het genootschap Kunstliefde, 1807–1947* [The Kunstliefde society, 1807–1947] (Utrecht, 1947)

C. H. de Jonge: *Centraal Museum Utrecht: Catalogus der schilderijen* (Utrecht, 1952)

J. Juffermans: *Met stille trom: Beeldende kunst in Utrecht sinds 1900* [With silent trumpet: visual art in Utrecht from 1900] (Utrecht, 1976)

J. A. L. de Meyere: 'Utrechtse schilderkunst in de tweede helft van de 16de eeuw', *Jb. Oud-Utrecht* (1978), pp. 106–91

L. van Tilborgh and A. Hoogenboom: *Tekenen destijds: Utrechts tekenonderwijs in de 18e and 19e eeuw* [Drawing in the past: the teaching of drawing in Utrecht during the 18th and 19th centuries] (Utrecht and Antwerp, 1982)

The Golden Age of Dutch Manuscript Painting (exh. cat., intro. J. Marrow; New York, Pierpont Morgan Lib.; Utrecht, Catharijneconvent; 1989–90)

M. Langenbach: *Onbekend talent: Leerlingen van de Utrechtse Fundatie van Renswoude* (Zutphen, 1991)

M. J. Bok: *Vraag en aanbod op de Nederlandse Kunstmarkt, 1580–1700* [Supply and demand in the Dutch art market, 1580–1700] (diss., U. Utrecht, 1994), pp. 165–202

MARTEN JAN BOK

Utrecht, Adriaen van (*b* Antwerp, 12 Jan 1599; *d* Antwerp, 1652). Flemish painter. He was apprenticed to Herman de Ryt in 1614 and later visited France, Italy and Germany before returning to Antwerp by 1625. He painted pantry scenes, farmyards with poultry, fish markets, game pieces, garlands and diverse still-lifes of fruit and vegetables. Game paintings are most frequent and reflect the influence of Frans Snyders. Adriaen adopted the same abundant displays of game, fruit and vegetables, usually set on a table parallel to the picture plane. Compositions typically fall in horizontal and vertical lines in contrast to the dynamic diagonals of Snyders. In large works, such as the *Still-life with Game, Vegetables, Fruit and a Cockatoo* (1650; Malibu, CA, Getty Mus.), Adriaen's accessories overflow the table on to the floor below. Baroque devices, such as a sweeping curtain and background window view, add movement and depth. Van Utrecht favoured warm earthen tones, especially grey-green, and a strong chiaroscuro light in his still-lifes; the latter may derive from his knowledge of Italian painting. The artist's style changed little during his career, save for the gradual elimination of figures in his paintings. The influence of Jan de Heem and Jan Fyt can also be seen in his later work. Van Utrecht is known to have collaborated with Jacob Jordaens, Thomas Willeboirts Bosschaert (1613/14–54) and Erasmus Quellinus (ii).

BIBLIOGRAPHY

E. Greindl: *Les Peintres flamands de nature morte au XVIIe siècle* (Brussels, 1956, rev. 2/1983), pp. 90–93, 315–20

SCOTT A. SULLIVAN

Utrecht, Jacob (Claesz.) van. *See* JACOB VAN UTRECHT.

Utrecht Caravaggisti. Group of painters from Utrecht who travelled to Rome at the beginning of the 17th century and were profoundly influenced by the work of Caravaggio. On their return to the northern Netherlands, they developed these new artistic ideas into a style known as Utrecht Caravaggism. This trend had a short-lived but intense development that lasted from 1620 to 1630. The first generation and initiators were Hendrick ter Brugghen, Gerrit van Honthorst and Dirck van Baburen, who introduced Caravaggism into Utrecht painting *c.* 1620 with immediate success. Such older painters as Abraham Bloemaert, Paulus Moreelse and even the Mannerist Joachim Wtewael were affected.

The Utrecht Caravaggisti painted predominantly history scenes and genre pieces. These are life-size paintings with economical and powerful compositions; the impact of the scene is heightened by contrasting areas of light and dark, and a small number of figures who are abruptly cropped so that they seem to be portrayed in close-up.

Utrecht Caravaggism marked a break with the artificiality and fantasy of Mannerism. The Caravaggisti strove for realism. Through a life-size and lifelike presentation of figures, they stripped away the then customary elevation and detachment in painting's themes. This is most noticeable in religious subjects, where saints are often shown as ordinary types. Ter Brugghen and van Baburen were the most daring and expressive of the Utrecht Caravaggisti, both in choice of subject and spontaneity of technique. Other Caravaggisti, such as van Honthorst, Jan van Bijlert and Hendrick Bloemaert, had a more restrained style. Several themes were introduced into Dutch painting or revived by the Utrecht Caravaggisti, for example St Sebastian, the Calling of St Matthew or Heraclitus and Democritus. The genre scenes show a preference for half-length figure pieces with shepherds and shepherdesses, procuresses or merry companies.

Utrecht Caravaggism came to an end after the deaths of van Baburen and ter Brugghen in 1624 and 1629 respectively; van Honthorst had by then already turned more towards international Classicism, followed by, among others, Abraham Bloemaert and van Bijlert. Although Caravaggism ceased to predominate in Utrecht thereafter, painters continued to work in the style, as is evident in the paintings of Paulus Bor, Gerard van Kuijll (1604–73), Lumen Portengen (1608–49), Johan Baeck (*d* 1654/5) and Jan Gerritsz. van Bronchorst. Even in the 1650s such Utrecht painters as Johan de Veer (*c.* 1610–62) and Johannes Jansz. van Bronchorst were inspired by it.

Utrecht Caravaggism had an important influence on Dutch painting. Frans Hals, Jan Lievens and Rembrandt, among others, adopted various features of the style. Other painters in Amsterdam, Haarlem and Delft were also influenced; the early work of Johannes Vermeer, from the 1650s, was inspired by Utrecht Caravaggism. The style was thus more than a merely local phenomenon; it laid the groundwork for later developments of the 17th century.

BIBLIOGRAPHY

A. von Schneider: *Caravaggio und die Niederländer* (Marburg, 1933/R Amsterdam, 1967)

Caravaggio en de Nederlanden (exh. cat., Utrecht, Cent. Mus.; Antwerp, Kon. Mus. S. Kst.; 1952)

Nieuw Licht op de Gouden Eeuw: Hendrick ter Brugghen en tijdgenoten (exh. cat., ed. A. Blankert and L. J. Slatkes; Utrecht, Cent. Mus.; Brunswick, Herzog Anton Ulrich-Mus.; 1986–7)

Hendrick ter Brugghen und die Nachfolger Caravaggios in Holland: Braunschweig, 1987

PAUL HUYS JANSSEN

Utrecht Psalter. Illustrated manuscript (Utrecht, Bib. Rijksuniv., MS. 32) made between AD 816 and 834 at the Benedictine abbey of Hautvillers (Altumvillare) in the diocese of Reims, then held by Archbishop EBBO. It is one of the finest examples of Carolingian art. The early history of the manuscript is unknown, but several ivory carvings made between *c.* 850 and 870 for Emperor Charles the Bald are dependent on its illustrations (Zurich, Schweizer. Landesmus., AG.1311 and LM.21825; Paris, Bib. N., MS. lat. 1152; Rome, Vatican, Throne of St Peter). Three surviving 'copies' witness the manuscript's presence at Christ Church, Canterbury, from *c.* 1000 onwards (*c.* 1000, London, BL, Harley MS. 603; *c.* 1150, Cambridge, Trinity Coll., MS. R.17.1; *c.* 1200, Paris, Bib. N., MS. lat. 8846). After the Dissolution of the monasteries in the 1530s, the manuscript passed into private hands and eventually into the library of Sir Robert Cotton (1571–1631). Loaned to Thomas Howard (1585–1646), 2nd Earl of Arundel, it was brought to the Netherlands and, under obscure circumstances, came into the possession of Willem de Ridder, who in 1716 gave it to the University Library at Utrecht.

The manuscript contains the 150 psalms according to St Jerome's 'Gallican' version, 15 canticles and credos and the apocryphal psalm. It consists of 92 parchment folios in 11 (quaternion) gatherings, preceded by a single leaf and followed by one bifolium and one single leaf. The folios were cut to between 328–32×254–9 mm when the manuscript was rebound for Sir Robert Cotton, at which point 4 blank leaves and 12 leaves of a fragmentary 8th-century Hiberno-Saxon Evangeliary were added. The text is arranged on the pages in three columns of rustic capitals in brown ink. Headings and the initial letters of the verses are executed in red uncial script, while the first letter of each psalm is a square capital with the following first line written in uncial. Gold ink, now faded, was used in the first gathering for these initial lines, the rest being written in brown ink. Only Psalm 1 has a decorated initial. Each psalm, canticle or credo is preceded by pen drawings in brown ink, 166 in all, executed by several artists. The hands usually change with or after a decimal psalm number, such as psalms 11 (12), 30 (31), 51 (52), 60 (61), 70 (71), 81 (82), 101 (102), 121 (122), and with the canticle of Isaiah (van der Horst and Gaehde).

The fame of the Utrecht Psalter rests on this extensive sequence of spirited drawings, which, with layout and script, seem designed to recall Christian antiquity. They translate the poetical text of the psalms into pictorial compositions in three different ways. Some present narrative scenes of biblical events mentioned either in the headings of psalms or called forth by analogies between Psalter and Old Testament passages, as in the illustration to Psalm 105 (106):7–11 (fol. 61*v*), showing the Egyptian host drowning in the Red Sea. A few others give typological images, which are evoked either by Psalter citations and paraphrases in the New Testament, by their use in liturgy, or by exegetical commentaries; one such is the illustration to Psalm 115 (116): 13–15, representing the martyrdom

Utrecht Psalter, illustration to the opening of Psalm 11, red and brown ink on parchment, *c.* 145×247 mm, AD 816–34 (Utrecht, Bibliotheek der Rijksuniversiteit, MS. 32, fol. 6*v*)

of saints and the Crucifixion, with the psalmist holding a chalice and paten. However, the most common form of illustration is literal, where words and phrases are realized by an image. Thus, for Psalm 11 (12):5 ('For the oppression of the poor, for the sighing of the needy, now will I arise, saith the Lord . . .'), the Lord is shown stepping from his throne to hand a lance to an angel while the oppressed and needy rise to witness the event (see fig.). Verses 2 and 3 are represented by the angel below ramming the end of the lance into the mouth of the first of a group of men: 'They speak vanity every one with his neighbour: with flattering lips and with a double heart do they speak. The Lord shall cut off all flattering lips, and the tongue that speaketh proud things'. A representation of a smithy in the upper right depicts verse 6: 'The words of the Lord are pure words: as silver tried in a furnace of earth, purified seven times.' Below, to the left and centre, 'The wicked walk on every side [in circuitu] . . .', as described in verse 8.

The Utrecht Psalter is not unique in the use of such 'literal' illustrations. Although rarer than other methods, their use occurs also in Byzantine Psalters and in the Carolingian Stuttgart Psalter (Stuttgart, Württemberg. Landesbib., MS. bibl. fol. 23). It follows that most of the drawings must be indebted to a model or models that brought this, the oldest tradition of Psalter illustration, to Hautvillers (Mütherich). The verve, dexterity and seeming spontaneity of the style on the other hand have the unmistakable distinction of an original creation.

This apparent contradiction is reflected in the differing opinions as to whether and to what extent the drawings are copies. Among the many hypotheses advanced over the past 100 years or so, Tikkanen, Wormald, Engelbrecht and van der Horst argued that the drawings, although eclectic and indebted to earlier pictorial sources, are largely Carolingian creations. Others saw the drawings as copies from an earlier manuscript. In 1967 Tselos postulated a source in an 8th-century Greco-Italian Psalter that transmitted a late 4th- or early 5th-century archetype to northern Europe. On the strength of iconographic comparisons between all the images of the Utrecht Psalter and 14 other Psalters as well, Dufrenne suggested that a 4th- to 5th-century Psalter with painted miniatures had come into the hands of the Carolingian illuminators, but that they are nonetheless to be credited with additions derived from other pictorial sources and, above all, with the transformation of the putative model's Late Antique illusionistic style into the vibrant, expressive and highly wrought illustrations that distinguish both this work and the Ebbo Gospels (Epernay, Bib. Mun., MS. 1).

BIBLIOGRAPHY

J. J. Tikkanen: *Die Psalterillustration im Mittelalter* (Helsinki, 1895–1900/R Soest, 1975)
E. T. DeWald: *The Illustrations of the Utrecht Psalter* (Princeton, [1932])
F. Wormald: *The Utrecht Psalter* (Utrecht, 1953)
D. T. Tselos: *The Sources of the Utrecht Psalter Miniatures* (Minneapolis, 1955)
J. H. A. Engelbrecht: *Het Utrechts Psalterium: Een eeuw wetenschappelijke bestudering (1860–1960)* (Utrecht, 1965) [Eng. summary]
D. T. Tselos: 'Defensive Addenda to the Problem of the Utrecht Psalter', *A. Bull.*, xlix (1967), pp. 334–49
F. Mütherich: 'Die verschiedenen Bedeutungsschichten in der frühmittelalterlichen Psalterillustration', *Frühmittelalt. Stud.*, vi (1972), pp. 232–44

S. Dufrenne: *Les Illustrations du Psautier d'Utrecht: Sources et apport carolingien* (Paris, 1978)
——: *Tableaux synoptiques de quinze psautiers médiévaux à illustrations intégrales issues du texte* (Paris, 1978)
K. van der Horst and J. H. A. Engelbregt, eds: *Utrecht-Psalter: Vollständige Faksimile-Ausgabe im Originalformat der Handschrift 32 aus dem Besitz der Bibliotheek der Rijksuniversiteit te Utrecht*, Codices Selecti, lxxv (Graz, 1984)
J. E. Gaehde: 'The Draughtsmen of the Utrecht Psalter', *Studien zur mittelalterlichen Kunst, 800–1250: Festschrift für Florentine Mütherich* (Munich, 1985), pp. 49–52

JOACHIM E. GAEHDE

Utrechtsche Machinale Stoel- en Meubelfabriek. *See* UMS.

Utriainen, Raimo (Arvi Johannes) (*b* Kuopio, 24 Sept 1927; *d* 27 April 1994). Finnish sculptor. He attended the Turku Art Association School of Drawing in 1947, the Central School of Industrial Design, Helsinki, in 1948–9, the architecture department of the Technical Institute, Helsinki, between 1949 and 1953, and the School of the Academy of Fine Arts, Helsinki, from 1953 to 1956. His first large public sculpture, *Winter Navigation Memorial* (erected 1961; Turku, shore of River Aura), tends towards abstraction but clearly shows two men and a ship struggling against the frozen ice. *Newspaper Boy* (erected 1961; Kuopio) is similar in style. The abstract sculpture (1963) on the façade of the Scout Centre in Tel Aviv climbs straight and steadily up the wall and creates impenetrable shadows.

At the end of the 1960s Utriainen began a period of experimental constructivism, as can be seen in the imposing memorial to the actress *Ida Aalberg* (1960–72; Helsinki, Kaisaniemi Park) and the mechanically operated composition *Cosmos* (erected 1965–7; Tampere, Business Sch.), for which Utriainen used industrial parts and which he constructed on site. He described the correlation between water and dynamic motion in the steel fountain memorial to *Emil Aaltonen* (1966–9; Tampere, Tammela Park Street), which also reveals the artist's interest in architecture and mathematics. Utriainen also made use of transparent materials and his style became closer and closer to that of sculptors Naum Gabo and Antoine Pevsner. His passion for transparent effects was refined and developed in the kinetic lyricism of his aluminium strip compositions of the 1970s, of which the first notable example is the outdoor sculpture *Vogue* (erected 1974; Helsinki, State Alcohol Monopoly). The aluminium strip sculptures established Utriainen's reputation, and he held important one-man exhibitions in Finland in 1974, 1976 and 1980, as well as in Japan in 1982, where he produced *Ascending*, the central sculpture of the outdoor sculpture museum at Sapporo, in 1986.

BIBLIOGRAPHY

L. Ahtola-Moorhouse: 'Review of Finnish Sculpture 1910–80', *Suomalaista veistotaidetta/Finnish Sculpture* (Porvoo, 1980)
J. Pallasmaa: 'Raimo Utriainen—Builder of Form and Movement', *Sculptor Raimo Utriainen, Artist of the Year* (exh. cat., Helsinki, A. Exh. Hall, 1980), pp. 7–24
——: 'The Roots of Raimo Utriainen's Art', *Sculptor Raimo Utriainen, Artist of the Year* (exh. cat., Helsinki, A. Exh. Hall, 1980), pp. 94–6

LEENA AHTOLA-MOORHOUSE

Utrillo, Maurice (*b* Paris, 26 Dec 1883; *d* Dax, 5 Nov 1955). French painter, son of SUZANNE VALADON. He was entrusted to his grandmother while his mother posed as a model for such painters as Renoir and Puvis de Chavannes before discovering her own talent for drawing and painting. His father, the Spanish painter Miguel Utrillo (1862–1934), only admitted paternity eight years after Maurice's birth. Maurice Utrillo had no predisposition for art, but when he was 19 his mother took medical advice and urged him to adopt drawing and painting as a distraction from his need for alcohol. In search of a suitable subject, he went to the countryside around Montmagny, a village to the north of Paris, where, between the autumn of 1903 and the winter of 1904, he completed almost 150 paintings, sombre, heavily impasted landscapes, such as the *Roofs of Montmagny* (Paris, Pompidou). By 1906 the doctor felt that Utrillo could return to Montmartre. His pictures of the streets and suburbs were painted with a less heavy impasto and with lighter tones. He was attracted by ordinary houses, as in the *Rue du Mont-Cenis* (see fig.) and *Berlioz's House* (both 1914; Paris, Mus. Orangerie), and suburban churches, for instance the *Church of Villiers-le-Bel* (1909; priv. col., see Pétridès, i, p. 129). These themes, associated with painters such as Daumier, Pissarro and Caillebotte, became Utrillo's chief source of inspiration, but he soon turned to a more ambitious subject, cathedrals. He was concerned with the development of an ordered composition and a flattened treatment of space that suggested the artificial appearance of a theatre set, as in *Notre-Dame* (1909; Paris, Mus. Orangerie). Particularly during World War I he also found that such subjects allowed him to project strong emotions, as in *Rheims Cathedral in Flames* (1914; Basle, priv. col., see Pétridès, i, p. 67).

From 1909 until *c.* 1914 Utrillo mixed glue, plaster or cement with his paint to obtain the whites for which he became famous. His paintings of buildings show a striking contrast between the boldness of his colour and his painstaking draughtsmanship (traces of his having used a ruler and compass are often noticeable). Carried to their logical conclusion, these experiments led him to produce austere monochrome paintings in beige and grey.

His deteriorating health and social awkwardness led him gradually to withdraw from the streets of Montmartre into the relative safety of nursing homes. Here he developed the habit of painting from postcards (see Warnod, pp. 20, 26). His mother and stepfather, the painter André Utter (1886–1948), selected cards reproducing his favourite views of La Butte Montmartre. He worked from these either in their communal studio at 12 Rue Cortot, in the restaurant La Belle Gabrièle or in a bedroom above the Père Gay bistro. He exacted his revenge on the locals who had made his life difficult with their criticisms and jokes by depicting them in his paintings in rear view, as heavily outlined clumsy shapes and stereotyped silhouettes.

Maurice Utrillo: *Rue de Mont-Cenis*, oil on board, 760×1070 mm, 1914 (Paris, Musée de l'Orangerie)

There is no hint in Utrillo's work of the vicissitudes of his life: spells in homes; a move to the Château de Saint-Bernard in the Saône in 1923 with his mother and stepfather; his marriage to Lucie Pauwels (née Valore) in 1936 and consequent establishment in an orderly bourgeois existence at Vésinet; and various visits to the country. His late paintings, such as *Old House at Aubusson* (gouache on paper, 1935; Lausanne, Pal. Rumine) and *Village Street under Snow* (*c*. 1945; Albi, Mus. Toulouse-Lautrec), are characterized by rich colours and strong black contours and are almost entirely on landscape themes. From 1937 he was looked after by his friend and dealer Paul Pétridès at the request of his family. In spite of his wretched life he maintained a prolific output with a deep vein of poetic melancholy.

After his death his critical reputation declined, although he remained popular with collectors and the public.

BIBLIOGRAPHY

A. Tabarant: *Maurice Utrillo* (Paris, 1927)
A. Werner: *Utrillo* (New York, 1955)
P. Pétridès: *L'Oeuvre complet de Maurice Utrillo*, 5 vols (Paris, 1959–74)
J. Warnod: *Maurice Utrillo. V.* (Paris, 1983)
Centenaire d'Utrillo (exh. cat., ed. J. Warnod; Tokyo, Mitsukoshi, 1985)

COLETTE GIRAUDON

Utzon, Jørn (Oberg) (*b* Copenhagen, 9 April 1918). Danish architect. He was the son of a noted yacht designer, from whom he learnt an awareness of the relationship of design to performance. During the 1940s he studied both forms in nature and Islamic and oriental architecture, in which he was particularly interested in compositions based on the ordering of standard elements. He also took a special interest in the work of Gunnar Asplund and Alvar Aalto, for whom he worked in the mid-1940s. A scholarship to the USA in 1949 put him in contact with the important and contrasting contemporary architects Frank Lloyd Wright and Ludwig Mies van der Rohe, who both influenced his future development.

Utzon's competition entries had aroused interest, but the first opportunity to realize his ideas was the construction of his own house at Hellebæk, near Elsinore, in 1951. Probably the first open-plan house in Denmark, it is a narrow, one-storey structure with one long side completely closed and the other almost entirely glazed. Two years later he designed the very different, but equally uncompromising house at Lake Furesø in Holte, Sjælland. This was constructed with a strongly emphasized post-and-lintel system of reinforced concrete elements. Also in 1953 he designed the winning project for Langelinie Pavilion, a restaurant shaped as a tower with cantilevered terraces overlooking Copenhagen harbour.

Utzon gained international recognition in 1957 with the winning entry in the Sydney Opera House competition. This realized his generation's efforts to endow large projects with greatness and individuality, freed from both the reductionism of Modernism and traditional monumentality. The building was clearly and simply divided into two main parts: a substructure (known as the podium) with service accommodation surmounted by the seating tiers of the two auditoriums and a superstructure of concrete shells forming the roofs of the stages and public areas. This creates a tension between airiness and weight,

reminiscent of the relationship between sails and a ship's hull. During the detailed planning Utzon worked with the engineer OVE ARUP. This collaboration led to the modification of Utzon's shell structures into ribbed constructions based on sections of spheres, which, without changing the overall design, gave the curved shapes a steeper profile (see fig.). Before its completion the project drew widespread international acclaim: it was thought to promise a 20th-century *Gesamtkunstwerk* analogous to the synthesis of arts in a medieval cathedral. Utzon moved to Australia in 1963 to supervise the building of the Opera House, but political pressure forced him to resign from the work in 1966, and he subsequently acknowledged only the building's exterior as his design.

By this time Utzon had already distinguished himself with several projects in Denmark. Among these were the first- and third-prize designs for the Trade Union Congress High School in Helsingør in 1958, which, like the Opera House, were designed on the podium principle. Neither design was executed, but they had a more immediate influence than the unique Opera House. In 1958–60 Utzon built the Kingo Houses in Helsingør, a model housing development of low, closely constructed dwellings. The unit in this complex is an L-shaped house, which, with a patio, forms a quadratic ground plan. The houses open inwards and are almost closed to the outside, permitting great topographical adaptability in the arrangement of the units. The architecture is robust, based on traditional materials with common yellow brickwork and stepped roofs. The layout of the development is an example of Utzon's interpretation of the 'open form' concept, uniting open-ended clusters of uniform elements. This house type and arrangement were further developed in the courtyard complex, The Terraces (1962–3), in Fredensborg, Sjælland, in this instance set around a collection of facilities, including a restaurant. In 1963 Utzon built the Melhi Bank in Tehran in collaboration with Hans Munk Hansen (*b* 1929), but an outstanding series of projects from subsequent years remained on the drawing board. These include a museum for Silkeborg (1963), conceived as an underground cave, a theatre in Zurich (1964), a town plan for the centre of Farum, Sjælland (1966) and a stadium for Jiddah, Saudi Arabia (1969).

In 1969 Utzon developed a building system based on laminated wood sections called Espansiva. It was intended for a school building at Herning, Jutland, among other projects, but this was only built in prototype. Utzon coined the term 'additive architecture' to describe the varied possibilities of construction with industrially produced components. He also worked on a furniture system based on the same concept. In Bagsværd Church (1974–6), Sjælland, he used strongly articulated elements that also formed the constructional framework of the building: a curving, freely shaped concrete ceiling is supported by double outer walls, forming skylit corridors that merge into the halls of the complex. In 1973 Utzon won the competition for the Parliament Building in Kuwait, completed in 1985. It is based on a kasbah-like structure with internal light wells and suspended roofs covering the large halls. The sculpturally formed constructional components render the building an outstanding example of additive architecture. Early in his career Utzon evolved the idea of

Jørn Utzon: exterior of the Opera House, Sydney, 1957–73

the podium as the unifying architectural element. Later came the concept of additive architecture, in which elements were conjoined to form rich and complex wholes. In both cases his philosophy led to a freer and more positive view of the potential of industrialized building methods.

WRITINGS

'Nationaloperæn i Sydney', *Arkitektur* [Copenhagen], iii (1959), pp. 201–7

'The Zurich Theatre', *Zodiac*, 14 (1965), pp. 90–93

'Additiv arkitektur: Espansiva', *Arkitektur* [Copenhagen], xiv (1970), pp. 1–48

BIBLIOGRAPHY

T. Faber: 'Konkurrencen om en højskole ved Helsingør' [Competition for a high school at Helsingør], *Arkitekten* [Copenhagen], lxi (1959), pp. 101–7

Skriver: 'Plateau og element i Utzons arbejder' [Plateau and element in Utzon's works], *Arkitektur* [Copenhagen], lxvi (1964), pp. 97–105

T. Faber: *New Danish Architecture* (Stuttgart, 1968)

J. Yeomans: *The Other Taj Mahal* (London, 1968)

P. Drew: *The Third Generation: The Changing Meaning of Architecture* (New York, 1972)

V. Smith: *The Sydney Opera House*, (London, 1974)

T. Michaelsen: *Bibliografi vedr. Jørn Utzon* [Bibliography relating to Jørn Utzon] (Copenhagen, 1979)

C. Norberg-Schultz: 'Sydney Opera House', *Global Archit.*, 54 (1980)

——: 'Church at Bagsværd, near Copenhagen', *Global Archit.*, 61 (1981)

'Hotel og kongrescenter på Langelinie', *Arkitekten* [Copenhagen], lxxxvii (1985), pp. 454–5

JORGEN SESTOFT

Uwins, Thomas (*b* London, 24 Feb 1782; *d* Staines, Middx, 26 Aug 1857). English painter and illustrator. He was apprenticed to the line-engraver Benjamin Smith (*d* 1833) in 1797, but his greater interest in portrait painting led him to take life classes at the Royal Academy, London; he exhibited portraits there from 1799. Versatile and industrious, he painted miniature likenesses, taught drawing, designed and engraved illustrations for books in French, Portuguese and English, and wrote for and illustrated Rudolph Ackermann's *Repository*. His half-a-crown watercolours, known as 'pretty faces', were particularly popular, and he found employment as an assiduous copyist. In 1809 he was elected to the Society of Painters in Water-Colours and for the next nine years exhibited careful and colourful images of the countryside that provided views of the year's harvest. In 1817 Uwins travelled to France to record the Burgundian grape harvest, identifying the labour force more obviously as peasants than their English counterparts. In debt, he moved in 1820 to Edinburgh, where he illustrated books by Walter Scott and painted portraits. In 1824, his debt paid, he left for Italy, where he spent seven years; he sent highly valued copies of Italian works back to England (to Thomas Lawrence among others) and made studies of life in and around Rome and Naples, from which his later successes at the Royal Academy derived. An immodest Protestant, Uwins deplored but revelled in the 'polluted streams' of Catholic Italy, and provided London with oils renowned for their clarity and colour. *A Neapolitan Saint Manufactory* (exh. RA 1832; Leicester, Mus. & A.G.) shows monks haggling, women gazing and children playing amid carved and painted icons. Once back in England Uwins painted further images of Italy, such as *Italian Peasants* (1850; Manchester, C.A.G.), and was also employed as Keeper of the Queen's Pictures and, from 1847, of the National Gallery, London.

BIBLIOGRAPHY
S. Uwins: *A Memoir of Thomas Uwins RA* (London, 1858/R 1978)

LEWIS JOHNSON

Uxmal. Pre-Columbian MAYA site in the Puuc region of the Northern Maya Lowlands of Yucatán, Mexico, *c.* 80 km south-west of the modern city of Mérida. It flourished *c.* AD 800–*c.* 1000, at the end of the Late Classic period (*c.* AD 600–*c.* 900) and the beginning of the Early Post-Classic period (*c.* AD 900–*c.* 1200), but was also occupied earlier. Uxmal was one of the major Puuc sites that rose to prominence at a critical juncture in the development of Maya civilization, when the great sites of the Classic period (*c.* AD 250–*c.* 900) in the Southern Maya Lowlands collapsed and the cultural and geographic focus of Lowland civilization shifted to the Northern Maya Lowlands. Uxmal appears to have been the largest Puuc site and is certainly the most famous. Major construction there ceased by the end of the 11th century AD, after which the site presumably lost much of its former importance. However, it continued to be occupied until the Spanish Conquest in the 16th century.

The Late Classic architecture at Uxmal and other Puuc sites, and in certain buildings at some sites in the Northern Maya Lowlands (e.g. CHICHÉN ITZÁ), has several distinctive characteristics. Many scholars view the Puuc style as marking the height of Pre-Columbian Maya architectural

achievement. Among the principal components of the style are an emphasis on decorated walls above the medial mouldings or cornices, repetitive stone mosaic decorations with stylized geometric or naturalistic designs, stone mosaic masks above doorways, decorated roof-combs and carefully cut stone veneer masonry. At Uxmal, many buildings with such features are well preserved or have been completely or partially restored. Among the best-known structures, the names of which are all post-Spanish Conquest attributions, are the Palace (or House) of the Governor, the Temple (or Pyramid) of the Magician (El Adivino; *see* MESOAMERICA, PRE-COLUMBIAN, fig. 16) and the Nunnery Quadrangle (see fig.).

The beautiful proportions and design of the Palace of the Governor have long been admired. According to Harry Pollock (1980, p. 242), this 'magnificent building is thought by many to be the finest example of pre-Columbian architecture in the Americas'. The palace, a multi-roomed, rectangular building (*c.* 100 m long) with a symmetrical layout, sits on a large artificial platform. Covering the upper walls is an elaborate mosaic design consisting of stepped-frets and other geometrical motifs, masks of Chac (the rain god), serpents, Maya thatched huts and human busts. Research by Kowalski in the 1980s indicated that it may have been the 10th-century residence of 'Lord Chac', one of the last and most influential rulers of Uxmal. The Temple of the Magician consists of a large, sloping oval base with a structure on top. The temple went through a series of renovations after its earliest, 6th-century phase. The four subsequent reconstructions included one in the style of Maya buildings in the Chenes region to the south, in which the façade around an opening on the west side of the temple was decorated in the form of an open serpent mouth. The Nunnery Quadrangle, which lies immediately west of the Temple of the Magician, consists of four range structures or multi-roomed buildings. These are renowned for the mosaic friezes on the upper sections of their façades, which have naturalistic and geometric motifs and Chac masks (see fig.).

Uxmal reveals a great degree of formal planning, exceeding that of both its Classic-period predecessors and its contemporaries. The architect George Andrews (1975, p. 203) has argued that at Uxmal 'the Mayas succeeded in creating a truly monumental architecture—that completely denies its dependence on nature by its insistence on conforming to abstract rules of order and form as determined by man'. It is laid out primarily along a north–south axis and includes a series of large pyramid-temples, such as the Great Pyramid in the South Group and those in the Cemetery Group and in the North Group. Near the centre of the ceremonial area lies the Terrace of the Monuments, where 16 of the 17 stelae found at Uxmal were erected. Figures and hieroglyphic texts relating to Maya history, genealogy and political events were carved on the stelae, now in various locations, including the Museo Regional de Antropología de Yucatán in Mérida. The different buildings and groups are carefully aligned with each other, the lines of sight from one structure to another playing important roles. Research carried out at the end of the 1970s and in the 1980s indicated that astronomical orientations were also significant in the planning and layout, including the alignment of the Maya site of Cehtzuc

Uxmal, Nunnery Quadrangle, before AD 1000; view from the Temple of the Magician

(*c.* 4 km south-east of Uxmal) with the front of the Palace of the Governor. Moreover, Uxmal is connected by a raised causeway to the site of KABÁH, 18 km to the south-east. A free-standing monumental arch with a corbelled vault may mark the end of the causeway at Uxmal, as does a similar arch at the end of the causeway at Kabáh.

BIBLIOGRAPHY

T. Proskouriakoff: *An Album of Maya Architecture* (Cambridge, MA, 1946, rev. Norman, OK, 2/1963)

I. Marquina: *Arquitectura prehispánica* (Mexico City, 1950, 2/1964/*R* 1981)

G. F. Andrews: *Maya Cities: Placemaking and Urbanization* (Norman, OK, 1975)

A. F. Aveni: *Skywatchers of Ancient Mexico* (Austin, 1980)

H. E. D. Pollock: 'The Puuc: An Architectural Survey of the Hill Country of Yucatán and Northern Campeche, Mexico', *Mem. Peabody Mus. Archaeol. & Ethnol.*, xix (1980) [whole issue]

J. K. Kowalski: 'Lords of the Northern Maya: Dynastic History in the Inscriptions of Uxmal and Chichén Itzá', *Expedition*, xxvii (1985), pp. 50–60

I. Sprajc: 'Cehtzuc: A New Maya Site in the Puuc Region', *Mexicon*, xii (1990), pp. 62–3

JEREMY A. SABLOFF

Uylenburgh [Uilenburg; Ulenborch; Uylenborch; Uylenburch], **Gerrit** [Gerard] (*b* Amsterdam, *c.* 1626; *d* England, 1690). Dutch dealer and painter. He was the son of Hendrick van Uylenburgh (1584/9–*c.* 1660), the painter, art dealer and patron of Rembrandt, and a cousin of Saskia van Uylenburgh, Rembrandt's wife. Gerrit was himself a pupil of Rembrandt *c.* 1640. On 5 March 1660 Uylenburgh married Elisabeth Just from Königsberg (now Kaliningrad). As an art dealer, he had an international clientele and such painters as Gérard de Lairesse worked as copyists at his premises. In 1671 Uylenburgh was the subject of a scandal: he supplied 13 paintings to Frederick William, Elector of Brandenburg, 11 of them attributed to Italian Old Masters. When these arrived in Berlin, the court painter Hendrick de Fromantiou (1633/4–1694 or after 1700) pronounced them merely mediocre copies and the sale did not proceed. In 1672 both Uylenburgh and de Fromantiou invited artists from Amsterdam, Delft and The Hague to assess the disputed works. In November 1674 Uylenburgh went to Italy on business and by March of the following year he was declared bankrupt and an inventory of his possessions was drawn up. On 5 April he announced that he was travelling to England. There he made a living painting landscapes and draperies in Peter Lely's portraits. Gerrit's brother Abraham Uylenburgh (*d* Dublin, 1668) was a painter in the service of the Duke of Ormonde.

BIBLIOGRAPHY

Thieme–Becker

W. Bode and R. Dohme: 'Die Ausstellung von Gemälden älterer Meister im Berliner Privatbesitz', *Jb. Kön. Preuss. Kstsamml.*, iv (1883), pp. 126–7

FEMY HORSCH

Uyō. *See* ODANO NAOTAKE.

Uyŏm. *See* KWŎN TON-IN.

Uytenbogaardt, Roelof (Sarel) (*b* Cape Town, 23 June 1933). South African architect, urban planner and teacher. After graduating in architecture at the University of Cape Town (1956), he was an RIBA scholar at the British School in Rome. He then studied (1959–61) with Louis Kahn at the University of Pennsylvania, Philadelphia, taught at Harvard University, Massachusetts Institute of Technology and other universities and was Chief Planning Designer (1961–3) for the Boston Redevelopment Authority. He returned to practise in Cape Town in 1963. Among his numerous buildings and projects in South Africa, the best known are the Dutch Reformed Church (1964), Welkom, which shows the influence of Louis Kahn's First Unitarian Church (1959–67), Rochester, NY; the Werdmuller Commercial Centre (1973), Claremont, Cape Town, which is a spatially complex building organized around an internal spiral ramp; the Sports Centre (1977), University of Cape Town; and the Steinkopf Community Centre (1978), Steinkopf, which was published internationally as a leading example of South African late 20th-century architecture (see Beck). Later works include the Sports Complex (1981), University of the Western Cape, Bellville, and the Belhar Community Centre (1981), Cape Town, both of which received Awards of Merit from the Institute of South African Architects. Uytenbogaardt's work, some of it in association with other architects, shows great formal and spatial skills that reflect the tenets of the Modern Movement and the work of Le Corbusier, Louis Kahn and, to a certain extent, Alvar Aalto. In 1971 Uytenbogaardt was appointed Professor of Urban and Regional Planning, University of Cape Town, and he became an influential teacher, grounding urban planning in the act of design.

WRITINGS

with D. Dewar: 'Urbanization and City Management: The Case of South Africa', *UIA Int. Architect*, 8 (1985), p. 66

——: *South African Cities: A Manifesto for Change* (Cape Town, 1991), pp. 1–13

BIBLIOGRAPHY

D. Dewar and others: *Housing: A Comparative Evaluation of Urbanism in Cape Town* (Cape Town, 1977), pp. 1–207

H. Beck: 'Community Centre Steinkopf', *UIA Int. Architect*, 8 (1985), pp. 12–13

IVOR PRINSLOO

Uytewael, Joachim. *See* WTEWAEL, JOACHIM.

Uyttenbroeck [Wtenbrouck], **Moses** [Moyses] **(Matheusz.) van** (*b* The Hague, *c.* 1600; *d* The Hague, after 1646). Dutch painter and etcher. He was the younger brother of the painter Jan (Matheusz.) van Uyttenbroeck (*c.* 1581–1651), who was accepted into the Guild of St Luke in The Hague in 1614. Moses van Uyttenbroeck was a contemporary of the group of history painters now known as the PRE-REMBRANDTISTS, who were active in Amsterdam. However, compared with the varied repertoire of subjects depicted by the Pre-Rembrandtists, his range was limited, being mainly centred on themes from the Old Testament and Classical mythology, the latter usually based on Ovid's *Metamorphoses*. He also painted pastoral scenes, which are often difficult to distinguish clearly from the mythological works. Representations of bacchanalia with music, dancing and erotic scenes are particularly prevalent. A few portraits by him have also survived, including a picture thought to be a self-portrait (Doorn, priv. col., see Weisner, pl. 1).

Moses van Uyttenbroeck's earliest known work is the dated etching of *Peter Healing the Lame Man at the Door of the Temple* (1615); although it is still very awkward in

Moses van Uyttenbroeck: *Triumph of Bacchus*, oil on canvas, 1.25×2.06 m, 1627 (Brunswick, Herzog Anton Ulrich-Museum)

the way it is executed, it shows the influence of the Amsterdam painter Pieter Lastman. In 1620, six years after his brother, Moses himself entered the Guild of St Luke, The Hague, of which he was dean in 1627 and possibly again in 1633. He married Cornelia van Wyck by 1624. Probably dating from about the time he joined the guild is what is considered to be his earliest painting (Rennes, Mus. B.-A. & Archéol.), which depicts a spacious, very dramatic landscape with a riverbank in the foreground, a large, tree-covered range of hills and small figures. Van Uyttenbroeck then developed his compositional approach, building up his pictures from landscape elements placed close to one another rather in the manner of a stage set, often using boulders, running or still water and tall plants. Hills or trees delimit the pictures on either side, and the backgrounds consist of gentler, less precipitous wooded countryside, as in the *Mythological Scene* (1623; on dep. Basle, Kstmus.). The paintings from the mid-1620s are more peaceful and balanced; the scenery is flatter and therefore clearer, no longer distracting attention as much from the figures (e.g. *Old Testament or Mythological Scene*, 1625; The Hague, Gemeentemus.). For his figures, he preferred the calm profile or frontal view, and the individual forms became larger, heavier and sturdier, as can be seen in the *Judgement of Paris* (1626; Kassel, Schloss Wilhelmshöhe) and the *Triumph of Bacchus* (1627; Brunswick, Herzog Anton Ulrich-Mus.; see fig.).

No reliable chronology can be established for paintings dating from the 1630s and 1640s. Paintings apparently belonging to this period include the *Shepherds and Nymphs* (1631 or 1633; Algiers, Mus. N. B.-A.); the *Landscape with a Shepherd and his Flock* (?1633; London, priv. col.,

see Weisner, pl. 18); a *Mythological Scene* (1642; Berlin, Jagdschloss Grunewald), the only known commissioned work to have survived; and the *Two Nymphs* (1644; ex-art market, Düsseldorf, see Weisner, pl. 32). The oddly contrived branches on the trees conceal the landscape and provide a lively background for the figures, which, as in the paintings of the early 1620s, were again reduced to the size of staffage. There is little or no coherence in this group, either in terms of individual motif or in general subject-matter.

During his lifetime van Uyttenbroeck was highly regarded: Constantijn Huygens mentioned him with approval in his autobiography, and Prince Frederick Henry bought his paintings and involved him in the decoration of HONSELAARSDIJK. The merit of his oeuvre as a whole lies in the contribution it made to the depiction of Classical mythology. However, van Uyttenbroeck often repeated himself and did not achieve the same density or pithiness in his subject-matter as the Pre-Rembrandtist painters from Amsterdam. Dirk Dalens (*d* 1676) was his pupil, as probably was his son Matheus van Uyttenbroeck, also an artist.

BIBLIOGRAPHY
Thieme–Becker
U. Weisner: 'Die Gemälde des Moyses van Uyttenbroeck', *Oud-Holland*, lxxix (1964), pp. 189–228
The Pre-Rembrandtists (exh. cat., ed. A. Tümpel; Sacramento, CA, Crocker A. Mus., 1974), pp. 41–3, 115–25
Masters of 17th-century Dutch Landscape Painting (exh. cat. by P. C. Sutton and others, Amsterdam, Rijksmus.; Boston, MA, Mus. F.A.; Philadelphia, PA, Mus. A.; 1987–8), pp. 535–7

ASTRID TÜMPEL

Uzbekistan, Republic of. Central Asian country bounded by Kazakhstan to the north and west, Kyrgyzstan and

Tajikistan to the east and Turkmenistan to the south (see fig. 1). It contains in its north-west corner the autonomous republic of Karakalpak, largely made up of the Amu delta, facing the salt-water Aral Sea. Central and northern Uzbekistan is dominated by the Kyzylkum Desert, into which runs the Zarafshan River; much of the Ferghana Valley (*see* FERGHANA) occupies the eastern extremity of the country, and the south borders the Amu River. The capital, TASHKENT (formerly Binket), was rebuilt following an earthquake in 1966.

1. Introduction. 2. Architecture. 3. Painting and sculpture. 4. Decorative arts.

1. INTRODUCTION. Its position on a major overland trade route between East and West and the existence of well-watered oases in huge tracts of desert have resulted in a long history for what is now Uzbekistan. Prehistoric agriculture flourished along the great rivers for millennia; early settlements at BUKHARA and SAMARKAND (5th–2nd century BC) were walled settlements containing raised citadels. Successively the Achaemenids (including the satrap of Sogdiana centred on Ferghana; 6th–4th century BC), Seleucids (4th–3rd century BC), Greco-Bactrians (*c.* 250–*c.* 200 BC) and Parthians (3rd century BC–3rd century AD) contested control of it. By the 1st century AD it

was ruled by the Kushana until incorporated into the Sasanian empire in the 3rd century. The Sasanians were defeated by the Huns (Hepthalites) in 425. The evolution of the SILK ROUTE, on which Samarkand and Bukhara were key points, further focused attention on the area. The Ferghana Valley straddling the eastern border with Kyrgyzstan, always somewhat apart from the rest of the region, was a centre of Buddhism, with key sites at KUVA and Uzgend (Kyrgyzstan), until the rise of the Qarakhanid khanate (from 999). There were also some Buddhist foundations in South Uzbekistan.

By the mid-6th century AD power lay with the Turkish Qaghanate. The Arabs took Samarkand, then capital of Sogdiana, in 712. Throughout the Islamic period Samarkand and Bukhara were frequently capitals of ruling dynasties that ranged from small localized powers to empires covering much of Iran and western Central Asia. First came the Abbasids, then their erstwhile governors the Samanids (*reg* 875–1005 in Transoxiana, with their capital at Bukhara), the Qarakhanids (*reg* 992–1211, with their capital at Samarkand, overthrowing the Samanids in 999) and then Saljuk tribes, who arrived in the late 10th century and were in control of the area by the early 12th; they were defeated in 1141 by the Qara Khitay, who in turn lost to the Khwarazmshahs in the late 12th century.

Mongol invasions (with Samarkand, Bukhara and Urgench razed in 1220) under Genghis Khan (*d* 1227)

1. Map of Uzbekistan; those sites with separate entries in this dictionary are distinguished by CROSS-REFERENCE TYPE

disrupted urban life until it was restored under Ghenghis's eldest surviving son, Chaghatay, and his successors (*reg* 1227–1370). Around this time the White Horde began to lose control to the Nogai and Uzbek tribes; the latter, taking their name from Khan Uzbek (*reg* 1282–1342) under whom they had converted to Islam, became the Shaybanids (see below). Subsequent order was interrupted briefly by the TIMURID dynasty under Timur (*reg* 1370–1405), who made Samarkand his capital and Shahr-i Sabz his second city. In various forms Timurid rule lasted into the 16th century; then the Shaybanids (*reg* 1500–98, with their capital at Bukhara) and their successors controlled much of Central Asia until 1785, though increasing fragmentation led to the formation of many smaller khanates. By the 19th century the Khanate centred on Khiva ruled the area of modern Karakalpak; the Khanate centred on Bukhara most of Uzbekistan and Tajikistan; and the Khanate centred on Kokand the territories bordering the Syr and Amu rivers.

Russian expansion southward in the late 18th century and the 19th put an end to the declining khanates—the most important, the emirate of Bukhara, surrendered much of its eastern property, including Samarkand, in 1868 and became a Russian protectorate; Kokand was taken in 1876 and abolished—and thereafter Russian forts and new civil towns were established and linked by railways. Tashkent, taken in 1865, became the Russians' main city.

The Turkestan Territory created in 1886 was redefined in the Soviet period. In 1918 the area was contained in the Turkestan ASSR, but after internal fighting the emir of Bukhara and the *khān* of Khiva were deposed in 1920. The Uzbek SSR was created in 1924 out of former Bukharan lands between the Amu and Syr rivers—it contained Tajikistan until 1929—and the Karakalpak ASSR was combined with it in 1936. Drastic changes in land use led to the depletion of rivers to form the Karakumskiy Canal in Turkmenistan. Soviet architects and artists were prominent in urban renewal projects, especially the re-building of Tashkent in 1966. After the break-up of the USSR, Uzbekistan declared its independence on 21 August 1991. The following sections concentrate mainly on the arts of Uzbekistan from the period of Russian influence and control; for more extensive discussion of pre-19th-century art *see* CENTRAL ASIA, §I and ISLAMIC ART.

2. ARCHITECTURE. KHIVA, capital of the khanate of that name, and today a museum-city in the Khwarazm region embodies the concept of a late feudal Islamic capital city, with its monumental structures and complexes of buildings, both civic and religious, of different sizes and functions. Following the Central Asian tradition of towns with a tripartite structure, Khiva consists of the walled town (Ichan-kala); the trade and craft suburb (Dishan-kala); and the citadel (Kunya-ark). Many buildings are 19th- or early 20th-century, including court, religious and commercial structures, the caravanserai and houses; all are richly decorated with multicoloured surfaces, painting and the stucco and wood-carving for which Khiva is famous.

During the period under consideration, a few important buildings were added to the medieval capital city of Bukhara, such as the Char-minar ('Four Minarets') gateway (1807) to the Madrasa of the wealthy merchant khalif Niyazkul, with its unusual tetrapylon with four massive, circular corner towers; the traditionally styled complex of Bala-khauz, with its Winter (1712) and Summer (early 20th century) mosques, reservoir (Pers. *hawz*) and small minaret (1917; architect Shirin Muradov, 1880–1957); and the picturesque suburban palace of the Bukhara emirs, Sitoray-makhi-khasa (late 19th century to 1918), which combines European taste with the decorative style of Bukhara. The palace of Khudoyar Khan (1871) in Kokand, built and decorated by the finest masters of Ferghana, and the khan's palace of Tash Hawli (1830–38) in Khiva constitute the finest achievements of local building and decorative arts. Although there are regional variations, the architecture of Uzbekistan generally makes wide use of beamed roofs laid on elegant carved columns, carved wooden and stucco details in the decoration of façades, and bright ornamental wall painting and gilding.

At the end of the 19th century and the beginning of the 20th, Russian architects including Leonty Nikolayevich Benois and Georgy Mikhailovich Svarichevsky (1871–1935) worked in Uzbekistan. New towns (Skobelev, now Ferghana) and the European sections of old towns were built to a regular plan, though Russian architecture did not at this time have a noticeable influence on local forms. Significant changes came during the Soviet period, when architects from Moscow, Leningrad (now St Petersburg) and elsewhere, together with such local architects as Abdulla Babakhanov (*b* 1910) and Mutkhat Sagadatgino-vich Bulatov (*b* 1907), drew up general plans for the reconstruction, improvement and future development of Tashkent (1938 and 1954), Samarkand (1938–9 and 1954), Bukhara, Andizhan, Ferghana and many other towns, as well as plans for industrial complexes.

The architecture of public buildings in Uzbekistan from the 1920s to the 1950s followed the usual path of development for the eastern regions of the USSR, in which Constructivism and Neo-classicism fused with elements of national architecture and decoration (e.g. the Theatre of Opera and Ballet in Tashkent; 1940–47, by Aleksey Shchusev, with paintings by Chingiz Akhmarov (*b* 1912), stucco carving by masters from Bukhara, Khiva and elsewhere). The architecture of the town of Navoi, founded in the desert in the 1960s, and of Tashkent as restored after the earthquake of 1966, expressed the new principles of Soviet urban planning in regions with hot climates and high seismicity: a spacious siting of multi-storey buildings among squares and green areas, with reservoirs and fountains; an expressive use of ornamental sculpture and painting; and a subtle use of traditional decoration (e.g. the Palace of Friendship of the People, Tashkent, 1981; by Sabir Rahimovich Adylov (*b* 1932), and others; Alisher Navoi metro station, Tashenkt, 1981; by R. Faizullayer and Ya. Mansurov, with Chingiz Akh-marov and others).

3. PAINTING AND SCULPTURE. The figural arts in Uzbekistan arose at the turn of the 19th and 20th centuries as a result of the creative and educative work of Russian and Ukrainian painters and illustrators, including Vasily Vasil'yevich Vereshchagin, Sergey Ivanovich Svetoslavsky

(1857–1931) and Leon Leonardovich Bure (1887–1943). In the 1920s and 1930s the successors of the school of SOCIALIST REALISM, Ivan Semyonovich Kazakov (173–1935) and Maksim Yevtatyevich Novikov (1889–1974), as well as fine representatives of the Soviet avant-garde, such as ALEKSANDR VOLKOV, Oganes Karapetovich Tatevosyan (1889–1974), Aleksandr Vasilyevich Nikolayev (1895–1957), Nikolay Georgievich Karakhan (1990–70), Nadezhda Vasil'yevna Kashina (1896–1977) and URAL TANSYKBAYEV, worked in Uzbekistan. Their work from this period, which embraced a wide variety of artistic styles, and objectives, became known to the wider public only in the mid-1960s, thanks very largely to the activity of Igor Vital'yevich Savitsky (1915–?90), the Moscow connoisseur and artist, founder and Director of the Museum of Arts of the Karakalpaksky Autonomous SSR in Nukus (now Nukus, Karakalpakiya Mus. A.).

Many Central Asian artists of the 1930s and 1940s were taught by Pavel Petrovich Ben'kov (1879–1949), a master of landscape painting and a sensitive colourist (e.g. *Girl with Dutar*, 1947; Tashkent, Mus. A. Uzbekistan), by Aleksandr Volkov, who was influenced by Cubism (eg *Pomegranate Teahouse*, 1924; Moscow, Tret'yakov Gal.) e. g. the graphic artist Mikhil Ivanovich Kurzin 1888–1957), one of the organizers of the association Masters of the New East (1927–9, based in Tashkent) and the Association of Workers of IZO' (1929–31, based in Tashkent and Samarkand). In the period from the 1930s to the 1960s, the art of U. Tansykbayev and N. G. Karakhan showed the development of a specifically Central Asian approach—lyrical and full of emotion—to the genre of landscape painting. Socialist Realism was consistently adopted in the topical paintings and portraits of Zinaida Mikhailovna Kovalevskaya (1902–1979), Abdukhak Abdullayev (*b* 1928), Bahram Khamdami (1910–42), Lutfulla Abdullayev (*b* 1912) and Rashid Mukhamedovich Timurov (*b* 1912). The traditions of Central Asian manuscript painting were skilfully used by the graphic artist and illustrator Iskandr Ikramov (1904–72).

Painting, graphic art, sculpture, monumental art and stage design from the 1960s to the 1980s were enriched by a variety of creative trends, a search for original solutions to the problems of composition and colour, a desire to incorporate both national and universal traditions of art as well as noticeably wider range of artistic vocabulary. The major painters of the period were Dzhavalat Yusupovich Umarbekov (*b*1946), Ruzy Charyyev (*b* 1931) Charyyev, Kutkuk Basharov (*b* 1925), Shukrat Abdurashidov (1948–79) and and Telman Yaminovich Muhamedov (1935–76); the major sculptors were Anvar Kamilovich Akhmedov (*b* 1935), Abdumunin Baymatov (*b* 1934), Mukhtar Nabiyevich Musabayev (*b*1929) and Khakim Khodzha Khusnutdinkhodzhayev, (*b* 1948). Work done since the 1980s has been characterized by psychological upheaval as well as thematic and artistic variety (e.g. the painter Sagdulla Asadullayevich Abdullayev, *b* 1945 and the graphic artists Victor Olgovich Apukhtin, *b*1945 and Marat Faiziyevich, Sadykov, *b*1945). The most important collections of Uzbekistan art are in the Tashkent Museum of the Art of Uzbekistan, Taskent, the Karakalpakiya Museum of Art, Nukus, and the Museum of Oriental Art, Moscow.

4. DECORATIVE ARTS. In the 18th and 19th centuries the traditional types and shapes of articles, methods and character of decoration, and types of ornament continued to be used. In Bukhara, Samarkand, Margilan, Andizhan, Tashkent and Khiva, cotton, silk and half-silk ikat textiles (see fig. 2) were produced (known in Central Asia as *abr* ('cloud') because of the soft outlines of decorative pattern, a result of resist-dyeing the threads before weaving); as well as striped examples (*alocha*); plain and patterned velvets; brocades; and satins among others (*see* ISLAMIC ART, §VI, 2(iii)(d)). Shahr-i Sabz, Bukhara, Samarkand and Nurata were famous for their embroideries, especially that used as wall hangings (*syuzan*) with richly coloured patterns. Many centres produced embroidered Asian headgear in the shape of a circular or multifaceted little hat (*see also* CENTRAL ASIA, §I, 6(i)). Skilful gilding and jewellery came from the courtly workshops of Bukhara (*see* CENTRAL ASIA, §I, 8(vi)(b)). Pile carpets with diagonal patterns of motifs on a central field, and *palas*, smooth (without pile) carpet of simple weave decorated with coloured strips, were made everywhere as part of women's household work.

A particular development of this period was the embossing and engraving in metal and the artistic working of hide. Suede, *yuft* (a kind of leather made from bull or pig skin and used for shoes and saddles), elk-skin and coarse

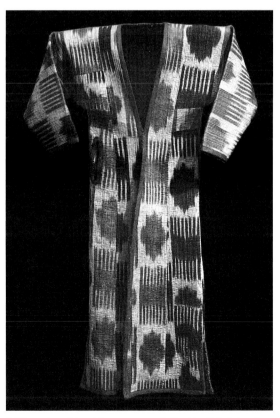

2. Woman's traditional dress, cotton and silk with relief stitches, from Khiva, Uzbekistan, early 20th century (Moscow, State Museum of Oriental Art)

shagreen were coloured by stamping, embroidery, appliqués of coloured hide, velvet, metal engraving with plates, small bells and tassels. One of the leading centres of glazed ceramics from the mid-19th century was Kislak Rishtan in the Ferghana Valley, producing dishes with elegant coloured painting on white slipe under a transparent smoke-coloured alkaline glaze (see CENTRAL ASIA, §I, 7(viii)). At the end of the 19th century and beginning of the 20th, under the influence of Russian culture, decorative motifs copied from manufactured articles such as periodicals, books, textiles, china and linoleum appeared in traditional ornament; nonetheless the diversity of colours used, the variety of shapes and the abundance of gilding remained characteristic. The introduction of aniline dyes had a detrimental effect on the quality of the carpets and embroidery but a beneficial influence on the development of multicoloured fabrics as designs and colour schemes became more diverse. In ceramics the resumption of the production of lead glazes (e.g. at Katta Kurgan) enriched the palette of the painters. In the Soviet period, contemporary forms of decorative and applied art developed alongside traditional types.

BIBLIOGRAPHY

A. Umarov: *Iskusstvo Uzbekskoy SSR* [Art of the Uzbek SSR] (Leningrad, 1972) [in Uzbek, Rus. and Eng.]

Iskusstvo Sovetskogo Uzbekistana, 1917–1972 [Art of Soviet Uzbekistan, 1917–72] (Moscow, 1976)

M. Miunts and D. Fakhretdinova: *Izobrazitel'noye iskusstvo Uzbekistana: Zhivopis', grafika, skul'ptura, dekorativno-prikladnoye iskusstvo* [Fine art of Uzbekistan: painting, graphic arts, sculpture, decorative and applied arts] (Tashkent, 1976) [In Uzbek, Rus. and Eng.]

M. S. Bulatov and T. F. Kadyrova: *Tashkent* (Leningrad, 1977) [in Rus. and Eng.]

A. S. Morozova, N. A. Avedova and S. M. Makhkamova: *Narodnoye iskusstvo Uzbekistana* [National art of Uzbekistan] (Tashkent, 1979) [in Uzbek, Rus. and Eng.]

Ye. M. Ismailova: *Iskusstvo oformleniya sredneaziatskoy rukopisnoy knigi, XVIII–XIX vekov* [Art of production of Central Asian manuscripts in the 18th and 19th centuries] (Tashkent, 1982)

V. A. Bulatova and G. V. Shishkina: *Samarkand: Muzei pod otkrytym nebom* [Samarkand: a museum beneath the open sky] (Tashkent, 1986) [in Uzbek, Rus. and Eng.]

I. Azimov: *Rospisi Uzbekistana* [Paintings of Uzbekistan] (Tashkent, 1987) [In Rus., Uzbek and Eng.]

T. J. Kadyrova : *Arkhitektura sovetskogo Uzbekistana* [Architecture of Soviet Uzbekistan] (Moscow, 1987)

T. KH. STARODUB

Uzgend [Uzgand; Uzgen]. Town in Kyrgyzstan. Located between the Kara and Yassa (Dzhaza) rivers in the eastern part of the Ferghana valley, Uzgend is set on three hills and comprises three free-standing towns and citadels surrounded by suburban estates and gardens. The town developed in the 8th and 9th centuries along the Silk Route as a border post on the frontier between the lands of Islam and the Turks. In the 10th and 11th centuries it became the major trading and administrative centre in the region and the fourth largest town in Ferghana, covering 12–15 sq. km. From the second half of the 11th century to the beginning of the 13th it was the capital of the Ferghana region of the Karakhanid khanate, and the major architectural ensemble of the town, comprising three dynastic mausolea, the Friday mosque and minaret, and the remains of a madrasa, dates from this period. Square chambers with *pīshtāq*s (monumental portals) facing the street, the mausolea are elaborately decorated with incised plaster and terracotta. The central mausoleum (8 m sq.) for Nasr ibn 'Ali (*d c*. 1012–13) contains one of the earliest known examples of strapwork decoration; the northern one (1152) for Jalal al-Din Husayn and the southern one (1186) are even more elaborate. North of the mausolea near a modern mosque stands the minaret. Set on an octagonal socle, it has a tapering cylindrical shaft (diam. at base 9 m; h. 17 m) decorated with bands of brick. It probably served as the model for other minarets built later by the Karakhanids at Bukhara (1127) and Vabkent (1197). Tombstones from the 11th to the 15th century document the local development of styles of calligraphy. In the 16th century the town declined to a village, but the modern town preserves some of the layout and narrow streets of the medieval city, with pisé houses and a network of bazaars and public baths.

BIBLIOGRAPHY

B. N. Zasypkin: *Pamyatniki Uzgenda* [Monuments of Uzgend] (Moscow, 1927)

E. Cohn-Wiener: *Turan* (Berlin, 1930)

A. Yu. Yakubovsky: 'Dve nadpisi na severnom mavzoleye v g. Uzgende' [Two inscriptions on the northern mausoleum in Uzgend], *Epig. Vostoka*, i (1947), pp. 27–32

Y. A. Zadneprowsky: 'Istoriko-arkheologicheskiye raboty v yuzhnoy Kirgizii' [Historical and archaeological work in southern Kyrgyzstan], *Trudy Kirgiz. Arkheol.–Etnog. Eksped.*, iv (1960), pp. 213–46

V. D. Goryacheva: *Srednevekovyye gorodskiye tsentry i arkhitekturnyye ansambli Kirgizii (Burana, Uzgen, Safid-Buland)* [Medieval urban centres and architectural ensembles of Kyrgyzstan (Burana, Uzgend, Safid-Bulan)] (Frunze, 1983), pp. 67–104

V. D. Goryacheva and V. N. Nastich: 'Epigrafischeskiye pamyatniki Uzgena, XII–XX vv.' [Epigraphical monuments of Uzgend, 12th–20th century], *Kirgiziya pri Karakhanidakh* [Kyrgystan under the Karakhanids] (Frunze, 1983), pp. 140–93

V. D. GORYACHEVA

Uzhhorod [Rus. Uzhgorod]. Ukrainian town in the south Carpathian mountains on the River Uzh. It grew up in the 8th and 9th centuries AD as a centre of the western Slavs, passing under Hungarian rule in the 11th century. From the 18th century it was included in the Austro-Hungarian empire, transferring to Czechoslovakia in 1919. It was annexed by the USSR in 1945 and became part of independent Ukraine in 1991. Architecturally the town is noted for its castle, which was already in existence in the 11th century and was rebuilt during the 15th–17th centuries, laid out round a courtyard, with three-storey ranges and four corner towers. The Orthodox, formerly Greek Catholic, cathedral is a basilican structure of 1644. The Baroque Roman Catholic church dates from 1762–7. The Transcarpathian Regional Museum has an archaeological collection, and the Museum of Art a collection of Ukrainian and Hungarian art of the 15th–20th centuries. There is also an open-air Transcarpathian Museum of Folk Architecture and Life.

The village of Goryany on the edge of Uzhhorod has the 13th-century round church of St Nicholas. Its 14th-century frescoes, which may have been painted by an Italian artist, reflect the dissemination of the spatial and compositional ideas of late medieval Italian painting.

BIBLIOGRAPHY

L. D. Godovanny: *Uzhgorod* (Kiev, 1970)

L. I. POPOVA

Uzunov, Dechko (*b* Kazanlŭk, 22 Feb 1899; *d* Sofia, 26 April 1986). Bulgarian painter, stained-glass designer, ceramicist, illustrator and teacher. He studied art under Karl von Maar at the Akademie der Bildenden Künste, Munich, and in 1924 under Stephan Ivanov (1875–1951) at the National Academy of Arts (Natsionalna Hudozhestvena Academia), Sofia. He became known as an artist who worked in a wide variety of media, executing paintings, book illustrations and stained glass. In 1922 he became the youngest member of the NATIONAL ART SOCIETY OF BULGARIA and later its chairman. He was also chairman of the Union of Bulgarian Artists for several terms. During the 1930s Uzunov became known as a master of portrait painting: among his best-known works are the *Poet Liliev* (1929), the *Theatre Director Masalitinov* (1931) and the *Actor Krustyo Sarafov in the Role of Falstaff* (1932; all Sofia, N.A.G.). From 1938 he was a professor of painting at the National Academy of Arts, Sofia. He represented Bulgaria at the Venice Biennale in 1942, 1948 and 1964. As a stained-glass artist, he executed commissions for the Bulgarian National Bank (1942), the Court House (1938–43) and the University of Sofia (1980), and he did a ceramic wall piece for the Opera House in Stara Zagora. His frescoes include those for the Hall of Culture in Karlovo and the National Theatre in Sofia, the latter done in 1976. His last large public commission was the fresco *Apotheosis of Bulgarian Culture* (1981) in Hall Nine of the National Palace of Culture, Sofia. In his late works, for example *Self-portrait* (1979; Sofia, N.A.G.) and *Cain and Abel* (1979; Samokov A.G.), he began to use abstract forms. In 1978 he became an academician at the Bulgarian Academy of Sciences (Balgarskara Akademija na Nankite). He was also a president of the International Association of the Plastic Arts at UNESCO in Paris.

BIBLIOGRAPHY

Natsionalna hudozhestvena galeriya [National Art Gallery], cat. (Sofia, 1970)

K. Stefanov and M. Kirov, eds: *Suvremenno bulgarsko monumentalno izkustvo, 1956–1986* [Contemporary Bulgarian monumental art] (Sofia, 1986) [Eng. Summary]

MARIANA KATZAROVA

V

Vaardt [Vandervaart], **Jan van der** (*b* Haarlem, *c*. 1653; *bur* London, 30 March 1727). Dutch painter and engraver, active in England. He was trained by Thomas Wijck and moved to England in 1674 as a painter of still-lifes and small landscapes with figures. He painted draperies for the fashionable portrait painter Willem Wissing from about 1685 to 1687. Their names appear together on several paintings and on several engravings after portraits. The portrait of *Frances Theresa Stuart, Duchess of Richmond and Lennox* (1687; London, N.P.G.; *see* DRESS, fig. 42) is a fine example of their collaboration. Van der Vaardt may also be the 'Landervart' who together with Wissing and others completed many of Lely's unfinished studio paintings after his death. According to Marshall Smith, he 'Paints a Face and Posture very well, Landskip, Foul &c. extraordinary fine and is to be Rank'd among the great Masters of the Age'. He occasionally collaborated with the German-born painter Johann Kerseboom (*see* KERSE-BOOM, (2)), one of their more notable pieces being *Thomas Osborne, 1st Duke of Leeds* (1704; London, N.P.G.). He also imitated the portrait types of his talented contemporaries: *Mr and Mrs Robert Bristow* (1713; Squerryes Court, Kent) is a typical late work in the manner of Godfrey Kneller. Although suffering from poor eyesight, which later forced him to reduce the number of his commissions, he established a picture restoration business. He also practised as a mezzotint-engraver, working for the publishers Richard Thompson and Edward Cooper, and is said to have taught the engraver John Smith (i). His painting of *Lot and his Daughters* (untraced) is recorded in Queen Anne's Kensington Palace inventory in the picture store, but it is not known if he painted any other subject pictures. He was buried at St Paul's, Covent Garden.

BIBLIOGRAPHY
E. K. Waterhouse: *Painting in Britain, 1530–1790*, Pelican Hist. A. (Harmondsworth, 1953, 4/1978), p. 145
M. K. Talley: 'Marshall Smith "The Art of Painting" 1692', *Portrait Painting in England: Studies in the Technical Literature before 1700* (Guildford, 1981), pp. 378–9

JOHN SHEERAN

Vác [formerly Ger. Weitzen]. Town in Hungary 35 km north of Budapest on the left bank of the Danube. In the 11th century an episcopal see was established there by Stephen I (*reg* 997–1038), who built a fortified Romanesque castle and cathedral. After the town was invaded by the Mongols in 1241, Béla IV (*reg* 1235–70) rebuilt the castle and had the fortifications strengthened. In the 14th century the cathedral was rebuilt in Gothic style, and at the end of the 15th century Bishop Miklós Báthori had the town redesigned in Renaissance style and a new cathedral built. From 1544 to 1686 Vác was ruled by the Turks. After they were driven out, the ruined town was again rebuilt in the 18th century by the bishops of Vác.

Plans for the 18th-century cathedral, the most important building in Vác, were drawn up by Franz Anton Pilgram under the direction of Bishop Károly Esterházy. Although construction did not begin until 1761, Pilgram's plans, which included a large square in front of the cathedral with a Bishop's Palace and Jesuit College, were not fully realized owing to the great cost involved. When Christoph Anton Migazzi became Bishop of Vác, he commissioned Isidore Canevale to design a new cathedral using the existing foundations. Canevale, having been influenced by the work of Jacques-Germain Soufflot in France, designed it in an early Neo-classical style. It was dedicated in 1772, although work on the interior continued until 1777. A portico of six colossal Corinthian columns supports a heavy attic and links two towers. Six statues by Joseph Bechert (*d* 1806) are on the parapet. The interior closely follows the model of Palladio's S Giorgio Maggiore, Venice, and has a square-ended chancel, transept arms and an organ-loft of three sections. The chancel's Renaissance balustrade (from the previous cathedral) was commissioned by Miklós Báthori. The frescoes on the interior of the dome and in the sacristy are by Franz Anton Maulbertsch. A crypt runs the entire length of the cathedral and contains a carved stone coat of arms (1485) of the Báthori family.

The Dominican church (now the Felsővárosi parish church) was commissioned by Bishop Dvornikovich from Márton Kalcher, a stonemason from Buda (now part of Budapest) and was begun in 1699. In 1774 it was damaged by fire and in 1784 was confiscated on an order of Joseph II (*reg* 1765–90). Its façade is decorated with pilasters and has a three-sectioned pediment and lyre-shaped Baroque gate. The first storey of the façade elevation has statues of *St Dominic* and *St Imre*; the second storey has a statue of the *Virgin* with a 'god's eye' circular window above. The chancel contains a Neo-classical high altar with the *Assumption of the Virgin* as its principal painting and *Christ and the Disciples* on its predella. There is also a figured pulpit (1776) with statues by Bechert. The altarpiece (*c*. 1770) behind the *St Anne* altar was painted by the Viennese artist Felix Ivo Leicher (1727–after 1811). Urban

Lincz was probably the architect of the towerless Franciscan church, the cornerstone of which was laid in 1721. Its chancel was dedicated in 1726, and the building finished in 1766. The façade is covered with smooth pilasters with corner volutes and has statues of *St Anthony of Padua*, *St Francis* and the *Virgin*. The high altar was built in 1729 by Regeli, a carpenter, and Joseph Hebenstreit (*bapt* 1698; *d* 1742), a sculptor from Pest. The altarpiece, by an unknown artist, represents the *Martyrdom of St Stephen*. The organ (1728) and the pulpit (1767) are the work of Brother Vitus, and the *Calvary* in the chancel was erected by Brother George Skursky.

The triumphal arch by Canevale is the only one in Hungary and is a fine example of early Neo-classicism in central Europe. It has a single opening and is decorated with pilasters, ten dentilled brackets and garlanded eagles. On one side is the Latin inscription AETERNAE DOMUI and on the other busts of *Maria-Theresa* and her husband *Francis I* (*reg* 1745–65) and an inscription stating that Bishop Migazzi commissioned the arch in 1764. It was built to commemorate Maria-Theresa's visit to Vác that year.

BARBRA RUCKRIEGEL EGERVÁRY

Vacca, Flaminio (*b* Rome, 1538; *d* Rome, 26 Oct 1605). Italian sculptor of Spanish descent. Although an accomplished artist, he has been neglected and at times categorically condemned by critics. His few surviving works reveal the influence both of Classical models, to which he was passionately devoted, and of the Florentine manner derived from Michelangelo. He studied with the Florentine Vincenzo de' Rossi, who was in Rome between 1546 and 1560, and at first worked on restorations and adaptations of antique sculptures. Around 1572 he was listed among the members of the Congregazione dei Virtuosi al Pantheon. His period of greatest creative productivity began in the last years of the pontificate of Pope Gregory XIII. In 1583 he carved the Pope's coat of arms in the two large marble escutcheons for the Collegio del Gesú, the rich curves of which are meticulously carved in the Florentine style of Bartolomeo Ammanati. In 1587–8 he worked with Pietro Paolo Olivieri to complete an *Angel* and a low relief of *Joshua and his Army* for the Acqua Felice fountain, the latter work showing his interest in late Roman reliefs. The two sculptors, together with Domenico Fontana (iii) and Leonardo Sormani, also took part in the restoration (1588–90) of *Castor and Pollux* in the Monte Cavallo Fountain in Piazza del Quirinale. During this period Vacca also sent a tabernacle (1589) to the church of S Lorenzo in Spello, outside Rome.

In 1588 Vacca produced one of his most demanding works, the *St Francis of Assisi*, for the Sistine Chapel in S Maria Maggiore, Rome. This work reveals a Mannerist taste, together with a certain stylized expressionism in the manner of de' Rossi. In contrast, the signed figures of *St John the Baptist* (see fig.) and *St John the Evangelist* (1592–3) in S Maria Vallicella (or Chiesa Nuova) display a soft, shadowy quality, modifying the Mannerist style that Vacca had learnt both from his teacher and from Baccio Bandinelli. On the other hand, the *Angel* in the Capella degli Angeli in Il Gesú, which dates from the end of the decade, is characterized by a freedom of modelling and an elegance

Flaminio Vacca: *St John the Baptist*, 1592–3 (Rome, S Maria Vallicella)

of line; another *Angel* in the same chapel was begun by Olivieri and completed by Vacca. Vacca also executed a signed *Lion* (between 1570 and 1590; now Florence, Loggia Lanzi), commissioned by Grand Duke Ferdinando I for the Villa Medici in Rome; it was moved to Florence in 1787. It is a finely made statue that shows a return to the classical mode, a work of great vitality and virtuoso realism. Vacca's passion for antiquity also found expression in his *Memorie di varie antichità trovate in diversi luoghi della città di Roma*, written in 1594 and published in 1704 as an appendix to a text by Famiano Nardini. These notes are particularly interesting as a history of archaeological excavations in Rome. Vacca also produced highly admired portraits, with a concern for accuracy in physiognomy and psychology. His *Self-portrait* (signed and dated 1599; formerly Rome, Pantheon; now Rome, Protomoteca Capitolina) is modelled with great sensitivity to the play of light, revealing an expression of contained anxiety and a rigorous simplicity. The same characteristics appear in the bust of *Baldassare Ginanni* (*c.* 1599; Rome, S Agostino), which has been attributed to Vacca. In 1599 he was elected head of the Accademia di S Luca in Rome.

WRITINGS

app.: F. Nardini: *Roma antica* (Rome, 1704)

BIBLIOGRAPHY

Thieme–Becker

G. Baglione: *Vite* (1642); ed. V. Mariani (1935), pp. 71–2

A. Venturi: *Storia* (1901–40), pp. 690–92

V. Martinelli: 'Flaminio Vacca, scultore e antiquario romano', *Stud. Romani*, ii (1954), pp. 154–64

C. D'Onofrio: *Le fontane di Roma* (Rome, 1986)

S. Lombardi: 'Flaminio Vacca', *Roma di Sisto V* (exh. cat., ed. M. L. Madonna; Rome, 1993)

ANA MARIA RYBKO

Vaccarini, Giovanni Battista (*b* Palermo, 1702; *d* Milazzo, Sicily, 1769). Italian architect. He was one of the major architects active in Sicily in the mid-18th century. He showed early promise by inventing hydraulic and pneumatic devices and was sent by the Senate of Palermo to Rome for his architectural training. There he won the favour of Cardinal Pietro Ottoboni and studied under Carlo Fontana and at the Accademia di S Luca. He was recalled to Catania in 1730 to complete the cathedral, and he was appointed architect to the city in 1735. Vaccarini brought new vitality and rigour to the reconstruction works then still being undertaken following the earthquake of 1693. He introduced the Late Roman Baroque manner, adapted to the local taste for exuberant form and exploiting the colour and texture of Catanian black lava stone. The façade (1730–68) of the cathedral (*see* CATANIA) was part of the rebuilding of the 11th-century structure. It is a dynamic composition: an undulating screen of free-standing columns contrasts with the straight wall behind. The composition may have had precedents in Rome, for example S Maria in Campitelli (1662–75) by Carlo Rainaldi, although the belfry with a third storey is typically Sicilian. In the Piazza del Duomo, Vaccarini also designed the Palazzo del Municipio (1732–50); the Fontana dell'Elefante (1736), the symbol of Catania; and the church of S Agata (1735–67). The Palazzo del Municipio reveals Vaccarini's sensibilities: he linked the existing ground floor, a rusticated structure typical of Catanian provincial exuberance, to two severe pilastered upper storeys in the Roman manner. He also provided a new layout for the city of a grid of wide tree-lined streets punctuated by squares, and he supervised the construction of the new building works, which provided a unified appearance. The church of S Agata, considered Vaccarini's most important work, was based on Francesco Borromini's plan of S Agnese in Agone (1653) in the Piazza Navona, Rome, consisting of a Greek cross with the crossing defined by three-quarter columns. The façade was of two storeys, the lower double-curved on plan, based on Borromini's S Carlo alle Quattro Fontane (1638–77), Rome, the upper of three concave bays. The inclusion of a covered belvedere integrated with the façade and the use of black lava make the design resolutely Catanian; the Rococo interior was completed after his death.

The church of S Giuliano (1739–57), Catania, was based on the elliptical plan of S Maria di Montesanto (1673), Rome, by Bernini, but with a convex façade and integrated belvedere; the interior was altered in the 19th century. Vaccarini added a similar belvedere to the church of S Chiara, Catania. His extensive rebuilding work for the Benedictine monastery (now incorporated into Catania University) included a library, refectories and a museum; the library (1733) shows an extraordinary austerity, with five bays of rectangular windows and oval clerestory windows in a plain brick façade. The Palazzo Valle (*c.* 1740–50) has a severe façade relieved by an elaborate portal and balcony on canted brackets; ornate wrought-iron balustrades, also a Catanian tradition, contrast with the stonework.

Vaccarini's later work shows the classicizing influence of his friend Luigi Vanvitelli. The circular arcaded courtyard of the austere Palazzo Cutelli (1754) reveals this, but it is enlivened by an intarsia pavement of black lava pebbles and limestone. The Palazzo Gravina (after 1755) has a loggia with paired pilasters between the arches, similar to the plan of Vaccarini's own house (1738). Vaccarini also took over the reconstruction of the university from 1730; in 1752 he completed the courtyard, with two storeys of elegant arcades, its severity offset by Vaccarini's characteristic intarsia pavement. In 1749 Vaccarini returned to Palermo, where he worked on the restoration (1752) of the cathedral. His prolific career was influential on the next generation of Catanian architects.

BIBLIOGRAPHY

F. Fichera: *Giovanni Battista Vaccarini e l'architettura del settecento in Sicilia*, 2 vols (Rome, 1934)

E. Rufini: 'Vaccarini e Vanvitelli: Spigolature d'archivo', *Palladio*, xi (1961), pp. 181–2

G. Gangi: *Il barocco nella Sicilia orientale* (Rome, 1964)

A. Blunt: *Sicilian Baroque* (London, 1968)

J. Varriano: *Italian Baroque and Rococo* (New York, 1986)

G. Pagnano: 'Vaccarini, Light and Lava', *Spazio & Soc.*, xiii/52 (1990), pp. 88–91

P. Blundel-Jones: 'Giancarlo De Carlo's renovation of, and master plan for, Catania University, Sicily', *Archit. Rev.* [London] (1993), pp. 30–32 [places Vaccarini's renovations at the Benedictine monastery in the context of later developments]

Vaccaro. Italian family of artists. (1) Lorenzo Vaccaro, primarily a sculptor, and (2) Domenico Antonio Vaccaro, a sculptor, architect and sometime painter, had much influence on Neapolitan style in the late 17th century and the early 18th.

BIBLIOGRAPHY

B. de Dominici: *Vite* (1742–3), iii, pp. 467ff

Civiltà del settecento a Napoli, 1734–1799, 2 vols (exh. cat., ed. N. Spinosa; Naples, Capodimonte, and elsewhere, 1979–80), i, p. 165; ii, pp. 40–45

The Golden Age of Naples: Art and Civilization under the Bourbons, 1734–1805 (exh. cat., Detroit, MI, Inst. A., 1981), i, p. 46, 152–5; ii, pp. 286–307, 322–4

(1) Lorenzo Vaccaro (*b* Naples, 10 Aug 1655; *d* Torre del Greco, 1706). Sculptor, architect, silversmith and painter. He was the son of a lawyer and began to study law, but a precocious gift for drawing led him to study both sculpture and architecture with Cosimo Fanzago. On Fanzago's death (1678) Vaccaro inherited several important commissions, one of which was the marble monument to *Francesco Rocco* in the church of the Pietà dei Turchini, Naples. In this powerfully realistic work (begun 1676 by Fanzago and completed by Vaccaro two years later) the portly Rocco kneels on a cushion, his left hand spread across his ample chest and his voluminous drapery overlapping the surrounding frame. Vaccaro's close attention to detail here was particularly admired by his 18th-century biographer de Dominici (p. 469). There followed commissions for several bronze and silver figures in S Gennaro, Naples (1679), marble putti in Santa Croce, Torre del Greco (1680), and stucco figures in the Gesù delle Monache, Naples (1681–5). The stucco decoration in the last, particularly the caryatid-angels, is reminiscent of Algardi's four allegorical marble figures on the tomb of *Leo XI* in St Peter's, Rome, which Vaccaro could have seen on a journey there recorded by de Dominici. The classicism of two terracottas of the *Labours of Hercules* (Naples, Mus. Civ. Gaetano Filangieri) is again indebted to sculpture in Rome. In the 1680s and 1690s Vaccaro and his growing workshop undertook many large-scale decorative schemes in Naples. They executed stucco decorations (1682) in S Giorgio, over life-size stucco statues of *St Helen* and *St Constantine* (both 1689) in S Giovanni Maggiore and the light and graceful stucco decoration (1693–8) of the transept and cupola of S Agostino degli Scalzi, which was one of the most successful decorative works of the period and of considerable influence. Vaccaro was in the forefront of the change from a High Baroque style to the more refined treatment known as *barocchetto*.

In 1689 Vaccaro won the commission for the large silver altarpiece in the Cappella delle Grazie in S Maria la Nova, Naples, decorated with scenes of the *Birth*, *Assumption* and *Presentation of the Virgin*, divided by caryatids. It was executed by the silversmith Matteo Treglia (*fl* 1685–1714), but de Dominici indicates that Vaccaro himself worked in silver. The success of this project led to commissions for other works in silver, among them allegories of the *Four Continents* (1692; Toledo Cathedral). In both these works the dominant influence is no longer Fanzago or Roman sculpture but the painter Francesco Solimena. The influence was mutual; de Dominici described them as 'the Solimena of sculpture' and 'the Vaccaro of painting', but Solimena was the dominant figure, and Vaccaro's increasing response to him can be seen in the eloquent gestures, complex compositions and rich use of drapery of his work in the 1690s. Vaccaro is known to have executed some paintings himself, such as the four recorded in 1690 for the Duca di Morciano (d'Addosio), but none has so far been identified. Until his death Vaccaro continued to work on architectural and decorative schemes, such as the decoration of chapels in the church of the Certosa di S Martino, as well as on monuments, such as the equestrian statue of *Philip V* (1702–5; destr. 1707), for which two bronze modelli survive in the Museo del Prado, Spain.

Vaccaro's son (2) Domenico Antonio Vaccaro inherited his father's workshop, but Lorenzo Vaccaro was also responsible for training a new generation of sculptors, including Matteo Bottiglieri, Bartolomeo Granucci, Domenico Catuogno and Domenico Lenmico (*d* 1700).

BIBLIOGRAPHY
G. B. d'Addosio: 'Documenti inediti di artisti napoletani del XVI e XVII secolo', *Archv Stor. Prov. Napolet.*, xliii (1918), pp. 133–64
E. Catello: 'Lorenzo Vaccaro scultore argentiere', *Napoli Nob.*, xxi (1982), pp. 8–16
V. Rizzo: 'Uno sconosciuto paliotto di Lorenzo Vaccaro e altri fatti coevi napoletani', *Stor. A.*, xlix (1983), pp. 211–33
Civiltà del seicento a Napoli, 2 vols (exh. cat., ed. S. Cassani; Naples, Capodimonte, 1984–5), ii, pp. 227–33

ALEXANDER KADER

(2) Domenico Antonio Vaccaro (*b* Naples, 3 June 1678; *d* Naples, 13 June 1745). Sculptor, architect and painter, son of (1) Lorenzo Vaccaro. He was a prolific and versatile artist who left his mark on the most important Neapolitan sculptural and architectural projects of the early 18th century and elicited special praise from the historian de Dominici for his contribution to the embellishment of the city.

1. PAINTING. He trained in the workshop of his father and then with Francesco Solimena. Among his earliest surviving paintings, executed during the 1690s, are the *Penitent St William of Aquitaine* (Naples, S Agostino degli Scalzi), a work of complex composition, charged colours and dramatic chiaroscuro inspired by Mattia Preti's work, and a *bozzetto* (Naples, Mus. N. S Martino) for the proposed vault decoration of the sacristy of S Domenico Maggiore. De Dominici suggested that it was Domenico's failure to secure the S Domenico commission, which went to Solimena, that dissuaded him from pursuing a career as a painter. Certainly, from around 1707 he appears to have practised almost exclusively as a sculptor and architect, until during the 1730s he resumed painting, executing large works in an individualistic Rococo style for the Collegiata at Marigliano, the Monteverginella in Naples, and for many other Neapolitan churches.

2. SCULPTURE. Domenico's earliest sculptures were made in collaboration with his father, whom he helped to complete the bronze equestrian monument to *Philip V* for the Piazza del Gesù in Naples (1702–5; destr. 1707). In 1707 he carved the marble antependium, the *Dead Christ with Angels*, for the high altar of S Giacomo degli Spagnoli. After Lorenzo's death Domenico completed his unfinished figures of *Providence* and *Divine Grace* (1708) for the Cappella di S Giovanni Battista in the church of the Certosa di S Martino. He continued his family's involvement in the major redecoration programme at the Certosa for another 13 years. He provided figures of *Solitude* (1707) and *Penitence* (1708) for the Cappella di S Bruno and monumental half-length busts of *St Januarius* and *St Martin* (1709) for the Chiostro Grande. In 1709–19 he made four reliefs of the *Evangelists* and the imposing high altar relief of the *Trinity and the Virgin Consigning the Keys of the City of Naples to St Januarius* for the Cappella di S Gennaro, and his colourful stucco and marble decoration of the Cappella di S Giuseppe (1718–19) is one of the most important early 18th-century decorative ensembles in Naples. Domenico's contemporary Cappella del Rosario, with graceful white stucco garland-bearing angels balanced on the architraves and putti and cherubs flitting over the walls, is characteristic of his light-hearted *barocchetto* architectural decoration. From 1719–24 he was occupied on the decoration of the crypt of S Paolo Maggiore, carving four atmospheric marble reliefs of the *Life of St Cajetan*. For the same church he executed one of his most appealing works, the tender and naturalistic marble group of the *Guardian Angel* (1724; *in situ*; see fig.), in which the influence of Solimena's painterly style is especially evident. Domenico's carved obelisk and its bronze statue of *St Dominic* in the Piazza S Domenico, Naples, date from 1737.

In addition to his religious commissions, Domenico Vaccaro also produced portrait busts for funerary monuments, among them those of *Vincenzo Petra* and his brother *Domenico Petra* (marble, 1701) for their chapel in

Domenico Antonio Vaccaro: *Guardian Angel*, marble, h. 1.90 m, 1724 (Naples, S Paolo Maggiore)

S Pietro a Maiella, and that of *Anna Maria Caterina Doria* (marble, 1730), in the same church. Like his father, he provided models for silversmiths, such as that for the monumental silver statue of the *Virgin Immaculate* (destr.), finished by 1724 for the high altar of the church of the Gesù Nuovo. He also made crib figures (e.g. Naples, Mus. N. S Martino; Munich, Bayer. Nmus.).

3. ARCHITECTURE. Domenico Vaccaro was among those artists who introduced the light-hearted *barocchetto* style of architectural decoration to Naples. At S Maria delle Grazie, Calvizzano, near Naples, he added transepts and a choir to an earlier church. His extensive use of white stucco rather than coloured decoration for the interior accentuates the impression of height, and is so applied as apparently to abolish the conventional architectonic elements. In the centralized church of S Maria della Concezione in Naples (1718–24), Domenico supervised the design and execution of the decoration, carved the sculpture and provided the painted altarpiece. Again all superfluous decoration is eliminated, and large windows in the elongated central octagon accentuate the brilliant light created by the white stucco decoration, whose forms are inspired by Cosimo Fanzago's. The towers and concave profiles of Domenico's church façades are related to those of Francesco Borromini, but are less inspired than his interiors. His most engaging architectural device, however, was his use of maiolica tiles in the redecoration of the Chiostro delle Clarisse (1739–42) at S Chiara, Naples. The coloured narrative tiles that clad the piers and benches dividing the original Gothic garden lend a brilliantly conceived bucolic note to this city cloister. Domenico's most ambitious secular architectural commission was the Palazzo Tarsia in Naples (1732–9). This magnificent palace, conceived on a larger scale than any hitherto in the city, was never completed and its elaborate terraces, ramps and gardens were destroyed in the 19th century. Its design perhaps owed something to Lucas von Hildebrandt's plans for the Belvedere in Vienna.

BIBLIOGRAPHY
A. Blunt: *Neapolitan Baroque and Rococo Architecture* (London, 1973), pp. 110–28, pls 172–93
R. Causa: *L'arte nella Certosa di San Martino* (Cava dei Tirreni, 1973)
T. Fittipaldi: *Scultura napoletana del settecento* (Naples, 1980), pp. 38–40, 82–7 [extensive bibliog.]

ANTONIA BOSTRÖM

Vaccaro, Andrea (*bapt* Naples, 8 May 1604; *d* Naples, 18 Jan 1670). Italian painter. He first studied literature but at an early age turned to painting. He was probably a pupil of the late-Mannerist painter Gerolamo Imparato, though there are no known works from this period. About 1620 he became a follower of Caravaggio; he copied Caravaggio's *Flagellation* (Naples, Capodimonte), and his copy and the original hung in S Domenico Maggiore, Naples (copy *in situ*). *David with the Head of Goliath* (Florence, Fond. Longhi) and *Sebastian* (Naples, Capodimonte) are early works indebted to Caravaggio's naturalism and chiaroscuro. After 1630 Vaccaro drew inspiration from Guido Reni, Anthony van Dyck and Pietro Novelli and made copies of their works for Neapolitan collectors and dealers such as Gaspar Roomer and Jan Vandeneyden. *Abraham and the Angels* (Naples, priv. col.; see 1984–5 exh. cat., p. 489) dates from this period; Reni's images of saints are the forerunners of his *St Rosalia* (mid-1630s; Madrid, Prado) and *Penitent Magdalene* (1636; Naples, Certosa di S Martino, chapel of St Martin).

Vaccaro was one of the most successful Neapolitan painters in his day, and in 1635 he began exporting many works to Spain for religious orders and for noble patrons; among such works were his canvases of saints for the Casón del Buen Retiro (Madrid, Prado), his *St Theresa's Vision of the Golden Necklet* (1642; Madrid, Real Acad. S Fernando) and the four scenes from the *Life of Tobias* (*c.* 1640; Barcelona, Mus. A. Catalunya; see fig.). After 1640 his workshop produced a vast number of devotional works. Yet in works by his own hand, such as the outstanding *Tobias* pictures, he achieved a perfect blend of the classicism of Reni, Domenichino and Poussin with rich colour and glimpses of distant landscape that are characteristically Neapolitan.

In the mid-1640s Vaccaro came into contact with Bernardo Cavallino, from whom he learned to soften the academic structure of his paintings by injecting an element of sentimentality. *Jonah Preaching to the Ninevites* (1640–50; Seville, Mus. B.A.), signed and painted on copper,

Andrea Vaccaro: *Tobias Curing his Father*, oil on canvas, 1.96×2.61 m, *c.* 1640 (Barcelona, Museu d'Art de Catalunya)

forms part of a series of paintings that included three works by Cavallino—*Mucius Scaevola before King Porsenna* (Fort Worth, TX, Kimbell A. Mus.), the *Shade of Samuel Invoked by Saul* (Malibu, CA, Getty Mus.) and the *Expulsion of Heliodorus from the Temple* (Moscow, Pushkin Mus. F.A.).

The years between 1650 and 1670 have been unjustly regarded as marking a period of decline for Vaccaro. Yet in this period, between the leadership of Massimo Stanzione and the rise of Luca Giordano, he exerted a considerable influence over Neapolitan painters. This was made possible by his role as founder and leader of the Congrega dei SS Anna e Luca (1665), an embryonic version of a Neapolitan public academy of painting. His two scenes from the *Life of St Hugo* (1652; Naples, Certosa di S Martino) are an original synthesis of the classical style of Stanzione, influenced by Domenichino and Reni, and the brilliant neo-Venetian colour of Novelli, Ribera, van Dyck and Rubens.

In his last period Vaccaro responded to the brilliant colour of Giordano and to the shifting patterns of light and shade that characterize the art of Mattia Preti. In the *Madonna Interceding for the Souls in Purgatory* (1660; Naples, S Maria del Pianto) the figures remain classical, yet the flickering, theatrical light is now far removed from a Caravaggesque chiaroscuro. The scenes from the life of

St Catherine of Alexandria (1659–60; Naples, S Maria della Sanità), *St Luke and the Virgin* (1666; Naples, S Giovanni Battista delle Monache) and the *Communion of St Mary of Egypt* (1668; Naples, S Maria Egiziaca all'Olmo) share these characteristics. Two works from Vaccaro's final years, *St Peter Tending St Agatha* and its pendant, *St Lucy Dragged by Bulls* (both Madrid, Real Acad. S Fernando), clearly reveal his source of inspiration in the art of Giordano and Preti. The style of his son, Nicola Vaccaro (?1634–1709), who completed the *St Martha* (Naples, S Marta) left unfinished on Vaccaro's death, is a less subtle development of these sources.

BIBLIOGRAPHY

Bolaffi; Thieme–Becker

B. de Dominici: *Vite* (1742–3), iii, pp. 135–57

G. A. Galante: *Guida sacra della città di Napoli* (Naples, 1872); ed. N. Spinosa and others (Naples, 1985)

R. Causa: *L'arte della Certosa di San Martino in Napoli* (Cava dei Tirreni, 1973), pp. 58–9, 65, 80

D. Vasseur: 'Lamentation over the Dead Christ by Andrea Vaccaro', *Bull. A. Inst. Chicago*, lxxi/5 (1977), pp. 14–17

Painting in Naples, 1606–1705; From Caravaggio to Giordano (exh. cat., ed. C. Whitfield and J. Martineau; London, RA, 1982), pp. 261–2

Il patrimonio artistico del Banco di Napoli (Naples, 1984), pp. 52–5 [entry by R. Lattuada]

Civiltà del seicento a Napoli (exh. cat., ed. S. Cassani; Naples, Capodimonte, 1984–5), i, pp. 130–31, 251–3

Pintura napolitana de Caravaggio a Giordano (exh. cat. by A. E. Pérez Sánchez, Madrid, Pal. Villahermosa, 1985), pp. 59, 318–42

L. Arbace, F. Capobianco and R. Pastorelli: *Museo della Certosa di San Martino: Il Quarto del Priore* (Naples, 1986), pp. 48, 90–93

Váchal, Josef (*b* Milaveč, 23 Sept 1884; *d* Studeňany u Jičína, 10 May 1969). Czech printmaker, illustrator and writer. He studied in the studios of Alois Kalvoda (1875–1934) and Rudolf Bém, but he was self taught in woodcut. He lived and worked in Prague and then in Studeňany u Jičína. His life was marked by his experiences as an illegitimate child, by psychotic exaggeration, and by the total lack of recognition for his work. The latter ensured constant financial difficulties. He alternated between a fervent Baroque form of Christianity on the one hand and blasphemous satanic mysticism, spiritism, anarchism etc. on the other. He was deliberately provocative and contemptuous in his social relations.

Váchal joined the artistic group Sursum (initiated 1910–11), where he associated with Jan Konůpek (1883–1950) and Jan Zrzavý, among others, but stylistically he was markedly different from his peers in the group. His work is infused with the atmosphere of picturesque medieval paintings, the visions of Hieronymus Bosch, and crudely worked Baroque prints from the Counter-Reformation and from folk art. Among modern trends he espoused Expressionism, as in the cycle of coloured woodcuts *At the Front* (1919; Prague, N.G., Kinský Pal.), Surrealism, and also Primitivism and naive art. Váchal produced fine prints, books (which he himself wrote, printed, ornamented, bound and published), graphic designs and book illustrations. He also drew and painted. He is noted for systematically developing the theory and the technique of coloured woodcuts. His versatility culminated, however, in the creation of his own books (often single copies or in limited editions), which he printed himself on a hand press with his own carved typeface and decorated with his own woodcuts. His greatest technical achievement was the printing of typeface and illustrations from a single plate. In form and content his books mostly recall Baroque prints, characterized by deliberate 'anti-artistic' treatment. Public indifference long prevented any recognition of his work, and his literary work remains unevaluated and largely unpublished.

WRITINGS
Krvavý román [Bloody novel] (Prague, 1990)

BIBLIOGRAPHY
Josef Váchal: Grafika a kresby [Josef Váchal: graphics and drawings] (exh. cat., Olomouc, Reg. Gal., 1967)
M. Bajerová: *Josef Váchal a kniha: Soupis knižního díla* [Josef Váchal and the book: list of his book production] (Prague, 1968)
J. Ballek: *Pekelník Josef Váchal* [Josef Váchal: hell's child] (Chlumec nad Cidlinou, 1970)
Zasloužilý umělec Josef Váchal: Volná a knižní grafika [Merited artist Josef Váchal: fine and book graphics] (exh. cat., Brno, House A., 1982)
Tschechische Kunst der 20er & 30er Jahre (exh. cat., Darmstadt, Inst. Mathildenhöhe, 1988–9)
J. Olič: *Readings on Josef Váchal* (Brno, 1991)

JIŘÍ BUREŠ

Václav IV, King of Bohemia. *See* LUXEMBOURG, (4).

Vacquerie, Auguste (*b* Villequier, Seine-Maritime, 1819; *d* Paris, 1895). French photographer and poet. He was a close friend and associate of Charles Hugo (*see* HUGO, (2)) and followed him and the Hugo family into exile in the Channel Islands in 1852. Along with Hugo, he dispelled the boredom of life in exile by working on a literary and photographic project about the life of the Hugo family. The albums they produced—perhaps as many as 67, but of which only 2 survive (Rochester, NY, Int. Mus. Phot., and Paris, Bib. N.)—were presented to friends as mementoes of the Hugo family. Although the photographs are technically poor, the subjects, which include family, friends, children and household pets, have all the charm of intimate snapshots of 19th-century family life.

BIBLIOGRAPHY
H. Gernsheim: *The Origins of Photography* (London, 1982), pp. 259, 262

PATRICIA STRATHERN

Vadasz, Christine (*b* Budapest, 1 March 1946). Australian architect of Hungarian birth. She came to Australia when she was three but was raised in Central European traditions that taught her a special appreciation of art and craftsmanship. She studied at the University of Adelaide, and, while still a student, worked in I. M. Pei's New York office. Graduating in 1971, she worked for the Sydney architect Bill Lucas in 1972–3, enjoyed the unconventional working environment, moved to the coastal town of Byron Bay in northern New South Wales in 1974 and began her own practice in similar style: 'If there is a lot of work we work hard. If there is a lull we go surfing'. In the 20 years from 1974 she produced a body of organic and often quite sculptural work that includes 30 houses and 18 commercial and tourism projects. Her approach to design is subtle and innovative (e.g. Bedarra Bay and Bedarra Hideaway resorts, 1985–6, Bedarra Island, North Queensland), and she frequently uses timber, stone and other natural materials. The Dunne/Vadasz House (1977) and Thorpe House (1987), both Byron Bay, and the Klinger House (1994), Port Douglas, are examples of her residential work in non-urban areas. She provides specialist architectural design and advice for the tourist industry when a high degree of environmental protection is required, as in the Carita Beach Resort (1987), West Java, and the Bakal Tourism Masterplan (1993), Kerala, India. She taught design at the University of Sydney (1985), lectured at most major Australian architectural schools, participated in many conferences and won various awards, including the Royal Australian Institute of Architects (RAIA) President's Award (New South Wales Chapter, 1984); the Queensland RAIA Non-Residential Award (1988) and the House of the Year Commendation (1988).

WRITINGS
'Making Waves in Byron Bay', *Archit. Bull.* (April 1984), pp. 3–5

BIBLIOGRAPHY
Australian Built: A Photographic Exhibition of Recent Australian Architecture (exh. cat., ed. M. Griggs and C. McGregor; Sydney, Des. A. Board Austral. Council, 1985), p. 21
B. Andresen: 'Bedarra Island Resorts', *Archit. Australia*, lxxviii/7 (1989), pp. 44–8
P. Drew: 'A House that Lives with Nature', *Business Rev. Wkly* (15 June 1990), pp. 116–17
C. Lorenz: *Women in Architecture: A Contemporary Perspective* (New York, 1990)
P. Middleton: 'Raise High the Roof-beam Carpenter: Vadasz and Addison at Tusculum', *Archit. Bull.* (June 1990), p. 10
C. Bull: *Sustainable Tourism in Remote Australia: Strategies for Physical Planning and Infrastructure* (diss., Cambridge, MA, Harvard U., 1991)

ANNA RUBBO

Vadder, Lodewijk [Lodewyk] **de** (*bapt* Brussels, 8 April 1605; *d* Brussels, 10 Aug 1655). Flemish painter, draughtsman, engraver and tapestry designer. He was received as a master in the Brussels Guild of St Luke on 15 May 1628, probably, like his brother Hubert de Vadder, after an apprenticeship to his elder brother, Philippe de Vadder (Coeckelberghs). Lodewijk is best known as a landscape painter, although he also executed landscape engravings and drawings. He was granted a privilege to make tapestry cartoons by the Brussels city magistrate in 1644. In this capacity he worked mainly for weavers such as Jean Courdijn and Baudouin van Beveren. The latter referred to him as the best landscape painter in the country and in 1644 paid him 1000 florins for a series of designs of the *Story of Diana and Pan*.

It used to be thought that de Vadder painted only small panels, usually bearing the monogram LDV, but it has been shown (e.g. by de Callatay) the he was also responsible for several large compositions previously attributed to Jacques d'Arthois. Like d'Arthois and Lucas Achtschellinck, de Vadder painted the rural surroundings of Brussels and the woods near Soignes, delighting especially in depicting thickly leaved trees and sunken paths amid dunes (e.g. *Landscape with Horsemen*, Brussels, Mus. A. Anc.). His works are distinguished by their free compositions and loose brushwork. The breadth of his touch, seen, for example, in the long brushstrokes used to render foliage, and his intense, often strongly contrasted colours are reminiscent of Rubens's style. De Vadder's work also has affinities with d'Arthois's early paintings, although his decorative sense seems to be supported by a more direct and heartfelt experience of nature, as in the *Wooded Landscape with Peasants* (Barnard Castle, Bowes Mus.). Ignatius van der Stock became his apprentice in 1653, and, according to de Bie though uncorroborated by the guild's registers, Achtschellinck also studied with him.

BIBLIOGRAPHY

Hollstein: *Dut. & Flem.*

C. de Bie: *Het gulden cabinet* (1661), p. 98

Y. Thiéry: *Le Paysage flamand au XVIIe siècle* (Paris and Brussels, 1953), pp. 133–6

E. de Callatay: 'Etudes sur les paysagistes bruxellois du XVIIe siècle', *Rev. Belge Archéol. & Hist. A./Belge Tijdschr. Oudhdknde & Kstgesch.*, xxix (1960), pp. 155–70

D. Coeckelberghs: 'Contribution à l'étude du paysage italianisant flamand et hollandais au XVIIe siècle: Oeuvre inédites de A. Goubau, L. de Vadder, J. Both', *Rev. Archéologues & Historiens A.* Louvain, viii (1975), pp. 109–14

O. Naumann: *Netherlandish Artists* (1980), 6 [v/i] of *The Illustrated Bartsch*, ed. W. L. Strauss (New York, 1978–)

HANS DEVISSCHER

Vadnagar [anc. Ānandapura]. Town and temple site in northern Gujarat, India. While the date of its foundation is uncertain, references in the ancient religious text known as the *Skanda purāṇa* and the writings of the Chinese pilgrim Xuanzang (7th century AD) indicate the considerable importance the town enjoyed by this date as a centre of Hindu and Jaina learning. Two elaborately carved monumental arched gateways (*toraṇa*s) dating to the 11th century and located just outside the northern walls are the major artistic remains. In form, sculptural style and trabeate construction technique they resemble the gateways at Modhera and Sidhpur. Nothing remains of the temple to which they were originally attached. Several stone-lined, stepped tanks of the 11th and 12th centuries also survive, the largest being the Sarmishta Tank; these were embellished with figurative relief sculptures. A stone inscription embedded in one of Vadnagar's six gates commemorates the building of the town's walls and dates to 1152. Several temples, originally built during the SOLANKI period (11th century) have been refurbished and expanded, as in the case of the Hatkeshvara Temple; there are also several Jaina temples, notably the 10th-century Adinatha Temple. In the *Āyin-i Akbarī* ('Annals of Akbar') of Abu'l Fazl (*c.* 1596–1602), Vadnagar is described as a thriving city of many temples populated mainly by Brahmins. It was plundered by the Marathas in 1762 and was subsequently ruled by the Gaekwads of Baroda (*see* VADODARA) until 1949.

BIBLIOGRAPHY

J. Burgess and H. Cousens: *The Architectural Antiquities of Northern Gujarat, More Especially of the Districts Included in the Baroda State* (London, 1903)

H. D. Sankalia: *The Archaeology of Gujarat* (Bombay, 1941)

S. B. Rajyagor, ed.: *Mehsana District*, Gujarat State Gazetteers (Ahmedabad, 1975)

□

Vadodara [Baroda]. City in Gujarat, India. Although artefacts from as early as the Palaeolithic and Mesolithic periods (*c.* 600,000–*c.* 5000 BC) have been found in the region, Vadodara only came to prominence after a Maratha family known as the Gaekwad won control of the city from the Mughals in 1732, ruling it virtually without interruption until Indian independence from British rule in 1947. The few Islamic remains in the city include the Jami' Masjid, built in the 16th century by the Mughal emperor Akbar (*reg* 1556–1605), and the mosque of Sakar Khan. North of the old city is the former British cantonment, with an Anglican church built in 1838. Examples of the *wada* form of residential dwelling survive (*see also* INDIAN SUBCONTINENT, §III, 7(ii)(c)).

Almost all surviving Gaekwad buildings in Vadodara were sponsored by Maharaja Sayaji Rao III (*reg* 1875–1936). A social reformer, he was very Westernized in his tastes, and his buildings exhibit a frank and bold eclecticism in which structural and decorative elements from the Western Gothic and classical traditions blend with those of Mughal, Rajput and Gujarati origin. This is epitomized in the Laxmi Vilas Palace (1890), designed by Charles Mant (*d* 1881) in the Indo-Saracenic style and completed by ROBERT FELLOWES CHISHOLM (*see also* INDIAN SUBCONTINENT, §III, 8(i)). The 150 m-long building comprises three distinct parts: the public rooms, primarily in Mughal style; the prince's private apartments, which emulate Rajput architecture; and the women's quarters, executed in the Gujarati regional style. Dominating the façade, a central cupola and tower rise above a scintillating array of decorative detail. The interior is almost completely Western in layout and furnishings, with billiard and dining rooms and a vast durbar hall decorated with a Venetian floor mosaic. Other works of Maharaja Sayaji Rao include the Makapura Palace (late 19th century), 6 km south of Vadodara, a three-storey Italianate building that includes a Mughal dome and a side entrance porch with a Bengali-style curved roof, the Pratap Vilas Palace (*c.* 1910) and several parks and tanks. The Kirti Mandir (Temple of Fame; early 20th century) contains the cenotaphs of the Gaekwad kings; in its vault are paintings by NANDALAL BOSE.

Vadodara has several museums. The Museum and Picture Gallery (founded 1894 and 1920 respectively) contain collections of sculptures from Shamalaji and Roda and of Indian and European paintings, while the Maharaja Fateh Singh Museum holds the royal collection of Asian and European art. At the Maharaja Sayajirao University two collections of Indian sculpture are held by the Departments of Museology and Archaeology respectively; the university is also noted for its outstanding art and art-history courses (*see also* INDIA, REPUBLIC OF, §X).

BIBLIOGRAPHY
B. Subharao: *Baroda Through the Ages* (Baroda, 1953)
S. B. Rajvagor, ed.: *Vadodara District*, Gujarat State Gazetteers (Ahmadabad, 1979)
Maharaja of Baroda: *The Palaces of India* (New York, 1980)
P. Davies: *The Penguin Guide to the Monuments of India*, ii (London, 1989)
G. H. R. Tillotson: *The Tradition of Indian Architecture* (New Haven, 1989)

WALTER SMITH

Vadstena Abbey. Mother church of the Brigittine Order, situated in the town of Vadstena on Lake Vättern, Sweden, *c*. 40 km west of Linköping. It is on the site of a fortified farm bequeathed for building an abbey by King Magnus IV Eriksson (*reg* 1319–65) in 1346.

The abbey, dedicated to the Virgin Mary, was legally established after the Brigittine Rule was confirmed by Pope Urban V (1362–70) in 1370. It was to be a double monastery with separate quarters for 60 nuns and 25 monks, superintended by an abbess. Building began *c*. 1369, but by 1384, when the first members of the Order were accepted, the convent was served only by a small wooden church or chapel, mentioned in the *Vadstena Diary* for 1388, when 'the entire wooden chapel and both stone houses as well as a great part of the sisters' quarters' were burnt down. The stone church may have been begun in the 1370s, but building began in earnest only after the fire. The nuns' buildings were arranged round a cloister, of which the north and west walks survive, on the north side of the church. The monks had one main building, south-west of the church, and the churchyard, surrounded by high walls and containing the stations of the cross, lay to the east.

St Bridget's *Revelations* (*see* BRIGITTINE ORDER) include instructions for building and arranging the abbey, which could be very precise:

> God's Son speaks: 'The church should be in the west, by the lake, and a high wall should lead from the brick house to the north along the lake to the clerks' yard. The brothers' choir should measure 22 cubits in length below a single vault, which reaches from the west wall to the high altar, so that this high altar finds itself beneath the vault and the clerks must stand between the high altar and the west wall. The vault should measure 20 cubit in width. This wall, which is behind the brothers' choir-stalls and faces the sisters' area to the north, should have five window openings near the floor, against which the sisters should make confession and receive the Lord's body. The church itself should have five lengthways vaults and three widthways, and each vault should measure 20 cubits in width and 20 in length' (*Revelations*, 28).

These instructions are reflected in most Brigittine buildings. Vadstena has a three-aisled hall church with five bays, and a separate western choir of one bay. The church (see fig.) is built of limestone and buttressed on the exterior. The interior is faced with limestone, which is now exposed but was probably originally plastered and whitewashed, like the brick vaults. The arcade has eight massive, octagonal columns with gently pointed arches, and a stellar vault. There are five entrances: two double portals in the east wall for the lay congregation, the nuns' door on the north side of the nave, a reconstructed door in the west of the south nave aisle and a door leading south from the brothers' choir to the sacristy. The *Vadstena Diary* records nearly all the building history of the church: the brothers' choir at the west was consecrated in 1405 when the vault was built; the outer walls of the entire church were built to their full height by 1414, and the arcade was begun in 1416. The east wall of the choir was finished in 1418, and the main vault was built in 1420 and 1421. The church was consecrated in 1430.

In accordance with St Bridget's instructions, no decoration was allowed, and the liturgical arrangement was designed more for the convenience of the members of the Order than for the laity. The brothers' choir, with the altar under the choir arch, was orientated towards the west. The altar of the Virgin, in an elevated position at the east end of the nave, could be used only by the sisters. Long galleries, with stairways giving access from the west, were built along both sides of the nave, those on the south for the monks, and the north for the nuns. The main vessel was screened from the laity by openwork iron gates. This arrangement became the prototype for the churches of

Vadstena Abbey Church, view from the east, consecrated 1430

the Order. Nothing remains of the original arrangement at Vadstena itself, except the position of the high altar at the west end of the church, but at Maribo Abbey in Denmark (now a Lutheran church) the long galleries of the nave survive.

Vadstena did not found a distinct architectural current, but it was the model for numerous Brigittine daughter houses in other European countries. Its history shows how the Order benefited from the king's power and the country's magnates. Although Bridget, who died in 1373, never visited the abbey, she performed a significant deed through its foundation. Vadstena became renowned both as a religious institution and as a humanist educational centre.

BIBLIOGRAPHY

B. Berthelson: *Studier i birgittinerordens byggnadsskick* [Studies in the building style of the Brigittine Order], Kun. Vitt., Hist. & Ant. Akad. Hand., lxiii (Stockholm, 1947)
I. Anderson: *Vadstena gård och kloster* [Vadstena farm and abbey], 2 vols (Uppsala, 1972)
C. Gejrot: *Diarium Vadstenense: The Memorial Book of Vadstena Abbey*, Acta U. Stockholm.: Stud. Lat. Stockholm., xxiii (Stockholm, 1988)
I. Anderson: *Vadstena klosterkyrka* [Vadstena abbey church], Sveriges Kyrkor, ccxiii (Stockholm, 1991)

ERLAND LAGERLÖF

Vaenius, Otto van. *See* VEEN, OTTO VAN.

Vaernewijck [Vaernewyck], **Marcus van** (*b* Ghent, 21 Dec 1516; *d* Ghent, 20 Feb 1569). South Netherlandish writer and poet. He was a public servant in Ghent: guardian of the poorhouse in 1563, alderman in 1564, headman of seven craft corporations, and in 1566 he became controller of the grain depot. He was a fervent Catholic and led the civic guard responsible for reporting to the authorities on the religious convictions of the people of Ghent and foreigners in the city. In 1560 he published *Vlaemsche audvremdigheyt*, a poem on Flemish history in four parts. *Den spieghel der Nederlandscher audtheyt* was published eight times between 1568 and 1829; in essence a history of Flanders from antiquity until 1568, this bizarre mixture of reality and fantasy is historically unreliable. However, the last chapters contain interesting information concerning the city of Ghent and its art treasures, including the Ghent Altarpiece by Jan and Hubert van Eyck. Vaernewijck's diary, consisting of 10 books written between 1566 and 1568, is historically more reliable and of more importance to the art historian. It provides information concerning the Protestant secret preachings (Flem. *Hagepreken*), the iconoclastic riots and a systematic review of the destruction of works of art in Ghent, the ill-fated attack by Prince William I of Orange-Nassau on Spanish forces in October–November 1568 and the subsequent repression of the Flemish people by the Duke of Alba and the Spanish. These books are an important primary source for factual evidence as well as for understanding the popular mentality that shaped Flemish culture in Ghent in a period of religious transformation.

WRITINGS

Vlaemsche audvremdigheyt [Old Flemish curiosities] (Ghent, 1560); rev. as *Nieu tractaet en curte bescrijvinghe van dat edel graefscap van Vlaenderen en ander omligghende landen* [New tract and concise description of the noble country of Flanders and other surrounding countries] (Ghent, 1562)

Den spieghel der Nederlandscher audtheyt [The mirror of Netherlandish antiquity] (Ghent, 1568); 2nd edn as *Die historie Belgis* (Ghent, 1574, 3–5/1619, 6/1665, 7/1784, 8/1829)
Van de beroerlicke tijden in de Nederlijden: En voornamelijk in Ghendt, 1566–1568 [About the troubled times in the Netherlands: in particular in Ghent, 1566–1568] (MS. diary in 10 vols; 1566–8; Ghent U.); ed. F. Vanderhaeghen (Ghent, 1872–81)

BIBLIOGRAPHY

NBW; Thieme–Becker
H. Van Nuffel: 'Marcus van Vaernewijck (1518–1569) en zijn kroniek over de beroerlicke tijden', *Standen & Landen*, xi (1966), pp. 113–45
——: 'De opstand van de Nederlanden in de literatuur', *Opstand en Pacificatie in de Lage Landen* (Ghent, 1976), pp. 147, 241

HANS J. VAN MIEGROET

Vafflard, Pierre(-Antoine)-Auguste (*b* Paris, 19 Dec 1777; *d* Paris, 1837). French painter. A pupil of Jean-Baptiste Regnault, he exhibited regularly in the Salon between 1800 and 1831. He executed a number of unremarkable academic works on Classical subjects, for example *Electra* (1804; exh. Salon 1814) and *Orestes Sleeping* (1819; both Dijon, Mus. B.-A.). Vafflard gained more success with his Troubadour pictures, which he began to paint in the early 19th century, at the outset of this fashion. They are remarkable for their absence of colour, their theatrical quality and contrasted lighting effects. One of his earliest Troubadour scenes was *Emma and Eginhard* (exh. Salon 1804; Evreux, Mus. Evreux), based on an episode in the history of Charlemagne's court and painted at a time when the Holy Roman Empire was in fashion in official French circles. In this sentimental painting Vafflard demonstrated his historicizing intentions by emphasizing medieval costume and Gothic architecture and seeking to create an atmosphere similar to the *romans de la chevalerie*, so highly thought of in France at the end of the 18th century. In the same Salon he exhibited a strange and novel painting, *Young Holding his Dead Daughter in his Arms* (Angoulême, Mus. Mun.), taken from Edward Young's *Night Thoughts* (pubd in French in 1769–70). This English poet was a rare source of inspiration for painters seeking romantic subjects, who tended to prefer Gessner or Ossian. Vafflard's emphasis on the fantastic and the morbid was also unusual at this period, and these effects were further accentuated by leaden tones and a strange lunar chromaticism.

Vafflard established his reputation with the *Hospice Dog* (exh. Salon 1810; Arenenberg, Napoleonmus.), which was bought by Empress Josephine for her gallery at Malmaison. As in *Young Holding his Dead Daughter*, although in a less dramatic way, Vafflard exploited contrasts of light that were accentuated by the presence of snow. The subject, a lost, sleeping child brought back by a dog, was the ideal choice for a public, with a taste for charming, sentimental anecdote, that enjoyed scenes showing children with devoted pets by such artists as Jeanne-Elisabeth Chaudet and Henriette Lorimier (*fl* 1800–54).

Like many Troubadour painters, Vafflard attempted a large painting halfway between the grand style and historical anecdote. He won a Prix d'Encouragement for the *Last Respects Paid to Duguesclin* (exh. Salon 1806; Rennes, Mus. B.-A. & Archéol.). The work was inspired by Nicolas-Guy Brenet's *Death of Duguesclin* (1778; Grenoble, Mus. Peint. & Sculp.) and was intended to re-create the famous and mythical 'age of chivalry'. To achieve authenticity,

Vafflard crowded the composition with knights in armour and banners, which were attacked by the critics who also disliked the dark tonality and the absence of any chiaroscuro that might enliven this stiff and awkward scene. During the Empire, Vafflard also painted incidents from contemporary history, for example *Rosbach's Column Defeated by the French Army* (exh. Salon 1810; Versailles, Château).

After 1815 Vafflard's career went into decline. He restored paintings in Versailles and executed a number of religious compositions, which were brighter and more animated than his earlier work, including *St Margaret Driven out by her Father* (exh. Salon 1817; Paris, Ste-Marguerite) and *St Ambrose Saving a Priest from the People's Rage* (exh. Salon 1819; Paris, St Ambroise). However, he often lacked work, as he wrote to the Minister of the Maison du Roi when he attempted, unsuccessfully, to get a commission for ceilings in the Louvre (Paris, Archvs N., 0^3 1426). In his last years he abandoned historical subjects to paint a few portraits and intimist scenes in the style of Eugène Devéria, for example *Rest* (1830) and *Waiting* (1831; both Evreux, Mus. Evreux). He made several drawings to be engraved in Godefroy Engelmann's *Galerie militaire dédiée aux braves*.

BIBLIOGRAPHY

P. Marmottan: *L'Ecole française de peinture (1789–1830)* (Paris, 1886), pp. 306, 334–5
H. Béraldi: *Les Graveurs du XIXe siècle*, v (Paris, 1889), pp. 167–8
F. Benoit: *L'Art français sous la Révolution et l'Empire* (Paris, 1897/R 1975), pp. 323, 392–3
De David à Delacroix: La Peinture française de 1774 à 1830 (exh. cat., Paris, Grand Pal., 1974), pp. 625–7

MARIE-CLAUDE CHAUDONNERET

Vaga, Perino del. *See* PERINO DEL VAGA.

Vagedes, Adolph von (*b* Münster, 26 May 1777; *d* Düsseldorf, 27 Jan 1842). German architect. He may have studied architecture in Paris, and his work shows the influence of Jean-Nicolas-Louis Durand. He first worked as an architect in Münster, but by 1808 he had moved to Düsseldorf, then capital of the Grand Duchy of Berg, where he became Baudirektor (1812). When the Grand Duchy was absorbed by Prussia (1815) he became Baurat, effectively a demotion, in the regional administration. Thereafter he had to suffer his designs being altered by his superiors in Berlin, particularly by Karl Friedrich Schinkel. Vagedes adhered closely to classical precedent, as in the most beautiful of his surviving buildings, the Ratinger Tor (1812–14) in Düsseldorf, which was based on the Doric propylaeum of the Acropolis at Athens, whereas Schinkel used classical elements with greater freedom. The Ratinger Tor consists of twin Greek Doric hexastyle temples flanking the road to Ratingen. Vagedes's ideas on urban planning appear to have been inspired by the example of Paris. For Elberfeld (preliminary drafts 1817; unexecuted) he designed a circular platz 100 m across, with a Rathaus and Bourse situated on an axis to give the composition importance and grandeur. The city council rejected the design as too costly and unsuited for a modest bourgeois town. For the extensions to the medieval city of Krefeld (1819; executed from 1824 in a modified form) he suggested a grid plan with streets of varying widths to avoid monotony, strict building regulations to limit building heights and palace façades masking the many units of housing behind. Schinkel disapproved, preferring street frontages of individual single houses. Of Vagedes's five churches not one was built without intervention by others. Only the ground-plan and parts of the exterior of the Protestant church (1825) of Solingen-Wald are his own work, the design having been altered considerably by the Oberbaudeputation in Berlin. Although begun by him, the Laurentiuskirche (1829–35; destr. 1944, rebuilt with modifications) in Elberfeld was completed by Otto van Lassaulx. Despite numerous alterations, his basic design was retained, consisting of a square nave, divided by four high piers, and a shallow, rectangular chancel alcove with a twin-towered façade surmounted by spires. From the 1830s Vagedes was director of the office of weights and measures and as an architect was almost forgotten by the time of his death.

BIBLIOGRAPHY

T. Rensing and W. Kordt: 'Adolph von Vagedes', *Z. Westfälen*, xxvi (1941), pp. 243–4
W. Kordt: *Adolph von Vagedes* (Ratingen, 1961)
W. Zimmermann: *Adolph von Vagedes und seine Kirchenbauten* (Cologne, 1964)
W. Weyres: 'Das Ratinger Tor in Düsseldorf', *Beiträge zur rheinischen Kunstgeschichte und Denkmalpflege*, ed. G. Borchers, ii (Düsseldorf, 1974), pp. 213–26
E. Trier and W. Weyres, eds: *Kunst des 19. Jahrhunderts im Rheinland* (Düsseldorf, 1980), Architektur, i, pp. 81–92, 278–81; ii, pp. 503–23

WILLY WEYRES

Vagharshapat. *See* ĒDJMIADZIN.

Vagkat. *See* URA TYUBE.

Vágó. Hungarian family of architects and urban planners. László Vágó (*b* Nagyvárad [now Oradea, Romania], 30 March 1875; *d* Budapest, 30 Dec 1933) received his diploma in architecture from the State Architects' High School, Budapest. His brother József Vágó (*b* Nagyvárad, 23 Dec 1877; *d* Salies-de-Béarn, 7 June 1947) obtained his diploma in 1900 from the Hungarian Palatine Joseph Technical University, Budapest. László worked first on construction design and urban planning, while József worked successively with Ödön Lechner, whose influence appears in József's competition design for a High School (1903), Nagykanizsa; with Ignác Alpár (1855–1928) on the Stock Exchange (now Hungarian Television Building) and the Austro-Hungarian Bank (now National Bank of Hungary), both built in 1905 in Szabadság Square, Budapest; and with Zsigmond Quittner on the Secessionist-style Gresham Life Assurance Company building (1903–6), Roosevelt Square, Budapest.

In 1902 the brothers formed a partnership in which they created their most original work. The Book Printers' and Typesetters' Cultural Centre (1906–7), Gutenberg Square, Budapest, has rich decoration on the upper levels with animated façades and Secessionist decorated gables, mansard roofs and curved balconies on the corner towers; the influence of developments in Munich and Vienna is clear. The building also houses the Secessionist 'Intimate Theatre'. The brothers' most important joint work is the Arcade Bazaar (1909; now Metroclub), Dohány Street, Budapest, which originally contained a residential block, offices and a large toyshop. Here they emphasized the corners, where they placed the entrances and curved windows. The whole building is rendered in white maiolica, including imitation structural elements in line with the separation of structure and decoration introduced by Otto Wagner in Vienna. The three-storey pilasters are echoed in the divisions of the corner windows, and a decorative frieze of children playing is placed below the cornice.

Following the dissolution of the partnership in 1910, László Vágó worked on rebuilding and renovating theatres, planning residential blocks and urban planning. He re-modelled the Parisiana Music-hall (1921), Budapest, orig-inally to a plan of 1909 by Béla Lajta, and the National Theatre (1925), Miskolc. He also built, with Ferenc Faragó (*b* 1902), the Cultural Centre and Synagogue (late 1920s), Dohány Street, Budapest. His urban planning (1895–1932) includes work on Clark Ádám Square, Roosevelt Square and Vigadó Square, all in Budapest.

József Vágó designed the Police Academy (1912), Nagyvárad, a symmetrical composition of a central block with high-pitched roof, flanked by two wings with terrace roofs. The simple unornamented façade with a tall stone plinth shows Viennese influence. His summer casino (1912), an enlargement of the Lipótváros Casino, Buda-pest, is in a similarly classicizing vein, partly derived from Josef Hoffmann. His villa designs show an increasingly geometric form and are also characterized by their lack of ornament, large terraces and terrace roofs, as in the Schiffer Villa (1911), Munkácsy Street, Budapest. The interiors were intended to complement the architecture to create a *Gesamtkunstwerk*. In 1914 József Vágó represented Hun-gary at the German Werkbund conference in Cologne. During the Republic of Councils (1919) his socialist sympathies led him to be appointed Director of the Building Directorate, and when forced to leave Hungary he lived in Italy and Switzerland (1920–27) before settling in France. He won first prize for his historicizing design (1926; with others) for the Palace of the League of Nations, Geneva. Later he frequently returned to Hungary, where he designed a modernist villa (1933), Városmajor Street, Budapest, with stone cladding and a front courtyard of Tuscan columns, which recalls Viennese and Mediter-ranean models. His numerous designs for the city plan of Budapest show the influence of Italian urban planning of the 1930s.

WRITINGS
L. Vágó: *Az újjáépülő Tabán* [The newly built Tabán] (Budapest, 1934)
J. Vágó: *Városokon keresztül* [Across the cities] (Budapest, 1939)

BIBLIOGRAPHY
K. Lyka: 'Vágó László', *Magyar Müvészet*, x (1934), p. 21
P. Nádai: 'Vágó József építészeti kiállítása' [József Vágó's architectural exhibition], *Magyar Iparmüvészet*, xxxix (1936)
F. Merényi: *A magyar építészet, 1867–1967* [Hungarian architecture, 1867–1967] (Budapest, 1970), pp. 58–9
Á. Moravánszky: *Die Architektur der Jahrhundertwende in Ungarn und ihre Beziehungen zu der Wiener Architektur der Zeit* (diss., Vienna, Tech. U., 1983)

ÁKOS MORAVÁNSZKY,
KATALIN MORAVÁNSZKY-GYŐNGY

Vahland, W(illiam) C(harles) [Wilhelm Carl] (*b* Nien-burg, 2 Oct 1828; *d* Bendigo, Victoria, 22 July 1915). British architect of German birth. He studied architecture at the Baugewerkeschule, Holzminden, during which time he worked in architects' offices in Bremen and Hamburg. He qualified in 1852, and although he had been appointed engineer to a section of railway between Hannover and Kassel, he resigned to practise as an architect at Diepholz. Dissatisfaction with German politics, combined with the lure of the gold rushes, attracted him to Melbourne in 1854 and to the Bendigo goldfields. Unsuccessful as a miner, he worked as a carpenter until 1857, when he took British citizenship, built a house for himself and entered practice in partnership with Robert Getzschmann (*d* 1875). In 1862–3 Vahland practised at Dunedin, New Zealand, in partnership with W. H. Monson while Getzschmann continued the practice at Bendigo. Vahland is generally taken to be the partnership's principal designer and to be responsible for its distinctive characteristics, which include many Greek details, such as the acroteria on his own house and others. Many of his churches, for example St Peter's, Eaglehawk (1863), show distinctive characteristics that are possibly of German origin, as well as personal quirks such as the desperately overhanging belfry on the front gable of St John's, Heathcote (1868). Vahland's work is ubiquitous in the central goldfields and as far north as Echuca on the Murray River. He retired from practice in 1900 and made his only trip to Germany in 1902.

BIBLIOGRAPHY
G. Lawler: *The Vahland School*, 2 vols (diss., U. Melbourne, 1980)

MILES LEWIS

Vaillant, Wallerant (*b* Lille, 30 May 1623; *d* Amsterdam, 28 Aug 1677). Dutch painter, draughtsman, mezzotint-engraver and etcher of French birth. He was the son of a merchant who established himself in Amsterdam about 1642. Vaillant was apprenticed to Jan Erasmus Quellinus in Antwerp, and in 1647 he was registered as a member of the Guild of St Luke in Middelburg. In 1649 he was in Amsterdam, where he painted the portrait of *Jan Six* (Amsterdam, Col. Six). Vaillant lived in Paris between 1659 and 1665 before returning to Amsterdam, where he remained for the rest of his life, although he was also registered in Middelburg. Vaillant first learnt the technique of mezzotint-engraving during a visit to Frankfurt am Main in 1658. There he met Prince Rupert of the Rhine, who was then experimenting with mezzotint. As the first professional mezzotint-engraver, Vaillant achieved re-markable results and had a great following (*see* MEZZO-TINT, §2): his more than 200 prints were copied until well into the 18th century. He took his designs from his own paintings (e.g. the portrait of *Jan Six*, Hollstein, no. 194) but also from Italian Renaissance artists and the work of contemporaries. Of the last group the wash drawings of Jan de Bisschop were particularly suitable for translation into mezzotint because of their tonal character.

As a painter Vaillant specialized in portraits (e.g. *Maria van Oosterwijck*, 1671; Amsterdam, Rijksmus.), but there are also genre scenes and one or two *trompe-l'oeil* still-lifes (e.g. Dresden, Gemäldegal.). He is known primarily for his studio interiors showing apprentices learning to draw (e.g. *Boy Seated Drawing*, 1658; Paris, Louvre). His work as a draughtsman consists mainly of life-size portrait studies in chalk.

BIBLIOGRAPHY

Hollstein: *Dut. & Flem.*; Thieme–Becker

J. E. Wessely: *Wallerant Vaillant: Verzeichnis seiner Kupferstiche und Schabkunstblätter* (Wenen, 1865, rev. 2/1881)

M. Vandalle: 'Les Frères Vaillant', *Rev. Belge Archéol. & Hist. A.*, vii (1937), pp. 341–60

N. MacLaren and C. Brown: *The Dutch School, 1600–1900*, London, N.G. cat. (London, 1991), pp. 438–40

G. Luijten: 'Jan de Bisschop and Wallerant Vaillant', *Prt Q.* (1994)

GER LUIJTEN

Vaishali [Vaiśālī; Vesāli]. Ancient Indian city that flourished from *c.* 6th century BC to *c.* 5th century AD. The site, in Muzaffarpur District, Bihar, spans several villages, including Basarh and Kolhua. By the 6th century BC Vaishali was the capital of the Vrjis (Lichchavis). It is important in JAINISM as the birthplace of Mahavira, the last Jaina saviour, and in Buddhism (*see* BUDDHISM, §§I and III, 1) as a place where the Buddha visited and taught. Its most important monumental remain is a pillar with a lion capital dating to the 3rd century BC. The shaft has no inscription, but the design is similar to the pillars erected by the MAURYA dynasty at LAURIYA NANDANGARH and elsewhere. An adjacent mound, the likely location of a stupa, has yielded an image of the Buddha, shown crowned and seated (Vaishali Mus.). Excavations at Vaishali have uncovered numerous terracotta sculptures from the Kushana and Gupta periods (all Vaishali Mus.), among them a superbly rendered mother goddess image (*c.* 5th century AD). Stone sculptures of the 6th to 8th centuries are enshrined in temples in the area. These include a Shiva linga with four faces at Kamman Chapra and a Karttikeya figure at the Hari Katori temple at Basarh.

BIBLIOGRAPHY

W. Hoey: 'On the Identification of Kusinara, Vaishali, and Other Places Mentioned by the Chinese Pilgrims', *J. Asiat. Soc. Bengal*, lxix/1 (1900), pp. 74–88

V. A. Smith: 'Vaisāli', *J. Royal Asiat. Soc. GB & Ireland* (1902), pp. 267–88

Krishna Deva and V. Mishra: *Vaiśālī Excavations, 1950* (Vaishali, 1961)

Y. Mishra and Sita Ram Roy: *A Guide to Vaishali and the Vaishali Museum* (Vaishali, 1964)

B. P. Sinha and Sita Ram Roy: *Vaiśālī Excavations, 1958–1962* (Patna, 1969)

FREDERICK M. ASHER

Vaison-la-Romaine. *See* VASIO VOCONTIORUM.

Vajda, Lajos (*b* Zalaegerszeg, Aug 1908; *d* Budakeszi, 7 Sept 1941). Hungarian painter, draughtsman, collagist and printmaker. He studied in 1927–30 at the Art School in Budapest under István Csók. At this stage he was committed to Constructivism, left-wing political ideas and the Munka-kört (workers' circle), run by Lajos Kassák. From 1930 to 1934 he lived in Paris, where Cubism and Surrealism impressed him, but his greatest interest was Soviet avant-garde film, which influenced the politically committed Surrealist simultaneous photomontages that he made in Paris. In 1935–6 he worked in the SZENTENDRE COLONY, near Budapest, and in Szigetmonostor with Dezső Korniss: the artistic programme they worked out there was a visual version of Béla Bartók's musical theory. Through the painterly transformation of the material and spiritual remnants of peasant culture, Vajda wanted to construct a modern art style that reconciled the icons of eastern European art with the western avant-garde. Using elements of Constructivism and Surrealism, and building on the principle of simultaneity, he made drawings and coloured collages using forms drawn from Serbian Orthodox Church traditions and modern trends. In 1937–8 he made a series of masks based on the rituals of tribal cultures. His late work blended biomorphic Surrealist and non-figurative elements; he made prints expressing the suffering of the people during those tragic times. His work was rarely exhibited during his lifetime, but a retrospective was held in 1943 in the Creative Circle Art Gallery in Budapest. In 1987 a museum of his work was opened in Szentendre.

BIBLIOGRAPHY

Vajda Lajos emlékkiállítás [Lajos Vajda commemorative exhibition] (exh. cat. by É. Körner, Székesfehérvár, István Király Mus., 1969)

Vajda Lajos emlékkönyv [Lajos Vajda album] (Budapest, 1972)

Vajda Lajos, 1908–1941, emlékkiállítás [Lajos Vajda, 1908–1941, commemorative exhibition] (exh. cat. by É. Bálint and L. Haulisch, Budapest, N.G., 1978)

S. Mándy: *Vajda Lajos* (Budapest, 1983)

LAJOS NÉMETH

Vajdahunyad [Vajda-Hunyad]. *See* HUNEDOARA CASTLE.

Vajrayogini. *See under* SANKHU.

Vakataka [Vākāṭaka]. Indian dynasty that ruled portions of Maharashtra, Gujarat and Madhya Pradesh, flourishing from the mid-3rd to late 5th century AD. The Vakataka house was founded by Vindhyashakti I who ruled in the mid-3rd century. Pravarasena I (*reg c.* 270–330), responsible for significantly advancing the Vakatakas, conquered large parts of the western Deccan. After his death, the kingdom was apparently divided into four parts; the history of each branch is not entirely clear. Those descended from Pravarasena through Gautamiputra are considered the main branch and are best known for their matrimonial alliance with the imperial GUPTA dynasty, King Rudrasena II (*reg c.* 385–90) marrying Prabhavatigupta, daughter of Chandragupta II (*reg c.* 380–415). With the death of Rudrasena, Prabhavatigupta served as regent (*c.* 390–410). Whether these events led to more northern influence in Maharashtra than would have occurred in the ordinary course of events is a subject that has not been satisfactorily explored. The Vakataka branch at Basim (anc. Vatsagulma) controlled the Vidarbha region and is associated with AJANTA, one of the leading Buddhist sites in India. Inscriptions indicate that Cave 16 and Cave 17 were excavated during the time of Harishena (*reg c.* 460–77). The patron of Cave 16 was Varahadeva, a minister of Harishena, and the patron of Cave 17 was Upendragupta, who was a Vakataka feudatory king until *c.* 472. The Vakatakas themselves were probably not Buddhists but devotees of Shiva and occasionally Vishnu.

BIBLIOGRAPHY

V. V. Mirashi: *Inscriptions of the Vākāṭakas*, Corp. Inscr. Indic., v (Ootacamund, 1963)

W. Spink: 'Ajanta: A Brief History', *Aspects of Indian Art*, ed. P. Pal (Leiden, 1972), pp. 49–58

——: 'The Splendour of India's Crown: A Study of Mahayava Developments at Ajanta', *J. Royal Soc. A.*, cxxii/5219 (1974), pp. 743–67

S. L. Weiner: *Ajanṭā: Its Place in Buddhist Art* (Berkeley, 1977)

J. G. Williams: *The Art of Gupta India: Empire and Province* (Princeton, 1982) [App. on Ajanta, pp. 181–7]

J. MARR

Valabhi. Former capital of the Maitraka dynasty near Bhavnagar on the eastern coast of the Saurashtra Peninsula in Gujarat, India. Having ruled the Saurashtra Peninsula from the 5th century AD, the Maitrakas under Dharasena IV (*reg c.* mid-7th century) extended their power to the whole of Gujarat, Malava in Rajasthan and the Sahya region of Maharashtra. From the remaining temples and numerous finds of *linga*s and Nandi images, it can be inferred that Shaivism was the predominant cult in the Valabhi region. However, the large number of Buddhist caves, stupas, monasteries and donative inscriptions indicate that Valabhi was a great centre of Buddhist learning comparable to the famous university of Nalanda. Although Jaina literary sources refer to the existence of Jainism in Valabhi during the Maitraka period, no art-historical remains survive. The Arab invasion that destroyed Valabhi in 788 seems to have ended its rich cultural and religious heritage.

BIBLIOGRAPHY

M. Meister, M. A. Dhaky and K. Deva, eds: *North India: Foundations of North Indian Style, c. 250 BC–AD 1100* (1988), ii/1 of *Encyclopaedia of Indian Temple Architecture* (New Delhi and Philadelphia, 1983–)

JUTTA JAIN-NEUBAUER

Valade, Jean (*b* Poitiers, *bapt* 27 Nov 1710; *d* Paris, 13 Dec 1787). French painter. He was the son of the painter Léonard Valade (*d* 1720) and trained with his father before moving to Paris; there he worked in the studios of the portrait painters Charles-Antoine Coypel and Louis Tocqué, who influenced his portrait style. Valade's portrait of *François Rivard*, a professor of mathematics and philosophy (before 1745; Poitiers, Mus. B.-A.), already shows elements that were to be typical of his later portraits. The subject is depicted in his customary surroundings, as if interrupted in the middle of his ordinary occupations; the objects around him are not purely emblematic but are such as he would normally use. However, the naturalness in portraiture demanded by contemporary art theory remained, in Valade's case, somewhat restricted; the composition and expression give a rather static effect.

In 1750 Valade was approved (*agréé*) by the Académie Royale, and in 1754 he was received (*reçu*) as a member. His *morceaux de réception* were portraits of the painter *Louis de Silvestre* and the sculptor *Jean-Baptiste Lemoyne* (both Versailles, Château). Both artists are depicted in their studios beside one of their works, yet they are elegantly dressed and in a studied pose. In these portraits Valade's particular strengths are the subtle harmonies of his colours and the precise reproduction of the textures of the objects depicted. A favourite medium of his was pastel, as in his portrait of *Etienne Borot des Cottais* (1753; Dijon, Mus. B.-A.). Valade seldom worked as a history painter, and the allegorical portrait of *Maréchal Charles-Louis-Auguste Fouquet, Duc de Belle-Isle* (1767; version, Versailles, Château) follows a time-honoured formula, with the oval framed half-length portrait of the Maréchal being presented by Minerva and Fame.

BIBLIOGRAPHY

R. Crozet: 'Notes sur le pastelliste Jean Valade (1710–1787)', *Bull. Soc. Hist. A. Fr.* (1941–4), pp. 35–46 [incl. provisional cat. of Valade's works]

H. Baderou: 'Le Portrait de François Rivard par Jean Valade au Musée des Beaux-Arts de Poitiers', *Dibutade* (suppl. to *Bull. Amis Mus. Poitiers*), ii (1955), pp. 29–35

P. Ratouis de Limay: 'Un Pastel de Jean Valade au Musée des Beaux-Arts de Poitiers', *Dibutade* (suppl. to *Bull. Amis Mus. Poitiers*, ii (1955), pp. 36–8

Diderot et l'art de Boucher à David (exh. cat., ed. M.-C. Sahut and N. Volle; Paris, Hôtel de la Monnaie, 1984), pp. 364–7

CATHRIN KLINGSÖHR-LE ROY

Valadier. Italian family of artists, of French descent. Andrea Valadier (*b* Aramont, 1695; *d* Rome, 23 July 1759), a goldsmith from Provence, settled in Rome in 1714. He established a workshop in Via Babuino that continued operating under the control of successive generations of the family until the mid-19th century and was the precursor of the modern Valadier factory employing some 150 craftsmen. Andrea's workshop produced decorative objects in a variety of media that had a profound influence on prevailing taste and established a distinctive style characterized by classically inspired Rococo elements. Andrea's son, Luigi Valadier I (*b* Rome, 26 Feb 1726; *d* Rome, 15 Sept 1785), took over his father's workshop in 1759 and started working for the Vatican in 1769. In 1779 Pope Pius VI appointed him superintendent of the restoration of the bronzes in the papal collection and gave him responsibility for the collection of ancient cameos. Luigi Valadier's greatest religious work, aside from the silver and lapis lazuli chalice (Paris, Louvre), given by Pius VI to Prince Stanisław Poniatowski, was the gold- and silver-plated bronze altar (*in situ*) with depictions from the *Life of the Virgin* for Monreale Cathedral, executed in Rome between 1770 and 1773. Luigi also produced a large number of secular items, in which his extraordinary technical skill in all media is evident; these include silver and bronze pieces (e.g. mirror in the Salone d'Oro in the Palazzo Chigi, Rome) and jewellery. He also engraved cameos and hardstones and worked as a cabinetmaker (e.g. cupboards in Rome, Vatican, Mus. Profano Bib. Apostolica). He became well known for his silver dinner services, pendulum clocks and centrepieces; his tableware incorporating architectural features and made of gilt bronze combined with rare marble and hardstones was particularly successful. His suicide in 1785 was supposedly linked to the founding of the monumental bell of St Peter's, which was completed by his son (1) Giuseppe Valadier, an architect working in the Neo-classical style, who took over the family workshop and became the silversmith of the Sacro Palazzo Apostolico and head of the Vatican foundry. As Giuseppe became increasingly occupied in his work as an architect, he turned over his workshop to the Spagna family in 1817, but the goldsmithing tradition continued in the Valadier family through Luigi's younger brother Luigi Giovanni Valadier (1732–1805) and Luigi Giovanni's three sons Filippo Valadier (*b* 1770), Tommaso Valadier (*b* 1772) and Luigi Valadier II (*b* 1781). The last member possessed considerable technical skill and invention and developed an eclectic and original style that assimilated various historical motifs and that remained an important influence in the European Neo-classical movement.

For bibliography see ITALY, §IX, 1 and 2.

ANGELA CATELLO

(1) Giuseppe Valadier (*b* Rome, 14 April 1762; *d* Rome, 1 Feb 1839). Architect, urban planner, designer and writer. He was one of the most important exponents of international Neo-classicism in central Italy. Although he was expected to follow his father's profession and indeed subsequently took over the family workshop (see above), he pursued his own vocation from an early age. In 1775 he won a prize at the Concorso Clementino of the Accademia di S Luca with a design for a façade for the church of S Salvatore in Lauro, Rome, and two years later, still aged only 15, he won the Concorso Balestra for architecture. In 1781, before he was 20, he was appointed Architetto dei Sacri Palazzi, no doubt assisted by the influence of his father, who enjoyed papal patronage. In the same year he embarked on a study tour that took him north to Milan and France, although it seems he went no further than Marseille.

Valadier's first architectural commission (1784) was from the nobleman Alessandro Pinciani, for a villa and separate chapel at Spoleto. Following the death in 1786 of Carlo Marchionni, Valadier was promoted to the post of Architetto Camerale and coadjutor to St Peter's, Rome. He was immediately given the responsibility of overseeing reconstruction following an earthquake in the homeland of Pope Pius VI in the Romagna. The most important of these projects was the rebuilding of the cathedral at Urbino, undertaken in collaboration with Camillo Morigia (1743–95), whose buildings in Ravenna are thought to have had some influence on the young Valadier. At Urbino, a façade type used several times by Valadier made its first appearance: with its monumental double gable, it was derived from Palladio's S Giorgio Maggiore (1566), Venice. The large coffers of the interior vault followed the more recent precedent of Giacomo Quarenghi's internal reconstruction of S Scolastica (1771–7) at Subiaco. In the same period (1788–90), Valadier submitted designs for the Palazzo Braschi, Rome, to be built on a triangular site that had been acquired by Pope Pius VI. Valadier's solution to the irregularity of the site was to arrange three blocks at tangents to a central circular courtyard. The less spatially dramatic design of Cosimo Morelli (1732–1812) proved a cheaper alternative, however, and was chosen in preference to that of Valadier.

In the 1790s Valadier undertook some religious commissions in the Marches, including the enlargement of the church of SS Paolo, Pietro e Donato at Mont'Olmo (now Corridonia) and the collegiate church at Monte S Pietrangeli, near Macerata. In 1796 he was involved in the first of his numerous publications; he supplied eight designs for a *Raccolta di diverse invenzioni*, mostly of small churches and villas aimed at an international clientele.

The occupation of Rome by the French from 1798 and the death in 1799 of Pius VI resulted in a loss of secure patronage for Valadier, who was forced briefly to leave the city. In 1800, however, he began a 17-year association with Prince Stanisław Poniatowski with the building of the Villa Poniatowski on the Via Flaminia, Rome. The villa, which was partly rebuilt in the 19th century, is an important example of Neo-classical Italian villa architecture. Soon after the election in 1800 of Pius VII, Valadier was put in charge of works on the River Tiber, including the restoration of the Ponte Milvio, a symbolic monument

for the papacy as it was the scene of Constantine's great victory over Emperor Maxentius (AD 312). The decayed bastion was turned into a monumental gateway with severe rustication, reminiscent of Claude-Nicolas Ledoux's *Barrières* (1784–9) in Paris. Similar rustication completely covers the narrow but monumental façade of S Pantaleo, Rome (see fig.), which Valadier executed for the TORLONIA family from 1806. The two-storey façade is articulated to suggest a pair of massive pilasters supporting an arch that embraces a thermal window. The two storeys are divided by a deep sculpted frieze, the whole façade being surmounted by a shallow pediment.

Following the annexation of the papal states by the French in 1809, Valadier was appointed Direttore dei Lavori Pubblici di Beneficenza, in which capacity he investigated the navigability of the Tiber and produced proposals for the restoration of the antiquities of Rome. Of greater significance, however, was the project to ennoble the Piazza del Popolo, Valadier's triumphant experiment in urban design. As early as 1793 Valadier had considered the problem of unifying the various elements of this incoherent ensemble: the 15th-century church of S Maria del Popolo, the 16th-century Porta del Popolo and the twin churches by Carlo Rainaldi, Gianlorenzo Bernini and Carlo Fontana that had been commissioned by Alexander VII and built in the 1660s. Valadier originally proposed a treatment not unlike Michelangelo's Piazza del

Giuseppe Valadier: façade (begun 1806) of S Pantaleo, Rome

Campidoglio (1539–64; completed in the 17th century by others), with two long columnar façades converging towards the Porta del Popolo to produce a trapezoidal piazza. The schemes he drew up from 1812, however, were much more ambitious, involving the demolition of a large area to the west of the piazza and the laying out of extensive gardens. The trapezoidal form was initially retained, although flanked by semicircular areas. In later projects, the semicircles were further emphasised until the piazza itself took on the oval form that was finally adopted. To the east, a series of ramps lead up the Pincian Hill to a formal garden of some complexity. Many different schemes exist for the siting of a monumental building on this hill, but all that was finally built was a coffee house, the Casina Valadier. In the piazza itself, the four corners were anchored by two speculative residential blocks to the south, a barracks to the north-west and a monastery adjoining S Maria del Popolo. The asymmetrically placed 16th-century fountain was replaced by four stone lions spouting water at the four corners of the existing obelisk. The work was approved by Pope Pius VII in 1816 and completed in 1824.

Pius VII also engaged Valadier for the construction of a church (1814–25) in his home town of Cesena, dedicated to S Christina. Externally unpretentious, the circular church has a brick façade with an unpedimented Tuscan Doric portico. The interior features a coffered dome supported by coupled Ionic columns. Valadier subsequently worked on the tomb of *Pius VII* in St Peter's, Rome (1824–31; for details *see* THORVALDSEN, BERTEL). Valadier then became embroiled in the controversy that raged over the rebuilding of the church of S Paolo fuori le Mura, destroyed by fire in 1823. He proposed rebuilding the church along the axis of the old transept, thus considerably reducing its size. This was opposed by Abbot Angelo Uggeri and the church architects, one of whom, Pasquale Belli, finally received the commission. In the last two decades of his life, Valadier became increasingly involved in restoration work, most notably of the Arch of Titus (1819–21; *see* TRIUMPHAL ARCH, fig. 1), remarkable for the care taken to distinguish the new work from the original by using travertine rather than marble, and the Temple of Fortuna Virilis (1829–35; now the Temple of Fortunus). Valadier was professor of architectural theory (1821–37) at the Accademia di S Luca, later publishing his lectures.

WRITINGS

Raccolta di diverse invenzioni (Rome, 1796)
Progetti architettonici (Rome, 1807)
Narrazione artistica dell'operato finora nel restauro dell'Arco di Tito (Rome, 1822)
Della basilica di S Paolo sulla via Ostiense (Rome, 1823)
L'architettura pratica dettata nella scuola e cattedra dell'insigne Accademia di S Luca, 5 vols (Rome, 1828–39)
Opere di architettura e di ornamento (Rome, 1833)

BIBLIOGRAPHY

E. Schulze-Battman: *Giuseppe Valadier: Ein klassizistischer Architekt Roms, 1762–1839* (Dresden, 1939)
S. Giedion: *Space, Time and Architecture* (Cambridge, MA, 1943), pp. 84–90
P. Marconi: *Giuseppe Valadier* (Rome, 1964)
E. Debenedetti: *Valadier: Diario architettonico* (Rome, 1979)
——: *Valadier: Segno e architettura* (Rome, 1985)

RICHARD JOHN

Valadon, René. *See under* BOUSSOD, VALADON & Cie.

Valadon, Suzanne (*b* Bessines-sur-Gartempe, nr Limoges, 23 Sept 1865; *d* Paris, 7 April 1938). French painter and artist's model. She led a lonely childhood in Paris as the daughter of an unmarried and unaffectionate maid, seeking refuge from her bleak circumstances by living in a dream world. While residing in the Montmartre district of Paris, she became an artist's model, working in particular with those painters who frequented the Lapin Agile. From 1880 to 1887, for example, she sat regularly for Pierre Puvis de Chavannes, posing for both the male and female figures in the *Sacred Wood* (1884–6; Lyon, Mus. B.-A.). She also modelled for Renoir, Luigi Zandomeneghi, Théophile Steinlein, Jean-Louis Forain, Giuseppe De Nittis and Jean-Jacques Henner. No longer able to tolerate the passive role of the model, she became a full-time painter in 1896, making use, however, of the working methods that she had observed in the studios of these painters.

Valadon is thought to have taught herself to draw at the age of nine. In 1883, the year of her first signed and dated work, a *Self-portrait* (pastel, Paris, Pompidou), she gave birth to Maurice Utrillo, who later achieved fame as a painter in his own right. She entrusted him to his grandmother so that she could return to her work as a model. She was encouraged to continue with her own art by Renoir's enthusiastic response to one of her pastels and by a visit to Degas instigated by Toulouse-Lautrec. The appreciation shown by Degas for one of her red chalk drawings, and his subsequent purchase of three drawings from the Salon de la Nationale in 1894, renewed her determination to draw. Degas introduced her to various collectors, including Paul Durand-Ruel and Ambroise Vollard, and taught her drypoint, etching and soft-ground etching techniques in the hope that she could earn her living through printmaking; she produced just over 30 prints.

Valadon's marriage to Paul Mousis in 1896 finally gave her the financial support to abandon her work as a model in order to devote herself full-time to painting in a studio at 12 Rue Cortot in Montmartre. Her favourite subjects were realistically depicted nudes in a decorative setting, as in *Adam and Eve* and *After the Bath (Neither Black nor White)* (both 1909; Paris, Pompidou). Like Puvis de Chavannes and Matisse, she also undertook large allegorical compositions as the *Joy of Life*, a hymn to the happiness and love that she found with the French painter André Utter (1886–1948), whom she met in 1909 and who became her companion after she left Mousis; she married him in 1914 after divorcing Mousis. Her later paintings, such as the *Blue Room* (1923; Paris, Pompidou) and *Still-life with Violin* (1923; Paris, Mus. A. Mod. Ville Paris), are characterized by a richer use of colour and by a preference for extremely crowded decorative backgrounds. Her eventual critical and commercial success was signalled by such society portraits as that of *Mme Mauricia Gustave-Coquiot* (1915; Menton, Mus. Pal. Carnolès), wife of the art critic Gustave Coquiot. Her happiness, however, continued to be marred by personal problems and excesses that eventually ruined her health.

BIBLIOGRAPHY

R. Rey: *Suzanne Valadon* (Paris, 1922)
A. Basler: *Suzanne Valadon* (Paris, 1929)
C. Roger-Marx: *Les Dessins de Suzanne Valadon* (Paris, 1932) [with 18 original prints dating from 1895 to 1910]
N. Jacometti: *Suzanne Valadon* (Geneva, 1947)
Suzanne Valadon (exh. cat., ed. P. Georgel; Paris, Mus. N. A. Mod., 1967)
P. Petrides: *Catalogue raisonné de l'oeuvre de Suzanne Valadon* (Paris, 1971)
S. Prou: *Suzanne Valadon* (Stockholm, 1978)
J. Warnod: *Suzanne Valadon* (Paris, 1981)

COLETTE GIRAUDON

Valbudea [Ionescu-Valbudea], **Ştefan** (*b* Bucharest, Aug 1856; *d* Bucharest, 21 May 1918). Romanian sculptor. He studied at the Fine Arts School, Bucharest (1872–81), under Karl Storck, then in Paris at the Ecole des Beaux-Arts (1882–85) under Alexandre Falguière and in the studio of Emmanuel Fremiet. For a time he attended the course of the alienist Benjamin Ball (1833–93) at the Hospice Sainte-Anne. Observations made there helped him to achieve his masterpiece, *Michael the Madman* (plaster, 1.3 m, 1885; Bucharest, N. Mus. A.), in which the naturalist element is transfigured by the Romantic vision of the artist. An impetuous dynamism, creating strong contrasts of light and shadows, animates this symbolic expression of the human drama. In the same period he executed the *Frightened Man* (plaster, 1.14 m, 1885; Bucharest, N. Mus. A.), an attempt to solve the problems of a complex spatial composition. Valbudea continued his studies in Rome, where he produced *The Victor* (plaster, 1.7 m, 1886; Bucharest, N. Mus. A.), and he then moved to Florence, where in 1887 he dedicated a series of works to childhood and adolescence (e.g. *Sleeping Child;* marble, 0.44×1.58 m, 1893; Bucharest, N. Mus. A.). After his return to Bucharest, Valbudea's studies for the statue of *Miron Costin* (1887; destr.), sacrificing the illustrative function to sculptural expression, were rejected by the initiator of the monument, the historian V. A. Urechia (1834–1901). Thereafter Valbudea rarely received official commissions. Among these, however, were the statues of *Mercury* and *Vulcan* (both marble, *c.* 1888) on the façade of the National Bank in Bucharest and a part of the decorative sculptures for the University Palace in Iaşi, consisting of an allegorical group and a set of reliefs representing historical figures (marble, 1895). He also modelled some of his contemporaries, such as the painter *Eugen Voinescu* (terracotta, 0.50m, *c.* 1890; Bucharest, N. Mus. A.). Disenchanted with official neglect, Valbudea remained an independent, although isolated, force for the last years of his life.

BIBLIOGRAPHY

I. Frunzetti: *St. Ionescu-Valbudea* (Bucharest, 1940)
G. Oprescu: *Ştefan Ionescu-Valbudea* (Bucharest, 1955)
A. Botez: *Valbudea* (Bucharest, 1982)

REMUS NICULESCU

Valcin, Gérard (*b* Port-au-Prince, 10 July 1927; *d* Port-au-Prince, 15 May 1988). Haitian painter. He came from a poor family and was forced to leave school after only three years. He began to paint after coming into contact with the Centre d'Art in Port-au-Prince and became a full-time artist as soon as he began to earn enough from his pictures to abandon his work as a tile-setter. He joined the Centre d'Art in 1959. He was a fervent adept of Vodoun, from which he took much of his subject-matter. He was attracted by the life of the countryside, usually situating his ceremonial scenes amid lush tropical foliage. Leaves, rows of tilled earth and the movements of water or human figures all conform to simplified motifs arranged in rhythmic repetition. In his pictures the embodied spirits are provided with symbolic dress and attributes; details of costume and draperies are highly stylized, falling into neatly parallel and rhythmic folds, and hands and faces are conventionalized. Using precisely delineated contours and enamel-like surfaces similar to those of the patterned tiles with which he worked in his youth, he arranged figures in circles, squares or horizontal registers across the picture plane. They have little individuation. With their pure colours and stylized but precise rendering, his pictures sometimes resemble the illuminations of medieval manuscripts.

BIBLIOGRAPHY

Haitian Art (exh. cat. by U. Stebich, New York, Brooklyn Mus., 1978)
M. P. Lerrebours: *Haïti et ses peintres,* i (Port-au-Prince, 1989)

DOLORES M. YONKER

Valck [Valk], **Gerard** (*b* Amsterdam, 1651–2; *d* Amsterdam, 21 Oct 1726). Dutch mezzotint engraver and publisher. He was the son of Leendert Gerritsz. Valck, a silversmith from Amsterdam, and the pupil, brother-in-law and business partner of Abraham Blooteling, with whom he went to London in 1672. Valck's earliest dated mezzotint, *Sleeping Cupid* (1677; Hollstein, no. 40), is after a painting by Guido Reni. Valck's 67 engravings and mezzotints were mostly based on designs by other artists, for example Peter Lely, Gérard de Lairesse (Hollstein, nos 1–2 and 22–3) and Philipp Tidemann (e.g. illustrations for an unpublished Danish translation of Ovid's *Metamorphoses*; Hollstein, nos 32–8); they were often published by Valck himself. In Amsterdam he worked in partnership with his brother-in-law Pieter Schenck and later with his son Leonardus Valck. Gerard Valck's publications include atlases, separate maps and printed globes, as well as series of prints with views of houses belonging to the Orange-Nassau family, trades and professions, fountains, chimneys and birds.

BIBLIOGRAPHY

Hollstein: *Dut. & Flem.*; Thieme–Becker
C. Koeman: *Atlantes Neerlandici,* iii (Amsterdam, 1969), pp. 107–8, 136–40
P. van der Krogt: *Old Globes in the Netherlands* (Utrecht, 1984), pp. 220–54

CHRISTIAAN SCHUCKMAN

Valckenborch, van. Flemish family of artists. The family was originally from Leuven but was one of many families who, for political or religious reasons, left the Spanish-occupied southern Netherlands and settled in the more tolerant German imperial cities, particularly Frankfurt am Main, where they often strongly influenced artistic developments. Of the 14 known painters in the family, only (1) Marten van Valckenborch I, his brother (2) Lucas van Valckenborch I and Marten's sons (3) Frederik van Valckenborch and Gillis (Egidius) van Valckenborch (1570–1622) have so far been identified as significant from surviving works. The origins of Lucas's and Marten's painting are found in Antwerp and Mechelen, where landscape paintings in watercolour on canvas (*waterschilderijen*) were especially popular as a substitute for tapestry. One later artist in the family, Johan Jacob van Valckenborch (1625–75), was a goldsmith.

BIBLIOGRAPHY

W. K. Zülch: 'Die Künstlerfamilie van Valckenborch nach den Urkunden im Frankfurter Stadtarchiv,' *Oud-Holland*, xlix (1932), pp. 221–8

J. Stiennon: *Les Sites mosans de Lucas I et Martin I van Valckenborch* (Liège, 1954)

H. F. Friederichs: 'Die flämische Malersippe van Valckenborch in Frankfurt a.M.', *Forsch. Hess. Fam.- & Heimatknd.*, xv (1955) [whole issue]

C. C. van Valkenburg: 'Het Vlaamse schildersgeslacht van Valckenborch, *Oud-Holland*, lxxxvi (1971), pp. 43–6

A. Wied: *Lucas I und Marten I van Valckenborch* (Freren, 1990)

(1) Marten van Valckenborch I (*b* Leuven, 1534; *d* Frankfurt am Main, 27 Jan 1612). Painter. He joined the Guild of St Luke in Mechelen on 13 August 1559 and on 3 December 1563 was recorded as having a pupil named Gysbrecht Jaspers. In 1564 Marten went to Antwerp, where he taught his brother Geraard van Valckenborch until 1568. In 1573 Marten became a citizen of Aachen but returned to Antwerp *c*. 1575–6 and in 1584 is mentioned as an *ouderman* (elder) in the Antwerp Guild of St Luke. For the final period of their lives, after an existence disrupted by war and religious persecution, the brothers Marten I and (2) Lucas van Valckenborch I were united in Frankfurt am Main, where they ran a flourishing workshop. On 7 July 1586 Marten became a citizen of Frankfurt, the same time as his son-in-law, Hendrick van Steenwijk the elder.

Marten's work has been overshadowed until now by that of his brother Lucas I. Initially their styles were very similar, although Marten's earlier landscapes can be distinguished from those of his brother mainly by their composition: Lucas favoured rocky landscape or views with a distant prospect on one side, whereas Marten preferred uniform terrain with shallow undulations, always with oak trees as an articulating element and sometimes with large or numerous incidental figures, as in his 11 paintings showing the *Labours of the Months* (all Vienna, Ksthist. Mus.). Around 1600, probably influenced by his sons Gillis I and (3) Frederik van Valckenborch I, Marten developed a Late Mannerist landscape style, with dramatically agitated clouds and large mountains. Many of these late landscapes are lost or in private collections and thus not easily seen. Of the few in public collections, the following deserve special mention: the *Tower of Babel* (two versions: Dresden, Gemäldegal. Alte Meister; Gaasbeek, Kasteel); an altarpiece in the Wallfahrtskirche of Deggingen, Germany; and oil paintings in Dessau (Staatl. Gal.), Enschede (Rijksmus. Twenthe), Poitiers (Mus. B.-A.) and Monte Carlo (Mus. N.). There are also watercolour paintings in Coburg (Veste Coburg) and Amsterdam (Hist. Mus.).

BIBLIOGRAPHY

A. Laes: 'Marten van Valckenborch', *Annu. Mus. Royaux B.-A. Belgique*, i (1939), pp. 123–41

H. G. Franz: *Niederländische Landschaftsmalerei im Zeitalter des Manierismus*, 2 vols (Graz, 1969), i, pp. 208–9; ii, pls 375–84

See also bibliography above.

(2) Lucas van Valckenborch I (*b* Leuven, in, or, more likely, after 1535; *d* Frankfurt am Main, 2 Feb 1597). Painter and draughtsman, brother of (1) Marten van Valckenborch I.

1. LIFE. On 26 August 1560 he joined the painters' guild in Mechelen; Jaspar van der Linden is recorded as his pupil on 30 August 1564. Lucas married and had a son, Marten van Valckenborch II (*b* before 1566; *d* Vienna, 1597), also a painter, before fleeing to Liège in 1566 and then to Aachen, where his brother Marten I had settled. In 1574–5 Lucas returned to Antwerp and, in 1579, became court painter to the Habsburg archduke, Matthias, governor of the Spanish Netherlands in Brussels from 1577 to 1582 and later Emperor (*reg* 1612–19). In or after 1582 he followed Matthias to Linz, finally rejoining his relatives in Frankfurt in 1592–3.

In his art Lucas was close to Pieter Bruegel the elder, who was about ten years his senior, yet he did not become a copyist, like Pieter Brueghel the younger. His art drew on the same Flemish tradition, modifying it in a highly personal way, without recourse to then current Mannerist tendencies. Although he did not have Bruegel's skill, he never lapsed into mediocrity, and thematically his work is more varied than was formerly supposed. While his most significant achievements are undoubtedly his landscape paintings, he also made an interesting contribution to late 16th-century portraiture and subject painting, the latter with his large-scale allegories of seasonal labours. His works, many of which bear his monogram LVV and the date (with the L placed under the two Vs until 1570 and above them thereafter), always show solid craftsmanship and sometimes a brilliant technique. Unlike that of Marten I, Lucas's style did not change significantly. Judging from the relatively large number of paintings dating from his last years, he probably had a flourishing workshop, which may have included other, as yet unidentified family members. About 100 oil paintings and *c*. 10 drawings by Lucas I are known.

2. WORK.

(i) Landscapes. Lucas adhered to the old conventions of composition, depicting panoramic scenes from a high viewpoint but, more than his predecessors, basing his work on first-hand observation of nature. There are painted views of actual places, including Liège (1567; ex-Kaiser-Friedrich Mus., Berlin; destr. 1945; and Reims, Mus. St-Denis), Burtschied-Aachen (1570; Brussels, Mus. A. Anc.), Antwerp (1575 and ?1589), Linz (1593; all Frankfurt am Main, Städel. Kstinst. & Städt. Gal.) and the newly built Schloss in Vienna (159(?); Vienna, Ksthist. Mus.). It is thought that Joris Hoefnagel used his topographical drawings, for instance the drawn *View of Linz* (1593; Paris, Ecole N. Sup. B.-A.), when supplying G. Braun and F. Hogenberg with illustrations for their six-volume atlas, the *Civitates orbis terrarum* (Cologne, 1572–1618). Lucas often mixed invention with genuine topography, as in the *Spring Landscape with the Palais Royal of Brussels* (1587; Vienna, Ksthist. Mus.; see fig.), in which the palace has been transplanted into a fantasy landscape. This mixture of realism and fantasy is quite distinct from the Mannerist tradition, being a blend of imaginary landscapes based on earlier prototypes (for example the landscapes of Jan and Cornelis Massys, Mathijs Cock and Lucas Gassel) with the naturalistic depiction of real places, the resulting 'hybrid' often being embellished with narrative details taken from everyday life. This free approach

Lucas van Valckenborch I: *Spring Landscape with the Palais Royal of Brussels*, oil on canvas, 1.16×1.98 m, 1587 (Vienna, Kunsthistorisches Museum)

to topographical accuracy undermines attempts to localize his views and explains why, for instance, none of the many furnaces and forges that Lucas painted in expertly observed detail has ever been identified. His preference was for rocky landscapes into which he would set these ironworks or small religious or peasant scenes. Fairs and rustic entertainments were another favourite feature, as in the *Mountain Landscape with Peasants Dancing and a Furnace in the Background* (1577; St Petersburg, Hermitage) or the two versions of the *Landscape with a Peasant Wedding and Dance* (both 1574; Copenhagen, Stat. Mus. Kst.).

In the mid-1580s Lucas painted a series of large pictures showing the labours of the months, probably for Archduke Matthias. These compositions, of which seven survive (five in Vienna, Ksthist. Mus.; two in Brno, Morav. Gal.), present the traditional activities in an apparently realistic setting and thus are also of documentary interest. In this they differ from earlier Flemish examples and from the work of Pieter Bruegel the elder, who otherwise provided Lucas with an influential model. The careful brushwork, always technically correct, is never dry or monotonous in effect. Fore-, middle- and background are not divided in a mannered or schematic way but blend delicately in a soft triad of brown, green and blue hues, often with a sensitively calculated touch of colour, such as a piece of red clothing, accentuating the foreground.

Lucas also painted close-up views of forest landscapes, a subject that reached its apogee *c.* 1600 in the work of such painters as Gillis van Coninxloo III and Jan Breughel I. Van Valckenborch produced striking and original compositions, such as *Cattle Pasture under Trees* (1573; Frankfurt am Main, Städel. Kstinst. & Städt. Gal.), *Woody Landscape with Peasants and Nobility* (*c.* 1575; Frankfurt am Main, priv. col.) and *Angler at a Woodland Pool* (1590;

Vienna, Ksthist. Mus.), but did not pursue the form further.

(ii) Portraits and allegories. According to van Mander, it was Lucas's skill as a portrait painter that attracted Archduke Matthias's attention, a claim supported by six portraits of *Archduke Matthias*—some life-size, some miniature—and two portraits of *Duchess Sibylle von Cleve* (all Vienna, Ksthist. Mus.). Lucas also demonstrated skill as a miniaturist in his self-portraits (e.g. St Petersburg, Hermitage; Frankfurt am Main, Städel. Kstinst. & Städt. Gal.; Oldenburg, Landesmus.; Vienna, Ksthist. Mus.) and in the miniaturized portraits of others that he inserted in his landscapes: for example, the *Landscape with Peasants Dancing* (St Petersburg, Hermitage) shows Abraham Ortelius, Joris Hoefnagel and Lucas himself among the throng.

Lucas has become better known as a figure painter with the rediscovery of nine allegories of the seasons, all painted in Frankfurt from 1592 onwards, several having come to light in Czech collections and two (formerly untraced) in a Swedish private collection (Djursholm, T. Fischer priv. col.). In this series Lucas developed the tradition of art market scenes pioneered by Pieter Aertsen and Joachim Beuckelaer in his own way, striving for a synthesis of still-life with landscape and with what is now called genre. Some show market scenes with large figures (e.g. *Meat and Fish Market (Winter)*, after 1592; Montreal, Mus. F.A.), while others represent harvest scenes (e.g. *Scene with Vegetables and Fruit (Summer)*, 1592; Count Sternberg priv. col., Častolovice Castle). Georg Flegel probably contributed the still-life elements to these; it was undoubtedly he who painted the food and luxurious tableware in two interesting banquet paintings (Opava, Siles. Mus.; St Gilgen-Salzburg, H. Wiesenthal priv. col.).

BIBLIOGRAPHY

K. van Mander: *Schilder-boeck* ([1603]–1604), fol. 260
H. G. Franz: *Niederländische Landschaftsmalerei im Zeitalter des Manierismus*, 2 vols (Graz, 1969)
A. Wied: 'Lucas van Valckenborch', *Jb. Ksthist. Samml. Wien*, lxvii (1971), pp. 119–231
S. Grieten: 'De iconografie van der Toren van Babel bij Pieter Bruegel: Traditie, vernienwing en navolging', *Jb.: K. Mus. S. Kst* (1988), pp. 97–136

ALEXANDER WIED

(3) Frederik van Valckenborch (*b* Antwerp, 1566; *d* Nuremberg, 1623). Painter and draughtsman, son of (1) Marten van Valckenborch I. He must have received his first training in Antwerp, possibly from his father, although his earliest works, two drawings—the *Deluge* (1588; London, BM) and *Moses Drawing Water from the Rocks* (1589; Brunswick, Herzog Anton Ulrich-Mus.)—contain figures of a completely different type from Marten's. This has prompted the theory that, whereas he studied landscape painting with his father, he must also have worked with an Antwerp figure painter. Gerszi (1974, pp. 63–5) has compared Frederik's painting of the *Last Judgement* (Munich, Alte Pin.) with Jacob de Backer's version of the same theme (Antwerp, Kon. Mus. S. Kst.): similar in both works are the structure of the composition and the representation of the figures, especially their rounded bodies and oval faces, their gestures and stances. De Backer certainly influenced the young master strongly, but it would be premature to assume that Frederik was his pupil.

In the 1590s Frederik and his brother Gillis probably left for Italy, although there is no evidence for this beyond the existence of a drawing, *Fantastic River Landscape* (Stockholm, Nmus.), signed, dated and inscribed GILLIS VAN VALCKENBORCH, ROMA 1595. Frederik's work does reveal an Italian influence, as, for example, in a drawing with a *View of Venice* on the *recto* and a *River Landscape* on the *verso* (Budapest, Mus. F.A.). The *View of Venice* with its sketchy and selective character seems to have been drawn from nature, while the *River Landscape* has definite Venetian characteristics: the shape of the whimsical overgrown rocks, their use as a frame and the motif of the tall inclining trees. Gerszi (1974, pp. 65–6) indicated that in this drawing, as in a signed *Mountainous Landscape* (Vienna, Albertina), the decorative composition, the calligraphic rendering of the foliage and the slightly stylized technique demonstrate the influence of Lodewijk Toeput. Whether Frederik went to Italy or not, by the beginning of 1597 he was back in Frankfurt am Main, where he became a citizen on 24 February. Presumably in the same year he married, for on 23 April 1598 twin sons, Frederik

1. Frederik van Valckenborch: *Mountainous Landscape*, oil on copper, 270×350 mm, 1605 (Amsterdam, Rijksmuseum)

2. Frederik van Valckenborch: *Inn Valley near Tratzberg Castle*, pen and brown ink, with brown and blue wash, heightened with white, 191×287 mm, late 1590s (London, British Museum)

and Wilhelm, were baptized in Frankfurt. Frederik had two more sons, both of whom became painters: Moritz (*bapt* 17 Aug 1600; *d* 1632) and Nicolaus (*b c.* 1603). In 1602 Frederik the elder left Frankfurt to settle in Nuremberg, and in 1607 he received a commission from Archduke Maximilian for a copy (untraced) of Albrecht Dürer's *Assumption of the Virgin*, formerly in the Dominican monastery in Frankfurt (now Städel. Kstinst. & Städt. Gal.), a six-month task in which he was assisted by the Nuremberg painter Paul Juvenel. In 1612 Frederik was commissioned by the Nuremberg authorities to design an arch for the Triumphal Entry of Archduke Matthias.

Only a small number of paintings signed or monogrammed by him are known, which may explain his relative obscurity. Much of his work is characterized by violent contrasts between light and dark and by animated forms that lend a dynamic, if somewhat threatening, quality to the whole (e.g. *Mountainous Landscape*, 1605; Amsterdam, Rijksmus.; see fig. 1). In this they are typical of late Mannerism, a feature of which was the novel treatment of the foreground, which, instead of being a limited zone leading the eye into the distance, now takes up most of the composition and functions independently of the background. These characteristics are displayed in Frederik's earliest surviving work, the drawing of the *Deluge*. The whole, rather dark foreground of rocks, trees and bizarrely shaped, gesticulating figures forms a semicircular frame for a distant view of a light, mistily drawn and almost visionary background, in which Noah's ark and a

number of figures are standing on a spit of land. These two contrasting spatial planes are quite unconnected to each other: there are no roads or rivers linking the foreground and the background, which is accessible only to the eye of the viewer.

The same features are present in the drawing of a *Fantastic Landscape with Two Pilgrims* (1597; Vienna, Albertina) and a painting of a *Landscape with Hunters* (1612; Antwerp, Kon. Mus. S. Kst.), in which the dark group of trees on the right is connected to the tree that completes the composition on the left by a dark foreground zone with figures. Opening beyond this dark area is a wide prospect with a brightly lit church and a few cottages, their shapes blurred by the fierce light. The introduction of a horizontal bridge over the river decisively separates foreground from background. In his *Last Judgement* the dark foreground, with its many closely packed figures and sombre clouds with angels, surrounds a view on to a more brightly lit background containing extremely slender figures with blurred contours.

A number of paintings, such as the *Shipwreck of Aeneas* (Rotterdam, Mus. Boymans–van Beuningen), the *Pilgrim by a Country Chapel* and the *Approaching Thunderstorm* (both Budapest, Mus. F.A.) and the *Burning Town* (Prague, N.G., Šternberk Pal.), reveal Frederik's interest in depicting the forces of nature. The stormy interplay of forms, combined with a smooth and flowing brush technique and violent contrasts between light and dark, creates a dynamic, almost visionary, quality. The impression is of intentionally unbalanced compositions constructed for expressive ends.

By contrast, many of Frederik's drawings seem to demonstrate a quest for realism in depicting nature. Most belong to the so-called Travelling Sketchbook, originally attributed to Lucas when in the collection of the Archduke Frederick of Austria (1856–1936; the book was subsequently broken up and its contents dispersed). Most of the sketches it contained, objectively descriptive and topographically accurate, were produced during the last years of the 16th century, when the artist was travelling in the Alps and the Danube area. The difference between these drawings and Frederik's late Mannerist works is most marked in the handling of space, as can be seen in his views of the *Inn Valley near Tratzberg Castle* (London, BM; see fig. 2; Amsterdam, Rijksmus.), and also in the *View of a Country Hut* (1597; Budapest, Mus. F.A.), which while not part of the Travelling Sketchbook is stylistically and technically very close to it. The impulse towards topographical accuracy forced him to create serene and simple scenes that were true to appearances in the coherent portrayal of space and in the faithful depiction of individual motifs. Frederik is thus an artist of contrasted aspects: in his late Mannerist style producing vividly imagined but contrived effects and in his travel drawings aiming for an unadorned realism. Faggin called him, justifiably, an artistic genius—one of the most temperamental personalities of the transitional period from Mannerism to Baroque: an artist with a fertile imagination, an excellent draughtsman of the human figure and an exceptional landscape artist.

BIBLIOGRAPHY

A. Pigler: 'Zum Werk des Frederik van Valckenborch', *Oud-Holland*, lxxvii (1962), pp. 127–9
G. T. Faggin: 'De gebroeders Frederik en Gillis van Valckenborch', *Bull.: Mus. Boymans–van Beuningen*, xiv (1963), pp. 2–14
T. Gerszi: 'Dessins maniéristes néerlandais', *Bull. Mus. Hong. B.-A.*, xxiv (1964), pp. 65–78
H. G. Franz: 'Meister der spätmanieristischen Landschaftsmalerei in den Niederländen', *Jb. Ksthist. Inst. Graz*, iii–iv (1968–9), pp. 24–32, pls 1, 5–10, 12, 16
T. Gerszi: 'Quelques problèmes que pose l'art du paysage de Frederik van Valckenborch', *Bull. Mus. Hong. B.-A.*, xlii (1974), pp. 63–89
O. Benesch: *From an Art Historian's Workshop* (Lucerne, 1979), pp. 45–76, 90–98; pls 40–68

HANS DEVISSCHER

Valckert, Werner (Jacobsz.) van den (*b* ?in or nr The Hague, *c.* 1580–85; *d* ?Amsterdam, in or after 1627). Dutch painter, etcher, woodcutter, draughtsman and writer. On 6 November 1605 he married Jannetje Cornelis, the daughter of Cornelis Sybertsz. Monicx van Montvoort, a stained-glass painter from The Hague. He received his first artistic training from his father-in-law and probably not during the journey he is supposed to have made to Italy. Between 1600 and 1605 he was registered at the Guild of St Luke in The Hague, in 1612 as a master. During this period he probably made all but two of his etchings, a woodcut of the *Inspiration of St Jerome* (1613) and a painting of *Venus as Temptress* (Haarlem, priv. col., see van Thiel, 1983, no. 6). Despite his skilled etching technique, evident in his refined use of hatching, cross-hatching and dots, and his experiments with plate tone, van den Valckert applied himself almost exclusively to painting after 1613. His history paintings are similar in their academic formalism to those of Adriaen van Nieulandt and Pieter Isaacsz., two of the artist's rivals in Amsterdam, while his idealized, historicizing portraits resemble those of Cornelis van der Voort (*c.* 1576–1624). His patrons were mainly Amsterdam Remonstrants and Catholics but also included Christian IV of Denmark and presumably also the Stadholder, Prince Frederick Henry of Orange Nassau. The only known piece of writing by the artist is an exhortation written for St Luke's Day in 1618 and illustrated with one of his etchings. A similar moralizing tone underlies his painting of the *Goat as an Unsuitable Leader of the Young* (1616; untraced; see van Thiel, 1983, no. 8), which bears the initials of members of Amsterdam's Guild of St Luke.

Van Thiel's catalogue of van den Valckert's paintings comprises 33 items dating from 1616 to 1625, including the tentative attribution of the *Anatomy Lesson of Sebastiaen Egbertsz. de Vrij* (*c.* 1619; Amsterdam, Hist. Mus.), a group portrait traditionally attributed to Thomas de Keyser (*see* KEYSER, DE, (3)) but now reattributed to Nicolaes Eliasz. Pickenoy (see 1993 exh. cat., no. 268). A recent addition to van den Valckert's prints are two etchings, *Allegory of Death and Time* (1624; Hollstein, no. 8) and *Fool Holding a Foolscap* (Hollstein, no. 14). There are four known drawings by van den Valckert, three made for *alba amicorum*; the fourth drawing, *Head of a Grimacing Man* (Leiden, Rijksuniv., Prentenkab.), is closely related to two woodcuts based on van den Valckert's designs, one of *Plato* (1620) and the other of *Charon*.

BIBLIOGRAPHY

Hollstein: *Dut. & Flem.*
P. J. J. van Thiel: 'Houtsneden van Werner van den Valckert en Moses van Uyttenbroeck' [Woodcuts by Werner van den Valckert and Moses Uyttenbroeck], *Oud-Holland*, xcii (1978), pp. 7–42
——: 'Werner Jacobsz. van den Valckert', *Oud-Holland*, xcvii (1983), pp. 128–95
Dawn of the Golden Age: Northern Netherlandish Art, 1580–1620 (exh. cat. by R. Ekkart, Amsterdam, Rijksmus., 1993)

CHRISTIAAN SCHUCKMAN

Valckx [Valck], **Pieter** [Peeter] (*b* Mechelen, 1 March 1734; *d* Mechelen, 3 May 1785). Flemish sculptor. He was the son of a painter and trained with the sculptors Theodor Verhaegen and Jan-Baptist Mooriaen (*fl c.* 1750). He also studied at the Academy of Fine Arts of Antwerp and in the studio of Alexander Schobbens (1720–81). In 1761 he returned to Mechelen, where he became a master sculptor. He produced many pieces of church furnishings after designs by Verhaegen, such as the pulpit (1774) for Ste Catherine, Mechelen. In 1780 he became dean of the Guild of St Luke. The panels (1784) carved in relief of the choir stalls in the St Janskerk, Mechelen, are thought to be his finest work, displaying a feeling for naturalistic detail in the tradition of Verhaegen.

BIBLIOGRAPHY

BNB; Thieme–Becker; Wurzbach
C. H. Immerzeel: *De Levens en werken der Hollandsche en Vlaamsche Kunstschilders, Beeldhouwers, Graveurs, Bouwmeesters van het begin der XVe eeuw tot heden*, iii (Amsterdam, 1843), pp. 172–3

IRIS KOCKELBERGH

Valdambrino, Francesco di. *See* FRANCESCO DI VALDAMBRINO.

Valde-Iñigo, Marqués de [Saenz de Santa María, José Marcos] (*b* Veracruz, Mexico, 25 April 1738; *d* Cádiz, 4 Sept 1804). Spanish priest and patron. He came from a family of *hidalgo* (noblemen) originally from Rioja, whose wealth derived from trade with South America. After a period articled as a clerk to a foreign trader in Cádiz, the Marqués was ordained a priest in 1761. He spent a short time in Madrid, where he claimed the naked figures on the ceilings of the Palacio Real were too upsetting for him to contemplate, before returning to Cádiz and settling there. His religious life and his artistic patronage became closely linked to the church of Nuestra Señora del Rosario and particularly to a penitential cult conducted in an underground cavern adjacent to the church. The Marqués acquired a plot of land above the cavern, improved it and between 1793 and 1796 built over it a spacious elliptical chapel, designed by the City Architect, Torcuato José de Benjumeda (1757–1836), in the classical style. No expense was spared to enrich the interior with sculpture, paintings, marble and porphyry. Subjects relating to the Mass were depicted in a series of five semicircular paintings for the pendentives and two stucco medallions. *St Carlo Borromeo Giving the First Communion to St Luigi Gonzaga* was the subject of one medallion by Zacarías González Velázquez; an *Angel Giving the Host to St Stanislas Kostka* that of the other by the leading Cádiz sculptor Cosme Velázquez (*b* 1755). The paintings, which contrasted Old and New Testament subjects and depicted the *Last Supper* and the *Miracle of the Loaves and Fishes*, were executed by Goya, José Camarón y Boronat and Zacarías González Velázquez.

BIBLIOGRAPHY

Carta edificante o relación sumaria de la vida del ejemplar sacerdote y obrero apostólico infatigable: Sr D. Josef Saenz de Sta María, Marqués de Valde-Iñigo, y fundador en Cádiz de la actual Santa Cueva . . . escrita por otro sacerdote (Cádiz, 1807)

J. Ezquerra del Bayo: 'Las pinturas de Goya en el oratorio de la Santa Cueva de Cádiz', *A. Esp.*, ix/3 (1928), pp. 388–91

R. Moreno Criado: *La Santa Cueva y sus Goyas* (Cádiz, 1977)

NIGEL GLENDINNING

Valdelvira [Valdevira], **Andrés de.** *See* VANDELVIRA, ANDRÉS DE.

Valdés, Manuel. *See under* EQUIPO CRÓNICA.

Valdés, Sebastián de Llanos y. *See* LLANOS Y VALDÉS, SEBASTIÁN DE.

Valdés Leal. Spanish family of artists. They were active principally in Seville but also in Córdoba and Cádiz. (1) Juan de Valdés Leal, the most important member of the family, was the last of the great Baroque painters of Seville. His wife Isabel de Carrasquila (1630–91) is said to have painted in oils, but no works by her have been recorded. Luisa Raphaela Morales (née de Valdés) (*bapt* Córdoba, 27 Dec 1654), their eldest child, is documented as a gilder and etcher. (2) Lucas de Valdés, their only son, was a painter, printmaker and teacher who was his father's principal assistant during the 1680s. Another daughter, María de Valdés (*b* Seville, 1664; *d* Seville, 1730), became a nun and was a portrait and miniature painter. Lucas de Valdés's son, Juan de Valdés the younger (*b* 1684; *fl c.* 1700–1730s), was an engraver who continued the family tradition in Seville well into the 18th century. His modest prints are sometimes confused with the far greater work of his grandfather.

(1) Juan de Valdés Leal (*b* Seville, 4 May 1622; *d* Seville, 15 Oct 1690). Painter, draughtsman, sculptor and etcher. The last of the great Baroque painters of Seville, he was also a sculptor and etcher of considerable ability and was praised as an architect by his contemporaries, although no buildings by him are known. In addition, he wrote on art, though none of his writings is extant. With the exception of rare portraits, his paintings are entirely religious. The visual excitement of his style reflects his religious fervour. He is thus the antithesis of Bartolomé Esteban Murillo, his more famous colleague.

1. To 1670. After his baptism in Seville, Valdés Leal is next documented in Córdoba in 1647. The identity of his master in Seville is not known, and it is improbable that he was trained by Antonio del Castillo in Córdoba, as has been suggested. He probably arrived in Córdoba *c.* 1644 and remained in the city until his return to Seville in 1650. He married in 1647, the year in which he signed and dated his first work, *St Andrew* (Córdoba, S Francisco). The impasto and the dark tonalities in the painting, and the realistic and yet static treatment of the figure, are characteristic of his early work. In 1650 and 1651 he is documented in Seville, where he probably remained until the end of 1653. During this period his work was strongly influenced by the paintings of Francisco de Herrera the elder, Murillo and, to a lesser extent, those of Francisco de Zurbarán. In 1653 he signed and dated the *Death of St Clare* (Palma de Mallorca, Col. March), the last in the series of the life of the saint painted for the Franciscan convent in Carmona, near Seville. The composition is taken from Murillo's work of the same subject (1646; Dresden, Gemäldegal. Alte Meister), but the brushwork and figural types show that he had studied the work of Herrera the elder. The most impressive of the paintings of this period is the *Miraculous Rout of the Saracens* (Seville, Alcázar), which demonstrates Valdés Leal's ability to depict form in motion, his love of elaborate decorative detail and his strong sense of bright colour.

In 1654 Valdés Leal returned to Córdoba, where the first of his five children was baptized. On 18 February 1655 he signed the contract for the pictures on the high altar of the church of the Carmelitas Descalzas in Córdoba. These paintings are his only retable series still in their original setting, and they include some of his finest works. The large central canvas depicts the *Ascension of Elijah* and is the first work in his mature style, while the paintings in the predella and the upper section of the altar are more conservative. Valdés Leal probably studied the works of Tintoretto, Titian, Rubens and the leading Spanish painters in Madrid in 1655 to prepare for the *Elijah*, which is marked by a new lightness in brushwork, an open composition and a general lightening of the palette. The Carmelite retable was, for some reason, not completed until 1658.

By 15 July 1656 Valdés Leal had returned to Seville, where he remained for the rest of his life with the exception of a few brief trips. His first important commission of this period for the Hieronymite monastery of Buenavista outside Seville consists of scenes from the *Life of St Jerome* and single figures of monks and saints of the Hieronymite Order. Several of the canvases are signed and dated 1657. The composition of the *Temptation of St Jerome* (Seville, Mus. B.A.; see fig. 1) is derived from the same subject painted by Zurbarán for the Hieronymite monastery at Guadalupe (1638–9; *in situ*), but the style of the two works is completely different. That by Valdés Leal is active, colourful and lightly brushed and shows the influence of Titian's *Penitent St Jerome* (*c.* 1650; Madrid, Escorial). The *Marriage of the Virgin* (1657; Seville Cathedral) was probably Valdés Leal's first work to include an elaborate architectural setting. Unlike Murillo, he painted few landscapes, and his interest in architecture is related to his close contacts with the Ribas brothers, who were retable architects and sculptors working in Seville; the Salomonic columns in the *Marriage* are taken directly from the type used by Francisco Dionisio de Ribas (1617–71). The composition of the painting is reminiscent of Mannerism;

the space recedes rapidly and the bodily proportions are distorted, traits possibly derived from Valdés Leal's study of Domenico Tintoretto, who was in Madrid in 1655.

Also in 1655 Francisco de Herrera the younger had returned to Seville. His activities there led to the establishment of the High Baroque style as the dominant new manner, although he painted relatively little in the city himself. It was Valdés Leal who received the lion's share of the commissions from 1656 to 1660 and who disseminated the new style, but the feelings engendered by his dominance led to complaints in 1658 that he had never passed the painter's examination in Seville. In 1659 he was commissioned to paint the altarpieces for the church of the Order of Calatrava (Seville, church of the Magdalene), and in 1660 he painted the series of the *Life of St Ignatius* (Seville, Mus. B.A.) for the Jesuits. The *Vanitas* (Hartford, CT, Wadsworth Atheneum) and its pendant, the *Allegory of the Crown of Life* (York, C.A.G.), also date from 1660 and are now among his most famous works. Valdés Leal derived his *Vanitas* from a study of Antonio de Pereda's

1. Juan de Valdés Leal: *Temptation of St Jerome*, oil on canvas, 1657 (Seville, Museo de Bellas Artes)

work while in Madrid. In 1660 the Real Academia de Belles Artes de Sta Isabel de Hungria opened in Seville; Valdés Leal was a founder-member and in 1663 was elected president. He also served as an officer in the Guild of Painters. Murillo dominated painting in Seville from 1665 until his death, commanding higher prices than Valdés Leal. From 1664 Valdés Leal turned increasingly to gilding, sculpture and printmaking in order to support his large family.

2. FROM 1670. The early 1670s were a productive period. In 1671 Valdés Leal designed the enormous ephemeral monument erected in Seville Cathedral for the celebrations in honour of the canonization of Ferdinand III of Castile (1217–52). The structure, known as 'el Triunfo', was recorded by Valdés Leal in an etching included in the book (Seville, 1671) that commemorated the events (see SEVILLE, fig. 4). At the end of 1672 an inventory of the Hermandad de la Caridad, to which he belonged, listed the *In ictu oculi* (see fig. 2) and *Finis gloriae mundi*, two outstanding *vanitas* paintings by Valdés Leal. Located in their original setting below the raised choir in the church of the Hospital de la Caridad in Seville, they were probably painted earlier that year. The iconographic programme of the church decoration was devised by Don MIGUEL MAÑARA VICENTELO DE LECA, the head of the Hermandad, and the works by Valdés Leal express Mañara's pessimistic theology. *In ictu oculi* ('in the twinkling of an eye') shows a skeleton extinguishing a candle and trampling on objects symbolizing power, wealth and fame; death ends life and mocks all worldly pursuits. *Finis gloriae mundi* depicts the interior of a crypt with corpses that vividly represent the decay of the flesh after death.

Through the gloom appears the hand of Christ holding a pair of scales in balance; on the left are emblems of the seven mortal sins and on the right symbols of prayer and penance. The scales would be weighed in favour of all those who followed the rules of the Hermandad as written by Mañara. The programme of decoration was completed with six paintings by Murillo and the high altarpiece sculpture depicting the *Entombment* by Pedro Roldán (1670–72). These works represent the biblical seven acts of mercy—the life of righteousness that would tip the scales in one's favour on the Day of Judgement. Valdés Leal also painted his largest altarpiece in 1672, the *Franciscan Allegory* (Cabra, Colegio S José Escolapias), for which a finished drawing exists (Paris, Ecole B.-A.). The drawing serves as a touchstone for his graphic work, which is closer to the style of Murillo than might be expected. In 1673 Valdés Leal painted the *Life of St Ambrose* for an oratory in the Archiepiscopal Palace in Seville, and in October of the same year he signed a contract to gild and paint Bernardo Simon de Pineda's high altar retable of the church of the Hospital de la Caridad. He was then the leading practitioner of gilding in Seville and may well have earned more from gilding than from the sale of his pictures.

In 1680 Valdés Leal began to paint in fresco, working principally in this medium during the last decade of his life. As his health began to fail, most of the programmes were realized with the help of his son (2) Lucas de Valdés. The programmes include the frescoes in the church of the Hospital de la Caridad (1680–82), those in the church of the Convento de S Clemente el Real (1680–90) and those in the church of the Hospital de los Venerables Sacerdotes (1686–8). Unlike the fresco tradition in Madrid with its emphasis on *quadratura*, the frescoes of Valdés Leal accentuate the surface of the vaults and walls with a brightly coloured, dense, decorative schema and with figural scenes most often set within painted fictive frames. The style was continued in Seville after his death by his son. In 1680 Valdés Leal also executed his only extant sculpture, the full-length *Virgin of the Rosary*, still in the hospital of the Hospital de la Caridad. In 1681 he painted the remarkable portrait, *Don Miguel Mañara Presiding over a Meeting of the Hermandad de la Caridad* (Seville, church of the Hospital de la Caridad). His remaining oil paintings show increasing intervention by his son and the deterioration of his own hand, for example the *Immaculate Conception* (1682; Dallas, TX, S. Methodist U., Meadows Mus. & Gal.) and the gigantic *Exaltation of the Cross* (c. 1684; Seville, church of the Hospital de la Caridad). Valdés Leal's fame did not abate despite the decline of his work. The portrait of *Don Miguel Mañara* (Málaga, priv. col.), commissioned in 1683, was extravagantly praised in a contemporary letter and compared with works in Spanish royal collections. Several apprentices are documented for Valdés Leal, but none achieved fame. Of the painters said to have been his pupils, such as Matías de Arteaga y Alfaro or Clemente Fernández de Torres, none were trained by Valdés, although Palomino acknowledged help from Valdés Leal in Córdoba in 1672 and was proud to consider himself a pupil.

2. Juan de Valdés Leal: *In ictu oculi*, oil on canvas, 2.20×2.16 m, 1672 (Seville, Church of the Hospital de la Caridad)

BIBLIOGRAPHY

Ceán Bermúdez

El manuscrito de la Academia de Murillo (Seville, 1660–74); ed. A. de la Banda y Vargas (Seville, 1982)

F. de la Torre y Farfán: *Fiestas de la S iglesia metropolitana y patriarcal de Sevilla al nuevo culto del Señor Rey S Fernando* (Seville, 1671)

A. A. Palomino de Castro y Velasco: *Museo pictórico* (1715–24/R 1947), iii, pp. 387, 436–8, 456

J. Gestoso y Pérez: *Biografía del pintor sevillano, Juan de Valdés Leal* (Seville, 1916)

E. du Güe Trapier: *Valdés Leal: Spanish Baroque Painter* (New York, 1960)

D. Angulo Iñiguez: *Pintura del siglo XVII*, A. Hisp. (Madrid, 1971)

D. Kinkead: *Juan de Valdés Leal (1622–90): His Life and Work* (New York, 1978) [cat. rais. and full bibliog.]

E. Valdivieso and J. M. Serrera: *El Hospital de la Caridad de Sevilla* (Seville, 1980)

D. Kinkead: 'Juan de Valdés Leal: Nueva documentación y obras', *Actas del symposium internacional 'Murillo y su época': Sevilla, 1982*

L. de Moura Sobral: 'Deux nouveaux Valdés Leal', *Rev. Louvre*, xxxi (1982), pp. 356–62

E. Sullivan and N. Mallory: *Painting in Spain, 1650–1700* (Princeton, NJ, 1982)

E. Valdivieso and J. M. Serrera: *La época de Murillo* (Seville, 1982)

E. Paéz Ríos: *Repertorio de grabados españoles*, iii (Madrid, 1983), §2188–90

D. Luengo Pedrero: 'Un lienzo de Valdés Leal adquirido por el Prado y otra nueva atribución al artista', *Bol. Mus. Prado*, v (1984), pp. 113–18

L. de Moura Sobral: 'Le Roi "San Fernando": Deux nouveaux tableaux de Valdés Leal', *Racar*, xii (1985), pp. 45–9

E. Valdivieso: 'La pintura de la Catedral de Sevilla: Siglos XVII al XX', *La catedral de Sevilla* (Seville, 1985)

A. E. Pérez Sánchez: *Historia del dibujo en España de la edad media a Goya* (Madrid, 1986)

E. Valdivieso: *Juan de Valdés Leal* (Seville, 1988)

D. Kinkead: *Juan de Valdés Leal* (in preparation)

DUNCAN KINKEAD

(2) Lucas de Valdés (*b* Seville, 1661; *d* Cádiz, 1725). Painter, printmaker and teacher, son of (1) Juan de Valdés Leal. He studied under his father, beginning to paint at an early age and acquiring an excellent humanist training. His early works included four pictures (1671; destr.) for the feast day of the canonization of St Ferdinand; these were published as prints in Fernando de la Torrey Farfán's *Fiestas de la Santa Iglesia Metropolitana y Patriarcal de Sevilla al nuevo culto del Sr Rey San Fernando* (Seville, 1671). The *Martyrdom of St James* (1677; Córdoba, Mus. Prov. B.A.) is also another early work of Valdés's. In the 1680s, because of his father's deteriorating health, he took complete charge of his workshop, being responsible for the completion of many fresco cycles in Seville, such as those in S Clemente el Real (1680–90) and the church of the Hospicio de los Venerables Sacerdotes (1686–8). He dominated contemporary art in Seville with his vigorous and decorative style that showed little influence of Murillo and his followers. His style is not as well-developed as his father's, although occasionally his paintings exhibit a Baroque complexity comparable to the large illusionistic frescoes that were popular in Seville. Examples of his frescoes, now destroyed, were those for the chapel of S Laureano in Seville Cathedral and for the dome of the monastery church of S Diego, Seville. He also received commissions to decorate the cloister and staircase of the Trinitarios and to paint frescoes in S María Magdalena (*c.* 1710–15) and S Luis (*c.* 1715–19), all in Seville. All of these paintings contain images of complex iconography rendered in rich colours that stand out against the white walls. His series of *St Francis of Paola* (Seville, Mus. B.A.) is carelessly executed yet has meticulous detail in places. He also painted allegories (e.g. *Allegory of the Paths of Life*, Seville, priv. col., see Valdivieso, p. 295), portraits (e.g.

Admiral Don Pedro Corbet, *c.* 1699; Seville, Hospicio Venerables Sacerdotes) and architectural scenes (e.g. *View of the Ribera Sepulchres in the Cartuja de las Cuevas in Seville*, 1714; Seville, Casa Dueñas). From 1719 until his death in 1725 he lived in Cádiz, where he taught mathematics at the Colegio Naval.

BIBLIOGRAPHY

E. Valdivieso: *Historia de la pintura sevillana: Siglos XIII al XX* (Seville, 1986), pp. 283–95

ISMAEL GUTIÉRREZ PASTOR

Valdivia. Pre-Columbian culture of Ecuador that flourished between *c.* 4000 BC and *c.* 1500 BC. It was the first major cultural manifestation along the south and south-western coasts of Ecuador and was defined by E. Estrada in 1956 from excavations at site G-31 near the modern coastal town of Valdivia, Guayas Province, from which it takes its name. It is classed archaeologically as part of the Intermediate area (*see* SOUTH AMERICA, PRE-COLUMBIAN, §II). Valdivia remains have since been found in the lower Gulf of Guayaquil, northward through coastal areas, the Guayas Basin and in the north of Manabí Province. Early pottery with similar stylistic affinities has been found in northern Peru, in the southern and northern highlands of Ecuador and in areas east of the Andes. Study of the highly distinctive Valdivia pottery, particularly from the south coast of Ecuador, has led archaeologists to develop an eight-phase cultural sequence. It has been suggested that Valdivia is ancestral to the subsequent Machalilla phase (*c.* 1500–*c.* 900 BC). Judging from the competent manufacturing techniques and wide range of complex ornamentation associated with the ceramic assemblages of the earliest phase (*c.* 2600–*c.* 2500 BC), the Valdivia culture appears to have been already highly developed, without apparent local antecedents. An earlier style found at the Valdivia site, and known as San Pedro, is technically superior and probably unrelated to the style associated with the Valdivia culture.

From their earliest appearance, and continuing for *c.* 2000 years, the coiled, sand-tempered wares associated with Valdivia fall into three generally distinct vessel categories with attendant decorative motifs: spherical pots with tall, decorated concave necks; short-necked shouldered pots with varying rim treatment; and red-slipped hemispherical bowls with elaborately incised or excised designs thought to imitate the general shape of halved gourds. An early feature of Valdivian ceramic art is the selection of separate sets of geometric designs and decorative motifs for bowls, and for jars and pots. Bowls often have designs created by excising wide bands, whereas jars and pots have designs filled in with incised hatching and cross-hatching. There are subtle chronological changes in bowl design and manufacture (overall form, rim treatment, the appearance of bowl supports such as legs, carination, changes in the composition and execution of stylistic motifs and the subsequent use of red, yellow and white, or trichrome painting after firing) and in jars and pots (forms and attendant decoration, rim and neck development, and the appearance of additions such as loop handles).

The ceramic chronology is supported by a parallel development in the Valdivia figurine tradition. The earliest examples include simple, carved stone pieces, generally under 100 mm long, with stylized features in low relief, such as T-shaped noses, brow lines, squared eyes, mouths and cheeks, head notches, hands placed on the midriff directly above the waist, occasional lower body decoration, and leg incisions or notches, sometimes including feet. By the Valdivia III phase (*c.* 2300 BC), small red-slipped clay figurines predominate. They are frequently hand-modelled on a base of clay coils. They often have faces surrounded by elaborate coiffures, appliqué arms and modelled breasts. Figurines from later phases are defined in part by increasingly elaborate hair treatment, breast exaggeration and stylization of facial features. In the middle phases the prevalent forms were pregnant figures, double-headed figures, male figures and rattles. By Valdivia VII (*c.* 1700 BC), figurine manufacture appears to have waned in the south, although later northern variants are known and have been recovered at REAL ALTO.

Inland Valdivia sites were usually located near alluvial areas, where the bulk of agricultural activities probably took place. Associated tools include *manos* and *metates* (grinding stones and slabs), eared stone axes and stone bladelets that could have been used in the processing of root crops. At the early inland site of Loma Alta, mammals, birds and reptiles formed part of the diet; bone points, stone saws, hammerstones, reamers, pebble choppers, scrapers, knives and gravers are all the evidence that remains in an environment otherwise hostile to preservation. At other sites mangrove and ocean resources were exploited. Coastal sites have produced large amounts of shell refuse and such artefacts as abraders, polishers, spoons and bowls. Associated tools include shell fish-hooks, stone reamers, net weights and a Valdivia IV (*c.* 2200 BC) ceramic vessel that is thought to represent a dugout canoe.

The earliest Valdivia villages, such as Loma Alta, appear to have been arranged concentrically around a clearing, a pattern of great social, ceremonial and cosmographical significance to contemporary indigenous South Americans. This pattern continued to be used at Real Alto in Valdivia III, where the evolution of Valdivia settlement morphology is best documented. Here two centrally located and opposing ceremonial mounds represent early examples of ceremonial architecture in the Pre-Columbian Americas. Other early examples of ceremonial paraphernalia include miniature ceramic depictions of stools used by shamans, plain and decorated lime vessels used for coca consumption, representations of figurines with snuff tablets and possibly coca mastication, and feline effigy mortars, probably used in the preparation of hallucinogenic substances. It is suggested that the motifs typical both of Valdivia bowls and of the related figurine tradition are associated with the ritual use of psychoactive substances. There are good examples of Valdivia figurines and pottery in the archaeological collection of the Banco Central del Ecuador, Quito, and figurines in the Museo Chileno de Arte Precolombino, Santiago.

BIBLIOGRAPHY

E. Estrada: *Valdivia: Un sitio arqueológico formativo en la costa de la provincia de Guayas, Ecuador* (Guayaquil, 1956)

B. J. Meggers, C. Evans and E. Estrada: *The Early Formative Period of Coastal Ecuador: the Valdivia and Machalilla Phases*, Smithsonian Contrib. Anthropol., i (Washington, DC, 1965)

Ancient Ecuador: Culture, Clay and Creativity, 3000–300 BC (exh. cat. by D. W. Lathrap, D. Collier and H. Chandra, Chicago, IL, Field Mus. Nat. Hist., 1975)

PETER W. STAHL

Valdivieso, Raúl (*b* Santiago, 9 Sept 1931). Chilean sculptor. He studied at the Escuela de Bellas Artes in Santiago under the Chilean sculptors Julio Antonio Vásquez (*b* 1900), Lily Garáfulic (*b* 1914) and Marta Colvin. He left Chile in 1958 for Spain, France and Morocco, settling in Spain in 1961 but returning to Chile in 1974 to produce a number of works, including an important commission for the Parque de las Esculturas in Santiago (*Bandaged Torso*; stone, h. 1.62 m, installed 1989), before leaving again for Spain.

Valdivieso worked in bronze and also in granite, limestone, diorite and basalt. Much of his work was concerned with natural forms, conveyed with a directness of feeling. Approaching mass through a process of gradual abstraction, Valdivieso sought a balance between the visual and tactile qualities of his materials and the meanings implicit to their forms. He often formulated his sculptures first in easily moulded, ductile materials, which he then translated into the final work. He particularly favoured chrome-plated bronze for its accentuation of the surface with its brilliant finish.

In one of his most characteristic series, *Seeds* (*Emerging Seed*; marble, h. 400 mm, 1985; Santiago, Mus. N. B.A.), Valdivieso simplified natural forms into masses of great formal purity, establishing an intimate dialogue between the material (stone or bronze) and the suggestions of fruit, seeds and doves. In his sculptures of the 1980s he combined such forms with shapes related to sexual organs (*Kiss*; bronze, h. 330 mm, 1982; artist's col.).

BIBLIOGRAPHY

Raúl Valdivieso: Esculturas (exh. cat., Madrid, Gal. Nebli, 1963)

M. Ivelič: *Escultura chilena* (Santiago, 1979), pp. 57–62

W. Sommer: *Plástica chilena* (Santiago, 1985), pp. 64–7

CARLOS LASTARRIA HERMOSILLA

Vale. Portuguese family of artists. They belong to a period of transition in northern Portugal, from Baroque to Rococo, when structural elements adhered to the earlier style and the elegance of form depended on the new. Their training and architectural practice were closer to those of artisans, but they did have access to Augsburg engravings that were circulating among the monastic orders in the region. For these reasons their work often reflects the conflict apparent in Portuguese art of the second half of the 18th century, which fluctuated in form and decoration between Baroque and Rococo.

(1) José da Cunha Correia Vale (*fl* Guimarães, *c.* 1748). Architect. He designed the impressive façade of the Lobo Machado mansion (1750–75), Guimarães. Here the lintel forms, as well as the carved, voluted and inverted pediment forms of the window cornices, are derived directly from the work of Nicolau Nasoni in Oporto, though the forms have been rearranged and given a more powerful expression; the swinging line of the cornice comes from the architecture of the neighbouring city of

Braga. A related design by the same architect is seen on the façade of the church of S Domingos, the Third Order of St Dominic, Guimarães, built before 1784.

(2) António da Cunha Correia Vale (*fl* Guimarães, *c*. 1756–81). Wood-carver, brother of (1) José da Cunha Correia Vale. He was one of the most successful wood-carvers in Guimarães, and, in collaboration with his brother Manuel da Cunha Correia Vale (*fl c*. 1756), he executed there the two lateral retables (*c*. 1760) in the former convent of S Rosa de Lima. From 1762 António was working for the church of the Misericórdia, Guimarães, where his most important and finest work was the retable for the high altar; its structure is Baroque but it has a decorative vocabulary that is Rococo. His other carvings for the same church were the organ cases (1775) and the two pulpits (1781), as well as the choir of the same date, which was done in collaboration with Manuel Fernandes Novais. He also worked on the retable of Nossa Senhora do Rosário (*c*. 1770; untraced) for the church of S Domingos, Guimarães, and carried out work in carved and gilded wood (1756), after designs by José Álvares de Araújo, for the church of the Franciscan Tertiaries, Ponte de Lima, again in collaboration with his brother Manuel.

BIBLIOGRAPHY

R. Smith: *The Art of Portugal, 1500–1800* (London, 1968), p. 106
F. Goncalves: *A talha na arte religiosa de Guimarães* [Wood-carving in the religious art of Guimarães] (Guimarães, 1982)

JOSÉ FERNANDES PEREIRA

Vale [Valle]**, Amaro do** (*fl* 1584–1619). Portuguese painter and draughtsman. He was trained in Rome and from 1612 was court painter (*pintor régio*) to Philip II of Portugal (III of Spain). We know that he worked in the circle of the Procaccini family in Milan, probably after his stay in Rome. The style of his work reflects the Mannerism of the Escorial, suggesting that Amaro do Vale had studied the works of Luca Cambiaso, Bartolomé Carducho or Orazio Borgianni, and seems to be more evolved in comparison with the Mannerist style of his contemporaries. His finest works have been destroyed or remain untraced; these include an *Assumption of the Virgin* (early 17th century; destr. 1755) from a retable in Lisbon Cathedral; a *Calvary* (early 17th century) for the Franciscan convent, Lisbon; and a fresco of the *Nativity* (late 16th century) painted for the refectory of the Hieronymite monastery, Belém, of which only fragments exist. Amaro do Vale's drawings and preparatory studies (Lisbon, Mus. N.A. Ant.) show his confident draughtsmanship and give an idea of his delicate line, luminous brushstroke and careful mastery of naturalism. One drawing, *St Luke Painting the Virgin* (*c*. 1610), a study for the panel in the chapel of S Luke in the convent church of the Anunciada (untraced), was commissioned by the Irmandade dos Pintores de Lisboa (Fraternity of the Painters of Lisbon) in 1610 and is a particularly fine bistre sketch of vibrant plasticity and sensitive line.

The few surviving paintings by Amaro do Vale are in poor condition: six canvases depicting the *Agony in the Garden*, *St Peter*, *St Paul*, the *Baptism*, *St John the Evangelist* and *St Augustine* (Leiria, Semin. Maior) were painted for an altar of 1605–6 in Leiria Cathedral; the panel of the *Miracle of the Relics of St Vincent* (early 17th century;

Lisbon, Mus. N.A. Ant.) from a series, now dispersed, for Lisbon Cathedral; *Our Lady of the Safe Harbour Guarding the City of Lisbon* (*c*. 1610), a vast canvas in S Luis dos Franceses, Lisbon, of iconographic interest; and the large panel of the *Adoration of the Heavenly Court* (*c*. 1615–18; Lisbon, Mus. N.A. Ant.). The last includes, beneath groups of saints, martyrs and angels gathered around Christ and the Virgin, portraits of the principal members of the nobility at court who supported the Spanish monarch, surrounding Philip III, and the effigies of Charles V and Pope Paul V, together with Trinitarian and Dominican friars; all these were executed with great delicacy of line, feeling for colour and skill in portraiture. It is possible that this painting adorned the altar in the chapel of the old royal palace, the Palácio da Ribeira (destr. 1755), which was restored after 1615 in preparation for the state entry of Philip III into Lisbon in 1619.

BIBLIOGRAPHY

F. da Costa Meesen: *Antiguidade da arte da pintura* (MS.; 1696), ed. G. Kubler (New Haven and London, 1967), p. 267
J. Martínez: *Discursos praticables del nobilíssimo arte de la pintura* (Zaragoza, 1866)
V. Serrão: *A pintura maneirista em Portugal* (Lisbon, 1982), pp. 84–8
——: *A pintura maneirista e o desenho*, História da Arte em Portugal, Alfa vii (Lisbon, 1986), pp. 78–82

VITOR SERRÃO

Valencia. Capital city of the province of Valencia, Spain, on the River Turia in the fertile Huerta, an alluvial plain. It has a university and a population of *c*. 752,000.

1. History and urban development. 2. Art life and organization.

1. HISTORY AND URBAN DEVELOPMENT. The first reference to Valencia was made by Livy, who indicated that Valentia was founded *c*. 138 BC by the Roman consul Decius Julius Brutus after the defeat of the Lusitanian leader Viriato. Roman Valencia had an irregular layout and was enclosed by a wall with four gates. It had a typically Roman plan with two principal roads (the cardo and decumanus); the forum was situated at their intersection (now the area between the Plaza de la Virgen and the Palacio Arzobispal). Under the Visigoths (AD 413–714) Valencia was the seat of a bishop, although it was not a major urban centre. In the Islamic period (from 711), although initially neglected, it gradually acquired greater importance; on separating from the caliphate of Córdoba, the city was the capital of a *taifa* ('splinter kingdom').

In 1094 Valencia was conquered by Rodrigo Díaz de Vivar, known as El Cid (1043–99), and in 1102 it came into the possession of the Almoravids. The 11th-century Arabic wall had seven gateways and the Medina at the heart of the enclosure was larger than the old Roman forum. Outside the Arabic wall were the suburbs, among them Boatella (south), Xerea (east) and Roteros (west). In 1238 the city was incorporated into Aragon by James the Conqueror (1213–76). Following the Reconquista new churches, such as S Agustín, were built, and mosques were converted for Christian use, including S Nicolás (rebuilt 1693 by Juan Pérez Castiel (*c*. 1650–*c*. 1707)) and the cathedral (from 1262; extended 1480). A wall was built in 1356 that incorporated the suburbs. Later additions to the cathedral include a chapter house (1369) with an octagonal vault, and the Miguelete or Micalet (h. *c.* 68 m; 1380–1420; see fig. 1), a free-standing, octagonal bell-tower.

After a period of political agitation and social and economic crisis, partly due to the plague, Valencia became in the 15th century the most important city in Aragon, its population rising from 36,000 in 1418 to 67,500 in 1483. Surviving medieval secular buildings include a Gothic mansion (the Casa del Almirante), the Palacio de la Generalidad, or Audiencia (begun 1482; completed 1581 in the Renaissance style), and the Lonja de la Seda (1482–98; see fig. 2), both by PERE COMPTE. The city's various phases of development can still be seen in the Seu, Carme and Xerea districts. During the 16th century the city deteriorated as economic activity was attracted from the Mediterranean towards the Atlantic; the failure of the Revolt of the Germanias (1521–3) worsened the situation, but the Expulsion of the Moors (1609) dealt the hardest blow.

In the War of the Spanish Succession (1701–14) Valencia backed the Habsburgs, for which the Bourbon king, Philip V, abolished its privileges (1707). Throughout the 18th century the city participated in the Spanish economic and cultural revival. Monasteries, parish churches and chapels of the Military Orders were built, all shown in a plan (1705) of the city by Tomás Vicente Tosca (1651–

1723). Many buildings were altered in Baroque style (e.g. the Gothic S Martín), and the cathedral's interior was redecorated both by Pérez (planned 1671; executed 1674–82) and, in the late 18th century, by Antonio Gilabert (1716–92). Such buildings as the Colegio S Pio (now Museo de Bellas Artes) by Pérez (designed 1683), the Palacio del Marqués de Dos Aguas (*c.* 1740; now Museo Nacional de Ceramica y de las Artes Suntuarias), the Ayuntamiento (1763; 20th-century façade; now Museo Paleontológico Municipal), the Aduana (1756–1802; now Palacio de Justicia) by Felipe Rubio (*d* 1767) and the temple church (rebuilt 1770) are evidence of the economic prosperity of the 18th century and of a new urban concept. By 1794 the population of the city had reached *c.* 112,500.

During the Peninsular War (1808–14) Valencia was occupied (1812) by Major General Suchet and was liberated in 1813 by General Elío. Under the First Spanish Republic (1873–4) the city was aligned with the Cantonalista movement and proclaimed itself independent in 1873. Important changes in urban layout were made in the 19th century. In 1865 the demolition of the walls began, leaving only the Torre de Serranos (1391–8, by Pedro Balaguer) and the Torre de Cuarte (1441–60, by Pedro Bonfill). A ring-road was built that separated the

1. Valencia Cathedral (from 1262), view from the south-east, showing the *cimborio* with alabaster panes (left), the rose window surmounting the Puerta de los Apóstoles (centre) and the Miguelete

2. Valencia, Lonja de la Seda by Pere Compte, view from the west, 1482–98

old, inner city from the planned districts, and the immediately outlying areas were also incorporated into the city. The development plan approved in 1887 endeavoured to organize the area outside the ring-road by dividing it into a grid pattern. The Paseo al Mar project dates from 1898. Parallel with suburban development were projects to redevelop the inner city, notably the unexecuted plan (1910–12) by Federico Aymaní and that (1928) by Javier Goerlich Lleo (1886–1972).

During the Civil War (1936–9) Valencia was the capital of the Republican government, and many churches, including the cathedral, were damaged. In 1946 Germán Valentín Gamazo directed the implementation of an urban plan that introduced functional zoning. The diversion of the Turia caused by the flood of 1957 made it necessary to modify this plan and draw up another in 1966. Late 20th-century Valencia is characterized by contrasts in planning and facilities between the various districts. Attempts have been made to conserve the deteriorated Seu–Xerea district, the site of the original Roman nucleus.

2. ART LIFE AND ORGANIZATION. After the reconquest of Valencia (1094), painted devotional icons of the Virgin were imported into the city, which were evocative of Byzantine art (e.g. the *Virgin of Grace*, S Augustín). The earliest Valencian works, however, date from well into the 14th century (e.g. paintings in the secret chamber over the steps of the sacristy in Valencia Cathedral). In the mid-14th century the Tuscan style was influential, and this facilitated the creation of an individual Valencian style, which was fully developed by *c.* 1400. The reconquest also brought sculptural images of the Virgin in the Romanesque tradition (e.g. the 'Morenata' in the convent of the Incarnation, 13th century). Notable from the 14th century are the image of the *Hospital de Sacerdotes Pobres*, for the church of the Milagro de Valencia, and the mutilated image of *St John of the Hospital* (Mus. Catedralicio–Dioc.). In monumental sculpture, the figurative elements of the Palau portal in the cathedral belong to the Early Gothic of the 13th century, although Romanesque solutions continued to be used; the sculpture on the Puerta de los Apóstoles in the cathedral perhaps dates from the first quarter of the 14th century.

Valencian painting reached its first peak in the 15th century, inspired by the visits of Gherardo Starnina, documented between 1395 and 1401, and probably that of Jan van Eyck, who toured the Peninsula in 1428–9. Their influence can be seen in anonymous works of extraordinary quality. In the second half of the century Jacomart and Juan Rexach worked in this Hispano-Flemish style. Under Alfonso V (*reg* 1416–58) Valencian art and culture flourished. Compared to the rest of Spain, Valencia adopted Renaissance forms early, undoubtedly due to the presence from 1472 of the Italian artists PAOLO DA SAN LEOCADIO and Francisco Pagano, who were patronized by Rodrigo Lenzuoli-Borgia, the future Pope Alexander VI. The Borgia family were important patrons, particularly Popes Calixtus III and Alexander VI, who were benefactors of such churches as the cathedral and S Nicolás. The Renaissance reached its peak in the city at the beginning of the 16th century owing to the presence of the artists LLANOS AND YÁÑEZ, whose work contains many references to that of Leonardo da Vinci. Between 1507 and 1510 they executed the paintings on the wings of the main retable in the cathedral. Some paintings by Sebastiano del Piombo were brought to the city by Ambassador Jerónimo de Vich (*c.* 1459–1534) and had a considerable impact on the development of Valencian painting at the beginning of the 16th century. Sebastiano's style impressed Vicente Maçip, whose son, Juan de Juanes (*see* MAÇIP, (2)), inherited his father's influences and softened them, creating a style that appealed to popular taste and was much imitated by his followers. The most renowned Renaissance sculptor from Valencia was Damián Forment, though he mostly worked in Aragon and Catalonia. JUAN SARIÑENA brought realism to Valencian painting, and this was refined by Francisco Ribalta (*see* RIBALTA, (1)). The presence of Pedro Orrente influenced the development of painting in Valencia significantly.

Valencian artists enjoyed a great deal of patronage: Ambassador Vich built an Italianate palace (*c.* 1507–20) in Valencia; its remains are now integrated into the Convento del Carmen. Mencia de Mendoza had the tomb of her parents, the *Marqués and Marquesa de Cenete* (1564–5), carved in Genoa and placed in the Capilla de los Reyes in the monastery of S Domingo, Valencia. The dukes of Calabria were benefactors to the monastery of S Miguel de los Reyes (1578–1645). Archbishop Juan de Ribera was a collector and patron; he built and decorated the Colegio de Patriarca (1586–1610; now a museum; *see* RIBERA (i), (3)). Diego de Vich y Mascó (*d* 1657) inherited and extended his family collections and befriended such artists as Ribalta, JERONIMO JACINTO ESPINOSA and Orrente.

Between 1607 and 1617 attempts were made to establish a Colegio de Pintores resembling a guild. Its function was to protect its professional interests from both outsiders and the untalented. Half a century later an academy was established in the monastery of S Domingo (before 1667), while some painters maintained private academies. By the time the Real Academia de Bellas Artes de S Carlos (1768) was officially founded, art in the city was largely centred on and taught in the lecture halls of the academies.

After a period of decadence, Valencian sculpture prospered in the 18th century with the arrival in the late 17th century and the early 18th of Italian works by D. Solavo (1649–c. 1726) and J. A. Ponzanelli (1654–1735), and of Italian and German–Italian sculptors: J. Bertessi, Antonio Aliprandi (fl early 18th century), Konrad Rudolf (d 1732) and Francisco Stolf, who greatly contributed to the establishment of Italianate Baroque sculpture. Such local artists as Ignacio Vergara (1715–76) and José Esteve Bonet maintained these high standards throughout the 18th century. Sculptors belonged to the carpenters' guild until the rise of the academies and usually lived in the fishing district of the city. Engraving also flourished between the late 18th century and the first half of the 19th, notably through the work of Tomás López Enguidanos and Rafael Esteve Vilella.

The most famous Valencian painters between the end of the 18th century and the mid-19th were Mariano Salvador Maella and Vicente López y Portaña, both of whom worked mostly in Madrid. In the second half of the 19th century and the first decades of the 20th painting flourished once more, led by such artists as IGNACIO PINAZO, Francisco Domingo y Marqués and Joaquín Sorolla y Bastida. At the end of the 19th century the great sculptor Mariano Benlliure (1862–1947) became famous and was succeeded by Andreu Alfaro. In the late 20th century several internationally recognized painters were active in Valencia, for example Francisco Lozano Sanchis (b 1912), Jordi Teixidor (b 1941), Javier Calvo (b 1941), Manuel Boix (b 1942), Arturo Heras (b 1948) and Ximo Amigó (b 1965).

The city's most important museums include the Museo Nacional de Cerámica y de las Artes Suntuarias Gonzáles Marti (founded 1954), the Museo de Bellas Artes (1837), the Museo del Patriarca, the IVAM Centro Julio González (1986), the Museo Catedralicio–Diocesano (1954), the Museo Histórico de la Ciudad (1927) and the Casa–Museo Benlliure (1957). The Feria de Anticuarios and Interarte, a sale of contemporary art, is held annually in Valencia.

BIBLIOGRAPHY

Marques de Alcahali: Diccionario biográfico de artistas valencianos (Valencia, 1897)
M. Sanchis Guarner: La ciutat de Valencia (Valencia, 1972)
Gran enciclopedia de la región valenciana, xii (Valencia, 1973), pp. 63–104
F. M. Garin y Ortiz de Taranco: Catalogo monumental de la ciudad de Valencia (Valencia, 1983)
——: Historia del arte de Valencia (Valencia, 1983)
M. J. Teixidor and A. Prades: 'Valencia: Conjunto histórico artístico a favor de seis zonas de la ciudad', Catálogo de monumentos y conjuntos de la comunidad valenciana, ii (Valencia, 1983), pp. 224–342
V. Aguilera Cerni, ed.: Historia del arte valenciano (Valencia, 1985)
A. E. Pérez Sánchez: 'Valencia: Arte', Tierras de España: Valencia (Madrid, 1985)
Historia de l'art al país Valencia (Valencia, 1988)
M. González Baldovi, ed.: Guia de museos de la comunidad valenciana (Valencia, 1991), pp. 201–81
For further bibliography see SARALEGUI Y LÓPEZ-CASTRO, LEANDRO DE.

ANA MARÍA BUCHÓN CUEVAS

Valencia, Felipe Gómez de. See GÓMEZ DE VALENCIA, FELIPE.

Valenciennes. French town in the Nord département, c. 46 km south-east of Lille, and formerly a centre of lace production. The introduction of lacemaking in Valenciennes is traditionally attributed to Françoise Badar, who learnt both bobbin and needle lacemaking during an apprenticeship in Antwerp (1640–44). The industry flourished, but declined sharply in the severe slump of c. 1700, the number of lace merchants falling from about fifty in the 1680s to only one in 1714. Despite the corresponding loss of skilled lacemakers, the industry began to revive in the 1720s and reached its peak between 1735 and the 1780s, the period of the classic Valenciennes bobbin lace. The industry's fortunes are mirrored in those of the Tribout firm, with its many contacts in Paris and elsewhere. Designs were obtained from Brussels and Paris, and other laces, including Brussels, Mechlin (Mechelen; Malines) and even needle lace, were produced alongside Valenciennes. The industry at Valenciennes was irrevocably ruined by the Napoleonic wars, but Valenciennes lace itself survived to be revived in various centres in Belgium in the 19th century.

BIBLIOGRAPHY

A. Maletot: La Dentelle de Valenciennes (Paris, 1927)
P. Guignet: 'The Lacemakers of Valenciennes in the Eighteenth Century', Textile Hist., x (1979), pp. 96–113

PATRICIA WARDLE

Valenciennes, Jean de [Valenchine, Jean van]. See JEAN DE VALENCIENNES.

Valenciennes, Pierre-Henri (de) (b Toulouse, 6 Dec 1750; d Paris, 16 Feb 1819). French painter. He trained at the academy in Toulouse under the history painter Jean-Baptiste Despax (1709–73). In 1769 he went to Italy for the first time, with Mathias Du Bourg, a councillor at the Toulouse parliament. Du Bourg introduced him to Etienne-François, Duc de Choiseul, a keen patron of the arts, who in turn recommended him to Gabriel-François Doyen, one of the leading history painters in Paris, whose studio he entered in 1773. Doyen gave his pupil a sense of the elevated ideals of history painting but was also sympathetic to the lesser genre of landscape. Valenciennes presumably frequented Choiseul's country seat at Chanteloup, near Amboise, meeting there the landscape painters Hubert Robert and Jean Hoüel, both protégés of Choiseul. His early interest in the native landscape can be seen in his sketchbooks (Paris, Louvre), especially one dated 1775 that contains drawings made at Amboise, Compiègne and Fontainebleau, and in a later series of oil studies on paper made in Brittany, at the mouth of the River Rance and around St Malo.

In 1777 Valenciennes made a second trip to Italy, remaining there until 1784 or 1785. Among the earliest records of this stay are three precise drawings of rocks and trees, dated 1780 in Rome (Paris, Louvre). It was probably on a return trip to Paris in 1781 that Valenciennes met Joseph Vernet, who taught him a broader manner of working that was responsive to the effects of aerial perspective, as he later acknowledged (*Elémens de perspective*, p. xviii). It was probably Vernet's advice and practice that encouraged Valenciennes on his return to Rome to make the studies in oil on paper, many of them done in the open air (e.g. *Study of Clouds, from the Quirinal*; see fig.), that seem to have been his chief occupation in Italy. The mistaken notion that following his return from Italy, Valenciennes travelled in Greece, Asia Minor, North Africa and the East stems from passages in his treatise *Elémens de perspective* exhorting the modern artist to travel as widely as possible; but both the date of his return from Italy and his movements during the next two or three years are uncertain.

Valenciennes's public career began in 1787, when he was approved (*agréé*) by the Académie Royale on 31 March and, in unusually rapid succession, received (*reçu*) on 28 July. His reception piece was *Cicero Uncovering the Tomb of Archimedes* (Toulouse, Mus. Augustins), a historical subject set in an imaginary landscape intended to evoke ancient Sicily in the vicinity of Syracuse. This painting and the *Ancient City of Agrigentum* (Paris, Louvre), another landscape with a classical theme, were shown at the Salon of 1787. The latter shows servants sent out to welcome travellers approaching the city, an ancient hospitable custom. In the background is the Temple of Concord, the ruins of which Valenciennes had visited during a trip to Sicily in 1779. These large-scale Salon paintings, which

represent ideal and imaginary visions of the ancient world, use the study of nature only in the most indirect way. They reflect fashionable interest in Sicily but are remote in concept from the everyday observations of Hoüel's series of Sicilian prints published in the same decade. Moreover, they lack the verisimilitude of Vernet's calm or dramatic landscapes and marines. Instead they represent a vain Neo-classical attempt to regain the arcadian world of Poussin's late landscapes, using an updated archaeology. Valenciennes continued to send similar landscapes to the Salon from 1787 until the year of his death.

Valenciennes's major contribution to the history of art lies in his theory and practice as a teacher and in his efforts to raise the status of landscape. His successful official career did much to raise its low standing, as did his treatise, *Elémens de perspective*, in which he gave landscape painting the full practical and theoretical discussion it deserved but had been previously denied. Indeed, this treatise was to remain the basic handbook for French landscape painters up to the time of the Realists and Impressionists. Valenciennes thought that the landscape painter should be as learned as any history painter, combining his wide general knowledge with the close study of nature to improve the academic credibility and intellectual standing of landscape. In 1812 he became Professeur de Perspective at the Ecole Impériale des Beaux-Arts, helping to form a generation of Neo-classical landscape painters, such as Achille Michallon, Pierre-Athanase Chauvin, Jean-Baptiste Deperthes and Nicolas Bertin. His aspirations were vindicated in 1816, when a special Prix de Rome for landscape was

Pierre-Henri Valenciennes: *Study of Clouds, from the Quirinal*, oil on paper, 256×381 mm, *c.* 1783 (Paris, Musée du Louvre)

established at the Académie to encourage 'historical landscape' (*paysage historique*) based on historical and literary subject-matter. Indeed, Valenciennes had the pleasure of seeing his pupil Michallon become the first recipient of this prize. There was little demand for elevated landscapes in the manner of Poussin, however, and his followers generally made a living from attractive small-scale arcadian and Italianate scenes.

Valenciennes is also notable for having encouraged artists to paint oil studies in the open, thus training them to match in paint the visual effects of nature, especially transient light, atmosphere and aerial perspective. He urged repeated studies of one view in different lights but saw such works purely as training exercises; they bore no direct relation to finished studio works. His own oil studies were not seen publicly until 1930, when they were donated to the Musée du Louvre. The critical response to Valenciennes was not very complimentary from the 1820s onwards, as the new aesthetics of Romanticism, Realism and Impressionism were not sympathetic to his classical ideal. Had his critics examined the full range of his work, including the oil studies, they might have recognized his importance as a student of nature; instead, he came to be misunderstood as a poor pasticheur of Poussin, with little observation or truth in his art.

WRITINGS

Elémens de perspective pratique à l'usage des artistes (Paris, 1799–1800)

BIBLIOGRAPHY

J.-B. Deperthes: *Histoire de l'art du paysage* (Paris, 1822)
Oeuvres provenant des donations faites par Madame la Princesse Louise Croÿ et Monsieur Louis Devillez (exh. cat., ed. J. Guiffrey; Paris, Mus. Orangerie, 1930), no. 134
Pierre-Henri de Valenciennes (exh. cat., ed. R. Mesuret; Toulouse, Mus. Dupuy, 1956)
C. Sterling and H. Adhémar: *Musée national du Louvre: Peintures, école française, XIXe siècle*, iv (Paris, 1961)
P. Conisbee: 'Pre-Romantic *Plein-air* Painting', *A. Hist.*, ii (1969), pp. 413–28
W. Whitney: 'Pierre-Henri Valenciennes: An Unpublished Document', *Burl. Mag.*, cxviii (1976), pp. 225–7
Les Paysages de Pierre-Henri de Valenciennes, 1750–1819 (exh. cat., ed. G. Lacambre; Paris, Louvre, 1976)
P. R. Radisich: *Eighteenth-century Landscape Theory and the Work of Pierre Henri de Valenciennes* (Ann Arbor, 1981)

PHILIP CONISBEE

Valente, Pietro (*b* Naples, 1796; *d* Naples, 10 Aug 1859). Italian architect and writer. He was a pupil of D. Chelli and G. Santacroce at the Accademia di Belle Arti in Naples and from 1814 to 1821 in Rome on a scholarship from the Real Istituto di Belle Arti. In 1817 he won the competition to build the votive church of S Francesco di Paola in the present Piazza Plebiscito, Naples, designed on a Greek cross plan, which Valente considered 'the most suitable in terms of beauty, regularity and decorum'. Controversy over the competition result, however, led to all the designs being sent to the Accademia di S Luca in Rome, the members of which preferred the designs of PIETRO BIANCHI (ii), to whom Valente lost the commission. He designed and supervised the completion of the Palazzo De Rosa (1826–34) on the Via Toledo, Naples, which is astylar with a rusticated basement. In 1827 he was commissioned to build the Villa Acton (now the Museo Diego d'Aragona Pignatelli Cortes) on the Riviera di Chiaia, Naples, for Sir Ferdinand Richard Acton (1801–

37). The imposing Neo-classical villa is set in an English-style landscaped park. Other works included the Palazzo Mautone, intended for rented housing, on the Via S Teresa in Naples and the cemeteries at Aversa and Santa Maria Maggiore. In 1834 he designed the highly praised theatre (destr.) at Messina and in the same year was appointed professor of civil architecture at the Regia Università di Napoli, but the post was abolished in 1840. In that year Valente became director of the Scuola di Scenografia, which had just been annexed to the Real Istituto di Belle Arti, and in 1849 he succeeded Antonio Niccolini as director of the institute. He was one of the leaders of Neapolitan Neo-classicism, a measured and sober style that borrowed elements from the architecture of Pompeii, the Italian Renaissance and the French Empire style brought to Naples by French architects working there during Napoleon's occupation.

WRITINGS

Osservazione dell'architetto Pietro Valente napoletano: nell'invenzione di un monumento il più opportuno per decorare la piazza della reggia di Napoli in dilucidazione di tre progetti dal medesimo fatti per questo (Rome, 1819)
Dell'istituzione degli architetti e del miglioramento dell'architettura (Naples, 1832)
Dello stato presente delle teorie di architettura e della necessità di una istituzione teorica (Naples, 1835)
Dell'essenza e dignità dell'architettura e dei doveri di un'architetto (Naples, 1836)
Relazione dell'architetto Pietro Valente sulle risaie di Cocuruzzo, Napoli a di 31 marzo 1839 (Naples, 1840)

BIBLIOGRAPHY

Portoghesi; Thieme–Becker
C. N. Sasso: *Storia dei monumenti di Napoli e degli architetti che li edificarono dallo stabilimento della Monarchia sino ai nostri giorni* (Naples, 1856)
C. Lorenzetti: *L'Accademia di Belle Arti di Napoli (1752–1952)* (Florence, [1953])
B. Molajoli: *Il Museo Principe Diego Aragona Pignatelli Cortes* (Naples, 1960)
A. Venditti: *Architettura neoclassica a Napoli* (Naples, 1961)
E. Catello: 'Architettura neoclassica a Napoli. La Basilica di San Francesco di Paola', *Napoli Nob.*, xvii (1978), pp. 81–92
R. De Stefano: 'Storia, architettura ed urbanistica', *Stor. Napoli*, ix (1971), pp. 645–743

GIOVANNA CASSESE

Valenti Gonzaga, Cardinal **Silvio.** *See* GONZAGA, (21).

Valentim, Mestre. *See* FONSECA E SILVA, VALENTIM DA.

Valentin, Curt (*b* Hamburg, 5 Oct 1902; *d* Forte dei Marmi, nr Viareggio, 19 Aug 1954). German dealer, active in the USA. After leaving school he trained at the Galerie Kahnweiler in Paris, then at the Galerie Kommiter in Hamburg and after 1927 at the Galerie Flechtheim in Berlin, where he helped to organize exhibitions and where he co-edited the gallery's magazine *Omnibus*. After the gallery was closed in 1934, he worked at the Buchhandlung Buchholz, running his own gallery in the art department. The bookseller's efforts to expand his market overseas led Valentin to visit New York. In 1936, when the Nazis placed restrictions on artists and their dealers, Valentin decided to emigrate there. In 1937 he founded the Buchholz Gallery, Curt Valentin, on West 46th Street; in 1939 it was moved to modest premises on 57th Street. Although the early stages of dealing were difficult, he was helped by MOMA in New York and by some wealthy friends. His exhibitions were successful, as were his small and original catalogues. His great advantage as a dealer was to have close personal links with many European artists, whose work he helped to promote in the USA. These included Arp, Brancusi, Braque, Max Beckmann (a particular enthusiasm of Valentin's), Chagall, Lyonel Feininger, Kirchner, Klee and a number of German Expressionists, Wilhelm Lehmbruck Léger, Miró, Henry Moore and Picasso, as well as lesser known American painters and sculptors whose reputations he established. In 1951 the Buchholz Gallery was renamed the Curt Valentin Gallery; it operated until 1955.

Valentin was conspicuous among dealers for his confidence, his deep knowledge and his unselfish commitment to artists, collectors and museum directors. He helped to overcome the dominance of French art in the USA by introducing the work of British, Italian and German artists. He was particularly keen on exhibiting sculpture, and his achievement in reviving an appreciation of sculpture in the USA was considerable. In addition to his work as a dealer in New York, he helped to organize exhibitions in Chicago, Seattle, St Louis, Buffalo and Cincinnati, often loaning them works, as with the Beckmann exhibition of 1948 at the Art Museum in St Louis, MO. He was also an enthusiastic and knowledgeable book collector, and he edited many art books and selected writings of authors that he admired, for example Novalis's *The Apprentices of Sais* (New York, 1949).

BIBLIOGRAPHY
In Memory of Curt Valentin, 1902–1954: Exhibition of Modern Masterpieces Lent by American Museums (exh. cat. by P. T. Rathbone, New York, Curt Valentin Gal., 1954)
Artist and Maecenas: A Tribute to Curt Valentin (exh. cat., intro. W. Grohmann and R. Colin; New York, Marlborough–Gerson Gal., 1963)
INGRID SEVERIN

Valentin de Boulogne. *See* BOULOGNE, VALENTIN DE.

Valentiner, Wilhelm [William] **R(einhold)** (*b* Karlsruhe, 2 May 1880; *d* New York, 6 Sept 1958). American art historian and museum director of German birth. He made his mark as a Rembrandt scholar with the publication of his thesis *Rembrandt und seine Umgebung* in 1905. Appointed assistant to Wilhelm von Bode at the Kaiser-Friedrich Museum, Berlin, in 1906, he gained an encyclopedic knowledge of museums and their organization, which was matched by his appetite for writing. His influence was felt especially in American museums, first as curator at the Metropolitan Museum of Art, New York, from 1908 and then as director of the Detroit Institute of Arts, the Los Angeles County Museum of Art, the J. Paul Getty Museum, Malibu, and the North Carolina Museum of Art, Raleigh. He was friend and adviser to two generations of collectors, reaching new audiences for German Expressionist painting, and he organized important loan exhibitions devoted to Rubens and van Dyck, Rembrandt and Frans Hals. He also mastered specialized areas from Italian Renaissance sculpture to Islamic pottery. Although he was often unduly generous in his attributions, his publications are notable for their insights and enthusiasm.

WRITINGS
Rembrandt und seine Umgebung (diss., Heidelberg, Ruprecht-Karls-U., 1904; Strasbourg, 1905)
Studies of Italian Renaissance Sculpture (London, 1950)

Regular contributions to *Art in America* (1913–47) and *A. Q.* [Detroit] (1938–58), both of which he founded

BIBLIOGRAPHY
Masterpieces of Art: In Memory of William R. Valentiner, 1880–1958 (exh. cat., Raleigh, NC Mus. A., 1959), pp. 295–319 [with list of writings]
M. Sterne: *The Passionate Eye: The Life of William R. Valentiner* (Detroit, 1980)
JAMES DAVID DRAPER

Valentinis [Valentini]**, Sebastiano de'** (*fl* Udine and Gorizia, *c.* 1540–60). Italian etcher, painter and gilder. He was formerly identified as Sebastiano d'Ul because of a misreading of the signature 'SEBASTIANO D'.VL' that appears in one of his prints. His etchings are in certain aspects akin to the contemporary graphic art of Paolo Farinati (1524–1606) and Battista del Moro (1514–74) in Verona, but with obvious northern European influences, perhaps from the Danube school. Only three of his works are known: the *Rest on the Flight into Egypt* (see exh. cat., 1983, no. 45) and *Prometheus* (1558; see exh. cat., 1983, no. 46), both of which are signed, and the recently discovered large print of the *Turkish Army* (1558; London, BM).

BIBLIOGRAPHY
Bolaffi
V. Rossitti: *Dizionario degli incisori friulani* (Udine, 1981), pp. 85–7
D. Landau: 'Printmaking in Venice and the Veneto', *The Genius of Venice* (exh. cat., ed. J. Martineau and C. Hope; London, RA, 1983), pp. 342–3
FELICIANO BENVENUTI

Valentino, Duca di. *See* BORGIA, (3).

Valentis, Thoukididis (*b* Cairo, 1 Nov 1908; *d* Athens, 4 April 1982). Greek architect and teacher. He studied at the School of Architecture, National Technical University of Athens (1925–30), and worked for the technical departments of the Ministry of Education (1930–32) and of the Greek Air Force (1935–40), where he later became director of the Design Department (1952–60). His projects for the Ministry of Education's Programme of New School Buildings in the 1930s are characterized by simple, compact prismatic volumes, regular openings and a fusion of classical elements with Modernist ones. These principles are most evident in his largest school (1930–32) on Krystalli, Syngrou and Amvrosiou Episkopou Mediolanou streets, Thessaloniki. His pre-war blocks of flats, for example the one (1933) designed with Polyvios Mihailidis (1907–42) on Zaimi and Stournara streets, Athens, are similar to the buildings of the Italian Rationalists. In his post-war projects, however, such as the office buildings (1953–5) at Patission 4, Athens, he favoured a visible Functionalist expression of the concrete load-bearing structure, resulting in an exposed grid on the façades that became influential in speculative office buildings in Greece. He was Professor of Architectural Design at the Aristoteleion University of Thessaloniki (1961–5) and at the National Technical University of Athens (1965–74).

BIBLIOGRAPHY
F. Loyer: *Architecture de la Grèce contemporaine* (diss., U. Paris III, 1966)
A. Giacumakatos and E. Godoli: *L'architettura delle scuole e il razionalismo in Grecia* (Florence, 1985)
ALEXANDER KOUTAMANIS

Valeriano, Giuseppe (*b* L'Aquila, Aug 1542; *d* Naples, 15 July 1596). Italian architect and painter. He was in

Rome from the early 1560s and *c*. 1570 executed the decoration of the Cappella dell'Ascensione, including an altarpiece showing the *Ascension*, in Santo Spirito in Sassia, Rome. His painting style, though provincial, shows the influence of Mannerism and of the successors in Rome of Pellegrino Tibaldi and Michelangelo. Also characteristic is an exaggerated expressiveness and a peculiar imbalance in the depiction of figures and space. He worked partly in collaboration with Scipione Pulzone and Gaspare Celio (1571–1640). Valeriano, however, is more important for his work as an architect. The first buildings that can be securely attributed to him were designed in Spain, where he went in 1573, becoming a member of the Jesuit Order there in 1574. These included the church in Villagarcìa de Campos and projects for the Jesuits at Seville, Granada, Córdoba, Málaga and Trigueros (all unexecuted or only partially executed). He came into contact with Juan de Herrera, whose work on the Escorial clearly influenced him in his own work on the Collegio Romano in Rome after he returned to Italy in 1580. Despite the traditional attribution to Bartolomeo Ammanati, the design of the Collegio Romano, founded by Pope Gregory XIII, is now regarded as Valeriano's, in collaboration with a team that included Giacomo della Porta. In 1584 Valeriano produced plans for the new building of the Collegio Massimo (now the University), Naples, and started work there on his masterpiece, the Gesù Nuovo, the largest Jesuit church in southern Italy. The building has a basically centralized plan, with a dome over the crossing, tunnel-vaulted transepts and cupolas over the corner chapels; the longitudinal axis was emphasized by a one-bay extension of the nave on both entrance and choir sides. Originally painted white, with features picked out in *piperno*, the local volcanic stone, they have since been covered in rich marble. His Chiesa del Gesù (begun 1589), Genoa, has a similar plan, and the wall surfaces of its spacious interior are articulated with pilasters. In 1591 Valeriano worked on the enlargement of the Michaelskirche, Munich, and in 1592 he produced plans for Jesuit buildings in Lisbon, Malta, L'Aquila, Marsala and Palermo.

BIBLIOGRAPHY

G. Baglione: *Vite* (1642); ed. V. Mariani (1935), pp. 83–4
A. Rodriguez y Guttiérrez de Ceballos: 'Juan de Herrera y los Jesuitas Villalpando, Valeriano, Ruiz, Tolosa', *Archv Hist. Soc. Iesu*, xxxv (1966), pp. 285–321
P. Pirri: *Giuseppe Valeriano S.I.: Architetto e pittore, 1542–1596* (Rome, 1970)
A. Blunt: *Neapolitan Baroque and Rococo Architecture* (London, 1975), pp. 37–9
A. Ceccarelli: 'Giuseppe Valeriano, padre gesuita: Architetto progettista della Chiesa e Collegio di S Ignazio di Cosenza', *Boll. A.*, xliv/2 (1979), pp. 29–60
R. Bösel: *Jesuitenarchitektur in Italien (1540–1773): Die Baudenkmäler der römischen und der neapolitanischen Ordensprovinz* (Vienna, 1985)
S. Benedetti: 'La prima architettura gesuitica a Roma: Note sulla chiesa dell'Annunziata e sul Collegio Romano', *L'architettura della Compagnia di Gesù in Italia, XVI-XVIII secolo: Milan, 1990*, pp. 57–68
I. Di Resta: 'Il Collegio Romano', *L'architettura della Compagnia di Gesù in Italia, XVI-XVIII secolo: Milan, 1990*, pp. 81–5

RICHARD BÖSEL

Valéry, Paul (Ambroise) (*b* Sète, 30 Oct 1871; *d* Paris, 20 July 1945). French writer. One of the greatest French poets of the early 20th century and one of its most original minds, he had a lifelong interest in the visual arts. Edgar Degas introduced Valéry to his future wife, Jeannie Gobillard, in the house of his friend, the collector Henri Rouart. Valéry's marriage brought him into a family of artists: his wife was a niece of Berthe Morisot and was an accomplished musician and a talented watercolour painter; her sister, Paule Gobillard, was also a gifted painter. In 1902 Paul and Jeannie Valéry moved into the house Berthe Morisot had built in 1884 at 40 Rue Villejust (now Rue Paul Valéry) in Paris. 'The house smelt of turpentine', Agathe, Valéry's daughter, once said, so pervasive was the presence of painting, new and old. Paul Valéry himself illustrated his poem 'Le Cimetière marin' with seven fine etchings; the 26,600 pages of his 261 notebooks, the famous *Cahiers*, covering the years 1894 to 1945, include numerous drawings, sketches and (from the 1920s onwards) watercolours, sometimes related to the text, sometimes independent of it.

Although Valéry rightly disclaimed any pretension to being an art historian or critic, his writings on art are an important part of his work. At 19 he proclaimed the unity of architecture and music in his 'Paradoxe sur l'architecte' (1891). At 23 he published his 'Introduction à la méthode de Léonard de Vinci' (1895), an article elaborated in close discussion with Stéphane Mallarmé and later completed by the important 'Note et digression' (1919) and 'Léonard et les philosophes' (1929). Valéry believed that the universal genius Leonardo had found 'the central attitude from which the undertakings of knowledge and the operations of art are equally possible'. Valéry brought a boundless curiosity to his scrutiny of the workings of the mind; the endless probing of the problems of mental creativity is the central theme of the *Cahiers* (initially inspired by Leonardo's notebooks) and underlies all his varied writings on art. Architecture and music were for him the supreme arts; he regarded construction and composition as the mainspring of all the arts, including painting and poetry. His prose dialogues, *L'Ame et la danse* (1921) and *Eupalinos ou l'architecte* (1923), gave poetic expression to his principles; his 'mélodrame' *Amphion* (1931) evoked the creation of Thebes to the music of the lyre.

Valéry wrote occasional pieces, generally commissioned, notably on Degas, Honoré Daumier, Edouard Manet, Jean-Baptiste-Camille Corot and Berthe Morisot. His *Degas, danse, dessin* (1936), drawing largely on his personal memories of Degas in old age, is anecdotal and wide-ranging but full of penetrating and illuminating remarks on the nature of drawing (which Degas defined as not form but the way of seeing form), the dance and problems of general aesthetics (although Valéry regarded this as a rather fruitless enquiry). Unlike Mallarmé, Valéry was out of touch with his artistic contemporaries and regarded 20th-century art with blanket disapproval as decadent. His gods were those of Mallarmé, together with the Old Masters. He blamed the rise of landscape and still-life painting for the disappearance of 'Great Art', involving all the faculties of man, as exemplified in Leonardo and Michelangelo, Veronese and Rembrandt. That was the theme of his *Préambule* to the catalogue of the 1935 exhibition of Italian art from Cimabue to Tiepolo at the Petit Palais in Paris. Whether positive or negative, whether fruitful or perverse, Valéry's ideas are generally expressed in prose of great precision, elegance and distinction, always stimulating, perhaps most of all when most provocative.

WRITINGS
J. Hytier, ed.: *Oeuvres*, 2 vols (Paris, 1957–60, rev. 2/1980–84)
Cahiers, 29 vols (Paris, 1957–61); extracts, ed. J. Robinson, 2 vols (Paris, 1973–4)
Degas, Monet, Morisot; Eng. trans. by D. Paul, intro. by D. Cooper, as *The Collected Works of Paul Valéry*, xii (New York, 1960)
N. Celeyrette-Pietri and J. Robinson-Valéry, eds: *Cahiers, 1894–1919* (Paris, 1987–)

BIBLIOGRAPHY
R. Pelmont: *Paul Valéry et les beaux-arts*, Harvard Studies in Romance Languages, xxiii (Cambridge, MA, 1949)
F. Fosca: *De Diderot à Valéry: Les Ecrivains et les arts visuels* (Paris, 1960)
LLOYD JAMES AUSTIN

Valesi, Dionigi (*b* Parma, *c.* 1730; *d* Venice, *c.* 1780). Italian printmaker. He worked in Verona and Venice, where he produced etchings and engravings of sacred and secular subjects after Veronese, Francesco Guardi, Francesco Battaglioli, Pietro Antonio Rotari and Adriano Cristofali (1717–88), among others. His most renowned prints are three Venetian views: the *Grand Canal at Riva di Biasio*, the *Island of S Giorgio Maggiore* and an architectural capriccio. All three are derived from Guardi and were executed *c.* 1778 for the Venetian bookseller–publisher Marchiò Gabrieli. Valesi also engraved a *Map of the City of Verona Showing the Flood of 2 December 1752*, various portraits of notable Venetian citizens, and illustrations for books. He collaborated with other artists on a *Road to Calvary*, with a rich decorative border, which was published (*c.* 1778) by the Bassano branch of the Remondini printing and publishing firm.

BIBLIOGRAPHY
Thieme–Becker
D. Succi: *Da Carlevarijs ai Tiepolo: Incisori veneti e friulani del settecento* (Venice, 1983), pp. 412–14
——: *Guardi, metamorfosi dell'immagine* (Venice, 1987), pp. 179–84, 280–82
DARIO SUCCI

Valī Jān. *See* VELI CAN.

Välikangas, Martti (*b* Kuopio Province, 1 Aug 1893; *d* Helsinki, 9 May 1973). Finnish architect. Having qualified in 1917, he set up his practice in 1920. During the 1920s his housing projects in Helsinki were his most important work, in particular the workers' housing suburb Puu-Käpylä (1920–25), built with municipal assistance. For Puu-Käpylä, Välikangas designed one- and two-storey wooden houses, built of vertical planks with low saddle-back roofs, in the style of old Finnish farmhouses. They were erected quickly and cheaply by using standardized components: doors and windows, in a classical style. The houses followed simple plans found in Finnish 18th-century architecture. They were individualized with details such as garlands and acroteria derived from the Empire style, which Välikangas also used for blocks of flats (1920s) in Helsinki. Puu-Käpylä combined the English concept of the garden suburb and the most successful ideas from contemporary Swedish public housing. His small buildings, most housing two to eight families each, were complemented with large gardens, with outbuildings, arranged on a variety of plans.

Välikangas was sympathetic to new trends in architecture; in the 1930s he designed an important group of Functionalist buildings in Mikkeli. Although the bus station (1934) is of this group, it is still dominated by classical symmetry. His later work includes a number of large hospitals in different parts of Finland, notable for the interesting use of colour and materials, as well as refined detailing, which create an intimate environment.

BIBLIOGRAPHY
N. E. Wickberg: *Byggnadskonst i Finland* [Finnish architecture] (Helsinki, 1959, 2/1962), pp. 122, 220–22
J. M. Richards: *800 Years of Finnish Architecture* (Newton Abbot, 1966, rev. 1978), pp. 138, 140–41
R. Weston: 'Classical Excursions', *Architects' J.*, clxxxvii/7 (1988), pp. 48–53, 55
T. Keinären and K. Paatero, eds: *Martti Välikangas, 1893–1973: Arkkitehti* (Helsinki, 1993)
RIITTA NIKULA

Valkenauer [Valckenawer]**, Hans** [Hanns] (*b* ?Regensburg, ?1448; *d* ?Regensburg, ?1518). German sculptor. He was the most important Late Gothic sculptor in Salzburg, where he was granted citizenship on 18 October 1479. Despite his probable origins in Regensburg (Martin Valkenauer, his father (?), is documented in 1465 in Regensburg), he worked in a tradition of tomb sculpture found in Salzburg, Wiener Neustadt and Vienna. The artists who influenced him most were Master E. S. and Nicolaus Gerhaert.

Valkenauer's first tomb slab was that of *Lukas Lamprechtshauser* (shortly before 1480; Regensburg, St Blasius). The figures of the Virgin and saints are developed using the whole space between the background and the projecting canopy. The same is true of the figures on two epitaphs: that of *Kunz Horn* (*c.* 1502; Nuremberg, St Lorenz), where the enthroned Christ is surrounded by angels of different sizes and adored by Horn and his wife, and the *Keutschach* epitaph (Maria Saal, Pilgrimage Church). Similarities between the head of God the Father on both these epitaphs and the limewood reliquary bust of *St Sebastian* (Munich, Bayer. Nmus.; original colouring lost) show that the latter may be by Valkenauer.

The tomb monument of *Archbishop Leonhard of Keutschach* (*d* 1519) was destroyed when Salzburg Cathedral was rebuilt in 1614, but several important sculptures by Valkenauer or his shop survive. The sculpture of the Archbishop and some red marble reliefs with saints are in the Georgskirche, Hohensalzburg Castle, and the Castle also contains interesting examples of architectural sculpture in the form of seven busts in spotted red marble. Funerary monuments include those of *Hans Herzheimer* (Bad Aussee, St Paul), *Wolfgang Panicher* (*d* 1507; Kuchl, SS Maria und Pankraz), *Gregor Rainer* (Berchtesgaden, Abbey Church), *Michael Scherringer* (*d* 1517; Salzburg, St Peter, cemetery) and *Wolfgang von Polheim* (Oberthalheim, Parish Church).

Valkenauer was among the important group of artists, including Albrecht Dürer, who were employed to glorify Emperor Maximilian I (*see* HABSBURG, §I(3)). On 5 February 1514 Maximilian concluded an agreement with Valkenauer for a grand monument in the choir of Speyer Cathedral. The idea was for a huge corona supported by 12 round or polygonal columns, with attached figures of 12 emperors, kings, empresses and queens who were buried in the crypt beneath the monument. According to the agreement, which is preserved, Valkenauer did not actually draw up the design (possibly made by the Emperor's architect, Joerg Koelderer). The monument was never completed, and when Maximilian died in 1519 work stopped. The surviving fragments (Salzburg, Mus. Carolino Augusteum) give an idea of how fantastic the concept was. The surviving crown circle is 6 m in diameter: one point of the crown, in the shape of a palm leaf, is 1.55 m high; and one of the eight surviving figures of an emperor is 1.78 m high. That the fragments contain much shop work is of no particular significance. In design, the monument was more Gothic than Renaissance: the faces and bodies of the figures are deeply reflective, expressing mourning and sorrow. This is in contrast to the gigantic crown, which was intended to remind the spectator of the glory of the Holy Roman Empire and of German nationhood (the figures are in contemporary dress). Another notable aspect of the design was the open arrangement, which allowed the spectator to look through the columns and sculpture to the choir with the altar beyond it.

BIBLIOGRAPHY
Thieme–Becker
P. M. Halm: *Studien zur süddeutschen Plastik*, i (Augsburg, 1926), pp. 176–224
W. Pinder: *Die deutsche Plastik vom ausgehenden Mittelalter bis zum Ende der Renaissance* (Wildpark-Potsdam, 1929), p. 410
T. Müller: *Alte bairische Bildhauer* (Munich, 1950), p. 39
A. Legner: 'Beiträge zur Salzburger Bildnerei im frühen 16. Jahrhundert', *Jschr.: Salzburg. Mus. Carolino Augusteum* (1957), pp. 47–70
G. van der Osten and H. Vey: *Painting and Sculpture in Germany and the Netherlands, 1500–1600*, Pelican Hist. A. (Harmondsworth, 1969), p. 43
Maximilian I (exh. cat., Innsbruck, Tirol. Landesmus., 1969), i, p. 156
G. F. Fehring and A. Ress: *Die Stadt Nürnberg* (Munich, 1977), p. 81
P. E. Schramm and H. Fillitz: *Denkmale der deutschen Könige und Kaiser*, ii (Munich, 1978), p. 104
W. Czerny: *Hans Valkenauer und die spätgotische Grabmalplastik in der Diözese Salzburg* (diss., Vienna, 1982)
A. Schädler: 'Eine geschnitzte Reliquienbüste von Hans Valkenauer', *Festschrift Kurt Rossacher* (Salzburg, 1983), pp. 281–90

VINCENT MAYR

Valkenburg [Valke], **Johannes von.** *See* JOHANNES VON VALKENBURG.

Valkot, V. F. *See* WALCOT, WILLIAM.

Valladolid. Spanish city and administrative capital of the province of Castile and León. It is situated in north central Spain, at the confluence of the River Pisuerga with the Esgueva, and has a population of *c.* 400,000. It flourished during the Renaissance and Baroque periods, when it was an important centre for work in gold and silver.

1. HISTORY AND URBAN DEVELOPMENT. Valladolid was founded in the mid-8th century BC by the Vaccii, a Celtic–Iberian people from Soto de la Medinilla. From the 1st century AD the area was occupied by the Romans, who established such villas as the Villa de Prado, reconstructed in the 4th century (mosaics and remains in Valladolid, Mus. Arqueol.). There is evidence of Germanic settlements from the 5th century, and some Visigothic groups remained after the Muslim invasion. In 1072 the site was given to Conde Pedro Ansúrez (*d* 1119) by Alfonso VI, King of León and Castile (*reg* 1065–1109). The Villa Condal consisted of a palace, a bridge over the River Pisuerga, a hospital, the church of Maria la Antigua and the collegiate church of S Maria la Mayor (11th–12th century; Romanesque remains *in situ*). In the 11th century Valladolid was a typical medieval walled city, with streets radiating from the church of S Pelaya (destr.; now Plaza de S Miguel) and an alcázar in the west, all between the Esgueva and Pisuerga rivers. With the increase in population under Conde Pedro Ansúrez in the 12th century, the town expanded to the south, and a new encircling wall was built. By the end of the Middle Ages Valladolid was the seat of the counts of Castile. The church of S Maria la Antigua was rebuilt in the early 13th century; from this period, only the fine campanile and the north portico survive; the Gothic style of the remainder is from the late 13th century. The tower of S Martín also dates from the beginning of the 13th century. During this same century the collegiate church was enlarged under Abbot J. Domínguez; it retains elements of the Cistercian style and several chapels from the 13th to 15th centuries; the rest was demolished in the 16th and 17th centuries in order to build the cathedral. There are few other important medieval remains in the city except for the brick *Mudéjar* door from the palace (destr.) of Queen Maria de Molina (*d* 1321), wife of Sancho IV of Castile (*reg* 1284–95).

Between the second half of the 15th century and the first half of the 17th Valladolid prospered, and artistic activity flourished. During this period it could boast a law court (the Real Chancillería), a prestigious university (founded 14th century) and a printing house (1481), as well as markets and fairs that attracted merchants and the nobility from all over the empire, many of whom built prestigious mansions. It was in Valladolid that the marriage took place in 1469 of Ferdinand of Aragón and Isabella of Castile and León, creating the first Spanish state. The Spanish Renaissance is represented in Valladolid by some important buildings: the Colegio de S Gregorio, with a fine façade (see fig.), by Gil de Siloé and Juan Guas, founded by Fray Alonso de Burgos; and S Pablo by Simon de Colonia (for illustration *see* HISPANO-FLEMISH STYLE); S Benito (the mother house of the Benedictines in Spain, Central Europe and South America), built by Juan de Arandia (1497), with a portal by Rodrigo Gil de Hontañón; and the Colegio Mayor de Santa Cruz (1486–94) by Lorenzo Vázquez under the patronage of Cardinal Pedro González del Mendoza (for illustration *see* MENDOZA, (1)). Among the many important Renaissance sculptors active in Valladolid were ESTEBAN JORDÁN, Alonso Berruguete (*see* BERRUGUETE, (2)), who executed a retable for the church of S Benito (1532; Valladolid, Mus. N. Escul.), and JUAN DE JUNI, who executed a retable for the church of S Maria la Antigua (1556; *in situ*).

In 1561 a fire destroyed the centre of Valladolid; it was subsequently rebuilt with the support of Philip II (a native of the city) and according to designs by Juan Bautista de Toledo, the royal architect. These were executed by Francisco de Salamanca, the city architect, with the help of Juan de Herrera, Juan Escalante, Juan de Nates and Diego de Praves. The urban plan centred on the Plaza Mayor, while the adjacent streets and squares were designed to give unrestricted views and broad open spaces. It was the most important example of urban planning in Renaissance Spain and included separate areas for such functions as municipal and commercial activities, festivals,

Valladolid, façade (1487) of the Colegio de S Gregorio (now the Museo Nacional de Escultura Religiosa)

public executions and proclamations, and religious activities. Among the outstanding building works from this period are: the Palacio Real by Luis de Vega; the palace of Fabio Nelli (*d c.* 1612) by P. Mazuecos (now Mus. Arqueol.); additions to S Benito, which was enlarged by Juan del Ribero Rada, who also designed the convent of Las Huelgas Reales (1579–1600); Nuestra Señora de las Angustias (1604) by Juan de Nates; and the façade of the church of La Vera Cruz (begun 1595) by Diego de Praves. The cathedral was also begun by Praves to designs (1580) by Juan de Herrera (*see* HERRERA, JUAN DE, fig. 3), but was left unfinished in 1598.

Under Philip III, Valladolid was briefly (1601–5) the capital of the Spanish empire. Diego de Praves continued work on the Palacio Real and also began the churches of the Descalzas Franciscas (founded *c.* 1600–15) and S Augustín (from 1619), while in the second half of the 17th century Felipe Berrojo de Isla built the church of La Pasión (1671; now Mus. Pint.). During the 17th century some notable sculptors were also active in Valladolid, including GREGORIO FERNÁNDEZ (e.g. *St Teresa*, 1627; Valladolid, Mus. N. Escul.), while among the significant painters working in the city was DIEGO VALENTÍN DÍAZ.

In the 18th century new public spaces such as the Espolón, Prado de la Magdalena and the Campo de Marte were created. From this period the Baroque style was employed for the university (from 1715) by Pedro de la Visitación, Narciso Tomé and Diego Tomé, for the central façade (1730–33) of the cathedral by Alberto de Churriguera, and for S Juan de Letrán by M. Machuca. Later in the century Neo-classicism appeared in the design for the monastery of the Agustinos Filipinos (1759) by VENTURA RODRÍGUEZ, and for the convent of S Ana (1780) by FRANCESCO SABBATINI.

From 1835 the monasteries were expropriated and their grounds cleared to create new streets and blocks of buildings. The Castile Canal and the railway were constructed (1860), as well as the Ayuntamiento (begun 1892), numerous new schools and theatres, and houses for the middle classes. Towards the end of the 19th century the branches of the River Esgueva were covered over and infilling of the spaces in the heart of the city took place. The Campo Grande, containing a picturesque Anglo-Indian garden, with Oriental features, was also created around this time.

After the Civil War (1936–9) the population of Valladolid increased with an influx of immigrants, and from the 1950s to the 1970s industrialization resulted in the creation of workers' residential districts in the suburbs. Undistinguished buildings gradually replaced those in the city centre. In the last two decades of the 20th century important Post-modern and late Modern works were designed by such architects as P. Rodriguez, S. Mata, R. Valle, P. Puente and L. S. Polo.

BIBLIOGRAPHY
J. Marti y Monso: *Estudios histórico-artísticos* (Valladolid, 1901)
J. Agapito y Revilla: *La obra de los maestros de la escultura vallisoletana* (Valladolid, 1929)
E. Garcia Chico: *Documentos para la historia del arte en Castilla* (Valladolid, 1940–63)
J. J. Martin González: *La arquitectura doméstica del renacimiento en Valladolid* (Valladolid, 1948)
F. Chueca: *La catedral de Valladolid* (Madrid, 1957)
J. J. Martin González: *La escultura barroca castellana* (Valladolid, 1959)
——: *La arquitectura barroca vallisoletana* (Valladolid, 1969)
M. A. Virgili Blanquet: *Desarrollo urbanístico y arquitectónico de Valladolid, 1851–1936* (Valladolid, 1979)
J. Rivera: *El Palacio Real de Valladolid* (Valladolid, 1981)
A. Bustamante: *La arquitectura classicista del foco vallisoletano, 1561–1640* (Valladolid, 1983)
J. J. Martin González: *Catálogo monumental de la provincia de Valladolid*, xiii (1983); xv (1985–7)
A. Rucquoi: *Valladolid en la edad media* (Valladolid, 1987)
S. Mata and J. Rivera: *Arquitecturas en Valladolid: Tradición y modernidad, 1900–1950* (Valladolid, 1989)
B. Bennasar: *Valladolid en el siglo de oro* (Valladolid, 1990)
M. D. Merino: *Urbanismo y arquitectura de Valladolid en los siglos XVII y XVIII* (Valladolid, 1990)
J. Rivera and others: *VI centenario: Monasterio de San Benito el Real, 1939–1990* (Valladolid, 1990)

JAVIER RIVERA

2. CENTRE OF GOLD AND SILVER PRODUCTION. There was organized activity by gold- and silversmiths in Valladolid from the beginning of the 15th century, although the earliest guild regulations date from 1452. During the reign of Ferdinand and Isabella a wide variety of elaborate works in the Gothic style were produced: chalices and crosses decorated with reliefs; small, naturalistic statues; and monumental pieces (*see* GOTHIC, §V, 8).

Gold- and silversmithing in the Renaissance style (*see* SPAIN, fig. 52) increased with the arrival of the goldsmith Antonio de Arfe in 1547, and the establishment of the court in Valladolid from 1601 to 1606 resulted in the production of splendid pieces in the Mannerist style by numerous craftsmen, whose work influenced that made in neighbouring centres. One particular type of silverware developed in Valladolid at this time and used throughout Spain was a ewer with a spout. Most 17th-century products follow the style of those made in Madrid, with well-proportioned geometric forms and enamel decoration. Although a considerable number of craftsmen were active in the 18th century, production declined in the 19th. The town mark consists of the coat of arms of the city (which depicts flying pennants); makers' and assayers' marks were also used, and date marks were introduced in the 17th century (*see* SPAIN, §IX, 1).

BIBLIOGRAPHY

J. C. Brasas Egido: *La platería vallisoletana y su difusión* (Valladolid, 1980)

JOSÉ MANUEL CRUZ VALDOVINOS

Vallari [Valéry; Vallarie; Wallerij], **Nicolas (de)** (*fl* Stockholm, 1646; *d* after 1673). French painter and sculptor, active in Sweden. In the service of Magnus Gabriel De la Gardie and Christina, Queen of Sweden, from 1646 until 1673, he became Sweden's leading artist in the field of temporary feast decorations and of monumental pictures of allegorical and mythological content, before David Klöcker Ehrenstrahl emerged as the unsurpassed master of such works. Among the few extant works attributed to Vallari, the ceiling painting '*Deus temperavit corpus*' in the main stair-well of Venngarn Castle in Uppland (1660s), an elegant composition of a female figure in the clouds of a light sky, surrounded by putti, is still *in situ*; another ceiling painting in the Princess's bedchamber in Läckö Castle, Västergötland, depicting *Bacchus, Ceres and Venus* (1667), seems to have been repainted or at least restored by another artist (1679) because of water damage. Vallari also executed a series of ceiling paintings in Karlberg Castle outside Stockholm (all three castles were residences of Magnus Gabriel De la Gardie). These were early examples in Sweden of paintings combined with lavish stucco decorations; the stucco is well preserved, but the paintings are lost. All of these ceiling paintings were executed in oil on canvas. Vallari also produced oil paintings for the altarpiece in the German church, Stockholm, for which he was paid in 1658. Of these, the *Last Supper* was replaced in 1743, but scenes from the *Passion*, the *Baptism* and the *Crucifixion* may be the originals by Vallari. A series of allegorical paintings for a feast in honour of Queen Christina (1650), executed in gouache on paper in a sketchy, fluent style, preserved in the Lyceum of Borgå, Finland, have also been connected with Vallari. He worked in a French–Venetian Baroque style, with vivid figures and rather light, fleeting colours.

SVKL

BIBLIOGRAPHY

J. Böttiger: *Hedvig Eleonoras Drottningholm* (Stockholm, 1897)

K. E. Steneberg: *Kristinatidens måleri* [Painters of the reign of Queen Christina] (Malmö, 1955)

TORBJÖRN FULTON

Vallayer-Coster [née Vallayer], **Anne** (*b* Paris, 21 Dec 1744; *d* Paris, 28 Feb 1818). French painter. She spent her childhood at the Gobelins, where her father was a goldsmith. Though she thus belonged to artistic circles, when received (*reçue*) by the Académie Royale in 1770, on presentation of the still-lifes *Attributes of Painting* and *Musical Instruments* (both Paris, Louvre), she was known to have neither a teacher nor an official patron.

She exhibited for the first time at the Salon the following year and achieved a success that never deserted her. She showed still-lifes (which were compared to those of Jean-Siméon Chardin), imitation low reliefs and genre scenes, the last reminiscent of those by Jean-Baptiste Greuze. From 1775 onwards her flower paintings attracted greatest attention: many of these remain in private collections (see Roland Michel), but among others on public view are those in Nancy (Mus. B.-A.) and New York (Met.). She also drew, painted miniatures (see Roland Michel, nos 361–86) and executed life-size portraits. Her portraits were admired by her contemporaries, as is shown by the commissions she received for those of Louis XVI's aunt *Mme Sophie* and of *Queen Marie-Antoinette* (both 1780). Among her surviving portraits is that of a *Lady Writing, and her Daughter* (1775; Barnard Castle, Bowes Mus.). One of her series of portraits of *Vestals* belonged to Marie-Antoinette, who obtained lodgings for her in the Louvre and in 1781 signed her contract of marriage with the lawyer Jean-Pierre-Sylvestre Coster. However, the appearance of the portrait painters Adélaïde Labille-Guiard and Elisabeth Vigée-Lebrun led to comparisons unfavourable to Vallayer-Coster, who then devoted herself to the genre in which her superiority was recognized. In her last Salon in 1817 she showed a large still-life, *Vase, Lobster, Fruit and Game* (Paris, Louvre), which belonged to Louis XVIII.

Vallayer-Coster had a very personal way of grouping flowers, fruit, animal trophies, plate and domestic objects in a perfectly organized space over which the chromatic subtleties of her palette could play. With particular arrangements of selected forms such as flowers and fruit she built up a repertory, which, over the years, though hardly changing, became increasingly subtle. This unsentimental art sometimes achieved, in her assemblages of flags and drums, corals and shells, a strength unrivalled by any of the painters of her generation.

BIBLIOGRAPHY

M. Roland Michel: *Anne Vallayer-Coster, 1744–1818* (Paris, 1970)

L. Nochlin and A. Sutherland Harris: *Women Artists, 1550–1950* (Los Angeles, 1976)

MARIANNE ROLAND MICHEL

Valle, Andrea da (*b* Koper, Istria; *d* Venice, ?1577). Italian architect. He worked principally in Padua, where he is first recorded in 1531, when he began a long association with the basilica of S Giustina. In 1533 he assisted Giovanni Maria Falconetto, then working on the chapel of the Santo at the basilica of S Antonio; by 1539 he had established his own workshop. His work at the Villa dei Vescovi (the villa of the bishops of Padua), Luvigliano, executed under the supervision of Bishop Alvise Cornaro, dates from the same period. Da Valle's first important works date from the 1540s and show his developing style more clearly. The first of these was the cloister of S Gregorio, Bologna, which was followed by the double cloisters (completed by 1562) at S Vitale, Ravenna. Both latter cloisters are harmonious essays in a refined style similar to that of Palladio, which was to remain characteristic of da Valle's work. In 1547 he proposed a scheme for the completion of the choir and apses of Padua Cathedral. He was not immediately successful, but following opposition to the proposed appointment of Jacopo Sansovino, the chapter asked da Valle to execute the work, which was loosely based on an original proposal by Michelangelo. Work began in 1551 on da Valle's appointment as *proto* (chief architect).

The clarity and monumentality of form of the cathedral apses were even more clearly expressed in da Valle's most important work, the grandiose basilica of S Giustina. Work had begun on the basilica in 1532, to a model (1521–2) by Alessandro Leopardi, with Matteo da Valle (probably a relative) as *proto*. Matteo died shortly afterwards and was replaced as *proto* by Andrea Moroni. Andrea da Valle, who had been associated with the project since 1531, worked as Moroni's assistant until the latter's death in 1560, when he himself became *proto*, a title he retained until his own death. Da Valle's contribution to the early stages of S Giustina cannot, however, be accurately gauged. The original Greek cross plan was modified at an early stage to form the complex Latin cross that was built. The plan has a central nave and two aisles, flanked by rows of side chapels. Beyond the crossing there is a deep central apse, flanked in turn by smaller apsidal chapels, while the transepts also have apsidal ends and are flanked by smaller chapels. The overall form is loosely modelled on S Antonio, but on a considerably grander scale. The interior is most imposing, with a highly unified appearance; the whole is finished in a refined classical style that has affinities with Palladio's churches, although on a more monumental scale. The east end is surmounted by a cluster of four domes (again referring to the basilicas of S Antonio and S Marco, Venice), all set on high drums containing windows. The choir and apses are thus brightly lit, in contrast with the nave, which is roofed with three large, shallow, windowless domes and where the light is far more subdued. The complex east end is almost certainly da Valle's work, as are the domes, although the roof was not complete at his death.

In 1577 da Valle, together with other leading architects of the day, was invited by the Venetian government to inspect and report on the damage inflicted on the Doge's Palace by the fires of 1574 and 1577. However, this is the last record of him, and he must have died shortly thereafter. Although highly regarded in his own time, his reputation did not extend much beyond his native Republic and was later eclipsed by that of Palladio, with whose work that of da Valle has some affinity.

Portoghesi

BIBLIOGRAPHY
G. Cappelletti: *Storia di Padova dalle sue origini fino al presente*, 2 vols (Padua, 1872 and 1875)
A. Venturi: *Storia* (1901–40)
E. Lovarini: 'Di Andrea da Valle, architetto', *Riv. Italia*, xiii/6 (1910)
E. Rigoni: *L'architetto Andrea Moroni* (Padua, 1939)
R. Pepi: *L'abbazia di S Giustina* (Padua, 1966)
G. Bresciani Alvarez: *La basilica di S Giustina* (Castelfranco Veneto, 1970)

RICHARD J. GOY

Valle, Cardinal **Andrea della** (*b* 30 Dec 1463; *d* Rome, 4 Aug 1534). Italian prelate and patron. From a Roman family of jurists, physicians and scholars linked to the nobility, he became Bishop of Cotrone in 1496 and of Mileto in 1508. He enlarged the complex of family properties in the centre of Rome in order to reconstruct the della Valle palazzo, which had been razed in 1484 at the order of Pope Sixtus IV. The new palazzo on the Via Papale (now Corso Vittorio Emmanuele) was built (1517) by Lorenzo Lotti. The architrave of the entrance portal still bears della Valle's name. Originally the Palazzo della Valle presented a well-designed principal façade (later extended by several bays by the Bufalo family) built on three storeys with a series of handsome aedicule windows and an interior courtyard with a Doric arcade. Within the palazzo, the rooms on the *piano nobile* are embellished with capitals and fireplaces sculpted with the della Valle coat of arms. The ceilings were decorated with fine stuccowork and illusionistic paintings, attributed to Raffaello dal Colle, of which some in the principal reception room survive.

After his election as cardinal in 1517, della Valle began a second palazzo, which was largely completed by 1536, after his death. Although most of this palazzo was later subsumed in the Teatro della Valle (1819–22), part of it survives in the Palazzo Capranica, which displays on its exterior façade finely worked rustication and handsome ground-floor windows, the sills of which are supported by carved brackets. Two plans for this palazzo by Antonio Sangallo the younger survive (Florence, Uffizi, A.982, A.1274), but from *c.* 1526 work was directed by Lorenzo Lotti. The statue garden in the second palazzo is well documented in 16th-century prints and drawings, notably the drawing by Francisco de Holanda (Madrid, Escorial) and the engraving by Hieronymus Cock (Bober and Rubinstein, p. 480) after Maarten van Heemskerck's drawing (untraced) of *c.* 1530. The della Valle collection was highly prized by contemporaries, including Vasari, both for the quality of individual pieces and for the decorative unity of the display. The inventory, drawn up in 1584, when Ferdinand I de' Medici purchased the sculpture, indicates the scope and extent of the collection, which included celebrated pieces such as the hanging *Marsyas*, a Roman copy of a Greek statue of the 3rd century BC (Florence, Uffizi), *Apollo*, a Roman copy of a Hellenistic work (Florence, Poggio Imp.), and *Minerva*, a Roman copy of a Greek statue of the 4th century BC (Florence, Pitti). Antique reliefs from the collection were installed on the rear façade of the Villa Medici, Rome; della Valle's famous coin collection was dispersed.

BIBLIOGRAPHY
DBI
G. Vasari: *Vite* (1550, rev. 2/1568); ed. G. Milanesi (1878–85), iv, pp. 579–80
G. A. Mansuelli: *Galleria degli Uffizi: Le sculture*, i–ii (Florence, 1958–61)
C. L. Frommel: *Der römische Palastbau der Hochrenaissance* (Tübingen, 1973), ii, pp. 336–54
P. P. Bober and R. Rubinstein: *Renaissance Artists and Antique Sculpture* (Oxford, 1986), pp. 479–80

DIANA NORMAN

Valle, Angel Della. *See* DELLA VALLE, ANGEL.

Valle, Filippo della (*b* Florence, 26 Dec 1698; *d* Rome, 29 April 1768). Italian sculptor. He was trained by his uncle Giovanni Battista Foggini, from whom he first learnt the style of late Baroque Florentine sculpture, best exemplified in Foggini's reliefs for the Corsini Chapel in S Maria del Carmine, Florence. On Foggini's death in 1725, della Valle went to Rome and worked for several years in the studio of Camillo Rusconi. He shared with Pietro Bracci first prize for sculpture at the Accademia di S Luca in 1725. After Rusconi's death in 1728, della Valle established his own studio near the church of S Nicolò da Tolentino. He was elected to the Accademia di S Luca in 1730.

Throughout the 1730s and 1740s della Valle collaborated on and himself received many of the artistic commissions sponsored by Clement XII (*reg* 1730–40) and Benedict XIV (*reg* 1740–58). These were for the rebuilding of the façade of S Giovanni in Laterano (and, within the Lateran, the erection of the Corsini Chapel), the construction of the new Palazzo della Consulta (Piazza del Quirinale) and later the building of a new façade for S Maria Maggiore, as well as extensive refurbishing of that church. In the mid-1740s and early 1750s della Valle completed three of his most significant works, all for St Peter's. The statue of *St John of God* (designed by Pietro Branchi) was dedicated in 1745, the tomb of *Innocent XII* (*reg* 1691–1700) in 1746 and the figure of *St Teresa* in 1754. His most important commission also came during these years: the relief of the *Annunciation* in S Ignazio, Rome (1750).

Like many of his contemporaries in Rome, della Valle profited from the desire of the British for copies of antiquities. In 1743 Horace Walpole received della Valle's marble portrait of his mother, *Catherine, Lady Walpole, as Livia* (London, Westminster Abbey), a design after the *Venus pudica* (Rome, Vatican, Mus. Pio-Clementino). He also sent figures to Thomas Watson-Wentworth, 1st Earl of Malton, at Wentworth Woodhouse, S. Yorks (e.g. a marble copy of 1750 after the Farnese *Flora*), and to Hugh Percy, 1st Duke of Northumberland, at Syon House, London. Even when working after the Antique, della Valle never completely suppressed his own style, which is evident in the soft modelling of facial features and a characteristic angular drapery style.

Della Valle valued intimacy over grandeur. Although the locations of his sculptures in Baroque churches of Rome invited large gestures, the rhetoric of art had changed, and scale was no longer as highly prized. Della Valle valued the sensuality, the surface and realistic potential of sculpture more than its noble, symbolic and transcendent qualities. Even in a large-scale work such as the tomb of *Innocent XII*, small accents of drapery and detail, the feminine sensibilities of his allegorical figures and the innocence of his putti reveal the introversion and sensitivity of a graceful but unheroic artist. In the last decade of his life della Valle produced little more than two statues for the Trevi Fountain, *Salubrity* and *Fecundity*, because of declining patronage and, probably, poor health.

Along with Pietro Bracci, della Valle achieved prominence in Roman public sculpture of the 18th century, but his influence did not long survive his death. His only known pupils were the Spaniard Francesco Bergara (or

Vergara, 1681–1753) and the Roman Tommaso Righi (1717–1802); neither had much impact on the subsequent development of Roman sculpture. With his death came the end of the rhetorical *Barocchetto* style of Italian sculpture, soon to be replaced by the Neo-classicism of Antonio Canova.

BIBLIOGRAPHY

DBI
F. Baldinucci: *Vite di pittori* (Florence, Bib. N. Cent., Cod. Palatino 565, 1725–*c*. 1730), i, fol. 70*v* [appended to Baldinucci's life of Camillo Rusconi]; ed. A. Matteoli as *Vite di artisti dei secoli XVII–XVIII* (Rome, 1975), pp. 98, 387
N. Gabburri: *Vite* (Florence, Bib. N. Cent., Cod. Palatino E.B.9.5., *c*. 1734–7), fol. 955
Serie degli uomini i più illustri nella pittura, scultura e architettura (Florence, 1775), xii, p. 74
V. Moschini: 'Filippo Della Valle', *L'Arte*, xxviii (1925), pp. 177–90
A. Riccoboni: *Roma nell'arte: La scultura nell'evo moderno da quattrocento ad oggi* (Rome, 1942), pp. 288–91
H. Honour: 'Filippo Della Valle', *Connoisseur*, cxliv (1959), pp. 172–9
V. Minor: 'Filippo Della Valle's Monument to Sampaio: An Attribution Resolved', *Burl. Mag.*, cxvii (1975), pp. 659–63
——: 'Della Valle and G. B. Grossi Revisited', *Antol. B.A.*, ii (1978), pp. 233–47
——: 'Della Valle's Last Commission', *Burl. Mag.*, cxxii (1980), pp. 44–5
——: 'Filippo Della Valle as Metalworker', *A. Bull.*, lxvi (1984), pp. 511–14
——: 'Della Valle or Cayot?: The Art of Deceiving Well', *Apollo*, cxxiii (1986), pp. 418–21

VERNON HYDE MINOR

Valle, Francisco Perez del. *See* PEREZ DEL VALLE, FRANCISCO.

Valle, Gino (*b* Udine, 7 Dec 1923). Italian architect and designer. He graduated from the Istituto Universitario di Architettura in Venice (1948) and then studied urban planning at the Graduate School of Design of Harvard University, Cambridge, MA (1951–2). After his studies he joined his father Provino Valle and sister Nani Valle in practice in Udine; until the end of the 1950s his first works, mostly private houses and office buildings in the Friuli area, were signed also by his father and his sister. In works such as the combined housing and office building (1955–7) in Trieste, the Via Marinoni flats (1958–60) in Udine and even in the emotive poetry of the Monument to the Resistance (1959; executed 1967–9) in Udine, he gradually developed a vocabulary based upon the formal possibilities of constructional expression. It brought him international recognition in the offices (1959–61) for the Zanussi Rex factory at Porcia, Pordenone. Constructional form and function are expressed on the face of the building, which also demonstrates clearly his affinity with the Friuli landscape, in which much of his work is executed. The best-known of his industrial buildings include the Dapres factory (1973–4) at Portogruaro, Venice, and the Fantoni offices (1973–9) at Osoppo, Udine.

Valle rejected a preconstituted style or methodology in such buildings as the offices (1963–5) in Via Mercatovecchio and his thermal plant for Arta Terme (1962–3), both in Udine, preferring to treat each solution with individual care for context or function. These qualities characterize his later work in Italy and abroad: the offices of the Banca Commerciale Italiana (1986), Manhattan, New York, the offices of IBM (1989) in La Défense, Paris, and in particular the housing complex (1986) on La Giudecca,

Venice. Valle taught at home and abroad and was a professor in his own university from 1977.

BIBLIOGRAPHY

J. Rykwert: 'The Work of Gino Valle', *Archit. Des.*, iii (1964), pp. 112–39

Gino Valle, architetto, 1950–1978 (exh. cat., Milan, Padiglione A. Contemp., 1979)

P. Fumagalli: 'Arbeiten von Gino Valle', *Werk, Bauen & Wohnen*, vii–viii (1983), pp. 18–31

P. A. Croset: 'Edifici per uffici di Gino Valle alla Défense a Parigi', *Casabella*, 69 (1985), pp. 4–17

——: 'Sul progetto di Gino Valle alla Giudecca', *Lotus Int.*, li (1987), pp. 108–28

ANDREA NULLI

Valle, Julio Rosado del. *See* ROSADO DEL VALLE, JULIO.

Valle, Lázaro Díaz del. *See* DÍAZ DEL VALLE, LÁZARO.

Valle, Pietro della (*b* Rome, 11 April 1586; *d* Rome, 21 April 1652). Italian nobleman, traveller, writer, composer and antiquary. He was a notable figure in the cultural life of 17th-century Rome. His fame rested chiefly on his travels in Asia, which earned him the nickname il Pellegrino. In June 1614 he sailed from Venice to Constantinople, then visited Egypt, Palestine, Syria, Persia and India, sending to his friend Mario Schipano in Naples letters containing detailed descriptions, which he later began to publish. He became known as an authority on the architecture of the Holy Land and Asia Minor (in Constantinople he admired the Süleymaniye Mosque, and suggested Italian architects might learn from mosque design) and for his interest in archaeology. He sent back the first Mesopotamian cuneiform writing tablets seen in Europe, and at Saqqara in Egypt he bought mummies, which were later displayed at his residence in Rome, which adjoined the palace (101 Corso Vittorio Emanuele) where Cardinal Andrea della Valle had organized his antiquities collection in the 16th century.

Pietro della Valle returned to Rome in March 1626 and the following year was elected a member of the literary academy of the Umoristi. His diary reveals that he took a lively interest in the arts and sciences, and the respect he enjoyed among contemporaries and the breadth of his intellectual interests are reflected in the names of his friends and correspondents, including the scientists Galileo Galilei, Athanasius Kircher (a Jesuit) and Nicolas Claude Fabri de Peiresc, the antiquary Francesco Angeloni and the biographer and art theorist Giovanni Pietro Bellori.

UNPUBLISHED SOURCE

Rome, Vatican, Archv Segreto [Archivio della Valle-Del Bufalo]

WRITINGS

Viaggi (Rome, 1650–62) [with biog. by G. P. Bellori, 1662]; ed. F. Gaeta and L. Lockhart (Rome, 1972); Eng. trans., abridged, with intro. by G. Bull as *The Pilgrim: The Journeys of Pietro Della Valle* (London, 1989)

BIBLIOGRAPHY

G. P. Bellori: *Nota delli musei, librerie, galerie et ornamenti di statue e pitture ne' palazzi, nelle case e ne' giardini di Roma* (Rome, 1664); ed. E. Zocca (Rome, 1976), pp. 118–20

I. Ciampi: 'Della vita e delle opere di Pietro della Valle il Pellegrino', *Nuova Antol.* (Sept–Dec 1879); as booklet (Rome, 1880)

W. Blunt: *Pietro's Pilgrimage* (London, 1953)

JANET SOUTHORN

Vallejo y Galeazo, José (*b* Málaga, 15 Aug 1821; *d* Madrid, 19 Feb 1882). Spanish lithographer, illustrator and painter. In 1859 he enlisted for the African Campaign in Morocco, and the studies he did in Africa led to drawings for an atlas of the battles in Africa (Madrid, 1860), as well as those for *Crónicas de la guerra de África* (Madrid, 1859) by Emilio Castelar and for *Diario* (Madrid, 1859–60) by the novelist Pedro Antonio de Alarcón (1833–91). He promoted a section for lithography at the Escuela de Artes y Oficios in Madrid. An excellent portraitist, he also made numerous drawings and illustrations for newspapers, royal chronicles and for *Iconografía española* (Madrid, 1855–64) by Valentín Carderera y Solano, as well as lithographs of bullfights. He provided decorative works for various public buildings in Madrid and the provinces.

BIBLIOGRAPHY

A. Canovas: *Pintores malagueños del siglo XIX* (Málaga, 1908)

A. Gallego: *Historia del grabado en España* (Madrid, 1979), p. 356

E. Paez Rios: *Repertorio* (1981–3)

BLANCA GARCÍA VEGA

Vallemput, Remigius. *See* LEEMPUT, REMI VAN.

Vallen de la Motte [Vallin de la Mothe]**, Jean-Baptiste-Michel** (*b* Angoulême, 1729; *d* Angoulême, 7 May 1800). French architect and teacher, active in Russia. He was a nephew and pupil of Jacques-François Blondel, became an external student at the French Academy in Rome and studied the works of Palladio in Vicenza (1750–52). In 1759 he was invited to Russia as professor of architecture at the new Academy of Arts on the recommendation of Jacques-Germain Soufflot. He was one of the first to introduce the ideas of Neo-classicism to Russia, but the retention of certain Baroque features lent his works a particular grace and beauty. In 1761 he took over the design of the Gostinyy Dvor (1758–85) in St Petersburg, a trading market of 200 shops with a central courtyard, which had been started by Bartolomeo Francesco Rastrelli (*see* RASTRELLI, (2)). Vallen de la Motte achieved a clarity of concept and rationality that dispensed with Rastrelli's planned Rococo decoration; only the handsome composition of the rounded corners hints at the Baroque. In the Roman Catholic church of St Catherine (1762–83) on the Nevsky Prospect, the spatial effect of a portal in the form of an immense arch is combined with shallow decorative detail in the French Rococo style.

The Academy of Arts (1764–88; with ALEKSANDR KOKORINOV) and the Small Hermitage (1764–75; *see* ROMANOV, (3)) demonstrate Vallen de la Motte's mastery of Neo-classicism. The sides of the latter building, which adjoins Rastrelli's Winter Palace, are articulated so as to complement Rastrelli's Rococo façades, but the river façade is a Neo-classical composition, based on the combination of a portico of six free-standing Ionic columns with statues along its sides, a severe entablature and delicate enrichment of the walls. Neo-classical features also distinguish a number of houses and palaces in St Petersburg attributed to Vallen de la Motte. These include the Yusupov Palace (1760s) on the banks of the River Moyka, embellished by a hexastyle portico; the Chernyshev Palace (1766–8; incorporated in the Mariya Palace), near the Blue Bridge (Siny Most), reminiscent of French designs; and the Aleksandrino house (mid-1770s) on the Peterhof road. With other prominent artists, he directed work on refashioning the interiors of the Winter Palace and Tsarskoye Selo Palace (1760s–70s; with Yury Fel'ten) in a Neo-classical style. Vallen de la Motte also carried out projects in Moscow (e.g. the Foreign Ministry in the Kremlin; destr.) and in Pochep, near Bryansk, where he designed the church of the Resurrection (1765–71) and a palace for Count Kirill Razumovsky (built by Aleksey Yanovsky (*b* 1742) in the 1780s). His finest works include New Holland (begun 1761 by Savva Chevakinsky; not completed), St Petersburg, incorporating vast warehouses and docks, in which the calm rhythm of the arches and the effective, austere treatment of the centre create a majestic impression. Vallen de la Motte's educational activities played an important role in the development of Russian architecture. His pupils included Vasily Bazhenov, Il'ya Neyelov (1745–93) and Ivan Starov. After leaving Russia in 1775 he acted as mentor to Russian students sent by the Academy of Arts on scholarships to France.

BIBLIOGRAPHY

L. Réau: 'Un Grand Architecte français en Russie: Vallen de la Motte, 1729–1800', *Architecture* [Paris], xxxv/12 (1922), pp. 173–80
P. D. Ettinger: 'Novyye dannyye k biografii Vallena De-lya-Mot' [New biographical details about Vallen de la Motte], *Arkhit. SSSR*, 1–2 (1923), pp. 23–6
V. Nechayev: 'Rastrelli i Delamot: Iz istorii postroyki Gostinogo dvora' [Rastrelli and de la Motte: from the building history of the Gostiny Dvor], *Starina i iskusstvo* (Leningrad, 1928), pp. 3–21
A. F. Krasheninnikov: 'Nachalo tvorcheskogo puti arkhitektora Dela-mota' [The beginning of the creative career of the architect de la Motte], *XVIII nauchnaya konferentsiya LISI: Doklady arkhitekturnykh sektsiy: Leningrad, 1960*
I. E. Grabar, S. S. Bronshteyn and G. G. Grimm: 'U istokov russkogo klassitsizma' [At the sources of Russian classicism], *Istor. Rus. Isk.*, vi (Moscow, 1961), pp. 60–68 [proc. of the 22nd scientific confer. (of LISI)]
A. F. Krasheninnikov: 'O tvorchestve pozdnego Delamota' [The late works of de la Motte], *Doklady XXII nauchnoy konferentsii [LISI]: Leningrad, 1964*

N. A. YEVSINA

Vallet, Edouard (*b* Geneva, 12 Jan 1876; *d* Geneva, 1 May 1929). Swiss painter, draughtsman and printmaker. He left the Ecole des Arts Industriels in Geneva before completing his studies and instead drew and painted from nature in the countryside. He also experimented with wood-engraving and produced illustrations for a local publisher. In 1899 he exhibited his work for the first time. In 1900 Vallet began to make etchings and lithographs. After travelling through Germany, France and Italy in 1903–5, he settled first near Geneva, then, in 1908, in the Valais. In 1909 he presented to the Swiss section of the tenth Internationale Kunstausstellung in Munich *Sunday Morning* (1908–9; Zurich, Ksthaus), which combined fresh colour with firm drawing and composition in the depiction of a Valais peasant woman in national dress looking out over the valley from the balcony of her chalet; this large figure was influenced by primitivism, albeit recognizably in the HEIMATSTIL. The work earned him his reputation. Thereafter Vallet's work, comprising both paintings and engravings and including a considerable number of self-portraits (e.g. 1916; St Gall, Kstmus.), was characterized by his constant fidelity to these subjects, although after 1920 he also executed a number of monumental views of the Valais.

BIBLIOGRAPHY
Edouard Vallet (1896–1929) (exh. cat. by B. Wyder, Geneva, Mus. Rath; Chur, Bündner Kstmus.; Schaffhausen, Mus. Allerheiligen; Martigny, Manoir; 1976)
J.-C. Giroud and M. Jean-Petit-Matile: *Edouard Vallet, maître de la gravure suisse* (Lausanne, 1991) [cat. rais., bibliog.]
G. Germann: 'A "Sunday Morning" (1908–1909) by Edouard Vallet', *1000 Years of Swiss Art*, ed. H. Horat (New York, 1992), pp. 301–10

□

Valley of the Kings. *See under* THEBES (i), §IX.

Vallgren, Ville [Wallgren, Carl Wilhelm] (*b* Porvoo, 15 Dec 1855; *d* Helsinki, 13 Oct 1940). Finnish sculptor. He began studying sculpture in Helsinki as a pupil of Carl Eneas Sjöstrand. In 1877 he moved to Paris, which was to prove much more significant for his studies. During his years there Vallgren followed the instruction of Pierre-Jules Cavelier at the Ecole des Beaux-Arts. Vallgren's progress was leisurely. He spent the early part of the 1880s sketching figures and practising portrait sculpture. He was clearly attracted by the realist tendencies of the decade, as well as by the study of movement. The life-size marble sculpture *Echo* (1885; Helsinki, Athenaeum A. Mus.) marks a turning point in his work; it combines the familiarity of drawing-room realism with the serenity of a lyrical depiction of nature. Towards the end of the 1880s Vallgren was greatly influenced by Auguste Rodin, and at the same time he moved closer to both decorative and Symbolist expression. His works dating from this period, such as the reliefs *Ophelia* and *Volubilis* (Helsinki, Athenaeum A. Mus.), also reflect contemporary interest in early Renaissance art. Vallgren was awarded a gold medal at the Paris Exposition of 1889 for his relief *Christ* (Helsinki, Athenaeum A. Mus.).

In the 1890s, an important period for Vallgren's work, he shifted to a smaller scale that particularly suited his style and specialized in miniature bronze figurines and *objets d'art*. The tear phials, miniature urns and vases that he exhibited at the Salon de la Rose + Croix and Champ de Mars gallery at the beginning of the 1890s brought him recognition all over Europe as a representative of Art Nouveau. In this period Vallgren received several exhibition offers and he participated in the Berlin, Munich and Vienna Secessions, among others, as well as exhibiting with La Libre Esthétique in Brussels. The main subject of his small sculptures is the female figure, naked or loosely draped, generally expressive of powerful emotions, often grief, melancholy or pain, as in, for example, *Resurrection, Spring* (h. 285 mm, 1895; Helsinki, Athenaeum A. Mus.). His works also evince a Nordic unaffectedness and proximity to nature. Vallgren's creativity in the 1890s was closely linked to the Art Nouveau movement in France, from which he drew, for example, his flower symbolism. In the latter half of the decade he produced a series of figurines using the motif of the woman and the flower, for example *Rose Dance* (bronze, h. 285 mm, 1899; Helsinki, Athenaeum A. Mus.). He returned to Finland in early 1910.

Vallgren produced a quantity of portrait and other larger sculptures. *Albert Edelfelt* and *August Strindberg* (both Helsinki, Athenaeum A. Mus.) were among his subjects.

At the beginning of the 1900s he also received commissions for several monuments, such as the tomb of *Baryatinsky* at Tsarskoye selo (now Pushkin) and the memorial at the grave of *Aurora Karamzin* in Helsinki. In 1908 he completed *Havis Amanda*, the lively fountain figure that was erected at the market square in Helsinki; it was one of the most popular and powerful images of women in Finnish art. Towards the end of his life Vallgren continued to produce smaller sculptures using Finnish clay. During this period he also wrote several volumes of memoirs.

WRITINGS
Ville Vallgrens ABC-bok (Helsinki, 1916)

BIBLIOGRAPHY
M. Supinen: 'Vallgren's objets d'art of the 1890s', *Ateneumin Taidemuseo Museojulkaisu* (1983), pp. 44–55

MARJA SUPINEN

Vallin, Eugène (*b* Herbeviller, Meurthe-et-Moselle, 13 July 1856; *d* Nancy, 21 July 1922). French architect and cabinetmaker. He learnt his trade in the carpentry business belonging to his uncle Charles-Auguste Claudel (1827–93), a specialist in church furniture, in Nancy. Although he only spent a year at the municipal drawing school, through his uncle he discovered Eugène-Emmanuel Viollet-le-Duc's famous *Dictionnaire raisonné de l'architecture française du XIe au XVe siècle* (Paris, 1854–68). He had been managing the business for six years when in 1887 he completed work on the great organ of the church of St Léon at Nancy where their passion for neo-medievalism made the sculptor voluble and the carpenter bold. The enthusiastic proselytizing of Emile Gallé and Victor Prouvé converted a developing love of Gothic into an engagement with Modernism, and by 1896 Vallin had designed a house for his own use—the first in the Ecole de Nancy manner. The décor is naturalist and the composition anti-classical, with a façade of which the features are differentiated by interior functions.

In 1902 Vallin collaborated with architect Georges Biet (1869–1955) on an Art Nouveau house for Biet; its lively street façade boasts an open loggia, a porch and a high gallery. The critic Emile Nicolas (1871–1940) compared it to a plant and saw in it the victory of botanical naturalism over classical anthropomorphism. For the Nancy Exposition Internationale de l'Est de la France in 1909 Vallin built a pavilion of reinforced concrete, which, paradoxically, was symmetrical in design (unfinished; destr.). The Musée de l'Ecole de Nancy houses several pieces of furniture and a furnished dining-room (1904) that illustrate the nature of Vallin's work, and there is also an astonishing multi-functional bookcase (1902) decorated with a sculpture by his son Auguste Vallin (1881–1967).

BIBLIOGRAPHY
E. Nicolas: 'Un Cabinet de travail de M. Vallin', *Lorraine Artiste* (15 Sept 1902), pp. 276–87
——: 'Eugène Vallin et son oeuvre', *Lorraine Artiste* (1–15 Sept 1904), pp. 257–75
F. Loyer: 'Viollet-le-Duc to Tony Garnier: The Passion for Rationalism', *Art Nouveau Architecture*, ed. F. Russel (London, 1979), pp. 102–35
F. T. Charpentier and others: *Art nouveau: L'Ecole de Nancy* (Paris, 1987)
J.-C. Vigato: 'L'Architecture', *Nancy 1900: Rayonnement de l'art nouveau*, ed. H. Claude and others (Thionville, 1989), pp. 120–55

JEAN-CLAUDE VIGATO

Vallmitjana y Barbany. Spanish family of sculptors. Venancio Vallmitjana y Barbany (*b* Barcelona, 1828; *d* Barcelona, 1919) and Agapito Vallmitjana y Barbany (*b* Barcelona, 1830; *d* Barcelona, 1905) were brothers who collaborated closely, making it difficult to distinguish between their individual styles and personalities. Their father was a weaver, and they were enrolled in the Escuela de la Lonja, Barcelona, through the intervention of a secularized Jesuit, Father Gattés, who admired their work in clay. There they completed their studies, under the Catalan sculptor Damián Campeny y Estrany, and then turned to the traditional Catalan activity of making small clay figures for Christmas crèches (*belenes*); later they made popular religious sculptures, such as the *Four Evangelists* and *Faith* (both 1854), commissioned for the parish church of SS Justo y Pastor, Barcelona. They also worked with glazed pottery.

There was a change of direction when the brothers' friendship with the architect José Oriol Mestres led to commissions for sculptural decorations for some of his buildings, such as their allegories (1858) for the Banco de Barcelona. Another important event was the visit in 1860 of Isabella II to the brothers' studio in the chapel of S Agueda; she commissioned from Venancio a marble sculpture of *St George* (Barcelona, Mus. A. Mod.). On this occasion Agapito presented the Queen with a fine statue of herself holding the future Alfonso XII in her arms (Barcelona, Pal. Pedralbes). The original clay model, in which the Queen appears naked, displays a freshness and spontaneity that are lacking in the finished piece. Venancio and Agapito also worked together on a project to decorate the façade of the University of Barcelona. For this they executed a series of statues of Spanish intellectuals, including the Catalan writer *Ramón Llull* (*c.* 1235–1315), the scholar and churchman *St Isidore of Seville* (*c.* 570–636), the humanist scholar *Juan Luis Vives* (1492–1540) and the writer and king of Castile and León *Alfonso X the Wise*.

In 1873 Venancio Vallmitjana achieved popular success with a small statue of the *Barber of Seville* (Barcelona, Mus. A. Mod.), made for a competition sponsored by the Parisian newspaper *Le Figaro*. He did not win the prize but through the contest met leading French sculptors such as Jean-Baptiste Carpeaux and Jean-Paul Laurens. Venancio also received acclaim for his striking and realistic *Birth of Venus* (1888), which decorates the main waterfall in the Parc de la Ciutadella in Barcelona. Agapito was for a time overshadowed by the success of his brother, but his work, especially his religious art, was later considered to be of equal value. His statue of *St John of God* (Barcelona, Asilo S Juan de Dios) carrying a sick child is a deeply felt work, and the saint has been compared with the monks in the paintings of Francesco de Zurbarán. It seems to have been intended to halt the decline into decadence of contemporary religious sculpture. Agapito's marble reclining *Christ* (1872; Madrid, Casón Buen Retiro) is another work notable for its originality of conception.

BIBLIOGRAPHY
M. Rodríguez Codolá: *Venancio y Agapito Vallmitjana Barbany* (Madrid)
J. A. Gaya Nuño: *Arte del siglo XIX*, A. Hisp., xix (Madrid, 1966)
C. Perez Reyes: *Escultura del neoclasicismo al modernismo* (Madrid, 1980)

JUAN NICOLAU

Vallotton, Félix(-Emile-Jean) (*b* Lausanne, 28 Dec 1865; *d* Paris, 28 Dec 1925). Swiss printmaker, painter and critic, active in France. He attended school in Lausanne, then moved to Paris in 1882 and enrolled as an art student at the Académie Julian. Paris remained his main base for the rest of his life, although he returned regularly to Switzerland to see his family. He became a close friend of Charles Cottet and Charles Maurin, who was his teacher and mentor. As a student, copying in the Louvre, Vallotton was drawn to the minute realism of the earlier masters, in particular Holbein, whose work he sought to emulate. He succeeded in having portraits accepted by the Salon jury in 1885 and 1886.

Vallotton was primarily a printmaker. He first made a drypoint etching in 1881. Between 1888 and 1892, to make ends meet, he produced reproductive etchings after such artists as Rembrandt and Millet, and from 1891 to 1895 he worked as Paris art correspondent for the *Gazette de Lausanne*: he showed sympathy for independent artists such as Puvis de Chavannes, Whistler and Toulouse-Lautrec and praised the innovations of his contemporaries in the avant-garde. In 1892 he produced his first woodcut, and it was in this medium, largely neglected until its revival in the 1890s, that Vallotton was to excel. His work appeared regularly in the *Revue Blanche*. In 1892 he joined the NABIS group. That year he exhibited woodcuts at the first Salon de la Rose+Croix, in the company of Maurin, and participated in the second Nabis group exhibition at Saint-Germain-en-Laye. From this date he exhibited regularly with the Nabis in Paris and elsewhere. In the favourable climate of Art Nouveau, Vallotton's woodcuts awakened international interest; examples appeared in *The Studio* (1893), the American *Chap Book* (1894) and the German periodicals *Pan* and *Jugend* (1895–6) and he had a substantial influence on the German woodcut revival at the beginning of the 20th century.

Vallotton's woodcut style is extremely simple; it makes play with contrasts between pure blocks of black and white and stark contours, exaggerated almost to the point of caricature. Unlike the other key exponents of the woodcut in the 1890s, Gauguin and Munch, Vallotton did not exploit the irregularities of the wood grain for artistic effect but relied on icy precision, a quality he also cultivated in his painting.

Vallotton found the subjects of his woodcuts in the tense and humorous spectacles of modern city life, both public and private. In *The Demonstration* (see fig.), for instance, which was included in *L'Estampe originale* (1893–5), an album dedicated to promoting the original print, Vallotton bore witness, as an anarchist sympathizer, to the street violence that frequently resulted from social unrest in the early 1890s in Paris. In the celebrated series *Intimacies* (1898), ten woodcuts depicting the traumatic disintegration of a love affair, Vallotton found inspiration in a contemporary novel by his friend Jules Renard; his stark use of the woodcut medium added a mood of Symbolist intensity to these private interior scenes.

Following his marriage in 1899 to Gabrielle Rodrique-Henriques, a member of the Bernheim-Jeune family, Vallotton's financial security was assured. He continued to produce illustrations for journals such as *L'Assiette au beurre* (1901) and demonstrated his social views in the

Félix Vallotton: *The Demonstration*, woodcut, 229×320 mm, 1893 (Paris, Bibliothèque Nationale); from *L'Estampe originale* (1893–5), pl. 8

album *C'est la guerre*, a series of anti-German propagandist woodcuts published in 1917. After 1902 Vallotton concentrated mainly on painting highly finished studies of interiors and nudes, such as *Models Resting* (1905; Winterthur, Kstmus.). He continued to exhibit regularly, though with less success after 1914. His brother Paul, an art dealer in Lausanne, assisted in promoting Vallotton's work in Switzerland.

BIBLIOGRAPHY

M. Vallotton and C. Georg: *Félix Vallotton: Catalogue Raisonné of the Printed Graphic Work* (Geneva, 1972)

G. Guisan and D. Jakubec: *Félix Vallotton: Documents pour une biographie et pour l'histoire d'une oeuvre*, 3 vols (Lausanne, 1973–5)

The Graphic Work of Félix Vallotton, 1865–1925 (exh. cat., ACGB and Pro Helvetia, 1976)

Félix Vallotton (exh. cat. by R. Koella, Winterthur, Kstmus., 1978)

G. Busch, B. Dorival and D. Jakubec: *Félix Vallotton: Leben und Werk* (Freuenfeld, 1982; Fr. trans., Lausanne, 1985)

S. M. Newman: *Félix Vallotton* (New Haven and New York, 1991)

BELINDA THOMSON

Vallou de Villeneuve, Julien (*b* Boissy-Saint-Léger, 12 Dec 1795; *d* Paris, 4 May 1866). French lithographer, photographer and painter. From his début at the Salon of 1814 as a painter he regularly exhibited lithographed images of daily life, fashion, regional costumes and erotica, many done after the work of English and Dutch artists. He also published his own lithographed compositions, mostly 'female types'. With Achille Deveria and others he contributed to the compendium of romantic erotica called *Imagerie galante* (Paris, 1830), which provocatively updated an erotic mode found in 18th-century engravings. The subjects were pictorial versions of stock characters from popular novels and plays.

Vallou turned to photography in 1842 after nearly 30 years of popular lithography. By 1851 he was using the paper negative exclusively. He belonged to the Société Héliographique and was a founder-member of the Société Française de Photographie. It is not known how and why he changed to the new medium, except that he may have seen its market potential in providing artists with photographic studies (*académies*); he had a large repertory of nudes and draped models he called 'études d'après nature'. As with other painters who used the paper negative, his style obfuscates detail and boldly organizes masses of light and shade. Even in their small scale (negatives *c.* 180×130 mm), meant for albums and intimate viewing, the images show figures with a strong physical presence. His studies liberated the nude from classical poses and theatricality, with sensuality of a different order. Courbet drew inspiration from them for his *Bathers* of 1853, undoubtedly attracted to the figures' solid construction, abstract simplicity of design, chaste mood and Vallou's penchant for healthy-looking country girls, which distinguish his images from similar studies of the 1850s. Vallou smoothed the contours of the female form by retouching his negatives with hundreds of tiny pencil marks, which suggests that even as a photographer he continued to draw, ever correcting and perfecting his classical lines. He also made a number of portraits of actors and actresses (Paris, Bib. Comédie Fr.; Paris, André Jammes priv. col.; Rochester, NY, Int. Mus. Phot.).

BIBLIOGRAPHY

E. Durieu: 'Rapport présenté au nom de la commission chargée de l'examen de l'exposition ouverte dans les salons de la Société Française de Photographie, du 1er août au 15 novembre 1855', *Bull. Soc. Fr. Phot.* (Feb 1856), no. 1, pp. 37–72 (67)

E. P. Janis: 'Photography', *The Second Empire, Art in France under Napoleon III* (exh. cat., Philadelphia, PA, Mus. A.; Paris, Réunion Musées N.; 1978–9), pp. 401–33 (432–3)

A. Jammes and E. P. Janis: *The Art of French Calotype, with a Critical Dictionary of Photographers, 1845–1870* (Princeton, 1983), pp. 252–3

EUGENIA PARRY JANIS

Valmarana. Italian family of patrons. First noted in Vicenza in the 11th century, the family was among the oldest and most powerful of the city's ruling dynasties; the title Count was awarded in 1540 by the Holy Roman Emperor Charles V, and in 1648 the family was inscribed in the patriciate of Venice. The family occupied an important position in the Lisiera region, where, by 1555, it had control over the rivers and bridges. Giovanni Francesco Valmarana (*d* 1566) commissioned from AN-DREA PALLADIO the Villa Valmarana (1563–?4; now Villa Scagnolari; partly destr. 1945; reconstr.) at Lisiera. The drawings show a block with a two-storey loggia, but the villa was only partly constructed, probably due to the death of Giovanni Francesco. His brother Giovanni Alvise (Luigi) Valmarana (*d* 1558) was a friend of Palladio, whose design for the loggia of the Palazzo della Ragione (also known as the Basilica) in Vicenza he supported in 1549. Giovanni Alvise's widow was responsible for the family's principal act of patronage: the commissioning of Palazzo Valmarana (1565–71; now Palazzo Braga) in Vicenza, one of the most important of Palladio's palazzi. The façade (*see* PALLADIO, ANDREA, fig. 6) is dominated by a giant order of pilasters, and the planning is functional; however, only the front part was executed. The Valmarana family had owned a house there since 1487, and Palladio's work incorporated parts of the existing building.

Giovanni Alvise's son, Leonardo Valmarana (?1548–?1613), who inherited the estates of both his father and uncle, played an important part in the completion and decoration of the Palazzo Valmarana, later commissioning Domenico Fontana to execute the statues on the façade. He also involved Palladio in the design of the Valmarana funerary chapel (1576) in the church of Santa Corona, Vicenza. As director of Vicenza's Accademia Olimpica in 1583, he commissioned the statues for Palladio's Teatro Olimpico (1580; *see* THEATRE, fig. 4). Giuseppe di Bernardino Valmarana (1524–80), from a different branch of the family, commissioned the Villa Valmarana (1541–3; now Villa Bressan) in Vigardolo. This is an early work by Palladio, with an unarticulated pedimented brick façade with a single central Serlian motif opening to a loggia; it differs slightly from his drawing (*see* ARCHITECTURAL DRAWING, fig. 6). The Valmarana family, still resident in Vicenza and Venice, has owned the Villa Rotonda (*c.* 1565/6–70; *see* PALLADIO, ANDREA, fig. 5, and VICENZA, §2) since 1911 and has recently undertaken its restoration.

BIBLIOGRAPHY

Libro d'oro della nobilità italiana, iii (Rome, 1914–15)

G. Arnaldi, ed.: *Storia di Vicenza*, iii (Vicenza, 1989)

Valmaseda, Juan de. *See* BALMASEDA, JUAN DE.

Valmier, Georges (*b* Angoûleme, 4 April 1885; *d* Paris, 25 March 1937). French painter, collagist, draughtsman and stage designer. A few years younger than most of the Cubists with whom he became associated, he received a traditional art education at the Ecole Nationale des Beaux-Arts in Paris from 1906 to 1910. He did not participate in any of the manifestations of Cubism that took place before World War I. His interest in the movement appears to have developed under the influence of Albert Gleizes, who painted his portrait while both served near the front in the 167th regiment at Toul in 1914–15. By 1916 Valmier was making small and very delicate collages markedly different from those of Picasso, Braque or Gris, composed of minutely fragmented surfaces.

In 1919 Valmier signed a contract with the dealer Léonce Rosenberg, for whose *Bulletin de l'effort moderne* he later designed a cover. Rosenberg gave him his first one-man exhibition at his Galerie de l'Effort Moderne, Paris, in 1921. He had by now developed his characteristic style of simplified, flat planes articulated by graceful, linear arabesques. By 1922, when Valmier became involved with the theatre, designing sets and costumes for Max Jacob's *Isabelle et Pantalon*, he was a master of decorative Cubism, an adroit manipulator of elegant shapes that often masked humorous observations about life, love, art and theatre. He created stage designs for six productions of Art et Action in Paris, including works by Georges Pillement, Paul Claudel, Filippo Tommaso Marinetti and Jules Romains; he also designed for productions by the Ballets Russes staged in New York. In demand as an interior decorator, he experimented occasionally with oddly shaped formats destined to fit over doors or mantles. His work on the interior of Rosenberg's apartment in 1931 was instantly famous.

As early as the mid-1920s Valmier's paintings had become more curvilinear, and organic references in them multiplied. A series of pictures combining motifs borrowed from fruit still-lifes with hands or faces demonstrate that he was not hostile to the formal inventions of André Masson and Miró, although he eschewed Surrealist imagery and automatism, always holding to a deliberate look. In 1931 he was a founder member of ABSTRACTION–CRÉATION, with whom he exhibited. From 1932 to 1937 his painting grew steadily more monumental and abstract; the mood is no longer witty but grave and measured. A group of gouaches and paintings collectively known as *Forms in Space* (1933–5) are the immediate prelude to three large mural compositions executed for the French Railways Pavilion at the 1937 Exposition Internationale at Paris. These, with gouaches to illustrate Pillement's poem, *Entre la vie et le rêve*, were Valmier's last works.

BIBLIOGRAPHY

Georges Valmier: Oeuvres de 1917 à 1935 (exh. cat., essay G. Pillement; Paris, Gal. Melki, 1973)

D. Robbins: 'Georges Valmier', *The Société Anonyme and Dreier Bequest at Yale University: A Catalogue Raisonné*, ed. R. L. Herbert (New Haven, 1984), pp. 671–3

C. Green: *Cubism and its Enemies* (London and New Haven, 1987)

For further bibliography *see* CUBISM.

DANIEL ROBBINS

Valois, House of. French family of rulers, patrons and collectors. The Counts of Valois, a branch of the Capet dynasty, succeeded to the French throne in 1328. Their claim was disputed by the kings of England (*see* PLANTAGENET), giving rise to the Hundred Years' War. The seat of the dynasty was the Ile-de-France, roughly between Soissons and Senlis. The direct Valois line (see fig.) began with Philip VI (*reg* 1328–50), son of Charles (1270–1325), Comte d'Alençon. Charles was the younger son of the Capetian king Philip III (*reg* 1270–85), from whom he received the county of Valois in 1285. In accordance with the salic law that excludes sisters and daughters of sovereigns, when the direct Capetian line died out Philip VI succeeded his cousin Charles IV (*reg* 1322–8). Under Philip's reign the Valois acquired (1349) the Dauphiné. Both Philip's first wife, Joanna of Burgundy (*d* 1348), and his second wife, Blanche of Navarre (*d* 1398), were known for their literary patronage and commission of illuminated manuscripts.

Philip's son (1) John II founded the Order of the Star and, in addition to literary commissions, he and his wife, Bonne of Luxembourg, employed such artists as Girard d'Orléans and Jean Le Noir. John was held hostage in England after the Battle of Poitiers (1356) until 1360 and again in 1364. His son (2) Charles V was one of the most important Valois patrons. Charles built up the royal library and had new walls constructed around Paris. His three brothers were also outstanding patrons of the late medieval period: Louis, Duke of Anjou (*see* ANJOU, §II(2)); (3) Jean, Duc de Berry, and Philip the Bold, Duke of Burgundy (*see* BURGUNDY, (1)), both of whom were particularly notable for their interest in manuscripts, employing such outstanding illuminators as the Limbourg brothers, and for their many building commissions. Artists such as Jean d'Orléans and Jean du Vivier, who had worked for Charles V, continued in the service of his son (4) Charles VI. Despite suffering attacks of madness from 1392, Charles VI commissioned several buildings, including the completion of the Sainte-Chapelle at Vincennes, and other, smaller, luxury items. In 1385 he married (5) Isabeau of Bavaria, whose collection included manuscripts, jewels and precious metalwork. Her brother-in-law (6) Louis, Duke of Orléans, proved an effective rival to the hostile Dukes of Burgundy. Louis commissioned building work from such architects as Raymond du Temple and acquired textiles, metalwork and manuscripts; after 1393 he was actively associated with the Celestine Order. After his assassination in 1407, his son (7) Charles, Duke of Orléans, was prominent in the Armagnac–Angoulême faction and established a court at Blois that attracted literary figures.

Charles VI was succeeded by his fifth son, (8) Charles VII. Although the latter's patronage was limited, such artists as Jean Fouquet received royal commissions. Charles VII's son (9) Louis XI was founder of the Order of St Michael. He commissioned several royal portraits and the construction of the château of Langeais. His second wife, Charlotte of Savoy (1445–83), employed important illuminators, including Jean Colombe and Jean Bourdichon. Louis's brother (10) Charles, Duc de Berry, was also a keen patron of illuminators, retaining Fouquet and several of his followers in his service. (11) Charles VIII, Louis XI's son, was involved in improving the royal

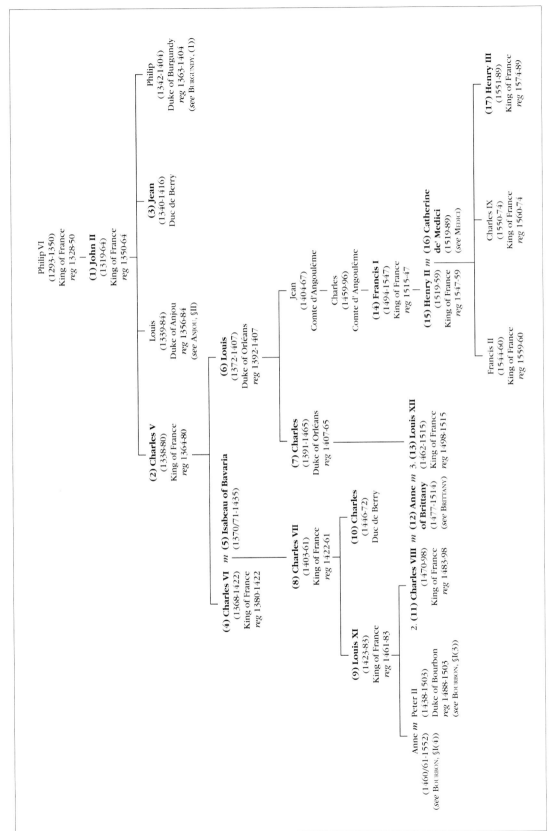

Family tree of the House of Valois

residence at Amboise. His patronage was influenced by his campaigns in Italy from 1494, after which Italian artists, craftsmen and engineers were persuaded to work in France. His wife, (12) Anne of Brittany, attempted to preserve the independence of Brittany from the French Crown, a concern reflected in several aspects of her patronage. Her most renowned commission was a lavish Book of Hours from Bourdichon.

Charles and Anne had no surviving heir, and the throne passed to the Valois–Orléans branch with (13) Louis XII, son of (7) Charles of Orléans. As a keen bibliophile, Louis added numerous manuscripts to the royal library at the château of Blois, which he extended. His conquest of Milan in 1499 resulted in contacts with Italian artists, including Leonardo da Vinci. As Louis XII also had no heir, the throne passed to the Valois–Angoulême line with (14) Francis I, who had married Claude, the eldest daughter of Louis XII. Francis I was a protector of humanists and a founder of the institution eventually known as the Collège de France; he brought Leonardo to his court and was involved with several important architectural projects that included a number of châteaux, notably that at Fontainebleau. His son (15) Henry II and Henry's wife, (16) Catherine de' Medici, both continued Francis's work on the royal châteaux, as well as at the palaces of the Louvre and the Tuileries, both in Paris. They had three sons: Francis II (*reg* 1559–60), Charles IX (*reg* 1560–74) and (17) Henry III, who founded the Order of the Holy Spirit, for which sumptuous silverwork was commissioned, and who instigated several architectural projects on the royal residences around Paris. He left no heirs, and with him the House of Valois was extinguished and the Crown passed to the Bourbon family (see BOURBON, §I).

BIBLIOGRAPHY
A. de Sainte-Marie: *Histoire généologie et chronologique de la maison royale de France*, i (Paris, 1726)
L. Delisle: *Le Cabinet des manuscrits de la Bibliothèque imperiale* (Paris, 1868–81)
——: *Le Cabinet des manuscrits de la Bibliothèque nationale*, 2 vols (Paris, 1868–81)
G. Sirjean: *Encyclopédie généologique des maisons souveraines du monde*, iv (Paris, 1960)
Y. Botineau: 'Architecture des premiers Valois' *Gaz. B.-A.*, lxxxii (1973), pp. 237–62

(1) John II [Jean le Bon; John the Good], King of France (*b* 26 April 1319; *reg* 1350–64; *d* London, 8 April 1364). The son of Philip VI (*reg* 1328–50) and Joanna of Burgundy (1293–1348), he was the second ruler of the Valois line. He married Bonne of Luxembourg (*d* 1349) in 1332 and Joanna of Boulogne (*d* 1360) in 1349. His sons, (2) Charles V, Louis I, Duke of Anjou (see ANJOU §II(2)), Philip the Bold, Duke of Burgundy (see BURGUNDY, (1)), and (3) Jean, Duc de Berry were all active patrons. John's own interest in music, literature and the visual arts is often attested. He commissioned several translations, including a Bible from Jean de Sy (see below) and Livy's *Decades* from Pierre Bersuire (1352–6). Gace de La Buigne was commissioned to compose his *Roman des déduits de la chasse* (1360–77). Of the painters in the royal service, the most renowned was GIRARD D'ORLÉANS who provided many items for the household as well as panel paintings. Others were Guillaume Bernier (*fl* 1350) and Jean de Coste (*fl* 1349–67) who, from 1349 to 1356,

assisted primarily by Jean Quarré (*fl* 1349), produced at the castle of Le Vaudreuil (Normandy) wall paintings (destr.) of the *Life of Julius Caesar*, hunting scenes and, in the chapel there, saints' lives, *Passion* scenes in simulated marble frames, the *Annunciation*, the *Coronation of the Virgin* with the faces of angels in relief, and a triptych (untraced). Records show that King John purchased a Sienese panel in 1349 in Paris, by an unknown painter. Under his directive, painting was consciously employed to uphold the new Valois dynasty. A panel once in the Sainte-Chapelle, Paris, painted in 1342–3, possibly by Matteo Giovannetti, depicted him in Avignon receiving an Italo-Byzantine diptych from the future Pope Clement VI (untraced; recorded in a drawing, Paris, Bib. N., Est. Oa 11, fols 85–8). John appeared kneeling in a painting of the *Crucifixion* (*c.* 1360; untraced; recorded in a drawing, Paris, Bib. N., Est. Oa 11, fol. 89), once at Saint-Denis Abbey. The bust-length profile portrait inscribed *jehan roy de france* (Paris, Louvre; see GOTHIC, fig. 66), sometimes attributed to Girard d'Orléans, is the earliest extant medieval portrait on panel. The authenticity of the inscription has been questioned, and the sitter, depicted without regal attire, has been identified as John's son, the future Charles V; but it may indeed be John before his accession.

Joanna of Boulogne's inventory of 1360 records many Parisian goldsmiths' and carved works in royal holdings. For the abbey church of Poissy, John commissioned a silver-gilt reliquary (1351) of *St Louis* with kneeling figures of his parents, himself and his consort (untraced). His third son, Jean, Duc de Berry, inherited a gold ring with 'the likeness of King John' in silver (untraced). John II is known to have borrowed 'romans' and zealously collected manuscripts. He fostered the activity, in Paris, of Franco–Flemish illuminators who replaced the idealized forms of the circle of Jean Pucelle with more naturalistic renderings. In 1349 he acquired a *Roman des moralités de la Bible* (untraced) from the bookseller Thomas de Maubeuge. He commissioned a book of motets (untraced) illustrated by Jean de Wirmes (*fl* 1349–50), a copy of the *Histoire des croisades*, a partially extant *Miroir historial* in four volumes (Leiden, Bib. Rijksuniv., MS. Voss. gall. 3A; Paris, Bib. Arsenal, MS. 5080), a copy of the *Grandes chroniques de France* (London, BL, Royal MS. 16. G. IV) and the Bible of Jean de Sy (Paris, Bib. N., MS. fr. 15397), the first six quires of which are deftly illustrated by the MASTER OF THE BOQUETEAUX (see MASTERS, ANONYMOUS, AND MONOGRAMMISTS, §I). A large *Bible historiale* (London, BL, Royal MS. 19. D. II) and a volume of the *Miracles de Notre Dame* by Gauthier de Coincy (Paris, Bib. N., n. a. fr. 24541) were looted from John's camp at Poitiers (1356). From 1349 to 1353, Jean de Montmartre (*fl* 1349–53) produced, with collaborators, over 5000 grisaille illustrations in a *Bible moralisée* (Paris, Bib. N., MS. fr. 167) for the King. Other illuminators named in the royal accounts are Jean le Noir, Jean Susanne (*fl* 1350) and Guillaume Castaigne (*fl* 1349–50). In 1351 John founded at Saint-Ouen the chivalric Order of the Star, of which miniatures illustrating the first chapter have survived (Paris, Bib. N., MS. fr. 2813, fol. 394).

BIBLIOGRAPHY
L. C. Doüet d'Arcq: *Comptes de l'argenterie des rois de France au XIVe siècle* (Paris, 1851)

R. Cazelles: 'Jean II le Bon; Quel homme? Quel roi?', *Rev. Hist.*, ccli (1974), pp. 6–25

——: 'Peinture et actualité politique sous les premiers Valois: Jean le Bon ou Charles, dauphin', *Gaz. B.-A.*, xcii (1978), pp. 53–65

Les Fastes du gothique: Le Siècle de Charles V (exh. cat. by J. Favier and others, Paris, Grand Pal., 1981)

F. Avril: 'Un Moment méconnu de l'enluminure française: Le Règne de Jean le Bon', *Archeologia*, clvii (1982), pp. 24–31

PATRICK M. DE WINTER

(2) Charles V [Charles le Sage; Charles the Wise], King of France (*b* Bois de Vincennes, 21 Jan 1338 *reg* 1364–80; *d* Beauté, Nogent-sur-Marne, 16 Sept 1380). Son of (1) John II. His early attitudes to the visual arts were formed during a period of political turmoil following the capture of his father by the English in 1356. Although these threats to the French monarchy were eventually overcome, they forced Charles as regent to rethink the defences of Paris and the suitability of his residences. Around the north of Paris, where expansion had left the late 12th-century line of fortification obsolete, Charles built a new, much taller wall, with deep outer trenches (*see* PARIS, fig. 1). Abandoning the Palais de la Cité, he took up residence in the Hôtel St Pol in the east of the city, a vicinity protected by the Bastille, a massive new fortress, consisting of eight conjoined towers. This complemented the older fortress of the Louvre in the west of the city, which, like the château of St Germain-en-Laye (Seine-et-Oise), was remodelled under the supervision of RAYMOND DU TEMPLE, Charles's director of works. These projects were begun *c.* 1360, but after his accession (8 April 1364), Charles's plans for the château of Vincennes (Seine-et-Oise) proved to be on a still grander scale (*see* VINCENNES, §1). Work on its enlargement began in 1362 with the appointment of a treasurer, and was completed *c.* 1369. The workforce comprised 500 masons, workers and servants, one of the highest-paid being the stonecutter Guillaume d'Arondel, perhaps an Englishman. According to Christine de Pisan, Charles's first biographer (1404), the King, whom she called 'a true architect', intended Vincennes to function as a kind of royal town, a new concept, where members of government would live in mansions tax free.

Although little remains of Charles V's building projects, documentation and descriptions record some of the decorative schemes favoured by the King. At the Hôtel St Pol, for example, a gallery was painted to represent a forest, full of fruit trees and flowers, in which children played. In the vault, branches gave way illusionistically to the sky, painted in blue and white. Nearby, the King's gardener, Philippart Persant, created a pleasure park, featuring a labyrinth and trellised pavilions. In the great hall of the Louvre, wall paintings (1360s) depicted a landscape filled with birds and other wildlife. The most spectacular of the sculptural schemes was the spiral staircase in the Louvre, created *c.* 1365 by Raymond du Temple, which consisted of ten statues, mostly representing members of the royal family, including two by Jean de Saint-Romain (*fl* 1364–1403), who designed the stained glass in the Hôtel St Pol, and others by Jean de Liège. This ensemble, which served to emphasize the strength of the Valois dynasty, was later destroyed, but fine statues of *Charles V* and his wife *Joanna of Bourbon* (Paris, Louvre) have survived, which were possibly part of the original

decoration of the Louvre's east entrance. Statues of the royal couple also decorated the portal of the church of the Celestines (destr.) in Paris, Charles's principal ecclesiastical foundation. Charles laid the foundation stone in 1365 and two years later gave the considerable sum of 1000 francs d'or to complete the work. In 1378 the sculptor Jean de Thoiry received 30 francs from the King for making a statue of *St Celestine V* for the trumeau.

Among Charles's other projects promoting Valois interests were the tomb effigies (three *in situ*) of the first Valois monarchs and of his father and himself, commissioned in 1364 from the Netherlandish sculptor, ANDRÉ BEAUNEVEU, for Saint-Denis Abbey. In 1368 Charles ordered another effigy for his heart tomb in Rouen Cathedral, the work of Jean de Liège, now known only from a drawing (Paris, Bib. N., MS. Clairambault 633, fol. 31*r*). Charles's will of 1374 refers to another effigy (Paris, Louvre) for the tomb of his entrails in Maubuisson Abbey. Charles's desire to promote his authority by propagating his own image can also be seen in many other portraits. Perhaps the finest is by Jan Boudolf, 'painter to the King', executed in 1371 in a *Bible historiale* commissioned as a gift to the king (The Hague, Rijksmus. Meermanno-Westreenianum, MS. 10. B. 23, fol. 2*r*; for illustration *see* BOUDOLF, JAN). Another excellent portrait appears in an altar hanging, the *Parement de Narbonne* (Paris, Louvre), which was painted *c.* 1375 and probably made for one of the royal chapels (*see* MASTERS, ANONYMOUS, AND MONOGRAMMISTS, §I: MASTER OF THE PAREMENT DE NARBONNE). The artist has sometimes been identified as JEAN D'ORLÉANS, the King's favourite painter, who executed panel and wall paintings (all untraced) for several royal residences and collaborated with the King's goldsmith, Jean du Vivier (*fl* 1378–1401).

Charles's most outstanding cultural achievement was the formation of the royal library, which, by the time of the inventory of 1380, comprised 900 volumes, mostly housed in a special tower in the Louvre run by the librarian Gilles Malet. Among the older illuminated manuscripts in the collection were the Ingeborg Psalter (*c.* 1195; Chantilly, Mus. Condé, MS. 1695; *see* TRANSITIONAL STYLE, fig. 2) and the Peterborough Psalter (*c.* 1300; Brussels, Bib. Royale Albert 1er, MSS 9961–2). Charles's particular taste in illumination is shown from his acquisition of older manuscripts by the Parisian illuminator JEAN PUCELLE, including the Hours of Jeanne d'Evreux (*c.* 1325–8; New York, Cloisters, MS. 54.1.2), attributed to this artist and bequeathed to Charles in 1371 by its original owner. Charles's Breviary (before 1380; Paris, Bib. N., MS. lat. 1052; see fig.), probably by Jean le Noir, closely follows the iconography and style of the earlier BELLE-VILLE BREVIARY (1323–6; Paris, Bib. N., MSS lat. 10483–4), attributed to Pucelle and his circle. An illuminator used frequently by Charles was the Master of the Jean de Sy Bible (alias the MASTER OF THE BOQUETEAUX, *see* MASTERS, ANONYMOUS, AND MONOGRAMMISTS, §I), a less slavish follower of the Pucelle style. His works for Charles include the anonymous *Songe du verger* (1378; London, BL, Royal MS. 19.C.IV), a treatise that includes a defence of Charles's building projects on the grounds that their magnificence was a reflection of the monarchy's strength, and therefore in the interests of the people and peace.

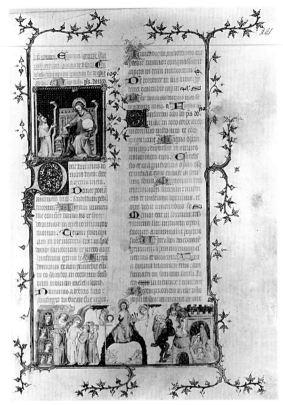

Charles V before God the Father and the *Last Judgement*, illustrations to Psalm 109, probably by Jean Le Noir, from the Breviary of Charles V, 230×178 mm, before 1380 (Paris, Bibliothèque Nationale, MS. lat. 1052, fol. 261*r*)

Another favoured illuminator was the Master of the Coronation Book of Charles V, whose illustrations in a copy of the coronation ceremony (1365; London, BL, Cotton MS. Tiberius B. VIII), form a unique record of Charles's coronation (for an illustration of Charles's coronation *see* CHRONICLES AND HISTORIES, MANUSCRIPT, fig. 2).

Most of Charles V's collection of 20 religious paintings, 200 tapestries and numerous *objets d'art* has been lost, but the items that survive suggest his interest in the past. An ancient agate bust of a Roman emperor, for example, was incorporated *c.* 1365 into the top of a baton (Paris, Bib. N., Cab. Médailles), and a new cover for an Ottonian Gospel book (Paris, Bib. N., MS. lat. 8551) dated 1379 imitates the style of *c.* 1200. As with much of Charles's patronage, these antiquarianisms were probably devised in an attempt to strengthen the monarchy after the crises of the 1350s.

BIBLIOGRAPHY

Christine de Pisan: *Le Livre des faits et bonnes meurs du sage roi Charles V* (1404); ed. S. Solente, 2 vols (Paris, 1936–40)
H. Sauval: *Histoires et recherches des antiquités de la ville de Paris*, 2 vols (Paris, 1733)
J. Labarte: *Inventaire du mobilier de Charles V, roi de France* (Paris, 1879)
R. Delachenal: *Histoire de Charles V*, 5 vols (Paris, 1909–31)
P. Pradel: 'Art et politique sous Charles V', *Rev. A.*, i (1951), pp. 89–93
——: 'Les Tombeaux de Charles V', *Bull. Mnmtl*, cix (1951), pp. 273–96
La Librairie de Charles V (exh. cat., ed. F. Avril and J. Lafaurie; Paris, Bib. N., 1968)
F. Avril: 'Trois manuscrits napolitains de Charles V', *Bib. Ecole Chartes*, cxxvii (1969), pp. 291–328
C. R. Sherman: *The Portraits of Charles V of France* (New York, 1969)
F. Avril: 'Une Bible historiale de Charles V', *Jb. Hamburg. Kstsamml.*, xiv–xv (1970), pp. 45–76
C. R. Sherman: 'Representations of Charles V as a Wise Ruler', *Med. & Human.*, n. s., ii (1971), pp. 83–96
A. Erlande-Brandenburg: 'Aspects du mécénat de Charles V: La Sculpture décorative', *Bull. Mnmtl*, cxxx (1972), pp. 303–45
——: 'Jean de Thoiry, sculpteur de Charles V', *J. Sav.* (1972), pp. 210–27
P. Henwood: 'Jean d'Orléans, peintre des rois Jean II, Charles V et Charles VI', *Gaz. B.-A.*, xcv (1980), pp. 137–40
D. Byrne: 'Rev imago Dei: Charles V of France and the *Livre des propriétés des choses*', *J. Med. Hist.*, vii (1981), pp. 97–115
A. D. Hedeman: 'Valois Legitimacy: Editorial Changes in Charles V's *Grandes chroniques de France*', *A. Bull.*, lxvi (1984), pp. 97–117
——: 'Reconstructing the Narrative: The Function of Ceremonial in Charles V's *Grandes chroniques de France*', *Stud. Hist. A.*, xvi (1985), pp. 171–81
J. Mesqui: *Les Demeures seigneuriales*, ii of *Ile de France gothique*, Monuments de France Gothique (Paris, 1988)

(3) Jean [Jean de France], Duc de Berry (*b* Vincennes, nr Paris, 30 Nov 1340; *d* Paris, 15 June 1416). Son of (1) John II. He became one of the most prolific patrons of the late Middle Ages. His early interests concerned the acquisition or construction of important buildings. Later, however, he became increasingly interested in fine illuminated manuscripts, to the extent that he not only persuaded many illuminators to work exclusively in his service, but also encouraged artists who were not principally illuminators to work in that medium. For example, the sculptor ANDRÉ BEAUNEVEU, who started working for Jean de Berry *c.* 1385, soon found himself illuminating miniatures in the Duc's Psalter (Paris, Bib. N., MS. fr. 13091), partly imitating the grisaille technique first used in the 1320s by Jean Pucelle, one of the Duc's favourite artists, whose work he avidly collected. Jean de Berry's passion for the visual arts is evident in a passage from Froissart's *Chronicles*, which also comments on his relationship with Beauneveu. When describing the political situation in France, Froissart wrote that instead of undertaking his duties, the Duc preferred to spend time at his château at Mehun-sur-Yèvre (Cher):

> one of the handsomest castles in the world; for the Duke had spent upwards of 3000 francs in building and ornamenting it. . .he remained at Mehun-sur-Yèvre more than three weeks, planning new improvements with his master of the works, André Beauneveu, in sculpture and painting; for in such arts he [Berry] took great delight, and was skilled in them.

Although little remains of the decoration at Mehun-sur-Yèvre, an early example of a château designed as much for comfort as defence, it was clearly out of the ordinary since artists from as far afield as Troyes and Dijon were sent to see it. Something of André Beauneveu's large-scale work, however, survives from another building constructed for Jean de Berry, the Sainte-Chapelle at Bourges, built to house his tomb and dedicated in 1405 (*see* BOURGES, §II, 2). The structure itself was designed by Guy de Dammartin (*see* DAMMARTIN, DE, (1)), the Duc's Master of Works, who was a member of a family also employed by Jean de Berry's brother, Philip the Bold, Duke of Burgundy. Like many of Jean's architectural projects, the Sainte-Chapelle was destroyed in the 18th century, but some of the surviving sculptures, for example elements from the Duc's tomb, commissioned from JEAN DE CAMBRAI, and the kneeling figures of the Duc and his wife praying to the Virgin and Child (restored; Bourges Cathedral), were inspired by Claus Sluter's work for Philip the Bold at the Charterhouse of Champmol, Dijon.

Other large-scale decorative schemes created for Jean de Berry imply a taste for novelty and variety. The *Chronique du religieux de Saint-Denys*, for example, describes a series of painted portraits of the pope, his cardinals, various kings, emperors and princes, which decorated the Duc de Berry's castle of Bicêtre (destr. 1411) in Paris. In the hall of the palace at Poitiers, reconstructed in the 1380s, a magnificent triple fireplace is embellished with Flamboyant tracery, heraldry, and fine statues representing *Jean Duc de Berry, Joanna of Boulogne, Charles VI* and *Isabeau of Bavaria*. The façade of the adjacent Tour Maubergeon originally displayed 19 statues placed at a high level, apparently representing the Duc and his ancestors. Although some residences displayed wall paintings, the interiors of most were decorated with hangings, both embroidered and woven. The subjects of Jean's tapestries included ancient battles, the lives of his patron saints, Andrew and John, and religious themes such as the Seven Deadly Sins and the Coronation of the Virgin. The only extant tapestry cycle, datable *c.* 1385, represents the *Nine Worthies* (New York, Cloisters; *see* GOTHIC, fig. 114). Other hangings featured landscapes filled with animals. One set, intended to decorate an entire room, showed several swans (a de Berry emblem), including one in flight on the ceiling. The Duc also collected embroidered altar hangings of Italian origin, many adorned with precious stones. Most of these were given in 1404–5 to the Sainte-Chapelle in Bourges with much of his collection of jewels. Two of Jean's *joyaux* survive: the Royal Gold Cup (*c.* 1380–90; London, BM; *see* ENAMEL, colour pl. III, fig. 1) tells the *Legend of St Agnes* in delicate translucent enamel, while the Reliquary of the Sacred Thorn (*c.* 1400; London, BM) features *Christ in Judgement*, the figures sculpted and enamelled in white.

Knowledge of Jean de Berry's collection comes from inventories compiled in 1401–3, 1413–14 and 1416 by Robinet d'Etampes, 'keeper of *joyaux*'. The Duc clearly delighted in objects of great antiquity or that purported to be antiques. He possessed about 33 cameos and in 1402 acquired mock antique medals of four Roman emperors, each set with precious stones, two of which he had copied. By 1416 Berry owned over 20 panel paintings, mostly religious in subject-matter. A work in seven panels showed six scenes from the Life of St Lawrence with a Crucifixion in the middle; one secular work was a quadriptych consisting of four portraits of monarchs (both untraced). Much of Jean's energies went into building up his library, beginning with four romances purchased in 1371. Eventually he possessed about 300 manuscripts, which by 1415 were cared for by Pierre de Verone, a bookseller. Unlike his brother Charles V, Jean frequently seems to have interested himself in the illumination of his manuscripts. The many Books of Hours he possessed suggest that he was more concerned with their decoration than with their text. Some manuscripts, such as those illuminated by Jean Pucelle, were acquired from earlier collections or by gift. Others were apparently specially commissioned from

leading artists in Paris, such as the Josephus *Antiquités judaïques* (*c.* 1410; Paris, Bib. N., MS. fr. 6446) by the Master of the Cité des Dames. The most lavishly decorated manuscripts, however, were executed by the Duc's own artists. The earliest illuminators in Jean de Berry's service worked in styles derived from that of Pucelle. Often these artists had previously worked for older relatives, suggesting that the Duc based his taste on theirs. Jean Le Noir, whom the Duc employed in the 1370s, had worked earlier for Charles V. Le Noir may be identified with the Passion Master, the artist responsible for some of the most fussy and highly decorative work in Jean's Petites Heures (Paris, Bib. N., MS. lat. 18014; for illustration *see* JEAN LE NOIR), executed at this time. Another Book of Hours begun during this period, the main fragment of the TURIN–MILAN HOURS, known as the Très Belles Heures de Notre-Dame (Paris, Bib. N., MS. nouv. acq. lat. 3093), contains miniatures by the Master of the Parement de Narbonne, who had also worked for Charles V.

By 1400 Jean de Berry's taste favoured artists working in more naturalistic styles originating in Italy. The full-page miniatures in the Très Belles Heures (Brussels, Bib. Royale Albert 1er, MSS 11060–1), for example, show clear influence from Tuscan frescoes. They were probably executed *c.* 1400 by JACQUEMART DE HESDIN, first recorded as the Duc de Berry's 'painter' in 1384. The textual decorations are the work of a Bolognese artist, the Master of the Brussels Initials, whose feeling for space influenced much French illumination of the early 1400s. Jean de Berry's interest in Italian art is confirmed by attempts made on his behalf in 1408 to obtain the services of an unnamed Sienese intarsia worker. In his Grandes Heures (Paris, Bib. N., MS. lat. 919), completed in 1409, some of the illumination reproduces designs by Pucelle and the Master of the Parement de Narbonne, indicating that older French traditions were still appreciated. On the other hand, the only extant full-page miniature to have been identified from the Grandes Heures, the *Road to Calvary* (Paris, Louvre; for illustration *see* JACQUEMART DE HESDIN), is witness to the increasing importance of interest in Italian styles. Italian art seems to have been particularly admired for the range of emotions it presented and the solutions it offered to the representation of three-dimensional space.

The last of the major illuminators to work for Jean de Berry, the Limbourg brothers (Herman, Jean and Pol; *see* LIMBOURG, DE), continued these interests. At least one of them was well versed in a wide range of Italian sources, while another was able to capture vividly many aspects of courtly life, making much use of elaborate costumes and aspects of pageantry, a combination of talents that seems to have been much to the Duc's taste. Jean de Berry obtained the Limbourgs' services after the death of his brother Philip the Bold, Duke of Burgundy, their former patron. Their first work for Jean de Berry was a charter dated 1405 (untraced), followed by the Belles Heures (*c.* 1405–8; New York, Cloisters; *see* LIMBOURG, DE, fig. 3) and the Très Riches Heures (Chantilly, Mus. Condé, MS. 65), left unfinished in 1416. They also made additions to such earlier manuscripts as the Petites Heures. The calendar of the Très Riches Heures seems to have been particularly designed to appeal to the Duc. Some of its

The Limbourg brothers, *January*, 241×153 mm; miniature from the Très Riches Heures of Jean, Duc de Berry, *c.* 1411/13–16 (Chantilly, Musée Condé, Château de Chantilly, MS. 65, fol. 1*v*)

miniatures appear to record events connected with him or his family (see fig.), which are contrasted with scenes depicting life in the country. Many of the miniatures feature topographical portraits of Jean's châteaux, a clear indication that towards the end of his life the Duc favoured more naturalistic modes of representation. In the *Temptations of Christ* (fol. 161*v*; *see* MILITARY ARCHITECTURE AND FORTIFICATION, fig. 1), the kingdoms with which Satan tempts Christ are depicted as a landscape with the château of Mehun-sur-Yèvre in the foreground, thus flattering the Duc by implying that the château was the finest in the world.

Jean de Berry's relations with his artists seem to have been particularly enlightened for this period. Instead of treating them as ordinary craftsmen, he recognized their individuality and creativity by honouring them with special titles. Many artists became Valets de Chambre, beginning with Etienne Lannelier (*fl* 1369–91) who was 'painter to the duke' by 1369. In the case of some of his artists, such as André Beauneveu, Jean de Berry's relations with them were conducted along exceptionally friendly lines, anticipating aspects of 16th-century patronage. On New Year's Day 1411, for example, the Limbourgs gave their patron what appeared to be a finely bound book, complete with gilded silver clasps enamelled with the Duc's arms. The 'book' was only a block of wood, but it indicates that the brothers and Jean de Berry were on terms that made it possible for them to share a joke. The Duc presented valuable gifts to several of his artists. In 1402, for instance, he gave a diamond ring to Milet le Cavelier (*fl* 1414–16), who worked in stained glass. Pol de Limbourg was especially honoured, receiving many fine jewels and a house in Bourges, in which Guy de Dammartin had previously lived, said to be fit for a prince. Even artists' wives were treated in this fashion. In 1414–15 Jean gave a diamond to the wife of Michelet Saumon, who between 1401 and 1415 was one of his favourite painters. Another aspect of the Duc's patronage, which looked forward to later developments, was a sense that a collection of small but precious objects seen as a whole could make an aesthetic effect, like displays in museums. Although most of the items donated to the Sainte-Chapelle in Bourges had religious significance, there can be little doubt that part of the Duc's intention was for them to create a lasting impression of magnificence, which would help to safeguard his memory. Jean continued to collect such objects until the end of his life. Almost all the creditors in evidence after his death were purveyors of precious items or works of art.

BIBLIOGRAPHY

Chronique du religieux de Saint-Denys, contenant le règne de Charles VI, de 1380 à 1422, ed. M. L. Bellaguet, 6 vols (Paris, 1839–52)
J. Froissart: *Chronicles* (*c.* 1369–1400); Eng. trans. by J. Johnes (London, 1849)
A. Hiver de Beauvoir: 'Description . . . du trésor . . . donné par Jean duc de Berry, à la Sainte-Chapelle de Bourges', *Mém. Soc. Hist., Litt. & Sci. Cher*, i (1857), pp. 1–128; ii (1860), pp. 255–80
——: *La Librairie de Jean duc de Berry au château de Mehun-sur-Yèvre, 1416* (Paris, 1860)
A. de Champeaux: 'Les Relations du duc Jean de Berry avec l'art italien', *Gaz. B.-A.*, xxxviii (1888), pp. 409–15
A. de Champeaux and P. Gauchery: *Les Travaux d'art exécutés pour Jean de France, duc de Berry, avec une étude biographique sur les artistes employés par ce prince* (Paris, 1894)
J. Guiffrey: *Inventaires de Jean duc de Berry (1401–1416)*, 2 vols (Paris, 1894–6)
P. Durrieu: *Heures de Turin: Quarante-cinq Feuillets à peintures provenant des Très Belles Heures de Jean de France duc de Berry* (Paris, 1902)
——: 'La Bible du duc Jean de Berry conservée au Vatican', *Rev. A. Anc. & Mod.*, xxvii (1910), pp. 58–71
——: 'Les "Très Belles Heures de Notre-Dame" du duc Jean de Berry', *Rev. Archéol.*, xvi (1911), pp. 30–51, 246–79
——: 'Les Tableaux des collections du duc Jean de Berry', *Bib. Ecole Chartes*, lxxix (1918), pp. 265–90
P. Gauchery: 'Le Palais du duc Jean et la Sainte-Chapelle', *Mém. Soc. Antiqua. Cent.*, xxxix (1919–20), pp. 37–77
L. Labande-Mailfert: 'Le Palais de Justice de Poitiers', *Congr. Archéol. France* (1951), pp. 27–43
H. Bober: 'André Beauneveu and Mehun-sur Yèvre', *Speculum*, xxviii (1953), pp. 741–53
B. Gagnabin: 'Le Boccace du duc de Berry', *Genava*, v (1957), pp. 129–48
P. Pradel: 'Nouveaux documents sur le tombeau de Jean de Berry', *Mnmt Piot*, xlix (1957), pp. 141–57
B. Gagnabin: 'Le Tite Live du duc de Berry', *Genava*, vii (1959), pp. 193–214
L. M. Delaissé: 'Remaniements dans quelques manuscrits de Jean de Berry', *Gaz. B.-A.*, lxii (1963), pp. 123–46
F. Lehoux: *Jean de France, duc de Berri: Sa vie, son action politique, 1340–1416*, 2 vols (Paris, 1966–8)
M. Meiss: *French Painting in the Time of Jean de Berry: The Late Fourteenth Century and the Patronage of the Duke*, 2 vols (London, 1967, 2/1969)
P. Pradel: 'Les Sculptures du palais ducal de Bourges et du château de Mehun', *Humanisme actif: Mélanges d'art et de littérature offerts à Julien Cain* (Paris, 1968), pp. 359–63
J. Longnon, R. Cazelles and M. Meiss: *The Très Riches Heures of Jean Duke of Berry* (New York, 1969)
M. Thomas: *Les Grandes Heures of Jean Duke of Berry* (New York, 1971)
M. Meiss: *French Painting in the Time of Jean de Berry: The Limbourgs and their Contemporaries*, 2 vols (London, 1974)
M. Meiss and E. H. Beatson: *Les Belles Heures de Jean Duc de Berry* (London, 1974)
S. K. Scher: 'Notes sur les vitraux de la Sainte-Chapelle de Bourges' *Cah. Archéol. & Hist. Berry*, xxxv (1974), pp. 23–44
A. Erlande-Brandenburg: 'Jean de Cambrai, sculpteur de Jean de France duc de Berry', *Mnmt Piot*, lxiii (1980), pp. 143–86
St-J. Bourdin: *Analyses des Très Riches Heures du Duc de Berry: Identifications des personnages figurant dans le calendrier* (Paris, 1982)
Les Petites Heures du duc de Berry (Lucerne, 1988–) [facs. and commentary]

THOMAS TOLLEY

(4) Charles VI, King of France (*b* Paris, 3 Dec 1368; *reg* 1380–1422; *d* Paris, 21 Oct 1422). Son of (2) Charles V. Charles VI was crowned in Reims on 4 November 1380 before he was 12. He inherited the prodigious collections of his father. Early in his reign, his uncles, the regent Louis I, Duke of Anjou, (3) Jean, Duc de Berry, Philip the Bold, Duke of Burgundy, and Louis II, Duke of Bourbon, made the first inroads into this inheritance. Following his marriage in 1385 to (5) Isabeau of Bavaria, and a brief majority rule, Charles VI was afflicted from 1392 by attacks of madness. France was divided by civil war between the rival Armagnac and Burgundian parties, led by the King's brother (6) Louis, Duke of Orléans, and John the Fearless, Duke of Burgundy. By the end of Charles VI's reign, the Anglo-Burgundian government of Philip the Good, Duke of Burgundy, and Henry V, King of England, ruled Paris and northern France.

Losses from the royal collections throughout the reign of Charles VI resulted from the demands of the King's uncles and other acquisitive princes and courtiers, from the festivals of an intensely luxurious court and, above all, from the costs of war. The dismembering of the residue (goldsmiths' work, embroideries, tapestries and the books of the great Louvre library) took place after 1422, during the regency of John, Duke of Bedford (*see* LANCASTER,

(1)), for his nephew, Henry VI of England. This process can be followed in detail from the surviving inventories.

Charles was King of France at a time when Paris was unrivalled as a centre for the luxury trades. Given the King's precarious mental state, the element of personal patronage after 1392 remains questionable, but commissions for building works and for the minor arts flowed from the crown, especially during the years 1389–1405. The most important surviving building work from the reign is the Sainte-Chapelle at Vincennes. Begun in 1379 under Charles V, building continued under Charles VI to the archivolts of the windows and to below the level of the rose window in the west façade. The sculpture of the west portal and other elements of the decorative programme probably date from his reign. Besides financing royal building works, Charles made substantial donations (some recorded in stained glass), for projects including the rebuilding of the nave of Troyes Cathedral after 1389. The tomb of *Bertrand du Guesclin* (*d* 1380) at Saint-Denis Abbey (chapel of St Jean-Baptiste) was completed by Thomas Privé and Robert Loisel under Charles VI in 1397, and erected by Raymond du Temple, who had built the 'grand vis' at the Louvre. As master mason to Charles VI, Raymond undertook many of the King's works, including the temporary structures erected in 1389 for the jousts at Saint-Denis. The King's painters included JEAN D'ORLÉANS and Colard de Laon, his goldsmiths Jean du Vivier (*fl* 1359–1401) and Hermann Ruissel. The careers of many of the King's artists began in the reigns of John II and Charles V, and they also worked for the royal dukes.

Surviving goldsmiths' work includes the Goldenes Rössl (Altötting, SS Philipp & Jacob, Schatzkam.; *see* GOTHIC, fig. 95), given to the King by Isabeau of Bavaria for New Year 1404, and the chalice given by Charles to the monastery of St Catherine, Sinai, in 1411 (*in situ*). The reliquary (destr.) of the Holy Nail (Saint-Clou), commissioned by Charles for Saint-Denis Abbey in 1397, resembled the Goldenes Rössl in its creation of a *tableau vivant* in *ronde bosse* enamel, with a kneeling image of the King. In 1392 Charles commissioned a copper *entablement*, a sort of ciborium (destr.), for the newly completed gold image of *St Louis* ordered by his father, Charles V, from Jean du Vivier for Saint-Denis Abbey. It was finished in 1398 and is depicted behind the high altar in the *Mass of St Giles* (London, N.G.; for illustration *see* MASTERS, ANONYMOUS, AND MONOGRAMMISTS, §I: MASTER OF ST GILES).

None of the secular and liturgical textiles ordered for Charles VI is known to have survived, but documents emphasize the scale of expenditure on such embroideries as those ordered from Robert de Varennes: *pourpoints* (or coats) for the entry of Isabeau in 1389, a set of hangings sent to the church of the Holy Sepulchre, Jerusalem, in 1393, and a fantastically valuable jewelled set of vestments and chapel hangings made for the state visit to Paris of Manuel Palaiologos in 1400. High-weave tapestries, some ordered from Paris, included sets recording the great pageants of the reign: the jousts of Saint-Inglevert and Saint-Denis. Many textiles incorporated the King's motto, *Jamais*, his heraldic supporter, the *cerf volant*, and his devices, including broom-cods. These can be seen in such manuscripts as the *Réponses à Pierre Salmon*, written for

Charles in 1409, and known in two copies (Paris, Bib. N., MS. fr. 23279 and Geneva, Bib. Pub. & U., MS. fr. 165; *see* MASTERS, ANONYMOUS, AND MONOGRAMMISTS, §I: BOUCICAUT MASTER, fig. 2). A bacinet in the treasury of Chartres Cathedral and a *chapel* (helm) recovered in 69 fragments from the well of the donjon Philippe Auguste in the Louvre in 1985 are associated with them.

Apart from manuscripts, seals and the Goldenes Rössl, images of Charles VI include sculptures. Cardinal Jean de La Grange commissioned (*c.* 1375) a standing figure for the Beau Pilier (N.-W. buttress) of Amiens Cathedral and a kneeling alabaster figure (Avignon, Mus. Calvet) for his lost tomb ensemble (*c.* 1402) for St Martial, Avignon. Another figure is in place in the Palais de Justice, Poitiers. The effigy survives from the double tomb with Isabeau of Bavaria (*c.* 1425–9; Saint-Denis Abbey; fragments of lost ensemble, Paris, Louvre) by Pierre de Thoiry. François d'Orléans (son of the painter, Jean) modelled a death mask in wax (destr.), the first recorded in France.

BIBLIOGRAPHY
J. Labarte: *Inventaire du mobilier de Charles V, roi de France* (Paris, 1879)
J. Guiffrey: 'Inventaire des tapisseries du roi Charles VI vendues par les Anglais en 1422', *Bib. Ecole Chartes*, xlviii (Paris, 1887), pp. 59–110, 396–444
L. Delisle: *Recherches sur la librairie de Charles V*, 2 vols (Paris, 1907)
B. de Montesquiou-Fezensac and D. Gaborit-Chopin: *Le Trésor de Saint-Denis*, 3 vols (Paris, 1973–7)
Y. Grandeau: 'La Mort et les obsèques de Charles VI, *Bull. Philol. & Hist. Cté Trav. Hist. & Sci.* (1974), pp. 133–86
P. Henwood: 'Le Trésor royal sous le règne de Charles VI, 1380–1422: Etude sur les inventaires, les orfèvres parisiens et les principaux artistes du roi', *Ecole nationale des Chartes. Positions des thèses* (1978), pp. 91–8
——: 'Les Orfèvres parisiens pendant le règne de Charles VI (1380–1422)', *Bull. Archéol. Cté Trav. Hist. & Sci.*, n.s. 15 (1979), pp. 85–180
——: 'Administration et vie des collections d'orfèvrerie royales sous le règne de Charles VI, 1380–1422', *Bib. Ecole Chartes*, cxxxviii (1980), pp. 179–215
F. Autrand: *Charles VI: La Folie du roi* (Paris, 1986)
U. Heinrichs-Schreiber: 'La Sculpture de la Sainte-Chapelle de Vincennes et sa place dans l'art parisien à l'époque de Claus Sluter', *Actes des journées internationales Claus Sluter: Dijon, 1990*, pp. 97–114
J.-B. de Vaivre: 'Deux défenses de tête de Charles VI', *Bull. Mnmtl*, cxlix (1991), pp. 91–100
J. Stratford: *The Bedford Inventories: The Worldly Goods of John, Duke of Bedford, Regent of France, 1389–1435* (London, 1993)
JENNY STRATFORD

(5) Isabeau [Isabella] **of Bavaria**, Queen of France (*b* Munich, 1370–71; *d* Paris, 28 Sept 1435). Wife of (4) Charles VI. She was the daughter of Duke Stephen III Wittelsbach of Bavaria (*reg* 1347–75) and Tadea Visconti and married Charles VI in 1385. His long bouts of insanity (from 1392), led, however, to her being entrusted with political responsibilities. She facilitated the ambitions of her brother-in-law (6) Louis, Duke of Orléans, and after his assassination (1407) supported the Armagnac faction. Subsequently quarrelling with them and her son, the future (7) Charles VII, Isabeau sided with the Burgundians, recognizing King Henry V of England, consort of her daughter, as legitimate heir to the French throne (Treaty of Troyes, 1420).

While not an innovative patron, Isabeau presided over a court famous for its commissions. She amassed a large collection of jewels, pearls, precious stones, silverware and religious 'tableaux', stored from 1394 at the Bastille St Antoine in Paris. As was customary, Isabeau also made many lavish gifts, some produced by her goldsmith Jean du Vivier (*fl* 1378–1401), to pilgrimage sites and individuals. Her brother Ludwig the Bearded (1368–1447; *reg* as Duke Ludwig VII of Bavaria, 1395–1447), then courtier and chamberlain of the dauphin Louis, and notoriously greedy, was her frequent beneficiary. Isabeau gave him a *joyau* of *St Michael* (painted copy, Munich, Bayer. Nmus.) and he received in pawn several objects from the royal holdings, including the enamelled Goldenes Rössl shrine (Altötting, SS Philipp & Jakob, Schatzkam.; *see* GOTHIC, fig. 95), originally presented by Isabeau to Charles VI on New Year's Day 1404, another shrine with the royal couple kneeling (copy also Munich, Bayer. Nmus.), and manuscripts such as the *Miroir historial* (Paris, Bib. Arsenal, MS. 5080). In 1401 Isabeau was granted the Hôtel Barbette in Paris as her private residence. She owned land in Normandy and north of Paris where in 1397 she took possession of the Hôtel de la Chevalerie (Saint-Ouen), transforming it into a model farm named Hôtel des Bergeries. She also commissioned some structural works at the royal palaces in Paris and Saint-Germain-en-Laye.

In 1396–7 the painter Jean Malouel was in Isabeau's service and Colart de Laon painted for her figures on a reliquary chest, a panel with *SS Louis of France and Louis of Toulouse* and also restored a panel from Germany; in 1400 he produced tapestry cartoons for her (all untraced). Isabeau acquired several manuscripts, mostly Books of Hours, Breviaries and devotional texts, produced by Geoffroi Chose (*fl* 1397), Gervaisot de Dueil (*fl* 1402), Jean de Chastillon (*fl* 1396–9), Pierre Le Portier (*fl* 1397–1404) (including *Cents Ballades* in 1399 and the *Golden Legend* in 1400), Robin de Fontaines (*fl* 1398), Alain Sebèce (*fl* 1398), Jean de Jouy (*fl* 1399) and others; in 1403 the illuminator Haincelin de Hagenau (probably the Bedford Master) was working for her. In 1387 Isabeau gave Margaret, Duchess of Burgundy, a Book of Hours. In 1397–8 she borrowed a *Grandes chroniques de France* (probably Paris, Bib. Arsenal, MS. 5523) from Philip the Bold, Duke of Burgundy, returning it with new silver-gilt clasps and his enamelled arms. Around 1398 Isabeau presented her husband with an illuminated *Passion Nostre Seigneur* (untraced). Christine de Pisan offered the Queen her works and in exchange received gilt-silver cups. The frontispiece of a volume of Christine's poems (*c.* 1412–15; London, BL, Harley MS. 4431, fol. 2*r*; for illustration *see* CHRISTINE DE PISAN) by the Master of the Cité des Dames provides a realistic rendering of the Queen: she is shown wearing an elaborate headdress picked out with pearls, seated on a couch surrounded by her ladies-in-waiting. The most exact rendering extant of the Queen is the statue (one of four) by an unknown sculptor, commissioned by Jean, Duc de Berry, shortly before 1400 (Poitiers, Pal. Justice). The tomb (1425–9) at Saint-Denis Abbey that Isabeau commissioned for herself and Charles VI from Pierre de Thoiry (*fl* 1425–9) is conventional both in workmanship and conception.

BIBLIOGRAPHY

A. Vallet de Vireville: 'La Bibliothèque d'Isabeau de Bavière, reine de France', *Bull. Bibliogh. & Bibliothécaire* (1858), pp. 663–87

——: 'Isabeau de Bavière, reine de France', *Rev. Fr.*, xv (1858–9), pp. 41–53, 113–20, 233–41, 297–305

M. Thibault: *Isabeau de Bavière, reine de France: La Jeunesse, 1370–1405* (Paris, 1903)

M. Rey: *Les Finances royales sous Charles VI: Les Causes du déficit, 1388–1413* (Paris, 1965)

P. de Winter: 'Copistes, éditeurs et enlumineurs de la fin du XIVe siècle, la production à Paris de manuscrits à miniatures', *Actes du 100e congrès national des sociétés savantes: Paris 1975*, pp. 173–98

PATRICK M. DE WINTER

(6) Louis, Duke of Orléans (*b* Paris, 13 March 1372; *reg* 1392–1407; *d* Paris, 23 Nov 1407). Son of (2) Charles V. While his elder brother, (4) Charles VI, proved a weak monarch unable to limit the growing power of Philip the Bold, Duke of Burgundy, Louis proved an increasingly significant rival to the Duke, acquiring important territories between 1391 and 1402. After Philip's death in 1404, his son John the Fearless and Louis competed for power with growing hostility until 1407 when Louis was murdered in Paris by Burgundian partisans.

Profuse documentation reveals that Louis also rivalled Philip the Bold in expenditure on art and architecture. At many of the castles in his newly acquired lands, he undertook the building work necessary to establish a network of castles fit for habitation by both himself and his garrisons; he also spent very heavily on the building of the castles of Pierrefonds (begun after *c.* 1396) and La Ferté-Milon (begun *c.* 1399). At Paris, his most favoured place of residence, he acquired no less than seven hôtels. Among these, the Hôtel de Bohème (or de Behaigne; destr.), which was given to Louis by Charles VI in 1388, came to rival in splendour the nearby Palais du Louvre after undergoing major improvements (1394–5) under RAYMOND DU TEMPLE and Colart de Laon. Another residence in the Rue de la Poterne was scarcely less splendid, especially after improvements by Colart and others (1398–9).

Significant contributions to the splendour surrounding Louis were made by his extensive acquisitions, mainly by purchase, of the principal luxury goods of his time. Between 1389 and 1399 he spent large sums on acquiring fine tapestries from merchants in Paris and Arras, including NICOLAS BATAILLE, from whom he bought a huge and extremely expensive hanging of the *History of Theseus* (untraced). Besides abundant fine clothes, jewellery and plate, Louis also purchased, mainly from Parisian booksellers, illuminated manuscripts on which he subsequently spent even more on their adornment with costly textiles and metalwork. Surviving examples include Jean de Vignay's French translation of Vincent of Beauvais's *Speculum historiale* (1395–7; Paris, Bib. N., MSS fr. 312–14); Nicolas Oresme's French translation of Aristotle's *Ethics, Politics and Economics* (Chantilly, Mus. Condé, MS. 1327; Paris, Bib. N., MS. fr. 9106) purchased in 1397; Christine de Pisan's *Collected Works* (Paris, Bib. N., MSS fr. 606, 835–6); and Sallust's *Jugurtha and Catilina* (*c.* 1403–4; Paris, Bib. N., MSS lat. 5747 and 9684), produced for his sons' education. Louis also funded the continuation of work on the Bible of Jean de Sy, begun under his grandfather (1) John the Good in 1355 (fragment of the earlier part, Paris, Bib. N., MS. fr. 15397).

After the Bal des Ardents in January 1393, in which Charles VI was nearly burnt to death, Louis also became actively associated with the Celestine Order both in and outside Paris. By 1394, under the direction of Raymond du Temple, he had built the Orléans family chapel at the

Celestine church (both destr.) in Paris, for which in 1396–7 Colart de Laon was paid for painting the altarpiece (destr.). Louis also presented the Celestines of Paris with two Bibles (Paris, Bib. Arsenal, MSS 578–9 and 590; St Petersburg, Rus. N. Lib., MS. lat. F. v. I, 24), one of which had belonged to his father. Louis's will of 1403 instructed that his tomb in the chapel there should show him dressed as a Celestine monk. It also made provision for the erection of modest, but well endowed, chapels in each of the Celestine houses in France. The Benedictine abbey of Cluny also had a chapel founded by Louis, on which he spent a very large sum for glass in 1397. Images of the Duke are preserved in several illuminated manuscripts (e.g. Paris, Bib. N., MS. fr. 606, fol. l*r*, and London, BL, Harley MS. 4431, fol. 95*r*) and in a fragment from the tomb of *Cardinal Jean de La Grange* (*c*. 1402; Avignon, Mus. Calvet).

BIBLIOGRAPHY

A. Champollion-Figeac: *Louis et Charles, ducs d'Orléans: Leur influence sur les arts, la littérature et l'esprit de leur siècle* (Paris, 1844)
J. Roman: 'Inventaires et documents relatifs aux joyaux et tapisseries des princes d'Orléans-Valois', *Recl Anc. Inventaires*, i (1896), pp. 79–314
F. M. Graves: *Quelques pièces relatives à la vie de Louis I, duc d'Orléans, et Valentine Visconti sa femme*, Bibliothèque du XVe siècle, xix (Paris, 1906)
——: *Deux inventaires de la maison d'Orléans, 1389 et 1408*, Bibliothèque du XVe siècle, xxxi (Paris, 1926)
F. D. S. Darwin: *Louis d'Orléans, 1372–1407: A Necessary Prologue to the Tragedy of La Pucelle d'Orléans* (London, 1936), pp. 91–110
P. Pradel: 'Le Visage inconnu de Louis d'Orléans, frère de Charles VI', *Rev. A.*, ii (1952), pp. 93–8
C. Ribéra-Pervillé: 'Aspects du mécénat de Louis Ier d'Orléans (*d* 1407)', *Jeanne d'Arc. Colloque d'histoire médiévale: Orléans, 1979*, pp. 139–48
J. Mesqui and C. Ribéra-Pervillé: 'Les Châteaux de Louis d'Orléans et leurs architectes, 1391–1407', *Bull. Mnmtl*, cxxxviii (1980), pp. 293–345

SCOT MCKENDRICK

(7) Charles, Duke of Orléans (*b* Paris, 24 Nov 1391; *reg* 1407–65; *d* Amboise, 4 Jan 1465). Son of (6) Louis, Duke of Orléans. He gained prominence in the Armagnac–Orléans faction after the murder of his father by the Burgundians in 1407. He was a prisoner in England after the Battle of Agincourt (1415) until 1440, when he unsuccessfully pursued his claim to the Duchy of Milan. Charles retired to Blois where he ordered some construction work to the château. There his court attracted such poets as Gilles des Ourmes, François Villon (*fl* 1431–62) and René I, Duke of Anjou. Charles of Orléans is himself remembered as a prolix poet whose autobiographically inspired verses are replete with expressions of love and nostalgia. The original collection of his works, bearing revisions, survives (Paris, Bib. N., MS. fr. 25458). The Duke's library was one of the most diversified of its time in France; his ex-libris and notes documenting origin appear in many volumes. Illuminators documented in Charles's service are Yvonnet de la Motte (*fl* 1426), Jean Haincelin of Blois (*fl* 1445), Colinet de Marties (*fl* 1454), Jean Moreau (*fl* 1455) and Angelot de la Presse (*fl* 1464). In 1472 Jean Fouquet was commissioned to decorate a Book of Hours for the Duke's third wife, Mary of Cleves (1426–86). Charles and Mary are depicted in a miniature by a follower of the Bedford Master in the *Livre de la Passion* (Paris, Bib. N., MS. fr. 966). More conventional portrayals of Charles are found in other manuscripts (e.g. Paris, Bib. N., MS. lat. 1196). Charles's court painter was PIÈTRE ANDRÉ, his goldsmith, Jean Lessayer, and his tapestry maker, Jean Petit.

BIBLIOGRAPHY

P. Champion: *La Libraire de Charles d'Orléans*, 2 vols (Paris, 1910)
——: *Vie de Charles d'Orléans* (Paris, 1911)
G. Ouy: 'Recherches sur la librairie de Charles d'Orléans et Jean d'Angoulême', *Acad. Inscr. & B.-Lett.: C. R. Séances* (1955), pp. 273–88

(8) Charles VII, [Charles the Victorious], King of France (*b* Paris, 22 Feb 1403; *reg* 1422–61; *d* Mehun-sur-Yèvre, 22 July 1461). Son of (4) Charles VI and (5) Isabeau of Bavaria. First Comte de Ponthieu and Duc de Touraine, Charles became dauphin in 1417. At the Treaty of Troyes (1420), however, he was disinherited in favour of Henry V of England, through the latter's marriage with Charles's sister Catherine. On the death of Charles VI, only the Armagnac faction acknowledged Charles as king, but his fortunes changed in 1429 after Joan of Arc led him to be crowned at Reims. Charles VII was unprepared for a court life on a grand scale and his patronage also remained confined.

To underscore his dynastic rights, shortly after 1436 Charles VII had statues of his father and of himself (untraced) erected at the main portal of the Louvre in Paris; they were made by Philippe de Foncières (*fl* 1436–40) and Guillaume Jasse (*fl* 1438). A statue of *Charles VII* (untraced) was also placed at the royal residence, the Hôtel St Pol in Paris. The King ordered the completion of Jean, Duc de Berry's cenotaph in Bourges Cathedral, the tomb of his favourite, Agnès Sorel (*d* 1450), at St Ours, Loches (moved to the Logis du Roi in the 19th century) and works at his residences of Montil-les-Tours (Indre-et-Loire; destr.) and Mehun-sur-Yèvre (Cher; ruined). Henri d'Aubersque (*fl* 1423–9) was the initial Peintre du Roi in 1423; Hames Polvoir (*fl* 1420–36), on royal command, painted Joan of Arc's standards in 1429; Henri Mellein (*fl* 1431–40) was Charles's painter for a decade beginning in 1431, followed until 1459 by the more noteworthy Conrad de Vulcop. Conrad's brother, Henri de Vulcop, was painter to Charles's consort, Marie of Anjou (*d* 1463), for whom he produced a Book of Hours (1454–5; untraced). At Charles VII's death, his painter was Jacques de Litemont (*fl* 1453–69). Although JEAN FOUQUET held no court position, he painted an unflattering panel portrait of the King (*c*. 1450; Paris, Louvre), shown in half length and inscribed LE TRES VICTORIEUX ROY DE FRANCE. Another royal portrait (untraced), perhaps by a different painter, was in the royal chapel at St Martin, Tours. The portrait (Versailles, Château) representing Charles when younger and perhaps, as suggested by drawings made for Roger de Gaignières (see Reynaud, p. 16), part of a diptych with a picture of Marie of Anjou, is probably a copy of a lost original by Fouquet, possibly the example that Vasari states was copied by Bramantino for the Vatican.

Charles VII probably owned the sumptuous Breviary (Châteauroux, Bib. Mun., MS. 2) that contains illumination by the Bedford and Boucicaut Masters. Martial d'Auvergne's testimony in his *Vigilles de Charles VII* (1461) that the King 'aymoit les clercs, genz lettrez et science' is demonstrated by Nicolas l'Asteran's dedication to him of a history of Milan (Paris, Bib. N., MS. lat. 6166) and by translations made for his use of Frontinus's *Stratagems*

(Paris, Bib. N., MS. fr. 1233) and Leonardo Bruni's *History of the First Punic War* (Paris, Bib. N., MS. fr. 23085). Around 1458 Gilles Le Bouvier (*b c.* 1386; *fl* 1418–58) completed for the King his famed *Armorial* with xylographs (Paris, Bib. N., MS. fr. 4985); shortly afterwards a copy of the *Grandes chroniques de France* (Paris, Bib. N., MS. fr. 6465) with miniatures by Fouquet probably entered the royal collection. A number of goldsmiths are recorded in Charles VII's service, including Jean Lambert (*c.* 1427–91), who in 1454 made the silver chasse (destroyed) of St Martin, Tours. Jean Cochet was the King's embroiderer. In 1461, the sculptor Pierre de Hannes (*fl* 1461) and the painters Litemont and Colin d'Amiens brought to Paris Charles's death mask, which Fouquet had painted 'comme au vif' before the translation of the King's body to Saint-Denis Abbey.

BIBLIOGRAPHY

G. du Fresne de Beaucourt: *Histoire de Charles VII*, 6 vols (Paris, 1881–91)

M. Vale: *Charles VII* (Berkeley, 1974)

Jean Fouquet (exh. cat. by N. Reynaud, Paris, Louvre, 1981)

(9) Louis XI, King of France (*b* Bourges, 3 July 1423; *reg* 1461–83; *d* Plessis-lès-Tours, 30 Aug 1483). Son of (8) Charles VII. He married Margaret of Scotland (*d* 1445) in 1436 and Charlotte of Savoy (1445–83) in 1451. He was dubbed 'universal spider' for his tortuous politics, which led to the return of Anjou, Provence, Maine and Burgundy to the French crown. In 1462 he ordered the construction of the austere fortress of Langeais (Indre-et-Loire), and in 1474 the rebuilding of the château at Plessis-lès-Tours (Indre-et-Loire) in stone and brick, a building method that was to prove influential on subsequent Loire Valley architecture. Louis's artistic commissions were pragmatic, and portraiture was used as a tool of government. A medal cast by Francesco Laurana around the time of Louis's accession is an incisive depiction (diam. 85 mm; e.g. Paris, Bib. N., Cab. Médailles). JEAN FOUQUET, Louis's Peintre du Roi, produced the frontispiece of the statutes of the Order of St Michael (1469/70; Paris, Bib. N., MS. fr. 19819) depicting the King presiding over a meeting of knights of the Order; Fouquet also painted panels with arms for the same Order. Late copies of a profile portrait of *Louis XI* wearing the collar of his Order, best exemplified by a copy (New York, Brooklyn Mus.), are considered to be after an original by Fouquet, as is a drawing (Paris, Bib. N., MS. Clairambault 1242, p. 1411) depicting Louis a few years older. Roger de Gaignières's record of a full-length portrait (see Bouchot, p. 219) may relate to a commission from Jean Bourdichon, successor to Fouquet as Peintre du Roi (1481). In 1478–80 Bourdichon had already executed paintings in the château at Plessis-lès-Tours; these are mostly unspecified, but they included a large view of Caudebec in Normandy and 24 subjects with maidens and sailors on parchment (all untraced). In 1461 while in Brussels he settled a discord between the painter Rogier van der Weyden and his Milanese pupil Zanetto Bugatto, from whom he acquired, in 1468, portraits of *Francesco Sforza* and his wife.

Louis XI made numerous gifts to sanctuaries of the Virgin: a monstrance including a representation of himself to Notre-Dame-de-Hal; paintings by Jacques de Litemont (*fl* 1453–69) to St Jacques, Compiègne (Oise); and silver nefs to Notre-Dame, Cléry-Saint-André (Loiret), where, departing from royal tradition, he chose to be buried. Other offerings were made to St Martin, Tours: a large silver kneeling statue of the King, a silver reredos and stained glass—perhaps designed by Fouquet—depicting the King in the guise of the Merovingian king Clovis. For Saint-Michel-en-l'Herm (Vendée) the sculptor Michel Colombe executed a marble relief that included a depiction of Louis XI. None of these works is known to survive. Louis XI did not share the taste of some of his predecessors for aesthetic libraries. His Book of Hours (Fort Worth, TX, A. Haddaway priv. col.) had been illuminated by the workshop of the Guise Master and by a follower of the Limbourg brothers. But his consort Charlotte of Savoy was far more sensitive to the enchantment of the illuminated page and to panel paintings. Jean Colombe produced miniatures for her in the *Livre des douzes périlz d'enfer* (Paris, Bib. N., MS. fr. 449) and Guillaume Piquereau (*fl* 1480–3) of Tours illuminated a *Vita Christi* (Paris, Bib. N., MSS fr. 407–8). In 1483–4 Bourdichon painted for Charlotte miniatures of *St Gregory*, the *Pietà* and 19 'riches histoires' in a *Papaliste*, a manuscript of prophecies about the pope (untraced). At her death, Bourdichon was paid for the portrait (untraced) that hung above her tomb. Louis XI's cenotaph at Notre-Dame, Cléry, was the one monument of his reign for which there was considerable planning (from 1467). Fouquet drew two designs and supplied cartoons for stained-glass windows, while independently a model in stone was commissioned from Michel Colombe. The painter and illuminator Colin d'Amiens, recorded in the King's service in 1464, was instructed (Paris, Bib. N., MS. fr. 20493) to model a life-size 'statue' (destr. 1662) of the King, which was then cast in bronze by his gunner, Laurens Wrines of Tours and the goldsmith Conrad of Cologne.

BIBLIOGRAPHY

P. Grandmaison: *Procès-verbal du pillage par les Huguenots des reliques et joyaux de Saint-Martin de Tours en mai et juin 1562* (Tours, 1863)

A. Tuetey: 'Inventaires des biens de Charlotte de Savoie', *Bib. Ecole Chartes*, 6th ser., i (1865), pp. 338–66, 423–42

H. Bouchot: 'Les Portraits de Louis XI', *Gaz. B.-A.*, xxix (1903), pp. 213–27

P. Durrieu: 'Les Manuscripts des statuts de l'ordre de Saint-Michel', *Bull. Soc. Fr. Repr. MSS Peint.*, i (1911), pp. 19–57

P. Pradel: *Michel Colombe* (Paris, 1953)

Jean Fouquet (exh. cat. by N. Reynaud, Paris, Louvre, 1981)

PATRICK M. DE WINTER

(10) Charles, Duc de Berry [Charles de France; Charles of France] (*b* Montil-les-Tours, 28 Dec 1446; *d* Bordeaux, 24 May 1472). Son of (8) Charles VII and brother of (9) Louis XI. In 1461 he became Duc de Berry, which made him head of the League of the Public Weal. During the League's uprising against the King in 1465, Charles sided with the rebels and became Duke of Normandy. In the hope of succeeding his childless brother Louis XI to the French throne, he undertook not to marry Mary of Burgundy, the sole heiress of Charles the Bold, in return for the title Duc de Guyenne (1469). After the birth of Louis XI's son in 1470, however, Charles entered into new coalitions against the King. He was buried in the choir of Bordeaux Cathedral.

As Duc de Berry, Charles founded Bourges University (1463) and commissioned several manuscripts. A copy of

Dante's *Divine Comedy* (Paris, Bib. N., MS. ital. 72) contains miniatures by the MASTER OF COËTIVY (*see* MASTERS, ANONYMOUS, AND MONOGRAMMISTS, §I), who may be Henri de Vulcop, documented in Charles's service in Bourges from 1463. Charles also commissioned work to be continued on a richly illustrated Book of Hours, subsequently known as the Hours of Charles of France (Paris, Bib. Mazarine, MS. 473; New York, Cloisters, 58.71 a–b), which was only partially completed. The miniature of the *Betrayal of Christ* (MS. 473, fol. 13*v*) by Jean Fouquet bears Charles's arms as Duc de Berry and must have been painted first; the other arms in the book are his as Duke of Normandy (1465–9). The completed illumination of the later part of the book, which includes the two detached leaves in the Cloisters, dated 1465, are by a follower of Fouquet, the MASTER OF CHARLES OF FRANCE (*see* MASTERS, ANONYMOUS, AND MONOGRAMMISTS, §I), who is probably identifiable with Jean de Laval, an illuminator and painter recorded in Charles's service from 1463 to 1468. A portrait of Charles appears in another manuscript (Paris, Bib. N., MS. 19819).

DBF

BIBLIOGRAPHY

H. Stein: *Charles de France, frère de Louis XI* (Paris, 1919)
The Last Flowering: French Painting in Manuscripts, 1420–1530, from American Collections (exh. cat. by J. Plummer and G. Clark, New York, Pierpont Morgan Lib., 1982)

L. VAN MEERBEEK

(11) Charles VIII, King of France (*b* Amboise, 30 June 1470; *reg* 1483–98; *d* Amboise, 6 Dec 1498). Son of (9) Louis XI. Crowned on 30 August 1483, he soon showed his sensitivity to the value of the visual arts in the service of kingship. As early as 1485, he ordered and subsequently funded the restoration of one of the most significant buildings associated with the French monarchy, the Sainte-Chapelle in Paris. The most spectacular part of the work was a new rose window with stained glass depicting the *Apocalypse* attributable to the MASTER OF THE UNICORN HUNT (*see* MASTERS, ANONYMOUS, AND MONOGRAMMISTS, §I), the leading Parisian artist of the late 15th century. After his minority he put into effect a distinctive policy for aggrandizing his favourite residence at Amboise. After his marriage to (12) Anne of Brittany

in 1491 the old château proved inadequate for the court and plans for a new palace were ready by 1493. Raimond de Dezest was in charge of the works and Colin Biart was the master mason. The chronicler Philippe de Commines called Amboise 'the largest edifice begun by a king in over a hundred years' (see fig.). Charles was so keen to complete the structure that work on it was maintained day and night throughout the year, with large fires to provide heat and light during winter. The most impressive survival of Charles's work at Amboise is the chapel of St Hubert, originally part of the Queen's apartments and a fine example of Flamboyant Gothic architecture, with windows containing elaborate, flowing tracery. The lintel above the doorway, showing two scenes from the *Lives of SS Hubert and Christopher*, is the most impressive sculpture to survive and is probably the work of Netherlandish sculptors, including Casin d'Utrecht. Charles was also concerned with the decoration of the interiors. The principal painter responsible for the main rooms, Antoine Bryant, was surprisingly paid at a higher rate than the master mason. Tapestries were an even greater expense. As early as 1487 Charles purchased a series of eight south Netherlandish verdure tapestries and at Moulins around December 1490 he acquired a *Destruction of Jerusalem* in six pieces and a *History of Hercules* in seven pieces. The large tapestry known as the *Glorification of Charles VIII* (New York, Cloisters) includes an inscription that has been interpreted as the signature of the Brussels designer Jan van Róome. Not all of Charles's tapestries, however, were new: the *Trojan War* tapestries hung at Amboise in 1492–3, probably designed in France during the 1460s, were re-emblazoned with Charles's device of the sun for the reception of the Queen soon after their marriage. In 1494 230 tapestries were recorded at Amboise.

In 1494 Charles marched through Italy to renew an old French claim to the kingdom of Naples. Although the campaign ultimately failed, Charles's experience of Italy had a profound effect on his attitude to the arts. In Florence he saw Donatello's emotional *St Mary Magdalene* (Florence, Mus. Opera Duomo; *see* DONATELLO, fig. 5) and attempted to purchase it. The Florentines gave him instead a splendid manuscript of Petrarch's poems made

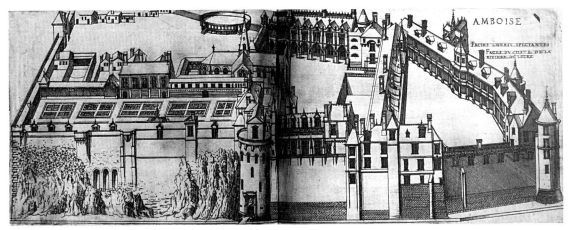

Château of Amboise, begun 1493, mostly destr. 19th century; illustration from Jacques Androuet Du Cerceau: *Les Plus Excellents Bastiments de France*, ii (Paris, 1576–9)

in 1476 for Lorenzo de' Medici and illuminated by Francesco di Antonio del Cherico. The chroniclers of the campaign record how in Rome the King was awestruck by ancient monuments such as Hadrian's tomb; but it was Naples that made the greatest impact. The King wrote to his brother-in-law:

> . . . you cannot believe what exquisite gardens there are in this city . . . I have also found here some skilful painters, and will send some of them to you; they will paint you the most beautiful ceilings. The ceilings of Beauce, Lyon, and other places in France do not compare in beauty and richness with the ones here, so I shall engage some of these artists, and take them to work at Amboise.

Among the Italians who were persuaded to work in France for Charles were the architect Fra Giovanni Giocondo from Verona, who later advised on the construction of the Pont Notre-Dame in Paris, and the garden designer Pacello da Mercogliano, who created at Amboise something of the effect of the gardens Charles had admired in Naples. Perhaps the most favoured artist to make the journey was the sculptor GUIDO MAZZONI, whose uncompromisingly emotional style seems to have particularly appealed to the King. In 1496 Mazzoni was knighted and allowed to display an heraldic device, perhaps the first time an artist had received such an honour in France; however, what he actually achieved at Amboise is uncertain.

Charles also arranged for huge quantities of booty to be sent from Naples to Amboise, including the bronze doors of the Castelnuovo and a stained-glass window from the church of the Annunziata. A document of December 1495 recorded the transport of 43 tons of works of art to France, including 130 tapestries, 172 carpets and 1140 volumes from the library of the Aragon kings of Naples, as well as marbles, paintings and furniture. On his way back to France, many of Charles's personal possessions were captured by Francesco Gonzaga at the Battle of Fornovara. The list of spoils indicates the kind of objects Charles chose to keep near him. Apart from a number of reliquaries, arms and other precious items, there was the portrait of his son *Charles-Orland* (Paris, Louvre) painted by the MASTER OF MOULINS (*see* MASTERS, ANONYMOUS, AND MONOGRAMMISTS, §I), a magnificent set of embroidered hangings (the subject of a letter written by Isabella d'Este) and a collection of drawings of women from different parts of Italy. Charles's practice of having portraits taken of pretty women is referred to in other correspondence of the period. One such portrait is also mentioned by Margaret of Navarre in the *Heptaméron* (1558), where the artist is named as JEAN PERRÉAL. JEAN BOURDICHON, who had worked for Charles's parents, was called Peintre en Titre to the King from 1484. Like Perréal, he painted portraits 'from life', including, in 1491, two of the King (untraced), one described as showing just a head and shoulders, the other full-length, an early example of this portrait type in France. Bourdichon was, however, principally required for painting banners and religious pictures. His workshop also illuminated one of Charles's many Books of Hours (Paris, Bib. N., MS. lat. 1370). Another splendid Book of Hours (Madrid, Bib. N., MS. Vit. 24-1) originally made for Charles was illuminated by an artist known as the Chief Associate of Master François, who also illuminated a number of other books for the King, both secular and devotional, including a *Vie abrégée de St Denis* (Paris, Bib. N., MS. fr. 5868). Indeed, Charles made a significant contribution to the royal library through commissions, gifts and acquisitions. His signature and devices may be found in a considerable number of illuminated manuscripts.

BIBLIOGRAPHY

A. de Montaiglon: 'Etat des gages des ouvriers italiens employés par Charles VIII', *Archvs A. Fr.*, i (1851–2), pp. 94–128

B. Fillon: 'Ouvriers italiens employés par Charles VIII', *Archvs A. Fr.*, i (1851–2), pp. 273–6

C. Grandmaison: 'Comptes du château d'Amboise de 1493', *Bull. Soc. Archéol. Touraine*, i (1873), pp. 253–304

E. Muntz: *La Renaissance en Italie et en France à l'époque de Charles VIII* (Paris, 1885)

A. Paz y Melia: 'El libro de horas de Carlo VIII de Francia', *Rev. Archvs, Bib. & Mus.* (1897), pp. 348–63

P. Pélecier, ed.: *Charles VIII, roi de France: Lettres*, 5 vols (Paris, 1898–1905)

P. Lesueur: 'Les Italiens à Amboise au début de la Renaissance', *Bull. Soc. Hist. A. Fr.* (1929), pp. 7–11

——: 'Fra Giocondo en France', *Bull. Soc. Hist. A. Fr.* (1931), pp. 115–45

——: *Le Château d'Amboise*, Petites monographies des grands édifices de la France (Paris, 1935)

J. Rorimer: 'The Glorification of Charles VIII', *Bull. Met.*, xii (1954), pp. 282–90

G. Souchal: 'Charles VIII et la tenture de la guerre de Troie', *Rev. Belge Archéol. & Hist. A.*, xxxix (1970), pp. 187–98

Y. Labande-Mailfert: *Charles VIII et son milieu, 1470–1498* (Paris, 1975)

R. Scheller: 'Imperial Themes in Art and Literature of the Early French Renaissance: The Period of Charles VIII', *Simiolus*, xii (1981–2), pp. 5–69

(12) Anne of Brittany, Queen of France (*b* Nantes, 25 Jan 1477; *d* Blois, 9 Jan 1514). Wife of (11) Charles VIII and (13) Louis XII. She succeeded her father, Francis II, Duke of Brittany (*d* 1488), and despite her youth attempted to maintain the traditional independence of Brittany from the kingdom of France. Although this ultimately failed after she was besieged at Rennes and then compelled to marry Charles VIII of France (6 Dec 1491), she continued to insist on the recognition of Brittany's separateness. By the terms of her first marriage contract, after the death of Charles VIII Anne was obliged to marry his successor Louis XII (8 Jan 1499). For the remainder of her life Anne occupied herself with the affairs of her duchy, which she still hoped would resist French domination. She was forced to consent to the betrothal (21 May 1506) of her daughter and heir, Claude, to Francis of Angoulême, who succeeded as (14) Francis I in 1515, thus finally paving the way for Brittany to become indisputably part of the realm of France.

It is not surprising that much of Anne's patronage helped to give expression to Breton independence. At Nantes, the capital of Brittany, she continued the ducal castle begun in 1466 by her father, building the upper part of the Grand Logis, with its five ornate dormer windows, and the Tour de la Couronne d'Or, which features twin loggias with some fine flamboyant decoration and carving. In 1499 Anne commissioned the tomb of her parents for the Carmelite church in Nantes (now in the cathedral). Finished in 1507, this was one of the most important monuments of the early Renaissance in France and remained a focal point for Breton feeling for centuries.

Designed by Jean Pérreal, Peintre du Roi, and executed in the workshop of Michel Colombe (*see* COLOMBE, (1)), the tomb is distinguished by its rich decorative programme and imaginative use of coloured marbles.

After her marriage to Charles VIII, Anne became a particular patron of the illuminator JEAN BOURDICHON, another artist in the King's service. His commissions from Anne included designs for Breton coinage, a portrait of her 'from life', as well as manuscript illumination. On 14 March 1508 the Queen ordered the staggering sum of 1050 livres tournois to be paid to Bourdichon for a large Book of Hours (Paris, Bib. N., MS. lat. 9474), 'richly and sumptuously illuminated and historiated'. In contrast to the *trompe l'oeil* borders, the style of the miniatures emphasizes devotional appeal at the expense of naturalism. Landscapes, for example, make much use of bright blue aerial perspective and figures tend to be softly modelled with sweet features, lacking individual characterization. Anne also possessed several other splendid Books of Hours, including the Très Petites Heures (*c.* 1492–8; Paris, Bib. N., MS. nouv. acq. lat. 3120) by the Master of the Unicorn Hunt, the leading artist in Paris in the late 15th century, and the Petites Heures of Anne of Brittany (*c.* 1499–1514; Paris, Bib. N., MS. nouv. acq. lat. 3027) by an illuminator active in Rouen, known as the Master of Petrarch's Triumphs. The Book of Hours she commissioned in 1497 from the illuminator JEAN POYET is unidentified, but it has been suggested that illumination in a prayerbook probably made for Anne in the 1490s (New York, Pierpont Morgan Lib., MS. M. 50) is Poyet's work. One of the miniatures (fol. 10*v*) shows *Anne at Confession*, an unusual portrayal which suitably expresses her enthusiasm for devotion. In the same miniature she wears a robe trimmed with ermine, symbolic of Brittany, and a girdle in the form of a knotted cord with tassel, a device of the Order of the *Cordelière*, which Anne founded for young women in honour of St Francis of Assisi, her father's patron saint. Heraldic ermine and knotted cords are abundantly used as decorative features in many works made for the Queen, for example her little oratory at Loches.

In 1492 Jean de Cormont, a painter living in Paris, was paid for a large picture of the Virgin for use in the Queen's chapel. Several such pictures are listed in inventories of the Queen's possessions between 1492 and 1507, which also itemize extensive collections of jewels, reliquaries and tapestries. One painting not mentioned is the portrait which she probably commissioned in 1494 from the Master of Moulins of her son *Charles-Orland* (Paris, Louvre), which was dispatched to Charles VIII in Italy. Anne also paid for stained-glass windows at the convent of the Minim Friars at Chaillot (destr.), considered incomparable examples of work in this medium. After about 1499 Anne collected Italian panel paintings, favouring devotional works with idealized styles. An inventory of 1498–9 mentions a painting that has been identified with the *St Jerome* (Caen, Mus. B.-A.) attributable to Perugino. Another inventory (1500) lists 27 Italian paintings, mostly portraits of Milanese origin, probably taken as booty after Louis XII captured Milan in 1499. One of these was inscribed with the word *Genevra*, which has led to speculation that it may have been Leonardo da Vinci's portrait of *Ginevra de' Benci* (Washington, DC, N.G.A.). Correspondence from 1509–10 shows that Anne was negotiating to obtain a work by Lorenzo Costa, perhaps identifiable as the *Holy Family* (Toledo, OH., Mus. A.). There is some evidence that Anne also developed an interest in Italian humanism. Some representations depict her with the attributes of the goddess Juno. One of the last works associated with her is the gold reliquary in the shape of a heart (Nantes, Mus. Dobrée) with inscriptions in red and green enamel, which was made to contain her own heart and which she desired should be deposited with the remains of her parents in Brittany.

BIBLIOGRAPHY

A. Le Roux de Lincy: *Vie de la reine Anne de Bretagne, femme des rois de France Charles VIII et Louis XII: Suivie de lettres inédites et documents originaux*, 4 vols (Paris, 1861)

P. Arnauldet: 'Tapisseries du château de Blois aux XVe et XVIe siècles', *Bull. Soc. N. Antiqua. France* (1905), pp. 346–52

H. Omont: *Heures d'Anne de Bretagne* (Paris, 1907)

C. Couderc: 'Les Miniatures du voyage de Gênes', *Trésors Bibs France*, vi (1927), pp. 39–55

R. Grand: 'Anne de Bretagne et le premier humanisme de la Renaissance en France', *Mém. Soc. Hist. & Archéol. Bretagne*, xxix (1949), pp. 44–70

Anne de Bretagne en son temps (exh. cat., Nantes, Mus. Dobrée, 1961)

J. Babelon: 'Monnaies et médailles d'Anne de Bretagne', *Congrès national des sociétés savantes: Rennes, 1966*, pp. 383–7

P. Quarré: 'Les Pleurants du tombeau de François II duc de Bretagne', *Congrès national des sociétés savantes: Nantes, 1972*, pp. 275–85

J. Adhémar: 'Une galerie des italiens à Amboise en 1500', *Gaz. B.-A.*, lxxxvi (1975), pp. 99–104

J. Biejon de Lavergnée: 'L'Emblématique d'Anne de Bretagne d'après les manuscrits à peintures (XVe–XVIe siècles)', *Mém. Soc. Hist. & Archéol. Bretagne*, lv (1978), pp. 83–95

M. Jones: 'Les Manuscrits d'Anne de Bretagne', *Mém. Soc. Hist. Archéol. Bretagne*, lv (1978), pp. 43–81

C. Brown: 'Una immagine de Nostra Donna: Lorenzo Costa's Holy Family for Anne of Brittany', *Cultura figurativa ferrarese tra XVe e XVIe secolo: Arte e grafica*, i (Ferrara, 1981), pp. 53–73

A.-C. Dere: 'Anne de Bretagne et son château de Nantes', *Bull. Soc. Archéol. & Hist. Nantes & Loire-Atlantique*, cxix (1983), pp. 55–77

(13) Louis XII [le Père du Peuple], King of France (*b* Blois, 27 June 1462; *reg* 1498–1515; *d* Paris, 1 Jan 1515). Son of (7) Charles, Duke of Orléans. Like his father, Louis was a great bibliophile, with a taste for finely decorated books. One of his first acts as King was to add the royal library from Amboise to that of his ancestors in their château at BLOIS, which after considerable work (1498–1508) became the King's favourite residence. In an illuminated copy of Xenophon (Paris, Bib. N., MS. fr. 7140), made *c.* 1503 for presentation to Louis, the translator Claude de Seyssel described the library at Blois as especially magnificent. The King took every opportunity to augment it. In 1504 Gilles Hannequin bound 126 volumes, mostly works by Classical authors, for Louis; those that survive are elaborately decorated with Louis's devices and mottoes. Perhaps the most spectacular manuscript made for the King is a French translation of Petrarch's *Trionfi* (Paris, Bib. N., MS. fr. 594), with several large allegorical miniatures by an artist active in Rouen, the Master of Petrarch's Triumphs. Louis's passion for books is best illustrated by his acquisition of two major libraries. The first, assembled in the 1470s and 1480s by Louis de Gruuthuse, Lord of Bruges, was an outstanding collection of books illuminated by artists of the Ghent–Bruges school. Some of the volumes were partly redecorated for Louis. For example, one of Louis's principal painters, Jean Perréal, added a fine miniature showing the King kneeling in prayer to a copy of Ptolemy's *Cosmographia* (Paris, Bib. N., MS. lat. 4804). In 1499 Louis overran Lombardy, claiming the title of Duke of Milan as part of his inheritance, and acquired the splendid ducal library. The King sent back to Blois several Lombard panel paintings, listed in an inventory of the Queen's possessions drawn up in 1500. One of these was signed by the Milanese painter Ambrogio da Predis.

Louis's patronage was considerably affected by his experience of art in Italy, but he rarely commissioned works totally at the expense of French traditions. Although the tomb he ordered in 1502 for the Dukes of Orléans (ex-church of the Celestines, Paris; Saint-Denis Abbey), was made by four Italian sculptors, it features recumbent effigies and appears to be based on a French design. In architecture, Louis's taste seldom departed from French Flamboyant: intricate, flowing forms may be seen, for example, on the work he sponsored on the south façade at Senlis Cathedral and also at Blois. Many of the structures he built, however, such as the exterior staircase (destr.) at the Sainte-Chapelle in Paris and the loggia with classical pilasters in the courtyard at Blois, suggest Italian sources although they are Gothic in detail. The encouragement Louis gave to developing Paris as a suitable capital also attracted Italians of international standing to the city. The sculptor GUIDO MAZZONI, who made the tomb of Louis's predecessor (destr.), was treated with particular honour. Described in several documents between 1507 and 1515 as 'the King's painter', Mazzoni lived at Louis's expense in the Hôtel de Nesle, Paris. Another Italian pensioned by Louis was the architect Fra Giovanni Giocondo of Verona who advised on the reconstruction of the Pont Notre-Dame in Paris. Both Italians seem to have been employed at Blois. Fra Giocondo's hydraulic works for the gardens were even known to Leonardo da Vinci. Louis's relationship with Leonardo represents one of the most uncertain aspects of his patronage. His admiration for Leonardo's *Last Supper* (Milan, S Maria della Grazie), which he saw in 1499, is known from early sources. By 1506 Leonardo is referred to by the King as 'our dear and good friend' and 'our painter and good friend in ordinary', and drew a regular salary while resident in Italy. Louis certainly requested paintings from Leonardo, though none can be identified with certainty. The cartoon of the *Virgin and Child with St Anne* (the Burlington House Cartoon; London, N.G.) has been connected with a royal commission, but the evidence for this is inconclusive. Jean Bourdichon, best known as an illuminator, was, like Perréal, Valet de Chambre to the King. In 1511 he was paid for making the King an image of St Michael.

BIBLIOGRAPHY

H. de Tschudi: 'Le Tombeau des ducs d'Orléans à Saint-Denis', *Gaz. Archéol.*, x (1885), pp. 93–8
R. Maulde La Clavière: *Histoire de Louis XII*, 4 vols (Paris, 1889–93)
P. Arnauldet: 'Tapisseries du château de Blois aux XVe et XVIe siècles', *Bull. Soc. N. Antiqua. France*, (1905), pp. 346–52
H. Omont: 'Répertoire de la librairie royale de Blois rédigé en 1518', *Anciens inventaires et catalogues de la Bibliothèque nationale* (Paris, 1908), pp. 1–154
G. Ritter and J. Lafond: *Manuscrits à peintures de l'école de Rouen* (Rouen, 1913)
M. Cermenati: 'Le Roi qui voulait importer en France la Cène de Léonard de Vinci', *Léonard de Vinci, 1519–1919*, ed. M. Mignon (Rome, 1919), pp. 8–26
M. Melot: 'Politique et architecture, essai sur Blois et le Blésois sous Louis XII', *Gaz. B.-A.*, lii (1967), pp. 317–28
F. Lesueur: *Le Château de Blois* (Paris, 1970)
J. Wasserman: 'The Dating and Patronage of Leonardo's Burlington House Cartoon', *A. Bull.*, liii (1971), pp. 312–24
M. Sherman: 'Pomp and Circumstance: Pageantry, Politics and Propaganda during the Reign of Louis XII', *16th C. J.*, ix/4 (1978), pp. 13–33
J. Snow-Smith: *The Salvator Mundi of Leonardo da Vinci* (Seattle, 1982), pp. 11–25
R. Scheller: 'Ensigns of Authority: French Royal Symbolism in the Age of Louis XII', *Simiolus*, xiii (1983), pp. 75–141
——: 'Gallia cisalpina: Louis XII and Italy, 1499–1508', *Simiolus*, xv (1985), pp. 5–60
B. Quilliet: *Louis XII père du peuple* (Paris, 1986)

THOMAS TOLLEY

(14) Francis [François] **I**, King of France (*b* Cognac, 12 Sept 1494; *reg* 1515–47; *d* Fontainebleau, 31 March 1547). Great-great grandson of (2) Charles V. He was the son of Charles d'Angoulême. Louis XII, who had no sons, made him Duke of Valois and his heir: he ascended the throne at the age of 18. His early reign was dominated by continuing war with Italy, which Charles VIII had begun in 1494. Francis's dynastic claim to the Duchy of Milan led to a military campaign in northern Italy and victory at Marignano (1515); however, his attempt to reclaim Milan after the expulsion of the French in 1522 resulted in disastrous defeat at Pavia (1525) and a two-year imprisonment in Spain. In the later part of his reign (after 1527) Francis centralized royal power in the Ile-de-France and created a personal absolutism that was thereafter to mark the French monarchy. He also gave increased attention to artistic patronage, especially in his preferred residence, the château of Fontainebleau (*see* §1 below). Known even in his own time as 'father of the arts', he used patronage as a means of achieving power and fame and making his court a focal point of culture that would equal those of Italy and (after 1519) that of his personal rival, the Emperor Charles V. The administrative structure of Francis's patronage was flexible by contrast with that of later French monarchs, such as Louis XIV, and remained under his personal control, with privileged artists being appointed Peintre du Roi or Architecte du Roi. His accomplishment as patron extended to all areas of culture, including literature and learning.

Because Francis was convinced of the supremacy of the taste and art of Italy, his patronage of the arts and letters bore an unmistakably Italian stamp. In his *Autobiography*, Benvenuto Cellini (whom Francis brought to his court in 1540) represents the King as boasting of his knowledge of Italian art: 'I well remember having inspected all the best works, and by the greatest masters of all Italy'. Francis was the first French king who could make such a claim. The Italian bias had stemmed from (11) Charles VIII and (13) Louis XII, who had hired Italian artisans to work at the French court after their Italian campaigns had brought them into close contact with Italian art. But it was only with Francis, a connoisseur who imported major Italian artists and art works to France on a grand scale, that a fundamental change came about in the direction of French art and culture.

1. Architecture. 2. Painting, sculpture and other arts.

1. ARCHITECTURE. While Francis also patronized painting and sculpture at Fontainebleau, he was primarily a patron of architecture—one 'marvellously addicted to buildings', as the architect Jacques Androuet Du Cerceau the elder characterized him. The most visible evidence of this passion is in his great châteaux, which mark the change in French architecture from the country house to the palace, and from late medieval to Renaissance style (see Printz and Kecks). In the first decade of his rule he focused on châteaux in the Loire valley: he had additions made at Amboise, but his first great monument was at the château of BLOIS, to which he added the structure known as the Francis I Wing (1515–24), with an exterior spiral staircase and a façade of tiered loggias. The château of CHAMBORD (designed in 1518–19; completed after 1550) has a more Italianate character and monumentality, with a central plan and a roof adorned with motifs borrowed from the vocabulary of the Italian Renaissance. Francis's architectural patronage shifted about 1528 to the Ile-de-France, where (besides Fontainebleau, see below) he commissioned a group of related designs. These included the château in the Bois de Boulogne later called Madrid (begun 1528; destr.), the original design of which is documented by Du Cerceau's engraving of 1579, and the château of SAINT-GERMAIN-EN-LAYE (1539–49; much altered). The precise authorship of Francis's châteaux is unknown, but all were the result of cooperation between local French and imported Italian architects and artisans.

After 1528, Fontainebleau (see FONTAINEBLEAU, §1) was the focus of Francis I's architectural patronage, as well as the site of its dramatic expansion to include painted and sculptured decoration (documented in the *Comptes des Bâtiments du Roi*, i). The original medieval hunting lodge consisted of a loosely circular cluster of buildings around the Cour de Donjon, with a Trinitarian abbey to the west. The Parisian architect and mason GILLES LE BRETON was in charge of the work, which first concentrated around the Cour de Donjon, with the Porte Dorée (completed 1535) as a new ceremonial entrance to the château and a gallery 60 m in length built to connect the old structures with the abbey. A second phase of the rebuilding of the château began after the King's marriage in 1530 to Eleanor, daughter of Philip I of Spain, and the death (1531) of his mother Louise of Savoy. In the Cour de Donjon, Le Breton built the Chapelle St Saturnin (completed 1545) and a grand exterior stairway (destr.) in a newly classicizing style; he also made additions to the gallery wing that permitted the construction of the King's Appartement des Bains on the ground floor. About 1535 activity shifted beyond the gallery wing to the lower court (later the Cour de Cheval Blanc), which had been begun earlier: at the north end of the east wing was the Pavillon des Armes (since rebuilt), where the King's armour and ancient statues were stored, while at the south end was the Pavillon des Poêles (destr.). The central block of the façade and its definitive conception belong to the 1550s. The Galerie d'Ulysse was built on the second floor of the south wing (1537–40), of which the only surviving part is the Grotte du Jardin des Pins (1543), attributed to Francesco Primaticcio. During this last phase of Francis's

building activities at Fontainebleau, a new wave of Italian influence transformed the hybrid architectural style of the King's earlier reign to a classicism based on Italian High Renaissance models. This was largely due to the presence at the court (from 1541) of SEBASTIANO SERLIO, who dedicated to the King Book III (Venice, 1540) and Books I and II (Paris, 1545) of his treatise on architecture. Francis placed him in charge of building operations as Architecte du Roi, but his role at Fontainebleau was rather that of adviser, his influence being exerted mainly through his treatise and unexecuted projects.

Francis's efforts as patron of extensive decorative ensembles were concentrated at Fontainebleau (see 1972 exh. cat.). The château became the chief artistic monument of his reign and the locus of works in Italian Mannerist style that were to be a catalyst for French Renaissance art: in choosing for them Italian artists and largely mythological subjects, his taste was ever more directed towards Italy, at a time when his personal ties with Florence were being strengthened by the marriage of his son, the future (15) Henry II, to (16) Catherine de' Medici (1533). To carry out an ever-expanding decorative programme, Italian artists were imported, chief among them being ROSSO FIORENTINO and Primaticcio, who arrived respectively in 1530 and 1532. These artists transformed the rooms and galleries in the château with a novel kind of decoration, consisting of painting combined with high-relief stucco ornament. The most important decorative ensemble commissioned by Francis, and the only one that survives in approximately its original condition, is Rosso's Galerie François I (1533–40). Its complex iconographical programme, which combines mythology, history and religious elements, is full of enigmas, but it is essentially a panegyric to Francis and his rule. Of this scheme, Primaticcio's fireplace in the Chambre de la Reine (1534–7), with stuccos framing a *Venus and Adonis*, and his frescoes of *Stories of Hercules* on the Porte Dorée (1535) alone survive. The other decorations (destr.) included the *History of Psyche* in the Chambre du Roi (1533–5), the *Stories of Vertumnus* in the Pavillon de Pomone (c. 1535; in collaboration with Rosso) and, in the Appartement des Bains, frescoes of the *Loves of Jupiter and Callisto* combined with stuccos framing paintings from the King's collection (1534–40).

In the last phase of Francis's patronage at Fontainebleau, Primaticcio, following Rosso's death in 1540, was his chief decorator in fresco and stucco in the Chambre de la Duchesse d'Etampes, where he painted frescoes of the *History of Alexander* with large, framing nude caryatids (1541–4) and *Stories of the Olympian Gods* (1541–4) in the vestibule of the Porte Dorée. His other works, no longer extant, included an extensive cycle of the *History of Ulysse* in the Galerie d'Ulysse (1541–7, completed under Henry II); the *Cardinal Virtues and Heroes* and other works in the Cabinet du Roi (1541–5); *Juno, Venus, Minerva* and *Mars* in the Galerie Basse (1538–40); and tondi of *Juno* and *Minerva* in the vault of the Grotte du Jardin des Pins (1541–3). Contemporaneously, Cellini undertook architectural sculpture for this gateway, of which only the *Nymph of Fontainebleau* (1543; Paris, Louvre) was completed. The only major building that Francis commissioned in his later years was the Palais du Louvre, the transformation of which from a medieval fortress he initiated. Serlio made a design for it; however, the commission was ultimately given in 1546 to Pierre Lescot, whose west façade of the Cour Carrée (1548–56) was erected after Francis's death (*see also* PARIS, §V, 6(ii)).

2. PAINTING, SCULPTURE AND OTHER ARTS. Descriptions of Fontainebleau from the 17th century, ranging from John Evelyn's restrained appraisal ('a sumptuous palace of the King's, like ours at Hampton Court') to the account by Père Pierre Dan (1594/5–1649) of a 'trésor des merveilles' were based on the château's architecture and decoration, but they also took note of the King's magnificent art collection. Francis was the first French monarch to bring together a significant collection of major art works beyond the tapestries, *objets d'art*, manuscripts and books that he and his predecessors routinely commissioned. He owned some Flemish pictures, mainly drawn and painted portraits by Jean Clouet and François Clouet, who often portrayed him (e.g. François Clouet's *Francis I on Horseback*; see fig.); however, he concentrated, as in his other patronage, on Italian art. He did not assemble his collection systematically, but depended somewhat haphazardly on a variety of Italian sources. Among these were Florentine merchants, who combined art dealing with other business in France, and diplomatic donors—from the Venetian state, the Este rulers of Ferrara, the Gonzagas of Mantua, the Medici popes Leo X and Clement VII, and Cosimo I de' Medici. Other sources were artists, such as Leonardo da Vinci, Andrea del Sarto, Rosso Fiorentino and Cellini; and art agents, such as Giambattista della Palla and Pietro Aretino, who sought the King's

favour with gifts of works of art. The latter commissioned from Titian a portrait of *Francis I* (*see* PORTRAITURE, fig. 13).

Francis's collection was not a gallery of paintings in the modern sense, and there were no official inventories of it. In imitation of the combination of baths and paintings in antiquity, he integrated his pictures into an overall decoration in elaborate stucco frames in his Appartement des Bains. The humidity of the baths was doubtless responsible for the loss of many paintings, the titles of which are known from 17th-century descriptions of the collection. Under Henry IV the surviving paintings were moved to the Cabinet des Peintures in the château; in the later 17th century they formed the basis of the royal collections at Versailles, ultimately becoming the nucleus of the Italian paintings collection at the Musée du Louvre, Paris. Among the most important paintings there that Francis had owned are Leonardo's *Virgin of the Rocks* and '*Mona Lisa*' (*see* DRESS, fig. 22); Fra Bartolommeo's *Noli me tangere*; Andrea del Sarto's *Charity* and *Holy Family with Angels*; Raphael's *Self-portrait with a Friend*, *Madonna with St John* (*La Belle Jardinière*), *Holy Family* and *St Michael Fighting the Devil*; Giulio Romano's *St Margaret* and *Giovanna d'Aragon*; Sebastiano del Piombo's *Visitation*; and Giovanni Girolamo Savoldo's *Self-portrait with Mirrors*. He may also have owned an important work by Bronzino, the *Allegory of Venus, Cupid, Folly and Time* (*c.* 1544–5; London, N.G.; *see* BRONZINO, fig. 2). Francis's collection included Italian sculpture such as Michelangelo's colossal *Hercules* and Cellini's silver *Jupiter*, but these and many other works are untraced. The only evidence of this once luxurious part of the collection are a marble sculpture, Niccolò Tribolo's *Goddess of Nature* (Fontainebleau, Château), and two *objets d'art*, Cellini's salt (Vienna, Ksthist. Mus.; *see* CELLINI, BENVENUTO, fig. 4) and Valerio Belli's casket, with scenes from the *Life of Christ* (Florence, Pitti). Francis also had casts made from famous antiquities from the Cortile del Belvedere of the Vatican, by Primaticcio in 1540; the bronzes made from these (Fontainebleau, Château) were displayed in the gardens of the château and influenced the turn to classicism in French art. After Francis's death, reports reached Italy of his glorious patronage at Fontainebleau, which Giorgio Vasari declared to be 'a kind of new Rome'.

BIBLIOGRAPHY
P. Dan: *Fontainebleau: Le Trésor des merveilles de la maison royale* (Paris, 1642/*R* 1990)
L. de Laborde: *Les Comptes des Bâtiments du Roi (1528–71): Suivis de documents inédits sur les châteaux royaux et les beaux-arts au XVIe siècle*, 2 vols (Paris, 1877–80)
F. Herbet: *Le Château de Fontainebleau* (Paris, 1937)
J. Adhémar: 'The Collection of Paintings of Francis I', *Gaz. B.-A.*, n. s. 5, xxx (1946), pp. 5–16
——: 'Aretino: Artistic Adviser to Francis I', *J. Warb. & Court. Inst.*, xvii (1954), pp. 311–18
La Collection de François Ier (exh. cat. by J. Cox-Rearick, Paris, Louvre, 1972)
L'Ecole de Fontainebleau (exh. cat., Paris, Grand Pal., 1972)
Rev. A., xvi–xvii (1972) [issue dedicated to 'La Galerie François Ier au château de Fontainebleau']
S. Favier: 'Les Collections de marbres antiques sous François Ier', *Rev. A.*, xxiv (1974), pp. 153–6
S. Pressouyre: 'Remarques sur le devenir d'un château royal: Fontainebleau au XVIe siècle', *Inf. Hist. A.*, xix (1974), pp. 25–37
K. Wilson Chevalier: *Le Trésor des merveilles de Pierre Dan: Une étude critique* (diss., U. Paris IV, 1980)

Francis I on Horseback by François Clouet (Florence, Galleria degli Uffizi)

W. Prinz and R. G. Kecks: *Das französische Schloss der Renaissance: Form und Bedeutung der Architectur, ihre geschichtlichen und gesellschaftlichen Grundlagen* (Berlin, 1985)

C. Scailliérez: *François Ier et ses artistes dans les collections du Louvre* (Paris, 1992)

C. Elam: 'Art in the Service of Liberty: Battizta della Palla, Art Agent for Francis I', Tatti Stud., v (1993), pp. 33–109

J. Cox-Rearick: 'Sacred to Profane: Diplomatic Gifts of the Medici to Francis I', *J. Med. & Ren. Stud.*, xxiv (1994), pp. 239–58

R. J. Knecht: *Renaissance Warrior and Patron: The Reign of Francis I* (Cambridge, 1994)

J. Cox-Rearick: *The Collection of Francis I: Royal Treasures* (New York, 1995)

JANET COX-REARICK

(15) Henry [Henri] **II**, King of France (*b* Saint-Germain-en-Laye, 31 March 1519; *reg* 1547–59; *d* Paris, 10 July 1559). Son of (14) Francis I. Undeservedly overshadowed by the reputation of his father, Henry carried on his father's artistic undertakings, but also launched new ones and seems to have had a more sophisticated taste. In 1548 he put PHILIBERT DE L'ORME in charge of the Bâtiments du Roi, his authority extending to the château of Anet (Eure-et-Loire) belonging to the royal mistress DIANE DE POITIERS. De L'Orme brought a new and more developed classical style to the various royal works in progress, for example at the château of Fontainebleau, where he completed the Salle de Bal with a coffered ceiling. The new and more severe taste, which seems to have been Henry's own, is even more apparent in such new works as Anet (1547–55), the tomb of *Francis I* at Saint-Denis Abbey (begun 1547; *in situ*), the château of Saint-Léger-en-Yvelines (1547–57; destr.), the Château Neuf at Saint-Germain-en-Laye (begun 1553; destr.; for illustration *see* SAINT-GERMAIN-EN-LAYE) and the centrally planned chapels at the châteaux of Villers-Cotterêts, near Soissons (1552; destr.) and Saint-Germain (1555; destr.), all designed by de L'Orme. At the Palais du Louvre, Henry left Francis I's architect PIERRE LESCOT in charge, but he had him modify his design by the creation of the Pavillon du Roi, at the south-west corner, which resulted in a more monumental handling of the façades (*see* PARIS, §V, 6(ii)). If the appellation 'le style Henri II' has become synonymous with this phase of French Renaissance architecture, the influence of Henry's personal taste can also be felt in two spheres of the decorative arts, where his commissions resulted in works of exceptional quality: bookbinding, in which coloured so-called *cuirs* ornaments in the style of the School of Fontainebleau were adopted (numerous examples Paris, Bib. N.), and arms and armour, where works of unequalled refinement with historiated decoration in low relief, derived from designs by Etienne Delaune, were produced for the King (examples Paris, Louvre; New York, Met.; Windsor Castle, Royal Col.). In 1533 he married (16) Catherine de' Medici. He died as a result of a wound received at a tournament.

BIBLIOGRAPHY

B. Thomas: 'Die Münchner Harnischvorzeichnungen', *Jb. Ksthist. Samml. Wien*, lvi (1960), pp. 7–62; lviii (1962), pp. 101-65; lxi (1965), pp. 41-90

I. Cloulas: *Henri II* (Paris, 1985)

(16) Catherine de' Medici, Queen of France (*b* Florence, 13 April 1519; *reg* 1559–74; *d* Blois, 5 Jan 1589). Wife of (15) Henry II. She was the daughter of Lorenzo de' Medici, Duke of Urbino (*reg* 1512–19), and Madeleine de La Tour d'Auvergne. Without influence during the reign of her husband, she ruled France from his death in 1559 until the first years of her son Henry III's reign, continuing to spend lavishly on her properties and collections in emulation of her father-in-law (14) Francis I, whom she greatly admired. In 1547 she acquired the château of Montceaux-en-Brie (Seine-et-Marne), and in 1560 she compelled her husband's mistress Diane de Poitiers to surrender the château of Chenonceau (Indre-et-Loire) to her. In 1563 she acquired the château of Saint-Maur-Les-Fossés (destr.), near Charenton, and began to assemble the lands at the gates of Paris that were to constitute her estate of the Tuileries. In 1570 she bought another property in Paris in the parish of St Eustache.

Her favoured architect was at first PHILIBERT DE L'ORME, who added a pavilion with a grotto (destr.) to Montceaux in 1557. At the death of Henry II, however, she replaced de L'Orme with FRANCESCO PRIMATICCIO as head of the Bâtiments du Roi, and he built the Aile de la Belle Cheminée (1568; *see* FONTAINEBLEAU, fig. 1) at the château of Fontainebleau and designed the circular, domed Chapelle des Valois (before 1570; not completed, destr.) at Saint-Denis Abbey as a funerary chapel for the royal family. She continued to employ de L'Orme, however: from 1563 he added pavilions at the unfinished Saint-Maur, and in 1564 she asked him to design her villa in the Tuileries (destr.). After his death in 1570 she turned to his former associate JEAN BULLANT (1572–92), to continue work at the Tuileries, the Maison de St Eustache, and the Chapelle des Valois (1572–8), and to complete her Paris town house near St Eustache (of which only the astonishing observatory in the form of a colossal Doric column survives). Bullant also enlarged Saint-Maur to a new design (1575–9), altered the façade of Chenonceau, constructed the famous gallery supported on arches over the River Cher (1576–7) and designed an immense trapezoid forecourt (not built). Catherine was probably also responsible for the construction at the Palais du Louvre, Paris, of the flat-roofed Basse Galerie (1566), the forerunner of the Petite Galerie designed to connect the Louvre with the Tuileries.

Catherine's major sculptural commissions were given to Germain Pilon, who executed for her the monument for the heart of Henry II for the church of the Celestines in Paris (marble, 1561–65; Paris, Louvre), the bronze figures (1562–70) for Henry's tomb designed by Primaticcio at Saint-Denis (*see* SAINT-DENIS ABBEY, fig. 8), as well as the *Risen Christ* (marble, begun 1572; Paris, Louvre) and the *Virgin of Sorrows* (marble, begun 1586; Paris, St Paul–St Louis; *see* PARIS, fig. 16) intended for the Chapelle des Valois. She also had numerous pictures and had a particular liking for portraits, of which she owned 341. Her favoured artists were the Italians employed at Fontainebleau, Nicolò dell'Abate and Rugiero de Ruggieri (*d* 1596), as well as the French Dumonstier family and Antoine Caron. The inventory drawn up after Catherine's death reveals the extent of her collections, which included, among other objects, a library of 4500 volumes, 259 painted enamels, including 32 portraits set into the panelling of a room, 141 pieces of ceramics by Bernard Palissy (who had also created a rustic grotto (destr.) for the Jardins des Tuileries), tapestries, antiquities and all kinds of precious objects. Among surviving objects from her collection are a triptych of painted enamel representing her in her oratory (Ecouen, Mus. Ren.), an emerald pendant (Paris, Bib. N., Cab. Médailles) by the goldsmith François Dujardin (*fl* mid-16th century) and the enamelled gold covers for her Book of Hours (Paris, Bib. N.) and a set of elaborately worked crystal vases (Florence, Pitti).

BIBLIOGRAPHY

E. Bonaffé: *Inventaire des meubles de la reine Catherine de Médicis en 1589* (Paris, 1974)
I. Cloulas: *Catherine de Médicis* (Paris, 1979)

BERTRAND JESTAZ

(17) Henry [Henri] **III**, King of France [Duc d'Anjou] (*b* 19 Sept 1551; *reg* 1574–89; *d* Saint-Cloud, 2 Aug 1589). Son of (15) Henry II and (16) Catherine de' Medici. He was the elected King of Poland from 1573–4 and in 1574 succeeded his brother Charles IX (*reg* 1560–74) to the French throne. His contribution to the cultural life of France in the 16th century has been eclipsed by the condemnation he received as a ruler. As Duc d'Anjou he received a humanist education at the court of Henry II and took an active interest in both theatre and music. In July 1574, he was in Venice where he was welcomed with a lavish fête comprising a triumphal arch and loggia designed by Andrea Palladio and painted by Jacopo Tintoretto, Paolo Veronese and Antonio Vassillacchi. He purchased a gem-encrusted sceptre at the Fugger bank on the Fondaco de' Tedeschi and three paintings from Tintoretto. One was possibly a portrait of Henry, of which a painting in the Doge's Palace, Venice, may be a copy. He returned to France and was crowned at Rheims on 13 February 1575.

During his reign Henry III instigated a number of large-scale architectural projects. Several fine residences outside Paris were built or remodelled for his 'mignons' (favoured courtiers), including the Château de Tournanfy (begun 1581), now the Château de Graville (Seine-et-Marne), the Château de Grange-le-Roi (begun after 1579), Grisy-Suisnes (Seine-et-Marne) and the château of Liancourt (*c.* 1581). The chief designer is identified as Baptiste Androuet Du Cerceau, architect to the King. In Paris Henry instigated the building of the Pont Neuf (begun 1577), work in the Palais du Louvre, including the Grande Gallerie (1578) and a chapel (begun 1580), and, from 1578, the continuation of the Chapelle des Valois in Saint-Denis Abbey. Towards the end of his reign he employed at court the painters Pierre Dumonstier the elder and Benjamin Foulon (*c.* 1550–1612). Henry's unpopularity led to his assassination by Jacques Clément, a Dominican monk. The King's likeness is preserved in François Clouet's portrait drawing (1571; Paris, Bib. N., Cab. Est.) and a portrait panel (*c.* 1573–4; Chantilly, Mus. Condé), and two portrait drawings (*c.* 1573 and *c.* 1580; both Paris, Bib. N., Cab. Est.) attributed to Jean Decourt (*c.* 1530–after 1585). Germain Pilon and Claude de Héry (*c.* 1525–82) produced portrait medals of the King (e.g. London, BM; Paris, Bib. N.).

BIBLIOGRAPHY

F. Yates: *The French Academies of the Sixteenth Century* (London, 1947)
N. Ivanoff: 'Henri III à Venise', *Gaz. B.-A.*, lxxx (1972), pp. 313–30
W. Wolters: 'Le architetture erette al Lido per l'ingresso di Enrico III a Venezia nel 1574', *Boll. Cent. Int. Stud. Archit. Andrea Palladio*, xxi (1979), pp. 273–89
J. Boucher: *La Cour de Henri III* (Rennes, 1986)
D. Thomson: 'Baptiste Androuet du Cerceau: Architecte de la cour de Henri III', *Bull. Mnmtl*, cxlviii (1990), pp. 47–81

Valori, Baccio [Bartolomeo] (*b* Florence, 1477; *d* Florence, 20 Aug 1537). Italian politician and patron. From a noble Florentine family, he was the son of Filippo Valori, a rector of the university of Pisa and a friend of Angelo Poliziano and Marsilio Ficino. Baccio Valori was active in political affairs, in opposition to the government of Piero Soderini, and later served as a councillor to Cardinal Silvio Passerini (1470–1529), who was regent in Florence under Cardinal Ippolito de' Medici and Alessandro de' Medici. He then went to Rome, where Clement VII appointed him as his general commissioner. He supported the surrender to the Medici of the army of the Florentine republic in 1530 and achieved his greatest political power as a councillor during the reign of Alessandro de' Medici as Duke of Florence. After the assassination of the Duke, he allied himself with other Florentine exiles against the rise to power of Cosimo I de' Medici. Their forces were defeated in the battle of Montemurlo in 1537, and he was imprisoned and condemned to death by Cosimo. He is depicted as a prisoner in a fresco in the Sala di Cosimo in the Palazzo Vecchio in Florence.

Valori had contacts with some of the most important artists of his time. According to Vasari, in 1530–31 he commissioned from Michelangelo a marble figure of Apollo taking an arrow from his quiver. This work (Florence, Bargello) later entered the collection of Cosimo I, probably at the time of Valori's execution. Valori's frequent contacts with Michelangelo are confirmed by their correspondence. In a letter of 1532 he asked the artist for some drawings for his house and referred to a work thought to be the *Apollo*: 'I do not wish to solicit you further about my statue, because I am quite certain, because of the affection I know you have for me, that there is no need to ask about it.' The *Apollo* was probably in Valori's house in Florence, in Borgo degli Albizi, which was later described, with the works of art it contained, by Borghini. In Rome, Valori knew Benvenuto Cellini, who mentions him in his autobiography, and patronized Sebastiano del Piombo, who painted an intense portrait of him on slate (Florence, Pitti). According to Vasari, he was also painted by Giuliano Bugiardini, with Clement VII.

BIBLIOGRAPHY

G. Vasari: *Vite* (1550, rev. 2/1568); ed. G. Milanesi (1878–85), v, p. 576; vi, p. 206; viii, p. 190
R. Borghini: *Il Riposo* (Florence, 1584); ed. M. Rosci (Milan, 1967), i, pp. 587–8, 621–2
P. Barocchi and R. Ristori, eds: *Il carteggio di Michelangelo* (Florence, 1973), iii, pp. 301, 329, 331–2, 335, 344, 348, 364, 386; iv, p. 394
C. de Tolnay: *Michelangelo, Sculptor, Painter, Architect* (Princeton, 1975), pp. 201–2
Palazzo Vecchio: Committenza e collezionismo medicei (exh. cat., Florence, Pal. Vecchio, 1980), p. 265, n. 495
M. Hirst: *Sebastiano del Piombo* (Oxford, 1981), pp. 103, 110–11, 113

DONATELLA PEGAZZANO

Valori plastici. Italian magazine edited by the critic and painter Mario Broglio (1891–1948), published in 15 issues in Rome between 1918 and 1921 in both Italian and French editions. Following its first issue, dated 15 November 1918, it was published monthly until September 1920 and then bi-monthly; the final issue, dated September–October 1921, was distributed in 1922. It also served as a publishing house and as a focal point for a loose association of artists who exhibited together in Berlin, Dresden and Hannover in 1921 and in Florence in 1922. Broglio's closest collaborators were his wife, the Lithuanian painter Edita Walterowna zur Muehlen (1886–1977), Roberto Melli, Alberto Savinio, Giorgio de Chirico and Carlo Carrà.

There were many affinities between *Valori plastici* and other journals concerned with the creation of a language based on solid 'classical' foundations in opposition to the rapid succession of styles that characterized the avant-garde. There were particularly close parallels with literary journals such as *La Ronda* in Italy and with art magazines such as *L'Esprit nouveau* in France and *De Stijl* in the Netherlands, but *Valori plastici* was far less homogeneous in its approach, providing a platform for lively polemics and disputes among its collaborators. Its strongest and most positive element, however, was provided by de Chirico, Carrà and Savinio, all of whom were involved at that moment with the creation of PITTURA METAFISICA as a way of escaping the banality of naturalistic mimicry by embracing the mystery of everyday objects. Their position attracted artists already linked with the magazine, such as Giorgio Morandi and Arturo Martini, and went on to exercise a vast influence in Italy and elsewhere in Europe.

Valori plastici's other important contribution lay in its new way of understanding tradition. While Futurism and the avant-garde in general had given the impression of wanting to burn the bridges linking contemporary art with the past, *Valori plastici* proposed to use antique art as a powerful vehicle for the new. The complexity of tradition in this sense was well reflected in the variety of the magazine's related publishing activities: a series of monographs on the Old Masters, from Byzantine painting to Giotto, from Piero della Francesca to Titian; a series devoted to heterodox traditions, looking towards African, Chinese and Mexican art; and lastly a series on modern art from the 19th century to the latest developments in Cubism and Expressionism. In their art as well as in their writings the artists associated with *Valori plastici* showed a tremendous freedom in their interpretation of the past. The renewed passion for geometry and craft led them all back to the Italian Quattrocento and other historical sources, but each in his own way and without imitating academic models: de Chirico preferred the nervous style of Signorelli and Hans Holbein II, Carrà looked back to Giotto, Martini explored the Etruscan world, and Morandi in his still-lifes evoked Ingres.

Gino Severini, Jean Cocteau, André Breton, Louis Aragon, Theo van Doesburg and Vasily Kandinsky were among the notable contributors to *Valori plastici* during its brief existence. They were among the many artists and writers who became associated with the magazine and its return to classicism, sometimes referred to as a 'rappel à l'ordre' in Cocteau's words, after having participated in the evolution of various avant-garde movements.

BIBLIOGRAPHY
M. Carrà: *Gli anni del ritorno all'ordine* (Milan, 1967)
M. Fagiolo dell'Arco: *Giorgio de Chirico: Il tempo di 'Valori plastici', 1918/1922* (Rome, 1980)
P. Fossati: *Valori plastici, 1918–22* (Turin, 1981)
VALERIO RIVOSECCHI

Valory [Valori], **Louis-Guy-Henri**, Marquis de (*b* Menin [now Menen], 11 Nov 1692; *d* Oct 1774). Flemish soldier and diplomat. After a distinguished military and diplomatic career which took him to the court of Frederick the Great at Berlin, where he met Voltaire and had his portrait (untraced) painted by Antoine Pesne, he was elected to the Académie Royale de Peinture et de Sculpture on 30 September 1747 as an *associé libre*, the category reserved for distinguished amateurs. In September 1765 he was made an *amateur honoraire*, an even greater mark of distinction for an art lover. He gave a number of lectures at the Académie, including one on 6 February 1762 on the life of his friend Jean-François de Troy who, according to Pierre-Jean Mariette, had taught Valory to draw and paint. On 8 January 1763 he had addressed the question 'whether it is more advantageous to an artist to live in retreat or to mingle in the world'. On 7 January 1764 he lectured on the life of the sculptor René Frémin, whom he admitted never having known.

BIBLIOGRAPHY
F. Peukert: *Die Memoiren des Marquis von Valory, deren Form, Verfasser, und Abfassungszeit, Tendenzen und Quellewerth* (Berlin, 1883)
THIERRY BAJOU

Valparaíso. Chilean city with a population of *c.* 280,000, on the coast *c.* 100 km west of Santiago, for which it served as a port for centuries. The city's shore and hillside areas are connected by tortuous streets and by several funicular railways installed between 1883 and 1914. First reconnoitred by the Spaniard Juan de Saavedra in 1536, Valparaíso was founded in 1544, and it remained a tiny settlement until the commercial expansion of the 19th century. The population rose from *c.* 5000 in 1800 to 100,000 in 1875, and the port assumed a notably cosmopolitan character with the arrival of numerous foreign merchants. The British, in particular, imprinted a characteristic tone on the business district and on the hillside suburb of Cerro Alegre, where English-style villas proliferated (although few survive). A more traditional Chilean atmosphere prevailed in the Almendral district north along the coast. Urban improvements such as street-paving were initiated in the 1850s. Public buildings constructed during these years include the modestly handsome Intendencia (*c.* 1855), the church of La Matriz (1842), the Casa de la Aduana (1855) and a series of plain but imposing public warehouses. Much rebuilding was needed after the savage bombardment of the city by a Spanish naval squadron in March 1866, but Francisco Echaurren, the city's Intendant from 1870 to 1876, sponsored further improvements.

In August 1906 Valparaíso was almost completely devastated by the worst in a long series of earthquakes, and *c.* 4000 people died. A further economic setback occurred in 1914 with the opening of the Panama Canal, which ended Valparaíso's dominance as a port. From the 1960s its traditional role was also challenged by the new container-port at San Antonio, 110 km to the south. The steady growth of Viña del Mar, the smart and fashionable ocean resort adjoining Valparaíso to the north, lessened the port's attractiveness as a place of residence for the wealthier classes. By the early 1990s Viña del Mar's population was approaching Valparaíso's, and the two cities effectively formed a single conurbation (although Valparaíso retains a more 'popular' and raffish character than its affluent neighbour). In 1990, on a whim of the outgoing dictator Augusto Pinochet (*b* 1915), Valparaíso was made the seat of the National Congress, for which the most extravagant public building in the city's history was hurriedly erected in the Almendral district (1991). It is perhaps best described as half neo-Babylonian, half Post-modernist. The Museo Municipal de Bellas Artes in the Art Nouveau Palacio Baburizza, Cerro Alegre district, houses a collection of Chilean paintings.

BIBLIOGRAPHY

E. Pereira Salas: *La arquitectura chilena en el siglo XIX* (Santiago, n.d.)

SIMON COLLIER

Valpuesta, Pedro de (*b* Burgos de Osma, Soria, 1614; *d* Madrid, 1688). Spanish painter. Like many other Spanish Baroque painters, Valpuesta was also a priest. He was active in both capacities in Madrid during the second third of the 17th century. He was a disciple of the Madrid painter Eugenio Cajés (*see* CAJÉS, (2)) and followed his style closely. Palomino mentioned numerous paintings by Valpuesta in various churches in Madrid. These have not been identified for lack of signatures and only three works are known. *St Ignatius of Loyola*, signed and dated 1658, belongs to the Hospital de Antezana in Alcalá de Henares. It is a conventional, frontal portrait representing the saint full-length in a stiff and inexpressive pose. The effect of perspective developed in the background architecture is the most striking feature of the work. Four episodes from the life of the saint are represented in small-scale pictures on the side panels of the painting. The other two known works by Valpuesta are *Philip V Swearing to Defend the Immaculate Conception* (*c*. 1661; Madrid, Mus. Mun.) and the *Virgin Presenting the Rule to the Founder of the Convento de la Latina* (Madrid, Convento de la Latina).

BIBLIOGRAPHY

A. A. Palomino de Castro y Velasco: *Museo pictórico* (1715–24/*R* 1947), pp. 954–5
D. Angulo Iñiguez and A. E. Pérez Sánchez: *Pintura madrileña del segundo tercio del siglo XVII* (Madrid, 1983), pp. 355–60
A. E. Pérez Sánchez: *Pintura barroca en España (1600–1750)* (Madrid, 1992), pp. 97–9

ENRIQUE VALDIVIESO

Valsamakis, Nikos [Nicos] (*b* Athens, 1925). Greek architect. He studied at the School of Architecture, National Technical University of Athens (1945–7; 1950–53). His early buildings, all in Athens, such as the simple block of flats (1951) at Semitelou 5, formalized the prototypes of urban residential and office buildings in post-war Greece. These buildings are cage-like structures of exposed concrete, similar to those of Giuseppe Terragni, placed on recessed, darker bases comprising the ground floor and mezzanine. The use of colour and natural materials was equally bold for the time. A similar approach is evident in the office building (1958) at Ermou and Plateia Kapnikareas 9, Athens; its curtain wall was the first one to be executed in Athens and is considered the most elegant in Greece. In contrast to his solemn and prismatic urban structures, his early private residences, such as his own house (1961) in Philothei, Athens, are among the most daring introductions of Modernism to Greek architecture: they are technically advanced constructions with deep recesses under or between dramatic cantilevers, extensive glazed surfaces and fluid, free-plan spaces around isolated columns and linear partition walls of heavy masonry, all elements being regulated by strict grids. The Amalia Hotel (1963) at Delphi and the White Rocks Hotel (1967–70) at Argostolion, Kefallinia, marked an important transition towards an additive process of prismatic cellular units, later manifested most clearly in the Amalia Hotel (1977) at Olympia. The stripped-down neo-classical complex of the Hotel Amalia (1980) at Navplion is an example of his later tendency to exhibit more explicitly historicist and vernacular elements and concepts of organization.

WRITINGS

'Hotel Amalia, Nauplion, Peloponnesus', *Archit. Des.*, lvii/5–6 (1987), pp. 20–22

BIBLIOGRAPHY

D. Porphyrios: 'Modern Architecture in Greece, 1950–1975', *Des. Greece*, x (1979), pp. 14–33
E. Constantopoulos, ed.: *Nicos Valsamakis, 1950–83* (London, 1984)

ALEXANDER KOUTAMANIS

Valtat, Louis (*b* Dieppe, 8 Aug 1869; *d* ?Paris, 2 Jan 1952). French painter, printmaker and stage designer. He spent much of his youth in Versailles, moving in 1887 to Paris, where he studied under Gustave Moreau at the Ecole des Beaux-Arts and under Jules Dupré at the Académie Julian. There he met Maurice Denis, Pierre Bonnard, Edouard Vuillard and Albert André. With a keen interest in both artistic precedents and contemporary trends, he absorbed in the mid-1890s the chief tenets of Impressionism, van Gogh's work and Pointillism before slowly developing his own style. In 1895 he collaborated with Henri de Toulouse-Lautrec and André on the set of Aurélien-François Lugné-Poë's play *Chariot de terre cuite*, performed at the Théâtre de l'Oeuvre, Paris. Under Toulouse-Lautrec's influence, his own works darkened both in colour and sentiment, for example *Chez Maxim's* (1895; Geneva, Petit Pal.), in which he depicted two gaunt, severe-looking women seated in a murky café. By 1896 he painted contemporary French life with an overall sunnier, more optimistic air, as in *Water Carriers at Arcachon* (1897; Geneva, Petit Pal.), in which he referred to van Gogh, also looking to Fauvism for his use of bold colours.

From 1899 to 1914 Valtat divided much of his time between Paris and a house he built in Anthéor, near le Lavandou, but early on he also travelled and considerably broadened his contacts with other artists. In 1894 or early 1895 he spent time with Aristide Maillol in Banyuls and Collioure, at the point when Maillol abandoned a career in textiles for sculpture. In 1895 he went to Spain with Georges-Daniel de Monfreid and through him learnt more about Paul Gauguin's work. He visited Auguste Renoir several times between 1900 and 1905 at Magagnosc, near Grasse. Their portraits of each other included a wood-engraving of *Renoir* (1904–5; Bagnols-sur-Cèze, Mus.), and they collaborated on a sculpted bust of *Cézanne* (bronze, 1905; Aix-en-Provence, Bib. Méjanes). A work that reveals Renoir's stylistic influence is *Bathers* (1905; Geneva, Petit Pal.). In 1902 in Venice Valtat translated his direct observations of southern light into a striking group of broadly painted works. He visited Signac at St Tropez in 1903 and 1904 and recorded North African street life in *Algiers* (1906; Paris, Dr Jean Valtat priv. col., see Cogniat, p. 61), an oil sketch in which flickering paint strokes of intense colour convey the crowd movement rather than solidity of forms. He also explored Normandy in 1907.

As early as 1893 Valtat exhibited at the Salon des Indépendants, La Libre Esthétique in Brussels in 1900, and the Salon d'Automne in 1903. Among the reproductions in Louis Vauxcelle's review of the Salon d'Automne of 1905 (*L'Illustration*, 4 Nov 1905, p. 295), in which the term 'Fauve' was first used, was a loosely brushed marine scene by Valtat (untraced). Valtat, however, always remained detached and on the fringe of the Fauvist circle. His palette then was bright, but the distortions of colour and line were never as bold nor as masterful as those achieved by Henri Matisse.

Valtat's career suffered from a lack of aggressive marketing by Ambroise Vollard, his dealer from 1900 to 1912, and from a decline in his own creativity. He made prints, of which the wood-engravings are the most interesting, for example *Seated Woman with Two Cats on her Lap* (see J. Bailly-Herzberg: *Dictionnaire de l'estampe en France, 1830–1950* (Paris, 1985), p. 325), but apart from a show in February 1896 at the Galerie Vivienne, Paris, they went relatively unnoticed during his lifetime. After 1914 he divided his time between Paris and regions near Rouen and Versailles. His interest turned to scenes of contemporary French life, flowers, sea and landscape. In many instances he experimented with colours and shapes as abstract intertwining patterns. In his flower paintings, for instance, the flowers are almost overwhelmed by the strong patterns or intense colours of the backgrounds. In 1948 he went blind from glaucoma.

BIBLIOGRAPHY

Louis Valtat (exh. cat., Dieppe, Château-Mus., 1959)
Paintings by Louis Valtat (exh. cat., New York, Acquavella Gals, 1962)
R. Cogniat: *Louis Valtat* (Neuchâtel, 1963)
Valtat et ses amis Albert André, Charles Camoin, Henri Manguin, Jean Puy (exh. cat., Besançon, Mus. B.-A. & Archéol., 1964)
Louis Valtat: Rétrospective centenaire (1869–1969) (exh. cat., Geneva, Petit Pal., 1969)
J. Valtat: *Louis Valtat, catalogue de l'oeuvre peint, 1869–1952* (Neuchâtel, 1977)

LYNN BOYER FERRILLO

Valters, Jānis Teodors [Valter, Ivan (Fyodorovich); Walter-Kurau, Johann] (*b* Mitava [now Jelgava], 3 Feb 1869; *d* Berlin, 19 Dec 1932). Latvian painter. He took painting and drawing lessons at the Mitava Gymnasium, where his teachers included the portrait and history painter Julius Döring (1818–98), then he studied at the St Petersburg Academy of Arts (1889–97) under Aleksey Kivshenko (1851–95) and Vladimir Makovsky. During his St Petersburg years he joined and later became chairman of the first Latvian group of artists, THE GNOME (Rūķis). After graduating from the Academy and briefly travelling through western Europe he established his own studioschool in Mitava (1898–1905). There his students included Ģederts Eliass (1887–1975) and Sigismunds Vidbergs

(1890–1970), important members of the next generation of Latvian artists, as well as the Lithuanian Petras Kalpokas. Active as both a participant in and organizer of exhibitions (in Russia, Latvia and Germany) during this period, Valters's own work consists mainly of Impressionist landscapes (*Rippling Water, c.* 1898), figure scenes (*Peasant Girl* and *Boys Bathing*, both 1900) and portraits (*Woman in Yellow*, n.d.; all Riga, Latv. Mus. F.A.). Having expressed his primary concern with colour and light in such works, he then adopted a more decorative approach to composition, as in *Landscape with Four Trees* (n.d.) and *Forest* (*c.* 1904; both Riga, Latv. Mus. F.A.), later a defining characteristic of his work, before he left Latvia in 1906 to live permanently in Germany. There, his painting, as if in accordance with his new work as a violinist in the Dresden Opera Orchestra, gained a heightened sense of musicality. Thus such canvases of his German period as *Violinist* (1914) and *Trees* (1925; both Riga, Latv. Mus. F.A.) are marked by rhythmic stylizations of forms, emphatic lines and bright colours, while also being derivative of both *Jugendstil* and the Expressionism of Die Brücke, Franz Marc and Vasily Kandinsky.

BIBLIOGRAPHY

A. Lapiņš and E. Eglītis: *Jānis Valters* (Riga, 1958)
M. Ivanovs and K. Sūniņš: *Jānis Valters* (Riga, 1978)
E. Sierer: *Objektive Wertgruppierung: Kunstmonographische Übersicht über das Werk des Walter-Kurau* (Berlin, n.d.)
J. Siliņš: *Latvijas māksla, 1800–1914* [Latvian art, 1800–1914], ii (Stockholm, 1980)

JEREMY HOWARD

Valvassori, Gabriele (*b* Rome, 21 Aug 1683; *d* Rome, 7 April 1761). Italian architect. He trained at the Accademia di S Luca, Rome, and first worked as a draughtsman and engraver for such architectural publications as the third volume of the *Studio di architettura civile* (1721), published by Domenico de Rossi. Valvassori's first documented work as an architect was for the spa buildings (begun 1713) in Bagni di Nocera Umbra. In 1715 he was commissioned to design the small church of S Giuseppe alle Fornaci in Foligno, where he made use of Rococo ornamentation. In 1717 Valvassori entered the service of the Pamphili princes, first as an assistant to Carlo Bizzaccheri, under whom he designed unusually decorative railings for the Villa Pamphili, becoming architect to the Pamphili in 1720. In 1723 he built the high altar of the church of S Agnese in Piazza Navona, Rome, for Cardinal Benedetto Pamphili. In 1732 Valvassori executed the garden portals, outer walls and fountains for the Villa Doria-Pamphili in Rome. He also remodelled the courtyard front (1731–5) of the Palazzo Doria-Pamphili in Rome, closing off the upper loggias and turning them into galleries. Their decoration is among the finest Roman interior ornamentation of its time. He rebuilt the 17-bay main façade on the Corso, enlivening it with a battery of close-set windows embellished with Rococo pediments, while projecting portals and balconies introduced elements of controlled movement. Valvassori's link with the Pamphili family was broken off in 1739, for unknown reasons. His other commissions included festival decorations for the 'Chinea' for Prince Colonna (1729–30) at the Palazzo Colonna, Rome, and about 1730 he designed the new building of the Roman church of S Maria della Luce (now

S Salvatore in Corte). It has an idiosyncratic ground-plan with two pairs of transepts, probably dictated by the layout of the previous building, which give rise to an unusual rhythmic sequence of lower and higher volumetries and changed lighting effects. In 1731 he built the Collegio Cerasoli on the Piazza di Pietra for the Bergamasques in Rome, although his designs for their church of SS Bartolommeo e Alessandro, in a style showing the influence of Filippo Juvarra, were never carried out. Between 1747 and 1750 Valvassori designed the chapel of S Giovanni Battista in S Maria dell'Orto. His last known work was the new building (1750–53) for the convent of SS Quirico e Giulitta.

Despite his slender output, Valvassori is one of the finest architects of the Roman Rococo, surpassed only by Juvarra, from whom he seems to have learnt much. In a similar way to Juvarra, Valvassori experimented with the interpenetration of the wall and cupola zones in church architecture and with the largest possible openings in the wall zones (Rome, Pal. Doria-Pamphili and projects for SS Bartolommeo e Alessandro). Valvassori was elected an *accademico di merito* (1737) of the Roman Academy and rose to be *reggente* of the *Virtuosi al Pantheon*. With sparse means he gave elegance even to such simple buildings as colleges and convents. By the time of his death, however, the Roman Rococo style that he had represented with talent and creativity had already fallen into disrepute.

BIBLIOGRAPHY

Macmillan Enc. Architects
A. Rava: 'Gabriele Valvassori: Architetto romano, 1683–1761', *Capitolium*, x (1934), pp. 385–98
F. Fasolo: 'Disegni inediti di un architetto romano del settecento', *Palladio*, iv (1951), pp. 186–9
P. Portoghesi: *Roma barocca* (Rome, 1966, rev. 3/Rome and Bari, 1978)
G. Carandente: *Il Palazzo Doria-Pamphili* (Milan, 1975)
L. Barroero: 'Per Gabriele Valvassori', *Boll. A.*, 5th ser., 3–4/lx (1975), pp. 235–8
N. A. Mallory: *Roman Rococo Architecture from Clement XI to Benedict XIV, 1700–1758*, Outstanding Diss. F. A. (New York and London, 1977)
A. Gambardella: *Architettura e committenza nello stato pontificio tra barocco e rococo: Un amministratore illuminato: Giuseppe Renato Imperiali* (Naples, 1979)
F. Gualdi Sabatini: 'Opere giovanili di Gabriele Valvassori', *Storia architettura*, 1/v (1982), pp. 39–52
M. G. Filingeri: 'Un aspetto illuminista del Valvassori minore: I cancelli di Villa Doria-Pamphili', *Annu. Ist. Stor. A.* [Rome], n. s., ii (1982–3), pp. 23–31
C. Benocci: 'Gabriele Valvassori "architetto di giardini": Gli interventi nella Villa Doria Pamphili a Roma e nella Villa Aldobrandini a Frascati', *Architettura, città, territorio: Realizzazioni e teorie tra illuminismo e romanticismo*, Studi sul settecento romano, ed. E. Debendotti, viii (1992), pp. 51–92

ELISABETH KIEVEN

van [van den; van der]. For Netherlandish, Dutch and pre-19th-century Flemish proper names with this prefix, *see under* the first part of the name for individuals active before *c.* 1500 (when the last part of the name indicates a place of origin, domicile, patronym or profession); *see under* the second part of the name for those active after *c.* 1500.

Vanacken [Vanaken], **Joseph.** See AKEN, JOSEPH VAN.

Van Alen, William (*b* Brooklyn, NY, 1888; *d* New York, 24 May 1954). American architect. While studying at the Pratt Institute in Brooklyn, he was apprenticed to Clarence True, a speculative builder in New York, after which he joined the local firm of Copeland & Dole and later Clinton & Russell. Van Alen also studied under Donn Barber (1871–1925) at the Beaux-Arts Institute in New York and in 1908 won a fellowship to the Ecole des Beaux-Arts in Paris, where he studied under Victor A. F. Laloux. From 1911 to 1925 he was in partnership with H. Craig Severance (1879–1941) in Manhattan.

Van Alen established the firm's reputation for progressive skyscraper design. However, his most notable buildings, all in New York, were executed after the partnership ended. Among these were the headquarters for the Childs Restaurant chain (1926), as well as the Reynolds Building (1928) and, the most spectacular, the Chrysler Building (1928–30; *see* SKYSCRAPER, fig. 2). The exterior decoration of this 77-storey building incorporates elaborate iconography based on automobiles, including hub caps, mud flaps and a stainless steel spire that figures prominently on the skyline. The interiors are embellished with murals, marquetry and metalwork; it is the foremost Art Deco skyscraper in New York. In a celebrated race for skyline priority, Van Alen surpassed Severance's 282.55 m Bank of Manhattan in November 1929. He had the 56.39 m Chrysler spire assembled inside the building and in 90 minutes had hoisted it into position, before an unsuspecting public. At 318.52 m, it remained the tallest building in the world until the Empire State Building (381 m) opened in 1931.

BIBLIOGRAPHY

Macmillan Enc. Architects
F. S. Swales: 'Draughtsmanship and Architecture, V, as Exemplified by the Work of William Van Alen', *Pencil Points*, x (1929), pp. 515–26

JANET ADAMS

Van Assche, Auguste (*b* Ghent, 26 July 1826; *d* Ghent, 24 Feb 1907). Belgian architect, writer and restorer. He was the son of a carpenter-builder, and his studies at the Academie voor Schone Kunsten in Ghent under the direction of Louis Joseph Adrien Roelandt, J. Van Hoecke (1803–1862) and Adolphe Pauli were crowned by a first prize in 1855–6. His first works included several designs for houses and a published project for a museum ('Ontwerp van een Museum van beeldende kunsten', in *Album uitgegeven door hat kunstlievend geselschap der Gentsche Academie* (Ghent, 1856)) in the classical taste, as well as work in the *Rundbogenstil* advocated by his teachers. When JEAN-BAPTISTE CHARLES FRANÇOIS BETHUNE settled in Ghent in 1858, Van Assche became his pupil and collaborator, teaching at the St Luke Schools and becoming a member of the archaeological society, the Gilde de St Thomas et de St Luc. Under Bethune's influence, from *c.* 1865 he increasingly developed his own practice as a protagonist of the Gothic Revival movement. His personal interpretation of Bethune's architectural principles, distinguished by a preference for a strong visual impact sometimes resulting in a striking constructional polychromy, are evident in St Joseph's (1880–83) in Ghent, the Dominican Church (1883) in Ostend and the abbey churches of Maredret (1891–1907) and Dendermonde (1901–2). As a restorer Van Assche was responsible for work on many medieval monuments, such as churches in Ghent, Liège,

Oudenaerde, Deinze, Veurne, Tirlemont, Zoutleeuw, Dinant, Halle, Hoogstraten and Lissewege. In the spirit of the times he preserved a unity of style even if this required extensive reconstruction. The results of his archaeological research were published, sometimes in collaboration with the painter and archaeologist Jules Helbig (1821–1906), in a series of monographs called *Recueil des églises du Moyen-Age*.

BNB

BIBLIOGRAPHY

L. C.: 'Auguste Van Assche', *Rev. A. Chrét.*, l (1907), p. 143
Obituary, *Bull. Comm. Royale A. & Archéol.*, 46 (1907), pp. 37–9
J. G. E.: 'M. Auguste Van Assche', *Bull. Gilde St Thomas & St Luc*, xx (1908), p. 76–8
J. van Cleven: 'Vlaamse neogotiek in Europees perspectief', *Vlaanderen*, xxix/174 (Jan–Feb 1980), p. 14
——: '19th-century Architecture', *Flemish Art*, ed. H. Liebaers (Antwerp, 1985), p. 509
M. Van Helleputte: *August Van Assche (1826–1907): Een aspect van zijn werk: Restauraties en vergrotingen van dorpskerken* (diss., Ghent U., 1985)
J. van Cleven: 'Sint-Lucasateliers in de plastische kunsten en de toegepaste kunst', *De Sint-Lucasscholen en de neogotiek*, ed. J. De Maeyer (Leuven, 1988), p. 339

JEAN VAN CLEVEN

Van Averbeke, Emiel (Leo Josephus) (*b* Antwerp, 10 July 1876; *d* Antwerp, 1 Feb 1946). Belgian architect. His father was a carpenter and he was forced to interrupt his architectural studies at the Koninklijke Academie voor Schone Kunsten in Antwerp in order to earn his living. He went to work for Emile Thielens, a German architect who had settled in Antwerp and designed the buildings in the zoological garden. In 1898, at the age of 22, Van Averbeke collaborated with the architect Jan Van Asperen on the Help U Zelve building in Antwerp, whose remarkable Art Nouveau façade can be entirely attributed to Van Averbeke. He was one of the most original Art Nouveau designers in Belgium and developed a style that was at once lyrical and geometrical, coloured by Scottish and Viennese influences. He was also a talented draughtsman and several of his projects were published in the German review *Moderne Bauformen*. In 1905 he joined the municipal architects' department of Antwerp, ultimately becoming Chief Architect in 1920. About 1910 he turned towards Dutch architecture and the work of H. P. Berlage in particular for inspiration, investing his version of the latter's style with a greater spirit of rationality; an example is the fire station (1913), Rue de Visé, Antwerp. After World War I Van Averbeke was put in charge of the delicate restoration work (1926–30) on the cathedral in Antwerp, and he built both the town pavilion and the Flemish art pavilion, as well as two concrete bridges, for the Antwerp colonial exhibition (1930). At this time his work was imbued with a lyricism that suggested the work of Frank Lloyd Wright and W. M. Dudok and he became a pioneer of modernist architecture in the years between the two World Wars. Later works include the Ecole Centrale d'Application, the Galeries du Bon Marché (1937) and the kiosks at the entrances to the tunnel under the river Escaut, all in Antwerp. He devoted the last years of his life to the restoration of Rubens's house.

BIBLIOGRAPHY

L. D. M.: 'In Memoriam: Architect Van Averbeke, Emiel, Leo, Josephus, 1876–1946', *Bouwen*, 2 (1946)

F. Borsi, R.-L. Delevoy and H. Wieser-Benedetti: *Bruxelles 1900: Capitale de l'art nouveau* (Rome, 1972) pl. 65, 76

MARIE DEMANET

Vanboucle, Pieter. See BOUCLE, PIERRE.

Van Brée. Flemish family of artists. The Antwerp painter Andreas Van Brée was the father of (1) Mathieu Ignace Van Brée and (2) Philippe Jacques Van Brée.

(1) Mathieu Ignace Van Brée (*b* Antwerp, 22 Feb 1773; *d* Antwerp, 15 Dec 1839). Painter, draughtsman, sculptor and teacher. From 1783 to 1794 he studied at the local academy. His first known work, *Venus and Cupid* (1794; untraced), is in the French Neo-classical style. At this time Van Brée must also have painted landscapes and portraits. After the closing of the academy in September 1794, following the French invasion, he left for Paris, where he took lessons from François André Vincent. In 1797 he took part in the Prix de Rome competition and won a second prize with *Death of Cato* (untraced; preparatory drawing, priv. col., see 1985 exh. cat., p. 149). Shortly afterwards he returned to Antwerp, where he became a teacher at the reopened Akademie in 1804. From 1801 onwards he executed, on commission from the city council, an allegory on the glory of Napoleon (untraced), which in turn won him an important commission from Josephine de Beauharnais: the *Arrival of the First Consul Napoleon Bonaparte at Antwerp, 18 June 1803* (1807; Versailles, Château). This large narrative piece was followed by similar commissions, such as the *Launching of the 'Friedland' on 2 May 1810 at Antwerp* (1810; Versailles, Château) and the *Presentation of the Keys of Amsterdam to Napoleon* (1812; Amsterdam, Hist. Mus.). During the period of French rule, he also painted portraits, and more traditional subjects from Classical history and mythology, in an austere Neo-classical style indebted to both David and Vincent (e.g. the *Departure of Regulus for Carthage*, 1804–7, and *Drawing Lots for the Sacrificial Victims of the Minotaur*, *c*. 1807–11; both untraced; sketches in Brussels, Mus. Royaux A. & Hist.).

Van Brée was one of the first Flemish painters to choose themes from the history of the Netherlands; for example, in 1813 he exhibited a sketch in Amsterdam of the *Self-sacrifice of Burgomaster van der Werff* (untraced), a scene from the siege of Leiden in 1574. After the fall of Napoleon, the new head of state, William I of Orange Nassau, commissioned a large version of this sketch, which was placed in the Leiden Town Hall (now Leiden, Stedel. Mus. De Lakenhal) in 1818. This commission demonstrated Van Brée's unreserved acceptance by the new Dutch government. He had engineered this state of affairs by making a timely show of his anti-French sentiments and his sympathy for the Dutch royal family in prints and drawings; important works in this area were the engravings by Reinier Vinkeles and Phillipus Velyn (1787–1836) of designs by Van Brée, which appeared in a number of Orangist publications from the publisher Johannes Allart in The Hague from 1815 to 1818. After 1815 Classical subjects disappeared entirely from Van Brée's repertory, and his paintings were devoted exclusively to scenes from Dutch and Flemish history; examples include *Prince William of Orange Pleading the Case of the*

Roman Catholics in Ghent in 1578 (Ghent, Stadhuis) and the *Deathbed of Peter Paul Rubens* (1827; Antwerp, Kon. Acad. S. Kst.). Through their series of scenes from the life of Rubens, Van Brée and his brother did much to revive contemporary interest in Rubens. Van Brée was a member of the commission responsible for recovering works of art confiscated from the Netherlands by the French and as a result was able to retrieve many works by Rubens. His interest in Rubens was also expressed stylistically: after 1813 he turned away from the French Neo-classical style and tended increasingly to adopt Rubens's looser brush-work and warmer palette. He had an important influence as a teacher on the development of 19th-century Belgian art. He published his ideas on art in *Leçons de dessin* in 1821, the year in which he also visited Italy with his student Ferdinand De Braekeleer. In 1827 he succeeded Willem Herreyns (1743–1827) as Director of the Antwerp Akademie. Among his other pupils, to whom he transmit-ted his admiration for Rubens and van Dyck, were Gustaf Wappers, Antoine Wiertz and Nicaise de Keyser, who were the leading members of the following generation of Belgian colourists.

Although Van Brée's large narrative paintings were highly regarded in his own time and for much of the 19th century, it has subsequently been his small-scale, delicately drawn and colourful oil sketches that have been most esteemed. He also produced a few sculptures, including busts of *Peter Paul Rubens* (1816) and *Baron de Keverberg* (both untraced).

WRITINGS
Leçons de dessin (Antwerp, 1821)

(2) Philippe Jacques Van Brée (*b* Antwerp, 13 Jan 1786; *d* Brussels, 16 Feb 1871). Painter and etcher, brother of (1) Mathieu Ignace Van Brée. He studied under his brother at the Antwerp Akademie. Between 1805 and 1811 he exhibited history paintings in Antwerp and Brussels. In 1811 he went to Paris to complete his studies under Anne-Louis Girodet. In this period he painted large anecdotal narrative pieces, often from the life of Rubens (e.g. *Rubens Presenting a Horse to Anthony van Dyck on the Occasion of the Latter's Departure for Italy*, 1814; Antwerp, Rubenshuis). In 1816 Philippe, accompanied by Louis Ricquier (1792–1884), left for Rome, where, due to a private scholarship, he was able to remain for two years. After having worked in Paris again between 1818 and 1820, he returned to Rome in 1821, where he subsequently was a respected member of the Belgian–Dutch artists' colony for more than ten years. In Rome he painted mostly narrative and genre pieces in the polished and saccharine manner of Léopold Robert. Good examples of his work from this Italian period are *Capt. Bontekoe* (1822; priv. col.), *Interior of Van Brée's Workshop in Rome* (*c.* 1830; priv. col., see Coekelberghs, 1976, p. 371) and the *Youth of Sixtus V* (1832; Brussels, Mus. Royaux A. & Hist.). After having undertaken many trips from Rome through-out Europe, he settled around 1834 in Brussels. There he produced mostly Italian and oriental genre pieces, as well as numerous Madonnas and a few portraits (e.g. *Portrait of a Child*; Ghent, Oudhdknd. Mus. Bijloke). Seven of his etchings also survive.

BIBLIOGRAPHY
D. Coekelberghs: *Les Peintres belges à Rome de 1700 à 1830* (Brussels and Rome, 1976)
A. Monballieu: 'M. I. Van Brée en de restauratie van Rubens' schilderijen in het Museum van Antwerpen', *Jb. Kon. Mus. S. Kst., Antwerpen* (1977), pp. 325–59
Het vaderlandsch gevoel [The sense of a fatherland] (exh. cat., Amsterdam, Rijksmus., 1978)
G. Jansen: 'De vergankelijke glorie van Matthijs Van Bree (1773–1839)' [The transitory glory of Matthijs Van Bree (1773–1839)], *Oud-Holland*, xcv (1981), pp. 228–57
1770–1830: Autour du néo-classicisme en Belgique (exh. cat., ed. D. Coekelberghs and P. Loze; Brussels, Mus. Ixelles, 1985), pp. 148–64 [Mathieu], pp. 225–30 [Philippe]
Quelques aspects de l'art en Belgique aux XVIIIe et XIXe siècles (exh. cat., ed. D. Coekelberghs; Brussels, Gal. Arenberg, 1988)

G. JANSEN

Vanbrugh, Sir John (*b* London, *bapt* 24 Jan 1664; *d* London, 26 March 1726). English architect and writer. He was the most important country-house designer in Eng-land at the beginning of the 18th century and, with Nicholas Hawksmoor and Christopher Wren, a leading figure in the English Baroque. Vanbrugh first emerged as a successful writer of comedies; taking up architecture in his thirties, he quickly made himself a professional in that field despite being self-taught, and in May 1702 he obtained the post of Comptroller of the Queen's Works, the second office in royal building in England, a position he took seriously. Vanbrugh's dramatic sense and his enthusiasm for large buildings, seen especially at Blenheim Palace and Eastbury, earned him a reputation for extravagance, even megalomania, but he understood and exploited the differ-ence between size and scale in architecture. His work was not much to the taste of the mid-18th century, but it was praised by both Robert Adam and Joshua Reynolds, and he has come to be recognized as a figure of excellence in both comedy and architecture.

1. Early life, before *c.* 1700. 2. Architectural work, *c.* 1700–*c.* 1722. 3. Last works, after *c.* 1722.

1. EARLY LIFE, BEFORE *c.* 1700. Vanbrugh was born, probably on the day of his baptism, the eldest surviving son of a London merchant of Flemish descent. His mother was a great-niece of Dudley Carleton, 1st Viscount Dor-chester, and was distantly related to a number of noble families; some of these connections were of importance for the progress of Vanbrugh's career. The family probably left London at the time of the Great Plague (1665); by October 1667 they were established in Chester, where Vanbrugh's father carried on a business in finance and property. The direction of Vanbrugh's life seems still to have been quite undecided when he was in his early twenties; he was employed by various kinsmen, including a cousin in the wine trade in London (1681), and for seven months from January 1686 he served as an ensign in the foot regiment commanded by Theophilus Hastings, 7th Earl of Huntingdon. Around September 1688, while in France with another relative, Robert Bertie, 4th Earl of Lindsey, he was arrested on spurious charges and then became involved, after the outbreak of war between England and France, in the tedious business of hostage exchange. Because he was not a spy and was of little significance, he remained in prison, first at Calais, then at Vincennes and finally in the Bastille until November 1692, when an exchange was finally arranged. At Vincennes he

saw the new royal pavilions designed by Louis Le Vau, and a period of several weeks on parole in Paris after his release from the Bastille afforded him a visitor's view of French architecture. But the story that he studied architecture in France is extremely improbable, and the chief effect of his experiences concerned the formation of his character: serious, stoical, determined to succeed and totally Whig in his politics: his portrait was among the series painted of members of the Kit-Cat Club, at the centre of Whig society (*see* KNELLER, GODFREY, fig. 2). Vanbrugh's political antipathy to France was strong enough for him to join a marine regiment some time after returning to England in April 1693, and he took part in the naval attack at Camaret Bay in June 1694.

By 1696 the Anglo-French war was coming to a close, and Vanbrugh was increasingly involved with the London stage. On 21 November 1696 his masterly first comedy, *The Relapse*, opened at the Theatre Royal, Drury Lane. The bawdy and profane aspects of Vanbrugh's play, and of its brilliant successor *The Provok'd Wife* (April 1697), have been stressed by critics as often as the notion that he purged his several other plays, which are adaptations and not innovations, of such supposed defects; the antithesis is false, and it is important to remember that, in the theatre as in architecture, Vanbrugh was more a late Restoration figure than an early Georgian one. By the standards of the time his claim to have completed *The Relapse* in six weeks indicates concentration, not haste, in a play that is essentially a farce in the modern sense and composed empirically rather than by rule.

2. ARCHITECTURAL WORK, *c.* 1700–*c.* 1722.

(i) Castle Howard. (ii) Blenheim Palace. (iii) The 'castle air'. (iv) Vanbrugh and Palladio.

(i) Castle Howard. By 1707 Vanbrugh's career as a dramatist was virtually over, but already by 1699 he had found his final, most permanent, and perhaps his true vocation in architecture. Untried and untaught, 'without thought or lecture' in Jonathan Swift's phrase (*The History of Vanbrug's House*, London, 1706), he embarked in the summer of that year on no less than the design of a country palace, Castle Howard, for Charles Howard, 3rd Earl of Carlisle. The possibility and the achievement of this first commission were due not only to the understanding between Vanbrugh and Carlisle—another kinsman and Whig—but also to their conjunction with two other persons, William Talman and NICHOLAS HAWKSMOOR. Talman, who had been Carlisle's first choice as architect, provided a catalyst for Vanbrugh's invention and for his desire, as in the theatre, to surpass his prototype. It was Talman whom Vanbrugh subsequently replaced as Comptroller of the Queen's Works in 1702, a position also obtained through Carlisle. Hawksmoor was Vanbrugh's collaborator on Castle Howard and other early works; his experience in draughtsmanship, detailing and management was essential if Vanbrugh was to present and realize the products of his imagination. Although it was of a later commission (Blenheim) that Hawksmoor afterwards claimed 'when the building began all of them [the builders] put together could not stir an inch without me', in the first years of Vanbrugh's architectural career he certainly learnt principally from Hawksmoor.

1. John Vanbrugh: entrance hall of Castle Howard, North Yorkshire, 1700–12

Carlisle wanted a house appropriate in scale to the Yorkshire estates on which he practised agriculture and forestry and to his status as a leading member of the Whigs, the party of the 1688 Revolution and the Protestant succession to the throne. Talman had begun to rebuild Chatsworth House, Derbys, in 1687 for William Cavendish, 1st Duke of Devonshire, one of the principal agents of the Revolution, and, although it was Blenheim that Vanbrugh later described as 'beyond all comparison more magnificent' than Chatsworth, Castle Howard undoubtedly held in his mind a middle place between them. It was planned not only with matching state suites as in a royal palace ('king's side' and 'queen's side'), but also with more emphasis on state rooms than on bedchambers. This aspect of its planning must have been the patron's choice; in order to provide it Vanbrugh designed a long house with two pairs of wings, most of the main rooms facing south to the gardens, and an entrance hall rising into a tall dome like the crossing of an Italian church (see fig. 1). The dome, an addition to the initial design, is by conventional standards too large in scale for the house, but its effect both outside and within is startling.

Construction began in 1701 with the north-east wing; the dome had been added to the design by 1702, when work started on the centre block, and by 1712 the house was finished except for the west wings, which were never completed to Vanbrugh's design but were built in 1753–9 by Thomas Robinson (i). Several interiors were decorated by the Italian stuccoist Giovanni Bagutti (1681–after 1730) and by the painters Giovanni Antonio Pellegrini and

Sebastiano Ricci; of these only the hall survived a serious fire in 1940, the painting now in the dome being a replica of the original. (For further discussion and illustration *see* CASTLE HOWARD.)

(ii) Blenheim Palace. Meanwhile, Vanbrugh had quickly become involved in his second great masterpiece. The victory of the British and Imperial forces, led by John Churchill, 1st Duke of Marlborough, over those of France and Bavaria at Blenheim (now Blindheim) on the Danube in August 1704 was felt worthy of a singular reward. Marlborough was given the royal manor of Woodstock, Oxon, and, apparently, the added favour of a mansion to be built there at state expense. He chose Vanbrugh as his architect and asked for a house similar to Castle Howard but with some additions such as a gallery. The foundation stone of Blenheim Palace was laid on 18 June 1705; four days later Vanbrugh recorded an alteration almost as momentous as the addition of the dome to his earlier house: the hall was to be raised into a clerestory and fronted by a projecting giant portico (see fig. 2). Subsequent alterations included moving the flanking service wings further from the main house to enlarge the forecourt, building service courts behind these wings and increasing the whole exterior height. This increase was made after some 18 months' work, when the diameters of the columns had already been determined; proportional rather than iconographic reasons, therefore, necessitated a change in the order from the martial Doric to the celebratory and more slender Corinthian (for further discussion and illustration *see* BLENHEIM PALACE).

Work on the project was interrupted in 1710, however, and then ceased altogether in 1712, when the Marlboroughs, fallen from royal favour, prepared for exile. Vanbrugh's personal loyalty to the Duke led to his own disgrace early in 1713, and his patent as Comptroller was revoked. The arrival of George I as King of England in 1714 brought the restoration of both Duke and architect, as well as Vanbrugh's knighthood under the Duke's patronage and new royal offices, but in 1716 the behaviour of the Duchess so provoked Vanbrugh that he resigned from the work at Blenheim and it was completed by others, including Hawksmoor. The original interior planning, with state suites on either side of the central axis, was never realized.

Blenheim and Castle Howard both largely depend externally on the selective and knowledgeable use—undoubtedly worked out by Hawksmoor—of the giant order in the main block, with a smaller order used or implied in the flanking buildings. Of the two, Blenheim is the more complex, the two orders being interwoven. The one-storey Doric, used explicitly in the quadrants and wings of the entrance (north) front, reappears in pilaster form in the middle of the east and west sides, but its entablature extends in a simplified form around the whole house and runs through the giant orders that front the central block. It is even implied in the corner towers by raised panels at the same level, under the upper windows. These towers also have heavy block cornices that continue the line of the giant order entablature. These interrelations recall one of the Parisian buildings most likely to have influenced Vanbrugh, Louis Le Vau's Collège des Quatre Nations (begun 1662); Le Vau's portico may also be the prototype for the form used by Vanbrugh at Blenheim and elsewhere, in which two widely spaced columns are flanked on either side by a closely coupled pair.

The liberal use of giant pilasters in Vanbrugh's first two great houses was perhaps demanded by his patrons; certainly he inclined increasingly towards an architecture that depended less on the regular articulation of an order and more on variety of shape and projection in both plan and silhouette, and on sudden dramatic accents. The towers, attics and finials of Blenheim were the first fruits of this conception of architecture and are the most

2. John Vanbrugh: entrance front of Blenheim Palace, Oxfordshire, 1705–16

revealing of the sources of Vanbrugh's inspiration. The geometrical elaboration of their invention betrays Hawksmoor's hand, but the conception and boldness of forms must be Vanbrugh's. Architecture as colossal solid geometry was a concept derived by Hawksmoor from the theories of Wren and in turn offered to Vanbrugh; but Blenheim also evokes memories of the flamboyant houses of such designers as Robert Smythson a century or so earlier, which themselves recall the towers and castles of the late Middle Ages.

The corner finials, with their ducal coronets, inverted fleurs-de-lis and cannonballs, suggest in both form and allusion the mind of Hawksmoor, but Vanbrugh was probably responsible for suggesting the carved groups on the gateways to the service courts, depicting the British lion savaging the French cockerel. This device drew the disapproval of Addison (*The Spectator*, lix, 1711) as lacking decorum as much as 'a Pun in an Heroic Poem'—just the sort of similarity that would appeal to Vanbrugh. But one of the most remarkable features of Blenheim is the enormous bridge (or rather viaduct) that carries the northern approach avenue across the valley. Both its ruggedly primitive and simplified versions of classical details and its scenic contribution to the landscape of the park are due to Vanbrugh alone.

(iii) The 'castle air'. In 1700 Vanbrugh had obtained permission to build a small free-standing brick house for himself in the ruins of Whitehall Palace, London: Goose-Pie House, as it came to be known after the 1708 version of Swift's lampoon *Vanbrug's House*, which was completed in 1701 (destr. 1906). It was square in plan, symmetrical and astylar, and it had a rusticated three-arch front loggia and a cresting parapet. As a house designed and built for his own use, the Goose-Pie may fairly be taken as exemplifying the architect's ideas about both the general appearance and the details of his art. Before the walls of Blenheim were finished these ideas had been developed and explicitly expressed. In July 1707 Charles Montagu, 4th Earl (later 1st Duke) of Manchester (*see* MONTAGU, (2)), consulted Vanbrugh after the collapse of part of Kimbolton Castle, Cambs. He quickly prepared a design for reconstructing and regularizing the south range of this courtyard house and soon persuaded the Earl to rebuild most of the outside (the courtyard fronts having been rebuilt about 20 years before). Vanbrugh explained in letters to the Earl that, for reasons not only of practical economy but of context and aesthetic preference, his design was astylar.

The 'castle air', the phrase he coined for it, embraced not only the mock battlements with which he crested the new elevations of Kimbolton but also an architectural style of which both the language and the message it expressed depended on qualities of shape and massing and not on the use of the Classical orders. Vanbrugh also revealed in a letter to the Earl his general conception of his art: '[I]t is certainly the Figure and Proportions', he wrote, 'that make the most pleasing Fabrick, And not the delicacy of the Ornaments'. Internal alterations and a change of use have vitiated Vanbrugh's internal planning at Kimbolton, but he commented on his own ability to reconcile external 'regularity' with internal convenience. The giant Doric

3. John Vanbrugh: Vanbrugh Castle, Greenwich, London, 1718–25

portico by Alessandro Galilei on the east front was added by Lord Manchester on his elevation to a dukedom in 1719; he felt that his astylar house was out of keeping with the growing Italianate fashion.

Meanwhile Vanbrugh had continued to develop the 'castle air'. Chargate (1709–10; destr.), near Esher, Surrey, built for himself on the site of a large farmhouse, had windows with segmental heads like those at Kimbolton but entirely without architraves. It also had on a small scale the variety of outline that characterizes Blenheim: in elevation this was achieved with battlements and an attic above the central hall, and in plan also by boldly projecting porches, chimney-stacks and square flanking turrets. Vanbrugh sold this house to Thomas Pelham-Holles, Duke of Newcastle, and from 1715 to 1720 expanded it to form CLAREMONT (destr. 1769; for illustration *see* BELVEDERE).

Kings Weston (*c.* 1710–14; interior by Robert Mylne, 1760s), near Bristol, is a stone-faced mansion house commanding a wide view over the Avon estuary, from which in turn can be seen its crowning feature, a battlemented arcade composed of linked chimneys. Many windows here again are without architraves, but the bold prismatic simplicity of the house is relieved on the entrance (south) façade by an unfluted Corinthian pilaster temple-front and on the east side by a very Serlian rusticated and pedimented Doric garden door.

The ultimate realization of the 'castle air' was the group of small houses Vanbrugh designed and built for himself and some of his family at Greenwich between 1718 and 1725. The first of these, and the only one to survive, is his own house, Vanbrugh Castle (see fig. 3). As initially built in 1718–19, it was a small, tall, symmetrical building of London stock brick, with a round stair tower flanked by two square turrets on the front, and a central bow window overlooking Greenwich and the lower reaches of the Thames at the back. On his marriage in January 1719 Vanbrugh added a second block, again symmetrical in itself, to make an asymmetrical whole.

(iv) Vanbrugh and Palladio. Vanbrugh's continuing enthusiasm for castles was only one component of his mature conception of architecture, and his medievalism should not be overemphasized. The accepted use of the term 'Palladian' for the Anglo-Italianate style that supplanted the English Baroque should not be taken to imply that Wren, Vanbrugh and Hawksmoor were uninterested in Palladio or ignorant of the ideas and designs contained in his *Quattro libri*. Through the accidental survival of his letters we know that in 1703 Vanbrugh saw Roland Fréart's scholarly and accurate French edition of Palladio of 1650 and that he subsequently owned a copy; he mentioned specifically and significantly that it contained 'the Plans of most of the Houses he built'. It is a truism that Vanbrugh's houses share with Palladio's villas a symmetrical arrangement of front and back rooms on the main axis flanked by staircases; in the light of Vanbrugh's comment this resemblance may be seen not only as deliberate but as an instance of Vitruvian *utilitas*, the convenience and practicality that Vanbrugh found in his own houses when describing them to patrons. Palladio's woodblock illustrations also convey the prismatic and sometimes astylar simplicity of his exteriors, which appealed increasingly to

Vanbrugh's sense of what in reference to Kimbolton he had called 'manly beauty'. There is a connection too between the 'castle air' and Vanbrugh's admiration for the rationalistic plans and romantically towered skylines of Robert Smythson's Wollaton Hall (begun 1580) and Hardwick Hall (1590–97). But by 1715 the scope of Vanbrugh's interest in Palladio, like Hawksmoor's, had widened as English architectural taste in general moved away from France towards Renaissance Italy.

All these features are combined in the designs of Vanbrugh's last decade: exciting outlines, rational plans, evocation rather than imitation of the past, and Italianate detail. The first design for Eastbury (*c.* 1715), Dorset, uses the Serliana or Venetian window that became a cliché of English Palladianism. Eastbury, begun in 1718 and unfinished at Vanbrugh's death, would have approached Blenheim in scale; most of it was dismantled in 1775. At the other end of England, Seaton Delaval (1719–28), Northumberland, narrowly escaped a comparable destruction; it was gutted by fire in 1822, but the shell survives, re-roofed and glazed, as the most complete of Vanbrugh's later exteriors (see fig. 4). The main house at Seaton Delaval stands at the end of a deep arcaded courtyard, but, like Vanbrugh Castle, it is a relatively tall, compact building. Octagonal turrets mark the four corners, and square towers containing the oval staircases flank and rise above the side elevations. A giant order appears sporadically, in ringed Doric pillars on the entrance side and a tetrastyle Ionic portico facing the garden. The bold massing is emphasized by variations in texture from smooth freestone to deep rustication, and over the centre of the house a huge attic

4. John Vanbrugh: north front of Seaton Delaval, Northumberland, 1719–28

room takes the place of the clerestory at Blenheim. The elegance of the garden portico is echoed by the orthodox window architraves, some pedimented, and the Venetian windows that light the stair towers. Seaton is the epitome of Vanbrugh's style, an indivisible amalgam of seemingly disparate elements.

3. LAST WORKS, AFTER *c.* 1722. Vanbrugh's last works in architecture were the rebuilding of Grimsthorpe (begun 1722, abandoned at his death), Lincs, and the Belvedere Temple at Castle Howard (1725–8; completed under Hawksmoor's supervision; interior, 1738–9, by Francesco Vassali). The north (entrance) range of Grimsthorpe carries on the elegant alchemy of the Seaton Delaval portico: ringed Doric columns, round-headed arcades, rusticated basement windows with exaggerated keystones, and pedimented upper windows of a Cinquecento purity. In the unexecuted south front, known from an engraving, Vanbrugh reworked Colen Campbell's porticoed project for Houghton (1722) almost motif for motif, to produce something livelier and more dramatic, less dogmatic and more empirical. The Belvedere Temple at Castle Howard, intended as a summer-house for Lord Carlisle, is a conscious re-creation on a small scale of Palladio's Villa Rotonda, Vicenza, consisting of a domed cube with porticos on all four sides. Paradoxically, the temple is closer in spirit both to the Antique and to the Villa Rotonda than such overtly 'Palladian' versions as Campbell's Mereworth.

When Vanbrugh died in 1726, aged 62, of a throat infection, he was in mid-career and still had much to say. He left an unfinished comedy, *A Journey to London*, which would have shown (as he no doubt intended) that the easy flow, subtle characterization and farcical brilliance of his early plays were no less lively or appropriate over 20 years later. The question remains whether he designed stage scenery or gardens. Although he designed the Queen's Theatre, Haymarket, London (1704–5; burnt 1789), there is no evidence that he designed theatre sets. His own plays require stock scenes of rooms, streets and gardens, and his interest lay on the one hand in real buildings and places and on the other in characters and words. As far as gardens are concerned, his reputation as a designer rests on slender evidence. A correspondent in 1703 noted casually that Vanbrugh had designed a lake for Welbeck (London, BL, MS. Stowe 748, fols 9–10), and Vanbrugh's belief that he could do well whatever he took up must have extended to landscape soon after he first became involved with Castle Howard. In 1715 Lord Carlisle had obtained for him the new administrative post of Surveyor of Gardens and Waters to George I, but this was far from onerous although it entailed making surveys of royal gardens. He was constantly aware of the setting of architecture, and in 1709 he urged the preservation of old Woodstock Manor as part of the Blenheim scenery. Yet even at Castle Howard and later, *c.* 1719–20, at STOWE, in both of which he certainly gave advice as well as designing garden buildings, professional garden designers—for example George London, Stephen Switzer and (at Stowe) Charles Bridgeman—are known to have been involved. The idea that his appreciation of garden prospects derived from experience of stage perspectives is simplistic.

As a draughtsman Vanbrugh became proficient but never professional. Hawksmoor, and subsequently less august assistants, drew out his sketches, but the sporadic surviving drawings suggest that his empirical approach to architectural design depended far less than Hawksmoor's on the drawing board. Vanbrugh, the creator of *The Relapse* and Blenheim Palace, has seldom been out of public notice and has never lacked both admirers and detractors. The publication of about 300 letters and (in Downes, 1977) of his account book for 1715–26, added greatly to the knowledge and understanding of Vanbrugh's work; other research has shown not only how, and how much, he depended on Hawksmoor, but also that the ebullient and apparently casual Vanbrugh had a character as strong as, and talents scarcely less valuable than, those of his learned and indefatigable colleague. Castle Howard and Blenheim were their joint achievement, but Vanbrugh's later houses stand comparison with Hawksmoor's churches among the great works of their time.

For further illustration *see* ORANGERY.

WRITINGS
Works, 4 vols (London, 1927–8); [i–iii, *The Plays*, ed. B. Dobrée; iv, *The Letters*, ed. G. Webb]

BIBLIOGRAPHY
H. A. Tipping and C. Hussey: *The Work of Sir John Vanbrugh and his School* (1928), iv/2 of *English Homes* (London, 1912–37)
L. Whistler: *Sir John Vanbrugh, Architect and Dramatist* (London, 1938)
F. Kimball: 'Romantic Classicism in Architecture', *Gaz. B.-A.*, n.s. 6, xxv (1944), pp. 95–112
D. Green: *Blenheim Palace* (London, 1951)
L. Whistler: *The Imagination of Vanbrugh and his Fellow Artists* (London, 1954)
H. M. Colvin and M. J. Craig: *Architectural Drawings in the Library of Elton Hall* (Oxford, 1964)
K. Downes: 'The Kings Weston Book of Drawings', *Archit. Hist.*, x (1967), pp. 9–88
H. M. Colvin, ed.: *The History of the King's Works*, v (London, 1976)
K. Downes: *Vanbrugh* (London, 1977)
M. Gibbon: 'Stowe, Buckinghamshire: The House and Garden Buildings and their Designs', *Archit. Hist.*, xx (1977), pp. 31–44
D. Cast: 'Seeing Vanbrugh and Hawksmoor', *J. Soc. Archit. Hist.*, xliii (1984), pp. 310–27
K. Downes: *Sir John Vanbrugh: A Biography* (London, 1987)

KERRY DOWNES

Van Brunt, Henry (*b* Boston, MA, 5 Sept 1832; *d* Milton, MA, 8 April 1903). American architect and writer. Educated at Harvard University (1850–54), Cambridge, MA, and trained in the studio of Richard Morris Hunt, New York, he formed a partnership in Boston (1863) with fellow trainee William Robert Ware (*see* WARE, (1)). In 1865 Ware and Van Brunt were awarded their best-known commission, Memorial Hall at Harvard University, in a limited competition. The building incorporated in an ecclesiastical plan two functional components—a dining-hall (nave) and a theatre (chancel)—as well as a Civil War memorial (transept). Influenced by John Ruskin, Viollet-le-Duc, and Hunt's teaching of Beaux-Arts composition, the design was derived from a number of English precedents, both medieval and contemporary Gothic Revival.

Following the lead of Hunt's professionalism, Van Brunt served as Secretary (1860) and as President (1899) of the American Institute of Architects (AIA), and was a founder of the Boston Society of Architects. Ware and Van Brunt set up a studio to pass on Hunt's teachings from the lessons delivered at the Ecole des Beaux-Arts. Ware became increasingly engaged in education, and when he left for New York in 1881, Van Brunt formed a new partnership, Van Brunt and Howe, with Frank Howe (1849–1909), who had joined the previous partnership in 1868.

Despite his exceptional training, Van Brunt never developed into an innovative designer. He adapted to the changing styles of his era while gaining a reputation for attention to the needs and preferences of clients, and for the design of libraries. As his importance in Boston architecture began to diminish, he found new opportunities in the West, moving to Kansas City, MO, in 1887, where again his training placed him to the fore. There he adopted the style of H. H. Richardson, as the mainstay of his practice (other than residential work) shifted from churches and libraries to railway stations and commercial buildings. Upon joining the group of architects of the World's Columbian Exposition in Chicago in 1893 (he designed the Electricity building), he converted somewhat awkwardly to the new régime of Beaux-Arts classicism. He retired from active practice in 1900 and took his only trip to Europe to see the architecture he knew from photographs and drawings.

Of more lasting importance than his buildings are Van Brunt's prolific writings, which reflect the changing conditions, ideals and controversies that affected his practice. His first published essay, 'Cast Iron in Decorative Architecture' (1859), challenged the basis of Ruskin's utopian vision on philosophical, pragmatic and theoretical grounds, arguing for control over the forces of modernity rather than avoidance of them in handcraft. In 'Greek Lines' (1861) Van Brunt advocated a romantic individualistic idealism inspired by Henri Labrouste, to balance the regimentation of the Ecole des Beaux-Arts, thus introducing the juxtaposition that was to occupy much of his later writing. 'Architectural Reform' (1866), a review of the first volume of Viollet-le-Duc's *Entretiens sur l'architecture*, proclaimed in Viollet a new hero-antagonist within the French system. Van Brunt began a translation in the hope that Viollet could provide a critical standard lacking in the USA, but by the time the first volume was published (Boston, 1875), Van Brunt's faith in individual innovation had waned markedly. His emphasis had shifted to institutions, the training and professionalism of the schools and the AIA. To undisciplined American architecture, the Ecole des Beaux-Arts offered a system of rules and precedents that could serve as a model for education and practice. By the time Van Brunt's translation of the second volume was published (Boston, 1881), he had turned away from theory entirely in favour of accepting architecture as a cultural index. Thus his participation in the Court of Honour buildings at the World's Columbian Exposition (*see* BURNHAM, DANIEL H.) marked a shift of emphasis in what he believed. He now thought architects should provide a collective reaction to the public's requirements rather than imposing their individual innovations.

WRITINGS

'Cast Iron in Decorative Architecture', *The Crayon*, vi (1859), pp. 15–20
Greek Lines, and Other Architectural Essays (Boston, MA, 1893)
W. Coles, ed.: *Architecture and Society: Selected Essays of Henry Van Brunt* (Cambridge, MA, 1969) [incl. 'Architectural Reform']

BIBLIOGRAPHY

W. J. Hennessey: *The Architectural Works of Henry Van Brunt* (diss., New York, Columbia U., 1979)

SAMUEL BERKMAN FRANK

Vancouver. Canadian city in the province of British Columbia. It is situated to the east of Vancouver Island and linked by the Strait of Georgia to the Pacific Ocean. The third largest city in Canada, it is the leading commercial and cultural centre in the west of the country. Its site was discovered by Captain George Vancouver, of the British Navy, in 1792. Permanent European settlement dates from the 1860s, when logging camps became the villages of Moodyville, Hastings and Granville. In 1884 the Canadian Pacific Railway (C.P.R.) selected Vancouver as the western terminus of the transcontinental railway line. Vancouver's scenic qualities, with open water, wooded hills and the mountain backdrop of the Coastal Range, added to its attractiveness as a development site. The railway line was completed in 1887, and early architecture is associated with C.P.R. officials, who commissioned buildings mainly in the Queen Anne Revival and Scottish Baronial-cum-Château styles, exemplified respectively by J. M. Browning's house and the first Vancouver Station (1896–7) by Edward Maxwell (*see* MAXWELL). Commercial and residential development was centred on the West End, adjacent to Stanley Park (est. 1888), while the C.P.R. also promoted construction in lower-income areas, such as Yale Town, Fairview and Mount Pleasant around the industrialized False Creek. From 1907 SAMUEL MACLURE developed an original Arts and Crafts idiom in the prestigious Shaughnessy Heights district. Before World War I many fine buildings were erected, the results of commercial or civic patronage. The second C.P.R. Hotel (1901) by FRANCIS MAWSON RATTENBURY was a neo-Renaissance design, and his second court-house (1906; completed by Thomas Hooper; now Vancouver, A.G.) brought academic classicism to the city. The firm of Sharp and Thompson (*see* SHARP, THOMPSON, BERWICK, PRATT, & PARTNERS) was active in domestic and institutional architecture. The Neo-classical tradition was well represented, particularly in the Canadian Bank of Commerce (1906–8) by DARLING & PEARSON and the second Vancouver Station (1912–14) by Barrott, Blackader and Webster. Impressive also are the initial skyscrapers, such as the Imperial Trust Co. (now Dominion) Building (1908–10) by J. S. Helyer. By 1912 the population had reached 122,000, consequent on increasing fish and lumber exports.

The impact of the USA, in both finance and design, burgeoned during the inter-war years despite the continued popularity of English taste in housing and for institutions, such as the neo-Gothic University of British Columbia planned from 1914 by Sharp and Thompson. The period was dominated by this firm and those of McCARTER NAIRNE and TOWNLEY AND MATHESON, responsible respectively for the Marine Building (1929–30), a superb Art Deco tower block, and the neatly articulated 'Modern Gothic' Stock Exchange Building (1928–9). Modernist tendencies affected each firm, as in the austerely Gothic reinforced-concrete St James Anglican Church (1935–7) by Sharp and Thompson with Adrian Gilbert Scott (*see*

SCOTT (ii), (5)) and the severely geometric City Hall (1935–6) by Townley and Matheson. Albeit slowed by the Depression, urban expansion across Burrard Inlet to North and West Vancouver occurred in the 1930s.

After 1945 full-scale Modernism was introduced to Vancouver in such projects as the functionalist War Memorial Gymnasium (1949–50) at the University of British Columbia and the tapered glass and steel BC Hydro Building (1956–7), both by R. A. D. Berwick and C. E. Pratt, partners of an expanded Sharp and Thompson. Site-sensitive but functional 'West Coast'-style houses are typified by the Copp House (1952) by RON THOM. Other adept exponents of Modernism were C. B. K. Van Norman and Associates, responsible for the pioneering Park Royal Shopping Centre (1950) in West Vancouver, and Semmens and Simpson. Eastern Canadian architects conceived a majority of the larger commercial schemes, the most controversial being the Miesian Pacific Centre (begun 1969) by Victor Gruen and Associates with McCarter Nairne and Partners. A more imaginative Modernism is associated with ARTHUR ERICKSON, designer of the innovative Simon Fraser University (1963–5; with Geoffrey Massey) on Burnaby Mountain, layered, cubic houses (1965–87) on the woodland slopes of West Vancouver and the Museum of Anthropology (1973–6) at the University of British Columbia. His Robson Square development (1974–83), including law courts, a provincial government office complex and the conversion of the adjacent Rattenbury/Hooper court-house into the Vancouver Art Gallery, succeeded in countering the typical mechanistic bulk of modern downtown development. An effective heritage policy inspired the revitalization (late 1960s) of the Gastown district and Chinatown. Other exceptional schemes included the suspended West Coast Building (1968–9) by Rhone and Iredale, and Picturesque single- and multi-dwelling housing (from 1973) along the south bank of False Creek, based on a scheme by Thompson, Berwick, Pratt and Partners, including contributions by Downs/Archambault and Henriquez and Todd. Corporate patrons adopted High Tech, for example in the Canadian Broadcasting Corporation Regional Centre (1971–2) by Thompson, Berwick, Pratt and Partners. Developers favoured the visual glitter of Late and Post-modernism as land values rose steeply in the 1980s. For Expo 86 EBERHARD ZEIDLER built the spectacular Canada Place complex, with roofs rising like sails above the shoreline, while Paul Merrick clothed advanced structure with contextual Neo-Gothic and château detail in Cathedral Place (1989–91). Post-modernist contextualism has assumed three forms in Vancouver architecture since the mid-1980s: associational historicism, epitomized by the populist neo-classical monumentality of the Public Library and Government Office complex (Moshe Safdie with Downs/Archambault, 1993–5); the more profound search for a sense of place through memory of Richard Henrique, notably the Eugenia Apartments (1990–92); and the formal and cultural relationship established in such works as Merrick's Cathedral Place. However, Modernist concepts persist in the technically inventive and imaginatively functionalist designs of Nigel Baldwin, Peter Busby, Peter Cardew, Roger Hughes and John and Patricia Patkau, as well as in the blend of parks with high-density, high-rise residential development on the Expo' Lands (Downs/Archambault et al., from 1992).

Organization of the other arts in Vancouver began in 1908 with the founding of the British Columbia Society of Fine Arts by Thomas Fripp (1864–1931). Together with his brother Charles Fripp (1854–1906), he was an exponent of Impressionistic landscape painting. FRED VARLEY taught at the Vancouver School of Art (founded 1920s), and a more abstract idiom, still centred on landscape, emerged with the painters JOCK MACDONALD, JACK SHADBOLT and Donald Jarvis (b 1923).

BIBLIOGRAPHY

M. Picken: *City of Vancouver: Terminus of the Canadian Pacific Railway* (Vancouver, 1887)
A. P. Morley: *Vancouver, from Milltown to Metropolis* (Vancouver, 1969, 2/1974)
E. Mills and W. Sommer: *Vancouver Architecture, 1886–1914* (Ottawa, 1975)
W. McKee: *The History of the Vancouver Park System, 1886–1929* (Victoria, 1976)
L. J. Evenden, ed.: *Vancouver: Western Metropolis* (Victoria, 1978)
P. Roy: *Vancouver: An Illustrated History* (Toronto, 1980)
L. Rombout, ed.: *Vancouver: Art and Artists, 1931–1983* (Vancouver, 1983) [col. of essays]
R. E. Allen: *A Pictorial History of Vancouver* (Winnipeg, 1986)
D. W. Holdsworth: 'Cottages and Castles for Vancouver Home-seekers', *Vancouver Past: Essays in Social History* (Vancouver, 1986)
H. Kalman: *A History of Canadian Architecture*, 2 vols (Toronto, 1994)

R. WINDSOR LISCOMBE

Van de Cappelle, Jean-Baptiste (*b* Ghent, 28 Oct 1772; *d* Ghent, 3 Dec 1833). Flemish architect. He was the son of the architect Adriaan Van de Cappelle and was trained at the Academie in Ghent, where he won the first prize for architecture (1794). He completed his studies under the architect Jean-Baptiste Pisson and practised as an architect and builder, as well as becoming director of the architecture department of the Ghent Academie in 1805. Apart from his work as a contractor, he was particularly occupied in civil and church architecture, including the restoration and extension of the village churches at Zomergem, Vinderhoute (1821) and Lovendegem (choir, 1822). His most important civil works, many of which are difficult to date, include the châteaux of Moerkerke and Oostakker (Slotendries); additions to the châteaux of Vinderhoute and Kluizen; country houses in Destelbergen and Nevele (the latter jointly with Jacques Goetghebuer); and a number of mansions in Ghent, St Nicholas and Aalst. The town hall (1833–4) of Ninove was designed jointly with Lewis Joseph Adrian Roelandt and was executed by the latter. It is a characteristic example of the late Neo-classical style, of which Van de Cappelle was one of the most prominent exponents in the province of East Flanders. His work was generally symmetrical and of refined design.

BNB

BIBLIOGRAPHY

P. J. Goetghebuer: *Choix des monuments, édifices et maisons les plus remarquables du royaume des Pays-Bas* (Ghent, 1827)
P. Devos: *De gemeentehuizen van Oost-Vlaanderen: Inventaris van het kunstpatrimonium* [The town halls of East Flanders: inventory of the arts inheritance], xvii/2 (Ghent, 1982)

FRIEDA VAN TYGHEM

Vandelli, Domenico [Domingos] **Agostino** (*b* Padua, *c.* 1730; *d* Lisbon, 27 June 1816). Portuguese scientist, potter and writer of Italian birth. He was one of several Italians brought to Portugal in the second half of the 18th century by Sebastião Carvalho e Mello, 1st Marquês de Pombal, to promote the arts and sciences in Portugal. Vandelli arrived in Lisbon *c.* 1764–5 and was immediately appointed lecturer in chemistry and natural sciences at Coimbra University and director of the Jardim Botânico. In 1784 he founded the Fábrica do Rocio de Santa Clara in Coimbra, which was later considered to produce some of the best faience in Portugal. Wares included jugs, pitchers, bowls, teapots, coffeepots and jardinières decorated with finely painted floral sprays. A decree issued on 7 February 1787 gave Vandelli the exclusive right to raw materials found in the Beira and Minho regions of Portugal, and in 1788 he was given more land for his Coimbra factory. While in Coimbra Vandelli also manufactured stoneware and experimented with hard-paste porcelain and creamware; in 1786 he had founded a special factory for the production of creamware at the Real Fábrica do Cavaquinho in Vila Nova de Gaia, near Oporto (*see* OPORTO, §2). In about 1793 Vandelli returned to Lisbon, where he became the first director of the new Jardim Botânico at the Palácio da Ajuda.

BIBLIOGRAPHY

A. A. Gonçalves: *Breve noção sobre a história da cerâmica em Coimbra* (Coimbra, 1889)
J. Queirós: *Cerâmica portuguesa* (Lisbon, 1907, rev. in 2 vols, 1948/*R* 1987)
V. Valente: *Porcelana artística portuguesa* (Oporto, 1949)
R. dos Santos: *Oito séculos de arte portuguesa: História e espírito*, iii (Lisbon, 1970)
A. de Sandão: *Faiança portuguesa, séculos XVIII, XIX*, 2 vols (Oporto, 1976–85)

BERNADETTE NELSON

Vandelvira [Valdelvira; Valdevira; Vandaelvira], **Andrés de** (*b* Alcaraz, nr Albacete, 1509; *d* Jaén, after 16 April 1575). Spanish architect. He was trained amid the increased architectural activity that occurred from 1510 in Alcaraz, where he is documented in connection with the building of La Lonja between 1523–4 and 1526–7. During this period he was a pupil of the Maestro de Obras Francisco de Luna (*d* 1551), whom he accompanied to Uclés, where he is recorded as a stonecutter at work on the church of the Casa Maestral of the Order of Santiago. He married Luna's daughter Luisa *c.* 1536, and on 18 September 1536, together with a stonecutter named Alonso Ruiz, he was contracted to execute the plans made by Diego de Siloé (*see* SILOÉ, (2)) for El Salvador at Ubeda—the church and circular pantheon of the Imperial Secretary FRANCISCO DE LOS COBOS. After an interruption, work was resumed there on 12 June 1540, when Vandelvira assumed responsibility for the construction, still according to Siloé's plans, but with an enlarged sacristy (see fig.). For this Vandelvira designed a space (10.5×8×*c.* 7 m) based on a rectangular ground-plan with three blind vaulted niches, to house vestments and images, along each of the longer sides and a ceiling consisting of a series of finely decorated sail vaults. This was all inserted obliquely into the square-based area between the main body of the church and the rotunda of the chancel that Siloé had originally intended for the sacristy. The portal giving access to the church is set at an angle; in its style, with canephors at each side and a marked overhang of the cornices over the architrave, it

Andrés de Vandelvira: interior of the sacristy of El Salvador, Ubeda, after 1540

anticipates the Baroque. During the 1540s Vandelvira also designed the Benavides Chapel in the church of the monastery of S Francisco (partially destr.) in Baeza, Jaén, a version with a square ground-plan of the chancel of El Salvador and characterized by the use of a giant order to resolve the corners and to support the great sail vault.

In May 1547 Francisco de los Cobos died, but Vandelvira's considerable reputation had already been consolidated by the interest aroused by his buildings in Ubeda and in Baeza. Also in 1547 he assisted in the building of the parish church of Huelma, Jaén, and on 27 August 1548 he was called to Jaén, along with Pedro Machuca and Jerónimo Quijano, by the Council of Canons of the Cathedral. As a result of this meeting, and on his return to Ubeda, Vandelvira stipulated the conditions needed to create a setting for the church of the Hospital de los Honrados Viejos, which flanked the site of the church of El Salvador in Ubeda. In 1549, in competition with Diego de Vergara (*d* 1582), who was already the Maestro Mayor there, he proposed plans for the choir of Málaga Cathedral, but Hernán Ruiz the younger, Maestro de Córdoba Cathedral, decided in favour of those by Vergara. In 1554 Vandelvira was commissioned to renovate the parish church of Santiago Apóstol at San Clemente, Cuenca. In that same year, and following his meetings with the Council of Canons in 1548, he became Maestro of Jaén Cathedral, a post that he held until his death. At Jaén the Gothic sanctuary (early 16th century) had been demolished except for the east wall, but work on the cathedral had not started until 1540. The new building has three aisles, two lateral chapels, a square apse and a cupola mounted on spandrels and shows a remarkable compositional unity. The quality and use of the orders and the rigorous treatment of space all indicate theoretical links with contemporary Roman architecture, with which Vandelvira experimented. This is also apparent in his additions to the cathedral—the sacristy (from 1555; for illustration see JAÉN), chapter house and crypt—where he employed and developed the device of a rectangular ground-plan covered by a barrel vault.

During the 1560s Vandelvira's chief patrons in Ubeda were Francisco de los Cobos's heirs. He designed a palace (c. 1560) for Juan Vázquez de Molina, Cobos's nephew and the king's secretary, with a square ground-plan, a two-storey arcaded patio and a classical façade articulated with three orders. He completed the palace (1561) of Francisco Vela de los Cobos, using an arcaded loggia, and for Diego de los Cobos, the Bishop of Jaén, he built the Hospital de Santiago (1562–76; for illustration see UBEDA). The severity of this structure—with its fine colonnaded patio, its church (also based on a square ground-plan), sacristy, grand staircase and façade flanked by towers extended at the sides to give access to the patio—anticipates the rigorous style of Juan de Herrera. From 1560 until 1567 Vandelvira was also Maestro de Obras at Cuenca, where he planned a cathedral cloister (not erected) and directed the completion of the bridge of S Pablo (destr. 1895)—the work of Francisco de Luna, which had been interrupted after the construction of the five great supporting piers. In Baeza the chancel (c. 1562) of S Andrés was built to his designs as were the Fuente de S María (1564) and the cathedral (1567–93).

During the following years much of Vandelvira's activity was linked with the construction of parish churches. In 1568 he built the small church of the Dominican convent at La Guardia, Jaén, and in Alcaraz he was involved with the building of the Torre del Tardón (1568). In Huelma in 1569 he was responsible for the building work on the parish church. In 1572 he solved the problem of providing a roof over the elliptical chapter house of Seville Cathedral, an alternative to that designed by Hernán Ruiz the younger. At Linares in 1573 he replaced the apse of the Gothic church of S María de la Asunción with one in the form of a Latin cross, covered by a sail vault and contained within a cube measuring 20 m on each side.

Vandelvira's reputation led to a diffusion of his style in various centres in upper Andalusia, where his influence was felt until the end of the 18th century. His eldest son, Alonso Vandelvira (1544–c. 1625), was active in Sabiote (Jaén), Baeza, Seville and Cádiz and was responsible for spreading his father's style. He compiled a *Libro de trazas de cortes de piedras* (c. 1580), in which he collected his father's notes concerning methods of stonecutting and an extensive catalogue of designs for vaults, which, although unpublished, was widely circulated in manuscript form. It was, however, Alonso Barba (c. 1524–95) who, after more than 20 years of collaboration, took up the master's architectural legacy and, as Maestro de Obras of Jaén Cathedral, faithfully continued Vandelvira's work.

See also UBEDA.

BIBLIOGRAPHY
F. Chueca Goitía: *Andrés de Vandelvira, arquitecto* (Jaén, 1971)
A. Pretel Marín: *Arquitectos de Alcaraz a principios del siglo XVI* (Albacete, 1975)
G. Barbé-Coquelin de Lisle, ed.: *Tratado de arquitectura de Alonso de Vandelvira*, 2 vols (Albacete, 1977)
M. Tafuri: *La arquitectura del humanismo* (Madrid, 1978), pp. 91–7
M. L. Rokiski Lázaro: *Arquitectura del siglo XVI en Cuenca* (Cuenca, 1985)

CRISTIANO TESSARI

Van den Berghe, Frits [Fredericus] (*b* Ghent, 3 April 1883; *d* Ghent, 23 Sept 1939). Belgian painter and printmaker. He studied at the Académie des Beaux-Arts in Ghent (1891–1903) and grew up in an intellectual environment. Like his friend Gustave De Smet, with whom he worked closely, almost until the end of his life, he began his painting career with a compromise between Symbolism and Impressionism, working sometimes in Ghent, sometimes near the artists' colony at Laethem-Saint-Martin. He painted primarily portraits, interiors and landscapes. During World War I he moved to the Netherlands and stayed there with De Smet and other Flemish artists in Amsterdam and Blaricum successively. In the Netherlands, he became acquainted with Dutch painters including Leo Gestel and the French émigré, Henri Le Fauconnier. Under the influence of Fauvism, Cubism, German Expressionism and Futurism, Van den Berghe painted a series of important canvases, mostly figure compositions and portraits, in which one can note the gradual development of a cubistic-expressionistic formal language. He also made woodcuts such as *The Wait* (1919; see Haesaerts, p. 319) and brush drawings that show the influence of German Expressionism.

In 1921 Van den Berghe returned to Belgium. After a visit to Constant Permeke in Ostend he went to live with De Smet near Laethem-Saint-Martin. Both artists were under contract to Paul-Gustave Van Hecke (1887–?1965), a gallery-owner in Brussels, and could work in peace in their rustic setting. The galleries Sélection and Le Centaure distributed their work. During this period, Van den Berghe evolved towards a controlled Expressionism in balanced compositions with a clear palette. He painted people in urban or rural settings, usually portraying his subjects with a highly contemplative approach. In addition to large canvases in oil, he painted series of gouaches on the themes of woman and fairs. In the work of this mature period (from 1924), more ironic and fantastic elements gradually appeared, and a depressive quality sometimes dominated. Van den Berghe himself was a restless, philosophically inclined personality with a strong tendency to bitterness, a quality that was in no way unfamiliar in his unstable personal life. Around 1926 Van den Berghe's art began to take a completely different direction, towards Surrealism, with which he had come to sympathize (e.g. *The Creation*; Deurle, Mus. J. Dhondt-Dhaenens, see Haesaerts, p. 325). In 1927 he became the secretary of a circle founded by Van Hecke, L'Epoque, from which a gallery and a periodical (*Variétés*, 1928–30) developed, both concerned with Surrealism. His first Surrealistic works were ink drawings and small paintings on paper, in which he experimented with new techniques such as *frottage*. The influence of Max Ernst is very much in evidence in these works. His experimentation led him to new themes and forms, which he then worked out in large paintings. In this last period Van den Berghe achieved remarkable creative power. His critical vision of humanity was expressed in strange Surrealistic works, such as *Strange Beings* (India ink, 1935; see Haesaerts, p. 318), in which he juxtaposed poetic and monstrous beings. Their exact meaning is not always clear, and the artist himself left no explanation. In his last years, Van den Berghe was also active as a political cartoonist and caricaturist for the socialist newspaper *Vooruit* ('Forward'), published in Ghent.

BIBLIOGRAPHY

Sélection Cahier, 12 (1931) [issue devoted to Van den Berghe]

E. Langui: *Frits Van den Berghe, teekenaar* [Frits Van den Berghe, draughtsman] (Ghent, 1933)

A. De Ridder: *Laethem-Saint-Martin, colonie d'artistes* (Brussels and Paris, 1945)

P. Haesaerts: *Laethem-Saint-Martin: Le Village élu de l'art flamand* (Brussels, 1963, 5/1970)

E. Langui: *Frits Van den Berghe* (Brussels, 1966)

——: *Frits Van den Berghe. De mens en zijn werk* (Antwerp, 1968)

——: *L'Expressionnisme en Belgique* (Brussels, 1970)

Frits Van den Berghe (exh. cat., Ghent, Mus. S. Kst., 1983)

ROBERT HOOZEE

Van den Broek & Bakema. Dutch architectural partnership formed in Rotterdam in 1948 by J(ohannes) H(endrik) van den Broek (*b* Rotterdam, 4 Oct 1898; *d* The Hague, 6 Sept 1978) and Jacob (Berend) Bakema (*b* Groningen, 8 March 1914; *d* Rotterdam, 20 Feb 1981). They were among the leading Dutch modernists of the 1950s and 1960s: through their membership of CIAM and Team Ten they were at the forefront of contemporary architectural debate, and their work reflected trends in European architecture in the first two decades after World War II. Van den Broek studied at the Technische Hogeschool, Delft (1919–24), and worked in private practice in Rotterdam from 1927 to 1937, building several housing schemes and achieving a reputation as a practitioner of the International Style with his Netherlands Pavilion at the Exposition Internationale des Arts et Techniques dans la Vie Moderne (1937), Paris. From 1937 to 1948 he worked in partnership with J. A. Brinkman (*see* BRINKMAN, (2)), who was an important and elegant exponent of the Modern Movement. Bakema studied at the Rijksuniversiteit, Groningen (1932–7), the Academie van Bouwkunst in Amsterdam (1937–41), where his teachers included Mart Stam, and at the Technische Hogeschool, Delft (1939–40). He then worked in the offices of Cornelis van Eesteren (1937–41), Willem van Tijen and H. A. Maaskant (1941), and in the municipal housing department in Rotterdam (1945) before joining van den Broek. This experience confirmed him in his support of Modernism and his rejection of the craft-based tradition of the Delft school (ii).

The partnership of Van den Broek & Bakema was formed at a time when the Netherlands was engaged in post-war reconstruction and the alleviation of the housing shortage. It subsequently became one of the largest and most prolific practices in the country, employing up to 200 people and producing housing schemes, schools and industrial, commercial and public buildings. Both architects were concerned with developing an architecture that was appropriate to the new conditions and that would serve social needs and human values. Such ideas were discussed at the post-war meetings of CIAM, which van den Broek and Bakema had both joined in 1947. Bakema

subsequently played an important role in the formation of Team Ten, the group of younger members of CIAM who caused the collapse of CIAM at meetings in 1956 and 1959, the latter—at Otterlo—coordinated by Bakema (*see* CIAM, §2; *see also* TEAM TEN). Bakema was a prolific writer, and through his writings and his position as joint editor of the influential Dutch architectural journal *Forum* (1959–64; with Aldo van Eyck and Herman Hertzberger) he promoted Team Ten's ideas on urban planning and architecture; these rejected the rigid zoning and functionalism of CIAM in favour of human scale and association, individual identity and Bakema's 'space-qualities'—fitting particular people in particular situations.

Despite this theoretical position, however, much of the work of Van den Broek & Bakema reflected the functionalist approach of *Nieuwe Bouwen* and the pre-war generation, particularly in the planning of large-scale housing, and it remained considerably indebted to the formal ideals of De Stijl and the International Style. Many of the partnership's early housing schemes, including the Klein Driene development (1956–8), Hengelo, reiterated the established form of repetitive terraces, although here designed around a central space; at Leeuwarden Noord (1959–62) a heavier look was introduced to the terraced house concept, with blocks set in dense landscaping. A modular layout was seen in studies (1953–6) carried out for the Alexanderpolder Housing Estate, Rotterdam, in which housing was grouped in neighbourhoods around shops, schools and other public amenities. This approach was echoed in their planning proposals for the Kennermerland area, presented at the Otterlo meeting of CIAM, while their project for Tel Aviv (1963; unexecuted) adopted the concept of superblocks running through the city like a spine, which had been proposed by Le Corbusier in his Plan Obus (1930) for Algiers.

One of the best-known works of Van den Broek & Bakema is the Lijnbaan Centre (1949–53; extended 1962), built in the centre of Rotterdam as an early version of the modern pedestrian shopping mall. Here a series of low, rectilinear buildings line a broad, paved and landscaped urban street, with roofed walkways along the sides and bridging across the street. Linked to the Beaux-Arts town hall, the development came to serve an important function as an urban centre. The partnership built a number of schools, including two at Brielle (1949–53 and 1955–7) and the Montessori School (1955–60) at Rotterdam, as well as several buildings for the Technische Hogeschool in Delft (lecture blocks for the schools of engineering and architecture, 1959–64; auditorium, 1961–2). They also designed austere buildings for the Reformed church at Schiedam (1954–8) and Nagele (1958–60), the latter featuring heavy concrete work. Their public buildings included town halls at Marl (1958–62), Germany, and Terneuzen (1963–72; see fig.), a terraced structure with large-scale sculptural elements that reflects the monumental style of modernism seen in other work of the period, notably in Britain. Other work included the Netherlands pavilions at the World's Fair, Brussels (1958; with Gerrit Rietveld and Joost Willem Cornelis Boks), and Expo 70, Osaka (1970; with Carel Weeber), and a psychiatric hospital (1973–4) at Middelharnis, which features long,

Van den Broek & Bakema: Terneuzen Town Hall, 1963–72

narrow, rectilinear two-storey blocks raised on massive, eccentric piers.

Both van den Broek and Bakema were influential teachers, the former becoming Professor of Town Planning at the Technische Hogeschool in Delft (1947–64) and the latter Extraordinary Professor of Architecture there (1963–80) and Professor in Urban Design at the Staatliche Hochschule für Bildende Künste, Hamburg (1965–80); Bakema also taught at the Internationale Sommerakademie, Salzburg (1965–9, 1973–5). In his teachings at universities in the USA (1970–72) Bakema played an important role in introducing to American students the ideas of Team Ten.

WRITINGS

J. H. van den Broek: *Habitation*, 3 vols (Rotterdam, 1945–65)
——: *Creative krachten in de architectonische conceptie* (Delft, 1948)
J. Bakema: *Towards an Architecture for Society* (Delft, 1963)
——: *From Doorstep to Town* (Zeist, 1964)
——: *Städtebauliche Architektur* (Salzburg, 1965)
A. Smithson, ed.: *Team Ten Primer* (London, 1968) [contains writings by Bakema]

BIBLIOGRAPHY

'Van den Broek und Bakema', *Bauen + Wohnen*, 10 (1959) [whole issue]
B. Housden: 'Brinkman, Brinkman, van der Vlugt, van den Broek, Bakema', *Archit. Assoc. J.* (Dec 1960) [special issue]
O. Newman, ed.: *CIAM '59 in Otterlo* (Stuttgart, 1961)
J. Joedicke, ed.: *Architektur und Städtebau: Das Werk der Architekten van den Broek und Bakema* (Stuttgart, 1963)
C. Gubitosi and A. Izzo: *Van den Broek/Bakema* (Rome, 1976)
J. Joedicke, ed.: *Architectengemeenschap van den Broek en Bakema: Architektur und Urbanism* (Stuttgart, 1976)
W. Röling: 'J. B. Bakema: Zijn bestemming en zijn blijvende betekenis' [J. B. Bakema: his destiny and his remaining significance], *Bouw: Cent. Wkbld Bouwwzn Nederland & België*, 6 (1981), pp. 14–17
VALERIE A. CLACK

Vandenhove, Charles (*b* Teuven, Liège, 3 July 1927). Belgian architect, urban planner, furniture designer and teacher. He graduated from the Ecole Nationale Supérieure des Arts Visuels de la Cambre, Brussels, in 1952 and went into partnership with his fellow student Lucien Kroll until 1957. In his early career he adhered to the rationalist aesthetic of the Modern Movement: simplicity of volumes, strong geometricization and legibility of structure were the hallmarks of this early conviction. From 1958 to 1986, the Université de Liège was his main client. The first project he undertook for this institution, a mortuary clinic, belongs to his 'Cubist' period, characterized by the massive expanses of brick wall to which the style of his own house (1961; enlarged in 1972) in Liège and other university buildings are related. The Institut d'Education Physicale (1963), Liège, is in some ways a related work: without departing from Vandenhove's characteristic approach, it has a very powerful unifying form, generated by the arrangement of the interior plans. It also, however, heralded Vandenhove's second 'period', which was characterized by geometric structure, simplified as much as possible, and by archetypal forms: large sloping roofs, enclosing walls and colonnades. This evolution was evident in the Standard sports hall (1965), Liège, and became more marked in the seven private houses he built between 1967 and 1978. The return to classical principles of composition that characterize this decade was accompanied by a progressive incorporation of architectonic elements, inspired by tradition, such as capitals, entablatures, friezes and cornices. The reception centre La Maison Blanche (1981), Esneux, near Liège, and the Delforge house (1983), Namur, represent the culmination of this approach.

Vandenhove's restoration (1979) of the Hôtel Torrentius (built in 1565), Liège, belongs to his late period, characterized by his interest in the architectural context provided by the site, and attempts to reconcile respect for the past with contemporary creation. The same attitude governed the first urban renewal project he undertook, in 1978, in the historic Hors-Château district of Liège, where he interspersed renovated homes with new ones, around a small square, incorporating the scale and language of the traditional urban fabric into the new building work. Another project (1985; unexecuted), for the reclamation of waste land created by the Musée d'Art Moderne, Brussels, confirmed his flair for urban planning and his willingness to enter into contemporary debates on architecture.

The university hospital centre at Sart-Tilman (1962–86), Liège, encapsulates Vandenhove's entire development: a deliberately neutral overall structure, typical of polyvalent functional architecture, is wedded to highly detailed interior architecture, violently rejecting the industrial standards of much medical building. The collaboration of artists in the project indicates the importance Vandenhove accorded the relationship between art, decoration and architecture. His other attempts to integrate these disciplines, with the collaboration of painters Daniel Buren, Sam Francis and Sol LeWitt, include the Hôtel Torrentius (1979) and the design (1986) for the Salon Royal of the Théâtre de la Monnaie in Brussels. In the late 1980s his work was given retrospective exhibitions at Paris, Aix-la-Chapelle, Amsterdam, Liège and Brussels. Among his later projects were an urban renewal project (1986), Montmartre, Paris, and a marine museum (1987; unexecuted) in Hellevoetshuis, the Netherlands, as well as several urban reconstructions, including social housing, public spaces and public buildings in The Hague (1991–2) and Amsterdam (1992). From 1970 he was a teacher at the Faculté Polytechnique de Mons.

BIBLIOGRAPHY

G. Bekaert and F. Strauven: *La Construction en Belgique, 1945–1970* (Brussels, 1971), pp. 358, 359
Charles Vandenhove: Une Architecture de la densité (exh. cat. by F. Chaslin, L. Guyon and F. Mutterer, Liège and Paris, 1985)
Charles Vandenhove: Projets choisis (exh. cat., Brussels, 1986)
Charles Vandenhove: Samenstelling (exh. cat. by R. Brouwers and L. Hermans, Amsterdam, 1986)
G. Bekaert: *Charles Vandenhove: Centre Hospitalier Universitaire* (Antwerp, 1988)
Visie op de stad (The Hague, 1988) [small pubn on two urb. proj.]

C. MIEROP

Vanderbank, John [Van der Banck, Johan], the younger (*b* London, 9 Sept 1694; *d* London, 23 Dec 1739). English painter and illustrator of Dutch origin. He was first instructed in drawing by his father, John Vanderbank the elder (*d* 1717), a tapestry-weaver of Soho, London. He worked at Kneller's Academy from its foundation in 1711 but broke away in 1720 and with Louis Chéron set up a new school in St Martin's Lane, London, at which a greater emphasis was placed on life drawing. He had begun as a portrait painter and in the 1720s attracted sitters who included *Isaac Newton* (1725; version, London, Royal Soc.), *Martin Folkes* (untraced; mezzotint by J. Faber, 1737) and *Thomas Guy* (London, Guy's Hosp.). Royal commissions included *George I* (1726; Windsor Castle, Berks, Royal Col.) and *Queen Caroline* (1736; Goodwood House, W. Sussex). At that time he also did some decorative painting, executing designs on a staircase at 11 Bedford Row, London (*c.* 1720); this commission included an equestrian portrait of *George I* surrounded by allegorical figures, as well as an allegory of the Arts and of Britannia receiving the commerce of the world. Some of his drawings, such as *Cybele* (version, Chicago, IL, A. Inst.) and *St Michael in Combat with Lucifer* (Vienna, Albertina), similarly show an interest in Baroque decorative design, but he did not develop this further.

Vanderbank's career as a book illustrator began with the publication of his *Twenty-five Actions of the Manage Horse* (1729). His skilled and loose drawing style led to many of his works being mistaken for those of William Hogarth. Indeed the drawings that Hogarth submitted for John, Baron Carteret's edition of Cervantes's *Don Quixote* (1738; Eng. trans., 1742, 5/1788) were rejected in favour of Vanderbank's. This edition contains 68 designs (engraved by Gerard Vandergucht), which Vanderbank had begun as early as 1723. Four different sets of drawings for *Don Quixote* reveal the care with which he worked out

John Vanderbank: *Duenna's Night Visit*, preliminary drawing for *Don Quixote*, pen and ink with brown wash over black lead, 216×176 mm, 1729 (London, British Museum)

the design: while his initial sketches are schematic (e.g. series, London, BM; see fig.), his second attempts are more elaborate; the third and fourth sets are worked out in greater detail, obviously with the engraver in mind. Among the most important examples of 18th-century book illustration, these drawings represent an early attempt to relate text with image in a considered and satisfying way. He also provided frontispieces for plays, such as John Vanbrugh's and Colley Cibber's *Provok'd Husband* (1729; pen and wash drawings, London, BM).

Vanderbank's success was undermined by his profligacy. He kept a coach and horses as well as a country house for his mistress, and in May 1724 he was compelled to dodge arrest for debt by crossing over to France. After his return he was seized in 1729 and forced to live within the liberties of the Fleet Prison for debtors. While there he continued to work on his *Don Quixote* designs, painting small panels (1730–39; e.g. London, Tate; San Marino, CA, Huntingdon A.G.) that were purported to be for his landlord in lieu of rent.

Vanderbank's brother Moses (*c.* 1695–after 1745) executed three altarpieces for Adel Church, near Leeds, W. Yorks (1745).

BIBLIOGRAPHY

H. A. Hammelmann: 'A Draughtsman in Hogarth's Shadow: The Drawings of John Vanderbank', *Country Life*, cxli (5 Jan 1967), pp. 32–3
——: 'Eighteenth-century English Illustrators: John Vanderbank (1694–1739)', *Bk Colr*, xvii (1968), pp. 285–94
——: 'Two 18th-century Frontispieces', *J. Warb. & Court. Inst.*, xxxi (1968), pp. 448–9
——: 'John Vanderbank's "Don Quixote"', *Master Drgs*, vii (1969), pp. 3–15
H. A. Hammelmann and T. S. R. Boase: *Book Illustrators in Eighteenth-century England* (New Haven and London, 1975), pp. 79–86

SHEARER WEST

Vanderbilt, William Henry (*b* New Brunswick, NJ, 8 May 1821; *d* New York, 8 Dec 1885). American financier, patron and collector. He was the eldest surviving son of Cornelius Vanderbilt (1798–1877) and inherited £100 million (made from steam navigation and transport) which he doubled by the time of his death. He was educated at Columbia College Grammar School and began to work for a banking firm at the age of 18. His first paintings were purchased in Italy in 1853. Once back in New York he bought works by such American artists as James Mac-Dougal Hart, Arthur Fitzwilliam Tait, William Holbrook Beard (1823–1900), Jasper Francis Cropsey, John George Brown and Samuel Colman (ii). Eastman Johnson painted Vanderbilt's portrait (Nashville, TN, Vanderbilt U.) and Seymour Joseph Guy (1824–1910) depicted him surrounded by his family at his home on the corner of Fifth Avenue at 40th Street (1873; Asheville, NC, Biltmore Estate). In 1879 Vanderbilt decided to build homes for himself and his daughters. John Butler Snook designed the twin brownstone mansions that were built on the west side of Fifth Avenue between 51st and 52nd Street (destr. 1927). Christian Herter supervised the interiors, which were described in a book by Earl Shinn and functioned as a showcase for works of the Aesthetic Movement. John La Farge designed two major stained-glass windows for the main staircase depicting allegories of *Commerce* and *Hospitality* and an elaborate glass décor for the Japanese parlour. Along with an outstanding display of oriental porcelain, Vanderbilt's mansion had a picture gallery filled with paintings bought with the advice of Samuel P. Avery. It contained works by such celebrated contemporary European artists as William-Adolphe Bouguereau, Jules Breton, Thomas Couture, Jean-Léon Gérôme, Ludwig Knaus, Ernest Meissonier and Jean-François Millet, including Millet's *The Sower* (1850; Boston, MA, Mus. F.A.). On occasion Vanderbilt invited large groups of friends to view his collection. Liberal in his charities, in 1881 he underwrote the cost of transporting to Central Park, New York, a 22 m high granite obelisk, known as Cleopatra's Needle, which had been given to the city by the Khedive of Egypt. In 1884 he commissioned Richard Morris Hunt to design a family mausoleum on a one-acre plot in the Moravian cemetery at New Dorp, Staten Island. Completed in 1889, its details were inspired by the Romanesque church of St Gilles-du-Gard, near Arles. Shortly before his death, Vanderbilt sat for a portrait bust by John Quincy Adams Ward (New York, Columbia U.). Among other bequests Vanderbilt left £100,000 to the Metropolitan Museum of Art, New York.

BIBLIOGRAPHY

E. Strahan [E. Shinn]: *Mr. Vanderbilt's House and Collection*, 2 vols (Boston and New York, 1883–4)
W. A. Croffut: *The Vanderbilts and the Story of their Fortune* (New York, 1886)
W. Andrews: *The Vanderbilt Legend: The Story of the Vanderbilt Family* (New York, 1941)

MADELEINE FIDELL-BEAUFORT

Vandercruse, Roger [pseud. Lacroix] (*b* Paris, 1728; *d* Paris, 19 May 1799). French cabinetmaker. He became a *maître-ébéniste* on 6 February 1755 and about this time he took over the workshop of his father, François Vandercruse. He was related to the cabinetmakers Jean-Henri Riesener, Martin Carlin, Etienne Levasseur, Pioniez, Nicolas-Jean Marchand and the brothers Jean-François Oeben and Simon Oeben (*d* 1786). He stamped his work R.V.L.C. He was very successful and worked for Louis-Philippe, 4th Duc d'Orléans, the Comtesse Du Barry and the Garde Meuble de la Couronne through Gilles Joubert and Riesener. He moved with ease from the Louis XV to the Neo-classical style and mastered all types of marquetry: geometric, floral (e.g. secrétaire à abattant, *c.* 1770; Paris, Petit Pal.) and a trellis design known as 'à la Reine' on a citrus-wood ground (London, V&A). He also used mahogany veneering (Paris, Mus. Carnavalet) and porcelain from the factory of Sèvres to embellish some secrétaires (e.g. New York, Met.) and many small tables (e.g. worktable, *c.* 1760; London, Wallace). His furniture, while often ingenious, displays great rigour and elegance.

BIBLIOGRAPHY

F. de Salverte: *Les Ebénistes du XVIIIème siècle: Leurs oeuvres et leurs marques* (Paris 1923, rev. 5/1962)
J. Viaux: *Bibliographie du meuble (Mobilier civil français)*, 2 vols (Paris, 1966–88)

JEAN-DOMINIQUE AUGARDE,
JEAN NÉRÉE RONFORT

Vandergucht [Gucht, van der]. English family of artists of Flemish origin. (1) Michael Vandergucht left Antwerp for London before 1700. He trained his sons (2) Gerard Vandergucht and (3) John Vandergucht, both of whom, like their father, were primarily active as book illustrators. Gerard had at least thirty children, but only one, (4) Benjamin Vandergucht, pursued an artistic career, becoming a painter and picture dealer.

(1) Michael Vandergucht (*b* Antwerp, 1660; *d* London, 16 Oct 1725). Illustrator and painter. He studied with Frederick Bouttats (*d* 1676) in Antwerp and by 1700 was in London, where he studied with the artist David Loggan and began contributing engravings to illustrated books. These usually adopted the designs of other artists; for example, his engravings for Jacob Tonson's edition (1697) of Virgil were based on works by Wenzel Hollar, William Faithorne and others. His speciality was the portrait frontispiece, for instance that for Daniel Defoe's *Jure divino* (1706). He also engraved allegorical subjects, including the *Story of Phaethon* and *Transformation of Scylla*, which accompanied Tonson's edition (1717) of Ovid's *Metamorphoses*. Although his figures often appear wooden and uninspired, he had great success, partly because of the lack of competent engravers in London at the time. Some oil portraits at Knole, Kent, have also been tentatively attributed to him. He died of gout at his home in Bloomsbury, London. George Vertue was among his pupils.

(2) Gerard Vandergucht (*b* London, 1696; *d* London, 18 March 1776). Illustrator and picture dealer, son of (1) Michael Vandergucht. He studied with his father and Louis Chéron and became a prolific book illustrator. Among his numerous engravings are his frontispiece for Josiah Burchett's *Complete History of the Most Remarkable Transactions at Sea* (1720), based on a rare book design by James Thornhill, and his illustrations for Samuel Croxall's *Select Collection of Novels* (2/1729) based on works by Joseph Highmore and John Vanderbank. He contributed to some of the more ambitious and unusual illustrated books, such as Lewis Theobald's edition (2/1740) of Shakespeare, in which Gravelot's light Rococo designs belie the hearty Englishness of many of Shakespeare's characters. He also engraved designs after Vanderbank for John, Baron Carteret's large illustrated edition (1738; Eng. trans., 1742, 5/1788) of Cervantes's *Don Quixote*. The growing popularity of a French style of engraving practised by Charles Grignion and Bernard Baron gradually depleted his own commissions, and he gave up engraving to become a picture dealer and supplier of artists' materials, working from a shop in Lower Brook Street, London.

(3) John Vandergucht (*b* London, 1697; *d* London, ?1732). Illustrator, son of (1) Michael Vandergucht. His brief artistic career began with training under his father and Louis Chéron. Among his works were engravings after William Hogarth, Bartholomew Dandridge and others for an English edition of Molière (*Select Comedies*, 1732) and designs for William Cheselden's *Osteologie* (1733). He was also reported to have been a caricaturist.

(4) Benjamin Vandergucht (*b* London, 1753; *d* Chiswick, London, 21 Sept 1794). Painter and picture dealer, son of (2) Gerard Vandergucht. Having studied at the St Martin's Lane Academy, London, he was one of the first students to enter the new Royal Academy Schools in 1769 and won a silver medal there in 1774. He exhibited

Benjamin Vandergucht: *Moody and Parsons in a Scene from 'The Register Office' by Joseph Reed*, oil on canvas, 1.06×1.13 m, exhibited Royal Academy 1773 (Leicester, Leicestershire Museum and Art Gallery)

portraits at the Free Society (1767–70) and at the Royal Academy (1771–87), including a number of theatrical portraits such as *Henry Woodward as Petruchio* (exh. RA 1774; London, Garrick Club) and *David Garrick as Steward of the Stratford Jubilee* (1772, exh. RA 1776; Althorp House, Northants). He also painted theatrical conversation pieces such as *Moody and Parsons in a Scene from 'The Register Office' by Joseph Reed* (exh. RA 1773; Leicester, Mus. & A.G.; see fig.), which shows the influence of Johan Zoffany in its lively characterization and simple spatial construction. His adoption of this formula was possibly in self-conscious rivalry of Zoffany, who was in Italy at the time and unable to accept such commissions.

In 1787 Vandergucht gave up painting to become a picture cleaner and dealer. In this role he was involved in several controversies. When a dispute between William Beechey and the Royal Academy council resulted in a rejection of Beechey's paintings, Vandergucht defied the Academy by displaying them among his collection of Old Masters. Also in 1787 the rival dealer Noël Desenfans successfully sued him for £700—the price of a picture that Vandergucht had falsely sold to Desenfans as by Nicolas Poussin. The painting was denounced as a fake by a distinguished panel of artists, including Thomas Gainsborough, Benjamin West and John Singleton Copley. Despite such difficulties, Vandergucht became affluent and respected. He died by drowning in a boating accident on the Thames, and his picture collection was sold at Christie's, 11–12 March 1796.

BIBLIOGRAPHY
E. Edwards: *Anecdotes of Painters* (London, 1808/*R* 1970), pp. 229–32
W. T. Whitley: *Artists and their Friends in England*, 2 vols (London, 1928/*R* 1968)
H. A. Hammelmann: 'A Family of Book Illustrators', *TLS* (26 July 1957)

H. A. Hammelmann and T. S. R. Boase: *Book Illustrators in Eighteenth-century England* (New Haven and London, 1975), pp. 86–96

SHEARER WEST

Vanderlyn, John (*b* Kingston, NY, 15 Oct 1775; *d* Kingston, 24 Sept 1852). American painter. The grandson of Pieter Vanderlyn (1687–1778), a portrait painter active in the Hudson River Valley, Vanderlyn manifested an early talent for penmanship and drawing. During his late youth he moved to New York where he worked in a frame shop and studied in Archibald Robertson's drawing academy. His copy of a portrait by Gilbert Stuart brought him to the attention of that artist, with whom he then worked in Philadelphia.

Under the patronage of the politician Aaron Burr (1756–1836), Vanderlyn went to France in 1796, becoming the first American painter to study in Paris. He gained a reliable Neo-classical technique and aspirations after 'the Grand Manner' from his teacher François-André Vincent. Exhibits at the Paris Salons over several years—beginning with the notable *Self-portrait* of 1800 (New York, Met.)—reflected his growing ambitions. In 1804 he produced a history painting with an American subject, the *Murder of Jane McCrea* (Hartford, CT, Wadsworth Atheneum; see fig.), taken from a poem describing an incident in the Revolutionary War. *Caius Marius on the Ruins of Carthage* (1808; San Francisco, CA, de Young Mem. Mus.) won him a *médaille d'encouragement* from Napoleon. *Ariadne Asleep and Abandoned by Theseus on the Island of Naxos* (1812; Philadelphia, PA Acad. F.A.) was the first monumental female recumbent nude painted by an American-born artist. Painted within the traditions of 19th-century salon art, the solidly modelled figure of Ariadne, reclining in a lush American landscape, did not arouse the immediate

acclaim or controversy for which Vanderlyn had hoped. Asher B. Durand made an engraving of the painting in 1835.

Vanderlyn had ambitions as an entrepreneur but was not always successful. On a return visit to America in 1801 he painted several views of the Niagara Falls, intending to capitalize on the Falls' vast appeal by having his oils engraved in order to reach the general public. In 1815, returning from Europe more permanently, he displayed a panorama made of enlarged sketches of the palace and gardens of Versailles (New York, Met.). Later he sent exhibitions to such places as Charleston, New Orleans and Havana.

The popularity of these ventures waned, so Vanderlyn had to earn a living by painting portraits. The quality of these works reflected the status of the subject: he treated ordinary citizens casually, especially during the 1830s, while state portraits of presidents and the powerful stimulated a certain inventiveness. When the Congress commissioned a portrait of George Washington, to be based on Gilbert Stuart's *Atheneum Washington* (1796; jointly owned by Washington, DC, N.G.A. and Boston, MA, Mus. F.A.), for the House of Representatives, Vanderlyn was awarded the task because of his ability as a copyist and because Congressmen from his home state lobbied effectively for him.

The *Landing of Columbus* for the Rotunda of the US Capitol in Washington was his last and largest (3.60×5.49 m) public commission. It was painted in Paris between 1839 and 1846. He built up the painting step by step in the Neo-classical manner, using vegetation studies he had made in San Salvador, and exercising care in the accuracy of the costumes. This characteristically bold achievement did not match contemporary taste; Vanderlyn ended his career embittered and neglected.

BIBLIOGRAPHY

L. Hunt Averill: *John Vanderlyn, American Painter* (diss., Yale U., 1949) [incl. unfinished biography by R. Gosman, much of which was written during the artist's lifetime]
M. Schoonmaker: *John Vanderlyn, Artist* (Kingston, NY, 1950)
S. Edgerton: 'The Murder of Jane McCrea: The Tragedy of an American Tableau d'Histoire', *A. Bull.*, xlvii (1965), pp. 481–92
K. C. Lindsay: *The Works of John Vanderlyn: From Tammany to the Capitol* (exh. cat., Binghamton, SUNY, 1970)
——: 'John Vanderlyn in Retrospect', *Amer. A. J.*, vii (1975), pp. 79–90
W. T. Oedel: *John Vanderlyn: French Classicism and the Search for an American Art* (diss., U. Delaware, 1981) [incl. documentary data relating to the artist's activities in France]

KENNETH C. LINDSAY

John Vanderlyn: *Murder of Jane McCrea*, oil on canvas, 813×673 mm, 1804 (Hartford, CT, Wadsworth Atheneum)

Van der Nüll & Siccardsburg. Austrian architectural partnership formed by Eduard Van der Nüll (*b* Vienna, *bapt* 9 Jan 1812; *d* Vienna, 4 April 1868) and August Sicard von Siccardsburg (*b* Pest, 6 Dec 1813; *d* Weidling, nr Klosterneuburg, 11 June 1868). They first met as students at the Polytechnic Institute in Vienna between 1828 and 1832. They subsequently completed the architectural course at the academy (Siccardsburg in 1835; Van der Nüll in 1838). In 1838 they both won, each with a separate design, high academy awards and were granted a joint scholarship for a study trip (1839–43) to Italy, France, England and Germany. This was a surprising departure from the traditional visit to Rome made by academy graduates. During their travels they acquired a profound knowledge of medieval and Renaissance architecture, which formed the basis of their search for a new style. In 1844 they became professors at the academy. They held these positions for over 20 years, influencing future generations of architects. Among their students was HEINRICH VON FERSTEL.

In their architectural partnership Siccardsburg supervised the technical and commercial aspects while Van der Nüll was responsible for artistic design. Their first important work in Vienna, the Carl-Theater (1847; destr.), clearly displayed their new architectural style, which differed greatly from both the dry Neo-classicism of the period and from the Romantic vision of Early Christian Revival architecture, as represented by Karl Rösner. Van der Nüll and Siccardsburg were mainly interested in adapting elements of early Renaissance architecture to contemporary demands. Thus, 14th- and 15th-century Italian details dominated the front of the Carl-Theater, which in its plastic and decorative richness was unique in Vienna at that time. In 1849 they won the Arsenal competition (see VIENNA, §II, 3) and designed the main buildings of the vast military complex south of Vienna (completed 1856). The bulky brick cube of the Headquarters building with its heavy battlements and dominant central gateway successfully combines northern Italian and English military architecture. Another important early work was Van der Nüll's inner decoration (ornamental wall paintings and furnishings, 1853–60) of the new parish church in Vienna-Altlerchenfeld. In contrast to the architects' rather dry neo-Gothic competition design for the same church, this interior is among the finest examples of early historicism in Vienna.

When the urban reorganization of Vienna finally came close to realization (1858) Van der Nüll and Siccardsburg were among the main prizewinners in the international competition for the layout of the Ringstrasse (see FÖRSTER, LUDWIG). In July 1860 Van der Nüll and Siccardsburg also won the international competition to design the first public building on the new Ringstrasse, the Staatsoper (1861–9). The most prominent feature of their design is the clever arrangement of massive cubes of different dimensions. The structure is dominated by the huge central block that houses the auditorium and stage. This vigorous handling of large architectural masses as well as the extensive decorative treatment of the surface with its continual changes of light and shade, give the building an extraordinary dynamic tension, innovative in contemporary Viennese architecture. For the decorative forms the architects adapted various sources, especially 14th-century Venetian architecture and the French Renaissance architecture of the 15th and 16th centuries, but the final result was a very individual achievement. The Opera was soon used as the model for other opera houses in the provincial capitals of the Austro-Hungarian Empire, including Prague (1868–81) and Budapest (1875–84). By the time of its completion, however, the Opera had been subject to much criticism, for changing artistic tastes demanded stylistic purity rather than the mixture of styles visible at the Opera.

BIBLIOGRAPHY

Thieme–Becker
R. von Eitelberger: *Eduard van der Nüll und August von Sicardsburg, Kunst und Künstler Wiens* (Vienna, 1879)
A. von Wurm-Arnkreuz: 'Eduard von der Nüll und August von Sicardsburg, die Schöpfer moderner Architektur', *Z. Österreich. Ingen.-& Architekten-Ver.*, lxv (1913), pp. 833–7, 849–55
H.-C. Hoffmann: 'Die Architekten van der Nüll und August von Sicardsburg', *Das Wiener Opernhaus, Die Wiener Ringstrasse: Bild einer Epoche*, viii/1 (1972)

SUSANNE KRONBICHLER-SKACHA

Van der Ouderaa, Piet Jan [Pierre Jean] (*b* Antwerp, 13 Jan 1841; *d* Antwerp, 5 Jan 1915). Belgian painter. He enrolled at the age of 15 at the Academie in Antwerp where he studied first under Jacob Jacobs (1812–79), then Joseph Van Lerius (1823–76) and finally Nicaise De Keyser. In 1865 he came second in the Grand Prix de Rome, which enabled him to travel for three years at the expense of the Belgian government and study the works of Raphael in Italy. Works from this period include his portrait of *Julius II, after Raphael* (1865; ex-Mus. A. Mod., Brussels). Motivated by a taste for the exotic probably imparted by Jacobs, who had brought back with him from his wide travels in the Orient and Europe a large number of paintings and drawings, Van der Ouderaa accompanied Albert Cogels (1842–84) to Algiers, Tunis, Oran and Spain. On his return to Belgium in 1869 he devoted himself to history painting. He produced romantic fantasies in the manner of Henri Leys and De Keyser and gradually turned to the large, dramatic compositions, usually connected with the history of his native Antwerp, that established his reputation, for example *Tanchelin's Sermon* (1870; untraced) and the *Last Resort* (1885; Brussels, Mus. A. Mod.). In 1890 he completed a large and very colourful academic triptych, *Jean Berchmans Lying in State* (Antwerp Cathedral).

In 1893 Van der Ouderaa travelled to Palestine with Max Rooses and Karel Ooms (1845–1900). Thenceforth he devoted himself almost exclusively to religious painting, using the landscape of Palestine to create what he felt was an authentic setting for his biblical compositions. These paintings are, however, rendered insipid by the same academic correctness that was present in his history pictures; examples include the *Holy Women Returning from the Saviour's Tomb* (1893) and the *Return from Calvary* (1905; both Antwerp, Kon. Mus. S. Kst.). He was more successful with the picturesque everyday scenes of Palestine in which he explored the colour effects produced by the warm local light, as in the *Wailing Wall in Jerusalem* (1899; Charleroi, Mus. Com. B.-A.). Van der Ouderaa was appointed Professor at the Hoger Instituut voor Schone Kunsten in Antwerp in 1896. In 1913, at the age of 72, he travelled to Assisi to study the setting for his last big composition, *St Francis at the Start of his Vocation*. He was also a sought-after portrait painter whose works in this genre include his portrait of *David Col* (1897) and a *Self-portrait* (1904; both Antwerp, Kon. Mus. S. Kst.).

BIBLIOGRAPHY

Bénézit; Thieme–Becker
H. Hymans: *Belgische Kunst des 19. Jahrhunderts* (Leipzig, 1906), pp. 176–8
E. H. Van Heurck: 'Notice nécrologique sur M. Pierre Van der Ouderaa', *Bull. Acad. Royale Archéol. Belgique*, n.s., ii (1919), p. 34
L'Orientalisme et l'africanisme dans l'art Belge: 19e et 20e siècles (exh. cat.; Brussels, Gal. CGER, 1984), pp. 60–61

ALAIN JACOBS

Vander Roost, Jan [Janni; Giovanni]. *See* ROST, JAN.

Van der Stappen, Charles (*b* Brussels, 19 Dec 1843; *d* Brussels, 21 Oct 1910). Belgian sculptor. He studied at the Académie des Beaux-Arts in Brussels from 1859 to around 1868 under Louis Jéhotte (1803/4–84) and Louis-Eugène Simonis, and later at the studio of Jean-François Portaels. He first exhibited at the Brussels Salon in 1866, with the allegorical figure group, *Birth of Crime* (untraced). In 1871 he visited Florence where the example of the work of the Quattrocento prompted him towards an elegant Naturalism, in contrast to the academic Neo-classicism prevalent in sculpture at the time. In 1873 he went to Naples, where he was impressed by the Antique bronzes in the Museo di Capodimonte. The influence of Italian sculpture can be seen in the statue of *Alexandre Gendebien* (1874) in the Place Frère-Orban, Brussels. At this time he also sculpted a pediment, *Orchestration*, for the Conservatoire Royal de Musique in Brussels. From 1876 to 1879 he lived in Rome, where he produced a *David* (Antwerp, Kon. Mus. S. Kst) that clearly reveals his debt to the art of Donatello and of Michelangelo in the treatment of both structure and pose.

Van der Stappen was in Paris from 1879 to 1881, and in 1882 settled in Brussels. He opened a studio and among his pupils were Paul Dubois (ii) and Guillaume Charlier. In 1883 he succeeded Simonis as Professor of Sculpture at the Académie Royale des Beaux-Arts, moving in the same year to a new studio, which became a regular meeting-place for such poets as Emile Verhaeren and such art critics as Camille Lemonier, as well as for artists. Van der Stappen continued to receive public commissions; there are more than ten outdoor monuments by him in Brussels. In 1887 he completed a monumental group, the *Teaching of Art* (1882–7), for the entrance of the Musée d'Art Ancien in Brussels (studies; Brussels, Mus. A. Mod.).

In the late 1880s Van der Stappen's work took a new direction, noted by contemporary critics, as he adopted the populist themes then in vogue. He responded to the influence of his friends Auguste Rodin and Constantin Meunier. He took his subjects from the life of the poor and the workers, and the result was informed by social preoccupations, as in the *Death of Ompdrailles* (1892), in the Avenue Louise, Brussels, an epic group inspired by a novel by the French writer Léon Cladel. The influence of Rodin is discernible in this piece. In 1894 Van der Stappen was a founder-member of the group L'Art, whose purpose was to promote the application of the arts to industry. He became closely associated with this cause and in 1905 was chosen in preference to Meunier to design a *Monument to Work* for the provincial government of Brabant; Van der Stappen died, however, before he could complete this work.

BIBLIOGRAPHY

A. Goffin: 'Notice sur Charles Van der Stappen', *Annu. Acad. Royale Sci., Lett. & B.-A. Belgique* (1926), pp. 1–41

Cent Cinquante Ans de vie artistique (exh. cat., Brussels, Pal. Acad., 1980), pp. 59–60

J. Van Lennep: 'Van der Stappen, Charles', *Académie royale des beaux-arts de Bruxelles: 275 ans d'enseignement* (exh. cat., Brussels, Mus. A. Mod., 1987), pp. 380–85

H. Lettens: 'Van der Stappen, Charles', *La Sculpture belge au 19ième siècle* (exh. cat., Brussels, Gén. de Banque, 1990), pp. 574–82

RICHARD KERREMANS

Van der Straeten, Charles (*b* Brussels, 14 June 1771; *d* Ixelles, Brussels, 17 June 1834). Flemish architect. Nothing is known of his professional training, but throughout his career he worked in a Neo-classical style derived from France. Most of his work was for the Dutch royal family and in 1820 he succeeded Ghislain-Joseph Henry (1754–1820) as architect to William I, King of Holland. As royal architect in Brussels (which alternated annually with The Hague as capital of the Low Countries), he erected or decorated many official buildings, of which the majority have been destroyed or altered. His earlier work included altering the former Hôtel du Conseil de Brabant (now the Palais de la Nation) to accommodate the States General and adding a large room to house the upper chamber (1815; interior destr. 1820 and reconstructed by the architect); the Château de Tervueren (begun 1817; destr. 1879) for the Prince of Orange; the archbishop's palace at Mechelen (1818; destr. 1914) and headquarters for the Société de Commerce (1820; later the Bourse; destr. 1882). After his royal appointment he built the royal palace in Brussels (1821; altered 1826); a residence (1823–6; completed by other hands; now the Palais des Académies) for the Prince of Orange, also in Brussels, and the Butte de Lion (1824), a commemorative monument on the battlefield of Waterloo. Following accusations of overspending, Van der Straeten was dismissed from his post in 1825, but not, apparently, disgraced. Later works included the châteaux of La Hulpe and Schiplaken (destr. 1914); the restoration of Brussels Cathedral (1828), and the building of a new rood screen and the addition of one bay and an aisle (1833) to the church of Notre Dame des Riches-Claires, Brussels.

BNB
BIBLIOGRAPHY

P. J. Goetghebuer: *Choix des monuments, édifices et maisons les plus remarquables du royaume des Pays-Bas* (Ghent, 1827), pp. 15–17, pls 23–6

S. Ansiaux: 'Charles Van der Straeten, architecte de Guillaume 1er' *Perspectives*, i (1937), pp. 14–16

V. G. Martiny: 'Charles Van der Straeten, architecte des palais royaux, 1771–1834', *Industrie* (1971); as booklet (Brussels, 1972)

V. G. MARTINY

Van der Swaelmen, Louis (*b* Brussels, 18 Oct 1883; *d* Montreux, 12 Oct 1929). Belgian urban planner, landscape designer and painter. He was trained as a landscape designer by his father, Louis-Léopold Van der Swaelmen, and took an active part in the foundation of the Union Internationale des Villes during the Exposition Universelle et Internationale at Ghent (1913). There he met Patrick Geddes who had a deep influence on his ideas about urban planning. During World War I Van der Swaelmen was exiled in the Netherlands where he became close to H. P. Berlage; during this time he prepared for the reconstruction of his country by centralizing research and documentation in the Comité Néerlando-belge d'Art Civique, which he founded in 1916. In that year he also published his ideas as *Préliminaires d'art civique*, which was one of the first explicit theories on functionalist urban planning to be published in Belgium. Having returned there after the war, he organized modernist urban planners into the Société Belge des Urbanistes et Architectes Modernistes, which produced the magazine *La Cité*. With the Société he arranged the *Exposition de la Reconstruction*

(1919) at the Palais d'Egmont in Brussels and promoted the construction of low-cost housing and garden cities. He played a major role in planning the first garden cities in Belgium, including Selzaete, near Ghent (1921–3), le Kapelleveld (1923–6) in collaboration with Antoine Pompe, Le Logis and Floréal (1921–30) in collaboration with Jean-Jules Eggericx, the last three in the region of Brussels. He was also an important proponent of modernism in the 1920s. From 1927 he was Professor of Urban Planning at the Institut Supérieur des Arts Décoratifs in Brussels. Van der Swaelmen was also a self-taught painter and associated with the group Les XX. In 1927 he built a tomb-memorial of the poet Emile Verhaeren in St Amands.

WRITINGS

Préliminaires d'art civique (Leiden, 1916)

BIBLIOGRAPHY

Antoine Pompe et l'effort moderne en Belgique, 1890–1940 (exh. cat., ed. M. Culot and F. Terlinden; Brussels, Mus. Ixelles, 1969), pp. 174–5 [with bibliog.]

M. Smets: *L'Avènement de la cité-jardin en Belgique* (Liège, 1977)

H. Stynen: *Urbanisme et société: Louis Van der Swaelmen, 1883–1929: Animateur du mouvement moderne en Belgique* (Brussels and Liège, 1979)

HERVÉ PAINDAVEINE

Vandervaart, Jan. See VAARDT, JAN VAN DER.

Van Der Zee, James (*b* Lenox, MA, 29 June 1886; *d* Washington, DC, 15 May 1983). American photographer. America's first eminent black photographer, he lived in Harlem, New York, and there in 1916 opened his own photographic studio, Guarantee Photos (later called GGG Photo Studio), which he ran until 1968. He worked on commission as a photo-reporter and as a portrait and society photographer. In his work he sought to uncover glamour in Harlem, the cultural capital of black America, picturing it not as a ghetto but as a characterful part of the city. He succeeded in producing a cumulative view of the social structure of Harlem during the 1920s and 1930s; however romanticized, his photographs form an important historical archive, which is now kept at the Metropolitan Museum of Art, New York.

PHOTOGRAPHIC PUBLICATIONS

The World of James Van Der Zee: A Visual Record of Black Americans (New York, 1969)

BIBLIOGRAPHY

The Legacy of James Van Der Zee: A Portrait of Black Americans (exh. cat., preface G. Rodriguez; New York, Altern. Cent. Int. A., 1979)

ERIKA BILLETER

Van de Velde, Henry (*b* Antwerp, 3 April 1863; *d* Zurich, 25 Oct 1957). Belgian designer, architect, painter and writer. He was one of the leading figures in the creation of ART NOUVEAU in the 1890s.

1. PAINTINGS. From 1880 to 1883 Van de Velde studied at the Academie voor Schone Kunsten in Antwerp, exhibiting for the first time in 1882. In 1883 he was a founder-member of the art group Als Ik Kan, which fostered the position of the artist outside of the Salon. His earliest paintings, such as the *Guitar-player* (1883; Brussels, priv. col., see Canning, p. 100), are in a Realist vein with sombre tones. In October 1884 Van de Velde travelled to Paris. Although he entered the studio of the academic painter Carolus-Duran, where he remained until the spring of 1885, he was strongly attracted to the works of Jean-François Millet (ii). His works after his stay in Paris, such as *Still-life with Fruit Dish* (1886; Otterlo, Kröller-Müller), display the characteristic broken brushstroke of the Impressionists, although this style is often combined with subjects drawn from Millet, seen in the *Potato Gatherers* (1886; Brussels, priv. col., see Canning, p. 126). Leaving Paris, he visited Barbizon and once back in Belgium joined Wechelderzande, an artists' colony patterned after the Barbizon group. The Belgian *plein-air* painters who worked there included Joseph Heymanns and Jacob Rosseels (1828–1912).

In 1886 Heymanns, who had shown at the première season of Les XX (*see* VINGT, LES) in Brussels in 1884, first recommended Van de Velde to membership. However, he was not elected until 1888 and first showed with Les XX in 1889. Van de Velde's discovery of Georges Seurat's works produced a radical change in his style, and in 1888 he painted his first Neo-Impressionist pictures, including *Bathing Huts on the Beach at Blankenberghe* (Zurich, Ksthaus). It was these pointillist works that he chose to exhibit at his début with Les XX. The exhibitions brought him into contact with the works of James McNeill Whistler, Auguste Rodin, Jean-François Raffaëlli, Claude Monet and Auguste Renoir, while the rhetoric of the group's critical support, the periodical *Art moderne*, appealed to his growing sense of personal mission. In his last canvases (e.g. the *Garden at Kalmthout, c.* 1891; Munich, Neue Pin.), dating from 1890–92, Van de Velde experimented with the emotive power of parallel lines. Developed from Seurat's theory of line, they are clearly related to Vincent van Gogh's empirical approach to convulsive linearity.

Impressed with Paul Gauguin's *Vision after the Sermon* (Edinburgh, N.G.), shown at Les XX in 1889, Van de Velde designed an appliqué and embroidered wall panel, *Angels' Vigil* (1892–3; Zurich, Mus. Bellerive), which is similarly abstract, flat and decorative; this work effectively marks Van de Velde's turn from the fine arts to the decorative arts.

2. DECORATIVE ARTS AND ARCHITECTURE. Inspired by the ideals of the Arts and Crafts Movement and its precocious introduction into Belgium through his friend, the artist Georges Lemmen, Van de Velde called for reform in the design of everyday objects. In 1892 he produced his first book decorations for Max Elskamp's *Dominical*. His woodcuts for the Flemish magazine *Van nu en straks* (1893) are dynamic, non-figural compositions. When Van de Velde's fiancée, Maria Sèthe, returned from a trip to England with samples of wallpapers and fabrics from Morris & Co. and Jeffrey & Co., Van de Velde used them to illustrate his lecture course on the industrial arts at the Université de Bruxelles (1894–5).

Van de Velde's interest in a unity of the arts led him inexorably to architecture, and in 1895 he designed Bloemenwerf, a house for Maria and himself in the Brussels suburb of Uccle. At Bloemenwerf, completed in 1896, Van de Velde turned to English sources for its stucco and half-timber construction although the ungainly plan reflects its designer's inexperience. For his new showpiece,

Van de Velde created all the interior furnishings, including Maria's dresses (for illustration, see Hammacher, p. 91). Van de Velde's output was prodigious at this time. In order to manufacture his rugs, furniture and metalwork, he established a company, the Société Van de Velde, in Brussels (*see* BELGIUM, fig. 33). In addition to designing and promoting his work, he wrote and lectured. In such theoretical tracts as *Déblaiement d'art* (1894) and *Aperçus en vue d'une synthèse d'art* (1895), Van de Velde argued against the use of historic styles in architecture, for the unification of all the arts, and for the value of art as an instrument of social reform.

After he was visited by the art dealer Siegfried Bing and the critic Julius Meier-Graefe in 1895, Van de Velde was invited to design three rooms for Bing's new Parisian gallery, L'Art Nouveau. Although at Bloemenwerf he had eschewed the curvilinear style of his rival Victor Horta, Van de Velde now employed his own sinuous decoration in his architectural as well as graphic work. In his later writings, including *Vom neuen Stil* (1907), Van de Velde argued that ornament should not be applied but should grow naturally from the structure it enriched. However, his own forms often seem to take on an independent life, as if in response to his earlier dictum that 'line is a force'. When the Bing rooms were exhibited in 1897 in Dresden, Van de Velde's name became synonymous with *Jugendstil* in Germany and Austria. A series of commissions in Berlin for art galleries and small shops, often created in conjunction with Georges Lemmen, led to Van de Velde's move to Berlin in 1900. Typical of his mature *Jugendstil* works

are his remodellings of the Keller & Reiner Gallery (Berlin, 1898) and the Havana Cigar Shop (Berlin, 1899; see fig. 1).

In 1900 Van de Velde met the German patron Karl Ernst Osthaus, and there followed a fruitful 20-year association between them. For Osthaus, Van de Velde remodelled and completed the Folkwang Museum (1902) and Osthaus's own house, Hohenhof (1907–8), both in Hagen. In 1920 Osthaus wrote an important biography of Van de Velde. Van de Velde's friendship with the aesthete Graf Harry Kessler and Elisabeth Förster-Nietzsche, sister of the philosopher, led to his move to Weimar in 1902, where he remained until 1917. In 1904, the year he designed a new Kunstschule for the duchy, Van de Velde was appointed by Wilhelm Ernst, Grand Duke of Saxe-Weimar (1876–1923), to head the new Kunstgewerbe-schule. Construction began the following year on a new building for this school as well. During the Weimar period he produced a large number of architectural designs and graphic work, including the monumental edition of *Zarathustra* (1908), and theoretical tracts, such as the autobiographical *Amo* (1909). Van de Velde gradually reduced the ornamentation on his buildings, while investing the bulky masses that he preferred with remembrances of Classical forms, seen in the Abbe Monument (Jena, 1909).

An early member of the Deutscher Werkbund, in 1913 Van de Velde was invited to create a theatre for their exhibition, planned for Cologne in 1914. The commission resulted in one of his most famous buildings (see fig. 2), its curving, animate form contrasting with the classicism of Peter Behrens's festival hall and the emerging International Style of Walter Gropius's model factory. The

1. Henry Van de Velde: Havana Cigar Shop, Berlin, 1899

2. Henry Van de Velde: Werkbund Theater, Cologne, 1914

Werkbund exhibition was the scene of a confrontation between Van de Velde and Hermann Muthesius over the role of the artist in industrial design. The polemics of both sides turned the misunderstanding into a forum in which Van de Velde affirmed his belief in the significance of the individual creative spirit in contrast to Muthesius's call for uniformity in the industrial arts. (For a discussion of this conflict *see* DEUTSCHER WERKBUND.)

At the outbreak of World War I Van de Velde was dismissed as a foreigner by the Grand Duke and his work temporarily ceased. In 1917 he moved to Switzerland, where he remained until 1920. In that year he began work for his last great patrons, Hélène Kröller-Müller and her family, and moved to the Netherlands. Although he started immediately to enrich the Kröllers' enormous estate, the Hoge Veluwe Park, Otterlo, his greatest work for them was not begun for some 15 years. The Rijksmuseum Kröller-Müller, constructed between 1936 and 1944, reveals Van de Velde's adherence to a severe International style in his last years.

In 1925 Van de Velde returned to Belgium as professor of architecture at the University of Ghent. In 1926, to great local acclaim, King Albert appointed him to head the new Institut Supérieur des Arts Décoratifs, Brussels, where he worked and taught for the next 20 years. He received many state commissions at this time, including the Belgian pavilions at the Exposition Universelle of 1937 in Paris and the World's Fair of 1939 in New York. Van de Velde retired to Switzerland in 1947 to complete his autobiography and died there ten years later. His influence on architectural theory and design in the years before World War I surpassed that of any architect of his generation.

WRITINGS
Déblaiement d'art (Brussels, 1894/*R* 1979)
Aperçus en vue d'une synthèse d'art (Brussels, 1895)
Die Renaissance im modernen Kunstgewerbe (Berlin, 1901)
Vom neuen Stil (Leipzig, 1907)

C. Rességuier, ed.: *Die Schriften Henry Van de Veldes* (New York, 1955)
Geschichte meines Lebens (Munich, 1962/*R* 1986)
Cahiers Henry Van de Velde (Brussels, 1962–76)

BIBLIOGRAPHY
Dek. Kst, ii (1898) [issue ded. to Van de Velde; incl. article by J. Meier-Graefe]
K. E. Osthaus: *Henry Van de Velde: Leben und Schaffen des Künstlers* (Hagen, 1920/*R* 1984)
P. M. Shand: 'Henry Van de Velde: Extracts from his Memoirs', *Archit. Rev.*, cxii (1952), pp. 143–55
A. M. Hammacher: *Le Monde de Henry Van de Velde* (Antwerp, 1967) [with cat. rais.]
L. Tannenbaum: 'Henry Van de Velde: A Re-evaluation', *ARTnews Annu.*, xxxiv (1968), pp. 134–47
G. Stamm: *Studien zur Architektur und Architekturtheorie Henry Van de Veldes* (diss., U. Göttingen, 1969)
F. Aubry: 'Henry Van de Velde et le Bloemenwerf', *Maison Hier & Aujourd'hui*, xli (1979), pp. 48–59
W. Pecher: *Möbel und Kunstgewerbe* (1981), i of *Henry Van de Velde: Das Gesamtwerk Gestaltung* (Munich, 1981–)
L. Ploegaerts and P. Puttemans: *L'Oeuvre architecturale de Henry Van de Velde* (Brussels, 1987)
S. Canning: *Henry Van de Velde (1863–1957): Schilderijen en tekeningen* (Antwerp, 1988)
B. Schulte, G. Breuer and K.-J. Sembach: *Henry Van de Velde: Ein europäischer Künstler seiner Zeit* (Cologne, 1992)
F. Van de Kerckhove and others: *Henry Van de Velde dans les collections de la Bibliothèque royale Albert 1er* (Brussels, 1993)

JANE BLOCK, PAUL KRUTY

Van de Voorde, Oscar(-Henri) (*b* Ghent, 1871; *d* Ghent, 1935). Belgian architect, exhibition designer and teacher. He studied at the Koninklijke Academie voor Schone Kunsten in Ghent, where he won the first prize in architecture in 1894. He then travelled to Paris and Vienna (1896–8) and his discovery of the works shown at the Viennese Secession exhibition made a deep impression on his subsequent work. His career as a designer began when he took part in the Esposizione Internazionale d'Arte Decorativa in Turin (1902) and Milan (1906), and the reputation he acquired at the Exposition d'Art Religieux in Paris (1911) led to him being chosen as the principal architect and coordinator of the international exhibition at Ghent in 1913. He built its main pavilions in a classically inspired style tinged with echoes of Vienna; the Palais des Fêtes et des Floralies is the only building that remains. In 1920 Van de Voorde was appointed Director of the Koninklijke Academie voor Schone Kunsten in Ghent where he was already teaching architecture, the history of ornament and decorative art, and where he continued to teach until the end of his life. He reorganized the architectural curriculum to cover both stylistic vocabulary and contemporary building techniques, and his school became one of the best in the country. He continued to work as an architect on a variety of buildings including public commissions, restoration projects, garden city planning and low-cost housing, blocks of flats, industrial buildings and large houses, mainly in the region of Ghent. Some works were executed in collaboration with his brother, A. Van de Voorde, including the Banque Belge du Travail (1923) in Ghent. He was one of the most important architectural figures in Ghent during the first half of the 20th century.

BIBLIOGRAPHY

E. De Seyn: *Dictionnaire biographique des sciences, des lettres et des arts en Belgique* (Brussels, 1936)

MARIE DEMANET

Van de Woestyne, Gustave (*b* Ghent, 2 Aug 1881; *d* Uccle, 21 April 1947). Belgian painter. He studied at the Koninklijke Akademie voor Schone Kunsten in Ghent from 1895 to 1899. In 1901, under the influence of his brother the poet Karel Van de Woestyne, he settled in LAETHEM-SAINT-MARTIN as part of the first group of artists to form a colony there. Between the years 1902 and 1906 he worked as a nurse, and he resided for some months in a Benedictine monastery in Leuven in 1905, thereafter staying in Laethem-Saint-Martin, Leuven and from 1913 in Tiegem. His admiration for the work of the Flemish 'Primitives', which he saw at an exhibition in Bruges in 1902, and for the art of the English Pre-Raphaelites is apparent in his paintings and drawings. They are thematically very varied: farmers from the region, pastoral scenes, allegorical representations, religious events set in a rural scene, portraits and, after World War I, still-lifes. His technique also varied: on the one hand works painted in a linear manner in delicate, flat colours; on the other slightly hazy paintings in which the colours and outlines become blurred. There is nevertheless a great uniformity in the ever-present atmosphere of alienation and unreality. Figures are outlined against a golden background or against a stylized rural scene; they are introspective and mutually isolated by their attitudes, expressions and gestures, for example *The Two Springs* (1910; Antwerp, Kon. Mus. S. Kst.).

In 1913 Van de Woestyne travelled to Italy and lived in England from 1914 to 1919. In 1921 Cubist elements and Expressionist distortions pervaded his restrained and sensitive Symbolist paintings. This was pushed to its most extreme in *Christ Offering his Blood* (1925; Brussels, Mus. A. Mod.). In 1925 he became director of the Koninklijke Akademie voor Beeldende Kunsten in Mechelen and in 1928 he became a lecturer at the Hoger Instituut voor Sierkunsten in Ter Kameren. He became a member of the Académie Royale des Beaux-Arts of Belgium. He was a member of the artists' group Art Contemporain and the Groupe des IX.

BIBLIOGRAPHY

K. Van de Woestyne: *Gustave Van de Woestyne* (Brussels, 1931)
F. Van Hecke: *Gustave Van de Woestyne* (Antwerp, 1949)
P. Haesaerts: *Laethem-Saint-Martin: Le Village élu de l'art flamand* (Brussels, 1963, 5/1970)
Gustave Van de Woestyne (exh. cat., Mechelen, Cult. Cent., 1967)
Gustave Van de Woestyne (exh. cat., Antwerp, Kon. Mus. S. Kst, 1981)

D. CARDYN-OOMEN

Vandières, Abel-François Poisson de. *See* POISSON, (2).

Vandoni, Giuseppe (*b* Milan, 29 Dec 1828; *d* Milan, 16 April 1877). Italian architect. He studied engineering at Pavia and architecture at the Accademia di Belle Arti, Milan, qualifying as an architectural engineer in 1853. In 1854 he entered the Ufficio delle Pubbliche Costruzioni, Milan, where, after 1858, he worked with Giacomo Tazzini (1785–1861), from whom he took over as Ispettore dei Palazzi di Corte in 1863. In 1861, on Tazzini's advice, Vandoni was appointed Architetto della Fabbrica del Duomo di Milano and held both positions until his death. As Ispettore dei Palazzi di Corte, Vandoni was responsible for the furnishing and maintenance of the Palazzo Reale in Milan, the Villa Reale in Monza and the castle of Cassano Magnago, Lombardy. He was also responsible for minor alterations to the fabric of these buildings. As Architetto della Fabrica del Duomo, he directed the continuation of work on the crowning of the flanks of the building, the restoration of the stained glass and began the south-east turret containing the bells which was completed after his death by Paolo Cesa Bianchi. He designed the façade of the church at Lomagna, Lombardy, and between 1852 and 1871 was engaged several times on S Maria presso S Satiro, Milan, where he restored (from 1855) Bramante's rotunda, linking it with the inside of the church, restored the external wall along the Via del Falcone, and designed the new façade (1869–71) on the Via Torino in an early 16th-century Lombard style. In 1872 he was engaged in the completion of Galeazzo Alessi's Palazzo Marino, which had become the seat of the city authorities in Milan.

In his restoration work he sought not only to complete the appearance of the building but also to be practical. He did not favour one particular style, but adapted easily to that of the work in hand.

WRITINGS

Relazione al Consiglio Comunale sull'esito del concorso pubblicato con avviso municipale 14 novembre 1872 per il progetto della facciata del Palazzo Marino (Milan, 1873)

BIBLIOGRAPHY

Portoghesi
A. Legnani: *Ricordo dell'ingegnere architetto cav. Giuseppe Vandoni* (Milan, 1877)
G. Lise: *Santa Maria presso San Satiro* (Milan, 1975)
G. Mulazzani: 'Trasformazione e vicende della villa dall'epoca austriaca al 1923', *La Villa Reale di Monza* (Monza, 1984), pp. 144–183
M. T. Fiorio, ed.: *Le chiese di Milano* (Milan, 1985), p. 325

STEFANO DELLA TORRE

Vaneau, Pierre (*b* Montpellier, 31 Dec 1653; *d* Le Puy, 27 June 1694). French sculptor. He probably trained in the workshop of his father, a carpenter and sculptor. From

1680 or 1681 he was in the service of Armand de Béthune (1635–1703), Bishop of Le Puy, to whose collection of drawings and engravings he probably had access. His career seems to have been spent almost entirely in what is now the département of the Haute-Loire. He worked in a Baroque style moderated by classical influences. He excelled in low relief, as in the surviving fragments of his monument to *John III Sobieski, King of Poland* (1683–7; Le Puy, Mus. Crozatier and Trésor A. Rélig.) and in the decoration of the Chapelle St Maurice, Le Puy (1687, destr.; fragments Le Puy, Trésor A. Rélig.). Among his extensive production of free-standing statues, both secular and religious, are two *Theban Soldiers* (Le Puy, Trésor Cathédrale Notre-Dame). He also executed church furnishings, such as the pulpit and organ-case (1690 and 1692) in Le Puy Cathedral, and the carved altarpiece (1693) in the church of St Julien, Brioude. The great number of works known to be by Vaneau suggests that he ran a large workshop, while the numerous anonymous works close to his style to be found in the Haute-Loire make it clear that he was at the head of a considerable local school.

BIBLIOGRAPHY

Lami

M. Vachon: *La Vie et l'oeuvre de Pierre Vaneau* (Paris, 1883)
E. Gautheron: *Peintres et sculpteurs du Velay* (Le Puy, 1927), pp. 182–257
P. Vitry: 'Trois Bas-reliefs de Pierre Vaneau', *Bull. Mus. France* (1930), pp. 163–7
——: 'Monuments élevés en France à la gloire de Jean III Sobiesky', *La France et la Pologne dans leurs relations artistiques*, i/1 (1938), pp. 425–9
R. Gounot: 'De Vaneau à Julien', *Cah. Haute-Loire* (1967), pp. 51–66
Pierre Vaneau: La Sculpture française au XVIIème siècle (exh. cat. by F. Vialet and Y. Soulingeas, Le Puy, Baptistère St Jean, 1980)

FRÉDÉRIQUE VIALET

Van Gierdegom, Josephus Franciscus [Joseph François] (*b* Bruges, 12 Oct 1760; *d* Bruges, 7 May 1844). Belgian architect. The son of a master carpenter called Joseph Van Gierdegom (*c.* 1729–*c.* 1795), he is often confused with his father and with his half-brother Jean-Népomucène Van Gierdegom (1785–1865). The latter was town architect in Bruges and, like Josephus, a teacher at the Vrije Academie voor Schone Kunsten; however in 1825 he became a municipal architect in Mons. Josephus was trained in architecture at the Bruges Academie and won a prize there in 1778; in 1779 he obtained a second prize in Brussels. Apart from his practice as an architect and master carpenter, he was primarily a teacher at the Vrije Academie voor Schone Kunsten in Bruges, where he was a professor from 1802 to 1838 and headmaster from 1832 to 1835. His best-known work, which establishes him as one of the more interesting Belgian Neo-classical architects, is the Château de Peellaert (1813–17) at Sint Andries near Bruges; it was never finished and survives in a fragmentary state. The plans published by Goetghebuer show the monumental conception, with a main building composed of a cupola-crowned rotunda and flanked by long colonnades interrupted by gates in the form of triumphal arches. He was also a pioneer of the Gothic Revival style and was involved with works in Bruges such as the rebuilding of the Lanchals chapel (1812–16), the furnishing of the baptistery (1830) in the church of Onze Lieve Vrouw, the enlargement of the 15th-century Poortersloge (1818–25) and the rebuilding of the stairs of the chapel of the Holy Blood (1832) in the basilica of the Holy Blood (Heilig Bloedbaziliek).

BIBLIOGRAPHY

BNB

P. Goetghebuer: *Choix des monuments, édifices et maisons les plus remarquables du royaume des Pays-Bas* (Ghent, 1827), pp. 8–9
J. Immerzeel jr: *De levens en werken der hollandsche en vlaamsche kunstschilders, beeldhouwers, graveurs en bouwmeesters, van het begin der vijftiende eeuw tot heden*, i (Amsterdam, 1842), pp. 278–9
A. Schouteet: 'Beknopte geschiedenis van de vrije academie voor schone kunsten en van de stedelijke academie voor schone kunsten te Brugge', *250 jaar Academie voor Schone Kunsten te Brugge, 1717–1967* (Bruges, 1970), p. 31
J. van Cleven: 'Van Gierdegom, Josephus Franciscus', *Nationaal biografisch woordenboek*, xi (Brussels, 1985), cols 284–8
——: *Het centrum Brugge en de opkomst van de archeologische neogotiek in België* (diss. in preparation)

JEAN VAN CLEVEN

Van Hoeydonck, Paul (*b* Antwerp, 8 Oct 1925). Belgian painter. He studied history of art and archaeology at the Kunsthistorisch Institut in Antwerp (1949–53). Though self-taught as a painter, he received early encouragement from Georges Vantongerloo and Ossip Zadkine. He made his début in 1952 as a figurative painter in the tradition of Rik Slabbinck (*b* 1914) and other representatives of the Jeune Peinture Belge. He moved on to geometric abstraction and joined artists' groups with the same ideals, such as ART ABSTRAIT. He produced collages and reliefs with perspex fragments on canvas, followed by monochrome white paintings. In 1958 he was one of the co-founders of the group G-58 in Antwerp, which had close ties with the German Zero group. Subsequently he moved towards figurative assemblages, a technique that he continued to use. From 1961, the time of his first stay in New York, his work showed an unabashed reverence for space exploration as an attempt to explore and exploit the cosmos, as in *Spacescape* (white relief, 2.10×1.22 m, 1961; Brussels, Mus. A. Mod.). This attitude is directly related to his childhood love of Jules Verne's writings and *Flash Gordon* comic strips. The varying success of his career was in direct proportion to society's opinion of space exploration. One example of this is the controversy around his miniature sculpture *Fallen Astronaut* (aluminium, 80×20× 15 mm, 1971; see Van den Busche, pl. 35), which was placed by the crew of the Apollo 15 on the surface of the moon as a 'memorial' to the 'martyrs of space exploration'. Drawing on his rich imagination, Van Hoeydonck introduced a kind of metaphorical and anecdotal iconography of space exploration into post-war art; in 1964 the critic Pierre Restany called him the 'archaeologist of the future'. Using mass-produced articles from department stores, he made small monochromatic white scenes and figures, mutants and astronauts, as well as a life-size Icarus and cybernetic figures (e.g. *Cybernetic Christ*, h. 1.8 m, 1968; Antwerp, priv. col., see Fryns, p. 137). He frequently used plastics, and after 1974 he also worked with chrome-plated steel and patinated bronze. After 1970 he added brilliant colours to his work. In 1976 he started to paint images in which wildlife and space exploration were combined. In the 1980s he made series of images incorporating drawing and photography, in which familiar landmarks (e.g. *New York Guggenheim Exit One Way*, 1981; artist's col., see Van den Bussche, p. 61) were transmuted into visions of impossible structures.

BIBLIOGRAPHY

M. Fryns: *Paul Van Hoeydonck: Space Art* (Brussels, 1970)

W. Van den Busche: *Paul Van Hoeydonck* (Brussels, 1982)

HERWIG TODTS

Van Horne, Sir **William (Cornelius)** (*b* Chelsea, IL, 3 Feb 1843; *d* Montreal, 11 Sept 1915). Canadian businessman and collector. He worked for several American railway companies and then emigrated to Canada in 1881 to become General Manager of the Canadian Pacific Railway. He expanded it to a transcontinental line and became its President in 1888. He also developed a steamship line and a chain of hotels for the Canadian Pacific Railway. He had been interested in collecting since his youth, and set about building a collection with the same astuteness and single-mindedness with which he built his railways. He was strongly influenced by collecting trends in New York and Chicago but relied on his own judgement to assemble a large collection of Oriental porcelain and European painting. He maintained ties with the Montreal collectors Sir George A. Drummond and James Ross (1848–1913) and with dealers and collectors in Europe. Among those paintings acquired at auction in New York and in Europe was Alexandre-Gabriel Decamps's *Saul Pursuing David* (1853; Montreal, Mus. F.A.). In the 1890s he depended particularly closely upon the New York dealer Daniel Cottier (1838–91) and his partner James Inglis (1852–1907) for advice on purchases. In *c.* 1892 he acquired nine canvases from Paul Durand-Ruel in Paris that were among the first Impressionist paintings to enter Canadian collections, including Alfred Sisley's *Seine at Bougival* (originally titled *Autumn: Banks of the Oise*, 1873; Montreal, Mus. F.A.). By 1910 he was making such avant-garde purchases as Toulouse-Lautrec's *The Hangover* (1887–9; Cambridge, MA, Fogg) and *Red-headed Woman Sitting in M. Forest's Garden* (1899; sold New York, Christie's, 5 Nov 1991, lot 33), as well as Cézanne's portrait of *Mme Cézanne* (Geneva, H. Berggruen priv. col., see Rewald, p. 156). In 1913 he loaned these paintings to the Armory Show in New York. His collection in Montreal was housed in a large mansion and was made available to artists and scholars and to the Art Association of Montreal, to which he donated funds and of which he was Vice-President from 1894 to 1897. The quality, breadth and coherence of his collection made it among the first of international significance to be formed in Canada. He was also a landscape painter (e.g. *Steelworks at Sydney, Cape Breton*, Montreal, Mus. F.A.). After the death of his daughter Adaline Van Horne in 1941 his collection was divided between the surviving heirs and the Art Association of Montreal, the latter obtaining such paintings as Giambattista Tiepolo's *Apelles Painting the Portrait of Campaspe* (*c.* 1730) and Honoré Daumier's *Nymphs Pursued by Satyrs* (*c.* 1850; both Montreal, Mus. F.A.).

UNPUBLISHED SOURCES

Montreal, Mus. F.A., Archv Dept [notebooks]

BIBLIOGRAPHY

J. La Farge and A. Jaccaci, eds: *Noteworthy Paintings in American Private Collections* (New York, 1907)

M. Conway: 'Sir William Van Horne's Collection at Montreal', *Connoisseur*, xii (1909), pp. 135–42

W. Vaughan: *The Life and Work of Sir William Van Horne* (New York, 1920)

A Selection of Paintings from the Collection of Sir William Van Horne, K.C.M.G. (exh. cat., Montreal, Mus. F.A., 1933)

Canada Collects, 1860–1960: European Paintings (exh. cat. by E. H. Turner, Montreal, Mus. F.A., 1960)

J. Rewald: *Cézanne* (New York, 1986)

Discerning Tastes: Montreal Collectors, 1880–1920 (exh. cat. by J. Brooke, Montreal, Mus. F.A., 1989)

JANET M. BROOKE

Van Huffel, Albert (*b* Ghent, 20 Jan 1877; *d* Brussels, 17 March 1935). Belgian architect. He came from a modest background and at first worked in a number of trades and crafts; for example, he was a painter and decorator, cabinetmaker, mason and glassworker between 1896 and 1912. His artistic horizons were greatly extended through his membership of the Kunst en Kennis circle (1895–1904), whose members sought to stimulate locally a spirit similar to that of the Arts and Crafts Movement in England among building craftsmen. His interest in the botanical work of Julius Mac Léod (1857–1919), a departmental head at the Rijksuniversiteit of Ghent, also stimulated his studies of ornament in the context of Art Nouveau, the style of the Viennese Secession and Art Deco. He received no formal architectural training but established himself as an architect and built several private town houses in Ghent. From 1912 to 1920 he was artistic director of Céline Dangotte, a furnishing company in Brussels. He then embarked on his major work, the Basilique Nationale du Sacré Coeur in Koekelberg, Brussels, a national monument begun in 1908 by the architect Pieter Langerock. Its original plan was too ambitious and in 1921 Van Huffel started work on a scaled-down version, continuing until his death. His modified design expressed the traditional forms of the basilica in the Art Deco style. The building, which was completed in 1970, demonstrates the diverse interests and professionalism of this self-trained architect. Van Huffel also taught a course on applied ornamentation at the Institut Supérieur des Arts Décoratifs in Brussels from 1927 to 1935.

BIBLIOGRAPHY

M. Dubois: *Albert Van Huffel, 1877–1935* (Ghent, 1983)

HERVÉ PAINDAVEINE

Vanishing point. Point towards which perspective lines (orthogonals) converge (*see* PERSPECTIVE, §II).

Vanitas [Lat.: 'emptiness']. Type of painting concerned with the fragility of man and his world of desires and pleasures in the face of the inevitability and finality of death. It is essentially a biblical term, referring to the vanity of earthly possessions: the corresponding Hebrew term means 'smoke' or 'vapour'. The *vanitas* tradition, which also appears in Western literature and other representational arts, was a particularly important element in paintings in the Netherlands in the 17th century.

1. Origins. 2. The Netherlands. 3. Elsewhere in Europe.

1. ORIGINS. The term *vanitas* first appears in early 17th-century European inventories: like the term *trompe l'oeil*, it is used to describe a type of painted still-life (*see* STILL-LIFE, §2). *Vanitas* comes from the passage in Ecclesiastes (1:2) in which the Greek-inspired Hebrew superlative 'vapour of vapours' is used to indicate man's

insubstantiality. This is a vivid expression of the 'vanity of vanities' and of analogous biblical quotations explicitly asserting the weakness, fragility and transitory nature of human life compared with Time, the power of God and History (Psalms 39: 6–7; 94: 11; 102: 4–12; 103: 15–17; 109: 23; Ecclesiastes 41: 11 and Isaiah 40: 6–8).

The theme of the vanity of man's life and actions has a long literary history: from Attic Greece to Horace, from patristic literature and the sacred and moralizing writings of the 14th and 15th centuries (e.g. Petrarch's *Triomfi* and Torquato Tasso's *Gerusalemme liberata*) to the religious propaganda of the Reformation and Counter-Reformation.

The contrast between love of life and sentiment of death constitutes one of the most descriptive and significant themes in all extant *vanitas* paintings. Yet the whole *vanitas* tradition, as a distinct and separate category of still-lifes that emerged in the Netherlands in the early 17th century, was contradictory, loaded with a heavy verbal and symbolic inheritance and hence not truly unprecedented. The interest in devices and emblems derived from purely heraldic and aristocratic origins but soon became a space of interchange for traditions of illustrations and allegory, as well as for literary and encyclopedic erudition. By the first half of the 17th century an extensive emblematic vocabulary based on Italian precedents had developed in the Netherlands, giving *vanitas* associations to all sorts of actions and occurrences as well as to fruits, flowers and other objects from daily life. Such popular EMBLEM BOOKS as Roemer Visscher's *Sinnepoppen* (Amsterdam, 1614), Johan de Brune's *Emblemata of Sinnewerck* (Amsterdam, 1624), Zacharias Heyns's *Emblemata* (Rotterdam, 1625) and Jacob Cats (i)'s *Sinne- en minnebeelden* (Amsterdam, 1627) were based on Netherlandish proverbs and common sayings. Many of these emblems preferred to make their point with common domestic images rather than the classical esoterica of Renaissance emblems. The *vanitas* still-life combined the two strands of moralizing, the consciously erudite with the deliberately homespun.

A *vanitas* still-life is distinguished by the presence of traditional symbols such as the skull and other human remains (*memento mori*). These appear in earlier south Netherlandish prototypes of the 15th century, such as the *verso* of Rogier van der Weyden's Braque Triptych (Paris, Louvre), and in the 16th century, such as the *verso* of the right wing of Jan Gossart's diptych of *Jean Carondelet* (1517; Paris, Louvre). A skull, as symbol of mortality, and a carnation, emblem of the hope for eternal life, appear in Dirk Jacobsz.'s portrait of the banker, merchant and humanist *Pompeius Occo* (?1531; Amsterdam, Rijksmus.). In Bartholomaeus Bruyn (i)'s *Vanitas Still-life* on the back of the portrait of *Jane-Loyse Tissier* (1524; Otterlo, Kröller-Müller) the skull and candle symbolize the shortness of life, and the inscription reads: *Omnia morte cadut, mors ultima linia rerum* ('Everything is conquered by death, death is the end of things'). A putto blowing bubbles, another way of indicating the fragility of human existence, is found on the back of Cornelis Ketel's *Portrait of a Man* (1574; Amsterdam, Rijksmus.). The *verso* is inscribed in Greek: 'Man is a soap bubble', of which the Latin variant is *Homo bulla*.

Undoubtedly, portrait *versos* in the 15th and 16th centuries were instrumental in the rise of the independent *vanitas* still-life at the beginning of the 17th century; however, a survey of the representation of the macabre is not enough to explain the wide popularity of the *vanitas* still-life. It is found in Calvinist areas such as the northern Netherlands, in particular Leiden and its university, and in areas influenced by the Counter-Reformation, the southern Netherlands, France and Spain, where it sometimes reached extreme proportions. Many theories have been advanced to explain the origins and the sudden rise of the *vanitas* still-life. Some scholars have seen its source in the Counter-Reformation (Mâle and Knipping), others in 16th-century symbolism and Calvinism (Bergström), and still others in the then new conception of the importance of painting as an art form, a direct development of the Italian Renaissance (Sterling). In fact, these theories are more complementary than opposed. The *vanitas* exemplifies—more than any other narrative or allegorical theme—the paradox of earthly life as contemplated by the growing middle class in the Netherlands: there was a concern that man should not be seduced by sensual experiences, but at the same time theologians had begun to celebrate the blessings of God's creation, the extraordinary riches and beauty of the natural world. The two strands of thought were conflicting yet interrelated. The purchaser of a *vanitas* still-life could enjoy the beauty of the work but simultaneously be reminded of its sombre message.

2. THE NETHERLANDS. The first independent *vanitas* still-lifes (i.e. those not combined with a portrait) were probably painted in the northern Netherlands *c.* 1600. Among the earliest examples is a signed *Vanitas* by Jacques de Gheyn II, with the inscription *Humana vana* (1603; New York, Met.; see fig. 1). In a central niche is a skull, placed on a few stalks of grain; above it floats a transparent ball (a well-established reference to *homo bulla*), in which are reflected many objects relating to transience and vanity, including playing cards and a tric-trac game; a vase of flowers (with the expensive yet quickly decaying tulip) on the left, some coins in the middle and a smoking urn on the right reinforce the explicit reference to the transience of earthly things; and in the spandrels above are images of Democritus laughing at human folly and Heraclitus bemoaning it. Another early example (untraced) was painted by Abraham Bloemaert and, with the still-life by de Gheyn, was mentioned by Karel van Mander as being in the possession of the Amsterdam art collectors Jacques Rozet and Reynier Anthonissen. Bloemaert's composition is known from an engraving by Jan Saenredam, with a particularly rich border decorated with all the panoply and attributes of death, from the reclining skeleton to hour-glasses and blazing torches with curls of smoke. In an engraving of 1626 by Hendrik Hondius I a *vanitas* still-life has books, flowers, hour-glasses, a candle and a skull arranged on a table in a room, but in the foreground are attributes pertaining to the arts. The print's inscription reads: *Finis coronat opus* ('The end crowns the work'), which is one of the many variants of the well-known *vanitas* maxim *Vita brevis, ars longa* ('Life is short, but art endures').

1. *Vanitas* by Jacques de Gheyn II, oil on panel, 825×540 mm, 1603 (New York, Metropolitan Museum of Art)

David Bailly also played an important part in the development of the *vanitas* theme in the Netherlands. Three *vanitas* works by him survive, including a small pen-and-ink drawing in the *Album amicorum* of Cornelis de Montigny de Charges (1624; The Hague, Kon. Bib.) and the painting *Vanitas Still-life with a Portrait of a Young Painter* (1651; Leiden, Stedel. Mus. Lakenhal; for illustration *see* BAILLY, DAVID). The earlier drawing contains the standard ensemble of didactic *vanitas* still-life objects, as well as a paper scroll with the inscription *Quis evadet* and a smoking pipe, signifying ephemerality as well as the futility of the material life. Three of Bailly's pupils, Harmen van Steenwyck (1612–after 1655), his younger brother Pieter van Steenwyck (*fl* 1632–54) and Pieter (Symonsz.) Potter (i), all specialized in *vanitas* still-lifes. Paintings depicting the contemplation of a skull, which stem from 16th-century images of St Jerome meditating in his study by such artists as Marinus van Reymerswaele, Joos van Cleve (ii) and Jan Sanders van Hemessen, began to give way to the depiction of more everyday objects, such as books, candles, hour-glasses, watches, globes, astrolabes, flowers and fruit. These all refer to the measurement and the passage of time, wisdom accumulated in study, the fragile treasures of the earth and the human senses. Flowers and fruit were particularly frequent in Dutch and Flemish *vanitas* images, their flowering, withering and death being

a highly effective illustration of beauty's fragility, brevity and desirability (*see* FLOWER PAINTING, §2). The association between flowers (e.g. carnation, rose, lily etc) and moral qualities (e.g. incarnation, transience, purity etc) derives from 15th- and 16th-century symbolism, and the *vanitas* still-life often functions as a visual metaphor for a biblical quotation: 'He comes forth like a flower, and is cut down. And he, as a rotten thing, consumed, as a garment that is moth-eaten' (Job 14:2). The tulip was especially popular in this respect owing to its short flowering season and the fact that it was the centre of a spectacular financial crash in 1637; it thus came to represent the dangers of financial greed and speculation. The *vanitas* tradition was already firmly vested in the flower still-lifes of Jan Breughel I and also noticeable in various degrees in the oeuvre of early 17th-century still-life painters, including Ambrosius Bosschaert, Balthasar van der Ast and Osias Beert the elder.

The prominent Haarlem still-life painters Pieter Claesz. and Willem Claesz. Heda also painted *vanitas* still-lifes, but it was Jan Davidsz. de Heem (*see* HEEM, DE, (1)) who had a decisive influence on the further development of *vanitas* still-life paintings. Between 1625 and 1631 in Leiden, de Heem painted a number of small still-lifes with books, so-called *vanitas-studium* still-lifes, in greyish and brownish tones. Sometimes he added a skull and a globe and sometimes a musical instrument, as in the different versions of his *Still-life with Books* (e.g. Amsterdam, Rijksmus.; see fig. 2), which are early examples of a disordered composition with books bearing distinct *vanitas* connotations. The variety of objects found in the *vanitas* paintings and their symbolic meanings has led to the subdivision of the genre. Another type of *vanitas* painting contained arms and armour, books and references to arts and sciences. Thus, the hollow trophies of war were balanced against the peaceful values of *studium*. Jacques de Gheyn II's *vanitas* (1621; New Haven, CT, Yale U. A.G.) is an example of the *vanitas* trophy. Yet another type were the ostentatious *vanitas* still-lifes (Dut. *pronkstilleven*: 'ornate still-lifes'), characterized by a display of rare, exotic and luxurious objects. The ornate *vanitas* still-life was developed by de Heem in the 1640s and was carried to further extremes by Willem Kalf and Abraham Hendricksz. van Beyeren.

3. ELSEWHERE IN EUROPE. *Vanitas* themes also enjoyed particular popularity in Paris from the 1620s (e.g. Jacques Linard's *Vanitas Still-life with a Skull, Book and Carnation*, Madrid, Prado; and Sebastien Stoskopff's *Vanitas Still-life*, Rotterdam, Mus. Boymans–van Beuningen). The influence of de Heem's ornate still-lifes is also unmistakable in Stoskopff's *La Grande Vanité* (1641; Strasbourg, Mus. Oeuvre Notre-Dame; for illustration *see* STOSKOPFF, SEBASTIEN), a *vanitas* still-life with glass goblets and silver beakers symbolizing the transience of wealth and power. An engraving after Jacques Callot in the foreground depicts Zani, a clown from the *opera buffa*. The text appropriately reinforces the *vanitas* association: *Kunst, Reichthum, Macht und Kühnheit stirbet, Die Welt und all ihr thun verdirbet, Ein ewiges komt nach dieser Zeit, Ihr Thoren, flieht die Eitelkeit . . .* ('Art, riches, power and courage die. The world with its activities decays. After this

2. *Vanitas Still-life with Books* by Jan Davidsz. de Heem, oil on panel, 265×415 mm, *c.* 1625–31 (Amsterdam, Rijksmuseum)

time comes eternity. You fools, escape from vanity'). From the middle of the 17th century the theme also enjoyed popularity in France among such painters as Philippe de Champaigne and Simon Renard de Saint-André (1613–77), but the latter mainly continued the iconographic tradition of the previous century.

In Spain the allegorical *vanitas*, with a strongly dramatic setting dedicated to the triumph of death, was to find its greatest exponent in the paintings of Juan de Valdés Leal (e.g. *Finis gloria mundi*, 1672; Seville, Hosp. Caridad). It was a genre also found in Naples, a city where Spanish influence was significant. In other parts of Italy the *vanitas* tradition can be found in the works of Francesco Solimena, Cristoforo Munari, Giuseppe Ghislandi, Evaristo Baschenis and Cerano, among others. Baschenis, for instance, specialized in still-lifes with dust-covered musical instruments, which—given the impermanence of their tones—were also well-known *vanitas* symbols (for illustration *see* BASCHENIS, EVARISTO). Musical and nautical instruments also figured largely in the work of the Dutch-born artist Edwart Collier, who may have introduced *vanitas* subject-matter into England during his stay there some time between 1688 and 1706.

By the beginning of the 18th century the impetus of *vanitas* still-lifes was different from that of the previous century: their focus began to shift away from the scientific, religious and philosophical foundation that had so characterized the earlier development towards greater displays of extraordinary virtuosity. In short, still-lifes became more decorative than didactic.

BIBLIOGRAPHY

E. Mâle: *L'Art religieux après le Concile de Trente* (Paris, 1931)
B. Knipping: *De iconografie van de Contra-Reformatie in de Nederlanden*, 1 (Hilversum, 1939–40; Eng. trans., Leiden, 1974)
I. Bergström: *Dutch Still-life Painting in the Seventeenth Century* (New York, 1956)
C. Sterling: *La Nature-morte de l'antiquité à nos jours* (Paris, 1959)
E. de Jongh: *Zinne- en minnebeelden in de schilderkunst van de zeventiende eeuw* (Amsterdam and Antwerp, 1967)
B. Haak: 'De vergankelijkheidssymboliek in zestiende-eeuwse portretten en zeventiende-eeuwse stillevens in Holland', *Antiek*, i (1968), pp. 23–30; ii (1969), pp. 399–411
Ijdelheid der ijdelheden: Hollandse vanitas-voorstellingen uit de zeventiende eeuw (exh. cat., ed. I. Bergström and M. L. Wurfbain; Leiden, Stedel. Mus. Lakenhal, 1970)
N. Popper-Voskuil: 'Self-portraiture and Vanitas Still-life in 17th-century Holland in Reference to David Bailly's Vanitas Oeuvre', *Pantheon*, xxxi (1973), pp. 58–74
Stilleben in Europa (exh. cat., ed. C. Klemm; Münster, Westfäl. Landesmus.; Baden-Baden, Staatl. Ksthalle; 1979–80)
Vanitas: Il simbolismo del tempo (exh. cat., ed. A. Veca; Bergamo, Gal. Lorenzelli; 1981) [with Eng. summary]
Een bloemrijk verleden: Overzicht van de Noord- en Zuidnederlandse bloemschilderkunst, 1600-heden/A Flowery Past: A Survey of Dutch and Flemish Flower Painting from 1600 until the Present (exh. cat., ed. S. Segal; Amsterdam, P. De Boer; 's Hertogenbosch, Noordbrabants Mus.; 1982)
Still-life in the Age of Rembrandt (exh. cat., ed. E. de Jongh; Auckland, C.A.G.; 1982)
B. Haak: *The Golden Age: Dutch Painters of the Seventeenth Century* (New York, 1984), pp. 125–8
Still-lifes of the Golden Age: Northern European Paintings from the Heinz Family Collection (exh. cat., ed. A. K. Wheelock; Washington, DC, N.G.A.; 1989)

HANS J. VAN MIEGROET

Van Lau [Wen Lou] (*b* Xinhui County, Guangdong Province, 15 Sept 1933). Chinese sculptor and printmaker, active in Hong Kong. Van moved with his family to Vietnam in 1935 and studied architecture and fine arts in Taiwan from 1953 to 1958; in 1960 he settled in Hong Kong. He became an influential figure in the local arts scene, not only assuming a leading role as a sculptor of the modern school, but also active in arts administration, publishing, design, education and politics. In the 1960s, inspired by contemporary international movements, Van experimented in different styles and media. He subsequently returned to his native tradition for imagery and aesthetic concepts, though retaining a Western approach in formal organization. Thereafter, his focus has been metal sculpture in geometric formations suggesting vitality and organic growth. His fascination with movement, particularly flight, inspired his *Space Form* (Hong Kong, Space Mus.), completed in 1980, followed by numerous public commissions.

BIBLIOGRAPHY

Wen Lou/The Art of Van Lau (exh. cat., intro. C. Chu; Hong Kong, Mus. A., 1987)

MAYCHING KAO

Van Leemputten. Belgian family of painters.

(1) Cornelis Van Leemputten (*b* Werchter, 25 Jan 1841; *d* Brussels, 23 Nov 1902). He was totally self-taught, except for a few lessons from his father, Jan-Frans Van Leemputten. He made studies from nature, working mainly in Brabant and Campine, near Antwerp. His vast landscapes with grazing sheep, such as *Sheep* (1871; Brussels, Mus. A. Mod.) and *Flock of Sheep* (Antwerp, Kon. Mus. S. Kst.), have a poetic quality influenced by the works of Charles Jacque. He became fairly successful through participating in international exhibitions, winning a gold medal in Ghent in 1883 and another in Berlin in 1896. He was made a Chevalier de l'ordre de Léopold in 1895.

(2) Frans Van Leemputten (*b* Werchter, 29 Dec 1850; *d* Antwerp, 26 Nov 1914). Brother of (1) Cornelis Van Leemputten. He studied with the landscape painter Paulus Lauters at the Académie Royale de Beaux-Arts in Brussels, and he also attended the free studio known as 'La Patte de Dindon' with Constantin Meunier and Frans Courtens (1854–1943). He took part in exhibitions organized by La Chrysalide, a group in Brussels that championed the Realist movement. He was influenced by the writings of the Realist novelist Hendrik Conscience and devoted his career to portraying life in Campine, emphasizing the resignation and monotony of rural life. His work shows him to have been an attentive observer, although his pictures always evince an atmosphere of gentle melancholy, as in *Peasants on their Way to Work* (1887; Brussels, Mus. A. Mod.) and *Distribution of Bread in the Village* (1892; Antwerp, Kon. Mus. S. Kst.). From 1888 he was influenced by Luminism, and his paintings became brighter, although his subjects did not change. He participated in many international exhibitions and received numerous medals. He was appointed Professor of Animal Painting at the Nationaal Hoger Instituut en Koninklijke Academie Voor Schone Kunsten in Antwerp, the city in which he settled and pursued his academic career.

BIBLIOGRAPHY

Bénézit; *BNB*

Catalogus schilderijen 19de en 20ste eeuw (exh. cat. by J. B. Buyck, Antwerp, Kon. Mus. S. Kst., 1977)

SIBYLLE VALCKE

Vanlimpitt, Remigeus. *See* LEEMPUT, REMI VAN.

Vanloo. *See* LOO, VAN.

Vanni. Italian family of artists.

(1) Francesco Vanni (*b* Siena, 1563; *d* Siena, 26 Oct 1610). Painter, draughtsman and printmaker. He studied first in Siena with his stepfather Arcangelo Salimbeni (*d* 1580), and then in Rome (1579–80) with Giovanni de' Vecchi. The stylistic sources of his earliest works, such as the *Baptism of Constantine* (1586–7; Siena, S Agostino), lie both in the art of Salimbeni, which represented a reaction against the artificiality of Mannerism, and in the art of the Counter-Reformation in Rome, particularly that of Federico Zuccaro. From 1585 the strongest influence on his work is the art of Federico Barocci. This is particularly evident in the sharp and acid colours, rich in clear and iridescent tones, of *Christ Appearing to St Catherine* (Siena, Santuario Cateriniano) and of the *Baptism* (1587; ex-S Giovannino e Gennaro, Siena). It is also evident in his handling of facial types in the *Immaculate Conception* (1588; Montalcino Cathedral) and still more marked in the *Annunciation* (1589; Siena, S Maria dei Servi), commissioned by the Servi Order in Siena, which is directly based on Barocci's *Annunciation* (Rome, Pin. Vaticana). Vanni also responded to the art of the Carracci, which he may have assimilated during a probable apprenticeship with Bartolomeo Passarotti in Bologna, or while on a visit to that city. *St Francis Receiving the Child from the Virgin* (Florence, Uffizi) has long been attributed to Ludovico Carracci but is in fact the bozzetto for Vanni's *St Anthony Receiving the Child from the Virgin* (Amsterdam, Rijksmus.).

In the 1590s Vanni became the leading figure in the artistic life of Siena. He received many commissions from churches and confraternities which, in line with the new dictates of the Counter-Reformation, were renewing the decoration of ancient churches. Altarpieces such as *St Ansano Baptizing the Sienese* (1593; Siena Cathedral) and *St Hyacinth Reviving a Drowned Child* (1596; Siena, Santa Spirito) show that Vanni was searching for more spacious compositions and clearer narrative, with intensely naturalistic portraits and details, as were contemporary Florentine painters. This new realism aroused the interest of Cardinals Cesare Baronio (1538–1602) and Paolo Emilio Sfondrati (1560–1618), distinguished representatives of the oratory of the Filippini in Rome and dedicated worshippers of the early Christian martyrs. It was to them that Vanni owed the numerous commissions he received *c.* 1600 from Roman patrons. The most celebrated of these works is the lunette painting the *Death of St Cecilia* (1600), painted in Siena for S Cecilia in Trastevere, Rome (*in situ*). This masterpiece is distinguished by the deeply felt yet restrained emotion, and an archaizing classical quality. In 1603 Baronio secured for Vanni the highly prized commission for one of the altarpieces for St Peter's, Rome: the *Fall of Simon Magus* (Rome, St Peter's, Depositi), which was soon broken up. The painting's magniloquent scenic effect makes it comparable with the nearby altar-pieces by the Tuscans Lodovico Cigoli, Cristoforo Roncalli and Domenico Passignano, who were involved in the same commission, and emphasizes the fidelity of all these artists to the Tuscan ideal of *disegno*.

On his return to Siena, Vanni devoted himself to local commissions, of which the best known are the *Return of the Holy Family from Egypt* (1603; Siena, SS Quirico e Giulitta) and the *Disputation over the Sacrament* (1609; Pisa Cathedral). In these last works his colours became harsher and he began to fill the entire surface area with figures. Nevertheless his art, in its opposition to Mannerism and its allegiance to the Roman art of Raphael, and to Barocci and the Carracci, remained fundamental to the development of Sienese painting at the end of the 16th century.

Vanni was an able draughtsman and made painstaking preparatory drawings for his works. Representative collections are held at the Uffizi in Florence and the Louvre, Paris. Three prints by him are known (B. 1–3), all on religious subjects.

BIBLIOGRAPHY

A. von Bartsch: *Le Peintre–graveur* (1803–21), pp. 195–7 [B.]

G. Bianchi Bandinelli: 'Catalogo delle opere del pittore Francesco Vanni', *Bull. Sen. Stor. Patria*, 1 (1943), pp. 139–55

P. A. Riedl: 'Zu Francesco Vanni und V. Salimbeni', *Mitt. Ksthist. Inst. Florenz*, ix (1959–60), pp. 60–90

L. Salmina Haskell: 'Drawings by Francesco Vanni in the Hermitage', *Master Drgs*, iv/1 (1966), pp. 32–6

S. Pepper: 'Baglione, Vanni and Cardinal Sfrondato', *Paragone*, xviii/221 (1967), pp. 69–74

A. Nava Cellini: 'S. Maderno, F. Vanni e G. Reni a S Cecilia in Trastevere', *Paragone*, xx/227 (1969), pp. 18–41

W. C. Kirwin: 'The Oratory of the Sanctuary of St Catherine in Siena', *Mitt. Ksthist. Inst. Florenz*, xvi (1972), pp. 199–220

P. A. Riedl: 'Francesco Vanni als Zeichner', *Münchn. Jb. Bild. Kst*, xx (1979), pp. 81–106

L'arte e Siena sotto i Medici, 1555–1609 (exh. cat., Siena, Pal. Pub., 1979), pp. 120–42

(2) Raffaele Vanni (*b* Siena, 4 Oct 1587; *d* 29 Nov 1673). Painter, son of (1) Francesco Vanni. He studied first in Siena with his father, whose sweetness of style remained a constant influence. After his father's death he went to Rome, where he was apprenticed first to Guido Reni and later to Antonio Carracci. It seems that subsequently he spent a few years in Venice studying colour. His earliest documented work, the *Virgin and Child* (1644; Siena, Monte Paschi; see Bisogni and Ciampolini, fig. 33), combines the influence of Siena with the restrained classicism of Antonio Carracci. Later he responded enthusiastically to the Baroque art of Pietro da Cortona and in subsequent years was involved in major projects in Rome, where he worked with the most distinguished artists of the day while still retaining links with Tuscany. His earliest recorded works include *SS Flora and Lucilla* (1651; Arezzo, Chiesa della Badia), a fresco of the *Victory of Clovis over Alaric* (1652; Siena, Santa Trinità) and the frescoes featuring scenes from the *Life of St John the Baptist* (Siena, S Giovanni Battista della Staffa), in which he collaborated with Rutilio Manetti. His best Sienese work (della Valle) is the *Road to Calvary* (1656) in S Giorgio, in which he successfully created a new and personal style from Bolognese classicism and the lyricism of Siena, transformed by the Roman Baroque of Cortona. The *St Ivo in Glory between SS Sebastian and Agnes* (Siena, S Martino), a more mature work, also reveals a response

to Roman Baroque painting. His sweet and tender *Holy Family with St John* (Florence, Uffizi), however, re-creates the poetic spirit of his father's painting.

In Rome, Vanni had succeeded in gaining entry to the Accademia di S Luca and was Principal from 1658 to 1660. Among his Roman works are two canvases in S Maria in Publicolis: the *Birth of the Virgin* on the high altar and *St Helen before the Cross* on a side-wall (both 1643; *in situ*). In 1656–7 he was commissioned to paint the *Birth of the Virgin* for the decoration of the walls of the octagon in S Maria della Pace, Rome (*in situ*), where Pietro da Cortona was directing the restoration. Vanni's work, magnificent and grandly composed, is dominated by the influence of Cortona (who may have won him the commission), although there remain echoes of Bolognese classicism.

In 1665 Vanni was one of a group of artists selected by Bernini to paint altarpieces for the Collegiata dell'Assunta at Ariccia, a building that Bernini had designed. Vanni's *Death of St Thomas of Villanueva* is a grave and clearly structured work that reflects his training with Antonio Carracci. In the last decades of his life he painted for private collectors and for churches in Tuscany, especially in Siena. His *Dream of St Robert's Mother* (Rome, Santa Croce in Gerusalemme) is a late work from the 1670s, arranged on two levels, and including the miraculous appearance of the Virgin. It is Vanni's parting tribute to Roman Baroque painting, particularly to Pietro da Cortona, whose example so dominated his mature oeuvre.

BIBLIOGRAPHY

G. della Valle: *Lettere senesi*, iii (Venice and Rome, 1786), pp. 405–9

G. Milanesi: *Sulla storia dell'arte toscana* (Siena, 1873), p. 63

V. Mengozzi: 'Il Monte di Paschi (Siena): Lavori artistici', *Bull. Sen. Stor. Patria*, xi (1904), p. 435

Bernardino Mei e la pittura barocca a Siena (exh. cat. by F. Bisogni and M. Ciampolini, Siena, Pal. Chigi–Saraceni, 1987), ii, pp. 83–107

SIMONETTA PROSPERI VALENTI RODINÒ

Vanni, Andrea. *See* ANDREA VANNI.

Vanni, Lippo. *See* LIPPO (DI) VANNI.

Vanni, Mariano. *See* TACCOLA, MARIANO.

Vanni [Besprosvanni], **Sam(uel)** (*b* Viipuri [now Vyborg, Russia], 6 July 1908; *d* Helsinki, 20 Oct 1992). Finnish painter. He studied at the School of the Fine Arts Association (later the Academy of Fine Arts), Helsinki (1927–8) and at the Accademia di Belle Arti, Florence. In 1930 he was a private student of the sculptor Wäinö Aaltonen and assisted him in his great public commissions, notably the decoration of the new Parliament building in Helsinki. In 1931 Vanni exhibited a work publicly for the first time—a *Still-life with Violin* (1931; priv. col., see Kruskopf), characterized by rigorously constructed plastic forms. In 1938 and 1939 he was resident in London and in France, where he attended the Académie Julian and the Académie de la Grande Chaumière in Paris and, on the suggestion of the Finnish painter Ragnar Ekelund (1892–1960), travelled to Chevreuse, diligently drawing and painting urban themes. This period was of great significance for Vanni, although he still exhibited in Finland, where he was commended for his use of colour. Henri

Matisse and Pierre Bonnard were important early influences.

Vanni belonged to the first generation of Finnish painters who adopted abstraction after World War II. For Vanni this was a gradual process, and as early as 1942 in his first one-man exhibition his landscapes, still-lifes and portraits show a simplification of form, as in the *Still-life with Book* (1942; priv. col., see Kruskopf). On his travels to Italy and France in 1947 and 1948 Vanni was able to see more abstract art, but the old models were still important. In his painting *Parisian Woman* (1948; priv. col., see Kruskopf), for example, features of Matisse's decorative expression are noticeable. However, many of Vanni's portraits from the late 1940s already tended towards abstraction. He finally abandoned representational art in 1952, when he painted a series of abstract gouaches (e.g. *Autumn*; see Kruskopf). In that same year the influential exhibition *Clear Form* was held in the Art Exhibition Hall, Helsinki, in cooperation with the Galerie Denise René in Paris. Vanni was again tempted by the international atmosphere in Paris and worked there in 1953 and 1954. In Vanni's early abstract works there is no depth of field, but movement is an important factor in the composition. His early works were already dynamic, but colour and later, form, were of major importance.

In 1948 Vanni was joint winner in a competition in monumental painting for Kauttua, with *Dance on the Jetty* (1947; sketches in Lund, Kstmus., Arkv Dek. Kst), but the commission went to Birger Carlstedt (1907–75). In the late 1950s and 1960s Vanni gained several public assignments, the most important being the oil painting *Contrapunctus* (1959; Helsinki, Fin. Workers' Inst.; collage model, Helsinki, Athanaeum A. Mus.), which has the people's struggle with matter as the theme. Here, he successfully united figurative elements with an abstract composition and made use of a limited colour-scale of black, white and brown with accents in red. He continued to paint large public commissions, one of the largest being the abstract *Work and Family* (1.7×9.7 m, 1965) for a branch of the Postal Savings Bank in Fredrikinkatu, Helsinki.

Vanni joined the artists' group Prisma in 1956, along with Unto Pusa (1913–73), Sigrid Schauman (1877–1979) and Ragnar Ekelund, among others. These artists were united in remaining open to influences from Europe and counterbalancing the strong nationalist tendencies of post-war Finnish art. In the early 1960s Vanni took an interest in optical and kinetic effects in his painting and executed, among others, *Multidimensional Space* (1961; see Kruskopf), based on the interior of his studio, following many studies on the same theme. Optical effects are also apparent in *Beneath the Flicker of the Northern Lights* (1964), which he produced for the Lapland Central Vocational School in Rovaniemi. This period culminated in the exhibitions he held in 1967 in Tampere and in Jyväskylä, where the best results from this period were presented, for instance the oil painting *Helsinki* (1966; Helsinki, Anderson Mus. A.; see FINLAND, fig. 7). Vanni spent many years teaching, first at the Free Art School and subsequently at the Art Academy School in Helsinki, and he created a movement of young non-figurative artists. For his services Vanni was chosen as Wäinö Aaltonen's successor at the Finnish Academy in 1964, a post that he held until 1978 when he retired, although he continued to paint.

BIBLIOGRAPHY
E. Kruskopf: *Sam Vanni: Ikkuna Eurooppaan/Ett fönster mot Europa/Window on Europe* (Espoo, 1978)
Ehdotuksia ja vaihtoehtoja/Projekt och alternativ/Projects and Alternatives, 1950–1993 (exh. cat. by L.-G. Nordström, Helsinki, City A. Mus., 1993)
Väri-Muoto-Muunnelma/Färg-Form-Variation/Couleur-Forme-Variation (exh. cat., ed. T. Hihnala and P. Raippalinna; Jyväskylä, Alvar Alto Mus., 1994)
                                        BENGT VON BONSDORFF

Vanni, Turino di. *See* TURINO DI VANNI.

Vannini, Ottavio (*b* Florence, 16 Sept 1585; *d* Florence, 25 Feb 1644). Italian painter. He studied with Domenico Passignano in Florence and with Anastasio Fontebuoni (1580–1626) in Rome. In 1605, together with the Sienese painter Pietro Sorri (1556–1621/2), he executed one of his first commissions by completing the decoration of the Brunaccini Chapel in the church of the SS Annunziata in Florence. Probably he then moved to Rome as Passignano's assistant, which makes his work of this period difficult to isolate and identify confidently. Nonetheless, under the influence of his studies of Raphael and Michelangelo, he developed a personal style based on 16th-century classicism. He returned to Florence, where in 1618 he matriculated at the Accademia del Disegno and was fully employed on numerous commissions and in making copies. From *c.* 1619 he was involved in several important decorative schemes in Florence: in the Palazzo dell'Antella (*Three Virtues* (1619–20; part destr.) in the cycle of frescoes on the façade); in 1622–3 at the Villa di Poggio Imperiale (four panels in the small vault of the Sala di Cosimo II and lunettes in other rooms); in the Casino Mediceo (decorations of the vault of the Sala di Francesco I). His most prestigious commission (1638–42) was executed at the Palazzo Pitti in Florence, where he completed the Salone degli Argenti (left unfinished by Giovanni di San Giovanni) with *Lorenzo the Magnificent among the Florentine Artists* (*in situ*). For his most important patron, Andrea del Rosso (1640–1715), he frescoed the private chapel (destr.) at his palace in the Via Chiara, executed at least 14 paintings (e.g. the *Gathering of the Manna* and *Moses Drawing Water from the Rock*, both Florence, priv. col.) for Rosso's collection (works that are judged to be among his finest), and also produced other works intended for public places. Among his most notable paintings are *Judith* (*c.* 1625–30; Pisa Cathedral), the *Virgin and Saints* (1630s; Poppi, in Arezzo, S Fedele) and *Rebecca at the Well* (*c.* 1626–7; Vienna, Ksthist. Mus.).

BIBLIOGRAPHY
Bolaffi; Thieme–Becker
F. Baldinucci: *Notizie* (1681–1728); ed. F. Ranalli (1845–7), iv, pp. 430–47
M. Campbell: 'The Original Program of the Salone di Giovanni da San Giovanni', *Ant. Viva*, xv/4 (1976), pp. 3–25
Il seicento fiorentino: Arte a Firenze da Ferdinando I a Cosimo III, 3 vols (exh. cat. by A. Parronchi and A. Brook, Florence, Pal. Strozzi, 1986), i, *Pittura*, pp. 232–7; ii, *Biographie*, pp. 180–83
A. Perissa: 'Un disegno di Ottavio Vannini', *Prospettiva* [Florence], 48 (1987), p. 86
C. Pizzorusso: 'Ottavio Vannini', *La pittura in Italia: Il seicento*, M. Gregori and E. Schleier, ii (Milan, 1989), p. 914 [with bibliog.]

A. Matteoli: 'Il *Battesimo di Cristo* nel duomo di S Miniato al Tedesco dei pittori Vannini e Domminioti', *Boll. Accad. Eutelèti Città San Miniato*, lvii (1990), pp. 37–64

W. Siemoni: 'Appunti su Ottavio Vannini: L'attività empolese', *Ant. Viva*, xxix/4 (1990), pp. 5–11

ANA MARIA RYBKO

Vannocci, Oreste. *See* BIRINGUCCI, (2).

Vannucci, Pietro di Cristoforo. *See* PERUGINO.

Vannuccio, Francesco di. *See* FRANCESCO DI VANNUCCIO.

Van Osdel, John Mills (*b* Baltimore, MD, 31 July 1811; *d* Chicago, IL, 21 Dec 1891). American architect. In about 1840 he moved to New York, where he studied architecture by reading at the Apprentice Library. In 1836 William B. Ogden, a prosperous merchant from Chicago, commissioned him to design an elaborate Neo-classical residence in Chicago, then a town of only several hundred inhabitants with no other architects. His designs included residences and blocks of houses, the Rush Medical College (1844), the first Chicago City Hall (1844; destr.) and the second Cook County Court House (1853; destr.), all in a variant of the Greek Revival style. Chicago grew rapidly in the 1860s and 1870s. After 1865 Van Osdel's stylistic range broadened; his Second Presbyterian Church (1869; destr.) was Gothic Revival in style. He designed a number of hotels, including the third Tremont House (1850; destr.) and the large Palmer House (1869–70; destr.) in the popular Second Empire style. His Kendall Building (1872–3) had fireproofing applied by George H. Johnson (*b* 1830) to the internal iron structure. One of his last buildings was the imposing third Palmer House (1873–5; destr.). Although few of Van Osdel's buildings are extant, he was an inspiration to the architects who created the Chicago school in the late 19th century.

WRITINGS
The Carpenter's Own Book (Baltimore, 1834)

BIBLIOGRAPHY
DAB; *Macmillan Enc. Architects*
J. Van Osdel: *A Quarter Century of Chicago Architecture* (Chicago, 1898)
T. E. Tallmadge: *Architecture in Old Chicago* (Chicago, 1941)
F. A. Randall: *History of the Development of Building Construction in Chicago* (Urbana, 1949)
C. W. Condit: *The Chicago School of Architecture: A History of Commercial and Public Building in the Chicago Area* (Chicago, 1964)
D. Lowe: *Lost Chicago* (Boston, 1975)

LELAND M. ROTH

Van Overstraeten, Henri [Hendrik] **Désiré Louis** (*b* Leuven, 23 May 1818; *d* Ghent, 24 July 1849). Belgian architect. He was one of the most promising Belgian architects of the mid-19th century, and his early death during a cholera epidemic contributed to the growth of his romantic reputation among his contemporaries. A favourite pupil of Louis Joseph Adrien Roelandt at the Academie voor Schone Kunsten at Ghent, he was promoted by his master, whose daughter he married. The church of Ste Marie (1845–53) at Porte de Schaerbeek, Brussels, established Van Overstraeten's reputation. In contemporary publications it was praised for its originality and harmonious style and its integration into the urban setting. Composed of a combination of Romanesque,

Byzantine, Gothic and Renaissance elements, it introduced the *Rundbogenstil* into Belgium. Today it is still an important landmark along the ceremonial way leading from the Place Royale to the royal funerary church at Laken, its cupola-crowned silhouette, now somewhat altered by the tower added by Gustave Hansotte (1827–86), making the best use of the irregular site. The churches that he built at Middelkerke (1848), Lokeren (1849–53) and Sint Niklaas (1841–9) were also interesting contributions to the Gothic Revival style and the *Rundbogenstil*, whereas his unexecuted, prize-winning project for the 'Bas Fonds' of the Rue Royale (1847) in Brussels was remarkable for its use of structural iron.

In Van Overstraeten's theoretical work, the *Architectonographie des temples chrétiens*, of which one part was posthumously published by Roelandt (1850), he advocated eclecticism as a possible solution for 19th-century architecture, proposing his church at Schaarbeek as a model. As well as an architect he was a musician, and he studied painting under the direction of Edouard de Vigne (1808–66), dedicating to Count Philip of Flanders an album with watercolours of his designs for a historical pageant at Ghent in 1849.

WRITINGS
Architectonographie des temples chrétiens, ou étude comparative et pratique des différents systèmes d'architecture applicables à la construction des églises, spécialement en Belgique (Mechelen, 1850)

BIBLIOGRAPHY
BNB
C. Kramm: *De levens en werken der hollandsche en vlaamsche kunstschilders, beeldhouwers, graveurs en bouwmeesters*, iv (Amsterdam, 1857–64), p. 1242 [app.; p. 116]
C. F. A. Piron: *Algemeene levensbeschrijving der mannen en vrouwen van België* (Mechelen, 1860), p. 290
Poelaert en zijn tijd (exh. cat., text V. G. Martiny and others; Brussels, Pal. Justice, 1980), pp. 197–9
J. van Cleven: '19th Century: Architecture', *Flemish Art*, ed. H. Liebaers (Antwerp, 1985), p. 505

JEAN VAN CLEVEN

Vanpook, Karel van. *See* POUCKE, KAREL VAN.

Van Rensselaer, Mariana Griswold [Mrs Schuyler] (*b* New York, 21 Feb 1851; *d* New York, 20 Jan 1934). American writer. She was educated at home by tutors and travelled in Europe, chiefly in Germany. In 1873 she married Schuyler Van Rensselaer, an engineer. They lived in New Brunswick, NJ, until her husband's death in 1884. Mrs Van Rensselaer then lived with her mother in New York while pursuing the writing career she had begun shortly before her husband's death. Some of her essays had already appeared in *American Architect* and the popular *Century Magazine*. From May 1884 to July 1886 *Century Magazine* published six extended illustrated essays in which she examined the current state of American architecture. A writer on all the visual arts, she published numerous books on painting, architecture, photography and landscape architecture, as well as two of her own poetry. In her writing she addressed a broad popular audience, particularly potential patrons of architecture. She published a small book on this topic, *Client and Architect*. A keen admirer of the work of H. H. Richardson, she wrote *Henry Hobson Richardson and his Works*, which was the first monograph on a modern American architect. For her efforts in cultivating the public awareness of architecture she was made an honorary member of the American Institute of Architects and the American Society of Landscape Architects.

WRITINGS

American Etchers (New York, 1886)
Book of American Figure Painters (New York, 1886)
Henry Hobson Richardson and his Works (Boston, MA, 1888)
Client and Architect (Chicago, 1891)
English Cathedrals (New York, 1892, 6/1914)
Art out of Doors (New York, 1893, 2/1914)
Jean-François Millet: Painter-etcher (New York, 1901)
Art of Gardening (Amherst, MA, 1907)
History of the City of New York in the Seventeenth Century, 2 vols (New York, 1909)

BIBLIOGRAPHY

L. M. Roth: *America Builds: Source Documents in American Architecture and Planning* (New York, 1983), pp. 242–3

LELAND M. ROTH

Van Rysselberghe [Van Rijsselberghe]. Belgian family of artists.

(1) Octave Van Rysselberghe (*b* Antwerp, 22 July 1855; *d* Nice, 30 March 1929). Architect. He studied at the Koninklijke Academie voor Schone Kunsten in Ghent and was trained by Adolphe Pauli in the neo-classical tradition, which he freely interpreted by drawing his inspiration from the Italian Renaissance. On his return from a two-year stay in Italy, he received his practical training with Joseph Poelaert on the Palais de Justice site in Brussels before building the Observatoire Royal and a town house (both 1882) for Comte Goblet d'Alviella in Brussels. In 1893 he built a studio for his brother (2) Théo Van Rysselberghe, and it was through the latter's circle of acquaintances that he met the internationalist Paul Otlet (1868–1944), for whom he designed a town house (1894) in Brussels in the Art Nouveau style; here he was assisted by Henry Van de Velde, who was responsible for the interiors. Van Rysselberghe subsequently came to be considered one of the more original exponents of the Art Nouveau style in Belgium. He began to work for the Compagnie des Grands Hôtels Européens, for which, between 1895 and 1905, he built several tourist establishments in Ostend, Cherbourg, Monte Carlo, St Petersburg and Tunis, among other places, and these gave him a wide reputation. The Hotel Belle-Vue (1905) on the sea-front at Westende was designed on a curvilinear plan and exhibited a Mediterranean spirit in its ornamental refinement. Otlet also commissioned from Van Rysselberghe a design for a bathing resort development (1900–03) at Westende, where he built the Kursaal, a development of villas and housing, in a plastic and expressive style using large areas of roofing. He also built three large villas—Le Pachy (1906) at Bellecourt, Le Beukenhoek (1907) in Uccle and the Kreutzberg residence (1908) in Dudelange—that constitute the most finished works in this style, described as a 'regional' style in architectural debate of the period.

BIBLIOGRAPHY

L. Van der Swaelmen: 'Octave Van Rysselberghe, architecte', *La Cité*, xi (1929), pp. 145–8
Antoine Pompe et l'effort moderne en Belgique, 1890–1940 (exh. cat., eds M. Culot and F. Terlinden; Brussels, Mus. Ixelles, 1969), p. 178 [with bibliog.]

J. Stevens and E. Henvaux: 'Octave Van Rysselberghe, 1855–1929', *A+*, xvi (1978), pp. 17–56

HERVÉ PAINDAVEINE

(2) Théo(phile) Van Rysselberghe (*b* Ghent, 23 Nov 1862; *d* St-Clair, Manche, France, 13 Dec 1926). Painter, designer and sculptor, brother of (1) Octave Van Rysselberghe. He was enrolled in the Academie van Beeldende Kunsten in Ghent at an early age. In 1879 he became a pupil of Jean-François Portaels, director of the Académie Royale des Beaux-Arts in Brussels, whose Orientalist works he admired. Van Rysselberghe first exhibited at the Salon in Brussels in 1881. The next year he won a travelling scholarship and, following in the footsteps of Portaels, visited Spain and Morocco. With fellow artists Darío de Regoyos and Constantin Meunier, Van Rysselberghe recorded picturesque scenes of everyday life. He exhibited these Mediterranean pictures in 1883 at L'Essor. He attended the historic meeting on 28 October 1883 at which the avant-garde exhibition society Les XX was created, and at their exhibition in 1885 he showed the results of a second Moroccan trip, including the exotic *Fantasia* (Brussels, Mus. A. Mod.).

Membership of Les XX brought Van Rysselberghe into contact with the most radical European art. He quickly fell under the influence of James McNeil Whistler, who had exhibited at Les XX in 1884, an influence apparent in the portrait of *Octave Maus* (1885; Brussels, Mus. A. Mod.; *see* BELGIUM, fig. 51). Van Rysselberghe's *Madame Picard in her Loge* (1886; Brussels, priv. col.) was painted after Monet and Renoir had exhibited at Les XX in 1886 and reveals Impressionist influences in both form and content. Because of his growing ties with the Parisian art world, Van Rysselberghe became an important adviser to Octave Maus, secretary of Les XX.

In 1886, with the poet Emile Verhaeren, Van Rysselberghe saw Seurat's *Sunday Afternoon on the Island of La Grande Jatte* (Chicago, IL, A. Inst.) at the 8th Impressionist exhibition in Paris. The following year, when Seurat also exhibited at Les XX, Van Rysselberghe adopted Seurat's pointillist technique for the portrait of *Alice Sèthe* (Saint-Germain-en-Laye, Mus. Dépt. Prieuré). He followed this with a series of Neo-Impressionist portraits, which are psychological studies of their sitters: *Mme Charles Maus* (1890; Brussels, Mus. A. Mod.), *Maria Van de Velde at the Harmonium* (1890; Antwerp, Kon. Mus. S. Kst.) and *Mme Van Rysselberghe* (Otterlo, Rijksmus. Kröller-Müller). This genre culminated in the group portrait *The Reading* (Ghent, Mus. S. Kst.), which deftly portrays the symbiosis between Belgian and French literary and artistic circles. His Neo-Impressionist paintings were admired in Germany and Austria, and his exhibitions at the Keller & Reiner Gallery, Berlin (1898), and at the Vienna Secession (1899), were particularly successful. After 1903 his pointillist technique became more relaxed and was eventually abandoned.

During the 1890s Van Rysselberghe turned his attention to the decorative arts. For the Libre Esthétique he created the stylized cyclamen catalogue cover (1894) and several posters. In 1895 he worked for S. Bing's Parisian gallery, L'Art Nouveau, and he created furniture, jewellery, stained glass and mural decorations for a variety of clients. In 1902 he painted a decorative mural for Victor Horta's Hôtel Solvay House in Avenue Louise, Brussels. Van

Rysselberghe's striking Art Nouveau designs grace the pages of Verhaeren's *Almanach* (1894), G. Flé's *Poésies mises en musique* (1898) and Philippe-Auguste, Comte de Villiers de l'Isle-Adam's *Histoires souveraines* (1899).

In 1889 Van Rysselberghe married Maria Monnom, heiress to the Monnom firm, which published *Jeune Belgique* and *L'Art moderne*. Extensive travels in the 1890s to Athens, Constantinople, Hungary, Romania, St Petersburg and Moscow seem not to have disrupted his output of paintings and decorative art objects. He maintained a strong friendship with Signac and frequently spent time at Signac's home in St Tropez. After 1905 he continued to paint commissioned portraits, decorative murals and, more frequently, monumental nudes. Late in his career he turned also to portrait sculpture.

BIBLIOGRAPHY

E. Verhaeren: 'Théo Van Rysselberghe', *Ver Sacrum*, ii/11 (1899), pp. 1–31

G. van Zype: 'Notice sur Théo Van Rysselberghe', *Annu. Acad. Royale Belgique/Jb. Kon. Akad. België*, xcviii (1932), pp. 96–134

P. Fierens: *Théo Van Rysselberghe* (Brussels, 1937)

F. Maret: *Théo Van Rysselberghe* (Antwerp, 1948)

Rétrospective Théo Van Rysselberghe (exh. cat., ed. P. Eeckhout; Ghent, Mus. S. Kst., 1962)

M. J. Chartrain-Hebbelinck: 'Théo Van Rysselberghe: Le Groupe des XX et la Libre Esthétique', *Rev. Belge Archéol. & Hist. A.*, xxxiv (1965), pp. 99–134

——: 'Les Lettres de Van Rysselberghe à Octave Maus', *Bull. Mus. Royaux B.-A.* [Belgique], xv (1966), pp. 55–118

Théo Van Rysselberghe: Néo-impressionniste (exh. cat., intro. R. Hoozee and H. Lauwert; Ghent, Mus. S. Kst., 1993) [essays by J. Block, A. Fontainas and L. Fontainas]

JANE BLOCK

Vansanzio, Giovanni. *See* VASANZIO, GIOVANNI.

Vanson, Adrian [Son, Adriaen van] (*fl* 1570s–1602; *d* before 1610). Netherlandish painter, active in Scotland. He is first recorded in Edinburgh in June 1581, when James VI's treasurer paid him for two small paintings that had been sent to the Calvinist reformer Theodore Beza (1519–1605) in Geneva. Beza's *Icones* (Geneva, 1580), a book of engravings depicting heroes of the Reformation, contains portraits of the young *James VI* and the reformer *John Knox*, which are probably taken from Vanson's paintings (untraced); there is evidence that Vanson also sent a portrait of *George Buchanan* (untraced), the King's tutor (*c.* 1506–82), although there is not an engraving of him in the book. The engraved portrait of the King is close to the image on Scottish coins of 1575 and 1582, which are known to be derived from portraits by a painter employed by the courtier George Seton, 5th Lord Seton (*c.* 1533–85). Seton frequently travelled in France and the Low Countries (where he had been painted by Frans Pourbus (i)), and it is probable that his painter and Vanson are the same person.

In 1584 Vanson succeeded Arnold Bronckorst as official painter to the Scottish court: it is reasonable to assume that the principal royal images after that year are his work, notably the brooding, sharp-eyed portrait of *James VI* (1595; Edinburgh, N.P.G.). A colourful, complex portrait of *Lord Seton* (Edinburgh, N.G.; see fig.) has some of the same provincial qualities, allied to aspects of the northern Mannerist tradition, and is likely to be this painter's finest surviving work. Vanson is also recorded as painting

Adrian Vanson (attrib.): *George Seton, 5th Lord Seton*, oil on panel, 1.20×1.06 m, 157(?) (Edinburgh, National Gallery of Scotland)

banners and miniatures. In 1590 he provided the trumpeters' banners used at the coronation of Anne of Denmark as Queen of Scotland, while in 1601 he painted a miniature of *James VI* (untraced) that, attached to a gold chain made by the royal goldsmith George Heriot (1563–1624), was dispatched to the Queen's grandfather Ulrich III, Herzog von Mecklenburg.

Vanson became a free burgess of the city of Edinburgh on the undertaking that he would train apprentices. By this means he prepared the ground for the development of an indigenous school of painting, although this inevitably received a setback when the Scottish court moved to London in 1603, on the King's accession to the English throne as James I. Vanson is last noted (at a baptism) in 1602; in 1610 his widow Susanna de Colone petitioned for payments due to her late husband. Their son ADAM DE COLONE became a painter, a significant rival to George Jamesone.

BIBLIOGRAPHY

Painting in Scotland, 1570–1650 (exh. cat. by D. Thomson, Edinburgh, N.P.G., 1975), pp. 25–33

DUNCAN THOMSON

Vantongerloo [van Tongerloo], **Georges** (*b* Antwerp, 24 Nov 1886; *d* Paris, 5 Oct 1965). Belgian sculptor and painter. He trained at the Academy of Fine Arts in Antwerp (1900–04) and at the Académie Royale des Beaux-Arts in Brussels (1906–9). During World War I he moved to The Hague as a refugee. In 1915 he met Jules Schmalzigaug, who introduced him to Cubism and Futurism. His sculpture of this period consists of impressionistic representations of the human body, while his painting reflects a debt to Pointillism (e.g. *Sitting Man*, 1917; priv. col., see Gast, p. 234).

In 1918 Vantongerloo became associated with the journal *De Stijl*; in two of its issues he published a series of articles titled 'Réflections', in which he formulated theories about art and the role of the artist. These articles reveal his absolute belief in abstraction and a predilection for mystic and pseudo-scientific theories and concepts. Largely derived from his interest in the writings of the philosopher M. H. J. Schoenmaekers, these beliefs led Vantongerloo to visualize space as a combination of the volumes of objects and the voids that surround them.

After meeting Theo van Doesburg in 1918, Vantongerloo moved towards greater geometric and biomorphic abstraction in his sculpture. Familiarity with van Doesburg's work and ideas led Vantongerloo to construct four small sculptures collectively titled *Construction in the Sphere* (version, priv. col., on loan to The Hague, Gemeentemus.), in which Impressionism has given way to geometric abstraction, without, however, totally relinquishing recognizable motifs. In these works the human figure is reduced to geometric forms, such as the sphere, cube and pyramid. In one instance the figure is transformed into an amorphous, bulging mass with which Vantongerloo suggests movement; he appears to have been influenced by Boccioni, although there is no evidence that he knew that sculptor. After World War I Vantongerloo returned to Brussels and in 1919 he produced two stone sculptures, *Interrelation of Volumes* (version, London, Tate; for illustration *see* STIJL, DE), constructed from horizontal and vertical interlocking rectangular forms; van Doesburg recognized these works as the three-dimensional realization of the principles of De Stijl.

In 1920 Vantongerloo moved to Menton in southern France and there developed a theory of colour in which the three primary colours favoured by De Stijl artists were exchanged for the seven main colours of the spectrum. In addition, mathematical formulae and equations played an increasingly important part in his work. His sculptures still consisted of rectangular forms, but their construction was more open. A similar development took place in his paintings, where some of the rectangular blocks produced by the irregular grid were left white. At this time Vantongerloo began designing interiors, furniture and ceramics, as well as utopian architectural projects (villas, airports and bridges) that were never realized.

Vantongerloo gradually began to move away from De Stijl, although he remained true to most of its principles. In 1928 he moved to Paris and became a driving force behind the emergent movements Cercle et Carré (1930) and Abstraction-Création (1931–6). Although Vantongerloo gradually distanced himself from De Stijl and went so far, after van Doesburg's death, as to deny that he had ever been associated with the movement, it was not until 1937 that dramatic changes occurred in his paintings: his reliance on a rectilinear grid was replaced by rounded forms (circle segments and ovals), drawn as thin coloured lines against a white background, softening the severe character of his compositions.

From 1937 to 1945 Vantongerloo produced only paintings. When he took up sculpture again, his compositions became progressively more playful, comprising loose constructions of painted wire, reminiscent of atomic nuclei and the orbits of electrons around them. In this period he favoured such modern materials as perspex and plastic, in the form of imaginary heavenly bodies and comets, reflecting his continuing preoccupation with the concept of space.

WRITINGS
Regular contributions to *De Stijl* (1918–20)
L'Art et son avenir (Antwerp, 1924)
Paintings, Sculptures, Reflections (New York, 1948)

BIBLIOGRAPHY
Georges Vantongerloo (exh. cat., London, Marlborough F.A., 1962)
E. Bergen: 'Georges Vantongerloo', *Bull. Mus. Royaux B.-A. Belgique*, iv (1966), pp. 271–99
Georges Vantongerloo: Retrospective Exhibition (exh. cat. by J. Livingston, Washington, DC, Corcoran Gal. A., 1980)
V. Anker: 'Vantongerloo', *A. Int.*, xxiv/5–6 (1981), pp. 158–93
G. Baines: 'Georges Vantongerloo, de invloed van het werk van Wouters en het onstaan van de eerste abstracte beelden' [Georges Vantongerloo, the influence of the work of Wouters and the rise of the first abstract statues], *Wonen TA–BK* (1981), pp. 6–15
A. T. Jankowski: 'Georges Vantongerloo, 1886–1965', *Du*, 4 (1981), pp. 64–6
N. Gast: 'Georges Vantongerloo', *De Stijl: The Formative Years*, C. Blotkamp and others, eds (Cambridge, MA, and London, 1986), pp. 229–57

NICOLETTE GAST

Vanuatu [Ripablik Blong Vanuatu; formerly the New Hebrides]. Archipelago in the South Pacific Ocean comprising 82 islands totalling 12,190 sq. km in area. The major islands are Vanua Lava, Espiritu Santo, Maewo, Pentecost, Ambae, Malakula, Ambrym, Epi, Efate, Erromango, Tanna and Aneityum. The total population numbers 143,370 (1989 census). The capital is Port-Vila on Efate. The former Anglo-French Condominium of the New Hebrides became an independent republic in 1980. Vanuatu is characterized by enormous cultural diversity, demonstrated by its 113 distinct indigenous languages. Despite such variety, the islands of Vanuatu are culturally linked by the materials, craft techniques and traditions that occasion the production of indigenous art.

Although little archaeological work has been done, it is known that Lapita pottery-making settlements existed in north-central Vanuatu by 3500 BP, and by *c.* 2500 years ago 'Mangaasi' pottery was being used throughout the central and northern parts of Vanuatu (*see also* PACIFIC ISLANDS, §II, 4(ii)). Although spasmodic Western contacts took place from the beginning of the 17th century, most of the islands were first mapped only in 1774 by Capt. James Cook, who also named them the New Hebrides. From 1825 the people of Vanuatu were in contact with sandalwood traders, whalers, labour recruiters and land grabbers. Although conversion to Christianity had less impact than in some other Pacific areas, the introduction of European diseases, alcohol and firearms, labour recruitment and the psychological depression caused by abrupt cultural changes significantly diminished the population so that by the early 1930s only *c.* 40,000 Ni-Vanuatu survived, and many languages and cultures had died out completely. (It is difficult to gauge the pre-European contact population of Vanuatu, but estimates range from 150,000 to 1,500,000.)

While the visual and material arts of Vanuatu are spectacular and diverse, they are also often of a deeply religious nature. Consequently, much information about certain objects and their ritual use is restricted by traditional law to initiates and cannot be freely discussed or written about. More than 35,000 objects from Vanuatu are held in various collections, including those of museums in Europe (e.g. U. Cambridge, Mus. Archaeol. & Anthropol.; London, BM; Paris, Mus. Homme; Paris, Mus. A. Afr. & Océan.; Basle, Mus. Vlkerknd.), the USA (e.g. Chicago, IL, Field Mus. Nat. Hist.) and Australia (e.g. Sydney, Austral. Mus.; Melbourne, Mus. Victoria), as well as in Vanuatu itself (e.g. Port-Vila, N. Mus. Vanuatu Cult. Cent.).

1. Ritual and funerary arts. 2. Architecture. 3. Body arts. 4. Domestic arts. 5. Musical instruments.

1. RITUAL AND FUNERARY ARTS. Although some of the ceremonies that occasion the production of art in Vanuatu are secular, much art is concerned with such rituals as those of male initiation, men's secret societies, ranking systems and death. The creation and use of ritual objects are limited to those with inherited, or purchased, rights. In northern Vanatu objects are usually made from strong bamboo or tree-fern bases, covered in spiders' webs and overmodelled with a paste made from vegetable fibre mixed with mud-slip mixture. They are frequently painted with vegetable-, mineral- or marine-based colourings and may incorporate pigs' tusks. Objects are made in a secluded and sacred area singly or by groups of men, and mass production may be supervised by ritual 'assessors' who ensure that standards are maintained. The range of objects produced is enormous. A single area such as southern Malakula, for example, may have as many as a thousand different Nalawan (male secret society) rituals, and each would need several dozen pieces. Similarly, each area has its own type of headdresses and masks for use in men's grading rituals, Nimangi, or even more than one type, and particular objects and masks are required for each of the grades. Figures for the lower grades are made of plant material, tree fern is used for the middle grades and stone for the higher grades. In some areas of southern Malakula woven materials and wood, tree fern and stone carvings are used in women's grading rituals: all except the woven types being made by men. In central Pentecost, as many as two hundred red-dyed money mats are displayed and danced with as part of one of the women's higher grade rituals. The mats hang from four bamboo poles, each of which carries fifty mats. On Ambrym, grade figures represent generalized ancestral spirits associated with the grade, and additional paintings on them may link them to the natural world.

In southern Malakula entry into Nalawan rituals and the purchase of grades are important in determining an individual's funerary rituals and its associated objects. The most well-known funeral object is the male mortuary effigy (*rambaramp*), which contains the deceased's overmodelled skull (see fig. 1). After public display in the final stages of the funeral rituals, these are placed in the men's sacred hut. On the island of Maewo dance batons made from wood and barkcloth and painted with designs associated with the creation hero, Tagaro, are used in the funerary rituals of high-ranking men. Some items made for ritual

1. Vanuatu overmodelled skull, painted in light brown and black, with spider-web headdress, 160×250 mm, from southern Malakula (Paris, Musée de l'Homme)

use in Vanuatu are seldom seen, because they are intentionally destroyed after use. Others (e.g. the *botmolmoli* headdresses made for the dance that closes male grade rituals on Atchin Island) are fragile, being made of a light-wood framework with feather decoration, and consequently few examples reach the outside world. Rarity is not only caused by fragility or intentional destruction. Although Tamate societies on the Banks Islands use a variety of headdresses and masks, representing aspects of the spirit world, sea snakes, fish, sharks and crocodiles as well as ships and aeroplanes, production of these decreased with the decline of the Tamate societies following the publication in the 1890s of many of their secrets. The spectacular Aneityumese decorated litters made for carrying chiefs during rituals are also rare.

Vanuatu graphic art includes large petroglyphs at Aname and Unmej on Aneityum and the undated charcoal cave paintings in the cave of Feles on Leleppa showing hands, spirit figures and lunar counting marks. In north-east Malakula knowledge of particular continuous line sand drawings is essential in order to ensure the passage of one's spirit to its place of rest. On north Ambrym such drawings are known as *tu netan*, and several hundred different styles are found throughout northern Vanuatu. Cave paintings and ancient large stone carvings are found in the Torres.

2. ARCHITECTURE. The centre of much of Vanuatu's ritual life is the men's sacred house, from which women are excluded. These may be more than 30 m in length, are

often highly decorated and have arched or sloped roofs reaching to the ground. On Efate the oblong houses are constructed using highly decorated coconut-fibre binding, while men's houses in the Banks Islands have intricately carved posts, particularly on the front exterior, and paintings of spirits or mythical heroes on flat boards. Beautifully decorated sacred ladders are built up the sides of men's huts in southern Pentecost for male grade-taking rituals. On Tanna, a 4–5 m high pole symbolizing the power of a chief comprises a long reed bundle covered in feathers with a crown into which hawk feathers are inserted. In southern Pentecost Island massive towers, 25 m or more high, are built for the annual land dive ceremonies that celebrate the sprouting of the first yams.

3. BODY ARTS. Personal adornment is widely practised in Vanuatu and includes not only the wearing of elaborate garments but also face painting, nasal perforation, ear-piercing for shell segment earrings and puberty-related scarification of women's backs to enhance beauty, indicate status and promote good health. Rank is often indicated by both dress and ornament. Until the late 1920s, women in Ambae were tattooed with extremely elaborate patterns all over their bodies in preparation for marriage to high-ranking men. On Erromango, once married, decorated leaf dresses were used to indicate rank, and so many might be worn at one time that movement was impeded. The twined and extended hairstyles worn by some men to enhance their ritual power were also restrictive. To ensure that the hair was not disturbed during sleep, carved wooden neckrests were used. Decorated beaded armbands are common and on Efate are made of white shell and black coconut wood beads, worn with a heavy, circular white shell on the chest. On Espiritu Santo men wore polished lozenge-shaped pieces of hardwood on a beaded belt as buttock ornaments, while in the Banks Islands finely woven chest, shoulder and back coverings indicate status. A circular, pierced greenstone neck pendant, symbolizing lineage power, was worn by men on Tanna during rituals. Tapa belts with black-, brown- and red-painted designs were worn also on Tanna, with red being restricted to the more important men. Penis wrappers made of barkcloth may be worn strapped upright, as on Tanna, where wrappers are undifferentiated, or hanging down, as on Erromango, where a large white cowrie-like shell at the end of the wrapper indicated status. On Malakula, Ambrym and southern Pentecost Island men normally wore woven penis wrappers, woven mat loincloths being worn widely elsewhere in the northern central islands.

4. DOMESTIC ARTS. Vanuatu pottery-making declined from the 13th century, possibly with the introduction of new cooking techniques, the destruction of trade links and the demise of pottery-making groups. By the 1990s only a few villages, all on Espiritu Santo, retained the right to make pottery. Two such villages are Wusi and Olpoe on the west coast of Santo. Here women continue to produce pottery, some of which is similar to the ancient Lapita style. Domestic items made from hardwood are often finely carved and include breadfruit pounders, wooden plates (including large plates in the form of stylized turtles)

and different types of bowls and troughs. During presentations and rituals, prepared kava is drunk, formerly from miniature carved wooden canoes in southern Vanuatu, but in modern times from large, undecorated coconut shells. Northern Malakula has a tradition of intricate stone carvings that includes large and ancient stone kava containers, which often take the form of pigs. These are kept hidden to protect them from foreigners.

Tapa cloth was produced both for clothing and household use. It may be plain, decorated with agricultural, religious or status symbols or even, as on Efate, fringed with feathers. Motifs used for body tattoo may be reproduced on *tapa*. *Tapa* played an important part in many rituals, especially that accompanying the death of some Erromangan chiefs, in which hundreds of *tapa*s were hung from bamboo fences that radiate from the base of yam towers and were burnt.

Other Vanuatuan textiles include fine, decorated pandanus mats and baskets made by the women of central and northern Pentecost. These women also weave large mats that are dyed red in various designs and used in funeral rituals and as money. Finely made stringed shell money was also used on Malo and northern Vanuatu, while on Erromango fossilized, carved, giant clam shells, provided by the ancestral spirits, were used in marriage and blood payments and are kept hidden in the ground, only being brought out for exchanges.

5. MUSICAL INSTRUMENTS. Bamboo flutes, panpipes, horizontal and vertical slit- drums (*c.* 2–5 m tall) are carved from wood. The drums are found at the edges of dancing grounds throughout the northern half of the country, with many local variations in form and style, and are made by

2. Vanuatu slit-drum, North Ambrym, 20th century; from a photograph by David Attenborough, 1959

groups of specialist carvers sponsored by individuals who have purchased the right to the drum. Many made in the late 20th century (see fig. 2) display far higher standards of craftsmanship than those carved in the 19th century, and, while some traditional styles are no longer evident, many have survived. The carvings feature the faces of ancestral spirits, sometimes in conjunction with clan and power symbols. On Ambrym two or three faces may be carved one above the other, one style having five such faces. Smaller, hand-held wooden drums may take the form of fish. In the Banks and Torres Islands, a rare upright hollow drum is made from light wood with a mat or leaf membrane.

6. WEAPONS AND CANOES. Much artistic endeavour went into the production of such weapons as boomerangs and clubs. The latter may be finely carved of wood or roughly shaped from coral stone and were used in hand-to-hand fighting, for throwing or in dances. Spears between 3 and 4 m in length might be intricately carved, or barbed with marine spines. Arrows sometimes have carved, detachable hardwood points. The only feathered arrows in the Pacific are produced on Espiritu Santo. In common with other Pacific areas, canoes were important in Vanuatu for both peaceful and martial purposes. The most common form is the outrigger, and on Fotuna these have vertically extended sides. In Tongoa and the Shepherds Islands group large outrigger canoes often have a platform built over the outrigger for transport purposes. Small Islands canoes from north-east Malakula often have prow pieces carved in the shape of birds with styles that denote social status.

BIBLIOGRAPHY

R. H. Codrington: *The Melanesians: Studies in their Anthropology and Folklore* (Oxford, 1891/R New Haven, CT, 1957)

F. Speiser: *Ethnographische Materialien aus den Neuen Hebriden und Banks-Inseln* (Berlin, 1923); Eng. trans. by D. Q. Stephenson as *Ethnology of Vanuatu: An Early Twentieth Century Study* (Bathurst, Australia, 1990)

J. W. Layard: 'Degree-taking Rites in South West Bay, Malekula', *J. Royal Anthropol. Inst. GB & Ireland*, lviii (1928), pp. 139–223, pls xiv–xix

A. B. Deacon: 'Geometrical Drawings from Malekula and Other Islands of the New Hebrides', *J. Royal Anthropol. Inst. GB & Ireland*, xiv (1934), pp. 129–75, pl. xiii

——: *Malekula: A Vanishing People in the New Hebrides*, ed. C. H. Wedgwood (London, 1934/R Oosterhout, 1970)

J. Layard: *Stone Men of Malekula: Vao* (London, 1942)

Arts of the South Seas (exh. cat. by R. Linton and S. Wingert, with R. d'Harnoncourt, New York, MOMA, 1946), pp. 83–90

J. Guiart: 'Les Effigies religieuses des Nouvelles-Hébrides: Etude des collections du Musée de l'Homme', *J. Soc. Océanistes*, v (1949), pp. 51–85

——: 'Société, rituels et mythes du Nord Ambrym', *J. Soc. Océanistes*, vii/7 (1951), pp. 5–103

——: *The Arts of the South Pacific*, The Arts of Mankind (London, 1963), pp. 229–51

D. Attenborough: *The Tribal Eye* (London, 1976), pp. 106–11

K. Huffman: 'The Hidden World of Mbotgot', *Austral. Nat. Hist.*, xviii/11 (1976), pp. 414–19

R. Guidieri and F. Pellizzi: 'Shadows: Nineteen Tableaux on the Cult of the Dead in Malekula, Eastern Melanesia', *Res*, 2 (1981), pp. 5–69

J. MacClancy: 'Vao Concepts', *Res*, 2 (1981), pp. 70–90

K. Huffman: 'An Exhibition of Bark Cloths from Vanuatu', *COMA*, 16 (1985), pp. 49–50

J. Guiart: 'Art as a Means of Communication in Pre-literate Societies', *Art as a Means of Communication in Pre-literate Societies* (exh. cat., Jerusalem, Israel Mus., 1990), pp. 217–43

K. W. HUFFMAN

Vanvitelli, Gaspare. *See* WITTEL, GASPAR VAN.

Vanvitelli, Luigi (*b* Naples, 12 May 1700; *d* Caserta, 1 March 1773). Italian architect, draughtsman and painter. His work represents the transition from Baroque to Neoclassicism, and his correspondence and the number of his extant drawings make him perhaps the best-documented Italian architect of the 18th century. Vanvitelli's father was the Dutch *vedute* painter GASPAR VAN WITTEL, and his mother was Roman. Luigi began his career as a history painter, and from 1724 he was employed as a copyist in the *fabbrica* of St Peter's in Rome. The extent of his academic training is not clear, but under Antonio Valeri (1648–1736), who succeeded Carlo Fontana as *architetto soprastante*, Vanvitelli discovered his talent as an architect. Ultimately, however, Valeri was a less significant influence on his work than Fontana or Filippo Juvarra. His first patron was the prefect Cardinal Annibale Albani. As a member of the latter's retinue, in the 1720s, Vanvitelli went to Urbino, where he participated in the decoration of the Albani Chapel (*c.* 1729) in the church of S Francesco (*in situ*), the staircase and corridors of the Palazzo Albani and the fountain in front of the palazzo. Although the extent of his involvement in the work is not known with certainty, these decorations with their isolation of fanciful single forms are clearly derived from the Roman *Barocchetto* of the early 18th century or directly from Borromini. Forms typical of Borromini, such as garlands, palm branches and herm pilasters, continue to appear discreetly throughout Vanvitelli's later work. Many drawings testify to Vanvitelli's interest, from the 1720s onwards, in designing decorative ceilings and ciboria. The early fountains, however, are in a restrained decorative style and are clearly executed. In Urbino he may also have been involved in building the churches of S Francesco and S Domenico.

After being engaged in engineering works in and around Rome, designing the Vermicino aqueduct with a fountain (*c.* 1730) below Albano, in 1732 Vanvitelli was a finalist in the competitions for the façade of S Giovanni in Laterano and for the Trevi Fountain. These designs are of a monumental and academic character that is unusual for their date and in parts resemble the work of Vanvitelli's friend and collaborator Nicola Salvi. These designs led to Vanvitelli's being admitted to the Accademia di S Luca. He was also commissioned to develop the port of Ancona by building a pentagonal lazaretto (see fig. 1) and lengthening the quay with a triumphal arch (from 1733), the Arco Clementino, in honour of Pope Clement XII. Subsequently, for the most part in the service of the Camera Apostolica (the Papal Office of Works), he acquired wide experience in the Marches and Umbria, both in engineering projects and in architecture, including the construction in Ancona of Il Gesù (the Jesuit church, completed 1743) and the reliquary chapel (1739; partly destr.) in the cathedral there. In the lazaretto and its chapel, in the Arco Clementino and in the façade of Il Gesù, Vanvitelli arrived for the first time at his own style, characterized by concise, harmoniously modulated reliefs and displaying the ability to take on very diverse kinds of work and use them as a basis for invention. Among his other works of this period are the construction of the church and monastery of Montemorcino (1739–62; now the university) for the Olivetan Order in Perugia. In the interior here, with its centralizing longitudinal space inspired by Palladio, he achieved for the first time the clarity and plasticity characteristic of his mature work and in contrast to his previous church designs, in which he had experimented with designs in a rather unsatisfactory manner; important motifs were columns and pendentive domes with ribs and coffers in the manner of Bernini.

During the 1740s Vanvitelli became increasingly active in Rome. Although originally subordinate to Filippo Barigioni (1690–1753), he began to take over the effective direction of the *fabbrica* of St Peter's, arguing for the highly controversial restoration of the dome, which he executed in 1742–8 in accordance with the calculations of the mathematician Giovanni Poleni. With Nicola Salvi he also carried out the enlargement (*c.* 1745) of the Palazzo Chigi-Odescalchi, doubling the width of the central section and thereby upsetting the finely balanced proportions of Bernini's original scheme. He also collaborated with Salvi on the design, execution and furnishing of St John's Chapel for the Jesuit church of S Roque in Lisbon, which was built in Rome between 1743 and 1745 and which is an extreme example of material splendour encased in a strict architectonic form. In 1745 he was also commissioned to design a façade for Milan Cathedral, but his plans (preserved) were not executed. Also in the 1740s, Vanvitelli restored the Villa Rufinella (1741–5) at Frascati for the Jesuits and began a collaboration with the Augustinians

that continued into the 1750s and included the construction of the sacristy and large monastery (1746–56) of S Agostino in Rome, the construction of S Agostino in Siena (1747–55; only the nave built according to his plans), the construction of S Agostino in Ancona (1760–64; destr.), and the restoration of S Agostino in Rome (from 1756). The exterior of the monastery is particularly austere. Inside, however, Vanvitelli gave rein to his decorative imagination; particularly interesting architectural features are the courtyard with Renaissance-style windows set in arcades and the vestibule of the side entrance. His most spectacular work in Rome, however, was the reworking of Michelangelo's Carthusian church of S Maria degli Angeli (1748–65), where he converted the nave into a transept, relocating the entrance on the west side. Here—as at S Agostino, Rome, and in his plans for the modernization (1750–54) of Foligno Cathedral—Vanvitelli was inspired by the halls of Roman baths (*thermae*), and he conferred the most elaborate decoration on the *tepidarium* of what had formerly been the Baths of Diocletian, which Michelangelo had left unadorned.

In 1750 Charles VII, King of Naples, later Charles III of Spain, summoned Vanvitelli, and in 1751 the planning of the Palazzo Reale at Caserta, 33 km north of Naples, was basically completed. The most important part of Vanvitelli's remaining career was devoted to supervising

1. Luigi Vanvitelli: lazaretto, Ancona, 1733–8; aerial view

the work there (*see also* CASERTA, PALAZZO REALE). He himself was responsible for the completion of the palace's staircase, chapel and theatre (not part of the original plans); the first of the state apartments and the fountains in the garden were executed to his plans after his death. The Palazzo Reale is an enormous block (253×190 m), and despite the overall simplicity of its appearance it is a complex creation. Some of its basic ideas are derived, thanks to Charles III, from Spanish and French Bourbon palaces: in particular the ground-plan with its four internal courtyards formed by crossed wings is derived from Robert de Cotte's unexecuted projects for the Cason del Buen Retiro, Madrid, while the chapel is influenced by that at Versailles. The functional and rational working out of the plan (for example, the placing of the staircase and the chapel), however, are Vanvitelli's distinctive contribution. The radiating visual effect of the upper central vestibule (including the splayed corners of the courtyards) is splendid, as is the visual axis extending from the road through the centre of the palace and the length of the entire park; both are ideas derived from Vanvitelli's experiments with scenography. Further scenographic effects are achieved with the majestic staircase (see fig. 2), which opens from the central octagon.

Subsequently Vanvitelli was engaged in numerous civil engineering and technical works, including the aqueduct for the gardens at Caserta, with the tunnelling works and the archi della Valle (1753–69). He also completed the barracks begun by military engineers at the Ponte della Maddalena on the outskirts of Naples (from 1754; partly destr.). Here the ennoblement of a utilitarian building by the application of geometry and a unifying order demonstrate Vanvitelli's affinities with early Neo-classicism. His next major scheme, undertaken as court architect, was the Foro Carolino in Naples (from 1758; now the Piazza Dante), a hemicycle backed by a curved building with a palace front that is articulated by a giant Tuscan order, interrupted in the centre by a *nicchione* that originally held an equestrian statue of *Charles III*. This statue was commissioned in 1761. Although never executed in bronze, a plaster model was set up in 1765 and destroyed in 1799. The use of a colonnade here again foreshadows Neo-classicism. Another important project in Naples was the rebuilding from 1760 of the church of SS Annunziata, which had been damaged by fire in 1757, and the church of the Albergo dei Poveri, under royal patronage. Here Vanvitelli produced a splendid variation on the theme of the large aisleless church with side chapels, an amply architraved colonnade and dome. The church also has a characteristic concave façade in two tiers; in addition there is a striking crypt with a circular colonnade. In Naples he was also involved in work on the Calabritto and Casacalenda palaces, and he drew up plans for the Palazzo d'Angri; he also completed the Villa Campolieto (after 1762) at Ercolano. Apart from SS Annunziata, however, his ecclesiastical works in Naples were few: the building of the Vincentian missionary church in Via Vergini (from *c*. 1760); the decoration of SS Marcellino e Festo (*c*. 1765), with the oratory of the Scala Santa (1772); and the sacristy of S Luigi in Palazzo (completed in 1766; destr.). SS Marcellino e Festo has the appearance of being sheathed

2. Luigi Vanvitelli: staircase (1756–66) of the Palazzo Reale, Caserta

in coloured marble, with elegant decorative details. Generally, however, Vanvitelli's later style is characterized by a reductive and more abstract resumption of old themes with strict organization, chiefly by means of flat pilasters and lesenes: for example in the oratory of the Scala Santa, the staircase and vestibule of the Villa Campolieto and, above all, the scenographic sequence of three central spaces (the middle one of which is inspired by the Roman church of S Maria in Montesanto) in the Vincentian missionary church and monastery, where the influence of Borromini is also evident.

Throughout his career Vanvitelli made important designs for altars and tabernacles, notable examples of which include the high altar of Terni Cathedral (1751–4), executed with Carlo Murena (1713–64); the high altar of S Pantaleo in Rome (1751–68); and the altar of the Sampajo Chapel in S Antonio dei Portoghesi, Rome (1752–6). He was also commissioned to produce a design for the grand staircase (1745) of the Palacio Real in Madrid, and in 1769 he went to Milan for the replanning of the Palazzo Regioducale (unexecuted); during his visit he also provided plans for the Loggia dei Commercianti in Brescia (partly destr.) and for private dwellings. In his last years there were important opportunities for festive architecture. He designed a false façade and temporary grand hall for the Palazzo Teora (for the Austrian Ambassador) in 1768, on the betrothal of Ferdinand IV to Maria Carolina of Austria, and for the Spanish Ambassador in 1772, when the King's first son was born. Again, Vanvitelli's treatment of festive decorations as ideal architecture with antique overtones can be regarded as an early example of Neo-classicism.

After his death, Vanvitelli continued to be regarded as the greatest architect of his day. His pupils did much to disseminate his style, especially Giuseppe Piermarini in Lombardy, his son Carlo Vanvitelli in Naples, Carlo Murena in Rome and Francesco Sabbatini in Spain, and his own contribution is sometimes difficult to distinguish from those of his immediate successors in Naples and Rome. His work can nevertheless be characterized by the recurrent use of some distinctive elements: concave forms (as in such church façades as S Maria degli Angeli and the SS Annunziata in Naples or Il Gesù in Ancona); reinforcing arches and coffers; lunettes or oval medallions in the vaulted areas and over the doors; and, in his decorative details, seashell-shaped niches and motifs derived from Borromini. He also made frequent use of columns, but always taking into consideration the architectural context rather than seeing them as absolute values.

For further illustration *see* LORETO, fig. 1.

WRITINGS

Dichiarazione dei disegni del Reale Palazzo di Caserta (Naples, 1756)
ed. F. Strazzullo: *Le lettere di Luigi Vanvitelli nella biblioteca palatina di Caserta*, 3 vols (Galatina, 1976)

BIBLIOGRAPHY

L. Vanvitelli: *Vita dell'architetto Luigi Vanvitelli* (Naples, 1823); ed. M. Rotili (Naples, 1975)
F. Fichera: *Luigi Vanvitelli* (Rome, 1937)
J. Garms: 'Die Briefe des Luigi Vanvitelli an seinen Bruder Urbano in Rom: Kunsthistorisches Material', *Röm. Hist. Mitt.*, xiii (1971), pp. 201–85
R. de Fusco and others: *Luigi Vanvitelli* (Naples, 1973)
Disegni di Luigi Vanvitelli nelle collezioni pubbliche di Napoli e di Caserta (exh. cat., ed. J. Garms; Naples, Pal. Reale, 1973)
J. Garms: 'Altäre und Tabernakel von Luigi Vanvitelli', *Wien. Jb. Kstgesch.*, xxvii (1974), pp. 140–57
——: 'Beiträge zu Vanvitellis Leben, Werk und Milieu', *Röm. Hist. Mitt.*, xvi (1974), pp. 107–90
C. de' Seta: 'I disegni di Luigi Vanvitelli per la reggia di Caserta ed i progetti di Carlo Fontana per il palazzo del principe di Liechtenstein', *Stor. A.*, xxii (1974), pp. 267–76
L'attività di Luigi Vanvitelli nelle Marche e i suoi epigoni: Convegno vanvitelliano: Ancona, 1974
G. Fiengo: *Gioffredo e Vanvitelli nei palazzi dei Casacalenda* (Naples, 1976)
P. Carreras: 'Studi su Luigi Vanvitelli', *Stor. A.*, xxiv, xxv (1977) [suppl.]
C. de' Seta: 'Luigi Vanvitelli: L'antico ed il neoclassico', *Prospettiva* [Florence], xv (1978), pp. 40–46
Luigi Vanvitelli e il '700 europeo: Convegno internazionale di studi: Naples and Caserta, 1973 (Naples, 1979)
J. Garms: 'Ultimi contributi Vanvitelliani', *Arti e civiltà del settecento a Napoli*, ed. C. de' Seta (Bari, 1982)
G. L. Hersey: *Architecture, Poetry and Number in the Royal Palace at Caserta* (Cambridge, MA, 1983)
L'esercizio del disegno: I Vanvitelli (exh. cat. by A. Pampalone, Caserta; Madrid; Rome; 1992–3)
J. Garms: 'The Church of the Annunziata in Naples', *Parthenope's Splendor: Art in the Golden Age in Naples*, ed. J. Chenault Porter and S. Scott Munshower (University Park, PA, 1993), pp. 396–429
——: 'Zwei unbekannte Zeichnungen Vanvitellis in österreichischem Privatbesitz: Von der Bauforschung zur Denkmalpflege', *Festschrift Alois Machatschek* (Vienna, 1994), pp. 65–77

JÖRG GARMS

Van Ysendyck, Jules-Jacques (*b* Paris, 17 Oct 1836; *d* Uccle, Brussels, 17 March 1901). Belgian architect. He was the son of the painter Antoine Van Ysendyck (1801–75), and he was educated at the Académie du Dessin, Mons, the Académie Royale des Beaux-Arts, Brussels, and finally at the Ecole des Beaux-Arts, Paris, where he studied with Eugène-Emmanuel Viollet-le-Duc, Louis-Hippolyte Lebas and Jean-Baptiste-Cicéron Lesueur. Returning to Belgium, from 1861 he worked for a number of years in the office of Jean-Pierre Cluysenaar in Brussels before establishing his own architectural practice there. During the 1870s Van Ysendyck supervised the restoration of some important monuments in Brussels dating from the Gothic period to the Baroque. His first important new architectural commission was the town hall (1875–9) of Anderlecht, a suburb of Brussels. The interiors of this building were carried out by Charle-Albert, a noted decorative designer with whom Van Ysendyck collaborated on several projects. He went on to produce numerous other public buildings, town houses and country seats, typically in Flemish Renaissance Revival or Gothic Revival styles, in Brussels and the Flemish provinces. Examples include the town hall in Schaerbeek (1885–7), which was destroyed by fire and restored (1911) by his son Maurice Van Ysendyck (1868–1941), who was also successful as an architect in Brussels; the town hall in Jette (1899); and the villa La Clairière (1875), Boulevard de Waterloo 868–76, Brussels. Many of his works were published in *L'Emulation*, the journal of the Société Centrale d'Architecture (from 1874), and *Academy Architecture*, which spread his reputation as a talented and successful architect throughout Belgium and abroad. His interest in the historical architecture and applied arts of Flanders and the Netherlands culminated in the publication (1880–90) of a five-volume compendium on the subject, comprising 725 plates.

WRITINGS

Documents classés de l'art dans les Pays-Bas du Xe au XIXe siècle, 5 vols (Antwerp, 1880–90)

BIBLIOGRAPHY

J. Brunfaut: 'Notice sur Jules-Jacques Van Ysendyck', *Annu. Acad. Royale Sci., Lett. & B.-A. Belgique*, lxxvii (1911), pp. 165–75

ALFRED WILLIS

Vapheio. *See under* SPARTA, §1.

Vaprio, Giovanni Zenone da. *See* GIOVANNI ZENONE DA VAPRIO.

Vaquet, Jean. *See under* MASTERS, ANONYMOUS, AND MONOGRAMMISTS, §III: MASTER I♀V.

Varakhsha [Barakhshah, Farakhshah, Warakhshah; Dakhfandun]. Site in Uzbekistan, 40 km west-north-west of Bukhara, which flourished *c.* 1st century BC–12th century AD. According to tradition it served for more than 1000 years as the residence of the Bukhar-khudat, rulers of Bukhara. The 9 ha site was excavated in 1938–9 and 1949–54 under V. A. Shishkin. Varakhsha originated in the first centuries BC as the last halt before crossing the desert between Bukhara and Khwarazm. The fortified city was triangular in plan, with walls built of square mud-bricks and incorporating semi-elliptical bastions and numerous loopholes. A citadel mound (h. 20 m) crowned by buildings and surrounded by a wide moat remained a constant feature of the southern part of the city throughout its history. Surrounding the city was an area of cultivated land farmed by adjacent village settlements. An oasis with irrigation canals conveyed water from Zarafshan River. The site was abandoned from the first centuries AD until the 5th century, when insubstantial new defences of rammed earth were constructed. In the late 5th century and early 6th a new perimeter wall was built (extant h. 10 m), with bastions 30 m apart. The foundation of the rebuilt citadel comprised a 15 m high platform with an incised mud-brick facing, which simulated block construction. The walls of the citadel were of compressed mud-brick and had friezes of clay roundels with a prominent fretted pattern and possibly also crenellations. A later building abutting the east side of the citadel contained narrow rooms with arched doorways, embrasure windows and vaulted ceilings.

On the west side of the citadel was the palace of the Bukhar-khudat. Fragments have survived in the earliest palace buildings of whitewashed clay sculpture and large terracotta reliefs of fantastic animals, human figures and plant motifs. The later rooms were decorated with paintings: that in the Eastern Hall depicts the conventional subject of the adoration of a deity; those in the Red Hall, in which a royal huntsman-like figure riding an elephant features prominently, are a remarkable, rhythmic composition with austere red and yellow colouring (*see* CENTRAL ASIA, §I, 4(iv) and fig. 33). A large iwan was possibly used for ceremonial receptions. It had a triple portal comprising a central arch (w. 7.75 m) flanked by two smaller arches (w. 3.25 m), which were supported by brick columns and pilasters 2 m in diameter. Four steps extending the length of the façade led down to a courtyard. The surfaces of the columns and walls were entirely covered with repeated stucco relief panels and borders of stylized vegetal motifs and hunting scenes (*see also* CENTRAL ASIA, §I, 3(iii)(a)). Above the arches were figures (possibly female) with haloes. The palace was redecorated several times. The paintings were retouched or completely repainted, and the ornate stucco decoration was replaced with simplified geometric designs.

According to the historian Narshakhi (*d* 959; see Barthold, pp. 13–15) Varakhsha was an important economic centre similar in size to Bukhara (*c.* 12 sq. km). During the Arab conquest in the 760s, the Bukhar-khudat ruler Sukan was assassinated and buried in the palace. A later Bukhar-khudat, Buniat (*reg* 782–4), was beheaded in his newly built palace for supporting the uprising of the 'men in white clothes' against Arab rule. A 10th-century building on the citadel had a central courtyard paved with yellow and red brick in a parquet pattern with a multi-petalled rosette of alternatively coloured shaped bricks encircling a drinking well in the centre. Houses were built against the city walls and on the central mound. Numerous wells in the inhabited quarters were roofed either with brick corbelled vaults or several vessels placed one above the other. These wells were temporary shallow constructions that had to be frequently replaced. An area up to 2 km in extent surrounding the town appears also to have been densely populated, to judge from the profusion of scattered sherds, predominantly of the 10th–12th centuries. Occupation of the site ceased in the second half of the 12th century, before the Mongol invasions.

BIBLIOGRAPHY

W. Barthold: *Turkestan v epokhu mongol'skago nashestviya* (Moscow, 1900); rev. Eng. trans. as *Turkestan down to the mongol Invasion*, ed. C. E. Bosworth (London, 3/1963), pp. 13–15, 115–16

S. K. Kabanov: 'Raskopi zhilogo kvartala v zapadnoy chasti gorodishsha Varakhsha' [Excavations on the inhabited quarter in the west part of the city site of Varakhsha], *Trudy Inst. Istor. & Arkheol. Akad. Nauk UzSSR*, viii (Tashkent, 1956)

V. A. Nil'sen: 'Varakhshskaya tsitadel'' [The citadel of Varakhsha], *Trudy Inst. Istor. & Arkheol. Akad. Nauk UzSSR*, viii (Tashkent, 1956)

E. Knobloch: *Beyond the Oxus: Archeology, Art and Architecture of Central Asia* (London, 1972), pp. 169–71, figs 13, 102

V. A. SHISHKIN

Varallo, Sacro Monte. Observant Franciscan foundation and pilgrimage site in Piedmont, Italy.

1. Architecture. 2. Decoration.

1. ARCHITECTURE. Situated in the diocese of Novara, the Sacro Monte occupies about 12 wooded ha on top of a spur rising *c.* 160 m above the town of Varallo (see fig. 1). The monument's primary feature is 44 chapels, in which scenes from or associated with the Life of Christ are rendered as life-size dioramas, consisting of groups of figures in various materials against painted background scenes. These chapels are either free-standing or grouped within secondary structures to suggest their scenes' shared locations, are evenly distributed around the summit, and are connected in approximately chronological order of their events by a main path. Their sequence concludes at a central piazza and the monument's secondary feature, a basilica dedicated to the Virgin of the Assumption. Reflecting a succession of conceptions and programmes, the whole combines a monastic retreat, a delightful park and a penitential vehicle.

The earliest architecture of the Sacro Monte was designed by Brother Bernardino Caimi (*d* 1499), whose intention was to re-create the plans and salient features of the holy sites of Jerusalem in a series of chapels. An early source (the acts of concession) confirms that three structures were complete by 1493: the reproduction of the Holy Sepulchre and a contiguous hermitage, and two additional chapels. A pilgrim's guide to the sanctuary (1514) describes some two dozen chapels ('*capeleta*' or '*lucco*'), of which there survive the complexes of Nazareth, Bethlehem and the Sepulchre (with modifications); the chapels of the Way to Calvary and the Stone of Unction (with different subjects); those of the Last Supper and the Pentecost (with entirely different functions); and the Sepulchre of the Virgin (abandoned). These earliest structures, simple in construction (of rock-faced rubble and hewn timber) and vernacular in style, provided little more than shelter for their ensembles and passageways for the visitor.

The chapels of the Procession of the Magi and Calvary (begun before 1519; completed by 1528) signalled a departure from the earlier style towards a more generic and grand representation of the sites. Caimi's scheme became confused, and progress was halted until Giacomo d'Adda commissioned Galeazzo Alessi to reorganize the entire Sacro Monte (*see* ALESSI, GALEAZZO). Prepared between 1565 and 1569, Alessi's studies of a comprehensive plan and 34 new or redesigned chapels, along with an articulate preface and careful notations, are contained in the *Libro dei misteri* (Varallo, Bib. Civ.), a single volume of 318 folios. The project generally respects the earliest structures and even acknowledes the topographic conceit, but it subsumes these within a textually based, temporally ordered narrative from the Fall to the Last Judgement and phrases it with an unprecedented formal sophistication. Contemporary with the *Libro*, the monumental portal and the first chapel in this new scheme, that of the Fall of Man (or of Adam and Eve), were the only structures carried out according to Alessi's plans. Built between 1572 and 1576 with funds provided by d'Adda, most of the new chapels in the Sacro Monte's lower area (from the Fall to the Entry into Jerusalem) correspond to the *Libro* at least in subject and location. And several conceptions—the

1. Varallo, Sacro Monte, view from the north

temporal sequence, the urbanistic entity in the upper area, the isolation and regulated viewing of the ensembles by screens—became principles of the Sacro Monte's later development. But, as Alessi himself recognized, the scheme was inherently difficult, its materials (now marble and carved stone) costly, and the requisite skills lacking in the local builders. Worse, by submerging the monastic sense in one of Mannerist delectation, his brilliant solution exacerbated conflicts with the Observants and conflicted with a Counter-Reformation desire for clarity, simplicity and directness. There were two different efforts to address these practical, but also increasingly ideological, problems. The first was initiated by d'Adda himself, who, sometime during the 1570s (but probably 1578–80; Longo, 1985) engaged Martino Bassi to draw up versions of the *Libro*'s plans for the overall organization, especially the upper area (which became 'Jerusalem' explicitly) and several individual chapels. Bassi's studies (Milan, Bib. Ambrosiana) considerably simplify, clarify and (as their preface notes) avoid anything that might distract from the devotional purpose.

The balance of the architecture was planned during the episcopate of Carlo Bascapè (1593–1615); Bascapè, influenced by S Carlo Borromeo's views on religious art and by his belief in direct episcopal intervention in artistic as well as administrative matters, gave precise instructions for the sanctuary's remaining arrangement. His architectural consultants were Domenico Alfani (1593 to 1602) and then, probably, Giovanni d'Enrico (d 1644). The six interior chapels of Pilate's Palace were ready for decoration by 1608, and the basilica—its presbytery and crossing complete—was dedicated in 1649. Realized after Bascapè's death, but hardly less determined by him, were those of the Arrest and First Presentation to Pilate (before 1617);

two of the three free-standing chapels that form the Piazza dei Tribunali, the Second Presentation to Pilate and the marble reproduction of the Scala Santa (before 1628); the Crucifixion (before 1637); the Deposition (before 1641); and, protracted from a foundation around 1570, the Transfiguration (after 1647). Uniform in style and consistent in relation to the site and their ensembles, these structures represent a final tempering of Alessi's project in the light of Observant tradition, Counter-Reformation ideology and practicality. Even when departing considerably in style, the later architecture of the Sacro Monte, which includes the chapel of Annas (1737), the basilica's nave (1708–20s), tribune and crypt (designed by Benedetto Innocente Alfieri; executed by Giovanni Battista Morondi, 1730s) and façade (designed by Giovanni Ceruti, 1891–6), still reflects the basic scheme and ideas promoted by Bascapè.

2. DECORATION. The earliest decoration of the Sacro Monte was intended to reinforce identification of its chapels with the holy sites of Jerusalem and to encourage visualization of their relative events. Initially, in the three structures completed by 1493, this seems to have included reproductions of objects and relics (first mentioned in the guide of 1514 and purportedly then extant). An early source suggests that by 1495 the decoration featured figural representations that brought to mind the religious dramas or *misteri*, and the guide of 1514 mentions sculpted representation at three sites, painted representation at another four, and, in one instance, to both forms. Corresponding to these citations, there survive wooden statues of two types: earlier and more conventional in style, the carved and polychromed figures of the *Stone of Unction*

group (Varallo, Pin.) and, with modifications, the Sepulchre's *Christ* (to which can be added the Calvary's *Christ* and the *Risen Christ* of the piazza's fountain); somewhat later and more distinctive are the cloth-draped and wigged mannequins of the *Annunciation* and *Last Supper* (to which can be added the basilica's *Death of the Virgin*). None of the cited paintings was preserved much beyond the 16th century, but there remain traces of fresco ornament on the interior and exterior of several chapels and, unique as a record of the earliest figural painting, the frescoes of the *Sepulchre of the Virgin* (Varallo, Pin.). This early decoration is essentially vernacular: the first type of sculpture is an elaboration of a regional type, the second apparently an adaptation of a popular and ephemeral one, and the painting a provincial interpretation of recent Milanese style.

In the second decade of the 16th century there is a new concern with completeness and consistency as well as a new stylistic sophistication. This can be seen in the more differentiated description and characterized expression of such wooden figures as the *Disrobing of Christ*, in the introduction of polychromed terracotta in the figures of the *Nativity* and *Adoration of the Shepherds*; and in the frescoes of the *Disrobing* (presently surrounding the *Pietà*), which are compatible in style and increasingly coordinated in scale and composition with the sculpture. These developments, traditionally and convincingly attributed to Gaudenzio Ferrari, most likely date to *c.* 1514–20 and culminate in his decoration of the *Crucifixion* (begun probably *c.* 1520; *see* SACROMONTE, fig. 1) and the *Adoration of the Magi* (largely completed by 1528), in which terracotta figures and panoramic frescoes are combined in ensembles of extraordinary size (37 figures and 200 sq. m of painting in the former), narrative richness and visual coherence. With these ensembles, which provided the model for later decoration, figural representation displaced topographic reproduction as the primary significance of the Sacro Monte.

In the following period decoration was interrupted, with the exception of some works that can be dated to the early 1540s and that are still legible to varying degrees. In one interior space of the original Pilate's Palace, Bernardino Lanino painted a fresco of *Christ before Pilate* (surviving sections, Varallo, Pin.); in the other interior space of the palace, an anonymous sculptor returned to completely carved wood for the three figures of a *Flagellation* (one destr.; two integrated into the later version of the subject). At the same time, Lanino added a fresco version of the *Pentecost* (Varallo, Pin.), a virtual altarpiece, to the chapel dedicated to that event. These exceptions suggest an attempt, albeit a limited one, to revive the decoration at Varello: Ferrari's style is the basis of Lanino's frescoes and even of the statues' types, but they revert to conventional formats, differing scales and separate existences.

A true revival of the decoration began with the implementation of Galeazzo Alessi's plan. Between 1570 and the early 1580s painted plaster figures loosely based on the vignettes in his *Libro dei misteri* (*see* §I above) were introduced to the new chapels, from the *Fall of Man* to the *Entry into Jerusalem*, as they were completed (the latest figures of this type, included in the *Miracle of the Widow's Son*, date from 1589). Accompanying frescoes followed between the late 1570s and 1594. These ensembles, however, remain modest works in a provincial Mannerist style, secondary to both Gospel and the abstract order of Alessi's scheme.

The decoration of one chapel in this series, depicting the *Massacre of the Innocents*, signalled a further stage in the revival. Set up between 1587 and 1590 and attributed to Giacomo Paracca (*b c.* ?1557), its figures are many (originally about 36), startlingly rude in the characterization of soldiers, mutilated babies and desperate mothers, and, although relatively coarse in finish, they are again in polychromed terracotta. Its frescoes, commissioned from Giovanni Battista della Rovere (1561–1627/30) in 1590 (and executed in collaboration with his brother Giovanni Mauro della Rover, 1575–1640), cover every surface, including the vault (*c.* 100 sq. m); the complex and illusionistic composition suggests an agitated crowd about a large atrium and asserts the contemporary Milanese style.

After Bascapè's appointment as Bishop of Novara in 1593, the revival of artistic ambitions for Varallo coincided with a Tridentine concern for accuracy and respect for stylistic precedent and visual continuity, quickly returning the decoration to the highest level. The renovation or repair of extant ensembles included the definitive revision of the *Fall* and the addition of figures to the *Massacre* (*c.* 1594–5; both with statues by Michele Prestinari (*fl* 1594–1634) and paintings by Domenico Alfani), and modifications of the *Visitation* and *Temptation* (*c.* 1598) by Jean de Wespin, called Tabacchetti. The decoration of the new chapel of the Way to Calvary was the first to be realized entirely according to Bascapè's orders. Between 1599 and *c.* 1601 Tabacchetti created the requisite procession with 44 terracotta figures and 9 horses. They are almost caricatural in type and extravagant in attitude, but superb in manufacture and are arranged relative to three principal viewpoints. The ensemble was completed by Morazzone with frescoes that augment the crowd below and fill the vault above with illusionistically framed Old Testament archetypes (this was largely executed by *c.* 1605, but was still awaiting completion in 1616). Throughout, as Bascapè had instructed, there are references to the scene that now properly followed, Ferrari's *Crucifixion*.

The next 30 years were the most active and best organized in the history of the decoration. The principal agent was Giovanni d'Enrico (*c.* 1559–1644), who virtually became the sole contractor *c.* 1605: every one of the hundreds of statues set up during the period is indebted to his hand or that of his assistant Giacomo Ferro (*fl* 1620s–after 1647), with their polychromy often undertaken by his younger brother Melchiorre d'Enrico (*c.* 1570/75–after 1640). With Tabacchetti's eccentricities tempered, these figures are more simply handsome, rhetorically precise and suited to repertory performance. The most important works were for the newly created chapels within Pilate's Palace and around the adjacent Piazza dei Tribunali: Giovanni's own two collaborations with Morazzone (the *Ecce homo*, with figures started by 1608 and frescoes of 1609–*c.* 1616; see fig. 2; and the *Sentencing of Christ* with figures in place by 1610 and frescoes of 1610–*c.* 1616) and subsequent three with his younger brother Tanzio da Varallo (*Christ Presented to Pilate*, with figures

2. Varallo, Sacro Monte, Pilate's Palace, *Ecce homo*, with statues by Giovanni d'Enrico (begun 1608) and frescoes by Morazzone (1609–
c. 1616)

and frescoes executed simultaneously, before 1617; *Pilate Washing his Hands*, in progress in 1617 and completed *c.* 1620; and *Christ before Herod*, in progress in 1628). In these, the most coherent of all ensembles at Varallo, there is an almost complete coincidence of the chapel's architecture with the representation, coordination of sculpture and painting (at points they merge), unity of composition and integrity of expression. Throughout the 1620s most of the other ensembles echo these effects. Giovanni's three collaborations with a distinctive local follower of Morazzone, Cristoforo Martinolo (1599–after 1642), called Rocca (the new but poorly preserved *Flagellation*, with figures completed by 1617 and frescoes dated 1620; *Christ Healing the Paralytic*, *c.* 1621; and *Christ before Caiaphas*, with figures completed by 1628 and frescoes dated 1642) are particularly successful. With their large casts of figures and elaborate settings remaining harmonious, these scenes work coherently both in sequence and individually.

By the 1630s, however, as the Tridentine impulse weakened, funds dwindled and work slowed, such coherence could not be maintained. In the late ensembles in the area of Calvary (e.g. the sprawling *Crucifixion*, with figures commissioned in 1627 and completed by 1637, and with frescoes executed in 1637–41 by Melchiorre Gherardini, 1607–68), the figures began to be banal, the frescoes separate backdrops and the compositions dissipated. Lavish efforts were occasionally mounted and sustained: the long-delayed *Transfiguration* (figures begun by Ferro but competed by Giacomo Soldo after 1671; frescoes by Guiseppe Danedi and Giovanni Antonio Danedi (called Montalto), 1665–after 1671); the grandiose *Assumption of the Virgin* in the basilica's choir and cupola (frescoes principally by the Montalto brothers, before 1671; the 142 statues principally by Dionigi Bussola and Cesare Bussola, *c.* 1661–before 1701); and, the last ensemble in the traditional sense, *Christ before Annas* (figures by Carlantonio Tandarini; their polychromy and frescoes by Sigismondo Betti, 1763). But, even when satisfying Bascapè's orders, the results pertain much less to the preceding style at the Sacro Monte than to the Piedmontese Baroque generally.

Since the late 18th century decoration at the Sacro Monte has consisted mainly of restoration. Only once, in the case of the *Lamentation*, were figures simply replaced (in 1823, by a tepid Neo-classical group by Luigi Marchesi (*fl* 1823–63); later furnished by Francesco Burlazzi (1846–1908) with a fresco landscape). Frequently, however, frescoes were repainted: the *Fall* was given scenes of Adam and Eve by Burlazzi in 1885; the *Flight into Egypt*, with a panorama again by Burlazzi, was repainted in the late 19th century. Part vintage, part mediocre *arte sacra*, the resulting ensembles are confused in stylistic identity and lend themselves to misinterpretation. By the late 19th century, however, the emphasis had begun to shift to conservation. Although not without contoversy, this process was continued during the late 20th century.

BIBLIOGRAPHY

Pre-19th-century guides are excluded except important ones that have been reprinted. Also excluded are writings on the principal artists, which can be found under the individual biographies.

G. Alessi: *Libro dei Misteri: Progetto di pianificazione urbanistica, architettonica e figurativa del Sacro Monte di Varallo in Valsesia* (1565–9); ed. S. Stefani Perrone, intro. A. M. Brizio, 2 vols (Bologna, 1974)

G. B. Fassola: *La Nuova Gierusalemme o sia il Santo Sepolcro di Varallo* (Milan, 1671/*R* 1973)

M. Cusa: *Nuova guida storica, religiosa ed artistica al Sacro Monte di Varallo ed alle sue adiacenze* (Varallo, 1857–63/*R* 1984)

F. Tonetti: *Museo storico ed artistico valsesiano*, 4 vols (Varallo, 1883–91/*R* vols ii–iv, 1973)

S. Butler: *Ex voto: An Account of the Sacro Monte or New Jerusalem at Varallo Sesia* (London, 1888)

E. Motta: *Il beato Bernardino Caimi fondatore del Sacro Monte di Varallo: Documenti e lettere inedite* (Milan, 1891)

P. Galloni: *Sacro Monte di Varallo: Atti di fondazione; B. Caimi fondatore* (Varallo, 1909/*R* 1973)

——: *Sacro Monte di Varallo: Origine e svolgimento delle opere d'arte* (Varallo, 1914/*R* 1973)

A. Durio: 'Francesco Sesalli e la prima "Descrittione" del Sacro Monte di Varallo', *Boll. Stor. Prov. Novara*, xxi (1927), pp. 167–379

——: *Bibliografia del Sacro Monte di Varallo e della chiesa di Santa Maria della Grazie annessa al Santurario* (Novara, 1930)

——: 'Bibliografia del Sacro Monte di Varallo: Omissioni e aggiornamento, 1600–1943', *Boll. Sezione Novara*, xxxvii (1943), pp. 75–100

M. Bernardi: *Il Sacro Monte di Varallo* (Turin, 1960)

M. L. Gatti Perrer: 'Martino Bassi, il Sacro Monte di Varallo e S Maria presso San Celso a Milano', *A. Lombarda*, ix/2 (1964), pp. 21–57

C. Debiaggi: *Dizionario degli artisti valsesiani dal secolo XIV al XX* (Vorallo, 1968)

——: 'Le cappelle dell'Ascensione, dell'Apparizione di Gesù ai Discepoli e l'originaria topografia del Sacro Monte di Varallo', *Boll. Stor. Prov. Novara*, lxix/2 (1978), pp. 56–81

——: *A cinque secoli dalla fondazione del Sacro Monte di Varallo: Problemi e ricerche* (Varallo, 1980)

M. Cometti: 'Bibliografia del Sacro Monte di Varallo', *Aspetti storici ed artistici del Sacro Monte di Varallo* (exh. cat., ed. M. G. Cagna and others; Varallo, Bib. Civ. and Archv Stato, 1980)

J. Bober: 'Storia e storiografia del S Monte di Varallo: Osservazioni sulla "prima pietra" del S Sepolcro', *Novarien*, xiv (1984), pp. 3–18

G. Gentile: 'La storia del Sacro Monte nei documenti: Note per una lettera della mostra', *Il Sacro Monte di Varallo: Mostra documentaria* (exh. cat., ed. M. G. Cagna Pagnone; Varallo, Archv Stato, 1984), pp. 79–93

W. Hood: 'The Sacro Monte of Varallo: Renaissance Art and Popular Religion', *Monasticism and the Arts*, ed. T. G. Verdon (Syracuse, NY, 1984), pp. 291–311

P. G. Longo: 'La proposta religiosa del Sacro Monte di Varallo', *Novarien*, xiv (1984), pp. 19–98

——: 'Il Sacro Monte di Varallo nella seconda metà del XVI secolo', *Da Carlo Borromeo a Carlo Bascapè: Atti della giornata culturale: Arona, 1984*, pp. 83–182

Iconografia del Sacro Monte di Varallo: Disegni, dipinti e incisioni dal XVI al XX secolo (exh. cat., ed. M. Cometti Valle; Varallo, Bib. Civ., 1984)

G. Gentile: 'Il Sacro Monte di Varallo nella pietà di Carlo Borromeo: Sviluppi spirituali e catechetici di una tradizione devozionale', *Boll. Stor. Prov. Novara*, lxxvi (1985), pp. 201–31

G. Testori and S. Stefani Perrone: *Artisti del legno: La scultura in Valsesia dal XV al XVIII secolo* (Borgosesia, 1985)

P. G. Longo: 'Fonti documentarie sui Francescani a Varallo tra XV e XVI secolo', *Sacro Monte di Varallo: Spunti storici e devozionalei: Atti del convegno culturale: Varallo, 1986*, pp. 29–108

S. Stefani Perrone, ed.: *Questi sono li Misteri che sono sopra el Monte di Varalle (in una 'Guida' poetica del 1514)* (Borgosesia, 1987)

J. Bober: 'Sulla "preistoria" del Sacro Monte di Varallo', *Sacri Monti: Devozione, arte e cultura della Controriforma: Atti del convegno internazionale: Gazzada (Varese), 1990*, pp. 119–30

S. Stefani Perrone: 'La Gerusalemme delle origini nella secolare vicenda edificatoria del Sacro Monte di Varallo', *Sacri Monti: Devozione, arte e cultura della Controriforma: Atti del convegno internazionale: Gazzada (Varese), 1990*, pp. 27–57

For further bibliography *see* SACROMONTE.

JONATHAN BOBER

Varallo, Tanzio da. *See* TANZIO DA VARALLO.

Varamin [Varāmān; Waramin]. Town in Iran 60 km south-east of Tehran. It was an agricultural satellite of Rayy until the 1220s, when Rayy was irreparably destroyed by the Mongols. When economic life began to revive under the Mongol Ilkhanid dynasty (*reg* 1256–1353), Varamin developed into a major urban centre. Between 1322 and 1326 Hasan al-Quhadhi, a vizier from the region, built a splendid congregational mosque in the town (*see* ISLAMIC ART, §II, 6(i)(a) and MOSQUE, fig. 2). It is an almost perfect example of the classical Iranian mosque: four iwans are set around a central courtyard, one of which leads to a domed area in front of the mihrab. Other work done under the Ilkhanids includes a number of tombs—the Imamzada Yahya (1261–3; restored 1305–7), the mausoleum of 'Ala al-Din (1289) and the Imamzada Shah Husayn (*c.* 1330)—and the portal of the Sharif Mosque (1307). Numerous fragments of lustre tiles of the 1260s and 1300s that once decorated the Imamzada Yahya are now in collections in London (V&A), St Petersburg (Hermitage) and elsewhere. At the turn of the 14th century Varamin was subjected to devastating attacks by the armies of Timur (Tamerlane), so that the Spanish traveller Clavijo found the town mostly deserted in 1405. Its subsequent recovery is marked by minor restorations to the congregational mosque (1412–19) and the construction of the tomb of Husayn Riza (1437), known for its retardataire stucco decoration. From the 16th century onwards Varamin was overtaken by Tehran as the major city of the region.

BIBLIOGRAPHY

Enc. Islam/1: 'Waramin'
D. Wilber: *The Architecture of Islamic Iran: The Il-Khanid Period* (Princeton, 1955)
O. Grabar: 'The Visual Arts, 1050–1350', *The Saljuq and Mongol Periods*, ed. J. A. Boyle, v of *The Cambridge History of Iran* (Cambridge, 1968), pp. 629–36 [detailed disc. of the congregational mosque]
B. O'Kane: 'The Imamzada Husain Riza at Varamin', *Iran*, xvi (1978), pp. 175–7
O. Watson: *Persian Lustre Ware* (London, 1985)

ABBAS DANESHVARI

Varanasi [anc. Kāsī: 'City of Light'; Kashi; Vārānasī; Banāras; Benares]. Sacred city and pilgrimage centre on the banks of the Ganga River between the Barna, or Varuna, and Asi rivers in Uttar Pradesh, India. It is the most holy of the seven sacred cities of Hinduism (the others being Ayodhya, Mathura, Hardwar, Kanchipuram, Ujjain and Dwarka) and has been the focus of Brahmanical learning and religious pilgrimage from ancient times.

1. HISTORY AND URBAN DEVELOPMENT. The existence of the city from earliest times is attested by myriad references in the sacred texts. The kingdom of Kashi is mentioned in the Vedas, and the kings of Kashi are referred to in the *Mahābhārata*, although not until the Puranas is Varanasi mentioned as the capital city of Kashi. Around the time of the Buddha (600 BC) 16 great city states flourished in north India, the three most prominent being Maghada, Koshala and Varanasi. Owing to its strategic position at the confluence of the Ganga and Varuna rivers, Varanasi was a significant trading and commercial centre. In many tales of the previous lives of Buddha (Skt *jātaka*s), Varanasi is described as a city of much splendour and an important commercial centre. It was first suggested in 1868 (Sherring) that ancient Varanasi was situated north of the present city on both sides of the confluence of the Varuna and Ganga rivers. Excavations carried out at Rajghat in 1940 by Krishna Deva for the

Archaeological Survey of India revealed an enormous clay rampart, 10 m high, datable to between *c.* 600 and 200 BC and similar to the early fortifications at Kaushambi and Vaishali. Within the city were baked-brick structures equipped with drainage systems. Terracotta and other artefacts are in the Bharat Kala Bhavan at Banaras Hindu University.

Varanasi's urban development is an indication of its religious significance. By the time of the Buddha it was already famous as a place for seekers of religious knowledge and spiritual experience. After attaining Enlightenment at Bodhgaya, Shakyamuni, the historical Buddha preached the first sermon in the Deer Park at nearby Sarnath, thereby founding the Buddhist faith. In the 7th century AD Xuanzang, the Chinese Buddhist pilgrim, visited Varanasi; he noted that, while Buddhism was still flourishing at Sarnath, it was not a force in Varanasi proper. Mahavira, contemporary of Buddha and the inaugurator of JAINISM, also preached in Varanasi. Kashi was known as the City of Shiva. However, it is most famous as the City of Death. According to the Hindu theory of reincarnation, one must travel through myriad existences in order to be released from the eternal round of birth and death to achieve union with the Divine. The conditions and status of the present life depend on the actions performed in the previous life so one is constantly struggling through many rebirths. However, Kashi is so potent that simply to die there is to achieve instant liberation (Skt *mokṣa*) and for centuries pilgrims from all over India have journeyed there to die. The *ghāt*s and their environs are crowded with buildings devoted to religious purposes: *āshram*s for the thousands of widows who come from all over India to devote their lives to piety and austerity and for the old and sick who come here to die; accommodation for the crowds of holy men (*sādhu*s) and renouncers (*sannyāsin*s) as well as for the masses of pilgrims who crowd the city. The most famous *ghāt* is Manikarnika (Burning Ghat) with its sacred ever-burning flame to light the cremation pyres (see fig. 1). The sacred texts enumerate five traditional pilgrimage routes entailing the circumambulation (*pradakṣiṇā*) of the five sacred zones that extend outwards in circles from the devotional heart of Varanasi, the Shaivite Vishvanatha Temple; the nearer it is to the core, the more sacred and more potent is the zone. Pilgrimages involve bathing at particular *ghāt*s and *kuṇḍ*s (sacred pools) and visiting auspicious sites and temples to worship. The largest takes in the entire area of Varanasi, beginning at Manikarnika Ghat and ending at Vishvanatha; 108 sites are visited over a period of four days.

In 1194 the forces of Muhammad ibn Sam, the Ghurid sultan, attempted to crush the faith by demolishing the most sacred temples and building their own religious structures on the ruins, a practice that continued for over 500 years.

From ancient times Varanasi was famous for its sages and philosophers. In the 2nd century BC Patanjali, founder of the *yoga* school of philosophy, wrote his famous treatise on Sanskrit grammar here. Kabir, one of India's most famous poets, was born in Varanasi, and Tulsi Das translated the *Rāmāyaṇa* from Sanskrit to Hindi at Tulsi Ghat. In 1585 a formal school of Sanskrit studies was

1. Varanasi, Manikarnika Ghat, 18th century

inaugurated by Raja Jai Singh II of Jaipur (*reg* 1693-1743); destroyed by the Moghul emperor Aurangzeb (*reg* 1658–1707) to build his Great Mosque. It was rebuilt by Jonathan Duncan of the East India Company in 1791 as the Sanskrit College and today owns a large collection of Sanskrit manuscripts. In 1916 Banaras Hindu University was founded by Madan Malaviya (helped by Annie Besant, founder of the Theosophical Besant) to teach traditional knowledge, including ancient herbal medicine (*ayurveda*), astronomy and philosophy, with modern medicine and science.

The city has a reputation for fine textiles; Buddhist literature frequently mentions the delicacy and fineness and that Kashi cloth was the finest of all (Singh, pp. 111–12). The famous 'cloth of gold' called *kamkhwab* (brocade) was described by T. N. Mukharji when he collected objects for the Glasgow International Exhibition of 1888 (Mukharji, pp. 366–7). He estimated that upwards of 2750 people were employed making silk and gold and silver brocade. In the late 20th century artisans, usually Muslim, maintain the basic 'pre-industrial' techniques but adapted to produce mainly the celebrated Varanasi *sārī*s. In other craft fields, most metalworkers are Hindu, making mainly sacrificial articles, *pūja* utensils and images, and such decorative articles as trays, pan (betel) boxes, bowls, palanquins etc. The local brassware was praised particularly by Mukharji (pp. 192–3). The Muslims introduced carpet-weaving, and their patronage and opulent lifestyle greatly boosted production of all crafts.

2. BUILDINGS. Royal families from all over India built palaces on the *ghāt*s, the Marathas in particular being responsible for much building after the decline of Muslim rule. Manikarnika Ghat (see fig. 1 above) is regarded as the oldest and most sacred, because of its relationship with the Manikarnika Well (mentioned in the *Kasikhanda purāṇa*), water from which is said to wash away all sins of the soul. Also known as the Cremation Ghat, it is slowly subsiding into the water, and one of its three temples has been completely claimed by the River Ganga.

Most of the standing temples at Varanasi were constructed in the 18th century. The conventional style for the temple of this period is in typical northern (*nagara*) style and characterized by an emphasis on the vertical and a central soaring spire (*śikhara*) flanked by minor spires (*śikharikā*s), which in turn are clustered with even smaller spires topped by silver, gold or brass finials. A classic example of this style is the small, pale honey-coloured sandstone Lakshmi Narayana Temple (18th century) with a main central spire and four flanking *śikharikā*s, each crowned by exceedingly tall gilded finials (see fig. 2). Also in the typical Varanasi style is the 19th-century deep-red sandstone Durga Kund Temple (erected on ancient foundations by the Marathi Rani Bhawani) with elaborately carved columns, multiple spires and a wide, intricately carved entrance. The temple complex consists of an open courtyard surrounded by a colonnade, which opens on to the tank (*kund*) on one side; the Durga Kund is one of the many tanks or sacred pools included in various pilgrimage routes as an obligatory site for bathing and performing worship. The complex has several small shrines, including one to Mahadeva (Shiva) and one to Ganesha. The 19th-century Durga temple (h. *c.* 30 m) of Maharaja Cheit Singh is elaborately carved with myriad figures of elephants and lions, the three river goddesses Ganga, Yumna and Saraswati, plus a whole host of images of deities. Although the temple is dedicated to Durga and

2. Varanasi, Lakshmi Narayana Temple, 18th century

is therefore of the Shaiva sect, the Maharaja seems to have included almost every recognized Indian deity to magnify the sanctity of his construction.

Just as many Hindu temples were built on the ruins of Buddhist temples and monasteries, so the Muslims in turn demolished both, using the masonry available to create the many mosques that are now interspersed among the temples and *ghāt*s. The Vishvanatha Temple was destroyed in the late 17th century by the Mughal emperor Aurangzeb, who built his Great Mosque on the site reusing columns. The temple was rebuilt many times. The present version (1777) is remarkable for its golden steeple, which was plated with gold by Ranjit Singh in 1839. The Great Mosque of Aurangzeb is composed of masonry not only from the Vishvanatha Temple but also from an earlier Buddhist complex and possibly also a Jaina temple (Sherring, pp. 317–18). The two colossal octagonal minarets (h. 70.7 m) of the mosque tower above all other buildings and form the most distinctive landmark of the river skyline. It is situated next to the sacred Hindu Jnana Vapi (Well of Wisdom), water from which is believed to be the essence (*amrita*) of enlightenment. Other Muslim buildings include Lat Bhairon, Ganj-i-Shahid Mosque and Alamgir's Mosque, all built on Buddhist ruins, and the Arhai Kangura Mosque, which bears a Hindu inscription of 1190 although some of the masonry belongs to an earlier period. The Ramnagar Fort Palace of the Maharaja of Banaras has massive battlements built down into the

water, overhung by finely carved, bracketed balconies. The outer ramparts date to the 17th century.

In the city Queen's College (the former Sanskrit College; *see* §1 above) designed by Major Kittoe in 1847–52, is constructed in a Perpendicular Gothic style of Chunar sandstone. Banaras Hindu University, founded in 1916, is set in a spacious tree-shaded compound and includes the Bharat Kala Bhavan, a museum with a very fine collection of paintings as well as representative stone sculpture from north India. Also in the compound is the recently completed Visvanatha Temple, built in marble in the revivalist northern (*nāgara*) style (*see also* INDIAN SUBCONTINENT, §III, 8(ii)).

BIBLIOGRAPHY
M. A. Sherring: *The Sacred City of the Hindus: An Account of Benares in Ancient and Modern Times* (London, 1868)
T. N. Mukharji: *Art Manufactures of India (Specially Compiled for the Glasgow International Exhibition, 1888)* (Calcutta, 1888/*R* 1974)
E. B. Havell: *Benares, the Sacred City: Sketches of Hindu Life and Religion* (London, [1905])
——: *Indian Architecture: Its Psychology, Structure, and History from the First Muhammadan Invasion to the Present Day* (London, 1913/*R* 1927)
D. L. Eck: *Banaras: City of Light* (London, 1983)
B. P. Singh: *Life in Ancient Varanasi (An Account Based on Archaeological Evidence)* (Delhi, 1985)
J. Keay: *Banaras: City of Shiva* (New Delhi, 1987) [photography by R. Bedi]
N. Kumar: *The Artisans of Banaras: Popular Culture and Identity, 1880–1986* (Princeton, 1988)
G. Michell: *Buddhist, Jain, Hindu*, i of *The Penguin Guide to the Monuments of India* (Harmondsworth, 1989)
P. Davies: *Islamic, Rajput, European*, ii of *The Penguin Guide to the Monuments of India* (Harmondsworth, 1989)

M. A. CLARINGBULL

Varano. Italian family of patrons. They emerged as Lords of Camerino, a commune in the Marches, a province of the Papal States, in the second half of the 13th century. Their ascendancy was built on property held in the city and its surrounding *contado*, or jurisdiction, on occasional high public offices and on their alliance with the Guelph cause. Despite Camerino's importance as a market town and a centre of production for textiles and, later, paper, much of the Varano wealth depended on their service as condottieri, often for the papacy. The dynasty tried to buttress its position through marriage with other ruling dynasties in the region; in 1451 Giulio Cesare da Varano (*reg* 1444–1502) married Giovanna Malatesta. The family received formal recognition as papal vicars (hereditary vicars after 1468) and then dukes (from 1515), but it never became one of the major Italian powers, and its lordship over Camerino was interrupted by family rivalry, internal dissent and foreign interference. Divisions within the dynasty and external intervention drove them into exile between 1433 and 1444, and Alexander VI ousted them from the city between 1502 and 1503. The principal male line ended with Giovanni Maria da Varano (*reg* 1503–27), and, after brief periods of rule by the della Rovere and Farnese families, Camerino returned to direct papal rule in 1545.

The Varano attracted many artists, craftsmen and men of letters to Camerino. During the 14th century the family's properties in the centre of the city and next to the cathedral were converted into a palace, which was greatly extended in two campaigns (1465–75 and 1489–99) by Giulio Cesare.

Craftsmen were imported from elsewhere in the Marches and from Tuscany, while labour services were demanded of the local population. The second phase was possibly directed by Baccio Pontelli and Rocco da Vicenza (*fl c.* 1500). The Palazzo Ducale, which now houses part of the University and the Biblioteca Valentiniana, has been much modified and largely stripped of its furnishings and decorations, but early descriptions and inventories suggest that it was intended to rival the palaces of contemporary and neighbouring dynasties, such as the Montefeltro of Urbino. Tapestries and intarsia panelling formed part of its decoration; some of the latter, the work of Luca di Firenze (1471) is preserved in the Museo Diocesano. Under the direction of Giulio Cesare and his son Giovanni Maria, its principal public rooms were frescoed with representations of members of the Varano family, its allies, dynastic coats of arms and laudatory captions (*elogie*) composed by the churchman and scholar Varino Favorino (*c.* 1450–1537). The courtyard is decorated with the devices of the Varano and Malatesta families, and a bust of *Giulio Cesare* crowned the main entrance. Following contemporary fashion, the lord of Camerino had a *studiolo* in his palace, commissioned a portrait medal and attracted the praise of men of letters. He also contributed to work on the façade of S Venanzio (1480) and embellished the Varano chapel, dedicated to S Ansovino, in the cathedral; both church and cathedral were largely rebuilt in the 19th century. Giulio Cesare's other projects included the central hospital of S Maria della Misericordia (1479) and the monastery of S Pietro di Muralto (1484), for which he commissioned an altarpiece from Crivelli.

The Varano family directed and inspired enough architectural, artistic and literary activity in the city to ensure that their lordship (especially the rule of Giulio Cesare) was long regarded as a 'golden age' in the region, but their resources, and those of the other leading families of Camerino, were insufficient to create a distinct school.

BIBLIOGRAPHY
P. Litta: *Famiglie celebri italiani*, vii (Milan, 1819), table 4
B. Feliciangeli: 'Cenni storici sul palazzo dei Varano a Camerino', 'Sulle condizioni economiche e demografiche di Camerino e sulla ricchezza della famiglia Varano', *Atti & Mem. Reale Deput. Stor. Patria Marche*, n.s., viii (1912), pp. 21–61
R. Romani: 'Il Palazzo Varano a Camerino', *Rassegna Marchigian*, vi (1927–8), pp. 374–84
S. Corradini: 'Il palazzo di Giulio Cesare Varano e l'architetto Baccio Pontelli', *Stud. Maceratesi*, iv (1969), pp. 186–220
P. Zampetti: *Paintings from the Marches* (London, 1971), pp. 67–130
A. Bittarelli: 'Varino Favorino e i suoi "Elogia"', *Stud. Picena*, xliv (1977), pp. 215–29
——: *Camerino: Viaggio dentro la città* (Macerata, 1978)
J. E. Law: 'City, Court and *contado* in Camerino, *c.* 1500', *City and Countryside in Late Medieval and Renaissance Italy: Essays Presented to Philip Jones*, ed. T. Dean and C. Wickham (London, 1990), pp. 171–82

JOHN LAW

Varbanov, Marin (*b* Oriahovo, nr Ruse, 22 Sept 1932; *d* Beijing, 22 July 1989). Bulgarian tapestry and textile designer, carpet-weaver and teacher. In 1959 he graduated from the Central Academy of Art and Design in Beijing, where he specialized in textile design. On his return to Bulgaria he established himself as an innovative tapestry designer, primarily using motifs drawn from Bulgaria's history and artistic iconography. Drawing on the legacy of the ancient Bulgarian art of woven textiles, he collected a school of followers. In 1960 he became a professor of textiles at the National Academy of Arts (Natsionalna Hudozhestvena Academia) in Sofia. From 1974 he lived and worked in Paris with his wife, the Chinese artist Sun Huaikuei-Varbanova (*b* 1937), whom he had met in Beijing. He combined his knowledge of Bulgarian weaving techniques with that of the ancient Chinese practice of weaving rugs from crude unspun wool and sheer silk thread. This resulted in striking constrasts, which lend a quality of sculptural relief to his tapestries. He received commissions for wall hangings for several major buildings in European cities: examples are *Kuker* (1969) for the Palazzo del Quirinale in Rome, *A Rodophi Song* (1969) for the Ministry Council Building in Warsaw, *Old Icons* (textile and metal, 1981) for the National Palace of Culture in Sofia and *Ancient Bulgaria* (1973–83), a series of six carpets for the residence of the President of Bulgaria in Boyana, near Sofia. One of his last commissions was the Gobelins tapestry *Impulses* (1990), designed for the interior of Pierre Cardin's restaurant Maxim's in Beijing.

BIBLIOGRAPHY
V. Angelov: 'Goblen' [Tapestry], *Suvremenno bulgarsko monumentalno izkustvo, 1956–1986* [Contemporary Bulgarian Monumental art], ed. K. Stefanov and M. Kirov (Sofia, 1986), pp. 180–279 [with Eng. summary]

JULIANA NEDEVA-WEGENER

Varchi, Benedetto (*b* Florence, March 1503; *d* Florence, Dec 1565). Italian humanist and theorist. After travels in the 1530s during which he studied Aristotle and frequented the circle of Pietro Bembo he settled permanently in Florence in 1543. A chronicler and writer, he became one of the most active members of the Accademia Fiorentina, writing many commentaries on the works of Dante and Petrarch. He was in close contact with artists: he exchanged numerous sonnets with Agnolo Bronzino and Bartolomeo Ammanati and, according to Vasari, advised Niccolò Tribolo on iconographic matters. He also helped Benvenuto Cellini revise the manuscript of his *Vita*. Varchi's writings on art comprise a short discourse of unknown date entitled *Della beltà e grazia* ('Of beauty and grace'); two lectures delivered in 1547 in S Maria Novella, Florence, and published in 1549 as *Due lezzioni*; an unpublished treatise on proportion; and the funeral oration for Michelangelo (Florence, 1564).

Della beltà e grazia synthesizes commonplaces of Renaissance aesthetics stemming from Marsilio Ficino's commentary on Plato's *Symposium* and disseminated in the 16th century through various *trattati d'amore* and commentaries on Petrarch's *Canzoniere*. The funeral oration for Michelangelo summarizes his life, describes his Platonic standpoint and presents his work as crowning the development of Tuscan art from the time of Cimabue. The two lectures are Varchi's most important contribution to art history. In the first, a commentary on Michelangelo's sonnet *Non ha l'ottimo artista alcun concetto*, Varchi expounds the principles of natural creation after the example of artistic creation, which he defines as the reproduction of an image retained in the artist's imagination. He concludes with a eulogy of Michelangelo based on the Platonic doctrine of love. The second lecture, a series of three discussions based on Book VI of Aristotle's *Nicomachean Ethics*, sets out to assess the nobility of the various arts, the operations of which, according to Aristotelian psychology, are situated in the lower part of the rational soul, their domain being confined to the universe of particulars. In the first discussion medicine triumphs over the arts in general. In the second, despite the unifying principle of *disegno*, Varchi invokes the Aristotelian concept of substance—the fusion of form and matter (*Metaphysics*, 1029a)—in declaring himself in favour of sculpture. The last discussion compares painting and poetry, opposing the two disciplines in terms of content but underlining their common imitative properties. The text concludes with eight letters from artists, including Vasari, Bronzino, Tribolò, Jacopo Pontormo, Benvenuto Cellini, Francesco da Sangallo, Battista di Marco del Tasso and Michelangelo, whose views on the matter Varchi had requested.

While bearing witness to the immense reputation of Michelangelo, the two lectures present a theory as yet ill defined, halfway between traditional Aristotelianism and empirical admiration. They nevertheless had considerable influence on subsequent comparative discussions of the arts (*see* PARAGONE), and their introduction of Aristotelian categories in this debate prepared the way for the ideas of Vincenzo Danti and Federico Zuccaro.

UNPUBLISHED SOURCES

Florence, Bib. Riccardiana, fols 84–108 [*Trattato della proportioni e proportionalità*]

WRITINGS

Due lezzioni di M. Benedetto Varchi (Florence, 1549); ed. in part by P. Barocchi in *Trattati d'arte del cinquecento* (Bari, 1962), i, pp. 1–82; also in P. Barocchi, ed., *Scritti d'arte del cinquecento* (Milan, 1971–3), i, pp. 493–544

Orazione funerale . . . nell'essequie di Michelagnolo Buonarroti (Florence, 1564)

Libro della beltà e grazia; in *Lezzioni di M. Benedetto Varchi* (Florence, 1590); ed. P. Barocchi, *Trattati d'arte del cinquecento* (Bari, 1962), i, pp. 83–91

BIBLIOGRAPHY

E. Panofsky: *Idea: Ein Beitrag zur Begriffgeschichte der älteren Kunsttheorie* (Leipzig, 1924; Eng. trans., 1968), pp. 115–21

U. Pirotti: *Benedetto Varchi e la cultura del suo tempo* (Florence, 1971)

S. Rossi: *Dalle botteghe alle accademie* (Milan, 1980), pp. 83–122

L. Mendelsohn: *Paragone: Benedetto Varchi's Due Lezzioni and Cinquecento Art Theory* (Ann Arbor, 1982)

F. Quiviger: 'Benedetto Varchi and the Visual Arts', *J. Warb. & Court. Inst.*, 1 (1987)

FRANÇOIS QUIVIGER

Vardy, John (*b* Durham, *bapt* 20 Feb 1718; *d* London, 17 May 1765). English architect, engraver and furniture designer. The son of a gardener, he was appointed Clerk of the Works at the Queen's House, Greenwich, in 1736 and was clerk at a succession of royal buildings, notably at the London palaces of Whitehall, Westminster and St James's (1746–54). In this capacity he became closely associated with William Kent, whose Horse Guards scheme he was responsible for executing and possibly modifying (1750–59). He engraved and published a number of Kent's designs (notably in *Some Designs of Mr Inigo Jones and Mr William Kent*, 1744). Not surprisingly, Kent's influence is strongly felt in Vardy's own work, such as the 'New Stone Building' adjoining Westminster Hall (begun 1755; destr. 1883) and the unexecuted scheme (1754) for a building for the new British Museum in Old Palace Yard, Westminster.

Vardy's private commissions included the remodelling (1761–3) of Hackwood Park (destr. in later alterations,

1805–13), Hants, for Charles Paulet, 5th Duke of Bolton, and Milton (later Dorchester) House (begun 1751; completed by William Chambers; destr. 1850) in Park Lane, London, for Joseph Damer, 1st Baron Milton and subsequently 1st Earl of Dorchester. His Rococo–Gothic scheme of *c.* 1755 for Milton Abbey in Dorset, also for Lord Milton, was inspired by Kent's Esher Place (*c.* 1733), Surrey. It was executed in modified form after his death by Chambers. Although Vardy could be impeccably Palladian, many of his designs develop motifs from Kent in a more Rococo direction. This is also true of his important contribution to furniture design—as seen in the design (1749; London, V&A) for a state bed for St James's Palace and items for Hackwood (*c.* 1763), in which he collaborated with his brother Thomas Vardy (*b* 1724), a carver.

Much of Vardy's work has been altered or destroyed, and still more was never executed. Spencer House, London, where he was allowed to complete the exterior and ground-floor rooms (1755–60), gives an idea of the range of his talent; he was subsequently supplanted there by the more fashionable Neo-classicist James 'Athenian' Stuart.

BIBLIOGRAPHY

Colvin

R. White: 'John Vardy, 1718–65', *The Architectural Outsiders*, ed. R. Brown (London, 1985), pp. 63–81

ROGER WHITE

Vardzia. Site on the north bank of the Kura River in the Aspindza district of the Republic of Georgia. A rock-cut complex, it consists of the village of Ananauri (10th–12th century) and a monastery (12th–13th century). An investigation into the site was first undertaken in the 1920s, revealing many layers of occupation. Ananauri lies on the west of the complex, with dwellings and terraces for orchards and vineyards. On the uppermost terrace is a single-nave church (10th century) with 16th-century wall paintings. The monastery (ded. 1185) is one of the most important and impressive monuments of Georgian medieval architecture. It was mostly built between 1156 and 1203 during the reigns of King Giorgy III (*reg* 1156–84) and his daughter Queen Tamar (*reg* 1184–1213). There are over 400 houses, comprising 120 residential complexes, several refectories, churches and administrative buildings, all carved into the rock and divided between 13 storeys with interconnecting passageways and staircases: a pipe (3.5 km long) supplied the monastery with water.

In the centre of the monastery is the single-aisled church of the Assumption, in front of which stands a portico with two broad arches, built rather than cut from the rock. In the late 13th century to the early 14th a bell-tower was erected in front of the portico. The cathedral's interior walls are decorated with frescoes (1184–6) paid for by Eristave Rati Surameli, whose portrait and dedicatory inscription are on the north wall. The master painter was a certain Giorgy, whose compositions include scenes from the *Life of Christ* and *Life of the Virgin* (e.g. the *Virgin and Child with the Archangels Michael and Gabriel* in the apse) and figures of *Rati Surameli* and *King Giorgy III and Queen Tamar* (see fig.), the latter being in the place of honour near the sanctuary.

The monastery served as an important centre of education and manuscript production until its destruction in 1551 by Iranian forces under Shah Tahmasp I (*reg* 1524–

Vardzia, monastery, church of the Assumption, fresco of *King Giorgy III and Queen Tamar*, 1184–6

76). Between 1578 and 1828 Vardzia was under Turkish control, and the site remained neglected until the 1920s, becoming a museum in 1938.

BIBLIOGRAPHY
F. Gaprindashvili: *Peshchernyy ensembl' Vardzia* [The cave ensemble of Vardzia] (Tbilisi, 1960)
K. Melitauri: *Arkitekturuli strukturuli sakitkhebis shestsavla Vardiziashi* [Questions of architectural constructional study at Vardzia] (Tbilisi, 1961)
F. Gaprindashvili: *Vardzia* (Leningrad, 1975)
E. Privalova: *Vardzia* (Tbilisi, 1982)

V. BERIDZE

Varela, Francisco (*b* Seville, *c.* 1580; *d* Seville, 1645). Spanish painter. He is first documented in Seville in 1605, when he was already a master painter. Few of his works survive, which makes it difficult to study his stylistic development, but it would seem that he oscillated between Mannerism and naturalism. His draughtsmanship is firm and meticulous and his figures expressive and sober.

Varela's earliest known painting is a portrait of the sculptor *Juan Martínes Montañez* (1616; Seville, Ayuntamiento). A small *Immaculate Conception* is dated 1618 (San Sebastián, priv. col.). Varela's most important works are the *Last Supper* (1622; Seville, Hermandad Sacramental S Bernardo) and the *Archangel Michael* (1629; Seville, priv. col.). The paired female saints, *St Catherine and St Ines* and *St Elizabeth of Hungary and a Martyr* (Seville, S Teresa), are lateral panels from a dismembered altarpiece, as are the panels in the Museo de Bellas Artes, Seville.

BIBLIOGRAPHY
E. Valdivieso and J. M. Serrera: *Pintura sevillana del primer tercio del siglo XVII* (Madrid, 1985), pp. 228–59
A. E. Peréz Sánchez: *Pintura barroca en España, 1600–1750* (Madrid, 1992), p. 169

Vargas, Andrés (*b* Cuenca, 1614; *d* Cuenca, 1674). Spanish painter. He began his training in 1648 in the Madrid workshop of Francisco Camilo, with whom he collaborated on the series of paintings (dispersed) that decorated the convent of the Capuchinos de la Paciencia in Madrid. Vargas's *Fireside Hymn* (Pontevedra, Ayuntamiento Porriños) from the series shows that he developed a pictorial style similar to that of Camilo, in both its use of line and its warm tonalities. Between 1652 and 1655 Vargas completed a series of frescoes for the vaults of the Sagrario Chapel of Cuenca Cathedral, where he also executed the main altarpiece depicting the *Assumption of the Virgin* as well as two side panels. The first section of the right-hand side panel represents the *Birth of the Virgin*, the second the *Presentation of the Virgin*. On the first section of the left panel is the *Appearance of the Virgin to St Julian*, with the *Assumption of Mary Magdalene* on the second. Vargas also painted the *Transfixion of St Teresa* (1644; Guadalajara, church of the Carmelites) and the *Immaculate Conception* (destr. 1936), which was kept in the small town of Iniesta.

BIBLIOGRAPHY
D. Angulo Iñiguez: 'Pintura del siglo XVII', *A. Hisp.* (1971), pp. 239
D. Angulo Iñiguez and A. Pérez Sánchez: *Pintura madrileña del segundo tercio del siglo XVII* (Madrid, 1984), pp. 361–70

ENRIQUE VALDIVIESO

Vargas, Luis de (*b* Seville, *c.* 1505; *d* Seville, 1567). Spanish painter. He was the son of an undistinguished painter, Juan de Vargas, who was probably his first master. Luis de Vargas spent many years in Italy and probably trained with Perino del Vaga; he is recorded as being back in Seville in 1553. His works in Spain show a direct knowledge of Mannerist painting in Florence and Rome in the 1540s, especially that of Giorgio Vasari, Francesco Salviati and Perino del Vaga, and represent the triumph of Italianate forms in Seville. The altarpiece of the *Nativity* (1555) in Seville Cathedral, Vargas's earliest documented work, combines an Italianate style with expressive naturalistic passages. His most celebrated work is the *Allegory of the Immaculate Conception* (1561; Seville Cathedral), which follows Vasari's version of the same subject (1540–41; Florence, SS Apostoli) and represents the genealogy of Christ from Adam to the Virgin Mary. Also known as *La Gamba*, because of the foreshortened leg of the nude figure of Adam in the lower left, the painting exemplifies Vargas's mastery of the Italian *maniera*, with its pastel colours, crowded space and complexity of forms and poses. Pacheco called him the father of Sevillian painting, and he was reputed to be the first Sevillian painter to use the new Italian technique of fresco painting. Much of his work in this medium has been destroyed, however, although there is a painting of the *Road to Calvary* (1563) in the old Sagrario, Seville Cathedral, in poor condition.

BIBLIOGRAPHY
F. Pacheco: *Arte* (1649); ed. F. Sánchez Cantón (1956)
A. Camón Aznar: *La pintura española del siglo XVI*, Summa A. (Madrid, 1970)

J. M. Serrera: 'Pinturas y pintores del siglo XVI en la catedral de Sevilla', *La catedral de Sevilla* (Seville, 1985, 2/1991), pp 353–7, 398–404

E. Valdivieso: *Historia de la pintura sevillana: Siglos XIII al XX* (Seville, 1986), pp. 67–73

J. Brown: *The Golden Age of Painting in Spain* (New Haven and London, 1991), pp. 47–8

DOLORES LE FANU

Varignana, Domenico da. *See* AIMO, DOMENICO.

Varin, Jean. *See* WARIN, JEAN.

Varin [Warin], Quentin (*b* Beauvais, *c.* 1570; *d* Paris, 27 March 1634). French painter. He was the son of a shoemaker and from 1597 to 1600 was in the papal territory of Avignon, where he worked with a local painter, Pierre Duplan (*fl* late 16th century), enrolling also in the local painters' guild. By 1607 he had returned to northern France, and he was married that year at Amiens. In 1612 he was working in the Norman village of Les Andelys, and there he became Nicolas Poussin's first master. For the Gothic church of Notre-Dame, Le Grand Andely, he produced in 1612 a *Martyrdom of St Vincent*, a *Martyrdom of St Clarus* and a *Regina Coeli* (all *in situ*), the works that provided Poussin with his first contact with contemporary painting. These are the earliest fixed points in Varin's oeuvre, although a ruined *Rock of the Philosophers* (Rouen, Mus. B.-A.), reminiscent of such late 16th-century French Mannerist painters as Antoine Caron, and his *Flagellation* (Beauvais, Cathedral), another painting inferior to those at Les Andelys, presumably date from earlier in his career.

In 1612 Varin moved to Paris, and in 1613 he was freed from the restrictions of his guild by his appointment as Peintre Ordinaire du Roi to Louis XIII. He was presented to the Regent, Marie de' Medici, and was commissioned to produce decorations for the Palais du Luxembourg, Paris, which were never executed, possibly because of his association with the engraver and poet Etienne Durand, who was executed for treason in 1618. Among the surviving works from Varin's years in Paris are the *Marriage at Cana* for the high altar of SS Gervais et Protais (*c.* 1618–20; Rennes, Mus. B.-A. & Archéol.), the *Presentation of the Virgin in the Temple*, which was given by Anne of Austria to the Convent of the Discalced Carmelites (1642; *in situ*, now called St Joseph-des-Carmes), and *St Carlo Borromeo Giving Alms* for S Jacques-de-la-Boucherie (1627; Paris, St Etienne-du-Mont). The *Entombment* (Paris, Louvre) shows the influence of Jacques Bellange and Georges Lallemand and confirms Varin as both a Mannerist and an eclectic who had studied paintings by or engravings after such late 16th-century Italian and Flemish masters as Taddeo Zuccaro, the Cavaliere d'Arpino, Giorgio Vasari (i) and Marten de Vos.

Varin preferred acid colours and discordant and jarring effects, such as the oblique perspective recession of *St Carlo Borromeo* and the contrast in the *Marriage at Cana* between the beauty of the female guests and the rusticity of the servants. He was an important contributor to the late flowering of Mannerism in France, but, in spite of being based in Paris, he remained a provincial artist practising an outdated style.

BIBLIOGRAPHY

E. Delignières: 'Notes complémentaires sur Quentin Varin, peintre picard (vers 1580–1627)', *Réun. Soc. B.-A. Dépt.*, xxvii (1903), p. 262

G. Varenne: *Essai sur la vie et l'oeuvre du peintre Quentin Varin* (Beauvais, 1905)

Y. Pruvost: 'Un Tableau de Quentin Varin: *La Présentation au temple*', *Rev. des A.*, ix (1959), p. 47

P. Ramade: *Quentin Varin: Le Christ aux 'Noces de Cana' (l'oeuvre du mois 19)* (exh. cat., Rennes, Mus. B.-A. & Archéol., 1982)

SIMON LEE

Varley. English family of artists. The most influential member was (1) John Varley, known particularly for his landscape watercolours. He was the eldest of five children, of whom (2) Cornelius Varley became a scientist as well as a watercolour painter. Two other members of that generation were also active as painters: their sister Elizabeth Varley (1798–1864), who married William Mulready in 1802; and their brother William Fleetwood Varley (1785–1856), whose work is similar to that of (1) John Varley. Of John Varley's ten children, two became painters: Albert Fleetwood Varley (1804–76) and Charles Smith Varley (1811–87). Other artists in the family were Cromwell Fleetwood Varley (1828–83), son of Cornelius; Edgar John Varley (1839–88), son of Charles Smith; and John Varley jr (1850–1933), son of Albert Fleetwood, who painted watercolours of Egypt, India and Japan.

(1) John Varley (*b* London, 17 Aug 1778; *d* London, 17 Nov 1842). Painter and draughtsman. At the age of 15 he attended an evening drawing school in Holborn, London, run by J. C. Barrow. Throughout his career he worked primarily in watercolour. His first exhibited work was a *View of Peterborough Cathedral* (exh. RA 1798). In between sketching expeditions to Wales (1798 or 1799, 1800 and 1802) and Yorkshire (1803) he executed topographical views of towns—particularly of half-timbered buildings in Hereford, Leominster, Conway and Chester—drawn in the picturesque idiom of the late 18th century. From 1800 until as late as 1820 he attended evening classes at Dr Monro's 'Academy' in London and also visited Monro's cottage at Fetcham, Surrey. In company with Monro he executed the watercolour *View from Polsden, Surrey* (1800; Newcastle upon Tyne, Laing A.G.), which shows the influence of Thomas Girtin. This painting is inscribed *Study from Nature*, an inscription that recurs on some of his work as late as 1831.

Varley's early watercolours have been seen as his most inspired. They often combine naturalistic qualities with the influence of other artists, forming striking and original compositions, as in *Sunrise from the Top of Cader Idris* (1804; England, priv. col., see Lyles, pp. 12–13), which is remarkable for its glowing light effects and owes much to J. R. Cozens; another example is *Harlech Castle and Tygwyn Ferry* (1804; Upperville, VA, Paul Mellon priv. col., see Lyles, pp. 14–15), in which the broad, unmodulated wash layers resemble the contemporary work of J. S. Cotman, with whom Varley became acquainted in 1802 at meetings of the Sketching Society.

In 1805 Varley became a founder-member of the Society of Painters in Water-Colours. His contributions to its early exhibitions furnished 'the very backbone of its landscape art' (Roget). In the ensuing years he wished his watercolours to rival oils and they became larger, more varied in technique and more aspiring in content. Varley helped to create this taste and increasingly adapted his work to suit

John Varley: *Distant View of Bamburgh Castle, Northumberland, and Holy Island*, watercolour, 252×475 mm, *c*. 1810 (Edinburgh, National Gallery of Scotland)

it, for example *Suburbs of an Ancient City* (702×940 mm, 1808; London, Tate).

As Varley became more prolific, exhibiting about 20 watercolours a year (he had a large family to support, having married in 1803), he increasingly worked to a formula, often painting Welsh scenes interpreted through the eyes of the Old Masters, for example *Landscape with Harlech Castle* (*c*. 1825; London, V&A).

Varley's finest and most characteristic watercolours date from the early years of the Society of Painters in Water-Colours, *c*. 1805–20. They are models of those 'clear skies, distances and water' that he claimed 'are the beauties most sought after in the art of watercolours'. Such features are often best seen in the watercolours of a long horizontal format, which he first adopted after his trip to Northumberland in 1808, for example the *Distant View of Bamburgh Castle, Northumberland, and Holy Island* (see fig.). Such broad and luminous works contrast with his later ones, which from 1837 were executed on coarse paper and more densely painted, using deep blues, purples and pinks over a brown ground (cologne earth), often with gum (e.g. London, V&A). He also worked with the Patent Graphic Telescope invented by his brother (*see* (2) below).

Varley was a gifted and successful teacher, renowned for his phenomenal enthusiasm and engaging personality. He wrote a number of drawing manuals, mainly intended for the amateur, in which he explained the value of tints and set out rules of composition, many of which are evident in his own work. His pupils included William Henry Hunt, William Mulready, John Linnell, David Cox, Copley Fielding, Peter De Wint, Francis Oliver Finch and Samuel Palmer, all of whom he encouraged to sketch from nature. In 1818 Linnell introduced Varley to William Blake, who, for Varley's benefit, drew his famous visionary heads in two of Varley's sketchbooks; some of these,

including the *Head of the Ghost of a Flea*, were engraved by Linnell for Varley's *Treatise on Zodiacal Physiognomy* (1828), a publication that reflects Varley's life-long interest in astrology. Despite his success as an artist and teacher, Varley was always short of money and spent much of his later life in debtors' prison.

WRITINGS

A Practical Treatise on the Art of Drawing in Perspective (London, 1815–20)

A Treatise on the Principles of Landscape Design (London, 1816–21)

(2) Cornelius Varley (*b* London, 21 Nov 1781; *d* London, 21 Oct 1873). Painter, draughtsman and printmaker, brother of (1) John Varley. Primarily a scientist, he painted watercolours for pleasure. He was less prolific than his brother. Although he was also a founder-member of the Society of Painters in Water-Colours, he exhibited few watercolours there from 1805 to 1820 and even fewer at the Royal Academy and the Society of British Artists between 1820 and 1859 and 1826 and 1844 respectively.

Most of Cornelius's work dates from 1800 to the 1820s. Between 1800 and 1805 he produced a number of sketches from nature, often deliberately left unfinished, which in their sensitive and evocative qualities reveal Cornelius as an important exponent of early 19th-century English naturalism. Many of these, such as *Evening at Llanberis* (1805; London, Tate), record the atmospheric effects he observed on his sketching tours in Wales (1802, 1803 and 1805), which he described in an unpublished autobiographical fragment, *Cornelius Varley's Narrative Written by Himself*; other works include tree, sky and cloud studies.

Most of his watercolours are executed in a restrained palette of blues, greys, fawns and soft greens, enlivened by brighter colours such as yellow and orange—a similar palette to that used by John in his early career and in his more informal views of the London suburbs. Like John,

Cornelius painted classical and pastoral subjects, albeit with more prominent figures, while his later watercolours, again recalling those of John, tend to be more heavily painted, often with gouache, in a more garish palette based on purples and strong greens, for example in the two views of *Regent's Canal* (1827, 1843; London, Mus. London).

Having been brought up by his uncle Samuel Varley, a watch and instrument maker, Cornelius became increasingly absorbed in scientific pursuits. He invented lenses and scientific instruments, including a type of *camera lucida*, which he patented in 1811 as the Patent Graphic Telescope (e.g. London, Sci. Mus.). By means of a simple inverting telescope and a series of reflecting mirrors this instrument could project on to paper an erect, reduced image that could then be traced by hand. It was used by Cornelius to make landscape drawings such as *Patshull, Staffordshire* (1820) and *View from Ferry Bridge, Yorkshire* (both London, BM), both inscribed *PGT*, and by both John and Cornelius for drawing portrait heads. The most famous examples are those by Cornelius of *John Sell Cotman* and ?*J. M. W. Turner* (both Sheffield, Graves A.G.), and those by John of *Walter Fawkes (1769–1825)*, one of Turner's patrons, and of *Dr Monro* (both London, V&A). Cornelius may also have used the telescope to make the preliminary drawings for his *Etchings of Shipping, Barges, Fishing Boats* published by the two brothers in 1809. This work contains some of the earliest independent examples of lithography (known as 'polyautography') in England.

UNPUBLISHED SOURCES
Cornelius Varley's Narrative Written by Himself (London, V&A; extensively quoted in 1973 exh. cat.)

BIBLIOGRAPHY
R. Redgrave and S. Redgrave: *A Century of Painters of the English School*, 2 vols (1866)
J. L. Roget: *A History of the Old Water-Colour Society* (London, 1891)
S. D. Kitson: 'Notes on a Collection of Portrait Drawings Formed by Dawson Turner', *Walpole Soc.*, xxi (1932–3), pp. 67–104
A. Bury: *John Varley of the 'Old Society'* (Leigh-on-Sea, 1946) [pls]
M. Butlin: *The Blake-Varley Sketchbook of 1819 in the Collection of M. D. E. Clayton-Stamm* (London, 1969)
M. Pidgley: 'Cornelius Varley, Cotman and the Graphic Telescope', *Burl. Mag.*, cxiv (1972), pp. 781–6
Cornelius Varley (exh. cat. by M. Pidgley, London, Colnaghi's, 1973)
Works of Splendor and Imagination: The Exhibition Watercolor, 1770–1870 (exh. cat. by J. Bayard, New Haven, CT, Yale Cent. Brit. A., 1981)
C. M. Kauffmann: *John Varley (1778–1842)* (London, 1984)
A. Lyles: 'John Varley's Early Work, 1800–1804', *Old Wtrcol. Soc. Club*, lix (1984), pp. 1–22
The Larger Blake-Varley Sketchbook, London, Christie's: 21 March 1989
C. Ryskamp: 'A Cornelius Varley Sketchbook in the Morgan Library', *Master Drgs*, xxviii/3 (1990), pp. 344–59
A. Lyles: 'John Varley's Thames: Varieties of Picturesque Landscape, *c.* 1805–1835', *Old Wtrcol. Soc. Club*, lxiii (1994), pp. 1–37

ANNE LYLES

Varley, Fred(erick Horseman) (*b* Sheffield, 2 Jan 1881; *d* Toronto, 8 Sept 1969). Canadian painter of English birth. He studied at Sheffield School of Art (1892–1900) and at the Koninklijk Akademie voor Schone Kunsten, Antwerp, from 1900 to 1902. He began working as an illustrator and teacher in Sheffield, where he befriended Arthur Lismer. Lismer emigrated to Canada in 1911 and in 1912 encouraged Varley to move there. Through him, Varley found work in Toronto as an illustrator and met Tom Thomson as well as painters who later banded together as the GROUP OF SEVEN. He and Lismer joined Thomson and A. Y. Jackson on a sketching trip to Algonquin Provincial Park in the autumn of 1914. Varley wrote at the time of their shared desire to rid themselves of preconceived ideas, so as to convey nature in all its greatness just as they found it. In February 1918 Varley was appointed to the War Art programme of the Canadian War Records and was sent to England, where he joined Jackson, who was there for the same purpose. Varley was in France during the last two months of the war and again in early 1919, returning that summer to Canada, where he continued with the War Records programme until March 1920.

Varley joined the Group of Seven as a founder-member in 1920. Although he painted a large number of landscape pictures, such as *The Cloud, Red Mountain* (*c.* 1928; Toronto, A.G. Ont.), he had neither the same interest nor commitment to the genre as the other members of the Group. His main interest was in portraits: his subjects included *Vincent Massey* (1920; U. Toronto, Hart House), who supported him as a patron, and members of Massey's family. Unable to make a living from his art in spite of Massey's patronage, Varley moved to Vancouver, where he taught at the Vancouver School of Decorative and Applied Arts. In 1933 he and another painter teaching there, Jock Macdonald, opened their own school, the British Columbia College of Arts, but they were forced to close it for lack of funds in 1935. Always strongly drawn to unorthodox religious mysticism, Varley became part of a small circle of artists and intellectuals in Vancouver who were interested in theosophy, an interest to which he alluded clearly in portraits such as *Vera* (1930; Ottawa, N.G.) and *Dhârâna* (1932; Toronto, A.G. Ont.). The title of the latter painting, which represents a woman with eyes upraised ecstatically against a deserted landscape, refers to a Buddhist term for spiritual union with nature.

Varley left Vancouver in 1936, thereafter living in Ottawa, Montreal and Toronto. Disappointed in his hope of regenerating his career as a portrait painter, he produced less during the 1940s and 1950s but recovered his enthusiasm for landscapes from 1957, when he began to make regular sketching trips to British Columbia. A fine draughtsman and an energetic painter, he did not fully achieve the promise of his talent, perhaps most disappointingly in not finding the support to be able to pursue his interest in portrait painting.

BIBLIOGRAPHY
F. H. Varley (exh. cat., Toronto, A.G., 1954)
F. H. Varley: Retrospective, 1964 (exh. cat. by K. Saltmarche, Windsor, Ont., Willistead A.G., 1964)
F. H. Varley: A Centennial Exhibition (exh. cat. by C. Varley, Edmonton, Alta A.G., 1981)

For further bibliography *see* GROUP OF SEVEN.

DAVID BURNETT

Varlin [Guggenheim, Willy] (*b* Zurich, 16 March 1900; *d* Bondo, nr Chiavenna, 30 Oct 1977). Swiss painter and draughtsman. Like many Swiss artists, he left his homeland at an early age. After a fairly brief period in Berlin (1921–2), where he was a pupil of Emil Orlik, he settled in Paris in 1923. There he attended the Académie Julian and associated with painters based in the Montparnasse district, such as Jules Pascin and Chaïm Soutine. On the advice of the dealer Léopold Zborowski he adopted the pseudonym Varlin, exhibiting his work in Paris at the Salon des Humoristes et de l'Araignée and regularly also at the Salon d'Automne. He also contributed cartoons to the Swiss magazine *Nebelspalter* and to the Parisian magazines *Candide, Gringoire, Aux écoutes* and the *Petit parisien.*

For political and personal reasons Varlin returned to Switzerland in 1935, settling in Zurich. From then on he painted Switzerland and the Swiss, living the classic life of a Bohemian and *enfant terrible* and becoming a social outsider and outlaw as far as art criticism was concerned. His main distinguishing features were humour, irony and a distaste for ideology and the idyllic that set him apart from even his great models, Soutine and Maurice Utrillo. Although much of his work had an Expressionist directness and emphasis on gesture, he was also a talented portraitist. His best-known portraits include those of Swiss writers such as *Max Frisch* (1958; Basle, Kstmus.) and Friedrich Dürrenmatt (1963; priv. col., see Vachtova, p. 120), who valued and wrote about his work, but his studies of ordinary people, such as *Clochard Wolz* (1944; priv. col., see Vachtova, p. 143), are also convincing because of their profound humanity and their portrayal of the tragedy of life as comedy. Varlin also applied his observational skills to the façades of public buildings such as hospitals, barracks and abattoirs, and to townscapes. He represented Switzerland at the Venice Biennale in 1960, winning the Guggenheim Award.

BIBLIOGRAPHY
Varlin (exh. cat., intro. F. Dürrenmatt, Basle, Ksthalle, 1967)
H. Lötscher, ed.: *Varlin: Der Maler und sein Werk* (Zurich, 1969)
L. Vachtova: *Varlin* (Zurich, 1978)

URS-B. FREI

Varma, (Raja) Ravi (*b* Kilimanoor, 29 April 1848; *d* Kilimanoor, 2 Oct 1906). Indian painter. He was the most important and one of the earliest Indian artists of the 19th century to work in oil paints. The subjects of his paintings were often mythological, but they were produced in a European historicist style. He absorbed the influence of such French 19th-century academic painters as William-Adolphe Bouguereau and Gustave Boulanger and of Indian contemporary popular theatre, specializing in the type of mythological paintings that found favour with Indian rajas and British administrators. His successful exploitation (from 1894) of the lithographic reproduction of his paintings ensured, for the first time in India, that the work of an individual artist could reach a mass market. He was also a proficient portrait painter, adjusting his style to suit the taste of his patrons. He was assisted by his brother C. Raja Raji Varma, a talented *plein-air* painter.

For illustration of work *see* INDIAN SUBCONTINENT, fig. 316.

BIBLIOGRAPHY
K. P. P. Tampy: *Ravi Varma: A Monograph* (Trivandrum, 1934)
K. Chaitanya: *Ravi Varma* (New Delhi, 1960)

K. M. Varma: *Ravi Varma: A Sketch* (Trivandrum, 1964)
E. M. J. Venniyoor: *Raja Ravi Varma* (Trivandrum, 1981)

R. SIVA KUMAR

Varna. Site of Neolithic cemetery of the 5th millennium BC on the Black Sea coast of eastern Bulgaria. It is famous for its spectacular grave goods, including artefacts in copper, clay, stone, flint, bone, shell and gold, which exhibit an exuberant range of craft skills. A settlement may have existed near by. The cemetery was discovered by chance in 1972 during construction work and was excavated by Ivan Simeonov Ivanov and others from 1973 to the early 1980s. The material recovered from the site was removed to Varna Archaeological Museum; in 1989 a new museum for finds from the cemetery was under construction. The cemetery comprised at least 190 simple earth-cut pit graves containing individual burials of both men and women. Many contained just a few simple grave goods, or none at all. However, one grave (no. 43) was much richer, yielding over a thousand gold objects. There were also *c.* 30 cenotaphs, some with sun-dried clay masks apparently representing human faces. These mask cenotaphs contained rich inventories of grave goods; other cenotaphs have also yielded large quantities of gold artefacts and other material. Although other contemporary cemeteries are known in the region, none has produced such a quantity and range of finds.

The gold, which may have been imported from across the Black Sea, was mainly worked by beating to produce an extraordinary range of decorative and symbolic items (*see* PREHISTORIC EUROPE, fig. 25). These included beads, pins, plaques (some in the form of horned animals with *repoussé* decoration), discs, arm-rings, ribbed tubing, strips representing facial features for attachment to clay masks and solid shafted sceptres imitating contemporary copper axes. Gold was also laid on to the inner surface of two open ceramic bowls in delicate curvilinear and zigzag motifs. Other decorated pottery included graphite painted vessels of the type found at KARANOVO, but some of the pottery is rather plain. Further craft skills are illustrated by beaten and cast copper tools including pins, chisels and perforated axe-hammers. In addition to gold, beads were made in *Dentalium* and *Spondylus* shell, various minerals and skilfully cut and perforated quartz. Stone was also cut into dishes and rhyta. Struck flint blades, supreme examples of the knapper's craft, measure up to 440 mm long. Bone was used for pins and for highly stylized anthropomorphic figurines, which were probably cult objects.

For further discussion of the arts and architecture of Neolithic Europe *see* PREHISTORIC EUROPE, §IV.

BIBLIOGRAPHY
I. Ivanov: *Treasures of the Varna Chalcolithic Necropolis* (Sofia, 1978)
——: 'Les Fouilles archéologiques de la nécropole chalcolithique à Varna (1972–1975)', *Stud. Praehist.*, i–ii (1978), pp. 13–26
——: 'Le Chalcolithique en Bulgarie et dans la nécropole de Varna', *Ancient Bulgaria*, ed. A. Poulter (Nottingham, 1983), pp. 154–63
A. Whittle: *Neolithic Europe: A Survey* (Cambridge, 1985)

ALASDAIR WHITTLE

Illustration Acknowledgements

We are grateful to those listed below for permission to reproduce copyright illustrative material and to those contributors who supplied photographs or helped us to obtain them. The word 'Photo:' precedes the names of large commercial or archival sources who have provided us with photographs, as well as the names of individual photographers (where known). It has generally not been used before the names of owners of works of art, such as museums and civic bodies. Every effort has been made to contact copyright holders and to credit them appropriately; we apologize to anyone who may have been omitted from the acknowledgements or cited incorrectly. Any error brought to our attention will be corrected in subsequent editions. Where illustrations have been taken from books, publication details are provided in the acknowledgements below.

Line drawings, maps, plans, chronological tables and family trees commissioned by the *Dictionary of Art* are not included in the list below. All of the maps in the dictionary were produced by Oxford Illustrators Ltd, who were also responsible for some of the line drawings. Most of the line drawings and plans, however, were drawn by one of the following artists: Diane Fortenberry, Lorraine Hodghton, Chris Miners, Amanda Patton, Mike Pringle, Jo Richards, Miranda Schofield, John Tiernan, John Wilson and Philip Winton. The chronological tables and family trees were prepared initially by Kate Boatfield and finalized by John Johnson.

Tino di Camaino *1–2* Photo: Archivi Alinari, Florence

Tintoretto: (1) Jacopo Tintoretto *1* Kunsthistorisches Museum, Vienna; *2* Photo: Osvaldo Böhm, Venice; *3, 5* Photo: Archivi Alinari, Florence; *4* Gabinetto Fotografico, Soprintendenza ai Beni Artistici e Storici, Venice; *6* Trustees of the National Gallery, London

Tiraz Photo: Centre de Documentation du Petit Palais, Avignon

Tiryns Photo: Deutsches Archäologisches Institut, Athens

Tischbein: (2) Friedrich Tischbein Hamburger Kunsthalle, Hamburg

Tissot, James Tate Gallery, London

Titian *1* Photo: Gabinetto Fotografico Nazionale, Istituto Centrale per il Catalogo e la Documentazione, Rome; *2* Photo: Scala, Florence; *3, 6* Photo: Bridgeman Art Library, London; *4* Trustees of the National Gallery, London; *5* Museo del Prado, Madrid; *7* Photo: Archivi Alinari, Florence; *8* Isabella Stewart Gardner Museum, Boston, MA; *9* Soprintendenza per i Beni Artistici e Storici, Naples; *10* Gabinetto Fotografico, Soprintendenza ai Artistici e Storici, Venice

Titicaca Basin *1* South American Pictures, Woodbridge, Suffolk/Photo: Tony Morrison

Title-page *1* Domschatz, Trier; *2* Bodleian Library, Oxford

Titles *1* Musées Royaux des Beaux-Arts de Belgique, Brussels; *2* Los Angeles County Museum of Art, Los Angeles, CA (Purchased with funds provided by the Mr and Mrs William Preston Harrison Collection)/© ADAGP, Paris, and DACS, London, 1996

Tito, Santi di *1–2* Photo: Archivi Alinari, Florence

Tivoli *3* J. Paul Getty Museum, Malibu, CA; *4* Photo: Archivi Alinari, Florence; *5* British Library, London

Tlatelolco Photo: D. Donne Bryant, DDB Stock Photo, Baton Rouge, LA

Tobey, Mark Museum of Modern Art, New York/© ARS, New York, and DACS, London, 1996

Tocqué, Louis Photo: © RMN, Paris

Toeput, Lodewijk Museo Civico Luigi Bailo, Treviso

Togo Yale University Art Gallery, New Haven, CT/Photo: Susan Vogel

Tokelau Photo: Judith Huntsman

Tok-kala Hermitage Museum, St Petersburg

Tokoname Ceramic Art Research Institute, Tokoname

Tokyo *1* Japan National Tourist Organisation; *2* Eye Ubiquitous, Hove, E. Sussex/Photo: Paul Seheult

Toledo *1* Paisajes Españoles, Madrid; *2–4* Photo: Ampliaciones y Reproducciones MAS, Barcelona; *6* Photo: Conway Library, Courtauld Institute of Art, London

Toledo, Juan Bautista de Photo: Patrimonio Nacional Archivo Fotografico, Madrid

Toltec Photo: Henri Stierlin, Geneva

Tomar Abbey Photo: Conway Library, Courtauld Institute of Art, London

Tomasino da Vimercate Syndics of the Fitzwilliam Museum, Cambridge

Tomaso da Modena *1* Photo: Foto d'Arte G. Fini, Treviso; *2* Státní Ústava Památkové Péče, Prague

Tomb *2* Photo: Sheila S. Blair; *3* Photo: Bernard O'Kane; *4* Photo: W. Denny; *5, 20* Photo: Robert Harding Picture Library, London; *8, 10, 13–14* Photo: Archivi Alinari, Florence; *9, 11* RCHME/© Crown Copyright; *12* Photo: © RMN, Paris; *15* Photo: © ACL Brussels; *16* Photo: Archivio Fotografico Vasari, Rome; *17* Warburg Institute, London; *18* Photo: Oxfordshire Photographic Archive, D.L.A., O.C.C; *19* Royal Collection, Windsor Castle/© Her Majesty Queen Elizabeth II

Tomioka Tessai Yamato Bunkakan, Nara

Tonga *1* Pitt Rivers Museum, Oxford; *2* Marischal Museum (University Anthropological Museum), Marischal College, University of Aberdeen

Toorop: (1) Jan Toorop Kröller-Müller Stichting, Otterlo

Topiary Photo: Brent Elliott

Topography *2* Ashmolean Museum, Oxford; *3* Bayerische Staatsgemäldesammlungen, Munich

Toprakkale Trustees of the British Museum, London

Torana Photo: © American Institute of Indian Studies, Varanasi

Torcello Photo: Osvaldo Böhm, Venice

Torii: (2) Torii Kiyomasu I Nelson–Atkins Museum of Art, Kansas City, MO

Torii: (8) Torii Kiyonaga Honolulu Academy of Arts, Honolulu, HI (Gift of James A. Michener, 1992; no. HAA 24.452)

Toronto *1* Metropolitan Toronto Library Board (J. Ross Robertson Collection); *2* Photo: Steven Evans, Toronto

Torralva, Diogo de *1* Photo: Conway Library, Courtauld Institute of Art, London; *2* Art Archive of the Calouste Gulbenkian Foundation, Lisbon (Legacy of Robert C. Smith)/Photo: Robert Chester Smith

Torrelobatón Castle Photo: Felipe Valbuena

Torres García, Joaquín Museo Nacional de Artes Plásticas e Visuales, Montevideo

Torres Strait Islands Trustees of the British Museum, London

Torrigiani, Pietro *1* Photo: RCHME/© Crown Copyright; *2* Museo de Bellas Artes, Seville

Torriti, Jacopo Photo: Archivi Alinari, Florence

Tortoiseshell Board of Trustees of the Victoria and Albert Museum, London

Toruń Photo: Marian Kutzner

Tosa: (1) Tosa Mitsunobu Ishiyamdera Temple Treasury, Ōtsu, Shiga Prefecture

Tosa school Freer Gallery of Art, Smithsonian Institution, Washington, DC

Tōshūsai Sharaku Trustees of the British Museum, London

Toulouse *1, 3* Photo: Conway Library, Courtauld Institute of Art, London; *2, 4* Photo: Thomas W. Lyman; *5* Musée des Augustins, Toulouse

Art, Washington, DC/Photo: Art Resource, New York; *14* Corcoran Gallery of Art, Washington, DC (Museum Purchase, Gallery Fund); *15* Amon Carter Museum of Western Art, Fort Worth, TX; *16* National Gallery of Art, Washington, DC (Gift of the Avalon Foundation); *17* Photo: Christie's, New York; *18* National Gallery of Victoria, Melbourne/© Helen Frankenthaler, 1992; *19* Tate Gallery, London; *21* Boston Picture File, Fine Arts Department, Boston Public Library, MA; *22, 37* Museum of Modern Art, New York; *23* Albright–Knox Art Gallery, Buffalo, NY (Gift of Seymour H. Knox, 1957)/© David Smith/DACS, London/VAGA, New York, 1996; *24* Musée National d'Art Moderne, Paris; *25* Metropolitan Museum of Art, New York (Sage Fund, 1926; no. 26.290); *26* Metropolitan Museum of Art, New York (Rogers Fund, 1918; no. 18.87.1-4); *27* Metropolitan Museum of Art, New York (Gift of Sirio D. Molteni and Rita M. Pooler, 1965; no. Inst. 65.4); *28* Metropolitan Museum of Art, New York; *29* Metropolitan Museum of Art, New York (Purchase, Bequest of Emily Crane Chadbourne, 1972; no. 1972.60.1; installation through the generosity of Saul P. Steinberg and Reliance Group Holdings, Inc.); *30* Metropolitan Museum of Art, New York (Gift of Mrs J. Insley Blair, 1950; no. 50.20.3); *31* Metropolitan Museum of Art, New York (Rogers Fund, 1925; no. 25.115.18)/Photo: Richard Cheek; *32* Metropolitan Museum of Art, New York (Rogers Fund, 1915; no. 15.21.2); *33* Metropolitan Museum of Art, New York (Kennedy Fund, 1918; no. 18.110.4); *34* Metropolitan Museum of Art, New York (Purchase, 1969, gift of Mrs Russell Sage, 1910, and other donors; no. 69.203); *35* Metropolitan Museum of Art, New York (Gift of Mrs Charles Reginald Leonard, 1957, in memory of Edgar Welch Leonard, Robert Jarvis Leonard and Charles Reginald Leonard; no. 57.130.1); *36* Metropolitan Museum of Art, New York (Purchase, Edgar J. Kauffman Jr Foundation Gift, 1968; no. 68.100.1); *38* Photo: Domore Corporation, Elkhart, IN; *39* Brooklyn Museum, Brooklyn, NY (Museum Collection Fund; 45.174); *40* Brooklyn Museum, Brooklyn, NY (Dick S. Ramsay Fund; no. 49.100.la-c); *41* New Jersey State Museum, Trenton, NJ (Brewer Collection); *42* Metropolitan Museum of Art, New York (Gift of Wells M. Sawyer, 1945; no. 45.147); *43* Detroit Institute of Arts, Detroit, MI (Founders Society Purchase, Miscellaneous Memorials Fund); *44–6* Corning Museum of Glass, Corning, NY; *47–9, 51* Yale University Art Gallery, New Haven, CT; *50* Metropolitan Museum of Art, New York (Gift of Edward D. Adams, 1904; no. 04.1); *52* Photo: Catherine B. Thompson, Georgetown, MA; *53* Photo: Wartski Jewellers Ltd, London; *54–5* Museum of American Textile History, North Andover, MA; *56* © Michelle Lester, New York

University palace Photo: Bildarchiv Foto Marburg

Unkoku Tōgan National Museum, Kyoto. All rights reserved

Unterberger: (1) Michael Angelo Unterberger Photo: Bundesdenkmalamt, Vienna

Upholstery *1, 3, 5* Board of Trustees of the Victoria and Albert Museum, London; *2* Statens Konstmuseer, Stockholm; *4* Stiftung Preussische Schlösser und Gärten Berlin-Brandenburg/Photo: Jörg P. Anders

Upjohn: (1) Richard Upjohn *1* Upjohn Family Collection, Avery Architectural and Fine Arts Library, Columbia University, New York; *2* New-York Historical Society

Uppsala Photo: Sören Hallgren

Ur *2* Trustees of the British Museum, London

Uragami Gyokudō Spencer Museum of Art, University of Kansas, Lawrence, KS

Urartian *1* Trustees of the British Museum, London; *2* Museum of Anatolian Civilizations, Ankara

Urban life *1* Rijksmuseum, Amsterdam; *2* Photo: © RMN, Paris

Urban planning *1* British Library, London (no. Kings Top.LXX.5a); *3* British Library, London (no. Maps c7.d.1); *4* Photo: AKG Ltd, London; *5* Warden and Fellows of All Souls College, Oxford; *6* British Library, London (no. Maps 16625 (7)); *7* Archives Nationales, Centre des Archives d'Outre-Mer, Paris; *8* Photo: Overseas Agenzia Fotografica, Milan; *9, 13* Museums of the City of New York; *10* British Library, London (no. 10827.df.17); *11* British Library, London (no. 8205.d.18); *12* Art Institute of Chicago, Chicago, IL/Photo: © 1996. All rights

reserved; *14* Photo: Landesbildstelle Berlin; *15* Architectural Association, London; *16, 19* Photo: David Gosling; *17* © Kawasumi Architectural Photograph Office; *18* Arcaid, London/Photo: Richard Bryant

Urbino *1* Photo: Scala, Florence; *2* Syndics of the Fitzwilliam Museum, Cambridge; *3* Photo: James Austin, Cambridge; *5* Yale University Press Photo Library, London/Photo: Istituto Nazionale Luce, Rome

Urnes *1* Riksantikvaren, Oslo; *2* Photo: Arne Emil Christensen

Uruguay *2* South American Pictures, Woodbridge, Suffolk/Photo: Tony Morrison; *3* Museum of Modern Art, New York; *4* Photo: Alicia Haber

Uruk Department of Antiquities and Heritage, Baghdad/Photo: Hirmer Fotoarchiv, Munich

Utagawa: (2) Utagawa Toyokuni I Board of Trustees of the Victoria and Albert Museum, London

Utagawa: (5) Utagawa Kunisada I Trustees of the British Museum, London

Utrecht Photo: Tarq Hoekstra

Utrecht Psalter Bibliotheek der Rijksuniversiteit, Utrecht

Utrillo, Maurice Photo: © RMN, Paris

Utzon, Jørn Photo: British Architectural Library, RIBA, London

Uxmal Photo: Henri Stierlin, Geneva

Uyttenbroeck, Moses van Herzog Anton Ulrich-Museum, Brunswick

Uzbekistan *2* Oriental Museum, Moscow

Vacca, Flaminio Photo: Archivi Alinari, Florence

Vaccaro: (2) Domenico Antonio Vaccaro Photo: Archivi Alinari, Florence

Vaccaro, Andrea Photo: Ampliaciones y Reproducciones MAS, Barcelona

Vadstena Abbey Photo: Erland Lagerlöf

Valadier: (1) Giuseppe Valadier Photo: Alessandro Vasari, Rome

Valckenborch: (2) Lucas van Valckenborch I Kunsthistorisches Museum, Vienna

Valckenborch: (3) Frederik van Valckenborch *1* Rijksmuseum, Amsterdam; *2* Trustees of the British Museum, London

Valdés Leal: (1) Juan de Valdés Leal *1* Museo de Bellas Artes, Seville; *2* Photo: Ampliaciones y Reproducciones MAS, Barcelona

Valencia *1–2* Photo: Conway Library, Courtauld Institute of Art, London

Valenciennes, Pierre-Henri Photo: © RMN, Paris

Valladolid Photo: Ampliaciones y Reproducciones MAS, Barcelona

Vallotton, Félix Bibliothèque Nationale de France, Paris

Valois: (2) Charles V Bibliothèque Nationale de France, Paris

Valois: (3) Jean Photo: Giraudon, Paris

Valois: (11) Charles VIII Photo: British Architectural Library, RIBA, London

Valois: (14) Francis I Photo: Scala, Florence

Vanbrugh, John *1* Country Life Picture Library, London/Photo: Henson; *2–4* Photo: RCHME/© Crown Copyright

Vandelvira, Andrés de Photo: Ampliaciones y Reproducciones MAS, Barcelona

Van den Broek & Bakema Architectenbureau Van den Broek en Bakema, Rotterdam/Photo: Geljon, Rotterdam

Vanderbank, John Trustees of the British Museum, London

Vandergucht: (4) Benjamin Vandergucht Leicestershire Museums, Arts and Records Service, Leicester

Vanderlyn, John Wadsworth Atheneum, Hartford, CT/Photo: Joseph Szaszfai

Van de Velde, Henry *1–2* Photo: Bildarchiv Foto Marburg

Vanitas *1* Metropolitan Museum of Art, New York (Charles B. Curtis, Marquand, Victor Wilbour Memorial and Alfred N. Punnett Endowment Funds, 1974; no. 1974.1); *2* Rijksmuseum, Amsterdam

Vanson, Adrian Scottish National Portrait Gallery, Edinburgh

Vanuatu *1* Phototèque du Musée de l'Homme, Paris; *2* Photo: David Attenborough

Vanvitelli, Luigi *1–2* Photo: Archivi Alinari, Florence

Varallo, Sacro Monte *1–2* Photo: Archivi Alinari, Florence

Varanasi *1* Photo: © American Institute of Indian Studies, Varanasi; *2* Photo: David McCutcheon

Vardzia Photo: VAAP, Moscow

Varley: (1) John Varley National Gallery of Scotland, Edinburgh